# THE ROUGH GUIDE TO

# France

written and researched by

David Abram, Nikki Bayley, Ruth Blackmore, Brian
Catlos, Mary Anne Evans, Emma Gibbs, Norm Longley,
John Malath~~~
Walker and

ROUGH
GUIDES

roughguides.com

# Contents

# Introduction to
# France

The sheer physical diversity of France would be hard to exhaust in a lifetime of visits. Landscapes range from the fretted coasts of Brittany and the limestone hills of Provence to the canyons of the Pyrenees and the half-moon bays of Corsica, and from the lushly wooded valleys of the Dordogne and the gentle meadows of the Loire valley to the glaciated peaks of the Alps. Each region looks and feels different, has its own style of architecture, its own characteristic food and often its own dialect. Though the French word *pays* is the term for a whole country, people frequently refer to their own region as *mon pays* – my country – and this strong sense of regional identity has persisted despite centuries of centralizing governments, from Louis XIV to de Gaulle.

Industrialization came relatively late to France, and for all the millions of French people that live in cities, the idea persists that theirs is a rural country. The importance of the land reverberates throughout French culture, manifesting itself in areas as diverse as regional pride in local cuisine and the state's fierce defence of Europe's agricultural subsidies. Perhaps the most striking feature of the French countryside is the sense of space. There are huge tracts of woodland and undeveloped land without a house in sight, and, away from the main urban centres, hundreds of towns and villages have changed only slowly and organically over the years, their old houses and streets intact, as much a part of the natural landscape as the rivers, hills and fields.

Despite this image of pastoral tranquillity, France's history is notable for its extraordinary vigour. For more than a thousand years the country has been in the vanguard of European development, and the accumulation of wealth and experience is evident everywhere in the astonishing variety of **things to see**, from the Dordogne's prehistoric cave paintings and the Roman monuments of the south, to the Gothic cathedrals of the north, the châteaux of the Loire, and the cutting-edge architecture of

**RIGHT** CHÂTEAU LAROSE TRINTAUDON, MÉDOC

the *grands projets* in Paris. This legacy of history and culture – **le patrimoine** – is so widely dispersed across the land that even the briefest of stays will leave you with a powerful sense of France's past.

The importance of these traditions is felt deeply by the French state, which fights to preserve and develop its national **culture** perhaps harder than any other country in the world, and by private companies, which also strive to maintain French traditions in arenas as diverse as haute couture, pottery and, of course, food. The fruits of these efforts are evident in the subsidized **arts**, notably the film industry, and in the lavishly endowed and innovative **museums and galleries**. From colonial history to fishing techniques, aeroplane design to textiles, and migrant shepherds to manicure, an array of impressive collections can be found across the nation. Inevitably, however, first place must go to the fabulous displays of fine art in Paris, a city which has nurtured more than its fair share of the finest creative artists of the last century and a half, both French – Monet and Matisse for example – and foreign, such as Picasso and Van Gogh.

There are all kinds of pegs on which to hang a holiday in France: a city, a region, a river, a mountain range, gastronomy, cathedrals, châteaux. All that open space means there's endless scope for outdoor activities, from walking, canoeing and cycling to skiing and sailing, but if you need more urban stimuli – clubs, shops, fashion, movies, music – then the great cities provide them in abundance.

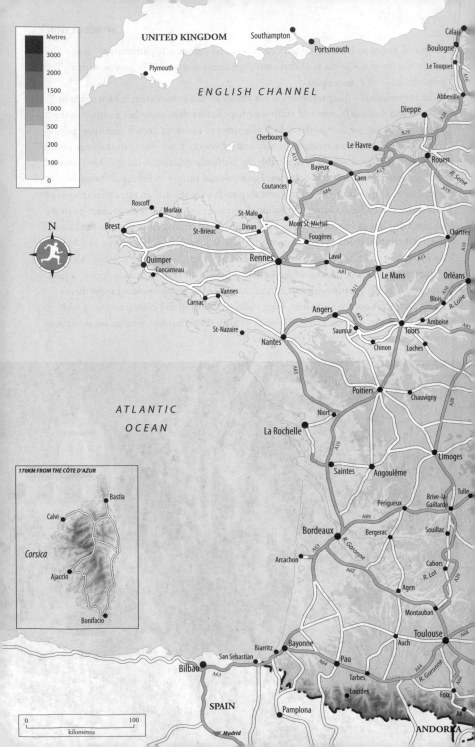

## FACT FILE

- With a land area of 547,000 square kilometres, France is the largest country in the EU; its population of 66 million is second only to that of Germany.

- France has a long secular republican tradition dating back to the revolution of 1789. Yet the majority of its population is Roman Catholic – nominally, at least – and there's a substantial Muslim minority of around 8–10 percent.

- Annual GDP per capita is around $44,000, making France one of the world's richest countries, but unemployment is a persistent problem, at around 10 percent. Taxes are high, at around 43 percent, but so is social spending, at almost 30 percent.

- France remains by far the most popular tourist destination in the world, with some 82 million visitors annually.

- The French film industry is the world's third most prolific, after the US and India, with around 215 million tickets sold annually.

- France is no longer the bastion of popular gastronomy it once was. Frogs' legs, horse flesh and snails do indeed still appear on many restaurant menus, but contrary to its self-image, the country is also the second largest consumer of McDonalds' burgers after the US, flipping more than a million Big Macs daily.

- A great source of confusion when meeting and greeting French people is the double kiss, or *bise*. When it is appropriate, and how many times to do it, which cheek to start with, whether to touch or air kiss, what to do with your hands, or whether it's better to shake hands instead, are all matters that vex the French just as much as foreign visitors – not least because norms vary between regions, social situations and age groups. When in doubt, hang back, copy what everyone else does, and go left for the first one.

- In 1910, a law was passed in France forbidding couples from kissing on train platforms to avoid delayed departures. The law is still in place, though no longer enforced.

# Where to go

Travelling around **France** is easy. Restaurants and hotels proliferate, many of them relatively inexpensive when compared with other developed Western European countries. Train services are admirably efficient, as is the road network – especially the (toll-paying) *autoroutes* – and cyclists are much admired and encouraged. Information is highly organized and available from tourist offices across the country, as well as from specialist organizations for walkers, cyclists, campers and so on.

As for specific destinations, **Paris**, of course, is the outstanding cultural centre, with its impressive buildings and atmospheric backstreets, its art, nightlife and ethnic diversity, though the great **provincial cities** – Lyon, Bordeaux, Toulouse, Marseille – all now vie with the capital and each other for prestige in the arts, ascendancy in sport and innovation in attracting visitors.

For most people, however, it's the unique characters of the **regions** – and not least their cuisines – that will define a trip. Few holiday-makers stay long in the largely flat, industrial **north**, but there are some fine cathedrals and energetic cities to leaven the mix. The picture is similar in **Alsace-Lorraine** where Germanic influences are strong, notably in the food. On the northern Atlantic coast, **Normandy** has a rich heritage of cathedrals, castles, battlefields and beaches – and, with its cream-based sauces, an equally rich cuisine. To the west, **Brittany** is more renowned for its Celtic links, beautiful coastline, prehistoric sites and seafood, while the

# Author picks

Our authors travelled the length and breadth of France, exploring indecently pretty villages and busy markets, sipping heady red wines in Bordeaux and tackling myriad walking trails. Here are their (off-the-beaten-track) highlights:

**Wild swimming** The iconic Pont d'Arc (see p.718), a natural limestone arch spanning the River Ardèche, forms a magnificent backdrop for a river swim.

**Must-see masterpiece** The Romanesque carving of Isaiah in Souillac's twelfth-century Church of Sainte-Marie (see p.559) captures a moment of pure ecstasy.

**Awesome castle** With its turreted towers soaring from a wooded hilltop in Alsace, Haut Koenigsbourg (see p.231) is like a vision from a medieval fairy tale.

**Mountain road** Panoramic views to the distant Alps extend from the spectacular Route des Crêtes (see p.238) in the Vosges – one of France's most scenic drives.

**Easy riding** The anthithesis of the Tour de France, the tow path lining the Canal de Bourgogne (see p.436) between Migennes and Dijon offers a gentle ride though classically beautiful French scenery.

**Small-town festival** Scores of hot-air balloons and thousands of spectators converge on the northern French town of Chalon-sur-Saône (see p.462) over the weekend of Pentecost for this lively balloon fest.

**Terrace with a view** A chilled Corsican muscat on the sun-drenched terrace of the *Hotel des Roches Rouges* (see p.958) in Piana is a delectable treat.

**Rotten tipple** One of France's most succulent dessert wines, Muscat de Beaumes de Venise (see p.964), is made from mouldy grapes – a particular kind of fungus imparts a heavenly aroma of honey and apricot.

**Chilled campsite** On a shaded bank of the Moselle, the municipal campsite in Metz (see p.246) sits next to a sandy town beach that's re-created every summer.

> Our author recommendations don't end here. We've flagged up our favourite places – a perfectly sited hotel, an atmospheric café, a special restaurant – throughout the book, highlighted with the ★ symbol.

## PÉTANQUE

For your average Frenchman, any recipe for a relaxing summer's evening would have to include the three Ps: plane trees (or palms at a pinch); *pastis*; and that most quintessentially French of games, **pétanque**. You'll see this Gallic version of **bowls** played on countless squares across the country, where groups of mostly middle-aged men in baggy shorts congregate around gravel-and-dirt bouldromes to lob heavy metal *boules* at diminutive wooden ones called *cochonnets* (literally "piglets"). *Pétanque* matches played after work and on weekends are part and parcel of the daily rhythm of life, especially in the south.

The game was invented in 1907 in the town of La Ciotat on the Côte d'Azur by an enthusiastic bowler whose rheumatism prevented him from making the usual extended run up. Instead, he devised a version of his favourite sport in which the bowler's feet stayed planted firmly on the ground (*pieds tanqués*). The pitch was shortened accordingly, and after the local bar owner firmed up a set of rules, the new game quickly caught on. A whole **lexicon** has evolved around *pétanque* to describe different throws and scenarios. Each team, for example, has a mix of "pointeurs" (pointers), players who place the ball as closely as possible to the jack, and "tireurs" (shooters), whose job it is to displace the opposition's balls with spectacular lobs. If the throw falls short, it's a "palouf". If it nudges one of the other team's balls, it's made a "biberon", or "baby's bottle". "Faire la Micheline" means to turn up for a game without your own set of boules. "Faire la chanson" refers to attempts to distract the opposition by chatting between points. And, most insulting of all for wannabe *pétanque* players from the UK, "faire de l'anglais" describes a totally hopeless throw.

Finally, if you're lucky enough to spectate at a complete whitewash, you'll experience the most ribald of all *pétanque* traditions, "Kissing the Fanny". When a team or individual player loses by 13 points to zero they have to kiss the bare buttocks of a statue or framed picture of a lady named "Fanny", usually kept in the nearest bar expressly for the purpose.

**Loire** valley, extending inland towards Paris, is famed for soft, fertile countryside and a marvellous parade of châteaux. Further east, the green valleys of **Burgundy** shelter a wealth of Romanesque churches, and their wines and food are among the finest in France. More Romanesque churches follow the pilgrim routes through rural **Poitou-Charentes** and down the Atlantic coast to **Bordeaux**, where the wines rival those of Burgundy. Inland from Bordeaux, visitors flock to the gorges, prehistoric sites and picturesque fortified villages of the **Dordogne** and neighbouring **Limousin**, drawn too by the truffles and duck and goose dishes of Périgord cuisine. To the south, the great mountain chain of the **Pyrenees** rears up along the Spanish border, running from the Basque country on the Atlantic to the Catalan lands of **Roussillon** on the Mediterranean; there's fine walking and skiing, as well as beaches at either end. Further along the Mediterranean coast, **Languedoc** offers dramatic landscapes, medieval towns and Cathar castles, as well as more beaches, while the **Massif Central**, in the centre of the country, is undeveloped and little visited, but beautiful nonetheless, with its rivers, forests and the wild volcanic uplands of the **Auvergne**. The **Alps**, of course, are prime skiing territory, but a network of signposted paths makes walking a great way to explore too; to the north, the wooded mountains of the **Jura** provide further scope for outdoor adventures. Stretching down from the Alps to the Mediterranean is **Provence**, which, as generations of travellers have discovered, seems to have everything: Roman ruins, charming villages, vineyards and lavender fields – and legions of visitors. Its cuisine is similarly diverse, encompassing fruit, olives, herbs, seafood and lamb. Along the Provençal coast, the

## "LA GRAND BOUCLE"

Each year, in the sweltering heat of July, millions of people take up positions on roadsides around France to cheer, shout and bellow cries of encouragement to a peloton of nearly 200 cyclists as they speed past in a stream of day-glo lycra. Millions more watch on television – though few of them are cycling aficionados. Because the Tour de France is far more than a mere bike race. For the French, it's a national institution; a symbol of unity; a chance, as the riders pit themselves against the toughest terrain the mighty *héxagone* can throw at them, to admire the scenic splendour of the country in all its summer glory, with the fields of the Garonne's sun flowers in full bloom, the Côte d'Azur at its most sleek, and the craggy Alps basking under boundless blue skies.

Started in 1903, the Tour was born out of the **rivalry** between two sporting papers, *L'Auto* and *Le Vélo*, as a ruse to boost sales. The passion it incited nearly scuppered the event in its second year, when riders were beaten up by rival fans and cheating was rife (racers were spotted jumping into cars and taking trains). These days, in the wake of a series of high-profile doping scandals, performance-enhancing drugs pose the main threat to the survival of the 3600-km (2200-mile) race, though **La Grand Boucle** (the "Great Loop"), as it's known, still casts a powerful spell over the nation. And it's not just an obsession for the French; in 2012, Britain's own Bradley Wiggins clinched the title – the Tour's first British winner – successfully ensuring a new and ardent fan base just across the Channel.

beaches, towns and chic resorts of the **Côte d'Azur** form a giant smile extending from the down-at-heel but vibrant city of **Marseille** to the super-rich Riviera hotspots of Nice and Monaco. For truly fabulous beaches, however, head for the rugged island of **Corsica**, birthplace of Napoleon and home to an Italian-leaning culture and cuisine and some fascinating Neolithic sculptures.

# When to go

The single most important factor in deciding when to visit France is tourism itself. As most French people take their holidays in their own country, it's as well to consider avoiding the main **French holiday** periods – mid-July to the end of August. At this time almost the entire country closes down, except for the tourist industry itself. Easter, too, is a bad time for Paris: half of Europe's schoolchildren seem to descend on the city. For the same reasons, ski buffs should keep in mind the February school ski break. And no one who values life, limb and sanity should ever be caught on the roads during the last weekend of July or August, and least of all on the weekend of August 15.

Generally speaking, **climate** (see p.50) needn't be a major consideration in planning when to go. Northern France, like nearby Britain, is wet and unpredictable. Paris has a marginally better climate than New York, rarely reaching the extremes of heat and cold of that city, but only south of the Loire does the weather become significantly warmer. West coast weather, even in the south, is tempered by the proximity of the Atlantic, and is subject to violent storms and close thundery days even in summer. The centre and east, as you leave the coasts behind, have a more continental climate, with colder winters and hotter summers. The most reliable weather is along and behind the Mediterranean coastline and on Corsica, where winter is short and summer long and hot.

# 30

# things not to miss

It's not possible to see everything that France has to offer in one trip – and we don't suggest you try. What follows, in no particular order, is a selective taste of the country's highlights, including wonderful architecture, breathtaking landscapes and delectable food and wine. All entries have a page reference to take you straight into the Guide, where you can find out more.

**2**

### 1 LES GORGES DU VERDON
Page 849
The mighty gorges are Europe's answer to the Grand Canyon, and offer stunning views, a range of hikes, and colours and scents that are uniquely, gorgeously Provençal.

### 2 AIX-EN-PROVENCE
Page 843
Aix is Provence's regional capital, and with its wonderful market, top-class restaurants and lively bars, it makes a very satisfying stop.

### 3 THE LOUVRE
Page 71
The palace of the Louvre cuts a grand Classical swathe through the centre of Paris and houses what is nothing less than the gold standard of France's artistic tradition.

### 4 PREHISTORIC CAVE ART
Page 554

The most impressive prehistoric art in France is found at Lascaux, Dordogne.

### 5 DINING OUT IN A LYON BOUCHON
Page 788

Famed for its gastronomy, Lyon offers no end of wonderful eating places, not least the old-fashioned bouchons.

### 6 MONT ST-MICHEL
Page 290

One of France's best-loved landmarks, Mont St-Michel is a splendid union of nature and architecture.

### 7 AMIENS CATHEDRAL
Page 188

The largest Gothic building in France, this lofty cathedral has a clever son et lumière show.

### 8 ANNECY
Page 746

One of the prettiest towns in the Alps, Annecy has a picture-postcard quality which even the crowds can't mar.

### 9 MEDIEVAL PROVENÇAL VILLAGES
Page 839

Provence's hilltop villages attract visitors by the score. Gordes is one of the most famous.

### 10 GORGES DE L'ARDÈCHE
Page 718

The fantastic gorges begin at the Pont d'Arc and cut their way through limestone cliffs before emptying into the Rhône valley.

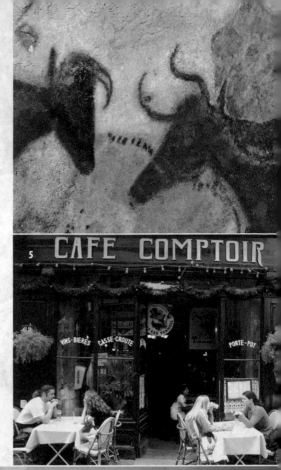

**11 CANAL DU MIDI**
Page 660
Cycling, walking or drifting along the Canal du Midi is the most atmospheric way of savouring France's southwest.

**12 BASTIDE TOWNS**
Page 545
Monpazier is the best preserved of Dordogne's medieval fortified towns – *bastides* – built when there was fierce conflict between the French and English.

**13 JARDIN DU LUXEMBOURG**
Page 97
Paris's most beautiful park, in the heart of the laid-back Left Bank, is the ideal spot for relaxing.

**14 ABBAYE DE FONTENAY**
Page 438
This complex Burgundian monastery has a serene setting in a stream-filled valley.

**15 THE ISSENHEIM ALTARPIECE, COLMAR**
Page 234
Grünewald's amazing altarpiece is one of the most extraordinary works of art in the country.

**16 CYCLING**
Page 36
Cycling is an ideal way to explore France's scenic back roads, and there are some great long-distance cycle routes, too, such as those that lace the Alps.

### 17 THE GR20
Page 952

Arguably France's most dramatic – and most demanding – long-distance footpath climbs through and over Corsica's precipitous mountains.

### 18 CHAMPAGNE TASTING AT ÉPERNAY
Page 207

Dom Pérignon is the most famous, but there are plenty of other bubblies to try in the cellars of Épernay's *maisons*.

### 19 CARCASSONNE
Page 660

So atmospheric is this medieval fortress town that it manages to resist relentless commercialization and summer's visitors.

### 20 CARNAC
Page 346

Archeologically, Brittany is one of the richest regions in the world and the alignments at Carnac rival Stonehenge.

### 21 CHÂTEAUX OF THE LOIRE
Page 367

The River Loire is lined with gracious châteaux, of which Azay-le-Rideau is the most staggeringly impressive.

### 22 LES CALANQUES
Page 877

The cliffs between Marseille and Cassis offer excellent hiking and isolated coves that are perfect for swimming.

### 23 BAYEUX TAPESTRY
Page 281

This 70-metre-long tapestry is an astonishingly detailed depiction of the 1066 Norman invasion of England.

**28**

### 24 BORDEAUX
Page 503

Bordeaux was the principal English stronghold in France for years, and is still known for its refined red wines.

### 25 BASTILLE DAY
Pages 85

July 14 sees national celebrations commemorating the beginning of the French Revolution, with fireworks and parties.

### 26 ST-OUEN FLEA MARKET
Page 110

It's easy to lose track of an entire weekend morning browsing the covetable curios at St-Ouen, the mother of Paris's flea markets.

### 27 WAR MEMORIALS
Pages 158, 183–185

World Wars I and II left permanent scars on the French countryside. The dead are remembered in solemn, overwhelming cemeteries.

### 28 CATHAR CASTLES
Page 618

These gaunt fortresses are relics of the brutal crusade launched by the Catholic church and northern French nobility against the heretic Cathars.

### 29 WINTER SPORTS IN THE ALPS
Page 733

The French Alps are home to some of the world's most prestigious ski resorts, offering a wide range of winter sports.

### 30 CORSICAN BEACHES
Page 979

Some of France's best beaches are found on Corsica, with its white shell sand and turquoise water.

**29**

**30**

# Itineraries

The following itineraries are designed to lead you up, down and round about *la belle France* – picking out the crème de la crème of the country's cities, valleys and mountains, vineyards and coastline.

## LE GRAND TOUR

❶ **Paris** Crossing off the iconic sights takes up most visitors' first few days, but leave time for soaking up that legendary Parisian chic while relaxing in pavement cafés and squares. **See p.60**

❷ **Normandy** The chocolate-box port of Honfleur makes the obvious base for day-trips to the Bayeux tapestry (see p.272), D-Day Beaches (see p.282) and Le Mont St-Michel (see p.290).

❸ **Loire Valley** Use Amboise as your pied-à-terre in the beautiful Loire Valley, famed for its fairy-tale castles. **See p.396**

❹ **Dordogne** An abundance of medieval clifftop castles, prehistoric cave art and sublime local cuisine account for the enduring popularity of the Dordogne. **See p.537**

❺ **Carcassone** Take in a couple of the southern Lot's *bastide* towns and Cathar castles en route to the magnificently turretted Carcassonne. **See p.660**

❻ **Arles, West Provence** The elegant Pont du Gard (see p.644) and beautifully preserved theatre at Orange (see p.807) are just two of the many Roman vestiges within reach of Arles.

❼ **Gorges du Verdon, East Provence** String together as many *villages perchés* as you can on the high road across the Var to the awesome Gorges du Verdon. **See p.849**

❽ **The Alps** A jaw-dropping journey north through the heart of Europe's highest mountains culminates with the snowfields of Mont Blanc. **See p.752**

❾ **Nancy, Lorraine** A serene and refined city, Nancy has one of the most elegant *places* in Europe – Place Stanislas. **See p.240**

❿ **Verdun** Travel back to the capital via the sobering monument to World War I's fallen at Verdun. **See p.250**

## VITICULTURAL ODYSSEY

❶ **Saumur, Loire** Known for its cool-climate-style whites, such as Sancerre, Vouvray and Muscadet, the Loire's varied wines are best sampled from the pretty town of Saumur. **See p.404**

❷ **St-Émilion, Bordeaux** St-Émilion is an ideal springboard for visiting the famous châteaux around Bordeaux. **See p.514**

❸ **St-Jean-Pied-de-Port, Pays Basque** In the Pyrenean foothills, St-Jean is a delightfully picturesque medieval town where you can taste the luscious sweet wines of nearby Jurançon. **See p.595**

❹ **Béziers, Languedoc** The sun-drenched land sweeping from the Mediterranean coast is the world's largest wine-producing region, and Béziers, its capital, is perfectly placed for tasting forays to Collioure, Banyuls and Faugères. **See p.653**

❺ **Bandol, Côte d'Azur** Low rainfall and oodles of sunshine are the hallmarks of the region to the east of Marseille, where the fishing village of Bandol is home to the flagship wine; reds and rosés rule the roost here. **See p.897**

**ABOVE** TARPAN PONIES, LASCAUX CAVE, DORDOGNE; ALPINE TRAIN, CHAMONIX

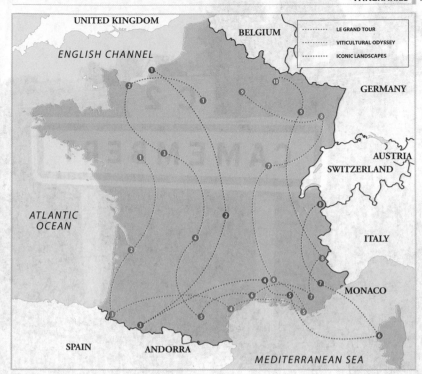

**⑧ Châteauneuf-du-Pape, Provence** The wines produced around this ancient village in the southern Rhône are legendary – and expensive. **See p.810**

**❼ Beaune, Bourgogne** Burgundy boasts more AOP designation wine than anywhere else and the medieval town of Beaune is the recommended base. **See p.459**

**❽ Colmar, Alsace** The Fecht Valley, just west of Colmar, is striped with steeply shelving vines – source of Alsace's finest Rieslings and Gewürtztraminers. **See p.233**

**❾ Épernay, Champagne** France's champagne capital, Épernay, is the place to sample the country's best bubbly. **See p.207**

## ICONIC LANDSCAPES

**❶ Les Falaises d'Etretat, Normandy** The chalk cliffs, needles and arches of Étretat inspired Monet, Courbet, Flaubert and Maupassant in their day, and now offer a superb, if dizzying, coastal walk. **See p.261**

**❷ Les Volcans d'Auvergne** With their grassy slopes, cratered summits and ridgetops, the extinct volcanoes running across the Massif

Central create a mountain environment unlike any other. **See p.691**

**❸ Grande Cascade de Gavarnie, Pyrenees** France's tallest waterfall crashes 423 metres from the awesome Cirque de Gavarnie in the Pyrenees. **See p.609**

**❹ Gorge de l'Ardèche** Kayak down the magnificent Gorge de l'Ardèche, lined by 300-metre-tall limestone cliffs. Famous landmarks include the Pont d'Arc, the largest natural bridge in Europe. **See p.718**

**❺ Lavender fields, Provence** Immortalized in the paintings of Van Gogh and Cézanne, the lavender fields of the southeast are at their most fragrant in early summer. **See p.840**

**❻ Golfe de Porto, Corsica** The red porphyry cliffs of Corsica's wild northwest coast rise from a bay of exquisite cobalt blue to a wall of snow-streaked granite mountains. **See p.954**

**❼ Les Gorges du Verdon, Vaucluse** France's own Grand Canyon forms a spectacular trench in the Provençal limestone. **See p.849**

**❽ Mer de Glace, French Alps** Hop on the rack railway from Chamonix for a stupendous view of Europe's largest glacier. **See p.757**

CAMEMBERT ROAD SIGN

# Basics

# Getting there

The quickest way to reach France from most parts of the United Kingdom and Ireland is by air. From southern England, however, the Eurostar provides a viable alternative, making the journey from London to Paris in as little as two and a quarter hours. The Channel Tunnel is the most flexible option if you want to take your car to France, though cross-Channel ferries are usually cheaper. From the US and Canada a number of airlines fly direct to Paris, from where you can pick up onward connections. You can also fly direct to Paris from South Africa, while the best fares from Australia and New Zealand are generally via Asia.

Whether you are travelling by air, sea or rail, prices increasingly depend on how far in advance you book, but will also depend on the **season**. Fares are at their highest from around early June to the end of August, when the weather is best, drop during the "shoulder" seasons – roughly September to October and April to May – and are at their cheapest during the low season, November to March (excluding Christmas and New Year when prices are hiked up and seats are at a premium). Note also that flying at weekends can be more expensive; price ranges quoted below assume midweek travel, and include all taxes and surcharges.

## Flights from the UK and Ireland

Flights between the UK, Ireland and France are plentiful, even from regional airports, though industry consolidation and high oil prices mean that the bargain-basement fares of the budget airlines' heyday are much rarer than they were – so look out for special offers advertised on the airline websites or in the media. The main budget airlines are easyJet, flyBE and Ryanair, which between them cover forty or so airports across France, including Bergerac, Carcassonne, Chambéry, La Rochelle, Montpellier, Nantes, Perpignan, Toulon and Tours, as

well as more established hubs such as Paris, Lyon and Nice. Routes change frequently and some destinations are not served all year round, so again keep an eye on the airlines' websites. It's also worth double-checking exactly where the airport is in relation to your destination; Ryanair claims to fly to Paris, for example, but in reality flies to Beauvais, a 1hr 15min coach journey from Porte Maillot, west of the city. **Tickets** work on a quota system, and it's wise to book ahead for the cheapest fares. In theory it's still possible to travel for as little as £50/€62 return including taxes, if you're prepared to be flexible about routes and to go out of season – but surcharges for checked-in baggage, priority boarding or paying by credit card can all bump up the price considerably, so the price you actually pay will probably be higher than these figures.

It's worth checking out the **traditional carriers**, such as Air France, British Airways and Aer Lingus, which have streamlined their schedules and lowered prices in response to the budget airline challenge. Low-season return fares to Paris start at around £110 from London, £130 from Edinburgh and €105 from Dublin; to Nice you'll pay upwards of £100 from London and €125 from Dublin.

**Air France** flies direct to Paris Charles-de-Gaulle (CDG) several times daily from London Heathrow, Dublin and regional airports such as Birmingham and Manchester; its subsidiary Cityjet flies from London City to Paris Orly (ORY). Flights to most other French destinations involve a change at Paris. **British Airways** has several flights a day to Paris CDG from London Heathrow but its flights from provincial airports to Paris involve a change at London. BA also operates flights from London to Bordeaux, Lyon, Marseille, Nice and Toulouse. In Ireland, **Aer Lingus** offers nonstop flights from Dublin and Cork to Paris CDG; from Dublin to Bordeaux, Lyon, Marseille, Nice, Perpignan and Toulouse; and from Cork to Nice.

## Flights from the US and Canada

Most major airlines operate scheduled flights to Paris from the US and Canada. Air France has the most

---

## A BETTER KIND OF TRAVEL

At Rough Guides we are passionately committed to travel. We believe it helps us understand the world we live in and the people we share it with – and of course tourism is vital to many developing economies. But the scale of modern tourism has also damaged some places irreparably, and climate change is accelerated by most forms of transport, especially flying. All Rough Guides' flights are carbon-offset, and every year we donate money to a variety of environmental charities.

frequent service, with good onward regional connections and competitive fares that sometimes undercut US carriers; it also operates a codeshare with Delta. One possible disadvantage, if your destination is not Paris, is that while Air France transatlantic flights often terminate at Charles-de-Gaulle, domestic connections frequently depart from Orly, entailing an inconvenient transfer between the two airports. Other airlines offering **nonstop** services to Paris from a variety of US cities include: American Airlines from New York, Boston, Chicago, Dallas and Miami; Delta from Atlanta and Cincinnati; United from Chicago, Philadelphia and Washington DC and US Airways from Charlotte. Air Canada offers nonstop services to Paris from Montréal and Toronto, while Air Transat offers good-value scheduled and **charter flights** to Paris from a number of bases and to other destinations from Montréal, Québec or Toronto. Another option is to fly with a European carrier – such as British Airways, Iberia or Lufthansa – to its European hub and then continue on to Paris or a regional French airport.

Transatlantic **fares** to France have risen sharply of late, reflecting high fuel costs. An off-season midweek direct return flight to Paris can be US$940 before taxes from New York, US$1070 from Los Angeles and US$1080 from Houston. From Canada, prices to Paris start at around CAN$928 from Montréal or Toronto.

## Flights from Australia, New Zealand and South Africa

Most travellers from **Australia and New Zealand** choose to fly to France via London, although the majority of airlines can add a Paris leg (or a flight to any other major French city) to an Australia/New Zealand–Europe ticket. Flights via Asia or the Gulf States, with a transfer or overnight stop at the airline's home port, are generally the cheapest option; those routed through the US tend to be slightly pricier. Return **fares** start at around AUS$1900 from Sydney, AUS$1870 from Perth, AUS$1890 from Melbourne and NZ$2725 from Auckland.

From **South Africa**, Johannesburg is the best place to start, with Air France flying direct to Paris from around R8000 return; from Cape Town, they fly via Johannesburg or Amsterdam and are more expensive, starting at around R9000. BA, flying via London, costs upwards of R9000 from Johannesburg and R10,000 from Cape Town. SAA operates a codeshare with Lufthansa, routing via Frankfurt or Munich to Paris for around R9700.

## By train

**Eurostar** operates high-speed passenger trains daily from St Pancras International to France through the **Channel Tunnel**; many but not all services stop at either Ebbsfleet or Ashford in Kent (15min and 30min from London, respectively). There are 1–2 services an hour from around 5.30am to 9.15pm for Paris Gare du Nord; fast trains take 2hr 15min; Brussels-bound trains stop at Lille (1hr 20), where you can connect with TGV trains heading south to Bordeaux, Lyon and Marseille; some also stop at Calais (1hr). In addition, Eurostar runs direct trains from London to Disneyland Paris (daily during UK school holidays; otherwise daily except Tues & Sat; 2hr 40min), to Avignon (mid-July to early Sept; Sat; 5hr 30min), and a special twice-weekly ski service to Moutiers, Aime-la-Plagne and Bourg-St-Maurice in the French Alps (mid-Dec to mid-April; 7hr 5min–7hr 20min).

Standard **fares** from London to Paris or Lille start at £69 (£109 to Avignon) for a non-refundable, non-exchangeable return; availability is limited so it's best to book as early as possible. Another option is the non-refundable "semi-flexible" ticket (from £250/290 respectively), where you can change the dates for a fee. Similar non- and semi-flexible terms are offered at slightly higher prices (including a meal) if you book Standard Premier. Otherwise, you're looking at £490/480 for a fully refundable Business Premier ticket with no restrictions. Return fares to Disneyland Paris start at £69 for adults. Child fares apply for 4–11-year-olds while under-4s travel for free provided they travel on the lap of a fare-paying passenger.

**Tickets** can be bought online or by phone from Eurostar, as well as through travel agents and websites like ⓦlastminute.com. InterRail and Eurail **passes** (see p.29) entitle you to discounts on Eurostar trains. Under certain circumstances, you can also take your bike on Eurostar (below).

### By car via the Channel Tunnel

The simplest way to take your car to France from the UK is on one of the drive-on drive-off shuttle trains operated by **Eurotunnel**. The service runs continuously between Folkestone and Coquelles, near Calais, with up to four departures per hour (one every 1hr 30min from midnight–6am) and takes 35 minutes. It is possible to turn up and buy your ticket at the check-in booths, though you'll pay a premium and at busy times booking is strongly recommended; if you have a booking, you must arrive at least thirty minutes before departure. Note that Eurotunnel does not transport cars fitted with LPG or CNG tanks.

Standard **fares** start at £60 one-way if you book far enough ahead and/or travel off peak, rising to £157. Fully refundable and changeable FlexiPlus fares cost £149 each way for a short stay (up to 5 days) and £199 for longer periods. There's room for only six **bicycles** on any departure, so book ahead in high season – a standard return costs £32 for a bike plus rider.

### Rail passes

There is a variety of rail passes useful for travel within France, some of which need to be bought in your home country (for details of railcards that you can buy in France, see p.34). **Rail Europe** (see p.31) the umbrella company for all national and inter-national rail purchases, is the most useful source of information on availability and cost.

### InterRail Pass

**InterRail Passes** are only available to European residents, or those who have lived in a European country for at least six months, and you will be asked to provide proof of residency (and long-stay visa if applicable) before being allowed to buy one. They come in first or second-class senior (over 60), first- or second-class over-26 or second-class under-26 versions, and cover thirty European countries. Children from 4–12 years pay half; those under 4 travel free, though they may not get a seat.

There are two types of passes: **global** and **one-country**. The global pass covers all thirty countries with various options: five days travel in a ten-day period (under-26 £155/over-26 £237); ten days travel within a 22-day period (£228/£338); 15 days (£264/£374); 22 days (£292/438); and one month (£374/£565) continuous travel. Similarly, the one-country pass allows you to opt for various periods, ranging from three days in one month (£124/£182) to eight days in one month (£187/283). In each case, first-class passes are also available.

Inter Rail Passes do not include travel within your country of residence, though pass-holders are eligible for discounts on Eurostar and on ferries from Rosslare.

### Eurail Pass

**Eurail Passes** are not available to European residents but can once ordered can be delivered to a European address. Again, there are various options; the most useful are likely to be the **regional passes**, covering France with Benelux, Germany, Italy, Spain or Switzerland. The France-Italy pass offers four days of unlimited train travel

### TRAVELLING WITH PETS FROM THE UK

If you wish to take your dog (or cat) to France, the **Pet Travel Scheme (PETS)** enables you to avoid putting it in quarantine when re-entering the UK as long as certain conditions are met. Current regulations are available on the Department for Environment, Food and Rural Affairs (DEFRA) website ⓦdefra.gov.uk/wildlife-pets/pets/travel/index.htm or through the PETS Helpline (☎0870 241 1710).

within two months for €191 under-26/€252 adult travelling second class, or up to ten days within two months for €325 under-26/€424 adult. The Saverpass offers the same benefits for between two and five people travelling together.

## Ferries

Though slower than travelling by plane or via the Channel Tunnel, the ferries plying between Dover and Calais offer the cheapest means of travelling to France **from the UK** and are particularly conven-ient if you live in southeast England. If you're coming from the north of England or Scotland, you could consider the overnight crossing from Hull (13hr) to Zeebrugge (Belgium) operated by P&O Ferries. It's also worth bearing in mind that if you live west of London, the ferry services to Roscoff, St-Malo, Cherbourg, Caen, Dieppe and Le Havre can save a lot of driving time. **From Ireland**, putting the car on the ferry from Cork (14hr) or Rosslare (17hr 30min) to Roscoff in Brittany, or Rosslare to Cherbourg (19hr) in Normandy cuts out the drive across Britain to the Channel.

Ferry **prices** are seasonal and, for motorists, depend on the type of vehicle. In general, the further you book ahead, the cheaper the fare and it's well worth playing around with dates and times to find the best deals: midweek and very early or late sailings are usually cheapest. At the time of writing, one-way fares for a car and up to four passengers are available for £29 with DFDS on the Dover–Dunkerque and Dover-Calais routes. One-way fares from Ireland kick off at around €119 for a car and two adults.

Some ferry companies (but not DFDS) also offer fares for **foot passengers**, typically £40–50 return on cross-Channel routes; accompanying **bicycles** can usually be carried free.

## Buses

**Eurolines** runs regular services from London Victoria to forty French cities (fewer in winter), with up to eleven a day to Paris, crossing the Channel by ferry or Eurotunnel. Prices are lower than for the same journey by train, with adult return "Advance" fares (must be booked at least ten days in advance) starting at around £46 to Paris or Lille. If you're travelling frequently, a Eurolines Discount Card (three months £23/six months £43) will give you 25 percent off fares subject to certain restrictions. There's also a Eurolines Pass which offers Europe-wide travel between 50 European cities for fifteen or thirty days. Prices range from £159 for a fifteen-day youth pass in low season to £389 for a peak-season thirty-day adult pass.

## Airlines, agents and operators

There are a vast number of travel agents and tour operators offering holidays in France, with options varying from luxury, château-based breaks to adventure trips involving skiing and hiking. The following pages list the most useful contacts.

### AIRLINES

**Aer Lingus** Ⓦ aerlingus.com.
**Air Canada** Ⓦ aircanada.com.
**Air France** Ⓦ airfrance.com.
**Air Transat** Ⓦ airtransat.com.
**American Airlines** Ⓦ aa.com.
**British Airways** Ⓦ ba.com.
**Cathay Pacific** Ⓦ cathaypacific.com.
**Delta** Ⓦ delta.com.
**easyJet** Ⓦ easyjet.com.
**Emirates** Ⓦ emirates.com.
**flyBE** Ⓦ flybe.com.
**Jet2** Ⓦ jet2.com.
**KLM** Ⓦ klm.com.
**Lufthansa** Ⓦ lufthansa.com.
**Qantas** Ⓦ qantas.com.
**Ryanair** Ⓦ ryanair.com.
**Singapore Airlines** Ⓦ singaporeair.com.
**South African Airways** Ⓦ flysaa.com.
**United Airlines** Ⓦ united.com.
**US Airways** Ⓦ usairways.com.

### AGENTS AND OPERATORS

**Allez France** Ⓦ allezfrance.com. UK tour operator offering accommodation only as well as short breaks and other holiday packages throughout France.
**Arblaster & Clarke** UK ☎ 01730 263 111, Ⓦ winetours.co.uk. Wine-themed tours to all the great wine regions, from Champagne to Bordeaux.

**Austin-Lehman Adventures** US ☎ 1 800 575 1540, Ⓦ austinlehman.com. Good range of bike and walking tours all over France for family groups or solo travellers.
**Belle France** UK ☎ 01580 214 010, Ⓦ bellefrance.co.uk. Walking, cycling and boating holidays throughout France.
**Bonnes Vacances Direct** UK ☎ 0844 804 2000; Ⓦ bvdirect.co.uk. Agent for property owners in France for self-catering and B&B accommodation.
**Canvas Holidays** UK ☎ 0845 268 0827, Ⓦ canvasholidays.co.uk. Tailor-made caravan and camping holidays.
**Chez Nous** UK ☎ 0845 268 1102, Ⓦ cheznous.com. Thousands of self-catering and B&B properties online, including ski rentals.
**Corsican Places** UK ☎ 0845 330 2059, Ⓦ corsica.co.uk. Corsica specialists.
**Cycling for Softies** UK ☎ 0161 248 8282, Ⓦ cycling-for-softies .co.uk. Easy-going cycle holiday operator to rural France.
**Discover France** US ☎ 1-800-960-2221, Ⓦ discoverfrance.com. Self-guided cycling and walking holidays throughout France.
**Eurocamp** UK ☎ 0844 406 0402, Ⓦ eurocamp.co.uk. Camping holidays with kids' activities and single-parent deals.
**European Waterways** ☎ 0808 189 9777, Ⓦ ewaterways.co.uk. Wide range of river cruise options, from hotel barge cruises through Burgundy to boat hire or trips on the Loire.
**Fields Fairway** France ☎ +33 (0)3 21 33 65 64, Ⓦ fieldsfairway .co.uk. British-run, France-based company offering all-inclusive golfing holidays.
**France Afloat** UK ☎ 0870 011 0538, Ⓦ franceafloat.com. Canal and river cruises across France.
**French Affair** UK ☎ 020 7616 9990, Ⓦ frenchaffair.com. Wide range of self-catering accommodation in southern France and Corsica.
**French Travel Connection** Australia ☎ 02 9966 1177, Ⓦ frenchtravel.com.au. Offers large range of holidays to France.
**Headwater** UK ☎ 0845 154 5253, US ☎ 843 856 97716286, Australia ☎ 1300 363 055, Ⓦ headwater.com. UK-based operator offering walking, cycling, and canoeing tours throughout France, and cross-country skiing.
**Holiday France** Ⓦ holidayfrance.org.uk. Website that allows you to search for French tour operators by holiday type and location.
**HouseTrip** UK ☎ 0203 463 0087, Ⓦ housetrip.com. Holiday home rental website offering a wide range of affordable family accommodation with thousands of properties across rural France.
**Inntravel** UK ☎ 01653 617 001, Ⓦ inntravel.co.uk. Broad range of activity holidays, including riding, skiing, walking and cycling, as well as property rental.
**Keycamp Holidays** UK ☎ 0844 406 0200, Republic of Ireland ☎ 021 425 2300; Ⓦ keycamp.com. Caravan and camping holidays, including transport to France.
**Le Boat** US ☎ 1-866 734 5491, UK ☎ 0845 463 3594 Ⓦ leboat .com. Self-drive canal holidays all over France.
**Locaboat** UK ☎ 01756 706517, US ☎ 401 849 1112; Ⓦ locaboat .com. French company specializing in holidays on *pénichettes* (scaled-down replicas of commercial barges).
**North South Travel** UK ☎ 01245 608 291, Ⓦ northsouthtravel .co.uk. Friendly, competitive travel agency, offering discounted fares

worldwide. Profits are used to support projects in the developing world, especially the promotion of sustainable tourism.

## RAIL, CHANNEL TUNNEL AND BUS CONTACTS

**Eurail** Ⓦ eurail.com.
**Eurolines** UK Ⓣ 08717 818178, Ⓦ eurolines.co.uk.
**European Rail** UK Ⓣ 020 7619 1083, Ⓦ europeanrail.com.
**Eurostar** UK Ⓣ 08432 186 186, Ⓦ eurostar.com.
**Eurotunnel** UK Ⓣ 08443 35 35 35, Ⓦ eurotunnel.com.
**International Rail** UK Ⓣ 0871 231 0790, Ⓦ international
-rail.com.
**Rail Europe** (SNCF French Railways) UK Ⓣ 08448 484 064; US
Ⓣ 1-800 622 8600, Canada Ⓣ 1-800 361 7245, Ⓦ raileurope.com.
**Rail Plus** Australia Ⓣ 1300 555 003, New Zealand Ⓣ 09 377 5415;
Ⓦ railplus.com.au.
**Trainseurope** UK Ⓣ 0871 700 7722, Ⓦ trainseurope.co.uk.
**World Travel** South Africa Ⓣ 011 628 2319, Ⓦ worldtravel.co.za.

## FERRY CONTACTS

**Brittany Ferries** UK Ⓣ 0871 244 0744, Ⓦ brittany-ferries.co.uk;
Republic of Ireland Ⓣ 021 427 7801, Ⓦ brittanyferries.ie.
**Condor Ferries** UK Ⓣ 0845 609 1024, Ⓦ condorferries.co.uk.
**DFDS** UK Ⓣ 0871 574 7235 (Dover-Calais, Dover-Dunkerque),
Ⓦ dfdsseaways.co.uk.
**Direct Ferries** UK Ⓣ 08718 900 900 Ⓦ directferries.co.uk.
**EuroDrive** UK Ⓣ 0844 371 8021, Ⓦ eurodrive.co.uk.
**Ferry Savers** UK Ⓣ 0844 371 8021, Ⓦ ferrysavers.com.
**Irish Ferries** Republic of Ireland Ⓣ 0818 300 400,
Ⓦ irishferries.com.
**LD Lines** UK Ⓣ 0844 576 8836, Ⓦ ldlines.com.
**MyFerryLink** UK Ⓣ 0844 248 2100, Ⓦ myferrylink.com.
**P&O Ferries** UK Ⓣ 08716 64 21 21, Ⓦ poferries.com.

# Getting around

**With the most extensive train network in Western Europe, France is a great country in which to travel by rail. The national rail company, SNCF (Société Nationale des Chemins de Fer), runs fast, efficient trains between the main towns. Buses cover rural areas, but services can be sporadic, with awkward departure times. If you want to get off the beaten track the best option is to have your own transport.**

## By train

**SNCF** (Ⓣ 3635, €0.34/min; Ⓦ voyages-sncf.com) operates one of the most efficient, comfortable and user-friendly railway systems in the world. Staff are generally courteous and helpful, and its trains – for the most part, fast, clean and reliable – continue, in spite of the closure of some rural lines, to serve most of the country.

### Trains

Pride and joy of the French rail system is the high-speed **TGV** (*train à grande vitesse*), capable of speeds of up to 300kph, and its offspring Eurostar. The continually expanding TGV network has its main hub at Paris, from where main lines head north to Lille, east to Strasbourg and two head south: one to Marseille and the Mediterranean, the other west to Bordeaux and the Spanish frontier. Spur lines service Brittany and Normandy, the Alps, Pyrenees and Jura.

Bookable online only, **iDTGV** (Ⓦ idtgv.com) trains compete with low-cost airlines and have quiet areas, a bar, facilities to watch DVDs and play computer games. Available on routes to more than 30 destinations from Paris including Bordeaux, Mulhouse, Marseille, Nice, Perpignan, Toulouse, Strasbourg and Hendaye, travel times can be changed for an additional fee. **Intercité** is the catch-all brand name for trains providing intercity services on routes not yet upgraded to TGV. Though not as fast, they have decent facilities including restaurant cars. Intercité sleeper services link Paris, Toulouse, the Alps and the south. Local services are covered by **TER** regional express trains.

Aside from the regular lines there are a number of special **tourist trains**, usually not part of the SNCF system or covered by normal rail passes, though some offer a discount to rail-pass holders. One of the most popular is the spectacular Petit Train Jaune, which winds its way up through the Pyrenees (see p.632).

### Tickets and fares

**Tickets** can be bought online (see above) or at train stations (*gare SNCF*). If you have language problems or there are long queues at the counter, note that touch-screen vending machines with instructions in English sell tickets for express services in most stations; separate vending machines for regional (TER) services have basic English labelling. All tickets – but not passes or computerized tickets printed out at home – must be validated in the orange machines located beside the entrance to the platforms, and it's an offence not to follow the instruction *Compostez votre billet* ("validate your ticket").

**Timetables** covering particular destinations are available free at stations. The word *Autocar* (often

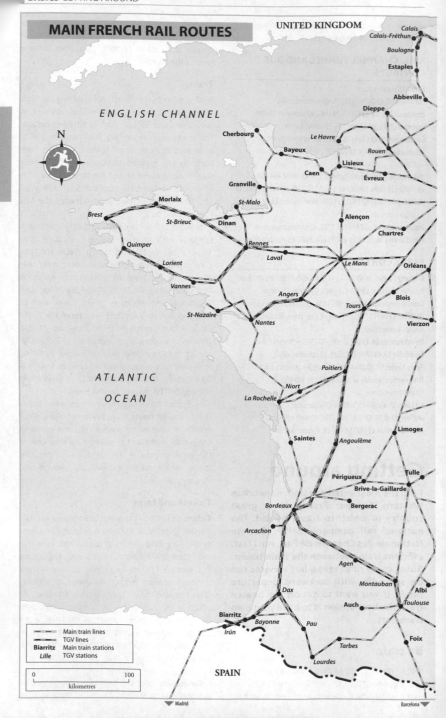

**MAIN FRENCH RAIL ROUTES**

UNITED KINGDOM

Calais
Calais-Fréthun
Boulogne
Estaples
Abbeville

ENGLISH CHANNEL

Dieppe

Cherbourg
Le Havre
Bayeux
Rouen
Lisieux
Caen
Évreux
Granville
Alençon
Chartres
St-Malo
Dinan
Morlaix
St-Brieuc
Rennes
Le Mans
Orléans
Brest
Laval
Quimper
Lorient
Blois
Angers
Tours
Vannes
Vierzon
St-Nazaire
Nantes

ATLANTIC
OCEAN

Poitiers

Niort
La Rochelle

Limoges

Saintes
Angoulême

Périgueux
Tulle
Brive-la-Gaillarde

Bordeaux
Bergerac

Arcachon

Agen

Montauban
Albi
Dax
Toulouse
Auch
Biarritz
Bayonne
Pau
Foix
Irún
Tarbes

Lourdes

SPAIN

N

Main train lines
TGV lines
**Biarritz** Main train stations
*Lille* TGV stations

0 — 100
kilometres

Madrid

Barcelona

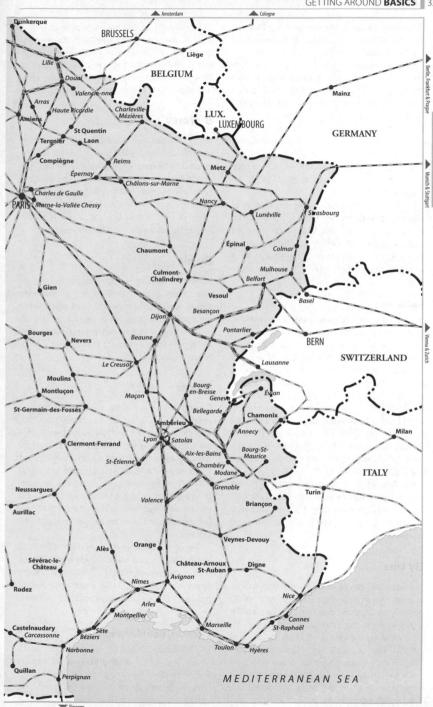

Dunkerque

Amsterdam     Cologne

BRUSSELS

Lille     Liège

Douai     BELGIUM

Valencie-nne

Arras     Haute Picardie     Charleville-Mézières     Mainz

Amiens     St Quentin     LUX.     GERMANY
Tergnier     Laon     LUXEMBOURG

Compiègne     Reims     Metz

Épernay     Châlons-sur-Marne

Charles de Gaulle     Nancy
PARIS     Marne-la-Vallée Chessy     Lunéville     Strasbourg

Chaumont     Épinal     Colmar

Gien     Culmont-Chalindrey     Mulhouse
     Belfort
     Vesoul     Basel

Dijon     Besançon

Bourges     Nevers     Beaune     Pontarlier     BERN

Le Creusot     Lausanne     SWITZERLAND

Moulins
Montluçon     Maçon     Bourg-en-Bresse     Évian
     Genève
St-Germain-des-Fossés     Bellegarde     Chamonix

     Ambérieu     Annecy     Milan
Clermont-Ferrand     Lyon     Satolas
     St-Étienne     Aix-les-Bains     Bourg-St-Maurice
     Chambéry     ITALY
Neussargues     Modane
     Valence     Grenoble     Turin
Aurillac
     Briançon

     Veynes-Devouy

     Orange     Château-Arnoux
Alès     St-Auban     Digne
Sévérac-le-Château     Nîmes     Avignon
Rodez     Nice
     Arles
Castelnaudary     Montpellier     Cannes
Carcassonne     Sète     Marseille     St-Raphaël
     Béziers
     Narbonne     Toulon     Hyères
Quillan
     Perpignan

MEDITERRANEAN SEA

Figueres

Berlin, Frankfurt & Prague

Munich & Stuttgart

Vienna & Zürich

abbreviated to *car*) on the timetable signifies that the service is covered by an SNCF bus, on which rail tickets and passes are valid.

**Fares** are cheaper if you travel off-peak (*période bleue* or blue period) rather than during peak hours (*période blanche* or white period); peak period generally means Monday mornings and Friday and Sunday evenings. One-way iDTGV fares from Paris to Nice start at around €45, and from as little as €26 one-way to Toulouse. Tickets are sold a maximum of three months in advance on national trains and four months in advance on TER. You can choose your seat on TGV; reservation is obligatory on certain Intercité services.

On certain mainline routes a limited number of **discount tickets**, known as *tarifs Prems* can be bought up to ninety days in advance; these are non-refundable and cannot be changed. Prices start at €25. It's worth checking the Voyages SNCF website (ⓦvoyages-sncf.com) for last-minute offers, too.

### Rail passes

SNCF offers a range of **travel cards**, which are valid for one year, and can be purchased online, by phone (☏3635), through accredited travel agents and from main *gares SNCF*. Anyone aged 26 to 59 years, for example, is eligible for the Carte Escapades (€76). This guarantees a minimum reduction for journeys of at least 200km of 25 percent on standard peak fares, rising to 50 percent off-peak; you need to either travel at weekends or stay away for a Saturday or Sunday night. Similar deals are available for 12- to 25-year olds (Carte 12–25; €50), over-60s (Carte Senior; €57) and families with children under the age of 12 (Carte Enfant +; €71).

Non-Europeans also have the option of picking up the **France Rail Pass** (starting from $242/$178 for three days unlimited travel in one month) before arriving in France. The pass is available from 3 to 9 day periods.

## By bus

SNCF operates bus services between train stations in areas no longer accessible by rail. Additionally, private, municipal and departmental buses can be useful for local and cross-country journeys – for instance along the long coast of the Var, much of which is not served by train. If you want to see much outside the main towns be prepared for early starts and careful planning – the timetable is often constructed to suit market and school hours. As a rule, buses are cheaper and slower than trains.

Larger towns usually have a *gare routière* (bus station), often next to the *gare SNCF*. However, the private bus companies don't always work together and you'll frequently find them leaving from an array of different points (the local tourist office should be able to help locate the stop you need).

## By ferry

Most of France's coastal islands, which are concentrated around Brittany and the Côte d'Azur can only be reached by **ferry**. Local companies run services, with timetables and prices varying according to season. Some routes have a reduced schedule or cease to operate completely in winter months, while in high season booking ahead is recommended on all but the most frequent services.

## By air

Arriving by air from outside Europe, you may be able to get a good deal on add-on **domestic flights**. Air France operates the most routes within the country, although competition is hotting up, with the likes of easyJet running internal discount flights from Paris or Lyon to Biarritz, Brest, Corsica, Nice and Toulouse.

## By car

**Driving** in France can be a real pleasure, with a magnificent network of *autoroutes* providing sweeping views of the countryside. If you're in a hurry, it's worth paying motorway tolls to avoid the often congested toll-free *routes nationales* (marked, for example, RN116 or N116 on signs and maps), many of which have been reclassified as *routes départmentales* in recent years. Many of the more minor *routes départementales* (marked with a D) are uncongested and make for a more scenic – if slow – drive.

There are times when it's wiser not to drive at all: in big cities; around major seaside resorts in high season; and at peak holiday migrations such as the beginning and end of the month-long August holiday, and the notoriously congested weekends nearest July 14 and August 15.

### Licences, petrol and tolls

US, Canadian, Australian, New Zealand, South African and all EU **driving licences** are valid in France for up to twelve months, though an International Driver's Licence makes life easier. The minimum driving age is 18 and you must hold a full licence. Drivers are required to carry their licence with them when driving, and you should also have the insurance and registration documents with you in the car.

All the major car manufacturers have garages and service stations in France, which can help if you run into mechanical difficulties. You'll find them listed in the Yellow Pages of the phone book under "*Garages d'automobiles*"; for breakdowns, look under "*Dépannages*". If you have an accident or theft, contact the local police – and keep a copy of their report in order to file an insurance claim. Within Europe, most car **insurance policies** cover taking your car to France; check with your insurer. However, you're advised to take out extra cover for motoring assistance in case your car breaks down.

Note that **petrol stations** in rural areas tend to be few and far between, and those that do exist usually open only during normal shop hours – don't count on being able to buy petrol at night and on Sunday. Some stations are equipped with automated 24-hour pumps, but many of these only accept French bank cards. Most sell unleaded (*sans plomb*), and diesel (*gazole* or *gasoil*); some also sell LPG and an increasing number are selling SP95-E10, a form of unleaded which includes 10 percent ethanol. Not all cars can run on this, so check with the manufacturer before using it.

Most *autoroutes* have **tolls**: rates vary, but to give you an idea, travelling by motorway from Calais to Montpellier costs roughly €63; pay in cash or by credit card (get in a lane marked CB at the toll-gates). You can work out routes and costs of both petrol and tolls online at the useful ⓦviamichelin.com. UK motorists can use the Liber-T automatic tolling lanes if their cars are fitted with the relevant transponder; to register in advance for a transponder and for more information see ⓦsaneftolling.co.uk.

### Rules of the road

Since the French **drive on the right**, drivers of right-hand-drive cars must adjust their **headlights** to dip to the right. This is most easily done by sticking on glare deflectors, which can be bought at most motor accessory shops, at the Channel ferry ports or the Eurostar terminal and on the ferries. It's more complicated if your car is fitted with High-Intensity Discharge (HID) or halogen-type lights; check with your dealer about how to adjust these well in advance. Dipped headlights must be used in poor daytime visibility.

All non-French vehicles must display their **national identification letters** (GB, etc) either on the number plate or by means of a sticker, and all vehicles must carry a red warning triangle, a reflective safety jacket and (since July 2012) a single use breathalyser. You are also strongly advised to carry a spare set of bulbs, a fire extinguisher and a first-aid kit. **Seat belts** are compulsory and children under 10 years must travel in an approved child seat, harness or booster appropriate to their age and size.

In built-up areas the law of *priorité à droite* – **giving way** to traffic coming from your right, even when it is coming from a minor road – still sometimes applies, including at some roundabouts. A sign showing a yellow diamond on a white background indicates that you have right of way, while the same sign with a diagonal black slash across it warns you that vehicles emerging from the right have priority. *Cédez le passage* means "Give way"; *vous n'avez pas la priorité* means "You do not have right of way".

If you have an **accident** while driving, you must fill in and sign a *constat d'accident* (declaration form) or, if another car is also involved, a *constat aimable* (jointly agreed declaration); in the case of a hire car, these forms should be provided with the car's insurance documents.

Unless otherwise indicated **speed limits** are: 130kph (80mph) on *autoroutes*; 110kph (68mph) on dual carriageways; 90kph (55mph) on other roads; and 50kph (31mph) in towns. In wet weather, and for drivers with less than two years' experience, these limits are 110kph (68mph), 100kph (62mph) and 80kph (50mph) respectively, while the town limit remains constant. Many towns and villages have introduced traffic calming and 30kph limits particularly in town centres where there are lots of pedestrians. Fixed and mobile radars are now widely used. The **alcohol limit** is 0.05 percent (0.5

---

### ROAD INFORMATION

Up-to-the-minute information regarding traffic jams and road works throughout France can be obtained from the Bison Futé free-dial recorded information service (☎0800 100 200; French only) or their website ⓦwww.bison-fute.equipement.gouv.fr. For information regarding *autoroutes*, you can also consult the bilingual website ⓦautoroutes.fr. Once on the *autoroute*, tune in to the national 107.7FM information station for 24-hour music and updates on traffic conditions.

grams per litre of blood), and random breath tests and saliva tests for drugs are common. There are stiff **penalties** for driving violations, ranging from on-the-spot **fines** for minor infringements to the immediate confiscation of your licence and/or your car for more serious offences. Note that radar detectors and SatNav systems that identify the location of speed traps are illegal in France.

## Car rental

To rent a car in France you must be over 21 (25 with some agencies) and have driven for at least a year. Car rental costs upwards of €80 a day and €150–250 for a week for the smallest car; reserve online well in advance to get the best price. You'll find the big-name international firms – Avis, Hertz and so on – represented at airports and in most major towns and cities, though. Local firms can be cheaper but they won't have the agency network for one-way rentals and you should check the small print. Unless you specify otherwise, you'll get a car with manual (stick shift) transmission.

### CAR-RENTAL AGENCIES

**Avis** Ⓦ avis.com.
**Argus Car Hire** Ⓦ arguscarhire.com.
**Auto Europe** Ⓦ autoeurope.com.
**Europcar** Ⓦ europcar.com.
**Europe by Car** Ⓦ europebycarblog.com.
**Hertz** Ⓦ hertz.com.
**Holiday Autos** Ⓦ holidayautos.com.

## By scooter and motorbike

**Scooters** are ideal for pottering around locally. They're easy to rent – places offering bicycles often also rent out scooters. Expect to pay in the region of €35 and up a day for a 50cc machine. If you are over 24 years old, you don't need a licence for a 50cc moped – just passport/ID – but otherwise you'll need a driving licence. For anything 50cc–125cc you'll need to have held a driving licence for at least

two years regardless of your age, and for anything over 125cc you need a full **motorbike** licence. Rental prices are around €60–70 a day for a 125cc bike and expect to leave a hefty deposit by cash or credit card – over €1000 is the norm – which you may lose in the event of damage or theft. Crash helmets are compulsory on all bikes, and the headlight must be switched on at all times. For bikes over 125cc it is compulsory to wear reflective clothing. It is recommended to carry a first-aid kit and a set of spare bulbs.

# By bicycle

**Bicycles** (*vélos*) have high status in France, where cyclists are given respect both on the roads and as customers at restaurants and hotels. In addition, local authorities are actively promoting cycling, not only with urban cycle lanes, but also with comprehensive networks in rural areas (often on disused railways). Most towns have well-stocked repair shops, but if you're using a foreign-made bike with non-standard wheels, it's a good idea to carry spare tyres.

You can take your bike free of charge without reservation on many TER and Intercité trains; look out for trains marked on the timetable with a bicycle symbol. Folding bikes travel free on TGV and Intercité trains if they're packed into a bag no more than 90cm x 120cm; for non-folding bikes you'll have to pay a €10 fee and it may be necessary to book a space in advance. Another option is to have your bicycle delivered to your destination for a fee of €80. Eurostar has similar arrangements. On ferries, bikes count as your "vehicle" and attract much lower charges than taking a car across. Some airlines, such as British Airways, will not charge an additional fee for a bicycle if it's within your free baggage allowance; others now charge – check when making your booking.

Bikes – usually mountain bikes (*vélos tout-terrain* or VTT) or hybrid bikes (*vélos tout-chemin* or VTC) – are often available to **rent** from campsites and

---

## BUY-BACK LEASING SCHEMES

If you are not resident in an EU country and will be touring France for between 17 days (21 in the case of Peugeot and Renault) and six months, it's worth investigating the special **buy-back leasing schemes** operated by Peugeot ("Peugeot Open Europe"), Citroën ("Citroën DriveEurope") and Renault ("Renault Eurodrive"). Under these deals, you purchase a new car tax-free and the manufacturer guarantees to buy it back from you for an agreed price at the end of the period. In general, the difference between the purchase and re-purchase price works out considerably less per day than the equivalent cost of car hire. Further details are available from Peugeot, Citroën and Renault dealers and online at Ⓦ peugeot-openeurope .com, Ⓦ citroendriveeurope.com.au and Ⓦ renault-eurodrive.com.

## CANAL AND RIVER TRIPS

With over 7000km of navigable rivers and canals, **boating** is one of the most relaxed ways of exploring France. Expect to pay between around €800 and €2500 per week, depending on the season and level of comfort, for a four- to six-person boat. There are many companies (see p.30) offering boating holidays or you could contact the Fédération des Industries Nautiques (📞01 44 37 04 00, 🌐france-nautic.com). If you want to bring your own boat, contact Voies Navigables de France (VNF) (📞0800 863 000, 🌐vnf.fr) has information in English on maximum dimensions, documentation, regulations and so forth. The **principal areas** for boating are Brittany, Burgundy, Picardy-Flanders, Alsace and Champagne. The eighteenth-century Canal de Bourgogne and 300-year-old Canal du Midi in particular are fascinating examples of early canal engineering, the latter being a UNESCO World Heritage site.

hostels, as well as from specialist cycle shops and some tourist offices for around €15 per day. Many cities, including Lyon, Marseille, Nice and Paris, have public self-service bike hire schemes with hire points scattered widely throughout the city.

# Accommodation

**At most times of the year, you can turn up in any French town and find a room or a place in a campsite. Booking a couple of nights in advance can be reassuring, however, as it saves you the effort of trudging round and ensures that you know what you'll be paying; many hoteliers, campsite managers and hostel managers speak at least a little English. In most places, you'll be able to get a simple double for €35–40, though expect to pay at least €50 for a reasonable level of comfort. Paris and the Côte d'Azur are more expensive, however, with equivalent rates of roughly €60 and €100. We've detailed a selection of hotels throughout this book, and given a price for each (see box, p.38); as a general rule the areas around train stations have the highest density of cheap hotels.**

**Problems** may arise between mid-July and the end of August, when the French take their own vacations en masse. During this period, hotel and hostel accommodation can be hard to come by, particularly in the coastal resorts, and you may find yourself falling back on local tourist offices for help.

All **tourist offices** can provide lists of hotels, hostels, campsites and bed-and-breakfast possibilities, and some offer a booking service, though they can't guarantee rooms at a particular price. With campsites, you can be more relaxed about finding an empty pitch, though it may be more difficult

with a caravan or camper van or if you're looking for a place on the Côte d'Azur.

## Hotels

French hotels are graded in six bands, from zero for the simplest through one, two, three and four to five for the most exclusive. The price more or less corresponds to the number of stars, though the system is a little haphazard, having more to do with ratios of bathrooms per guest and so forth than genuine quality; some unclassified and single-star hotels can be very good. Single rooms – if the hotel has any – are only marginally cheaper than doubles, so sharing slashes costs, especially since many hotels willingly provide rooms with extra beds for three or more people.

Big cities tend to have a good variety of cheap establishments; in small towns and rural areas, you may not be so lucky, particularly as the cheaper, family-run hotels find it increasingly hard to survive. Swanky resorts, particularly those on the Côte d'Azur, have very high **prices** in July and August, but even these are still cheaper than Paris, which is far more expensive than the rest of the country. If you're staying for more than three nights in a hotel it's sometimes possible to negotiate a lower price, particularly out of season.

**Breakfast** will often add anything between €6 and €30 per person to a bill – though there is no obligation to take it.

Note that many **family-run hotels** close for two or three weeks a year in low season. In smaller towns and villages they may also close for one or two nights a week, usually Sunday or Monday. Details are given where relevant in the text, but dates change from year to year; the best precaution is to phone ahead to be sure.

A very useful option, especially if you're driving and are looking for somewhere late at night, are the **chain hotels** located at motorway exits and on the

## ACCOMMODATION PRICES

Throughout this book we give a headline price for every accommodation reviewed. This indicates the **lowest rack rate price for a double/twin room during high season** (usually July & August). Single rooms, where available, usually cost between 60 and 80 percent of a double or twin; in many budget chain hotels in particular there is no discount for single occupancy of a double or triple bed room. At **hostels**, where relevant, we have given the price of a double room and of a dormitory bed – and at **campsites**, the cost of two people, a pitch and a vehicle, unless otherwise stated.

outskirts of major towns. They may be soulless, but you can usually count on a decent and reliable standard. Among the cheapest (from around €30 for a three-person room with communal toilets and showers) is the one-star Formule 1 chain (☎0892 685 685, ⓦhotelformule1.com). Other budget chains include B&B (☎0298 337 529, ⓦhotel-bb .com), the slightly more comfortable Première Classe (☎0892 688 123, ⓦpremiereclasse.fr) and Ibis Budget (formerly Etap; ☎0892 688 900 ⓦetaphotel.com). Slightly more upmarket are Ibis (☎0892 686 686, ⓦibishotel.com) and Campanile (ⓦcampanile.fr), where en-suite rooms with satellite TV and often broadband internet access cost from around €60–120.

There are a number of well-respected **hotel federations** in France. The biggest and most useful of these is Logis de France (☎01 45 84 70 00, ⓦlogishotels.com), an association of over 2800 hotels nationwide. They produce a free annual guide, available in French tourist offices, from Logis de France itself and from member hotels. Two other, more upmarket federations worth mentioning are Châteaux & Hôtels de France (☎01 72 72 92 02, ⓦchateauxhotels.com) and the Relais du Silence (☎01 70 23 81 63, ⓦrelaisdusilence.com), both of which offer high-class accommodation in beautiful older properties, often in rural locations.

## Bed and breakfast and self-catering

In country areas, in addition to standard hotels, you will come across **chambres d'hôtes** – bed-and-breakfast accommodation in someone's house, château or farm. Though the quality varies widely, on the whole standards are pretty high, and the best can offer more character and greater value for money than an equivalently priced hotel. If you're lucky, the owners may also provide traditional home cooking and a great insight into French life. Prices generally range between €50 and €120 for two people including breakfast; payment is almost always expected in cash. Some

offer meals on request (*tables d'hôtes*), usually evenings only.

If you're planning to stay a week or more in any one place it's worth considering renting self-catering accommodation. This will generally consist of self-contained country cottages known as *gîtes*. Many *gîtes* are in converted barns or farm outbuildings, though some can be quite grand. "Gîtes Panda" are *gîtes* located in a national park or other protected area and are run on environmentally friendly lines.

You can get lists of both *gîtes* and *chambres d'hôtes* from the government-funded agency Gîtes de France (☎01 49 70 75 75; ⓦgites-de-france .com), or search on their website for accommodation by location or theme (for example, *gîtes* near fishing or riding opportunities). In addition, every year the organization publishes a number of national guides, such as *Nouveaux Gîtes* (listing new addresses); these guides are available to buy online or from departmental offices of Gîtes de France, as well as from bookstores and tourist offices. Tourist offices will also have lists of places in their area which are not affiliated to Gîtes de France.

## Hostels

At around €12–26 per night for a **dormitory bed**, usually with breakfast thrown in, youth hostels – *auberges de jeunesse* – are invaluable for single travellers of any age on a budget. Some now offer rooms, occasionally en suite, but they don't necessarily work out cheaper than hotels – particularly if you've had to pay a taxi fare to reach them. However, many allow you to cut costs by eating in the hostels' cheap canteens, while in a few you can prepare your own meals in the communal kitchens. In the text we give the cost of a dormitory bed.

In addition to those belonging to the two French hostelling associations listed below, there are now also several independent hostels, particularly in Paris (for example MIJE ⓦmije.com). At these, dorm beds cost €30–40, with breakfast sometimes extra.

## Youth hostel associations

Slightly confusingly, there are two rival **French hostelling associations** – the *Fédération Unie des Auberges de Jeunesse* (FUAJ: ☎01 44 89 87 27, 🖥fuaj .org) and the much smaller *Ligue Française* (LFAJ: ☎01 44 16 78 78, 🖥auberges-de-jeunesse.com). In either case, you normally have to show a current Hostelling International (HI) **membership card**. It's usually cheaper and easier to join before you leave home, provided your national youth hostel association is a full member of HI. Alternatively, you can purchase an HI card in certain French hostels (€7 HI Welcome tariff for foreign visitors at FUAJ hostels, €11 under 26/€16 over 26 at LFAJ hostels).

## Gîtes d'étape and refuges

In the countryside, another hostel-style option exists in the form of **gîtes d'étape**. Aimed primarily at hikers and long-distance bikers, *gîtes d'étape* are often run by the local village or municipality and are less formal than hostels, providing bunk beds and primitive kitchen and washing facilities for around €15–25 per person. They are marked on the large-scale IGN walkers' maps and listed in the individual Topo guides. In addition, mountain areas are well supplied with **refuge huts**, mostly run by the Fédération Français des Clubs Alpins et de Montagne (FFCAM; ☎01 53 72 87 00, 🖥ffcam.fr). These huts, generally staffed only in summer, offer dorm accommodation and meals, and are the only available shelter once you are above the villages. Costs are around €17–26 for the night, or half of this if you're a member of a climbing organization affiliated to FFCAM, plus around €20–25 for breakfast and dinner, which is good value when you consider that in some cases supplies have to be brought up by mule or helicopter. Outside the summer season, some refuges offer very limited, basic shelter at reduced cost.

More information can be found online at 🖥gites -refuges.com, where you can download four printable regional *Gîtes d'Étape et Réfuges* guides for €5 per region.

## Camping

Practically every village and town in France has at least one **campsite** to cater for the thousands of people who spend their holiday under canvas. Most sites open from around Easter to September or October. Most are graded – from one to four stars – by the local authority. One-star sites are basic, with toilets and showers (not necessarily with hot water) but little else, and standards of cleanliness are not always brilliant. Facilities improve with more stars: at the top end of the scale, four-star sites are far more spacious, have hot-water showers and electrical hook-ups; most will also have a swimming pool (sometimes heated), washing machines, a shop and sports facilities, and will provide refreshments or meals in high season. A further designation, **Camping Qualité** (🖥campingqualite.com), indicates campsites with particularly high standards of hygiene, service and privacy, while the **Clef Verte** (🖥laclefverte.org) label is awarded to sites (and also hostels and hotels) run along environmentally friendly lines. For those who really like to get away from it all, **camping à la ferme** – on somebody's farm – is a good, simple option. Lists of sites are available at local tourist offices or from Gîtes de France (see p.38).

The Fédération Française de Camping et de Caravaning has some 1200 affliated sites and (☎01 42 72 84 08, 🖥ffcc.fr) publishes an annual **guide** (€12.50) details of which can also be found online on the excellent Camping France website (🖥campingfrance.com), which lists 11,000 sites. If you'd rather have everything organized for you, note that there are a number of companies that specialize in camping holidays (see p.30).

Most campsites charge per emplacement and per person, usually including a car, with extra charges for electricity. As a rough guide, two people with a tent and car might pay as little as €10 per day at an out-of-the-way rural one-star site, or as much as €45 at a four-star on the Côte d'Azur in July or August. In peak season it's wise to book ahead, and note that at many of the big sites the emphasis is more on letting caravans or chalet bungalows.

Lastly, a word of caution: always ask permission before **camping rough** (*camping sauvage*) on anyone's land. If the dogs don't get you, the guns might – farmers have been known to shoot first, and ask later. Camping on public land is not officially permitted and is often strongly discouraged, particularly in the south where in summer the risk of forest fires is high.

# Food and drink

**France is famous for producing some of the most sublime food in the world, whether it's the rarefied delicacies of haute cuisine or the robust, no-nonsense fare served up at country inns. Nevertheless, French cuisine has taken a bit of a**

**knocking in recent years. The wonderful ingredients are still there, as every town and village market testifies, but those little family restaurants serving classic dishes that celebrate the region's produce – and where the bill is less than €25 – are increasingly hard to find. Don't be afraid to ask locals for their recommendations; this will usually elicit strong views and sound advice.**

In the complex world of **haute cuisine**, where the top chefs are national celebrities, a battle has long been raging between traditionalists, determined to preserve the purity of French cuisine, and those who experiment with different flavours from around the world. At this level, French food is still brilliant – in both camps – but can be astronomically expensive: at a three-star Michelin restaurant, even the set lunch menu is likely to cost €90, though you might get away with less than half that at a – still very impressive – one-star restaurant.

As for **foreign cuisines**, North African is perhaps the best bet, but you'll also find Caribbean (known as *Antillais*), Vietnamese, Chinese and Indian, though French versions of spicy favourites tend to be more bland than you may be used to.

## Breakfast and lunch

A croissant or *pain au chocolat* (a chocolate-filled, light pastry) in a café or bar, with tea, hot chocolate or coffee, is generally the most economical way to eat breakfast, costing from €4. If there are no croissants left, it's perfectly acceptable to go and buy your own at the nearest bakery or patisserie. The standard hotel breakfast comprises bread and/or pastries, jam and a jug of coffee or tea, and orange juice if you're lucky, from around €6. More expensive places might offer a breakfast buffet or even hot dishes cooked to order.

The main meal of the day is traditionally eaten at **lunchtime**, usually between noon and 2pm. Midday, and sometimes in the evening, you'll find places offering a *plat du jour* (daily special) for €8.50–13, or *formules* (or simply *menus*), limited menus typically offering a main dish and either a starter or a dessert for a set price. **Crêpes**, or pancakes with fillings, served at ubiquitous crêperies, are popular lunchtime food. The savoury buckwheat variety (*galettes*) provide the main course; sweet, white-flour crêpes are dessert. **Pizzerias**, usually *au feu du bois* (baked in wood-fired ovens), are also very common. They are somewhat better value than crêperies, but quality and quantity vary greatly.

For **picnics**, the local outdoor market or supermarket will provide you with almost everything you need, from tomatoes and avocados to cheese and pâté. Cooked meat, prepared snacks, ready-made dishes and assorted salads can be bought at charcuteries (delicatessens), which you'll find even in most small villages, and at supermarket cold-food counters. You purchase by weight, or you can ask for *une tranche* (a slice), *une barquette* (a carton) or *une part* (a portion) as appropriate.

---

## CHEESE

Charles de Gaulle famously commented "How can you govern a country that has 246 kinds of cheese?" For serious **cheese**-lovers, France is the ultimate paradise. Other countries may produce individual cheeses which are as good as, or even better than, the best of the French, but no country offers a range that comes anywhere near them in terms of sheer inventiveness. In fact, there are officially over 350 types of French cheese, and the methods used to make them are jealously guarded secrets. Many cheese-makers have successfully protected their products by gaining the right to label their produce **AOP** (*appellation d'origine protégée*), covered by laws similar to those for wines, which – among other things – controls the amount of cheese that a particular area can produce. As a result, the subtle differences between French local cheeses have not been overwhelmed by the industrialized uniformity that has plagued other countries.

The best, or most traditional, restaurants offer a well-stocked *plateau de fromages* (cheeseboard), served at room temperature with bread, but not butter. Apart from the ubiquitous Brie, Camembert and numerous varieties of goat's cheese (*chèvre*), there will usually be one or two local cheeses on offer – these are the ones to go for. If you want to buy cheese, local markets are always the best bet, while in larger towns you'll generally find a *fromagerie*, a shop with dozens of varieties to choose from. We've indicated the best regional cheeses throughout the book.

## Snacks

Outside tourist areas the opportunities for snacking on the run are not always as plentiful or obvious in France as in Britain or North America; the local boulangerie is often the best bet. Popular snacks include croques-monsieur or croques-madame (variations on the toasted cheese-and-ham sandwich) – on sale at cafés, brasseries and many street stands – along with frites (fries), crêpes, galettes, gauffres (waffles), glaces (ice creams) and all kinds of fresh-filled baguettes (which usually cost between €3 and €7 to take away). For variety, in bigger towns you can find Tunisian snacks like brick à l'œuf (a fried pastry with an egg inside), merguez (spicy North African sausage) and Middle Eastern falafel (deep-fried chickpea balls served in flat bread with salad). Wine bars are good for regional sausages and cheese, usually served with brown bread (pain de campagne).

## Regional dishes

French cooking is as varied as its landscape, and differs vastly from region to region. In **Provence**, in close proximity to Italy, local dishes make heavy use of olive oils, garlic and tomatoes, as well as Mediterranean vegetables such as aubergines (eggplant) and peppers. In keeping with its close distance to the sea, the region's most famous dish is bouillabaisse, a delicious fish stew from Marseille. To the southwest, in **Languedoc** and **Pays Basque**, hearty cassoulet stews and heavier meals are in order, with certain similarities to Spanish cuisine. **Alsace**, in the northeast, shows Germanic influences in dishes such as choucroute (sauerkraut), and a hearty array of sausages. **Burgundy**, famous for its wines, is the home of what many people consider classic French dishes such as coq au vin and boeuf bourguignon. In the northwest, **Normandy** and **Brittany** are about the best places you could head for seafood, as well as for sweet and savoury crêpes and galettes. Finally, if you're in the **Dordogne**, be sure to sample its famous foie gras or pricey truffles (truffes).

For more on which regional dishes to try, see the boxes at the start of each chapter.

## Vegetarian food

On the whole, **vegetarians** can expect a somewhat lean time in France. Most cities now have at least one specifically vegetarian restaurant, but elsewhere your best bet may be a crêperie, pizzeria or North African restaurant. Otherwise you may have to fall back on an omelette, salad or crudités (raw vegetables) in an ordinary restaurant. Sometimes restaurants are willing to replace a meat dish on the fixed-price menu (menu fixe); at other times you'll have to pick your way through the carte. Remember the phrase Je suis végétarien(ne); est-ce qu'il y a quelques plats sans viande? ("I'm a vegetarian; are there any non-meat dishes?"). **Vegans**, however, should probably stick to self-catering.

## Drink

In France, drinking is done at a leisurely pace whether it's a prelude to food (apéritif) or a sequel (digestif), and **café-bars** are the standard places to do it. By law the full price list, including service charges, must be clearly displayed. You normally pay when you leave, and it's perfectly acceptable to sit for hours over just one cup of coffee, though in this case a small tip will be appreciated.

### Wine

French wines, drunk at just about every meal and social occasion, are unrivalled in the world for their range, sophistication, diversity and status. With the exception of the northwest of the country and the mountains, wine is produced almost everywhere. Champagne, Burgundy and Bordeaux are the most famous wine-producing regions, closely followed by the Loire and Rhône valleys, and the up-and-coming Languedoc region.

**Choosing wine** is an extremely complex business and it's hard not to feel intimidated by the seemingly innate expertise of all French people. Many appellations are mentioned in the text, but trusting your own taste is the best way to go. The more interest you show, the more helpful advice you're likely to receive.

The best way of **buying wine** is directly from the producers (vignerons) at their vineyards or at Maisons or Syndicats du Vin (representing a group of wine-producers), or Coopératifs Vinicoles (producers' co-ops). At all these places you can usually sample the wines first. It's best to make clear at the start how much you want to buy (particularly if it's only one or two bottles) and you'll not be popular if you drink several glasses and then fail to make a purchase. The most economical option is to buy en vrac, which you can do at some wine shops (caves), filling an easily obtainable plastic five- or ten-litre container (usually sold on the premises) straight from the barrel. Supermarkets often have good bargains, too.

## FINE FRENCH WINES

The most obvious guide to the quality of a wine is its **classification**, and in 2012 the system used to classify French wines changed. At the lowest level is now **vin de France**, suitable for everyday drinking, replacing the old **vin de table** but now allowing growers to provide information on vintage and grape variety. Then there's **Indication Géographique Protégée** (IGP), a new intermediate category indicating quaffable fare. IGP replaces the old Vin de Pays category. AOP – **appellation d'origine protégée** – is the highest category, taking the place of the old AOC classification. Within this category a number of exceptional wines qualify for the superior labels of **Premier Cru** or **Grand Cru**.

### WINE REGIONS

Within each wine region there's enormous diversity, with differences generated by the type of grape grown (there are over sixty varieties), the individual skill of the *vigneron* (producer) and something the French refer to as *terroir*, an almost untranslatable term meaning the combination of soil, lie of the land and climate.

**Burgundy's** luscious reds and crisp white wines can be truly sublime. The best wines come from the Côte de Nuits, producing Burgundy's headiest reds, made from the richly fruity Pinot Noir grape, and the Côte de Beaune, which yields the region's great white burgundy, made from the buttery Chardonnay grape. To the south, the Côte Chalonnaise and the Mâconnais also produce good-quality whites, while further south still the Beaujolais region is famous for its light, fruity reds. Out on its own, further north, is the Chablis region, known for its wonderfully fresh, flinty whites.

**The Bordeaux** wine-producing region, three times the size of Burgundy, produces a huge quantity of very fine, medium-bodied reds, delicious sweet whites, notably Sauternes, and dry whites of varying quality. The best-known area is the Médoc, known for its long-lived, rich reds, including such legendary names as Margaux and Lafitte, made from a blend of wines, chiefly the blackcurranty Cabernet Sauvignon. Graves produces the best of the area's dry white wines, while St-Emilion, where the Merlot grape thrives, yields warmer, fruitier wines.

**Champagne's** status as *the* luxury celebration drink goes back to a time when it was used to anoint French kings, and at its best is an extraordinarily complex and rich sparkling wine. This far north – Champagne is just an hour from Paris – where good weather cannot be relied on year in year out, the only way to achieve consistent quality is by blending the produce of different vineyards and vintages. The leading Champagne houses, known as *maisons*, such as Bollinger and Moët et Chandon, blend up to sixty different wines and allow them to age for some years before selling. Needless to say, they produce the best and most expensive champagnes; those of smaller growers are more variable in quality.

**The Loire's** wines tend to be rather overlooked, probably because their hallmark is subtlety and elegance rather than intensity and punch. Sauvignon Blanc is the dominant white grape variety, as manifested in the dry, fragrant Sancerre and the smoky Pouilly-Fumé, arguably the region's finest whites. Steely Muscadet, made from the hardy Melon de Bourgogne grape, is not to everyone's taste, but the best (try Sèvre-et-Maine) make a great accompaniment to seafood. The region's top reds include the light, aromatic Chinon and Bourgueil.

**The Rhône** is best known for its warm, flavoursome reds such as the blackberry-scented Hermitages, the peppery Gigondas and most famously of all the rich, spicy Châteauneuf-du-Pape.

**The Languedoc** has the largest area of vineyards in the world, too many of them, unfortunately, producing rather mediocre wine, though recently some great-quality wines have been emerging, such as the heady, full-bodied reds from Faugères and Collioure.

The basic wine terms are: *brut*, very dry; *sec*, dry; *demi-sec*, sweet; *doux*, very sweet; *mousseux*, sparkling; *méthode champenoise*, mature and sparkling.

### Beer and spirits

Familiar light Belgian and German brands, plus French brands from Alsace, account for most of the **beer** you'll find. Draught beer (*à la pression*) – very often Kronenbourg – is the cheapest drink you can have next to coffee and wine; *un pression* or *un demi* (0.33 litre) will cost around €3. For a wider choice of draught and bottled beer you need to go to the special beer-drinking establishments such as the English- and Irish-style pubs found in larger towns and cities. A small bottle at one of these places can set you back double what you'd pay in an ordinary café-bar. Buying bottled or canned bear in supermarkets is, of course, much cheaper.

**Spirits**, such as cognac and armagnac, and liqueurs are consumed at any time of day, though in far smaller quantities these days thanks to the clampdown on drink-driving. *Pastis* – the generic name of aniseed drinks such as Pernod and Ricard – is served diluted with water and ice (*glace* or *glaçons*). It's very refreshing and not expensive. Among less familiar names, try Poire William (a pear-flavoured eau de vie) or Marc (a spirit distilled from grape pulp). Measures are generous, but they don't come cheap: the same applies for imported spirits like whisky (*Scotch*). Two drinks designed to stimulate the appetite – *un apéritif* – are *pineau* (cognac and grape juice) and kir (white wine with a dash of Cassis – blackcurrant liqueur – or with champagne instead of wine for a Kir Royal). Cognac, armagnac and Chartreuse are among the many aids to digestion – *un digestif* – to relax over after a meal. Cocktails are served at most late-night bars, discos and clubs, as well as upmarket hotel bars and at every seaside promenade café; they usually cost upwards of €8.

### Soft drinks, tea and coffee

You can buy cartons of unsweetened **fruit juice** in supermarkets, although in cafés the bottled (sweetened) nectars such as apricot (*jus d'abricot*) and blackcurrant (*cassis*) still hold sway. Fresh orange (*jus d'orange*) or lemon juice (*citron pressé*) is much more refreshing – for the latter, the juice is served in the bottom of a long ice-filled glass, with a jug of water and a sugar bowl to sweeten it to your taste. Other soft drinks to try are syrups (*sirops*) – mint or grenadine, for example, mixed with water. The standard fizzy drinks of lemonade (*limonade*), Coke (*coca*) and so forth are all available, and there's also no shortage of bottled mineral **water** (*eau minérale*) or spring water (*eau de source*) – whether sparkling (*gazeuse*) or still (*plate*) – from the big brand names to the most obscure spa product. But there's not much wrong with the tap water (*l'eau de robinet*), which will usually be brought free to your table if you ask for it. The only time you shouldn't drink the tap water is if the tap is labelled *eau non potable*.

**Coffee** is invariably espresso – small, black and very strong. *Un café* or *un express* is the regular; *un crème* is with milk; *un grand café* or *un grand crème* are large versions. *Un déca* is decaffeinated, now widely available. Ordinary **tea** (*thé*) – Lipton's, nine times out of ten – is normally served black (*nature*) or with a slice of lemon (*limon*); to have milk with it, ask for *un peu de lait frais* (some fresh milk). *Chocolat chaud* – **hot chocolate** – unlike tea, lives up to the high standards of French food and drink and is very commons in cafés and bars. After meals, herb teas (*infusions* or *tisanes*), offered by most restaurants, can be soothing. The more common ones are *verveine* (verbena), *tilleul* (lime blossom), *menthe* (mint) and *camomille* (camomile).

# The media

**French newspapers and magazines are available from newsagents (maisons de la presse) or any of the ubiquitous street-side kiosks, while TV, satellite and otherwise, is easy to track down in most forms of accommodation. A limited range of British and US newspapers and magazines is widely available in cities and occasionally in even quite small towns.**

## Newspapers and magazines

Of the **French daily papers**, *Le Monde* (Ⓦ lemonde.fr) is the most intellectual; it's widely respected, and somewhat austere, though it does now carry such frivolities as colour photos. Conservative, and at times controversial, *Le Figaro* (Ⓦ lefigaro.fr) is the most highly regarded of the more Right-wing papers. *Libération* (Ⓦ liberation.fr), founded by Jean-Paul Sartre in the 1960s, is moderately Left-wing, pro-European, independent and more colloquial, while rigorous Left-wing criticism of the government comes from *L'Humanité* (Ⓦ humanite.fr), the Communist Party paper, though it is struggling to survive. The top-selling **tabloid**, predictably more readable and a good source of news, is *Aujourd'hui* (Ⓦ aujourdhui-en-france.fr, published in Paris as *Le Parisien*), while *L'Équipe* (Ⓦ lequipe.fr) is dedicated to sports coverage. The widest circulations are enjoyed by the **regional dailies**, of which the most important is the Rennes based *Ouest-France* (Ⓦ ouest-france.fr). For visitors, these are mainly of interest for their listings.

Weekly **magazines** of the *Newsweek/Time* model include the wide-ranging and Left-leaning *Le Nouvel Observateur* (ⓦnouvelobs.com), its Right-wing counterpoint *L'Express* (ⓦlexpress.fr) and the centrist with bite, *Marianne* (ⓦmarianne2.fr). The best investigative journalism is found in the weekly satirical paper *Le Canard Enchaîné* (ⓦlecanardenchaine.fr), while *Charlie Hebdo* (ⓦcharliebedo.fr) is roughly equivalent to the UK's *Private Eye*. There's also *Paris Match* (ⓦparismatch.com), for gossip about stars and royalty, and, of course, the French versions of *Vogue*, *Elle* and *Marie-Claire*, and the relentlessly urban *Biba*, for women's fashion and lifestyle.

**English-language** newspapers which are printed locally, such as the *International Herald Tribune*, are available on the day of publication. Others usually arrive the following day, and the prices are all heavily marked up.

## Television and radio

French **terrestrial TV** has six channels: three public (France 2, France 3 and Arte/France 5); one subscription (Canal Plus – with some unencrypted programmes); and two commercial (TF1 and M6). Of these, TF1 (ⓦtf1.fr) and France 2 (ⓦfrance2.fr) are the most popular channels, showing a broad mix of programmes.

In addition there are any number of **cable and satellite channels**, including CNN, BBC World, Euronews, Eurosport, Planète (which specializes in documentaries) and Jimmy (*Friends* and the like in French). The main French-run music channel is MCM.

**Radio France** (ⓦradiofrance.fr) operates eight stations. These include France Culture for arts, France Info for news and France Musique for classical music. Other major stations include Europe 1 (ⓦeurope1.fr) for news, debate and sport. Radio France International (RFI, ⓦrfi.fr) broadcasts in French and various foreign languages, including English; programmes are broadcast on FM to Africa or you can listen on the website or through your mobile phone.

# Festivals

**It's hard to beat the experience of arriving in a small French village, expecting no more than a bed for the night, to discover the streets decked out with flags and streamers, a band playing in the square and the entire population out celebrating the feast of their patron saint. As well as nationwide celebrations such as the Fête de la Musique (around June 21; ⓦfetedelamusique. culture.fr), Bastille Day (July 14) and the Assumption of the Virgin Mary (Aug 15), there are any number of festivals – both traditional and of more recent origin – held in towns and villages throughout France. For more information see ⓦculture.fr and ⓦviafrance.com.**

## Festival calendar

### JANUARY AND FEBRUARY

**Nantes** La Folle Journée (late Jan to early Feb; ⓦfollejournee.fr).

### FEBRUARY TO APRIL

**Menton** Fête du Citron (two weeks following Mardi Gras, forty days before Easter; ⓦfeteducitron.com).
**Nice Carnival** (Feb–March; ⓦnicecarnaval.com).

### MAY

**Cannes** Festival de Cannes (ⓦfestival-cannes.com); international film festival.
**Les Saintes-Maries-de-la-Mer** Fête de Ste Sarah (May 24–25); Romany festival.
**Nîmes** La Féria de Nîmes (Pentecost, seven weeks after Easter); bullfights.

### JUNE

**Annecy** Festival International du Film d'Animation (early June; ⓦannecy.org); animated films.
**Bordeaux** Fête le Vin (late June in even-numbered years; ⓦbordeaux-fete-le-vin.com).
**Châlons-en-Campagne** Festival Furies (early June; ⓦfestival-furies.com); circus and street theatre.
**Lyon** Les Nuits de Fourvière (June and July; ⓦnuitsdefourviere.fr); performance arts.
**Montpellier** Montpellier Danse (mid-June to early July; ⓦmontpellierdanse.com).
**Paris** La Marche des Fiertés Lesbienne, Gai, Bi & Trans (late June; ⓦinter-lgbt.org).
**Samois-sur-Seine** Festival Django Reinhardt (late June; ⓦfestivaldjangoreinhardt.com); jazz.
**Paris** Festival de St-Denis (May–June; ⓦfestival-saint-denis.com); classical and world music festival.
**Strasbourg** Festival de Musique de Strasbourg (ⓦfestival-strasbourg.com); classical music.
**Uzès** Uzès Danse (ⓦuzesdanse.fr); contemporary dance.
**Vienne** Jazz à Vienne (late June to early July; ⓦjazzavienne.com).

### JULY

**Aix-en-Provence** Festival International d'Art Lyrique (ⓦfestival-aix.com); classical music and opera.

**Alès** Cratère/Surfaces (early July; 🕸 lecratere.fr); street theatre.

**Arles** Les Suds à Arles (mid-July; 🕸 suds-arles.com); world music.

**Avignon** Festival d'Avignon (🕸 festival-avignon.com); contemporary dance and theatre.

**Beaune** Festival International d'Opéra Baroque (🕸 festival beaune.com).

**Belfort** Eurockéennes (late June to early July; 🕸 eurockeennes.fr); rock and indie music.

**Carhaix** Festival des Vieilles Charrues (mid-July; 🕸 vieillescharrues .asso.fr); rock music festival.

**Chalon-sur-Saône** Chalon dans la Rue (third week July; 🕸 chalondanslarue.com); street theatre.

**Colmar** Festival International de Colmar (early July; 🕸 festival-colmar.com); classical music.

**Gannat** (near Vichy) Les Cultures du Monde (late July; 🕸 gannat.com).

**Grenoble** Rencontres du Jeune Théâtre Européen (early July; 🕸 crearc.fr); contemporary theatre.

**Juan-les-Pins** Jazz à Juan (mid-July; 🕸 jazzjuan.com).

**La Rochelle** Festival International du Film (late June to early July; 🕸 festival-larochelle.org); Francofolies (mid-July; 🕸 wwwfrancofolies.fr); contemporary French music.

**La Roque d'Anthéron** Festival International de Piano (mid-July to mid-Aug; 🕸 festival-piano.com).

**Nice** Jazz Festival (late July; 🕸 nicejazzfestival.fr).

**Orange** Chorégies d'Orange (July; 🕸 choregies.asso.fr); opera.

**Prades** Festival Pablo Casals (late July to mid-Aug; 🕸 prades-festival-casals.com); chamber music.

**Reims** Flâneries Musicales d'Été (late June to mid-July: 🕸 flaneriesreims.com); open-air concerts.

**Rennes** Les Tombées de la Nuit (early July; 🕸 lestombeesdelanuit .com); concerts, cinema and performance arts.

**Saintes** Festival de Saintes (mid-July; 🕸 abbayeauxdames.org); classical music.

**Vaison-la-Romaine** Vaison Danse (mid- to late July; 🕸 vaison-danses.com); contemporary dance.

## AUGUST

**Aurillac** Festival International de Théâtre de Rue (🕸 aurillac.net); street theatre.

**Lorient** Festival Interceltique (early Aug; 🕸 festival-interceltique .com); Celtic folk festival.

**Menton** Festival de Musique (late July to early Aug: 🕸 musique-menton.fr); chamber music.

**Mulhouse** Festival Météo (mid- to late Aug; 🕸 festival-meteo.fr); jazz.

**Paris** Rock en Seine (late Aug; 🕸 rockenseine.com).

**Périgueux** Mimos (late July to early Aug; 🕸 mimos.fr); international mime festival.

**Quimper** Semaines Musicales (🕸 semaines-musicales-quimper .org); baroque, classical and contemporary music.

**St-Malo** La Route du Rock (mid-Aug; 🕸 laroutedurock.com).

## SEPTEMBER

**Limoges** Les Francophonies en Limousin (late Sept to early Oct; 🕸 lesfrancophonies.com); contemporary francophone theatre, dance and music.

**Lyon** Biennale de la Dance (next in 2014; 🕸 biennaledeladanse.com).

**Paris** Biennial des Antiquaires (next in 2014; 🕸 www.sna-france .com) antiques fair; Jazz à la Villette (late Aug to early Sept; 🕸 citedelamusique.fr); Festival d'Automne (mid-Sept to mid-Dec; 🕸 festival-automne.com); theatre, concerts, dance, films and exhibitions.

**Perpignan** Visa pour l'Image (early to mid-Sept; 🕸 visapourlimage.com); international photojournalism.

**Puy-en-Velay** Fête Renaissance du Roi de l'Oiseau (mid-Sept; 🕸 roideloiseau.com); historical pageants, fireworks and re-creations.

**Strasbourg** Musica (late Sept to early Oct; 🕸 festival-musica.org); contemporary music.

## OCTOBER

**Bastia** Les Musicales (🕸 musicales-de-bastia.com); chanson and world music.

**Nancy** Jazz Pulsations (🕸 nancyjazzpulsations.com).

**Paris** Foire International d'Art Contemporain (mid- to late Oct; 🕸 fiac.com).

## NOVEMBER AND DECEMBER

**Rennes** Rencontres Transmusicales (early Dec; 🕸 lestrans.com); contemporary music.

**Strasbourg** Jazz d'Or (Nov; 🕸 www.jazzdor.com).

# Sports and outdoor activities

**France has much to offer sports fans, whether spectator or participant. It's not difficult to get tickets for football and rugby matches, while the biggest event of all, the Tour de France, is free. And if you prefer to participate, there's a host of activities and adventure sports available.**

## Spectator sports

More than any cultural jamboree, it's **sporting events** that excite the French – particularly cycling, football, rugby and tennis. In the south, bullfighting and the Basque game of pelota are also popular. At the local, everyday level, the rather less gripping but ubiquitous game of *boules* is the sport of choice.

### Cycling

The sport the French are truly mad about is **cycling**. It was, after all, in Paris's Palais Royale gardens in

1791 that the precursor of the modern bicycle, the *célerifère*, was presented; the French can also legitimately claim the sport of cycle racing as their own, with the first event, a 1200-metre sprint, held in Paris in 1868 – won by an Englishman.

The world's premier cycling race is the **Tour de France**, held over three weeks in July and covering around 3500 kilometres. The course changes each year, but always includes some truly arduous mountain stages and time trials, and ends on the Champs-Élysées. An aggregate of each rider's times is made daily, the overall leader wearing the coveted yellow jersey (*maillot jaune*). Huge crowds turn out to cheer on the cyclists and the French president himself presents the jersey to the overall winner. The last French cyclist to win the Tour was Bernard Hinault in 1985, while Bradley Wiggins, the 2012 winner, was the first Brit to clinch the title since 1903.

Other classic long-distance bike races include the **Paris–Roubaix**, instigated in 1896 and held in April, which is reputed to be the most exacting one-day race in the world; the **Paris–Brussels** (Sept), held since 1893; and the rugged seven-day **Paris–Nice** event (March). Details for all the above can be found at ⓦletour.fr.

## Football

**Football** (soccer) is France's number one team sport. After its legendary win at the 1998 World Cup, the national team's chequered recent history reached its nadir at the 2010 World Cup in South Africa, when the players refused to train after Nicolas Anelka was expelled from the squad for verbally abusing coach Raymond Domenech; a disastrous World Cup performance subsequently ended with defeat 2-1 by the host nation and an ignominious exit from the competition in the first round. In the Euros in 2012, they were equally diffident, knocked out by eventual victors Spain in the quarter finals.

The **domestic game** has been on the up in recent years, and average attendances have improved. The leading club sides include AS Monaco, Olympique Lyonnais and Olympique de Marseille. For the latest information visit the website of the *Ligue de Football Professionel* at ⓦlfp.fr.

**Tickets** to see domestic clubs are available either from specific club websites, or in the towns where they are playing; ask at local tourist offices. To watch the national team, you can get tickets online at ⓦfff.fr (Fédération Française de Football), or try ⓦfrancebillet.com. Prices tend to start at around €10–15.

## Rugby

Although most popular in the southwest, **rugby** enjoys a passionate following throughout France. The France rugby team is continually successful in European tournaments while in the **World Cup** clash they have reached the final three times, losing to New Zealand in 1987 and 2011, and to Australia in 1999. More international compitition is provided by the **Six Nations** tournament – the other five nations being England, Ireland, Italy, Scotland and Wales. France has been the most consistent team in recent years, having won the competition sixteen times, shared it a further eight times and gained the Grand Slam title in 2002, 2004 and 2010.

**Domestic clubs** to watch out for include Toulouse (record-breaking four-time winners of the Europe-wide Heineken Cup), Paris's Stade Français, Perpignan and Brive, Agen, and the Basque teams of Bayonne and Biarritz, which still retain their reputation as keepers of the game's soul.

**Tickets** for local games can be bought through the clubs themselves, with prices starting around €10. For bigger domestic and international games, they are available online at ⓦfrancebillet.com. Information can be found on the Fédération Française de Rugby's website (ⓦwww.ffr.fr).

## Pelota

In the Basque country (and also in the nearby Landes), the main draw for crowds is **pelota**, a lethally (sometimes literally) fast variety of team

---

## SPORTING CALENDAR

**January** Monte Carlo Car Rally (ⓦacm.mc).
**February–March** Six Nations rugby tournament (Paris; ⓦrbs6nations.com).
**April** Paris Marathon (ⓦparismarathon.com)
**May** Roland Garros International Tennis Championship (Paris; ⓦrolandgarros.com); Monaco Formula 1 Grand Prix (ⓦacm.mc).
**June** Le Mans 24-hour car rally (ⓦlemans.org).
**July** Tour de France (ⓦletour.fr).
**September:** Le Mans 24-hour motorcycle rally (ⓦlemans.org).
**October** Grand Prix de l'Arc de Triomphe (Paris; ⓦprixarcdetriomphe.com).

handball or raquetball played in a walled court with a ball of solid wood. The most popular form today is played with bare hands in a two-walled court called a *fronton*. In other varieties wooden bats are used or wicker slings strapped to the players' arms. Ask at local tourist offices for details of where to see the game played.

### Bullfighting

In and around the Camargue, the number-one sport is **bullfighting**. Different from the Spanish version, the *course camarguaise* (W ffcc.info) involves variations on the theme of removing cockades from the base of the bull's horns, and it's generally the fighters, rather than the bulls, who get hurt. Further west, particularly in the Landes *département*, you'll come across the similar *courses landaises (W www .courselandaise.org)*, where men perform acrobatics with the by no means docile local cows.

Spanish bullfights, known as *corridas*, do take place – and draw capacity crowds – in southern France. The major events of the year are the Féria de Nîmes (see p.641) at Pentecost (Whitsun) and the Easter *féria* at Arles (p.830). See the local press or ask at tourist offices for details of where to pick up tickets.

### Boules

In every town or village square, particularly in the south, you'll see beret-clad men playing *boules* or its variant, *pétanque* (in which contestants must keep both feet on the ground when throwing). Although more women are taking up *boules*, at competition level it remains very male-dominated: there are café or village teams and endless championships.

## Outdoor activities

France provides a fantastically wide range of outdoor activities. Most have a national federation (listed in the text where relevant), which can provide information on local clubs.

### Walking and climbing

France is covered by a network of some 180,000km of long-distance footpaths, known as *sentiers de grande randonnée* or **GRs**. They're signposted and equipped with campsites, refuges and hostels (*gîtes d'étape*) along the way. Some are real marathons, like the GR5 from the coast of Holland to Nice, the trans-Pyrenean GR10 and the magnificent GR20 in Corsica (see p.952). There are also thousands of shorter *sentiers de promenade et de randonnée*, the **PRs**, as well as nature walks and many other local

footpaths. Note that in the south, many routes are subject to closure in summer at times of high forest fire risk.

Each GR and many PRs are described in the **Topo-guide series** (available outside France in good travel bookshops), which give a detailed account of each route, including maps, campsites, refuges, sources of provisions, and so on. In France, the guides are available from bookshops and some tourist offices, or direct from the principal French walkers' association, the Fédération Française de la Randonnée Pédestre (T 01 44 89 93 90, W ffrandonnee.fr). In addition, many tourist offices have guides to local footpaths.

**Mountain climbing** is possible all year round, although bear in mind that some higher routes will be snowbound until quite late in the year, and require special equipment such as crampons and ice axes; these shouldn't be attempted without experience or at least a local guide. Accommodation when mountain climbing comes in the form of refuges (see p.39).

No matter where you are walking, make sure you have your own water supplies, or find out locally if you'll be able to fill up your water bottles on the way. You'll also need decent footwear, waterproofs and a map, compass and possibly GPS system. Finally, don't forget sunblock, sunglasses and a hat.

In mountain areas associations of professional **mountain guides**, often located in the tourist office, organize walking expeditions for all levels of experience. In these and more lowland areas, particularly the limestone cliffs of the south and west, you'll also find possibilities for **rock climbing** (*escalade*). For more information contact the Fédération Française de la Montagne et de l'Escalade (W ffme.fr).

**Walking holidays** are popular in France, and there are many tour operators (see p.30) offering enticing packages.

### Cycling

There are around 60,000km of marked cycle paths (*pistes cyclables*) in France. Many towns and cities have established cycle lanes, while in the country-side there are an increasing number of specially designated **long-distance cycle routes** (*véloroutes* and *voies vertes*). Burgundy is particularly well served, with an 800km circuit, while the Loire à Vélo cycle route runs the length of the Loire valley from Nevers to St Nazaire. The Fédération Française de Cyclisme website (W ffc.fr) has useful information in French on mountain-biking sites and tourist offices can provide details of local cycle ways; the Fédération Française de Cyclo-tourisme website (**W** ffct.org) provides links to local cycling clubs, and lists local trips by region. IGN sells various cycling guides through its website; their France-wide 1:100,000 maps are the best option for cyclists (see p.53).

A large number of tour operators (see p.30) specialize in French cycle holidays.

## Skiing and snowboarding

Millions of visitors come to France to go **skiing** and **snowboarding**, whether its downhill, cross-country or ski-mountaineering. It can be an expensive sport to arrange independently, however, and the best deals are often from package operators (see p.30). These can be arranged in France or before you leave (most travel agents sell all-in packages). Though it's possible to ski from early November through to the end of April at high altitudes, peak season is February and March.

The best skiing and boarding is generally in the **Alps** (see box, p.733). The higher the resort the longer the season, and the fewer the anxieties you'll have about there being enough snow. The foothills of the Alps in **Provence** offer skiing on a smaller scale; snow may be not as reliable. The **Pyrenees** are a friendlier range of mountains, less developed (though that can be a drawback if you want to get in as many different runs as possible per day) and warmer, which means a shorter season and – again – less reliable snow.

**Cross-country skiing** (*ski de fond*) is being promoted hard, especially in the smaller ranges of the Jura and Massif Central. It's easier on the joints, but don't be fooled into thinking it's any less athletic. For the really experienced and fit, though, it's a good way of getting about, using snowbound GR routes to discover villages still relatively uncommercialized. Several independent operators organize **ski-mountaineering courses** in the French mountains (see p.30).

Lift **passes** start at around €30 a day, but can reach €50 in the pricier spots; six-day passes cost from €140 to around €250. **Equipment** hire is available at most resorts, and comes in at around €20 per day for skis and boots, while a week's hire will generally set you back anything from €60–130, but can climb to €200 for the most high-tech or stylish gear.

The Fédération Française de Ski (**T** 04 50 51 40 34, **W** ffs.fr) provides links to local clubs, while **W** france-montagnes.com is a good overall source of **information** in English, with links to all the country's ski resorts.

## Adventure sports

**Hang-gliding** and **paragliding** are popular in the Hautes-Alpes of Provence, the Pyrenees and Corsica. Prices start at around €60 for a tandem trip; contact local tourist offices for more information.

**Caving** is practised in the limestone caverns of southwest France and in the gorges and ravines of the Pyrenees, the Alps and the Massif Central. You'll need to make an arrangement through a local club; they usually organize beginner courses as well as half- or full-day outings. For more information, contact the Fédération Française de Spéléologie (**T** 04 72 56 09 63, **W** ffspeleo.fr).

As for all adventure sports, it is important to make sure that your **insurance** (see p.52) covers you for these rather more risky activities.

## Horseriding

**Horseriding** is an excellent way to explore the French countryside. The most famous and romantic region for riding is the flat and windswept Camargue at the Rhône Delta, but practically every town has an equestrian centre (*centre équestre*) where you can ride with a guide or unaccompanied. **Mule-** and **donkey-trekking** are also popular, particularly along the trails of the Pyrenees and Alps. An hour on horseback costs from around €20; a day's horse- or donkey-trekking will cost €50 or more. Lists of **riding centres** and events are available from the Comité National de Tourisme Équestre (**W** ffe.com/tourisme), or from local tourist offices.

## Watersports and activities

France's extensive coastline has been well developed for recreational activities, especially in the south. In the towns and resorts of the Mediterranean coast, you'll find every conceivable sort of beachside activity, including boating, sea-fishing and diving, and if you don't mind high prices and crowds, the clear-blue waters and sandy coves are unbeatable. The wind-licked western Mediterranean is where **windsurfers** head to enjoy the calm saltwater inlets (*étangs*) that typify the area. The Atlantic coast is good for **sailing**, particularly around Brittany, while the best **surfing** (Fédération Française de Surf; **W** surfingfrance.com) is in Biarritz; further north, Anglet, Hossegor and Lacanau regularly host international competitions. Corsica and the Côte d'Azur – which has a number of World War II-era wrecks – are popular for **diving**; contact the Fédération Française d'Études et de Sports Sous-Marins (**T** 04 91 33 99 31, **W** ffessm.fr) for more information.

Most towns have a **swimming pool** (*piscine*), though outdoor pools tend to open only in the height of summer. You may be requested to wear a bathing cap and men to wear trunks (not shorts), so come prepared. You can also swim at many river beaches (usually signposted) and in the real and artificial lakes that pepper France. Many lakes have leisure centres (*bases de plein airs* or *centres de loisirs*) at which you can rent pedaloes, windsurfers and dinghies, as well as larger boats and, on the bigger reservoirs, jet-skis.

**Canoeing** (Fédération Française de Canoë-Kayak; @ ffck.org) is very popular in France, and in summer practically every navigable stretch of river has outfits renting out boats and organizing excursions. The rivers of the southwest (the Dordogne, Vézère, Lot and Tarn) in particular offer tremendous variety. **Canal-boating** (see p.436), particularly in the Loire and Burgundy, is also a favourite water-based activity.

# Shopping

**France in general is a paradise for shoppers. Even outside Paris, most main towns have excellent department stores – usually a Galeries Lafayette – as well as a host of independent shops which make superb targets for window-shopping (known as lèche-vitrines, or literally "window-licking" in French).**

**Food** is a particular joy to shop for; well-stocked supermarkets are easy to find, while on the outskirts of most towns of any size you'll come across at least one *hypermarché*, enormous supermarkets selling everything from food to clothes and garden furniture. The most well-known chains include Auchan, Carrefour, Leclerc and Casino. Every French town worth its salt holds at least one **market** (*marché*) a week. These tend to be vibrant, mostly morning affairs when local producers gather to sell speciality goods such as honey, cheese and alcohol, alongside excellent quality vegetable, meat and fish stalls. Boulangeries are the best places to buy bread, while patisseries offer a broader range of pastries, cakes and sometimes also sandwiches and other snacks.

**Regional specialities** are mostly of the edible kind. If you're travelling in Brittany, be sure to pick up some of the local cider (*cidre*), while Normandy is famous for its calvados, and the south for its *pastis*. Provence is well known for its superb olive oil (*huile d'olive*) and pricey truffles (*truffes*), as is

the Dordogne. No matter where you go, each region will produce at least one local cheese, and wine of course also varies from region to region. Cognac (p.499) and the Champagne region (p.200) are also obvious destinations if you're looking to stock up.

Other items to look out for include **lace** (*dentelle*) in the north, **pottery** in Brittany and **ceramics** in Limoges. The northeast, especially Lorraine, is renowned for its **crystal** production, while Provence, particularly the town of Grasse on the Côte d'Azur (p.902), is *the* place in France to buy **perfume**.

Non-EU residents are able to claim back **VAT** (*TVA*) on purchases that come to over €175. To do this, make sure the shop you're buying from fills out the correct paperwork, and present this to customs before you check in at the airport for your return flight.

# Travel essentials

## Costs

France can be one of the more expensive European countries to visit, but how much a visit will cost depends on where in the country you go and when. Much of France is little or no more expensive than its Eurozone neighbours, with reasonably priced accommodation and restaurant food. But in prime tourist spots hotel prices can go up by a third during July and August, and places like Paris and the Côte d'Azur are always more expensive than other regions. If you're visiting a chic tourist hotspot like St Tropez, be prepared for a wallet-bashing.

For a reasonably comfortable existence – staying in hotels, eating lunch and dinner in restaurants, plus moving around, café stops and museum visits – you need to allow a **budget** of around €100 (£81/$125) a day per person, assuming two people sharing a mid-range room. By counting the pennies – staying at youth hostels or camping and being strong-willed about extra cups of coffee and doses of culture – you could probably manage on €60 (£48/$75) a day.

**Admission charges** to museums and monuments can also eat into your budget, though many state-owned museums have one day of the month when they're free or half-price. Reductions are often available for those under 18 (for which you'll need your passport as proof of age) and for

## AVERAGE DAILY TEMPERATURES AND RAINFALL

| | Jan | Feb | Mar | Apr | May | Jun | Jul | Aug | Sep | Oct | Nov | Dec |
|---|---|---|---|---|---|---|---|---|---|---|---|---|
| **PARIS** | | | | | | | | | | | | |
| Max/min (°C) | 6/2 | 7/2 | 11/4 | 14/6 | 18/9 | 21/12 | 24/14 | 23/14 | 20/12 | 16/9 | 10/5 | 7/2 |
| Max/min (°F) | 43/35 | 45/35 | 51/39 | 57/42 | 64/49 | 70/54 | 74/58 | 74/57 | 68/53 | 60/47 | 49/40 | 44/36 |
| Rainfall (mm) | 54 | 46 | 52 | 45 | 62 | 57 | 54 | 51 | 57 | 59 | 59 | 55 |
| **ST-MALO** | | | | | | | | | | | | |
| Max/min (°C) | 8/3 | 9/3 | 11/4 | 13/6 | 17/9 | 20/11 | 22/13 | 22/13 | 20/12 | 16/10 | 12/6 | 9/4 |
| Max/min (°F) | 47/38 | 48/38 | 52/40 | 56/43 | 62/48 | 67/53 | 71/56 | 71/56 | 68/54 | 61/49 | 53/43 | 48/40 |
| Rainfall (mm) | 82 | 68 | 63 | 50 | 57 | 48 | 41 | 48 | 62 | 75 | 95 | 89 |
| **LYON** | | | | | | | | | | | | |
| Max/min (°C) | 6/0 | 8/1 | 12/3 | 15/6 | 19/9 | 23/13 | 27/15 | 26/14 | 23/12 | 17/8 | 10/4 | 6/1 |
| Max/min (°F) | 42/32 | 47/34 | 53/37 | 60/42 | 67/49 | 74/55 | 80/59 | 78/58 | 73/53 | 62/46 | 50/38 | 43/33 |
| Rainfall (mm) | 58 | 58 | 66 | 69 | 89 | 78 | 61 | 77 | 78 | 79 | 73 | 64 |
| **TOULOUSE** | | | | | | | | | | | | |
| Max/min (°C) | 9/2 | 11/3 | 14/4 | 16/7 | 20/10 | 24/13 | 28/15 | 27/15 | 24/13 | 19/10 | 13/5 | 10/3 |
| Max/min (°F) | 49/35 | 52/37 | 56/39 | 61/44 | 68/49 | 75/55 | 82/60 | 80/59 | 76/55 | 67/49 | 56/41 | 49/37 |
| Rainfall (mm) | 59 | 59 | 57 | 67 | 77 | 71 | 44 | 57 | 67 | 58 | 63 | 69 |
| **NICE** | | | | | | | | | | | | |
| Max/min (°C) | 11/3 | 11/4 | 13/6 | 15/8 | 19/12 | 22/15 | 26/18 | 26/18 | 23/16 | 19/12 | 14/7 | 12/5 |
| Max/min (°F) | 51/38 | 52/39 | 55/42 | 60/47 | 66/53 | 72/59 | 78/64 | 78/64 | 73/60 | 67/54 | 58/45 | 53/40 |
| Rainfall (mm) | 77 | 79 | 74 | 66 | 61 | 46 | 22 | 43 | 65 | 104 | 101 | 78 |

students under 26, while many are free for children under 12, and almost always for kids under 4. Several towns and regions offer multi-entry tickets covering a number of sights (detailed with in the text).

### Discount cards

Once obtained, various official and quasi-official youth/student ID cards soon pay for themselves in savings. Full-time students are eligible for the **International Student ID Card** (ISIC, Ⓦisic.org or Ⓦstatravel.co.uk in the UK) which entitles you to special air, rail and bus fares and discounts at museums and for certain services. You have to be 25 or younger to qualify for the **International Youth Travel Card (IYTC)**, while teachers are eligible for the **International Teacher Card (ITIC)**. A **university photo ID** might open some doors, but is not always as easily recognizable as the above cards.

Some cities issue their own discount cards, offering free or reduced price entry to museums or on public transport. These are mentioned in the relevant sections of the book.

## Crime and personal safety

### Theft and assault

While violent crime involving tourists is rare in France, **petty theft** is endemic in all the big cities, on beaches and at major tourist sights. In Paris, be especially wary of pickpockets at train stations and on the métro and RER lines; RER line B, serving Charles de Gaulle airport and Gare du Nord, has recently been the scene of several serious assaults. There has also been a spate of violent express kidnappings around the Channel ports in the early hours, often involving armed Eastern European gangs in British-registered vehicles and targeting lone drivers outside all-night stores or filling stations. Another recent trend, particularly in the south, is the targeting at night of foreign drivers on unlit sections of *autoroute* by fake police equipped with uniforms and flashing blue lights. Having stopped the drivers for some "offence", they make off with their documentation and a considerable "fine". Violence has sometimes been involved.

It obviously makes sense to take the normal **precautions**: don't flash wads of notes around;

carry your bag or wallet securely and be especially careful in crowds; never leave valuables lying in view; and park your car overnight in a monitored parking garage or, at the very least, on a busy and well-lit street. Be wary of unmanned *aires* (rest areas) on the *autoroute* at night. It's also wise to keep a separate record of cheque and credit card numbers and the phone numbers for cancelling them. Finally, make sure you have a good insurance policy (see p.52).

To **report a theft**, go to the local gendarmerie or Commissariat de Police (addresses are given in accounts for major cities). Remember to take your passport, and vehicle documents if relevant. The duty officer will usually find someone who speaks English if they don't themselves.

### Drugs

**Drug use** is just as prevalent in France as anywhere else in Europe – and penalties for use remain harsh by European standards, despite public agitation for a softening of the law. The authorities make no distinction between soft and hard drugs. People caught smuggling or possessing drugs, even just a few grams of marijuana, are liable to find themselves in jail. Should you be arrested on any charge, you have the right to contact your consulate, though don't expect much sympathy.

### Racism

Though the self-proclaimed home of "liberté, égalité, fraternité", France has an unfortunate reputation for **racism**. The majority of racist incidents are focused against the Arab community, although black and Asian visitors may also encounter an unwelcome degree of curiosity or suspicion from shopkeepers, hoteliers and the like. Anti-semitic violence has had a high profile in France since the torture and murder of a young Jewish man, Ilan Halimi, in a Paris banlieue in 1996. An attack on a school in Toulouse in March 2012 left

four dead and another in Villeurbanne saw young yarmulke-wearing Jews attacked with hammers. If you suffer a **racial assault**, contact the police, your consulate or one of the local anti-racism organizations (though they may not have English-speakers); SOS Racism (W sos-racisme.org) and Mouvement contre le Racisme et pour l'Amitié entre les Peuples (MRAP; W mrap.fr) have offices in most regions of France. Alternatively, you could contact the **English-speaking helpline** SOS Help (T 01 46 21 46 46, daily 3–11pm; W soshelpline.org). The service is staffed by trained volunteers who not only provide a confidential listening service, but also offer practical information for foreigners facing problems in France.

### Road safety

**Pedestrians** should take great care when crossing roads. Although the authorities are trying to improve matters, many French drivers pay little heed to pedestrian/zebra crossings. Never step out onto a crossing assuming that drivers will stop. Also be wary at traffic lights: check that cars are not still speeding towards you even when the green man is showing.

## Electricity

**Voltage** is officially 230V, using **plugs** with two round pins. If you need an adapter, it's best to buy one before leaving home, though you can find them in big department stores in France.

## Entry requirements

Citizens of **EU countries** can enter France freely on a valid passport or national identity card, while those from many **non-EU countries**, including Australia, Canada, New Zealand and the United States, among others, do not need a visa for a stay of **up to ninety days**. South African citizens require a short-stay visa for up to ninety days, which should be applied for in advance and costs €60.

All non-EU citizens who wish to remain **longer than ninety days** must apply for a long-stay visa, for which you'll have to show proof of – among other things – a regular income or sufficient funds to support yourself and medical insurance. Be aware, however, that the situation can change and it's advisable to check with your nearest French embassy or consulate before departure. For further information about visa regulations consult the Ministry of Foreign Affairs website: W diplomatie .gouv.fr.

---

**EMERGENCY NUMBERS**

**Police** T 17
**Medical emergencies/ambulance (SAMU)** T 15
**Fire brigade/paramedics** T 18
**Emergency calls from a mobile phone** T 112
**Rape crisis** (Viols Femmes Informations) T 0800 05 95 95
All emergency numbers are toll-free.

## FRENCH EMBASSIES AND CONSULATES

**Australia** Canberra ☎ 02 6216 0100, ✆ ambafrance-au.org.
**Britain** London ☎ 020 7073 1000; Edinburgh ☎ 0845 0060 200; ✆ ambafrance-uk.org.
**Canada** Montréal ☎ 514 878 4385, ✆ consulfrance-montreal.org; Toronto ☎ 416 847 1900, ✆ consulfrance-toronto.org.
**Ireland** Dublin ☎ 01 277 5000, ✆ ambafrance-ie.org.
**New Zealand** Wellington ☎ 04 384 2555, ✆ ambafrance-nz.org.
**South Africa** Johannesburg ☎ 011 77 85 600, ✆ consulfrance -jhb.org.
**USA** Washington ☎ 202 944 6000, ✆ ambafrance-us.org.

# Gay and lesbian France

In general, France is as liberal as other western European countries. The age of consent is 15, and same-sex couples have been able to form civil partnerships, called PACs, since 1999.

Gay male communities thrive, especially in Paris and southern towns such as Montpellier and Nice. Nevertheless, gay men tend to keep a low profile outside gay communities and specific gay venues, parades, and the prime gay areas of Paris and the coastal resorts. Lesbian life is rather less upfront, although Toulouse has a particularly lively lesbian community. The biggest annual event is the Gay Pride march in Paris (✆ gaypride.fr), which takes place every June. Other cities with Pride celebrations in early summer include Lille, Lyon, Marseille, Montpellier, Strasbourg and Toulouse.

## USEFUL CONTACTS

**Spartacus** Published by Bruno Gmünder Verlag, the English-language *Spartacus International Gay Guide* has an extensive section on France and contains some information for lesbians.
**Têtu** ✆ tetu.com. France's best-selling gay/lesbian magazine with events listings and contact addresses; you can buy it in bookshops or through their website, which is also an excellent source of information.

# Health

Visitors to France have little to worry about as far as health is concerned. No vaccinations are required, there are no nasty diseases, and tap water is safe to drink. The worst that's likely to happen to you is a case of sunburn or an upset stomach from eating too much rich food. If you do need treatment, however, you should be in good hands: the French healthcare system is rated one of the best in the world.

Under the French health system, all services, including doctors' consultations, prescribed medicines, hospital stays and ambulance call-outs, incur a charge which you have to pay upfront. **EU** citizens are entitled to a refund (usually 70 percent) of medical and dental expenses, providing the doctor is government-registered (*un médecin conventionné*) and provided you have a European Health Insurance Card (EHIC; *Carte Européenne d'Assurance Maladie*). Present your EHIC card to avoid upfront charges if you're admitted to hospital; you'll generally only have to pay a 20 percent co-payment for treatment you receive there. Note that everyone in the family, including children, must have their own EHIC card, which is free. In the UK, you can apply for them online (✆ ehic.org.uk), by phone (☎ 0845 606 2030) or by post – forms are available at post offices. Even with the EHIC card, however, you might want to take out some additional insurance to cover the shortfall. All **non-EU visitors** should ensure they have adequate medical insurance cover. For minor complaints go to a **pharmacie**, signalled by an illuminated green cross. You'll find at least one in every small town and even in some villages. They keep normal shop hours (roughly 9am–noon & 3–6pm), though some stay open late and in larger towns at least one (known as the *pharmacie de garde*) is open 24 hours according to a rota; details are displayed in all pharmacy windows, or the local police will have information.

**Condoms** (*préservatifs*) are widely available in pharmacies, supermarkets and coin-operated street dispensers. The pill (*la pilule*) is available only on prescription but emergency contraception (*la pilule du lendemain*) can be obtained at pharmacies.

For anything more serious you can get the name of a **doctor** from a pharmacy, local police station, tourist office or your hotel. Alternatively, look under "Médecins" in the Yellow Pages of the phone directory. The consultation fee is in the region of €23 to €25; note that some practitioners charge an additional fee on top of the official rate. You'll be given a *Feuille de Soins* (Statement of Treatment) for later insurance claims. Any prescriptions will be fulfilled by the pharmacy and must be paid for; little price stickers (*vignettes*) from each medicine will be stuck on the *Feuille de Soins*.

In serious **emergencies** you will always be admitted to the nearest general hospital (*centre hospitalier*). Phone numbers and addresses of hospitals in all the main cities are given in the text.

# Insurance

Even though EU citizens are entitled to health-care privileges in France, they would do well to take out an **insurance policy** before travelling in order to cover against theft, loss, illness or injury. Before paying for a new policy, however, it's worth checking whether you are already covered: some all-risks home insurance policies may cover your possessions when overseas, and many private medical schemes include cover when abroad.

After investigating these possibilities, you might want to contact a **specialist travel insurance** company. A typical travel insurance policy usually provides cover for the loss of baggage, tickets and – up to a certain limit – cash or cheques, as well as cancellation or curtailment of your journey. Most exclude so-called **dangerous sports** unless an extra premium is paid.

Rough Guides has teamed up with World Nomads to offer you **travel insurance** that can be tailored to suit the length of your stay. There are also annual **multi-trip** policies for those who travel regularly. You can get a quote on our website (ⓦ roughguides.com/website/shop).

## Internet

Wireless internet (wi-fi) is increasingly the norm in even the cheapest French hotels and is often – though not invariably – free. Many hotels will also have a computer terminal in a public area for those who do not have laptops or smartphones. Internet cafés are less common than they were but can still be found in big cities, sometimes also offering cheap international calls or other services such as photocopying. Unless specified otherwise, all accommodation establishments listed in this guide have wi-fi.

## Laundry

Self-service **laundries** are common in French towns – just ask in your hotel or the tourist office, or look in the phone book under "*Laveries automatiques*" or "*Laveries en libre-service*". Most **hotels** forbid doing laundry in your room, though you should get away with just one or two items.

## Mail

French **post offices**, known as La Poste and identified by bright yellow-and-blue signs, are generally open from around 9am to 6pm Monday to Friday, and 9am to noon on Saturday. However, these hours aren't set in stone: smaller branches and those in rural areas are likely to close for lunch (generally noon to 2pm) and finish at 5pm, while big city centre branches may be open longer.

You can **receive letters** using the poste restante system available at the central post office in every town. They should be addressed (preferably with the surname first and in capitals) "Poste Restante, Poste Centrale, Town x, post code". You'll need your passport to collect your mail and there'll be a charge of €0.60 per item. Items are kept for 15 days.

For **sending mail**, standard letters (20g or less) and postcards in France and beyond cost €0.57; to other European Union countries a charge of €0.05 per 10g is added to the basic fee for heavier letters and of €0.11 per 10g to all other countries. You can also buy stamps from *tabacs* and newsagents. To post your letter on the street, look for the bright yellow postboxes.

For **further information** on postal rates, among other things, log on to the post office website ⓦ laposte.fr.

## Maps

In addition to the maps in this guide and the various free town plans and regional maps you'll be offered along the way, the one extra map you might want is a good, up-to-date **road map** of France. The best are those produced by Michelin (1:200,000; ⓦ viamichelin.fr) and the Institut Géographique National (IGN; 1:250,000; ⓦ ign.fr), either as individual sheets or in one large spiral-bound *atlas routier*.

## Money

France's **currency** is the euro, which is divided into 100 cents (often still referred to as *centimes*). There are seven notes – in denominations of 5, 10, 20, 50, 100, 200 and 500 euros – and eight different coins – 1, 2, 5, 10, 20 and 50 cents, and 1 and 2 euros. At the time of writing, the **exchange rate** for the euro was around €1.24 to the pound sterling (or £0.80 to €1) and €0.81 to the dollar (or $1.23 to €1). See ⓦ xe.com for current rates.

You can change cash at **banks** and main **post offices**, and travellers' cheques at post offices and some BNP Paribas branches. Rates and commission vary, so it's worth shopping around. There are **money-exchange counters** (*bureaux de change*) at French airports, major train stations and usually one or two in city centres as well, though they don't always offer the best exchange rates.

By far the easiest way to access money in France is to use your credit or debit card to withdraw cash from an **ATM** (known as a *distributeur* or *point argent*); most machines give instructions in several European languages. Note that there is often a transaction fee, so it's more efficient to take out a sizeable sum each time rather than making lots of small withdrawals.

**Credit and debit cards** are also widely accepted, although some smaller establishments don't accept cards, or only for sums above a certain threshold. Visa – called Carte Bleue in France – is widely recognized, followed by MasterCard (also known as EuroCard). American Express ranks a bit lower.

# Opening hours and public holidays

Basic **hours of business** are Monday to Saturday 9am to noon and 2 to 6pm. In big cities, **shops** and other businesses stay open throughout the day, as do most **tourist offices** and museums in July and August. In rural areas and throughout southern France places tend to close for at least a couple of hours at lunchtime. Small food shops may not reopen till halfway through the afternoon, closing around 7.30 or 8pm, just before the evening meal. The standard **closing day** is Sunday, even in larger towns and cities, though some food shops and newsagents are open in the morning. Some shops and businesses, particularly in rural areas, also close on Mondays.

**Banking hours** are typically Monday to Friday 8.30am to 12.30 and 1.30/2 to 5 or 6pm. Some branches, especially those in rural areas, close on Monday, while those in big cities may remain open at midday and may also open on Saturday morning. All are closed on Sunday and public holidays.

**Museums** tend to open from 9 or 10am to noon and from 2 or 3pm to 5 or 6pm, though in the big cities some stay open all day and opening hours tend to be longer in summer. Museum closing days are usually Monday or Tuesday, sometimes both. **Churches** are generally open from around 8am to dusk, but may close at lunchtime and are reserved for worshippers during services (times of which will be posted on the door).

France celebrates eleven **public holidays** (*jours fériés*), when most shops and businesses (though not necessarily restaurants), and some museums, are closed.

# Phones

Payphones (*cabines*) are increasingly rare due to the proliferation of mobile phones. You can make and receive calls – look for the number in the top right-hand corner of the information panel. The vast majority of public phones require a prepaid phonecard (*télécarte*) available from *tabacs* and newsagents; they come in units of 50 and 120 units (€7.50 and €15 respectively). Alternatively, a more flexible option is one of the many prepaid phonecards which operate with a unique code (*tickets téléphoniques*) on sale at Orange outlets, post offices, *tabacs*, newsagents and many supermarkets, which can be used from both private and public phones. Orange's Ticket France Europe, for example, for domestic and European calls is available in €5 and €10 denominations, while the prices for the Ticket International are €7.50 and €15. The €15 card buys up to 1000 minutes to landlines in the US and Canada. You can also use credit cards in many call boxes.

### Calling within France

For calls within France – local or long distance – simply dial all ten digits of the number. Numbers beginning ☎0800 and ☎0805 are free-dial numbers; those beginning ☎081 are charged as a local call; numbers beginning ☎086 cost €0.1 for the first minute and €0.02 per minute thereafter. Note that some of these ☎08 numbers cannot be accessed from abroad. Numbers starting ☎06 and 07 are mobile numbers and are therefore more expensive to call.

### Mobile phones

If you want to use your **mobile/cellphone**, contact your phone provider to check whether it will work in France and what the call charges are – they tend to be pretty exorbitant, and remember you're likely to be charged extra for receiving calls. French mobile phones operate on the GSM standard; if you're travelling from the US your cellphone may not work if it is not tri-band or from a supplier that has switched to GSM. If you are going to be in France for any length of time and will be making and receiving a lot of local calls, it may be worth

> ## PUBLIC HOLIDAYS
>
> **January 1** New Year's Day
> **Easter Monday**
> **Ascension Day** (forty days after Easter)
> **Whit Monday** (seventh Monday after Easter)
> **May 1** Labour Day
> **May 8** Victory in Europe (VE) Day 1945
> **July 14** Bastille Day
> **August 15** Assumption of the Virgin Mary
> **November 1** All Saints' Day
> **November 11** Armistice Day
> **December 25** Christmas Day

buying a pay-as-you-go **French SIM card** from any of the big mobile providers (Orange, SFR and Bouygues Telecom), all of which have high-street outlets. SFR does a SIM-only deal aimed at visitors for around €20 including a limited amount of call time and texts, while Bouygues and Orange both do very low cost SIM cards; you can then decide how much prepaid time to buy. Remember you'll need either a plug adapter for your phone charger or a charger compatible with French power sockets – phone shops stock the most popular models. One other option, of course – if your hotel has free wi-fi – is to use your Skype account.

## Smoking

**Smoking** is banned in all indoor public places, including public transport, museums, cafés, restaurants and nightclubs.

## Time

France is in the Central European Time Zone (GMT+1). Daylight Saving Time (GMT+2) in France lasts from the last Sunday in March to the last Sunday in October.

## Tipping

At restaurants you only need to leave an additional cash **tip** if you feel you have received service out of the ordinary, since restaurant prices always include a service charge. It's customary to tip porters, tour guides, taxi drivers and hairdressers a couple of euros.

## Tourist information

The **French Government Tourist Office** (Maison de la France; ⓦfranceguide.com) generally refers you to their website for information, though they still produce a free magazine, *Traveller in France*, and dispense the *Logis de France* book (see p.38). For more detailed information, such as hotels, campsites, activities and festivals in a specific location, it's best to contact the relevant regional or departmental tourist offices; contact details can be found online at ⓦfncrt.com and ⓦrn2d.net respectively.

In France itself you'll find a tourist office – usually an **Office du Tourisme** (OT) but sometimes a **Syndicat d'Initiative** (SI, run by local businesses) – in practically every town and many villages. Addresses, contact details and opening hours are detailed throughout the book,

or try ⓦtourisme.fr. All local tourist offices provide specific information on the area, including hotel and restaurant listings, leisure activities, car and bike rental, bus times, laundries and countless other things; many can also book accommodation for you. If asked, most offices will provide a town plan (for which you may be charged a nominal fee), and will have maps and local walking guides on sale. In mountain regions they display daily meteorological information and often share premises with the local hiking and climbing organizations. In the big cities you can usually pick up free *What's On* guides.

### TOURIST OFFICES AND GOVERNMENT SITES

**Australia and New Zealand** ⓦau.franceguide.com.
**Canada** ⓦca-en.franceguide.com.
**Ireland** ⓦie.franceguide.com.
**South Africa** ⓦza.franceguide.com.
**UK** ⓦuk.franceguide.com.
**USA** ⓦus.franceguide.com.

## Travellers with disabilities

The French authorities have been making a concerted effort to improve facilities for **disabled travellers**. Though haphazard parking habits and stepped village streets remain serious obstacles for anyone with mobility problems, ramps or other forms of access are gradually being added to hotels, museums and other public buildings. All hotels are required to adapt at least one room to be wheelchair accessible and a growing number of *chambres d'hôtes* are doing likewise. Hotels, sights and other facilities are inspected under the nationwide "Tourisme & Handicap" scheme and, if they fulfil certain criteria, issued with a certificate and logo. A supplementary scheme, "Destination pour tous" was rolled out in 2011 to recognize communities that promote disabled access to tourism.

For **getting to France**, Eurotunnel (see p.28) offers the simplest option for travellers from the UK, since you can remain in your car. Alternatively, Eurostar trains have dedicated wheelchair spaces in Standard Premier and Business Premier carriages; fares cost £69 return to Paris or Lille. A companion can also travel at a discounted rate. It's wise to reserve well in advance, when you might also like to enquire about the special assistance that Eurostar offers. If you're flying, it's worth noting that, while airlines are required to offer access to travellers with mobility problems, the level of service provided by some discount airlines may be fairly basic. All cross-Channel ferries have lifts for getting to and from the car deck, but moving between the different passenger decks may be more difficult.

**Within France**, most train stations now make provision for travellers with reduced mobility. SNCF produces a free booklet outlining its services, which is available from main stations or to download from SNCF's dedicated website for travellers with disabilities: ⓦ accessibilite.sncf.com, where you can also find information on accessible stations. Note that you need to give 48 hours advance warning to gain assistance from the beginning to the end of your trip.

Specially adapted **taxi** services (such as Taxis G7's Horizon in Paris) are available in some towns: contact the local tourist office for further information or one of the organizations listed below. All the big **car hire** agencies can provide automatic cars if you reserve sufficiently far in advance. while Hertz offers cars with hand controls – again, make sure you give them plenty of notice.

As for finding suitable **accommodation**, guides produced by *Logis de France* (see p.38) and *Gîtes de France* (see p.38) indicate places with specially adapted rooms, though it's essential to double-check when booking that the facilities meet your needs.

Up-to-date **information** about accessibility, special programmes and discounts is best obtained before you leave home from the organizations listed below. French readers might want to get hold of the *Handitourisme* guide, published by Petit Futé (ⓦ petitfute.com), available online or from major bookstores.

## USEFUL CONTACTS

**Access in Paris** ⓦ accessinparis.org. Comprehensive (if slightly dated) information on accessible Paris in book form or online.

**Association des Paralysés de France (APF)** ⓦ apf.asso.fr. National association that can answer general enquiries and put you in touch with their departmental offices.

**Door to Door** ⓦ dptac.independent.gov.uk/door-to-door. General online travel information from the UK's Disabled Persons Transport Advisory Committee.

**Fédération Française Handisport** France ⓦ handisport.org. Among other things, this federation provides information on sports and leisure facilities for people with disabilities.

**Irish Wheelchair Association** Ireland ⓦ iwa.ie. Useful information about travelling abroad with a wheelchair, and good links.

**Mobile en Ville** France ⓦ mobile-en-ville.asso.fr. Information on getting around, mainly in Paris (French only).

**Mobility International USA** US ⓦ miusa.org. Provides information and referral services and international exchange programmes.

**Tourism for All** UK ⓦ toursimforall.org.uk. Masses of useful information.

# Travelling with children

France is a relatively easy country in which to travel with children. They're generally welcome everywhere and young children and babies in particular will be fussed over. There are masses of family-oriented theme parks and no end of leisure activities geared towards kids, while most public parks contain children's play areas.

Local **tourist offices** will have details of specific activities for children, which might include anything from farm visits, nature walks or treasure hunts to paintball and forest ropeways for older children. In summer most seaside resorts organize clubs for children on the beach, while bigger campsites put on extensive programmes of activities and entertainments. Children under 4 years travel free on public transport, while those between 4 and 11 pay half-fare. Museums and the like are generally free to under-12s and half-price or free up to the age of 18; in some cases, citizens of the European Union aged under 26 get in free too.

**Hotels** charge by the room, with a small supplement for an additional bed or cot, and family-run places will sometimes babysit or offer a listening service while you eat or go out. Some youth hostels also now offer family rooms. Nearly all **restaurants** offer children's menus. Disposable **nappies/diapers** (*couches à jeter*) are available at most pharmacies and supermarkets, alongside a vast range of **baby foods**, though many have added sugar and salt. **Milk powders** also tend to be sweet, so bring your own if this is likely to be a concern. You can **breastfeed** in public.

### FURTHER INFORMATION

**Family Travel** ⓦ family-travel.co.uk. Slightly outdated but useful for basic information on where to go, health and what to pack.

**The Rough Guide to Travel with Babies and Young Children**. Comprehensive guide to hassle-free family travel.

# Women travellers

Despite a relatively strong feminist movement, France can still feel like a very male-dominated country, with many men still holding rather strong chauvinist ideas. While change is in the air, with female politicians starting to take a higher profile and giving the male ruling class a run for their money, for the moment many women still suffer the double burden of being housewife and earner.

French men tend to be on the predatory side, but are usually easily brushed off if you don't want the attention. It's not unusual, however, to be chatted up regularly, or have men (more often boys) call at you from cars in the street, and make comments as they pass you. The best way to deal with this is simply to avoid making eye contact and fail to react, and they'll soon get the message. On the beaches, especially on the Riviera, women young and old tend to go **topless**. Be sensitive though; if on the rare occasion you find you're the only one baring all on the beach, do cover up.

# Work and study in France

**EU citizens** are able to work in France on the same basis as a French citizen. This means that you don't have to apply for a residence or work permit except in very rare cases – contact your nearest French consulate for further information (see p.52). You will, however, need to apply for a **Carte du Séjour** from a police station within three months of your arrival – consular websites have details. Non-EU citizens are not allowed to work in France unless their prospective employer has obtained an "autorisation de travail" from the Ministry of Labour before they arrive in France. Under the "Compétences et Talents" scheme, a three-year renewable work permit may be issued to individuals with specific skills. Students who have completed one academic year in France can work on renewable three-month work permits under strict conditions, subject to obtaining prior permission from the Ministry of Labour. Au pair visas must also be obtained before travelling to France. Contact your nearest French consulate for more information on what rules apply in your particular situation.

When **looking for a job**, a good starting point is to read one of the books on working abroad published by Crimson Publishing (Ⓦcrimsonbooks .co.uk). You might also want to search the online recruitment resource Monster (Ⓦmonster.fr) and Job Etudiant (Ⓦjobetudiant.net) which focuses on jobs for students. In France, try the youth information agency CIDJ (Ⓦcidj.com), or CIJ (Centre d'Information Jeunesse) offices in main cities, which have information about temporary jobs and about working in France.

A degree and a TEFL (Teaching English as a Foreign Language) or similar qualification are normally required for **English-language teaching** posts. The online *EL Gazette* newsletter (Ⓦelgazette.com) is a useful source of information; so too is the annual *Teaching English Abroad* published by Vacation Work and the TEFL website (Ⓦtefl.com), with its database of English-teaching vacancies.

Foreign **students** pay the same as French nationals to enrol for a course, and you'll be eligible for subsidized accommodation. French universities are relatively informal, but there are strict entry requirements, including an exam in French for undergraduate courses if you don't already have a degree in French. If you're not a citizen of the EU or European Economic Area you'll also need a one-year extended-stay visa and residency permit. For 31 countries including the United States, enrolment is through a compulsory online process. See the Campus France website (Ⓦcampusfrance.org) for more information.

Should you wish to study French in France, you can search online for language courses meeting recognized quality criteria at Ⓦlabelqualitefle.org.

## Further contacts

**AFS Interncultural Programs** Ⓦafs.org. Opportunities for high-school students to study in France for a term or full academic year, living with host families.

**American Institute for Foreign Study** US Ⓦaifs.com. Language study and cultural immersion for the summer or school year.

**Council on International Educational Exchange (CIEE)** US Ⓦciee.org. A non-profit organization with summer, semester and academic-year programmes in France.

**Erasmus** UK Ⓦbritishcouncil.org/erasmus. EU-run student exchange programme enabling students at participating EU universities to study in another European member country.

**Experiment in International Living** US Ⓦexperimentinternational.org. Summer programmes for high-school students.

**World Wide Opportunities on Organic Farms (WWOOF)** Ⓦwwoof.fr. Volunteer to work on organic farm in return for board and lodging.

# Paris

THE LOUVRE

# Paris

Long considered the paragon of style, Paris is perhaps the most glamorous city in Europe. It is at once deeply traditional – a village-like metropolis whose inhabitants continue to be notorious for their hauteur – and famously cosmopolitan. The city's reputation as a magnet for writers, artists and dissidents lives on, and it remains at the forefront of Western intellectual, artistic and literary life. The most tangible and immediate pleasures of Paris are found in its street life and along the banks and bridges of the River Seine. Cafés, bars and restaurants line every street and boulevard, and the city's compactness makes it possible to experience the individual feel of the different *quartiers*.

You can move easily, even on foot, from the calm, almost small-town atmosphere of **Montmartre** and parts of the **Quartier Latin** to the busy commercial centres of the **Bourse** and **Opéra-Garnier** or the aristocratic mansions of the **Marais**. The city's lack of open space is redeemed by unexpected havens like the **Mosque**, **Arènes de Lutèce** and the **place des Vosges**, and courtyards and gardens of grand houses like the **Hôtel de Soubise**. The gravelled paths and formal beauty of the **Tuileries** create the backdrop for the ultimate Parisian Sunday promenade, while the islands and quaysides of the Left and Right Banks of the **River Seine** and the Quartier Latin's two splendid parks, the **Luxembourg** and the **Jardin des Plantes**, make for a wonderful wander.

   Paris's architectural spirit resides in the elegant streets and boulevards begun in the nineteenth century under Baron Haussmann. The mansion blocks that line them are at once grand and perfectly human in scale, a triumph in city planning proved by the fact that so many remain residential to this day. Rising above these harmonious buildings are the more arrogant monuments that define the French capital. For centuries, an imposing Classical style prevailed with great set pieces such as the **Louvre**, **Panthéon** and **Arc de Triomphe**, but the last hundred years or so has seen the architectural mould repeatedly broken in a succession of ambitious structures, the industrial chic of the **Eiffel Tower** and **Pompidou Centre** contrasting with the almost spiritual glasswork of the Louvre **Pyramide** and **Institut du Monde Arabe**. Paris is remarkable, too, for its **museums** – there are more than 150 of them, ranging from giants of the art world such as the Louvre, **Musée d'Orsay** and Pompidou Centre to lesser-known gems such as the Picasso, Rodin and Jewish museums – and the diversity of **entertainment**, from cinema to jazz music, on offer.

Brief history

Paris's **history** has conspired to create a sense of being apart from, and even superior to, the rest of the country. To this day, everything beyond the capital is known quite ordinarily as *province* – the provinces. Appropriately, the city's first inhabitants, the **Parisii**, a Celtic tribe that arrived in around the third century BC, had their settlement on an island: Lutetia, probably today's Île de la Cité. The **Romans** conquered the city two centuries later, and preferred the more familiar hilly ground of the Left Bank. Their city, also called Lutetia, grew up around the hill where the Panthéon stands today.

# Highlights

**❶ Sainte-Chapelle** The stunning stained-glass windows of the Sainte-Chapelle rank among the finest achievements of French High Gothic. **See p.66**

**❷ The Louvre** Quite simply, one of the world's greatest art museums. **See p.71**

**❸ Marais** Arguably the city's most lively and attractive district, characterized by narrow streets, fine Renaissance mansions and trendy bars. **See p.80**

**❹ Musée d'Orsay** After its major revamp, the Musée d'Orsay's fabulous collection of Impressionist paintings are displayed to better effect than ever. **See p.93**

**❺ Jardin du Luxembourg** These lovely gardens capture Paris at its most warm-hearted. **See p.97**

**❻ Palais de Tokyo** This cool 1930s structure houses two of Paris's most exciting art spaces. **See p.99**

**❼ Musée Rodin** Rodin's intense sculptures are displayed to powerful effect in his eighteenth-century townhouse. **See p.103**

**❽ Puces de St-Ouen** Even if it's less of a flea market now, and more of a mega-emporium for arty bric-a-brac and antiques, the St-Ouen market is a wonderful place for relaxed weekend browsing. **See p.110**

**HIGHLIGHTS ARE MARKED ON THE MAP ON PP.64–65**

**1**

This hill, now known as the Montagne Ste-Geneviève, gets its name from Paris's first patron saint, who, as legend has it, saved the town from the marauding army of Attila in 451 through her exemplary holiness. Fifty years later **Geneviève** converted another invader to Christianity: Clovis the Frank, the leader of a group of Germanic tribes, went on to make the city the capital of his kingdom. His newly founded Merovingian dynasty promptly fell apart under his son Childéric II.

Power only returned to Paris under **Hugues Capet**, the Count of Paris. He was elected king of France in 987, although at the time his territory amounted to little more than the Île de France, the region immediately surrounding Paris. From this shaky start French monarchs gradually extended their control over their feudal rivals, centralizing administrative, legal, financial and political power as they did so, until anyone seeking influence, publicity or credibility, in whatever field, had to be in Paris – which is still the case today. The city's cultural influence grew alongside its **university**, which was formally established in 1215 and swiftly became the great European centre for scholastic learning.

The wars and plagues of the fourteenth and fifteenth centuries left Paris half in ruins and more than half abandoned, but with royal encouragement, the city steadily recovered. During the **Wars of Religion** the capital remained staunchly Catholic, but Parisians' loyalty to the throne was tested during the mid-seventeenth-century rebellions known as the Frondes, in which the young Louis XIV was forced to flee the city. Perhaps this traumatic experience lay behind the king's decision, in 1670, to move the court to his vast new palace at **Versailles**. Paris suffered in the court's absence, even as grand Baroque buildings were thrown up in the capital.

Parisians, both as deputies to the Assembly and mobs of sans-culottes, were at the forefront of the **Revolution**, but many of the new citizens welcomed the return to order

## PARIS ORIENTATION

Finding your way around Paris is remarkably easy, as the centre is fairly small for a major capital city, and very **walkable**. The city proper is divided into twenty **arrondissements**, or districts, and are included as an integral part of addresses. Arrondissements are abbreviated as 1$^{er}$ (premier = first), 2$^{e}$ (deuxième = second), 3$^{e}$, 4$^{e}$ and so on; the numbering spirals out from the centre.

The **Seine** flows in a downturned arc from east to west, cutting the city in two. In the middle of the Seine lie two islands, the **Île de la Cité**, ancient heart of Paris and home of the cathedral of **Notre-Dame**, and the elegant **Île Saint-Louis**. North of the river is the busy, commercial **Right Bank**, or *rive droite*. Most of the city's sights are found here, within the historic central arrondissements (1$^{er}$ to 4$^{e}$). Here you can take in the Arc de Triomphe and walk down the glamorous **Champs-Élysées** to the Louvre palace. Immediately north is the expensive **Opéra district**, home of the shopping arcades (*passages*), ritzy Place Vendôme and the tranquil gardens of the Palais Royal. East, the bustle and tacky shops of **Les Halles** and **Beaubourg** give way to the aristocratic and fashionable **Marais** and trendy **Bastille** quarters. To the north lie **Montmartre** and the northern arrondissements, while the grittier eastern end of the city incorporates the vast Père-Lachaise cemetery.

South of the river is the relatively laidback **Left Bank**, or *rive gauche* (arrondissements 5$^{e}$ to 7$^{e}$). Here you'll find the studenty **Quartier Latin** and the elegant and international **St-Germain**, along with the aristocratic, museum-rich area around the **Eiffel Tower**, a short hop across the river from the **Trocadéro** quarter. The **outer arrondissements** (8$^{e}$ to 20$^{e}$) were mostly incorporated into the city in the nineteenth century. Generally speaking, those to the east accommodated the working classes while those to the west were, and still are, the addresses for the aristocracy and new rich. Neighbourhoods here include **Montparnasse** in the south, and to the west, the wealthy **Beaux Quartiers**, the green space of the Bois de Boulogne and the business district of La Défense.

Paris proper is encircled by the *boulevard périphérique* ring road. The sprawling conurbation beyond is known as the **banlieue**, or suburbs. There are few sights for the tourist here, and only one of significant interest: St-Denis, with its historic cathedral.

under Napoleon I. The emperor adorned the city with many of its signature monuments, Neoclassical almost-follies designed to amplify his majesty: the Arc de Triomphe, Arc du Carrousel and the Madeleine. He also instituted the Grandes Écoles, super-universities for the nation's elite administrators, engineers and teachers. At the fall of the Empire, in 1814, Paris was saved from destruction by the arch-diplomat Talleyrand, who delivered the city to the Russians with hardly a shot fired. Nationalists grumbled that the occupation continued well into the Restoration regime, as the city once again became the playground of the rich of Europe, the ultimate tourist destination.

The greatest shocks to the fabric of the city came under Napoléon III. He finally completed the Louvre, rebuilding much of the facade in the process, but it was his Prefect of the Seine, **Baron Haussmann**, who truly transformed the city, smashing through the slums to create wide boulevards that could be easily controlled by rifle-toting troops – not that it succeeded in preventing the **1871 Commune**, the most determined insurrection since 1789. It was down these large boulevards, lined with grey bourgeois residences, that **Nazi troops** paraded in June 1940, followed by the Allies, led by General Leclerc, in August 1944.

Although riotous street protests have been a feature of modern Parisian life – most famously in **May 1968**, when students burst onto the streets of the Quartier Latin – the traditional barricade-builders have long since been booted into the depressing satellite towns, known as la banlieue, alongside the under-served populations of immigrants and their descendants. Integrating these communities, riven with poverty, unemployment and discontent, is one of the greatest challenges facing the city. Meanwhile, the city's Socialist mayor, **Bertrand Delanoë**, who has held the post since 2001, has been keen on promoting a greener, happier Paris. His vision has resulted in the introduction of **Paris Plages**, which sees a swathe of the Seine's *quais* converted into a beach every summer, along with the inexpensive Velib' bike rental and Autolib' car rental schemes, the huge expansion of cycle and bus lanes and the building of tramways on the outskirts – all of which are having some success in easing traffic congestion.

# The islands

There's nowhere better to start a tour of Paris than the two islands at its centre. The Île de la Cité is where Paris began, and boasts a number of important sights. The smaller Île St-Louis, linked to the Île de la Cité by a footbridge, is often considered the most romantic part of Paris. There are no particular sights on this little island, just austerely handsome seventeenth-century houses on single-lane streets, tree-lined *quais*, a church, restaurants, cafés and interesting little shops. It is particularly atmospheric in the evening, when an arm-in-arm wander along the *quais* is a romantic must.

## Île de la Cité

The earliest settlements were built here, followed by the small Gallic town of Lutetia, overrun by Julius Caesar's troops in 52 BC. A natural defensive site commanding a major east–west river trade route, it was an obvious candidate for a bright future. In 508 it became the stronghold of the Merovingian kings, then of the counts of Paris, who in 987 became kings of France.

The Frankish kings built themselves a splendid palace at the western tip of the island, of which the **Sainte-Chapelle** and **Conciergerie** survive today. At the other end of the island, they erected the great cathedral of **Notre-Dame**. By the early thirteenth century this tiny island had become the bustling heart of the capital, though it's hard to imagine this today: virtually the whole medieval city was erased by Baron Haussmann in the nineteenth-century and replaced by four imposing Neoclassical edifices, including the Palais de Justice.

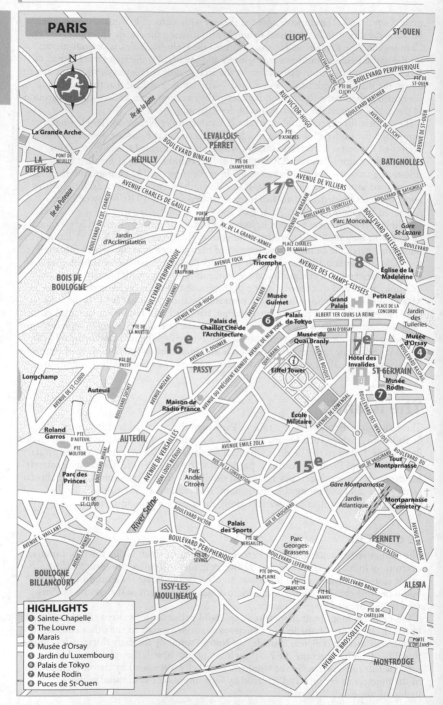

# PARIS

N

La Grande Arche

LA DÉFENSE

PONT DE NEUILLY

Ile de la Jatte

Ile de Puteaux

CLICHY

ST-OUEN

BOULEVARD PERIPHERIQUE

PTE DE ST-OUEN

PTE DE CLICHY

BOULEVARD BERTHIER

AVENUE DE CLICHY

RUE VICTOR-HUGO

BOULEVARD BINEAU

LEVALLOIS-PERRET

NEUILLY

PTE D'ASNÈRES

PTE DE CHAMPERRET

AVENUE DE VILLIERS

17e

BATIGNOLLES

AVENUE CHARLES DE GAULLE

BOULEVARD DU LOT. CHARIOT

Jardin d'Acclimatation

BOIS DE BOULOGNE

BOULEVARD PERIPHERIQUE

AVENUE VICTOR-HUGO

BOULEVARD LANNES

PTE DAUPHINE

AVENUE FOCH

AVENUE DE WAGRAM

BOULEVARD DE COURCELLES

Parc Monceau

BOULEVARD DE BATIGNOLLES

Gare St-Lazare

BOULEVARD MALESHERBES

BOULEVARD

PORTE MAILLOT

AV. DE LA GRANDE-ARMÉE

PLACE CHARLES DE GAULLE

Arc de Triomphe

AVENUE DES CHAMPS-ELYSEES

8e

Église de la Madeleine

PTE DE LA MUETTE

AVENUE KLEBER

Musée Guimet

Palais de Tokyo

Grand Palais

Petit Palais

PLACE DE LA CONCORDE

Jardin des Tuileries

16e

AVENUE P. DOUMER

Palais de Chaillot Cité de l'Architecture

6

ALBERT 1ER COURS LA REINE

Musée d'Orsay

4

PTE DE PASSY

PASSY

Musée du Quai Branly

QUAI D'ORSAY

7e

Hôtel des Invalides

ST-GERMAIN

BOULEVARD RASPAIL

Longchamp

Auteuil

AVENUE DE ST-CLOUD

BOULEVARD SUCHET

AVENUE MOZART

Maison de Radio France

Eiffel Tower

i

École Militaire

AVENUE DE LOWENDAL

BOULEVARD DES INVALIDES

Musée Rodin

7

Roland Garros

PTE D'AUTEUIL

PTE MOLITOR

BOULEVARD MURAT

AUTEUIL

QUAI LOUIS BLERIOT

AVENUE DE VERSAILLES

AVENUE EMILE ZOLA

RUE DE LA CONVENTION

15e

RUE DE VAUGIRARD

Tour Montparnasse

BOULEVARD DU

Parc des Princes

PTE DE ST-CLOUD

Parc André Citroën

Gare Montparnasse

Jardin Atlantique

Montparnasse Cemetery

AVENUE DU MAINE

River Seine

BOULEVARD VICTOR

Palais des Sports

RUE DE VAUGIRARD

Parc Georges-Brassens

PERNETY

RUE D'ALESIA

ALESIA

AVENUE E. VAILLANT

AVENUE P. KREBER

BOULEVARD PERIPHERIQUE

PTE DE VERSAILLES

PTE DE LA PLAINE

BOULEVARD LEFEBVRE

BOULEVARD BRUNE

BOULOGNE BILLANCOURT

PTE DE SÈVRES

ISSY-LES-MOULINEAUX

PTE DE LA PLAINE

PTE BRANCION

PTE DE VANVES

PTE DE CHÂTILLON

PORTE D'ORLEANS

AVENUE P. BROSSOLETTE

MONTROUGE

## HIGHLIGHTS

1. Sainte-Chapelle
2. The Louvre
3. Marais
4. Musée d'Orsay
5. Jardin du Luxembourg
6. Palais de Tokyo
7. Musée Rodin
8. Puces de St-Ouen

1

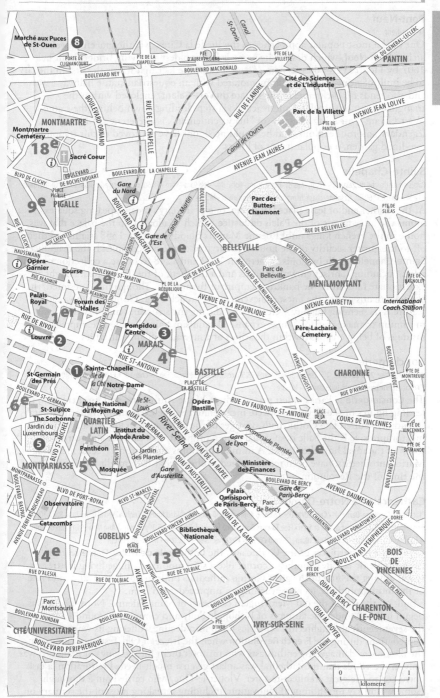

**1**

## Pont-Neuf
M° Pont-Neuf

One of the most popular approaches to the Île de la Cité is via the graceful, twelve-arched **Pont-Neuf**, which despite its name is Paris's oldest surviving bridge, built in 1607 by Henri IV. It takes its name ("new") from the fact that it was the first in the city to be built of stone. Henri is commemorated with an equestrian statue halfway across, and also lends his nickname to the **square du Vert-Galant**, enclosed within the triangular stern of the island and reached via steps leading down behind the statue. "Vert-Galant", meaning a "green" or "lusty gentleman", is a reference to Henri's legendary amorous exploits, and he would no doubt have approved of this tranquil, tree-lined garden, a popular haunt of lovers.

## Sainte-Chapelle
Palais de Justice, bd du Palais, 1ᵉʳ • Daily: March–Oct 9.30am–6pm; Nov–Feb 9am–5pm • €8.50, combined admission to the Conciergerie €12.50 • ☎ 01 53 60 80, ⓦ sainte-chapelle.monuments-nationaux.fr • M° Cité

At the further end of leafy **place Dauphine**, one of the city's most appealing squares, looms the huge facade of the **Palais de Justice**, which swallowed up the palace that was home to the French kings until Étienne Marcel's bloody revolt in 1358 frightened them off to the greater security of the Louvre. A survivor of the old complex is the magnificent **Sainte-Chapelle**, built by Louis IX between 1242 and 1248 to house a collection of holy relics, including Christ's crown of thorns and a fragment of the True Cross, bought at extortionate rates from the bankrupt empire of Byzantium. Though much restored, the chapel remains one of the finest achievements of French High Gothic. Its most radical feature is its seeming fragility – created by reducing the structural masonry to a minimum to make way for a huge expanse of exquisite stained glass. The impression inside of being enclosed within the wings of a myriad brilliant butterflies.

## Conciergerie
Palais de Justice, 2 bd du Palais, 1ᵉʳ • Daily 9.30am–6pm • €8.50, combined ticket with Sainte-Chapelle €12.50 • ☎ 01 53 40 60 80, ⓦ conciergerie.monuments-nationaux.fr • M° Cité

The **Conciergerie** is Paris's oldest prison, where Marie-Antoinette and, in their turn, the leading figures of the Revolution were incarcerated before execution. Inside are several splendidly vaulted late Gothic halls, vestiges of the old Capetian kings' palace. The most impressive is the Salle des Gens d'armes, originally the canteen and recreation room of the royal household staff. A number of rooms and prisoners' cells, including Marie-Antoinette's, have been reconstructed to show what they might have been like at the time of the Revolution.

## Cathédrale de Notre-Dame
Place du Parvis Notre-Dame, 4ᵉ • **Cathedral** Daily 8am–6.45pm; free 60–90min guided tours in English Wed & Thurs 2pm, Sat 2.30pm; free organ recitals Sun around 4pm or 5pm • Free **Towers** April–June & Sept daily 10am–6.30pm; July & Aug Mon–Fri 10am–6.30pm, Sat & Sun 10am–11pm; Oct–March daily 10am–5.30pm • €8.50 • ⓦ cathedraledeparis.com • M° St-Michel/Cité

One of the masterpieces of the Gothic age, the **Cathédrale de Notre-Dame** rears up from the Île de la Cité's southeast corner like a ship moored by huge flying buttresses. It was among the first of the great Gothic cathedrals built in northern France and one of the most ambitious, its nave reaching an unprecedented 33m.

Built on the site of the old Merovingian cathedral of Saint-Étienne, Notre-Dame was begun in 1160 under the auspices of Bishop de Sully and completed around 1345. In the seventeenth and eighteenth centuries it fell into decline, suffering its worst depredations during the **French Revolution** when the frieze of Old Testament kings on the facade was damaged by enthusiasts who mistook them for the kings of France. It was only in the 1820s that the cathedral was at last given a much-needed restoration, a task entrusted to the great architect-restorer, Viollet-le-Duc, who carried out a thorough (some would say too thorough) renovation, including remaking most of the statuary on the facade – the originals can be seen in the Musée National du Moyen Âge (see p.89) – and adding the steeple and baleful-looking gargoyles.

## Visiting the cathedral

The cathedral's **facade** is one of its most impressive exterior features; the Romanesque influence is still visible, not least in its solid H-shape, but the overriding impression is one of lightness and grace, created in part by the delicate filigree work of the central rose window and gallery above. Of the magnificent **carvings**, the oldest, dating from the twelfth century, are those in the right portal, depicting the Virgin Enthroned, elegantly executed and displaying all the majesty of a royal procession.

**Inside**, the immediately striking feature is the dramatic contrast between the darkness of the nave and the light falling on the first great clustered pillars of the choir. It's the end walls of the transepts that admit all this light: they are nearly two-thirds glass, including two magnificent rose windows coloured in imperial purple. These, the vaulting and the soaring columns are all definite Gothic elements, though there remains a strong sense of Romanesque in the stout round pillars of the nave.

For good views, and to see the gargoyles close up, you can brave the ascent of the **towers**, for which there is a separate entrance outside. Queues for the towers often start before they open, so it pays to get here early or to come in the evening, when it's often quieter. The same goes for visiting the cathedral itself.

## The Crypte Archéologique

Place du Parvis Notre-Dame, 4ᵉ • Tues–Sun 10am–6pm • €4 • ☎ 01 55 42 50 10, ⓦ crypte.paris.fr • M° Cité

Beneath the large windswept square in front of the cathedral, known as the **Parvis** (from "paradise"), is the atmospheric **Crypte Archéologique**, a large excavated area revealing the remains of the original cathedral, as well as remnants of the streets and houses that once clustered around Notre-Dame. Most are medieval, but some date as far back as Gallo-Roman times and include parts of a Roman hypocaust (heating system).

## Le Mémorial de la Déportation

Square de l'Île de France, 4ᵉ • Daily 10am–noon & 2–5pm • Free • M° Cité/Pont Marie

At the eastern tip of Île de la Cité is the symbolic tomb of the 200,000 French who died in Nazi concentration camps during World War II – Resistance fighters, Jews and forced labourers among them. The stark and moving **Mémorial de la Déportation** is scarcely visible above ground; stairs hardly shoulder-wide descend into a space like a prison yard and then into the crypt, off which is a long, narrow, stifling corridor, its wall covered in thousands of points of light representing the dead. Floor and ceiling are black, and it ends in a raw hole, with a single naked bulb hanging in the middle. Above the exit are the words "Pardonne, n'oublie pas" ("Forgive, do not forget").

# The Champs-Élysées and around

Synonymous with Parisian glamour, the **Champs-Élysées** cuts through one of the city's most exclusive districts, studded with luxury hotels and top fashion boutiques. The avenue forms part of a grand, 9km-long axis that extends from the Louvre, at the heart of the city, to the Grande Arche de la Défense, in the west. Referred to as the Voie Triomphale, or Triumphal Way, it offers impressive vistas all along its length and incorporates some of the city's most famous landmarks – not only the Champs-Élysées but also the **Tuileries** gardens, **place de la Concorde**, and the **Arc de Triomphe**. The whole ensemble is so regular it looks as though it was laid out by a single town planner rather than by successive kings, emperors and presidents, all keen to add their stamp and promote French power and prestige.

Note that **rue de Lévis** (a few blocks up rue Berger from M° Monceau) has one of the city's most colourful and appetizing **markets** (daily except Mon).

1

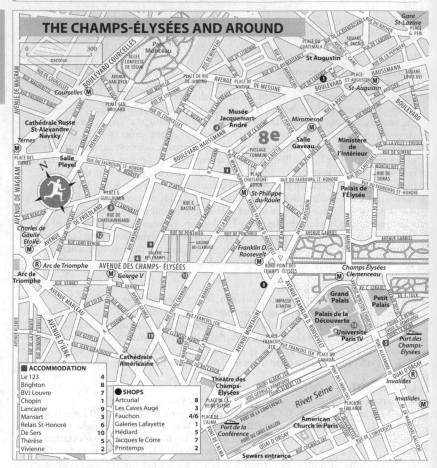

# THE CHAMPS-ÉLYSÉES AND AROUND

**■ ACCOMMODATION**

| Le 123 | 4 |
|---|---|
| Brighton | 8 |
| BVJ Louvre | 7 |
| Chopin | 1 |
| Lancaster | 9 |
| Mansart | 3 |
| Relais St-Honoré | 6 |
| De Sers | 10 |
| Thérèse | 5 |
| Vivienne | 2 |

**● SHOPS**

| Artcurial | 8 |
|---|---|
| Les Caves Augé | 3 |
| Fauchon | 4/6 |
| Galeries Lafayette | 1 |
| Hédiard | 5 |
| Jacques le Corre | 7 |
| Printemps | 2 |

## The Arc de Triomphe

Place Charles-de-Gaulle; access is via underground stairs from the north corner of the Champs-Élysées • Daily: April–Sept 10am–11pm;
Oct–March 10am–10.30pm • €9.50 • ☎ 01 55 37 73 77, ⓦ arc-de-triomphe.monuments-nationaux.fr • M° Charles-de-Gaulle-Étoile

The **Arc de Triomphe** towers above the traffic in the middle of **place Charles-de-Gaulle**,
better known as l'Étoile ("star") on account of the twelve avenues radiating out from it.
The arch was started by Napoleon as a homage to the armies of France and himself, but
it wasn't actually finished until 1836 by Louis-Philippe, who dedicated it to the French
army in general. The names of 660 generals and numerous French battles are engraved
on the inside of the arch, and reliefs adorn the exterior: the best is François Rude's
extraordinarily dramatic *Marseillaise*, in which an Amazon-type figure personifying the
Revolution charges forward with a sword, her face contorted in a fierce rallying cry. A
quiet reminder of the less glorious side of war is the **tomb of the unknown soldier**
placed beneath the arch and marked by an eternal flame that is stoked up every evening
at 6.30pm by war veterans. Climbing the 280 steps to the top will be amply rewarded
by the panoramic views; the best time to come is towards dusk on a sunny day, when
the marble of the Grande Arche de la Défense sparkles in the setting sun and the
Louvre is bathed in warm light.

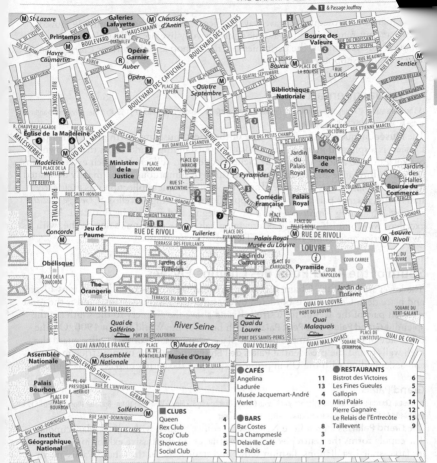

| CAFÉS | | RESTAURANTS | |
|---|---|---|---|
| Angelina | 11 | Bistrot des Victoires | 6 |
| Ladurée | 13 | Les Fines Gueules | 5 |
| Musée Jacquemart-André | 4 | Gallopin | 2 |
| Verlet | 10 | Mini Palais | 14 |
| | | Pierre Gagnaire | 12 |
| CLUBS | | Le Relais de l'Entrecôte | 15 |
| Queen | 4 | Taillevent | 9 |
| Rex Club | 1 | | |
| Scop' Club | 3 | BARS | |
| Showcase | 5 | Bar Costes | 8 |
| Social Club | 2 | La Champmeslé | 3 |
| | | Delaville Café | 1 |
| | | Le Rubis | 7 |

## The Champs-Élysées

The celebrated **avenue des Champs-Élysées**, a popular rallying point at times of national crisis and the scene of big military parades on Bastille Day, sweeps down from the Arc de Triomphe towards the place de la Concorde. Seen from a distance it's an impressive sight, but close up can be a little disappointing, with its constant stream of traffic, fast-food outlets and chain stores. Over the last decade or so, however, it's been steadily regaining something of its former cachet as a chic address: top fashion stores have moved in, once dowdy shops have undergone stylish makeovers and acquired cool bar-restaurants, while new, fashionable cafés and restaurants in the streets around have injected fresh buzz and glamour. Just off the avenue, **rue Francois 1er** and **avenue Montaigne**, part of the *"triangle d'or"* (golden triangle), are home to the most exclusive names in fashion: Dior, Prada, Chanel and many others.

The Champs-Élysées began life as a leafy promenade, an extension of the Tuileries gardens. It was transformed into a fashionable thoroughfare during the Second Empire when members of the *haute bourgeoisie* built themselves splendid mansions along its length and high society would come to stroll and frequent the cafés and theatres. Most mansions subsequently gave way to office blocks and the beau monde moved where, but remnants of the avenue's glitzy heyday live on at the *Lido* cabaret, *...quet's* café-restaurant, the perfumier Guerlain's shop and the former *Claridges* hotel, ...ow a swanky shopping arcade.

## Musée Jacquemart-André

158 bd Haussmann, 8ᵉ • Daily 10am–6pm • €11; free audioguides available in English • ☎ 01 45 62 11 59, ⓦ musee-jacquemart-andre .com • Mᵒ Miromesnil/St-Philippe-du-Roule

The **Musée Jacquemart-André**, just one of the select museums north of the Champs-Élysées, is a splendid mansion laden with the outstanding works of art that its owners, banker Édouard André and his wife Nélie Jacquemart, collected on their extensive trips abroad. Informative audioguides take you through sumptuous *salons*, mainly decorated in Louis XV and Louis XVI style. The pride of the couple's collection was their early Italian Renaissance paintings, on the upper floor, including Uccello's *St George and the Dragon*, a haunting *Virgin and Child* by Mantegna, and another by Botticelli. An excellent way to finish off a visit is a reviving halt at the museum's **salon de thé**, with its lavish interior and ceiling frescoes by Tiepolo.

## South of the Rond-Point des Champs-Élysées

The lower stretch of the Champs-Élysées, between the Rond-Point des Champs-Élysées and place de la Concorde, is bordered by chestnut trees and flowerbeds and is the most pleasant part of the avenue for a stroll. Rising above the greenery to the south are the splendid **Grand Palais** and **Petit Palais**, both built for the World Fair in 1900. On the other side of the avenue, to the north of place Clemenceau, combat police guard the high walls round the presidential **Palais de l'Élysée** and the line of ministries and embassies ending with the US in prime position on the corner of place de la Concorde.

### Grand Palais

Av Winston Churchill; Galeries nationales entry at 3 av du General Eisenhower, 8ᵉ • Mon & Wed–Sun 10am–8pm, till 10pm on Wed • €12 • ☎ 01 44 13 17 17, ⓦ grandpalais.fr • Mᵒ Champs-Elysees-Clemenceau

The **Grand Palais** is a grandiose Neoclassical edifice topped with a huge glass cupola. The cupola forms the centrepiece of the *nef* (nave), an impressive exhibition space, used for large-scale installations, fashion shows and trade fairs. In the Grand Palais' north wing is the **Galeries nationales**, the city's prime venue for blockbuster art exhibitions, while its western wing houses the **Palais de la Découverte** science museum.

#### Palais de la Découverte

Av Franklin D. Roosevelt, 8ᵉ • Tues–Sat 9.30am–6pm, Sun 10am–7pm • €8 • ☎ 01 56 43 20 20, ⓦ palais-decouverte.com • Mᵒ Champs-Elysees-Clemenceau

The **Palais de la Découverte** is Paris's original science museum, dating from 1937. The emphasis, as its name suggests, is very much on discovery and experiment; there are plenty of interactive exhibits and working models to help you, for example, discover the properties of electro-magnets, or find out how ants and spiders communicate. In addition, there is an excellent planetarium and engaging temporary exhibitions.

#### Petit Palais

Av Winston Chuchill, 8ᵉ • Tues–Sun 10am–6pm • Free • ☎ 01 53 43 40 00, ⓦ petitpalais.paris.fr • Mᵒ Champs-Elysees-Clemenceau

The **Petit Palais**, facing the Grand Palais, is hardly "petit" but certainly palatial, boasting beautiful spiral wrought-iron staircases, ceiling frescoes and a grand gallery on the lines of Versailles' Hall of Mirrors. At first sight it looks like it's mopped up the leftovers discarded by the city's other galleries, but there are some real gems here, such as Monet's *Sunset at Lavacourt* and Courbet's provocative *Young Ladies on the Bank of the Seine*.

## Place de la Concorde

At the lower end of the Champs is the vast **place de la Concorde**, where crazed traffic makes crossing over to the middle a death-defying task. As it happens, some 1300 people did die here between 1793 and 1795, beneath the Revolutionary guillotine – Louis XVI, Marie-Antoinette, Danton and Robespierre among them. The centrepiece of the square is a stunning gold-tipped **obelisk** from the temple of Luxor, offered as a favour-currying gesture by the viceroy of Egypt in 1829. From here there are sweeping vistas in all directions; the Champs-Élysées looks particularly impressive, and you can admire the alignment of the Assemblée Nationale in the south with the church of the Madeleine – sporting an identical Neoclassical facade – to the north.

## Jardin des Tuileries

East of place de la Concorde lies the **Jardin des Tuileries**, the formal French garden *par excellence*. It dates back to the 1570s, when Catherine de Médicis had the site cleared of the medieval warren of tilemakers (*tuileries*) to make way for a palace and grounds. One hundred years later, Louis XIV commissioned renowned landscape artist Le Nôtre to redesign them and the results are largely what you see today: straight avenues, formal flowerbeds and splendid vistas. Shady tree-lined paths flank the grand central alley, and ornamental ponds frame both ends. The much-sought-after chairs strewn around the ponds are a good spot from which to admire the landscaped surroundings and contemplate the superb statues executed by the likes of Coustou and Coysevox, many of them now replaced by copies, the originals transferred to the Louvre.

### The Jeu de Paume

1 place de la Concorde, 1ᵉʳ · Tues noon–9pm, Wed–Fri noon–7pm, Sat & Sun 10am–7pm · €8.50 · ☎ 01 47 03 12 50, ⓦ jeudepaume.org · Mᵒ Concorde

At the Concorde end of the Jardin des Tuileries is the **Jeu de Paume**, once a royal tennis court and now a venue for major exhibitions of photography and video art; recent retrospectives included Martin Parr and Edward Steichen. There's also a small café and good bookshop.

### The Orangerie

Jardin des Tuileries, 1ᵉʳ · Daily except Tues 9am–6pm · €7.50 · ☎ 01 44 77 80 07, ⓦ musee-orangerie.fr · Mᵒ Concorde

Originally designed to protect the Tuileries' orange trees, the **Orangerie**, an elegant Neoclassical-style building, now houses a private art collection including eight of Monet's giant water-lily paintings, vast, mesmerizing canvases executed in the last years of the artist's life. On the lower floor of the museum is a fine collection of paintings by Monet's contemporaries. Highlights include a number of Cézanne still lifes, sensuous nudes by Renoir and vibrant landscapes by Derain.

# The Louvre

The palace of the **Louvre** cuts a magnificent Classical swathe right through the centre of the city – a fitting setting for one of the world's grandest art galleries. Originally little more than a feudal fortress, the castle was rebuilt in the new Renaissance style from 1546, under François I. Over the next century and a half, France's rulers steadily aggrandized their palace without significantly altering its style, and the result is an amazingly harmonious building. Admittedly, Napoleon's pink marble Arc du Carrousel, standing at the western end of the main courtyard, looks a bit out of place, but it wasn't until the building of IM Pei's controversial Pyramide in 1989, followed by the new Islamic arts department in 2012, with its sinuous glass and gold roof, that the museum saw any significant architectural departure.

e origins of the art gallery, the **Musée du Louvre**, lie in the French kings' personal collections. The royal academy mounted exhibitions, known as salons, in the palace early as 1725, but the Louvre was only opened as a public **art gallery** in 1793, in the midst of the Revolution. Within a decade, Napoleon's wagonloads of war booty transformed the Louvre's art collection into the world's largest – and not all the loot has been returned.

## The Musée du Louvre

It's easy to be put off by tales of long queues outside the Pyramide, endless foot-wearying corridors amd multilingual jostles in front of the *Mona Lisa*, but there are ways around such hassles: you can use a back entrance, stop at one of the cafés or make for a less well-known section. Ultimately, the draw of the mighty collections of the **Musée du Louvre** is irresistible.

A **floor plan**, available free from the information booth in the Hall Napoléon, will help you find your way around. It's wise not to attempt to see too much – even if you spent the entire day here you'd only see a fraction of the collection. The museum's size does at least make it easy to get away from the crowds – beyond the Denon wing you can mostly explore in peace. You can always step outside for a break, but three moderately expensive **cafés** (see p.126) are enticing and open all day.

From the Hall Napoléon under the **Pyramide**, stairs lead into each of the three wings: Denon (south), Richelieu (north) and Sully (east, around the giant quadrangle of the Cour Carré). Few visitors will be able to resist the allure of the *Mona Lisa*, in the **Denon** wing, housed along with the rest of the Louvre's Italian paintings and sculptures and its large-scale French nineteenth-century canvases. A relatively peaceful alternative would be to focus on the grand chronologies of French painting and sculpture, in the **Richelieu** wing. For a complete change of scene, descend to the **Medieval Louvre** section on the lower ground floor of Sully where you'll find the dramatic stump of Philippe-Auguste's keep and vestiges of Charles V's medieval palace walls.

### Antiquities

The **Antiquities** galleries cover the sculptures, stone-carved writings, pottery and other relics of the ancient Near East, including the Mesopotamian, Sumerian, Babylonian, Assyrian and Phoenician civilizations, plus the art of ancient Persia. The highlight of this section is the boldly sculpted stonework, much of it in relief. Watch out for the statues and busts depicting the young Sumerian prince Gudea, and the black, 2m-high Code of Hammurabi, a hugely important find from the Mesopotamian civilization, dating from around 1800 BC.

**Egyptian Antiquities** contains jewellery, domestic objects, sandals, sarcophagi and dozens of examples of the delicate naturalism of Egyptian decorative technique, such as the wall tiles depicting a piebald calf galloping through fields of papyrus, and a duck taking off from a marsh. Among the major exhibits are the Great Sphinx, carved from a single block of pink granite, the polychrome Seated Scribe statue, the striking, life-size wooden statue of Chancellor Nakhti, a bust of Amenophis IV and a low-relief sculpture of Sethi I and the goddess Hathor.

The collection of **Greek and Roman Antiquities**, mostly statues, is one of the finest in the world. The biggest crowd-pullers in the museum, after the *Mona Lisa*, are here: the *Winged Victory of Samothrace*, at the top of Denon's great staircase, and the *Venus de Milo*. Venus is surrounded by hordes of antecedent Aphrodites, from the graceful marble head known as the "Kaufmann Head" and the delightful *Venus of Arles* to the strange *Dame d'Auxerre*. In the Roman section a sterner style takes over, but there are some very attractive mosaics from Asia Minor and vivid frescoes from Pompeii and Herculaneum.

## Islamic arts

In 2012 an entirely new section of the museum, the department of **Islamic arts**, was opened in the restored Cour Visconti. More than 2500 objects, many never before displayed, have been gathered here from the Louvre's own collections and the Musée des Arts Décoratifs. Under a stunning rippling glass-and-gold roof, meant to evoke a silk headscarf, you can admire anything from early Islamic inscriptions to intricate Moorish ivories, and from ninth-century Iraqi moulded glass to exquisite miniature paintings from the court of Mughal India.

## French Sculpture

The **French Sculpture** section is arranged on the lowest two levels of the Richelieu wing, with the more monumental pieces housed in two grand, glass-roofed courtyards: the four triumphal *Marly Horses* grace the Cour Marly, while Cour Puget has Puget's dynamic *Milon de Crotone* as its centrepiece. The surrounding rooms trace the development of sculpture in France from painful Romanesque Crucifixions to the lofty public works of David d'Angers. The startlingly realistic Gothic pieces – notably the Burgundian *Tomb of Philippe Pot*, complete with hooded mourners – and the experimental Mannerist works are particularly rewarding, but towards the end of the course you may find yourself crying out for an end to all those gracefully perfect nudes and grandiose busts. You'll have to leave the Louvre for Rodin, but an alternative antidote lies in the intense **Italian and northern European** sections, on the lower two floors of Denon, where you'll find such bold masterpieces as two of Michelangelo's writhing *Slaves*, Duccio's virtuoso *Virgin and Child Surrounded by Angels*, and some severely Gothic Virgins from Flanders and Germany.

## Objets d'Art

The vast **Objets d'Art** section, on the first floor of the Richelieu wing, presents the finest tapestries, ceramics, jewellery and furniture commissioned by France's wealthiest and most influential patrons. Walking through the entire 81-room chronology affords a powerful sense of the evolution of aesthetic taste at its most refined and opulent. The exception is the **Middle Ages** section, which is of a decidedly pious nature, while the apotheosis of the whole experience comes towards the end, as the circuit passes through the breathtakingly plush **apartments** of Napoléon III's Minister of State.

## Painting

The largest section by far is **Painting**. A good place to start a tour of **French painting** is in the Sully wing with the master of French Classicism, Poussin, whose profound, mythological themes influenced artists such as Lorrain, Le Brun and Rigaud. After this grandly Classical suite of rooms, the more intimate paintings of Watteau come as a relief, followed by Chardin's intense still lifes and the inspired Rococo sketches by Fragonard known as the *Figures of Fantasy*. From the southern wing of Sully to the end of this section, the chilly wind of Neoclassicism blows through the paintings of Gros, Gérard, Prud'hon, David and Ingres, contrasting with the more sentimental style that begins with Greuze and continues into the Romanticism of Géricault and Delacroix. The final set of rooms takes in Millet, Corot and the Barbizon school of painting, prefiguring the Impressionists.

The nineteenth century is most dramatically represented in the second area of the Louvre devoted to painting, on the first floor of the Denon wing. A pair of giant rooms is dedicated to Nationalism and Romanticism, respectively, featuring some of France's best-known works including such gigantic, epic canvases as David's *Coronation of Napoleon in Notre Dame*, Géricault's *The Raft of the Medusa*, and Delacroix's *Liberty Leading the People*, the icon of nineteenth-century revolution.

Denon also houses the frankly staggering **Italian collection**. The high-ceilinged Salon Carré – which has been used to exhibit paintings since the first "salon" of the Royal Academy in 1725 – displays the so-called Primitives, with works by Uccello, Giotto,

Cimabue and Fra Angelico. To the west of the Salon, the famous Grande Galerie stretches into the distance, parading all the great names of the Italian Renaissance – Mantegna, Filippo Lippi, Leonardo da Vinci, Raphael, Coreggio, Titian. The playfully troubled Mannerists kick in about halfway along, but the second half of the Galerie dwindles in quality and representativeness as it moves towards the eighteenth century. Leonardo's *Mona Lisa*, along with Paolo Veronese's huge *Marriage at Cana*, hangs in the Salle des États, a room halfway along the Galerie. If you want to catch *La Joconde* – as she's known to the French – without a swarm of admirers, go first or last thing in the day. At the far end of Denon, the relatively small but worthwhile **Spanish** collection has some notable Goya portraits.

The western end of Richelieu's second floor is given over to a more selective collection of **German**, **Flemish** and **Dutch** paintings, with a brilliant set of works by Rubens and no fewer than twelve Rembrandts, including some powerful self-portraits. Interspersed throughout the painting section are rooms dedicated to the Louvre's impressive collection of **prints and drawings**, exhibited in rotation.

---

**INFORMATION**                                    **THE MUSÉE DU LOUVRE**

**Website** ⊚ louvre.fr.

**Opening hours** The permanent collection is open daily except Tuesday, from 9am to 6pm. On Wednesdays and Fridays, it stays open till 9.45pm – these "nocturnes" are an excellent time to visit. Note that almost a quarter of the museum's rooms are closed one day a week on a rotating basis, though the most popular rooms are always open.

**Admission** The entry fee is €10, free on the first Sunday of each month, and free to under-18s and under-26s from the EU (with proof of residency) at all times. You may leave and re-enter as many times as you like throughout the day.

**Tickets** You can buy tickets in advance online, by phone (☎ 01 46 91 57 57), or from branches of FNAC and Virgin Megastore (conveniently, there's one right outside the entrance under the Arc du Carrousel).

**Access** The Pyramid is the main entrance, although the often lengthy lines can be avoided by using one of the alternative entrances: Porte des Lions, just east of the Pont Royal; Arc du Carrousel, 99 rue de Rivoli; or directly from the métro station Palais Royal-Musée du Louvre (line 1 platform). If you've already got a ticket or a museum pass you can also enter from the passage Richelieu.

---

## Les Arts Décoratifs

Entrance at 107 rue de Rivoli • Tues, Wed & Fri–Sun 11am–6pm, Thurs 11am–9pm • €9 • ☎ 01 44 55 57 50, ⊚ lesartsdecoratifs.fr

The westernmost wing of the Louvre palace houses **Les Arts Décoratifs**, an umbrella for three separate museums, the **Musée des Arts Décoratifs**, the **Musée de la Mode et du Textile** and the **Musée de la Publicite**.

### Musée des Arts Décoratifs

The **Musée des Arts Décoratifs** has an eclectic collection of art objects and superbly crafted furnishing. The works in the "historical" rooms (from the medieval period through to Art Nouveau) may seem humble in comparison with those in the Louvre's Objets d'Art section, but these furnishings were made to be used, and feel more accessible as a result. There are curious and beautiful chairs, dressers and tables, religious paintings, Venetian glass and some wonderful tapestries. A number of "period rooms" have been reconstituted top-to-toe in the style of different eras; there's even an entire 1903 bedroom by Hector Guimard, the Art Nouveau designer behind Paris's métro stations. The topmost floors show off designer furnishings from the 1940s through to the present day, with some great examples from the prince of French design, Philippe Starck. Separate galleries focus on jewellery and toys.

### Musée de la Mode et du Textile

The **Musée de la Mode et du Textile** holds high-quality exhibitions demonstrating the most brilliant and cutting-edge of Paris fashions from all eras. Recent exhibitions have included couture handbags, a history of fashion curated by Christian Lacroix, and a retrospective of the Parisian designer, Sonia Rykiel.

### Musée de la Publicité

Immediately above the Musée de la Mode et du Textile, the **Musée de la Publicité** shows off its collection of advertising posters through cleverly themed, temporary exhibitions. Designed by the French über-architect Jean Nouvel, the space mixes exposed brickwork and steel panelling with crumbling Louvre finery.

# The Opéra district

Between the Louvre and **boulevards Haussmann, Montmartre, Poissonnière** and **Bonne-Nouvelle** to the north lies the city's main commercial and financial district. Right at its heart stand the solid institutions of the Banque de France and the Bourse, while just to the north, beyond the glittering **Opéra-Garnier**, are the large department stores **Galeries Lafayette** and **Printemps**. More well-heeled shopping is concentrated on the rue **St-Honoré** in the west and the streets around aristocratic place Vendôme, lined with top couturiers, jewellers and art dealers. Scattered around the whole area are the delightful, secretive **passages** – nineteenth-century arcades that hark back to shopping from a different era.

## The Opéra-Garnier

Cnr rues Scribe & Auber, 9ᵉ • Daily 10am–4.30pm • €9 • Ⓦ operadeparis.fr • Mᵒ Opéra

Set back from the boulevard des Capucines and crowning the avenue de l'Opéra is the dazzling **Opéra-Garnier**, which was constructed from 1860 to 1875 as part of Napoléon III's new vision of Paris. The architect, Charles Garnier, whose golden bust by Carpeaux can be seen on the rue Auber side of his edifice, pulled out all the stops to provide a suitably grand space in which Second Empire high society could parade and be seen. The facade is a fabulous extravaganza of white, pink and green marble, colonnades, rearing horses, winged angels and niches holding gleaming gold busts of composers. You can look round the equally sumptuous **interior**, including the plush auditorium – rehearsals permitting – the colourful ceiling of which is the work of Chagall, and which depicts scenes from well-known operas and ballets. The visit includes the small **Bibliothèque-Musée de l'Opéra**, dedicated to the artists connected with the Opéra throughout its history, and containing model sets, paintings and temporary exhibitions on operatic themes.

## Église de la Madeleine

Place de la Madeleine, 8ᵉ • Ⓦ eglise-lamadeleine.fr • Mᵒ Madeleine

Dominating place de la Madeleine, the imperious-looking **Église de la Madeleine** is

---

### THE PASSAGES

Among the most attractive of the Opéra's **passages** is the **Galerie Vivienne**, between rue Vivienne and rue des Petits-Champs, its decor of Grecian and marine motifs providing a suitably flamboyant backdrop for its smart shops, including a branch of Jean-Paul Gaultier. But the most stylish examples are the three-storey **passage du Grand-Cerf**, between rue St-Denis and rue Dussoubs, and **Galerie Véro-Dodat**, between rue Croix-des-Petits-Champs and rue Jean-Jacques-Rousseau, named after the two pork butchers who set it up in 1824. This last is the most homogeneous and aristocratic *passage*, with painted ceilings and faux marble columns. North of rue St-Marc, the several arcades making up the **passage des Panoramas** are more workaday, although they do retain a great deal of character and an air of nostalgia about them: there's an old restaurant (*L'Arbre à Cannelle*) with fantastic carved wood panelling, and a printshop with its original 1867 fittings, as well as bric-a-brac shops, and stamp and secondhand postcard dealers. **Passage Jouffroy**, across boulevard Montmartre, harbours a number of quirky shops, including one selling antique walking sticks and another stocking exquisite dolls' house furniture.

the parish church of the cream of Parisian high society. Modelled on a Greek classical temple, it's surrounded by 52 Corinthian columns and fronted by a huge pediment depicting the Last Judgement. Originally intended as a monument to Napoleon's army, it narrowly escaped being turned into a railway station before finally being consecrated to Mary Magdalene in 1845. Inside, a wonderfully theatrical sculpture, *Mary Magdalene Ascending to Heaven*, draws your eye to the high altar, and its organ, once regularly played by Gabriel Fauré, is one of the best in Paris.

The rest of the square is largely given over to Paris's top gourmet food stores. On the east side of the Madeleine church is one of the city's oldest **flower markets** dating back to 1832 (daily except Mon).

## Place Vendôme

A short walk east of the Madeleine along ancient rue St-Honoré, a preserve of top fashion designers and art galleries, lies **place Vendôme**, one of the city's most impressive set pieces. Built by Versailles' architect Hardouin-Mansart, it's a pleasingly symmetrical, eight-sided *place*, enclosed by a harmonious ensemble of elegant mansions, graced with Corinthian pilasters, *mascarons* and steeply pitched roofs. Once the grand residences of tax collectors and financiers, they now house such luxury establishments as the *Ritz* hotel, Cartier, Bulgari and other top-flight jewellers, lending the square a decidedly exclusive air. No. 12, now occupied by Chaumet jewellers, is where Chopin died in 1849.

Somewhat out of proportion with the rest of the square, the centrepiece is a towering triumphal **column**, surmounted by a statue of Napoleon dressed as Caesar, raised in 1806 to celebrate the Battle of Austerlitz – bronze reliefs of scenes of the battle, cast from 1200 recycled Austro-Russian cannons, spiral their way up the column.

## The Palais Royal

Place du Palais Royal, 1er • M° Palais-Royal-Musée-du-Louvre

At the eastern end of rue St-Honoré stands the handsome, colonnaded **Palais Royal**, built for Cardinal Richelieu in 1624, though much modified and renovated since. The current building houses various governmental bodies and the **Comédie Française**, a long-standing venue for the classics of French theatre.

To its rear lie gardens lined with stately three-storey houses built over arcades housing quirky antique and designer shops. It's an attractive and peaceful oasis, with avenues of limes, fountains and flowerbeds. You'd hardly guess that this was a site of gambling dens, brothels and funfair attractions until the Grands Boulevards took up the baton in the 1830s. Folly, some might say, has returned in the form of Daniel Buren's **art installation**, which consists of black-and-white striped pillars, all of varying heights, dotted about the palace's main courtyard.

## Bibliothèque Nationale

Quai François-Mauriac, 1er • Exhibitions Tues–Sat 10am–7pm, Sun noon–7pm • €7 • ☎ 01 53 79 59 59, ⓦ bnf.fr • M° Bourse

North of the Palais Royal looms the huge **Bibliothèque Nationale**, the French National Library, dating back to the 1660s. It's currently undergoing major renovation, due to be completed in 2017. Parts of the library will remain open for exhibitions, though it's best to check the website for the latest updates.

You can enter free of charge and peer into the atmospheric reading rooms, though some look rather bereft, as many books have now been transferred to the new François Mitterrand site on the Left Bank (see p.106).

### Cabinet des Monnaies, Médailles et Antiques

Mon–Fri 9–6pm, Sat 9–5pm • Free

Within the Bibliothèque Nationale is a small museum, the **Cabinet des Monnaies, Médailles et Antiques**, a rich display of coins and ancient treasures, such as Charlemagne's ivory chess set, built up by successive kings from Philippe-Auguste onwards. The Cabinet will close in 2014, probably for a couple of years, during which period it will be transferred to grander rooms in the building as part of the library's extensive revamp.

# Beaubourg and around

The **Beaubourg** quartier centres on the **Centre Pompidou,** one of the city's most popular and recognizable landmarks and one of the twentieth century's most radical buildings. The area around the Centre Pompidou is home to more contemporary art. Jean Tinguely and Niki de Saint-Phalle created the colourful moving sculptures and

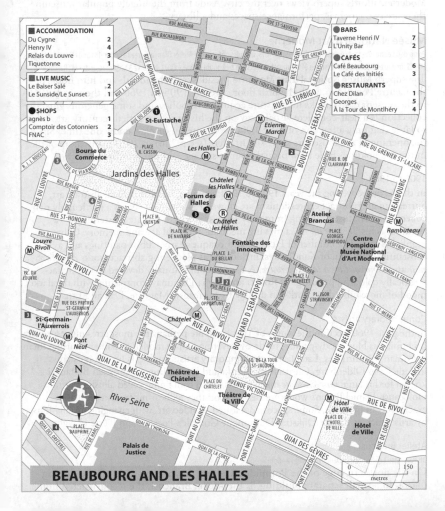

BEAUBOURG AND LES HALLES

fountains in the pool in front of Église St-Merri on **place Igor Stravinsky**. This squirting waterworks pays homage to Stravinsky – each fountain corresponds to one of his compositions (*The Firebird*, *The Rite of Spring* and so on) – and shows scant respect for passers-by. To the north are numerous commercial **art galleries**, occupying the attractive old *hôtels particuliers* on pedestrianized **rue Quincampoix**, while to the west is the rather less alluring **Les Halles** underground shopping and leisure complex.

## Centre Pompidou

The opening of the **Centre Pompidou** in 1977 gave rise to some violent reactions; since then, however, it has won over critics and public alike. Architects Renzo Piano and Richard Rogers freed up maximum space inside by placing all infrastructure outside: utility pipes and escalator tubes, all brightly colour-coded according to their function, climb around the exterior in crazy snakes-and-ladders fashion. The transparent escalator on the front of the building, giving access to the **Musée National d'Art Moderne**, affords superb views over the city. Aside from the hugely popular museum there are two cinemas, performance spaces and a library.

### Musée National d'Art Moderne

Pompidou Centre, 4e • Daily except Tues 11am–9pm • €13, includes entry to the Atelier Brancusi; free to under-18s and EU residents aged 18–25; free to everyone on the first Sun of the month; tickets can be bought online • ☎ 01 44 78 12 33, ⓦ cnac-gp.fr • Mo Rambuteau

The superb **Musée National d'Art Moderne** presides over the fourth and fifth floors of the Centre Pompidou, with the fifth floor covering 1905 to 1960 and the fourth 1960 to the present day. Thanks to an astute acquisitions policy and some generous gifts, the collection is a near-complete visual essay on the history of twentieth-century art and is so large that only a fraction of the 50,000 works are on display at any one time. Since the opening of the museum's sister site in Metz (see p.246) in 2010 many more of the museum's holdings have been brought out of storage and put on display.

#### 1905 to 1960

In the section covering the years **1905 to 1960** Fauvism, Cubism, Dada, abstract art, Surrealism and abstract expressionism are all well represented. There's a particularly rich collection of Matisses, ranging from early Fauvist works to his late masterpieces – a standout is his *Tristesse du roi*, a moving meditation on old age and memory. Other highlights include a number of Picasso's and Braque's early Cubist paintings and a substantial collection of Kandinskys, including his pioneering abstract works *Avec l'arc noir* and *Composition à la tache rouge*. A whole room is usually devoted to the characteristically colourful paintings of Robert and Sonia Delaunay, contrasting with the darker mood of more unsettling works on display by Surrealists Magritte, Dalí and Ernst.

#### Contemporary artists

In the post-1960s section the works of Yves Klein are perhaps the most arresting, especially his luminous blue "body prints", made by covering female models in paint and using them as human paintbrushes. Established **contemporary artists** you're likely to come across include Claes Oldenburg, Christian Boltanski and Daniel Buren. Christian Boltanski is known for his large *mise-en-scène* installations, often containing veiled allusions to the Holocaust. Daniel Buren's works are easy to spot: they all bear his trademark stripes, exactly 8.7cm in width. Some space is dedicated to **video art**, with changing installations by artists such as Rineke Dijkstra, Dominique Gonzalez-Foerster and Pierre Huyghe.

#### Atelier Brancusi

Off Pompidou Centre piazza • Daily except Tues 2–6pm

On the northern edge of the Pompidou Centre, down some steps off the sloping piazza, in a small separate building, is the **Atelier Brancusi**, the reconstructed home and studio of Constantin Brancusi. The sculptor bequeathed the contents of his workshop to the state on condition that the rooms be arranged exactly as he left them, and they provide a fascinating insight into how he lived and worked. Studios one and two are crowded with Brancusi's trademark abstract bird and column shapes in highly polished brass and marble, while studios three and four comprise the artist's private quarters.

## Hôtel de Ville

Place de l'Hôtel de Ville, 4ᵉ • **Guided tours** Once a week (days and times vary); book ahead on ☎ 01 42 76 50 49 or at the Salon d'Accueil at 29 rue de Rivoli **Exhibitions** Entrance usually at 5 rue de Lobau • Mon–Sat 10am–7pm • Free **Ice rink** Dec–Feb Mon–Fri noon–10pm, Sat & Sun 9am–10pm • Skate hire €5 • Mᵒ Hôtel de Ville

South of the Pompidou Centre, rue Renard runs down to the **Hôtel de Ville**, the seat of the city's government. It's a mansion of gargantuan proportions in florid neo-Renaissance style, modelled pretty much on the previous building that was burned down in the Commune in 1871. Guided tours allow you to see some of the lavish reception rooms, decorated with murals by artists such as Puvis de Chavannes and Henri Gervex. The Hôtel de Ville also stages regular free exhibitions on Parisian themes. In front, the huge square – a notorious guillotine site in the French Revolution – transforms into a popular ice-skating rink in winter.

## Les Halles

**Les Halles** was the city's main food market for more than eight hundred years until it was moved out to the suburbs in 1969 amid widespread opposition from city residents. It was replaced by a large underground shopping and leisure complex, known as the **Forum des Halles**, and an RER/métro interchange. Unsightly, run-down, even unsavoury in parts, the complex is now widely acknowledged as an architectural disaster – a major facelift, due to be completed in 2014, will, hopefully, give it a little more lustre. A vast glass roof, dubbed **La Canopée**, will be suspended over the forum, allowing light to flood in, while overground a promenade on the model of Barcelona's Ramblas will be created, as well as ponds and playgrounds.

### Forum des Halles

Mᵒ Les Halles/Châtelet/RER Châtelet Les Halles

The **Forum des Halles** centre stretches underground from the Bourse du Commerce rotunda to rue Pierre-Lescot and is spread over four levels. The overground section comprises aquarium-like arcades of shops, arranged around a sunken patio, and landscaped gardens. The shops are mostly devoted to high-street fashion and there's also a large FNAC bookshop and the Forum des Créateurs, an outlet for young fashion designers. It's not all commerce, however: there's scope for various diversions including swimming, billiards and movie-going at the **Forum des Images** (see p.138).

Although little now remains of the former working-class quarter, you can still catch a flavour of the old Les Halles atmosphere in some of the surrounding bars and bistros and on the lively market street of **rue Montorgueil** to the north, where traditional grocers, horse butchers and fishmongers continue to ply their trade.

### St-Eustache

2 Impasse St-Eustache, 1ᵉʳ • ⓦ saint-eustache.org • Mᵒ Les Halles

At the foot of rue Montorgueil stands the beautiful, gracefully buttressed church of **St-Eustache**. Built between 1532 and 1637, it's a glorious fusion of Gothic and Renaissance styles, with soaring vaults, Corinthian pilasters and arcades. It was the scene of Molière's baptism, and Rameau and Marivaux are buried here.

**1**

# The Marais

The **Marais** is one of the most seductive districts of Paris. Having largely escaped the heavy-handed attentions of Baron Haussmann, and unspoiled by modern development, the *quartier* is full of handsome Renaissance *hôtels particuliers*, narrow lanes and inviting cafés and restaurants.

There's a significant, if dwindling, Jewish community here, established in the twelfth century and centred on **rue des Rosiers**, and with its long-lasting reputation for tolerance of minorities, the area has become popular with gay Parisians. Prime streets for wandering are **rue des Francs-Bourgeois**, lined with fashion and interior design boutiques, **rue Vieille-du-Temple** and **rue des Archives**, with their buzzy bars and cafés, and **rue Charlot and rue de Poitou** in the so-called Haut Marais, home to sleek art galleries and chic young fashion outlets. The Marais' animated streets and atmospheric old buildings would be reason enough to visit, but the *quartier* also boasts a high concentration of excellent museums, not least among them the **Musée Picasso**, the **Carnavalet** history museum, the **Musée d'Art et d'Histoire du Judaïsme**, and the **Musée de l'Histoire de France**, all set in fine mansions.

## Musée de l'Histoire de France

60 rue des Francs-Bourgeois, 3ᵉ • Mon & Wed–Fri 10am–12.30pm & 2–5.30pm, Sat & Sun 2–5.30pm • €4, exhibitions €6 • ⓦ archivesnationales.culture.gouv.fr • Mᵒ Rambuteau/St-Paul

A fine place to start exploring the Marais is the eighteenth-century magnificence of the **Palais Soubise**, which houses the Archives Nationales de France and the **Musée de l'Histoire de France**. The palace's fabulous rococo interiors are the setting for changing exhibitions drawn from the archives, as well as a permanent collection of documents including Joan of Arc's trial proceedings, with a doodled impression of her in the margin, and a Revolutionary calendar where "J" stands for Jean-Jacques Rousseau and "L" for Labourer. The palace's interior gardens make for a pleasant stroll.

## Musée Carnavalet

23 rue de Sévigné, 4ᵉ • Tues–Sun 10am–6pm • Free; entry to special exhibitions varies • ☎ 01 44 59 58 58, ⓦ carnavalet.paris.fr • Mᵒ St-Paul

The **Musée Carnavalet** presents the history of Paris from its origins up to the *belle époque* through an extraordinary collection of paintings, sculptures, decorative arts and archeological finds. The museum's setting in two beautiful Renaissance mansions, Hôtel Carnavalet and Hôtel Le Peletier, surrounded by attractive gardens, makes a visit worthwhile in itself. There are 140 rooms in all, with hardly a dull one among them. The **collection** begins with nineteenth- and early twentieth-century shop and inn signs (beautiful objects in themselves) and fascinating models of Paris through the ages. Other highlights on the ground floor include the renovated orangery, which houses a significant collection of Neolithic finds such as wooden pirogues unearthed during the 1990s redevelopment of the Bercy riverside area.

On the **first floor** is a succession of richly decorated Louis XV and Louis XVI salons and boudoirs rescued from buildings destroyed to make way for Haussmann's boulevards, and remounted here more or less intact. Rooms 128 to 148 are largely devoted to the *belle époque*, evoked through vivid paintings of the period and some wonderful Art Nouveau interiors, among which is the sumptuous peacock-green interior designed by Alphonse Mucha for Fouquet's jewellery shop in the rue Royal. José-Maria Sert's Art Deco ballroom, with its extravagant gold-leaf decor and grand-scale paintings, including one of the Queen of Sheba with a train of elephants, is also well preserved. Nearby is a section on literary life at the beginning of the twentieth century, including a reconstruction of Proust's cork-lined bedroom.

The **second floor** is full of mementos of the **French Revolution**: models of the Bastille, the original *Declaration of the Rights of Man and the Citizen*, tricolours and liberty caps, sculpted allegories of Reason, crockery with Revolutionary slogans, models of the guillotine and execution orders to make you shed a tear for royalists as well as revolutionaries.

## Musée Picasso

5 rue de Thorigny, 3ᵉ • ☎ 01 42 71 25 21, ⓦ musee-picasso.fr • Mᵒ Filles du Calvaire/St-Paul

The **Musée Picasso**, closed until 2013 for a major renovation, is set in the magnificent seventeenth-century Hôtel Salé and is the largest collection of Picassos anywhere, representing almost all the major periods of the artist's life from 1905 onwards. Many of the works were owned by Picasso and on his death in 1973 were seized by the state in lieu of taxes owed. The result is an unedited body of work, which, although not including the most recognizable of Picasso's masterpieces, does provide a sense of the artist's development and an insight into the person behind the myth. In addition, the collection includes paintings Picasso bought or was given by contemporaries such as Matisse and Cézanne, his African masks and sculptures and photographs of him in his studio taken by Brassaï.

The **exhibition** covers the artist's blue period; his experiments with Cubism and Surrealism; larger-scale works on themes of war and peace; and numerous paintings of the Minotaur and bullfighting, reflecting his later preoccupations with love and death. Perhaps some of the most striking works on display are Picasso's more personal ones – those of his children, wives and lovers – such as *Olga Pensive* (1923), in which his first wife is shown lost in thought, the deep blue of her dress reflecting her mood.

The museum also holds a substantial number of Picasso's **engravings**, **ceramics** and **sculpture**, showcasing the remarkable ease with which the artist moved from one medium to another. Some of the most arresting sculptures are those he created from recycled household objects, such as the endearing *La Chèvre* (Goat), whose stomach is made from a basket, and *Tête de Taureau*, an ingenious pairing of a bicycle seat and handlebars.

## The Jewish quarter

One block south of the rue des Francs-Bourgeois, the area around narrow **rue des Rosiers** has traditionally been the **Jewish quarter** of the city, though recent incursions by trendy fashion boutiques are changing the character of the place. Some Jewish shops survive, however, such as the odd kosher food shop, a Hebrew bookstore and falafel takeaways, testimony to the influence of the North African Sephardim, who replenished Paris's Jewish population, depleted when its Ashkenazim were rounded up by the Nazis and the French police and transported to the concentration camps.

### Musée d'Art et d'Histoire du Judaisme

71 rue de Temple, 3ᵉ • Mon–Fri 11am–6pm, Sun 10am–6pm • €6.80 • ☎ 01 53 01 86 53, ⓦ mahj.org • Mᵒ Rambuteau

The attractively restored Hôtel de St-Aignan, just northeast of the Centre Pompidou, is home to the **Musée d'Art et d'Histoire du Judaisme**, which traces the culture, history and artistic endeavours of the Jewish people from the Middle Ages to the present day. The focus is on the history of Jews in France, but there are also many artefacts from the rest of Europe and North Africa. Some of the most notable exhibits are a Gothic-style Hanukkah lamp, one of the very few French Jewish artefacts to survive from the period before the expulsion of the Jews from France in 1394; an Italian gilded circumcision chair from the seventeenth century; and a completely intact late nineteenth-century Austrian *sukkah*, a brightly painted wooden hut built as a temporary dwelling for the celebration of the harvest. One room is devoted to the **Dreyfus affair**, documented with letters, postcards and press clippings. There's also a significant collection of paintings

1

**3e**

RUE DE TURBIGO

RUE REAUMUR

RUE AU MAIRE

SQUARE
DU TEMPLE

RUE DE BRETAGNE

RUE DE TURENNE

RUE RAMBUTEAU

RUE BEAUBOURG

RUE DES GRAVILLIERS

RUE CHAPON

RUE DU TEMPLE

RUE DES ARCHIVES

Marché
des Enfants
Rouges

RUE ST-MARTIN

RUE DU GRENIER ST-LAZARE

RUE DE MONTMORENCY

RUE M. LE COMTE

Musée d'Art et
d'Histoire
du Judaïsme

RUE DES HAUDRIETTES

RUE CHARLOT

RUE DE POITOU

Atelier
Brancusi

Ⓜ Rambuteau

RUE RAMBUTEAU

RUE DE BRAQUE

Musée
de l'Histoire
de France

PL. GEORGES
POMPIDOU

RUE BEAUBOURG

RUE G. L'ANGEVIN

RUE DE BRAQUE

Centre
Pompidou/
Musée National
d'Art Moderne

RUE DU TEMPLE

RUE DES 4 FILS

Musée
Picasso

RUE AUBRY LE BOUCHER

RUE SIMON LE FRANC

R. DES BLANCS MANTEAUX

RUE DE LA PERLE

RUE COUTURES
ST GERVAIS

PLACE
E. MICHELET

PL. IGOR
STRAVINSKY

RUE ST-MERRI

RUE DU PLÂTRE

RUE DES FRANCS BOURGEOIS

PLACE DE
THORIGNY

RUE DU PARC ROYAL

RUE BARBETTE

RUE PERNELLE

RUE DU TEMPLE

RUE STE-CROIX DE LA BRETONNERIE

Musée
Carnavalet

RUE DE RIVOLI

RUE ST-DENIS

RUE DE LA VERRERIE

**4e**

RUE DES ARCHIVES

RUE VIEILLE DU TEMPLE

RUE DES FRANCS BOURGEOIS

Hôtel
de Ville

Ⓜ

RUE DE MOUSSY

RUE DU ROI DE SICILE

RUE DES ROSIERS

AVENUE VICTORIA

PLACE DE
L'HÔTEL DE VILLE

Hôtel
de Ville

RUE DU TRÉSOR

PL. DU
MARCHÉ
STE-CATHERINE

Mairie de
Paris

PLACE
ST-GERVAIS

RUE FRANÇOIS MIRON

RUE DE RIVOLI

Ⓜ St-Paul

RUE ST-ANTOINE

QUAI DE LA CORSE

QUAI DE L'HÔTEL DE VILLE

St-Gervais
St-Protais

RUE DU PONT LOUIS PHILIPPE

Maison
Européenne de la
Photographie

✚ Hôtel
Dieu

PONT DE L'HÔTEL DE VILLE

Mémorial de
la Shoah

VOIE GEORGES POMPIDOU

Quai de l'Hôtel
de Ville

PL. DU
BATAILLON
FRANÇAIS
DE L'O.N.U.
EN CORÉE

RUE DE L'HÔTEL DE VILLE

SQUARE
A SCHWEITZER

RUE CHARLEMAGNE

RUE NEUVE ST-PIERRE

RUE DE L'AVE MARIA

Pont Marie

Ⓜ

RUE DU CLOÎTRE NOTRE-DAME

River Seine

Cathédrale de
Notre-Dame

SQUARE
JEAN XXIII

QUAI DE BOURBON

QUAI DES CELESTINS

Quai de
Montebello

SQUARE
DE L'ÎLE DE
FRANCE

PONT ST-LOUIS

PORT DES CELESTINS

QUAI D'ANJOU

SQUARE DE
L'AVE MARIA

SQUARE
H GALLI

Île St-Louis

St-Louis-
en-l'Île

Sully
Morland Ⓜ

QUAI D'ORLÉANS

QUAI DE BÉTHUNE

BOULEVARD

PORT DE LA TOURNELLE

QUAI DE LA TOURNELLE

River Seine

PONT DE SULLY

SQUARE
BARYE

Préfecture
de Paris

QUAI HENRI IV

BOULEVARD SAINT-GERMAIN

N

# MARAIS, ÎLE ST-LOUIS AND BASTILLE

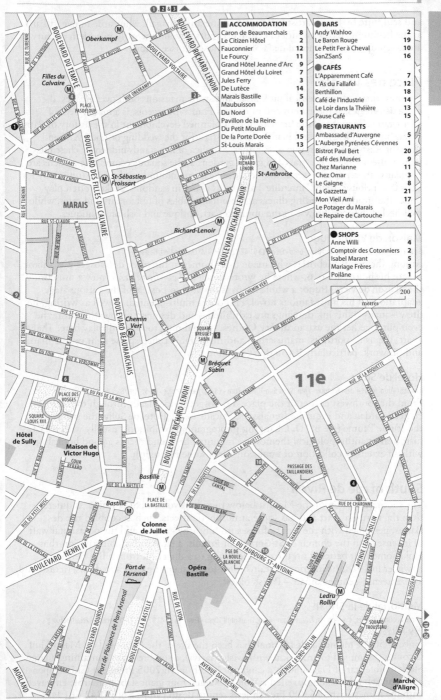

**■ ACCOMMODATION**

| | |
|---|---|
| Caron de Beaumarchais | 8 |
| Le Citizen Hôtel | 2 |
| Fauconnier | 12 |
| Le Fourcy | 11 |
| Grand Hôtel Jeanne d'Arc | 9 |
| Grand Hôtel du Loiret | 7 |
| Jules Ferry | 3 |
| De Lutèce | 14 |
| Marais Bastille | 5 |
| Maubuisson | 10 |
| Du Nord | 1 |
| Pavillon de la Reine | 6 |
| Du Petit Moulin | 4 |
| De la Porte Dorée | 15 |
| St-Louis Marais | 13 |

**● BARS**

| | |
|---|---|
| Andy Wahloo | 2 |
| Le Baron Rouge | 19 |
| Le Petit Fer à Cheval | 10 |
| SanZSanS | 16 |

**● CAFÉS**

| | |
|---|---|
| L'Apparement Café | 7 |
| L'As du Fallafel | 12 |
| Berthillon | 18 |
| Café de l'Industrie | 14 |
| Le Loir dans la Théière | 13 |
| Pause Café | 15 |

**● RESTAURANTS**

| | |
|---|---|
| Ambassade d'Auvergne | 5 |
| L'Auberge Pyrénées Cévennes | 1 |
| Bistrot Paul Bert | 20 |
| Café des Musées | 9 |
| Chez Marianne | 11 |
| Chez Omar | 3 |
| Le Gaigne | 8 |
| La Gazzetta | 21 |
| Mon Vieil Ami | 17 |
| Le Potager du Marais | 6 |
| Le Repaire de Cartouche | 4 |

**● SHOPS**

| | |
|---|---|
| Anne Willi | 4 |
| Comptoir des Cotonniers | 2 |
| Isabel Marant | 5 |
| Mariage Frères | 3 |
| Poilâne | 1 |

**1**

and sculpture by Jewish artists, such as Soutine and Chagall, who came to live in Paris at the beginning of the twentieth century. Events beyond the early twentieth century are taken up at the Mémorial de la Shoah's museum (see below).

## Place des Vosges

A grand square of symmetrical pink brick and stone mansions built over arcades, the **place des Vosges**, at the eastern end of rue des Francs-Bourgeois, is a masterpiece of aristocratic elegance and the first example of planned development in the history of Paris. It was built by Henri IV and inaugurated in 1612 for the wedding of Louis XIII and Anne of Austria; Louis's statue – or, rather, a replica of it – stands hidden by chestnut trees in the middle of the grass and gravel gardens at the square's centre. The gardens are popular with families on weekends – children can run around on the grass (unusually for Paris the "pelouse" is not "interdite") and mess about in sandpits. Buskers often play under the arcades, serenading diners at the outside tables of restaurants and cafés, while well-heeled shoppers browse in the upmarket art, antique and fashion boutiques.

### Maison de Victor Hugo

6 place des Vosges, 4ᵉ · Tues–Sun 10am–6pm · Free · ☎ 01 42 72 10 16 · Mᵒ Chemin-Vert/Bastille

Among the many celebrities who made their homes in the place des Vosges was Victor Hugo: his house, at no. 6, where he wrote much of *Les Misérables*, is now a museum, the **Maison de Victor Hugo**; a whole room is devoted to posters of the various stage adaptations of his most famous novel. Hugo was multi-talented: as well as writing, he drew – many of his ink drawings are exhibited – and designed his own furniture; he even put together the extraordinary Chinese-style dining room on display here. That apart, the usual portraits, manuscripts and memorabilia shed sparse light on the man and his work, particularly if you don't read French.

### Hôtel de Sully

62 rue St-Antoine, 4ᵉ · Tues–Fri noon–7pm, Sat & Sun 10am–7pm · €5 · ⓦ jeudepaume · Mᵒ St-Paul/Bastille

From the southwest corner of the place des Vosges, a door leads through to the formal château garden and exquisite Renaissance facade of the **Hôtel de Sully**, the sister site to the Jeu de Paume (see p.71). Changing photographic exhibitions, usually with social, historical or anthropological themes, are mounted here, and there's a good bookshop with an extensive collection of books on Paris, some in English.

## South of rue de Rivoli

The southern section of the Marais, below rues de Rivoli and St-Antoine, is quieter than the northern part and has some atmospheric streets, such as cobbled rue des Barres, perfumed with the scent of roses from nearby gardens and the occasional waft of incense from the church of **St-Gervais-St-Protais**, a late Gothic construction that looks somewhat battered on the outside owing to a direct hit from a Big Bertha howitzer in 1918. Its interior contains some lovely stained glass, carved misericords and a seventeenth-century organ – Paris's oldest.

### Mémorial de la Shoah

17 rue Geoffroy-l'Asnier, 4ᵉ · Mon–Fri & Sun 10am–6pm, Thurs until 10pm · Free · ☎ 01 42 77 44 72, ⓦ memorialdelashoah.org · Mᵒ St-Paul/Pont-Marie

Since 1956 the **Mémorial de la Shoah** has been the site of the Mémorial du Martyr Juif Inconnu (Memorial to an Unknown Jewish Martyr), a sombre crypt containing a large black marble star of David, with a candle at its centre. In 2005 President Chirac opened a new **museum** here and unveiled a Wall of Names: four giant slabs of marble engraved with the names of the 76,000 French Jews sent to death camps from 1942 to 1944.

The museum gives an absorbing and moving account of the history of Jews in France, especially Paris, during the German occupation. There are last letters from deportees to their families, videotaped testimony from survivors, numerous ID cards and photos. The museum ends with the Mémorial des Enfants, a collection of photos, almost unbearable to look at, of 2500 French children, each with the date of their birth and the date of their deportation.

# Bastille

A symbol of revolution since the toppling of the Bastille prison in the 1789, the **Bastille** quarter was a largely working-class district up until the construction of the new opera house in the 1980s. Since then, it has attracted artists, fashion folk and young people, who have brought with them stylish shops and an energetic nightlife, concentrated on rue de Lappe and rue de la Roquette.

## Place de la Bastille and around

**Place de la Bastille**, a large, traffic-choked square, is where the notorious Bastille prison once stood. The only visible remains of the prison have been transported to square Henri-Galli at the end of boulevard Henri-IV. The square is the scene of partying on the evening of July 13 to celebrate Bastille Day, and at other times of the year it's often used as a rallying point for left-wing demonstrations. In the centre towers a column topped with the gilded "Spirit of Liberty", erected not to commemorate the surrender of the prison, but the July Revolution of 1830 that replaced the autocratic Charles X with the "Citizen King" Louis-Philippe. On the eastern side of the square looms the **Opéra-Bastille**, built in 1989 to mark the 200th anniversary of the French Revolution. Likened by one critic to "a hippopotamus in a bathtub", the sprawling building with its semicircular glass facade is difficult to warm to, but its high-calibre performances are nearly always a sell-out (see p.137).

# The 12ᵉ arrondissement

South of Bastille, the relatively unsung **12ᵉ arrondissement** offers an authentic slice of Paris, with its neighbourhood shops and bars and traditional markets, such as the lively **Marché d'Aligre**. Among the area's attractions are the **Promenade Plantée**, an ex-railway line turned into an elevated walkway running from Bastille to the green expanse of the **Bois de Vincennes**, and **Bercy**, once the largest wine market in the world, its handsome old warehouses now converted into cafés and shops.

## Bercy

The riverside **Bercy** quartier, which extends southeast from the Gare de Lyon, was where the capital's wine supplies used to be unloaded from river barges. Much of the area has been turned into a welcome green space, the extensive **Parc de Bercy**.

### Bercy village
M° Cour St-Emilion

**Bercy village** is a complex of handsome old wine warehouses stylishly converted into shops, restaurants and, appropriately enough, wine bars – popular places to come before or after a film at the giant Bercy multiplex cinema at the eastern end of Cour Saint Emilion.

**1**

### Parc de Bercy

M° Cour St-Emilion

The contemporary **Parc de Bercy** incorporates elements of the old warehouse site, such as disused railway tracks and cobbled lanes. The western section of the park is a fairly unexciting expanse of grass, but the area to the east has arbours, rose gardens, lily ponds and an orangerie.

### Cinémathèque

51 rue de Bercy, 12ᵉ • **Museum** Mon & Wed–Sat noon–7pm, Sun 10am–8pm • €6.50 • ☎ 01 71 19 33 33, ⓦ cinematheque.fr • M° Bercy

Overlooking the Parc de Bercy, the **Cinémathèque**, a striking glass, zinc and stone building designed by Guggenheim architect Frank Gehry, houses a huge archive of films dating back to the earliest days of cinema. Along with cinema screens (see p.138) it also has an engaging museum, with lots of early cinematic equipment and silent-film clips.

## Promenade Plantée

M° Bastille/Ledru-Rollin

The **Promenade Plantée** is a stretch of disused railway line, much of it along a viaduct, which has been converted into an elevated walkway and planted with a profusion of trees and flowers. The walkway starts near the beginning of avenue Daumesnil, just south of the Bastille opera house, and is reached via a flight of stone steps – or lifts – with a number of similar access points all the way along. It takes you to the Parc de Reuilly, then descends to ground level and continues nearly as far as the *périphérique*, from where you can follow signs to the Bois de Vincennes. The whole walk is around 4.5km long, but if you don't feel like doing the entire thing you could just walk the first part – along the viaduct – which also happens to be the most attractive stretch, running past venerable old mansion blocks and giving a bird's-eye view of the area below and of small architectural details not seen from street level. The arches of the viaduct itself have been ingeniously converted into spaces for artisans' ateliers and craftshops, collectively known as the **Viaduc des Arts**.

## Bois de Vincennes

Main entrance on av de Paris, Vincennes • **Parc Floral** Daily: summer 9.30am–8pm; winter 9.30am–dusk • June–Sept Wed, Sat & Sun €5; all other times free • ⓦ parcfloraldeparis.com • M° Château-de-Vincennes then bus #112 or a 15min walk

The **Bois de Vincennes** is a favourite family Sunday retreat and the largest green space in the city, aside from the Bois de Boulogne in the west. It's rather crisscrossed with roads, but there are some very pleasant corners, including the picturesque Lac Daumesnil, where you can hire boats, and the **Parc Floral**, perhaps Paris's best gardens, with an adventure playground attached. Flowers are always in bloom in the Jardin des Quatres Saisons; you can picnic amid pines and rhododendrons, then wander through concentrations of camellias, cacti, ferns, irises and bonsai trees. Just north of Lac Daumesnil is the city's largest **zoo**, due to reopen in 2014 after major renovations.

### Château de Vincennes

Daily: May–Aug 10am–6pm; Sept–April 10am–5pm • €8.50 • ☎ 01 48 08 31 20, ⓦ chateau-vincennes.fr • M° Château-de-Vincennes

On the northern edge of the *Bois de Vincennes* lies the **Château de Vincennes**, the country's only surviving medieval royal residence, built by Charles V, subsequently turned into a state prison, then porcelain factory, weapons dump and military training school. Enclosed by a high defensive wall and still preserving the feel of a military barracks, it presents a rather austere aspect on first sight, but it's worth visiting for its Gothic **Chapelle Royale**, decorated with superb Renaissance stained-glass windows; and the restored fourteenth-century **donjon** (keep), where you can see some fine vaulted ceilings, Charles V's bedchamber, and graffiti left by prisoners, whose number included one Marquis de Sade.

**CLOCKWISE FROM TOP LEFT** ABBESSES MÉTRO; THE ARC DE TRIOMPHE (P.68); MUSÉE RODIN (P.103); EIFFEL TOWER (P.98) >

# 1 | Quartier Latin

South of the river, the **Rive Gauche** (Left Bank) has long maintained an "alternative" identity, opposed to the formal ambience of the Right Bank. Generally understood to describe the 5$^e$ and 6$^e$ arrondissements, the Left Bank was at the heart of *les évènements*, the revolutionary political "events" of May 1968. Since that infamous summer, however, gentrification has transformed the artists' garrets and beatnik cafés into designer pads and top-end restaurants, and the legend is only really kept alive by the student population of the **Quartier Latin** – so-called for the learned Latin of the medieval scholars who first settled here, or possibly for the abundant Roman ruins. It is in fact one of the city's more palpably ancient districts.

The pivotal point is **place St-Michel**, where the tree-lined **boulevard St-Michel** begins. It's a busy commercial thoroughfare these days, but the universities on all sides still give an intellectual air to the place, and the cafés and shops are still jammed with young people. Meanwhile, on the riverbank you'll find old books, postcards and prints on sale from the **bouquinistes**, whose green boxes line the parapets of the **riverside quais**. It's a pleasant walk upstream to **Pont de Sully**, which leads across to the Île St-Louis and offers a dramatic view of Notre-Dame.

## Around St-Séverin

The Quartier Latin's touristy scrum is at its most intense around **rue de la Huchette**, just east of place St-Michel. Hemmed in by cheap bars and Greek restaurants, the tiny Théâtre de la Huchette (see p.139) is the last bastion of the area's postwar beatnik heyday, still showing Ionesco's absurdist plays more than fifty years on. Connecting rue de la Huchette to the riverside is **rue du Chat-qui-Pêche**, a narrow slice of medieval Paris as it was before Haussmann got to work. At the end of rue de la Huchette, **rue St-Jacques** follows the line of the main street of Roman Paris, and was the road up which millions of medieval pilgrims trudged at the start of their long march to Santiago (Saint Jacques, in French) de Compostela in Spain. Across rue Lagrange from the square Viviani, rue de la Bûcherie is the home of the celebrated English-language bookshop **Shakespeare and Co** (see p.141), a huge tourist attraction in its own right.

### St-Séverin

1 rue des Prêtres St-Séverin, 5$^e$ • Mon–Sat 11am–7.30pm, Sun 9am–8.30pm • Free • M° St-Michel/Cluny–La Sorbonne

One block south of rue de la Huchette, just west of rue St-Jacques, is the mainly fifteenth-century church of **St-Séverin**. It's one of the city's more intense churches, its Flamboyant (distinguished by *flamboyant*, or flame-like, carving) choir resting on a virtuoso spiralling central pillar and its windows filled with edgy stained glass by the modern French painter Jean Bazaine.

## Institut du Monde Arabe

1 rue des Fossés-St-Bernard, 5$^e$ • Sept–June Tues–Sun 10am–6pm, July & Aug from 1–6pm • Museum €8, temporary exhibitions €12.20 • ℡ 01 40 51 38 38, ⬡ imarabe.org • M° Jussieu/Cardinal-Lemoine

Opposite Pont de Sully, you can't miss the bold glass and aluminium mass of the **Institut du Monde Arabe**, a cultural centre built to further understanding of the Arab world. Designed by Paris's favourite architect, Jean Nouvel, its broad southern facade, which mimics a *moucharabiyah*, or traditional Arab latticework, is made up of thousands of tiny, photo-sensitive metallic shutters. Inside, its **museum** aims to present a broad history of the Arab world, going back as far as prehistoric times (the oldest exhibit, a statuette of an earth goddess from Jordan, dates from the seventh century BC). If the collection feels sparse in places and slightly confusingly arranged (by theme, rather than chronologically), you do at least get a sense of the cultural diversity and richness of the

1

Arab peoples. The institute also puts on temporary exhibitions and concerts of Arab music, and there's a library and specialist bookshop. The rooftop **café-restaurant** is a fantastic place to enjoy a mint tea and the view towards the apse of Notre-Dame.

## The Musée National du Moyen Age

6 place Paul-Painlevé, 5ᵉ • Daily except Tues 9.15am–5.45pm • €8.50 • ☎ 01 53 73 78 16, ⓦ musee-moyenage.fr • Mᵒ Cluny-La Sorbonne

The area around the slopes of the **Montagne Ste-Geneviève**, the hill on which the Panthéon stands, is good for a stroll. The best approach is from **place Maubert** (which has a market on Tues, Thurs & Sat mornings) or from the St-Michel/St-Germain crossroads, where the walls of the third-century **Roman baths** are visible in the garden of the **Hôtel de Cluny**, a sixteenth-century mansion built by the abbots of the powerful Cluny monastery as their Paris pied-à-terre. It now houses the richly rewarding **Musée National du Moyen Age**, a treasure house of medieval sculpture, stained glass, books and *objets d'art*. The real beauties here, however, are the **tapestries**, and supreme among them is *La Dame à la Licorne* ("The Lady with the Unicorn"), a fifteenth-century masterpiece depicting the five senses along with an ambiguous and distinctly erotic image that may represent the virtue in controlling them. You can also see the vaults of the former Roman cold room, or *frigidarium*, which now shelter the beautifully carved Gallo-Roman *Pillar of St-Landry*. The museum puts on high-quality **concerts** of medieval music throughout the week.

## The Sorbonne

Mᵒ Cluny-La Sorbonne/RER Luxembourg

The elite educational institutions of the **Sorbonne**, **Collège de France** and the prestigious **Lycée Louis-le-Grand** number Molière, Robespierre, Sartre and Victor Hugo among its pupils. The hub of the quarter is **place de la Sorbonne**, overlooked by the dramatic Counter-Reformation facade of the Sorbonne's chapel, which was built in the 1640s by the great Cardinal Richelieu, whose tomb it houses. With its lime trees, fountains and cafés, the square is a lovely place to sit.

## The Panthéon

Place du Panthéon, 5ᵉ • Daily: April–Sept 10am–6.30pm; Oct–March 10am–6pm • €8.50 • ☎ 01 44 32 18 00, ⓦ pantheon.monuments -nationaux.fr • RER Luxembourg/Mᵒ Cardinal-Lemoine

The Montagne Ste-Geneviève is topped by the grandly domed and porticoed **Panthéon**, Louis XV's grateful response to Ste-Geneviève, patron saint of Paris, for curing him of illness. The Revolution transformed it into a mausoleum, and the remains of giants of French culture such as Voltaire, Rousseau, Hugo and Zola are entombed in the vast, barrel-vaulted crypt below, along with Marie Curie (the only woman), and Alexandre Dumas, of musketeers fame, who was only "panthéonized" in 2002. The interior is overwhelmingly monumental, bombastically Classical in design – and has a working model of **Foucault's Pendulum** swinging from the dome. The French physicist Léon Foucault devised the experiment to demonstrate vividly the rotation of the earth: while the pendulum appeared to rotate over a 24-hour period, it was in fact the earth beneath it turning. Huge crowds turned up here in 1851 to watch the ground move beneath their feet, and you can do the same today. In summer, regular guided tours take groups up into the vertiginous cupola and out onto the high balcony running round the outside of the dome.

## St-Étienne-du-Mont

Place Ste-Geneviève, 5ᵉ • Sept–June Tues–Sun 8.45am–noon & 2.30–7.45pm; July & Aug Tues–Sun 10am–noon & 4–7.15pm • Free • ⓦ saintetiennedumont.fr • RER Luxembourg/M Cardinal-Lemoine

The remains of Pascal and Racine, two seventeenth-century literary giants who didn't

1

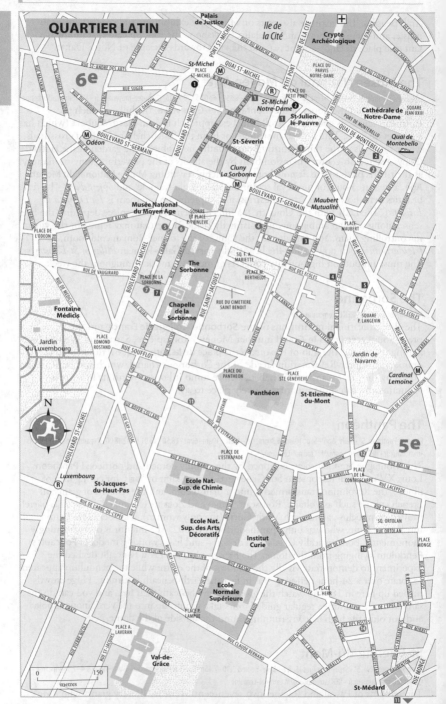

1

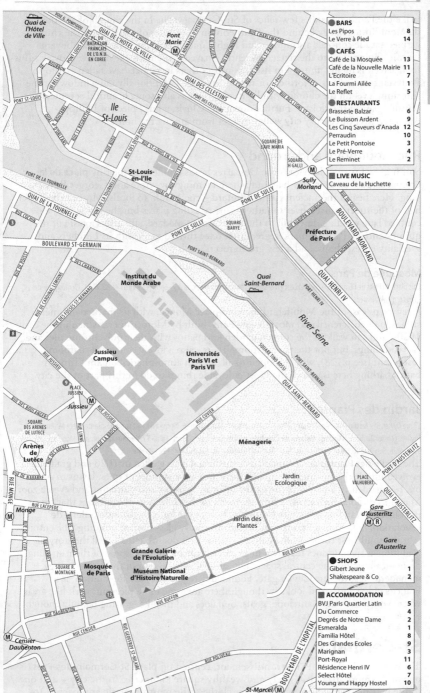

**● BARS**

| Les Pipos | 8 |
| Le Verre à Pied | 14 |

**● CAFÉS**

| Café de la Mosquée | 13 |
| Café de la Nouvelle Mairie | 11 |
| L'Ecritoire | 7 |
| La Fourmi Ailée | 1 |
| Le Reflet | 5 |

**● RESTAURANTS**

| Brasserie Balzar | 6 |
| Le Buisson Ardent | 9 |
| Les Cinq Saveurs d'Anada | 12 |
| Perraudin | 10 |
| Le Petit Pontoise | 3 |
| Le Pré-Verre | 4 |
| Le Reminet | 2 |

**■ LIVE MUSIC**

| Caveau de la Huchette | 1 |

**● SHOPS**

| Gibert Jeune | 1 |
| Shakespeare & Co | 2 |

**■ ACCOMMODATION**

| BVJ Paris Quartier Latin | 5 |
| Du Commerce | 4 |
| Degrés de Notre Dame | 2 |
| Esmeralda | 1 |
| Familia Hôtel | 8 |
| Des Grandes Ecoles | 9 |
| Marignan | 3 |
| Port-Royal | 11 |
| Résidence Henri IV | 6 |
| Select Hôtel | 7 |
| Young and Happy Hostel | 10 |

**1**

make the Panthéon, and a few relics of Ste-Geneviève, lie in the church of **St-Étienne-du-Mont**, immediately behind the Panthéon on the corner of rue Clovis. The church's garbled facade conceals a stunning and highly unexpected interior, its Flamboyant Gothic choir linked to the sixteenth-century nave by a remarkable narrow catwalk. This rood screen is highly unusual in itself, as most others in France have fallen victim to Protestant iconoclasts, reformers or revolutionaries. Exceptionally tall windows at the triforium level fill the church with light, and there is also some beautiful seventeenth-century glass in the cloister. Further down rue Clovis, a huge piece of Philippe-Auguste's twelfth-century **city walls** emerges from among the houses.

## Rue Mouffetard and around

South of St-Étienne-du-Mont, rue Descartes heads uphill onto the tiny **place de la Contrescarpe** – once an arty hangout where Hemingway wrote and Georges Brassens sang. Here begins the ancient **rue Mouffetard** – rue Mouff' to locals. Most of the upper half of the street is given over to rather touristy eating places but the lower half, a cobbled lane winding downhill to the church of **St-Médard**, still offers a taste of the quintessentially Parisian market street that once thrived here, with its butchers and speciality cheese shops, and a few greengrocers' stalls.

### Mosquée de Paris

2bis place du Puits de l'Ermite, 5ᵉ • Daily except Fri & Muslim holidays 9am–noon & 2–6pm • €3 • ☎ 01 45 35 97 33, ⓦ mosquee-de -paris.org • Mᵒ Jussieu

A few steps east of rue Mouffetard, beyond place Monge, with its market and métro stop, stands the crenellated **Mosquée de Paris**, built by Moroccan craftsmen in the early 1920s. You can walk in the sunken garden and patios with their polychrome tiles and carved ceilings, but not the prayer room. There's also a lovely courtyard **tearoom/restaurant** (see p.128), which is open to all, and an atmospheric **hamam** (Turkish bath); bathing here is one of the most enjoyable things to do in this part of the city.

## Jardin des Plantes

57 rue Cuvier, 5ᵉ • **Jardin** Daily: April–Aug 7.30am–7.45pm; Sept–March 8am–5.30pm • Free • ⓦ jardindesplantes.net • Mᵒ Austerlitz/ Jussieu/Censier Daubenton **Grande Galerie de l'Évolution** Daily except Tues 10am–6pm • €7 **Menagerie** Summer Mon–Sat 9am–6pm, Sun 9am–6.30pm; winter daily 9am–5pm • €10, under-26s €8, under-4s free • ⓦ mnhn.fr

The **Jardin des Plantes** was founded as a medicinal herb garden in 1626 and gradually evolved into Paris's botanical gardens. There are shady avenues of trees, lawns to sprawl on, rose gardens, a sunken alpine garden, historic glasshouses, museums and even a zoo. Magnificent floral beds make a fine approach to the collection of buildings that forms the **Muséum National d'Histoire Naturelle**. Best of the lot is the **Grande Galerie de l'Évolution**, housed in a dramatic nineteenth-century glass-domed building (the entrance is at the southwest corner of the gardens). Though it doesn't actually tell the story of evolution as such, it does feature a huge cast of stuffed animals, some of them striding dramatically across the central space. Live animals can be seen in the rather mangy **ménagerie** near the rue Cuvier gate. Founded here just after the Revolution, it is France's oldest zoo – and looks it, though there are some more pleasant, park-like areas where you can see deer, antelope, goats, buffaloes and the like, grazing happily enough.

# St-Germain

The northern half of the 6ᵉ arrondissement, centred on **place St-Germain-des-Prés**, is one of the most attractive, lively and wealthy square kilometres in the city – and one of the best places to shop for upmarket clothes. The most dramatic approach is to cross the river from the Louvre by the footbridge, the **Pont des Arts**, from where there's a classic upstream view of the Île de la Cité, with barges moored at the quai de Conti, the Tour St-Jacques and Hôtel de Ville breaking the skyline of the Right Bank. The dome and pediment at the end of the bridge belong to the **Institut de France**, seat of the Académie Française, an august body of writers and scholars whose mission is to safeguard the purity of the French language. This is the most grandiose part of the Left Bank riverfront: to the left is the **Hôtel des Monnaies**, redesigned as the Mint in the late eighteenth century; to the right is the **Beaux-Arts**, the School of Fine Art, whose students throng the *quais* on sunny days, sketchpads on knees. Inspiration for budding artists is in plentiful supply at the stunning **Musée d'Orsay**, just a little further west along the river. The perfect place to unwind after a little sightseeing is the lovely **Jardin du Luxembourg**, which borders the Quartier Latin towards the southern end of the *sixième*.

## Musée d'Orsay

1 rue de la Légion d'Honneur, 7e • Tues–Sun 9.30am–6pm, Thurs till 9.45pm • €9; free to under-18s and EU residents aged 18–25; free to everyone on the first Sun of the month • ☎ 01 40 49 48 14, Ⓦ musee-orsay.fr • M° Solférino/RER Musée-d'Orsay

Behind the stony facade of a former railway station is the **Musée d'Orsay**, famed for its electrifying collection of **Impressionist** works. The museum recently underwent a major revamp; the results are stunning and show the paintings as never before. As well as the Impressionists, the museum showcases French painting and sculpture between 1848 and 1914, thus bridging the gap between the "Classical" Louvre and the "modern" art of the Centre Pompidou. You could spend half a day meandering through in chronological order, but the layout makes it easy to confine your visit to a specific section.

The museum has two fine – if pricey – places to take stock: the **café** on the upper level, the decor of which is inspired by the dreamlike artworks of Art Nouveau artist Emile Gallé, with a summer terrace and wonderful view of Montmartre through the giant railway clock, and a resplendent café-restaurant on the middle level, gilded in stunning period style.

### The ground level

The **ground floor**, under the great glass arch, is devoted mostly to pre-1870 work, with a double row of sculptures running down the central aisle like railway tracks, and paintings in the odd little bunkers on either side. You'll find works by Ingres, Delacroix and the serious-minded painters and sculptors acceptable to the mid-nineteenth century salons (rooms 1–3), as well as the relatively unusual works of Puvis de Chavannes and Gustave Moreau (Galerie Symboliste), and the younger Degas (room 13). The influential **Barbizon school** and the **Realists** (rooms 4–7) are showcased alongside works by Daumier, Corot and Millet. Gentler essays in Realist and early Impressionist landscape hang nearby (18), with works by Pissarro, Sisley and Monet. A whole room (room 10) is devoted to **Toulouse-Lautrec**'s deliciously smoky caricatures; don't miss his *Danse Mauresque* (hanging nearby in the Galerie Symboliste), a work that depicts the celebrated cancan dancer La Goulue entertaining a washed-up and obese Oscar Wilde. At the far end is a high-ceilinged room hung with Courbet's impressive large-format paintings, including *A Burial at Ornans*, a stark depiction of a family funeral; these large-format works were groundbreaking in their day for depicting everyday scenes on a scale that was usually reserved for "noble" subjects, such as historic or mythical scenes.

### The Pavillon Amont

The Courbet room on the ground floor is part of the renovated **Pavillon Amont**, the station's former engine room, which has been radically restructured to create five different levels.

1

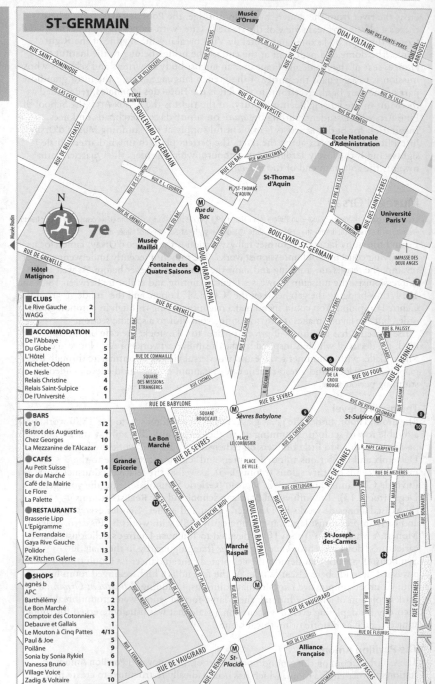

## ST-GERMAIN

Musée d'Orsay

7e

**CLUBS**
Le Rive Gauche 2
WAGG 1

**ACCOMMODATION**
De l'Abbaye 7
Du Globe 5
L'Hôtel 2
Michelet-Odéon 8
De Nesle 3
Relais Christine 4
Relais Saint-Sulpice 6
De l'Université 1

**BARS**
Le 10 12
Bistrot des Augustins 4
Chez Georges 10
La Mezzanine de l'Alcazar 5

**CAFÉS**
Au Petit Suisse 14
Bar du Marché 6
Café de la Mairie 11
Le Flore 7
La Palette 2

**RESTAURANTS**
Brasserie Lipp 8
L'Epigramme 9
La Ferrandaise 15
Gaya Rive Gauche 1
Polidor 13
Ze Kitchen Galerie 3

**SHOPS**
agnès b 8
APC 14
Barthélémy 2
Le Bon Marché 12
Comptoir des Cotonniers 3
Debauve et Gallais 1
Le Mouton à Cinq Pattes 4/13
Paul & Joe 5
Poilâne 9
Sonia by Sonia Rykiel 6
Vanessa Bruno 11
Village Voice 7
Zadig & Voltaire 10

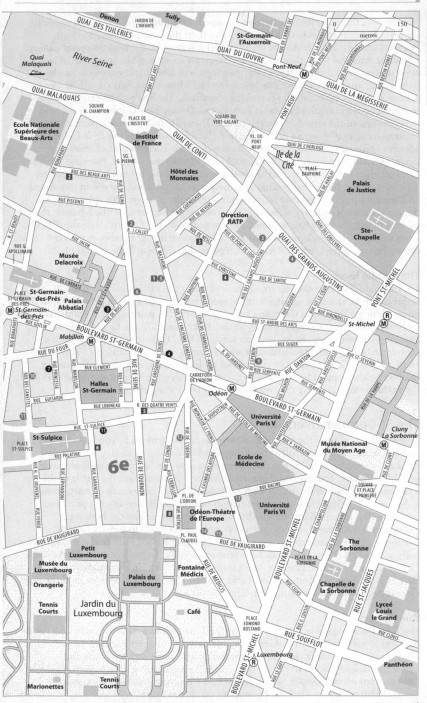

Levels two, three and four are devoted to superb **Art Nouveau** furniture and *objets*, for the first time displayed together with paintings from the same period by Vuillard, Bonnard and Maurice Denis. On the fifth level you come to the **Impressionists' gallery**, where the results of the museum's recent revamp are most tangible. In a series of large, open spaces, painted charcoal grey, the paintings, well spaced and warmly lit, make a tremendous impact – even the almost-too-familiar Monets and Renoirs – their vibrant colours and vigorous brushstrokes striking you afresh. The first painting to greet you, magnificent in its isolation, is Manet's scandalous *Déjeuner sur l'herbe*, the work held to have announced the arrival of Impressionism. Thereafter follows masterpiece after masterpiece: Degas' *Dans un café (L'Absinthe)*, Renoir's *Bal du Moulin de la Galette*, Monet's *Femme à l'ombrelle*, Cézanne's *Joueurs de cartes*. There's a host of small-scale landscapes and outdoor scenes by Renoir, Sisley, Pissarro and Monet, paintings which owed much of their brilliance to the novel practice of setting up easels in the open to capture the light. Degas' ballet dancers demonstrate his principal interest in movement and line as opposed to the more common Impressionist concern with light, while his domestic scenes of ordinary working life are touchingly humane. Berthe Morisot, the first woman to join the early Impressionists, is represented by her famous *Le Berceau* (1872), among others. The development of Monet's obsession with light is shown with five of his extraordinary Rouen Cathedral series, each painted in different light conditions.

### The middle level

On the middle level, rooms 69 to 72 are devoted to the various offspring of Impressionism, and have an edgier, more modern feel, with a much greater emphasis on psychology. You'll find **Gauguin**'s ambivalent Tahitian paintings and **Pointillist** works by Seurat (the famous *Cirque*, 1891), Signac and others. On the far side, in rooms 55 and 58, overlooking the Seine, you can see a less familiar side of late nineteenth-century painting, with epic, naturalist works such as Detaille's stirring *Le Rêve* (1888) and Cormon's *Caïn* (1880). On the parallel sculpture terraces, nineteenth-century marbles on the Seine side face early twentieth-century pieces across the divide, while the **Rodin terrace** bridging the two puts almost everything else to shame.

## The St-Germain riverside

The riverside chunk of the 6$^e$ arrondissement is cut lengthwise by **rue St-André-des-Arts** and **rue Jacob**. It's an area full of bookshops, commercial art galleries, antique shops, cafés and restaurants, and if you poke your nose into the courtyards and side streets, you'll find foliage, fountains and peaceful enclaves removed from the bustle of the city. The houses are four to six storeys high, seventeenth- and eighteenth-century, some noble, some bulging and skew, all painted in infinite gradations of grey, pearl and off-white. Broadly speaking, the further west you go the posher the houses get.

**Historical associations** are legion: Picasso painted *Guernica* in rue des Grands-Augustins; Molière started his career in rue Mazarine; Robespierre et al split ideological hairs at the *Café Procope* in rue de l'Ancienne-Comédie. In rue Visconti, Racine died, Delacroix painted and Balzac's printing business went bust. In the parallel rue des Beaux-Arts, Oscar Wilde died, Corot and Ampère (father of amps) lived, and the poet Gérard de Nerval went walking with a lobster on a lead.

### Rue de Buci

You'll find numerous places to eat on **place** and **rue St-André-des-Arts** and along **rue de Buci**, up towards boulevard St-Germain. Rue de Buci preserves a strong flavour of its origins as a market street, with food shops, delis and some excellent cafés and brasseries. Before you get to rue de Buci, there is an intriguing little passage on the left, **Cour du Commerce St-André**, where Marat had a printing press and Dr Guillotin perfected his notorious machine by lopping off sheep's heads.

# St-Germain-des-Prés and around

**Place St-Germain-des-Prés**, the hub of the *quartier*, has the famous *Deux Magots* café (see p.129) on its corner, *Flore* (see p.129) adjacent and *Lipp* (see p.129) across the boulevard St-Germain. All three are renowned for the number of philosophical and literary backsides that have shined – and continue to shine – their banquettes, along with plenty of celebrity-hunters. Picasso's bust of a woman, dedicated to the poet Apollinaire, recalls the district's creative heyday.

## St-Germain-des-Prés

Place St-Germain-des-Pres, 6ᵉ • Daily 7.30am–7.30pm • Free • Mᵒ St-Germain-des-Prés

The tower opposite the *Deux Magots* café belongs to the church of **St-Germain-des-Prés**, all that remains of an enormous Benedictine monastery. Inside, the transformation from Romanesque to early Gothic is just about visible under the heavy green-and-gold nineteenth-century paintwork. The last chapel on the south side contains the tomb of the philosopher René Descartes.

## Musée Delacroix

6 rue du Furstemburg, 6ᵉ • Daily except Tues 9.30am–5pm • €5 • ☎ 01 44 41 86 50, ⓦ musee-delacroix.fr • Mᵒ Mabillon/
St-Germain-des-Prés

Halfway down rue du Furstemburg, opposite a tiny square and backing onto a secret garden, is Delacroix's old studio now the **Musée Delacroix**, which has a small collection of the artist's personal belongings as well as minor exhibitions of his work. This is also the beginning of some very upmarket shopping territory, in rue Jacob, rue de Seine and rue Bonaparte in particular.

# St-Sulpice

Place St-Sulpice, 6ᵉ • Daily 7am–7.30pm • Free • Mᵒ St-Sulpice

South of boulevard St-Germain, the streets round **place St-Sulpice** are calm and classy. The enormous, early eighteenth-century church of **St-Sulpice** is an austerely Classical building with Doric and Ionic colonnades and Corinthian pilasters in the towers. On the south tower centuries-old uncut masonry blocks protrude from the top, still awaiting the sculptor's chisel. Three Delacroix murals can be seen in the first chapel on the right, but most visitors these days come to see the **gnomon**, a kind of solar clock whose origins and purpose were so compellingly garbled by *The Da Vinci Code*.

# Jardin du Luxembourg

**Gardens** Daily dawn to dusk **Musée du Luxembourg** 19 rue de Vaugirard, 6ᵉ • Mon, Fri, Sat & Sun 9am–10pm, Tues–Thurs 10am–8pm •
€10–15 • ☎ 01 42 34 25 95, ⓦ museeduluxembourg.fr • Mᵒ Odeon/RER Luxembourg

The **Jardin du Luxembourg** offers formal lawns, gravel paths and resplendent floral parterres, all dotted with sculptures, citrus and olive trees in giant pots (taken inside in winter) and elegant sage-green chairs. Sprawling on the lawns is strictly forbidden, except on the southernmost strip, which gets fantastically crowded on sunny days. The shady **Fontaine de Médicis,** in the northeast corner, is a pleasant place to sit, and there's a delightful **café** roughly 100m northeast of the central pond. The pond is overlooked by the Palais du Luxembourg, seat of the French Senate. The western side of the park is the more active area, with tennis courts and a **puppet theatre** that has been in the same family for the best part of a century, and still puts on enthralling shows (Wed, Sat, Sun and daily during school holidays at 3.30pm; €4.70). The quieter, wooded southeast corner ends in a miniature orchard of elaborately espaliered pear trees.

On the north side of the park, the **Musée du Luxembourg** hosts some of the city's largest and most exciting temporary art exhibitions. Recent successes have included an exhibition on Cézanne and Paris, and works by Cima da Conegliano.

# 1

# The Eiffel Tower quarter

The stretch of Paris in the shadow of the **Eiffel Tower** is so sweepingly grand that it can take the fun out of exploration: the avenues are just too long, the pavements somehow too hard and the buildings too forbiddingly monumental. Most visitors drop in by métro (or sail in by Batobus), to climb the Tower and perhaps call in at one of the quarter's fine museums, in the **Trocadéro**, a hop away on the north bank. The area at the Eiffel Tower's feet, to the east, is the **septième** (7e) arrondissement, mostly dominated by monumental military and government buildings.

## The Eiffel Tower

Daily: mid-June to Aug 9am–12.45am; Sept to mid-June 9.30am–11.45pm; last entry 45min before closing time; Sept to mid-June access to stairs closes at 6pm; ticket sales for the top level stop at 10.30pm (or 11pm mid-June to Aug); save queuing time by buying tickets online • Top level (accessible by lift only) €13.40; second level €8.20, €4.70 by stairs; stairs then lift to top level €9.90 • **ⓦ** tour-eiffel.fr • RER Champ de Mars–Tour Eiffel

It's hard to believe that the **Eiffel Tower**, the quintessential symbol both of Paris and of the brilliance of industrial engineering, was designed to be a temporary structure for a fair. Late nineteenth-century Europe had a decadent taste for such giant-scale, colonialist-capitalist extravaganzas, but the 1889 Exposition was particularly ambitious, and when completed the tower, at 300m, was the tallest building in the world. Reactions were violent. Outraged critics protested "in the name of menaced French art and history" against this "useless and monstrous" tower. "Is Paris", they asked, "going to be associated with the grotesque, mercantile imaginings of a constructor of machines?"

Curiously, Paris's most famous landmark was only saved from demolition by the sudden need for "wireless telegraphy" aerials in the first decade of the twentieth century. The tower's role in telecommunications – its only function apart from tourism – has become increasingly important, and the original crown is now masked by an efflorescence of antennae. After dark, the tower is particularly spectacular, an urban lighthouse illuminated by a double searchlight and, for the first ten minutes of every hour, by thousands of effervescent lights that fizz across its gridlines.

Though you may have to wait a while for the lifts, it's arguable that you simply haven't seen Paris until you've seen it from the top. While the views are almost better from the second level, especially on hazier days, there's something irresistible about going all the way to the top, and looking down over the surreally microscopic city below.

## Trocadéro

On the Trocadéro heights of the north bank of the river, facing the Eiffel Tower, stand the brutally resplendent **Palais de Tokyo** and **Palais de Chaillot**. They house some of the city's best art museums: the **Site de Création Contemporaine**, the **Musée d'Art Moderne de la Ville de Paris** and the **Cité de l'Architecture**.

### Cité de l'Architecture et du Patrimoine

Palais de Chaillot, 1 place du Trocadéro et du 11 Novembre, 16e • Mon, Wed & Fri–Sun 11am–7pm, Thurs 11am–9pm • €8 • **ⓣ** 01 58 51 52 00, **ⓦ** citechaillot.fr • M° Trocadéro

The northern wing of the ugly **Palais de Chaillot** is occupied by the superb **Cité de l'Architecture et du Patrimoine**, a stunningly put-together museum of architecture. On the loftily vaulted ground floor, the **Galerie des Moulages** displays giant plaster casts taken from the greatest French buildings (chiefly churches) at the end of the nineteenth century, before pollution and erosion dulled their detail. The Galerie des Peintures Murales, with its radiant, full-scale copies of French frescoes and wall paintings, is equally impressive. The top floor offers a sleek rundown of the modern and contemporary, with models, photographs and a reconstruction of an entire apartment from **Le Corbusier**'s Cité Radieuse, in Marseille. Restore yourself afterwards on the terrace of the ground-floor **café**, with its eye-popping views of the Eiffel Tower.

## Musée d'Art Moderne de la Ville de Paris

Palais de Tokyo, av du Président-Wilson, 16ᵉ • Tues–Sun 10am–6pm • Free • ☎ 01 53 67 40 00, ⓦ mam.paris.fr • M° Iéna/Alma-Marceau

The **Palais de Tokyo**, contemporary with the nearby Chaillot, houses the **Musée d'Art Moderne de la Ville de Paris**. While it's no competition for the Pompidou Centre, the cool modernist setting is more fitting – and more contemplative – for a collection focused on early twentieth-century, Paris-based artists. Braque, Chagall, Delaunay, Derain, Léger and Picasso are well represented, and many works were expressly chosen for their Parisian themes. The enormous centrepieces are the two versions of Matisse's glorious mural, *La Danse*, and Dufy's gigantic *La Fée Électricité*, a mural commissioned by the electricity board to illustrate the story of electricity from Aristotle to the then-modern power station. Temporary exhibitions fill the ground-floor space.

## Site de Création Contemporaine

Palais de Tokyo, av du Président-Wilson, 16ᵉ • Tues–Sun noon–midnight • €8 • ☎ 01 47 23 54 01, ⓦ palaisdetokyo.com • M° Iéna/Alma-Marceau

The western wing of the Palais de Tokyo is occupied by the **Site de Création Contemporaine**, a cutting-edge gallery whose semi-derelict interior focuses exclusively on contemporary and avant-garde art. A constantly changing flow of exhibitions and events – anything from a concept show by Turner Prize-winning Jeremy Deller to a temporary "occupation" by squatter-artists – keeps the atmosphere lively, with a genuinely exciting countercultural buzz.

## Musée de la Mode de la Ville

Palais Galliera, 10 av Pierre 1er de Serbie, 16ᵉ • ☎ 01 56 52 86 00, ⓦ galliera.paris.fr • M° Iéna/Alma-Marceau

Behind the Palais de Tokyo, the stately, Italianate Palais Galliera is home to the **Musée de la Mode de la Ville de Paris**, which rotates its magnificent collection of clothes and accessories from the eighteenth century to the present day in a few themed exhibitions a year.

## Musée National des Arts Asiatiques-Guimet

6 place d'Iéna, 16ᵉ • Daily except Tues 10am–6pm • €7.50 • ☎ 01 56 52 53 00, ⓦ guimet.fr • M° Iéna

The remarkable **Musée National des Arts Asiatiques-Guimet** boasts a stunning display of Asian and especially Buddhist art. Four floors groan under the weight of statues of Buddhas and gods, while a roofed-in courtyard provides an airy space in which to show off the museum's world-renowned collection of **Khmer sculpture**.

# The 7ᵉ arrondissement

Most imposing of the 7ᵉ arrondissement's many monumental buildings is the **Hôtel des Invalides**, with its impressive war museum and tomb of Napoleon. Tucked away in the more intimate streets to the east, towards St-Germain, the **Musée Rodin** and **Musée Maillol** show off the two sculptors' works in handsome private houses. One tiny neighbourhood in this area, between rue St-Dominique and rue de Grenelle, is full of appealingly bijou shops, hotels and restaurants, with the lively market street of **rue Cler** at the centre of it all.

## Musée du Quai Branly

37 quai Branly, 7ᵉ • Tues, Wed & Sun 11am–7pm, Thurs–Sat 11am–9pm • €8.50 • ☎ 01 56 61 71 72, ⓦ quaibranly.fr • M° Iéna/RER Pont de l'Alma

A short distance upstream of the Eiffel Tower stands the intriguing **Musée du Quai Branly**, which gathers together hundreds of thousands of non-European objects bought or purloined by France over the centuries. The museum was the pet project of President Chirac, whose passion for what he would no doubt call *arts primitifs* ("primitive art")

1

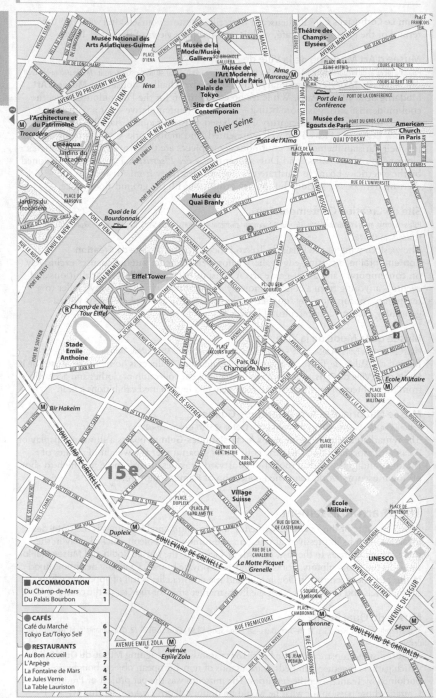

**Muséé National des Arts Asiatiques-Guimet**
PLACE D'IENA
**Musée de la Mode/Musée Galliera**
**Théâtre des Champs-Elysées**
AVENUE MONTAIGNE
AVENUE KLEBER
RUE DE LONGCHAMP
RUE DE LA POMPE
RUE BOISSIERE
AVENUE PIERRE 1ER DE SERBE
RUE GOETHE
RUE L. REYNAUD
AVENUE MARCEAU
AVENUE GEORGE V
RUE JEAN GOUJON
PLACE FRANÇOIS 1ER
101 BRIGNOLE GALLIERA
**Musée de l'Art Moderne de la Ville de Paris**
Alma Marceau
PLACE DE L'ALMA
PLACE DE LA REINE ASTRID
COURS ALBERT 1ER
COURS ALBERT 1ER
Iéna
**Palais de Tokyo**
**Site de Création Contemporain**
AVENUE DU PRESIDENT WILSON
AVENUE D'IENA
Port de la Conférence
PORT DE LA CONFERENCE
**Cité de l'Architecture et du Patrimoine**
Trocadéro
RUE FRESNEL
AVENUE DE NEW YORK
River Seine
PONT DE L'ALMA
**Musée des Egouts de Paris**
PORT DU GROS CAILLOU
QUAI D'ORSAY
**American Church in Paris**
**Cinéaqua**
**Jardins du Trocadéro**
Pont de l'Alma
PLACE DE LA RESISTANCE
PORT DEBILLY
RUE COGNACO JAY
R. DU COLONEL COMBES
Jardins du Trocadéro
PLACE DE VARSOVIE
QUAI BRANLY
RUE DE L'UNIVERSITE
AVENUE DES NATIONS-UNIES
Quai de la Bourdonnais
PONT D'IENA
QUAI BRANLY
**Musée du Quai Branly**
RUE DE PASSY
PORT DE PASSY
AVENUE DE NEW YORK
RUE LE NOTRE
PORT DE LA BOURDONNAIS
AV. FRANCO RUSSE
AVENUE RAPP
AVENUE BOSQUET
RUE DE L'UNIVERSITE
CITE DE L'UNIVERSITE
**Eiffel Tower**
AV. DE LA BOURDONNAIS
RUE DE MONTTESSUY
RUE F. VALENTIN
DUPONT DES LOGES
RUE CLER
AV. RAPP
RUE DU GEN. CAMOU
AV. S. DE LA CLERC
AVENUE ELISEE RECLUS
RUE SAINT-DOMINIQUE
AVENUE DE SUFFREN
AV. OCTAVE GREARD
AVENUE CHARLES FLOQUET
AVENUE DE LA MOTTE-PICQUET
AVENUE E. POUVILLON
**Champ de Mars-Tour Eiffel**
PL. DU GEN. GOURAUD
AVENUE JOSEPH BOUVARD
AVENUE ANATOLE FRANCE
**Stade Emile Anthoine**
RUE JEAN REY
PLACE JACQUES RUEFF
**Parc du Champs de Mars**
AVENUE DE LA BOURDONNAIS
AVENUE EMILE DESCHANEL
RUE DU CHAMP DE MARS
AVENUE BOSQUET
RUE DE GRENELLE
**Ecole Militaire**
PLACE DE L'ECOLE MILITAIRE
AVENUE BOSQUET
Bir Hakeim
PONT DE SUFFREN
RUE NELATON
RUE SAINT-SAENS
RUE DE LA FEDERATION
AVENUE CHARLES RISLER
AVENUE PIERRE LOTI
AVENUE HENRI THIERRY
PLACE JOFFRE
**Ecole Militaire**
PLACE DE FONTENOY
**15e**
RUE DU DOCTEUR FINLAY
RUE D. STERN
AVENUE DU GEN. DETRIE
AVENUE DE SUFFREN
AVENUE DE LA MOTTE PICQUET
BOULEVARD DE GRENELLE
RUE DUPLEIX
**Village Suisse**
AVENUE DE LOWENDAL
AVENUE DE SAXE
**UNESCO**
RUE VIALA
Dupleix
PLACE DUPLEIX
PLACE DU GARO AMETTE
RUE DU GEN. DE LARMINAT
RUE DE LA CAVALERIE
AVENUE DE SUFFREN
AVENUE DE SEGUR
BOULEVARD DE GRENELLE
**La Motte Picquet Grenelle**
Ségur
SQUARE CAMBRONNE
PLACE CAMBRONNE
Cambronne
ST. JEAN THEBAUD
BOULEVARD DE GARIBALDI
AVENUE EMILE ZOLA
**Avenue Emile Zola**
RUE FREMICOURT

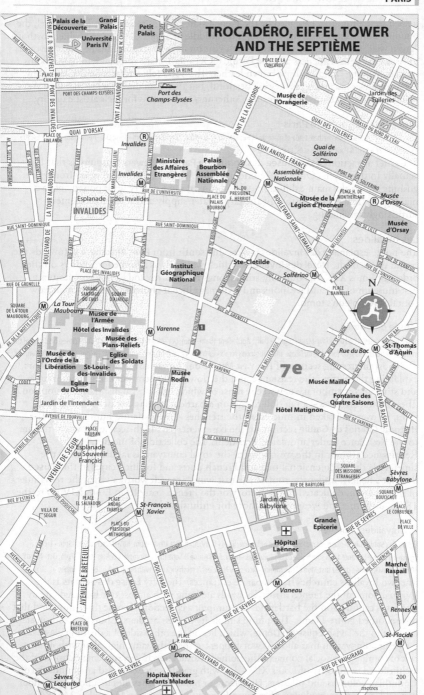

# TROCADÉRO, EIFFEL TOWER AND THE SEPTIÈME

Palais de la Découverte
Grand Palais
Petit Palais
Université Paris IV

AVENUE F. D. ROOSEVELT
RUE FRANÇOIS 1ER
AVENUE W. CHURCHILL
PLACE DE LA CONCORDE

PLACE DU CANADA
COURS LA REINE

PONT DES INVALIDES
PORT DES CHAMPS-ELYSÉES
PONT ALEXANDRE III
Port des Champs-Elysées
Musée de l'Orangerie
Jardin des Tuileries

QUAI D'ORSAY
PLACE DE FINLANDE
Invalides (R)
PONT DE LA CONCORDE
QUAI DES TUILERIES
TERRASSE DU BORD DE L'EAU

AV. DE SÉLITY-PRUDHOMME
RUE SURCOUF
RUE FABERT
LA TOUR MAUBOURG
RUE DE CONSTANTINE
AVENUE DE MARECHAL GALLIENI
RUE ROBERT ESNAULT PELTERIE
Invalides (M)
Ministère des Affaires Etrangères
Palais Bourbon Assemblée Nationale
QUAI ANATOLE FRANCE
Quai de Solférino
PORT DE SOLFÉRINO
Musée d'Orsay (R)
RUE DE LILLE
Musée d'Orsay

RUE DE L'UNIVERSITÉ
PL. DU PRÉSIDENT E. HERRIOT
Assemblée Nationale (M)
Musée de la Légion d'Honneur
PLACE H. DE MONTHERLANT

Esplanade des Invalides
avenue des Invalides
PLACE DU PALAIS BOURBON
BOULEVARD SAINT-GERMAIN

RUE SAINT-DOMINIQUE
INVALIDES
RUE SAINT-DOMINIQUE
RUE DE BELLECHASSE
RUE DE VERNEUIL

BOULEVARD DE LA TOUR MAUBOURG
RUE FABERT
RUE DE GRENELLE
PLACE DES INVALIDES
Institut Géographique National
Ste-Clotilde
RUE LAS CASES
Solférino (M)
RUE DE VILLERSEXEL
RUE DE L'UNIVERSITÉ
N

RUE DE GRENELLE
SQUARE SANTIAGO DU CHILI
SQUARE D'AJACCIO
RUE CASIMIR PERIER
RUE DE BOURGOGNE
PLACE J. BAINVILLE

SQUARE DE LA TOUR MAUBOURG
La Tour Maubourg (M)
Musée de l'Armée
Hôtel des Invalides
Musée des Plans-Reliefs
Varenne (M)
RUE DE GRENELLE
RUE DE BELLECHASSE
Rue du Bac
St-Thomas d'Aquin
RUE DU BAC

AV. DE LA MOTTE PICQUET
RUE CHEVERT
RUE J. CODET
RUE GRENIER
Musée de l'Ordre de la Libération
Eglise des Soldats
St-Louis-des-Invalides
RUE DE VARENNE
7e
Rue du Bac
BOULEVARD RASPAIL

RUE CLER
Eglise du Dôme
Musée Rodin
RUE DE VARENNE
Musée Maillol
RUE DE GRENELLE

Jardin de l'Intendant
AVENUE DE TOURVILLE
Fontaine des Quatre Saisons
Hôtel Matignon
RUE DE VARENNE

AVENUE DE LOWENDAL
AVENUE DE SÉGUR
PLACE VAUBAN
Esplanade du Souvenir Français
BOULEVARD DES INVALIDES
RUE DE CHANALEILLES
SQUARE DES MISSIONS ETRANGÈRES
Sèvres Babylone (M)

RUE D'ESTRÉES
AVENUE DUQUESNE
RUE DE BABYLONE
RUE DE BABYLONE
SQUARE BOUCICAUT
PLACE LE CORBUSIER

VILLA DE SÉGUR
PLACE EL SALVADOR
PLACE ANDRÉ TARDIEU
St-François Xavier (M)
Jardin de Babylone
Grande Epicerie
RUE DE SÈVRES
PLACE DE VILLE

AVENUE DE SAXE
AVENUE DE BRETEUIL
PLACE DU PRÉSIDENT MITHOUARD
RUE OUDINOT
Hôpital Laënnec ✚
RUE DE SÈVRES
Marché Raspail

AVENUE DE SAXE
VILLA DE SAXE
RUE EBLÉ
RUE ROUSSELET
RUE DU CHERCHE MIDI
Vaneau (M)
Rennes (M)

RUE PÉRIGNON
RUE CÉSAR FRANCK
AV. C. COQUELIN
RUE DE SÈVRES
St-Placide (M)

RUE DE BRETEUIL
PLACE DE BRETEUIL
AV. D. LESUEUR
PLACE F. FARGUE

RUE ROSA BONHEUR
RUE V. HUGO
BOULEVARD DES INVALIDES
Duroc (M)
BOULEVARD DU MONTPARNASSE
RUE DE VAUGIRARD

RUE BARTHÉLEMY
Sèvres Lecourbe (M)
RUE DE SÈVRES
Hôpital Necker Enfants Malades ✚

0    200
metres

**1**

helped secure funding. Designed by the French state's favourite architect, Jean Nouvel, the building unfurls in a sleek curve through the middle of a splendid **garden** – which, with its "green wall" and exotic plantings is worth a visit on its own account. Inside, areas devoted to Asia, Africa, the Americas and the Pacific ("Oceania") snake through semi-dark rooms lined by curving "mud" walls in brown leather. The 3500 **folk artefacts** on display at any one time are as fascinating as they are beautiful, but there's an uneasy sense that they are being presented in terms of their exotic "otherness" as much as for their artistic quality.

## Musée des Egouts de Paris

Quai d'Orsay, 7ᵉ; entrance on northeast side of place de la Résistance • Sat–Wed: May–Sept 11am–5pm; Oct–April 11am–4pm • €4.30 • ☎ 01 53 68 27 81 • RER Pont de l'Alma/ Mᵒ Place d'Iéna

The chief attraction of the **Musée des Egouts de Paris**, or **Sewers Museum**, is that it is actually in the sewers. Once you're underground it's dark, damp and noisy from the gushing water; the main exhibition, which runs along a gantry walk poised above a main sewer, renders the history of the city's water supply and waste management surprisingly fascinating.

## Les Invalides

The noble **Esplanade des Invalides** strikes due south from **Pont Alexandre III** towards the proud dome of the **Hôtel des Invalides**, which was built as a home for soldiers on the orders of Louis XIV. The building still belongs to the army today, but now houses a vast museum of war and weapons and two magnificent **churches**, one of which now contains **Napoleon's tomb**.

### Musée de l'Armée

Hôtel des Invalides, 51 bd de la Tour-Maubourg, 7ᵉ • Daily: April–Sept 10am–6pm; Oct–March 10am–5pm; Oct–June closed first Mon of the month • €9 ticket also valid for Église du Dôme and Napoleon's tomb • ☎ 01 44 42 38 77, ⓦ invalides.org • Mᵒ La Tour-Maubourg/Varenne

The most interesting section of the vast **Musée de l'Armée** covers the two World Wars, explaining the battles, the resistance and the slow, final liberation using memorabilia and stirring contemporary newsreels, most of which have an English-language option. The simplest artefacts – a rag doll found on a battlefield, plaster casts of mutilated faces, an overcoat caked in mud from the trenches – tell a stirring human story. The **Historial Charles de Gaulle** section, in the basement, pays high-tech audiovisual tribute to the Resistance leader and, later, President. The collection of medieval and Renaissance armour in the west wing of the royal courtyard is fabulous, while the super-scale three-dimensional maps of French ports and fortified cities in the **Musée des Plans-Reliefs**, under the roof of the east wing, are well worth a visit. The remainder of the museum, dedicated to the history of the French army from Louis XIV up to the 1870s, uniforms and weaponry, is more for enthusiasts.

### The Invalides churches

**Église des Soldats** entrance from main courtyard of Les Invalides • Daily: April–Oct 10am–6pm; Nov–March 10am–5pm • Free
**Église du Dôme** Entrance from south side of Les Invalides • Daily: April–June & Sept 10am–6pm; July & Aug 10am–7pm; Oct–March 10am–5pm; Oct–June closed first Mon of the month • Access to Napoleon's tomb included with ticket to Musée de l'Armée

The two Invalides churches have separate entrances. The lofty **Église des Soldats** is the spiritual home of the French army. The walls are hung with almost one hundred enemy standards captured on the battlefield, the rump of a collection of some three thousand that once adorned Notre-Dame. The proud simplicity of this "Soldiers' Church" stands in stark contrast to the lavish **Église du Dôme**, which lies on the other side of a dividing glass wall – a design innovation that allowed worshippers to share the same high altar without the risk of coming into social contact. The domed "Royal church" is a supreme example of the architectural pomposity of Louis XIV's day, with grandiose frescoes and an abundance of Corinthian columns and pilasters. **Napoleon**, or rather his ashes, lies in a hole in the floor in a cold, smooth sarcophagus of red porphyry, installed there on December 14, 1840.

### Musée Rodin

79 rue de Varenne, 7ᵉ • House Tues–Sun 10am–5.45pm; garden Tues–Sun: Oct–March 10am–5pm; April–Sept 10am–6pm • House and gardens €7, gardens €1 • ☎ 01 44 18 61 10, ⓦ musee-rodin.fr • Mᵒ Varenne

The **Musée Rodin**, arguably Paris's loveliest museum, occupies a beautiful eighteenth-century mansion that the sculptor leased from the state in return for the gift of all his work at his death. Today, major projects like *The Burghers of Calais*, *The Thinker*, *The Gate of Hell* and *Ugolino* are exhibited in the extensive and peaceful gardens – the latter forming the centrepiece of the ornamental pond. Indoors, the mould-breaking, stormy vigour of the sculptures sits beautifully with the time-worn elegance of the wooden panelling. Well-loved works like the touchingly erotic *The Kiss* and *The Hand of God* get most of the attention, but you can explore quieter rooms full of tortured clay figures that still bear the imprint of the artist's hands. Don't miss the room dedicated to Camille Claudel, Rodin's ill-starred pupil, muse and lover.

### Musée Maillol

61 rue de Grenelle, 7ᵉ • Sat–Thurs 10.30am–7pm, Fri 10.30am–9.30pm • €11 • ☎ 01 42 22 59 58, ⓦ museemaillol.com • Mᵒ Rue-du-Bac

Amid the aristocratic mansions of rue de Varenne and its parallel rue de Grenelle stands the **Musée Maillol**, a handsome eighteenth-century house stuffed with Aristide Maillol's endlessly buxom sculpted female nudes – copies of which can be seen to better effect in the Louvre's Jardin du Carrousel. His paintings follow a similar theme, and there are also minor works by contemporaries like Picasso, Degas, Cezanne, Gauguin and Suzanne Valadon, as well as some excellent exhibitions.

# Southern Paris

The entertainment nexus of **Montparnasse**, with its evocative literary and artistic associations, divides the well-heeled opinion-formers and powerbrokers of St-Germain and the 7ᵉ from the relatively anonymous populations to the south. The three arrondissements to the south of Montparnasse have suffered from large-scale housing developments, most notably along the riverfronts to both east and west, but villagey areas such as **rue du Commerce** in the 15ᵉ, **Pernety** in the 14ᵉ and the **Buttes-aux-Cailles** in the 13ᵉ are worth a foray. On the fringes of the city proper, hard up against the *périphérique* ring road, are three fantastic **parks**: André Citroën, Georges-Brassens and Montsouris.

## Montparnasse

Like other Left Bank *quartiers*, Montparnasse trades on its association with the wild characters of the interwar artistic and literary boom. Many were habitués of the cafés *Select*, *Coupole*, *Dôme*, *Rotonde* and *Closerie des Lilas*. The cafés are all still going strong on **boulevard du Montparnasse**, while the glitterati have mostly ended up in the nearby **Montparnasse cemetery**. The quarter's artistic traditions are maintained in a couple of fascinating art museums, while elsewhere you can ascend the **Tour Montparnasse**, Paris's first and ugliest skyscraper, and descend into the bone-lined **catacombs**.

### Tour Montparnasse

33 av du Maine, 15ᵉ • Daily: April–Sept 9.30am–11.30pm; Oct–March 9.30am–10.30pm • €13 • ☎ 01 45 38 52 56, ⓦ tourmontparnasse56.com • Mᵒ Montparnasse-Bienvenüe

At the station end of boulevard du Montparnasse, the colossal **Tour Montparnasse** has become one of the city's principal and most despised landmarks. Although central Paris is more distant, the view from the top is better than the one from the Eiffel Tower in that it includes the Eiffel Tower – and excludes the Tour Montparnasse. Alternatively, you could sit down for an expensive drink in the 56th-storey café-gallery, from where you get a tremendous view westwards. Sunset is the best time to visit.

## Musée Bourdelle

16–18 rue Antoine Bourdelle, 15ᵉ • Tues–Sun 10am–6pm • Free • ☎ 01 49 54 73 73, ⓦ bourdelle.paris.fr • Mᵒ Montparnasse-Bienvenüe/Falguière

One block northwest of the Montparnasse tower, a garden of sculptures invites you into the fascinating **Musée Bourdelle**, which has been built around the sculptor's atmospheric, musty and slightly ghostly old studio. Bourdelle, Rodin's pupil and Giacometti's teacher, moved sculpture on from naturalism – as in the wonderful series of Beethoven busts – towards a more geometric, modernist style. Some of his better-known, monumental sculptures are dotted around the garden.

## Jardin Atlantique

Access via lifts on rue du Commandant Mouchotte and bd Vaugirard, or by the stairs alongside Montparnasse station platform #1 • Daily 9am–dusk • Free • Mᵒ Montparnasse-Bienvenüe

Montparnasse station was once the great arrival and departure point for travellers heading across the Atlantic, a connection commemorated in the unexpected **Jardin Atlantique**, suspended above the train tracks behind the station. Hemmed in by cliff-like high-rise apartment blocks, the park is a wonderful example of French design, with fields of Atlantic-coast grasses, wave-like undulations in the lawns (to cover the irregularly placed concrete struts below) – and well-hidden ventilation holes that reveal sudden glimpses of TGV roofs and rail sleepers below.

## Montparnasse cemetery

Bd Edgar Quinet, 14ᵉ • Mid-March to Nov 5 Mon–Fri 8am–6pm, Sat 8.30am–6pm, Sun 9am–6pm; Nov 6 to mid-March closes 5.30pm • Free • Mᵒ Raspail/Gaîté/Edgar Quinet

Just south of boulevard Edgar-Quinet (which has a good food market) is the main entrance to the **Montparnasse cemetery**. Second in size and celebrity to Père-Lachaise, its ranks of miniature temples pay homage to illustrious names from Baudelaire to Beckett and Gainsbourg to Saint-Saëns; pick up a free map at the entrance gate to track down your favourites. The simple joint grave of Jean-Paul Sartre and Simone de Beauvoir lies immediately right of the main entrance; a couple of poignant monuments are marked by artist Niki de Saint-Phalle's distinctive mosaic sculptures. In the southwest corner is an old windmill, remains of one of the seventeenth-century taverns frequented by the carousing students who caused the district to be named after Mount Parnassus, the legendary home of the muses of poetry and song, and of Bacchus's drunken revels.

## Fondation Henri Cartier-Bresson

2 Impasse Lebouis, 14ᵉ • Sept–July Tues, Thurs, Fri & Sun 1–6.30pm, Wed 1–8.30pm, Sat 11am–6.45pm • €6 • ☎ 01 56 80 27 00, ⓦ henricartierbresson.org • Mᵒ Gaîté

The slender steel-and-glass **Fondation Henri Cartier-Bresson** houses the archive of the grand old photographer of Paris. Exhibitions of work by HCB himself, and his contemporaries, alternate with exhibitions promoting younger photographers.

## The catacombs

1 av du Colonel Henri Rol-Tanguy, 14ᵉ • Tues–Sun 10am–4pm • €8 • ☎ 01 43 22 47 63, ⓦ catacombes-de-paris.fr • Mᵒ Denfert-Rochereau

For a surreal, somewhat chilling experience, head down into the **catacombs** in place Denfert-Rochereau, formerly place d'Enfer (Hell Square). Abandoned quarries stacked with millions of bones, which were cleared from overstocked charnel houses and cemeteries between 1785 and 1871, the catacombs are said to hold the remains of around six million Parisians. Lining the gloomy passageways, long thigh bones are stacked end-on, forming a wall to keep in the smaller bones and shards, which can just be seen in dusty, higgledy-piggledy heaps behind. These high femoral walls are further inset with gaping, hollow-eyed skulls and plaques carrying macabre quotations. It's undeniably fascinating, but note that there are a good couple of kilometres to walk – it's 500m through dark, damp, narrow passageways before you even get to the ossuary – and it can quickly become claustrophobic in the extreme.

## Fondation Cartier pour l'Art Contemporain

261 bd Raspail, 14ᵉ • Tues 11am–10pm, Wed–Sun 11am–8pm • €9.50 • ☎ 01 42 18 56 50, ⓦ fondation.cartier.com • Mᵒ Raspail

Rue Schoelcher and boulevard Raspail, on the east side of Montparnasse cemetery, have some interesting examples of twentieth-century architecture, from Art Nouveau to the modern glass-and-steel façade of the **Fondation Cartier pour l'Art Contemporain**. Built in 1994 by Jean Nouvel, this presents contemporary installations, videos and multimedia in high-quality temporary exhibitions.

## Observatoire de Paris

Av de l'Observatoire, 14ᵉ • Mᵒ Denfert-Rochereau/RER Port Royal

The classical **Observatoire de Paris** sat on France's zero meridian line from the 1660s, when it was constructed, until 1884. After that date, they reluctantly agreed that 0° longitude should pass through a small village in Normandy that happens to be due south of Greenwich. You can see one of the bronze markers of the "Arago line" set into the cobbles of the observatory's courtyard.

# The 15ᵉ arrondissement

Though it's the largest and most populous of them all, the **15ᵉ arrondissement** falls off the agenda for most visitors as it lacks a single important building or monument. It does have a pleasant villagey heart, however, in the **rue du Commerce**, and an appealing offbeat riverside walk on the narrow midstream island, the **Allée des Cygnes**, which you can reach in a short stroll south of the Eiffel Tower, via the Pont de Bir-Hakeim. The chief landmarks of the 15ᵉ, however, are its **parks**.

## Parc André-Citroën

Quai André-Citroën, 15ᵉ • **Park** Daily 9am–dusk **Balloon** Fine days only: 9am to roughly 1hr before dusk • Mon–Fri €10, Sat & Sun €12 • Mᵒ Balard

In the southwest corner of the 15ᵉ lies the hyper-designed **Parc André-Citroën**, so named because the site used to be the Citroën motor works. Its best features are the glasshouses full of exotic-smelling shrubs, the dancing fountains – which bolder park-goers run through on hot days – and the tethered hot air **balloon**, which offers spectacular views.

## Parc Georges-Brassens and around

Entrance on rue des Morillons, 15ᵉ • Daily dawn to dusk • Mᵒ Convention/Porte-de-Vanves

The **Parc Georges-Brassens**, in the southeast corner of the 15ᵉ, is a delight, with a garden of scented herbs and shrubs (best in late spring), puppets and merry-go-rounds for kids, a mountain stream with pine and birch trees, beehives and a tiny terraced vineyard. On the west side of the park, in a secluded garden in passage Dantzig, off rue Dantzig, stands an unusual polygonal studio space known as **La Ruche**. Home to Fernand Léger, Modigliani, Chagall, Soutine and many other artists at the start of the twentieth century, it's still used as studios. A **book market** is held every Saturday and Sunday morning in the sheds of the old horse market between the park and rue Brançion.

**1**

# The 13ᵉ arrondissement

The 13ᵉ is one of the most disparate areas of the city. **Place d'Italie**, with the ornate *mairie* and vast Gaumont cinema, is the hub, with each of the major roads radiating out into very different *quartiers*. To the north, the genteel neighbourhood around the ancient **Gobelins** tapestry works has more in common with the adjacent Quartier Latin. Between boulevard Auguste-Blanqui and rue Bobillot, meanwhile, is the lively hilltop quarter of the **Butte-aux-Cailles**. If you're looking for unpretentious, youthful and vaguely lefty restaurants and nightlife, this area is well worth the short métro ride out from the centre. The easiest route is to walk up rue Bobillot from place d'Italie.

Over to the east, in the middle of a swathe of high-rise social housing, is the **Chinese quarter** of Paris. Avenues de Choisy and d'Ivry are full of Vietnamese, Chinese, Thai, Cambodian and Laotian restaurants and food shops, as is **Les Olympiades**, a weird semi-derelict pedestrian area seemingly suspended between giant tower blocks. Along the riverside, the old quays, mills and warehouses have been transformed into an upmarket new *quartier* called **Paris Rive Gauche**, centred on the flagship **Bibliothèque Nationale**.

## Bibliothèque Nationale de France

Quai François-Mauriac, 13ᵉ • Tues–Sat 9am–8pm, Sun 1–7pm • €3.50 for a reading room pass • ☎ 01 53 79 40 43, ⓦ bnf.fr • Mᵒ Quai-de-la-Gare/Bibliothèque-François Mitterrand

The impressive **Bibliothèque Nationale de France** has four enormous towers – intended to look like open books – framing a sunken pine copse. Jaw-dropping as it is, architect Dominique Perrault's design attracted widespread derision after shutters had to be added to the towers to protect the books and manuscripts from sunlight. It's worth wandering around inside, in order to see the pair of wonderful globes that belonged to Louis XIV and occasional small-scale exhibitions; the garden level is reserved for accredited researchers only.

## Passerelle Simone de Beauvoir and around

From the Bibliothèque Nationale down to the *boulevard périphérique*, almost every stick of street furniture and square metre of tarmac is shiny and new. The still-underpopulated cafés and apartment blocks, and the **Passerelle Simone de Beauvoir**, a €21-million footbridge that crosses the Seine in a hyper-modern double-ribbon structure, give the area a futuristic frontier-town feel. Between the bridge and the pont de Bercy, several tethered **barges** have made the area a nightlife attraction; among them, the floating swimming pool **Piscine Josephine Baker**, on its own barge, is wonderful.

## Les Frigos

19 rue des Frigos, 13ᵉ • ⓦ les-frigos.com • Mᵒ Quai de la Gare/Bibliothèque François Mitterrand

Immediately south of rue Tolbiac is the giant, decaying warehouse of **Les Frigos** which was once used for cold-storage of meat and fish destined for Les Halles, but was taken over, immediately after the market's closure, by artists and musicians. It has been run as an anarchic studio space ever since, with a bar-restaurant on site and open-door exhibitions once or twice a year.

## Docks en Seine

ⓦ paris-docks-en-Seine.fr • Mᵒ Austerlitz/Quai de la Gare

Newest of all the Paris Rive Gauche developments is the **Docks en Seine** complex on the bleak Quai d'Austerlitz. The ugly concrete warehouses have been rebuilt as the **Cité de la Mode et du Design**, a fashion institute – its intrusive design of twisting, lime green tubes, by Dominique Jacob and Brendan MacFarlane, is supposed to recall the sinuous shape of the river. Inside, the **Institut Français de la Mode** (ⓦ ifm-paris.com), a new fashion school, is expected to host frequent exhibitions, and has a floating café-restaurant, *Petit Bain*.

# The Beaux Quartiers

Commonly referred to as the **Beaux Quartiers**, Paris's well-manicured western arrondissements, the 16$^e$ and 17$^e$, are mainly residential and have few specific sights, the chief exception being the **Musée Marmottan**, with its dazzling collection of late Monets. Bordering the area to the west is the **Bois de Boulogne**, with its trees, lakes, cycling trails and the beautiful floral displays of the Parc de Bagatelle. Further west still bristle the gleaming skyscrapers of the purpose-built commercial district of **La Défense**, dominated by the enormous Grande Arche.

## Musée Marmottan

2 rue Louis-Boilly, 16$^e$ • Tues, Wed & Fri–Sun 10am–6pm, Thurs 10am–8pm • €10 • ☎ 01 44 96 50 33, ⓦ marmottan.com • M$^o$ Muette

The **Musée Marmottan** showcases Impressionist works, the highlight of which is a dazzling collection of canvases from Monet's last years at Giverny, including several *Nymphéas* (Water Lilies). The collection also features some of his contemporaries – Manet, Renoir and Berthe Morisot.

## Bois de Boulogne

M$^o$ Porte-Maillot/Porte Dauphine

The **Bois de Boulogne** is an area of extensive parkland running down the west side of the 16$^e$. The "bois" of the name is somewhat deceptive, though it does contain some remnants of the once great Forêt de Rouvray. Once the playground of the wealthy, it also established a reputation as the site of the sex trade and its associated crime. The same is true today and you should avoid it at night. By day, however, the park is an extremely pleasant spot for a stroll.

### Parc de Bagatelle

Bois de Boulogne • Daily 9.30am to dusk • €5 • Bus #244 from M$^o$ Porte-Maillot, or bus #43 from M$^o$ Pont-de-Neuilly

One of the Bois de Boulogne's main attractions is the **Parc de Bagatelle**, which features beautiful displays of tulips, hyacinths and daffodils in the first half of April, irises in May, and water lilies and roses at the end of June.

### Jardin d'Acclimatation

Bois de Boulogne • Daily: April–Sept 10am–7pm; Oct–March 10am–6pm • €2.90 or €5.60 including return train ride from métro; rides from €2.70 • ☎ 01 40 67 90 82, ⓦ jardindacclimatation.fr • M$^o$ Les Sablons/Porte-Maillot; the best way to get there is via the *petit train* (every 15min from rue de la Porte des Sablons au Porte Maillot, near Porte Maillot métro station)

The highlight of the Bois de Boulogne for children is the **Jardin d'Acclimatation**, a cross between a funfair, zoo and amusement park. Temptations range from bumper cars, merry-go-rounds and a mini canal ride to birds, bears and llamas. It is also the location for a new contemporary arts space, the **Fondation Louis Vuitton pour la Création**, designed by Frank Gehry and due for completion at the end of 2013.

## La Défense

An impressive complex of gleaming skyscrapers, **La Défense** is Paris's prestige business district and a monument to late twentieth-century capitalism. Its most popular attraction is the huge **Grande Arche** (M$^o$/RER Grande-Arche-de-la-Défense), an astounding 112m-high hollow cube clad in white marble, standing 6km out from the Arc de Triomphe at the far end of the Voie Triomphale. It's no longer possible to take a lift up to the rooftop, but it's no great loss, as the views from the base of the arch are impressive enough – from here you can see as far as the Louvre on a clear day.

**1**

# Montmartre and around

Perched on Paris's highest hill, towards the northern edge of the city, **Montmartre** was famously the home and playground of artists such as Renoir, Degas, Picasso and Toulouse-Lautrec. The crown of the Butte Montmartre, around place du Tertre, is a scrum, overrun with tourists these days, but the steep streets around **Abbesses** métro preserve an attractively festive, village-like atmosphere – and seem to become more gentrified and more fashionable every year. Even **Pigalle**, the brassy sprawl at the southern foot of the Butte, is turning trendy, with fashionable shops and boutique hotels springing up around rue des Martyrs. The **Goutte d'Or**, to the east, remains vibrantly multi-ethnic. Out at the northern city limits, the mammoth **St-Ouen market** hawks everything from extravagant antiques to the cheapest flea-market hand-me-downs.

## The Butte Montmartre

In spite of being one of the city's chief tourist attractions, the **Butte Montmartre** manages to retain the quiet, almost secretive, air of its rural origins. The most popular access route is via the rue de Steinkerque and the steps below the Sacré-Coeur (the funicular railway from place Suzanne-Valadon is covered by normal métro tickets). For a quieter approach, wind your way up via **place des Abbesses,** the hub of a lively neighbourhood full of clothes shops, buzzing wine bars and laidback restaurants, or rue Lepic.

One quiet and attractive way to get from place des Abbesses to the top of the Butte is to climb up rue de la Vieuville and the rue Drevet stairs to the minuscule **place du Calvaire**, a route with a lovely view back over the city; you could also head up rue Tholozé, turning right below the **Moulin de la Galette** – the last survivor of Montmartre's forty-odd windmills, immortalized by Renoir – into rue des Norvins. Artistic associations abound hereabouts: Zola, Berlioz, Turgenev, Seurat, Degas and Van Gogh lived in the area. Picasso, Braque and Gris invented Cubism in an old piano factory in place Émile-Goudeau, known as the **Bateau-Lavoir**; it still serves as artists' studios, though the original building burnt down years ago. Toulouse-Lautrec's inspiration, the **Moulin Rouge**, survives too, albeit as a shadow of its former self, on the corner of boulevard de Clichy and place Blanche.

### Musée de Montmartre

12 rue Cortot, 18e • Daily 10am–6pm • €8 • ☎ 01 49 25 89 37, ⓦ museedemontmartre.fr • M° Lamarck-Caulaincourt

The intriguing little **Musée de Montmartre** recaptures something of the feel of the quarter's bohemian days, with its old posters, paintings and photos and recreations of period rooms. The house, rented at various times by Renoir, Dufy, Suzanne Valadon and her alcoholic son Utrillo, also offers views over the neat terraces of the tiny **Montmartre vineyard** – which produces some 1500 bottles a year – on the north side of the Butte. The lovely little cabaret *Le Lapin Agile* (see p.135) is very nearby.

### Place du Tertre

The **place du Tertre**, the core of old Montmartre, is today best avoided. It's been sucked dry of all interest, clotted with tour groups, overpriced restaurants, tacky souvenir stalls and jaded artists knocking out garish paintings. Between place du Tertre and the Sacré-Coeur, the old church of **St-Pierre** is all that remains of the Benedictine abbey that occupied the Butte Montmartre from the twelfth century on.

## MONTMARTRE & THE NEUVIÈME

0    200
metres

## Sacré-Coeur

**Church** Daily 6.45am–10.30pm • Free **Dome** Daily: April, May, Sept & Oct 9.30am–6.45pm; June–Aug 9.30am–8pm • €6 • M° Abbesses/Anvers

Crowning the Butte is the **Sacré-Coeur** with its iconic ice-cream-scoop dome. Construction of this French–Byzantine confection was started in the 1870s on the initiative of the Catholic Church to atone for the "crimes" of the Commune. **Square Willette**, the space at the foot of the monumental staircase, is named after the local artist who turned out on inauguration day to shout "Long live the devil!". Today the staircase acts as impromptu seating for visitors enjoying the views over Paris, munching

**1**

on picnics and watching the street entertainers; the crowds only increase as night falls. You can also get stunning **views** from the top of the dome, which takes you almost as high as the Eiffel Tower.

## Montmartre cemetery

Entrance on av Rachel under rue Caulaincourt, 18ᵉ • Mid-March to Nov 5 Mon–Fri 8am–6pm, Sat 8.30am–6pm, Sun 9am–6pm; Nov 6 to mid-March closes 5.30pm • Free • Mᵒ Blanche/Place-de-Clichy

West of the Butte lies the **Montmartre cemetery**. It's a melancholy place, tucked down below street level in the hollow of an old quarry, its steep tomb-dotted hills creating a sombre ravine of the dead. The graves of Nijinsky, Zola, Stendhal, Berlioz, Degas, Feydeau, Offenbach and Truffaut, among others, are marked on a free map available at the entrance.

## St-Ouen flea market

Officially open Sat–Mon 9am–6.30pm – unofficially, from 5am; many stands are closed on Mon; Mᵒ Porte-de-Clignancourt

**Puces de St-Ouen** claims to be the largest flea market in the world, though nowadays it's predominantly a proper – and expensive – antiques market (mainly furniture, but including old café-bar counters, traffic lights, jukeboxes and the like), with many quirky treasures to be found. Of the twelve or so individual markets, you could concentrate on Marché **Dauphine**, good for movie posters, chanson and jazz records, comics and books, and Marché **Vernaison** for curios and bric-a-brac.

## Pigalle

From place Clichy in the west to Barbès-Rochechouart in the east, the hill of Montmartre is underlined by the sleazy **boulevards de Clichy and Rochechouart**. In the middle, between place Blanche and place **Pigalle**, sex shows, sex shops, girly bars and streetwalkers (both male and female) vie for custom. Only a few steps south of the Pigalle maelstrom, the atmosphere shifts as you enter the so-called SoPi, or "South of Pigalle" district; it still has its gritty elements, but bohemian shops and bars are moving in, especially in the streets around rue des Martyrs, long known for its neighbourhood food shops and fast acquiring a hot reputation for boutique clothes shops too.

### Musée de l'Erotisme

72 bd Clichy, 18ᵉ • Daily 10am–2am • €10 • ☎ 01 42 58 28 73, ⓦ musee-erotisme.com • Mᵒ Blanche

Appropriately set among the sex shops and shows of Pigalle, the surprisingly classy **Musée de l'Erotisme** bristles with sacred, ethnographic and ribald erotic art and sculpture from around the world. There's also a fascinating history of Parisian brothels, and regular, high-quality themed exhibitions.

## Goutte d'Or

Along the north side of the grotty boulevard de la Chapelle, between boulevard Barbès and the Gare du Nord rail lines, stretches the quartier of the **Goutte d'Or** ("Drop of Gold"), a name that derives from the medieval vineyard that occupied this site. After World War I, when large numbers of North Africans were first imported to replenish the ranks of Frenchmen dying in the trenches, the area gradually became an immigrant ghetto. Today, while the quartier remains poor, it is a vibrant place, home to a host of mini-communities, predominantly West African and Congolese, but with pockets of South Asian, Haitian, Turkish and other ethnicities as well. Countless shops sell ethnic music and, and on rue Dejean, a few steps east of métro Château-Rouge, is the Marché Dejean (closed Sun afternoon and Mon), which sells African groceries. Another, more general market takes place in the mornings twice weekly (Wed & Sat) beneath the métro viaduct on the boulevard de la Chapelle.

# La Villette and around

The **Bassin de la Villette** and the **canals** at the northeastern gate of the city were for generations the centre of a densely populated working-class district, whose main source of employment were the La Villette abattoirs and meat market. These have long gone, replaced by the huge complex of La Villette, a postmodern park of science, art and music.

The Villette complex stands at the junction of the **Ourcq** and **St-Denis canals**. The first was built by Napoleon to bring fresh water into the city; the second is an extension of the Canal St-Martin built as a short cut to the great western loop of the Seine around Paris. The canals have undergone extensive renovation, and derelict sections of the *quais* have been made more appealing to cyclists, rollerbladers and pedestrians. A major new arts centre, **Le 104**, has also helped to regenerate the area.

## Canal St-Martin

The **Canal St-Martin** runs underground at Bastille to surface again in boulevard Jules-Ferry by rue du Faubourg-du-Temple. The canal still has a slightly industrial feel, especially along its upper stretch. The lower part is more attractive, with plane trees, cobbled *quais* and elegant, high-arched footbridges, as well as lively bars and stylish boutiques frequented by artsy, media folk. The area is particularly lively on Sunday afternoons, when the *quais* are closed to traffic, and pedestrians, cyclists and rollerbladers take over the streets; on sunny days a young crowd hangs out along the canal's edge, nursing beers or strumming guitars.

### La Rotonde de la Villette

6–8 place de la Bataille de Stalingrad, 19ᵉ • ☎ 01 80 48 33 40, ⓦ larotonde.com • Mᵒ Stalingrad/Laumière/Riquet

On place de la Bataille de Stalingrad, where the Canal St Martin disappears underground, stands the beautifully restored Palladian-style **Rotonde de la Villette**, a former tollhouse, built by Ledoux in 1788. Its atrium, roofed with glass, has been elegantly converted into an exhibition space, concert venue and stylish bar-brasserie. The outside tables on the square are a pleasant spot for a day-time or evening drink.

### Bassin de la Villette

Mᵒ Stalingrad/Laumière/Riquet

Beyond the place de la Bataille de Stalingrad extends the **Bassin de la Villette** dock, once France's premier port. It's been recobbled and the dockside buildings have been converted into brasseries and a multiplex cinema (the MK2), which has screens on both banks, linked by a boat shuttle. In August, as part of the Paris Plages scheme (see p.63 & p.137), there are canoes, pedaloes for children and other boating activities. At rue de Crimée a unique hydraulic bridge marks the end of the dock and the beginning of the Canal de l'Ourcq. If you keep to the south bank on quai de la Marne, you can cross directly into the **Parc de la Villette**.

## Parc de la Villette

Between avs Corentin-Cariou and Jean-Jaurès, 19ᵉ • Daily 6am–1am • Free • ⓦ villette.com • Mᵒ Porte-de-la-Villette/Porte-de-Pantin

The futuristic **Parc de la Villette**, a highly stimulating music, art and science complex, is so large in scope and size, it can feel a little overwhelming at first. It's best to start at the

**1**

information centre by the M° Porte-de-Pantin entrance where you can pick up a free map and get your bearings. The park's main visitor attractions are the **Cité des Sciences et de l'Industrie**, the **music museum** within the **Cité de la Musique** (the city's music academy) and its ten themed **gardens**, mostly aimed at children, such as the *Jardin du Dragon*, with its huge dragon slide.

## Cité des Sciences et de l'Industrie

Parc de la Villette, 30 av Corentin-Cariou, 19ᵉ • Tues–Sat 10am–6pm, Sun 10am–7pm • €8 or €11 with the planetarium **Cité des Enfants** 90min sessions Tues–Fri 10am, 11.45am, 1.30 & 3.15pm; Sat & Sun 10.30am, 12.30, 2.30 & 4.30pm; €6; book in advance during busy holiday periods via the website or on ☏ 08 92 69 70 72 • ☏ 01 40 05 70 00, ⓦ cite-sciences.fr • M° Porte-de-la-Villette

The Parc de la Villette's dominant building is the **Cité des Sciences et de l'Industrie**, an enormous, glass-walled, high-tech science museum, four times the size of the Pompidou Centre, built into the concrete hulk of an abandoned abattoir. Inside are crow's-nests, cantilevered platforms, bridges and suspended walkways, the different levels linked by lifts and escalators around a huge central space open to the full forty-metre height of the roof. The permanent exhibition, called Explora, covers subjects such as sound, robotics, energy, light, ecology, maths, medicine, space and language, using interactive computers, videos, holograms, animated models and games. You can have your head spun further in the **planetarium**.

The Cité des Sciences has a special section for children called the **Cité des Enfants**, with areas for 2- to 7-year-olds and 5- to 12-year-olds (all must be accompanied by an adult). It's hugely engaging; children can play about with water, construct buildings on a miniature construction site, manipulate robots and race their own shadows.

## Cité de la Musique

221 av Jean Jaurès, 19ᵉ **Musée de la Musique** Tues–Sat noon–6pm, Sun 10am–6pm • €8 • ⓦ cite-musique.fr

The **Cité de la Musique** occupies two fine contemporary buildings to either side of the Parc de la Villette's Porte-de-Pantin entrance. To the west is the national music academy, while to the east are a concert hall, the chic *Café de la Musique* and the excellent **Musée de la Musique**, presenting the history of music from the end of the Renaissance to the present day, both visually – through a collection of 4500 instruments – and aurally, with headsets and interactive displays.

## Le 104

5 rue Curial, 19ᵉ • ☏ 01 53 35 50 00, ⓦ 104.fr • M° Riquet

Located in a former grand nineteenth-century funeral parlour, **Le 104** is a huge arts centre, with an impressive glass-roofed central hall (*nef curial*) and numerous artists' studios. It hosts exhibitions and installations, dance and theatre, with an emphasis on presenting "avant-premières" of new plays and extended runs of sell-out performances from other theatres. The complex also houses a good bookshop, charity and fair-trade shops, a café and restaurant.

# The eastern districts

Traditionally working class, with a history of radical and revolutionary activity, the gritty **eastern districts** of Paris, particularly the old villages of **Belleville** and **Ménilmontant**, are nowadays among the most diverse and vibrant parts of the city, home to sizeable ethnic populations, as well as students and artists, attracted by the low rents. The main visitor attraction in the area is the **Père-Lachaise cemetery**, final resting place of many well-known artists and writers. Visiting the modern **Parc de Belleville** will reveal the area's other main asset – wonderful views of the city below. Another park well worth seeing is the fairy-tale-like **Parc des Buttes-Chaumont**.

# Parc des Buttes-Chaumont

M° Buttes-Chaumont/Botzaris

At the northern end of the Belleville heights, a short walk from La Villette, is the **parc des Buttes-Chaumont**, constructed by Haussmann in the 1860s to camouflage what until then had been a desolate warren of disused quarries and miserable shacks. Out of this rather unlikely setting a wonderfully romantic park was created – there's a grotto with a cascade and artificial stalactites, and a picturesque lake from which a huge rock rises up topped with a delicate Corinthian temple.

# Belleville and Ménilmontant

The route from Buttes-Chaumont to Père-Lachaise will take you through the one-time villages of **Belleville** and **Ménilmontant**. Absorbed into Paris in the 1860s and subsequently built up with high-rise blocks to house migrants from rural districts and the ex-colonies, this area might not be exactly "belle", but it's certainly vibrant and happening. The main street, rue de Belleville, abounds with Vietnamese, Thai and Chinese shops and restaurants, and numerous artists live and work in the area, attracted by the availability of affordable and large spaces; the best time to view their work is during the **Journées portes ouvertes ateliers d'artistes de Belleville** in mid-May (ⓦateliers-artistes-belleville.org).

You get fantastic views down onto the city centre from the higher reaches of Belleville and Ménilmontant: the best place to watch the sun set is the **Parc de Belleville** (M° Couronnes/Pyrénées), which descends in a series of terraces and waterfalls from rue Piat. And from **rue de Ménilmontant**, by rues de l'Ermitage and Boyer, you can look straight down to the Pompidou Centre. Rue de Ménilmontant's extension, **rue Oberkampf**, and parallel rue Jean-Pierre Timbaud are the hub of the city's nightlife, where you can hear anything from live rock to gypsy jazz.

## Père-Lachaise cemetery

Main entrance on bd de Ménilmontant, 20ᵉ • Mon–Fri 8am–5.30pm, Sat 8.30am–5.30pm, Sun 9am–5.30pm • Free • ⓦ pere-lachaise .com • M° Gambetta/Père-Lachaise/Alexandre-Dumas/Phillipe-Auguste

**Père-Lachaise cemetery**, final resting place of numerous notables, is an atmospheric, eerily beautiful haven, with little cobbled footpaths, terraced slopes and magnificent old trees which spread their branches over the tombs as though shading them from the outside world. The cemetery was opened in 1804, after an urgent stop had been put to further burials in the overflowing city cemeteries and churchyards. The civil authorities had Molière, La Fontaine, Abelard and Héloïse reburied here, and to be interred in Père-Lachaise quickly acquired cachet. A free **map** of the cemetery is available at all the entrances or you can buy a more detailed one at the Père-Lachaise shop at 45 boulevard de Ménilmontant. Among the most visited graves is that of **Chopin** (Division 11), often attended by Poles bearing red-and-white wreaths and flowers. Fans also flock to the ex-Doors lead singer **Jim Morrison** (Division 6), who died in Paris at the age of 27, and to **Oscar Wilde**'s tomb (Division 89), which is topped with a sculpture by Jacob Epstein of a mysterious Pharaonic winged messenger. You can also visit the graves of Edith Piaf, Marcel Proust, Corot, Balzac and Modigliani.

In Division 97 are the memorials to the victims of the Nazi **concentration camps** and executed **Resistance fighters**. Marking one of the bloodiest episodes in French history is the Mur des Fédérés (Division 76), the wall where the last troops of the Paris Commune were lined up and shot in the final days of the battle in 1871.

## ARRIVAL AND DEPARTURE                                                                                     PARIS

### BY PLANE

The two main international ariports are Roissy-Charles de Gaulle – usually referred to as Charles de Gaulle (CDG or Paris CDG) – 23km northeast of the city, and

Orly, 14km south. Both are well connected to the centre. The more distant Beauvais Airport, some 65km northwest of Paris, is used by some budget airlines, including Ryanair.

**1**

## ROISSY-CHARLES DE GAULLE AIRPORT

**Information** Detailed information in English at ⓦadp.fr, or ☎33 1 48 62 22 80 for 24hr English-language information.

**Terminals** Charles de Gaulle has two main terminals, CDG 1 and CDG 2, with a third, CDG 3 (sometimes called CDG-T3), handling various low-cost airlines, including easyJet.

**TGV links** A TGV station links the airport (CDG 2) with Bordeaux, Brussels, Lille, Lyon, Nantes, Marseille and Rennes, among other places.

**RER into Paris** The least expensive and probably quickest way into the centre of Paris is to take the suburban train line RER B3, sometimes called Roissy-Rail (every 10–15min 5am–midnight; 30min; €9.25 one way, no return tickets). To get to the RER station from CDG 1 you have to take a free shuttle bus (*navette*) to the RER station, but from CDG 2 and CDG-T3 it's simpler to take the pedestrian walkway, though the station is also served by a shuttle bus. The RER train stops at stations including Gare du Nord, Châtelet-Les Halles and St-Michel, at all of which you can transfer to the ordinary métro system – your ticket is valid through to any métro station in central Paris. Note that if your flight gets in after midnight your only means of transport is a taxi or the minibus.

**Minibuses** The Paris Blue door-to-door minibus service costs from €32 for two people, with no extra charge for luggage. Bookings must be made at least 24 hours in advance (☎01 30 11 13 00 or, for the best rates, ⓦparis-blue-airport-shuttle.fr).

**Taxis** Taxis into central Paris (50min–1hr) cost around €50 on the meter, plus a small luggage supplement (€1 per item).

**Buses** Various bus companies provide services from the airport direct to various city-centre locations, but they're slightly more expensive than Roissy-Rail, may take longer, and don't run at night.

## ORLY AIRPORT

**Information** Detailed information in English at ⓦadp.fr, or call ☎01 49 75 15 15 (daily 6am–11.30pm).

**Terminals** Orly Sud (South; international flights) and Orly Ouest (West; domestic flights), linked by shuttle bus but easily walkable.

**Trains into Paris** The easiest way into the centre is via Orlyval, a fast train shuttle link to the suburban RER station Antony, where you can pick up RER line B trains to the central RER/métro stations Denfert-Rochereau, St-Michel and Châtelet-Les Halles; Orlyval runs (every 4–7min 6.10am–11pm; 35min to Châtelet; €10.90 one way).

**Shuttle buses** The useful Orlybus shuttle bus takes you direct to RER line B station Denfert-Rochereau, on the Left Bank, with good onward métro connections (every 15–20min 6am–11pm, midnight Fri & Sat; €7 one-way; total journey around 30min).

**Taxis** Taxis take about 35min to reach the centre of Paris (around €35).

## BEAUVAIS AIRPORT

**Information** ⓦaeroportbeauvais.com, ☎08 92 68 20 66.

**Coaches** Coaches (depart 15–30min after flights arrive, around 3hr before the flight leaves on the way back; €15 one-way) shuttle between the airport and Porte Maillot (around 1hr), at the northwestern edge of Paris, where you can pick up métro line 1 to the centre.

## BY TRAIN

Paris has seven mainline train stations. All of them have left luggage (*consignes*) facilities.

**Gare du Nord** Eurostar (☎08 92 35 35 39, ⓦeurostar.com), along with trains from Calais and other north European countries, terminate at the busy Gare du Nord, on rue Dunkerque, in the northeast of the city. As you come off the train, turn left for the métro, the RER and the tourist office, and right for taxis (around €10 to central Paris). Just short of the taxi exit, head down the escalators for left luggage and car rental desks. There are two *bureaux de change* (neither offer a good deal) and cash machines.

**Gare de l'Est** Near the Gare du Nord, at place du 11-Novembre-1918, 10ᵉ, Gare de l'Est serves eastern France and central and eastern Europe.

**Gare St-Lazare** Serving the Normandy coast and Dieppe, St-Lazare is the most central, at place du Havre, 8ᵉ close to the Madeleine and the Opéra-Garnier.

**Gare de Lyon** On the southeast edge of the Right Bank, at place Louis-Armand, 12ᵉ, Lyon is the terminus for trains to Italy and Switzerland and TGV lines to southeast France.

**Gare Montparnasse** South of the river on Bd de Vaugirard, 15ᵉ; the terminus for Chartres, Brittany, the Atlantic coast and TGV lines to Tours and southwest France.

**Gare d'Austerlitz** Bd de l'Hôpital, 13ᵉ, serves the Loire Valley and the Dordogne.

**Gare de Paris-Bercy** The motorail station is down the tracks from the Gare de Lyon on Bd de Bercy, 12ᵉ. It is also the terminus for trains from Avallon, Auxerre and Sens.

## BY BUS

Almost all the buses coming into Paris – whether international or domestic – arrive at the main *gare routière* at 28 av du Général-de-Gaulle, Bagnolet, at the eastern edge of the city; métro Gallieni (line 3) links it to the centre.

## BY CAR

If you're driving in yourself, don't try to go straight across the city to your destination. Use the ring road – the *boulevard périphérique* – to get around to the nearest *porte*: it's much quicker, except at rush hour, and far easier to navigate, albeit pretty terrifying. For information on car parks in Paris, see ⓦparkingsdeparis.com.

## GETTING AROUND

While walking is undoubtedly the best way to discover Paris, the city's integrated public transport system of bus, me
and trains – the RATP (Régie Autonome des Transports Parisiens; ⓦ ratp.fr) – is cheap, fast and meticulously signpostec
The métro, combined with the RER (Réseau Express Régional) suburban express lines, is the simplest way of getting
around. Free métro and bus maps of varying sizes and detail are available at most stations, bus terminals and tourist
offices: the largest and most useful is the *Grand Plan de Paris numéro 2*, which overlays the métro, RER and bus routes
on a map of the city so you can see exactly how transport lines and streets match up. If you just want a handy pocket-
sized métro/bus map ask for the *Petit Plan de Paris* or the smaller *Paris Plan de Poche*. You can also download maps,
including a wallet-sized version of the métro map and a very useful searchable interactive online version of *Grand
Plan de Paris numéro 2* at ⓦ ratp.fr.

### THE MÉTRO AND RER

**Hours** The métro runs from 5.20am to 1.20am, RER trains
from 4.45am to 1.30am.

**Stations** Stations (abbreviated M° Concorde, RER
Luxembourg, etc) are evenly spaced and you'll rarely find
yourself more than 500m from one in the centre, though
the interchanges can involve a lot of legwork, including
many stairs.

**The network** In addition to the free maps available (see
above), every station has a big plan of the network outside
the entrance and several inside, as well as a map of the local
area. The lines are colour-coded and designated by numbers
for the métro and by letters for the RER, although they are
signposted within the system with the names of their
terminus stations: for example, travelling from Montparnasse
to Châtelet, you follow the sign "Direction Porte-de-
Clignancourt"; from Gare d'Austerlitz to Grenelle on line 10
you follow "Direction Boulogne–Pont-de-St-Cloud". For RER
journeys beyond the city, make sure the station you want is
illuminated on the platform display board.

## TICKETS AND PASSES

Useful for a short stay in the city, **carnets** of ten tickets can be bought from any station or
*tabac* (€12.70, as opposed to €1.70 for an individual ticket). The RATP is divided into **five
zones**, and the métro system itself more or less fits into zones 1 and 2. The same tickets are
valid for the buses (including the night bus), métro and, within the city limits and immediate
suburbs (zones 1 and 2), the RER express rail lines, which also extend far out into the Île de
France. Only one ticket is ever needed on the métro system, and within zones 1 and 2 for any
RER or bus journey, but you can't switch between buses or between bus and métro/RER on
the same ticket. For RER journeys beyond zones 1 and 2 you must buy an RER ticket. In order
to get to La Défense on the RER rather than on the métro, for example, you need to buy a RER
ticket, as La Défense is in zone 3. Children under 4 travel free and from ages 4 to 10 at
half-price. Don't buy from the touts who hang round the main stations – you may pay well
over the odds, quite often for a used ticket – and be sure to keep your ticket until the end of
the journey as you'll be fined on the spot if you can't produce one.

### PASSES

If you're doing a fair number of journeys in one day, it might be worth getting a **Mobilis day
pass** (€6.40 for zones 1 & 2), which offers unlimited access to the métro, buses and, depending
on which zones you choose, the RER. Other possibilities are the **Paris Visite** passes (ⓦ ratp
.info/touristes/), one-, two-, three- and five-day visitors' passes at €9.75, €15.85, €21.60 and
€31.15 for Paris and close suburbs, or €20.50, €31.15, €43.65 and €53.40 to include the airports,
Versailles and Disneyland Paris (make sure you buy this one when you arrive at Roissy-Charles
de Gaulle or Orly to get maximum value). A half-price child's version is also available. You can
buy them from métro and RER stations, tourist offices and online from ⓦ helloparis.co.uk. Paris
Visite passes can begin on any day and entitle you to unlimited travel (in the zones you have
chosen) on bus, métro, RER, SNCF and the Montmartre funicular; they also allow you discounts
at certain monuments and museums.

   If you arrive early in the week and stay more than three days, it's more economical to buy a
**Navigo weekly pass** (*le passe Navigo découverte*). It costs €19.15 for zones 1 and 2 and is valid
for an unlimited number of journeys from Monday morning to Sunday evening. You can only
buy a ticket for the current week until Thursday; from Friday you can buy a ticket to begin the
following Monday. A monthly pass costs €62.90 for zones 1 and 2. The Navigo swipe card itself
costs €5, and you'll also need a passport photo.

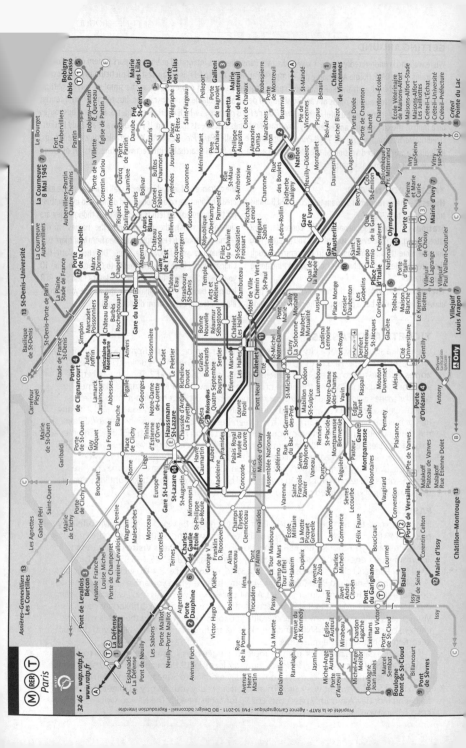

## BUSES

**City buses** The city's buses (roughly 5.30am–8.30pm with some services continuing to 1.30am) are not difficult to use. Every bus stop displays the name of the stop, the numbers of the buses that stop there, a map showing all the stops on the route, and the times of the first and last buses. You can buy a single ticket (€1.90 from the driver), or use a pre-purchased carnet ticket or pass (see box, p.115); validate your ticket by inserting it into one of the machines on board. Press the red button to request a stop and an *arrêt demandé* sign will then light up. Most buses are easily accessible for wheelchairs and prams. Around half the lines don't operate on Sundays and holidays – the *Grand Plan de Paris* (see p.115) lists those that do. You can download a map of the most useful tourist routes from ⓦ ratp.fr.

**Balabus** An orange-and-white Balabus service (not to be confused with Batobus, see below) passes all the major tourist sights between the Grande Arche de la Défense and Gare de Lyon (mid-April to mid-Sept Sun and holidays every 15–20min noon–9pm). Bus stops are marked "Balabus", and you'll need one to three bus tickets, depending on the length of your journey: check the information at the bus stop or ask the driver. The Paris Visite and Mobilis passes are all valid too.

**Night buses** Night buses (Noctilien; ⓦ noctilien.fr) ply 47 routes (at least hourly 12.30am–5.30am) between place du Châtelet, west of the Hôtel de Ville, and the suburbs.

## TAXIS

**Fares** Taxi charges are fairly reasonable: between €7 and €12 for a central daytime journey, though considerably more if you call one out; there's a pick-up charge of €2.30. The minimum charge for a journey is €6.30, and you'll pay €1 for each piece of luggage carried. Taxi drivers do not have to take more than three passengers (they don't like people sitting in the front); if a fourth passenger is accepted, an extra charge of €3 will be added. A tip of ten percent will be expected.

**Taxi ranks** Waiting at a rank (*arrêt taxi* – there are around 470 of them) is usually more effective than hailing a cab from the street. If the large green light on top of the vehicle is lit up the taxi is free; the red light means it's in use.

**Taxi firms** Taxis can be rather thin on the ground at lunchtime and any time after 7pm, when you might prefer to call one out – the three main firms, Alpha, Taxis Bleues and G7, can all be reached on ☎ 01 45 30 30 30.

## VÉLIB'

Parisians took enthusiastically to the self-service bike scheme set up in 2007. More than 24,000 sleek, modern – and heavy – bicycles are stationed at some 17,500 locations around the city and close suburbs; you simply pick one up at one rack, or *borne*, ride to your destination, and drop it off again. Vélib' passes (one-day €1.70, weekly €8) are sold from meters at bigger bike stations, or any shop that displays the Vélib' logo, or online at ⓦ velib .paris.fr; plug in your credit card details (which will also secure a €150 deposit, not cashed unless you damage the bike). Once your card is paid up, you simply press it against the automatic readers to release a bike. The first 30min on top of the cost of the pass are free, but after that costs mount; €1 for the next 30min, €2 for the next, and €4 for every further 30min. Helmets are not provided. There are between twelve and twenty bike stands at each *borne*, which are around 300m apart. Maps of the network are displayed at the *bornes*, and available to print in advance from the Vélib' website.

## BATOBUS

One of the most enjoyable ways to get around Paris is on the Batobus (April–Aug every 20min 10am–9.30pm; Sept–Dec, Feb & March every 25min 10am–7pm; ☎ 08 25 05 01 01, ⓦ batobus.com), which stops at eight points along the Seine, including the Eiffel Tower and the Louvre. To do the entire circuit takes around 1hr 40min, and you can hop on and off as many times as you like – a day pass costs €15, two days €18 and five days €21 (there are no single tickets; children are half price).

## AUTOLIB'

A pioneering electric car rental scheme (ⓦ autolib.eu), launched in 2011, operates on the same model as Velib'. Some three thousand cars are available to rent from stands all over the city; cars can be picked up at one station and deposited at another. As with Velib', you need to buy a subscription card first, either online or from one of the 75 Espaces Autolib' in the city. Cards are valid for a day (€10) or a week (€15). The first 30min costs €7, the second €6 and subsequent ones €8. The scheme is open to anyone with a driving licence over the age of 18, and, unlike with most car rental companies, you don't have to have been driving for a couple of years before you're eligible.

## INFORMATION

**Tourist offices** At all the city's tourist offices (ⓦ parisinfo .com) you can pick up maps and information, book accommodation and buy travel passes and the Paris Museum Pass (see p.118). The most usefully located branches are at 25 rue Pyramides, 1er (daily: May–Oct 9am–7pm; Nov–April 10am–7pm, Sun 11am–7pm; M° Pyramides), and in the Carrousel du Louvre, accessed from 99 rue de Rivoli, 1er (daily 10am–6pm; M° Palais Royal-Musée du Louvre). The latter also has information on the region around Paris, the Île de France. Montmartre has its

## BOAT TRIPS

Most tourists are keen, rightly, to take a **boat trip** on the Seine. The faithful old **Bateaux-Mouches** is the best-known operator (April–Sept every 45min 10.15am–6.30pm, every 20min 7–11pm; fewer departures in winter; 1hr 10min; €11, €5.50 for children and over-65s; reservations and information ☎01 42 25 96 10, ☻bateaux-mouches.fr; M° Alma-Marceau). Leaving from the Embarcadère du Pont de l'Alma on the Right Bank in the 8ᵉ boats take you past the major Seine-side sights, such as Notre-Dame and the Louvre. The night-time cruises use lights to illuminate the streetscapes that are so bright they almost blind passers-by – much more fun on board than off – and at all times a narration in several languages blares out. The outrageously priced lunch and dinner trips, for which "correct" dress is mandatory, are probably best avoided. Bateaux-Mouches has many competitors, all much of a muchness and detailed in *Pariscope* under "Croisières" in the "Promenades et Loisirs" section.

Another option, which takes you past less-visited sights, is to take a **canal boat trip** run by Canauxrama (2hr 30min; €16, children €8.50; reservations advisable on weekends; ☎01 42 39 15 00; ☻canauxrama.com) on the Canal St-Martin in the east of the city. They depart from the Port de l'Arsenal (opposite 50 bd de la Bastille; M° Bastille, exit Opéra; May–Sept daily 9.45am & 2.30pm), and from the Bassin de la Villette (M° Jaurés; May–Sept daily 9.45am & 2.45pm); trips run less frequently from October to April – email or phone for information and reservations during this period. **Paris Canal** (☻pariscanal.com) also runs canal trips (mid-March to mid-Nov daily; 2hr 30min; €19, 12–25s and over-60s €16, 2–11s €12; reservations online) between the Musée d'Orsay (quai Anatole-France by the Pont Solférino, 7ᵉ; M° Solférino; departure 9.30am) and the Parc de la Villette ("La Folie des Visites du Parc", on the canal by the bridge between the Grande Salle and the Cité des Sciences, 19ᵉ; M° Porte-de-Pantin; departure 2.30pm).

---

own little office at 72 bd Rochechouart (daily 10am–6pm; M° Anvers) and there are booths at the Gare du Nord (daily 8am–6pm), Gare de l'Est (Mon–Sat 8am–7pm) and Gare de Lyon (Mon–Sat 8am–6pm).

**Reduced museum admissions** The permanent collections at all municipal museums are free all year round, while all national museums (including the Louvre, Musée d'Orsay and Pompidou Centre) – see ☻rmn.fr for a full list – are free on the first Sun of the month and to under-18s. Elsewhere, the cut-off age for free admission varies between 18, 12 and 4. Reduced admission is usually available for 18 to 26-year-olds and those over 60 or 65; you'll need to carry your passport or ID card around with you as proof of age. Some discounts are available for students with an ISIC Card (International Student Identity Card; ☻isic.org).

**Paris Museum Pass** If you're planning to visit a great many museums in a short time it might be worth buying the Paris Museum Pass (€39 two-day, €54 four-day, €69 six-day; ☻parismuseumpass.fr). Available from the tourist office and participating museums, it's valid for 35 or so of the most important museums and monuments including the Louvre (but not special exhibitions) inside Paris, and allows you to bypass ticket queues (though not the security checkpoints).

**Listings magazines** Of Paris's inexpensive weekly listings mags, sold at newsagents and kiosks, *Pariscope* has the edge, with a comprehensive section on films. On Wednesdays, *Le Monde* and *Le Figaro* also bring out free listings supplements.

**Webzines** *Paris Voice* (☻parisvoice.com) and *GoGo Paris* (☻gogoparis.com) cover the latest events and trends.

**Maps** For a comprehensive A–Z map, your best bet is one of the pocket-sized "*L'indispensable*" series booklets, sold throughout the city.

## ACCOMMODATION

**Prices** Hotels in the budget and mid-range category are less expensive than those in many other European capitals. By contrast, the city's four- and five-star hotels are among Europe's most expensive. Smaller three-star hotels typically charge between €75 and €150 for a double room, though for something with a bit of style you'll probably have to pay in the region of €120–240. Bargains exist in the 10ᵉ, especially around place de la République, and you can also get good deals in quieter areas further out, in the 13ᵉ and 14ᵉ, south of Montparnasse.

**Reservations** If you want to secure a really good room it's worth booking a couple of months or more ahead, as even the nicer hotels often leave their pokiest rooms at the back for last-minute reservations, and the best places will sell out well in advance in all but the coldest months. If you find yourself stuck on arrival, the main tourist office (see p.117) who will find you a room in a hotel or hostel free of charge. The tourist office also offers a free online reservation service (☻paris-info.com), with discounts on some hotels.

**Hostels** Most hostels take advance bookings, including the hostel groups: FUAJ (⊛fuaj.fr), which is part of Hostelling International, and MIJE (⊛mije.com), which runs three excellent hostels in historic buildings in the Marais. (There is a third big hostel group, UCRIF, but it caters largely to groups; full details can be found online at ⊛ucrif.asso.fr.)

### THE ISLANDS

**Henri IV** 25 place Dauphine, Ile de la Cité, 1$^{er}$ ☎01 43 54 44 53, ⊛henri4hotel.fr; M° Pont-Neuf/Cité; map p.77. An ancient, slightly ramshackle cheapie on a beautiful square right in the centre of Paris. A squeaky, narrow staircase winds its way up to fifteen basic rooms spread over five storeys (no lift). Book well in advance. €67
**De Lutèce** 65 rue St-Louis-en-l'Île, 4$^e$ ☎01 43 26 23 52, ⊛paris-hotel-lutece.com; M° Pont-Marie; map pp.82–83. Twenty-three tiny but appealing rooms, decorated in contemporary style and equipped with sparkling white bathrooms, are eked out of this old wood-beamed townhouse situated on the most desirable island in France. €210

### THE CHAMPS-ÉLYSÉES AND AROUND

**Le 123** 123 rue du Faubourg-Saint-Honoré, 8$^e$ ☎01 53 89 01 23, ⊛astotel.com; M° Saint-Philippe-du-Roule; map pp.68–69. A giant puffball light greets you in the lobby of this stylish hotel, a 5min walk from the Champs-Élysées. Rooms are a good size with high ceilings, laminate floors and bathtubs. Each one has at least one antique – a chaise longue, nest of tables or desk – to take the edge off the minimalism. Frequent special offers bring the quoted rates down by around €80. €238
★ **Brighton** 218 rue de Rivoli, 1$^{er}$ ☎01 47 03 61 61, ⊛paris-hotel-brighton.com; M° Tuileries; map pp.68–69. An elegant hotel dating back to the late nineteenth century and possessing a certain period charm. The "classic" rooms, with internal views and striped walls, are fine but nothing special; the "superior" rooms are much better, particularly those on the upper floors, with magnificent views of the Tuileries gardens and nice touches such as double sinks in the bathrooms. Classic €180, superior €240
**Lancaster** 7 rue de Berri, 8$^e$ ☎01 40 76 40 76, ⊛hotel-lancaster.fr; M° George-V; map pp.68–69. Once the pied-à-terre for the likes of Garbo, Dietrich and Sir Alec Guinness, this elegantly restored nineteenth-century townhouse remains a favourite hideout for anyone fleeing the paparazzi. The rooms retain original features and are chock-full of Louis XVI and rococo antiques, but with a touch of contemporary chic. To top it all off, there's a Michelin-starred restaurant and zen-style interior garden. €416
**Relais St-Honoré** 308 rue St-Honoré, 1$^{er}$ ☎01 42 96 06 06, ⊛relaissainthonore.com; M° Tuileries; map pp.68–69. A snug little hotel set in a stylishly renovated

seventeenth-century townhouse. The pretty wood-beamed rooms are decorated in warm colours and rich fabrics. €229
**De Sers** 41 av Pierre 1er Serbie, 8$^e$ ☎01 53 23 75 75, ⊛hoteldesers.com; M° George-V; map pp.68–69. A seriously chic boutique hotel, just off the Champs-Élysées, offering minimalist rooms with rosewood furnishings and white, grey, deep red and pink decor; facilities include CD/DVD player and huge TV. The two suites on the top floor have fabulous panoramic terraces. €300

### THE LOUVRE

**BVJ Louvre** 20 rue Jean-Jacques Rousseau, 1$^{er}$ ☎01 53 00 90 90, ⊛bvjhotel.com; M° Louvre/Châtelet-Les-Halles; map pp.68–69. With 200 beds, the *BVJ Louvre* attracts an international studenty crowd, though dorms (sleeping eight) have a slightly institutional feel. Single rooms are available. Dorms €30, doubles €70
**Thérèse** 5–7 rue Thérèse, 1$^{er}$ ☎01 42 96 10 01, ⊛hoteltherese.com; M° Palais-Royal-Musée-du-Louvre; map pp.68–69. A very attractive boutique hotel, on a quiet street within easy walking distance of the Louvre, offering more expensive "traditional" rooms, which are pared-down and stylish, with dark wood fittings, and "classic" rooms, which are small but good value. Book well in advance as it's very popular, especially during the fashion shows. €165

### THE OPÉRA DISTRICT

★ **Chopin** 46 passage Jouffroy, entrance on bd Montmartre, near rue du Faubourg-Montmartre, 9$^e$ ☎01 47 70 58 10, ⊛bretonnerie.com/chopin; M° Grands-Boulevards; map pp.68–69. A lovely period building hidden away at the end of an elegant 1850s *passage*, with quiet and pleasantly furnished rooms, though the cheaper ones are on the small side and a little dark. €98
**Mansart** 5 rue des Capucines 1$^{er}$ ☎01 42 61 50 28, ⊛paris-hotel-mansart.com; M° Opéra/Madeleine; map pp.68–69. This gracious hotel is on the corner of place Vendôme, just a stone's throw from the *Ritz*, but with rooms at a fraction of the price. While they're not quite in the luxury bracket, rooms are attractively decorated in Louis XIV style, with antique furniture, old prints and quality fabrics – most are fairly spacious by Parisian standards. €150
**Vivienne** 40 rue Vivienne, 2$^e$ ☎01 42 33 13 26, ⊛hotel-vivienne.com; M° Grands-Boulevards; map pp.68–69. A 10min walk from the Louvre, this is a friendly, family-run budget hotel, with good-sized, simple, but cheery rooms (some en suite, others with shower only and shared toilet) and modern bathrooms – a pretty good deal considering the location. €83

### BEAUBOURG AND AROUND

**Du Cygne** 3–5 rue du Cygne, 1$^{er}$ ☎01 42 60 14 16, ⊛cygne-hotel-paris.com; M° Etienne-Marcel; map p.77. A six-storey, seventeenth-century townhouse, with a measure of charm, is the setting for this friendly budget hotel, harbouring twenty very small, cheerily decorated rooms. There's no lift, just a narrow twisty staircase. It's on a lively pedestrianized street in the heart of the Les Halles district, so can get noisy at night. Five singles, from €67 a night. **€122**

**Relais du Louvre** 19 rue des Prêtres St-Germain l'Auxerrois, 1$^{er}$ ☎ 01 40 41 96 42, ⓦ relaisdulouvre .com; M° Palais-Royal-Musée-du-Louvre; map p.77. A small, discreet hotel set on a quiet back street opposite the church of St-Germain l'Auxerrois. The decor is traditional but not stuffy, with rich, quality fabrics, old prints, Turkish rugs and solid furniture. The cheaper rooms are rather small. **€141**

**Tiquetonne** 6 rue Tiquetonne, 2$^e$ ☎ 01 42 36 94 58; M° Etienne-Marcel; map p.77. On a pedestrianized street a block away from Montorgueil street market and around the corner from the rue Saint Denis red-light district, this excellent-value budget hotel dates back to the 1920s and looks as though it's probably changed little since. The rooms are very simply furnished; some are quite spacious, though walls are thin. Non-en-suite rooms have a sink and bidet. There are no TVs and breakfast is served in your room. **€60**

### THE MARAIS

**Caron de Beaumarchais** 12 rue Vieille-du-Temple, 4$^e$ ☎ 01 42 72 34 12, ⓦ carondebeaumarchais.com; M° Hôtel-de-Ville; map pp.82–83. A pretty boutique hotel, named after the eighteenth-century French playwright, who lived just up the road. Everything – down to the original engravings and Louis XVI-style furniture, not to mention the pianoforte in the foyer – evokes the refined tastes of high-society pre-Revolutionary Paris. Rooms overlooking the courtyard are small but cosy, while those on the street are more spacious, some with a balcony. **€145**

**Fauconnier** 11 rue du Fauconnier, 4$^e$ ☎ 01 42 74 23 45, ⓦ mije.com; M° St-Paul/Pont Marie; map pp.82–83. MIJE hostel in a superbly renovated seventeenth-century building. Dorms sleep three to eight, and there are some single (€51) and en-suite doubles. Dorms **€31**, doubles **€76**

**Le Fourcy** 6 rue de Fourcy, 4$^e$ ☎ 01 42 74 23 45; M° St-Paul; map pp.82–83. Excellent MIJE hostel housed in a beautiful mansion, this place has a garden and an inexpensive restaurant. Dorms sleep three to eight, and there are singles, en-suite doubles and triples. Dorms **€31**, doubles **€76**

**Grand Hôtel Jeanne d'Arc** 3 rue de Jarente, 4$^e$ ☎ 01 48 87 62 11, ⓦ hoteljeannedarc.com; M° St-Paul; map pp.82–83. A recent makeover has brightened up this old Marais townhouse, just off lovely place du Marché-Ste-Catherine. The small, simple, clean en-suite rooms have yellow, orange or mauve walls and often clashing carpets and duvets, but it all seems to work. The triple at the top has nice views over the rooftops. **€81**

**Grand Hôtel du Loiret** 8 rue des Mauvais Garçons, 4$^e$ ☎ 01 48 87 77 00, ⓦ hotel-du-loiret.fr; M° Hôtel-de-Ville; map pp.82–83. A budget hotel, grand in name only. The rooms are essentially uneventful and very small, but acceptable for the price; cheaper ones have washbasin only, all have TV and telephone. **€80**

**Maubuisson** 12 rue des Barres, 4$^e$ ☎ 01 42 74 23 45; M° Pont Marie/Hôtel de Ville; map pp.82–83. A MIJE hostel in a magnificent medieval building on a quiet street. Shared use of the restaurant at *Le Fourcy* (see p.120). Dorms only, each sleeping four. **€31**

**Pavillon de la Reine** 28 place des Vosges, 3$^e$ ☎ 01 40 29 19 19, ⓦ pavillon-de-la-reine.com; M° Bastille; map pp.82–83. A perfect honeymoon hideaway in a beautiful ivy-covered mansion secreted away off the adorable place des Vosges. It preserves an intimate ambience, with friendly, personable staff. The rooms mostly have a distinctively 1990s "hip hotel" feel, and could probably use another makeover. **€330**

★ **Du Petit Moulin** 29–31 rue du Poitou, 3$^e$ ☎ 01 42 74 10 10, ⓦ paris-hotel-petitmoulin.com; M° Saint-Sébastien-Froissart/Filles du Calvaire; map pp.82–83. An ultra-stylish boutique hotel, set in an old bakery and designed top to bottom by Christian Lacroix. Each room bears the designer's hallmark flamboyance and is a fusion of different styles, from elegant Baroque to Sixties kitsch. **€190**

**St-Louis Marais** 1 rue Charles-V, 4$^e$ ☎ 01 48 87 87 04, ⓦ saintlouismarais.com; M° Sully-Morland; map pp.82–83. Formerly part of the seventeenth-century Célestins Convent, this cosy place retains its period feel, with stone walls, exposed beams and tiled floors. Rooms are done out with terracotta-coloured fabrics and old maps of Paris; the cheaper ones are very small. Its annexe round the corner is less appealing. A major plus is its location on a very quiet road, just a short walk from the Left Bank and all the Marais action further north. **€169**

### BASTILLE

**Marais Bastille** 36 bd Richard-Lenoir, 12$^e$ ☎ 01 48 05 75 00, ⓦ maraisbastille.com; M° Bréguet-Sabin/Bastille; map pp.82–83. Part of the *Best Western* chain, this 37-room hotel has recently undergone a stylish refurbishment by interior designer Michel Jouannet. The rooms are small but bright, done out in beige, taupe and moss green, with splashes of orange **€125**

**De la Porte Dorée** 273 av Daumesnil, 12$^e$ ☎ 01 43 07 56 97, ⓦ hoteldelaportedoree.com; M° Porte-Dorée; map p.82–83. A good-value hotel, a considerable step above the two-star norm: all rooms have private shower or bath, cable TV, comfy beds and pleasant decor. Traditional features such as ceiling mouldings, fireplaces and the elegant main staircase have been retained and many of the furnishings are antique. It's a little out of the centre, near the

Bois de Vincennes, but Bastille is only 7min away by métro or a pleasant 20min walk along the Promenade Plantée. **€68**

## QUARTIER LATIN

**BVJ Paris Quartier Latin** 44 rue des Bernardins, 5ᵉ ☎01 43 29 34 80, ⓦbvjhotel.com; Mᵒ Maubert-Mutualité; map pp.90–91. Spick-and-span hostel in a good location. Single rooms (€49) and dorm beds are good value; for double rooms you can do better elsewhere. Dorms **€30**, doubles **€70**

**Du Commerce** 14 rue de la Montagne-Ste-Geneviève, 5ᵉ ☎01 43 54 89 69, ⓦcommerce-paris-hotel.com; Mᵒ Maubert-Mutualité; map pp.90–91. Business-like but very central budget hotel with a range of rooms from washbasin-only cheapies (around €10 less than the others) up to modern en suites and family rooms. Communal kitchen and free internet access. **€64**

★ **Degrés de Notre Dame** 10 rue des Grands Degrés, 5ᵉ ☎01 55 42 88 88, ⓦlesdegreshotel.com; Mᵒ St-Michel/Maubert-Mutualité; map pp.90–91. This charming, superbly idiosyncratic hotel has just ten rooms, so book in advance. The building is ancient and the rooms all very different, with prices corresponding to size. Unique, personal touches are everywhere: hand-painted murals, antique mirrors and curious nooks. Perhaps the loveliest room of all is under the roof, with its own stairs. Breakfast included. **€115**

**Esmeralda** 4 rue St-Julien-le-Pauvre, 5ᵉ ☎01 43 54 19 20, ⓦhotel-esmeralda.fr; Mᵒ St-Michel/Maubert-Mutualité; map pp.90–91. Dozing in an ancient house on square Viviani, this rickety old hotel offers a deeply old-fashioned, faded feel, with resolutely unmodernized en-suite rooms done up in worn red velvet or faded florals. A few rooms have superb views of Notre-Dame. **€100**

**Familia Hôtel** 11 rue des Ecoles, 5ᵉ ☎01 43 54 55 27, ⓦfamiliahotel.com; Mᵒ Cardinal-Lemoine/Maubert-Mutualité/Jussieu; map pp.90–91. Big, friendly, family-run hotel on a busy road. Rooms are small but attractive, with beams and *toile de Jouy* wallpaper; some have views of Notre-Dame, others have balconies. **€102**

★ **Des Grandes Ecoles** 75 rue du Cardinal-Lemoine, 5ᵉ ☎01 43 26 79 23, ⓦhotel-grandes-ecoles.com; Mᵒ Cardinal-Lemoine; map pp.90–91. Follow the cobbled alleyway to a large, peaceful garden and this tranquil hotel, with its pretty, old-fashioned rooms. Reservations are taken three months in advance, on the 15th of the month; don't be even a day late. **€120**

**Marignan** 13 rue du Sommerard, 5ᵉ ☎01 43 54 63 81, ⓦhotel-marignan.com; Mᵒ Maubert-Mutualité; map pp.90–91. Great-value place, totally sympathetic to the needs of rucksack-toting foreigners, with laundry, ironing and kitchen facilities, a library of guidebooks – and rooms for up to five people. The cheapest share bathrooms with one other room. No credit cards except for payments over €400. **€75**

**Port-Royal** 8 bd Port-Royal, 5ᵉ ☎01 43 31 70 06, ⓦhotelportroyal.fr; Mᵒ Gobelins; map pp.90–91. A friendly, good-value one-star that has been in the same family since the 1930s. Doubles, though small, are attractive and very clean; those with shared bath are considerably cheaper. It's in a quiet, residential area at the rue Mouffetard end of the boulevard, near the métro and the Quartier Latin. No credit cards. **€84**

★ **Résidence Henri IV** 50 rue des Bernardins, 5ᵉ ☎01 44 41 31 81, ⓦresidencehenri4.com; Mᵒ Maubert-Mutualité; map pp.90–91. A discreet and elegant hotel with classically styled rooms, set back from busy rue des Écoles on a cul-de-sac. Some have period features such as fireplaces, and all have miniature kitchenettes. **€120**

**Select Hôtel** 51 place de la Sorbonne, 5ᵉ ☎01 46 34 14 80, ⓦselecthotel.fr; Mᵒ Cluny-Sorbonne; map pp.90–91. This hotel, right on the *place*, has had the full designer makeover, with exposed stone walls, leather and recessed wood trim much in evidence. **€218**

**Young and Happy Hostel** 80 rue Mouffetard, 5ᵉ ☎01 47 07 47 07, ⓦyoungandhappy.fr; Mᵒ Monge/Censier-Daubenton; map pp.90–91. Noisy, basic and studenty independent hostel in a lively, touristy location. **€19**

## ST-GERMAIN

★ **De l'Abbaye** 10 rue Cassette, 6ᵉ ☎01 45 44 38 11, ⓦhotelabbayeparis.com; Mᵒ St-Sulpice; map pp.94–95. An atmosphere of hushed, luxurious calm presides over this four-star hotel. The rooms have swathes of floral fabric and brass fittings, and there's a fair-sized courtyard garden and conservatory out back. **€265**

**Du Globe** 15 rue des Quatre-Vents, 6ᵉ ☎01 43 26 35 50, ⓦhotel-du-globe.fr; Mᵒ Odéon; map pp.94–95. Welcoming hotel in a tall, narrow, seventeenth-century building decked out with four-posters, stone walls, roof beams and the like. Rooms can be small, but aren't expensive for the location. **€99**

**L'Hôtel** 13 rue des Beaux-Arts, 6ᵉ ☎01 44 41 99 00, ⓦl-hotel.com; Mᵒ Mabillon/St-Germain-des-Prés; map pp.94–95. Extravagant designer hotel, with twenty sumptuous rooms accessed by a wonderful spiral staircase, and with a tiny pool in the basement. Oscar Wilde died here, "fighting a duel" with his wallpaper. **€270**

★ **Michelet-Odéon** 6 place de l'Odéon, 6ᵉ ☎01 53 10 05 60, ⓦhotelmicheletodeon.com; Mᵒ Odéon; map pp.94–95. A serious bargain for a hotel so close to the Jardin du Luxembourg. Rooms are unusually attractive (especially those facing onto the *place*) and larger than most at this price. **€120**

**De Nesle** 7 rue de Nesle, 6ᵉ ☎01 43 54 62 41, ⓦhoteldenesleparis.com; Mᵒ St-Michel; map pp.94–95. Eccentric and sometimes chaotic hotel whose tiny rooms are decorated with cartoon historical murals that you'll either love or hate. It's inexpensive for the central location. **€75**

**Relais Christine** 3 rue Christine, 6ᵉ ☎01 40 51 60 80, ⓦrelais-christine.com; Mᵒ Odéon; map pp.94–95. Elegant, romantic four-star in a sixteenth-century former convent set around a deliciously hidden courtyard. It's well worth paying the 20 percent premium for one of the *supérieure* rooms. **€320**

**Relais Saint-Sulpice** 3 rue Garancière, 6ᵉ ☎01 46 33 99 00, ⓦrelais-saint-sulpice.com; Mᵒ St-Sulpice/St-Germain-des-Prés; map pp.94–95. Set in an aristocratic townhouse immediately behind St-Sulpice's apse, this is a discreet and classy small hotel with well-furnished rooms painted in cheerful Provençal colours. The sauna is a nice touch. **€222**

**De l'Université** 22 rue de l'Université, 7ᵉ ☎01 42 61 09 39, ⓦuniversitehotel.com; Mᵒ Rue du Bac; map pp.94–95. Cosy, quiet boutique three-star with antique details, including beamed ceilings and fireplaces in the larger, slightly pricier rooms. **€190**

### EIFFEL TOWER QUARTER

★ **Du Champ-de-Mars** 7 rue du Champ-de-Mars, 7ᵉ ☎01 45 51 52 30, ⓦhotelduchampdemars.com; Mᵒ École-Militaire; map pp.100–101. Cosy, colourful, excellent-value rooms in a well-run hotel. The location is great, too, in a nice neighbourhood just off the lively rue Cler market. **€115**

★ **Du Palais Bourbon** 49 rue de Bourgogne, 7ᵉ ☎01 44 11 30 70, ⓦhotel-palais-bourbon.com; Mᵒ Varenne; map pp.100–101. This substantial, handsome old building on a quiet street in the hushed, posh district near the Musée Rodin offers spacious, prettily furnished rooms, with parquet floors and plenty of period detail. Some homely family rooms, too. Breakfast included. **€190**

### SOUTHERN PARIS

**De la Loire** 39bis rue du Moulin-Vert, 14ᵉ ☎01 45 40 66 88, ⓦhoteldelaloire-paris.com; Mᵒ Pernety/Alésia. This delightful family hotel is on a pedestrianized street. En-suite doubles, with spotless, if tiny, bathrooms, are a bargain. There are cheaper options (with shared WC) in the slightly darker rooms in the annexe, which runs the length of the peaceful garden. Each room is different, and all have charming personal touches. **€72.50**

**Mistral** 24 rue Cels, 14ᵉ ☎01 43 20 25 43, ⓦhotel-mistral-paris.com; Mᵒ Pernety/Alésia. Welcoming, cosy and pleasantly refurbished hotel on a very quiet street, with a little courtyard garden and a shared dining room/kitchen. Some rooms come with showers and shared WC facilities only (€70). **€90**

**Oops** 50 av des Gobelins, 13ᵉ ☎01 47 07 47 00, ⓦoops-paris.com; Mᵒ Gobelins. This "design hostel" is brightly decorated with funky patterns. All dorms are en suite,

there's a/c and a basic breakfast, and it's open 24hr. Unexceptional location, but just a couple of métro stops south of the Quartier Latin. Dorms **€28**, doubles **€8**

**Solar Hôtel** 22 rue Boulard, 14ᵉ ☎01 43 21 08 20, ⓦsolarhotel.fr; Mᵒ Denfert-Rochereau. Set on an old-fashioned Montparnasse street, this budget hotel has paintings by local artists on the walls, cultural events in the back garden and strives to be ecological, with low-energy fittings, organic breakfasts and free bike rental. Don't be put off by the exterior: rooms are basic, but comfortable, bright and well-equipped. **€69**

### BEAUX QUARTIERS

**Camping du Bois de Boulogne** Allée du Bord-de-l'Eau, 16ᵉ ⓦcampingparis.fr. This campsite is reasonably close to central Paris, by the Seine; there's a free shuttle bus to the Porte-Maillot métro station. It gets booked out in summer. Some bungalow accommodation. **€19**

### MONTMARTRE AND AROUND

**Amour** 8 rue Navarin, 9ᵉ ☎01 48 78 31 80, ⓦhotelamourparis.fr; Mᵒ Pigalle; map p.109. Designer hotel for a cool clientele, with old parquet, new paintwork and a deliberately boho Pigalle porn theme. Every room is decorated differently – one is all black with disco balls above the bed – but none has phone or TV, and all have iPod speakers. There's also a spacious dining area and a vodka bar. **€155**

★ **Des Arts** 5 rue Tholozé, 18ᵉ ☎01 46 06 30 52, ⓦarts-hotel-paris.com; Mᵒ Blanche/Abbesses; map p.109. Homely but efficient, with the family dog lolling at the reception desk and courteous staff. Rooms are a little small and bland, but cosy and the location on a romantic cobbled Montmartre street is fantastic. **€95**

★ **Bonséjour Montmartre** 11 rue Burq, 18ᵉ ☎01 42 54 22 53, ⓦhotel-bonsejour-montmartre.fr; Mᵒ Abbesses; map p.109. Rooms are basic and old-fashioned (with shower, but WC down the hall), but the location and price are superb. Ask for the corner rooms 23, 33, 43 or 53, which have balconies. **€68**

★ **Eldorado** 18 rue des Dames, 17ᵉ ☎01 45 22 35 21, ⓦeldoradohotel.fr; Mᵒ Place-de-Clichy; map p.109. Idiosyncratic hotel in the bohemian Batignolles village. Rooms with some vintage fittings are brightened up with vivid colour schemes and furnishings, and there's a secluded annexe at the back of the courtyard garden. Good bistro. **€58**

**Ermitage** 24 rue Lamarck, 18ᵉ ☎01 42 64 79 22, ⓦermitagesacrecoeur.fr; Mᵒ Anvers; map p.109. Hushed, family-run hotel set on the lofty heights behind Sacré-Coeur. Rooms are old-fashioned and chintzy; those at the back have views across northern Paris.

mplementary breakfast served in rooms. Approach via
ne funicular to avoid a steep climb. No credit cards. **€96**

★ **Langlois** 63 rue St-Lazare, 9ᵉ ☎01 48 74 78 24,
ⓦhotel-langlois.com; M° Trinité; p.109. Despite having
all the facilities of a two-star, this genteel hotel in an
untouristy quarter has barely changed in the last century,
with antique furnishings and some spacious, handsome
rooms. **€140**

★ **Particulier Montmartre** 23 av Junot, 18ᵉ ☎01 53
41 81 40, ⓦhotel-particulier-montmartre.com; M°
Abbesses/Lamarck-Caulaincourt; p.109. An exceptional
hotel for a treat – or perhaps a retreat, given its secluded
location in a garden off a private passage set back from one
of Paris's most exclusive streets. Set in an elegant
Neoclassical mansion, this discreet boutique hotel has just
five rooms, all *très* designer. **€390**

**Plug-inn Boutique Hostel** 7 rue Aristide Bruant,
18ᵉ ☎01 42 58 42 58, ⓦplug-inn.fr; M° Blanche/
Abbesses; p.109. This friendly hostel has a cool designer
decor, in parts, and offers breakfast (and no curfew), but
the best thing is the location on the slopes of
Montmartre. Dorms **€25**, doubles **€60**

**Style Hôtel** 8 rue Ganneron, 18ᵉ ☎01 45 22 37 59;
M° Place-de-Clichy; p.109. An unpromising exterior in
Batignolles hides a good budget place, with wooden floors,
marble fireplaces and a secluded courtyard. Great value,
especially the rooms with shared bathrooms (€40). **€60**

**Le Village Hostel** 20 rue d'Orsel, 18ᵉ ☎01 42 64
22 02, ⓦvillagehostel.fr; M° Anvers; p.109. Attractive
independent hostel in a handsome building, with good
facilities, doubles and triples available, and a view of
Sacré-Coeur from the terrace. Rates include breakfast.
Small discounts in winter. Dorms **€28**, doubles **€80**

**Woodstock Hostel** 48 rue Rodier, 9ᵉ ☎01 48 78 87 76,
ⓦwoodstock.fr; M° Anvers/St-Georges; map p.109. A
reliable hostel with its own bar, set in a great location on a
pretty street near Montmartre. Breakfast included. Dorms
**€25**, twins **€54**

## EASTERN PARIS

**Le Citizen Hôtel** 96 quai de Jemmapes, 10ᵉ ☎01 83 62
55 50, ⓦlecitizenhotel.com; M° Jacques Bonsergent;
map pp.82-83. The *Citizen* is an eco-friendly hotel with just
twelve rooms, each with iPad. The Zen-style decor of light
wood and pale tones is nice and airy, and rooms overlook
the Canal St Martin. The cheaper options are compact, the
more expensive twice as big. **€175**

**Jules Ferry** 8 bd Jules-Ferry, 11ᵉ ☎01 43 57 55 60,
ⓦfuaj.fr; M° République; map pp.82-83. Fairly central
HI hostel, in a lively area at the foot of the Belleville hill.
Difficult to get a place, but they can help find a bed
elsewhere. Two to four people in each room. **€25.80**

★ **Mama Shelter** 109 rue de Bagnolet, 20ᵉ ☎01 43
48 48 48, ⓦmamashelter.com; M° Alexandre-Dumas.
Philippe Starck-designed, with a hip, industrial-chic
theme, and extremely good value. The sharp en suites
come with an arty graffiti motif, swanky bathrooms, iMacs
and decorative superhero masks. **€89**

**Du Nord** 47 rue Albert Thomas, 10ᵉ ☎01 42 01 92 10,
ⓦhoteldunord-leparivelo.com; M° Jacques Bonsergent/
République; map pp.82-83. A pretty, ivy-strewn entrance
leads into a cosy hotel with 23 simple en-suite rooms. The
cheaper ones look on to the courtyard and are smaller and
darker. Ten bicycles are available to use for
free. **€71**

**St Christopher's Paris** 68–74 quai de la Seine, 19ᵉ
☎01 40 34 34 40, ⓦst-christophers.co.uk/paris-hostels;
M° Crimée/Laumière; map p.109. Massive new hostel
overlooking the waters of the Bassin de la Villette. Rooms
sleep six to eight and are pleasant in a functional, cabin-like
way, but there's a great bar, inexpensive restaurant. Dorm
beds **€27**, doubles **€84**

## EATING AND DRINKING

**Cuisine** An incredible number of restaurants remain
defiantly traditional, offering the classic *cuisine bourgeoise*
based on well-sauced meat dishes, or regional French
cuisines, notably from the southwest. You can find a
tremendous variety of foods, from Senegalese to Vietnamese,
however, and contemporary French gastronomy is
increasingly willing to embrace spices and exotic ingredients.
Spin-off bistros of Michelin-starred celebrity chefs like Alain
Ducasse, Pierre Gagnaire and Guy Savoy are something of a
fashion at the moment, and well worth considering.

## PARIS FOR VEGETARIANS

The chances of finding vegetarian main dishes on the menus of traditional French restaurants
are not good, though these days some of the newer, more innovative establishments will
often have one or two on offer. It's also possible to put together a meal from vegetarian
starters, omelettes and salads. Your other option is to go for a Middle Eastern or Indian
restaurant or head for one of the city's handful of proper vegetarian restaurants – they do tend
to be based on a healthy diet principle rather than haute cuisine, but at least you get a choice.
Try *Les Cinq Saveurs d'Anada* (see p.128) and *Le Potager du Marais* (see p.127).

**Where to eat** There is a huge diversity of ambiences to choose from: luxurious, hushed restaurants decked with crystal and white linen; noisy, elbow-to-elbow bench-and-trestle-table joints; intimate neighbourhood bistros with specials on the blackboard; grand seafood brasseries with splendid, historic interiors; and artfully distressed cafés serving dishes of the day. Our reviews are divided into restaurants, including brasseries and bistros, and bars and cafés, a term used to incorporate anywhere you might go for a drink or a lighter meal – cafés, ice-cream parlours and *salons de thé*. There are more bars, which have less emphasis on eating, listed under "Nightlife" (see p.132).

**Prices** Eating out in restaurants is expensive, with evening meals rarely costing less than €30. Lunchtime set menus (known as *menus* or *formules*) can still cost as little as €13–16, however. The big boulevard cafés and brasseries, especially those in more touristy areas, can be significantly more expensive than those a little further removed. If you can, it's worth budgeting for at least one meal in one of Paris's spectacular Michelin-starred gourmet restaurants. You'll need to dress smartly; most prefer men to wear a jacket and perhaps a tie. Prices are often significantly lower at weekday lunchtimes; otherwise count on €110–150 as a minimum, and there's no limit on the amount you can pay for wine. Note that a surprising number of places don't accept credit cards.

**Reservations** It's best to reserve for evening meals, especially from Thursday to Saturday; for many places it's usually enough to book on the day, though for the top gourmet restaurants you'll need to book at least two or three weeks in advance.

## THE ISLANDS
### BARS AND CAFÉS
**Berthillon** 31 rue St-Louis-en-l'Île, 4ᵉ ☎01 43 54 31 61, ⊛berthillon.fr; M° Pont-Marie; map pp.82–83. You may well have to queue for one of *Berthillon's* exquisite ice creams or sorbets – arguably the best in Paris. Wed–Sun 10am–8pm.

**Taverne Henri IV** 13 place du Pont-Neuf, Île de la Cité, 1ᵉʳ ☎01 43 54 27 90; M° Pont-Neuf; map p.77. An old-style wine bar that's probably changed little since Yves Montand used to come here with Simone Signoret. It's especially lively at lunchtime when lawyers from the nearby Palais de Justice drop in for generous platters of meats and cheeses and toasted sandwiches. Mon–Fri 11.30am–9.30pm, Sat noon–5pm; closed Aug.

### RESTAURANT
★ **Mon Vieil Ami** 69 rue St-Louis-en-l'Ile, 4ᵉ ☎01 40 46 01 35, ⊛mon-vieil-ami.com; M° Pont-Marie; map pp.82–83. Charming little bistro, with appealing contemporary decor of chocolate browns and frosted-glass panels. The excellent cuisine is bold and zesty, with seasonal ingredients, and the wine list includes some choice vintages. Three courses cost around €45. Wed–Sun noon–2pm & 7–11pm; closed three weeks in Jan & Aug.

## THE CHAMPS-ÉLYSÉES AND AROUND
### BARS AND CAFÉS
**Ladurée** 75 av des Champs-Élysées, 8ᵉ ☎01 40 75 08 75, ⊛laduree.fr; M° George-V; map pp.68–69. This Champs-Élysées branch of the *Ladurée* tearooms, with its luxurious gold and green decor, is perfect for a shopping break. Try the delicious macaroons or the thick hot chocolate. Daily 7.30am–11.30pm.

**Musée Jacquemart-André** 158 bd Haussmann, 8ᵉ ☎01 45 62 11 59, ⊛musee-jacquemart-andre.com; M° St-Philippe-du-Roule/Miromesnil; map pp.68–69. Part of the museum but with independent access, this is the most sumptuously appointed *salon de thé* in the city. Admire the ceiling frescoes by Tiepolo while savouring fine pastries or salads. Daily 11.45am–5.30pm.

### RESTAURANTS
**Mini Palais** Av Winston Churchill ☎01 42 56 42 42, ⊛minipalais.fr; M° Champs-Élysées-Clemenceau; map pp.68–69. A meal at the Grand Palais's lofty dining room or out on the colonnaded terrace is a real treat. The menu is a sophisticated mix of French classics and more international dishes. You can also just come for a snack, or a drink at the bar. Mains €15–35. Daily 10am–2am.

**Le Relais de l'Entrecôte** 15 rue Marbeuf, 8ᵉ ☎01 49 52 07 17, ⊛relaisentrecote; M° Franklin-D.-Roosevelt; map pp.68–69. No reservations are taken at this bustling diner, so you may have to queue for the single main course on the menu: *steak-frites*. This is no ordinary steak though – the secret is in the delicious, buttery sauce. Around €30 for three courses. Daily; closed Aug.

**La Table Lauriston** 129 rue Lauriston, 16ᵉ ☎01 47 27 00 07, ⊛restaurantlatablelauriston.com; M° Trocadéro; map pp.100–101. A slightly older, well-off crowd from the neighbourhood usually dines at this traditional bistro run by chef-to-the-stars Serge Rabey. Game terrine with chanterelle mushrooms and *poularde fondante au vin jaune* (chicken croquettes with Arbois wine) are indicative of the upscale dishes here, and be sure to taste their famed *Baba au Rhum*. The lunch *menu* is €26, dinner is à la carte, with mains at €25–30. Closed Sat lunch, all day Sun & Aug.

**Taillevent** 15 rue Lamennais, 8ᵉ ☎01 44 95 15 01, ⊛taillevent.com; M° Charles-de-Gaulle; map pp.68–69. One of Paris's finest gourmet restaurants. The Provençal-influenced cuisine and wine list are exceptional, the decor classy and refined. There's a set *menu* for €82 at lunch only, otherwise reckon on an average of €160 a head, excluding wine, and book well in advance. Closed Sat, Sun & Aug.

## THE LOUVRE
### BARS AND CAFÉS

**Angelina** 226 rue de Rivoli, 1$^{er}$ ☎01 42 60 82 00, ⓦangelina-paris.fr; M° Tuileries; map pp.68–69. This elegant old *salon de thé*, with its murals, gilded stuccowork and comfy leather armchairs, does the best hot chocolate in town – a generous jugful with whipped cream on the side is enough for two. Mon–Fri 7.30am–7pm, Sat & Sun 8.30am–7pm; closed Tues in July & Aug.

★ **Verlet** 56 rue St-Honoré, 1$^{er}$ ☎01 42 60 67 39, ⓦcafesverlet.com; M° Palais-Royal/Musée du Louvre; map pp.68–69. A heady aroma of coffee greets you as you enter this charming old-world coffee merchant's and café done out with wood furnishings and green-leather benches. You can dither over 25 varieties of coffee, and there's a selection of teas and light snacks, too. Mon–Sat 9.30am–6.30pm, closed Aug.

## THE OPERA DISTRICT
### BARS AND CAFÉS

**Le Rubis** 10 rue du Marché-St-Honoré, 1$^{er}$ ☎01 42 61 03 34; M° Pyramides; map pp.68–69. This very small and very crowded wine bar is one of the oldest in Paris, known for its excellent wines – mostly from the Beaujolais and Loire regions – and home-made *rillettes* (a kind of pork pâté). Mon–Fri 7.30am–9pm, Sat 9am–3pm; closed mid-Aug.

### RESTAURANTS

**Bistrot des Victoires** 6 rue de la Vrillère, 1$^{er}$ ☎01 42 61 78; M° Bourse; map pp.68–69. This charming old-fashioned bistrot is one of a dying breed and serves good old standbys such as confit de canard and roast chicken for around €10, as well as huge salads and *tartines* – the *savoyarde*, with bacon, potatoes and gruyere, is a nice hearty one. Daily 9am–11pm.

★ **Les Fines Gueules** 43 rue Croix des Petits Champs, 1$^{er}$ ☎01 42 61 35 41, ⓦlesfinesgueules.fr; M° Bourse; map pp.68–69. An elegant little wine bar, one of a new breed that is branching out to provide much more than just the usual cold meats and cheese to complement some choice wines. You might start with white asparagus with truffle sauce, followed by saddle of pork, and finish with a *café gourmand* (coffee with a selection of four mini desserts). Or you can just get a glass of really good wine at the bar. Count on around €50 a head for three courses, including wine. Daily noon–11.30pm.

**Gallopin** 40 rue Notre-Dame-des-Victoires, 2$^e$ ☎01 42 36 45 38, ⓦbrasseriegallopin.com; M° Bourse; map pp.68–69. An utterly endearing old brasserie, with all its original brass and mahogany fittings and a beautiful painted glass roof in the back room. The classic French

dishes, especially the *foie gras maison*, are well above par. Lunch *menu* is from €19.90, evening from €38. Daily noon–midnight.

## BEAUBOURG AND AROUND
### BARS AND CAFÉS

**Café Beaubourg** 43 rue St-Merri, 4$^e$ ☎01 48 87 63 96, ⓦmaisonthierrycostes.com; M° Rambuteau/Hôtel-de-Ville; map p.77. Seats under the expansive awnings of this stylish café command frontline views of the Pompidou piazza and are great for people-watching. It's also good for a relaxing Sunday brunch. Daily 8am–midnight.

**Le Café des Initiés** 3 place des Deux-Ecus, 1$^{er}$ ☎01 42 33 78 29, ⓦlecafedesinities.com; M° Châtelet-Les-Halles/Louvre; map p.77. A smart yet intimate and comfortable café, with dark-red leather banquettes, wooden floor, arty photos on the wall and a popular terrace. Locals gather round the zinc bar or tuck into tasty dishes such as grilled king prawns and steak *tartare* (around €16) and home-made apple crumble. It's also a good spot for an evening drink. Mon–Fri 7.30am–2am, Sat & Sun 9am–2am.

### RESTAURANTS

★ **À la Tour de Montlhéry (Chez Denise)** 5 rue des Prouvaires, 1$^{er}$ ☎01 42 36 21 82; M° Louvre-Rivoli/Châtelet; map p.77. A quintessential old-style Parisian bistro, going back to the Les Halles market days. Diners sit elbow to elbow at long tables in a narrow dining room and tuck into substantial meaty dishes, such as *andouillette* (tripe sausage), offal and steak, accompanied by perfectly cooked *frites*. Mains around €25. Mid-Aug to mid-July Mon–Fri noon–3pm & 7.30pm–5am.

**Chez Dilan** 13 rue Mandar, 2$^e$ ☎01 40 26 81 04; M° Les Halles/Sentier; map p.77. Excellent-value Kurdish restaurant, strewn with kilims and playing taped Kurdish music. Starters include melt-in-your mouth *babaqunuc* (stuffed aubergines) and mains feature *beyti* (spiced minced beef wrapped in pastry, with yoghurt, tomato sauce and bulgar wheat). Mains from €13. Mon–Fri noon–2.30pm & 7.30–11pm, Sat 7.30–11pm.

**Georges** Centre Georges Pompidou, 4$^e$ ☎01 44 78 47 99, ⓦcentrepompidou.fr; M° Rambuteau/Hôtel-de-Ville; map p.77. On the top floor of the Pompidou Centre, this trendy, minimalist restaurant with outdoor terrace commands stunning views over Paris and makes a stylish place for lunch or dinner. The international cuisine is pretty good, if overpriced. Main courses from around €30. Daily except Tues noon–midnight.

## THE MARAIS
### BARS AND CAFÉS

**L'Apparement Café** 18 rue des Coutures-St-Gervais, 3$^e$ ☎01 48 87 12 22; M° St-Sébastien-Froissart; map pp.82–83. A chic and cosy café resembling a series of comfortable sitting rooms, with quiet corners and deep sofas. The salads, which you compose yourself by ticking off your chosen ingredients and handing your order to the waiter, are recommended, as is the popular Sunday brunch (from €16.50). Mon–Fri noon–2am, Sat 4pm–2am, Sun 12.30pm–midnight.

**L'As du Fallafel** 34 rue des Rosiers, 4ᵉ ☎01 48 87 63 60; Mᵒ St-Paul; map pp.82–83. The best falafel shop in the Jewish quarter. Falafels to take away cost only €5, or you can pay a bit more and sit in the little dining room. Sun–Thurs noon–midnight, Fri closed in the evening.

**Le Loir dans la Théière** 3 rue des Rosiers, 4ᵉ ☎01 42 72 90 61; Mᵒ Saint-Paul; map pp.82–83. A very popular *salon de thé* where you can sink into comfy sofas and feast on enormous portions of home-made cakes and vegetarian quiches. Come early, or be prepared to queue, for the popular Sunday brunch. Mon–Fri 11am–7pm, Sat & Sun 10am–7pm.

### RESTAURANTS

**Ambassade d'Auvergne** 22 rue de Grenier St-Lazare, 3ᵉ ☎01 42 72 31 22, 🖥ambassade-auvergne.com; Mᵒ Rambuteau; map pp.82–83. Suited, mustachioed waiters serve scrumptious Auvergnat cuisine that would have made Vercingétorix proud. There's a set *menu* for €28, but you may well be tempted by some of the house specialities, like the roast guinea fowl with garlic. Daily noon–2pm & 7.30–10pm.

★ **Café des Musées** 49 rue de Turenne, 4ᵉ ☎01 42 72 96 17; Mᵒ Chemin Vert; map pp.82–83. A relaxed, attractive old bistro (with a less appealing basement room) popular with locals drawn by the reasonably priced, hearty food, such as *steak-frites*, *terrines* and crème caramel. There's always a vegetarian dish on the menu, too. The evening set *menu* is a bargain €22, otherwise mains cost around €20. Mon–Fri 8am–3pm & 7–11pm, Sat 10.30am–3pm & 7–11pm, Sun 10.30am–noon & 7–11pm.

**Chez Marianne** 2 rue des Hospitalières-St-Gervais, 4ᵉ ☎01 42 72 18 86; Mᵒ St-Paul; map pp.82–83. A Marais institution, this homely place with cheery red awnings specializes in Middle Eastern and Jewish delicacies. A platter of meze (from €12) might include tabbouleh, aubergine purée, chopped liver and hummus, and there's a good selection of wines. Daily noon–midnight.

**Chez Omar** 47 rue de Bretagne, 3ᵉ ☎01 42 72 36 26; Mᵒ Arts-et-Métiers; map pp.82–83. No reservations are taken at this popular North African couscous restaurant, so it's best to arrive early, though it's no hardship to wait at the bar for a table, taking in the handsome old brasserie decor and the buzzy atmosphere. Portions are copious and reasonably priced, and the couscous light and fluffy. No credit cards. Daily except Sun noon–2.30pm & 7–11.30pm.

**Le Gaigne** 12 rue Pecquay, 3ᵉ ☎01 44 59 86 72, 🖥restaurantlegaigne.fr; Mᵒ Rambuteau; map pp.82–83. Run by young chef Mickaël Gaignon, this small contemporary bistro with just nine tables serves beautifully presented inventive cuisine, with a slant towards fish. Considering the quality of the food, it's very good value, at €45 for the five-course tasting menu, or €64 with specially chosen accompanying wines. Tues–Sat 12.15–2pm & 7.30–10.30pm.

**Le Potager du Marais** 22 rue Rambuteau, 4ᵉ ☎01 42 74 24 66; Mᵒ Rambuteau; map pp.82–83. Come early or book in advance for a place at this tiny vegetarian restaurant, which has only 25 covers at a long communal table. The ingredients are all organic and there's plenty for vegans and those with gluten allergies, too. Dishes include goat's cheese with honey, "crusty" quinoa burger, and ravioli with basil. Allow around €30 a head for three courses. Daily except Tues noon–4pm & 7–10.30pm.

## BASTILLE

### BARS AND CAFÉS

**Le Baron Rouge** 1 rue Théophile-Roussel, corner of place d'Aligre market, 12ᵉ ☎01 43 43 14 32; Mᵒ Ledru-Rollin; map pp.82–83. This traditional bar à vin is perfect for a light lunch or aperitif after shopping at the place d'Aligre market. If it's crowded inside (as it often is), join the locals standing around the wine barrels on the pavement lunching on *saucisson* or mussels washed down with a glass of Muscadet. Tues–Sat 10am–2pm & 5–9.30pm, Sun 10am–2pm.

★ **Café de l'Industrie** 16 rue St-Sabin, 11ᵉ ☎01 47 00 13 53; Mᵒ Bastille; map pp.82–83. One of the best Bastille cafés (actually two cafés, across the road from each other), packed out at lunch and every evening. There are rugs on the floor around solid old wooden tables, mounted rhinoceros heads, old black-and-white photos on the walls and a young, unpretentious crowd enjoying the comfortable absence of minimalism. Simple *plats du jour* such as sausage and mash and pasta dishes cost around €10. The waitresses are charming, though service can be slow. Daily 10am–2am.

**Pause Café** 41 rue de Charonne, 11ᵉ ☎01 48 06 80 33; Mᵒ Ledru-Rollin; map pp.82–83. Or maybe "Pose Café" – given its popularity with the *quartier's* young and fashionable (sunglasses are worn at all times) who bag the pavement tables at lunch and aperitif time. *Plats du jour* around €13. Mon–Sat 8am–2am, Sun 8.45am–8pm.

### RESTAURANTS

**Bistrot Paul Bert** 18 rue Paul Bert, 11ᵉ ☎01 43 72 24 01; Mᵒ Faidherbe-Chaligny; map pp.82–83. A quintessential Parisian bistro, with the menu chalked up on the board. A mix of locals and visitors flock here for the cosy, friendly ambience and high-quality simple fare such as *poulet rôti* as well as more sophisticated dishes like guinea fowl with morel mushrooms. Save room for one of the substantial desserts, such as the perfectly cooked Grand Marnier soufflé. Around €50 a head for three courses and wine in the evening. Sept–July Tues–Sat noon–2pm & 7.30–11pm.

★ **La Gazzetta** 29 rue de Cotte, 12e ☎01 43 47 47 05, ⓦlagazzetta.fr; M° Ledru-Rollin; map pp.82–83. A nonchalently stylish place, with sleek Art Deco decor, dim lighting, romantic ambience and imaginative, well-executed food. The five-course *menu* is fixed and the portions on the dainty side, but at €42 it's a bargain when you consider the quality of the food. You might start with oysters, rosehip *sablé*, broad beans and peas, followed by perfectly cooked lamb, topped off with not just one, but two divine desserts. Tues–Sat noon–3pm & 7–11pm.

**Le Repaire de Cartouche** 8 bd des Filles du Calvaire, 11e ☎01 47 00 25 86; M° Filles du Calvaire; map pp.82–83. Supposedly the house where eighteenth-century brigand Cartouche once hid away, this cosy, rustic-style restaurant is a popular bolthole with locals, who come for the excellent classic French cuisine and the exceptional wine list of more than 400 vintages. Around €60 a head for three courses and wine. Closed Mon & Sun.

## QUARTIER LATIN

### BARS AND CAFÉS

**Café de la Mosquée** 39 rue Geoffroy-St-Hilaire, 5e ☎01 43 31 38 20; M° Monge; map pp.90–91. Drink mint tea and eat sweet cakes in the Algerian-styled courtyard haven of the Paris mosque. Consider the hammam-massage-meal option. Daily 9am–11pm.

★ **Café de la Nouvelle Mairie** 19 rue des Fossés-St-Jacques, 5e ☎01 44 07 04 41; M° Cluny-La Sorbonne/RER Luxembourg; map pp.90–91. Sleek café-wine bar with a university clientele. Serves satisfying mains like linguine or lamb steaks, as well as *assiettes* of cheese or charcuterie (all around €10). On warm days there are outside tables on the picturesque square. Mon–Fri 8am–midnight.

**L'Ecritoire** 3 place de la Sorbonne, 5e; ☎01 43 54 60 02, ⓦlecritoirecafe.com; M° Cluny-La Sorbonne/RER Luxembourg; map pp.90–91. This classic university café has outside tables right beside the Sorbonne. Good for a coffee and people-watching. Daily 7am–midnight.

★ **La Fourmi Ailée** 8 rue du Fouarre, 5e ☎01 43 29 40 99, ⓦparisresto.com; M° Maubert-Mutualité; map pp.90–91. Simple, filling food is served in this relaxed *salon de thé*. A high, mural-painted ceiling and background jazz contribute to the atmosphere. Around €13 for a *plat*. Daily noon–11pm.

**Les Pipos** 2 rue de l'École-Polytechnique, 5e ☎01 43 54 11 40, ⓦles-pipos.com; M° Maubert-Mutualité/Cardinal-Lemoine; map pp.90–91. This antique bar has a decor that's heavy on old wood, and a local clientele. Serves wines from €5 a glass along with simple plates of Auvergnat charcuterie, cheese and the like (€10–15). Mon–Sat 8.30am–1am; closed 2 weeks in Aug.

**Le Reflet** 6 rue Champollion, 5e ☎01 43 26 14 93; M° Cluny-La Sorbonne; map pp.90–91. This cinema café has a pleasingly scruffy black decor, and its rickety tables are packed with artsy film-goers. Perfect for a pre-film drink, perhaps accompanied by a steak or quiche from the blackboard specials. Daily 11am–2am.

**Le Verre à Pied** 118bis rue Mouffetard, 5e; ☎01 43 31 15 72, ⓦleverreapied.fr; M° Monge; map pp.90–91. Deeply old-fashioned market bar where traders take their morning *vin rouge*, or sit down to eat an inexpensive *plat du jour*. Some have been doing it so long they've got little plaques on their tables. Tues–Sat 9am–9.30pm, Sun 9am–4pm.

### RESTAURANTS

**Brasserie Balzar** 49 rue des Écoles, 5e ☎01 43 54 13 67, ⓦbrasseriebalzar.com; M° Maubert-Mutualité; map pp.90–91. This classic, high-ceilinged brasserie with its attentive, suited waiters feels almost intimidatingly Parisian– though if you're unlucky, or eat early, the tourist clientele can spoil the Left Bank mood. À la carte is around €40. Daily 8am–11.45pm.

★ **Le Buisson Ardent** 25 rue Jussieu, 5e ☎01 43 54 93 02, ⓦlebuissantardent.fr; M° Jussieu; map pp.90–91. Generous helpings of first-class cooking with vivacious touches: think *velouté* of watermelon followed by a perfectly cooked sea bream. The dining room is high-ceilinged, panelled and muralled and the atmosphere convivial. Lunch *menu* €17.90, dinner €36. Mon–Sat noon–2pm & 7.30–10pm, Sun noon–4pm; closed two weeks in Aug.

**Les Cinq Saveurs d'Anada** 72 rue du Cardinal-Lemoine, 5e ☎01 43 29 58 54, ⓦanada-5 saveurs.com; M° Cardinal-Lemoine; map pp.90–91. Airy and informal restaurant serving delicious organic vegetarian food. Salads are good, as are more robust dishes such as tofu soufflé with ginger (around €14–18). Tues–Sun noon–2.30pm & 7.30–10.30pm.

**Perraudin** 157 rue St-Jacques, 5e ☎01 46 33 15 75, ⓦrestaurant-perraudin.com; RER Luxembourg; map pp.90–91. One of the classic bistros of the Left Bank, featuring enjoyable homely cooking. The place is brightly lit, packed and thick with Parisian chatter. Lunch *menu* at €17.50, evening *menu* at €31.90. Daily noon–2.30pm & 7.30–10.30pm.

**Le Petit Pontoise** 9 rue de Pontoise, 5e ☎01 43 29 25 20; M° Maubert-Mutualité; map pp.90–91. This relaxed, young bistro is as authentically Parisian as you can get this close to the river: lace café-curtains, little wooden tables, a bar in one corner and blackboard specials like haricot bean salad with prawns, or duck breast. Puddings are outstanding. Around €50 a head. Mon–Fri & Sun noon–2.30pm & 7.30–10.30pm, Sat 7.30–10.30pm.

★ **Le Pré-Verre** 8 rue Thénard 5ᵉ ☎01 43 54 59 47, ⓦlepreverre.com; Mᵒ Maubert-Mutualité; map pp.90–91. This sleek *bistro à vin* has a great wine list, and interesting modern French food with a few judiciously oriental touches – you might find swordfish on blue poppy seeds and artichoke, or chicken with avocado and ginger. *Menus* at €29.50, or just €13.90 at lunch. Tues–Sat noon–2pm & 7.30–10.30pm.

**Le Reminet** 3 rue des Grands-Degrés, 5ᵉ ☎01 44 07 04 24, ⓦlereminet.com; Mᵒ Maubert-Mutualité; map pp.90–91. This artful, chandelier-hung little bistro-restaurant graces high-quality traditional French ingredients with imaginative sauces. Gastronomic *menu* at €55, with a bargain lunch *menu* at €14.40 (weekends only). Daily noon–2.30pm & 7–10.30pm.

## ST-GERMAIN

### BARS AND CAFÉS

**Au Petit Suisse** 16 rue de Vaugirard, 6ᵉ ☎01 43 26 03 81; RER Luxembourg/Mᵒ Cluny-La Sorbonne; map pp.94–95. The perfect retreat from the Jardin du Luxembourg, with everything you'd need from a café, including a lovely outdoor terrace. Mon–Sat 7am–midnight, Sun 7am–11.30pm.

★ **Bistrot des Augustins** 39 quai de Grands-Augustins, 6ᵉ ☎01 43 54 04 41; Mᵒ St-Michel; map pp.94–95. That a wine bar this friendly and traditional should be found on the riverbank between the Pont Neuf and Place St-Michel is quite incredible. Serves good charcuterie, salads and hot *gratins*, all for around €10. Daily 10am–midnight.

★ **Café de la Mairie** 8 place St-Sulpice, 6ᵉ ☎01 43 26 67 82; Mᵒ St-Sulpice; map pp.94–95. A peaceful, pleasant café on the sunny north side of this gorgeous square, right opposite the church of St-Sulpice. Perfect for basking at an outdoor table, admiring the neighbourhood's beautiful people. Mon–Sat 7am–1am.

**Chez Georges** 11 rue des Canettes, 6ᵉ ☎01 43 25 36 72; Mᵒ Mabillon; map pp.94–95. This dilapidated wine bar is one of the few authentic addresses in an area dominated by big, noisy theme pubs (you'll find plenty in the vicinity if you're in the market). The young, studenty crowd gets good-naturedly rowdy later on in the cellar bar. Sept–July Tues–Sat 2pm–2am.

★ **Le Flore** 172 bd St-Germain, 6ᵉ ☎01 45 48 55 26, ⓦcafedeflore.fr; Mᵒ St-Germain-des-Prés; map pp.94–95. The great rival and immediate neighbour of the equally famous (and rather similar) *Les Deux Magots*. There's a unique hierarchy: tourists on the *terrasse*, beautiful people inside, intellectuals upstairs. Sartre, de Beauvoir, Camus and Marcel Carné used to hang out here. Try the hot chocolate. Daily 7.30am–1.30am.

**Bar du Marché** 75 rue de Seine, 6ᵉ ☎01 43 26 55 15; Mᵒ Mabillon; map pp.94–95. A thrumming, fashionable café where the *serveurs* are cutely kitted out in flat caps and aprons, and the rue de Buci market bustles on the doorstep. Lively by night or day. Daily 8am–1.45am.

**La Palette** 43 rue de Seine, 6ᵉ ☎01 43 26 68 15, ⓦcafelapetteparis.com; Mᵒ Odéon; map pp.94–95. This once-famous Beaux-Arts student hangout is now frequented by art dealers, though it still attracts a trendy young crowd in the evenings. There's a roomy *terrasse* outside, and some good daily specials on the *menu*. Mon–Sat 9am–1am.

### RESTAURANTS

★ **Brasserie Lipp** 151 bd St-Germain, 6ᵉ ☎01 45 48 53 91, ⓦgroupe-bertrand.com; Mᵒ St-Germain-des-Prés; map pp.94–95. One of the most celebrated of all the classic Paris brasseries, with a wonderful 1900s wood-and-glass interior. There are decent *plats du jour*, including the famous *choucroute* (sauerkraut), from €20, but exploring à la carte gets expensive. Daily noon–12.30am

**L'Epigramme** 9 rue de l'Eperon, 6ᵉ ☎01 44 41 00 09; Mᵒ Odéon; map pp.94–95. This tiny, simple restaurant offers quality French cooking, stripped bare of pretensions. Prices from around €40, plus wine. Tues–Sun noon–2.30pm & 7.30–11.30pm.

★ **La Ferrandaise** 8 rue de Vaugirard, 6ᵉ ☎01 43 26 36 36, ⓦlaferrandaise.com; Mᵒ St-Germain-des-Prés; map pp.94–95. Relaxed, airy restaurant near the Jardin du Luxembourg offering rich dishes such as crab ravioli, oven-steamed pikeperch or the richest shoulder of lamb. Evening *menu* €34. Mon 7–10.30pm, Tues–Thurs noon–2.30pm & 7–10.30pm, Fri noon–2.30pm & 7–11pm. Sat 7–11pm.

**Gaya Rive Gauche** 44 rue du Bac, 6ᵉ ☎01 45 44 73 73, ⓦpierre-gagnaire.com; Mᵒ Rue du Bac; map pp.94–95. This hyper-designed, upscale mini-restaurant is the fishy satellite of celebrity chef Pierre Gagnaire's empire. Imagine *pressé* of skate with a Bloody Mary sauce, or grilled swordfish on a bed of caramel, soya and Asian mushrooms. Around €100 a head with wine. Mon–Sat noon–2.30pm & 7.30–11pm.

**Polidor** 41 rue Monsieur-le-Prince, 6ᵉ ☎01 43 26 95 34, ⓦpolidor.com; Mᵒ Odéon; map pp.94–95. Open since 1845, this Left Bank classic is still bright and bustling with aproned waitresses and noisy regulars dining until late. Serves solid French classics like *confit de canard* or guinea fowl with lardons, from around €14. Mon–Sat noon–2.30pm & 7pm–midnight, Sun noon–2.30pm & 7pm–11pm.

**Ze Kitchen Galerie** 4 rue des Grands-Augustins, 6ᵉ ☎01 44 32 00 32, ⓦzekitchengalerie.fr; Mᵒ St-Michel; map pp.94–95. Hovering halfway between restaurant and trendy art gallery in atmosphere, this place mixes

**1**

Asian influences with contemporary Mediterranean cuisine – try gnocchetti with squid and *nori*, or pork croquettes with Thai herbs. At dinner, expect to pay around €70, without wine. Mon–Fri noon–2.30pm & 7–11pm, Sat 7–11pm.

## EIFFEL TOWER QUARTER
### BARS AND CAFÉS

**Café du Marché** 38 rue Cler, 7ᵉ ☎ 01 47 05 51 27; Mᵒ La Tour-Maubourg; map pp.100–101. Big, busy café-brasserie in the middle of the rue Cler market, serving reasonably priced meals and chunky salads. There's outdoor seating, or a covered *terrasse* in winter. Mon–Sat 7am–midnight, Sun 7am–4pm.

**Tokyo Eat/Tokyo Self** Palais de Tokyo, 16ᵉ ☎ 01 47 20 00 29, ⓦ palaisdetokyo.com; Mᵒ Iéna/Alma-Marceau; map pp.100–101. The restaurant inside the Site de Création Contemporaine is a self-consciously cool place to eat, with its futuristic, colourful decor, arty clientele and Mediterranean fusion menu. The more dressed-down *Tokyo Self* café is a reliable bet for a drink and a snack. Tues–Sun noon–1am, bar till 2am.

### RESTAURANTS

**L'Arpège** 84 rue de Varenne, 7ᵉ ☎ 01 47 05 09 06, ⓦ alain-passard.com; Mᵒ Varenne; map pp.100–101. Alain Passard is one of France's great chefs – and he really pushes boundaries here by giving vegetables the spotlight. Dishes such as grilled turnips with chestnuts or duck with black sesame and orange brandy are astounding. The lunch *menu* costs €120, the incredible *menu dégustation* €360. Mon–Fri noon–2.30pm & 8–11pm.

★ **Au Bon Accueil** 14 rue de Monttessuy, 7ᵉ ☎ 01 47 05 46 11, ⓦ aubonaccueilparis.com; Mᵒ Duroc/Vaneau; map pp.100–101. A relaxed, modern wine bar-bistro, where you might enjoy well-turned-out dishes like a delicate salad of prawns, salmon and lemon verbena, followed by a perfectly cooked veal liver with Jerusalem artichoke purée. There are a few outside tables. Lunch *menu* €32; in the evening expect to pay upwards of €50 with wine. Mon–Fri noon–2.30pm & 7–10.30pm, Sat 7–10.30pm; closed Sat in Aug.

★ **La Fontaine de Mars** 129 rue Saint-Dominique, 7ᵉ ☎ 01 47 05 46 44, ⓦ fontainedemars.com; Mᵒ La Tour-Maubourg; map pp.100–101. Heavy, pink-checked tablecloths, leather banquettes, tiled floor, attentive service: this quintessentially French restaurant serves reliable, meaty southwestern French cuisine, and has lovely outside tables – no wonder President Obama ate here. *Plat du jour* around €20. Daily noon–3pm & 7.30–11pm.

**Le Jules Verne** Pilier Sud, Eiffel Tower, 7ᵉ ☎ 01 45 55 61 44, ⓦ lejulesvernes-paris.com; Mᵒ Bir-Hakeim; map pp.100–101. Dining halfway up the Eiffel Tower is enough

of a draw in itself, but since Alain Ducasse's team took over in 2007, the gastronomic food is worthy of the setting. Best at dinner (€210), but cheaper for a weekday lunch (a mere €88). Reserve months in advance, and don't expect a window table. Daily noon–2pm & 7–10pm.

## SOUTHERN PARIS
### BARS AND CAFÉS

★ **L'Entrepôt** 7–9 rue Francis-de-Pressensé, 14ᵉ ☎ 01 45 40 07 50, ⓦ lentrepot.fr; Mᵒ Pernety. A spacious, relaxed café – part of an arty cinema – with lovely seats in its green courtyard. Serves a great Sunday brunch (€26), has *plats du jour* for around €15–25, and holds occasional evening concerts. Daily noon–2am.

**Le Select** 99 bd du Montparnasse, 6ᵉ ☎ 01 45 48 38 24; Mᵒ Vavin. If you want to visit one of the great Montparnasse cafés, as frequented by Picasso, Matisse, Henry Miller and F. Scott Fitzgerald, make it this one. It has changed least; only the brasserie-style food is disappointing. Daily 7am–2am, Fri & Sat till 4am.

### RESTAURANTS

★ **L'Avant Goût** 37 rue Bobillot, 13ᵉ ☎ 01 45 81 14 06, ⓦ lavantgout.com; Mᵒ Place d'Italie. Small neighbourhood restaurant with bright-red leather banquettes and a reputation for exciting modern French cuisine. Superb value at around €15 for lunch and €35 for dinner. Tues–Sat 12.30–2pm & 7.45–10.45pm.

★ **Le Bambou** 70 rue Baudricourt, 13ᵉ ☎ 01 45 70 91 75; Mᵒ Tolbiac. Tiny Asian-quarter restaurant crammed with local punters tucking into giant, inexpensive *pho* soups and Vietnamese specialities. Last orders at 10.30pm, but you can stay till midnight. Tues–Sun 11.30am–3.30pm & 6–10.30pm.

**Chez Gladines** 30 rue des Cinq-Diamants, 13ᵉ ☎ 01 45 80 70 10; Mᵒ Corvisart. This little, Basque-run corner bistro is always warm, welcoming and packed with young people. Serves rich Basque and southwest dishes such as *magret de canard*. Giant salads cost less than €10, *plat du jour* €10. Mon & Tues noon–3pm & 7pm–midnight, Wed–Sun noon–3pm & 7pm–1am.

★ **Le Café du Commerce** 51 rue du Commerce, 15ᵉ ☎ 01 45 75 03 27, ⓦ lecafeducommerce.com; Mᵒ Emile-Zola. Once a 1920s workers' canteen, this is still a buzzing place to eat, with tables set on three storeys of galleries. Honest, high-quality meat is the speciality, but there's always a fish and vegetarian dish too. Expect to pay €15–20 for a *plat*, though the lunch *menu* is a bargain €15.50. Daily noon–3pm & 7pm–midnight.

**La Coupole** 102 bd du Montparnasse, 14ᵉ ☎ 01 43 20 14 20, ⓦ lacoupole-paris.com; Mᵒ Vavin. The largest and most enduring arty-chic Parisian brasserie, *La Coupole* still buzzes with conversation and clatter under its high, chandeliered roof. The menu runs from oysters to Welsh rarebit, with plenty of fishy and meaty classics in between. *Menus* €28 and €32.50. Mon–Wed & Sun 8.30am–midnight, Thurs–Sat 8.30am–1am.

★ **L'Os à Moelle** 3 rue Vasco-de-Gama, 15ᵉ ☎01 45 57 27 27, ⓦparis-restaurant-osamoelle.com; Mᵒ Lourmel. The highlight of this relaxed bistro is the €55 four-course *menu*, which brings you everything from Jerusalem artichoke and black truffle soup to fine steaks, via scallops and giant snails. You can also dine across the road at the cheaper, no-frills *La Cave de l'Os à Moelle*, where you sit at communal tables, helping yourself to a steaming pot of stew or the like. Reserve well in advance at either. Tues–Sat noon–2.30pm & 7.30–10.30pm; closed 3 weeks in Aug.

## MONTMARTRE AND AROUND
### BARS AND CAFÉS

**Aux Négociants** 27 rue Lambert, 18ᵉ ☎01 46 06 15 11; Mᵒ Château-Rouge; map p.109. An intimate and friendly *bistro à vin* with a selection of well-cooked *plats*, home-made charcuterie and excellent Loire wines by the glass. It's wise to book if you plan to eat – count on around €30 for a full meal, without wine. The clientele is resolutely local, with a smattering of arty-intellectual types. Sept–July Mon–Fri noon–2.30pm & 7–10.30pm.

**Café des Deux Moulins** 15 rue Lepic, 18ᵉ ☎01 42 54 90 50; Mᵒ Blanche; map p.109. Having seen its early-2000s heyday of fans on the trawl of *Amélie* lore (she waited tables here in the film), this diner-style café is now back to what it always was: a down-to-earth neighbourhood hangout, preserved in a bright, charming 1950s interior. Sunday brunch is popular. Daily 7.30am–1am.

**L'Été en Pente Douce** 23 rue Muller, 18ᵉ ☎01 42 64 02 67, ⓦparisresto.com; Mᵒ Château-Rouge; map p.109. The big salads and *plats* (around €14) are unspectacular, but the big outdoor terrace alongside the steps leading up to Sacré-Coeur is delightful on a sunny day. Daily noon–midnight.

**Wepler** 14 place de Clichy, 18ᵉ ☎01 45 22 53 24, ⓦwepler.com; Mᵒ Place-de-Clichy; map p.109. Now over a hundred years old, and still a beacon of conviviality amid the hustle of place de Clichy. Its clientele has moved upmarket since it was depicted in Truffaut's *Les 400 Coups*, but as palatial brasseries go, *Wepler* has remained unashamedly *populaire*. Serves honest brasserie food and classic seafood platters (from €33). Daily noon–1am, café from 8am.

### RESTAURANTS

**À la Pomponnette** 42 rue Lepic, 18ᵉ ☎01 46 06 08 36, ⓦpomponnette-montmartre.com; Mᵒ Blanche/Abbesses; map p.109. A genuine old Montmartre bistro, with posters, drawings and a zinc-top bar. The traditional French food is just as it should be, with an evening *menu* at

€37. Tues–Thurs noon–2.30pm & 7–11pm, Fri & Sat noon–2.30pm & 7pm–midnight.

**Au Grain de Folie** 24 rue de La Vieuville, 18ᵉ ☎01 42 58 15 57; Mᵒ Abbesses; map p.109. A tiny, simple and colourfully dilapidated vegetarian place where all the food is inexpensive and organic and there's always a vegan option. Tues–Sat 12.30–2.30pm & 7.30–10.30pm, Sun 12.30–10.30pm.

★ **Café Burq** 6 rue Burq, 18ᵉ ☎01 42 52 81 27; Mᵒ Abbesses; map p.109. Ultra-relaxed bar-restaurant offering (from 8pm to midnight) zesty-flavoured dishes such as an asparagus velouté, veal with lime cream sauce, or honey-roast camembert. You'll jostle elbows with a trendy clientele, whose noisy conversation competes with the DJ soundtrack. Mon–Sat 7pm–2am.

★ **Chez Casimir** 6 rue de Belzunce, 10ᵉ ☎01 48 78 28 80; Mᵒ Gare du Nord; map p.109. It's astonishing to find a restaurant this good so close to the Gare du Nord. Serves inexpensive (€24 at lunch, or €32 in the evening) but well-cooked dishes in basic, unrenovated *bistro* surroundings. The Sunday "brunch" (€26) is more scallops and cod casserole than eggs and ham. Mon–Fri noon–2pm & 7.30–10.30pm, Sat & Sun 10am–7pm.

**Le Mono** 40 rue Véron, 18ᵉ ☎01 46 06 99 20; Mᵒ Abbesses; map p.109. Welcoming, family-run Togolese restaurant. Mains (around €14) are mostly grilled fish or meat served with sour, hot sauces, with rice or cassava on the side. Enjoyable atmosphere, with soukous on the stereo, Afro-print tablecloths and Togolese carvings on the walls. Thurs–Tues 7.30–11pm.

**Le Relais Gascon** 6 rue des Abbesses, 18ᵉ ☎01 42 58 58 22, ⓦlerelaisgascon.fr; Mᵒ Abbesses; map p.109. Serving hearty, filling meals all day, this two-storey restaurant provides a welcome blast of straightforward Gascon cuisine in this alternately trendy, run-down and touristy part of town. There are good-value enormous warm salads, *plats* and lunch *menus*. There's a second branch, just around the corner at 13 rue de Joseph Maistre, with the same opening hours. Mon–Thurs 10.30am–midnight, Fri–Sun 10.30am–12.30am.

## EASTERN PARIS
### CAFÉ

**Chez Prune** 36 rue Beaurepaire, 10ᵉ ☎01 42 41 30 47; Mᵒ Jacques-Bonsergent. Named after the owner's grandmother (a bust of whom is inside), friendly, laid-back *Chez Prune* is popular with an arty and media crowd, who bag the outside tables overlooking the canal. Lunchtime dishes around €14; evening snacks like platters of cheese or charcuterie around €11. Daily 10am–2am.

### RESTAURANTS

**Flo** 7 cour des Petites-Écuries, 10ᵉ ☎01 47 70 13 59 ⓦfloparis.com; Mᵒ Château-d'Eau. Tucked away down a

**1**

secret side alley, this is a dark, handsome and extremely atmospheric old-time brasserie. Sound but not scintillating fish and seafood are the specialities, along with snooty wait-staff. From around €30. Daily noon–3pm & 7pm–12.30am.

★ **Julien** 16 rue du Faubourg-St-Denis, 10ᵉ ☎ 01 47 70 12 06, ⊛ julienparis.com; Mᵒ Strasbourg-St-Denis. So splendid is the decor – globe lamps, brass, murals, white linen and polished wood, with frescoes of flowery Art Deco maidens – that not even the patchy service and crammed-in clientele can spoil it. Satisfying if unsophisticated fish and seafood dishes are served, with *menus* from €33. Daily noon–3pm & 7pm–1am.

**Lao Siam** 49 rue de Belleville, 19ᵉ ☎ 01 40 40 09 68; Mᵒ Belleville. The surroundings are nothing special, but the excellent Thai and Laotian food, popular with locals, makes up for it. Dishes from around €10. Mon–Fri noon–3pm & 6–11.30pm, Sat & Sun noon–12.30am.

**Pooja** 91 passage Brady, 10ᵉ ☎ 01 48 24 00 83; Mᵒ Strasbourg-St-Denis/Château-d'Eau. Not quite London, let alone Mumbai, but friendly and located in a glazed passage that is lined with Indian restaurants, all offering good if rather similar food. Costs around €20 in the evening, not including drinks. Daily noon–3pm & 7–11pm.

★ **Le Train Bleu** Gare de Lyon, 12ᵉ ☎ 01 43 43 09 06, ⊛ le-train-bleu.com; Mᵒ Gare de Lyon. The sumptuous decor of what must be the world's most luxurious station buffet is straight out of a bygone golden era – everything drips with gilt, and chandeliers hang from high ceilings frescoed with scenes from the Paris–Lyon–Marseilles train route. The traditional French cuisine has a hard time living up to all this, but is still pretty good, if a tad overpriced. *Menus* from €56, including half a bottle of wine. Daily 11.30am–3pm & 7–11pm.

**Waly Fay** 6 rue Godefroy-Cavaignac, 11ᵉ ☎ 01 40 24 17 79; Mᵒ Charonne. A moderately priced West African restaurant with a cosy, stylish atmosphere, the dim lighting, rattan and old, faded photographs creating an intimate, faintly colonial ambience. Smart young Parisians come here to dine on perfumed, richly spiced stews and other West African delicacies. Mains €13–18. Mon–Sat noon–2pm & 7–11pm.

## NIGHTLIFE

Paris's fame as the home of decadent, hedonistic nightlife has endured for centuries. That reputation is sustained today by a vibrant bar and club scene and a world-class live music programme. World music and jazz are particularly strong, but you'll find everything from house and electro-lounge to home-grown rock and chanson. For listings, *Pariscope* (see p.118) is the traditional first port of call. For more detail, try *Nova* magazine (⊛ novaplanet.com), also available from newsstands, or specialist websites such as ⊛ radiofg.com and ⊛ triselectif.net. To find the latest club nights seek out flyers – or word-of-mouth tips – in one of the city's trendier bars. The best place to get tickets is FNAC – the main branch is in the Forum des Halles, 1–5 rue Pierre-Lescot, 1ᵉʳ (Mon–Sat 10am–8pm; ☎ 08 25 02 00 20, ⊛ fnac.com; Mᵒ Châtelet-Les Halles).

### BARS

Drinking venues range from the many cafés that move seamlessly from coffees to cocktails as evening approaches, to the tiny, dedicated wine bars offering little-known vintages from every region of France. Many bars have happy hours, but prices can double after 10pm, and any clearly trendy, glitzy or stylish place is bound to be expensive. There are cavernous beer cellars, designer bars with DJ soirées at weekends and the ubiquitous Irish/British/Canadian pubs. We've reviewed a number of bars that are particularly good for food in our "Eating and Drinking" section (see p.124).

### THE LOUVRE

**Bar Costes** Hôtel Costes, 239 rue St-Honoré, 8ᵉ ☎ 01 42 44 50 00, ⊛ hotelcostes.com; Mᵒ Concorde/Tuileries; map pp.68–69. A favourite haunt of fashionistas and celebs, this is a romantic place for an aperitif or late-night drinks amid decadent nineteenth-century decor of red velvet, swags and columns, set around an Italianate courtyard. Cocktails around €20. Daily until 2am.

### THE OPERA DISTRICT

**Delaville Café** 34 bd de la Bonne Nouvelle, 10ᵉ ☎ 01 48 24 48 09, ⊛ delavillecafe.com; Mᵒ Bonne-Nouvelle; map pp.68–69. This ex-bordello, with grand staircase, gilded mosaics and marble columns, draws in crowds of hipsters, who sling back a mojito or two before moving on to one of the area's clubs. Daily 11am–2am.

### THE MARAIS

★ **Andy Wahloo** 69 rue des Gravilliers, 3ᵉ ☎ 01 42 71 20 38, ⊛ andywahloo-bar.com; Mᵒ Arts-et-Métiers; map pp.82–83. A very popular bar decked out in original Pop Art-inspired Arabic decor. Tasty meze appetizers are available until midnight and the bar serves a few original cocktails, including the Wahloo Special (rum, lime, ginger, banana and cinnamon). DJs play a wide range of dance music. Tues–Sat noon–2am.

**Le Petit Fer à Cheval** 30 rue Vieille-du-Temple, 4ᵉ ☎ 01 42 72 47 47; Mᵒ St-Paul; map pp.82–83. A very attractive small drinking spot with original *fin-de-siècle* decor, including a marble-topped bar in the shape of a

**1**

horseshoe (*fer à cheval*). You can snack on sandwiches or something more substantial in the little back room furnished with old wooden métro seats. Mon–Fri 9am–2am, Sat & Sun 11am–2am; food noon–midnight.

## BASTILLE

**SanZSanS** 49 rue du Faubourg-St-Antoine, 11ᵉ ☎01 44 75 78 78, ⓦsanzsans.com; Mᵒ Bastille; map pp.82–83. Gothic get-up of red velvet, oil paintings and chandeliers, popular with a young crowd, especially on Fri & Sat evenings, when DJs play funk, Brazilian beats and house. Drinks are reasonably priced. Daily 9am–5am.

## ST-GERMAIN

**Le 10** 10 rue de l'Odéon, 6ᵉ ☎01 43 26 66 83; Mᵒ Odéon; map pp.94–95. Classic Art Deco-era posters line the walls of this small, dark, studenty bar. The atmospherically vaulted cellar bar gets noisy in the small hours. Daily 5.30pm–2am.

**La Mezzanine de l'Alcazar** 62 rue Mazarine, 6ᵉ ☎01 53 10 19 99, ⓦalcazar.fr; Mᵒ Odéon; map pp.94–95. Cool, expensive cocktail bar set on a mezzanine level overlooking Conran's *Alcazar* restaurant. Most nights start off relaxed and finish with dancing, with hardcore types moving on to the *WAGG* club below. DJs Wed–Sat. Daily 7pm–2am.

## SOUTHERN PARIS

**Café Tournesol** 9 rue de la Gâité, 14ᵉ ☎01 43 27 65 72; Mᵒ Edgar Quinet. This corner café-bar attracts bohemian twenty-somethings for its distressed chic, outside tables and cool playlists. Fashionable yet welcoming – a rare combination. Daily 8am–2am.

**La Folie en Tête** 33 rue Butte-aux-Cailles, 13ᵉ ☎01 45 80 65 99; Mᵒ Place-d'Italie/Corvisart. Surveying the Butte-aux-Cailles from its prime corner spot, this vibrant, friendly and distinctly lefty café-bar is a classic. The walls are littered with bric-a-brac and musical instruments and there's usually something cool playing on the system – laidback underground beats, perhaps, or a young singer-songwriter's latest album. Mon–Sat 7pm–2am, Sun 7pm–midnight.

**Le Merle Moqueur** 11 rue Butte-aux-Cailles, 13ᵉ ☎01 45 65 12 43; Mᵒ Place-d'Italie/Corvisart. This bohemian Butte-aux-Cailles bar once saw the Paris debut of Manu Chao. It maintains an alternative edge, though most days serves up 1980s French rock CDs and home-made flavoured rums to young Parisians. If you don't fancy the playlist when you arrive, you can always try the very similar *Le Diapason*, two doors along. Daily 5pm–2am.

**Le Rosebud** 11bis rue Delambre, 14ᵉ ☎01 43 35 38 54; Mᵒ Vavin. A hushed, faintly exclusive Art Nouveau bar just

off the bd Montparnasse, serving wonderful Martinis from €13. Daily 7pm–2am.

## MONTMARTRE AND AROUND

⭐ **La Fourmi** 74 rue des Martyrs, 18ᵉ ☎01 42 64 70 35; Mᵒ Pigalle/Abbesses; map p.109. The glamorous decor, long bar and high-ceilinged spaciousness draw the discerning bourgeois-bohemians of Abbesses and the 10ᵉ for cocktails, wine and chatter, to the tune of lounge music. Mon–Thurs 8am–2am, Fri & Sat 8am–3am, Sun 10am–1am.

**Le Relais de la Butte** 12 rue Ravignan, 18ᵉ ☎01 79 97 32 05; Mᵒ Abbesses; map p.109. Come for the outdoor café tables on the expansive terrace, with its amazing views over Paris. The drinks come with a moderate mark-up, but don't bother with the overpriced, indifferent food. Daily 8.30am–midnight.

**Le Sancerre** 35 rue des Abbesses, 18ᵉ ☎01 42 58 08 20; Mᵒ Abbesses; map p.109. A much-loved and always thrumming hangout under the southern slope of Montmartre, with a row of outside tables perfect for watching the world go by. The food can be disappointing, though. Daily 7am–2am.

## EASTERN PARIS

⭐ **L'Autre Café** 62 rue Jean-Pierre Timbaud, 11ᵉ ☎01 40 21 03 07, ⓦlautrecafe.com; Mᵒ Parmentier. Amid the heaving throng of bars on this popular nightlife stretch, this attractive *fin-de-siècle* café-bar-restaurant stands slightly apart, perhaps because it seems to welcome all comers and has no trace of pretension, and yet still has a great vibe. It also stands out for its size – it's very spacious, with high ceilings and a long zinc bar. Drinks are reasonably priced, and the food isn't bad either, especially if you stick to the blackboard specials (around €10). Daily 8am–2am.

**Aux Folies** 8 rue de Belleville, 20ᵉ ☎01 46 36 65 98; Mᵒ Belleville. *Aux Folies* offers a real slice of Belleville life: its outside terrace and 1930s long brass bar, with mirrored tiles and red neon lights, are packed day and night with a cosmopolitan and artsy crowd sipping inexpensive cocktails and beer. Daily 6.30am–1am.

**Café Charbon** 109 rue Oberkampf, 11ᵉ ☎01 43 57 55 13, ⓦlecafecharbon.com; Mᵒ St-Maur/Parmentier. The place that pioneered the rise of the Oberkampf bar scene is still going strong and continues to draw in a fashionable mixed crowd. Part of the allure is the attractively restored *fin-de-siècle* decor. Thurs–Sat 9am–4am, Sun–Wed 9am–2am.

## LIVE MUSIC VENUES

Most of the venues listed here are primarily concert venues, though some double up as clubs on certain nights, or after-hours. The majority host bands on just a couple of nights a week. Note too that some clubs host gigs earlier on in the evening, and jazz venues (see opposite) often branch out into world music and folk.

## MONTMARTRE AND AROUND

**La Cigale** 120 bd de Rochechouart, 18ᵉ ☎01 49 25 81 75, ⓦlacigale.fr; M° Pigalle; map map p.109. Since 1987 and a Philippe Starck renovation this historic, 1400-seat Pigalle theatre has become a leading venue for French rock, world music and indie acts. You might see anything from Rock dinosaur Marc Lavoine to electro superstars Beat Torrent, or from actress/chanteuse Charlotte Gainsbourg to Ivory Coast reggae star Tiken Jah Fakoly.

**Le Divan du Monde** 75 rue des Martyrs, 18ᵉ ☎01 40 05 06 99, ⓦdivandumonde.com; M° Anvers; map p.109. A youthful venue in a café whose regulars once included Toulouse-Lautrec. One of the city's most diverse and exciting programmes, ranging from techno to Congolese rumba, with dancing till dawn on weekend nights.

**Elysée Montmartre** 72 bd de Rochechouart, 18ᵉ ☎01 55 07 06 00, ⓦelyseemontmartre.com; M° Anvers; map p.109. A cavernous historic Montmartre nightspot that pulls in a young, excitable crowd with its rock, soul, R&B and hip-hop acts – the Pharcyde, the Hives, Public Enemy. Also hosts up-tempo Latin and club nights.

## EASTERN PARIS

**Le Bataclan** 50 bd Voltaire, 11ᵉ ☎01 43 14 00 30, ⓦbataclan.fr; M° Oberkampf. Classic pagoda-styled, ex-theatre venue (seats 1200) with one of the best and most eclectic line-ups covering anything from international and local dance and rock acts – Francis Cabrel, Chemical Brothers, Khaled, Hole – to chanson, opera, comedy and techno nights.

★ **La Bellevilloise** 19–21 rue Boyer, 20ᵉ ☎01 46 36 07 07, ⓦlabellevilloise.com; M° Gambetta/Ménil-montant. There's always something interesting going on at this former workers' co-op, now a dynamic bar, club, live concert venue and exhibition space, all rolled into one. Its attractive terrace is a good place for drinks or tapas-style meals before settling into an evening of Balkan gypsy music or Afro jazz. Jazz brunch on Sunday (€29). Generally Wed & Thurs 7pm–1am, Fri 7pm–2am, Sat 6pm–2am, Sun 11.30am–midnight.

**Café de la Danse** 5 passage Louis-Philippe, 11ᵉ ☎01 47 00 57 59, ⓦcafedeladanse.com; M° Bastille; map p.82–82. Rock, pop, world, folk and jazz music played in an intimate and attractive space. Open nights of concerts only.

**Maroquinerie** 23 rue Boyer, 20ᵉ ☎01 40 33 35 05, ⓦlamaroquinerie.fr; M° Gambetta. The smallish concert venue is the downstairs part of a trendy arts centre. The line-up is rock, folk and jazz, with a particularly good selection of French musicians.

**Point Ephemère** 200 quai de Valmy, 10ᵉ ☎01 40 34 02 48, ⓦpointephemere.org; M° Jaurès. Run by an arts collective in a disused warehouse, this superbly dilapidated venue lives up to its reputation as a nexus for alternative and underground performers of all kinds. There are gigs most nights, covering anything from electro to Afro-jazz via folk-rock, as well as dance studios, rehearsal spaces and the like.

## JAZZ VENUES

**Le Baiser Salé** 58 rue des Lombards, 1ᵉʳ ☎01 42 33 37 71, ⓦlebaisersale.com; M° Châtelet; map p.77. Small, crowded upstairs room with live music every night from 10pm – usually jazz, rhythm & blues, fusion, reggae or Brazilian. The downstairs bar is great for just chilling out. Admission up to €22. Mon–Sat 5.30pm–6am.

**Caveau de la Huchette** 5 rue de la Huchette, 5ᵉ ☎01 43 26 65 05, ⓦcaveaudelahuchette.fr; M° St-Michel; map p.90–91. One of the city's oldest jazz clubs, dating back to the mid-1940s. Live jazz, usually trad and big band, to dance to on a floor surrounded by tiers of benches. Admission Sun–Thurs €12, Fri & Sat €14; drinks around €8. Daily 9.30pm–2am or later.

**New Morning** 7–9 rue des Petites-Écuries, 10ᵉ ☎01 45 23 51 41, ⓦnewmorning.com; M° Château-d'Eau. This cavernous, somewhat spartan venue, an ex-printing press, is *the* place to hear the big international names on the circuit. It's often standing room only unless you get here early. Admission around €20. Usually Mon–Sat 8pm–1.30am (concerts start around 8.30pm).

**Le Sunside/Le Sunset** 60 rue des Lombards, 1ᵉʳ ☎01 40 26 46 60, ⓦsunset-sunside.com; M° Châtelet-Les Halles; map p.77. Two clubs in one: *Le Sunside* on the ground floor features mostly traditional jazz, whereas the downstairs *Sunset* is a venue for electric and fusion jazz. The *Sunside* concert usually starts at 9 or 9.30pm and the *Sunset* at 10pm, so you can sample a bit of both. Admission €20–28. Daily 8pm–2.30am.

## CHANSON VENUES

**Au Lapin Agile** 22 rue des Saules, 18ᵉ ☎01 46 06 85 87, ⓦau-lapin-agile.com; M° Lamarck-Caulaincourt; map p.109. Famous Montmartre cabaret painted and patronized by Picasso, Utrillo and other leading lights of the early twentieth-century Montmartre scene. It's an adorable little building, hidden behind shutters and a pretty garden, and still puts on old-fashioned cabaret shows featuring French chanson and poetry. €24. Tues–Sun 9pm–1am.

**Au Limonaire** 18 Cité Bergère, 9ᵉ ☎01 45 23 33 33, ⓦlimonaire.free.fr; M° Grands Boulevards. Tiny back-street venue, perfect for Parisian chanson nights showcasing young singers and zany music/poetry/performance acts. Dinner beforehand – traditional, inexpensive and fairly good – guarantees a seat for the show, otherwise you'll be

**1**

crammed up against the bar, if you can get in at all. Shows Tues–Sat 10pm.

**Casino de Paris** 16 rue de Clichy, 9ᵉ ☎01 49 95 99 99, ⓦ casinodeparis.fr; Mᵒ Trinité; map p.109. This decaying, once-plush former casino in one of the seediest streets in Paris is a venue for all sorts of performances – including chanson, poetry, flamenco and cabaret. Tickets from €25. Most performances start at 8.30pm.

**Les Trois Baudets** 64 bd de Clichy, 18ᵉ ☎01 42 62 33 33, ⓦ lestroisbaudets.com; Mᵒ Blanche/Pigalle; map p.109. Refitted in 2009, this chanson venue has already found a proud place on the Pigalle nightlife scene. It specializes in developing young, upcoming French musicians, so concerts are something of a lucky dip, but tickets are inexpensive at around €12–15. The venue is pleasingly intimate (250 seats), and there are often after events with DJs at the lively bar/restaurant. Tues–Sat 6.30pm–1.30am.

## CLUBS

The clubs listed here support good programmes and attract interesting crowds, but it really depends who is running the individual *soirée*. It's worth also checking the listings for live music venues (see p.134), which often hold DJ-led sessions after hours, as well as gay and lesbian clubs (see p.139). Most clubs open between 11pm and midnight, but venues rarely warm up before 1 or 2am. Entry prices and admission vary, and may be free or reduced before midnight, but almost always include one "free" drink (*consommation*). Trendier places may turn away the scruffier or less fashionably dressed, though booking online in advance and being very obviously a tourist can prevent problems.

### THE CHAMPS ELYSÉES AND AROUND

★ **Showcase** Pont Alexandre III, 8ᵉ ☎01 45 61 25 43, ⓦ showcase.fr; Mᵒ Champs-Elysées-Clemenceau/Les Invalides; map pp.68–69. This big club underneath the Alexandre III bridge is spacious and atmospheric, with its stone arches. Committed to showcasing (geddit) good electronic music. Entry up to €20.

### THE OPÉRA DISTRICT

★ **Rex Club** 5 bd Poissonnière, 2ᵉ ☎01 42 36 10 96; Mᵒ Bonne-Nouvelle; map pp.68–69. The iconic *Rex* is the clubbers' club: spacious and serious about music, which is strictly electronic, notably techno, played through a top-of-the line sound system. Refreshingly, not a style-fest. Attracts big-name DJs too. Entry up to €20. Wed–Sat 11.30pm–5am.

## ENTERTAINMENT

## CLASSICAL MUSIC

Paris is a stimulating environment for classical music, both established and contemporary. The former is well

**Scop' Club** 5 av de l'Opéra ☎01 42 60 64 45, ⓦ lescopclub .com; Mᵒ Pyramide/Palais Royal; map pp.68–69. Currently one of the cooler small clubs in town, pulling in a designer-scruffy Parisian crowd. The entrance fee varies, with gigs earlier on, and lots of free nights. Mon–Sat 8pm–5am.

**Social Club** 142 rue Montmartre, 2ᵉ ☎01 40 28 05 55, ⓦ parissocialclub.com; Mᵒ Palais de la Bourse; map pp.68–69. Despite the forbidding black exterior, and interior, this unpretentious yet cool club is packed with a mixed clientele, from local students to lounge lizards. Here, it's all about the music, with everything from electro to jazz and hip-hop to ska on the playlist. Free–€20. Wed 11.30pm–3am, Thurs–Sat 11pm–6am.

### SAINT GERMAIN

**WAGG** 62 rue Mazarine, 6ᵉ ☎01 55 42 22 00, ⓦ wagg.fr; Mᵒ Odéon; map pp.94–95. Adjoining Terence Conran's flashy *Alcazar* restaurant and bar, the *WAGG* offers glossy good times, with Seventies-themed "Carwash" nights on Fri, Eighties and Nineties grooves on Sat, and Latino/salsa on Sun. Entry €12, Sun and Fri & Sat before midnight free. Fri & Sat 11.30pm–6.45am, Sun 5pm to midnight.

### SOUTHERN PARIS

★ **Batofar** Opposite 11 quai François Mauriac, 13ᵉ ☎01 56 29 10 33, ⓦ batofar.org; Mᵒ Etienne-Marcel. This old lighthouse boat moored at the foot of the Bibliothèque Nationale is a small but classic address. The programme is electro, house, techno, hip-hop, whatever – with the odd experimental funk night or the like thrown in. Entry €8–13. Tues–Thurs 8pm–2am, Fri 11pm–dawn, Sat 11pm–noon.

### EASTERN PARIS

**Glaz'art** 7–15 av de la Porte de la Villette, 19ᵉ ☎01 40 36 55 65, ⓦ glazart.com; Mᵒ Porte de la Villette. Artsy, alternative-leaning venue which is serious about its music – hugely eclectic range of live acts and DJ sets covering everything from punk to jungle. Quite a trek from the centre, but it's spacious and in summer there's a glorious outdoor "beach". Entry €10–20. Times vary, but weekend club nights usually 11pm–5am.

**Le Nouveau Casino** 109 rue Oberkampf, 11ᵉ ☎01 43 57 57 40, ⓦ nouveaucasino.net; Mᵒ Parmentier. Right behind *Café Charbon* (see p.134), this adventurous concert venue makes way for a relaxed, dancey crowd later on, with music ranging from electro-pop or house to rock and world music. Entry €5–20. Tues & Wed 9pm–2am, Thurs–Sat midnight–5am.

represented in performances within churches – sometimes free or very cheap – and in an enormous choice of commercially promoted concerts held every day of the

## PARIS FESTIVALS

Paris has an extraordinarily vibrant festival schedule; just a few are listed here. For details of the following and more, check at tourist offices or ⓦ parisinfo.com.

### MARCH

**Festival de Films des Femmes** ⓣ 01 49 80 38 98, ⓦ filmsdefemmes.com. Held at the Maison des Arts in Créteil, just southeast of Paris (M° Créteil-Préfecture).
**Festival Exit** ⓦ maccreteil.com. International contemporary dance, performance and theatre, at the Créteil's Maison des Arts.

### JUNE/JULY

**Festival Chopin** ⓦ frederic-chopin.com. Held from mid-June to mid-July in the lovely setting of the Bois de Boulogne's Orangerie.
**Fête de la Musique** ⓦ fetedelamusique .culture.fr. Free concerts and street performers all over Paris to coincide with the summer solstice (June 21).
**Gay Pride** Held on the last Sat of June.

### JULY/AUG

**Festival du Cinéma en Plein Air** ⓦ cinema.arbo.com. Free films in the Parc de la Villette from July to mid-Aug.
**Bastille Day** July 14 is celebrated with official pomp in parades of tanks down the Champs-Élysées, followed by firework displays; the evening before there is dancing on the place de la Bastille.
**Paris Quartier d'Été** ⓦ quartierdete.com. A programme of free music, theatre and cinema events around the city from mid-July to mid-Aug.
**Tour de France** The race finishes along the Champs-Élysées on the third or fourth Sun of July.
**Paris Plages** For four weeks from the end of July, the *quais* are transformed into a sandy beach along the Seine.

### SEPT–DEC

**Festival d'Automne** ⓦ festival-automne .com. Traditional and experimental theatrical, musical, dance and multimedia productions from all over the world.

### SEPT–DEC

**Nuit Blanche** In early Oct, the "sleepless night" persuades Parisians to stay up all night for an energetic programme of arts events and parties all over the city.
**Festival d'Art Sacré** ⓦ festivaldartsacre. new.fr. Concerts and recitals of early sacred music, from end Nov to mid-Dec.

week. Tickets are best bought at the box offices, though for big names you may find overnight queues, and a large number of seats are always booked by subscribers.

### CONCERT HALLS

**Philharmonie de Paris** Parc de la Villette, 19ᵉ ⓦ philharmoniedeparis.com; M° Porte-de-Pantin. This major state-of-the-art 2400-seater auditorium is currently under construction, due to be completed in 2014.
**Salle des Concerts** Cité de la Musique, 221 av Jean-Jaurès, 19ᵉ ⓣ 01 44 84 44 84, ⓦ cite-musique.fr; M° Jaurès. Concert hall with seating for 800–1200, which hosts anything from traditional Korean music to the contemporary sounds of the Ensemble Intercontemporain.
**Salle Gaveau** 45 rue de la Boétie, 8ᵉ ⓣ 01 49 53 05 07, ⓦ sallegaveau.com; M° Saint-Augustin. This atmospheric and intimate concert hall, built in 1907, is a major venue for piano recitals, as well as chamber music and full-scale orchestral works.
**Salle Pleyel** 252 rue du Faubourg-St-Honoré, 8ᵉ ⓣ 01 42 56 13 13, ⓦ sallepleyel.fr; M° Concorde. Distinguished concert hall, dating back to 1927. The Orchestre de Paris (ⓦ orchestredeparis.com) performs here most frequently, along with visiting international performers.
**Théâtre des Champs-Elysées** 15 av Montaigne, 8ᵉ ⓣ 01 49 52 50 50, ⓦ theatrechampselysees.fr; M° Alma-Marceau. Two-thousand-seat capacity in this historic modernist theatre with sculptures by Bourdelle and paintings by Vuillard. Home to the Orchestre National de France and Orchestre Lamoureux, it also hosts international superstar conductors and ballet troupes. Offers bargain tickets for seats with no view, but you can pay up to €150 or so for star performers.
**Théâtre Musical de Paris** Théâtre du Châtelet, 1 place du Châtelet, 1ᵉʳ ⓣ 01 40 28 28 40, ⓦ chatelet-theatre .com; M° Châtelet. A prestigious concert hall with a varied programme of high-profile operas, ballets, concerts, musicals and solo recitals. Wide range of tickets from around €10.

### OPERA

**Opéra-Bastille** 120 rue de Lyon, 12ᵉ ⓣ 08 92 89 90 90 or ⓣ 331 71 25 24 23 from abroad, ⓦ opera-de-paris .fr; M° Bastille. The city's main opera house, opened in

**1**

1989. Opinions differ over the acoustics, but the well-designed stage allows the auditorium uninterrupted views. Director Nicolas Joel concentrates on the mainstream repertoire, with A-list performers. Tickets (€5–180) can be bought online, by phone (Mon–Fri 9am–6pm, Sat 9am–1pm), or at the ticket office (Mon–Sat 11am–6.30pm). There are 32 standing tickets (€5) sold 90min before the curtain goes up; 15min before curtain, unfilled seats are sold at a discount to under-28s and retired people.

**Opéra-Comique** Salle Favart, 5 rue Favart, 2<sup>e</sup> ☎ 01 42 44 45 46, ⓦ opera-comique.com; M° Richelieu-Drouot. Here they concentrate on the rich, yet largely forgotten French opera of the nineteenth century, reviving such obscure composers as Hérold and Auber, with largely successful and surprising results.

**Opéra-Garnier** Place de l'Opéra, 9<sup>e</sup> ☎ 08 92 89 90 90 or ☎ 331 71 25 24 23 from abroad ⓦ opera-de-paris.fr; M° Opéra. Operas are still staged at this old opera house, though these days it hosts mostly ballets. As with Opéra-Bastille, you can buy tickets online, by phone (Mon–Fri 9am–6pm, Saturday 9am–1pm), or at the box office (Mon–Sat 11am–6.30pm). Tickets €10–150.

## FILM

Around three hundred films are shown in Paris in any one week. The plethora of little arts cinemas screen unrivalled programmes of classic and contemporary films, and you can find mainstream movies at almost any time of the day or night.

**Venues** The city is littered with fine cinemas, from the megaplexes on the boulevards to the small venues in the Quartier Latin. In addition to those listed below, there is a cluster of venues around rue Champollion and rue des Écoles, 5<sup>e</sup> – check out in particular the mini-chains operated by the Reflet Médicis (ⓦ lesecransdeparis.fr) and the Action chain (ⓦ actioncinemas.com). Many cultural institutions and embassies also offer regular screenings.

**Listings** You can find film listings online at sites including ⓦ allocine.fr, but the handiest guide is still *Pariscope* (see p.118). Its *Reprises* section lists British or American classics, often one-off afternoon screenings. Note that foreign films shown in the original language are listed as *version originale* or *v.o.*; films dubbed into French are *v.f.*

**Tickets** Average cinema ticket prices are around €9, but there are many reduced-rate periods, especially for students; you rarely need to book in advance.

### CINEMAS

**Cinémathèque Française** 51 rue de Bercy, 12<sup>e</sup> ☎ 01 71 19 33 33, ⓦ cinemathequefrancaise.com; M° Bercy. This Gehry-designed cinema is the best in Paris, showing around two dozen films and shorts every week, with regular retrospectives of French and foreign films screened in its four cinemas. Tickets €6.50.

**L'Entrepôt** 7–9 rue François Pressensé, 14<sup>e</sup> ☎ 01 45 40 07 50, ⓦ lentrepot.fr; M° Pernety. One of the best alternative Paris cinemas, with three screens dedicated to the obscure, the subversive and the brilliant.

**Forum des Images** 2 Grande Galerie, Porte St-Eustache, Forum des Halles ☎ 01 44 76 63 00, ⓦ forumdesimages.net; M° Châtelet-Les Halles. This refitted hall shows several films or projected videos daily, with tickets at just €5. Its unique feature, though, is the Salle des Collections, which has individual terminals with digital access to the huge archive, and private, rentable screens for up to seven people (Tues–Fri 1–10pm, Sat & Sun 2–10pm; €5/person/2hr session).

**Le Grand Rex** Bd Poissonnière, 2<sup>e</sup> ⓦ legrandrex.com. A huge Art Deco cinema showing big-screen movies – dubbed, if the film is foreign.

**Max Linder Panorama** Bd Poissonnière, 2<sup>e</sup> ⓦ maxlinder .cine.allocine.fr. This Art Deco cinema always shows films in the original language and has state-of-the-art sound.

**La Pagode** 57bis rue de Babylone, 7<sup>e</sup> ☎ 01 46 34 82 54, ⓦ etoile-cinemas.com; M° François Xavier. An Orientalist folly, built in 1895 for the wife of a director of Paris's elegant Le Bon Marché department store and turned into an arts cinema in the 1930s – in 1959 it premiered Jean Cocteau's *Le Testament d'Orphée*.

**Le Studio 28** 10 rue de Tholozé, 18<sup>e</sup> ☎ 01 42 54 18 11, ⓦ cinemastudio28.com; M° Blanche/Abbesses. Avant-garde premieres, followed occasionally by discussions with the director.

## THEATRE

Looking at the scores of métro posters advertising theatre in Paris, you might think bourgeois farces form the backbone of French theatre. To an extent, that's true, though the classics – Molière, Corneille and Racine – are also staple fare, and well worth a try if your French is up to it. You can easily get by with quite basic French, however, at one of the frequent performances of plays by the great postwar generation of Francophone dramatists, including Genet, Camus, Sartre, Ionesco, Cocteau and Beckett. For monolingual visitors, the most rewarding theatre in Paris is likely to be the genre-busting, avant-garde, highly styled and radical kind best represented by Ariane Mnouchkine and her Théâtre du Soleil, based at the Cartoucherie in Vincennes, and the Bouffes du Nord theatre.

**Listings** Productions are detailed in *Pariscope* and *L'Officiel des Spectacles* with brief résumés or reviews.

**Prices** Around €15–30, though you may pay less in smaller venues, and more for many commercial and major state productions (most closed Sun & Mon). Half-price previews are advertised in *Pariscope* and *L'Officiel des Spectacles*, and there are weekday student discounts.

**Tickets** Buy directly from the theatres, from FNAC shops or the Virgin Megastore (52–60 av des Champs-Élysées, 8ᵉ; M° Franklin-D.-Roosevelt; Mon–Sat 10am–midnight, Sun noon–midnight), or at the kiosks on place de la Madeleine, 8ᵉ, opposite no. 15, and on the parvis of the Gare du Montparnasse, 15ᵉ (Tues–Sat 12.30–7.45pm, Sun 12.30–3.45pm). They sell half-price same-day tickets and charge a small commission, but be prepared to queue.

#### VENUES

**Bouffes du Nord** 37bis bd de la Chapelle, 10ᵉ ☏ 01 46 07 34 50, ⓦ bouffesdunord.com; M° La Chapelle. Peter Brook resurrected the derelict Bouffes du Nord in 1974 and though he has officially retired, is still regularly invited back by his successors. Outstanding performances of opera and chamber music are also put on here.

**Cartoucherie** Rte du Champ-de-Manoeuvre, 12ᵉ; M° Château-de-Vincennes. Home to several interesting theatre companies including workers' co-op Théâtre du Soleil, set up by Ariane Mnouchkine (☏ 01 43 74 24 08, ⓦ theatre-du-soleil.fr).

**Comédie Française** 2 rue de Richelieu, 1ᵉʳ ☏ 01 44 58 15 15, ⓦ comedie-francaise.fr; M° Palais-Royal. This venerable national theatre stages mainly Racine, Molière and other classics, but also twentieth-century greats such as Anouilh and Genet.

**Odéon Théâtre de l'Europe** 1 place Paul-Claudel, 6ᵉ ☏ 01 44 41 36 36, ⓦ theatre-odeon.fr; M° Odéon. Contemporary plays and foreign-language productions in the theatre that became an open parliament during May 1968.

**Théâtre de la Huchette** 23 rue de la Huchette, 5ᵉ ☏ 01 43 26 38 99, ⓦ theatre-huchette.com; M° Saint-Michel. Almost sixty years on, this intimate little theatre, seating ninety, is still showing Ionesco's *La Cantatrice Chauve* (*The Bald Prima Donna*; 7pm) and *La Leçon* (8pm), two classics of the Theatre of the Absurd.

**Théâtre National de Chaillot** Palais de Chaillot, place du Trocadéro, 16ᵉ ☏ 01 53 65 30 00, ⓦ theatre-chaillot.fr; M° Trocadéro. An exciting programme and frequent foreign productions; Deborah Warner and Robert Lepage are regular visitors.

#### DANCE
The status of dance in Paris received a major boost with the inauguration in 2004 of the Centre National de la Danse, committed to promoting every possible dance form from classical to contemporary, and including ethnic traditions. While the city itself has few home-grown companies it makes up for this by regularly hosting all the best contemporary practitioners. Names to look out for are Régine Chopinot's troupe from La Rochelle, Maguy Marin's from Rilleux-le-Pape and Angelin Preljocaj's from Aix-en-Provence. Plenty of space and critical attention are also given to tango, folk and visiting traditional dance troupes from all over the world. Some of the venues listed under "Theatre" (see p.138) also host dance productions.

**Centre National de la Danse** 1 rue Victor Hugo, Pantin ☏ 01 41 83 27 27, ⓦ cnd.fr; M° Hoche/RER Pantin. The capital's major dance centre occupies an impressively large building, ingeniously converted from a disused 1970s monolith into an airy high-tech space. Though several of its eleven studios are used for performances, the main emphasis of the centre is to promote dance through training, workshops and exhibitions.

**Opéra-Garnier** Place de l'Opéra, 9ᵉ ☏ 08 36 69 78 68, ⓦ opera-de-paris.fr; M° Opéra. Main home of the Ballet de l'Opéra National de Paris, directed by Brigitte Lefèvre, and which still bears the influence of Rudolf Nureyev, its charismatic, if controversial, director from 1983 to 1989. They frequently revive his productions, such as *Swan Lake* and *La Bayadère*.

**Théâtre des Abbesses** 31 rue des Abbesses, 18ᵉ ☏ 01 42 74 22 77, ⓦ theatredelaville-paris.com; M° Abbesses. The Théâtre de la Ville's sister company, with a slightly more risk-taking programme – including Indian and other international dance.

**Théâtre de la Ville** 2 place du Châtelet, 4ᵉ ☏ 01 42 74 22 77, ⓦ theatredelaville-paris.com; M° Châtelet. Specializes in avant-garde dance by top European choreographers, such as Anne Teresa de Keersmaeker.

## GAY AND LESBIAN PARIS

Paris is one of Europe's great centres for gay men, with the scene's focal point in the Marais, the "pink triangle" around rue Sainte-Croix-de-la-Bretonnerie. Lesbians have fewer dedicated addresses, but the community is becoming more energetic and visible.

The high spots of the festival calendar are the annual Marche des Fiertés LGBT, or gay pride march, which normally takes place on the last Saturday in June, and the Bastille Day Ball – open to all – held on the quai de Tournelle, 5ᵉ (M° Pont-Marie) on July 13. For information, check *Têtu* (ⓦ tetu.com), France's main gay monthly magazine.

#### BARS
**Café Cox** 15 rue des Archives, 3ᵉ ☏ 01 42 72 08 00, ⓦ cox.fr; M° Hôtel-de-Ville; map p.82. Muscular types up for a seriously good time pack out this loud, riotous

neon-coloured bar. Friendly – if your face fits – with DJs at weekends. Mon–Thurs 12.30pm–2am, Fri–Sun 1.30pm–2am.

**La Champmeslé** 4 rue Chabanais, 2ᵉ ☏ 01 42 96 85 20,

**1**

ⓦlachampmesle-wifeo.com; M° Pyramides; map pp.68–69. Long-established, community-oriented lesbian address in a handsome old building. Popular among thirty-somethings, though it packs everyone in for the live music or cabaret nights Thurs–Sat. Daily 4pm–4am.

★ **Le Duplex** 25 rue Michel-le-Comte, 3ᵉ ☎01 42 72 80 86, ⓦduplex-bar.com; M° Rambuteau; map pp.82–83. Arty little gay men's bar that's popular with intellectual or media types for its relatively relaxed and chatty atmosphere. Mon–Thurs & Sun 8pm–2am, Fri & Sat 8pm–4am.

**Le Free DJ** 35 rue Ste-Croix de la Bretonnerie, 4ᵉ ☎01 42 78 26 20, ⓦfreedj.fr; M° Hôtel-de-Ville; map pp.82–83. This stylish, fairly recent addition to the gay men's scene draws the young and *très looké* – beautiful types – and offers house and disco-funk in the basement club. Mon–Wed & Sun 6pm–3am, Fri & Sat 6pm–4am.

**L'Open Café** 17 rue des Archives, 3ᵉ ☎01 48 87 80 25, ⓦopencafe.fr; M° Arts-et-Métiers; map pp.82–83. The first gay café-bar to have tables out on the pavement, and they're still there, with overhead heaters in winter. Expensive and now touristy, but still good fun. Mon–Thurs & Sun 11am–2am, Fri & Sat 11am–4am.

★ **Le Raidd** 23 rue du Temple, 4ᵉ ☎01 42 77 04 88, ⓦraiddbar.com; M° Hôtel-de-Ville. One of the city's biggest, glossiest (and most expensive) bars, famous for its beautiful staff, topless (male) waiters and go-go boys' shower shows every hour. Daily 5pm–2am.

**Le So What** 30 rue du Roi de Sicile, 4ᵉ ☎06 98 75 45 46; M° St Paul; map pp.82–83. A recent arrival on the scene, aimed mainly at thirtysomethings, this is an intimate and cosy mainly lesbian bar that hots up on Fri and Sat with dancing till the early hours. Tues–Thurs 9.30pm–2am, Fri & Sat 10pm–4am.

**L'Unity Bar** 176 rue St-Martin, 3ᵉ ☎01 42 72 70 59, ⓦunity.bar.free.fr; M° Rambuteau. Predominantly butch lesbian bar where life is centred on the beer tap and the pool table. Daily 4pm–2am.

## CLUBS

A few classic club addresses are given here, but many, if not most, mainstream clubs (see p.136) run gay *soirées*. Club opening hours are largely irrelevant: they're all pretty empty before at least 1am and keep going till at least dawn. Entry prices are generally around €10–20 (usually including a *conso*, or "free" drink).

**CUD** 12 rue des Haudriettes, 3ᵉ ☎01 42 77 44 12, ⓦcud-paris.com; M° Rambuteau; map pp.82–83. The "Classic Up and Down" is just that: bar upstairs, miniature club below. Low-key: no queues, door policies or overpriced drinks. More for bears than boys, though it's pretty mixed.

**Queen** 102 av des Champs-Elysées, 8ᵉ ☎01 53 89 08 90, ⓦqueen.fr; M° George V; map p.69. The legendary gay club of the 1980s has bounced back from its inevitable fall, though it's still a bit packed out with eager provincials – except on the kitsch Sun nights.

**Le Rive Gauche** 1 rue du Sabot, 6ᵉ ☎01 40 20 43 23, ⓦlerivegauche.com; M° St-Germain-des-Près; map pp.94–95. Currently very fashionable among gorgeous young gamines, this pocket-sized club is a historic 1970s address preserving some of its gold mirror-mosaic decor. Sat 11pm–5am.

**Le Tango** 13 rue au-Maire, 3ᵉ ☎01 42 72 17 78, ⓦboite-a-frissons.fr; M° Arts-et-Métiers; map p.82–83. Unpretentious and inexpensive gay and lesbian club with a traditional Sunday-afternoon *bal* from 7pm, featuring proper slow dances as well as tangos and disco classics. Turns into a full-on club later on, and on Fri and Sat nights.

## SHOPPING

The Parisian love of style and fierce attachment to small local traders have kept alive a wonderful variety of speciality shops. The nineteenth-century arcades, or *passages*, in the 2ᵉ and 9ᵉ arrondissements, are particularly rich in intriguing boutiques, while the square kilometre around place St-Germain-des-Prés is hard to beat for anything from books to shoes, and from antiques to artworks. Other atmospheric and rewarding places for browsing include the aristocratic Marais, the trendy Bastille quartier, the quirky Abbesses quarter of Montmartre, and the broadly bohemian Oberkampf and Canal Saint-Martin areas of northeastern Paris. For haute couture the traditional bastions are avenue Montaigne, rue François 1ᵉʳ and the upper end of rue du Faubourg-St-Honoré in the 8ᵉ. The traditional shopping heart of the city, Les Halles, is very commercial, and mostly downmarket. The most atmospheric places for book shopping are the Seine *quais*, with their rows of mostly secondhand bookstalls perched against the river parapet. The *quartier Latin* is the home of most of the city's best independent bookshops.

### BOOKS

**Artcurial** 7 du rond-point des Champs-Elysées, 8ᵉ ☎01 42 99 20 20, ⓦartcurial.com; M° Franklin-D.-Roosevelt; map p.68. The best art bookshop in Paris, set in an elegant townhouse. Sells French and foreign editions, and there's also a gallery and stylish

café. Mon–Sat 10.30am–7pm; closed two weeks in Aug.

**FNAC** Forum des Halles, niveau 2, Porte Pierre-Lescot, 1ᵉʳ (M°/RER Châtelet-Les Halles); 136 rue de Rennes, 6ᵉ (M° Montparnasse) ☎08 25 02 00 20, ⓦfnac.com; map p.77 Not the most congenial of bookshops, but it's

## CLOTHES SHOPPING IN PARIS

If you're looking for a one-stop hit of Paris fashion, the **department stores** (see p.142) are probably the place to go. For more picturesque browsing, make for the streets around **St-Sulpice métro**, on the Left Bank: you'll find rich pickings if you wander down rues du Vieux Colombier, de Rennes, Madame and du Cherche-Midi – the last is particularly good for shoes. The home of couture and designer labels is the wealthy, manicured "**golden triangle**" off the Champs-Élysées, especially av François 1$^{er}$, av Montaigne and rue du Faubourg-St-Honoré. Younger designers have colonized the lower reaches of the latter street, between rue Cambon and rue des Pyramides. On the **eastern side of the city**, around the Marais, Canal St Martin and Bastille, the clothes, like the residents, are younger, cooler and more relaxed. Chic boutiques cluster on rue Charlot, rue du Poitou and rue Saintonge in the **Haut Marais**, and young, trendy designers and hippy outfits congregate on **Bastille** streets rue de Charonne and rue Keller. There's also a good concentration of one-off designer boutiques around the foot of **Montmartre** – try rue des Martyrs, and the streets around rue des Trois-Frères. For more streetwise clothing, the area surrounding the **Forum des Halles** is a good place to browse; Rue Etienne Marcel and (pedestrianized) rue Tiquetonne are good for clothes with a young, urban edge.

the biggest and covers everything. Mon–Sat 10am–7.30pm.

**Gibert Jeune** 5 place St-Michel, 5$^e$ ⓦgibertjeune.fr; M° St-Michel; map pp.90–91. A Latin Quarter institution for student/academic books, with eight, slightly chaotic, stores on and around place St-Michel. There's a second-hand selection at 2 pl St-Michel, and foreign-language titles at 10 pl St-Michel. Mon–Sat 9.30am–7.30pm; closed first 2 weeks of Aug.

**Shakespeare & Co** 37 rue de la Bûcherie, 5$^e$ ☎01 43 25 40 93, ⓦshakespeareandcompany.com; M° Maubert-Mutualité; map pp.90–91. The original shop with the Shakespeare name – owned by Sylvia Beach, the first publisher of Joyce's *Ulysses* – was on rue de l'Odéon, but even the replacement has become a classic. A cosy, welcoming literary haunt that acts as an informal hostel for wannabe Hemingways who sleep on lumpy divans on the top floor, it sells the best selection of English-language books in town and run regular readings and events. Mon–Fri 10am–11pm, Sat & Sun 11am–11pm.

★ **Village Voice** 6 rue Princesse, 6$^e$ ☎01 46 33 25 34, ⓦvillagevoicebookshop.com; M° Mabillon; map pp.94–95. A welcoming neighbourhood bookstore in St-Germain, with a good selection of contemporary titles and British and American classics. Frequent readings and author signings. Mon 2–7.30pm, Tues–Sat 10am–7.30pm, Sun noon–6pm.

## CLOTHES

**agnès b** 6 rue du Jour, 1$^{er}$ (M° Châtelet-Les Halles), 6 & 10 rue du Vieux Colombier, 6e (M° St-Sulpice) ☎01 40 03 58 44, ⓦeurope.agnes-b.com; map pp.94–95. The queen of classic understatement, for men and women. Relatively affordable for designer gear. Mon–Sat 10.30am–7.30pm.

**Anne Willi** 13 rue Keller, 11$^e$ ☎01 48 06 74 06, ⓦannewilli.com; M° Ledru-Rollin/Voltaire; map pp.82–83. Original pieces of clothing in gorgeous fabrics that respect classic French sartorial design. Prices from around €70 upwards. Mon 2–8pm, Tues–Sat 11.30am–8pm.

**APC** 38 rue Madame, 6$^e$ (☎01 42 22 12 77; M° St-Sulpice); 112 rue Vieille-du-Temple, 3$^e$ (☎01 42 78 18 02; M° St-Sébastien Froissart) ⓦapc.fr; map pp.94–95. Effortlessly classic but youthful fashion – like a Parisian take on Gap, and all the better for it. Mon–Sat 11am–7.30pm.

**Cancan** 30 rue Henry Monnier, 9$^e$ ☎01 42 80 30 41, ⓦ30cancan.com; M°Pigalle; map p.109. In the last few years a handful of boutiques have sprung up on rue Monnier, all stocking choice selections of women's clothes by French *créateurs* – Cancan usually has some quirky, stylish dresses that won't break the bank and that you won't find back home. Tues–Sat 11.30am–7.30pm.

**Comptoir des Cotonniers** 30 rue de Buci 6$^e$ (☎01 43 54 56 73; M° Mabillon); Forum des Halles, 1$^{er}$ (☎01 53 40 82 41; M° Les Halles); 33 rue des Francs-Bourgeois, 4$^e$ (☎01 42 76 95 33; M° St-Paul) ⓦcomptoirdes cotonniers.com; map p.77. Utterly reliable chain (there are some thirty shops in Paris) stocking comfortable, well-cut women's basics that make well-judged concessions to contemporary fashions without being modish. Trousers, shirts and dresses for around €100. Generally Mon–Sat 10am–7pm.

**Isabel Marant** 16 rue de Charonne, 11$^e$ ☎01 49 29 71 55, ⓦisabelmarant.fr; M° Bastille; map p.82–83. Marant excels in feminine and flattering clothes in quality fabrics such as silk and cashmere. Prices from around €100 upwards. Mon–Sat 10.30am–7.30pm.

**Jacques Le Corre** 193 rue Saint-Honoré, 1$^{er}$ ☎01 42 60 37 27; M° Tuileries; map p.68–69. Creative, original hats,

**1**

footwear and handbags. The stylish, unisex hats here come in interesting colours and shapes; Jacques is famed for his classic cotton *cloche*, perfecting the vagrant-chic look. Mon–Sat 11am–7pm.

**Le Mouton à Cinq Pattes** 138 bd St-Germain, 6ᵉ ☎01 43 26 49 25, ⓦmoutonacinqpattesparis.com; M° Odéon/Mabillon; map pp.94–95. You might just find a Gaultier among the racks of last-season bargains – though often the labels are cut out so you'll have to trust your judgement. There's a branch at 18 rue St-Placide, 6ᵉ, and one just for women's clothes at 8 rue St-Placide, 6ᵉ (both ☎01 45 48 86 26; M° Sèvres-Babylone). Mon–Sat 10am–7pm.

★ **Paul & Joe** 62–66 rue des Saints-Pères, 7ᵉ ☎01 42 22 47 01, ⓦpaulandjoe.com; M° Sèvres-Babylone; map pp.94–95. Quintessential Parisian chic: classic but quirky, feminine (and that goes for the men's clothes too) but with an edge. Mon–Sat 10.30am–7.30pm.

**Sonia by Sonia Rykiel** 6 rue de Grenelle, 6ᵉ ☎01 49 54 61 00, ⓦsoniarykiel.com; M° Sèvres-Babylone; map pp.94–95. Sonia Rykiel has been a St-Germain institution since opening a store on bd St-Germain in 1968; "Sonia" is a younger, less expensive offshoot. Mon–Sat 10.30am–7pm.

★ **Spree** 16 rue de la Vieuville, 18ᵉ ☎01 42 23 41 40, ⓦspree.fr; M° Abbesses; map p.109. Funky, feminine clothing store/gallery led by designers such as Vanessa Bruno, Isabel Marant and Christian Wijnants. Also vintage pieces, accessories, furniture and beauty products. Clothing mostly falls in the €100–250 range. Mon–Sat 11am–7.30pm, Sun 3–7pm.

**Vanessa Bruno** 25 rue St-Sulpice, 6ᵉ ☎01 43 54 41 04, ⓦvanessabruno.com; M° Odéon; map pp.94–95.

Effortlessly beautiful women's fashions with a hint of floaty, hippy chic. Branch at 100 rue Vieille du Temple, 4ᵉʳ (☎01 42 77 19 41; M° St-Sébastien/Froissart). Mon–Sat 10.30am–7.30pm.

**Zadig & Voltaire** 1 & 3 rue du Vieux Colombier, 6ᵉ ☎01 43 29 18 29, ⓦzadig-et-voltaire.com; M° St-Sulpice; map pp.94–95. The women's clothes at this moderately expensive Parisian chain are pretty and feminine: not a million miles from agnès b, but with a more wayward flair. Branches all over Paris. Generally Mon–Sat 10.30am–7pm.

## DEPARTMENT STORES

★ **Le Bon Marché** 38 rue de Sèvres, 7ᵉ ☎01 44 39 80 00, ⓦlebonmarche.fr; M° Sèvres-Babylone; map pp.94–95. The world's oldest department store, founded in 1852, is a beautiful building and a classy place to shop, with a legendary food hall. Mon–Wed & Sat 10am–8pm, Thurs & Fri 10am–9pm.

**Galeries Lafayette** 40 bd Haussmann, 9ᵉ ☎09 69 39 75 75, ⓦgalerieslafayette.com; M° Havre-Caumartin; map pp.68–69. Three floors are given over to high fashion for women, while an adjoining three-storey store is devoted to men's clothing. Then there's a huge *parfumerie* and a host of big names in mens' and women's accessories – all under a superb 1900 dome. Lafayette Maison, the huge, impressive home store, is just up the road at 35 bd Haussmann. Mon–Wed, Fri & Sat 9.30am–8pm, Thurs 9.30am–9pm.

**Printemps** 64 bd Haussmann, 9ᵉ ☎01 42 82 50 00, ⓦprintemps.com; M° Havre-Caumartin; map pp.68–69. Printemps has an excellent fashion collection for men and women, a whole floor devoted to shoes and a *parfumerie*

---

## FOOD MARKETS

Many of Paris's most historic market streets, such as **rue Mouffetard** (5ᵉ) and **rue des Martyrs** (9ᵉ) are lined with food shops, now, not stalls, but this is still one of the world's great cities for outdoor food shopping. A few of the more classic or unusual markets are recommended here; for a full list, arranged by arrondissement, see the town hall site, ⓦparis.fr, under "Marchés Parisiens".

**Marché Barbès** Bd de la Chapelle, 18ᵉ; M Barbès Rochechouart. Wed & Sat 7/8am–1/2.30pm.

**Belleville** Bd de Belleville, 20ᵉ; M° Belleville/ Ménilmontant. Tues & Fri 7/8am–1/2.30pm.

**Enfants-Rouges** 39 rue de Bretagne, 3ᵉ; M° Filles-du-Calvaire. Tues–Sat 9am–2pm & 4–8pm, Sun 9am–2pm.

**Maubert** Place Maubert, 5ᵉ; M° Maubert-Mutualité. Tues, Thurs & Sat 7/8am–1/2.30pm.

**Monge** Place Monge, 5ᵉ; M° Monge. Wed, Fri & Sat 7/8am–1/2.30pm.

**Montorgueil** Rue Montorgueil & rue Montmartre, 1ᵉʳ; M° Châtelet-Les Halles/Sentier. Tues–Sat 8am–1pm & 4–7pm, Sun 9am–1pm.

**Place d'Aligre** 12ᵉ; M° Ledru-Rollin. Tues–Sun until 12.30pm.

**Raspail** Bd Raspail, between rue du Cherche-Midi & rue de Rennes, 6ᵉ; M° Rennes. Tues & Fri 7/8am–1/2.30pm, organic market Sun 9am–3pm.

**Richard Lenoir** Bd Richard Lenoir, 11ᵉ; M° Bastille/ Richard Lenoir. Thurs & Sun 7/8am–1/2.30pm.

**Ternes** (flowers) Rue Lemercier, 17ᵉ; M° Ternes. Tues–Sun 8am–7.30pm.

even bigger than that of rival Galeries Lafayette. Mon–Wed, Fri & Sat 9.35am–8pm, Thurs 9.35am–10pm.

## FOOD AND DRINK

**Barthélémy** 51 rue de Grenelle, 7ᵉ ☎01 45 48 56 75; Mᵒ Bac; map pp.94–95. Purveyors of carefully ripened and meticulously stored seasonal cheeses to the rich and powerful. Delivery available. Sept–July Tues–Fri 8.30am–1pm & 4–7.15pm, Sat 8.30am–1.30pm & 3–7pm.

**Les Caves Augé** 116 bd Haussmann, 8ᵉ ☎01 45 22 16 97, ☷cavesauge.com; Mᵒ St-Augustin; map pp.68–69. This old-fashioned, wood-panelled shop is the oldest *cave* in Paris and sells not only fine wines, but also a wide selection of port, armagnac, cognac and champagne. Mon 1–7.30pm, Tues–Sat 9am–7.30pm.

**Debauve et Gallais** 30 rue des Sts-Pères, 7ᵉ ☎01 45 48 54 67, ☷debauve-et-gallais.fr; Mᵒ St-Germain-des-Prés/Sèvres-Babylone; map pp.94–95. A beautiful, ancient shop specializing in ambrosial chocolates. Mon–Sat 9am–7pm.

**Fauchon** 26 place de la Madeleine, 8ᵉ ☎01 70 39 38 00, ☷fauchon.com; Mᵒ Madeleine; map pp.68–69. A dazzling range of exquisite groceries and wine; just the place for presents of tea, jam, truffles, chocolates, exotic vinegars and mustards etc. There's a *traiteur* (deli) which stays open until 9pm and a swish restaurant. Mon–Sat 9am–7pm.

**Hédiard** 21 place de la Madeleine, 8ᵉ ☎01 43 12 88 88, ☷hediard.fr; Mᵒ Madeleine; map pp.68–69. The aristocrat's grocer since 1850; there are several other branches throughout the city. Mon–Sat 9am–8.30pm.

**Mariage Frères** 30 rue du Bourg-Tibourg, 4ᵉ ☎01 42 72 28 11, ☷mariagesfreres.com; Mᵒ Hôtel-de-Ville;

map pp.82–83. Hundreds of teas, neatly packed in tins, line the floor-to-ceiling shelves of this 100-year-old emporium. There's a *salon de thé* in the back with exquisite pastries (daily noon–7pm). Daily 10.30am–7.30pm.

**Poilâne** 8 rue du Cherche-Midi, 6ᵉ ☎01 45 48 42 59, ☷poilane.fr; Mᵒ Sèvres-Babylone; map pp.82–83. You can order the famous, traditionally made sourdough *pain Poilâne* online, or visit the delicious-smelling store for loaves and baked goods. Branches at 49 bd de Grenelle, 15ᵉ (☎01 45 79 11 49; Mᵒ Duplex), and 38 rue Debelleyme, 3ᵉ (☎01 44 61 83 39; Mᵒ Filles du Calvaire). Main branch Mon–Sat 7.15am–8.15pm; others Tues–Sun 7.15am–8.15pm.

## FLEA MARKETS

**Place d'Aligre** 12ᵉ; Mᵒ Ledru-Rollin. A small flea market and the only one located in the city proper, peddling secondhand clothes and bric-a-brac – anything from old gramophone players to odd bits of crockery. Tues–Sun 7.30am–12.30pm.

**Porte de Montreuil** 20ᵉ; Mᵒ Porte-de-Montreuil. The most junkyard-like of all the *marchés aux puces*, and the best for secondhand clothes – it's cheapest on Mon when leftovers from the weekend are sold off. Also good for old furniture and household goods. Sat–Mon 7am–7.30pm.

**Porte de Vanves** Av Georges-Lafenestre/av Marc-Sangnier, 14ᵉ; Mᵒ Porte-de-Vanves. The best for bric-a-brac and Parisian knick-knacks. Sat & Sun 7am–1pm (Marc-Sangnier), all day (Georges-Lafenestre).

**St-Ouen/Porte de Clignancourt** 18ᵉ; Mᵒ Porte-de-Clignancourt. The biggest and most touristy flea market, with nearly a thousand stalls selling new and used clothes, shoes, records, books and junk of all sorts, along with expensive antiques. Sat–Mon 7.30am–6pm.

## DIRECTORY

**Banks and exchange** Cash machines (ATMs) are located at all airports and mainline train stations, and at most of the banks in town. Beware of money-exchange bureaus and automatic exchange machines, however, which may advertise the selling rather than buying rate and add on hefty commission fees.

**Embassies/Consulates** Australia, 4 rue Jean-Rey, 15ᵉ ☎01 40 59 33 00, ☷france.embassy.gov.au, Mᵒ Bir-Hakeim; Canada, 35 av Montaigne, 8ᵉ ☎01 44 43 29 00, ☷amb-canada.fr, Mᵒ Franklin-D.-Roosevelt; Germany, 13–15 av Franklin D. Roosevelt, 8ᵉ ☎01 53 83 45 00, ☷paris.diplo.de, Mᵒ Franklin D. Roosevelt; Ireland, 4 rue Rude, 16ᵉ ☎01 44 17 67 00, ☷embassyofireland.com, Mᵒ Charles-de-Gaulle-Étoile; New Zealand, 7ter, rue Léonardo-de-Vinci, 16ᵉ ☎01 45 01 43 43, ☷nzembassy .com/france, Mᵒ Victor-Hugo; South Africa, 59 Quai d'Orsay, 7ᵉ ☎01 53 59 23 23, ☷afriquesud.net, Mᵒ Invalides; UK, 35 rue du Faubourg-St-Honoré, 8ᵉ ☎01 44

51 31 00, ☷http://ukinfrance.fco.gov.uk, Mᵒ Concorde; US, 2 av Gabriel, 8ᵉ ☎01 43 12 22 22, ☷france.usembassy .gov, Mᵒ Concorde.

**Health** The private association SOS Médecins (☎36 24) offers 24hr medical help. In emergencies, call an ambulance on ☎15, or the Sapeurs-Pompiers on ☎18. If you require longer-term outpatient care, perhaps, or if you prefer not to avail yourself of France's superb healthcare system, then consider one of the English-speaking private, not-for-profit hospitals. These include the Hertford British Hospital, 3 rue Barbès, Levallois-Perret (☎01 46 39 22 22, ☷british -hospital.org; Mᵒ Anatole-France) and the American Hospital, 63 bd Victor-Hugo, Neuilly-sur-Seine (☎01 46 41 25 25, ☷american-hospital.org; Mᵒ Porte-Maillot then bus #82 to terminus).

**Left luggage** Lockers are available at all train stations.

**Lost property** Your first port of call should be the Commissariat de Police for the arrondissement where you think the loss took place; the next step is the central police Bureau des Objets Trouvés, 36 rue des Morillons, 15e; Mº Convention (☎08 21 00 25 25; Mon–Thurs 8.30am–5pm, Fri 8.30am–4.30pm). If you lose your passport, report it to a police station and then your embassy.

**Pharmacies** 24hr service at: Dhéry, 84 av des Champs-Élysées, 8e; Mº George-V (☎01 45 62 02 41); 6 place Clichy,

9e; Mº Blanche (☎01 48 74 65 18). All pharmacies, if closed, post the address of one nearby that stays open late (*pharmacie de garde*).

**Police** ☎17 (☎112 from a mobile) for emergencies. To report a theft, go to the Commissariat de Police of the arrondissement in which the theft took place.

# Around Paris

The region around the capital – the **Île de France** – and the borders of the neighbouring provinces are studded with large-scale **châteaux**. Many were royal or noble hunting retreats, while some – like gargantuan **Versailles** – were for more serious state show. **Vaux-le-Vicomte** has perhaps the most harmonious architecture, **Chantilly** the finest art collection and **Fontainebleau** the most gorgeous interiors. Two of the world's loveliest cathedrals also lie within easy reach of Paris: at **St-Denis**, on the edge of Paris, the Gothic style was born; at **Chartres**, it reached its exquisite pinnacle. St-Denis also offers a fascinating collection of royal tombs, while Chartres rises from a delightful medieval town. The most popular attraction by far, however, is **Disneyland Paris**, out beyond the satellite town of **Marne-la-Vallée**. All of the places detailed here are easily accessible from Paris by public transport.

## Basilique St-Denis

St-Denis, 10km north of the centre of Paris; 300m south of the Basilique-de-Saint-Denis métro stop • April–Sept Mon–Sat 10am–6.15pm, Sun noon–6.15pm; Oct–March Mon–Sat 10am–5pm, Sun noon–5.15pm • €7.50 • Mº St-Denis-Basilique

**ST-DENIS**'s chief claim to fame is its magnificent cathedral. Begun in the first half of the twelfth century, the **Basilique St-Denis** is generally regarded as the birthplace of the Gothic style in European architecture. With its two towers (the northern one collapsed in 1837), three large sculpted portals and high rose window, the west front set the pattern of Gothic facades to come, but it's in the choir that you best see the emergence of the new style: the use of the pointed arch, the ribbed vault and the long shafts of half-column rising from pillar to roof. It's beautifully lit, thanks to the transept windows – so big that they occupy their entire end walls – and the clerestory, which is almost entirely made of glass – another first.

Legend holds that the first church here was founded by a mid-third-century Parisian bishop, later known as St-Denis. The story goes that after he was beheaded for his beliefs at Montmartre (Mount of the Martyr), he picked up his head and walked to St-Denis, thereby establishing the abbey. The site's **royal history** began with the coronation of Pepin the Short in 754, but it wasn't until the reign of Hugues Capet, in 996, that it became the customary burial place of the kings of France. Since then, all but three of France's kings have been interred here, and their fine tombs and effigies are distributed about the **necropolis** (closed during services) in the transepts and ambulatory.

Immediately on the left of the entrance, in the south transept, is one of the most bizarre sights: the bare feet of **François 1er** and his wife Claude de France peeking out of their enormous Renaissance memorial. Beside the steps to the ambulatory lies **Charles V**, the first king to have his funeral effigy carved from life, on the day of his coronation in 1364. Alongside him is his wife Jeanne de Bourbon, who clutches the sack of her own entrails to her chest – a reminder that royalty was traditionally eviscerated at death, the flesh boiled away from the bones and buried separately. Up the steps and round to the right, a florid Louis XVI and busty **Marie-Antoinette** – often graced by bouquets of flowers – kneel in prayer. The pious scene was sculpted in 1830, long after their execution.

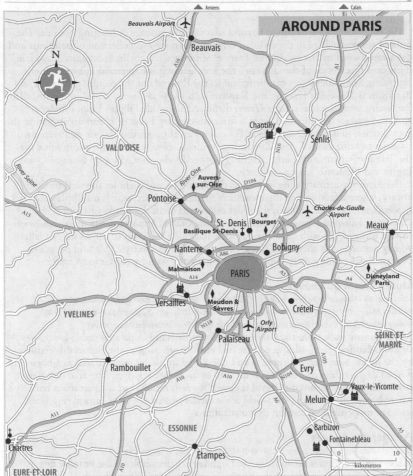

# Chantilly

**CHANTILLY**, a small town 40km north of Paris, is famous for its horses. Scores of thoroughbreds can be seen thundering along the forest rides of a morning, and two of the season's classiest flat races, the Jockey Club and the Prix de Diane, are held here.

### Chantilly Château

Daily except Tues: château April–Oct 10am–6pm, Nov–March 10.30am–5pm; park April–Oct 10am–8pm, Nov–March 10.30am–6pm • Château and park €14, park only €7 • Ⓦ chateaudechantilly.com • Trains almost every hour from Gare du Nord to Chantilly Gouvieux station (30min); free shuttle buses meet some trains, otherwise it's a pleasant 2km stroll through the forest – turn right outside the station, then left at the major roundabout on the signposted footpath

The Chantilly estate used to belong to two of the most powerful clans in France: first the Montmorencys, then, through marriage, to the Condés. The present **Château** was built in the late nineteenth century on the ruins of the Grand Château, for the Grand Condé, who helped Louis XIV smash Spanish power in the mid-seventeenth century. It's a beautiful structure, graceful and romantic, surrounded by water and looking out over a formal arrangement of pools and pathways designed by Le Nôtre,

Louis XIV's gardener.

The entrance is across a moat, beyond two realistic bronzes of hunting hounds. The bulk of what you'll see in the château is from the enormous collection of **paintings and drawings** owned by the Institut de France. Stipulated to remain as organized by Henri d'Orléans (the donor of the château), the arrangement is haphazard but immensely satisfying. Some highlights can be found in the Rotunda of the picture gallery – Piero di Cosimo's *Simonetta Vespucci* and Raphael's *La Vierge de Lorette* – and in the so-called Sanctuary, with Raphael's *Three Graces* displayed alongside Filippo Lippi's *Esther et Assuerius* and forty miniatures from a fifteenth-century Book of Hours attributed to the great French Renaissance artist Jean Fouquet. Pass through the Galerie de Psyche, with its series of sepia stained glass illustrating Apuleius' *Golden Ass*, to the room known as the Tribune, where Italian art, including Botticelli's *Autumn*, takes up two walls, and Ingres and Delacroix have a wall each.

The sixteenth-century wing known as the Petit Château includes the well-stocked **library**, where a facsimile of the museum's single greatest treasure is on display, *Les Très Riches Heures du Duc de Berry*, the most celebrated of all the Books of Hours. The remaining half-dozen rooms on the tour of the **Grands Appartements** mostly show off superb furnishings, with exquisite *boiseries* panelling the walls of the Monkey Gallery, wittily painted with allegorical stories in a pseudo-Chinese style. A grand parade of canvases in the long gallery depicts the many battles won by the Grand Condé.

### Musée Vivant du Cheval

7 rue Connétable • **Museum** Closed for renovation until 2014, check website for updated opening hours **Demonstrations** Most days 2.30pm, often at 11am too, but check online • €11, €18 combined ticket with château and park • ☎ 03 44 27 31 80, ⓦ museevivantducheval.fr • Trains almost every hour from Gare du Nord to Chantilly Gouvieux station (30min)

A five-minute walk from the Château de Chantilly stands a palatial stable block, **Les Grandes Ecuries**. The building was erected at the beginning of the eighteenth century by the incumbent Condé prince, who believed he would be reincarnated as a horse and wished to provide accommodation for 240 of his future relatives. The actual museum part of the **Musée Vivant du Cheval** is closed for restoration, but the vast main hall, where breeds from around the world are stalled, remains open; its central ring is the scene of meticulous equestrian **demonstrations**.

### Potager des Princes

17 rue Faisanderie • April–Oct daily 2–7pm • €8.50 • ☎ 03 44 57 39 66, ⓦ potagerdesprinces.com

A few hundred metres down from the Grandes Ecuries stables is the **Potager des Princes**, or "kitchen garden of the princes" – a huge horticultural haven of herbs, salad plants and artistically planted vegetables, as designed for the Grand Condé by the ubiquitous Le Nôtre.

## Disneyland Paris

Children will love **Disneyland Paris** – and most adults too, for all the rampant commercialism. If you're not staying in one of the resort hotels, in Disney Village, it's easy to visit in a day-trip from the capital, 25km away. There are two main areas: **Disneyland Park**, which has most of the really big rides, and **Walt Disney Studios Park**, which offers more technological rides based on animation – though there are plenty of thrill rides too.

### Disneyland Park

**Disneyland Park** has a variety of good thrill rides, though the majority of attractions remain relatively sedate. The Magic Kingdom is divided into four "lands" radiating out from **Main Street USA**. **Fantasyland** appeals to the tinies, with "It's a Small World", Sleeping Beauty's Castle, Peter Pan's Flight and Dumbo the Flying Elephant among its attractions. **Adventureland** has the most outlandish sets and two of the best rides – Pirates of the Caribbean and Indiana Jones and the Temple of Peril. **Frontierland**, loosely set in the Wild West, features the hair-raising roller coaster Big Thunder Mountain, modelled on a runaway mine train, and the gothic Phantom Manor. In **Discoveryland** there's a 3-D experience called "Honey, I Shrunk The Audience", an interactive Buzz Lightyear laser battle, and the terrifyingly fast Space Mountain roller coasters. The grand **parade** of floats representing all your favourite characters sallies down Main Street USA at about 7pm every day, with smaller events, special shows and fireworks displays occurring regularly.

### Walt Disney Studios Park

Though it has its share of big rides – among them the Rock 'n' Roller Coaster Starring Aerosmith, a corkscrew-looping, metal-playing white-knuckler, and the Twilight Zone Tower of Terror, with its gut-churning elevator drop – the **Walt Disney Studios Park** largely focuses on what Disney was and is still renowned for – animation. You can try your hand at drawing, be part of the audience in a mocked-up film or TV set, and enjoy special effects and stunt shows. The virtual reality Armageddon ride is genuinely thrilling – your space station is bombarded by meteors – the tram tour through the collapsing Catastrophe Canyon is good fun, and smaller children will be bowled over by their live interactions with that alarmingly crazed blue alien, Stitch.

#### ARRIVAL AND DEPARTURE                                           DISNEYLAND PARIS

**By train** From Paris, take RER line A from Châtelet-Les Halles, Gare-de-Lyon or Nation to Marne-la-Vallée/Chessy station, which is opposite the main park gates (40min; €7.10 one way). Marne-la-Vallée/Chessy also has its own TGV train station, linked to Lille and Lyon, as well as London (via special Eurostar trains).
**From the airport** Shuttle buses from Charles de Gaulle

and Orly (every 20min–1hr from 8.30am; 45min; €19 one-way, €15 for children aged 3 to 12; ⓦ vea.fr/uk).
**By car** Disneyland Paris is a 32km drive east of Paris along the A4: take the "Porte de Bercy" exit off the *périphérique*, then follow "direction Metz/Nancy", leaving at exit 14. From Calais follow the A26, changing to the A1, the A104 and finally the A4.

#### INFORMATION

**Website** ⓦ disneylandparis.co.uk
**Admission passes** Most people buy their tickets online, but you can also get them at tourist offices. A "1-day/1-Park" ticket costs €53, or €48 for children aged 3–11; the ticket allows entry to either the Disneyland Park or Walt Disney Studios Park. One-day tickets

allowing access to both parks cost €64/57; multi-day tickets are also available. The website details various seasonal offers.
**Opening hours** Hours vary, and should be checked when you buy your ticket, but are usually 9/10am–6/8pm, or until 11pm in high summer.

#### ACCOMMODATION

Disney's six themed, heavily designed hotels are a mixed bag, and only worth staying in as part of a multi-day package booked through an agent, or through Disneyland. To really economize, you could camp.

**Camping du Parc de la Colline** Rte de Lagny, Torcy ⓦ camping-de-la-colline.com. On the RER line A4, this campsite, near Disneyland, is open all year and provides

shuttle service to the parks. Some bungalow accommodation. **€32.80**

## Vaux-le-Vicomte

46km southeast of Paris, 7km east of Melun • **Château** Mid-March to mid-Nov daily 10am–6pm • €14, €16 including Apartements Privés de Fouquet; garden only €8 **Candlelight evenings** May to early Oct Sat 8pm–midnight • €17 **Fountains** April to mid-Oct 2nd & last Sat of the month 4–6pm • ☎ 01 64 14 41 90. ⓦ vaux-le-vicomte.com • Trains from Gare de Lyon to Melun (every 30min; 25min); from where an infrequent shuttle (April–Oct Sat & Sun; €7 return) heads to the château (7km); a taxi from Melun station costs around €16

Of all the great mansions within reach of a day's outing from Paris, the classical **Château of Vaux-le-Vicomte** is the most architecturally harmonious and aesthetically

**1**

pleasing – and the most human in scale. Louis XIV's finance minister, Nicholas Fouquet, had the château built between 1656 and 1661 at colossal expense, using the top designers of the day – architect Le Vau, painter Le Brun and landscape gardener Le Nôtre. The result was magnificence and precision in perfect proportion, and a bill that could only be paid by someone who occasionally confused the state's accounts with his own. In September 1661, weeks after his sumptuous and showy house-warming party, he was arrested – by d'Artagnan of **Musketeer** fame – charged with embezzlement, of which he was certainly guilty, and clapped into jail for life. Thereupon, the design trio was carted off to build the king's own piece of one-upmanship, the palace of Versailles.

Seen from the entrance, the château is an austere grey pile surrounded by an artificial moat. It's only when you go through to the south side – where clipped box and yew, fountains and statuary stand in formal gardens – that you can look back and appreciate the very harmonious and very French combination of steep, tall roof and central dome with classical pediment and pilasters. Inside, the main artistic interest lies in the work of Le Brun. He was responsible for the two fine **tapestries** in the entrance, made in the local workshops set up by Fouquet specifically to adorn his house, as well as numerous **painted ceilings** including the one in the Salon des Muses, *Sleep* in the Cabinet des Jeux, and the so-called King's Bedroom, whose decor is the first example of the style that became known as "Louis Quatorze".

Other points of interest are the **kitchens**, which have not been altered since construction, and a room displaying letters in the hand of Fouquet, Louis XIV and other notables. The **Musée des Equipages** in the stables comprises a collection of horse-drawn vehicles, complete with model horses.

On Saturday evenings in summer the château's state rooms and gardens are illuminated with two thousand **candles**, as they probably were on the occasion of Fouquet's fateful party; the classical music, sadly, is no longer live. The **fountains** can be seen in action twice a month.

## Fontainebleau Château

70km from Paris, 16km from the A6 *autoroute* (exit Fontainebleau) • **Château** Daily except Tues: April–Sept 9.30am–6pm; Oct–March 9.30am–5pm • €10 **Petits Appartements** Call on the day for timetables of guided tours • €6.50 • ☎ 01 60 71 50 70 or ☎ 01 60 71 50 60 for Petits Appartements, ⓦ musee-chateau-fontainebleau.fr • Trains from Gare de Lyon to Fontainebleau-Avon station (40min), from where shuttle buses take you to the château gates (15min)

The ramblingly magnificent **Fontainebleau Château** owes its existence to the surrounding forest, which made it the perfect base for royal hunting expeditions. A lodge was built here as early as the twelfth century, but it only began its transformation into a luxurious palace during the 1500s on the initiative of François I, who imported a colony of Italian artists – most notably Rosso il Fiorentino and Niccolò dell'Abate – to carry out the decoration. Their work is best seen in the celebrated **Galerie François I** – a sumptuously decorated long gallery that had a seminal influence on the development of French aristocratic art and design – and the dazzlingly frescoed **Salle de Bal**. A few years later, Henri IV commissioned the resplendent decoration of the **chapelle de la Trinité**.

Utterly contrasting in style to the rest of the château are the sober but elegant **Petits Appartements**, the private rooms of Napoleon, his wife and their intimate entourage. You have to buy a separate ticket to join the (obligatory) guided tour, but a tour of the **Musée Napoléon** – which displays a wide variety of personal and official souvenirs – is included in the main château ticket.

The **gardens** are equally splendid, but if you want to escape to the relative wilds, note that the surrounding **forest** of Fontainebleau is full of walking and cycling trails, all marked on the Michelin map *Environs de Paris*.

# Château de Versailles

Some 20km southwest of Paris lies Louis XIV's extraordinary **Château de Versailles**. With 700 rooms, 67 staircases and 352 fireplaces alone, Versailles is, without doubt, the apotheosis of French regal indulgence. While it's possible to see the whole complex in one day, it's undeniably tiring. The best plan to avoid the worst of the crowds is to head in the morning through the glorious **gardens** (free), with their perfectly symmetrical lawns, grand vistas, statuary, fountains and pools, to **Marie Antoinette's estate**, leaving the main palace to the tour buses. You can then work your way backwards, leaving the palace, and in particular the Hall of Mirrors, till as late as possible.

## The palace

Driven by envy of his finance minister's château at Vaux-le-Vicomte (see p.147), the young Louis XIV recruited the same design team – architect Le Vau, painter Le Brun and gardener Le Nôtre – to create a **palace** a hundred times bigger. Construction began in 1664 and lasted virtually until Louis XIV's death in 1715. Second only to God, and the head of an immensely powerful state, Louis was an institution rather than a private individual. His risings and sittings, comings and goings, were minutely regulated and rigidly encased in ceremony, attendance at which was an honour much sought after by courtiers. Versailles was the headquarters of every arm of the state, and the entire court of around 3500 nobles lived in the palace (in a state of squalor, according to contemporary accounts).

Following the king's death, the château was abandoned for a few years before being reoccupied by Louis XV in 1722. It remained a residence of the royal family until the Revolution of 1789, when the furniture was sold and the pictures dispatched to the Louvre. Thereafter Versailles fell into ruin until Louis-Philippe established his giant museum of French Glory here – it still exists, though most is mothballed. In 1871, during the Paris Commune, the château became the seat of the nationalist government, and the French parliament continued to meet in Louis XV's opera building until 1879.

Without a guide you can visit the **State Apartments**, used for the king's official business. A procession of gilded drawing rooms leads to the dazzling **Galerie des Glaces** (Hall of Mirrors), where the Treaty of Versailles was signed after World War I. More fabulously rich rooms, this time belonging to the **queen's apartments**, line the northern wing, beginning with the queen's bedchamber, which has been restored exactly as it was in its last refit, of 1787, with hardly a surface unadorned with gold leaf.

## The Domaine de Marie-Antoinette

Hidden away in the northern reaches of the gardens is the **Domaine de Marie-Antoinette**, the young queen's country retreat, where she found relief from the stifling etiquette of the court. Here she commissioned some dozen or so buildings, sparing no expense and imposing her own style and tastes throughout (and gaining herself a reputation for extravagance that did her no favours).

The centrepiece of the Domaine de Marie-Antoinette is the elegant Neoclassical **Petit Trianon** palace, built by Gabriel in the 1760s for Louis XV's mistress, Mme de Pompadour, and given to Marie-Antoinette by her husband Louis XVI as a wedding gift. The interior boasts an intriguing *cabinet des glaces montantes*, a pale-blue salon fitted with sliding mirrors that could be moved to conceal the windows, creating a more intimate space.

Also included in the ticket for the Domaine is the Italianate **Grand Trianon** palace, which was designed by Hardouin-Mansart in 1687 as a country retreat for Louis XIV and refurbished in Empire style by Napoleon, who stayed here intermittently between 1805 and 1813.

**1**

The gardens

West of the Petit Trianon, in the formal **Jardin français**, is the **Petit Théâtre** where Marie-Antoinette would regularly perform, often as a maid or shepherdess, before the king and members of her inner circle. On the other side of the palace lies the bucolic **Jardin anglais**, impossibly picturesque with its little winding stream, grassy banks and grotto, and the enchanting, if bizarre, **Hameau de la Reine**, a play village and farm where the queen indulged her fashionable Rousseau-inspired fantasy of returning to the "natural" life.

## ARRIVAL AND INFORMATION
## CHÂTEAU DE VERSAILLES

**By train** Take the RER line C5 from Champ de Mars or another Left Bank station to Versailles-Rive Gauche (35min); the palace is an 8min walk away.

**Website** ⓦ chateauversailles.fr.

**Opening hours** Château Tues–Sun: April–Sept 9am–6.30pm; Oct–March 9am–5.30pm; Domaine de Marie Antoinette Tues–Sun: April–Oct noon–6.30pm; Nov–March noon–5pm.

**Tickets** The Passeport Versailles (April–Oct Tues–Fri €18, Sat & Sun €25; Nov–March €18; under-26s resident in the EU and under-18s free) is a one-day pass that gives you access to all the main sights, including the Trianons, and includes audioguides. Tickets for the château alone cost €15, including audioguide, while admission to

Marie-Antoinette's estate, including both Trianon palaces, is €10. All tickets, including the Passeport, can be bought and printed out from the website. You can also buy the Passeport at the château itself up until 3pm on the day, though this of course means queuing.

**Guided tours** Excellent, English-language tours (€16) take you to wings that you wouldn't otherwise get to see; they can be booked online or in the morning at the information point – turn up early to make sure of a place.

**Getting around** Distances in the estate are considerable, so you may want to make use of the *petit train* that shuttles between the terrace in front of the château and the Trianons. You could also rent a buggy (you'll need a driving licence) or a bike.

# Chartres

About 80km southwest of Paris, **CHARTRES** is a modest but charming market town whose existence is almost entirely overshadowed by its extraordinary Gothic **cathedral**. One of the world's most astounding buildings, the cathedral is best experienced early or late in the day when visitors are fewer and the low sun transmits the stained-glass colours to the interior stone.

## Chartres cathedral

Cloître Notre-Dame • **Cathedral** Daily 8.30am–7.30pm **North tower** May–Aug 9.30am–noon & 2–5.40pm, Sun 2–5.30pm; Sept–April Mon–Sat 9.30–noon & 2–4.30pm, Sun 2–4.30pm • Free • ☏ 02 37 21 75 02, ⓦ diocesechartres.com/cathedrale

Built between 1194 and 1260, the **Chartres cathedral** was one of the quickest ever constructed and, as a result, preserves a uniquely harmonious design. The cathedral's official name, Notre-Dame (Our Lady), and its staggering size and architectural richness are owed to its holiest relic, the **Sancta Camisia** – supposed to have been the robe Mary wore when she gave birth to Jesus – which was discovered here, miraculously unharmed, three days after an earlier Romanesque structure burnt down in 1194. In the heyday of the pilgrimage to Santiago de Compostela hordes of medieval pilgrims would stop here on their way to Spain – note the sloping floor, which allowed it to be washed down more easily. The Sancta Camisia still exists, though it has been rolled up and put into storage.

The geometry of the building is unique in being almost unaltered since its consecration, and virtually all of the magnificent **stained glass** is original thirteenth-century work. But the paint and gilt that once brought the portal sculptures to life has vanished, while the walls have lost the whitewash that reflected the vivid colours of the stained glass. Worse still, the high altar has been brought down into the body of the church, and chairs usually cover the thirteenth-century **labyrinth** on the floor of the nave. The cathedral's **stonework**, however, is still captivating, particularly the **choir screen**, which curves around the ambulatory. Like the south tower and spire that abuts it, the mid-twelfth-century **Royal Portal** actually survives from the earlier Romanesque church. You have to pay extra to visit the crypt and treasury, though these are relatively unimpressive. Crowds permitting, it's worth climbing the **north tower** for its bird's-eye view of the sculptures and structure of the cathedral.

## Musée des Beaux Arts

29 Cloître Notre-Dame • May–Oct Mon & Wed–Sat 10am–noon & 2–6pm, Sun 2–6pm; Nov–April Mon & Wed–Sat 10am–noon & 2–5pm, Sun 2–5pm • €3.10

The **Musée des Beaux Arts**, in the former episcopal palace just north of the cathedral, has some beautiful tapestries, work by the French Fauvist Vlaminck, and the Spanish Baroque painter Zurbarán's *Sainte Lucie*. Behind the museum, rue Chantault leads past old townhouses to the River Eure and Pont du Massacre.

| ARRIVAL AND INFORMATION | CHARTRES |
|---|---|

**By train** Trains run from Paris's Gare du Montparnasse (Mon–Fri at least hourly; 1hr). The *gare SNCF* is 5min walk from the cathedral, and from the old town.
**Tourist office** Maison du Saumon, Place de la Poissonnerie, right by the cathedral (April–Sept Mon–Sat 9am–7pm, Sun 9.30am–5.30pm; Oct–March Mon–Sat 9am–6pm, Sun 9.30am–5.30pm; ☎ 02 37 18 26 26, ⓦ chartres-tourisme.com).

### EATING

For a snack, there are lots of places with outside tables on rue Cloître-Notre-Dame, opposite the south side of the cathedral.

**Les Feuillantines** 4 rue Bourg ☎ 02 37 30 22 21. This welcoming restaurant Just down the road from the tourist office, has some outside tables; the traditional food on the €26 *menu* is good enough to satisfy even locals. Mon 7–9.30pm, Tues–Sat noon–1.30pm & 7–9.30pm.

# The north

MONTREUIL-SUR-MER

# The north

When conjuring up exotic holiday locations, you're unlikely to light upon the north of France. Even among the French, the most enthusiastic tourists of their own country, it has few adherents. Largely flat Artois and Flanders include some of the most heavily industrialized parts of the country, while across the giant fields of sparsely populated Picardy, a few drops of rain are all that is required for total gloom to descend. Coming from Britain it's probable, however, that you'll arrive and leave France via this region, possibly through the busy ferry port of Calais, and there are several good reasons to stop off in the area. Dunkerque offers a bustling, university atmosphere and poignant war memorials, and just inland, the delightful village of Cassel is a rare example of a Flemish hill settlement. St-Omer and Montreuil-sur-Mer are also strong contenders in terms of charm and interest.

Northern France has always been on the path of various invaders into the country, from northern mainland Europe as well as from Britain, and the events that have taken place in Flanders, Artois and Picardy have shaped both French and world history. The bloodiest battles were those of World War I, above all the **Battle of the Somme**, which took place north of Amiens, and **Vimy Ridge**, near Arras, where the trenches have been preserved in perpetuity; a visit to any of these is highly recommended in order to understand the sacrifice and futility of war.

    **Picardy**, meanwhile, boasts some of France's finest cathedrals, including those at **Amiens**, **Beauvais** and **Laon**. Other attractions include the bird sanctuary of **Marquenterre**; the wooded wilderness of the **Ardennes**; industrial archeology in the Lewarde coalfields around **Douai**, where Zola's *Germinal* was set; the great medieval castle of **Coucy-le-Château**; and the battle sites of the Middle Ages, **Agincourt** and **Crécy**, familiar names in the long history of Anglo–French rivalry. In city centres like **Lille**, you'll find your fill of food, culture and entertainment.

---

**GETTING THERE AND AROUND**                                                    **THE NORTH**

The Channel Tunnel emerges at Sangatte, 5km southwest of Calais. The "Chunnel" has reduced crossing times (see p.28) from the UK to just 30min, with the efficient but pricey *autoroute* waiting to whisk you away to your ultimate destination.

**By train** Eurostar will get you to Calais or Lille from London, Brussels and Paris and a comprehensive local train network serves both large and small towns (ⓦ ter-sncf.com).

**By bus** There is a good local bus network operating in and around the main towns, but long distance bus routes only operate between large centres.

---

# Dunkerque and around

Less reliant than Boulogne-sur-Mer (see p.166) or Calais (see p.162) on the cross-channel ferry trade, **DUNKERQUE** is the liveliest of the three big Channel ports,

FRENCH MILITARY CEMETERY, PICARDY

# Highlights

**❶ La Coupole** This vast complex built to launch the V2 bombs on London takes you from the 1930s through to the Cold War and the space race. **See p.161**

**❷ Cité Internationale de la Dentelle et de la Mode de Calais** Housed in a former factory, this entertaining museum tells the story of lace-making in Calais through films, machines and glorious fashions. **See p.163**

**❸ Parc Ornithologique du Marquenterre** From geese and godwits to storks and spoonbills, a huge variety of birds make their home amid briny meres and tamarisk-fringed dunes. **See p.171**

**❹ Lillois cuisine** Eat anything from the ubiquitous *moules-frites*, washed down with micro-brewed beer, to fried *escargots* with onions roasted in lavender oil in the historic centre of Lille, the cultural capital of northern France. **See p.177**

**❺ World War I monuments in the Somme** Moving memorials by Lutyens and others to the victims of the trenches. **See p.182**

**❻ Son et lumière at Amiens Cathedral** The biggest Gothic building in France, brought to life by sound and light shows on summer evenings. **See p.188**

HIGHLIGHTS ARE MARKED ON THE MAP ON P.156

a university town with an appealing, boat-filled inner harbour, the **Bassin du Commerce**. It was from the shores of **Malo-les-Bains**, an attractive beachfront suburb, that the evacuation of Allied troops took place in 1940. Dunkerque remains France's third largest port and a massive industrial centre, its oil refineries and steelworks producing a quarter of the total French output. Devastated during World War II, central Dunkerque is largely the brick-built product of postwar reconstruction, slightly more ambitious and stylish than the rebuild of Calais or Boulogne-sur-Mer. But among the 1950s architecture, you come across some

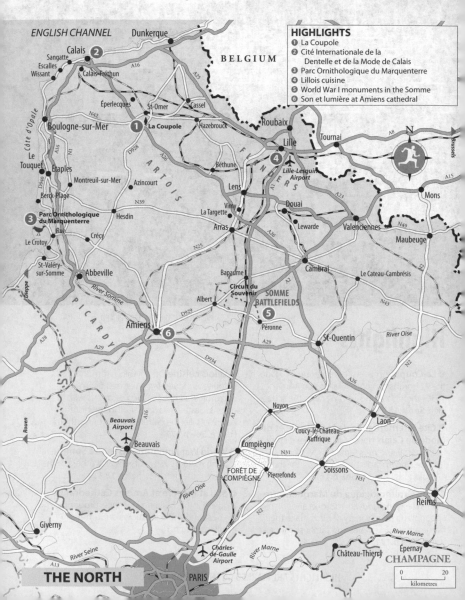

**HIGHLIGHTS**

❶ La Coupole
❷ Cité Internationale de la Dentelle et de la Mode de Calais
❸ Parc Ornithologique du Marquenterre
❹ Lillois cuisine
❺ World War I monuments in the Somme
❻ Son et lumière at Amiens cathedral

THE NORTH

delightful Art Nouveau-style villas with curving forms and balconies.

Among the few buildings of any significance that survived World War II (or were rebuilt afterwards) are the tall medieval brick **belfry**, the town's chief landmark; the impressive, bullet-ridden fifteenth-century **church of St-Éloi** opposite, to which the belfry belonged; and, a few blocks north of the church on place Charles-Valentin, the early twentieth-century **Hôtel de Ville**, a giant Flemish fancy to rival that of Calais.

## Musée des Beaux-Arts

Place du Géneral-de-Gaulle • Tues–Sun 10am–12.15pm & 2–6pm • €4.50 • ☎ 03 28 59 21 65

With notable Flemish, Dutch, French and Italian paintings and sculptures from the fourteenth to the twentieth-century, the impressive **Musée des Beaux-Arts** includes works such as Corot's *A Dune at Dunkirk*. Don't miss the room dedicated to the local hero, seventeenth-century privateer Jean Bart.

## Bassin du Commerce

The **Bassin du Commerce** is a lively and attractive stretch of water, housing not just fishing boats and yachts but some attractive preserved historic ships. Tours take you around the three-masted sailing ship **Duchesse Anne**, built in Germany in 1901, the Sandettie light ship and the Guild barge. They're all part of the **Musée à Flot** (daily July & Aug; guided tours 2.30pm, 3.30pm, 4.30pm; Sept–June guided tours Wed & Sun at 3.30pm, €7.50, or €10 joint ticket with Musée Portuaire, see below) – the "floating" half of the Musée Portuaire.

## Musée Portuaire

9 quai de la Citadelle • Daily except Tues: July & Aug 10am–6pm; Sept–June 10am–12.45pm & 1.30–6pm • €5 or €10 joint ticket with Bassin du Commerce (see above) • ☎ 03 28 63 33 39, ⓦ museeportuaire.com

The **Port Museum**, housed in a restored brick warehouse on the Bassin du Commerce, is particularly child-friendly. Engaging ship models, panoramas and period film footage lead you through the main events of Dunkerque's history, from its beginnings as a fishing hamlet. It's an easily digestible size and mounts good temporary exhibitions on related themes.

---

### REGIONAL FOOD AND DRINK

**French Flanders** has one of northern France's richest regional cuisines. Especially on the coast, the **seafood** – oysters, shrimps, scallops and **fish**, and above all, sole and turbot – are outstanding, while in Lille *moules-frites* are appreciated every bit as much as in neighbouring Belgium. Here, too, **beer** is the favourite drink, with pale and brown Pelforth the local brew. Traditional *estaminets* or brasseries also serve a range of dishes cooked in beer, most famously *carbonnade flamande*, a kind of beef stew; rabbit, chicken, game and fish may also be prepared *à la bière*. Other pot–cooked dishes include *hochepot* (a meaty broth), *waterzooi* (chicken in a creamy sauce) and *potjevlesch* (white meats in a rich sauce). In addition to *boulette d'Avesnes*, the **Flemish cheese** *par excellence* is the strong-flavoured *maroilles*, used to make *flamiche*, a kind of open tart of cheese pastry also made with leeks (*aux poireaux*). For the sweet-toothed, *crêpes à la cassonade* (pancakes with muscovado sugar) are often on menus, but **waffles** (*gaufres*) are the local speciality and come in two basic varieties: the thick honeycomb type served with sugar or cream, or the wafer-like biscuit filled with jam or syrup. Game looms large on menus in the Ardennes, with *pâté d'Ardennes* being the most famous dish and juniper berries used to flavour food *à l'Ardennaise*.

## Mémorial du Souvenir

32 Courtines du Bastion • April–Sept daily 10am–noon & 2–5pm • €4 • ☎ 03 28 66 79 21, ⓦ dynamo-dunkerque.com

The **Mémorial du Souvenir** is the place to discover more about the 1940 evacuations of Operation Dynamo that rescued 350,000 allied soldiers. It all starts with the short film in English that sets the scene, then a wander through vaults displaying photographs, maps, uniforms and military equipment of the time. It's a private museum run by volunteers and you'll possibly meet the elderly enthusiasts who were there during the evacuation – they'll recount a rare tale or two.

## LAAC

Jardin des Sculptures, Pont Lucien-Lefol • Tues–Sun 10am–12.15pm & 2–6pm • €4.50 • ☎ 03 28 29 56 00

In a park of sculptures just south of the Mémorial du Souvenir in the Pont Lucien-Lefol area, the worthwhile **LAAC** (**Lieu d'Art et Action Contemporaine**) specializes in the period from 1950 to 1980 and features works by the likes of Andy Warhol, Pierre Soulages and César.

## Malo-les-Bains

**Malo-les-Bains** is a pleasant nineteenth-century seaside suburb on the east side of Dunkerque, from whose vast sandy beach the Allied troops embarked in 1940. Digue des Alliés is the urban end of an extensive beachfront promenade lined with cafés and restaurants, though things are rather nicer further east along Digue de Mer, away from Dunkerque's industrial side. Much of the promenade's attractive architecture survived wartime destruction; there's more *fin-de-siècle* charm a few blocks inland, along avenue Faidherbe and its continuation avenue Kléber, and around leafy place Turenne with its dainty old-fashioned bandstand.

In high season a free bus, the Étoile de Mer, runs from the Port du Grand Large north of the Bassin du Commerce along the Digue de Mer to La Licorne on the east side of Malo. To get to Malo from Dunkerque all year round, take bus #3 from Place République in the centre to Parc des Sports in east Malo.

### ARRIVAL AND INFORMATION DUNKERQUE

**By train** Dunkerque's *gare SNCF* is on place de la Gare, a 10min walk from the town centre.
Destinations Calais-Ville (12 daily; 45min); Cassel (16 daily; 25min); Lille Europe (approx 2 hourly; 35min).
**By bus** The *gare routière* is located next to the *gare SNCF*. Information on ⓦ ligne-bcd.com.

Destinations Boulogne (5 daily; 1hr 30min); Calais (12 daily; 45min).
**Tourist office** Beffroi St-Eloi, rue de l'Amiral Ronarc'h (Mon–Fri 9.30am–12.30pm & 1.30–6.30pm, Sat 9.30am–6.30pm, Sun & public hols 10am–noon & 2–4pm; ☎ 03 28 66 79 21, ⓦ dunkirk-tourism.com).

### ACCOMMODATION

**Borel** 6 rue L'Hermite ☎ 03 28 66 51 80, ⓦ hotelborel .fr. Predominantly a business hotel, the *Borel* has good-sized rooms with conventional furnishings of dark wood and impressive bathrooms. It's a comfortable but rather anonymous three-star option, right on the Bassin du Commerce. €92
**Hirondelle** 46/48 av Faidherbe, Malo-les-Bains ☎ 03 28 63 17 65, ⓦ hotelhirondelle.com. Very near the beach, this bright *Logis de France* hotel occupies two buildings with newly renovated, comfortable en-suite rooms, including three adapted for people with limited mobility. The restaurant offers regional fish and shellfish with *menus* from €13.80–28.50, and a children's *menu*. €94

**La Licorne** 1005 bd de l'Europe Malo-les-Bains ☎ 03 28 69 26 68, ⓦ campingdelalicorne.com. On the eastern end of Digue de Mer, accessible by the #3 bus, you can pitch your tent or take your campervan near the beach. You can also book comfortable and spacious eco-lodges by the week. Closed Dec–March. Camping €12, lodges from €342.80
**Welcome** 37 rue Raymond-Poincaré ☎ 03 28 59 20 70, ⓦ hotel-welcome.fr. In the centre of town, the *Welcome* is basic but comfortable. The clean, small rooms are good for a one-night stay and the downstairs bar and colourful *L'Écume Bleue* restaurant offer good-value *menus* and a friendly, casual atmosphere. €80

2

**2**

## DUNKERQUE'S 1940 EVACUATION

The evacuation of 350,000 Allied troops from the beaches of **Dunkerque** from May 27 to June 4, 1940, has become legendary, concealing the fact that the Allies, through their own incompetence, almost lost their entire armed forces in the first weeks of the war.

The German army had taken just ten days to reach the English Channel and could easily have cut off the Allied armies. Hitler, unable to believe the ease with which he had overcome a numerically superior enemy, ordered his generals to halt their advance, giving Allied forces trapped in the Pas-de-Calais time to organize **Operation Dynamo**, the largest wartime evacuation ever undertaken. Initially it was hoped that around 10,000 men would be saved, but thanks to low-lying cloud and more than 1750 vessels – including pleasure cruisers, fishing boats and river ferries – 140,000 French and more than 200,000 British soldiers were successfully shipped back to England. The heroism of the boatmen and the relief at saving so many British soldiers were the cause of national celebration.

In France, however, the ratio of British to French evacuees caused bitter resentment, since Churchill had promised that the two sides would go *bras dessus, bras dessous* ("arm in arm"). Meanwhile, the British media played up the "remarkable discipline" of the troops as they waited to embark, the "victory" of the RAF over the Luftwaffe and the "disintegration" of the French army all around. In fact, there was widespread indiscipline in the early stages as men fought for places on board; the battle for the skies was evenly matched; and the French fought long and hard to cover the whole operation, some 150,000 of them remaining behind to become prisoners of war. In addition, the Allies lost seven destroyers and 177 fighter planes and were forced to abandon more than 60,000 vehicles. After 1940, Dunkerque remained occupied by Germans until the bitter end of the war. It was the last French town to be liberated in 1945.

## EATING AND DRINKING

**L'Atelier de Steff** 3 place Jeanne-D'Arc ☎03 28 61 60 14, ⓦatelierdesteff.com. The decor of tiled floors and smart striped chairs suits the locals who pack the place regularly for good value, inventive cooking. *Menus* from €19 take in creamy mushroom soup with foie gras sorbet, monkfish with garlic jus and caramelized apple scented with rosemary. Tues–Fri noon–2pm & 7–9pm, Sun noon–2pm.

**L'Auberge de Jules** 9 rue de la Poudrière ☎03 28 63 68 80. Funky modern restaurant just off the Bassin du Commerce, with plenty of fish on offer, freshly caught by members of the family. *Menus* run from €25–32. Mon–Fri 11.30am–2pm & 6.30–10.30pm, Sat 6.30–10.30pm.

**Au Bon Coin** 49 av Kléber, Malo-les-Bains ☎03 28 69 12 63, ⓦauboncoinrestaurant.fr. Oysters, lobster and a selection of *plateaux de fruits de mer* (€35) are the dishes to go for here. To reinforce the seaside feel in the restaurant, a large sea scene featuring Jean Bart, the local buccaneer dominates one wall. Tues–Sat noon–2.30pm & 7.30pm–10.30pm, Sun noon–2.30pm.

**La Cocotte** 55 Digue de Mer, Malo-les-Bains ☎03 28 29 15 18. The restaurant plays on "cocotte", which is both a

chicken and a way of cooking in a small pot. Try the fish mix of shellfish and whitefish or the chicken in a pot. It's a cheerful place with red gingham tablecloths, plenty of decorative chicken artefacts and a good terrace for windsurf-watching. *Menus* €17.90–22.90, mains from €15. Daily 11.45am–3pm & 7–11.30pm (closed Mon & Tues out of season).

**Le Corsaire** 97 Entrée du Port ☎03 28 59 03 61, ⓦlecorsaire-dk.com. The sparkling, glass-fronted restaurant which looks out onto the quayside is owned and run by Arnaud Tétard who previously worked at *The Ritz* in Paris. Tétard is known for his fish dishes such as crab with flaky pastry and Granny Smith apple (€12), and scallops with spring vegetables and lobster jus (€26). Alternatively, go for the good-value *menus* ranging €20–42. Daily noon–2pm & 7–10pm.

**Le Désirade** 6 quai de la Citadelle ☎03 28 61 53 85, ⓦledesirade.com. A bright, modern restaurant right on the harbour with a great view of the boats, and with plenty on the menu for those wanting meat rather than fish. *Menus* at €20 and €29. Mon–Sat noon–2pm & 7–10pm.

# Cassel

The tiny hilltop town of **CASSEL** is just 30km southeast of Dunkerque. Hills are rare in Flanders, so Cassel was fought over from Roman times onwards. It was supposedly to the top of Cassel's hill that the "Grand Old Duke of York" marched his ten thousand men in 1793, though, as implied in the nursery rhyme, he failed to take the town. In more recent history, during World War I, Marshal Foch spent some of the "most distressing hours" of his life here.

The town was originally a Flemish-speaking community – until use of the language was suppressed by the authorities – and it still boasts a very Flemish **Grand'Place**, lined with some magnificent mansions, from which narrow cobbled streets fan out to the ramparts.

## Musée de Flandres

26 Grand'Place • April–Sept daily 10am–12.30pm & 2–6pm; Oct–March Sat, Sun & school hols 10am–12.30pm & 2–6pm • €3 • ☎ 03 59 73 45 60, ⓦ museedeflandre.cg59.fr

Housed in the splendid Flemish/Renaissance Hôtel de la Noble, the **Musée de Flandres** mixes everyday *objets* and odd collectables from the Flemish past with contemporary art. Exhibits are beautifully displayed in wood-panelled rooms straight out of a Flemish Old Master painting. The museum stages interesting temporary shows; past exhibitions have included the *Splendours of Mannerism in Flanders*, which showed odd and exotic sixteenth-century Flemish paintings.

### ARRIVAL AND INFORMATION | CASSEL

**By train** Cassel's *gare SNCF* is 3km west of the town near Oxelaëre and there are no taxis so those without transport will have to walk into town.
Destinations Dunkerque (16 daily; 27min); Lille (20 daily; 40min).
**By bus** Buses arrive in central Cassel on the Dunkerque to Hazebrouck route, bus #105.
Destinations Dunkerque (5 daily Mon–Sat, 2 daily Sun; 50min)

**Tourist office** 20 Grand'Place (April, May, Sept & Oct Mon–Sat 8.30am–noon & 1.30–5.45pm, Sun 2–5.45pm; June Mon–Sat 8.45am–noon & 1.30–5.45pm, Sun 2–6.30pm; July & Aug Mon–Sat 8.45am–noon & 1.30–6pm, Sun 2–6.30pm; Nov–March Mon–Fri 8.30am–noon & 1.30–5.30pm, Sat 9am–noon; ☎03 28 40 52 55, ⓦ cassel-horizons.com).

### ACCOMMODATION AND EATING

**Châtellerie de Schoebeque** 32 rue Foch ☎ 03 28 42 42 67, ⓦ schoebeque.com. A former eighteenth-century château where Marshal Foch met Britain's George V in World War I, this delightful hotel has intriguing themed rooms: those after a touch of Edith Piaf might take "La Vie en Rose", or indulge your inner gypsy in the old wooden caravan in the garden. Views from the dining room are spectacular. **€187**
**La Taverne Flamande** 34 Grand'Place ☎03 28 42 42 59, ⓦ taverne-flamande.fr. Try this cosy restaurant with its wooden panelling and red gingham-checked tablecloths for a typical Flemish experience. Hearty dishes like large plates of charcuterie or *carbonnade flamande* start at €12. The terrace has great views. Thurs–Mon noon–2pm & 6.30–10pm, Tues 6.30–10pm.
★ **T'Kasteel Hof** 8 rue Saint-Nicolas ☎03 28 40 59 29. If it wasn't so well-executed, this might verge on the kitsch, but instead this lovely, crowded *estaminet* is a real find, with hops and pots hanging from the ceiling, games to play, an open fire and good Flemish dishes from €10. Wash them down with local beers. Thurs–Sun 11am–10pm.

# St-Omer

**ST-OMER**, a popular stop for many away from the ports, is an attractive old Flemish town of yellow-brick houses, 43km southeast of Calais. The Hôtel de Ville on place Foch and the chapel of the former Jesuit college on rue du Lycée are genuine flights of architectural fancy, but for the most part the style is simple but handsome. For a little greenery, head to the pleasant **public gardens** to the west of town or to the nearby **marais**, a network of Flemish waterways cut between plots of land on reclaimed marshes along the river.

## Cathédralé Notre-Dame

Enclos Notre-Dame • Daily 8.30am–12.30pm & 2.30–6pm • Free

It's hard to miss the Gothic **cathedral**, founded in the thirteenth century, and stuffed full of treasures such as an astronomical clock, an eighteenth-century organ and a rather odd shrine to St Erkembode – patron saint of children – that's covered with pairs of shoes.

## Musée de l'Hôtel Sandelin

14 rue Carnot • Wed–Sun 10am–noon & 2–6pm • €4.50 • ☎ 03 21 38 00 94

The centrepiece of the delightful **Musée de l'Hôtel Sandelin**, housed in an eighteenth-century mansion, is the suite of panelled rooms on the ground floor. The museum displays focus on eleventh- to fifteenth-century Flemish art (including a Breughel) and ceramics. Look out for the glorious piece of medieval goldsmithing known as the *Pied de Croix de St-Bertin*.

## The Blockhaus at Éperlecques

Rue de Sart, 12km north of St-Omer off the D300 • Daily: March 11am–5pm; April & Oct 10am–6pm; May–Sept 10am–7pm; Nov 2.15–5pm • €9 • ☎ 03 21 88 44 22, ⓦ leblockhaus.com

The Forêt d'Éperlecques feels remote, making it the perfect place for the largest ever **Blockhaus**, the German concrete bunker, built in 1943–44 by six thousand half-starved prisoners of war. It was designed to launch V2 rockets against London, but the RAF and French Resistance attacked it so heavily – killing many Allied prisoners at the same time – that it was never ready for use. Walk around the massive bunker, which has special spots for commentaries in different languages blaring out the story.

## La Coupole

Just off the D928 (A26 junctions 3 & 4) • Daily: July & Aug 10am–7pm; Sept–June 9am–6pm; closed mid-Dec to Jan 2 • €9.50 • Visits last 2hr 30min • ☎ 03 21 12 27 27, ⓦ lacoupole-france.com

Of all the World War II museums, **La Coupole**, 5km southwest of St-Omer, is the best. As you walk around the site of the intended V2 rocket launch pad, individual, multilingual infrared headphones tell you the story of the occupation of northern France by the Nazis, the use of prisoners as slave labour, and the technology and ethics of the first liquid-fuelled rocket – advanced by Hitler and later developed for the space race by the Soviets, the French and the Americans. Four excellent films cover all aspects.

### ARRIVAL AND INFORMATION                                      ST-OMER

**By train** The exuberant 1903 St-Omer railway station is on rue Saint-Martin, about a15min walk south into the town centre.
**Destinations** Calais-Ville (16 daily; 30min); Hazebrouck (2 per hour; from 12 min); Lille (21 daily; 50min).
**Tourist office** 4 rue Lion d'Or (Easter–Sept Mon–Sat 9am–6pm, Sun 10am–1pm; Oct–Easter Mon–Sat

9am–12.30pm & 2–6pm; ☎ 03 21 98 08 51, ⓦ tourisme -saintomer.com).
**Boat trips** Société Isnor (☎ 03.21.39.15.15, ⓦ isnor.fr). Boat trips leave from the church in nearby Clairmarais. For information and details of kayak and canoe rental, contact the tourist office (see above).

### ACCOMMODATION

**Le Bretagne** 2 place du Vainquai • ☎ 03 21 38 25 78, ⓦ hotellebretagne.com. Near the railway station, this hotel with 69 rooms is decorated in dark colours and feels more business- than leisure-orientated. Comfortable and convenient for the town centre with a good restaurant. €80

**Château Tilques** Rue de Chateau, Tilques • ☎ 03 21 88 99 99, ⓦ chateautilques.com. Originally a seventeeth-century manor house, this rebuilt red-brick château is the best hotel in the region. Set in a delightful park, you can choose from rooms in the main château, some with four-poster beds and classic grand furniture, or more contemporary choices in the Pavilion. The restaurant in the former stables is expensive, but offers good-value *menus*

(€35–50). Leisure facilities include tennis and indoor swimming pool. €220

**Le Clair Marais** Rue du Romelaër • ☎ 03 21 38 34 80, ⓦ camping-clairmarais.com. Near the Forêt de Clairmarais, 4.5km east of St-Omer, and in the heart of the Marais, this countryside campsite has simple facilities and offers fishing and boating. Note there's no transport between it and the town. Closed mid-Dec to Jan. €15

**St-Louis** 25 rue d'Arras • ☎ 03 21 38 35 21, ⓦ hotel -saintlouis.com. Comfortable, simply decorated hotel in a quiet street near the cathedral with pretty fabrics brightening up the rooms. Some overlook the gardens, with more modern rooms in the annexe. Good, popular restaurant and bar. €78

★ **Chez Tante Fauvette** 10 rue Ste Croix ☎ 03 21 11 26 08. Tiny restaurant with a wood floor, red gingham tablecloths and quirky artefacts. The patron runs it single-handed, producing a changing menu of good-value dishes. Try home-made soup or a fish gratin (around €5), pork sautéed with curry powder and rice, or cod with creamy sorrel sauce (€13–16), plus great desserts. Booking essential. Wed–Sat noon–2.30pm & 7–9.30pm, Sun noon–2.30pm.

**Le Cygne** 8 rue Caventou ☎ 03 21 98 20 50, ⑩ restaurantlecygne.fr. Elegantly decorated and offering seasonal dishes, this is a favourite with well-to-do Brits who drop by for the likes of fish terrine (€6) or a dozen *escargots* (€12), followed by beef in Maroilles cheese sauce (€22). Tues–Sat 11.45–1.45pm & 6.30–9.15pm.

**De Drie Kalders** 18 place du Maréchal Foch ☎ 03 21 39 72 52, ⑩ restaurantles3caves.fr. Vaulted brick cellar for the winter, ground floor and terrace for summer months, this old-fashioned restaurant is a busy, cheerful place with hearty Flemish specialties chalked up on a blackboard. *Menus* from €18.50. Tues, Thurs–Sun noon–2pm & 7–11pm.

# Calais and around

**CALAIS** is less than 40km from Dover – the Channel's shortest crossing – and is by far the busiest French passenger port. In World War II, the British destroyed Calais to prevent it being used as a base for a German invasion, but the French still refer to it as "the most English town in France", an influence that began after the battle of Crécy in 1346, when Edward III seized it for use as a beachhead in the Hundred Years' War. It remained in English hands for over two hundred years until 1558, when its loss caused Mary Tudor to say: "When I am dead and opened, you shall find Calais lying in my heart." The association has continued over the centuries, and today Calais welcomes more than nine million British travellers and day-trippers per year.

## Calais-Nord

**Calais-Nord** (or Old Town), was originally a fortified town on an island. It was rebuilt after World War II, with drab place d'Armes and more appealing rue Royale as its focus. The **Tour du Guet**, on place d'Armes, is the only medieval building on the square to have survived wartime bombardment. From here, rue de la Paix leads east to the **church of Notre-Dame**, where Charles de Gaulle married local girl Yvonne Vendroux in 1921. It's currently being restored and will be a major attraction as the only church in English Perpendicular style in Europe.

Walk north up rue Royale over the bridge to the city's **beaches**, where the chilly waters are swimmable, and from which on a fine day a white strip of English shore is visible; get a panoramic view from the top of the 59m **lighthouse** (daily 2–5.30pm, also Sat & Sun 10am–noon; closes 6.30pm June–Sept; €4.50) at place Henri-Barbusse.

### Musée des Beaux-Arts

25 rue Richelieu • Tues–Sat 10am–noon & 2–5pm, Sun 2–5pm; closes 6pm June–Sept • €4 • ☎ 03 21 46 48 40, ⑩ calais.fr/-Le-musee-des-beaux-arts

Since the lace exhibition moved to its new venue (see opposite), there's more space here for the collection of sixteenth- to twentieth-century art, which includes paintings by Picasso and Dubuffet, and a Rodin sculpture exhibition, plus good temporary exhibitions.

## Calais-Sud

Just over the canal bridge, **Calais-Sud**, a nineteenth-century extension of the old town, is now the main **city centre**. Here the town's landmark, the **Hôtel de Ville**, raises its belfry over 60m into the sky; this Flemish extravaganza was finished in 1926, and

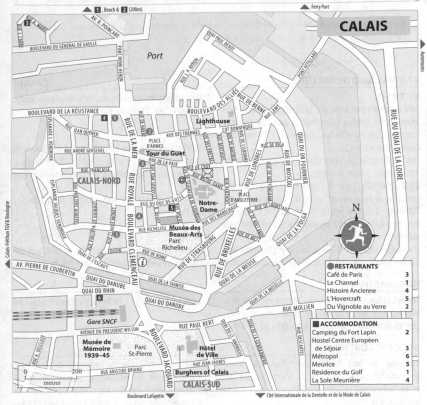

miraculously survived World War II. Nearby, Rodin's famous bronze, the *Burghers of Calais*, records for ever the self-sacrifice of local dignitaries, who offered their lives to assuage the blood lust of the victor at Crécy, Edward III – only to be spared at the last minute by the intervention of Queen Philippa, Edward's wife.

### Cité Internationale de la Dentelle et de la Mode de Calais

135 quai du Commerce • Daily except Tues April–Oct 10am–6pm, Nov–March 10am–5pm • €5 (permanent or temporary exhibition) €8 (both exhibitions) • ☎ 03 21 00 42 30, ⓦ cite-dentelle.fr

Housed in a former lace factory, the extensive Cité Internationale de la Dentelle et de la Mode guides visitors from the early days of hand-made lace – when it was worn only by the aristocracy – to the Industrial Revolution, when machines were smuggled in from England, and up to the present day. The working machines are particularly engrossing, as are the interactive exhibits and videos showing off the complex lace-making process itself. Models display early seventeenth-century costumes, the elegant clothes of the twentieth century and finally the futuristic inspirations of tomorrow's design names.

### Musée de Mémoire 1939–45

Parc Saint-Pierre • Feb–April & Oct–Nov daily except Tues 11am–5pm; May–Sept daily 10am–6pm • €6 • ☎ 03 21 34 21 57, ⓦ museeguerrecalais.free.fr

For a record of Calais' wartime travails, don't miss this museum dedicated to World War II, set in the ivy-covered former German *blockhaus* (bunker) in the Parc Saint-Pierre. It's quaintly old-fashioned with its faded newspaper cuttings, stiff models in uniform and models, but it gives a good picture of occupied Calais.

**2**

Drivers keen to **avoid Calais** should take a left out of the ferry terminal – the *autoroute* bypass begins almost immediately, leading to the A26 and the N1.

## ARRIVAL AND DEPARTURE
CALAIS

### BY TRAIN
**TGV** Eurostar trains from and to London, Lille and Paris arrive at the outlying Calais-Fréthun *gare TGV*. Take the *navette*, usually a shuttle bus, occasionally a TER train, into Calais-Ville station (€2).
Destinations Lille (2 hourly; 30min); London (3 daily; 1hr 10min); Paris (5 daily; 1hr 30min).
**SNCF** Calais-Ville, on av du President Wilson, is the main station for regional services on the TER network and some TGV trains. A daytime bus (€1.50 one-way) runs from the ferry terminal to place d'Armes and the central Calais-Ville *gare SNCF*.
Destinations Abbeville (10 daily; 1hr 25min); Boulogne-Ville (approx. hourly; 30min); Dunkerque (12 daily; from 45min);

Étaples-Le Touquet (approx. hourly; 1hr); Lille (approx. hourly; 1hr 30min); Paris (7 daily; 1hr 40min).

### BY BUS
BCD buses arrive and depart from in front of the Calais-Ville station (☎ 0800 62 00 59, ⓦ ligne-bcd.com) for Dunkerque, Boulogne-sur-Mer and out-of-town shopping centres (see opposite).
Destinations Boulogne (5 daily; 40min); Dunkerque (12 daily; 1hr 45min).

### BY CAR
From the Tunnel exit, road connections to Calais and the *autoroutes* are well signposted and straightforward.

## INFORMATION
**Tourist office** 12 bd Clémenceau (April to mid-June daily 10am–7pm; mid-June to mid-Sept daily 9am–7pm; mid-Sept to March Mon–Sat 10am–6pm; ☎ 03 21 96 62 40,

ⓦ calais-cotedopale.com). For free accommodation booking service.

## ACCOMMODATION
**Camping du fort Lapin** Route Nationale D940, Sangatte-Blériot ☎ 03 21 97 67 77. A large, exposed site at the harbour end of Calais' adults beach; closed Nov to mid-April. **€15**
**Hostel Centre Européen de Séjour** Av du Maréchal-de-Lattre-de-Tassigny ☎ 03 21 34 70 20, ⓦ auberge -jeunesse-calais.com. This modern, well-appointed hostel is just one block from the beach. Dorm beds are in two-or three-bed rooms, plus there are single rooms available. Breakfast is included, while the good on-site restaurant offers meals from €14 to €25. Dorms from **€20.80**, singles **€27.50**
**Métropol** 45 quai du Rhin ☎ 03 21 97 54 00, ⓦ metropolhotel.com. Situated beside the canal close to the train station, and popular with the British, this looks like a grand seaside hotel, albeit a slightly faded one. The oldest hotel in Calais, it's comfortable with conventionally decorated rooms and a bar with an English pub feel. **€99**
**Meurice** 5 rue Edmond-Roche ☎ 03 21 34 57 03,

ⓦ hotel-meurice.fr. Feeling rather *fin-de-siècle*, this comfortable three-star hotel has spacious lounges on the ground floor and a club-like bar that gets crowded with British guests after dinner. A grand staircase (or lift) takes you up to bedrooms decorated with antique furniture. The most expensive bedrooms have jacuzzis in the bathroom. It's in a quiet street behind the Musée des Beaux-Arts (see p.163). **€162**
**Résidence du Golf** 745 Digue G. Berthe ☎ 03 21 96 88 99, ⓦ hoteldugolf-calais.com. The neat, bright motel-style rooms might lack character, but they have kitchenettes and sea views. Rooms accommodating up to 4 people, and proximity to the beach make this a good family choice. **€87**
**La Sole Meunière** 1 bd de la Résistance ☎ 03 21 96 83 66, ⓦ solemeuniere.com. Well situated near the ferry port, beach and the lighthouse, this friendly hotel has 18 basic but comfortable rooms and a restaurant with a good local reputation. **€71**

## EATING AND DRINKING
Calais has enough good restaurants to make eating here worthwhile, mainly on place d'Armes and rue Royale. Drinking establishments, ranging from Gaelic theme pubs to trendier offerings, are concentrated on rue Royale and rue de la Mer.

**Café de Paris** 72 rue Royale ☎ 03 21 34 76 84, ⓦ cafedeparis-calais.com. This lively Calais-Nord brasserie swings along late into the night. It's popular with

locals and tourists for its inexpensive, straightforward dishes; *plats du jour* €9, *menus* range €12.50–35. Sun–Thurs 9am–1am, Fri & Sat 9–2am.

**Le Channel** 3 bd de la Résistance ☎ 03 21 34 42 30, ⓦ restaurant-lechannel.com. Stylish, gourmet restaurant overlooking the yacht basin, with wooden floors, a wall of wine bottles, bright red chairs and a classic menu that doesn't short-change on quality and flavour. The à la carte is expensive, but set meals (€21–54) are skilfully cooked. Closed 2 weeks in summer; booking recommended. Wed–Sat & Mon noon–2.30pm & 6–10pm, Sun noon–2.30pm.

★ **Histoire Ancienne** 20 rue Royale ☎ 03 21 34 11 20, ⓦ histoire-ancienne.com. Family-run brasserie with a charming, vaguely Art Deco interior, well-spaced tables and a warm welcome. On the menu, bistro dishes with a twist include crab soup with liquorice cream (€12) while classics range from flambéed pepper fillet steak (€26) to sea bass (€21). Generous *menus* from €18.90. Tues–Sat noon–2pm & 6.30–11pm, Mon noon–2pm.

**L'Hovercraft** 11 place Foch ☎ 03 21 34 59 73. This popular bar and brasserie gets even busier when football matches are shown on a giant screen. It's a friendly spot – even British-French matches are watched in an entente cordiale spirit. Mon–Thurs 9–1am Fri & Sat 9am–2am.

**Du Vignoble au Verre** 43 place d'Armes ☎ 03 21 34 83 29, ⓦ duvignoble-calais.com. The cosy interior matches the traditional French cooking – including pâté made on the premises alongside classics like steak with pepper sauce and scallops in white wine sauce. There's an emphasis on wine, including a reasonable selection by the glass. *Menus* from €14.50–31.50. Mon–Sat noon–2pm & 7–10pm, Sun 7–10pm.

## SHOPPING

**Hypermarkets** Auchan, avenue Roger Salengro, west of town (Mon–Sat 8.30am–9.30pm, open till 10pm Fri & Sat; bus #1); Carrefour/Mi-Voix, on the east side of town, on avenue Georges-Guynemer (Mon–Sat 8.30am–9pm; bus #2 or #4); Cité Europe, a vast shopping mall on boulevard du Kent by the Channel Tunnel terminal (bus #1), offers another Carrefour (Mon–Sat 8.30am–9pm, open till 10pm Fri & Sat) plus high-street clothing and food shops (Mon–Thurs 10am–8pm, Fri 10am–9pm, Sat 10am–8pm).

**Clothes** Marques Avenue outlet centre, on boulevard du Parc (Mon–Sat 10am–7pm; bus #1) for discounted brands including Adidas, Nike and Puma.

**Wine and cheese** For cheap wine, head for the British-run Majestic Wine on the eastern side of town at rue de Judée, Zone Marcel Doret (daily 8am–8pm; bus #7). For help and tastings try Calais Vins at junction 44 of the A16 where you can also get cheese from Philippe Olivier, bread and a good snack (Mon–Sat 9am–7pm, Sun 9.30am–6pm). In downtown Calais, La Maison du Fromage et des Vins (daily except Tues, Mon am and Sun pm; 8.30am–12.30pm & 3–7.30pm) on place d'Armes has a good selection of cheeses and wine.

**Markets** Street markets are around place d'Armes (Wed & Sat am) and place Crèvecoeur (Thurs & Sat am).

# Wissant

**WISSANT**, some 20km from Calais south along the coast, is a small, attractive place, popular with windsurfers and weekending Britons drawn to its enormous beach. It's long been a preferred beach – indeed Julius Caesar launched his expedition to England from here in 55 BC. The drive from Wissant along the D940 towards Boulogne-sur-Mer is lined with beautiful and undeveloped dunes with frequent turn-offs for **walking paths** to the shore, each of which is tempting on a fine day.

## INFORMATION                                                                            WISSANT

**Tourist office** Place de la Mairie (Mon–Sat 9.30am–noon & 2–6pm, Sun 10am–1pm & 3–6pm; ☎ 08 20 20 76 00, ⓦ terredes2caps.fr).

## ACCOMMODATION

**Escale** Rue de la Mer, Escalles, 6km from Wissant ☎ 03 21 85 25 00, ⓦ hotel-lescale.com. In the little village of Escalles, this creeper-covered modern hotel has pretty rooms, many for three or four people. Facilities like tennis, a children's playground and a restaurant menu of tried and tested favourites make this a solid family choice. **€82**

**De la Plage** 1 place Édouard-Houssin ☎ 03 21 35 91 87, ⓦ hotelplage-wissant.com. Old seaside hotel, very simply refurbished. Rooms have no telephone or TV, and it's not well sound-proofed, but it's friendly and family-orientated, and the restaurant serves excellent seafood. A good bet for a cheap and cheerful stay. **€81.80**

**La Source** 62179 Wissant ☎ 03 21 35 92 46. No reservations here; just turn up and pitch your tent in the municipal campsite just off the rue des Goërlans a short walk from the sea. Basic facilities but it's near the beach and Wissant's small restaurants. Closed mid-Nov to mid-March. **€14.70**

2

**2**

# Boulogne-sur-Mer

**BOULOGNE-SUR-MER** is the smallest of the three main channel ports. The *ville basse* is pretty unprepossessing but rising above the lower town is a diminutive, cobbled medieval quarter, the *ville haute*, contained within the old town walls and dominated by a grand, domed basilica. The main tourist street in the *ville haute* is **rue de Lille**, where you'll find the **Hôtel de Ville**, whose twelfth-century belfry is the most ancient monument in the Old Town (only accessible via guided tour arranged with the tourist office, see opposite).

The most impressive sight in the *ville haute* is the **medieval walls** themselves, set out with rose beds, gravel paths and benches, and providing panoramic views of the city below; it takes about 45 minutes to walk around them. Within the walls, the domed **Basilique Notre-Dame** (April–Aug 9am–noon & 2–6pm; Sept–March 10am–noon & 2–5pm) is an odd building – raised in the nineteenth century by the town's priest without any architectural knowledge or advice – yet it seems to work. The vast medieval **crypt** (Tues–Sun 2–5pm; €2) contains frescoed remains of the Romanesque building and various sacred objects.

## Château Musée

Rue du Bernet • Mon & Wed–Sat 10am–12.30pm & 2–5.30pm, Sun 10am–12.30pm & 2.30–6pm • €4.50 • ☎ 03 21 10 02 20

The **Château Musée** is one of the more surprising discoveries in Boulogne, containing the largest collection of Greek and Etruscan vases outside the Louvre, Egyptian funerary objects including a mummy, an unusual set of Eskimo masks and paintings including works by Corot and Fantin-Latour. The underground ramparts are also worth a walk around.

| ■ ACCOMMODATION | |
| --- | --- |
| Auberge de Jeunesse | 5 |
| Enclos de L'Evêché | 2 |
| Faidherbe | 4 |
| Hamiot | 3 |
| La Matelote | 1 |

| ● RESTAURANTS | |
| --- | --- |
| Chez Jules | 4 |
| La Grillardine | 3 |
| La Matelote | 1 |
| Les Terrasses de l'Enclos | 2 |

BOULOGNE-SUR-MER

# Nausicaá

Bd Ste-Beuve • Daily: July & Aug 9.30am–7.30pm; Sept–June 9.30am–6.30pm; closed for 3 weeks in Jan • €17.40 • ☎ 03 21 30 99 99, ⓦ nausicaa.fr

Boulogne's number one attraction – and one of the most visited in northern France – is the Centre National de la Mer, or **Nausicaá**. You can wander from tank to tank while hammerhead sharks, giant conger eels and jellyfish float and circle over your head. There are up-close-and-personal-experiences with turbot and rays, and feeding time with the sea lions and predictably exuberant penguins. Environmental issues are touched on in some of the display materials and as you'd expect in France, there's an emphasis on the sea as a source of food – the restaurant offers appropriately caught fresh fish. In May and June the place is crawling with French and British school groups, and you may find it best to avoid.

**2**

# Around Boulogne

Three kilometres north of Boulogne on the N1 stands the **Colonne de la Grande Armée** where, in 1803, Napoleon is said to have changed his mind about invading Britain and turned his troops east towards Austria. The column was originally topped by a bronze figure of Napoleon symbolically clad in Roman garb – though his head, equally symbolically, was shot off by the British navy during World War II; a replacement statue now tops the column.

For a pleasant excursion on a fine day, take bus #1 10min north to **Wimereux**, a charming seaside village with a broad promenade and a network of walking paths leading up into the wind-swept headlands.

## ARRIVAL AND INFORMATION

**BOULOGNE-SUR-MER**

**By train** The *gare SNCF* (Boulogne-Ville) is on bd Voltaire, a 10min walk to the centre.

**Destinations** Abbeville (11 daily; 1hr); Amiens (12 daily; 1hr 20min); Arras (4 daily; 2hr); Calais-Ville (approx. hourly; 30min); Étaples-Le Touquet (24 daily; from 15min); Lille (10 daily; 2hr); Montreuil-sur-Mer (9 daily; 40min); Paris (10 daily; 2hr 40min).

**By bus** The bus station is on place de France, bd Mitterand; the centre is just a few minutes' walk.

**Destinations** Calais (4 daily; 40min); Dunkerque (4 daily; 1hr 20min); Le Touquet (5 daily; 1hr 20min).

**Tourist office** Bd Sainte Beuve, Parvis de Nausicaà (July & Aug Mon–Sat 10am–7pm, Sun 10am–1pm & 2.30–6pm; Sept to mid-Nov, April & May Mon–Sat 10am–12.30pm & 1.45–6pm, Sun 10.30am–1pm & 2.30–5pm; mid-Nov to March 10.30am–12.30pm & 2–5pm; ☎ 03 21 10 88 10, ⓦ tourisme-boulognesurmer .com).

## ACCOMMODATION

**Auberge de Jeunesse** Place Rouget-de-Lisle ☎ 03 21 99 15 30, ⓦ fuaj.org. Opposite the *gare SNCF* in the middle of a housing estate, this friendly modern HI hostel has en-suite rooms for 2–4 people. Breakfast included. Dorms **€20.97**

★ **Enclos de L'Evêché** 6 rue de Pressy ☎ 03 91 90 05 90, ⓦ enclosdeleveche.com. Classy *chambres d'hôte* of five individually and beautifully decorated large rooms and spacious bathrooms, set in a nineteenth-century townhouse in the heart of the medieval quarter. Around the corner from the cathedral and looking out onto the ramparts, the peaceful hotel has its own internal courtyard. **€120**

**Faidherbe** 12 rue Faidherbe ☎ 03 21 31 60 93, ⓦ hotelfaidherbe.fr. Don't be put off by the rather grim exterior, this is a great-value two-star near the sea and

shops, with pretty rooms, a small bar-cum-breakfast room and friendly proprietors. **€69**

**Hamiot** 1 rue Faidherbe, cnr bd Gambetta ☎ 03 21 31 44 20, ⓦ hotelhamiot.com. Harbour-side hotel over a large popular bistro. With a rather more business feel than the *Faidherbe* (see above), this is another good-value hotel above in the centre of town. Renovated rooms have double-glazing; some have balconies and baths. **€69**

**La Matelote** 80 bd Ste-Beuve ☎ 03 21 30 33 33, ⓦ la-matelote.com. Boulogne's most celebrated hotel has recently been enlarged and now has a swimming pool, jacuzzi, hammam and sauna. Smartly decorated and supremely comfortable, bedrooms come with minibar, a/c, and cable TV. Some have private balconies and all look towards the sea and Nausicaá (see above) directly opposite. **€155**

**2**

## THE CÔTE D'OPALE

The **Côte d'Opale** is the stretch of Channel coast between Calais and the mouth of the River Somme, characterized by huge, windswept beaches. Along the northern stretch, as far as Boulogne, the beaches are fringed by white chalk cliffs, as on the English side of the Channel. Just here, between the prominent headlands of **Cap Blanc-Nez** and **Cap Gris-Nez**, the D940 coast road winds high above the sea, allowing you to appreciate the "opal" in the name – the sea and sky merging in an opalescent, oyster-grey continuum. The southern part of the coast is flatter, and the beach, uninterrupted for 40km, is backed by pine-anchored dunes and brackish tarns, punctuated by German pillboxes toppled over by the shifting sands. To help you appreciate the area even more, join a guided walk with Eden 62, an organization that protects natural areas, based at 2 rue Claude, Desvres (☎03 21 32 13 74, ⓦwww.eden62.fr).

### EATING AND DRINKING

As a fishing port, Boulogne is a good spot to eat fish and seafood, with plenty of possibilities around place Dalton and a scattering in the *ville haute* (mostly on rue de Lille). There's a handful of bars in the *ville haute* and a rather livelier selection in place Dalton.

**Chez Jules** 8–10 place Dalton ☎03 21 31 54 12, ⓦchez-jules.fr. On the main square of the *ville basse* this jolly brasserie is perfect for families, with a pizza oven, a fish tank, cheerful waiters and typical brasserie dishes. The terrace outside is perfect for people-watching. Set *menus* €22.50–32. Mon–Sat 10am–10pm, Sun 10am–3pm.

**La Grillardine** 30 rue de Lille ☎03 21 80 32 94. Bright, small and cheerful restaurant in the *ville haute*. It has a growing and glowing reputation for its focus on offering limited menus of bistro dishes, using locally sourced meat. At this level of cooking, the €20 *menu* is particularly good value. Tues–Sat noon–2pm & 6–10.30pm, Sun noon–2pm.

**La Matelote** 80 bd Ste-Beuve ☎03 21 30 17 97, ⓦla-matelote.com. In the eponymous hotel down by the sea, this restaurant is high end, though a little stuffy with it. Fish is a speciality and the cooking has a complex mix of ingredients, so expect dishes like basil-filled monkfish that comes with piperade or grated artichokes all in a creamy courgette jus. *Menus* from €31 to €75 are pretty decently priced for this high quality. Daily 7.30–9.30pm, plus Fri–Wed noon–2pm.

**Les Terrasses de l'Enclos** 6 rue de Pressy ☎03 91 90 05 90, ⓦenclosdeleveche.com. At the restaurant of the excellent *chambres d'hotes* in the *ville haute*, the concentration is on fresh, seasonal ingredients and surprising dishes like sea bass with chocolate, or lamb cutlets with tapenade. *Menus* €14–46. Tues–Sat noon–2pm & 7–10.30pm, Sun noon–2pm.

### SHOPPING

**Markets** On Wednesday and Saturday mornings place Dalton hosts a general market.

**Meat and cheese** Boulogne has some good food shops around the Grande Rue, including Charcuterie Bourgeois, 1 Grande Rue (☎ 03 21 31 53 57, ⓦbourgeois-traiteur.eu), which is the locals' favourite. ★ Philippe Olivier, 43 rue Thiers (☎03 21 31 94 74, ⓦphilippeolivier.fr) is quite simply the best cheese shop in northern France with over 200 varieties in various states of maturation.

**Wine** Le Chais, 49 rue des Deux-Pont (☎03 21 31 65 42 ⓦlechais.com) in the Bréquerecque district by the *gare SNCF*, is where you can buy wines in bulk.

**Hypermarket** For the enormous Auchan, catch bus #8 along the N42 towards St-Omer, or bus #20 for the Leclerc.

# Le Touquet

Nestled among dunes and wind-flattened tamarisks and pines, leafy **LE TOUQUET** (officially called Le Touquet-Paris-Plage) resembles some of the snootier places on the English south coast. This is no real surprise, given its interwar popularity with the British smart set: Noel Coward spent weekends here, while the author P.G. Wodehouse lived in the town from 1934 to 1940. He was captured here by the rapidly advancing Germans, then interned, later making his notorious wartime broadcasts from Berlin. Though the town's seafront has been colonized by modern apartments, magnificent villas still hide behind the trees a few blocks inland.

## ARRIVAL AND INFORMATION

**By train and bus** Take the train from Boulogne to Étaples, then a local bus covers the last four kilometres. Alternatively, take the slow bus (Mon–Sat only; timetable from local tourist offices) directly from Boulogne down the coast through Le Touquet to Berck-sur-Mer.

**Tourist office** Palais de l'Europe, place de l'Hermitage (April–Sept Mon–Sat 9am–7pm, Sun 10am–7pm; Oct–March Mon–Sat 9am–6pm, Sun 10am–6pm; ☎03 21 06 72 00, ⓦletouquet.com).

## ACCOMMODATION

**Bristol** 17 rue Jean Monnet ☎03 21 05 49 95, ⓦhotelbristol.fr. Near the beach but very central, this 1920 villa-style hotel has renovated rooms decorated in pretty pastel colours with good bathrooms, a quiet inner courtyard, the comfortable *Ascot Bar* and a lounge with a fireplace for cosy winter evenings. **€190**

**Le Manoir** Av du Golf ☎03 21 06 28 28, ⓦlemanoirhotel.com. You don't get much more English than this manor-house-style hotel, loved by golfers for the course on its doorstep and its good-value golf breaks (see website for details). Bedrooms vary in size, with the largest having a huge window area, sofa and comfortable chairs.

It's full of tasteful old-fashioned furniture, is comfortable and has a tinge of the club feel. **€210**

**Le Westminster** Av du Verger ☎03 21 05 48 48, ⓦwestminster.fr. The best hotel in the area is a grand old lady with impressive public spaces, traditional furnishings and good rooms. The list of past guests reads like a *Who's Who*, from Winston Churchill to Sean Connery. *Le Pavillon* restaurant is Michelin-starred (see below). **€300**

**Le Windsor** 7 rue St Georges ☎03 21 05 05 44, ⓦhotel -windsor.fr. In a quiet street in the centre of town and near the beach, this hotel is a comfortable, affordable option with a good bar but no restaurant. **€70**

## EATING AND DRINKING

**Côté Sud** 187 bd Docteur Jules-Poujet ☎03 21 05 41 24, ⓦle-touquet-cote-sud.com. The only independent restaurant in Le Touquet with a sea view. Oysters, foie gras, sole or smoked sea bass as well as beef fillet with morels are on offer on *menus* from €15.50–54. Summer daily except Wed lunch noon–2.30pm & 7–10pm; winter closed Wed, Mon lunch & Sun dinner.

**Le Café des Arts** 80 rue de Paris ☎03 21 05 21 55, ⓦrestaurant-lecafedesarts.com. Specializing in fish dishes, this is the place for mussels, grilled scallops and haddock. Meat dishes, like steak and potatoes smashed in olive oil, follow the classic route. *Menus* €18–35. Daily noon–2pm & & 7.30–10pm.

**Le Pavillon** Le Westminster (see above), av du Verger

☎03 21 05 48 48, ⓦwestminster.fr. The best restaurant in the region, *Le Pavillon* is smart, with classic decor and an outside terrace. Exciting, inventive, modern cooking ups the ante with starters like a perfect lobster in a vegetable *bouillon* (€40) and turbot with burnt onion, orange and powdered *speculoos* (€44). Meat is equally impressively sourced and prepared. *Menus* from €55 to €85. Tues–Sun 7.30–9.30pm; July & Aug open nightly.

**Les Sports** 22 rue St-Jean ☎03 21 05 05 22, ⓦbrasserieslessports.fr. Both bar and brasserie have been serving classic French cuisine since 1912; this popular down-to-earth place has a good-value *menu* from €18. Order the speciality, fish with "Ratte", Le Touquet's famous potato. Daily 7am–4am.

# Étaples and around

Facing Le Touquet on the other side of the River Canche is the workaday **ÉTAPLES**, a fishing port whose charm lies in its relaxed air. To discover more about the local fishing industry, visit the engaging **Maréis La Coderie** (April–Sept daily 10am–1pm & 2–6.30pm; Oct–March Tues–Sun 10am–12.30pm & 2–6pm; €6; ☎03 21 09 04 00, ⓦmareis.fr), which shares the former rope factory with the tourist office (see above). Apart from **Étaples**, the seaside towns in this area are only interesting in that they provide access to the beaches. Their eerie beauty is best experienced by walking the coastal GR path or any of the marked trails promoted by the local tourist offices. For drivers, the D119 between Boulogne and just north of Dannes provides turn-offs directly into the dunes.

## ARRIVAL AND INFORMATION

**By train** The station is on place de Huckeswagen, a few minutes walk from the centre.
Destinations Boulogne (24 daily; from 15min).

**Tourist office** La Corderie, bd Bigot Descelers (April–Sept daily 10am–1pm & 2–6.30pm; Oct–March Mon–Sat 10am–noon & 2–6pm, Sun 2–6pm; ☎03 21 09 56 94,

ⓦetaples-tourisme.com).

**Boat trips** Depart from the port between April and September. A 45min sea jaunt costs €6.50, and a more

rigorous twelve-hour fishing stint with experienced fishermen is €49. Book via the tourist office.

## EATING

**Aux Pêcheurs d'Étaples** Quai de la Canche ☎03 21 94 06 90, ⓦauxpecheursdetaples.fr. Set above the bustling fish market on the quayside, this restaurant is the perfect place for the freshest fish caught by the local fishing

cooperative. From a long menu, the generous-sized fish soup (€7) is outstanding; otherwise go for grilled sole or a seafood platter. Daily noon–2.30pm & 7–9.30pm.

# Montreuil-sur-Mer

Once a port, **MONTREUIL-SUR-MER** is now stranded 13km inland, after the River Canche silted up in the sixteenth century. Perched on a hilltop above the river and surrounded by ancient walls, it's compact and easily walkable, with fine views from its hilltop ramparts. Laurence Sterne spent a night here on his *Sentimental Journey*, and it was the scene of much of the action in Victor Hugo's *Les Misérables*, best evoked by the steep cobbled street of Cavée St-Firmin, first left after the Porte de Boulogne.

Two heavily damaged Gothic churches grace the main square: the **church of St-Saulve** and a tiny wood-panelled **chapelle** tucked into the side of the red-brick hospital. To the south cobbled lanes are lined with little artisan houses. In the northwestern corner of the walls lies Vauban's **Citadelle** (daily except Tues: mid-April to mid-Oct 10am–noon & 2–6pm; Feb to mid-April & mid-Oct to Nov 10am–noon & 2–5pm; Dec 2–5pm; €4), ruined and overgrown, with subterranean gun emplacements and a fourteenth-century tower that records the coats of arms of the French noblemen killed at Agincourt. Don't miss the World War I exhibition in the vaulted underground rooms of the tower.

## INFORMATION MONTREUIL-SUR-MER

**Tourist office** 21 rue Carnot (April–June, Sept & Oct Mon–Sat 10am–12.30pm & 2–6pm, Sun 10am–12.30pm; July & Aug Mon–Sat 10am–6pm, Sun 10am–12.30pm & 3–5pm; Nov–March Mon–Sat 10am–12.30pm & 2–5pm; ☎03 21 06 04 27,

ⓦtourisme-montreuillois.com).

**Festivals** In mid-August, Montreuil stages a lively mini arts festival of opera, theatre and dance, Les Malins Plaisirs (ⓦlesmalinsplaisirs.com).

## ACCOMMODATION

**Château de Montreuil** 4 Chaussée ☎03 21 81 53 04, ⓦchateaudemontreuil.com. The best hotel in the region is a pretty, low white building surrounded by gardens and an old wall. Individually decorated rooms are beautifully done and have spacious bathrooms. For a treat, book a room with a four-poster bed and old tapestries on the walls. Look out for special deals. **€235**

**Le Coq Hotel** 2 place de la Poissonnerie ☎0321 81

05 61 ⓦcoqhotel.fr. This red-brick hotel on a square has simple, comfortable rooms in the annexe and a courtyard garden. A convivial bar and good restaurant (*menus* from €25) complete a satisfying package. **€154**

**La Hulotte** La Citadelle ☎03 21 06 10 83. Small, basic hostel (bedding provided) in one of the citadelle's outbuildings. Closed Nov–Feb; reception 10am–6pm. Dorms **€11.60**

## EATING

**Château de Montreuil** 4 Chaussée ☎03 21 81 53 04, ⓦchateaudemontreuil.com. Superb food served in the pretty dining room at this impressive hotel (see above) might include imaginative dishes like warm foie gras with rhubarb followed by lamb with cloves. *Menus* €35–95. July & Aug Tues, Wed & Fri–Sun noon–2pm & 7–10pm plus Thurs 7–10pm; Sept–June Tues 7–10pm, Thurs 7–10pm plus Wed, Fri–Sun noon–2pm.

**Le Darnétal** Place Darnétal ☎03 21 06 04 87, ⓦdarnetal-montreuil.com. Cosy restaurant full of odd objects, from plaster Buddhas to antique bags and rugby caps hanging from the ceiling, offers a bistro menu of favourites. *Menus* €21–40. Wed–Sun noon–2pm & 7–9pm.

**Le Jeroboam** 1 rue des Juifs ☎03 21 86 65 80, ⓦlejeroboam.com. In the vaulted buildings of the *Hermitage* hotel, this unexpectedly chic restaurant, run by the owners of the *Château de Montreuil*, aims high and succeeds with top modern cooking and a superb wine list.

*Menus* €17–66. Tues–Sat noon–2pm & 7–9.15pm, plus Mon eve in July & Aug.

# Crécy and Agincourt battlefields

**Agincourt** and **Crécy**, two of the bloodiest Anglo–French battles of the Middle Ages, took place near the attractive little town of **HESDIN** (familiar to Simenon fans from the TV series *Inspector Maigret*). Twenty kilometres southwest of Hesdin, at the **Battle of Crécy**, Edward III inflicted the first of his many defeats of the French in 1346. This was the first appearance on the continent of the new English weapon, the six-foot longbow, and reputedly the first use in European history of gunpowder. Today you just see the **Moulin Édouard III** (now a watchtower), 1km northeast of **Crécy-en-Ponthieu** on the D111 to Wadicourt, site of the windmill from which Edward watched the hurly-burly of battle. Further south, on the D56 to Fontaine, the battered **croix de Bohème** marks the place where King John of Bohemia died fighting for the French, having insisted on leading his men into battle despite his blindness.

Ten thousand more died in the heaviest defeat ever of France's feudal knighthood at the **Battle of Agincourt** on October 25, 1415. Forced by muddy conditions to fight on foot in heavy armour, the French, though more than three times as numerous, were easy prey for the lighter, mobile English archers. The rout took place near present-day **AZINCOURT**, about 12km northeast of Hesdin off the D928. Agincourt Centre Historique Médiéval (April–Oct daily 10am–6pm; Nov–March daily except Tues 10am–5pm, €7.50, ☎03 21 47 27 53, ⓦazincourt-medieval.fr) uses video and interactive facilities to bring the story to life and a map takes you for a circular drive around the English and French lines, including an orientation point by the crossroads of the D104 and the road to Maisoncelle.

# Parc Ornithologique du Marquenterre

30km south of Étaples off the D940 between the Canche and Somme estuaries • Daily: Feb, March & Oct to mid-Nov 10am–6pm; April–Sept 10am–7.30pm; mid-Nov to Jan 10am–5pm • €9.90 • ☎03 22 25 68 99, ⓦparcdumarquenterre.com

If you know nothing about birds, the **Parc Ornithologique du Marquenterre** will be a revelation. The landscape is beautiful and strange: all dunes, tamarisks and pine forest, full of salty meres and ponds thick with water plants.

You can hire binoculars (€4); otherwise, rely on the guides at some of the observation huts, who set up portable telescopes and will tell you about the nesting birds. There's a choice of itineraries – two longer, more interesting walks (2–3hr) and a shorter one (roughly 1hr 30min). On both you can see dozens of species – ducks, geese, oyster-catchers, terns, egrets, redshanks, greenshanks, spoonbills, herons, storks, godwits – most taking a breather from their epic migratory flights. In April and May they head north, returning from the end of August to October; in early summer the young chicks can be spotted.

Keen natural historians might also want to drop into the **Maison de la Baie de Somme et de l'Oiseau** (daily: March–June, Sept & Oct 9.30am–6pm; July & Aug 9.30am–7pm; mid-Oct to March 10am–5pm, €6.90, ☎03 22 26 93 93) on the other side of the bay, which has displays relating to birds and seals of the Somme bay and organizes seal excursions.

# The Somme estuary

After Marquenterre, the D940 meanders through yet more silted-up fishing hamlets. Some, like **LE CROTOY**, have enough sea still to attract the yachties, and have enjoyed a boom in second homes. Le Crotoy's south-facing beach has attracted numerous writers and painters over the years: Jules Verne wrote *Twenty Thousand Leagues under the Sea* here.

## St-Valéry-Sur-Somme

**ST-VALÉRY-SUR-SOMME**, on the opposite side of the bay from Le Crotoy, is where William, Duke of Normandy, set sail to conquer England in 1066. With its intact medieval citadelle and brightly painted quays, St-Valéry is the jewel of the coast. The main sight is the **Écomusée Picarvie**, 5 quai du Romerel (April–Sept Wed–Sun 10am–12.30pm & 1.30–6pm; €5.90), with its interesting collection of tools and artefacts relating to vanished trades and ways of life. Otherwise, **activities** include boat trips, cycling and guided walks, led by the Maison des Guides (see below). Digging for shellfish is also popular, but be extremely careful about the tide: when it's high it reaches up to the quays, but withdraws 14km at low tide, creating a dangerous current; equally, it returns very suddenly, cutting off the unwary.

### GETTING THERE AND INFORMATION                                    ST-VALÉRY-SUR-SOMME

**By train** St-Valéry-sur-Somme is accessible from April to Oct on the Baie de la Somme steam train from Le Crotoy and Noyelles-sur-Mer on its way to Cayeux-sur-Mer (see website for timetables; return €9; w cfbs.eu).

**Tourist office** 2 place Guillaume-le-Conqérant (daily

9.30am–12.30pm & 2–6pm, closed Mon Sept–May; ☏ 03 22 60 93 50 w saint-valery-sur-somme.fr). For activities, go to the Maison des Guides at Quai Jeanne d'Arc (☏ 06 18 42 71 16, w guides-baiedesomme.com).

### ACCOMMODATION

**Picardia** 41 quai Romerel ☏ 03 22 60 32 30, w picardia .fr. The gracious nineteenth-century building at the foot of the medieval quarter and a few steps from the water is a delightful family-owned hotel. Pretty rooms follow the contours of the old house, many with beamed ceilings. **€98**

**Du Port et des Bains** 1 quai Balvet ☏ 03 22 60 80 09, w hotelhpb.fr. Right on the estuary and offering simple, brightly coloured rooms and a friendly welcome, this long, low, 15-roomed hotel is particularly popular with families. **€85**

### EATING

**Du Port et des Bains** 1 quai Balvet ☏ 03 22 60 80 09, w hotelhpb.fr. The bright dining room looking onto the water buzzes with contented locals and visitors tucking into seafood and shellfish specialities using the freshest local ingredients. *Menus* €16–35. Daily noon–2.30pm & 7–10pm.

**Relais Guillaume de Normandy** 46 quai Romerel

Balvet ☏ 03 22 60 82 36, w relais-guillaume-de -normandy.com. Away from the crowds, this *Logis de France* red-brick manor-house hotel is known particularly for its food. There are three dining rooms as well as a covered terrace. Try specialities like sweet local saltmarsh lamb or a perfect sole meunière. *Menus* €19.50–45. Daily noon–2pm & 7–10pm; closed Tues Sept–June.

# The Flemish cities

From the Middle Ages until the late twentieth century, great Flemish cities like **Lille**, **Roubaix**, **Douai** and **Cambrai** flourished, mainly thanks to their textile industries. The other dominating – now virtually extinct – presence in this part of northern France was the **coalfields** and related industries, which, at their nineteenth-century peak stretched from Béthune in the west to Valenciennes in the east. At **Lewarde** you can visit one of the pits, while in the region's big industrial cities you can see what the masters built with their profits: noble townhouses, magnificent city halls, ornate churches and some of the country's finest art collections.

## Lille

**LILLE** (Rijsel in Flemish), northern France's largest city, surprises many visitors with its impressive architecture, the winding streets of its tastefully restored **old quarter** (Vieux Lille), its plethora of excellent restaurants and bustling nightlife. It boasts a large university, a modern métro system and a serious attitude to culture, with some great museums.

Historically the main stop on the rich trading route between Flanders and Paris, Lille was first and foremost a merchant city: instead of a soaring Gothic cathedral, taking pride of place are secular temples like the Flemish Renaissance jewel of the **Ancienne Bourse**. The focal part of central Lille is the place du Général de Gaulle, always referred to as the **Grand'Place**, marking the southern boundary of Vieux Lille. South of this, the pedestrianized shopping area runs along rue de Béthune to the squares of place Béthune and place de la République. The city's **museums** are a short walk from the centre and the top museums are outside: La Piscine in Roubaix and the Museum of Modern Art in Villeneuve d'Ascq. The city spreads far into the countryside in every direction, a jumble of suburbs and factories, and for the French it remains the symbol of the country's heavy industry and working-class politics.

## Ancienne Bourse

The east side of the Grand'Place is dominated by the lavishly ornate **Ancienne Bourse**. To the merchants of seventeenth-century Lille, all things Flemish were the epitome of wealth and taste and they lavished money on the Bourse and the imposing surrounding mansions. The courtyard holds a book **market** in the afternoons. A favourite Lillois pastime is lounging around the fountain at the centre of the Grand'Place, in the middle of which is a **column** commemorating the city's resistance to the Austrian siege of 1792, which is topped by *La Déesse* (the goddess), modelled on the wife of the mayor at the time.

## Place du Théâtre and the Nouvelle Bourse belfry

Next to the Ancienne Bourse, in **place du Théâtre** you can see how Flemish Renaissance architecture was assimilated and Frenchified in grand flights of Baroque extravagance – above all at the **Opéra** (closed July–Sept; ☎08 20 48 90 00, ⓦopera-lille.fr), built at the turn of the twentieth century by Louis-Marie Cordonnier, who also designed the extravagant **belfry** of the neighbouring Nouvelle Bourse – now the regional chamber of commerce.

## Vieux Lille

The smart shopping streets, rues Esquermoise and Lepelletier, lead towards the heart of **Vieux Lille**, a warren of red-brick terraces on cobbled lanes and passages. It's an area of great character and charm, having been successfully reclaimed and reintegrated into the mainstream of the city's life. To experience the atmosphere, head up towards rue d'Angleterre, rue du Pont-Neuf and the Porte de Gand, rue de la Monnaie and place du Lion d'Or. Everywhere restaurants and bars are interspersed with chic boutiques.

Amid the city's secular pomp, Lille's ecclesiastical architecture is rather subdued. Exceptions include the facade of the cathedral, **Notre-Dame-de-la-Treille**, just off rue de la Monnaie. The body of the cathedral is a Neo-Gothic construction begun in 1854, but the new facade, completed in 1999, is a translucent marble skin supported by steel wires, best appreciated from inside, or at night when lit up from within. More traditional, but also impressive, is the **church of St-Maurice**, close to the station on rue de Paris, whose white stone front hides a classic Flemish Hallekerke, its five aisles characteristic of the style.

### Musée de l'Hospice Comtesse

32 rue de la Monnaie • Mon 2–6pm, Wed–Sun 10am–12.30pm & 2–6pm • €3.50 • ☎03 28 36 84 00

Vieux Lille's main sight is the **Hospice Comtesse**. Twelfth century in origin, though much reconstructed in the eighteenth, the former hospital became an orphanage after World War I. The Hospice is the setting for a collection of paintings, tapestries and porcelain of the region, recreating the ambience of a seventeenth-century Flemish convent, and its medicinal garden, a riot of poppies and verbena, is a delight.

2

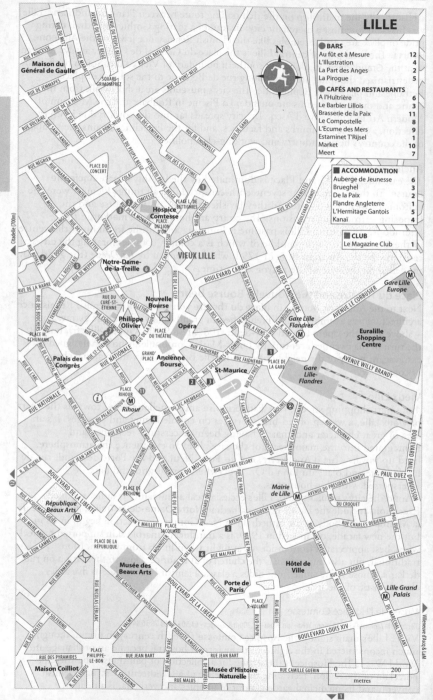

LILLE

● BARS
Au fût et à Mesure          12
L'Illustration              4
La Part des Anges           2
La Pirogue                  5

● CAFÉS AND RESTAURANTS
A l'Huîtrière               6
Le Barbier Lillois          3
Brasserie de la Paix        11
Le Compostelle              8
L'Ecume des Mers            9
Estaminet T'Rijsel          12
Market                      10
Meert                       7

■ ACCOMMODATION
Auberge de Jeunesse         6
Brueghel                    3
De la Paix                  2
Flandre Angleterre          1
L'Hermitage Gantois         5
Kanaï                       4

■ CLUB
Le Magazine Club            1

## Maison du Général de Gaulle

9 rue Princesse • Sept–June Wed–Sat 10am–noon & 2–5pm, Sun 1.30–5pm; July & Aug Wed–Sun 10am–noon & 2–5pm •€6 •
☎ 03 28 38 12 05, ⓦ maison-natale-de-gaulle.org

The house where **Charles de Gaulle** was born in 1890 is now a museum exhibiting keepsakes and personal objects in rooms that give a very real idea of a bourgeois home in the nineteenth century. A multimedia display takes you through his life and there are interesting temporary exhibitions on related subjects like the story of Anne Frank.

**2**

## Citadelle

Rue de la Barre • **Guided tour** Sept–March plus third Fri of the month; May–Aug Thurs, Fri & Sun; two tours daily depart from the citadelle's Porte Royale at 3pm & 4pm • €7

A must for military buffs, the **citadelle** overlooks the old quarter to the northwest, constructed in familiar star-shaped fashion by Vauban in the seventeenth century. Still in military hands, it can only be visited by guided tour.

## Musée des Beaux-Arts

Place de la République • Mon 2–6pm, Wed–Sun 10am–6pm • €6.50 • ☎ 03 20 06 78 00, ⓦ pba-lille.fr

Just south of the Grand'Place, **place Rihour** is a largely modern square flanked by brasseries and the remains of an old palace that now houses the tourist office, hidden behind a war memorial of gigantic proportions. The **Musée des Beaux-Arts** on place de la République is France's second museum after the Louvre in Paris with the core of its collection from Napoleon's looting of art from the rest of Europe. The late 1990s redesign is sleek and spacious, and the museum contains some important works. Flemish painters form the bulk of the collection, from "primitives" like Dirck Bouts, through the northern Renaissance to Ruisdael, de Hooch and the seventeenth-century greats, including several painted by Rubens for the Capuchin convent in Lille. French works include paintings by Delcroix, Courbet and Monet.

## Musée d'Histoire Naturelle

19 rue de Bruxelles • Mon & Wed–Fri 9am–noon & 2–5pm, Sun 10am–5pm • €3 • ☎ 03 28 55 30 80

Located near the green avenue Jean-Baptiste Lebas, the charming **Musée d'Histoire Naturelle** is a manageable size for children, and has a lovely collection of dinosaur bones, fossils, as well as an impressive array of stuffed birds, including a dodo.

## Maison Coilliot and Hôtel de Ville

West of the Musée des Beaux-Arts, on rue de Fleurus, lies **Maison Coilliot**, one of the few houses built by Hector Guimard, who made his name designing the Art Nouveau entrances to the Paris métro – it's worth taking a look at the facade. East of the museum, near the triumphal arch of Porte de Paris, is the city's odd but serviceable **Hôtel de Ville**, executed in a Flemish-modernist style not unlike German *jugendstil*, and which has an extremely tall belfry.

## Euralille

Thanks to Eurostar and the international extension of the TGV network, Lille has become the transport hub of northern Europe, a position it is trying to exploit by turning itself into an international business centre: hence **Euralille**, the burgeoning complex of shops and offices behind the old *gare SNCF*. Some of the structures are by big-name architects like Rem Koolhaas and Jean Nouvel, but some of the glitter is already coming off this "new" Lille: the TGV station is bustling and audacious, but the shopping mall opposite is dull, the brutal concrete expanse between the two stations is popular only with drunks and vagrants, and the weed-infested kerbs and dirty fountains point to a lack of adequate maintenance.

**2**

## Villeneuve d'Ascq: Lille Métropole Musée d'Art Modern (LaM)
Tues–Sun 10am–6pm, park open Tues–Sun 9am–7pm • €7 • ☎ 03 20 19 68 68, ⓦ musee-lam.fr

The suburb of Villeneuve d'Ascq is a mark of Lille's cultural ambition. Acres of parkland, an old windmill or two, and a whole series of mini-lakes form the setting for the renovated **Musée d'Art Moderne**. The ground floor holds exhibitions by contemporary French artists, while the permanent collection, on the first floor, contains canvases by Picasso, Braque, Modigliani and Rouault. The museum also has the largest collection of *art brut* ("raw art") in France, which includes graffitti and pieces by primitive artists working outside the fine art tradition.

## ARRIVAL AND DEPARTURE                                     LILLE

### BY AIR
If you arrive by air at Lille-Lesquin Airport, a shuttle-bus service (hourly on the hour; ☎ 08 91 67 32 10; €7 one way) can whisk you to Euralille (see p.175), just by Gare Lille-Flandres, in 20min.

### BY TRAIN
**Gare Lille-Flandres** Situated in central Lille, a few minutes walk from Grand'Place, this station serves regional trains plus a regular service to Paris. It was originally Paris's Gare du Nord, which was brought here brick by brick in 1865.
Destinations Arras (approx. every 1–2hr; 40min); Boulogne (approx. hourly; 1hr 30min); Brussels (TGV 7 daily; 40min); Charleville-Mézières (3 daily; 2hr);

Dunkerque (approx. hourly; 1hr); Lyon (TGV approx. 2 to 3 hourly; from 2hr 57min); Marseille (TGV 6 daily; 4hr 30min); Paris (TGV 23 daily; from 59 min).
**Lille-Europe** This station services TGV and Eurostar trains from London, Brussels and further afield. Trains also connect with Lille-Flanders.
Destinations Brussels (16 daily; from 34min); London (Eurostar 11 daily; from 1hr 22min); Paris (TGV 23 daily; from 59min).

### BY BUS
Eurolines buses from the UK and Europe pull into Lille-Europe (see above).
Destinations London (6 daily; 5hr 30min).

## GETTING AROUND

Lille's centre is small enough to walk around, and unless you choose to visit the modern art museum at Villeneuve-d'Ascq (see above) or La Piscine in Roubaix (see p.178), you won't even need to use the city's public transport system.

**By metro** Two VAL (Véhicule Automatique Léger, or automatic light vehicle) lines go from central Lille to the suburbs including Villeneuve-d'Ascq and Roubaix.
**By bus** Citadine route is a continuous loop running past

the principal sights, from 5.30am to 9.30pm.
**Tickets** Public transport tickets are €1.40 single; €11.40 for a book of 10 tickets, and €4.10 for a day pass.

## INFORMATION

**Tourist office** Place Rihour (Mon–Sat 9am–6pm, Sun & public hols 10am–noon & 2–5pm; ☎ 08 91 56 20 04, ⓦ lilletourism.com).
**Passes and tours** The tourist office runs regular city tours by bus and walking tours, plus 4hr tours of the surrounding world war battlefields every Saturday (April–Dec at 1pm; €42 per person). It can help book hotels, and sells a City Pass (one day €20, two days €30 and three days €45), which offers free entry to various

sites and attractions and free use of public transport.
**Festivals** The major festival of the year, the Grande Braderie, takes place over the first weekend of September, when a big street parade and vast flea market fill the streets of the Old Town by day, and the nights see a *moules-frites* frenzy in all the restaurants.
**Health** SOS Médecins ☎ 03 20 29 91 91.
**Police** Commissariat Central, 5 bd du Maréchal Vaillant ☎ 03 20 62 47 47.

## ACCOMMODATION

**Auberge de Jeunesse** 12 rue Malpart, off rue de Paris ☎ 03 20 57 08 94, ⓦ fuaj.org. HI hostel in a fairly central position. Kitchen facilities and internet access available. Breakfast included. Closed Jan. Dorms €21
**Brueghel** 3–5 parvis St-Maurice ☎ 03 20 06 06 69, ⓦ hotel-brueghel.com. Tucked down a pedestrianized side street, this charming hotel with small but well-decorated

rooms full of antique furniture and fresh flowers, is a real find. Prices are as attractive as the welcome. €140
**De la Paix** 46bis rue de Paris ☎ 03 20 54 63 93, ⓦ hotel-la-paix.com. In a great central location just off the Place du Théâtre, this hotel has standard rooms called after artists (Modigliani, Picasso and the like), each one livened up with classy posters and reproductions on the walls. €125

**Flandre Angleterre** 13 place de la Gare ☎ 03 20 06 04 12, ⊛ hotel-flandre-angleterre.fr. Near the train station, the 2-star hotel has good-sized rooms with standard fittings but pretty textiles. Double-glazed windows effectively keep out the noise outside. €92

**L'Hermitage Gantois** 224 rue de Paris ☎ 03 20 85 30 30, ⊛ hotelhermitagegantois.com. This mellow red-brick hotel is housed in a charity hospital dating back to 1462. Now a hotel, it successfully bridges the centuries, mixing medieval and modern. Large luxurious bedrooms look out onto peaceful cobbled courtyards and you feel you're far from the city, though the location is central. Splash out on the room and economize by eating in the casual *Estaminet* restaurant (mains from €18). €390

**Kanaï** 10 rue du Faubourg de Béthune ☎ 03 20 57 14 78 ⊛ hotelkanai.com. Near place Rihour, this thoroughly modern hotel has rooms decorated with dramatic colours and has good bathrooms. It's a pleasant contrast to other, older hotels. €110

## EATING, DRINKING AND ENTERTAINMENT

A Flemish flavour and a taste for mussels characterize the city's traditional cuisine, with the main central concentration of cafés, brasseries and restaurants around place Rihour and along rue de Béthune. Vieux Lille has a reputation for gastronomic excellence, particularly on the eastern side towards and along rue de Gand, where you'll find most of the worthwhile places. The student quarter along rues Solférino and Masséna is good for ethnic eating – the former mostly Chinese or Japanese, the latter dominated by cheap kebab shops. The cafés around the Grand'Place and place Rihour buzz with life. Up near the cathedral in Vieux Lille, rue Royale, rue de la Barre, rue Basse and place Louise-de-Bettignies have trendier spots, with a few stretched out along rue de la Monnaie. West of the centre, Celtic-style pubs dominate in studenty rue Masséna, attracting a young crowd. Art and music events are always worth checking up on – there's a particularly lively jazz scene. Pick up a copy of the free weekly listings magazine, *Sortir*, from the tourist office, or look in the local paper, *La Voix du Nord*.

### CAFÉS AND RESTAURANTS

**Le Barbier Lillois** 69 rue de la Monnaie ☎ 03 20 06 99 35, ⊛ le-barbier-lillois.com. A butcher's shop selling meat and meals to take away is on the ground floor, while the restaurant sits above. Decorated with grand eighteenth-century carved wood panelling, it specializes in classic dishes like smoked salmon, charcuterie, steaks and regional Flemish specialities such as *carbonnade flamande*. A good beer list, including some from their own brewery, completes a thoroughly satisfying experience. Mains €13.50–26. Tues–Sun noon–2.30pm & 7–10.30pm.

**Brasserie de la Paix** 25 place Rihour ☎ 03 20 54 70 41, ⊛ paix.restaurantsdelille.com. Red velvet banquettes, wooden tables, Art Deco stained glass and brass lamps decorate this bustling 1930s brasserie. Expect classic dishes of thyme and garlic lamb and their specialities of platters of seafood, a good French wine list and Belgian beer. *Menus* €15–29. Mon–Sat noon–12.30pm & 7–11.30pm.

**Le Compostelle** 4 rue St-Étienne ☎ 03 28 38 08 30 ⊛ lecompostelle-lille.fr. In a renovated Knights Templar Renaissance palace, this airy restaurant is the place for refined versions of traditional French specialities, including vegetarian options. *Menus* from €19.90–48. Daily noon–2pm & 7–10.30pm.

**L'Ecume des Mers** 10 rue de Pas ☎ 03 20 54 95 40, ⊛ ecume-des-mers.com. Large space with a pristine all-white decor sets the scene for top fish dishes from a daily changing menu. From tuna carpaccio with fresh leaf salad (€15) to rich bouillabaisse (€24), this is the place for pescatorial *delicies*. *Menus* €18–25. Daily noon–2.30pm & 7–11pm.

**Estaminet T'Rijsel** 25 rue de Gand ☎ 03 20 15 01 59. If you want the true Flemish *estaminet experience*, this is the place. Decorated with hops, old photos and candles on the tables, this crowded bistro serves the whole gamut of regional dishes, and over 40 beers. *Plats* from €10.50. Mon 7–1.30pm, Tues–Sun noon–2.30pm & 7–10.30pm.

★ **A l'Huîtrière** 3 rue des Chats-Bossus ☎ 03 20 55 43 41, ⊛ huitriere.fr. A wonderful shop (worth a visit just for the mosaics and stained glass) with an expensive, chandelier-hung restaurant at the back specializing in fish and oysters. If you can, splash out on the impressive €110 *menu*, or sit at the oyster bar for a lighter meal. Daily noon–2pm & 7–9.30pm.

**Market** 6 Sq Maurice Schumann ☎ 03 20 54 98 02. Chic red-bricked walled restaurant and bar with an up-to-date simple menu such as sea bass with oriental spices or New York strip steak, and a very good wine list. *Menus* from €23. Tues–Sat noon–2pm & 7–10.30pm.

★ **Meert** 27 rue Esquermoise ☎ 03 20 57 07 44 ⊛ meert.fr. Join Lille society in this old-fashioned *salon de thé* and shop, which has provided the locals (including General de Gaulle) with *gaufrettes* (crispy waffles) since 1761. At lunch the restaurant behind the shop is packed with people ordering traditional *blanquette de veau* (veal stew) and finishing with wildly sweet desserts. Main dishes from €12. Tues & Wed noon–3pm, Thurs–Sat noon–3pm & 8–10.30pm.

### BARS AND CLUBS

**Au fût et à mesure** 5 rue du Faisan ☎ 03 20 48 20 66, ⊛ aufutetamesure.com. The concept, imported from Spain, is simple: you pay in advance for a special card, and

2

**2**

then have access to the beer tap on your table to fill up as you want. A good range of beers and big screens for sports events ensure its popularity. Daily 5–10.30pm.

**L'Illustration** 18 rue Royale ☎ 03 20 12 00 90, ⓦbar -illustration.fr. The place to sample Trappist beers from Belgium or the bar's specialist cocktails. Suitably shabby and atmospheric with changing art on the walls, it's a meeting place for artists, both genuine and wannabes. Mon–Fri 12.30pm–2am, Sat 2pm–3am, Sun 3pm–2am.

**Le Magazine Club** 84 rue de Trévise ⓦmagazineclub .fr. Superstar DJs of world electro music plus great live acts

in three comfortable bars make this one of Lille's most popular clubs. Fri, Sat and evenings before public holidays 11pm–7am.

**La Part des Anges** 50 rue de la Monnaie ☎ 03 20 06 44 01. Trendy wine bar with an enviable cellar (20,000 bottles), serving simple meals and oysters to accompany the wine. Daily noon–2.30pm & 7.30–10.30pm.

**La Pirogue** 16 rue Jean-Jacques Rousseau ☎ 03 20 31 70 82. Antilles-themed bar and suitably hot atmosphere with reasonably priced cocktails, especially popular with local students. Mon–Thurs 5pm–2am, Fri & Sat 3pm–2am.

### SHOPPING

**Books** Le Furet du Nord, 15 place Général-de-Gaulle, is Europe's largest bookshop. It fills eight floors and has a wide selection of books in English.

**Cheese** Foodies should head to Philippe Olivier's *fromagerie* with its three hundred cheeses, on 3 rue du Curé-St-Étienne.

**Market** Place de la Nouvelle Aventure. Wazemmes market is a loud and colourful flea market in the west of central Lille, selling food and clothes in a market hall and the streets around. Its main day is Sun but it's also open Tues–Sat (6am–late afternoon).

# Roubaix

Accessed by metro (line 2 to Gare Jean Lebas) and just 15km northeast of Lille, right up against the Belgian border, **ROUBAIX** is a once-great Flemish textile city that fell into decline and is striving to rejuvenate itself. The city centre is not especially attractive and even the modest outlet shopping mall on its southern fringe is somehow dispiriting. Nevertheless, Roubaix is worth a visit to see its showpiece museum, **La Piscine**.

### La Piscine – Musée d'Art et d'Industrie

23 rue de l'Espérance • Tues–Thurs 11am–6pm, Fri 11am–8pm, Sat & Sun 1–6pm; temporary and permanent collection €7; permanent collection only €4.50 • ☎ 03 20 69 23 60, ⓦ roubaix-lapiscine.com

Halfway between the *gare SNCF* and the Grand'Place, the magnificent **La Piscine – Musee d'Art et d'Industrie** was opened in 2001, and is in the improbable setting of one of France's most beautiful swimming pools and bath complexes, originally built in the early 1930s for the poor of the city. Architect Paul Philippon's contemporary conversion retains various aspects of the baths – part of the pool, the shower-cubicles, the changing rooms and the bathhouses – and uses each part to display a splendid collection of mostly nineteenth- and early twentieth-century sculpture and painting, plus haute couture clothing, textiles and photographs of the pool in its heyday.

# Douai

Right in the heart of mining country, 40km south of Lille, **DOUAI** is an unpretentious, surprisingly attractive town, despite being badly damaged in both world wars. Its handsome streets of eighteenth-century houses are cut through by the River Scarpe and a canal. Once a haven for English Catholics fleeing Protestant oppression in Tudor England, Douai later became the seat of Flemish local government under Louis XIV, an aristocratic past evoked in the novels of Balzac.

### Hôtel de Ville

83 rue de la Mairi • **Guided tours** through the tourist office: July & Aug daily 10am, 11am & hourly 2–6pm; Sept–June Mon 3pm, 4pm & 5pm, Tues–Sun 11am, 3pm, 4pm & 5pm • €3.80

Most of Douai's sights are west of the central place d'Armes, from which rue de la Mairie leads to the splendid fifteenth-century Gothic **Hôtel de Ville**, which is topped by a belfry of fairy-tale fabulousness, popularized by Victor Hugo and renowned for its carillon of 62 bells – the largest single collection in Europe. There are concerts every Saturday at 10.45am.

## Church of St-Pierre
One block north of the town hall, on **rue Bellegambe**, an outrageous Art Nouveau facade fronts a very ordinary children's store. At the end of the street, rising above the Old Town, is the **church of St-Pierre**, its Baroque nave bracketed by a stone west tower, begun in 1513 but not finished until 1690, and by a dumpy round tower and dome at the opposite end. The church contains – among other treasures – a spectacular carved Baroque organ case.

## Ancienne Chartreuse
Daily except Tues: 10am–noon & 2–6pm • €6, free first Sun of the month • ☎ 03 27 71 38 80

With the exception of the 1970s extension to the old Flemish Parliament, the riverfront west of the town hall is pleasant to wander along; across the river to the west are quiet streets of handsome two-storey houses. Here, at 130 rue des Chartreux, the **Ancienne Chartreuse** has been converted into a wonderful **museum**, with a fine collection of paintings by Flemish, Dutch and French masters, including Van Dyck, Jordaens, Rubens and Douai's own Jean Bellegambe. The adjacent chapel displays an array of sculptures including a poignant *Enfant prodige* by Rodin.

## Lewarde
A visit to the colliery at **LEWARDE**, 7km east of Douai, is a must for admirers of Zola's *Germinal*. It offers visitors a fascinating insight into the gruelling conditions of a nineteenth-century coal mine. Surrounded by flat, featureless beetroot fields, Lewarde's dour brick dwellings line streets named after Pablo Neruda, Jean-Jacques Rousseau, Georges Brassens and other luminaries of the Left. This is the traditional heart of France's coal-mining country, though you'll look in vain for winding towers or slag heaps hereabouts, demolition and landscaping having removed almost all visible traces.

### Centre Historique Minier de Lewarde
Guided tours: March–Oct daily 9am–5.30pm; Nov, Dec & Feb Mon–Sat 1–5pm, Sun 10am–5pm; 1hr 30min • €11.50 • ☎ 03 27 95 82 82, ⓦ chm-lewarde.com • From Douai's place de Gaulle, take tram A to Bougival then bus #1 one stop or 20min walk on the D132 towards Erchin.

The largest mining museum in France is in the former Delloye pithead where 1000 miners worked. You can tour the exhibition and surface installations with an English-language audioguide, but the tours of the mine itself are led by retired miners. These pits were deep and hot, with steeply inclined narrow seams that forced the miners to work on slopes of 55 degrees and more, just as Étienne and the Maheu family do in Zola's story. After a simulated ride you see mining machinery, photographs, and the stables where the pit ponies were kept. There's a lot for children to see and do, and you should allow half a day to do it justice.

## ARRIVAL AND INFORMATION                                        DOUAI

**By train** The *gare SNCF* is on bd de Liège, a 5min walk from the centre.
Destinations Lille (2 hourly; from 18min); Arras (2–3 hourly; from 13min).

**Tourist office** 70 place d'Armes (April–Sept Mon–Sat 10am–1pm & 2–6.30pm, Sun 3–6pm; Oct–March Mon–Sat 10am–12.30pm & 2–6.30pm; ☎ 03 27 88 26 79, ⓦ ville-douai.fr).

## EATING AND DRINKING

**Aux Grès** 2 place Saint-Amè ☎ 03 27 86 83 53. With its old fireplace, brick walls and tiled bar, this is a convivial place for a drink and occasional live music into the small hours. Tues–Thurs 6pm–1am, Fri 6pm–2am, Sat 8pm–3am.

**Le Prévert** 28 rue de la Comedie ☎ 03 27 98 59 51. Cosy bistro, with dishes chalked up on a blackboard and simple cooking in a friendly, umpretentious atmosphere. *Menus* from €14. Sun–Fri noon–2pm, Tues, Thurs–Sat 7–10pm. Closed Aug.

**La Terrasse** 36 terrasse St-Pierre ☎ 03 27 88 70 04, ⓦ laterrasse.fr. The food here is in the grand French tradition, with everything made in their own kitchens, from the breakfast croissants to the foie gras. Both Flemish (*potjevleich*) and classic French dishes (steak with pepper sauce) make an appearance. Old-fashioned maybe, but very reliable and well regarded. *Menus* €18–90. Daily noon–2pm & 7–10pm.

# Cambrai

Despite the tank battle of November 1917 to the west of the town (see box below), and the fact that the heavily defended Hindenburg Line ran through the town centre for most of World War I, **CAMBRAI** has kept enough of its character and cobbled streets to make a fleeting visit worthwhile, though it is less attractive than either Douai or Arras.

The large, cobbled, main **place Aristide-Briand** is dominated by the Neoclassical Hôtel de Ville. The imposing building hints at the town's former wealth, which was based on textiles and agriculture. Cambrai's chief ecclesiastical treasure is the **Church of St-Géry**, off rue St-Aubert west of the main square, worth a visit for a celebrated *Mise au Tombeau* by Rubens.

## Musée des Beaux-Arts

15 rue de l'Épée • Wed–Sun 10am–noon & 2–6pm • €3.10, free entry first weekend of the month • ☎ 03 27 82 27 90, ⓦ musenor.com/Les-Musees/Cambrai-Musee-des-Beaux-Arts

The appealingly presented **Musée des Beaux-Arts** is worth a visit. Paintings by Velázquez, Utrillo and Ingres feature prominently alongside works by various Flemish old masters, plus great twentieth-century artists like Zadkine and Van Dongen. Take the audioguided tour and be sure to check out the archeological display in the basement, where you can see some fascinating exhibits including elegant statues rescued from Cambrai's cathedral which was decimated after the Revolution.

### INFORMATION

**Tourist office** Maison Espagnole, 48 rue de Noyon (March–Nov Mon–Sat 9.30am–12.30pm & 2.30–5.30pm, Sun 2.30–5.30pm (except Dec–March); ☎ 03 27 78 36 15, ⓦ tourisme-cambrai.fr).

### ACCOMMODATION AND EATING

**Château de la Motte Fenelon** Square du Val du Château ☎ 03 27 85 25 84, ⓦ cambrai-chateau-motte-fenelon.com. The château is oddly located within a suburban area of Cambrai, but its surrounding parkland shuts off the world. Inside it's stately with large well decorated rooms and good bathrooms (ask for one in the château). The restaurant in the vaulted castle caves offers classic dishes and a good value three-course *menu* (€26). **€300**

**Le Clos St-Jacques** 9 rue St Jacques ☎ 03 27 74 37 61, ⓦ leclosstjacques.com. Delightful bed and breakfast with five individually themed rooms decorated with flair and imagination. All rooms can accommodate families. **€136**

---

#### CAMBRAI 1917

At dawn on November 20, 1917, the first full-scale **tank battle** in history began at Cambrai, when more than four hundred British tanks poured over the Hindenburg Line. In just 24 hours, the Royal Tank Corps and British Third Army made the biggest advance by either side since the trenches were dug in 1914. A fortnight later, however, casualties had reached 50,000, and the armies were back where they'd started.

Although the tanks were ahead of their time, they still relied on cavalry and plodding infantry as backup. The primitive tanks were operated by a crew of eight who endured almost intolerable conditions – with no ventilation, the temperature inside could reach 48°C. The steering alone required three men, each on separate gearboxes, communicating by hand signals through the mechanical din. Maximum speed (6kph) dropped to barely 1kph over rough terrain, and refuelling was necessary every 55km. Of the 179 tanks lost at Cambrai, few were destroyed by the enemy; most broke down and were abandoned by their crews.

---

**CLOCKWISE FROM TOP LEFT** *MOULES MARINÈRE*; RIDING ON THE CÔTE D'OPALE (P.168); AMIENS CATHEDRAL AT NIGHT (P.188) >

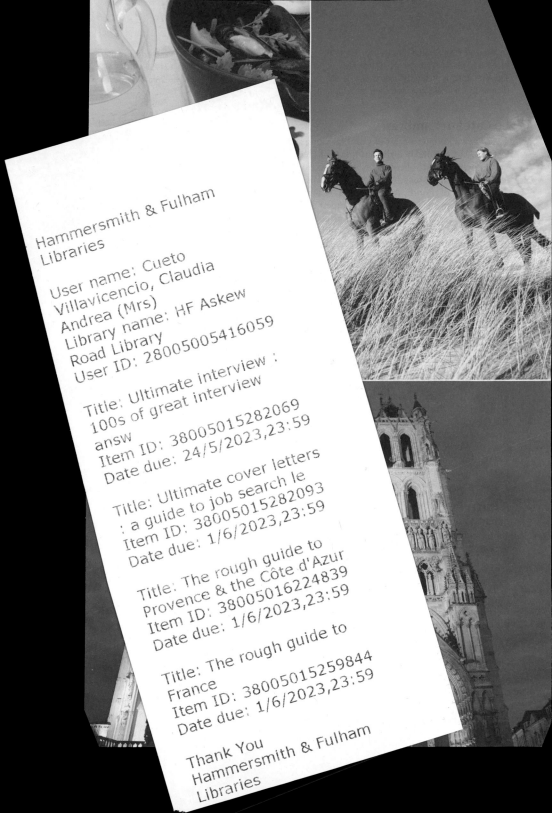

**Mouton Blanc** 33 rue d'Alsace-Lorraine ☎03 27 ⬤1 30 16, ⓦmouton-blanc.com. Moderately priced and with smartly decorated rooms, this family-run Flemish-style hotel is conveniently near the station. The restaurant features regional cooking and extensive use of local ingredients. *Menus* from €24–50. Tues–Sat noon–2pm & 7–9.30pm, Sun noon–2pm.

## Le Cateau–Cambrésis

Twenty-two kilometres east of Cambrai along an old Roman road, the small town of **LE CATEAU-CAMBRÉSIS** is the birthplace of Henri Matisse (1869–1954). As a gift to his home town, the artist bequeathed it a collection of his works, some of which are displayed in the remarkable **Musée Matisse** in the Palais Fénelon (daily except Tues 10am–6pm; €5, free first Sun of month, ☎03 27 84 64 50 ⓦmusematisse.cg59.fr). Although it contains no major masterpieces, this is the third-largest Matisse collection in France, with many attractive and interesting paintings. The collection includes several studies for the chapel in Vence, plus a whole series of his characteristically simple pen-and-ink sketches. The work of local Cubist Auguste Herbin, particularly his psychedelic upright piano, and the magazines and books published by the editor-poet, Tériade, add to the collections.

**ACCOMMODATION AND EATING**　　　　　　　　　　　　　　　　**LE CATEAU–CAMBRÉSIS**

**Des Digues** 13–15 rue Charles Seydoux ☎03 27 84 12 07, ⓦhoteldesdigues.eu. Welcoming, and with nine bright, individually decorated rooms, themed according to colours, this former old inn is a charming choice. *Les Digues* restaurant offers bistro dishes such as a gratin of apple and local Maroilles cheese (€9) and caramelized pork with creamed maize (€14). Otherwise go for the equally good-value *menus* (€16–33). €̲6̲5̲

# The Somme battlefields

Picardy, Artois and Flanders are littered with the monuments, battlefields and cemeteries of the two world wars, but they are nowhere as intensely concentrated as in the region northeast of Amiens, between **Albert** and the appealing market town of **Arras**. It was here, among the fields and villages of the Somme, that the main battle lines of World War I were drawn. You can get a real feel of trench warfare at **Vimy Ridge**, north of Arras, where the trenches have been left in situ. Lesser sites, often more poignant, dot the countryside around Albert along the **Circuit de Souvenir**.

## Arras

**ARRAS** is one of the most architecturally striking towns in northern France, the cobblestoned squares of its old centre surrounded by ornate Baroque townhouses that hark back to its Flemish past. It was renowned for its tapestries in the Middle Ages, giving its name to the hangings behind which Shakespeare's Polonius was killed by Hamlet. The town later fell under Spanish control. Only in 1640 was Arras returned to French control, with the help of Cyrano de Bergerac. During World War I, British and New Zealand miners dug tunnels under the town to surprise the Germans to the northeast, while the Germans bombarded the town. Only one of the famous medieval Arras tapestries survived the centuries of wartime destruction; it's now on display in a cathedral in Belgium.

Reconstruction after the war was meticulous, and the townhouses lining the grand arcaded Flemish- and Dutch-style squares in the central **Grand'Place** and the smaller **Place des Héros** preserve their historic character. Both were once lively market squares, but now the centre is covered with parking spaces. The architecture is impressive; on every side are restored seventeenth- and eighteenth-century mansions.

Inside the grandly ornate **Hôtel de Ville** (daily during tourist office hours, see p.184), on place des Héros, old photographs provide an interesting history of the town's wartime destruction and subsequent reconstruction.

## THE BATTLE OF THE SOMME

On July 1, 1916, the British and French launched the **Battle of the Somme** to relieve pressure on the French army defending Verdun. The front ran roughly northwest–southeast, 6km east of Albert across the valley of the Ancre and over the almost treeless high ground north of the Somme. The windy terrain had no intrinsic value, nor was there any long-term strategic objective; the region around Albert was the battle site simply because it was where the two Allied armies met.

There were 57,000 British casualties on the first day alone, approximately 20,000 of them fatal, making it the costliest defeat the British army has ever suffered. **Sir Douglas Haig** is the usual scapegoat, yet he was only following the military thinking of the day, which is where the real problem lay. As historian A.J.P. Taylor put it, "Defence was mechanized: attack was not." Machine guns were efficient, barbed wire effective, and, most important of all, the rail lines could move defensive reserves far faster than the attacking army could march. The often ineffective heavy bombardment before an advance only warned the enemy of an offensive and churned the trenches into a giant muddy quagmire.

Despite the bloody disaster of the first day, the battle wore on until bad weather in November made further attacks impossible. The cost of this futile struggle was roughly 415,000 British, 195,000 French and 600,000 German casualties.

For a panoramic view of the town and countryside, go up to the **belfry** (€2.90) viewing platform, 150m high. A lift, then 43 steps takes you to the top. From bird's eye to mole's eyes, guided tours (ask for times in the tourist office; €5.70) take you round Les Boves – cold, dark passageways and spacious vaults beneath the city centre, tunnelled since the Middle Ages and completed by the British during World War I. The rooms – many of which have fine, tiled floors, pillars and stairways – were used as a British barracks and hospital.

### La Carrière Wellington

Rue Deletoillé • Daily 10am–12.30pm & 1.30–6pm • €6.80 • ☎ 03 21 51 26 95, 🖰 carriere-wellington.com

A few minutes' walk from the centre of town, the **La Carrière Wellington** is a particularly moving and impressive exhibition involving a descent into the network of medieval chalk quarries adapted by British and New Zealand miners and engineers to create secret underground quarters for the 24,000 allied troops awaiting the start of the Battle of Arras, a diversionary attack in preparation for the Chemin des Dames assaults. The troops emerged to mount their surprise attack on April 9, 1917. The visit is accompanied but there are also individual audioguides. Film footage on small screens, inscriptions on the walls and the words of poets such as Wilfred Owen bring the horrors to life. The visit finishes with a hauntingly effective film on the battle.

### Benedictine Abbaye St-Vaast

**Musée des Beaux–Arts** 22 rue Paul-Donnier • Daily except Tues 9.30am–noon & 2–5.30pm • €4 • ☎ 03 21 71 26 43

Next to its enormous cathedral, the eighteenth-century **Benedictine Abbaye St-Vaast** houses **the Musée des Beaux–Arts.** The grey-stone classical building, still pockmarked by wartime shrapnel, contains an impressive collection, with works by seventeenth-century French and Dutch artists including Jordaens, Brueghels and Rubens – surprising to find outside Paris. Remnants of the history of Arras include medieval sculpture, porcelain and a unique Arras tapestry. One room is filled with vivid seventeenth-century paintings by Philippe de Champaigne and his contemporaries, including his own *Présentation de la Vierge au Temple*.

### The war cemetery and Mémorial des Fusillés

Thirty minutes away by foot along boulevard Général-de-Gaulle from the Vauban barracks is a **war cemetery** and memorial by the British architect Sir Edwin Lutyens.

**2**

It's a movingly elegiac, classical colonnade of brick and stone, commemorating 35,928 missing soldiers, their names inscribed on the walls. Around the back of the barracks, alongside an overgrown moat, is the stark **Mémorial des Fusillés** where two hundred Resistance fighters were shot by firing squad during World War II – many of them of Polish descent, nearly all of them miners, and most of them Communists.

## ARRIVAL AND INFORMATION
ARRAS

**By train** Gare Arras, place du Marechal Foch, is a five-minute walk away from the centre.
Destinations Albert (every 1–2hr; 25min); Boulogne (6 daily; 1hr 50min); Calais (24 daily; from 1hr 11min); Douai (2–3 hourly; from 13min); Étaples-Le Touquet (9 daily; 1hr 30min); Lille (approx. every 1–2hr; 1hr); Paris (17 daily; from 49min).
**Tourist office** Hôtel de Ville (April to mid-Sept Mon–Sat

9am–6.30pm, Sun 10am–1pm & 2.30–6.30pm; mid-Sept to March Mon 10am–noon & 2–6pm, Tues–Sat 9am–noon & 2–6pm, Sun 10am–1pm & 2.30–6.30pm; ☎ 03 21 51 26 95, ⓦ ot-arras.fr).
**Festivals** On the last Sunday of August the town transforms itself into an open-air bistro for La Fête de l'Andouillette, with parades, colourful costumes and tasting of the sausage itself.

## ACCOMMODATION

**Les 3 Luppars** 49 Grand'Place ☎ 03 21 60 02 03, ⓦ hotel-les-3luppars.com. Go for the location in the Grand'Place where the small rooms are comfortable rather than luxurious. The ancient building has a superb Gothic facade on the front, but ask for a room at the back for peace and quiet. **€77**
**Moderne** 1 bd de Faidherbe ☎ 03 21 23 39 57, ⓦ hotel-moderne-arras.com. Opposite the station and just a

short walk from the Grand'Place, this 1920 red-brick hotel has reasonable-sized rooms simply decorated but jazzed up with bright curtains and bedcovers. **€95**
**De l'Univers** 3 & 5 place de la Croix Rouge ☎ 03 21 71 34 01, ⓦ univers.najeti.fr. The best hotel in town is set in a former seventeenth-century Jesuit monastery built around a paved courtyard. Choose from a variety of rooms, all spacious and full of pretty fabrics and good furniture. **€159**

## EATING

There's a good *fromagerie*, *L'Alpage*, just off the Grand'Place on rue de la Taillerie. Saturday is the best day for food and wine, when the squares are taken over by a morning market.

**Le Between Terre et Mer** 12 rue de la Taillerie ☎ 03 21 73 57 79, ⓦ betweenterreetmer.fr. Contemporary decoration in an old vaulted cellar and an imaginative menu of dishes like roast duck with pears or salmon with ginger, pineapple, coriander and mango set this cheerful restaurant apart from its neighbours. *Menus* at €25 and €32. Mon–Fri noon–2.30pm & 7–10.30pm, Sat 7–10.30pm, Sun noon–2pm.
**La Faisanderie** 45 Grand'Place, ☎ 03 21 48 20 76, ⓦ restaurant-la-faisanderie.com. Gourmet restaurant in a knock-out Flemish Baroque building; the adventurous cooking provides another revelation. Foie gras and *magret*

*de canard* on the cheapest €29 *menu* (they go up to €45) make this a real affordable treat. Noon–2.30pm & 6.30–10pm; closed Mon, Thurs lunch & Sun dinner.
**La Rapière** 44 Grand'Place ☎ 03 21 55 09 92, ⓦ larapiere.fr. Like many restaurants on the main square, the dining room is underground in a vaulted, red-brick seventeenth-century cellar, part of the old quarries under Arras. Typically, there are outside terrace tables for summer dining off an excellent regional menu. You can't get more local than a tart made with local Maroilles cheese followed by *andouillette*. *Menus* €17.50–29.50. Daily noon–2pm & Mon–Sat 7–10pm.

# Vimy Ridge

Eight kilometres north of Arras on the D49 • Daily: March–Oct 10am–6pm; Nov–March 9am–5pm • Free • Tours daily except Mon; call to pre-book, as they are heavily over-subscribed • ☎ 03 21 50 68 68, ⓦ veterans.gc.ca

**Vimy Ridge**, or Hill 145, was the scene of some of the fiercest trench warfare of World War I: almost two full years of battle, culminating in its capture by the Canadian Corps in April 1917. It's a vast site, given in perpetuity by the French to the Canadian people out of respect for their sacrifices, and the churned land has been preserved, in part, as it was during the conflict. Of all the battlefields, this is the best place to gain an impression of the lay of the land, and to imagine how it may have felt to be part of a World War I battle.

Near the information centre, long veins of neat, sanitized **trenches** wind through the earth, still heavily pitted by shells beneath the planted pines. Under the ground lie countless rounds of unexploded ammunition – visitors are warned not to stray from the paths. Free guided **tours** of the trenches are run by friendly, bilingual Canadian students, who supervise the visitor centre. An exhibition in the visitor centre illustrates the well-planned Canadian attack and its importance for the Canadians: this was the first time they were recognized as fighting separately from the British, which hugely influenced their growing sense of nationhood.

On the brow of the ridge to the north, overlooking the slag-heap-dotted plain of Artois, a great white **monument** reaches for the heavens, inscribed with the names of 11,285 Canadians and Newfoundlanders whose bodies were never found. Back from the ridge lies a memorial to the **Moroccan Division** who also fought at Vimy, and in the woods behind, on the headstones of another exquisitely maintained **cemetery**, you can read the names of half the counties of rural England.

## La Targette and around

The **Musée de la Targette** (irregular hours: officially daily 9am–8pm; €4; ☉03 21 59 17 76) at La Targette, 8km north of Arras at the crossroads of D937/D49 contains an interesting collection of World War I and II artefacts. It's the private collection of one David Bardiaux, inspired by his grandfather, a veteran of Verdun. Its appeal lies in the precision with which the mannequins of British, French, Canadian and German soldiers are dressed and equipped, down to their sweet and tobacco tins and such rarities as a 1915 British cap with earflaps – very comfortable for the troops but withdrawn because the top brass thought it made their men look like yokels. All the pieces exhibited have been under fire; some have stitched-up tears of old wounds.

North and south of La Targette along the D937 are several **cemeteries,** including a small British one, and south of the crossroads is the vast and moving German Neuville-Saint-Vaast cemetery, containing the remains of 44,833 Germans, some four to a cross, others singly under a Star of David. To the north, a Polish memorial and a Czech cemetery face each other across the D937 between La Targette and Souchez.

### Notre-Dame de Lorette

Albain-Nazaire, 5km north of La Targette • March 8am–5pm; April & May 8am–6pm; June–Sept 8am–7pm; Oct 8.30am–5pm; Nov–Feb 9am–5.30pm • Free

On a bleak hill a few kilometres further north of the cemeteries is the church of **Notre-Dame de Lorette**, which stands on the site of a costly French offensive in May 1915. The Neo-Byzantine church was built in 1937, grey and dour outside but rich and bejewelled within. Around it stretches a vast graveyard with more than 20,000 crosses laid out in pairs, back to back. There are 20,000 more buried in the ossuary. The small **Musée Vivant 1914–1918** (daily 9am–8pm, €4), behind the church, displays photographs, uniforms and other paraphernalia.

## Albert

The church at **ALBERT**, 40km south of Arras and 30km northeast of Amiens, was one of the minor landmarks of World War I. Its tall tower was hit by German bombing early on in the campaign, leaving the statue of the Madonna on top leaning at a precarious angle. The British, entrenched over three years in the region, called it the "Leaning Virgin". The superstition that when she fell the war would end inspired frequent pot shots by disgruntled troops. The town itself was completely rebuilt after the war in Art Deco style.

### Musée "Somme 1916"

Rue Anicet Godin • Daily: Feb–May & Oct to mid-Dec 9am–noon & 2–6pm; June–Sept 9am–6pm • €5.50 • ☎ 03 22 75 16 17, ⓦ musee-somme-1916.eu

This underground museum contains re-enactments of fifteen different scenes from life

2

in the Somme trenches in 1916. The mannequins look slightly too jolly but it does go some way to bringing the war to life. The final section recreates the actual battle, complete with flashing lights and the sound of exploding shells.

## ARRIVAL AND INFORMATION

**By train** The train station is on place du Maréchal-Foch and is a few minutes' walk from the centre. Destinations Amiens (15 daily; from 20min); Arras (hourly; 20min).
**Tourist office** 9 rue Gambetta (April–Oct Mon–Fri

### ALBERT

9am–12.30pm & 1.30–6.30pm, Sat 9am–noon & 2–6.30pm, Sun 10am–12.30pm; Nov–March Mon–Sat 9am–12.30pm & 1.30–5pm; ☏03 22 75 16 42, ⓦ paysducoquelicot.com).

## ACCOMMODATION & EATING

**De la Paix** 43 rue Victor-Hugo ☏03 22 75 01 64, ⓦ hoteldelapaix-albert.fr. The small rooms are simply decorated and have basic bathrooms, but you get a good welcome here and it makes a good base. The old-fashioned comfortable dining room offers *menus* from €16.50. **€78**

## The Circuit du Souvenir

*Was it for this the clay grew tall?*
*O what made fatuous sunbeams toil*
*To break earth's sleep at all?*

Wilfred Owen, Futility

The **Circuit du Souvenir** takes you from graveyard to mine crater, trench to memorial. There's little to show the scale of the destruction nor do you get much sense of battle tactics. But you will find that, no matter what the level of your interest in the Great War, you have embarked on a sort of pilgrimage, as each successive step uncovers a more harrowing slice of history.

The **cemeteries** are deeply moving, with the grass perfectly mown and flowers by every gravestone. Tens of thousands of them stand in precise rows, all identical, with a man's name if it's known (nearly half the British dead have never been found), his rank and regiment and, often, a personal message chosen by the bereaved family. In the lanes between Albert and Bapaume you'll see cemeteries everywhere: at the angle of copses, halfway across a field, in the middle of a wood.

### Lochnagar to the Memorial to the Missing

The Circuit du Souvenir heads east from Albert to the giant mine crater of **Lochnagar** at La Boisselle before swinging north to **BEAUMONT-HAMEL**, where, pipes playing, the 51st Highland Division walked abreast to their deaths. On the hill where most of them died, a series of trenches, now grassed over and eroding, is preserved. You'll get a good sense of the battle at the **Newfoundland Memorial visitor centre** (daily: Nov–March 9am–5pm; April–Oct 10am–6pm), a few minutes' walk south; of 800 Newfoundlanders who took part in the push, just 86 returned. Across the river, near the village of **THIEPVAL**, the 5000 Ulstermen who died in the Battle of the Somme are commemorated by the **Ulster Memorial** (café and exhibition open May–Sept Tues–Sun 10am–6pm; March–April & Oct–Nov Tues–Sun 10am–5pm; closed Dec–Feb), a replica of Helen's Tower at

---

### GETTING AROUND THE CIRCUIT DE SOUVENIR

Only the truly dedicated would try to see all four hundred Commonwealth cemeteries in the area. The easiest way to explore the circuit is by car, though the distances are short enough to do it by bicycle. Both Albert to the West and Péronne to the southeast (see opposite) make good starting points, their tourist offices and museums offering free **maps** of the circuit. The route is marked (somewhat intermittently) by arrows and poppy symbols, with Commonwealth graves also indicated in English.

Clandeboyne near Belfast. Probably the most famous of Edwin Lutyens' many memorials is also at Thiepval: the colossal **Memorial to the Missing** (daily 10am–6pm), inscribed with the names of the 73,367 British troops whose bodies were never recovered at the Somme, is visible for miles around. Here, too, an informative **visitor centre** has a poignant photo wall of some of the missing, an exhibition on the Somme Offensive and short films in English on related themes.

### Devil's Wood

Delville Wood, known as "**Devil's Wood**", lies some 10km to the east at **LONGUEVAL**. Here, where thousands of **South Africans** lost their lives, there's a memorial to the dead from both world wars and a **museum** (daily except Mon: April–Oct 10am–5.45pm; Nov & March 10am–3.45pm). It describes not just the battle in France but also the longest march of the war, thousands of kilometres away, when South African troops walked 800km to drive the Germans out of East Africa (now Tanzania). The display is brought up to date with a short section documenting the armed struggle against apartheid.

### Péronne

The excellent **Historial de la Grande Guerre** museum is in Péronne's Château (daily 10am–6pm, closed mid-Dec to mid-Jan, €6.50, ☎03 22 83 14 18, ⌨historial.org) explains the political and cultural tensions before 1914, the conflict and the consequences of World War I for civilians and the soldiers through an imaginative display of uniforms and accessories, posters, newsreel, film footage, Otto Dix drawings, artificial limbs and weaponry.

#### ARRIVAL AND INFORMATION

**By train** The Gare Haute Picardie TGV station is 15km from Péronne (30min from the Lille-Europe Eurostar stop). For a taxi to or from the station, call Confort Taxi (☎03 22 84 40 00) or Taxi Nico (☎03 22 84 59 22), both based in Péronne.

#### CIRCUIT DU SOUVENIR: PÉRONNE

**Tourist office** Place André Audinot, Péronne (July & Aug Mon–Sat 9am–noon & 2–6.30pm, Sun 10am–noon & 2–5pm; April–June & Sept Mon–Sat 10am–noon & 2–6.30pm; Oct–March Mon–Sat 10am–noon & 2–5pm; ☎03 22 84 42 38, ⌨ville-peronne.fr).

#### ACCOMMODATION

**Le St-Claude** 42 place du Cdt-L-Daudré, Péronne ☎03 22 79 49 49, ⌨hotelsaintclaude.com. Perfect for visiting the Historial as it's right opposite, this nineteenth-century former inn has spacious rooms and a fairly ordinary but handy restaurant, with *menus* from €16–29. **€140**

### Villers-Bretonneux and The Australian Memorial

Near the village of **VILLERS-BRETONNEUX**, 18km from Albert near the River Somme, another Lutyens creation dominates. As at Vimy, the landscaping of the **Australian Memorial** is dramatic – for the full effect, climb up to the viewing platform of the stark white central tower. The monument was one of the last to be inaugurated, in July 1938, when the prospects for peace were again looking bleak, and it was damaged during World War II – bullet holes are still visible. There's a small **Franco–Australian Museum** (Mon–Sat: Nov–Feb 9.30am–4.30pm; March–Oct 9.30am–5.30pm, €5, ☎03 22 96 80 79, ⌨museeaustralien.com/en) on the first floor of the village school, just south of the memorial.

# Picardy

To the southeast of the Somme, away from the coast and the main Paris through-routes, the often rainwashed province of Picardy becomes considerably more inviting. **Amiens** is a friendly city whose life revolves around its canals, while both the Amiens and Beauvais cathedrals are highlights of the region. In the *départements* of **Aisne** and **Oise**, where Picardy merges with neighbouring Champagne (see Chapter 3), there are some real attractions amid the lush wooded hills. **Laon**, **Soissons** and **Noyon** all have handsome Gothic cathedrals, while at **Compiègne**, Napoleon Bonaparte and Napoléon III enjoyed the luxury of a magnificent château. The most rewarding overnight stop is off the beaten track in the tiny fortified town of **Coucy-le-Château-Auffrique**, which is perched on a hill between Soissons and Laon.

# Amiens

**AMIENS** was badly scarred during both world wars, but sensitively restored. Most people visit for the cathedral, but there's much more to the city: **St-Leu**, the renovated medieval artisans' quarter north of the cathedral with its network of canals, is charming, while the *hortillonnages* (see below) transport you into a peaceful rural landscape. A sizeable student population ensures enough evening entertainment to make an overnight stay worthwhile.

## Cathédrale Notre-Dame

Daily: April–Sept 8.30am–6.30pm; Oct–March 8.30am–5.30pm • **Son et lumière** Daily mid-June to mid-Sept & Dec starts at dusk & in Dec at 7pm • Free • **Towers** Daily except Tues & Sun am: April–June & Sept 2.30–5.15pm, Sat & Sun 2.30–4pm; July & Aug 11am; guided tours July & Aug Mon–Fri 4pm Sat 11am; other times check with the tourist office • €5.50 • ☎ 03 22 71 60 50

The **Cathédrale Notre-Dame** dominates the city by sheer size – it's the biggest Gothic building in France – but its appeal lies mainly in its unusually uniform style. Begun in 1220 under architect Robert de Luzarches, it was effectively finished by 1269. The west front shows traces of the original polychrome exterior, in stark contrast to its sombre modern appearance. A spectacular summer evening **sound and light show** vividly shows how the west front would have looked, with an explanation of the various statues on the facade in French and then in English. The interior, on the other hand, is a light, calm and unaffected space. Later embellishments, like the sixteenth-century choir stalls, are works of breathtaking virtuosity, as are the sculpted panels depicting the life of St Firmin, Amiens' first bishop, on the right side of the choir screen. The choir itself can be visited at 3.30pm daily but is otherwise locked. Those with strong legs can mount the cathedral's front **towers**. One of the most atmospheric ways of seeing the cathedral is to attend a Sunday morning Mass (9am and 10.30am), accompanied by sublime Gregorian chants.

## Quartier St-Leu

Just north of the cathedral, the **quartier St-Leu** is a Flemish-looking network of canals and cottages that was once the centre of Amiens' textile industry. The city still produces much of the country's velvet, but the factories moved out to the suburbs long ago, leaving St-Leu to rot in peace. Today the former slums have been transformed into neat brick cottages on cobbled streets, and the waterfront has been colonized by restaurants and bars.

## Hortillonnages

Boat trips: Association des Hortillonnages, 54 bd de Beauvillé • April–Oct daily 1.30–5pm • €5.70 • ☎ 03 22 92 12 18

On the edge of the city, the canals still serve as waterways for the **hortillonnages** – fertile market gardens cultivated since Roman times in the marshes of the Somme. Farmers travel between them in black, high-prowed punts and a few still take their produce into the city by boat for the Saturday morning **market** at place Parmentier. Each June farmers dress up in traditional garb and load their punts with produce for a festive *marché sur l'eau*.

## Musée de Picardie

48 rue de la République • Tues–Sun 10am–12.30pm & 2–6pm • €5

Five minutes' walk down rue de la République you come to an opulent nineteenth-century mansion which houses the splendidly laid-out **Musée de Picardie**, whose star exhibits are the Puvis de Chavannes paintings on the main stairwell, the room created by Sol LeWitt, and a collection of rare sixteenth-century paintings on wood donated to the cathedral by a local literary society. It is partly closed for a huge renovation.

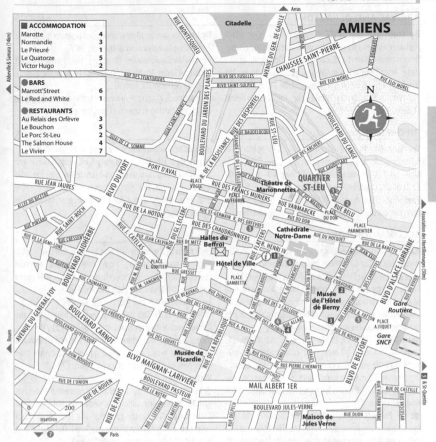

**ACCOMMODATION**
| Marotte | 4 |
| Normandie | 3 |
| Le Prieuré | 1 |
| Le Quatorze | 5 |
| Victor Hugo | 2 |

**BARS**
| Marrott'Street | 6 |
| Le Red and White | 1 |

**RESTAURANTS**
| Au Relais des Orfèvre | 3 |
| Le Bouchon | 5 |
| Le Porc St-Leu | 2 |
| The Salmon House | 4 |
| Le Vivier | 7 |

## House of Jules Verne

2 rue Charles Dubois • Mid-April to mid-Oct Mon & Wed–Fri 10am–12.30pm & 2–6.30pm, Tues 2–6.30pm, Sat & Sun 11am–6.30pm; mid-Oct to mid-April Mon & Wed–Fri 10am–12.30pm & 2–6pm, Sat & Sun 2–6pm • €7 • ☎ 03 22 45 45 75, Ⓦ jules-verne.net/maison-jules-verne.html

**Jules Verne** (1828–1905) spent most of his life in Amiens, and died here. Recently restored, his four-storey former house is a historic and attractive building, and a must for Jules Vernes' fans. It's laid out as a prosperous townhouse dating from the nineteenth century, with one room exactly as it was when the Verne family lived here. Large maps, posters, illustrations and models give an idea of the inspiration behind the writer and his science fiction works like *Twenty Thousand Leagues under the Sea* and *Around the World in Eighty Days*. They appear even more extraordinary when set against this evocation of life in a provincial French city.

## Samara

La Chaussée-Tirancourt, Tirancourt off the N1 to Abbeville • Mid-March to June & Sept to mid-Nov Mon–Fri 9.30am–5.30pm, Sat & Sun 10am–6pm; July & Aug daily 10am–6.30pm; closed mid-Nov to mid-March • €9 • ☎ 03 22 51 82 83, Ⓦ samara.fr

**Samara** (from "Samarobriva", the Roman name for Amiens), a large museum-cum-park, re-creates the life of prehistoric man in northern Europe. The open-air park is full of reconstructions of dwellings and displays illustrating the way of life – how people farmed, made oil lamps, cooked their dinners and coped with the weather.

2

## ARRIVAL AND DEPARTURE

**By train** The *gare SNCF* (Amiens-Nord) is at place Alphonse Fiquet a five-minute walk west into the centre. Destinations Albert (15 daily; from 20min); Arras (12 daily; from 44min); Compiègne (21 daily; from 1hr 02min); Laon (8 daily; 1hr 40min); Lille (19 daily; from 1hr 19min); Paris (every 30min–1hr; 1hr 30min); Reims (7 daily; 3hr).

**By bus** The *gare routière* is concealed beneath the Amiens 2 shopping complex next to the *gare SNCF*. Destinations Abbeville (2 daily; 1hr 25min); Albert (4 daily; 45min–1hr 8min); Beauvais (14 daily; 1hr 20min); Péronne (2 daily; 1hr 40min).

**By car** Much of central Amiens is traffic-free – the rest is full of cars circling in search of parking spaces.

## INFORMATION

**Tourist office** 40 place Notre-Dame (April–Sept Mon–Sat 9.30am–6.30pm, Sun 10am–noon & 2–5pm; Oct–March Mon–Sat 9.30am–6pm, Sun 10am–noon & 2–5pm; ☎ 03 22 71 60 50, ⌨ amiens-tourisme.com).

**Pass** The Pass Amiens (€8) provides reductions on everything from museum entry to city transport, bicycle

hire and restaurants and is available at the tourist office.

**Festivals** In late March and early April, Amiens bursts into life with its annual international jazz festival; on the third weekend in June, the local costumes come out for the Fête d'Amiens, which is the best time of year to visit the *hortillonnages*.

## ACCOMMODATION

**Marotte** 3 rue Marotte ☎ 03 60 12 50 00, ⌨ hotel -marott.com. The latest hotel to open in Amiens is causing quite a stir. A classic Flemish-style red-brick house built for an Amiens doctor has been converted into a 4-star property where Art Nouveau touches fill the rooms. A new-build annexe (*the Cube*) was built on to high 'green' standards and has three huge suites with private saunas. **€450**

**Normandie** 1bis rue Lamartine ☎ 03 22 91 74 99, ⌨ hotelnormandie-80.com. This comfortable two-star hotel in a little side street in an Art Deco building is close to the *gare SNCF*. It makes a good choice for a sightseeing base on a budget. Not all rooms have en-suite bathrooms; check when you book. **€70**

★ **Le Prieuré** 17 rue Porion ☎ 03 22 71 16 71, ⌨ hotel-prieure-amiens.com. You could be in Paris in this chic, beautifully renovated hotel very close to the cathedral.

Each room of the former canon's house is different – with varying styles ranging from cosy antique to cool contemporary – so you can choose to match your mood and taste; there's even a chapel room. **€90**

**Le Quatorze** 14 ave du Dublin ☎ 03 22 47 50 85, ⌨ lequatorze.fr. This delightful bed and breakfast in the former English quarter is beautifully decorated by the artist owner with her own whimsical works. There's a kitchen you can use for meals and a small garden. The owner lives elsewhere so you really feel it's your own. **€70**

**Victor Hugo** 2 rue de l'Oratoire ☎ 03 22 91 57 91, ⌨ hotel-a-amiens.com. This pretty renovated hotel has just 10 rooms, each differently decorated and with good bathrooms. It's near the cathedral and feels more like a rural bed and breakfast than a city hotel. Old photos and pictures give the place real character. **€60**

## EATING, DRINKING AND ENTERTAINMENT

If you're stocking up for a picnic or fancy some gourmet food shopping, the Les Halles du Beffroi (Mon–Sat 10am–7pm; ☎ 02 33 91 96 22) is the place to head; it's a large covered market hall full of top producers and individual cheesemongers, like Julien Planchon who encourages local makers to produce new cheeses.

### RESTAURANTS

**Au Relais des Orfèvres** 14 rue des Orfèvres ☎ 03 22 92 36 01, ⌨ restaurant-relais-orfevres.fr. Contemporary decor accompanies Jean-Michel Descloux's renowned cooking. Go for one of the *menus* (€25–54) for dishes like cheese ravioli in *petit pois* soup, *boudin blanc* of crab and a selection of superb cheeses and desserts. Tues–Fri noon–2.30pm & 7–10.30pm, Sat 7–10.30pm.

**Le Bouchon** 10 rue A-Faton ☎ 03 22 92 14 32, ⌨ lebouchon.fr. Simple bistro menu of staples like terrine and snails, leg of lamb with thyme and chicken fricassee, alongside more ambitious dishes, from foie gras with spiced sauce to pikeperch with sorrel polenta, keep the locals happy at this popular restaurant.

*Menus* are €14–42 and there's a seriously good wine list. Mon–Sat noon–2.30pm & 6.30–10.30pm, Sun noon–2.30pm.

**Le Porc St-Leu** 45/47 rue Bélu ☎ 03 22 80 00 73. More traditional than its trendy neighbours, this brasserie-style restaurant has banquette seating, brass lamps and a tiled floor. It's the place for hearty meat dishes like *cochon de lait* (suckling pig) and shoulder of lamb on *menus* running from €19–29.50. Mon–Fri noon–2pm & 7–10pm, Sat & Sun noon–2pm & 7–10pm.

**The Salmon House** 14/16 rue Cormont ☎ 03 22 91 27 83. Located right by the south door of the cathedral, this restaurant, with a summer terrace for people-watching, offers salmon in every conceivable form (main dishes

€12–19), plus a few meat dishes. *Menus* €19–24. Mon–Sat noon–2pm & 7–10pm, Sun noon–2pm.
**Le Vivier** 593 rte de Rouen ☎ 03 22 89 12 21, ⓦ levivier. It's definitely worth the slight trek to this pretty restaurant where you can eat in the glass extension. Dishes like prawn carpaccio with lime, groaning platters of seafood (from €29 to an eye-watering €160) to share, and red mullet cooked in salt with a *piperade* make this the best fish restaurant in Amiens. *Menus* €30–€75. Tues–Sat noon–2.30pm & 7–10.30pm.

### BARS
**Marott'Street** 1 rue Marotte ☎ 03 22 91 14 93. Chic champagne bar housed in a former insurance office, designed by Eiffel's architectural firm in 1892. It's an atmospheric spot next to the *Marotte* (see opposite), with wood panelling, stained glass and funky tables and chairs. The wine list is excellent. Mon–Sat 11am–1am.
**Le Red and White** 9 rue de la Dodane ☎ 08 92 02 36 83. The best gay bar in Amiens, which is busy and lively right into the small hours with live music. Tues–Sat 10pm–3am.

### THEATRE
**Théâtre de Marionnettes Chés Cabotans d'Amiens** 31 rue Edouard-David ☎ 03 22 22 30 90, ⓦ ches-cabotans-damiens.com. Traditional Picardy marionette (*cabotans*) performances are suitable for children as well as adults. Tickets €8 to €10. You can buy the handmade marionettes at Jean-Pierre Facquier's workshop at 67 rue du Don (☎ 03 22 92 49 52).

# Beauvais
As you head south from Amiens towards Paris, the countryside becomes broad and flat; **BEAUVAIS**, 60km from Amiens, seems to fit into this landscape. Rebuilt in tasteful but dull fashion after World War II, it's not a town for aimless wandering.

### Cathédrale St-Pierre
Daily: June–Sept 9am–6.30pm; May & Oct 9am–12.30pm & 2–6.30pm; Nov–April 9am–12.30pm & 2–5.30pm • ☎ 03 44 48 11 60, ⓦ cathedrale-beauvais.fr

Beauvais is redeemed by its audacious, eccentric Gothic cathedral which rises above the town. It perfectly demonstrates the religious materialism of the Middle Ages – its main intention was to be taller and larger than its rivals. The choir, completed in 1272, briefly 5m higher than that of Amiens, collapsed in 1284. Its replacement also fell and, the authorities having overreached themselves financially, the church remained as it is today: unfinished, mutilated and rather odd. At over 155m high, the interior vaults are impressive, seemingly on a larger scale than at Amiens; though the props and brackets reinforcing the structure internally show its fragility. The building's real beauty lies in its glass, its sculpted doorways and the remnants of the so-called Basse-Oeuvre, a ninth-century Carolingian church incorporated into (and dwarfed by) the Gothic structure. It also contains a couple of remarkable **clocks**: a 12m-high astronomical clock built in 1865, with figures mimicking scenes from the Last Judgement on the hour; and a medieval clock that's been working for seven hundred years.

### Galerie Nationale de la Tapisserie
Daily 10.30am–5.30pm • Free • ☎ 03 44 15 39 10

Beside the cathedral, the **Galerie Nationale de la Tapisserie** houses a collection of furniture and textiles from the fifteenth century to the present day. Louis XIV founded the royal tapestry works here in 1664; in 1939 they were transferred to Aubusson then brought back here in 1989. You can see the colourful products at the Manufacture Nationale de la Tapisserie on 24 rue Henri Brisport (☎ 03 44 14 41 90).

### Musée Départemental de l'Oise
1 rue du Musée • Daily except Tues: 10am–noon & 2–6pm • Free • ☎ 03 44 10 40 50

The **Musée Départemental de l'Oise** is devoted to painting, local history and archeology, and is housed in the former Bishop's Palace. The magnificent Renaissance building is being renovated but you can see part of the collection; worth seeing are French paintings from the sixteenth century, plus works by nineteenth-century artists like

**2**

Corot. The Art Nouveau dining room is full of ceramics and there's a good representation of artists active between the two world wars.

## ARRIVAL AND INFORMATION
### BEAUVAIS

**By air** The Paris-Beauvais airport – served by Ryanair from the UK and Ireland – is just outside the town (shuttle bus €4; 8 daily; 17min to cathedral).
**By train** The train station is on Avenue de la Republique, and is a 10min walk from the centre.

Destinations Paris (every 45min–1hr; 1hr 10min).
**Tourist office** 1 rue Beauregard (Mon–Sat 9.30am–12.30pm & 1.30–6pm; April–Oct also Sun 10am–5pm; ☎ 03 44 15 30 30, ⓦ beauvaistourisme.fr).

## ACCOMMODATION

**Cygne** 24 rue Carnot ☎ 03 44 48 68 40, ⓦ hotelducygne-beauvais.com. Serviceable small hotel in the centre of town makes a good base for sightseeing, with its simple rooms and a warm welcome. **€84**
**Hostellerie St-Vincent** 241 rue de Clermont ☎ 03 44 05 49 99, ⓦ stvincent-beauvais.com. Near the

Paris–Calais *autoroute* and five minutes from Beauvais Airport, this modern hotel is a good out of town spot. Rooms are large, well decorated and adapted for people with disabilities, and the restaurant serves traditional cooking (menus €19–36). **€86**

## EATING

**L'Auberge de la Meule** 8 rue du 27 juin ☎ 03 44 45 87 24. This restaurant in one of Beauvais' few surviving streets of half-timbered houses, specializes in salads and cheese dishes and is well known for its fondues (from €12.50). Tues–Sat noon–2pm & 7.30–10pm.
**La Maison Haute** 128 rue de Paris ☎ 03 44 02 61 60,

ⓦ lamaisonhaute.fr. Beauvais' best food is served in a contemporary, smart restaurant. Try well-prepared dishes like roast scallops and Parmesan-flavoured polenta followed by fillet of beef with shallots. Menus €34–44. Tues–Fri noon–2.30pm & 7.30–10pm.

# Laon

Looking out over the plains of Champagne and Picardy from the spine of a high narrow ridge, still protected by its gated medieval walls, **LAON** (pronounced "Lon") is one of the highlights of the region. Dominating the town, and visible for miles around, are the five great towers of one of the earliest and finest Gothic cathedrals in the country. Of all the cathedral towns in the Aisne, Laon is the one to head for.

## Cathédrale Notre-Dame

Daily 9am–7pm; guided tours at 2.30pm or 4pm; different tours available – enquire at tourist office (see above)

The magnificent **Cathédrale Notre-Dame,** built in the second half of the twelfth century, was a trendsetter in its day. Elements of its design – the gabled porches, the imposing towers and the gallery of arcades above the west front – were repeated at Chartres, Reims and Notre-Dame in Paris. The creatures craning from the uppermost ledges, looking like reckless mountain goats borrowed from a medieval bestiary, are reputed to have been carved in memory of the valiant horned steers which lugged the cathedral's masonry up from the plains below. Inside, the effects are no less dramatic – the high white nave is lit by the dense ruby, sapphire and emerald tones of the medieval stained glass.

Crowded in the cathedral's lee is a quiet jumble of grey stone streets. South of the cathedral on rue Ermant is the crumbly little twelfth-century octagonal **Chapelle des Templiers** – the Knights Templar – set in a secluded garden. The rest of the *ville haute*, which rambles along the ridge to the west of the cathedral, is enjoyable to wander around, with sweeping views from the **ramparts**.

## Musée de l'Art et de l'Archéologie

32 rue Georges-Ermant • June–Sept Tues–Sun 11am–6pm; Oct–May Tues–Sun 2–6pm • €3.60 • ☎ 03 23 22 87 00

The **Musée de l'Art et de l'Archéologie** contains a rather stuffy collection of classical antiquities, albeit with some fine Grecian ceramics among them, and a jumble of furniture and paintings including an acclaimed seventeenth-century work, *Le Concert*, by local lad Mathieu Le Nain.

## ARRIVAL AND DEPARTURE

**LAON**

**By train** The train station is in the lower town (*ville basse*). To get to the upper town – *ville haute* – without your own transport, you face either the stiff climb up the steps at the end of avenue Carnot, or the easier option of the Poma 2000 (Mon–Sat 7am–8pm every 5min; same-day return ticket €1.10), a fully automated, rubber-tyred cable railway; you board next to the train station and alight by the town hall (Terminus "Hôtel de Ville") on place Général-Leclerc; from there, a left turn down rue Sérurier brings you to the cathedral.

Destinations Paris (hourly; 1hr 45min); Soissons (every 1–2hr; 30min).

## INFORMATION

**Tourist office** (April–Sept daily 9.30am–1pm & 2–6.30pm; Oct–March Mon–Sat 9.30am–12.30pm & 2–5.30pm, Sun 2–5.30pm; ☎03 23 20 28 62, ⓦ tourisme-paysdelaon.com) is housed in the impressive Gothic Hôtel-Dieu, built in 1209; ask for information about local *gîtes* and guesthouses.

## ACCOMMODATION

**Bannière de France** 11 rue Franklin-Roosevelt ☎03 23 23 21 44, ⓦ hoteldelabannieredefrance.com. This comfortable hotel in the old town very near the cathedral, has 18 renovated rooms and a restaurant serving traditional food making it a good-value option. *Menus* €22–56. **€86**

**La Chênaie** Allée de la Chênaie ☎03 23 20 25 56. Laon's well-established campsite is on the northwest side of town, just a few minutes from the centre, and has shady trees and just 55 spaces. May–Sept. Two adults per tent **€12.90**

**Les Chevaliers** 3–5 rue Sérurier ☎03 23 27 17 50, ⓔ hotelchevaliers@aol.com. Near the Poma stop in the old town, this is a charming hotel, though ask for a room at the back for a peaceful night. **€63**

★ **La Maison des 3 Rois** 17 rue Martin ☎03 23 20 74 24, ⓦ lamaisondes3rois.com. In the middle of the old town, this bed and breakfast has more than a medieval slant, with its wooden floors, creaking staircases and bathrooms with floor tiles dating from the fourteenth century. Some may find the simplicity of the rooms too austere but there are spectacular views and profound peace. **€98**

## EATING, DRINKING AND ENTERTAINMENT

**Crêperie Agora** 8 place du Marché ☎03 23 20 29 21, ⓦ creperieagora.fr. Just the place, after a visit to the cathedral opposite, for a cheap lunch, snack, salad (from €14.50) or a full menu. Good summer terrace. *Menu* €12–16.90. Mon 11.30am–2.30pm, Tues–Sun 11.30am–2.30pm & 6.30pm–10.30pm.

**La Petite Auberge** 45 bd Pierre-Brossolette ☎03 23 23 02 38, ⓦ zorn-lapetiteauberge.com. Located in the *ville basse* near the station, this Michelin-starred restaurant is far above average. Scallops done three different ways (€22); pan-seared thinly sliced veal with parsnip purée and onion and hazelnut chutney (mains €29) and superb desserts (€15) are served in a refreshingly contemporary space. The adjacent *Bistrot St-Amour* under the same ownership, offers more casual eating. Mon noon–2.30pm, Tues–Sat noon–2.30pm & 7–10pm, Sat 7–10pm, Sun noon–2.30pm.

**Restaurant Arsenic et Vielles Dentelles** 3 rue St Pierre au Marché ☎03 23 29 08 58. *Arsenic and Old Lace* is a delightful teashop and restaurant in a brocante-filled room. Weekly changing menus and top pastries draw in the locals. Tues–Sat 11.45am–2pm, Fri & Sat 7–9pm.

## THEATRE

**Maison des Arts de Laon** Place Aubry ☎ 03 23 22 86 86. MAL is based in a theatre to the north of the cathedral, and puts on concerts, drama and lots of other events during Les Médiévales de Laon in May and the Festival de Laon in October, either in the cathedral or at MAL venues (details from the tourist office).

# Soissons

Half an hour by train, or 30km down the N2, **SOISSONS** has a long and highly strategic history. Before the Romans arrived it was already a town, and in 486 AD the last Roman ruler, Syagrius, suffered a decisive defeat here at the hands of Clovis the Frank, making Soissons one of the first real centres of the Frankish kingdom. Napoleon, too, considered it a crucial military base, a judgement borne out in the twentieth century by extensive war damage.

### Cathédrale St Gervais-St Protais

Rue des Déportées et Fusilliées • Daily 9.30am–noon & 2–5.30pm (May–Sept until 6.30pm)

Once one of the most beautiful gothic cathedrals of north France, the mainly thirteenth-century **Cathédrale St Gervais-St Protais** stands at the west end of the oversized main square and dominates the countryside despite huge damage in World War I. Inside it's remarkable for the stone vaulting in the choir, majestic glass and the *Adoration of the Shepherds* by Rubens.

2

### Abbaye de St-Jean-des-Vignes

More impressive than the cathedral is the ruined **Abbaye** to the south of place Marquigny. The gaping west front of the tremendous Gothic abbey rises sheer and grand, impervious to the empty space behind it – you get a superb view of it from the peaceful abbey precincts, but the ruin itself is in crumbly condition and fenced off. The rest of the complex, save for remnants of a **cloister** and **refectory** (free to visit), was dismantled in 1804.

#### ARRIVAL AND INFORMATION — SOISSONS

**By train** The train station is at place de la Gare from where it's 20min walk west into the centre.

Destinations Laon (approx every 2hr; 30min); Paris (12 daily; from 1hr 16min).

**By bus** The bus station is on avenue de l'Aisne, a few minutes walk from the centre.

Destinations Compiègne (9 daily; 1hr 15min); Coucy (5 daily; 25min).

**Tourist office** Place Fernand Marquigny (July–Aug Mon–Sat 9am–7pm, Sun 10am–12.15pm & 1.15–5pm; Sept–June Mon–Sat 9am–5pm, Sun 10.30am–12.15pm & 1–3.30pm; T 03 23 53 17 37, W tourisme-soissons.fr).

#### ACCOMMODATION

**Francs** 62 bd Jeanne-d'Arc T 03 60 71 40 00, W **hoteldesfrancs.fr.** This new, modern hotel is strong on up-to-date facilities and eco practices. Good-sized rooms may lack period charm but the hotel is opposite the old abbey of St-Jean-des-Vignes, and has great views. There's also a chic brasserie with good *menus* from €18. **€165**

**Le Terminus** 56 av du Général-de-Gaulle T 03 23 53 33 59. Above a bar and conveniently near the station, this hotel with small rooms serves for a quick stop. **€89**

#### EATING

**L'Arthé** 16 rue de la Bannière T 03 23 76 29 64. Simple, casual *salon de thé* and restaurant on a side street between the cathedral and the river. On offer are simple *menus* from €12, or just coffee and desserts. Tues–Sat 9.30am–6pm.

**L'Assiette Gourmande** 16 av de Coucy T 03 23 93 47 78, W **agourmande.fr.** Elegant decor and classy cooking, which involves a good value €31 *menu* offering foie gras with fig and apricot compote, along with deliciously sweet lamb with *petit pois* and mushrooms. Mon noon–2pm, Tues–Sat noon–2pm & 7.30–9pm, Sun noon–2pm.

## Coucy-le-Château-Auffrique

About 30km west of Laon and 15km north of Soissons, in hilly countryside on the far side of the forest of St-Gobain, lie the straggling ruins of one of the greatest castles of the Middle Ages, **Coucy-le-Château** (daily: May to early Sept 10am–1pm & 2–6.30pm; early Sept to April 10am–1pm & 2–5.30pm; €5). The castle's walls still stand, encircling the attractive village of **COUCY-LE-CHÂTEAU-AUFFRIQUE**. In the past this was a seat of great power and the influence of its lords, the Sires de Coucy, rivalled and often even exceeded that of the king. The retreating Germans capped the destruction of World War I battles by blowing up the castle's keep as they left in 1917, but enough remains, crowning a wooded spur, to be extremely evocative.

Enter the village through one of three original gates, squeezed between powerful, round flanking towers – there's a footpath around the outside which is open even when the castle is not. A display of photographs in the museum (Wed–Sun 2–6pm; free) at the Porte de Soissons, shows how the castle looked pre-1917. Go onto the roof to compare with today's post-war reconstruction. Also here are costumed characters and explanations of medieval life.

## ARRIVAL AND INFORMATION

**COUCY-LE-CHÂTEAU-AUFFRIQUE**

**By bus** It's hard to get to Coucy-le-Château without a car, though there are around five buses a day from Soissons. Buses on the Soissons–St Quentin route (line 10) stop in Coucy-le-Chateau at the *Café des Sports* and the *Hotel Lion Rouge*.

Destinations Soissons (6 daily; 25min).

**Tourist office** Place de l'Hotel-de-Ville (Mon–Fri 9am–6pm, Sat & Sun 2–6pm; ☎ 03 23 52 44 55, ⓦ coucy .com).

**Festivals** Check out the many medieval spectacles (such as Coucy à la Merveille) on ⓦ coucyalamerveille.com; note that you'll have to book in advance.

## ACCOMMODATION

**Belle Vue** 2 Porte de Laon ☎ 03 23 52 69 70, ⓦ hotel -bellevue-coucy.com. Rather faded grandeur in the bedrooms fits in perfectly with the romantic feel of being within the medieval walls. The restaurant specializes in Picardy cuisine (*menus* from €21.90), and serves special "medieval" meals to get you in the right frame of mind. **€47**

# Compiègne

Thirty-eight kilometres west of Soissons, **COMPIÈGNE** owes its reputation as a tourist centre to a vast royal palace, built at the edge of the Forêt de Compiègne so that generations of French kings could play at "being peasants", in Louis XIV's words. It's an attractive and lively town of pale stone houses, white shutters and dark slate roofs, and makes a good base for seeing the sites associated with the two world wars and for walks in the surrounding forest.

## Château de Compiègne

Place du Général de Gaulle • Daily except Tues 10am–6pm, last admission 5.15pm • €6.50–€7.50, more during temporary exhibitions • **Musée de la Voiture** Same ticket • **Palace gardens** Daily: March to mid-April & mid-Sept to Oct 8am–6pm; mid-April to mid-Sept 8am–7pm; Nov–Feb 8am–5pm • Free • ☎ 03 44 38 47 00, ⓦ musee-chateau-compiegne.fr

The town of Compiègne plays foil to its star attraction, the opulent **Château de Compiègne**, with extensive gardens that make excellent picnicking territory. The eighteenth-century château, two blocks east of the Hôtel de Ville along rue des Minimes, inspires a certain fascination despite its pompous excess. Napoleon commissioned a renovation of the former royal palace in 1807, and the work was completed in time for the emperor to welcome his second wife, Marie-Louise of Austria – a relative of Marie-Antoinette – here in 1810. The ostentatious post-revolutionary apartments stand in marked contrast to the more sober Neoclassicism of the few surviving late royal interiors, a monument to the unseemly haste with which Napoleon I moved in, scarcely a dozen years after the Revolution. The **Théâtre Impérial** was first planned by Napoléon III in the historic apartments of the Second Empire. It was only completed with a restoration project in 1991 at a cost of some thirty million francs. Originally designed with just two seats for Napoleon and his wife, it now seats nine hundred and is used for concerts.

To see the **Musée de la Voiture** in another part of the vast palace, you have to join a one-hour guided tour. It contains a wonderful array of antique bicycles, tricycles and aristocratic carriages, as well as the world's first steam coach.

You can visit the **palace gardens** separately. Much of the original French-style garden was replanted on Napoleon's orders after 1811. The result is monumental; the great avenue that extends 4.5km into the Forêt de Compiègne (see p.196) was inspired by the Austrian imperial summer residence at Schönbrunn on the outskirts of Vienna.

## Place de l'Hôtel-de-Ville

The centre of town is more handsome than picturesque, though several half-timbered buildings remain on rue Napoléon and rue des Lombards, south of the main place de l'Hôtel-de-Ville. The **Hôtel de Ville** itself – Louis XII Gothic – features ebullient nineteenth-century statuary including the image of Joan of Arc, who was captured in this town before being handed to the English.

## Musée de la Figurine Historique

Tues–Sat 9am–noon & 2–6pm, Sun 2–6pm; closes 5pm in winter • €3 • ☎ 03 44 20 26 04, ⓦ musee-figurine.fr

Beside the Hôtel-de-Ville, the **Musée de la Figurine Historique** reputedly holds the world's largest collection of toy soldiers in mock-up battles; the huge diorama of the Battle of Waterloo is the most impressive.

## Mémorial de l'Internement et de la Déportation

2bis av des Martyrs de la Liberté • Daily except Tues 10am–6pm • €3 • ☎ 03 44 96 37 00, ⓦ memorial-compiegne.fr

Southwest of the town centre, the sombre **Mémorial de l'Internement et de la Déportation** occupies the former barracks of Royallieu, transformed into a prisoner of war camp by the German army in 1940 and later used as a transit camp for political prisoners, Jews and others. It was from here in March 1942 that the first deportation from France to Auschwitz took place.

### ARRIVAL AND INFORMATION                                   COMPIÈGNE

**By train** The train station is a few minutes' walk from the centre of town: cross the River Oise and go up rue Solférino to place de l'Hôtel-de-Ville.
Destinations Paris (approx. 3 hourly; from 39min); Amiens (21 daily; from 56min).
**By bus** The bus station is next to the train station.

**Tourist office** Place de l'Hotel de Ville (April–Sept Mon–Sat 9.15am–12.15pm & 1.45–6.15pm; Oct–March Mon 1.45–5.15pm, Tues–Sat 9.15am–12.15pm & 1.45–5.15pm; open Sun Easter–Oct 10am–12.15pm & 2.15–5pm; ☎ 03 44 40 01 00, ⓦ compiegne-tourisme.fr).

### ACCOMMODATION

**Les Beaux-Arts** 33 cours Guynemer ☎ 03 44 92 26 26, ⓦ compiegne-hotel.com. A mix of bedrooms and apartments, with fresh, pretty decorations near the town centre and overlooking the river. The bistro on the ground floor is very popular (*menus* from €22). **€129**

**Flandre** 16 quai de la République ☎ 03 44 83 24 40, ⓦ hoteldeflandre.com. Between the station and the centre and overlooking the river, this hotel has some good-value, simple doubles with hall showers alongside its more expensive, plusher suites. **€75**

### EATING AND DRINKING

**Le Bistrot de Flandre** 2 rue Amiens ☎ 03 44 83 26 35, ⓦ bistrotdeflandre.fr. Modern bistro with summer terrace and tasty dishes, from terrine of hare (€8) to a thoroughly satisfying roast beef with potato gratin. *Menus* from €20.50–€27. Mon–Sat noon–2.30pm & 7–10pm, Sun 7–10pm.
**Le Nord** Place de la Gare ☎ 03 44 83 22 30. Just by the station, this restaurant serves traditional dishes in a huge dining room which has an open kitchen at one end

so you can watch the action. *Menus* from €25. Daily noon–2pm & 7–10.30pm (closed Sat lunch & Sun eve).
**Le Saint Clair** 6 rue des Lombards ☎ 03 44 40 58 18. Sitting on a pedestrianized street, you're guaranteed a good meal here, along with a big selection of Belgian beers and a warm welcome. There's live music on some nights and the bar becomes a gay meeting place after 1am. Daily 3pm–3am.

# The Forêt de Compiègne

Very ancient, and cut through by a succession of hills, streams and valleys, the **Forêt de Compiègne**, with the GR12 running through it, is ideal stomping ground for walkers and cyclists. East of Compiègne, some 6km into the forest and not far from the banks of the Aisne, is the green, sandy clearing known as the **Clairière de l'Armistice**. Here, in what was a rail siding for rail-mounted artillery, World War I was brought to an end on November 11, 1918. A plaque commemorates the deed: "Here the criminal pride of the German empire was brought low, vanquished by the free peoples whom it had sought to enslave." To avenge this humiliation, Hitler had the French sign their capitulation on June 22, 1940, on the same spot, in the same rail carriage. The original car was taken to Berlin and destroyed by fire in the last days of the war. Its replacement, housed in a small **museum** (Daily April to mid-Oct 10am–5.30pm; mid-Oct to March Wed–Mon 10am–5.30pm; last admission 30min before closing, €5), is similar, and the objects inside are the originals.

## Pierrefonds

Some 13km southeast of Compiégne, Pierrefonds is home to a classic medieval **château** (May–Aug daily 9.30am–6pm; Sept–April Tues–Sun 10am–1pm & 2–5.30pm, €7.50, ☎03 44 42 72 72, ⓦpierrefonds.monuments-nationaux.fr/en), built in the twelfth century, dismantled in the seventeenth and restored by order of Napoléon III in the nineteenth to create a fantastic fairy-tale affair of turrets, towers and moat. The nearby picturesque villages of **Vieux-Moulin** and **St-Jean-aux-Bois** are in the heart of the forest, the latter retaining part of its twelfth-century fortifications.

## Noyon

Around twenty kilometres north of Compiègne – and a possible day-trip – **NOYON** is another of Picardy's cathedral towns. Its quiet provinciality belies a long, illustrious history, first as a Roman prefecture, then as seat of a bishopric from 531. Here, in 768, Charlemagne was crowned king of Neustria, largest of the Frankish kingdoms; in 987, Hugues Capet was crowned king of France; and John Calvin was born here in 1509.

Rowing along the Oise on his *Inland Journey* of 1876, Robert Louis Stevenson stopped briefly at Noyon, which he described as "a stack of brown roofs at the best, where I believe people live very respectably in a quiet way". It's still like that, though the **cathedral**, to which Stevenson warmed, is impressive enough. Spacious and a little stark, it successfully blends Romanesque and Gothic, and is flanked by the ruins of thirteenth-century cloisters and a strange, exquisitely shaped Renaissance library.

### Musée du Noyonnais

1-7 rue de l'Évêche • Tues–Sun 10am–noon & 2–6pm; Nov–March closes 5pm • €3

On the south side of the cathedral, the old episcopal palace houses the **Musée du Noyonnais**, a small, well-presented collection of local archeological finds and cathedral treasures. Close by, signs direct you to the **Musée Calvin** (Tues–Sun 10am–noon & 2–6pm; Nov–March closes 5pm, €3, same ticket as for the Musée du Noyonnais), ostensibly on the site of the reformer's birthplace. The respectable citizens of Noyon were never among their local boy's adherents and tore down the original building long before its tourist potential was appreciated.

### INFORMATION

**Tourist office** Hôtel de Ville, place Bertrand Labarre (Mon 2–6.15pm, Tues–Sat 9am–noon & 2–6.15pm, Sun 10am–noon; closed Sun Nov–March; ☎03 44 44 21 88, ⓦnoyon-tourisme.com).

### ACCOMMODATION

**Le St-Éloi** 81 bd Carnot ☎03 44 44 01 49, ⓦhotelsainteloi.fr. An elegant brick and half-timbered turreted building of 1870 (along with a newer annexe) houses stately rooms equipped with atmospheric carved headboards. Rooms in the annexe are smartly decorated and cheaper. Tradition also rules in the dining room which has columns, fancy striped wallpaper, crisp linen and *menus* from €30. **€110**

### NOYON

# Champagne and the Ardennes

CHAMPAGNE CORKS READY FOR USE

# Champagne and the Ardennes

The bubbly stuff is the reason most people visit Champagne, drawn to the vineyards and cellars of the region's capital, the cathedral city of Reims. Some of the most extravagant champagne houses are here, the *caves* beneath them notable for their vaulted ceilings and kilometres of bottles. Épernay, a smaller town set in the scenic heart of the region, is dominated by an avenue of champagne *maisons*, where visitors can float from one to another like the bubbles they're drinking.

The cultivation of vines here was already well established in Roman times, when Reims was the capital of the Roman province of Belgae (Belgium), and by the seventeenth century still wines from the region had gained a considerable reputation. Contrary to popular myth, however, it was not Dom Pérignon, cellar master of the Abbaye de Hautvillers near Épernay, who "invented" champagne. He was probably responsible for the innovation of mixing grapes from different vineyards, but the wine's well-known tendency to re-ferment within the bottle was not controllable until eighteenth-century glass-moulding techniques produced vessels strong enough to contain the natural effervescence.

The region's other major attraction is **Troyes**, some way to the southwest, a town of cobbled streets, half-timbered houses and cut-price shopping. Further south still, the small, far-flung towns of **Chaumont** and **Langres** also merit a stop.

Many people miss out the **Ardennes** in the far north on the Belgian border, which is a mistake: it's a breathtakingly wild landscape offering nature-lovers a tempting array of hiking, cycling and boating opportunities. The region's main town, **Charleville-Mézières,** is thrust into the limelight every three years by an international puppet festival but is worth a visit at other times for its lovely seventeenth-century palace.

## Reims

Laid flat by the shells of World War I, **REIMS** (pronounced like a nasal "Rance", and traditionally spelled Rheims in English) was rebuilt afterwards with tact and touches of Art Nouveau and Art Deco, but lacks any great sense of antiquity. It makes up for this with a walkable centre, beneath which lies its real treasure – kilometre upon kilometre of bottles of fermenting champagne. The old centre of Reims clusters around one of the most impressive Gothic cathedrals in France – formerly the coronation church of dynasties of French monarchs going back to Clovis, the first king of the Franks, and later painted obsessively by Monet. The northernmost section of the old town was protected by the place de la République's triumphal Roman arch, the **Porte de Mars**, reached via the grand squares of place Royale, place du Forum and place de l'Hôtel-de-Ville. To the west, place Drouet d'Erlon is the focus of the city's nightlife and an almost-complete example of the city's 1920s reconstruction. To the south, about fifteen minutes' walk from the cathedral, is the other historical focus of the town, the **Abbaye St-Remi**, with the Jesuits' College nearby. Most of the champagne houses are to the east of here, and still further east, there's a museum of cars. These attractions, plus a handful

Champagne: the facts p.203
Champagne-tasting in Reims p.207
Clothes shopping in Troyes p.210

It takes guts ... p.212
Puppets in charleville p.216

# Highlights

**❶ Champagne-tasting at Épernay or Reims**
Taste vintage bubbly in the atmospheric cellars
of world-famous sparkling wine emporia.
**See p.207 & p.200**

**❷ Troyes** Delightful medieval town with historic
churches and fascinating museums, from an old
apothecary to a personal collection of modern
art. **See p.209**

**❸ Colombey-les-Deux-Églises** Find out more
about the man who said "No" to British

membership of the Common Market – Général
de Gaulle – in this charming house museum.
**See p.214**

**❹ Langres** Walk around the impressive
fortified walls and towers of the town where
the French philosopher Diderot was born.
**See p.214**

**❺ The Ardennes** Explore the spectacular
scenery and forested hills of the rugged Meuse
river valley. **See p.215**

**HIGHLIGHTS ARE MARKED ON THE MAP ON P.202**

of interesting museums and a big city buzz unusual in this part of France, make it worth a day or two's stopover.

## Cathédrale Notre-Dame

Daily 7.30am–7.30pm • **Towers** Guided tour only; mid-March to May 5/6 & Sept–Oct Sat at 10 & 11am, 2, 3 & 4pm; May 6/7 to Sept Tues–Sat every 30min from 10am–11.30am, 2–5pm • €7.50, or combined ticket with the Palais du Tau €11

The glorious Gothic thirteenth-century **Cathédrale Notre-Dame** features prominently in

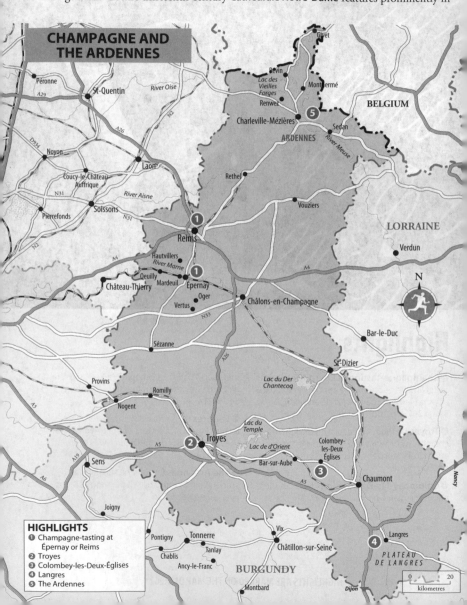

**CHAMPAGNE AND THE ARDENNES**

HIGHLIGHTS
1. Champagne-tasting at Épernay or Reims
2. Troyes
3. Colombey-les-Deux-Églises
4. Langres
5. The Ardennes

## CHAMPAGNE: THE FACTS

Nowhere else in the world are you allowed to make a drink called **champagne**, though many people do, calling it "champan", "shampanskoye" and all manner of variants. You can blend grape juice harvested from chalk-soil vineyards, double-ferment it, store the result for years at the requisite constant temperature and high humidity in sweating underground *caves*, turn and tilt the bottles little by little to clear the sediment, add some vintage liqueur, and finally produce a bubbling golden (or pink) liquid; but according to international law you may refer to it only as "*méthode champenoise*". The jealously guarded monopoly helps keep the region's sparkling wines in the luxury class, although the locals will tell you the difference comes from the squid fossils in the chalk, the lay of the land and its climate, the evolution of the grapes, the regulated pruning methods and the legally enforced quantity of juice pressed.

Three authorized **grape varieties** are used: chardonnay, the only white grape, grown best on the Côte des Blancs and contributing a light and elegant element; pinot noir, grown mainly on the Montagne de Reims slopes, giving body and long life; and pinot meunier, cultivated primarily in the Marne valley, adding flowery aromas.

The **vineyards** are owned either by *maisons*, who produce the *grande marque* champagne, or by small cultivators called *vignerons*, who sell the grapes to the *maisons*. The *vignerons* also make their own champagne and will happily offer you a glass and sell you a bottle at two-thirds the price of a *grande marque* (ask at any tourist office in the Champagne region for a list of addresses). The difference between the two comes down to capital. The *maisons* can afford to blend grapes from up to sixty different vineyards and to tie up their investment while their champagne matures for several years longer than the legal minimum (one year for non-vintage, three years vintage). So the wine they produce is undoubtedly superior.

If you could visit the head offices of Cartier or Dior, you'd probably find the atmosphere similar to that of the champagne *maisons*, whose palaces are divided between Épernay and Reims. Visits to the handful that organize regular **tours** are not free, and most require appointments, but don't be put off – their staff all speak English and a generous *dégustation* is thrown in. Their audiovisuals and (cold) cellar tours are on the whole very informative, and do more than merely plug brand names. Local tourist offices can provide full lists of addresses and times of visits.

If you want to work on the harvest, contact any of the *maisons* direct or Pôle Employ Vendanges (☎03 177 86 39 49, ⊕pole-emploi.fr)

French history: in 1429 Joan of Arc managed to get the Dauphin crowned here as Charles VII – an act of immense significance when France was more or less wiped off the map by the English and their allies. In all, 26 French kings were crowned here.

The chief draw inside the cathedral is the kaleidoscopic patterns in the stained glass, with fantastic **Marc Chagall** designs in the east chapel, and champagne processes glorified in the south transept. The exterior is also fabulous: an inexplicable joke runs around the restored but still badly mutilated statuary on the west front – the giggling angels who seem to be responsible for a prank are a delight. Not all the figures on the cathedral's west front are originals – some have been removed to spare them further erosion and are now at the former bishop's palace, the Palais du Tau. The **towers** of the cathedral are open to the public; as well as a walk round the transepts and chevet, you get to see inside the framework of the cathedral roof; tickets available from the Palais du Tau.

## Palais du Tau

Daily: early May to early Sept 9.30am–6.30pm; early Sept to early May 9.30am–12.30pm & 2–5.30pm • €7.50, or combined ticket with the towers €11 • ☎03 26 47 81 79, ⊕palais-tau.monuments-nationaux.fr

At the **Palais du Tau**, next door to the cathedral, you can appreciate the expressiveness of the statuary from close up. Apart from the grinning angels, there is also a superb Eve, shiftily clutching the monster of sin, while embroidered tapestries of the Song of Songs line the walls. The palace also preserves the paraphernalia of Charles X's coronation in 1824, right down to the Dauphin's hat box and cathedral treasures.

## Musée des Beaux-Arts

Rue Chanzy • Daily except Tues & public hols 10am–noon & 2–6pm • €3 • ☏ 03 26 35 36 00

West of the cathedral, the **Musée des Beaux-Arts** is the city's principal art museum, which, though ill-suited to its ancient building, effectively covers French art from the Renaissance to the present. Few of the works are among the artists' best but the collection includes one of David's replicas of his famous Marat death scene, 27 Corots, two great Gauguin still lifes, and some beautifully observed sixteenth-century portraits by the German artists Lucas Cranach the Elder and Younger.

## Musée-Hôtel Le Vergeur

36 place du Forum • Tues–Sun 2–6pm • €5 • ☏ 03 26 47 20 75, Ⓦ mhlv.free.fr • **Crypto portique Gallo-Romain** June to mid-Oct Tues–Sun 2–6pm • Free

Just north of the cathedral is the **Musée-Hôtel Le Vergeur**, a treasure house stuffed with all kinds of beautiful objects, including two sets of Dürer engravings – an *Apocalypse* and *Passion of Christ* – but you have to go through a long guided tour to see them. Opposite the museum there's access to sections of the partly submerged arcades of the **crypto portique Gallo-Romain**, which date back to 200 AD. Reims's other Roman monument, the quadruple-arched **Porte de Mars**, on place de la République, belongs to the same era.

## Musée de la Reddition

Rue Franklin-Roosevelt • Daily except Tues & public hols 10am–noon & 2–6pm • €3 • ☏ 03 26 47 84 19

West of the Porte behind the train and bus station, the "Museum of the Surrender" is based around an old schoolroom that served as Eisenhower's HQ from February 1945. In the early hours of May 7, 1945, General Jodl agreed to the unconditional surrender of the German army here, thus ending World War II in Europe. The room has been left exactly as it was (minus the ashtrays and carpet), with the Allies' battle maps on the walls.

## The Abbaye St-Remi

Rue Simon Basilique St-Remi Daily 8am–7pm, closed during service • Son et lumière show July–Sept Sat 9.30pm • Free • **Musée St-Remi** Mon–Fri 2–6.30pm, Sat & Sun 2–7pm • €3 • ☏ 03 26 35 36 91

Most of the early French kings were buried in Reims's oldest building, the eleventh-century **Basilique St-Remi**, part of a former Benedictine abbey named after the 22-year-old bishop who baptized Clovis and three thousand of his warriors. An immensely spacious building, it preserves its Romanesque transept walls and ambulatory chapels, some of them with modern stained glass that fits in beautifully. Albert Nicart, the bell-ringer of St-Remi, was the inspiration for Victor Hugo's fictional Quasimodo in *The Hunchback of Notre Dame;* Hugo met Nicart and the gypsy girl Esméralda in 1825 while visiting Reims to attend Charles X's coronation.

The spectacular abbey buildings alongside the church house the **Musée St-Remi**, the city's rather dry archeological and historical museum that includes the reconstructed facade of a thirteenth-century house destroyed by World War I German shelling. The museum's twelfth- to thirteenth-century chapterhouse has been listed as a UNESCO World Heritage Site.

## Musée de l'Automobile

84 av Georges-Clemenceau • Daily except Tues: April–Oct 10am–noon & 2–6pm; Nov–March 10am–noon & 2–5pm; also open Tues July & Aug • €8 • ☎ 03 26 82 83 84, ⓦ musee-automobile-reims-champagne.com

If you have even a passing interest in old cars don't miss the **Musée de l'Automobile**, fifteen minutes' walk southeast of the cathedral. The collection contains many prototypes and rarities; highlights include a string of sleek, powerful Delahaye coupés designed by Philippe Charbonneaux in the 1940s and 1950s, and a stunning Panhard et Levassor Dynamic 130 Coupé from 1936 – pure Art Deco on wheels.

### ARRIVAL AND INFORMATION
REIMS

**By train** Reims main station is on bd Joffre, a few minutes' walk from the centre.
**Destinations** Charleville-Mézières (almost hourly; 50min); Épernay (16 daily; from 20min); Laon (7 daily; 45min); Paris (TGV 16 daily; 45min).
**By bus** The *gare routière* is on rue Pingat, beside the train station.

**Destinations** Laon (1 daily; 1hr 30min); Troyes (5 daily; 2hr 10min).

**Tourist office** 2 rue Guillaume-de-Machault (April to first week Oct Mon–Sat 9am–7pm, Sun & public hols 10am–6pm; second week Oct to March Mon–Sat 9am–6pm, Sun 10am–1pm; ☎ 08 92 70 13 51, ⓦ reims -tourisme.com).

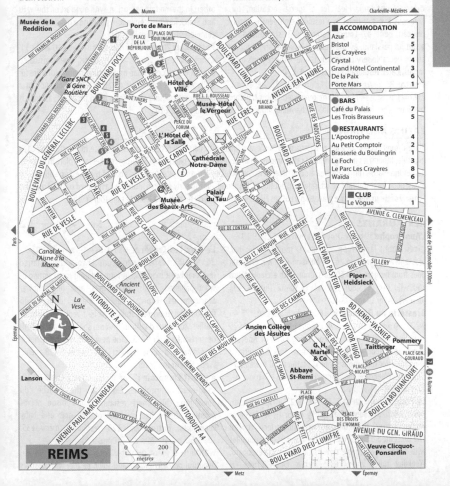

**3**

**Passes** Reims City Card (€16) includes entry to various museums, two audioguides and a tour of a champagne cellar. English audioguides (€6) to the city are available from the tourist office.

## ACCOMMODATION

**Azur** 9 rue des Ecrevées ⊕03 26 47 43 39, ⓦhotel-azur-reims.com. This charming small hotel, five minutes' from the station, is friendly, has spotless simple rooms, and is in the up-and-coming Boulingrin area, with its restaurants, shops and renovated market. In summer, take breakfast in the little courtyard. **€86**

**Bristol** 70 place Drouet d'Erlon ⊕03 26 40 52 25, ⓦbristol-reims.com. New owners have refurbished this 2-star hotel minutes from the cathedral. Comfortable, traditional rooms and the welcoming, bistro-like *Bristol Café* with a good-value breakfast make this a dependable choice. **€79**

**Les Crayères** 64 bd Henry-Vasnier ⊕03 26 24 90 00, ⓦlescrayeres.com. Ideal for a special occasion, this gorgeous five-star hotel in a restored eighteenth-century château built by Louise Pommery is surrounded by beautiful parkland. As you'd expect it has luxurious rooms and impeccable service, as well as one of the region's most sophisticated restaurants (see below). **€700**

**Crystal** 86 place Drouet-d'Erlon ⊕03 26 88 44 44, ⓦhotel-crystal.fr. Most of the renovated rooms here are spacious and look out onto a charming flower-filled courtyard garden where you can eat breakfast in the summer months. The garden also blocks out much of the noise from the local nightlife. **€84**

**Grand Hôtel Continental** 93 place Drouet-d'Erlon ⊕03 26 40 39 35, ⓦgrandhotelcontinental.com. This three-star hotel has rather grand public areas, with a splendid staircase and rooms that are either traditionally furnished, or sport a contemporary look. It's welcoming and very central but avoid the rooms overlooking bd du Général Leclerc. **€189**

**De la Paix** 9 rue Buirette ⊕03 26 40 04 08, ⓦhotel-lapaix.fr. In the same family for a century, this hotel has smart, contemporary rooms, some in the old building, others in the modern extension, with good art on the walls and Starck furniture. An indoor pool and a good restaurant completes the package. **€220**

**Porte Mars** 2 place de la République ⊕03 26 40 28 35, ⓦhotelportemars.com. Cosy rooms, well insulated against noise, a good bar, and a sitting room with a fire for chilly evenings make this an attractive option. Add in a grass-roofed dining room for a good breakfast, as well as friendly staff. **€105**

## EATING AND DRINKING

Place Drouet-d'Erlon, a wide pedestrianized boulevard lined with bars and restaurants, is the place for most of the city's nightlife, though it's more pavement café lounging than high-octane partying. A big Saturday market takes place in place du Boulingrin (6am–1pm). The area around here, between Hotel de Ville and Porte du Mars, is one of the latest up and coming areas, good for restaurants, bars, cafes and boutiques. From mid-June to early August, more than a hundred classical concerts – many of them free – take place as part of Les Flâneries Musicales d'Été; pick up a leaflet at the tourist office.

### RESTAURANTS

**L'Apostrophe** 59 place Drouet d'Erlon ⊕03 26 79 19 89, ⓦrestaurant-lapostrophe.fr. Smart, modern café, bar, brasserie and terrace in an old building with a menu that goes from burgers (€14.60) to salmon with a creole sauce and wild rice (€15.80). *Menus* €13.50–18 (lunch), €33 (dinner). Daily 10am–1am.

**Brasserie du Boulingrin** 48 rue de Mars ⊕03 26 40 96 22, ⓦboulingrin.fr. *Belle époque* glamour from 1925 including a wall-length fresco depicting a bucolic vineyard scene and good-value classics make this brasserie a winner. Order its famous seafood platters and *fondant au chocolat*. Weekday *menu* at €18.50. Mon–Sat noon–2.30pm & 7–11.30pm.

**Le Foch** 37 bd Foch ⊕03 26 47 48 22, ⓦlefoch.com. Never mind the somewhat quirky decor (is it classic or contemporary?), this is the place to savour perfectly cooked and presented dishes. Foie gras hamburger; grilled mullet with tempura courgette flowers; a superb cheeseboard. Weekday lunch *menu* €31; *menus* €48–80. Tues–Fri noon–2pm & 7–9.30pm, Sat 7–9.30pm, Sun noon–2pm.

**Le Parc Les Crayères** 64 bd Henry-Vasnier ⊕03 26 24 90 00, ⓦlescrayeres.com. Two-Michelin-starred restaurant in a magnificent formal dining room setting of wood-panelled walls, chandeliers and huge flower arrangements. Expect exquisite classic dishes with fashionable touches: scallop vol-au-vent with black truffles, cod dusted with shavings, and superb desserts. *Menus* €65–185. The new brasserie in the hotel, *Le Jardin*, is a more modest affair with a €28 *menu*. Wed–Sun noon–2pm & 7–9.30pm.

**Au Petit Comptoir** 17 rue de Mars ⊕03 26 40 58 58, ⓦau-petit-comptoir.fr. Close to the Marché du Boulingrin, this smart restaurant and bistro serves inventive dishes like couscous of foie gras and baby vegetables. Bistro *menu* €20, restaurant *menu* €35. Tues–Sat noon–2pm & 7–10pm.

**Waïda** 3–5 place Drouet-d'Erlon ⊕03 26 47 44 49. Beautiful *patissier-glacier* and *salon de thé*, with pastries

## CHAMPAGNE-TASTING IN REIMS

**Tours** of the Reims champagne houses and *caves* generally need to be pre-booked but in summer it may be worth showing up on the off chance. Those in the southern part of town near the Abbaye St-Remi tend to have the most impressive cellars – some have been carved in cathedral-esque formations from the Gallo–Roman quarries used to build the city, long before champagne was invented. This is not a comprehensive list of all the *maisons* in the city, but includes the most visitor-friendly.

### NON-APPOINTMENT HOUSES

**Lanson** 66 rue de Courlancy ✆ 03 26 78 50 50, ⓦ lanson.fr. Worth the trip across the river because the in-depth tours take you into the factory, and demonstrate the mechanized process of champagne-making. Most days you'll see the machines degorging the bottles, as well as labelling and filling them in preparation for the second fermentation. Mon–Fri; closed Aug; €15.

**Taittinger** 9 place St-Niçaise ✆ 03 26 85 45 35, ⓦ taittinger.fr. Starts with a film show before a guided stroll through the ancient cellars, some of which have doodles and carvings added by more recent workers; there are also statues of St Vincent and St Jean, patron saints respectively of *vignerons* and cellar hands. Mid-March to mid-Nov daily 9.30–1pm & 2–5.30pm (last tour at 11.30am & 4.30pm); mid-Nov to mid-March Mon–Fri same hours; closed Sat & Sun; tour 1hr; €16.

### APPOINTMENT HOUSES

**G.H.Martel & Co** 17 rue des Créneaux, near the Basilique St-Remi ✆ 03 26 82 70 67, ⓦ champagne martel.com. This good-value tour with a *dégustation* of three champagnes as well as a film show and guided visit taking in the old equipment. Daily 10am–7pm, last tour at 5.45pm; €11.

**Mumm** 34 rue du Champ-de-Mars ✆ 03 26 49 59 70, ⓦ mumm.com. Known for its red-slashed Cordon Rouge label, Mumm's un-French-sounding name is the legacy of its founders, German winemakers from the Rhine Valley who established the business in 1827. The guided tour includes a short film, and ends with a glass of either Cordon Rouge, the sweeter Cordon Vert, or the Extra Dry. March–Oct daily 9–11am & 2–5pm; Nov–Feb by appointment only on weekdays, Sat 9–11am & 2–5pm; €10–20.

**Pommery** 5 place du Général-Gouraud ✆ 03 26 61 62 55, ⓦ pommery.fr. The creator of the cute one-eighth size "Pop" bottles has excavated Roman quarries for its cellars – it claims to have been the first *maison* to do so. Take a train for part of the tour. Daily: April–Oct 9.30am–7pm; mid-Nov to March 10am–6pm; from €12.

**Ruinart** 4 rue des Crayères ✆ 03 26 77 51 51, ⓦ ruinart.com. The fanciest of the champagne producers, housed in a swanky mansion was founded in 1729. The 45-minute tour is followed by a tasting of two prestige cuvées. Jan–Oct Tues–Sat 10am–4pm; Nov & Dec Tues–Sat 10am–4pm; €35.

**Veuve Clicquot-Ponsardin** 1 place des Droits-de-l'Homme ✆ 03 26 89 53 90, ⓦ veuve-clicquot.com. In 1805 the widowed Mme Clicquot not only took over her husband's business – *veuve* means "widow" in French – but also later bequeathed it to her business manager rather than to her children. The *maison* is one of the least pompous, and its *caves* some of the most spectacular, sited in ancient Gallo-Roman quarries. 10am–6pm (last tour at 4.15pm): April–Oct Tues–Sat; Nov–March Tues–Fri; from €25.

and ice cream made on the premises, plus one of the best original Art Deco interiors in Reims. Tues–Sun 7.30am–7.30pm.

### BARS AND CLUBS

**Café du Palais** 14 place Myron-Herrick ✆ 03 26 47 52 54, ⓦ cafedupalais.fr. Long-running large brasserie and bar stuffed full of improbable artefacts in its grand Art Deco setting. Mon–Sat 8am–10.30pm.

**Les Trois Brasseurs** 77 place Drouet-d'Erlon ✆ 03 26 47 86 28, ⓦ les3brasseurs-reims.com. Large restaurant with good bar for beers brewed on the premises. Summer terrace. Sun–Thurs noon–11pm, Fri & Sat noon–midnight.

**Le Vogue** 93 bd du Général Leclerc ✆ 03 26 47 34 29, ⓦ levogue.fr. The place to go clubbing into the small hours and dance to the excellent DJs. Minimum age 18. Cover charge €12 after 1am on some nights. Wed–Sat 10.30pm or 11.30pm–5am or 7am.

# Épernay

There's no question that **ÉPERNAY**, 26km south of Reims, is a single-industry town. But it's beautifully situated below rolling, vine-covered hills, and the industry in question – champagne production – is a compelling reason for a visit. The town contains some of the most famous champagne *maisons* as well as several smaller houses so start at the appropriately named **avenue de Champagne**, running east from place de la République. Dubbed "the most drinkable street in the world" by Winston Churchill, it's worth strolling along for its imposing eighteenth- and nineteenth-century champagne *maisons*. You can tour some of the *maisons*, and many others welcome visitors to taste and buy. The town makes a sensible base for exploring the surrounding villages and vineyards.

## Moët et Chandon

18 av de Champagne • Daily 9.30–11.30am & 2–4.30pm; mid-Nov to March closed Sat & Sun; closed Jan • From €16.50, including *dégustation* of the Brut Impérial • Ⓦ moet.com

The largest, and probably the most famous *maison*, though neither the most beautiful nor necessarily the most interesting to tour, is **Moët et Chandon**, one of the keystones of the LVMH (Louis Vuitton, Moët and Hennessy) empire which owns Mercier, Veuve Clicquot, Dior perfumes and other luxury brands. The house is also the creator of the iconic **Dom Pérignon** label. The tour is rather generic, beginning with a mawkish video, followed by a walk through the cellars adorned with mementos of Napoleon (a good friend of the original M. Moët), and concluding with a tasting of their truly excellent champagne.

## Mercier

70 av de Champagne • End-March to mid-Nov 9.30–11am & 2–4pm; closed Tues & Wed out of season • €11, including *dégustation* • Ⓣ 03 26 51 22 23, Ⓦ champagnemercier.fr

**Mercier** runs a fairly rewarding tour around its cellars in an electric train. Nowadays the wine producer is known for being at the lower end of the champagne market in terms of price, demonstrating that M. Mercier was achieved his ultimate goal: he founded the house, aged 20, in 1858 with a plan to make champagne more accessible to the French people. In 1889 he carted a giant barrel that held 200,000 bottles' worth to the Paris Exhibition – only to be upstaged by the Eiffel Tower. The barrel is on display in the lobby.

## Castellane

57 rue de Verdun • April–Dec daily 10am–noon & 2–6pm • €10 including *dégustation* • Ⓣ 03 26 51 19 19, Ⓦ castellane.com

**Castellane**, by the train station, provides Épernay with its chief landmark: a pastel edifice resembling a kind of Neoclassical water tower. Along with the cellars, the visit shows off the working assembly lines that fill the champagne bottles, and the huge vats that hold the grape juice prior to fermentation. After the tour you can wander the little museum and climb the tower for a great view of the surrounding vineyards.

## Around Épernay

The villages in the appealing **vineyards** of the Montagne de Reims, Côte des Blancs and Vallée de la Marne surrounding Épernay are home to a range of curiosities, including the world's largest champagne bottle and cork in **Mardeuil** and a traditional *vigneron*'s house and early twentieth-century school room at **Oeuilly**. Many of the villages have a sleepy, old-stone charm: **Vertus**, 16km south of Épernay, is particularly pretty, and so too is **Hautvillers**, 6km north of town, where you can see the abbey of Dom Pérignon fame (closed to the public), and visit the church where he is buried.

## ARRIVAL AND INFORMATION

**By train and bus** Épernay's *gare SNCF* and *gare routière* are in place de la Gare, a 5min walk from the centre.

**Tourist office** 7 av de Champagne (mid-April to mid-Oct Mon–Sat 9.30am–12.30pm & 1.30–7pm, Sun 11am–4pm; mid-Oct to mid-April Mon–Sat 9.30am–12.30pm & 1.30–5.30pm; ☎03 26 53 33 00, ⊚ ot-epernay.fr). Their *guide*

**ÉPERNAY**

*touristique* has details about champagne-tasting and *maison* tours.

**Vineyard tours (VTT)** Tours are run independently or in an organized group; contact Bulleo, Parc Roger Menu (☎03 26 53 35 60; ⊚ bulleo.com from €11 per half-day).

## ACCOMMODATION

**Les Berceaux** 13 rue des Berceaux ☎03 26 55 28 84, ⊚ lesberceaux.com. Right in the heart of town in the old eighteenth-century quarter, the restaurant (see below) here is one of the main reasons people stay in Épernay. But don't dismiss the hotel side of things, which has individually decorated, sound-proofed rooms, and good-sized bathrooms. **€95**

**Jean Moët** 7 rue Jean-Moët ☎03 26 32 19 22, ⊚ hoteljeanmoet.com. The *Jean Moët* opened in 2010 in a beautifully restored eighteenth-century mansion. Twelve smart air-conditioned rooms, named after the sizes of Champagne bottles, have wooden floors, pastel-coloured walls and luxury fabrics. With a spa, chic champagne bar and a conservatory for drinks and snacks in the internal courtyard, it's a welcome addition to Épernay's hotel scene. **€225**

**Royal Champagne** Champillon, 5km north of Épernay ☎03 26 52 87 11, ⊚ royalchampagne.com. Set high on

a hill overlooking some of the world's most famous Champagne names, this whitewashed hotel was once a coaching inn that welcomed both Napoleon and Queen Elizabeth (the Queen Mother). Now a luxury hotel, its 28 sumptuously decorated rooms are in a smart modern annexe, while the main house has comfortable lounges, a library and several dining rooms. If you're staying elsewhere but want a real treat, book a meal here. Breakfast is a feast in its own right (with champagne for the dedicated). *Menus* from €39–90. **€610**

**La Villa St-Pierre** 1 rue Jeanne-d'Arc ☎03 26 54 40 80, ⊚ villasaintpierre.fr. In a quiet street away from the centre but near the main Champagne houses, this good-value, welcoming hotel has rooms decorated in fresh pale blues and greens. Some rooms have very small bathrooms; some are not en-suite, so check when you book. **€61**

## EATING AND DRINKING

**Les Berceaux** 13 rue des Berceaux ☎03 26 55 28 84, ⊚ lesberceaux.com. Concentrating on classic bourgeois cooking and using seasonal, local ingredients where possible, this wonderful restaurant is the place for dishes like wild turbot braised in champagne, warm foie gras with peach, and roast wild pigeon. It's pricey, but always busy and the elegant setting of a large dining room with fireplace, flowers and crisp linen adds to the sense of occasion. The hotel's second restaurant, the good-value *Bistrot le 7* has *menus* at €20–29. *Menus* in *Les Berceaux*

€39–81. Wed–Sun noon–2pm & 7–9.30pm.

**La Table Kobus** 3 rue Dr-Rousseau ☎03 26 51 53 53, ⊚ latablekobus.com. Delightful brasserie, with traditional marble-topped tables and banquette seating, that's locally popular for dishes like poached egg with snails and ham, and duck roasted with lime and pear poached in Champagne. Unusually you can take your own wine, at no extra cost (though their wine list is good value). *Menus* €19.50–45. Tues, Wed, Fri & Sat noon–2pm & 7–10pm, Thurs & Sun noon–2pm.

# Troyes

It is easy to find charm in the leaning medieval half-timbered houses and churches of **TROYES**, the ancient capital of the Champagne region. The town also offers top-quality museums and shopping outlets, and is a good place to try the regional speciality, *andouillette* (see box, p.212).

## The churches

The centre of Troyes between the station and cathedral is scattered with marvellous **churches**, four of which are open to the public. The first you come to is the sumptuous, high-naved **St-Pantaléon** (May–Sept Mon–Sat 10am–noon & 2–7pm, Sun 2–7pm; Oct–April 10am–noon & 2–5pm, Sun 2–5pm) on rue de Vauluisant, which is filled with sixteenth-century sculpture, stored here away from the ravages of the Revolution. A short walk to the north is Troyes' oldest church, twelfth-century **Ste-Madeleine**, on the road of the same name and remodelled in the sixteenth century, when the delicate stonework rood screen – used to keep the priest separate from the congregation – was added. A lovely garden provides a peaceful oasis in the summer. A short way to the southeast, between rues Émile-Zola and Champeaux, is **St-Jean-au-Marché**, the church where Henry V of England married Catherine of France after being recognized as heir to the French throne in the 1420 Treaty of Troyes. Between it and the cathedral is the elegant Gothic **Basilique St-Urbain** (May–Sept Mon–Sat 10am–noon & 2–7pm, Sun 2–7pm; Oct–April 10am–noon & 2–5pm, Sun 2–5pm), on place Vernier, its exterior dramatizing the Day of Judgement.

## Musée d'Art Moderne

May–Sept Tues–Fri 10am–1pm & 2–7pm, Sat & Sun 11am–7pm; Oct–April Tues–Fri 10am– 1pm & 2–5pm, Sat & Sun 11am–6pm • €5, or part of museum pass (see p.211) • ☏ 03 25 76 26 80

Across the Canal de la Haute Seine lies the city's most outstanding museum, the **Musée d'Art Moderne**, housed in the old bishops' palace next to the cathedral on place St-Pierre. The museum displays the private collection built up by industrialist Pierre Lévy (1907–2002) and his wife Denise. Lévy developed a strong friendship with the Fauvist André Derain, and it's Derain's work (including the famous paintings of Hyde Park and Big Ben) that forms the collection's core. For the rest, there are works by Degas, Courbet, Gauguin and Max Ernst, but it's in no sense a greatest hits of modern art and therein lies its charm: entire rooms are devoted to a particular theme or to the works of lesser-known artists. Another room is given over to a beautiful collection of African carvings.

## Quartier de la Cité

The ancient **quartier de la Cité**, across the canal from the centre, is home to many of the city's oldest buildings. They all huddle around the **Cathédrale St-Pierre-et-St-Paul** (May–Sept Mon–Sat 10am–1pm & 2–7pm; Sun 2–7pm; Oct–April Mon–Sat 9am–noon & 1–5pm, Sun 2–5pm), whose pale Gothic nave is mottled with reflections from the wonderful stained glass. On the other side of the cathedral from the Musée d'Art Moderne (see above), the once glorious **Abbaye St-Loup** houses the **Musée Saint-Loup** (May–Sept Tues–Fri 10am–1pm & 2–7pm, Sat, Sun 11am–7pm; Oct–April Tues–Fri 10am–noon & 2–5pm, Sat, Sun 11am–6pm; €5, or part of museum pass ☏03 25 76 21 68) seemingly endless galleries of mostly French paintings, including a couple by Watteau and an impressive collection of medieval sculpture.

---

### CLOTHES SHOPPING IN TROYES

Troyes made its name in the clothing trade, and today the industry still accounts for more than half of the town's employment. **Factory outlets** are one of the chief attractions here: designer-label clothes can be picked up at two-thirds or less of the normal shop price. The best array is at the giant **Marques Avenue**, avenue de la Maille, St-Julien-les-Villas, a couple of kilometres south of the city on the N71 to Dijon or on bus #2 (Mon–Fri 10am–7pm, Sat 9.30am–7pm; ⊛marquesavenue.com); there's also a special "shed" for household goods at 230 faubourg Croncels, including luxury glass and chinaware. At Pont-Ste-Marie, a short way to the northeast of Troyes between the D677 to Reims and the D960 to Nancy, are **Marques City** (Mon–Fri 10am–7pm, Sat 9.30am–7pm; ⊛marquescity.fr) and **McArthur Glen** (same hours as Marques City; ⊛mcarthurglen.fr). Buses for the outlets depart from the bus stops by Marché les Halles (ask at the tourist offices for details).

# Apothicairerie

May–Sept Wed 2–7pm, Thurs, Fri 10am–1pm & 2–7pm, Sat & Sun 11am–1pm & 2–7pm; Oct–April Wed & Thurs 2–7pm, Fri–Sun 10am–noon & 2–5pm • €2 or part of museum pass (see below) • ☎ 03 25 80 98 97

Down rue de la Cité (entrance on quai des Comtes de Champagne), the **Apothicairerie**, a richly decorated sixteenth-century pharmacy, occupies a corner of the majestic eighteenth-century **Hôtel-Dieu-le-Comte**. Rows of painted wooden "silènes" boxes dating from the eighteenth century adorn its shelves, each illustrating the medicines once found inside.

# Maison de l'Outil et de la Pensée Ouvrière

7 rue de la Trinité • April–Sept daily 10am–6pm; Oct–Feb daily except Thurs 10am–6pm • €6.50, or part of museum pass (see below) • ☎ 03 25 73 28 26, ⓦ maison-de-l-outil.com

Despite being raked by numerous fires since the Middle Ages, Troyes' Old Town has retained many timber-framed buildings. The most infamous fire, in 1524, led to a massive rebuilding scheme giving Troyes a wealth of Renaissance palaces. An outstanding example, just east of the church of St-Pantaléon, is the sixteenth-century Hôtel de Mauroy, once an orphanage, then a textile factory, and now the **Maison de l'Outil et de la Pensée Ouvrière**. Troyes' most original museum, it exhibits traditional tools of a myriad of trades, ranging from chair-caning to glove-making. Its beautifully lit displays provide a window into the world of the workers, while video monitors throughout the museum demonstrate how the tools were used. Be sure to pick up the English-language guide at the entrance.

# Hôtel de Vauluisant

4 rue de Vauluisant • **Musée de la Bonneterie** Wed 2–7pm, Thurs, Fri 10am–1pm & 2–7pm, Sat, Sun 11am–1pm & 2–7pm • €3, or part of museum pass (see below) • **Musée Historique de Troyes et de la Champagne Méridionale** Wed 2–7pm, Thurs & Fri 10am–1pm & 2–7pm, Sat & Sun 11am–1pm & 2–7pm • €3, or part of museum pass (see below) • English-language leaflet available at entrance

Hosiery ("bonneterie") and woollens have been Troyes' most important industry since the late Middle Ages. Some of the old machines and products used for creating garments can be seen in the sixteenth-century palace, the **Hôtel de Vauluisant**. The **Musée de la Bonneterie** displays an array of looms, sewing machines and the like, as well as historic photographs and a collection of socks and stockings from the nineteenth and twentieth centuries. The stone Renaissance palace is also home to the more compelling **Musée Historique de Troyes et de la Champagne Méridionale**, which contains some gorgeous sixteenth-century sculptures of the Troyes school as well as some fine winged triptychs.

## ARRIVAL AND DEPARTURE          TROYES

**By train** The *gare SNCF* is off boulevard Carnot, a 5min walk into the centre.

**Destinations** Chaumont (approx. every 1–2hr; 50min); Langres (9 daily; 1hr 15min); Paris (frequent; 1hr 30min).

**By bus** The *gare routière* is beside the train station.

**Destinations** Reims (approx. 5 daily; 2hr).

## INFORMATION

**Tourist office** Station branch: 16 bd Carnot (mid-Sept to mid-June Mon–Sat 9am–12.30pm & 2–6.30pm; mid-Sept to mid-June 9am–12.30pm & 2–6pm, Sun 10am–1pm; ☎ 03 25 82 62 70). Town centre branch: rue Mignard (April–June & mid-Sept to Oct Mon–Sat 10am–1pm & 2–6pm, Sun 10am–noon & 2–5pm; July to mid-Sept daily 10am–7pm; Nov–March closed; ☎ 03 25 73 36 88). Both on ⓦ tourisme-troyes.com.

**Passes** The museum pass (€12), available at the tourist office, includes entry to all Troyes' museums, two champagne *dégustations*, a chocolate tasting, and discount vouchers for the factory outlets.

**Festivals and events** From late June to late July, the city organizes free Ville en Musique concerts in picturesque locations in the historic centre; the programme ranges from classical and jazz to rock and hip-hop – pick up a schedule at the tourist office.

**3**

## ACCOMMODATION

**Arlequin** 50 rue Turenne ☎03 25 83 12 70, ⓦhotel arlequin.com. Tucked away in the rambling alleyways of the Old Town, this newly renovated hotel has sunny, individually decorated rooms. Some are small, so check on booking. **€88**

**Camping municipal** 7 rue Roger-Salengro, Pont Ste-Marie ☎03 25 81 02 64, ⓦtroyescamping.net. Set in a wooded area, 5km out on the N60 to Châlons, with good facilities including washing machines and children's play area. Minimum two-night reservation, closed mid-Oct to March. **€15.40**

**Les Comtes de Champagne** 54 rue de la Monnaie ☎03 25 73 11 70, ⓦcomtesdechampagne.com. In the middle of the old quarter, but down a quiet street, this charming two-star in a twelfth-century house has odd-shaped rooms, fireplaces, slanted floors and creaking staircases. Friendly proprietors and covered parking. **€90**

★ **La Maison de Rhodes** 18 rue Linard-Gonthier ☎03 25 43 11 11, ⓦmaisonderhodes.com. Walk through the heavy wooden gate into an inner courtyard surrounded by medieval half-timbered buildings with staircases that seem to belong more to a theatre set than a five-star boutique hotel. With antique furniture and beamed rooms, this gorgeous hotel with links to the Templars lives up to its reputation as one of France's most romantic hotels. **€235**

**Le Relais St–Jean** 51 rue Paillot-de-Montabert ☎03 25 73 89 90, ⓦhotel-relais-saint-jean.com. Behind the facade of a half-timbered building in the centre of the old town, you'll find a smart hotel, elegantly decorated with contemporary furniture and fabrics. The bar is a local meeting place and fills up in the evenings. **€150**

**Le Royal** 22 bd Carnot ☎03 25 73 19 99, ⓦroyal-hotel -troyes-com. Decent, pleasantly restored hotel in a rather drab building near the station. Don't be put off – it's pleasant and welcoming; rooms have spacious bathrooms and there's a copious breakfast. **€120**

## EATING, DRINKING AND NIGHTLIFE

Self-caterers should head for the Marché les Halles, a daily covered market on the corner of rue Général-de-Gaulle and place St-Rémy, close to the Hôtel de Ville. Central Troyes is sprinkled with places to eat, but quality is uneven. Most of the restaurants cluster in the narrow streets around St-Jean.

### RESTAURANTS

**Aux Crieurs de Vins** 4 place Jean-Jaurès ☎03 25 40 01 01, ⓦauxcrieursdevin.com. Delightfully unpretentious wine bar and shop with *andouillettes* on the menu and a jumble of different furniture. A good selection of wines come by the glass, with emphasis on bio wines; *plats du jour* from €11. Tues–Sat noon–2pm & 7.30–10pm.

**Le Bistroquet** Place Langevin ☎03 25 73 65 65, ⓦbistroquet-troyes.fr. A classic brasserie with just the right decor of stained glass, brass, and banquette seating and a small terrace, slightly removed from the main drag. This is the place to trust the regional speciality (an acquired taste) of *andouillette*. Otherwise reliable well-cooked classics like lamb with haricots beans will satisfy. *Menus* from €20.90–32.90. Daily noon–2.15pm, & 7–10pm (Fri, Sat to 10.30pm); closed Sun eve.

**La Mignardise** 1 ruelle des Chats ☎03 25 73 15 30, ⓦlamignardise.net. Troyes' most celebrated restaurant is set in a sixteenth-century building looking onto a quiet courtyard where you can eat on balmy summer evenings. Come here for the classics: duck terrine with dried apricots; fillet of beef with Bordelaise sauce. *Menus* €36–85. Tues–Sat noon–2pm & 7–9.30pm, Sun noon–2pm.

**Le Valentino** 35 rue Paillot de Montabert (entrance cours de la Rencontre) ☎03 25 73 14 14. This chic and intimate restaurant with a pretty paved courtyard makes for a rather romantic dinner. Reasonable prices, local ingredients and emphasis on fish has earned it a top local reputation. Reservations essential; *menus* €25–55. Tues–Sat noon–2pm & 7–10pm.

### BARS AND CLUBS

**Au Coeur du Bouchon** 14 rue Colbert ☎03 10 95 20 06. Smart new champagne bar with a well-to-do young clientele, offering a good selection and five weekly specials at €5 a glass. Tues & Wed 11am–11pm, Thurs & Fri 11am–1.30am, Sat 10am–1.30am, Sun 10am–6pm.

---

### IT TAKES GUTS …

Troyes is famed for its **andouillette**. Translated euphemistically into English as "chitterling sausage", *andouillette* is an intestine crammed full of more intestines, all chopped up. It's an acquired taste (and texture), but it's better than it sounds – look out for the notation AAAAA, a seal of approval awarded by the Amicable Association of Amateurs of the Authentic Andouillette. Game looms large on menus in the Ardennes, with *pâté d'Ardennes* being the most famous dish and juniper berries used to flavour food *à l'ardennaise*.

**Bar des Bougnats des Pouilles** 29 rue Paillot-de-Montaubert ☎03 25 73 59 85, ⓦbougnat despouilles.com. Quirky decor with contributions from local artists, always packed, good wine list, concerts and exhibitions. Mon–Wed 5pm–1.30am, Thurs–Sat 5pm–3am.

**Cotton Club** 8 rue Charbonnet. Popular and lively bar in the centre of town, with a disco and a good line-up of live music in the vaulted cellars. Sat 6.30–11.30pm plus cellar Thurs 11.30pm–3.30am, Fri & Sat 11.30pm–4am.

**L'Illustré** 8 rue Champeaux ☎03 25 40 00 88, ⓦlillustre .com. Restaurant, café, bar and club downstairs in an old half-timbered building. Café daily 2.30–7pm; restaurant Mon–Sat noon–2.30pm & 7–11pm; bar Sun–Wed 6.30–11.30pm, Thurs–Sat 6.30pm–1.15am; club Thurs–Sat 7.30–midnight (Thurs) and to 1am (Fri, Sat).

# The Plateau de Langres

The Seine, Marne, Aube and several other lesser rivers rise in the **Plateau de Langres** between Troyes and Dijon, with main routes between the two towns skirting this area. To the east, the N19 (which the train follows) takes in **Chaumont** and **Langres**, two towns that could briefly slow your progress if you're in no hurry, and the home village of Charles de Gaulle, **Colombey-les-Deux-Églises**.

**3**

## Chaumont

Situated on a steep ridge between the Marne and Suize valleys, **CHAUMONT** (Chaumont-en-Bassigny, to give its full name), lies 93km southeast of Troyes. Approach by train to cross the town's stupendous mid-nineteenth-century viaduct, which took an average of 2500 labourers working night and day two years to construct. It's also possible to walk across the viaduct, which gives you fine views of the Suize valley.

The town's most interesting historic building is the **Basilique St-Jean-Baptiste**. Though built with the same dour, grey stone of most Champagne churches, it has a wonderful Renaissance addition to the Gothic transept of balconies and turreted stairway, and a superb church organ. The decoration includes an *Arbre de Jessé* of the early sixteenth-century Troyes school, in which all the characters are sitting in the tree, dressed in the style of the day.

You shouldn't leave without taking a look at **Les Silos**, 7–9 av Foch, near the *gare SNCF* (Tues, Thurs & Fri 2–7pm, Wed & Sat 10am–6pm; free, ☎03 25 03 86 80, ⓦcig-chaumont.com), a 1930s agricultural co-op transformed into a graphic arts centre and *médiathèque*. As well as hosting temporary exhibitions, it's the main venue for Chaumont's international **poster festival** (Festival de l'Affiche), which is held every year from mid-May to mid-June. As for the rest of the Old Town, there's not much to do except admire the twelfth-century castle keep of the Comtes de Champagne, the delightfully named **Tour d'Arse** at the foot of the vieille ville – all that remains of the thirteen-century town gate – and the strange, bulging stair towers of the houses.

### ARRIVAL AND INFORMATION
CHAUMONT

**By train** The *gare SNCF* is just off place Général de Gaulle, from where it's a 10min walk into the centre along Place Emile Goguenheim.
Destinations Paris (10 daily; 4hr 33min); Reims (11 daily; from 2hr); Troyes (10 daily; from 43min).

**By bus** The *gare routière* is beside the train station.
**Tourist office** Place Charles de Gaulle (Mon–Sat 9.30am–12.30pm & 2.30–6pm; also June–Aug Sun 10am–noon & 2–5pm; ☎03 25 03 80 80, ⓦtourisme -chaumont-champagne.com).

### ACCOMMODATION

**Le Terminus Reine** Place Charles de Gaulle ☎03 25 03 66 66, ⓦrelais-sud-champagne.com. Once the residence of the Counts of Champagne, this old-fashioned hotel has great charm. The hotel is known for its special truffle weekends and the restaurant is a good place to eat; during the game season, it gets very booked up. **€126**

## Colombey-les-Deux-Églises

Twenty-seven kilometres northwest of Chaumont, on the N19 to Troyes, is **COLOMBEY-LES-DEUX-ÉGLISES**, the village where Gaullist leaders come to pay their respects at the grave of **Général Charles de Gaulle**. The former president's family home, **La Boisserie** opens its ground floor to the public (April–Sept daily 10am–1pm & 2–6.30pm; Oct–March daily except Tues 10am–12.30pm & 2–5.30pm; €4.50), but more impressive are the pink-granite **Cross of Lorraine**, symbol of the French Resistance movement, standing over 40m high on a hill just west of the village, and the **Mémorial Charles de Gaulle** (May–Sept daily 9.30am–7pm; Oct–April daily except Tues 10am–5.30pm; €12.50; €14.50 including La Boisserie; ⓦmemorial-charlesdegaulle.fr), an exhaustive chronicle of the man's life and times in an ultra-sleek museum beneath the cross. It was inaugurated in 2008 with much pomp by Nicolas Sarkozy and German Chancellor Angela Merkel on the fiftieth anniversary of the rapprochement between de Gaulle and then-German Chancellor Konrad Adenauer.

### ACCOMMODATION AND EATING      COLOMBEY-LES-DEUX-ÉGLISES

**La Grange du Relais** 26 Route Nationale 19 ⓣ 03 25 02 03 89, ⓦ lagrangedurelais.fr. It may be on the RN19 but the charming, simply decorated rooms face towards the fields or are around the outdoor swimming pool. A dining room crowded with artefacts, most for sale, offers honest, classic dishes. *Menus* €17.90–39.90. **€85**

**Hostellerie La Montagne** Rue de Pisseloup ⓣ 03 25

01 51 69, ⓦ hostellerielamontagne.com. Run by a father and son team, this gracious mansion is really a restaurant with rooms – chef Jean-Baptiste Natali worked previously at a Michelin-starred restaurant in Cannes. Rooms are individually designed and top-notch, as is the Michelin-starred cooking which uses local ingredients. *Menus* €28–53. **€150**

## Langres

**LANGRES**, 35km south of Chaumont and just as spectacularly situated above the Marne, retains its near-complete encirclement of gateways, towers and ramparts. If you're just here for an hour or so, the best thing to do is to walk this circuit, with its great views east to the hills of Alsace and southwest across the Plateau de Langres. Don't miss the **St-Ferjeux tower** with its beautiful metal sculpture, *Air and Dreams*. Wandering inside the walls is also rewarding – Renaissance houses and narrow streets give the feel of a place time has left behind, swathed in the mists of southern Champagne. Langres was home to the eighteenth-century Enlightenment philosopher **Diderot** for the first sixteen years of his life, and people like to make the point that, were he to return to Langres today, he'd have no trouble finding his way around. The **Musée d'Art et Histoire** (daily except Tues: April–Oct 10am–noon & 2–6pm; until 5pm Nov–March; €4; ⓣ 03 03 25 86 86 86) on place du Centenaire near the cathedral, duly devotes a section to Diderot, including his encyclopedias and various other first editions of his works, plus a portrait by Van Loos. The highlight of the museum is the superbly restored Romanesque **chapel of St-Didier** in the old wing, which houses a fourteenth-century which houses painted ivory *Annunciation*.

Other attractions worth visiting are the sixteenth-century tiles from Rouen, on display in one of the nave chapels of the **Cathédrale St-Mammès** (daily 2–6pm), where you'll also find an amusing sixteenth-century relief of the *Raising of Lazarus*, in which the apostles watch, totally blasé, while other characters look like kids at a good horror movie. Look out also for the **Hôtel du Breuil de St-Germain** at 2 rue Chambrûlard, one of the best of the town's sixteenth-century mansions, though it can only be viewed from outside.

### ARRIVAL AND INFORMATION      LANGRES

**By train** The *gare SNCF* is on avenue de la gare, a 10min walk into town.
Destinations (Rheims 6 daily; 3hr 30min; Dijon 2 direct daily; 1hr).

**Tourist office** Porte des Moulins, place Bel'Air (April–Sept daily 9am–noon & 1.30–6.30pm; Oct–March Mon–Sat 9am–noon & 1.30–6pm, Sat 9.30am–noon & 1.30–6pm; ⓣ 03 25 87 67 67, ⓦ tourisme-langres.com).

## ACCOMMODATION

**Cheval Blanc** 4 rue de l'Estrés ☎ 03 25 87 07 00, ⓦ hotel-langres.com. Once part of an ancient abbey church, this mellow stone building has been an inn since the 1790s. Huge windows, wooden floors and exposed stone retain the ecclesiastical feel, but rest assured, bedrooms and bathrooms are firmly twenty-first century. **€100**

**Grand Hôtel de l'Europe** 23–25 rue Diderot ☎ 03 25 87 10 88, ⓦ relais-sud-champagne.com. The large, high-ceilinged, modestly decorated rooms and an inner courtyard recall the days when this was an old coaching inn in the centre of town. Comfortable and welcoming. **€120**

## EATING AND DRINKING

Langres has its own highly flavourful, strong-smelling – and excellent – cheese, which you can buy at the Friday market on place Bel'Air.

**Auberge des Voiliers** 1 rue des Voiliers, Lac de la Liez ☎ 03 25 87 05 74, ⓦ hotel-voiliers.com. Just outside town, overlooking a lake, this hotel/restaurant has two restaurants, one for casual eating, and *Les Voilliers* for more serious meals. *Menus* from €23.50–36. Daily noon–2pm & 7–9pm.

**Restaurant Diderot** Cheval Blanc, 4 rue de l'Estrés ☎ 03 25 87 07 00, ⓦ hotel-langres.com. The restaurant is as elegant as the hotel, with high-beamed ceilings and polished wood floors. Classic dishes with inventive twists are the order of the day: roast veal with spiced vegetable blinis and mushroom tart; millefeuille of strawberries and almonds with minted strawberry coulis. *Menus* €32–45. Daily noon–2pm & 7–9.30pm (closed Wed lunch).

# The Ardennes

To the northeast of Reims, the scenery of the **Ardennes** region along the Meuse valley knocks spots off any landscape in Champagne. Most of the hills lie over the border in Belgium, but there's enough of interest on the French side to make it well worth exploring.

In war after war, the people of the Ardennes have been engaged in protracted last-ditch battles down the valley of the Meuse, which, once lost, gave invading armies a clear path to Paris. The rugged, hilly terrain and deep forests (frightening even to Julius Caesar's legionnaires) helped World War II Resistance fighters, but during peacetime life here has never been easy. The land is unsuitable for crops, and the slate and ironworks, the main source of employment during the nineteenth century, closed in the 1980s. The only major investment in the region has been a nuclear power station, to which locals responded by etching "Nuke the Élysée!" high on a half-cut cliff of slate just downstream. This said, tourism, the main growth industry, is developing apace – there are walking and boating possibilities, plus good train connections – though the isolated atmosphere of this region still lingers.

## Charleville-Mézières

CHARLEVILLE-MÉZIÈRES – an agglomeration of former stand-alone towns Charleville and Mézières – provides a good base for exploring the northern part of the region, which spreads across the meandering Meuse before the valley closes in and the forests take over.

The splendid seventeenth-century **place Ducale**, in the centre of town, was the result of the local duke's envy of the contemporary place des Vosges in Paris, which it somewhat resembles. Despite the posh setting, the shops in the arcades remain down-to-earth and the cafés charge reasonable prices to sit outside.

### Musée de l'Ardenne

Accessed from 31 place Ducale • Tues–Sun 10am–noon & 2–6pm • €4, combined ticket with Musée Arthur Rimbaud (see p.216)

A complex of old and new buildings houses the **Musée de l'Ardenne**, a typically eclectic local museum which includes archeological finds from a local Merovingian cemetery, fascinating historic models of Charleville and Mézières in the seventeenth century, and paintings on nineteenth-century industrial and political themes by Paul Gondrexon.

**3**

## PUPPETS IN CHARLEVILLE

Charleville is a major international puppetry centre (its school is justly famous), and every three years it hosts one of the largest puppet festivals in the world, the **Festival Mondial des Théâtres de Marionnettes** (ⓦfestival-marionnette.com). Up to 150 professional troupes – some from as far away as Mali and Burma – put on around fifty shows a day on the streets and in every available space in town. Tickets are cheap, and there are shows for adults as well as the usual stuff aimed at kids. If you miss the festival you can still catch one of the puppet performances year-round at the **Institut de la Marionnette** on place Winston Churchill (ⓣ03 24 33 72 50, ⓦwww.marionette.com; tickets free to €35). If you're passing by here during the day, you can see one of the automated episodes of the *Four Sons of Aymon* enacted on the facade's clock every hour, or all twelve scenes on Saturday at 9.15pm.

## Musée Arthur Rimbaud

Tues–Sun 10am–noon & 2–6pm • €4, combined ticket with Musée de l'Ardenne (see p.215)

The most famous person to emerge from Charleville was Arthur Rimbaud (1854–91), who ran away from the town four times before he was 17, so desperate was he to escape its provincialism. He is honoured in the **Musée Arthur Rimbaud**, housed in a very grand stone windmill – a contemporary of the place Ducale – on quai Arthur-Rimbaud, two blocks north of the main square. It contains paintings and sketches of him and his contemporaries, including his lover Verlaine, as well as facsimiles of his writings and related documents. A few steps down the quayside is the spot where he composed his most famous poem, *Le Bateau Ivre*. After penning poetry in Paris, journeying to the Far East and trading in Ethiopia and Yemen, Rimbaud died in a Marseille hospital. His body was brought back to his home town – probably the last place he would have wanted to be buried – and true Rimbaud fanatics can visit his **tomb** in the cemetery west of the place Ducale at the end of avenue Charles Boutet.

### ARRIVAL AND INFORMATION                    CHARLEVILLE-MÉZIÈRES

**By train** The *gare SNCF* is on avenue du Général Leclerc, a 10min walk to place Ducale.
Destinations Reims (almost hourly; 50min).
**By bus** The *gare routière* is a couple of blocks west of the square, by the Marché Couvert.
**Destinations** Reims (2 weekly, Mon & Sat; 2hr 30min); Troyes (2 weekly 3hr; 10min)

**Tourist office** Ardennes regional tourist office is on 24 place Ducale (Mon–Sat: May–Sept 10am–12.30pm & 1.30–7pm; Oct–April closes 6pm; ⓣ03 24 56 06 08, ⓦgb .ardennes.com) while Charleville-Mézières' own tourist office is on 4 place Ducale (Mon–Sat 9.30am–noon & 1.30–6pm, July & Aug open Sun and closes 7pm; ⓣ03 24 55 69 90, ⓦcharleville-tourisme.org).

### ACCOMMODATION

**Camping du Mont Olympe** ⓣ03 24 33 23 60. On a bend in the river and just a few minutes' walk into town, this small campsite is open April–Sept and has a snack bar, wi-fi and laundry. **€14.26**
**Dormeur du Val** 32 rue de la Gravière ⓣ03 24 42 04 30, ⓦdormeur.fr. Four-star, seventeen-room boutique hotel with large, colourful and stylish rooms. Adding to the

lively atmosphere is a bar with industrial steel girders and more mix-and-match contemporary furniture. **€169**
**De Paris** 24 av Georges Corneau ⓣ03 24 33 34 38, ⓦhoteldeparis08.fr. An early twentieth-century hotel near the station on a busy road, but sound-proofed, with conventional, pleasantly decorated rooms, some with fireplaces. **€78**

### EATING AND DRINKING

**La Clef des Champs** 33 rue du Moulin ⓣ03 24 56 17 50, ⓦlaclefdeschamps.fr. Attractive, Michelin-listed restaurant in a seventeenth-century building with wood floors, brick walls and beams. Classic dishes are enlivened with gentle Japanese spicing. *Menus* €19–65. Daily noon–2pm & 7–9.30pm, closed Sun eve.

**La Côte à l'Os** 11 cours Aristide-Briand ⓣ03 24 59 20 16, ⓦrestaurant-charleville-lacotealos.fr. Pretty restaurant in a tree-lined avenue with warm red walls, plenty of flowers and a menu that favours both fish, shellfish and classic meat dishes. A local favourite. *Menus* €22.50 to €28.50. Daily noon–2pm & 7–11pm.

# North of Charleville-Mézières

Writing about the stretch of the Meuse that winds through the Ardennes, George Sand said: "its high wooded cliffs, strangely solid and compact, are like some inexorable destiny that encloses, pushes and twists the river without permitting it a single whim or any escape". What all the tourist literature emphasizes, however, are the legends of medieval struggles between Good and Evil whose characters have given names to some of the curious rocks and crests. The grandest of these, where the schist formations have taken the most peculiar turns, is the **Roc de la Tour**, also known as the "Devil's Castle", up a path off the D31, 3.5km out of **Monthermé**.

The **GR12** is a good **walking route**, circling the **Lac des Vieilles Forges**, 17km northwest of Charleville-Mézières, then meeting the Meuse at Bogny and crossing over to Hautes-Rivières in the even more sinuous **Semoy Valley**. There are plenty of other tracks, too, though beware of *chasse* (hunting) signs – French hunters tend to hack through the undergrowth with their safety catches off and are notoriously trigger-happy. They're mostly after the local wild boar, who are nowhere near as dangerous as their pursuers, and would seem to be more intelligent, too, rooting about near the crosses of the Resistance memorial near **Revin**, while hunters stalk the forest. The abundance of wild boar is partly explained when you rummage around on the forest floor yourself and discover, between the trees to either side of the river, an astonishing variety of mushrooms, and, in late summer, wild strawberries and bilberries. For a quaint insight into life in the forest, stop at the **Musée de la Forêt**, situated right on the edge of the Ardennes, 2km north of **Renwez** on the D40 (daily 9am–7pm; €8; ☎03 24 54 82 66, ⓦrenwez.fr). All manner of wood-cutting, gathering and transporting is enacted by wooden dummies along with displays of utensils and flora and fauna of the forest; it's also a tranquil spot for a picnic.

**3**

## GETTING AROUND                                    AROUND CHARLEVILLE-MÉZIÈRES

Journeys in this neck of the woods are best tackled on foot, on skis, by bike or on a boat.

**By train** Trains follow the Meuse towards Belgium, while local buses run as far as Nouzonville.

**By boat** There are various different kinds of pleasure boats, some just for the day and some to rent by the week or weekend – not wildly expensive if you can split the cost four or six ways. South of Charleville-Mézières at Pont à Bar, Ardennes Nautisme (☎03 24 27 05 15, ⓦardennes-nautisme.com.) provides boats for weekly and weekend rent; while north of

Charleville-Mézières at Haybes, Au Fil de Flo (☎06 74 57 79 51, ⓦcroisiereardennes.fr) has trips ranging from 1 hour to 8 hours along the Meuse.

**By bicycle** The Trans-Ardennes Green Track provides over 80km of off-road bike trails following the Meuse Valley; the regional tourist office at Charleville-Mézières (see p.216) can provide free route maps, as well as information on hiking, canoeing or riding.

## ACCOMMODATION                                                                REVIN

**François-1er** 46 quai Camille-Desmoulins ☎03 24 40 15 88, ⓦfrancois1.eu. Modern hotel with standard rooms but the bonus of overlooking the river Meuse in a town

which proudly claims to be the St Tropez of the forest. Restaurant, *boules*, good parking and proximity to walking and biking trails make this popular with families. **€72**

# Alsace and Lorraine

TRADITIONAL ALSACIEN HOUSES

# Alsace and Lorraine

Disputed for centuries by French kings and the princes of the Holy Roman Empire, and subsequently embroiled in a bloody tug-of-war between France and Germany, France's easternmost provinces, Alsace and Lorraine, share a tumultuous history. It's no surprise then that almost everything, from the architecture to the cuisine and the language, is an enticing mixture of French and German – so much so that you might begin to wonder which country you're actually in.

Cute Hansel-and-Gretel-type houses – higgledy-piggledy creations with oriel windows, carved timberwork, toy-town gables and geranium-filled window boxes – are a common feature in **Alsace**, especially along the winding **Route des Vins**, which traces the eastern margin of the forests of the Vosges mountains. This road also represents the region's chief tourist *raison d'être* – wine – best accompanied with a regional cuisine that's more Germanic than French: think hefty portions of pork, cabbage and pungent cheese. Ruined medieval castles are scattered about, while outstanding churches and museums are concentrated in the handsome regional capital of **Strasbourg** and in smaller, quirkier **Colmar**. Bustling **Mulhouse** stands out for its industrial heritage and entertaining nightlife. A noticeably wealthy province, Alsace has historically churned out cars and textiles, not to mention half the beer in France.

Alsace's less prosperous and less scenic neighbour, **Lorraine**, shares borders with Luxembourg, Germany and Belgium. The graceful former capital, **Nancy**, is home to a major school of Art Nouveau and is well worth a visit, as is leafy **Metz**, with its sparkling new contemporary art gallery. The bloody World War I battlefields around **Verdun** attract a large number of visitors, as so does the zoo in Amnéville, one of the largest in France. Gastronomically no less renowned than other French provinces, Lorraine has bequeathed to the world one of its favourite savoury pies, the *quiche lorraine*, and an alcoholic sorbet, the *coupe lorraine*.

**GETTING AROUND**                                                          **ALSACE AND LORRAINE**

While the cities in Alsace and Lorraine – Strasbourg, Nancy and Metz, for example – are easy and small enough to navigate on foot, it's best to have your own wheels to explore the countryside areas.

**By train and bus** Strasbourg and Metz are connected to Paris by speedy TGV, while the rest of Alsace and Lorraine is crisscrossed by a regional train network (W ter-sncf.com).

TER buses fill in the gaps, but the Route des Vins is served by a relatively sporadic service, so again it's best to have your own car or motorcycle in this area.

# Strasbourg

**STRASBOURG** is a hybrid city: part medieval village, characterized by lovely half-timbered houses, soaring Gothic cathedral and narrow winding streets, and part modern European powerhouse, with sleek, glassy buildings inhabited by important

STRASBOURG CATHEDRAL

# Highlights

**① Strasbourg cathedral** Climb the lofty spire of this magnificent Gothic cathedral for stunning views as far as the Black Forest. See p.224

**② The Route des Vins** Surrounded by a sea of vines, Alsace's picturesque wine villages are overlooked by a wealth of ruined castles, perched on pine-clad fringes of the Vosges. See p.230

**③ The Issenheim Altarpiece, Colmar** Luridly expressive, this early Renaissance masterpiece alone makes quaint Colmar worth a visit. See p.234

**④ Bugattis at Mulhouse's Cité de l'Automobile** A matchless collection of vintage motors in the city of many unique museums. See p.239

**⑤ Place Stanislas, Nancy** Along with some outstanding Art Nouveau furniture and glassware, elegant Nancy is home to one of the most grandiose eighteenth-century squares in all France. See p.240

**⑥ Centre Pompidou-Metz** Explore the brand new branch of the famous Parisian Centre Pompidou. See p.246

HIGHLIGHTS ARE MARKED ON THE MAP ON PP.222–223

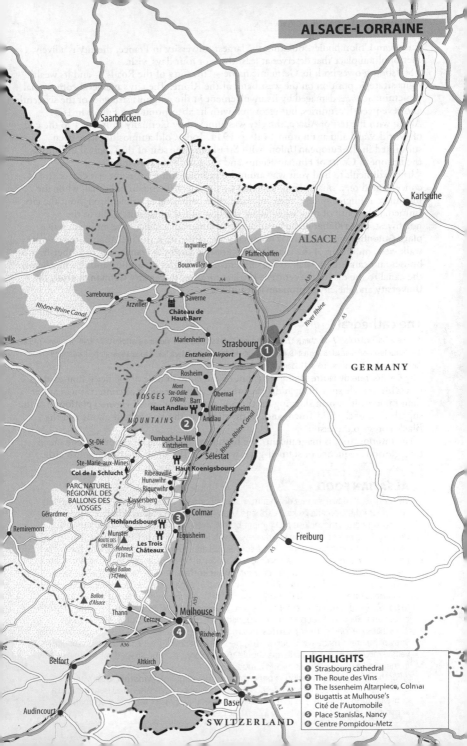

# ALSACE-LORRAINE

Saarbrücken

Karlsruhe

ALSACE

GERMANY

Ingwiller

Bouxwiller

Pfaffenhoffen

A4

A35

Sarrebourg

Arzviller

Saverne

Rhône-Rhine Canal

Château de
Haut-Barr

Marlenheim

Strasbourg ❶

Entzheim Airport

River Rhine

A5

ville

Rosheim

VOSGES

Mont
Ste-Odile
(760m)

Barr

Obernai

Mittelbergheim

Haut Andlau ❦

Andlau

MOUNTAINS

❷

St-Dié

Dambach-La-Ville

Kintzheim

Sélestat

Haut Koenigsbourg

Rhône-Rhine Canal

Ste-Marie-aux-Mines

Col de la Schlucht

Ribeauvillé

Hunawihr

Riquewihr

PARC NATUREL
RÉGIONAL DES
BALLONS DES
VOSGES

Kaysersberg

Gérardmer

Hohlandsbourg

Colmar ❸

Remiremont

Munster

ROUTE DES
CRÊTES

Hohneck
(1361m)

Les Trois
Châteaux

Eguisheim

Grand Ballon
(1424m)

Freiburg

A5

Ballon
d'Alsace

Thann

Cernay

Mulhouse

Rixheim

❹

Belfort

Altkirch

A36

A35

A3

Audincourt

Basel

SWITZERLAND

A36

**HIGHLIGHTS**

❶ Strasbourg cathedral
❷ The Route des Vins
❸ The Issenheim Altarpiece, Colmar
❹ Bugattis at Mulhouse's
   Cité de l'Automobile
❺ Place Stanislas, Nancy
❻ Centre Pompidou-Metz

European Union bodies. Boasting the largest university in France, the city is a lively, metropolitan place that deserves at least three or four days' visit.

Strasbourg owes both its Germanic name – "the City of the Roads" – and its wealth to its strategic position on the west bank of the Rhine. The city's medieval commercial pre-eminence was damaged by its involvement in the religious struggles of the sixteenth and seventeenth centuries, but recovered with its absorption into France in 1681. Along with the rest of Alsace, the city was annexed by Germany from 1871 to the end of World War I and again from 1940 to 1944. Today, old animosities have been subsumed in the **European Union**, with Strasbourg the seat of the Council of Europe, the European Court of Human Rights and the European Parliament.

It isn't difficult to find your way around Strasbourg on foot, as the flat city centre is concentrated on a small island encircled by the River Ill and an old canal, while the magnificent filigree spire of the pink sandstone **cathedral** is visible throughout the city. Immediately south of the cathedral are the best of the museums, while to the northwest, **place Kléber** is the heart of the commercial district. The more attractive **place Gutenberg** to the south is nominally the city's main square. About a ten-minute walk west, on the tip of the island, is picturesque **La Petite France**, where timber-framed houses and canals hark back to the city's medieval trades of tanning and dyeing. Across the canal to the east of the centre is the late nineteenth-century **German quarter**, the **University** and the city's **European institutions**.

## The cathedral

Place de la Cathédrale • Daily 7–11.20am & 12.35–7pm; closed during services • Free **Viewing platform** Daily: April–Sept 9am–7.15pm; Oct–March 10am–5.15pm; July & Aug until 9.45pm Fri & Sat • €5 **Astrological clock** Tickets bought from the postcard stand 9–11am, then at the cash desk at the south door 11.35am–noon • €2

The **Cathédrale de Notre-Dame** soars out of the close huddle of medieval houses at its feet with a single spire of such delicacy that it seems the work of confectioners rather than masons. It's worth slogging up the 332 steps to the spire's **viewing platform** for the superb view of the Old Town, and, in the distance, the Vosges to the west and the Black Forest to the east.

The **interior**, too, is magnificent, the high nave a model of proportion enhanced by a glorious sequence of stained-glass windows. The finest are in the south aisle

---

### ALSATIAN FOOD

The cuisine of Alsace is quite distinct from that of other regions of France. The classic dish is *choucroute*, the aromatic pickled cabbage known in German as **sauerkraut**. The extra ingredient here is the inclusion of juniper berries in the pickling stage and the addition of goose grease or lard. Traditionally it's served with large helpings of smoked pork, ham and sausages, but some restaurants offer a succulent variant replacing the meat with fish (*choucroute aux poissons*), usually salmon and monkfish. The qualification *à l'alsacienne* after the name of a dish means "with *choucroute*". **Baeckoffe**, a three-meat hotpot, comprising layers of potato, pork, mutton and beef marinated in wine and baked for several hours, is a speciality. **Onions**, too, crop up frequently on menus, either in the guise of a tart (*tarte à l'oignon*), made with a béchamel sauce, or as *flammeküche* (*tarte flambée*), a mixture of onion, cream and pieces of chopped smoked pork breast, baked on a thin, pizza-like base.

Alsatians are fond of their **pastries**. In almost every patisserie, you'll find a mouthwatering array of fruit tarts made with rhubarb (topped with meringue), wild blueberries, red cherries or yellow *mirabelle* plums. Cake-lovers should try *kugelhopf*, a dome-shaped cake with a hollow in the middle made with raisins and almonds.

For the classic Alsatian eating experience, you should go to a **winstub**, loosely translated as a "wine bar", a cosy establishment with bare beams, wood wall panels and benches and a convivial atmosphere. The food revolves around Alsatian classics, such as *choucroute*, all accompanied by local wines (or, in a *bierstub*, beer).

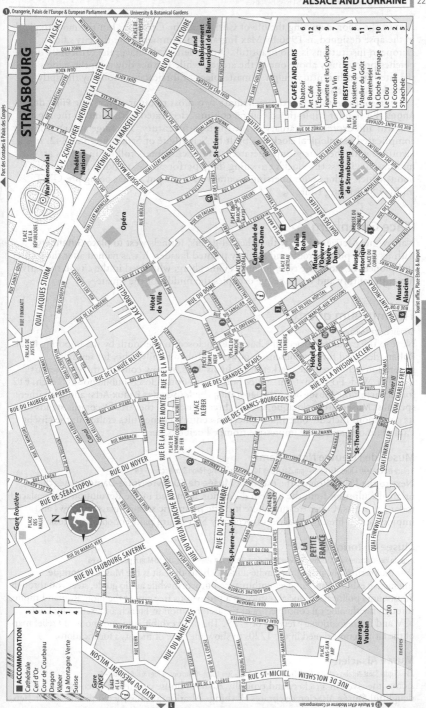

**STRASBOURG**

**CAFÉS AND BARS**
| | |
|---|---|
| L'Abattoir | 6 |
| Art Café | 12 |
| L'Épicerie | 4 |
| Jeanette et les Cycleux | 9 |
| Terres à Vin | 7 |

**RESTAURANTS**
| | |
|---|---|
| L'Assiette du Vin | 8 |
| L'Atelier du Goût | 11 |
| Le Buerehiesel | 1 |
| La Cloche à Fromage | 10 |
| Le Clou | 3 |
| Le Crocodile | 2 |
| S'Kaechele | 5 |

**ACCOMMODATION**
| | |
|---|---|
| Cathédrale | 3 |
| Cerf d'Or | 6 |
| Cour de Courbeau | 5 |
| Dragon | 7 |
| Kléber | 2 |
| La Montagne Verte | 1 |
| Suisse | 4 |

Gare Routière

Gare SNCF

War Memorial

Théâtre National

Opéra

Hôtel de Ville

Palais de Justice

Palais Rohan

Cathédrale de Notre-Dame

Musée de l'Œuvre Notre-Dame

Musée Historique

Musée Alsacien

Sainte-Madeleine de Strasbourg

St-Étienne

St-Pierre-le-Vieux

St-Thomas

Hôtel du Commerce

LA PETITE FRANCE

Barrage Vauban

PLACE KLÉBER

PLACE DE LA RÉPUBLIQUE

PLACE DES HALLES

Parc des Contades & Palais des Congrès

Tourist office, Place Étoile & Airport

① & Musée d'Art Moderne et contemporain

0    metres    200

next to the door, depicting the life of Christ and the Creation, but the modern glass in the apse designed in 1956 by Max Ingrand to commemorate the city's first European institutions is also beautiful. On the left of the nave, the cathedral's organ perches precariously above one of the arches, while further down on the same side is the late fifteenth-century pulpit, a masterpiece of intricacy in stone by the aptly named Hans Hammer.

In the south transept are the cathedral's two most popular sights. The **Pilier des Anges** is a slender triple-tiered central column, decorated with some of the most graceful and expressive statuary of the thirteenth century. The huge and enormously complicated **astrological clock** was built by Schwilgué of Strasbourg in 1842. It is a favourite with the tour-group operators, whose customers roll up in droves at midday to witness the clock's crowning daily performance, striking the hour of noon, which it does with unerring accuracy at 12.30pm – that being pre-GMT midday Strasbourg time.

## Place Gutenberg

Narrow rue Mercière, busy with cathedral-gazers, funnels west to **place Gutenberg**, with its steep-pitched roofs and brightly painted facades. It was named after the printer and pioneer of moveable type, Johannes Gutenberg, who lived in the city in the early fifteenth century and whose statue occupies the middle of the square.

## 4 The museum quarter

Ⓦ musees.strasbourg.eu

Next to the cathedral, place du Château is enclosed to the south by the imposing **Palais Rohan**, designed for the immensely powerful Rohan family, who, for several generations, cornered the market in cardinals' hats. It now contains three museums (Mon & Wed–Fri noon–6pm, Sat & Sun 10am–6pm; closed public hols; €6 each, €12 for all three): the **Musée des Arts Décoratifs**; the **Musée des Beaux-Arts**; and the rather specialist **Musée Archéologique**. Of the three museums, the Arts Décoratifs stands out; its collections include some fine eighteenth-century faïence tiles crafted in the city by Paul Hannong and some impressive trompe l'oeil crockery.

### Musée de l'Oeuvre Notre-Dame

3 place du Château • Tues–Fri noon–6pm, Sat & Sun 10am–6pm; closed Mon & public hols • €6

Next to the Palais Rohan, the excellent **Musée de l'Oeuvre Notre-Dame** houses the original sculptures from the cathedral exterior, damaged in the Revolution and replaced today by copies. Other treasures here include mesmeric stained-glass windows and impressive still lifes by the sixteenth-century Strasbourg painter Sebastian Stoskopff.

### Musée Historique

2 rue du Vieux Marché aux Poissons • Tues–Fri noon–6pm, Sat & Sun 10am–6pm; closed Mon & public hols • €6

Past the picturesque place du Marché-aux-Cochons-de-Lait is the **Musée Historique**. Interactive exhibits, and an over-enthusiastic but worthwhile audio guide, steer you through Strasbourg's political and social history, as a prosperous free city of the Holy Roman Empire, through the theological controversies of the Reformation to French annexation by Louis XIV and the revolutionary fervour of 1789. The prize exhibit is an enormous 3D relief map of the city, commissioned in the 1720s to show the state of the city's fortifications.

### Musée Alsacien

23–25 quai Saint-Nicolas • Mon & Wed–Fri noon–6pm, Sat & Sun 10am–6pm; closed Tues & public hols • €6

Across the river, in a rickety and typically Alsatian house on quai St-Nicolas, the delightful **Musée Alsacien** celebrates all things Alsatian: reconstructed rooms – a kitchen, nursery, bedroom, even a *winstub* and a farmyard – are packed with local artefacts, which come together to paint a vivid picture of Alsatian life in the eighteenth and nineteenth centuries.

## Musée d'Art Moderne et Contemporain

1 place Hans Jean Arp • Tues, Wed & Fri noon–7pm, Thurs noon–9pm, Sat & Sun 10am–6pm • €7

Housed in a purpose-built, glass-fronted building overlooking the river and Vauban's dam (see below), the light and airy **Musée d'Art Moderne et Contemporain** hosts temporary exhibitions, alongside its well-presented permanent collections. Most interesting is the ground floor, which confronts the themes of modern European art from the late nineteenth century through to the 1950s. Starting with a small group of impressionist paintings by the likes of Pissarro and Renoir, the collection features Kandinsky's studies for the ceramic *salon de musique*, a couple of Picassos, plus a good section on Surrealism, with plenty of folkloric, mystical paintings by Brauner. Finally, there's a room devoted to the voluptuous, smooth curves sculpted by Strasbourg's own Jean Arp, who was influenced by Dada and Surrealism before turning to sculpture.

# La Petite France and the rest of the old city

The attractive Pont St-Martin marks the beginning of the district known as **La Petite France**, where the city's millers, tanners and fishermen used to live. At the far end of a series of canals are the so-called **Ponts Couverts** (they are in fact no longer covered), built as part of the fourteenth-century city fortifications. Just beyond is the **barrage Vauban** (daily 9am–7.30pm; free), a dam built by Vauban to protect the city from waterborne assault. The whole area is picture-postcard pretty, with winding streets – most notably rue du Bain-aux-Plantes – bordered by sixteenth- and seventeenth-century houses adorned with flowers and elaborately carved woodwork.

## Place du Marché-Gayot and place Broglie

The area east of the cathedral, where rue des Frères leads to place St-Étienne, is good for a stroll. **Place du Marché-Gayot**, tucked away off rue des Frères behind the cathedral, is a lively cobbled square lined with café-bars and is one of the city's top nightspots. From the north side of the cathedral, rue du Dôme leads to the eighteenth-century **place Broglie**, with the Hôtel de Ville, the bijou **Opéra** and some imposing eighteenth-century mansions.

# The German quarter (Neustadt) and the European institutions

Across the canal from the cathedral, **place de la République** is surrounded by vast German Neo-Gothic edifices erected during the Prussian occupation, one example being the main **post office** on avenue de la Marsellaise. At the other end of avenue de la Liberté, across the confluence of the Ill and Aar, is the city's **university**, where Goethe studied. From in front of the university, alleé de la Robertsau, flanked by handsome *fin-de-siècle* bourgeois residences, leads to the headquarters of three major European institutions: the bunker-like **Palais de l'Europe**, the 1970s-built home of the 44-member Council of Europe; the glass and steel curvilinear **European Parliament building**, opened in 1999; and the glass entrance and silver towers of Richard Rogers' **European Court of Human Rights**, completed in 1995. Individuals can arrange to visit the European Parliament during plenary sessions (free; ⓦeuroparl.europa.eu); the European Court of Human Rights has public court hearings (free; ⓦechr.coe.int). Booking is also required to visit the Council of Europe (free; ⓦcoe.int). Opposite the Palais de l'Europe, the **Orangerie**, Strasbourg's best bit of greenery, hosts a variety of exhibitions and free concerts. There's also a small zoo with monkeys and exotic birds.

## ARRIVAL AND DEPARTURE

STRASBOURG

**By plane** Entzheim International Airport (ⓦstrasbourg .aeroport.fr) lies 15km outside the city and is connected with the *gare SNCF* via a shuttle that makes the journey in 9min around every 15min (€3.80).

**By train** The *gare SNCF* lies on the west side of the city centre, a 15min walk from the cathedral. It is a terminus for the TGV high-speed train.

Destinations Barr (1–2 hourly; 50min); Colmar (1–2 hourly; 30min); Lille (1 daily; 3hr 20min); Nantes (2 daily;

5hr 10min); Obernai (1–2 hourly; 30min); Metz/Nancy (9–13 daily; 1hr 15min); Mulhouse (1–2 hourly; 50min); Paris Gare de l'Est (1–2 hourly; 2hr 20min); Rennes (1–2 daily; 5hr 15min); Sélestat (10 daily; 30min).

**By bus** Eurolines has an office at place d'Austerlitz (ⓣ03 90 22 14 60); its international coaches depart from the Parc de l'Etoile. Buses to destinations in Alsace leave from the place des Halles.

## GETTING AROUND

**By tram** While the compact centre can easily be explored on foot, the city boasts an efficient public transport system, which includes five tram lines (€4 unlimited 24hr pass; ⓦcts-strasbourg.fr).

**By boat** Batorama (ⓣ03 88 84 13 13, ⓦbatorama.fr) runs cruises on the Ill, which depart from in front of the Palais Rohan (daily: April–Oct every 30min 9.30am–9pm; rest of year at least four sailings). The itinerary includes La Petite France, the Vauban dam, the European Parliament and the Palais de l'Europe. The trip lasts 1hr 10min and costs €9.20 (discounts for students and children).

**By car and motorcycle** There are several car hire firms operating in the main station while ⓦrhinocarhire.com

can pick the best price among all firms. Although much of the city centre is geared for pedestrian use, there are enough car parks available (ⓦparcus.com).

**By bicycle** Strasbourg is a very bicycle-friendly city, and its 300km of cycle lanes make bike hire a tempting option. Velhop is at the train station and at 23 bd de la Victoire (daily 8am–7pm, Sat–Sun closed 12.30pm–1.30pm; ⓣ09 69 39 36 67, ⓦvelhop.strasbourg.eu). The city's own rental stations are open 24/7. All bikes cost €5 per day, €15 week, €150 deposit.

**By taxi** Taxis-11 (ⓣ03 88 22 11 11) are available all through the day and night.

## INFORMATION

**Tourist office** The main tourist office is at 17 place de la Cathédrale (daily 9am–7pm; ⓣ03 88 52 28 28, ⓦotstrasbourg.fr), which can provide you with a map (€1 for one with museums and sights marked on it; free otherwise). There's another branch in the underground shopping complex just in front of the train station (Mon–Sat 9am–7pm; Sun 9am–12.30pm & 1.45–7pm) and a third one at Place de l'Etoile near the international bus terminus.

**Tourist pass** Depending on your itinerary, it may be worth investing in a Strasbourg Pass (€14), which entitles you to one free museum entry, one half-price museum entry, a boat

tour, a half-day of bike hire, and the cathedral tower and clock and many more reductions; it's valid for three days.

**Internet** *Linky's*, 22 rue Fréres (daily 9.30am–9pm, Sun & holidays noon–9pm; ⓣ03 88 35 08 31, ⓦlinkys -strasbourg.com).

**Markets** Place Broglie hosts a large market of produce and bric-a-brac every Wed & Fri (7am–6pm); there are fruit, vegetable and local produce markets every Tues and Sat am on bd de la Marne and in the place du Vieux-Marché aux Poissons on Sat. The flea market is on Wed and Sat on rue du Vieil-Hôpital (near the cathedral).

## ACCOMMODATION

When looking for a place to stay, bear in mind that once a month (except Aug, but twice in Oct) the European Parliament is in session for the best part of a week, bringing hundreds of MEPs and their entourages into town. To find out in advance when the parliament is sitting, check the calendar at ⓦeuroparl.europa.eu.

**Cathédrale** 12–13 place de la Cathédrale ⓣ03 88 22 12 12, ⓦhotel-cathedrale.fr. Bang next to the cathedral, the location of this charming hotel can't be beaten. If you can, fork out for the pricier rooms, which have wonderful cathedral views. €140–180

**Cerf d'Or** 6 place de l'Hôpital ⓣ03 88 36 20 05, ⓦcerf -dor-strasbourg.fr. Attractive, family-run place in a

sixteenth-century building, with a small swimming pool/ sauna and its own restaurant (lunch *menu* €29). Closed mid-Dec to mid-Jan and (restaurant only) for three weeks in July. Breakfast €10.50. €95

★ **Cour de Courbeau** 6–8 rue des Couples ⓣ03 90 00 26 26, ⓦcour-corbeau.com. Housed in an exquisite sixteenth-century building with an intricate wooden courtyard and 300-year-old cobbles in the dining room, *Cour de Courbeau* lays claim to being the oldest hotel in Europe, mentioned first in 1538 (although it was a factory between 1854 and 2007). The pale, whitewashed rooms, some with views of the cathedral, are luxurious and spacious and the service is suitably attentive. Breakfast €22. **€250**

**Dragon** 2 rue de l'Écarlate ☎03 88 35 79 80, ⓦdragon .fr. Painted in a pleasing shade of red ochre, this seventeenth-century house situated near the river has a little cobbled courtyard and comfortable rooms in soothing shades of grey. Buffet breakfast €12. **€92**

**Kléber** 29 place Kléber ☎03 88 32 09 53, ⓦhotel -kleber.com. Thirty quirky, "bijou" rooms named after enticing flavours, fruits and puddings; take your pick from

almond, rose, damson, pavlova, honey and cappuccino, among others. Very central, so choose one of the rooms higher up for the occasional – but never intrusive– street noise. Breakfast €8.50. **€76**

**La Montagne Verte** 2 rue Robert-Forrer ☎03 88 30 25 46, ⓦ aquadis-loisirs.com. Well-equipped campsite; take bus #2 from train station, direction "Campus d'Illkirch", to stop "Nid des Cigognes", or tram B or C from place Homme de Fer to "Montagne Verte" then bus #2, #13 or #15 to "Nid des Cigognes". **€14.90**

**Suisse** 2–4 rue de la Râpe ☎03 88 35 22 11, ⓦhotel -suisse.com. Friendly hotel in a labyrinthine old house just a stone's throw from the cathedral. It's a superb location, although the rooms (with the exception of the family rooms) are rather cramped. Buffet breakfast €9.90. **€77**

## EATING AND DRINKING

Traffic-free Place du Marché-Gayot near the cathedral is one of the best spots for café-bars, most of which stay open until 1.30am. In summer, when the sun comes out, the floating cafés and deckchairs along the quai des Pêcheurs make great hangouts. There's a good selection of less touristy restaurants, ranging from upmarket *winstubs* to simple neighbourhood eateries, along the quai des Pêcheurs and on surrounding streets, such as rue de Zürich and rue de la Krutenau.

### RESTAURANTS

**L'Assiette du Vin** 5 rue de la Chaîne ☎03 88 32 00 92, ⓦassietteduvin.fr. A superb wine list and tasty food in this bright, cheery restaurant specializing in seafood – especially lobster. Four-course *menu* at €65 includes half a bottle of champagne. Noon–1.30pm & 7pm–10pm; closed Sat & Mon lunch, Sun & Aug.

**L'Atelier du Gout** 17 rue des Tonneliers ☎03 88 21 01 01. A mix of modern and old – lime green banquettes and slick lighting along with wood-panelled walls and dried flowers – this restaurant places heavy emphasis on serving fresh, locally sourced food. Starters could include

smoked tuna *tarte flambée* (€14) and fried foie gras (€17). Noon–1.30pm & 7pm– 9.30pm; closed Sat & Sun.

**Le Buerehiesel** 4 parc de l'Orangerie ☎03 88 45 56 65, ⓦbuerehiesel.com. Run by Eric Westermann, son of the much-lauded, Michelin-starred chef Antoine Westermann, *Buerehiesel* is housed in a delightful, rustic farmhouse in the Parc de l'Orangerie. It's pricey – *menus* start at €65, and à la carte mains hover around the €30 mark. Noon– 1.30pm & 7.30pm–9.30pm; closed Sun & Mon, first three weeks in Aug & Jan.

**La Cloche à Fromage** 27 rue des Tonneliers ☎03 88 23 13 19. Don't come here if you don't like cheese: everything

**4**

## THE WINES OF ALSACE

Despite the long, tall bottles and Germanic names, Alsatian wines are unmistakably French in their ability to complement the region's traditional cuisine. This is white wine country – if you do spot a local red, it will invariably be a Pinot Noir. Winemakers take advantage of the long, dry autumns to pick extremely ripe grapes producing wines with a little more sweetness than elsewhere in France, but good wines will have a refreshing natural acidity, too. Each of the three main grape varieties listed below can be made with a sweetness level ranging from off-dry right through to *"Sélection des Grains Nobles"* for the most highly prized dessert wines (*vendages tardives* being the label for the slightly less sweet late-harvested wines). *Grand Cru* labelled wines come from the best vineyard sites.

**Riesling** The ultimate thirst-quencher, limey, often peachy, excellent with fish dishes and *choucroute*.

**Gewurztraminer** Alsace's most aromatic grape, with roses, lychees, honey, spices and all manner of exotic flavours. Try with pungent Munster cheese or rich pâté.

**Pinot Gris** Rich, fruity, smoky and more understated than Gewurztraminer. A versatile food wine; try with white meat in creamy sauces and milder cheeses.

Other wines you're likely to come across include the grapey **Muscat**, straightforward **Sylvaner**, and delicate **Pinot Blanc/Auxerrois**, which also forms the base of the region's excellent sparkling **Crémant d'Alsace**. **Pinot Noir** is used for light, fruity reds and rosés.

on the menu centres around it, from the delicious oven-baked goats' cheese platters (€19) to the *raclettes* (from €25.90) and fondues (from €23.90). They also have an excellent cheese shop across the road at number 32. Noon–2pm & 7pm–12.30am; closed Sun.

**Le Clou** 3 rue du Chaudron ☎ 03 88 32 11 67. Reliable, ever-popular *winstub* tucked away close to the cathedral, serving hearty meals such as *choucroute* (€16) and *pot-au-feu* (€19.50). Mon–Sat 11.45am–2pm & 5.30pm–midnight; closed Sun.

**Le Crocodile** 10 rue de l'Outre ☎ 03 88 32 13 02, ⊛ au-crocodile.com. Named after the stuffed beast above the entrance, this elegant restaurant has earned a Michelin star for its excellent cuisine: exquisite *plats* could include pork trotters with truffles (€50) or lobster cannelloni (€76). It has a very affordable dinner menu at €38. 11.45am–1.30pm & 7–9.30pm; closed Sun.

★ **S'Kaechele** 8 rue de l'Argile ☎ 03 88 22 62 36, ⊛ skaechele.com. Alsatian couple Karine and Daniel have gained a quick reputation as *the* winstub to visit when in Strasbourg. *Jambonneau*, *choucroute* (€15), *escargots* and plenty of desserts served in a cosy, half-timbered building where the house wine means wine from its own vineyard. Book in advance. Mon–Fri 11.45am–1.45pm & 7pm–9.30pm; closed public holidays.

### CAFÉS AND BARS

**L'Abattoir** 1 quai Charles Altorffer ☎ 03 88 32 28 12. With its funky lamps, painted black walls and wooden benches, *L'Abattoir* is a very relaxed café-bar. Delicious snacks are on offer – for a sugary pick-me-up, try the strawberry crumble or the waffles (from €3.50) – all day, as well as shisha pipes. There's a lounging area with strange circular beds as well as two outside areas for a drink in the sunshine. Daily 11am–2am; Sat to 3am, Sun to 1am.

**Art Café** 1 rue Hans-Jean Arp (inside the musée d'Art Moderne, see p.227) ☎ 03 88 22 18 88, ⊛ artcafé-restaurant.com. You don't have to get a ticket to the museum to come up to its superb café-restaurant which serves everything from teas and coffees to light snacks; tarts from €9.50. There's a large terrace that looks out over the whole of Strasbourg, perfect for brunch (Sun only; €12). Tues–Fri 11am–7pm, Thurs until 9pm, Sat–Sun 10am–6pm. Closed Mon.

**L'Épicerie** 6 rue du Vieux Seigle ☎ 03 88 32 52 41, ⊛ lepicerie-strasbourg.com. This fun café-bar is a reconstructed grocers, with jolly tablecloths, ramshackle wooden furniture, and vintage advertisements. It's always packed out with people enjoying very reasonably priced *tartines* (open sandwiches), served daily until midnight. Tartine with prunes and *fourme d'ambert* cheese €5.20. Daily noon–midnight.

★ **Jeanette et les Cycleux** 30 rue des Tonneliers ☎ 03 88 23 02 71, ⊛ lenetdejeannette.com. A cycling theme dominates at this trendy little bar that serves a variety of coffees (€3) cocktails, milkshakes and wines. Substantial snacks on offer include salads (€9.50) and delicious planchettes of cold meat and cheese (from €5.70). Free alcotests and condoms offered for those that need them. Daily 11am–1am.

**Terres à Vin** 1 rue du Miroir ☎ 03 88 25 60 20, ⊛ terresavin.com. Excellent boutique wine-shop/bar, brainchild of wine connoisseur Eric Demange, stocking over 2500 different wines from high-quality producers around France, with an emphasis on bio-dynamic wines and *vins naturelles*. There are a variety of snacks to accompany your tipple (glass from €2.50). Daily 10.30am–10pm.

## ENTERTAINMENT

Strasbourg usually has lots going on, particularly when it comes to music. Pick up the free monthly magazine *Spectacles à Strasbourg et alentours* (⊛ spectacles-publications.com) for entertainment info and listings.

**Festivals** There are theatre, dance and musical festivals throughout the summer, with a particular emphasis on classical music in mid-June, jazz in July, and "contemporary classical" music at the Musica festival (⊛ festivalmusica.org) from mid-September to early October. If you happen to be in town from July to the first week of August don't miss the impressive illumination of the cathedral facade, accompanied by music (10.30pm–1am).

**Christmas market** At the Marché de Noël (last weekend in Nov to Dec 31), an increasingly commercial event dating back over 400 years, central Strasbourg is taken over by wooden stalls selling mulled wine, crafts of varying quality and spicy Christmas cookies known as *bredele*.

# The Route des Vins

Flanked to the west by the rising forests of the southern Vosges, which stretch all the way down to Belfort, Alsace's picturesque **Route des Vins** ("Wine Route") follows the foot of the mountains along the western edge of the wide and flat Rhine valley. Beginning in Marlenheim, west of Strasbourg, the route, on or around the D35, snakes its way over 180km to Thann, near Mulhouse, through exquisitely preserved medieval towns and villages characterized by half-timbered houses, narrow cobbled streets and neighbouring ancient ruined castles – testimony to the province's turbulent past. The route is blanketed with neat terraces of vines, which produce the famous white wines (see box, p.229). Tasting opportunities are plentiful, particularly during the region's countless wine festivals that mainly coincide with the October harvest.

## Obernai

Picturesque little **OBERNAI** on the Strasbourg–Molsheim–Sélestat train line is the first place most people head for when travelling south from Strasbourg. Miraculously unscathed by the last two world wars, Obernai has retained almost its entire **rampart system**, including no fewer than fifteen towers, along with street after street of carefully maintained medieval houses, two Michelin-starred restaurants and four wine producers offering tastings a short stroll away from the centre. True, it gets more than its fair share of visitors, but with good reason.

## Barr and around

Every bit as charming as Obernai, **BARR**, only 6km south, is for some reason overlooked by mass tourism. Still, it is easy to while away a couple of hours wandering its twisting cobbled streets, at their busiest during the lively mid-July **wine festival**, when you can taste over two hundred local wines in the town hall. To break up the

**4**

---

### FOUR FABULOUS ALSACE FORTRESSES

Alsace is dotted with medieval fortresses, heirlooms from a quarrelsome past. Here's a rundown of the very best castles in the region:

**Bernstein** Explore the marvellous ruins of this castle perched 552m up on a rock overlooking Dambach-la-Ville. It's a 45-minute walk from the village past the chapel of St-Sébastien or a drive up the D35, turning left at Blienschwiller towards Villé on the D203 and then following the sign to Bernstein on the GR5 until the Schulwaldplatz car park. From there it's a gentle 20min walk uphill through a spruce forest. Free access.

**Haut Koenigsbourg** A massive pile of honey-coloured sandstone that sits astride a 757m bluff, this castle dates from the twelfth century. It was heavily restored in the twentieth century under the tenacious management of Kaiser Wilhelm II and is today one of the most visited monuments in France – try to come midweek or out of season to avoid the crowds. It is a stunning spot with fantastic views on a clear day. Daily: March & Oct 9.30am–5pm; April, May & Sept 9.15am–5.15pm; June, July & Aug 9.15am–6pm; Nov–Feb 9.30am–noon & 1–4.30pm; guided tour in English daily June–Sept at 11.45am. €7 50; ⓦ haut-koenigsbourg.fr.

**Château Hohlandsbourg** Six kilometres outside Eguisheim, this enormous castle surrounded by massive walls is the largest in the region. It was extensively damaged during the Thirty Years' War but there's still plenty to see, including beautiful gardens. The castle is also a venue for cultural activities, music concerts and children's workshops – check the website for events. July & Aug daily 10am–7pm; April, June & Sept Mon–Sat 2–6pm, Sun 11am–6pm; May Sat & Sun 11am–6pm; Oct Sat 2–6pm, Sun 11am–6pm; €4 20; ⓦ chateau-hohlandsbourg.com.

**Château Kintzheim** Small but wonderful ruined castle built around a cylindrical refuge-tower and located just south of Haut Koenigsbourg (see above). Today Kintzheim is an aviary for birds of prey – the Volerie des Aigles – and puts on magnificent displays of aerial prowess by resident eagles and vultures. Daily: April–May 2–5.30pm; June to mid-July 2–6.30pm; mid-July to mid-Aug 10.30am–6.30pm; mid-Aug to late-Aug 1.30pm–6.30pm; Sept to mid-Nov 2pm–5.30pm. March–May & Sept–Nov Mon–Fri demonstrations twice daily, three demonstrations Sat & Sun; June–Aug three or four demonstrations daily – consult website for demonstration times; €9.5 (under 14s €6); ⓦ voleriedesaigles.com.

wine and the walking, you might like to drop into La Folie Marco (30 rue du Docteur-Sultzer; June & Oct Sat & Sun 10am–noon & 2–6pm; July–Sept daily except Tues 10am–noon & 2–6pm; €5) an eighteenth-century mansion on the northern outskirts of town, which has interesting displays of furniture from the Renaissance to the late nineteenth century.

There are several delightful stops south of Barr, such as **Gertwiller** – virtually next door – the world capital of gingerbread-making, where there are still two workshops making traditional *pain d'epices* today; **Mittelbergheim**, a peaches-and-cream cluster of houses lining narrow, undulating streets; **Andlau**, in the middle of a green ridge with a venerable abbey that dates back to 880 AD; the south-facing **Itterswiller**, which offers some of the best views on the Route des Vins; and the impossibly picturesque **Dambach-la-Ville** where the road enters from one village gate and leaves from the other. The focus in every village is wine; virtually every other house is a wine cellar offering tastings.

## Bergheim

From Dambach you'll drive through a few medieval villages of varying attractiveness to reach the peaceful walled town of **BERGHEIM**, for many the most beautiful village in the Route des Vins and certainly not one to drive by without stopping. Just by the car park is one of the most easily accessible grand cru Alsatian cellars, that of **Gustave Lorentz**, established in 1836 and still in the same family.

## Hunawihr

**Reintroduction centre** April, May & Sept 10am–12.30pm & 2–5.30pm; Sat & Sun 10.30am–5.30pm; June–July 10am–6.30pm; Aug 10am–7pm, plus late opening the first three Thurs; Oct 2–5.30pm, Sat–Sun 10.30am–12.30pm & 2pm–5.30pm; Nov & March Sat & Sun 10.30am–12.30pm & 2–4.30pm • Show times are always in the afternoons, check website for times • €8.50 • ☎ 03 89 73 72 62, ⓦ cigogne-loutre.com **Butterfly Garden** April–Sept 10am–6pm; Oct 10am–5pm • €7.50 • ⓦ jardinsdespapillons.fr

Around 8km south of Bergheim lies the beguiling hamlet of **HUNAWIHR**, with its fourteenth-century walled church standing proud amid the green vines. Hunawihr is at the forefront of the Alsatian ecological movement aimed at protecting the stork – the *cigogne* – of the region, and there's a **Reintroduction Centre** for them, along with otters, to the east of the village, as well as a Butterfly Garden (Jardins des Papillons).

## Riquewihr

**Museum** Château des Princes de Wurtemberg-Montbéliard • Daily: April–Oct & Dec 10am–5.30pm • €4.50 • ⓦ shpta.com

An exceptionally well-preserved medieval town a couple of kilometres south of Hunawihr, **RIQUEWIHR** has its fair share of visitors but is still a lovely place to stay a night or two. To distract you from the tempting tastings at wine cellars that dot Riquewihr's cobbled streets, there's a small museum investigating the development of communications – the **Musée de la Communication en Alsace**.

## Kaysersburg

**Museum** 126 rue du Général de Gaulle • April–Nov plus weekends in December; daily 9am–noon & 2–6pm • €2 • ⓦ ville-kaysersberg.fr

Considered one of the most striking villages on the Route des Vins, **KAYSERSBURG** suffers from a deluge of summertime visitors, thanks to its houses clustered in chocolate-box fashion around the River Weiss and its fortified bridge. Along with a wonderful sixteenth-century altarpiece in its Gothic church, the town's main claim to fame is as the birthplace of Nobel Peace Prize-winner Albert Schweitzer, who founded a leprosy hospital at Lambaréné in French Equatorial Africa. He is honoured with the **Musée du docteur Schweitzer**.

## ACCOMMODATION

## THE ROUTE DES VINS

### ANDLAU

**Zinck** 13 rue de la Marne ☎03 88 08 27 30, ⓦzinckhotel.com. This quirky hotel occupies a former windmill and each room has a different theme, from the 1930s browns and beiges in "Jazzy" to the more traditional "Vigneronne" and the colourful "Zen" suites. **€60**

### BARR

**Les Hortensias** 19 rue Docteur Sultzer ☎03 88 58 56 00, ⓦhortensias-hotel.com. Both charming and pleasant from the outside, set in the middle of a large park, *Les Hortensias* manages to have a cool, contemporary feel in its rooms inside. The swimming pool is a great draw in the summer months. Breakfast €10. **€115**

**Manoir** 11 rue St-Marc ☎03 88 08 03 40, ⓦhotel-manoir.com. Light and spacious rooms, furnished with elegant drapes and antiques, housed in a nineteenth-century winemaker's villa. There's also an excellent restaurant (noon–1.30pm & 7pm–9.30pm; closed Mon & Sat lunch) with great *tartes flambées* (€9) and a rare vegetarian menu. **€80**

### BERGHEIM

**La Cour du Bailli** 57 Grand'Rue, Bergheim ☎03 89 73 73 46, ⓦcour-bailli.com. A cheerful little place with studios and rooms housed in a charming lavender-coloured building – there's also a rather incongruous, but most welcome, spa. Breakfast €10. **€86**

### OBERNAI

**À la Cour d'Alsace** 3 rue de Gail ☎03 88 95 07 00, ⓦcour-alsace.com. This four-star grand hotel is tucked away next to the rampart walls; it has a pool, garden terrace, a sauna, a Turkish bath, two restaurants, closed parking and some excellent half-board deals. Breakfast €12.50. **€140**

**La Diligence** 23 place du Marché ☎03 88 95 55 69, ⓦhotel-diligence.com. Slap bang in the centre of town with spotless, neat rooms and geranium-brimming balconies, above a pleasant *salon de thé* (Thurs–Mon 11.30am–6pm). Parking €9 per day. Buffet breakfast €8.70. **€60**

**Le Gouverneur** 13 rue de Sélestat ☎03 88 95 63 72, ⓦhotellegouverneur.com. A wonderful sixteenth-century building named after Louis the XIV's military governor who ensconced himself here when Alsace was conquered by France. It has 32 comfortable and peaceful rooms set around an old horse carriage entrance. **€70**

## EATING AND DRINKING

### BERGHEIM

**Auberge de l'Ill** ☎03 89 71 89 00, ⓦauberge-de-l-ill.com. A Michelin three-starred restaurant that's the star of Illhaeusern, a small agglomeration of houses south of Bergheim: behind a traditional, half-timbered facade, the restaurant's decor is a modern medley of camouflage carpet, crystal chandeliers, and cream-coloured furniture, while the food and wines are pretty spectacular. Expect a fair dent in your bank account, with dishes starting at €43 and rising to €65 – menus are €121 at lunch and €158 at dinner. Noon–1.45pm & 7–9pm; closed Mon & Tues all day, Feb–March eves only.

**Eglantine de Bergheim** 10 place Walter ⓦbergheim-confitures.com. Home-made jams and chutneys packed all around every empty space in this tiny shop whose house speciality, and namesake, is a sticky, sweet rosehip jam (*confiture d'eglantine*). 10am–1pm & 2.30–7pm; closed Sun afternoon.

★ **La Mosaique** Place Walter. Stop by for a bite to eat with the locals in this diminutive café where the *plat du jour* is extremely good value and their house speciality, *matafan* – thick crêpes covered with a bechamel sauce and filled with onions, bacon and cheese – is particularly delicious (€8). Daily 8am–8pm (summer to 10pm).

### OBERNAI

**Le Bistrot des Saveurs** 35 rue de Sélestat ☎03 88 49 9 0 51. One-star Michelin restaurant by chef Thierry Schwartz, with few tables, small menu with local produce and excellent service, notable for making its own bread. It is generally not busy at lunch during weekdays so reservations might not be necessary. Menu at €88 with four glasses of wine. 12.15–2pm & 7.15–9.30pm; closed Sun & Mon.

**La Dime** 5 rue des Pèlerins ☎03 88 95 54 02, ⓦladime.fr. Busy, popular and very friendly restaurant. The artichoke beer on offer – full of iron, apparently – prepares you for its cheerful *menus* that start from €15.65. Noon–2pm, 7pm–9.30pm; closed Wed.

**La Fourchette des Ducs** 6 rue de la Gare ☎03 88 48 33 38, ⓦlafourchettedesducs.com. One of the great restaurants in Alsace under chef Nicolas Stamm, situated very conveniently opposite the station and well worth travelling from Strasbourg for a meal. Contemporary decor and dishes, but limited hours, so make reservations well in advance. Mains from €48, *menu dégustation* €95 and €130. Tues–Sat 7–9pm & Sun noon–1.30pm.

4

# Colmar and around

The old centre of **COLMAR**, a fifty-minute train ride south of Strasbourg and lying east of the main Route des Vins villages, is *echt* Alsatian, with crooked half-timbered and painted houses. Its small canals and picturesque narrow streets are a flaneur's paradise. This is prime Elsässisch-speaking country, a German dialect known to philologists as Alemannic, which has waxed and waned during the province's chequered history. As the proud home of Mathias Grünewald's magnificent Issenheim altarpiece, the town is a magnet for tourists all year round.

### Musée d'Unterlinden

1 rue d'Unterlinden • May–Oct daily 9am–6pm; Nov–April daily except Tues 9am–noon & 2–5pm; closed public hols • €7 • ⓦ musee-unterlinden.com

Colmar's foremost attraction, the **Musée d'Unterlinden** is housed in a former Dominican convent with a peaceful cloistered garden. The museum's *pièce de résistance* is the **Issenheim altarpiece**, thought to have been made between 1512 and 1516 for the monastic order of St Anthony at Issenheim, whose members dedicated themselves to caring for those afflicted by ergotism and other nasty skin diseases. The extraordinary painted panels are the work of Mathias Grünewald (1480–1528). The luridly expressive centre panel depicts the Crucifixion: a tortured Christ of exaggerated dimensions turns his outsize hands upwards, fingers splayed in pain, flanked by his pale, fainting mother and saints John and Mary Magdalene. The face of St Sebastian, on the right wing, is believed to have been modelled on Grünewald's own likeness. The reverse panels depict the annunciation, Christ's resurrection, the nativity and a vivid, flamboyant orchestra of angels, all splendidly bathed in transcendental light. On the rest of the painted panels, you'll find a truly disturbing representation of the temptation of St Anthony, who is engulfed by a grotesque pack of demons; note the figure afflicted with the alarming symptoms of ergotism. Altarpieces by Martin Schongauer, in the same room as the *Issenheim*, are also worth a quick look, as is the museum's collection of modern paintings, which includes some Impressionist works and a couple of Picassos.

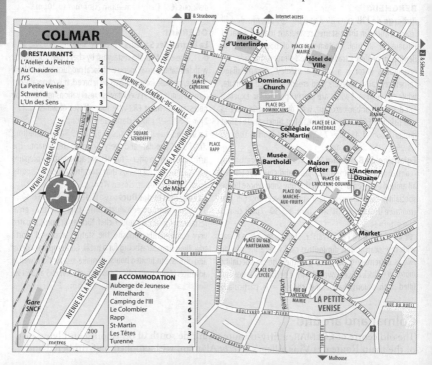

## Dominican church and the Collégiale St-Martin

**Church** April–Dec daily 10am–1pm & 3–6pm • €1.50 **Collégiale St-Martin** Daily except Sun am 8am–6pm • Free

The austere **Dominican church** on rue des Serruriers has some fine glass and a beautiful altarpiece known as *The Virgin in a Bower of Roses*, painted in 1473 by Schongauer. At the other end of the street you reach the **Collégiale St-Martin** on a busy café-lined square. It's known locally as "the cathedral" because for a short period it served as one; peek in to see its stonework and stained glass. The sixteenth-century **Maison Pfister**, with external painted panels, is on the south side of the church.

## Musée Bartholdi

30 rue des Marchands • March–Dec daily except Tues 10am–noon & 2–6pm; closed public hols • €4.50 • ⓦ musee-bartholdi.com

Frédéric Auguste Bartholdi, the sculptor of New York's Statue of Liberty, was born at 30 rue des Marchands, which now houses the **Musée Bartholdi**. It contains Bartholdi's personal effects and the original designs for the statue, along with 1870s memorabilia and scale models of his greatest works.

## Ancienne Douane and La Petite Venise

Rue des Marchands continues south to the **Ancienne Douane** or Koïfhus, its gaily painted roof tiles loudly proclaiming the town's medieval prosperity. This is the heart of Colmar's Old Town, a short step away from the canal quarter down the Grand'Rue known as **La Petite Venise** (Little Venice). The dolly-mixture colours of the old fishing cottages on quai de la Poissonnerie contrast with the much taller, black-and-white, half-timbered tanners' houses on **rue des Tanneurs**, which leads off from the Koïfhus.

**4**

### ARRIVAL AND INFORMATION COLMAR

**By train** The *gare SNCF* is a 10min walk from the centre of town, along avenue de la République.

Destinations Mulhouse (1–2 hourly; 50min); Munster (1 hourly; 30min); Sélestat (1–3 hourly; 10–12mins); Strasbourg (1–2 hourly; 32min).

**Tourist office** Place d'Unterlinden (Jan–March Mon–Sat 9am–noon & 2pm–5pm; April–Oct Mon–Sat 9am–6pm (July and Aug till 7pm), Sun 10am–1pm; Nov to Christmas markets Sat 9am–noon & 2pm–6pm, Sun 10am–1pm; during Christmas markets Mon–Sat 9am–6pm, Sun 10am–1pm & 2pm–5pm;ⓣ 03 89 20 68 92, ⓦ ot-colmar.fr).

**Internet** Available at Cyber Didim (Mon–Sat 10am–10pm, Sun 2–10pm; €2.50/hr), 9 rue du Rempart, on the first floor above a kebab shop.

### GETTING AROUND

**Boat trips** You can get up close to the charming half-timbered houses in La Petite Venise by taking a peaceful boat trip with either La Krutenau (April–Oct Tues–Sun 10am–6.30pm; €6; ⓣ 03 89 41 18 80) from 1 rue de la Poissonnerie, or with Sweet Narcisse (April–Oct daily 10am–noon & 1.30–7pm; €6; ⓣ 03 89 41 01 94, ⓦ sweetnarcisse.com) which has a 30min commentary, from 10 rue de la Herse; English is spoken.

**By bike** Colmar Vélo Vélodocteurs by the train station (Fri–Sun 8am–noon & 2–5pm; €6/half-day, €8/day, €14/2 days and €40/week).

**By car** Colmar has a one-way system around the town which is not easy to manage. Hotels in the centre do not often offer parking and rates are high. There is a small free car park signposted "Vielle Ville" by the canal on the southeast side of the city, but cars are left overnight at your own risk.

### ACCOMMODATION

**Auberge de Jeunesse Mittelhardt** 2 rue Pasteur ⓣ 03 89 80 57 39, ⓔ auberge.jeunesse@ville-colmar .com. The town's only youth hostel is perfectly adequate but gets extremely busy in summer. It's 1km from town; take bus #4, #5 or #15 to Pont Rouge. Closed Jan. Breakfast €4.40. Dorms (up to 9 beds) **€9.60**

**Camping de L'Ill** Rte de Neuf-Brisach ⓣ 03 89 41 15 94, ⓦ campingdelill.com. Inexpensive but excellent campsite 2km east of Colmar by the river Ill. It offers wi-fi and bike rental. Take bus #1 from the station, direction "Wihr", stop "Plage de l'Ill". Closed Jan & Feb. **€15.10**

★ **Le Colombier** 7 rue Turenne ⓣ 03 89 23 96 00, ⓦ hotel-le-colombier.fr. Colmar's best-known boutique hotel in the heart of the Petite Venise quarter. Modern rooms are swathed in cool lavender tones and back onto a calm internal courtyard. Large family suites available, too. **€89**

**Rapp** 1–5 rue Weineimer ⓣ 03 89 41 62, 10 ⓦ rapp -hotel.com. Central three-star hotel with rooms rather on the small side but with a great swimming pool and sauna in the basement. Traditional restaurant on the ground floor with a good choice of wines. **€102**

**St-Martin** 38 Grand'Rue ☎03 89 24 11 51, ⍟hotel -saint-martin.com. A riot of flowery wallpaper, flounces and painted headboards, for those who like the Renaissance style of decoration. In the shadow of the cathedral, the hotel couldn't be more central yet it's remarkably quiet. Breakfast €12. **€89**

**Les Têtes** 19 rue des Têtes ☎03 89 24 43 43,

⍟maisondestetes.com. Well-appointed seventeenth-century house with a wonderful facade covered in grimacing faces. The rooms are clad in wood panelling. There's a refined restaurant downstairs (mains around €20, breakfast €15). **€126**

**Turenne** 10 rte de Bâle ☎03 89 21 58 58, ⍟turenne .com. Functional, multicoloured rooms in a jolly little hotel, overflowing with balcony geraniums in the heart of Petite Venise. Breakfast €8.50. **€60**

## EATING AND DRINKING

**L'Atelier du Peintre** 1 rue Schongauer ☎03 89 29 51 57, ⍟atelier-peintre.fr. French contemporary cuisine that finally earned chef Lefebvre a Michelin star in 2011. It is all served up in an attractive authentic ambiance, all lime green and distressed wood, with some tables al fresco. Wide range of menus from €20 to €72, while à la carte dishes start at €10 and go no further than €35. Noon–2pm 7–9.30pm. Closed Sun & Mon, mid-Feb for two weeks & last two weeks in Aug.

★ **Au Chaudron** 5 rue de Conseil Souverain ☎03 89 24 42 21, ⍟auchaudron.fr. Affable French restaurant inspired by classic Alsatian food but served with a modern twist. Its *presskopf* (pigs' cheeks in aspic along with foie gras) is a must in the hors d'oevres list. Mains around €18. Noon–1.45pm & 7–9.45pm; closed Sun all day, Tues & Thurs lunch.

**JYS** 17rue de la Poissonnerie ☎03 89 21 53 60, ⍟jean -yves-schillinger.com. Sitting by the canal and with a lovely outdoor terrace, this is one of the top gastronomic restaurants in Colmar with a Michelin star. Inside, the decor is cool and contemporary, and the food simply sublime.

Reasonable menus start at €33 (lunch) €76 (dinner). Noon–2pm & 7–9.45pm; closed Sun, Mon & winter school holidays.

**La Petite Venise** 4 rue de la Poissonnerie ☎03 89 41 72 59, ⍟restaurantpetitevenise.com. It's like eating dinner in an old Alsatian house in this charming *winstub*: pots and pans, wooden benches and even an old oven adorn the interior. Alsatian classics prevail, starting from €8. Noon–2pm &7–9.45pm; closed first two weeks in July.

**Schwendi** 23–25 Grand Rue ☎03 89 23 66 26. Exposed wooden beams, tightly packed tables and vintage posters on the wall give this place a warm, convivial feel. The menu is varied and good value; salads (from €8), onion soup (€5), and the house speciality is a hearty and deliciously salty potato rösti (€18). Daily noon–10.30pm.

**L'Un des Sens** 18 rue Berthe-Molly ☎03 89 24 04 37. Excellent *cave à vins*, where you can taste a wide range of wines and nibble on plates of cold meat and cheese (€5–16). Buy the wines you liked at the front from the boutique. Tues–Thurs 3–10pm, Fri–Sat 10am–late.

# Sélestat

Less touristy and much larger than the pretty little villages that surround it, **SÉLESTAT** has nevertheless an interesting centre to amble around in. It's worth dropping into the town's two churches, the romanesque **Ste-Foy**, much restored since its construction by the monks of Conques and, close by, the attractive Gothic **St-Georges**, which sports spectacularly multicoloured roof tiles and some very beautiful stained glass. For a brief period in the late fifteenth and early sixteenth centuries, Sélestat was the intellectual centre of Alsace; its Latin School attracted a group of humanists led by Beatus Rhenanus, whose personal library was one of the most impressive collections of its time. Rhenanus' library is now on display in the **Bibliothèque Humaniste** (Mon & Wed–Fri 9am–noon & 2–6pm; Sat 9am–noon; July & Aug also Sat–Sun 2–5pm; €4.10) which is housed in the town's former corn exchange. Alongside Rhenanus' humanist texts, the library holds rare books and manuscripts dating back to the seventh century, including the 1507 *Cosmographiae Introductio*, the first document ever to use the word "America".

## EATING AND DRINKING                                                   SÉLESTAT

★ **L'Acoustic** 5 place du Marché Vert ☎03 88 92 29 40, ⍟restobiolacoustic.com. A dinky organic café-bar just by

the church of Ste-Foy, which serves tasty snacks and main meals – *plats* around €8, menus from €12; on Saturday

evenings twice a month there are amateur performances ranging from jazz and classical concerts to comedy and drama (*menu* €19 for two courses, plus €6 for the show). Mon–Sat 9am–3pm, Fri & Sat also 7.30–10pm. **La Vieille Tour** 7–8 Rue de la Jauge ☎ 03 88 92 15 02,

ⓦ vieille-tour.com. Gourmand restaurant with immaculate service and food inspired from all regions of France; despite the variety, *choucroute* at €19 is their biggest hit, but maybe that's because the locals love it. Noon–2pm & 7–9.30pm; closed Mon.

## Munster

Some 19km west of Colmar, and accessible by train, the peaceful town of **MUNSTER** owes its existence and its name to a band of Irish monks who founded a successful monastery (monasterium = Munster) here in the seventh century. Today its name is associated with a rich, creamy and exceedingly smelly **cheese**, the crowning glory of many an Alsatian pretzel – or even meal. Overlooked by Le Petit Ballon (1272m) and Le Hohneck (1363m), among the highest peaks of the Vosges, the town itself is not as picturesque as the wine villages further east but nevertheless makes a pleasant day-trip from Colmar.

# Mulhouse

A large, sprawling, industrial city 35km south of Colmar, **MULHOUSE** was Swiss until 1798 when, at the peak of its prosperity (founded on printed textiles), it voted to become part of France. Today it bills itself as a "museum town", with at least four that might grab your interest. It's much cheaper to stay here than in neighbouring Colmar (or Basel), plus it offers the best nightlife in Alsace should you find yourself there over a weekend. The **Hôtel de Ville** on the central Place de la Réunion contains a beautifully presented history of the city in the **Musée Historique** (daily except Tues 1.30–6.30pm; free). The Neo-Gothic cathedral opposite the museum was built in 1866, replacing a twelfth-century church, yet its fourteenth-century stained glass is considered the most beautiful in the Upper Rhine; this is the only Protestant cathedral standing in a main square in France.

## Écomusée d'Alsace

Chemin Grosswald, Ungersheim • April–Nov, generally open 10am–6pm; July & Aug 10am–7pm, but check the online calendar for odd closing dates and staff holidays (normally mid-Nov and Feb–March) • €13; family with two children €38 • ⓦ ecomusee-alsace.fr

Around 18km outside Mulhouse, the **Écomusée d'Alsace** is a successful reconstruction of a typical early twentieth-century Alsatian village – the seventy or so half-timbered huts were dismantled from elsewhere in the region and rebuilt in fields here, using Alsatian building methods. Visitors can wander at will around the farmyard and stables – complete with farm animals – pottery, school, bakery, ironmongers and buzzing apiary. There's even a barber, where brave souls can treat themselves to a shave and haircut *à l'alsacien*. Enthusiastic staff dressed in traditional Alsatian garb – white

---

### THE ROUTE DES CRÊTES

Above Munster, the main road west to the little town of Gérardmer crosses the mountains by the principal pass, the Col de la Schlucht, where it intersects the "**Route des Crêtes**" (Crest Road), built for strategic purposes during World War I to facilitate the movement of munitions and supplies. It's a spectacular road traversing thick forest and open pasture, and in winter it becomes one long cross-country ski route. Starting in Cernay, 15km west of Mulhouse, it follows the main ridge of the Vosges, including the highest peak of the range, the **Grand Ballon** (1424m), north as far as Ste-Marie-aux-Mines, 20km west of Sélestat; a great experience especially if you are travelling on a motorbike. From Munster it's also accessible by a twisting minor road through Hohrodberg, which takes you past beautiful glacial lakes and the eerie World War I battlefield of Linge, where the French and German trenches, once separated by just a few metres, are still clearly visible; there is a small museum nearby.

aprons, ribboned headdresses and the like – are on site to help explain the ins and outs of the history. Throughout the year, usually on Sundays, there are festivals and various workshops, ranging from pottery to stone-masonry. Note that information signs are all in French or German, but don't let this put you off – there's still plenty to feast your eyes on, and you could easily spend a couple of hours here. Note that you need your own wheels to drive to Écomusée, but the way there is very well signposted.

### Cité de l'Automobile, Musée National-Collection Schlumpf

192 av de Colmar • Daily: April–Oct 10am–6pm; Nov–Dec 10am–5pm; Jan to mid-Feb closed weekdays am • €11, combined ticket with Cité du Train, €17.50 • Free audioguide in English • Take tram #1 from *gare SNCF* to stop "Musée Auto" • Ⓦ citedelautomobile.com

A couple of tram stops north of Mulhouse's city centre, the **Cité de l'Automobile, Musée National-Collection Schlumpf**, houses an overwhelming collection of over six hundred cars, originally belonging to local brothers Hans and Fritz Schlumpf, who made their fortunes running a nearby spinning mill. Lined up in endless rows, the impeccably preserved vehicles range from the industry's earliest attempts, like the extraordinary wooden-wheeled Jacquot steam "car" of 1878, and the very first attempt at an environmentally friendly, solar-powered car made in 1942 to the 1968 Porsche racers. The highlights are the locally made Bugatti models: dozens of alluringly displayed, glorious racing cars, coupés and limousines, the pride of them being the two Bugatti Royales, out of only seven that were constructed. There's also the most expensive Bugatti in the world today, priced at a cool €1.6 million.

### Cité du Train – Musée Français du Chemin de Fer

2 rue Alfred-de-Glehn • Daily: April–Oct 10am–6pm; Nov–Dec & Feb–March 10am–5pm; Jan to mid-Feb closed weekdays pm • €10, combined ticket with Cité de l'Automobile, €18.50 • Free audioguide in English • Take tram #3 from *gare SNCF* to stop "Musees" • Ⓦ citedutrain.com

Several tram stops to the west of the town centre is the multicoloured corrugated iron building that houses the city's fantastic train museum. Slick and interactive, the museum has impressive railway rolling stock on display. A small train (what else?) transports you round from the earliest 1840s locomotives to today's TGV.

### Musée de l'Impression sur Etoffes

14 rue Jean-Jacques-Henner • Daily except Mon 10am–noon & 2–6pm • €8 • Ⓦ musee-impression.com

Sitting close to the *gare SNCF*, the wallpaper and textile museum is rather more fun than the name would suggest. Mostly displayed in temporary exhibitions, the museum's vast collection of sumptuous fabrics includes the eighteenth-century Indian and Persian imports that revolutionized the European ready-to-wear market and made Mulhouse a prosperous manufacturing centre. It's worth trying to coincide with one of the daily demonstrations of fabric printing (consult the website).

### ARRIVAL AND DEPARTURE                                        MULHOUSE

**By air** The international airport (Ⓦ euroairport.com) Basel-Mulhouse-Freiburg is 30min by car outside Mulhouse (still in France, but near the Swiss/German border). Take the shuttle bus to the train station in St Louis and change onto a train there. It is a 15min non-stop ride to the *gare SNCF*.
**By train** The main square, place de la Réunion, is five minutes' walk north of the *gare SNCF*. It is a terminus for the TGV.

Destinations Colmar (1–2 hourly; 20–25min); Lyon (6 daily; 2hr 50min); Marseille (1 daily; 4hr 40min); Nice (1 daily; 10hr 30min); Paris Gare de Lyon (10 daily; 2hr 40min); Sélestat (1–3 hourly; 30–40min); Strasbourg (1–2 hourly; 50min).

### INFORMATION

**Tourist office** Ground floor of the Hôtel de Ville (July, Aug & Dec daily 10am–7pm; Jan–June & Sept–Nov 10am–noon & 1–6pm; 10am–1pm Sun Jan–March, Oct & Nov; ☏ 03 89 66 93 13, Ⓦ tourisme-mulhouse.com). The 3-day ticket City Pass is valid for all public transport, a free visit to one museum and to a second at a reduced rate, plus other reductions.
**Bicycle rental** Vélocité, the city's bicycle self-service scheme, has 35 stands all over town, open 24/7 (€1 per day and €1/hr but you must pre-register at Ⓦ velocite .mulhouse.fr).

## ACCOMMODATION

★ **Kyriad** 15 rue Lambert ☎ 03 89 66 44 77, ⓦ kyriad.com. Good-value hotel in the middle of the shopping area that's comfortable and modern, with little touches which make a big difference: own lift to (public) parking below, safe, fast wi-fi, Turkish bath and fitness room, varied buffet breakfast (€9.50). Worth checking out its occasional special offers (under €50 for a double). **€71**

## EATING AND DRINKING

**Au Caves du Vieux Couvent** 23 rue de Convent ☎ 03 89 46 28 79, ⓦ cavesduvieuxcouvent.com. Good traditional home-cooking in this friendly restaurant with filling *menus* at €17 and a great *assiette de fromages* (€7.50) if you just want to try some of the wines in its excellent wine list. Noon–2.30pm & 6.30–9.30pm; closed Mon all day, Sun & Wed eves.

**O2** 2 Passage de l'Hotel de Ville ☎ 03 89 45 17 12. Stylish black-and-white wine bar/restaurant with late opening hours that attracts a young, trendy clientele. You can either taste the wines on offer or try its bistro-type food. Its signature dish is a remarkable seafood *choucroute* (€16). Daily 7am–midnight (kitchen: 11.30am–2pm & 7–10pm).

## NIGHTLIFE

**Bar 'a' Normal** 3 rue des Halles ☎ 03 89 43 25 78. Starts as a café in the morning with smooth jazz and ambient tones, which become more lively as the day progresses, playing anything from blues and rock to hip-hop and metal. It encourages clients to use a USB stick to transfer their MP3s and play them in the venue. Daily Mon–Sat 7.30am–1.30am, Sun 3–9pm.

**Jet7** 47 rue de la Sinne ☎ 06 71 98 95 19, ⓦ jet7club .fr. Medium-sized club on two floors; although it started as a gay club, it now has many different nights catering for everyone. Open weekends from midnight onwards.

# Nancy

The city of **NANCY**, on the River Meurthe, is renowned for the magnificent place Stanislas, cited as a paragon of eighteenth-century urban planning and today the finest in France. For its spectacularly grand centre, Nancy has the last of the independent dukes of Lorraine to thank: the dethroned king of Poland and father-in-law of Louis XV, Stanislas Leszczynski. During the twenty-odd years of his office in the mid-eighteenth century, he ordered some of the most successful construction of the period in all France. The city is also home to some impressive examples of Art Nouveau furniture and glassware hailing from the days of the **École de Nancy**, founded at the end of the nineteenth century by glass-master and furniture-maker, Émile Gallé.

## Place Stanislas and around

From the *gare SNCF*, walk through **Porte Stanislas**, straight down rue Stanislas to reach the rococo **place Stanislas**. Both this gate and Porte St-Catherine opposite are meticulously aligned with place Stanislas's solitary statue – that of the portly **Stanislas Leszczynski**, who commissioned architect Emmanuel Héré to design the square in the 1750s. On the south side of the square stands the imposing **Hôtel de Ville**, its roof topped by a balustrade ornamented with florid urns and winged cupids. Along its walls, lozenge-shaped lanterns dangle from the beaks of gilded cockerels; similar motifs adorn the other buildings bordering the square – look out for the fake, two-dimensional replacements. The square's entrances are enclosed by magnificent wrought-iron gates; the particularly impressive railings on the northern corners frame fountains dominated by statues of Neptune and Amphitrite.

## Musée des Beaux-Arts

Place Stanislas • Daily except Tues 10am–6pm; closed public holidays • €6, €10 combined ticket with Musée Lorrain and École de Nancy • ⓦ mban.nancy.fr

In the corner where rue Stanislas joins the square, the **Musée des Beaux-Arts** presents some excellent nineteenth- and twentieth-century French art, including a number of beautiful paintings by Émile Friant and Nancy's own Victor Prouvé. The layout of the basement – where works from Nancy's glass company, Daum, are beautifully lit – follows the shape of fortifications constructed from the fifteenth century through to Vauban's seventeenth-century alterations, discovered during the museum's 1990s renovation. For a glimpse of Daum's contemporary creations you can visit their shop on place Stanislas.

## Musée Lorrain

64 Grande-Rue • Daily except Mon 10am–12.30pm & 2–6pm, closed public hols • €4 or €5.50 combined ticket with Musée des Cordeliers (see p.242)

On its north, place Stanislas opens into the long, tree-lined **place de la Carrière**. Its far end is enclosed by the classical colonnades of the **Palais du Gouvernement**, former residence of the governor of Lorraine. Behind it, housed in the fifteenth-century Palais Ducal, is the **Musée Lorrain**. It displays local treasures – pottery, sculptures, Renaissance painting – along with a worthwhile annexe showing off a collection of Gallo-Roman skeletons found in the

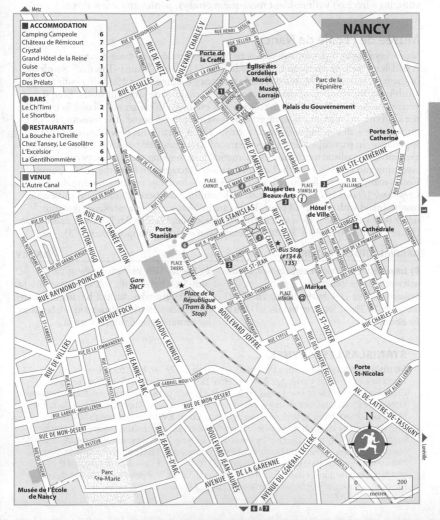

Lorraine region. Back in the main building there's also a room full of superb etchings by the Nancy-born artist, Jacques Callot, whose concern with social issues, evident in series such as *The Miseries of War*, presaged much nineteenth- and twentieth-century art.

## Musée des Cordeliers

64 Grande-Rue • Daily except Mon 10am–12.30pm & 2–6pm, closed public hols • €3.50 or €5.50 combined ticket with Musée Lorrain (see p.241)

Next to the Musée Lorrain, in the Église des Cordeliers et Chapelle Ducale, the **Musée des Cordeliers** illustrates the history of rural life in the region. You can access the church and adjacent octagonal chapel, which contain a few tombs belonging to various dukes of Lorraine. As a descendant of these dukes, Prince Otto von Habsburg (1912–2011) claimed the right to marry here in 1951 (and celebrate his golden jubilee in 2001). On the other side of the Palais du Gouvernement, you can collapse with exhaustion on the green grass of the attractive **Parc de la Pépinière**, which also contains a free zoo with resident macaque monkeys, ponies and a few sheep.

## Musée de l'École de Nancy

36 rue du Sergent-Blandan • Wed–Sun 10.30am–6pm • €6; free the first Sunday of each month • ⓦ ecole-de-nancy.com

A half-hour walk or a ten-minute bus ride (bus #123; stop "Nancy-Thermal") southwest of the train station, the **Musée de l'École de Nancy** is housed in a 1909 villa built for the Corbin family, founders of the Magasins Réunis chain of department stores. Even if you're not into Art Nouveau, this collection is exciting. Although not all of it belonged to the Corbins, the museum is arranged as if it were a private house. The furniture is outstanding – all swirling curvilinear forms – and the standards of workmanship are superlative. In particular, there's some extraordinary glassware by Émile Gallé, whose expressive naturalistic motifs and experimental glass-making techniques, particularly in colouring and etching, brought him international recognition from the 1880s. Some of Gallé's marquetry and furniture is also on display – look out for the stunning *Aube et Crépuscule* (*Dawn and Dusk*) bed, with its beautifully curvaceous headboard and exotic moths, inlaid with mother of pearl. If you are in Nancy during a weekend, put your name down at the desk for a visit at the **Villa Majorelle**, Nancy's Art Nouveau masterpiece (1 rue Majorelle ☎03 83 4 30 00; weekends 2pm or 4pm by appointment; €3).

### ARRIVAL AND DEPARTURE                                    NANCY

**By train** The *gare SNCF* is at the centre of town, a 15min walk west from place Stanislas.
Destinations Metz (2–4 hourly; 35min); Paris-Est (1 hourly; TGV; 1hr 30min); Strasbourg via Saverne (1 hourly; 1hr 20min).

**By bus** The STAN information centre at the *gare SNCF* (Mon–Sat 7am–7.30pm; ⓦreseau-stan.com) has timetables and tickets for local bus and tram routes. Nancy's main public transport hub is place de la République, just around the corner from the train station.

### STANISLAS LESZCZYNSKI

**Stanislas Leszczynski**, born in the Polish–Ukrainian city of Lemberg (now Lviv) in 1677, lasted just five years as the king of Poland before being forced into exile by Tsar Peter the Great. For the next twenty-odd years he lived on a French pension in northern Alsace, but after fifteen years Stanislas's luck changed when he managed, against all odds, to get his daughter, Marie, betrothed to the 15-year-old king of France, **Louis XV**. Marie was not so fortunate: married by proxy in Strasbourg Cathedral, having never set eyes on the groom, she gave birth to ten children, only to be rejected by Louis, who preferred the company of his mistresses, Madame de Pompadour and Madame du Barry. Bolstered by his daughter's marriage, Stanislas had another spell on the Polish throne from 1733 to 1736, but gave it up in favour of the comfortable dukedom of Barr and Lorraine. He lived out his final years in aristocratic style in the capital, Nancy, which he transformed into one of France's most beautiful towns.

## INFORMATION

**Tourist office** South side of Place Stanislas in the Hôtel de Ville (April–Oct Mon–Sat 9am–7pm, Sun & public hols 10am–5pm; Nov–March Mon–Sat 9am–6pm, Sun 10am–1pm; ☏ 03 83 35 22 41, ⦿ ot-nancy.fr).

**Internet** Cybercafé, 11 rue des Quatre-Églises (Mon 11am–9pm, Tues–Fri 9am–9pm & Sat 11am–9pm; €5/hr).

## ACCOMMODATION

**Camping Campeole** ☏ 03 83 27 18 28, ⦿ camping -brabois.com. Set in a large park near the hostel. To get there take bus #126 direction "Villers Clairlieu", stop "Camping". April to mid-Oct. Reception open 8am–12.30pm & 2–9pm; Mon, Tues 3–9pm. **€11.50**

**Château de Rémicourt** 149, rue de Vandoeuvre, Villers-les-Nancy ☏ 03 83 27 73 67, ⦿ aubergeremi court@mairie-nancy.fr. Spacious and pretty hostel, set in a sixteenth-century castle, but a fair trek from the centre in the suburb of Villers-lès-Nancy. To get there, take tram #1 from the station to "Le Reclus", then it's a 10min walk; bus #134 or #135 to terminus "Lycée Stanislas", or bus #126 in the direction of "Villers Clairlieu", stop "St-Fiacre". Two-bed private rooms including breakfast from **€15**

**Crystal** 5 rue Chanzy ☏ 03 83 17 54 00, ⦿ bwcrystal .com. Modern, no-nonsense three-star hotel with spotless large rooms decorated with brown and purple furnishings, comfortable beds, flat LSD TVs, private parking and easy-to-use wi-fi connection. Excellent weekend deals. The huge buffet breakfast is a steal at €12. **€81**

★ **Grand Hôtel de la Reine** 2 place Stanislas ☏ 03 83 35 03 01, ⦿ hoteldelareine.com. The grandest hotel in Nancy, situated on the elegant main square, is surprisingly affordable. Marie Antoinette stayed here en route from Vienna to Paris and the service is as regal as it was then. You have to register electronically for free wi-fi. Breakfast €16. **€125**

★ **Guise** 18 rue de Guise, just off Grande-Rue ☏ 03 83 32 24 68, ⦿ hoteldeguise.com. An eighteenth-century seigneurial residence, atmospherically furnished with antiques and tucked away on a quiet side street off the lively, restaurant-lined Grande-Rue. Wi-fi around reception area. Breakfast €9. **€75**

**Portes d'Or** 21 rue Stanislas ☏ 03 83 35 42 34, ⦿ hotel -lesportesdor.com. Located just a few steps from place Stanislas, this is an absolute bargain. Each room is adorned in a different, rather lurid colour – take your pick from lavender, pink, orange and green. Breakfast €6 in the restaurant, €9 in the room. **€55**

**Des Prélats** 56 place du Monseigneur-Ruch ☏ 03 83 30 20 20, ⦿ hoteldesprelats.com. Attractive, classic rooms in a light and airy seventeenth-century house. Breakfast (€12) is served in the elegant conservatory. **€110**

## EATING, DRINKING AND ENTERTAINMENT

There's a cluster of restaurants along and around the Grande-Rue, the rue des Maréchaux and the rue des Ponts, although some of the latter cater primarily to tourists. The cafés on place Stanislas are good for a drink and make great people-watching points. At night, head up the Grande-Rue towards place St-Epvre with its various lively bars.

### RESTAURANTS

**La Bouche à l'Oreille** 42 rue des Carmes ☏ 03 83 35 17 17. Hearty Alsatian food using lots of cheese is on offer in this adorable restaurant covered ceiling to floor in knick-knacks – think old clocks, earthenware pots, faded pictures, wonky lamps and so on. *Tartiflette*, omelettes and crêpes are on the large and varied menu (all from €9). Another slightly less festooned branch is at 17 rue Stanislas (☏ 03 83 37 22 87). Both noon–3pm & 7–10pm (weekends 10.30pm); closed Mon lunch, Sat lunch & Sun.

★ **Chez Tansey, Le Gastrolâtre** 23 Grande-Rue ☏ 03 83 35 51 94. Wonderful little restaurant run by jovial chef Patrick Tansey. *Plats* are tasty and unusual – try the melt-in-the-mouth scallops served on a rhubarb compote (€28). The high-quality food is reflected in the *menu* price – from €45. Booking recommended. 11am–2pm & 6pm–midnight. Closed Sun, Mon & Tues lunch.

★ **L'Excelsior** 50 rue Henri-Poincaré ☏ 03 83 35 67 44, ⦿ brasserie-excelsior.com. A lively 1911 Art Nouveau brasserie worth visiting for the grandeur of the interior alone; now part of the *Flo* brasserie chain, but managing to retain its good classic food (mains from €20). Mon–Sat 8am–12.30am, Sun 8am–11pm.

**La Gentilhommière** 29 rue des Maréchaux ☏ 03 83 32 26 44. By far the trendiest establishment on this street of restaurants, with a busy terrace and generous portions, specializing in fish. Set *menus* at €23 and €38. Noon–2pm & 7–10.30pm; closed Sat lunch & Sun.

### BARS AND VENUES

**L'Autre Canal** 45 bd d'Austrasie ☏ 03 83 38 44 88, ⦿ lautrecanalnancy.fr. The main live venue for bands that are not quite stadium material, as well as an outlet for rap artists and electronica DJs from all over Europe. Prices and times vary, but there are at least ten events per month.

**Le Ch'timi** 17 place St-Epvre ☏ 03 83 32 82 76. An institution in Nancy for 30 years under the stewardship of

**4**

the formidable Natalie, offering sixteen beers on tap, 150 bottles ones and numerous beer cocktails from €5. Mon 11am–2am, Tues–Sat 10am–2am, Sun 9.30am–9pm.

**Le Shortbus** 2 ter rue de la Citadelle (behind Porte de la Graffe). Gay bar that has been embraced by the mainstream student population en masse since its opening in April 2011. Packed to the rafters, loud and youthful, with a DJ spinning the decks after 10pm. Beers from €3. Wed–Sun 6pm–2am.

# Metz

**METZ** (pronounced "Mess"), the capital of Lorraine, lies on the east bank of the River Moselle, close to the Autoroute de l'Est linking Paris and Strasbourg, and the main Strasbourg–Brussels train line. Today the city has another connection to the capital in the much-awaited and much-lauded satellite branch of the Centre Pompidou. Along with its rather splendid cathedral, a strong dining scene (inspired by the Renaissance writer and famous gourmand, Rabelais, who lived here for two years), large and beautiful flower-lined public spaces and riverside setting, the honey-coloured city of Metz is something of an undiscovered gem.

The city's origins go back at least to Roman times, when, as now, it stood astride major trade routes. On the death of Charlemagne it became the capital of Lothar's portion of his empire. By the Middle Ages it had sufficient wealth and strength to proclaim itself an independent republic, which it remained until its absorption into France in 1552. Caught between warring influences, Metz has endured more than its share of historical hand-changing; reluctantly ceded to Germany in 1870, it recovered its liberty at the end of World War I, only to be re-annexed by Hitler until the Liberation.

Metz is, in effect, two towns: the original French quarters of the **Vieille Ville**, gathered round the cathedral and encompassing the **Île de la Comédie**, and the **Quartier Impérial**, undertaken as part of a once-and-for-all process of Germanification after the Prussian occupation in 1870. Developing with speed and panache is a third section: the **Quartier de l'Amphithéâtre**, south of the train station, heralded by the **Centre Pompidou** and the adjacent sports stadium – shops and offices are slowly following.

## Vieille Ville

From the north side of place de la République, **rue des Clercs** cuts through the attractive, bustling and largely pedestrianized heart of the **Vieille Ville**. Past the place St-Jacques, with its numerous outdoor cafés, you come to the eighteenth-century **place d'Armes**, where the lofty Gothic **Cathédrale Saint-Étienne** (daily 8am–6pm) towers above the colonnaded classical facade of the **Hôtel de Ville**. Its nave is the third tallest in France – after Beauvais and Amiens cathedrals – but its best feature is without doubt the stained glass, both medieval and modern, including windows dating from the thirteenth century. Pride of place, however, goes to **Chagall's** 1963 masterpiece in the western wall of the north transept, representing the Garden of Eden, while his slightly earlier works in the ambulatory vividly depict Old Testament scenes – Moses and David, Abraham's Sacrifice and Jacob's Dream.

Some ten-minutes' walk to the east of the cathedral along **En-Fournirue** is the popular drinking spot **place St-Louis**, with its Gothic arcades. On the way, wander up the Italianate streets climbing the hill of **Sainte-Croix** to your left, the legacy of the Lombard bankers who came to run the city's finances in the thirteenth century. It's also worth continuing east down the rue des Allemands to have a look at the **Porte des Allemands** – a massive, fortified double gate that once barred the eastern entrances to the medieval city. For the city's most compelling townscape, go down to the riverbank and cross over to the tiny **Île de la Comédie** which is dominated by its classical eighteenth-century square and theatre (the oldest in France) and a rather striking Protestant church erected under the German occupation.

## Musées de la Cour d'Or

2 rue du Haut-Poirier • Mon & Wed–Fri 9am–5pm, Sat & Sun 10am–5pm; May–Oct until 6pm; closed public holidays • €4.60, free first Sun of month • Ⓦ musees.metzmetropole.fr

From the cathedral, a short walk up rue du Chanoine Collin brings you to the city's main museum complex, the labyrinthine **Musées de la Cour d'Or**, a conglomeration of the town's old Roman baths, a Carmelite church and a medieval granary. It is a treasure trove of Gallo-Roman sculpture, with the original remains of the city's Roman baths, excavated during an extension in the 1930s. There are objects from the Middle Ages including a fantastic painted ceiling, as well as special sections showcasing local painters from the fifteenth century onwards and artefacts illustrating the city's Jewish community.

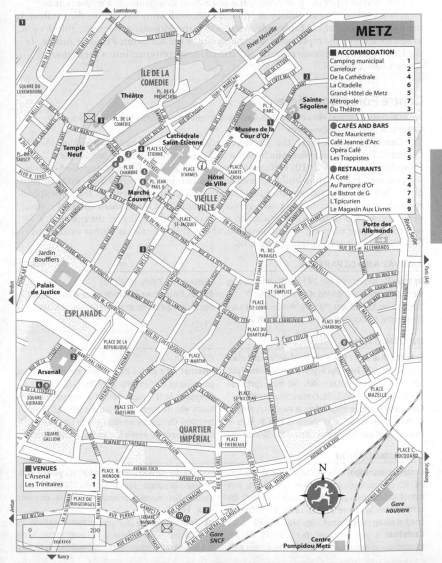

**METZ**

■ **ACCOMMODATION**
| | |
|---|---|
| Camping municipal | 1 |
| Carrefour | 2 |
| De la Cathédrale | 4 |
| La Citadelle | 6 |
| Grand-Hôtel de Metz | 5 |
| Métropole | 7 |
| Du Théâtre | 3 |

● **CAFÉS AND BARS**
| | |
|---|---|
| Chez Mauricette | 6 |
| Café Jeanne d'Arc | 1 |
| Opéra Café | 3 |
| Les Trappistes | 5 |

● **RESTAURANTS**
| | |
|---|---|
| À Coté | 2 |
| Au Pampre d'Or | 4 |
| Le Bistrot de G | 7 |
| L'Epicurien | 8 |
| Le Magasin Aux Livres | 9 |

■ **VENUES**
| | |
|---|---|
| L'Arsenal | 2 |
| Les Trinitaires | 1 |

## Quartier Impérial

The **Quartier Impérial** makes up the southern section of the city, an elegant and stately collection of rose and yellow sandstone buildings, unmistakably Teutonic in style: the **gare SNCF** sets the tone, a vast and splendid granite structure of 1870 in Rhenish Romanesque, a bizarre cross between a Scottish laird's hunting lodge and a dungeon. Its gigantic dimensions reflect the Germans' long-term intention to use it as the hub of their military transport system. It's matched in style by the **post office** opposite and by some imposing bourgeois apartment buildings on the surrounding streets. The whole quarter was meant to serve as a model of superior town planning, in contrast to the squalid Latin hugger-mugger of the old French neighbourhoods further north.

To the northwest of the *gare SNCF*, the place de la République is a major parking area, bounded on the east side by shops and cafés, with army barracks to the south and the formal gardens of the **Esplanade**, overlooking the Moselle, to the west. To the right, as you look down the esplanade from the square, is the handsome **Palais de Justice**. To the left, a gravel drive leads past the old arsenal, now converted into a prestigious concert hall, **L'Arsenal**.

## Centre Pompidou-Metz

1 parvis des Droits de L'Homme • Mon & Wed–Fri 11am–6pm; Sat 10am–8pm; Sun 10am–6pm; €7, free for under 26-year-olds • ☎ 03 87 15 39 39 • ⓦ centrepompidou-metz.fr

The **Centre Pompidou-Metz**, the first decentralized branch of the Georges Pompidou Centre in Paris, opened with much pomp and ceremony in Metz's *Quartier de l'Amphithéâtre* in May 2010. Designed by architects Shigeru Ban and Jean de Gastines, it's a curious, bright white building resembling a swimming stingray and, with its huge glass windows and wooden scaffolding, is extremely light and inviting. The same spirit reigns here as in Paris: showing off a varying percentage of the Parisian stock, the aim of the museum is to bring modern art to the masses, and judging by the queues it's working. Expect to spend around two hours here; there's a café, as well as workshops for children (ask at reception for details).

### ARRIVAL AND DEPARTURE                                                    METZ

**By train** The huge granite *gare SNCF* stands centre stage in the Quartier Impérial at the end of rue Gambetta. Destinations Luxembourg (10 daily; 40min–1hr); Nancy (2–4 hourly; 35min); Paris Est (10 daily; TGV 1hr 20min); Strasbourg (6–8 daily; 1hr 25min).

**By bus** The *gare routière*, where regional buses depart, is east of the train station on avenue de l'Amphithéâtre.

### INFORMATION

**Tourist office** By the side of the Hôtel de Ville at 2 place d'Armes in the Old Town (April–Sept Mon–Sat 9am–7pm, Sun 10am–5pm; Oct–March Mon–Sat 9am–7pm, Sun 10am–3pm; ☎ 03 87 55 53 76, ⓦ tourisme-metz.fr).

**Car rental** There are rental offices at *gare SNCF*; book at ⓦ rhinocarhire.com for all of them. Parking in Metz is relatively easy and the car parks have a flat 50-cent rate during 8pm–1am.

**Internet** There are two internet cafés opposite the main post office on Rue Gambetta (daily 10am–8pm; €3/hr).

**Shopping** Metz is much more of a shopper's city than Nancy, with the streets off the Rue des Clercs full of trendy boutiques. On Saturday mornings, nearby place Jean Paul II is taken over by the weekly fruit and vegetable market.

### ACCOMMODATION

**Camping municipal** Allée de Metz-Plage ☎ 03 87 68 26 48, ✉ campingmetz@mairie-metz.fr. Quiet, very central and luxurious campsite, a 10min walk from the centre of town by the river and near where the city's sandy beach is put up every summer. May–Sept. **€12.50**

**Carrefour** 6 rue Marchant ☎ 03 87 75 07 26, ⓦ carrefour-metz.asso.fr. Large HI hostel, a 5min walk north of the museums and cathedral; it's packed with teenagers in summer. Four-bed dorms €16.70; €21 for a double. The en-suite private rooms are excellent value. **€24**

★ **De la Cathédrale** 25 place de Chambre ☎ 03 87 75 00 02, ⓦ hotelcathedrale-metz.fr. Lovely, friendly hotel in a seventeenth-century townhouse, wonderfully located opposite the cathedral. Parquet floors, original beams and elegant furnishings give this place bags of character. Breakfast €11. **€75**

**La Citadelle** 5 av Ney ☎03 87 17 17 17, ⓦcitadelle-metz.com. Extremely stylish four-star hotel housed in an impeccably converted fifteenth-century military building overlooking a peaceful little park. The rooms are chic, spacious and contemporary, with a touch of Japanese decor about them. Breakfast €21. **€205**

**Grand-Hôtel de Metz** 3 rue des Clercs ☎03 87 36 16 33, ⓦgrandhotelmetz.com. Centrally located hotel on the main pedestrian shopping district with welcoming staff. Common areas look fussy but never overbearing – the paintings around reception are by local artist Denis

Gaudinot – while the rooms are surprisingly business-like. Breakfast €11. **€71**

**Métropole** 5 place du Général de Gaulle ☎03 87 66 26 22, ⓦhotelmetropole-metz.com. A decent two-star option near the station with cheerful, soundproofed rooms with special floors for smokers. Look out for the resident chirping budgies in their cage by the staircase and for the large aquarium in the breakfast room (€8). **€52**

**Du Théâtre** 3 rue du Pont-St-Marcel ☎03 87 31 10 10, ⓦhoteldutheatre-metz.com. Upmarket hotel with pastel-hued decor in a pretty location on the Île de la Comédie. There's an outdoor swimming pool, jacuzzi, Turkish bath and sauna. Breakfast €12.50. **€95**

## EATING AND DRINKING

Metz celebrates Lorraine specialities with enthusiasm – you'll find quiche and *maribelle* (yellow plum) tarts everywhere, as well as many a *menu rabelais*, involving such earthy delights as pigs' trotters, foie gras and snails. Place de Chambre, beside the cathedral, place St-Jacques and place St-Louis all have their fair share of restaurants and bars. For a picnic or snack, head to the covered market (Tues–Sat 8am–6pm).

### RESTAURANTS

**Á Côté** 43 place de Chambre ☎03 87 66 38 84. Excellent regional fare offered by chef Eric Maire in an unusual seating arrangement with high chairs around a central open *cuisine* with a decor of red and black. *Plat du jour* €10, *menu couverte* (three tapas and one dessert €38). 11.30am–2pm 7.30–10pm; closed Sun, Mon.

★ **Au Pampre d'Or** 31 place de Chambre ☎03 87 74 12 46, ⓦpampredor.fr. If you want Michelin-starred quality at reasonable prices, look no further. Chef Jean-Claude Lamage returned his Michelin star in protest and returned to serving excellent food without the pressure the star brings. Starched tablecloths, smart decor and attentive service with menus from €27 and €40 (including a glass of wine). Noon–2pm 7–10pm; closed Mon, Wed lunch & Tues.

**Le Bistrot de G** 9 rue du Faisan ☎03 87 37 06 44, ⓦrestaurant-bistrotdeg.com. Atmospheric Parisian-style bistro serving anything from *tartines au jambon* (€9.50) to an expensive *menu* at €51 involving an intense chocolate fondue. For a light lunch try the *tartines* at €12. Tues–Sat noon–2pm & 7–10.30pm; closed Sun & Mon.

★ **L' Épicurien** 33 rue Vigne Saint-Avold ☎03 87 36 69 11. Jan from Yorkshire will serve you her French husband's creations with a beaming English smile. Their set menu three-course lunch for €15.50 can't be beaten. Great choice of wines, too. Noon–1.30pm & 7.30–9pm; closed Wed eve, Sat noon & Sun.

★ **Le Magasin aux Livres** 5 av Ney ☎03 87 17 17 17. Metz's own Michelin-starred establishment under chef Christophe Dufossé. It belongs to Hotel Citadelle and offers cookery, patisserie or wine-tasting afternoons (usually Saturday) starting from €60 per person. *Menu dégustation* is 10 dishes for €110 and a lunch menu for €45. Noon–2pm

& 7.30–10pm; closed Sat lunch, Sun dinner & Mon.

### CAFÉS, BARS AND VENUES

**L'Arsenal** Avenue Ney ☎03 87 74 16 16, ⓦarsenal-metz.fr. The principal live venue in Metz offering rock, classical and jazz concerts in a great environment. All performances start at 8pm.

**Café Jeanne d'Arc** Place Jeanne-d'Arc ☎03 87 37 39 94. Medieval beams and frescoes inside, and an attractive terrace centred around a trickling fountain. An ideal spot to catch one of the free jazz concerts which take place in the square every Thursday evening in summer. Mon–Fri 11.45am–midnight, Sat 3pm–2am; closed Sun.

**Chez Mauricette** Marché couvert, place de la Cathédrale ☎03 87 36 37 69, ⓦchezmauricette.com. Serves vast sandwiches, made with the finest local cheese and charcuterie on crusty rustic bread; eat in or take away from €2. 9am–6.30pm; closed Sun & Mon.

**Opéra Café** 39 place de Chambre. One of the most popular drinking spots on this lively square – it stays open till late and attracts the barflies from all over town; the place to come if you want to have an impromptu chat with a stranger. Summer only: Mon–Sat 10am–2am; Sun 6pm–midnight.

**Les Trappistes** 20 place de Chambre ☎03 87 36 71 17. Charming bar with friendly, chatty locals that has outside seating in the best people-watching spot by the cathedral. 8am–11pm (lunch noon–2pm; only snacks in the evening for around €5); closed Sun.

**Les Trinitaires** 10–12 rue des Trinitaires ☎03 87 20 03 03, ⓦlestrinitaires.com. The place to go for jazz, rock, folk and chanson on Thursday, Friday and Saturday nights (from 8.30pm; tickets from €6).

**4**

# Amnéville

A 30min drive north of Metz lies **Amnéville,** an easy-to-overlook town off the A31 motorway. But, just outside, in the Parc **Amnéville-Les-Thermes**, there is a gigantic tourist site with a conglomeration of attractions, cinemas, restaurants, spas and hotels which you expect to see in North America rather than Europe. There are three large spas, Centre Thermal St Eloy (with a more therapeutic-medical orientation), Waterland (fun for the family) and Villa Pompéi (offering massage and beauty treatments), which have been built over natural thermal springs; sports arenas that include the largest indoor ski slope in Europe, an 18-hole golf and mini-golf course, a "Fitnessium", an ice-skating rink and an Olympic-size swimming pool. There's also an IMAX cinema, a bowling alley, a dinosaur exhibition, a discotheque and a live venue – the list is endless. But the main attraction is the **zoo** – one of the largest in France. You need a car to get there – and to move around the site.

## Amnéville Zoo

1 rue du Tigre • Daily: April–Sept 9.30am–7.30pm (8pm Sun & holidays); Oct–March 10am–sunset • Adults and children over 12 €30; children under 3 free; children between 3–11 €24 • ⓦ zoo-amneville.com

Amnéville Zoo, rated one of the three largest in France, is alone worth travelling to Amnéville for because of the number of rare species on display. Many of them are photogenic mammals, such as snow leopards, Siberian tigers, dwarf hippos, a big number of monkey species and, since 2012, a family of very active gorillas. Feeding of animals takes place several times a day; the wolf-pack feed is the biggest draw.

### ACCOMMODATION AND EATING

**Amnéville Plaza** Parc de Coulange ⓣ 03 87 71 82 86, ⓦ amneville-plaza.com. Italian-managed modern and minimalist four-star hotel with pleasing curves and lines. As well as large rooms with plasma TV, that rises majestically with the press of the button, and superfast wi-fi, it also offers a gym, a pool and immaculate service. Check the excellent weekend deals on its website. Breakfast €16. **€125**

★ **La Forêt** Bois de Coulange ⓣ 03 87 70 34 34, ⓦ restaurant-laforet.com. Nicely set apart in a forested turn, far from the rest of the rather touristy restaurants, this is one of the best family restaurants in Lorraine, combining local produce in creative, yet familiar dishes (€15–20). The wine list is superb and the service impeccable. Reservation recommended. Noon–1.45pm & 7–9.30pm; closed Sun eve & Mon.

---

#### CHÂTEAU MALBROUCK

Only 2km from France's border with Germany, the imposing and impregnable **Château Malbrouck** (April–Dec Mon 2–5pm, Sat & Sun and public hols 10am–6pm, June–Aug until 6pm, weekends until 7pm; €7; ⓦ chateau-malbrouck.com) is a restoration marvel. Every brick and turret has been placed in the medieval manner, with masons having had to be re-schooled in bygone techniques.

The castle's history is pretty dramatic: it was built by the Sierck family between 1419–36 and, then called Meinsberg Castle, it passed on through generations until the French Revolution. A change in fortune came during the War of Spanish Succession (1701–14) when, after the Battle of Blenheim, the **Duke of Marlborough** decided to invade France through the Moselle and reached the castle. On June 4 1705 it surrendered without resistance and the Duke set his headquarters there. His adversary, the **Duke of Villars**, one of Louis XIV's best generals, assembled a massive army and waited outside the castle. The one who blinked was the Duke of Marlborough; after long deliberation he withdrew from the castle during the night of June 16/17, thus abandoning his plans for the invasion of France. Even though he was there for only two weeks, the castle's name has remained in folk memory as **Malbrouck**, a Francification of Marlborough.

# Verdun

VERDUN lies in a bend of the River Meuse, some 70km west of Metz. Of no great interest in itself, what makes this sleepy provincial town remarkable is its association with the horrific battle that took place on the bleak uplands to the north between 1916 and 1918. In 1916, aiming to break the stalemate of trench warfare, the German General Erich von Falkenhayn chose Verdun as the target for an offensive that ranked among the most devastating ever launched in the annals of war. His troops advanced to within 5km of Verdun, but never captured the town. Gradually the French clawed back the lost ground, but final victory came only in the last months of the war with the aid of US troops. The price was high: hundreds of thousands of men died on both sides. To this day, memorials in every village, hamlet and town of France are inscribed with the names of men slaughtered at Verdun. Near Verdun's railway station, the **Rodin memorial**, a disturbing statue of winged Victory, stands beside a handsome eighteenth-century gateway at the northern end of rue St-Paul where it joins avenue Garibaldi. Nearby, a simple engraving lists all the years between 450 and 1916 that Verdun has been involved in conflict. The fourteenth-century **Porte Chaussée** guards the river-crossing in the middle of town. Beyond it, further along rue Mazel, a flight of steps climbs up to the **Monument de la Victoire**, where a helmeted warrior leans on his sword in commemoration of the 1916 battle, while in the crypt below a roll is kept of all the soldiers, French and American, who took part.

## Cathédrale Notre-Dame de Verdun around

The rue de la Belle Vierge leads round to the **Cathédrale de Notre-Dame** (8.45am–6pm; summer to 7pm), whose outward characteristics are Gothic; its earlier Romanesque origins were only uncovered by shell damage in 1916. The elegant **bishop's palace** behind it has been converted into the **Centre Mondial de la Paix et des Droits de l'Homme** (Tues–Sun 9.30am–noon & 2–6pm; July & Aug 9.30am–7pm; entry price variable depending on events), which hosts exhibitions on themes such as peacekeeping and human rights.

## The Citadelle

Av du 5ème R.A.P • Daily: Feb 10am–noon & 2–5pm; March, Oct & Nov 9.30am–5.30am; April–June & Sept 9am–6pm; July & Aug 9am–7pm; Dec 10am–12.30pm & 2–5pm • €6

Rue du Rû, the continuation of rue Mazel, takes you to the underground galleries of the **Citadelle**, used as shelter for thousands of soldiers during the battle. The Unknown Soldier, whose remains now lie under the Arc de Triomphe in Paris, was chosen from among the dead who lie here. A small train takes visitors around the site that reconstitutes the lives of soldiers in World War I.

### ARRIVAL AND DEPARTURE                                        VERDUN

**By car** It is best to reach Verdun and drive around the battlefields by car (1hr from Metz on the A4 motorway; exit 30).

**By train** Verdun's *gare SNCF*, on avenue Garibaldi, is poorly served; the TGV stops at Gare de Meuse about 30km from the city. You need to change there to reach Verdun (35min).

### INFORMATION

**Tourist office** Pavillon Japiot, avenue du Général Mangin (Jan, Feb & Dec Mon–Sat 10am–12.30pm & 2–5pm, Sun & public hols 10am–12.30pm; March–June & Sept–Nov Mon–Sat 9.30am–12.30pm & 1.30–6pm, Sun & public hols 10am–noon & 2.30–5pm; July & Aug Mon–Sat 9am–7pm, Sun & public hols 10am–noon & 2–6pm;

☎ 03 29 84 55 55, ⓦ tourisme-verdun.fr) lies just across the River Meuse from the Porte Chaussée and is well stocked with free information on the battlefields. For specific information and guided tours (see below) round the battlefields, head to the Maison du Tourisme on place de la Nation (☎ 03 29 86 14 18, ⓦ verdun-tourisme.com).

**4**

**Pass Musées** The Maison du Tourisme (see p.249) sells the Pass Musées (€18.50 or €13.50 without the Citadelle), which allows discounted entry to the Citadelle, Fort de Vaux, Fort de Douaumont, Ossuaire de Douaumont and the Mémorial de Verdun.

**Guided tours** The Maison du Tourisme (see p.249) runs a variety of guided minibus tours in French (April–Oct; booking advised if English is requested; €27 for half-day) around some of the battlefields, memorials and forts.

## ACCOMMODATION

★ **Chateau des Monthairons** Le Petit Monthairon, 26 rue de Verdun ☎ 03 29 87 78 55, ⓦ chateaudes monthairons.fr. Superb-value hostellerie in a plush nineteenth-century château, 18km south of Verdun, offering enormous apartment-rooms overlooking its own forest and lake with wading herons. The excellent restaurant (noon–1.30pm 7.30–9pm) open to non-residents has four-course menus at €58. Breakfast €16.

Pay extra to have a view of the garden in front. **€100**

**Coq Hardi** 8 av de la Victoire ☎ 03 29 86 36 36, ⓦ coq -hardi.com. Eighteenth-century half-timbered coach inn that has somehow survived the vicissitudes of history to emerge as the highest-rated hotel in Verdun. It is blessed with good luck and its opulent interior never lets you forget it. Breakfast €18. **€95**

## EATING

**Le Chantaco** 2 av de la Victoire ☎ 03 29 87 57 01. Smart no-nonsense bistro with a large terrace which is always busy in the summer. This is the best place locally to try

exotic Gallic fare such as snails on toast or frog soup. Lunch *menus* €13. Noon–2pm & 7–9.30pm; closed Sun eve (& Tues Sept–May).

# The battlefields

The **Battle of Verdun** opened on the morning of February 21, 1916, with a German artillery barrage that lasted ten hours and expended two million shells. The battle concentrated on the forts of Vaux and Douaumont, which the French had built after the 1870 Franco–Prussian War. By the time the main battle ended ten months later, nine villages had been pounded into oblivion; not a single trace of them is detectable in aerial photos taken at the time.

The most visited part of the battlefield extends along the hills north of Verdun, but the fighting also spread to the west of the Meuse, to the hills of Mort-Homme and Hill 304, to Vauquois and the Argonne, and south along the Meuse to St-Mihiel, where the Germans held an important salient until dislodged by US forces in 1918. Unless you take an organized tour the only viable way to explore the area is with your own transport. The main sights are reached via two minor roads that snake through the battlefields, forming a crossroads northeast of Verdun: the D913 and D112.

## Memorial de Verdun and Fort de Vaux

Fleury • Daily: Feb & March 9am–noon & 2–6pm; April to mid-Nov 9am–6pm; mid-Nov to mid-Dec 9am–noon & 2–6pm • €7 • ⓦ memorial-de-verdun.fr **Fort de Vaux** Daily: Feb, March, Oct & Nov 10am–5pm; April 10am–5.30pm; May–Aug 10am–6.30pm; Sept 10am–5.30pm; Dec 10am–4.30pm • €4

The full horror of the battle is graphically documented at **FLEURY**, in the **Memorial de Verdun**, where, alongside contemporary newsreels and photos, a section of the shell-torn terrain that was once the village of Fleury has been reconstructed as the battle left it.

Another major monument is the **Fort de Vaux**, 4km east of Fleury. After six days' hand-to-hand combat in the gas-filled tunnels, the French garrison were left with no alternative but to surrender. On the exterior wall, a plaque commemorates the last messenger pigeon sent to the command post in Verdun asking, in vain, for reinforcements. Having delivered its message, the pigeon expired, poisoned by the gas-filled air above the battlefield. It was posthumously awarded the Légion d'Honneur.

## ST-MIHIEL AND THE VOIE SACRÉE

As early as 1914, the Germans captured the town of **St-Mihiel** on the River Meuse to the south, which gave them control of the main supply route into Verdun. The only route left open to the French was the N35 (now downgraded to the D1916), winding north from Bar-le-Duc over the open hills and wheat fields. In memory of all those who kept the supplies going, the road is called **La Voie Sacrée** (The Sacred Way) and marked with milestones capped with the helmet of the *poilu* (the slang term for infantryman). In St-Mihiel itself, the **Église St-Michel** contains the **Sépulcre** or *Entombment of Christ*, by local sculptor **Ligier Richier** – a set of thirteen stone figures, carved in the mid-sixteenth century and regarded as one of the masterpieces of the French Renaissance. Just beyond the town to the east, on the Butte de Montsec, is a **memorial** to the Americans who died here in 1918.

## Ossuaire de Douaumont

Douaumont • Daily: Feb 2–5pm; March & Oct 9am–noon & 2–5.30pm; April 9am–6pm; May–Aug 9am–6.30pm; Sept 9am–noon & 2–6pm; Nov 9am–noon & 2–5pm; Dec 2–5pm • €3.50, tower €5 • ⓦ verdun-douaumont.com

The principal memorial to the carnage stands in the middle of the battlefield a short distance along the D913 beyond Fleury. The **Ossuaire de Douaumont** is a vast ossuary, with a central tower and two horizontal galleries shaped like a sword with its blade buried in the earth. Its vaults contain the bones of thousands upon thousands of unidentified soldiers, some of them visible through windows set in the base of the building. When the battle ended in 1918, the ground was covered in fragments of corpses; 120,000 French bodies were identified, perhaps a third of the total killed. Across the road, a separate memorial honours the 15,000 fallen Muslims of the French colonial regiments; while a nearby wall, beneath an eerily tree-less ridgetop, commemorates the Jewish dead.

## Fort de Douaumont

Douaumont • Daily: Dec, Feb & March 10am–1pm & 2–5pm; April & Sept 10am–6pm; May–June 10am–6.30pm; July–Aug 10am–7pm; Oct–Nov 10am–5pm; Jan closed • €3

The **Fort de Douaumont** is 900m down the road from the cemetery. Completed in 1912, it was the strongest of the 38 forts built to defend Verdun. Inexplicably, however, the armament of these forts was greatly reduced in 1915, and when the Germans attacked in 1916, twenty men were enough to overrun the garrison. The fort is on three levels and its claustrophobic, dungeon-like galleries are hung with stalactites. The Germans held the fort for eight months while under continuous siege, housing 3000 men in these cramped, unventilated quarters, infested with fleas and lice and plagued by rats that attacked the sleeping and the dead indiscriminately.

## American Cemetery

Romagne-sous-Montfoucon • Daily: no tours. The American superintendent is available Mon–Fri during office hours

The only other war site worth making a detour for is the **American cemetery** in Romagne-sous-Montfocon, near Argonne – at 40 hectares the biggest US graveyard in Europe – with 14,246 graves. Solemn, dignified and throught-provoking, it lies on ground leased to the US in perpetuity and is overseen by an American superintendent who lives in the house overlooking the chapel on the top of the burial slope. There, on its Wall of the Disappeared, you can read the engraved names of 954 US soldiers whose bodies were never recovered.

**4**

# Normandy

MONT ST-MICHEL

**5**

# Normandy

Now firmly incorporated into the French mainstream, the seaboard province of Normandy has a history of prosperous and powerful independence. Colonized by Vikings from the ninth century onwards, it went on to conquer not only England but as far afield as Sicily and areas of the Near East. Later, as part of France, it was instrumental in the settlement of Canada.

Normandy's wealth has always depended on its ports: **Rouen**, on the Seine, is the nearest navigable point to Paris, while **Dieppe**, **Le Havre** and **Cherbourg** have important transatlantic trade. Inland, it is overwhelmingly agricultural – a fertile belt of tranquil pastureland, where the chief interest for many will be the groaning restaurant tables of regions such as the **Pays d'Auge**. While parts of the coast are overdeveloped, due either to industry, as with the huge sprawl of Le Havre, or tourism – as along the "Norman Riviera", around **Trouville** and **Deauville** – ancient harbours such as **Honfleur** and **Barfleur** remain irresistible, and numerous seaside villages lack both crowds and affectations. The banks of the Seine, too, hold several delightful little communities.

Normandy also boasts extraordinary Romanesque and Gothic **architectural treasures**, although only its much-restored capital, Rouen, retains a complete medieval centre. Elsewhere, the attractions are more often single buildings than entire towns. Most famous of all is the spectacular *merveille* on the island of **Mont St-Michel**, but there are also the monasteries at **Jumièges** and **Caen**, the cathedrals of Bayeux and **Coutances**, and Richard the Lionheart's castle above the Seine at **Les Andelys**. **Bayeux** has its vivid and astonishing tapestry, while more recent creations include Monet's garden at **Giverny**. Furthermore, Normandy's vernacular architecture makes it well worth exploring inland – rural back roads are lined with splendid centuries-old half-timbered manor houses. It's remarkable how much has survived – or, less surprisingly, been restored – since the D-Day landings in 1944 and the subsequent **Battle of Normandy**, which has its own legacy in war museums, memorials and cemeteries.

---

**GETTING AROUND**                                 **NORMANDY**

**By train** The main towns and cities are well served, though many routes in Haute Normandie require a change at Rouen, and services are less frequent at weekends.

**By bus** Services vary by *département*: the best served is Calvados, where Bus Verts (ⓦbusverts.fr), for example, link Caen to the D-Day beaches, and Honfleur to Le Havre.

Services to rural areas such as the Pays d'Auge are infrequent or nonexistent.

**By car** To explore the countryside, you'll need a car. A car is also useful for the coast, although there are tours from Bayeux and Caen to the D-Day beaches.

---

# Seine Maritime

The *département* of Seine Maritime comprises three distinct sections: Normandy's dramatic **northern coastline**, home not only to major ports like Dieppe and Le Havre but also to such delightful resorts as **Étretat**; the meandering course of the **River Seine**, where unchanged villages stand both up- and downstream of the provincial capital of

---

MONET'S GARDEN AT GIVERNY

# Highlights

**❶ Rouen** This fine old medieval city would still seem familiar to Joan of Arc, whose life came to a tragic end in its main square. **See p.264**

**❷ Château Gaillard** Richard the Lionheart's sturdy fortress, at Les Andelys, commands superb views of the River Seine. **See p.271**

**❸ Giverny** Claude Monet's house and garden remain just as he left them. **See p.271**

**❹ The Bayeux Tapestry** One of the world's most extraordinary historical documents, embroidering the saga of William the Conqueror in every colourful detail. **See p.280**

**❺ The war cemeteries** Memories of D-Day abound in Normandy, but nowhere more so than in the American cemetery at Colleville-sur-Mer. **See p.284**

**❻ Mont St-Michel** Second only to the Eiffel Tower as France's best-loved landmark, the *merveille* of Mont St-Michel is a magnificent spectacle. **See p.290**

**❼ The Pays d'Auge** With its luscious meadows and half-timbered farmhouses, the Pays d'Auge is a picture-perfect home for Camembert and other legendary cheeses. **See p.293**

**HIGHLIGHTS ARE MARKED ON THE MAP ON P.256**

Rouen; and the flat, chalky **Caux plateau**, which makes for pleasant cycling country but holds little of note to detain visitors.

Dieppe in particular offers an appealing introduction to France, and with the impressive white cliffs of the **Côte d'Albâtre** (Alabaster Coast) stretching to either side it makes a good base for a long stay. The most direct route to Rouen from here is simply to head south, but it's well worth tracing the shore west to **Le Havre**, then following the Seine inland.

Driving along the D982 on the northern bank of the Seine, you'll often find your course paralleled by mighty container ships out on the water. Potential stops en route include the medieval abbey of **Jumièges**, but **Rouen** itself is the prime destination, its association with the execution of Joan of Arc the most compelling episode in its fascinating history. Further upstream, Monet's wonderful house and garden at **Giverny** and the English frontier stronghold of Château Gaillard at **Les Andelys** also justify taking the slow road to Paris.

## Dieppe

Squeezed between high cliff headlands, **DIEPPE** is an enjoyably small-scale port that used to be more of a resort. During the nineteenth century, Parisians came here by train to take the sea air, promenading along the front while the English indulged in the peculiar pastime of swimming.

---

### THE FOOD OF NORMANDY

The **food of Normandy** owes its most distinctive characteristic – its gut-bursting, heart-pounding richness – to the lush orchards and dairy herds of the region's agricultural heartland, especially the area southeast of Caen known as the Pays d'Auge. Menus abound in **meat** such as veal (veau) cooked in vallée d'Auge style, which consists largely of the profligate addition of **cream** and **butter**. Many dishes also feature orchard fruit, either in its natural state or in successively more alcoholic forms – either as apple or pear cider, or perhaps further distilled to produce brandies.

Normans relish blood and guts. In addition to gamier meat and fowl such as rabbit and duck (a speciality in Rouen, where the birds are strangled to ensure that all their blood gets into the sauce), they enjoy such intestinal preparations as andouilles, the sausages known in English as chitterlings, and tripes, stewed for hours à la mode de Caen. A full blowout at a country restaurant will also traditionally entail one or two pauses between courses for the trou normand: a glass of the apple brandy Calvados to let you catch your breath before struggling on with the feast.

Normandy's long coastline ensures that it is also renowned for its **seafood**. Waterfront rows of restaurants in its ports and resorts compete for attention, each with its "copieuse" assiette de fruits de mer. **Honfleur** is probably the most enjoyable, but **Dieppe**, **Étretat** and **Cherbourg** also offer endless eating opportunities. The menus tend to be much the same as those on offer in Brittany, if perhaps slightly more expensive.

The most famous products of Normandy's meadow-munching cows are, of course, their **cheeses**. Cheese-making in the Pays d'Auge started in the monasteries during the Dark Ages. By the eleventh century the local products were already well defined; in 1236, the Roman de la Rose referred to Angelot cheese, identified with a small coin depicting a young angel killing a dragon. The principal modern varieties began to emerge in the seventeenth century – **Pont l'Evêque**, which is square with a washed crust, soft but not runny, and **Livarot**, which is round, thick and firm, and has a stronger flavour. Although Marie Herel is generally credited with having invented **Camembert** in the 1790s, a smaller and stodgier version of that cheese had already existed for some time. A priest fleeing the Revolution stayed in Madame Herel's farmhouse at Camembert, and suggested modifications in her cheese-making in line with the techniques used to manufacture Brie de Meaux – a slower process, gentler on the curd and with more thorough drainage. The rich full cheese thus created was an instant success. In the market at Vimoutiers, and the development of the railways (and the invention of the chipboard cheesebox in 1880) helped to give it a worldwide popularity.

**5**

Though ferry services have diminished in recent years, Dieppe remains a nice little place, and you won't regret spending time here. If you have kids in tow, the aquariums of the **Cité de la Mer** and the strip of pebble **beach** are the obvious attractions; otherwise, you could settle for admiring the cliffs and the **castle** as you stroll the seafront lawns.

## The château

June–Sept daily 10am–noon & 2–6pm; Oct–May Mon & Wed–Sat 10am–noon & 2–5pm, Sun 10am–noon & 2–6pm • €4 • ☎ 02 35 06 61 99, ⓦ dieppe.fr/mini-sites/chateau-musee

Overlooking the seafront from the clifftops to the west, Dieppe's medieval **château** is home of the **Musée de Dieppe**, where the permanent collection includes carved ivories – virtuoso pieces of sawing, filing and chipping of the plundered riches of Africa, shipped back to the town by early Dieppe explorers. It also holds paintings of local scenes by artists such as Pissarro, Renoir, Dufy, Sickert and Boudin, and works by Georges Braque, the co-founder of **Cubism**, who went to school in Le Havre, spent summers in Dieppe and is buried not far west at Varengeville-sur-Mer. A separate, much newer wing of the castle stages temporary exhibitions.

## Boulevard de Verdun and around

Modern Dieppe is laid out along the three axes dictated by its eighteenth-century town planners. The **boulevard de Verdun** runs for more than 1km along the seafront, from

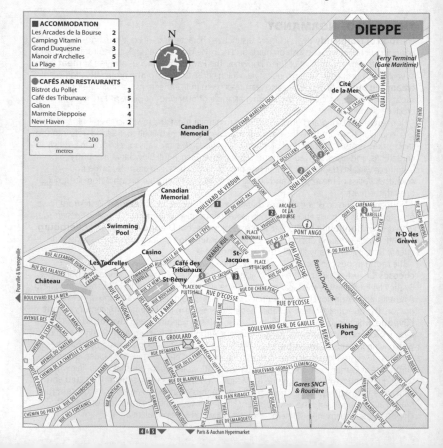

just below the fifteenth-century **château** in the west, to the port entrance in the east. The **square du Canada**, at its western end, was originally named in commemoration of the role played by Dieppe sailors in the colonization of Canada. Now a small plaque is dedicated to the Canadian soldiers who died in the suicidal 1942 raid on Dieppe, justified later as a trial run for the 1944 Normandy landings.

West from there, the boulevard de Verdun passes the Casino; "Les Bains", a large complex of indoor and outdoor **swimming pools**; and the town's grandest and oldest hotels.

## Cité de la Mer

37 rue de l'Asile-Thomas • Daily 10am–noon & 2–6pm • €7 • ☎ 02 35 06 93 20, ⍾ estrancitedelamer.free.fr

Tucked into the back streets at the eastern end of town, just back from the harbour, Dieppe's **Cité de la Mer** is a museum and scientific research centre for all things sea-related. Unless you are a maritime history or marine biology enthusiast, little is likely to hold your attention for long: the small museum races through the history of seagoing vessels, including a Viking *drakkar* reconstructed using methods depicted in the Bayeux Tapestry, and an exhibition details Dieppe's relationship with the sea, with a pungent display of dried, salted fish. Visits culminate with the large **aquariums**, filled with the marine life of the Channel: flatfish with bulbous eyes and twisted faces, retiring octopuses, battling lobsters, and hermaphrodite scallops.

## Grande Rue and around

Not far inland from the Boulevard de Verdun, Dieppe's main shopping streets – the **rue de la Barre** and its pedestrianized continuation, the **Grande Rue**, scene of Saturday's all-day open-air **market** – run parallel to the seafront. At the centre of the Old Town, the *Café des Tribunaux*, on place du Puits-Salé, is a landmark (see p.260), while along the harbour's edge, an extension of the Grande Rue, **quai Henri IV**, has a colourful backdrop of cafés, brasseries and restaurants.

### ARRIVAL AND INFORMATION                                    DIEPPE

**By train** The gare SNCF, with services from Paris-St-Lazare (19 daily; 2hr 10min) via Rouen (16 daily; 50min), is 500m south of the tourist office, on bd Clemenceau.

**By bus** The gare routière, on bd Clemenceau, alongside the train station, sees services from Fécamp (4 daily; 2hr 20min).

**By ferry** LD Lines (☎ 0800 650 100, ⍾ ldlines.co.uk) sail between Dieppe's gare maritime, east of the centre, and Newhaven in England (2 daily; 4hr).

**Tourist office** Pont Ango (May, June & Sept Mon–Sat 9am–1pm & 2–6pm, Sun 9.30am–1pm & 2–5.30pm; July & Aug Mon–Sat 9am–7pm, Sun 9.30am–1pm & 2–5.30pm; Oct–April Mon–Sat 9am–12.30pm & 1.30–5pm; ☎ 02 32 14 40 60, ⍾ dieppetourisme.com).

### ACCOMMODATION

**Les Arcades de la Bourse** 1–3 arcades de la Bourse ☎ 02 35 84 14 12, ⍾ lesarcades.fr. Long-established central hotel under the arcades facing the port; you couldn't ask for a more convenient location. Cheaper rooms face the street. Restaurant with full, good-value *menus* from €19. **€69**

**Camping Vitamin** Chemin des Vertus ☎ 02 35 82 11 11, ⍾ camping-vitamin.com. Three-star site, well south of town in an unremarkable setting in St-Aubin-sur-Scie. It's really only convenient for motorists, though it is served by bus #2. Closed mid-Oct to March. **€19.90**

**Grand Duquesne** 15 place St-Jacques ☎ 02 32 14 61 10, ⍾ augrandduquesne.free.fr. This small, central hotel is unusually plain for the *Logis de France*

organization, offering twelve slightly old-fashioned en-suite rooms at bargain rates, and good food in the downstairs restaurant. **€40**

**Manoir d'Archelles** Rte de Neufchâtel, Arques-La-Bataille ☎ 02 32 83 40 51, ⍾ www.manoir-darchelles .fr. Simple rooms, including some large family options, in an eccentric old château set in gorgeous gardens, 6km southeast of central Dieppe; restaurant next door. **€75**

**La Plage** 20 bd de Verdun ☎ 02 35 84 18 28, ⍾ plagehotel.fr.st. Seafront hotel with rooms to suit all budgets, from the upmarket sea-view options to smaller but perfectly pleasant courtyard-facing doubles. No restaurant. **€55**

**5**

## EATING AND DRINKING

The most promising area to look for restaurants in Dieppe is along the quai Henri IV, which faces the fishing port rather than the open sea, and makes a lovely place to stroll and compare *menus* of a summer's evening. The beach itself, by contrast, offers no formal restaurants. The café-lined Place St-Jacques, dominated by the Gothic Église St-Jacques, is an ideal spot for a relaxed drink.

**Bistrot du Pollet** 23 rue de la Tête du Boeuf ☎ 02 35 84 68 57, ⓦbistrotdupollet.fr. Little local restaurant just east of Pont Ango, especially cosy on a winter's evening, selling fresh seafood at low prices. Tues–Sat noon–2pm & 7–9pm; closed second fortnight in April and second fortnight in Aug.

**Café des Tribunaux** Place du Puits-Salé ☎ 02 32 14 44 65. The place du Puits-Salé, is dominated by this cavernous café, built as an inn towards the end of the seventeenth century. Two hundred years later, it was favoured by painters and writers such as Renoir, Monet, Sickert, Whistler and Pissarro, but for English visitors, its most evocative association is with the exiled and unhappy Oscar Wilde, who drank here regularly. It's popular with students. Daily 8am–8pm.

**Galion** 83 quai Henri IV ☎ 02 35 82 71 87. Harbourfront bistro, entirely indoors but with a bright conservatory decked out with parasol lightshades. You can enjoy anything from a bowl of mussels to the cheapest *menu* (€11.80) or a €28 all-scallop feast; less adventurous kids can opt for sausages and chips. Daily noon–9.30pm.

**Marmite Dieppoise** 8 rue St-Jean ☎ 02 35 84 24 26. Rustic, busy little restaurant between St-Jacques church and the arcades de la Bourse. *Menus* are on the pricey side, starting at €30, while €38 buys the local speciality *marmite Dieppoise* (seafood pot, with shellfish and white fish), followed by apple tart. Tues–Sat noon–2pm & 7–9.30pm, Sun noon–2pm; closed Thurs eve in low season.

**New Haven** 53 quai Henri IV ☎ 02 35 84 89 72, ⓦrestaurantdieppe.fr. Reliable seafood specialist, towards the quieter end of the quayside, with good *menus* from €18. Mon & Wed–Sun noon–9.30pm, Tues noon–3pm; closed Mon & Wed in winter.

## The Côte d'Albâtre

West of Dieppe, the shoreline of the **Côte d'Albâtre** ("Alabaster Coast") is eroding at such a ferocious rate that small resorts like **Fécamp** and **Étretat**, tucked among the cliffs at the ends of its successive valleys, may not last more than another century or so. For the moment, however, they are quietly prospering, with casinos, sports centres and yacht marinas ensuring a modest but steady summer trade.

### Varengeville

The lovely rural village of **VARENGEVILLE** sprawls to either side of the D75 8km west of Dieppe, 1km or so inland from the steep coastal cliffs. Its main attractions are the **Bois des Moutiers** (mid-March to mid-Nov daily: house 10am–noon & 2–6pm, gardens 10am–8pm; €10; ☎ 02 35 85 10 02, ⓦboisdesmoutiers.com), where a house built by English architect **Edwin Lutyens** features magnificent **gardens**, designed by owner Guillaume Mallet with Gertrude Jekyll, and the château-like **Manoir d'Ango** (first half of April & Oct Sat & Sun 10am–12.30pm & 2–6pm; mid-April to Sept daily 10am–12.30pm & 2–6pm; €5; ☎ 02 35 83 61 56, ⓦmanoirdango.fr), the splendid "summer palace" of sixteenth-century Dieppe shipbuilder Jean Ango.

Artist **Georges Braque** lies buried in Varengeville's clifftop church, where his marble **tomb** is topped by a sadly decaying mosaic of a white dove in flight. More impressive is his vivid blue *Tree of Jesse* stained-glass window inside the church, through which the sun rises in summer.

### St-Valéry-en-Caux

Open-air stalls beside the narrow harbour in the rebuilt but still attractive port of **ST-VALÉRY-EN-CAUX**, 30km west of Dieppe, sell fresh fish daily. Crumbling brown-stained cliffs soar to either side of its long shingle beach, busy with tourists in summer.

### Fécamp

Halfway between Dieppe and Le Havre, **FÉCAMP** is a serious fishing port with a pleasant seafront promenade. Guided tours of its most distinctive attraction, the rambling **Benedictine Distillery**, 110 rue Alexandre-le-Grand (daily: early Feb to March & mid-Oct to Dec 10.30–11.45am & 2–5pm; April to mid-July & Sept to mid-Oct 10am–noon & 2–5.30pm; mid-July to Aug 10am–6pm; 90min tours €7; ⓦbenedictine.fr), culminate with boxes of herbs being flung into copper vats and alembics, and a *dégustation* of the liqueur itself in their bar across the street.

### Musée des Terres-Neuvas et de la Pêche

27 bd Albert 1er • July & Aug daily 10am–7pm; Sept–June daily except Tues 10am–noon & 2–5.30pm • €3 • ☎ 02 35 28 31 99

Adorned with miniature model boats and amateur paintings, the seafront **Musée des Terres-Neuvas et de la Pêche** focuses on the long tradition whereby the fishermen of Fécamp decamp en masse each year to catch cod in the cold, foggy waters off Newfoundland. Sailing vessels continued to make the trek from the sixteenth century right up until 1931; today vast refrigerated container ships have taken their place.

## Étretat

In delightful little **ÉTRETAT**, the alabaster cliffs are at their most spectacular – their arches, tunnels and the solitary "needle" out to sea adorn countless tourist brochures – and the town itself has grown up simply as a pleasure resort. There isn't even a port of any kind: the seafront consists of a sweeping unbroken curve of concrete above a shingle beach. In the town itself, a lovely architectural ensemble surrounds the central **place Foch**. The old wooden market *halles* still dominate the square; the ground floor is now converted into souvenir shops, but the beams of the balcony and roof are bare and ancient.

### The cliffs

Footpaths climb the stunning **cliffs** to either side of town. The **Falaise d'Aval** to the south is a straightforward walk. Lush lawns and pastures stretch away inland, while German fortifications on the shore side extend to the point where the turf abruptly stops. From the windswept top you can see further rock formations and sometimes even glimpse Le Havre. However, it's the views back to the town sheltered in the valley, and the **Falaise d'Amont** on its northern side – an idyllic green hillside, topped by the little chapel of Notre-Dame – that stick in the memory.

---

| INFORMATION | THE CÔTE D'ALBÂTRE |

**ST-VALÉRY-EN-CAUX**
**Tourist office** Quai d'Amont (April–Sept daily 9.30am–12.30pm & 2–6.30pm; Oct–March Mon–Sat 9.30am–12.30pm & 2–6pm; ☎ 02 35 97 00 63, ⓦ ville-saint-valery-en-caux.fr).

**FÉCAMP**
**Tourist office** Quai Sadi-Carnot (Sept–March Mon–Fri 9am–12.30pm & 2–5.30pm, Sat 10am–1pm & 3–5pm, Sun 9.30am–12.30pm in school hols only; April–June

Mon–Fri 9am–6pm, Sat & Sun 10am–6.30pm; July & Aug daily 9am–6.30pm; ☎ 02 35 28 51 01, ⓦ fecamp tourisme.com).

**ÉTRETAT**
**Tourist office** Place Maurice Guillard (mid-March to mid-June & mid-Sept to mid-Nov Mon–Sat 10am–noon & 2–6pm; mid-June to mid-Sept daily 10am–7pm; mid-Nov to mid-March Fri & Sat 10am–noon & 2–6pm; ☎ 02 35 27 05 21, ⓦ etretat.net).

---

## ACCOMMODATION

**VARENGEVILLE**
★ **De la Terrasse** Rte de Vastérival ☎ 02 35 85 12 54, ⓦ hotel-restaurant-la-terrasse.com. Irresistible *Logis de France*, perched high above the cliffs at the end of a dead-end right turning just west of town. Fish *menus* in its panoramic dining room start at €22, and you can follow footpaths down through narrow cracks in the cliffs to

reach the rocky beach below. Some large family rooms. Closed mid-Oct to mid-March. Rates include breakfast and dinner. **€124**

**ST-VALÉRY-EN-CAUX**
**La Maison des Galets** 22 rue le Perrey ☎ 02 35 97 11 22, ⓦ lamaisondesgalets.com. Though housed in the

5

unremarkable concrete block that lines St-Valery's beach, this charming hotel has a distinct pre-war, Art Deco flavour. All the simple tasteful rooms, of which half enjoy sea views, have good bathrooms, and there's a decent restaurant-cum-tearoom downstairs. **€60**

### FÉCAMP

**Camping de Reneville** Chemin de Nesmond ☏ 02 35 28 20 97, ⓦ campingdereneville.com. Lovely campsite, with beautiful views along the coast, located just a short walk out of town on the western cliffs. Closed early Nov to March. **€15.70**

**De la Mer** 89 bd Albert 1er ☏ 02 35 28 24 64, ⓦ hotel -dela-mer.com. Eight plain but good-value rooms above a seafront bar, the cheapest of which have toilet but no bath. **€60**

**De la Plage** 87 rue de la Plage ☏ 02 35 29 76 51,

ⓦ hoteldelaplage-fecamp.com. Behind its somewhat drab exterior, this hotel holds some surprisingly genteel rooms, including larger family options. Only the higher ones have sea views, while the cheapest have showers but not toilets. All are comfortable, and the location is quiet. **€60**

### ÉTRETAT

**Camping Municipal** 69 rue Maupassant ☏ 02 35 27 07 67. Spacious individual pitches in Étretat's campsite spread amid the trees to the east of the D39, 1km inland from the town centre. Closed mid-Oct to March. **€19.80**

**La Résidence** 4 bd René-Coty ☏ 02 35 27 02 87, ⓦ hotels-etretat.com. Guest rooms in this dramatic half-timbered old mansion vary enormously; the cheapest option has a toilet but no other en-suite facilities, while others are positively luxurious. **€42**

### EATING

### ST-VALÉRY-EN-CAUX

**Du Port** 18 quai Amont ☏ 02 35 97 08 93. Stand-alone quayside restaurant that specializes in whisking deliciously fresh fish from boat to table with only the most minimal, subtle intervention. Dinner *menus* €25.50 and €46. Tues, Wed, Fri & Sat noon–1.45pm & 7.30–9.30pm; Thurs & Sun noon–1.45pm.

### FÉCAMP

**La Marée** 77 quai Bérigny ☏ 02 35 29 39 15. Well-priced quayside fish restaurant, attached to a fish shop and

offering a recommended €29 *menu* as well as assorted seafood platters. Tues, Wed, Fri & Sat noon–2pm & 7–9.30pm; Thurs & Sun noon–2pm.

### ÉTRETAT

**Le Galion** Bd René-Coty ☏ 02 35 29 48 74, ⓦ etretat -legalion.fr. Étretat's finest restaurant, adjoining the *Résidence* hotel just off the square, serves classic Norman dishes in a gloriously weathered medieval hall, on *menus* from €25. Daily noon–1.30pm & 7.30–9pm; closed Tues & Wed in winter.

# Le Havre

While **LE HAVRE** may hardly be picturesque or tranquil, neither is Normandy's largest town the soulless sprawl some travellers suggest. Its port, the second-largest in France, takes up half the Seine estuary, but the town itself, home to almost 200,000 people, is a place of pilgrimage for fans of contemporary **architecture**.

Built in 1517 to replace the ancient ports of Harfleur and Honfleur, then silting up, Le Havre – "The Harbour" – swiftly became the principal trading post of northern France. Following its near-destruction during World War II, it was rebuilt by a single architect, **Auguste Perret**, between 1946 and 1964.

The sheer sense of space can be exhilarating: the showpiece monuments have a winning self-confidence, and the few surviving relics of the old city have been sensitively integrated into the whole. While the endless mundane residential blocks can be dispiriting, even those visitors who fail to agree with Perret's famous dictum that "concrete is beautiful" may enjoy a stroll around his city.

## Hôtel de Ville

One reason visitors often dismiss Le Havre out of hand is that it's easy to get to and from the city without ever seeing its downtown area. For those who make the effort, the Perret-designed central **Hôtel de Ville** is a logical first port of call, a long, low, flat-roofed building topped by a seventeen-storey concrete tower. Sitting in an attractive, lively square, surrounded by pergola walkways, flowerbeds and fountains, it hosts imaginative exhibitions.

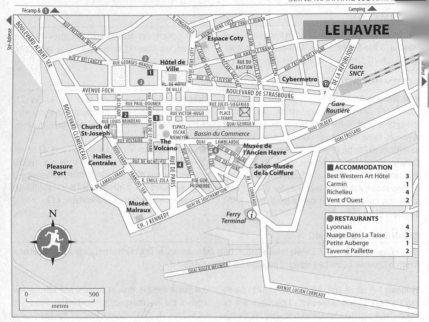

## Church of St-Joseph

From the outside, Perret's major creation, the **church of St-Joseph**, is a mass of speckled concrete, the main doors thrown open to hint at dark interior spaces within. When you get inside it all makes sense: the altar is right in the centre, with the 100m bell tower rising directly above. Simple patterns of stained glass, extending right the way up the tower, create a bright interplay of coloured light, focusing on the altar.

## The Volcano

Le Havre's boldest specimen of modern architecture is a post-Perret creation – the cultural centre known as the **Volcano** (or, less reverentially, the "yoghurt pot"), dominating the Espace Oscar Niemeyer. Niemeyer, the Brazilian architect who oversaw the construction of Brasilia, was still hard at work, aged 104, at the time of writing. He designed this slightly asymmetrical gleaming white cone in the 1970s.

## Musée Malraux

2 bd Clemenceau • Mon & Wed–Fri 11am–6pm, Sat & Sun 11am–7pm • €5 • ☎ 02 35 19 62 72, ⓦ musee-malraux.lehavre.fr

The **Musée Malraux** ranks among the best-designed art galleries in France, making full use of the natural light afforded by its seafront location to display an enjoyable array of nineteenth- and twentieth-century French paintings. Its highlights are more than two hundred canvases by Eugène Boudin, including greyish landscapes produced all along the Normandy coastline, as well as an entire wall of miniature cows. A lovely set of works by Raoul Dufy make Le Havre seem positively radiant, whatever the weather outside.

## ARRIVAL AND DEPARTURE                                    LE HAVRE

**By train** The *gare SNCF* is a 10min walk from the centre down bd de Strasbourg, not far from the ferry port.
Destinations Paris (11 daily; 2hr 30min); Rouen (15 daily; 50min).

**By bus** The *gare routière* stands alongside the *gare SNCF*.
Destinations Étretat (12 daily; 45min); Fécamp (11 daily; 1hr 20min); Honfleur (7 daily; 30min).

**By ferry** Daily sailings from Portsmouth are operated by LD Lines (☎ 08 25 30 43 04, ⓦ ldlines.co.uk).

**...rist office** 186 bd Clemenceau, on the main seafront ...g (July & Aug daily 9am–7pm; April–June & Sept Mon–...at 9.30am–12.30pm & 2–6.30pm, Sun 10am–12.30pm & 2.30–6.30pm; Oct–March Mon–Sat 9.30am–12.30pm & 2–6pm, Sun 10am–12.30pm & 2.30–5pm; ☎02 32 74 04 04, ⓦlehavretourisme.com).

## ACCOMMODATION

**Best Western Art Hôtel** 147 rue Louis Brindeau ☎02 35 22 69 44, ⓦwww.art-hotel.fr. Very smart, comfortable hotel on the north side of the Espace Oscar Niemeyer, facing the Volcano cultural centre. All rooms have flatscreen TVs; the largest have outdoor terraces. €79
**Carmin** 15 rue Georges Braque ☎02 32 74 08 20, ⓦhotelcarmin.com. Good-value hotel in a relatively quiet neighbourhood, not too far back from the sea; the large rooms may not be fancy, but they're comfortable. Buffet breakfasts €8.20. €65

**Richelieu** 135 rue de Paris ☎02 35 42 38 71, ⓦhotellerichelieu.fr. For a mid-priced hotel in a very central location with bright, comfortable rooms, this hotel is hard to beat. €56
★ **Vent d'Ouest** 4 rue de Caligny ☎02 35 42 50 69, ⓦventdouest.fr. Le Havre's smartest hotel is a stylishly designed boutique affair, with comfortable, well-equipped rooms decorated on a nautical or mountain theme. Apartments sleeping four are also available. €92

## EATING AND DRINKING

The area around the *gare SNCF* is where to head for bars, cafés and brasseries, while all sorts of restaurants, from traditional French to Japanese, fill the back streets of the waterside St-François district.

**Lyonnais** 7–9 rue de Bretagne ☎02 35 22 07 31. Small, cosy restaurant with chequered tablecloths and a welcoming atmosphere. The speciality is baked fish, though dishes from Lyon, such as *andouillettes*, are also available on *menus* that start at €13 at lunch, €17.50 at dinner. Mon noon–2pm, Tues–Sat noon–2pm & 7–10pm.
**Nuage Dans La Tasse** 93 av Foch ☎02 35 21 64 94. Huge salads and simple, good-value bistro meals – or you can simply drop in for a cup of tea – near the town hall. Mon–Wed 4–7pm, Thurs–Sat 11am–7pm.
**Petite Auberge** 32 rue de Ste-Adresse ☎02 35 46 27 32. High-class traditional French cooking, aimed more at local businesspeople than at tourists, and offering few surprises but no disappointments. Tues & Thurs–Sat noon–2pm & 7.30–9pm, Wed 7.30–9pm, Sun noon–2pm.
**Taverne Paillette** 22 rue Georges Braque ☎02 35 41 31 50, ⓦtavern-paillette.com. This venerable Bavarian brasserie can trace its roots – and its beer – back to the sixteenth century, even if its present incarnation is a postwar reconstruction. The twin specialities are *choucroute* and elaborate seafood platters; there's also a changing daily lunch *menu* for €13. Daily noon–midnight.

# Rouen

**ROUEN**, the capital of Upper Normandy, is one of France's most ancient cities. Standing on the site of Rotomagus, built by the Romans at the lowest point where they could bridge the Seine, it was laid out by Rollo, the first duke of Normandy, in 911. Captured by the English in 1419, it became the stage in 1431 for the trial and execution of Joan of Arc, before returning to French control in 1449.

After bombing during World War II destroyed all Rouen's bridges, the area between the cathedral and the *quais*, and much of the left bank's industrial quarter, the city was rebuilt, turning its inner core of streets, a few hundred metres north of the river, into the closest approximation to a medieval city that modern imaginations could conceive.

Rouen today can be very seductive, its lively and bustling centre well equipped with impressive churches and museums. North of the Seine at any rate, it's a real pleasure to explore. As well as some great sights – **Cathédrale de Notre-Dame**, all the delightful twisting streets of timbered houses – there's history aplenty too, most notably the links with **Joan of Arc**.

While Rouen proper is home to a population of 110,000, its metropolitan area holds five times that number, and it remains the fourth-largest port in the country. The city spreads deep into the loop of the Seine, with its docks and industrial infrastructure stretching endlessly away to the south.

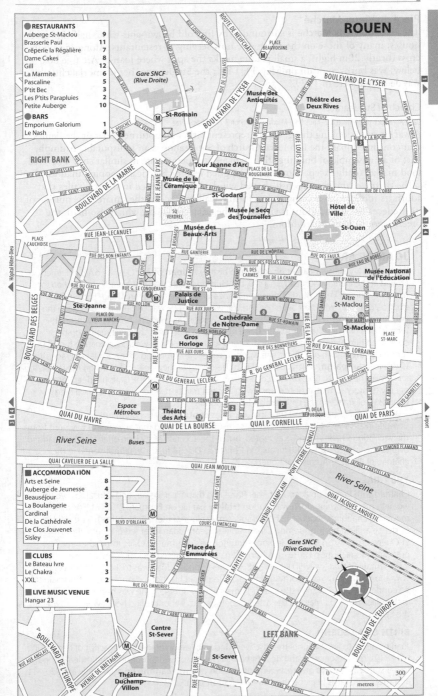

**RESTAURANTS**
| | |
|---|---|
| Auberge St-Maclou | 9 |
| Brasserie Paul | 11 |
| Crêperie la Régalière | 7 |
| Dame Cakes | 8 |
| Gill | 12 |
| La Marmite | 6 |
| Pascaline | 5 |
| P'tit Bec | 3 |
| Les P'tits Parapluies | 2 |
| Petite Auberge | 10 |

**BARS**
| | |
|---|---|
| Emporium Galorium | 1 |
| Le Nash | 4 |

**ACCOMMODATION**
| | |
|---|---|
| Arts et Seine | 8 |
| Auberge de Jeunesse | 4 |
| Beauséjour | 2 |
| La Boulangerie | 3 |
| Cardinal | 7 |
| De la Cathédrale | 6 |
| Le Clos Jouvenet | 1 |
| Sisley | 5 |

**CLUBS**
| | |
|---|---|
| Le Bateau Ivre | 1 |
| Le Chakra | 3 |
| XXL | 2 |

**LIVE MUSIC VENUE**
| | |
|---|---|
| Hangar 23 | 4 |

**ROUEN**

**5**

## Place du Vieux-Marché

The **Place du Vieux-Marché** is surrounded by fine old brown-and-white half-timbered houses, many of those on the south side now serving as restaurants. Alongside a huge cross (nearly 20m high), a small plaque marks the spot where Joan of Arc (see box below) was burnt to death on May 30, 1431; the **Ste-Jeanne**, her memorial church, was dedicated here in 1979.

### Church of Ste-Jeanne

Daily: April–Oct 10am–noon & 2–6pm; Nov–March 10am–noon & 2–5.30pm • Free

A wacky, spiky-looking thing, said to represent either an upturned boat or the flames that consumed Joan, the memorial **Church of Ste-Jeanne** is an indisputable triumph, part of an ensemble of buildings that manages to incorporate in similar style a covered food market (daily except Mon) that's designed less for practical shopping than for show.

The theme of the church's fish-shaped windows is continued in the scaly tiles that adorn its roof, which is elongated to form a walkway across the square. The outline of its predecessor's foundations is visible on the adjacent lawns, which also mark the precise spot of Joan's martyrdom.

---

### JOAN OF ARC

When the 17-year-old peasant girl known to history as **Joan of Arc** (Jeanne d'Arc in French) arrived at the French court early in 1429, the Hundred Years' War had already dragged on for more than ninety years. Most of northern France was in the grip of an Anglo–Burgundian alliance, but Joan, who had been hearing voices since 1425, was certain she could save the country, and came to present her case to the as-yet-uncrowned Dauphin. Partly through recognizing him despite a simple disguise he wore to fool her at their first meeting, she convinced him of her Divine guidance. After a remarkable three-week examination by a tribunal of the French *parlement*, she went on to secure command of the armies of France. In a whirlwind **campaign**, which culminated in the raising of the siege of Orléans on May 8, 1429, she broke the English hold on the Loire Valley. She then escorted the Dauphin deep into enemy territory so that, in accordance with ancient tradition, he could be crowned King Charles VII of France in the cathedral at Reims, on July 17.

Within a year of her greatest triumph, Joan was **captured** by the Burgundian army at Compiègne in May 1430, and held to ransom. Chivalry dictated that any offer of payment from the vacillating Charles must be accepted, but in the absence of such an offer Joan was handed over to the English for 10,000 ducats. On Christmas Day, 1430, she was imprisoned in the château of Philippe-Auguste at Rouen.

#### THE TRIAL

Charged with heresy, on account of her "false and diabolical" visions and refusal to give up wearing men's clothing, Joan was put on **trial** for her life on February 21, 1431. For three months, a changing panel of 131 assessors – only eight of them English-born – heard the evidence against her. Condemned, inevitably, to death, Joan recanted on the scaffold in St-Ouen cemetery on May 24, and her sentence was commuted to life imprisonment. The presiding judge, Bishop Pierre Cauchon of Beauvais, reassured disappointed English representatives that "we will get her yet". The next Sunday, Joan was tricked into breaking her vow and putting on male clothing, and taken to the archbishop's chapel in rue St-Romain to be condemned to death for the second time. On May 30, 1431, she was burned at the stake in the place du Vieux-Marché; her ashes, together with her unburned heart, were thrown into the Seine.

#### BIRTH OF A LEGEND

Joan passed into legend, until the discovery and publication of the full transcript of her trial in the 1840s. The forbearance and devout humility she displayed throughout her ordeal added to her status as France's greatest religious heroine. She was **canonized** as recently as 1920, and soon afterwards became the country's patron saint.

**5**

## Gros Horloge

Rue du Gros-Horloge • Daily except Mon: June–Sept 10am–1pm & 2–7pm; Oct–May 2–6pm; last admission 1hr before closing • €6 •
☎ 02 32 08 01 90, ⓦ rouen.fr/gros-horloge

Until it was lowered to straddle the rue du Gros Horloge in 1529, to allow the citizens of
Rouen to see it better, the colourful one-handed clock known as the **Gros Horloge** used to
adorn the Gothic belfry alongside. Visitors now climb, via several rooms that explain the
history of both clock and city, up a stone spiral staircase, to emerge on a narrow but safely
railed boardwalk around the very top. Here you can admire the clock's intricate workings,
and enjoy marvellous views of the old city, with its startling array of towers and spires.

## Cathédral de Notre-Dame

**Cathedral** April–Oct Mon 2–7pm, Tues–Sat 7.30am–7pm, Sun 8am–6pm; Nov–March Mon 2–6pm, Tues–Sat 7.30am–noon & 2–6pm,
Sun 8am–6pm; crypt closed on Sun and during services **La Cathédrale de Monet aux Pixels** Daily: July 11pm, August 10.30pm • Free
• ⓦ cathedrale-rouen.net

Despite the addition of all sorts of towers, spires and vertical extensions, Rouen's
**Cathédral de Notre-Dame** remains at heart the Gothic masterpiece that was built in
the twelfth and thirteenth centuries. The west facade of the cathedral, intricately
sculpted like the rest of the exterior, was Monet's subject for more than thirty studies of
changing light, several of which now hang in the Musée d'Orsay in Paris. Monet might
not recognize it today, however – in the last few years, it's been scrubbed a gleaming
white, free from the centuries of accreted dirt he so carefully recorded.

On summer nights, colours inspired by Monet's cathedral paintings are projected
onto the building's facade in a thirty-minute light show known as **La Cathédrale de
Monet aux Pixels**, transforming it quite magnificently into a series of giant Monet-
esque canvases. Inside the cathedral, the **ambulatory** and **crypt** hold the assorted tombs
of various recumbent royalty, such as Duke Rollo, who died "enfeebled by toil" in 933
AD, and the actual heart of Richard the Lionheart.

## St-Ouen

Place du Général-de-Gaulle • Tues–Thurs, Sat & Sun: April–Oct 10am–noon & 2–6pm; Nov–March 10am–noon & 2–5.30pm • Free

The **church of St-Ouen**, next to the Hôtel de Ville (which itself occupies buildings that
were once part of the abbey), is larger than Rouen's cathedral and has far less
decoration. From the outside, therefore, there's nothing to diminish the instant impact
of its vast Gothic proportions and the purity of its lines. Inside, it holds some stunning
fourteenth-century stained glass, though much was destroyed during the Revolution.

## Aître St-Maclou

188 rue Martainville • Daily: April–Oct 8am–8pm; Nov–March 8am–7pm • Free

Built as a cemetery for plague victims, **Aître St-Maclou** was originally an integral part of the
complex that centred on the light, graceful **church of St-Maclou**. On first glance, it now
appears simply to be the tranquil garden courtyard of the Fine Arts school; take a look at
the ornate carvings that line the lower storey of the surrounding buildings, however, and
you'll find all sorts of chilling symbols of death and decay. Look out, too, for a genuine
mummified cat.

## Musée des Beaux-Arts

Esplanade Marcel-Duchamp • Daily except Tues 10am–6pm • €5; there may be an extra charge for temporary exhibitions •
☎ 02 35 71 28 40, ⓦ rouen-musees.com/Musee-des-Beaux-Arts

Rouen's imposing **Musée des Beaux-Arts** commands the square Verdrel from just east of
the central rue Jeanne-d'Arc. The grand edifice is home to an absorbing permanent
collection, as well as regular temporary exhibitions. Unexpected highlights include dazzling
Russian icons from the sixteenth century onwards, and an entertaining eighteenth-century
crib from Naples. Many of the biggest names among the painters – Caravaggio (the
centrepiece *Flagellation of Christ*), Velázquez, Rubens – tend to be represented by a single

**5**

minor work, but there are several Modiglianis and a number of Monets, including *Rouen Cathedral* (1894), the *Vue Générale de Rouen* and *Brume sur la Seine* (1894). The central sculpture court, roofed over but very light, holds a small tearoom.

## Musée da la Céramique

I rue Faucon • Daily except Tues 10am–6pm • €3 • ☎ 02 35 71 28 40, ⓦ rouen-musees.com/Musee-de-la-Ceramique

Rouen's history as a centre for *faïencerie*, or earthenware pottery, is recorded in the **Musée de la Céramique**, raised above the north side of the square Verdrel. A series of beautiful rooms, some of which incorporate sixteenth-century wood panelling rescued from a demolished nunnery of St-Amand, display specimens from the 1600s onwards. Assorted tiles and plates reflect the eighteenth-century craze for *chinoiserie*.

## Musée Le Secq des Tournelles

2 rue Jacques-Villon • Daily except Tues 10am–1pm & 2–6pm • €3 • ☎ 02 35 71 28 40, ⓦ rouen-musees.com/Musee-le-Secq-des-Tournelles

Housed in the old, barely altered church of St-Laurent, behind the Beaux-Arts, the **Musée Le Secq des Tournelles** consists of a gloriously eccentric and uncategorizable collection of wrought-iron objects of all dates and descriptions. Prize exhibits include nutcrackers and door knockers, a huge double bed from sixteenth-century Italy, spiral staircases that lead nowhere and hideous implements of torture.

## Musée des Antiquités

Rue Beauvoisine • Tues–Sat 1.30–5.30pm, Sun 2–6pm • €3 • ☎ 02 35 98 55 10, ⓦ www.museedesantiquites.fr

The **Musée des Antiquités** provides a dry but comprehensive run-through of ancient artefacts found in or near Rouen. Starting with an impressive Bronze Age helmet and an assortment of early iron tools, it continues with some remarkably complete and beautifully presented Roman mosaics from local villas. Then comes a long gallery filled with woodcarvings rescued from long-lost Rouen houses – including a lovely bas-relief of sheep that served as the sign for a medieval draper's shop – and also some fine fifteenth-century tapestries.

## Tour Jeanne d'Arc

Rue Bouvreuil • April–Sept Mon & Wed–Sat 10am–12.30pm & 2–6pm, Sun 2–6.30pm; Oct–March Mon & Wed–Sat 10am–12.30pm & 2–5pm, Sun 2–5.30pm • €1.50 • ☎ 02 35 98 16 21, ⓦ www.tourjeannedarc.fr

The tall, sharp-pointed **Tour Jeanne d'Arc**, a short way southeast of the *gare SNCF*, is all that remains of the castle of Philippe-Auguste, built in 1205 and scene of the imprisonment and trial of Joan of Arc (see p.266). It served as the castle's keep and entrance-way, and was itself fully surrounded by a moat. Joan's actual prison, however, was the Tour de la Pucelle, demolished in 1809, while the trial took place first of all in the castle's St-Romain chapel, and then later in its great central hall, both of which were destroyed in 1590. After seeing a small collection of Joan-related memorabilia, visitors can climb a steep spiral staircase to the very top, but you can't see out over the city, let alone step outside into the open air.

### ARRIVAL AND INFORMATION

**ROUEN**

**By train** The main *gare SNCF*, Gare Rive Droite, stands at the north end of rue Jeanne-d'Arc.

Destinations Paris-St-Lazare (25 daily; 1hr 20min); Vernon (12 daily; 30min).

**By bus** The *gare routière* is tucked away behind the riverfront on rue des Charrettes one block west of rue Jeanne-d'Arc.

Destinations Le Havre (hourly; 2hr 45min), via Jumièges (30min); Lisieux (2 daily; 2hr 30min).

**By car** Rouen is a difficult and unpleasant city to drive into. All traffic is funnelled into the hideous multi-lane highways that line either bank of the river, while many of the central streets, north of the river, have been pedestrianized. It's best to park as soon as you can – there are plenty of central underground car parks, especially near the cathedral and the place du Vieux-Marché – and explore the city on foot.

**Tourist office** 25 place de la Cathédrale (May–Sept Mon–Sat 9am–7pm, Sun 9.30am–12.30pm & 2–6pm; Oct–April Mon–Sat 9.30am–12.30pm & 1.30–6pm; ☎ 02 32 08 32 40, ⓦ rouentourisme.com).

## GETTING AROUND

**By métro** Rouen's métro system (ⓦtcar.fr) is more useful to commuters than tourists. It follows the line of the rue Jeanne-d'Arc south from the *gare SNCF*, making two stops before resurfacing to cross the river by bridge. Individual journeys cost €1.50; a book of ten tickets is €12.30, or you can buy a 24hr pass for €4.30.

**By bus** All buses from the *gare SNCF* except #2A run down rue Jeanne-d'Arc to the centre, which takes 5min. From the fifth stop, the "Théâtre des Arts" by the river, the *gare routière* is one block west in rue des Charrettes, tucked away behind the riverfront buildings.

**By bike** The city-sponsored Cy'clic network (ⓦcyclic .rouen.fr ) enables credit-card holders to unlock a simple bike from "stations" scattered along the streets, and leave it at any other station; journeys of less than 30min are free.

## ACCOMMODATION

**Arts et Seine** 6 rue St-Étienne-des-Tonneliers ☎02 35 88 11 44, ⓦartsetseine.com. Inexpensive hotel, a block north of the river not far from the cathedral, smartened up by friendly new owners and offering clean, well-equipped rooms of varying levels of comfort, plus good €7.60 breakfasts. **€64**

**Auberge de Jeunesse** 3 rue du Tour, rte de Darnetal ☎02 35 08 18 50, ⓦfuaj.org/rouen. Housed in an eighteenth-century dyers' works, beside the little Robec river well east of the centre, Rouen's new youth hostel offers dorm beds in rooms that sleep from two to six, plus bright and friendly communal areas. **€21.80**

**Beauséjour** 9 rue Pouchet ☎02 35 71 93 47, ⓦhotel -beausejour-rouen.fr. Good-value, revamped hotel near the station (turn right as you come out). Beyond the orange facade and nice garden courtyard, the rooms are nothing fancy, but they're crisply decorated with large-screen TVs; one cheaper single room lacks its own shower. Closed second half of July. **€65**

**La Boulangerie** 59 rue St-Nicaise ☎06 12 94 53 15, ⓦlaboulangerie.fr. Very welcoming three-room B&B, just north of St-Ouen and set above a half-timbered, red-painted boulangerie where the owners bake bread and serve breakfast. Bedrooms feature exposed beams, comfy beds, and in two instances bathtubs open to the room. **€75**

**Cardinal** 1 place de la Cathédrale ☎02 35 70 24 42, ⓦcardinal-hotel.fr. Very good-value hotel in a stunning location – albeit potentially noisy –facing the cathedral. Rooms are spacious and clean, with good en-suite facilities and flatscreen TVs. Two family rooms available. All have views of the cathedral (the higher ones from balconies). Ample buffet breakfasts for €9. **€85**

**De la Cathédrale** 12 rue St-Romain ☎02 35 71 57 95, ⓦhotel-de-la-cathedrale.fr. Attractive hotel, in a pedestrian lane beside the cathedral, with a pleasant olde-worlde theme, nice breakfast room and flower-filled courtyard. The rooms are plainer than the public spaces might suggest, but it's a still a peaceful haven. Discounts at public car park nearby. Buffet breakfasts €9.50. **€76**

★**Le Clos Jouvenet** 42 rue Hyacinthe Langlois ☎02 35 89 80 66, ⓦleclosjouvenet.com. Four beautifully decorated, comfortable rooms in an immaculate nineteenth-century house a 10min walk east of the train station. Breakfast is served in the conservatory, overlooking the enclosed garden. **€110**

**Sisley** 51 rue Jean-Lecanuet ☎02 35 71 10 07, ⓦhotelsisley.fr. Very central little budget hotel, an easy walk from the station, where each of the thirteen bright, comfortable double rooms is decorated in keeping with a different Impressionist painter, and has shower rather than bath. **€50**

## EATING AND DRINKING

Rouen's busiest bars and restaurants are especially concentrated around the streets that radiate out from the place du Vieux-Marché. Rue Martainville offers some excellent, often less touristy alternatives.

### RESTAURANTS

**Auberge St-Maclou** 224–226 rue Martainville ☎02 35 71 06 67. Half-timbered building in the shadow of St-Maclou church, with outdoor tables on a busy pedestrian street, and an old-style ambience. Well-priced traditional French *menus* – lunch is €12.50/€15.50, dinner €21/€27. Tues–Sat noon–2pm & 7–9.30pm, Sun noon–2pm; closed 2 wks in Feb and 3 wks in Aug.

**Brasserie Paul** 1 place de la Cathédrale ☎02 35 71 86 07, ⓦbrasserie-paul.com. Rouen's definitive bistro, an attractive *belle époque* place facing the cathedral. Daily lunch specials, with a €16 *formule* or Simone de Beauvoir's favourite goat's cheese and smoked duck salad for €12.50. Mon–Thurs & Sun 10am–11pm, Fri & Sat 10am–midnight.

**Crêperie la Régalière** 12 rue Massacre ☎02 35 15 33 33. This quaint, inexpensive but good-quality crêperie, with some outdoor seating just off the place du Vieux-Marché, is one of central Rouen's best bargains, with *menus* at €10 and €15. Tues–Sat 11.45am–11pm.

**Dame Cakes** 70 rue St-Romain ☎02 35 07 49 31, ⓦdamecakes.fr. Elegant tearoom, with a little garden, on a quiet street next to the cathedral, tempting the tastebuds with delicious desserts, savoury tarts and salads. Mon–Fri 10.30am–7pm, Sat 10am–7.30pm.

**5**

**Gill** 8–9 quai de la Bourse ☎ 02 35 71 16 14, ⓦ gill.fr. A showcase for celebrated local chef Gilles Tournadre, this ultra-smart quayside restaurant boasts two Michelin stars. The Asian-influenced food is presented with all the fancy trimmings and extras that might suggest, and it can be hard to tell what you're eating, but it tastes sublime. Weekday lunch *menus* start at €37; dinner ranges from €68 to €150. Tues–Sat noon–1.45pm & 7.30–9.45pm; closed 2 wks in April and 3 wks in Aug.

★ **La Marmite** 3 rue de Florence ☎ 02 35 71 75 55, ⓦ lamarmiterouen.com. Romantic little place just north of the place du Vieux-Marché, offering beautiful, elegantly presented gourmet dishes on well-priced *menus* at €29, €39 and €56. Tues 7–9.30pm, Wed–Sat noon–2pm & 7–9.30pm, Sun noon–2pm.

**Pascaline** 5 rue de la Poterne ☎ 02 35 89 67 44, ⓦ pascaline.fr. Classic bistro, north of the Palais de Justice, near the flower market, with a green wooden enclosure attached to the front of a half-timbered house. Set *menus* at €15.50–29.50, and live jazz some Thursdays. Daily noon–2.30pm & 7–11pm.

**P'tit Bec** 182 rue Eau-de-Robec ☎ 02 35 07 63 33. Friendly brasserie that's especially popular at lunchtime. Simple *menus* at €12.50 and €16 include a fish or meat main course, plus vegetarian options, or you can get a salad for €11. There's seating indoors as well as out on the pedestrianized street, in view of several fine half-timbered mansions. June–Aug Mon noon–2.30pm, Tues–Sat noon–2.30pm & 7–10.30pm; Sept–May Mon–Wed noon–2.30pm, Thurs–Sat noon–2.30pm & 7–10.30pm.

★ **Les P'tits Parapluies** 46 rue Bourg-l'Abbé, place de la Rougemare ☎ 02 35 88 55 26, ⓦ lesptits -parapluies.com. Elegant, secluded half-timbered restaurant not far north of the Hôtel de Ville, on the edge of an attractive little square. Counting your calories (or your pennies) is not really an option; set *menus* start at €32 and include foie gras and oysters. Just €6 extra buys two glasses of wine per person. Tues–Fri noon–2.45pm & 7.45– 10pm, Sat 7.45–10pm, Sun noon–2.45pm.

**Petite Auberge** 164 rue Martainville ☎ 02 35 70 80 18, ⓦ restaurant-petite-auberge.fr. Attractive, old-fashioned, indoor restaurant, serving delicious traditional Norman cuisine at very reasonable prices; they're very proud of their snails, but there are plenty of alternatives. Weekday lunch *formule* €12.50, dinner *menus* from €16 on weekdays, €20.50 at weekends. Tues–Fri noon–2.45pm & 7.45–10pm, Sat 7.45–10pm, Sun noon–2.45pm.

### BARS

**Emporium Galorium** 151 rue Beauvoisine ☎ 02 35 71 76 95, ⓦ emporium-galorium.com. Busy, half-timbered student-dominated bar, a short walk north of the centre, hosting small-scale gigs and theatrical productions. Tues & Wed 8pm–2am, Thurs–Sat 8pm–3am; closed 2 weeks in Aug.

**Le Nash** 97 rue Écuyère ☎ 02 35 98 25 24. Relaxed bar that's popular with locals. The interior has a lounge-like feel with its mood lighting and zebra stripes, while the outdoor terrace is much more akin to a classic French café, and serves light snacks. Music from ambient to Latin. Mon–Fri 11am–2am, Sat 6pm–2am.

## NIGHTLIFE AND ENTERTAINMENT

### CLUBS

**Le Bateau Ivre** 17 rue des Sapins ☎ 02 35 70 09 05, ⓦ bateauivre.rouen.free.fr. Low-key but atmospheric hangout a long way northeast of the centre. Mostly rock-oriented programme of music and performance, with some open-mic nights. Sept–July Tues–Sat 10pm–4am.

**Le Chakra** 4 bd Ferdinand-de-Lesseps ☎ 07 61 08 89 19, ⓦ lechakra.fr. Busy, sweaty club, beside the Seine a couple of kilometres west of the centre, where big-name DJs play hip-hop on Fri and electro on Sat, to a young crowd. Fri 11pm–4am, Sat 5–9pm & 11pm–4am, Sun 5–9pm.

**XXL** 25–27 rue de la Savonnerie ☎ 02 35 88 84 00, ⓦ xxl-rouen.com. Gay (very largely male) club near the river, just south of the cathedral, with theme nights and a small basement dancefloor. Tues–Sat 9pm–4am, Sun 9pm–2am.

### LIVE MUSIC

**Hangar 23** Presqu'île Waddington, pied du Pont Flaubert ☎ 02 32 18 28 10, ⓦ hangar23.fr. Rouen's premier concert venue, on the right bank a couple of kilometres west of the centre, also hosts plays and touring companies as well as big-name musical events.

### THEATRE

**Théâtre des Arts** 7 rue du Dr-Rambert ☎ 02 35 98 74 78, ⓦ operaderouen.com. This highbrow venue puts on a varied programme of opera, ballet and concerts.

**Théâtre des Deux Rives** ☎ 02 35 70 22 82, ⓦ cdr2rives .com. Home to an adventurous repertory company, this small theatre, opposite the Antiquités museum at the top end of rue Louis Ricard, also hosts touring productions.

# Along the Seine from Rouen

As well as idyllic pastoral scenery, the banks of the Seine in either direction of Rouen hold some unmissable historical and cultural attractions. **Upstream**, high cliffs on the north bank of the river look down on green woodlands and scattered river islands. By the time you reach the splendid castle at **Les Andelys**, 25km southeast of Rouen, you're within 100km of Paris, while another 30km brings you to Monet's former home in the village of **Giverny**. **Downstream**, on the other hand, the highlight of the lovely riverside route has to be the intriguing ruins of **Jumièges abbey**.

## Château Gaillard

Les Andelys • Mid-March to mid-Nov daily except Tues 10am–1pm & 2–6pm • €3, grounds free all year • ⓦ lesandelys.com
/chateau-gaillard

The most dramatic sight anywhere along the Seine has to be Richard the Lionheart's **Château Gaillard**, perched high above **LES ANDELYS**. Constructed in a position of impregnable power, it looked down over all movement on the river at the frontier of the English king's domains. Built in less than a year (1196–97), the castle might have survived intact had Henri IV not ordered its destruction in 1603. As it is, the stout flint walls of its keep, roughly 4m thick, remain reasonably sound, and the outline of most of the rest is still clear, arranged over assorted green and chalky knolls. To reach it on foot, climb the steep path that leads off rue Richard-Coeur-de-Lion in Petit Andely.

## Monet's house at Giverny

84 rue Claude Monet, Giverny • April–Oct daily 9.30am–6pm; last entry 5.30pm • €9 • ☎ 02 32 51 28 21, ⓦ fondation-monet.fr

The house where **Claude Monet** lived from 1883 until his death in 1926 remains much as he left it – complete with water-lily pond – at **GIVERNY**, 20km south of Les Andelys near the north bank of the Seine. While the **gardens** that Monet laid out are still lovingly tended, none of his original paintings is on display, so art lovers who make the pilgrimage here tend to be outnumbered by garden enthusiasts.

Visits start in the huge **studio**, built in 1915, where Monet painted the last and largest of his many depictions of water lilies (*nymphéas*). It now serves as a well-stocked book- and gift shop. The **house** itself is a long two-storey structure, painted pastel pink with green shutters. Almost all the main rooms are crammed floor-to-ceiling with Monet's collection of Japanese prints. Most of the furnishings are gone, but you get a real sense of how the dining room used to be, with its walls and fittings painted a glorious bright yellow.

The flower-filled **gardens** stretch down towards the river, though these days the footpath that drops to the **water-lily pond** burrows beneath the road. Once there, paths around the pond, as well as arching Japanese footbridges, offer differing views of the water lilies, cherished by gardeners in rowing boats. May and June, when the rhododendrons flower and the wisteria is in bloom, are the best times to visit.

## Abbaye de Jumièges

24 rue Guillaume le Conquérant, Jumièges • Daily: mid-April to mid-Sept 9.30am–6.30pm; mid-Sept to mid-April 9.30am–1pm &
2.30–5.30pm • €5 • ☎ 02 35 37 24 02, ⓦ www.abbayedejumieges.fr

Nestled into an especially delightful loop of the river, 23km west of Rouen, the majestic **abbey** of **JUMIÈGES** is said to have been founded by St Philibert in 654 AD. Now a haunting ruin, the abbey was burned by Vikings in 841, rebuilt a century later, then destroyed again during the Revolution. Its main surviving outline dates from the eleventh century – William the Conqueror himself attended its reconsecration in 1067. The twin towers, 52m high, are still standing, as is one arch of the roofless nave, while a one-sided yew tree stands amid what were once the cloisters.

| INFORMATION | ALONG THE SEINE FROM ROUEN |
|---|---|

**LES ANDELYS**
**Tourist office** 24 rue Philippe-Auguste, Petit Andely (March Mon–Fri 2–6pm, Sat 10am–1pm & 2–5pm; April & May Mon–Sat 10am–noon & 2–6pm, Sun 10am–1pm; June–Sept Mon–Sat 10am–noon &

2–6pm, Sun 10am–noon & 2–5pm; Oct Mon–Fri 2–6pm, Sat 10am–noon & 2–5pm; Nov–Feb Mon–Fri 2–6pm, Sat 10am–1pm; ☎ 02 32 54 41 93, ⓦ ville-andelys.fr).

**5**

## ACCOMMODATION AND EATING

### LES ANDELYS

★ **Chaîne d'Or** 27 rue Grande ☎ 02 32 54 00 31, ⓦ hotel-lachainedor.com. Les Andelys' most upscale hotel, this luxurious old coaching inn is arrayed around a courtyard beside the river, opposite the thirteenth-century St-Sauveur church; Seine-view rooms cost from €30 extra. Its restaurant (closed Wed all year, plus Sun eve & Tues in winter) serves wonderful food on *menus* priced €46 and up. **€94**

**L'Île des Trois Rois** ☎ 02 32 54 23 79, ⓦ camping -troisrois.com. Lovely – and lively – three-star campsite, stretching out beside the river far below the château. Closed mid-Nov to mid-March. **€24**

### GIVERNY

**Musardière** 123 rue Claude-Monet ☎ 02 32 21 03 18, ⓦ lamusardiere.fr. Giverny's one hotel offers ten comfortable en-suite rooms in a fine old townhouse a couple of hundred metres from Monet's house. Dinner *menus* in its restaurant start at €26. Closed Christmas– Jan. **€83**

### ABBAYE DE JUMIÈGES

**Auberge des Ruines** 17 place de la Mairie ☎ 02 35 37 24 05, ⓦ auberge-des-ruines.fr. A relaxing and truly superb restaurant, with outdoor seating on a shaded terrace across from the abbey. Its wide range of *menus* starts at €25. Mon, Tues & Thurs–Sat noon–2pm & 7–9pm, Sun noon–2pm.

# Basse Normandie

Heading west along the coast of the region known as Basse Normandie, which starts west of the mouth of the Seine, you come to a succession of somewhat exclusive resorts: **Trouville** and **Deauville** are the busiest centres, while **Honfleur** is a delightful medieval port. Continuing west brings you to the beaches where the Allied armies landed in 1944, and then to the wilder, and in places deserted, shore around the **Cotentin Peninsula**.

## Honfleur

**HONFLEUR**, the best preserved of the old Norman ports and the most easterly on the Calvados coast, is a near-perfect seaside town, but for its lack of a beach. It used to have one, but with the accumulation of silt from the Seine the sea has steadily withdrawn, leaving the eighteenth-century waterfront houses of **boulevard Charles-V** stranded and a little surreal. The ancient port, however, still functions – the channel to the beautiful Vieux Bassin is kept open by regular dredging – and though only pleasure craft now use the harbour moorings, fishing boats tie up alongside the pier nearby.

While picturesque enough to attract hundreds of visitors daily, Honfleur remains recognizable as the fishing village that so appealed to nineteenth-century artists. Its compact size, quaint waterside setting and abundance of restaurants make it an ideal destination for a weekend break. Visitors inevitably gravitate towards the old centre, around the **Vieux Bassin**, where slate-fronted houses, each one or two storeys higher than seems possible, harmonize despite their tottering and ill-matched forms. They create a splendid backdrop for the **Lieutenance** at the harbour entrance, the former dwelling of the King's Lieutenant, which has been the gateway to the inner town since at least 1608, when Samuel Champlain sailed from Honfleur to found Québec.

### Musée de la Marine

Quai St-Étienne • Mid-Feb to March, Oct & Nov Tues–Fri 2.30–5.30pm, Sat & Sun 10am–noon & 2 30–5.30pm; April–Sept Tues–Sun 10am–noon & 2–6.30pm • €3.60, €4.80 with Musée d'Ethnographie, €9.50 with Musée d'Ethnographie, Musée Eugène Boudin and Les Maisons Satie • ☎ 02 31 89 14 12, ⓦ musees-honfleur.fr

Honfleur's **Musée de la Marine** somehow manages to squeeze into the fourteenth-century church of **St-Étienne**, on the eastern side of the *basin*. Exhibits tracing the story of the town's intimate association with the sea include assorted model sailing ships, displays on the local shipbuilding industry, and a cumbersome early diving suit.

## Musée d'Ethnographie

Rue de la Prison • Mid-Feb to March, Oct & Nov Tues–Fri 2.30–5.30pm, Sat & Sun 10am–noon & 2.30–5.30pm; April–Sept Tues–Sun 10am–noon & 2–6.30pm • €3.60, €4.80 with Musée de la Marine, €9.50 with Musée de la Marine, Musée Eugène Boudin and Les Maisons Satie • ☎ 02 31 89 14 12, ⓦ musees-honfleur.fr

Alongside the Musée de la Marine, on tiny rue de la Prison, a nice little ensemble that once held Honfleur's prison now serves as the **Musée d'Ethnographie**, filling ten rooms with a fascinating assortment of everyday artefacts from old Honfleur.

## Musée Eugène Boudin

Place Érik-Satie • Mid-March to May & Sept Mon & Wed–Sun 10am–noon & 2–6pm; June–Aug Mon & Wed–Sun 10am–12.30pm & 2–6pm; Oct to mid-March Mon & Wed–Fri 2.30–5.30pm, Sat & Sun 10am–noon & 2.30–5.30pm • €5.80, €9.50 with Les Maisons Satie, Musée de la Marine and Musée du Vieux Honfleur • ☎ 02 31 89 54 00, ⓦ musees-honfleur.fr

Honfleur's artistic heritage – and its present concentration of galleries and painters – is primarily thanks to Eugène Boudin, forerunner of Impressionism. Born in the town, he worked here, trained the 18-year-old Monet, and was joined for various periods by Pissarro, Renoir and Cézanne. He was also among the founders of what's now the **Musée Eugène Boudin**, west of the port, and left 53 works to it after his death in 1898. His pastel seascapes and sunsets hold an especial resonance in this setting, where panoramic windows offer superb views of the Seine estuary.

## Ste-Catherine

**Church** Daily: summer 9am–6pm; winter 9am–5.30pm **Belfry** Mid-March to May & Sept Mon & Wed–Sun 10am–noon & 2–6pm; June–Aug Mon & Wed–Sun 10am–12.30pm & 2–6pm; Oct to mid-March Mon & Wed–Fri 2.30–5.30pm, Sat & Sun 10am–noon & 2.30–5.30pm • €2, or free with Musée Eugène Boudin

Honfleur's most remarkable building, the church of **Ste-Catherine**, is, like its distinctive detached **belfry**, built almost entirely of wood. The church itself has the added peculiarity of being divided into twin naves, with one balcony running around both. The belfry, a favourite subject for the young Monet, holds random ethnographic oddities; visitors are not permitted above ground level.

## Les Maisons Satie

67 bd Charles-V • Mon & Wed–Sun: mid-Feb to April & Oct–Dec 11am–6pm; May–Sept 10am–7pm; last entry 1hr before closing • €5.80, €9.50 with Musée Eugène Boudin, Musée de la Marine and Musée du Vieux Honfleur • ☎ 02 31 89 11 11, ⓦ musees-honfleur.fr

From the outside, the red-timbered former home of **Érik Satie** – open to visitors as **Les Maisons Satie** – looks unchanged since the composer was born there in 1866. Step inside, however, and you'll find yourself in Normandy's most unusual and eccentric museum. It's worth finding out a little about Satie before visiting, as the unconventional exhibits provide few facts. Instead, as befits a close associate of the Surrealists, the composer is commemorated by all sorts of weird and wonderful interactive surprises. It would be a shame to give too many of them away here; suffice it to say that you're immediately confronted by a giant pear, bouncing into the air on huge wings to the strains of his best-known piano series, *Gymnopédies*.

## ARRIVAL AND INFORMATION | HONFLEUR

**By train** The nearest train station, 20km south at Pont-l'Évêque, is connected to Honfleur by the Lisieux bus #50 (20min).

**By bus** The *gare routière*, a 10min walk east of the Vieux Bassin, is served by frequent buses from Caen and Le Havre (☎ 08 10 21 42 14, ⓦ www.busverts.fr).

**Tourist office** Quai Le Paulmier (Easter–June & Sept Mon–Sat 9.30am–12.30pm & 2–6.30pm, Sun 10am–12.30pm & 2–5pm; July & Aug Mon–Sat 9.30am–7pm, Sun 10am–5pm; Oct–Easter Mon–Sat 9.30am–12.30pm & 2–6pm, Sun 10am–1pm in school hols only; ☎ 02 31 89 23 30, ⓦ ot-honfleur.fr). The office offers cheap internet access.

## ACCOMMODATION

Honfleur is an expensive destination, especially in summer; budget travellers would do better simply to visit for the day. No hotels overlook the harbour itself, while motorists will find it hard to park anywhere near most central hotels.

**5**

**Les Cascades** 17 le cours des Fossés ☎ 02 31 89 05 83, ⓦ lescascades.com. Seventeen-room hotel-restaurant that opens onto both place Thiers and the cobbled rue de la Ville behind. Slightly noisy rooms upstairs, and a good-value restaurant with outdoor seating; menus €16.50–35. Closed Jan & Dec. €71

★ **La Cour Sainte-Catherine** 74 rue du Puits ☎ 02 31 89 42 40, ⓦ giaglis.com. Beautiful B&B tucked down a quiet street beyond Ste-Catherine church. Comfortable, well-decorated rooms around a plant-filled courtyard, with breakfast served in the old cider press. €120

**L'Ex Voto** 8 place Albert-Sorel ☎ 02 31 89 19 69. Four clean, well-priced rooms above a friendly family-run bistro, a short walk inland along the main road from the Vieux Bassin. Two are en suite, the others share a shower and toilet. Rates include breakfast. Closed Nov & Dec. €60

**Des Loges** 18 rue Brûlée ☎ 02 31 89 38 26, ⓦ www .hoteldesloges.com. Smart, brightly refurbished hotel, spread through three houses on a cobbled street 100m from Ste-Catherine church. It's run by helpful staff and offers good but expensive accommodation. Closed Jan. €114

**Les Maisons de Léa** Place Ste-Catherine ☎ 02 31 14 49 49, ⓦ lesmaisonsdelea.com. This magnificent hotel spreads through four seventeenth-century houses on Honfleur's central square. Rooms range from spacious doubles to family suites and a self-catering cottage; each has its own quirks and treasures, all are luxurious. No restaurant; only breakfast is served. €150

★ **Monet** Charrière du Puits ☎ 02 31 89 00 90, ⓦ hotel-monet-honfleur.com. Spruce, modern en-suite rooms, in a welcoming ivy-covered house in a very quiet spot 10min walk uphill from the centre. Courtyard parking available. €96

**Du Phare** Place Jean-de-Vienne, bd Charles V ☎ 02 31 89 10 26, ⓦ www.campings-plage.fr. Honfleur's relatively low-key two-star campsite is set just off the main road to the west, an easy walk from the heart of town. Closed Oct–March. €19.70

## EATING

With its abundance of visitors, Honfleur supports an astonishing number of restaurants, many specializing in seafood. Few face onto the harbour itself; instead, most of the narrow buildings around its edge are home to cafés and ice-cream parlours.

**Au P'tit Mareyeur** 4 rue Haute ☎ 02 31 98 84 23, ⓦ auptitmareyeur.fr. No distance from the centre, but all the seating is indoors and there are no views. Very good fish dishes, plus plenty of creamy pays d'Auge sauces and superb desserts. Menus from €30; the €38 option centres on a sumptuous bouillabaisse. Feb–Dec Mon & Thurs–Sun noon–2pm & 7.30–9.30pm.

**Le Bréard** 7 rue du Puits ☎ 02 31 89 53 49, ⓦ restaurant -lebreard.com. Highly creative, contemporary take on classic French cuisine, in a fine old mansion just off the church square that's been hollowed out and remodelled from the inside. Don't expect to be bludgeoned with heavy sauces and huge portions; here things are very much lighter and more delicate. Dinner menus €29–55. Wed 7–9.30pm,

Thurs–Sun noon–2pm & 7–9.30pm; closed 3 weeks in Dec.

**La Cidrerie** 26 place Hamelin ☎ 02 31 89 59 85, ⓦ creperie-lacidrerie-honfleur.com. This lively and convivial old cider bar also serves a wide range of crêpes and galettes, including on an €11 lunch menu. Daily noon–10pm; closed Tues & Wed in low season.

**L'Endroit** 3 rue Bréard ☎ 02 31 88 08 43. Hip modern bistro, not far inland from the tourist office, in a loft-like former industrial space with a large open kitchen. An inventive mélange of Mediterranean cuisines with the odd Asian tinge; look out for clams with chorizo, or the cider-based pork curry. Menus from €26. Wed 7.30–10pm, Thurs–Sun noon–2.30pm & 7.30–10pm.

# Trouville and Deauville

As you head west along the corniche from Honfleur, green fields and fruit trees lull the land's edge, and cliffs rise from sandy beaches all the way to the sister towns of **Trouville**, 15km away, and **Deauville**, just beyond.

Of the twin towns of Trouville and Deauville, **TROUVILLE** is more of a real town, with a constant population and industries other than tourism. But it's still a resort, with a tangle of pedestrian streets just back from the beach that are alive with restaurants and hotels, and a busy boardwalk running along a sandy beach.

**DEAUVILLE** is slightly larger than its neighbour, and significantly smarter, its sleek streets lined with designer boutiques and chic cafés. In summer, life revolves around the beach and the *planches*, 650m of boardwalk, beyond which rows of primary-coloured parasols obscure the view of the sea.

The town is best known for its **American Film Festival** (ⓦ www.festival-deauville.com), held in the first week of September. It's the antithesis of the snootier Cannes shindig, with public admission to a wide selection of previews.

## ARRIVAL AND DEPARTURE
### TROUVILLE AND DEAUVILLE

**By train and bus** Trouville and Deauville share their *gare SNCF* and *gare routière*, located between the two just south of the marina.

Destinations (train) Lisieux (5 daily in winter, much more frequently in summer; 20min); Paris (5 daily in winter, much more frequently in summer; 2hr).

Destinations (bus). Caen (hourly; 1hr 15min); Honfleur (10 daily; 30min).

**By plane** In summer only, CityJet (ⓦ cityjet.com) flies from London's City Airport direct to Deauville (4 weekly; 1hr).

## INFORMATION

**Trouville tourist office** 32 quai Fernand Moureaux (April–June, Sept & Oct Mon–Sat 9.30am–noon & 2–6.30pm, Sun 10am–1pm; July & Aug Mon–Sat 9.30am–7pm, Sun 10am–4pm; Nov–March Mon–Sat 9.30am–noon & 1.30–6.30pm, Sun 10am–1pm; ☎ 02 31 14 60 70, ⓦ trouvillesurmer.org).

**Deauville tourist office** 112 rue Victor Hugo (July & Aug Mon–Sat 9am–7pm, Sun 10am–6pm; Sept–June Mon–Sat 10am–6pm, Sun 10am–1pm & 2–5pm; ☎ 02 31 14 40 00, ⓦ deauville.org).

## ACCOMMODATION

★ **Flaubert** Rue Gustave-Flaubert, Trouville ☎ 02 31 88 37 23, ⓦ www.flaubert.fr. If you fancy staying right on the seafront, it's hard to beat this great-value faux-timbered mansion at the start of Trouville's boardwalk, where the spacious, comfortable rooms have large bathrooms and in many cases balconies. **€80**

**Des Sports** 27 rue Gambetta, Deauville ☎ 02 31 88 22 67. Nine well-priced, en-suite rooms above a popular local bar behind Deauville's fish market. Closed March & Nov, plus Sun in winter. **€65**

## EATING

**Chez Miocque** 81 rue Eugène-Colas, Deauville ☎ 02 31 88 09 52, ⓦ chez-miocque.fr. Everyone who's anyone in Deauville drops in at some point in this bustling, top-quality Parisian-style bistro, to snack on anything from hard-boiled eggs to steak and chips, or enjoy a full three-course meal for €40. Feb–Dec daily noon–11pm; closed Tues & Wed in winter.

**La Petite Auberge** 7 rue Carnot, Trouville ☎ 02 31 88 11 07, ⓦ lapetiteaubergesurmer.fr. Small, intimate restaurant a short walk inland from the beach, where seafood is the speciality but the *menus*, from €35 in the evenings, always include some hearty meat dishes too. Sept–July Mon & Thurs–Sun 12.15–1.45pm & 7.15–9.30pm; Aug Wed–Mon 12.15–1.45pm & 7.15–9.30pm.

# Caen

Few tourists go out of their way to visit **CAEN**, capital and largest city of Basse Normandie. It was devastated during the fighting of 1944, so busy roads now fill the wide spaces where prewar houses stood, circling ramparts that no longer have a castle to protect. However, the former home to William the Conqueror remains impressive in parts, adorned with the scattered spires and buttresses of two abbeys and eight old churches. It also makes a convenient base for exploring the D-Day beaches.

Most of the centre is taken up with shopping streets and pedestrian precincts, with branches of the big Parisian stores and local rivals. The main city **market** takes place on Friday, spreading along both sides of Fosse St-Julien. The **Bassin St-Pierre**, the pleasure port at the end of the canal that links Caen to the sea, is the liveliest area in summer.

## Château de Caen

Although almost nothing remains of the eleventh-century Château de Caen, its ancient **ramparts** are still in place. Walking the complete circuit gives a good overview of the city, with a particularly fine prospect of the reconstructed fourteenth-century facade of the nearby church of **St-Pierre**.

**5**

Within the walls, it's possible to visit the former **Exchequer**, which once hosted a banquet thrown by Richard the Lionheart en route to the Crusades, and inspect a garden planted with the herbs and medicinal plants that would have been cultivated here during the Middle Ages.

Two modern structures inside the castle precinct hold **museums**.

## Musée des Beaux-Arts

Daily except Tues 9.30am–6pm • €3.10; special exhibitions extra • ☎ 02 31 30 47 70, ⓦ www.mba.caen.fr

In the **Musé des Beaux-Arts**, upstairs galleries trace a potted history of European art from Renaissance Italy to eighteenth-century France. Downstairs brings things up to date with diverse twentieth-century and contemporary art as well as paintings by Monet, Bonnard and Gustave Doré.

## Musée de Normandie

June–Oct daily 9.30am–6pm; Nov–May daily except Tues 9.30am–6pm • €3.10; special exhibitions extra • ☎ 02 31 30 47 60, ⓦ musee-de-normandie.eu

The **Musée de Normandie** provides a surprisingly cursory overview of Norman history, ranging from archeological finds from the megalithic period and glass jewellery from Gallo-Roman Rouen to artefacts from the Industrial Revolution. It also hosts regular temporary exhibitions.

## Abbaye aux Hommes

Rue St-Pierre • Mon–Sat 8.30am–12.30pm & 1.30–7pm, Sun 8.30am–12.30pm & 2.30–7pm; 1hr 15min guided tours leave adjacent Hôtel de Ville daily 9.30am, 11am, 2.30pm & 4pm; tours in English mid-July to Aug only, times vary • Free; tours €4, free on Sun • ☎ 02 31 30 42 81, ⓦ caen.fr/abbayeauxhommes

The spectacular Romanesque monument known as the **Abbaye aux Hommes** was founded by William the Conqueror and designed to hold his tomb within the huge, austere Romanesque church of St-Étienne. However, his burial here, in 1087, was hopelessly undignified. The funeral procession first caught fire and was then held to ransom, as various factions squabbled over his rotting corpse for any spoils they could grab. During the Revolution the tomb was again ransacked, and now holds a solitary thigh-bone rescued from the river. The eighteenth-century abbey buildings adjoining the church now house the Hôtel de Ville.

## Abbaye aux Dames

Rue des Chanoines • Daily 2–5.30pm; guided tours 2.30pm & 4pm • Free

Corresponding to William the Conqueror's Abbaye aux Hommes, on the other side of the town centre, the **Abbaye aux Dames** holds the tomb of William's queen, Mathilda. She commissioned the building of the abbey church, La Trinité, well before the Conquest. It's starkly impressive, with a gloomy pillared crypt, superb stained glass behind the altar, and odd sculptural details like the fish curled up in the holy-water stoup.

## The Caen Memorial

Av Marshal-Montgomery • Late Jan to mid-Feb & mid-Nov to Dec daily except Mon 9.30am–6pm; mid-Feb to mid-Nov daily 9am–7pm; closed 3 weeks in Jan; last entry 1hr 15min before closing • May–Sept €18.80; Oct–April €18.30 • ☎ 02 31 06 06 44, ⓦ memorial-caen.fr • Bus #2 from stop "Tour le Roi" in central Caen

Just north of Caen, the **Caen Memorial** stands on a plateau named after General Eisenhower on a clifftop beneath which the Germans had their HQ in June and July 1944. A typically French, high-tech museum, its excellent displays are divided into several distinct sections. Originally a "museum for peace", its brief has expanded to cover history since the Great War; allow two hours at the very least for a visit. It begins with the rise of fascism in Germany, follows with resistance and collaboration in France, then charts all the major battles of World War II, with a special emphasis on D-Day and its aftermath.

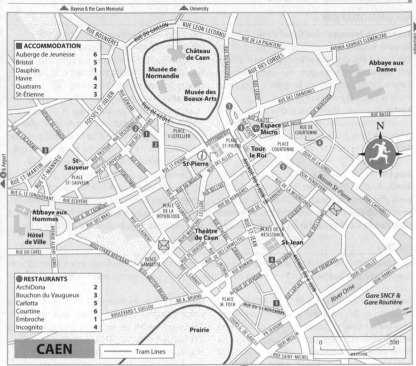

**CAEN**

▲ Bayeux & the Caen Memorial ▲ University ▶ Ouistreham ◀ & Airport ◀ & Airport

**ACCOMMODATION**
| | |
|---|---|
| Auberge de Jeunesse | 6 |
| Bristol | 5 |
| Dauphin | 1 |
| Havre | 4 |
| Quatrans | 2 |
| St-Étienne | 3 |

**RESTAURANTS**
| | |
|---|---|
| ArchiDona | 2 |
| Bouchon du Vaugueux | 3 |
| Carlotta | 5 |
| Courtine | 6 |
| Embroche | 1 |
| Incognito | 4 |

Tram Lines

Further areas examine the Cold War, and Berlin in particular. Most captions, though not always the written exhibits themselves, are translated into English. The memorial also hosts temporary exhibitions, and has a good-value self-service restaurant.

## ARRIVAL AND DEPARTURE
CAEN

**By train** Caen's *gare SNCF* is 1km south of the centre, across the river Orne.

Destinations Cherbourg (10 daily; 1hr 15min), via Bayeux (20min); Lisieux (21 daily; 30min); Le Mans (5 daily; 2hr), via Alençon (1hr 15min); Paris-St-Lazare (11 daily; 2hr 10min); Rennes (4 daily; 3hr), via St-Lô (50min), Coutances (1hr 15min) and Pontorson (2hr); Rouen (6 daily; 2hr).

**By bus** The *gare routière* is alongside the *gare SNCF*, 1km

south of the centre.

Destinations Arromanches (1 daily; 1hr 10min); Bayeux (3 daily; 50min); Clécy (4 daily; 50min); Falaise (7 daily; 1hr); Honfleur (13 daily; 2hr), via Cabourg (50min), Houlgate (1hr) and Deauville (1hr 51min), of which 5 continue to Le Havre (2hr 30min); Le Havre (3 daily express services; 1hr 20min), via Honfleur (1hr); Ouistreham (20 daily; 30min); Thury-Harcourt (5 daily; 40min).

## GETTING AROUND

**By bus and tram** Caen's buses and trams are run by TWISTO (☎ 02 31 15 55 55, ◍ twisto.fr). Single journeys cost €1.30, and a 24-hour pass €3.65 per adult, €5.40 per

family. The main tram route connects the southern and northern suburbs, running through the centre from the *gare SNCF* up av du 6-juin to the university and beyond.

## INFORMATION

**Tourist office** Place St-Pierre (March Mon–Sat 9.30am–1pm & 2–6.30pm; April–June & Sept Mon–Sat 9.30am–6.30pm, Sun 10am–1pm; July & Aug Mon–Sat 9am–7pm, Sun 10am–1pm & 2–5pm; Oct–Feb Mon–Sat 9.30am–1pm & 2–6pm; ☎ 02 31 27 14 14,

◍ www.tourisme.caen.fr).
**Internet** You can go online at Espace Micro, on place Courtonne at 1 rue Basse, or at the main post office on place Gambetta (Mon–Fri 8am–7pm, Sat 8.30am–12.30pm).

**5**

## ACCOMMODATION

**Auberge de Jeunesse** Foyer Robert-Remé, 68bis rue Eustache Restout, Grâce-de-Dieu ☏ 02 31 52 19 96, ⓦ fuaj.org/Caen. Lively and welcoming hostel in a sleepy area 2km southwest of the *gare SNCF*. Beds in four-bed dorms or two-bed private rooms. Reception 5–9pm. Closed Oct–May. Dorms €12; doubles €24

**Bristol** 31 rue du 11-Novembre ☏ 02 31 84 59 76, ⓦ hotelbristolcaen.com. Efficient, spruce, friendly and inexpensive hotel, in a quiet location an easy walk across the river from the train station. Rooms are small, but not bad for the price. €70

**Dauphin** 29 rue Gémare ☏ 02 31 86 22 26, ⓦ le-dauphin -normandie.com. Upmarket *Best Western* hotel behind the tourist office. The public areas are impressive, while the rooms are comfortable but relatively compact, at least at the lower end of the price scale. Sauna and fitness facilities are available

– for a price – and there's a grand restaurant. €140

★ **Havre** 11 rue du Havre ☏ 02 31 86 19 80, ⓦ hotelduhavre.com. Modern, cosy, welcoming and very good-value budget hotel, a block south of St-Jean church, close to the trams and with free parking. €65

**Quatrans** 17 rue Gémare ☏ 02 31 86 25 57, ⓦ hotel-des -quatrans.com. Fully renovated hotel in an anonymous modern setting, a very short walk from the tourist office and the château. The pastel theme of the facade continues inside; some might find it a bit cloying, but the service is friendly, and everything works well. All rooms are en suite. €80

**St-Étienne** 2 rue de l'Académie ☏ 02 31 86 35 82, ⓦ hotel-saint-etienne.com. Friendly budget hotel in a venerable stone house in the characterful St-Martin district, not far from the Abbaye aux Hommes. The cheapest rooms share bathrooms; en-suite ones cost a little more. €35

## EATING

Caen's town centre offers two major areas for eating, with cosmopolitan restaurants in the largely pedestrianized quartier Vaugueux and more traditional French restaurants on the streets off rue de Geôle, near the western ramparts.

**ArchiDona** 17 rue Gémare ☏ 02 31 85 30 30, ⓦ www .archidona.fr. This classy and atmospheric restaurant, adjoining the Quatrans hotel, serves delightfully fresh Mediterranean-influenced cuisine, ranging from simple entrée-plus-dessert meals at €16 up to the €37 "seduction" and €49 "emotion" *menus*. Tues–Thurs noon–2pm & 7–9.30pm, Fri & Sat noon–2pm & 7–10pm.

★ **Bouchon du Vaugueux** 12 rue Graindorge ☏ 02 31 44 26 26, ⓦ bouchonduvaugueux.com. Intimate little brasserie in the Vaugueux quarter, offering well-prepared French classics on just two *menus* (€19 and €28). Tues–Thurs noon–2pm & 7–10pm, Fri & Sat noon–2pm & 7–10.30pm.

**Carlotta** 16 quai Vendeuvre ☏ 02 31 86 68 99, ⓦ www .lecarlotta.fr. Smart, busy, fashionable Parisian-style brasserie beside the pleasure port, which serves good Norman cooking both à la carte and on *menus* at €24.50 (not Fri & Sat), €29.50 and €38. Mon–Thurs noon– midnight, Fri & Sat noon–11pm.

**Courtine** 16 rue Caponière ☏ 02 31 79 19 16. Behind a simple side-street shopfront, a short walk west of the Abbaye aux Hommes, this friendly local restaurant serves a different short *menu* daily; €19 buys excellent local cuisine, with an emphasis on fresh salads. Tues, Wed, Fri & Sat noon–2pm & 7.30–9.30pm, Thurs noon–2pm.

**Embroche** 17 rue de la Porte au Berger ☏ 02 31 93 71 31. Cosy little place, where the open kitchen whips up simple regional specialities in full view of appreciative diners, with lunch from €17.50 and dinner from €25; there are also a few outdoor tables. Tues–Fri noon–2pm & 7–9.30pm, Sat 7–10pm.

**Incognito** 14 rue de Courtonne ☏ 02 31 28 36 60, ⓦ stephanecarbone.fr. Stylish, up-to-the-minute, Michelin-starred restaurant, specializing in Asian-influenced cuisine with a flair for both presentation and flavour. The most expensive *menu*, at €96, is devoted entirely to lobster, but you can sample Stéphane Carbone's cooking on *menus* from €26 at lunchtime, €37 in the evening. Mon–Fri noon–2pm & 7.30–10pm, Sat 7.30–10pm.

# Bayeux

With its perfectly preserved medieval ensemble, magnificent **cathedral** and world-famous **tapestry**, BAYEUX is smaller and much more intimate than its near neighbour Caen, and a far more enjoyable place to visit. A mere 10km from the coast, Bayeux was the first French city to be liberated in 1944, the day after D-Day. Occupied so quickly that it escaped serious damage, it briefly became capital of Free France.

**CLOCKWISE FROM TOP LEFT** AÎTRE ST-MACLOU (P.267); CHÂTEAU GUILLAUME-LE-CONQUÉRANT (P.280); CHEESE AT A MARKET STALL; ABBAYE DE JUMIÈGES (P.271) >

**5**

## Centre Guillaume le Conquérant (Bayeux Tapestry)

Rue de Nesmond • Daily: first week of Jan & late Jan to mid-March 9.30am–12.30pm & 2–6pm; mid-March to April & Sept to mid-Nov 9am–6.30pm; May–Aug 9am–7pm; mid-Nov to Christmas 9am–6.30pm; closed middle fortnight of Jan; last admission 45min before closing • €7.80 • ☎ 02 31 51 25 50, ⓦ tapisserie-bayeux.fr

A grand eighteenth-century seminary, now remodelled as the **Centre Guillaume le Conquérant**, houses the extraordinary **Bayeux Tapestry**, known to the French as the *Tapisserie de la Reine Mathilde*. Unexpectedly, and unceremoniously, the first thing you see on entry is the tapestry itself, with an interesting audio-guided commentary to explain the events it so vividly depicts.

Only afterwards comes an exhibition detailing the theories that surround the tapestry's creation, and explaining more about its turbulent history, followed by a film (shown in English at least once an hour in summer) that gives more of the historical background.

## Cathédrale Notre-Dame

Daily: Jan–March 9am–5pm; April–June & Oct–Dec 9am–6pm; July–Sept 9am–7pm • Free

The **Cathédrale Notre-Dame**, the first home of the Bayeux Tapestry, stands just a short walk from its latest resting place. The original Romanesque plan of the building is still intact, although only the crypt and towers date from the original work of 1077. The crypt is a beauty, its columns graced with frescoes of angels playing trumpets and bagpipes, looking exhausted by their performance for eternity.

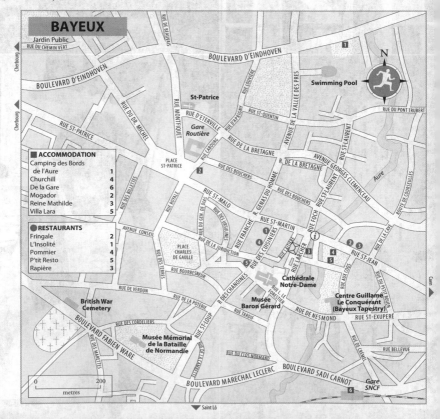

## THE BAYEUX TAPESTRY

Created more than nine centuries ago, the 70m strip of linen known as the **Bayeux Tapestry** recounts the story of the Norman Conquest of England. The brilliance of its coloured wools has barely faded, and the tale is enlivened throughout with scenes of medieval life, popular fables and mythical beasts; its draughtsmanship, and the sheer vigour and detail, are stunning. Commissioned by Bishop Oddo, William's half-brother, for the inauguration of Bayeux Cathedral in 1077, the work is thought to have been carried out by nuns in England, most likely in Canterbury.

The tapestry looks, and reads, like a modern comic strip. While it's generally considered to be historically accurate, William's justification for his invasion – that during an enforced sojourn after he was rescued by William following a shipwreck on the coast of northern France, Harold had sworn to accept him as King of England – remains in dispute.

In the tapestry itself, Harold is every inch the villain, with his dastardly little moustache and shifty eyes. At the point when he breaks his oath and seizes the throne, Harold looks extremely pleased with himself; however, his comeuppance swiftly follows, as William crosses the Channel and defeats the English armies at Hastings.

Alongside the cathedral, the former palace of the archbishops of Bayeux was at the time of research being remodelled to serve as a museum devoted to the extensive Episcopal collection of porcelain and lacework.

## Musée Mémorial de la Bataille de Normandie

Bd Fabian Ware • Daily: May–Sept 9.30am–6.30pm; Oct–April 10am–12.30pm & 2–6pm • €7 • ☎ 02 31 51 46 90

Set behind massive guns on the southwest side of town, Bayeux's **Musée Mémorial de la Bataille de Normandie** provides a readily accessible, visceral and highly visual overview of the Battle of Normandy. Rather than endless military hardware, it's filled with colour photos, maps and display panels that trace the development of the campaign, with good sections on German counter-attacks and the role of the press. The understated and touching **British War Cemetery** stands immediately across the road.

### ARRIVAL AND INFORMATION

BAYEUX

**By train** The *gare SNCF* is 15min walk southeast of the town centre, just outside the ring road.

**By bus** Buses stop both at the *gare SNCF* and across town, on the north side of place St-Patrice.

Destinations Arromanches (4 daily; 30min); Ouistreham (3 daily; 1hr 15min).

**Tourist office** On the arched pont St-Jean, in the town centre (Jan–March & Nov–Dec Mon–Sat 9.30am–12.30pm & 2–5.30pm; April, May, Sept & Oct Mon–Sat 9.30am–12.30pm & 2–6pm, Sun 10am–1pm & 2–6pm; June–Aug Mon–Sat 9am–7pm, Sun 9am–1pm & 2–6pm; ☎ 02 31 51 28 22, ⓦ bessin-normandie.com).

### ACCOMMODATION

**Camping des Bords de l'Aure** Bd d'Eindhoven ☎ 02 31 92 08 43, ⓦ camping-bayeux.fr. Large three-star municipal campsite, near the river on the northern ring road (RN13). Well-shaded tent sites, rental cabins, and free access to the local swimming pool alongside. Closed early Nov to early April. **€13.17**

★ **Churchill** 14–16 rue St-Jean ☎ 02 31 21 31 80, ⓦ hotel-churchill.fr. Perfectly situated in the heart of town, with its own free parking, this beautifully furnished 32-room hotel has no restaurant, but offers personal and friendly service. Closed Dec–Feb. **€115**

**De la Gare** 26 place de la Gare ☎ 02 31 92 10 70, ⓦ hotel -delagare-bayeux.fr. Set beside the station, a 15min walk

from the cathedral, this is a basic but perfectly adequate hotel, with fourteen en-suite rooms (showers not baths) and a simple brasserie. Tours of D-Day beaches arranged through Normandy Tours (see p.282), who are based here. **€44**

**Mogador** 20 rue Chartier ☎ 02 31 92 24 58, ⓦ hotel -mogador-bayeux.fr. Friendly little hotel facing Bayeux's main square; the fourteen varied rooms are simple but very presentable, with the quieter ones overlooking the inner courtyard. Some sleep three or four. **€57**

**Reine Mathilde** 23 rue Larcher ☎ 02 31 92 08 13, ⓦ hotel-reinemathilde.com. Simple but well-equipped en-suite rooms backing onto the canal, between the

**5**

tapestry and the cathedral. There's a nice open-air brasserie/crêperie downstairs. Closed Dec–Feb. **€85**
**Villa Lara** 6 place du Québec ☎02 31 92 00 55, ⓦhotel -villalara.com. Brand new luxury hotel, tucked away in a peaceful square close to the Tapestry. All its 28 large, exceptionally comfortable rooms enjoy cathedral views; there's no restaurant, but staff prepare and serve excellent breakfasts. **€155**

### EATING

**Fringale** 43 rue St-Jean ☎02 31 21 34 40. The nicest of the pavement restaurants along rue St-Jean, offering lunch *menus* from €16.50, generous salads and snacks, and formal fish dinners. Mon & Thurs–Sun noon–2pm & 7–9.30pm.
**L'Insolité** 16 rue des Cuisiniers ☎02 31 51 71 16. Cheap but chic crêperie serving an imaginative range of savoury *galettes* followed by sweet crêpes. Daily noon–2pm & 7–9.30pm; closed Mon in low season.
**Pommier** 38–40 rue des Cuisiniers ☎02 31 21 52 10, ⓦrestaurantlepommier.com. Traditional restaurant near the cathedral, with a tiny terrace. Meat- and dairy-rich Norman cuisine on *menus* from €14 (lunch only) up to €35, including a €27.45 vegetarian option that centres on a soya steak. Mid-March to Oct daily noon–2pm & 7–9.30pm.
**P'tit Resto** 2 rue Bienvenue ☎02 31 51 85 40, ⓦrestaurantbayeux.com. Tiny old place opposite the cathedral, where the "creative cuisine" extends to veal chop fried in wasabi, and rolled monkfish with tandoori stuffing. *Menus* from €17 at lunch, €22 at dinner. Tues–Sat noon–2pm & 7–9.30pm.
**Rapière** 53 rue St-Jean ☎02 31 21 05 45, ⓦlarapiere .net. Hidden away just off the main pedestrianized street, this cosy little restaurant feels as though it's been here forever – certainly its old-fashioned Norman cooking remains as dependable as ever, on copious €28.50 and €37 dinner *menus*. Mon, Tues, & Fri–Sun noon–1.30pm & 7–9.30pm.

## The D-Day beaches

At dawn on **D-Day**, June 6, 1944, Allied troops landed at points along the Normandy coast from the mouth of the Orne to the eastern Cotentin Peninsula. For the most part, the shore consists of innocuous beaches backed by gentle dunes, and yet this foothold in Europe was won at the cost of 100,000 lives. The ensuing **Battle of Normandy** killed thousands of civilians and reduced nearly six hundred towns and villages to rubble, but within a week of its eventual conclusion, Paris was liberated.

The various D-Day beaches are still widely referred to by their wartime code names. The British and Commonwealth forces landed on **Sword**, **Juno** and **Gold** beaches between Ouistreham and Arromanches; the Americans, further west on **Omaha** and **Utah** beaches. Substantial traces of the fighting are rare, the most remarkable being the remains of the astounding **Mulberry Harbour** at **Arromanches**, 10km northeast of Bayeux. Further west, at **Pointe du Hoc** on Omaha Beach, the cliff heights are deeply pitted with German bunkers and shell holes, while the church at **Ste-Mère-Église**, from whose steeple the US paratrooper dangled during heavy fighting throughout *The Longest Day*, still stands, and now has a model parachute permanently fastened to the roof.

World War II **cemeteries** dot the Normandy countryside. While most of the French dead were taken home for burial in the churchyards of their home towns, the remains of fallen foreigners were gathered into cemeteries devoted to the separate warring nations. In total, over 140,000 young men were disinterred; more than half of the 31,744 US casualties were repatriated. In addition, almost every coastal town has its own **war museum**, in which the wealth of incidental human detail can be overpowering.

---

### D-DAY TOURS

The Caen Memorial (see p.276) organizes informative bilingual **guided tours** of the beaches in summer (June–Aug Wed, Fri & Sat, plus Sun in high summer; departs 1pm; €39, ages 2–9 €30); the price includes admission to the Memorial, not necessarily on the same day.

Other operators offering D-Day tours, at typical prices of around €50/half-day and €80/day, include Normandy Sightseeing Tours (☎02 31 51 70 52, ⓦd-daybeaches.com), Victory Tours (☎02 31 51 98 14, ⓦvictorytours.com), and Normandy Tours (☎02 31 92 10 70, ⓦnormandy-landing-tour.com).

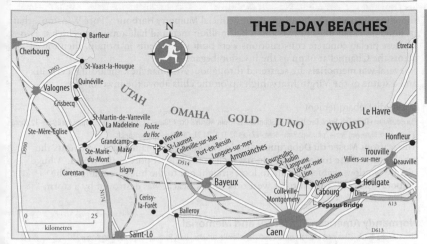

## Ouistreham

**OUISTREHAM-RIVA BELLA**, on the coast 15km north of Caen, is that rare thing, a cross-Channel ferry port that remains a small seaside resort. From the harbour, at its eastern end, it's easy to head straight out on the main road towards Caen. Head west instead, and you'll soon come to the handful of charming streets at the heart of the old town. The sea itself lies a couple of hundred metres north, along the semi-pedestrianized **avenue de la Mer**, home to several inexpensive snack bars and restaurants. Strictly speaking, the waterfront, backing a long straight beach, is a separate community known as **Riva Bella**. Its large central **casino**, on place Alfred-Thomas, has been remodelled as a 1930s passenger liner, housing an expensive restaurant and cocktail bar, while gloriously old-fashioned bathing huts face onto the sands.

### Musée du Mur de l'Atlantique

Av du 6-Juin • Daily: Feb, March & Oct–Dec 10am–6pm; April–Sept 9am–7pm • €7 • ☎ 02 31 97 28 69, ⓦ www.musee-grand-bunker.com

Also known as the Grand Bunker, the **Musée du Mur de l'Atlantique** is housed in a lofty bunker that was headquarters to several German batteries defending the mouth of the River Orne, and fell to Allied forces on June 9, 1944. Inside, displays re-create the living quarters, with newspapers, cutlery and cigarette packets adding a welcome human touch to the moderately interesting explanations of the generators, gas filters and radio room.

### Pegasus Bridge

5km south of Ouistreham • **Mémorial Pegasus** Daily: Feb, March, Oct & Nov 10am–5pm; April–Sept 9.30am–6.30pm • €6 • ☎ 02 31 78 19 44, ⓦ memorial-pegasus.org

South of Ouistreham, the main road towards Caen passes close by the site now known as **Pegasus Bridge**. On the night before D-Day, the twin bridges across the Caen canal and the River Orne here were the target of a daring but successful Allied glider assault. Replaced in 1994, the original bridge is the focus of the **Mémorial Pegasus** immediately east. This vaguely glider-shaped museum explains the attack in detail, accompanied by the expected array of helmets, goggles, medals and other memorabilia, most captioned in English, as well as photographs and models used to plan the attack.

### Arromanches

While basically a little seaside village, **ARROMANCHES**, cradled between high cliffs 31km west of Ouistreham, has the strongest identity of all the resorts along this

**5**

shoreline. This was the location of the artificial **Mulberry Harbour**, "Port Winston", that facilitated the landings of two and a half million men and half a million vehicles. Two of these prefab concrete constructions were built in segments in Britain, then towed across the Channel at 6kph as the invasion began.

Several **war memorials** are scattered throughout Arromanches, including a crucifix and a statue of the Virgin Mary, high up on the cliffs above the invasion site.

## Musée du Débarquement

Place du 6 Juin • Daily: Feb, Nov & Dec 10am–12.30pm & 1.30–5pm; March & Oct 9.30am–12.30pm & 1.30–5.30pm; April 9am–12.30pm & 1.30–6pm; May–Aug 9am–7pm; Sept 9am–6pm • €7 • ☏ 02 31 22 34 31, ⓦ musee-arromanches.fr

The seafront **Musée du Débarquement**, in Arromanches' main square, recounts the whole story of the town's three-month spell as the busiest port in the world. A huge picture window enables visitors to look straight out to the bulky remains of the harbour (the other one, further west on Omaha Beach, was destroyed by a storm within a few weeks).

## Normandy American Cemetery and Memorial

Above Omaha Beach, 21km west of Arromanches, outside Colleville-sur-Mer • Daily 9am–6pm • Free • ⓦ abmc.gov

In the vast **Normandy American Cemetery and Memorial**, near the Pointe du Hoc, neat rows of crosses cover the clifftop lawns. There are no individual epitaphs, just gold lettering for a few exceptional warriors. At one end, a muscular giant dominates a huge array of battlefield plans and diagrams covered with surging arrows and pincer movements. Barack Obama is the latest of many US presidents to have paid his respects here; another president's son, General Theodore Roosevelt Jr, is among those buried.

A high-tech visitor centre explains the events of 1944 and the American role in them. Poignant multimedia displays focus on the personal angle, highlighting the stories of both casualties and survivors.

## Utah Beach

The westernmost of the Invasion Beaches, **Utah Beach** stretches up the eastern shore of the Cotentin Peninsula, running 30km north towards St-Vaast (see p.287). From 6.30am onwards on D-Day, 23,000 men and 1700 vehicles landed here. A minor coast road, the D421, traces the edge of the dunes and enables visitors to follow the course of the fighting, though in truth there's precious little to see these days. Ships deliberately sunk to create artificial breakwaters are still visible at low tide, while markers along the seafront commemorate individual fallen heroes.

In the comprehensive **Musée du Débarquement d'Utah-Beach** in **STE-MARIE-DU-MONT**, huge sea-view windows lend immediacy to the copious models, maps, films and diagrams (daily: Feb, March & Nov 10am–5.30pm; April, May & Oct 10am–6pm; June–Sept 9.30am–7pm; last admission 45min before closing; €7.50; ☏02 33 71 53 35, ⓦutah-beach.com). The **Mémorial de la Liberté** in **QUINÉVILLE** focuses on everyday life for the people of Normandy under Nazi occupation (late March to mid-Nov daily 10am–7pm; €6; ☏02 33 95 95 95, ⓦwww.memorial-quineville.com).

| **GETTING AROUND** | **THE D-DAY BEACHES** |
|---|---|

**By bus** Bus Verts (☏08 10 21 42 14, ⓦ www.busverts.fr) run all along this coast. From Bayeux, bus #74 goes to Arromanches, Courseulles and Ouistreham, and bus #70 to the Pointe du Hoc, the US cemetery at Colleville-sur-Mer and Port-en-Bessin. From Caen, bus #30 runs inland to Bayeux, express bus #1 to Ouistreham, and express bus #3 to Courseulles.

| **INFORMATION** | |
|---|---|

**OUISTREHAM**
**Tourist office** Esplanade Lofi, alongside the casino (April–June & Sept daily 10am–12.30pm & 2–6.30pm; July & Aug daily 10am–1pm & 2–7pm; Oct–March Mon–Sat 10am–12.30pm & 2.30–6pm, Sun 2.30–5.30pm; ☏02 31 97 18 63, ⓦville-ouistreham.fr).

**Tourist office** 2 rue Maréchal-Joffre (Feb, March & Oct–Dec daily 10am–noon & 2–5pm; April & Sept Mon–Sat 9.30am–12.30pm & 2–6pm, Sun 10am–12.30pm & 2–6pm; May–Aug daily 9.30am–12.30pm & 2–7pm; ☎ 02 31 22 36 45, ⊛ ot-arromanches.fr).

## ACCOMMODATION AND EATING

### OUISTREHAM

**Normandie** 71 av Michel-Cabieu ☎ 02 31 97 19 57, ⊛ lenormandie.com. This smart hotel, very close to the ferry port, has pleasant, quiet rooms, while its restaurant (closed Sun eve, plus Mon Nov–March) serves good three-course *menus* from €23.50. Closed Jan. **€71**

### ARROMANCHES

**La Marine** 1 quai Canada ☎ 02 31 22 34 19, ⊛ hotel-de-la-marine.fr. At the centre of Arromanches' seafront, ideally placed for the D-Day sights and the beach, this comfortable hotel offers sizeable sea-view rooms and a high-class restaurant serving fishy *menus* from €24. **€106**

# Cherbourg

Though its heyday as a transatlantic passenger port is now long gone, the sizeable town of **CHERBOURG**, at the northern tip of the Cotentin peninsula, makes an appealing point of arrival in France. Its **Old Town**, immediately west of the quayside, is an intriguing maze of pedestrian alleys that abounds in shops and restaurants.

The tempting array of small shops and boutiques clustered around the place Centrale includes a place to buy the city's most famous product, the genuine **Cherbourg umbrella**, at 30 rue des Portes, while the excellent Thursday **market** is held on and off rue des Halles, near the majestic theatre with its *belle époque* facade. A pleasant stroll north of the commercial zone leads to the Basilique de la Trinité and the former town beach, now grassed over to form the **Plage Vert**.

## Cité de la Mer

Daily: May, June & Sept 9.30am–6pm; July & Aug 9.30am–7pm; Oct–Dec & Feb–April 10am–6pm, with variations including longer hours in school hols, and Mon closures in March, Nov & Dec; last entry 1hr before closing • April–Sept €18, Oct–March €15.50 • ☎ 02 33 20 26 69, ⊛ citedelamer.com

Just across the pleasure port from the town centre, the **Cité de la Mer** centres on Cherbourg's former Transatlantic ferry terminal. It's divided into several sections, the newest of which opened on April 10, 2012, a hundred years to the day since the Titanic called here for two hours on her maiden voyage. Almost 300 passengers joined the ill-fated ship at Cherbourg, including such famous names as John Jacob Astor IV, Benjamin Guggenheim, and "the unsinkable" Molly Brown. Rather than reconstruct the entire Titanic, superb mock-ups of her wireless room, mailroom, and a typical first-class cabin offer an "immersive experience" that fortunately stops short of a dunking in icy waters.

The complex includes a museum that tells the story of underwater exploration in history and fiction, along with fish tanks holding such species as jellyfish, seahorses and large squid, while walkways offer views into a vast cylindrical aquarium at ever-greater depths.

In a dry dock alongside is the *Redoutable*, France's first ballistic-missile **submarine**. Visitors can scramble through its labyrinth of tube-like walkways and control rooms, though as the nuclear generator that once powered it has been removed, there's a cavernous empty space at its heart. The cramped crew quarters will feel very familiar if you've just shared a cabin on an overnight ferry crossing.

## ARRIVAL AND INFORMATION                                    CHERBOURG

**By ferry** Brittany Ferries and Irish Ferries sail into Cherbourg's *gare maritime*, not far east of the town centre and served by regular shuttle buses.

**By train** The *gare SNCF* is on av J-F Millet, a short walk south of the town centre.

Destinations Paris (8 daily; 3hr), via Valognes (15min) and Caen (1hr 15min).

**By bus** The *gare routière* is opposite the *gare SNCF*.

Destinations St-Lô (3 daily; 1hr 30min); St-Vaast (3 daily; 1hr 10min) via Barfleur (1hr).

**Tourist office** 2 quai Alexandre III (mid-June to mid-Sept Mon–Sat 9.30am–7pm, Sun 10am–5pm; mid-Sept to mid-June Mon–Sat 10am–12.30pm & 2–6pm, Sun 10am–1pm; ☎ 02 33 93 52 02, ⊛ cherbourgtourisme.com).

5

**RESTAURANTS AND CAFÉS**

| Café de Paris | 3 |
| Café du Théâtre | 4 |
| Faitout | 1 |
| Le Pily | 2 |

**ACCOMMODATION**

| Ambassadeur | 3 |
| Auberge de Jeunesse | 1 |
| De la Gare | 5 |
| Moderna | 2 |
| Régence | 4 |

CHERBOURG

▼ Valognes & Paris

## ACCOMMODATION

**Ambassadeur** 22 quai de Caligny ☎02 33 43 10 00, ⓦambassadeurhotel.com. Inexpensive, good-value central hotel on the quayside, with four storeys of en-suite rooms, many with harbour views (there's a lift). Double-glazing keeps the noise down. Decent breakfasts cost €7. **€71**

**Auberge de Jeunesse** 55 rue de l'Abbaye ☎02 33 78 15 15, ⓦfuaj.org/Cherbourg-Octeville. Well-equipped red-brick hostel, a 15min walk west of the centre and on bus routes #3 and #5. Two rooms are designed for visitors with limited mobility. Breakfast included. Check-in 9am–1pm & 6–11pm, closed 3 wks over Christmas and early Jan. **€20.60**

**De la Gare** 10 place Jean Jaurès ☎02 33 43 06 81. This conspicuous blue-trimmed budget hotel is surprisingly quiet for such a convenient location, close to the *gares SNCF* and

*routière*. The rooms may not be exactly stunning, but have en-suite facilities, and family-sized rooms are available. **€51**

**Moderna** 28 rue de la Marine ☎02 33 43 05 30, ⓦmoderna-hotel.com. Friendly, small hotel, set slightly back from the harbour, with reasonably well-priced en-suite rooms of all sizes. **€66**

**Régence** 42–44 quai de Caligny ☎02 33 43 05 16, ⓦlaregence.com. Slightly more upmarket than Cherbourg's other offerings, with antique-style British furnishings, this family-run *Logis de France* has neat, well-equipped rooms overlooking the harbour. The dining room downstairs starts with a reasonable €21 *menu*, and ranges up to €36; it's not the best restaurant along the *quai*, but there's something to be said for eating where you sleep. **€98**

**EATING AND DRINKING**

Cherbourg's restaurants divide readily into the glass-fronted seafood places along the quai de Caligny, each with its "copious" *assiette de fruits de mer*, and the more varied, less expensive little places tucked away in the pedestrianized streets and alleyways of the Old Town. This is also where you'll find some animated bars, especially along rue de l'Union.

**Café de Paris** 40 quai de Caligny ☎ 02 33 43 12 36, ⓦ restaurantcafedeparis.com. As well as fish-heavy *menus* (€18.50–36.50), you can work your way up through the ranks of *assiettes de fruits de mer*, from the €18.50 *Matelot* to the *Corsaire* at €55 for two. Mon 7–9pm, Tues–Sat noon–2pm & 7–9pm.

**Café du Théâtre** 8 place de Gaulle ☎ 02 33 43 01 49, ⓦ lecafedutheatre.com. Attractive setup adjoining the theatre, with a café behind plate-glass windows on the ground floor and a full-scale brasserie upstairs. It's a place used by the community as a whole rather than being a typical tourist restaurant, and the varied *menus*, from €13, offer more than just seafood. Mon–Sat 11am–11pm.

**★ Faitout** 25 rue Tour-Carrée ☎ 02 33 04 25 04, ⓦ restaurant-le-faitout.com. Stylish, faux-rustic fishing-themed restaurant that offers traditional French cuisine, including mussels prepared with celery, apples and the like for around €15, and has good *menus* at €21 and €35. Reservations advised in summer. Mon 7–10.30pm, Tues–Sat noon–2pm & 7–10.30pm.

**Le Pily** 39 rue Grande Rue ☎ 02 33 10 19 29, ⓦ restaurant-le-pily.com. This tiny but smart little Michelin-starred restaurant, in the tangled heart of the old town, is a showcase for imaginative contemporary Norman cuisine, with a focus on fish and meat. Weekday lunch *menu* €28, dinner from €39.50. Mon, Tues, Thurs & Fri noon–1.45pm & 7–9pm, Sat 7–9pm, Sun noon–1.45pm.

# The Cotentin Peninsula

Hard against the frontier with Brittany, and cut off from the rest of Normandy by difficult marshy terrain, the **Cotentin Peninsula** has traditionally been seen as something of a backwater, far removed from the French mainstream. By sea, on the other hand, it's very easily accessible. Beyond the peninsula's major port, **Cherbourg** (see p.285), little ports such as **Barfleur** and **St-Vaast** on the indented northern headland presage the rocky Breton coast, while **La Hague** to the west offers a handsome array of heather-clad cliffs and stone-wall-divided patchwork fields.

For many visitors the Cotentin's long western flank, with its flat beaches, serves primarily as a prelude to **Mont St-Michel**, with hill towns such as **Coutances** and **Avranches** cherishing architectural and historical relics associated with the abbey. Halfway down, however, the walled port of **Granville**, a popular destination with French holiday-makers, is a sort of small-scale mirror-image of Brittany's St-Malo.

## Barfleur

The pleasant harbour village of **BARFLEUR**, 25km east of Cherbourg, was the biggest port in Normandy seven centuries ago. Its population having dwindled along with its fortunes, it's now a surprisingly low-key place, where the sweeping crescent of the picturesque grey-granite quayside sees little tourist activity.

## St-Vaast

Pretty **ST-VAAST-LA-HOUGUE**, 11km south of Barfleur, is a relaxed resort that comes alive in summer. Countless tiny Channel-crossing yachts moor in the bay where Edward III landed on his way to Crécy, overlooked by a string of fortifications that date from Vauban's time.

## Barneville-Carteret

Backed by sand dunes that resemble miniature mountain ranges, the **beaches** along the Cotentin's northwestern coast rank among the finest in Normandy. The twinned villages known as **BARNEVILLE-CARTERET** make the best overnight halt. **Carteret** itself, sheltered by a rocky headland, is the nearest harbour to the English-speaking island of **Jersey**, just 25km away across seas made treacherous by the fast Alderney current.

**5**

Visitors who prefer to stay right beside a beach should head instead for **Barneville**, directly across the mouth of the bay. Here, an endless exposed stretch of clean, firm sand is backed by a long row of weather-beaten villas and the occasional hotel.

## Coutances

The hill town of **COUTANCES**, 65km south of Cherbourg, confined by its site to just one main street, is crested by the landmark **Cathédrale de Notre-Dame**. Essentially Gothic, it remains very Norman in its unconventional blending of architectural traditions, and the octagonal lantern crowning the nave is nothing short of divinely inspired. The son et lumière on Sunday evenings and throughout the summer is a true complement to the light stone building. Also illuminated on summer nights (and left open) are the formal fountained **public gardens**.

## Granville

The striking fortified coastal town of **GRANVILLE**, 25km southwest of Coutances, is the Norman equivalent of Brittany's St-Malo, with a similar history of piracy and an imposing, severely elegant citadel – the **haute ville** – that guards the approaches to the bay of Mont St-Michel across from Cancale. Here, however, the fortress was originally built by the English, early in the fifteenth century, as the springboard for an attack on Mont St-Michel that never came to fruition.

The great difference between Granville and St-Malo is that Granville's walled citadel stands separate from the modern town, an intriguing enclave that remains resolutely uncommercialized. Sheltered behind a rocky outcrop that juts into the Channel, it's reached by steep stairs from alongside the beach and casino, or circuitous climbing roads from the port. Once up there, you'll find three or four long narrow parallel streets of grey-granite eighteenth-century houses – some forbidding and aloof, some adorned with brightly painted shutters – that lead to the church of Notre-Dame.

Granville today is a deservedly popular tourist destination. Thanks in part to the long beach that stretches away north of town, which disappears almost completely at high tide, it's the area's busiest resort. Traffic in the maze-like new town, down below the headland, can be nightmarish, but the beaches are excellent, with facilities for watersports of all kind.

## Avranches

Perched high above the bay on an abrupt granite outcrop, **AVRANCHES** is the closest large town to Mont St-Michel, and has always had close connections with the abbey. The Mont's original church was founded by a bishop of Avranches, spurred on by the Archangel Michael, who became so impatient with the lack of progress that he prodded a hole in the bishop's skull.

Robert of Torigny, a subsequent abbot of St-Michel, played host in the town on several occasions to Henry II of England, the most memorable being when Henry was obliged, barefoot and bareheaded, to do public penance for the murder of Thomas Becket, on May 22, 1172.

### Scriptorial d'Avranches

Place d'Estouteville • Feb–April & Oct–Dec Tues–Fri 10am–12.30pm & 2–5pm, Sat & Sun 10am–12.30pm & 2–6pm; May–June & Sept daily except Mon 10am–12.30pm & 2–5pm; July & Aug daily 10am–7pm • €7 • ☎ 02 33 79 57 00, ⍟ scriptorial.fr

For a vivid evocation of Normandy's medieval splendours, be sure to examine the illuminated manuscripts, mostly created on the Mont, displayed in the state-of-the-art museum known as the **Scriptorial d'Avranches**. Additional exhibits trace the history of Avranches, and bring the story up to date by covering modern book-production techniques.

## ARRIVAL AND DEPARTURE

### COUTANCES

**By train** Coutances's *gare SNCF*, which meets trains from Caen (7 daily; 1hr 15min) and Rennes (7 daily; 1hr 45min), is 1.5km southeast of the centre, at the bottom of the steep hill.

### GRANVILLE

**By train and bus** Trains from Coutances (7 daily; 30min) arrive at the *gare SNCF*, well east of the centre on av du Maréchal-Leclerc; buses stop here, too.

### THE COTENTIN PENINSULA

### AVRANCHES

**By train** Avranches's *gare SNCF* is a long way below the town centre; the walk up discourages most rail travellers from stopping here at all.
Destinations Granville (2 daily; 55min); St-Malo (2 daily; 45min) via Pontorson (for Mont St-Michel; 15min).

**By bus** Buses to Mont St-Michel (1 daily; 1hr) stop on the main town square, and also outside the *gare SNCF*.

## INFORMATION

### COUTANCES

**Tourist office** Place Georges-Léclerc, behind the Hôtel de Ville (July & Aug Mon–Fri 9.30am–6pm, Sat 10am–12.30pm & 2–6pm, Sun 10am–1pm; Sept–June Mon–Fri 9.30am–12.30pm & 2–6pm, Sat 10am–12.30pm & 2–5pm; ☏ 02 33 19 08 10, ⦿ tourisme-coutances.fr).

### GRANVILLE

**Tourist office** 4 cours Jonville, below the citadel (July & Aug Mon–Sat 9am–6.30pm, Sun 10am–1pm & 2–5pm;

April–June & Sept Mon–Sat 9am–12.30pm & 2–6pm, Sun 10am–1pm & 2–5pm; Oct–March Mon–Sat 9am–12.30pm & 2–5.30pm; ☏ 02 33 91 30 03, ⦿ granville-tourisme.fr).

### AVRANCHES

**Tourist office** 2 place Général-de-Gaulle (July & Aug Mon–Sat 9.30am–12.30pm & 2–7pm, Sun 9.30am–12.30pm & 2–6pm; Sept–June Mon–Fri 9.30am–12.30pm & 2–6pm, Sat 10am–12.30pm & 2.30–5pm; ☏ 02 33 58 00 22, ⦿ ot-avranches.com).

## ACCOMMODATION AND EATING

### BARFLEUR

★ **Comptoir de la Presqu'Île** 30 quai Henri Chardon ☏ 233 203751. Relaxed and extremely friendly waterfront brasserie, near the end of Barfleur's main street, with lots of seating both indoors and out. With no set *menus*, the temptation is to settle for a simple and succulent €10 *moules-frites*, but the whole grilled fish, at €20 and up, is sublime. Daily noon–2.30pm & 7.30–10pm.

★ **Le Conquérant** 16–18 rue St-Thomas-à-Becket ☏ 02 33 54 00 82, ⦿ hotel-leconquerant.com. Welcoming family-owned hotel, set in an elegant old stone-built townhouse on the main street, a few steps inland from the harbour. Pleasant rooms overlooking a peaceful garden courtyard; no restaurant. Closed mid-Nov to mid-March. **€85**

**La Ferme du Bord du Mer** 23 rte du Val de Saire, Gatteville-le-Phare ☏ 02 33 54 01 77. This basic but appealing campsite, a couple of kilometres north of town, is exactly what its name suggests: a farm beside the sea, alongside a scruffy flat beach. **€11.50**

### ST-VAAST

**De France et des Fuchsias** 18 rue du Maréchal-Foch ☏ 02 33 54 40 41, ⦿ france-fuchsias.com. Sprawling back from the main road a few blocks short of the sea, this popular hotel has splendid gardens and an excellent restaurant, and with rooms of all sizes and degrees of comfort it makes an ideal stopover for ferry passengers. Closed Jan–Feb, plus Mon in winter. **€55**

### BARNEVILLE-CARTERET

★ **Des Isles** 9 bd Maritime, Barneville ☏ 02 33 04 90 76, ⦿ hoteldesisles.com. Very classy beachfront hotel, which following a cool makeover resembles a bright and relaxing New England coastal inn. All the rooms have sea views, and there's a heated outdoor swimming pool plus a superb restaurant. **€132**

### COUTANCES

**Cositel** Rte de St Malo ☏ 02 33 19 15 00, ⦿ hotelcositel .com. Large and exceptionally comfortable modern hotel, architecturally uninspiring but equipped with stylish rooms and roomy gardens, halfway up the hill towards Agon on the western outskirts of town. **€87**

**Taverne du Parvis** 18 place du Parvis ☏ 02 33 45 13 55, ⦿ hotel-restaurant-taverne-du-parvis.com. Unexciting but adequate rooms, several of them family-sized, above a reasonable brasserie in the cathedral square. Restaurant closed Sun. **€48**

**Les Vignettes** 27 rte de St Malo ☏ 02 33 45 43 13, ⦿ ville-coutances.fr/campingtcpc.php. Excellent little year-round municipal campsite, offering lush pitches on a wooded hill just west of town. **€11.60**

### GRANVILLE

**Centre Régional de Nautisme** bd des Amiraux ☏ 02 33 91 22 62, ⦿ crng.fr. This modern, oceanfront building, 1km south of the station in the town centre, serves as Granville's hostel, with dorms and private rooms. Closed Sat & Sun Nov–Feb. Dorms **€16.70**, doubles **€43.20**

**5**

**Logis du Roc** 13 rue St-Michel ☎02 33 50 75 71, ⓦlelogisduroc.com. The three attractive and spacious en-suite rooms in this nicely furnished townhouse B&B, run by a fluent English-speaker, are the only accommodation option in Granville's peaceful old citadel. **€60**

**Mer et Saveurs** 49 rue du Port ☎02 33 50 05 80, ⓦmeretsaveurs.fr. The pick of the fine crop of waterfront restaurants that face Granville's commercial port; its mouthwatering assortment of fishy *menus*, from €13.50 for lunch, €24 dinner, changes daily. Tues–Sun noon–2pm &

7–9.30pm; closed Sun eve in low season.

**AVRANCHES**
★ **Croix d'Or** 83 rue de la Constitution ☎02 33 58 04 88, ⓦhoteldelacroixdor.fr. Gloriously old-fashioned hotel, consisting of a rambling former coaching inn plus a newer annexe hidden away in the beautiful hydrangea-filled gardens at the back. Good-value rooms, and the best restaurant in town, where dinner *menus* start at €26. Closed Jan, plus Sun eve in winter. **€80**

# Mont St-Michel

Deservedly the most famous French landmark outside Paris, the stupendous abbey of **MONT ST-MICHEL** was first erected on an island at the very frontier of Normandy and Brittany more than a millennium ago. In recent years, that island had become attached to the mainland by a long causeway, topped by a road. As of 2012, however, a lengthy hydraulic and reconstruction project – aimed ultimately at detaching the island once more, and restoring at least a little of the isolation and mystery that has made it such a major destination for pilgrims and tourists alike – has closed that road to private cars. For the moment, visitors still use it to reach the island, in shuttle buses or on foot; in due course it will be replaced by a bridge.

### Brief history
The 80m-high rocky outcrop on which the abbey stands was once known as "the Mount in Peril from the Sea". Many a pilgrim in medieval times drowned while trying to cross the bay to reach it. The Archangel Michael was its vigorous protector, with a marked propensity to leap from rock to rock in titanic struggles against Paganism and Evil.

The abbey itself dates back to the eighth century, when the archangel appeared to Aubert, bishop of Avranches, who duly founded a monastery on the island. Since the eleventh century – when work on the sturdy church at the peak commenced – new buildings have been grafted to produce a fortified hotchpotch of Romanesque and Gothic buildings clambering to the pinnacle of the graceful church, forming probably the most recognizable silhouette in France after the Eiffel Tower. Although the abbey was a fortress town, home to a large community, even at its twelfth-century peak it never housed more than sixty monks.

When the Revolution came the monastery was converted into a prison, but in 1966, exactly a thousand years after Duke Richard the First originally brought the order to the Mont, the Benedictines were invited to return. They departed again in 2001, after finding that the present-day island does not exactly lend itself to a life of quiet contemplation. In their place, a dozen nuns and monks from the Monastic Fraternity of Jerusalem now maintain a presence.

## The island
The **island of Mont St-Michel** is almost entirely covered by medieval stone structures, encircled by defensive walls. Amazingly enough, less than a third of all visitors climb high enough to reach the abbey itself at the summit; the rest stay in the commercialized town lower down.

Accessing the town via the heavily fortified **Porte du Roi**, you find yourself on the narrow **Grande Rue**, which spirals steadily upwards, passing top-heavy gabled houses amid the jumble of souvenir shops and restaurants.

Large crowds gather each day at the **North Tower** to watch the tide sweep in across the bay. Seagulls wheel away in alarm, and those foolish enough to be wandering too late on the sands have to sprint to safety.

## The abbey

**Abbey** Daily: May–Aug 9am–7pm; Sept–April 9.30am–6pm; last admission 1hr before closing; closed Jan 1, May 1 and Dec 25 • €9, ages 18–25 €5.50, under-18s free; fee includes optional 1hr 15min guided tour, available in English all year **Night visits** July & Aug Mon–Sat 7pm–midnight • €9, or €13.50 with daytime admission; ages 18–25 €5.50/€8 • ☎ 02 33 89 90 00, ⓦ mont-saint-michel .monuments-nationaux.fr

Although the **abbey**, an architectural ensemble that incorporates the high-spired, archangel-topped church and the magnificent Gothic buildings known since 1228 as the **Merveille** ("The Marvel") – which in turn includes the entire north face, with the cloister, Knights' Hall, Refectory, Guest Hall and cellars – is visible from all around the bay, it becomes, if anything, more awe-inspiring the closer you get.

The Mont's rock comes to a sharp point just below what is now the transept of the **church**, a building where the transition from Romanesque to Gothic is only too evident in the vaulting of the nave. In order to lay out the church's ground plan in the traditional shape of the cross, supporting crypts had to be built up from the surrounding hillside, and the Chausey granite sculpted to match the exact contours of the hill. Space was always limited, and yet the building has grown through the centuries, with an ingenuity that constantly surprises – witness the shock of emerging into the light of the cloisters from the sombre Great Hall.

Not surprisingly, the building of the **monastery** was no smooth progression: the original church, choir, nave and tower all had to be replaced after collapsing. The style of decoration has varied, too, along with the architecture. That you now walk through halls of plain grey stone is a reflection of modern taste. In the Middle Ages, the walls of public areas such as the refectory would have been festooned with tapestries and frescoes, while the original coloured tiles of the cloisters have long since been stripped away to reveal bare walls.

## ARRIVAL AND DEPARTURE                                        MONT ST-MICHEL

**By car** All visitors have to park on the mainland (cars €8.50, motorbikes €3.50). Rates include the shuttle ride to the island, but you may prefer to walk.
**By train** The nearest *gare SNCF* is at Pontorson, 6km south; shuttle buses timed to coincide with trains take 15min to

make the trip to Mont St-Michel (€2).
**By bus** Buses from Rennes (5 daily; 1hr 20min) and St-Malo (4 daily; 1hr 30min) arrive at the information centre, on the mainland.

## INFORMATION

**Information centre** The main information centre is on the mainland, on the east side of the D976 (April–June & Sept Mon–Fri 9am–7pm, Sat & Sun 9am–8pm; July & Aug daily 9am–8pm; Oct to mid-Nov Mon–Fri 9am–6pm, Sat & Sun 9am–7pm; mid-Nov to March daily 10am–6pm; ☎ 02 14 13 20 15, ⓦ accueilmontsaintmichel.com).

**Tourist office** The island has its own tourist office, in the lowest gateway (April–June & Sept Mon–Sat 9am–12.30pm & 2–6.30pm, Sun 9am–noon & 2–6pm; July & Aug daily 9am–7pm; Oct–March Mon–Sat 9am–noon & 2–6pm, Sun 10am–noon & 2–5pm; ☎ 02 33 60 14 30, ⓦ ot-montsaintmichel.com).

## ACCOMMODATION AND EATING

Mont St-Michel holds a surprising number of hotels, albeit not enough to cope with the sheer number of visitors. Most are predictably expensive, and all charge extra for a view of the sea. Many visitors choose instead to stay on the mainland, where the D976 is lined with large and virtually indistinguishable hotels and motels, or in Pontorson or other nearby towns. Sadly, the restaurants on the island, both independent and in the hotels, are consistently worse than almost anywhere in France. It's impossible to make any confident recommendations, other than that ideally you should aim to eat elsewhere.

### MONT ST-MICHEL

**Du Guesclin** Grande Rue ☎ 02 33 60 14 10, ⓦ hotelduguesclin.com. The cheapest option on the

island, a *Logis de France* with ten old-fashioned and generally small en-suite rooms, of which five have sea views. Closed mid-Nov to March. **€89**

**5**

**Croix Blanche** Grande Rue ☎02 33 60 14 04, ⓦhotel-la-croix-blanche.com. This little hotel is the nicest on Mont St-Michel itself, with nine sprucely decorated rooms, but there's a hefty premium for a sea view. **€170**

**Mouton Blanc** Grande Rue ☎02 33 60 14 08, ⓦlemoutonblanc.fr. Wood-panelled fourteenth-century house, now a hotel with fifteen small and somewhat plain rooms, and a large old-fashioned restaurant. **€99**

**ON THE MAINLAND**

**Formule Verte** La Caserne, rte de Mont-St-Michel ☎02 33 60 14 13, ⓦhotelformuleverte-montsaintmichel .com. Sprawling, inexpensive motel/restaurant, on the approach road just short of the island. Closed mid-Nov to early Feb. **€66**

**Vert** La Caserne, rte de Mont-St-Michel ☎02 33 60 09 33, ⓦhotelvert-montsaintmichel.com. Low-slung, anonymous but perfectly adequate motel, offering 54 pastel-toned rooms of varying sizes, plus the *Rôtisserie* restaurant and bar. **€78**

# Inland Normandy

Seeking out specific highlights is not really the point when you're exploring **inland Normandy**. The pleasure lies not so much in show-stopping sights, or individual towns, as in the feel of the landscape – the lush meadows, orchards and forests of the Norman countryside. On top of that, the major attraction in these rich dairy regions is the **food**. To the French, the **Pays d'Auge** and the **Suisse Normande** are synonymous with cheeses, cream, apple and pear brandies, and ciders.

This is also a place to be active. The Suisse Normande is canoeing and rock-climbing country, and there are countless good walks in the stretch along the southern border of the province. Of the towns, **Falaise** is inextricably associated with the story of William the Conqueror, while **Lisieux** was home to France's most popular modern saint.

## South of the Seine

Heading south from the Seine you can follow the River Risle from the estuary just east of Honfleur, or the Eure and its tributaries from upstream of Rouen. The lowest major crossing point over the Risle is at **Pont-Audemer**, where medieval houses lean out at alarming angles over the crisscrossing roads, rivers and canals. From here, perfect cycling roads lined with timbered farmhouses follow the river south.

### Abbaye de Bec-Hellouin

Daily 8am–9pm; guided tours Mon & Wed–Sat 10.30am, 3pm & 4pm, plus 5pm June–Sept only; Sun & hols noon, 3pm & 4pm • Free; tours €5 • ☎02 32 43 72 62, ⓦabbayedubec.com

The size and tranquil setting of the **Abbaye de Bec-Hellouin**, upstream from Pont-Audemer just before Brionne, lend a monastic feel to the whole Risle valley. Bells echo across the water and white-robed monks go soberly about their business. From the eleventh century onwards, the abbey was an important intellectual centre; the philosopher Anselm was abbot here before becoming Archbishop of Canterbury in 1093. Thanks to the Revolution, most of the monastery buildings are recent – the monks only returned in 1948 – but some have survived amid the appealing clusters of stone ruins, including the fifteenth-century **bell tower of St-Nicholas** and the cloister. Visitors are welcome to wander through the grounds for no charge; to get a better sense of what you're seeing, join a **guided tour**.

#### ACCOMMODATION AND EATING                          SOUTH OF THE SEINE

**Auberge de l'Abbaye** 12 place Guillaume le Conquérant, Bec-Hellouin ☎02 32 44 86 02, ⓦhotel bechellouin.com. Pretty, half-timbered hotel-restaurant in the tiny and rather twee village adjacent to the Abbaye de Bec-Hellouin, bedecked in flowers and offering ten rooms of varying degrees of luxury, plus a spa. **€80**

# The Pays d'Auge

The rolling hills and green twisting valleys of the **Pays d'Auge**, stretching south of Lisieux, are scattered with magnificent manor houses. The lush pastures here are responsible for the world-famous **cheeses** of Camembert, Livarot and Pont L'Evêque. They are intermingled with orchards yielding the best of Norman **ciders**, both apple and pear (*poiré*), as well as Calvados apple brandy.

For really good, solid Norman cooking visit one of this area's *fermes auberges*, working farms which welcome paying visitors to share their meals. Local tourist offices can provide copious lists of these and of local producers from whom you can buy your cheese and booze.

### Lisieux

**LISIEUX**, the main town of the Pays d'Auge, is most famous as the home of **Ste Thérèse**, the most popular French spiritual figure of the modern era, who was born here in 1873 and lived just 24 years. Passivity, self-effacement and a self-denial that verged on masochism were her trademarks, and she is honoured by the gaudy and gigantic **Basilique de Ste-Thérèse**, on a slope southwest of the centre. The huge modern mosaics that decorate the nave are undeniably impressive, but the overall impression is of a quasi-medieval hagiography. The faithful can ride on a white, flag-bedecked fairground train around the holiest sites, which include the infinitely restrained and sober **Cathédrale St-Pierre**.

Lisieux's large street **market**, on Wednesday and Saturday, is a great opportunity to get acquainted with its cheeses and ciders.

### Crèvecoeur-en-Auge

While it's always fun to stumble across dilapidated old half-timbered farms in the Pays d'Auge, here and there it's possible to visit prime specimens that have been beautifully restored and preserved. An especially fine assortment has been gathered just west of **CRÈVECOEUR-EN-AUGE**, 17km west of Lisieux on the N14, in the grounds of a small twelfth-century **château** (April–June & Sept daily 11am–6pm; July & Aug daily 11am–7pm; Oct Sun 2–6pm; €7; ⓦchateau-de-crevecoeur.com). Around the pristine lawns of a recreated village green, circled by a shallow moat, this photogenic group of golden adobe structures includes a manor house, a barn and a tall thin dovecote that date from the fifteenth century. The little twelfth-century chapel that adjoins the château holds a fascinating exhibition on the music and instruments of the Middle Ages, although almost all the explanatory captions are in French.

### Beuvron-en-Auge

By far the prettiest of the Pays d'Auge villages is **BEUVRON-EN-AUGE**, 7km north of the N13 halfway between Lisieux and Caen. It consists of an oval central *place*, ringed by a glorious ensemble of multicoloured half-timbered houses, including the yellow-and-brown sixteenth-century Vieux Manoir.

### Orbec

The town of **ORBEC**, 19km southeast of Lisieux, epitomizes the simple pleasures of the Pays d'Auge. Along the rue Grande, you'll see several houses in which the gaps between the timbers are filled with intricate patterns of coloured tiles and bricks. Debussy composed *Jardin sous la pluie* in one of these, and the oldest and prettiest of the lot – a tanner's house dating back to 1568, known as the **Vieux Manoir** – holds a museum of local history. On the whole, though, it's more appealing just to walk down behind the church to the river, its watermill and paddocks.

### Livarot

In venerable **LIVAROT**, at the centre of cheese country, the **Fromagerie Graindorge**, 42 rue Général-Leclerc (April–June, Sept & Oct Mon–Sat 9.30am–1pm & 2–5.30pm; July &

**5**

Aug Mon–Sat 9.30am–1pm & 2–5.30pm, Sun 1.30am–1pm & 3–5.30pm; Nov–
March Mon–Fri 10am–noon & 2–5pm, Sat 9.30am–noon; free; ☏02 31 48 20 10,
ⓦgraindorge.fr) gives visitors a closer look at how the town's eponymous cheese is made.

For superb views of the valley, climb up to the thirteenth-century church of **St-Michel
de Livet**, just above town.

## Vimoutiers

The pretty little town of **VIMOUTIERS** is home to the **Musée du Camembert**, 10 av
Général-de-Gaulle (April–Oct Thurs–Mon 2–5.30pm; €3; ☏02 33 39 30 29,
ⓦvimoutiers.fr), a rather homespun affair which explains the production process of the
famous cheese, with tastings at the end.

A statue in the town's main square honours **Marie Harel**, who, at the nearby village of
Camembert, developed the original cheese early in the nineteenth century, promoting
it with a skilful campaign that included sending free samples to Napoleon. Marie is
confronted across the main street by what might be called the statue of the Unknown
Cow. Vimoutiers hosts a **market** on Monday afternoons.

## Camembert

The tiny, hilly, very rural and world famous village of **CAMEMBERT**, 3km southeast of
Vimoutiers, is home to far more cows than humans. In its little central square, the
largest Camembert producers, **La Ferme Président**, run a museum, aptly called **La
Maison du Camembert** (March Thurs–Sun 10am–5pm; April, Sept & Oct Wed–Sun
10am–6pm; May–Aug daily 10am–7pm; €3; ☏02 33 12 10 37, ⓦfermepresident.com),
which whirls through the history of the cheese and the methods, both traditional and
modern, used to make it. Afterwards comes a cheese tasting, in their café.

## Falaise

The historic town of **FALAISE**, 40km southwest of Lisieux, was almost entirely
destroyed during the climax of the **Battle of Normandy** in August 1944. In the
desperate struggle to close the so-called "Falaise Gap", the Allied armies sought to
encircle the Germans and cut off their retreat. By the time the Canadians entered the
town on August 17, they could no longer tell where the roads had been and had to
bulldoze a new 4m strip straight through the middle. As a result, although its mighty
**château**, the birthplace of William the Conqueror, still stands as a fascinating
monument, the town itself has lost its former charm.

### Château Guillaume-le-Conquérant

Daily 10am–6pm • €7.50 • T02 31 41 61 44, ⓦ chateau-guillaume-leconquerant.fr

Firmly planted on the massive rocks of the cliff (*falaise*) that gave Falaise its name, and
towering over the **Fontaine d'Arlette** down by the river, the keep of the **Château
Guillaume-le-Conquérant** is as evocative an historic sight as one could imagine.
Nonetheless, it was so heavily damaged during the war that it took more than fifty
years to reopen for regular visits.

Huge resources have been lavished on restoring the central **donjon**, reminiscent of the
Tower of London with its cream-coloured Caen stone. Steel slabs, concrete blocks, glass

---

### WILLIAM THE BASTARD AND THE LAUNDRYWOMAN

William the Conqueror, or William the Bastard as he is more prosaically known in his homeland,
was born in **Falaise**. William's mother, Arlette, a laundrywoman, was spotted by his father,
Duke Robert of Normandy, at the washing place below the château. She was a shrewd
woman, scorning secrecy in her eventual assignation by riding publicly through the main
entrance to meet him. During her pregnancy, she is said to have dreamed of bearing a mighty
tree that cast its shade over Normandy and England.

floors and tent-like canvas awnings have been slapped down atop the bare ruins, and metal staircases squeezed into the wall cavities. The raw structure of the keep, down to its very foundations, lies exposed to view, while the newly created rooms are used for changing exhibitions that focus on the castle's fascinating past.

| INFORMATION | THE PAYS D'AUGE |
|---|---|

### LISIEUX

**Tourist office** 11 rue d'Alençon (mid-June to Sept Mon–Sat 8.30am–6.30pm, Sun 10am–12.30pm & 2–5pm; Oct to mid-June Mon–Sat 8.30am–noon & 1.30–6pm; ☎ 02 31 48 18 10, ⓦ lisieux-tourisme.com).

### FALAISE

**Tourist office** Bd de la Libération (May to late June Mon–Sat 9.30am–12.30pm & 1.30–6.30pm; late June to mid-Sept also open Sun 10am–12.30pm & 2–4pm; mid-Sept to April Mon–Sat 9.30am–12.30pm & 1.30–5.30pm; ☎ 02 31 90 17 26, ⓦ falaise-tourisme.com).

## ACCOMMODATION AND EATING

### LISIEUX

**St-Louis** 4 rue St-Jacques ☎ 02 31 62 06 50, ⓦ hotelsaintlouis-lisieux.com. The friendly and ultra-enthusiastic new owners have transformed this budget hotel, which has seventeen individually decorated rooms – of which the cheapest lack en-suite facilities – and serves excellent organic breakfasts for €8. **€55**

### BEUVRON-EN-AUGE

**Pavé d'Auge** ☎ 02 31 79 26 71, ⓦ pavedauge.com. Top-notch restaurant in Beuvron's timber-framed medieval market hall, in the central square, serving rich and opulent Norman cuisine on changing *menus* from €37.50; it also offers five comfortable rooms in the separate *Pavé d'Hôtes*. Restaurant July & Aug daily except Mon noon–1.45pm & 7.30–9.30pm; Sept–June Wed–Sun noon–1.45pm & 7.30–9.30pm. **€95**

### VIMOUTIERS

**La Couronne** 9 rue du 8 mai ☎ 02 33 67 21 49, ⓦ hotel-restaurant-la-couronne.com. Little hotel, above a bar/restaurant on the main square in the centre of Vimoutiers, which offers the best-value rooms in town, and makes a convivial base, as well as serving good brasserie food and full *menus* from €16. **€50**

**L'Escale du Vitou** Rte d'Argentan ☎ 02 33 39 12 04, ⓦ domaineduvitou.com. Attractive half-timbered hotel, in a delightful rural setting not far south of Vimoutiers towards Camembert, where the lake known as the Escale du Vitou offers everything you need for windsurfing, swimming and horseriding. Seventeen rooms, a couple of rental cottages, and a decent restaurant, closed Mon. **€60**

### FALAISE

**Camping Municipal** Rue du Val d'Ante ☎ 02 31 90 16 55, ⓦ falaise-tourisme.com. This well-equipped three-star municipal campsite is in a superb location, immediately below the castle, next to Arlette's fountain and the local swimming pool complex. Closed Oct–April. **€14.30**

**Poste** 38 rue Georges-Clemenceau ☎ 02 31 90 13 14, ✉ hotel.delaposte@orange.fr. Falaise's best-value rooms, in an imposing white-painted hotel near the tourist office, which also serves good food on *menus* from €16. Hotel closed Jan, restaurant closed Fri eve, Sun eve & Mon. **€70**

# The Suisse Normande

The area known as the **Suisse Normande** starts roughly 25km south of Caen, along the gorge of the River Orne, between Thury-Harcourt and Putanges. While the name is a little far-fetched – there are certainly no mountains – the region is quite distinctive, with cliffs, crags and wooded hills at every turn. There are plenty of opportunities for **outdoor pursuits**: you can race along the Orne in canoes and kayaks, cruise more sedately on pedalos, or dangle on ropes from the sheer rock faces high above. For mere walkers the Orne can be frustrating: footpaths along the river are few and far between, and often entirely overgrown.

## Thury-Harcourt

**THURY-HARCOURT** is really two separate towns: a little village around a bridge across the Orne, and a larger market town on the hill that overlooks it. In summer, the grounds of the local manor house are open to visitors, providing access to the immediate riverside.

**5**

## Clécy

The small village of **CLÉCY**, 10km south of Thury-Harcourt, is perched on a hill about 1km up from the point where the D133A crosses the River Orne by means of the Pont du Vey. On the way up, the Parc des Loisirs holds a **Musée du Chemin de Fer Miniature**, featuring a gigantic model railway certain to appeal to children (March–Easter, Oct & Nov Sun 2–5.30pm; Easter–June daily except Mon 10am–noon & 2–6pm; July & Aug daily 10am–6pm; second half of Sept daily except Mon 2–6pm; €6.80; ⓦchemin-fer -miniature-clecy.com).

Across from Clécy, the east bank of the Orne is dominated by the exposed rock face of the giant **Pain de Sucre**, or Sugarloaf, looming above the river. Small footpaths, and the tortuous Route des Crêtes, wind up to its flat top, making for some fabulously enjoyable walks. Picnic sites and parking places along the crest hold orientation maps so weather-beaten as to be almost abstract, but the views down to the flat fields of the Orne Valley are stupendous.

## Pont d'Ouilly

**PONT D'OUILLY**, at the point where the main road from Vire to Falaise crosses the river, makes a good central base for walkers and cyclists. It's just a village, with a few basic shops, an old covered market hall and a promenade (with bar) slightly upstream alongside the weir. As you continue upstream, a pleasant walk leads for 3.5km to the pretty little village of Le Mesnil Villement.

A short distance south of Pont d'Ouilly, the **Roche d'Oëtre** is a high rock with a tremendous view into the deep and totally wooded gorge of the Rouvre, a tributary of the Orne. The river widens soon afterwards into the **Lac de Rabodanges**, formed by the many-arched Rabodanges Dam.

### ARRIVAL AND INFORMATION

### THE SUISSE NORMANDE

**By bus** Bus Verts #34 stops in Thury-Harcourt and Clécy en route between Caen and Flers.

**Thury-Harcourt tourist office** 2 place St-Sauveur (May, June & Sept Tues–Sat 10am–12.30pm & 2.30–6.30pm, Sun 10am–12.30pm; July & Aug also open Mon; Oct–April Tues–Fri 10am–12.30pm & 2.30–5pm, Sat 10am–12.30pm; ☏02 31 79 70 45, ⓦot-suisse-normande.com).

**Clécy tourist office** Place du Tripot, behind the church (May, June & first half of Sept Tues–Sat 10am–12.30pm & 2.30–6.30pm, Sun 10am–12.30pm; July & Aug also open Mon; second half of Sept Tues–Fri 10am–12.30pm, Sat 10am–12.30pm & 2.30–5pm; ☏02 31 69 79 95, ⓦwww .suisse-normande.com).

### ACCOMMODATION AND EATING

### THURY-HARCOURT

**Relais de la Poste** 7 rue de Caen ☏02 31 79 72 12, ⓦhotel-relaisdelaposte.com. Elegant old country-house hotel, holding a dozen rooms of all shapes and sizes, plus an opulent restaurant (closed Thurs & Fri lunchtimes in summer, Fri and Sun evenings in winter) that's perfect at the end of a long day. Dinner menus start at €28. **€69**

### CLÉCY

**Au Site Normand** 2 rue des Châtelets ☏02 31 69 71 05, ⓦhotel-clecy.com. Village hotel, facing the church, with pleasant, comfortable rooms in a modern annexe, and

a stylish modern dining room in the main timber-framed building, serving good menus from €24. The river is 1km away, down the hill. **€55**

### PONT D'OUILLY

**Auberge St-Christophe** Rte du Thury-Harcourt ☏02 31 69 81 23, ⓦauberge-st-christophe.fr. Just 1km north of the village centre, this attractive rural hotel, covered with ivy and geraniums, offers seven en-suite rooms in a beautiful setting on the right bank of the Orne. Closed Sun eve, Mon & three weeks in Feb–March. **€60**

# Southern Normandy

Drivers heading west from Paris towards Brittany can cut directly across southern Normandy by following the N12 through **Alençon** and then continuing on the N176 and N976. Much of the terrain along Normandy's southern border is taken up by the dense woodlands of the **Forêt d'Écouves** and the **Forêt des Andaines**, so there's plenty of good walking, while the hill towns of **Carrouges** and **Domfront** make great stopovers.

## Alençon and around

**ALENÇON**, a medium-sized and lively town, is known for its traditional – and now pretty much defunct – lacemaking industry. Wandering around the town will take you to St Thérèse's birthplace on rue St-Blaise, just in front of the **gare routière**.

### Musée des Beaux-Arts et de la Dentelle

Cour Carrée de la Dentelle • July & Aug daily 10am–noon & 2–6pm; Sept–June closed Mon • €4 • ☎ 02 33 32 40 07, ⓦ museedentelle-alencon.fr

Housed in a former Jesuit school, the **Musée des Beaux-Arts et de la Dentelle** has all the best trappings of a modern museum. The highly informative history of lacemaking upstairs, can, however, be tedious for anyone not already riveted by the subject. It also contains an unexpected collection of gruesome Cambodian artefacts like spears and lances, tiger skulls and elephants' feet, gathered in the nineteenth century. The paintings in the adjoining Beaux-Arts section are nondescript, except for a few works by Courbet and Géricault.

### Forêt d'Écouves

Starting 10km north of Alençon, the **Forêt d'Écouves** is a dense mixture of spruce, pine, oak and beech. Unfortunately, though, it's a favoured spot of the military – and, in autumn, deer hunters, too. You can usually ramble along the cool paths, happening upon wild mushrooms and even the odd wild boar.

## Mortagne-Au-Perche

Famous for the percheron horses who derive their name from this rural region, **Le Perche** is an ideal retreat for a few days' relaxation. An obvious base from which to explore southern Normandy's countryside is the pretty town of **MORTAGNE-AU-PERCHE**, 38km east of Alençon. Its historic centre includes the sixteenth-century **Église Notre-Dame**, as well as an impressive **Hôtel de Ville** set in some lovely formal gardens, from where there is an excellent view of the countryside beyond.

## Carrouges

The hill town of **CARROUGES**, perched along a high ridge at the western end of the Forêt d'Écouves, is noteworthy for its impressive moat-encircled **château**, set in spacious grounds at the foot of the hill.

### Carrouges château

Daily: April to mid-June & Sept 10am–noon & 2–6pm; mid-June to Aug 9.30am–noon & 2–6.30pm; Oct–March 10am–noon & 2–5pm • €7.50 • ☎ 02 33 27 20 32, ⓦ carrouges.monuments-nationaux.fr

The twin highlights of **Carrouges' château** are a superb restored brick staircase, and a room in which hang portraits of fourteen successive generations of the Le Veneur family, an extraordinary illustration of the processes of heredity. Local craftsmen sell their work in the **Maison de Métiers**, the former castle chapel.

## Bagnoles-de-l'Orne

The quaint spa town of **BAGNOLES-DE-L'ORNE** is quite unlike anywhere else in this part of the world, attracting the moneyed sick and convalescent from all over France to its thermal baths, along with mainly elderly visitors wanting to indulge themselves in the various spas. The layout is formal and spacious, centring on a lake surrounded by well-tended gardens. With so many visitors to keep entertained, there are also innumerable cultural events of a restrained and stress-free nature, such as tea dances and stage shows.

**5**

> ### THE BOCAGE
>
> The region that centres on **St-Lô**, just south of the Cotentin, is known as the **Bocage**; the word describes a type of cultivated countryside common in western France, where fields are cut by tight hedgerows rooted into walls of earth well over 1m high. An effective form of smallhold farming in pre-industrial days, it also proved to be a perfect system of anti-tank barricades. When the Allied troops tried to advance through the region in 1944, it was almost impenetrable – certainly bearing no resemblance to the East Anglian plains where they had trained. The war here was hand-to-hand slaughter, and the destruction of villages was often wholesale.

Anyone looking for more active pursuits has the choice of mini golf or a pedalo trip around the lake. The town as a whole operates to a **season** that lasts roughly from early April to the end of October; arrive in winter, and you may find everything shut.

### Domfront

**DOMFRONT** is a pretty hilltop town, dominated by the ruins of a redoubtable **castle**, perched at its very apex on an isolated rock. Eleanor of Aquitaine was born here in October 1162, and Thomas Becket came to stay for Christmas 1166, saying Mass in the **Notre-Dame-sur-l'Eau** church down by the river, which has sadly been ruined by vandals. The views from the flower-filled gardens that surround the mangled keep are spectacular, including an impressive panorama of the ascent you've made to get up here. A slender footbridge connects the castle with the narrow little village itself, which has an abundance of half-timbered houses.

### St-Lô

The city of **ST-LÔ**, 60km southeast of Cherbourg and 36km southwest of Bayeux, is still known as the "Capital of the Ruins". Memorial sites are everywhere and what is new speaks as tellingly of the destruction as the ruins that have been preserved. In the main square, the gate of the old prison commemorates Resistance members executed by the Nazis, people deported east to the concentration camps and soldiers killed in action. When the bombardment of St-Lô was at its fiercest, the Germans refused to take measures to protect the prisoners; this gate was all that survived.

The newness of so much in St-Lô reveals the scale of fighting. It took sixty years for the canalized channel of the Vire, running between the *gare SNCF* and the castle rock, to be re-landscaped. Now known as **Port-St-Lô**, it's an attractive area to walk around, and pedalos are available for rent. But the most visible – and brilliant – reconstruction is the **Cathédrale de Notre-Dame**. The main body of this, with its strange southward-veering nave, has been conventionally repaired and rebuilt. Between the shattered west front and base of the collapsed north tower, however, a startling sheer wall of icy green stone makes no attempt to mask the destruction.

By way of contrast, a lighthouse-like 1950s folly spirals to nowhere on the main square. Should you feel the urge, you can climb its staircase and make your way into the new and even more pointless labyrinth of glass at its feet for a €1.50 admission fee.

### ARRIVAL AND DEPARTURE                                        SOUTHERN NORMANDY

#### ALENÇON

**By train** The *gare SNCF* is northeast of the centre, on rue Denis Papin.

Destinations Caen (8 daily; 1hr 10min); Le Mans (11 daily; 40min).

**By bus** The *gare routière* is a little short of the *gare SNCF*, northeast of the centre.

Destinations Bagnoles (3 daily; 1hr); Mortagne (2–3 daily;

1hr); Vimoutiers (1–3 daily; 1hr 30min).

#### ST-LÔ

**By train** The *gare SNCF* is on av Briovère, across the Vire river from the town centre.

Destinations Caen (12 daily; 50min); via Bayeux (25min); Rennes (4 daily; 2hr 10min); via Coutances (20min) and Pontorson (1hr 15min).

## INFORMATION

### ALENÇON
**Tourist office** Place La Magdelaine (April–June Mon–Sat 9.30am–12.30pm & 1.30–6.30pm; July & Aug Mon–Sat 9.30am–7pm, Sun 10am–12.30pm & 2–4.30pm; Oct–March Mon–Sat 9.30am–12.30pm & 2–6pm; ☎02 33 80 66 33, ⓦ paysdalencontourisme.com).

### MORTAGNE-AU-PERCHE
**Tourist office** 36 place Général de Gaulle (mid-May to mid-June & 2nd half of Sept Tues–Sat 9.30am–12.30pm & 2.30–6pm; mid-June to mid-Sept Mon 10am–12.30pm & 2.30–6pm, Tues–Sat 9.30am–12.30pm & 2.30–6pm, Sun 10am–12.30pm; Oct to mid-May Tues–Sat 10am–12.30pm & 3–6pm; ☎02 33 83 34 37, ⓦ ot-mortagneauperche.fr).

### BAGNOLES-DE-L'ORNE

**Tourist office** Place du Marché (April–Oct Mon–Sat 9.30am–12.30pm & 2–6pm, Sun 10am–12.30pm & 2.30–6.30pm; Nov–March Mon–Sat 9.30am–12.30pm & 2–6pm; ☎02 33 37 85 66, ⓦ bagnolesdelorne.com).

### DOMFRONT
**Tourist office** 12 place de la Roirie (April–Oct Mon–Sat 10am–12.30pm & 2–6pm; also open Sun 10.30am–12.30pm & 1.30–4.30pm in midsummer; Nov–March Tues–Sat 10am–noon & 2–5pm; ☎02 33 38 53 97, ⓦ ot-domfront.com).

### ST-LÔ
**Tourist office** 60 rue de la Poterne (Mon 2–6pm, Tues–Fri 9.30am–12.30pm & 2–6pm, Sat 10am–1pm & 2–5pm; ☎02 14 29 00 17, ⓦ saint-lo.fr).

## ACCOMMODATION AND EATING

### ALENÇON
**Le Hangar** 12 place à l'Avoine ☎02 33 82 04 27. This popular local rendezvous, near the lace museum, serves high-quality but affordable Normand cusine, à la carte or on *menus* from €23. Mon–Fri noon–2pm & 7.30–10pm.
**De Paris** 26 rue Denis-Papin ☎02 33 29 01 64, ⓦ hoteldeparis-alencon.com. Perfectly presentable rooms in a simple hotel above a bar facing the *gare SNCF*. All rooms have showers, but some don't have toilets. **€37**

### MORTAGNE-AU-PERCHE
★ **Ferme du Gros Chêne** Le Gros Chêne ☎02 33 25 02 72, ⓦ fermedugroschene.com. This working farm, just outside Mortagne on the D8 towards Logny-au-Perche, has five comfortable, colourful and imaginatively decorated guest rooms in a converted barn, plus the option of a three-course dinner for €23. **€68**
★ **Du Tribunal** 4 place du Palais ☎02 33 25 04 77, ⓦ hotel-tribunal.fr. The nicest hotel in Mortagne, on a sleepy little tree-lined square, offering very tasteful if slightly old-fashioned rooms with good updated bathrooms, and also a good restaurant. **€62**

### CARROUGES
**Du Nord** Rue Ste-Marguerite ☎02 33 27 20 14. On the narrow street that runs through the heart of Carrouges – a noisier location than it might look – this unassuming hotel offers reasonably large en-suite rooms at low rates, and delicious local cuisine on *menus* from €19.50. Restaurant closed Fri eve, plus Sun eve Sept–June; hotel closed mid-Dec to mid-Jan. **€55**

### BAGNOLES-DE-L'ORNE
**Ô Gayot** 2 av de la Ferté-Macé ☎02 33 38 44 01, ⓦ ogayot.com. Bagnoles' nicest hotel, alongside the tourist office, offers a contemporary take on the spa experience with its minimalist rooms, and has a pleasant bistro/restaurant (closed Thurs) with outdoor seating. **€55**

### DOMFRONT
**France** 7 rue du Mont St-Michel ☎02 33 38 51 44, ⓦ hoteldefrance-fr.com. Old-fashioned but perfectly comfortable *Logis*, one of two very similar hotels side by side on the main road below the old town, where they're somewhat exposed to traffic noise. Affordable rooms above a nice bar and good-value restaurant, with a garden at the back. **€52**

### ST-LÔ
**La Crémaillère** 8 rue de la Chancellerie ☎02 33 57 14 68, ⓦ la-cremaillere-50.com. Economical hotel up in town, holding fifteen plain en-suite rooms, plus a good-value restaurant, where all the *menus*, which start at €9.50 for lunch and €12.50 for dinner, include a buffet of hors d'oeuvres. **€46**
**Mercure Saint-Lô** 1 av Brivère ☎02 33 05 10 84, ⓦ mercure.com. St-Lô's largest hotel, ranged atop a ridge beside the *gare SNCF*, just across the river. As well as 67 modern motel-style rooms, it's home to the *Tocqueville* restaurant, open for all meals on weekdays only, and serving *menus* from €19. **€90**

# Brittany

ÎLE D'OUESSANT

# Brittany

Long before Brittany became subsumed into France, the inhabitants of this rugged Atlantic region were risking their lives fishing and trading on the violent seas, and struggling with the arid soil of the interior. Today this toughness and resilience continues to define the region, which is deeply infused with Celtic culture: mystical, musical, sometimes morbid and defeatist, sometimes vital and inspired. Archeologically, Brittany is among the richest regions in the world – the alignments at Carnac rival Stonehenge. It first appeared in history as the quasi-mythical "Little Britain" of Arthurian legend, and in the days when travel by sea was safer and easier than by land, it was intimately connected with "Great Britain" across the water. Settlements such as St-Malo, St-Pol and Quimper were founded by otherwise unrecorded Welsh and Irish missionary saints.

Brittany remained **independent** until the sixteenth century; after its last ruler, Duchess Anne, died in 1532, François I took her daughter and lands, and sealed the **union with France** with an act supposedly enshrining certain privileges. The successive violations of this treaty by Paris, and subsequent revolts, form the core of Breton history since the Middle Ages.

Many Bretons continue to regard France as a separate country. Few, however, actively support Breton nationalism much beyond displaying Breizh (Breton for "Brittany") stickers on their cars. But the Breton **language** remains very much alive, and the economic resurgence since the 1970s, helped partly by summer tourism, has largely been due to local initiatives, like Brittany Ferries re-establishing the old trading links with Britain and Ireland. At the same time a Celtic artistic identity has consciously been revived, and local festivals – above all August's **Inter-Celtic Festival** at Lorient – celebrate Breton music, poetry and dance, with fellow Celts treated as comrades.

For most visitors, the Breton **coast** is the dominant feature. Apart from the Côte d'Azur, this is France's most popular resort area, for both French and foreign tourists. Its attractions are obvious: warm white-sand beaches, towering cliffs, rock formations and offshore islands and islets, and everywhere the stone dolmens and menhirs of a prehistoric past. The most frequented areas are the **Côte d'Émeraude** around **St-Malo**; the **Côte de Granit Rose** in the north; the **Crozon peninsula** in far western **Finistère**; the family resorts such as **Bénodet** just to the south; and the **Morbihan coast** below **Vannes**. Hotels and campsites here are plentiful, if pushed to their limits from mid-June to the end of August.

Be sure not to leave Brittany without visiting one of its many **islands** – such as the **Île de Bréhat**, the **Île de Sein**, or **Belle-Île** – or taking in cities like **Quimper** or **Morlaix**, testimony to the riches of the medieval duchy. Allow time, too, to explore the interior, even if the price you pay for the solitude is sketchy transport and a shortage of accommodation.

CÔTE DE GRANIT ROSE

# Highlights

**❶ Dinan** Brittany's most complete walled medieval town, perched in a gorgeous setting above the Rance river. **See p.315**

**❷ Cancale** The stalls and restaurants in Cancale's little harbour will have oyster-lovers in raptures. **See p.315**

**❸ The Côte de Granit Rose** With its bizarre pink rock formations and gem-like beaches, this memorable stretch of coastline is perfect for kids. **See p.322**

**❹ Île de Sein** Misty and mysterious island, barely rising from the Atlantic; a great day-trip from western Finistère. **See p.322**

**❺ The Inter-Celtic Festival** Celebrate the music and culture of the Celtic nations at Lorient's summer festival. **See p.345**

**❻ Carnac** France's most extraordinary megalithic monuments, predating even the Egyptian pyramids. **See p.346**

**❼ Belle-Île** The aptly named island offers a microcosm of Brittany, with wild coast in the south, beaches in the north, and beautiful countryside between. **See p.350**

**HIGHLIGHTS ARE MARKED ON THE MAP ON P.304**

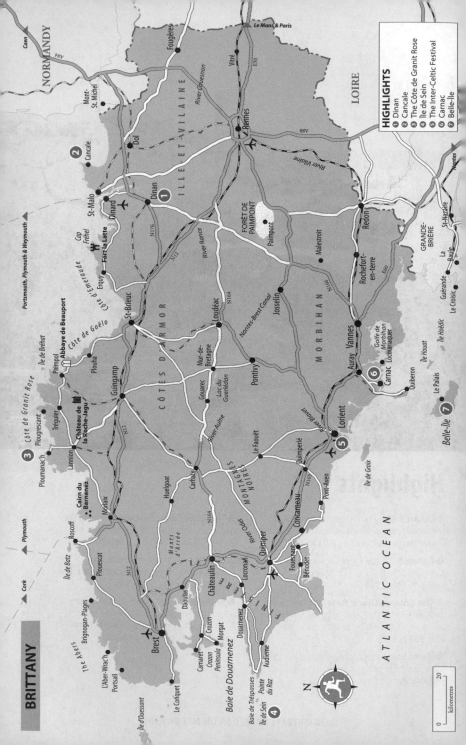

## A BRETON GLOSSARY

Although estimates of the number of **Breton-speakers** range from 400,000 to 800,000, you're unlikely to encounter it spoken as a first, day-to-day language. Learning Breton is not really a viable prospect for visitors without a grounding in Welsh, Gaelic or some other Celtic tongue. However, as you travel through the province, it's interesting to note the roots of Breton place names, many of which have a simple meaning in the language. Below are some of the most common:

| | | | |
|---|---|---|---|
| **aber** | estuary | **lann** | heath |
| **argoat** | land | **lech** | flat stone |
| **armor** | sea | **mario** | dead |
| **avel** | wind | **men** | stone |
| **bihan** | little | **menez** | (rounded) mountain |
| **bran** | hill | **menhir** | long stone |
| **braz** | big | **meur** | big |
| **coat** | forest | **nevez** | new |
| **cromlech** | stone circle | **parc** | field |
| **dol** | table | **penn** | end, head |
| **dolmen** | stone table | **plou** | parish |
| **du** | black | **pors** | port, farmyard |
| **enez** | island | **roc'h** | ridge |
| **goaz** | stream | **ster** | river |
| **gwenn** | white | **stivel** | fountain, spring |
| **hir** | long | **traez henn** | beach |
| **ker** | village or house | **trou** | valley |
| **kozh** | old | **ty** | house |
| **lan** | holy place | **wrach** | witch |

If you're looking for traditional Breton fun, and you can't make the Lorient festival (or the smaller Quinzaine Celtique at Nantes in June/July), look out for gatherings organized by **Celtic folklore groups** – Circles or Bagadou. You may also be interested by the **pardons**, pilgrimage festivals commemorating local saints. Bear in mind, though, that despite local attempts to promote these as exciting spectacles, they're not phoney affairs kept alive for tourists, but deeply serious and rather gloomy religious occasions.

### GETTING AROUND                                                                 BRITTANY

Brittany is well served by public transport. Separate TGV train lines from Paris – one ending at Brest, the other at Quimper – serve the major cities along the north and south coasts respectively, and high-speed trains also connect Lille with Rennes. All are complemented by local buses and trains. Driving too is straightforward, and none of Brittany's *autoroutes* charges tolls.

# Eastern Brittany and the north coast

All roads in Brittany curl eventually inland to **Rennes**, the capital. East of Rennes, the fortified citadel of **Vitré** protected the eastern approaches to medieval Brittany, which vigorously defended its independence against incursors. Along the north coast, west of Normandy's Mont St-Michel, stand some of Brittany's finest old towns. A spectacular introduction to the province greets ferry passengers: the **River Rance**, guarded by magnificently preserved **St-Malo** on its estuary, and beautiful medieval **Dinan** 20km upstream. Further west stretches a varied coastline that culminates in the seductive **Île de Bréhat**, and the colourful chaos of the **Côte de Granit Rose**.

**6**

## FOOD IN BRITTANY

Brittany's proudest contribution to world cuisine has to be the **crêpe**, and its savoury equivalent the **galette**; crêperies throughout the region attempt to pass them off as satisfying meals, serving them with every imaginable filling. However, gourmet types are more likely to be enticed by the magnificent array of **seafood**. Restaurants in resorts such as St-Malo and Quiberon jostle to attract fish connoisseurs, while some smaller towns – like Cancale, widely regarded as the best place in France for oysters (*huîtres*), and Erquy, with its scallops (*coquilles St-Jacques*) – depend on one specific mollusc for their livelihood.

Although they can't claim to be uniquely Breton, two appetizers feature on every self-respecting menu – **moules marinière**, giant bowls of succulent orange mussels steamed in white wine, shallots and parsley (and perhaps enriched with cream or crème fraîche to become *moules à la crème*), and **soupe de poissons** (fish soup), traditionally served with garlicky *rouille* mayonnaise (coloured with sweet red pepper), a mound of grated gruyère, and a bowl of croutons. Jars of fresh *soupe de poissons*, sold in seaside *poissonneries*, make an ideal way to take a taste of France home with you. Paying a bit more in a restaurant – typically on *menus* costing €25 or more – brings you into the realm of the **assiette de fruits de mer**, a mountainous heap of langoustines, crabs, oysters, mussels, clams, whelks and cockles, most raw and all delicious.

**Main courses** tend to be plainer than in neighbouring Normandy. Fresh local fish is prepared with relatively simple sauces. Skate served with capers, or salmon baked with a mustard or cheese sauce, are typical, while even the **cotriade**, a stew containing sole, turbot or bass, as well as shellfish, is less rich than its Mediterranean equivalent, the bouillabaisse. Brittany is also better than much of France in its respect for fresh **vegetables**, thanks to local-grown peas, cauliflowers, artichokes and the like. Only with the **desserts** can things get a little heavy; **far Breton**, considered a great delicacy, is a baked concoction of sponge and custard dotted with chopped plums, while *îles flottantes* are soft meringue icebergs adrift in a sea of *crème anglaise*, a light egg custard.

Strictly speaking, no **wine** is produced in Brittany; although they're often regarded as Breton, the dry whites Muscadet and Gros-Plant are produced in the neighbouring *département* of Loire-Atlantique.

# Rennes

The capital and power centre of Brittany since its 1532 union with France, **RENNES** is – outwardly at least – uncharacteristic of the region, with its Neoclassical layout and pompous major buildings. Any potential it had as a picturesque tourist spot was destroyed in 1720, when a drunken carpenter managed to set light to virtually the whole city. Only the area known as **Les Lices**, at the junction of the canalized Ille and the River Vilaine, was undamaged.

Rennes' subsequent remodelling left the city, north of the river at any rate, as a muddle of grand eighteenth-century public squares interspersed with intimate little alleys of half-timbered houses. It's a lively enough place though, with around sixty thousand university **students** to stimulate its cultural life, and a couple of major annual **festivals**, the Tombées de la Nuit and the Transmusicales, to lure in visitors.

## The medieval quarter

Rennes' surviving **medieval quarter**, bordered by the canal to the west and the river to the south, radiates from the **Porte Mordelaise**, the old ceremonial entrance to the city. Immediately northeast of the *porte*, the **place des Lices** is dominated by two usually empty market halls, but comes alive every Saturday for one of France's largest **street markets**. In a jousting tournament on this very spot in 1337, the hitherto unknown Bertrand du Guesclin, then aged 17, fought and defeated several older opponents. That set him on his career as a soldier, during which he was to save Rennes when it was under siege by the English. However, after the Bretons were defeated at Auray in 1364, he fought for the French, and twice invaded Brittany.

## Palais du Parlement

Rue Hoche

The one central building to escape Rennes' 1720 fire was the **Palais du Parlement** on rue Hoche downtown. In 1994, however, the Palais was all but ruined by a mysterious conflagration, sparked by a flare during a demonstration by Breton fishermen. Now rebuilt and restored, the entire structure is once more topped by an impressive array of gleaming gilded statues. Inside, its lobby stages temporary exhibitions.

## Musée des Beaux-Arts

20 quai Émile-Zola • Tues 10am–6pm, Wed–Sun 10am–noon & 2–6pm • €5.95 • ☎ 02 23 62 17 45, ⓦ mbar.org

The south bank of the **River Vilaine**, which flows through the centre of Rennes, narrowly confined into a steep-sided channel, is home to the **Musée des Beaux-Arts**. Unfortunately many of its finest artworks – which include drawings by Leonardo da Vinci, Botticelli, Fra Lippo Lippi and Dürer – are not usually on public display. Instead you'll find indifferent Impressionist views of Normandy by the likes of Boudin and Sisley, interspersed with the occasional treasure such as Veronese's depiction of a flying *Perseus Rescuing Andromeda*. Picasso makes a cameo appearance,

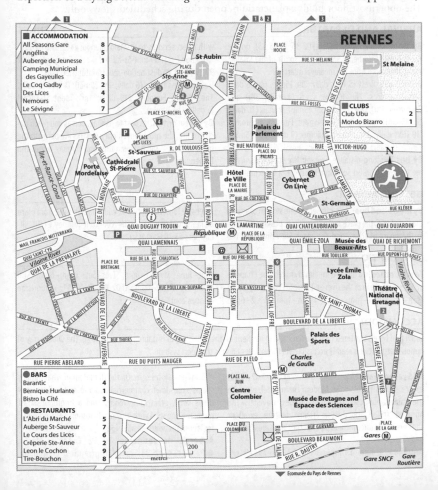

with a nude from 1923, a simple *Baigneuse à Dinard* from 1928, and a very late and surprisingly Cubist canvas from 1970. The museum also hosts a succession of high-quality temporary exhibitions.

## Musée de Bretagne and Éspace des Sciences

10 cours des Alliés • July & Aug Tues–Fri 1–7pm, Sat & Sun 2–7pm; Sept–June Tues noon–9pm, Wed–Fri noon–7pm, Sat & Sun 2–7pm • Musée de Bretagne €4, Éspace des Sciences €4.50; €7 for both • ☎ 02 23 40 66 00, ⓦ www.musee-bretagne.fr

The showpiece **Musée de Bretagne**, housed in the modern Champs Libres, 500m south on the cours des Alliés, provides a high-tech overview of Breton history and culture. It starts with a hearth used by humans in a Finistère sea cave half a million years ago that ranks among the oldest evidence of fire in the world. From here on, a quick, entertaining skate through regional history covers the dolmens and menhirs of the megalith builders, some magnificent jadeite axes and Bronze Age swords, and the arrival of first the Celts, next the Romans, and later still the spread of Christianity from the fifth century onwards. Labels are in English as well as French and Breton.

Under the same roof, the **Éspace des Sciences** is a peculiar sort of scaly volcano that contains two floors of rather dry scientific displays, this time with no English captions. The uppermost floor holds a planetarium, open during scheduled shows only.

## ARRIVAL AND DEPARTURE

RENNES

**By train** Rennes' *gare SNCF* (☎ 08 36 35 35 35), on the Paris–Brest TGV line, is 15min walk south of the Vilaine, and a little more from the medieval quarter.

Destinations Brest (5 TGVs daily; 2hr 15min, plus 6 daily slower services, 2hr 40min); Caen (4 daily; 3hr) and Pontorson (1hr); Lille (2 daily; 3hr 45min); Morlaix (10 daily; 1hr 45min); Nantes (10 daily; 45min); Paris-Montparnasse (10 TGVs daily; 2hr 10min); Quimper (9 daily; 2hr 15min); Vannes (6 daily; 1hr); Vitré (5 daily; 20min).

**By bus** The long-distance *gare routière* stands alongside the *gare SNCF* on bd Solférino. Rennes is a busy junction,

with direct services to St-Malo (Illenoo: ☎ 02 99 82 26 26, ⓦ illenoo.fr), and Mont-St-Michel (Keolis Emeraude: ☎ 02 99 19 70 80, ⓦ destination-montsaintmichel.com).

Destinations Dinan (6 daily; 1hr 20min); Dinard (5 daily; 1hr 40min); Fougères (10 daily; 1hr); Mont St-Michel (5 daily; 1hr 30min).

**By car** For drivers, it's best to park as soon as you reach the city centre; the most convenient car parks are beneath the place des Lices, and between the *quais* Duguay-Trouin and Lamennais.

## GETTING AROUND

**By metro and bus** A fast, efficient métro system connects the *gare SNCF*, the place de la République beside the canal in the heart of town, and the place Ste-Anne. Like the

extensive local bus network, which radiates out from place de la République, it's run by STAR (one journey €1.40, all-day pass €3.70; ⓦ star.fr).

## INFORMATION

**Tourist office** In a disused medieval church, the Chapelle St-Yves, just north of the river at 11 rue St-Yves (July & Aug Mon–Sat 9am–7pm, Sun 11am–1pm & 2–6pm;

Sept–June Mon 1–6pm, Tues–Sat 10am–6pm, Sun 11am–1pm & 2–6pm; ☎ 02 99 67 11 11, ⓦ tourisme -rennes.com).

## ACCOMMODATION

You'll find hotels scattered near the river and in old Rennes, the best area for restaurants and nightlife. The wider array of options further out is readily accessible via the excellent public transport system.

**All Seasons Gare** 15 place de la Gare ☎ 02 99 67 31 12, ⓦ all-seasons-hotels.com. Modern chain hotel, opposite the train station, used largely by business travellers. The hundred stylish, good-value rooms feature excellent showers, while rates include a buffet breakfast plus free hot and cold drinks. **€70**

**Angélina** 1 quai Lammenais ☎ 02 99 79 29 66,

ⓦ angelina-hotel.com. On the third floor of what initially seems a run-down commercial building, this budget hotel offers large, great-value rooms, and a bright breakfast room; the one snag with its central location is the potential for late-night noise outside. **€58**

**Auberge de Jeunesse** 10–12 Canal St-Martin ☎ 02 99 33 22 33, ⓦ fuaj.org/rennes. Welcoming, attractively positioned HI hostel, 3km north of the centre by the Canal d'Ille et Rance (bus #8 from place Ste-Anne métro station). It has a cafeteria and a laundry; hostelling association membership is compulsory. Closed Xmas to mid-Jan. **€21**

**Camping Municipal des Gayeulles** Rue du Prof-Maurice-Audin ☎02 99 36 91 22, ⓦcamping-rennes .com. An appealingly verdant site, 1km east of central Rennes (bus #3, direction "St-Laurent"), in a park that offers good shade and a pool and sporting facilities nearby. Open all year. **€13**

**Le Coq Gadby** 156 rue d'Antrain ☎02 99 38 05 55, ⓦlecoq-gadby.com. Family-run for four generations, this self-styled "urban resort" is in a somewhat inconvenient location, in a humdrum neighbourhood around 1.5km north of the centre. Spread between the original seventeenth-century building and a modern annex, it holds 24 comfortable rooms, an open-fire lounge, a pool

and spa, and a Michelin-starred restaurant. Reserve online for the best rates. **€120**

**Des Lices** 7 place des Lices ☎02 99 79 14 81, ⓦwww .hotel-des-lices.com. Forty-eight rooms, all with balcony, in a very comfortable and friendly modern hotel in the prettiest part of old Rennes, handy for the place des Lices car park. **€74**

★ **Nemours** 5 rue de Nemours ☎02 99 78 26 26, ⓦhotelnemours.com. Recast as a boutique hotel, this central option has spotless, stylish, and well-lit rooms in white and green tones, with flatscreen TVs and comfortable beds. Friendly and professional service, and you can take good breakfasts (€10) in bed. **€62**

**Le Sévigné** 47 av Jean-Janvier ☎02 99 67 27 55, ⓦhotellesevigne.fr. Smart, upmarket establishment 100m north of the *gare SNCF* en route to the centre, with buffet breakfasts, and a large brasserie next door. All rooms have good en-suite bathrooms, plus satellite TV; discounts at weekends. **€69**

## EATING AND DRINKING

Most of Rennes' more interesting bars and restaurants are in the streets just south of the place Ste-Anne, with the bar-lined rue St-Michel and rue Penhoët, each with a fine assemblage of ancient wooden buildings, forming the epicentre. Ethnic alternatives are concentrated along rue St-Malo just to the north, and also on rue St-Georges near the place du Palais. Rue Vasselot, south of the river, is similar.

**L'Abri du Marché** 9 place des Lices ☎02 99 79 73 87, ⓦcreperie-moulerie.com. Nothing but the Breton staples of *moules* (€10) and *galettes* (€3–9) are served at this local favourite, where the pleasant dining room is smothered in old Breton trinkets, and there's also seating outdoors. Daily noon–2pm & 7–10.30pm.

**Auberge St-Sauveur** 6 rue St-Sauveur ☎02 99 79 32 56. Classy, romantic restaurant, in an attractive medieval house near the cathedral, with light lunches for €13 and richer, meaty dinner *menus* at €19.50 and €29.50. Mon & Sat 7–11pm, Tues–Fri noon–3pm & 7–11pm.

★ **Le Cours des Lices** 18 place des Lices ☎02 99 30 25 25, ⓦlecoursdeslices.fr. Top-notch French restaurant, perfectly positioned to take advantage of the fresh produce in the adjoining market. Dinner *menus* at €19 (weekdays only), €29 and €41; the latter includes such dishes as roasted lobster and de-boned pigeon. Tues–Fri noon–2pm & 7.30–10pm, Sat 11.30am–2pm & 7.30–10pm.

**Crêperie Ste-Anne** 5 place Ste-Anne ☎02 99 79 22 72, ⓦcreperiesainteanne.com. Appealing crêperie nicely situated on the place Ste-Anne opposite the church, with plenty of outdoor seating and a good selection of *galettes* for €5–8. Mon–Sat 11.45am–10.30pm.

**Leon le Cochon** 1 rue Maréchal-Joffre ☎02 99 79 37 54, ⓦleonlecochon.com. Tasteful, contemporary but classically French restaurant; as the name suggests, there's a heavy emphasis on pigs, and their trotters in particular. The simple €12.50 lunch *menu* includes wine, while the dinner *menu* costs €23 on weekdays, €25 at weekends. Mon–Thurs & Sun noon–2pm & 7.30–10.30pm, Fri & Sat noon–2pm & 7.30–11pm. Closed Sun in July & Aug.

**Tire-Bouchon** 2 rue de Chapitre ☎02 99 79 43 43. Part bistro, part wine bar, this friendly local rendezvous chalks up a simple array of fresh-cooked dishes on its blackboard each day, from *tartines* to meat with pasta, and also offers ample plates of cheese or charcuterie. Mon–Fri noon–2pm & 7–10.45pm.

---

### RENNES FESTIVALS

Rennes is at its best in the first week of July, when the **Festival des Tombées de la Nuit** takes over the whole city to celebrate Breton culture with music, theatre, film, mime and poetry (ⓦlestombeesdelanuit.com). A pocket version of the same festival is also held in the week between Christmas and New Year.

In the first week of December, the **Transmusicales** rock festival attracts big-name acts from all over the world, though still with a Breton emphasis (ⓦlestrans.com).

## NIGHTLIFE AND ENTERTAINMENT

### BARS

**Barantic** 4 rue St-Michel ☎02 99 79 29 24. One of the city's favourite bars, putting on occasional live music for a mixed crowd of Breton nationalists and boisterous students; if it's too full, you can head to half a dozen similar alternatives within spitting distance. Daily noon–1am.

**Bernique Hurlante** 40 rue St-Malo ☎02 99 38 70 09. This popular yellow-painted haunt ranks among Rennes' most gay-friendly bars, and also serves as a rendezvous for local artists and activists. Tues–Sun 5pm–2am.

★ **Bistro la Cité** 7 rue St-Louis ☎02 99 79 24 34. This great little bar/bistro, with art on the walls and friendly staff and clientele, is the ideal place for a cider, a stronger house brew, or a quick meal. They host live music to suit a range of tastes on Saturday nights. Tues–Sun 5pm–1am.

### LIVE MUSIC

**Club Ubu** 1 rue St-Helier ☎02 99 31 12 10, ⓦubu-rennes.com. The city's principal venue for big rock concerts, open year round, in a separate auditorium on the same site as the Théâtre National de Bretagne.

**Mondo Bizarro** 264 av Général-Patton ☎02 99 87 22 00, ⓦmondobizarro.free.fr. Rock, metal and especially punk club, 1km northeast of the centre (bus line #5), and kept busy most nights with local bands and international punk stalwarts, plus a leavening of tribute bands, ska, reggae and jazz. Tues–Sat 5pm–3am.

### THEATRE

**Théâtre National de Bretagne** 1 rue St-Helier ☎02 99 31 12 31, ⓦt-n-b.fr. A stimulating programme of varied events – with dance and music as well as theatre – throughout the year, except in July and Aug.

# Vitré

**VITRÉ**, 30km east of Rennes, rivals Dinan as the best-preserved medieval town in Brittany. While its walls are not quite complete, the thickets of medieval stone cottages that lie outside them have hardly changed. The towers of the **castle**, which dominates the western end of the ramparts, have pointed slate-grey roofs in best fairy-tale fashion, looking like freshly sharpened pencils, but sadly the municipal offices and **museum** of shells, birds, bugs and local history inside are not exactly thrilling (April–Sept daily 10.30am–12.30pm & 2–6.30pm; Oct–March Mon & Wed–Sat 10.30am–12.15pm & 2–5.30pm, Sun 2–5.30pm; €4, ☎02 99 75 04 54).

Vitré's principal **market** is held on Mondays in the square in front of **Notre-Dame church**. The old city is full of twisting streets of half-timbered houses, a good proportion of which are bars – **rue Beaudrairie** in particular has a fine selection.

## ARRIVAL AND INFORMATION VITRÉ

**By train** The *gare SNCF* is on the southern edge of the centre, where the ramparts disappear and the town blends into its newer sectors.

**Tourist office** Place Général de Gaulle, left from the station (July & Aug Mon–Sat 9.30am–12.30pm & 2–6.30pm, Sun 10am–12.30pm & 3–6pm; Sept–June Mon 2.30–6pm, Tues–Fri 9.30am–12.30pm & 2.30–6pm, Sat 10am–12.30pm & 3–5pm; ☎02 99 75 04 46, ⓦot-vitre.fr); they run an intricate schedule of guided tours in summer.

## ACCOMMODATION AND EATING

**Du Château** 5 rue Rallon ☎02 99 74 58 59, ⓦhotelduchateauvitre.fr. Inexpensive hotel, down below the castle just outside the walls. All rooms are acceptable, but it's worth paying a little extra for those on the upper floors, which have views of the ramparts. €52

**Petit Billot** 5bis place du Général-Leclerc ☎02 99 75 02 10, ⓦpetit-billot.com. Very friendly, good-value hotel, facing the station, offering clean simple rooms of all shapes and sizes. €60

**La Soupe aux Choux** 32 rue Notre-Dame ☎02 99 75 10 86, ⓦlasoupe-auxchoux.fr. Fine old house, with exposed stone walls, converted into a smart restaurant that offers simple but classic French food, with the occasional eccentricity like kangaroo cooked in cider (€14) thrown in. Dinner *menu* €24. Mon–Fri noon–2pm & 7–10pm, Sat 7–10pm.

# St-Malo

Walled with the same grey granite stone as Mont St-Michel, the elegant, ancient, and beautifully positioned city of **ST-MALO** was originally a fortified island at the mouth of the Rance, controlling not only the estuary but also the open sea beyond. Now inseparably attached to the mainland, it's the most visited place in Brittany, thanks partly to its superb **old citadelle** and partly to its ferry service to England, and the lively streets that lie within the walls – the area known as *intra-muros* – are packed with restaurants, bars and shops. Yes, the summer crowds can be oppressive, but even then a stroll atop the walls should restore your equilibrium, while the vast, clean **beaches** beyond are a huge bonus, especially if you're travelling with kids.

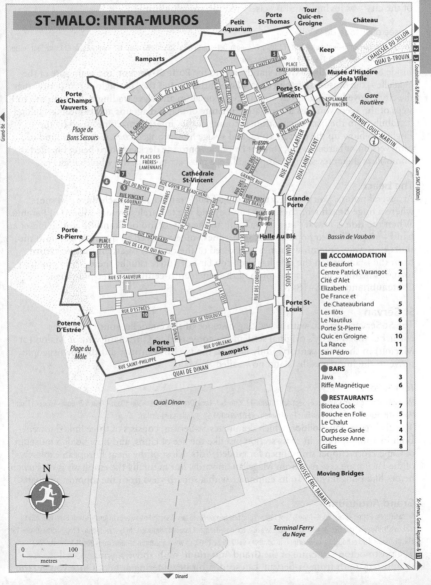

## ST-MALO: INTRA-MUROS

**ACCOMMODATION**

| | |
|---|---|
| Le Beaufort | 1 |
| Centre Patrick Varangot | 2 |
| Cité d'Alet | 4 |
| Elizabeth | 9 |
| De France et de Chateaubriand | 5 |
| Les Ilôts | 3 |
| Le Nautilus | 6 |
| Porte St-Pierre | 8 |
| Quic en Groigne | 10 |
| La Rance | 11 |
| San Pédro | 7 |

**BARS**

| | |
|---|---|
| Java | 3 |
| Riffe Magnétique | 6 |

**RESTAURANTS**

| | |
|---|---|
| Biotea Cook | 7 |
| Bouche en Folie | 5 |
| Le Chalut | 1 |
| Corps de Garde | 4 |
| Duchesse Anne | 2 |
| Gilles | 8 |

## The citadelle

The **citadelle** of St-Malo was long joined to the mainland only by a causeway; then the construction of the harbour basin concealed the original line of the coast forever. Although its streets of restored seventeenth- and eighteenth-century houses tend to be packed with visitors in high season, away from the more popular thoroughfares random exploration is fun, and you can always escape to the **ramparts** – first erected in the fourteenth century – to enjoy wonderful all-round views.

Ancient as they look, the **buildings** within the walls are almost entirely reconstructed; following the bombardment that forced the German surrender in 1944, eighty percent of the city was lovingly and precisely rebuilt, stone by stone.

### Musée d'Histoire de la Ville

St-Malo Château • April–Sept daily 10am–12.30pm & 2–6pm; Oct–March Tues–Sun 10am–noon & 2–6pm • €6, or €11 with Tour Solidor; free on first Fri of month • ☎ 02 99 40 71 57, ⓦ ville-saint-malo.fr

Inside St-Malo's **castle** – which stands next to the **Porte St-Vincent**, the main gate of the citadelle – the **Musée d'Histoire de la Ville** commemorates the "prodigious prosperity" that the city enjoyed during its days of piracy, colonialism and slave trading. Climbing the 169 steps of the keep, you pass a fascinating mixture of maps, diagrams and exhibits – chilling handbills from the Nazi occupation, accounts of the "infernal machine" used by the English to blow up the port in 1693, and savage four-pronged *chausse-trapes* (a kind of early version of barbed wire), thrown by pirates onto the decks of ships being boarded to immobilize their crews. At the top a gull's-eye prospect takes in the whole citadelle.

## The beach

At several points, you can pass through St-Malo's ramparts to reach the open shore, where a huge **beach** stretches away east beyond the featureless resort-suburb of **Paramé**. When the tide is low, it's safe to walk out to the tiny island of **Grand-Bé**, much closer at hand – the walk is so popular that sometimes you even need to queue to get onto the short causeway. Solemn warnings are posted of the dangers of attempting to return from the island when the tide has risen too far – if you're caught there, there you have to stay. The one "sight" is the tomb of the nineteenth-century writer-politician **Chateaubriand** (1768–1848).

## St-Servan

The **St-Servan** district, within walking distance of the citadelle, south along the corniche, was the city's original settlement, converted to Christianity by St Malou (or Maclou) in the sixth century. Only later, in the twelfth century, did the townspeople move to the impregnable island now called St-Malo.

### Tour Solidor

**Museum** 90min guided tours April–Sept daily 10am–12.30pm & 2–6pm; Oct–March Tues–Sun 10am–noon & 2–6pm • €6, or €11 with Musée d'Histoire de la Ville; free on first Fri of month • ☎ 02 99 40 71 57, ⓦ ville-saint-malo.fr

The distinctive **Tour Solidor**, which dominates St-Servan, consists of three linked towers. Built in 1382, it looks in cross-section just like the ace of clubs, and now holds a **museum** of Cape Horn clipper ships, open for guided visits. Most of the great European explorers of the Pacific are covered, from Magellan onwards, but naturally the emphasis is on French heroes like Bougainville. Tours culminate with a superb view from the topmost ramparts.

## Grand Aquarium

Av du Général-Patton • Daily: April–June & Sept 10am–7pm; first two weeks in July & second two weeks in Aug 9.30am–8pm; mid-July to mid-Aug 9.30am–10pm; Oct–March 10am–6pm as a rule, but closed most of Jan; last admission 1hr before closing • €16, children (under-15) €12, discounts if ticket bought a week or more in advance • ☎ 02 99 21 19 00, ⓦ www.aquarium-st-malo.com • Bus #5 from *gare SNCF*

The postmodern structure of the **Grand Aquarium**, high above town and well signposted south from St-Servan, can seem a bit bewildering at first. Once you get the hang of it, though, it's an entertaining place, where you can either learn interesting facts about slimy monsters of the deep or simply pull faces back at them. Its eight fish tanks, which hold fish from all over the world, include one shaped like a Polo mint, where dizzy visitors stand in the hole in the middle as myriad fish whirl around them.

## ARRIVAL AND DEPARTURE                                          ST-MALO

**By cross-channel ferry** From the Terminal Ferry du Naye, Brittany Ferries (☎02 99 40 64 41, ⊛brittany -ferries.com) sails to Portsmouth, while Condor Ferries (☎02 99 40 78 10, ⊛www.condorferries.co.uk) connects with Portsmouth and Poole (via Jersey or Guernsey) during spring and summer (see p.29).

**By river ferry** Between April and early Nov, regular passenger ferries (10min) to Dinard operate from the quai Dinan, just outside the southernmost point of the ramparts (€4.60 single, €7 return; bikes cost double; ☎08 25 13 80 35, ⊛compagniecorsaire.com).

**By train** St-Malo's *gare SNCF* is 2km inland from the citadelle, convenient neither for the old town nor the ferry. Destinations Rennes (14 daily; 50min; connections for Paris on TGV).

**By bus** Almost all local and long-distance buses stop at the *gare SNCF* as well as on the esplanade St-Vincent, just outside the citadelle. Illenoo (☎02 99 82 26 26, ⊛illenoo.fr) runs services to Dinard, Rennes and Mont-St-Michel; Tibus (☎08 10 22 22 22, ⊛www.tibus.fr) serves Dinan and Dinard.

Destinations Cancale (6 daily; 45min); Dinan (6 daily; 45min); Dinard (10 daily; 30min); Fougères (3 daily; 2hr 15min); Mont St-Michel (4 daily; 1hr 30min); Pontorson (4 daily; 1hr 15min); Rennes (3 daily; 1hr 30min).

## INFORMATION

**Tourist office** Esplanade St-Vincent, just outside the citadelle (April–June & Sept Mon–Sat 9am–1pm & 2–6.30pm, Sun 10am–12.30pm & 2.30–6pm; July & Aug Mon–Sat 9am–7.30pm, Sun 10am–6pm; Oct–March Mon–Sat 9am–1pm & 2–6pm; ☎08 25 13 52 00, ⊛saint -malo-tourisme.com). You can get online here, or in Cyber' Com, west of the *gare SNCF* at 26bis bd des Talards (☎02 99 56 05 83, ⊛www.cybermalo.com).

**Bike hire** Bicycles can be rented from Les Velos Bleus, 19 rue Alphonse-Thébault (☎02 99 40 31 63, ⊛velos-bleus .fr; closed Nov–March), or Espace Nicole, 11 rue R-Schuman, Paramé (☎02 99 56 11 06, ⊛cyclesnicole.com).

**Markets** St-Malo, in the Halle au Blé within the walls (Tues & Fri); St-Servan (Mon & Fri); Paramé (Wed & Sat). St-Malo's fish market is on Saturday in the place de la Poissonerie, within the walls.

## ACCOMMODATION

St-Malo boasts more than a hundred hotels, including the seaside boarding houses just off the beach, along with several campsites and a hostel. In high season it needs every one of them, so make reservations well in advance. Some *intra-muros* hotels take advantage of summer demand by insisting you eat in their own restaurants. Cheaper rates can be found by the *gare SNCF*, or in suburban Paramé.

### IN THE CITADELLE

**De France et de Chateaubriand** 12 place Chateaubriand ☎02 99 56 66 52, ⊛www.hotel-fr-chateaubriand.com. This imposing old hotel, in prime position behind a courtyard just off the main square, has been partially renovated. While the standard *confort* rooms are pretty ordinary, the *supérieure* – especially those with sea views – are well worth the extra, and the old-fashioned public spaces are ideal for lazy days. Choose between a large well-priced bistro downstairs, and the fancier modern top-floor restaurant, *Le 5*. Breakfast costs €12 and parking €15. *Confort* **€95**, *supérieure* **€113**

**Elizabeth** 2 rue des Cordiers ☎02 99 56 24 98, ⊛st-malo-hotel-elizabeth.com. Seventeenth-century mansion, just back from the walls and grandly furnished on a Far Eastern theme. Ten spacious guest rooms with rather small bathrooms, plus cheaper but modern and comfortable rooms in "the Skippers", an annexe 100m away. Breakfast €11. *Skippers* **€75**, *Elizabeth* **€145**

★ **Le Nautilus** 9 rue de la Corne de Cerf ☎02 99 40 42 27, ⊛lenautilus.com. Colourfully refitted hotel (with a lift), not far in from the Porte St-Vincent, with small, bright, good-value rooms, all with shower and WC. Friendly staff ensure it's hugely popular with younger travellers in particular, but it's welcoming to all. Bar but no restaurant. Closed mid-Nov to early Feb. **€70**

**Porte St-Pierre** 2 place du Guet ☎02 99 40 91 27, ⊛hotel-portestpierre.com. Comfortable *Logis de France*, peeping over the walls of the citadelle, near the small Porte St-Pierre and very handy for the beach; the recently modernized rooms have new floors and in many cases sea views. One family room sleeps five. The owners also run a restaurant across the alley, recommended for seafood lovers. Closed mid-Nov to Feb. **€78**

★ **Quic en Groigne** 8 rue d'Estrées ☎02 99 20 22 20, ⊛quic-en-groigne.com. Friendly little hotel at the far end of the citadelle, with attractive en-suite rooms, recently refreshed with good bathroom fittings, and helpful owners. Closed mid-Nov to late Jan. **€79**

**San Pédro** 1 rue Ste-Anne ⓣ 02 99 40 88 57, ⓦ sanpedro-hotel.com. Twelve compact but tastefully and stylishly furnished rooms in a nice quiet setting, just inside the walls in the north of the citadelle. Great breakfasts and friendly advice. Higher rooms (reached via a minuscule lift) enjoy sea views, and cost €10 extra. Closed Dec to mid-March. **€69**



### OUTSIDE THE WALLS

**Le Beaufort** 25 chaussée du Sillon, Coutoisville ⓣ 02 99 40 99 99, ⓦ www.hotel-beaufort.com. Grand seaside hotel, half-an-hour's walk along the beach from the citadelle. Beautifully restored rooms – some with lovely sea-view balconies – and a fine restaurant. **€147**

★ **La Rance** 15 quai Sébastopol, St-Servan ⓣ 02 99 81 78 63, ⓦ larancehotel.com. Small, tasteful and airy option in sight of the Tour Solidor, with eleven spacious and freshly spruced-up rooms, and a much more tranquil atmosphere than St-Malo itself. **€65**

### HOSTEL AND CAMPSITES

**Centre Patrick Varangot** 37 av du Père-Umbricht, Paramé ⓣ 02 99 40 29 80, ⓦ centrevarangot.com. One of France's busiest hostels, near the beach 2km northeast of the *gare SNCF*, and usually dominated by lively young travellers. Dorm beds in shared en-suite rooms which can also be rented privately; hostelling association membership required. Rates include breakfast, and there's also a cut-price cafeteria, kitchen facilities and tennis courts. No curfew, open all year. Dorms **€21**

★ **Cité d'Alet** Allée Gaston Buy, St-Servan ⓣ 02 99 81 60 91, ⓦ www.ville-saint-malo.fr/tourisme/les-campings. The nicest local campsite is also by far the nearest to the citadelle, a municipally run gem in a dramatic location on the headland southwest of St-Malo, overlooking the city from within the wartime German fortified stronghold. Bus #1 from *gare SNCF* or Porte St-Vincent. Closed Oct to late April. **€14.40**

**Les Ilôts** Av de la Guimorais, Rothéneuf ⓣ 02 99 56 98 72, ⓦ www.ville-saint-malo.fr/tourisme/les-campings. Green little municipal site, a 5min walk inland from either of two crescent beaches, roughly 5km east of the citadelle. Closed Dec to early April. **€14.40**

## EATING AND DRINKING

*Intra-muros* St-Malo boasts even more restaurants and bars than hotels, but prices are probably higher than anywhere else in Brittany, especially on the open café terraces – apart from the *Duchesse Anne*, avoid all those around rue Jacques-Cartier and Porte St-Vincent. Bear in mind that most crêperies also serve *moules* and similar snacks.

### RESTAURANTS

**Biotea Cook** 8 rue des Cordiers ⓣ 02 99 20 08 36, ⓦ www.restaurant-st-malo-bioteacook.com. Step beyond the deli and classy daytime tea lounge to find a dinner-only, all-organic restaurant – even the wine is organic – which serves the town's best choice for vegetarians, but also offers fresh meat and fish options, on *menus* priced from €19 to €37. Tues–Sat 7.30–10pm.

**Bouche en Folie** 14 rue du Boyer ⓣ 06 72 49 08 89, ⓦ boucheenfolie.eresto.net. This tiny little place offers classic, seasonal French dishes, with a good lunch *menu* for €13, and excellent dinner *menus* for €22 and €28. Some outdoor seating. Wed–Sun noon–1.30pm & 7.30–10pm.

**Le Chalut** 8 rue de la Corne de Cerf ⓣ 02 99 56 71 58. Quite an exclusive dining room, in a blue-painted fish-themed bistro a short way in from the Porte St-Vincent. All the *menus* offer a limited choice, with perhaps one or two exclusively fishy main courses, and the odd meaty appetizer. The €25 weekday lunch *menu* centres on the catch of the day; otherwise you can pay €38 or €55 for a gourmet fish dinner, designed to be not quite as rich as the traditional norm, or €70 for a three-course *menu* consisting entirely of lobster. Reservations preferred. Wed–Sun noon–1.30pm & 7–9.30pm.

**Corps de Garde** 3 montée Notre Dame ⓣ 02 99 40 91 46, ⓦ le-corps-de-garde.com. The only restaurant that's right up on St-Malo's ramparts is a simple crêperie, serving delicious but far from unusual crêpes (€3–10). However, the views from its large open-air terrace (covered when necessary) are sensational, looking out over the beach to dozens of little islets. Mid-Dec to mid-Nov daily noon–2pm & 7–9pm; July & Aug daily noon–9.30pm.

**Duchesse Anne** 5–7 place Guy-la-Chambre ⓣ 02 99 40 85 33. Despite a recent change of ownership, the old-fashioned elegance of St-Malo's best-known upmarket restaurant, beside Porte St-Vincent, remains unchanged. You can get a two-course lunch for €24, or the full three-course option for €34.50, but dinner will cost well over twice that. Whole baked fish is the speciality. Feb–Nov Tues & Thurs–Sat 12.15–1.30pm & 7.15–9.30pm, Sun 7.15–9.30pm.

**Gilles** 2 rue de la Pie-qui-Boit ⓣ 02 99 40 97 25, ⓦ restaurant-gilles-saint-malo.com. Bright, modern, good-value restaurant, just off the central pedestrian axis. The €17.50 lunch *menu* is fine; for dinner, €26 brings you duck sausage or smoked salmon, and a scallop risotto. Mon, Tues & Fri–Sun noon–1.30pm & 7.30–9.30pm.

### BARS

**Java** 3 rue Ste-Barbe ⓣ 02 99 56 41 90, ⓦ lajavacafe.com. Among its many eccentric features, this entertaining and unique cider bar – to give it its full official name, *Le Cafe duCoin d'en Bas de la Rue du Bout de la Ville d'en Face du*

*Port... La Java* – boasts a row of swings at the bar, old dolls on the wall, and an elevator door into the toilet. All is designed to keep the conversation flowing as smoothly as the drinks. Mon–Fri 8.31am–9.44pm, 11.42pm, or 12.52am "depending on the flexibility of the tail of the dog"; Sat & Sun opens 8.33am.

**Riffe Magnétique** 20 rue de la Herse ☎ 02 99 40 85 70, ⓦleriffmagnetique.com. Lively, friendly bar, with a fine choice of wines plus regular café-concerts, and DJs at the weekend. Tues–Sat 6pm–2am.

## Cancale

The delightful harbour village of **CANCALE**, across the peninsula less than 15km east of St-Malo, is not so much a one-horse as a one-mollusc town – the whole place is obsessed with the **oyster**, and with "*ostréiculture*". It consists of two distinct halves: the old town up on the hill, and the very pretty and smart port area of **La Houle** down below. Glass-fronted hotels and restaurants stretch the length of the waterfront, always busy with visitors, while fishing boats bob in the harbour itself. At its northern end, demarcated by a stone jetty, local women sell fresh oysters by the dozen from stalls with bright striped canvas awnings.

In the old church of St-Méen at the top of the hill, the town's obsession is documented with meticulous precision by the small **Musée des Arts et Traditions Populaires** (May, June & Sept Mon & Fri–Sun 2.30–6.30pm; July & Aug daily 10am–noon & 2.30–6.30pm; €3.50; ⓦmuseedecancale.fr).

Just north of town, the perilous and windy heights of the headland known as the **Pointe du Grouin** offer spectacular views of the pinnacle of Mont St-Michel and the bird sanctuary of the **Îles des Landes** to the east.

### ACCOMMODATION AND EATING

★ **Au Pied de Cheval** 10 quai Gambetta ☎ 02 99 89 76 95. A ramshackle, gloriously atmospheric little place to sample a few oysters, with great baskets of bivalves spread across its wooden quayside tables. While *menu* prices have crept up, a dozen raw oysters on a bed of seaweed can cost just €5. July & Aug Mon–Fri 9am–10pm, Sat & Sun 9am–6pm; Sept, Oct & mid-April to June Mon, Tues, Thurs & Fri 9am–10pm, Sat & Sun 9am–6pm.

**Auberge de Jeunesse** Port Picain ☎ 02 99 89 62 62, ⓦfuaj.org/cancale-baie-de-saint-michel. Modern hostel, very close to the beach 2km north of town, where rates include breakfast, and camping space and kitchen facilities are also available. Closed Nov–March. Dorms €22

★ **La Houle** 18 quai Gambetta ☎ 02 99 89 62 38. The cheapest rooms in Cancale's best budget hotel lack en-suite facilities, but paying a little more gets you an excellent bathroom, and more still a sea-view balcony. €35

## Dinan

The wonderful citadel of **DINAN**, 30 km south of St-Malo just before the river Rance begins to broaden towards the sea, has preserved almost intact its 3km encirclement of protective masonry, along with street upon colourful street of late medieval houses. However, despite its slightly unreal perfection, it's seldom overrun with tourists. There are no essential museums, the most memorable architecture is vernacular rather than monumental, and time is most easily spent wandering from crêperie to café and down to the pretty port. At the end of July, every other (even-numbered) year, the **Fête des Remparts** is celebrated with medieval-style jousting, banquets, fairs and processions, culminating in an immense fireworks display (ⓦfete-remparts-dinan.com).

### Port du Dinan

Like most of St-Malo, Dinan is ideally seen when arriving by boat up the Rance. By the time the ferries reach the lovely **port du Dinan**, down below the thirteenth-century ramparts, the river has narrowed sufficiently to be spanned by a small but majestic old stone bridge. High above it towers a former railway viaduct. The steep, cobbled lane that twists up from the quayside makes a wonderful climb, passing ancient flower-festooned edifices of wood and stone, as well as several crêperies and even a half-timbered poodle parlour, before it enters the city through the **Porte du Jerzual**.

## St-Sauveur church

On a little square not far above the imposing gateway of the Porte du Jerzual, **St-Sauveur church** sends the skyline of Dinan even higher. It's a real hotchpotch, with a Romanesque porch and an eighteenth-century steeple. Even its nine Gothic chapels feature five different patterns of vaulting in no symmetrical order; the most complex pair, in the centre, would make any spider proud.

The one small stretch of Dinan's medieval **ramparts** that's open to visitors leads from behind St-Sauveur church to just short of Tour Sillon, overlooking the river.

## Place du Guesclin and around

Dinan's large, central **place du Guesclin** hosts a large **market on Thursdays**, and serves as Dinan's main car park for the rest of the week. In 1364, the Breton warrior **Bertrand du Guesclin** fought and defeated the English knight Thomas of Canterbury in single combat here.

The true heart of town these days consists of two much smaller squares nearby, the **place des Merciers** and the **place des Cordeliers**, which hold a wonderful assortment of medieval wood-framed houses.

## Château de Duchesse Anne

Daily: June–Sept 10am–6.30pm; Oct–Dec & Feb–May 1.30–5.30pm • €5

What's now known as the **Château de Duchesse Anne** is not so much a castle as the fourteenth-century keep that once protected Dinan's southern approach, along with two separate towers to which it offers access. The keep itself, or *donjon*, consists of four

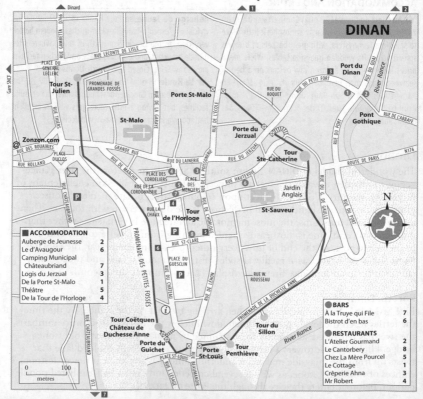

**DINAN**

**ACCOMMODATION**

| | |
|---|---|
| Auberge de Jeunesse | 2 |
| Le d'Avaugour | 6 |
| Camping Municipal Châteaubriand | 7 |
| Logis du Jerzual | 3 |
| De la Porte St-Malo | 1 |
| Théâtre | 5 |
| De la Tour de l'Horloge | 4 |

**BARS**

| | |
|---|---|
| À la Truye qui File | 7 |
| Bistrot d'en bas | 6 |

**RESTAURANTS**

| | |
|---|---|
| L'Atelier Gourmand | 2 |
| Le Cantorbery | 8 |
| Chez La Mère Pourcel | 5 |
| Le Cottage | 1 |
| Crêperie Ahna | 3 |
| Mr Robert | 4 |

0   100
metres

storeys, each of which holds an unexpected hotchpotch of items, including two big old looms and assorted Greek and Etruscan perfume jars; at ground level, well below the walls, there's a slender, closed drawbridge.

The more intriguing of the two neighbouring towers, the ancient **Tour Coëtquen**, is all but empty. If you descend the spiral staircase to its waterlogged bottom floor, however, you'll find a group of stone fifteenth-century notables resembling some medieval time capsule, about to depetrify at any moment.

## ARRIVAL AND INFORMATION  DINAN  6

**By train and bus** Both the Art Deco *gare SNCF* – with trains to Dol (8 daily; 23min), for connections to Caen and Brest – and the *gare routière* (6 daily buses to St-Malo; 45min; ☎08 10 22 22 22, ⓦtibus.fr) are in the rather gloomy modern quarter, on place du 11-Novembre, 10min walk west of the walls.

**By boat** Between May and Oct, boats sail along the Rance between Dinan's port and Dinard and St-Malo (Compagnie Corsaire: ☎08 25 13 81 20, ⓦcompagniecorsaire.com). The trip takes 2hr 45min, with the exact schedule varying according to the tides (adults €24.80, under-16s €14.90). It's only possible to do a day return by boat (adults €31, under-16s €18.60) if you start from St-Malo or Dinard; starting from Dinan, you have to come back by bus or train.

**Tourist office** 9 rue du Château, just off the place du Guesclin; internet access available (July & Aug Mon–Sat 9.30am–7pm, Sun 10am–12.30pm & 2.30–6pm; Sept–June Mon–Sat 9am–12.30pm & 2–6pm; ☎02 96 87 69 76, ⓦwww.dinan-tourisme.com).

## ACCOMMODATION

Many of Dinan's hotels lie within the walled town or down by the port. Both locations are convenient if you're on foot, but motorists should note that parking can be difficult in summer. Most hotels are mid-range, with only a couple of genuine budget options.

**Auberge de Jeunesse** Moulin de Méen, Vallée de la Fontaine-des-Eaux ☎02 96 39 10 83, ⓦfuaj.org/dinan. Attractive, rural former watermill, beside the river in green fields below the town centre. No bus access: to walk there, follow the quay downstream from the port on the town side. Breakfast €4. Camping is permitted in the grounds. Closed Oct–Feb. Dorms €14.30, doubles €28.60

★ **Le d'Avaugour** 1 place du Champ ☎02 96 39 07 49, ⓦavaugourhotel.com. Smart, elegant hotel, entered from the main square but backing onto the ramparts, with very tasteful renovated rooms, lovely gardens, and exceptionally helpful staff. Closed Nov–Feb, plus Sun in low season. €125

**Camping Municipal Châteaubriand** 103 rue Châteaubriand ☎02 96 39 11 96. Verdant, minimally equipped little campsite, in a quiet spot just outside the western ramparts, offering just fifty pitches. Closed late Sept to late May. €11

**Logis du Jerzual** 25–27 rue du Petit Fort ☎02 96 85 46 54, ⓦlogis-du-jerzual.com. Friendly B&B, with a lovely garden terrace, halfway up the exquisite little lane that leads from the port. The five rooms have wonderful character, with four-poster beds, modern bathrooms and romantic views over the rooftops. €80

**De la Porte St-Malo** 35 rue St-Malo ☎02 96 39 19 76, ⓦhotelportemalo.com. Simple but very comfortable rooms in a welcoming and tasteful small hotel just outside the walls, beyond the Porte St-Malo, away from the bustle of the centre. €65

**Théâtre** 2 rue Ste-Claire ☎02 96 39 06 91. Nine very basic rooms above a friendly bar, right by the Théâtre des Jacobins; the cheapest come only with a sink, but even those with en-suite bathrooms still cost less than €30, which is amazing for such a central location. Closed Mon Oct–May. €23

**De la Tour de l'Horloge** 5 rue de la Chaux ☎02 96 39 96 92, ⓦhotel-dinan.com. You have to climb forty-plus stairs to reach the rooms in this nice and very central little hotel, but they're spacious, clean and good value; the bells on the namesake clock tower start ringing at 7am. €72

## EATING AND DRINKING

All sorts of specialist restaurants, including several ethnic alternatives, are tucked away in the old streets of Dinan. Take an evening stroll through the town and down to the port, and you'll pass at least twenty places. For bars, explore the series of tiny parallel alleyways between place des Merciers and rue du Marchix. Along rue de la Cordonnerie, the busiest of the lot, the various hangouts define themselves by their taste in music.

### RESTAURANTS

**L'Atelier Gourmand** 4 rue de Quai ☎02 96 85 14 18. This delightful riverside spot, beside the bridge with indoor and outdoor seating, serves a well-priced menu of *tartines*

(€9), *moules* (€10–13), and assorted main courses (€12–15). July–Sept Mon–Sat noon–1.30pm & 6.30–9.30pm, Sun noon–1.30pm; Oct–June closed Mon.

**Le Cantorbery** 6 rue Ste-Claire ☎ 02 96 39 02 52. High-class food served in an old stone house with rafters, a spiral staircase and a real wood fire. Lunch from €14, while traditional dinner *menus* start with a good €27 option that includes fish soup and veal kidneys. June–Sept Mon–Sat noon–1.45pm & 7–9.30pm, Sun noon–1.45pm; Oct–May closed Wed.

**Chez La Mère Pourcel** 3 place des Merciers ☎ 02 96 39 03 80, ⓦ chezlamerepourcel.com. Beautiful half-timbered fifteenth-century house in the central square. Good à la carte options are served all day, while the dinner *menus* (€23–35), are gourmet class. June–Sept daily noon–1.30pm & 7.30–9pm; Oct–May closed Sun eve.

**Le Cottage** 78 rue du Petit Fort ☎ 02 96 87 96 70. Welcoming, cellar-like restaurant at the foot of pretty pedestrian alley, just a few steps up from the river bridge, with three outdoor tables but at its cosiest with a log fire blazing in winter. Good fishy *menus* from €19.50; be sure to sample the marmite de pecheur. Daily noon–2.30pm & 6.45–10.30pm.

**Crêperie Ahna** 7 rue de la Poissonnerie ☎ 02 96 39 09 13. Smart central crêperie, with limited outdoor seating, that's hugely popular with lunching locals. Savoury pancakes cost €3.50–8.50, and they also serve potato blinis and grilled meats, including nice big sausages. Mon–Sat noon–2pm & 7–9.30pm.

**Mr Robert** 11 place des Cordeliers ☎ 02 96 85 20 37, ⓦ www.mrrobertrestaurant.fr. Named for its Irish chef-owner, this excellent central option offers a handful of tables on the square itself but plenty of room indoors. Classic French cuisine with subtle Asian-influenced flavourings, on dinner *menus* from €20.50. Tues–Sat noon–1.30pm & 7.30–9.30pm, Sun noon–1.30pm.

**BARS**

**À la Truye qui File** 14 rue de la Cordonnerie ☎ 02 96 39 72 29. A long-standing stalwart of Dinan nightlife, one of several similar hangouts along the ever-lively rue de la Cordonnerie, this contemporary folky Breton dive continues to attract nightly crowds of drinkers. Tues–Sun 5pm–1am.

★ **Bistrot d'en bas** 20 rue Haute Voie ☎ 02 96 87 34 71. This lively little pub and wine bar hosts popular jazz and folk performances, and serves salads and *tartines* too. Tues–Sat 10.30am–1am, Sun 11.30am–3pm.

## The north coast from Dinard to Lannion

The coast that stretches from the resort of **Dinard** to Finistère at the western end of Brittany is divided into two distinct regions, either side of the bay of **St-Brieuc**. Between Dinard and St-Brieuc lie the exposed green headlands of the **Côte d'Émeraude**, while beyond St-Brieuc, along the **Côte de Goëlo**, the shore becomes more extravagantly indented, with countless secluded little bays and an increasing proliferation of huge pink-granite boulders, seen at their best on the **Côte de Granit Rose** near Tréguier.

### Dinard

Originally a fishing village, now a smart little resort blessed with several lovely beaches, **DINARD** sprawls around the western approaches to the Rance estuary, just across the water from St-Malo but a good twenty minutes' drive by road. With its casino, spacious shaded villas and social calendar of regattas and ballet, it might not feel out of place on the Côte d'Azur. Although Dinard is a hilly town, undulating over a succession of pretty coastal inlets, it attracts great numbers of older visitors; as a result, prices tend to be high, and pleasures sedate.

Central Dinard faces north to the open sea, across the curving bay that holds the attractive **plage de l'Écluse**. Hemmed in by venerable Victorian villas rather than hotels or shops, the beach itself has a low-key atmosphere, despite the casino and summer crowds. An unexpected statue of **Alfred Hitchcock** dominates its main access point. Standing on a giant egg, with a ferocious-looking bird perched on each shoulder, he was placed here to commemorate the town's annual festival of English-language films.

#### Coastal footpaths

Enjoyable **coastal footpaths** lead off in either direction from the principal beach, enlivened by notice boards holding reproductions of paintings produced at points along the way. Surprisingly, Pablo Picasso's *Deux femmes courants sur la plage* and *Baigneuses sur la plage*, both of which look quintessentially Mediterranean with their blue skies and golden sands, were in fact painted here in Dinard during his annual summer visits throughout the 1920s.

## ARRIVAL AND INFORMATION DINARD

**By plane** Dinard's small airport, 4km southeast of the town centre, off the D168 near Pleurtuit, is served by Ryanair flights from London Stansted (6wkly, 1hr 10min) and St-Malo (6 daily; 45min). Connecting Illenoo bus #990 (€4) runs via Dinard's tourist office to St-Malo.

**By boat** Companie Corsaire boats arrive from St-Malo (see p.313).
**Tourist office** 2 bd Féart (July & Aug daily 10am–12.30pm & 2.30–6pm; Sept–June Tues–Sat 10am–12.30pm & 2.30–6pm; ☎02 99 46 94 12, ⓦot-dinard.com).

## ACCOMMODATION AND EATING

Dinard is a relatively expensive place to stay, but it does at least have a wide selection of hotels, many of which are listed on ⓦdinard-hotel-plus.com.

★ **Didier Méril** 1 place du Général-de-Gaulle ☎02 99 46 95 74, ⓦrestaurant-didier-meril.com. High-quality gourmet restaurant, beside the main road on the edge of Dinard, just above a great beach, which offers fancy lunches from €22 and dinners from €29, and holds half a dozen exceptionally stylish designer bedrooms, including two sumptuous sea-view suites. **€140**
**Port Blanc** Rue du Sergent-Boulange ☎02 99 46 10 74, ⓦcamping-port-blanc.com. Dinard's finest campsite, run by the municipality, has the plage du Port-Blanc west of the centre almost to itself, with shady pitches right by the beach. Closed Oct–March. **€20**
**Printania** 5 av Georges-V ☎02 99 46 13 07, ⓦprintaniahotel.com. Good mid-range hotel, poised on a quiet street that drops down to the port. A great restaurant, serving a particularly good €40 *menu*, looks out towards St-Malo. Closed mid-Nov to mid-March. **€83**

## The Côte d'Émeraude

The splendidly attractive **Côte d'Émeraude**, west of Dinard, is one of Brittany's most traditional family resort areas, with old-fashioned holiday towns, and safe sandy beaches. It also offers wonderful camping, at its best around the heather-backed beaches near **Cap Fréhel**, a high, warm expanse of heath and cliffs where views can extend as far as Jersey and the Île de Bréhat.

### Fort la Latte

2km southeast of Cap Fréhel • Early July to late Aug daily 10.30am–7pm; April to early July & late Aug to Sept daily 10.30am–12.30pm & 2–6pm; Oct–March Sat, Sun & hols 1.30–5.30pm • €5.10 • ☎02 96 41 57 11, ⓦcastlelalatte.com

The fourteenth-century **Fort la Latte**, at the tip of a small headland 2km southeast of Cap Fréhel, is a gorgeous little gem. Visitors enter across two drawbridges; outbuildings scattered within include a cannonball factory, and there's also a medieval herb garden, but the highlight is the keep, which contains historical exhibits. Precarious walkways climb to its summit, for superb coastal views.

### Erquy

In the delightful little family resort of **ERQUY**, 20km west of Cap Fréhel, a perfect crescent beach nestles into a vast natural bay. At low tide, the sea disappears way beyond the harbour entrance, leaving gentle ripples of sand. You can walk right across its mouth, from the grassy wooded headland on the left side to the picturesque little lighthouse on the right.

## INFORMATION ERQUY

**Tourist office** 3 rue du 19 Mars (April–June Mon–Sat 9.30am–12.30pm & 2–6pm, Sun 10am–12.30pm; July & Aug Mon–Sat 9.30am–1pm & 2–7pm, Sun 10am–1pm & 4–6pm; first fortnight of Sept Mon–Sat 9.30am–12.30pm & 2–6pm; mid-Sept to March Mon–Sat 9.30am–12.30pm & 2–5pm; ☎02 96 72 30 12, ⓦerquy-tourisme.com).

## ACCOMMODATION AND EATING

★ **Beauséjour** 21 rue de la Corniche ☎ 02 96 72 30 39, ⓦ beausejour-erquy.com. Set in a seaside villa above the southern end of the beach, and festooned with dungaree-wearing teddies, the *Beauséjour* represents Erquy at its most quirky. The rooms are nice, though, and its panoramic restaurant is excellent. Closed mid-Nov to March. **€69**

**Camping de la Plage de St-Pabu** Plage de St-Pabu ☎ 02 96 72 24 65, ⓦ saintpabu.com. The pick of the local campsites, right by the sea just beyond the second promontory southwest of town. The garden-like location incorporates a kids' playground but not a pool. Closed mid-Nov to March. **€20**

★ **La Villa Nazado** 2 rue des Patriotes ☎ 02 96 63 67 14, ⓦ villanazado.com. Four very tasteful B&B rooms, in a grand, pastel-yellow nineteenth-century villa a couple of blocks back from the seafront in the heart of Erquy. **€65**

## The Côte de Goëlo

As you move northwest from Erquy towards Paimpol along the **Côte de Goëlo**, the shoreline becomes wilder and harsher and the seaside towns tend to be crammed into narrow rocky inlets or set well back in river estuaries.

### Abbaye de Beauport

2km south of Paimpol · Daily: mid-June to mid-Sept 10am–7pm, with regular 1hr 30min guided tours; mid-Sept to mid-June 10am–noon & 2–5pm · €6 · ☎ 02 96 55 18 58, ⓦ abbaye-beauport.com

South of Paimpol, in a superbly romantic waterfront setting, the D786 passes the substantial ruins of the **Abbaye de Beauport**, established in 1202 by Count Alain de Goëlo. Its stone walls are covered with wild flowers and ivy, the central cloisters are engulfed by a huge tree, and birds fly everywhere. The Norman Gothic chapterhouse is the most noteworthy building to survive, and its roofless halls hold relics from all periods of its history. In summer, the abbey hosts occasional evening concerts, usually of Breton music.

### Paimpol

At the top of the Côte de Goëlo, the attractive town of **PAIMPOL** consists of a tangle of cobbled alleyways and fine grey-granite houses. It centres on a port that has been stripped of much of its character in its transition from working fishing port to pleasure harbour. This was once the base for a cod and whaling fleet that sailed to Iceland each February. From then until September the town would be empty of its young men. Thanks to naval shipyards and the like, the open sea is not visible from Paimpol; a maze of waterways leads to its two separate **harbours**. Both are usually filled with the high masts of yachts, but are still also used by the fishing vessels that keep a fish market and a plethora of *poissonneries* busy.

## ARRIVAL AND INFORMATION                                          PAIMPOL

**By train and bus** The *gare SNCF* and *gare routière* are side by side on av du Général-de-Gaulle.

**Tourist office** Place de la République, 100m from the pleasure port (July & Aug Mon–Sat 9.30am–7.30pm, Sun 10am–12.30pm & 4.30–6.30pm; Sept–June Mon–Fri 9.30am–12.30pm & 2–6.pm, Sat 9.30am–12.30pm & 2–6.30pm; ☎ 02 96 20 83 16, ⓦ paimpol-goelo.com).

## ACCOMMODATION AND EATING

**La Cotriade** 16 quai Armand-Dayot ☎ 02 96 20 81 08, ⓦ la-cotriade.com. Paimpol's best seafood restaurant, close to the water on the far side of the harbour, serves a changing daily array of authentic fish dishes, with lunch *menus* from €21, and a dinner *menu* at €41. Mid-June to mid-Sept Mon 7.15–9.30pm, Tues–Sun 12.15–1.45pm & 7.15–9.30pm; mid-Sept to mid-June Tues–Sat 12.15–1.45pm & 7.15–9.30pm.

★ **K'Loys** 21 quai Morand ☎ 02 96 20 40 01, ⓦ k-loys .com. This grand old mansion, overlooking the small-boat harbour and crammed with oddities, houses an eccentric but extremely welcoming hotel. The comfortable rooms vary in price according to size and view; the wonderful top-floor Captain's suite, with its retractable ceiling, is highly recommended. A good bistro stretches from the front courtyard into the street. **€90**

### The Île de Bréhat

Hugely popular with French visitors in summer, the little **ÎLE DE BRÉHAT** – 2km offshore from Pointe de l'Arcouest, 6km northwest of Paimpol – is one of the most beautiful places in Brittany. Renowned as a sanctuary for rare species of wild flowers, including blue acanthus, it abounds in birds of all kinds.

Consisting, in truth, of two islands, joined by a tiny bridge, Bréhat appears to span great latitudes. On its north side are windswept meadows of hemlock and yarrow, sloping down to chaotic erosions of rock; on the south, you find yourself amid palm trees, mimosa and eucalyptus. All around is a multitude of little islets – some accessible at low tide, others *propriété privée*, most just pink-orange rocks.

**6**

#### Port-Clos

Boats to Bréhat (see below) arrive at the small harbour of **PORT-CLOS**, though depending on the tide passengers may have to walk several hundred metres before setting foot on terra firma. **Cars** are banned, so many visitors rent **bikes** at the port, for around €15 per day. However, it's easy enough to explore on foot; walking from one end to the other takes less than an hour.

#### Le Bourg

Each batch of new arrivals heads first to Bréhat's village, **LE BOURG**, 500m up from the port. Besides a handful of hotels, restaurants and bars, it also holds a limited array of shops, and hosts a small **market** most days. In high season, the attractive central square tends to be packed fit to burst, with exasperated holiday-home-owners pushing their little shopping carts through the throngs of day-trippers.

#### The northern island

A short distance north of Le Bourg, the slender **Pont ar Prat** bridge leads across to the northern island, where the crowds thin out, and countless little coves offer opportunities to sprawl on the tough grass or clamber across the rugged boulders. At the northernmost tip, the **Paon lighthouse** stands erect over the rock-scattered waters – girls of the island used to throw rocks into the wash, believing that if it landed in the water without hitting a rock they would marry their love, but if it hit a rock, it would be a cold bed for another year. Though the coastal footpath around this northern half offers the most attractive walking on the island, the best **beaches** line the southern shores, with the **Grève du Guerzido** at its southeastern corner being the pick of the crop.

#### ARRIVAL AND INFORMATION                    ÎLE DE BRÉHAT

**By ferry** Bréhat is connected regularly by ferry from the Pointe de l'Arcouest, which is 6km northwest of Paimpol, and served by summer buses from its *gare SNCF*. Broadly speaking, sailings, with Les Vedettes de Bréhat (☏ 02 96 55 79 50, ⊛ vedettesdebrehat.com), are every 30min at peak times between April and September, and every 1hr 30min between October and March, with the first boat out to Bréhat at 8.15am year round, and the last boat back at 7.45pm in summer, 6pm in winter. The return trip costs €9

(bikes, €15 extra, are only allowed outside peak crossing times). The same company also offers crossings in summer from Erquy, Binic and St-Quay-Portrieux, and boat tours of the island (€13).

**Tourist office** In Le Bourg's main square (July & Aug Mon–Sat 10am–1pm & 2–5pm, Sun 10am–1pm; March–June & Sept Mon, Tues & Thurs–Sat 10am–12.30pm & 1.30–4.30pm; Oct–Feb Mon & Thurs–Sat 10am–12.30pm & 1.30–4.30pm; ☏ 02 96 20 04 15, ⊛ brehat-infos.fr).

#### ACCOMMODATION

High demand has made the island's hotels lackadaisical about service and quality; all tend to be booked throughout the summer, and to insist on *demi-pension*.

**Bellevue** Port-Clos ☏ 02 96 20 00 05, ⊛ hotel -bellevue-brehat.fr. This twenty-room hotel, right by the *embarcadère*, has been nicely modernized; the best rooms have sea-view balconies and whirlpool baths. Compulsory *demi-pension* mid-July to Aug; closed mid-Nov to mid-Feb. **€84**, demi-pension **€176**

**Camping Municipal** Goareva ☎02 96 20 02 46, ⓦiledebrehat.fr. This wonderful municipal campsite is set in the woods high above the sea at the southwest tip of the island. Camping wild elsewhere is strictly forbidden. Closed mid-Sept to May. **€10.60**

## The Côte de Granit Rose

The northernmost stretch of the Breton coast, between Bréhat and Ploumanac'h, has loosely come to be known as the **Côte de Granit Rose**. Great pink-granite boulders jut from the sea around the island of Bréhat, and are scattered along the various headlands to the west. Perhaps the most memorable stretch of coast lies north of **Tréguier**, where the pink-granite rocks are eroded into fantastic shapes.

### Tréguier

West of Paimpol, the D786 passes over a green ria on the bridge outside Lézardrieux before arriving at **TRÉGUIER**, one of Brittany's very few hill towns. Its central feature is the **Cathédrale de St-Tugdual**, which contains the tomb of St Yves, a native of the town who died in 1303 and – for his incorruptibility – became the patron saint of lawyers. Attempts to bribe him continue to this day; his tomb is surrounded by marble plaques and an inferno of candles invoking his aid.

### Jardins de Kerdalo

Near Trédarzec, 2km east of Tréguier • July & Aug Mon–Sat 2–6pm; April–June & Sept Mon & Sat 2–6pm • €8 • ☎ 02 96 92 35 94

Originally planted by Russian Peter Wolkonsky, who died in 1997, the **Jardins de Kerdalo** rank among the finest in France. Rare and exotic breeds ramble through the grounds, making a joyful change from the exacting straight-line gardening of so many châteaux.

### Château de la Roche-Jagu

D787, 10km southeast of Tréguier • Easter hols, June, Sept, Oct & Nov hols daily 10am–noon & 2–6pm; May Sat & Sun 10am–noon & 2–6pm; July & Aug daily 10am–1pm & 2–7pm • Park access €2, château €4, or €5 during special exhibitions • ☎ 02 96 95 62 35, ⓦ www.larochejagu.fr

The fifteenth-century **Château de la Roche-Jagu** stands on a heavily wooded slope above the meanders of the Trieux river. A really gorgeous building, it hosts lavish **annual exhibitions**, usually on some sort of Celtic theme. Outside, the modern landscaped park is traced through by several **hiking trails**.

### Ploumanac'h

For anyone in search of a beach holiday, the best base along the Granit Rose coast has to be the tiny resort of **PLOUMANAC'H**, a couple of kilometres west of the missable town of Perros-Guirec. A great walk along the **Sentier des Douaniers** pathway winds round the clifftops from Ploumanac'h to the plage Trestraou in Perros-Guirec, passing an astonishing succession of deformed and water-sculpted rocks. Birds wheel overhead towards the offshore bird sanctuary of **Sept-Îles**, and battered boats shelter in the narrow inlets or bob uncontrollably out on the waves. There are patches and brief causeways of grass, clumps of purple heather and yellow gorse. The small golden yellow beach here is a surreal treat, in an alcove of soft-shaped and smooth pink granite

---

## LA PETITE MAISON DE PLOUGRESCANT

Perhaps the best-known photographic image of Brittany is of a small seafront cottage somehow squeezed between two mighty pink-granite boulders. Surprisingly few visitors, however, see the house in real life. It stands 10km north of Tréguier, and just 2km out from the village of **Plougrescant**. The precise spot tends to be marked on regional maps as either **Le Gouffre** or Le Gouffre du Castel-Meuru. Although you can't visit the cottage itself – which actually faces inland, across a small sheltered bay, with its back to the open sea – the shoreline nearby offers superb short walks, and a summer-only café sells snacks.

formations protected by numerous other outcrops in the bay, one of which barely separates a glorious private house from the waves.

## INFORMATION                                                CÔTÉ DE GRANIT ROSE

### TRÉGUIER

**Tourist office** 67 rue Ernest-Renan, down by the commercial port (mid-June to mid-Sept Mon–Sat

9am–7pm, Sun 10am–1pm & 2–6pm; mid-Sept to mid-June Tues–Sat 10am–12.30pm & 2–6pm; ☎ 02 96 92 22 33, ⓦ paysdetreguier.com).

## ACCOMMODATION AND EATING

**6**

### TRÉGUIER

**Aigue-Marine** Port de Plaisance ☎ 02 96 92 97 00, ⓦ aiguemarine.fr. Smart, welcoming hotel down by the port in Tréguier, with swimming pool, private parking, whirlpool spa, good buffet breakfasts and a top-notch restaurant. **€105**

★ **Manoir de Troezel Vras** Kerbors ☎ 02 96 22 89 68, ⓦ troezel-vras.com. Irresistibly tranquil rural B&B, set in a sensitively converted old farmhouse 8km northeast of Tréguier. The five large guest rooms are splendidly furnished, and the friendly hosts serve an excellent nightly dinner for €24; there's no menu, you just eat what you're given. No credit cards. Closed mid-Oct to March. **€82**

★ **Poissonnerie Moulinet** 2 rue Ernest-Renan ☎ 02 96 92 30 27. Tasting room above a fish shop just below the cathedral, where you can buy superb seafood platters at low prices; you can also take them away and eat in the square. Daily noon–2.30pm & 6–9pm.

### PLOUMANAC'H

**Castel Beau Site** Plage de Saint Guirec ☎ 02 96 91 40 87, ⓦ castelbeausite.com. Lavish luxury hotel in prime beachfront position, recently modernized and enlarged to offer 33 ultra-chic sea-view rooms, plus a delicious, expensive restaurant. **€200**

**Le Ranolien** ☎ 02 96 91 65 65, ⓦ leranolien.fr. Four-star campsite in a superb position near a little beach halfway along the Sentier des Douaniers, boasting a great array of swimming pools, waterslides, a spa and a cinema. Rental cabins also available. Closed late Sept to early April. **€30**

**Saint Guirec et de la Plage** Plage de Saint Guirec ☎ 02 96 91 40 89, ⓦ hotelsaint-guirec.com. Freshly upgraded hotel, facing the perfect little beach at Ploumanac'h; all the rooms have wetroom showers, some have spacious private terraces, and there's an excellent family suite. The unfortunately named *Coste Mor* restaurant is actually reasonably priced. Compulsory *demi-pension* June–Sept. *Demi-pension* **€205**

## The Bay of Lannion

Despite being set significantly back from the sea on the estuary of the River Léguer, **Lannion** gives its name to a huge coastal bay – and it's the bay rather than the town that is most likely to impress. One enormous beach stretches from **St-Michel-en-Grève**, which is little more than a bend in the road, as far as **Locquirec**; at low tide you can walk hundreds of metres out on the sands.

## Lannion

Set amid plummeting hills and stairways, **LANNION** is a historic city with streets of medieval housing and a couple of interesting old churches. As a centre for high-tech telecommunications, this is one of modern Brittany's real success stories – hence its self-satisfied nickname, *ville heureuse* or "happy town". In addition to admiring the half-timbered houses around the **place du Général-Leclerc** and along **rue des Chapeliers**, it's well worth climbing from the town up the 142 granite steps that lead to the twelfth-century Templar **Église de Brélévenez**. The views from its terrace are stupendous.

## INFORMATION                                                BAY OF LANNION

**Tourist office** 2 quai d'Aiguillon (July & Aug Mon–Sat 9am–6.30pm, Sun 10am–1pm; Sept–June Mon–Sat

9.30am–12.30pm & 2–6pm; ☎ 02 96 46 41 00, ⓦ www .ot-lannion.fr).

## ACCOMMODATION AND EATING

**Auberge Les Korrigans** 6 rue du 73e Territorial, Lannion ☎ 02 96 37 91 28, ⓦ fuaj.org/lannion-les -korrigans. Well-kept hostel, close to the station. Open

year-round, it has a restaurant and bar, and the enthusiastic staff can arrange a wide array of activities, including kayaking. Rates include breakfast. **€21**

**6**

**Grand Hotel des Bains** 15bis rue de l'Église, Locquirec ☎02 98 67 41 02, ⓦgrand-hotel-des-bains.com. Grand indeed, this imposing seafront hotel stands in private gardens close to the heart of the little resort of Locquirec. Spacious rooms, many with terraces, plus a good restaurant and spa. €250

**Ibis** 30 av du Général-de-Gaulle, Lannion ☎02 96 37 03 67, ⓦibishotel.com. The only central hotel in Lannion, facing the station, has seventy well-equipped modern rooms, but no restaurant. €86

## The Cairn du Barnenez

13km northeast of Morlaix • May & June daily 10am–6pm; July & Aug daily 10am–6.30pm; Sept–April Tues–Sun 10am–12.30pm & 2–5.30pm • €5.50 • ☎02 98 67 24 73, ⓦbarnenez.monuments-nationaux.fr

In a glorious position at the mouth of the Morlaix estuary, the prehistoric stone **Cairn du Barnenez** surveys the waters from the summit of a hill. As on the island of Gavrinis in the Morbihan, its ancient masonry has been laid bare by excavations, and provides a stunning sense of the architectural prowess of the megalith builders. Dated by radiocarbon testing to 4500 BC, this is one of the oldest large monuments in the world.

The site consists of two stepped **pyramids**, rising in successive tiers, and built of large flat stones chinked with pebbles. The second was added onto the side of the first, and the two are encircled by a series of terraces and ramps. The whole thing measures roughly 70m long by 15–25m wide and 6m high. Both pyramids were long buried under the same 80m-long earthen mound. While the actual cairns are completely exposed to view, most of the passages and chambers that lie within them are sealed off. The two minor corridors that are open simply cut through the edifice from one side to the other but visitors are not permitted to pass through. Local tradition has it that one tunnel runs right through this "home of the fairies", and continues out deep under the sea.

# Finistère

It's hard to resist the appeal of the **Finistère coast**, with its ocean-fronting cliffs and headlands. Summer crowds may detract from the best parts of the **Crozon peninsula** and the **Pointe de Raz**, but elsewhere you can enjoy near-solitude. Explore the semi-wilderness of the **northern stretches** west of the appealing little Channel port of **Roscoff**, where each successive estuary or **aber** shelters its own tiny harbour, or take a ferry to the misty islands of **Ouessant** and **Sein**. From the top of **Ménez-Hom** visitors can admire the anarchic limits of western France, while the cities of **Brest** and **Quimper** display modern Breton life as well as ancient splendours.

## Morlaix

**MORLAIX**, one of the great old Breton ports, thrived on trade with England during the "Golden Period" of the late Middle Ages. Built up the slopes of a steep valley with sober stone houses, the town was originally protected by an eleventh-century castle and a circuit of walls. Little is left of either, but the centre remains in part medieval with its cobbled streets and half-timbered houses. The present grandeur comes from the pink-granite **viaduct**, carrying trains from Paris to Brest, that towers above the town centre.

### Musée de Morlaix

Place des Jacobins • July–Sept daily 10am–12.30pm & 2–6pm; Sept–June Tues–Sat 10am–noon & 2–5pm, plus first Sun of month 2–5pm • €4.10 with Maison à Pondalez • ☎02 98 88 07 75, ⓦmusee.ville.morlaix.fr

The **Jacobin convent** that fronts place des Jacobins, which once housed the five-year-old Mary Queen of Scots on her way to the French court, now houses the **Musée de Morlaix**, which hosts two temporary exhibitions per year.

Maison à Pondalez

9 Grand'Rue • July–Sept daily 10am–12.30pm & 2–6pm; Sept–June Tues–Sat 10am–noon & 2–5pm, plus first Sun of month 2–5pm • €4.10 with Musée de Morlaix

Tickets for the Musée de Morlaix also entitle you to a guided tour of the **Maison à Pondalez**, a fabulously restored, sixteenth-century house that takes its name from the Breton word for the sculpted wooden internal gallery that dominates the ground floor.

### ARRIVAL AND INFORMATION                                                MORLAIX

**By train** The *gare SNCF* is on rue Armand-Rousseau, high above the town at the western end of the viaduct.

**By bus** All buses conveniently depart from place Cornic, right under the viaduct.

**Tourist office** Place des Otages, all but beneath the viaduct (June & Sept Mon–Sat 9am–12.30pm & 2–6.30pm; July & Aug Mon–Sat 9am–7pm, Sun 10.30am–12.30pm; Oct–May Mon–Sat 9am–12.30pm & 2–6pm; ☎ 02 98 62 14 94, ⓦ tourisme.morlaix.fr).

### ACCOMMODATION AND EATING

**De l'Europe** 1 rue d'Aiguillon ☎ 02 98 62 11 99, ⓦ hotel-europe-com.fr. Grand if eccentric old hotel in the centre of Morlaix, with a fabulous wooden staircase and rooms of varying standards – some plush, some plain – above a simple but good brasserie. **€75**

**Du Port** 3 quai du Léon ☎ 02 98 88 07 54, ⓦ lhotelduport.com. Good-value little hotel, facing the port, with presentable, recently refreshed rooms; the quietest are around the back, looking over the pleasant courtyard. No restaurant, but plenty close by. **€69**

# Roscoff

The opening of the deep-water port at **ROSCOFF** in 1973 was an integral component of a successful bid to revitalize the Breton economy. Its cross-Channel **ferry services** were designed not just to bring tourists, but also to revive the ancient trading links between the Celtic nations of Brittany, Ireland and southwest England. Roscoff had long been a significant port. Mary Queen of Scots landed here in 1548 on her way to Paris to be engaged to François, the son of Henri II of France, as did Bonnie Prince Charlie, the Young Pretender, in 1746, after his defeat at Culloden.

Roscoff itself is still just a small resort, mixing an economy based on fishing with relatively low-key pleasure trips to the **Île de Batz**. Almost all activity is confined to **rue Gambetta** and to the lively old port. The sixteenth-century church, **Notre-Dame-de-Croas-Batz**, at the far end of rue Gambetta, is embellished with an ornate Renaissance belfry, complete with sculpted ships and a protruding stone cannon. Some way beyond is Roscoff's best **beach**, at Laber, surrounded by expensive hotels and apartments.

### ARRIVAL AND INFORMATION                                                ROSCOFF

**By boat** Boats from Plymouth, Cork and Rosslare dock not in Roscoff's original natural harbour, but at the Port de Bloscon, a couple of kilometres east (and just out of sight) of the town.

**By train** From the *gare SNCF*, a few hundred metres south of the town centre, a restricted rail service (often replaced by buses) runs to Morlaix (4 daily; 35min, with connections beyond.

**By bus** Year-round, local buses leave from the *gare SNCF*. In summer, direct buses to Morlaix (5 daily; 1hr) and Quimper (1 daily; 3hr) also leave from the ferry terminal (Penn-ar-Bed; ☎ 08 10 81 00 29, ⓦ viaoo29.fr).

**Tourist office** The helpful tourist office, which also offers free internet access, is on the quayside in town, at 46 rue

---

### THE JOHNNIES OF ROSCOFF

In 1828, Henri Ollivier took **onions** to England from Roscoff, thereby founding a trade that flourished until the 1930s. The story of the "Johnnies" – that classic French image of men in black berets with strings of onions hanging over the handlebars of their bicycles – is told at **La Maison des Johnnies et de l'Oignon Rosé de Roscoff**, 48 rue Brizeux, near the *gare SNCF* (mid-June to mid-Sept Mon, Tues, Thurs & Fri 11am, 3pm & 5pm, Wed 11am; Feb to mid-June & mid-Sept to Dec Tues, Thurs, Fri & Sun 3pm; €4).

Gambetta (July & Aug Mon–Sat 9am–12.30pm & 1.30–7pm, Sun 10am–12.30pm & 2–7pm; Sept–June Mon–Sat 9.15am–noon & 2–6pm; ☎02 98 61 12 13, ⓦroscoff-tourisme.com).

## ACCOMMODATION

For a small town, Roscoff is well equipped with hotels, which are accustomed to late-night arrivals from the ferries. However, many close for some or all of the winter. There's also a hostel on the Île de Batz (see opposite).

**Aux Quatre Saisons** Perharidy ☎02 98 69 70 86, ⓦcamping-aux4saisons.com. Two-star seafront campsite, 2km west of Roscoff, just off the route de Santec. There's no pool, but the adjacent beach is perfect. Closed early Oct to March. **€14.20**

**Des Arcades** 15 rue de l'Amiral-Réveillère ☎02 98 69 70 45, ⓦhotel-les-arcades-roscoff.com. Sixteenth-century building with superb views from half of its modernized rooms, as well as from the restaurant, which has economical *menus* at €11, with a good €28.50 option. En-suite rooms cost around €12 extra. Closed mid-Nov to mid-Feb. **€49**

**Du Centre** 5 rue Gambetta ☎02 98 61 24 25, ⓦchezjanie.com. Family hotel above the café-bar *Chez Janie*, entered via the main street but looking out on the port. Modern, tastefully furnished rooms; sea views cost €25 extra. Closed mid-Nov to mid-Feb. **€99**

★ **Les Chardons Bleus** 4 rue de l'Amiral-Réveillère ☎02 98 69 72 03, ⓦroscoffhotel.com. Very friendly hotel in the heart of the old town, with a good restaurant (closed Thurs & Sun eve Sept–June) where dinner *menus* start at €22. Closed three weeks in Feb. **€70**

★ **Le Temps de Vivre** 19 place Lacaze-Duthiers ☎02 98 19 33 19, ⓦletempsdevivre.net. Ultra-stylish contemporary hotel, in an old mansion near the Notre-Dame church. Luxuriously spacious rooms with designer bathrooms, some with wonderful close-up sea views, but no restaurant. Off-season rates are at least €60 lower. **€156**

## EATING

The obvious places to eat in Roscoff are the dining rooms of the hotels themselves, but the town does hold a few specialist restaurants, plus appealing crêperies around the old harbour. Note that if you're arriving on an evening ferry out of season, it can be difficult to find a restaurant still serving any later than 9.15pm.

**Crêperie de la Poste** 12 rue Gambetta ☎02 98 69 72 81, ⓦcreperiedelaposte.fr. Cosy old stone house, just back from the port in the heart of town, offering inexpensive à la carte meals of sweet and savoury pancakes; more exotic seafood crêpes cost up to €11. They also serve fish soup, mussels and other simple meals. Sept to mid-Nov & mid-Jan to June Thurs–Sun 11.30am until late; July & Aug Mon & Wed–Sun 11.30am until late.

**L'Écume des Jours** Quai d'Auxerre ☎02 98 61 22 83, ⓦecume-roscoff.fr. Romantic restaurant in a grand old house halfway around the town harbour towards the ferry port, where good-value set lunches go for €19.50 on weekdays, and dinner *menus*, from €31, feature such delights as braised oysters or scallops with local pink onions. Jan to mid-Dec Mon & Thurs–Sun noon–1.30pm & 7–9pm.

# Île de Batz

The long, narrow, and very lovely **ÎLE DE BATZ** (pronounced "Ba") mirrors Roscoff across the water, separated from it by a sea channel that's barely 200m wide at low tide but perhaps five times that when the tide is high. Appearances from the mainland are deceptive: the island's old town fills much of its southern shoreline, but those areas not visible from Roscoff are much wilder and more windswept. With no cars permitted, and some great expanses of sandy beach, it makes a wonderfully quiet retreat for families in particular.

Ferries from Roscoff arrive at the **quayside** of the old town. A nice small beach lines the edge of the harbour, but it turns into a morass of seaweed at low tide. All arriving passengers make the obvious 500m walk towards the town.

Turning left when you get to the **church** will bring you to the hostel (see below), and the 44m-high **lighthouse** on the island's peak, all of 23m above sea level (second half of June & first half of Sept Thurs–Tues 2–5pm; July & Aug daily 1–5.30pm; €2). Turning right, on the other hand, leads you towards the best beach, the white-sand **Grève Blanche** at the eastern end of the island.

## ARRIVAL AND DEPARTURE

**By ferry** Three rival ferry companies make the 10min crossing from Roscoff to Batz (frequent services daily: July & Aug 8am–8pm; Sept–June 8.30am–6.30pm; 10min; €8 return; bikes €8). Compagnie Maritime Armein (☎02 98 61 75 47, ⓦarmein.fr), CFTM (☎02 98 61 78 87,

### ÎLE DE BATZ

ⓦvedettes-ile-de-batz.com), and Armor Excursions (☎02 98 61 79 66, ⓦvedettes.armor.ile.de.batz.fr) sell tickets at the landward end of Roscoff's long pier; in summer only, tickets are valid on any ferry. At low tide, the boats sail from the far end of the pier, a good 5min walk further.

## ACCOMMODATION AND EATING

**Auberge de Jeunesse Marine** Creach ar Bolloc'h ☎02 98 61 77 69, ⓦaj-iledebatz.org. The evocatively named Creach ar Bolloc'h makes a beautiful setting for this hostel, which faces south towards Roscoff from near the port. Two separate cottages hold dorm beds, with a lovely beach just a few steps away. Closed Oct–March. **€17**

**Les Couleurs du Temps** ☎02 98 61 75 75, ⓦles -couleurs-du-temps.net. Quirky little crêperie-restaurant,

near the ferries, which sells sweet and savoury pancakes for €5–7, and prepares the Breton speciality *kig ha farz*, seafood stew topped by a crêpe. Easter–Sept daily noon–2pm & 6–8pm.

**Ti Va Zadou** ☎02 98 61 76 91, ⓦtivazadou-iledebatz .fr. Run as a B&B, this pretty, peaceful cottage, in sight of the port, offers five attractive and comfortable guest rooms at varying prices, with great views and big breakfasts. **€50**

# The abers

The coastline west of Roscoff is among the most dramatic in Brittany, a jagged procession of **abers** – deep, narrow estuaries – that hold numerous small, isolated resorts. It's a little on the bracing side, especially if you're making use of the many **campsites**, but that just has to be counted as part of the appeal. In summer, at least, the temperatures are mild enough, and things grow more sheltered as you move around towards Le Conquet and Brest. The first real resort west of Roscoff, **PLOUESCAT**, is not quite on the sea itself, but there are **campsites** nearby on each of three adjacent beaches. Roscoff to Brest **buses** stop at Plouescat before turning inland. Pretty little **BRIGNOGAN-PLAGES**, on the first *aber* west of Plouescat, holds a small natural harbour, once the lair of wreckers, with beaches and weatherbeaten rocks to either side, as well as its own menhir. The *aber* between Plouguerneau and **L'ABER-WRAC'H** has a stepping-stone crossing just upstream from the bridge at Lannilis, built in Gallo-Roman times, where long cut stones still cross the three channels of water. L'Aber-Wrac'h itself, perched over the western side of the vast mouth of the Baie des Anges, is a small and attractive resort within reach of several sandy beaches.

## ACCOMMODATION AND EATING

THE ABERS

### PLOUESCAT

**La Baie du Kernic** Rue Pen an Théven ☎02 98 69 86 60, ⓦcampings.village-center.com/bretagne. For families who want a full-on resort campsite, with on-site restaurant, summer nightlife, and rental cabins available, this is the best choice along this stretch of coast, right beside a pretty beach but also offering a pool and whirlpool spa. Closed mid-Sept to mid-April. **€22**

**Roc'h-Ar-Mor** 18 rue Ar Mor, Porsmeur ☎02 98 69 63 01, ⓦrocharmor.com. Even though this exceptionally cheap little hotel is right on the beach at Porsmeur, none of its six simple but perfectly acceptable rooms has sea views, and neither are they en suite. The food is good, though, and it's the most affordable base you could hope to find. Closed Mon & Tues outside July & Aug; closed Mon Fri in winter. **€28**

### BRIGNOGAN-PLAGES

**Côte des Legendes** Rue Douar ar Pont, Brignogan-Plages ☎02 98 83 41 65, ⓦcampingcotedeslegendes .com. This two-star municipal campsite may be a little short of shade, but it's perfectly poised right by a lovely beach. Closed Nov–Easter. **€15**

### L'ABER-WRAC'H

★**La Baie des Anges** 350 rte des Anges ☎02 98 04 90 04, ⓦbaie-des-anges.com. Peaceful and exceptionally comfortable place to stay, commanding a stunning view as the ria starts to open towards the sea. It has no dining room, but there's a classy bar with a small waterfront terrace, reserved for guests only. Closed mid-Jan to mid-Feb. **€160**

**Le Vioben** ar Palud, L'Aber-Wrac'h ☎02 98 04 96 77, ⓦvioben.fr. Entirely rebuilt following a recent fire, this excellent harbourfront restaurant is an offshoot of the owner's namesake fishing boat, and concentrates on fresh seafood, with lunch *menus* from €17 and dinner *menus* at €28 and €33. Feb–Nov Mon 7–10pm, Tues–Fri & Sun noon–2pm & 7–10pm.

## Le Conquet

**LE CONQUET**, at the far western tip of Brittany 24km beyond Brest, is a wonderful place, scarcely developed, with a long beach of clean white sand, protected from the winds by the narrow spit of the Kermorvan peninsula. It's very much a working fishing village, with grey-stone houses leading down to the stone jetties of a cramped harbour. It occasionally floods, causing great amusement to locals who watch the waves wash over cars left there by tourists taking the ferry out to Ouessant. A good walk 5km south brings you to the lighthouse at **Pointe St-Mathieu**, with its much-photographed view out to the islands from its site amid the ruins of a Benedictine abbey.

| ACCOMMODATION | LE CONQUET |
|---|---|
| **Les Blancs Sablon** Rue de la presqu'île Kermorvan ☎02 98 89 06 90, ⓦles-blancs-sablon.com. Well-equipped two-star campsite, in a lovely spot just across the harbour on the Kermorvan peninsula, with pool as well as access to a huge wild beach. Closed Oct–March. **€15.50** | **Relais du Vieux Port** 1 quai Drellac'h ☎02 98 89 15 91, ⓦlerelaisduvieuxport.com. Right by the jetty, this good-value hotel offers a handful of inexpensive but surprisingly attractive rooms, and has a colourful, squashed-up little restaurant that serves good salads and seafood. Closed Jan. **€49** |

## Île d'Ouessant

The **Île d'Ouessant** ("Ushant" to the English) lies 30km northwest of Le Conquet, and its lighthouse at **Creac'h** (said to be the strongest in the world) is regarded as the entrance to the English Channel. Ouessant is the last in a chain of smaller islands and half-submerged granite rocks. Most are uninhabited, or like Beniguet the preserve only of rabbits, though the **Île de Molène**, midway, has a village.

### Lampaul

Boats to **Ouessant** arrive at the modern **harbour** in the ominous-sounding Baie du Stiff. While there's a scattering of houses here, the only town is 4km distant at **LAMPAUL**, and that's where everyone heads, either by the bus that meets each arriving ferry, by bike, or in a long walking procession that straggles along the one road.

There's not a lot to Lampaul. The best beaches are sprawled around its bay, while the cemetery's **war memorial** lists all the ships in which townsfolk were lost, alongside graves of unknown sailors washed ashore and a chapel of wax "*proëlla* crosses" symbolizing the many islanders who never returned.

### Niou

At **NIOU**, 1km northwest of Lampaul, the **Maisons du Niou** – one's a museum of island history, the other a reconstruction of a traditional island house – jointly form the **Éco-Musée d'Ouessant** (April–June & Sept daily 11am–6pm in school hols, 11am–5pm otherwise; July & Aug daily 10.30am–6pm; Oct–March daily except Mon 1.30–5.30pm; €3.50, or €7 with Musée des Phares et Balises; ☎02 98 48 86 37).

### Créac'h lighthouse

1km west of Niou **Musée des Phares et Balises** April–June & Sept daily 11am–6pm in school hols, 11am–5pm otherwise; July & Aug daily 10.30am–6pm; Oct–March daily except Mon 1.30–5.30pm • €4.50, or €7 with Éco-Musée d'Ouessant

The **Créac'h lighthouse**, 1km west of Niou, boasts a 500-million-candlepower beam

CREUSES
de CANCALE
ÉLEVÉES EN FRANCE
4€ 20/Dz
N°2

capable of being seen from England's Lizard Point. You can't visit the lighthouse tower itself, but the complex at its base holds the **Musée des Phares et Balises**, a large museum devoted to lighthouses and buoys. None of the information is in English, however, and photography is not permitted.

The Créac'h lighthouse makes a good starting point from which to set out along the barren and exposed rocks of the north coast. Particularly in September and other times of migration, it's a remarkable spot for birdwatching, frequented by puffins, storm petrels and cormorants.

## ARRIVAL AND DEPARTURE                                    ÎLE D'OUESSANT

**By boat** There are sailings to Ouessant all year with Penn Ar Bed (☎ 02 98 80 80 80, ⓦ pennarbed.fr). The timetables are extremely intricate, but broadly speaking each day there's one departure from Brest in the winter, leaving at 8.20am, and an additional slightly earlier departure in summer, while there are between one and six from Le Conquet. The first sailing from Le Conquet is at 8am early July to late Aug, at 9am April–June and Sept, and at 9.45am otherwise. Between early July and early September, they also depart from Camaret to Ouessant at

8.15am daily except Sun, with some additional 11am sailings, while between early April and early July, and from early until late Sept, they sail from Camaret at 8.15am on Thurs only. Whether you leave from Brest, Le Conquet, or Camaret, the round-trip fare is the same (June–Sept €31.90, Oct–May Mon–Fri €21.80, Sat & Sun €26).

**By plane** Finist'Air (Mon–Sat 8.30am & 4.45pm, Sun 8.30am; one way €65; ☎ 02 98 84 64 87, ⓦ www .finistair.fr) fly to Ouessant in just 15min from Brest's Guipavas airport.

## GETTING AROUND

**By bus** A bus meets the ferry to take you into Lampaul (€4 return, €15 for a full island tour).

**By bike** Bike rental is a convenient option, as the island is

too big to explore on foot (€12–15/day; operators wait at the port).

## INFORMATION

**Tourist office** General information is available from Lampaul's central tourist office (mid-July to Aug Mon–Sat 9am–1pm & 1.30–7pm, Sun 9.30am–1pm; Sept to

mid-July Mon–Sat 10am–noon & 2–5pm, Sun 10am–noon; ☎ 02 98 48 85 83, ⓦ www.ot-ouessant.fr).

## ACCOMMODATION AND EATING

**Auberge de Jeunesse** La Croix Rouge ☎ 02 98 48 84 53, ⓦ auberge-ouessant.com. Ouessant's clean, functional little hostel stands in a renovated old house, just outside Lampaul town centre as you head north towards Niou. Rates include breakfast, and kitchen facilities are available. Closed Dec & Jan. **€19**

**Ti Jan Ar C'hafé** Lampaul ☎ 02 98 48 82 64, ⓦ tijan .fr. The nicest hotel on the island, in the middle of Lampaul away from the sea. Eight comfortable rooms – each decorated in a different bright colour – and a fine terrace, but no restaurant. Closed mid-Nov to mid-Feb. **€69**

# Brest

Set in a magnificent natural harbour, known as the Rade de Brest, the city of **BREST** is sheltered from ocean storms by the Crozon peninsula to the south. Now home to France's Atlantic Fleet, Brest has been a naval town since the Middle Ages. During World War II, it was continually bombed to prevent the Germans from using it as a submarine base and when liberated in September 1944, after a six-week siege, it was devastated beyond recognition. The architecture of the postwar town is raw and bleak and though there have been attempts to green the city, it has proved too windswept to respond. While it's reasonably lively, most visitors tend simply to pass through.

## Château de Brest

Daily: Feb, March & Oct–Dec 1.30–6.30pm; April–Sept 10am–6.30pm • €5.50 • ☎ 02 98 22 12 39, ⓦ www.musee-marine.fr

The one major site in Brest's city centre is its fifteenth-century **château**, perched on a headland where the Penfeld river meets the bay, and offering a tremendous panorama of both the busy port and the roadstead. Not quite as much of the castle survives as its impressive facade might suggest, though new buildings in the grounds still house the French naval headquarters. Three still-standing medieval towers, however, hold Brest's portion of the **Musée National de la Marine**. Collections include ornate carved figureheads and models, as well as a German "pocket submarine" based here during World War II, and visitors can also stroll the parapets to enjoy the views.

**6**

## Tour Tanguy

June–Sept daily 10am–noon & 2–7pm; Oct–May Wed & Thurs 2–5pm, Sat & Sun 2–6pm • Free • ☎ 02 98 44 24 96

Facing the chateau from the lower right bank of the Penfeld river, the **Tour Tanguy**, with its conical slate roof, was constructed in the fourteenth century. Thanks to a remarkable collection of large-scale dioramas – all the work of one man, Jim Sévellec, and featuring intricately modelled ceramic figures – it now serves as a **history museum-cum-memorial** of Brest before 1939.

## Océanopolis

Port de Plaisance du Moulin Blanc • Mid-Jan to March & mid-Sept to Dec Tues–Sun 10am–5pm, Sat & Sun 10am–6pm; April to early July & first half of Sept daily 9.30am–6pm; early July to Aug daily 9am–7pm • Adults €17.05, under-18s €11.85 • ☎ 02 98 34 40 40, ⓦ oceanopolis.com • Bus #3

A futuristic complex of **aquariums** and related attractions, **Océanopolis** sprawls a couple of kilometres east of the city centre. Its original white dome, now known as the **Temperate Pavilion**, focuses on the Breton littoral and Finistère's fishing industry, holding all kinds of fish, seals, molluscs, seaweed and sea anemones. To that has been added a **Tropical Pavilion**, with a tankful of ferocious-looking sharks plus a myriad of rainbow-hued smaller fish that populate a highly convincing coral reef; a **Polar Pavilion**, complete with polar bears and penguins; and a **Biodiversity Pavilion**. Everything's very high-tech, and perhaps a little too earnest for some tastes, but it's possible to spend a whole entertaining day here.

## ARRIVAL AND DEPARTURE
BREST

**By plane** Brest's airport, at Guipavas 9km northeast, is served by flights from City of London Airport on Cityjet, and from Birmingham and Southampton on Flybe, and also offers local connections to Ouessant (see p.330).

**By train** Brest's *gare SNCF* is on place du 19ème RI at the bottom of av Clemenceau.

Destinations Le Mans (2 daily; 3hr 50min); Morlaix (16 daily; 30min); Paris-Montparnasse (7 TGVs daily; 4hr 20min); Quimper (7 daily; 1hr 15min); Rennes (8 daily; 2hr 15min).

**By bus** The *gare routière* stands shoulder-to-shoulder with the train station.

Destinations Brignogan (8 daily; 1hr); Camaret (1–3 daily; 1hr 10min); Le Conquet (8 daily; 45min); Quimper (5 daily; 1hr 15min); Roscoff (5 daily; 1hr 45min).

**By boat** As well as the sailings to Ouessant (see p.330), in summer boats make the 25min crossing from Brest's Port de Commerce to Le Fret on the Crozon peninsula (April–Sept daily except Mon 2–3 sailings daily; €7 one way; ☎ 02 98 41 46 23, ⓦ azenor.fr). They also offer trips around the Rade de Brest (1hr 30min €15; 3hr €28).

## INFORMATION

**Tourist office** Av Clemenceau, facing place de la Liberté (July & Aug Mon–Sat 9.30am–7pm, Sun 10am–1pm; Sept–June Mon–Sat 9.30am–6pm; ☎ 02 98 44 24 96, ⓦ brest-metropole-tourisme.fr).

## ACCOMMODATION

Used more by business travellers than tourists, the vast majority of Brest's hotels remain open throughout the year, and many offer discounted weekend rates. Only a few, however, maintain their own restaurants.

★ **Abalys** 7 av Clemenceau ☎ 02 98 44 21 86, ⓦ abalys.com. Small but good-value accommodation (especially with weekend reductions) in a spruce little hotel above a bar near the station. All rooms have en-suite facilities, though the bathrooms can be tiny, and most have computers with free wi-fi. Rates drop at weekends. **€49**

**Citôtel de la Gare** 4 bd Gambetta ☎ 02 98 44 47 01, ⓦ hotelgare.com. Convenient, good-value option very near the stations. The cheapest rooms have a shower but no WC, while for a bit extra you can get a magnificent view of the Rade de Brest from the upper storeys. Cheaper weekend rates. **€64**

**Continental** Place de la Tour d'Auvergne ☎ 02 98 80 50 40, ⓦ oceaniahotels.com. Despite the dull concrete facade, this grand luxury hotel has some fine Art Deco features, and is very popular with business travellers. Spotless rooms; several on the fourth floor have large balconies. Huge reductions for advance online reservations, and good weekend rates too. **€137**

## EATING

As well as several low-priced places near the stations, Brest offers a wide assortment of restaurants. Rue Jean-Jaurès, climbing east from the place de la Liberté, has plenty of bistros and bars, while place Guérin to the north is the centre of the student-dominated quartier St-Martin.

★ **La Maison de l'Océan** 2 quai de la Douane ☎ 02 98 80 44 84, ⓦ restaurant-fruit-mer-brest.com. Blue-hued fish restaurant down by the port, with a terrace facing across to the island ferries. It serves wonderful seafood on *menus* from €17.20 – which features fresh grilled catch of the day – to €39. Daily noon–2pm & 7–11pm.

**Le Ruffé** 1bis rue Yves-Collet ☎ 02 98 46 07 70. Unpretentious, very reliable restaurant between the *gare SNCF* and the tourist office, entirely indoors, which prides itself on *menus* (€14–36) of tasty, traditional French seafood dishes, and a good-value wine list. Tues–Sat noon–2pm & 6–10pm, Sun noon–2pm.

# The Crozon peninsula

A craggy outcrop of land shaped like a long-robed giant, arms outstretched, the **Crozon peninsula** is the central feature of Finistère's jagged coastline. Much the easiest way for cyclists and travellers relying on public transport to reach the peninsula from Brest is via the **ferries** to Le Fret (see p.331).

As you approach the Crozon peninsula, it's well worth making a slight detour to climb the hill of **Ménez-Hom** ("at the giant's feet") for a fabulous preview of the alternating land and water across the southern side of the peninsula out to the ocean.

## Crozon

The main town on the peninsula, **CROZON**, has a nice little stone-built core that serves as the commercial hub for the surrounding communities, and plays host to a large-scale **market** on alternate Wednesdays. As it's also, unfortunately, a traffic hub, its one-way traffic system distributing tourists among the various resorts, and in any case it's set back from the sea, it's more of a place to pass through than to linger.

## Morgat

**MORGAT**, 1km down the hill from Crozon, makes a more enticing base. It has a long crescent beach that ends in a pine slope, and a sheltered harbour full of pleasure boats on the short haul from England and Ireland. The main attractions are **boat trips** around the various headlands, such as the **Cap de la Chèvre** (which is a good clifftop walk if you'd rather make your own way) and to the **Grottes**.

### The Grottes

April to late Sept daily, departure times depend on tides • €12 • ☎ 02 98 27 10 71, ⓦ grottes-morgat.fr

The most popular boat trip from Morgat is the 45-minute tour out to the **Grottes**. From these multicoloured caves in the cliffs, accessible only by sea but with steep "chimneys" up to the clifftops, saints are said to have emerged in bygone days to rescue the shipwrecked.

## Camaret

One of the loveliest seaside towns in all Brittany, the sheltered port of **CAMARET** nestles at the western tip of the peninsula. Its most prominent building is the pink-orange

**château de Vauban**, standing at the end of the long jetty that runs parallel to the main town waterfront. Walled, moated, and accessible via a little gatehouse reached by means of a drawbridge, it was built in 1689 to guard the approaches to Brest; these days it guards no more than a motley assortment of decaying half-submerged fishing boats, abandoned to rot beside the jetty. A short walk away, around the port towards the protective jetty, the quai du Styvel holds a row of excellent hotels.

There are two beaches nearby – a small one to the north and another, larger and more attractive, in the low-lying (and rather marshy) Anse de Dinan. There are also some good wreck dives and submerged islands for **scuba-diving** enthusiasts – head to *Léo-Lagrange*, 2 rue du Stade (ⓦclub-leo-camaret.net).

**6**

## ARRIVAL AND DEPARTURE                                    ### THE CROZON PENINSULA

**By ferry** In summer, ferries run from Camaret to the islands of Ouessant (see p.328) and Sein (see p.336). Ferries also run from Brest to the village of Le Fret on the north coast of the peninsula (see p.331).

## INFORMATION

### CROZON
**Tourist office** Bd de Pralognan-la Vanoise, west of the centre in the *gare routière* (July & Aug Mon–Sat 10am–1pm & 2–6pm, Sun 10am–1pm; Sept–June Mon–Sat 10am–noon & 2–5.30pm; ☎02 98 27 07 92, ⓦcrozon.com).

### CAMARET
**Tourist office** 15 quai Kléber (Mon–Sat 9am–noon & 2–6pm; ☎02 98 27 93 60, ⓦcamaret-sur-mer.com).

## ACCOMMODATION

### MORGAT
**Camping Plage de Goulien** Kernavéno ☎06 08 43 49 32, ⓦcamping-crozon-laplagedegoulien.com. Three-star campsite, just across from the headland from Morgat and a few steps from a huge sandy beach. Pitches amid the trees, with an on-site grocery. Closed mid-Sept to May. **€19**
**Kermaria** 1 bd de la Plage ☎02 98 26 20 02, ⓦkermaria.com. Luxury B&B, set in a grand, somewhat formal house and featuring high ceilings, leather armchairs and lots of polished wood, with gardens leading onto the beach. Closed Oct–March. **€95**

### CAMARET
**Camping Le Grand Large** Lambézen ☎02 98 27 91 41, ⓦcampinglegrandlarge.com. Four-star campsite, 500m up from the nearest beach but offering nicely secluded grass pitches, plus a pool with water slide and great views. Closed Oct–March. **€23.60**
**Du Styvel** 2 quai du Styvel ☎02 98 27 92 74, ⓦhotel-du-styvel.com. Friendly seaside hotel, with a decent restaurant. Ten of the thirteen small but comfortable en-suite rooms have harbour-view balconies. Closed Jan. **€59**
★ **Vauban** 4 quai du Styvel ☎02 98 27 91 36, ⓦwww.hotelvauban-camaret.fr. Plain but exceptionally hospitable and more than adequate quayside hotel, with a simple brasserie. Rooms at the front look right out across the bay. Rates remain constant year round; the very cheapest lack en-suite facilities, while the one family room does not have a sea view. **€40**

## EATING AND DRINKING

### MORGAT
**Saveurs et Marées** 52 bd de la Plage ☎02 98 26 23 18, ⓦsaveurs-et-maree.com. The pick of Morgat's crop of beachfront seafood restaurants, with the bonus of outdoor seating. Dinner *menus* €17.50–49. April–Sept daily noon–2pm & 7–10pm; Oct–March Wed–Sun noon–2pm & 7–10pm.

### CAMARET
**Les Frères de la Côte** 11 quai Toudouze ☎02 98 27 95 42, ⓦbreiz-ile.fr. Camaret's finest seafood restaurant, open to the harbour and serving fresh fish accompanied by sauces and spices influenced by the owner's Guadalupe origins. The €13 weekday lunch *menu* is a real bargain. Mid-March to Sept daily noon–1.30pm & 7.30–9.30pm.

# Southwest Finistère

Moving south of the Crozon peninsula, you soon enter the ancient kingdom of **Cornouaille**. The most direct route to the region's principal city, **Quimper**, leaves the sea behind and heads due south, passing close to the unchanged medieval village of **Locronan**. However, it's worth following the supremely isolated coastline instead around the Baie de Douarnenez to the **Pointe du Raz**, the western tip of Finistère. With a few exceptions – most notably its land's-end capes – this stretch of coast has kept out of the tourist mainstream. Nowhere does that hold more true than on the remote **Île de Sein**.

## Locronan

The beautifully preserved medieval town of **LOCRONAN** stands a short way from the sea on the minor road that leads down from the Crozon peninsula. From 1469 through to the seventeenth century, it thrived on trading in woven "lin" (linen), supplying sails to the French, English and Spanish navies accumulating a glorious ensemble of fine mansions. It was first rivalled by Vitré and Rennes, before suffering the "agony and ruin" so graphically described in its small **museum** (April–June & Sept Mon–Sat 10am–12.30pm & 1.30–6pm, Sun 11am–1pm & 3–6pm; July & Aug Mon–Sat 10am–6pm, Sun 11am–1pm & 3–6pm; €2; ☎02 98 91 70 14). Film directors love this sense of time warp, even if Roman Polanski, filming *Tess*, deemed it necessary to change all the porches, put new windows on the Renaissance houses, and bury the main square in mud to make it all look a bit more English.

Today Locronan prospers on tourism, but this commercialization shouldn't put you off making at least a passing visit, as the town itself is genuinely remarkable, centred around the focal **Église St-Ronan**. Be sure to take the time to walk down the hill of the **rue Moal**, to the lovely little stone chapel of Notre-Dame de Bonne Nouvelle.

### INFORMATION
LOCRONAN

**Tourist office** Alongside the museum (April–June & Sept Mon–Sat 10am–12.30pm & 1.30–6pm, Sun 11am–1pm & 3–6pm; July & Aug Mon–Sat 10am–6pm, Sun 11am–1pm & 3–6pm; ☎02 98 91 70 14, ⓦlocronan.org).

### ACCOMMODATION

**Du Prieuré** 11 rue du Prieuré ☎02 98 91 70 89, ⓦhotel-le-prieure.com. Locronan's one hotel, on the main approach street rather than in the old town proper, is unremarkable from the outside, but offers well-equipped rooms and a good restaurant. **€72**

## Douarnenez

Though it's still home to the largest fish canneries in Europe, the sheltered, historic port of **DOUARNENEZ** has been transformed over the last two decades into a superb living museum.

### Port-Rhû and the Musée du Bateau

**Musée du Bateau** Place de l'Enfer • Feb–June & Sept to early Nov daily except Mon 10am–12.30pm & 2–6pm, July & Aug daily 10am–7pm • Feb & March €5.50, April to early Nov €7.50 • ☎02 98 92 65 20, ⓦport-musee.org

Since 1993, **Port-Rhû**, on the west side of Douarnenez, has been designated as the **Port-Musée**. Its entire waterfront is taken up with fishing and other vessels gathered from throughout northern Europe, five of which you can roam through between April and November only.

Its centrepiece, the **Musée du Bateau** (Boat Museum) in place de l'Enfer, houses slightly smaller vessels, such as Gallic coracles and a Portugese *moliceiro*, and displays exhaustive explanations on boat construction techniques and a strong emphasis on fishing.

### Port du Rosmeur

Of the three separate harbour areas still in operation in Douarnenez, by far the most appealing is the rough-and-ready **port du Rosmeur**, on the east side, which is nominally the fishing port used by the smaller local craft. Its quayside, still far from commercialized, holds a reasonable number of relaxed waterside cafés and restaurants.

## INFORMATION

**Tourist office** 1 rue du Dr-Mével, a short walk up from the Port-Musée (April–June Mon–Sat 10am–12.30pm & 2–6pm, Sun 10.45am–12.45pm; July & Aug Mon–Sat 10am–7pm, Sun 10am–6.30pm; Sept Mon–Sat 10am–12.30pm & 2–6pm; Oct–March Mon–Sat 10am–12.30pm & 2–5.30pm; ☎02 98 92 13 35, ⓦ douarnenez-tourisme.com).

## ACCOMMODATION AND EATING

**Les Bigorneaux Amoureux** 2 bd Richepin ☎02 98 92 35 55, ⓦ bigorneau-amoureux.com. The best stand-alone restaurant in Douarnenez, serving good seafood *menus* and blessed with a terrace that enjoys a fabulous view over the plage des Dames. Tues–Sun noon–1.30pm & 7.30–9.30pm.

**Camping Croas Men** 27bis rue du Croas Men ☎02 98 74 00 18, ⓦ croas-men.com. Two-star campsite, a short walk west of town close to the nice beach at Tréboul/Les Sables Blancs, and offering well-shaded pitches. Closed Oct–Easter. €12

**De France** 4 rue Jean Jaurès ☎02 98 92 00 02, ⓦ lafrance-dz.com. Nicely restored central hotel, a short walk from the port, where the 23 large, smart rooms have good bathrooms. Dinner *menus* start at €29 in the excellent restaurant, *L'Insolité* (closed Sun eve & Mon). €65

6

## The Baie des Trépassés

The **Baie des Trépassés** ("Bay of the Dead"), 30km west of Douarnenez just north of the Pointe du Raz, gets its grim name from the shipwrecked bodies that used to be washed up here. However, it's actually a very attractive spot; green meadows, too exposed to support trees, end abruptly on the low cliffs to either side; there's a huge expanse of flat sand (in fact little else at low tide); and out in the crashing waves surfers and windsurfers get thrillingly thrashed to within an inch of their lives. Beyond them, you can usually make out the white-painted houses along the harbour on the Île de Sein, while the various uninhabited rocks in between hold a veritable forest of lighthouses.

In total, less than half a dozen scattered buildings intrude upon the emptiness, including the two parts of a **hotel**, both with tremendous views.

## ACCOMMODATION

### BAIE DES TRÉPASSÉS

★ **De la Baie des Trépassés** ☎02 98 70 61 34, ⓦ baiedestrepasses.com. A truly spectacular hideaway, standing on the grass just behind the magnificent fine-sand beach, with its sister property, the Relais de la Pointe du Van, off to the side. The comfortable, simply decorated rooms come in all sizes and shapes – one cheaper option lacks en-suite facilities, while several sleep three or four – and the restaurant serves *menus* of wonderfully fresh seafood (€20–61). Closed mid-Nov to mid-Feb. €70

## Pointe du Raz

**Information complex** Daily: April–June & Sept 10.30am–6pm; July & Aug 9.30am–7pm • Parking €5 cars, €3 motorcycles • ☎02 98 70 67 18, ⓦ www.pointeduraz.com

Thirty kilometres west of Douarnenez, the **Pointe du Raz** – the Land's End of both Finistère and France – is designated a "Grand Site National", and makes a magnificent spectacle, buffeted by wind and waves and peppered with deep gurgling fissures. It's quite a wild experience to walk to the end and back, but don't expect to have the place to yourself; with three million visitors every year, they've had to build a huge car park 1km short of the actual headland, alongside an information complex which serves as the starting point for regular guided tours. To get to the *pointe*, take the free *navette*, then walk the most direct route, along an undulating, arrow-straight track or take a longer stroll along the footpath that skirts the top of the cliffs.

## Île de Sein

Of all the Breton islands, the tiny **Île de Sein**, just 8km out to sea from the tip of the Pointe du Raz, has to be the most extraordinary. It's hard to believe anyone could survive here; nowhere does the island rise more than 6m above the surrounding ocean, and for much of its 2.5km length it's barely broader than the breakwater wall of bricks that serves as its central spine. In fact, Sein has been inhabited since prehistoric times,

**6**

nd was reputed to have been the very last refuge of the druids in Brittany. It also became famous during World War II, when its entire male population answered General de Gaulle's call to join him in exile in England. Today, more than three hundred islanders make their living from the sea, gathering rainwater and seaweed, and fishing for scallops, lobster and crayfish.

Never mind cars, not even bicycles are permitted on Sein. Depending on the tide, boats pull in at one or other of the two adjoining harbours that constitute Sein's one tight-knit village, in front of which a little beach appears at low tide. There is a **museum** of local history here (daily: June & Sept 10am–noon & 2–4pm; July & Aug 10am–noon & 2–6pm; €2.50), packed with black-and-white photos and press clippings, and displaying a long list of shipwrecks from 1476 onwards. The most popular activity for visitors, however, is to take a bracing walk, preferably to the far end of the island, from where you can see the **Phare Ar-men** lighthouse, peeking out of the waves 12km further west into the Atlantic.

## ARRIVAL AND DEPARTURE
ÎLE DE SEIN

**By boat** The principal departure point for boats to Sein is Ste-Evette beach, just outside Audierne; the crossing takes around 1hr. Services are operated by Penn Ar Bed (daily: early July to late Aug 3–5 daily, with first at 8.45am; late Aug to early July 1–2 daily, with first at 9.30am; ☎ 02 98 70 70 70, ⓦ pennarbed.fr). On Sun from late June to early Sept, Penn Ar Bed also runs trips to Sein from Brest (departs 9am; 1hr 30min) via Camaret (9.40am; 1hr). The round-trip fare on every route is the same (June–Sept €31.90; Oct–May Mon–Fri €21.80, Sat & Sun €26).

## ACCOMMODATION AND EATING

★ **D'Armen** 39 rue Fernand Crouton ☎ 02 98 70 90 77, ⓦ hotel-restaurant-d-armen-ile-de-sein.fr. The nicer of Sein's two good hotels is the very last building as you walk west out of town, which makes it the last restaurant in Europe. All its simple but lovely rooms face the sea, and the excellent €20 dinner *menu* features mussels in cider, skate, and delicious home-baked bread. Closed early Nov to mid-Feb. **€70**

**Trois Dauphins** 16 quai des Paimpolais ☎ 02 98 70 92 09, ⓦ hoteliledesein.com. Seven cosy and attractive wood-panelled rooms, not all en suite or with sea views, above a bar in the middle of the port. **€48**

# Quimper

Capital of the ancient diocese, kingdom and later duchy of Cornouaille, **QUIMPER** is the oldest city in Brittany. Its first bishop, St Corentin, is said to have come with the first Bretons across the English Channel at some point between the fourth and seventh centuries.

Still "the charming little place" known to Flaubert, Quimper takes at most half an hour to cross on foot. Though relaxed, it's active enough to have the bars and atmosphere to make it worth going out **café-crawling**. The word "kemper" denotes the junction of the two rivers, the Steir and the Odet, around which lie the cobbled streets (now mainly pedestrianized) of the **medieval quarter**. To the east of the Gothic **cathedral**, towering over place St-Corentin, ancient half-timbered buildings hold lively shops and cafés.

With no great pressure to rush around monuments or museums, the most enjoyable option may be to take a **boat** and drift down the Odet, "the prettiest river in France", to the open sea at Bénodet. Overlooking all is tree-covered **Mont Frugy**; climb to its 87m peak for good views over the city.

## Cathédrale St-Corentin

Quimper's focal point, the enormous **Cathédrale St-Corentin**, is the most complete Gothic cathedral in Brittany, though its Neo-Gothic spires date from 1856. When the nave was being added to the old chancel in the fifteenth century, the extension would either have hit existing buildings or the swampy edge of the then-unchannelled river. So the nave was placed at a slight angle – a peculiarity which, once noticed, makes it hard to concentrate on the other Gothic splendours within. The exterior, however, gives no hint of the deviation, with King Gradlon mounted in perfect symmetry between the spires.

## Musée Départemental Breton

1 rue du roi Gradlon • Daily 9am–6pm • €4 • ☎ 02 98 95 21 60, ⓦ museedepartementalbreton.fr

The quirky-looking Bishop's Palace, alongside Quimper's cathedral, holds the beautifully laid-out **Musée Départemental Breton**. Collections start with Bronze Age spear- and axe-heads and prehistoric golden jewellery, move rapidly through Roman and medieval statues, and culminate with a fascinating assortment of Breton oddments and objets d'art.

## Musée des Beaux Arts

40 place St-Corentin • April–June, Sept & Oct daily except Tues 9.30am–noon & 2–6pm; July & Aug daily 10am–7pm; Nov–March Mon & Wed–Sat 9.30am–noon & 2–5.30pm, Sun 2–5.30pm • €4.50 • ☎ 02 98 95 45 20, ⓦ mbaq.fr

Quimper's compelling **Musée des Beaux Arts** stands across the main square immediately north of the cathedral. Equipped by an impressive architectural transformation with new floors and suspended walkways, it focuses on an amazing assemblage of drawings by Max Jacob – who was born in Quimper – and his contemporaries. Look out also for the museum's solitary work by Gauguin, a goose he painted on the door of Marie Henry's inn in Pont-Aven itself.

## Halles St-Francis

Rue Astor

The **Halles St-Francis** marketplace is a delight, not just for the food, but for the view beyond the upturned boat rafters through the roof to the cathedral's twin spires. It's

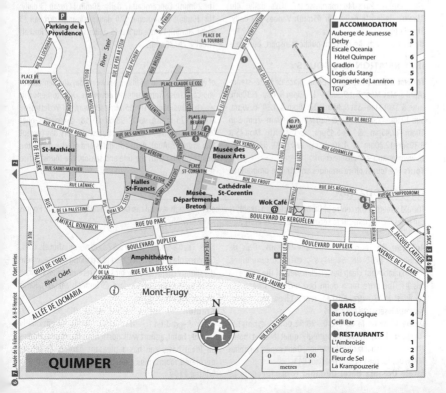

open from Monday to Saturday, with an extra-large market spreading into the surrounding streets on Saturdays.

## Musée de la Faïence

14 rue Jean-Baptiste Bousquet • Mid-April to Sept Mon–Sat 10am–6pm • €5, €7 with the H-B Henriot atelier • ☎ 02 98 90 12 72, ⓦ musee-faience-quimper.com

Visiting Quimper, it is impossible to ignore the local ceramic tradition of **faïence**, or tin-glazed earthenware. Having started here in the seventeenth century, its manufacture boomed from around 1875, when the coming of the railways brought Brittany's first influx of tourists, and some unknown artisan hit on the idea of painting ceramic ware with naive "folk" designs. The **Musée de la Faïence**, beside the river in the southwest corner of town, traces the history of the tradition.

## H-B Henriot

Rue Haute • Tours mid-April to mid-July 2pm & 4.15pm; mid-July to mid-Sept Mon–Sat 9.30am, 10.30am, 11.15am, 1.30pm, 2.15pm, 3.30pm, 4.15pm & 5pm • €5, or €7 with the Musée de la Faïence • ☎ 02 98 90 09 36, ⓦ hb-henriot.com

Right next door to the Musée de la Faïence, the major atelier **H-B Henriot** continues to produce hand-painted pottery, which it sells on site, and also offers tours that explain the entire process, from design through firing to completion.

## ARRIVAL AND DEPARTURE         QUIMPER

**By train** Quimper's *gare SNCF* is on av de la Gare 1km east of the centre, on bus route #6.
Destinations Lorient (6 daily; 40min); Nantes (5 daily; 2hr 30min); Paris-Montparnasse (7 TGVs daily; 4hr 15min); Redon (6 daily; 1hr 45min); Vannes (12 daily; 1hr 15min).
**By bus** To reach the coast on public transport, buses are

your only option (CAT: ☎ 02 98 90 68 40, ⓦ cat29.fr). The *gare routière* is beside the train station.
Destinations Bénodet (8 daily; 40min); Camaret (3 daily; 1hr 20min); Concarneau (7 daily; 30min); Crozon (3 daily; 1hr 10min); Douarnenez (10 daily; 40min); Locronan (3 daily; 20min); Pointe du Raz (5 daily; 1hr 30 min); Roscoff (1 daily; 2hr 30min).

## INFORMATION AND TOURS

**Tourist office** 7 rue de la Déesse, place de la Résistance (April & May Mon–Sat 9.30am–12.30pm & 1.30–6.30pm; June & Sept Mon–Sat 9.30am–12.30pm & 1.30–6.30pm; Sun 10am–12.45pm; July & Aug Mon–Sat 9am–7pm, Sun 10am–12.45pm & 3–5.45pm; Oct–March Mon–Sat 9.30am–12.30pm & 1.30–6pm; ☎ 02 98 53 04 05, ⓦ www.quimper-tourisme.com).
**Tours** The tourist office arranges an intricate programme

of walking tours. In addition, between May and September you can cruise from Quimper down the Odet to Bénodet, which takes about 1hr 15min each way, on Vedettes de l'Odet (€26 return; ☎ 02 98 57 00 58, ⓦ vedettes-odet .com). Between one and three boats sail every day (except Sun in July & Aug), with schedules and precise departure points varying with the tide and season; the tourist office sells tickets.

## ACCOMMODATION

The old streets in the centre of Quimper hold remarkably few hotels, though several can be found near the station. Rooms can be especially difficult to secure in late July or early August; so reserve ahead.

**Auberge de Jeunesse** 6 av des Oiseaux, Bois de Seminaire ☎ 02 98 64 97 97, ⓦ fuaj.org/quimper. Unremarkable but clean hostel, 2km west of the centre on bus #1. The price for a dorm bed includes sheets, but breakfast is €3 extra. Kitchen, rental bikes, and a quiet garden. Closed Oct–April. **€14**
**Derby** 13 av de la Gare ☎ 02 98 52 06 91, ⓦ hotel-le -derby.fr. Inexpensive, surprisingly quiet budget hotel, above a corner bar facing the station. Don't expect anything fancy, but for the price it's not bad. **€41**
**Escale Oceania Hôtel Quimper** 6 rue Théodore Le

Hars ☎ 02 98 53 37 37, ⓦ oceaniahotels.com. Comfortable central hotel, next to a parking garage, where the slightly characterless rooms have recently been spruced up to a pretty decent standard. €9 buffet breakfasts. Rates drop at weekends. **€100**
**Gradlon** 30 rue de Brest ☎ 02 98 95 04 39, ⓦ hotel-gradlon.fr. This quiet and exceptionally friendly hotel, a short walk north from the centre, makes an ideal base, and has a pleasant garden. Tastefully decorated rooms, plus a good bar, with an open fire in winter. **€109**

**THE FESTIVALS OF QUIMPER**

Having started in 1923, Quimper's **Festival de Cornouaille** is still going from strength to strength. This great jamboree of Breton music, costumes, theatre and dance is held in the week before the last Sunday in July, attracting guest performers from the other Celtic countries and a scattering of other, sometimes highly unusual, ethnic-cultural ensembles. The whole thing culminates in an incredible Sunday parade through the town. The official programme does not appear until July, but you can get provisional details in advance from the tourist office or at ⓦ www.festival-cornouaille.com. Accommodation is naturally at a premium during this period.

Not so widely known are the **Semaines Musicales**, which follow in the first three weeks of August (ⓦ www.semaines-musicales-quimper.org). Some events take place in the cathedral, others bring the rather stuffy nineteenth-century theatre on boulevard Dupleix alive. The music is predominantly classical, favouring French composers.

**6**

★ **Logis du Stang** Allée du Stang-Youen ☎ 02 98 52 00 55, ⓦ logis-du-stang.com. Delightful B&B, east of the centre in a nineteenth-century house, with four well-furnished en-suite rooms and a hortensia-filled garden. **€81**

**Orangerie de Lanniron** Rte de Bénodet ☎ 98 90 62 02, ⓦ lanniron.com. Five-star campsite, 4km south in the grounds of a château, with its own aquapark, restaurant and tennis court, and also chalets and stone cottages for rent. Closed mid-Sept to mid-May. **€30**

**TGV** 4 rue de Concarneau ☎ 02 98 90 54 00, ⓦ hoteltgv.com. Plain but clean rooms with shower and TV at bargain rates, opposite the station. Avoid the first floor, which gets a bit noisy. **€38**

## EATING AND DRINKING

Although the pedestrian streets west of the cathedral are unexpectedly short on places to eat, there are quite a few restaurants further east on the north side of the river, en route towards the *gare SNCF*. For crêperies, the place au Beurre, a short walk northwest of the cathedral, is a good bet.

### RESTAURANTS

**L'Ambroisie** 49 rue Élie-Fréron ☎ 02 98 95 00 02, ⓦ ambroisie-quimper.com. Upmarket French restaurant a short climb north from the cathedral, featuring fine seafood (including tuna) and meat dishes on *menus* from €25 for lunch, €38 for dinner. Tues–Sun noon–1.30pm & 7.30–9pm; closed Sun eve in winter.

**Le Cosy** 2 rue du Sallé ☎ 02 98 95 23 65, ⓦ lecosy -restaurant.fr. Pretty bistro just north of the cathedral, where the *menu* proudly insists they serve "pas de crêpes, pas de frites"; instead savoury *tartines* or daily *plats* cost €11–15, and there's a €15.50 lunch *menu*. Mon 7–9.30pm, Tues noon–2pm, Wed–Sat noon–2pm & 7–9.30pm.

**Fleur de Sel** 1 quai Neuf ☎ 02 98 55 04 71, ⓦ fleur-de -sel-quimper.com. Attractive little restaurant near the riverboat quay, not far west of the centre on the north bank. Despite looking like a chintzy café, it offers gourmet French cooking on largely fish-based €28 and €38 *menus*.

Tues–Fri 12.15–1.30pm & 7.30–9pm, Sat 12.15–1.30pm.

**La Krampouzerie** 9 rue du Sallé ☎ 02 98 95 13 08. Great crêperie, with outdoor seating on the place au Beurre. Most crêpes, such as the one with Roscoff onions and seaweed, cost around €4, though a wholewheat *galette* with smoked salmon and cream cheese is €6. Mon–Sat noon–2pm & 7–9pm; closed Mon in winter.

### BARS

**Bar 100 Logique** 9 rue des Réguaires ☎ 02 98 95 44 69, ⓦ le100logiquequimper.skyrock.com. Classy little bar that makes the most of being Quimper's only gay and lesbian hangout. Tues–Sun 7pm–1am.

**Ceili Bar** 4 rue Aristide Briand ☎ 02 98 95 17 61. This lively and convivial bar is the place to go for all things Breton: beer and opinionated conversation, plus live traditional Celtic bands and occasionally jazz. Mon–Sat 10.30am–1am, Sun 5pm–1am.

# South from Quimper

South of Quimper, no longer restrained into a narrow canalized channel, the Odet first broadens and then twists through successive tight corners to reach the sea. The southern coast here, and especially the string of wonderful **beaches** between the family-friendly resort of **Bénodet** and **La Forêt-Fouesnant**, is the most popular tourist destination in

Finistère. A little further east, the walled, sea-circled old town of **Concarneau** makes a perfect day-trip destination, though a prettier place to spend a night or two would be the flowery village of **Pont-Aven**, immortalized by Paul Gauguin, slightly further east.

## Bénodet and around

**BÉNODET**, at the mouth of the Odet, is a much-developed resort that comes alive in summer, when its many hotels and campsites are filled with holidaying families. The long, sheltered beach on its ocean side, perfect for children, is packed day after day.

East of Bénodet, the coast is rocky and repeatedly cut by deep valleys. Each seems to hold another little village, and there are plenty of further seafront communities tucked into the nearby coastal coves. **FOUESNANT** is the main commercial centre here, while **LA FORÊT-FOUESNANT**, clustered along the waterfront 12km out from Bénodet, at the foot of a hill so steep that caravans are banned from even approaching, is known for its beaches and cider. For a quiet seaside stay, the sleepy little beach town of **CAP-COZ**, languidly stretched along a sandspit facing Concarneau, is ideal.

### ACCOMMODATION AND EATING                                       BÉNODET AND AROUND

**Les Bains de Mer** 11 rue de Kerguélen, Bénodet ☎ 02 98 57 03 41, ⓦ lesbainsdemer.com. This down-to-earth hotel, near the port and beach, has comfortable, slightly staid rooms, a reasonable restaurant, and a heated outdoor pool. Closed Jan. **€75**

**Belle Vue** Cap-Coz, Fouesnant ☎ 02 98 56 00 33, ⓦ hotel-belle-vue.com. Classic seaside hotel, poised at the west end of a lovely long beach. Owned by the same family for almost a century, it's been energetically updated, with large and very pleasant sea-view bedrooms and a good-value restaurant. **€90**

**Camping du Letty** Rue du Canvez, Bénodet ☎ 02 98 57 04 69, ⓦ campingduletty.com. Large and very well-equipped four-star campsite, southeast of the centre alongside the plage du Letty, with an indoor/outdoor aquapark, gym, squash and tennis courts, and supermarket/deli. Closed early Sept to mid-June. **€18.50**

**Du Port** 4 corniche de la Cale, la Forêt-Fouesnant ☎ 02 98 56 97 33, ⓦ www.hotelduport.fr. Peaceful, smart little hotel a short walk from the port, with very reasonably priced and brightly furnished rooms and an attractive garden-view restaurant (closed Sun & Mon). **€67**

## Concarneau

Although **CONCARNEAU**, 25km southeast of Quimper, is the third most important fishing port in France, it does a reasonable job of passing itself off as a holiday resort. Its greatest asset is its small and very well fortified **old city**, located just a few metres offshore on an irregular rocky island.

### The ville close

Concarneau's walled core, the **ville close**, is a real delight. Like those of the citadelle at Le Palais on Belle-Île, its ramparts were completed by Vauban in the seventeenth century. The island itself, however, had been inhabited for at least a thousand years before that.

Concarneau boasts that it is a *ville fleurie*, and the flowers are most in evidence inside the walls, where climbing roses and clematis swarm all over the various gift shops, restaurants and crêperies. Walk the central pedestrianized street to the far end, and you can pass through a gateway to the shoreline to watch the fishing boats go by. The best views of all come from the promenade on top of the **ramparts**; you can't stroll all the way round to make a complete circuit of the walls, but here and there you can climb up for short stretches.

#### Musée de la Pêche

3 rue Vauban · Daily: July & Aug 9.30am–8pm; April–June & Sept 10am–6pm; mid-Feb to March, Oct and second half of Dec 10am–noon & 2–6pm · €6.50 · ☎ 02 98 97 10 20, ⓦ musee-peche.fr

By exploring the history of fishing all over the world, the **Musée de la Pêche**, immediately inside the *ville close*, provides an insight into the traditional life

Concarneau shared with so many other Breton ports. Oddities on show include a three-thousand-year-old anchor from Crete, the swords of swordfish and the saws of sawfish, and a genuine trawler, moored on the other side of the city walls behind the museum.

## ARRIVAL AND INFORMATION
CONCARNEAU

**By bus** While there's no rail service to Concarneau, SNCF buses connect it with Quimper, from the quai d'Aiguillon.

**Tourist office** Quai d'Aiguillon, just outside the *ville close* (May, June & first half of Sept Mon–Sat

9am–12.30pm & 1.30–6.30pm, Sun 10am–1pm; July & Aug daily 9am–7pm; mid-Sept to April Mon–Sat 9am–noon & 2–6pm; ☎02 98 97 01 44, ⓦtourismeconcarneau.fr).

## ACCOMMODATION

**Auberge de Jeunesse** Quai de la Croix ☎02 98 97 03 47, ⓦajconcarneau.com. Budget travellers will love this very central hostel, which enjoys magnificent ocean views just around the south tip of the headland from the town centre, and has a windsurfing shop nearby. Rates include breakfast. €17

**De France et d'Europe** 9 av de la Gare ☎02 98 97 00 64, ⓦhotel-france-europe.com. Bright, modernized and very central hotel near the main bus stop, which as well as well-furnished rooms has a garden terrace and a small gym. Closed mid-Dec to mid-Jan. €77

**Des Halles** Place de l'Hôtel de Ville ☎02 98 97 11 41, ⓦhoteldeshalles.com. Spruce pastel-orange hotel near

the fish market, across from the entrance to the *ville close*, offering light, recently refreshed rooms, with good showers, at reasonable rates. €65

★ **Ker Moor** 37 rue des Sables-Blancs ☎02 98 97 02 96, ⓦhotel-kermor.com. Classic, beautifully restored seafront hotel, nautically themed throughout, on the beach 2km west of town. All the rooms have sea views, but you can pay extra for a balcony. €107

★ **Prés Verts** ☎02 98 97 09 74, ⓦpresverts.com. This lovely, spacious, well-shaded campsite spreads through green fields at Kernous Plage at the far end of Sables-Blancs beach; facilities include pool and crazy golf. Closed mid-Oct to mid-March. €21

## EATING AND DRINKING

**Le Bélem** 2 rue Hélène Hascoët ☎02 98 97 02 78. Pretty little indoor restaurant, next to the market on the mainland, serving mussels for around €10 and good seafood *menus* from just over €20. Daily noon–2pm & 7–9.30pm; low season closed Wed, Thurs eve & Sun eve.

**La Coquille** 1 quai de Moros ☎02 98 97 08 52, ⓦlacoquille-concarneau.com. Sophisticated French cuisine, away from the crowds but with views of the *ville close* from a quayside terrace across the river, with a

bar-bistro as well as more formal dining. The *plat du jour* costs under €10, and a three-course lunch just under €20, while dinner *menus* run from €29 to €45. Tues–Sat noon–1.30pm & 7.30–9.30pm, Sun noon–1.30pm.

**Crêperie des Remparts** 31 rue Théophile Luarn ☎02 98 50 65 66. Good inexpensive crêpes, slightly off the beaten track behind the main street in the walled city, served either indoors or on a nice terrace. There's also a good €13 lunch *menu*. Daily noon–2pm & 6–9.30pm; low season closed Wed.

## Pont-Aven

**PONT-AVEN**, 14km east of Concarneau and just inland from the tip of the Aven estuary, is a delightful little port with a prominent place in art history. **Paul Gauguin** came here to paint during the 1880s, before he left for Tahiti, and inspired the **Pont-Aven School** of fellow artists, including Émile Bernard. Despite this, the town has no permanent collection of his work: the local **Musée des Beaux Arts**, temporarily closed pending a move to the town hall, holds changing exhibitions of the school and other artists active during the same period. Galleries abound on every street, though few show much connection with Pont-Aven's own traditions.

Gauguin aside, Pont-Aven is pleasant in its own right. Just upstream of the little granite bridge at the heart of town, the **promenade Xavier-Grall** crisscrosses the tiny river itself on landscaped walkways, offering glimpses of the backs of venerable mansions, dripping with ivy, and a little "chaos" of rocks in the stream itself. A longer walk – allow an hour – leads into the romantically named **Bois d'Amour**, wooded gardens which have long provided inspiration to painters, poets and musicians.

**6**

**INFORMATION**                                                    **PONT-AVEN**

**Tourist office** 5 place de l'Hôtel de Ville (Mon–Sat 10am–12.30pm & 2–6pm; ☏ 02 98 06 04 70, ⓦ pontaven.com).

**ACCOMMODATION**

**Ajoncs d'Or** 1 place de l'Hôtel de Ville ☏ 02 98 06 02 06, ⓦ ajoncsdor-pontaven.com. The actual bedrooms inside the very central, blue-and-white-painted hotel are adequate but very ordinary, but it's a great location, and the restaurant is pretty good, with a decent two-course dinner for €18 and full *menus* from €29. **€60**

**Castel Braz** 12 rue du Bois d'Amour ☏ 02 98 06 07 81, ⓦ castelbraz.com. Lovely and very good-value B&B, in a charming old townhouse with peaceful gardens, where each of the six rooms is decorated to a different theme. **€65**

# The Nantes–Brest canal

Completed in 1836, the meandering chain of waterways collectively known as the **Nantes–Brest canal** connects Finistère to the Loire. Interweaving rivers with stretches of canal, it was built at Napoleon's instigation to bypass the belligerent English fleets off the coast. As a focus for exploring **inland Brittany**, whether by barge, bike, foot, or all three, the canal is ideal. Not every stretch is accessible, but detours can be made away from it, such as into the wild and desolate **Monts d'Arrée** to the north of the canal in Finistère.

The canal passes through riverside towns, such as **Josselin**, that long predate its construction; the old port of **Redon**, a patchwork of water, where the canal crosses the River Vilaine; and a sequence of scenic splendours, including long, narrow **Lac de Guerlédan**, created by the construction of the **Barrage de Guerlédan**, near Mur-de-Bretagne.

## Carhaix

The sizeable market town of **CARHAIX**, on the eastern frontier of Finistère 50km southeast of Morlaix and 60km northeast of Quimper, has come to prominence in recent years as the host of France's biggest annual **rock festival**. The massive four-day **Vieilles Charrues** (ⓦ vieillescharrues.asso.fr) takes place during the third weekend of July; recent headliners have included Bruce Springsteen and Bob Dylan. Otherwise, the most interesting building in town, the granite Renaissance **Maison du Sénéchal** on rue Brizeux, houses the tourist office (see opposite).

## Huelgoat and its forest

**HUELGOAT**, next to its own small **lake** halfway between Morlaix and Carhaix on the minor road D769, makes a pleasant overnight stop. Spreading north and east from the village, the **Forêt de Huelgoat** is a landscape of trees, giant boulders and waterfalls tangled together in primeval chaos. Various paths lead into the depths of the woods, allowing for long walks amid spectacularly wild scenery.

## Le Lac de Guerlédan

For the 15km between Gouarec, 30km east of Carhaix, and Mur-de-Bretagne, the N164 skirts the edge of **Quénécan Forest**, within which is the artificial **Lac de Guerlédan** created by the dam of the same name completed in 1928. It's a beautiful stretch of river, peaceful enough despite the summer influx of campers and caravans.

Just off the N164 near the village of **ST-GELVEN**, 5km east of Gouarec, the beautiful **Abbaye de Bon-Repos** nestles beside the water at the end of an avenue of ancient trees. This twelfth-century Cistercian abbey was largely destroyed during the French

Revolution, but its ruins are open to visitors (March to mid-June & mid-Sept to Oct Mon–Fri & Sun 2–6pm; mid-June to mid-Sept daily 11am–7pm; E4; ⓦbon-repos .com), and play host to **son et lumière** spectacles on the first two weekends in August (€19; ☎02 96 24 85 28, ⓦpays-conomor.com). Its former outbuildings are home to a gorgeous little hotel, the *Jardins de l'Abbaye* (see p.344).

From just west of **CAUREL**, 7km east of St-Gelven, the brief loop of the D111 leads to tiny sandy beaches. **MÛR-DE-BRETAGNE**, set back from the eastern end of the lake, is a lively town with a wide and colourful pedestrianized zone around its church.

**6**

## Josselin

The historic riverside town of **JOSSELIN** is full of medieval splendours. Its gargoyle-studded **basilica**, Notre-Dame-du-Roncier – the focus of an important *pardon* each September 8 – is ringed by twisted streets of half-timbered houses. The major attraction for visitors, however, is the **château**, looming high over the Oust.

### Josselin château
April to mid-July daily 2–6pm; mid-July to Aug daily 11am–6pm; Sept daily 2–5.30pm; Oct Sat, Sun & hols 2–5.30pm • Tours €8, museum €7 • ☎ 02 97 22 36 45, ⓦ chateaujosselin.com

The three Rapunzel towers of the **château** at Josselin, embedded in a vast sheet of stone above the water, are the most impressive sight along the Nantes–Brest canal. However, they turn out on close inspection to be no more than a facade. The building behind was built in the last century, the bulk of the original castle having been demolished by Richelieu in 1629 in punishment for Henri de Rohan's leadership of the Huguenots. It's still owned by the Rohan family, which used to own a third of Brittany. Although tours of the castle's oppressively formal apartments are not very compelling, the duchess's collection of ancient **dolls**, housed in the **Musée des Poupées** behind, is something special.

## Redon

Situated at the junction not only of the rivers Oust and Vilaine and the canal, but also of the train lines to Rennes, Vannes and Nantes, and of six major roads, **REDON** is not easy to avoid. And you shouldn't try to, either. A wonderful mess of water and locks, it's a town with history, charm and life.

Until World War I, Redon was the seaport for Rennes. Its industrial docks – or what remains of them – are therefore on the Vilaine, while the canal, even in the very centre of town, is almost totally rural, its towpaths shaded avenues. Shipowners' houses from the seventeenth and eighteenth centuries can be seen along quai Jean-Bart by the *bassin* and quai Duguay-Truin next to the river. A rusted wrought-iron workbridge, equipped with a gantry, still crosses the river, but the main users of the port now are cruise ships heading down the Vilaine to La Roche-Bernard.

### Abbaye St-Sauveur
Redon's **Abbaye St-Sauveur**, founded in 832 by St Conwoion, remains its most prominent church. Its unique four-storeyed Romanesque belfry is squat, almost obscured by later roofs and the high choir, and best seen from the adjacent cloisters; the Gothic tower was entirely separated from the main building by a fire. In the crypt, you'll find the tomb of the judge who tried the legendary Bluebeard – Joan of Arc's friend, Gilles de Rais.

| INFORMATION | THE NANTES–BREST CANAL |
| --- | --- |
| **CARHAIX** | Mon–Sat 9am–noon & 2–6pm; Oct–May Mon 2–6pm, |
| **Tourist office** Rue Brizeux (July & Aug Mon–Sat | Wed–Sat 10am–noon & 2–5.30pm; ☎02 98 93 04 42, |
| 9am–12.30pm & 1.30–7pm, Sun 10am–1pm; June & Sept | ⓦtourismecarhaix.poher.com). |

**6**

## MÛR-DE-BRETAGNE

**Tourist office** 1 place de l'Église (July & Aug Mon–Thurs & Sat 10am–12.30pm & 2–6.30pm, Fri 10am–12.30pm & 2–7.30pm, Sun 10.30am–12.30pm; Easter–June & Sept Mon–Sat 10am–12.30pm & 2–5.30pm; Oct–Easter Mon–Fri 10am–12.30pm & 2–5pm, Sat 10am–12.30pm; ☎02 96 28 51 41, ⓦwww.guerledan.fr). They can organize bike rides, horseriding, canoeing and jet-skiing

## JOSSELIN

**Tourist office** Place de la Congrégation, in a superb old house by the castle entrance (April–June & Sept Mon 1.30–5.30pm, Tues–Sat 10am–noon & 1.30–5.30pm; July & Aug daily 10am–6pm; Oct–March Tues–Fri 10am–noon & 1.30–5.30pm, Sat 10am–noon; ☎02 97 22 36 43, ⓦjosselin-communaute.fr).

## REDON

**Tourist office** Place de la République, north across the railway tracks from the town centre (July & Aug Mon–Sat 9.30am–12.30pm & 1.30–6.30pm, Sun 10am–12.30pm & 3.30–5.30pm; Sept–June Mon & Wed–Fri 9.30am–noon & 2–6pm, Tues 2–6pm, Sat 10am–12.30pm & 2–5pm; ☎02 99 71 06 04, ⓦtourisme-pays-redon.com).

## ACCOMMODATION AND EATING

### ST-GELVEN

★ **Les Jardins de l'Abbaye** Abbaye de Bon Repos ☎02 96 24 95 77, ⓦabbaye.jardin.free.fr. Irresistible and inexpensive hotel-restaurant, housed in the cosy slate outbuildings of the twelfth-century abbey. Offering simple en-suite rooms with porthole-style windows, and a very pleasant no-frills restaurant, it makes a gloriously peaceful retreat. €45

### CARHAIX

**Noz Vad** 12 bd de la République ☎02 98 99 12 12, ⓦnozvad.com. This very central hotel, near the church, has en-suite rooms in all shapes and sizes, ranging from the tiny, plain "eco" rooms via plush "prestige" options to large family suites. It's also the venue for live concerts in the spring, and frequent exhibitions of art, sculpture and photography. €49

### HUELGOAT

**Camping du Lac** 800m from central Huelgoat towards Brest ☎02 98 99 78 80, ⓦtourismehuelgoat.fr /campingmunicipaldulac.htm. Two-star municipal campsite, in a gorgeous forested spot beside the lake. Closed Sept–June. €10.20

**Du Lac** 9 rue du Général-de-Gaulle ☎02 98 99 71 14, ⓦhoteldulac-huelgoat.com. Whatever its website might suggest, Huelgoat's only hotel is across the road from, rather than right beside, the lake. While the rooms are nothing fancy, they're fine for the price, and there's a bistro as well as a formal restaurant, both serving hearty local food. €70

**Laura's Chambres d'Hôtes** 2 Impasse des Cendres ☎02 98 99 91 62, ⓦbnbhuelgoatlauras.vpweb.co.uk. Very welcoming and good-value B&B, at the northern end of the village centre, offering six plain rooms with good en-suite facilities, including some family-sized suites. €55

### JOSSELIN

**Camping Domaine de Kerelly** Guégon ☎02 97 22 22 20, ⓦcamping-josselin.com. Very pleasant little three-star campsite, right beside the river a 30min walk west from the castle, with a mini golf course and simple rental chalets as well as pitches. Closed Nov–March. €13

★ **Du Chateau** 1 rue du Général-de-Gaulle ☎02 97 22 20 11, ⓦwww.hotel-chateau.com. Facing Josselin's fairy-tale castle from across the river, this lovely hotel makes a perfect place to stay. Though the slightly more expensive rooms, with château views, are not particularly luxurious, they're worth it – the whole place looks fabulous lit up at night – while the food, with dinner *menus* from €19, is first-rate. Closed 2 weeks in Nov, and 3 weeks Jan–Feb. €75

### REDON

**Chandouineau** 1 rue Thiers ☎02 99 71 02 04, ⓦhotel -restaurant-chandouineau.com. Smart hotel close to the station, with just seven comfortable bedrooms at great-value prices, and a gourmet restaurant. €70

# The southern coast

Brittany's **southern coast** is best known for mainland Europe's most famous prehistoric site, the megalithic alignments of **Carnac**, complemented by other ancient relics scattered around the beautiful, island-studded **Golfe de Morbihan**. While the beaches are not as spectacular as in Finistère, there are more safe places to swim and the water is warmer. Of the cities, **Lorient** has Brittany's most compelling **festival** and **Vannes** is a lively medieval centre, while you can also escape to the islands of **Belle-Île**, **Hoëdic** and **Houat**.

# Lorient

Brittany's fourth-largest city, **LORIENT**, lies on an immense natural harbour, sheltered by the Île de Groix. A functional, rather depressing port today, it was founded in the mid-seventeenth century by the Compagnie des Indes, an equivalent of the Dutch and English East India Companies. Apart from the name, little else remains to suggest the plundered wealth that once arrived here from France's far-flung colonial possessions.

## Cité de la Voile Éric Tabarly

Base de Sous-Marins de Keroman • Check website for the intricate calendar of opening hours, broadly summarized here: early Feb–June & Oct–Dec daily 10am–6pm during school hols, otherwise Tues–Fri 2–6pm, Sat & Sun 10am–6pm; July & Aug daily 10am–7pm; Sept Mon–Fri 2–6pm, Sat & Sun 10am–6pm; last admission 1hr 30min before closing • €11.90, children (ages 7–17) €8.60 • ☎ 02 97 65 56 56, ⓦ citevoile-tabarly.com

The **Cité de la Voile Éric Tabarly**, a couple of kilometres south of central Lorient at the mouth of the Ter river, is a large, modern, interactive museum of **sailing**. M Tabarly himself was a champion yachtsman and Breton hero who drowned in 1998. Several of his yachts – all of which were called *Pen Duick*, which roughly means "little black head" – are moored alongside, and can be visited.

## U-boat pens

Base de Sous-Marins de Keroman • July & Aug daily 10am–7pm; Feb–June & Sept–Dec school hols daily 10am–12.30pm & 2–6pm, closed Mon outside school hols • €8.10–16.20 depending on various possible visits and tours • ☎ 02 97 84 78 06, ⓦ la-flore.fr

During World War II, Lorient was a major target for the Allies; by the time the Germans surrendered, in May 1945, the city was almost completely destroyed. The only substantial traces to survive were the **U-boat pens**, which now stand alongside the Cité de la Voile in the port district of **Kéroman**. Subsequently expanded to hold French nuclear submarines, they're now open for **guided tours**, of which the highlight is the chance to visit the decommissioned sub La Flore.

## Musée de la Compagnie des Indes

Port-Louis • Feb–April & Sept to mid-Dec, daily except Tues 1.30–6pm; May–Aug daily 10am–6.30pm; closed mid-Dec to Jan • €6 • ⓦ musee.lorient.fr • Ferries Mon–Sat 5.30am–7.45pm, Sun 10am–7pm; €1.50; ☎ 02 97 21 28 29, ⓦ ctrl.fr

If you have time it's worth catching a ferry across the bay from Lorient's Embarcadère des Rades to **Port-Louis**. In the citadel here, the **Musée de la Compagnie des Indes** traces the history of French colonialism in Asia, with displays covering both the trading voyages and the goods they brought home.

**INFORMATION**                                                    **LORIENT**

**Tourist office** Beside the pleasure port on the quai de Rohan (early April to early July & late Aug to late Sept Mon–Fri 10am–noon & 2–6pm, Sat 10am–noon & 2–5pm; early July to late Aug Mon–Sat 9.30am–1pm & 2–7pm, Sun 10am–1pm, except during the festival, when it's daily 9am–8pm; late Sept to early April Mon–Fri

---

### THE INTER-CELTIC FESTIVAL

The world's largest Celtic event, Lorient's **Inter-Celtic Festival** takes place over ten days from the first Friday to the second Sunday in August. Representatives from all the Celtic nations of Europe – Brittany, Ireland, Scotland, Wales, Cornwall, the Isle of Man, Asturias and Galicia – come to celebrate cultural solidarity. Well over half a million people attend more than a hundred different shows, five languages mingle, and Scotch and Guinness flow with French and Spanish wines and ciders. There's a certain competitive element, with championships in various categories, but mutual enthusiasm and conviviality is paramount. Various activities – embracing music, dance and literature – take place all over the city, with mass celebrations around both the central place Jules-Ferry and the fishing harbour, and the biggest concerts at the local football stadium, the Parc du Moustoir. For full **schedules**, which are not usually finalized until June, see ⓦ festival-interceltique.com. **Tickets** for the largest events should be reserved well in advance.

6

10am–noon & 2–5pm, Sat 10am–noon; ☎ 02 97 84 78 00, ⓦ www.lorient-tourisme.fr). As well as providing full details on local boat trips, the office organizes some excursions itself.

## ACCOMMODATION

**Auberge de Jeunesse** 41 rue Victor-Schoelcher ☎ 02 97 37 11 65, ⓦ fuaj.org/lorient. Lorient's well-equipped, friendly hostel is in a plain, functional building beside the River Ter, 3km west of the centre (bus #C1 from the *gare SNCF*). Five-person dorms, with space for camping in summer. Closed Jan. **€15.40**

**Les Océanes** 17 av de la Perrière ☎ 02 97 37 14 66, ⓦ hotel-lesoceanes.com. Very presentable modern hotel, slightly removed from the centre near the sailing museum, with simple but bright and attractive rooms and some good-value family suites. **€66**

**Pecheurs** 7 rue Jean Lagarde ☎ 02 97 21 19 24, ⓦ hotel-lespecheurs.com. Basic but recently renovated and acceptable hotel, close to the town centre; the cheapest rooms lack en-suite facilities. **€28**

## EATING AND DRINKING

**Galway Inn** 18 rue Belgique ☎ 02 97 64 50 77, ⓦ pubgalway-lorient.com. Fine old stone pub, renowned for its fusion of Irish and Celtic traditions, with live music of all kinds at the weekend to go with its draught Guinness and cider. Mon–Sat 4pm–2am, Sun 5pm–2am.

**Le Pic** 2 bd Maréchal-Franchet-d'Esperey ☎ 02 97 21 18 29, ⓦ restaurant-lorient.com. Imaginative little restaurant, just south of the *gare SNCF*, with the look of a classy old-fashioned bistro and some outdoor seating.

Lunch from under €15, varied dinner *menus* of market-fresh produce from €27. Mon, Tues, Thurs & Fri noon–1.45pm & 7–9.30pm, Wed noon–1.45pm, Sat 7–9.30pm.

**Tavarn ar Roue Morvan** Place Polig-Monjarret ☎ 02 97 21 61 57. Infused with all things Breton, this lively old tavern serves good, hearty meat and fish dishes, as well as offering home-made cider and live traditional music. Mon–Sat 11am–1am.

# Carnac

**CARNAC** is the most important prehistoric site in Europe – in fact this spot is thought to have been continuously inhabited longer than anywhere else in the world. Its **alignments** of two thousand or so menhirs stretch over 4km, with great burial tumuli dotted amid them. In use since at least 5700 BC, the site long predates Knossos, the Pyramids, Stonehenge and the great Egyptian temples of the same name at Karnak.

## THE MEGALITHS OF BRITTANY

Along with Newgrange in Ireland, Stonehenge in England and the Ring of Brodgar in the Orkneys, the tumuli, alignments and single standing stones of Brittany are of pre-eminent status among the **megalithic sites** of Europe. Dated at 5700 BC, the tumulus of Kercado at Carnac is the earliest known stone construction in Europe. Little is known of the monuments' creators; the few skeletons unearthed indicate a short, dark, hairy race with a life expectancy of no more than the mid-30s. What is certain is that their civilization was long-lasting; the earliest and the latest constructions at Carnac are more than five thousand years apart.

Each megalithic centre had its own distinct styles and traditions. Brittany has relatively few stone circles, or **cromlechs**, and a greater proportion of free-standing stones, **menhirs**; fewer burial chambers, known as **dolmens**, and more evidence of ritual fires; and different styles of carving. Carnac's alignments are unique in their sheer complexity. As for their actual **purpose**, the most fashionable theory sees them as part of a vast astronomical observatory centred on the fallen Grand Menhir of Locmariaquer. However, controversy rages as to whether the Grand Menhir ever stood at all, or, even if it did, whether it fell or was broken up before the surrounding sites came into being. Moreover, sceptics say, these measurements ignore the fact that the sea level in southern Brittany 6600 years ago was 10m lower than it is today. Alternative theories interpret the menhirs as a series of territorial or memorial markers. This annual or occasional setting-up of a new stone is easier to envisage than the vast effort required to erect them all at once – in which case the fact that they were arranged in lines, mounds and circles might have been of peripheral importance.

Divided between the original **Carnac-Ville** and the seaside resort of **Carnac-Plage**, the modern town of Carnac has a special charm, especially in late spring and early autumn. For most, the alignments are, if anything, only a sideshow. The town and seafront remain well wooded, and the tree-lined avenues and gardens are a delight, the climate being mild enough for evergreen oak and Mediterranean mimosa to grow alongside native stone pine and cypress.

## The megaliths

Rte des Alignements, 1km north of Carnac-Ville • **Site** April–Sept tours only (some in English); Oct–March daily 10am–5pm • April–Sept €4.50; Oct–March free **Visitor centre** Daily: May & June 9am–7pm; July & Aug 9am–8pm; Sept–April 10am–5pm • ☎ 02 97 52 29 81, ⓦ carnac.monuments-nationaux.fr

Carnac's **megaliths** form three distinct major alignments, running roughly in the same northeast–southwest direction, but each with a slightly separate orientation. These are the **Alignements de Menec**, "the place of stones" or "place of remembrance", with 1169 stones in eleven rows; the **Alignements de Kermario**, "the place of the dead", with 1029 stones in ten rows; and the **Alignements de Kerlescan**, "the place of burning", with 555 stones in thirteen lines. All three are sited parallel to the sea alongside the **Route des Alignements**, north of Carnac-Ville.

Visitors can only walk freely around the best-preserved sites in winter. In summer, access is on guided tours only, some of which are in English – it's worth joining one of these if this is your first exposure to the subject, as otherwise you can feel as though you're simply staring at rocks in a field. They start from the official visitor centre, the **Maison des Mégalithes**, across the road from the Alignements de Menec, which also holds some interesting displays, plus a model of the entire site.

## Musée de Préhistoire

10 place de la Chapelle, Carnac-Ville • April–June & Sept Wed–Mon 10am–12.30pm & 2–6pm; July & Aug daily 10am–6pm; Oct–March Wed–Mon 10am–12.30pm & 2–5pm • €5 • ☎ 02 97 52 22 04, ⓦ www.museedecarnac.com

The rather dry **Musée de Préhistoire** traces the history of the Morbihan from earliest times, starting with 450,000-year-old chipping tools and leading by way of the Neanderthals to the megalith builders and beyond. Captions are in French only. As well as authentic physical relics, it holds reproductions and casts of the carvings at Locmariaquer, a scale model of the Alignements de Menec, and diagrams of how the stones may have been moved into place.

## The beaches

Carnac's five **beaches** extend for a total of nearly 3km. The two most attractive, usually counted as one of the five, are **plages Men Dû** and **Beaumer**, which lie east towards La Trinité beyond Pointe Churchill. They're especially popular these days with **kite surfers**.

### ARRIVAL AND INFORMATION CARNAC

**By train** In July and Aug, when the Tire-Bouchon rail link runs between Auray and Quiberon, trains call at Plouharnel, 4km northwest of Carnac.

**By bus** Buses from Auray (9 daily; 30min) and Vannes (7 daily; 1hr 20min) stop at the tourist office.

**Tourist office** Slightly back from the main beach, at 74 av des Druides (July & Aug Mon–Sat 9am–7pm, Sun 3–7pm; Sept–June Mon–Sat 9.30am–12.30pm & 2–6pm; ☎ 02 97 52 13 52, ⓦ ot-carnac.fr).

**Bike rental** Bicycles can be rented from Le Randonneur, 20 av des Druides, Carnac-Plage (☎ 02 97 52 02 55), or local campsites like the *Grande Métairie* (see p.348), which also arranges horseback tours.

### ACCOMMODATION

Prices for hotels in Carnac are among the most expensive in all Brittany, and at a premium in July and August. As befits such a family-oriented place, Carnac features as many as twenty campsites.

**6**

### HOTELS

**Celtique** 82 av des Druides, Carnac-Plage ☎ 02 97 52 14 15, ⓦ hotel-celtique.com. Luxurious option, by the beach and affiliated to *Best Western*, with an indoor pool, spa and billiard room. Look for deals on multi-night stays on their website. €107

★ **Plume au Vent** 4 venelle Notre-Dame, Carnac-Ville ☎ 06 16 98 34 79, ⓦ plume-au-vent.com. Central, welcoming and brilliantly decorated B&B, where the two suites draw tastefully on the nautical theme (for once), with pastel colours and some great found artefacts. €90

**Râtelier** 4 chemin de Douët, Carnac-Ville ☎ 02 97 52 05 04, ⓦ le-ratelier.com. Old, ivy-clad stone hotel with comfortable rooms characterized by rustic colours and open wooden beams; some have showers but not toilets. Top-quality food on *menus* from €23. Closed mid-Nov to mid-Dec & all Jan. €56

### CAMPSITES

**Camping Le Dolmen** Just north of Carnac-Plage ☎ 02 97 52 12 35, ⓦ campingledolmen.com. Three-star campsite, an easy walk from the sea, with grocery, snack bar, and seafood platters on demand, as well as heated swimming pool. Closed Oct–March. €28

**Camping Grande Métairie** Rte des Alignements de Kermario ☎ 02 97 52 24 01, ⓦ lagrandemetairie.com. Upscale four-star campsite, in a lovely tree-shaded spot near the Kercado tumulus, with its own extensive waterpark. Closed early Sept to late March. €43

### EATING AND DRINKING

**Chez Marie** 3 place de l'Église, Carnac-Ville ☎ 02 97 52 07 93. An old favourite in Carnac-Ville, this busy stone-clad crêperie offers good €12 *menus* with a *galette* as the main course. Mid-Feb to Oct daily noon–2pm & 7–9pm.

**La Côte** 3 impasse Parc-er-Forn, Carnac-Ville ☎ 02 97 52 02 80, ⓦ restaurant-la-cote.com. Inside this venerable stone cottage, a very smart dining room serves inventive, modern gourmet cuisine, which you can sample at lunch for just €25, or from €36 in the evening. July & Aug Tues 7.15–9.15pm, Wed–Sun 12.15–2.15pm & 7.15–9.15pm; Sept–June Tues 7.15–9.15pm, Wed–Sat 12.15–2.15pm & 7.15–9.15pm, Sun 12.15–2.15pm.

## Locmariaquer

**LOCMARIAQUER** stands right at the narrow mouth of the Gulf of Morbihan. On the ocean side, there's a long sandy beach; on the Gulf side, a small tidal port. As with Carnac, however, the main reason to go out of your way to visit Locmariaquer is to see its fine crop of **megaliths**.

### Site des Mégalithes

Daily: May & June 10am–6pm; July & Aug 10am–7pm; Sept–April 10am–12.30pm & 2–5.15pm • €5.50, under-18s free • ☎ 02 97 57 37 59, ⓦ locmariaquer.monuments-nationaux.fr

Locmariaquer's principal **Site des Mégalithes** was thought until 1991 to hold two monuments – the broken fragments of the **Grand Menhir Brisé**, which having originally stood 20m tall is the largest ever discovered, and a massive dolmen, the **Table des Marchands**. Then archeologists realized that the car park had inadvertently been created atop a third, even larger relic. Now known as **Er Grah**, it consists of a series of partially reconstructed stone terraces, the purpose of which remains unknown.

### ACCOMMODATION                                    LOCMARIAQUER

**Camping La Ferme Fleurie** Kerlogonan ☎ 02 97 57 34 06, ⓦ campinglafermefleurie.com. Excellent little campsite, not far from the beach on the way into town from the north, with peaceful pitches and its own farm shop. Closed mid-Oct to mid-March. €16

**Des Trois Fontaines** Rte d'Auray ☎ 02 97 57 42 70, ⓦ hotel-troisfontaines.com. Pretty, modern hotel, looking out over the bay from the road into town, near the Table des Marchands. Several of the colourful, comfortable rooms have balconies. Closed mid-Nov to mid-Feb. €85

## The Presqu'île de Quiberon

The **Presqu'île de Quiberon**, south of Carnac, is as close to being an island as any peninsula could conceivably be; the long causeway of sand that links it to the mainland narrows to as little as 50m in places. In summer, it attracts tourists in abundance, who come not so much for the towns, which, other than lively **Quiberon**, are generally featureless, but to use them as a base for trips out to **Belle-Île** or around the peninsula's contrasting coastline. The ocean-facing shore, known as the **Côte Sauvage**, is wild and highly unswimmable, where the stormy seas look like snowy mountain tops. The sheltered eastern side has safe and calm sandy beaches, and plenty of campsites.

## Quiberon

Despite recent construction on its namesake peninsula, **QUIBERON**, at the southern tip, is still the only real town. Its most active area, **Port-Maria**, is home to the **gare maritime** for the islands of Belle-Île, Houat and Hoëdic, and also has a sardine-fishing harbour of former glory. At Quiberon's centre is a busy little park and miniature golf course, but few of the streets further back hold anything of great interest. The exception is the little hill that leads down to the port from the **gare SNCF**, where browsing around is rewarded with some surprisingly good clothes and antique shops. Stretching away to the east of the harbour is a long curve of fine sandy **beach**, lined for several hundred metres with bars, cafés and restaurants.

### ARRIVAL AND INFORMATION                                    QUIBERON

**By train** Between mid-June and mid-Sept, the special Tire-Bouchon ("corkscrew") train links Quiberon's *gare SNCF*, a short way above the town proper, with Auray.
**By bus** Bus #1 (TIM; ☎ 02 97 24 26 20, ⓦ lactm.com) runs to the *gare maritime* from Vannes, via Auray and Carnac (8 daily; 1hr 30min).
**Tourist office** 14 rue de Verdun (July & Aug daily 9am–1pm & 2–7pm; Sept–June Mon–Fri 9am–12.30pm & 2–5.30pm, Sat 9am–12.30pm & 2–5.30pm; ☎ 08 25 13 56 00, ⓦ quiberon.com). A digital display outside shows which hotels are full, hour by hour.
**Bike rental** Cycl'omar, 47 place Hoche (☎ 02 97 50 26 00, ⓦ cyclomar.fr).

### ACCOMMODATION

For most of the year, it's hard to get a room in Quiberon. In July and August, the whole peninsula is packed, while in winter it's so quiet that virtually all its facilities close down. The nicest area to stay is along the seafront in Port-Maria, where several good hotel-restaurants face the Belle-Île ferry terminal.

**Au Bon Accueil** 6 quai de Houat ☎ 02 97 50 07 92. This freshly spruced up seafront hotel is Port-Maria's best option for budget travellers, with basic rooms and a good restaurant downstairs. Closed mid-Nov to mid-Feb. **€55**
★ **Neptune** 4 quai de Houat ☎ 02 97 50 09 62, ⓦ hotel-neptune-quiberon.com. Great-value hotel, where twelve of the 21 bright, cheery rooms have sea-view balconies – though the bathrooms are drab – and there's a very good restaurant (see below) with a terrace overlooking the water. Closed Jan to mid-Feb, plus Mon in low season. **€75**
**Port Haliguen** 10 Place de Port Haliguen ☎ 02 97 50 16 52, ⓦ hotel-port-haliguen.com. Very peaceful seafront hotel facing the pleasure port across the peninsula from the town centre. Recently modernized rooms have been stripped of all superfluities to leave them stylish and still comfortable, it's well worth paying the small supplement for a sea-view balcony. Closed mid-Nov to mid-March. **€73**

### EATING AND DRINKING

**La Chaumine** 79 rue de Port Haliguen ☎ 02 97 50 17 67, ⓦ restaurant-lachaumine.com. This lovely little fish restaurant, away from the sea on the main road into Port Haliguen, serves *menus* from €20 at lunch, and from €28 for dinner; the latter features salmon braised in champagne. Mid-March to mid-Nov Tues–Sun noon–2pm & 7–9pm; closed Sun eve in low season.
★ **De la Criée** 11 quai de l'Océan ☎ 02 97 30 53 09, ⓦ maisonlucas.net. Superb local fish restaurant, serving whatever may be fresh from the morning's catch; choose from the overflowing baskets of shellfish, the daily €20–25 specials, or the two good-value set *menus*, at €18 and €21. Feb–Dec Tues–Sun 12.15–2pm & 7.15–10pm; closed Sun eve in winter.
**Neptune** 4 quai de Houat ☎ 02 97 50 09 62, ⓦ hotel-neptune-quiberon.com. Hotel dining room that serves exceptionally good seafood *menus* at €21 and €26. The portions are small, but the food is exquisite. Closed Jan & Mon in low season. Feb–Dec daily noon–2pm & 7–9.30pm; closed Mon in winter.

6

## Belle-Île

Considerably larger than the other Breton islands, at 17km from east to west, gorgeous **BELLE-ÎLE**, 15km south of Quiberon, feels significantly less isolated than the rest. However, its towns – fortified **Le Palais**; **Sauzon**, arrayed along one side of a long estuary; and **Bangor**, inland – are consistently lovely, and it offers wonderful opportunities for walking and cycling. At different times in its turbulent history the island belonged to the monks of Redon, the English – who in 1761 swapped it for Menorca – and Lorient's Compagnie des Indes.

### Le Palais

Docking at the port and main town of **LE PALAIS**, the abrupt star-shaped fortifications of the **citadelle** are the first thing you see. Built along stylish and ordered lines by the great fortress-builder, Vauban, it is startling in size – filled with doorways leading to mysterious cellars and underground passages and deserted cells. Much of it has recently been converted into an expensive hotel, but it still houses a **museum** (daily: April–June, Sept & Oct 9.30am–6pm; July & Aug 9am–7pm; Nov–March 9.30am–5pm; €8; ☎02 97 31 85 54, ⓦ citadellevauban.com), documenting the island's history in fiction as much as in fact.

### Côte Sauvage

Belle-Île is far too large to stroll round, but a coastal footpath runs on bare soil for the length of the exposed **Côte Sauvage** with its sparse heather-covered cliffs facing out into the sea. To appreciate this and the rich and fertile landward side, some form of transport is advisable – **rental bikes** are widely available in Le Palais (see below).

### Grotte de l'Apothicairerie and around

Near the west end of the island, the **Grotte de l'Apothicairerie** is a cliff-face cave that earned its name because it was once full of cormorants' nests, arranged like the jars on a pharmacist's shelves. Inland, on the D25 back towards Le Palais, you pass the two **menhirs**, Jean and Jeanne, said to be lovers petrified as punishment for wanting to meet before their marriage. Another larger menhir used to lie near these two; it was broken up to help construct the road that separates them.

### ARRIVAL AND DEPARTURE                                                            BELLE-ÎLE

#### BY BOAT
**Compagnie-Océane** All year, Compagnie-Océane (☎08 20 05 61 56 or ☎02 97 35 02 00, ⓦ www .compagnie-oceane.fr) sends at least six ferries daily – and up to fifteen in high summer – from Port-Maria on the Quiberon peninsula to Le Palais on Belle-Île. The first departure is around 8am, and the crossing normally takes 45min, though the high-speed vessel *Kerdonis* makes up to five crossings daily between mid-April and August in just 30min. The return fare is €29.65. Small cars can be taken on the slower crossings only, for €134.30 return, while bikes cost €17.60 return. Reserve in advance during peak periods. Between early

July and the end of August, the same company also sends the *Kerdonis* on one daily trip to Sauzon from Port-Maria, for the same fare.

**Navix** Navix (☎08 25 13 21 00, ⓦ navix.fr; €30–44) sails to Le Palais on Belle-Île from Port-Maria (early April to mid-Sept, Mon, Wed & Fri–Sun 8.45am; boat continues to Sauzon; €16 one way, €27 return), and also from Vannes and Port-Navalo (May to late Sept Tues–Thurs, Sat & Sun; times vary; €19 one way, €30 return), with a connecting service from Locmariaquer. They also offer excursions to Belle-Île from Le Croisic (see p.419) and La Turballe, between Piriac and Guérande on the coast not far north of La Baule, in July and Aug only (€42 return).

#### GETTING AROUND
**By bus** Belle-Île's bus system offers around eight daily connections in summer from Le Palais to each of Sauzon, Bangor and Locmaria (☎02 97 31 32 32, ⓦ cars-verts.fr

/taolmor.html).
**By car** Locatourisle (☎02 97 31 83 56, ⓦ locatourisle.com) rents cars from around €70/day in summer.

**By bike** Several waterfront outlets in Le Palais, including Didier Banet (☎02 97 31 84 74, ⓦlocation2roues.com), rent bikes at around €12/day, as well as scooters from €45/day.

## INFORMATION

**Tourist office** Next to the *gare maritime* in Le Palais (July & Aug Mon–Sat 8.45am–7pm, Sun 8.45am–1pm; Sept–June Mon–Sat 9am–12.30pm & 2–6pm; ☎02 97 31 81 93, ⓦwww.belle-ile.com).

## ACCOMMODATION

**Atlantique** Le Palais ☎02 97 31 80 11, ⓦhotel -atlantique.com. Cheerful, yellow-and-blue hotel in prime position on the quayside facing the ferries, offering great-value accommodation and an excellent restaurant with a panoramic terrace. The cheapest rooms are in a separate annexe, but even in summer a sea-view room in the main building costs less than €100. **€65**

**Auberge de Jeunesse** Haute-Boulogne, Le Palais ☎02 97 31 81 33, ⓦfuaj.org/belle-ile-en-mer. Hugely popular hostel on the heights above town, behind the citadelle a 15min walk from the port. Small dorms, with cooking facilities and breakfast. Advance bookings essential. Closed Oct. **€15.40**

**Camping de Port Andro** Locmaria ☎02 97 31 73 25, ⓦlocmaria-belle-ile.com/heb_campings. Belle-Île holds plenty of fancier campsites, but if you like to camp close to the beach, there's no beating this secluded little municipal site, beside its own perfect strand 3km from Locmaria, towards the southeast tip of the island. Closed mid-Sept to April. **€10.90**

**Le Clos Fleuri** Rte de Sauzon, Le Palais ☎02 97 31 45 45, ⓦhotel-leclosfleuri.com. This exceptionally welcoming and peaceful hotel, just ourtside Le Palais on the road towards Sauzon, offers spacious, comfortable and tastefully furnished rooms at reasonable prices, with private terraces but no restaurant. Closed Christmas to mid-Feb. **€85**

6

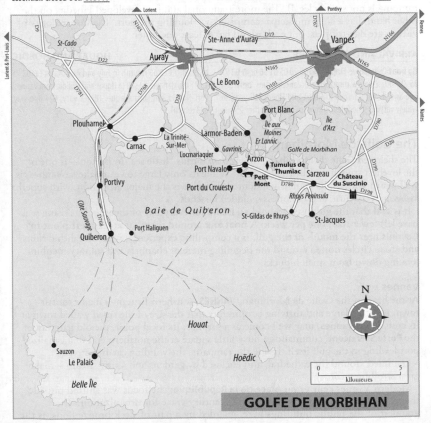

**GOLFE DE MORBIHAN**

**6**

---

### GULF TOURS

In season, dozens of boats leave for **gulf tours** each day from Vannes, Port Navalo, La Trinité, Locmariaquer, Auray, Le Bono and Larmor-Baden.

**Izenah Croisières** ☎ 02 97 57 23 24 or ☎ 02 97 26 31 45, ⓦ www.izenah-croisieres.com. Gulf tours from Port Blanc at Baden in summer, and a year-round ferry service to the Île aux Moines (daily every 30min: July & Aug 7am–10pm, Sept–June 7am–7.30pm; €4.30 return).

**Navix** ☎ 08 25 13 21 00, ⓦ navix.fr. Between mid-April and Sept, cruises from Vannes include half-day (€21.20) and full-day (€29) trips around the gulf, and

also lunch and dinner cruises, where the cost depends on your choice of *menu* (total €63–71). Similar tours at similar prices also depart from Port Navalo, Locmariaquer, Auray, Le Bono, Port Haliguen and La Trinité.

**Vedettes Angelus** ☎ 02 97 57 30 29, ⓦ vedettes-angelus.com. Up to five gulf tours of varying lengths daily from Locmariaquer (mid-April to Sept; first departure 10am; €14–26).

---

## Houat and Hoëdic

You can't take your car to Belle-Île's two smaller sisters, **HOUAT** and **HOËDIC**. Known as the *"îles de silence"*, both islands have a feeling of being left behind by the passing centuries. However, the younger fishermen of Houat have revived the island's fortunes by establishing a successful fishing cooperative, and it also has **beaches** – as ever on the sheltered (eastern) side – that fill up with campers in the summer (even though camping is not strictly legal). The more traditional and less developed Hoëdic, on the other hand, has a large municipal **campsite**, overlooking the port. The vast majority of visitors are day-trippers, but each island has at least one hotel.

### ARRIVAL AND DEPARTURE                                              HOUAT AND HOËDIC

**By boat** Compagnie-Océane (☎ 08 20 05 61 56 or ☎ 02 97 35 02 00, ⓦ www.compagnie-oceane.fr) runs between one and six daily ferries to Houat and Hoëdic all year, to widely varying schedules (40min to Houat, another 25min

to Hoëdic; €29.65 return). In July and Aug, Navix (☎ 08 25 13 21 00, ⓦ navix.fr) sail to Houat and Hoëdic from Vannes, Port-Navalo and Locmariaquer (times vary; €24 one way, €33 return).

## The Golfe de Morbihan

The sheltered **Golfe du Morbihan** – *mor bihan* means "little sea" in Breton – is one of the loveliest stretches of Brittany's coast. While its only large town, medieval **Vannes**, is well worth visiting, its endlessly indented shoreline is the major attraction, with superb vistas at every turn, and countless secluded **beaches**.

It is said that the gulf used to hold an **island** for every day of the year, but rising seas have left fewer than one per week. A **boat tour** around them, or at least a trip out to **Gavrinis** near the mouth of the gulf, is a compelling experience, with megalithic ruins and stone circles dotted around the beguiling maze of channels and solitary menhirs looking down from small hillocks.

## Vannes

At the head of the Golfe de Morbihan, **VANNES**, southern Brittany's major tourist town, is such a large and thriving community that the size of the small walled town at its core, **Vieux Vannes**, may well come as a surprise. Its focal point, the old gateway of the **Porte St-Vincent**, commands a busy little square at the northern end of a canalized port leading to the gulf itself. Inside the ramparts, the winding car-free streets – crammed around the cathedral, and enclosed by gardens and a tiny stream – make great strolling territory.

Modern Vannes centres on **place de la République**; the focus was shifted outside the medieval city during the nineteenth-century craze for urbanization. The grandest of the public buildings here, guarded by a pair of sleek bronze lions, is the

**Hôtel de Ville** at the top of rue Thiers. By day, however, the streets of the old city, with their overhanging, witch-hatted houses and busy commercial life, are the chief source of pleasure.

### La Cohue/Musée des Beaux Arts

9 place St-Pierre • Daily: June–Sept 10am–6pm; Oct–May 1.30–6pm • €6 with Musée d'Histoire et Archéologie • ☎ 02 97 01 63 00

It was in the impressive medieval building known as **La Cohue** that the Breton *États* assembled in 1532 to ratify the Act of Union with France. It currently houses the **Musée des Beaux Arts**, of interest primarily for its temporary exhibitions.

### Cathédrale St-Pierre

Place St-Pierre

Facing La Cohue, the **Cathédrale St-Pierre** is a rather forbidding place, with a stern main altar almost imprisoned by four solemn grey pillars. Light, tinted purple through the new stained glass, spears in to illuminate the desiccated finger of the Blessed Pierre Rogue, who was guillotined on the main square in 1796.

### Musée d'Histoire et Archéologie

2 rue Noé • Daily: mid-May to mid-June 1.30–6pm; mid-June to Sept 10am–6pm • €6 with Musée des Beaux Arts • ☎ 02 97 01 63 00

A sombre fifteenth-century mansion holds Vannes' summer-only **Musée d'Histoire et Archéologie**. Its collection of prehistoric artefacts is said to be one of the world's finest, but they're tediously arrayed in formal patterns in glass cases, and the Middle Ages exhibit on the upper floors is more entertaining.

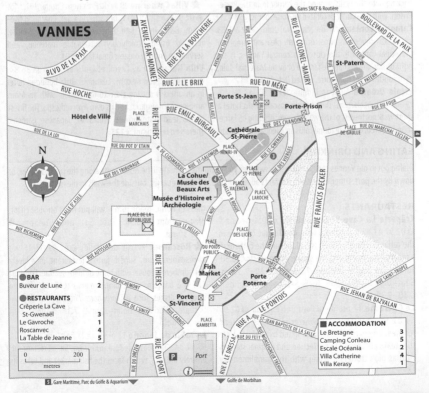

**VANNES**

| BAR | |
|---|---|
| Buveur de Lune | 2 |

| RESTAURANTS | |
|---|---|
| Crêperie La Cave St-Gwenaël | 3 |
| Le Gavroche | 1 |
| Roscanvec | 4 |
| La Table de Jeanne | 5 |

| ACCOMMODATION | |
|---|---|
| Le Bretagne | 3 |
| Camping Conleau | 5 |
| Escale Océania | 2 |
| Villa Catherine | 4 |
| Villa Kerasy | 1 |

**6**

## Parc du Golfe: L'Aquarium du Golfe and Jardin aux Papillons

21 rue Daniel Gilard • Daily: April–June & Sept 10am–noon & 2–6pm; July & Aug 9am–7.30pm; Oct–March 2–6pm, except school hols 10am–noon & 2–6pm • Aquarium: adults €12, under-12s €8.40; Jardin aux Papillons: adults €10, under-12s €6.90; combined ticket €17.50/€12.30 • ☏ 08 10 40 69 01, ⊛ aquarium-du-golfe.com

Vannes' major tourist attraction, its modern **aquarium**, 500m south of place Gambetta in the **Parc du Golfe**, claims to hold Europe's finest collection of tropical fish. Certainly it holds some pretty extraordinary specimens, including a type of fish from Venezuela with four sexes and four eyes; cave fish from Mexico that have no eyes at all; and *arowana* from Guyana, which jump 2m out of the water to catch birds.

Alongside, the separate **Jardin aux Papillons**, or Butterfly Garden, consists of a huge glass dome containing hundreds of free-flying butterflies.

### ARRIVAL AND INFORMATION     VANNES

**By train** Vannes' *gare SNCF* is 25min walk north of the centre.

**By bus** The *gare routière*, with buses to Carnac (7 daily; 1hr 20min) and Quiberon (7 daily; 2hr) faces the *gare SNCF* (☏ 02 97 01 22 01, ⊛ lactm.com).

**By car** Parking can be a problem, but there's plenty of space on Quai Tabarly on the port's west side.

**Tourist office** Quai Tabarly, on the west side of the port (July & Aug Mon–Sat 9.30am–7pm, Sun 10am–6pm; Sept–June Mon–Sat 9.30am–noon & 1.30–6pm; ☏ 08 25 13 56 10, ⊛ tourisme-vannes.com).

**Festivals** At the end of July, the open-air concerts of the Vannes Jazz Festival take place in the Théâtre de Verdure.

### ACCOMMODATION

**Le Bretagne** 36 rue du Méné ☏ 02 97 47 20 21, ⊛ hotel-lebretagne-vannes.com. Reasonable and friendly hotel, backing onto the walls, around the corner from the Porte-Prison, with pleasantly decorated en-suite rooms. **€58**

**Camping Conleau** Av du Maréchal-Juin ☏ 02 97 63 13 88, ⊛ flowercampings.com. Very pleasant three-star municipal campsite, the closest to central Vannes, is set right beside the gulf at the far end of av du Maréchal-Juin, 2km southwest of the centre. Closed Oct–March. **€17**

**Escale Océania** Av Jean-Monnet ☏ 02 97 47 59 60, ⊛ oceaniahotels.com. Dependable upscale chain hotel a short walk northwest of the walled town, offering 65 large, soundproofed, en-suite rooms, plus an adequate restaurant

that's closed at weekends, when hotel rates are cheaper. Book online for best rates. **€72**

★ **Villa Catherine** 89 av du Président Édouard-Herriot ☏ 02 97 42 48 59, ⊛ villa-catherine.net. Charming five-room B&B, in a late nineteenth-century townhouse, restored using ecologically sustainable materials, and serving an entirely organic breakfast. **€101**

**Villa Kerasy** 20 av Favrel et Lincy ☏ 02 97 68 36 83, ⊛ www.villakerasy.com. Luxurious little boutique hotel in an unlikely setting close to the station, with an Asian ambience throughout and its own Ayurvedic spa. The finest rooms lead onto private, miniature Japanese gardens. There's no restaurant. **€123**

### EATING AND DRINKING

Dining out in old Vannes can be expensive, whether you eat in the intimate little restaurants along the rue des Halles, or down by the port. Other, cheaper restaurants abound in the St-Patern quarter, outside the walls in the northeast.

#### RESTAURANTS

**Crêperie La Cave St-Gwenaël** 23 rue St-Gwenaël ☏ 02 97 47 47 94. Atmospheric, good-value crêperie in the cellar of a lovely old house, alongside the cathedral; a meal of one sweet and one savoury crêpe costs €10.30. July & Aug Mon–Sat noon–2.30pm & 6.30–9.30pm; Sept–Dec & Feb–June Tues–Sat noon–2.30pm & 6.30–9.30pm.

**Le Gavroche** 17 rue de la Fontaine Pasteur ☏ 02 97 54 03 54, ⊛ restaurant-legavroche.com. A godsend for meat-lovers in a region dominated by seafood. Here the steaks are cooked to perfection and original starters such as pig's trotters – along with the complimentary

glass of home-made rum – will put hairs on your chest. *Menus* from €16.50. Tues–Sat noon–1.45pm & 7–9.30pm.

★ **Roscanvec** 17 rue des Halles ☏ 02 97 47 15 96, ⊛ roscanvec.com. Superb formal restaurant, in a lovely half-timbered house, with some outdoor seating. Lunch at €25 is a bargain, while dinner *menus* (€45–65), feature unusual dishes such as *carbonara d'huîtres*. Tues 7.15–9.30pm, Wed–Sat noon–2pm & 7.15–9.30pm, Sun noon–2pm.

**La Table de Jeanne** 13 place de la Poissonnerie ☏ 02 97 47 34 91, ⊛ latabledejeanne.com. Smart restaurant, entirely indoors, which faces the fish market and takes its inspiration from the changing daily catch. There's a good-value €16 lunch *menu*, while dinner is entirely à la carte, with most main courses around €20. Tues, Wed & Sun noon–2pm, Thurs–Sat noon–2pm & 7–9.30pm.

**BAR**
**Buveur de Lune** 8 rue Saint-Patern ☏ 02 97 54 32 32. A relaxed and good-natured spot for fairly priced drink with the night sky painted across the ceiling. Wed–Sun 6pm–2am.

## Gavrinis

The reason to visit the island of **GAVRINIS**, which can only be reached on guided boat tours from Larmor-Baden, the closest spot on the mainland immediately north, is its **megalithic site**. The most impressive and remarkable in Brittany, it stands comparison with Newgrange in Ireland and – in shape as well as size and age – with the earliest pyramids of Egypt.

The megalithic structure is essentially a **tumulus**, an earth mound covering a stone cairn and "passage grave". However, half of the mound has been peeled back and the side of the cairn that faces the water was reconstructed to make a facade resembling a step-pyramid. Inside, every stone of both passage and chamber is covered in carvings, with a restricted "alphabet" of fingerprint whorls, axe-heads and other conventional signs, including the spirals that, although familiar in Ireland, are seen only on this spot in Brittany.

### ARRIVAL AND DEPARTURE                                    GAVRINIS

**By ferry** Gavrinis can be reached between March and November only. Tides permitting, ferries leave Larmor-Baden at half-hourly intervals, and the cost includes a 45-minute guided tour of the cairn (April, June & Sept daily 9.30am–12.30pm & 1.30–6.30pm; May Mon–Fri 1.30–6.30pm, Sat & Sun 9.30am–12.30pm & 1.30–6.30pm; July & Aug daily 9.30am–12.30pm & 1.30–7pm; Oct daily except Wed 1.30–5pm; €12; ☏ 02 97 57 19 38, ⓦ gavrinis .info). The last boats of the morning and afternoon leave Larmor-Baden 90min before the closing time.

# The Loire

THE GARDENS AT VILLANDRY

# The Loire

The Loire has a justifiable reputation as one of the greatest, grandest and most striking rivers anywhere in Europe. In its most characteristic stretch, from the hills of Sancerre to the city of Angers, it flows past an extraordinary parade of castles, palaces and fine mansions; unsurprisingly, when it came to choosing which should be awarded the title of World Heritage Site, UNESCO simply bestowed the label on the entire valley. Although the most striking feature is the beautiful views, there are simpler pleasures, such as the outstanding food and drink and the noticeably gentler pace of life.

**7**

The region's heartland, **Touraine**, long known as "the garden of France", has some of the best wines, the tastiest goat's cheese, and the most regal history in France, including one of the finest châteaux, in Chenonceau. Touraine also takes in three of the Loire's pleasantest tributaries: the **Cher**, **Indre** and **Vienne**. If you have just a week to spare for the region, then these are the parts to concentrate on. The attractive towns of **Blois** and **Amboise**, each with their own exceptional châteaux, make good bases for visiting the area upstream of Tours. Numerous grand **châteaux** dot the wooded country immediately south and east of Blois, including Chambord, the grandest of them all, while the wild and watery region of the Sologne stretches away further to the southeast. Downstream of Tours, around handsome Saumur, quirky troglodyte dwellings have been carved out of the rock faces.

Along with its many châteaux, the region has a few unexpected sights, most compelling of which are the gardens at **Villandry**, outside Tours, and the abbey at **Fontevraud**. The major towns of **Angers**, **Tours**, **Nantes**, **Le Mans** and **Orléans** have their own charms, from Orléans' astonishing cathedral, to Angers lively nightlife.

The Loire itself is often called the last wild river in France, mostly because unpredictable currents and shallow water brought an end to commercial river traffic as soon as the railways arrived, and the many quays remain largely forgotten, except by the occasional tour boat. Such an untamed river also makes for dramatic floods, but for most of the year it meanders gently past its shifting sandbanks, shaded by reeds and willows, and punctuated by long, sandy islands beloved by birds.

## GETTING AROUND                                                    THE LOIRE

Though most sites are accessible by public transport, buses and trains can be rather limiting. It's a good idea to hire some means of transport, at least for occasional forays away from the crowds. Hiring a bike is perhaps the most enjoyable option of all: this is wonderful and easy cycling country, especially on the dedicated cycle routes that make up the Loire à Vélo network (see box, p.363).

# Highlights

❶ **Châteaux à vélo** 300km of bike paths that ramble through forests, fields and pretty stone villages, an idyllic way to visit the stunning châteaux around Blois. **See p.363**

❷ **Stained glass at Bourges cathedral** Some of France's finest stained-glass windows are preserved in Bourges's extravagant Gothic cathedral. **See p.375**

❸ **Château de Blois** A brilliantly conceived building with an epic history – a must-see for all visitors. **See p.384**

❹ **Amboise** Beautiful, archetypal Loire Valley town, and a brilliant base for an exploration of the outlying regions. **See p.396**

❺ **The gardens at Villandry** These superb gardens are home to allegorical Renaissance hedge-work. **See p.399**

❻ **The Tapestry of the Apocalypse** Dramatically displayed in Angers' half-ruined fortress, this is an astonishingly well-preserved piece of medieval doom-mongering. **See p.408**

❼ **Les Machines de L'Île, Nantes** Thrilling steam-punk extravaganza, where visitors can ride on a twelve-metre-tall mechanical elephant. **See p.416**

**HIGHLIGHTS ARE MARKED ON THE MAP ON PP.360–361**

# Orléans and around

**ORLÉANS** is the northernmost city on the Loire, sitting at the apex of a huge arc in the river as it switches direction and starts to flow southwest. Its proximity to Paris, just over 100km away, has always shaped this ancient city. Nowadays Orléans' glory days are over, but high-speed train and motorway links to the capital and a rash of cosmetics factories in the suburbs have still brought a certain measure of prosperity. It's an attractive place; the ancient riverside quays have been redeveloped, and ultramodern trams provide a perfect foil to the handsome eighteenth- and nineteenth-century streets of the old centre.

Upstream from Orléans, the rambling Forêt d'Orléans spreads north. Along the river are plenty of lesser-known attractions, most notably the **abbey at St-Benoît**, the château at **Sully-sur-Loire**, the small town of **Gien**, the aqueduct at **Briare** and the hilltop town of **Sancerre**, where the famous dry white wines are produced.

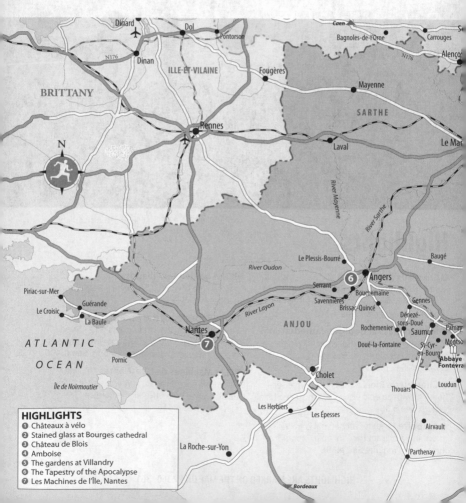

## HIGHLIGHTS

1. Châteaux à vélo
2. Stained glass at Bourges cathedral
3. Château de Blois
4. Amboise
5. The gardens at Villandry
6. The Tapestry of the Apocalypse
7. Les Machines de l'Île, Nantes

# Cathédrale Sainte-Croix

Place du Martroi • Daily 9.15am–5pm

In pride of place in the large, central **place du Martroi**, a mostly pedestrianized square at the end of rue de la République, rises a mid-nineteenth-century likeness of St Joan (see box, p.365) on horseback. Just beyond place du Martroi, the grand nineteenth-century stretch of rue Jeanne-d'Arc marches arrow-straight up to the doors of the **Cathédrale Sainte-Croix**, where Joan celebrated her victory over the English – although the uniformly Gothic structure actually dates from well after her death. Huguenot iconoclasts destroyed the transepts in 1568, and in 1601 Henri IV inaugurated a rebuilding programme that lasted until the nineteenth century. The lofty towers of the west front, which culminate in a delicate stone palisade, were only completed at the time of the Revolution. Inside, skeletal columns of stone extend in a single vertical sweep from the cathedral floor to the vault. Joan's canonization in 1920 is marked by a garish monumental altar next to the north transept, supported by two jagged golden leopards that represent the English. In the nave, the late nineteenth-century stained-glass

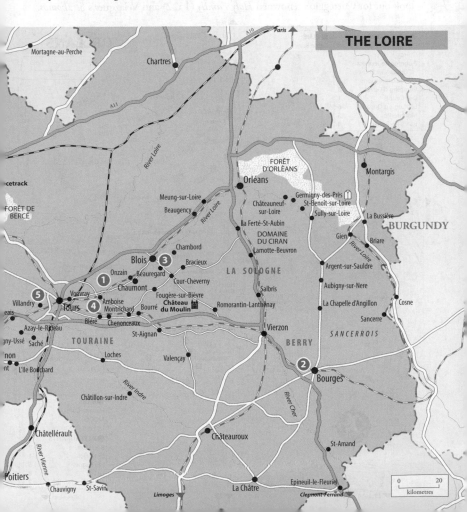

windows tell the story of her life, starting from the north transept. Across place d'Étape from the cathedral, outside the red-brick Renaissance Hôtel Groslot, the old Hôtel de Ville, Joan appears again, in pensive mood, her skirt flecked by World War II bullets.

## Musée des Beaux-Arts

1 rue Fernand Rabier • Tues–Sun 10am–6pm • ☎ 02 38 79 21 55 • €3; same ticket for Hôtel Cabu (see opposite) • ⓦ www.orleans.fr

The **Musée des Beaux-Arts**, opposite the Hôtel Groslot, is probably the cultural high point of the city. The highlights of the main French collection on the first floor include Claude Deruet's *Four Elements*, the Le Nain brothers' dream-like and compelling *Bacchus Discovering Ariane on Naxos*, and an exquisite collection of eighteenth-century pastel portraits. The suite of rooms on the mezzanine level leads from nineteenth-century Neoclassicism through Romanticism and on to a large chamber devoted to the early Realists, dominated by Antigna's taut, melodramatic *The Fire*. Foreign art, mainly Flemish and Italian sixteenth- and seventeenth-century works, is on the second floor – look out for Correggio's renowned *Holy Family* (1522) and Velázquez's *St Thomas*.

**7**

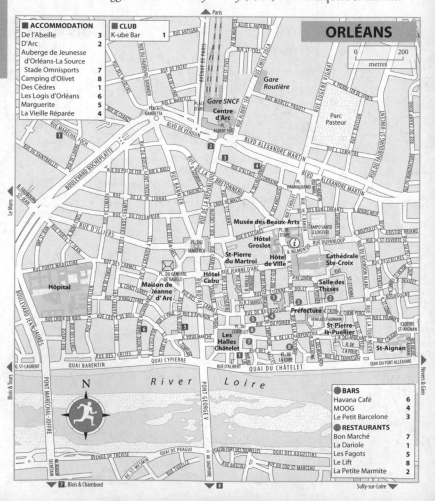

ORLÉANS

| ∎ ACCOMMODATION | |
|---|---|
| De l'Abeille | 3 |
| D'Arc | 2 |
| Auberge de Jeunesse d'Orléans-La Source Stade Omnisports | 7 |
| Camping d'Olivet | 8 |
| Des Cèdres | 1 |
| Les Logis d'Orléans | 6 |
| Marguerite | 5 |
| La Vieille Réparée | 4 |

| ∎ CLUB | |
|---|---|
| K-ube Bar | 1 |

| ● BARS | |
|---|---|
| Havana Café | 6 |
| MOOG | 4 |
| Le Petit Barcelone | 3 |

| ● RESTAURANTS | |
|---|---|
| Bon Marché | 7 |
| La Dariole | 1 |
| Les Fagots | 5 |
| Le Lift | 8 |
| La Petite Marmite | 2 |

## THE LOIRE BY BIKE

Thanks to the **Loire à Vélo** scheme (@loire-a-velo.fr), the Loire valley is now one of the most charming places in the world to have a cycling holiday or take a day out on a hired bike. A mix of dedicated cycle paths and meticulously signposted routes along minor roads now runs all the way along the Loire from Orléans to beyond Angers – a distance of more than 300km. The region around Blois offers an additional 300km network, **Châteaux à vélo** (@chateauxavelo.com). These routes thread inland among the forests, linking the area's many châteaux.

Tourist offices provide detailed maps and other information, and you can download most details, including maps, online. French villages are accustomed to cyclists, and most importantly, car-drivers are too.

### BIKE HIRE

All larger towns have at least one hire agency. Bikes can also be hired at hotels, campsites, tourist offices, train stations and even restaurants along the way. Orléans and Angers have share-bike schemes like the Paris Vélibs. Many have signed up to the **Détours de Loire** scheme (@02 47 61 22 23, @locationdevelos.com), which allows you to pick up a bike in one place and drop it off in another, paying inexpensive drop-off costs per zone crossed – on top of the bike rental charge.

**7**

Twentieth-century art lurks in the basement, where the big names include Picasso and Gauguin; a small inner chamber has a number of African-influenced sculptures by Henri Gaudier-Brzeska (1891–1915), who was born just outside Orléans at St-Jean-de-Braye. English information sheets are supplied in each room.

## Hôtel Cabu

Place Abbé-Desnoyers • May, June & Sept Tues–Sat 1.30–5.45pm, Sun 2–6pm; July & Aug Tues–Sat 9.30am–12.15pm & 1.30–5.45pm, Sun 2–6pm; Oct–April Wed 1.30–5.45pm, Sun 2–6pm • Same ticket as Musée des Beaux-Arts (see opposite)

Follow rue Jeanne-d'Arc west from the cathedral and turn left down rue Charles-Sanglier and you'll find the ornate **Hôtel Cabu**, whose three tiers faithfully follow the three main classical orders in strict Renaissance style. Inside, a small historical and archeological museum houses the extraordinary **Trésor de Neuvy-en-Sullias**, a collection of bronze animals and figurines found near Orléans in 1861. The cache was probably buried in the second half of the third century AD, either to protect it from Germanic invaders or to stop it being melted down for coinage at a time of rampant inflation, and possibly represents the last flourishing of Celtic religion at the end of the Gallo-Roman period. The floors above house various medieval oddities and Joan-related pieces, as well as exhibits on the history of Orléans. The entrance is on place Abbé-Desnoyers.

## Maison de Jeanne d'Arc

3 place du Général-de-Gaulle • Tues–Sun: May–Oct 10am–12.30pm & 1.30–6.30pm; Nov–April 1.30–6pm • €2 • @02 38 52 99 89

An entertaining enough diversion for an hour, the semi-timbered **Maison de Jeanne d'Arc** is a 1960s reconstruction on the site where Joan stayed during the siege of Orléans. Despite the hundreds of images of Joan, many with the pageboy haircut and demure little face, there is no contemporary portrait of her, save for a clerk's doodle in the margin of her trial proceedings, kept in the National Archives in Paris, and you can see a copy here.

## The riverfront and around

The scattered vestiges of the old city are to the east, down towards the river. Rue de Bourgogne was the Gallo-Roman main street, and is now lined with lively bars and restaurants. The Salles des Thèses is all that remains of the medieval university of Orléans where the hardline Reformation theologian Calvin studied Roman law.

**7**

## FOOD AND DRINK OF THE LOIRE

The Loire is renowned for the softness of its climate and the richness of its soil, qualities that help produce some of the best **fruit** and **vegetables** you'll find anywhere. From Anjou's orchards come greengages, named Reine Claude after François I's queen, and the succulent Anjou pear, Doyenné du Comice. Market stalls overflow with seasonal fruits, particularly local tiny sweet strawberries. Tours is famous for its French beans and Saumur for its potatoes and shallots. Asparagus, particularly the fleshy white variety, appears in soufflés, omelettes and other egg dishes as well as on its own, accompanied by vinaigrette made (if you're lucky) with local walnut oil. Finally, from Berry, comes the humble lentil, whose green variety often accompanies salmon or trout.

Given the number of rivers that flow through the region, it's hardly surprising that **fish** features on most restaurant menus, though this doesn't guarantee that it's from the Loire itself. Favourites are *sandre* (pikeperch, a fish native to Central Europe), usually served in the classic Loire *beurre blanc* sauce; stuffed bream; *matelote* (a kind of stew) of local eels softened in red wine and little smelt-like fishes served deep-fried (*la friture*).

The favoured **meat** of the Loire is game, and pheasant, guinea fowl, pigeon, duck, quails, young rabbit, venison and even wild boar are all hunted in the Sologne. They are served in rich sauces made from the wild mushrooms of the region's forests or the common *champignon de Paris*, cultivated on a huge scale in caves cut out of the limestone rock near Saumur. Both Tours and Le Mans specialize in *rillettes*, or potted pork (*rillauds* in Anjou); in Touraine charcuteries you'll also find *pâté au biquion*, made from pork, veal and young goat's meat.

Touraine makes something of a cult of its **goat's cheese**, and a local *chèvre fermier* (farm-produced goat's cheese) can be a revelation. Four named goats' cheeses are found on most boards: Ste-Maure is a long cylinder with a piece of straw running through the middle; Pouligny-St-Pierre and Valençay are pyramid-shaped; and Selles-sur-Cher is flat and round.

### WINE

Though not as famous as the produce of Bordeaux and Burgundy, the Loire valley has some of the finest **wines** in France. Sancerre, the easternmost Loire appellation, produces perhaps the best white wines in the region from the great Sauvignon grape, and the whites of Muscadet around Nantes are a great accompaniment to the local shellfish. Touraine's finest reds – Chinon, Bourgeuil and St-Nicolas de Bourgeuil – get their ruby colour from the Cabernet Franc grape, while many of its attractive white wines are made from the Chenin Blanc including the highly fashionable Jasnières. At the other end of the spectrum is the honeyed complexity of Côteaux du Layon's dessert wines – best with blue cheese or foie gras rather than pudding. Saumur and Vouvray both have sparkling varieties, a fraction of the price of champagne and easily equal to the taste. The orange-y liqueur **Cointreau** is made in a distillery close to Angers and appears in many cocktails and puddings in the region.

To the south, the attractive narrow streets of the old industrial area lead to the river. Once semi-derelict, this neighbourhood is now the focus of a campaign to make the riverfront once more the focus of the city. On the place de la Loire, which slopes down to the river from a nine-screen cinema complex, the flagstones are inset with a pattern that's supposed to suggest waves.

## The churches of St-Aignan and St-Pierre-le-Puellier

At least two of the quarter's churches are on the list of precious monuments: the remains of **St-Aignan** and its well-preserved eleventh-century crypt; and the Romanesque **St-Pierre-le-Puellier**, a former university church now used for concerts and exhibitions. St-Aignan was destroyed during the English siege and rebuilt by the Dauphin, then grew to become one of the greatest churches in France under Louis XII. More sieges of the city during the Wars of Religion took their toll, leaving just the choir and transepts standing. Tours of the crypt, which was built in the early eleventh century to house the relics of St-Aignan, are occasionally conducted by the tourist office.

## ARRIVAL AND INFORMATION

## ORLÉANS

**By train** The *gare SNCF* leads straight into the modern shopping centre on place d'Arc, which fronts onto a huge swathe of busy roads; the Old Town centre lies on the far side. Destinations Beaugency (frequent; 20min); Blois (frequent; 40min); La Ferté-St-Aubin (frequent; 15–25min); Meung-sur-Loire (frequent; 15min); Paris (at least hourly; 1hr); Tours (frequent; 1hr–1hr 30min).

**By bus** The *gare routière*, on rue Marcel-Proust, is just north of place d'Arc.
Destinations Beaugency (10 daily; 1hr); Chartres (9 daily; 1hr 10min–1hr 45min); Germigny-des-Près (3 daily; 1hr); Gien (8 daily; 1hr 50min); Meung-sur-Loire (10 daily; 35min); St-Benoît-sur-Loire (3 daily; 1hr); Sully-sur-Loire (8 daily; 1hr 20min).

**Tourist office** 2 place de l'Étape (Mon–Sat: March 10am–1pm & 2–5.30pm; April 10am–1pm & 2–6pm; May & Sept 9.30am–1pm & 2–6pm; June 9.30am–1pm & 2–6.30pm; July & Aug 9am–7pm, also Sun 10am–1pm & 2–5pm; Oct–Feb 10am–1pm & 2–5pm; ☏ 02 38 24 01 69, ⓦ tourisme-orleans.com).

## ACCOMMODATION

★ **De l'Abeille** 64 rue Alsace Lorraine ☏ 02 38 53 54 87, ⓦ hoteldelabeille.com. Just off the buzz of the main shopping street this gorgeous little hotel with original antique furniture has bags of charm. There's a spacious terrace and an organic breakfast to look forward to in the morning. Breakfast €11. **€89**

**D'Arc** 37 rue de la République ☏ 02 38 53 10 94, ⓦ hoteldarc.fr. This long-established Art Nouveau hotel has touches of grandeur, though it's now a *Best Western* and was refurbished in 2011. The most attractive rooms have small balconies with window boxes looking down onto the pedestrianized street below. Buffet breakfast €14. **€132**

**Auberge de Jeunesse d'Orléans-La Source Stade Omnisports** 7 rue Beaumarchais ☏ 02 38 53 60 06. Clean, decent hostel, with modern facilities, but far from the centre underneath a stand of Orléans' football stadium: take tram A from the train station to "Université l'indien" (30min), then walk 500m east down av du Président-Kennedy. Reception open Mon–Fri 8am–7pm, Sat & Sun 9am–noon. **€14.30**

**Camping d'Olivet** Rue du Pont Bouchet, Olivet ☏ 02 38 63 53 94, ⓦ camping-olivet.org. This is the closest site to town, 5km away by the river. There's free bike and canoe hire, ping pong, badminton and wet-weather games. To get there take Tram A, "Lorette" stop. Closed mid-Oct to end-March. **€26.40**

**Des Cèdres** 17 rue Maréchal-Foch ☏ 02 38 62 22 92, ⓦ hotelcedresorleans.com. Five minutes walk from the station away from town. Comfortable and clean with a courtyard out back where you can have breakfast under the trees. Breakfast €8.50. Cheaper week rates. **€85**

**Les Logis d'Orléans** 18 rue Notre Dame de Recouvrance ☏ 02 36 47 55 47, ⓦ chambre-hote-orleans.com. A beautifully preserved house dating from the 1700s, just a few steps from the church and a minute from the river, sheltering two *chambres d'hôtes*. The "Jeanne" is an open-plan romantic attic with claw-foot bath, dining, lounge space and huge bed. The "Chambre Dunois" is in a Louis XV period style and is a little smaller, but still impressive. Home-cooked breakfast included. **€95**

**Marguerite** 14 place du Vieux-Marché ☏ 02 38 53 74 32, ⓦ hotel-orleans.fr. Central (just a minute from the river), friendly and well run. Rooms are large and immaculate, painted in cheery shades. There's a lovely breakfast room with a tree-lined view. Breakfast €7. **€85**

**La Vieille Réparée** 17 rue des Hugenots ☏ 02 38 51 95 16, ⓦ lavieillereparee.com. You'll get a friendly welcome at this large and sunny *chambres d'hôtes* apartment overlooking a leafy garden. Separate lounge-dining area, bathroom and teeny tiny sitting room. The free parking in the middle of the city make this one of the best deals in town. Breakfast included. **€80**

7

---

## JOAN OF ARC

Orléans is most famous for its heroine, **Joan of Arc**, and her deliverance of the city in May 1429. This was the turning point in the Hundred Years' War (1337–1453), when Paris had been captured by the English and Orléans, as the key city in central France, was under siege. The legend says that Joan, a 17-year-old peasant girl in men's clothing, had talked her way into meeting Charles, the heir to the French throne, and persuaded him to reconquer his kingdom. The reality may be a little different as it seems that Joan was in fact born of nobility. The myth may have coloured her actual achievements, but she was undeniably an important symbolic figure. Less than three years later she was captured in battle, tried as a heretic, and burnt at the stake. Today, the Maid of Orléans is an omnipresent feature, whether in museums, hotels or in the stained glass of the vast Neo-Gothic cathedral. One of the best times to visit is on May 8 (Joan of Arc Day) or the evening before, when the city is filled with parades, fireworks and a medieval fair.

## EATING AND DRINKING

Rue de Bourgogne is the main street for restaurants and nightlife. You can choose from among French, Spanish, North African, Middle Eastern, Indian and Asian cuisines, all of which can be sampled at very reasonable prices. You can buy your own provisions in the covered market halls on place du Châtelet, near the river.

### RESTAURANTS

★ **Bon Marché** 12 place Châtelet ☎ 02 38 53 04 35, ⓦ aubonmarche-orleans.com. Superb service, delicious food and a cosy atmosphere in this family friendly restaurant on the corner of the Châtelet square. *Menus* start at €13.90; the pork braised in Chinon wine and rosemary is superb. They also have a small *cave à vin*, so you can buy any wines that took your fancy over dinner. Daily noon–2.30pm & 7–10.30pm, Sat till 11pm.

**Le Dariole** 25 rue Étienne-Dolet ☎ 02 38 77 26 67. Tearoom-cum-restaurant in a picture-postcard half-timbered building that serves good-quality food at inexpensive prices (*menus* from €17.50). It's fairly small so reserve if you want to be sure of grabbing a table. Mon–Fri 12.30–2pm, Tues & Fri 7.30–9.30pm.

**Les Fagots** 32 rue du Poirier ☎ 02 38 62 22 79. Wonderfully convivial place that looks as if it has been crammed into someone's grandmother's kitchen. Traditional mains and grilled meats feature on the €15 *menus*. There's a small terrace for al fresco dining, but you'll miss the charm of the fireplace if you opt for outside. Tues–Sat noon–2.30pm, 7–10.30pm.

**Le Lift** Place de la Loire ☎ 02 38 53 63 48. Run by a renowned chef, Philippe Bardau, this modern restaurant features finely prepared cuisine and a terrace with views of the Loire. As it's a little pricey, a good way to try Bardau's food is to go for a lunch *menu* (*formules* start from €18 including a glass of perfectly matched Loire wine). Evening *menus* from €48. Reservation required. Daily noon–2pm & 7.30–11pm.

**La Petite Marmite** 178 rue de Bourgogne ☎ 02 38 54 23 83. The most highly regarded restaurant on this busy street combines a stylish but homely atmosphere with excellent regional cuisine. The €22 *menu du terroir* features local produce, such as rabbit and mushrooms from the Sologne. Daily noon–2.30pm & 7–10.30pm, closed Tues.

### BARS AND CLUBS

**Havana Café** 28 place Châtelet ☎ 02 38 52 16 00. Packed and popular, with a terrace that's perfect for people-watching. If there's not a table immediately, it's worth hanging around near the bar as people come and go fairly often. Fresh-squeezed juices, milkshakes and rum cocktails. Daily till around 1am.

**K-ube Bar** 2 rue Alibert ☎ 02 38 53 34 28. A little out of the way on a small street leading down to the river, this small but friendly bar-club has DJs, is open late till 3am most weekends, and plays a bouncy blend of electro, hip hop, drum and bass and dub step. Tues–Fri 6pm–2am & Sat 7pm–3am.

**MOOG** 33 rue de l'Empereur ☎ 02 38 62 98 80. Excellent cocktails and a roomy terrace, just off the rue de Bourgogne. If you arrive around *apéro* time just after opening, you will be served a small complementary tray of savoury snacks like olives and a delicious baked salmon-bread. Perfect for lining the stomach, as the drinks are very strong. Tues–Sat 6pm–2am.

**Le Petit Barcelone** 218 rue de Bourgogne. Friendly, informal bar, popular with students on a budget, with cheapish drinks (around €3–4 for a beer or glass of wine) and serving meals and tapas. Daily till 2am in summer.

## DIRECTORY

**Bike hire** Orléans has a shared bike scheme (ⓦ agglo-veloplus.fr) with stands across the city. It's €1 for a day and €3 for the week, and free for rides of 30min or less. Many central hotels have bikes to lend free of charge if you call in advance.

**Car rental** Avis, *gare SNCF* ☎ 02 38 62 27 04; Rent-a-Car, 3 rue Sansonnières ☎ 02 38 62 22 44; Europcar, 17 av de Paris ☎ 02 38 63 88 00.

**Festivals** Fête de Jeanne d'Arc is a series of period-costume parades held at the end of April and in May. The Festival de Jazz d'Orléans (ⓦ orleansjazz.fr) is held right through June, culminating in concerts held in the Campo Santo. Every September in odd years, the Loire Festival (ⓦ www.orleans .fr/festival-de-loire-2013) takes place, with five days of concerts and shows beside the Châtelet quay.

**Health Centre** Hospitalier, 1 rue Porte-Madeleine ☎ 02 38 51 44 44; emergencies ☎ 15.

**Police** Courtyard of Hôtel Groslot, place de l'Étape ☎ 02 38 79 29 44; emergencies ☎ 17.

# Meung-sur-Loire

Little streams known as *les mauves* flow between the houses in the village of **MEUNG-SUR-LOIRE**, 14km southwest of Orleans, on the Blois train line; during the summer months they leave slimy green high-water marks, but the sound of water is always pleasant, and Meung is an agreeable place to spend an afternoon, having accumulated a number of literary associations over the centuries. In the late thirteenth century, Jean

**7**

## MUST-SEE CHÂTEAUX

First things first; though it is tempting to try and pack in as many châteaux as you can in a short period of time, this is counter-productive and frustrating. It's far better to aim to visit three or four of the best in the area in which you're staying, possibly with a one-day trip to one of the most spectacular set-piece châteaux.

### ADMISSIONS

Entry prices are undeniably steep, particularly for the châteaux that have remained in private hands – and there are a surprising number of French aristocrats still living in their family homes. This means that picking and choosing the best really will help you. There is no consistency in concessions offered, and children rarely go free. If you're over 65, under 25, a student or still at school, check for any reductions and make sure you've got proof of age or a student card with you. Here's a rundown of the very best châteaux to aim for:

**Chenonceau** (see p.376). Renaissance-period château in a glorious setting by the river.

**Azay-le-Rideau** (see p.400). A marvellous encapsulation of a long-gone period of grandeur and power, in a beautifully serene setting (surrounded by a moat).

**Blois** (see p.384). With its four wings representing four distinct eras, Blois is extremely impressive.

**Chambord** (see p.389). A monstrously huge château, the triumph of François I's Renaissance. The key feature here is the dual-spiral staircase; legend has it this was designed by Leonardo da Vinci.

**Cheverny** (see p.388). A prime example of seventeenth-century magnificence.

**Amboise** (see p.396). Urban château which rears above the Loire like a cliff; it's one of the most compelling and striking Loire châteaux, even if the interior decoration leaves something to be desired.

**Loches** (see p.382). For an evocation of medieval times, the citadelle of Loches is hard to beat.

**Langeais** (see p.399). Impressive interiors are the main attraction here, especially the tapestries and intricate tile work.

Other châteaux are more compelling for their contents than for their architecture:

**Valençay** (see p.380). The interior of this Renaissance château is Napoleonic – and it's a great spot for children.

**Beauregard** (see p.389). Most famous for its wonderful portrait gallery.

**La Bussière** (see p.371). Witness the obsessive nineteenth-century decoration, entirely dedicated to freshwater fishing.

**Angers** (see p.408). This stark, largely ruined medieval castle houses the *Tapestry of the Apocalypse*, the greatest work of art in the Loire valley, and worth a visit in itself.

de Meun, or de Meung, added eighteen thousand lines to the already four thousand line-long *Roman de la Rose*, a poetic hymn to sexuality written half a century earlier (by Guillaume de Lorris, from the town of the same name in the nearby Forêt d'Orléans). Inspired by the philosophical spirit of the times, de Meun transformed the poem into a finely argued disquisition on the nature of love, and inspired generations of European writers. Most recently, the town featured in the works of Georges Simenon – his fictional hero, Maigret, takes his holidays here.

## Château de Meung

April–May & Sept–Oct Tues–Sun 2–6pm; June–Aug Tues–Sun 10am–6pm • €8.50 • ⓦ chateau-de-meung.com

Looming at the western edge of Meung-sur-Loire is the **Château de Meung**, which remained in the hands of the bishops of Orléans from its construction in the twelfth century right up to the Revolution, though since then it has passed through seven or eight private owners. The exterior of the château on the side facing the old drawbridge looks grimly defensive with its thirteenth-century pepper-pot towers, while the park side presents a much warmer facade, its eighteenth-century windows framed by salmon-pink stucco. You can explore the older part on your own, even poking around under the roof, but bear in mind that most of this pleasantly shambolic section of the building was remodelled in the nineteenth century, and little sense of its history remains. More impressive is the eighteenth-century wing, where the bishops entertained their guests in relative comfort. Below here are the cellars where criminals condemned by the Episcopal courts were imprisoned. The most famous of the detainees was the poet François Villon, who was kept under lock and key between May and October 1461.

## Beaugency

**BEAUGENCY**, Six kilometres southwest of Meung along the Loire, is a pretty little town, which, in contrast to its innocuous appearance today, played its part in the conniving games of early medieval politics. In 1152 the marriage of Louis VII of France and Eleanor of Aquitaine was annulled by the Council of Beaugency in the church of Notre-Dame, allowing Eleanor to marry Henry Plantagenet, the future Henry II of England. Her huge land holdings in southwest France thus passed to the English crown – which already controlled Normandy, Maine, Anjou and Touraine – and the struggles between the French and English kings over their claims to these territories, and to the French throne itself, lasted for centuries.

Liberated by the indefatigable Joan of Arc on her way to Orléans in 1429, Beaugency was a constant battleground during the Hundred Years' War due to its strategic significance as the only bridge crossing point of the Loire between Orléans and Blois. Remarkably, the 26-arch bridge still stands. The once heavily fortified medieval heart of the town clusters tightly around a handful of central squares. Place St-Firmin, with its statue of Joan, is overlooked by the only remaining tower of a church destroyed during the Revolution, while place Dunois is bordered by the massive eleventh-century **Tour de César**, formerly part of the rather plain, fifteenth-century Château Dunois (which is closed to visitors for major structural works). The square is completed by the severe Romanesque abbey church of Notre-Dame, the venue for the council's fateful matrimonial decision in 1152. Shady place du Docteur-Hyvernaud, two blocks north of place Dunois, is dominated by the elaborate sixteenth-century facade of the Hôtel de Ville. Inside, the main council chamber is graced by eight fine embroidered wall hangings from the era of Louis XIII, but you'll have to ask at the tourist office (see below) to be allowed inside to have a look. One set illustrates the four continents as perceived in the seventeenth century, with the rest dramatizing pagan rites such as gathering mistletoe and sacrificing animals.

### INFORMATION
BEAUGENCY

**Tourist office** Place Docteur-Hyvernaud (April–Sept Mon–Sat 10am–12.30pm & 2–6.30pm, Sun 10am–noon; Oct–March Mon–Sat 9.30am–12.30pm & 2–5.30pm; ☎02 38 44 54 42, ⓦ beaugency.fr).

### ACCOMMODATION

**De l'Abbaye** 2 quai de l'Abbaye ☎02 38 45 10 10, ⓦ grandhoteldelabbaye.com. Set in a beautiful seventeenth-century abbey with painted ceilings and huge fireplaces, this charming places offers traditional luxury with prime Loire river views. The bar and lounge are redolent with the scent of wood smoke. Breakfast €16. **€119**

**Auberge de Jeunesse** 152 rue de Châteaudun, 2km north of town ☎02 38 44 61 31, ⓦ fuaj.org. Decent youth hostel but unfortunately there's no bus into town. Closed Dec. **€14.90**

**Relais de Templiers** 68 rue du Pont ☎02 38 44 53 78, ⓦ hotelrelaistempliers.com. Family-run, inexpensive concern that's a little faded, but there's a friendly feel. Rooms 25 and 21 are the largest and most modern. Breakfast €8. **€62**

**De la Sologne** 6 place St-Firmin ☎02 38 44 50 27, ⓦ hoteldelasologne.com. A small and delightful hotel with pleasantly chintzy rooms topped with timbered ceilings. Some rooms have views of the Tour de César and others offer a pleasing view over pretty shady gardens at the back. Breakfast €9. Closed Christmas and early Jan. **€66**

### EATING AND DRINKING

**Chez Henri** 43 rue du Pont ☎02 38 44 16 65. Good-value classic French cuisine with cheerful waiting staff and a shaded terrace area just off the narrow street. Lunch *menus* from €10. Mon–Sat noon–2pm & 7–10pm.

**La Crep'zeria** 32 rue due Pont ☎02 38 44 55 07. Perched on one of the little waterways that dot the streets in Beaugency, this is the place for decent and inexpensive pizzas and crêpes on the sunny terrace; with lunchtime

*menus* from €12. Closed Mon.
**L'Idée** 3 Place du Petit Marché ☎ 02 45 48 24 78. Classic *terroir* cooking with a modern twist in this stone and timber

restaurant with funky decor, overlooking the market square. Seasonal and local food plays a big part in the cuisine here. *Menus* from €12–29. Mon–Sat noon–3pm & 7–9.30pm.

## Château de la Ferté-St-Aubin

Daily: mid-Feb to March & Oct to mid-Nov 2–6pm; April–Sept 10am–7pm • €9 • ⓦ chateau-ferte-st-aubin.com

The **Château de la Ferté-St-Aubin** lies 20km south of Orléans, at the north end of the village of **LA FERTÉ-ST-AUBIN**. The late sixteenth- and early seventeenth-century building presents an enticing combination of salmon-coloured brick, creamy limestone and dark slate roofs, while the interior is a real nineteenth-century home – and you are invited to treat it as such, which makes a real change from the stuffier attitudes of most grand homes. You can wander freely into almost every room, playing billiards or the piano, picking up the old telephone, sitting on the worn armchairs or washing your hands in a porcelain sink; only the rather fancier grand salon is cordoned off. Roughly every hour there are demonstrations down in the kitchens of how to make Madeleine cakes – the sweet spongy biscuit that so inspired Proust. At the rear of the château, also enclosed by the moat, there's a play fort with sponge balls supplied for storming it, little cabins with dummies acting out fairy tales, and a toy farm.

**7**

### ARRIVAL AND DEPARTURE

### CHÂTEAU DE LA FERTÉ-ST-AUBIN

**By train** The *gare SNCF* is roughly 200m southwest of the village square.

**Destinations** Bourges (hourly; 1hr); Orléans (frequent; 15min); Vierzon (frequent; 30min).

## Germigny-des-Près

Heading east of Orléans on the D960, you pass through Châteauneuf-sur-Loire – whose château has very pleasant gardens of rhododendrons and magnolias and a museum of traditional Loire shipping – en route to **GERMIGNY-DES-PRÈS**, 30km from the city.

The small **church** (daily: June–Sept 9am–7pm; Oct–May 9am–5pm; guided tour €3) incorporates at its east end one of the few surviving buildings from the Carolingian Renaissance, a tiny, perfectly formed church in the shape of a Greek cross. The oratory's sheer antiquity could be said to have been spoiled by too-perfect restoration work, but the unique gold and silver mosaic on the dome of the eastern chapel preserves all its rare beauty. There are concerts here throughout the spring and summer. Call the tourist office (see below) to book a guided tour.

### INFORMATION

### GERMIGNY-DES-PRÈS

**Tourist office** Next to the church (April–Sept Tues–Sun 9am–12.30pm & 1.30–7pm; Oct–May Tues–Sun 9am–12.30pm & 1.30–5pm; ☎ 02 38 35 79 00). It has a

gallery of local artists' work, a shop selling specialities such as saffron and pralines, and there's also free wi-fi and a computer to use.

## St-Benoît-sur-Loire

**ST-BENOÎT-SUR-LOIRE**, five kilometres further upstream from Germigny-des-Près, along the D60, is home to the striking edifice of the Romanesque **Abbaye de Fleury** (Daily 6.30am–10pm; Mass daily noon, Sun 11am; ⓦ abbaye-fleury.com), populated by a small community of some forty Benedictine monks who still observe the original Rule – poverty, chastity and obedience – and whose Gregorian chants can be heard at Mass. Built in warm, cream-coloured stone between 1020 and 1218, the church dates from the abbey's greatest epoch. The oldest part, the porch tower, illustrates St John's vision of the New Jerusalem in Revelation – foursquare, with open gates on each side. The fantastically sculpted capitals of the heavy pillars are alive with acanthus leaves, birds and exotic animals. Three of them depict scenes from the Apocalypse, while another shows Mary's flight into Egypt. Inside, the choir is split into two levels: above, a marble mosaic of Roman origin covers the chancel floor; in the ancient crypt below lie the relics of St-Benoît.

## Sully-sur-Loire

**SULLY-SUR-LOIRE** lies on the south bank of the Loire, 7km east of St-Benoît and accessible by bus from Orléans. The grand château here (April–June & Sept Tues–Sun 10am–6pm; July & Aug daily 10am–6pm; Oct–Dec & Feb–March Tues–Sun 10am–noon & 2–5pm; €7; wsully-sur-loire.fr) is pure fantasy, despite savage wartime bombing that destroyed the nearby bridge. From the outside, rising massively out of its gigantic moat, it has all the picture-book requirements of pointed towers, machicolations and drawbridge.

The village of Sully itself is uninteresting, but the quiet riverbank roads are worth exploring by bike, or you can venture north into the Forêt d'Orléans on the far bank.

### ARRIVAL AND INFORMATION                                          SULLY-SUR-LOIRE

**By train** The *gare SNCF*, on the Bourges–Étampes line, is a 10min walk from the centre of the village.

**By bus** The #7 route from Orléans drops you off by the château.

**Tourist office** Place de Gaulle (May–Sept Mon–Sat 9.45am–12.15pm & 2.30–6.30pm, Sun 10.30am–1pm; Oct–April Mon 10am–noon, Tues, Wed, Fri & Sat 10am–

noon & 2–6pm, Thurs 2–6pm; ☎02 38 36 23 70, wsully -sur-loire.fr).

**Bike hire** Passion Deux Roues, 10 rue des Épinettes ☎02 38 35 13 13.

**Festivals** Sully's international Music Festival (wfestival -sully.com) runs through June, featuring classical concerts held in a huge marquee in the château grounds.

### ACCOMMODATION AND EATING

**Burgevin** 11 rue du Fbg St Germain ☎02 38 38 13 12, whotelburgevin.com. Minutes from the château, this stylish and modern small hotel has spacious rooms with original wooden ceiling beam features. The owners are helpful and friendly. Don't forget to ask to try the sparkling wine "house special" in the little bar. Breakfast €12.50. **€105**

**Camping Hortus** ☎02 38 36 35 94, wcamping -hortus.com. On the banks of the Loire; there's a swimming pool and paddling pool for little ones and café-bar-style restaurant. **€15**

★ **La Closeraie** 14 rue Porte Berry ☎02 38 05 10 90, whotel-la-closeraie.fr. Nine individually decorated rooms, which feature a mix of hardwood floors, bathtubs and fireplaces. There's an unusual touch: a jacuzzi and sauna in the brick-ceiling cave. Breakfast €9. **€67**

**Studio 5-Le Trevi** 5 rue Fbg St Germain ☎02 38 36 26 92. Join the throngs of locals at this movie-themed restaurant for reasonably priced and delicious pizzas, grills and salads. The menu is full of witty movie references like "Le Silence des Agneaux" or pasta listed under "Vacances Romaines". Wed–Mon noon–2pm & 7–10.30pm.

## Gien

The pretty town of **GIEN** has been restored to its late fifteenth-century quaintness after extensive wartime bombing, and the sixteenth-century stone bridge spanning the river gives excellent views as you approach from the south.

### Musée international de la Chasse et de la Nature

Feb, March & Oct–Dec Mon & Wed–Sun 2–5pm; April–June & Sept Mon & Wed–Sun 1.30–6pm; July & Aug daily 1.30–6pm; closed Jan • €3 • ☎02 38 67 69 69

The fifteenth-century château above the town centre – where the young Louis XIV and his mother, Anne of Austria, hid during the revolts against taxation known as the Frondes (see p.992) – has been turned over to the **Musée International de la Chasse et de la Nature**, with the emphasis more on *la chasse* – hunting horns, tapestries, exquisite watercolours of horseback hunts, guns and falconers' gear – than *la nature*. One of the significant consequences of the French Revolution for rural people was the right to hunt, a right still jealously guarded today. The château itself is modest, but unusual in its brick construction, a pattern of dark red interrupted by geometric inlays of grey. At the time of writing the château is being renovated; it should be finished by 2014, but until then various rooms may be closed during works.

## Musée de la Faïencerie

78 place de la Victoire • Mon–Sat 9am–noon & 2–6pm; Sun & holidays (except in Jan & Feb) 10am–noon & 2–6pm • €4 • ☎ 02 38 05 21 06

Gien is famous for its fine china, and it's worth paying a visit to the **Musée de la Faïencerie**, adjacent to the factory shop (where you can buy beautiful dinner sets and other china goodies direct at vastly discounted prices), which displays the more extravagant ceramic knick-knacks produced over the last 180-odd years.

## ARRIVAL AND INFORMATION                                        GIEN

**By bus** Bus #3, which runs between Briare and Orléans seven times daily, stops at place Leclerc, at the north end of the bridge.

**Tourist office** Place Jean-Jaurès (Oct–April Mon–Sat

9.30am–noon & 2–5.30pm; May, June & Sept Mon–Sat 9.30am–12.30pm & 2–6pm; July & Aug Mon–Sat 9.30am–6.30pm, Sun 10am–12.30pm; ☎ 02 38 67 25 28, ⓦ gien.fr).

## ACCOMMODATION AND EATING

**La Bodega** 17 rue Bernard Palissy ☎ 02 38 67 29 01. This two-bed apartment with its fresh, clean lines has a lounge and kitchenette. Rooms are also available above the very decent and friendly pizza and tapas restaurant. Breakfast €5. Apartment €90; rooms €37

**Campsite** ☎ 02 38 67 12 50, ⓦ camping-gien.com. Adjacent to the *Hôtel du Rivage*. Has a swimming pool and offers a number of outdoor activities, including bike hire and canoe trips. Closed mid-Nov to Feb. €15

**Le P'tit Bouchon** 66 rue Bernard Palissy ☎ 02 38 67 84

40. Although the restaurants lining the river on the quai have that wonderful Loire view, none can match the classic French cooking you'll find here, which is why the locals love it. Tues–Sat noon–1.45pm & 7–9pm.

**Du Rivage** 1 Quai de Nice ☎ 02 38 37 79 00. Just a minute's walk out of town, across from the river, this hotel has some lovely rooms and the staff are friendly. Decide whether you want a room with a bath or a room with a Loire view, as those at the front only have showers. Breakfast €10.50. €79

# La Bussière

Twelve kilometres northeast of Gien is a surprising château dedicated to fishing: the so-called **Château des Pêcheurs** (April–June & Sept to mid-Nov Mon & Wed–Sun 10am–noon & 2–6pm; July & Aug daily 10am–6pm, €7.50; ☎ 02 38 35 93 35, ⓦ chateau-labussiere.com) at **LA BUSSIÈRE**. Initially a fortress, the château was turned into a luxurious residence at the end of the sixteenth century, but only the gateway and one pepper-pot tower are recognizably medieval. Guided tours are available, but you're free to wander around, soaking up the genteel atmosphere evoked by the handsome, largely nineteenth-century furnishings and the eccentrically huge collection of freshwater fishing memorabilia bequeathed by Count Henri de Chasseval.

# Briare

The small town of **BRIARE**, 10km southeast of Gien on the Orléans–Nevers road and the Paris–Nevers rail line, is notable for its *belle époque* iron aqueduct, the **Pont Canal**. It links the Canal de Briare to the north with the Canal Lateral à la Loire, making it the longest bridge-canal in Europe. The design of the Pont Canal came from the workshops of Gustav Eiffel (of Tower fame), but parts of the canal scheme date back to the early seventeenth century. Stop at the **Hervé Roussel Chocolatier** (☎ 02 38 37 10 58; Tues–Sun 10am–12.30pm & 2.30–6.30pm), in the old lock-keeper's cottage on the bridge for a sweet treat.

## Museums

On the opposite side of town from the canal, at the northern end, is the tiny **Maison des Deux Marines** on 58 bd Buyser (March–May & Oct to mid-Nov daily 2–6pm; June–Sept 10am–12.30pm & 2–6.30pm; ☎ 02 38 31 28 27; €5) which is dedicated to the rival boatmen who plied the Loire and the Canal Lateral; its basement houses a modest aquarium of Loire species. Just across the street, the **Musée de la Mosaïque et des Emaux**, 1 bd Loreau (daily: June–Sept 10am–6.30pm; Oct–Dec & Feb–May 2–6pm; ☎02 38 31 20 51; €5), has a small collection of reproduction and contemporary mosaics made using locally manufactured tiles.

## INFORMATION                                                          BRIARE

**Tourist office** 1 place Charles-de-Gaulle (April to mid-Aug Mon–Sat 10am–noon & 2–6pm; mid-Aug to Sept Mon–Sat 10am–noon & 2–6pm, Sun 10am–noon; Oct–March Mon 2–5pm, Tues–Sat 10am–noon & 2–5pm; ☎02 38 31 24 51, ⓦ briare-le-canal.com) can provide details of canal boats rental as well as maps of footpaths, towpaths and the locks.

## ACCOMMODATION

**Le Cerf** 22 bd Buyser ☎02 38 37 00 80, ⓦ hotelducerf .com. Basic and clean, offering garages to store your bike, a garden with clothes-drying space and BBQ. The rooms are reasonably well-sized, but expect no frills. Breakfast €8. **€55**

# 7

# Sancerre

Huddled at the top of a steep, round hill with vineyards below, **SANCERRE** could almost be in Tuscany. The village trades heavily on its famous wines – there are endless *caves* offering tastings – rather than any particular sights or attractions, but it's certainly picturesque and the rolling hills of the Sancerrois, to the northwest, make an attractive venue for walks and cycle rides.

## ARRIVAL AND INFORMATION                                               SANCERRE

**By bus** The town is difficult to access by public transport, save for an infrequent bus service to and from Bourges, which leaves no more than twice a day.

**Tourist office** Nouvelle Place (daily: July–Sept 10am–6.30pm; Oct–March 10am–12.30pm & 2–5pm; April–June 10am–12.30pm & 2–6pm; ☎02 48 54 08 21, ⓦ sancerre.fr).

## ACCOMMODATION

**La Belle Époque** Rue St-André ☎02 48 78 00 04. Quirky, charming rooms, some with romantic canopies, others up creaky wooden stairs. The garden is a lovely spot to while away a few hours. Breakfast included. **€65**

**Le Cep en Sancerrois** 2 rue Maréchal Macdonald ☎06 85 71 72 20, ⓦ lecepensancerrois.com. Newly renovated

rectory, with three large suites suitable for families. The brightly painted rooms feature furniture crafted by the hosts, and the largest offers dazzling views. Breakfast included. **€80**

**Le Clos Saint-Martin** 10 rue Saint-Martin ☎02 48 54 21 11, ⓦ leclos-saintmartin.com. The freshened-up *Clos* is in the middle of town, just around the corner from the

---

### THE VINEYARDS OF SANCERRE

If you're going to be staying in Sancerre, your first priority is probably going to be the wine, and so it makes sense during your visit to have an idea of which are the best vineyards in the area. There are numerous quirks of wine production here; for instance, wines aren't allowed to carry an individual vineyard's name, instead being sold under the name of the producer or, very occasionally, the cuvée.

First port of call for wine enthusiasts should be the Maison des Sancerre on 3 rue du Méridien (April, May, Oct & Nov 10am–6pm; June–Sept 10am–7pm; €7; ☎02 48 54 11 35, ⓦ maison-des -sancerre.com) a fourteenth-century townhouse with a great view over the vine-clad hills around. With its entertaining film shows and interactive exhibits, you'll get a comprehensive picture of winemaking in Sancerre and a tasting is included. The Maison also organizes bespoke tours of wine- and cheese-makers in the region combined with cycling or canoeing activities.

To accompany your wines, try the local *crottin de Chavignol*, a goat's cheese named after the neighbouring village just 4km away in which it's made; Dubois-Boulay (☎02 48 54 15 69, ⓦ dubois-boulay.fr) offers the best selection. Henri Bourgeois (☎02 48 78 53 20, ⓦ henribourgeois.com), up the hill, have been making wine for 10 generations. Call ahead to book a 2-hour tour with a *dégustation* (€10) or stop by for a free tasting.

main square. Patio rooms are clean and bright, and have showers. Breakfast €10.50. **€77**
**La Côte des Monts Damnés** Bourg de Chavignol ☎ 02 48 54 01 72, ⓦ montsdamnes.com. In the heart of goats' cheese country and nestled in a quiet village – which looks like the last place you'd find this modern, well-designed hotel – is the boutique-style *Côte*. It's a fun mix of traditional on the outside and funky on the inside. Breakfast €13.50. **€110**

### EATING AND DRINKING

**Auberge L'Ecurie** 31 Nouvelle Place, downstairs ☎ 02 48 54 16 50, ⓦ auberge-ecurie.fr. A more casual, affordable option than *La Tour* (see below) just above it, *Auberge L'Ecurie* serves a tasty range of pizzas, grills, crêpes and salads. Mon–Thurs & Sun noon–2pm & 7–10pm; Fri & Sat noon–2pm & 7–11pm.

**La Tour** 31 Nouvelle Place, upstairs ☎ 02 48 54 00 81, ⓦ la-tour-sancerre.fr. Offering wonderful cooking and a phonebook-length wine list, *La Tour* is one of the best restaurants in the Loire. Splash out on the *dégustation menu* with wine for €100. If that's beyond your budget, then book in for lunch as the *menus* start at €25. Tues–Sun noon–2pm & 7.30–9.30pm.

# Bourges

**7**

**BOURGES**, the chief town of the region of Berry, is some way from the Loire valley proper but linked historically. It has one of the finest Gothic cathedrals in France, rising gloriously out of the well-preserved medieval quarter, which provides enough reason for making a detour.

## Musée des Arts Décoratifs and Musée Estève

Bourges's museums may be modest, but they are housed in some beautiful medieval buildings. Rue Bourbonnoux is worth a wander for the early Renaissance Hôtel Lallemant, richly decorated in an Italianate style. It contains the **Musée des Arts Décoratifs** (Jan–March 10am–noon & 2–5pm; April–June & Sept–Dec 10am–noon & 2–6pm; July & Aug 10am–12.30pm & 1.30–6pm; closed Mon & Sun am; free; ☎ 02 48 57 81 17, ⓦ ville-bourges.fr), a diverting enough museum of paintings, tapestries, furniture and *objets d'art*, including works by the Berrichon artist Jean Boucher (1575–1633).

Not far from the Musée des Arts Décoratifs is the fifteenth-century Hôtel des Échevins, home to the **Musée Estève** (13 rue Édouard Branly; Mon, Wed–Sat 10am–noon & 2–6pm; closed Tues & Sun am; Free; ☎ 02 48 24 75 38), which is dedicated to the highly coloured, mostly abstract paintings and tapestries by the locally born artist Maurice Estève, who died in 2001.

## Palais de Jacques-Coeur

Daily: May & June 9.30am–noon & 2–6.15pm; July & Aug 9.30–12.30pm & 2–6.30pm; Sept–April 9.30am–noon & 2–5.15pm • €7 •
Guided tours every 30min–1hr, depending on the season

**Rue Jacques-Coeur** was the site of the head office, stock exchange, dealing rooms, bank safes and home of Charles VII's finance minister, Jacques Coeur (1400–56). A medieval shipping magnate, moneylender and arms dealer, Coeur dominates Bourges as Joan of Arc does Orléans. The **Palais de Jacques-Coeur** is one of the most remarkable examples of fifteenth-century domestic architecture in France. There are hardly any furnishings, but the house's stonework recalls the man who had it built, including a pair of bas-reliefs on the courtyard tower that may represent Jacques and his wife, and numerous hearts and scallop shells inside that playfully allude to his name.

## Musée du Berry

Steps lead down beside the Palais de Jacques-Coeur to rue des Arènes, where the sixteenth-century Hôtel Cujas houses the **Musée du Berry** (4 rue des Arènes; Jan–March

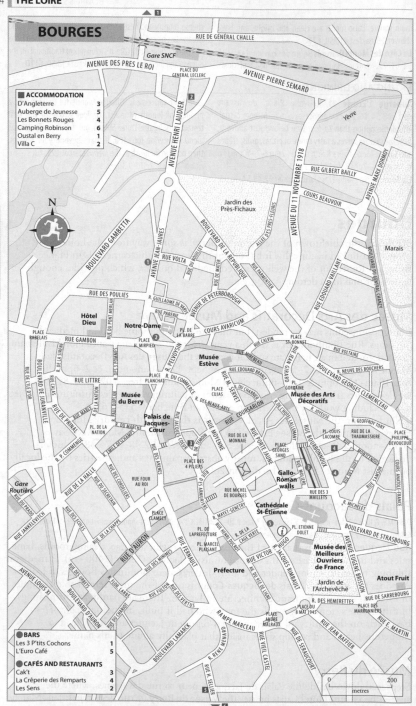

**BOURGES**

7

**■ ACCOMMODATION**

| | |
|---|---|
| D'Angleterre | 3 |
| Auberge de Jeunesse | 5 |
| Les Bonnets Rouges | 4 |
| Camping Robinson | 6 |
| Oustal en Berry | 1 |
| Villa C | 2 |

**● BARS**

| | |
|---|---|
| Les 3 P'tits Cochons | 1 |
| L'Euro Café | 5 |

**● CAFÉS AND RESTAURANTS**

| | |
|---|---|
| Cak't | 3 |
| La Crêperie des Remparts | 4 |
| Les Sens | 2 |

10am–noon & 2–5pm; April–June & Sept–Dec 10am–noon & 2–6pm; July & Aug
10am–12.30pm & 1.30–6pm; closed Tues & Sun am; free), which has a collection of
local artefacts, most notably ten of the forty *pleurants* (mourners) that survived the
breaking up of Jean de Berry's – or John the Magnificent, uncle of Jean sans Peur and
the Duke of Orléans – tomb; Rodin considered these weeping statues so beautiful that
he paid six thousand francs for one shortly before his death.

## The cathedral

Daily: April–Sept 8.30am–7.15pm; Oct–March 8.15am–5.45pm • **Tour de Beurre** Daily except Sun am: April & Sept 9.45–11.45am &
2–5.30pm; May & June 9.30–11.30am & 2–5.30pm; July & Aug 9.30am–12.30pm & 2–6pm; Oct–March 9.30–11.30am & 2–4.45pm •
€7, or €9 with the crypt and Palais de Jacques-Coeur (see p.373)

Renovation work on the roof is due to be completed in 2016, but despite the
scaffolding, **Cathédrale St-Étienne** still captivates. The exterior of the twelfth-century
cathedral is characterized by the delicate, almost skeletal appearance of its flying
buttresses. A much-vaunted example of Gothic architecture, it's modelled on Notre-
Dame in Paris but incorporates improvements on the latter's design, such as the
astonishing height of the inner aisles.

The interior's top feature is the twelfth- to thirteenth-century **stained glass**. The best
windows, with their astonishing deep colours, surround the choir, and were all created
between 1215 and 1225. You can follow various stories – the Prodigal Son, the Good
Samaritan, Christ's Crucifixion and the Apocalypse; binoculars come in handy for
picking up the exquisite detail. The painted decoration of the astronomical clock in the
nave celebrates the wedding of Charles VII, who married Marie d'Anjou here on April
22, 1422. On the northwest side of the nave aisle is the door to the **Tour de Beurre**,
which you can climb for fantastic views over the old city. There are guided tours of the
**crypt** (same hours and ticket; tours roughly every hour), which shelters the alabaster
statue of a puggish Jean de Berry, a small bear, symbol of strength, lying asleep at his
feet. The same ticket allows you to climb unsupervised to the top of the north tower,
rebuilt in flamboyant style after the original collapsed in 1506.

### ARRIVAL AND DEPARTURE                                          BOURGES

**By train** The *gare SNCF* lies 1km north of the centre; it's a
straightforward walk along avenues Henri Lauder and
Jean-Jaurès to place Planchat, from where rue du
Commerce connects with the main street, rue Moyenne.
Destinations Nevers (frequent; 50min); Orléans (frequent;

1hr 15min); Tours (frequent; 1hr 40min).
**By bus** The *gare routière* is west of the city beyond
boulevard Juranville on rue du Prado.
Destinations Sancerre (1–2 daily; 1hr 15min).

### INFORMATION

**Tourist office** Just off the top end of rue Moyenne, at 21
rue Victor-Hugo (April–Sept Mon–Sat 9am–7pm, Sun
10am–6pm; Oct–March Mon–Sat 9am–6pm, Sun
2–5pm; ☎ 02 48 23 02 60, ⓦ bourges-tourisme.com).
**Festivals** Un Eté à Bourges (ⓦ ville-bourges.fr) lasts from
the end of June until late September and involves free

concerts every night in unusual settings, from bandstands
to boats. Les Printemps de Bourges (ⓦ printemps-bourges.
com) features hundreds of contemporary music acts and
lasts for a week in the Easter holidays; finally, atmospheric
lighting transforms the Old Town every evening in July and
August (Thurs–Sat in May, June & Sept).

### ACCOMMODATION

**D'Angleterre** Place des Quatre-Piliers ☎ 02 48 24
68 51, ⓦ bestwestern-angleterre-bourges.com. This is
the old, traditional town-centre hotel, with an excellent
location right next to the Palais de Jacques-Coeur. Ask for a
street-facing room as they have been most recently
renovated. Breakfast included. **€122**
**Auberge de Jeunesse** 22 rue Henri-Sellier ☎ 02 48 24

58 09, ⓦ fuaj.org. Decent hostel located a short way
southwest of the centre, with a garden on the River Auron. Bus
#1 from the station towards "Golf", stop "Condé"; or a 10min
walk from the cathedral or *gare routière*. Reception hours mid-
Jan to mid-Dec daily 8–10am & 6–10pm. Dorms **€15.60**
★ **Les Bonnets Rouges** 3 rue de la Thaumassière
☎ 02 48 65 79 92, ⓦ bonnets-rouges.bourges.net. Five

beautifully furnished *chambres d'hôtes* in a striking seventeenth-century house with views of the cathedral from the attic rooms. Breakfast included. The "Suite Romance" is beautiful and definitely worth the extra few euros (€85). **€74**

**Camping Robinson** 26 bd de l'Industrie ☎02 48 20 16 85. Decent-sized three-star site located south of the hostel (see p.375). Bus Beugnon, from Nation, stop "Val D'Avron", or a 10min walk from the *gare routière*. Closed mid-Nov to mid-March. **€13.70**

**Oustal en Berry** 7 rue Félix Chédin ☎02 48 70 26 64, ⓦoustalenberry.fr. Two minutes from the station and set in a nineteenth-century merchant's house with spacious gardens, these four themed *chambres d'hôtes* are inspired by the lives of famous French women including Colette and Coco Chanel. Genuine and friendly hosts. Breakfast included. **€82**

**Villa C** 20 av Henri Laudier ☎02 18 15 04 00, ⓦhotelvillac.com. In the street across from the train station, this is a stylish boutique hotel with just ten rooms; ask for the "Villa Privilege 2" downstairs, which has a small private patio and large bathroom. Breakfast €12. **€115**

## EATING AND DRINKING

Bourges's main centre for eating is along rue Bourbonnoux. Pick up picnic goodies at the Halles St-Bonnet market (Tues–Sat 8am–12.30pm, 3.30–7pm, Sun 8am–1pm) and head to the nearby, Art Deco-inspired Jardin des Prés Fichaux on bd de la République; there are often free concerts in the park to accompany your picnic.

### CAFÉS AND RESTAURANTS

★ **Cak't** Promenade des Remparts ☎02 48 24 94 60. Tucked under the old ramparts just off rue Bourbonnoux, this deliciously refined tearoom serves home-made quiches and tarts at lunchtime and is a local favourite for afternoon tea. It's just off the main street, so look out for the sign. Tues–Sun noon–2pm & 3–6pm.

**La Crêperie des Remparts** 59 rue Bourbonnoux ☎02 48 24 55 44, ⓦcreperiedesremparts.com. Great value, freshly made crêpes, *galettes* and salads, best enjoyed in the sun-trap garden at the back of the restaurant. Tues–Sat 11.30am–10.30 pm.

**Les Sens** 4 place Henri Mirpied ☎02 48 68 30 36. Classic French food with a modern twist at superb prices – three courses with wine for around €40. *Les Sens* is hugely popular with the locals and no wonder. Leave room for the flaming chocolate-vanilla, caramel liquor-soaked crème brûlée. Tues–Sun noon–2pm & 7–11pm.

### BARS AND CLUBS

**Les 3 P'tits Cochons** Av Jean Jaurès ☎02 48 65 64 96, ⓦwww.3ptitscochons.com. Head here for a lively locals vibe and some great bistro-style and tapas cooking. Mains from around €13. DJs spin anything from electro to pop at weekends, special nights come with a door charge of usually no more than €3. Mon–Wed noon–2pm & 7–10pm, Thurs 7pm–1am, Fri noon–2pm & 7pm–1am, Sat 7pm–1am.

**L'Euro Café** 41 rue Moyenne ☎02 48 70 10 38. On warm nights, this is a good spot to try a "Berrychon" (red wine mixed with Monin Crème de Mûre) out on the terrace, which is perfect for people-watching. Daily 9.30am–noon; closed Sun during winter.

# The Cher and Indre

Of all the Loire's many tributaries, the slow-moving **Cher** and **Indre** are closest to the heart of the region, watering a host of châteaux as they flow northwest from this little-visited region to the south. Twenty kilometres southeast of Tours, spanning the Cher, the **Château de Chenonceau** is perhaps the quintessential Loire château for its architecture, site, contents and atmosphere. Further upstream, **Montrichard** and **St-Aignan** make quieter diversions from the endless stream of castle tours. To the south is the **Château de Valençay**, with its exquisite Empire interiors. A short drive west of here, on the River Indre itself, the lovely town of **Loches** possesses the most magnificent medieval citadelle in the region.

## Château de Chenonceau

Daily: April & May 9am–7pm; June & Sept 9am–7.30pm; July & Aug 9am–8pm; Oct 9am–6.30pm; Nov–Jan 9.30am–5pm; Feb & March 9.30am–5.30m • Château and gardens €8.50, plus waxworks museum €10.50, plus iPod audioguide €13.50 • ☎02 47 23 90 07, ⓦ chenonceau.com

Unlike the Loire, the gentle River Cher flows so slowly and passively between the exquisite arches of the **Château de Chenonceau** that you're almost always assured of a perfect reflection. The château is not visible from the road so you have to pay before even getting a peek at the residence. While the tree-lined path to the front door is dramatic, wind your way through the gardens for a more intimate approach; they were laid out under Diane de Poitiers, mistress of Henri II. The **waxworks museum** by the self-service restaurant is rather unimpressive, and there's a gastronomic **restaurant** in the grounds with prices to match the stunning settings. During summer the place teems with people and it can become uncomfortably crowded, so aim to visit first thing in the morning if possible.

## Inside the château

Visits are unguided – a relief, for there's an endless array of arresting tapestries, paintings, ceilings, floors and furniture on show (although you could opt for the worthwhile iPod guided tour).

On the **ground floor**, the François I room features two contrasting images of the goddess Diana; one is a portrait of Diane de Poitiers by Primaticcio, and the other represents a relatively aristocratic Gabrielle d'Estrées. The room also features works by or attributed to Veronese, Tintoretto, Correggio, Murillo and Rubens, among others. The tiled floors throughout, many original, are particularly lovely. There are some unique decorative details as well, such as the seventeenth-century window frame in the César de Vendôme room, supported by two carved caryatids, and the moving ceiling in the bedroom of Louise de Lorraine, which mourns her murdered husband Henri III in black paint picked out with painted tears and the couple's intertwined initials. The vaulted **kitchens**, poised above the water in the foundations, are also well worth a look.

The section of the château that spans the Cher is relatively empty. The seemingly incongruous chequerboard flooring of the elegant **long gallery** is in fact true to the Renaissance design, though potted plants have replaced the classical statues that Louis XIV carried off to Versailles. Catherine de Médicis used to hold wild parties here, all naked nymphs and Italian fireworks. She intended the door on the far side to continue into another building on the south bank, but the project was never begun, and these days the gallery leads to quiet, wooded gardens. During the war, the Cher briefly formed the boundary between occupied and "free" France, and the current proprietors, who rode out Nazi occupation, claim the château's gallery was much used as an escape route. Every Friday, Saturday and Sunday in June and every evening in July and August, as part of the "Nocturne à Chenonceau", the gardens and château are lit up between 9.30pm and 11pm, and classical music is played through speakers (€5). You can take boats out onto the Cher in the summer months.

**ARRIVAL AND DEPARTURE** **CHENONCEAUX**

Trains run from Tours almost hourly from 6am and take 30min. The station is next door to the château.

**ACCOMMODATION**

The tiny village of Chenonceaux – spelt with an "x" on the end – has been almost entirely taken over by a handful of well-appointed hotels. All of them are on rue du Docteur-Bretonneau, within easy reach of the *gare SNCF* and the château.

**Auberge du Bon Laboureur** 6 rue du Docteur-Bretonneau ❶02 47 23 90 02, ❿bonlaboureur.com. Spread around five former village houses, the rooms here are decked out in antique furniture. There's a swimming pool and small petting zoo, so children will be entertained. Free parking. Buffet breakfast €14.50. €125

**Hostel du Roy** 9 rue du Docteur-Bretonneau ❶02 47 23 90 17, ❿hostelduroy.com. *Hostel du Roy*, at the turn of the road leading out of town, offers small, faded rooms. However, they are spotlessly clean, the staff are cheerful and friendly and you won't find cheaper in town. Free parking. Buffet breakfast €7.50. €43

**Municipal campsite** ❶02 47 23 62 80. Between the railway line and the river. There's no pool but there are hot showers and electrical hook ups. Closed Oct–May. €8.80

**La Roseraie** 7 rue du Docteur-Bretonneau ❶02 47 23 90 09. A welcoming spot with slightly old-fashioned but spacious rooms. It also has a more than decent restaurant, extensive gardens to picnic in and a swimming pool. Free parking. Breakfast €11. €85

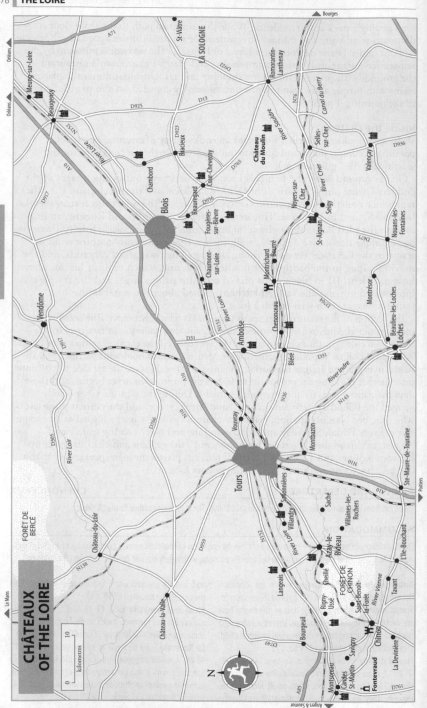

CHÂTEAUX OF THE LOIRE

# Montrichard

In many ways just a laidback market town, **MONTRICHARD** also happens to have a full complement of medieval and Renaissance buildings, plus a hilltop fortress, of which just the keep remains after Henri IV broke down the rest of the defences at the end of the sixteenth century. At any time, you can climb up the hill for the view of the Cher – though the keep itself is out of bounds. Montrichard's Romanesque church was where the disabled 12-year-old princess, Jeanne de Valois, who would never be able to have children, married her cousin the Duc d'Orléans. When he became King Louis XII, after the unlikely death of Charles VIII at Amboise, politics dictated that he marry Charles VIII's widow, Anne of Brittany. Poor Jeanne was divorced and sent off to govern Bourges, where she founded a new religious order and eventually took the veil herself, before dying in 1505.

## INFORMATION

MONTRICHARD

**Tourist office** Maison Ave Maria (April & May Mon–Sat 10am–noon & 2–6pm, Sun 10am–1pm; June & Sept daily 10am–6pm; daily July & Aug 10am–7pm; Oct–March Mon–Sat 10am–noon & 2–5pm; ☎ 02 54 32 05 10, ⓦ officetourisme-montrichard.com), an ancient house with saints and beasts sculpted down its beams, on rue du Pont.

**Watersports** In summer, you can rent pedalos and kayaks (July & Aug; ☎ 02 54 71 49 48) at the pleasant artificial beach on the opposite bank of the Cher. Some hardy locals swim from here, but be sure to seek advice before entering the water.

## ACCOMMODATION AND EATING

**Le Belleview** 24 quai de la Republique ☎ 02 54 32 06 17, ⓦ hotel-le-bellevue41.com. Located down by the river, *Le Belleview* offers basic modern rooms, some with river views – it's definitely worth asking for one of these. Breakfast €9.50. **€98**
**L'Étourneau** ☎ 02 54 32 10 16. A shaded, one-star campsite on large grounds, located 1km from the centre of Montrichard. Caravans are available for rent. Closed mid-Sept to April. **€8.60**

**La Tête Noire** 24 rue de Tours ☎ 02 54 32 05 55. A budget choice with bright rooms, which although rather faded, are spotlessly clean in a slightly atmosphere-free old building. Breakfast €7.50. **€53.50**
**La Villa** 34 rue de Sully ☎ 02 54 32 07 34. Serves relatively good-value dishes with *menus* from €15; there's a good range of *galettes*, salads, grills and traditional French food. Upstairs, although quieter, has tables with a good view over the square. Tues–Sun noon–2pm & 7–10pm.

# Bourré

Three kilometres to the east of Montrichard, the hills around **BOURRÉ** are riddled with enormous, cave-like quarries, dug deep to get at the famous château-building stone that gets whiter as it weathers.

Some of the caves are now used to cultivate mushrooms, a peculiar process that you can witness at the **Caves Champignonnières** (mid-March to mid-Nov guided visits daily at 10am, 11am, 2pm, 3pm, 4pm & 5pm; also at noon & 6pm July & Aug; €6.50, subterranean city tour €6.50, or €10.50 for both tours; ☎ 02 54 32 95 33, ⓦ le-champignon.com) at 40 rte des Roches. A second tour takes you to a "subterranean city" sculpted in recent years as a tourist attraction, and there's an excellent shop including rare varieties of mushrooms, mushroom soup, dried mushrooms, and so on.

You can visit a troglodyte dwelling at **La Magnanerie,** 4 chemin de la Croix-Bardin (guided visits only: April–Aug daily except Tues at 11am, 3pm, 4pm & 5pm; Sept daily except Tues & Wed at 3pm, 4pm & 5pm; Oct Fri–Sun at 4pm; €7; ☎ 02 54 32 63 91), where the owner demonstrates how his ancestors lived a troglodyte life here, quarrying the soft stone using huge saws, and producing silk in a chamber riddled with pigeonhole-like niches and stocked with living silkworms.

# St-Aignan

**ST-AIGNAN**, 15km southeast of Montrichard, is a small town comprising a cluster of houses below a huge Romanesque collegiate church and sixteenth-century private château. The lofty **Collégiale de St-Aignan** (daily 9am–7pm, Sun closed during services at 11am & 5.30pm) features some fine capitals carved in the twelfth century, though many more are nineteenth-century recreations. The crypt is renowned for its remarkably preserved, brightly coloured twelfth- and thirteenth-century frescoes, some of which show the beginnings of naturalistic Gothic tendencies.

A flight of 144 steps climbs from the collégiale to the grand gravelled terrace of the **château**, enclosed on one side by the L-shape of the Renaissance logis, and on the other by the remnants of the eleventh-century fortress. Private ownership means it's closed to visitors, but you're free to stroll around – the far corner of the terrace leads through to a great view of the river, which you can reach via a flight of steep steps.

One of the region's biggest tourist attractions in the region is the excellent **Zoo Parc Beauval** (daily: 9am–dusk; adult €24, child €18; ☎02 54 75 50 00, ⓦzoobeauval.com), 2km to the south of town on the D675. The space given to the animals is ample and it's part of a Europe-wide programme for breeding threatened species in captivity.

## INFORMATION                                                        ST-AIGNAN

**Tourist office** 60 rue Constant-Ragot (Oct–May Mon–Sat 9.30am–12.30pm & 2–6pm; June & Sept Mon–Sat 9.30am–12.30pm & 2–6.30pm, Sun 10am–1pm; mid-July to mid-Aug Mon–Sat 9am–7pm; ☎02 54 71 77 23, ⓦtourisme-valdecher-staignan.com), just off the car-park-like place Président-Wilson, in the upper part of town.

**Boat trips** The tourist office has details of various boat trips on the Cher: AVAC (daily July & Aug Sat, Sun & holidays in May, June & Sept; ☎02 54 71 40 38) leave from St Aignan on hour-long guided cruises. The tourist office can also give information about hiring out windsurfers, canoes and sailing boats at the lake a couple of kilometres upstream in Seigy.

## ACCOMMODATION AND EATING

**Camping des Cochards** 1 rue du Camping, Seigy ☎02 54 75 15 59, ⓦlescochards.com. On the bank of the river near Seigy. Amenities include grocery store, bar with a small restaurant, games and TV room, washing machines and dryers. Closed mid-Oct to March. **€19**

**Le Grand Hôtel St-Aignan** 7 quai Jean-Jacques Delorme ☎02 54 75 18 04, ⓦgrand-hotel-saint-aignan.com. This hotel in town is a good bet; it was refurbished in 2012, so ignore the rather scuffed hallways as the rooms are more than fine. Room 20 has a gorgeous river view and there's also a good restaurant (*menus* €13–36). Breakfast €9.50. **€60**

★ **Les Jardins de Beauval** ☎02 54 75 60 00, ⓦjardinsdebeauval.com. This hostel, next to the zoo is an impressive piece of modern design. Inspired by Thai and Indonesian architecture, large, comfortable rooms housed in pavilions are dotted around a landscaped lake, complete with wildfowl paddling around. Package deals, which include a trip to the zoo, are good-value and the buffet food is very reasonable. Breakfast included. **€150**

**Mange-Grenouille** 10 rue Paul-Boncour ☎02 54 71 74 91, ⓦlemangegrenouille.fr. An alternative to the hotel restaurants, this little spot has delightful sixteenth-century decor and outside seating in its courtyard. *Menus* range €25–30. Leave room for the strawberry *macarons*. Tues–Fri noon–2pm & 7–9pm, Sat 7–9.30pm, Sun noon–2pm.

# Château de Valençay

20km southeast of St-Aignan on the main Blois–Châteauroux road • Daily: mid-March to April 10.30am–6pm; May & Sept 10am–6pm; June 9.30am–6.30pm; July & Aug 9.30am–7pm; Oct to mid-Nov 10.30am–5.30pm • Château €11.50, car museum and château €15, audioguide free • ⓦchateau-valencay.fr

There is nothing medieval about the fittings and furnishings of the **Château de Valençay**, for all its huge pepper-pot towers and turreted, decorated keep. This refined castle was originally built to show off the wealth of a sixteenth-century financier, but the lasting impression of a visit today is the imperial legacy of its greatest owner, the Prince de Talleyrand.

One of the great political operators and survivors, Talleyrand owes most of his fame to his post as Napoleon's foreign minister. A bishop before the Revolution, with a reputation for having the most desirable mistresses, he proposed the nationalization of

church property, renounced his bishopric, escaped to America during the Terror, backed Napoleon and continued to serve the state under the restored Bourbons. One of his tasks for the emperor was keeping Ferdinand VII of Spain entertained for six years here after the king had been forced to abdicate in favour of Napoleon's brother Joseph. The Treaty of Valençay, signed in the château in 1813, put an end to Ferdinand's forced guest status, giving him back his throne. The interior is consequently largely First Empire: elaborately embroidered chairs, Chinese vases, ornate inlays to all the tables, faux-Egyptian details, finicky clocks and chandeliers. A single discordant note is struck by the leg-brace and shoe displayed in a glass cabinet along with Talleyrand's uniforms – the statesman's deformed foot was concealed in every painting of the man, including the one displayed in the portrait gallery that runs the length of the graceful Neoclassical wing.

### Car museum

Daily: June 10am–12.30pm & 2–6.30pm; July & Aug 10am–12.30pm & 1.30–7pm; April, May, Sept & Oct 10.30am–12.30pm & 2–6pm • €5.50 • ⓦ musee-auto-valencay.fr

In Valençay village, about 100m from the château gates, the **car museum** houses an excellent collection of sixty-odd mostly prewar cars, with the oldest dating from 1898. Each year there's a temporary exhibition, focusing on a different marque.

## Loches

**LOCHES**, 42km southeast of Tours, is the obvious place to head for in the Indre valley. Its walled citadelle is by far the most impressive of the Loire valley fortresses, with its unbreached ramparts and the Renaissance houses below still partly enclosed by the outer wall of the medieval town. Tours is only an hour away by bus, but Loches makes for a quiet, relatively un-touristy base for exploring the Cher valley, or the lesser-known country to the south, up the Indre.

### The Old Town

The **Old Town**, ringed by the sturdy **citadelle** (Jan–March & Oct–Dec 9.30am–5pm; April–Sept 9am–7pm) is dominated by the Tour St-Antoine belfry, close to the handsome place du Marché that links rue St-Antoine with Grande Rue. Two fifteenth-century gates to the Old Town still stand: the **Porte des Cordeliers**, by the river at the end of Grande Rue, and the **Porte Picois** to the west, at the end of rue St-Antoine. Rue du Château, lined with Renaissance buildings, leads to the twelfth-century towers of **Porte Royale**, the main entrance to the citadelle.

#### Musée Lansyer

April, May & Oct Wed–Fri 2–5pm, Sat & Sun 10.30am–12.30pm & 2–5pm; June–Sept daily 10.30am–12.30pm & 2–6pm, closed Tues; closed Jan–March, Nov–Dec • Free • ☎ 02 47 59 05 40

Behind the Porte Royale, the **Musée Lansyer** occupies the house of local nineteenth-century landscape painter Emmanuel Lansyer, done up prettily in period style.

#### Collégiale de St-Ours

In front of the Musée Lansyer is the Romanesque church, the **Collégiale de St-Ours**, with its distinctively odd roofline – the nave bays are capped by two octagonal stone pyramids, sandwiched between more conventional spires. The porch has some entertainingly grotesque twelfth-century monster carvings, and the stoup, or basin for holy water, is a Gallo-Roman altar. But the church's highlight is the shining white tomb of Agnès Sorel, the mistress of the Dauphin Charles VII, a beautiful recumbent figure tenderly watched over by angels. The alabaster is rather more pristine than it should be, as it had to be restored after anticlerical revolutionary soldiers mistook her for a saint – an easy error to make.

Logis Royal

Daily: Jan–March & Oct–Dec 9.30am–5pm; April–Sept 9am–7pm • €7.50 including the donjon • **Donjon** Daily: Jan–March & Oct–Dec 9.30am–5pm; April–Sept 9am–7pm

The northern end of the citadelle is taken up by the **Logis Royal**, or Royal Lodgings, of Charles VII and his three successors. It has two distinct halves; the older section was built in the late fourteenth century as a kind of pleasure palace for the Dauphin Charles and Agnès Sorel. A copy of Charles's portrait by Fouquet can be seen in the antechamber to the Grande Salle, where in June 1429 the Dauphin met Joan of Arc, who came here victorious from Orléans to give the defeatist Dauphin another pep talk about coronations.

From the Logis Royal, cobbled streets lined with handsome townhouses wind through to the far end of the elevated citadelle, to the donjon, the best preserved of its kind in Europe. You can climb up to the top of the massive keep, but the main interest lies in the dungeons and lesser towers. The Tour Ronde was built under Louis XI and served as a prison for his adviser, Cardinal Balue, who was kept locked up in a wooden cage in one of the upper rooms. Perhaps he was kept in the extraordinary graffiti chamber on the second floor, which is decorated with an enigmatic series of deeply carved, soldier-like figures that may date from the thirteenth century. From the courtyard, steps lead down into the bowels of the Martelet, which was home to a more famous prisoner: Ludovico "il Moro" Sforza, duke of Milan, patron of Leonardo da Vinci and captive of Louis XII. In the four years he was imprisoned here, from 1500, he found time to decorate his cave-like cell with ruddy wall paintings, still faintly visible. The dungeons peter out into quarried-out galleries which produced the stone for the keep.

## The Caravaggios of Philippe de Béthune

Daily 10am–6.45pm • Free • ⓦ ville-loches.fr/caravage.php

Loches is home to one of the art world's many scandals: in 2006, art historians discovered **two paintings** in the loft of the Church of Saint-Anthony which were believed to be the work of Caravaggio, brought from Rome by Philipe de Béthune, baron and minister of King Henry IV's court. After extensive testing, some experts declared that yes, the two paintings – *La Cène à Emmaüs* and *L'Incrédulité de Saint Thomas* – were indeed the work of the old Master. However, local gossip has it that after Loches' mayor refused to let the pictures go to Paris to be displayed in the Louvre, preferring instead to keep them for the town, experts since have declared them to be fake.

### ARRIVAL AND INFORMATION

### LOCHES

**By train and bus** From Tours, trains and buses arrive at the *gare SNCF* on the east side of the Indre. Trains from Tours run hourly (taking around 50min), less frequently on weekends. Buses from Tours also leave hourly (1hr).

**Tourist office** Housed in a modern wood-topped building on Place de la Marne (March & April Mon–Sat 9.30am–12.30pm & 2–6pm; May & June Mon–Sat 9am–12.30pm & 1.30–6pm, Sun 10am–12.30pm & 2.30–5pm; July & Aug Mon–Sat 9am–7pm, Sun 9.45am–12.30pm & 2.15–6pm; Sept Mon–Sat 9.30am–12.30pm & 1.30–6.30pm, Sun 9.45am–12.30pm & 2.15–6pm; Oct–Feb Mon–Sat 10am–12.30pm & 2.30–6pm; ⓣ 02 47 91 82 82, ⓦ loches-tourainecotesud.com).

### ACCOMMODATION

**La Citadelle** ⓣ 02 47 59 05 91. Right next to the abbey in Beaulieu-les-Loches, 1km across the river, the municipal campsite *La Citadelle* is between two branches of the Indre, by the swimming pool and stadium. Closed mid-Oct to mid-March. **€16**

★ **La Closerie Saint Jacques** 37 rue Balzac ⓣ 02 47 91 63 12, ⓦ lacloseriesaintjacques.com. Three dazzling designer rooms, named after the city *portes*. Truly jaw-dropping attention to detail with antiques, original art, timber beamed ceilings and luxurious fabrics. Owned by a charming and welcoming couple who also offer delicious evening meals (24hr notice required). Breakfast included. **€95**

**De France** 6 rue Picois ⓣ 02 47 59 00 32, ⓦ hotelde franceloches.com. Old-fashioned and characterful, with a beautiful ivy-covered courtyard and a good restaurant. The bedrooms are all large with spacious bathrooms. A little faded, but great value. Breakfast €9. **€62**

**Luccotel** 12 Rue Lézards ⓣ 02 47 91 30 30, ⓦ luccotel .com. Around ten minutes' walk above the old town, but boasting a covered pool, loungers, tennis court, a superb terrace with beautiful views and bright clean rooms. Restaurant *menus* from €15. Breakfast €10. **€75**

**Les Logis du Bief** 21 rue Quintefol ☎ 02 47 91 66 02, ⓦ logisloches.com. Four individually decorated rooms, with antiques, backing out over the river and park. Welcoming hosts and a lovely patio. Breakfast included. **€90**

### EATING AND DRINKING

For picnic items, stock up at the superb market, held on Wednesday and Saturday mornings in the winding streets just above the château gate.

**Le Caravage** 2 rue des Ponts ☎ 02 47 91 62 07, ⓦ lecaravage.fr. Live music, dancing and karaoke in a stone-walled fourteenth-century building, with generous fruit mojitos. Cheese and charcuterie plates available. Mon–Fri 6pm–midnight, Sat & Sun 4pm–2am; closed Mon in winter.

**Gerbe d'Or** 22 rue Balzac ☎ 02 47 91 67 63, ⓦ restaurantlagerbedor.fr. Organic, local and seasonal food is the name of the game here at this welcoming restaurant with a small outdoor terrace. Vegetarians are well-catered for (rare in France). *Menus* range €12.50–39. Daily noon–2pm, plus Thurs–Tues 7.30–9pm.

**Isabeau de Touraine** 33 rue Thomas Pactius ☎ 06 45 46 71 61. Excellent, hearty home-cooked meals, smoothies, ice creams and cakes at this friendly restaurant by the citadelle. Live music in Sept & Oct. April–May daily 12.15–10pm; June & Sept Mon–Fri 12.15–10pm; July & Aug daily 12.15–10pm; Oct Tues–Sat, 12.15–10pm; Nov–March Sat & Sun noon–10.30pm.

**Le Vicariat** Next to the château on place Charles-VII ☎ 02 47 59 0879. The recreations of medieval recipes here, such as *Hochepot (pot-au-feu) de saumon boucané à l'auberge* or *Pasté nourri de limassons*, can be fun if you don't expect any culinary fireworks and there is a great outside terrace. "Medieval *menu*" €35. Closed Mon & Sun eve, Tues lunch.

# Blois and around

The château at **BLOIS**, the handsome former seat of the dukes of Orléans, is magnificent; it's the main reason for visiting the town. The château's great facade rises above the modern town like an Italianate cliff, with the dramatic esplanade and courtyard behind and the rooms within steeped in (sometimes bloody) history. There are several stretches of woodland within striking distance including the **Forêt de Blois** to the west of the town on the north bank of the Loire, and the **Parc de Chambord** and **Forêt de Boulogne**, further upstream. To the south and east, the forested, watery, game-rich area known as the **Sologne** lies between the Loire and Cher, stretching beyond Orléans almost as far as Gien.

A good reason to use Blois as a base is its proximity to several **châteaux**. By car you could call at all of them in a couple of days, but they also make ideal cycling or walking targets if you arm yourself with a map and strike out along minor roads and woodland paths.

## The château

Daily: April–June & Sept 9am–6.30pm; July & Aug 9am–7pm; Oct 9am–6pm; Nov–March 9am–12.30pm & 1.30–5.30pm • €9.50 **Visite insolite** April–Sept every Sun at 10.30am; also Tues & Thurs in July & Aug • €12 **Son et lumière** April–Sept daily at dusk • €7.50, or €13 including château entry • In English on Wed • ☎ 02 54 90 33 33, ⓦ chateaudeblois.fr

The **Château de Blois** was home to six kings, and countless more aristocratic and noble visitors. The impression given is one of grandiloquent splendour, mixed with awe-inspiring spectacle, especially the way in which the predominantly Renaissance **north wing** is dominated by a superb spiral staircase. The grandly Classical **west wing** was built in the 1630s by François Mansart for Gaston d'Orléans, the brother of Louis XIII. Turning to the south side, you go back in time 140-odd years to Louis XII's St-Calais chapel, which contrasts with the more exuberant brickwork of his flamboyant Gothic **east wing**.

Mansart's breathtaking staircase leads you round to the less interesting **François I wing**; the garish decor here dates from Félix Duban's mid-nineteenth-century efforts to turn an empty barn of a château into a showcase for sixteenth-century decorative motifs. One of the largest rooms is given over to paintings of the notorious murder of the Duke of Guise and his brother, the Cardinal of Lorraine, by Henri III. As leaders of the radical Catholic League, the Guises were responsible for the summary execution of Huguenots at Amboise. The king had summoned the States-General to a meeting in the Grande Salle, only to find that an overwhelming majority supported the Duke, along with the stringing up of Protestants, and aristocratic over royal power. Henri had the Duke summoned to his bedroom in the palace, where he was ambushed and hacked to death, and the cardinal was murdered in prison the next day. Their deaths were avenged a year later when a monk assassinated the king himself.

The château was also home to Henri III's mother and manipulator, Catherine de Médicis, who died here a few days after the murders in 1589. The most famous of her suite of rooms is the study, where, according to Alexandre Dumas' novel, *La Reine Margot*, she kept poison hidden in secret caches in the skirting boards and behind some of the 237 narrow carved wooden panels; they now contain small Renaissance *objets d'art*. In the nineteenth century, revolutionaries were tried in the Grande Salle for conspiring to assassinate Napoléon III, a year before the Paris Commune of 1870. You can return to the courtyard via the vast space of the Salle des États, where the arches, pillars and fireplaces are another riot of nineteenth-century colour.

Across the courtyard to the ground floor of the François I wing, you'll find the **archeological museum**, which displays original stonework from the staircase and dormer windows, as well as carved details rescued from other châteaux.

**7**

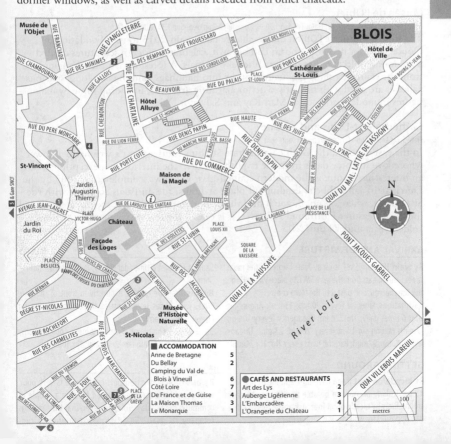

**BLOIS**

■ **ACCOMMODATION**
Anne de Bretagne 5
Du Bellay 2
Camping du Val de
  Blois à Vineuil 6
Côté Loire 7
De France et de Guise 4
La Maison Thomas 3
Le Monarque 1

● **CAFÉS AND RESTAURANTS**
Art des Lys 2
Auberge Ligérienne 3
L'Embarcadère 4
L'Orangerie du Château 1

French-speakers may want to take the two-hour guided **visite insolite**, which explores parts of the château you won't normally see, such as the roof and cellars. You can usually just turn up at the gate for the **son et lumière** – it's one of the best in the region, rising above the usual mix of melodrama, light and musical effects by making the most of the château's fascinating history and lovely courtyard setting, and thrillingly re-creates the murder of the Duc de Guise.

## The rest of the town

Just below the château on rue St-Laumer is the **church of St Nicholas** (April–Nov 9am–6.30pm; Nov–March 9am–5pm) which once belonged to an abbey. The choir is a handsome example of the humble Benedictine treatment of the Romanesque style.

### Maison de la Magie

1 place du Château • April–Aug daily 10am–12.30pm & 2–6.30pm; Sept Mon–Fri 2–6.30pm, Sat & Sun 10am–12.30pm & 2–6.30pm • €8 or €14.50 with château entry • ☎ 02 54 90 33 33, ⓦ maisondelamagie.fr

The **Maison de la Magie** faces the château on the far side of the esplanade. With three floors of interactive illusions, magic tricks and live performances throughout day, it offers an excellent few hours distraction. Highlights include learning how to perform card tricks and a section devoted to Houdini.

### Musée de l'Objet

6 rue Franciade; April–June & Sept–Nov Fri–Sun 1.30–6.30pm; July & Aug Wed–Sun 1.30–6.30pm • €4

The superb **Musée de l'Objet**, due to change name mid-2013 to the "Fondation du Doute", and located at the north end of town, celebrates modern sculptures created from found objects rather than traditional materials. A forest of hammers hanging from the staircase ceiling gradually morphs into handbags, and the two long, spacious galleries are filled with similarly witty or alarming artworks, including some by major figures in modern art such as Man Ray and Salvador Dali.

### Cathédrale St-Louis and around

Place Saint-Louis • Sun– Fri 8am–7pm; Sat 9am–6pm

In the east of town, the Gothic **Cathédrale St-Louis** leans against a weighty bell tower whose lowest storey dates from the twelfth century. The interior is unexceptional, but an interesting feature is the modern stained-glass windows, completed in 2003 by the Dutch artist Jan Dibbets. Leading off place St-Louis, rue du Palais connects with rue St-Honoré, where, at no. 8, you'll find the elaborate Hôtel Alluye; the private house of the royal treasurer Florimond Robertet, it is one of the few surviving relics of Blois' golden years under Louis XII.

### ARRIVAL AND DEPARTURE                                            BLOIS

**By train** The *gare SNCF* is on av Jean-Laigret – the main street leading east from the *gare SNCF* to place Victor-Hugo and the château, and past it to the town centre.
Destinations Amboise (every 20min; 13min); Angers (at least 6 times daily; 1hr 22min); Beaugency (every 40min; 17min); Meung-sur-Loire (every 20min; 23min); Orléans (every 20min; 27min); Paris (at least every 2hr; 1hr 24min);

Saumur (at least 6 times daily; 1hr); Tours (at least hourly; 36min).
**By bus** The *gare routière* is directly in front of the gare SNCF, with buses leaving up to three times a day for Cheverny and Chambord.
Destinations Chambord (3 daily; 45min); Cour-Cheverny (7 daily; 20min); St-Aignan (2–3 daily; 1hr 10min).

### GETTING AROUND

**By bicycle/on foot** If you have time and the inclination, it's particularly pleasant to be able to visit the châteaux around Blois by bicycle or on foot. Ask at the tourist office (see opposite) for walking and cycling maps.

**By bus** Local public transport in the area is very poor, with even the main routes served by only a couple of commuter buses a day. Note, however, that the local bus company TLC (☎ 02 54 58 55 55, ⓦ tlcinfo.net) runs return coach trips to Chambord, Cheverny and Beauregard from April–Sept, with two morning departures from Blois' *gare SNCF* (April–Aug; €6); tickets can be bought at the tourist office (see below) and give a discount to châteaux entry.

**By taxi** Taxi Radio Blois ☏ 02 54 78 07 65; expect to pay at least €29 one-way, more if the driver waits for you at the château.

## INFORMATION

**Tourist office** 23 place du Château (daily: April–Sept 9am–6pm; Oct–March 10am–5pm; ☏ 02 54 90 41 41, ⓦ bloischambord.com). The office organizes hotel rooms for a small fee and has information on day coach tours of Chambord and Cheverny. It also sells combined tickets to various local châteaux (tickets range €23–93.50).

Regional information is available online at ⓦ bloischambord.com

**Bike hire** Détours de Loire, 3 rue de la Garenne (April–Oct; ☏ 02 54 56 07 73), and Traîneurs de Loire, 12bis rue St-Lubin (April to mid-Nov; ☏ 02 54 79 36 71, ⓦ traineursde loire.com).

## ACCOMMODATION

There are some real bargain hotels in Blois and a lovely *chambres d'hôtes* too; with so many châteaux in the area, you will probably find yourself spending at least one night here.

**Anne de Bretagne** 31 av Jean-Laigret ☏ 02 54 78 05 38, ⓦ annedebretagne.free.fr. Charming, vine-covered hotel set a little way back from the station, more peaceful than many others in its category. Excellent wheelchair-friendly room and a quaint breakfast room. Buffet breakfast €8.50. **€56**

**Du Bellay** 12 rue des Minimes ☏ 02 54 78 23 62, ⓦ hoteldubellay.free.fr. Comfortable budget option in a fifteenth-century building with twelve well-worn but clean little rooms, much cheered up by pictures of local sights and the odd wooden beam. Good location at the top of the hill, above the town centre. Rooms 6 and 15 are the best. Continental breakfast costs €6. **€55**

**Camping du Val de Blois à Vineuil** ☏ 08 00 30 04 10, ⓦ onlycamp.fr/valdeblois. On the south bank of the river, 4km from the town centre. Bus #3C (stop "Mairie Vineuil") only runs twice a day during the summer, but the campsite offers bike hire. Closed Oct–May. **€14.20**

**Côté Loire** 2 place de la Grève ☏ 02 54 78 07 86, ⓦ coteloire.com. Charming boutique hotel, tucked away in a quiet corner by the river, with a breakfast terrace. Rooms have antique furnishings and brand-new bathrooms, and those at the front have views of the river. Breakfast €9.50. **€57**

**De France et de Guise** 3 rue Gallois ☏ 02 54 78 00 53. Dating from the nineteenth-century, this sprawling old hotel provides a pleasant mix of old-world charm and modern amenities. Rooms on the lower floors can be noisy, but the owners are friendly and the location is hard to beat. Ask for a room overlooking the park. Breakfast €7. **€59**

★ **La Maison Thomas** 12 rue Beauvoir ☏ 02 54 46 12 10, ⓦ lamaisondethomas.fr. On a pedestrian street in the heart of town, this delightful B&B, run by a wonderfully hospitable couple, has stylishly decorated rooms with original timber beams and quirky touches. Monsieur Thomas also runs a *cave à vin*, so ask for a wine tasting with snacks (from €11) before a night out. Breakfast included. **€85**

**Le Monarque** 61 rue Porte Chartraine ☏ 02 54 78 02 35, ⓦ annedebretagne.free.fr. Professional and energetically managed hotel with rooms cheerfully renovated in a modern style. Posters of Tintin and 1950s American cartoon heroes decorate the walls. Conveniently located at the top end of town. Buffet breakfast €8.50. **€58**

## EATING AND DRINKING

**Art des Lys** 42 rue Saint Lubin ☏ 02 54 78 30 03, ⓦ artdeslys.fr. Fun and friendly late-night tapas bar with a superb local wine selection, which you can also buy to take away. The calamari are to die for and the cheese plate selection is huge. Tues–Sat 6pm–2am.

**Auberge Ligérienne** 2 place de la Grève ☏ 02 54 78 07 86. Downstairs from the *Côté Loire* (see below), tucked away near the river, you'll find classic *terroir* French cooking in a friendly, cosy atmosphere. *Menus* from €29.50. There's a lovely little garden terrace at the back – perfect for a drink before or after your meal. Daily noon–2pm & 7–10pm.

**L'Embarcadère** 16 Quai Ulysse Besnard ☏ 02 54 78 31 41, ⓦ lembarcadere.fr A little distance out of town but absolutely worth the effort, this river-view locals' favourite serves zingingly fresh seafood, juicy grills and show-stopper desserts. *Menus* from €29. Mon–Thurs & Sun noon–2pm & 7–10pm, Fri, & Sat noon–2pm & 7–11pm.

**L'Orangerie du Château** 1 av Jean-Laigret ☏ 02 54 78 05 36. Offers the best gastronomic experience in town with acclaimed Michelin-starred cuisine. Expect the attitude and price points to match. *Menus* €33–77. Daily noon–2pm, 7–10pm.

## Château de Chaumont

Daily: April–June & Sept 10am–5.45pm; July & Aug 10am–6.15pm; Oct 10am–5.15pm; Nov–March 10am–4.15pm • €10 • ☎ 02 54 20 99 22, ⊛ domaine-chaumont.fr

Catherine de Médicis forced Diane de Poitiers to hand over Chenonceau in return for the **Château de Chaumont**, 20km downstream from Blois. Diane got a bad deal, but this is still one of the lovelier châteaux.

The original fortress was destroyed by Louis XI in the mid-fifteenth century in revenge for the part its owner, Pierre d'Amboise, played in the "League of Public Weal", an alliance of powerful nobles against the ever-increasing power of the monarch. But Pierre found his way back into the king's favour, and with his son, Charles I of Amboise, built much of the quintessentially medieval castle that stands today. Proto-Renaissance design is more obvious in the courtyard, which today forms three sides of a square, the fourth side having been demolished in 1739 to improve the spectacular views over the river. Inside, the heavy nineteenth-century decor of the ground-floor rooms dates from the ownership of the Broglie family, but a few rooms on the first floor have been remodelled in Renaissance style. The large council chamber is particularly fine, with seventeenth-century majolica tiles on the floor and its walls adorned with wonderfully busy sixteenth-century tapestries showing the gods of each of the seven planets known at the time.

### The grounds

Daily 9.30am–dusk • Free

The Broglie family also transformed the **landscaped park** into the fashionable English style and built the remarkable *belle époque* **stables**, with their porcelain troughs and elegant electric lamps for the benefit of the horses at a time before the château itself was wired – let alone the rest of the country. A corner of the château grounds now plays host to an annual **Festival des Jardins** (May to mid-Oct daily 9.45am to dusk; €11, or €15.50 with château entry), which shows off the extravagant efforts of contemporary garden designers.

### Boat trips

Contact the Association Millière Raboton ☎ 06 88 76 57 14, ⊛ milliere-raboton.net • 1hr 30min • €16

On weekends in summer, you can secure the best view of the château from the deck of a traditional Loire boat, which leave from the quay immediately below the château. The regular dawn excursions are best for wildlife-spotting, and you can organize longer-trips – even camping out overnight on an island sandbank.

## Château de Cheverny

Daily: April–June & Sept 9.15am–6.15pm; July & Aug 9.15am–6.45pm; Oct 9.45am–5.30pm; Nov–March 9.45am–5pm • €8.70; combined ticket for château, grounds and Tintin exhibition €13.20, free for under 7s • ⊛ chateau-cheverny.fr

Fifteen kilometres southeast of Blois, the **Château de Cheverny** is the quintessential seventeenth-century château. Built between 1604 and 1634, and little changed since, it presents an immaculate picture of symmetry, harmony and the aristocratic good life. This continuity may well be because descendants of the first owners still own, live in and go hunting from Cheverny today. Its stone, from Bourré on the River Cher, lightens with age, and the château gleams in its acres of rolling parkland. The interior decoration has only been added to, never destroyed, and the extravagant display of paintings, furniture, tapestries and armour against the gilded, sculpted and carved walls and ceilings is extremely impressive. The most precious objects are hard to pick out from the sumptuous whole, but some highlights are the painted wall panels in the dining room telling stories from Don Quixote; the vibrant, unfaded colours of the Gobelin tapestry in the arms room; and the three rare family portraits by François I's court painter, François Clouet, in the gallery.

Inspired by the Château de Cheverny, Hergé created Marlinspike Hall as a country home for Captain Haddock in the *Adventures of Tintin*. The Hergé Foundation has a small but fascinating permanent **exhibition**, which is worth a visit.

You can explore the elegant **grounds** on foot, or take a sedate tour on a little train and by boat (April to mid-Nov; €17.90 including château and museum entry). The **kennels** near the main entrance are certainly worth a look: a hundred lithe hounds mill and loll about while they wait for the next stag, and feeding time (5pm) is something to be seen. Cheverny's hunt culls around thirty deer a year, a figure set by the National Forestry Office.

## Château de Beauregard

April, May daily 10.30am–6pm; June–Sept daily 10am–7pm; Oct–March daily 2–6pm; Dec & Jan daily except Wed 9.30am–noon & 2–5pm; Feb & March daily except Wed 9.30am–12.30pm & 2–5pm • €12 • ☎ 02 54 70 41 65, ⓦ beauregard-loire.com

A pleasant cycle ride from Blois, the little-visited **Château de Beauregard**, 7km south of Blois on the D956 to Contres, lies in the Forêt de Russy. It was – like Chambord – one of François I's hunting lodges, but its transformation in the sixteenth century was one of beautification rather than aggrandizement. It was added to in the seventeenth century and the result is sober and serene, very much at ease in its manicured geometric park.

The highlight of the château is a richly decorated, long **portrait gallery**, whose floor of Delft tiling depicts an army on the march. The walls are entirely panelled with 327 portraits of kings, queens and great nobles, including European celebrities such as Francis Drake, Anne Boleyn and Charles V of Spain. All of France's kings are represented, from Philippe VI (1328–50), who precipitated the Hundred Years' War, to Louis XIII (1610–43), who occupied the throne when the gallery was created. Kings, nobles and executed wives alike are given equal billing – except for Louis XIII, whose portrait is exactly nine times the size of any other.

It's worth strolling down through the grounds to the sunken Jardin des Portraits, a Renaissance-influenced creation by contemporary landscaper Gilles Clément, who was responsible for Paris's futuristic Parc André Citroën (see p.105). It could be better tended, but the garden's formal arrangement – by colour of flower and foliage – is fascinating.

## Château de Chambord

Daily: April–Sept 9am–6pm; Oct–March 10am–5pm • April–Sept €9.50, Oct–March €8.50 • ☎ 02 54 50 40 00, ⓦ chambord.org

The **Château de Chambord**, François I's little "hunting lodge", is the largest and most popular of the Loire châteaux and one of the most extravagant commissions of its age. If you are going to visit – and it's one of the region's absolute highlights – try to arrive early, and avoid weekends, when the crush of visitors can be both unpleasant and overwhelming. Its patron's principal object – to outshine the Holy Roman Emperor Charles V – would, he claimed, leave him renowned as "one of the greatest builders in the universe"; posterity has judged it well.

Before you even get close, the gargantuan scale of the place is awe-inspiring: there are more than 440 rooms and 85 staircases, and a petrified forest of 365 chimneys runs wild on the roof. In architectural terms, the mixture of styles is as outrageous as the size. The Italian architect Domenico da Cortona was chosen to design the château in 1519 in an effort to establish prestigious Italian Renaissance art forms in France, though the labour was supplied by French masons. The château's plan (attributed, fancifully, to da Vinci) is pure Renaissance: rational, symmetrical and totally designed to express a single idea – the central power of its owner. Four hallways run crossways through the central keep, at the heart of which the Great Staircase rises up in two unconnected spirals before opening out into the great lantern tower, which draws together the confusion on the roof like a great crown.

The cold, draughty size of the château made it unpopular as an actual residence – François I himself stayed there for just 42 days in total – and Chambord's role in history is slight. A number of rooms on the first floor were fitted out by Louis XIV and his son, the Comte de Chambord, and as reconstructed today they feel like separate apartments within the unmanageable whole. You can explore them freely, along with the adjacent eighteenth-century apartments, where the château was made habitable by lowering ceilings, building small fireplaces within the larger ones, and cladding the walls with the fashionable wooden panelling known as boiseries.

The second floor houses a rambling Museum of Hunting where, among the endless guns and paintings that glorify hunting, are two superb seventeenth-century tapestry cycles: one depicts Diana, goddess of the hunt; another, based on cartoons by Lebrun, tells the story of Meleager, the heroic huntsman from Ovid's *Metamorphoses*.

The **Parc de Chambord** around the château is an enormous walled game reserve – the largest in Europe. Wild boar roam freely, though red deer are the beasts you're most likely to spot. You can explore on foot, or by bike or boat – both rentable from the jetty where the Cosson passes alongside the main facade of the château.

## ACCOMMODATION AND EATING

**Au Relais d'Artemis** 1 av de Chambord ☎ 02 54 46 41 22, ⓦ restaurant-relais-artemis-41.fr. A popular choice with locals and visitors alike, with light and airy rooms. Classic French *terroir* cooking served in its leafy garden, with *menus* from €18. Tues–Sun noon–9.45pm.

**De la Bonnheure** 9 rue René Masson ☎ 02 54 46 41 57, ⓦ hoteldelabonnheur.com. Various rooms and apartments with terraces set around floral gardens, run by a charming young couple. €10 home-cooked breakfast. **€67**

**Du Grand St-Michel** Chambord village, opposite the château ☎ 02 54 20 31 31, ⓦ saintmichel-chambord .com. Pretty much the only place to stay in town and with only 40 rooms, it can get booked up. There are no design fireworks here but the rooms are clean, reasonably sized and the more expensive ones give uninterrupted views of the château. In fine weather, taking the buffet breakfast €9.50 (on the terrace is a rare pleasure), with direct château views. No wi-fi, but there is a free computer to use. **€75**

# The Sologne

Stretching southeast of Blois, the **Sologne** is one of those traditionally rural regions of France that help keep alive the national self-image. Depending on the weather and the season, it can be one of the most dismal areas in central France: damp, flat, featureless and foggy. But at other times its forests, lakes, ponds and marshes have a quiet magic – in summer, for example, when the heather is in bloom and the ponds are full of water lilies, or in early autumn when you can collect mushrooms. Wild boar and deer roam here, not to mention the ducks, geese, quails and pheasants, who far outnumber the small human population. It was this remote, mystical landscape that provided the setting for Alain Fournier's novel *Le Grand Meaulnes*; Fournier himself spent his childhood in La Chapelle d'Angillon, 34km north of Bourges, and the story's famous "fête étrange" certainly took place in the Sologne. It's worth passing through by bike on a fine day, but there's little to see otherwise.

## GETTING AROUND AND INFORMATION

**Roads and paths** Two *grandes randonnées* lead through the Sologne, both variants of the main GR3 along the Loire. The northern GR3C runs through Chambord and east mostly along forest roads to Thoury and La Ferté-St-Cyr, where it rejoins the southern branch, the GR31, which takes a more attractive route through Bracieux and along footpaths through the southern part of the Forêt de Chambord. There are numerous other well-signposted walking paths.

**Tourist offices** There are tourist offices in most of Sologne's towns and villages, and they can provide maps and details of bike rental or horseriding, as well as accommodation details.

**Visiting** If you're exploring the Sologne during the hunting season (Oct 1 to March 1), don't stray from the marked paths: there are depressingly frequent stories of people being accidentally shot.

# Tours and around

Straddling a spit of land between the rivers Loire and Cher, the ancient cathedral city of **TOURS** is the chief town of the Loire valley. It has the usual feel of a mid-sized provincial city, with some discordant shifts between the strikingly grand and stripped-down modern. It has its charms, however, with some good bars and restaurants. It also has some unusual museums – of wine, crafts, stained glass and an above-average Beaux-Arts museum – and a great many fine buildings, not least St-Gatien cathedral.

The city's two distinct old quarters lie on either side of rue Nationale, a busy shopping street which forms the town's main axis. The quieter centre part is around the cathedral, while the main tourist area lies around picturesque place Plumereau, some 600m to the west. Tours is also the main transport link to the great châteaux of **Villandry**, **Langeais**, **Azay-le-Rideau** and **Amboise**.

## The cathedral quarter

7

The great west towers of the **Cathédrale St-Gatien**, standing on the square of the same name, are visible all over the city. Their surfaces crawl with decorated stone in the flamboyant Gothic style, and even the Renaissance belfries that cap them share the same spirit of refined exuberance. Inside, the style moves back in time, ending with a relatively severe High Gothic east end – built in the thirteenth century – and its glorious stained-glass windows.

A door in the north aisle leads to the **Cloître de la Psalette** (closed for renovations at the time of writing). It has an unfinished air, with the great foot of a flying buttress planted in the southeast corner and a missing south arcade – lost when a road was driven through in 1802 by the same progressive, anticlerical prefect who destroyed the basilica of St-Martin. The area behind the cathedral and museum, to the east, is good for a short stroll. There's a fine view of the spidery buttresses supporting the cathedral's painfully thin-walled apse from place Grégoire de Tours. Overlooking the square is the oldest wing of the archbishop's palace, whose end wall is a mongrel of Romanesque and eighteenth-century work, with an early sixteenth-century projecting balcony once used by clerics to address their flock.

To the side of the cathedral, between rue Albert-Thomas and the river, just two towers remain of the ancient royal **château** of Tours. You can get inside when an exhibition is on but there's nothing much left of the interior.

## Musée des Beaux-Arts

18 place François Sicard • Daily except Tues 9am–12.45pm & 2–6pm • €4 • ☎ 02 47 05 68 73

The **Musée des Beaux-Arts,** just south of the cathedral, is housed in the former archbishop's palace. There are pretty formal gardens in the grounds, and, rather bafflingly, in the stable by the museum entrance, a recreation of Fritz, the Barnum and Bailey elephant who died in Tours in 1904. Other than Mantegna's intense, unmissable *Agony in the Garden* (1457–59) in the basement, there are few celebrity works in the large collection. Even Rembrandt's much-advertised *Flight into Egypt* is a small oil study rather than a finished work. But the stately, loosely chronological progression of palatial seventeenth- and eighteenth-century rooms, each furnished and decorated to match the era of the paintings it displays, is extremely attractive. Local gems include Boulanger's portrait of Balzac, and the engravings *The Five Senses* by the locally born Abraham Bosse, which have been interpreted as full-size canvases in the handsome Louis XIII room.

## Rue Nationale

At the head of **rue Nationale**, Tours' main street, statues of Descartes and Rabelais – both Touraine-born – overlook the scruffy walkways running along the bank of

**TOURS**

N

**ACCOMMODATION**

| | |
|---|---|
| Des Arts | 5 |
| Auberge de Jeunesse | 3 |
| Colbert | 7 |
| Criden | 2 |
| Du Cygne | 6 |
| Du Manoir | 4 |
| L'Usine à Rêves | 1 |
| Val de Loire | 8 |

**BARS**

| | |
|---|---|
| Académie de la Bière | 3 |
| Le Strapontin | 11 |
| Le Vieux Mûrier | 9 |

**CAFÉS AND RESTAURANTS**

| | |
|---|---|
| L'Atelier Gourmand | 8 |
| Comme Autre-Fouée | 10 |
| Au Lapin qui Fume | 2 |
| Melting Pot | 7 |
| L'Oparavant | 6 |
| Le Petit Patrimoine | 5 |
| Le Saint Honoré | 1 |
| Scarlett | 4 |

**CLUB**

| | |
|---|---|
| Les Trois Orfèvres | 1 |

Orléans
St-Pierre-des-Corps

QUAI D'ORLEANS
RUE DES MAURES
RUE ALBERT THOMAS
Château
Cathédrale St-Gatien
Musée des Beaux-Arts
RUE DU GENERAL MEUSNIER
RUE DES URSULINES
RUE FLEURY
RUE JULES-SIMON
RUE TRAVERSIÈRE
BOULEVARD HEURTELOUP
RUE DU REMPART
RUE EDOUARD-VAILLANT
Gare SNCF
metres
200
0

RUE LAVOISIER
RUE DE LA TOUR DE GUISE
RUE JULES MOINAUX
RUE AUBERT
RUE DE LA BARRE
PLACE F-SICARD
RUE BERNARD-PALISSY
Préfecture
Jardin de la Préfecture
Gare Routière
RUE CHARLES GILLE
RUE CHARLES GILLE

RUE DES AMANDIERS
RUE DU CYGNE
RUE DE LA SCELLERIE
RUE BUFFON
RUE BALZAC
RUE MICHELET

AVENUE ANDRÉ MALRAUX
RUE DES JACOBINS
RUE FOIRE LE ROI
RUE COLBERT
RUE DES CORDELIERS
RUE CORNEILLE
RUE ÉMILE-ZOLA
Église Réformée
RUE DES MINIMES
RUE DE BORDEAUX

RUE VOLTAIRE
RUE BERTHELOT
Grand Théâtre
R. PIMBERT
RUE CHAPTAL
Hôtel de Ville
AV. DE GRAMONT
RUE DE LA DOVE
RUE VICTOR HUGO

Musée des Vins
Jardin de Beaune-Semblançay
RUE JULES-FAVRE
RUE LUCE
RUE NATIONALE
Palais de Justice
PLACE JEAN JAURÈS

PLACE ANATOLE-FRANCE
Musée de Compagnonnage
St-Julien
RUE NATIONALE
FOCH
RUE DES DÉPORTES
RUE RICHELIEU
RUE ETIENNE PALLU
RUE MARCEAU
RUE G-SAND

PONT WILSON
PLACE DE LA RÉSISTANCE
RUE DU MARÉCHAL
RUE DE CLOCHEVILLE
RUE DE SULLY

River Loire

Le Mans, Saumur & Angers

River Cher & Loches

RUE DE CONSTANTINE
RUE PAUL-LOUIS COURIER
RUE DU COMMERCE
HALLES
RUE DE JÉRUSALEM
RUE MARCEAU
RUE DE LA GRANDIÈRE
BOULEVARD BÉRANGER

RUE LITTRÉ
RUE DE LA LAMPROIE
RUE DE LA PAIX
RUE BRIÇONNET
Jardin de St-Pierre-le-Puellier
PLACE FOIRE-LE-ROI
PLACE DE CHÂTEAUNEUF
RUE DU PETIT SOLEIL
RUE BALESCHOUX
Basilique de St-Martin
RUE DESCARTES
RUE NÉRICAULT-DESTOUCHES
RUE RAPIN
RUE BARBELAIS
RUE DE COMEILLE
RUE CHANNOINEAU
RUE DE COURSET

RUE DES TANNEURS
RUE DE LA MONNAIE
PLACE DE LA ROTISSERIE
RUE DU CHANGE
RUE DU PETIT SOLEIL
PLACE NUMÉRAU
Tour de Charlemagne
RUE DE CHÂTEAUNEUF
Halles
PLACE DES HALLES

VIEILLE VILLE
RUE DES CERISIERS
RUE DU MÛRIER
RUE BRETONNEAU
P. RUE DU GRAND MARCHÉ
RUE DU GRAND MARCHÉ
P. DU GRAND MARCHÉ
RUE DES HALLES
CHARPENTIER

QUAI DU PONT NEUF
PLACE DE PICOU
RUE ÉTIENNE MARCEL
RUE DES BALAIS
RUE ROUGET-DE-L'ISLE
PLACE DES HALLES
RUE DE LA SERPE
RUE DE LA BÔNNE

PONT NAPOLEON
RUE DE BALZAC
RUE CHANTELOUP
RUE EUGÈNE SUE
RUE DE LA GROSSE TOUR
RUE GEORGES DELPERIER

RUE ALLERON
PLACE RABELAIS
QUATRE VENTS
RUE DE LA VICTOIRE
PLACE DE LA VICTOIRE
RUE JULES

Prieuré de St-Cosme

the Loire. A short walk back from the river brings you to the Benedictine church of St Julien, whose old monastic buildings are home to two fairly missable museums, the Musée des Vins and the Musée de Compagnonnage. At the southern end of rue Nationale, the huge, traffic-ridden place Jean-Jaurès is the site of the grandiose Hôtel de Ville and Palais de Justice. To the west of place Jean-Jaurès, a giant **flower market** takes over boulevard Béranger on Wednesdays and Saturdays, lasting from 8am into the early evening.

## The old quarter

The pulse of the city quickens as you approach **place Plumereau** – or place Plum' as it's known locally. The square's tightly clustered, ancient houses have been carefully restored as the city's showpiece, transforming what was once a slum into the epicentre of social life. On sunny days, the square is packed almost end-to-end with café tables, and students and families drink and dine out until late in the evening.

The slightly less touristy **rue Colbert** is where you'll find any number of excellent bars and restaurants and on Sundays there's an all-day street market from 6am–7pm, the street closes and stalls line the road.

If you're looking for peace, slip down **rue Briçonnet** into a miniature maze of quiet, ancient streets. Opposite an oddly Venetian-looking, fourteenth-century house, at no. 41 rue Briçonnet, a passageway leads past a palm tree and an ancient outdoor staircase to the quiet and insulated **Jardin de St-Pierre-le-Puellier**, laid out around the dug-out ruins of a conventual church.

To the south lay the pilgrim city once known as **Martinopolis** after St Martin, the fourth-century bishop of Tours who went on to become a key figure in the spread of Christianity through France. He is usually remembered for giving half his cloak to a beggar, an image repeated in stained-glass windows all over the region. The Romanesque basilica stretched along rue des Halles from rue des Trois-Pavés-Ronds almost to place de Châteauneuf: the outline is traced out in the street, but only the north tower, the **Tour de Charlemagne**, and the western clock tower survived the iconoclastic Huguenot riots of 1562. The new **Basilique de St-Martin**, on rue Descartes, is a late nineteenth-century neo-Byzantine affair built to honour the relics of St Martin, rediscovered in 1860. They are now housed in the crypt, watched over by hundreds of votive prayers carved into the walls. A short distance away, down rue des Halles, lies the huge, modern **Halles**, or covered market – an excellent place to browse for a picnic in the morning.

## Prieuré de St-Cosme

Mid-March to April & Sept to mid-Oct daily 10am–6pm; May–Aug daily 10am–7pm; mid-Oct to mid-March daily except Tues 10am–12.30pm & 2–5pm • €4.50 • Take bus #3 from immediately outside the Palais de Justice, on place Jean-Jaurès, towards La Riche-Petit Plessis; get off at the "La Pléiade" stop

In May, when the roses are in full bloom, the **Prieuré de St-Cosme**, 3km west of the centre, is one of the most appealing sights in the area even if it is hemmed in by suburbs and barred off from the nearby Loire by a trunk road. Once an island priory, now a semi-ruin, it was here that Pierre de Ronsard, France's greatest Renaissance poet, lived as prior from 1565 until his death in 1585. Vestiges of many monastic buildings survive but the most affecting sight is the lovingly tended **garden of roses**, which has some two thousand rose bushes, and 250 varieties – including the tightly rounded pink rose called "Pierre de Ronsard".

| **ARRIVAL AND DEPARTURE** | **TOURS** |
|---|---|
| **By air** The Aéroport Tours Val de Loire (☎ 02 47 49 37 00, ⓦ tours.aeroport fr) is situated 6km northeast of Tours. | A shuttle bus runs to the airport from the centre of town (€5). |

**By train** The *gare SNCF* is situated a short way southeast of the cathedral district, facing the futuristic Centre de Congrès Vinci. Most TGVs stop at St-Pierre-des-Corps station, in an industrial estate outside the city, which is a 5min train or bus ride away to the main station.

Destinations Amboise (frequent; 20min); Azay-le-Rideau (8 daily; 30min); Blois (frequent; 40min); Chenonceaux (8 daily; 30min); Chinon (8 daily; 45min); Langeais (10 daily; 20min); Le Mans (8 daily; 1hr); Montrichard (11 daily; 40min); Orléans (frequent; 1hr 30min); Paris (hourly; 2hr 30min, TGVs via St-Pierre-des-Corps 1hr); Saumur (frequent; 45min).

**By bus** The *gare routière* is directly outside the train station.

Destinations Amboise (8 daily; 50min); Azay-le-Rideau (3 daily; 50min); Chinon (3 daily; 1hr 10min); Loches (12 daily; 50min); Richelieu (3 daily; 1hr 50min); Villandry (July & Aug only; 2 daily; 30min).

## INFORMATION

**Tourist office** On the corner of rue Bernard-Palissy and busy bd Heurteloup (April–Sept Mon–Sat 8.30am–7pm, Sun 10am–12.30pm & 2.30–5pm; Oct–March Mon–Sat 9am–12.30pm & 1.30–6pm, Sun 10am–1pm; ☎ 02 47 70 37 37, ⓦ ligeris.com), just across the square from the train and bus stations; it offers information on château tours.

## ACCOMMODATION

**Des Arts** 40 rue de la Préfecture ☎ 02 47 05 05 00, ⓦ hoteldesartstours.com. Warmly decorated hotel with a choice of en-suite rooms next to the Musée des Beaux-Arts (see p.391) and 5 minutes from the station. It has a half-timbered breakfast room. Breakfast €6.45. **€51**

**Auberge de Jeunesse** 5 rue Bretonneau ☎ 02 47 37 81 58, ⓦ fuaj.org. Large, modern youth hostel with an excellent central location near place Plumereau. Inexpensive bicycle hire available for guests. Reception 8am–noon & 5–11pm. Singles or twin-bed rooms **€21.60**

**Colbert** 78 rue Colbert ☎ 02 47 66 61 56, ⓦ tours -hotel-colbert.fr Run by friendly hosts and right in the heart of the action on rue Colbert, *Colbert* was newly refurbished in 2012 and has a quiet sun-trap garden at the back. Buffet breakfast €7. **€61**

**Criden** 65 bd Heurteloup ☎ 02 47 20 81 14, ⓦ criden -tours.com. Fun, Paris-themed reception, with rooms of a standard chain-hotel type; bright, clean and reasonably spacious. There's a large sunny terrace where you can enjoy breakfast for €7.50. Parking is available in the underground car park (€8). **€66**

**Du Cygne** 6 rue du Cygne ☎ 02 47 66 66 41, ⓦ hotel -cygne-tours.com. Pleasantly old-fashioned and well-run hotel on a quiet street in the centre. The rooms are dated but comfortable, the larger rooms are unbeatable for families. Garage parking available. Buffet breakfast €7. **€59**

**Du Manoir** 2 rue Traversière ☎ 02 47 05 37 37, ⓦ site .voila.fr/hotel.manoir.tours. Set in a nineteenth-century townhouse, in a peaceful location between the cathedral and train station, the rooms here are perfectly comfortable. Organic breakfast served in the cave downstairs at €9.50. **€67**

★ **L'Usine à Rêves** 59bis rue Pierre Semard, Saint Pierre des Corps ☎ 02 47 54 56 00, ⓦ lusineareves.fr. Ten minutes from Tour city centre, the commuter town of Saint Pierre des Corps is fairly unremarkable, however these *chambre d'hôtes* are ultra-modern, hugely comfortable and offer a warm welcome from the friendly hosts. There's even a small swimming pool and the home-cooked breakfasts are delicious. **€100**

**Val de Loire** 33 bd Heurteloup ☎ 02 47 05 37 86. Charming, antique-laden townhouse hotel close to the station, and a real bargain at the price. The rooms, with wooden floors, are decked out in an assortment of chaise longues, raffia chairs and fireplaces, and a few have garden views. Buffet breakfast €8. **€68**

---

### CHÂTEAU TOURS

It's possible to get to most of the more-visited châteaux by public transport, but if you're short of time it's worth considering a **minibus** trip. The main drawback is that you're usually limited to fairly brief visits. A number of companies run excursions from Tours, and on most schedules you'll find the following châteaux: Amboise, Azay-le-Rideau, Blois, Chambord, Chenonceau, Cheverny, Clos-Lucé (in Amboise), Fougères-sur-Bièvre, Langeais, Ussé and Villandry. **Ticket prices** are steep: usually around €20 for a morning trip, taking in a couple of châteaux, and €40–60 for a full-day tour. These prices do not usually include entrance fees or lunch. Ask at tourist offices or contact the following Touraine-based agencies directly: Acco Dispo (☎ 06 82 00 64 51, ⓦ accodispo-tours.com); Saint-Éloi Excursions (☎ 06 70 82 78 75, ⓦ chateauxexcursions.com) and Quart de Tours (☎ 06 30 65 52 01, ⓦ quartdetours.com). There's little to choose between them, and most pick up from the tourist office in Tours or from your hotel.

## EATING

**L'Atelier Gourmand** 37 rue Etienne Marcel ☎ 02 47 38 59 87, ⊛ lateliergourmand.fr. One of the trendiest addresses in town, ultra-modern atmosphere, gay-friendly and superb fresh cuisine not far from rue Colbert. Tues–Fri noon–2pm & 7–10pm; closed Mon lunch.

**Au Lapin qui Fume** 90 rue Colbert ☎ 02 47 66 95 49. Tiny, relaxed but elegant restaurant serving a good menu that's half Loire and half south of France. Lots of tasty *lapin* (rabbit) – it comes as a terrine, as a fricassée with rosemary, or confit – but it's not obligatory. Evening *menus* around the €19 mark. Tues–Sat noon–2pm & 7–10pm; July–Aug & holidays open Mon.

**Comme Autre-Fouée** 11 rue de la Monnaie ☎ 02 47 05 94 78. The food served here is a revival of the archaic *fouace* (or *fouée*) breads immortalized by Rabelais, a kind of pitta bread, served hot and heavily garnished with local titbits. An excellent option for a unique meal, with a good-value lunch *menu* for €10. Tues–Sat 7–10pm, Thurs–Sat noon–2.30pm.

**Melting Pot** 95 rue Colbert. Excellent coffee, organic juices, shakes and bubble tea, as well as bagels from New York are all on the menu at this friendly cafe with graffiti art out the back. Sunday brunch is available from €14. Tues noon–5pm, Wed noon–8pm, Thurs–Sat noon–10.30pm & Sun noon–3pm.

**L'Oparavant** 46 rue Colbert ☎ 02 47 66 74 96. Superb value and heaped plates at this friendly "à la plancha" bar-restaurant: juicy steaks come served on a wooden board with crisp fries and grilled veg. Daily specials around €12. Mon–Sat noon–2pm & 7–11pm, Sun noon–7pm.

**Le Petit Patrimoine** 58 rue Colbert ☎ 02 47 66 05 81. Romantic little place serving rich, lovingly prepared Loire dishes and good Loire wines. House speciality is a traditional goat cheese dish macerated in olive oil, "Le Bocal de St Maure en Maceration". *Menus* €18–22. Tues–Sat noon–2pm & 7–10pm.

★ **Le Saint Honoré** 7 place des Petites Boucheries ☎ 02 47 61 93 82. In an old bakery, near the cathedral, this friendly cosy restaurant is making quite a name for itself, thanks to its hearty *terroir* cuisine and fruit and veg straight from the chef's own kitchen garden. Try the famous *pâté du Tours*. *Menus* from €28. Mon–Fri noon–3pm & 7–10pm.

**Scarlett** 70 rue Colbert ☎ 02 47 66 94 09. If you fancy a quiet cuppa, make for this peaceful teashop, which has almost 100 different kinds of tea, a good range of coffees and some really decadent cakes. Mon–Fri 11am–7pm; Sat 10am–7pm.

## DRINKING, NIGHTLIFE AND ENTERTAINMENT

### BARS AND CLUBS

**Académie de la Bière** 41 rue Lavoisie ☎ 02 47 05 32 88. The dream location for beer fans, just around the corner from the cathedral. Serving around 170 different varieties of beer, it's a lively, student-friendly place with a bar and also a dance space. Wed–Sat 8pm –5am.

**Le Strapontin** 23 rue de Châteauneuf ☎ 02 47 47 02 74. Clashing walls hung with funky art along with a well-deserved reputation for having the best wine list in town makes this a cool, but slightly more grown-up hangout. Make sure you try the delicious local cheese and pork specialities. Daily 5pm–2am.

**Les Trois Orfèvres** 6 rue des Orfèvres ☎ 02 47 64 02 73, ⊛ 3orfevres.com. Even in summer, when local students are away, the nightclubs just off place Plumereau fill up with backpackers, locals and language students. This is a small and relatively unpretentious club that may not really get going till after midnight, but certainly rocks when it does, playing more rocky-guitar breaks than house or disco. Wed–Sat 11pm–6am.

**Le Vieux Mûrier** 11 place Plumereau ☎ 02 47 61 04 77. The oldest bar in the area and in prime "Plum" position. Cosy, retro scarlet and smoky-yellow interiors and an always-packed terrace, make this one of the most popular choices for solo or group outings. Tues–Fri noon–2am, Sat & Sun 2pm–2am.

### MUSIC AND EVENTS

For details of classical music concerts, stop by the tourist office to pick up *Détours des Nuits*, a free monthly magazine of exhibitions, concerts and events in Touraine.

**Le Palais** 15 place Jean-Jaurès ⊛ brasserielepalais tours.fr. If you're around during the university term, it might be worth dropping in here on a Monday night, when you can speak in a variety of different languages to the students during an event called "Café des Langues". For more details, ask at the tourist office (see opposite).

## DIRECTORY

**Bike hire** Détours de Loire, 35 rue Charles Gille ☎ 02 47 61 22 23, ⊛ locationdevelos.com. Runs the Détours de Loire scheme (see p.363), which allows you to drop off the bike at various locations along the river, for a small extra charge. The *Hôtel Moderne* at 1 rue Laloux also rents bikes to the public ☎ 02 47 05 32 81.

**Car hire** Avis, gare de Tours ☎ 02 47 20 53 27; Europcar, 194 av Maginot ☎ 02 47 85 85 85; Hertz, 57 rue Marcel-Tribut ☎ 02 47 75 50 00. All offer pick-up and drop-off at Tours Airport, at St-Pierre-des-Corps TGV station or near the *gare SNCF* in Tours.

**Health** Ambulance ☎ 15; different hospital departments

7

**7**

## STAYING IN A CHÂTEAU

One of the great privileges of visiting the Loire is that there are a variety of châteaux that accommodate visitors. The standards range enormously: at the top end of the market, you are guaranteed deluxe accommodation, with room service, all mod cons, excellent food and all the amenities you would expect from a top-class hotel; at the other end, you are effectively staying in a bed and breakfast in someone's house, which can be pot luck. The following are the pick of the hotels in the Tours area:

**Château D'Artigny** Nr Montbazon (take D17 from there) ☎02 47 34 30 30, ⓦgrandesetapes.fr/en /Chateau-hotel-artigny. Stunning, beautifully restored château originally owned by the perfumier François Coty, and decorated in a Neoclassical style. The rooms are all large, lavishly appointed and very comfortable, and the excellent restaurant has sweeping views across the Loire valley. You can take cookery classes and enjoy wine tastings. If that all sounds too tiring, note that there's a pool, jacuzzi, steam room and sauna to relax in, along with spa treatments. **€165**
**Domaine de Beauvois** Nr Luynes ☎02 47 55 50 11, ⓦgrandesetapes.fr/en/Chateau-hotel-beauvois

/index.html. Much of the appeal of this beautiful sixteenth-century mansion comes from its peaceful seclusion, with long country walks and beautiful bike rides the order of the day. There are some lovely, quirky touches in the rooms, too, which have beamed ceilings and painted frescoes, and the restaurant offers excellent food. **€157**
**Domaine de la Tortinière** Nr Montbazon ☎02 47 34 35 00, ⓦtortiniere.com. Delightful family-run hotel, with friendly bilingual owners. Rooms range from the modestly comfortable to the spectacularly luxurious (such as the suites in the turrets, complete with circular bedrooms) and very good food is served in the dining room, overlooking an open-air swimming pool. **€115**

---

are spread around the city – call ☎02 47 47 47 47 to check where to head.
**Internet** Central options include: Cyber Gate, 11 rue Merville (Mon–Sat 10am–midnight, Sun 3–9pm); and Top

Communication, 129 rue Colbert (Mon–Sat 9am–10pm, Sun 2–10pm).
**Police** Commissariat Général, 70–72 rue Marceau ☎02 47 33 80 69.

# Amboise

Twenty kilometres upstream of Tours, **AMBOISE** is one of the highlights of the Loire region, with its beguiling mix of beauty, excellent food and drink and a genuine sense of history. The château dominates the town, but there are many other attractions, most famously Leonardo da Vinci's residence of **Clos-Lucé**, with its exhibition of the great man's inventions. Amboise draws a busy tourist trade, which may detract from the quieter pleasures of strolling around town, but does mean it's a lively destination.

## Château d'Amboise

Daily: April–June 9am–6.30pm; July & Aug 9am–7pm; Sept 9am–6pm; first 2 weeks Nov & March 9am–5.30pm; mid-Nov to Jan 9am–12.30pm & 2–4.45pm; Feb 9am–12.30pm & 1.30–5pm • €10.20, tours extra €4–14.70 • ⓦ chateau-amboise.com

Rising above the river are the remains of the château, once five times its present size, but much reduced by wars and lack of finance; it still represents a highly impressive accomplishment. It was in the late fifteenth century, following his marriage to Anne of Brittany at Langeais, that Charles VIII decided to turn the old castle of his childhood days into an extravagant palace, adding the flamboyant Gothic wing that overlooks the river and the chapelle de St-Hubert, perched incongruously atop a buttress of the defensive walls. But not long after the work was completed, he managed to hit his head, fatally, on a door frame. He left the kingdom to his cousin, Louis XII, who spent most of his time at Blois (see p.384) but built a new wing at Amboise (at right angles to the main body) to house his nearest male relative, the young François d'Angoulême, thereby keeping him within easy reach. When the young heir acceded to the throne as François I he didn't forget his childhood home. He embellished it with classical stonework (visible on the east facade of the Louis XII wing), invited Leonardo da Vinci to work in Amboise under his protection, and eventually died in the château's collegiate church.

Henri II continued to add to the château, but it was during the reign of his sickly son, François II, that it became notorious. The **Tumult of Amboise** was one of the first skirmishes in the Wars of Religion. Persecuted by the young king's powerful advisers, the Guise brothers, Huguenot conspirators set out for Amboise in 1560 to "rescue" their king and establish a more tolerant monarchy under their tutelage. But they were ambushed by royal troops in the woods outside the town, rounded up and summarily tried in the Salle des Conseils. Some were drowned in the Loire below the château, some were beheaded in the grounds, and others were hung from the château's balconies.

After such a colourful history, the interior of the château is comparatively restrained, though the various rooms still retain some sense of their historical grandeur. The last French king, Louis-Philippe, also stayed in the château, hence the abrupt switch from the solid Gothic furnishings of the ground floor to the 1830s post-First Empire style of the first-floor apartments. The most recently renovated part of the château are the **underground passageways**, which have been both dungeons and larders in their time. The **Tour des Minimes**, the original fifteenth-century entrance, is architecturally the most exciting part of the castle. With its massive internal ramp, it was designed to allow the maximum number of fully armoured men on horseback to get in and out as quickly as possible. These days it leads down to the pleasant gardens, which in turn lead to the exit.

## Clos-Lucé

Daily: Jan 10am–6pm; Feb–June, Sept & Oct 9am–7pm; July & Aug 9am–8pm; Nov & Dec 9am–6pm; March to mid-Nov • €13.50, mid-Nov to Feb €10.50 • Last entry one hour before close • Son et lumière shows are held July–Sept Wed–Sat from around 10pm at the château • Adults €17, children 6–12 €7 • ⓦ renaissance-amboise.com

Following his campaigns in Lombardy, François I decided that the best way to bring back the ideas of the Italian Renaissance was to import one of the finest exponents of the new arts. In 1516, **Leonardo da Vinci** ventured across the Alps in response to the royal invitation, carrying with him the Mona Lisa among other paintings. For three years before his death in 1519, he made his home at the **Clos-Lucé**, at the end of rue Victor-Hugo. Leonardo seems to have enjoyed a semi-retirement at Amboise, devoting himself to inventions of varying brilliance and impracticability, and enjoying conversations with his royal patron, but it seems that no work of any great stature was produced there. The house – an attractive brick mansion with Italianate details added by Charles VIII – is now a museum to Leonardo.

There's plenty to see and do in the museum and its grounds, which are dotted about with models of his inventions – including wooden flying machines. Most recently, a fresco of the *Annunciation of Mary*, thought to be either his work, or that of one of his disciples, has been restored in the Oratory.

## ARRIVAL AND INFORMATION                                    AMBOISE

**By train** The *gare SNCF* is on the north bank of the river, at the end of rue Jules-Ferry, about 1km from the château. There are frequent connections to Tours (at least 4 hourly; 17min) and Blois (2 hourly; 20min).

**By bus** Touraine Fil Vert's line C1 runs between Tours and Amboise (9 daily Mon–Sat).

**Tourist office** Information on Amboise and its environs, including the vineyards of the Touraine-Amboise *appellation*, is available at the tourist office on quai du Général-de-Gaulle, on the riverfront (June & Sept

Mon–Sat 9.30am–6.30pm, Sun 10am–1pm & 2–5pm; July & Aug Mon–Sat 9am–8pm, Sun 10am–6pm; Oct–May Mon–Sat 10am–1pm & 2–6pm; ☏ 02 47 57 09 28, ⓦ amboise-valdeloire.com).

**Bike hire** Cycles Richard, 2 rue Nazelles, near the station (☏ 02 47 57 01 79), or Locacycle, on 2bis rue Jean-Jacques-Rousseau (☏ 02 47 57 00 28).

**Canoe hire** Club de Canoë-Kayak, at the Base de l'Île d'Or (☏ 02 47 23 26 52, ⓦ loire-aventure.com), hire out canoes and also run guided trips.

## ACCOMMODATION

**Au Charme Rabelasien** 25 Rue Rabelais ☏ 06 86 14 10 68, ⓦ au-charme-rabelaisien.com. Only three rooms at this charming B&B that used to be a girls' school,

but they are stunners. Individually designed, with huge bathrooms boasting bathrobes, minibar and other boutique hotel mod-cons. There's a pool and shady

7

**7**

garden too. Breakfast included. **€167**

**Belle-Vue** 12 quai Charles-Guinot ☏ 02 47 30 32 78. Long-established *Logis de France* three-star just below the château, with comfortable, old-fashioned bedrooms. Currently undergoing renovation, due to be finished in 2013. Some rooms at the front overlook the Loire – and the main road. Closed mid-Nov to mid-March. Breakfast €7.50. **€80**

**Le Blason** 11 place Richelieu ☏ 02 47 23 22 41, ⓦ leblason.fr. Very smartly kept but homely hotel in a quiet corner a few minutes out of the centre. The furnishings are modern, but all rooms have pretty, exposed beams. Triples and quads available. Breakfast €7.50. **€63**

**Café des Arts** Place Michel-Debré ☏ 02 47 57 25 04. Simple backpacker-oriented place – think pine bunkbeds and hard-wearing carpet – set up above a popular local café directly opposite the châteaux. Noisy, but you're right in the heart of it all. Breakfast €6.50. **€27**

**Camping de l'Île d'Or** Île d'Or ☏ 02 47 57 23 37, ⓦ camping-amboise.com. Pleasant, leafy campsite, with access to the pool. Closed Oct–March. **€9.30**

**Le Choiseul** 36 quai Charles-Guinot ☏ 02 47 30 45 45, ⓦ le-choiseul.com. Widely acknowledged to be the best hotel in Amboise, this luxurious place has grandly appointed and very comfortable rooms, an excellent restaurant and all the other touches you'd expect including a pool, stunning views and exceptionally helpful staff. Breakfast €12. **€137**

**Le Clos d'Amboise** 27 rue Rabelais ☏ 02 47 30 10 20, ⓦ leclosamboise.com. A real oasis in the heart of the city with a pool and lovely park-like garden in which to relax and listen to the birdsong. Reasonable rooms with classic french decor and good-sized bathrooms. Breakfast €12. **€110**

★ **Le Vieux Manoir** 13 rue Rabelais ☏ 02 47 30 41 27, ⓦ le-vieux-manoir.com. Run by an utterly charming American couple, this lovingly restored manor house is one of the best bed and breakfasts in the region. Lots of lovely touches abound, from the glass of Loire wine waiting on your arrival to the sweet self-contained cottage. In summertime there's a delicious scent of flowers from the beautiful garden. Breakfast included. **€160**

## EATING AND DRINKING

### RESTAURANTS

**L'Ambacia** 12–14 place Michel-Debré ☏ 02 47 23 21 44. Funky brasserie on the square opposite the château, specializing in burgers, salads and grills. There's a whole street of restaurants here and this is one of the best. *Menus* from €9.80. Daily noon–10pm, Sat until 11pm.

**Anne de Bretagne** 1 Rampe du Château ☏ 02 47 57 05 46, ⓦ restaurant-annedebretagne-amboise.fr. With chairs on the ramp leading up to the château, facing Place Michel-Debré, this is in the heart of the action. Friendly service and excellent crêpes. *Menus* from €9.80. Daily noon–10pm.

**Restaurant Le 36** ☏ 02 47 30 45 45. The best restaurant in town is the celebrated dining room of *Le Choiseul* (see above); the food is expensive but excellent, and the views over the Loire are stunning. Book in for lunch to try the superb food at a far more wallet-friendly price. *Menus* €47–82. Daily noon–2pm & 7–9pm; mid-Nov to mid-March closed Tues & Wed.

### BARS

**Caveau des Vignerons d'Amboise** At the base of the château. If you're keen to taste some of the local wine,

head to this welcoming place, which offers a wide variety of local wines to sip and buy. Daily 10am–7pm; closed Nov–March.

**Caves Duhard** Rue Rocher des Violettes ☏ 02 47 57 20 77, ⓦ caves-duhard.fr. Tucked away deep in a sixteenth-century *cave*, three generations of enthusiastic specialists have dedicated themselves to the wines of the Loire valley. Drop by for a tasting. Tues–Sat 10am–noon & 2–6pm.

**Galland Epicerie de Terroirs** 27 rue Nationale ☏ 02 47 23 14 79. This welcoming local delicacies shop stocks more than 1000 different products from small producers and specializes in Loire valley wines, local cheeses and charcuterie. You're welcome to stop by for a tasting in the wine section at the back of the shop. Call ahead if you're in a group. Daily 9am–7pm; July–Aug till 8pm.

**Le Shaker** 3 quai François Tissard, Île d'Or. The place to go for a late cocktail. There's a great outside terrace with wonderful views across to the château. Their mixologist recently won an international award for his creations; try a White Lady (gin, cointreau and egg white) or put him through his paces with what he calls a "Fancy Cocktail" – but beware, they pack a punch. Tues–Sun 6pm–3am.

# Château de Villandry

Daily: March 9am–5.30pm; April–June, Sept & Oct 9am–6pm; July & Aug 9am–6.30pm; first 2 weeks Nov & Feb 9am–5pm; last 2 weeks Dec 9.30am–4.30pm; closed mid-Nov to mid-Dec & Jan • €9.50 château and gardens, €6.50 gardens only • ⓦ chateauvillandry .com • Some of minibus companies make the trip from Tours, usually stopping in Azay-le-Rideau (see p.400); they leave from the tourist office and cost around €20 return; in July and August, there are also two local buses a day from Tours' *gare routière*.

Even if gardens aren't normally your thing, those at the Château de Villandry are unmissable. Thirteen kilometres west of Tours along the Cher, this recreated

Renaissance **garden** is as much symbolic as ornamental or practical. At the topmost level is a large, formal water garden in the elevated Classical spirit. Next down, beside the château itself, is the ornamental garden, which features geometrical arrangements of box hedges symbolizing different kinds of love: tender, passionate, fickle and tragic. But the highlight, spread out at the lowest level across 12,500 square metres, is the *potager*, or Renaissance kitchen garden. Carrots, cabbages and aubergines are arranged into intricate patterns, while rose bowers and miniature box hedges form a kind of frame. Even in winter, there is almost always something to see, as the entire area is replanted twice a year. At the far end of the garden, overlooked by the squat tower of the village church, beautiful vine-shaded paths run past the medieval herb garden and the maze.

The elegant château was erected in the 1530s by one of François I's royal financiers, Jean le Breton, though the keep – from which there's a fine view of the gardens – dates back to a twelfth-century feudal castle. It's worth a quick visit, but pales in comparison to its gardens. Le Breton's Renaissance structure is arranged around three sides of a *cour d'honneur*, the fourth wing having been demolished in the eighteenth century.

## Château de Langeais

Daily: Feb & March 9.30am–5.30pm; April–June & Sept to mid-Nov 9.30am–6.30pm; July & Aug 9am–7pm; mid-Nov to Jan 10am–5pm • €8.50 • ⓦ chateau-de-langeais.com

Twenty-three kilometres west of Tours, the small riverside town of **LANGEAIS** huddles in the shadow of its forbidding château, which was built to stop any incursions up the Loire by the Bretons. This threat ended with the marriage of Charles VIII and Duchess Anne of Brittany in 1491, which was celebrated in the castle, and a diptych of the couple portrays them looking less than joyous at their union – Anne had little choice in giving up her independence. The event is also recreated in waxworks in the wedding hall. The main appeal here is in the way that the interior has resisted modernization, to give a genuine sense of what life would have been like in the fifteenth century. There are fascinating tapestries, some rare paintings, cots and beds and a number of *chaires* (seigneurial chairs). The banqueting hall has a large U-shaped table, piled high with imitation food, while in the huge marriage chamber, the gilded and bejewelled wedding coffer of Charles and Anne is carved with a miniature scene of the Annunciation and figures of the apostles, the wise and foolish virgins depicted on the lid.

### ARRIVAL AND INFORMATION

**By train** The *gare SNCF* is 5 minutes away on foot from the castle and has a regular service to Tours (10 daily; 20min) and Saumur (9 daily; 25min).

### ACCOMMODATION AND EATING                              LANGEAIS

**Au Coin Des Halles** 9 rue Gambetta ⓣ 02 47 96 37 25, ⓦ aucoindeshalles.com. This is a surprisingly modern addition to this pleasantly old-fashioned town; it serves gastronomic food in a decidedly funky dining room space. There's a good-sized terrace at the back so you can eat al fresco in fine weather. *Menus* €16–49. Fri–Tues 12.15–2pm & 7.15–8.45pm.

**Errard Hosten** 2 rue Gambetta ⓣ 02 47 96 82 12, ⓦ errard.com. On the small road leading to the château, this is a classic, old-fashioned and welcoming place to stay. Rooms are spacious, with most offering a good view over the square. There's a decent restaurant, which serves a bistro *menu* for lunch (except Sun; *menus* from €19.50) and a gastronomic *terroir menu* in the evening. *Menus* €29–59. Breakfast €13.50. **€74**

**La Maison de Rabelias** 2 lace Pierre de Brosse ⓣ 02 47 96 82 20. A delightful tearoom opposite the château which serves snacks and salads and specializes in ice-cream sundaes, along with a delicious cherry-chocolate confection, "Les Muscadins". Daily 8.30am–7pm in summer, closed Mon rest of the year.

7

# Azay-le-Rideau

Even without its striking château, the quiet village of **AZAY-LE-RIDEAU** would bask in its serene setting, complete with an old mill by the bridge and curious, doll-like Carolingian statues embedded in the facade of the church of St Symphorien. Perhaps unsurprisingly, it has become a magnet for tourists. On its little island in the Indre, the **château** (daily: April–June & Sept 9.30am–6pm; July & Aug 9.30am–7pm; Oct–March 10am–12.30pm & 2–5.30pm, €8; **son et lumière** July & Aug daily 9pm, €10, or €14 with daytime château entry) is one of the loveliest in the Loire: perfect turreted early Renaissance, pure in style right down to the blood-red paint of its window frames. Visiting the interior, furnished in mostly period style, doesn't add much to the experience although the grand staircase is worth seeing, and it's fun to look out through the mullioned windows across the moat and park and imagine yourself the *seigneur*. In summer, the château's grounds are the setting for a restrained and rather lovely **son et lumière**.

## ARRIVAL AND INFORMATION

AZAY-LE-RIDEAU

**By train** The *gare SNCF* is awkwardly situated a 15min walk west of the centre, along avenue Adélaïde-Riché. Trains from Tours (Mon–Fri 9 daily, Sat & Sun 5 daily; 30min) call at Azay-le-Rideau on their way to Chinon (Mon–Fri 10 daily, Sat & Sun 6 daily; 20min) roughly every two hours (some services are replaced by SNCF buses).

**By bus** The bus stop is next to the tourist office on the main road.

**Tourist office** Just off the village's main square, place de la République (May, June & Sept Mon–Sat 9am–1pm & 2–6pm, Sun 10am–1pm & 2–5pm; July & Aug Mon–Sat 9am–7pm, Sun 10am–6pm; Oct–April Mon–Sat 9am–1pm & 2–6pm; ☎02 47 45 44 40, ⦿azaylerideau-tourisme.com).

**Bike hire** Cycles Leprovost, 13 rue Carnot (☎02 47 45 40 94).

**Canoe hire** In summer, canoes can be hired from beside the bridge on the road out towards Chinon (June–Aug daily 1–7pm; ☎02 47 45 39 45).

## ACCOMMODATION

**De Biencourt** 7 rue Balzac ☎02 47 45 20 75, ⦿hotelbiencourt.com. Welcoming and friendly, attracting a slightly older crowd of châteaux fans. Rooms are a good size, with modern bathrooms. No parking, but there are plenty of spaces on the nearby square. Buffet breakfast €9. Closed mid-Nov to mid-March. **€62**

**Camping du Sabot** 813 rte du Stade, signposted off the D84 to Saché ☎02 47 45 42 72, ⦿campingdusabot.fr. This large and well-organized campsite, upstream from the château, has a grocery store, with bread and pastries to order, plus washing machines, picnic tables, hot showers, and free wi-fi. Closed Nov–March. **€16**

**Charitha Marambe** 2 rue Victor Hugo ☎06 23 86 23 07, ⦿chambresdhoteazaylerideau.com. An original choice, with two lovely double rooms in a Sri Lankan expat's home. Modern, comfortable and friendly, there's even a small "secret garden" terrace. Breakfast included. **€49**

**Le Grand Monarque** 3 place de la République ☎02 47 45 40 08, ⦿legrandmonarque.com. As the name suggests, this option is indeed rather grand, and has a wide range of rooms, some with exposed beams and stone walls. There's a shady terrace to enjoy breakfast or a pre-supper drink if it's warm. Buffet breakfast €12. **€95**

**Les Trois Lys** 2 rue du Château ☎02 47 45 34 36. Set right on the square, this budget hotel is relatively no frills, but good value. Divided between a "new" and old building, the rooms in the newer section are modern, bright and have timber beam ceilings, while the rooms in the older side are rather small. There's a basic brasserie-style restaurant too. Buffet breakfast €7.50. **€52**

**Troglododo** 9 chemin des Caves Mecquelines ☎02 47 45 31 25, ⦿troglododo.fr. The unusual rooms offered by M. et Mme Sarrazin are housed in troglodyte chambers hollowed out of the rock. Bright splashes of colour, stylish lighting and funky fabrics make this a unique spot, and it can get booked up a fair way in advance; don't even think about turning up in summer without a reservation. Breakfast included. **€65**

## EATING AND DRINKING

**L'Aigle d'Or** 10 av Adélaïde-Riché ☎02 47 45 24 58. This friendly, elegant and traditional restaurant serves French cuisine classics and some fabulous desserts. If the chocolate cherries are on the menu, snap them up. In the summertime, you can eat in its delightful garden. *Menus* €27–42. Daily noon–2pm & 7–9pm, closed Sun & Mon eve.

**Côté Cour** 19 rue Balzac ☎02 47 45 30 36, ⦿cotecour-azay.com. Probably the best restaurant in town, serving a small menu of local seasonal products. The house speciality is a delicious dried pear salad. *Menus* €16 and €22. Daily noon–2pm & 7.30–10pm, closed Tues eve & Wed (except July & Aug).

7

**Les Grottes** 23 rue de Pineau ☎ 02 47 45 21 04. This offers the novel sensation of dining in a cave or on its terrace. It's a short walk from the centre of town and it's a bit of a favourite with tourists, but pleasingly, there's friendly service and good traditional French cuisine. *Menus* €19–26. Daily noon–3pm & 7–10pm, closed Thurs in low season.

## Château d'Ussé

Daily: mid-Feb to March & Sept–Nov 10am–6pm; April–Aug 10am–7pm; Sept to mid-Nov 10am–6pm; closed Dec–Jan • €14 • ☎ 02 47 95 54 05, ⓦ chateaudusse.fr

Fourteen kilometres west of Azay-le-Rideau, as the Indre approaches its confluence with the Loire, is the Château d'Ussé in **RIGNY-USSÉ**. With its shimmering white towers and terraced gardens, this is the ultimate fairy-tale château – so much so that it's supposed to have inspired Charles Perrault's classic retelling of the Sleeping Beauty myth. The exterior resembles nothing so much as a Disney fantasy; you half expect to see Beauty and the Beast emerge. Inside, things are more restrained, apart from the rather kitsch tableaux telling the story of Sleeping Beauty. The most recent renovations are the attic areas, which are now open to visitors where you can see antiques and paintings. The château's vineyards are also now producing wine, a sparkling Cuvée Prestige Brut, which is for sale in the grounds. The gardens, designed by Le Nôtre, are pleasant to wander in. The loveliest feature of all is the Renaissance chapel in the grounds, shaded by ancient cedars.

7

| ACCOMMODATION AND EATING | RIGNY-USSÉ |

**Le Clos d'Ussé** Rigny-Ussé ☎ 02 47 95 55 47. The tiny village of Rigny-Ussé is home to a family-run hotel-restaurant with seven simple rooms just minutes walk from the château. The warm welcome that you receive from the friendly hostess more than makes up for the lack of frills. Breakfast €7. **€55**

**Domaine de la Juranvillerie** 15 rue des Fougères ☎ 02 47 95 57 85, ⓦ lajuranvillerie.com. Behind the château, in a tranquil, wooded fold of the valley, *Domaine de la Juranvillerie* almost opens the time-travelling door back into medieval times, but, thankfully, with modern, up-to-date comforts. Breakfast is served in medieval costume, and if you book for dinner (reserve in advance) you'll be given the chance to dress up too. Run by a charming older couple, this is an atmospheric gem. Breakfast included. **€80**

# Chinon and around

**CHINON** lies on the north bank of the Vienne, 12km from its confluence with the Loire, and is surrounded by some of the best vineyards in the Loire valley. While the cobbled medieval streets give a marvellous sense of history, it's a quiet town, and the actual sights won't keep you occupied for any more than a day or two. Chinon's medieval streets with their half-timbered and sculpted townhouses are pleasant enough to wander through, or you could duck into one of the town's low-key **museums**.

## The fortress

Daily: May–Aug 9.30am–7pm; March–April 9.30am–6pm; Jan, Feb, Nov, Dec 9.30am–5pm • €7.50 • To get there, walk from town or take the free lift from the car park at its base

Chinon's château, strictly speaking, is actually a fortress, rather than a typical Renaissance castle. High on a hill over the town, with a stunning view over the Vienne, the fortress was closed for years but after a lengthy restoration process is now fully open for business.

A fortress existed here from the Iron Age until the time of Louis XIV, the age of its most recent ruins. Henry Plantagenet added a new castle to the first medieval fortress on the site, built by his ancestor Foulques Nerra, and died here, crying vengeance on his son Richard, who had treacherously allied himself with the French king Philippe-Auguste. After a year's siege in 1204–5, Philippe-Auguste finally took the castle, from the English King John, ending the Plantagenet rule over Touraine and Anjou.

Over two hundred years later, Chinon was one of the few places where the Dauphin Charles, later Charles VII, could safely stay while Henry V of England held Paris and the title to the French throne. When Joan of Arc arrived here in 1429, she was able to talk her way into meeting him. The story depicted in a tapestry on display on the site is that as Joan entered the great hall, the Dauphin remained hidden anonymously among the assembled nobles, as a test, but Joan picked him out straight away. Joan herself claimed that an angel had appeared before the court, bearing a crown. She begged him to allow her to rally his army against the English. To the horror of the courtiers, Charles said yes. The reality is rather more prosaic: records show that Joan attended a small meeting with the king, so already knew who he was.

The fortress has been sensitively and impressively restored. The **Logis Royal**, or royal quarters, used to be spread over three buildings but now the only surviving part is the south wing which housed the apartments of Charles VII and Mary of Anjou. From the Logis, you go on to explore the **middle castle**, the **fort Coudray** and its towers and the **Fort Saint George**. Video projections, film and lighting provide good atmosphere and there are excellent information points which you can access via a modern smart-chip swipe-card information booklet. The site includes also a very good **Joan of Arc museum** dedicated to the many images of Joan and to false relics, including fragments of bone said to have been rescued from under the stake where she died.

## Musée d'Art et d'Histoire de Chinon

44 rue Haute St-Maurice • May to mid-Sept daily except Tues 2.30–6.30pm; March, April & mid-Sept to mid Nov Fri–Mon 2–6pm • €3

The **Musée d'Art et d'Histoire de Chinon** has some diverting oddments of sculpture, pottery and paintings related to the town's history, as well as a fascinating recreation of a room in a sixteenth-century inn. There's also a painting by Delacroix of Rabelais.

### ARRIVAL AND DEPARTURE          CHINON

**By train** The *gare SNCF* lies to the east of the town, from where rue du Dr-P.-Labussière and rue du 11-novembre lead to place Jeanne-d'Arc, where Joan is carved in mid-battle charge. Keep heading west and you'll soon reach the old quarter. Frequent trains to Tours depart daily (45min–1hour).

### INFORMATION

**Tourist office** Place d'Hofheim, on the central rue Jean-Jacques-Rousseau (May–Sept daily 10am–7pm; Oct–April Mon–Sat 10am–12.30pm & 2.30–6pm; ☎02 47 93 17 85, ⊕chinon-valdeloire.com). The office can provide addresses of local vineyards where you can taste Chinon's famous red wine.

**Canoe hire** Just beside the campsite, Chinon Loisirs Activités Nature (☎06 23 82 96 33, ⊕loisirs-nature.fr; April–Oct) hires out canoes and kayaks, and runs half-day and full-day guided trips in summer.

**Market** An antiques and flea market takes place every third Sunday of the month, while regular market day is Thursday.

### ACCOMMODATION

**Agnès Sorel** 4 quai Pasteur ☎02 47 93 04 37, ⊕hotel-agnes-sorel.com. Down by the main road, at the western edge of the Old Town, opposite the river, this bright modern boutique hotel has great views from some of its rooms. Breakfast €8. **€50**

**Belle Epoque** 14 av Gambetta ☎02 47 93 00 86, ⊕hotelchinon.com. Located opposite the station and with a friendly host, rooms at this small hotel are basic but clean; the least expensive rooms (€49) share a shower and loo just down the hallway. Good option for an early train. It has a cheap-but-cheerful restaurant too. Breakfast €8.50. **€60**

**Camping de l'Île Auger** ☎02 47 93 08 35. Overlooks the Old Town and château from the south bank of the

---

### WINE TASTING IN CHINON

Though it's better with a good meal, if you want to try a glass of Chinon you could visit the **Caves Painctes**, off rue Voltaire, a deep cellar carved out of the rock where a local winegrowers' guild runs tastings. "Paincte" was supposedly the name of a wine cellar owned by the father of Rabelais, who was born at the manor farm of La Devinière, 6km southwest of town, where there's a good but rather dry museum on Rabelias' life. Tastings take place July & Aug daily except Mon, 11am, 3pm, 4.30pm & 6pm and cost around €3.

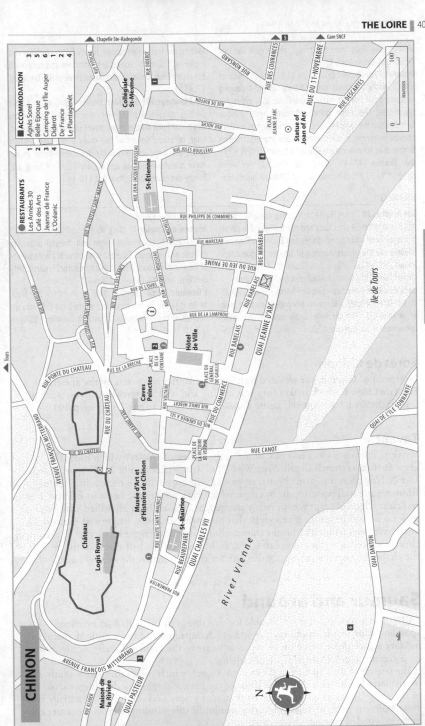

CHINON

RESTAURANTS
Les Années 30    3
Café des Arts    5
Jeanne de France 6
L'Océanic        1

ACCOMMODATION
Agnès Sorel          1
Belle Epoque         2
Camping de l'île Auger 3
Diderot              1
De France            2
Le Plantagenêt       4

7

Chapelle Ste-Radegonde

Gare SNCF

Collégiale St-Mexme

St-Étienne

RUE DIDEROT
RUE PITOCHE
RUE DES COURANCES
RUE DU 11-NOVEMBRE
RUE RONSARD
RUE DE BUFFON
RUE DESCARTES
PLACE JEANNE D'ARC
Statue of Joan of Arc
RUE HOCHE
RUE JULES ROULLEAU
RUE JEAN-JACQUES ROUSSEAU
RUE PHILIPPE DE COMMINES
RUE MARCEAU
RUE MIRABEAU
RUE DU JEU DE PAUME
RUE DE L'OURS
RUE DU PUY DES BANCS
RUE JEAN-JACQUES ROUSSEAU
RUE DE LA LAMPROIE
RUE RABELAIS
QUAI JEANNE D'ARC
RUE RABELAIS
RUE DU COLLÈGE SAINT-MARTIN
RUE DU COLLÈGE SAINT-MARTIN
RUE RODIEUR
RUE PORTE DU CHATEAU
RUE DE LA BRECHE
PLACE DE LA FONTAINE
Hôtel de Ville
PLACE DU GÉNÉRAL DE GAULLE
Caves Peinctes
RUE DE LA BRECHE
RUE DU CHATEAU
RUE VOLTAIRE
RUE EMILE HÉBERT
RUE DU GRENIER À SEL
RUE DU COMMERCE
AVENUE FRANÇOIS MITTERRAND
RUE DU CHATEAU
RUE JEANNE D'ARC
RUE DU CHATEAU
Château
Logis Royal
Musée d'Art et d'Histoire de Chinon
RUE HAUTE SAINT-MAURICE
St-Maurice
PLACE DE LA VICTOIRE DE VERDUN
RUE CANOT
RUE BEAUREPAIRE
QUAI CHARLES VII
RUE PARMENTIER
AVENUE FRANÇOIS MITTERRAND
Maison de la Rivière
RUE KLÉBER
QUAI PASTEUR
QUAI DANTON
QUAI DE L'ÎLE SONNANTE
River Vienne
Ile de Tours

Tours

N

0  100
metres

**7**

Vienne; turn right from the bridge along quai Danton. Closed mid-Oct to April. **€5.10**

**Diderot** 7 rue Diderot ☎02 47 93 18 87, ⓦhoteldiderot.com. Solidly bourgeois hotel offering an old-fashioned welcome from the jam-making proprietor in a venerable townhouse. Has some grand old rooms with antique furnishings in the main building, and some brighter modern ones in the annexe. Home-made jams and products from no further than 50km away are served for breakfast (€9). **€77**

**De France** 47–49 place du Général-de-Gaulle ☎02 47 93 33 91, ⓦbestwestern.fr. Historic hotel over-looking the leafy main square, handy for the fortress and exploring the town. Rooms are attractive and cosy, with big comfy beds, beams and exposed stone walls. Breakfast €7. **€111**

**Le Plantagenêt** 12 place Jeanne-d'Arc ☎02 47 93 36 92, ⓦhotel-plantagenet.com. Decent, welcoming three-star hotel on the large market square on the eastern edge of town. Rooms in the main nineteenth-century house are large and pleasantly decorated; those in the more motel-like garden annexe are cosy and have a/c. Family rooms available. Breakfast €10. **€61**

### EATING

**Les Années 30** 78 rue Haute St-Maurice ☎02 47 93 37, ⓦ18 lesannees30.com. Cosy and old-fashioned in decor, but with some adventurous dishes and Eastern-influenced flavours like the ginger, honey and sesame langoustines. *Menus* (€27–43). Daily noon–2pm & 7.30–9.30pm, closed Tues & Wed; July & Aug open for Tues dinner.

**Café des Arts** 4 rue Jean-Jacques-Rousseau ☎02 47 93 09 84. Offers reliable and reasonably priced brasserie grub at around €15. Popular with locals and visitors alike; specializes in local products. Daily noon–2pm & 7.30–9.30pm, closed Wed.

**Jeanne de France** 12 place du Général-de-Gaulle ☎02 47 93 20 12. Good value, bright and cheerful pizza and crêperie on the square. Excellent sundaes with a wide variety of ice-cream flavours; the salt-butter caramel is particularly delicious. Daily 11.30am–2.30pm & 7–10.30pm.

**L'Océanic** 13 rue Rabelais ☎02 47 93 44 55. The place to go if you're in the mood for some local fish; has an impressive cheese selection as well. Daily noon–1.30pm & 7.30–9.30pm.

## Forêt de Chinon

Northeast of Chinon, the elevated terrain of the landes is covered by the ancient **Forêt de Chinon**, which makes for great cycling and walking territory. If you want to stay in the area, base yourself at the *chambre d'hotes* near Rigny-Ussé (see p.401).

## Tavant

Sixteen kilometres southeast of Chinon is the village of **TAVANT** which hides the great **St-Nicolas church** (April–Sept Wed–Sun 10am–12.30pm & 2.15–6pm; March, Oct & Nov Mon–Fri, same hours, crypt €3). The appeal lies in the twelfth-century Romanesque wall paintings in its crypt, which rank among the finest in Europe. It's not clear why this crypt was so richly painted, as it hasn't been identified with any major relic cult or tomb. It's thought that the entire structure, inside and out, would once have been painted in bright colours, but today just fragments survive in the upper church, as well as a giant figure of Christ in Majesty on the half-dome of the apse. If the chapel isn't open when you arrive, ask for the guardian at the nearby *mairie*.

# Saumur and around

**SAUMUR** is a good-sized town notable for two things in particular: its excellent **sparkling wine** (some would say as good as Champagne) and the wealth of aristocratic **military** associations, based on its status as home to the French Cavalry Academy and its successor, the Armoured Corps Academy.

The stretch of the Loire from Chinon to Angers, which passes through Saumur, is particularly lovely, with the added draw of the bizarre troglodyte dwellings carved out of the cliffs. The land on the south bank, under grapes and sunflowers, gradually rises away from the river, with long-inactive windmills still standing. Across the water cows graze in wooded pastures.

## The château

April–May & Sept to early Nov Tues–Sun 10am–1pm & 2–5.30pm • €5 • June & Aug Tues–Sun 10am–6.30pm • €9 • **Son et lumière** July & Aug Thurs–Sat 10.30pm • Adult €18, child €14 • ☎ 02 41 83 31 31, ⓦ chateau-saumur.com

Set high above town, Saumur's impressive **château** may seem oddly familiar, but then its famous depiction in *Les Très Riches Heures du Duc de Berry*, the most celebrated of all the medieval illuminated prayer books, is reproduced all over the region. It was largely built in the latter half of the fourteenth century by Louis I, Duc d'Anjou, who wanted to compete with his brothers Jean de Berry and Charles V. The threat of marauding bands of English soldiers made the masons work flat out – they weren't even allowed to stop for feast days.

Part of the château has been closed since April 2001, when a huge chunk of the star-shaped outer fortifications collapsed down the hill towards the river. In the aftermath, the alarmed authorities decided to embark on a major renovation programme. However, the first floor of the north wing is open and shows a collection of decorative and fine arts.

## Notre-Dame de Nantilly and the church of St-Pierre

Down by the public gardens south of the château, Saumur's oldest church, **Notre-Dame de Nantilly** (daily 9am–6pm, closes 5pm in winter; ☎02 41 83 30 31), houses a large tapestry collection in its Romanesque nave, which is put on display in the summer. The original Gothic church of **St-Pierre**, in the centre of the Old Town, is closed for renovation works; once it re-opens it's worth taking a look at the Counter-Reformation facade, built as part of the church's efforts to overawe its persistently Protestant population – Louise de Bourbon, abbess of Fontevraud, called the town a "second Geneva", horrified at the thought that Saumur might become a similarly radical Calvinist power base.

## Musée des Blindés

1043 rte de Fontevraud • Daily: Jan–April & Oct–Dec Mon–Fri 10am–5pm, Sat & Sun 11am–6pm; May, June, Sept daily 10am–6pm; July & Aug daily 9.30am–6.30pm • Free guided tours throughout July & Aug • €7.50, "photo pass" €5 • ☎ 02 41 83 69 95, ⓦ museedesblindes.fr

The history of the tank – traditionally considered as cavalry not infantry – is covered in the **Musée des Blindés**, to the southeast of Saumur's centre. Around 250 vehicles are on display in an exhibition room showing tanks from 1917 to present day. Note you need to buy a "photo pass" if you want to take pictures inside.

## St-Hilaire-St-Florent

To get to St-Hilaire-St-Florent, take bus #5 from rue Portail Louis and ask for stop "Petit Souper/ENE"

A large number of manufacturers of the famous Saumur sparkling wine cluster in the suburb of **St-Hilaire-St-Florent**, and are especially prominent along the main stretch of the riverside road, along rue Ackerman and rue Leopold-Palustre: particularly good cellars include Ackerman-Laurance, Bouvet-Ladubay, Langlois-Château, Gratien & Meyer, Louis de Grenelle and Veuve Amiot; choosing between them is a matter of personal taste, and possibly a question of opening hours, though most are open all day every day throughout the warmer months (generally 10am–6pm, though most close for a couple of hours at lunchtime out of season). Buy a couple of bottles to take away, and you'll probably be impressed by both the taste and the price difference between this inexpensive wine and champagne.

Saumur's cavalry heritage is displayed in all its glory at the **École Nationale d'Équitation** (closed Sat afternoon, Sun, Mon morning and holidays: mid-Feb to March tours at 9.30am, 11am, 2pm & 4pm; April to mid-Oct tours every 30min 9.30–11.30am & 2–4pm; €7; ☎02 41 53 50 50, ⓦcadrenoir.fr), just south of St-Hilaire-St Florent at BP 207, Terrefort. The Riding School provides guided tours during which you can watch training sessions (mornings are best but there are none on the weekend in August) and

7

view the stables. Displays of dressage and anachronistic battle manoeuvres by the crackshot Cadre Noir, the former cavalry trainers, are regular events.

## ARRIVAL AND DEPARTURE
SAUMUR

**By train** The *gare SNCF* is on Saumur's north bank: turn right onto avenue David-d'Angers and either take bus #30 to the centre or cross the bridge to the island on foot.
Destinations Angers (frequent; 30min); Nantes (frequent; 60–90min); Tours (frequent; 40min).

**By bus** The *gare routière* is situated on the south bank, on place Balzac.

## INFORMATION

**Tourist office** 8bis Quai Carnot (mid-May to mid-Oct Mon–Sat 9.15am–7pm, Sun 10.30am–5.30pm; mid-Oct to mid-May Mon–Sat 9.15am–12.30pm & 2–6pm, Sun 10am–noon; ☎ 02 41 40 20 60, ⓦ saumur-tourisme.com). The old quarter, around St-Pierre and the castle, lies immediately behind the Hôtel de Ville, on the riverbank just east of the bridge.
**Useful website** ⓦ ville-saumur.fr

**Maison des Vins** 7 quai Carnot (May–Sept Mon 2–7pm, Tues–Sat 9.30am–1pm & 2–7pm, Sun 10.30am–1pm; Oct–April Tues–Fri 10.30am–12.30pm, 3–6pm, Sat 10.30am–12.30pm, 2.30–6.30pm; closed mid-Jan to mid-Feb, plus May 1, Dec 25, Jan 1; free to individuals, groups €2; ☎ 02 41 38 45 83, ⓦ vinsdeloire.fr). The Maison provides addresses of wine growers and *caves* to visit.

## ACCOMMODATION

**Anne d'Anjou** 32 quai Mayaud ☎ 02 41 67 30 30, ⓦ hotel-anneanjou.com. Comfortable hotel, with a wide range of attractively decorated, if rather uniform, rooms in a grand eighteenth-century listed building. The rooms at the back have exceptional château views and are quiet. Breakfast €13.50. **€115**

**Camping de l'Île d'Offard** Rue de Verden, Île d'Offard ☎ 02 41 40 30 00, ⓦ flowercampings.com. Large well-run site right next door to the hostel. March to mid-Nov. **€13**

★ **Château de Verrières** 53 rue Alsace ☎ 02 41 38 05 15, ⓦ châteauchâteau-verrieres.com. One of the finest buildings in the town is given over to this exceptional B&B. The rooms are ornate and lavish, the atmosphere luxurious, there's a little garden to potter around and a terrace on which to enjoy a glass of the local sparkling wine. No restaurant, but meals are prepared for groups by special request. Breakfast €15, free parking. **€170**

**Hostel Rue de Verden** Île d'Offard ☎ 02 41 40 30 00, ⓦ flowercampings.com. Large hostel at the east end of the island with laundry facilities, swimming-pool access and views of the château. Breakfast included. Reception 9am–noon & 2.30–7pm. Closed Nov–Feb. Dorms **€16.20**, singles **€24.50**

**St-Pierre** 8 rue Haute-St-Pierre ☎ 02 41 50 33 00, ⓦ saintpierresaumur.com. Charming boutique hotel in a refurbished seventeenth-century stone building, just around the corner from the busy main square, with individually decorated rooms complete with chandeliers and fireplaces. Breakfast €13. **€115**

**Le Volney** 1 rue Volney ☎ 02 41 51 25 41, ⓦ levolney .com This simple budget hotel on the south side of town has cheerful management and some inexpensive but cosy little rooms under the roof. Some rooms have shared showers. Breakfast €7.50. **€45**

## EATING AND DRINKING

**L'Alchimiste** 6 rue Lorraine ☎ 02 41 67 65 18. Exceptionally good gastronomic restaurant specializing in local and seasonal foods offering unbelievable value. If it's a warm night, they put tables outside on the road on a little strip of astroturf. Try the sweet digestifs – the *whisky carambar* is delicious. *Menus* from €16. Daily 12.15–1.30pm & 7.30–9pm, closed Sun lunch.

**Auberge Reine de Sicile** 71 rue Waldeck-Rousseau, Île d'Offard ☎ 02 41 67 30 48. This is over the bridge on the Île d'Offard, and has an atmospherically ancient dining room. Stick to the excellent local fish and you're unlikely to be disappointed. *Menus* at €19–35. Tues–Sat noon–1.15pm & 7.15–9.15pm.

**Bistrot Les TonTons** 1 place Saint-Pierre ☎ 02 41 59 59 40, ⓦ bistrotlestontons-saumur.blogspot.com. The place to go to enjoy charcuterie (from €18) and cheese

plates at any time, plus a delicious selection of grills and seasonal dishes. The portions are more than generous – the foie gras starter feeds at least two greedy people – and there's a superb wine list as the owner also offer wine tours and tastings of the wonderful Domaine de la Paleine. Tues–Sat noon–2pm & 7–10pm.

**Le Grand Bleu** 6 rue du Marché ☎ 02 41 67 41 83. Specializes in sea fish – Brittany is, after all, not so far away. Pleasant situation on a miniature square, with outside seating in summer. *Menus* €15–27. Daily noon–2pm & 7–9pm.

**Le Pot de Lapin** 35 rue Rabelais ☎ 02 41 67 12 86. Relaxed, contemporary bistro-restaurant on the way out towards the church of Notre-Dame des Ardilliers. There's a sleek bar area, a pleasant summer terrace and a focus on fresh game and tapas. Mains around €12. Tues–Sat lunch & dinner.

## The Abbaye de Fontevraud

Late Jan to early April & Sept to early Nov daily except Mon 10am–5pm; early April to June daily 9.30am–6.30pm; July & Aug daily 9.30am–7.30pm; early Nov to Dec daily except Mon 10am–5pm; closed most of Jan • €9 • ☎ 02 41 51 73 52, ⓦ abbayedefontevraud.com • Bus #1 runs from Saumur to Fontevraud, but it's not a frequent service and certain times have to be booked in advance (see ⓦ agglobus.fr)

At the heart of the stunning Romanesque complex of the **Abbaye de Fontevraud**, 13km southeast of Saumur, are the tombs of the Plantagenet royal family, eerily lifelike works of funereal art that powerfully evoke the historical bonds between England and France. A religious community was established in around 1100 as both a nunnery and a monastery with an abbess in charge – an unconventional move, even if the post was filled solely by queens and princesses. The remaining buildings date from the twelfth century and are immense, built as they were to house and separate not only the nuns and monks but also the sick, lepers and repentant prostitutes. There were originally five separate institutions, of which three still stand in graceful Romanesque solidity. In 1804 Napoleon decided to transform the building into a prison which continued till 1963. It was an inspiration for the writer Jean Genet, whose book *Miracle of the Rose* was partly based on the recollections of a prisoner incarcerated here.

The abbey church is an impressive space, not least for the four tombstone **effigies**: Henry II, his wife Eleanor of Aquitaine, who died here, their son Richard the Lionheart and daughter-in-law Isabelle of Angoulême, King John's queen. The strange domed roof, the great cream-coloured columns of the choir and the graceful capitals of the nave add to the atmosphere. Elsewhere in the complex you can explore the magnificent cloisters, the chapterhouse, decorated with sixteenth-century murals, and the vast refectory. All the cooking for the religious community, which would have numbered several hundred, was done in the – now perfectly restored – Romanesque kitchen, an octagonal building as extraordinary from the outside (with its 21 spikey chimneys) as it is from within.

**7**

### INFORMATION

**Tourist office** Place Saint-Michel (April Tues–Sat 9am–1pm & 2.30–6pm; May Tues–Sat 9.30am–1pm & 2.30–6pm, Sun & holidays 10.30am–1pm; June Mon–Sat 9.30am–1pm, 2–6.30pm, Sun & holidays 10.30am–1pm & 2.30–5pm; July & Aug Mon–Sat 9.30am–1pm & 2–7pm, Sun & holidays 10am–1pm, 2–7pm; early to mid-Sept Mon–Sat 9.30am–1pm, 2.30–5pm, Sun 10.30am–2.30–5pm; mid to late-Sept Mon–Sat

### ABBAYE DE FONTEVRAUD

9.30am–1pm & 4.30–6pm; closed Oct to Easter; ☎ 02 41 51 79 45, ⓦ saumur-tourisme.com). The abbey is now the Centre Culturel de l'Ouest (CCO), the cultural centre for western France, and one of Europe's most important centres of medieval archeology; it is used for a great many activities, from concerts to lectures, art exhibitions and theatre. Programme details are available at the abbey or from the tourist office (see above).

### ACCOMMODATION AND EATING

**Croix Blanche** 7 place des Plantagenets ☎ 02 41 51 71 11, ⓦ hotel-croixblanche.com. Opposite the Abbaye, this historic seventeenth-century coaching inn with slate roofs and tufa walls has been bought bang up to date with boutique hotel-standard cosy rooms with colour-splash accented decor, bath robes and flatscreen TVs. You can have breakfast or a drink before dinner on the little sun-trap patio. There's a fine dining restaurant in the hotel, which is one of the best in the region, with an innovative chef whipping up delicious gourmet creations. The cod with a preserved-lemon risotto is particularly good. *Menus* €24–39. There's also a brasserie on site, which is open for lunch and dinner and serves classic French dishes *menus* from €19.50–23. **€75**

# Angers and around

**ANGERS**, capital of the ancient county of Anjou, is a hugely likeable, vibrant town which seems to happily straddle the ancient and modern worlds. For fans of heritage tourism, it has two stunning **tapestry** series, the fourteenth-century *Apocalypse* and the twentieth-century *Le Chant du Monde* and the **château**. Along with its interesting cultural aspects, the city has a strong collection of shops, bars and restaurants as well as some nightlife spots.

## The château and Apocalypse tapestry

Daily: May–Aug 9.30am–6.30pm; Sept–April 10am–5.30pm • €6.50 • Audioguide €4.50

The **Château d'Angers** is a formidable early medieval fortress. The sense of impregnability is accentuated by its dark stone, the purple-brown schist characteristic of western Anjou. The château's mighty kilometre-long curtain wall is reinforced by seventeen circular towers, their brooding stone offset by decorative bands of pale tufa. Inside are a few miscellaneous remains of the counts' royal lodgings and chapels, but the chief focus is the astonishing *Tapestry of the Apocalypse*. Woven between 1373 and 1382 for Louis I of Anjou, it was originally 140m long, of which 100m now survives. From the start, it was treated as a masterpiece, and only brought out to decorate the cathedral of Angers on major festival days. The sheer grandeur of the conception is overwhelming but the tapestry's reputation rests as much on its superb detail and stunning colours, preserved today by the very low light levels in the long viewing hall. If you plan to follow the apocalypse story right through, the English-language audio guide comes in handy, but a Bible would be even better. In brief: the Day of Judgement is signalled by the breaking of the seven seals – note the four horsemen – and the seven angels blowing their trumpets. As the battle of Armageddon rages, Satan appears first as a seven-headed red dragon, then as the seven-headed lion-like Beast. The holy forces break the seven vials of plagues, whereupon the Whore of Babylon appears mounted on the Beast. She is challenged by the Word of God, seen riding a galloping horse, who chases the hordes of Satan into the lake of fire, allowing the establishment of the heavenly Jerusalem. It's spellbinding, operatic stuff, and will appeal whatever your religious views.

## The cathedral

The most dramatic approach to the **Cathédrale St-Maurice** is via the quayside, from where a long flight of steps leads straight up to the mid-twelfth-century portal, which shows another version of the apocalypse. Built in the 1150s and 1160s, the cathedral exemplifies the Plantagenet style – in fact, it's probably the earliest example in France of this influential architectural development. The interior is somewhat prosaic, but the fifteenth-century windows are impressive.

## Galerie David d'Angers

37bis rue Toussaint • June–Sept daily 10am–6.30pm; Oct–May Tues–Sun 10am–noon & 2–6pm • €4 • ☎ 02 41 05 38 00, Ⓦ musees-angers.fr

Arguably the greatest stoneworks in Angers are the creations of the famous local sculptor **David d'Angers** (1788–1856), whose *Calvary* adorns the cathedral. His great civic commissions can be seen all over France, but the large-scale marbles and bronzes on the cathedral are almost all copies of the smaller plaster of Paris works created by the artist himself. These plaster originals are exhibited in the **Galerie David d'Angers**, set impressively in the glazed-over nave of a ruined thirteenth-century church, the Église Toussaint.

## Musée des Beaux-Arts

10 rue du Musée • June–Sept daily 10am–6.30pm; Oct–May Tues–Sun 10am–noon & 2–6pm • €4

The **Musée des Beaux-Arts** is housed in the Logis Barrault, a proudly decorated mansion built by a wealthy late fifteenth-century mayor. Eighteenth- and nineteenth-century paintings dominate the collection, with works by Watteau, Chardin and Fragonard, as well as Ingres' operatic *Paolo et Francesca* – the same subject depicted by Rodin in *The Kiss* – and a small collection devoted to Boucher's *Les génies des Arts*.

## La Doutre

The district facing the château across the Maine is known as **La Doutre** (literally, "the other side"), and still has a few mansions and houses dating from the medieval period, despite redevelopment over the years.

### Musée Jean Lurçat et de la Tapisserie Contemporaine

In the north of La Doutre, is the **Hôpital St-Jean**, built by Henry Plantagenet in 1174 as a hospital for the poor, a function it continued to serve for nearly 700 years. Today it houses the **Musée Jean Lurçat et de la Tapisserie Contemporaine** (June–Sept daily 10am–6.30pm; Oct–May Tues–Sun 10am–noon & 2–6pm; €4) which contains the city's great twentieth-century tapestry, *Le Chant du Monde*. The tapestry sequence was designed by Jean Lurçat in 1957 in response to the Apocalypse tapestry, though he died nine years before its completion. It hangs in a vast vaulted space, the original ward for the sick, or **Salle des Malades.**

The first four tapestries deal with La Grande Menace, the threat of nuclear war: first the bomb itself; then Hiroshima Man, flayed and burnt with the broken symbols of belief dropping from him; then the collective massacre of the Great Charnel House; and the last dying rose falling with the post-Holocaust ash through black space – the End of Everything. From then on, the tapestries celebrate the joys of life: Man in Glory in Peace; Water and Fire; Champagne – "that blissful ejaculation", according to Lurçat; Conquest of Space; Poetry; and Sacred Ornaments. Subject matter and treatment are intense, and

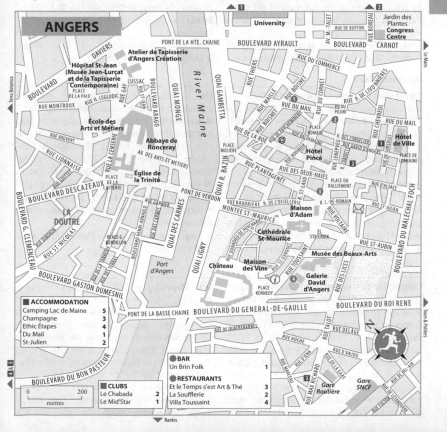

the setting helps: it's a huge echoey space, with rows of columns supporting soaring Angevin vaulting. The artist's own commentary is available in English. The Romanesque cloisters at the back, with their graceful double columns, are also worth a peek.

There are more modern tapestries in the building adjoining the Salle des Malades, where the collection includes several of Lurçat's paintings, ceramics and tapestries, along with the highly tactile but more muted abstract tapestries of Thomas Gleb and Josep Grau Garriga. With four local ateliers, Angers is a leading centre for contemporary tapestry. The neighbouring **Atelier de Tapisserie d'Angers Création** (☎02 41 88 31 92) can put you in touch with local artists and let you know where to find private exhibitions, though they are only open by appointment.

## Abbaye de Ronceray and Église de la Trinité

On La Doutre's central square, place de la Laiterie, is the church of the ancient **Abbaye de Ronceray** which is used to mount art exhibitions, and is worth visiting just to see the Romanesque galleries of the old abbey and admire their beautiful murals. When there's no exhibition, you can only visit as part of the tourist office's weekly tour of La Doutre; enquire at the tourist office (below). Inside the adjacent twelfth-century **Église de la Trinité**, an exquisite Renaissance wooden spiral staircase fails to mask a great piece of medieval bodging used to fit the wall of the church around a part of the abbey that juts into it.

### ARRIVAL AND DEPARTURE
ANGERS

**By train** The *gare SNCF* is just south of the centre, 1 Esplanade de la Gare. Trams run regularly from outside into town.
Destinations Le Mans (frequent; 36min–1hr 20min); Nantes (frequent; 40min); Paris (frequent; 1hr 40min); Saumur (frequent; 20–30min); Tours (frequent; 1hr–1hr 25min).

**By bus** The *gare routière* is near the train station on Place Pierre Semard.
Destinations Doué-la-Fontaine (5 daily; 50min); St-Georges-sur-Loire (3 daily; 45min).

### INFORMATION

**Tourist office** Place Kennedy (May–Sept Mon 10am–7pm, Tues–Sat 9.30am–7pm, Sun 10am–6pm; Oct–April Mon 2–6pm, Tues–Sat 10am–6pm, Sun 10am–1pm; ☎02 41 23 50 00, ⓦangersloiretourisme.com), facing the château; it sells a city pass (€12.50 for 24hr, €22 for 48hr), which allows access to the tapestries as well as the city's museums, galleries and other tourist spots.

**Festivals and events** Throughout summer, during the Festival Tempo Rives (ⓦtemporives.fr), there are free outdoor concerts performed on the Maine riverbanks, near le Quai theatre, opposite the castle, featuring everything from electro and rock to disco and reggae. In early Sept, the festival Les Accroche Coeurs (ⓦangers.fr/accrochecoeurs) brings in a host of theatrical companies, musicians and street performers for three days of surreal entertainment.

**Maison des Vins** Just across from the castle and a minute from the Tourist office centre, Maison des Vins de Loire (5bis place Kennedy; April Tues–Sat 10am–1pm & 2.30–6.30pm; May–Sept Mon 2.30–7pm, Tues–Sat 10am–12.30pm & 2.30–7pm; Oct–March Tues–Fri 10.30am–12.30pm & 3–6pm, Sat 2.30–6.30pm), is staffed with helpful wine experts, who can guide you through tastings and can provide lists of local wine growers and *caves* to visit.

**Listings** check local *What's On Le Chabada* (ⓦlechabada .com) for details.

### ACCOMMODATION

**Camping Lac de Maine** 49 av du Lac de Maine ☎02 41 73 05 03, lacdemaine.fr. Agreeably situated next to a lake, across from *Ethic Étapes*, complete with extensive sports facilities and heated pool. Closed Oct–March. **€14.20**

**Champagne** 34 av Denis Papin ☎02 41 25 78 78, ⓦhoteldechampagne.com. Handily placed next to the bus station and across the street from the station, this two-star friendly hotel has modern bright rooms with splashes of colour. The rooms at the back are noisy, but have a/c so you can keep the windows closed. Breakfast €8.90. Special offers from €55. **€70**

**Ethic Étapes** Lac de Maine 49, av du lac de Maine ☎02 41 22 32 10, ⓦethic-etapes-angers.fr. No frills but reliable budget youth and group hostel chain, with rooms sleeping up to 4, situated a short distance from town in a 200-acre park. From the train station, take the Line 6 bus (stop "Lac de Maine Accueil") or the Line 11 (stop "Pérussaie"). It's Line 1S bus in the evening, and Line 1D on Sundays and holidays. Breakfast €4.95. **€46.50**

★ **Du Mail** 8 rue des Ursules ☎02 41 25 05 25, ⓦhotel-du-mail.com. The ultramodern foyer with its trompe l'oeil painting behind the reception desk is a

misleading precursor to the cosy, simple and inexpensive rooms. There's a leafy terrace to enjoy an *apéro* in the courtyard. Parking available for €6. Breakfast €10. **€65**
**St-Julien** 9 place du Ralliement ☎02 41 88 41 62, ⓦhotelsaintjulien.com Large hotel right in the centre of

the city, on the large square a few steps away from the tram stop (Place du Ralliement). There is a decent choice of rooms available and some of the pretty little ones under the roof have views over the square (room 439 has the best). It's cosy and the staff are friendly. Breakfast €9. **€66**

## EATING

**Et le temps s'est art & thé** 7 rue Chaperonnière ☎02 41 34 06 31. Superb café serving flavoured coffees, artisan hot chocolate and more than 40 varieties of tea. Quiches and salads are well-priced and the mini-cakes are a particularly cute touch: enjoy them while curled up in one of the comfy chesterfields hidden at the back of the shop. Mon 3–6.30pm, Tues–Sat 10am–7pm.
**La Soufflerie** 8 place du Pilori ☎02 41 87 45 32. Popular café specializing in soufflés, both large and savoury (at around €12) and small and sweet (around €10). Closed

Sun, Mon & 4 weeks in July/Aug. Tues–Sat noon–2pm & 7–10pm.
**Villa Toussaint** 43 rue Toussaint ☎02 41 88 15 64. Funky restaurant around the corner from the château, focusing on Asian-themed dishes as well as some excellent puddings – The *cremet d'Anjou* (a local delicacy of whipped fromage blanc, cream and vanilla) is just delicious. There's a leafy terrace – with a tree squarely in the centre – which makes for a lovely spot in summer. Tues & Wed noon–2pm & 7.15–10.30pm, Thurs–Sat noon–2pm & 7.15–11pm.

## DRINKING AND NIGHTLIFE

**Un Brin Folk** 26 rue du Mail ☎02 44 85 58 04. Stripped-down hipster bar, playing an excellent playlist of anything from old-skool country to new-skool breaks, this is one of the few places open for food on a Monday. Serves an eclectic menu of piled-high *tartines* with toppings from smoked duck to local organic cheese, plus a wide range of desert specials. Once a month there are live music nights. Arrive after 8pm to stoke up before clubbing. Mon–Fri noon–2.30pm & 7–11pm.

**Le Chabada** 56 bd du Doyenné ⓦlechabada.com.Try this spot for less mainstream music; they have plenty of live music events – pick up their quarterly magazine for listings. Daily till late.
**Le Mid'Star** 25 quai Félix-Faure ⓦmidstar.fr. The biggest and best-known clubbing venue, playing electro, pop and disco. Free for women Thurs–Sat (before 2am); €9–10 Thurs–Sat for men; free for all on Sun. Thurs–Sun till late.

## DIRECTORY

**Bike hire** The tourist office (see p.410) rents out bikes.
**Boat hire** Numerous companies hire out canoes and run guided kayak trips on the five rivers in the vicinity of Angers. Try: Canoe Kayak Club d'Angers, 75 av du Lac de Maine (on the Maine and Lac de Maine) ☎02 41 72 07 04, ⓦckca.fr; Club Nautique d'Écouflant, rue de l'Île St-Aubin, Écouflant (Sarthe, Mayenne, Loire, Maine) ☎02 41 34 56 38, kayakecouflant.com; and Club de Canoe Kayak les Ponts de Cé, 30 rue Maximin-Gélineau, Les Ponts de Cé (on the Loire) ☎02 41 44 65 15, ⓦcanoe-kayak-lespontsdece.fr.

The tourist office has details of more sedate trips on sightseeing boats.
**Car hire** Avis, Gare SNCF ☎02 41 88 20 24; Europcar, Gare SNCF ☎02 41 87 87 10; Hertz, Gare SNCF ☎02 41 88 15 16.
**Market** There's a flower market on place Leclerc and an organic produce market on place Molière, both on Sat.
**Police** Commissariat, 15 rue Dupetit-Thouars ☎02 41 43 98 38.
**Health** Ambulance ☎15; Centre Hospitalier, 4 rue Larrey (☎02 41 35 36 37); for late-night pharmacies, phone ☎3915.

# Château du Plessis-Bourré

Mid-Feb to end March, Oct & Nov daily except Wed 2–6pm; April–June & Sept Mon, Tues & Fri–Sun 10am–noon & 2–6pm, Thurs 2–6pm; July & Aug daily 10am–6pm; closed Dec–Feb • €9.50 • ⓦplessis-bourre.com • No public transport

Five years' work at the end of the fifteenth century produced the fortress of **Le Plessis-Bourré**, between the Sarthe and Mayenne rivers. Despite the vast, full moat, spanned by an arched bridge with a still-functioning drawbridge, it was built as a luxurious residence rather than a defensive castle. The treasurer of France at the time, Jean Bourré, received important visitors here, among them Louis XI and Charles VIII.

Given the powerful medieval exterior, the first three rooms on the ground floor come as a surprise; they are beautifully decorated and furnished in the Louis XVI, XV and Régence styles, respectively, though things revert to type in the Gothic Salle du Parlement. The highlight of the tour comes in the Salle des Gardes, just above, where the original, deeply coffered ceiling stems from Bourré's fashionable interest in alchemy. Every inch is painted with allegorical scenes: sixteen panels depict alchemical symbols such as the phoenix, the pregnant siren and the donkey singing Mass, while eight cartoon-like paintings come with morals attached – look out for "Chicheface", the hungry wolf that only eats faithful women, whose victim is supposed to be Jean Bourré's wife.

## Château de Serrant

Guided tours only, departing on the hour; mid-March to June & mid-Sept to mid-Nov Wed–Sat 1.30–5.15pm, Sun & holidays 9.45am–noon & 1.30–5.15pm; June to mid-Sept daily 9.45am–5.15pm. English-speaking tour 1pm (July & Aug) • €9.50 • ⓦ chateau-serrant.net • To get there, take the infrequent #7 bus from Angers – the tourist office (see p.410) has timetables

At the Château de Serrant, 15km west of Angers beside the N23 near **ST-GEORGES-SUR-LOIRE**, the combination of dark-brown schist and creamy tufa give a rather pleasant cake-like effect to the exterior. But with its heavy slate bell-shaped cupolas pressing down on massive towers, the exterior is grandiose rather than graceful. The building was begun in the sixteenth century and added to up until the eighteenth century. In 1755 it belonged to an Irishman, Francis Walsh, to whom Louis XV had given the title Count of Serrant as a reward for Walsh's help against the old enemy, the English. The Walsh family married into the ancient La Trémoille clan, whose descendants – via a Belgian offshoot – still own the château. The massive rooms of the interior are packed with all the trappings of old wealth. Much of the decor dates from the late nineteenth and early twentieth centuries, but it's tastefully – and expensively – done, and you are also shown the Renaissance staircase, the sombre private chapel designed by Mansart, a bedroom prepared for Napoleon (who only stopped here for a couple of hours), and the attractive vaulted kitchens.

# Nantes and around

Over the last decade, the rejuvenated, go-ahead city of **NANTES** has transformed itself into a likeable metropolis that deserves to figure on any tourist itinerary. At the heart of this ambitious regeneration project stands a must-see attraction, the **Machines de l'Île** – home of the Grand Éléphant – but the city as a whole is also scrubbed, gleaming, and suffused with a remarkable energy.

As the capital of an independent Brittany, Nantes was a considerable medieval centre. Great wealth came later, however, with the growth of Atlantic trade; by the end of the eighteenth century, it was the principal port of France. An estimated 500,000 Africans were carried into **slavery** in the Americas in vessels based here, and even after abolition in 1817 the trade continued illegally. Subsequently the port declined, and heavy industry and wine production became more important. For fifty years now, since it was transferred to the Pays de la Loire in 1962, Nantes has no longer even been in Brittany.

Recent redevelopment schemes have shifted the focus of the city back towards the **Loire** itself. For visitors, nonetheless, once you've seen the machines, the main areas you're likely to spend time in are the older **medieval city**, concentrated around the cathedral, with the **Château des Ducs** prominent in its southeast corner, and the elegant **nineteenth-century town** to the west.

## Château des Ducs

**Courtyard and ramparts** July & Aug Mon–Fri & Sun 9am–8pm, Sat 9am–11pm; Sept–June daily 10am–7pm • Free **Musée d'Histoire de Nantes** July & Aug daily 10am–7pm, Sept–June daily except Mon 10am–6pm • €5, €8 combined with temporary exhibitions • ☎ 08 11 46 46 44 • ⓦ chateau-nantes.fr

Though no longer on the waterfront, the **Château des Ducs** still preserves the form in

**CLOCKWISE FROM TOP LEFT** CAFÉS IN TOURS (P.395); DETAIL FROM THE TAPESTRY OF THE APOCALYPSE (P.408); CHÂTEAU D'AMBOISE (P.396) >

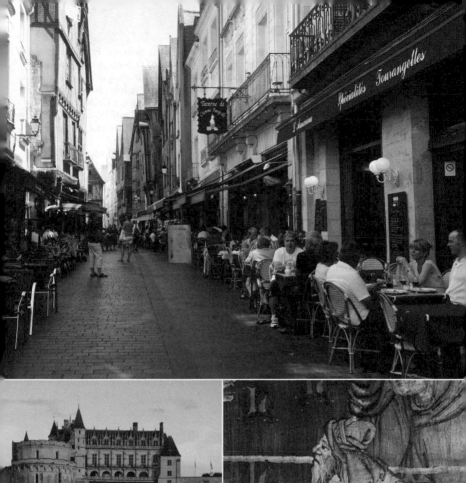

which it was built by two of the last rulers of independent Brittany, François II, and his daughter Duchess Anne, born here in 1477. The list of famous people who have been guests or prisoners, defenders or belligerents, of the castle includes Gilles de Rais (Bluebeard), publicly executed in 1440; Machiavelli, in 1498; John Knox as a galley-slave in 1547–49; and Bonnie Prince Charlie preparing for Culloden in 1745. In addition, the **Edict of Nantes** was signed here in 1598 by Henri IV, ending the Wars of Religion by granting a degree of toleration to the Protestants. It had far more crucial consequences when it was revoked, by Louis XIV, in 1685.

The stout **ramparts** of the château remain pretty much intact, and most of the encircling moat is filled with water, surrounded by well-tended lawns that make a popular spot for lunchtime picnics. Visitors can pass through the walls, and also stroll atop them for fine views over the city, for no charge.

The incongruous potpourri of buildings that encircle the courtyard within includes a major exhibition space used for year-long displays on differing subjects; the pleasant *Oubliettes* café/restaurant (see p.417); and the high-tech **Musée d'Histoire de Nantes**. The latter covers local history in exhaustive detail. Highlights include a fascinating scale model of the city in the thirteenth century, and a determined attempt to come to terms with Nantes' slave-trading past, displaying pitiful trinkets used to buy slaves in Africa.

## Cathédrale de St-Pierre-et-St-Paul

The fifteenth-century **Cathédrale de St-Pierre-et-St-Paul** has had an unfortunate history. It was used as a barn during the Revolution, while in 1800 the Spaniards Tower, the arsenal of the château 200m south, exploded and shattering its stained glass. The building was then bombed during World War II, and damaged by fire in 1972. Restored and reopened, its soaring height and lightness are emphasized by its clean white stone. It contains the tomb of François II and his wife Margaret – with symbols of Power, Strength and Justice for him and Fidelity, Prudence and Temperance for her.

## Musée des Beaux-Arts

10 rue Clemenceau • Mon, Wed & Fri–Sun 10am–6pm, Thurs 10am–8pm • €3.50, €2 after 4.30pm • ☎ 02 51 17 45 00, ⓦ museedesbeauxarts.nantes.fr

Nantes' **Musée des Beaux-Arts**, east of the cathedral, has a respectable compilation and good temporary exhibitions. Highlights of its permanent collection include *David Triumphant* by Delaunay, Chagall's *Le Cheval Rouge* and Monet's *Nymphéas*. It was closed for extensive restoration as this book went to press; check the website for the latest news.

## The nineteenth-century town

The financier Graslin took charge of the development of the western part of Nantes in the 1780s, when the city was at its richest. **Place Royale**, with its distinctive fountain, was laid out at the end of the eighteenth century, and has been rebuilt since it was bombed in 1943; the 1780s also produced the nearby **place Graslin**, with the elaborately styled **Grand Théâtre**, whose Corinthian portico contrasts with the 1895 Art Nouveau of the not-to-be-missed *La Cigale* brasserie (see p.417) on the corner.

The **Musée d'Histoire Naturelle**, west of the place Graslin at 12 rue voltaire (daily except Tues 10am–6pm; €4; ☎ 02 40 41 55 00, ⓦ nantes.fr), is a Victorian-era anachronism were among the eccentric assortment of oddities you'll find rhinoceros toenails, a coelecanth, an Aepyornis egg and an Egyptian mummy. There's even a complete tanned human skin, taken in 1793 from the body of a soldier whose dying wish was to be made into a drum.

7

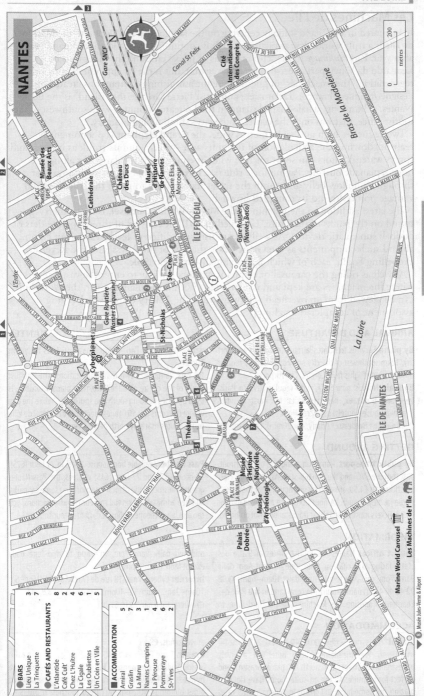

NANTES

BARS
Lieu Unique 3
La Trinquette 7

CAFÉS AND RESTAURANTS
L'Atlantide 8
Café Cult' 2
Chez L'Huître 4
La Cigale 6
Les Oubliettes 1
Un Coin en Ville 5

ACCOMMODATION
Amiral 5
Graslin 7
La Manu 3
Nantes Camping 1
La Pérouse 4
Pommeraye 6
St-Yves 2

## Les Machines de l'Île

Inaugurated in 2007, and initially centring on the fabulous **Grand Éléphant**, the **Machines de l'Île** is a truly world-class attraction, which is continuing to develop and expand year after year. Part *hommage* to the sci-fi creations of Jules Verne and the blueprints of Leonardo da Vinci, part street-theatre extravaganza, this is the lynchpin of Nantes' urban regeneration. The "machines" in question are the astonishing contraptions created by designer/engineer François Delarozière and artist Pierre Orefice; the "island" is the Île de Nantes, a 3km-long, whale-shaped island in the Loire, ten minutes' walk southwest of the tourist office, that was once the centre of the city's shipbuilding industry.

Twelve metres high and eight metres wide, the **Grand Éléphant** is phenomenally realistic, down to the articulation of its joints as it "walks", and its trunk as it flexes and sprays water. Visitors can see it for free when it emerges for regular walks along the huge esplanade outside. Paying for a ride (see box opposite) enables you to wander through its hollow belly and climb the spiral stairs within to reach the balconies and vantage points around its canopied howdah.

The latest addition to the machines, the **Marine Worlds Carousel**, is a vast merry-go-round on the banks of the Loire. Unveiled in 2012, it consists of three separate tiers of oddball subaquatic devices. As well as exploring the different levels, riders can climb aboard such components as the Giant Crab, the Bus of the Abyss, and the Reverse-Propelling Squid, each of which is individually manoeuvrable.

As well as riding the carousel or elephant, visitors can pay to enter the vast hangars where the machines are kept and constructed. Within the main hangar, the **Workshop** can be viewed from an overhead walkway, while the **Gallery** displays a changing assortment of completed machines.

### ARRIVAL AND DEPARTURE                                        NANTES

**By plane** Services to Nantes' airport (w nantes.aeroport .fr), 12km southwest of the city and connected by regular buses, include flights from London City Airport.

**By train** Nantes' *gare SNCF*, with regular TGVs to Paris, Lyon and Bordeaux, has two exits; for most facilities (tramway, buses, hotels) use Accès Nord.

Destinations Bordeaux (2 daily; 4hr 20min); Le Croisic (10

daily; 1hr 10min); Paris-Montparnasse (6 TGVs daily; 2hr 10min).

**By bus** Nantes has two main bus stations. The one just south of the centre on allée Baco, near place Ricordeau, is used by buses heading south and southwest, while the one where the cours des 50 Otages meets rue de l'Hôtel de Ville serves routes that stay north of the river.

### GETTING AROUND

**By public transport** Trams run along the old riverfront, past the *gare SNCF* and the two bus stations (w tan.fr). Flat-fare tickets, at €1.50, are valid for one hour, rather than just a single journey, though 24-hour tickets are also available for €4.30. Tickets must be bought at tram stations, not on board.

**Pass Nantes** Available from tourist offices in 24-hour (€25), 48-hour (€35) and 72-hour (€45) versions, the Pass Nantes grants unrestricted use of local transport and some car parks, and free admission to several museums and attractions; you can also buy it cheaper online at w nantes-tourisme.com.

### INFORMATION

**Tourist offices** Nantes has tourist offices at 9 rue des États, facing the château (mid-June to mid-Aug daily 9am–7pm, mid-Aug to mid-June daily 10am–6pm; ☏ 08 92 46 40 44, w nantes-tourisme.com), and in the Parc des Chantiers alongside the Machines de l'Île (mid-June to

mid-Aug daily 9am–7pm, mid-Aug to mid-June daily except Mon 11am–7pm).

**Internet** Cyberpl@net, 18 rue de l'Arche Sèche (Mon–Sat 10am–2am, Sun 2–10pm; ☏02 51 82 47 97, w cyberplanet-nantes.fr; €3/hr).

### ACCOMMODATION

**Amiral** 26bis rue Scribe ☏02 40 69 20 21, w hotel -nantes.fr. Well-maintained little hotel on a lively pedestrianized street just north of place Graslin, and perfect for nightlife. All the en-suite rooms have double-glazing, but some noise still creeps in. Much cheaper rates

at weekends. **€84**

**Graslin** 1 rue Piron ☏02 40 69 72 91, w hotel-graslin .com. Stylish, inexpensive hotel in the city centre, a minute's walk south of place Graslin, in a re-modelled older building with some Art Deco touches. It offers 47 rooms arranged over five themed floors. Friendly management and good breakfasts, albeit served in a subterranean dining room. **€70**

**La Manu** 2 place de la Manufacture ☎02 40 29 29 20, ⓦfuaj.org/nantes. Nantes' hostel, which has a cafeteria, is housed in a postmodern former tobacco factory a few hundred metres east of the *gare SNCF*, five minutes from the centre on tramway #1. Beds in 4- or 6-bed dorms; rates include breakfast. Reception daily 8am–noon & 3.30–10.30pm, closed mid-Dec to early Jan. **€20.45**

**Nantes Camping** 21 bd du Petit-Port ☎02 40 74 47 94, ⓦnantes-camping.fr. Well-managed five-star campsite, with a pool, in a pleasant tree-shaded setting north of the city centre on tram route #2 (stop "Morrhonnière"). Open all year. **€25.60**

★ **La Pérouse** 3 allée Duquesne ☎02 40 89 75 00,

ⓦhotel-laperouse.fr. Superb contemporary building ingeniously integrated with the older architecture that surrounds it. The interior is decorated with 1930s furniture, stucco walls and high-tech touches like flatscreen TVs. An original, comfortable and friendly place to stay, with excellent breakfasts. **€79**

★ **Pommeraye** 2 rue Boileau ☎02 40 48 78 79, ⓦhotel-pommeraye.com. Extremely good-value modern boutique hotel with large, designer-decor rooms, beautiful bathrooms and free parking; good buffet breakfast for €10.40. **€81**

**St-Yves** 154 rue du Général Buat ☎02 40 74 48 42, ⓦhotel-saintyves.fr. Very attractive, great-value little ten-room hotel, a twenty-minute walk north of the railway station, with friendly staff, a nice garden and big breakfasts. **€55**

## EATING AND DRINKING

### CAFÉS AND RESTAURANTS

**L'Atlantide** Centre des Salorges, 16 quai Ernest-Renaud ☎02 40 73 23 23, ⓦrestaurant-atlantide.net. Designer restaurant, with big river views from the fourth floor of a modern block, serving the contemporary French cuisine of chef Jean-Yves Gueho. Fish is the speciality, but expect quirky twists like the bananas braised in beer. *Menus* €32–95. Mon–Fri noon–2pm & 8–9.45pm, Sat 8–9.45pm.

**Café Cult'** 2 rue des Carmes ☎02 40 47 18 49, ⓦcafe-cult.com. Friendly, good-value café housed in a beautiful old half-timbered house. They serve two-course lunches for just €13.50, dinner for €21, and cheap drinks later on, when it becomes a lively bar. Mon–Sat noon–2pm &7pm–2am.

**Chez L'Huître** 5 rue des Petites-Écuries ☎02 51 82 02 02. Much as the name suggests, this lovely little restaurant, with outdoor seating on a pedestrian street, specializes in

oysters of all sizes and provenance. The *apérihuître* consists of six oysters and a glass of Muscadet for €8; there's also a €18.50 set *menu*. Mon–Sat noon–2pm & 7–10.30pm, Sun noon–3pm & 7–10.30pm.

★ **La Cigale** 4 place Graslin ☎02 51 84 94 94, ⓦwww.lacigale.com. Fabulous *belle époque* brasserie, offering fine meals in opulent surroundings, with seating either at tiled terrace tables or in a more formal indoor dining room. Fish is a speciality, and assorted set *menus* are served until midnight. Daily 7.30am–12.30am.

**Les Oubliettes** 4 place Marc Elder ☎02 51 82 67 04, ⓦlesoubliettes.fr. Despite the address, this little daytime-only restaurant is splendidly and very spaciously set in the château courtyard, far from the traffic, with indoors and open-air seating. Breakfast, tea and good-value lunches, with large *plats* and specials for around €10. July & Aug daily 10am–8pm; Sept–June Tues–Sun 10am–6pm.

---

## MACHINES DE L'ÎLE TIMES AND TICKETS

Opening hours for the Machines de l'Île vary enormously throughout the year; check ⓦlesmachines-nantes.fr or ☎08 10 12 12 25 for up-to-date information.

**Early Jan to mid-Feb**: closed
**Mid-Feb to late April**: Tues–Fri 2–5pm, Sat & Sun 2–6pm.
**Late April to mid-June**: Tues–Fri 10am–5pm, Sat & Sun 10am–6pm.
**July & Aug**: daily 10am–7pm.
**Sept to early Nov**: Tues–Fri 10am–6 pm, Sat & Sun 10am–7pm.
**Early Nov to late Dec**: Tues–Fri 2–5pm, Sat & Sun 2–6pm.
**Late Dec to early Jan**: Wed–Sun 2–6pm.

**Tickets** for an elephant ride *or* the Marine Worlds Carousel *or* the gallery cost €7 for adults and €5.50 for under-18s. All tickets gives access to the Workshop. Rides cannot be reserved in advance; tickets are sold for same-day rides only, with a limit per elephant ride of 49 passengers. Provided those times fall within that day's opening hours, elephant rides are scheduled for 10.30am, 11.15am, noon, 12.45pm, 3.30pm, 4.15pm, 5pm & 5.45pm. Only the Gallery is free with the Pass Nantes (see p.416), and holders still have to queue. The ticket office shuts an hour before the site closes.

**Un Coin En Ville** 2 place de la Bourse ☎ 02 40 20 05 97, ⓦ uncoinenville.com. This hip, cellar-like restaurant serves classic French cuisine with a fusion edge. Lunchtime *plats* for around €10, or set lunch with carpaccio for €14; the full dinner *menu* is €27. Tues–Thurs noon–1.30pm & 7.30–11pm, Fri noon–1.30pm & 7.30–11.30pm, Sat 7.30–11.30pm.

### BARS AND VENUES

**Lieu Unique** Quai Ferdinand Favre ☎ 02 51 82 15 00, ⓦ www.lelieuunique.com. As unique as its name proclaims, this former LU biscuit factory now plays host to concerts, theatre, dance, art exhibitions, a bookshop, a fair brasserie and a great bar. Mon 11am–8pm, Tues–Thurs 11am–midnight, Fri & Sat 11am–3am, Sun 3–8pm.

**La Trinquette** 3 quai de la Fosse ☎ 02 51 72 39 05. This youthful central bar, with friendly English-speaking owners, serves *tartines* and *croques monsieur* to go with its fine *aperitifs*, and gets especially lively on market day, Sat, when DJs play. Mon–Fri 8.30am–10pm, Sat 7.30am–8pm.

# Guérande

About 80km west of Nantes (an hour or so's drive), the wonderful walled town of **GUÉRANDE** stands on the southwestern edge of the Grande-Brière marshes. Guérande derived its fortune from controlling the saltpans that form a chequerboard across the surrounding inlets. This "white country" is composed of bizarre-looking *oeillets*, each 70 to 80 square metres, in which sea water has been collected and evaporated since Roman times, leaving piles of white salt.

A tiny little place, Guérande is still entirely enclosed by its stout fifteenth-century **ramparts**. A spacious promenade leads right the way around the outside, passing four fortified gateways; for half its length, the broad old moat remains filled with water. Within the walls, pedestrians throng the narrow cobbled streets during high season; the main souvenir on sale is locally produced salt, but abundant shops sell trinkets from all over the world, and there are lots of restaurants and crêperies. So long as the crowds aren't too oppressive, it makes a great day out, with the old houses bright with window-boxes. On Wednesdays and Saturdays, a market is in full swing in the centre, next to the **church of St-Aubin**.

### INFORMATION                                                    GUÉRANDE

**Tourist office** 1 place du Marché aux Bois, just outside the Porte St-Michel (June & Sept Mon–Sat 9.30am–6pm; July & Aug Mon–Sat 9.30am–7pm; Oct–May Mon–Sat 9.30am–12.30pm & 1.30–6pm; ☎ 08 20 15 00 44, ⓦ ot-guerande.fr).

### ACCOMMODATION

★ **La Guérandière** 5 rue Vannetaise ☎ 02 40 62 17 15, ⓦ guerande.fr. Hugely attractive four-room B&B, in a beautifully restored and decorated manor house beside the Porte Vannetaise in the old town. Breakfast is served in a pleasant garden. **€82**

★ **Roc-Maria** 1 rue des Halles ☎ 02 40 24 90 51, ⓦ hotel-creperie-rocmaria.com. This pretty fifteenth-century townhouse, tucked out of sight behind the market, offers nine cosy rooms above a crêperie, plus a delightful garden. Closed Mon in low season. **€64**

# Piriac-sur-mer

Still readily recognizable as an old fishing village, but lively all through summer with holidaying families, **PIRIAC-SUR-MER**, 13km west of Guérande, is a ravishing old-fashioned seaside resort that knocks the socks off its giant neighbour La Baule (see opposite). Although the adjacent headland offers fine sandy **beaches** within a couple of minutes' walk from the centre, the village itself turns its back on the Atlantic, preferring to face the protective jetty that curls back into the little bay to shield its small fishing fleet and summer array of yachts.

### ACCOMMODATION                                              PIRIAC-SUR-MER

★ **De la Plage** 2 place du Lehn ☎ 02 40 23 50 05, ⓦ hoteldelaplage-piriac.com. The most perfect French seaside hotel imaginable, this red-striped beauty overlooks a square on a quiet stretch of the seafront. The cheapest rooms lack en-suite facilities, but all are cheery and comfortable, and almost all have views of the sea. **€52**

# La Baule

With its dramatic crescent of superb sandy beach, and endless Riviera-style oceanfront boulevard, lined with palm-tree-fronted hotels and residences, the upscale resort of **LA BAULE** firmly imagines itself in the south of France. It can be fun if you feel like a break from the more subdued Atlantic-coast attractions – and the beach is undeniably impressive. It's not a place to imagine you're going to enjoy strolling around in search of hidden charms, however; the backstreets have an oddly rural feel, but hold nothing of any interest.

## ARRIVAL AND INFORMATION                                   LA BAULE

**By train** La Baule's *gare SNCF*, served by TGVs from Paris, is on place Rhin-et-Danube, away from the seafront.
**Tourist office** 8 place de la Victoire, close to both the *gare SNCF* and the *gare routière* (July & Aug daily 9.30am–7.30pm;

Sept–June Mon & Wed–Sat 9.15am–12.30pm & 2–6pm, Tues 10.15am–12.30pm & 2–6pm, Sun 10am–1pm; ☏02 40 24 34 44, ⓦlabaule.fr).

## ACCOMMODATION

**Lutetia** 13 av Olivier Guichard ☏02 40 60 25 81, ⓦlutetia-rossini.com. Right in the centre, less than 50m back from the sea and not far from the tourist office, this hotel has crisp, clean modern rooms as well as the excellent if expensive *Rossini* restaurant, which serves magnificent fish

cuisine (closed Mon & Tues). **€120**
**Marini** 22 av Clemenceau ☏02 40 60 23 29, ⓦle-marini.fr. The best of various lower-priced options near the station, with comfortable but unremarkable rooms, a restaurant, and indoor pool. **€82**

# Le Croisic

The small port of **LE CROISIC** – 10km west of La Baule, sheltering from the ocean around the corner of the headland, but with its built-up area stretching right across the peninsula – makes an attractive and more peaceful alternative base to La Baule. These days it's basically a pleasure port, but fishing boats do still sail from its harbour, near the very slender mouth of the bay, and there's a modern **fish market** near the long Tréhic jetty, where you can watch the day's catch being auctioned.

## ACCOMMODATION                                             LE CROISIC

**Camping l'Océan** 15 rte de la Maison-Rouge ☏02 40 23 07 69, ⓦcamping-ocean.com. Much the fanciest of the array of campsites along the rocky sea coast known as the Grande Côte, with its own aquapark and restaurant, and mobile homes for rent along with traditional camping pitches. Closed Oct–March. **€45**
**Castel Moor** Baie du Castouillet ☏02 40 23 24 18, ⓦcastel-moor.com. Modern seaside villa, 500m beyond the centre on the sheltered side of the headland, where

several of the tastefully furnished rooms have sea-view balconies, and there's a good semicircular restaurant. Closed Jan. **€68**
**Les Nids** 15 rue Pasteur ☏02 40 23 00 63, ⓦhotellesnids.com. Very friendly modern hotel, set slightly back from the ocean at the pretty little plage de Port-Lin. All rooms and suites have balconies, and there's a small indoor swimming pool but no restaurant. Closed Nov–Easter. **€74**

# Le Mans

**LE MANS**, the historic capital of the Maine region, is synonymous with its famous 24-hour car race in June. During the rest of the year, it's a much quieter place; what it lacks in obvious beauty it makes up for in historical background, being the favourite home of the Plantagenet family, the counts of Anjou, Touraine and Maine. The old quarter, in the shadow of the magnificent cathedral, is unusually well preserved, while outside town you can visit the serene Cistercian abbey of Épau and, of course, the racetrack, a must-see pilgrimage for petrolheads. There are a range of fun family activities just ten minutes drive from the centre of town, including **Tepacap D3**.

## The old quarter

The complicated web of the **old quarter** lies atop a minor hill above the River Sarthe, to the north of the central place de la République. Its medieval streets, a hotchpotch of intricate Renaissance stonework, medieval half-timbering, sculpted pillars and beams, and grand classical facades, are still encircled by the original third-century Gallo-Roman walls, supposedly the best preserved in Europe and running for several hundred metres. Steep, walled steps lead up from the river, and longer flights descend on the southern side of the enclosure, using old Gallo-Roman entrances. If it all looks familiar, that's because it's often used in films; both Leonardo di Caprio in *The Man in the Iron Mask* and Gérard Depardieu in *Cyrano de Bergerac* stomped up its cobbled streets.

## Le Carré Plantagenêt

2 rue Claude Blondel · Daily except Mon, 10am–6pm · €4 · ☎ 02 43 47 46 45, ⓦ lemans.fr

This earnest **archeological museum** details the history of Le Mans, from prehistoric times to the fifteenth century. The highlights are an exquisite enamel portrait of Henry II's father, Geoffroi Le Bel, a room of religious sculptures and six beautifully preserved and rather eerie slumbering statues. There's also a rather ghoulish skeleton of a child, aged between 7 and 9 years old, left in soil.

## Cathédrale St-Julien

Mon–Sat 9am–noon & 2–4.30pm, Sun 8am–6pm

The high ground of the Old Town has been sacred since ancient times, as testified by a strangely human, pink-tinted menhir now propped up against the southwest corner of the very impressive **Cathédrale St-Julien**, which crowns the hilltop. The nave of the cathedral was only just completed when Geoffroi Plantagenet, the count of Maine and Anjou, married Matilda, daughter of Henry I of England, in 1129, thus founding the English dynastic line. Inside, for all the power and measured beauty of this Romanesque structure, it's impossible not to be drawn towards the vertiginous High Gothic choir, filled with coloured light filtering through the stained-glass windows. At the easternmost end of the choir, the vault of the chapelle de la Vierge is painted with angels singing, dancing and playing medieval musical instruments.

## Musée de Tessé

Tues–Sun 10am–12.30pm & 2–6pm · €4, every Sun entry €2

In the 1850s a road was tunnelled under the old quarter – a slum at the time – helping to preserve its self-contained unity. Usually, on the north side of the quarter, the road tunnel comes out by an impressive monument to Wilbur Wright – who tested an early flying machine in Le Mans – which points you into place du Hallai. (Note, however, that until mid-2014 the monument will be under wraps until the tram line work is completed). From here, you can walk northeast alongside the park to the **Musée de Tessé**, on avenue de Paderborn. It's a mixed bag of paintings, furnishings and sculpture – the highlight being in the basement, where there are two full-scale reconstructions of ancient Egyptian tombs, one of which is of Queen Nefertari. There are mummies too.

## Tepacap D3

Rte de L'Isle en Dodon · May, Sept Wed–Sun 10am–7pm; June–Aug daily 10am–7pm; Oct to mid-Nov Wed–Sun 10am–6pm · Tariff varies on activities but around €20 · ☎ 05 62 14 71 61, ⓦ tepacap.fr · Take the #9 bus (direction Rainier)

Just a 10min drive from Le Mans, **Tepacap D3** is an outstanding wilderness adventure with Wild West-themed paintball, zipwire through the trees, orienteering and other

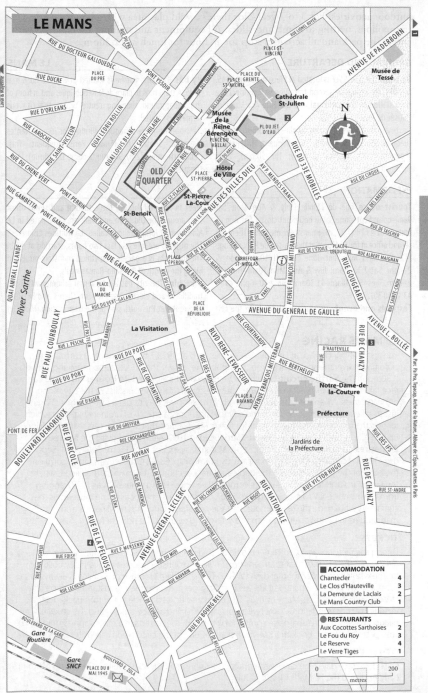

# LE MANS

7

**ACCOMMODATION**

| | |
|---|---|
| Chantecler | 4 |
| Le Clos d'Hauteville | 3 |
| La Demeure de Laclais | 2 |
| Le Mans Country Club | 1 |

**RESTAURANTS**

| | |
|---|---|
| Aux Cocottes Sarthoises | 2 |
| Le Fou du Roy | 3 |
| Le Reserve | 4 |
| Le Verre Tiges | 1 |

outdoor activities. For 3 to 7 year-olds there's a wild play area with a bouncy castle, trampolines, netting to climb and slides. All equipment and training are included with entry. The park and all activities stop for an hour for lunch at 12.30pm.

## ARRIVAL AND DEPARTURE
### LE MANS

**By train** The *gare SNCF* is located at Place du 8 mai 1945. In 2014, the complete second tram line will connect the train station to the cathedral and the Fine Art Museum (Musée de Tessé).

**Destinations** Angers (frequent 40min–1hr 20min); Nantes (frequent 55min–1hr 45min); Paris (frequent; 1hr); Rennes (frequent; 2hr); Saumur (2 daily; 1hr 50min); Tours (frequent; 1hr).

**By bus** The *gare routière* is located at 8 place du 8 mai 1945. A tram runs to place de la République, and in front of the underground shopping centre where the city bus terminal is located.

**Destinations** Angers (frequent 40min–1hr 20min); Nantes (frequent; 55min–1hr 45min); Paris (frequent; 1hr); Rennes (frequent; 2hr); Saumur (2 daily; 1hr 50min); Tours (frequent; 1hr).

## INFORMATION

**Tourist office** Rue de l'Étoile (July & Aug Mon–Sat 9am–6pm; Sept–June same hours but closed Sat noon–2pm; ☎ 02 43 28 17 22, ⓦ lemanstourisme.com). There is a second office in the Old Town at the Maison de Pillier Rouge (41–43 Grand Rue Sept–June Sun–Fri 10am–noon & 2–6pm, Sat 2.30–6pm; July & Aug Mon 10am–noon & 2–6pm, Tues–Sat 10am–11.30pm, Sun 2.30–6pm; ☎ 02 43 47 40 30).

**Festivals and events** On summer nights from the last week in June till August, the cathedral and seven other sites around the Old Town and walls are illuminated in Le Mans' son et lumière show, called "La Nuit des Chimères". The displays are free and last two hours, starting at dusk. The highlight is a parade of mythical monsters projected along the length of the Gallo-Roman walls.

**Bike hire** The city has a bike rental scheme with both traditional and electric bikes to rent. There's also SETRAM bike rental at the north side of the train station (Mon–Fri

## LE MANS RACING

The first 24-hour car race at Le Mans was run as early as 1923, on the present 13.6km Sarthe circuit, with average speeds of 92kph (57mph) – these days, the drivers average around 210kph (130mph). The **Sarthe circuit**, on which the now world-renowned **24 Heures du Mans** car race takes place every year in mid-June, stretches south from the outskirts of the city, along ordinary roads. When the competition isn't on, the simplest way to get a taste of the action is just to take the main road south of the city towards Tours, a stretch of ordinary highway which follows the famous Mulsanne straight for 5.7km – a distance that saw race cars reach speeds of up to 375kph, until two chicanes were introduced in 1989. Alternatively, visit the **Musée des 24 heures** (Jan Fri–Sun 11am–5pm; Feb & March daily except Tues 11am–5pm; April–Sept daily 10am–6pm; Oct–Dec daily except Tues 11am–5pm; €8.50; ⓦ musee24h.sarthe.com) on the edge of the Bugatti circuit – the dedicated track section of the main Sarthe circuit, where the race starts and finishes. It parades some 150 vehicles dating as far back as 1873, ranging from the humble 2CV to classic Lotus and Porsche race cars. The focus of the museum is the characters who made the race famous. Vintage newsreel along with newspapers and mannequins in period costume keep this interesting even for the non-car fans.

### TICKETS

During the race weekend, you'll need a ticket to get anywhere near the circuit. Buy them direct from the organizers at ⓦ lemans.org, or via the tourist office (see above); they cost €65 for the whole event, €27 for trial days (Wed & Thurs), and €42 for race day, which is always on a Sunday. You'll need a separate ticket (€62–105) to get access to the grandstands, and be sure to book well in advance. Many enthusiasts' clubs and ticket agencies offer tour packages including accommodation – otherwise impossible to find at race times – and the crucial parking passes; try ⓦ clubarnage.com or look through the adverts in a motor-sports magazine. True petrolheads can book themselves a place at one of the circuit-side campsites.

### OTHER EVENTS

Outside of race days, you can watch practice sessions, and there's the bikers' 24 Heures Moto in early April and the Le Mans Classic in July.

8.30–11.30am & 2.30–7pm; Sat 10am–midday & 2–7pm. ☎ 02 43 88 33 26, ⓦ setram.fr).

**Markets** There's a daily market in the covered halls on place du Marché, plus a bric-a-brac market on Wednesday, Friday (when there's also food) and Sunday mornings on place du Jet-d'Eau, below the cathedral in the new town.

## ACCOMMODATION

**Chantecler** 50 rue de la Pelouse ☎ 02 43 14 40 00, ⓦ hotelchantecler.fr. Quiet, professionally run hotel, offering spacious and well-fitted-out rooms and free parking. Good choice for the station as it's only a five-minute walk away, or ten minutes' stroll to place de la République. Breakfast €10.50. **€85**

**Le Clos d'Hauteville** 2 rue d'Hauteville ☎ 02 43 23 26 80, ⓦ leclosdhauteville.jimdo.com. A tranquil garden and welcoming couple make this a good budget choice B&B. The three large rooms are individually decorated, very much in a family, cosy home-style. The largest room is in the attic, complete with a child's room. Free private parking and breakfast included. **€80**

**La Demeure de Laclais** 4bis Place du Cardinal Grente.

Charming *chambre d'hotes* with three rooms to choose from right across from the cathedral. Smart dove-grey walls, fireplaces and wooden floors are the order of the day in this boutique hotel-like B&B. There is a small garden with a peerless view of the cathedral. Breakfast is included, with home-made yoghurt and jams. **€110**

★ **Le Mans Country Club** Château de la Ragotterie ☎ 02 43 82 11 00, ⓦ lemans-countryclub.com This surprisingly affordable château, ten minutes' drive away from the centre of the town is in the heart of the countryside. Thoroughly modernized and renovated inside, but with some original beams to add atmosphere. Rooms inside the château cost €20 more than those in the annexe in the park. Excellent restaurant. Breakfast €14.50. **€109**

## EATING AND DRINKING

**Aux Cocottes Sarthoises** 77 Grand Rue ☎ 02 43 28 65 24. Quirky restaurant that specializes in dishes cooked and presented in little casserole pots, such as curried sea bass with basmati. Leave room for the almond cream with berries and sorbet. *Menus* from €8.90–20.50. Tues–Sat noon–2.30pm & 7–10pm.

**Le Fou du Roy** 2 Impasse Sainte-Catherine ☎ 02 43 28 45 03. One of the very few establishments open on a Monday in the old town, this atmospheric restaurant has tapestries on its walls and a small terrace for eating outside on fine days. Traditional French cuisine with decent grills. *Menus* from €18. Thurs–Mon noon–1.30pm & 7–10pm.

**Le Reserve** 34 place République ☎ 02 43 52 82 82. This the hippest restaurant on the huge place de la République, serves exceptional steaks, good fish dishes and enormous salads. There's a daily changing menu; mains start at €11. Watch out for some funky twists on dessert, like raspberries with basil – try the "Café Gourmand" for a tiny selection of the day's puddings. They do excellent cocktails, too – the Candyfloss Mojito is really tasty. Reserve a table on the huge terrace or cosy up in the dark interior with its stylish decor and ornate chairs. Tues–Sat 7–10pm.

**Le Verre Tiges** 48 Grand Rue ☎ 02 43 28 39 00. This quaint restaurant in the old town, specializes in *tartines*, plates of charcuterie and cheese and good salads. The "Tartiflette" *tartine* is particularly good, piled high with reblochon cheese and bacon bits for €12.50. Tues–Sun 10am–late.

# The Abbaye de L'Épau

May–Oct daily 9am–noon & 2–6pm; Nov, Dec, March & April Wed–Sun 10am–noon & 2–5pm; closed Jan–Feb • €3 • ☎ 02 43 84 22 29, ⓦ sarthe.com • Take the tram to "Epau"

If car racing holds no romance, there's another outing from Le Mans of a much quieter nature, to the Cistercian **Abbaye de l'Épau**, 4km out of town off the Chartres–Paris road. The abbey was founded in 1229 by Queen Berengaria, consort of Richard the Lionheart, and it stands in a rural setting on the outskirts of the Bois de Changé more or less unaltered since its fifteenth-century restoration after a fire. The visit includes the dormitory, with the remains of a fourteenth-century fresco, the abbey church and the scriptorium, or writing room. The church contains the recumbent figure of Queen Berengaria over her tomb.

# Burgundy

VÉZELAY

# Burgundy

At the very heart of the country, Burgundy is one of France's most prosperous regions. Its peaceful way of life, celebrated wine, delicous food and numerous outdoor activities all combine to make this region the ideal place to discover and appreciate la vie française. Wine is, of course, the region's most obvious attraction, and devotees head straight for the great vineyards, whose produce has played the key role in the local economy since Louis XIV's doctor prescribed wine as a palliative for the royal dyspepsia. Wine tasting is particularly big business around Chablis, Mâcon and Beaune.

For centuries Burgundy's powerful **dukes** remained independent of the French crown, and during the Hundred Years War they even sided with the English, selling them the captured Joan of Arc. By the fifteenth century their power extended over all of Franche-Comté, Alsace and Lorraine, Belgium, Holland, Picardy and Flanders, and their state was the best-organized and richest in Europe. Burgundy finally fell to the French kings when Duke Charles le Téméraire (the Bold) was killed besieging Nancy in 1477.

There's evidence everywhere of this former wealth and power, both secular and religious: the dukes' capital of **Dijon**, the great abbeys of **Vézelay** and **Fontenay**, the ruins of the monastery of **Cluny** (whose abbots' influence was second only to the pope's), and a large number of imposing châteaux. During the Middle Ages, Burgundy – along with Poitou and Provence – became one of the great church-building areas in France. Practically every village has its Romanesque church, especially in the country around **Cluny** and **Paray-le-Monial**, and where the Catholic Church built, so had the Romans before, with their legacy visible in the substantial Roman remains at **Autun**. There's more history on show at Alesia, the scene Julius Caesar's epic victory over the Gauls in 52 BC.

Between bouts of gastronomic indulgence, you can engage in some moderate activity: for **walkers** there's a wide range of hikes, from gentle walks in the Côte d'Or to relatively demanding treks in the Parc Régional du Morvan.

## GETTING AROUND

**By bus and train** Burgundy has a pretty good transport network, with departmental buses filling in most of the gaps left by the SNCF, albeit with somewhat skeletal timetables (ⓦmobigo-bourgogne.com). For the smaller towns and villages you usually need to reserve the day before you want to travel and it's not always possible to do a round trip on the same day.

**By boat** The region's many canals can be explored by rented barge (ⓦleboat.co.uk).

**By bike** Many of the canal towpaths form part of a rapidly expanding network of cycle paths (ⓦburgundy-by-bike.com).

8

# Highlights

**❶ Cuisine** Gourmands, prepare to indulge – Burgundy has given us *boat bourguignon*, *escargots*, *gougères*, *jambon persillé* and many other delectable dishes; for some of the best food around, head to the Côte Saint-Jacques restaurant in Joigny. **See p.429**

**❷ Noyers-sur-Serein** Buried in beautiful countryside east of Auxerre, this stunningly unspoilt medieval town has the added bonus of an impressive museum. **See p.435**

**❸ Vézelay** One of France's earliest UNESCO sites, this small village with the gigantic Romanesque basilica of Mary Magdalene features among Burgundy's most historic locations. **See p.443**

**❹ Dijon** This affluent and cosmopolitan city is a great destination for a flaneur. **See p.451**

**❺ The Côte d'Or** Home to Burgundy's most renowned vineyards, the towns and villages that line the road from Dijon to Beaune are full of possibilities for wine tasting. **See p.458**

**❻ Beaune's Hôtel-Dieu** Topped by a myriad of glazed, multicoloured tiles, the medieval hospice at Beaune also houses Rogier van der Weyden's *Last Judgement*. **See p.459**

HIGHLIGHTS ARE MARKED ON THE MAP ON P.428

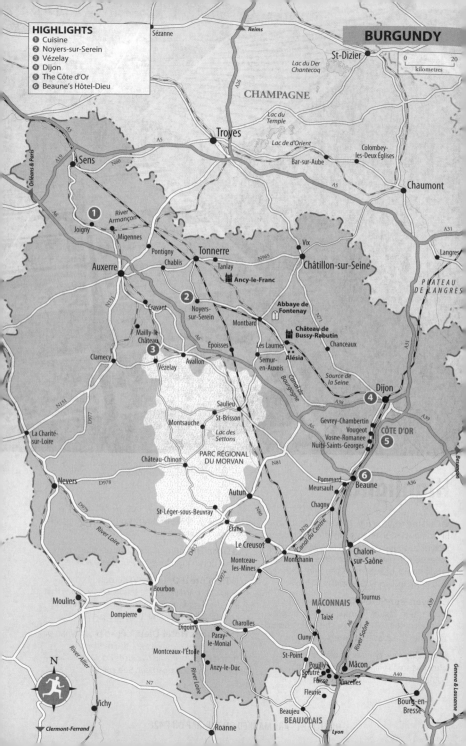

## THE FOOD OF BURGUNDY

The richness of Burgundy's **cuisine** is largely due to two factors: the region's wines and its possession of one of the world's finest breeds of beef cattle, the Charollais. **Wines** are often used in the preparation of sauces, especially *à la bourguignonne*. Essentially, this means that the dish is cooked in a red wine sauce to which baby onions, mushrooms and *lardons* (pieces of bacon) are added. The classic Burgundy dishes cooked in this manner are *bœuf bourguignon* and *coq au vin*. Another term that frequently appears on menus is *meurette*, which is also a red wine sauce but made without mushrooms and flambéed with a touch of marc brandy. It's used with eggs, fish and poultry as well as red meat.

**Snails** (*escargots*) are hard to avoid in Burgundy, and the local style of cooking involves stewing them for several hours in white wine with shallots, carrots and onions, then stuffing them with garlic and parsley butter and finishing them off in the oven. **Other specialities** include the parsley-flavoured ham (*jambon persillé*); calf's head (*tête de veau*, or *sansiot*); and a *pauchouse* of river fish (that is, poached in white wine with onions, butter, garlic and *lardons*).

Like other regions of France, Burgundy produces a variety of **cheeses**. The best known are the creamy white Chaource, the soft St-Florentin from the Yonne valley, the orange-skinned Époisses and the delicious goat's cheeses from the Morvan. And then there is **gougère**, a savoury pastry made with cheese, best eaten warm with a glass of Chablis.

# Auxerre and around

Most travellers to Burgundy arrive in **AUXERRE**, the chief population and industrial centre in the north of Burgundy – and with good reason. A very pretty and historic town of narrow lanes and lovely open squares, it looks its best from **Pont Paul-Bert** over the river **Yonne** and the riverside quays. From here you get a lovely view of moored houseboats and barges, with churches soaring dramatically and harmoniously above the surrounding rooftops.

To enjoy some local colour, and pick up some local produce, try the **market** in place de l'Arquebuse (Tues & Fri morning).

## St-Germain

Place Saint Germain • **Abbey** Daily Oct–April 10am–noon & 2–5pm; May–Sept 9.45am–6.45pm • Free **Museum** Daily Oct–April 10am–noon & 2–5pm; May–Sept 10am–6.30pm • Free **Crypt** Guided tours only hourly 10am–noon & 1.45–3.45pm (1.45–5.45pm in summer) • €6 • ☎ 03 86 18 02 90, ⓦ auxerre.com

The most interesting of Auxerre's many churches is the airy, light abbey church of **St-Germain**, famous for its ten-ribbed vaults, containing three of only five in existence worldwide. The monks' former dormitories, around a classical cloister, now house a historical and archeological **museum**, but the real highlight is the **crypt** where the tomb of St Germain, fourth bishop of Auxerre (378–448), was the epicentre of the bishops' burial catacombs. The tomb is empty – St Germain's remains were used for various reliquaries and what was left was desecrated by Huguenots in 1567. The crypt is one of the few surviving examples of Carolingian architecture, with its plain barrel vaults still resting on their thousand-year-old oak beams. Its wonderfully vivid and expressive ochre **frescoes** are the oldest in France, dating back to around 850 AD.

## Cathedral St-Etienne

Place St-Etienne • April–Oct Mon–Sat 7.30am–7pm, Sun 8.30am–7pm; Nov–March closes 5pm **Crypt** Nov 1 to Palm Sunday Mon–Sat 10am–5pm; Palm Sunday to Nov 1 Mon–Sat 9am–6pm, Sun 2–6pm • €3 **Treasury** Palm Sunday Mon–Sat 10am–5pm; Palm Sunday to Nov 1 Mon–Sat 9am–6pm, Sun 2–6pm • €1.90 • ☎ 03 86 52 23 29; ⓦ cathedrale-auxerre.com

The **cathedral** was built between 1215 and 1560 but remains unfinished; the southernmost of the two west front towers has never been completed. Look out for the

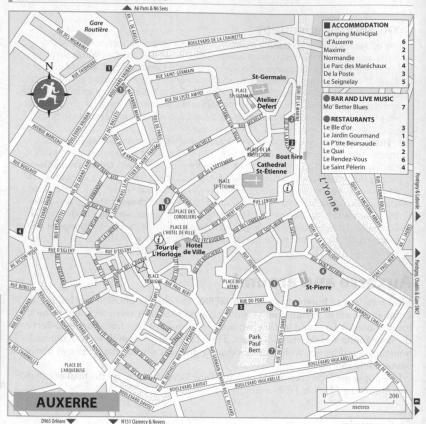

richly detailed sculpture of the porches and the glorious colours of the original thirteenth-century glass that still fills the windows of the choir, despite the savagery of the Wars of Religion and the Revolution. There has been a church on the site since about 400 AD, though nothing visible survives earlier than the eleventh-century **crypt**. Among its frescoes is a unique depiction of a warrior Christ mounted on a white charger, accompanied by four mounted angels. Upstairs, manuscripts, chalices and a number of interesting ivory ornaments are displayed in the **treasury**.

## St-Sauveur-en-Puisaye

An interesting side trip from Auxerre, about twenty minutes away by car, is the village of **ST-SAUVEUR-EN-PUISAYE**, the birthplace, in 1873, of the French novelist Colette (1873–1954). The **Musée Colette**, in the château (April–Oct Wed–Mon 10am–6pm; €6; ☎03 86 45 61 95, ⓦmusee-colette.com) includes a reconstruction of her apartment in Paris, as well as personal items and original manuscripts.

### ARRIVAL AND DEPARTURE

### AUXERRE AND AROUND

**By train** The *gare SNCF*, on rue Paul-Doumer, is across the river from the town; take bus #1 (every 20min; €1.20) which circles the centre until arriving at the *gare routière*.

Destinations Avallon (6 daily; 1hr 30min); Clamecy (4–6 daily; 1hr–1hr 20min); Dijon (10–15 daily; 2hr; change at Laroche-Migennes); Joigny (35min–50min); Laroche-Migennes (every 30min–1hr; 30min); Montbard

(5 daily; 1hr 30min); Paris Bercy (6 daily; 1hr 30min–2hr 30min); Sens (6 daily; 1hr).
**By bus** The *gare routiére* is on the north side of town, on rue de Migraines.

Destinations Avallon (1–2 daily; 1hr 20min); Chablis (2–5 daily; 35min); Sens (40min); Tonnerre (2–5 daily; 1hr 10min). Book in advance at ☎ 0800 303 309.

## GETTING AROUND

**Bike rental** You can rent bikes from the tourist office (€10/3hr; €18/day; subsequent days €16).
**Car rental** There are car hire firms all over town, including a few near the *gare SNCF*. Try ⓦ rhinocarhire.com to get the best price.
**Taxis** Taxis are difficult to get hold of in Auxerre; for 24hr service, call ☎ 03 86 46 78 78.

## INFORMATION

**Tourist office** The tourist office (mid-June to mid-Sept Mon–Sat 9am–1pm & 2–7pm, Sun 9.30am–1pm & 2.30–6.30pm; mid-Sept to mid-June Mon–Sat 9.30am–12.30pm & 2–6pm, Sun 10am–1pm; ☎ 03 86 51 03 26, ⓦ ot-auxerre.fr) stands by the river at 2 quai de la République with an annexe on place de l'Hôtel de Ville.

**Passes** The Auxerre Privilèges card (€2), sold at the tourist office, gives reductions to most of the sights in Auxerre.
**Internet** Speed Informatique, 32 rue du Pont (Mon–Fri 2–9pm; €5/hr).
**Boat rental** The tourist office rents electric boats for jaunts on the river (€20/hr up to €85/day). A €150 deposit and proof of ID is required.

## ACCOMMODATION

**Camping Municipal d'Auxerre** 8 rte de Vaux ☎ 03 86 52 11 15, ⓔ camping.mairie@auxerre.com. Next to the riverside football ground, this is a pleasant and quiet site on the south side of town. Closed Oct to mid-April. **€13.30**

**Maxime** 2 quai de la Marine ☎ 03 86 52 14 19, ⓦ lemaxime.com. Stylish and luxurious monochrome rooms (all have a/c, wi-fi, flatscreen TV and modern furnishings). Those with river views are not necessarily more expensive. Free parking, but reserve at time of booking. Breakfast €12. **€112**

**Normandie** 41 bd Vauban ☎ 03 86 52 57 80, ⓦ hotel normandie.fr. Just outside the old town centre, this fairly swanky, creeper-covered hotel occupies a former nineteenth-century country house, with elegant old furniture throughout and modern trimmings in the guest rooms. Facilities include a sauna, a gym and a billiards room. Buffet breakfast €9.50. **€69**

**Le Parc des Maréchaux** 6 av Foch ☎ 03 86 51 43 77, ⓦ hotel-parcmarechaux.com. An oasis of quiet just off one of the main roads radiating from the centre, this nineteenth-century mansion has a large garden with ancient trees to breakfast under. The decor is golden and brown, with each room named after a French marshal. A Victorian bar and a heated pool complete the picture. Breakfast €12. **€113**

**De la Poste** 9 rue d'Orbandelle ☎ 03 86 52 12 02, ⓦ hotel-de-la-poste-auxerre.federal-hotel.com. The bizarre coconut-matting-clad walls in the corridors lead to charmingly decorated, airy, modern rooms as idiosyncratic as the joss sticks and the bonsai tree at reception. A great central location and a high-quality restaurant to boot (*menu* €15; Mon dinner to Sat dinner noon–1.30pm & 7.30–8.30pm). **€56**

**Le Seignelay** 2 rue du Pont ☎ 03 86 52 03 48, ⓦ leseignelay.com. A good mid-range choice with friendly staff and a restaurant which is also popular with non-residents. Closed mid-Feb to mid-March. Breakfast €7.50. **€62**

## EATING AND DRINKING

If you fancy an aperitif, Place de l'Hôtel de Ville is a good spot to head, especially in summer, as there are several bars and cafés with sunny terraces.

**Le Ble d'Or** 5 rue d'Orbandelle ☎ 03 86 48 16 84. Packed wooden tables and wicker chairs in this cheerful Bretonne crêperie, offering filling, tasty food at fair prices. Salads, *galettes* and crêpes all €7–8. Oct to mid-Sept Tues–Fri 11.45am–2pm & 7–10pm; Sat 11.30am–2pm & 6.30–11pm.

**Le Jardin Gourmand** 56 bd Vauban ☎ 03 86 51 53 52, ⓦ lejardingourmand.com. Sparkling glass, crisp linen and immaculate decor; this is truly fine dining.

Although the *menu* changes regularly, you are guaranteed gastronomic dishes made from locally sourced ingredients. The *formule* is €52, while the full works, including wine, goes for €115. Reserve in advance. Wed–Sat noon–1.45pm & 7.30–9.15pm, Sun noon–1.45pm.

**La P'tite Beursaude** 55 rue Joubert ☎ 03 86 51 10 21, ⓦ beursaudiere.com. With exposed beams and waitresses wearing traditional Morvan dress, this rather romantic restaurant has a rustic feel to it. Specializing in regional cuisine, it has *menus* from €20.50 (lunch) and €26 (dinner). Reservations advised. Thurs–Mon noon–2pm & 7–9pm.

★ **Le Quai** Place St-Nicholas ☎ 03 86 51 66 67, ⓦ lequai-auxerre.com. Grab a seat on the outdoor terrace of this well-liked brasserie, which overlooks a pretty square. Reasonably priced *plats* and pizzas (€10–12) have a light, modern feel, with more accent on salads and less on rich Burgundy sauces. Daily: April–Oct 10am–midnight; Nov–March closed in the afternoon.

**Le Rendez-Vous** 37 rue de Pont ☎ 03 86 51 46 36, ⓦ restaurant-lerendezvous.fr. Old-fashioned family cuisine in very untraditional surroundings; the paintings on the wall might make you think you stumbled into Picasso's atelier. You won't stop gazing while you're eating from the multi-course set *menu* at €32. Mon–Fri noon–2pm & 7.30–9.30pm.

**Le Saint Pèlerin** 56 rue St-Pèlerin ☎ 03 86 52 77 05. The centrepiece of this quiet, relaxed dining room is the wood fire on which the restaurant's specialty *grillades* are prepared. Good choice of meats and fish, with *menus* from €15–35. Tues–Sat noon–2pm & 7.15–10pm.

### NIGHTLIFE

**Mo' Better Blues** 36–38 rue du Puits des Dames ☎ 03 86 51 36 64, ⓦ mobetterblues.fr. This lively jazz bar has regular live music, with concerts every weekend. Entry is usually free. Wed & Thurs 9pm–midnight, Fri & Sat 10pm–2am.

# The Yonne valley

Burgundy begins just south of Fontainebleau, near where the river **Yonne** joins the Seine, and follows the Yonne valley through the historic towns of **Sens** and **Joigny** before it reaches Auxerre. Scattered in a broad corridor to the east and west in the riverbanks of the Yonne's tributaries – the **Armançon**, **Serein**, **Cure** and **Cousin** – is a fascinating collection of abbeys, châteaux, towns, villages and other sites as ancient as the history of France. They all deserve a visit, for reasons ranging from architecture (**Pontigny**) and wine (**Chablis**) to sheer secluded beauty (**Noyers sur Serein**).

## Sens

The northernmost town in Burgundy, **SENS** is a relaxed place on the banks of the Yonne, but surprisingly lively at night when restaurants stay open well beyond the 9pm curfew encountered in many French provincial cities. Because of its **Monday market**, restaurants and museums stay open on Monday, too, unlike other cities in the Yonne; Tuesday tends to be a rest day.

The town's name commemorates the Senones, the Gallic tribe who all but captured Rome in 390 BC; they were only thwarted by the Capitoline geese cackling and waking the garrison. Sens' heyday as a major ecclesiastical centre was in the twelfth and thirteenth centuries, when **Thomas Becket** spent four years in exile here under the protection of Louis IX of France. Sens is proud of this connection: from the stained glass in the cathedral to its local microbrewery with its Thomas Becket beer, there are numerous reminders of the "English saint".

### Cathedral of St-Étienne

Place de la Republique • **Cathedral** Mon–Sat 8am–6pm; July & Aug • Daily guided tours of the cathedral (2.30pm), treasury (3.30pm) and museum (4.30pm); €5/€8 per tour or €12 for all three **Musée de Sens** June–Sept daily except Tues 10am–noon & 2–6pm; Oct–May Wed, Sat & Sun 10am–noon & 2–6pm, Thurs & Fri 2–6pm • €4.20, or included on guided tour • ☎ 03 86 64 15 27

The town's ancient centre is dominated by the **Cathedral of St-Étienne**. Built between 1130–80, this was the first of the great French Gothic cathedrals, and having been built without flying buttresses – these were added later for stability – its profile is relatively wide and squat. The architect who completed it, William of Sens, went on to rebuild the choir of Canterbury Cathedral in England. The story of Thomas Becket's murder is told in the twelfth-century windows in the north aisle of the choir. The **treasury** contains a number of rich tapestries and vestments – including those of Becket himself.

## Musée de Sens

Originally designed to accommodate the ecclesiastical courts next to the cathedral, the thirteenth-century **Palais Synodal** now houses part of the **Musée de Sens**, built over the old Roman Baths, which you can visit in the basement. The highlight is an extensive **art collection** including statues by Rodin and a lively crowd scene by Brueghel the Younger.

### ARRIVAL AND INFORMATION
SENS

**By train** The *gare SNCF* is on place François Mitterrand beyond the Yonne. Change at Laroche-Migennes for Auxerre.

**Destinations** Dijon (15 daily; 1hr); Joigny (18–21 daily; 30min); Laroche-Migennes (18–21 daily; 40 min); Paris Bercy (15 daily; 50min); Tonnerre (8–10 daily; 1hr 10min).

**Tourist office** Place Jean-Jaurès (July & Aug Mon–Sat

9.30am–1pm & 2–6.30pm; Sept–April Mon–Sat 9.30am–12.30pm & 2–6pm; May–Oct Mon–Sat 9.30am–12.30pm & 2–6pm, Sun 10.30am–1pm & 2–4.30pm; ☏ 03 86 65 19 49, ⓦ office-de-tourisme-sens .com). They rent audio-guides in English (€5), which can also be downloaded them their website for free.

### ACCOMMODATION

**Brennus** 21 rue de Trois Croissants ☏ 03 86 64 04 40, ⓦ hotel-brennus-89.com. A small family hotel tucked away in the edge of the centre. Some of the charmingly decorated rooms offer views of the cathedral. Reception closed for lunch, Fri eves and Sun. Buffet breakfast €8.10. €60

**Camping Entre-deux-Vannes** 191 av de Sénigallia ☏ 03 86 65 64 71, ⓔ espacesverts@mairie-sens.fr. The local campsite is a short ride away on bus #4 (stop by the tourist office) or a 20min walk south of town next to the

award-winning municipal gardens of Moulin à Tan. Closed mid-Sept to mid-May. €16

★ **De Paris et de la Poste** 97 rue de la République ☏ 03 86 65 17 43, ⓦ hotel-paris-poste.com. The grandest hotel in Sens, opposite the elaborate facade of the 1904 town hall, with large, comfortable rooms around a sizeable garden, each one decorated on different themes. The lively bar downstairs is worth popping into even if you're not a guest. Breakfast €15, parking €8. €75

### EATING AND DRINKING

The café terraces on place de la République are a great spot for a drink or light meal and are open quite late by French provincial standards.

**Au P'tit Creux** 3 rue de Brennus ☏ 03 86 64 99 29. This friendly, bustling crêperie on the doorstep of the cathedral has substantial *menus* from €19.50 and a great selection of salads. Thurs–Mon noon–2pm & 7–10pm.

**La Madeleine** 1 rue d'Alsace Lorraine ☏ 03 86 65 09 31, ⓦ restaurant-lamadeleine.fr. Sens' best restaurant,

under Patrick Gaultier, a gregarious personality even for a one-star Michelin chef. Classic setting, superb service and heavenly food (*menus* €49–110). Booking essential well in advance. Tues 8–9.15pm, Wed–Sat 12.30–1.15pm & 8–9.15pm; closed two weeks in June, two weeks in Aug and two weeks around Christmas.

# Joigny

As you travel south from Sens, the next place of any size on the Yonne is **JOIGNY,** a mini-Auxerre with the river dividing an old, hilly medieval quarter from the more modern, post eighteenth-century town. The first fort was constructed here at the end of the tenth century, but much of the original settlement was destroyed by a fire in 1530. Joigny is worth an overnight visit and makes a pleasant rest stop, particularly on market days (Wed & Sat).

Buildings worthy of attention are the classical **Château des Gondi**, built by Cardinal Gondi in the sixteenth century, the church of **St-Thibault** (daily 9am–6pm), which is in late Gothic flamboyant style, and the remains of the twelfth-century ramparts on Chemin de la Guimbard.

On **rue Montant-au-Palais** – the street leading up to the sixteenth-century church of **St-Jean** (daily 9am–6pm), with its masterpiece of a ceiling – there are several remarkable half-timbered houses that somehow escaped the 1530 conflagration. They include the best known, **Maison du Pilori**, which combines Gothic and Renaissance styles, with some carvings strangely reminiscent of crocodile heads, and the **Maison Jesse** that has Christ's own family tree carved on its ridge. Down by the bridge, there is a wonderful Victorian closed market hall (1887).

## ARRIVAL AND INFORMATION

**By train** The *gare SNCF* is way south in the new town. It's a straight 20min walk up avenues de Gaulle and Gambetta to the bridge over the river to the old town.
Destinations Dijon (12 daily; 1hr 50min); Paris Bercy (15 daily; 1hr 10min); Sens (15 daily; 20min).

**Tourist office** 4 quai Henri Dagobert (July–Sept Mon 2–5pm, Tues–Fri 9am–12.30pm & 2–7pm, Sat 9am–1pm & 2–6pm, Sun 10am–1pm; Oct–June Mon 2–5pm, Tues–Sat 9am–noon & 2–5/6pm; ☎03 86 62 11 05, ✆tourisme-joigny.fr).

## ACCOMMODATION AND EATING

★ **La Côte Saint-Jacques** 14 Faubourg de Paris ☎03 86 62 55 12, ✆cotesaintjacques.com. A four-star marvel of a hotel with wonderful views over the Yonne and a three-star Michelin restaurant (*menus* from €150) under chef Jean-Michel Lorain, (who offers one- or two-day cookery courses from €190, once a month). Apartments and suites range from the secluded and romantic to penthouse extravaganzas; ask for a river-view room if you can. An award-winning spa, unbeatable service and a memorable breakfast feast (€32, and worth every euro) make this hotel really stand out.

Restaurant Tues 7.30–9.30pm, Wed–Sun noon–2pm & 7.30–9.30pm. Annexe rooms **€225**; river-view rooms **€310**

**Paris-Nice** Rond-point de la Resistance ☎03 86 62 06 72. The food is good value, and the portions enormous, in this restaurant with bright orange decor and kitchen furniture scattered around the interior; the shady tables in the garden are almost always filled by locals on summer lunchtimes. They also have reasonably priced double rooms to rent for €66 including breakfast. Daily noon–2pm & 7.30–9pm.

# Pontigny

**PONTIGNY** lies 25km east of Joigny, and has a beautifully preserved twelfth-century Cistercian **abbey church** (daily: May–Oct 9am–6pm; Nov–April 10am–5pm; free), standing on the edge of the village. There's no tower, no stained glass and no statuary to distract from its austere lines, though the sombre effect is somehow compensated for by the seventeenth-century choir that occupies much of the nave.

Three Englishmen played a major role in the abbey's early history, all of them archbishops of Canterbury. Thomas Becket took refuge from Henry II in the abbey in 1164, before moving to Sens in 1166; Stephen Langton similarly hid here during an argument over his eligibility for the primacy from 1207 to 1213; finally, Saint Edmund of Abingdon retired here in 1240, after unsuccessfully trying to stand up to Henry III. Saint Edmund's relics lie in a seventeenth-century tomb inside the abbey.

# Chablis and around

Some 16km south of Pontigny, the pretty red-roofed village of **CHABLIS** is home to the region's famous dry white wines. Lying in the valley of the River **Serein**, the town is surrounded by rows of vines, interspersed with yellow splashes of fields full of sunflowers. While wandering around the wealthy, modern village take a look at the side door of the **church of St-Martin**, which is decorated with ancient horseshoes belonging to sick horses left by visiting pilgrims – St-Martin being the protector of horsemen.

The wacky **Corkscrew and Vineyard Museum** (Mon–Fri 8am–noon & 2–5pm; Sat by appointment; ☎03 86 42 43 76; €1.50) at **Beine**, a ten minutes' drive west of Chablis, is great fun; spot the phallic and occasionally X-rated bottle-openers and corkscrews, and indulge in a little wine tasting.

## CHABLIS WINES

The combination of fossilized/limestone Jurassic soil, as well as a perfect vineyard climate with hard, wet winters and dry, sunny summers have made the village of Chablis one of the best-known names in dry white wines. Chablis follows the four Burgundy denominations in its own, particular way: the plots on a plateau are the cheapest, denominated as **Petit-Chablis**. The ones with a northern or eastern orientation (and thus limited sun exposure) are simply called **Chablis**. Those facing south or west are much more expensive and classified into 79 **premiers crus**. At the top of the pyramid are 103 hectares on the west side of the Serein facing south and comprising just seven **grand crus** that many believe produce the finest dry white wine in France: Blanchot, Bougros, Le Clos, Grenouilles, Preuses, Valmur and Vaudésirs. You can pick up a premier cru bottle in local cellars for €12 and a grand cru for less than €30.

## TASTINGS AND TOURS

For **tastings** try domain Jean-Marc Brocard in Préhy (☎03 86 41 49 00, ⓦbrocard.fr); they use a unique biodynamic model of viniculture which they are happy to explain to you (in English). **Vititours** offer English-speaking tours that end in tastings (3hr; €45; ☎06 11 47 82 98, ⓦchablis-vititours.fr). They can pick you up from any hotel within a 35km radius of Chablis, which includes Auxerre. The hotel *Du Vieux Moulin* (see below) also offers tastings of its own domain Laroche.

### ARRIVAL AND INFORMATION

**By bus** Buses stop at Place St-Martin in the middle of town. There are very few daily buses to Tonnerre (20min) and Auxerre (45min); they have to be reserved in advance (☎0800 303 309).
**Tourist office** 1 rue du Maréchal de Lattre de Tassigny (Easter to mid-June & mid-Sept to Oct daily 10am–12.30pm & 1.30–6pm; mid-June to mid-Sept daily 10am–12.30pm

### CHABLIS AND AROUND

& 1.30–7pm; Nov–Easter Mon–Sat 10am–12.30pm & 1.30–6pm; ☎03 86 42 80 80, ⓦwww.chablis.net). They can provide lots of information about local vineyards and wine tasting.
**Taxis** Public transport runs at awkward times and you may have to book a taxi on ☎03 86 42 11 15. It costs around €30 to the nearest train station in Tonnerre.

### ACCOMMODATION

★ **Bergerand's** 4 rue des Moulins ☎03 86 18 96 08, ⓦilovechablis.com. The chirpy owner is a passionate Chablis lover, and a fluent English-speaker – if you are into Chablis, this is *the* place to stay. Rooms are large and comfortable, though the WC is on the small side. Breakfast included, parking €10. **€88**
**Camping de Chablis** Just outside Chablis ☎03 86 42 44 39, ⓦchablis.net/camping. A beautiful site beside the River Serein just outside the village. It's small,

and the cheapest place to stay in the area, and so gets booked well in advance; call the tourist office outside the season to secure a place. Closed mid-Sept to May. **€11**
**Du Vieux Moulin** 18 rue des Moulins ☎03 86 42 47 30, ⓦlarochehotel.fr. A luxurious mix of traditional and contemporary architecture, with stylish rooms, excellent service and an outstanding restaurant. Closed mid-Dec to mid-Jan & Sun. **€140**

### EATING AND DRINKING

**Le Syracuse** 19 ave du Maréchal de Lattre de Tassigny ☎03 86 42 19 45. Dine either in the garden, soaking up the sun, or in the thirteenth-century vaulted dining room, and choose a pizza (€9) or a *menu du jour* for €12.50. Tues–Sun 11am–2pm & 7–9pm.
**La Cuisine Au Vin** 16 rue Auxerroise ☎03 86 18 98 52.

Priding itself on the freshness of its ingredients, this restaurant occupies a vigneron's tenth-century cellars and specializes in sauces based on Chablis; have *andouillette au Chablis* with Chablis mustard and a glass of Chablis to top it all off. *Menus* from €22. Wed–Sun noon–2pm, Mon & Tues noon–2pm & 6–9pm.

## Noyers-sur-Serein

Around 23km southeast of Chablis – you'll need to drive, or take a taxi (about €35 from Tonnerre or Montbard train stations) – you come to the beautiful little town of **NOYERS-SUR-SEREIN** (ⓦnoyers-et-tourisme.com). Half-timbered and arcaded houses, ornamented with rustic carvings – particularly those on place de la Petite-Étape-aux-Vins and around place de l'Hôtel de Ville – are corralled inside a loop of the river and the town walls; you can pass a few pleasant hours wandering the path between the river and the irregular walls with their robust towers. The Serein here is as pretty as in Chablis, but Noyers, being remarkably free of commercialism, has more charm.

### Musée d'Art Naïf

25 rue de l'Église • July & Aug daily except Tues 10am–6.30pm; June & Sept daily except Tues 11am–12.30pm & 2–6pm; Oct–Dec & Feb– May Sat & Sun 2.30–6.30pm • €4 • ☎ 03 86 82 89 09

For a small town museum, the **Musée d'Art Naïf** certainly punches above its weight. It comprises one of the best collections in the country of "art naïf" – that is, works by painters who had no formal training and were often manual workers lacking even basic schooling. One, Augustine Lesage, worked as a miner for sixty years before he started painting. Some star exhibits include Gérard Lattier's morbid comic-strip-style work, the excellent collages of Louis Quilici and the dreamy early twentieth-century paintings of Jacques Lagrange.

| ACCOMMODATION AND EATING | NOYERS-SUR-SEREIN |
|---|---|

**La Vieille Tour** Place du Grenier-à-Sel ☎ 03 86 82 87 69. The best place to stay and eat in town is this ivy-covered seventeenth-century hotel/restaurant owned by a Dutch art historian. The five beautifully furnished and charmingly rustic rooms enjoy views across the gardens to the river. April–Oct. **€55**

**Restaurant la Vieille Tour** 1 rue de la Porte Peinte ☎ 03 86 82 87 36. This highly regarded restaurant, linked to the hotel down the road (see opposite), has three-course *menus* from €14.50 and a good-value wine list. Reservations are a must. April–Oct Mon–Wed, Sat & Sun noon–3pm & 7–10pm, Fri 7–10pm.

# The Canal de Bourgogne

East of Joigny, and, conveniently close to the TGV stop of Laroche-Migennes, the **Canal de Bourgogne** branches off to the north of the River Yonne southeast towards Dijon. Along or close to the canal are several places of interest: the beautiful town of **Tonnere**, the Renaissance châteaux of **Tanlay** and **Ancy-le-Franc**, the **Abbaye de Fontenay**, and the site of Julius Caesar's victory over the Gauls at **Alésia**. Just east of the canal, perched above the River Armançon, lies the picturesque town of **Semur-en-Auxois**. Further east the Canal encompasses the upper reaches of the River Seine: at **Châtillon-sur-Seine** is the famous Celtic Treasure of Vix.

## Tonnerre and around

On the Paris–Sens–Dijon TGV train route, **TONNERRE** is a great base for exploring this corner of the region, and far cheaper than Chablis, just 18km away; the local golden, fruity Chardonnay is the newest appellation contrôlée in Burgundy, recognized in 2006. Although not as prosperous as its world-renowned neighbour, it is much prettier,

---

### CHEVALIER D'ÉON: THE CROSS-DRESSING DIPLOMAT

Tonnerre's quirkiest claim to fame is that it was the birthplace of the great eighteenth-century cross-dresser, **Chevalier d'Éon**. Born in the **Hôtel d'Uzès** in 1728, still the most magnificent structure in Tonnerre, d'Éon went about his important diplomatic missions for King Louis XV dressed in women's clothes. He fell out with the king, however, and, when he was in exile in London, wore a (male) dragoon's uniform – yet still bookmakers took bets on his sex. When Louis XVI ascended to the throne he allowed him to return to France – but exiled in Tonnerre – and also recognized his claim to be a woman and to dress as such. After the Revolution Chevalier d'Éon slowly slid into debt, and died penniless in London in 1810. An autopsy determined that he was undoubtedly a man.

since it was not bombed during the war – unlike Chablis – and it has several sights well worth a look.

Tonnerre is also an excellent starting point for **cycling** along the **Canal de Bourgogne**; from here to Dijon it's four or five days of easy cycling through some superb countryside. You don't even have to worry about luggage: Bag Transfer (☎03 86 41 43 22, ⓦ Bagtransfert.com) will pick up your bags and take it to your next stop for €6 per piece.

## Hôtel-Dieu

Entrance through the tourist office, Place Marguerite-de-Bourgogne • April–Oct Mon–Sat 9.30am–noon & 1.30–6pm; Sun 10am–12.30pm & 2–6pm; Nov–March Mon, Tues & Thurs–Sat 9.30am–noon & 1.30–6pm • €4.50; the admission ticket gives you a discount in several châteaux in the area, including Tanlay

The **Hôtel-Dieu**, a huge medieval hospice founded in 1293 by Marguerite de Bourgogne, has a grand 100m-long column-free hall that is used today for village functions and the occasional concert. Don't miss the eighteenth-century sundial forming an elongated figure of eight. The first floor houses the town's museum, where interesting exhibits include a papal bull to Marguerite de Bourgogne and a wonderfully realistic sculpture of the *Entombment of Christ* by Klaus Sluter (1454).

## Fosse Dionne

Rue de la Fosse Dionne

Tonnerre's most unlikely attraction sits at the foot of the steep hill crowned by the church of St-Pierre. The **Fosse Dionne** is a fascinating blue-green "mystic" pool encircled by a wash house that dates from 1758. A number of legends are attached to the spring (the name derives from Divona, Celtic goddess of water), including suggestions that it was a gateway to hell or the lair of a ferocious basilisk slain by bishop St-Jean de Réôme. Divers have penetrated 360m along a narrow underwater passageway and 61m in depth with no end in sight, but further exploration was banned in 1996, after several explorers died in these attempts.

## Château de Tanlay

8km southeast of Tonnerre • April–Nov Wed–Mon 10am–12.30pm & 2.15–6pm; guided tours 10am, 11.30am & hourly 2.15–5.15pm • €9 • ☎ 03 86 75 70 61, ⓦ chateaudetanlay.fr

The romantic **Château de Tanlay** is a pleasant 8km cycle along the canal south-east from Tonnerre. This early sixteenth-century construction, very French in feel, is only slightly later in date than its near-neighbour, but those extra few years were enough for the purer Italian influences visible in Ancy to have become Frenchified. Encircling the château are water-filled moats and standing guard over the entrance to the first grassy courtyard is the grand lodge, from where you enter the château across a stone drawbridge.

# Château d'Ancy-le-Franc

25km southeast of Tonnerre • April to mid-Nov Tues–Sun 10.30am–12.30pm & 2–5pm; July & Aug 10.30am–5pm; guided tours 10.30am, 11.30am, 2pm, 3pm & 4pm; plus April–Sept 5pm • Château €9; château & park €13 • ⓦ chateau-ancy.com • No public transport

The **Château d'Ancy-le-Franc** was built in the mid-sixteenth century for the brother-in-law of the notorious Diane de Poitiers, mistress of Henri II. More Italian than French, with its textbook classical countenance, it is the work of the Italian Sebastiano Serlio, one of the most important architectural theorists of the Renaissance, who was brought to France in 1540 by François I to work on his palace at Fontainebleau. The exterior is elegant but austere, but the inner courtyard is a refined embodiment of the principles of classical architecture. Some of the apartments are sumptuous, decorated by the Italian artists Primaticcio and Niccolò dell'Abbate, both of whom also worked at Fontainebleau. **Concerts** are occasionally held in the courtyard, the price of which includes a tour of the château.

## Musée du Pays Châtillonnais

14 rue de la Libération, Châtillon-sur-Seine • Sept–June Wed–Mon 9am–noon & 2–6pm; July & Aug daily 10am–7pm • €7 •
☎ 03 80 91 24 67, 🖰 musee-vix.fr

For anyone interested in pre-Roman France, there is one compelling reason to visit
**CHÂTILLON-SUR-SEINE**, around 30km east of Tonnerre: the so-called **Treasure of Vix**,
discovered in 1953 6km northwest of Châtillon. The finds, from the sixth-century BC
tomb of a Celtic princess buried in a four-wheeled chariot, include the famous **Vase of
Vix**, which, weighing 208kg and 1.64m high, is the largest bronze vase of Greek origin
known from antiquity, with a superbly modelled high-relief frieze round its rim, and
Gorgons' heads for handles. The treasure is displayed in the **Musée du Pays
Châtillonnais**, which also boasts an impressive collection of objects from Celtic,
Gallo-Roman and medieval periods found in the Châtillonnais region.

## Montbard and around

One base worth knowing about if you're counting on **public transport** in the area is the
rather unexciting hillside town of **MONTBARD**, on the main line between Dijon and
Paris and where buses leave for both Chatillon and Semur. It may even be worth an
overnight stop if you're heading to the **Abbaye de Fontenay** and the site of **Alésia**.

### Abbaye de Fontenay

6km from Montbard • Daily: April–Oct 10am–6pm; guided visits hourly except 1pm; mid-Nov to mid-April 10am–noon & 2–5pm • €9.20 •
🖰 abbayedefontenay.com

The UNESCO World Heritage Site of **Abbaye de Fontenay** is the biggest draw in the
area. Founded in 1118, it's the only Burgundian monastery to survive intact, despite
conversion to a paper mill in the early nineteenth century. It was restored in the early
1900s to its original form, while the gardens were re-landscaped in 2008 in full
harmony with its Romanesque structure. It is one of the world's most complete
monastic complexes, including a caretaker's lodge, guesthouse and chapel, dormitory,
hospital, prison, bakery, kennels and abbot's house, as well as a church, cloister,
chapterhouse and even a forge.

On top of all this, the abbey's setting, at the head of a quiet stream-filled valley
enclosed by woods of pine, fir, sycamore and beech, is superb. There's a bucolic calm
about the place, particularly in the graceful cloister, and in these surroundings the
spartan simplicity of Cistercian life seems appealing. Hardly a scrap of decoration
softens the church and there's no direct lighting in the nave, just an otherworldly glow
from the square-ended apse.

## Alésia and around

A few kilometres south of Montbard, on Mont Auxois, above the village of **ALISE-STE-
REINE** is **Alésia** (closed Dec & Jan). It was here in 52 BC that the Gauls, united under
the leadership of Vercingétorix, made their last stand against the military might of
Rome. Julius Caesar himself commanded the Roman army, which surrounded the final
Gallic stronghold and starved the Gauls out, bloodily defeating all attempts at escape.
Vercingétorix surrendered to save his people, was imprisoned in Rome for six years
until Caesar's formal triumph, and then strangled. The **battle** was a fundamental
turning point in the fortunes of the region, as Gaul remained under Roman rule for
four hundred years.

### Muséoparc d'Alésia

1 rte des Trois Ormeaux, Alise-Ste-Reine • Daily: Oct–March 10am–5pm; April–June & Sept 9am–6pm; July & Aug 9am–7pm; museum
closes Jan & Feb • €9 • ☎ 03 80 96 96 23, 🖰 alesia.com

The modern **Muséoparc d'Alésia**, inaugurated in March 2012, brings the battle of

Alésia to life with a visitor centre, a museum and a multimedia exhibition about Gallo-Roman life. You can also visit excavations, including the theatre and a Gallo-Roman house.

### Vercingétorix statue

On the hilltop opposite the Muséoparc d'Alésia, and visible from far and wide, is a great bronze **statue of Vercingétorix**. Erected by Napoleon III, whose influence popularized the rediscovery of France's pre-Roman roots, the statue represents Vercingétorix as a romantic Celt – half virginal Christ, half long-haired 1970s heartthrob. On the plinth is inscribed a quotation from Vercingétorix's address to the Gauls as imagined by Julius Caesar: "United and forming a single nation inspired by a single ideal, Gaul can defy the world." Napoleon III signs his dedication, "Emperor of the French", inspired by a vain desire to gain legitimacy by linking his own name to that of a "legendary" Celt.

### Château de Bussy-Rabutin

8km east of Alésia, on the D954 • Daily: mid-May to mid-Sept 9.15am–1pm & 2–6pm; mid-Sept to mid-May 9.15am–noon & 3–5pm • €7.50 • ☎ 03 80 96 00 03, Ⓦ bussy-rabutin.monuments-nationaux.fr

The handsome **Château de Bussy-Rabutin**, a French National monument, was built for Roger de Rabutin, a member of the Academy in the reign of Louis XIV and a notorious womanizer. The scurrilous tales of life at the royal court told in his book *Histoires Amoureuses des Gaules* earned him a spell in the Bastille, followed by years of exile in this château. There are some interesting portraits of great characters of the age, including its famous female beauties, each underlined by an acerbic little comment such as: "The most beautiful woman of her day, less renowned for her beauty than the uses she put it to".

### Semur-en-Auxois

Sitting on a rocky bluff, **SEMUR-EN-AUXOIS**, an extraordinarily beautiful small fortress town, is a place of cobbled lanes, medieval gateways and ancient gardens tumbling down to the River Armançon, 13km west of Alésia. All roads here lead to Place Notre-Dame, a handsome square dominated by the large thirteenth-century **church of Notre-Dame**, characterized by its huge entrance porch and the narrowness of its nave. Inside, the windows of the second chapel on the left commemorate the dead of World War I – Semur was the general headquarters of the American 78th division, and the battlefields were not far away.

In front of the church are the four sturdy towers of Semur's once-powerful **castle**, all that remains after the body of the fortress was dismantled in 1602 because of its usefulness to enemies of the French crown. You can explore the winding streets around the castle – there's scarcely a lane in town without some building of note – and continue down to the delightful stretch of river between the Pont Pinard and the Pont Joly, from where there are beautiful views of the town.

### Époisses

Cheese connoisseurs might like to take a 12km hop west of Semur on the Avallon road to the village of **ÉPOISSES**, not only for its château (gardens year-round; €2; castle July & Aug daily except Tues 10am–noon & 3–6pm; €7; Ⓦ chateaudepoisses.com), but also for its distinctive, soft orange-skinned cheese of the same name, washed in *marc de Bourgogne*.

### The source of the Seine

The **source of the Seine** lies some 15km southeast of Alésia. No more than a trickle here, it rises in a tight little vale of beech woods. The spring is now covered by an artificial grotto complete with a languid nymph, Sequana, spirit of the Seine. In Celtic

8

times it was a place of worship, as is clear from the numerous votive offerings discovered there, including a neat bronze of Sequana standing in a bird-shaped boat, now in the Dijon archeological museum.

## ARRIVAL AND INFORMATION

CANAL DE BOURGOGNE

### TONNERRE

**By train** The *gare SNCF* is just a 10min walk from the centre of town.

Destinations Alésia/Les Laumes (15 daily; 35min); Dijon (15 daily; 1hr); Laroche Migennes (15 daily; 20min); Montbard (15 daily; 25min); Paris Bercy (15 daily; 1hr 50min).

**By bus** Buses stop in front of the train station. Book in advance at ☎0800 303 309.

Destinations Auxerre (4–6 daily; 1hr 10min); Chablis (4–6 daily; 20min); Noyers-sur-Serein (4 daily; 40min); Tanlay (4 daily; 15min).

**Tourist office** Place Marguerite-de-Bourgogne (April–Sept Mon–Sat 9.30am–noon & 1.30–6pm; Sun 10am–12.30pm & 2–6pm; Nov–March Mon, Tues & Thurs–Sat 9.30am–noon & 1.30–6pm; ☎03 86 55 14 48, ⓦtonnerre.fr). They rent bikes (€2.50/hr; €18/day) and offer a free town trail leaflet.

### MONTBARD

**By train** The *gare SNCF* is at place Henri Vincenot, south of town.

Destinations Auxerre (5 daily; 1hr 30min); Dijon (every 30min–1hr, 35min); Laroche-Migennes (9–10 daily; 50min); Les Laumes-Alésia (hourly; 8min); Tonnerre (15 daily; 25min).

**By bus** Buses stop by the *gare SNCF*.

Destinations Chatillon-sur-Seine (6–9 daily; 40min); Dijon (2–5 daily; 35min).

### ALÉSIA

**By train** Trains go as far as the station of Les Laumes–Alésia, from where it's a 3km ascent to the site.

**By taxi** You can book or order taxis from Montbard station to Alésia (☎06 08 82 20 61 or ☎03 80 92 31 49).

## ACCOMMODATION

### TONNERRE

**Du Centre** 63–64 rue de l'Hôpital ☎03 86 55 10 56, ⓦhotel-tonnerre.com. Located opposite the *Hotel Dieu* in the centre of town, this is a relaxed, provincial hotel with a reasonable little restaurant (*menus* from €10.50). Breakfast €7. **€50**

★ **Ferme de la Fosse Dionne** 11 rue de la Fosse Dionne ☎03 86 54 82 62, ⓦferme-fosse-dionne.fr. A sensitively restored former farm, with lovely rooms in bright colours and a beamed, covered balcony overlooking a small courtyard directly opposite the spring. The friendly owners also offer a three-course meal for €20 in the evening. Parking free, breakfast included. **€68**

### MONTBARD

**De la Gare** 10 av Foch ☎03 80 92 02 12, ⓦhotel-de-la-gare-montbard.com. Just opposite the station, this

two-star hotel offers reasonably priced rooms with parking. The restaurant has *menus* (€11–29), salads and sandwiches. Breakfast €9. **€53**

### SEMUR-EN-AUXOIS

**Du Commerce** 19 rue de la Liberté ☎03 80 96 64 40, ⓦhotel-du-commerce.fr. The cheapest option for miles around, this hotel has clean but rather basic rooms with a bar-restaurant downstairs offering internet access (€4/hr) and *menus* for €12.50. Breakfast €6. The half-board option at €66 is good value. **€49**

**Des Cymaises** 7 rue du Renaudot ☎03 80 97 21 44, ⓦhotelcymaises.com. Traditional hotel in the medieval city proper, housed in a grand old mansion with a walled courtyard. Rooms – some with sloping roofs – are of high standard with flatscreen TV. Breakfast €8.50. **€68**

## EATING AND DRINKING

### TONNERE

★ **Autour du Pressoir** Place Marguerite ☎03 86 54 81 05. A bar á vin in the lovely central town square offering large *assiettes* of local produce and an extensive wine list including Chablis, Tonnerrois and Aligoté. Eat and drink, then buy the ingredients and wines from the shop inside. July & Aug daily 10am–late; Sept–May Tues–Sun 10am–late.

**Saint Père** 2 rue Georges Pompidou ☎03 86 55 12 84, ⓦle-saint-pere.com. The place to try Burgundy

cuisine, this is family cooking at its best, served in splendid country mansion surroundings. Lunch *menus* start from €11, but the five-course dinner with wine at €50 is hard to beat. Mid-June to mid-Aug Mon & Wed–Sun noon–1.30pm & 7.30–9pm, Tues noon–1.30pm; mid-Aug to mid-June Mon & Wed–Sat noon–1.30pm & 7.30–9pm, Tues & Sun noon–1.30pm. Closed last week in Aug, last week of April and two weeks after Christmas.

# The Morvan

The **Morvan** region (Ⓦmorvan.com) lies in the middle of Burgundy between the valleys of the Loire and the Saône, stretching roughly from **Clamecy**, **Vézelay** and **Avallon** in the north to **Autun** in the south. It's a land of wooded hills and, with poor soil and pastures only good for a few cattle, villages and farms are few and far between. In the nineteenth century, supplying firewood and charcoal to Paris was the main business and large tracts of hillside are still covered in coniferous plantations. Wet nursing was also an important part of the economy, with local peasant women leaving their homes and families to feed the children of the French aristocracy and Parisian bourgeoisie, a practice that continued well into the twentieth century.

The World War II Occupation was felt profoundly in the Morvan, firstly because it was stripped of its machinery, equipment and forestry products; and secondly because it became a centre for the **Resistance**. As a result the locals suffered terribly from reprisals and forced labour programmes.

The creation of a **parc régional** in 1970 did something to promote the area as a place for outdoor activities, but it was the election of François Mitterrand, local politician and former mayor of **Château-Chinon**, as president of the Republic that rescued the Morvan from oblivion. In addition to lending it some of the glamour of his office, he took concrete steps to beef up the local economy. West of the Morvan, the landscape softens as it descends towards the River Loire and the fine medieval town of **Nevers**, on Burgundy's western border.

**8**

## Avallon

Approaching **AVALLON** along the N6 from the north, you might not give the place a second look. The southern aspect is altogether more promising, a small, ancient town clustered high on a ridge above the wooded valley of the River Cousin, looking out over the hilly, sparsely populated country of the Morvan regional park. Once a staging post on the Roman Via Agrippa from Lyon to Boulogne, it's an attractive place of stone facades and sleepy cobbled streets, and well worth a visit.

Bisecting the town north to south, the narrow **Grande-Rue Aristide-Briand** leads past the arch of the fifteenth-century **Tour de l'Horloge** – the 49m spire of which dominates

---

### CHÂTEAU LIVING

Burgundy – and in particular the area to the east and south of the Morvan – is one of the prime **château** regions in France. Whether still in the hands of old families like the **château Bazoches du Morvan** (Ⓦchateau-de-vauban.com) whose current owner is related to Vauban, the great French fortification builder, or state-owned and -maintained like the **château de Castellux** (Ⓦchateaudechastellux.com), their remoteness and association with a feudal aristocratic class places them several steps above a simple stately mansion.

As the upkeep of such massive structures becomes more and more expensive, many château owners rent their properties to large families or groups. Depending on numbers, costs can be as low as £300 per week, but take note: wi-fi may not penetrate the thick stone walls, and you will almost invariably need your own car; some places come with a cook and a maid, and occasionally the owners may still live on the premises (though you might never even bump into them). The range of experiences is broad, however, and you should be able to find something to suit your tastes – from **Château de Missery** near Saulieu (Ⓦchateaudemissery.com), who offer weekend cookery courses and wine tastings for about a dozen people, to **Château de Tailly** (Ⓦchateaudetailly.com), which is split into three buildings and can accommodate smaller parties of guests. Check Ⓦsimplychateau.com for a selection of options.

the town – to the pilgrim church of **St-Lazare**, on whose battered Romanesque facade you can still decipher graceful carvings of the zodiac signs; inside, in the southeastern chapel, there is a wonderful trompe l'oeil of the Virgin Mary.

Take a stroll down to the lime-shaded **Promenade de la Petite Porte**, where you can walk the perimeter of the outside walls, affording precipitous views across the plunging valley of the Cousin.

## Musée de l' Avallonnais

5 rue du Collège • April–Sept Wed–Mon 2–6pm; Oct, Nov & Jan–March Sat & Sun 2–6pm • €3 • ☎ 03 86 34 03 19, ⓦ museeavallonnais.com

The archeological section of the **Musée de l'Avallonais** includes a second-century mosaic from a Gallo-Roman villa, while the highlight of the fine arts department is Alfred Boucher's sculpture of a very life-like Jason pinching the Golden Fleece.

## Musée du Costume

6 rue Belgrand • April–Nov daily 10.30am–12.30pm & 1.30–5.30pm • €4 • ☎ 03 86 34 19 95

The rather quaint **Musée du Costume**, housed in a seventeenth-century mansion just off Grande-Rue, features a collection of regional dresses among furniture and *objets d'art* of this period. They host a special exhibition every summer concentrating on historical fashions.

### ARRIVAL AND INFORMATION

AVALLON

**By train** The *gare SNCF* is to the northeast of town about a 15min walk from the centre.
Destinations Autun (1–2 daily; 1hr 50min); Auxerre (1–2 daily; 1hr 10min); Montbard (1–2 daily; 1hr 50min); Saulieu (1–2 daily; 50min).
**By bus** Trans-Yonne buses stop at Place Vauban.
Destinations Auxerre (1–2 daily; 1hr 10min); Dijon (1–3 daily; 2hr–2hr 30min); Semur-en-Auxois (1–3 daily; 1hr); Vézelay (summer only 1–3 daily; 30min).

**Tourist office** In a fifteenth-century house at 6 rue Bocquillot, between the clock tower and St-Lazare (July & Aug Mon–Sat 9.30am–12.30pm & 1.30–6.30pm, Sun 10am–noon & 2–6pm; Sept–June Mon–Sat 9.30am–12.30pm & 2–6pm; ☎ 03 86 34 14 19, ⓦ avallon-tourisme.fr).
**Bike rental** Sarl Gueneau Frères, 26 rue de Paris (☎ 03 86 34 28 11; ⓦ touvelo.fr; €4/hr, €18/day).

### ACCOMMODATION

**Camping Municipal de Sous-Roche** Rue Sous-Roche ☎ 03 86 34 10 39, ⓔ campingsousroche@ville-avallon .fr. Attractive, classy riverside site 2km south of town inside the Parc du Morvan, close to many hiking and mountain biking trails. Closed mid-Oct to March. **€9.30**
**Les Capucins** 6 av Doumer ☎ 03 86 34 06 52, ⓦ avallonlescapucins.com. Delightful mid-range *hôtel de charme* housed in a nineteenth-century mansion close to the train station, with pleasant en-suite rooms all boasting a/c and some offering disabled access. Breakfast €8.50. **€60**
**Hostellerie de la Poste** 13 place Vauban ☎ 03 86 34 16 16, ⓦ hostelleriedelaposte.com. A former coaching inn turned into a four-star hotel with sumptuous,

exquisitely furnished rooms set around a cobbled courtyard. It also has a restaurant (Mon–Sat noon–2pm & 7.30–9.45pm), which serves a five-course "Menu 1707" – the date the inn was built – for €48. Breakfast included. Closed Jan to mid-March. **€150**
★ **Le Moulin des Ruats** 4km west of Avallon ☎ 03 86 34 97 00, ⓦ moulindesruats.com. If you have a car, try this eighteenth-century former flour mill on the scenic valley road to Vézelay. Some of the calm, elegant rooms have a view of the river Cousin, and the restaurant is the best in the area (from €29.50), specializing in regional cuisine. Breakfast €13. Closed mid-Nov to mid-Feb. Restaurant 7–9pm Tues–Sat, Sun noon–2pm & 7–9pm. **€85**

### EATING AND DRINKING

**Dame Jeanne** 59 Grande-Rue ☎ 03 86 34 58 71, ⓦ www.damejeanne.fr. This refined tea-room and café in a seventeenth-century house, which has long opening hours, offers an excellent breakfast and does light dishes for around €8 in a flowery courtyard. Its specialities are

*gougères* with spices. Fri–Wed 8am–6.30pm.

★ **Pizzeria de la Tour** 84 Grande-Rue ☎ 03 86 34 24 84, ⓦ latouravallon.com. Excellent-value and centrally located restaurant offering pizzas for €8, and recommended regional *plats du jour* for €7. Portions are on

the large side. Daily noon–3pm & 7–10pm.
**Relais des Gourmets** 47 rue de Paris ☎ 03 86 34
18 90, ⊛ relaisdesgrourmets.com. This restaurant of
thirty-odd years' standing has a large choice of *menus* –

for under €20 you get the regional classics, snails
and beef, while €42 involves more upmarket cuisine.
Mid-July to Aug daily; Sept to mid-July closed Sun eve
& Mon.

# Vézelay

The tourist buses winding their way up the steep incline to **VÉZELAY** should not deter
you from visiting this attractive hilltop hamlet, surrounded by ramparts and with some
of the most picturesque, winding streets and crumbling buildings in Burgundy. While
the main draw is undeniably the **Basilica of Ste-Mary La Madeleine**, Vézelay is also a
popular destination for art-lovers, with many small galleries and antique shops on rue
St-Pierre, and an impressive art collection in the **Musée Zervos**.

## Basilica of Ste-Mary La Madeleine

Top of rue St-Pierre • Daily sunrise–sunset (usually 8pm) • Free • ☎ 03 86 33 39 53, ⊛ basiliquedevezelay.org

Pilgrims journey to Vézelay to venerate the relics of Mary Magdalene (1120), housed in
one of the seminal buildings of the Romanesque period, the **Basilica of Ste-Mary La
Madeleine,** one of the first UNESCO-inscribed sites in France. On the church's west
front the colossal narthex was added to the nave in 1140 to accommodate the swelling
numbers of pilgrims. Inside, your eye is drawn to the sculptures of the central doorway,
on whose tympanum a Pentecostal Christ is shown swathed in exquisitely figured
drapery. From Christ's outstretched hands, the message of the Gospel shoots out to the
apostles in the form of beams of fire, while the frieze below depicts the converted and
the pagans – among those featured are giants, pygmies (one mounting his horse with a
ladder), a man with breasts and huge ears, and dog-headed heathens. The arcades and
arches are edged with fretted mouldings, and the supporting pillars are crowned with
finely cut capitals, depicting scenes from the Bible, classical mythology, allegories and
morality stories. The orientation of the church is such that, during the summer solstice,
the sun coming through the south windows creates a line of nine luminous spots
bisecting the nave floor.

## Musée de l'Oeuvre Viollet-le-Duc

Place du cloître • Easter–June & Sept Sat–Sun 2–6pm; July & Aug daily 2–6pm • €3 • ☎ 03 86 33 24 62

The **Musée de l'Oeuvre Viollet-le-Duc,** which takes up two rooms of the old monks'
dormitory, houses the best sculptures from the Ste-Mary La Madeleine basilica as well
as the mouldings created by Viollet-le-Duc during the basilica's restoration.

## Musée Zervos

Rue Saint-Étienne • Mid-March to June & Sept to mid-Nov Wed–Mon 10am–6pm; July & Aug daily 10am–6pm • €3 • ☎ 03 86 32 39 26,
⊛ musee-zervos.fr

Occupying the house where Romain Rolland, the Nobel prize for literature winner,
lived and died in 1944, the **Musée Zervos** is well worth a visit. Exhibits include a
number of interesting modernist works, including pieces by Picasso, Kandinsky, Miró,
Calder and Giacometti.

### ARRIVAL AND INFORMATION                                                                          VÉZELAY

**By bus** A shuttle operates from Avallon station (Easter–
June & Sept, Sat, Sun & holidays 11am & 5pm; July & Aug
daily 9.40am, 2.45pm & 5pm; 30min; €2); it heads back to
Avallon 40min later.

**By train** From Paris Bercy take the train to Avallon and
stop at Sermizelles (10km away) where you can continue to
Vézelay by pre-booked taxi (Cyril Taxi, ⊛ taxi-vezelay.com

or Cathy Taxi, ☎ 03 86 42 51 56; €20).

**By car** Vézelay is 14km from Avallon on the D957 and
48km away from Auxerre on the N6 and then the N151.
There are car parks at the bottom of the hill, including a
free one (which is always full); but keep climbing up,
because the largest car park is to the left of the basilica
right at the top.

**Tourist office** 12 rue St-Etienne (May–Sept daily 10am–1pm & 2–6pm; Oct–April Fri–Wed 10am–1pm & 2–6pm; mid-Nov to Easter Fri, Sat & Mon–Wed 10am–1pm & 2–6pm; ☎ 03 86 33 23 69, ⓦ vezelaytourisme.com).

## ACCOMMODATION

**L'Espérance** Grande-Rue, Saint-Père ☎ 03 86 33 39 10, ⓦ marc-meneau-esperance.com. Some 2km below Vézelay, in the village of Saint-Pére, this hotel-restaurant is truly extraordinary. Filled with antique furniture, but providing all modern conveniences, including disabled access, it has 34 luxurious rooms and suites in three locations: *Le Moulin* (the mill), *Le pré des marguerites* (the daisy field) and the main house above the restaurant. Good deals offer half board in its celebrated restaurant. Closed mid-Jan to early March. **€310**

★ **Les Glycines** Rue St Pierre ☎ 03 86 32 35 30, ⓦ glycines-vezelay.com. This beautiful mid-eighteenth century hotel looks crumbling but is very comfortable and charming; check out the Zervos suite with its 250-year-old wallpaper. The appealing courtyard faces the main street, while inside there's a cosy, atmospheric restaurant (*menus* €20.50). Breakfast included. Restaurant Sun–Tues 12.15–2pm, Fri & Sat 12.15–2pm & 7–9pm. **€72**

**De la Poste et du Lion d'Or** Place du Champ de Foire ☎ 03 86 33 21 23, ⓦ laposte-liondor.com. A grand and luxurious choice whose plush rooms have imposing old wooden furniture and great views of either the old town or the sweeping valley behind. Restaurant *menus* from €25. Breakfast €12. Closed Jan & Feb. **€96**

## EATING AND DRINKING

**Le Bougainville** 28 rue St-Pierre ☎ 03 86 33 27 57. Good regional cuisine served in a genteel dining room with *menus* from €25. The house terrine, made with *époisses* cheese, ham and artichoke, is delicious. March to mid-Nov Thurs–Mon Noon–2pm & 7–9pm.

**L'Espérance** Grande-Rue, Saint-Père ☎ 03 86 33 39 10, ⓦ marc-meneau-esperance.com. Chef Marc Meneau's two-star Michelin restaurant adds modern touches to traditional dishes – try, for example roasted lobster with sea urchins followed by Granny Smith apple cake with orange confit. *Menus* from €96, wine included. Bookings only, and well in advance. March to mid-Jan; closed Mon lunch, Tues & Wed lunch; they will allocate your dining time when you call.

★ **Le Saint Etienne** 39 rue St-Pierre ☎ 03 86 33 27 34, ⓦ le-saint-etienne.fr. Owned by Gilles Lafontaine, former chef of the well-known *George V* in Paris, this gourmet restaurant specializes in traditional French cuisine. Mains are around €15 and are served by the owner's wife who is happy to advise diners about the food, explain how dishes are made, and even disclosing a few of the chef's secrets. Reservations essential. March–Dec Fri, Sat, Mon & Tues noon–3pm & 7–8.30pm, Sun noon–3pm.

# Clamecy

**CLAMECY**, 23km west of Vézelay on the banks of the River Yonne, has less to offer than its rustic neighbours, but is worth a day-trip. It was the centre of the Morvan's logging trade from the sixteenth century up until the completion of the Canal du Nivernais in 1834; woodcutting gangs working in the hills floated their logs down the river as far as Clamecy, where they were made up into great rafts for shipment on to Paris.

Winding your way up the narrow streets that lead to the well-preserved historic town centre, you'll pass a number of fifteenth- to eighteenth-century buildings, particularly on **rue de la Monnaie**, **rue de la Tour** and **rue Bourgeoisie**. At the top of the hill is the church of **St Martin**, a veritable gem of flamboyant Gothic architecture, parts of which date back to the twelfth century.

## Romain Rolland Art and History Museum

Av de la République • April–Sept Wed–Sat & Mon 10am–noon & 2–6pm, Sun 2–6pm; Oct–Dec, Feb & March Wed–Sat 10am–noon & 2–6pm, Sun 2–6pm • €3 • ☎ 03 86 27 17 99

Clamecy's **Romain Rolland Art and History Museum** has a broad range of things to see, including three whole rooms of Gallo-Roman objects and a fine art collection that spans the last five centuries. The modernist posters designed by renowned poster artist Charles Loupot and the collection of paintings donated by President Mitterrand are particularly worth seeking out.

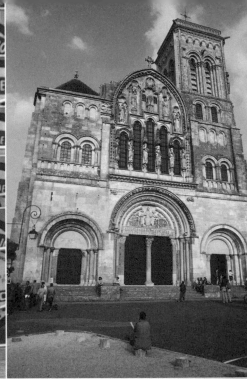

## Saulieu

An old market town with a reputation for its gastronomy, **SAULIEU** suffered as a result of the depopulation of the Morvan. Every year the town waits hungrily for its **Gourmet festival** on the third weekend of May – featuring mountains of meat, rivers of wine and all manner of local produce. Saulieu is a good springboard for the cycling, hiking and riding possibilities in the Parc du Morvan (see p.449), but unless you come during the festival it's not overly exciting as a base.

### Basilique St-Andoche

Nov–Easter Tues–Sat 9am–noon & 2–4.30pm; Easter–Nov Tues–Sat 9am–noon & 2–6.30pm, Sun 2–6.30pm • Free

The main sight of Saulieu old town is the twelfth-century **Basilique St-Andoche**, noted for its lovely Romanesque capitals of the school of Gislebertus, the master sculptor of Autun, as well as its impressive church organ.

### Musée François-Pompon

3 rue du Docteur Roclore• April–Sept Mon 10.30am–12.30pm, Wed–Sat 10am–12.30pm & 2–5pm, Sun & public holidays 10.30am–noon & 2.30–6pm; Oct–Dec & March Mon 10.30am–12.30pm, Wed–Sat 10am–12.30pm & 2–5pm, Sun & public holidays 10.30am–noon & 2.30–5.30pm • €3 • ☎ 03 80 64 19 51

Next door to the basilica, the **Musée François-Pompon** is fun to visit, with good local folklore displays and a large collection of works by the local nineteenth-century animal sculptor, François Pompon. One room is devoted to the gourmet past of the town with a particular dedication to local Michelin chef **Bernard Loiseau** who committed suicide in 2003.

**8**

### ARRIVAL AND INFORMATION
SAULIEU

**By train** A 10min walk from the train station up av de la Gare (10min) brings you to the main street, rue Argentine, which runs through the town north–south. Turn right for the tourist office (5min).

Destinations There are commuter trains in the morning and in the evening to Autun only (5 daily; 50min).

**By bus** Buses stop in front of the *gare SNCF*. Book in advance (☎ 0800 21 32 33).

Destinations Autun (2–4 daily; 50min); Avallon (4 daily; 1hr); Montbard (4 daily; 1hr).

**Tourist office** 24 rue d'Argentine (Oct–March Mon–Sat 10am–noon & 2–5pm; April Mon–Sat 10am–1pm & 2–6pm; May & Sept Mon–Sat 10am–noon & 2–5pm, Sun 10am–1pm & 2–5pm; June–Aug Mon–Sat 10am–noon & 2–7pm, Sun 10am–1pm & 2–7pm; ☎ 03 80 64 00 21, ⓦ saulieu.fr).

### ACCOMMODATION AND EATING

**La Borne Imperiale** 16 rue d'Argentine ☎ 03 80 64 19 76, ⓦ borne-imperiale.com. Run by a charming couple, with rooms facing a peaceful garden and a great restaurant (closed Mon eve & Tues) that has an attractive terrace and classic Burgundian *menus* from €18. Breakfast €9.50. €62

★ **La Côte d'Or (Le Relais Bernard Loiseau)** 2 rue d'Argentine ☎ 03 80 90 53 53, ⓦ bernard-loiseau.com.

This five-star hotel-restaurant-spa was created by the famed chef Bernard Loiseau (and made even more famous after his suicide in 2003 following a long bout of depression). It is an elegant, beyond-luxurious place of rich woods, stone arches and plush furnishings that exude wealth. *Menus* at the three-star Michelin restaurant (closed Tues & Wed), which has been continued by his widow, start at €66 for lunch. Free parking. Breakfast €22. €195

## Autun

With its Gothic spire rising against the backdrop of the Morvan hills, **AUTUN** is scarcely bigger than the circumference of its **walls**; most of the enclosure still consists of Roman fortifications that have been maintained through the centuries. The emperor Augustus founded the town in about 10 BC as part of a massive and, ultimately, highly successful campaign to pacify the brooding Celts of defeated Vercingétorix. The splendour of Augustodunum, as it was called, was designed to eclipse the memory of Bibracte, the neighbouring capital of the powerful tribe of the Aedui. Autun did indeed become one of the leading cities of Roman Gaul until it was sacked by the Arabs in 725 AD. Today, it is a picturesque provincial town, and an excellent base for exploring the surrounding countryside, particularly the Parc du Morvan.

### The Gallo-Roman remains

This town's past remains very tangible, and two of its four Roman gates survive: **Porte St-André**, spanning rue de la Croix-Blanche in the northeast, and **Porte d'Arroux** in the northwest. In a field just across the River Arroux stands a lofty section of wall known as the **Temple of Janus**, which was probably part of the sanctuary of an unknown deity. On the east side of town, on avenue du 2ème Dragons, you can see the remains of what was the largest **Roman theatre** in Gaul, with a capacity of fifteen thousand – in itself a measure of Autun's importance at that time. The most enigmatic of the Gallo-Roman remains in the region is the **Pierre de Couhard**, off Faubourg St-Pancrace to the southeast of the town. It's a 27m-tall stone pyramid situated on the site of one of the city's necropolises, thought to date from the first century, and most probably a cenotaph.

## Cathédrale St-Lazare

Place du Terreau • Daily 8am–7pm • Free

Autun's great twelfth-century **Cathédrale St-Lazare** was built nearly a thousand years after the Romans had departed, and its greatest claim to artistic fame lies in its sculptures, the work of Gislebertus, generally accepted as one of the most outstanding Romanesque sculptors.

The tympanum of the **Last Judgement** above the west door bears his signature – *Gislebertus hoc fecit* ("Gislebertus made this") – beneath the feet of Christ. To his left are the Virgin Mary, the saints and the apostles, with the saved rejoicing below them; to the right the Archangel Michael disputes souls with Satan, who tries to cheat by leaning on the scales, while the damned despair beneath. During the eighteenth century the local clergy decided the tympanum was an inferior work and plastered over it, saving it from almost certain destruction during the Revolution. The interior of the cathedral, whose pilasters and arcading were modelled on the Roman architecture of the city's gates, was also decorated by Gislebertus, who carved most of the capitals himself. Some of the finest are now exhibited in the old chapter library, up the stairs on the right of the choir, among them a beautiful *Flight into Egypt* and *The Death of Cain*.

## Musée Rolin

3 rue des Bancs • Oct–March Tues–Sat 10am–noon & 2–5pm, Sun 10am–noon & 2.30–5pm; April–Sept Tues–Sun 9.30am–noon & 1.30–6pm • €5.15 • ☎ 03 85 52 09 76

Just outside the cathedral is the **Musée Rolin** which occupies a Renaissance hôtel that was once home to Nicolas Rolin, Chancellor of Philippe le Bon. In addition to interesting Gallo-Roman (and even Greek) pieces, the star attractions are Gislebertus's representation of Eve as an unashamedly sensual nude, and Jean Hey's brilliantly coloured *Nativity*.

### ARRIVAL AND INFORMATION
AUTUN

**By train** The *gare SNCF* is a short walk from the central square of the Champs-de-Mars.

Destinations Etang (10–15 daily; 25min) for all connections to Dijon and Beaune; Saulieu (2–4 daily; 50min).

**By bus** The *gare routière* is very near the train station. Book buses 24hr in advance (☎ 0800 853 000).

Destinations Avallon (Fri–Sun 3 daily; 1hr 50min); Chalon-sur-Saône (2–4 daily; 1hr 15min); Epinac (3–5 daily; 25min); Saulieu (2–4 daily; 50min).

**Tourist office** The tourist office is at 13 rue Général-Demetz on Champs-de-Mars (Mon–Sat 9.30am–12.30pm & 2–6.30pm; ☎ 03 85 86 80 38, ⓦ autun-tourisme.com). However, there is better online information (French only) at ⓦ autun.info.

**Internet** You can get online at the stylish *Elgé*, which also serves tea and coffee, 6 rue Chauchien (€4/hr; Oct–May Mon–Sat 2–6.30pm; June–Sept Tues–Fri 10.30am–noon & 2–6.30pm, Mon & Sat 2–6.30pm).

### ACCOMMODATION

**De France** 18 av de la République ☎ 03 85 52 14 00, ⓦ hotel-de-france-autun.fr. Family-run hotel opposite the station that provides basic, clean rooms, the cheapest of which have shared facilities. Closed two weeks in Aug & three weeks in Feb. **€56**

**Maison Sainte Barbe** 7 place Sainte-Barbe ☎ 03 85 86 24 77, ⓦ maisonsaintebarbe.com. Run by a charming woman, this former fifteenth-century rectory has four spacious and beautifully furnished *chambres d'hôtes*, and a lovely garden with a view of the neighbouring chapel.

Breakfast included. **€72**

**St-Louis** 6 rue de l'Arbalète ☎ 03 85 52 01 01, ⓦ hotelsaintlouis.net. The now slightly faded but once magnificent *St-Louis* is Autun's most historic hotel. Napoleon and Josephine stayed here twice in 1802 and 1805, while Napoleon himself was here for New Year's Eve in 1807 and on the march from Elba on 15 March 1815. For €150 you can sleep in the emperor's suite itself, still containing much of its original furniture (but thankfully not the bed itself). Closed mid-Nov to mid-Feb. Breakfast €12. **€50**

### EATING AND DRINKING

**L'Atmosphère** 9 rue Deguin ☎ 03 85 82 36 07. A small, cosy bar with mock leather furniture, coloured

tiles and cheap draft beer. DJs at weekends. Daily 7.30pm–1am.

**Le Chalet Bleu** 3 rue Jeannin ☎03 85 86 27 30, ⓦlechaletbleu.com. Innovative, distinctly stylish and with a bar as comfortable to wait at as the dining room itself, this is a great place to dine; *menus* €16.50–58. Wed–Sat 10am–2pm & 7.30–9pm, Sun & Mon 10am–2pm.

★ **Le Petit Rolin** 1 Parvis du Chanoine Denis Grivot ☎03 85 86 15 55, ⓦle-petit-rolin.fr. If you care for quick service in good surroundings, check out this little crêperie – its walls form part of the old ramparts and a Roman column

props up the roof – where you can dine on *cuisine bourguignonne* (€12) or crêpes (€8). April–Oct daily 11am–2pm & 7–10pm; Nov & Dec Wed–Sun 11am–2pm & 7–10pm.

**Des Remparts** 17 rue Mazagran ☎03 85 52 54 02. A convivial family restaurant serving great-value *menus* (from €14 at lunch, €21 for dinner) featuring regional specialities. Wed 10am–2.30pm, Thurs–Mon 10am–2.30pm & 6–10pm.

# Parc Régional du Morvan

Carpeted with forest and etched by cascading streams, the **Parc Régional du Morvan** was officially created in 1970, when 170,000 hectares of hilly countryside were set aside in an attempt to protect the local cultural and physical environment with a series of nature trails, animal reserves, museums and local craft shops. It's an excellent place for **outdoor activities**, especially cycling and walking, with a good network of simple accommodation.

## Château-Chinon

Although it nestles in beautiful countryside dotted with evergreens, lakes and limestone deposits, **CHÂTEAU-CHINON** – the most substantial community in the Parc du Morvan – is a place to drive through rather than stay overnight. It is of interest, however, for its President Mitterrand connections; he was mayor here from 1959 to 1981, and thanks largely to him, the village now boasts a major hosiery factory and military printing works, both of which have provided much-needed employment to an isolated and often forgotten region.

**8**

### Musée du Septennat

6 rue du Château • July & Aug daily 10am–1pm & 2–7pm; May–June & Sept–Dec Wed–Mon 10am–1pm & 2–6pm; Feb–April & Oct–Dec daily 10am–noon & 2–6pm • €4 • ☎ 03 86 85 19 23

The **Musée du Septennat,** housed in the converted eighteenth-century convent of St Claire, displays the gifts Mitterrand received as head of state, including carpets from the Middle East, ivory from Togo, Japanese puppets, and a bizarre table decorated with butterfly wings.

| INFORMATION AND ACCOMMODATION | PARC RÉGIONAL DU MORVAN |
|---|---|

**Information centre** The park's main information centre, the Maison du Parc, is 13km from Saulieu in beautiful grounds about 1km outside St-Brisson on the D6 (April to mid-Nov Mon–Fri 9.30am–12.30pm & 2–5.30pm, Sat 10am–12.30pm & 2–5.30pm, Sun and public holidays 10am–1pm; July & Aug Mon–Fri 9.30am–6.30pm, Sat 10am–1pm & 2–6pm, Sun & public hols 10am–1pm & 3-6.30pm; mid-Nov to March Mon–Fri 9.30am–12.30pm & 2–5.30pm; ☎03 86 78 79 57).

**Website** You can download cycling, walking and activities brochures from ⓦ tourisme.parcdumorvan.org.

**Accommodation** Every other village in the park seems to have its own campsite and the larger ones often have a couple of simple hotels as well. There are five campsites and several small hotels around the large, wooded Lac des Settons, the main resort in the heart of the park, which has watersports facilities, café-restaurants and small beaches. The plain, modern village of Montsauche, 4km northwest of the lake, is a good base for provisions, including camping gas, and has a municipal campsite; Moux, a similar distance to the southeast, is another possible alternative.

### ACTIVITIES

**Cycling** There is a plethora of cycle routes in the Parc du Morvan, and tourist offices throughout the Morvan region

sell large-scale maps for €15 each. Bikes are available from most campsites in the area: for a complete list ask at any tourist office, or check online.

**Hiking** For walkers, the most challenging trip is the three-to four-day hike along the GR13 footpath, crossing the park from Vézelay to Mont Beuvray and taking in the major lakes, which are among the park's most developed attractions. There are also numerous less strenuous possibilities including the 4km walk from Saulieu to Lac Chamboux.

**Climbing** There is excellent rock climbing near Avallon and Dun les Places.

**Horseriding** Horseriding is a fairly popular way of seeing the park, and numerous *gîtes* offer pony trekking.

**Kayaking** The River Cure (ⓦamck.org) is good for kayaking.

# Nevers

Some 60km west of the Parc du Morvan, **NEVERS**, on the confluence of the rivers Loire and Nièvre, is a strange place, where motorbikers and boy racers drawn to the Formula One racing ring nearby at **Magny-Cours** mingle in the streets with religious pilgrims come to pay their respects to **Bernadette of Lourdes**, gourmands attracted by the local **nougatine** sweets, and shoppers out to buy fine hand-painted pottery. **Faïence**, as it's called, has been a hallmark of Nevers since the seventeenth century, painted in the deep colour known as *bleue de Nevers*; you can still see artisans at work in **Faïence Bleue** at 22 rue du 14 Juillet or **Fayencerie d'Art de Nevers** at 11 and 88b avenue Colbert.

Place Carnot is the hub of the centre; nearby, just above the tourist office you'll find the fifteenth-century **Palais Ducal** (Mon–Sat 9am–12.30pm & 2–6pm), former home of the dukes of Nevers, which has octagonal turrets and a central tower adorned with elegantly carved hunting scenes.

That aside, Nevers' main attractions are its religious monuments. The stunning **Cathédrale de St-Cyr** (daily 9am–noon & 2–6pm), with its wonderful display of jutting gargoyles, reveals French architectural styles from the tenth to the sixteenth centuries and, with its modern stained-glass windows, brings things right up to the present. The cathedral even manages to have two apses, one Gothic, the other Romanesque.

On the far side of the commercial pedestrian precinct around rue Mitterrand is the even more interesting and aesthetically satisfying late eleventh-century **church of St-Étienne** (daily 9am–noon & 2–6pm).

## Espace Bernadette (old convent of St-Gildard)

34 Rue St Gildard • **Convent** Daily: Nov–March 8am–noon & 2–6pm; April–Oct 8am–12.30pm & 3.30–7.30pm • Free **Museum** Daily: Nov–March 8am–noon & 2–6pm; April–Oct 8am–12.30pm & 3.30–7.30pm • Free • ☎03 86 71 99 50

Of spiritual rather than architectural appeal is the **Espace Bernadette**, in the old **convent of St-Gildard**, where Bernadette of Lourdes ended her days. A steady flow of pilgrims comes to visit her tiny, embalmed body, displayed in a glass-fronted **shrine**, in the convent chapel. A small but very engaging **museum** displays some of her belongings and correspondence.

### ARRIVAL AND INFORMATION                                                    NEVERS

**By train and bus** The train and bus stations are next to each other at the west of the town centre; from here, av de Gaulle leads east to place Carnot (15min).

Destinations (train) Clermont-Ferrand (5–7 daily; 1hr 45min); Le Creusot (5–7 daily; 1hr 30min); Dijon (5–7 daily; 2hr 20min); Lyon (3–4 daily; 3hr); Paris Bercy (6–9 daily; 2–3hr).

**Tourist office** Below the Palais Ducal (Oct–March Mon

2–6pm, Tues–Sat 10am–12.30pm & 2–6pm; April & May Mon–Sat 10am–12.30pm & 2–6pm, Sun 10am–1pm & 2–6pm; June–Sept Mon–Sat 9.30am–6.30pm & 2–6pm; ☎03 86 68 46 00, ⓦnevers-tourisme.com).

**Racing and karting** You can go karting on the Magny-Cours circuit on certain dates (☎03 86 21 26 18, ⓦcircuitmagnycours.com). Check also the website for details of races.

## ACCOMMODATION

Accommodation is at an absolute premium on rally days, so check your dates carefully or book well in advance.

**Beauséjour** 5bis rue Saint-Gildard ☎ 03 86 61 20 84, ⓦ hotel-beausejour-nevers.com. Close to the station and opposite the convent of St-Gildard, this hotel offers very reasonably priced rooms (the cheaper ones have shared facilities) and friendly service. Breakfast €5. **€54**

**Camping de Nevers** Rue de la Jonction ☎ 06 84 98 69 79, ⓦ campingnevers.com. The municipal campsite, next to the river across the Pont de Loire, offers a splendid view of the Palais Ducal and Cathédrale de St-Cyr. There's a bar, internet access and bike hire at €8/day. Closed mid-Oct to mid-April. **€13.50**

**De Cleves** 8 rue St Didier ☎ 03.86.61.15.87, ⓦ hoteldecleves.fr. A quiet and comfortable hotel in the centre of town, run by friendly and energetic owners. The pleasant rooms all have wi-fi; you pay on arrival, as reception is not always open. Breakfast €7; garage €6. **€67**

**Diane** 38 rue de Midi ☎ 03 86 57 28 10, ⓦ bestwesterndiane-nevers.com. Just a short walk from the station, this is an excellently situated hotel, with good, friendly service, tennis court, indoor pool and a golf course. Closed parking available €8. Buffet breakfast €11.50. **€96**

## EATING AND DRINKING

**L'Agricole** 10 place Carnot ☎ 03 86 71 65 30. Not a place for a full-on gastronomic experience, but the long hours and easy-to-find central location make it a good standby. Brasserie *menus* start at €12. Daily 7.30am–1am.

**La Botte de Nevers** Rue du peitit Chateau ☎ 03 86 61 16 93, ⓦ labottedenevers.fr. Easily spotted due to the wonderful wrought-iron sign outside, this is a place of many *menus* – they start at €18.50, but it's worth paying more for the best Charollais steaks this side of the Morvan. Tues 7–9pm, Wed–Sat noon–1.30pm & 7–9pm, Sun noon–1.30pm.

**La Cour St-Étienne** 33 rue St-Étienne ☎ 03 86 36 74 57, ⓦ restaurant-la-cour.com. Attractive restaurant with an elegant half-timbered dining room, which serves high-quality, traditional food, with *menus* starting at €19.50. Sun & Tues noon–1.30pm, Wed–Sat noon–1.30pm & 7.30–9pm.

**Jean-Michel Couron** 21 rue St-Étienne ☎ 03 86 61 19 28, ⓦ jm-couron.com. Located in a former chapel, Jean-Michel Couran's restaurant gives traditional dishes a modern edge, offering gourmet French cuisine at reasonable prices. *Menus* €35, €48 and €56. Sun noon–1.15pm, Tues 7.45–9pm, Wed–Sat noon–1.15pm & 7.45–9pm.

**8**

# Dijon

In Celtic times, **DIJON** held a strategic position on the tin merchants' route from Britain to the Adriatic. It became the capital of the dukes of Burgundy around 1000 AD, and in the fourteenth and fifteenth centuries, under the auspices of dukes Philippe le Hardi (the Bold – as a boy, he had fought the English at Poitiers), Jean sans Peur (the Fearless), Philippe le Bon (the Good – he sold Joan of Arc to the English), and Charles le Téméraire (also the Bold), Dijon flourished. The dukes used their tremendous wealth and power – especially their control of Flanders, the dominant manufacturing region of the age – to make this one of the greatest centres of art, learning and science in Europe. It lost its capital status on incorporation into the kingdom of France in 1477, but has remained one of the country's pre-eminent provincial cities. Today, it's an affluent university city: elegant, modern and dynamic, especially when the students are around.

Dijon is not enormous and the area you'll want to see is confined to the eminently walkable centre. The two **tram lines** that started service in the winter of 2012/13 have transformed the place, with cars being forced out onto the outskirts; if you have driven to Dijon, you are advised to leave the car at your hotel and forget about it until you leave. **Rue de la Liberté** forms the spine of the city, running east from the wide, attractive **place Darcy** and the eighteenth-century triumphal arch of **Porte Guillaume** – once a city gate – past the **palace** of the dukes of Burgundy on the semicircular **place de la Libération**. From this elegant, classical square, rue Rameau continues directly east to place du Théâtre, from where rue Vaillant leads on to the **church of St Michel**. Most places of interest are within ten minutes' walk to the north or south of this main axis, which is lined with smart shops, mammoth department stores and elegant old houses.

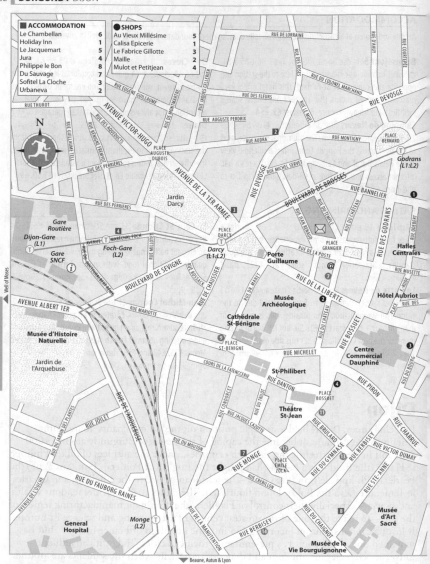

■ **ACCOMMODATION**
| | |
|---|---|
| Le Chambellan | 6 |
| Holiday Inn | 1 |
| Le Jacquemart | 5 |
| Jura | 4 |
| Philippe le Bon | 8 |
| Du Sauvage | 7 |
| Sofitel La Cloche | 3 |
| Urbaneva | 2 |

● **SHOPS**
| | |
|---|---|
| Au Vieux Millésime | 5 |
| Calisa Epicerie | 1 |
| Le Fabrice Gillotte | 3 |
| Maille | 2 |
| Mulot et Petitjean | 4 |

Beaune, Autun & Lyon

## The Palais des Ducs

Place de la Libération • **Tour Philippe-le-Bon** Guided tours only April–Nov 11 daily; Dec–March 6 tours Sat & Sun, 3 tours Wed • €2.30
**Musée des Beaux-Arts** Daily except Tues: May–Oct 9.30am–6pm; Nov–April 10am–5pm • Free

The focus of a visit to Dijon is inevitably the seat of its former rulers, the **Palais des Ducs**, which stands at the hub of the city. Facing the main courtyard is the relaxed **place de la Libération**, built by Jules Hardouin-Mansart, one of the architects of Versailles, towards the end of the seventeenth century. It's now something of a suntrap on a good day, and the decision to close it to traffic has stimulated a boom in café trade. The fourteenth-century Tour de Bar dominates the courtyard in front of the east wing, and now houses the **Musée des Beaux-Arts**, while the loftier, fifteenth-century

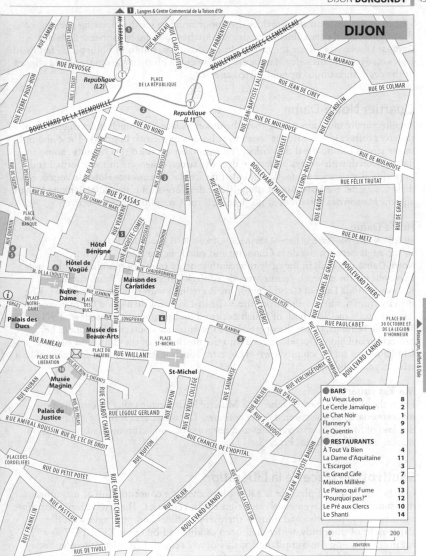

**Tour Philippe-le-Bon** can be visited only on guided tours. The vista from the top is particularly worthwhile for the views of the glazed Burgundian tiles of the Hôtel de Vogüé and the cathedral; on a clear day the Jura mountains loom on the horizon.

### Musée des Beaux-Arts

The **Musée des Beaux-Arts** has an interesting collection of works from the Middle Ages to the twentieth century; among the highlights are the Flemish paintings, particularly the *Nativity* by the so-called Master of Flémalle, a shadowy figure who ranks with van Eyck as one of the first artists to break from the chilly stranglehold of International Gothic, Burgundy's homespun phase of Gothic art.

Visiting the museum also provides the opportunity to see the surviving portions of the original ducal palace, including the vast **kitchen** and the magnificent **Salle des Gardes**. Displayed here are the lavish, almost decadent, **tombs** of Philippe le Hardi and Jean sans Peur and his wife, Marguerite de Bavière, with their startling, painted effigies of the dead, surrounded by gold-plated angels.

## Quartier Notre-Dame

Architecturally more interesting than the dukes' palace, and much more suggestive of the city's former glories, are the lavish townhouses of the rich burghers. These abound in the streets behind the duke's palace, most notably on **rue de la Chouette**. Some are half-timbered, with storeys projecting over the street, others are in more formal and imposing Renaissance stone. Particularly fine are the Renaissance **Hôtel de Vogüé**, 8 rue de la Chouette, the **Hôtel Auriot** at no.40 rue des Forges, plus the **Hôtel Benigne Malyot** and the **Maison des Cariatides** at no. 1 and 28 rue Chaudronnière respectively.

### Notre-Dame

Rue de la Préfecture • Tues–Thurs & Sat 10am–12.30pm & 1.30–4.30pm; Fri 10–11.30am & 2.30–4.30pm • Free

In the angle between rue de la Chouette and rue de la Préfecture, the church of **Notre-Dame** was built in the early thirteenth century in the Burgundian Gothic style. Look out for the eleventh-century wooden "black" Virgin in the south transept. Known as "Our Lady of Good Hope", she is credited with twice miraculously saving the city from fighting – once from the Swiss in 1513 and then when German troops left peacefully in 1944, both of which occurred on the now notorious date of 9/11. The **Tapisserie Terribilis**, below the organ above the entrance door, commemorates her protection of Dijon. Outside, carved into the north wall of the church on rue de la Chouette, is a small, sculpted owl – chouette. Touch it with your left hand and make a wish as you walk past.

### Market square

From the church of Notre-Dame, rue Musette leads west, passing just south of the **market square** and the covered *halles centrales*. The whole area is full of sumptuous displays of food and attractive cafés and restaurants, and is thronged with crowds on market days (Tues, Thurs, Fri & Sat).

## South of the place de la Libération

On the south side of place de la Libération, there's a concentration of magnificent **mansions** from the seventeenth and eighteenth centuries. These were built, for the most part, by men who had bought themselves offices and privileges with the Parliament of Burgundy, which had been established by Louis XI in 1477 as a means of winning the compliance of this newly acquired frontier province. Today a couple of them hold **museums**, while a few noteworthy houses around **rue Vauban** show the influence of sculptor Hugues Sambin in their decorative details (lions' heads, garlands of fruit, tendrils of ivy and his famous *chou bourguignon*, or "Burgundy cabbage"), notably, nos. 3, 12 and 21. To see more work by Sambin, head to Place Bossuet.

### Musée Magnin

4 rue des Bons-Enfants • Tues–Sun 10am–noon & 2–6pm • €3.50 • ☎ 03 80 67 11 10, ⊕ musee-magnin.fr

The **Musée Magnin**, installed in a seventeenth-century *hôtel particulier* (town house) – complete with its original furnishings – holds an assembly of French and Italian paintings that was bequeathed to the State by two collectors in 1938.

## Musée d'Art Sacré

15 rue Ste-Anne • Daily except Tues May–Sept 9am–12.30pm & 1.30–6pm; Oct–April 9am–noon & 2–6pm • Free • ☎ 03 80 48 80 90

One of two museums housed in the Monastère de Bernardine, the **Musée d'Art Sacré** contains an important collection of church treasures. Highlights include a seventeenth-century statue of St Paul, the first in the world to be restored using an extraordinary technique that involves injecting the stone with resin and then solidifying the resulting compound using gamma rays. Formerly crumbling to dust, the statue is now completely firm.

## Musée de la Vie Bourguignonne

17 rue Ste-Anne • Daily except Tues May–Sept 9am–12.30pm & 1.30–6pm; Oct–April 9am–noon & 2–6pm • Free • ☎ 03 80 48 80 90

The **Musée de la Vie Bourguignonne**, which, like the Musée d'Art Sacré is in the Monastère de Bernardine, explores nineteenth-century Burgundian life, and features costumes, furniture and a number of fun reconstructions of rooms and shops.

# Jardin de l'Arquebuse and around

Below the train station the small, landscaped **Jardin de l'Arquebuse** provides an oasis of calm in the town, with joggers and boules players sharing the space with families enjoying a leisurely stroll. The **Natural History Museum** stands by its gate, while the city's **Botanical Garden** dominates its middle.

# The Well of Moses

Centre Hospitalier Spécialisé de la Chartreuse, av Albert 1ᵉʳ • Daily: April–Oct 9.30am–12.30pm & 2–5.30pm; Nov–March 9.30am–12.30pm & 2–5pm • Free • Bus #3, stop Av Albert 1ᵉʳ

Around 1km west of Dijon train station lies the old **Carthusian Monastery of Champmol**, built by Philippe le Hardi, which was destroyed in the Revolution and is now a medical centre. However, many make the long journey on foot or by bus to visit one of Burgundy's masterpieces: the **Well of Moses**, a magnificent medieval sculpture in the grounds.

**8**

### ARRIVAL AND DEPARTURE                                                    DIJON

**By train** The *gare SNCF* is at the end of the tram line B. A few minutes' walk outside the station on Av Foch is the stop for tram line A.
Destinations Beaune (1–3 hourly; 25min); Besançon (1–3 hourly; 1hr); Bourg-en-Bresse (5 daily; 1hr 45 min); Chalon-sur-Saône (1–3 hourly; 40min); Laroche-Migennes (10–12 daily; 1hr 30min); Lyon (hourly; 2hr 10min); Mâcon (hourly; 1hr 10min); Nevers (5–7 daily; 2hr 20min); Nuits

St-Georges (1–3 hourly; 20min); Paris Bercy (6 daily 3hr); Paris Gare de Lyon (every 30min–1hr; 1hr 30min); Reims (every 30min–1hr; 3hr 20min); Tonnerre (10–12 daily; 1hr); Troyes (daily; 2hr 10min).
**By bus** The *gare routière* is next door to the train station.
Destinations Avallon (1–3 daily; 2hr–2hr 30min); Montbard (5 daily; 40min).

### GETTING AROUND

**By tram** Dijon has a brand new tram system (🌐 letram -dijon.fr).
**Bike rental** The city is very bicycle-friendly; rent bicycles from the tourist office (€13/half-day, €18/day).
**Car rental** Many people rent a car from Dijon to explore the nearby vineyards. Car companies at the train station

include Hertz (☎ 03 80 53 14 00) and Europcar (☎ 03 80 45 90 60); try 🌐 rhinocarhire.com to compare prices.
**By taxi** Taxis are few in Dijon and queues at the station stand are long. If you get no response from the town's main taxi company (☎ 03 80 41 41 12), try Michel's cab at ☎ 06 87 41 07 66.

### INFORMATION

**Tourist office** The central office is near Place Notre-Dame at 11 rue des Forges (April–Sept Mon–Sat

9.30am–6.30pm, Sun & public hols 10am–6pm; Oct–March Mon–Sat 9.30am–1pm & 2–6pm, Sun & public hols 10am–4pm; ☎08 92 70 05 58, ⍵visitdijon.com). There's a second office near the train station at 15 Cour de la Gare (same hours).

**Tours** You can book guided city tours that include the Well of Moses (€6), or longer minibus tours of local vineyards (from €48) at the tourist office.

**Passes** The tourist office sells the Dijon Pass (from €18), which offers significant reductions on museum entry fees and a number of free guided tours.

**Internet** Cybersp@ce21, 46 rue Monge (Mon–Sat 11am–midnight, Sun 2pm–midnight; €4/hr; ⍵cybersapce21.fr) is in the centre of the old town.

## ACCOMMODATION

**Le Chambellan** 92 rue Vannerie ☎03 80 67 12 67, ⍵hotel-chambellan.com. Relaxing rooms with sparkling bathrooms, clustered around a pretty seventeenth-century courtyard. The cheapest rooms (€36) have shared facilities. Breakfast €6. Special deal with nearby parking, €5/day. **€53**

★ **Holiday Inn** 1 place Marie de Bourgogne ☎03 80 60 46 00, ⍵holiday-inn-dijon.com. This is the best place to stay if you have a car; the tram just outside takes you into town in ten minutes. Next to the shopping centre Toison d'Or, it's a very competitively priced four-star with all the excellent service you would expect from a *Holiday Inn*. Rates include breakfast. **€114**

**Le Jacquemart** 32 rue Verrerie ☎03 80 60 09 60, ⍵hotel-lejacquemart.fr. Run by the same charming management as *Le Chambellan* (see above), this elegant hotel has comfortable and quiet high-ceilinged rooms. Breakfast €6.50, parking €6. **€58**

★ **Jura** 14 av Foch ☎03 80 41 61 12, ⍵oceaniahotels .com. By far the best of the huddle of options in the av Foch opposite the *gare SNCF*, this mid-nineteenth-century hotel is a famous Dijon landmark. The spacious, comfortable rooms have been modernized and are surprisingly quiet. The much-photographed old lift with its clocks will charm you even as you enter the reception. Breakfast €11, garage €12.50. **€134**

**Philippe le Bon** 18 rue Ste-Anne ☎03 80 30 73 52, ⍵hotelphilippelebon.com. Elegant old building in an agreeable garden opposite the Musée de la Vie Bourguignonne. The most expensive rooms are lovely; full of character and beautifully restored, the others are plush but a little bland in comparison. Great restaurant in the garden below; you can buy its wines at reception. Breakfast €15. **€97**

**Du Sauvage** 64 rue Monge ☎03 80 41 31 21, ⍵hotellesauvage.com. A delightful former coaching inn with large and elegant rooms overlooking a vine-draped courtyard. Despite being in the liveliest quarter of town, it's quiet. Breakfast €7.50, parking €5. **€56**

**Sofitel La Cloche** 14 place Darcy ☎03 80 30 12 32, ⍵hotel-lacloche.com. You get über-luxurious rooms and a gourmet restaurant in this grand luxury hotel, built in 1882. It has entertained Napoleon III, Rodin, Saint Saëns, Maurice Chevalier and Grace Kelly among others and it shows. Breakfast €20. **€230**

★ **Urbaneva** 4 rue Audra ☎03 80 50 08 08, ⍵urbaneva.com. Self-contained, comfortable studios, with kitchenette in the heart of town; ask for a room facing the pretty garden. Rates decrease the longer you stay. Breakfast €6 Mon–Fri only, when reception is open. **€77**

## EATING

Dijon has a number of excellent restaurants, particularly around rue Monge, while pretty place Émile Zola is packed with the open-air tables of reasonably priced brasseries.

**À Tout Va Bien** 12 rue Quentin ☎03 80 49 15 36. A friendly, brightly decorated restaurant with a lively ambience, particularly on market days. Specializing in traditional cuisine (such as *tête de veau*), with a *menu du jour* for €12.50. Tues–Thurs noon–3pm & 7pm–midnight, Fri & Sat noon–4pm & 7pm–1am.

★ **La Dame d'Aquitaine** 23 place Bossuet ☎03 80 30 45 65, ⍵ladamedaquitaine.fr. Possibly the best restaurant in Dijon, according to the locals; it's set in the twelfth-century crypt of the magnificent seventeenth-century Perreney de Balleure hotel. It has everything: ambience, friendly service, good food and *menus* starting at €17. Booking recommended. Tues–Sat noon–1.30pm & 7–9.30pm, Mon 7–9.30pm.

**L'Escargot** 43 rue J.J. Rousseau ☎03 80 73 33 85, ⍵restaurantlescargot-dijon.com. Attractive restaurant with surprisingly low prices, making it a great place to try the local classics. The *oeufs en meurette* are particularly delicious. Three courses from €22. Mon–Thurs noon–2pm & 7.30–9.30pm, Fri & Sat noon–2pm & 7.30–10pm, Sun 7.30–9.30pm.

**Le Grand Café** 5 rue de Chateau ☎03 80 30 97 26, ⍵www.legrandcafedijon.fr. A Dijonnais institution, this is a very popular, grand bar/brasserie/wine bar/restaurant depending on the time of day. You can have dishes for €15, salads for €6 or just sip a coffee and relax. Daily 11am–11pm.

★ **Maison Milliére** 10 rue de la Chouette ☎03 80 30 99 99, ⍵maison-milliere.fr. Don't miss out on

8

dining in this 1483 building – so photogenic that part of the film *Cyrano de Bergerac*, starring Gérard Depardieu, was filmed here. The back garden is almost as delightful as the €27 *menu Bourgogne*. After you've sampled the local food, you can pop into the adjoining shop and stock up on ingredients. Booking is a must. Tues–Sun: restaurant noon–2pm & 7–9.30pm; shop 10am–7pm.

**Le Piano qui Fume** 36 rue Berbisey ☎03 80 30 35 45, ⓦlepianoquifume.fr. A restaurant that prides itself on the freshness and topicality of its menus, made with seasonal ingredients. Its motto is "Cuisine is an art and art is patience". *Menus* from €29. Mon & Tues noon–2pm, Thurs–Sat noon–2pm & 7–10pm.

**"Pourquoi pas?"** 13 rue Monge ☎03 80 50 11 77. A simple but highly sophisticated restaurant that serves classic French cuisine with a short, but good-value wine list. Lunch from €14.50, or try the four-course *menu surprise* where the chef chooses the dishes for you (€45). Tues–Fri 7–9pm, Sat noon–1.30pm & 7–9pm.

**Le Pré aux Clercs** 13 place de la Libération ☎03 80 38 05 05, ⓦle-pre-aux-clercs.com. The *crème de la crème* of Dijon restaurants; under the direction of chef Jean-Pierre Billoux, this one-star Michelin establishment serves gourmet cuisine in an elegant dining room and in the square outside. Lunch *menu* €35, dinner €59/€95. Tues–Sat noon–2pm & 5.30–9.15pm, Sun noon–2pm.

**Le Shanti** 69 rue Berbisey ☎09 81 09 09 31, ⓦleshanti .unblog.fr. Great little hookah joint, decked out with divans and South Asian decor, serving delicious teas, non-alcoholic cocktails, *lassis* and flavoured shisha. Dishes around €6. Mon–Sat noon–midnight.

## DRINKING AND NIGHTLIFE

Dijon is an important university city as well as one of France's main conference centres, with a nightlife to span the spectrum. Rue Berbisey is a good place to start a night out.

**Au Vieux Léon** 52 rue Jeannin ☎03 80 67 78 93. Decorated like an old-fashioned French café on acid, this alternative – and strictly antifascist, as it proudly proclaims – café-bar is a student favourite, with a lively, friendly atmosphere. Mon–Sat 6pm–1.30am.

**Le Cercle Jamaïca** 14 place de la République ☎03 80 73 52 19, ⓦlecerclejamaique.com. With its pricey cocktails and burlesque decor, this place is popular with a trendy thirty-something crowd. They have live bands most evenings at 11pm. Thurs–Sat 10.30pm–4am.

★ **Le Chat Noir** 20 av Garibaldi ☎03 80 73 39 57, ⓦlechatnoir.fr. Just off place de la République, this is Dijon's main club, with special themed parties and big-name DJs. Beers €7, entry €5–7. Thurs–Sat 11.30pm–4am.

**Flannery's** 4 place St Benigne ☎03 80 44 94 33. A popular Irish bar (which one isn't?) with a particularly good selection of whiskeys behind the bar. Big-screen sport attracts many students. Guinness €5.60 a pint. Daily 4.30pm–2am.

**Le Quentin** 6 rue Quentin ☎03 80 30 15 05. Cool café-bar with lounge music inside and a terrace outside that looks onto the market. Ideal for people-watching on market days or for an *apero* on a sunny evening. Mon, Tues, Fri & Sat 9am–2am, Wed & Thurs 11am–2am, Sun 5–10pm.

## SHOPPING

Dijon, with its range of gastronomic specialties, from spicy condiments to sticky, sweet pastries, is a particularly good place to buy foodie gifts. Listed here are the best shops in their own genre.

**Au Vieux Millésime** 82 rue Monge ☎03 80 41 28 79 ⓦauvieuxmillesime.com. As capital of the Burgundy region, Dijon presides over some great winemaking country: sommelier Ludovic Flexas offers helpful advice on wines from the region and further afield; prices start at around €5. Mon–Sat 10am–12.30pm & 2–7pm.

**Calisa Epicerie** 12 rue Bannelier ☎03 80 30 86 21. Teas, coffees, chocolate, honey, *confitures*, truffles, oils, foie gras and mustards – all in one place. Best leave your credit card at home. Tues & Fri 8.30am–7pm, Wed & Thurs 10am–noon & 2–7pm, Sat 8.30am–6.30pm.

**Le Fabrice Gillotte** 21 rue du Bourg ☎03 80 30 38 88, ⓦfabrice-gillotte.fr. One of Dijon's numerous foodie specialities is chocolate, and Gillotte is the city's most famous *chocolaterie*. Mon–Sat 9.15am–noon & 2–7pm.

**Maille** 30 rue de la Liberté ☎03 80 30 41 02, ⓦmaille.com. Dijon is, of course, the high temple of mustard, and Maille its leading producer. This store sells a wide range, from mild-tasting to cauterizing. Mon–Sat 10am–7pm.

**Mulot et Petitjean** 13 place Bossuet ☎03 80 30 07 10 ⓦmulotpetitjean.fr. Visit the headquarters of this renowned producer of *pain d'épices*, a gingerbread made with honey and spices and eaten with butter or jam. Mon 2–7pm, Tues–Sat 9am–noon & 2–7pm.

**8**

# The Côte d'Or

South of Dijon, the attractive countryside of the **Côte d'Or** is characterized by the steep scarp of the *côte*, wooded along the top and cut by sheer little valleys called *combes*, where local rock climbers hone their skills. Spring is a good time to visit this region; you can avoid the crowds and the landscape is a dramatic symphony of browns – trees, earth and vines – punctuated by millions of bone-coloured vine stakes, standing like crosses in a vast war cemetery. The main administrative and shopping centre is the beautiful city of **Beaune,** south of which the **Great Wine Route** checks off the big names in Burgundy winemaking.

## The Great Wine Route

The place names that line the legendary **Great Wine Route** National 74 – Gevrey-Chambertin, **Vougeot**, Vosne-Romanée, Nuits-St-Georges, **Pommard**, Volnay, **Meursault** – are music to the ears of wine buffs. These prosperous villages are full of wine cellars where you can get good advice on different vintages; you can taste and buy direct from the source at most of the **vineyards** by just turning up and asking.

### Château du Clos-de-Vougeot

Clos de Vougeot, some 20km south of Dijon between Gévry-Chambertin and Nuits-St-Georges • Daily: April–Sept 9am–6.30pm; Oct–March 9–11.30am & 2–5.30pm • €4.10 • ☏ 03 80 62 86 09, ⓦ closdevougeot.fr

If you're interested in French wine culture, it's worth visiting the **Château du Clos-de-Vougeot** to see the winemaking process. Particularly impressive are the mammoth thirteenth-century winepresses installed by the Cistercian monks who owned these vineyards for nearly seven hundred years. The land now belongs to more than eighty different owners, each growing and marketing their own wine.

---

**THE WINES OF BURGUNDY**

Burgundy farmers have been growing grapes since Roman times, and Burgundy's **wines** are some of the most renowned in the world. In recent years, though, Burgundy's vineyards, and those in other regions of France, have suffered due to competition from the southern hemisphere. However, because of stringent legal restrictions banning watering and other interference, French wines, more than others, remain a faithful reflection of the *terroir* where they are produced, and Burgundy experts remain confident that the climate and soil of their region will fight off any temporary economic challenges.

Burgundy's best wines come from a narrow strip of hillside called the **Côte d'Or** that runs southwest from Dijon to Santenay, and is divided into two regions, Côte de Nuits (the better reds) and Côte de Beaune (the better whites). High-quality wine is certainly produced further south as well though, in the **Mâconnais** and on the **Côtes Chalonnaises**. Reds from the region are made almost exclusively from the Pinot Noir grape, while whites are largely from Chardonnay. Fans of bubbly should look out for the often highly regarded **sparkling** whites, which crop up across the region and won't set you back half as much as a bottle of Champagne.

The single most important factor determining the "character" of wines is the **soil**. In both the Côte d'Or and **Chablis** (see p.434), its character varies over very short distances, making for an enormous variety of taste. Chalky soil makes a wine drier and more acidic – while clay brings more fruitiness and body to it.

For an **apéritif** in Burgundy, you should try *kir*, named after the man who was both mayor and MP for Dijon for many years after World War II – two parts dry white wine, traditionally *aligoté*, and one part cassis. To round the evening off there are many **liqueurs** to choose from, but Burgundy is particularly famous for its marcs, of which the best are matured for years in oak casks.

### Château de la Tour

Clos de Vougeot, some 20km south of Dijon between Gévry-Chambertin and Nuits-St-Georges • Mon–Sat 10am–6pm • Free • ☎ 03 80 62 86 04, ⓦ chateaudelatour.com

Just down the road from the Château du Clos-de-Vougeot is the nineteenth-century **Château de la Tour**, one of the greatest names in winemaking, where they sell their own grands crus and other Cote d'Or wines. Theirs is the only Clos-Vougeot grand cru to be harvested, vinified and bottled in the centuries-old monks' fashion.

### Le Cassissium

On the outskirts on Nuits-St-Georges • April to mid-Nov daily 10am–1pm & 2–7pm; mid-Nov to March Tues–Sat 10.30am–1pm & 2–5.30pm; 90min guided tours • €8 • ☎ 03 80 62 49 70, ⓦ cassissium.fr

Fans of cassis (blackcurrant liqueur) should drop by **Le Cassissium**, where you can enjoy a comprehensive guided tour of the cassis factory and learn about the history of the blackcurrant.

### Château de Pommard

15 rue Marey Mange, near Beaune • Daily 9.30am–6.30pm; 45min guided tours • €21 (min 6 people) • ☎ 03 80 22 12 59, ⓦ chateaudepommard.com

Apart from being one of the great names in Burgundy, having been established in 1726 to furnish the tables of Louis XV, the **Château de Pommard** offers a very informative tour of the vineyards and the cellars as well as a tasting of three whites and one red. When it was restored in 2003, the new owner Maurice Giraud brought a couple of Dalí sculptures (the *Unicorn* and the *Rhinoceros*) which can be admired in the courtyard.

### Maison d'Oliver Leflaive

Place du Monument, Puligny-Montrachet • Mon–Sat 12.30–7.30pm • Free; tastings €15 for five wines; €40 for ten; meals €25; lodgings €160 for double • ☎ 03 80 21 37 65, ⓦ olivier-leflaive.com

The Leflaive family has been making wine for more than 370 years, but **Oliver Leflaive**, the current family head, was the first in 2007 to combine the concept of a vineyard tour, wine tastings, a gourmet meal (*menu* €25) and four-star lodgings all in one location, including several premiers and grands crus.

### Château de Meursault

Meursault • Daily 9.30am–noon/12.30pm & 2/2.30–6pm • Free • ☎ 03 80 26 22 75, ⓦ chateau-meursault.com

The **Château de Meursault** in Meursault is one of the oldest estates in Burgundy, with extensive and beautiful grounds. It is the most prestigious producer of Burgundy Chardonnay, and is open to the public for tastings, wine walks, vineyard trails and more.

## Beaune

**BEAUNE**, the principal town of the Côte d'Or, manages to maintain its attractively ancient air, despite a near-constant stream of wine aficionados using the place as their base. Narrow cobbled streets and sunny squares dotted with cafés make it a lovely, albeit expensive, spot to sample the region's wine.

### Hôtel-Dieu

Place de la Halle • Daily: April to mid-Nov 9am–6.30pm; mid-Nov to March 9–11.30am & 2–5.30pm; last admission 1hr before closing • €7, combined ticket with the Musée du Vin and Musée de Beaux-Arts €11 • ☎ 03 80 24 45 00

Beaune's chief attraction is the fifteenth-century hospital, the **Hôtel-Dieu**. As grateful ex-patients or their families donated vine plots to the hospital, the town prospered quickly to become the centre of the local wine trade. The cobbled courtyard is surrounded by a wooden gallery overhung by a massive roof patterned with

diamonds of variegated tiles – green, burnt sienna, black and yellow – and similarly multicoloured steep-pitched dormers and turrets. Inside is a vast paved hall with a glorious arched timber roof, the Grande Salle des Malades, with the original enclosed wooden beds. Passing through two smaller, furnished wards, one with some stunning seventeenth-century frescoes, then the kitchen and the pharmacy, you reach a dark chamber housing the splendid fifteenth-century altarpiece of the *Last Judgement* by Rogier van der Weyden and the tapestry of St Eloi, which is comparable to the *Lady and the Unicorn* in the museum of Cluny in Paris (see p.89).

## Marché aux Vins

Rue Nicholas Rolin • Daily 9.30am–11.45am & 2–5.45pm • €9 allows you to sample 12 wines • ☎ 03 80 25 08 23, ⓦ marcheauxvins.com

If you're keen to indulge in a **wine-tasting** session, head to the **Marché aux Vins**, where you can wander freely through the atmospheric Église des Cordeliers and its caves, sampling the wines. Note, however, that the operative word here is "sample".

## Dalineum

26 place Monge • Daily 11am–7pm • €7 • ☎ 03 80 22 63 13

After a few rounds of tasting wine, pop into Beaune's latest museum, the **Dalineum**, inaugurated in November 2011. Here you can see a private collection of Dalí works belonging to collector Jean Amiot, whose mother was a local girl. There are some famous pieces on display, including an Impressionist painting from a 15-year-old Dalí, a lip-shaped sofa, the Minotaur statue and the stereoscopic version of the *Christ of Gala*.

## Musée du Vin

Rue d'Enfer • April–Nov daily 9.30am–6pm; Dec–March daily except Tues 9.30am–5pm • €4.50, combined ticket with the Hôtel-Dieu and Musée de Beaux-Arts €11

The former residence of the dukes of Burgundy now houses the **Musée du Vin**, featuring, among other things, giant winepresses, a collection of traditional tools of the trade and a relief map of the vineyards that helps to make sense of it all.

## Fallot Moutarderie

31 rue du Faubourg Bretonnière • Tours mid-March to mid-Nov Mon–Sat 10am & 11.30am; June–Aug 10am, 11.30am, 3.30pm & 5pm • €10 • ☎ 03 80 22 63 13, ⓦ fallot.com

Surprisingly, French mustard – even Dijon – cannot be termed appellation contrôlée because all mustard seeds are imported from Canada nowadays. Only Fallot – established in 1840 – can claim to produce some brands with all ingredients (including seeds and verjuice) that are sourced locally with old-fashioned recipes. The **Fallot Moutarderie** offers a quirky and fun tour of the factory, finishing off with a hefty plate of mustard-related amuse-bouches at the end.

## ARRIVAL AND INFORMATION                                    BEAUNE

**By train** The *gare SNCF* is east of the centre on av du 8 Septembre, a 5min walk from the old walls. Local buses also stop here.

Destinations Chalon-sur-Saône (1–3 hourly; 20min); Dijon (1–3 hourly; 25min); Lyon (hourly; 1hr 10min); Mâcon (1–3 hourly; 50min).

**Tourist office** The well-managed tourist office, who organize a number of tours, is at 6 bd Perpreuil (April–Oct

Mon–Sat 9am–6.30/7pm, Sun 9am–6pm; Nov–March Mon–Sat 9am–noon & 1–6pm, Sun 10am–12.30pm & 1.30–5pm; ☎ 03 80 26 21 30, ⓦ beaune-tourisme.fr). There is a smaller information point by the Hôtel-Dieu.

**Bike rental** Bourgogne Randonnées, av 8 Septembre near the train station (Mon–Sat 9am–noon & 1.30–7pm; Sun 10am–noon & 2–7pm; €5/hr, €18/day; ☎ 03 80 22 06 03).

## ACCOMMODATION

★ **Abbaye de Maizières** 19 rue Maizières ☎ 03 80 24 74 64, ⓦ hotelabbayedemaizieres.com. Located in a twelfth-century abbey, this hotel has beautifully decorated rooms with exposed stone walls, wall hangings and medieval-style tapestries. Air-conditioned and with a great restaurant (dinner only 7–9pm); the only minor quibble is the lack of a lift. Beware the steep stairs and watch your head as you come in. Breakfast €10, parking €10, 400m away. **€118**

**Les Cent Vignes** 10 rue Auguste Dubois ☎ 03 80 22 03 91. This pretty campsite with a tennis court and swimming pool is about 1km north of town, off rue du Faubourg-St-Nicolas (the N74 to Dijon), before the

bridge over the *autoroute*. Booking is advisable. Closed Nov–Feb. **€17.40**

**La Cloche** 40 rue du Faubourg Madeleine ☎ 03 80 24 66 33, ⓦ hotel-lacloche-beaune.com. Near the station, this recently refurbished hotel offers brightly decorated, modern rooms which complement the elegant old building. Breakfast €9.70, parking €4.80. **€70**

**Des Remparts** 48 rue Thiers ☎ 03 80 24 94 94, ⓦ hotel -remparts-beaune.com. Run by Elyane, a delightful former headmistress, this is a wonderful hotel, sensitively restored and full of old beams and ancient stone. You can still see the ramparts that give it its name from the windows of some of the more expensive rooms. **€89**

## EATING

★ **Le Bistrot Bourguignon** 8 rue Monge ☎ 03 80 22 23 24. This relaxed and friendly bistro and wine bar specializes in regional cuisine (main courses around €18) and prides itself on having been the first wine bar in Burgundy to serve wine by the glass. Tues–Sat 12.15–2pm & 7.15–10pm.

**Caveau des Arches** 10 bd Perpreuil ☎ 03 80 22 10 37, ⓦ caveau-des-arches.com. Excellent dining, in a cellar, and surprisingly affordable given the plush surroundings. *Menus* start at €16; even the great-value *menu bourguignon*

costs just €23.50. Booking recommended. Tues–Sat noon–1.30pm & 7–9.30pm.

**Le Comptoir des Tontons** 22 rue du Faubourg Madeleine ☎ 03 80 24 19 64. Just outside the town walls, this down-to-earth restaurant serves a lot of organic produce, including wine. *Menus* from €33. Booking recommended. Tues–Sat noon–1pm & 7.30–8.30pm.

**Le Gourmandin** 8 place Carnot ☎ 03 80 24 07 88, ⓦ hotellegourmandin.com. One of the more upmarket

8

establishments on place Carnot, this sophisticated restaurant has an excellent *menu bourguignon* for €37 and a lunch *menu* for €19.50. *Plats du jour* are around €13 and its wine list has several grands crus. Daily noon–2pm & 7–10pm.

**Ma Cuisine** Passage Ste-Hélène ☎ 03 80 22 30 22. A simple yet stylish restaurant serving traditional French cuisine, with a *menu* at €24 and a wine list with no fewer than 900 wines. Mon, Tues, Thurs & Fri 12.30–1.30pm & 7.15–9.15pm.

# The Saône valley

The **Saône valley** south from **Chalon-sur-Saône** via **Tournus** all the way to **Mâcon** is prosperous and modern, nourished by tourism, industry (especially metal-working), and the wine trade. But turn your back on the river and head west and you immediately enter a different Burgundy, full of hilly pastures and woodland. This country is best known for its produce: the white wines of the **Mâconnais** are justly renowned, and the handsome white cattle that luxuriate in the green fields of the **Charollais** are an obvious sign that this is serious beef territory.

In the past, the region was famed for its religious institutions; almost every village clusters under the tower of a Romanesque church, spawned by the authority of the great abbey at **Cluny**. Many large and powerful abbeys were established in the eleventh and twelfth centuries under the aegis of Cluny.

## Chalon-sur-Saône

**CHALON** is a sizeable port and bustling town on a broad meander of the Saône. Its old riverside quarter has an easy charm, and the town itself makes a cheap and cheerful base for exploring the more expensive areas of the Côte d'Or.

The highlight of the **old town**, set just back from the river, is the lively **place St-Vincent**, where you can sit outside a café and admire the twin towers of the Romanesque cathedral, surrounded by medieval timber-framed houses. The Saône **quays**, meanwhile, provide some nice, though not always shaded, walking opportunities.

### Musée Niépce

28 quai des Messageries • Daily except Tues: July & Aug 10am–6pm; Sept–June 9.30am–11.45am & 2–5.45pm • Free • ☎ 03 85 48 41 98, ⓦ museeniepce.com

Not far from the tourist office is the unusual **Musée Niépce**. Nicéphore Niépce, who was born in Chalon, is credited with inventing photography in 1816 – though he named it "heliography". The museum possesses a fascinating range of cameras, from the first machine ever to the Apollo moon mission's equipment, plus an interesting selection of photographs.

### ARRIVAL AND INFORMATION

CHALON-SUR-SAÔNE

**By train** *Gares SNCF* and *routière* are a 15min walk from the centre, following av Jaurès and bd de la République. Destinations (train) Dijon (1–3 hourly; 40min); Lyon (hourly; 1hr 20min); Mâcon (hourly; 20min).

Destinations (bus) Autun (2–4 daily; 1hr 15min); Cluny (5 daily; 1hr 20min); Le Creusot (2–5 daily; 1hr 20min); Mâcon (5 daily; 2hr).

**Tourist office** 4 place du Port Villiers, by the riverside (July

---

**CHALON FESTIVALS**

You may be tempted to visit Chalon during the pre-Lent **carnival** (Feb or March), which features a parade of giant masks and a confetti battle, or for one of the most remarkable festivals in Burgundy, the three-day **Montgolfiades** which has a display and a race of dozens of multicoloured hot-air balloons, it take place in the last weekend of May (ⓦ montgolfiades71.com). As most of the sponsors are wine producers, the event is a great excuse to drink and be merry.

& Aug Mon–Sat 9am–12.30pm & 1.30–7pm, Sun 10am–noon & 3–7pm; Sept–June Mon–Sat 9am–12.30pm & 2–6.30pm; June & Sept Sun 3–6pm; ☎ 03 85 48 37 97, ⓦchalon-sur-saone.net).

## ACCOMMODATION

★ **A La Villa Bouciaut** 33bis av Boucicaut ☎ 03 85 90 80 45, ⓦla-villa-boucicaut.fr. Undoubtedly the nicest place to stay in Chalon, this peaceful hotel is a few minutes' walk from the stations. Run by a charming couple, who designed each of the beautifully furnished and decorated rooms themselves. Breakfast €11.50, parking €7. **€99**

**Camping du Pont de Bourgogne** Rue Julien Leneveu, St-Marcel ☎ 03 85 48 26 86, ⓦcamping-chalon.com. Cross the northern of Chalon's bridges and head east – the campsite is 1km out of town on the south bank of the Saône in St-Marcel. It offers cycles for hire, and a bar-restaurant. Reception closes 11am–2pm (3pm off-season). Closed Oct–March. **€22.40**

**St-Jean** 24 quai Gambetta ☎ 03 85 48 45 65, ⓦhotelsaintjean.fr. Right on the riverbank, this hotel offers classic rooms, some of which are rather old-fashioned in their decor. Ask for a room with a view of the Saône. Breakfast €7, Parking €8. **€57**

## EATING AND DRINKING

Rue de Strasbourg, on the so-called île aux restos, is lined with excellent places to eat, while the small river island of St-Laurent across the eponymous bridge is the nightlife centre, filled with good bars.

**Le Bistrot** 31 rue de Strasbourg ☎ 03 85 93 22 01. Tomato-red outside and chic to an almost Parisian degree inside, this restaurant is not difficult to spot. Chef Patrick Meziere offers serious quality for around €30, with lunch *menus* at €22. Some premiers crus on the wine list, which is highly commendable. Mon–Fri noon–1.30pm & 7–9pm.

**Chez Jules** 11 rue de Strasbourg ☎ 03 85 48 08 34, ⓦrestaurant-chezjules.com. This husband and wife enterprise is a good choice for traditional favourites, with special focus on fish and seafood. *Menus* €19. Mon–Thurs noon–1.30pm & 7–9.30pm, Fri noon–1.30pm & 7–10pm, Sat 7–10pm.

**Le Majorelle** 13 place St-Vincent ☎ 03 85 94 04 16. You get good, solid *menus* with some great desserts in this unassuming brasserie, but also the fastest service in the laidback square of St-Vincent. Long opening hours, too. Daily 8am–11pm.

**8**

# Tournus

Graced by ancient, golden buildings, **TOURNUS** is a beautiful little town on the banks of the Saône, 28km south of Chalon. Its main attraction is the old abbey church of **St-Philibert**, one of the earliest and thus most influential Romanesque buildings in Burgundy. Its construction began around 900 AD but the present building dates back to the first half of the eleventh century. The facade, with its powerful towers and simple decoration of Lombard arcading, is somewhat reminiscent of a fortress.

## Hôtel-Dieu

April–Oct daily except Tues 10am–1pm & 2–6pm • €5

To the south of town is the **Hôtel-Dieu**, a seventeenth-century charity hospital. You can still see the rows of solid, oak beds, in which patients lay until 1982, but the real highlight is the elaborate dispensary, complete with a host of faïence pots and hand-blown glass jars. The building also houses the **Musée Greuze**, which pays homage to one of Tournus' best known citizens, the Enlightenment painter Jean-Baptiste Greuze.

## ACCOMMODATION                                         TOURNUS

**Greuze** 5 place de l'Abbaye ☎ 03 85 51 77 77, ⓦhotelgreuze.com. Four-star hotel that offers plush rooms with all luxuries and three different breakfasts: from a simple café-croissant for €6 to a veritable gourmet experience at €16. The most expensive rooms offer a stunning view of the abbey. Check the website for two-nights/third-night-free deals. **€165**

# Mâcon

**MÂCON** is a lively, prosperous town on the banks of the River Saône, 58km south of Chalon and 68km north of Lyon, with excellent transport connections between the two. A centre for the wine trade, with a surprisingly relaxed, seaside atmosphere, thanks to its long café-lined **riverbank** and free outdoor concerts in late June, July and August, it also boasts the best **nightlife** between Dijon and Lyon. It is, however, a nightmare to drive around and parking is problematic, so it's not recommended as a base for a regional wine-tasting tour for anyone renting a car.

## Musée Lamartine

41 rue Sigorgne • Tues–Sat 10am–noon & 2–6pm, Sun 2–6pm • €2.50; combined ticket with Musée des Ursulines €3.40 • ☏ 03 85 38 96 19

Lamartine, the nineteenth-century French Romantic poet (see box below), was born in Mâcon in 1790 and you will see his name everywhere. He is remembered in the handsome eighteenth-century mansion, the Hôtel Senecé, the old Academy of Arts and Sciences of which he was president. Today it houses the **Musée Lamartine**, part of which is dedicated to documents and other memorabilia relating to his personal, political and poetic lives.

## Musée des Ursulines

5 rue des Ursulines • Tues–Sat 10am–noon & 2–6pm, Sun 2–6pm • €2.50; combined ticket with Musée Lamartine €3.40 • ☏ 03 85 38 90 38

Very near the Musée Lamartine, the **Musée des Ursulines** is housed in a seventeenth-century convent with a chequered history, having served not only as a convent but also as a prison and then as a barracks.

The museum itself features Gallo-Roman artefacts, an exhibition dedicated to Mâcon's history, and a collection of sixteenth- to twentieth-century paintings.

## ARRIVAL AND INFORMATION

MÂCON

**By train** The *gare SNCF* lies on rue Bigonnet at the southern end of rue Victor-Hugo; TGV trains leave from Mâcon-Loché station 6km out of town. There is a shuttle between the two train stations (Line E) or it's a short taxi ride (€15).
Destinations Bourg-en-Bresse (12 daily; 30min); Chalon-sur-Saône (1–3 hourly; 20min); Dijon (1–3 hourly; 1hr–1hr 20min); Lyon (hourly; 1hr).
**By bus** The *gare routière* is next to the train station.
Destinations Charolles (2–3 daily; 1hr 10min); Cluny (2–3 daily; 30min); Paray-le-Monial (2–3 daily; 1hr 30min); Tournus (1 daily; 50min).

**Tourist office** 1 place St Pierre (Nov–April Tues–Sat 10am–noon & 2–6pm; May–June, Sept & Oct Mon–Sat 9.30am–12.30pm & 2–6.30pm; July & Aug daily 9am–12.30pm & 2–7pm; ☏ 03 85 21 07 07, ⓦ macon-tourism.com). Among their many brochures and information on the local area they offer a free walking map of the city with all sights clearly marked.

**Cruises** Book at the tourist office for day-long (€67 with lunch) or half-day (€15) cruises on the River Saône (mid-April to June & Sept to mid-Oct 10.30am; July & Aug 10.30am & 2.30pm).

---

### ALPHONSE LAMARTINE: THE GREAT ROMANTIC

Often compared to Lord Byron, **Alphonse Lamartine** (1790–1869) is one of the best-known of the French Romantic poets. He was born and grew up in Milly (now called Milly-Lamartine), about 15km west of Mâcon, and published his first poetic work, *Méditations poétiques*, in 1820. After the 1830 Revolution in Paris, he became involved in politics and was elected to the Chambre des Députés in 1833.

Lamartine, having acquired a reputation as a powerful orator on the weighty questions of the day, like the abolition of slavery and capital punishment, had his finest hour was as the leading figure in the provisional government of the Second Republic, which was proclaimed from the Hôtel de Ville in Paris on February 23, 1848. He withdrew from politics when reactionary forces let the army loose on the protesting workers of Paris and Marseille in June 1848. Retiring to St-Point, he continued to write and publish until his death in 1869.

## ACCOMMODATION

**De Bourgogne** 6 rue Victor Hugo ☎03 85 21 10 23, ⓦhoteldebourgogne.com. Central hotel offering luxurious rooms and grandly decorated common areas. Some rooms get street-noisy during the day so ask for one at the back. Another big plus: the hotel organizes bus tours of the Mâconnais. Breakfast €11, private parking €10. **€96**

**Camping Municipal** 1 rue des Grandes-Varennes ☎03 85 38 16 22, ⓔcamping@ville-macon.fr. This large, local campsite, with excellent facilities including heated pool, bar and a good restaurant, is a better base for touring the Mâconnais with a car than the city itself. It's about 3km north of town off the Boulevard du Général de Gaulle, a continuation of the N6. Closed mid-Oct to mid-March. **€15.70**

**D'Europe d'Angleterre** 92–109 quai Jean-Jaurès ☎03 85 38 27 94, ⓦhotel-europeangleterre-macon.com. Although it's obvious that it has seen better times (Colette and the Aga Khan were visitors) this still-characterful hotel has finely furnished, high-ceilinged rooms, some of which have river views. Breakfast €8. Parking €8. **€65**

## EATING AND DRINKING

**Les Arts** 219 quai Lamartine ☎03 85 32 08 49. The most popular of the many bars on quai Lamartine, with friendly service, large MTV screen and cocktails at €6. Sun–Wed 7am–midnight, Thurs–Sat 7am–2am.

**Le Carline** 266 quai Lamartine ☎03 85 37 10 98, ⓦrestaurantlecarline.fr. Offering classic French cuisine, including a large *filet Charollais* with *frites* (€23), this restaurant has a laidback atmosphere and reasonable prices. The Bourgogne *menu* is a snip at €20.30, and the desserts are a meal in themselves. Mon–Sat noon–2pm 7.30pm–9.30pm.

**Dundee** 37 rue Victor Hugo ☎09 63 43 19 34. A bar and internet café with Australiana galore, from didgeridoos to kangaroo photos and "Koalas Ahead" signs –a little piece of France that will always hang down under. Fosters €2.50. Mon–Thurs 8am–11pm, Fri & Sat 9am–3am.

**La Perdrix** 6 rue Victor Hugo ☎03 85 21 10 23. The excellent restaurant of *De Bourgogne* hotel has some of the best-value *menus* in town – including low-calorie options – from €20. Mon–Fri noon–2pm & 7–10pm, Sat 7–10pm.

**8**

# The Mâconnais

The **Mâconnais** wine-producing country lies to the west of the Saône, a 20km-wide strip stretching from Tournus to just south of Mâcon. The region's best white wines, including all the grands crus and some of the best white grands crus, labelled **Pouilly-Fuissé**, come from the southern part of this strip, around the pretty villages of **Pouilly**, **Vinzelles** and **Fuissé**.

## Musée Départemental de Préhistoire

Solutré-Pouilly • Daily: April–Sept 10am–6pm; Oct, Nov & Jan–March 10am–noon & 2–5pm • €3.50 • ☎03 85 35 85 24

Directly above the villages of Pouilly, Vinzelles and Fuissé rises the distinctive and precipitous 500m rock of **Solutré**, which served as an ambush site for hunters in prehistoric times – around 20,000 BC. The bones of 100,000 horses have been found in the soil beneath the rock, along with mammoth, bison and reindeer carcasses. The history and results of the excavations are displayed in a museum at the foot of the rock, the **Musée Départemental de Préhistoire**.

A steep path climbs to the top of the rock, where, on a clear day, you get a superb view as far as Mont Blanc and the Matterhorn. As you look down on the huddled roofs of **Solutré-Pouilly** the slopes beneath you are covered with the vines of the Chardonnay grape, which makes the exquisite greenish Pouilly-Fuissé wine.

## ACCOMMODATION                                               THE MÂCONNAIS

**La Source des Fées** Rte du May, Fuissé ☎03 85 35 67 02, ⓦlasourcedesfees.com. A distinctive farmhouse *gîte*, whose name, "Fairy Source", alludes to a nearby spring where fairies were supposed to have appeared. Convenient (only a 5min drive from the TGV station at Mâcon-Loché) and comfortable, with enormous rooms and suites plus three-course dinners (€28) that are renowned in the area. Rates include wine tasting, breakfast and parking. **€118**

# Cluny

Scattered among the houses of the attractive modern-day town, the **abbey of CLUNY** is the Saône Valley's major tourist destination. The monastery was founded in 910 in response to the corruption of the existing church, and it took only a couple of vigorous early abbots to transform the power of Cluny into a veritable empire. Second only to that of the pope, the abbot's power in the Christian world made even monarchs tremble. However, Cluny's spiritual influence gradually declined and the abbey became a royal gift in the twelfth century. Centuries later, in the wake of the Revolution, Hugues de Semur's vast and influential eleventh-century **church**, which had been the largest building in Christendom until the construction of St Peter's in Rome, was dismantled. The most exciting thing that has happened since has been the burial of Mme Danielle Mitterrand, the President's wife, in the town cemetery; her grave attracts many visitors.

## The abbey

Place de l'Abbaye • **Abbey** Daily: April, May, June & Sept 9.30am–6pm; July & Aug 9.30am–7pm; Oct–March 9.30am–5pm • €8.50, €9.50, includes entrance to Musée d'Art et d'Archaeologie **Musée d'Art et d'Archaeologie** May & June daily 9am–noon & 2–6pm; July & Aug daily 9am–7pm; Sept daily 9am–6pm; Oct–April 9.30am–noon & 2–5pm • €6, €9.50 combined ticket with Abbey **Haras de Cluny** Guided tours April–June & Sept Tues–Sat 2pm & 4pm; July & Aug Tues–Sat 2pm, 3.30pm & 5pm; Oct & Nov Wed & Sun 2pm; Feb & March Wed, Fri & Sun 2pm • €6 • ☎ 06 22 94 52 69, ⓦ haras-mationaux.fr **Tour des Fromages** May–Aug daily 9.30am–7pm; April Mon–Sat 9.30am–12.30pm & 2.30–7pm; Sept daily 9.30am–12.30pm & 2.30–7pm; Oct daily 9.30am–12.30pm & 2.30–6pm Nov–March Mon–Sat 10am–12.30pm & 2.30–5pm • €2

What you see of the former **abbey** today is an octagonal belfry and the huge south transept. Standing amid these fragments of a once huge construction gives a tangible and poignant insight into the Revolution's enormous powers of transformation. Access to the belfry is through the Grand École des Ingénieurs, one of France's elite higher-education institutions, and you can often see the students in their grey lab coats. At the back of the abbey is one of France's national stud farms, **Haras de Cluny**, which you can visit, but only on a guided tour. The **Musée d'Art et d'Archaeologie**, in the fifteenth-century palace of the last freely elected abbot, helps to flesh out the ruins by renting tablet PCs which provide a representation of what the abbey looked like as you stand on particular spots; from the top of the **Tour des Fromages** (entered via the tourist office) an amazing virtual reality screen projects the old buildings onto a live cam that shows the street below.

## ARRIVAL AND INFORMATION

**By bus** Buses from both Mâcon (4–6 daily; 30min) and Chalon-sur-Saône (2–3 daily; 1hr 20min) stop on Portre-de-Paris, a 5min walk from the town centre.

**Tourist office** Beside the Tour des Fromages, 6 rue Mercière (May–Aug daily 9.30am–7pm; April Mon–Sat 9.30am–12.30pm & 2.30–7pm; Sept daily 9.30am–12.30pm & 2.30–7pm; Oct daily 9.30am–12.30pm & 2.30–6pm Nov–March Mon–Sat 10am–12.30pm & 2.30–5pm; ☎ 03 85 59 05 34, ⓦ cluny-tourisme.com).

## ACCOMMODATION

**De Bourgogne** Place de l'Abbaye ☎ 03 85 59 00 58, ⓦ hotel-cluny.com. Right in the centre of Cluny, built in the walls of the old abbey, this hotel has luxurious rooms, including one with disabled access, which look either onto the abbey or the pretty breakfast garden. If you can, splash out for the suite Lamartine at €163. Parking €10, breakfast €11. Great restaurant, too. Closed Dec & Jan. **€93**

★ **Le Clos de l'Abbaye** 6 place du Marché ☎ 03 85 59 22 06, ⓦ closdelabbaye.fr. A great mid-range choice, run by a friendly couple. There are four stylishly decorated rooms, three of which have a view of the abbey. Breakfast included. **€70**

**Le Potin Gourmand** 4 place du Champ de Foire ☎ 03 85 59 02 06, ⓦ potingourmand.com. A lovely, rambling old building, with charming and individually decorated rooms, set around a courtyard and garden. It also owns a beautiful rustic restaurant that combines local produce with exotic flavours (closed Mon lunch; *menus* from €22). Closed Jan. **€95**

**EATING AND DRINKING**

**Café du Centre** 4 rue Municipale ☎ 03 85 59 10 65. Right in the centre of town, with a charming terrace, this lively, old-fashioned bistro offers simple, tasty dishes and a great selection of salads from €8. Tues–Sat 6.30am–10pm, Sun until lunchtime.

**Le Cloître** 16 rue Municipale ☎ 3 85 59 00 17. With a nice garden and an even nicer dining room, this very busy bar-à-vins is open later than others. Great-value *pichet* (50cl for €6.60) and *menus* for €20. Daily noon–10pm.

**Nation** 21 rue Lamartine ☎ 03 85 59 05 45. A modern, spacious brasserie with outdoor seating, outstanding service and great *plats du jour*. The house *pichet* at €4 for 25cl is fantastic value. Daily 8am–10pm; food served noon–2pm & 7–9pm.

# The Charollais

The **Charollais** takes its name from the pretty little water-enclosed market town of **CHAROLLES**, with its 32 bridges, on the main N79 road. In turn, it gives its name to one of the world's most illustrious breeds of cattle: the white, curly-haired, stocky Charollais, bred for its lean meat. Throughout this region, scattered across the rich farmland, are dozens of small villages, all with Romanesque churches, the offspring of Cluny's vigorous youth.

## Paray-le-Monial

Some 14km west of Charolles, across countryside that becomes ever gentler and flatter as you approach the broad valley of the Loire, is **PARAY-LE-MONIAL**, whose major attraction is its **Basilique du Sacré-Coeur** (daily 9am–8pm). Not only is it an exquisite building in its own right, with a marvellously satisfying arrangement of apses and chapels stacking up in sturdy symmetry to a fine octagonal belfry, it's the best place to get an idea of what the abbey of Cluny looked like, as it was built shortly afterwards in devoted imitation of the mother church.

**8**

# Poitou-Charentes and the Atlantic coast

THE MARAIS POITEVIN

**9**

# Poitou-Charentes and the Atlantic coast

Newsstands selling *Sud-Ouest* remind you where you are: this is not the Mediterranean, certainly, but in summer the quality of the light, the warm air, the fields of sunflowers and the shuttered siesta-silence of the farmhouses give you the first exciting promises of the south. While foreign tourists flock to Paris or the Riviera when summer arrives, the discerning French head for the west coast. Straddling the regions of Poitou-Charentes, Aquitaine and Pays-de-la-Loire, it's an area of great variety, with Roman cities, rustling marshes, a beautiful wine region and miles of sandy coast, dotted with small islands and slumbering coastal villages.

The coastline is rich in **beaches**, which are especially lovely on the pine-covered, sandy **Côte d'Argent**, south of Bordeaux. The historic port **La Rochelle** is a pleasing mix of Renaissance mansions and ice-cream stalls, and the islands are delightful: **Noirmoutier**, small and idyllic; **Ré**, with long beaches, windswept plains and flashy Parisian guests; **Oléron**, unaffected and blue-collar; and romantic **Île d'Aix**, tiny and windswept. The islands are popular in July and August, but best in late spring or early autumn when the crowds slip away.

Inland, the cities make ideal weekend breaks: elegant **Bordeaux**, with unrivalled dining, nightlife and shopping; young and lively **Poitiers**; and cool, creative **Angoulême**, home to the comic strip. For walkers and cyclists there is the **Marais Poitevin**, a lace-like mass of intertwined canals, and for lovers of Romanesque piety, a long stretch of the church-lined **route to Santiago de Compostela**, the medieval pilgrim path to the shrine of St Jacques (also known as St James and Santiago) in Spain. The finest of the churches, among the best in all of France, are in the countryside around Saintes and Poitiers.

It is a region of seafood – fresh and cheap in markets, restaurants and oyster bars for miles inland. Around Bordeaux are some of the world's top **vineyards**, producing robust reds (claret) and sweet whites like Sauternes. Baked specialities include **macaroons**, invented in Saint-Émilion, and *canelé*, from Bordeaux.

## GETTING AROUND                                                POITOU-CHARENTES

Bigger towns are well connected by trains, and most smaller towns and villages are accessible by regular but infrequent buses. Off the main routes, particularly in the wine region and on the islands, having your own transport – car or bike – is a good idea.

# Poitiers and around

**POITIERS**, sitting on a hilltop overlooking two rivers, is a charming country town whose comes from a long and sometimes influential history – as the seat of the dukes of Aquitaine, for instance – is discernible in the winding lines of the streets and the

# Highlights

❶ **Marais Poitevin** A labyrinth of canals, marshes, pastures and ruins, dubbed "green Venice". **See p.479**

❷ **The Île de Ré** Misty beaches, glistening salt marshes, fishing boats, green-shuttered cottages and designer wellies. **See p.487**

❸ **Ile d'Aix** A miniscule island in the Bay of Biscay, where Napoleon made his final stand. **See p.490**

❹ **Angoulême** Maybe the best-kept secret in France – beautiful, historic, lively, full of

things to do, and hardly a tourist in sight. **See p.500**

❺ **Bordeaux** Known as "La Belle au bois dormant" (Sleeping Beauty), an elegant, serene city despite the bustling wine bars, cafés, shops and gourmet restaurants. **See p.503**

❻ **Wine country** Rolling vineyards, magnificent chateaux and the robust flavours of Margaux, Sauternes, St-Émilion, Pauillac, Cognac … the list goes on. **See p.511 & p.517**

**HIGHLIGHTS ARE MARKED ON THE MAP ON P.472**

# POITOU-CHARENTES AND THE ATLANTIC COAST

Pomic
Île de Noirmoutier
Cholet
Thouars
St-Jouin-de-Marnes
Les Herbiers
Les Épesses
Airvault
Châtellerault
A10
La Roche-sur-Yon
Parthenay
Poitiers
St-Sevin
Chauvigny
Les Sables-d'Olonne
A83
Luçon
**1 MARAIS POITEVIN**
Arçais
Coulon
Niort
N10
Île de Ré
**2**
La Rochelle Airport
St-Martin
River Vienne
La Rochelle
Surgères
A10
River Charente
Île d'Aix
**3**
Aulnay
Salle-lès-Aulnay
Ruffec
Conflans
Fouras
Rochefort
St-Mandé
Nouaillé-sur-Boutonne
Île d'Oléron
A837
St-Jean-d'Angély
Le Château
Brouage
Fenjoux
Migron
Marennes
Saintes
Burie
La Rochefoucauld
La Palmyre
N150
Chaniers
Cognac
Jarnac
Rioux
Bourg-Charente
**4 Angoulême**
Royan
Pointe de Grave
Talmont
Soulac
**6**
Barbezieux
**MÉDOC**
Nontron
**6**
St-Estèphe
Chalais
Ribérac
**ATLANTIC OCEAN**
Pauillac
La Roche-Chalais
Périgueux
St-Laurent-Médoc
Blaye
River Dronne
N21
Beychevelle (St-Julien)
Lamarque
N10
Lacanau-Ocean
Moulis-en-Médoc
A89
Côte d'Argent
Libourne
Bergerac
Limeuil
Bordeaux Airport
St-Émilion
River Dordogne
Parc Ornithologique du Teich
**Bordeaux**
Castillon-la-Bataille
**5**
A63
La Sauve-Majeure
Villeréal
Cap Ferret
Arcachon
La Brède
**ENTRE-DEUX-MERS**
Montflanquin
Pilat-Plage
Cadillac
A62
**Dune de Pyla**
St-Macaire
La Réole
River Lot
Villeneuve-sur-Lot
Biscarrosse-Plage
Sauternes
Uzeste
Villandraut
Bazas
A62
Agen
Labouheyre
Mimizan
Marquèze
Sabres
Nérac
Girons-Plage
**LES LANDES**
N10
N124
Mont-de-Marsan
Dax

**N**

## HIGHLIGHTS
**1** Marais Poitevin
**2** The Île de Ré
**3** Île d'Aix
**4** Angoulême
**5** Bordeaux
**6** Wine country

0    20
kilometres

breadth of architectural fashions represented in its buildings. Its pedestrian precincts and wonderful central gardens make for comfortable sightseeing, while the large student population ensures a lively atmosphere in the restaurants and pavement cafés.

**Place du Maréchal-Leclerc** is the heart of the café and restaurant scene, and to the north **place Charles-de-Gaulle** houses the food and clothes **market** (Mon–Sat 7am–1pm). Between is a rabbit warren of medieval streets.

## The church of Notre-Dame-la-Grande

Rue Gambetta cuts north past the old **Palais de Justice** (Mon–Fri 9am–6pm; free), whose nineteenth-century facade hides an older core, incluing a magnificent Gothic knights' hall. The Palais peers down on one of the most famous churches in France, **Notre-Dame-la-Grande**, built in the twelfth-century during the reign of Eleanor. The most exceptional thing about the church is the west front. The facade is not conventionally beautiful, squat and loaded as it is with detail to a degree that the modern eye could regard as fussy. And yet it's this detail which is enthralling, ranging from the domestic to the disturbingly anarchic. Such elaborate sculpted facades – and domes like pine cones on turret and belfry – are the hallmarks of the Poitou brand of Romanesque. Inside the church, the original Romanesque frescoes are gone, except in the apse vault above the choir, and the crypt. The columns and vaults were repainted by Joly-Leterme in 1851.

## Cathédrale St-Pierre

At the eastern edge of the old town stands the enormous, pale-faced **Cathédrale St-Pierre**. Some of the stained glass dates from the twelfth century, notably the Crucifixion in the central window of the apse, which supposedly features Henry II and Eleanor. The grand eighteenth-century organ, the Orgue Clicquot, is the cathedral's most striking feature – often put to good and deafening use in summer concerts.

## Baptistère St-Jean

April–June & Sept daily except Tues 10.30am–12.30pm & 3–6pm; July & Aug daily 10.30am–12.30pm & 3–6pm; Oct–March daily except Tues 2.30–4.30pm • €2

In the middle of rue Jean-Jaurès is the patched-up fourth-century **Baptistère St-Jean**, reputedly the oldest Christian building in France. The "font" is an octagonal pool sunk into the floor. Water pipes uncovered in the bottom suggest the water couldn't have been more than 30–40cm deep, which casts doubt on the popular belief that early Christian baptism was by total immersion.

## Musée Sainte-Croix

3bis rue Jean-Jaurès; June–Sept Tues–Fri 10am–noon & 1.15–6pm, Sat & Sun 10am–noon & 2–6pm; Oct–May Tues–Fri 10am–noon & 1.15–5pm, Sat & Sun 2–6pm • €4, free on Tues and 1st Sun of the month • ⓦ musees-poitiers.org

The town museum, the **Musée Sainte-Croix**, features an interesting Gallo-Roman section with some handsome glass, pottery and sculpture, notably a first-century white marble Minerva. Take the **riverside path** – on the right across Pont Neuf – upstream to Pont St-Cyprien for a picturesque amble.

| ARRIVAL AND DEPARTURE | POITIERS |
|---|---|

**By plane** Poitiers-Biard Airport (☎05 49 30 04 40 ⊕www.poitiers.aeroport.fr) is a short taxi ride (around €13) from the centre; almost half the flights are by Ryanair.
**By train** The *gare SNCF* on boulevard du Grand Cerf, part of

the ring road encircling Poitiers.
Destinations Angoulême (10–15 daily; 45min–1hr 15min); Bordeaux (3–15 daily; 1hr 45min–2hr 30min); Châtellerault (12 daily; 20min); La Rochelle (15 daily; 1hr

**9**

20min–1hr 45min); Limoges (6–9 daily; 2hr); Niort (6–14 daily; 45min); Paris-Montparnasse (10–16 daily; 1hr 45min); Surgères (10–14 daily; 1hr 15min).

**By bus** The *gare routière* is on the ground floor of next door's conference centre.

**Destinations** Châteauroux (2–3 daily; 2hr); Chauvigny (3–5 daily; 45min); Le Blanc (3–5 daily; 1hr 25min); Limoges (6–8 daily; 2hr 30min); Parthenay (6–10 daily; 1hr 30min); Ruffec (7–9 daily; 2hr 30min); St-Savin (3–5 daily; 1hr 30min).

## INFORMATION

**Tourist office** The tourist office (mid-June to mid-Sept Mon–Sat 9.30am–7pm, Sun 10am–6pm; Sept to mid-June Mon–Sat 10am–6pm; ☎ 05 49 41 21 24, ⓦ ot-poitiers.fr) is 15min by foot from the station, at 45 place Charles-de-Gaulle, and can supply walkers and cyclists with maps and guides. Maison du Tourisme, the tourist office for the Vienne region, is at 35 place Charles-de-Gaulle in Poitiers (☎ 05 49 37 48 58, ⓦ tourisme-vienne.com).

## ACCOMMODATION

**Auberge de Jeunesse** 1 allée Roger-Tagault ☎ 05 49 30 09 70, ⓔ poitiers@fuaj.org. Clean, modern hostel with a field for camping. Take bus #7 from the station to "Bellejouanne", 3km away. Well signposted, it's to the right off the N10 Angoulême road. Dorm **€14.30**

★ **Les Cours du Clain** 117 chemin de la Grotte Calvin ☎ 06 10 16 09 55, ⓦ lescoursduclain-poitiers.com. A beautiful early nineteenth-century château, surrounded by landscaped gardens with a pool, with five commodious rooms. The hostess is warm and helpful, and the atmosphere tranquil. **€85**

★ **Le Grand Hotel** 28 rue Carnot ☎ 05 49 60 90 60, ⓦ grandhotelpoitiers.fr. A very convenient central hotel, operated by *Best Western*, clean and comfortable, with off-street parking and a bar with sun terrace. Most rooms have a/c. **€73**

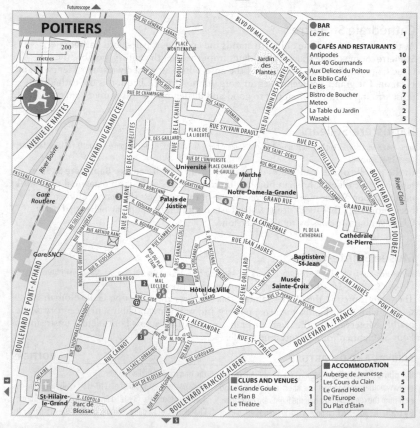

POITIERS

0 — 200 metres

| ● BAR | |
|---|---|
| Le Zinc | 1 |

| ● CAFÉS AND RESTAURANTS | |
|---|---|
| Antipodes | 10 |
| Aux 40 Gourmands | 9 |
| Aux Delices du Poitou | 8 |
| Le Biblio Café | 4 |
| Le Bis | 6 |
| Bistro de Boucher | 7 |
| Meteo | 3 |
| La Table du Jardin | 2 |
| Wasabi | 5 |

| ■ CLUBS AND VENUES | |
|---|---|
| Le Grande Goule | 2 |
| Le Plan B | 1 |
| Le Théâtre | 3 |

| ■ ACCOMMODATION | |
|---|---|
| Auberge de Jeunesse | 4 |
| Les Cours du Clain | 5 |
| Le Grand Hotel | 2 |
| De l'Europe | 3 |
| Du Plat d'Étain | 1 |

**De l'Europe** 39 rue Carnot ☎ 05 49 88 12 00, ⓦ hotel -europe-poitiers.com. A large old-fashioned hotel, once a coach house, in the centre of Poitiers, with 88 rooms. There's also a garden with a small playground. If you're a light sleeper avoid rooms on the road side. Parking €6. **€67**

**Du Plat d'Étain** 7 rue du Plat d'Étain ☎ 05 49 41 04 80, ⓦ poitiers-leplatdetain.com. A pleasant and inexpensive non-smoking hotel, on a quiet central street off the main shopping precinct. **€57**

## EATING AND DRINKING

Poitiers has the highest percentage of students of any city in France, which means lots of busy bars and cafés. You can ask about student and youth offers at the Centre Information Jeunesse (CIJ), 64 rue Gambetta (☎ 05 49 60 68 68).

### CAFÉS AND RESTAURANTS

★ **Antipodes** 65 rue Theophraste Renaudot ☎ 05 49 42 02 93, ⓦ restaurant-antipodes.fr. The name is a reference to the chef's tireless roving, which provides the inspiration behind the fusion menu at this delightful barrel-vaulted cellar restaurant. Ingredients are from its garden and local farms. Live jazz on Thursdays. Mon–Fri noon–2.30pm & 7–10pm, Sat 7–10pm.

**Aux 40 Gourmands** 40 rue Carnot ☎ 05 49 37 01 37. This cheerful family eatery is the place for *moules frites*. *Moules marinière* €12, curried *moules* €13. Mon 7–10pm, Tues–Sat noon–2pm & 7–10pm.

**Aux Delices du Poitou** 15 rue Magenta ☎ 05 49 41 14 69. A small central bakery, open on Sunday, with helpful staff, which performs the near-impossible feat by being the local favourite for bread and pastries too. Mon–Sat 7am–2pm, Sun 7am–1pm.

**Le Biblio Café** 71bis rue de la Cathédrale ☎ 05 49 47 13 70. A peppy student café dispensing stimulants (coffee), depressants (beer) and performance enhancers (books) to the local youth until 11pm. Closed Mon, early closing Sun (8pm).

**Le Bis** 4 rue Saint-Nicolas ☎ 05 49 50 77 91, ⓦ lebis -espritbistrot.fr. Back-lit origami stag-heads watch over smart 30-somethings eating trout with apples and cider, or duck cooked in rum. Dinner *menus* are €18–26, 3-course lunch *menu* is €13. Daily 10am–midnight.

★ **Bistrot du Boucher** 31 rue Carnot ☎ 05 49 03 37 02, ⓦ bistrotduboucher.fr. Food that's fresh, hearty and toothsome, at low prices, in an atmosphere so French it could be London. Daily *menus* €12–16. Daily noon– 1.45pm & 7–10pm.

**Meteo** 6 rue de la Marne ☎ 05 49 41 04 43, ⓦ lemeteo .fr. King of theatre café-bars, with panoramic views, live music, good coffee, a broad sunny terrace, and splendid

Scandinavian furniture, inherited from the European Council in Brussels. Tues–Sat 9am–1am.

**La Table du Jardin** 42 rue du Moulin au Vent ☎ 05 49 41 68 46. Creative reinterpretations of French classics served in a relaxed atmosphere, with outside seating in summer. There's a two-course €10 lunch *menu*, and evening menus in the late €20s to early €30s. Tues–Sat noon–2pm & 7–10pm.

**Wasabi** 11 rue du Chaudron d'Or ☎ 05 49 52 21 16, ⓦ wasabi-poitiers.com. A useful sushi bar with fresh, inexpensive sushi, sashimi and grilled meat (set *menus* around €12) and outdoor seating, popular with students. Daily noon–2.30pm & 7–11pm.

### BARS, CLUBS AND VENUES

**Le Grande Goule** 46 rue Pigeon Blanc ⓦ lagoule.fr. Where the freshers go – 3 storeys, 3 bars and 3 smoking rooms, free entry for girls every night and for students on Tuesdays. Tues–Thurs 11pm–4am, Fri & Sat 11pm–5am.

**Le Plan B** 30-32 bd du Grand Cer ⓦ barleplanb.fr. A retired warehouse couldn't decide whether to become a bar, café, club, gallery or theatre, so compromised with a shrug of fashionable *ennui*. From the station turn left and walk for five minutes. Thurs–Sat 8pm–2am.

**Le Théâtre** place du Maréchal-Leclerc ⓦ tap-poitiers .com. A glorious Art Deco cinema close to the town hall, showing old and new movies in their original language with French subs. June & July Mon–Fri 11am–7pm; Sept–Nov 11am–7pm & Sat 2–7pm; Nov–June 12.30– 6.30pm & Sat 2–7pm.

**Le Zinc** 196 Grand Rue ⓦ lezinc.net. Modelled on a Belgian brasserie, this place has a warm, rustic atmosphere, 20 kinds of beer (many Belgian), regular gigs and exhibitions, open till 2am. Tues–Sat 6pm–2am.

## DIRECTORY

**Bike rental** Cyclamen (☎ 05 49 8813 25) 60 bd Pont-Achard. Closed Sun & Mon.

**Car rental** National/Citer (☎ 05 49 58 51 58), 97 bd du Grand Cerf; Hertz (☎ 05 49 58 24 24) 105 bd Grand Cerf.

**Internet** Cybercorner, 18b rue Charles-Gide (daily 9am– late; €2 per hr).

**Police** 38 rue de la Marne (☎ 05 49 60 60 60).

**Taxis** Radio Taxi (☎ 05 49 88 12 34); Taxis Independants (☎ 05 49 01 10 01).

# Around Poitiers

North of Poitiers is the cinema theme park **Futuroscope** (see box below). There are also a number of safari parks; the best is monkey reserve **Vallée des Singes** ("Valley of the Apes"; daily March–Nov 10am–5pm; €14; ⓦla-vallee-des-singes.fr), thirty-minutes' drive south, near Romagne. More traditional attractions can be found east of Poitiers at **Chauvigny** and **St-Savin** – medieval towns with fine Romanesque churches. Both villages are accessible by bus, though you'll need an early start to see both in one day.

## Chauvigny

**Chauvigny** is a bustling market town on the banks of the Vienne. It is home to the imposing ruins of five **medieval castles** that stand atop a precipitous rock spur, and the Romanesque **church of St-Pierre,** with its magnificent sculpted capitals. If you take rue du Château from the central place de la Poste, you'll pass the ruins of the Château Baronnial, which once belonged to the bishops of Poitiers, and now hosts bird of prey shows, and the Château d'Harcourt, whose north tower houses exhibitions, before coming to the church, St-Pierre.

The choir capitals inside St-Pierre are gruesome and delightful, each depicting a vision of damnation. Monsters – bearded, winged, scaly, human-headed with burning manes – grab hapless humans – naked, struggling, puny – ripping their bowels out and crushing their heads. Counterbalancing these horrors are joyous depictions of the Nativity.

If you can, come on Thursday or Saturday and visit the **market** held between the church of Notre-Dame and the river; it sells a selection of local food – oysters, prawns, crayfish, cheeses galore and pâtés in aspic. The cafés are fun too, filled with noisy, vinous farmers.

## St-Savin

Scarcely more than a hamlet, **St-Savin** is worth visiting for the UNESCO-listed **abbey church**, which was built in the eleventh century. The vault is decorated with murals depicting scenes from Genesis and Exodus, including Noah with a three-decked ark, and Pharaoh's horses on the shores of the Red Sea. Next door is a very good multimedia **museum** (in French; Feb–June & Sept–Dec daily except Sun morn 10am–noon & 2–5pm; July & Aug daily 10am–7pm; €6; ⓦabbaye-saint-savin.fr) of Romanesque art history, medieval monastic life and architecture.

---

## FUTUROSCOPE

Since it opened in 1987, the enormous film themepark **Futuroscope** (ⓦfuturoscope.com), 8km north of the city, has attracted 40 million visitors. It houses ambitious virtual-reality rides, surrounded by lawns and green space, and a few play areas for kids to let off steam.

To see everything would take about nine hours, so some visitors come for more than a day. The films are in French, with English commentary via headphones.

### GETTING THERE

Get an early start to beat the queues. The Paris Montparnasse–Poitiers TGV stops at Futuroscope; there are also regular buses (line #9; €2.60 return, family ticket €4.80 one-way) from Poitiers' Hôtel de Ville or *gare SNCF*. The park is open all year apart from January, from 10am until shortly after sunset, when the laser show finishes.

### TICKETS

**Tickets** are valid for one or two days (adult one-day pass €38, child aged 5–16 €28; adult two-day pass €72, child €63) and to avoid queues at the park it's best to purchase tickets in advance from the Maison du Tourisme in Poitiers (see p.474). Once you're inside go to the translation kiosk with your ID or passport to borrow an iPod for translation – it's free, but bring your own earphones as there's a charge for those. It's a good idea to bring a picnic; there's plenty of lawn space, and food sold on-site is expensive. The hotels around Futuroscope are overpriced or grim or both, so it's best to stay in Poitiers and commute.

# Parthenay

Directly west of Poitiers is the small town of **PARTHENAY**, once an important stop on the pilgrim routes to Compostela. Its faded medieval splendour is worth a glance if you're heading north to Brittany, or west to the sea.

From the train station, avenue de Gaulle leads straight to the central place du Drapeau, from where you can cut through the shopping district to the Gothic **Porte de l'Horloge**, the fortified gateway to the old citadelle on a steep-sided neck of land above a loop in the River Thouet.

Through the gateway, on rue de la Citadelle, the Romanesque **church of Sainte-Croix** faces the *mairie* across a small garden. The view over the western ramparts and the **gully of St-Jacques**, with its muddle of medieval houses and vegetable plots, is spectacular. Further along rue de la Citadelle is a handsome but badly damaged Romanesque door, all that remains of the castle chapel of **Notre-Dame-de-la-Couldre**. The castle itself is gone, but from its site you can look down on the twin-towered **gateway**, and the **Pont St-Jacques**, a thirteenth-century bridge through which nightly flocks of pilgrims poured into the town for shelter and security. To reach it, turn left under the Tour de l'Horloge and down the medieval lane known as **Vaux St-Jacques**. The lane is very atmospheric, with crooked half-timber dwellings crowding up to the bridge.

There are three beautiful **Romanesque churches** within easy reach of Parthenay. One is a twenty-minute walk away at **Parthenay-le-Vieux**. The others are at **Airvault**, 20km northeast of Parthenay and accessible by the Parthenay–Thouars SNCF bus route, and **St-Jouin-de-Marnes**, 9km northeast of Airvault (no public transport).

## ARRIVAL AND DEPARTURE
PARTHENAY

**By train** The *gare SNCF* is on av Victor Hugo, a 15min walk from the tourist office.
Destinations Poitiers (6–12 daily; 50min); Nantes (2 daily; 2hr).

**By bus** Buses arrive at the *gare SNCF*.
Destinations Airvault (6 daily; 25min); Niort (8 daily; 50min); Thouars (at least 10 daily; 1hr).

## INFORMATION

**Tourist office** 8 rue de la Vau Saint-Jacques, next to the old bridge (May–Sept Mon–Fri 9am–12.30pm & 2–6pm, Sat 2.30–6.30pm; Oct–April Mon 2–6pm, Tues–Fri 9.30am–12.30pm & 2–6pm, Sat 9.30am–12.30pm; ☎ 05 49 64 24 24, ⓦ cc-parthenay.fr).

## ACCOMMODATION

**Le Bois Vert** ☎ 05 49 64 78 43, ⓦ camping-boisvert .com. Four-star site that's part of the huge Base de Loisirs riverbank recreation area, about 3km west of Parthenay on the D949. April–Oct. Wi-fi an extra €7 per day. **€21.50**

★ **Le Grand Logis** 7 rue Belisaire Ledain ☎ 05 49 70 22 00, ⓦ sliders.rock.pagesperso-orange.fr/hotes/ Site/Bienvenue.html. A bucolic medieval lodge, straight out of Arthurian legend, converted into a snug B&B sitting quietly in a leafy garden, breakfast included. **€52**

**Du Nord** ☎ 05 49 94 29 11, ⓦ hotel-restaurant -parthenay.com. Clean and decent no-frills hotel, with 9 rooms, TVs, friendly staff, rather tired bathrooms, a cheap restaurant and option of half-board; next to the station. **€62**

## EATING AND DRINKING

**La Citadelle** 9 place de Georges Picard ☎ 05 49 64 12 25, ⓦ restaurant-parthenay.com. A busy local bistro serving excellent wine and food (dishes start at €11) to hungry locals. *La Citadelle's* partner-restaurant, *L'Enoteka*, at 47 rue Jean-Jaurès, is more of the same for slightly less. Mon noon–1.30pm, Tues–Fri noon–1.30pm & 7.15–9.30pm, Sat 7.15–10pm.

**Le Fin Gourmet** 28 rue Ganne ☎ 05 49 64 04 53, ⓦ lefingourmet.com. High-quality traditional cuisine in a quaint, stone-walled medieval house. Everything is made on-site, even the bread. *Menus* from €20. Tues noon–1.30pm & 7.30–9pm, Wed 7.30–9pm, Thurs–Sat noon–1.30pm & 7.30–9pm, Sun 12.30–1.30pm.

**9**

# Niort

The medieval town of **NIORT**, built on two small hills, sits some 50km southwest of Poitiers and makes a useful stopover if your goal is the Marais Poitevin (see opposite). The most interesting part of the town is the mainly pedestrian area around **rue Victor-Hugo** and **rue St-Jean**, which is full of stone-fronted or half-timbered medieval houses. The old **town hall** on rue St Jean is a triangular building of the early sixteenth century with lantern, belfry and ornamental machicolations, perhaps capable of repelling drunken revellers but no match for catapult or sledgehammer. Along the tree-lined river **Sèvre Niortaise** lie the ruins of a glove factory, the last vestige of Niort's once thriving leather industry. At the time of the Revolution, it kept more than thirty cavalry regiments in breeches. Today Niort's bourgeois reputation is thanks to its new key industry: insurance. Accordingly, restaurants are usually packed at lunchtime, and well-heeled shoppers throng the pedestrianized streets, giving it an animated, affluent feel. Just downstream is the **market hall** and, beyond, vast and unmistakable on a slight rise, the keep of a **castle** begun by Henry II of England.

## ARRIVAL AND INFORMATION
NIORT

**By train** From the *gare SNCF* on Place Pierre Semard it's a 15min walk to the tourist office. Take rue de la Gare as far as rue du 14 Juillet, then turn right into place de la Brèche.
Destinations Paris Montparnasse (10 daily; 2–3hr); Nantes (6 daily; 40min) La Rochelle (10–15 daily; 35min).
**By bus** Buses leave and arrive at place de la Brèche; there are 6–8 buses daily to Coulon (20min).

**Tourist office** Place de la Brèche (daily 10am–6pm; ☎ 05 49 24 18 79, ⓦ niortmariaspoitevin.com). They have helpful maps of the town and plenty of information about walking itineraries around the Marais, and also sell large-scale maps of cycle routes (€1).
**Car rental** A number of car rental agencies line rue de la Gare by the station, including Avis at no. 89 (☎ 05 49 24 36 98).

## ACCOMMODATION

★ **Maison La Porte Rouge** 68 av de la Rochelle ☎ 05 49 28 41 62, ⓦ maisonlaporterouge.com. A dignified hotel-like B&B on a central residential street, with five stylish rooms and two apartments suitable for small families; new bathrooms, a leafy garden, swimming pool, table tennis and pool table. Breakfast included. Rooms **€65**, apartments **€85**
**Particulier** La Chamoiserie, 10 rue de l'Espingole ☎ 05 49 78 07 07, ⓦ hotelparticulierniort.com.

Boutique hotel close to the Donjon, with classic modern decor, 16 well-equipped rooms, a breakfast room overlooking the rocky garden, and free parking (book in advance). Breakfast included. **€98**
**Saint-Jean** 21 av St-Jean d'Angély ☎ 05 49 79 20 76, ⓦ niort-hotel-saint-jean.com. This friendly little budget hotel offers the best value for money in Niort, and is close to the medieval quarter. Breakfast €7.50. **€50**

## EATING AND DRINKING

**L'Adresse** 247 av de la Rochelle ☎ 05 49 79 41 06. Worth the 15min walk from the centre, with excellent food and an elegant atmosphere. Evening *menus* €28 and €36. Tues–Sat noon–2pm & 7.30–9.30pm.
**La Brûlerie des Halles** 12 rue du Rabot ☎ 05 49 28 54 00, ⓦ brulerie-deshalles.fr. Fifteen types of coffee roasted in-house and 150 teas. Tues–Fri 9am–7pm, Sat 9am–1.30pm & 3.30–7pm.
**La Dolce Vita** 46 rue St Jean ☎ 05 49 17 14 89. The kind of family-run Italian restaurant, with fresh, good food and a warm atmosphere, that every rainy night needs. Mains €9–17. Tues–Sat noon–1.45pm & 7–10pm.

**Le P'tit Rouquin** 92 rue de la Gare ☎ 05 49 24 05 34, ⓦ leptitrouquin.com. Everything a bistro should be – substantial and warm. The menu rotates with changing ingredients, and an organic wine-list. The steak tartare with basil and creamy seafood risotto with walnut oil are justly celebrated. Mains €15–23, 3-course lunch €14, 3 course-dinner €28. Mon–Thurs noon–2.30pm & 7–10pm, Fri noon–2.30pm.
**Restaurant du Donjon** 7 rue Brisson ☎ 05 49 24 01 32, ⓦ borelweb.com. The kind of place families go on a Saturday night, with good traditional cooking and convivial atmosphere. Mains €13–16, *plat du jour* €9. Mon–Sat noon–2pm & 7–10pm; closed Aug.

# The Marais Poitevin

An endless maze of green pools and streams, wild irises, ruined churches, hidden marshes and golden orioles, the **Marais Poitevin** is a beautiful part of the world. Known as "La Venise Verte" (Green Venice), it was created when seventeenth-century Dutch engineers drained a wet marsh by constructing a network of rigoles – tiny canals banked with poplars. You can explore by boat (below), bike (below) or by foot. The marshes lie across three départements, so getting information on the whole area, which is the size of the Isle of Wight, is difficult. Tourist offices stock an invaluable free map and guide called *Marais Poitevin: Carte Découverte*. When walking or cycling stick to the marked paths, as shortcuts end in wet socks.

## Coulon and around

You can access the eastern part of the marsh from pretty **COULON** (the "capital" of the Marais) 11km from Niort. Ten kilometres west is the quaint village of **ARÇAIS**, which is dominated by a nineteenth-century chôteau, and is another place to hire canoes and punts, or find accommodation.

### INFORMATION

**Tourist office** Place de la Coutume (Mon–Sat 10am–1pm & 2–7pm, ☎ 05 49 35 99 29, ⓦ marais-poitevin.fr); the office houses a free museum that explores the history of the area. They can provide a list of local campsites and *chambres d'hôtes*.

**Bike rental** La Libellule (☎ 05 49 35 83 42; €18 per day).
**Boat rental** La Pigouille boat rental on Quai Louis Tardy (☎ 05 49 35 80 99; 2–8 people with guide €25 per hour; up to 3 people without guide €10 per hour, €32 per day).

### ACCOMMODATION

**Camping Venise Verte** 178 rte des Bords de Sèvre ☎ 05 49 35 90 36, ⓦ camping-laveniseverte.com. Attractively situated in a meadow 2km and a 25min walk from Coulon. April–Oct. **€27.40**
**Central** 4 rue d'Autremont ☎ 05 49 35 90 20, ⓦ hotel-lecentral-coulon.com. Bright, pretty a/c rooms with phone and TV and private parking; dogs welcome (€5), and there's a traditional restaurant (see below). Breakfast €10. **€59**

**Le Fief du Marais** 6 impasse du Logis ☎ 05 49 35 92 43, ⓦ 2.marais-poitevin.com. A charming, rambling wisteria-clad fifteenth-century family home with a warm, charming hostess (speaks little English) and one en-suite guest room that's painted like a teacup. Breakfast included. **€50**
**Le Paradis** 29 Sainte-Sabine, Le Vanneau ☎ 05 49 35 33 95, ⓦ gite-le-paradis.com. Sitting deep into the marshes is this rustic house with five commodious rooms, a large garden and two rental cottages. Breakfast included. **€60**

### EATING AND DRINKING

★ **Central** 4 rue d'Autremont ☎ 05 49 35 90 20, ⓦ hotel-lecentral-coulon.com. A nostalgic, country hotel (see above) restaurant with an elegant dining room and superb cooking, perfect for long weekend lunches. Set lunch *menu* €20.

# Les Sables-d'Olonne and around

**LES SABLES-D'OLONNE** is an unpretentious seaside resort, a far cry from the boutiques and designer wellies of Île de Ré (see p.487), though they share the same stretch of coast. The town was founded in 1218, became a harbour under Louis XI, and peaked in the seventeenth century as the cod-fishing capital of France. Today the town is famous for **watersports** – the Vendée Globe sailing race (ⓦ vendeeglobe.org ) starts here, there's a big sailing school, and opportunities for windsurfing, kayaking, waterskiing and surfing. It's also a friendly place, with safe beaches and plenty of holiday rentals, making it perfect for families.

Les Sables-d'Olonne's **Musée de l'Abbaye Sainte-Croix** on rue Verdun (mid-June to mid-Sept Tues–Sun 1–7pm; mid-Sept to mid-June Tues–Sun 2.30–5.30pm; €5.10)

**9**

houses a respectable modern art collection. And don't miss a stroll up from the seafront to the Île Penotte quarter, where the houses are decorated with colourful seashell mosaics (*coquillages*).

## INFORMATION

**Tourist office** 1 promenade Joffre (July & Aug daily 9am–7pm; Sept–June Mon–Sat 9am–12.30pm & 1.30–6pm, Sun 10.30am–noon & 3.30–5.30pm; ☎02 51 96 85 85, ⓦ visitsablesdolonne.co.uk).

**Parking** The town has a one-way system and you have to pay at meters even on Sundays. The alternatives are to find parking in one of the residential streets at the eastern end of the beach, or park in quieter La Chaume, and take the passenger ferry over.

## ACCOMMODATION

**Antoine** 60 rue Napoléon ☎02 51 95 08 36, ⓦ antoinehotel.com. Clean and homely spot just three minutes from the port, with a private garage, plenty of fresh flowers, friendly owners and breakfast on the terrace. In July & August it's required half-board. Breakfast €7, dinner €24. March–Oct. **€85**

**Le Calme des Pins** 43 av Aristide Briand ☎02 51 21 03 18, ⓦ calmedespins.com. Gaudy red hallway but pleasant rooms at this three star family-run hotel five minutes from the beach, with 45 rooms (half of which overlook the sea), a generous, varied breakfast and services like babysitting and laundry. Breakfast €9, private parking €7. **€73**

**Camping La Dune des Sables** Rte de l'Aubrai ☎02 51 32 31 21, ⓦ chadotel.com/en/campsite -sables-olonne/la-dune-des-sables. Small site that's friendly and convenient rather than luxurious, with laundry, restaurant, shop, pools, great beaches (no lifeguards), kids' club, rental cabins with fridge and crockery. April–Sept. **€20**

**Les Ebruns** 33 rue du Lieutenant Anger ☎02 51 95 25 99, ⓦ hotel-sables-d-olonne.com. In the attractive La Chaume quarter, 400m from the beach. This place has clean, comfortable rooms (which look like the victims of a 90s home decoration show). Breakfast €8, parking €5. **€70**

## EATING AND DRINKING

There are good fish restaurants around the port, at quai Guiné, and opposite on quai des Boucanniers, reachable via shuttle ferry (daily 6am–midnight; €0.93). The covered market, Halles Centrales (June–Sept daily 8am–1pm, closed Mon Oct–May) stocks fresh local fish, dairy, fruit, vegetables, herbs and bread.

**Le Cabestan** 17 quai Guiné ☎02 51 95 07 50. A small quayside restaurant with freshly caught, nicely cooked fish, quick service and reasonable prices, popular with families. Two-course lunch *menu* €11. Fri–Tues noon–2pm & 7–10pm; closed Wed in summer, Wed–Thurs in winter.

**Le Fatra** 21 Quai George V ☎02 51 32 68 73. An excellent little restaurant with a terrace, changing seasonal menus, views of the port, friendly service and a wine list that carefully complements the menu. Reservation recommended. Lunch *menu* €14, dinner *menu* €25. Tues–Sun noon–2pm & 7.30–10pm; closed Sun & Thurs for dinner.

# Puy du Fou

June–Sept Fri & Sat 10.30pm • 1hr 40min • Adult €27, child €19, book in advance • ☎02 51 64 11 11, ⓦ puydufou.com

About 80km inland from Les Sables-d'Olonne is the "historical theme park", **Puy du Fou**, in **LES ÉPESSES** village. Highlights include *Gladiators*, staged in a rebuilt coliseum, with a re-enactment of the horse-racing scene from Ben Hur, and *Vikings*, featuring wild animals and a Viking warship. The show that tops them all is the *Cinéscénie* – a magical sound and light display with fireworks and a cast of hundreds, staged after sunset from June to September.

## ARRIVAL AND INFORMATION

**Public transport** To get to Les Épesses by public transport, you'll need to venture to Cholet (connected by train from Nantes) and take a bus south from there; Puy du Fou itself is 2.5km from Les Épesses on the D27 to Chambretaud.

**Tourist office** The tourist office in Cholet (☎02 41 49 80 00, ⓦ ot-cholet.fr) will provide information about transport.

## ACCOMMODATION

**Château de la Flocellière** 85700 la Flocellière ☎ 02 51 57 22 03, ⓦ chateaudelaflocelliere.com. This spectacular castle, 11km southeast of Puy de Fou overlooking miles of rolling farmland, was one of the first in a growing trend; B&Bs are not offering a holiday, but a social millieu. There are no swimming pools, bars or fitness rooms, but guests are greeted by a countess, and can dine with the gentry (€50). More B&Bs like this can be found at ⓦ bienvenueauchateau.com. **€155**

**La Crémaillère** 2 rue de la Libération ☎ 02 51 57 30 01.

An inexpensive village hotel, 3km from Puy du Fou, with eleven simple, comfortable rooms and a restaurant providing simply cooked traditional meals. **€42**

**La Libaudiere** Pouzauges ☎ 02 51 57 52 68, ⓦ chambresdhotesvendee.com. Children will love sleeping in a yurt or treehouse at this country B&B, 21km southeast from Puy du Fou, and a 30min drive away. The hosts are friendly and the breakfast is excellent. Yurt **€65**, treehouse **€98**, standard B&B **€49**

# The Île de Noirmoutier

The Impressionist painter, Renoir, loved **ÎLE DE NOIRMOUTIER**, an island of sandy inlets, pine forests and salt marshes. At 20km-long, and 60km north of Les Sables-d'Olonne (see p.479), Noirmoutier enjoys a warm microclimate, responsible for the figs and early-flowering mimosa. Although tourism is the island's main economy, it also produces salt, fine spring potatoes, and an abundance of cod, oysters, eels and squid.

The little village of **NOIRMOUTIER-EN-L'ÎLE**, the busiest of the island's six villages, has a twelfth-century **castle** once owned by the Black Prince (now containing a little museum), a **church** with a Romanesque crypt, an **aquarium**, a good **market** (Tues, Fri & Sun) on place de la République, and many of the island's restaurants, port-front bars and cafés.

Inland, the saltwater dykes are the only reminder that you're out to sea, while the pretty whitewashed and ochre-tiled houses in the villages are typical of La Vendée and southern Brittany. Spring weather is often stormy and the summer heat entices mosquitoes, so come prepared.

The most famous **beach**, Plage des Dames, with its painted bathing huts, is a ten-minute cycle east of Noirmoutier-en-l'Île. The beaches on the west and south coasts are the quietest in summertime. Near Fort Larron there is a bird reserve with Avocets, Egrets and Redshanks, and in La Guerinière a butterfly park.

### GETTING THERE AND AROUND                                            ÎLE DE NOIRMOUTIER

The best way to reach the island is via the spectacular, 4.5km-long causeway, "Le Gois", which is covered twice a day with water. Otherwise, there are daily buses from Nantes (p.412), taking 1hr 45min.

**By bike** Cycling is the ideal way to explore: there are paths around almost the entire perimeter, it's perfectly flat, and the traffic is regularly jammed. Of the dozens of bike rental outlets, Vel-hop, 55 av Joseph-Pineau (☎ 02 51 39 01 34,

ⓦ cyclhop.fr; €11 per day) will deliver to your hotel.
**By bus** In July and August Noirmoutier-en-l'Île has a free "park and ride" shuttle bus service from the town down to a number of beaches (daily 10am–7pm).

### INFORMATION

**Tourist office** Rue du Général Passaga, Noirmoutier-en-l'Île (Sept–June Mon–Sat 9.30am–12.30pm & 2–6pm; July & Aug daily 9am–7pm; ☎ 02 51 39 12 42,

ⓦ ile-noirmoutier.com). It can brief you on all the island's activities, from fishing to windsurfing, and provide lists of the island's campsites, and basic maps of cycle routes.

### ACCOMMODATION

**L'Île O Chateau** 11 rue des Douves ☎ 02 51 39 02 72, ⓦ ileochateau.com. In a prime location at the foot of the castle, this modish, good-value hotel, built around a central pool and courtyard, feels intimate despite the 24 rooms. **€73**

**Les Prateaux** 8 allee du Tambourin ☎ 02 51 39 12 52, ⓦ lesprateaux.com. A quiet, hotel in a pine wood, close to the beautiful beach Plage des Dames, in the heart of the

bois de la Chaise area, with prices at upper end of the scale. The bedrooms have balconies or terraces. **€130**

**Residence du Bois de la Chaize** 23 av de la Victoire ☎ 02 51 39 04 62, ⓦ hotel-noirmoutier.com. Good-value family hotel, close to shops and the beach, with fresh rooms (some family rooms) in motel-style freestanding units in the garden; private parking and a rental villa. **€70**

**9**

## EATING AND DRINKING

**Le Grand Four** 1 rue de la Cure ☎02 51 39 61 97, ⓦlegrandfour.com. A genteel country-house restaurant, serving fine local dishes to visitors since 1956. Two-course *menu* €23, three courses from €29. Closed Sun eve, all day Mon, Thurs lunchtime.

★ **La Marine** Port de Pêche de l'Herbaudière ☎02 51 39 23 09, ⓦrestaurantlamarine.blogspot.co.uk. Spectacular Michelin-starred cooking from celebrated chef Alexandre Couillon, who presents a *menu* that changes depending on the catch of the day. The daily *menus* cost between €56 (4 courses) and €130 (*dégustation* with wine). Mon & Thurs–Sat 12.15–1.30pm & 7.15–9pm, Sun 12.15–1.30pm.

**Le Roman Bleu** 1 rue Boucharde ☎02 51 39 03 88, ⓦleromanbleu.com. A warm, family-run restaurant with enthusiastic service, good food, and well-matched wines. Don't miss the cheese-platter or *babou* cake (made with museli, banana and nuts), made to a family recipe. Daily noon–2pm & 7–10pm.

**La Table d'Élise** rue Marie Lemonnie ☎02 28 10 68 35. The bistro version of *La Marine* (see opposite), next door, overseen by the same chef, it provides the chance to try simpler versions of the same food at a fraction of the price. Lunch *menu* €20, dinner *menu* €29. Daily noon–2pm & 5–9.30pm; closed Wed in July–Aug, also Sun night & Tues Sept–June.

# La Rochelle and around

Known as "La Ville Blanche" (the White City), **LA ROCHELLE** is a delicate concoction of pale limestone, warm light and sea air. The city was one of the most important ports in France during the Renaissance, and its rich past is visible in the city's grand arcades, turrets and timber-framed houses. Due to the foresight of mayor Michel Crépeau, the city's historic centre and waterfront were wrested from developers, and its streets freed of traffic in the 1970s. Controversial at the time, the policy has since been adopted across the country – even surpassing Crépeau's successful yellow bicycle plan, imitated in Paris and London.

Eleanor of Aquitaine gave La Rochelle a charter in 1199, releasing it from feudal obligations. This spurred rapid growth through salt and wine trade. The Wars of Religion devastated the town, which turned Protestant, and was ruthlessly besieged by Cardinal Richelieu in 1627. The English dispatched the Duke of Buckingham to their aid, but he was caught napping on the Île de Ré and suffered defeat. By the end of 1628 Richelieu had starved the city into submission. Out of the pre-siege population of 28,000, only 5000 survived. The walls were demolished and the city's privileges revoked. La Rochelle later became the principal port for trade with the French colonies in the Caribbean Antilles and Canada. Many of the settlers, especially in Canada, came from this part of France.

The area around **La Rochelle** is ideal for young families, with miles of safe, sandy beaches. Visiting in August is best avoided, unless you're camping, or book accommodation months in advance.

## The Vieux Port

The **Vieux Port**, where pleasure boats are moored, is the heart of the town. You can stroll very pleasantly for an hour or more along the seafront in either direction from the harbour: down to the **Port des Minimes**, a vast marina development 2km south of the centre, or west, along a promenade and strip of parkland, towards **Port Neuf**. Dominating the inner harbour, the heavy Gothic gateway of the **Porte de la Grosse Horloge** touches the entrance to the old town to the north, and to the south reaches towards the tree-lined pedestrianized cours des Dames, where sailors' wives used to await their husbands' return. Leading north from the Porte de la Grosse Horloge, rue du Palais runs towards the cathedral and museums on rue Thiers.

## The Towers

Daily: April–Sept 10am–6.30pm; Oct–March 10am–1pm & 2.15–5.30pm • €6 for one tower, €8 for all three

La Rochelle is home to three famous towers. **Tour St-Nicolas**, on the east side of the mouth of the harbour, is the most architecturally interesting, with two spiral staircases that intertwine but never meet. On the opposite bank is **Tour de la Chaine**, which houses an exhibition on seventeenth-century emigration to French Canada. You can climb along the old city walls to the third tower, just behind Tour de la Chaine, known as the **Tour de la Lanterne,** or Tour des Quatre Sergents – after four sergeants imprisoned and executed for defying the Restoration monarchy in 1822. All three towers have fine views back to the port, and the entry ticket includes a trip on the **electric ferry** (*passeur*), which tirelessly crosses the water all day (€0.75).

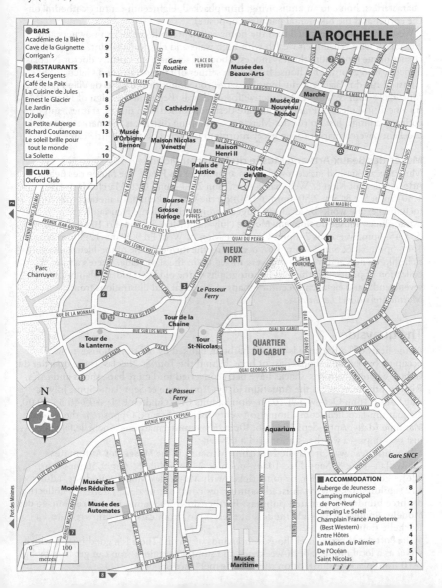

**9**

## The rue du Palais and around

The area around La Rochelle's main shopping street, **rue du Palais**, is beautiful. Lining the street are eighteenth-century houses, some grey-stone, some half-timbered, with distinctive Rochelais-style slates, overlapping like fish scales. The shops are a step back from the street beneath ground-floor arcades. Among the finest buildings are the **Hôtel de la Bourse** – actually the Chamber of Commerce – and the **Palais de Justice** with its colonnaded facade, both on the left-hand side. A few metres further on, in **rue des Augustins**, is **Maison Henri II**, built in 1555 and complete with loggia, gallery and slated turrets, where the regional tourist board has its offices. Place de Verdun itself is rather characterless, home to an uninspiring, humpbacked, eighteenth-century **cathedral** on the corner and the bike rental park (see opposite).

West of rue du Palais you'll find the homes of eighteenth-century shipowners and chandlers, who veiled their wealth with high walls and classical restraint, and on the corner of **rue Fromentin**, the less modest abode of seventeenth-century doctor Nicolas Venette, who adorned his house front with statues of Hippocrates and Galen.

East of rue du Palais, rue du Temple carries you alongside the **Hôtel de Ville**'s (guided tours daily 3pm & 4pm; €4) attractive fortified wall. Begun in the reign of Henri IV, it's a beautiful piece of Franco-Italianate design, adorned with niches, statues, and coffered ceilings. Just up rue des Merciers, a shopping district, is the **market square**; its excellent covered market (open every morning) is circled by simple little cafés.

### Musée des Beaux-Arts and Musée du Nouveau Monde

Museums are stashed inside townhouses around rue du Palais. The **Musée des Beaux-Arts** (April–Sept Mon & Wed–Sat 2–6pm, Sun 2.30–6pm; Oct–March Mon–Fri 1.30–5pm, Sat & Sun 2.30–6pm, €3.50) on rue Gargoulleau has a modest collection, including exotic works by local son Eugène Fromentin. On rue Fleuriau is the extraordinary **Musée du Nouveau Monde** (July–Sept Mon & Wed–Fri 10am–12.30pm & 1.45–6pm, weekends 2–6pm; Oct–June Mon & Wed–Fri 9.30am–12.30pm & 1.45–5pm, Sat & Sun 2–6pm, €4), occupying the former home of the Fleuriau family, rich ship-owners and traders who were mixed up in the slave trade. There's a fine collection of prints, paintings and photographs of the old West Indian plantations; seventeenth- and eighteenth-century maps of America; and illustrations from Marmontel's novel *Les Incas*.

## The quayside

At the heart of La Rochelle is the old harbour, banked by old stone houses now occupied by bars and shops. East of here, behind the Tour St-Nicolas, is the **quartier du Gabut**, where fishermens' shacks have been converted into more bars, shops and cafés. Right on the quayside is the **Aquarium** (daily: April–June & Sept 9am–8pm; July & Aug 9am–11pm; Oct–March 10am–8pm; adults €14, children €11; ☎05 46 34 00 00, ⓦaquarium-larochelle.com), home to twenty species of shark. Opposite is the **Musée Maritime** (daily: April–Sept 10am–6.30pm; €8; ⓦmuseemaritimelarochelle.fr) really just two ships – a weather station and a trawler.

Ten minutes', walk from the Maritime Museum is the **Musée des Automates** (daily: Jan–June & Sept–Dec 10am–noon & 2–6pm; July & Aug 9.30am–7pm; adults €8.50, children €6, or joint ticket with Musée des Modèles Réduits, adults €12, children €9; ⓦwww.museedesautomates.com) on rue de la Désirée, a collection of three hundred automated puppets. Further down the same street is the **Musée des Modèles Réduits**, with scale models of every kind, from cars to a shipwreck to La Rochelle train station.

The **Port des Minimes** itself houses thousands of yachts. There is a good beach, which serves as a local promenade at weekends and summer evenings. You can get here by bus (#10 from place Verdun), or on the "**bus de mer**" (see opposite).

## ARRIVAL AND DEPARTURE

**By plane** Ryanair serves La Rochelle daily from Stansted, which accounts for the large number of Brits who visit. Buses run every 30min between the airport and town centre (bus #7 Mon–Sat 7am–7.20pm & bus #47 Sun; €1.30; journey time 20min).

**By train** From the grandiose *gare SNCF* on boulevard Joffre, take avenue de Gaulle opposite to reach the town centre. Destinations Bordeaux (7–14 daily; 2hr 20min–3hr); La Roche-sur-Yon (4 daily; 1hr); Nantes (5 daily; 1hr 50min);

Paris-Montparnasse (15–20 daily; 3hr 10min–4hr); Rochefort (approximately every 30mins; 20min); Saintes (9 daily; 50min–1hr).

**By bus** The main bus station, or *gare routière*, is situated in place de Verdun, a 10-minute walk to the north of the old harbour. Most things you'll want to see are in the area behind the waterfront; between the harbour and place de Verdun.

By ferry Ferries serve the nearby island of St-Martin de Ré (6–16 daily; 1hr).

## INFORMATION

**Tourist office** Quai Georges Simenon (April & May Mon–Sat 9am–6pm, Sun 10.30am–5.30pm; June & Sept Mon–Sat 9am–7pm, Sun 10.30am–12.30pm; July & Aug Mon–Sat 9am–8pm, Sun 10.30am–6pm; Oct–March Mon–Sat 9am–6pm, Sun 10am–1pm; ☎05 46 41 14 68, ⊚larochelle-tourisme.com).

**Passes and tours** The tourist office (see above) sells the La Rochelle City Pass (2 days €6; 1 week €11.50), covering

all city transport and discount entry into attractions. The office also leads walking tours around the old town (July & Aug Mon–Sat 10.30am; adults €6.50, children €4.50), and rather more amusing two-hour evening tours of the city, led by a local in medieval garb (end of June to mid-Sept Thurs 8.30pm; adults €11.50, children €8).

**Internet** Continuum, rue Amelot (daily 10am–7.30pm; €2/hr; ⊚continuum-cybercafe.e-monsite.com).

## GETTING AROUND

**By bus** The "bus de mer" (April–June & Sept hourly 10am–7pm except 1pm; July & Aug half-hourly 9am–11.30pm; Oct–March Sat & Sun hourly 10am–6pm except 1pm; €1.30 one-way) shuttles visitors from the old port down to the Port des Minimes.

**By bike** There are two municipal bike parks, heirs to Michel Crépeau's original pick-up-and-leave scheme: one

in place de Verdun (all year), the other on quai Valin near the tourist office (May–Sept only). On handing over ID you get two hours of free bike time; after this it's €1.10 per hour.

**By car** Car rental is available from all major companies outside the station, such as Rent-A-Car, 29 av de Gaulle (☎05 46 27 27 27).

## ACCOMMODATION

Accommodation is expensive and scarce in summer, when booking is essential even for campers. There's no such thing as a budget hotel here, though an outstanding youth hostel goes some way to making amends. As an alternative to hotels, you might try the self-catering apartments that abound, particularly around Les Minimes – contact the tourist office (see above) for a list.

**Auberge de Jeunesse** Av des Minimes ☎05 46 44 43 11, ⊚fuaj-aj-larochelle.com. A convenient modern hostel overlooking the marina at Port des Minimes, with all facilities, including a bar, TV room, garden, laundry room, veranda, and a cafeteria serving dinner for €5. Bus #10 or walk from the train station, following the signs to the left. Dorms €17, singles €28

**Camping municipal de Port-Neuf** On the northwest side of town ☎05 46 43 81 20. This well-shaded but slightly shabby site is a 40min walk from the town centre or take bus #20 from place de Verdun, direction "Port-Neuf". Open all year. €14

**Camping Le Soleil** Av Michel Crépeau ☎05 46 44 42 53. In a good location near the hostel, and close to the beaches, this site is often crowded with raucous young holiday-makers. Take bus #10 from place de Verdun to Les Minimes. Open late June to late Sept. €14

★ **Champlain France Angleterre (Best Western)**

30 rue Rambaud ☎05 46 41 34 66 ⊚hotelchamplain .com. A splendid old mansion stuffed with polished mahogany and chandeliers, this is a three-star hotel that looks like it has two-stars more; reasonable prices, located five minutes from the port and surrounded by restaurants. Parking is an extra €7.50. €95

**Entre Hôtes** 8 rue Reaumur ☎05 16 85 93 33, ⊚entre -hotes.com. Impossibly luxurious B&B with five stylish rooms, garden, a good breakfast, and friendly but discreet hosts. It is less than 10min walk to the port; restaurants and bars are a few minutes away. €135

**La Maison du Palmier** 23 place du Marechal Foch ☎05 46 50 31 96, ⊚lamaisondupalmier.com. Elegant, tiny central B&B built around a central courtyard. It has three spacious rooms, decorated with love. There's an excellent breakfast and helpful, friendly service. No parking. €115

**De l'Océan** 36 cours des Dames ☎05 46 41 31 97, ⊚hotel-ocean-larochelle.com. Comfortable low-cost

**9**

two-star hotel in a central location, with a/c. Many rooms have views of the port. No parking provided. **€65**

**Saint Nicolas** 13 rue Sardinerie et place de la Solette ☎05 46 41 71 55, ⓦhotel-saint-nicolas.com. A convenient,

comfortable central hotel tucked away in a quiet courtyard, with a/c, private parking (€10), 24hr reception and a bar-lounge. **€125**

## EATING AND DRINKING

As long as you avoid the tourist-traps on cours des Dames, eating well is easy in La Rochelle. Rue St-Jean-du-Pérot is the stamping ground of high-end traditional restaurants, while there are cheaper, locals' places on and around the market square.

**Les 4 Sergents** 49 rue St-Jean-du-Pérot ☎05 46 41 35 80, ⓦles4sergents.com. This restaurant, which looks like a languid Victorian hothouse, excels in design and atmosphere. The food is nice, though not extraordinary. *Menus* from €21. Closed Mon.

**Café de la Paix** Place de Verdun ☎05 46 41 39 79. Opened in 1895, this gilded, plush *belle époque* café is ideal for lunchtime salads, or tea and cakes. Astonishingly, the prices are fair. Daily lunch & dinner.

★ **La Cuisine de Jules** 5 rue Thiers ☎05 46 41 50 91, ⓦlacuisinedejules.com. *La Cuisine de Jules* serves better food than other mid-range restaurants so it's popular; book in advance. Pleasant interior, excellent, well-presented food, good service. Three-course lunch €27. Tues–Sat noon–2pm & 7.15–10pm.

**Ernest le Glacier** 16 rue du Port/ 48 cours des Dames, ⓦernest-le-glacier.com. The best ingredients, imaginative flavours, large variety, friendly service and central locations make *Ernest* the only place in La Rochelle to buy your ice cream. Salted caramel, chocolate brownie, violet, mango, passion fruit, redcurrant ...

**Le Jardin** 16bis, rue Gargoulleau ☎05 46 41 06 42. A satisfying place for breakfast, with good tea and excellent hot chocolate, crêpes and pastries, a quiet courtyard and glassed-in veranda. Breakfast €6–8. Mon–Sat 9am–7pm.

**D'Jolly** 16 rue Chaudrier ☎05 46 41 26 95, ⓦdjolly.17 -flash.com. A well-stocked but badly lit cache of pastries, cakes and chocolates, where raspberry tarts and rose macaroons glint under glass cases, and Earl Grey and

caramel scents beckon in passers-by at teatime. Tues–Sat 8.30am–7.30pm, Sun 9am–1.30; open Mon July–Aug.

**La Petite Auberge** 25 rue St-Jean-du-Pérot ☎05 46 41 28 43. A champion seafood restaurant with crab, scallops, monkfish, sardines, salmon and the like, and a wine list stretching to Spain. Three-course *menu* €29 (Mon–Sat). Tues–Sun noon–2pm & 7.30–10.30pm, closed Wed lunchtime.

★ **Richard et Christopher Coutanceau** Plage de la Concurrence ☎05 46 41 48 19, ⓦcoutanceaularochelle .com. On the seafront west of the old harbour, with panoramic views over the beach and sea, this Michelin-starred restaurant is a veritable gallery of gastronomy. *Menus* €52–95. Mon–Sat 12.15–1.30pm & 7.30–9.30pm.

**Le soleil brille pour tout le monde** 13 rue des Cloutiers ☎05 46 41 11 42. Enjoyable home-cooked meals in a warm, family-run restaurant close to the market. It's built a reputation for top-of-the-line vegetarian tarts (€9), made – like everything else – from fresh market ingredients. Very popular, so book or arrive early. Tues–Sat 12.15–2pm & 7.30–10pm.

**La Solette** 11 place de la Fourche. On a cobbled square off rue St-Nicholas, this friendly café with a few tables inside and a lot on the terrace, serves a limited choice of fresh, tasty home-cooked meals at lunch and early dinner (salmon tartare, steak and chips, oysters) and a good wine list. From €15. Tues–Sat 10am–midnight.

## NIGHTLIFE AND ENTERTAINMENT

While nightlife along rue St-Nicolas is active all year round, the lively, late night student bars on the quai de Gabut, behind the tourist office, quieten in the holidays. The monthly magazine *Sortir* has listings for mainstream and classical music events, as well as theatre and film. In mid-July La Rochelle hosts the major festival of French-language music, Les Francofolies (ⓦfrancofolies.fr), which features musicians from overseas as well as France, and attracts around 100,000 visitors.

### BARS AND CLUBS

**Académie de la Bière** 10 cour du Temple, off rue des Templiers. A low-key beer bar containing ample *blondes*, *brunes* and *blanches*. Mon–Sat 9pm–2am.

**Cave de la Guignette** 8 rue St-Nicolas. With barrels for tables and low lighting, this well-stocked wine cellar, formerly frequented by sailors, is atmospheric or dingy depending on your taste. Closed Sun.

**Corrigan's** 20 rue des Cloutiers ⓦcorrigans.fr. Decisive proof that Irish pubs don't always have to be ghastly fakes. Near the market, popular with locals, live music every Sunday and occasional other nights. Daily 6pm–2am.

**Oxford Club** Promenade de la Concurrence ⓦoxford -club.fr. Two DJs, two dancefloors, techno/house line-up, girls free nights, 70s/80s music and karaoke Sundays. Admission €10. Summer only, Wed–Sun 11pm–5am.

# The Île de Ré

With misty beaches, green-shuttered cottages and lonely coves, **Île de Ré** is one of the loveliest places in western France. Out of season the economy rests on oysters and mussels, while in high season 400,000 visitors pass through, many of them rich Parisians, and the island is a little less tranquil. The Île de Ré is a rung higher on the French resort prestige ladder than Noirmoutier (see p.481), and three rungs above Oléron (see p.492), so designer boutiques, high-class restaurants, luxury hotels and white-trim Aigle wellies are the norm.

## St-Martin

The island's capital, **ST-MARTIN**, is the centre of tourist life. At its heart is a harbour, filled with a democratic mix of flat-bottomed oyster boats and gleaming yachts. Around the water are less democratic shops, bars and cafés. This is the main tourist drag, to be avoided at all cost on hot August afternoons. To the east of the harbour you can walk along the **fortifications** – redesigned by Vauban in the seventeenth century – to the citadelle. From 1860 to 1938, this was the departure point for the *bagnards* – prisoners sentenced to hard labour in French Guiana and New Caledonia.

## The rest of the island

The bird reserve, **Maison du Fier et Reserve Naturelle,** in the village of **LES PORTES-EN-RÉ** (daily except Sat morn: April to early July & mid-Sept 10am–12.30pm & 2.30–6pm; early July to Aug 10am–12.30pm & 2.30–7pm; €4, ⓦlilleau.niges.reserves-naturelles.org), is a must for nature-lovers. The **Écomusée du Marais Salant** (daily: mid-Feb to end-March & mid-Sept to mid-Nov 2.30–5.30pm, closed Sun & Mon except during school holidays; April to mid-June 2.30–6pm; mid-June to mid-Sept 10am–12.30pm & 2–7pm; adults €4.80, children €2.30–4.20; ⓦmarais-salant.com) near the village of **LOIX**, offers a glimpse into salt-harvesting. A little further inland, through a maze of salt and oyster beds, is the pretty village of **ARS-EN-RÉ**, recognizable by its distinctive church steeple, painted black and white to help sailors navigate the coastline.

### ARRIVAL AND INFORMATION

### ÎLE DE RÉ

**By bus** A regular bus service runs from place de Verdun in La Rochelle to St Martin.

**By car** You can drive over the toll bridge (€16.50 summer, €9 winter) near La Rochelle.

**By boat** Cruise companies in La Rochelle (see p.482) make boat trips to St-Martin (1hr; adults €19.50, children €12.50)

**Tourist office** Each village on the island has its own tourist office, but the branch by St-Martin harbour (April Mon–Sat 10am–1pm & 2pm–5.45pm, Sun 10am–noon; May, June & Sept Mon–Sat 10am–1pm & 2pm–5.45pm,

Sun 10am–1pm; Oct–March 10am–noon & 2–5.45pm; ⓣ5 46 09 20 06, ⓦsaint-martin-de-re.net), is the biggest and most comprehensive with useful maps of the island's numerous cycle routes.

**Bike rental** There are operators across the island like Cyclosurf (ⓣ 05 46 30 19 51, ⓦcyclo-surf.com) and Cycland (ⓣ 05 46 09 08 66, ⓦcycland.fr). A day's cycle hire for an adult is around €12 per day and for a child €7.50.

**Useful website** ⓦcampings-ile-de-re.com. A reliable and exhaustive source of the campsites on the island.

### ACCOMMODATION

**Camp du Soleil** Ars-en-Ré ⓣ05 46 29 40 62, ⓦcampdusoleil.com. A solid three-star campsite with grassy pitches, cabins and mobile homes of all varieties, TV room, games, playground and pool. Mid-March to mid-Nov. **€10.50**

**Le Clocher** 14 place Carnot, Ars-en-Ré ⓣ05 46 29 41 20, ⓦhotel-le-clocher.com. Modern and sleek with

free parking, family rooms, and low prices, this is Ré's version of a budget hotel. **€88**

**L'Ile Blanche** La Flotte ⓣ05 46 09 52 43, ⓦileblanche .com. Around 1.5km from the sea, this family-orientated site has outdoor and covered pools, tennis, volleyball, over 200 mobile homes and cottages, table tennis, football pitch and restaurant. Easter–Sept. **€15**

**9**

**Le Galion** Allée de la Guyane, St-Martin ☎05 46 09 03 19, ⊛hotel-legalion.com. Tucked away from the crowds, behind the harbour wall, with beautiful sea views from the upper floors. **€100**

**La Galiote Re** 7 rue du 8 Mai, La Flotte en Re ☎05 46 09 50 95, ⊛hotellagaliote.com. A charming and well-kept small hotel run with generosity and care; there's secure parking, and rooms decorated in jaunty naval style, and English spoken. Easy walking to the pretty village of La Flotte. **€115**

**Le Sénéchal** 6 rue Gambetta, Ars-en-Ré ☎05 46 29 40 42, ⊛hotel-le-senechal.com. As though a Berlin boutique hotel has been dropped into a rustic seaside village, *Le Sénéchal* has chic decor, a bright courtyard, small outdoor pool, lounge with board games, and a study with a Mac computer to use. Breakfast isn't worth the €15 – go to the bakery on Place de l'Eglise. Closed Jan. **€115**

**De Toiras** 1 quai Job Foran, St-Martin ☎05 46 35 40 32, ⊛hotel-de-toiras.com. A five-star splurge of unbridled Napoleonic decadence on the busy port in St Martin. Expect excellent service, a good restaurant, courtyard garden and effusive decor. **€280**

### EATING AND DRINKING

**Le Bistro Marin** 10 quai Nicolas Baudin-St-Martin ☎05 46 68 74 66. Fresh, well put-together meals in the heart of St-Martin, with a pleasant interior and seating on the quayside. Mains €12–19, desserts €6–8. Daily noon–2pm & 7.30–10.30pm.

**La Calanque** rue de la Pree ☎05 46 07 61 25. A €12 lunch? On Ré? Hard to be believe, but true; *La Calanque* is as out of place as a walrus in a monkey cage – inexpensive, friendly, good quality and popular with burly working types, with nary a Hermes keychain in sight. Lunch €12, three-course dinner €12, seafood platter (oysters, sea-snails, half a crab, shrimps) €20. Summer daily 11am–3pm & 6pm–10pm; winter Tues–Sat 11am–2pm & 6–8.30pm, Sun 11am–2pm.

**La Martinière** 12 rue de Sully in St-Martin/9 quai de Senac in La Flotte ⊛la-martiniere.fr. Thirty-three flavours of ice cream and 20 of sorbet using local ingredients (since 1970). Tastes like pineau, star anise, cinnamon, marshmallow and rum combine in strange and wonderful ways. Easter–Sept daily 11am–10pm.

**L'Ocean** Place de l'Eglise, Ars-en-Ré ☎05 46 29 24 70. A jovial crêperie popular with locals, serves hearty, inexpensive meals (*moules-frites*, goat's cheese and walnut crêpes, profiteroles). Crêpes €7–10, *moules* from €13. Closed Nov–Feb. Daily noon–10.30pm.

**La Poissonnerie du Port** 4 quai de Senac in La Flotte ☎05 46 09 04 14. This splendid fish restaurant proudly displays a sign reading "Restaurant sans congélateur" (Restaurant without freezer). Enough said. Pleasant outdoor seating, good atmosphere, prices high but quality to match. Around €55 for a full meal. March–Oct daily lunch & dinner.

# Rochefort and around

Colbert, Louis XIV's navy minister, built **ROCHEFORT** in the seventeenth century to repel the English and watch over Protestant-leaning La Rochelle (see p.482). It remained an important naval base for centuries, with its shipyards, sail-makers, munition factories and a hospital. Built on a strict grid plan, the town is a monument to the tidiness of the military mind. **Place Colbert** is just as the seventeenth century left it, complete with lime trees, and cobblestones brought from Canada as ships' ballast. The banks of the **Charente** river are beautiful, dominated by the eighteenth-century Royal Ropeworks and the stark, majestic Transporter Bridge, built in 1900.

## Musée d'Art et d'Histoire and Maison Pierre Loti

The explorers Pierre Loti – alias novelist Julien Viaud (1850–1923) – and the Lesson brothers haunt Rochefort's **Musée d'Art et d'Histoire** at 63 rue de Gaulle (Tues–Sun 10.30am–12.30pm & 2–6pm; free), which houses exotic objects brought back from expeditions, and nautical artworks. The **Maison Pierre Loti** (☎05 46 82 91 90) at 141 rue Pierre-Loti is closed for renovations at the time of writing, but once it's open a visit is essential. It's part of a row of modestly proportioned grey-stone houses, outwardly a model of petit bourgeois conformity and respectability, inside an outrageous and fantastical series of rooms decorated to exotic themes, from medieval gothic to an Arabian room complete with minaret. You can see how the house suited Loti's private life: he threw extravagant fancy dress parties and, rather more scandalously, fathered more children with his Basque mistress, kept in a separate part of the house, than with his French wife.

# Corderie Royal, Hermione and Museé National de la Marine

A **combined ticket,** available at both the museums and the tourist office, costs €18 and will get you into the three main museums. The first and grandest is the **Corderie Royale** (daily: April–June and Sept 10am–7pm; July– Aug 9am–7pm; Oct–March 10am–12.30pm & 2–6pm; Single ticket adults €9, children €5; ⓦcorderie-royale. com) or Royal Ropeworks, off rue Toufaire. It's a rare example of seventeenth-century industrial architecture, substantially restored after damage in World War II. Between 1660 and the Revolution it furnished the entire French navy with rope. From here, you can stroll through gardens by the river and examine the rest of the admirably restored **Arsenal.** After a few minutes, you will come to Rochefort's latest pride and joy: a shipyard, meticulously rebuilding the **Hermione** (daily: Feb–March 10am–12.30pm & 2–6pm; April–June & Sept 10am–7pm; July & Aug 9am–7pm; Adults €9, children €5; ⓦhermione.com), the frigate aboard which La Fayette set sail from here in 1780 to assist the American bid for independence from the British. When the ship is complete, which remains a matter of avid speculation, she will sail to America to retrace her original voyage. From the Hermione it is a further five-minute walk to the **Musée National de la Marine** (daily: May–June 10.30am–6.30pm; July–Sept 10am–8pm; Oct–April 1.30– 6.30pm; Adults €5.50, children and adults up to 26 years old free; ⓦmusee-marine.fr), which has a collection of sculptures and models of the Arsenal.

## ARRIVAL AND INFORMATION
ROCHEFORT

**By train** The *gare SNCF* is located at the northern end of avenue du Président Thomas Wilson, a 15min walk from the centre of town.

**By bus** The bus station is in the centre, in the wide, open space of place de Verdun, where it crosses De Gaulle. Lines D and F each run hourly from here to the *gare SNCF*.

Destinations Château d'Oléron (8 daily; 50min–1hr 10min); La Fumée-Île d'Aix (5–8 daily; 40min); Marennes (8 daily; 40min).

**Tourist office** The town has two tourist offices. The main one is on avenue Sadi-Carnot (Mon–Sat: July & Aug 9.30am–7pm; April–June & Sept 9.30am–12.30pm & 2–6.30pm; Jan–March & Oct–Dec 9.30am–12.30pm & 2–6pm; ☏05 46 99 08 60, ⓦrochefort-ocean.com). A smaller office is by the Musée National de la Marine (daily: July & Aug 9am–7pm; Sun & bank holidays only during low season 10am–1pm & 2–5pm and high season till 6pm).

**Bike rental** In July and August, you can hire bikes from the *gare routière* for just €1 per hour.

**Internet** Cybernet Copy 17, 38 rue du Dr-Peltier (Mon–Sat 9am–noon & 2–6pm; €4/hr).

## ACCOMMODATION

**La Caravelle** 34 rue Jean Jaures ☏04 95 65 00 03, ⓦhotel-la-caravelle.com. Fashionable boutique hotel opposite the beach, with oak floors, luxurious suites and a vibrant garden. In July and August prices double. Breakfast €15. **€162**

**Hostel Rochefort sur Mer** 20 rue de la République ☏05 46 99 74 62, ✉rochefort@fuaj.org. A basic HI hostel with clean rooms, communal kitchen, family rooms and a garden; no breakfast. Call beforehand if you'll be arriving on a Sunday, as reception closes. **€16.30**

**Municipal campsite** ☏05 46 82 67 70. Utilitarian-looking campsite with kids' club, wi-fi, barbecues and mobile home access. It's a long haul if you've arrived at the *gare SNCF*: take avenue du Président-Wilson and keep going straight, until you reach the bottom of rue Toufaire, where you turn right, then left – about half an hour all told. March–Nov. **€17.90**

★ **Palmier Sur Cour** 55 rue de la République, ☏05 46 99 55 54, ⓦpalmiersurcour.com. A magnificent, broad-halled townhouse B&B in the centre of town, with a sunny garden and three bedrooms, filled with paintings and antique books. Freshly baked biscuits for breakfast, made by the attentive hostess Mme Coulon. Breakfast included. **€76**

**Roca Fortis** 14 rue de la République ☏05 46 99 26 32, ⓦhotel-rocafortis.com. Reasonably priced two-star central hotel opposite *Palmier Sur Cour* (above) with comfortable modern rooms, a garden and comprehensive breakfast (€8.50). **€69**

## EATING AND DRINKING

**Barolo Ristorante** 15 rue Lesson ☏05 46 99 28 50. Excellent, inexpensive pizza (particularly the cuttlefish and garlic pizza) and good desserts at this simple Italian eatery in the heart of town. Tues–Sat noon–2pm & 7.30–10pm; Sept–June closed Sat lunchtime.

**Le Cap Nell** 1 quai Bellot ☏05 46 87 31 77, ⓦcapnell .com. Quayside dining, with a stylish modern interior,

**9**

outdoor terrace, and very good seafood. Three-course menus €20–26. Closed Tues eve & Wed.

**Les Jardins du Lac** Lac du Bois Fleuri, Trizay ☎ 05 46 82 03 56, ⓦ jardins-du-lac.com. A pale green country-hotel restaurant, with views over a lake, and delicate gourmet meals. It's 12km south-east from Rochefort, and a 20min drive. Drive out on a Sunday for a long walk and leisurely lunch. Three-course menu €55. Daily 12.30–2pm & 7.30–10pm.

★ **Pistache Chocolat** place Colbert ☎ 05 46 87 11 96. It's not even a café – just a bakery and chocolatiere, with a few tables on the street, but the sweets, cakes and bread (hand-kneaded because there's no room for a machine) are the best in town. Dive into hot milk with walnut, chocolate cupcakes, macaroons with chocolate ganache, apple and cinnamon macaroons or peppermint ice cream. Closed lunchtimes & weekends.

★ **La Rendez-Vous** 72 rue Jean Jaurès ☎ 05 46 99 07 11, ⓦ restaurant-rendezvous.com. The intimate atmosphere, fresh ingredients, specialities like tagliatelle with prawns and half-baked chocolate cake, make this restaurant a hot-spot with dating couples, so book in advance Friday or Saturday. Mains €13–18. Closed Sun.

**La Vilette** 15 av Generale de Gaulle ☎ 05 46 99 05 72. Inexpensive, good food in an old-fashioned bistro and bar, popular with workers from the nearby market. Mon–Sat noon–2pm.

## Fouras

The low-key seaside town of **FOURAS**, 30km south of La Rochelle, and accessible by bus G from Rochefort (35min), is the main embarkation point for Île d'Aix (see p.490). The ferry dock, **Pointe de la Fumée**, is at the tip of a 3km long peninsula. The finger of land is hemmed in by fortresses, originally intended to protect the Charente against Norman attack, later useful in repelling the Dutch and English.

### Fort Vauban and Île Madame

The seventeenth-century **Fort Vauban** (June–Sept daily except Mon am, 10am–noon & 3–6.30pm, Sept–May 2.30–5.30pm) now houses a small local history museum (€3.20). From its esplanade there's a panorama of neighbouring forts and islands, including **Île Madame**, accessible at low tide from Port des Barques, via the Passe aux Boeufs causeway. The island also has a grim history as the internment site, and in most cases death, of scores of priests from the region, victims of the anti-clerical terror unleashed in the 1790s.

**INFORMATION**

**FOURAS**

**Tourist office** Fouras's tourist office, which also serves the Île d'Aix, is situated on avenue du Bois Vert on the peninsula (Mon–Sat: July & Aug 9am–12.30pm & 1.30–6.30pm; April–June & Sept–Oct 9am–12.30pm & 2–6pm; Nov & March 9am–12.30pm & 2–5.30pm; ☎ 05 46 99 08 60 or ☎ 05 46 84 60 69, ⓦ fouras.net).

**ACCOMMODATION**

**Grand Hôtel Des Bains** 15 rue du General Brunche ☎ 05 46 84 03 44, ⓦ grandhotel-desbains.fr. Between the market and the beach, in a former coaching in, around a flowery courtyard; it has 31 likeable rooms. **€63**

★ **Roseraie** 2 rue Eric-Tabarly ☎ 05 46 84 64 89, ⓦ hotel-fouras.com. Cute as a button, neat as a pin, and a stone's throw from the beach; the owners are really friendly and there's a sweet garden. **€60**

**EATING AND DRINKING**

**L'Instant Thé** 33 rue de la Halle ☎ 05 46 82 76 56. Smashing quiches, tarts, cakes, salads and, of course, tea in this charming, faux-Granny teahouse. Closed Thurs.

**Ti Sable** Av Charles de Gaulle ☎ 05 46 84 61 10.

Jolly boat-like restaurant with value for money dishes, specializing in seafood. It's close to the beach and has a pleasant terrace. Three-course set lunch €14. Closed Tues.

## Île d'Aix

Lying in the Bay of Biscay like a forgotten croissant, **Île d'Aix** (pronounced "eel dex"), just 2km long, has a population of only 200. It's a romantic place – frequented by abdicating emperors, wild birds and hollyhocks. It's also well-defended, with forts and ramparts. Over the course of history the island, particularly **Fort Liédot**, has often served as a prison, notably during the Crimean and First World wars. The best time to visit is in spring or autumn, avoiding the midsummer crowds; hire a bicycle, cycle round the perimeter of the island in an hour or two, paddle in the sea, and enjoy a splendid lunch at *Hôtel Napoléon* (see below).

## Musée Napoléon and Musée Africain

Napoleon lived on Île d'Aix for three days in July 1815, planning his escape to America, only to find himself on the way to St Helena and exile. Now his former home, the **Musée Napoléon** (Nov–March daily except Tues: 9.30am–noon & 2–5pm; April–Oct daily except Tues: 9.30am–noon & 2–6pm; €4.50 with Musée Africain; Ⓦ musees-nationaux-napoleoniens.org), exhibits his clothing, art and arms. Napoleon's white dromedary camel, from whose back he conducted his Egyptian campaign, is lodged nearby at the **Musée Africain** (Nov–March daily except Tues: 9.30am–noon & 2–5pm; April–Oct daily except Tues: 9.30am–noon & 2–6pm; €4.50 with Musée Napoléon).

### ARRIVAL AND DEPARTURE                                                                 ÎLE D'AIX

**By ferry** Ferries connect Île d'Aix with Fouras (Pointe de la Fumée ❶ 08 20 16 00 17, Ⓦ service-maritime-iledaix.com) daily. Boats leave half-hourly in summer and a minimum of five times daily in winter; the journey takes approximately 30min. Buy tickets (adult return €8.90 in winter, €13.80 in summer) at the dock, arriving 30min before departure. In summer there are also ferries from La Rochelle and Oléron.

**Getting around** You can hire bikes on rue Gourgaud or rue Marengo, or pick up a horse and carriage from place Austerlitz.

### ACCOMMODATION

**Maeva** Fort de la Rade ❶ 01 58 21 55 50, Ⓦ pv -holidays.com. Camping and holiday rental cabins, with a heated pool and caravan rental, a few minutes' walk from the port. Cabin for two people per week €199, pitch per night €23

**Napoléon** rue Gourgaud ❶ 05 46 84 00 77, Ⓦ hotel-ile -aix.com. Sophisticated hotel with 18 rooms full of oak, slate and wicker. Enjoy views of the lighthouses and Fort Boyard from the rooms – just make sure you request a sea view. Breakfast €12. €120

### EATING AND DRINKING

**Les Paillots** ❶ 05 46 84 66 24. A simple seaside restaurant with a menu of fresh seafood, ship's galley decor and a terrace; a useful fallback if *Chez Joséphine* (see below) is full. Open for drinks and music until 2am in high season. Breakfast by reservation (€6.50), 2 courses €25, 3 courses €33. Sept–June Tues–Sun noon–2pm & 7.30–10pm.

**Restaurant Chez Joséphine** Hôtel Napoléon (see above) ❶ 05 46 84 00 77, Ⓦ hotel-ile-aix.com /restaurant-josephine. With a pleasing modern menu (of the French-classics-Asian-spices school) and modish design, *Chez Joséphine* is an urban island wrapped in a rural island. Three-course *menu* €26. Daily noon–2.30pm & 7.30pm–9.30pm, closed Nov to early spring (date dependent on weather).

# Brouage and around

Eighteen kilometres southwest of Rochefort is **BROUAGE**, another seventeenth-century military base. The way into the town is through the **Porte Royale** in the north wall of the original fortifications. Locked inside, Brouage seems abandoned and somnolent; even the sea has retreated, and all that's left of the harbour is a series of pools (*claires*), where oysters are reared (see box, p.492).

Brouage forms a tight grid lined with low two-storey houses. On the second street to the right is a memorial to Samuel de Champlain, the local boy who founded the French colony of Québec in 1608. In the same century, Brouage witnessed the last pangs of a royal romance when Cardinal Mazarin, successor of Richelieu, locked up his niece, Marie Mancini, to keep her from her young sweetheart, Louis XIV. The politics of the time made the Infanta of Spain a more useful consort for the King of France.

---

## OYSTERS

Marennes' speciality is fattening *creuses oysters*, a species bred in France since the 1970s. It's a lucrative but precarious business, vulnerable to storm damage, temperature changes, salinity in the water, the ravages of starfish and umpteen other natural disasters.

Oysters begin life as minuscule larvae, which are "born" about three times a year. When a birth happens, the oystermen are alerted by a special radio service, and they all rush out to place their "collectors" – usually arrangements of roofing tiles – for the larvae to cling to. They mature there for eight or nine months, and are then scraped off and moved to *parcs* in the tidal waters of the sea. Finally, they're taken to *claires* – shallow rectangular pools where they are kept permanently covered by water that's less salty than sea water. Here they fatten up and acquire the greenish colour the market expects. With "improved" modern oysters, the whole cycle, which used to take five years, now takes about two.

---

Louis gave in, while Marie pined on the battlements of Brouage. Returning from his marriage in St-Jean-de-Luz, Louis dodged his escort and stole away to see her. Finding her gone, he slept in her room and paced the battlements in her footsteps.

### Marennes

Half a dozen kilometres south of Brouages is the oyster village of **MARENNES**. It is the centre of production in a region that supplies over sixty percent of France's requirements (see box above).

#### INFORMATION

**Tourist office** Place Chasseloup-Laubat (April–June & Sept Mon–Fri 9.30am–noon & 2–5pm, Sat 9.30am–noon & 2–4pm; July & Aug Mon–Sat 9.30am–6.30pm; Oct–March Tues–Sat 10am–noon & 2–4pm; ☎ 05 46 85 04 36, ⓦ ile-oleron-marennes.com). There's a small art gallery here, too. Ask here about trips to the oyster beds (see box above).

#### ACCOMMODATION

**Les Cabanes de Nodes** 4 chemin des Oeillets ☎ 05 46 47 42 31, ⓦ lescabanesdenodes.site-pap.fr. Set at the foot of Île d'Oléron, this New England-looking wood-clad house has five quiet *chambres d'hôtes*, private parking, a terrace and a pool. **€67**

# The Île d'Oléron

Joined to the mainland by a bridge just north of Marennes, the **Île d'Oléron** is France's largest island after Corsica, a laidback, unaffected fishing island and coastal resort.

Outside the tourist season, the island is a peaceful retreat; a patchwork of little villages, pine forests and gleaming muddy tributaries lined with fishing boats. In July and August it is taken over by holiday-makers and their campervans, and much of the tranquillity is lost.

The main town in the south of the island, **LE CHÂTEAU**, is named after the **citadelle** that still stands, along with some seventeenth-century **fortifications**. The town thrives on its traditional oyster farming and boat building, and there's a lively **market** in place de la République every morning. The chief town in the north – and most picturesque of the island's settlements – is **ST-PIERRE**, whose market square has an unusual thirteenth-century monument, **La Lanterne des Morts**. The best beach is at **LA BRÉE LES BAINS**, in the northeast. Activities abound, from cycling to **surfing**, and a great **aqua park** opens between June and September in the village of Dolus d'Oléron in the centre of the island.

A pleasant place to spend an afternoon is **Le Marais aux Oiseaux** (daily: April–June & Sept 10am–1pm & 2–6pm; July & Aug 10am–7pm; €4.50; ⓦ centre-sauvegarde-oleron

.com), the bird park. Off the D126 between St-Pierre and Dolus, right in the middle of the island, it's a breeding centre with many rare and endangered species.

## GETTING THERE AND AROUND ÎLE D'OLÉRON

Oléron is reachable by bus #6 from Rochefort (1hr), and in July and August minibuses connect the main towns on the island; see w lesmouettes-transport.com for timetables.

## INFORMATION

**Tourist office** Place de la République in Le Château (daily: Mon–Sat 9.30am–12.30pm & 2.30–7pm, plus in July & Aug Sun 10am–12.30pm; ☎05 46 47 60 51, w ot -chateau-oleron.fr). Bikes can be rented from Vélos 17 (☎05 46 47 14 05, w velos17loisirs.com), which has outlets in all the towns on the island. A day's cycle hire for an adult is around €16 per day and for a child €12.

## ACCOMMODATION

What Île d'Oléron does best is mid-range family-orientated beach hotels. Prices rise by 30–50 percent in high season and most hotels are closed Nov–March. For stays of a week or longer, tourist offices have lists of rental apartments.

**L'Albatros** 11 bd du Dr-Pineau, St-Trojan-les-Bains ☎05 46 76 00 08, w albatros-hotel-oleron.com. A little gem of a seaside hotel with views of the sea and garden, very good restaurant, simple and convenient rooms. At €11 the simple breakfast is overpriced. **€95**

**Face aux Flots** 24 rue du Four, La Cotinière ☎ 05 46 47 10 05, w hotel-faceauxflots-oleron.com. A family-run star hotel in a freshly painted 1930's building, close to the beach, with balconies, a pool, bar and friendly service. No lift. **€95**

**De la Plage** 51 bd du Capitaine Leclerc, La Continiere ☎05 46 47 28 79, w oleronhotel.com. Quiet, simple family hotel in the suburbs of La Continiere, with rooms and studio flats (with kitchenette). All rooms have a terrace or a balcony; there's a heated pool (open April–Oct). The hotel is an easy 10min walk from the shops, restaurants and harbour. **€85**

**Pertuis d'Antioche** Off the D273 ☎05 46 47 92 00 w camping-antiochedoleron.com. A mere 150m from the beach, with mobile home rental, swimming pool, paddling pool, jacuzzi and solarium. April–Sept. **€32**

**Signol** Boyardville ☎05 46 47 01 22 w signol.com. Campsite with bar, restaurant, pool, sauna, fitness centre and even a hammam, near a pine forest, 800m from the beach. April–Sept. **€31**

**Le Square** Place des Anciens Combattants, St-Pierre ☎05 46 47 00 35, w le-square-hotel.fr. Bright, blue-and-white hotel minutes away from the restaurants and shops of St-Pierre, with 27 small but comfortable rooms, a heated pool, games room and free parking. Rooms at the back are quieter. **€75**

## EATING AND DRINKING

**Changement d'Ambiance** 3 rue du Marche St Pierre ☎05 46 36 87 45. Fresh, home-cooked food, prepared by a generous chef with a talent for sauces, served in a small convivial restaurant, at good prices. Approximately €20 for a meal including dessert and coffee. July–Sept Tues–Sun noon–10pm; Oct–June Wed–Sun noon–10pm.

**La Crêperie de St Denis d'Oléron** 3 rue du Port ☎05 46 47 90 63, w la-creperie-st-denis.blogspot .co.uk. A tip-top crêperie with well-stacked crêpes and galettes, tarts and salads and artisan ice-cream. The salted caramel and chocolate crêpe is a real treat. Menu including drink €10. April–Oct daily noon–2pm & 7–10pm.

★ **Les Jardins d'Alienor** 11 rue du Maréchal Foch Le Château d'Oleron ☎05 46 76 48 30, w lesjardins dalienor.com. A haute-rustic hotel and gourmet restaurant, with subtle, memorable food served in a bright, walled garden. Daily three-course menus €27–55. Daily noon–2pm & 7–10pm; closed Mon in summer, plus Mon & Tues in winter.

★ **La Pigouille-Bar à huitres** 20 rue du Port la Cotinière ☎05 46 47 13 77. A short walk from the fishing port of la Cotinière, this lunch bar and fishmonger sells the freshest cooked and raw seafood to eat in or take away. Oysters are from the family's farm at the port of Baudissière, and all the cooking is executed in traditional Oléron style, with garlic, parsley, shallots and cognac abounding. Sept–June Tues–Sun noon–2pm & 7–10pm; July & Aug daily 8am–11pm.

**Le Saint Pierre** 19 rue Republique St Pierre ☎05 46 47 14 39. A lovable cottage restaurant serving great seafood, like monkfish with preserved lemon, coriander and tomato and fricassee of cuttlefish with garlic cream sauce. It has a roaring fire in winter and a sunny terrace in summer, and good desserts. Three-course lunch (€14) and dinner (€26) menus. Sept–June Tues–Sat noon–2pm & 7–10pm; July & Aug daily.

**9**

# Royan

Before World War II, **ROYAN** was a glorious seaside resort, drawing the cream of society with its luxury hotels and casinos. The town is still popular, but the glory days are gone – a victim of Allied bombing and 1950's town planning. But Royan still has its **beaches**, which are lovely, particularly out towards the northern suburb of Pontaillac.

In a weather-beaten square behind the main waterfront is Gillet and Hébrard's uncompromising masterpiece, the **church of Notre-Dame** (1955–58). Tall concrete columns roar upwards, surging into a 65-metre bell tower, which looks rather like the prow of Noah's arc. The inside fulfils the promise of the outside with triangular columns and metres of stained glass. Royan's highlight is the area around **boulevard Garnier**, which leads southeast from Rond-Point-de-la-Poste along the beach. The area once housed Paris's good and great, including Émile Zola who lived at **Le Rêve**, 58 bd Garnier.

## Excursions from Royan

There are various **cruises** from Royan in season – ask at the tourist office (see below) – including one to the **Cordouan lighthouse**, built by the Black Prince. There's also a frequent 30min **ferry** (one-way: pedestrians €3.10, bicycles €1.60, motorbikes €10.40, cars €22.80) that crosses to the headland on the other side of the Gironde, **Pointe de Grave**. From there, a bicycle trail and the GR8 walking trail head down the coast through the pines and dunes to the bay of Arcachon.

An ideal bicycle or picnic excursion just over an hour's ride from Royan is to **TALMONT**, 16km up the Gironde on the GR360. Apart from a few ups and downs through the woods outside Royan, it's all level terrain. The low-lying village clusters around the beautiful twelfth-century **church of Ste-Radegonde**, which stands on a cliff above the Gironde.

### ARRIVAL AND INFORMATION                                                                  ROYAN

**By train** The *gare SNCF* is on place de la Gare near cours de l'Europe.
**Destinations** Saintes (5–10 daily; 30min).
**Tourist office** Bd de la Grandière (Jan–March Mon–Fri 9am–12.30pm & 2–6pm, closed weekends; April to mid-June Mon–Sat 9am–12.30pm & 2–6pm, Sun 10am–12.30pm; mid-June to Aug daily: 9am–7.30pm; Sept–Dec

Mon–Sat 9am–12.30pm & 2–6pm, closed Sun; ☎ 05 46 05 04 71, ⓦ royan-tourisme.com).
**Bicycle rental** You can hire bikes for €12 per day from Cycles Horseau at 107 cours de l'Europe (☎ 05 46 39 96 43).
**Car rental** The major car rental firms are based near the station.

### ACCOMMODATION

Accommodation in Royan is overpriced and scarce in high season, when you're best making a day visit from Saintes or Rochefort.

**Les Bleuets** 21 Façade de Foncillon ☎ 05 46 38 51 79, ⓦ hotel-les-bleuets.com. A good-value, nautical-themed hotel opposite Foncillon beach, with views of the Gironde and the Atlantic. Rooms are clean and for a little extra money you can get a sea view. **€51**
**Camping Clairefontaine** Off rue du Colonel Lachaud, on the outskirts Royan ☎ 05 46 39 08 11, ⓦ camping -clairefontaine.com. A four-star campsite with a range of cabins and chalets, 300m from the beach, with a swimming pool and faux beach in the grounds. May to mid-Oct. **€32.70**
**Family Golf Hotel** 28 bd Garnie ☎ 05 46 05 14 66, ⓦ family-golf-hotel.com. A bit pricier than the other

seafront hotels listed; what you're paying for is less functional but more welcoming interiors. Many rooms have balconies overlooking the sea. **€120**
★ **Ma Maison de Mer** 21 av du Platin, St Palais-Sur-Mer ☎ 05 46 23 64 86, ⓦ mamaisondemer.com. If you have a car, or don't mind a short train ride, *Ma Maison de Mer* (9km away) offers fantastic value for money, comfort and hospitality not available in Royan proper. A five-room B&B in an elegant family home, it's located in leafy suburbs, two minutes from the beach, and is close to the shops and restaurants in St Palais-Sur-Mer. A very good breakfast is included in the rate. **€120**

**FROM TOP** THE DUNE DU PYLA (P.520); NIGHTLIFE IN BORDEAUX (P.509) >

**9**

**Miramar** 173 av de Pontaillac ☎05 46 39 03 64, ⓦ miramar-pontaillac.com. Located right opposite the beach, this well-run hotel has large, comfortable rooms and a bar and a terrace with a sea view. **€97**

**Rêve de Sable** 10 place du Marechal Foch ☎05 46 06 52 25. Inexpensive and comfortable, this small three-star hotel is a few minutes' walk from the beach, and right in the heart of town. **€85**

### EATING AND DRINKING

**L'Aquarelle** 22 rte de Cande ☎05 46 22 11 38, ⓦ laquarelle.net. A Michelin-starred restaurant serving eccentric and delightful dishes, blending unusual flavours like foie gras with coconut or duck with sweet ginger. *Dégustation* menu €66–85. Tues 7–9.15pm, Wed–Sat noon–3.30pm & 7–9.15pm, Sun noon–3.15pm.

**Les Filets Bleus** 14 rue Notre-Dame ☎05 46 05 74 00. Near the cathedral, this traditional French restaurant with a maritime theme is a treat on any budget, with *menus* from €15–40. Tues–Sat noon–2pm & 7–10pm, Sun 7–10pm.

**Garden Ice Café** 3 bd de la Republique ☎05 46 05 02 89, ⓦ gardenicecafe.com. This versatile chain restaurant-bar serves food from noon till midnight every day – useful if you're caught hungry out of hours. Daily noon–midnight.

★ **Le Petit Bouchon** 8 quai Amiral Meyer ☎05 46 22 08 82, ⓦ lepetitbouchon17.com. In a town of overpriced eateries, *Le Petit Bouchon*, by the harbour, is a rare exception, with food that leaves the tastebuds happy and the wallet unharmed. The decor is the visual equivalent of a sea shanty, but not distracting, and the atmosphere is warm and unpretentious. A meal with drinks is around €25. Mid Feb to mid-Nov daily noon–2pm & 7–10pm.

# Saintes

**SAINTES** was once more important than its modest size suggests; the capital of the province of Saintonge and a little cog in the Roman machine. The city retains an atmosphere of grandeur and reminders of past greatness, including a marvellous amphitheatre and two Romanesque pilgrim churches.

## Abbaye aux Dames

Daily: April–Sept 10am–12.30pm & 2–7pm; Oct–March 2–6pm • Entry €2, guided tour €3.50, festival tickets from €10 • ⓦ abbayeauxdames.org

The abbey church, the **Abbaye aux Dames**, is as unique as Notre-Dame in Poitiers (see p.473). A sculpted doorway conceals the plain, domed interior. Its most unusual feature is the eleventh-century tower, by turns square, octagonal and lantern-shaped. A famous classical music festival takes place here in mid-July, and there are atmospheric concerts in the abbey.

## Arc de Germanicus and the Musée Archéologique

On the riverbank is the Roman **Arc de Germanicus**, a triumphal arch dedicated to Germanicus Caesar, as well as his uncle, the emperor Tiberius, and cousin Drusus, and built in 19 AD. Germanicus died later that year, most likely poisoned by Tiberius – he was becoming too popular. In a stone building next door is the **Musée Archéologique** (April–Sept Tues–Sat 10am–12.30pm & 1.30–6pm, Sun 1.30–6pm; Oct–March Tues–Sun 2–5pm; €1.70), which provides a glimpse into Roman Saintes.

## Cathédrale de St-Pierre and around

A footbridge crosses from the Musée Archéologique to the covered market on the west bank of the river. Nearby is place du Marché and the **Cathédrale de St-Pierre**, a tubby Romanesque church with an imposing Neoclassical facade, where John Calvin preached between 1536 and 1564.

North of the cathedral on rue Victor-Hugo is an early seventeenth-century mansion that houses the **Musée Présidial** (all museums: April–Sept Tues–Sat

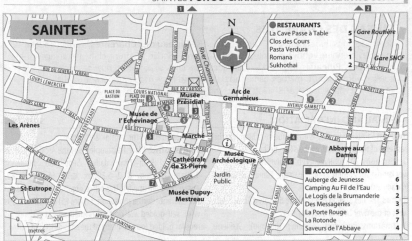

10am–12.30pm & 1.30–6pm, Sun 1.30–6pm; Oct–March Tues–Sun 2–5pm; €4.20 for access to all three museums), containing a collection of local pottery and fifteenth to eighteenth-century paintings. Just down the road is the **Musée de l'Echevinage**, that has nineteenth- and twentieth-century paintings, mainly by local artists of the Saintongaise and Bordelaise schools. The final museum nearby is **Musée Dupuy-Mestreau,** down on the riverbank, which houses a vast personal collection of turn-of-the-century objects ranging from model ships to headdresses.

## Les Arènes

June–Sept daily 10am–8pm; Oct–May Mon–Sat 10am–5pm, Sun 1.30–5pm · €2

Saintes' Roman heritage is best seen at **Les Arènes,** one of the finest amphitheatres in France. The remains are perhaps all the more extraordinary for their location: this monumental vestige from an ancient past, now a little grassy in parts, sits embedded in a valley almost completely surrounded by bland suburbia; a forgotten, sleeping relic dating from 40 AD, also the oldest surviving Romain ruins in France. To find it take the small footpath beginning by 54 cours Reverseaux. On the way back from the amphitheatre call in at the eleventh-century **church of St-Eutrope**, with its carved choir and atmospheric crypt, that houses the third-century tomb of Saintes' first bishop, Eutropius.

## Around Saintes

There are a number of marvellous Romanesque churches reachable by car from Saintes. In **FENIOUX**, 29km to the north towards St-Jean-d'Angély, there's St-Europe with its mighty spire, while the church at **RIOUX**, 12km south, has an intricate facade. Best of all is the twelfth-century pilgrim **church St-Pierre**, at **AULNAY**, 37km northeast of Saintes, with its facade depicting Christ in Majesty and St Peter, crucified upside down, with two lithe soldiers balancing on the arms of his cross to hammer nails into his feet.

Some 12km from Saintes, at Port d'Envaux, is the fantastic open-air gallery **Les Lapidiales** (Ⓦlapidiales.org). Here, many of Europe's best sculptors have carved into the face of a disused stone quarry, creating a magnificent permanent collection that grows each year.

**9**

## PINEAU DES CHARENTES

Roadside signs throughout the Charente advertise **Pineau des Charentes**, a sweet liqueur made by blending lightly fermented grape must and cognac. It's drunk chilled as an aperitif, or with oysters. **Pineau** is also used to make local specialities like *moules au Pineau* (mussels cooked with *Pineau*, tomatoes, garlic and parsley) and *lapin à la saintongeaise* (rabbit casseroled with *Pineau rosé*, shallots, garlic, tomatoes, thyme and bay leaves).

### ARRIVAL AND INFORMATION

**SAINTES**

**By train** Saintes' *gare SNCF* is on avenue de la Marne at the east end of the main road, avenue Gambetta.
Destinations Angoulême (20 daily Mon–Fri, 3–4 weekends; 1hr 20min); Cognac (9 daily; 20min); Rochefort (6 daily; 30min).
**By bus** The bus station is on Galerie du Bois d'Amour, just west of the river behind Quai de l'Yser.
Destinations Rochefort (4 daily; 1hr min); St-Pierre

d'Oléron (5 daily; 1hr 50min–2hr 20min).
**Tourist office** Place Bassompierre by the Arc Germanicus (July–Aug 9am–7pm daily; Sept–June Mon–Sat 9.30am–12.30pm & 2–5.30pm; ☎05 46 74 23 82, ⓦsaintes-tourisme.fr). The office organizes boat trips on the Charente during the summer (from €5) and offers maps with self-guided walking tours marked out as well as regular guided tours to many of the sites described below.

### ACCOMMODATION

**Auberge de Jeunesse** 2 place Geoffroy-Martel ☎05 46 92 14 92, ⓔsaintes@fuaj.org. In a superb location behind the Abbaye aux Dames, the facilities here are modern, and breakfast is included. Reception open 8am–noon & 5–10pm. **€18.60**
**Camping Au Fil de l'Eau** ☎05 46 93 08 00, ⓦcamping -saintes-17.com. This campsite occupies expansive grounds by the river Charentes, and has a laundrette, *Pétanque* and table tennis, mini-golf, river fishing and a restaurant. Mid-April to mid-Oct. **€13.50**
**Le Logis de la Brumanderie** 57 rte de la Brumanderie ☎05 46 93 38 35, ⓦlabrumanderie.com. Surrounded by vineyards, this family-run B&B 3km from Saintes is clean, comfortable and quiet, with English-speaking hosts, a separate entry for guests, and easy access to golf, tennis and riding. **€51**
**Des Messageries** rue des Messageries ☎05 46 93 64 99, ⓦhotel-des-messageries.com. A large, pleasant chain hotel with garage parking on a quiet central courtyard. Most rooms are a/c and all have TV and minibar. Ask for a

"trendy" rather than a "traditional" room – "traditional" is a euphemism for chipped paint. Breakfast €9. **€44**
**La Porte Rouge** 15 rue des Jacobins ☎05 46 90 46 71, ⓦsites.google.com/site/moniquepotel/home. An atmospheric sixteenth-century house, converted by friendly Franco-New Yorkers into a book-lined, art-filled home with guest rooms. The views of the town are spectacular, the location central, and there's a small walled garden. Prices can rise up to €140. **€85**
**La Rotonde** 2 rue Monconseil ☎05 46 74 74 44, ⓦchambres-hotes-saintes.com. A princely B&B which could give most luxury hotels a run for their money, with its open fires, fresh flowers, antique sideboards and the Charentes flowing beneath the windows. **€100**
**Saveurs de l'Abbaye** 1 place St-Pallais ☎05 46 94 17 91, ⓦsaveurs-abbaye.com. A sleek but inexpensive hotel opposite the Abbaye aux Dames, with parquet floors and light rooms – ask for one on the top floor. Downstairs is a decent restaurant (closed Sun & Mon) with set *menus* from €15. **€70**

### EATING AND DRINKING

**La Cave Passe à Table** 27 rue St Michel ☎05 46 74 05 01, ⓦlacavepasseatable.com. Half vintner's, half restaurant, pocket-sized *La Cave* sells 20 wines by the glass (€3), and a well-cooked three-course daily *menu* (€14.50) served at tables in the shop front. Closed Mon (except the first Mon of each month). Tues–Sat 10am–7pm.
**Clos des Cours** 2 place du Théâtre ☎05 46 74 62 62, ⓦclosdescours.com. An upmarket central restaurant with fantastic French cooking heated with Asian spices and warm service. Three-course lunch *menus* €13, dinner at €34. Mon–Sat noon–2pm & 7.30–10pm.
**Pasta Verdura** 7 rue du Rempart ☎05 46 74 98 22.

Quick, healthy lunch-bar with plenty of organic salads, serving food all day. A good option for vegetarians. Daily 9am–6.30pm.
**Romana** 89 av Gambetta ☎05 46 74 18 11, ⓦla-romana.fr. A cosy and affordable Italian, serving simple but flavoursome home-cooked meals to local families. Pizzas €10–13. Mon–Sat noon–2pm & 7–10pm, Fri & Sat till 10.30pm.
**Sukhothai** 113 av Gambetta ☎05 46 91 88 08, ⓦsukhothai.fr. Delicately presented, piquant Thai cooking served in a long bare room. Mains €12–16. Tues–Sat noon–2pm & 7–10pm.

# Cognac

Anyone who does not already know what **COGNAC** is about will quickly nose its quintessential air as they stroll about the medieval lanes of the town's riverside quarter. For here is the greatest concentration of *chais* (warehouses), where the high-quality brandy is matured, its fumes blackening the walls with tiny fungi. Cognac *is* cognac, from the tractor driver and pruning-knife wielder to the manufacturer of corks, bottles and cartons. Untouched by recession (eighty percent of production is exported), it is likely to thrive as long as the world has sorrows to drown – a sunny, prosperous, self-satisfied little place.

Cognac has a number of medieval stone and half-timbered buildings in the narrow streets of the old town, of which rue Saulnier and rue de l'Isle-d'Or make atmospheric backdrops for a stroll, while picturesque **Grande-Rue** winds through the heart of the old quarter to the *chais*, down by the river. The attractive Hôtel de Ville is set in pleasant gardens just to the east.

## Around Cognac

The gentle landscape around Cognac is good for walking and cycling. One good walk is the towpath or *chemin de halage* that follows the south bank of the Charente from Cognac upstream to Pont de la Trâche, then on to the idyllic village of **BOURG-CHARENTE** (about 8km in all), with its castle and Romanesque church. Alternatively, follow the GR4 the other way to the hamlet of **RICHEMONT**, 5km northwest of Cognac, where you can swim in the pools of the tiny River Antenne, below an ancient church on a steep bluff in the woods.

### Jarnac

One marvellous excursion is upstream to **Jarnac**, from where you can take boat trips on the Charente from €7.50, arranged by the Jarnac tourist office (place du Château; April–Oct; ☎05 45 81 09 30, ⓦjarnac-tourisme.com). The town proudly boasts its connection with the late President Mitterrand, who was born and buried here. The **Musée François-Mitterrand** 10 quai de l'Orangerie (July & Aug daily 10am–12.30pm & 2.30–6.30pm; Jan–June, Sept-Oct Wed–Sun 2–6pm; €5; ☎05 45 81 38 88), houses a permanent exhibition on Mitterrand's public works.

---

### COGNAC IN COGNAC

No trip to Cognac is complete without investigating the drink behind the town. All the major houses open their doors, and bottles, to visitors, so you can pick the one that appeals to your interests: **Otard** (127 bd Denfert-Rochereau; ☎05 45 36 88 86, ⓦbaronotard.com; 1hr; adults €9, children €4;) is historical – the birthplace of François I in 1494, and a prison for British prisoners after the Seven Years War; vast **Remi Martin** (20 rue de la Société Vinicole; ☎05 45 35 76 66, ⓦremimartin.com; 1hr 30min; adults €16) ferries visitors round on a little train; **Camus** (ⓦcamus.fr) is still a family-run outfit; at **Hennessy** (ⓦhennessy.com) you can cross the river on a boat to visit the storehouses; **Meukow** (ⓦmeukowcognac.com) is run by a family of Franco-Russian entrepreneurs; and at **Martell** (ⓦcognac.martell.com) you can visit the founder's home, and a replica of a traditional cognac barge. You will find more historical information at **Écomusée du Cognac** (April–Sept daily 10am–12.30pm & 2.30–6.30pm; adults €5, children €2; ☎05 46 94 91 16) an 18km drive northwest of Cognac, which shows the evolution of the distillation process and includes tasting of cognacs and liqueurs. Follow the D731 to St-Jean-d'Angély for 13km as far as Burie, then turn right onto the D131, 4km from Migron.

**9**

## ARRIVAL AND INFORMATION

**By train** To walk to the central place François I from the *gare SNCF* on bd de Paris, go down rue Mousnier, right on rue Taransaud, past the PTT and up rue du 14-Juillet. The square is dominated by an equestrian statue of the king rising from a bed of begonias; in fine weather the cafés here teem with locals.

**Tourist office** 16 rue du 14-Juillet (May, June & Sept Mon–Sat 9.30am–5.30pm; July & Aug Mon–Sat 9am–7pm, Sun 10am–4pm; Oct–April Mon–Sat 10am–5pm; ☎05 45 82 10 71, ⌨tourism-cognac.com), where you can ask about visiting the various *chais*, as well as get information on river trips. They sell large-scale maps of walks around Cognac for €3.50.

**Internet** Je Console, 24 allée de la Corderie (€3.50/hr).

## ACCOMMODATION

**Camping de Cognac** bd de Châtenay ☎05 45 32 13 32, ⌨campingdecognac.com. Four-star campsite on the tree-lined banks of the river. April–Sept. **€17.20**

**Le Cheval Blanc** 6 place Bayard ☎05 45 82 09 55, ⌨hotel-chevalblanc.fr. Clean, no-frills motel-style accommodation in the centre of town. Probably the best-value central option. **€60**

**Gites de Brives** 23 rte des Romains ☎05 46 93 15 34, ⌨gitesdebrives.com. Family rental cottages (for 2, 4–6 or 6–8) set in large grounds, 13km from town. There's a big swimming pool, children's play area, *boules* court, volleyball, badminton, table tennis and gym. Rental €400–1000 per week. Breakfast included in per-night cottage rental price of **€60**

★ **Quai des Pontis** 16 rue Pontis ☎05 45 32 47 40, ⌨quaidespontis.com. If you fell asleep reading *Wind In The Willows* and dreamt up a hotel, it might look like *Quai des Pontis*: a few acres of grassy land on a riverbank, singing birds, a handful of gypsy caravans, and long-legged fishing huts (priciest but best). A golf cart delivers luggage to the "rooms", and breakfast (€6.50 per person) is left in a hamper at your door. There's also a disused factory, converted into traditional B&B accommodation near the road. Caravans **€69**, fishing huts **€79**, B&B **€63**

**L'Yeuse** 65 rue de Bellevue ☎05 45 36 82 60, ⌨yeuse.fr. An old-fashioned château hotel located on the outskirts of town, with the heavy florals and truculent furniture popular in the 1960s, a hilly garden and a comfortable bar. Guests have free use of the mini-spa (hammam, sauna, jacuzzi). **€112**

## EATING

Picnickers should visit the food market, from 8am–1pm on Place d'Armes (closed Mon).

**Bistro de Claude** 55 rue Grande ☎05 45 82 60 32, ⌨bistro-de-claude.com. A Cognac institution, with fine food, knowledgable staff, 25 types of cognac and a smart, cosy interior. Dress is smart-casual, and it's not the place for quick eating, so allow a couple of hours for dinner. Three-course *menu* €29. Mon–Fri noon–2pm & 7–10pm.

**Brûlerie Marignan** 16 rue d'Angouleme ☎05 45 82 12 92. Suffused with the dark, warm smell of chocolate, coffee and apricots, this admirable coffeehouse stocks 300 kinds of tea and recently won the Best Coffee Roaster in France award. Tues–Sun 9.30am–7pm.

**Le Chantilly** 146 av Victor Hugo ☎05 45 32 43 07, ⌨le-chantilly-cognac.fr. King of bistros; friendly, simple, highly edible food, with an outdoor terrace and a first-rate chef. Three courses €12, two courses €9. Sept–July Mon–Fri noon–1pm.

**Le St Jacques** 8 rue Minotiers ☎05 45 82 25 78. Jolly worker's bistro with tables so close you can almost taste your neighbour's soup. Piquant, robust cooking and friendly service. Daily *menus* from €12. Tues–Sun dinner Fri & Sat.

# Angoulême and around

Perched on a plateau above a meander in the river Charente, hilly **ANGOULÊME** is the capital of its department. The town's splendid architectural muddle attests to a history of conquest and re-conquest stretching back to the sixth century, when the Franks took it from the Visigoths. An industrial powerhouse, Angoulême once manufactured paper for the whole of France, and although only a few mills struggled into the twenty-first century, its survival is still connected to paper through comic strips, illustration and animation. Every January 20,000 enthusiasts descend on Angoulême for the International Comics Festival, there is a celebrated animation museum (the **Cité Internationale de la Bande Dessinée** – see p.502) and murals decorate shop- and house-fronts through the city.

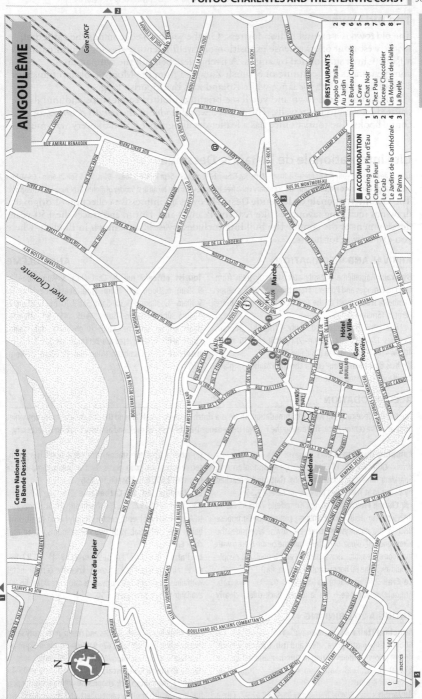

**ANGOULÊME**

Gare SNCF

Centre National de la Bande Dessinée

Musée du Papier

River Charente

Marché

Hôtel de Ville

Gare Routière

Cathédrale

N

0    100    metres

**RESTAURANTS**
| Angolo d'Italia | 2 |
| Au Jardin | 4 |
| Le Bruleau Charentais | 6 |
| La Cave | 5 |
| Le Chat Noir | 7 |
| Chez Paul | 3 |
| Duceau Chocolatier | 9 |
| Les Moulins des Halles | 8 |
| La Ruelle | 1 |

**ACCOMMODATION**
| Camping du Plan d'Eau | 1 |
| Champ Fleuri | 5 |
| Le Crab | 2 |
| Les Jardins de la Cathédrale | 4 |
| La Palma | 3 |

**9**

# The old town

The **old town** is a natural hilltop fortress. On the southern edge stands the **cathedral**, whose west front offers a dense exposition on twelfth-century theology, culminating in a Risen Christ surrounded by angels. A lively frieze beneath the tympanum commemorates the recapture of Spanish Zaragoza from the Moors; a bishop transfixes a Moorish giant with his lance while Roland kills the Moorish king.

Wandering the old town and you'll see brightly coloured **comic strips** and murals painted on various town walls. The city is a world leader of the *bandes dessinées*, or comic books. The tourist office has a leaflet detailing the location of every wall mural.

## Cité Internationale de la Bande Dessinée

121 rue de Bordeaux • July & Aug Tues–Fri 10am–7pm, Sat & Sun 2–7pm, June–Sept Tues–Fri 10am–6pm, Sat & Sun 2–6pm • €6.50 for the museum, library and reading room; free for library only; free for under 18s; free for all first Sunday of month Oct–June • ⓦ citebd.org

The **Cité Internationale de la Bande Dessinée** owns an impressive collection of original drawings including favourites like Astérix, Peanuts and Tintin, and traces the 150-year development of the comic. The building includes a vast library, much in English, where you can browse for hours.

### ARRIVAL AND INFORMATION

### ANGOULÊME

**By train** Angoulême is easily accessible by train from Cognac, Limoges and Poitiers. From the *gare SNCF*, avenue Gambetta leads uphill to the town centre through place Pérot, a 15min walk.

Destinations Bordeaux (20 daily; 1hr–1hr 30min); Limoges (7 daily; 1hr 30min–2hr); Poitiers (16 daily; 40min–1hr 10min); Royan (15 daily; 2hr).

**By bus** Buses leave from either the train station or place Bouillaud, at the top of the hill.

**Tourist office** 7 rue du Chat (July & Aug Mon–Sat 9.30am–6.30pm, Sun 10am–1pm; Sept–June Mon–Fri 9.30am–12.30pm & 1.30–6pm, Sat 9.30am–12.30pm & 1.30–5.30pm, closed Sun; ☎05 45 95 16 84, ⓦ angouleme-tourisme.co.uk), is on place des Halles, opposite the large covered market (mornings).

**Internet** 72 av Gambetta (Mon–Sat 10.30am–6.30pm, €2/hr).

### ACCOMMODATION

The tourist office can help with accommodation. There is a clutch of cheap hotels around the station and more upmarket options in the centre. Prices rise during the Festival de la Bande Dessinée (see above), and advance booking is necessary.

**Camping du Plan d'Eau** Impasse des Rouyères, St Yrieix ☎06 88 69 11 74, ⓦ camping-angouleme.fr. Sparkling three-star site with cabins, that can be reached by #3 bus to St Yrieix from the *gare routière*. €9.55

★ **Champ Fleuri** Chemin de l'Hirondelle ☎05 45 68 35 84, ⓦ champ-fleuri.com. Rambling, picturesque farmhouse B&B in the countryside above the town, alongside the Hirondelle golf course, only 3min from the centre by car, with five rooms, beautiful views, gardens and a pool. Tall people should avoid the BD Room. English spoken. €80

**Le Crab** 27 rue Kléber ☎05 45 93 02 93, ⓔ lecrab. angouleme@orange.fr. In a quiet backstreet, clearly

signposted from the station, this *Logis* hotel has clean, secure rooms at good prices, and a cheap three-course lunch (€12.50). Breakfast €6.50. €56

**Le Jardins de la Cathédrale** 35 rue Waldeck Rousseau ☎05 45 22 59 87, ⓦ lesjardinsdelacathedrale. fr. A spacious nineteenth-century family home slumbering below the cathedral, with two guest rooms; clean and cosy. €60

**La Palma** 4 rampe d'Aguesseau ☎05 45 95 22 89, ⓦ restaurant-hotel-palma.com. Friendly central hotel with nine a/c rooms and a private terrace. Breakfast €6.80, available in bed on request. €60

### EATING AND DRINKING

**Angolo d'Italia** 43 rue Genève ☎05 45 90 51 74. Good-quality pasta, pizza, meat and fish, friendly service, decent prices, outdoor seating in summer, and a 3-course €12.50 lunch. Tues–Sat noon–2pm & 7–10pm (till 11pm Sat & Sun).

**Au Jardin** 5 rue Ludovic Trarieux ☎05 45 90 07 97. Take a

quick break from French pastries and cream at this cosy salad and smoothie bar. DIY salad €7–9. Mon–Fri noon–2pm all year round, plus June–Aug Mon & Thurs 7–9pm.

★ **Le Bruleau Charentais** 10 Rue Beaulieu ☎05 45 69 72 17. An atmospheric chophouse with a roaring open fire from which molten camembert and juicy steaks are pulled by the pink-nosed chef. Rib-eye steak, chips and salad are ridiculously cheap at €9. Book in advance on Friday or Saturday night. Mon–Sat 7.45pm–midnight.

**La Cave** 13 rue Ludovic Trarieux ☏06 08 86 83 93, ⓦ lacaveangouleme.com. Most marvellous of things – a bar in love with wine. There is a vast array of Tariquet, Mainart, Michel Juillot, cognac and champagne to drink in, or take home. Tues–Sat 10.30–12.30 & 3–8pm.

**Le Chat Noir** 24 rue de Genève ☏05 45 95 26 27. Popular local meeting spot opposite the market that has inexpensive salads and omelettes at lunchtime, and a relaxed atmosphere. Mon & Tues 10am–11pm, Wed 3–8pm, Thurs & Fri 9am–1am, Sat 1–7pm & 11pm–1am, Sun 3–5pm & 9pm–1am.

**Chez Paul** 8 place Francis-Louvel ☏05 45 90 04 61, ⓦ restaurant-16.com. A high-class restaurant serving bistro-style dishes (*menus* from €20), with a large terrace

and garden, plus bar, open till midnight. Daily noon–2.30pm & 7–11.30pm, winter closed Sun.

**Duceau Chocolatier** Place de l'Hôtel-de-Ville ☏05 45 90 69 72. A truly delightful chocolate shop; founded in 1876, with more than 40 chocolates made in-house, an interior as delectable as the praline, and a celebrated pure chocolate ganache. Mon 2.30–7pm, Tues–Fri 9am–7pm, Sat 9am–1pm & 2–7pm.

**Les Moulins des Halles** 3 place des Halles ☏05 45 93 10 63. The best bread in Angoulême, with fresh sandwiches for picnicking. Tues–Sat 6.30am–8pm, Sun 5am–1.30pm.

★ **La Ruelle** 6 rue Trois Notre-Dame ☏05 45 95 15 19, ⓦ restaurant-laruelle.com. Delicate French favourites are souped up with Asian flavour like miso and lemon grass at this modern, urban restaurant. For best value go at lunchtime for the three-course €20 *menu*. Dinner *menus* from €38. Tues–Sat noon–2pm & 7.30–9.30pm.

## Around Angoulême

**LA ROCHEFOUCAULD**, 22km east of Angoulême, is home to a Renaissance **château** (April to Jan 2 except Tues 10am–7pm; adult €10, child €5) on the banks of the River Tardoire, which still belongs to the family that gave the town its name a thousand years ago. It stages a massive son et lumière with a brigade-sized cast in August.

Further east, the country becomes hillier and more wooded. One place to visit is the beautiful, if touristy, little town of **CONFOLENS**, about 40km northeast of La Rochefoucauld. Its ancient houses are stacked up a hillside above a broad brown sweep of the river Vienne, here crossed by a long narrow medieval bridge. Having come this far, it's worth continuing an extra 6km to the romantic little village of **St-Germain-de-Confolens** that's huddled by the riverside beneath the stark towers of a ruined castle.

# Bordeaux and around

The city of **BORDEAUX** cuts a fine figure, towering above the west bank of the River Garonne, a blend of neoclassical grandeur and modern innovation. The Romans set up a lively trading centre here, and the city still functions as the transport hub for Aquitaine. First-rate museums, excellent shopping, fine restaurants and lively nightlife make Bordeaux an absorbing place to spend a long weekend.

The hills of **Entre-Deux-Mers** and the medieval town of **St-Émilion** are well worth visiting in their own right. The vast pine forests of **Les Landes**, stretching towards the Dune de Pyla (the largest sand dune in Europe) and the glistening, wild Atlantic beaches of the **Côte d'Argent**, are magical, but you'll need your own transport to holiday there.

## Vieux Bordeaux

At the heart of the old town centre is **place de la Bourse**. Behind and to the west is the **Grand Théâtre** (☏05 56 00 85 95, ⓦ opera-bordeaux.com) on place de la Comédie. Built by the architect Victor Louis in 1780, on the site of a Roman temple, the lofty exterior is adorned with pillars, Muses and Graces. Inside are flamboyant trompe l'oeil paintings; to get in, attend an opera or ballet (seats in the gods from as little as €8), or ask at the tourist office (see p.508) about a guided tour (€6).

Smart streets radiate out from here: the city's main shopping streets, **rue Ste-Catherine** and the **cours de l'Intendance** to the south and west, and the sandy, tree-lined **allées de**

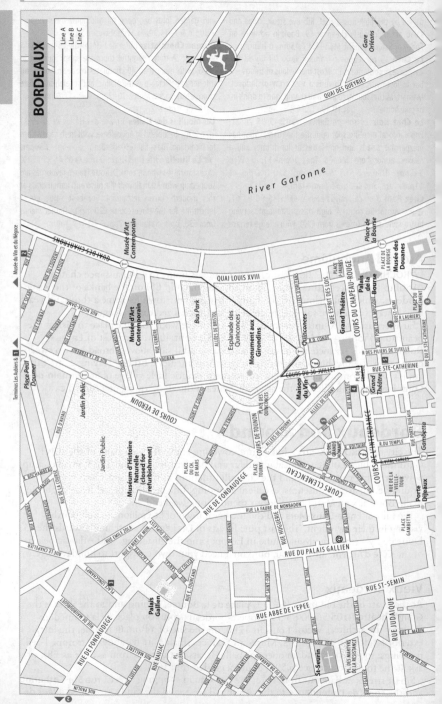

BORDEAUX

Line A
Line B
Line C

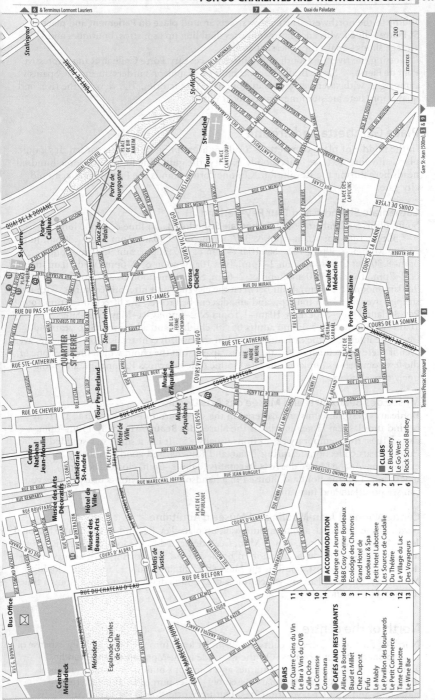

● **BARS**
| | |
|---|---|
| Aux Quatre Coins du Vin | 11 |
| Le Bar à Vins du CIVB | 4 |
| Calle Ocho | 6 |
| La Comtesse | 10 |
| Connemara | 14 |

● **CAFÉS AND RESTAURANTS**
| | |
|---|---|
| Ailleurs à Bordeaux | 8 |
| Baud et Millet | 3 |
| Chez Dupont | 1 |
| Fufu | 7 |
| Le Mably | 5 |
| Le Pavillon des Boulevards | 2 |
| Le Petit Commerce | 9 |
| Tante Charlotte | 12 |
| Le Wine Bar | 13 |

■ **ACCOMMODATION**
| | |
|---|---|
| Auberge de Jeunesse | 9 |
| B&B Cosy Corner Bordeaux | 8 |
| Ecolodge des Chartrons | 2 |
| Grand Hotel de | 4 |
| Bordeaux & Spa | |
| Petit Hotel Labottiere | 3 |
| Les Sources de Caudalie | 7 |
| Du Théâtre | 5 |
| Le Village du Lac | 1 |
| Des Voyageurs | 6 |

■ **CLUBS**
| | |
|---|---|
| Le Blueberry | 2 |
| Le Go West | 1 |
| Rock School Barbey | 3 |

**9**

**Tourny** to the northwest. The narrow streets around **place du Parlement** and **place St-Pierre** – lined with ancient townhouses doubling up as bistros, boutiques and vintage shops – make for a pleasant stroll.

Crossing the river just south of the fifteenth-century Porte Cailhau is the impressive **Pont de Pierre** – "Stone Bridge". It was built on Napoleon's orders during the Spanish campaigns, with seventeen arches in honour of his victories. The views of the river and quays from here are stunning, especially at dusk.

## Place Gambetta and around

In the middle of **place Gambetta** is a valiant attempt at an English garden. It's a quiet place, showing no trace of its bloody history; the guillotine lopped off three hundred heads here during the Revolution. On one corner stands the **Porte Dijeaux**, an old city gate.

### Cathédrale St-André and Tour Pey-Berland

South of place Gambetta is the **Cathédrale St-André** (daily: June & Sept Mon 3–7.30pm, Tues–Sat 10am–1pm & 3–7.30pm, Sun 9.30am–1pm & 3–7.30pm; July & Aug Mon 3–7.30pm, Tues–Sat 10am–1pm & 3–7.30pm, Sun 9.30am–1pm & 3pm–8.30pm; Oct–May Mon 2–7pm, Tues 10am–noon & 2–6pm, Wed 10am–noon & 2–7pm, Thurs–Fri 10am–noon & 2–6pm, Sat 10am–noon & 2–7pm, Sun 9.30am–noon & 2–6pm), built between the eleventh and fifteenth centuries, with twin steeples over the north transept, and an adjacent bell tower, the fifteenth-century **Tour Pey-Berland** (June–Sept daily 10am–1.15pm & 2–6pm; Oct–May Tues–Sun 10am–12.30pm & 2–5.30pm; adults €5.50, children and adults up to 26 years old free). The interior of the cathedral, begun in the twelfth century, is vast and impressive, even if there's not much of artistic interest apart from the choir, which provides one of the few complete examples of the late Gothic style known as Rayonnant, and some finely carved doors.

### Musée des Beaux-Arts and Musée des Arts Décoratifs

Bordeaux's best museums are scattered in the streets around the cathedral. Directly behind the classical Hôtel de Ville is the **Musée des Beaux-Arts** (daily 11am–6pm, closed Tues; free, temporary exhibitions usually €5). It has a small star-studded European art collection, featuring Titian and Rubens, and good temporary exhibitions. At the **Musée des Arts Décoratifs** (daily 2–6pm, closed Tues; free), two blocks north on rue Bouffard, housed in a handsome eighteenth-century house, you can see porcelain and furniture.

### Centre National Jean-Moulin and Musée d'Aquitaine

North of the cathedral, a four-minute walk up place Pey Berland, is the **Centre National Jean-Moulin** (daily 2–6pm, closed Mon; free), dedicated to the local Resistance, featuring a history of the occupation of Bordeaux and a harrowing permanent exhibit depicting the Holocaust. South is the **Musée d'Aquitaine** (daily 11am–6pm, closed Mon; free), on cours Pasteur, which traces the region's development since Roman times through objects and artworks.

## North of the centre

North of the Grand Théâtre, cours du 30-Juillet leads into the bare, gravelly expanse of the **esplanade des Quinconces**. On the west side is the **Monument aux Girondins**, a glorious *fin-de-siècle* ensemble of statues and fountains built in honour of the local deputies to the 1789 Revolutionary Assembly – later purged by Robespierre as moderates and counter-revolutionaries. During World War II the occupying Nazis made plans to to lower French morale by melting the monument down. Fortunately the local Resistance got there first and, under cover of darkness, dismantled the monument piece by piece, hiding it in a barn in the Médoc until after the war.

# Jardin Public and around

To the northwest of the city centre is the beautiful formal park, the **Jardin Public**, containing the city's botanical gardens as well as a small **natural history museum** (currently closed for refurbishment). Behind, to the west and north, lies a quiet, provincial quarter of two-storey stone houses including rue du Dr-Albert-Barraud, where you can see the **Palais Gallien**, a third-century arena and all that remains of Burdigala, Aquitaine's Roman capital. Nearby, on place Delerme, is the unusual round **market hall**.

## Musée d'Art Contemporain

Tues & Thurs–Sun 11am–6pm, Wed 11am–8pm, closed Mon • €5

To the east of the Jardin Public, close to the river, is the **Musée d'Art Contemporain** on rue Ferrère, occupying a converted nineteenth-century warehouse. The vast, arcaded hall is magnificent in its own right, and provides an ideal setting for the post-1960 sculpture and installations by artists like Richard Long and Sol LeWitt. The main space is used for temporary exhibitions. There's a superb collection of art books in the library and a café-restaurant on the roof (lunch only).

## Chartrons

Following the curve of the river north from the Musée d'Art Contemporain, you reach the down-at-heel but historic **Chartrons**, once the wine district. It's becoming increasingly cool, sprouting artists' studios, vintage shops and restaurants monthly. Every Sunday the quayside plays host to a bustling farmers' market. The **Musée du Vin et du Négoce** (Tues–Sat 10am–6pm, Sun 2–6pm, closed Mon; adults €7, children €3.50), on rue Borie, depicts the history of the wine trade, with an inevitable focus on Bordeaux.

## ARRIVAL AND DEPARTURE BORDEAUX

**By plane** Bordeaux-Mérignac airport is 12km west of the city and connected by shuttle buses (every 45min; €7) to the city.

**By train** Arriving by train, you'll find yourself at Gare St-Jean, 3km south of the city centre; bus #16 and tramline C run into town.

Destinations Angoulême (15 daily; 1hr–1hr 30min); Arcachon (20–30 daily; 50–55min); Bayonne (3–10 daily; 1hr 40min–2hr 10min); Bergerac (6–20 daily; 1hr 15–1hr 30min); Biarritz (6–12 daily; 2hr–2hr 45min); Brive (2–8 daily; 2hr 15min); Dax (15 daily; 1hr 10min–1hr 40min); Hendaye (3–5 daily; 2hr 30min); Irun (3 daily; 2hr 30min); La Rochelle (4–6 daily; 2hr–2hr 20min); Lourdes (3–10 daily; 2hr 20min–3hr); Marseille (5 daily; 4hr); Mont de Marsan (7 daily; 1hr 30min); Nice (3–8 daily; 9–10hr); Paris-Montparnasse (14–18 daily; 4hr); Périgueux (1–9 daily; 1hr–1hr 25min); Pointe de Grave (6–12 daily to

Lesparre; 1hr 45min; then bus 713 to Pointe de Grave 55min); Poitiers (5–10 daily; 2hr–2hr 30min); Saintes (5–10 daily; 1hr 30min); Sarlat (6 daily but not every day; 2hr 30min–3hr); St-Émilion (3–7 daily; 40 min); St-Jean-de-Luz (3–10 daily; 2hr–2hr 40min); Toulouse (10–17 daily; 2hr–2hr 40min).

**By bus** There's no central bus station, but bus stops congregate on the south side of the esplanade des Quinconces, on allées de Munich (where you'll also find the information centre – ☎ 05 56 43 68 43, ⦿ infotbc.com). Exceptions are the bus to Blaye, which leaves from "Buttinière" (take tram line A) and buses to Margaux and Pauillac, which leave from "place Ravezies" (tram line C). Destinations Blaye (4–10 daily; 1hr 45min); Cap Ferret (4–10 daily; 1hr 30min); Lacanau (5 daily; 1hr 25min); La Sauve-Majeure (1–4 daily; 50min); Margaux (4–10 daily; 45min–1hr); Pauillac (2–8 daily; 45min–1hr 10min).

## GETTING AROUND

**By tram** Tram services operate on the three lines regularly between 4.30am and midnight, and extend several kilometers into Bordeaux's suburbs. You can either purchase single tickets (€1.40) or packs of ten (€11.30)

from machines at tram stops or newsagents (tabacs). You can buy an unlimited-use pass, available for between one and seven days.

**Parking** There are numerous underground car parks in the

**9**

centre, though it's cheaper to use the ones next to the tram stations on the east bank of the Garonne: buy a round-trip park-and-ride ticket (€2.60) and hop on a tram to the centre.

## INFORMATION

**Tourist office** Bordeaux's main tourist office, near the Grand Théâtre on 12 cours du 30-Juillet (May–Oct Mon–Sat 9am–7pm, Sun 9.30am–6.30pm; Nov–April Mon–Sat 9am–6.30pm, Sun 9.45am–4.30pm; ☎05 56 00 66 00, Ⓦbordeaux-tourisme.com), will book your accommodation free of charge, has useful information on the city and surrounding vineyards, and can arrange city and vineyard tours (see box, p.511).

## ACCOMMODATION

It's better to lodge in the centre than venture out to rue Charles-Domercq and cours de la Marne, rife with grimy one- and two-star hotels. Rooms aren't hard to come by except during the week of the Vinexpo trade fair (in odd-numbered years) and Fête du Vin (in even-numbered years) in June, when Bordeaux is packed to the gunnels.

**Auberge de Jeunesse** 22 cours Barbey ☎05 56 91 59 51, Ⓦauberge-jeunesse-bordeaux.com. A slightly expensive private hostel with a warm, relaxed vibe. Located just off cours de la Marne, it's a 10min walk from *gare St-Jean*. Kitchen and laundry facilities are available. Breakfast included. **€22**

**B&B Cosy Corner Bordeaux** 241 cours de la Somme ☎05 56 31 96 85, Ⓦchambre-hotes-bordeaux.com. A quirky B&B with welcoming, helpful hosts (English spoken) about 15min walk from the centre, close to the bus and tram stations, with a very good breakfast (included). Rates drop to €65 for longer stays. **€85**

★ **Ecolodge des Chartrons** 23 rue Raze, Chartrons ☎05 56 81 49 13, Ⓦecolodgedeschartrons.com. On a quiet, shabby road in Chartrons, a 10min walk from the centre, *Ecolodge* is a beautifully restored eco-friendly B&B, with a glass-roofed courtyard, where splendid breakfasts are served. There are five rooms, with books, slate bathrooms, antique paintings, private parking, and a discreet but helpful hostess. Breakfast included. **€98**

**Grand Hotel de Bordeaux & Spa** ☎05 57 30 44 44, Ⓦghbordeaux.com. A great city hotel, right in the centre, in a grand old style, with brass-buttoned porters, a concierges service, three bars, a Michelin-starred restaurant, private parking (€35 per day), as well as an excellent buffet breakfast, spa, pool and jacuzzi on the roof and rooms equipped with everything imaginable. **€450**

**Petit Hotel Labottiere** 14 rue Francis Martin ☎06 75 67 86 21. Two small and tidy en-suite rooms in a modern annex of this beautiful eighteenth-century house, three minutes' walk from the Jardin Public. The main building, inhabited by the family who runs the B&B, is a living

mausoleum to eighteenth-century life, and the chatty proprietor Daniel, will conduct you around the house ('Le Monument') for an hour or two in French or English. **€190**

**Les Sources de Caudalie** Chateau Smith Haut Lafitte, Martillac ☎05 57 83 82 82, Ⓦsources-caudalie.com. Fifteen minutes' drive from Bordeaux, *Les Sources* is a four-star spar hotel, part of the Château Smith Haut Lafitte empire, that specializes in grape-based spa treatments. The setting is luxuriously faux-rustic, there's a Michelin-starred restaurant, tranquil grounds, and vineyards on every side, giving the air a vinous sweetness. Two-days half-board per person. **€262**

**Du Théâtre** 10 rue Maison-Daurade ☎05 56 79 05 26, Ⓦhotel-du-theatre.com. In the pedestrianized heart of town, off the main shopping street cours de l'Intendance, this place isn't stylish but it's pretty comfortable, with kitsch-themed rooms, 24-hr English-speaking reception, small clean bathrooms and good prices for the location. Breakfast €7.50. **€72**

**Le Village du Lac** Bd Jacques Chaban Delmas ☎05 57 87 70 60, Ⓦcamping-bordeauxlac.com. A campsite located 8km north of the centre near a lake and the tramline, with rental cottages (kitchenette, TV, a/c, bathroom, terrace) camping, camper vans, swimming pool, shops, laundrette, secure parking. **€18**

★ **Des Voyageurs** 3bis av Thiers ☎05 56 86 18 00, Ⓦhoteldesvoyageurs.net. This small, two star hotel is a short, picturesque walk from the centre across the Pont de Pierre, and represents the best value for money in Bordeaux. It has helpful staff and bright, soundproof en-suite rooms. Breakfast €6. **€61**

## EATING AND DRINKING

Bordeaux is packed with good restaurants to suit any budget, and because it's close to the coast there's excellent seafood. The streets around rue du Parlement St Pierre and rue St Remi are full of eateries, and upmarket options crowd around place de Parlement and towards Chartrons. For picnic supplies, head to the market on place des Grands-Hommes. At rue de Montesquieu (just off place des Grands-Hommes), Jean d'Alos runs the city's best fromagerie. Bordeaux's sweet speciality is the *canelés* – made from custard-like batter flavoured with rum and vanilla. The best place to buy them is Baillardran, on 55 cours de l'Intendance. The student population ensures a collection of young, lively bars, especially around place de la Victoire, and the city has a strong gay scene. Live music is ten a penny, and the weekend generally begins on Thursday.

## CAFÉS AND RESTAURANTS

**Ailleurs à Bordeaux** 3 place du Parlement Quartier St-Pierre ☎ 05 56 52 92 86, ⓦ ailleurs.bordeaux.free.fr. A gilded-teacup kind of teahouse, close to the shops, with carefully mismatched upholstery and 48 types of tea, as well as coffee, cake, ice cream and smoothies. Daily 10am–7pm.

**Baud et Millet** 19 rue Huguerie ☎ 05 56 79 05 77, ⓦ baudetmillet.fr. Customers pick a bottle from the shelves to accompany cheese and cold meat for €12.50 (or *raclette*), at this bar and vintners. Portions are generous – one goes a long way. Mon–Sat 10am–11pm.

**Chez Dupont** 45 rue de Notre-Dame ☎ 05 56 81 49 59. A bustling, old-fashioned restaurant in Chartrons, with wooden floors, vintage posters and waistcoated waiters. Prices are reasonable, with a *plat du jour*, fresh from the market, for €8.50. Mon–Sat noon–2pm & 7.30–11pm, Tues noon–2pm.

★ **Fufu** 37 rue St. Remi ☎ 05 56 52 10 29. A well-loved Japanese noodle bar in the heart of town; eat at the long bar, watching the chefs fry your noodles, or take away a hot box of *Ramen* and perch on a bench next to the Garonne, a few minutes' walk away. Mains €5–10. Tues–Sat noon–3pm & 7–11pm.

**Le Mably** 12 rue Mably ☎ 05 56 44 30 10, ⓦ le-mably .com. An elegant, popular restaurant with lots of rabbit, duck and atmosphere. The food is good and traditional, as is the decor. Daily *menus* from €22. Closed Sun & three weeks in Aug.

**Le Pavillon des Boulevards** 120 rue Croix-de-Seguey ☎ 05 56 81 51 02. This Michelin-starred restaurant is ideal for a special occasion. The cooking, by a self-taught chef, is creative and delightful, there's an elegant dining room and a quiet garden, and the service is exemplary. Daily *menu* €40; à la carte €80–100. Mon 7–10pm, Tues–Fri noon–2pm & 7–10pm, Sat 7–10pm.

**Le Petit Commerce** 22 rue Parlement St Pierre ☎ 05 56 79 76 58, ⓦ le-petit-commerce.com. A bustling, sociable seafood restaurant, open late, where everything's fresh – staff continuously re-stock from the fishmongers' opposite – popular with locals, with great tapas (€7 per dish). It gets busy so come early or expect a wait. Daily 10am–2am.

**Tante Charlotte** 7 rue des Bahutiers ☎ 09 82 60 13 12. This new central restaurant, small and stylish, is quickly gaining a reputation for good food, an impressive wine list and quality, affordable daily *menus*; the €35 set *menu* is three courses with an aperitif, half a bottle of wine and coffee. Tues–Sat 5pm–2am.

★ **Le Wine Bar** 19 rue des Bahutiers ☎ 05 56 48 56 99, ⓦ degustation-groupe33.com. A genial, thoroughly charming bar-restaurant near the river, run by two sisters and their husbands, with 60 types of wine (from 26 countries) sold by the glass and simple, delicious Italian snacks (cheese or ham and bread, salads, bruschetta, soup in winter). Their tiramisu (served Fri & Sat) is famous – customers pre-order. Wine served only when bought with food. Tues–Sat noon–2pm & 7pm–midnight.

## BARS, CLUBS AND VENUES

★ **Aux Quatre Coins du Vin** 8 rue de la Devise ☎ 05 57 34 37 29, ⓦ aux4coinsduvin.com. Where good grapes go when they die. There are 32 wines available, mostly red and mostly French, but a few whites and foreign wines, and you can taste by the glass, half-glass or quarter-glass. Pleasing tasting plates accompany the wine, big enough for two or three to share. Mon–Sat 6pm–2am.

**Le Bar a Vins du CIVB** 1 cours du 30-Juillet ☎ 05 56 00 43 47, ⓦ baravin.bordeaux.com/. On the ground floor of the Maison du Vin de Bordeaux, HQ of the Conseil Interprofessionnel des Vins de Bordeaux (Bordeaux Wine Council), this place offers two parts edification to one part intoxication. A full range of Bordeaux wines (reds, dry and sweet whites, rosés, clarets and sparkling whites) are available, with tips and advice to hand. Daily 11am–10pm.

**Le Blueberry** 61 rue Sauvageau ☎ 05 56 94 16 87. Jazz, blues, old-fashioned rock and gypsy jazz in this music-lovers' bar that has good cocktails. Mon–Sat 7pm–2am.

**Calle Ocho** 24 rue des Piliers-de-Tutelle ☎ 05 56 48 08 68, ⓦ calle-ocho.eu. Bordeaux's best-known salsa bar has an unrivalled party atmosphere and is packed out most nights till 2am. There's real Cuban rum and mojitos. Mon–Sat 5pm–2am.

**La Comtesse** 25 rue du Parlement ☎ 05 56 51 03 07. A fashionably old-fashioned music bar decorated with soft lighting, a jukebox and elegant people. Tues–Sat 9am–2am.

**Connemara** 18 cours d'Albret, ⓦ connemara-pub.com. As Irish a pub as ever you'll find. The Guinness is cold and the football always pulls a good crowd. Happy hour is 6–8pm daily, and they host weekly free live music and open-mic nights. Daily till late.

**Le Go West** 3 rue Duffour Deubergier ⓦ legowest.com. Modern gay club mostly for the boys, but welcomes lesbians and gay-friendly straights. Daily 6pm–2am.

**Rock School Barbey** 18 cours Barbey ⓦ rockschool -barbey.com. Bordeaux's premier venue for rock, which hosts well-known international bands. Daily 10pm–1am & 2–6am.

## DIRECTORY

**Bike rental** Liberty Cycles (☎ 05 56 92 77 18; closed Sat afternoon & Sun) at 104 cours d'Yser rents out bikes from €9 per day. Another option is Station Vélo Services, just down the road at 48 cours d'Yser. Both shops do repairs.

**Books and newspapers** Presse Gambetta, on place Gambetta, sells all the main English-language papers in addition to some regional guides and maps, while Bordeaux's largest bookstore, Mollat, 15 rue Vital Carles, has a wide selection. They also stock a few English-language titles, though there's more choice at helpful Bradley's Bookshop, 8 cours d'Albret.

**Car rental** Numerous rental firms are located in and around the train station, including Europcar ☎ 05 56 33 87 40; Hertz ☎ 05 57 59 05 95; and National/Citer ☎ 05 56 92 19 62. They all have outlets at the airport as well.

**Cinema** Original-language (*version originale* or *v.o.*) films at the wonderful art-house cinema Utopia, 5 place Camille-Jullian (☎ 05 56 52 00 03, ⓦ cinemas-utopia.org), in a converted church. For Hollywood blockbusters there's the vast, seventeen-screen Megarama (☎ 08 92 69 33 17,

ⓦ megarama.fr) across the Pont de Pierre in the old Gare d'Orléans. The free weekly *Bordeaux Plus* has details of other cinemas and full programmes.

**Consulate** UK, 353 bd du Président-Wilson ☎ 05 57 22 21 10; USA, 10 place de la Bourse ☎ 05 56 48 63 80.

**Health** Centre Hospitalier Pellegrin-Tripode, place Amélie-Raba-Léon (☎ 05 56 79 56 79), to the west of central Bordeaux.

**Internet** Iphone, 24 rue du Palais Gallien (daily 10am–midnight), or La Cyb, 23 cours Pasteur (daily), though the latter has the disadvantage of crowds of enthusiastic gamers.

**Police** Commissariat Central, 23 rue François-de-Sourdis (☎ 05 57 85 77 77 or ☎ 17 in emergencies).

# The Bordeaux wine region

Touring the local **vineyards** and sampling a few home-grown wines is one of the great pleasures of Bordeaux. The wine regions lie in a great semicircle around the city, starting with the **Médoc** in the north, then skirting east through **St-Émilion**, before finishing south of the city among the vineyards of the **Sauternes**. In between, the less prestigious districts are also worth investigating, especially **Blaye**, to the north of Bordeaux, and **Entre-Deux-Mers**, to the east.

You will quickly see that there's more to the region than wine. Many of the Médoc's eighteenth-century châteaux are architectural treasures, while a vast fortress dominates the town of Blaye, and there's an older, ruined castle at Villandraut on the edge of the Sauternes. St-Émilion, loved by tourists, is the prettiest of the wine towns, and has the unexpected bonus of a cavernous underground church. For scenic views you can't beat the green, gentle hills of Entre-Deux-Mers and its ruined abbey, **La Sauve-Majeur**.

## GETTING AROUND                                                    BORDEAUX WINE REGION

**By train** There are train lines from Bordeaux running north through the Médoc to Margaux and Pauillac, and south through the Garonne valley to St-Macaire and La Réole. St-Émilion lies on the Bordeaux–Sarlat line, but the station is a couple of kilometres from the town.

**By bus** There's a comprehensive regional bus network

– pick up timetables at the tourist office. Several different companies operate buses; the largest is Citram Aquitaine (ⓦ citram.fr).

**By bike** Cycling is an appealing mode of transport, and many of the towns are connected by well-marked tarmac cycle-paths.

## The Médoc

The landscape of **the Médoc**, a patch of land between the Atlantic coast forests and the Gironde, is monotonous: gravel plains, the brown water of the estuary, and gravelly soil. The D2 wine road, heading off the N15 from Bordeaux, passes through Margaux, St-Julien, Pauillac and St-Estèphe, where many of the famous châteaux reside.

### Château Margaux

By appointment only Mon–Fri; closed Aug and during harvest • ☎ 05 57 88 83 83, ⓦ chateau-margaux.com • Free

One of the loveliest châteaux in the Médoc, **Margaux** is an eighteenth-century villa set in extensive, sculpture-dotted gardens close to the west bank of the Gironde, 20km north of Bordeaux. Its wine, a classified Premier Grand Cru, already world-famous in the 1940s and 50s, went through a rough patch in the two succeeding decades but improved in the 1980s, after the estate was bought by a Greek family. The château does

## THE WINES OF BORDEAUX

The Bordeaux wine region circles the city, enjoying near-perfect climatic conditions and soils ranging from limestone to sand and pebbles. It's the largest quality wine district in the world, producing around 500 million bottles a year – over half of France's quality wine output and ten percent, by value, of the world's wine trade.

The Gironde estuary, fed by the Garonne and the Dordogne rivers, determines the lie of the land. The **Médoc** lies northwest of Bordeaux, between the Atlantic coast and the River Gironde. Its vines are deeply rooted in poor, gravelly soil, producing good, full-bodied red wines; the region's **eight appellations** are Médoc, Haut Médoc, St-Estèphe, Pauillac, St-Julien, Moulis en Médoc, Listrac-Médoc and Margaux. Southwest of Bordeaux are the vast vineyards of **Graves**, producing the best of the region's dry white wines, along with punchy reds, from some of the most prestigious communes in France, like Pessac, Talence, Martillac and Villenave d'Ornon. They spread down to Langon and envelop the areas of **Sauternes** and **Barsac**. The sweet white dessert wines produced there are considered among the best in the world.

East of the Gironde estuary and the Dordogne, the **Côtes de Blaye** produce some good-quality white table wines, mostly dry, and a smaller quantity of reds. The **Côtes de Bourg**, an area that spreads down to the renowned St Émilion region specialize in solid whites and reds. Here, there are a dozen producers who have earned the *Premiers Grands Crus Classés* classification. Their wines are full, rich reds that don't have to mature as long as the Médoc wines. Lesser-known neighbouring areas include the vineyards of **Pomerol**, **Lalande** and **Côtes de Francs**, all producing reds similar to St-Émilion but at more affordable prices.

Between the Garonne and the Dordogne is **Entre-Deux-Mers**, which yields large quantities of inexpensive, drinkable table whites, mainly from the Sauvignon grape. Stretching along the north bank of the Garonne, the vineyards of the **Côtes de Bordeaux** feature fruity reds and a smaller number of dry, sweet whites.

The **classification** of Bordeaux wines is a complex business. Apart from the usual *appellation d'origine protégée* (AOP) labelling, the wines of the Médoc châteaux are graded into five crus, or growths. These were established as early as 1855, based on the prices the wines had fetched over the last few hundred years. Four were voted the best or **Premier Grand Cru Classé**: Margaux, Lafitte, Latour and Haut-Brion. With the exception of Château Mouton-Rothschild, which moved up a class in 1973 to become the fifth Premier Grand Cru Classé, there have been no official changes, so divisions between the crus should not be taken too seriously.

### BUYING WINE AND VISITING CHATEAUX

If you're interested in **buying wine**, head for the châteaux, where you'll get the best price and the opportunity to sample and receive expert advice before purchasing. To **visit the châteaux**, ask at the Maison du Vin in each wine-producing village. In Bordeaux, the best place to sample wines is La Vinothèque (Mon–Sat 10am–7.30pm; ☏ 05 56 10 41 41, ⓦ la-vinotheque.com) next to the tourist office on 8 Cours du 30 Juillet. The tourist office runs **guided tours,** covering all the main wine areas (from €28 per person). The guide translates the wine-maker's commentary into English and answers any questions. Tastings are generous, and expert tuition is included.

not offer tastings or sell directly, but you can visit the grounds if you book a couple of weeks in advance.

In the small village of **MARGAUX** itself, there's a **Maison du Vin** (June–Sept Mon–Sat 10am–1pm & 2–6pm, Sun 11am–1pm & 2–5pm; Oct–May Mon–Sat 10am–1pm & 2–6pm; ☏ 05 57 88 70 82), which can help find accommodation, and advise on visits to the *appellation*'s châteaux. At the other end of the village is a cellar, La Cave d'Ulysse (daily 9am–7pm, closed Sun in winter; ⓦ caveulysse.com), which gives free tastings from a variety of Margaux châteaux. Prices range from a €5 run-of-the-mill Médoc to €2400 for a 1990 Petrus.

### Fort Médoc and Lamarque

The ruins of **Fort Médoc** sit between Margaux and St-Julien, on the D2 road with views over the estuary. It was designed by prolific military architect Vauban in the

**9**

seventeenth-century, and the ruins make good scrambling. Southwards is the pretty village of **LAMARQUE**, full of flowers, with a distinctive, minaret-like church tower. A couple of kilometres away is the port, where you can take a ferry (4–9 daily; one-way passengers €3.20, cycles €1.70, cars €13.70) across the muddy Gironde to Blaye (see opposite).

## Pauillac

**PAUILLAC** is the largest town in the Médoc, and close to the most important vineyards of Bordeaux: no fewer than three of the top five grand cru hale from here.

### INFORMATION PAUILLAC

**Maison du Tourisme et du Vin** On the waterfront (July & Aug Mon–Sat 9.30am–7pm, Sun 10am–1pm & 2–6pm; Sept–June Mon–Sat 9.30am–12.30pm & 2–6.30pm, Sun 10.30am–1pm & 2–6pm; ☎ 0556 59 03 08, ⓦ pauillac-medoc.com). They can provide a list of *gîtes*, info on bike hire, and, for a small fee, make appointments at the surrounding châteaux.

### ACCOMMODATION PAUILLAC

**Les Phoenix** 21 rue Jean Mermoz ☎ 05 56 59 62 48, ⓦ caruso33.net/les-phoenix-pauillac.html. A welcoming, good-value B&B with friendly hosts, spacious rooms, shared bathrooms, free parking and an excellent breakfast (included). **€50**

★ **Le V en Vertheuil** 5 rue de l'Abbaye, Vertheuil ☎ 06 42 55 49 59 ⓦ le-v-en-vertheuil.com. Imagine a simple country B&B, run like a luxury hotel, with some crêpes thrown in, and you have the quixotic *Le V*. Based in an 1850 bakery, *Le V* has three quiet rooms, views of the abbey, a long terrace, an attached crêperie, and a charming owner who left a successful career in five-star New York hotels. It's a 15min drive from Pauillac. **€56**

### EATING AND DRINKING

**Café Lavinal** P.Desquet, Bages ☎ 5 57 75 00 09. This pleasant bistro, a 5min drive from Pauillac in the village of Bages, serves nice food at prices only slightly higher than they should be, with a pleasant terrace. Daily noon–2.30pm & 7.30–9.30pm (5.30pm Sun).

**Château Cordeillan** Rte des Châteaux, Bages ☎ 05 56 59 24 24, ⓦ cordeillanbages.com. A first-rate gourmet restaurant in opulent surroundings, owned by the Bages set, run by Chef Rocha, who, according to restaurant publicity, "likes to simultaneously surprise and reassure with his cuisine." Prices are more likely to do the former (tasting *menu* €175) but there's a better-value lunch *menu* (€60). Dress smartly. Mid-Feb to mid-Dec Wed–Fri & Sun 12.30–1.30pm & 7.30–9.30pm, Tues & Sat 7.30–9.30pm; closed Mon.

## The Médoc châteaux

The most famous of the **Médoc châteaux** – Château Lafite-Rothschild (4km northwest of Pauillac; ☎ 05 56 59 73 18 18), and Château Latour (3km south of Pauillac; ☎ 05 56 73 19 80) – can be visited by appointment only, either direct or through the Maison du Vin.

## St-Estèphe

North of Pauillac is the wine commune of **ST-ESTÈPHE**, Médoc's largest *appellation*, consisting predominantly of crus bourgeois properties and growers belonging to the local *cave coopérative*, **Marquis de St-Estèphe**, on the D2 towards Pauillac (tastings July & Aug daily 10am–noon & 2–6pm; Sept–June by appointment; ☎ 05 56 73 35 30, ⓦ marquis-saint-estephe.fr). One of the *appellation*'s five crus classés is the distinctive **Château Cos d'Estournel**, with its flamboyant nineteenth-century pagoda; the *chais* (warehouses) can be visited by appointment (Mon–Fri 9am–12.30 & 2–5.30pm; ☎ 05 56 73 15 50, ⓦ estournel.com; English spoken, reserve a week ahead). St-Estèphe is a drowsy village dominated by the eighteenth-century **church of St-Étienne**, with its highly decorative interior. The small, homespun **Maison du Vin** (April–June & mid-Sept to early Nov Mon–Fri 10am–noon & 2pm-6pm, Sat 2–6pm; July to mid-Sept

> ## WINES OF BLAYE
>
> The green slopes north of the Garonne were planted long before the Médoc. Wine here is powerful, richly coloured, fruity, and cheaper than on the opposite riverbank. The **Côtes de Bourg** and **Côtes de Blaye** are quintessential pleasant, inexpensive reds. Visit the **Maison du Vin des Premières Côtes de Blaye** on cours Vauban (Mon–Sat 8.30am–12.30pm & 2–6.30pm) to stock up. You can get a good bottle for around €5.

Mon–Sat 10am–7pm; early Nov to March 10am–noon & 2–5pm; ☎05 56 59 30 59, ⓦvins-saint-estephe.com) is hidden in the church square.

## ACCOMMODATION ST ESTÈPHE

**Château les Ormes Pez** 29 rte des Ormes de Pez ☎05 56 73 24 00, ⓦlesormesdepez.com. A comfortable family hotel in a handsome chateau, with a pool (unheated) and large walled garden, surrounded by vineyards, just outside the village. **€200**

**Château Pomys** Rte de Poumey ☎05 56 59 73 44,

ⓦchateaupomys.com. Although it looks like a five-star hotel, with an imposing facade and manicured garden, this is a wine château, a long walk from the village, with a small restaurant and ten converted rooms – comfortable, clean and pleasant, but under-staffed and without amenities – which is reflected in the prices. **€100**

# Blaye

According to legend, the great Frankish hero Roland was buried in Blaye, which was a port of the Gaul Santones in pre-Roman times. The town played a crucial role in the wars against the English, and the French Wars of Religion. The citadelle was built by the great military engineer Vauban, but has never seen action. Blaye has a long history of viniculture, as the area was originally planted by the Romans, and is also known for a messy-looking sweet confectionery, praslines, made here since the seventeenth century. Another speciality is caviar; legend has it that it was introduced to residents by noble Russians who fled to France during the Revolution.

## INFORMATION

**Tourist office** The office on 33 allées Marines (April–Sept Mon–Sat 10am–6.30; ☎05 57 42 12 09,

ⓦtourisme-blaye.com) can reserve rooms and provide details on wine tasting/tours.

## ACCOMMODATION

**Camping Kernest** Citadelle de Vauban ☎05 57 42 00 20, ⓦcamping-kernest.com. Romantically situated inside the old citadelle, this is an old school campsite, with room for just 36 tents, electricity, bathrooms and a telephone box, in green, tree-lined grounds, ten minutes' walk from a pool, five minutes' from Blaye's shops and restaurants, with views of the Gironde. **€9.90**

★ **Château Bavolier** St Christoly de Blaye ☎05 57 42 59 74, ⓦchateau-bavolier.com. It's hard not to lavish praise on Bavolier, 15min by car from Blaye: an enchanting scale-model palace, run as a two-room B&B by its English owners. It was built in the seventeenth century by a consul to the king, and is packed with columns, nooks, frescoes and statues, and nestles in 5 acres of garden in the heart of wine country. Splendidly renovated, the interior is luxurious, the hostess is attentive, and the setting magical. Closed during winter. Book the Master Suite for a regal experience. Breakfast included. **€110**

**La Citadelle** 5 place des Armes ☎05 57 42 17 10, ⓦhotellacitadelle.com. A traditional hotel inside the old fort, with a restaurant and swimming pool overlooking the river, rather pricey but the best option if you want a hotel as opposed to a B&B. Avoid the overpriced breakfast. **€210**

**Domaine des Deux Cèdres** 26 rte des Astéries ☎05 57 64 88 65, ⓦdomainedesdeuxcedres.com. A very fine family-run B&B in the vineyards, with three inviting rooms and the option to eat in for €22–36. Breakfast included. **€75**

★ **Villa Saint Simon** 8 cours du General de Gaulle ☎55 74 29 99 66, ⓦbordeauxwinevilla.com. A splendid townhouse opposite Blaye port, built in 1860, skilfully renovated in the early 2000s, and run by a sociable South African couple. The man of the house is a zealous oenophile who runs tours and wine tastings (€15) for guests, the lady is an artist who runs a nearby gallery. If you're on a tight budget, ask about the ground-floor room. **€87**

### EATING AND DRINKING

**Au Sarment** 50 rue de la Lande ☎05 57 43 44 73. Michelin-starred restaurant in a small village halfway between Bordeaux and Blaye, with a good-value lunch *menu* (€26 for 3 courses), and dinner *menus* from €39. Tues–Fri noon–1.45pm & 8–9.45pm, Sat 8–9.45pm, Sun noon–1.45pm.

**Le Petit Port** 3 cours du Porte ☎05 57 42 99 95. Local's restaurant opposite the citadelle in Blaye, specializing in simple, nicely cooked seafood dishes. The seafood salad with citrus is a treat. Daily noon–2pm & 7.30–10pm.

**Le Plaisance au Port** Bourg sur Gironde ☎05 57 68 45 34. An urban-looking country restaurant 14km south-east of Blaye, with a long, curved windows overlooking the estuary, well-cooked dishes like monkfish with fresh pesto, or red snapper with peppers and olives. Go Thurs–Sat for live piano. Mains €14–20. Daily 11am–3pm & 7–11pm.

**La Popote de l'Antiquaire** 5 rue Anciens Combattants ☎05 57 68 26 44. A 20min drive away from Blaye in Pugnac, this family-run eatery serves one traditional home-cooked meal a day. Tues–Sat 10am–11pm.

# St-Émilion

**ST-ÉMILION**, 35km east of Bordeaux, and a short train trip, is an essential visit. The old grey houses of this fortified medieval town straggle down the steep south-hanging slope of a low hill, with the green froth of the summer's vines crawling over its walls. Many of the growers still keep up the old tradition of planting roses at the ends of the rows, which in pre-pesticide days served as an early-warning system against infection, the idea being that the commonest bug, oidium, went for the roses first, giving three days' notice of its intentions.

### The old town

The best way to see St Émilion is on a **guided tour** (see p.516). Tours begin at the **grotte de l'Ermitage**, where it's said that St Émilion lived as a hermite in the eighth century, sleeping on a stone ledge. The tour continues in the half-ruined **Trinity Chapel**, which was converted into a cooperage (barrel-makers') during the Revolution. Striking frescoes are still visible. Across the yard is a passage beneath the **belfry** leading to the **catacombs**, where three chambers dug out of the soft limestone were used as an ossuary between the eighth and eleventh centuries.

Below is the church itself. Simple and huge, the entire structure – barrel vaulting, great square piers and all – was hacked out of the rock. The interior was once painted, but only faint traces survived the Revolution, when it was used as a gunpowder factory. Every June the wine council – *La Jurade* – assembles here in red robes to judge last year's wine and decide whether each *viticulteur*'s produce deserves the *appellation contrôlée* rating.

Behind the tourist office is a grand view of the **moat** and old town **walls**. To the right is the twelfth-century **collegiate church**, with a handsome but mutilated doorway, and a fourteenth-century **cloister**, accessible through the tourist office (same hours; free).

### Local vineyards

Many local vineyards hold wine tastings: Château Fonplegade (☎05 57 74 43 11) is friendly and close to the train station, while Château Canon (☎05 57 55 23 45; appointment only), west of town, has splendid architecture. **Maison du Vin**, opposite the tourist office (daily 10am–12.30pm & 2–6.30pm; ⊕vins-saint-emilion.com), can advise you on which vineyards to visit, and sells local wines at a fair price.

### ARRIVAL AND INFORMATION

ST-ÉMILION

**By train** The small, unmanned Gare de Saint-Émilion is on the Sarlat–Bergerac–Libourne–Bordeaux rail route, and about 1.6km from the village (just turn right at the station and follow the road). The nearest mainline station is at Libourne (served by the TGV), a 40-minute walk from Saint-Émilion.

**Tourist office** Place des Créneaux by the belfry (Jan–March daily 10am–12.30pm & 2–5pm; April–June Mon–Fri 9.30am–12.30pm & 1.30pm–6/6.30pm, weekend 9.30am–6.30pm; July & Aug daily 9.30am–7.30pm; Sept–Nov Mon–Fri 9.30am–12.30pm & 1.30–5/6pm, weekend 9.30am–6pm; ☎05 57 55 28 28,

**9**

ⓦ saint-emilion-tourisme.com), organizes town tours (10am–5.30pm, one or two a day in English; adult €12, children €9) and vineyard tours (June–Sept; some in English; adults €9, children €6). They also have bikes for rent (€15 per day or €150 per month).

## ACCOMMODATION

**La Barbanne** ☎ 05 57 24 75 80, ⓦ camping-saint -emilion.com. Two kilometres northwest of St-Émilion, on the road to Montagne, this well-kept but over-priced three-star campsite has a restaurant and takeaway, corner-shop, internet point, pools, a lake with boats, bike rental and a free shuttle-bus to town. April–Sept €52

**Château Franc-Pourret** 1 Gomerie ☎ 06 70 21 00 24, ⓦ ouzoulias-vins.com. This family château, 15min by foot from St-Émilion, and set amid a sea of vines, has two homely guestrooms. The hostess is welcoming, breakfast (included) is good, and you can pay a few euros more for a wine tour (book in advance). €109

★ **La Gomerie** 5 Gomerie ☎ 05 57 24 68 85 ⓦ mf -favard.fr. Inexpensive and snug, *La Gomerie* is a rustic cottage in the vineyards, run as a B&B by a mother and daughter. Quiet, cosy rooms with en-suite bathrooms. Don't arrive after dark as the turn-off is easy to miss even in daylight; free parking. Breakfast included. €67

**Hostellerie de Plaisance** Place du Clocher ☎ 05 57 55 07 55 ⓦ www.hostellerie-plaisance.com. Those with trust funds to blow can do so with flair and expediency here; in the heart of town, with five stars, first-class dining, spectacular views, and handsome rooms. Breakfast €30. €300–600

## EATING AND DRINKING

St Émilion has a handful of excellent, reasonably priced restaurants, and a lot of dross, so do some research before eating out, and make reservations.

**Chai Pascal** 37 rue Gaudet ☎ 05 57 24 52 45, ⓦ chai -pascal.com. A welcoming family-run bistro with a concise, quality menu of traditional dishes. Mains around €10. Daily 11am–11pm.

**Lard & Bouchon** 22 rue Gaudet ☎ 05 57 24 28 53, ⓦ lardetbouchon.fr. An arched brick cellar-restaurant under rue Gaudet, with a bistro-style menu, a good chef, and a wide selection of local wines, cool even in blazing summer. Lunch €21 for 3 courses. Mon 12.30–1.30pm, Tues–Sat 12.30–1.30pm & 7.30–9.30pm, Sun 12.30–1.30pm.

★ **Macarons de St Émilion** 9 rue Gaudet ☎ 05 57 24 72 33, ⓦ macarons-saint-emilion.fr. Locals say that Nadia Fermingier, whose parents worked here before her,

makes the best *macarons* in France. She uses the original recipe, invented by nuns in the 1620s. The *canelés* are better than you will find in Bordeaux, and although unorthodox, the *macarons* with chocolate ganache are delectable. June–Oct Mon–Sat 8am–7.15pm, Sun 9am–7.15pm; Nov–May Mon–Fri 8am–12.30pm & 3–7pm, Sat 8am–7pm, Sun 9am–7pm.

**Restaurant Le Tetre** 5 rue du Tertre de la Tente ☎ 05 57 74 46 33, ⓦ restaurant-le-tertre.com. Stashed up a narrow central street, this wooden-beamed, cobble-walled restaurant may be the best in St Émilion, and with a 3-course regional *menu* for €23, is not too expensive. It's popular, so book in advance. Daily except Wed (mid-April to mid-Nov) & Thurs (Feb & March).

# Entre-Deux-Mers

**Entre-Deux-Mers** ("between two seas") lies between the tidal waters of the Dordogne and Garonne. It's the most attractive area in the wine region, with gentle hills and medieval villages. Its wines, including the Premières Côtes de Bordeaux, are mainly dry whites, produced by over forty *caves cooperatives*. They're considered good, but not up to the level of Médocs or dry Graves produced to the south.

## La Sauve-Majeure

June–Sept daily 10am–1.15pm & 2–6pm; Oct–May Tues–Sun 10.30am–1pm & 2–5.30pm • €7.50

Around 25km east of Bordeaux is the ruined eleventh-century abbey **LA SAUVE-MAJEURE**, an important stop for pilgrims en route to Santiago de Compostela in Spain. Thick woods once surrounded the abbey – in fact its name is from the Latin *silva major* (large forest). All that remains today are the Romanesque apse and apsidal chapels, and outstanding sculpted capitals in the chancel. The best illustrate stories from the Old and New Testaments; a pensive Daniel in the lions' den is particularly winning. There's a small **museum** at the entrance, with some keystones from the fallen roofs.

## St-Macaire and around

If you're heading south through Entre-Deux-Mers, Langon is the first town you come to, but it's best to postpone your rest stop until pretty **ST-MACAIRE**, across the Garonne. The village still has its original **gates** and **battlements**. There's a beautiful medieval church, the **Église-Prieuré**, with freshly restored wall paintings.

LA RÉOLE, 18km east, is full of medieval buildings on narrow, hilly streets – pick up a map from the tourist office on place Richard-Coeur-de-Lion. You can take a look at France's oldest **town hall**, constructed in the twelfth century by Richard the Lionheart, and the well-preserved **Abbaye des Bénédictins**, which has a fantastic view over the River Garonne and the surrounding countryside.

### INFORMATION
ST MACAIRE

**Tourist office** 8 rue du Canton (June–Sept daily 10am–1pm & 3–7pm; April & May Tues–Sun daily 10am–1pm & 3–7pm; March & Oct Tues–Fri 2–6pm, Sat & Sun 10am–noon & 2–6pm; Nov–Feb same hours but closed Tues; ☎ 05 56 63 32 14 ⓦ entredeuxmers.com), also sells delicious local produce, including wine and honey. Staff can arrange visits to the *chais*, and in season (July & Aug daily) tastings hosted by local winemakers.

### ACCOMMODATION AND EATING

**L'Abricotier** 2 rue François Bergoeing ☎ 05 56 76 83 63, ⓦ restaurant-labricotier.com. A genial local restaurant with a shady terrace and daily *menus* from €22. Closed all day Mon & Tues eve.

**Les Feuilles d'Acanthe** ☎ 05 56 62 33 75, ⓦ feuilles -dacanthe.fr. Opposite the tourist office, this stone-walled, wooden-beamed hotel has fine views out over the rooftops, a jacuzzi, a south-facing terrace, and one of the town's best restaurants, serving traditional meat-heavy dishes. Daily *menus* from €21. Closed mid-Dec to mid-Jan. **€95**

## Sauternes and around

SAUTERNES is a slumbering village surrounded by vines and dominated by the **Maison du Sauternes** (Mon–Fri 9am–7pm, Sat & Sun 10am–7pm; ☎ 05 56 76 69 83, ⓦ maisondusauternes.com) at one end of the village, and a pretty church at the other. The *maison* looks like a treasure-trove; the golden bottles with white labels are beautiful. A non-profit organization, the maison offers tastings, expert advice and good prices.

### ACCOMMODATION
SAUTERNES

★ **Peyraguey Maison Rouge Bommes** ☎ 05 57 31 07 55, ⓦ peyraguey-sauternes.com. This tiny B&B is a blessed island in the vines, with charming decoration, warm hosts, lounge, free use of bikes, good breakfast and a pool. Breakfast included. **€82**

**Relais du Château d'Arche** ☎ 05 56 76 67 67, ⓦ chateaudarche-sauternes.com. A luxurious château-hotel and vineyard on the D125 just outside Sauternes (heading north) with nine rooms. Breakfast €10. **€120**

---

### SAUTERNES

The **Sauternes** region, which extends southeast from Bordeaux for 40km along the left bank of the Garonne, is an ancient winemaking area, first planted during the Roman occupation. The distinctive golden wine of the area is sweet, round, full-bodied and spicy, with a long aftertaste. It's not necessarily a dessert wine, either; try it with Roquefort cheese. Gravelly terraces with a limestone subsoil help create the delicious taste, but mostly it's due to a peculiar microclimate of morning autumn mists and afternoons of sun and heat which causes *Botrytis cinerea* fungus, or "noble rot", to flourish on the grapes, letting the sugar concentrate and introducing some intense flavours. When the grapes are picked they're not a pretty sight: carefully selected by hand, only the most shrivelled, rotting bunches are taken. The wines of Sauternes are some of the most sought-after in the world, with bottles of **Château d'Yquem**, in particular, fetching thousands of euros. Sadly that particular château does not offer tastings, but you can wander around the buildings and grounds, two minutes' drive north of Sauternes.

**9**

## EATING AND DRINKING

**Auberge Les Vignes** 23 rue Principale ☎ 05 56 76 60 06. Regional specialities like *grillades aux Sauternes* (meats grilled on vine clippings), a good wine list and a lunch *menu* at €13. Mon noon–2pm, Tues–Sat noon–2pm & 7.30–9.30pm; closed Feb.

**Restaurant Saprien** 14 rue Principale ☎ 05 56 76 60 87. A pleasing country restaurant in the vines, with enjoyable food, view and atmosphere. Set *menus* from €15. Tues noon–2pm & 7.30pm–9pm, Wed noon–2pm, Thurs–Sat noon–2pm & 7.30pm–9pm, Sun noon–2pm.

### Around Sauternes

Ten kilometres south of Sauternes is the little town of **VILLANDRAUT**, overlooked by a great mammoth of a ruined château (July & Aug daily 10am–7pm; Sept–June 2–6pm; €3.50). It was built by Pope Clement V, who caused the Papal Schism (1378) by moving his papacy to Avignon. You can visit Clement's tomb in **UZESTE** en route to **BAZAS**, 15km east. At the heart of Bazas is the wide, arcaded place de la Cathédrale. The cathedral itself, **St-Jean-Baptiste**, is a harmonious blend of Romanesque, Gothic and classical styles.

## ACCOMMODATION AND EATING                                           AROUND SAUTERNES

**Les Remparts** Place de la Cathédrale ☎ 05 56 25 95 24. A high veranda with views over the countryside, and sophisticated cuisine. Three-course set *menu* for €35. Tues–Sat noon–1.30pm & 7.30–9.30pm, Sun noon–1.30pm.

★ **Le Sorbet** 3 Sorbet ☎ 05 56 25 08 83, ⓦ ausorbet .com. A delightfully countrified B&B with friendly hosts, toothsome breakfast and views of Bazas cathedral from the garden. Breakfast included. **€75**

# The Côte d'Argent

At over 200km, **Côte d'Argent** is the longest, straightest, sandiest stretch of coast in Europe. Behind the endless beaches, which reach from the mouth of the Gironde all the way to Biarritz, are high sand dunes, and the largest forest in Western Europe, **Les Landes**. There's no coast road, only a cycle path, built at the end of World War II. It winds through more than 75km of pine-forested dunes from the upmarket holiday town of Cap Ferret, to Soulac in the north. The lack of conventional tourist sights means that outside July and August the coast does not get many visitors, and away from the main resorts it's possible to find deserted stretches of coastline, even in August.

## Arcachon

On Friday nights in the summer, Bordeaux's residents flee the city, making for **ARCACHON**, the oldest beach resort on the Côte d'Argent. In August the white beaches bustle, and blue and yellow cruise boats buzz around the wooden jetties.

Many of Arcachon's houses date from that brief period in the nineteenth century when the public's taste resembled that of a seven year-old girl: extravagant, frilly bungalows sit in rose-filled gardens, inscribed with names like "Mirabelle" and "Claire de Lune" in curly italics. The town is made up of four little districts, named after the seasons. The seafront promenades and shopping streets of **ville d'été** (summer town) are full of ice-cream stalls and fishing nets. **Ville d'hiver** (winter town), south of the beach, is a place of broad, quiet streets and Second Empire mansions. To get there, follow the boulevard de la Plage west of Jetée Thiers until you reach the pedestrianized rue de Maréchal-de-Lattre-de-Tassigny; there a lift carries you up to the flower-filled, wooded **Parc Mauresque**, just below **ville d'hiver**. Residential **ville d'automne** (autumn town) stretches eastwards along boulevard de la Plage, a gentle 15min walk from the *ville d'été*; the beaches are a little quieter here.

### Parc Ornithologique du Teich

Daily 10am–6pm/8pm (winter/summer) • €7.60 • ⓦ parc-ornithologique-du-teich.com

At **LE TEICH**, about 14km east of Arcachon, one of the most important expanses of wetlands remaining in France has been converted into a bird sanctuary, the

**Parc Ornithologique du Teich.** There are no hotels in Le Teich, but there are campsites, and it's an easy day-trip from Arcachon by train.

## INFORMATION

**Tourist office** Esplanade Georges-Pompidou (April–June & Sept Mon–Sat 9am–6.30pm, Sun 10am–1pm & 2–5pm; July & Aug daily 9am–7pm; Oct–March Mon–Fri 9am–6pm, Sat 9am–5pm; ☎ 05 57 52 97 97; ⓦ arcachon .com) – it's a short, straight walk back from place Thiers.
**Boat trips** In summer boats leave the jetties of Thiers and

## ARCACHON

Eyrac on various cruises, including to the Île aux Oiseaux (1hr 45min; €14), and the Arcachon basin/ Dune de Pyla (2hr 45min; €21). There's also a regular boat service from here to Cap Ferret on the opposite peninsula (30min; €11.50 return). Discounted tickets for all excursions are available from the tourist office.

## ACCOMMODATION

**Le Camping Club** Allée de la Galaxie ☎ 05 56 83 24 15, ⓦ camping-arcachon.com. An excellent four-star campsite in town with a bar, restaurant, and shop (July & Aug only), playground, BBQs, volleyball, and bike rental. **€38**
**Du Parc** 5–7 av du Parc ☎ 05 56 83 10 58, ⓦ hotelduparc -arcachon.com. Neat, mostly spacious rooms with balconies a short walk from the beach and shops. **€99**
**La Plage** 10 av Nelly Deganne ☎ 05 56 83 06 23, ⓦ hotelarcachon.com. Long-halled, freshly painted hotel popular with families and business travellers, with 57 rooms, free parking (or garage parking for €10), fitness room, computer room. Breakfast €11. **€120**
**Saint-Christaud** 8 allee de la Chapelle ☎ 05 56 83 38 53, ⓦ hotel-saintchristaud.com. Right in the heart of

town and three minutes' walk from the beach, this free-spirited hotel has good prices and jolly little rooms. Large-scale renovations have damaged customer service in the last year, but workmen leave as this book goes to press, so standards will undoubtedly buck up. **€79**
★ **Ville d'hiver** 20 av Victor Hugo ☎ 05 56 66 10 36, ⓦ hotelvilledhiver.com. A unique and charming place – the main building (reception, lounge and restaurant) is a converted nineteenth-century water plant, surrounded by a little park with free-standing blocks of rooms (three levels, one room per level), which means quiet and privacy. There's a subterranean pool in the old purification tank in the garden. **€190**

## EATING AND DRINKING

**Au P'tit Ju** 27 av Gambetta ☎ 05 56 83 32 60. An uninspiring facade belies the small but well-chosen menu of tempting dishes. Lunch *menu* from €13. July & Aug daily 12.30–2pm & 7.30–10pm; Sept–June Tues–Fri 12.30–2pm, Sat & Sun 12.30–2pm & 7.20–10pm.
**Aux Délices Glacées** 257 bd Côte d'Argent ☎ 05 56 54 55 54. A selection of rich, flavourful ice creams and sorbets, light crêpes and crisp waffles. Mon–Fri 10am–7pm, Sat 9am–6pm.
**Le Cabestan** 6 bis av Gen de Gaulle ☎ 05 56 83 18 62. A straight-shooting fish restaurant with warm service, prime shellfish, and decor that's aging its way out of dowdy and into nostalgic. The prices aren't low but they're matched by quality. Three-course *menus* €24 and €32. Mid-Jan to mid Dec Wed–Sun noon–2pm & 7–9.30pm (9pm Sun), July–Aug also Tues 7–9pm.
★ **La Guérinière** 18 Cours Verdun ☎ 05 56 66 08 78, ⓦ lagueriniere.com. Top-drawer Michelin-starred hotel

restaurant. The focus is on fresh, organic products so the menu changes weekly. The tasting *menu* combines traditional and unexpected elements (duck tongues, roast beef, pea and mint *macarons*) in a manner that is highly enjoyable, and for tighter budgets there is a five-course weekend *menu* for €40. Daily noon–2pm & 7–10pm, closed Sat lunchtime.
**Pâtisserie Alain Guignard** 11 av Notre Dame des Passes. An Arcachon institution with a 20-year pedigree. Fruit crumble, *canelés*, layer cake, chocolate cake, biscuits, fruit tarts, coffee and éclairs. Mon–Fri 8am–7pm, Sat 8am–6pm.
**La Table du Boucher** 16 rue du Mal-de-Lattre-de-Tassigny ☎ 05 56 54 06 28. Perfect for the fish-phobic and weary, it serves meat only, except on Friday, to tourists and locals, with equal courtesy. The honeyed duck with spiced vegetables is especially good. July & Aug daily Tues–Sun noon–2pm & 7.30–10.30pm; Sept–June Tues–Sun noon–2pm & 7.30–10.30pm.

# Cap Ferret

The tiny peninsula town of **Cap Ferret** crashed onto the tourist scene in the 1920s, when Jean Cocteau began holidaying here: "We row, we nap, we roll in the sand, we stroll around naked, in a landscape like Texas", he wrote in Letters from Piquey (1923). Polite society wanted to join in, and Cap Ferret quickly became a well-heeled holiday

**9**

### THE DUNE DU PYLA

**The Dune du Pyla** is the largest dune in Europe – a vast white lunar landscape of windswept sand, 100m high, 12km south of Arcachon. The adventurous shouldn't miss the long, hair-raising slide down to the sea, over slopes as steep as an Olympic ski-jump. Bus #1 leaves from the *gare SNCF* in Arcachon every hour in July and August – two to five a day in other months. If you're driving, note that the car park costs €4. Three minutes away by car is *Hotel La Co(o)rniche* (46 bd Loius Gaume; ☎ 05 56 22 72 21, ⌨ lacoorniche-pyla.com; €325); the terrace, with views of the bay and dunes, is the ideal spot for cocktails or a plate of oysters.

resort. Luckily, surrounded by the Landes of Gascony and the Pays de Buch, it's never been fully civilized.

### ARRIVAL AND DEPARTURE — CAP FERRET

**By ferry** Cap Ferret is accessed by passenger ferry from nearby Arcachon (30min; €12 return; buy tickets at the jetty).

**By car** The town is accessible by road from the north.

### ACCOMMODATION

**Camping Bremontier** Grand Crohot ☎ 05 56 60 03 99. 10km north of Cap Ferret in a protected pine forest with a shop and bread delivery, bike rental, a supervised beach and a sailing club. June to mid-Sept. **€17.10**

**Chez Annie** 7 rue des Roitelets ☎ 05 56 60 66 25, ⌨ chezannie-capferret.com. Three spick-and-span furnished garden sheds in a suburban garden; two double rooms and one breakfast room, run by the very friendly Annie, who speaks no English but is happy to mime. **€120**

**La Maison du Bassin** 5 rue des Pionniers ☎ 05 56 03 72 46, ⌨ lamaisondubassin.com. Oak-floored chandelier-hung hotel with small but elegant rooms, a picturesque garden and veranda, impressive bar/restaurant, and the atmosphere of a bourgeoise summer home. Breakfast from €15. **€135**

★ **Des Pins** 23 rue des Fauvettes ☎ 05 56 60 60 11, ⌨ hoteldespins.eu. *Des Pins* feels like a genteel Edwardian boarding house, with fresh, pale rooms off a wood-panelled hall. There are sleeping cabins in the garden, and a gypsy caravan. The only downside is bad soundproofing. Closed mid-Nov to Jan. **€75**

**Yamina Lodge** 169 av de Bordeaux ☎ 05 56 60 14 89, ⌨ yamina-lodge.com. A romantic two-roomed B&B hidden in woods, five minutes from the town by bike. Has its own bicycles for hire as well as a spa. Closed winter. **€170**

### EATING AND DRINKING

**Pinasse Café** 2bis av de l'Ocean ☎ 05 56 03 77 87. Right next to Cap Ferret's main jetty, where the Arcachon boat disembarks, *Pinasse* should be an overpriced tourist trap, but against all odds it is an excellent little eatery, serving fresh seafood (dishes €8–35) and salads (€14–22) on the picturesque terrace. Daily noon–3pm & 7–11pm.

**So Phare Away** 32 av Nord du Phare ☎ 06 70 93 59 79. The quality-to-price ratio is high, with two- or three-course *menus* for €14/16 and fresh, piquant seafood. Delicious langoustines. Closed mid-Jan to mid-Feb. Summer daily, winter Sat & Sun only lunch & dinner.

## Les Landes

South of Bordeaux is **Les Landes**, the largest pine forest in Western Europe. Nearly 10,000 square kilometres long, it was declared a *parc naturel régional* in 1970. It's a beautiful place, but inhospitable and lonely; strong on outdoor pursuits but with few cultural attractions.

**MONT DE MARSAN** makes a good base for exploring the inland part of Les Landes. It's the administrative heart of the region, 100km south of Bordeaux, and served by regular trains. **Parc Jean Rameau**, on the north bank of the river Douze, is the prettiest part of the town. If you're lucky enough to be in the area in mid-July, you can enjoy Les Fêtes Madeleine (⌨ fetesmadeleine.fr), a week of parades, sports, flamenco and bullfighting, when the town's Basque identity asserts itself.

## INFORMATION

**Tourist office** Place du Général-Leclerc, Mont de Marsan (Jan–March & Nov–Dec Mon–Fri 9am–12.30pm & 1.30–6pm, Sat 9am–1pm; April–June & Sept–Oct Mon–Sat 9am–6pm; July & Aug Mon–Sat 9am–6.30pm, Sun 9am–1pm; ☎ 05 58 05 87 37, ⚅ tourisme -montdemarsan.com).

**Activities** The tourist office (see above) provides maps of local walking and cycling routes and also organizes a guided tour of Mont de Marsan in English (July & Aug, from the office daily 10.30am except Sun; adult €3.50). Another outdoor activity on offer is canoeing on one of the three rivers whose confluence is at the town. For canoe-hire try Canoë Loisir (☎ 05 58 45 62 21) in nearby Roquefort.

## ACCOMMODATION

**Le Renaissance** 225 av de Villeneuve ☎ 05 58 51 51 51, ⚅ le-renaissance.com. Quite a luxurious mid-size country hotel 1km from the centre, with a swimming pool and restaurant. **€84**

**Le Richelieu** 3 rue Wlérick ☎ 05 58 06 10 20, ✉ le .richelieu@orange.fr. In the heart of town, with a restaurant, paid parking, and comfortable, well-equipped rooms, part of the *Citodel* chain. **€68**

## EATING AND DRINKING

**Le Bistro de Marcel** 1 rue Pont du Commerce. A good choice of pleasing meals, professional service and a friendly atmosphere. Lunch *menu* €11. Mon 7.30–10.30am, Tues–Fri noon–2pm & 7.30–10.30pm, Sat 19.30–10.30pm.

**Brûlerie Montoise** 1, rue du 4-Septembre ☎ 05 58 75 02 63. The coffee is roasted daily, the teas are plentiful and the cakes are fresh. Tues–Fri 9am–noon & 2pm–7pm, Sat 8.30am–12.30pm & 2–7pm.

**Les Clefs d'Argent** 333 C Martyrs de la Resistance ☎ 05 58 06 16 45. A good gourmet restaurant with a light and elegant interior and delicate, tempting meals. Set *menus* €20–90. Tues–Sat noon–1.45pm & 7.45pm–9.45pm, Sun noon–1.45pm.

**La Rhumerie** 13 Place St Roch ☎ 05 58 75 76 83. Rum, cocktails, live music, snacks and a terrace. Tues–Fri 11am–1am, Sat & Sun 2pm–4am.

# The Limousin, Dordogne and the Lot

BEYNAC-ET-CAZENAC

# The Limousin, Dordogne and the Lot

The oval area bordered to the east by the uplands of the Massif Central and to the west by the Atlantic plains was the most contested between the English and the French during the Hundred Years' War, and has been most in demand among English visitors and second-home buyers in more recent times. Although it doesn't coincide exactly with either the modern French administrative boundaries or the old provinces of Périgord and Quercy, which constitute the core of the region, the land here has a physical and geographical homogeneity thanks to its great rivers: the Dordogne, the Lot and the Aveyron, all of which drain westwards from the Massif Central into the mighty Garonne.

From **Limoges** in the province of Limousin in the north to the Garonne valley in the south, the country is gently hilly, full of lush hidden valleys and miles of woodland, mainly oak. The northerly **Limousin** is slightly greener and wetter, the south more open and arid. But you can travel a long way without seeing a radical shift, except in the uplands of the **Plateau de Millevaches**, where the rivers plunge into gorges and the woods are beech, chestnut and conifer plantations. The other characteristic landscape is the *causses*, the dry scrubby limestone plateaux like the **Causse de Gramat** between the Lot and Dordogne and the **Causse de Limogne** between the Lot and Aveyron. Where the rivers have cut their way through the limestone, the valleys are walled with overhanging cliffs, riddled with fissures, underground streams and caves. And in these caves – especially in the valley of the Vézère around **Les Eyzies** – is some of the most awe-inspiring **prehistoric art** to be found anywhere in the world.

The other great artistic legacy of the area is the Romanesque sculpture, most notably adorning the churches at **Souillac** and **Beaulieu-sur-Dordogne**, but all modelled on the supreme example of the cloister of St-Pierre in the quiet town of **Moissac**. Hilltops through the region are marked by splendid **fortresses** of purely military design, such as **Bonaguil**, **Najac**, **Biron**, **Beynac** and **Castelnaud**, which more than compensate for the dearth of luxurious châteaux.

The charm of the area undoubtedly lies in the landscapes and the dozens of harmonious small towns and villages. Some, like **Sarlat** and **Rocamadour**, are so well known that they are overrun with tourists in the height of summer. Others, like **Figeac**, **Villefranche-de-Rouergue**, **Gourdon**, **Montauban**, **Monflanquin** and the many *bastides* (fortified towns) that pepper the area between the Lot and Dordogne, boast no single notable sight but are perfect organic ensembles.

The wartime Resistance was very active in these out-of-the-way regions, and the roadsides are dotted with memorials to those killed in ambushes or shot in reprisals. There is also one chilling monument to wartime atrocity: the ruined village of **Oradour-sur-Glane**, still as the Nazis left it after massacring the population and setting fire to the houses.

MONPAZIER

# Highlights

**❶ Brantôme** This old abbey town, scenically set on an island in the middle of the Dronne, makes a great base for leisurely boat trips on the river. **See p.538**

**❷ Cuisine** Foie gras, truffles and *pommes sarladaise* – Dordogne is the place to sample French country cooking at its best. **See p.538**

**❸ Monpazier** The finest of numerous *bastides* (fortified towns) in the region, particularly resplendent in the late afternoon sun. **See p.546**

**❹ Sarlat-la-Canéda** Wander the narrow lanes of this archetypal medieval town, with its lovely *vieille ville* of honey-coloured stone. **See p.548**

**❺ Grotte de Font-de-Gaume** Stunning examples of prehistoric cave art, including the spectacular frieze of five bison. **See p.552**

**❻ Jardins de Marqueyssac** Extraordinary gardens, perched on a rocky promontory, with astounding views over the Dordogne and its picturesque villages. **See p.557**

**❼ Montauban** A relaxed city with an atmospheric old centre, built around stately place Nationale – perfect for a spot of people-watching. **See p.577**

**HIGHLIGHTS ARE MARKED ON THE MAP ON P.526**

All of the region's main towns are linked by rail and/or bus services, while a fair number of smaller places have sporadic public transport links. To really make the most of the area, though, you'll need your own vehicle – car rental is available in all of the major towns.

# The Limousin

The **Limousin** – the country around **Limoges** – is hilly, wooded, wet and not particularly fertile: ideal pasture for the famous Limousin cattle. This is herdsman's country, and it's the widespread use of the shepherd's cape known as a *limousine* that gave its name to the car. The modern Limousin region stretches south to the Dordogne valley to include **Brive and Turenne**. But while these places, together with Limoges itself, are not without interest, the star of the show is the countryside – especially in the east on the **Plateau de Millevaches,** between **Eymoutiers** and **Meymac**.

## Limoges

**LIMOGES** is a pleasant city, if not one that calls for a long stay. It's famed for its crafts – enamel in the Middle Ages and, since the eighteenth century, exceptionally **fine china** – though the porcelain industry itself is pretty much spent, hard hit by recession and changing tastes. The local kaolin (china clay) mines that gave Limoges china its special quality are exhausted, and the workshops survive mainly on the tourist trade, though some are now successfully diversifying into high-tech ceramics. On first glance, its centre is rather blighted by the ugly concrete buildings of **place de la Republique**, but delving into the quiet streets beyond, particularly **rue de la Boucherie** and around, reveals a more atmospheric and charming side to Limoges.

### Cathédrale St-Étienne
Place St-Étienne

The **Cathédrale St-Étienne** was begun in 1273 and modelled on the cathedral of Amiens, though only the choir, completed in the early thirteenth century, is pure Gothic. The rest of the building was added piecemeal over the centuries, the western part of the nave not until 1876. The most striking external feature is the sixteenth-century facade of the north transept, built in full flamboyant style with elongated arches, clusters of pinnacles and delicate tracery in window and gallery. At the west end of the nave, the tower, erected on a Romanesque base that had to be massively reinforced to bear the weight, has octagonal upper storeys, in common with most churches in the region. It once stood as a separate campanile and probably looked the better for it. Inside, the effects are much more pleasing. The sense of soaring height is accentuated by all the upward-reaching lines of the pillars, the net of vaulting ribs, the curling, flame-like lines, and, as you look down the nave, by the narrower and more pointed arches of the choir.

### Musée des Beaux-Arts de Limoges
1 Place de l'Évêché • April–Sept daily except Tues 10am–6pm; Oct–March Mon & Wed–Sat 10am–noon & 2–5pm, Sun 2–5pm • Free • ⓦ museebal.fr

The best of the city's museums – with its showpiece collections of enamelware dating back to the twelfth century – is the **Musée des Beaux-Arts de Limoges** in the old bishop's palace next to the cathedral. The large, attractive exhibition space charts the progression from the simple Byzantine-influenced *champlevé* (copper filled with enamel) to seventeenth- and eighteenth-century work that uses a far greater range of colours and indulges in elaborate, virtuoso portraiture.

## The Botanical Garden

Daily sunrise to sunset • Free

Behind the cathedral, the **botanical garden** feels like a tucked away gem, descending gracefully towards the River Vienne and split into three different sections, including the historic garden, which, unsurprisingly, is the oldest of the three, with around 1500 beautifully presented plants spread out in neat – but not too ordered – lines.

## The old quarter

Stretching roughly north from the River Vienne to the ugly, modern place de la Republique, the partly renovated **old quarter** is a charmingly jumbled mix of predominantly timbered buildings. It's the best part of the city for a stroll, with the most interesting area lying immediately south and east of the market. Here you'll find rue de la Boucherie, for a thousand years the domain of the butchers' guild, and arguably the most attractive of Limoges' streets. The dark, cluttered **chapel of St-Aurélien** (daily 7am–7pm), halfway along, belongs to the guild, while one of their former shophouses at no. 36 makes an interesting little museum, the **Maison de la Boucherie** (July–Sept daily 10am–1pm & 2.30–7pm; free). At the top of the street, in

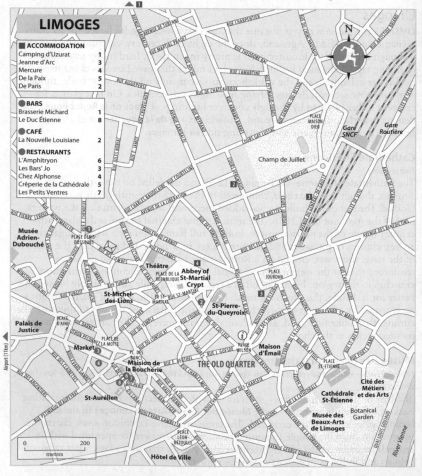

place de la Motte, is the attractive **market hall** (Mon–Sat 6am–2pm, Sun 7am–1pm), at its best and most lively during the week.

## St-Michel-des-Lions
Place St Michel

The fourteenth- and fifteenth-century **church of St-Michel-des-Lions**, tucked away near the market hall, is named after the two badly weathered Celtic lions guarding the south door and topped by one of the best towers and spires in the region. The inside is dark and atmospheric, with two beautiful, densely coloured fifteenth-century windows either side of the choir.

## Abbey of St-Martial crypt
Place de la République • July–Sept daily 9.30am–noon & 2.30–7pm • Free

The concrete swathes of place de la République conceal the fourth-century **crypt** of the long-vanished **Abbey of St-Martial**, containing the eponymous saint's massive sarcophagus, discovered during building work in the 1960s.

## St-Pierre-du-Queyroix
Rue St Pierre

The **church of St-Pierre-du-Queyroix** sits under a typically Limousin belfry, and the interior, partly twelfth-century, has the same slightly pink granite glow as the cathedral. There's more fine stained glass here, including an eye-catching window at the end of the south aisle depicting the Dormition of the Virgin, and signed by the great enamel artist Jean Pénicault in 1510.

## Musée Adrien-Dubouché
8bis place Winston-Churchill • Daily except Tues 10am–12.25pm & 2–5.40pm • €4.50 • ⓦ musee-adriendubouche.fr

Limoges's renowned **porcelain** is best displayed in the **Musée Adrien-Dubouché**, a short walk west of the old quarter. The well-presented collection includes samples of the local product and china displays from around the world, as well as various pieces from celebrity services ordered for the likes of Abraham Lincoln, Queen Elizabeth and sundry French royals.

## ARRIVAL AND INFORMATION
LIMOGES

**By plane** Limoges Bellegarde Airport (ⓦ aeroportlimoges .com) is 11km northwest of the city. From mid-June to Sept, a shuttle bus service runs into town (Mon–Fri 3 daily; 25min), stopping by the train station at place Maison-Dieu. Outisde of this period, the only way to get into the city is by taxi (€20–30).

**By train** Limoges's magnificent Art Deco *gare des Bénédictins* lies slightly northeast of the centre on av de-Gaulle, from where it's a 5min walk to central place de la Republique.
Destinations Aubusson (daily; 1hr 50min); Clermont Ferrand (1–2 daily; 4hr 15min); Eyemoutiers (3–7 daily; 1hr); St-Léonard-de-Noblat (4–7 daily; 25min).

**By bus** The *gare routière* is next to the train station; for local destinations, however, it's usually more convenient to use the bus stops on places Jourdan and Winston-Churchill.
Destinations Aubusson (1–2 daily; 45min); Oradour-sur-Glane (Mon–Sat 3 daily; 35min); St-Léonard-de-Noblat (2–4 daily; 30min).

**Tourist office** Place Wilson (May to mid-June & mid-Sept to end Sept Mon–Sat 9am–7pm; mid-June to mid-Sept Mon–Sat 9am–7pm, Sun 10am–5.30pm; Oct–April Mon–Sat 9.30am–6pm; ☎ 05 55 34 46 87, ⓦ limoges-tourisme .com); they offer free wi-fi and can help with accommodation booking.

## ACCOMMODATION

**Camping d'Uzurat** 40 av d'Uzurat ☎ 05 55 38 49 43, ⓦ campinglimoges.fr. About 5km north of Limoges's centre, this large campsite has a great setting right on a lake. Bus #20 from the *gare SNCF*. Closed Nov–Feb. **€14.60**
**Jeanne d'Arc** 17 av de-Gaulle ☎ 05 55 77 67 77,
ⓦ hoteljeannedarc-limoges.fr. The elegant entrance, tastefully decorated rooms and grand breakfast hall make this an appealing option. Rooms with showers can be a bit poky, however – better to upgrade to one with a bath, and overlooking the interior courtyard. **€82**

**10**

**Mercure** Place de la République ☏ 05 55 34 65 30, ⓦ mercure.com. Sitting on the edge of the old quarter, the *Mercure* is an unattractive, concrete affair, though the rooms are a decent size. More expensive rooms have balconies looking over the square. **€105**

★ **De la Paix** 25 place Jourdan ☏ 05 55 34 36 00, ⓦ hoteldelapaix87.fr. A wonderful old hotel, doubling as a museum of gramophones, which decorate the breakfast room in all shapes and sizes. The bedrooms might be a little old-fashioned, but are not devoid of charm, and are generally airy and pleasant. The cheapest are not en suite. **€63**

**De Paris** 5 cours Vergniaud ☏ 05 55 77 56 96, ⓦ hoteldeparis-limoges.com. You'll need to book ahead for this well-located budget hotel, where the good size of the rooms – the cheapest with washbasin only – make up for the rather worn furnishings. **€55**

## EATING AND DRINKING

Limoges has an abundance of good and not too expensive places to eat; however, if you're in town on a Sunday you'll find choices to be extremely limited. It's advisable to book on Saturday evenings when restaurants can quickly fill up.

### RESTAURANTS AND CAFÉS

**L'Amphitryon** 26 rue de la Boucherie ☏ 05 55 33 36 39. There's no better place for a real treat of subtle and sophisticated cuisine, well deserving its Michelin star. You'll be offered a good choice of seafood as well as beef, veal and other local food. The lunchtime *formule* is excellent value at just €25; evening *menus* start at €46. Closed one week in Jan, March & May, and two weeks in Aug/Sept. Tues–Sat 12.15–1.15pm & 7.45–9.15pm.

★ **Les Bars' Jo** Market hall, place de la Motte ☏ 05 55 32 32 79. For a good-value lunch and a lively atmosphere, head straight to the market hall to join the locals round the colourful communal tables here. Bright pictures of market life and animals adorn the walls, and the menu makes use of the best market produce, ranging from plates of cheese (€4.80) to seafood platters (€35), with excellent-value *menus* from €12.80. Mon–Sat 8am–2pm.

**Chez Alphonse** 5 place de la Motte ☏ 05 55 34 34 14. Welcoming and very popular bistro, complete with red-check tablecloths and bustling waiters, which specializes in local, seasonal dishes, such as roast veal or rabbit *chasseur* (both €15.20). Mon–Sat noon–2pm & 7–11pm.

**Crêperie de la Cathédrale** 3 rue Haute-Cité ☏ 05 55 32 09 75, ⓦ creperiedelacathedrale.fr. One of a cluster of places to eat and drink on this attractive pedestrianized street, this little crêperie has an interesting range of *galettes*, including the "Sancy" with bleu d'Auvergne cheese, potatoes, and cured ham (€8.60). Daily 11.30am–11pm.

**La Nouvelle Louisiane** Rue Dalesme ☏ 05 55 34 10 34. A charming, modern little café and teashop, tucked down a side street near the church of St-Pierre-du-Queyroix. The small menu includes delicious salads (from €10.90), cakes and ice-cream sundaes, plus a decent range of tea and coffee. Tues–Sat 9.30am–7pm.

**Les Petits Ventres** 20 rue de la Boucherie ☏ 05 55 34 22 90, ⓦ les-petits-ventres.com. This elegant restaurant in a timbered, seventeenth-century building will delight lovers of brain, brawn, tongue and other unmentionable cuts – though they also do plenty of less challenging dishes. Lunch *menus* from €12.80, dinner *menus* from €26.50. Tues–Thurs noon–2pm & 7.30–9.30pm, Fri & Sat noon–2pm & 7.30–10pm.

### BARS

★ **Brasserie Michard** 8 place Denis Dussoubs ⓦ bieres-michard.com. A friendly microbrewery bar serving their own very decent beers – the Ambrée is particularly nice (€2.70). Enjoy either inside the large but cosy interior, or on the terrace overlooking the square. Tues–Sat 3.30pm–1am.

**Le Duc Étienne** 19 rue de la Boucherie. A relaxed, wood-timbered bar in the old quarter, which gets very busy and spills out into place St Aurelien on warm evenings. Daily 7pm–1am.

---

## LIMOGES FESTIVALS

In late September, there's an interesting and important gathering of writers, dramatists and musicians from other French-speaking countries at the **Festival International des Francophonies** (ⓦ lesfrancophonies.com). For one week in mid-August brass instruments take pride of place in the **Cuivres en Fête** music festival (ⓦ cuivres-en-fete.com), while gourmets of a certain persuasion should make sure their visit coincides with the third Friday in October for the **Frairie des Petits Ventres food fair**, when the entire population turns out to gorge on everything from pig's trotters to sheep's testicles in the rue de la Boucherie. In addition, there's **Urbaka**, a festival of street theatre held at the end of June (ⓦ urbaka.com), and the **Danse Emoi** contemporary dance festival every two years in January, the next being in 2014.

# Around Limoges

The countryside **around Limoges** may not have quite the same appeal as that further south, but it's peppered with interesting small towns and villages that make great day-trips from the city.

## Solignac and around

A dozen kilometres south of Limoges in the lovely wooded valley of the Briance, the village of **SOLIGNAC** is notable for its Romanesque church, and the nearby Château de Châlucet.

**10**

### The abbey church

Daily 9am–5.30pm

With the tiled roofs of its octagonal apse and neat little brood of radiating chapels, the **abbey church** of Solignac is utterly charming in its simplicity, striking a sturdy pose beside the main road through the village. The twelfth-century facade has little adornment, as the granite is too hard to permit intricate carving. Inside it's beautiful, with a flight of steps leading down into the nave with a dramatic view of the length of the church. There are no aisles, just a single space roofed with three big domes – an absolutely plain Latin cross in design.

### Château de Châlucet

5km east of Solignac • Daily: mid-March to mid-June & mid-Sept to mid-Nov 9.30am–12.30pm & 1.30–6pm; mid-June to mid-Sept 11am–6.30pm • €2 • No public transport

The **Château de Châlucet** is a good 5km up the valley of the Briance to the east of Solignac. At the highest point of the climb there is a dramatic view across the valley to the romantic, ruined keep of the castle, rising above the woods. Built in the twelfth century, the château was in English hands during the Hundred Years' War and, in the lawless aftermath, became the lair of a notorious local brigand, Perrot le Béarnais. It was dismantled in 1593 for harbouring Protestants and has been much restored recently. You can borrow an explanatory guide from the visitors' centre on the path up to the ruins.

### ARRIVAL AND DEPARTURE                                    SOLIGNAC AND AROUND

Note that no combination of public transport allows you to see Solignac as a day-trip from Limoges.

**By train** Trains from Brive (1–3 daily; 1hr 10min) and Limoges (1–3 daily; 9min) pull in at Solignac-Le Vigen station, 1km northeast of the village.

**By bus** Buses from Limoges (1–3 daily except Sun; 45min) arrive at place Georges Lemaigre Dubreuil, just a few minutes' walk north of the abbey.

## St-Léonard-de-Noblat

**ST-LÉONARD-DE-NOBLAT**, 20km east of Limoges, is an appealing little market town of narrow streets and medieval houses with jutting eaves and corbelled turrets. There's a very lovely eleventh- and twelfth-century church, with a six-storey tower, high dome and simple, barrel-vaulted interior – the whole in grey granite.

### HistoRail

8 rue de Beaufort • July & Aug Mon–Fri 10am–noon & 2–6pm • €5 • ⊕ historail.com

The little railway museum of **Historail** is completely charming; run entirely by volunteers, it boasts a fun collection of both full-sized and model trains through the ages. Outside, a specially erected model train set meanders through the flowers and around a small pond.

### ARRIVAL AND INFORMATION                                  ST-LÉONARD-DE-NOBLAT

**By train** St-Léonard's train station, around a 20min walk from the old town, is on the Limoges–Clermont Ferrand line. Destinations Clermont Ferrand (1–2 daily; 3hr 50min);

Eymoutiers (3–7 daily; 30min); Limoges (4–7 daily; 25min); Meymac (3–5 daily; 1hr 30min).

**By bus** SNCF bus #9 between Limoges (from place

Churchill, place Jourdan & the train station) and Felletin stops at St-Léonard's train station and in the town itself. **Destinations** Aubusson (1–2 daily; 1hr 10min); Limoges (2–4 daily; 30min).

**Tourist office** Place du Champs-de-Mars (April–June & Sept Mon–Sat 10am–12.15pm & 2.15–5.30pm; July & Aug Mon & Sat 10am–1pm & 2.30–6pm, Tues–Fri 10am–6.30pm, Sun 10am–12.30pm; Oct–March Mon & Wed–Sat 10am–12.15pm & 2.15–5pm, Tues 2.15–5pm; ☎ 05 55 56 25 06, ⓦ otsi-noblat.fr).

## ACCOMMODATION AND EATING

**Camping de Beaufort** Lieu-dit Beaufort ☎ 05 55 56 02 79, ⓦ campingdebeaufort.fr. A rather spruce campsite, in a lovely riverside position a couple of kilometres out of town on the D39, with a swimming pool, canoeing and fishing on site. **€13**

**Relais St-Jacques** 6 bd Adrien Pressemane ☎ 05 55 56 00 25, ⓦ lerelaissaintjacques.com. On the main boulevard that encircles the old town, this small hotel has just nine rooms, decked out smartly in earthy tones. The good restaurant (*menus* from €19.50) serves regional dishes including home-made foie gras. Restaurant May–Sept daily noon–2pm & 7–9pm; Oct–April Mon 7–9pm, Tues–Sat noon–2pm & 7–9pm, Sun noon–2pm. **€59**

# Oradour-sur-Glane

Some 25km northwest of Limoges, the village of **ORADOUR-SUR-GLANE** stands just as the soldiers of the SS left it on June 10, 1944, after killing 642 of the inhabitants in reprisal for attacks by French *maquisards*. On arriving, the SS took the men of the village into barns, where they opened fire with machine guns, deliberately aiming low to wound rather then kill, before setting the barns alight – only six men escaped, one of whom was shot dead shortly after. Meanwhile, the women and children were shepherded into the church, where a gas bomb was set off – when this failed, the soldiers let loose with machine guns and grenades, before, again, setting the church, and its inhabitants, and then the rest of the village, on fire. The entire village, which sits to the southeast of the modern village, has been preserved as a shrine.

### The Centre de la Mémoire

Daily: Feb & Nov to 15 Dec 9am–5pm; March to 15 May & 16 Sept to Oct 9am–6pm; 16 May to 15 Sept 9am–7pm; closed 16 Dec–Jan • Exhibition €7.80; audioguide €2 • ⓦ oradour.org • Buses from Limoges (Mon–Sat 3 daily; 35min)

It's well worth taking the time to visit the exhibition at the **Centre de la Mémoire**, which sets the historical context for the events of June 1944 and attempts to explain how – and why – such acts of brutality took place. Most of the displays are in French, but there's enough English translation and photographs to give a good sense of the content.

### The village

Daily: Feb & Nov to mid-Dec 9am–5pm; March to mid-May & mid-Sept to Oct 9am–6pm; mid-May to mid-Sept 9am–7pm • Free

Access to the **village** is only possible through the Centre de la Mémoire, though it's not necessary to visit the exhibition in order to do so. An underground passage leads from beside the ticket desk into the village itself, where a sign admonishes *Souviens-toi* ("Remember"), and the main street leads past roofless houses gutted by fire. Telephone poles, iron bedsteads and gutters are fixed in tormented attitudes where the fire's heat left them; prewar cars rust in the garages; cooking pots hang over empty grates; last year's grapes hang wizened on a vine whose trellis has long rotted away. To the north of the village a dolmen-like slab on a shallow plinth covers a crypt containing relics of the dead, and the awful list of names, while to the southeast, by the stream, stands the church where the women and children – five hundred of them – were burnt to death.

# Rochechouart

**ROCHECHOUART**, a lovely little walled town roughly 45km west of Limoges, is most famous for being the site, two million years ago, of one of the largest **meteorites** ever to hit earth, a monster 1.5km in diameter and weighing some 6 billion tonnes. The traces of this cosmic calamity still attract the curiosity of astronomers, though the only evidence that a layman might notice is the unusual-looking breccia stone many of the region's older buildings are made of: the squashed, shattered, heat-transformed and reconstituted result of the collision.

## Musée Départemental d'Art Contemporain

Daily except Tues: March–Sept 10am–12.30pm & 1.30–6pm; Oct to mid-Dec 10am–12.30pm & 2–5pm • €4.60 • ⓦ musee-rochechouart.com

One building using the stone from the impact is the handsome **château** that stands at the town's edge. It started life as a rough fortress before 1000 AD, was modernized in the thirteenth century (the sawn-off keep and entrance survive from this period) and embellished with Renaissance additions in the fifteenth. Until it was acquired as the *mairie* in 1832, it had belonged to the de Rochechouart family for 800 years. Today it houses not only the town hall, but also the very well-regarded **Musée Départemental d'Art Contemporain**, which includes an important collection of works by the Dadaist Raoul Haussmann, who died in Limoges in 1971. In another room, decorated with its original sixteenth-century frescoes of the Labours of Hercules, the British artist Richard Long has created a special installation of white stones, while in the garden Giuseppe Penone's metal sculpture grapples with a tree.

10

### ARRIVAL AND INFORMATION ROCHECHOUART

**By bus** Buses between Limoges and Rochechouart (daily except Sun; 1hr 20min) stop on rue Maurice Thorez, a short walk southeast of central place Octave-Marquet.

**Tourist office** 6 rue Victor-Hugo (July & Aug Mon–Sat 10am–12.30pm & 2.30–6pm; Sept–June Mon–Sat 10am–noon & 2–5pm; ☎ 05 55 03 72 73, ⓦ rochechouart.com).

### ACCOMMODATION

**De France** Place Octave-Marquet ☎ 05 55 03 77 40, ⓦ hoteldefrance-rochechouart.fr. This lovely blue-shuttered building has simple, if rather unexciting, rooms

above a decent restaurant that serves a menu of Limousin specialities (€20). **€42**

## Aubusson

A neat grey-stone town in the bottom of a ravine formed by the River Creuse, **AUBUSSON**, 85km east of Limoges, is mainly of interest as a centre for weaving **tapestries** – second only to the Gobelins works in Paris. In 2009, the town's tapestry was recognised by UNESCO on its list of intangible cultural heritage, and as a result schools have started teaching the craft for the first time in almost twenty years.

Two museums provide a good background; **Musée Départemental de la Tapisserie**, 16 av des Lissiers (July & Aug daily 10am–6pm; Sept–Dec & Feb–June daily except Tues 9.30am–noon & 2–6pm; €5; ⓦcite-tapisserie.com) charts the history of Aubusson tapestries over six centuries, up to the modern-day works of Jean Lurçat (see p.564), while the **Maison du Tapissier**, next to the tourist office on rue Vieille (Mon–Sat 9.30am–12.30pm & 2–6pm, Sun 10am–noon & 2.30–5.30pm; €5), gives an overview of weaving techniques and local history, displayed in the sixteenth-century home of a master weaver.

### ARRIVAL AND INFORMATION AUBUSSON

**By train** Aubusson's train station is just under 1km (about 10min walk) from the town centre; daily trains run to Limoges (1hr 50min).
**By bus** All buses, including services to Limoges (1–3 daily; 2hr 25min) and St-Léonard-de-Noblat (1–3 daily; 1hr

50min), stop at the *gare routière*, on the south side of the river on av des Lissiers.
**Tourist office** Rue Vieille (Mon–Sat 9.30am–1pm & 2–6.30pm, Sun 10am–noon & 2.30–5.30pm; ☎ 05 55 66 32 12, ⓦ tourisme-aubusson.fr).

### ACCOMMODATION AND EATING

**Le France** 6 rue des Déportés ☎ 05 55 66 10 22, ⓦaubussonlefrance.com. A charming hotel offering elegant rooms decorated in an unfussy mix of traditional

and contemporary styles. They have a decent formal restaurant (*menus* from €20), atmospherically set among bare stone walls. **€68**

**10**

# The Plateau de Millevaches

Millevaches (ⓦpnr-millevaches.fr), the plateau of a thousand springs, is undulating upland country rising to 800–900m in altitude, on the northern edge of the Massif Central, with a wild and sparsely populated landscape and villages few and far between. Those that do exist appear small, grey and sturdy, inured to the buffeting of upland weather. It's a magnificent country of conifer plantations and natural woodland – of beech, birch and chestnut – interspersed with reed-fringed tarns, man-made lakes and pasture grazed by sheep and cows, much of it now designated a **natural regional park**. It's an area to walk or cycle in, or at least savour at a gentle pace, stopping in the attractive, country inns scattered across the plateau.

The small towns, like **Eymoutiers** and **Meymac**, have a primitive architectural beauty and an old-world charm. Near Eymoutiers, the **Lac de Vassivière** offers all sorts of sports activities and a beautiful setting for a contemporary art museum.

## Lac de Vassivière and around

The man-made **Lac de Vassivière**, with 45km of indented shoreline, provides some lovely spots for walking and cycling. In summer, it is a popular destination for watersports enthusiasts, with opportunities for sailing, windsurfing and water skiing, among other activities. The jumping-off point for the lake, **EYMOUTIERS**, 45km southeast of Limoges, is an upland town of tall, narrow stone houses crowding round a much-altered Romanesque **church**.

### Centre International d'Art et du Paysage

Ile de Vassivière • June–Oct daily 11am–7pm; Nov–June Tues–Sun 11am–1pm & 2–6pm • €3 • ☎ 05 55 69 27 27, ⓦ ciapiledevassiviere.com

An island in the Lac de Vassivière, accessible by causeway, provides a wonderful home for the **Centre International d'Art et du Paysage**, a contemporary art centre where many of the pieces lie scattered among the trees. There's also a hall hosting temporary exhibitions and a café where you can get light meals while admiring the views (May–Sept daily).

## ARRIVAL AND DEPARTURE                                  LAC DE VASSIVIÈRE AND AROUND

**By train** Eymoutiers-Vassivière train station, just a few minutes' walk north of Eymoutiers centre, is served by trains on the Limoges–Clermont Ferrand line.
Destinations Clermont Ferrand (2 daily; 3hr 15min); Limoges (3–7 daily; 1hr); Meymac (2–5 daily; 1hr); St-Léonard-de-Noblat (3–7 daily; 30min).
**Getting to the lake** Getting to Lac de Vassivière by public transport is only possible between 31 March and

4 November, when TER run "Passouvert" services from Limoges. The €5 fare includes the round-trip journey by train (depart 10am) to Eymoutiers, and then on by bus to the lake. It's also possible to pick up the Passouvert in Eymoutiers (€2; depart 11am). Buses make the return journey at 6.20pm, though you should check all times online (ⓦ lelacdevassiviere.com) for up-to-date details.

## INFORMATION

**Tourist office** Maison de Vassivière in Auphelle, on the western shore of the lake (April–Sept daily 9.30am–noon & 2–5pm; July & Aug daily 10am–12.30pm & 2.30–7pm;

Oct–March Mon–Fri 9.30am–noon & 2–5pm; ☎ 05 55 69 76 70, ⓦ lelacdevassiviere.com).

## ACCOMMODATION

There are six campsites around the lake, three of which are municipally run (ⓦ campings.lelacdevassiviere.com).

**La Caravelle** Port de Crozat ☎ 05 55 57 06 75, ⓦ la -caravelle-vassiviere.com. The rooms at this lakeside hotel are rather old-fashioned and fussy, but all benefit from their own private balcony or terrace with fabulous lake views. **€80**
**Les Cerisiers** 14 rue Pierre et Marie Curie, Eymoutiers

☎ 05 55 69 68 32, ⓦ lescerisiers87.com. A charming B&B run by two Brits, set in a lovely old townhouse just a short walk from the centre of Eymoutiers. There are just two simple but very pleasant bedrooms, plus a lovely garden and a dining room with a log-burning stove. Three-course dinners are available for €20. **€48**

**St-Pierre Château** Rue de Saint Pierre Château, 2km southeast of Eymoutiers off the Bugeat road ☎ 05 55 69 27 81, ✉ ot.eymoutiers@orange.fr. A simple campsite, magnificently sited on a hill, with lots of pleasant, shady spots beneath the trees. June–Sept. **€6.50**

**Les Terrasses du Lac** Vauveix ☎ 05 55 64 76 77, ⊛ campings.lelacdevassiviere.com. In a prime position right by the lake, with beautiful views from the best pitches, this quiet campsite is particularly popular with families, though it's generally quiet and relaxed. **€16.50**

## Meymac

**10**

Pepper-pot turrets and steep slate roofs adorn the ancient grey houses of **MEYMAC**, 50km southeast of Eymoutiers, on the southern fringes of the plateau. The village is packed tightly around its Romanesque church and the Benedictine **abbey**, whose foundation a thousand years ago brought the town into being. In the abbey, the innovative **Centre National d'Art Contemporain** (Tues–Sun: July to mid-Sept 10am–1pm & 2–7pm; mid-Sept to June 2–6pm; €4; ⊛ centre-art-contemporain-meymac.com), features changing exhibitions of young, local artists as well as big-name retrospectives. It's also worth popping into the adjacent **Musée de la Fondation Marius Vazeilles** (mid-April to June, Sept & Oct Tues, Wed & Fri–Sun 2.30–6pm; July & Aug Tues–Sun 10am–noon & 2.30–6.30pm; €4; ⊛ mariusvazeilles.fr) to learn about the history and traditions of the plateau.

### ARRIVAL AND DEPARTURE

MEYMAC

**By train** The station is 1km north of the town centre. To get into town, follow av du Jassonneix until you reach the first crossroads; a left onto rue des Horts de Celle will take you onto the Grande Rue.

Destinations Brive-la-Gaillarde (3–7 daily; 1hr 20min);

Clermont-Ferrand (2–3 daily; 1hr 45min); Eymoutiers (3–5 daily; 1hr); St-Léonard-de-Noblat (3–5 daily; 1hr 30min).

**Tourist office** Place de l'Hôtel de Ville (Mon–Sat 10am–12.30pm & 2–6.20pm, Sun 10–12.20pm; ☎ 05 55 95 18 43, ⊛ tourismemeymac.fr).

### ACCOMMODATION

**Chez Françoise** 24 rue Fotaine du Rat ☎ 05 55 95 10 63, ⊛ chezfrancoise.fr. This charming small hotel has just four rooms, attractively set in a sixteenth-century tower and decorated with antique furniture. They also run a

well-respected restaurant serving local specialities (menus €13.50–35), with a vast wine list. Restaurant Tues–Sat noon–2pm & 7–9pm, Sun noon–2pm. **€60**

# Brive-la-Gaillarde and around

**BRIVE-LA-GAILLARDE** is a major rail junction and the nearest thing to an industrial centre for miles around. Nevertheless, it has an attractive old centre and makes an agreeable base for exploring the Corrèze *département* and its beautiful villages, as well as the upper reaches of the Vézère and Dordogne rivers. Numerous streets fan out from the central square, **place du Général-de-Gaulle**, home to a number of turreted and towered houses, some dating back to the thirteenth century.

### Church of St-Martin

Place du Général-de-Gaulle

At Brive's centre is the much-restored **church of St-Martin**, originally Romanesque in style, though only the transept, apse and a few comically carved capitals survive from that era. St Martin himself, a Spanish aristocrat, arrived in pagan Brive in 407 AD on the feast of Saturnus, smashed various idols and was promptly stoned to death by the outraged onlookers.

### Musée Labenche

26bis bd Jules Ferry • Daily except Tues: April–Oct 10am–6.30pm; Nov–March 1.30–6pm • €5 • ⊛ brive.fr/12170.php

One of the town's most impressive buildings is the sixteenth-century Hôtel de Labenche, now the **Musée Labenche**. The museum traces the history of Brive with a number of different displays, including the town's archeological finds and a fine collection of seventeenth-century tapestries.

## Turenne

**TURENNE**, just 16km south of Brive, was capital of the viscountcy of Turenne, whose most illustrious seigneur was Henri de la Tour d'Auvergne – the "Grand Turenne", born 1611, whom Napoleon rated the finest tactician of modern times. Mellow stone houses crowd in the lee of the sharp bluff on whose summit sprout two towers, all that remains of the castle.

### The château

April–June, Sept & Oct daily 10am–noon & 2–6pm; July & Aug daily 10am–7pm; Nov–March Sun 2–5pm • €4.50 • ⓦ château-turenne.com

Though little remains of Turenne's **château**, it is possible to visit one of the towers, the Tour de César, and the beautiful gardens that surround it. The real reason to climb up here, however, is for the fabulous views over the surrounding countryside. Two routes lead to the château – the steepest leads directly through the pretty village, or follow the road that curves around the hill, which will take you past the attractive church before coming to the château itself.

## Collonges-la-Rouge

With its red-sandstone houses, pepper-pot towers and pink-candled chestnut trees, **COLLONGES-LA-ROUGE**, 7km east of Turenne, is the epitome of rustic charm – but make sure you get here early in the day, or after 5pm, to avoid the crowds. Though small-scale, there's a certain grandeur about the place, befitting the status of the resident Turenne administrators. On the main square a twelfth-century **church** testifies to the imbecility of shedding blood over religious differences: in the sixteenth century, Protestant and Catholic conducted their services here simultaneously, side by side. Outside, the covered **market hall** still retains its old-fashioned baker's oven.

## ARRIVAL AND DEPARTURE

### BRIVE-LA-GAILLARDE

**By plane** Brive Dordogne Valley Airport (ⓣ 05 55 22 40 00, ⓦ aeroport-brive-vallee-dordogne.com) is 13km south of town.

Destinations Ajaccio (21 April to 15 Sept weekly; 1hr 45min); London City (2–6 weekly; 1hr 35min); Paris Orly (Sun–Fri 1–3 daily; 1hr 25min).

**By train** The *gare SNCF* is at the top of av Jean-Jaurès, a 5min walk south of the Old Town.

Destinations Bordeaux (2–4 daily; 1hr 40min); Cahors (7–9 daily; 1hr 10min); Carcassonne (daily; 3hr 10min); Figeac (2–5 daily; 1hr 20min); Gourdon (7–9 daily; 40min); Limoges (12–14 daily; 1hr); Meymac (4–6 daily; 1hr 30min); Montauban (7–9 daily; 1hr 55min); Narbonne (daily; 3hr 45min); Paris Austerlitz (7 daily; 4hr 20min); Périgueux (2–4 daily; 15min); Perpignan (daily; 4hr 45min); Rocamadour-Padirac (2–5 daily; 40min);

## BRIVE-LA-GAILLARDE AND AROUND

Solignac-le-Vigen (Mon–Sat 3 daily; 1hr 10min); Souillac (7–9 daily; 25min); Toulouse (7–9 daily; 2hr 35min); Turenne (Mon–Sat daily; 15min)

**By bus** The *gare routière* is on place 14-juillet.

Destinations Beaulieu-sur-Dordogne (1–2 daily; 1hr); Collonges la Rouge (Mon–Fri 1–3 daily; 40min); Montignac (3 daily; 1hr 30min); Turenne (Mon–Fri 1–2 daily; 35min).

### TURENNE

**By bus** Buses to and from Brive (Mon–Fri 1–2 daily; 35min) and Collonges-la-Rouge (Mon–Fri 1–2 daily; 8min) stop on the main road, close to the tourist office.

### COLLONGES-LA-ROUGE

**By bus** Buses from Brive (Mon–Sat 1–3 daily; 40min) and Turenne (Mon–Fri 1–2 daily; 8min) stop on the main road at the top of the village, near the permit holders' car park.

## INFORMATION

### BRIVE-LA-GAILLARDE

**Tourist office** Place 14-juillet (April–June & Sept Mon–Sat 9am–12.30pm & 1.30–6.30pm; July & Aug Mon–Sat 9am–7pm, Sun 11–5pm; Oct–March Mon–Sat 9am–noon & 2–6pm; ⓣ 05 55 24 08 80, ⓦ brive-tourisme.com).

### TURENNE

**Tourist office** On the main road, close to the road that leads up into the village (June & Sept Tues–Sun 10am–12.30pm & 3–6pm; July & Aug daily 9.30am–12.30pm & 2.30–6.30pm; Oct–May Fri–Sun 10am–noon & 2–5pm; ⓣ 05 55 24 08 80).

## ACCOMMODATION

### BRIVE-LA-GAILLARDE

**L'Andréa** 39 av Jean-Jaurès ☎ 05 55 74 11 84, ⓦ hotel-andrea.fr. Just down the road from the station, this is one of Brive's better cheapies, with pleasant rooms, a small garden terrace and a cosy bar-restaurant. **€35**

**Auberge de Jeunesse** 56 av de Marechal Bugeaud ☎ 05 55 24 34 00, ⓦ FUAJ.org/Brive-la-Gaillarde. In a grand old mansion just a short walk from the centre, this is a fairly standard FUAJ hostel, with a kitchen for guests' use and dorms sleeping three or four people; the selling point, however, is the lovely garden. **€14.60**

**Le Collonges** 3 place Winston-Churchill ☎ 05 55 74 09 58, ⓦ hotel-collonges.com. A welcoming, family-run place, with comfortable, unfussy rooms, just across the ring road from the old town. The terrace is a good spot for a cold drink. **€63**

**La Truffe Noir** 22 bd Anatole-France ☎ 05 55 92 45 00, ⓦ la-truffe-noire.com. Brive's grandest hotel, though its position on the ring road around the old town leaves something to be desired. Despite the impressive lobby, the rooms are ordinary, though they're well equipped and air-conditioned. **€117**

### TURENNE

**La Maison des Chanoines** ☎ 05 55 85 93 43, ⓦ maison-des-chanoines.com. This lovely little hotel is housed in one of Turenne's most beautiful buildings, which dates back to the sixteenth century. The homely (if a little old-fashioned) rooms feature floral fabrics and dark wood furniture, with an attractive garden terrace on the other side of the small cobbled street. **€70**

## EATING AND DRINKING

### BRIVE-LA-GAILLARDE

★ **Bistrot Chambon** 8 rue des Echevins ☎ 05 55 22 36 83. Bustling, contemporary corner bistro serving elegant but unpretentious food. At lunch, the dish of the day, which ranges from veal escalope with tagliatelle to steak with bearnaise sauce, will set you back just €10 with coffee – though be sure to leave room for the heavenly desserts. Dinner *menus* from €28. Tues–Thurs noon–2pm & 7.15–9.30pm, Fri & Sat noon–2pm & 7.15–10.15pm.

**Le Corrèze** 3 rue de Corrèze ☎ 05 55 24 14 07. Usually packed with locals, this small restaurant offers a cheap and cheerful menu with lots of local specialities, includng the ubiquitous *magret de canard*. Lunch *menus* from €7.50. Mon–Sat noon–2pm & 7–10.15pm.

**Les Viviers St-Martin** 4 rue Traversière ☎ 05 55 92 14 15, ⓦ les-viviers.fr. Tucked down an alley near St-Martin, this cosy restaurant offers more interesting choices than most, with lots of fresh fish. Lunch menu from €12, dinner from €26. Daily noon–2pm & 7–10pm.

# The Dordogne

To the French, the **Dordogne** is a river. To the British, it is a much looser term, covering a vast area roughly equivalent to what the French call Périgord, which starts south of Limoges and includes the Vézère and Dordogne valleys. The Dordogne is also a *département*, with fixed boundaries that pay no heed to either definition. The central part of the *département*, around Périgueux and the River Isle, is known as **Périgord Blanc**, after the light, white colour of its rock outcrops; the southeastern half around Sarlat as **Périgord Noir**, said to be darker in aspect because of the preponderance of oak woods. To confuse matters further, the tourist authorities have added another two colours to the Périgord patchwork: **Périgord Vert**, the far north of the *département*, so called because of the green of its woods and pastureland; and **Périgord Pourpre** in the southwest, purple because it includes the wine-growing area around Bergerac.

This southern region is also known for its **bastides** – fortified towns – built during the turbulent medieval period when there was almost constant conflict between the French and English. In the reaches of the **upper Dordogne**, the colour scheme breaks down, but the villages and scenery in this less travelled backwater still rival anything the rest of the region has to offer.

## Périgord Vert

The close green valleys of **Périgord Vert** are very rural, with plenty of space and few people, large tracts of wood and uncultivated land. Less well known than the

Périgord Noir, its largely granite landscape bears a closer resemblance to the neighbouring Limousin than to the rest of the Périgord. It's partly for this reason that in 1998 the most northerly tip, together with the southwestern part of the Haute-Vienne, was designated as the **Parc Naturel Régional Périgord-Limousin** in an attempt to promote "green" tourism in this economically fragile and depopulated area.

It's undoubtedly in the countryside that the region's finest monuments lie. One of the loveliest stretches is the **valley of the Dronne**, from **Aubeterre** on the Charente border through **Brantôme** to the marvellous Renaissance château of **Puyguilhem** and the picture-postcard village of **St-Jean-de-Côle**, and on to the Limousin border, where the scenery becomes higher and less intimate.

## Brantôme

The picturesque old town of **BRANTÔME** sits on an island in the River Dronne, whose still, water-lilied surface mirrors the limes and weeping willows of the riverside gardens. The countryside that surrounds the town, along the **River Dronne**, remains largely undisturbed, though Brantôme itself is firmly on the tourist trail. This is one of the most tranquil and beautiful parts of the Dordogne, best savoured at a gentle pace, perhaps by bike, on a **boat trip**, or even by canoeing along the river.

---

### THE FOOD AND WINE OF PÉRIGORD

The two great stars of Périgord cuisine are **foie gras** and **truffles** (*truffes*). Foie gras is best eaten either chilled in succulent, buttery slabs, or lightly fried and served with a fruit compote to provide contrasting sweetness and acidity. Truffle is often dished up in omelettes and the rich *périgourdin* sauces which accompany many local meat dishes, but to appreciate the delicate earthy flavour to the full, you really need to eat truffle on its own, with just a salad and some coarse, country bread.

The other mainstay of Périgord cuisine is the grey Toulouse **goose**, whose fat is used in the cooking of everything, including the flavourful potato dish, *pommes sarladaises*. The goose fattens well: *gavé* or crammed with corn, it goes from six to ten kilos in weight in three weeks, with its liver alone weighing nearly a kilo. Some may find the process off-putting, but small local producers are very careful not to harm their birds, if for no other reason than that stress ruins the liver. Geese are also raised for their meat alone, which is cooked and preserved in its own thick yellow grease as *confits d'oie*, which you can either eat on its own or use in the preparation of other dishes, like cassoulet. **Duck** is used in the same way, both for foie gras and *confits*. *Magret de canard*, or duck-breast fillet, is one of the favourite ways of eating duck and appears on practically every restaurant menu.

Another goose delicacy is *cou d'oie farci* – goose neck stuffed with sausage meat, duck liver and truffles, while a favourite salad throughout the region is made with warm *gésiers* or goose gizzards. Try not to be apprehensive, or your palate will miss out on some delicious experiences – like *tripoux*, sheep's stomach stuffed with tripe, trotters, pork and garlic, which is really an Auvergnat dish but is quite often served in neighbouring areas like the Rouergue. Other less challenging specialities include stuffed *cèpes*, or wild mushrooms; *ballottines*, fillets of poultry stuffed, rolled and poached; the little flat discs of goat's cheese known as *cabécou* or *rocamadour*; and for dessert there's *pastis*, a light apple tart topped with crinkled, wafer-thin pastry laced with armagnac.

The **wines** should not be scorned, either. There are the fine, dark, almost peppery reds from Cahors, and both reds and whites from the vineyards of Bergerac, of which the sweet, white Monbazillac is the most famous. Pécharmant is the fanciest of the reds, but there are some very drinkable Côtes de Bergerac, much like the neighbouring Bordeaux and far cheaper. The same goes for the wines of Duras, Marmande and Buzet. If you're thinking of taking a stock of wine home, you could do much worse than make some enquiries in Bergerac itself, Ste-Foy, or any of the villages in the vineyard areas.

## The abbey

North bank of the river; access through the tourist office (see below) • Caves & museum Feb, March & mid-Oct to Dec daily except Tues 10am–noon & 2–7pm; April–June & Sept to mid-Oct daily 10am–6pm; July & Aug daily 10am–7pm • €4.50

Brantôme's former **Benedictine abbey** has been the town's focus ever since it was founded, possibly by Charlemagne. Its most notorious abbot, Pierre de Bourdeilles, was the sixteenth-century author of scurrilous tales of life at the royal court.

The first monastery on the site is thought to have been troglodytic in origin, and the caves against which the later abbey was built were initially very important for worship, but over time were relegated to outhouses and storage. The **caves** here are arguably the most fascinating feature of the abbey; they're hugely atmospheric, not least the Last Judgement Cave, where the origins of the huge bas-relief remain an enigma, but is thought to date back to the fifteenth century. Admission also includes entry to the **Musée Fernand Desmoulin**, dedicated to the illustrator and painter best remembered for the 75 drawings he did between 1900 and 1902, apparently under the influence of three different spirits – the drawings, especially compared to Desmoulin's non-spirit work, are surprisingly modern, and some are undeniably eerie.

10

### ARRIVAL AND DEPARTURE

### BRANTÔME

**By bus** Buses between Angoulême (1–3 daily; 1hr 5min) and Périgueux (1–3 daily; 35min) stop in front of the gendarmerie on av Docteur Devillard, just a couple of minutes' walk southeast of the town centre.

### INFORMATION AND TOURS

**Tourist office** Hôtel de Ville, next to the abbey church (Feb, March & mid-Oct to Dec daily except Tues 10am–noon & 2–5pm; April–June & Sept to mid-Oct daily 10am–6pm; July & Aug daily 10am–7pm; ☎05 53 05 80 52, ⓦperigord-dronne-belle.fr).

**Boat trips** One nice thing to do is hire a mini version of a traditional wooden river boat for a brief, leisurely trip up the Dronne. Pick them up at Les Petit Gabarres (Easter–June, Sept & Oct Sat & Sun 10.30am–6.30pm; July & Aug daily 10.30am–6.30pm; ☎05 53 06 93 17; €3/person) at the southern end of the shaded Monks' Gardens, on the west bank of the river.

**Canoe rental** Allo Canoës, bd Coligny (from €5/person; ☎05 53 06 31 85, ⓦallocanoes.com).

### ACCOMMODATION

**Coligny** 8 place de Gaulle ☎05 53 05 71 42, ⓦhotel-coligny.fr. A pleasant hotel facing the river, with eight surprisingly contemporary rooms, decked out in soothing earth colours. The restaurant has a lovely riverside terrace that's a great spot for a drink. **€60**

★ **Les Jardins de Brantôme** 33 rue de Mareuil ☎05 53 05 88 16, ⓦlesjardinsdebrantome.com. With elegant, individually decorated rooms staggered up a gentle hillside, just a short walk from the town centre, *Les Jardins de Brantôme* offers the kind of sophisticated, unstuffy accommodation that you don't often find in rural France, and there's a small, lovely pool that catches the afternoon sun. It's run by a friendly husband and wife team

– he's the chef at their restaurant (see below). **€130**

**Maison Fleurie** 54 rue Gambetta ☎05 53 35 17 04, ⓦmaison-fleurie.net. A charming, English-owned *chambres d'hôte* with sweet country-style rooms and a quiet courtyard garden and pool. They also have a small self-catering property (sleeps 2–3; €750/week) in a converted water mill nearby. **€70**

**Le Peyrelevade** 1km east of Brantôme on the D78 Thiviers road ☎08 25 00 20 30, ⓦcamping-dordogne.net. A very pleasant campsite, set among lovely wooded grounds, with both a heated swimming pool and its own private riverside beach. Closed mid-Sept to mid-May. **€19**

### EATING AND DRINKING

**Le Bar du Marché** 16 rue Victor Hugo ☎05 53 05 80 49. The colourful tables spilling out the front of this café across the river from the abbey make it a popular choice on sunny days. The menu covers all the usual Perigordian specialities, plus more basic lunch dishes like *croque monsieur* (€5). Daily 10am–10pm.

★ **Les Jardins de Brantôme** 33 rue de Mareuil ☎05 53 05 88 16, ⓦlesjardinsdebrantome.com.

Arguably the best place to eat in town, serving sublime, seasonal food beneath the trees in their lovely garden at lunch and in their unfussy beamed dining room at dinner. *Menus* (€26–40) may include seared scallops with chorizo, *magret de canard*, and warm chocolate and caramel cake, all set off by utterly charming service. Mon, Tues, Thurs & Fri 7–9pm, Sat & Sun noon–2pm & 7–9pm; call to check hours out of season.

## Bourdeilles

**BOURDEILLES**, 16km down the Dronne from Brantôme by a beautiful back road, is a sleepy backwater. Its shady riverbanks are perfect for picnics, with trees drooping leisurely into the water. The ancient village clusters round its château set on a rocky spur above the river; at the other end of rue d'Eglise, the lovely terraced gardens next to the church offer beautiful views over the water-lily-strewn river and the château and houses that line it.

### The château

11 Feb to 7 April & 8 Nov to 31 Dec Sun–Thurs 10am–12.30pm & 2–5pm; 8 April to 7 July & Sept to 7 Nov daily except Tues 10am–1pm & 2–6pm; 8 July–Aug daily 10am–7pm • €6 • ⍟ semitour.com

Bourdeilles' **château** consists of two buildings: one a thirteenth-century fortress, the other an elegant Renaissance residence begun by the lady of the house as a piece of unsuccessful favour-currying with Catherine de Médici – unsuccessful because Catherine never came to stay and the château remained unfinished. Climb the octagonal keep for a good view over the town's clustered roofs and along the valley of the Dronne.

The château is now home to an exceptional collection of **furniture** and **religious statuary** bequeathed to the state by its former owners. Among the more notable pieces are some splendid Spanish dowry chests and a sixteenth-century Rhenish Entombment with life-sized statues, embodying the very image of the serious, self-satisfied medieval burgher. The *salon doré*, the room in which de Médici was supposed to sleep, has also been preserved.

### ARRIVAL AND DEPARTURE                                       BOURDEILLES

**By car** There's no public transport to Bourdeilles; parking (free) is available outside the Hôtel de Ville, across the river from the *Hostellerie Les Griffons*.

### ACCOMMODATION AND EATING

**Hostellerie Le Donjon** Place de la Halle ☎ 05 53 04 82 81, ⍟ hostellerie-ledonjon.fr. This appealing hotel on the main street offers views of the château from some of its rooms, all of which are arranged around a charming courtyard. The courtyard restaurant is a lovely spot for dinner. Closed mid-Nov to Easter. Restaurant daily except Mon noon–2.30pm & 7–9.30pm. **€60**

**Hostellerie Les Griffons** ☎ 05 53 45 45 35, ⍟ griffons.fr. Bourdeilles' most upmarket option, set in a lovely sixteenth-century house beside the old bridge. Rooms are hugely atmospheric, with original features like wood beams and bare stone walls. The restaurant serves top-notch regional cuisine (*menus* from €35). Closed Nov–Easter. Restaurant Mon–Sat 7–9pm, Sun noon–2pm & 7–9pm. **€115**

## Aubeterre-sur-Dronne

Rather touristy, but very beautiful with its ancient galleried and turreted houses, **AUBETERRE-SUR-DRONNE** hangs on a steep hillside above the river some 30km downstream of Ribérac. South of Aubeterre the country gradually changes. Farmland gives way to an extensive forest of oak and sweet chestnut, bracken and broom, interspersed with sour, marshy pasture, and is very sparsely populated. It's ideal cycling and picnicking country.

### Église Monolithe

Daily 9.30am–12.30pm & 2–6pm • €5

Aubeterre's principal curiosity is the cavernous **Église Monolithe**, carved out of the soft rock of the cliff face in the twelfth century, with its rock-hewn tombs going back to the sixth. A (blocked-off) tunnel connects with the **château** on the bluff overhead.

### Church of St-Jacques

Following the road through the village and up the hill from central place Trarieur brings you to the extremely beautiful church of **St-Jacques**, with its eleventh-century facade sculpted and decorated in the richly carved Poitiers style. The interior is barely adorned, and all the more atmospheric in its simplicity.

**By bus** A daily bus runs to and from Angoulême, from a bus stop near the tourist office.

**Tourist office** 8 place du Champ de Foire, beside the main car park (April–June, Sept & Oct Mon–Sat 10am–noon & 2–6pm; July & Aug Mon 2–7pm, Tues–Sun 10am–12.30pm & 2–7pm; Nov–March Mon–Fri 2–6pm; ☎ 05 45 98 57 18, ⓦ aubeterresurdronne.com).

## ACCOMMODATION

**Aubeterre Plage Camping** Rte de Riberac ☎ 05 45 98 60 17, ⓦ camping-aubeterre.fr. This campsite has an enviable position by the river, at the foot of Aubeterre, with a sandy beach, pleasant pitches, and plenty of space to run around. **€15.90**

**Hostellerie du Périgord** Rte de Riberac, beside the bridge ☎ 05 45 98 50 46, ⓦ hostellerie-perigord .com. It's a steep walk up the hill to the centre of the village from here, but this is a lovely place to stay, with comfortable, modern rooms. There's an outdoor pool, spa and fitness room, and a smart restaurant serving local specialities. **€65**

## St-Jean-de-Côle

**ST-JEAN-DE-CÔLE**, 20km northeast of Brantôme, ranks as one of the loveliest villages in the Dordogne. Its ancient houses huddle together in typical medieval fashion around a wide sandy square dominated by the charmingly ill-proportioned eleventh-century **church of St-Jean-Baptiste** and the rugged-looking **Château de la Marthonie** (May–Sept 3 tours daily from the tourist office; €1.50). The château, which dates from the twelfth century, has acquired various additions in a pleasingly organic fashion.

**By car** There is no public transport to St-Jean-de-Côle. Parking is available along the main road or behind the *mairie*.

**Tourist office** On the main square (mid-June to mid-Sept daily 10am–12.30pm & 2–6.30pm; mid-Sept to mid-June Thurs–Sun 10am–1pm & 2–6pm; ☎ 05 53 62 14 15, ⓦ ville-saint-jean-de-cole.fr).

## EATING

**La Perla** Place de l'Eglise ☎ 05 53 52 38 11. An attractive restaurant opposite the château, with its outside tables the perfect place to soak up the sun over lunch. *Menus* (from €14.50), include the usual range of duck-based dishes. May, June & Sept Wed–Sun 10am–10pm, July & Aug daily 10am–10pm.

## Château de Puyguilhem

Villars, around 10km west of St-Jean-de-Côle · April & Sept 10am–12.30pm & 2–5.30pm; May–Aug daily 10am–12.30pm & 2–6.30pm; Oct–March Wed–Sun 10am–12.30pm & 2–5.30pm · €5.50 · ⓦ puyguilhem.monuments-nationaux.fr

Just outside the village of **VILLARS**, the **Château de Puyguilhem** sits on the edge of a valley backed by oak woods. It was erected at the beginning of the sixteenth century on the site of an earlier military fortress. With its octagonal tower, broad spiral staircase, steep roofs, magnificent fireplaces and false dormer windows, it's a perfect example of French Renaissance architecture. From the gallery at the top of the stairs you get a close-up of the roof and window decoration, as well as a view down the valley, which once was filled by an ornamental lake.

## Grotte de Villars

North of Villars · Daily: April–June & Sept 10am–noon & 2–7pm; July & Aug 10am–7.30pm; Oct 2–6.30pm · €7.50 · ⓦ grotte-villars.com

The **Grotte de Villars**, north or the village of the same name, boasts a few prehistoric paintings – notably of horses, and a still unexplained scene of a man and a bison. The main reason for coming here, however, is to see the impressive array of stalactites and stalagmites.

## Château de Hautefort

40km east of Périgueux · March & 1–11 Nov Sat & Sun 2–6pm; April & May daily 10am–12.30pm & 2–6.30pm; June–Aug daily 9.30am–7pm; Sept daily 10am–6pm; Oct daily 2–6pm · €8.50 · ⓦ château-hautefort.com

Forty kilometres east of Périgueux (take the D5 along the River Auvézère for the most

**10**

attractive route), the **Château de Hautefort** enjoys a majestic position at the end of a wooded spur above its feudal village. A magnificent example of good living on a grand scale, the castle has an elegance that is out of step with the usual rough stone fortresses of Périgord. The approach is across a wide esplanade flanked by formal gardens, over a drawbridge, and into a stylish Renaissance courtyard, open to the south. In 1968 a fire gutted the castle, but it has since been meticulously restored using traditional techniques; it's all unmistakably new, but the quality of the craftsmanship is superb.

**10**

# Périgueux

**PÉRIGUEUX**, capital of the *département* of the Dordogne and a central base for exploring the countryside of Périgord Blanc, is a small, busy market town with an attractive medieval and Renaissance core of stone-flagged squares and narrow alleys harbouring richly ornamented merchants' houses. The main hub of the modern town is the tree-shaded **boulevard Montaigne**, which marks the western edge of the *vieille ville*.

**Place de la Clautre** sits at the heart of the renovated streets of the medieval town, the most attractive of which is the narrow **rue Limogeanne**, lined with Renaissance mansions, now turned into boutiques and delicatessens, intermingled with fast-food outlets. Roman Périgueux, known as **La Cité**, lies to the west of the town centre towards the train station.

### Cathédrale St-Front
Place de la Clautre

The square, pineapple-capped belfry of the domed and coned **Cathédrale St-Front** surges far above the roofs of the surrounding medieval houses. It's no beauty, having suffered from the attentions of the nineteenth-century restorer Abadie, best known for the white elephant of Paris's Sacré-Coeur. The result is an excess of ill-proportioned, nipple-like projections – a pity, since when it was rebuilt in 1173 following a fire, it was one of the most distinctive Byzantine churches in France, modelled on St Mark's in Venice and the Holy Apostles in Constantinople. Nevertheless, the Byzantine influence is still evident in the interior in the Greek-cross plan – unusual in France – and in the massive clean curves of the domes and their supporting arches. The big Baroque altarpiece, carved in walnut wood in the gloomy east bay, is worth a look, too, depicting the Assumption of the Virgin, with a humorous little detail in the illustrative scenes from her life of a puppy tugging the infant Jesus's sheets from his bed with its teeth.

### Musée d'Art et d'Archéologie du Périgord
Cours Tourny • April–Sept Mon & Wed–Fri 10.30am–5.30pm, Sat & Sun 1–6pm; Oct–March Mon & Wed–Fri 10am–5pm, Sat & Sun 1–6pm • €4.50 • ⓦ musee-perigord.museum.com

The **Musée d'Art et d'Archéologie du Périgord** is best known for its extensive and important prehistoric collection and some beautiful Gallo-Roman mosaics. Exhibits include copies of a 70,000-year-old skeleton, the oldest yet found in France, and a beautiful engraving of a bison's head.

### Musée Gallo-Romain Vesunna
La Cité • April–June & Sept Tues–Fri 9.30am–5.30pm, Sat & Sun 10am–12.30pm & 2.30–6pm; July & Aug daily 10am–7pm; Oct–March Tues–Fri 9.30am–12.30pm & 1.30–5pm, Sat & Sun 10am–12.30pm & 2.30–6pm • €6 • ⓦ vesunna.fr

West of town, in **La Cité**, the most prominent vestige of Roman Périgueux is the high brick **Tour de Vésone**, the last remains of a temple to the city's guardian goddess, standing in a public garden just south of the train tracks. Beside the tower, the foundations of an exceptionally well-preserved Roman villa form the basis of the **Musée Gallo-Romain Vesunna**. This was no humble abode: the villa, complete with under-floor heating, thermal baths and colonnaded walkways around the central garden with its cooling pond and fountains, boasted at least sixty rooms. You can see the remains of

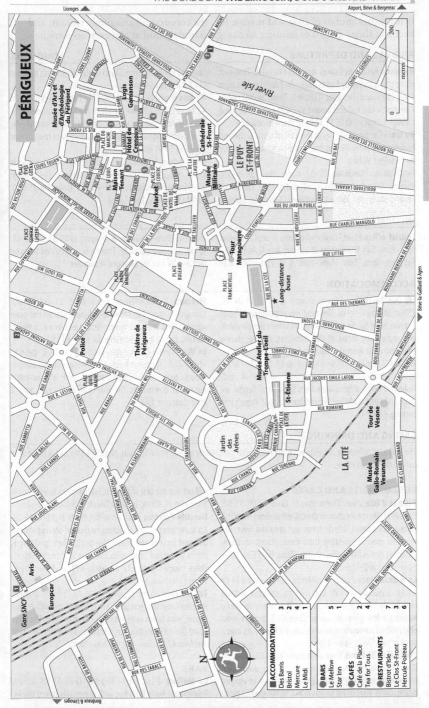

**PÉRIGUEUX**

Liomges ▲

Airport, Brive & Bergerac ▲

River Isle

**10**

Brive-la-Gaillard & Agen ▼

Gare SNCF

Bordeaux & Limoges ▼

**N**

0 — 200
metres

**ACCOMMODATION**
| | |
|---|---|
| Des Barris | 3 |
| Bristol | 2 |
| Mercure | 4 |
| Le Midi | 1 |

**BARS**
| | |
|---|---|
| Le Mellow | 5 |
| Star Inn | 1 |

**CAFÉS**
| | |
|---|---|
| Café de la Place | 4 |
| Tea for Tous | 1 |

**RESTAURANTS**
| | |
|---|---|
| Bistrot d'Isle | 7 |
| Le Clos St-Front | 3 |
| Hercule Poireau | 6 |

**10**

first-century murals of river and marine life, the colours still amazingly vibrant, and here and there, graffiti of hunting scenes, gladiatorial combat and even an ostrich.

## ARRIVAL AND DEPARTURE
PÉRIGUEUX

**By plane** Périgueux's small airport, at Bassilac, 7km east of the city, is served by flights (Mon–Fri 2 daily) to and from Paris (1hr) and Bergerac (35min). There is no public transport; a taxi will cost around €15, and cars can be hired through Europcar (☎ 05 55 30 81 57; book in advance).

**By train** The *gare SNCF* lies to the west of town at the end of rue des Mobiles-du-Coulmiers, the continuation of rue du Président-Wilson.

Destinations Bordeaux (6–12 daily; 1hr 15min–1hr 45min); Brive-la-Gaillarde (2–4 daily; 1hr); Clermont-Ferrand (daily; 4hr 35min); Les Eyzies (3–8 daily; 30min);

Limoges (3–7; 1hr 5min); Lyon (daily; 6hr 30min); Meymac (1–2 daily; 2hr 55min).

**By bus** Regional buses run by CFTA Périgord (☎ 05 53 08 43 13, ⌨ cftaco.fr) leave from both the train station and the more central rue de la Cité, behind place Francheville. Buses to Montignac and Sarlat require advance reservations (☎ 05 53 59 01 48).

Destinations Angoulême (1–3 daily; 1hr 40min); Bergerac (3–4 daily; 1hr–1hr 30min); Brantôme (1–3 daily; 35–45min); Montignac (Mon–Fri 1–2 daily; 1hr 25min); Sarlat (1–3 daily; 1hr 45min).

## INFORMATION

**Tourist office** Place Francheville (June & Sept Mon–Sat 9am–7pm, Sun 10am–1pm & 2–6pm; July & Aug Mon–Sat 9am–9pm, Sun 10am–1pm & 2–7pm; Oct–May

Mon–Sat 9am–12.30pm & 2–6pm; ☎ 05 53 53 10 63, ⌨ tourisme-perigueux.fr). Free wi-fi, and guided tours on foot and by bike are arranged in summer.

## ACCOMMODATION

★ **Des Barris** 2 rue Pierre-Magne ☎ 05 53 53 04 05, ⌨ hoteldesbarris.com. The most romantically sited hotel in town, right by the river. Rooms are simple but pleasant, and some have views of the cathedral; double-glazing keeps out noise from the main road. **€53**

**Bristol** 37 rue Antoine-Gadaud ☎ 05 53 08 75 90, ⌨ bristolfrance.com. A welcoming, somewhat old-fashioned hotel, a 5min walk from the centre. Rooms are large and fairly dark, but benefit from a/c and there's free parking. **€69**

**Mercure** 7 place Francheville ☎ 05 53 06 65 00, ⌨ mercure.com. This rather bland three-star on the main square offers spacious rooms decked out in earth tones. Parking and wi-fi are available, for a fee. **€115**

**Le Midi** 18 rue Denis-Papin ☎ 05 53 53 41 06, ⌨ hotel-du-midi.fr. A decent budget hotel opposite the station, though rooms are a little cramped, with a good-value restaurant downstairs. The collection of toy cars adds a little character. **€48**

## EATING AND DRINKING

The best area to look for places to eat is the *vieille ville*, particularly around place St-Louis, place St-Silain and in the streets behind the tourist office.

### RESTAURANTS AND CAFÉS

**Bistrot d'Isle** 2 rue Pierre-Magne ☎ 05 53 09 51 50. You can't beat the location or the cathedral views from this restaurant's terrace, which opens out onto the river. The menu is more interesting than most places in town, including dishes like scallop risotto. *Menus* from €26. Daily noon–2pm & 7–9pm.

**Café de la Place** 7 place du Marché-du-Bois ☎ 05 53 08 21 11. Scenically set café-bar, with an attractive interior and ample seating in the square. The extensive menu includes a few gourmet salads (from €10), but it's most enjoyable as somewhere to while away a few hours over a drink or two. Daily 9am–11pm.

★ **Le Clos St-Front** 5 rue de la Vertu ☎ 05 53 46 78 58, ⌨ leclossaintfront.com. High-quality *menus*, using local ingredients, served in a leafy, walled courtyard or elegant dining rooms. You can eat for less than €30, but the €63 *menu*

will get you the best of the best, with wine included. Tues & Sun noon–1.30pm, Wed–Sat noon–1.30pm & 7–9pm.

**Hercule Poireau** 2 rue de la Nation ☎ 05 53 08 90 76. An atmospheric, stone-vaulted restaurant serving serious gourmet food at very reasonable prices. Their speciality is *rossini de canard* (duck with foie gras in a truffle sauce). Three courses from €17 at lunch, €29 at dinner. Daily except Wed noon–2pm & 7–9pm.

**Tea for Tous** 28 rue Eguillerie ☎ 05 53 53 92 86. A sweet little teahouse that occupies a lovely spot on this picturesque square, with tables outside to make the most of it. The huge salads (from €8) are fabulous, and there's an excellent arrray of teas from €2.90. Tues–Sat 9.30am–7pm.

### BARS

**Le Mellow** 4 rue de la Sagesse ☎ 05 53 08 53 97. Relaxed but lively little bar, with reasonably priced drinks,

DJs most evenings and student nights on Thursdays. Wed 7pm–1am, Thurs–Sat 7pm–2am, Sun 8.30pm–1am. **Star Inn** 17 rue des Drapeaux ☏05 53 08 56 83, ⓦ hestarinnfrance.com. A cute little pub tucked just off rue St-Front, which is popular with both locals and expats.

Guinness, Kilkenny and Strongbow on tap, plus an excellent selection of bottled British beers. Thurs is fish and chips night. Also has a book exchange. Tues & Wed 7pm–1am, Thurs 6pm–2am, Fri & Sat 7pm–2am.

## Périgord Pourpre

**10**

The **Périgord Pourpre** takes its name from the wine-growing region concentrated in the southwest corner of the Dordogne *département*, most famous for the sweet white wines produced around **Monbazillac**. The only town of any size is **Bergerac**, which makes a good base for exploring the vineyards and the uplands to the south. These are peppered with *bastides*, medieval fortified towns (see box below), such as the beautifully preserved **Monpazier**, and here also you'll find the **Château de Biron**, which dominates the countryside for miles around.

### Bergerac

**BERGERAC**, "capital" of Périgord Pourpre, lies on the riverbank in the wide plain of the Dordogne. Once a flourishing port for the wine trade, it is still the main market centre for the surrounding maize, vine and tobacco farms. Devastated in the Wars of Religion, when most of its Protestant population fled overseas, Bergerac is now essentially a modern town with some interesting and attractive reminders of the past.

---

### BASTIDES

From the Occitan word *bastida*, meaning a group of buildings, **bastides** were the new towns of the thirteenth and fourteenth centuries. Although they are found all over southwest France, from the Dordogne to the foothills of the Pyrenees, there is a particularly high concentration in the area between the Dordogne and Lot rivers, which at that time formed the disputed "frontier" region between English-held Aquitaine and Capetian France.

That said, the earliest *bastides* were founded largely for economic and political reasons. They were a means of bringing new land into production – in an era of rapid population growth and technological innovation – and thus extending the power of the local lord. But as tensions between the French and English forces intensified in the late thirteenth century, so the motive became increasingly military. The *bastides* provided a handy way of securing the land along the frontier, and it was generally at this point that they were fortified.

As an incentive, anyone who was prepared to build, inhabit and defend the *bastide* was granted various benefits in a founding charter. All new residents were allocated a building plot, garden and cultivable land. The charter might also offer asylum to certain types of criminal or grant exemption from military service, and would allow the election of consuls charged with day-to-day administration – a measure of self-government remarkable in feudal times. Taxes and judicial affairs, meanwhile, remained the preserve of the representative of the king or local lord under whose ultimate authority the *bastide* lay.

The other defining feature of a *bastide* is its layout. They are nearly always square or rectangular in shape and are divided by streets at right angles to each other, producing a chequerboard pattern. The focal point is the market square, often missing its covered *halle* nowadays, but generally still surrounded by arcades, while the church is relegated to one side.

The busiest *bastide* founders were Alphonse de Poitiers, on behalf of the French crown, after he became Count of Toulouse in 1249, and King Edward I of England (1272–1307), who wished to consolidate his hold on the northern borders of his Duchy of Aquitaine. The former chalked up a total of 57 *bastides*, including **Villeneuve-sur-Lot** (1251) and **Monflanquin** (1252), while Edward was responsible for **Beaumont** (1272) and **Monpazier** (1284), among others. While many *bastides* retain only vestiges of their original aspect, both Monpazier and Monflanquin have survived almost entirely intact.

**10**

The vieille ville

The compact **vieille ville** is a beguiling area to wander through, with numerous late medieval houses and one or two beautiful squares. The splendid seventeenth-century Maison Peyrarède on Rue de l'Ancien-Pont houses the informative **Musée du Tabac** (April–Sept Tues–Fri 10am–noon & 2–6pm, Sat 10am–noon & 2–5pm, Sun 2.30–6.30pm; Oct–March Tues–Fri 10am–noon & 2–6pm, Sat 10am–noon; €4), which details the history of the plant, with collections of pipes and tools of the trade. Unsurprisingly, it rather skims over the negative side of tabacco use. Wine-lovers should make a beeline for the **Maison des Vins**, 1 rue des Récollets (Feb–June & Sept–Dec Tues–Sat 10.30am–12.30pm & 2–6pm; July & Aug daily 10am–7pm; free; ☎05 53 63 57 55, ⊛vins-bergerac.fr), which offers free tastings and beginners' courses (July & Aug; €5). It also sells a selection of local wines, many under €10, and provides information about visiting the surrounding vineyards.

## ARRIVAL AND INFORMATION                    BERGERAC

**By air** The airport (☎05 53 22 25 25) lies 5km southeast of Bergerac (roughly €15 by taxi); during the week there are two flights daily to Paris Orly on Twin Jet (26 March to 26 October; 1hr 50min; ⊛twinjet.fr).

**By train** The station is on av Du 108 Regiment D'infanterie, a 10min walk northeast of the old town, which is best reached by following bd Victor-Hugo to place de la République.

Destinations Bordeaux (9–15 daily; 1hr 20min); Sarlat (5–10 daily; 1hr 20min); Trémolat (5–10 daily; 45min).

**By bus** Buses to Périgueux (Mon–Fri 3–5 daily; 1hr 15min)

arrive and depart from the *gare SNCF*.

**Tourist office** 97 rue Neuve-d'Argenson (July & Aug Mon–Sat 9.30am–7.30pm, Sun 10.30am–1pm & 2.30–7pm; Sept–June Mon–Sat 9.30am–1pm & 2–7pm; ☎05 53 57 03 11, ⊛bergerac-tourisme.com). A second office opens in summer behind the Maison des Vins in the Cloître des Récollets (July & Aug daily 10.30am–1pm & 2.30–7pm).

**Bicycle and motorbike rental** Apolo Cycles, 31 Victor Hugo (bike €15/day, motorbike from €54; ☎06 20 64 59 25, ⊛apolo-cycles.com).

## ACCOMMODATION

**De Bordeaux** 38 place Gambetta ☎05 53 57 12 83, ⊛hotel-bordeaux-bergerac.com. Bergerac's poshest hotel, though the rooms feel a little old-fashioned, just a short walk north of the old town. A bonus is the outdoor swimming pool set in the attractive garden. **€69**

**Le Colombier de Cyrano et Roxanne** 17 rue du Grand Moulin ☎05 53 57 96 70, ⊛bluemoon2.freehost.pl. Ignore the rather tacky dummies decorating the exterior, this two-bedroom *chambre d'hôte* offers sweet, atmospheric rooms, one of which benefits from its own

hammock-strung terrace. **€73**

**Le Family** 3 rue du Dragon ☎05 53 57 80 90. Basic but not unpleasant rooms above a small bar-restaurant. Some of the rooms are a bit dark, but enlivened with splashes of colour, and its hard to beat the central location. **€36**

**La Pelouse** 8 rue Jean Jacques Rousseau ☎05 53 57 06 67, ⊛entreprisefrery.com/camping-la-pelouse. This shady campsite is on the south bank of the river, a pleasant 15min walk from the old town. **€9.75**

## EATING

**La Blanche Hermine** Place du Marché-Couvert ☎05 53 57 63 42. A cheerful crêperie opposite the covered market dishing up an imaginative range of buckwheat crêpes as well as copious salads – all at very reasonable prices (from €4.80). Tues–Sat noon–2pm & 7–9pm.

**Côté Noix** Place Pélissière ☎05 53 57 71 38, ⊛cotenoix.fr. Boasting arguably the prettiest position in town, with outdoor tables set against a small flowering garden, this little café makes a great pit-stop. The lunch

*menu* is a very reasonable €13, but the real reason to come is for the delicious cakes (from €5). April–Oct Tues–Sat 10am–6pm.

**La Table du Marché** 21 place de la Bardonnie ☎05 53 22 49 46, ⊛table-du-marche.com. This smart, modern bistro offers some of the more interesting dishes in town, including delights like hake with a tomato marmalade, on its daily *menus* (from €19). Mon–Sat 11.45am–1.30pm & 7.45–11.30pm.

## Monpazier and around

**MONPAZIER**, founded in 1284 by King Edward I of England (who was also Duke of Aquitaine), is one of the most complete of the surviving *bastides*. Picturesque and placid though it is today, the village has a hard and bitter history, being twice – in 1594 and 1637 – the centre of peasant rebellions provoked by the misery following the Wars of Religion. Both uprisings were brutally suppressed: the 1637 peasants' leader was broken on the wheel in the square.

Monpazier follows the typical *bastide* layout, with a grid of streets built around a gem of a central square. Deep, shady arcades pass under all the houses, which are separated from each other by a small gap to reduce fire risk; at the corners the buttresses are cut away to allow the passage of laden pack animals. There's also an ancient *lavoir* where women used to wash clothes, and a much altered church.

**10**

### Château de Biron

8km southwest of Monpazier • Feb, March, Nov & Dec Tues–Sun 10am–5pm; April–June, Sept & Oct daily 10am–6pm; July & Aug daily 10am–7pm; Sept & Oct Tues–Sun 10am–12.30pm & 2–6pm • €7; English-language audio-guide €2 • ⓦ semitour.com

The vast **Château de Biron** was begun in the eleventh century and added to piecemeal afterwards. You can take a guided tour (in French only), but it's better to use the audio-guide and wander at will around the rooms and the grassy courtyard, where there is a restored Renaissance chapel and guardhouse with tremendous views over the roofs of the feudal village below.

### ARRIVAL AND INFORMATION

**MONPAZIER AND AROUND**

**By car** There is no public transport to Monpazier; parking (free) is available on Foirail Nord, directly outside the north gate to the *bastide*.

**Tourist office** Place des Cornières (July & Aug daily 10am–12.30pm & 2–7pm; Sept–June Tues–Sat 10am–12.30pm & 2–6pm, Sun 10am–12.30pm; ☎ 05 53 22 68 59, ⓦ pays-des-bastides.com).

### ACCOMMODATION

There are just two hotels in Monpazier; once the tour buses go home it's easy to feel like you have the town to yourself.

★ **Edward 1ᵉʳ** 5 rue St-Pierre ☎ 05 53 22 44 00, ⓦ hoteledward1er.com. A gorgeous, stately hotel a few minutes' walk from the main square, with friendly and helpful Dutch owners. The rooms have a rustic chic, with lots of white furniture and luxurious fabrics, and are very comfortable. They also run two excellent restaurants (see below). Closed mid-Nov to mid-March. **€104**

**De France** 21 rue St-Jacques ☎ 05 53 22 60 06, ⓦ hoteldefrancemonpazier.fr. Just off the central square in an attractive old building, this friendly hotel has old-fashioned, but not unpleasant, bedrooms, and a restaurant that boasts a lovely terrace right on the square. Closed Nov–Feb. **€55**

**Moulin de David** 4km south of Monpazier, off the road to Villeréal ☎ 05 53 22 65 25, ⓦ moulindedavid.com. A very pleasant and well-equipped campsite, in a peaceful and shady setting by a brook. There's an outdoor pool, a wading pool, and a natural pool, the latter complete with slides. **€24**

### EATING

**Bistrot 2** Foirail Nord ☎ 05 53 22 60 64, ⓦ bistrot2.fr If *Eléonore* (see below) is full, try this lovely bistro, run by the same people; it's a more informal place, a few streets to the north, with *menus* from €15. Mon noon–2pm, Tues–Thurs & Sun noon–2pm & 7–9pm, Sat 7–9pm.

★ **Restaurant Eléonore** 5 rue St-Pierre ☎ 05 53 22 44 00, ⓦ hoteledward1er.com. The elegant restaurant at the Edward 1ᵉʳ hotel is the best and most atmospheric place to eat in town. On warm evenings, tables are set up outside, with swallows swooping overhead. The menu changes daily and reflects local, seasonal produce, with a choice of three to five courses (from €30). Reservations required. Mid-March to June & Sept to mid-Nov daily except Wed 7.30–9pm, July & Aug daily 7.30–9pm.

## Périgord Noir

**Périgord Noir** encompasses the central part of the valley of the Dordogne, and the valley of the Vézère. This is the distinctive Dordogne country: deep-cut valleys between limestone cliffs, with fields of maize in the alluvial bottoms and dense oak woods on the heights, interspersed with patches of not very fertile farmland. Plantations of walnut trees (cultivated for their oil), flocks of low-slung grey geese (their livers enlarged for foie gras) and prehistoric-looking stone huts called *bories* are all hallmarks of Périgord Noir.

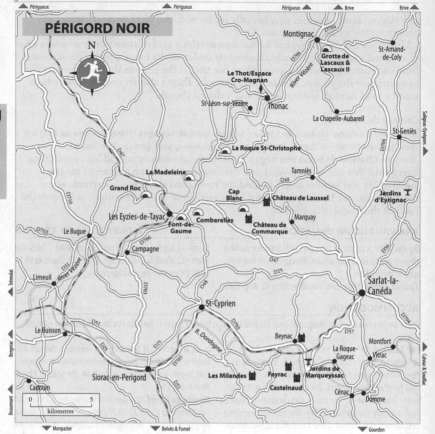

The well-preserved medieval architecture of **Sarlat**, the wealth of **prehistory** and the staggering cave paintings of the **Vézère valley**, and the stunning beauty of the château-studded **Dordogne** have all contributed to making this one of the most heavily touristed inland areas of France, with all the concomitant problems of crowds, high prices and tack. If possible, it's worth coming out of season, but if you can't, seek accommodation away from the main centres, and always drive along the back roads – the smaller the better – even when there is a more direct route available.

## Sarlat-la-Canéda

**SARLAT-LA-CANÉDA**, the "capital" of Périgord Noir, lies in a hollow between hills 10km or so back from the Dordogne River and is undoubtedly the big tourist draw of the region. You hardly notice the modern town, as it's the mainly fifteenth- and sixteenth-century houses of the *vieille ville* in mellow, honey-coloured stone that draw the attention.

The **vieille ville** is an excellent example of medieval organic urban growth. It was also the first town to benefit from culture minister André Malraux's law of 1962 which created the concept of a *secteur sauvegardé* (protected area), and boasts no fewer than 65 protected buildings and monuments. The old centre is violated only by the straight swath of the rue de la République which cuts through its middle. The west side, devoid of any standout sights, remains relatively quiet (and all the more atmospheric), whereas the east side, where most people wander, is full of sun-facing bars and restaurants.

## Cathédrale St-Sacerdos and around

Place du Peyrou

Sarlat's cathedral is rather large and unexciting, and mostly dates from its seventeenth-century renovation. Adjoining the cathedral is the more impressive facade of the seventeenth-century **Palais Episopal**, while opposite stands the town's finest house, the **Maison de La Boétie** (not open to the public) where the poet and humanist Étienne de La Boétie was born in 1530. It has gabled tiers of windows and a characteristic steep roof stacked with heavy limestone tiles (*lauzes*).

For a better sense of the medieval town, wander through the cool, shady lanes and courtyards – **cour des Fontaines** and **cour des Chanoines** – around the back of the cathedral. On a slope directly behind the cathedral stands the curious twelfth-century coned tower, the **Lanterne des Morts**, whose exact function has escaped historians, though the most popular theory is that it was built to commemorate St Bernard, who performed various miracles when he visited the town in 1147.

**10**

### ARRIVAL AND INFORMATION

SARLAT-LA-CANÉDA

**By train** The *gare SNCF* is just under 2km south of the old town, about a 20min walk.

Destinations Bergerac (6–10 daily; 1hr 10min–1hr 50min); Bordeaux (6–10 daily; 2hr 30min–3hr 10min); Trémolat (5–10 daily; 1hr 15min).

**By bus** Buses depart from place Pasteur, just south of place du 14-Juillet; most services require advance reservations (☎ 05 53 59 01 48).

Destinations Lascaux II (July & Aug Mon–Sat 2 daily; 45min); Montignac (1–3 daily; 30min); Périgueux (1–2 daily; 1hr 45min); Souillac (2–4 daily; 50min)

**Tourist office** 3 rue Tourny (March, Oct & Nov Mon–Sat 9am–noon & 2–5pm; April Mon–Sat 9am–noon & 2–6pm, Sun 10am–1pm & 2–5pm; May & June Mon–Sat 9am–6pm, Sun 10am–1pm & 2–5pm; July & Aug Mon–Sat 9am–7pm, Sun 10am–noon & 2–6pm; Sept Mon–Sat 9am–1pm & 2–7pm, Sun 10am–1pm & 2–5pm; ☎ 05 53 31 45 45, ⓦ sarlat-tourisme.com).

**Bike rental** Cycleo, 44 rue des Cordeliers (€17/day; May–Oct Mon–Sat 9am–7pm, reserve at least 4hr in advance; Nov–April shop closed but rental possible by reserving 24hr in advance; ☎ 05 53 31 90 05, ⓦ cycleo.fr).

### ACCOMMODATION

⭐ **Clos de Boetie** 95 av de Selves ☎ 05 53 29 44 18, ⓦ closlaboetie-sarlat.com. Sarlat's poshest hotel, just a few minutes' walk from the town centre, oozes decadent romance. Pick of the rooms is the Montaigne, with a gorgeous four-poster bed and a leafy private terrace. **€225**

**La Couleuvrine** 1 place de la Bouquerie ☎ 05 53 59 27 80, ⓦ la-couleuvrine.com. One of the nicest and most reasonable places to stay in Sarlat, occupying a tower in the former ramparts on the northeast side of the *vieille ville*. Most of the rooms are quite small, though cosily furnished with solid dark furniture and pretty fabrics. Its fine, bustling restaurant takes up most of the ground floor. **€66**

**Des Récollets** 4 rue Jean-Jacques Rousseau ☎ 05 53 31

36 00, ⓦ hotel-recollets-sarlat.com. A good-value place, set in an old cloister around a little courtyard, on an atmospheric side street on the quieter western side of the old town. The small rooms are modern and rather functional. **€49**

**Les Terrasses du Périgord** About 2.5km north of Sarlat near Proissans village ☎ 05 53 59 02 25, ⓦ terrasses-du-perigord.com. A really lovely campsite, with spacious pitches beneath the trees, and panoramic views of the surrounding countryside. Closed Oct–March. **€18.70**

⭐ **La Villa des Consuls** 3 rue Jean-Jacques Rousseau ☎ 05 53 31 90 05, ⓦ villaconsuls.fr. Smart, elegant rooms with original features like wooden beams, plus a

---

### SARLAT MARKET

In a region famous for its **markets**, Sarlat's twice-weekly (Wed & Sat) offering is particularly notable for its size and the range of produce on offer. Of the two, the Saturday market is the largest, spreading down from northerly av Gambetta to place du 14-Juillet. The stalls that crowd the main drag are a rather uninspired selection of clothes, shoes and mass-produced crafts; veer off towards place de la Liberté, however, and you'll find stalls selling everything from seasonal fruit and veg (not to mention truffles) to foie gras, walnut wine and nougat. It's an irresistible Sarlat experience, but get there early as most stalls start packing up around 12.30pm.

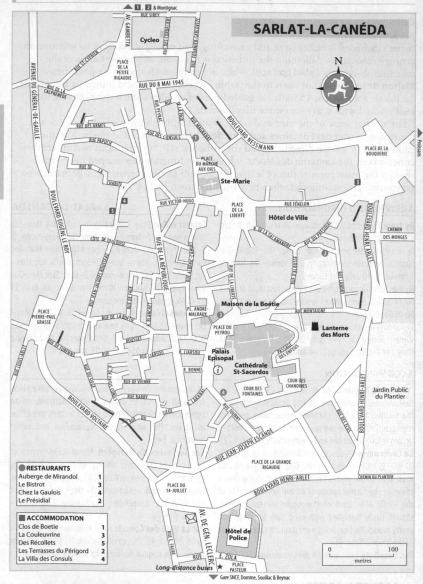

SARLAT-LA-CANÉDA

**RESTAURANTS**

| | |
|---|---|
| Auberge de Mirandol | 1 |
| Le Bistrot | 3 |
| Chez la Gaulois | 4 |
| Le Présidial | 2 |

**ACCOMMODATION**

| | |
|---|---|
| Clos de Boetie | 1 |
| La Couleuvrine | 3 |
| Des Récollets | 5 |
| Les Terrasses du Périgord | 2 |
| La Villa des Consuls | 4 |

handy kitchenette, and gorgeous apartments, most of which boast a private terrace or balcony. Most sleep up to four, some up to six, and there's substantial reductions for longer stays. Rooms €92, apartment €103

## EATING AND DRINKING

**Auberge de Mirandol** 7 rue des Consuls ☎05 53 29 53 89, ⓦlemirandol.fr. An attractive and popular restaurant serving reasonably priced local delicacies in a fourteenth-century house, complete with its own *cave*. *Menus* from €14.50. Mid-Feb to Nov daily noon–2pm & 7–9pm; closed Mon out of season.

**Le Bistrot** 14 place du Peyrou ☎05 53 28 28 40. Right opposite the cathedral, this little place is full of stereotypical French rustic charm – not least the checked tablecloths – but it's nonetheless a good choice for a meal. The gourmet salads are a highlight – the *salade Bistrot* (€13), with Comté, bacon, croutons and a poached egg, is particularly tasty. Mon–Sat noon–2pm & 7pm.

★ **Chez la Gaulois** 1 rue Tourny ✆ 05 53 59 50 64. A delightful little place specializing in cheese and charcuterie, with tables inside the cosy interior or outside on the cobbled street. There's a good choice of both hot (*fondue*) and cold dishes (most around €12). April–June &

Sept–Feb Tues–Sat noon–2pm & 7–9pm; July & Aug daily noon–2pm & 7–10pm.

**Le Présidial** 6 rue Landry ✆ 05 53 28 92 47. A beautiful setting, in a lovely seventeenth-century mansion, with tables out in the walled garden in summer. Expect the usual local dishes like *confit de canard*, plus more interesting options including giant mussels stuffed with salted butter (mains from €15, *menus* from €19). Tues–Sat noon–1.30pm, Mon–Sat 7.30–10pm.

## The Vézère valley

The **valley of the Vézère** River between **Limeuil** and **St-Amand-de-Coly** justifiably styles itself as the **prehistory** capital of the world. The high, rocky outcrops which overlook acres of thick forest are riddled with caves which have provided shelter for humans for tens of thousands of years. It was here that the first skeletons of **Cro-Magnon people** – the first Homo sapiens, tall and muscular with a large skull – were unearthed in 1868 by labourers building the Périgueux–Agen train line. Since then, an incomparable wealth of archeological and artistic evidence of late Stone Age people has been revealed, most famously in the breathtakingly sophisticated **cave paintings** of **Lascaux** and **Font de Gaume**.

Away from the throngs of visitors at the caves, there is much to appreciate in the peace and quiet of the Vézère valley. It's best enjoyed from a **canoe**, where you'll often find yourself alone in a bend of the river, rather than part of a vast armada, as tends to be the case on the Dordogne.

### Limeuil

Built into the steep slope at the confluence of the Dordogne and Vézère rivers, the beautiful village of **LIMEUIL** is a picturesque place to while away a couple of hours. From the riverbank – an ideal picnic spot, with a pebbly beach for those who fancy a dip – the narrow, cobbled rue du Port leads steeply uphill, winding in between medieval houses and through the old gateways. At the top, the best views out over the village and surrounding countryside have been monopolized by the **Parc Panoramique** (April–June & Sept–Nov Sun–Fri 10am–12.30pm & 2–6pm; July & Aug daily 10am–8pm; €7), a wilderness of trees, shrubs and crumbling stone walls.

### Trémolat and around

Set back from the river, the picturesque village of **TRÉMOLAT** is worth a stop for its two superlative dining opportunities, both of which are part of the luxurious *Le Vieux Logis* hotel (see p.556). Most people pass through the village on their way to the **Cingle de Trémolat**, a short drive west on the D31, where a viewpoint allows you to see the river as it meanders through the countryside. The best view, however, is just above this – to reach it, take the turning just after the car park for the Cingle (if coming from Trémolat), towards "Belvedere et Calvaire du Rocamadou", and pull over when you reach the tower. On clear days, the river takes on a mirror-like consistency, and you can see Trémolat's stately church rising up from the green fields that surround.

### Les Eyzies-de-Tayac

The main base for visiting many of the region's prehistoric painted caves is **LES EYZIES-DE-TAYAC**, a one-street village lined with gift shops and foie gras outlets. There are more prehistoric caves around Les Eyzies than you could possibly hope to visit in one day; in addition, the compulsory tours are tiring, so it's best to just do a couple rather than attempt them all. In town, it's worth visiting the excellent **Musée National de Préhistoire**

10

(June & Sept daily except Tues 9.30am–6pm; July & Aug daily 9.30am–6.30pm; Oct–May daily except Tues 9.30am–12.30pm & 2–5.30pm; €5; ⓦ musee-prehistoire-eyzies.fr), which contains many important prehistoric artefacts found in the various caves in the region. Look out for the oil lamp from Lascaux and the exhibits from La Madeleine, to the north of Les Eyzies, including a superb bas-relief of a bison licking its flank.

### Grotte de Font-de-Gaume

Daily except Sat: mid-May to mid-Sept 9.30am–5.30pm; mid-Sept to mid-May 9.30am–12.30pm & 2–5.30pm • €7; 120 tickets are sold per day; it's best to buy them in advance (€1.50 reservation fee) – at least a month ahead in high season – and note that tickets cannot be cancelled, though you can change the date and time if necessary; you could also try for one of the 30 same-day tickets sold each morning (in high season aim to be at the ticket office 1hr before opening) • ☏ 05 53 06 86 00, ✉ fontdegaume@monuments-nationaux.fr, ⓦ eyzies.monuments-nationaux.fr

Since its discovery in 1901, dozens of polychrome paintings have been found in the **Grotte de Font-de-Gaume**, 1.5km from Les Eyzies on the D47 to Sarlat. The **cave** was first settled by Stone Age people during the last Ice Age – about 25,000 BC – when the Dordogne was the domain of roaming bison, reindeer and mammoths. The entrance is no more than a fissure concealed by rocks and trees above a small lush valley, leading to a narrow twisting passage. The first painting you see is a frieze of bison, reddish-brown in colour, massive, full of movement and very far from the primitive representations you might expect. Further on comes the most miraculous image of all, a **frieze** of five bison discovered in 1966 during cleaning operations. The colour, remarkably sharp and vivid, is preserved by a protective layer of calcite. Shading under the belly and down the thighs is used to give three-dimensionality with a sophistication that seems utterly modern. Another panel consists of superimposed drawings, a fairly common phenomenon in cave painting, sometimes the result of work by successive generations, but here an obviously deliberate technique. A reindeer in the foreground shares legs with a large bison behind to indicate perspective.

Stocks of **artists' materials** have also been found: kilos of prepared pigments; palettes – stones stained with ground-up earth pigments; and wooden painting sticks. Painting was clearly a specialized, perhaps professional, business, reproduced in dozens of caves located in the central Pyrenees and northern Spain.

### Grotte des Combarelles

2km from Les Eyzies on the D47 towards Sarlat • Daily except Sat: mid-May to mid-Sept 9.30am–5.30pm; mid-Sept to mid-May 9.30am–12.30pm & 2–5.30pm • €7; tickets can only be purchased from the Font-de-Gaume ticket office

The **Grotte des Combarelles** was discovered in 1910. The innermost part of the cave is covered with **engravings** from the Magdalenian period (about 12,000 years ago).

---

### A PREHISTORY MYSTERY

Most of the **caves** around Les Eyzies were not used as permanent homes, and there are various theories as to the purpose of such inaccessible spots. Most agree that they were sanctuaries and, if not actually places of worship, at least had religious significance. One suggestion is that making images of animals that were commonly hunted – like reindeer and bison – or feared – like bears and mammoths – was a kind of sympathetic magic intended to help men either catch or evade these animals. Another is that they were part of a fertility cult: sexual images of women with pendulous breasts and protuberant behinds are common. Others argue that these cave paintings served educational purposes, making parallels with Australian aborigines who used similar images to teach their young vital survival information as well as the history and mythological origins of their people. But much remains unexplained – the abstract signs that appear in so many caves, for example, and the arrows that clearly cannot be arrows, since Stone Age arrowheads looked different from these representations.

---

Drawn over a period of two thousand years, many are superimposed one upon another, and include horses, reindeer, mammoths and stylized human figures – among the finest are the heads of a horse and a lioness.

### Abri du Cap Blanc

7km east of Les Eyzies • Daily except Sat: mid-May to mid-Sept 9.30am–5.30pm; mid-Sept to mid-May 9.30am–12.30pm & 2–5.30pm • €7 • ☎ 05 53 06 86 00, ⓦ eyzies.monuments-nationaux.fr

**10**

Not a cave but a natural rock shelter, the **Abri du Cap Blanc** lies on a steep wooded hillside. The shelter contains a **sculpted frieze** of horses and bison dating from the Middle Magdalenian period, about 14,000 years ago. Of only ten surviving prehistoric sculptures in France, this is undoubtedly the best. The design is deliberate, with the sculptures polished and set off against a pockmarked background. But what makes this place extraordinary is not just the large scale, but the high relief of some of the sculptures. This was only possible in places where light reached in, which in turn brought the danger of destruction by exposure to the air. Cro-Magnon people actually lived in this shelter, and a female skeleton some two thousand years younger than the frieze was found here.

### Grotte du Grand Roc

2km north of Les Eyzies, off the D47 • Mid-Feb to March, Nov & Dec Sun–Thurs 10am–noon & 2–5pm; April–June, Sept & Oct daily 10am–12.30pm & 2–6pm; July & Aug daily 10am–7pm • €7

As well as prehistoric cave paintings, you can see some truly spectacular **stalactites** and **stalagmites** in the area around Les Eyzies. Some of the best examples can be found in the **Grotte du Grand Roc**, whose entrance is high up in the cliffs that line much of the Vézère valley. There's a great view from the mouth of the cave and, inside, along some 80m of tunnel, a fantastic array of rock formations.

### La Roque St-Christophe

9km northeast of Les Eyzies along the D706 to Montignac • Daily: Jan 2–5pm; Feb, March & Oct 10am–6pm; April–June & Sept 10am–6.30pm; July & Aug 10am–8pm; Nov–Dec 2–5.30pm • €7.80 • ☎ 05 53 50 70 45, ⓦ roque-st-christophe.com

The enormous prehistoric dwelling site of **La Roque St-Christophe** is made up of about a hundred **rock shelters** on five levels, hollowed out of the limestone cliffs. The whole complex is nearly 1km long and about 80m above ground level, where the River Vézère once flowed. The earliest traces of occupation go back over 50,000 years. There are frequent guided visits in summer, or you could just take an English-language leaflet and wander at your own pace.

### Montignac

The small, attractive town of **MONTIGNAC** is the main base for visiting the **Lascaux cave**. It's a more attractive place than Les Eyzies, with several wooden-balconied houses leaning appealingly over the river, a good **market** (Wed & Sat) and a lively annual **arts festival** (third week of July), featuring international folk groups.

### Grotte de Lascaux and Lascaux II

2km south of Montignac • 40min guided tours (French or English) Feb, March, Nov & Dec Tues–Sun 10am–12.30pm & 2–5.30pm; April–June, Sept & Oct daily 9.30am–6pm; July & Aug daily 9am–8pm • €9.50, €12.50 with Espace Cro-Magnon; 2000 tickets are sold each day, but go fast in peak season – from April to Oct, you can only buy them from the office next to Montignac tourist office (see opposite), at other times, they're normally available at the site (check in Montignac first) • ⓦ semitour.com • Buses (July & Aug Mon–Fri 2 daily) run between Lascaux II and Sarlat (45min) and Souillac (1hr 30min)

The **Grotte de Lascaux**, 2km south of Montignac on the D704, was discovered in 1940 by four boys who stumbled across a deep cavern decorated with marvellously preserved **paintings** of animals. Executed by Cro-Magnon people 17,000 years ago, the paintings are among the finest examples of prehistoric art in existence. There are five or six identifiable styles, and subjects include bison, mammoths and horses, plus the biggest known prehistoric drawing, of a 5.5m bull with an astonishingly expressive head and face. In 1948, the cave was opened to the public, and over the next fifteen years more than a million tourists came to see it. Sadly, because of deterioration caused by the heat and breath of visitors, the cave had to be closed in 1963; now you have to be content with the replica known as **Lascaux II**.

Opened in 1983, Lascaux II was the result of eleven years' painstaking work by twenty artists and sculptors, using the same methods and materials as the original cave painters. While the visit can't offer the excitement of a real cave, the reconstruction rarely disappoints the thousands who trek here every year. For an enhanced appreciation of the cave itself, especially if you have children, it's worth visiting the museum at **Le Thot** first (see below).

### Espace Cro-Magnon

Le Thot • Feb, March, Nov & Dec Tues–Sun 10am–12.30pm & 2–5.30pm; April–June & Sept daily 10am–6pm; July & Aug daily 10am–7pm • €7, €12.50 with Lascaux II • ⓦ semitour.com

Around 5km down the Vézère from Lascaux II, at **Le Thot** near Thonac, **Espace Cro-Magnon** is a combined animal park and museum with a very interesting video showing the construction of Lascaux II along with mock-ups of prehistoric scenes and live examples of some of the animals featured in the paintings. Here you'll see European bison, long-horned cattle and Przewalski's horses, rare and beautiful animals from Mongolia believed to resemble the prehistoric wild horse – notice the erect mane.

### St-Amand-de-Coly

Nine kilometres east of Montignac, the village of **ST-AMAND-DE-COLY** boasts a superbly beautiful fortified Romanesque church, a magical venue for concerts in the summer. Despite its bristling military architecture, the twelfth-century church manages to combine great delicacy and spirituality, with its purity of line and simple decoration most evocative in the low sun of late afternoon or early evening. Its defences left nothing to chance: the walls are 4m thick, a ditch runs all the way round, and a passage once skirted the eaves, with numerous positions for archers to rain down arrows, and blind stairways to mislead attackers.

### ARRIVAL AND INFORMATION                    THE VÉZÈRE VALLEY

**LIMEUIL**

**By car** There is no public transport to Limeuil. Parking is available (for a fee) by the river, or at a larger car park (free) just before the turn-off to the village.

**Canoe rental** Canoes Rivieres Loisirs, just off the D51 (ⓣ 05 53 63 38 73, ⓦ canoes-rivieres-loisirs.com).

**TRÉMOLAT**

**By train** Trémolat's small train station is 1km south of town.
Destinations Bergerac (5–10 daily; 30min); Bordeaux (5–10 daily; 2hr); Sarlat (5–10 daily; 1hr 15min).

**LES EYZIES-DE-TAYAC**

**By train** The train station is about 0.5km northwest of town, on the Perigueux–Agen train line (Perigueux 6–11 daily; 35min).

**Tourist office** On the main street (April to mid-June Mon–Sat 9am–noon & 2–6pm, Sun 10am–noon & 2–5pm; mid-June to mid-Sept Mon–Sat 9am–7pm, Sun 10am–noon & 2–6pm; mid-Sept to March Mon–Fri 9am–noon & 2–6pm, Sat 10am–noon & 2–5pm; ⓣ 05 53 06 97 05, ⓦ tourisme-vezere.com). Bike rental is available (€20/day).

**Canoe rental** Canoës Vallée Vézère (ⓣ 05 53 05 10 11, ⓦ canoesvalleevezere.com), by the river near Les Glycines.

**MONTIGNAC**

**By bus** Buses stop at place Tourny, just off rue du 4 Septembre, south of the river. For Perigueux and Sarlat, you'll need to reserve in advance (ⓣ 05 53 59 01 48)
Destinations Brive-la-Gaillarde (Mon–Fri 1–3 daily; 2hr); Perigueux (2–3 daily; 1hr 15min); Sarlat (Mon–Sat 2–3 daily; 30min).

**Tourist office** Place Bertran-de-Born (Jan Mon–Fri 10.30am–12.30pm; Feb & March Mon–Sat 10.30am–12.30pm & 2–5pm; April Mon–Sat 10.30am–12.30pm & 2–6pm; May & June Mon–Sat 9.30am–12.30pm & 2–6pm; July & Aug daily 9am–7pm;

**10**

Sept Mon–Sat 9.30am–12.30pm & 2–5pm; Oct–Dec Mon–Sat 10am–noon & 2–4.30pm; ☎ 05 53 51 82 60, Ⓦ tourisme-montignac.com).

**Canoe rental** Les 7 Rives on the north side of the river, near place d'Armes (daily 9.30am–6.30pm; from €14; ☎ 05 53 50 19 26).

## ACCOMMODATION AND EATING

### LIMEUIL

**Au Bon Accueil** ☎ 05 53 63 30 97. Celebrated restaurant up on the hill near the park, with a small terrace. *Menus* start from €19 and include *tourain* – a garlic soup that's a speciality of the region – and rabbit casserole in mustard sauce. Daily noon–2pm & 7–9pm.

★ **Le Plassial** Coux et Bigaroque ☎ 05 53 04 47 62, Ⓦ home-away.co.uk. There's no better way to explore this beautiful area than by pretending you live here, and this gorgeous house, just a short drive from Limeuil, makes the perfect base. Sleeping up to four people, it's been beautifully decorated, and boasts an abundant private garden. Reservations essential. Weekly stays €870

### TRÉMOLAT AND AROUND

**Bistrot d'en Face** In the village ☎ 05 53 22 80 06, Ⓦ vieux-logis.com. The cheaper and more relaxed restaurant of *Le Vieux Logis* (see below), serving seasonal *menus* (from €20) that include delights like local asparagus and roast salmon. April to mid-Oct daily noon–1.30pm & 7.30–9pm; mid-Oct to March Wed–Sun noon–1.30pm & 7.30–9pm.

★ **Le Vieux Logis** ☎ 05 53 22 80 06, Ⓦ vieux-logis .com. A peaceful and intimate *Relais et Châteaux* property set among beautiful gardens. Rooms are luxurious and unfussy, but the real reason to come here is for its two eating options. The swankiest is the on-site Michelin-starred gourmet restaurant, which serves sublime food using local ingredients (*menus* from €48). Restaurant mid-April to mid-Oct daily noon–1.30pm & 7.30–9pm; mid-Oct to mid-April Mon & Thurs–Sun noon–1.30pm & 7.30–9pm. €190

### LES EYZIES-DE-TAYAC

Les Eyzies hotels are pricey and may require half-board in high season, while most are closed in winter. When it comes to eating, you're best off dining in one of the hotel restaurants.

**Des Falaises** Av de la Préhistoire ☎ 05 53 06 97 35, Ⓔ hotel-d-falaises@wanadoo.fr. At the quieter end of the main drag, this is the cheapest option in town. Rooms are fairly plain, but enlivened with colourful bed covers, and all are en suite. €42

**Les Glycines** Av de Laugerie ☎ 05 53 06 97 07, Ⓦ les -glycines-dordogne.com. Elegant hotel near the tiny

railway station, offering very pretty, romantic rooms with drapes and frills, some overlooking the extensive, beautiful grounds and swimming pool. The hotel's *potager* provides much of the produce used in the fine restaurant (*menus* from €45). Closed Nov–March. Restaurant daily 7.30–9pm. €115

★ **Le Moulin de la Beune** Rue du Moulin ☎ 05 53 06 94 33, Ⓦ moulindelabeune.com. In a glorious setting, right by the river Beune, this ivy-covered hotel offers calm, spacious rooms. The restaurant is one of the best in town, with a lovely garden terrace at the back (*menus* from €34). Closed Nov–March. Restaurant Mon, Thurs, Fri & Sun noon–1.30pm & 7–9.30pm, Tues, Wed & Sat 7–9.30pm. €64

**Du Passeur** Av de la Préhistoire ☎ 05 53 06 97 13, Ⓦ hostellerie-du-passeur.com. Centrally located, attractive hotel a stone's throw from the river, right in the centre of town. Rooms blend modern and traditional styles, but with varying success. Closed Dec–April. €92

### MONTIGNAC

Montignac hotels, as everywhere around here, get booked up quickly in summer. All of the hotels have restaurants – the one at *Hostellerie de la Roseraie* is particularly good.

**Bar des Arcades** Rue du 4-septembre. This friendly, no-frills café, with some tables out on the pavement, is a good lunch spot, offering light dishes like *croque monsieur* (€5.90) as well as larger meals. Mon–Sat 9am–10pm.

**De la Grotte** Rue du 4-septembre ☎ 05 51 80 48, Ⓦ hoteldelagrotte.fr. A good, reasonably priced hotel, with a restaurant and small but pleasant garden beside a stream. Rooms are decked out in floral fabrics but are otherwise quite plain; ask for one away from the main road. €56

**Le Moulin du Bleufond** Av Aristide Briand ☎ 05 53 51 83 95, Ⓦ bleufond.com. On the riverbank 500m downstream from the centre of Montignac, this is a well-tended and very popular three-star campsite, with a great pool. Closed mid-Oct to March. €22.50

**De la Roseraie** Place d'Armes ☎ 05 53 50 53 92, Ⓦ laroseraie-hotel.com. This ivy- and wisteria-clad hotel, in a nice location near the river on a quiet square, has pretty, period rooms, plus a pool and flower-filled garden, and a great restaurant. Closed Nov–March. €95

## The middle Dordogne valley

The most familiar images of the River Dordogne are those from around **Beynac** and **La Roque-Gageac**, where the scenery is at its most spectacular, with clifftop châteaux facing each other across the valley. The most imposing of these date from the Hundred

---

### CANOEING ON THE DORDOGNE AND VÉZÈRE

**Canoeing** is hugely popular in the Dordogne, especially in summer, when the Vézère and Dordogne rivers are shallow and slow-flowing – ideal for beginners. There are rental outlets at just about every twist in both rivers. Although it's possible to rent one-person kayaks or two-person canoes by the hour, it's best to take at least a half-day or longer (some outfits offer up to a week's rental), and simply cruise downstream. The company you book through will either take you to your departure point or send a minibus to pick you up from your final destination. **Prices** vary according to what's on offer; expect to pay around €17–25 per person per day. Most places function daily in July and August, on demand in May, June and September, depending on the weather, and are closed the rest of the year. All companies must provide life jackets (*gilets*) and teach you basic safety procedures, most importantly how to capsize and get out safely. You must be able to swim.

---

**10**

Years' War, when the river marked the frontier between French-held land to the north and English territory to the south. Further upstream, the hilltop *bastide* village of **Domme** offers stunning views, but is as crowded as Sarlat in summer.

Just south of the river, the **Abbaye de Cadouin** lies tucked out of harm's way in a fold of the landscape, hiding a lovely Gothic cloister. The train line from Bergerac to Sarlat runs along the river for this stretch, offering some wonderful views but unfortunately not stopping anywhere very useful; to appreciate the villages in this area, you need your own transport or, better still, a canoe.

### Abbaye de Cadouin

6km south of Le Buisson • **Cloister** Feb, March, Nov & Dec Mon–Thurs & Sun 10am–12.30pm & 2–5pm; April–June, Sept & Oct Sun–Fri 10am–1pm & 2–6pm; July & Aug daily 10am–7pm • €6 • ⓦ semitour.com

For eight hundred years, until 1935, the twelfth-century Cistercian **Abbaye de Cadouin** drew flocks of pilgrims to wonder at a piece of cloth first mentioned by Simon de Montfort in 1214 and thought to be part of Christ's shroud. In 1935 the two bands of embroidery at either end were shown to contain an Arabic text from around the eleventh century. Since then the main attraction has been the finely sculpted but badly damaged capitals of the Flamboyant Gothic **cloister**. Beside it stands a Romanesque **church** with a stark, bold front and wooden belfry roofed with chestnut shingles (chestnut trees abound around here – their timber was used in furniture-making and their nuts ground for flour during frequent famines). Inside the church, the nave is slightly out of alignment; this is thought to be deliberate and perhaps a vestige of pagan attachments, as the three windows are aligned so that at the winter and summer solstices the sun shines through all three in a single shaft.

### Jardins de Marqueyssac

Daily: Feb, March & Oct 10am–6pm; April–June & Sept 10am–7pm; July & Aug 9am–8pm; Nov–Jan 2–5pm; candlelit evenings Thurs dusk–midnight • €7.40, or €14 with Château de Castelnaud; candlelit evenings €12 • ☏ 05 53 31 36 36, ⓦ marqueyssac.com

The gorgeous **Jardins de Marqueyssac**, sitting on top of a wooded promontory that rises above a wide meander in the Dordogne, are one of the most magical sights in the region. At times, the gardens feel like a Tim Burton fantasy – quirky, maze-like topiary is the first thing that greets you upon entering – while at others it's like being in the heart of a forest, with only the rustle of birds in the trees above disturbing the peace. Though the gardens were originally laid out in the seventeenth century, what you see today is the result of extensive restoration work from the late 1990s.

Three paths lead through the grounds to the **Belvedere**, jutting out from the cliff with stupendous views over the river towards La Roque-Gageac and, in the opposite direction, Castelnaud. The gardens are even more magical during the special candlelit

**10**

evenings in July and August when you can explore to the accompaniment of a live jazz band.

### Château de Castelnaud

Daily: Feb, March & Oct 10am–6pm; April–June & Sept 10am–7pm; July & Aug 9am–8pm; Nov–Jan 2–5pm • €8.20, €14 with Jardins de Marqueyssac • ☯ castelnaud.com

The partially ruined **Château de Castelnaud** is a true rival to Beynac (see below) in terms of impregnability – although it was successfully captured by the bellicose Simon de Montfort as early as 1214. The English held it for much of the Hundred Years' War, and it wasn't until the Revolution that it was finally abandoned. Fairly heavily restored in recent years, it now houses a highly informative **museum of medieval warfare**. Its core is an extensive collection of original weaponry, including all sorts of bizarre contraptions, and a fine assortment of armour.

### Beynac-et-Cazenac

Clearly visible on an impregnable cliff on the north bank of the river, the eye-catching village and castle of **BEYNAC-ET-CAZENAC** was built in the days when the river was the only route open to traders and invaders. By road, it's 3km to the **château** (March–Nov daily 10am–6.30pm; €7.50) but a steep lane leads up through the village and takes only fifteen minutes by foot. It's protected on the landward side by a double wall; elsewhere the sheer drop of almost 200m does the job. The flat terrace at the base of the keep, which was added by the English, conceals the remains of the houses where the beleaguered villagers lived. Richard the Lionheart held the place for a time, until a gangrenous wound received while besieging the castle of Châlus, north of Périgueux, ended his term of blood-letting.

### La Roque-Gageac

The village of **LA ROQUE-GAGEAC** is almost too perfect, its ochre-coloured houses sheltering under dramatically overhanging cliffs. It inevitably pulls in the tourist buses, and since the main road separates the village from the river, the noise and fumes of the traffic can become rather oppressive in summer. The best way to escape is to slip away through the lanes and alleyways that wind up through the terraced houses.

### Domme

High on a cliff on the river's south bank, **DOMME** is an exceptionally well-preserved *bastide*. Its attractions, in addition to its position, include three original thirteenth-century **gateways** and a section of the old **walls**. From the northern edge of the village, marked by a drop so precipitous that fortifications were deemed unnecessary, you look out over a wide sweep of river country. Beneath the village is a warren of **caves** (daily: Feb to mid-Nov & Christmas hols; contact the tourist office for times & tickets; €8.20) in which the townspeople took refuge in times of danger. Unfortunately, the rock formations can't compare with the area's other caves; the only good point is the exit onto the cliff face with a panoramic lift up to the top.

---

### MESSING ABOUT ON THE RIVER

There are a number of watery pursuits available from Beynac-et-Cazenac.
**Gabarres de Beynac**, by the car park at the bottom of the hill (daily: April & Oct 11am–5pm; May–Sept 10am–12.30pm & 2–6pm; reserve ahead in July & Aug; €7.50; ☯ gabarre-beynac. com), offer a picturesque journey on the river on a replica *gabarre*, the traditional wooden river-boat, or you could rent a canoe from **Canoë Copeyre** (from €15; book ahead; ☏ 05 53 28 95 01, ☯ canoe-copeyre.com), by the river, next to *Restaurant Maleville*.

## INFORMATION

### DOMME

**Tourist office** Place de la Halle (Feb–June & Sept to mid-Nov daily 10am–noon & 2–6pm; July & Aug daily 10am–7pm;

mid-Nov to Dec Mon–Fri 10am–12.30pm & 1.30–4.30pm; closed Jan; ☎ 05 53 31 71 00, ⦿ ot-domme.com).

## THE MIDDLE DORDOGNE VALLEY

## ACCOMMODATION AND EATING

### ABBAYE DE CADOUIN

**De l'Abbaye** Place de l'Abbaye ☎ 05 53 63 40 93, ✉ delpech@orange.fr. A small restaurant with five simple en-suite bedrooms opposite the abbey. The restaurant serves hearty, reasonably priced meals (from €13), all starting with a complementary helping of the delicious house *touraine* (garlic soup). Restaurant Tues–Sat noon–1.30pm & 7–9pm, Sun noon–1.30pm. **€45**

★ **Auberge de Jeunesse** ☎ 05 53 73 28 78, ⦿ FUAJ .org. This excellent FUAJ hostel is situated in part of the abbey itself, with dorms in the monks' old sleeping quarters, and some great double rooms. There's a kitchen and bike hire. Closed mid-Dec to Jan. Dorms **€20.60**, doubles **€47.60**

### BEYNAC-ET-CAZENAC

**Du Château** On the D703 ☎ 05 53 29 19 20, ⦿ hotelduchâteau-dordogne.com. The best of Beynac's hotels, with fresh, bright rooms, a small pool and a good restaurant (*menus* from €19.50) with a terrace overlooking the river; though it's on the busy main road, rooms are double-glazed and some have a/c. Closed Dec to mid-Jan. **€87**

**Le Capeyrou** Off the D703 ☎ 05 53 29 54 95, ⦿ campinglecapeyrou.com. In an enviable position along the river, with the château making a rather magnificent backdrop, this leafy campsite is, unsurprisingly, a popular spot, with its own sandy beach and a large

swimming pool. Closed Oct to mid-April. **€20.30**

### LA ROQUE-GAGEAC

★ **La Belle Étoile** On the D703 ☎ 05 53 29 51 44, ⦿ belleetoile.fr. A really lovely small hotel in a prime position across the road from the river. Rooms are spacious and cool; it's worth splashing out an extra €20 for a river view. The restaurant serves good traditional cuisine and has a lovely river-view terrace. Closed Nov–March. Restaurant Tues & Thurs–Sun 12.30–1.30pm & 7.15–8.45pm; Wed 7.15–8.45pm. **€55**

### DOMME

**La Belvedere** Esplanade de la Barre. Soak up the fabulous views over the river from this popular restaurant's appealing covered terrace. Though it's undoubtedly touristy, the food is decent and reasonably priced (menus from €14.90). Daily 11.30am–3pm & 6–9.30pm.

**L'Esplanade** Esplanade de la Barre ☎ 05 53 28 31 41, ⦿ esplanade-perigord.com. The most luxurious place to stay in Domme, right on the cliff edge, with panoramic views from some of the rooms, which are rather sumptuously decorated. Closed Nov–March. **€108**

**Le Nouvel Hôtel** Grand'Rue ☎ 05 53 28 36 81, ⦿ domme-nouvel-hotel.com. This small hotel has simple, rather old-fashioned rooms, some of which have more character than others, with features like bare stone walls. Closed mid-Nov to Easter. **€49**

# The upper Dordogne valley

East of Sarlat and Domme, you leave the crowds of Périgord Noir behind, but the Dordogne valley retains all of its beauty and interest. **Martel** and **Carennac** are wonderfully preserved medieval villages, and there are exceptional examples of Romanesque sculpture in the churches at **Souillac** and **Beaulieu**. Travel is difficult without a car, but Souillac is reachable by train and has bus routes to Sarlat and Martel. Cyclists can follow the *voie verte*, a 23km-long cycle route from Sarlat to Souillac along a decommissioned train track.

## Souillac

The first place of any size east of Sarlat is **SOUILLAC**, at the confluence of the Borrèze and Dordogne rivers and on a major road junction. Virginia Woolf stayed here in 1937, and was pleased to meet "no tourists ... England seems like a chocolate box bursting with trippers afterward"; things have changed little today, and the town has an understated charm.

### Church of Ste-Marie

Rue Morlet

Roofed with massive domes like the cathedrals of Périgueux and Cahors, the spacious interior of the twelfth-century **church of Ste-Marie** creates just the atmosphere for cool reflection on a summer's day. On the inside of the west door are some of the most wonderful Romanesque sculptures, including a seething mass of beasts devouring each other. The greatest piece of craftsmanship, though, is a **bas-relief of Isaiah**, fluid and supple, thought to be by one of the artists who worked at Moissac.

## Musée de l'Automate

Rue Morlet • April–June & Sept Tues–Sun 10am–noon & 3–6pm; July & Aug daily 10am–6pm; Nov–March Wed–Sun 2.30–5.30pm • €6

The **Musée de l'Automate** contains an impressive collection of nineteenth- and twentieth-century mechanical dolls and animals, which dance, sing and perform magical tricks; look out for the irresistible laughing man.

## ARRIVAL AND INFORMATION                                         SOUILLAC

**By train** The train station is just over 1km northwest of the town centre.

**Destinations** Brive-la-Gaillarde (6–10 daily; 25min); Cahors (7–9 daily; 40min); Gourdon (5–7 daily; 15min); Montauban (4–6 daily; 1hr 25min); Sarlat (8–11 daily; 30min); Toulouse (7–9 daily; 2hr 10min–2hr 20min).

**By bus** Buses arrive and depart from both the train station and the more central av de Sarlat.

**Destinations** Lascaux II (July & Aug Mon–Sat 2 daily; 1hr

40min); Martel (1–4 daily; 30min); Sarlat (2–4 daily; 45min).

**Tourist office** Bd Louis-Jean-Malvy (July & Aug Mon–Sat 9.30am–12.30pm & 2–7pm, Sun 10am–noon & 3–6pm; Sept–June Mon–Sat 10am–12.30pm & 2–6pm; ☎ 05 65 37 81 56, ⊛ tourisme-souillac.com).

**Canoe rental** Copeyre Canoe, La Borgne (from €16; ☎ 05 65 32 72 61, ⊛ copeyre.com).

## ACCOMMODATION

**Les Ondines** La Borgne ☎ 05 65 37 86 44, ⊛ camping -lesondines.com. A large riverside campsite, just 1km south of the old town. Very family-orientated, with a heated pool, children's playground and a bouncy castle. May–Sept. **€18**

**Le Pavillon St-Martin** 5 place St-Martin ☎ 05 65 32 63 45, ⊛ tourisme-vallee-dordogne.com. Directly opposite the brooding church of St-Martin, this attractive, sixteenth-century shuttered building has beautifully renovated, sumptuous rooms, which are full of character. **€49**

## EATING

**Le Beffroi** 6 place St-Martin ☎ 05 65 37 80 33. Situated on a pretty square, in the shadow of the church of St-Martin, this friendly restaurant is a great choice for simple but tasty

meals, especially under the lovely, wisteria-shaded terrace. The sirloin steak is particularly recommended (€14). Closed Jan–March. Daily noon–2.30pm & 7–9.30pm.

## Martel

About 15km east of Souillac and set back even further from the river, **MARTEL** is a minor medieval masterpiece, built in a pale, almost white stone, offset by warm reddish-brown roofs. A Turenne-administered town (see p.536), its heyday came during the thirteenth and fourteenth centuries, when the viscounts established a court of appeal here.

### Place des Consuls

The main square, **place des Consuls**, is mostly taken up by the eighteenth-century **market hall** (market Sat & Wed), but on every side are reminders of the town's illustrious past, most notably in the superb Gothic **Hôtel de la Raymondie**. Begun in 1280, it served as the Turenne law courts, though it doubled as the town's refuge, hence the distinctive corner turrets. Facing it is the **Tour des Pénitents**, one of the medieval towers that gave the town its epithet, *la ville aux sept tours* ("the town with seven towers"). The Young King Henry, son of Henry II, died in the striking **Maison Fabri**, in the southeast corner of the square. One block south, rue Droite leads east to the town's main **church**, St-Maur, which was built in a fiercely defensive, mostly Gothic style, and has a finely carved Romanesque tympanum depicting the Last Judgement above the west door.

Tourist train

April–Sept • €9.50 return • ☏ 05 65 37 35 81, ⓦ trainduhautquercy.info

One way to soak up the scenery is on the **steam and diesel tourist trains** (*train à vapeur*) that run on a restored line between Martel and St-Denis. The trains, which depart from an old station about 200m south of town, afford wonderful views as they climb the steep cliffs overlooking the river valley.

## ARRIVAL AND INFORMATION                                      MARTEL

**By bus** Buses from Brive-la-Gaillarde (Mon–Sat 1–3 daily; 1hr 15min) and Souillac (Mon–Sat 1–5 daily; 20min) stop on the main road, just a short walk from the town square.

**Tourist office** Place des Consuls (☏ 05 65 37 43 44, ⓦ tourisme-martel.fr).

## ACCOMMODATION

**Auberge des 7 Tours** ☏ 05 65 37 30 16, ⓦ auberge7tours.com. The position of this small hotel, just a short walk north of the town centre, affords it lovely views of the surrounding countryside from its terrace. Rooms are plain but bright, and there's a decent restaurant on site (*menus* from €12.60). Restaurant Tues–Fri noon–2pm & 7pm–9pm, Sat 7–9pm, Sun noon–2pm. **€44**

**Camping les Falaises** Gluges, 5km from Martel ☏ 05 65 37 37 78, ⓦ camping-lesfalaises.com. In a lovely

position by the Dordogne, this pleasant campsite offers lots of shady pitches and canoeing and kayaking opportunities right on the doorstep. June–Aug. **€12.60**

★ **Relais Ste-Anne** Rue du Pourtanel ☏ 05 65 36 40 56, ⓦ relais-sainte-anne.com. The nicest place to stay is this ivy-covered former girls' boarding school, surrounded by attractive gardens with a small heated pool and a fine restaurant (*menus* from €16). The rooms are furnished in a tasteful mix of contemporary and modern styles, some with their own terrace. Closed Dec–Feb. **€95**

## EATING

**Plein Sud** Place des Consuls. A charming little place opposite the covered market, with tables out on the square, serving decent pizzas (from €6.50) and more interesting

mains like tuna steak (€14.50). April–June & Sept Tues–Sun noon–2pm & 7–9pm; July & Aug daily noon–2pm & 7–9pm.

## Carennac and around

**CARENNAC** is without doubt one of the most beautiful villages along the Dordogne River. Elevated just above the south bank, 13km or so east of Martel, it's best known for its typical Quercy architecture, its Romanesque priory, where the French writer Fénelon spent the best years of his life, and for its greengages.

### Church and cloisters

**Cloisters** April–June, Sept & Oct Mon–Sat 10am–12.30pm & 2–6pm; July & Aug daily 10am–1pm & 2–7pm; Nov–March Mon–Fri 10am–noon & 2–5pm • €2.50

Carennac's major feature, as so often in these parts, is the Romanesque tympanum – in the Moissac style – above the west door of its church, the **Église St-Pierre**. Christ sits in majesty with the Book of Judgement in his left hand, with the apostles and adoring angels below him. Next to the church, don't miss the old **cloisters and chapterhouse**, which contain an exceptionally expressive life-size *Entombment of Christ*.

### Château de Castelnau-Bretenoux

2.5km southwest of Bretenoux • April & Sept daily 10am–12.30pm & 2–5.30pm; May & June daily 10am–12.30pm & 2–6.30pm; July & Aug daily 10am–7pm; Oct–March daily except Tues 10am–12.30pm & 2–5.30pm • €7 • ⓦ monuments-nationaux.fr

Ten kilometres upstream from Carennac, the sturdy towers and machicolated red-brown walls of the eleventh-century **Château de Castelnau-Bretenoux** dominate a sharp knoll above the Dordogne. Most of the château has been restored, though the main reason to come here is for the view from the ramparts, which stretch as far as Turenne on a clear day.

### ARRIVAL AND DEPARTURE

**CARENNAC AND AROUND**

**By car** There is no public transport to Carennac. There are a number of free car parks just off the main road above the village.

**Tourist office** Cour du Prieuré (April–June, Sept & Oct

Mon–Sat 10am–12.30pm & 2–6pm; July & Aug daily 10am–1pm & 2–7pm; Nov–March Mon–Fri 10am–noon & 2–5pm; ☎05 65 33 22 00, ⓦtourisme -vallee-dordogne.com).

### ACCOMMODATION AND EATING

★ **La Farga** ☎05 65 33 18 97, ⓦlafarga.wordpress .com. Arguably the nicest place to stay in Carennac is this welcoming *chambres d'hôte* on the main street. There are five appealingly simple, tastefully decorated rooms and one apartment, some overlooking the garden with its heated pool and children's play area. Meals using local organic ingredients are available for around €20 in the

communal dining room. **€60**

**Hostellerie Fénelon** ☎05 65 10 96 46, ⓦhotel -fenelon.com. Old-fashioned but perfectly adequate rooms, the nicer ones overlooking the river. It also has a pool and a good restaurant specializing in traditional regional cuisine (*menus* from €19). Closed mid-Nov to mid-March. Restaurant daily noon–2pm & 7–9pm. **€59**

## Beaulieu-sur-Dordogne

In a picturesque spot on the banks of the Dordogne, 8km upriver from Castelnau-Bretenoux, **BEAULIEU-SUR-DORDOGNE** boasts one of the great masterpieces of Romanesque sculpture, on the porch of the **church of St-Pierre**. This doorway is unusually deep-set, with a tympanum presided over by an oriental-looking Christ with one arm extended to welcome the chosen. All around him is a complicated pattern of angels and apostles, executed in characteristic "dancing" style, similar to that at Carennac. The dead raise the lids of their coffins hopefully, while underneath a frieze depicts monsters crunching heads. Take the opportunity also to wander north along rue de la Chapelle past some handsome sculpted facades and down to the river.

### ARRIVAL AND INFORMATION

**BEAULIEU-SUR-DORDOGNE**

**By bus** Buses run to and from Brive (1–2 daily; 1hr 10min), alighting and departing from place du Champs-du-Mars, just west of place Marbot.

**Tourist office** Place Marbot (April–June & Sept Mon–Sat 9.30am–12.30pm & 2.30–6pm, Sun 9.30am–12.30pm;

July & Aug Mon–Sat 9.30am–1pm & 2.30–7pm, Sun 9.30am–1pm; Oct Mon–Sat 9.30am–12.30pm & 2.30–6pm; Nov–March Mon–Sat 10am–12.30pm & 2.30–5pm; ☎05 55 91 09 94, ⓦbeaulieu-tourisme.com).

### ACCOMMODATION AND EATING

**Camping des Îles** Bd Rodolphe de Turenne ☎05 55 91 02 65, ⓦcampingdesiles.fr. As its name suggests, this large campsite is set on its own island in the Dordogne, just a short walk from the old town. It's a great choice for families, with a swimming pool and adventure playground on site, plus bike and canoe hire. Closed mid-Oct to mid-April. **€23.50**

★ **Le Relais de Vellinus** 17 place du Champ-de-Mars ☎05 55 91 11 04, ⓦvellinus.com. One of the most

appealing hotels in town, decorated in warm, contemporary colours. Some rooms have a small balcony overlooking the square. **€68**

**Velouté** Rue de la Bridolle ☎05 55 91 14 51. A surprisingly contemporary restaurant in the old town, with a small covered terrace out front, serving an interesting range of dishes, such as cod back with rice and *moules marinière* (*menus* from €17.50). Tues noon–2.30pm, Wed–Sat noon–2.30pm & 7–9.30pm, Sun noon–3pm.

# The Lot

While the old provinces of **Haut Quercy** and **Quercy** – the land between the Dordogne and the Lot rivers and between the Lot and the Garonne, Aveyron and Tarn – largely correspond to the modern-day Lot *département*, it makes sense, for convenience's sake, to group them together with the gorges of the River **Aveyron** and Villefranche-de-Rouergue on the edge of the province of Rouergue.

The area is hotter, drier, less well known and, with few exceptions, less crowded than the Dordogne, though no less interesting. The cave paintings at **Pech-Merle** are on a par with those at Les Eyzies, while **Najac** has a ruined castle (and fabulous views) to rival those of the Dordogne. The towns of **Figeac** and **Villefranche-de-Rouergue** are without equal, as is the village of **St-Antonin-Noble-Val**, and stretches of country such as that below **Gourdon**, around **Les Arques** where Ossip Zadkine had his studio, and the **Célé valley**.

# Rocamadour and around

Halfway up a cliff in the deep and abrupt canyon of the Alzou stream, the spectacular setting of **ROCAMADOUR** is hard to beat. Since medieval times the town has been inundated by pilgrims drawn by the supposed miraculous ability of Rocamadour's Black Madonna. Nowadays, pilgrims are outnumbered by more secular-minded visitors, who fill the lanes lined with shops peddling incongruous souvenirs, but who come here mainly to wonder at the sheer audacity of the town's location, built almost vertically into its rocky backdrop.

## Brief history

Legend has it that the history of Rocamadour began with the arrival of **Zacchaeus**, a tax-collector in Jericho at the time of Christ. According to one legend he was advised by the Virgin Mary to come to France, where he lived out his years as a hermit. When in 1166 a perfectly preserved body was found in a grave high up on the rock, it was declared to be Zacchaeus, or **St Amadour**. The place soon became a major pilgrimage site and a staging post on the road to Santiago de Compostela in Spain. St Bernard, numerous kings of England and France and thousands of others crawled up the chapel steps on their knees to pay their respects and seek cures for their illnesses. Young King Henry, son of Henry II of England, was the first to plunder the shrine, but he was easily outclassed by the Huguenots, who tried in vain to burn the saint's corpse and finally resigned themselves simply to hacking it to bits. A reconstruction was produced in the nineteenth century, in an attempt to revive the flagging pilgrimage.

## Chapelle Notre-Dame

Rocamadour is easy enough to find your way around. There's just one street, rue de la Couronnerie, strung out between two medieval gateways. Above it, the steep hillside supports no fewer than seven churches. There's a lift dug into the rock face (€3 return), but it's far better to climb the 223 steps of the Via Sancta, up which the devout drag themselves on their knees to the little **Chapelle Notre-Dame** where the miracle-working twelfth-century Black Madonna resides. The tiny, crudely carved walnut statue glows in the mysterious half-light, but the rest of the chapel is unremarkable. From the rock above the entrance door hangs a rusty sword, supposedly Roland's legendary blade, Durandal.

## The ramparts

Daily 9am–7pm • €2

Just east of the Chapelle Notre-Dame you can either hop in a lift (€4.10 return) or take a winding, shady path, *La Calvarie*, past the Stations of the Cross, to the top of the hill, where you can walk around the ancient **ramparts** and enjoy vertiginous views across the valley.

## Gouffre de Padirac

20km east of Rocamadour • Daily guided tours (90min): April–June 9.30am–6.30pm; July 9.30am–8pm; Aug 8.30am–8.30pm; Sept to mid-Nov 10am–6pm • €9.80 • ⓦ gouffre-de-padirac.com

An enormous limestone sinkhole, about 100m deep and more than 100m wide, the **Gouffre de Padirac** gives access to an underground river network containing some spectacular rock formations and magical lakes, but is very, very popular. There is no system for reservations, so in summer you're advised to arrive before 10am. Visits are partly on foot, partly by boat, and in wet weather you'll need a waterproof jacket.

**10**

## ARRIVAL AND INFORMATION

**By car** Getting to Rocamadour without your own transport is awkward. The best place to park is in L'Hospitalet, on the hilltop above Rocamadour (which has the best view of the town).

**By train** Rocamadour-Padirac *gare SNCF* on the Brive-Capdenac line is 3.5km from Rocamadour; it's a fairly straightforward walk along the main road (D673), or you can call a taxi (☎ 06 73 44 79 98).

**Tourist office** There are two tourist offices: the main one in L'Hospitalet (Mon–Fri 10am–noon & 2–5pm; ☎ 05 65 33 22 00, ⓦ rocamadour.com), and a second next to the Hôtel de Ville, on rue de la Couronnerie (daily 10am–noon & 2–5pm; ☎ 05 65 33 62 59).

## ACCOMMODATION

Rocamadour's hotels close for the winter, and you need to book early in summer.

**Beau Site** Rue de la Couronnerie ☎ 05 65 33 63 08, ⓦ bw-beausite.com. Rocamadour's most luxurious hotel, in the heart of the village, offers surprisingly unexciting rooms in a beautiful old building. The sunny, tucked-away terrace is a real bonus. Closed mid-Nov to Easter. **€99**

**Belvédère** L'Hospitalet ☎ 05 65 33 63 25, ⓦ hotel -le-belvedere.fr. Though you're not in the medieval city here, you can benefit from some of the most fabulous views of it from a number of the bedrooms and the restaurant at this modern hotel. Closed mid-Nov to Easter. **€55**

**Lion d'Or** Rue de la Couronnerie ☎ 05 65 33 62 04, ⓦ liondor-rocamadour.com. A good-value choice, offering fairly small but bright rooms on the main drag. They have a decent restaurant across the road (*menus* from €12.80) which enjoys panoramic views. Closed mid-Nov to Easter. **€43.50**

## EATING

**Les Jardins de la Louve** Far end of rue de la Couronnerie ☎ 05 65 33 62 93. At the quieter end of the main street, this pleasant restaurant is one of the more appealing in town, with both a shady terrace and a lovely garden. The *plat du jour* is good value at €12.50, and lighter dishes are also on offer. Closed mid-Nov to Easter. Daily noon–2pm & 7–9.30pm.

**Le Jehan de Valon** Rue de la Couronnerie ☎ 05 65 33 63 08, ⓦ bw-beausite.com. The *Beau Site*'s gourmet restaurant provides fabulous views over the valley from its terrace, and serves up seasonal, local dishes like *magret de canard* with blackberry sauce. *Menus* from €19.60. Daily noon–2pm & 7.30–9.30pm.

# St-Céré

The medieval town of **ST-CÉRÉ**, full of ancient houses crowding around place du Mercadial, is dominated by the brooding ruins of the **Château de St-Laurent-les-Tours**, whose two powerful keeps were once part of a fortress belonging to the Turenne. During World War II, the artist Jean Lurçat operated a secret Resistance radio post here; after the war he turned it into a studio, and it's now a **museum** of his work, with mainly huge tapestries but also sketches, paintings and pottery (daily: two weeks at Easter & mid-July to Sept 9.30am–noon & 2.30–6.30pm; €2.50). At an altitude of more than 200m, the site is spectacular, with stunning views all around.

## ARRIVAL AND INFORMATION

**By bus** Buses arrive and depart from place de la République. Destinations Cahors (1–3 daily; 1hr 45min); Figeac (1–3 daily; 1hr); Martel (Mon; 55min).

**Tourist office** 31 av Francpos de Maynard (Mon–Sat 10am–12.30pm & 2–6pm; ☎ 05 65 33 22 00, ⓦ tourisme-vallee-dordogne.com).

**Bike rental** Velo Oxygen, 45 rue Faidherbe (€9/day; ☎ 05 65 38 03 23).

## ACCOMODATION AND EATING

**Victor-Hugo** 7 av des Maquis ☎ 05 65 38 16 15, ⓦ hotel-victor-hugo.fr. Boasting the best position in town, right by the river in a gorgeous old red-shuttered building, the *Victor-Hugo* has attractive, calm rooms and an unpretentious restaurant. **€55**

# Gourdon

**GOURDON** lies between Sarlat and Cahors, conveniently served by the Brive–Toulouse train line, and makes a quiet, agreeable base for visiting some of the major places in this part of the Dordogne and Lot. It's 17km south of the River Dordogne and pretty much at the eastern limit of the luxuriant woods and valleys of Périgord, which give way quite suddenly, at the line of the N20, to the arid limestone landscape of the **Causse de Gramat**.

It is a striking town, its medieval centre of yellow-stone houses attached like a swarm of bees to a prominent hilltop, neatly ringed by modern boulevards containing all the commerce. The main street through the Old Town, with a fortified **gateway** at one end, is rue du Majou. It's lined all the way up with splendid stone houses, some, like the **Maison d'Anglars** at no. 17, dating back to the thirteenth century. At the top you emerge into a lovely, intimate square in front of the massive but not particularly interesting fourteenth-century **church of St-Pierre**. From the square, steps climb to the top of the hill, where the castle once stood and from where there is a superb view stretching for miles.

10

## ARRIVAL AND INFORMATION

GOURDON

**By train** The station is roughly 1km northeast of the centre; from the station, walk south on av de la Gare, then turn right onto av Gambetta to reach the boulevard encircling the Old Town.

Destinations Brive-la-Gaillarde (1–9 daily; 40min); Cahors (5–9 daily; 30min); Montauban (5–9 daily; 50min); Souillac (1–9 daily; 15min).

**By bus** Buses from Souillac (Mon–Fri daily 50min) arrive and depart from place de la Libération, just a few minutes' walk southwest of the centre.

**Tourist office** 24 rue du Majou (March–June, Sept & Oct Mon–Sat 10am–noon & 2–6pm; July & Aug Mon–Sat 10am–7pm, Sun 10am–noon; Nov–Feb Mon–Sat 10am–noon & 2–5pm; ☎ 05 65 27 52 50, ⓦ tourisme -gourdon.com).

## ACCOMMODATION AND EATING

**Hostellerie de la Bouriane** Place du Foirail ☎ 05 65 41 16 37, ⓦ hotellabouriane.fr. A smart, traditional hotel, with comfortable rooms, though some are a little on the dark side. The restaurant is especially popular for Sunday lunch, with *menus* from €28. Closed Jan–May. Restaurant May to mid-Oct Tues–Sun 7.30–9pm, Sun 12.15–1.30pm; mid-Oct to April Sun 12.15–1.30pm & 7.30–9pm. **€83**

★ **Le Pot Occitan** 39 bd Mainiol ☎ 05 65 41 11 81. A charming, relaxed restaurant, decorated with bright cushions and books on Americana, serving up simple, hearty dishes like the *formule du boucher* – sirloin steak, chips, salad and a generous slice of Cantal – for around €13. Daily noon–2pm & 7–9pm.

**De la Promenade** 48 bd Galiot-de-Genouillac ☎ 05 65 41 41 44, ⓦ lapromenadegourdon.com. On the northwest side of the ring road, this is a cheerful place with well-priced rooms and an inexpensive pub-style restaurant (*menus* from €13). Restaurant Mon–Sat 7–10pm. **€57**

## Les Arques

The exquisite hamlet of **LES ARQUES**, 27km southwest of Gourdon, is set among quiet, remote, small-scale farming country, emptied of people by the slaughter of the two World Wars and by migration to the towns in search of jobs. The village itself is attractive, but notable mainly as the home of the Russian Cubist/Expressionist sculptor Ossip **Zadkine**, who bought an old house by the church here in 1934, and for its excellent restaurant (see p.566).

### Musée Zadkine

Tues–Sun April–Oct 10am–1pm & 3–7pm; Nov, Dec, Feb & March 2–6pm • €3

Even for those with no real interest in the sculptor's work, Les Arques' **Musée Zadkine** is a fascinating stop, with a compelling collection of his statues. It's the ones in the basement that really steal the show, with Orphée taking pride of place; awe-inspiring in its size, this wood-carved sculpture appears to change as you view it from different sides, and the attention to detail is quite astounding.

The church

Les Arques' small twelfth-century **church** is beautiful in its unadorned simplicity. Above the door, Zadkine's huge cruxification works perfectly against the bare stone walls and the simple stained-glass windows, while in the tiny crypt, his Pieta has been created in such a way that the shading on the figures makes them appear almost two dimensional.

**10**

### ARRIVAL AND DEPARTURE LES ARQUES

**By bus** There are weekly buses to Cahors (Wed; 1hr 5min) from the bus stop on the main road, opposite *La Récréation*.

### EATING

★ **La Récréation** ☎ 05 65 22 88 08. Set in the old village school, this wonderful restaurant serves up copious, delicious meals beneath the chestnut trees of the old school yard and in one of the converted classrooms (*menus* from €26). On a summer night, with the swifts flying overhead, it's idyllic. Reservations highly recommended. March–Oct Mon, Tues & Fri–Sun noon–1.30pm & 7–9pm.

# Cahors

**CAHORS**, on the River Lot, was the capital of the old province of Quercy. In its time, it has been a Gallic settlement; a Roman town; a briefly held Moorish possession; a town under English rule; a bastion of Catholicism in the Wars of Religion, sacked in consequence by Henri IV; a university town for 400 years; and birthplace of the politician Léon Gambetta (1838–82), after whom so many French streets and squares are named. Modern Cahors is a sunny southern backwater, with two interesting sights in its **cathedral** and the remarkable **Pont Valentré**. The city sits on a peninsula formed by a tight loop in the River Lot, and is small and easily walkable.

While you're in the Cahors area, don't miss out on the local **wine**, heady and black but dry to the taste and not at all plummy like the Gironde wines from Blaye and Bourg, which use the same Malbec grape.

## Cathedral

Place J. Chapou • St Gaubert's chapel closed to the public, though it is occasionally included on city tours – ask at the tourist office

Dominating the centre is the **Cathedral,** which, consecrated in 1119, is the oldest and simplest in plan of the Périgord-style churches. The exterior is not exciting: a heavy square tower dominates the plain west front, whose best feature is the north portal, where a Christ in Majesty dominates the tympanum, surrounded by angels and apostles, while cherubim fly out of the clouds to relieve him of his halo. Side panels show scenes from the life of St Stephen. The outer ring over the portal shows a line of naked figures being stabbed and hacked with axes.

Inside, the cathedral is much like Périgueux's St-Front, with a nave lacking aisles and transepts, roofed with two big domes; in the first are fourteenth-century frescoes of the stoning of St Stephen, while over the west door are faded but beautiful Creation scenes from the same era. To the right of the choir a door opens into a delicate **cloister** in the Flamboyant style, still retaining some intricate, though damaged, carving. On the northwest corner pillar the Virgin is portrayed as a graceful girl with broad brow and ringlets to her waist. In the cloister's northeast corner **St Gaubert's chapel** holds the Holy Coif, a cloth said to have covered Christ's head in the tomb, which according to legend was brought back from the Holy Land in the twelfth century by Bishop Géraud de Cardaillac.

## The old town

The area around the cathedral is filled by a warren of narrow lanes, most of them now handsomely restored. Many of the houses, turreted and built of thin, flat brick, date

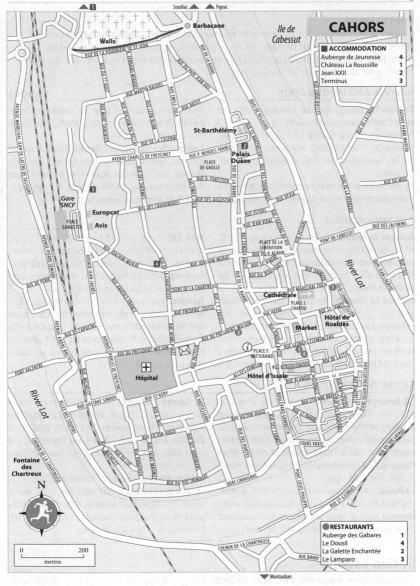

**CAHORS**

**10**

■ **ACCOMMODATION**

| | |
|---|---|
| Auberge de Jeunesse | 4 |
| Château La Roussille | 1 |
| Jean XXII | 2 |
| Terminus | 3 |

● **RESTAURANTS**

| | |
|---|---|
| Auberge des Gabares | 1 |
| Le Dousil | 4 |
| La Galette Enchantée | 2 |
| Le Lamparo | 3 |

from the fourteenth and fifteenth centuries. As you wander, look out for the many little "secret gardens" scattered round the town.

Immediately south of the cathedral, the lime-bordered **place Jean-Jacques-Chapou** commemorates a local trade unionist and Resistance leader, killed in a German ambush on July 17, 1944. Next to it is the covered **market** and a building still bearing the name Gambetta, where the family of the famous deputy of Belleville in Paris had their grocery shop.

## Pont Valentré

Cahors is best known for its dramatic fourteenth-century **Pont Valentré**, one of the finest surviving medieval bridges. Its three powerful towers, originally closed by portcullises and gates, made it effectively an independent fortress, guarding the river crossing on the west side of town.

### ARRIVAL AND INFORMATION

CAHORS

**By train** The station is on place Jouinot-Gambetta, just under 500m from central bd Gambetta.

Destinations Brive-la-Gaillard (7–9 daily; 1hr 5min); Gourdon (6–9 daily; 25min); Montauban (6–11 daily; 50min); Souillac (6–9 daily; 45min); Toulouse (7–12 daily; 1hr 25min).

**By bus** Most buses arrive and depart from both the train station and the more central place Charles-de-Gaulle.

Destinations Figeac (4–5 daily; 1hr 45min); Les Arques (weekly; 50min); Luzech (3–7 daily; 20min); Puy-l'Évêque (3–7 daily; 45min).

**Tourist office** Place François-Mitterrand (April, May & Oct Mon–Sat 9am–12.30pm & 1.30–6.30pm; June–Sept Mon–Sat 9am–7pm, Sun 10am–1pm & 1.30–5.30pm; Nov–March Mon–Sat 9.30am–12.30pm & 2–6pm; ☎ 05 65 53 20 65, ⓦ tourisme-cahors.com).

### ACCOMMODATION

**Auberge de Jeunesse** Rue Joachim Murat ☎ 05 65 35 64 71, ⓦ FUAJ.org. In an elegant old building in lovely grounds between the train station and the city centre, this FUAJ hostel offers the usual dorms, plus a small bar and canteen-restaurant. €14.70

**Château La Roussille** Chemin du Moulin, Labéraudie ☎ 05 65 22 84 74, ⓦ châteauroussille.com. This welcoming chambres d'hôte, a 5min drive from Cahors centre, has a large garden with a swimming pool. There are two rooms and two suites, all with their own character, plus a lounge and billiard room. Closed mid-Nov to end March. €75

**Jean XXII** 2 rue Edmond-Albe ☎ 05 65 35 07 66, ⓦ hotel-jeanxxii.com. Situated in the fourteenth-century buildings of the Palais Duèze, at the north end of bd Gambetta, this small, friendly hotel offers modern, fairly functional rooms done up in paisley. €62

**Terminus** 5 av Charles-de-Freycinet ☎ 05 65 53 32 00, ⓦ balandre.com. An elegant nineteenth-century house near the station, with a fine restaurant (menus €35–75). The rooms don't quite match up to the public areas, but boast all modern three-star comforts such as double-glazing and a/c. €70

### EATING AND DRINKING

★ **Auberge des Gabares** 24 place Champollion ☎ 05 65 53 91 47. One of the nicest and best-value places to eat in Cahors, serving hearty home cooking on its wisteria-covered terrace overlooking the Lot – there's just one five-course menu, with a certain amount of choice, which changes daily (€15, Sat eve €21). Wed–Mon noon–2pm & 7–9pm, Tues noon–2pm.

**Le Dousil** 124 rue Nationale ☎ 05 65 53 19 67. A small, cosy wine bar that's a great place to sample local wines, alongside plates of cheese and meat, or more substantial dishes like cassoulet (from €12.20). Daily 10am–1pm.

**La Galette Enchantée** 45 rue du Président Wilson ☎ 05 65 23 88 14. Friendly little crêperie tucked off the main drag, offering galettes from €6.20, such as La Basquaise with rataouille, chicken and Emmenthal, and sweet crêpes from just €2.80. Mon–Sat noon–2.45pm, Fri & Sat 7–10pm.

**Le Lamparo** 76 rue Georges Clémenceau ☎ 05 65 35 25 93. In a great position on the south side of the market square, this is a perennial favourite for its very reasonably priced menus, pizzas and generous portions (from €8.50). Mon–Sat noon–2pm & 7–10.30pm.

# St-Cirq-Lapopie

The pale stone houses of **ST-CIRQ-LAPOPIE**, staggered down the steep hillside above the south bank of the Lot, appear almost fairy-tale-like as you approach from the east. The village was saved from ruin when poet André Breton came to live here in the early twentieth century, and though it's now an irresistible draw for the tour buses, with its cobbled lanes, half-timbered houses and flower-strewn balconies, it's still well worth a visit, especially early or late in the day, when the buildings glow in the sunlight. From behind the tourist office (see opposite), a steep path leads up to the top of the cliff, once the site of the town's château, for commanding views over the river valley.

## ARRIVAL AND INFORMATION
ST-CIRQ-LAPOPIE

**By bus** The only way to get to St-Cirq-Lapopie by public transport is by bus from Cahors to Tour-de-Faure (3–8 daily; 30min), from where it's a steep 2km walk up the hill.

**Tourist office** Place du Sombral (Mon–Sat 10am–1pm & 2–6pm, Sun 11am–1pm & 2–6pm; ☏ 05 65 31 31 31, ⊚ saint-cirqlapopie.com).

## ACCOMMODATION

**Auberge du Sombral** Place du Sombral ☏ 05 65 31 26 08, ⊚ lesombral.com. This attractive auberge on the village's main square offers charming, if a little plain, rooms with surprisingly modern bathrooms, above a popular restaurant (*menus* from €15). Closed mid-Nov to March. Restaurant Sun–Thurs noon–2pm, Fri & Sat noon–2pm & 7–9pm. **€52**

**Camping de la Plage** ☏ 05 65 30 29 51, ⊚ campingplage.com. Down by the river, this well-run campsite has lovely pitches among the trees, and various activities on offer, including swimming, canoeing and horseriding. **€20**

**Château de Saint Cirq Lapopie** Just below the church ☏ 05 65 31 27 48. A lovely *chambres d'hôte*, set in an old château in the heart of the village, with appealing rooms that boast traditional features like wood beams and views over the valley. They often host interesting modern art exhibitions here. **€108**

## EATING AND DRINKING

**Le Cantou** Below the church ☏ 05 65 35 59 03. With its cosy, stone-walled interior, this appealing restaurant is excellent value, with *menus* starting at €12 and dishes ranging from the usual traditional options to a tasty prawn curry. April to mid-Nov Mon–Sat noon–2pm & 7–9pm.

**L'Oustal** Rue de la Pélissaria ☏ 05 65 31 20 17. Cute place tucked away just south of the church, with a handful of tables on an outside terrace. They offer dishes like trout persillade and rice (*menus* from €16). Daily except Wed noon–2pm & 7–9pm.

# Downstream from Cahors

West of Cahors the vine-cloaked banks of the Lot are dotted with ancient villages. The first of these, Luzech and the dramatic **Puy-l'Évêque**, are served by SNCF buses that thread along the valley from Cahors via Fumel to Monsempron-Libos, on the Agen–Périgueux train line. You'll need your own transport, however, to reach the splendid **Château de Bonaguil**, in the hills northwest of Puy-l'Évêque, worth the effort for its elaborate fortifications and spectacular position. From here the Lot valley starts to get ugly and industrial, though **Villeneuve-sur-Lot** provides a pleasant enough base for exploring the villages around. Prettiest are **Pujols**, to the south, which also has a number of excellent restaurants, and Penne-d'Agenais, overlooking the Lot to the east. **Monflanquin**, a *bastide* to the north of Villeneuve, is also well worth a visit for its hilltop location and almost perfect arcaded central square.

## Puy-l'Évêque

**PUY-L'ÉVÊQUE** is probably the prettiest village in the entire valley, with many grand houses built in honey-coloured stone and overlooked by both a **church** and the **castle** of the bishops of Cahors. The best view is from the bridge across the Lot.

## ARRIVAL AND INFORMATION
PUY-L'ÉVÊQUE

**By bus** Buses from Cahors (1–9 daily; 45min) depart and arrive at place du Rampeau, on the main road at the top of the village, and rue Platanes, just east of *Hotel Henry*.

**Tourist office** 12 Grand Rue (Tues & Thurs–Sat 9am–12.30pm & 2–5.30pm, Wed 9am–12.30pm; ☏ 05 65 21 37 63, ⊚ puy-leveque.fr).

## ACCOMMODATION AND EATING

**Bellevue** Place de la Truffière ☏ 05 65 36 06 60, ⊚ hotelbellevue-puyleveque.com. Perched on the cliff edge, this modern hotel has stylish rooms – some with a four-poster bed – and a good restaurant with panoramic views over the village and river. Restaurant daily noon–2pm & 7.30–10pm. **€70**

**Henry** 23 rue du Docteur Rouma ☏ 05 65 21 32 24, ⊚ hotel-henry.com. Pleasant, if plain, rooms, some of

which have a nice view over the attractive garden. **€38**
**Le Pigeonnier** Promenade de Héron ☎ 05 65 21 37 77. Situated directly across the river from the village, this simple crêperie boasts lovely views from its grassy terrace,

and serves *galettes* from €5.50 and large salads from €6.50. May–Sept Tues–Fri & Sun noon–2pm & 7–9pm, Sat 7–9pm; Nov–April Wed noon–2pm & 7–9pm, Sat & Sun 7–9pm.

## Château de Bonaguil

8km from Fumel • March–May & Oct daily 10am–12.30pm & 2–5.30pm; June & Sept daily 10am–12.30pm & 2–6pm; July & Aug daily 10am–7pm; Nov Sun 10.30am–12.30pm & 2–5pm; Dec–Feb during school holidays only daily 2–5pm • €7 • ☎ 05 53 71 90 33, ⓦ bonaguil.org

The imposing **Château de Bonaguil** is spectacularly perched on a wooded spur. Dating largely from the fifteenth and sixteenth centuries, with a double ring of walls, five huge towers and a narrow boat-shaped keep designed to resist artillery, Bonguil was the last of a dying breed, completed just when military architects were abandoning such elaborate fortifications. As it attracts around two thousand visitors a day during summer, it's advisable to get here early.

## Villeneuve-sur-Lot and around

**VILLENEUVE-SUR-LOT**, 75km west and downstream from Cahors, is a pleasant, workaday sort of town that makes a useful base. While there are no standout sights, the handful of attractive timbered houses in the old town and the arcaded central square go some way to compensate. A couple of towers alone survive from the fortifications of this originally *bastide* town, and to the south the main avenue, rue des Cieutats, crosses thirteenth-century **Pont des Cieutat**, which resembles the Pont Valentré in Cahors but is devoid of its towers.

### Church of St-Catherine

The town's most striking landmark is the red-brick tower of the **church of St-Catherine**, completed as late as 1937 in typically dramatic neo-Byzantine style. Beautiful friezes run along the length of the interior, depicting a procession of numerous saints, resplendent against a gold background, and evocative of early Christian art.

### Pujols

Just 3km south of Villeneuve, the tiny hilltop village of **PUJOLS** makes a popular excursion, partly to see the faded Romanesque frescoes in the **church of Ste-Foy** and partly for the views over the surrounding country. The main reason locals come here is for the quality of its **restaurants**.

### ARRIVAL AND INFORMATION
### VILLENEUVE-SUR-LOT AND AROUND

**By bus** Villeneuve's *gare routière* is next to the old train station; buses link up with Monsempron-Libos *gare SNCF* (1–5 daily; 35min) for trains to Perigueux and Agen and with Marmande for trains to Bordeaux (3 daily; 1hr 40min). Buses to Pujols run from place de la Libération (Mon–Sat 1–5 daily; 25min).

**Tourist office** 3 place de la Libération, just outside Villeneuve's northern gate (July & Aug Mon–Sat 9.30am–12.30pm & 2.30–7pm, Sun 9.30am–1pm; Sept–June Mon–Sat 9am–noon & 2–6pm; ☎ 05 53 36 17.30, ⓦ tourisme-villeneuvois.fr).

### ACCOMMODATION AND EATING

**L'Entracte** 30 bd de la Marine, Villeneuve-sur-Lot ☎ 05 53 49 25 50. An upmarket option, serving good-value regional cooking (*menus* from €13.90), with a lovely terrace under the plane trees. Thurs noon–2pm, Fri–Sun noon–2pm & 7–10pm.
**Pietro et Pâtes** 42 rue de Casseneuil, Villeneuve-sur-Lot ☎ 05 53 70 65 13. A very popular little Sicilian restaurant, tucked down a side street, with an

excellent-value lunch *formule* (€11) and delicious dishes like penne *alla Norma* (pasta with aubergines, bacon and tomatoes; €9.50). Tues–Sat noon–2pm & 7–9pm.
**Les Platanes** 40 bd de la Marine, Villeneuve-sur-Lot ☎ 05 53 40 11 40, ⓦ hoteldesplatanes.com. One of the best hotels in town, with unfussy but spacious and well-kept rooms, in a quiet position to the northwest of the old quarter. **€47**

**La Résidence** 17 av Lazare-Carnot, Villeneuve-sur-Lot ☎ 05 53 40 17 03, ⓦ hotellaresidence47.com. This basic hotel, near the *gare routière*, has slightly fussy bedrooms and an appealing plant-filled patio. **€34**

★ **La Toque Blanche** South of Pujols ☎ 05 53 49 00 30, ⓦ la-toque-blanche.com. Just south of Pujols, with views back to the village, this Michelin-starred restaurant is one of the best places to eat in the region. At €39, the "Repas Terroir" is excellent value, and includes delights like foie gras and roasted monkfish. Tues–Sat 11.45am–1.30pm & 7.45–11.30pm.

## Monflanquin

The pretty village of **MONFLANQUIN**, founded by Alphonse de Poitiers in 1256, is one of the region's perfectly preserved *bastides*, not too touristy and impressively positioned on the top of a hill that rises sharply from the surrounding country. It conforms to the regular pattern of right-angled streets leading from a central square to the four town gates. The square – **place des Arcades** – with its distinctly Gothic houses, derives a special charm from being tree-shaded on a slope.

### Musée des Bastides

Place des Arcades • May, June & Sept Mon–Sat 10am–noon & 2–5pm, Sun 10am–1pm; July & Aug Mon–Fri & Sun 10am–7pm, Sat 10am–1pm & 2–7pm; Oct–April Mon–Fri 10am–noon & 2–5pm • €4 • ☎ 05 53 36 40 19, ⓦ monflanquin-museedesbastides.jimdo.com

The surprisingly high-tech little **Musée des Bastides**, above the tourist office, details the life and history of *bastides*. Most of the information is in English, and the various models bring the *bastides* to life.

### ARRIVAL AND INFORMATION  MONFLANQUIN

**By bus** Buses stop on the main road, from where it's a short (but steep) walk up the hill to place des Arcades.

**Tourist office** Place des Arcades (May, June & Sept Mon–Sat 10am–noon & 2–5pm, Sun 10am–1pm; July & Aug Mon–Fri & Sun 10am–7pm, Sat 10am–1pm & 2–7pm; Oct–April Mon–Fri 10am–noon & 2–5pm; ☎ 05 53 36 40 19, ⓦ monflanquin-tourisme.com).

### ACCOMMODATION AND EATING

**La Bastide** Place des Arcades ☎ 05 53 36 77 05. This friendly little crêperie, decked out with old signs and potted plants, has tables outside on the shady terrace – grab one facing down the hill for views over the countryside. The *printemps* – ham, cheese, crème fraiche and asparagus (€6.50) – is especially recommended. Tues, Wed, Fri & Sat noon–11pm, Thurs 11am–11pm, Sun noon–3pm.

**Bastide des Oliviers** 1 tour de Ville ☎ 05 53 36 40 01, ⓦ labastidedesoliviers.fr. At the bottom of the hill, on the main road, this small hotel has attractive modern rooms decked out in earthy tones, with small bathrooms, above a decent restaurant. **€85**

## Figeac

**FIGEAC**, on the River Célé, 71km east of Cahors, is a beautiful town with an unspoilt medieval centre not too encumbered by tourism. Like many other provincial towns hereabouts, it owes its beginnings to the foundation of an abbey in the early days of Christianity in France, one that quickly became wealthy because of its position on the pilgrim routes to both Rocamadour and Compostela. In the Middle Ages it became a centre of tanning, which partly accounts for why many houses' top floors have *solelhos*, or open-sided wooden galleries used for drying skins and other produce. It was the Wars of Religion that pushed it into eclipse, for Figeac sided with the nearby Protestant stronghold of Montauban and suffered the same punishing reprisals by the victorious royalists in 1662. The **church of St-Sauveur**, near the river, maintains its lovely Gothic chapterhouse decorated with heavily gilded but dramatically realistic seventeenth-century carved wood panels illustrating the life of Christ.

### Hôtel de la Monnaie and around

In the Old Town centre, the **Hôtel de la Monnaie** surveys place Vival. It's a splendid building dating back to the thirteenth century, when the city's mint was located in this district. In the streets radiating off to the north of the square there's a delightful range of houses of the medieval and classical periods, both stone and half-timbered, adorned with carvings and colonnettes and interesting ironwork. At the end of these streets are the two adjacent squares of **place Carnot** and **place Champollion**, both of great charm. The former is the site of the old *halles*, under whose awning cafés now spread their tables.

## Musée Champollion

Place Champollion • April–June & Sept Tues–Sun 10.30am–12.30pm & 2–6pm; July & Aug daily 10.30am–6pm; Oct–March Tues–Sun 2–5.30pm • €4 • ☎ 05 65 50 31 08, ⓦ musee-champollion.fr

Jean-François Champollion, who cracked Egyptian hieroglyphics by deciphering the triple text of the Rosetta Stone, was born at 4 impasse Champollion, just off place Champollion. The house now forms part of the excellent **Musée Champollion**, dedicated to the history of writing, from the very earliest cuniform signs some 50,000 years ago. The most interesting exhibits relate to Champollion's life and work, including original manuscripts tracing his and others' progress towards cracking the hieroglyphs. Beside the museum, a larger-than-life reproduction of the Rosetta Stone forms the floor of the tiny **place des Écritures**, above which is a little garden planted with tufts of papyrus.

### ARRIVAL AND INFORMATION                                                    FIGEAC

**By train** The *gare SNCF* is a 5min walk to the south of the Old Town, across the river at the end of rue de la Gare and av des Poilus.

Destinations Brive-la-Gaillarde (3–7 daily; 1hr 15min); Najac (3–6 daily; 1hr 10min); Rocamadour-Padirac (3–7 daily; 35min); Villefranche-de-Rouergue (3–6 daily; 35min).

**By bus** Buses arrive and depart from the train station.

Destinations Cahors (3–6 daily; 2hr); Najac (weekly; 1hr 10min); Villefranche-de-Rouergue (1–6 daily; 40min).

**Tourist office** Hôtel de la Monnaie, place Vival (May, June & Sept Mon–Sat 9am–12.30pm & 2–6pm, Sun 10am–1pm; July & Aug daily 9am–7pm; Oct–April Mon–Sat 9am–12.30pm & 2–6pm; ☎ 05 65 34 06 25, ⓦ tourisme-figeac.com).

### ACCOMMODATION

**Des Bains** 1 rue du Griffoul ☎ 05 65 34 10 89, ⓦ hoteldesbains.fr. Just across the river from the old town, with lovely views from its restaurant terrace, in a building that used to house the town swimming baths. Rooms are light and airy, if a little spartan. **€48**

**Champollion** 3 place Champollion ☎ 05 65 34 04 37, ⓔ hotelchampollion@orange.fr. Small hotel on this bustling square, with surprisingly smart rooms above a popular café-bar. Two have views over the square. **€52**

**Château du Viguier du Roy** 52 rue Émile-Zola ☎ 05 65

50 05 05, ⓦ château-viguier-figeac.com. Right in the heart of the old town, this luxurious fourteenth-century château has huge rooms, a cloister garden, small (unheated) pool and a gourmet restaurant. Closed mid-Oct to mid-April. **€219**

**Les Rives du Célé** 2km east of Figeac ☎ 05 61 64 88 54, ⓦ lesrivesducele.com. This well-equipped riverside campsite has two pools (including water slides), and is a great choice for families. Bikes and canoes for hire. Closed Oct–March. **€22.50**

### EATING AND DRINKING

**Le 5** 5 place Champollion ☎ 05 65 50 10 81. In a lovely position on this attractive square, especially on sunny days when you can eat outside, this smart, unpretentious restaurant has a small but appealing menu that includes local produce like foie gras and onglet steak with a Bordeaux sauce. Daily noon–2.30pm & 7–9.30pm.

**Les Anges Gourmands** 4 rue Séguier ☎ 05 65 34 08 01. A very popular, quirky little place, serving up tasty assiettes de terroir that showcase local specialities (from

€9.50), plus delicious home-made cakes. Tues–Sat noon–2pm & 7–9pm.

**Pizzeria del Portel** 9 rue Orthabadial ☎ 05 65 34 53 60. A convivial pizzeria serving an extensive menu of pizzas, salad platters, *moules* and the like, with the benefit of outside seating; most dishes are under €12. Tues–Sat noon–2pm & 7.15–9.30pm, Sun 7.15–9.30pm.

## Grotte de Pech-Merle

April–Oct daily 9.15am–5pm • €9; visitors are limited to seven hundred per day – it's advisable to book ahead in July and Aug either by phone or online, three or four days ahead • ☎ 05 65 31 27 05, ⓦ pechmerle.com

Discovered in 1922, the **Grotte de Pech-Merle** is less accessible than the caves at Les Eyzies, well hidden on the scrubby hillsides above Cabrerets, which lies 15km from Marcilhac and 4km from Conduché. The cave itself is far more beautiful than those at Padirac or Les Eyzies, with galleries full of the most spectacular stalactites and stalagmites – structures tiered like wedding cakes, hanging like curtains, or shaped like discs or pearls.

The first **drawings** you come to are in the "Chapelle des Mammouths", executed on a white calcite panel that looks as if it's been specially prepared for the purpose. There are horses, bison – charging head down with tiny rumps and arched tails – and tusked, whiskery mammoths. Next comes a vast chamber where the glorious horse panel is visible on a lower level; it's remarkable how the artist used the relief of the rock to do the work, producing an utterly convincing mammoth in just two black lines. The ceiling is covered with finger marks, preserved in the soft clay. You pass the skeleton of a cave hyena that has been lying there for 20,000 years – wild animals used these caves for shelter and sometimes, unable to find their way out, starved to death. And finally, the most spine-tingling experience at Pech-Merle: the footprints of an adolescent preserved in a muddy pool.

The admission price includes an excellent film and **museum**, where prehistory is illustrated by colourful and intelligible charts, a selection of objects (rather than the usual 10,000 flints), skulls, and beautiful slides displayed in wall panels.

## The valley of the Aveyron

Thirty-odd kilometres south of Figeac, **Villefranche-de-Rouerge** lies on a bend in the River Aveyron, clustered around its perfectly preserved, arcaded market square. From here the Aveyron flows south through increasingly deep, thickly wooded valleys, past the hilltop village of **Najac**, and then turns abruptly west as it enters the **Gorges de l'Aveyron**. The most impressive stretch of this gorge begins just east of **St-Antonin-de-Noble-Val**, an ancient village caught between soaring limestone cliffs, and continues downstream to the villages of **Penne** and **Bruniquel**, perched beside their crumbling castles. Bruniquel marks the end of the gorges, as you suddenly break out into flat alluvial plains where the Aveyron joins the great rivers of the Tarn and Garonne.

### Villefranche-de-Rouergue

No medieval junketing, barely a craft shop in sight, **VILLEFRANCHE-DE-ROUERGUE** must be as close as you can get to what a French provincial town used to be like. It's a small place, lying on a bend in the Aveyron, 35km south of Figeac and 61km east of Cahors across the **Causse de Limogne**. Built as a *bastide* by Alphonse de Poitiers in 1252 as part of the royal policy of extending control over the recalcitrant lands of the south, the town became rich on copper from the surrounding mines and its privilege of minting coins. From the fifteenth to the eighteenth centuries, its wealthy residents built the magnificent houses that grace the cobbled streets to this day.

#### Place Notre-Dame

Villefranche is home to arguably the loveliest *bastide* square in the region, **place Notre-Dame**. It's built on a slope and you enter at the corners underneath the buildings. All the houses are arcaded at ground-floor level, providing for a **market** (Thurs) where local merchants and farmers spread out their weekly produce – the quintessential Villefranche experience. The houses are unusually tall and some are very elaborately decorated, notably the so-called **Maison du Président Raynal** on the lower side at the top of rue de la République.

The square's east side is dominated by the **church of Notre-Dame** with its colossal porch and bell tower, nearly 60m high. The interior has some fine late fifteenth-century stained glass, carved choir stalls and misericords.

### Chapelle des Pénitents-Noirs

Bd de Haute Guyenne • April–June & Oct Tues–Sat 2–5pm; July–Sept daily 2–6pm • €4

On the boulevard that forms the northern limit of the Old Town, the seventeenth-century **Chapelle des Pénitents-Noirs** boasts a splendidly Baroque painted ceiling and an enormous gilded retablo.

### Chartreuse St-Sauveur

1km out of town on the Gaillac road • April–June & Oct Tues–Sat 2–5pm; July–Sept daily 2–6pm • €5

The **Chartreuse St-Sauveur** was completed in the space of ten years from 1450, giving it a singular architectural harmony, and has a very beautiful cloister and choir stalls by the same master as Notre-Dame in Villefranche (which, by contrast, took nearly three hundred years to complete).

## ARRIVAL AND INFORMATION VILLEFRANCHE-DE-ROUERGUE

**By train** The *gare SNCF* lies a couple of minutes' walk south across the Aveyron from the Old Town and is served by regular trains to Figeac (4–7 daily; 45min).

**By bus** Buses pull in at the train station; those from Figeac also stop on the more central place de la Liberté. Destinations Figeac (2–6 daily; 40min); Najac (4–9 daily;

35min).

**Tourist office** Promenade du Guiraudet (May–June & Sept Mon–Fri 9am–noon & 2–7pm, Sat 9am–noon & 2–6pm; July & Aug also open Sun 10am–12.30pm; Oct–April Mon–Fri 9am–noon & 2–6pm, Sat 9am–noon; ☎ 05 65 45 13 18, ⓦ villefranche.com).

## ACCOMMODATION

**Auberge de Jeunesse** ☎ 05 65 45 09 68, ✉ fjt .villefranche@wanadoo.fr €15. Right next to the train station in a striking wooden building, offering basic dorm rooms, plus a simple restaurant with a €9 *menu*. **€22**

**Aveyron** 4 rue Lapeyrade ☎ 05 65 45 17 88, ✉ hotel -restaurant.aveyron@orange.fr. Convenient for the station but not terribly scenic, this cheapie offers simple rooms and a decent, inexpensive restaurant (*menu* €12). Closed Christmas & New Year hols and weekends out of season. **€36**

**Camping du Rouergue** 1.5km south of Villefranche

on the D47 to Monteil ☎ 05 65 45 16 24, ⓦ campingdurouergue.com. Attractive tree-shaded pitches, separated by hedges, plus a small swimming pool and children's playgound. Closed Oct to mid-April. **€14**

★ **Le Claux de la Bastide** 8 rue Ste-Émile-de-Rodat ☎ 06 70 74 61 57, ⓦ leclauxdelabastide.fr. A lovely *chambres d'hôte* in an elegant townhouse one block north of the tourist office, with peaceful, stylish rooms. On fine days, breakfast is served on the patio, surrounded by flowers and trees. **€80**

## EATING AND DRINKING

**L'Assiette Gourmande** Place André-Lescure ☎ 05 65 45 25 95. One of the best places to eat in town, *L'Assiette* specializes in local cuisine (*menus* from €15), such as a delicious salad of foie gras and smoked duck breast. Mon, Thurs–Sat noon–2pm & 7–9pm, Tues & Sun noon–2pm. **Le Dali's** Place Notre Dame ☎ 05 65 45 65 17. An

unbeatable location on the main square, with a sleek, modern interior and views of the cathedral from the terrace. The *menus* are good value (€11.50), though the Spanish-influenced food is fairly mediocre. July & Aug daily noon–2pm & 7–9pm; Sept, Oct & Dec–June Mon–Fri noon–2pm, Fri & Sat 7–9pm.

## Najac

**NAJAC** occupies an extraordinary site on a conical hill isolated in a wide bend in the deep valley of the Aveyron, 25km south of Villefranche-de-Rouergue. Its magnificent **castle**, which graces many a travel poster, sits right on the peak of the hill, while the half-timbered and stone-tiled village houses tail out in a single street along the narrow back of the spur that joins the hill to the valley side.

**10**

## Najac château

Daily: April, May, Sept & Oct 10.30am–1pm & 3–5.30pm; June to mid-July 10.30am–1pm & 3–6.30pm; mid-July to Aug 10.30am–7pm • €4.50 • W tourisme-najac.com

Najac's **château** is a model of medieval defensive architecture and was endlessly fought over because of its impregnable position in a region once rich in silver and copper mines. In one of the chambers of the keep are sculpted portraits of St Louis, king of France, his brother Alphonse de Poitiers and Jeanne, the daughter of the count of Toulouse, whose marriage to Alphonse was arranged in 1229 to end the Cathar wars by bringing the domains of Count Raymond and his allies under royal control. It was Alphonse who "modernized" the castle and made the place we see today – a model in one of the turrets shows his fortifications as they were in the castle's prime in 1253. The main reason to visit, however, is the magnificent all-round view from the top of the keep, a full 200m above the river.

## Church of St-Jean and around

April–Sept daily 10am–noon & 2–6pm; Oct Sun 10am–noon & 2–6pm • Free

In the centre of what was the medieval village, at the foot of the castle, stands the sturdy **church of St-Jean**, which the villagers of Najac were forced by the Inquisition to build at their own expense in 1258 as a punishment for their conversion to Catharism. In addition to a collection of reliquaries and an extraordinary iron cage for holding candles, the church has one architectural oddity: its windows are solid panels of stone from which the lights have been cut out in trefoil form. Below the church, a surviving stretch of **Roman road** leads downhill to where a thirteenth-century bridge spans the Aveyron.

### ARRIVAL AND INFORMATION                                         NAJAC

**By train** The train station is on the other side of the river from the village, 2km by road.
Destinations Figeac (6–7 daily; 55min); Villefranche-de-Rouergue (6–7 daily; 15min).
**By bus** The daily bus from Villefranche-de-Rouergue (Mon–Sat; 30min) arrives and departs from place du

Faubourg.
**Tourist office** 25 place du Faubourg (April–Sept Mon–Sat 9.30am–12.30pm & 2.30–6pm, Sun 10am–1pm; Oct–March Mon–Fri 9.30am–noon & 2.30–5.30pm, Sat 9.30am–noon; ☎ 05 65 29 72 05, W tourisme-najac.com).

### ACCOMMODATION AND EATING

**L'Oustal del Barry** 2 place Sol del Barry ☎ 05 65 29 74 32, W oustaldelbarry.com. This very comfortable hotel has simple but warmly decorated rooms with solid wood furnishings; the best room has a balcony with wonderful panoramic views of the château and countryside. Its restaurant is renowned for its subtle and inventive cuisine (menus from €17.50). Closed Nov–March. **€51**

**Tartines & Campagne** 31 rue du Bourguet ☎ 05 65 29 57 47. A sweet little café on the way to the château, with a street-side terrace that enjoys views over the countryside, serving light dishes like croque monsieur (€7.50) and salads (from €8.30). April–Oct Mon–Wed 10am–5.30pm, Fri–Sun 10.30am–10pm.

## St-Antonin-Noble-Val

One of the finest and most substantial towns in the valley is **ST-ANTONIN-NOBLE-VAL**, 30km southwest of Najac. It sits on the bank of the Aveyron beneath the beetling cliffs of the Roc d'Anglars, and has endured all the vicissitudes of the old towns of the southwest: it went Cathar, then Protestant, and each time was walloped by the alien power of the kings from the north. Yet, in spite of all this, it recovered its prosperity, manufacturing cloth and leather goods, and was endowed by its wealthy merchants with a marvellous heritage of medieval houses in all the streets leading out from the lovely **place de la Halle**. It's on this square that you'll find the town's finest building, the **Maison des Consuls**, whose origins go back to 1120.

| INFORMATION | ST-ANTONIN-NOBLE-VAL |
|---|---|

**Tourist office** Place de la Mairie (March & Oct Mon 2–5.30pm, Tues–Sun 10am–12.30pm & 2–5.30pm; April–June daily 9.30am–12.30pm & 2–6pm; July & Aug daily 9am–1pm & 2–7pm; Oct Mon 2–5.30pm, Tues–Sun 10am–12.30pm & 2–5.30pm; Nov–Feb Mon & Sat 2–5pm, Tues–Fri 10am–12.30pm & 2–5pm; ☎ 05 63 30 63 47, ⓦ saint-antonin-noble-val.com).

### ACCOMMODATION AND EATING

**Auberge Côté Pont** 6 bd des Thermes ☎ 05 63 30 63 75. This is without doubt one of the nicest places to eat in town, with an inventive and constantly changing *menu* (from €25). Tues–Sat 7–9pm, Wed–Sun noon–2pm.

**La Résidence** 37 rue Droite ☎ 05 63 67 37 56, ⓦ laresidence-france.com. Smart and welcoming, and arguably the best *chambres d'hôte* in St-Antonin. Rooms are large and airy, one with its own roof terrace, and meals are available for €27 a head. **€80**

10

# Montauban

The prosperous, provincial city of **MONTAUBAN** is capital of the largely agricultural *département* of Tarn-et-Garonne. It lies on the banks of the River Tarn, 53km from Toulouse, close to its junction with the Aveyron and their joint confluence with the Garonne. With an attractive old centre, interesting shops, some great places to eat, and a laid-back feel, it makes a particularly pleasant base for a few days. The greatest delight is simply to wander the streets of the compact city centre, with their lovely pink-brick houses.

## Brief history

The city's **history** goes back to 1144, when the count of Toulouse decided to found a *bastide* here as a bulwark against English and French royal power. In fact, it's generally regarded as the first *bastide*, and that plan is still clearly evident in the old city centre.

Montauban has enjoyed periods of great prosperity, as one can guess from the proliferation of fine townhouses. The first followed the suppression of the Cathar heresy and the final submission of the counts of Toulouse in 1229, and was greatly enhanced by the building of the Pont-Vieux in 1335, which made it the best crossing-point on the Tarn in these parts. The Hundred Years' War did its share of damage, as did Montauban's opting for the Protestant cause in the Wars of Religion, but by the time of the Revolution it had become once more one of the richest cities in the southwest, particularly successful in the manufacture of cloth.

## Place Nationale

Montauban's finest feature is **place Nationale**, the *bastide*'s central square, rebuilt after a fire in the seventeenth century and surrounded on all sides by exquisite double-vaulted arcades with the octagonal belfry of St-Jacques showing above the western rooftops.

## Church of St-Jacques
Rue de la République

First built in the thirteenth century on the pilgrim route to Compostela, the **church of St-Jacques** is a much more atmospheric prospect than the cathedral (see p.578). Inside, the church is dark and in need of repair, but its varying murals are testament to the fact that it was added to up until the eighteenth century.

## Musée Ingres
19 rue Hôtel de Ville • July & Aug daily 10am–6pm; Sept–June Tues–Sat 10am–noon & 2–6pm, Sun 2–6pm • €4.50 • ☎ 05 63 22 12 91

The former bishop's residence, by the Pont-Vieux, is a massive half-palace, half-fortress, begun in 1363 by the Black Prince, the son of King Edward III of England, but never finished because the English lost control of the town. It's now home to the **Musée**

**Ingres**, based on a collection of drawings and paintings that artist Jean-Auguste-Dominique Ingres, a native of Montauban, left to the city on his death. It's a collection the city is very proud of, though his hyper-realistic, luminous portraits aren't to everyone's taste. The museum also contains a substantial collection of sculptures by another native, Émile-Antoine Bourdelle.

## Cathédrale Notre-Dame
Place Notre-Dame

The **Cathédrale Notre-Dame** is a cold fish: an austere and unsympathetic building erected just before 1700 as part of the triumphalist campaign to reassert the glories of the Catholic faith after the cruel defeat and repression of the Protestants. Apart from being a rare example of a French cathedral built in the classical style, its most interesting features are the statues of the four evangelists that triumphantly adorn the facade. Those on show now are recent copies, but the weather-beaten originals can be seen just inside.

### ARRIVAL AND INFORMATION · MONTAUBAN

**By train** The *gare SNCF* is southeast of the old town, across the river on av Roger-Salengro.
Destinations Brive-la-Gaillarde (4–5 daily; 1hr 50min); Cahors (5–8 daily; 45min); Gourdon (4–5 daily; 1hr 10min); Moissac (4–6 daily; 20min); Souillac (4–5 daily; 1hr 25min); Toulouse (7–12 daily; 30min).

**Tourist office** 4 rue du Collège (mid-April to Oct Mon–Sat 9.30am–12.30pm & 2–6.30pm; July & Aug Mon–Sat 9.30am–6.30pm, Sun 10am–12.30pm; Nov to mid-April Mon–Sat 9.30am–12.30pm & 1.30–6pm; ☎ 05 63 63 60 60, ⓦ montauban-tourisme.com).

### ACCOMMODATION

**Du Commerce** 9 place Roosevelt ☎ 05 63 66 31 32, ⓦ hotel-commerce-montauban.com. Next to the cathedral, with small, simply furnished rooms; the buffet breakfast (€9) is surprisingly good value. €61
**Mercure** 12 rue Notre-Dame ☎ 05 63 63 17 23, ⓦ mercure.com. Chain hotel opposite the cathedral offering large rooms and three-star services, as well as a reasonably priced restaurant, but not a lot of character. €107
**D'Orsay** 32 rue Salengro ☎ 05 63 66 06 66, ⓦ hotel-restaurant-orsay. This old-fashioned hotel, opposite the train station, has dated but comfortable rooms and an excellent restaurant (*menus* from €23). €68

### EATING

**Le Contre Filet** 4 rue Princesse ☎ 05 63 66 28 72. Just off place National, this modern restaurant serves tasty and inexpensive platters of local produce and excellent *faux filet*. *Menus* from €18. Mon, Tues & Thurs–Sat noon–2pm & 7–9pm.
★ **Crumble Tea** 25 rue de la République ☎ 05 63 20 39 43. A delightful little teashop crammed with tea miscellanea (much of it for sale), in a small courtyard off rue de la République. There's an excellent array of homemade cakes (from €3.20), plus a good-value lunch *menu* (€11.20). Tues–Sat 9am–7pm.

# Moissac

**MOISSAC**, 30km northwest of Montauban, is remarkable only for its beautiful Romanesque abbey church. The town suffered terrible damage during the flood of March 1930, when the Tarn, swollen by a sudden thaw in the Massif Central, burst its banks, destroying 617 houses and killing 120 people. The modern town is rather bland, in great contrast to the outstanding church and its cloister, which has made Moissac a household name in the history of art.

## Abbey church of St-Pierre
Place Durand de Bredon • April–June & Oct Mon–Fri 9am–noon & 2–6pm, Sat & Sun 10am–noon & 2–6pm; July & Aug daily 9am–7pm; Sept daily 9am–6pm; Nov–March Mon–Fri 10am–noon & 2–5pm, Sat & Sun 2–5pm

The cloister and porch of the **abbey church of St-Pierre** is a supreme masterpiece of Romanesque sculpture. Indeed, the fact that it has survived numerous wars, including siege and sack by Simon de Montfort senior in 1212 during the crusade against the

Cathars, is something of a miracle. During the Revolution it was used as a gunpowder factory and billet for soldiers, who damaged many of the sculptures. In the 1830s it only escaped demolition to make way for the Bordeaux–Toulouse train line by a whisker.

Legend has it that Clovis the Frank first founded a monastery here, though it seems more probable that its origins belong in the seventh century, which saw the foundation of so many monasteries throughout Aquitaine. The first Romanesque church on the site was consecrated in 1063 and enlarged in the following century. The famous south **porch**, with its magnificent tympanum and curious wavy door jambs and pillars, dates from this second phase of building, and its influence can be seen in the decoration of porches on countless churches across the south of France. It depicts Christ in Majesty, right hand raised in benediction, the Book of Life in his hand, surrounded by the evangelists and the elders of the Apocalypse as described by St John in the Book of Revelation. There's more fine carving in the capitals inside the porch, and the interior of the church, which was remodelled in the fifteenth century, is interesting too, especially for some of the wood and stone statuary it contains.

## The abbey cloister

Enter through the tourist office, 6 place Durand de Bredon • April–June & Oct Mon–Fri 9am–noon & 2–6pm, Sat & Sun 10am–noon & 2–6pm; July & Aug daily 9am–7pm; Sept daily 9am–6pm; Nov–March Mon–Fri 10am–noon & 2–5pm, Sat & Sun 2–5pm • €5

The **cloister** adjoining the abbey is at its most peaceful first thing in the morning. It surrounds a garden shaded by a majestic cedar, and its pantile roof is supported by 76 alternating single and double marble columns. Each column supports a single inverted wedge-shaped block of stone, on which are carved with extraordinary delicacy all manner of animals and plant motifs, as well as scenes from Bible stories and the lives of the saints.

## ARRIVAL AND INFORMATION                                   MOISSAC

**By train** The train station is just over 500m southwest of the abbey church.
Destinations Montauban (4–7 daily; 25min); Toulouse (4–7 daily; 55min).
**Tourist office** 6 place Durand de Bredon (April–June &

Oct Mon–Fri 9am–noon & 2–6pm, Sat & Sun 10am–noon & 2–6pm; July & Aug daily 9am–7pm; Sept daily 9am–6pm; Nov–March Mon–Fri 10am–noon & 2–5pm, Sat & Sun 2–5pm; ☎ 05 63 04 01 85, ⊛ tourisme.moissac .fr).

## ACCOMMODATION AND EATING

★ **Auberge du Cloître** 5 place Durand de Bredon ☎ 05 63 04 37 50. In a really lovely setting with tables outside beneath a magnolia tree, overlooking the abbey, this restaurant serves interesting takes on local ingredients, such as an artichoke salad with foie gras and smoked duck breast. *Menus* from €18. Tues–Sat noon–2pm & 7–9pm.
**Camping du Bidounet** 2km south of Moissac ☎ 05 63 32 52 52, ⊛ camping-moissac.fr. In an enviable position on an island in the Tarn, this very attractive campsite offers lots of green space, plus a swimming pool, a kids' club and various water activities. Closed Oct–March. **€16.60**

**Le Chapon Fin** Place des Récollets ☎ 05 63 04 04 22, ⊛ lechaponfin-moissac.com. Simple but clean and comfortable rooms just a short walk from the abbey on a rather bland square, with an old-fashioned brasserie downstairs. **€65**
**Moulin de Moissac** ☎ 05 63 32 88 88, ⊛ lemoulindemoissac.com. Occupying a large, not particularly attractive former mill on the river, Moissac's top hotel has lovely, atmospheric rooms, many with bare stone walls and river views, and an excellent spa on site. **€89**

10

# The Pyrenees

TREKKING IN THE CIRQUE DE GAVARNIE

# The Pyrenees

Basque-speaking, wet and green in the west; craggy, snowy, Gascon-influenced in the middle; dry, Mediterranean and Catalan-speaking in the east – the Pyrenees are physically beautiful, culturally varied and less developed than the Alps. The whole range is marvellous walkers' country, especially the central region around the Parc National des Pyrénées, with its 3000-metre-high peaks, streams, forests and wildlife. If you're a committed hiker, it's possible to traverse these mountains, usually from the Atlantic to the Mediterranean, along the GR10.

**11**

As for the more conventional tourist attractions, the **Côte Basque** – peppered with fun-loving towns like **Bayonne** and **Biarritz** – is lovely, sandy but very popular, and suffers from seaside sprawl and a surfeit of caravan-colonized campsites. The foothill towns are on the whole rather dull, although **Pau** merits at least a day, while monstrously kitsch **Lourdes** has to be seen whether you're a devout pilgrim or not. **Roussillon** in the east, focused on busy **Perpignan**, has beaches every bit as popular as those of the Côte Basque, some nestled into the compact coves of its southern rocky coast, while its interior consists of craggy terrain split by spectacular canyons and sprouting a crop of fine Romanesque abbeys and churches – **St-Michel-de-Cuixà**, **St-Martin-de-Canigou** and **Serrabona** being the most dramatic – and a landscape bathed in Mediterranean light. Finally, the sun-drenched foothills just to the northwest harbour the famous **Cathar castles**, legacies of the once-independent and ever-rebellious inhabitants of south-western Languedoc.

## The Pays Basque

The three **Basque provinces** – Labourd (Lapurdi), Basse Navarre (Behe Nafarroa) and Soule (Zuberoa) – share with their Spanish neighbours a common language – Euskera – and a strong sense of identity. The language is widely spoken, and Basques refer to their country as Euskal-herri (or, across the border in Spain, Euskadi). You'll see bilingual French/Euskera toponym signage and posters throughout the region (sometimes only in Euskera), so in this section we have given the Euskera for all locations in brackets after the French.

Apart from the language and the traditional broad beret, the most obvious manifestations of Basque national identity are the ubiquitous *trinquets* (enclosed) or *frontons* (open) concrete courts in which the national game of **pelota** is played. Pairs of players wallop a hard leather-covered ball, either with their bare hands or a long basket-work extension of the hand called a *chistera* (in the variation known as *cesta punta*), against a high wall blocking one end of the court. It's extraordinarily dangerous – the ball travels at speeds of up to 200kph – and knockouts or worse are not uncommon.

SURF'S UP, BIARRITZ

# Highlights

**❶ Surfing the Côte Basque** Catch a wave at Biarritz Europe's top destination for both boogie-boarders and classic surfers. **See p.588**

**❷ Cauterets** Several lake-spangled valleys above this agreeable spa offer superb trekking, whether modest day-loops or more ambitious multi-day traverses. **See p.608**

**❸ The Cirque de Gavarnie** A vast alpine amphitheatre with wind-blown cascades and traces of glacier. **See p.610**

**❹ Niaux cave** The upper Ariège valley hosts a cluster of prehistoric caves painted by Cro-Magnon humans over 10,000 years ago;

Niaux contains the best preserved and most vivid of these images. **See box, p.615**

**❺ Cathar castles** The imposing castles of the upper Aude and Corbières region testify to southwestern Languedoc's era of independence. **See p.618**

**❻ Musée d'Art Moderne, Ceret** An astonishing collection of paintings from the prime movers of the early twentieth-century avant-garde. **See p.628**

**❼ Petit Train Jaune** Rumble up the dramatic Têt valley of Roussillon in an open-car, narrow-gauge train. **See p.632**

**HIGHLIGHTS ARE MARKED ON THE MAP ON PP.584–585**

## The Côte Basque

Barely 30km long from the Spanish frontier to the mouth of the Adour, the **Basque coast** is made up of scattered rocky outcrops and beautiful sandy beaches. Most surfers head for Biarritz, Hendaye (near the border) or Anglet (just north of Biarritz) which all offer surf hire and schooling. Reasonably priced accommodation is not difficult to find – except from mid-July and throughout August, when space should be reserved at least six weeks in advance.

### Biarritz

Up until the 1950s, **BIARRITZ** (Miarritze) was the Monte-Carlo of the Atlantic coast, transformed by Napoléon III during the mid-nineteenth century into a playground for monarchs, aristos and glitterati. With the 1960s rise of the Côte d'Azur, however, the place went into seemingly terminal decline, despite having been discovered by the first surfers in 1957. But from the early 90s, Biarritz was rediscovered by Parisian yuppies, a new generation of the international surfing fraternity and a slightly alternative family clientele, who together have put the place back on the map.

The focus of Biarritz is the **Casino Municipal**, just behind the Grande Plage, now restored to its 1930s grandeur, while inland the town forms a surprisingly amorphous, workaday sprawl, where you'll find fancy shops and restaurants on main drags and cosier eateries light up the otherwise tenebrous side streets after sundown.

The **halles**, divided into a seafood wing and a produce, cheese and ham division, is friendly and photogenic, the streets around it lined with places to eat and drink. To the west, **place de l'Atalaye**, high above the port and named for a nearby whalers' lookout tower, is fringed by elegant mansions; just below, characterful if touristy **rue du Port-Vieux** leads down to its namesake beach.

#### Musée Asiatica

1 rue Guy-Petit • Daily 2–7pm, July & Aug plus school holidays 10.30am–6.30pm • €7 • ☏ 05 59 22 78 79, ⓦ museeasiatica.com

Exhibiting the private collection of Chinese, Indian and Tibetan art specialist Michel

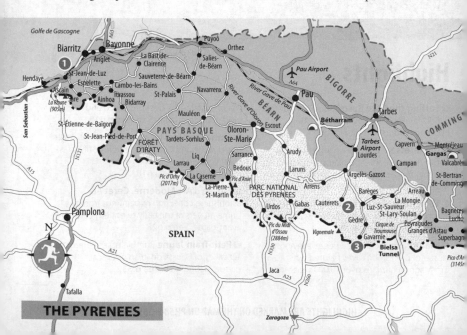

THE PYRENEES

Postel, the atmospherically presented **Musée Asiatica** holds eastern riches, including medieval jades, textiles and religious icons.

## Musée Historique de Biarritz

Rue Broquedis • Tues–Sat 10am–12.30pm & 2–6.30pm • €4 • ⊙ 05 59 24 86 28, Ⓦ musee-historique-biarritz.fr

Sited in a former Anglican church, **Musée Historique de Biarritz** holds a smallish collection of photos, clothing and other artefacts that trace the town's fortunes from its beginnings as a medieval whaling station to its *belle époque* heyday.

## Musée de la Mer

Plateau Atalaye • Nov–March Tues–Sun 9.30am–7pm, April–June & Sept–Oct daily 9.30am–8pm, July & Aug daily 9.30am–midnight • €13 • ⊙ 05 59 22 75 40, Ⓦ museedelamer.com

The **Musée de la Mer** is one of Europe's great aquarium collections, based on the life found throughout the course of the Gulf Stream from the Caribbean to the Bay of Biscay and beyond. The fifty tanks offer spectacular sub-aquatic views of deep sea, mangrove and coral habitats where you'll come face to face with hammerhead sharks, rays, turtles and seals as well as pretty, multicoloured coral fish and the less pretty but decidedly more interesting moray eels.

**11**

### ARRIVAL AND DEPARTURE                                      BIARRITZ

**By plane** Biarritz airport sits 4km inland from the town centre, just off the D810. Bus #14 from the airport heads into Biarritz. Flights are mostly domestic although a few no-frills routes exist to and from Ireland and England.

**By train** The *gare SNCF* is 4km southeast of the centre at the end of avenue Foch/avenue Kennedy in the *quartier* known as La Négresse (take bus A1 to or from square d'Ixelles). Around eight trains arrive from Bordeaux (2hr 15min) and Hendaye (35min) daily or from the Spanish

border town, Irún, three times daily (45min).

**By bus** There are no long-distance bus routes serving Biarritz but buses for local destinations Anglet (bus #10) and Bayonne (buses A1 & A2) can be picked up from avenues Edouard VII and Louis Barthou respectively, beside the tourist office.

**Public transport** There are two free shuttle buses (*navettes*): one makes a city centre circuit and another goes to the plage de la cote des Basques that can be boarded at av de Londres.

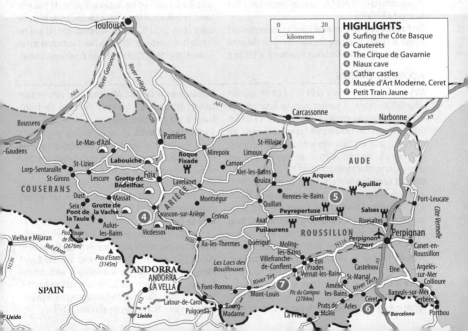

11

## BASQUE COUNTRY CUISINE

Although **Basque cooking** shares many of the dishes of the southwest and the central Pyrenees – in particular **garbure**, a thick potato, carrot, bean, cabbage and turnip soup enlivened with pieces of pork, ham or duck – it does have distinctive recipes. One of the best known is the Basque omelette, *pipérade*, made with tomatoes, peppers and often Bayonne ham, and actually more like scrambled eggs. Another delicacy is sweet red peppers, or piquillos, stuffed whole with *morue* (salt cod). *Poulet basquaise* is also common, especially as takeaway food: pieces of chicken browned in pork fat and casseroled in a sauce of tomato, ground Espelette chillis, onions and a little white wine. In season there's a chance of *salmi de palombe*, an onion-and-wine-based stew of wild doves netted or shot as they migrate north over the Pyrenees.

With the Atlantic adjacent, **seafood** is also a speciality. The Basques inevitably have their version of fish soup, called *ttoro*. Another great delicacy is elvers or piballes, caught as they come up the Atlantic rivers. Squid are common, served here as *txiperons*, either in their own ink, stuffed and baked or stewed with onion, tomato, peppers and garlic. All the locally caught fish – tuna (*thon*), sea bass (*bor*), sardines (*sardines*) and anchovies (*anchois*) – are regular favourites, too.

**Cheeses** mainly comprise the delicious ewe's-milk *tommes* and *gasna* from the high pastures of the Pyrenees. Puddings include the *Gâteau Basque*, an almond-custard pie often garnished with preserved black cherries from Itxassou. As for **alcohol**, the only Basque AOC wine is the very drinkable Irouléguy – as red, white or rosé – while the local digestif liqueur is the potent green or yellow Izzara.

## INFORMATION

**Tourist office** Situated just inland from Grande Plage on Square d'Ixelles (daily: July & Aug 8am–8pm; Sept–June Mon–Fri 9am–6pm, Sat & Sun 10am–5pm; ☎ 05 59 22 37 00, ✆ biarritz.fr).

**Bicycle and scooter rental** Cycle Océan at 24 rue Peyroloubilh (☎ 05 59 24 94 47, ✆ cycle-ocean.com) offers bicycles for €15 a day.

**Surf rental and surf lessons** There are numerous surf schools in Biarritz all offering the same thing for the same price. Expect to pay €17 a day to hire a surfboard or €15 for a bodyboard plus €10 for a wetsuit. If it's your first time, note that 90min group lessons cost €35 each. Kids can also learn (from aged seven and up provided they can swim) for €32 a lesson. To surf on Plage de la Côte des Basques (see box, p.588) head down to the shorefront and pick from any of the surf-hire tents that are just past the restaurants on bd du Prince de Galles. To book ahead try La Vague Basque, bd du Prince de Galles (☎ 05 59 52 22 26, ✆ vaguebasque.fr). To surf on Grande Plage (see box, p.588) go to Plums surf school on rue Gardères (☎ 05 59 24 10 79, ✆ touradour.com/shops/plums).

## ACCOMMODATION

**Alcyon** 8 rue Maison-Suisse ☎ 05 59 22 64 60, ✆ hotel -alcyon-biarritz.com. A modern four-star establishment in a listed nineteenth-century building a short stroll from Grande Plage. The moderately spacious rooms are impeccably clean and come with bathrooms and balconies. Unfortunately, the hotel offers no parking but staff can point you to possible parking spots. **€120**

**Biarritz Camping** 28 rte d'Harcet ☎ 05 59 23 0012, ✆ biarritz-camping.fr. 1km behind plage de la Milady and 3km south of town, this is a basic campsite that's nearest to Biarritz, with a small pool, play park and shop and a 10min walk to the beach. Also indoor accommodation (bungalow huts and static homes) available for four to six people. Early April to Sept. Camping **€32**, bungalow huts (weekly) **€525**

**De La Marine** 1 rue des Goélands ☎ 05 59 24 34 09, ✆ hotel-lamarine-biarritz.com. The best-value budget option in town offers a warm reception and has an ideal location near the old port. All rooms come with en-suite facilities but can get a tad noisy thanks to the hotel's brasserie/pub downstairs. **€60**

**Surf Hostel Biarritz** 27 av de Migron ☎ 05 59 22 55 70, ✆ surfhostelbiarritz.com. The hippest hostel on the west coast, with bikes, boards and a hearty breakfast all included in the price. Its Achilles heel is that it's a bit out of the way; however hostel shuttle buses run to and from the surf as well as the train station and airport. Booking essential. **€35**

**Villa Le Goeland** 12 plateau de l'Atalaye ☎ 05 59 24 25 76, ✆ villagoeland-biarritz.com. This eighteenth-century turreted manor house stands tall in the heart of the old port and has 180-degree views over the Bay of Biscay. Rooms are elegant and spacious with antique furniture, parquet floors and sumptuous bathroom suites. The pricier rooms have their own private terrace with jaw-dropping views. Private parking available. **€170**

## EATING, DRINKING AND NIGHTLIFE

**L'Atelier** 18 rue de la Bergerie ☎05 59 22 09 37, ⓦlatelierbiarritz.com. This slightly upmarket restaurant reaching for the Michelin stars serves fish and meat enhanced by fancy accompaniments like quinoasotto (risotto made from quinoa) and chanterelles or peppermint and pink grapefruit mousse. Finish up with the dessert trio of mango mousse, exotic fruits and spicy mango ice cream. *Menus* start at €25 (two courses) for lunch rising to €95 (five courses including wine) for the "*temptation menu*". Daily 12.15–1.30pm & 7.30–10.30pm; Sept–June closed Sat lunch, Sun eve & Mon; July & Aug closed Mon–Wed lunch.

★ **Bar Jean** 5 rue des Halles ☎05 59 24 80 38, ⓦbarjean-biarritz.com. Not to be confused with *Café Jean* on the same street, this semi-subterranean tapas bar serves creative bites and seafood meals to a lively clientele into the wee small hours. Noisy, yet intimate and with a lengthy list of fine Riojas, this is the perfect place to pass an evening. Tapas €2, paella €20. Daily 9am–3pm & 6.30pm–1.30am; Oct–May closed Tues & Wed; closed Jan.

**Chez Ospi** 6 rue Jean Bart ☎05 59 24 64 98, ⓦchezospi .com. Unpretentious backstreet restaurant providing an imaginative melding of *nouvelle* and *vieille cuisine* in a tasteful modern environment. Start with poached egg, morel sauce and Parmesan cream, or fresh crab ravioli (€12), then move onto fish with bean mousse or artichoke stew (€20). Weekday *menus* cost €14 for two courses or treat yourself to the five course tasting *menu* at €47. Mon, Thurs–Sun noon–2pm & 7.45–10.30pm.

**Miremont Patissier** Place Clémenceau ☎05 59 24 01 38, ⓦmiremont-biarritz.fr. Established in 1872, *Miremont* still sets the standard in patisserie arts. The cakes (ranging from €2.40–7.20) that greet you as you enter this opulent boutique-cum-tearoom-cum-restaurant are almost devastatingly pretty: their Beret Rouge, a white chocolate mousse covered with raspberry paste is a thing of beauty, while the tartlette of wild strawberries hits the mark. The café-restaurant through the back has nice sea views if you can take your eyes off your cake. Daily 9am–8pm.

**Le Surfing** Plage de Côte des Basques, 9 bd Prince de Galles ☎05 59 24 78 72, ⓦlesurfing.fr. A sea-view shrine to the sport positioned near the water's edge, this place is festooned with antique boards and serves tasty grilled fish from €16.50 or *risotto verde* with squid *a la plancha* for €15.50. Mon–Wed 9am–noon, Thurs–Fri 11am–1pm, Sat 9am–2pm & 6pm–midnight, Sun noon–11pm (continuous service during weekends in Aug).

**La Table d'Aranda** 87 av de la Marme ☎05 59 22 16 04, ⓦtabledaranda.fr. Basque slow food restaurant a 10min walk from the centre. First appearances are deceptive, with the tacky flashing neon sign and dated exterior, but all is forgiven when the top-quality food arrives – usually starting with an amuse-bouche. No expense is spared with the ingredients – Thai lobster spring

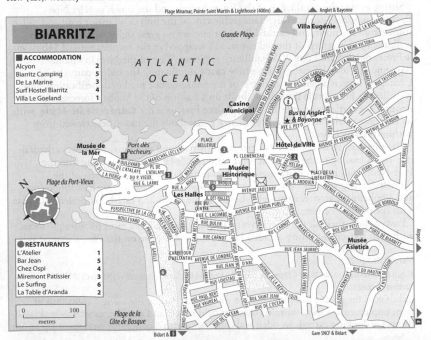

## BIARRITZ BEACHES

Of Biarritz's six beaches, three are **surfable**, although in summer months and especially at weekends there's not always a lot of space in the water. Parking is near impossible at any time of the year, let alone summer so consider taking the free *navette* service (see p.585).

**Grande Plage** is the legendary beach to show off your board and sun tan; it's sited on the north edge of the old town by the famous casino. With its golden sand, beautiful views and famous backdrop, people come in their droves to see and be seen. Consequently restrictions on the number of bathers and surfers come in to force at busier times. **Plage Miramar**, extending north east of Grande Plage, offers more space but deadly currents so there's no surfing here. **Plage Marbella** and **Plage de la Côte des Basques**, south of the rocky outcrop, have two clear kilometres of sand and surf although the latter loses its sandy beach at high tide leaving perilous rocks to circumnavigate the way back to land. A number of surf schools and board-hire companies can be found at the north end near the old town.

**Plage Port Vieux**, a petite little cove beach in the old town that has gentle waves and **Plage Milady** on the southern edge of town are ideal for non-surfing beachgoers and families. The latter has better parking provisions and a playground although the waves can still be pretty choppy.

11

rolls as a main course (€12) and white truffles broken over locally sourced beef and a port reduction (€22). *Menus* start at €15 for two plates. Daily noon–1.45pm & 7.45–9.45pm; Sept–June closed Sun & Mon.

## Bayonne

**BAYONNE** (Baïona) stands back some 5km from the Atlantic, a position that until recently protected it from any real touristic exploitation. The city is effectively the economic and political capital of the Pays Basque and to the lay person, at least, its Basque flavour predominates, with tall half-timbered dwellings and woodwork painted in the traditional green and red.

Sitting astride the confluence of the River Ardour and the much smaller Nive, Bayonne is a small-scale, easily manageable city, at the hub of all major road and rail routes from the north and east. Although there are no great sights, it's a pleasure to walk the narrow streets of the old town, still wrapped in the fortifications of **Sébastien le Preste de Vauban**, Louis XIV's military engineer. West of the Nive in Grand Bayonne, the town's fourteenth-century **castle** dominates. The oldest part, the Château-Vieux, is a genuine example of no-nonsense late medieval fortification. Just west lies the little **Jardin Botanique**, built on a bastion of the Vauban fortifications. Around the corner on magnolia-shaded place Pasteur is the **Cathédrale Ste-Marie**, with its twin towers and steeple rising with airy grace above the town, best viewed from within its own cloister.

The smartest, most commercial streets in town extend northeast from the cathedral: rue Thiers leading to the Hôtel de Ville, and rue de la Monnaie, leading into rue Port-Neuf, with its chocolate *confiseries* and restaurants. South and west of the cathedral, along rue des Faures and rue d'Espagne, there's exemplary half-timbering and a bohemian, artsy-craftsy feel, where antique shops and rare-book dealers alternate with the odd bar or restaurant.

East of the cathedral, the Nive's riverside quays are the city's most picturesque focus, with their sixteenth-century arcaded houses across the Nive on the Petit Bayonne side.

### Musée Basque

37 quai des Corsaires • Tues–Sun 10am–6.30pm, July & Aug also Mon; free first Sun of each month • €5.50 • ☎ 05 59 59 08 98, Ⓦ musee-basque.com

Exhibits in the **Musée Basque** illustrate traditional Basque life using a collection of farm implements – solid-wheeled oxcarts, field rollers and the like, as well as *makhilak* (innocent-looking carved, wooden walking sticks with a concealed steel spear tip at one end, used by pilgrims and shepherds for self-protection). The seafaring gallery features a superb rudder handle carved as a sea monster, a wood-hulled fishing boat, and a model of Bayonne's naval shipyards dating to 1805.

## ARRIVAL AND DEPARTURE
### BAYONNE

**By plane** Biarritz airport is 6km south west of Bayonne. From the airport, either buses #14 or C will take you into town.

**By train** The *gare SNCF* is just off place de la République on the north bank of the Adour. Destinations include Bordeaux with approximately eight trains daily (2hr) plus Biarritz,

St-Jean-de-Luz and Hendaye running every 10 to 30min and Pau (11 train Mon–Fri, 6 on Sat, 7 on Sun).

**By bus** The *gare routière* for destinations in Béarn, Basse Navarre and Soule is next to the train station. For Biarritz take either #A1 or #A2 (every 10–20min Mon–Sat and every 50min on Sun).

## INFORMATION

**Tourist office** Place des Basques (July & Aug Mon–Sat 9am–7pm, Sun 10am–1pm; Sept–June Mon–Fri 9am–6.30pm, Sat 10am–6pm; ☎ 08 20 42 64 64,

ⓦ bayonne-tourisme.com). Free bike hire is available here, provided you bring ID and €150 deposit.

**11**

## ACCOMMODATION

**Des Arceaux** 26 rue Port Neuf ☎ 05 59 59 15 53, ⓦ hotel-arceaux.com. Comfortable hotel with pastel-hued rooms furnished with an agreeable mishmash of

antique and faux-antique furniture. The ubiquitous bolster pillows might leave you with a sore neck in the morning, though. **€71**

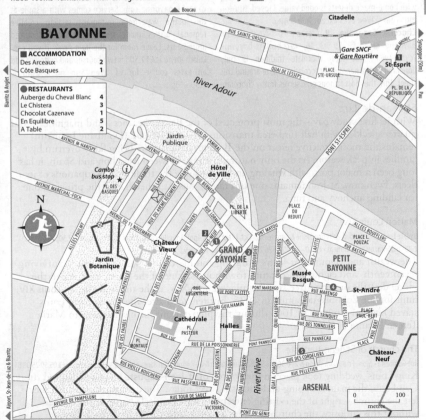

★ **Côte Basques** 2 rue Maubec ☎ 05 59 55 10 21, ⓦ hotel-cotebasque.fr. Tastefully modernized hotel in a central if a tad noisy location just across from the station. Family suites are available for an extra €23. €75

## EATING, DRINKING AND ENTERTAINMENT

The most popular areas for eating and drinking are along the right-bank of the Nive or along quai Jauréguiberry on the Grand Bayonne side.

**Auberge du Cheval Blanc** 68 rue Bourg-Neuf, Petit Bayonne ☎ 05 59 59 01 33, ⓦ cheval-blanc-bayonne .com. Formerly Michelin-starred, this seafood restaurant is still considered the best in town. While the menu lacks some of the complexity of typical fine dining, the flavour combinations are inventive and successful. Try their sea bream with braised fennel and aniseed. Lunch *menus* €25, evening from €46. Daily noon–1.30pm & 7.45–9.30pm; closed Sat noon, Sun eve, Mon & first week of July.

**Le Chistera** 42 rue Port-Neuf, Grand Bayonne ☎ 05 59 59 25 93, ⓦ lechistera.com. The best option out of a row of three similar restaurants under the arcades here, offering fish soup, Basque chicken and *piperade*. The €15.80 three-course *menu* culminating with home-made deserts is good value. Closed all Mon plus Tues & Wed eves except July & Aug.

**Chocolat Cazenave** 19 Arceaux Port-Neuf, Grand Bayonne ☎ 05 59 59 03 16, ⓦ chocolats-bayonne -cazenave.fr. The local chocolate tradition is duly honoured with a handful of chocolatiers on, or around this street. This, the most famous one, serves frothy chocolate beverages in flowery porcelain teacups at tables under the arcade or in its Art Nouveau interior. Mon–Sat 9.15am– noon & 2–7pm.

**En Equilibre** 19 rue des Cordeliers ☎ 05 59 59 46 98, ⓦ enequilibre.fr. Across the river Nive in Petite Bayonne, this unassuming little diner draws inspiration from the proprietor's Normandy cheese-making heritage. Naturally, cheese features heavily on the menu, be it roasted or in sauces accompanying meat dishes like *magret de canard* (€16). Rennet-tolerant vegetarians may seek refuge here. There's an enticing array to choose from including leek tart with *compté* gratin and vegetable crumble (both €7). Tues–Sat noon–2pm & 7.30–10pm.

**A Table** Quai Admiral Dubourdieu ☎ 05 59 56 79 22, ⓦ atablebayonne.com. Service comes with a smile at this petite waterfront restaurant serving creative regional dishes made from fresh locally sourced ingredients. Leave room for the *pain perdu* if you can. Lunch *menu* is €11.50 for two courses and coffee or add an extra course for €3. Wed–Sun noon–2pm & 7.30–10pm.

## St-Jean-de-Luz

With its fine sandy bay – the most protected of the Basque beaches – and magnificent old quarter speckled with half-timbered mansions, **ST-JEAN-DE-LUZ** (Donibane Lohitzun) remains the most attractive resort on the Basque coast, despite being fairly overrun by families in peak season. As the only natural harbour between Arcachon and Spain, it has long been a major port, with whaling and cod-fishing the traditional occupations of its fleets. Even now, St-Jean remains one of Frances' busiest fisheries, and the principal one for landing anchovy and tuna.

### Maison Louis XIV

6 place Louis XIV • Guided visits only: June & Sept to mid-Oct 11am, 3pm, 4pm, 5pm; July & Aug Mon–Sat 10.30am–12.30pm & 2.30–6.30pm; by appointment • €5.50 • ☎ 05 59 26 27 58, ⓦ maison-louis-xiv.fr

The wealth and vigour of St-Jean's seafaring and mercantile past is evident in surviving seventeenth- and eighteenth-century townhouses. One of the finest, adjacent to the Hôtel de Ville on plane-tree-studded place Louis-XIV, is the turreted **Maison Louis XIV**, built for the Lohobiague family in 1635, but renamed after the young King Louis stayed here for a month in 1660 during the preparations for his marriage to Maria Teresa, Infanta of Castile.

### The church of St-Jean-Baptiste

Rue Gambetta • Mon–Fri 8.30am–noon & 2–6.30pm, Sat 8.30am–noon & 2–7.45pm, Sun 8am–noon & 3–7.45pm • Free • ☎ 05 59 26 08 81

King Louis' wedding took place in the **church of St-Jean-Baptiste** on pedestrianized rue Gambetta, the main shopping-and-tourism street today. The door through which they left the church – right of the existing entrance – has been sealed up ever since. Even without this curiosity, the church deserves a look inside: the largest French Basque church, it has barn-like nave roofed in wood and lined on three sides with tiers of dark oak galleries accessed by wrought-iron stairways. The galleries, a distinctive feature of Basque churches, were reserved for the men, while the women sat at ground level. Equally Basque is the elaborate gilded retable of tiered angels, saints and prophets behind the altar. Hanging from the ceiling is an *ex voto* model of the Empress Eugénie's paddle steamer, the *Eagle*, which narrowly escaped being wrecked outside St-Jean in 1867.

## ARRIVAL AND INFORMATION                           ST-JEAN-DE-LUZ

**By train** St-Jean's *gare SNCF* is on av de Verdun on the southern edge of the town centre, 500m from the beach. There are regular services (every 10–30min) to Hendaye (10min) and north to Biarritz (12min) and Bayonne (22min).

**By bus** Buses arrive at the *halte routière* diagonally opposite the trains.

Destinations Hendaye (10 daily; 25min) Biarritz (12 daily; 25min) Bayonne (10 daily; 55min).

**Tourist office** Opposite the fish market on the corner of bd Victor Hugo and rue Bernard Jaureguiberry (April–June & Sept Mon–Sat 9am–12.30pm & 2–7pm, Sun 10am–1pm; July & Aug Mon–Sat 9am–7.30pm, Sun 10am–1pm & 3–7pm; Oct–March Mon–Sat 9am–12.30pm & 1.30–6.30pm, Sun 10am–1pm; ☎ 05 59 26 0 316, ⓦ saint-jean-de-luz.com).

## ACCOMMODATION

★ **Les Goëlands** 4–6 av d'Etcheverry ☎ 05 59 26 10 05, ⓦ hotel-lesgoelands.com. Consists of two *belle époque* villas 300m from the beach and old town, with jazzy interiors and en-suites plus some rooms with balconies and sea views. If you've got kids and a large budget opt for the "Family connecting rooms" (at €216). There's also a restaurant and well-tended gardens to relax in. Free parking. Easter–Oct. **€115**

**Kapa Gorry** 9 rue Paul Gelos ☎ 05 59 26 04 93, ⓦ hotel -kapa-gorry.com. A good budget option near the northern edge of the beach and 500m from the centre. The rooms are clean if a little unhomely. Downstairs there is a reading room, dining room and terrace where a simple breakfast can be taken (€6.50). Easter–Oct. **€89**

**La Marisa** 16 rue Sopite ☎ 05 59 26 95 46, ⓦ hotel -lamarisa.com. A stone's throw or two from the beach within the old town, this hotel oozes charm and eccentricity with its wood panelling and antique furniture complementing the seafaring artwork. There is a well-stocked reading/common room and rear garden to relax in. Closed mid-Dec to mid-Feb. **€118**

## EATING AND DRINKING

**Le Brouillarta** 48 Prom Jacques Thibaud ☎ 05 59 51 29 51, ⓦ restaurant-lebrouillarta.com. For a sea view try this fishy restaurant across the road from the middle section of the beach. The food here is rustic yet refined, using high quality, fresh ingredients and a dose of creative flair. The €23 *menu* has three courses that must include the €12 *plat du jour* or you can opt for the hefty €48 tasting *menu* available evenings and all day Sunday. Mon & Thurs–Sun 12.15–2pm & 7.30–10pm.

**Le Kaiku** 17 rue de la Republique ☎ 05 59 26 13 20. Basque/French cuisine romantically served in a lovely medieval old stone and timber building yards from the beach. Seafood features heavily on the menu while meat enthusiasts should opt for roasted Kintoa (a Basque breed of pig) served with gingered pak choi. Vegetarians are usually accommodated for with mainstays like aubergine and mushroom risotto. *Menus* range from €25 to the gourmet €55 with fancy amuse-bouches. Daily12.30– 2pm & 7.30–10pm.

★ **Zoko Moko** 6 rue Mazarin ☎ 05 59 08 01 23, ⓦ zoko-moko.com. Blazing a trail in fine cuisine, *Zoko Moko* has become a reason to visit this town. Expect vibrant, colourful platters based around crustaceans, fish or meat. Wash it all down with either the excellent Muga (rosé from Rioja region) at €19 a bottle or if you're feeling flush, try the regional Irouleguy Dom Brana (€34). *Menus* here start at €19 for a quick three-course lunch up to the tasting *menu* for €66 which includes amuse-bouche plus four courses and glasses of wine designed to accompany each plate. Tues–Sun 12.30–2pm & 7.30–10pm.

# Inland Labourd and Basse Navarre

Without your own transport, the simplest forays into the soft, seductive landscapes of the Basque hinterland – **Labourd** (Lapurdi) and **Basse Navarre** (Behe Nafarroa) – are along the St-Jean-de-Luz–Sare bus route past **La Rhune**, **Ascain** and **Sare**, or the Bayonne–St-Jean-Pied-de-Port train line through the **Vallée de Nive**. Both give a representative sample of the area.

**11**

**By bus** Three to four buses a day (Sunday service in July & Aug only), run by Le Basque Bondissant (ⓦbasque -bondissant.com) ply the route from St-Jean-de-Luz, stopping also at Ascain, Col de St-Ignace and Sare. For complete timetables consult ⓦhoraires.cg64.fr.

**Destinationas (by bus)** Ainhoa (from Cambo-Les-Bains) (2 daily; 25min); Cambo-Les-Bains (from Bayonne) (2–8

daily; 30min); Espelette (from Cambo-les–Bains) (3 daily; 10min); La Bastide-Clairence (from Bayonne) (1 daily; 35min); Sare (from St-Jean-de-Luz via Ascain) (2 Mon–Sat & 5 daily July & Aug; 30min).

**Destinations (by train)** Cambo-les-Bains (from Bayonne) (4 daily; 23min); St Jean Pied-de-Port (from Bayonne) (4 daily; 1hr 18min).

## La Rhune

The 905-metre cone of **La Rhune** (Larrun), straddling the frontier with Spain, is the westernmost skyward thrust of the Pyrenees before they decline into the Atlantic. As *the* landmark of Labourd, in spite of its unsightly multipurpose antennae, it's a predictably popular vantage point, offering fine vistas way up the Basque coast and east along the Pyrenees.

A rack-and-pinion **tourist train** (mid-Feb to June & Sept to mid-Nov every 35min between 9.30am & 11.30am & 2–4pm; July & Aug every 35min between 8.30am–5.30pm; €17; ☎05 59 54 20 26, ⓦrhune.com) runs up to the top of the cone from **Col de St-Ignace**, on the road to Sare. The railway line's steep gradient up (constructed between 1912 and 1924), ensures that the antediluvian carriages trundle at a leisurely 9km/hr; the ascent takes 35 minutes, but you should allow over two hours for the round trip. A free *navette* bus service to Col de St-Ignace is available from the St-Jean-De-Luz bus station.

## Ascain

Like so many Labourdan villages, **Ascain** (Azkaine), just southeast of St Jean de Luz, is postcard-perfect to the point of tweeness, with its galleried church, *fronton* and polychrome, half-timbered houses. It's the ideal base for exploring la Rhune although most visitors only stop briefly on their way to Sare and beyond.

**Tourist office** Across the road from the church (daily 9am–12.30pm & 2–5.30pm closed Sat pm & all Sun; ☎05 59 54 00 84).

**De la Rhune** Next to the church ☎05 59 54 00 04, ⓦhotel-rhune-ascain.com. This former village post office on place du Fronton was regularly visited in the early nineteenth century by writer Pierre Loti who, inspired by the window view of la Rhune, wrote the novel *Ramuntcho* in room 21. The bedrooms are comfortable but lack the charm and character that you might expect from a building of this vintage. The restaurant delivers two courses for €15 of simple home-made Basque cuisine served in the pleasant garden out back. **€84**

## Sare

Seven kilometres southeast from Ascain, **Sare** is a perfectly proportioned knoll-top village, with traditional half-timbered houses and typically Basque church with its three tiers of balconies. Centred around the place du Fonton with its pelota court at one end and restaurants at the other.

**Tourist office** Place Du Fronton (Nov–March Mon–Fri 9.30am–12.30pm & 1.30–5.30pm; April–mid-July & Sept– Oct, Mon–Fri 9.30am–12.30pm & 2–6pm plus Sat 9.30am–12.30pm except Oct; mid July & Aug 9.30am– 12.30pm & 2–6.30pm, Sat & Sun 10am–12.30pm & Sat 3–6.30pm; ☎05 59 54 20 14, ⓦsare.fr). Look for postings on the wall inside the tourist information office for upcoming pelota matches that take place in the court opposite. Games take place on Mondays at 8.30pm in summer but at irregular times throughout the rest of the year.

## ACCOMMODATION AND EATING

**Arraya** On the village square ☎ 05 59 54 20 46, ⓦ arraya .com. A former hospice on the Santiago de Compostela pilgrimage route dating back to the sixteenth century, *Arraya* is now a charming and unpretentious hotel as well as the village's most accomplished restaurant. Rooms are sumptuously presented with embroidered fabrics and antique furnishings, befitting of the ceiling's oak beams. The ground-floor restaurant makes a decent stab at haute cuisine, delivering pretty Basquaise platters of trout and smoked crab ravioli with *menus* from €17 that culminate with a slice of top-notch gateaux Basque. Restaurant open 12.30–2pm & 7.30–10pm, closed Sun eve, Mon & Tues lunch (except July to mid-Sept). Hotel open April–Oct. Rooms €104

**Camping La Petite Rhune** Follow the D406 for 1km south of Sare (campsite is signposted left) ☎ 05 59 54 23 97, ⓦ lapetiterhune.com. A nicely shaded three-star site with playground, tennis and the all-important pool. Also offers *gîtes* and chalets all year round. Mid-June to mid-Sept. Camping €22, chalets (four person) €80
**VVF** 200m north of the church ☎ 05 59 54 20 95, ⓦ vvfvillages.fr. A good, centrally located budget option if you're travelling in a group or en famille (a kids' club is included). The lodging offers four beds spread across two uncharming rooms plus a mini kitchen and balcony. Easter to mid-Oct. Minimum stay 2 nights. €66.50

## Ainhoa

**11**

A mere 8km east from Sare on the GR10 brings you to **Ainhoa**, a gem of a village. It consists of little more than a single street lined with substantial, mainly seventeenth-century houses, whose lintel plaques offer mini-genealogies as well as foundation dates. Take a look at the bulky towered **church** with its gilded Baroque altarpiece of prophets and apostles in niches, framed by Corinthian columns.

### INFORMATION                                                           AINHOA

**Tourist office** On the side street opposite the church (Tues–Fri 10am–12.30pm & 2–6pm; ☎ 05 59 29 93 99).

### ACCOMMODATION & EATING

**Auberge Alzate** On the main street ☎ 05 59 29 77 15. The village's most economical eatery (although still a bit pricey) with its €18 *menu* featuring Basque favourites, veal and duck. The cheapest lunch option is *omelette brebis* (sheep's cheese) for €8 enhanced by home-made *frites* (€3). Mon, Tues & Thurs–Sun 9am–7pm; July–Aug daily 9am–9pm; closed Dec & Jan.
**Chambre d'hôte Ohantzea** Rue Principale ☎ 05 59 29 57 17, ⓦ ohantzea.com. The cheapest accommodation in town by a long shot, this lovely old building (one of only two blue painted buildings in town) is perfectly pleasant, offering three spacious rooms with queen-sized beds, as well as an inviting back garden to unwind in. Breakfast

included. April–Oct. €70
**Ithurria** On the north edge of the village ☎ 05 59 19 92 11, ⓦ ithurria.com. The most luxurious option in the village, this seventeenth-century villa (originally built to house Santiago de Compostela pilgrims) ameliorated with a pool, sauna, and exotic garden, has well-equipped doubles and family apartments. The gourmet restaurant beneath holds a Michelin star for its perfect regional cuisine. The *menus* offer the best value, ranging from €39–62, and include beautifully embellished *piperade* or lobster and finish with regional cakes or cheese. Noon–1.45pm & 7.30–9pm, closed Wed & Thurs lunch (except July & Aug). Hotel open April–Oct. €165

## Espelette

Six kilometres north-east of Ainhoa, **Espelette** is a somewhat busy village of wide-eaved houses, with a church notable for its heavy square tower, painted ceiling and keyhole-shaped, inscribed-slab gravestones (the oldest are by the church, under the lime trees). The village's principal source of renown is its dark red **chilli peppers** – much used in Basque cuisine, and hung to dry in summer on many house fronts.

### INFORMATION                                                         ESPELETTE

**Tourist office** In the seventeenth-century château (Mon–Fri 9.30am–12.30pm & 2–6pm; June, Sept & Oct Sat

9am–12.30pm; July & Aug 9.30am–12.30pm & 2–6pm; ☎ 05 59 93 95 02, ⓦ espelette.fr).

### ACCOMMODATION AND EATING

**Artz Axoa** Rte Karrikalandako. This fast-food snack bar with outside tables is worthy of mention for its *talo*; thick

Basque pancakes made from cornmeal, used as a wrap encasing tasty local products (from €4). Opening times should be taken with a pinch of salt. April–Oct noon–2.30pm; earlier opening on market day (Wed).

**Euzkadi** 285 Karrika Nagusia ☎ 05 59 93 91 88, ⓦ hotel-restaurant-euzkadi.com. Newly renovated traditional hotel, with a facade proudly emblazoned with the local *piment* crop, offering stylish, spacious rooms with bathrooms. The quieter rooms face the pool to the rear while the downstairs restaurant offers Michelin-quality *piperade* and *elzekaria* (bean and cabbage soup) within *menus* of €18–35. Vegetarian meals provided on demand. Restaurant open

12.30–2pm & 7.30–8.45pm; closed Mon & Tues low season. €71

★ **Maison Eliza Bidea** Xerrendako karrika ☎ 05 59 93 96 51, ⓦ gueslot.com. Peacefully tucked away by a leafy riverbank and housed in a beautiful eighteenth-century building, this hotel is a bohemian embodiment of the proprietor's creativity. Minimalists beware – there are knick-knacks everywhere. Guests are permitted to prepare their own meals in the kitchen or the house restaurant (open to demand) will provide three-course Basque-style meals for €16. April–Oct. €58

## Cambo-les-Bains

Six kilometres east of Espelette is **Cambo-les-Bains** (Kanbo), an established spa resort with a favourable microclimate that made it ideal for the treatment of tuberculosis in the nineteenth century. Its other historical attribute is that it was the birthplace of the **Gâteau Basque** (see box, p.586), now ubiquitous throughout the region. The "new" town, with its ornate houses and hotels, radiates out from the baths over the heights above the River Nive, while the old quarter of Bas Cambo lies beside the river and *gare SNCF*.

### Villa Arnaga

1.5km northwest of town on the Bayonne road • mid-Oct to March 2.30–6pm; April–mid-Oct 9.30am–12.30pm & 2.30–7pm; July–Aug 10am–7pm • €6.50 • ☎ 05 59 29 83 92, ⓦ www.arnaga.com

The main sight around Cambo-les-Bains is the **Villa Arnaga**, built for Edmond Rostand, author of *Cyrano de Bergerac*, who came here to cure his pleurisy in 1903. This larger-than-life Basque house, painted in deep-red trim, overlooks an almost surreal formal garden with discs and rectangles of water and segments of grass punctuated by blobs, cubes and cones of topiary box, with a distant view of green hills. Inside it's very kitsch, with a minstrels' gallery, fake pilasters, allegorical frescoes, numerous portraits and various memorabilia.

### INFORMATION                                                                          CAMBO-LES-BAINS

**Tourist office** 3 av de la Marie (Mon–Sat 9am–12.30pm & 2–5.30pm; July & Aug Mon–Sat 9am–6.30pm; July–Sept Sun 9am–12.30pm; ☎ 05 59 29 70 25, ⓦ cambolesbains.com).

### ACCOMMODATION AND EATING

**Hostellerie du Parc** Av de la Marie ☎ 05 59 93 54 54, ⓦ hotel-parc-cambo.com. Homely, clean and central hotel with comfortable en-suite rooms equipped with TV and fridge. Out the back there is a lovely secluded garden with Black Rock chickens dust bathing in the shade. Closed first two weeks of Jan. €72

★ **Tarterie Au Dejeuner Sur l'Herbe** 17 place Duhalde, just off rue du Centre ☎ 05 59 42 67 17. A transfixingly beautiful window display of artisan pies, tarts and cakes greets you on entering this adorable café-restaurant. *Tourtes* (with a pastry top) at €7.90 and *tartes* (without) for €7.20 come with a wealth of different fillings including vegetarian options. For dessert, the rhubarb pie with meringue (€4.60) is as pretty as it is tasty, or you can stick to old favourites like apple crumble or Basque gâteau washed down with reasonably priced coffee. Sun–Fri noon–7pm.

## La Bastide-Clairence

Nineteen kilometres northeast of Cambo lies arguably the most perfectly preserved village in the Basque region, **La Bastide-Clairence** (Bastida), which dates back to the fourteenth century. Resting on the northeastern perimeter with Bearn, historically this predominantly Bascaise village has seen tolerant cohabitation of the two cultures – a progressive inclination that was put to good use in the sixteenth century by Spanish and Portuguese Jews who settled here after fleeing the Spanish inquisition. There is still a fascinating Jewish graveyard next to the Christian one by the fourteenth-century church. The main focus of the village however is its symmetrical arcaded square, with its bar/restaurants and an old forge open to the public gaze.

## INFORMATION

**LA BASTIDE-CLAIRENCE**

**Tourist office** In the arcaded square (Sept–June Mon–Fri 9.30am–12.30pm & 2–6pm, closes at noon on Wed; June & Sept Sat 10am–noon; July & Aug 10am–1pm & 3–7pm; ☎ 05 59 29 65 05, ⓦ labastideclairence-pays-basque.com).

## ACCOMMODATION & EATING

**Bar Restaurant Les Arceaux** Place des Arceaux ☎ 05 59 29 66 70. One of two restaurant options in the heart of the village, this friendly restaurant, which doubles as the village newsagent, has changing €8 and €10 *menus* of regional cuisine. Dine inside, or under shade in the lovely *place*. Mon & Wed–Sat 7.30am–9pm; closed Jan.

**Maison Marchand** Rue Notre Dame ☎ 05 59 29 18 27, ⓦ maison.marchand.pagesperso-orange.fr. In a lovely

old half-timbered house, this family B&B offers four characterful en-suite rooms and a well-tended garden, complete with resident cats. Breakfasts come with delicious warm bread, croissants, local cheese and jam. A hospitality tray in the rooms is also provided. On Mondays and Thursdays the proprietors cook a veritable feast for guests (€25pp including unlimited wine) using the finest regional produce. Closed mid-Nov to mid-March. **€70**

## St-Jean-Pied-de-Port

About 33km southeast of Cambo, the old capital of Basse Navarre, **ST-JEAN-PIED-DE-PORT** (Donibane Garazi), lies in a circle of hills at the foot of the Bentarte pass into Spain. Part of France since the 1659 Treaty of the Pyrenees, it was an important stop on the **Santiago de Compostela pilgrimage** in the Middle Ages.

The old town consists of a single cobbled street, **rue de la Citadelle**, which runs downhill from the fifteenth-century **Porte St-Jacques** – the gate by which pilgrims entered the town, St Jacques being French for Santiago – to the **Porte Notre-Dame**, commanding the bridge over the Nive, with its constantly photographed view of balconied houses overlooking the stream.

## ARRIVAL AND INFORMATION

**ST-JEAN-PIED-DE-PORT**

**By train** The *gare SNCF* is at the end of avenue Renaud, a 10min walk north of the centre.

**Tourist office** 14 place Charles de Gaulle (Sept–June Mon–Sat 9am–noon & 2–6pm; July & Aug Mon–Sat 9am–7pm, Sun 9.30am–1pm & 2.30–5pm ☎ 05 59 37 03 57, ⓦ pyrenees-basques.com).

## ACCOMMODATION

*Chambres d'hôtes*, as well as cheaper dormitory lodgings for pilgrims and hikers, are numerous: try along rue de la Citadelle.

**Chambre d'hôte Errecaldia** 5 chemin st Jacques ☎ 05 59 49 17 02 ⓦ errecaldia.com. Quietly situated beneath the grounds of the seventeenth-century citadelle, yet central enough to dip in and out of town. The spacious rooms within come with a cracking view over the modern town and beyond. **€65**

★ **L'Esprit du Chemin** 40 rue de la Citadelle ☎ 05 59 37 24 68, ⓦ espritduchemin.org. Delightful hostel run by

volunteers, with 14 bunks, offering moral support exclusively to pilgrims and walkers. April–Sept. Bunks **€8**

**Des Remparts** 16 place Floquet ☎ 05 59 37 13 79, ⓦ hoteldesremparts.fr. The best budget choice among the hotels, this relatively quiet place (when the windows are shut) is located just before you cross the Nive coming into town on the Bayonne road. Closed Nov to mid-Feb. **€58**

## EATING AND DRINKING

**Cave Des Etats De Navarre** Rue d'Espagne ☎ 05 59 49 10 48. This watering hole on the southern side of the Nive is an excellent place to sample local produce. Local ciders and wines sold by the glass (from €3) help to wash down the tasty Basquaise tapas accompaniments (from €3.50). Daily 9.30am–8pm; closed Tues.

**Paxkal Oillarruru** 8 rue de l'Église ☎ 05 59 37 06 44.

Offering three-course *menus* from €15.50, and excellent, well-proportioned rustic dishes that include *garbure* and Iraty trout in garlic butter. You may need to evoke the patience of St Jacques to dine in this very popular restaurant in busier times. Book ahead in summer. Mon & Wed–Sun 12.30–2.30pm & 7.30–8.45pm.

**Restaurant Les Pyrenees** Place Charles de Gaulle. The

town's gourmet option delivers exquisite, delicate plates using decadent ingredients. Beyond the reach of most budgets, the *menus* at this Michelin-starred restaurant range from €42 up to an eye-watering €100. Daily noon–2.30pm & 7.30–9pm; closed mid-Nov to Jan & closed Tues between mid-Sept & June.

## Haute Soule

East of the Nive valley, you enter largely uninhabited country, the old Basque county known as the **Haute Soule**, threaded only by the GR10 and a couple of minor roads. The border between Basse Navarre and Soule skims the western edge of the **Forêt d'Iraty**, one of Europe's largest surviving beech woods, a popular summer retreat and winter cross-country skiing area. There are no shops or proper hotels until you reach **Larrau**, the only real village hereabouts, though the scattered hamlet of Ste-Engrâce in the east of the district has accommodation, as do Licq and Tardets-Sorholus, foothill settlements some way down the valley.

Haute Soule is a land of open skies, where griffon vultures turn on the thermals high above countless flocks of sheep (their occasional corpses providing sustenance). It's not a great distance between the Nive valley and Béarn, but the slowness of the roads and the grandeur of the scenery seems to magnify it.

### The Forêt d'Iraty

To drive to the **Forêt d'Iraty** (Irati), follow the D301 east out of the Nive valley from the junction on the D428, where the forest is signposted. The road is steep, narrow and full of tight hairpins and ambling livestock but as you climb up the steep spurs and around the heads of labyrinthine gullies, ever more spectacular views open out over the valley of the Nive, St-Jean and the hills beyond. Solar-powered sheep ranches abound, with cheese on sale. Beech copses fill the gullies, shadowing the lighter grass whose green is so intense it seems almost theatrical – an effect produced by a backdrop of purplish rock outcrops.

### Larrau

The first thing you notice coming into **LARRAU** (Larraiñe) from the west is how different the architecture is from the villages in Labourd and Basse Navarre. In contrast to the usual painted, half-timbered facades and tiled roofs, the houses here are grey and stuccoed, with Béarnais-style, steep-pitched slate roofs to shed heavy snow. Despite its size, it's nonetheless very quiet – almost dead out of season.

#### Gorges d'Holzarte

The **Gorges d'Holzarte**, 4km southeast of Larrau, is one of several local gorges, cutting deep into northern slopes of the ridge that forms the frontier with Spain. A short track leads from Auberge Logibar (3km east of Larrau) across a lively, chilly stream to a car park, from where a steep path – a variant of the GR10 – climbs through beech woods in about 45 minutes to the junction of the Holzarte gorge with the **Gorges d'Olhadubi**. Slung across the mouth of the latter is a spectacular Himalayan-style **suspension bridge**, the *passerelle*, which bounces and swings alarmingly as you walk out over the 180-metre drop.

---

#### OSSAU-IRATY CHEESE

Native to the Basque country and Bearn, this AOC ewe's **cheese**, with its delightfully nutty flavour, is developed in the summer-grazing huts extending along the Basque coast up to the Col d'Aubisqe in the Pyrenees national park. Look out for **Route du Fromage** signs (Ⓦossau-iraty.fr) while travelling about the Basque hinterland and buy direct from the shepherds themselves. The true artisan cheese often has small holes and should not stick to the palate.

## Gorges de Kakuetta

15km east of Larrau on the D113 • Mid-March to mid-Nov 8am–nightfall • €5 (€3.80 in June) • ☎ 05 59 28 73 44

The **Gorges de Kakuetta** is truly dramatic and, outside peak season, not crowded at all; allow about two hours to visit. It pays to be well shod – the metal catwalk or narrow path, by turns, are slippery in places and provided with safety cables where needed. The walls of the gorge rise up to 300m high and are scarcely more than 5m apart in spots, so little sunlight penetrates except at midday from May to July. The air hangs heavy with mist produced by dozens of seeps and tiny waterfalls, nurturing tenacious ferns, moss and other vegetation that thrives in the hothouse atmosphere. Within an hour, the path brings you to a small cave beyond which only technical climbers need apply; just before it a twenty-metre waterfall (which you can walk behind) gushes out of a hole in the rock.

### ACCOMMODATION AND EATING                                                    LARRAU

**Auberge Logibar** 3km east of Larrau on the D26 ☎ 05 59 28 61 14, ⓦ auberge-logibar.com. Perfectly positioned for lay-walker hikes to the Gorges d'Holzarté, just over 1km to the south, this welcoming *gîte* has simple private rooms and dorms. The bar-restaurant downstairs has *menus* from €11.50 with lamb, trout, cèpes and other locally sourced ingredients served until 3pm. They also provide takeaway sandwiches and snacks throughout the day. Closed Dec–Feb. Dorms **€14.50**, doubles **€32**

**Camping Ibarra** Just off the D113, 13km east of Larrau near ☎ 05 59 28 73 59, ⓦ ibarra-chantina.com.

Attractive riverside campsite just 3km from the gorges de Kakuetta. Easter to mid Oct. **€11.50**

**Hôtel-Restaurant Etchémaïté** Just off the D26 on the east side of the village ☎ 05 59 28 61 45, ⓦ hotel -etchemaite.fr. Nicely renovated old hotel with bright spacious rooms, some with balconies and views over the town and mountains. The excellent restaurant is pretty good value, offering three courses for €18 or four for €24; it serves quail, fish and offal dishes. The vegetarian main of wild mushroom terrine celebrates the wild produce of the region. Food available 12.30–2.30pm & 7.30–9pm. Closed Jan to mid Feb. **€60**

# The Central Pyrenees

The **Central Pyrenees**, immediately east of the Pays Basque, hosts the range's highest mountain peaks, the most spectacular section by the border being protected within the **Parc National des Pyrénées**. Highlights – apart from the lakes, torrents, forests and 3000-metre peaks around **Cauterets** – are the cirques of **Lescun**, **Gavarnie** and **Troumouse**, each with its distinctive character. And for less *sportif* interests, there's many a flower-starred mountain meadow accessible by car, especially near **Barèges**, in which to picnic. The only real urban centres are **Pau**, a probable entry point to the area, the dull city of **Tarbes** and pilgrimage target, **Lourdes**.

## Pau

From humble beginnings as a crossing on the Gave de Pau (*gave* is "mountain river" in Gascon dialect), **PAU** became the capital of the ancient viscountcy of Béarn in 1464, and of the French part of the kingdom of Navarre in 1512. In 1567 its sovereign, Henri d'Albret, married the sister of French King François I, Marguerite d'Angoulême, who transformed the town into a centre of the arts and nonconformist thinking.

The least-expected thing about Pau is its **English connection**: seduced by its climate and persuaded (mistakenly) of its curative powers by Scottish doctor Alexander Taylor, the English flocked to Pau throughout the nineteenth century, bringing along their cultural idiosyncrasies – fox-hunting, horse racing, polo, croquet, cricket, golf (the first eighteen-hole course in continental Europe in 1860, and the first to admit women), tea salons and parks. When the railway arrived here in 1866, the French came, too: writers like Victor Hugo, Stendhal and Lamartine, as well as socialites. The first French rugby club opened here in 1902, after which the sport spread throughout the southwest.

Pau has few must-see sights or museums, so you can enjoy its relaxed elegance without any sense of guilt. The parts to wander in are the streets behind the **boulevard des Pyrénées**,

11

PARC NATIONAL DES PYRÉNÉES

▲ Campan

La Mongie

Pic du Midi
de Bigorre
(2877m) ▲

Col du
Tourmalet
(2115m)

Lourdes ◀

N21

Argelès-Gazost

St-Savin

Pierrefitte-Nestalas

Barèges

Luz-St-Sauveur

Cauterets

D920

VALLÉE DU LUTOUR

VALLÉE D'ESTAING

Lac
d'Estaing

Arrens-Marsous

D918

Moun Né
(2724m) ▲

Lac de
Gaube

Pont
d'Espagne

Gèdre

Gavarnie

Cirque

Héas

P. Néouvielle
(3091m) ▲

Lac
d'Orédon

Lac de
Cap-de-Long

Turon
(3035m) ▲

RESERVE
NATURELLE
DE NÉOUVIELLE

Pic de la
Munia (3133m) ▲

Cirque de
Troumouse

Grd. Astazou
(3077m) ▲

Marboré
(3248m) ▲

Brèche de
Roland

Mte. Perdido
(3355m) ▲

PARQUE
NACIONAL
DE ORDESA

Port de Gavarnie

Vignemale
(3298m) ▲

S P A I N

Col de
Soulor
(1475m)

Gourette

Col
d'Aubisque
(1709m)

VALLÉE D'ARRENS

Lac
d'Artouste

Lac de
Fabrèges

Le Petit Train
d'Artouste

Téléphérique

Pic de
la Sagette
(2031m) ▲

Sallent de Gállego

N260

Huesca ▶

Pau ◀

Aste-Béon

Béost

Laruns

Eaux-Bonnes

Eaux-Chaudes

Gabas

D934

Pic Du Midi
d'Ossau
(2884m) ▲

VALLÉE D'OSSAU

Lacs
d'Ayous

Col du
Pourtalet

Pau ◀

Sarrance

Bedous

Lourdios-Ichère

Osse-en-Aspe

Cirque de
Lescun

Lescun

Cette-Eygun

L'Estanguet

Etsaut

Borce

Urdos

Fort du
Portalet

VALLÉE D'ASPE

N134

Col du
Portalet

Col du
Somport
(1632m)

Candanchu

Canfranc

N330

Jaca ▶

N

0    10
kilometres

especially the western end, which stretches along the escarpment above the Gave de Pau, from the castle to the Palais Beaumont, now a convention centre, in the English-style **Parc Beaumont**. On a clear day, the view from the boulevard encompasses a broad sweep of the highest Pyrenean peaks, with the distinctive Pic du Midi d'Ossau slap in front of you. In the narrow streets between the castle and ravine-bed chemin du Hédas are numerous cafés, restaurants, bars and boutiques, with the main Saturday **market** in the *halles* just northeast on place de la République.

### The Château Musée National

Rue du Château • Daily guided tours: mid-June to mid-Sept 9.30am–12.30pm & 1.30–5.45pm; mid-Sept to mid-June 9.30–11.45am & 2–5pm • €8; free first Sun of month; exterior unenclosed gardens free • ☎ 05 59 82 38 02, ⓦ musee-chateau-pau.fr

The **château** is very much a landmark building, though not much remains of its original fabric beyond the southeastern brick keep built in 1370. Louis-Philippe renovated it in the nineteenth century after two hundred years of dereliction, and Napoléon III and Eugénie titivated it further with stellar vaulting, chandeliers and coffered ceilings. The **Musée National** inside is visitable by a French-only, one-hour guided tour, the only way to see the vivid eighteenth-century tapestries with their wonderfully observed scenes of rural life, or Henri IV memorabilia like the giant turtle shell that purportedly served as his cradle.

### Musée Bernadotte

6 rue Tran • Tues–Sun 10am–noon & 2–5pm • €3 • ☎ 05 59 27 48 42

A short distance northeast of the château, the mildly interesting **Musée Bernadotte** is the birthplace of the man who, having served as one of Napoleon's commanders, went on to become Charles XIV of Sweden. As well as fine pieces of traditional Béarnais furniture, the house contains some valuable works of art collected over his lifetime.

### Musée des Beaux-Arts

Rue Mathieu-Lalanne • Daily except Tues 10am–noon & 2–6pm • €3 • ☎ 05 59 27 33 02

Pau's second worthwhile museum, the **Musée des Beaux-Arts,** has an eclectic collection of little-known works from European schools spanning the fourteenth to twentieth centuries; the only really world-class items are Rubens' *The Last Judgement* and Degas' *The Cotton Exchange*, a slice of finely observed *belle époque* New Orleans life.

---

#### THE PARC NATIONAL DES PYRÉNÉES

The **Parc National des Pyrénées** was created in 1967 to protect at least part of the high Pyrenees from modern touristic development – ski resorts, paved roads, mountain-top restaurants, car parks and other inappropriate amenities. It extends for more than 100km along the Spanish border from Pic de Laraille (2147m), south of Lescun, in the west, to beyond Pic de la Munia (3133m), almost to the Aragnouet–Bielsa tunnel. Varying in altitude between 1070m and 3298m at the Pic de Vignemale, south of Cauterets, the park includes the spectacular Gavarnie and Troumouse cirques, as well as 220 lakes, more than a dozen valleys and about 400km of marked walking routes.

By the **banning of hunting** and all dogs and vehicles (except local herders), the park has also provided sanctuary for many rare, endangered species of birds and mammals. These include chamois, marmots, stoats, genets, griffon vultures, golden eagles, eagle owls and capercaillies, to say nothing of the rich and varied flora. The most celebrated animal – extinct as of 2004 – is the Pyrenean **brown bear**, whose pre-1940 numbers ran to as many as two hundred; the twenty plus current specimens are descended from introduced Slovenian brown bears. Although largely herbivorous, bears will take livestock opportunistically, and most mountain shepherds are their remorseless enemies. To appease them, local authorities pay prompt and generous compensation for any losses, but the restocking programme remains highly controversial, with pro- and anti-bear graffiti prominent on the road approaches to the park, and troublesome animals being shot illegally by aggrieved farmers or herders on a regular basis.

The **GR10** runs through the entire park on its 700-kilometre journey from coast to coast, starting at Banyuls-sur-Mer on the Mediterranean and ending at Hendaye-Plage on the Atlantic.

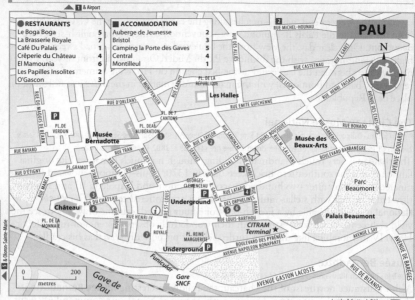

| ● RESTAURANTS | | ■ ACCOMMODATION | |
|---|---|---|---|
| Le Boga Boga | 5 | Auberge de Jeunesse | 2 |
| La Brasserie Royale | 7 | Bristol | 3 |
| Café Du Palais | 1 | Camping la Porte des Gaves | 5 |
| Crêperie du Château | 4 | Central | 4 |
| El Mamounia | 6 | Montilleul | 1 |
| Les Papilles Insolites | 2 | | |
| O'Gascon | 3 | | |

## Grottes de Bétharram

Guided visits only late March to Oct daily 9am–noon & 1.30–5.30pm; Feb to late March Mon–Fri 2.30–4pm • €13 •
ⓦ grottes-de-betharram.comat St-Pé-de-Bigorre

One worthwhile excursion from Pau, particularly for families, is to the **Grottes de Bétharram** just off the D937 between Pau and Lourdes (14km from the latter). Part of the eighty-minute tour around its spectacular stalactites and stalagmites takes place in a barge on an underground lake; the remaining kilometre is by miniature railway.

### ARRIVAL AND INFORMATION                                          PAU

**By plane** Pau airport is 6 miles northwest of Pau and served by routes from London City and Dublin and Amsterdam. The #20 bus runs from the airport to the *gare SNCF* hourly from 7.40am–7.40pm, while another runs from the *gare SNCF* to the airport hourly from 6.30am–7.50pm. The fare is €1.

**By train** The *gare SNCF* (trains and SNCF buses) is just south of the old centre, by the riverside. A free funicular links the train station to the boulevard des Pyrénées, opposite place Royale.
Destinations Bordeaux (6 daily; 2hr 15min); Oloron Ste-Marie (for the vallee d'Aspe change here) (8 daily, fewer at weekends; 35min); Paris (4 direct daily; 5hr 39min); Tarbes

(approx. hourly; approx. 40min).
**By bus** CITRAM buses leave from the *gare SNCF*.
Destinations Laruns and the Vallée d'Ossau (3 daily, 4 at weekends; 1hr).
**By car** Parking is predictably nightmarish; there are a few free spaces to the west of the centre around place de Verdun or to the east beyond Park Beaumont, otherwise shell out for kerbside meters or use the giant underground car park at place Georges-Clemenceau.
**Tourist office** Place Royale (July & Aug Mon–Fri 9am–6.30pm, Sat 9am–6pm, Sun 9.30am–1pm & 2–6pm; Sept–June Mon–Sat 9am–6pm, Sun 9.30am–1pm; ☏ 05.59.27.27.08, ⓦ pau-pyrenees.com).

### ACCOMMODATION

**Auberge de Jeunesse** 30 rue Michel Hounau ☏ 05 59 11 05 05, ⓦ habitat-jeunes-pau-asso.fr. It's not pretty to look at but this small youth hostel has a friendly, convivial atmosphere and is within easy reach of the town centre. Dorms are not too crowded, having either two beds or four beds per room, and all bedding is included in the bed rate.

The facilities available include kitchen, computer room and laundry, plus breakfast for just €3. Advance booking is advisable as there are only ten beds in the hostel. **€14**
**Bristol** 3 rue Gambetta ☏ 05 59 27 72 98 ⓦ hotelbristol -pau.com. Solid three-star comfort in the heart of the city, this nineteenth-century villa, renovated in 2006 with

modern fabrics and sober colours, provides well equipped rooms and a nice salon with a balcony in which to take breakfast for €10. Free parking. **€99**

**Camping la Porte des Gaves** Chemin de la Saligue ☎05 59 27 56 38, ⓦpaupyrenees-stadeeauxvives .co.uk. The nearest campsite (one mile walk) to town on the southern banks of the gave. Well equipped with a shop, wi-fi and child's playground, the campsite also offers year-round rafting for €20. **€15**

★ **Central** 15 rue Léon-Daran ☎05 59 27 72 75, ⓦhotelcentralpau.com. Offers 28 personalized rooms

– some more tasteful than others – with comfy beds, en-suites and, most importantly, soundproofing. The hotel can garage your car for €5.50 per day. Breakfast €7.50. **€58**

**Montilleul** 47 av jean Mermoz ☎05 59 32 93 53, ⓦhotel-montilleul.com. A nice cheap option although a good 30min walk north of the centre, this small, family-run hotel is simple and clean. The excellent continental breakfasts have a nice selection of jams worthy of the €7.50 price tag. The #5 bus passes by on its way to and from town and the *gare SNCF*; for those with their own transport, the hotel offers free parking. **€55**

## EATING AND DRINKING

**Le Boga Boga** 19 rue des Orphelines ☎05 59 83 71 44, ⓦlebogaboga.fr. One of three favoured bars on this narrow side street serving drinks and tapas late into the night. Allow €15–20 for tapas depending on how much alcohol you need to soak up. The Spanish wine menu starts at €14 a bottle or try the harder stuff, like a caffeine-laced Mojito Bull for €8. Tues–Sun 6pm–2am.

★ **La Brasserie Royale** 5 place Royale ☎05 59 27 72 12, ⓦbrasserie-royale.com Popular, upscale brasserie with *carte* and *menus* from €15 up – even the cheapest nets you a solid lamb-based main course, salad and dessert. There's been an establishment here since 1843, and the current interior with swirling fans and original art (larger parties can book the back room) vies for allure with tables on the *place* in fine weather. Noon–2.15pm & 7.30–10.15pm; closed Sun eve.

**Café Du Palais** 7 rue St Jacques ☎05 59 27 74 08, ⓦcafedupalaispau.com. Pavement café/brasserie just off the picturesque place de la liberation offering breakfasts from €7 and attractive hot plates and salads. Two-course menus with coffee are €14; make sure you go for the *clafoutis aux framboise* (an almond dessert speciality from Limousin) when available. If you just need a drink, note their happy "hour" between 6 & 6.45pm on Tues & Fri. Mon–Sat 8am–8pm.

**Crêperie du Château** 6 rue du Château ☎05 59 27 59 88.

Simple crêperie/cidrerie right opposite the castle with outside tables; a good option for vegetarians, with big salads for €7, crêpes from €4 or simply drink a cider for €2.20 and enjoy the château view. Tues–Sun 11am–midnight.

**El Mamounia** 7 rue des Orphelines ☎05 59 27 12 44, ⓦelmamounia.fr. Fine dining, Moroccan-style, with a pleasant colonial ambiance. Traditional tajines and couscous are on the set *menus* that start from €19. Don't miss out on the sweet fig wine aperitif for €5. Noon–2.30pm & 7.30–9pm; closed Mon lunch & Sun.

**Les Papilles Insolites** 5 rue Alexandre Taylor ☎05 59 71 43 79, ⓦlespapillesinsolites.blogspot.co.uk. An exciting option for wine lovers, this part-vintners, part-restaurant provides an intimate setting where you dine at dimly lit tables surrounded by the *cave's* stock. If you like a wine, take home a case. The menu offers fancy meat-focused dishes supported by seasonal veg; three courses for €18. Noon–2.30pm & 7.30–9.30pm; closed Sun–Tues.

**O'Gascon** 13 rue du Château ☎05 59 27 64 74. The most popular and reasonable of the four non-pizzerias on this touristy little *place* and the best to sample regional cuisine. The excellent trout with almonds is included in the €23 three-course menu. Noon–2pm & 7–9pm; closed Mon & Tues lunch and all Wed.

# Salies-de-Béarn

Fifteen kilometres northwest from Pau is **SALIES-DE-BÉARN**, a typical Béarnais village of winding lanes and flower-decked houses with brightly painted woodwork. The River Saleys, hardly more than a stream here, runs through the middle of it, separating the old village from the nineteenth-century quarter that sprang up to exploit the powerful saline spring for which it has long been famous. You can try the curative waters at the wonderful **thermal baths** at cours du Jardin Public (10am–noon & 2–7pm; closes at 6pm at weekends; 1hr entry includes use of the jacuzzi for €9.50; ☎05 59 38 10 11, ⓦthermes-de-salies.com), "curative" pools – one salty, one not – in an old but modernized thermal establishment.

## ARRIVAL AND INFORMATION

SALIÉS-DE-BEARN

**By bus** You can pick up the bus to Orthez (on the Pau-Bordeaux train line) by the Thermal pool on cours de Jardin Public (3 daily; 25min).

**Tourist office** Rue des Bains (Mon–Sat 9.30am–noon & 2–6pm; ☎05 59 38 00 33, ⓦtourisme-bearn -gaves.com).

## ACCOMMODATION AND EATING

**La Demeure Saint Martin** Rue St Martin ☎ 05 59 38 07 01, ⓦlademeuresaintmartin.com. A quasi sacro-bohemian retreat, this twelfth-century presbytery bears the hallmarks of its age as well as of its eccentric owner. Adorned with quirky personal effects, this building feels loved. Rooms are equipped with a sink and shower while the toilet is in the hall. Breakfast is served in your room: home-made cake, bread and jams for €10. €70

**La Terrasse** 2 rue Loume ☎ 05 59 38 09 83, ⓦlaterrasse.e-monsite.com. With its large terrace – hence the name – enviably positioned overlooking the Saleys river, its unsurprising that this restaurant-bar is so popular. The menu holds no great surprises; just hearty Béarnaise home cooking and quaffably good wine. Three courses for €22.50. Noon–2pm & 7–10pm; Oct–June closed Thurs & Sun eves & all Mon; July–Sept closed Mon.

# Sauveterre-de-Béarn

Heading south from Salies-de-Béarn, the D933 winds over hilly farming country to **SAUVETERRE-DE-BÉARN**, a pretty country town beautifully set on a bluff high above the Gave d'Oloron, just before it mingles with the Saison. From the terrace by the thirteenth-century **church of St-André** – over-restored but still retaining a fine west-portal relief of Christ in Glory – you look down over the river and the remains of fortified, half-ruined **Pont de la Légende**, while at the west end of the compact *cité médiévale* stand the ruins of a Gaston Fébus **château**. A pedestrian-only lane leads down to the bridge and river, full of bathers (and canoers/rafters: see ⓦaboste.com) on hot days despite its murky greenness.

### ARRIVAL                                          SAUVETERRE-DE-BÉARN

**By bus** The bus to Orthez (on the Pau-Bordeaux train line) stops by the main place Royal (3 daily Mon–Fri; 35min).

### ACCOMMODATION

**L'Auberge du Saumon** Across the river 2km south of town on the D933 ☎ 05 59 38 53 20. If you have a car try this cute detached cottage straddling the main road 2km from the centre. The timbered rooms are clean and comfortable yet refreshingly untouched by modernity. Downstairs dining room where you can find sustenance for €17pp if you don't fancy the long walk to town. Closed mid-Jan to mid-Feb. €65

# Navarrenx

From Sauveterre-de-Béarn, the D936 bears southeast along the flat valley bottom 20km away on the Pau–Mauléon bus route to **NAVARRENX**, a sleepy, old-fashioned market town built as a *bastide* in 1316 and still surrounded by its medieval walls. Having crossed the medieval bridge over the Gave d'Oloron – claimed here as the salmon-fishing capital of France – you enter from the west by the fortified Porte St-Antoine.

### ACCOMMODATION

**Du Commerce** Place des Casernes ☎ 05 59 66 50 16, ⓦwww.hotel-commerce.fr. The lovingly preserved exterior of this hotel with its grey-blue shutters and mansard roof contrasts with its modern, sometimes futuristic interior. It's a comfortable and friendly hotel offering substantial breakfasts for €8, or you can take the half-board option for €114 (for two) and sample the terraced restaurant's vibrant cuisine. Wi-fi is available here for a rather pointless €1 per day. Closed Jan. €72

# Lourdes

**LOURDES**, 37km southeast of Pau, has one principle function. Over seven million Catholic pilgrims arrive here yearly, and the town is totally dedicated to looking after and, on occasion, exploiting them. Lourdes was hardly more than a village before 1858,

**CLOCKWISE FROM TOP LEFT** PREHISTORIC CAVE PAINTING, NIAUX (P.615); PAINTING BY MIRÓ, MUSÉE D'ART MODERNE, CÉRET (P.628); CHÂTEAU DE QUÉRIBUS (P.619) >

when Bernadette Soubirous, 14-year-old daughter of a poor local miller, had the first of eighteen visions of the Virgin Mary in the Grotte de Massabielle by the Gave de Pau. Since then, Lourdes has become the most visited attraction in this part of France, many pilgrims hoping for a miraculous cure for conventionally intractable ailments.

Myriad shops are devoted to the sale of unbelievable religious kitsch: Bernadette and/or the Virgin in every shape and size, adorning barometers, thermometers, plastic tree trunks, empty bottles that you can fill with holy water, bellows, candles and illuminated plastic grottoes. Clustered around the miraculous grotto are the churches of the Domaine de la Grotte, an annexe to the town proper that sprang up in the century following Bernadette's visions. The first to be built was an underground crypt in 1866, followed by the flamboyant double **Basilique du Rosaire et de l'Immaculée Conception** (1871–83), and then in 1958 by the massive subterranean **Basilique St-Pie-X**, which can apparently fit 20,000 people at a time. The **Grotte de Massabielle** itself is the focus of pilgrimage – a moisture-blackened overhang by the riverside with a marble statue on high of the Virgin, where pilgrims queue to circumambulate, stroking the grotto wall with their left hand. To one side are taps for filling souvenir containers with the holy spring water; to the other are the *bruloirs* or rows of braziers where enormous votive candles burn, prolonging the prayers of supplicants.

## The château

**Musée Pyrénéen** Daily: April–Sept 9am–noon & 1.30–6.30pm, no lunch break mid-July to Aug; Oct–March daily 9am–noon & 2–6pm, 5pm on Fri • €5 • ☎ 05 62 42 37 37, ⓦ lourdes-visite.com

Lourdes' only secular attraction is its spectacular **château,** poised on a rocky bluff east of the Gave de Pau, and guarding the approaches to the valleys and passes of the central Pyrenees. Inside is the surprisingly excellent **Musée Pyrénéen**. Its collections include Pyrenean fauna, all sorts of fascinating pastoral and farming gear, and an interesting section on the history of Pyrenean mountaineering.

### ARRIVAL AND INFORMATION

LOURDES

**By plane** The Tarbes-Ossun-Lourdes airport is currently served by no-frills flights from Britain. Take the "Maligne Gave" #2 bus into town (€2).

**By train** Lourdes' *gare SNCF* is on the northeast edge of the town centre, at 33 av de la Gare.
Destinations Bayonne (6 daily; 1hr 40min); Pau (21 daily; 30min); Tarbes (21 daily; 15min).

**By bus** The *gare routière* is in central place Capdevielle. Destinations en-route to Cauterets (6 daily; 55min).

**Tourist office** Place Peyramale (Oct–March Mon–Sat 9am–noon & 2–5.30pm; April–June & Sept Mon–Sat 9am–12.30pm & 1.30–6.30pm, Sun 10am–12.30pm; July & Aug Mon–Sat 9am–7pm, Sun 10am–6pm; ☎05.62.42.77.40, ⓦ lourdes-infotourisme.com).

### ACCOMMODATION

Lourdes has more hotels than any city in France outside Paris and consequently competition is intense. For a good rate find an internet café and search for offers which could be considerably cheaper than turning up at a hotel.

**Au Berceau De Bernadette** 44 bd de la Grotte ☎05 62 42 76 58, ⓦ laresidencelourdes.com. Have a good old pray any time of the day at this *petite residence* with its own DIY chapel. Religious imagery is present throughout the building without being too overbearing while the rooms offer space, comfort and hot beverages in your room – a rarity in France. Closed Nov–March. **€48**

**Mediterane** 23 av du Paradis ☎05 62 94 72 15, ⓦ lourdeshotelmed.com. Overlooking the river, this modern hotel rises above the town's tatty norm. The rooms are bright and well equipped but lack the space you might expect for the price tag. The half-board option is a worthwhile €25 extra and covers all you can eat continental breakfast and reputable evening meals. **€101**

### EATING AND DRINKING

**Café Leffe** 16 place Marcadal ☎05 62 46 34 48, ⓦ cafeleffe.fr Part of a small chain of bar/brassieres specializing in strong Belgian beers. It's a popular haunt of the forty-something crowd and has outside tables in a

peaceful enough locality. The food here, although hardly haute cuisine, will please most palates; there's even a delicious vegetarian lasagne with salad for €10. Otherwise, there are various meat and fish dishes served with

11

beer-incorporated sauces. Mon–Thurs 7am–11pm, Fri & Sat 7am–2am & Sun 3–8pm.

**La Fine Escale** 9 Impasse du Fort ☎ 05 62 91 28 33, ⓦ finescale.e-monsite.com. This backstreet restaurant delivers substance over style with its communion of French and Asian cuisine. The regionally ubiquitous *magret de canard* is reinvented (roasted with pears, honey and spices) for €17.50 or you can play it safe with the salmon in mint and lemon sauce at €14. Three-course *menus* range from €13.50–31. Noon–1.30pm & 7–9.30pm; closed Sun eve, all Mon; Oct–April closed Tues.

**Le Palacio** 28 place Champ Commun ☎ 05 62 94 00 59, ⓦ restaurant-lourdes-palacio.fr. Just out of reach of the touristic concourse trappings, *Le Palacio* offers solid French cuisine served on the sunny *place*. You can dine on a budget here with their *plat du jour* for €8 or their pizzas starting at €6.50. Daily noon–1.30pm & 7–9.30pm.

# The Vallée d'Aspe

The **Vallée d'Aspe** presents the central Pyrenees at their most undeveloped, primarily because inappropriate topography and unreliable snow conditions have precluded ski-resort construction.

## GETTING AROUND AND INFORMATION                              THE VALLÉE D'ASPE

**11**

**By train** The train from Pau serves the grey town of Oloron-Ste-Marie (8 daily; 40min), which sits 45km west of Lourdes. From there, the bus that goes deeper into the valley is sometimes coordinated to depart from the train station eight minutes later.

**By bus** Five buses daily journey up the valley, through the Tunnel du Somport into Spanish territory. Destinations on the way include Bedous (33min), Cette Eygun (42min), Estaut (48min), Pont-de-Lescun (40min) and Urdos (55min).

## Lescun

Some 35km south of Pau, southwest of the N134 and valley floor, the ancient stone-and-stucco houses of **LESCUN** huddle on the northeast slopes of a huge and magnificent green **cirque**. The floor of the cirque and the lower slopes, dimpled with vales and hollows, have been gently shaped by generations of farming, while to the west the town is overlooked by the great grey molars of **Le Billare**, Trois Rois and Ansabère, beyond which rises the storm-lashed bulk of the **Pic d'Anie** (2504m).

## ARRIVAL AND INFORMATION                                         LESCUN

The bus from Oloron-Ste-Marie stops in the valley floor below Lescun; then it's a three-mile hike up the hill to the village. Alternatively, you can hop off a couple of stops early and take a taxi from Bedous. Taxis can be taken from the garage on the southern end of town. Ideally phone or email ahead to book ☎ 05 59 34 70 06 ✉ gerard.lepretre@wanadoo.fr.

## ACCOMMODATION

**Camping Le Lauzart** Turn left onto the D340 just before Lescun village and continue for one mile ☎ 05 59 34 51 77, ⓦ camping-lescun.com. This lush green campsite has a stupendous position with unimpeded views of the peaks. The site owners sell basic provisions and might even cook breakfast or dinner for you bearing in mind there's no restaurant in the village. May–Sept. **€11.50**

**Chambres d'Hôte Pic d'Anie** Place Centrale ☎ 05 59 34 71 54, ⓦ hebergement-picdanie.fr. A characterful old building full of plants and ancient wooden furniture that give insight into the house's past. The bedrooms are on the small side but at least come en-suite and there's also a reading room, handy for the frequent rain showers. Breakfast €6. April to mid-Sept. **€45**

**Gîte Pic d'Anie** Opposite the Chambres d'Hôte Pic d'Anie. Run by the same establishment as the *Chambres d'Hôte Pic d'Anie*, the simple and clean interior lacks the charm of its neighbouring accommodation but at least has cooking facilities in this restaurant-less town. Supplies can be bought from the shop across the road. Breakfast €6. **€16**

## Cette-Eygun

A couple of kilometres beyond the turn-off for Lescun is **CETTE-EYGUN**, a pretty little village with a few good walking opportunities, but the main reasons to come here are to dine and sleep it off at the beautiful *Château d'Arance* (see p.606) with its bird's-eye view of the valley.

11

★ **Au Château d'Arance** ☎ 05 59 34 75 50, ⊕ hotel -auchateaudarance.com. Converted and modernized twelfth-century stone manor house with spectacular, unhampered views. Internally, the hotel lacks the charm in places promised by its well-restored exterior, but the bedrooms come with all the conveniences you would expect for the price and are thus comfortable. The château's vaulted restaurant offers bounteous plates of fresh, locally sourced food like the trout with cèpes for €12 or lamb with wild mushrooms for €10, all washed down with a nice bottle of Béarnaise red at €15. Vegetarians are also catered for. Leisurely breakfasts (€9) can be taken on the terrace in front of the château overlooking the valley and the thermal seeking vultures that kettle below. Restaurant open noon–2pm & 7.30–9pm; closed Mon Nov–Feb. Reservation essential if not a guest. Gîte €55; hotel rooms €65

## Urdos

Some 10km south of Cette-Eygun, **URDOS** is the last village on the French side of the frontier, and has one of the best hotel-restaurants (see below) in the valley. From here, you (and the odd bus) can continue through the free tunnel under the **Col de Somport** and on to Canfranc in Spain, the terminus for trains from Jaca, though in fine weather the far more scenic road over the pass is not that strenuous a drive.

Further upstream – about two miles north of Urdos – at one of the narrowest, rockiest, steepest points of the Aspe squats the menacing nineteenth-century **Fort du Portalets** (July, Aug & school holidays 2–6pm; €3 reservation only ☎ 05 59 34 57 57). Built to defend against Spanish incursions, the garrison housed over four hundred men and could withstand a week's siege in total autonomy. In the 1940s it served as a prison for Socialist premier Léon Blum under Pétain's Vichy government, and then for Pétain himself after the liberation of France. Today the fort is undergoing major restoration work and visits are temporarily limited.

★ **Des Voyageurs** Route du Col du Somport ☎ 05 59 34 88 05, ⊕ hotel-voyageurs-aspe.com. Good old-fashioned hotel that has made a name for itself – at least locally – for its fine restaurant. Share a duck breast roasted with apples and cèpes for €30 (for two) or stick with the €13.50 *menu*. Restaurant 12.15–2pm & 7.30–9pm; closed Mon & Sun eve. Breakfast is €6. The hotel is closed mid-Oct to Nov. Doubles €40, half-board €80

# Vallée d'Ossau

A destination for hikers, cyclists and snow-sports enthusiasts rather than casual day-trippers, the route up the Ossau valley rises fast towards the gnarled eminence of the Pic du Midi and the Cirque d'Aneou on the Spanish border. Outside winter the landscape is lush and green, with high pastures grazed by the brebis sheep whose milk provides the distinctive Ossau-Iraty cheese (see box, p.596), a Bearn/Basque delicacy not to be missed. Near the Col, look out for marmots, that never stray far from their burrows. The villages on the way are little reason to stick around – except for unremarkable Laruns, in order to stock up on supplies, and the two spa resorts of Eaux-Chauds and Eaux-Bonnes, which retain charm even if they have seen more prosperous times.

**By bus** From Pau, four buses daily call at Gere Beleston (57min) opposite Béon and Laruns (1hr 5min) before turning east towards Eaux Bonnes (1hr 15min) and Gourette. For destinations south to the border change at Laruns for one of two coordinated buses that stop at Eaux-Chaudes (10min) and Gabas (25min).

**Tourist office** Place de la Mairie, in Laruns village (Mon–Sat 9am–noon & 2–6pm, except Thurs 9am–noon & 3–6pm; ☎ 05 59 05 31 41).
**Maison du Parc** Next to the tourist office (mid-June to mid-Sept Mon–Fri 9am–noon & 2–5.30pm closed Sat & Sun and every second Fri; ☎ 05 59 05 41 59).

## Eaux-Chaudes

The D934 road from Laruns towards the Spanish border winds steeply into the upper reaches of the Gave d'Ossau valley, passing through **EAUX-CHAUDES** spa village: an attractive ghost town of a place, somewhat run-down but unspoilt by development and an ideal base for climbers and walkers. The perfect place to rest weary bones is the **Thermes des Eaux Chaudes**, next to the river (May–Oct Mon–Sat 9am–noon & 3.30–6.30pm; ☎05 59 05 36 36, ⊚eauxchaudes.fr). It's in a lovely vintage building, and offers the usual spa facilities and treatments, from jet showers (€7) to massages (€26). Further en-route, the **Pic du Midi d'Ossau** comes into view, with its craggy, mitten-shaped summit (2884m) – it's a classic Pyrenean landmark.

## ACCOMMODATION AND EATING                                 EAUX-CHAUDES

**Auberge La Caverne** Southern edge of the village ☎05 59 05 34 40, ⊚aubergelacaverne.com. Run by a hard-working couple who offer both dorms and en-suite doubles in a jolly old building. Reasonably priced *table d'hôte* meals are also available starting from €6.50 for a crêpe, €11 for Basque chicken; or, if you're just passing through, stop for a drink on the flowery terrace. Service any time of the day. Closed Oct–

Nov. Dorms half-board €31; rooms half-board €80

★ **Chambre d'hôte Baudot** Place Henri IV ☎05 59 05 34 51, ⊚chambre-hote-baudot.com. Impeccably restored old hotel next to the spa offering understated charm and good value. The three-storey nineteenth-century building has large en-suite rooms and breakfasts by a log fire when the air gets a bit nippy. June–Sept. Rates include breakfast. €65

**11**

## Eaux-Bonnes

The only way of reaching the Gave de Pau by road without going back towards Pau is along the minor D918 east over the Col d'Aubisque, via Eaux-Bonnes and **Gourette**, 12km east of Laruns and the favourite **ski centre** of folk from Pau. The base development is ugly but the skiing, on 28 north-facing runs from a top point of 2400m, is more than respectable. You can of course stay here, but the once thriving spa village of **EAUX-BONNES**, 8km below Gourette, is more elegant and pleasant. Save for the unattractive tourist info hut, the village remains undeveloped and thus retains a certain charm especially out of high season when you practically have the town to yourself.

## INFORMATION                                             EAUX-BONNES

**Tourist office** In the central place (Mon–Fri 9.30am–12.15pm & 1.45–5.30pm; ☎05 59 05 12 17, ⊚gourette.com).

## ACCOMMODATION AND EATING

**De la Poste** 19 rue Louis-Barthou ☎05 59 50 33 06, ⊚hotel-dela-poste.com. This old-fashioned hotel offers spacious if dated rooms spread round a central indoor courtyard overlooking a quirky fish pond containing trout. Needless to say, trout appears on the

hotel's restaurant menu along with other regional mainstays. Unfortunately, not all the ingredients used here are as fresh as the trout and the hotel's labelled house wine is not local. The three-course *menu* costs €16.50. €45

## Arrens-Marsous

The **Col d'Aubisque** itself (1709m), a grassy saddle with a souvenir stall/café on top, usually sees the Tour de France come through, making the pass irresistible to any French cyclist worth his salt. Once over the next, lower Col de Soulor (1475m), the route descends, 18km in all, to attractive **ARRENS-MARSOUS**, at the head of the Val d'Azun.

---

### LE PETIT TRAIN ARTOUSTE

**Le Petit Train Artouste** (late May to early Sept 9am–5pm hourly (every 30min in July & Aug); €17 one-way; €27 return; ☎05 59 05 36 99 ⊚train-artouste.com) chugs along a spectacular miniature railway line that runs ten vertiginous kilometres southeast through the mountains from **Lac de Fabrèges**, 13km south of Eaux-Chaudes, to **Lac d'Artouste**. Built in the 1920s to service a hydroelectric project and later converted for tourist purposes, this is a beautiful trip, lasting about four hours there and back, including the initial télécabine ride from the base of **Pic de la Sagette** (2031m). Tickets can be purchased from the tourist office in the resort at Lac de Fabrèges and the *télécabine* leaves from next door.

### INFORMATION — ARRENS-MARSOUS

**Tourist office** Housed in the Maison du Val d'Azun in the village centre (mid June to mid-Sept only Mon–Sat 9am–noon & 2–6/7pm, Sun 9am–12.30pm; ☎ 05 62 97 49 49, ⓦ valdazun.com).

### ACCOMMODATION

**Chambre d'hôte La Condorinette** 3 rue de la Gourgoutiere, Marsous ☎ 05 62 92 06 39, ⓦ chambreshotes.pyrenees-65.com. Friendly B&B offering colourful double rooms plus a two-bed family suite. The wood-burning stove in the lounge/dining room makes for a pleasant backdrop to the substantial breakfasts provided and on warmer days you can eat outside in the orchard garden. Evening meals are also provided for €22 and offer regional favourites, duck in pepper sauce and *la garbure*. For pudding make a beeline for the Limousan speciality, *clafoutis de framboises*. May–Oct. Doubles €65 family suite €115

**Gîte Camélat** 8 rue de Cardet ☎ 05 62 97 40 94, ⓦ www.gite-camelat.com. A fine, rambling, nineteenth-century house with en-suite rooms and dormitory beds. Breakfast and a wholesome evening meal are included in the price as is the fine hiking recommendations from your hosts and fellow trekkers. Open all year. Dorms €35, doubles €90

11

## The Gave de Pau

From its namesake city, the **Gave de Pau** forges southeast towards the mountains, bending sharply south at Lourdes and soon fraying into several tributaries: the **Gave d'Azun**, the **Gave de Cauterets**, the **Gave de Gavarnie** and the **Gave de Bastan**, dropping from the Col du Tourmalet. **Cauterets**, 30km due south of Lourdes, and **Gavarnie** 37km southeast of Argelès, are busy, established resorts on the edge of the national park, but the countryside they adjoin is so spectacular that you forgive their deficiencies. If you want a smaller, more manageable base, then either **Barèges**, up a side valley from the spa resort of **Luz-St-Sauveur**, or Luz itself, are better bets. But pick your season – or even the time of day – right, and you can enjoy the most popular sites in relative solitude. At Gavarnie few people stay the night, so it's quiet early or late, and the **Cirque de Troumouse**, which is just as impressive (though much harder to get to without a car), has far fewer visitors.

### Cauterets

**CAUTERETS** is a pleasant if unexciting little town that owes its fame and rather elegant Neoclassical architecture (especially on boulevard Latapie-Flurin) to its spa, and more recently to its role as one of the main Pyrenean ski and mountaineering centres. The town is small and easy to get around; most of it is still squeezed between the steep wooded heights that close the mouth of the Gave de Cauterets valley.

### ARRIVAL AND INFORMATION — CAUTERETS

**By bus** Buses arrive at the lovely old *gare* on avenue de la Gare on the north edge of the centre from Lourdes (6 daily & one extra on Fri; 55min).

**Tourist office** Place Maréchal-Foch (Mon–Sat: July & Aug 9am–noon & 2–7pm; Sept–June 9am–noon & 2–6pm; ☎ 05 62 92 50 50, ⓦ cauterets.com).

**Maison du Parc** Avenue de la Gare, on the northern edge of the centre (Mon–Fri 9.30am–noon & 3–6.30pm; ☎ 05 62 92 52 56 ). A good source of walking maps and hiking route advice.

### ACCOMMODATION

**Camping La Prairie** Rte de Pierrefitte (D920) ☎ 05 62 92 07 04, ⓦ campinglaprairie.over-blog.com. A 5min walk north of the town centre – and one of a number of campsites on this side of town – *La Prairie* is predominantly a canvas site with a few basic facilities and consequently is the cheapest of the bunch. Mid-May to mid Oct. €11.60

**Cesar** 3 rue Cesar ☎ 05 62 92 52 57, ⓦ cesarhotel.com. Quiet, centrally located hotel with a modern/yesteryear decor melange. Closed late Sept to late Oct & late April to late May. €60

**Le Pas de l'Ours** 21 rue de la Raillère ☎ 05 62 92 58 07, ⓦ lepasdelours.com. Clean and warm hotel and *gîte d'etape* with so much pine cladding, it's almost a sauna. The double rooms don't offer particularly good value but if you're alone or on a budget, the six bed dorms are the town's best option. Dorm €22, doubles(B&B) €74

## EATING

**La Crêperie du Gave** Galerie Aladin, rue de Belfort ☏ 05 62 45 09 96, ⓦ lacreperiedugave.com. Located on the west side of the river, this small, economical restaurant serves *galettes* from €4.50 to €8.80 or three-course *menus* including wine/cider for €12. Noon–2pm & 7–9pm, closed Sun eve & Mon. During school holidays: daily noon–2pm, 4.30–5.30pm & 7–9pm.

**Les Halles de Cauterets** Av l'Eclerc. For tantalizing takeaway food, visit this indoor market with its rotisseries selling hot meals by the kilo. Stuff your picnic hamper with roast lamb €14.50/kg or vegetable gratin €10.50/kg or if you're off on a hike, get sandwiches made up for you €2.90. The *fromagerie* attached to the Halles sells wonderful aged brebis. Daily 9am–noon & 2–6pm.

## Luz-St-Sauveur

The only road approach to the cirques Gavarnie and Troumouse zones is through **LUZ-ST-SAUVEUR**, astride the GR10. Like Cauterets, this was a nineteenth-century spa, patronized by Napoléon III and Eugénie, and elegant Neoclassical facades in the left-bank St-Saveur quarter date from then.

The **St-André church** (approximately daily May 15 to Sept 30 3–6pm; free) on place de la Comporte at the top of Luz's medieval, right-bank quarter is the town's principal sight. Built in the late eleventh century, it was fortified in the fourteenth by the Knights of St John with a crenelated outer wall and two stout towers. The north entrance sports a handsome portal surmounted by a Christ in Majesty carved in fine-grained local stone.

### ARRIVAL AND INFORMATION
LUZ-ST-SAUVEUR

**By bus** One direct bus travels to and from Lourdes during school days and termtime. Otherwise change at Pierrefitte Nestallas a few kilometres north of Luz. The changeover is co-ordinated to leave five minutes after arrival in both directions. From Lourdes there are 5 indirect buses Mon–Sat and 4 on Sun (55min).

**Tourist office** On the edge of the central place du Huit-Mai (Mon–Sat 8.30am–7pm, Sun 8.30am–noon & 4–7pm; ☏ 05 62 92 30 30 ⓦ luz.org).

### ACCOMMODATION

★ **Le Montaigu** Rte de Vizos ☏ 05 62 92 81 71, ⓦ hotelmontaigu.com. This modern three-star hotel sits in a semi-rural position beneath the ruined tenth-century château Ste-Marie (a 5min uphill saunter). The rooms within have large balconies with cracking southwesterly views to the high Pyrenees. Breakfast included. Doubles **€103**; half-board **€138**

**Les Templiers** 6 place De La Comporte ☏ 05 62 92 81 52, ⓦ www.hotellestempliers.com. With en-suite rooms looking onto a beautiful eleventh-century church, this rustic gem, clad in Virginia creeper and climbing rose, is centrally located in a peaceful square. The hotel also runs an organic crêperie downstairs and provides a tasty €7.50 breakfast. **€65**

### EATING

★ **Chez Christine** 3 rue Dossun Prolongée ☏ 05 62 92 86 81. Although this is predominantly a pizzeria, the quality of the own-made pasta and desserts plus locally sourced meat dishes make this a superb all-rounder.

Vegetarians will find a lot to choose from here including cheesy fondues for €16 (min two persons) and pizzas starting at €7. April–Aug daily noon–2pm & 7–9pm; Sept–March open Thurs–Sat, except closed Nov.

## Gavarnie

Once poor and depopulated, **Gavarnie** village found the attractions of mass tourism – much of it excursions from Lourdes – too seductive to resist, and it's now filled with souvenir shops and snack bars.

### ARRIVAL AND INFORMATION
GAVARNIE

**By car** If you drive in, a parking fee (July to mid-Sept 8am–5pm; €5) is charged; otherwise there is ample free parking around the shops and hotels.

**By bus** Buses leave the *gare routière* in Lourdes at 8.55am, stop at Luz-St-Sauveur at 9.50am and head on to Gavarnie's tourist office. The bus back to Lourdes departs at 9.30am.

The journey takes 1hr 40min.

**Tourist office** By the car park (daily 9am–noon & 2–6pm; ☏ 05 62 92 49 10, ⓦ gavarnie.com).

**Maison du Parc** On the main drag past the car park (Mon–Thurs 8.30am–noon & 1.30–6pm & Fri 8.30am–noon; ☏ 05 62 92 42 48).

11

## ACCOMMODATION

**La Bergerie** Chemin du Cirque ☎05 62 92 48 41, ⓦ camping-gavarnie-labergerie.com. Surely one of the most stunningly located Pyrenean campsites, with views compensating for basic facilities. The site has a small bar serving wine and *pression* beer. June–Sept. **€10.90**

★ **Compostelle** Rue de l'Église ☎05 62 92 49 43, ⓦ compostellehotel.com. Thanks to its elevated position next to the beautiful old church, this pretty hotel has the best views in town onto the cirque. Inside, the decor may not be that of a deluxe hotel but it's all clean and functional. Breakfast €7. Closed Oct to mid-Jan. Doubles **€43**, half-board **€50.50pp**

**Gîte Auberge Le Gypaète** Below the main car park behind the tourist office ☎05 62 92 40 61, ⓦ legypaete .pagesperso-orange.fr. Nice little stone cottage with a wall humorously covered in climbing footholds. Inside there's a large dining area and, incredibly, 45 beds jammed in, literally to the rafters. Most guests opt for the hearty half-board option and wash it down with a €4 half-litre of house wine. There's free internet here and picnics on request for €8. Dorms **€14**, half-board **€33**

**Vignemale** Across the river at the end of the village ☎05 62 92 40 00, ⓦ hotel-vignemale.com. For three-star luxury, this hotel, astride the *gave*, offers spacious rooms and balconies with unimpeded views to the cirque. Closed mid-Oct to mid-May. **€150**

## EATING AND INFORMATION

★ **Les Cascades** Next to the Maison du Parc (see p.609) ☎05 62 92 40 17. A gastronomic highlight of the town, this restaurant presents fresh regional platters with low food-mile ingredients. All with the added benefit of tables overlooking the cirque. *Menus* range from €20–32. Mon–Sat noon–1.30pm & 7–8.30pm.

## The Cirque de Troumouse

Much bigger than Gavarnie and, in bad weather, rather intimidating, the **Cirque de Troumouse** forms a 10km wall of curved rock shorn by glacial action. A mere 22km by road from Gavarnie village, it would be inconceivable to visit one cirque and not the other. Just north of Gavarnie the D922 forks to the right leading up a wild valley whose only habitations are the handful of farmsteads and a pilgrimage chapel, with its ancient polychrome statuette of the Virgin and Child, that make up the scattered hamlet of **HÉAS** – among the loneliest outposts in France before the road in was constructed.

**GETTING THERE**                                                                                    **CIRQUE DE TROUMOUSE**

**By car** After 8km up the D922 from Gavarnie, vehicles need to pay a toll (€5) although only when the booth is open: May–Oct 9am–5pm, depending on the weather.

### THE CIRQUE DE GAVARNIE

Victor Hugo called it "Nature's Colosseum" – a magnificent, natural amphitheatre scoured out by glaciers. Over 1500m high, the Gavarnie cirque consists of three sheer bands of rock streaked by seepage and waterfalls, separated by sloping ledges covered with snow and glacier remnants. On the east, it's dominated by the jagged **Astazou** and **Marboré** peaks, both over 3000m. In the middle, a cornice sweeps round to the **Brèche de Roland**, a curious vertical slash, 100m deep and about 60m wide, said to have been hewn from the ridge by Roland's sword, Durandal. In winter, there's good beginner-to-intermediate **skiing** at the nearby 24-run resort of **Gavarnie-Gèdre**, with great views of the cirque from the top point of 2400m.

From Gavarnie village an unmade road follows the river towards the cirque, gradually narrowing as the gradient and the drama increases. It's a moderately easy hour's walk in each direction but if you prefer, hire a horse from the edge of town for €25. The broad track ends at the *Hôtel du Cirque et de la Cascade*, once a famous meeting place for mountaineers and now a popular snack bar in summer.

To get to the foot of the cirque walls, you face a steeper, final half-hour on a dwindling, increasingly slippery path which ends in a spray-bath at the base of the **Grande Cascade**, fed by Lago Helado on the Spanish side, and at 423m the highest waterfall in Europe. This plummets and fans out in three stages down the rock faces – a fine sight in sunny weather, with rainbows in the wind-teased plumes. For a bit of serenity the best time to see the cirque is at dusk when, even in summer, you could have it all to yourself.

## ACCOMMODATION & EATING

**Auberge de la Munia** Héas ☎05 62 92 48 39, ⓦaubergedelamunia.com. With a handful of plain rooms and an attractive garden this is the most appealing place to stay in this remote valley. Their restaurant offers *garbure*, trout with almonds and other regional stalwarts as well as a vegetarian omelette with cêpes. Three-course *menus* are €19.90. Food available noon–2pm & 7–8.30pm; closed when there is no B&B. **€65**, half-board **€48pp**

**Auberge du Maillet** 4km past the tollbooth ☎05 62 92 48 97, ⓦaubergedumaillet.free.fr. The closest accommodation to the cirque, this is a superb base for walkers, cyclists and mountaineers. The rooms are surprisingly fresh and naturally the views rob you of your breath. Although predominately a hostel, you can pay extra to have a private room. Mid-May to Oct. Dorms **€37**, private rooms **€96**

## Barèges

The only major village in the Cirque de Bastan is **BARÈGES**, primarily a skiing, mountaineering and paragliding centre, and the most congenial, low-key resort around the Gave de Pau.

## ARRIVAL AND INFORMATION                                          BAREGES

**11**

**By bus** One direct bus travels to and from Lourdes during school days and termtime. Otherwise change at Pierrefitte Nestallas. The changeover is co-ordinated to leave five minutes after arrival in both directions. From Lourdes (5 indirect Mon–Sat & 4 Sun; 1hr 5min).

**Tourist office** Place Urbain Cazaux (July & Aug Mon–Sat 9am–12.30pm & 2–6.30pm, Sun 10am–noon & 4–6pm; Sept–June closes 5pm; ☎05 62 92 16 00, ⓦgrand -tourmalet.com). Can supply ski-lift plans.

## ACCOMMODATION

**La Montagne Fleurie** 21 rue Ramon ☎05 62 92 68 50, ⓦhotel-tourmalet.fr. The best value out of the handful of hotels lining the main road, this eighteenth-century

building has been restored with dignity and thought. Evening meals are traditional, varied and inexpensive at €15. Breakfast included. **€68**

# The Comminges

Stretching from Luchon almost to Toulouse, the **Comminges** is an ancient feudal county encompassing the upper Garonne River valley. It also hosts one of the finest buildings in the Pyrenees, a magnificent cathedral built over three distinct periods in St-Bertrand-de-Comminges.

## St-Bertrand-de-Comminges

The grey fortress-like **cathedral** (daily 10am–noon & 2–6pm; May–Sept daily 9am–7pm, Sun 2–5pm; admission to cloister and choir €4) of **ST-BERTRAND-DE-COMMINGES** commands the plain from its knoll-top position, the austere white-veined facade and heavily buttressed nave totally subduing the clutch of fifteenth- and sixteenth-century houses huddled at its feet. To the right of the west door a Romanesque twelfth-century cloister with carved capitals looks out across a lush valley to the foothills, haunt of Resistance fighters during World War II. In the aisleless interior, the church's great attraction is the central choir, built by Toulousain craftsmen and installed 1523–35. The 66 elaborately carved stalls, each one the work of a different craftsman, are a feast of virtuosity, mingling piety, irony and satire. During the summer (mid-July to mid-Aug), the cathedral and St-Just in Valcabrère, both with marvellous acoustics, host the musical Festival du Comminges (ⓦfestival-du-comminges.com).

## St-Just de Valcabrère

June–Sept 9.30am–7pm; April–May & Oct 10am–noon & 2–6pm; Nov–March weekend only 2–5pm €2.50 ☎05 61 95 49 06

One mile east of St-Bertrand, there's an exquisite Romanesque church – the **St-Just de Valcabrère** – whose square tower rises above a cypress-studded cemetery. The north portal is girded by four elegant full-length sculptures and overtopped by a relief of Christ in Glory borne heavenward by angels. Both interior and exterior are full of

---

## SKIING AND HIKING AROUND BARÈGES

With its links to the adjacent, equal-sized *domaine* of **La Mongie** over 10km east on the far side of the Col du Tourmalet, Barèges offers access to the largest **skiing** area in the French Pyrenees, including downhill pistes totalling 125km (1850–2400m) and 31km of cross-country trails through the Lienz plateau forest (1350–1700m). Beginners' runs finishing in Barèges village are much too low (1250m) to retain snow; so all skiers usually have to start from the Tournaboup or Tourmalet zones. High-speed, state-of-the-art chair lifts are the rule at Barèges, and runs have been regraded to make the resort more competitive, and La Mongie over the hill, despite its hideous purpose-built development, offers even higher, longer pistes. For more information consult ⑩ tourmalet.fr.

The **GR10** passes through Barèges on its way southeast into the lake-filled **Néouvielle Massif**, part of France's oldest (1935) natural reserve, and a great **hiking** area. The best trailhead for **day-hikes** lies 3km east of Barèges on the D918 at **Pont de la Gaubie** (you'll see a small car park and an abandoned snack bar), from where the classic seven-hour day-loop takes in the Vallée des Aygues Cluses plus the lakes and peak of Madamète, followed by a descent via Lac Nère and Lac Dets Coubous back to Gaubie.

---

**11**

recycled masonry from the Roman **Lugdunum Convenarum**, whose remains are visible at the crossroads just beyond the village.

### The Grottes de Gargas

About 6km from St-Bertrand in the direction of St-Laurent (guided tours daily every 30min: July & Aug 10am–6pm; rest of year 10.30am–5.30pm Tues–Sun, but reservations usually necessary; €7; ☏ 05 62 98 81 50 ⑩ grottesdegargas.free.fr) are the **Grottes de Gargas**, renowned for their 231 prehistoric painted hand-prints outlined in black, red, yellow or white. The prints seem to be deformed – perhaps the result of leprosy, frostbite or ritual mutilation, though no one really knows why.

**INFORMATION**                                     ST-BERTRAND-DE-COMMINGES

**Tourist office** In the nineteenth-century Olivétain chapel and monastery on the cathedral square (Mon–Sat 9am–noon & 1.30–6pm; ☏ 05 61 95 44 44). The office doubles as a festival box office.

**ACCOMMODATION AND EATING**

**Chez Simone** Rue du Musée ☏ 05 61 94 91 05. Specializing in wood-pigeon stew, this friendly family-run restaurant serves hearty regional food with little concession for vegetarians. There's a lovely terrace outside and the beam-ceilinged interior has nice views and a fireplace. Three-course *menus* begin at €17. Daily noon–2pm plus mid-July–mid-Sept 7–9pm; closed Jan and when there's snow.

**Du Comminges** Place du Bout du Pont ☏ 05 61 88 31 43, ⑩ hotelducomminges.fr. This beautiful old building, part obscured by climbing plants, looks onto the cathedral. First impressions are good: there's a charming original oak front door and inside the exposed beams and heavy wood furniture add to the hotel's vintage atmosphere. The cheapest rooms have a shower but no toilet. The buffet breakfast costs €8. April–Sept. **€45**

# The Eastern Pyrenees

The dominant climatic influence of the **Eastern Pyrenees**, excluding the misty Couserans region, is the Mediterranean; the climate is warmer, the days sunnier, the landscape more arid than elsewhere in the Pyrenees. Dry-weather plants like cistus, broom and thyme make their appearance, and the foothills are planted with vines. The proximity of Spain is evident, with much of the territory definitively incorporated into France in 1659 previously belonging to historical Catalonia. Like the rest of the Pyrenees, the countryside is spectacular, and densely networked with hiking trails. Historical sights, except the painted caves of the **Ariège** and the Cathar castles and medieval towns of the **upper Aude**, are concentrated towards the coast in French Catalonia and along the Tech and Tet valleys.

# Val d'Ariège

Whether you're coming from the western Pyrenees or heading south from the major transport hub of Toulouse, the **Val d'Ariège** marks the start of the transition to the Mediterranean zone. The river, extending from high peaks along the Andorran border around the spa of Ax-les-Thermes down to agricultural plains north of **Foix**, forms the main axis of the eponymous *département*. In between lie a wealth of **caves**, most notably near Tarascon and Mas d'Azil. Transport is no problem as long as you stick to the valley.

## Foix

France's smallest *départemental* capital, **FOIX,** lies 82km south of Toulouse on the Toulouse–Barcelona train line. It's an agreeable country town of narrow alleys and sixteenth- to seventeenth-century half-timbered houses, with an old quarter squeezed between the rivers Ariège and Arget.

Built one millennia ago on top of an existing seventh-century fortification, Foix's **chateau** (July–Aug 10am–6.30pm; early May Mon–Fri 10.30am–noon & 2–5.30pm, Sat & Sun 10am–6pm; mid-May to June & early Sept 10am–6pm; Feb–April & Oct–Dec & Jan weekends 10.30am–noon & 2–5.30pm; €4.60; ☎05 34 09 83 83) with its three distinctive hilltop towers, has seen its fair share of controversy: Its counts sided against the Albigensians during their eleventh-century Cathar genocide and after the revolution it became a home to political prisoners. Today it houses the small Musée d'Ariège.

**11**

### ARRIVAL AND INFORMATION                                          FOIX

**By train** The *gares SNCF* and *routière* are together on avenue de la Gare, off the N20 on the right (east) bank of the Ariège. **Destinations** Ax-les-Thermes (12 daily, 45min); Latour-de-Carol (7 daily; 1hr 45min); Tarascon-sur-Ariège (11 daily; 15min); Toulouse (16 daily, 1hr 10min).

**Tourist office** Rue Théophile-Delcasse (Mon–Sat 9am–noon & 2–6pm; ☎05 61 65 12 12, ⓦ tourisme

-foix-varilhes.fr).
**Boat trips** 6km north of Foix on the D1, boat trips set off for a 1.5km trip along Europe's longest underground river, the Rivière Souterraine de Labouiche. The trips (April–June & Sept 10–11.15am & 2–5.15pm; July–Aug 9.30am–5.15pm; Oct to mid-Nov 2–4pm closed Mon; €9 ☎05 61 65 04 11) take in the usual stalagtites and stalacmites and a beautiful waterfall.

### ACCOMMODATION

**Auberge Léo Lagrange** 16 rue Nöel Peyrevidal ☎05 61 6509 04, ⓦ leolagrange-foix.com. More an activity centre (rafting and the like) than a hostel but ideal if you're on a budget. The rooms are basic and pokey but come with bathrooms attached and free parking outside. Economical weekday lunches (noon–2pm) are available downstairs

with traditional main courses costing €8. **€36**
**Lons** 6 place Duthil ☎05 34 09 28 00, ⓦ www.hotel-lons-foix.com. This hotel is the quietest and most comfortable option in town, with a respected restaurant attached (*menus* from €11.90). Restaurant open daily noon–2pm & 7.30–9pm. Closed late Dec to early Jan. **€62**

### EATING

A prime area for eating is rue de la Faurie and the lanes leading off it, the old blacksmiths' bazaar at the heart of the old town.

★ **Le Jeu de l'Oie** 17 rue de la Faurie ☎05 61 02 69 39. Does classic French country-bistro cuisine – cassoulet, duck dishes, terrines, offal, good desserts, Leffe draught beer – at low prices (two-course *menus* with a

glass of wine €9.80) which guarantees a lunch-time crush. Vegetarians can partake of the menu too with *tarte tatin* of vegetables followed by pesto tagliatelle. Tues–Sat noon–2.30pm & 7–10.30pm.

## Niaux

Some 21km south of Foix, the rather ordinary village of **Niaux** has found itself at the centre of the French Magdalenian era (approx 15,000 BC–7000 BC). Its surrounding hills of scrub-topped limestone conceal great cave systems (see box, p.615); rock carved by water over millennia, home to prehistoric hominids and the archeological treasures they left behind.

**ACCOMMODATION AND EATING**      NIAUX

**Le Petite Auberge de Niaux** Niaux, turn right as you enter the village from the north ☎ 05 61 05 79 79, aubergedeniaux.com. Although predominantly a fine restaurant, the owners offer a two bedroomed *gîte* with lounge, kitchenette and balconies overlooking the river. There's usually a 2-night minimum stay. The restaurant is nicely tucked away in an old stone building with al fresco

dining an option in the garden. A wide variety of *menus* are available with alluring names such as "Temptation", "Montagne" and "Terre d'Ariège" and a vegetarian *menu* even makes a rare appearance. All high-end, regional cooking in idyllic surroundings. *Menus* range from €21–45. Restaurant open noon–2pm & 7–9pm. Closed mid-Nov to mid-Feb. **€75**

## The Pays de Sault

The **Pays de Sault** – a magnificent upland bounded by the rivers Ariège and Aude, and the D117 road from Foix to Quillan – marks the start of "Cathar country" (see p.618). The region's main town, **Lavelanet**, is a nondescript place on the banks of the River Touyre, 28km from Foix and 35km from Quillan, that offers little beyond bus connections – including north to **Mirepoix** covered on p.615, though (it's not strictly in the *pays*).

### Roquefixade

**ROQUEFIXADE** sits roughly 19km east of Foix en route to Lavelanet; the ruined eleventh-century castle (free, unenclosed) towering above the village sets the scene for further Cathar exploration of the region.

**ACCOMMODATION**      ROQUEFIXADE

**Gîte d'étape** Just northeast of the village and well signposted ☎ 05 61 03 01 36, ⊛ www.gite-etape -roquefixade.com. Dorm beds and family rooms in a beautiful old house in idyllic countryside. Ideally located for

gentle hikes, although the *gîte* is also frequented by trekkers completing the final leg of the "Sentier Cathare", a 12-day route from the Mediterranean coast. The *gîte* does breakfasts for €5 and meals or packed lunches for €8. All year. **€25pp**

### Montségur

The tiny village of **MONTSÉGUR**, a small distance south of Lavelanet, straggles in long terraces at the foot of its castle-rock, a modified version of a *bastide* (the original settlement was up by the castle). The castle itself (daily: Feb, Nov & Dec 11am–4pm; March & Oct 10am–5pm; April–June & Sept 10am–6pm; July–Aug 9am–7pm; Dec 10am–4pm, closed Jan; €4.50; ⊛ montsegur.org) is not strictly Cathar but actually a remnant of a fortification built on Cathar ruins to protect France from southern raiders. A garrison remained there until the Treaty of the Pyrenees in the seventeenth century. All that remain today are the stout, now truncated curtain walls and keep. The space within is terribly cramped, and you can easily imagine the sufferings of the six hundred or so persecuted Cathars.

**INFORMATION**      MONTSÉGUR

**Tourist office** In the village *place* (July–Sept 10am–1pm & 2–6pm; ☎ 05 61 03 03 03, ⊛ montsegur.fr).

**ACCOMMODATION AND EATING**

★ **Auberge de Montségur** Rue du Village ☎ 05 61 01 10 24, ⊛ aubergemontsegur.com. Characterful hotel hosting generously proportioned rooms and rustically beamed dining room with log fires, hanging candelabras and faux-medieval artwork. The restaurant menu features the stodgy Languedocian comfort food as well as vegetarian dishes and classic regional/national favourites like *coq au vin*. *Menus* from €14.90–29.50. Restaurant open

noon–2pm & 7–10pm, closed Mon except July & Aug. Breakfast €8.50. **€45**

**Tindleys** 8km east of Montsegur in Fougax-et-Barrineuf ☎ 05 61 01 34 87, ⊛ tindleys.com. If Montségur is full, consider this English/Canadian-run *chambre d'hôte* opposite the post office which has three lovely en-suite rooms, and offers a copious breakfast and dinner on request for €22. **€65**

**PREHISTORIC PYRENEES**

The following are a selection of the best prehistoric sights in the Pyrenees:

**Grotte de Niaux** 22km south of Foix (45min guided visits: Jan weekends, Feb & March 3 daily 11am–4.15pm, closed Mon; April–June, 5 daily 11am–4.15pm (1.30pm in English); July & Aug 10 daily between 9.45am–5.30pm (9.45am & 12.15pm in English); Sept–June 7 daily 10.15am–4.30pm (10.15am & 1pm in English); Oct 5 daily between 11am–4.15pm (1.30pm in English); Nov & Dec 3 daily 11am–4.15pm, closed Mon & Tues; €9; advance reservations mandatory ☎ 05 61 05 10 10). A huge cave complex under an enormous rock overhang 2km north of the hamlet of Niaux. There are 4km of galleries in all, with paintings of the Magdalenian period scattered throughout, although tours see just a fraction of the complex. No colour is used to render the subjects – horses, ibex, stags and bison – just a dark outline and shading to give body to the drawings, executed with a "crayon" made of bison fat and manganese oxide.

**Grotte de la Vache** Alliat, 2km across the valley west from Niaux (90min guided tours: April–June, Sept & school holidays 2.30pm & 4pm; July & Aug daily 10am–5.30pm; otherwise by arrangement; €9; ☎ 05 61 05 95 06, ⓦ grotte-de-la-vache.org). A relatively rare example of an inhabited cave where you can observe hearths, embossed bones, tools and other remnants in situ that date back 14,000 years.

**Grotte de Bédeilhac** Above Bédeilhac village; take the D618 from Tarascon towards Saurat; after 5km, the cave entrance yawns in the Soudour ridge (75min guided tours: April–June, Sept & school holidays 2.30pm & 4pm plus Sun at 3pm, July & Aug daily 10am–5.30pm; €9; ⓦ grotte-de-bedeilhac.org). Inside are examples of every known technique of Paleolithic art; while not as immediately powerful as at Niaux, its diversity – including modelled stalagmites and mud reliefs of beasts – compensates.

**Parc de la Prehistoire** 2km west of Tarascon on the D23 (April–June & Sept–Oct 10am–6pm & weekends 10am–7pm, closed Mon in May, Sept & Oct; July & Aug 10am–8pm, last entry 5.30pm; €9.90; ☎ 05 61 05 10 10). This museum presents a circuit of discovery that shows the life and art of people from the Magdalenian period who lived in this area 14,000 years ago. Outdoor exhibits here feature engaging workshop demonstrations on archeology, prehistoric hunting, fire-making and art techniques; as well as a recreated encampment.

## The Gorges de la Frau to Comus

From either Montségur or Fougax-et-Barrineuf, you can take an impressive half-day walk through the **Gorges de la Frau**, emerging at Comus hamlet in the heart of the Pays de Sault. The route from Montségur initially follows the "Sentier Cathare" until linking up with the **GR107** in the valley of the Hers river, which has carved out the gorge. Starting from Fougax, just follow the minor D5 south along the Hers until, beyond Pelail, tarmac dwindles to a rough, steep track as you enter the gorges proper, where thousand-metre-high cliffs admit sunlight only at midday. The defile ends some 3.5km before Comus, where the track broadens and the grade slackens.

### ACCOMMODATION

**Gîte le Barry** Comus village ☎ 04 68 20 33 69, ⓦ gites-comus.com. Comus village has two good *gîte d'étapes*, *Barry du Haut* in the old rectory and *Barry d'en Bas* in the old town hall. You can also camp outside. All meals are provided: Breakfast €7, hot meal €18 and picnic €10. Here you're just 2.5km shy of the D613 road between Ax-les-Thermes and Quillan, with two daily buses (not weekends) to the latter. Camping €7, dorms €20

## Mirepoix

If you're heading north from Lavelanet towards Carcassonne, it's definitely worth stopping in at **MIREPOIX**, a late thirteenth-century *bastide* built around one of the finest surviving arcaded market squares – **Les Couverts** – in the country. The square is bordered by houses dating from the thirteenth to the fifteenth centuries, and a harmonizing modern *halle* on one side, but its highlight is the medieval **Maison des Consuls** (council house), whose rafter-ends are carved with dozens of unique portrayals of animals, and monsters, and caricatures of medieval social groups and professions, as well as ethnic groups from across the world. Just south of Les Couverts is the early Gothic cathedral of **St-Maurice** which is claimed to have the largest undivided nave in France, supported only by airy rib vaulting.

## THE FALL OF MONTSÉGUR

Between 1204 and 1232, Montségur's castle was reconstructed by Guilhabert de Castres as a strongpoint for the **Cathars** (see p.618). By 1232 it – and the village at the base of the *pog* or rock pinnacle – had become the effective seat of the beleaguered Cathar Church, under the protection of a garrison commanded by Pierre-Roger de Mirepoix, with a population of some five hundred, clergy as well as ordinary believers fleeing Inquisition persecution.

Provoked by de Mirepoix's raid on Avignonet in May 1242, in which the eleven chief Inquisitors were hacked to pieces, the forces of the Catholic Church and the king of France laid siege to the castle in May 1243. By March 1244, Pierre-Roger, despairing of relief, agreed to terms. At the end of a fortnight's truce, the 225 Cathar civilians who still refused to recant their beliefs were burnt on a communal pyre on March 16.

Four men who had escaped Montségur unseen on the night of March 15 recovered the Cathar "treasure", hidden in a cave for safekeeping since late 1243, and vanished. Two of them later reappeared in Lombardy, where these funds were used to support the refugee Cathar community there for another 150 years. More recent New Agey-type speculations, especially in German writings, identify this "treasure" as the Holy Grail, and the Cathars themselves as the Knights of the Round Table.

### ARRIVAL AND INFORMATION

**By bus** Buses stop on Cours Colonel Petit Pied, one block north of the central *place*.
**Destinations** Lavelanet (1–7 daily; 25min); Toulouse (1–3 daily; 1hr 50min).

**MIREPOIX**

**Tourist office** Place Maréchal Leclerc, the main square (Mon–Sat 9.15am–12.15pm & 2–6pm; ☎ 05 61 68 83 76, ⓦ tourisme-mirepoix.com).

### ACCOMMODATION AND EATING

**Camping Les Nysades** 2km east on the Limoux road (D626) ☎ 05 61 60 28 63, ⓦ camping-mirepoix-ariege .com. A small campsite that welcomes tents and caravans but with few facilities. Easter–Sept. **€15**

**Chambre d'hôte La Ferme de Boyer** 3km west of Mirepoix on the D119, the turning is on the left just past Besset village ☎ 05 61 68 93 41, ⓦ fermeboyer .iowners.net. In a lovely eighteenth-century farmstead set back from the main road, this B&B offers a relaxing environment with its large garden and pool. Families can opt for the self-contained two-bedroomed cottage and either use the good kitchen facilities or let the hosts provide dinner for around €30. Doubles **€80**, cottage **€150**

**Maison des Consuls** 6 place du Maréchal Leclerc ☎ 05 61 68 81 81, ⓦ maisondesconsuls.com. Extravagantly furnished hotel tucked into the medieval square with a small patio out back to relax away from the masses. The more expensive rooms have private terraces overlooking the *place*. Breakfast €12. **€99**

★ **Les Remparts** 6 cours Louis Pons Tande ☎ 05 61 68 12 15, ⓦ hotelremparts.com. The best value accommodation in town, if you're looking for a mid-range hotel. The building may be old but the bedroom decor is sympathetically modern and comfortable. The hotel's restaurant targets gourmands with its typically small but pretty portions on big plates. That said, the ingredients are very fresh, seasonal and mostly local; even the vegetarian options are more than an afterthought – try the smoked ravioli. *Menus* €17–49. Restaurant open 12.30–1.30pm & 7.15–9.30pm, closed Mon. **€70**

## Camon

Near enough to Mirepoix, 13km to the southeast, to make a pleasant day excursion, this walled medieval village is home to a twelfth to fourteenth-century **fortified Benedictine abbey** at the summit (now a *chambres d'hôte*).

### ACCOMMODATION AND EATING

★ **L'Abbaye-Château de Camon** ☎ 05 61 60 31 23, ⓦ chateaudecamon.com. A truly special retreat for those with deep pockets. There's a large pool, a part of the original cloister, eighteenth-century canvases in the lounge, a frescoed chapel, plus all the echoing galleries and spiral staircases you could want; the gourmet restaurant does dinner for all comers (€42 *table d'hôte*; closed Wed). Closed early Nov to mid-March. **€135**

# Vallée de l'Aude

South of Carcassonne, the D118 and the (mostly disused) rail line both forge steadily up the twisting **Vallée de l'Aude** between scrubby hills and vineyards, past **L'Abbaye de St-Hilaire** and its carved sarcophagus, river-straddling **Limoux** and sleepy **Alet-les-Bains**, before reaching **Quillan** where the topography changes. The route squeezes through awesome gorges either side of **Axat** before emerging near the river's headwaters on the Capcir plateau, east of the Carlit massif. It's a magnificent drive or slightly hair-raising cycle-ride up to isolated **Quérigut**, then easier going on to **Formiguères**.

## GETTING AROUND                                   VALLÉE DE L'AUDE

Transport is heavily subsidized in Languedoc and regional train and bus journeys cost just €1.

**By train** A train line runs south from Carcassonne. **Destinations** Alet-Les-Bains (2 Mon–Sat; 45min); Limoux (6 Mon–Sat; 30min); Quillan (2 Mon–Sat; 1hr 10min).

**By bus** The bus follows the same route as the train line from Carcassonne, covering the timetable gaps and part routes.

**Destinations** Alet-Les-Bains (3 daily; 40min); Limoux (3 daily; 30min); Quillan (3 daily; 1hr 10min).

**11**

## Limoux and around

Some 24km south of Carcassonne, **LIMOUX** life revolves around pretty **place de la République** in the heart of the old town, with its Friday market, brasseries and cafés, and the nineteenth-century **promenade du Tivoli**, in effect a bypass road on the west. Previously known for its wool and leather-tanning trades, Limoux's recent claim to fame is the excellent regional sparkling wine, Blanquette de Limoux, a cheaper alternative to champagne.

### Abbaye de St-Hilaire

16km south of Carcassonne • Daily: Nov–March 10am–noon & 2–5pm; April–June & Sept–Oct, same hours, closes 6pm; July & Aug 10am–7pm • €4 • ⓦ abbayedesainthilaire.pagesperso-orange.fr

Blanquette de Limoux sparkling wine was supposedly invented in 1531 at the **Abbaye de St-Hilaire**, which dominates the centre of the eponymous village (11km northeast by minor road). The Gothic cloister (always open) doubles as the village square, but the main attraction is the so-called **sarcophagus** in the south chapel of the thirteenth-century cathedral. This is one of the masterpieces of the mysterious **Maître de Cabestany**, an itinerant sculptor whose work – found across the eastern Pyrenees on both sides of the border – is distinguished by the elongated fingers, pleated clothing and cat-like, almond-eyed faces of the human figures. Here, the arrest of evangelizing **St Sernin** (Saturnin), patron of Toulouse, his martyrdom through dragging by a bull and burial by female disciples is portrayed on three intricately carved side panels of what's actually a twelfth-century marble reliquary too small to contain a corpse.

## ARRIVAL AND INFORMATION                           LIMOUX

**By train and bus** The train and bus stations are to the east of the town on Avenue de la Gare. Buses stop at Promenade du Tivoli.

**By car** Free parking is on the riverbanks by the picturesque old bridge.

**Tourist office** Avenue du Pont de France, inconveniently positioned north of the centre (Mon–Fri 9am–noon & 2–6pm, Sat–Sun 10am–noon & 2–5pm; ☏ 04 68 31 11 82, ⓦ www.limoux.fr).

## ACCOMMODATION AND EATING

Hotel accommodation is not in plentiful supply in Limoux and what there is does not inspire. Best go for a nearby B&B.

**Chambre d'hôte le Hothouse** 25 chemin Tour de la Badoque ☏ 04 68 31 66 83, ⓦ chambredhote -lehothouselimoux.blogspot.co.uk. A charming little

B&B just outside town with characterful rooms, hammocks next to the pool, and in lush surroundings. **€65**

**La Goutine** 10 rue de la Goutine ☏ 04 68 74 34 07.

A healthy option, this organic and vegetarian restaurant prides itself in its use of fresh and seasonal ingredients. The menus are inventive and ever-changing. Three courses for a very reasonable €14.80. Tues–Sat noon–2.30pm, plus Fri & Sat 7.30–10.30pm.

## Alet-les-Bains

South of Limoux, an essential halt is the small thermal resort of **ALET-LES-BAINS**; the spa on the outskirts is incidental to the unspoilt half-timbered houses and arcaded *place* inside the fortifications. The **Abbaye Ste-Marie d'Alet** (daily: 10am–12.30pm & 2.30–6pm; €3.50; ☎04 68 69 93 56, ⊛info.aletlesbains.free.fr) on av Nicolas Pavillon – attached to the tourist office (which has the keys) – is a sandstone Romanesque abbey that was sacked by the Huguenots in the sixteenth century. Today there remains only the church and chapterhouse overlooking the remains of a gallery of the cloisters and the northern gateway of the monastery.

### ACCOMMODATION AND EATING
ALET-LES-BAINS

**11**

★ **Hostellerie de l'Évêché** 2 rue Nicolas Pavillon, by the abbey ☎04 68 69 90 25, ⊛hotel-eveche.com. Occupying the old bishop's palace, this beautiful hotel and restaurant astride the river within its own parkland is a wonderful stopover. Dinner is served either in the atmospheric stonewalled annex or outside under the huge copper beech trees. Three-course *menus* start at €18 or you can sample a good cassoulet for €17. Children can play outside in the secure gardens in between courses. Vegetarian dishes on the menu. Service noon–2pm & 7.30–9pm. April–Oct. **€67**

## Quillan

Quillan, 28km upstream from Limoux is a useful staging post en route south into the mountains or east to the Cathar castles (see below). The only monument is the ruined castle, burnt by the Huguenots in 1575 and partly dismantled in the eighteenth century.

### ARRIVAL AND INFORMATION
QUILLAN

**By bus and train** The *gare SNCF* and *gare routière* sit together on the main bypass road.

**Tourist office** Square A. Tricoire, opposite the train station (Mon–Sat 9.30am–noon & 2.30–6pm; ☎04 68 20 07 78).

### ACCOMMODATION

**Camping Sapinette** 21 rue René-Delpech ☎04 68 20 13 52, ⊛camping-quillan.fr. A nice municipal site surrounded by pine trees on a hill, with moderately good leisure facilities including a pool and playground. April–Oct. **€7.95**
**Chambre d'hôte Nidelice** 28 bd jean Bourrel ☎09 63 40 15 10, ⊛nidelice.com. In a rather peaceful boulevard, this newly renovated B&B has rustic rooms with stripped pine floors. **€59**

**Hotel-Restaurant Cartier** 31 bd Charles de Gaulle ☎04 68 20 05 14, ⊛hotelcartier.com. Notable for its Art Deco facade, this hotel may not be a beacon of modernity, but it has comfortable and spacious rooms (including family suites) and a great restaurant. Rabbit is on the menu either roasted with garlic jus or in a cassoulet, while vegetarians will find wild mushroom options. Three-course *menus* start at €20. Late March to mid-Dec. **€65**

## The Cathar castles

Romantic and ruined, the medieval fortresses that pepper the hills between Quillan and Perpignan have become known as the **Cathar castles**, though many were built either before or after the Cathar era. Roussillon, Languedoc and the eastern Ariège were the twelfth-century sect's power base. Their name derives from the Greek word for "pure" – *katharon* – as they abhorred the materialism and worldly power of the established Church, and they were initially pacifist, denying the validity of feudal vows or allegiances. While the Cathars probably never accounted for more than ten percent of the population, they included many members of the nobility and mercantile classes, which alarmed the ruling powers.

Once disputational persuasion by the ecclesiastical hierarchy proved fruitless, Pope Innocent III anathemized the Cathars as heretics in 1208 and persuaded the French king to mount the first of many "Albigensian" crusades, named after Albi, a Cathar stronghold. Predatory northern nobles, led for a decade by the notoriously cruel Simon de Montfort, descended on the area with their forces, besieging and sacking towns, massacring Cathar and Catholic civilians alike, laying waste or seizing the lands of local counts. The effect of this brutality was to unite both the Cathars and their Catholic neighbours in southern solidarity against the barbarous north. Though military defeat became inevitable with the capitulation of Toulouse in 1229 and the fall of Montségur in 1244, it took the informers and torturers of the Holy Inquisition another 180 years to root out Catharism completely.

### Puilaurens

10km east of Axat • Daily: Feb, March weekends & April, Oct to mid-Nov 10am–5pm; May 10am–6pm; June & Sept 10am–7pm, July & Aug 9am–8pm • €4 • ☎ 04 68 20 65 26

The westernmost Cathar castle, **Puilaurens**, perches atop a hill at 700m, its fine crenelated walls sprouting organically from the rock outcrops. It sheltered many Cathars up to 1256, when Chabert de Barbera, the region's *de facto* ruler, was captured and forced to hand over this citadelle and Quéribus further east to secure his release. The castle remained strategically important – being close to the Spanish border – until 1659, when France annexed Roussillon and the frontier was pushed south. Highlights of a visit are the **west donjon** and **southeast postern gate**, where you're allowed briefly on the curtain wall for views, and the **Tour de la Dame Blanche**, with its rib-vaulted ceiling.

**11**

### Quéribus

Overlooks village of Cucugnan, halfway between Quillan and the sea • Daily: 10am–5pm; April & Oct 9.30am–6.30pm; May, June & Sept 9.30am; July–Aug 9am–8pm; closed Feb • €5.50 • ☎ 04 68 45 03 69

The history of **Quéribus** is similar to that of Puilaurens, and it too held holding out until 1255 or 1256; not reduced by siege, its role as a Cathar sanctuary ended with the capture of the luckless Chabert, though the garrison escaped to Spain. Spectacularly situated above the Grau de Maury pass 6km north of the Quillan–Perpignan road, the castle balances on a storm-battered rock pinnacle above sheer cliffs – access is forbidden in bad weather. Because of the cramped topography, the space within the walls is stepped in terraces, linked by a single stairway and dominated by the polygonal keep. The high point, in all senses, is the so-called **Salle du Pilier**, whose vaulted ceiling is supported by a graceful pillar sprouting a canopy of intersecting ribs. A spiral staircase leads to the roof terrace and fantastic views (best outside summer) in every direction, including Canigou, the Mediterranean and northwest to the next Cathar castle, Peyrepertuse.

### Peyrepertuse

Just west of Quéribus • Daily: Feb 10am–5pm; March & Oct 10am–6pm; April 9.30am–7pm; May, June & Sept 9am–7pm; July & Aug 9am–8pm • €8.50 (July & Aug) otherwise €6 • ☎ 04 82 53 24 07

If you only have time for one of the Cathar castles, make it the **Château de Peyrepertuse**, not only for the unbeatable site and stunning views, but also because it's unusually well preserved. The castle was obtained by treaty with the Kingdom of Aragón in 1258, and most of the existing fortifications were built afterwards, staying in use until 1789. The 3.5-km access road starts in Duilhac village or, alternatively, you can walk up from Rouffiac des Corbières village to the north via the GR36 – a tough, hot climb of over an hour. Either way the effort is rewarded, for Peyrepertuse is among the most awe-inspiring castles anywhere, draped the length of a jagged rock-spine with sheer drops at most points. Access is banned during fierce summer thunderstorms, when (as at Quéribus) the ridge makes an ideal lightning target.

Tickets are sold by the southerly car park, but you then walk fifteen minutes through thickets of box to the entrance on the north side. The bulkiest fortifications enclose the lower, eastern end of the ridge, with a **keep** and **barbican** controlling the main gate. Things get increasingly airy as you progress west along the ridge past and through various cisterns, chapels and bastions, culminating in a **stairway** of over a hundred steps carved into the living rock, which leads to a keep, tower and the **chapel of San Jordi** at the summit.

## Aguilar

Just east of Tuchan • Daily: April to mid-June 10am–6pm; mid-June to mid-Sept 9am–7pm; mid-Sept to Oct 11am–5pm; closed Nov–April • €3.50 • ☎ 04 68 45 51 00

Overlooking the Côtes de Roussillon-Villages wine *domaine* is the isolated, thirteenth-century **Château d'Aguilar**; perched at the end of a steep, one-lane drive, its hexagonal curtain wall shelters a keep, with the chatelain's lodge on the top floor.

### VISITING THE CASTLES

**By train** The Train du Pays Cathare et du Fenouillèdes (☎ 04 68 20 04 00, ☜ tpcf.fr) runs from Rivesaltes or Espira de Agly, just north of Perpignan, to Axat, stopping at the main towns along the Cathar way. The service (sometimes only St-Paul-de-Fenouillet to Axat) runs Sun & Wed, April–June & Sept–Oct; daily except Sat, July & Aug; and except Fri in Sept (adult fare €11–18 depending on direction and distance).

**Passeport des Sites du Pays Cathare** If you're planning on visiting several of the Cathar-related and other medieval sites in the Aude, consider purchasing the Le Passeport des Sites du Pays Cathare, available for €2 at any of the nineteen participating monuments in the *département*. The card (valid per calendar year) gives €1 off adult admission, and free child tickets, for the ramparts of Carcassonne, Lastours, Saissac, Caunes-Minervois, St-Hilaire, Lagrasse, Fontfroide, Puilaurens, Usson, Peyrepertuse, Quéribus, Aguilar and other sites. For more information see ☜ payscathare.org.

## Cucugnan

**Cucugnan**, fifty kilometres east of Quillan, half way to the coast, is a popular base for visiting Quéribus (and Peyrepertuse) and there's ample accommodation in *chambres d'hôtes* and hotels.

### ACCOMMODATION

CUCUGNAN

**Auberge de Cucugnan** 2 place de la Fontaine ☎ 04 68 45 40 84, ☜ auberge-de-cucugnan.com. The smallish, modern rooms (with en-suite) contrast with the building's stone facade and charming restaurant. The food is on the whole of a high standard but not particularly original. *Menus* from €18; closed Thurs. **€53**

★ **Auberge du Vigneron** 2 rue Achille-Mir ☎ 04 68 45 03 00, ☜ auberge-vigneron.com. Comfortable, timeless hotel above an excellent restaurant with a terrace overlooking the hills. The half-board option is excellent value; many of the restaurant ingredients come from the hotel's own garden. Restaurant closed Mon. Hotel closed mid-Nov to mid-Feb. **€67**; half-board **€85**

# Roussillon

The area comprising the eastern fringe of the Pyrenees and the lowlands down to the Mediterranean is known as **Roussillon**, or **French Catalonia**. Catalan power first emerged in the tenth century under the independent counts of Barcelona, who then became kings of Aragón as well in 1163. The Catalan zenith was reached during the thirteenth and fourteenth centuries, when the Franco–Catalan frontier traced the Corbières hills north of Perpignan. But Jaume I of Aragón and Valencia made the mistake of dividing his kingdom between his two sons at his death in 1276, thus ensuring continuous see-saw battles and annexations that ended only with the Treaty of the Pyrenees, negotiated by Louis XIV and the Spanish king in 1659.

Although there's no real separatist impetus among French Catalans today, their sense of identity remains strong: the language is very much alive (not least in bilingual place-signage), and their red-and-yellow flag is ubiquitous. The **Pic du Canigou**, which completely dominates Roussillon despite its modest (2784m) elevation, shines as a powerful beacon of Catalan nationalism, attracting hordes of Catalans from across the border to celebrate St John's Eve (June 23–24). At the feet of the Canigou the little town of **Prades**, place of exile from Franco's Spain of cellist Pablo (Pau) Casals, served as a focus of Catalan resistance until 1975.

Most of the region's attractions are easily reached by public transport from Roussillon's

capital, **Perpignan**. The coast and foothills between it and the Spanish frontier are beautiful, especially at **Collioure**, though predictably crowded and in most places overdeveloped. You'll find the finest spots in the **Tech** and **Têt valleys** which slice southwest towards the high peaks, among them the Romanesque monasteries of **Serrabona**, **St-Michel-de-Cuixà** and **St-Martin-du-Canigou**, the world-class modern art museum at **Céret**, and **Mont Canigou** itself, lapped by foothill orchards of peaches and cherries.

## Perpignan and around

This far south, climate and geography alone would ensure a palpable Spanish influence. Moreover, a good part of **PERPIGNAN**'s population is of Spanish origin – refugees from the Civil War and their descendants. The southern influence is further augmented by a substantial contingent of North Africans, including both Arabs and white French settlers repatriated after Algerian independence in 1962. Given its relatively grubby appearance, few will want to stay here for more than a day or two; if you have your own transport, you may prefer to base yourself somewhere in the surrounding area.

### Casa Païral

Place de Verdun • 10.30am–6pm; closed Mon & bank holidays • €4 • ☎ 04 68 35 42 05

The best place to begin explorations of Perpignan is at **Le Castillet**, built as a gateway in the fourteenth century and now home to the **Casa Païral**, an interesting museum of Roussillon's Catalan rural culture and the anti-French rebellions of 1661–74, when the tower held captured Catalan insurgents.

### Place de la Loge

A short distance down rue Louis-Blanc lies **place de la Loge**, focus of the pedestrianized heart of the old town, with a voluptuous Venus statue by Aristide Maillol (see p.627) in the centre. Dominating the cafés and brasseries of the narrow square is Perpignan's most interesting building, the Gothic **Loge de Mer** (1397). Designed to hold the city's stock exchange and maritime court, it features gargoyles, lancet windows and lacy balustrades up top. Adjacent stand the sixteenth-century **Hôtel de Ville**, with its magnificent wrought-iron gates and another Maillol (*La Méditerranée*) in the courtyard, and the fifteenth-century **Palais de la Députation**, once the parliament of Roussillon.

### Cathédrale St-Jean-Baptiste

Place Gambetta • Mon–Sat 7.30am–6pm, Sun 7.30am–7.30pm; June–Sept closes 7pm • Free • **Campo Santo** Oct–April Tues–Sun 11am–5pm; closed May–Sept

From place de la Loge, rue St-Jean leads northeast to the fourteenth-century **Cathédrale St-Jean** on place Gambetta, its external walls built of alternating bands of river stones and brick. The dimly lit interior is most interesting for its elaborate Catalan altarpieces and for the fourteenth-century, Rhenish polychrome Crucifixion known as the *Dévôt Christ*; it's in the fifth side chapel along the north wall, and was probably brought from the Low Countries by a travelling merchant. Out of the side door, a few steps on the

---

### CATALAN CUISINE

Characterized by the wide variety of ingredients that grow throughout the different climates between the mountains and the sea, Catalonia's distinctive food depends on its use of contrasting (sweet, savoury & sour) flavours within the five fundamental **sauces** of Catalan cuisine. The most important of these is **sofregit**, a tomato-based sauce with caramelized onion that's used ubiquitously. The most popular traditional dishes include *ollada* (pork stew), *bullinada* (similar to paella but with potatoes instead of rice) and regional favourite, *Boles de Picolat* (meatballs). Catalans have a sweet tooth too and produce a variety of custardy desserts like *Pa d'ous* (flan) and *crema catalane* as well as the wonderful sweet wines of Banyuls and Rivesaltes.

left you'll find the entrance to the **Campo Santo**, a vast enclosure that's one of France's oldest cemeteries, occasionally used for summer concerts.

### The Maghrebian and Romany quarters

South of the cathedral, rue de la Révolution-Française and rue de l'Anguille lead into the teeming, dilapidated **Maghrebian and Romany quarters**, where women congregate on the secluded inner lanes but are seldom seen on the busier thoroughfares. Here you'll find North African shops and cafés, especially on rue Llucia, and a daily market on place Cassanyes. Uphill and north from this stands the elegant church of **St-Jacques** (daily 8am–5.30pm; free) which was built in two phases in the fourteenth and eighteenth centuries; it abuts **La Miranda gardens**, atop a section of the old city walls.

### Palais des Rois de Majorque

Rue Archers • Daily: June–Sept 10am–6pm; Oct–May 9am–5pm • €4 • ☎ 04 68 34 48 29

A twenty-minute walk southwest through place des Esplanades brings you to the main entrance of the **Palais des Rois de Majorque**, crowning the hill that dominates the southern part of the old town. Although Vauban's walls surround it now, and it's suffered generally from on-going military use until 1946, the two-storey palace and its

**11**

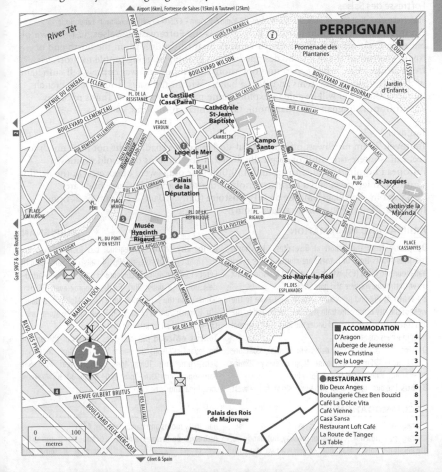

> **INTERSITE PASS**
>
> As with Aude's Passeport des Sites du Pays Cathare (see p.620), there's an **Intersite Pass**
> (Ⓦ reseauculturel.fr) scheme for Roussillon, with the same rules and discounts. The 44
> participating attractions include the abbeys of St-Martin-du-Canigou and St-Michel-de-Cuixà,
> the Palais des Rois de Majorque and the art museum in Céret.

partly arcaded courtyard date originally from the late thirteenth century. There are frequent worthwhile temporary exhibits in the former king's apartments.

### Musée Hyacinth Rigaud

16 rue de l'Ange near place Arago • Tues–Sun 10.30am–6pm • €4 • ☎ 04 68 35 43 40

The collection at the **Musée Hyacinth Rigaud** is largely devoted to Catalan painters, most notably Minorcan-born **Pierre Daura** (1896–1976), a Republican and godson of Pablo Casals long exiled in the US: his sympathies are evident in two symbolic canvases of the post-Civil-War Republican refugee camps at nearby Argelès. One room has a few Maillol sketches and statues, and three portraits by Picasso.

### Fortresse des Salses

Guided tours: April–Sept 10am–6.30pm; Oct–March 10am–12.15pm & 2–5pm • €7.50 • Ⓦ salses.monuments-nationaux.fr

An interesting stop 15km north of Perpignan is the **Forteresse de Salses**, in the town of Salses-le-Château. This late-fifteenth-century Spanish-built fort, on the north end of town, was one of the first to be designed with a ground-hugging profile to protect it from artillery fire. It housed around one thousand troops and was entirely self-sufficient with wells, irrigation systems and even a bakery within the walls. Tours are in French but afterwards you will be able to explore some parts on your own. Trains to Salses depart from Perpignan every half-hour, taking thirteen minutes.

### Tautavel

**Tautavel**, 25km northwest off the St-Paul-de-Fenouillet road, might not have much to see, but is interesting anthropologically. In 1971 the remains of the oldest known European hominid – dated to around 450,000 year old – were discovered in the nearby Caune d'Arago cave, and a reconstruction of the skull and other cave finds are displayed in the village's **Musée de la Préhistoire** (daily: 10am–12.30pm & 2–6pm; July–Aug 10am–7pm; €8; Ⓦ tautavel.com).

## ARRIVAL AND INFORMATION                                              PERPIGNAN

**By plane** From the airport at Rivesaltes, 6km north (no-frills flights from UK), there are shuttle buses every half-hour into town (€5), which call at bd St Assiscle to link up with the *gare routière* and *gare SNCF*.

**By train** At the end of avenue General-de-Gaulle to the west of the city centre; the train station is connected to the bus station by way of a tunnel under the tracks. All regional train journeys cost €1.

Destinations Barcelona (3 daily; 2hr 30min); Collioure (8–12 daily; 25min); Narbonne (approx every 30min; 30–45min); Villefranche (8 daily; 55min).

**By bus** The bus station is on bd Saint Assiscle, to the west

of the city centre. All regional bus journeys cost €1.

Destinations Banyuls-sur-Mer (4 daily not Sun; 45min); Céret (15 daily; 40min); Collioure (3 daily; 45min); Latour-de-Carol (2–3 daily; 2hr); Prades (approx every 30min; 55min); via the Tech valley to Prats-de-Molló (2–3 daily; 1hr 40min); Quillan (2 daily; 2hr); Tet valley to Mont-Louis (3–4 daily; 2hr 15min).

**Tourist office** In the Palais des Congrès at the end of boulevard Wilson (mid-June to mid-Sept Mon–Sat 9am–7pm, Sun 10am–4pm; rest of year Mon–Sat 9am–6pm, Sun 9am–1pm; ☎ 04 68 66 30 30, Ⓦ www .perpignantourisme.com).

## ACCOMMODATION

**D'Aragon** 17 av Gilbert Brutus ☎ 04 68 54 04 46, Ⓦ aragon-hotel.com. A bit out of the way, but handy for the Palais des Rois de Majorque, *Aragon* is a two-star with

non-fusty rooms and parking nearby. €59

**Auberge de Jeunesse** Av de la Grande-Bretagne ☎ 04 68 34 63 32, Ⓦ fuaj.org. Welcoming, if somewhat traffic-noisy hostel behind the Parc de la Pépinière by Pont Arago (entrance from avenue de Grande-Bretagne). Reception open 8–11am & 5–11pm. Closed mid-Nov to Feb. Breakfast included. **€18.50pp**

★ **New Christina** 51 cours Lassus ☎ 04 68 35 12 21, ⓦ hotel-newchristina.com. Sited a 5min stroll northeast of the old town centre and overlooking the attractive park of Square Bir Hakeim. The en-suite rooms within are comfortable if a little charmless, made up for by the irresistible-fifth floor plunge pool and sun terrace with views to the park. Disabled access. Closes Dec 20 for one month. **€99**

**De la Loge** 1 Fabriques d'en Nabot ☎ 04 68 34 41 02, ⓦ hoteldelaloge.fr. In the centre of town, this is a well-renovated medieval mansion with a central courtyard, on a quiet alley. Breakfast €10. **€55**

## EATING, DRINKING AND ENTERTAINMENT

For a place of Perpignan's size, restaurants are quite thin on the ground. There's also live street theatre, dance and music in the city centre during the Les Estivales in July. Perpignan hosts The Trobades festival celebrating the medieval heritage of the region (in late September), plus other events like the October-long Jazzèbre festival. But Perpignan's best-known spectacle is La Procession de la Sanch, the Good Friday procession of red-hooded penitents that goes from the church of St-Jacques to the cathedral between 3pm and 5pm. Nightlife is largely confined to wine/tapas bars in the narrow alleyways of the old centre while young clubbers journey to the modern coastal resort of Canet Plage at weekends.

**11**

**Bio Deux Anges** 39 rue des Augustins ☎ 04 68 08 78 32. Organic, vegetarian restaurant with nutritionally balanced *menus* from €12.50 based around whole grains such as quinoa and Camargue rice. Tues–Sat 9am–7pm.

★ **Boulangerie Chez Ben Bouzid** Place Cassanyes ☎ 04 68 67 09 58. Savour the scent of a true *boulanger* as you enter this gourmet tribute to France's colonial past. Serves a selection of French and North African breads plus irresistibly sticky pastries for little more than €1. Daily 8am–5pm.

**Café La Dolce Vita** Place de la Révolution Française ☎ 04 68 67 11 73. A delightful café on the edge of the North African quarter with shaded tables next to an old marble well. Daily noon till around 6pm; closes later at weekends according to demand.

**Café Vienne** 3 place Arago ☎ 04 68 34 80 00. Specializing in seafood, this large non-stop pavement restaurant churns out three courses for €17.50 rising to €24.50 in the evening. The €25 "Oyster Seller's Tray", with all manner of tasty crustaceans is the highlight. Fri–Sat noon–midnight; Sun–Thurs noon–11pm.

**Casa Sansa** 2 rue Fabriques-Couvertes ☎ 04 68 34 21 84. In a smart side street, this place, with bullfight posters and old photos on the wall, in traditional regional dishes such as *suquet-bouillabaise*, a Catalan take on the famous Marseillan fish broth. Evening *menus* for €22. Daily noon–2pm & 7–10.30pm.

★ **Restaurant Loft Café** 2 rue Fontfroide. Hosts live blues and novelty classical acts on Thursdays and Fridays. Also provides tapas starting from €3.60. Mon–Wed & Sun 8.45am–7.45pm; Thurs–Sat 8.45am–11.30pm.

**La Route de Tanger** 1 rue du Four St-Jean ☎ 04 68 51 07 57. Moreish North African tagines and couscous, and finished off with a pastry and traditional mint tea. Tasteful antique decor with old colonial posters framed on the wall. Three courses including tea €20. Tues–Sat noon–2pm & 7–9.30pm.

★ **La Table** 5 rue de la Poissonnerie ☎ 04 68 28 53 21, ⓦ latable-restaurant.com. Perpignan's gourmet choice delivers beautifully presented plates (and slates) in atmospheric surroundings. The three-course lunch *menu* costs €18 but it's worth paying the extra for the superb €25 "menu de la maison". A la carte options are eye-wateringly expensive. Mon 7–10pm, Tues & Wed noon–2pm & 7–10pm, Thurs noon–2pm & 7–10.30pm, Fri & Sat noon–2pm & 7–11.30pm.

## Castlenou

Twenty kilometres southwest of Perpignan, beyond the winemaking town of Thuir, Castlenou is one of the best-preserved villages in the Pyrenees. Surrounded by rolling hills of sun-baked scrub and oak, there's little sign of modernization for miles around, save for the road to the village. Through the pedestrianized fourteenth-century portal, the village rambles up towards the pentagon-shaped **Château Vicomtal** (Nov–March 11am–5pm; Sept, Oct, April & June 11am–6pm; July & Aug 10am–7pm; ☎ 04 68 53 22 91) – a worthwhile ascent for the views alone. First inhabited in 990 AD, the château served as the military and administrative capital to the Viscount of Vallespir until 1321. Despite its elevated position, it was besieged several times, notably by the Kings of Majorca and Aragon in 1285 and 1295. There's a car park at the base of the village or up the hill behind the castle.

★ **Chambre d'hôte/Crêperie la Figuera** 3 Carrer de la Fond D'Avall ☎ 04 68 53 18 42, ⓦ la-figuera.com. In a truly idyllic spot at the base of the village. The terrace cloaked with plants and flowers, and tables beneath rambling fig trees, softens the beautiful stone building in the background. The restaurant produces simple Catalan dishes and *galettes* from €8 or you can just stop by for a quick drink (Easter–Sept noon–2pm & 7–9pm; non-stop service at busier times). **€80**

# The Côte Vermeille

The **Côte Vermeille**, where the Pyrenees meet the sea, is the last patch of French shoreline before Spain, its seaside villages once so remote that the Fauvist painters of the early 1900s hid out here. Mass tourism may have ended any sense of exclusivity but outside of high season there is solitude and peace among the wide empty beaches; interspersed between modern resorts like **Port-Barcares** (north east of Perpignan), **Canet Plage** and **Argèles-sur-Mer**. The coastline remains sandy and straight almost until the border before being pushed east by the upsurging Pyrenean chain, where the prettier cove towns of **Collioure** and **Banyuls** are found.

## Collioure

Some thirty kilometres southeast of Perpignan, **COLLIOURE** is achingly picturesque. Palm trees line the curving main beach of **Port d'Avall**, while slopes of vines and olives rise to ridges crowned with ruined forts and watchtowers. Its setting and monuments inspired Henri Matisse and André Derain to embark in 1905 on their explosive Fauvist colour experiments.

Collioure is dominated by its twelfth-century **Château-Royal** (daily: 9am–5pm; July & Aug 10am–7pm; €4; ☎ 04 68 85 85 85), founded by the Templars and subject to later alterations by the kings of Mallorca and Aragón, and again after the Treaty of the Pyrenees gave Collioure to France. The mediocre permanent "collection" inside scarcely merits the entrance fee; attend instead a concert in the courtyard.

The second landmark in the town is the **Église Notre-Dame-des-Anges** (daily: 9am–noon & 2–6pm; free; ☎ 04 68 82 06 43), which features in every postcard and tourist brochure of the region. With its belfry dating back to the middle ages, this building served as a beacon for the port until the late seventeenth century when the rest of the church was adjoined. Behind it two small **beaches** are divided by a causeway leading to the **chapel of St-Vincent**, built on a former islet, while west from here a concrete path follows the rocky shore to the bay of **Le Racou**.

Just north of the château lies the **old harbour**, still home to a handful of brightly painted lateen-rigged fishing boats – now more likely used as pleasure craft – all that remains of Collioure's traditional fleet. Beyond this, the stone houses and sloping lanes of the old **Mouré** quarter are the main focus of interest.

**Tourist office** Place de 18-Juin (July & Aug Mon–Sat 9am–8pm & Sun 10am–6pm; April–June & Sept 9am–noon & 2–7pm; Oct–March 9am–noon & 2–6pm; closed Sun; ☎ 04 68 82 15 47, ⓦ collioure.com).

### ACCOMMODATION

★ **L'Arapede** Rte de Port-Vendres ☎ 04 68 98 09 59, ⓦ arapede.com. Drivers should note that Collioure can be a parking nightmare. This spacious, modern hotel fifteen minutes' walk away from the centre of the town has ample parking and a beautiful clifftop garden patio with pool. There's also a mini beach five minutes away. Half-board is available for an extra €32pp. Closed mid-Nov to mid-Feb. **€80**

**Caranques** Rte de Port-Vendres ☎ 04 68 82 06 68, ⓦ www.les-caranques.com. With the best view in town, this clifftop hotel looks down to the sea and Collioure. There's a private staircase down to an area suitable for swimming. The rooms are slightly basic for the level of the hotel but the balcony outlook compensates. Parking costs €10. Breakfast €10. Closed Nov–March. **€110**

**La Girelle** Plage d'Ouille ☎ 04 68 81 25 56, ⓦ campinglagirelle.unblog.fr. Enviably positioned next to a nice little sandy beach, this mostly tent-only site, ten minutes' walk from Collioure, offers a decent range of services including a snack-bar restaurant, grocery and fridge lockers. Three bed caravans can be rented by the week for €390 if you book well in advance. April–Sept. **€28**

**Hostellerie des Templiers** 12 av Camille-Pelletan ☏ 04 68 98 31 10, ☼ hotel-templiers.com. The most

central place to stay, this atmospheric hotel celebrates Collioure's art heritage (Picasso frequented the bar downstairs) with paintings screening the bar and corridor walls. The hotel itself rambles into an annex that backs on to an occasionally noisy nightclub. Closed for five weeks from first Sunday in January. **€70**

### EATING

**Le 5eme Péché** 18 rue Fraternité ☏ 04 68 98 09 76. Collioure's most innovative restaurant, providing colourful platters combining fruit and fish. Their desserts are no less adventurous; the caramelized artichokes with crème caramel works incredibly well. Two-course *menus* cost €18. 12.15–1.45pm & 7.30–9.30pm; closed Sun eve, Mon & Tues lunch.

**Le Parc aux Couleurs de Tahiti** 1 av de General-de Gaulle ☏ 04 68 82 22 08, ☼ auxcouleursdetahiti.free.fr. A solidly Catalan restaurant serving vibrant cuisine; mostly seafood. The appealingly quirky decor, with shell necklaces hanging from the rafters, remind the chef of his previous life cooking in the Caribbean. *Menus* from €17. Noon–2.30pm & 7–10.30pm; closed Tues.

## Banyuls-sur-Mer

South towards **BANYULS-SUR-MER**, 10km from Collioure, both the main highway and minor D914 wind through attractive vineyards, with the Albères hills rising steeply on the right. Make sure you sample the dark, full-bodied Banyuls dessert **wine**, an *appellation* that applies only to the vineyards of the Côte Vermeille. The town itself, facing a broad sweep of pebble beach, is pleasant but lacks the overt charm of Collioure.

On the seafront avenue du Fontaulé, the **Biodiversarium** (July–Aug 9.30am–12.30pm & 2–6pm; April–June & Sept Wed–Sun 2–6pm; closed winter; €5 ☏ 04 68 88 73 39, ☼ www.biodiversarium.fr) aquarium, run by Sorbonne university's marine biology department, has tanks containing a comprehensive collection of the region's submarine life; this is protected in a nearby *réserve marine*, France's best, which can be explored with local **scuba outfitters**.

Four kilometres southwest of town in the Vallée de Roume, signposted from the top of avenue de Gaulle, is the **Musée Maillol** (daily 10am–noon & 4–7pm; Oct–April closed Tues; May–Sept closed Mon; €3.50; ☏ 04 68 88 57 11 ☼ musee-maillol.com), which is devoted to the works of sculptor **Aristide Maillol** (1861–1944), who was born near Banyuls. He is buried under his statue *La Pensée* in Banyuls.

### INFORMATION

**Tourist office** Diagonally opposite the *mairie* on the seafront (Nov–March 9am–noon & 2–6pm; April–June & Sept–Oct 9am–noon & 2–7pm; July & Aug 9am–7pm; ☏ 04 68 88 31 58, ☼ banyuls-sur-mer.com).

### ACCOMMODATION

**Les Pieds dans l'Eau** Rue des Elmes ☏ 06 27 34 81 66, ☼ locations-vacances-banyuls.ch. A self-catering apartment complex ideal for couples and families. Right on the sandy beach and just far enough away from the main road, it's an extremely relaxing spot. In high season there is a minimum stay period of one week. **€500** per week

**Les Elmes** At the eponymous sandy cove 1.5km north

of town ☏ 04 58 88 03 12, ☼ hotel-des-elmes.com. Slap bang on the beachfront, this hotel has excellent facilities including a hot tub, sauna and terrace. The rooms are comfortable and well equipped but aim for the sea-view ones instead of the road outlook if you can afford extra. The hotel provides secure parking for €7 per day or you can park across the road for free. **€82**

### EATING

**Al Fanal** Av de Fontaule ☏ 04 68 55 35 24, ☼ alfanal .com. Classic French cuisine served al fresco on tables overlooking the marina. The service can be a little slow but it's well worth the wait. The three-course €19.50 *menu* includes a very fresh catch of the day and a mouthwatering raspberry pavlova. Daily

noon–2.30pm & 7.30–9.30pm; closed Tues & Wed Feb–June.

**Can Rastoll** 3 rue St-Pierre ☏ 04 68 88 18 00. Straightforward tapas bar, with dishes of tasty tapas for €15. Inside are original Maillol lithographs and photos of old Banyuls. Noon–2.30pm & 7–9.30pm; closed Tues.

11

## Vallée de Tech

The D115 winds its way through the beautiful Vallée de Tech starting at the border town, Le Boulou, then westwards through pretty little **Ceret**, capital of the Vallespir region. Further upstream, the road passes through dilapidated spa town, Amélie-les-Bains and scruffy Arles-sur-Tech, whose only attraction is the sumptuous **Abbaye de Ste-Marie**. Just past Arles, the narrow Gorges de la Fou is well worth an outing, before you continue west to the captivating medieval walled town of **Prats-de-Mollo**, which is guarded by a menacing Vauban fortification.

### GETTING AROUND                                         VALLÉE DE TECH

**By bus** Destinations to and from Perpignan along the Tech valley include Céret (15 daily; 40min); Amélie-les-Bain (10 daily; 55min) and Arles-sur-Tech (10 daily; 1hr) and Prats-de-Molló (2–3 daily; 1hr 40min).

### Céret

**11**

Céret is a delightful place, with a wonderfully shady old town overhung by huge plane trees; the central streets are narrow and winding, opening onto small squares like **Plaça de Nou Reigs** ("Nine Spouts" in Catalan), named after its central fountain; on avenue d'Espagne, two remnants of the medieval walls, the **Porte de France** and **Porte d'Espagne**, are visible. Céret is also known for its cherries from the surrounding orchards (June festival), plus July *corridas* (bullfights) and Pamplona-style running of bulls. Céret's main sight, however, is the remarkable **Musée d'Art Moderne** (July to mid Sept 10am–7pm; mid-Sept to June 10am–6pm; Oct–April closed Tues; €8; ☎04 68 87 27 76, ⊛musee-ceret.com) at 8 bd Maréchal Joffre. Between about 1910 and 1935, Céret's charms – coupled with the residence here of the Catalan artist and sculptor Manolo – drew a number of avant-garde artists to the town, including Matisse and Picasso, who personally dedicated a number of pictures to the museum. The holdings are too extensive to mount everything at once, but there are works on show by Chagall, Miró, Pignon, Picasso and Dufy, among others.

### INFORMATION                                                    CÉRET

**Tourist office** 1 av Clemenceau (June–Aug Mon–Sat 9am–1pm & 1.30–7pm, Sun 9am–1pm; Sept–May Mon–Sat 9am–12.30pm & 2–5pm; ☎04 68 87 00 53 ⊛ceret.fr).

### ACCOMMODATION AND EATING

**Restaurant La Fontaine** Plaça de Nou Reigs ☎04 68 87 23 47. Few could resist dining in this beautiful, traffic-free marbled square shaded by vast plane trees. If you have a family, this is the perfect place for a relaxing meal while the kids dip hands in and out of the marbled fountain. The *plat du jour* costs €9.90. Noon–2.30pm & 7–10pm; closed Tues.

★ **Vidal** 4 place Soutine ☎04 68 87 00 85, ⊛hotelceret. com. A tastefully converted eighteenth-century episcopal palace within the old town walls, *Vidal* is now a charming and unpretentious hotel that has a decent restaurant, *Del Bisbe*, attached. Its first-floor terraced restaurant, shaded by vines, serves tasty, if not ground-breaking, regional dishes including lamb roasted with pistachios. The three-course *menu* costs €28.50. Noon–2pm & 7.30–9.30pm; closed Tues & Wed. Hotel and restaurant closed Nov. **€50**

### Abbaye de Ste-Marie

July–Aug 9am–7pm; Sept–June Mon–Sat 9am–noon & 2–6pm; also Sun April–Oct 2–5pm • €4 • 04 68 83 90 66

The Romanesque **Abbaye de Ste-Marie**, in Arles-sur-Tech, 14km from Céret, has Carolingian origins, thought to account for the back-to-front alignment of altar at the west end and entrance at the east. Entry is via the pleasant thirteenth-century cloister. The unique and compelling feature of the massive church interior is a band of still-vividly coloured twelfth-century **frescoes** high up in the apse of the eastern anti-chapel dedicated to St-Michel and which, appropriately, feature the archangel.

### Gorges de la Fou

April–mid Nov daily 10am–6pm; July & Aug 9.30am–6.30pm • €9.50 • ☎04 68 39 16 21

The world's narrowest canyon, the **Gorges de la Fou**, spans a spectacular 2km cut through the southeastern flank of Pic du Canigou; at some parts the walls are only one metre apart. The not-overly-arduous ascent through the gorge is aided by a metal catwalk.

## Prats-de-Mollo

Beyond the Gorges de la Fou, the D115 climbs steadily, between valley sides thick with walnut, oak and sweet chestnut, 19km to **PRATS-DE-MOLLO**, the end of the bus line. Prats is the last French town before the **Spanish frontier**, 13km beyond at Col d'Ares, but it has none of the usual malaise of border towns and is the most attractive place in the valley since Céret. Hub of the newer quarter is **El Firal**, the huge square used for markets since 1308 (now on Fridays); the walled and gated **ville haute** just south makes for a wonderful wander, with its steep cobbled streets and a weathered church that has marvellous ironwork on the door. The old town's walls were rebuilt in the seventeenth century after the suppression of a local revolt against onerous taxation imposed by Louis XIV on his new, post-Treaty Pyrenees holdings.

Vauban's fortress, the **Fort Lagarde** (guided visits: April–June & Sept–Oct Tues–Sun 2–6pm; July & Aug daily 10.30am–1pm, 3.30pm & 5–6.30pm; €3.50; ☎ 04 68 39 70 83; enquire about guided tours at the tourst office) sits on the heights above the town. It was built in 1677 as much to intimidate the local population as to keep the Spanish out.

**11**

### INFORMATION
### PRATS-DE-MOLLO

**Tourist office** Place le Fioral (Mon–Sat 9am–noon & 2–6pm, closed Sun; ☎ 04 68 39 70 83 ⓦ pratsdemollolapreste.com).

### ACCOMMODATION AND EATING

**Le Bellevue** Rue el Firal ☎ 04 68 39 72 48, ⓦ hotel-le-bellevue.fr. Overlooking the *place*/Friday market, just outside the town wall, this appealing hotel offers private parking and rooms with balconies for a little extra. Its restaurant has seasonal *menus* from €20. Closed Dec to mid-Feb. €53

**Hostellerie Le Relais** 3 place Josep de la Trinxeria ☎ 04 68 39 71 30, ⓦ hostellerie-le-relais.com. Cheerful

pastel-hued rooms and a south-facing garden restaurant serving an exciting range to suit all budgets starting at €10, including paella and Catalan meatballs. €42

**Village Liberte** Rte Col d'Arès, 100m south of the old town ☎ 04 68 39 72 78, ⓦ vvf-villages.com. A small family holiday village with petite studios, two-room apartments and leisure facilities including a nice pool. Advance booking essential. Easter–Oct. €60

## Saint Marsal and around

The only direct route between the **valleys of the Tech and the Têt**, best covered by car or cycle, is the D618 from Amélie-les-Bains to Bouleternère. It's 44 slow kilometres of mountain road, twisting through hillside meadows and magnificent oak forest, past isolated *masies* (Catalan farmsteads). Half-way there is the tiny village of **Saint Marsal** which offers the first amenities en route and are well worth the stop.

### Prieuré de Serrabona

Daily except major holidays 10am–6pm • €4 • ☎ 04 68 84 09 30

On the D84 just past Boule d'Amont, you'll come across one of the finest examples – arguably *the* finest – of Roussillon Romanesque. The interior of the **Prieuré de Serrabona** (consecrated 1151) is starkly plain, making the beautifully carved column-capitals of its rib-vaulted tribune even more striking: lions, centaurs, griffins and human figures with Asiatic faces and hairstyles – motifs brought back from the Crusades – executed in pink marble from Villefranche-de-Conflent, by students of the Maître d'Cabestany, if not himself.

### ACCOMMODATION AND EATING

★ **Chambre d'hôte de Saint Marsal** Saint Marsal ☎ 04 68 98 17 72, ✉ auberge@saint-marsal.com. Recently updated, comfortable rooms with en-suite

bathrooms. Run by avid wild-mushroom hunters who bring their rich bounty and their love of Catalan cuisine together onto the plates they serve. Budget around €18. If you can't stay long, note that the terraced bar provides excellent regional beers and wines. Restaurant open noon–2pm & 7–9pm (non-stop service in summer); closed Jan & Feb and Mon & Tues out of season. **€45**

## The Têt valley

The upper **Têt valley**, known as the **Pays de Conflent**, is utterly dominated by the **Pic du Canigou**. The valley bottoms are lush with fields and orchards, but the vast and uncompromising mountain presides over all. As you continue upstream, the valley steepens and buckles as magnificent gorges carve in from the surrounding mountains and scalding water bleeds from the valley's northern flank. Ancient shepherd's villages, basking in Mediterranean glow, peer down on the road below. Crisscrossing the Têt, the vintage **Train Jaune** (see box, p.632) groans its way towards the Cerdagne plateau.

### Prades (Prada) and around

The chief valley town is **Prades**, easily accessible by train and bus on the Perpignan–Villefranche–Latour-de-Carol route, and one obvious starting point for all excursions in the Canigou region. Although there are no great sights beyond the **church of St-Pierre** (free entry) in central place de la République, the town enjoys a status disproportionate to its size. This is largely thanks to Catalan cellist Pablo (Pau) Casals, who settled here as an exile from and fierce opponent of the Franco regime in Spain. In 1950 he instituted the internationally renowned **chamber music festival** (ⓦprades-festival-casals.com), held annually from late July to mid-August, the usual venue being the abbey of St-Michel-de-Cuixà (see below). The thriving Tuesday morning market is not to be missed, with its produce strongly influenced by Catalan and north African culture; you'll find paella, churros and fresh Moroccan spices, traded to the sounds of accordion buskers and congregations of elderly men chatting in French-Catalan dialect.

### Abbaye St-Michel-de-Cuxà

May–Sept Mon–Sat 9.30–11.50am & 2–6pm; Oct–April Mon–Sat 9.30–11.50am & 2–5pm • €5 • ☏ 04 68 96 15 35

Three kilometres south of Prades stands one of the loveliest abbeys in France, the eleventh-century **St-Michel-de-Cuxà**. Although mutilated after the Revolution it is still beautiful, with its crenelated tower silhouetted against the wooded – sometimes snowy – slopes of Canigou. You enter via the labyrinthine, vaulted crypt, with its round central chamber, before proceeding to the church with its strange Visigothic-style "keyhole" arches. But the glory of the place is the **cloister** and its twelfth-century column capitals.

### ARRIVAL AND INFORMATION
PRADES AND AROUND

**By bus** The bus depot is on avenue Général-de-Gaulle on the east side of town.
Destinations Latour-de-Carol (2–3 daily; 1hr); Perpignan (approx. every half-hour; 55min).
**By train** The *gare* is two blocks south of the bus depot on bd de la Gare.

Destinations Perpignan (8 daily; 45min); Villefranche (8 daily; 10min).
**Tourist office** Place de la Republique (Mon–Sat 9am–noon & 2–6pm; mid-June to mid-Sept Sun 10am–noon; ☏ 04 68 05 41 02, ⓦprades-tourisme.fr).

### ACCOMMODATION

★ **Castell Rose** Chemin de la Litera ☏ 04 68 96 07 57, ⓦcastellrose-prades.com. Sumptuous *chambres d'hôtes* in a converted manor house set in extensive grounds with a pool and tennis court. The cheaper rooms are a bit cramped but still offer exceptional value. **€85**
**Chambre d'hôte Maison Prades** 51 av du Général-de-Gaulle ☏ 04 68 05 74 27, ⓦmaisonprades.com. With its big bright rooms looking up to Mt Canigou and down to the sunny garden, this *chambre d'hôte* looks after its guests

well. Breakfasts are copious, delicious and healthy. **€70**
**Le Grand Hôtel** Molitg-les-Bains, 6km north of Prades ☏ 04 68 05 00 50, ⓦgrandhotelmolitg.com. If money is no object and you have transport, then this old and charmingly dishevelled spa hotel, beautifully set in a secluded valley next to a river, is a fine choice. Bathe in the hotel's thermal waters, or more appealingly, the gentle flowing river below. The hotel's gourmet restaurant has high standards and prices; a two-course

meal costs €27. **€145**
**L'Oasis** Molitg-les-Bains, 6km north of Prades ☎ 04 68 05 00 92, ⓦ hoteloasis.e-monsite.com. More down to earth than *Le Grand Hôtel* across the road, this budget option offers exceptional value with its basic, but clean rooms. **€39**

## EATING

A number of appealing pavement café-restaurants ring the central *place* and while they offer a pleasant place to stop for a kir or two the food tends to be of poor quality.

★ **Café Alchemie** 3 rue de l'Hospice ☎ 04 68 05 77 54, ⓦ alchimie-prades.com. With its internet café and fresh juice bar to the fore, and phenomenally good restaurant through the back, *Alchemie* has built up a formidable reputation over recent years for exceptional, healthy, home cooking. Ingredients are organic, sourced directly from growers and of the three main courses on offer, two are always vegetarian. The three-course *menu* costs €16 or €20 including wine/juice and coffee. Tues–Sat: Sept–June 10am–4pm; July–Aug 10am–6pm; closed Jan.

## Eus

The village of **Eus**, a five-minute drive northeast of Prades, claims to be the sunniest in France; it's certainly one of the prettiest. Built amongst the massive granite boulders that litter these elevated slopes, narrow cobbled lanes wind up to the ruined château and imposing eighteenth-century church of St Vincent. A number of easy hikes begin from the entrance to the village through the olive groves and gnarled green oak forests.

## DRINKING

**Des Gouts et des Couleurs** Place de la Republic ☎ 06 09 53 32 4. No visit to Eus would be complete without visiting this convivial pavement bar occupying its own little *place*. Opening hours approximately: mid-March to mid-Nov daily 10am–7pm.

## Villefranche-de-Conflent

Some six kilometres up the Têt from Prades, the medieval garrison town of **Villefranche-de-Conflent** is dwarfed by sheer limestone escarpments, and is undoubtedly one of the most beautiful in France. Founded in 1092 by the counts of Cerdagne to block incursions from rivals in Roussillon, then remodelled by Vauban in the seventeenth century after annexation by France, its streets and fortifications have remained untouched by subsequent events. Worth a visit is St-Jacques church, with its primitively carved thirteenth-century baptismal font just inside the door; you can also walk the walls for €4 when the tourist office is open.

### Château-Fort Libéria

Daily: 10am–6pm; May & June 10am–7pm; July–Aug 9am–8pm • €10 or €7 if you fancy walking up • ⓦ fort-liberia.com

In 1681, Vauban constructed the **Château-Fort Libéria** on the heights above Villefranche-de-Conflent to protect it from "aerial" bombardment. Getting there involves taking the jeep, which leaves from near the town's main gate; you can return to Villefranche by descending a subterranean stairway of a thousand steps, emerging at the end of rue St-Pierre.

### St-Martin-du-Canigou

A 30min walk (no car access) above the hamlet of Casteil, itself eight kilometres south of Villefranche in the cul-de-sac Vallee de Cady. French guided tours: Mon–Sat 10am, 11am, 2pm, 3pm, 4pm; plus June–Sept noon & 5pm; Sun/hols 10am & 12.30pm; closed Jan & Mon Oct–May • €5 • ⓦ stmartinducanigou.org

The stunning abbey of **St-Martin-du-Canigou**, founded in 1001, resurrected from ruins between 1902 and 1982, and now inhabited by a working religious community, occupies a narrow promontory of rock surrounded by chestnut and oak woods, while above it rises the precipitous slopes of the Pic du Canigou. Below, the ground drops vertically into the ravine of the Cady stream rushing down from the Col de Jou. What you see is a beautiful little garden and cloister overlooking the ravine, a low-ceiling, atmospheric chapel beneath the church, and the main church itself.

## INFORMATION

**Tourist office** Rue St Jean, by the western gate (Feb, Oct & Nov 10.30am–noon & 2–5pm; March–May 10.30am–5pm; June & Sept 10am–7pm; July & Aug 10am–8pm; Dec 2–5pm; closed Jan; ☎04 68 96 22 96 ⓦ www.villefranchedeconflent.fr).

## ACCOMMODATION

**À l'Ombre du Fort** 2 Sainte-Eulalie ☎04 68 97 10 01, ⓦactivityholidayfrance.com. A grand nineteenth-century house cloaked in Virginia creeper with spacious rooms and parquet flooring. Outside there's a large, landscaped garden and sun-drenched swimming pool secluded by trees. Min stay 2 nights. **€85**

**Camping Les Cerisiers** Chemin de la Pena, Vernet-les-Bains (6km south of Villefranche) ☎04 68 05 60 38, ⓦ camping-lescerisiers.com. Unlike other campsites in the area, this pleasant little site is peacefully tucked away from any kind of main road. It's also well located for attempts to summit the Pic du Canigou. There are a few facilities here: sauna, hot tub, free wifi and little shop, while Vernet covers all other needs. Mid March-mid Oct. **€17**

## EATING

★ **Au Grill Restaurant la Senyera** 81 rue Saint Jean ☎04 68 96 17 65. This beautiful and atmospheric restaurant has the best reputation in town and is where the locals choose to dine. Don't be put off by the "Grill" title, this restaurant's dishes show the skill and finesse of a fine dining establishment, even if they are very meat orientated. Budget around €20 for a generous meal. Noon–2.30pm & 7.30–9.30pm; Nov–March closed Wed lunch & every evening except Sat; April–Oct closed Tues–Thurs eve; closed mid-Oct to mid-Nov & first week of July.

**Boulangerie Patisserie Miras** 13 rue Saint Jacques ☎04 68 96 37 06, ⓦboulangerie.miras.free.fr. Run by a genuine artisan boulanger (most French bakers claim to be artisan these days), this is the ideal place to sample the *Bunyete*, a Catalan speciality akin to a pancake and a doughnut (€2.50). This attractive little shop proudly bakes its breads and patisseries in a 1930s cast iron, wood-fired oven. Tues–Sun 7am–1pm & 2–7pm; July & Aug 6.30am–8.30pm.

## The upper Têt

Ten or so kilometres west of Villefranche, the mountains close in, dwarfing the valley and road below. As you turn right just past the village of **Olette**, the road leads to the picture-perfect shepherd's village of **Evol**, overlooked by the old fortress of the So Viscounts. Further up the Têt, most of the settlements are high on the mountainside, connected by ancient footpaths and dry stone terraces, the most breathtaking of which is **Canaveilles**; from the main road it's three kilometres of vertiginous single-track hairpins to reach this characterful old village. If you cross the main N166 road from the foot of Canaveilles and follow the well-trodden path to the river, you'll see a stone basin with scalding thermal water pouring in from the mountainside with a makeshift sluice gate in the river for temperature adjustment. Some 3km further on the south side of the valley, the wild, wooded **Gorges de Carança** (Thuès-Entre-Valls is the nearest village) cuts south through the mountains towards Spain.

One trip worth making, particularly after a heavy day's trekking, is to Les **Bains de St-Thomas** (daily 10am–7.40pm; July & Aug last admission 8.40pm; closed early June;

---

### PETIT TRAIN JAUNE

One of the most spectacular train rides in the world, the **Petit Train Jaune** runs between Villefranche-de-Conflent and La Tour-de-Carol (with onward links towards Toulouse or Barcelona) in the upper Cerdagne and is a wonder of early twentieth-century engineering. Built to link up the villages of the high Pyrenees with Perpignan, the antique narrow-gauge carriages now mostly carry tourists, cyclists and skiers. The most spectacular section of the route is in the upper Têt between Olette and Mont Louis where you'll trundle over gorges and massive viaducts. The summertime frequency of the trains makes it practical to hop off and on, allowing you to explore the areas around smaller, isolated stations, many of them *haltes facultatifs* (ask to be set down). Outside summer, the timetable is somewhat unreliable, as the aging train system needs regular maintenance.

€5.50; ☎04 68 97 03 13, ⓦbains-saint-thomas.fr). Signposted from Fontpedrouse, 11km west of Olette, these are three open-air thermal pools set at a pleasant 36–38°C, and located in a beautiful pine forest.

## ACCOMMODATION AND EATING — UPPER TET VALLEY

There is a real dearth of accommodation options in this well touristed area, except for holiday homes that usually rent by the week. There are no restaurants here either; the nearest are either back in Villefranche or up in Mont Louis.

**La Fontaine** In the centre of Olette ☎04 68 97 03 67, ⓦatasteofcatalonia.co.uk. An excellent, English-run *chambre d'hôte* with very tasteful rooms in an unexciting town. Closed Jan. **€79**

★ **Gîte de Canaveilles** Rue Des Treilles, at the western edge of Canaveilles ✉stellotape@yahoo.co.uk, ⓦwww .gitedecanaveilles.info. A beautiful, self-catering cottage built into the mountainside with space for five people. The part shaded (by walnut tree), part sun-drenched garden has incredible views and is peaceful thanks to the path outside being too narrow for cars. Mountain trekking routes begin from the door. Easter–Oct. Per week **€420–600**

## The Cerdagne

Twenty kilometres up from Olette, the Mediterranean climate slips away as the gradient flattens onto the wide, grassy **Cerdagne** plateau, whose once-powerful counts controlled lands from Barcelona to Roussillon. It's a region that's never been sure whether it is Spanish or French. After the French annexation of Roussillon, it was partitioned, with Spain retaining – as it still does – the enclave of Lliva. The Petit Train Jaune (see box opposite) snakes laboriously across the entire plateau, though stations aren't always convenient for the settlements they nominally serve.

### Mont Louis

Easterly gateway to the region, the little garrison town of **Mont Louis**, built by Vauban in 1679–82, is France's highest fortified town. The top citadelle is still a training school for paratroops and marines. Today the town is an attractive halfway station between the Mediterranean and Andorra, and has a few shops, bars and restaurants.

## ACCOMMODATION AND EATING — MONT LOUIS

**Chambre d'hôte La Volute** Place d'Armes ☎04 68 04 27 21, ⓦlavolute.monsite.orange.fr. Set in the seventeenth-century former governor's mansion, with a garden atop a section of the ramparts overlooking the moat and mountains beyond. **€80**

**Le Rucher de l'Ours** 6 bd Vauban ☎04 68 04 11 26. Welcoming little restaurant serving two courses with wine and coffee for €14.50. Expect cassoulet, pizzas and *galettes* served under a stone-vaulted roof or outside in the often-chilly wind. Wed–Sun noon–2.30pm & 7–9pm.

### Les Lacs des Bouillouses

The Têt ultimately has its source in the Carlit massif, which looms above the lovely **Lacs Des Bouillouses**. This huge park in the high Pyrenees is strikingly beautiful; the sky is a different, purer kind of blue and the river and lake waters are clear and fresh. There are moderately difficult, circular hikes around the lakes that feed into the main reservoir as well as idyllic picnic beaches along the banks of the gentle river. Wild swimming in the summer months is a more than appealing prospect. To get here, turn north from Mont Louis and from there it's well signposted.

**11**

# Languedoc

CARCASSONNE

# Languedoc

In many ways, Languedoc is more an idea than a geographical entity. The modern *région* covers only a fraction of the lands where Occitan or the *langue d'oc* – the language of *oc*, the southern Gallo-Latin word for *oui* – once dominated, which stretched south from Bordeaux and Lyon into Spain and northwest Italy. The heartland today is the Bas Languedoc – the coastal plain and dry, stony vine-growing hills between Carcassonne and Nîmes. It's here that the Occitan movement has its power base, demanding recognition of its linguistic and cultural distinctiveness.

Languedoc's long-contested history has left it with a tremendous variety of sights for the visitor. **Nîmes** has extensive Roman remains, while the medieval towns at **Cordes** and **Carcassonne** are must-sees, with the latter providing access to the romantic Cathar castles to the south. There's also splendid ecclesiastical architecture in **Albi** and **St-Guilhem-le-Désert**. **Montpellier**'s university ensures it has a buzz that outstrips the city's modest size, while **Toulouse**, the cultural capital of medieval and modern Languedoc, though officially outside the administrative *région*, is a high point of any itinerary.

The many other attractions include great swathes of **beach** where – away from the major resorts – you can still find a kilometre or two to yourself, along with wonderful dramatic landscapes and river gorges, from the **Cévennes** foothills in the east to the **Montagne Noire** and **Corbières** hills in the west.

# Eastern Languedoc

Heading south from Paris via Lyon and the Rhône valley, you can go one of two ways: east to Provence and the Côte d'Azur – which is what most people do – or west to **Nîmes**, Montpellier and the comparatively untouched Languedoc coast. Nîmes makes a good introduction to the area, a hectic modern town impressive for its Roman past and some scattered attractions, including the **Pont du Gard** nearby. **Montpellier** is also worth a day or two, not so much for historical attractions as for a heady vibrancy and easy access to the ancient villages, churches and fine scenery of the upper **Hérault valley**.

This is the heartland of Languedoc, a rural region that has resolutely resisted the power of Northern France since the Middle Ages. This resistance came in the form of medieval Catharism; early-modern Protestantism; its support of the revolutions of 1789 and 1848; the nineteenth-century revival of Occitan culture; war-time resistance against the Nazis, and finally a democratic populism that has found its voice both in the extreme Left and the extreme Right. Such resistance often provoked reprisals on the part of Paris and the north; this only helped cement a distinct Languedocian identity expressed as opposition to the status quo.

| | |
|---|---|
| **Bullfighting** p.641 | **The Canal du Midi** p.660 |
| **Occitan identity** p.642 | **Armagnac** p.676 |
| **Joutes nautiques** p.651 | |

**12**

THE CANAL DU MIDI

# Highlights

**❶ The bulls of Languedoc** Whether in a bullfight at Les Arènes or eaten as a succulent *boeuf à la gardienne*, the taureaux of the plains of Languedoc are famous. **See p.641**

**❷ Pont du Gard** This graceful aqueduct is an emblem of southern France and a tribute to Roman determination. **See p.644**

**❸ St-Guilhem-le-Désert** The ancient Carolingian monastery and the tiny hamlet at its feet present a quintessential Occitan panorama. **See p.649**

**❹ Water-jousting** A Setois tradition, in which teams of rowers charge at each other in gondolas. **See p.651**

**❺ Carcassonne** The Middle Ages come alive in this walled fortress town. **See p.660**

**❻ The Canal du Midi** Cycling, walking or drifting along this tree-shaded canal is the most atmospheric way of savouring France's southwest. **See p.660**

**❼ Les Abattoirs, Toulouse** This former slaughterhouse contains an important collection of modern and contemporary art. **See p.668**

**❽ Toulouse-Lautrec museum, Albi** The most comprehensive collection of Toulouse-Lautrec's work is in the former Bishop's Palace of his home town. **See p.672**

**HIGHLIGHTS ARE MARKED ON THE MAP ON PP.638–639**

# Nîmes

On the border between Provence and Languedoc, **NÎMES** is inescapably linked to two things – denim and Rome. The latter's influence resulted in some of the most extensive **Roman remains** in Europe, while the former (*de Nîmes*), was manufactured for the first time in this city's textile mills and exported to the southern USA in the nineteenth century to clothe slaves. The city is worth a visit, in part for the ruins and the narrow lanes of the compact old city, but also to experience its energy and direction, having enlisted the services of a galaxy of architects and designers – including Norman Foster, Jean Nouvel and Philippe Starck – in a bid to wrest southern supremacy from neighbouring Montpellier.

## Les Arènes

4 bd des Arènes • Daily: March & Oct 9am–5.30pm; April, May & Sept 9am–6pm; June 9am–6.30pm; July & Aug 9am–7.30/8pm; Nov–Feb 9.30am–4.30pm • €7.90 • ☎ 04 66 58 38 00, ⓦ ot-nimes.fr

The focal point of the city is a first-century Roman arena, known as **Les Arènes**, at the junction of boulevards de la Libération and Victor-Hugo. One of the best-preserved Roman arenas in the world, its arcaded two-storey facade conceals massive interior vaulting, riddled with corridors and supporting raked tiers of seats with a capacity of more than twenty thousand spectators, whose staple fare was the blood and guts of

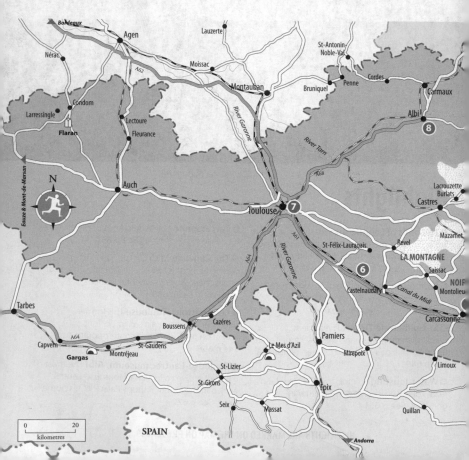

gladiatorial combat. When Rome's sway was broken by the barbarian invasions, the arena became a fortress and eventually a slum, home to an incredible two thousand people when it was cleared in the early 1800s. Today it has recovered something of its former role, with passionate summer crowds still turning out for some blood-letting – Nîmes has the most active bullfighting scene outside Spain.

### The Hôtel de Ville and around

Just to the north of the Roman arena lies the warren of narrow streets that makes up Nîmes' compact Old Town. Among the mostly seventeenth- and eighteenth-century mansions you'll find the **Hôtel de Ville**, set between rue Dorée and rue des Greffes, the interior of which has been redesigned by the architect Jean-Michel Wilmotte to combine high-tech design with classical stone. Look out for the stuffed crocodiles suspended from chains above the stairwells – a gift from wealthy eighteenth-century burghers.

A few minutes from the Hotel de Ville, at the eastern end of rue des Greffes, is the combined **Musée Archéologique** and **Muséum d'Histoire Naturelle** (Tues–Sun 10am–6pm; €5). Housed in a seventeenth-century Jesuit chapel at 13 bd Amiral Courbet, the museums are full of Roman bits and bobs, assorted curios, and stuffed animals.

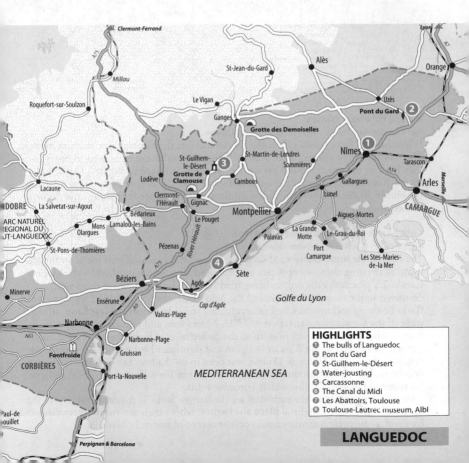

**HIGHLIGHTS**
1. The bulls of Languedoc
2. Pont du Gard
3. St-Guilhem-le-Désert
4. Water-jousting
5. Carcassonne
6. The Canal du Midi
7. Les Abattoirs, Toulouse
8. Toulouse-Lautrec museum, Albi

**LANGUEDOC**

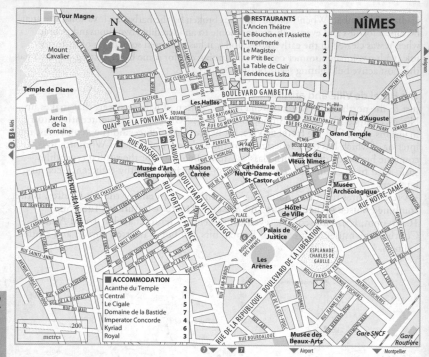

**12**

## Musée du Vieux Nîmes

Place aux Herbes • Tues–Sun 10am–6pm • €5 • ☎ 04 66 76 73 70, ⓦ nimes.fr

When banned from public office, the Protestants put their energy into making money. The results of their efforts can be seen in the seventeenth- and eighteenth-century *hôtels* they built in the streets around the cathedral – rues de l'Aspic, Chapitre, Dorée and Grand'Rue, among others. At the end of Grand'Rue, the former bishop's palace is now the **Musée du Vieux Nîmes**, which has displays of Renaissance furnishings and decor and documents relating to local history.

## Cathédrale Notre-Dame-et-St-Castor

Rue Saint-Castor • ☎ 04 66 67 27 72, ⓦ nimes.catholique.fr

The **Cathédrale Notre-Dame-et-St-Castor** sports a handsome sculpted frieze on the west front, illustrating the story of Adam and Eve, and a pediment inspired by the Maison Carrée. It's practically the only existing medieval building in town, as most were destroyed in the turmoil that followed the Michelade, the St Michael's Day massacre of Catholic clergy and notables by Protestants in 1567. Despite brutal repression in the wake of the Camisard insurrection of 1702, Nîmes was, and remains, a dogged Protestant stronghold. Apart from that, the cathedral is of little interest, having been seriously mutilated in the Wars of Religion and significantly altered in the nineteenth century. The author Alphonse Daudet was born in its shadow, as was Jean Nicot – a doctor, no less – who introduced tobacco into France from Portugal in 1560 and gave his name to the world's most widely consumed drug.

Meandering west from the cathedral are the narrow lanes of the medieval city, at the heart of which is the delightful **place aux Herbes**, where there are two or three cafés and bars and a fine twelfth-century house on the corner of rue de la Madeleine.

## Porte d'Auguste
Rue Nationale

North of the cathedral stands Nîmes' surviving Roman gate, **Porte d'Auguste** at the end of rue Nationale, the former Roman main street. Already a prosperous city on the Via Domitia, the main Roman road from Italy to Spain, Nîmes did especially well under Augustus. He gave the city its walls, remnants of which surface here and there, and its gates, as the inscription on the Porte records. He is also responsible for the chained crocodile, which figures on Nîmes' coat of arms. The image was copied from an Augustan coin struck to commemorate Augustus's defeat of Antony and Cleopatra after he settled veterans of that campaign on the surrounding land.

## Maison Carrée
14 rue de la Maison Carrée • Daily: March–June 10am–6/7pm; July & Aug 10am–8pm; Oct 10am–1pm & 2–6pm; Nov–Feb 10am–1pm & 2–4.30pm • €4.60 • ☎ 04 66 58 38 00, ⓦ ot-nimes.fr

One of the city's landmarks, the **Maison Carrée** is a neat, jewel-like temple celebrated for its integrity and harmonic proportions. Built in 5 AD, it's dedicated to the adopted sons of Emperor Augustus – all part of the business of inflating the imperial personality cult. No surprise, then, that Napoleon, with his love of flummery, took it as the model for the Madeleine church in Paris. The temple stands in its own small square opposite rue Auguste, where the Roman forum used to be, with pieces of Roman masonry scattered around.

## Musée d'Art Contemporain
Carré d'Art, Place de la Maison Carrée • Tues–Sun 10am–6pm • Free (€5 temporary exhibits) • ☎ 04 66 76 35 70, ⓦ nimes.fr

On the west side of place de la Maison Carrée stands a gleaming example of the architectural boldness characteristic of the city, the **Carré d'Art**, by British architect Norman Foster. In spite of its size, this box of glass, aluminium and concrete sits modestly among the ancient roofs of Nîmes, its slender portico echoing that of the Roman temple opposite. Light pours in through the walls and roof, giving it a grace and weightlessness that makes it not in the least incongruous.

Inside, the excellent **Musée d'Art Contemporain** contains an impressive collection of French and Western European art from the last four decades, focusing on French art since the 1960s, works relating to Mediterranean identity, and German and British artists. The roof-terrace café overlooks the Maison Carrée.

## Jardin de la Fontaine and around
Perhaps the most refreshing thing you can do in Nîmes is head east of the centre to the **Jardin de la Fontaine**, France's first public garden, created in 1750. Behind the formal entrance, where fountains, nymphs and formal trees enclose the **Temple de Diane**, steps

---

### BULLFIGHTING

Nîmes' great passion is **bullfighting**, and its *ferias* are attended by both aficionados and fighters at the highest level. The wildest and most famous is the **Feria de Pentecôte**, which lasts five days over the Whitsun weekend. A couple of million people crowd into the town (hotel rooms need to be booked a year in advance), and seemingly every city native opens a bodega at the bottom of the garden for dispensing booze. There are *corridas*, which end with the killing of the bull, *courses* where *cocards* are snatched from the bull's head, and semi-amateur *courses libres* when a small posse of bulls is run through the streets. Two other *ferias* take place: one at carnival time in February; the other, the Feria des Vendanges, in the third week of September at grape-harvest time. Recently, events have been marked by small but vocal protests and in 2006 several organizers of the local *tauromachie* world were injured by letter bombs. The **tourist office** can supply full details and advise about accommodation if you want to visit at *feria* time.

## OCCITAN IDENTITY

A good part of the political character of Languedoc derives from resentment of domination by remote and alien Paris, aggravated by the area's traditional poverty. In recent times this has been focused on Parisian determination to drag the province into the modern world, with massive tourist development on the coast and the drastic transformation of the cheap wine industry. It is also mixed up in a vague collective folk memory with the brutal repression of the Protestant Huguenots around 1700, the thirteenth-century massacres of the Cathars and the subsequent obliteration of the brilliant *langue d'oc* troubadour tradition. The resulting antipathy towards central authority has made an essentially rural and conservative population vote traditionally for the Left – except during the first decade of this century, which saw wide support for Le Pen's resurgent Front National. Although a sense of **Occitan identity** remains strong in the region, it has very little currency as a spoken or literary language, despite the popularity of university-level language courses and the foundation of Occitan-speaking elementary schools.

climb the steep wooded slope, adorned with grottoes and nooks and artful streams, to the **Tour Magne** (daily: March & Oct 9.30am–1pm & 2–6pm; April 9.30am–6pm; May–Aug 9am–6.10/7.40pm; Sept–March 9.30am–12.45pm & 2–4.15/6pm; €2.80). The 32m tower, left over from Augustus's city walls, gives terrific views over the surrounding country – as far, it is claimed, as the Pic du Canigou on the edge of the Pyrenees. At the foot of the slope flows the gloriously green and shady **Canal de la Fontaine**, built to supplement the rather unsteady supply of water from the *fontaine*, the Nemausus spring, whose presence in a dry, limestone landscape gave Nîmes its existence.

### Musée des Beaux-Arts

Rue de la Cité-Foulc • Tues–Sun 10am–6pm • Free • ☎ 04 66 28 18 32, ⓦ nimes.fr

The **Musée des Beaux-Arts**, in rue de la Cité-Foulc, prides itself on a huge Gallo-Roman mosaic showing the Marriage of Admetus. Originally housed in the tiny Maison Carrée, its collection now includes 3600 works from the fifteenth to the nineteenth centuries, including paintings by Rubens, Subleyras, and Delaroche.

### South of town

Out on the southern edge of town, you'll find examples of the revolutionary civic architecture for which Nîmes was once famed. Jean Nouvel's pseudo-Mississippi-steamboat housing project, named **Nemausus** after the deity of the local spring that gave Nîmes its name, squats off the Arles road behind the *gare SNCF*, and the magnificent sports stadium, the **Stades des Costières**, by Vittorio Gregotti, looms close to the *autoroute* along the continuation of avenue Jean-Jaurès.

### ARRIVAL AND INFORMATION                                             NÎMES

**By plane** The Camargue airport, shared by Nîmes and Arles, lies 20km southeast of the city. A shuttle service links it to the town centre (2–4 daily, timed with flights; ☎ 04 66 29 27 29; "Gambetta" or "Imperator" stop; €5). By taxi, the trip will cost at least €25 (€35 at night).

**By train** The *gare SNCF* (ⓦ ter-sncf.com) is 10min walk southeast of the city centre at the end of av Feuchères.

Destinations Arles (every 20–30min; 30–40min); Avignon (every 20–30min; 30min); Béziers (every 20–30min; 1hr 15min); Carcassonne (every 20–30min; 2hr 5min–3hr 10min); Clermont-Ferrand (every 20–30min; 5–6hr); Marseille (every 20–30min; 40min–1hr 15min); Montpellier (every 20–30min; 30min); Narbonne (every 20–30min; 1hr 45min); Paris (every 20–30min; 3hr–9hr 30min); Sète (every 20–30min; 48min); Perpignan (hourly; 2hr 45min).

**By bus** The *gare routière* (☎ 08 99 23 59 01) is just behind the train station.

Destinations Aigues-Mortes (hourly; 55min); Ganges (2–3 daily; 1hr 30min); La Grande-Motte (2–9 daily; 1hr 30min); Le Grau-du-Roi (hourly; 1hr 15min); Le Vigan (3–5 daily; 1hr 50min); Pont du Gard (8 daily; 45min); Sommières (8 daily; 45min); Uzès (30min–1hr).

**Tourist office** 6 rue Auguste (Mon–Fri 8.30am–7/8pm, Sat 9am–6.30/7pm, Sun 10am–5/6pm; ☎ 04 66 58 38 00, ⓦ ot-nimes.fr).

**Passes** If you're planning on making the rounds of museums and monuments, pick up the Billet Nîmes Romaine from the tourist office (€10).

## ACCOMMODATION

★ **Acanthe du Temple** 1 rue Charles Babout ☎ 04 66 67 54 61, ⓦ hotel-temple.com. A clean and economical hotel, with friendly staff, garage (€8), good amenities and 24hr access. This is one of the Old Town's best bargains, and lies within easy walking distance of the main sights. Closed Jan. **€60**

**Central** 2 place du Château ☎ 04 66 67 27 75, ⓦ hotel -central.org. Just behind the temple and the Porte d'Auguste, with English-speaking management, this small, cosy hotel features simple but comfortable rooms – although the top floor gets hot in summer. Secure parking available. **€65**

**Le Cigale** 257 chemin de l'Auberge de Jeunesse, 2km northwest of the centre ☎ 04 66 68 03 20, ⓦ fuaj.org. Set in airy, park-like surroundings this youth hostel's olive-tree-ed terrace provides quiet respite from the bustle of the old city, 2km to the southeast. Take bus #2 direction "Alès/ Villeverte" from the *gare SNCF* to stop "Stade" – the last bus goes at 8pm. July & Aug membership required; Sept–June no curfew. Dorms **€15.40**, doubles **€40**

**Domaine de la Bastide** Rte de Générac ☎ 04 66 62 05 82, ⓦ camping-nimes.com. 5km south of the city centre, beyond the modern Stade Costières and the *autoroute*, this well-equipped municipal campsite has a bar, playground and laundry. **€15.40**

**Imperator Concorde** Quai de la Fontaine ☎ 04 66 21 90 30, ⓦ hotel-imperator.com. The city's finest choice, and a favourite of Ernest Hemingway's, located by the Jardin de la Fontaine. Luxuriously appointed rooms, excellent service and private parking. Prices quadruple during *ferias*. **€110**

**Kyriad** 10 rue Roussy ☎ 04 66 76 16 20, ⓦ hotel-kyriad -nimes.com. A solid two-star option with an impressive range of amenities, including a generous breakfast buffet. Its location just outside the Old Town makes street parking a convenient possibility. **€71**

★ **Royal** 3 bd Alphonse-Daudet ☎ 04 66 58 28 27, ⓦ royalhotel-nimes.com. The *Royal* has a cool Spanish-style decor that draws in passing *toreros*. The rooms are individually decorated with an Iberian flavour, and the place exudes a certain chic. It's also home to the *Bodeguita* tapas bar. **€60**

## EATING AND DRINKING

The best places to hang out for coffee and drinks are the numerous little squares scattered through the Old Town: place de la Maison-Carrée, place du Marché and place aux Herbes.

**L'Ancien Théâtre** 4 rue Racine ☎ 04 66 21 30 75. Just a 5min stroll west from the Maison Carrée, with solid Gardoise cuisine, and home-made breads and pastries. *Menus* from €18. Tues–Fri noon–1.45pm & 6–9pm, Sat 6–9pm; closed early Aug.

**Le Bouchon et l'Assiette** 5bis rue de Sauve, ☎ 04 66 62 02 93. Come here for elaborate *gastronomique* variations on traditional *tarnaise* themes. Very reasonably priced, with *menus* at €17–45. Thurs–Mon noon–1.45pm & 5.45–9pm. Closed part of Jan & most of Aug.

**L'Imprimerie** 3 rue Balore ☎ 04 66 29 57 16. A favourite of local artists, this former printing shop features an ever-changing *carte* drawing on influences from as far away as North Africa. Mon–Fri noon–1.45.pm & 6–9pm; tapas till 10pm on Fri.

**Le Magister** 5 rue Nationale ☎ 04 66 76 11 00, ⓦ le -magister-a-table.com. Daring experimentation is the order of the day at this good *gastronomique* restaurant. A meal will cost around €25–37. Sept–June Mon–Sat noon–1.45pm & 56–9.45pm. Closed part of Feb.

**Le P'tit Bec** 87bis rue de la République ☎ 04 66 38 05 83. The best mid-range place for typical Gardoise cuisine. The dining room is pleasant and airy and the service is friendly. Expect to spend between €17 and €40. Tues–Fri 11.30am–1.15pm & 6.30–9.45pm

★ **La Table de Clair** Place des Esclafidous ☎ 04 66 67 55 61. This funky and unprepossessing restaurant features eclectic cuisine; everything is good. The house speciality is local beef, grilled and smothered in Cassis mustard sauce. *Menus* €25 and €45. Tues–Sat noon–2pm & 6–10pm.

★ **Tendences Lisita** 2b bd des Arènes ☎ 04 66 67 29 15, ⓦ lelisita.com. Hands-down, the city's best *gastronomique* restaurant, run by two former staff of Michel Roux's famous London restaurant *Le Gavroche*. Tues–Sat noon–2pm & 6–10pm.

# North of Nîmes

Some 20km to the northeast of Nîmes, the **Pont du Gard**, the greatest surviving stretch of a 50km-long Roman aqueduct, is a popular tourist destination, while 17km beyond, near the start of the aqueduct, the picturesque hilltop town of **Uzès** has a number of good places to stay.

## The Pont du Gard

Built in the middle of the first century AD to supply fresh water to the city, and with just a 17m difference in altitude between start and finish, the **Roman aqueduct** north of Nîmes was quite an achievement, running as it does over hill and dale, through a tunnel, along the top of a wall, into trenches and over rivers; the **Pont du Gard** carries it over the River Gardon. Today the bridge is a UNESCO World Heritage Site and something of a tourist trap, but is nonetheless a supreme piece of engineering and a brilliant combination of function and aesthetics; it made the impressionable Rousseau wish he'd been born Roman.

Three tiers of **arches** span the river, with the covered water conduit on the top rendered with a special plaster waterproofed with a paint apparently based on fig juice. A visit here used to be a must for French journeymen masons on their traditional tour of the country, and many of them have left their names and home towns carved on the stonework. Markings made by the original builders are still visible on individual stones in the arches.

### Site Pont du Gard

**Museum** 400 rte du Pont du Gard, Vers-Pont-du-Gard • Daily 9.30am–5/7pm • €10, or €18/vehicle • ☎ 04 66 37 50 99, ⊛ pontdugard.fr

The Pont du Gard features an extensive multimedia complex, the **Site Pont du Gard**, which includes a state-of-the-art **museum**, botanical **gardens** and a range of regular children's activities. With the swimmable waters of the Gardon and ample picnic possibilities available, you could easily spend a day here.

## Uzès

**UZÈS** is a lovely old town perched on a hill above the River Alzon. Half a dozen medieval towers – the most fetching is the windowed Pisa-like **Tour Fenestrelle**, tacked onto the much later cathedral – rise above its tiled roofs and narrow lanes of Renaissance and Neoclassical houses. The latter were the residences of the seventeenth- and eighteenth-century local bourgeoisie, who had grown rich, like their fellow Protestants in Nîmes, on textiles. From the mansion of Le Portalet, with its view out over the valley, walk past the Renaissance church of **St-Étienne** and into the medieval place aux Herbes, where there's a Saturday morning market, and up the arcaded rue de la République. The Gide family used to live off the square, and the young André spent summer vacations there with his granny.

### Le Duché castle

Place Duché • Daily guided tours (90min) 10am–noon/12.30 & 2–6/6.30pm • €17; tower only €12 • ☎ 04 66 22 18 96, ⊛ duche-uzes.fr

**Le Duché castle**, still inhabited by the same family a thousand years on, is dominated by its original keep, the **Tour Bermonde**. Guided tours take in exhibits of local history and vintage cars. Opposite, the courtyard of the eighteenth-century **Hôtel de Ville** holds summer concerts.

### ARRIVAL AND INFORMATION                                                  UZÈS

**By bus** Uzès is served by daily buses from Nîmes (2 daily; 50min).

**Tourist office** Place Albert-1er (June–Sept Mon–Fri 10am–6/7pm, Sat & Sun 10am–1pm & 2–5pm; Oct–May Mon–Fri 10am–12.30pm & 2–6pm, Sat & Sun 10am–1pm; ☎ 04 66 22 68 88, ⊛ uzes-tourisme.com).

### ACCOMMODATION

**Camping La Paillotte** Off av Maxime-Pascal ☎ 04 66 22 38 55. The municipal campsite is on the Bagnols-sur-Cèze road running northeast of town. Closed mid-Sept to mid-June. **€14**

**Hostellerie Provençale** 1 rue Grand Bourgade ☎ 04 66 22 11 06, ⊛ hostellerieprovencale.com. Set in two old row houses south of the church of St-Étienne, this hotel features air-conditioned, en-suite rooms, with wi-fi, and is fully accessible. Breakfast can be taken on the terrace, but is a rather pricey €16. **€118**

**La Maison d'Uzès**, 18 rue du Docteur Blanchard ☎ 04 66 20 07 00, ⊛ lamaisonduzes.fr. Spa-hotel set in a gorgeously renovated listed mansion dating from the seventeenth century and just a stone's throw from the

Duché. The nine rooms have spectacular views over the old town. **€245**

★ **La Taverne** 4 rue Xavier Sigalon ☎ 04 66 22 13 10, ✉ lataverne.uzes@wanadoo.fr. This small, welcoming

hotel with good amenities is just behind the tourist office. Rooms are basic but clean and well kept, and there is shady terrace for enjoying breakfast or an afternoon break. **€70**

# Montpellier

A thousand years of trade and intellectual activity have made **MONTPELLIER** a teeming, energetic city. Benjamin of Tudela, the tireless twelfth-century Jewish traveller, reported its streets crowded with traders from every corner of Egypt, Greece, Gaul, Spain, Genoa and Pisa. After the king of Mallorca sold it to France in 1349 it became an important university town in the 1500s, counting the radical satirist François Rabelais among its alumni. Periodic setbacks, including almost total destruction for its Protestantism in 1622, and depression in the wine trade in the early years of the twentieth century, have done little to dent its progress. Today it vies with Toulouse for the title of the most dynamic city in the south, a quality you'll appreciate as you explore the atmospheric pedestrianized streets of the **Old Town**. The reputation of its university especially, founded in the thirteenth century and most famous for its medical school, is a long-standing one: more than sixty thousand students still set the intellectual and cultural tone of the city, the average age of whose residents is said to be

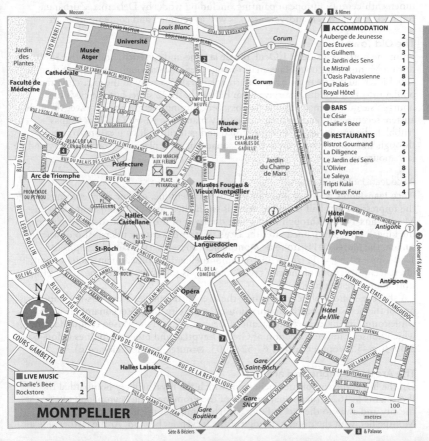

just 25. In many senses the best time to visit is during the academic year (Oct–May), when the city teems with students. The nearest **beaches** for a dip are at Palavas (tram direction "Odysseum" to Port Marianne, then bus #28), but the best are slightly to the west of the town.

Montpellier is renowned for its **cultural life**, and hosts a number of annual **festivals**, notably Montpellier Danse (late June to mid-July), and for music, Le Festival de Radio-France et de Montpellier (second half of July).

## Place de la Comédie

At the hub of the city's life, joining the old part to its newer additions, is **place de la Comédie**, or "L'Oeuf" ("the egg"). This colossal oblong square, paved with cream-coloured marble, has a fountain at its centre and cafés either side. One end is closed by the **Opéra**, an ornate nineteenth-century theatre; the other opens onto the **Esplanade**, a beautiful tree-lined promenade that snakes its way to the **Corum concert hall**, dug into the hillside and topped off in pink granite, with splendid views from the roof.

## Musée Fabre

39 bd Bonne Nouvelle • Tues–Sun 10am–6pm • €6 • ☎ 04 67 14 83 00, ⦿ museefabre.montpellier-agglo.com

South of the Corum, the city's most trumpeted museum, the **Musée Fabre**, has reopened after a major renovation. Its huge collection features seventeenth- to nineteenth-century European painting, including works by Delacroix, Zurbaran, Raphael, Jan van Steen and Veronese, as well as ceramics and contemporary art.

## The Old Town

From the northwest side of L'Oeuf, **rue de la Loge** and **rue Foch**, built in the 1880s during Montpellier's own Haussmann-izing spree, slice through the heart of the old city. Either side of them, a maze of narrow lanes slopes away to the encircling modern boulevards. Few buildings survive from before the 1622 siege, but the city's busy bourgeoisie quickly made up for the loss, proclaiming their financial power through austere seventeenth- and eighteenth-century mansions. Known as "Lou Clapas" (rubble), the area is rapidly being restored and gentrified. It's a pleasure to wander through and come upon secretive little squares like the places St-Roch, St-Ravy and de la Canourgue.

### Place Jean-Jaurès and around

**Place Jean-Jaurès** is a focal point in the city's student life: on fine early evenings you get the impression that half the population is sitting here and in the adjacent place du Marché-aux-Fleurs. Through the Gothic doorway of no. 10 is the so-called palace of the kings of Aragon, named after the city's thirteenth-century rulers. Also on the square, the **Musée de l'Histoire de Montpellier** (Tues–Sat 10.30am–12.30pm & 1.30–6pm; €1.50; ☎ 04 67 54 33 16, ⦿ montpellier.fr), housed in an ancient crypt, offers reconstructions of the city's past. Close by is the **Halles Castellane**, a graceful, iron-framed market hall.

A short walk from place Jean-Jaurès, the lively little rue des Trésoriers-de-France has one of the best seventeenth-century houses in the city, the **Hôtel Lunaret**, at no. 5, while round the block at 7 rue Jacques-Coeur you'll find the **Musée Languedocien**, which houses a mixed collection of Greek, Egyptian and other antiquities (Mon–Sat 2.30/3pm–5.30/6pm; €6; ☎ 04 67 52 93 03, ⦿ musee-languedocien.com).

## The Arc de Triomphe and around

On the hill at the end of rue Foch, from which the royal artillery bombarded the Protestants in 1622, the formal gardens of the **Promenade du Peyrou** look out across the city and away to the Pic St-Loup, which dominates the hinterland behind Montpellier, with the distant smudge of the Cévennes beyond. At the farther side a swagged and pillared water tower marks the end of an eighteenth-century aqueduct modelled on the Pont du Gard. Beneath the grand sweep of its double-tiered arches is a daily fruit and veg market and a huge Saturday **flea market**. At the city end of the promenade, the vainglorious **Arc de Triomphe** shows Louis XIV as Hercules, stomping on the Austrian eagle and English lion, forcefully reminding the locals of his victory over their Protestant "heresy".

### The cathedral

6 rue de-l'Abbé-Marcel-Montels • Free • ☎ 04 67 66 04 12, ⓦ catholique-montpellier.cef.fr

Montpellier's long-suffering **cathedral**, with its massive porch, sports a patchwork of styles from the fourteenth to the nineteenth centuries. Inside is a memorial to the bishop of Montpellier, who sided with the half-million destitute vine-growers who came to demonstrate against their plight in 1907 and were fired on by government troops.

### Around the cathedral

Across the road from the cathedral, on boulevard Henri-IV, the lovely but slightly run-down **Jardin des Plantes** (July & Aug noon–8pm; Sept–June 2–5pm; free; ⓦ univ-montp1.fr /patrimoine/jardin_des_plantes), is France's oldest botanical garden, founded in 1593, while above the cathedral, in the university's prestigious medical school on rue de l'École-de-Médecine, the **Musée Atger** has a distinguished academic collection of French and Italian drawings (Mon, Wed & Fri 1.30–5.45pm; free; ⓦ univ-montp1.fr).

## ARRIVAL AND INFORMATION

**By plane** Montpellier-Méditerranée Airport (ⓦ montpellier.aeroport.fr), is 8km southeast of town beside the Étang de Mauguio; from here a *navette* (timed for flights; 15min; €6) runs to the bus stop on rue de Crète (by the Léon Blum tram stop); a taxi will cost €20–30, depending on the time of day and traffic conditions.

**By train** The *gare SNCF* (no left luggage; ⓦ ter-sncf.com) is at the opposite end of rue Maguelone from the central place de la Comédie.

Destinations Arles (hourly; 1hr 20min); Avignon (every 20–30min; 1hr 15min–2hr); Béziers (every 20–30min; 40min); Carcassonne (every 20–30min; 1hr 15min); Lyon (every 20–30min; 1hr 40min–3hr 30min); Marseille (every 20–30min; 2hr 20min); Mende (every 20–30min; 3hr 40min–4hr 30min); Narbonne (every 20–30min; 45min–1hr 15min); Paris (every 20–30min; 3hr 15min–6hr); Perpignan (hourly; 2hr 15min); Sète (every 20–30min; 15–20min); Toulouse (every 20–30min; 2hr 15min–2hr 55min).

**By bus** The *gare routière* (☎ 04 67 92 01 43) is next to the train station.

Destinations Aigues-Mortes (2–4 daily; 1hr); Bédarieux (3–4 daily; 1hr 35min); Gignac (for St-Guilhem: 6–8 daily; 40min); La Grande-Motte (8–12 daily, hourly in summer; 1hr 5min); Grau-du-Roi (4–8 daily; 1hr 10min); Le Vigan (3–5 daily; 1hr 40min); Lodève (4 daily; 1hr 15min); Millau (2–8 daily; 2hr 20min); Palavas (local service); Rodez (1–3 daily; 3hr 55min); St-Pons-de-Thomières (1–3 daily; 2hr 55min).

**By car** Much of the city centre is pedestrianized, but you can park on the street outside the centre and there are many well-signed municipal garages.

**Tourist office** At the east end of place de la Comédie, opposite the Polygone shopping centre (July–Sept Mon–Fri 9am–7.30pm, Sat & Sun 9.30am–6pm; Oct–June Mon–Fri 10am–6pm, Sat & Sun 10am–5pm; ☎ 04 67 60 60 60, ⓦ ot-montpellier.fr). The tourist office sells the one-, two- and three-day City Card, which covers public transport and gives free admission to many sites as well as other discounts.

## GETTING AROUND

**By bus and tram** TAM city buses and trams run between the stations and outer districts as far as Palavas (€1.40; day ticket €3.80).

**By bike** There are more than 120km of bike paths running

throughout the city and to the sea. You can rent bikes at Montpellier's municipal *Vélomagg* (€0.50/30min; ⓦ tam-way.com) stations around town.

## ACCOMMODATION

**Auberge de Jeunesse** Impasse Petite Corraterie (off rue des Écoles Laïques), ☎ 04 67 60 32 22, ⓦ fuaj.org. This rather business-like hostel is located in the heart of the

old town. Breakfast and bike parking are available. Closed Dec. **€19.60**

**Des Étuves** 24 rue des Étuves ☎ 04 67 60 78 19,

Whoteldesetuves.fr. This family-run hotel (three generations since 1920) offers simple, spotless rooms in the south of the old city, all en suite. **€40**

**Le Guilhem** 18 rue Jean-Jacques Rousseau ☎04 67 52 90 90, Wleguilhem.com. Beautifully restored sixteenth-century townhouse, with cheerful rooms mostly overlooking quiet gardens, and a sunny breakfast terrace. A good alternative to the *Du Palais*. **€96**

★ **Le Jardin des Sens** 11 av St-Lazare ☎04 67 79 63 38, Wjardindessens.com. The best of the upper-bracket hotels, and the epitome of restrained and tasteful luxury, the four-star *Le Jardin* boasts a swimming pool, elegant rooms and one of the region's most acclaimed restaurants. **€215**

**Le Mistral** 25 rue Boussairolles ☎04 67 58 45 25, Whotel-le-mistral.com. Comfortable and clean, this is the city's best economy option; what it lacks in charm, it makes up for in value, offering satellite TV and garage parking (€5 extra). **€52**

**L'Oasis Palavasienne** Just south of town on the D21 to Palavas ☎04 67 15 11 61, Woasis-palavasienne.com. The closest campsite to town (bus #28) is one of the largest; it has just about every amenity imaginable, and also features a waterpark (admission included in the price). Closed mid-Oct to March. **€33**

**Du Palais** 3 rue du Palais ☎04 67 60 47 38, Whoteldupalais-montpellier.fr. Tastefully renovated eighteenth-century mansion on the west side of the Old Town, blending modern and antique touches. Cosy rooms, most of them en suite. An excellent mid-range option. **€82**

**Royal Hôtel** 8 rue Maguelone ☎04 67 92 13 36, Wroyalhotelmontpellier.com. Good amenities (including Canal Plus and 24hr reception) and an old-world ambience make this three-star hotel, between the Comédie and the *gare*, an excellent choice. **€70**

## EATING

**Bistrot Gourmand** 7 place de la Chapelle Neuve ☎04 67 66 08 09. Excellent-value Languedocian cuisine (both inland and coastal varieties) with a wonderful shaded terrace. The *pâtés de canard* are particularly notable, and the wine list is excellent. *Menus* €12 at lunch, €18 at dinner. Daily 10am–midnight. Closed Sun & Mon off season.

★ **La Diligence** 2 place Pétrarque ☎04 67 66 12 21, Wla-diligence.com. Atmospheric vaulted medieval setting for innovative dishes with Asian influences. A good-value dip into the finest French cuisine. *Menus* €36–60 (€23 at lunch). Sun & Tues–Fri noon–2pm & 7.30–11pm, Sat & Mon 7.30–11pm.

★ **Le Jardin des Sens** 11 av St-Lazare ☎04 67 79 63 38, Wjardindessens.com. One of the top restaurants in Languedoc and universally acclaimed as Montpellier's best. Excellent *terroir*-based creations from the famed Pourcel brothers, served in elegant surroundings. *Menus* €49–173. Reservations obligatory. Mon & Wed 8–10pm, Tues & Thurs–Sat noon–2pm & 8–10pm. Closed 1st week of Jan.

**L'Olivier** 12 rue Aristide-Olivier ☎04 67 92 86 28. Pretty little restaurant north of the station offering excellent-value, imaginative cuisine, such as salmon with oyster tartare or leg of rabbit stuffed with wild mushrooms. *Menus* €32–47. Sept–July Tues–Sat noon–2pm & 7–9.30pm.

**Le Saleya** Place du Marché aux Fleurs ☎04 67 60 53 92. A long-standing Montpellier institution. In fine weather, join the locals at the outdoor tables to feast on a daily selection of market-fresh fish and regional food. From €12. Mon–Sat noon–2pm & 7–10.30pm.

**Tripti Kulai** 20 rue Jacques-Coeur ☎04 67 66 30 51, Wtriptikulai.com. Quirky, friendly vegetarian/vegan restaurant. Dishes, including a good choice of salads, have oriental flair, and the lassis and home-made chai are superb. From €12. Mon–Sat noon–9.30pm.

**Le Vieux Four** 59 rue de l'Aiguillerie ☎04 67 60 55 95. Carnivores will love this cosy, candlelit place specializing in *grillades au feu de bois* – meats roasted on an open spit. The *andouillette* (offal sausage) is excellent. *Menus* €15–26. Thurs–Tues 7.45–10pm.

## NIGHTLIFE AND ENTERTAINMENT

In addition to its clubs, bars and live music, Montpellier has a very lively theatre scene, as well as a tradition of engaging *café-littéraires* on a variety of themes. For what's on at the various venues, look for posters around town or check the free weekly listings magazines, *Le Sortir* and *Olé*.

**Le César** 17 place Nombre-d'Or ☎04 67 20 27 02, Wcafecesar.com. This bistro in the modern Antigone district hosts concerts as well as two *café-littéraires* – check for days and times. Mon–Fri 9am–late.

**Charlie's Beer** 22 rue Aristide Olivier ☎04 67 58 89 86, Wcharlies-beer.com. More than forty beers on tap at this venerable, grungy old Montpellier institution. Live music on weekends. Daily 5pm–1/2am.

**Rockstore** 20 rue de Verdun ☎04 67 06 80 00, Wrockstore.fr. Montpellier's rock 'n' roll heart, featuring a regular slate of acts from Europe, North America and beyond. The bar, *Le Café Rock*, has a sophisticated, confident ambience. Daily 6pm–1am.

# St-Guilhem-le-Désert and around

The small town of **Gignac** lies amid vineyards 30km west of Montpellier. It is here that the highway (and buses) turn off for the glorious abbey and village of **ST-GUILHEM-LE-DÉSERT**, which lies in a side ravine, 6km further north up the Hérault beyond the famed medieval Pont du Diable. A ruined castle spikes the ridge above, and the ancient tiled houses of the village ramble down the banks of the rushing Verdus, which is everywhere channelled into carefully tended gardens.

## Abbaye de Gelone

Place de la Liberté • Daily 8am–12.10pm & 2.30–6.20pm • Free • ☎ 04 67 57 70 17, ⊚ saintguilhem-valleeherault.fr/l-abbaye-de-gellone

The grand focus of St-Guilhem-le-Désert is the tenth- to twelfth-century **Abbaye de Gelone**, founded at the beginning of the ninth century by St Guilhem, comrade-in-arms of Charlemagne. The church is a beautiful and atmospheric building, though architecturally impoverished by the dismantling and sale of its cloister – now in New York – in the nineteenth century. It stands on place de la Liberté, surrounded by honey-coloured houses and arcades with traces of Romanesque and Renaissance domestic styles in some of the windows. The interior of the church is plain and somewhat severe compared to the warm colours of the exterior, best seen from rue Cor-de-Nostra-Dama/Font-du-Portal, where you get the classic view of the perfect apse.

## Grotte de Clamouse

Rte de saint Guilhem-le-Désert • Daily 10.30am–6.20pm • €9 • ☎ 04 67 57 71 05, ⊚ clamouse.com

On the road between Gignac and St-Guilhem-le-Désert, cave enthusiasts will enjoy the **Grotte de Clamouse**, an extensive and beautiful stalactite cave entered along a subterranean river before opening up into three expansive grottoes.

## Grotte des Demoiselles

St Bauzille de Putois • Tours: March & Oct Mon–Sat 2.30–4.30pm, Sun 10am, 11am & 2–4.30pm; April–Sept daily 10am–5.30/6pm; Nov–Feb Mon–Fri 2–4pm, Sat & Sun 10am, 11am & 2–4pm • €9.50 • ☎ 04 67 73 70 02, ⊚ demoiselles.com

North of St-Guilhem, after passing through dramatic river gorges almost as far as Ganges, you reach the **Grotte des Demoiselles**, the most spectacular of the region's many caves: a set of vast cathedral-like caverns hung with stalactites descending with millennial slowness to meet the limpid waters of eerily still pools. Located deep inside the mountain, it's reached by an hourly funicular.

| ACCOMMODATION | ST-GUILHEM-LE-DÉSERT AND AROUND |
|---|---|
| **Domaine de Pélicain** 34150 Gignac ☎ 04 67 57 68 92, ⊚ domainedepelican.fr. The closest campsite to St-Guilhem is on this wine *domaine* near Aniane on the road back down to Gignac. They also have a B&B and restaurant. Closed Dec–April. **€13** | **Le Guilhaume d'Orange** 2 av Guillaume d'Orange ☎ 04 67 57 24 53, ⊚ guilhaumedorange.com. Set near the top of the old village, this welcoming hotel features ten unique and spacious rooms, tastefully appointed, if not long on amenities. Half- and full pension available. **€69** |

# Lodève

Around 25km northwest of Gignac, at the point where the swift A75 *autoroute* brings heavy traffic down from Clermont-Ferrand, sits **LODÈVE**, a town at the confluence of the Lergues and Soulondres rivers. In addition to being a pleasant, old-fashioned place to pause on your way up to Le Caylar or La Couvertoirade, it also has an **art museum** that puts on world-class temporary exhibitions. The **cathedral** – a stop on the pilgrim route to Santiago de Compostela – is also worth a look, as is the unusual World War I **Monument aux Morts**, in the adjacent park, by local sculptor Paul Dardé. This unsettling *mise en scène* of civilians mourning a soldier who has fallen on the field is a departure from the usual stiff commemorations of the "Morts pour la France". More of his work is displayed at the town **museum** in the **Hôtel Fleury** on place Georges Auric

**12**

(Tues–Sun: June–Sept 10am–6pm; Oct–May 9am–noon & 2–6pm; €4.50; ☎04 67 88 86 10) and the **Halle Dardé** (daily 9am–7pm; free; ☎04 67 88 86 00) off the place du Marché. There's a big market on Saturdays, and local farmers bring in their produce three times a week in summer.

## ARRIVAL AND INFORMATION
LODÈVE

**By bus** The *gare routière* (☎04 67 88 86 44) is next to the tourist office. There are services to Montpellier (4 daily; 1hr–1hr 15min) and Millau (4 daily; 55min) and connections to other destinations via Clermont l'Hérault (6 daily; 25min). **Tourist office** 7 place de la République (May, June & Sept

Mon–Sat 9.30am–12.30pm & 2–6pm; July & Aug Mon–Sat 9.30am–12.30pm & 2–6pm, Sun 10.30am–12.30pm & 3.30–6pm; Oct–April Mon–Fri 9.30am–12.30pm & 2–6pm, Sat 9.30am–12.30pm; ☎04 67 88 86 44, ⓦlodeve.com).

## ACCOMMODATION

**Du Nord** 18 bd de la Liberté ☎04 67 44 10 08, ⓦhoteldunord-lodeve.fr. This friendly, family-run establishment offers large air-conditioned rooms, each

with TV, private bath and balcony, and larger rooms for families and groups. **€50**

# The Languedoc coast

On the face of it, the **Languedoc coast** isn't particularly enticing, lined with bleak beaches and treeless strands, often irritatingly windswept and cut off from the sea by marshy *étangs* (lagoons). The area does, however, have long hours of sunshine, 200km of only sporadically populated sand and relatively unpolluted water. Resorts – mostly geared towards families who settle in for a few weeks at a time – have sprung up, sometimes engulfing once quiet fishing towns, but there's still enough unexploited territory to make this coast a good getaway from the crowds, and many of the old towns have managed to sustain their character and traditions despite the summer onslaught.

## The coast east of Montpellier

The oldest of the new resorts, on the fringes of the Camargue, **LA GRANDE-MOTTE** is a 1960s vintage beach-side Antigone – a "futuristic" planned community which has aged as gracefully as the bean bag and eight-track tape. In summer, its seaside and streets are crowded with semi-naked bodies; in winter, it's a depressing, wind-battered place with few permanent residents.

### Le Grau-Du-Roi

A little way east of La Grande-Motte are **Port-Camargue**, with a sprawling, modern marina, and **LE GRAU-DU-ROI**, which manages to retain something of its character as a working fishing port. Tourist traffic still has to give way every afternoon at 4.30pm when the swing bridge opens and lets in the trawlers to unload the day's catch onto the quayside, from where it's whisked off to auction – *la criée* – now conducted largely by electronic means rather than shouting.

### Aigues-Mortes

The town of **AIGUES-MORTES** ("dead waters") was built as a fortress port by Louis IX in the thirteenth century for his departure on the Seventh Crusade. Its massive walls and towers remain virtually intact. Outside the ramparts, amid drab modern development, flat saltpans lend a certain otherworldly appeal, but inside all is geared to tourism. If you visit, consider a climb up the **Tour de Constance** (daily 10am–5.30/7pm; €9; ☎04 66 53 61 55, ⓦmonuments-nationaux.fr) on the northwest corner of the town walls, where Camisard women were imprisoned (one such, Marie Durand, was incarcerated here for 38 years); or take and a walk along the wall, where you can gaze out over the weird mist-shrouded flats of the Camargue.

## ACCOMMODATION

**THE COAST EAST OF MONTPELLIER**

**Les Arcades** 23 bd Gambetta, Aigues-Mortes ☎ 04 66 53 81 13, ⓦ les-arcades.fr. This fine hotel is set within a renovated, listed sixteenth-century home tucked within the walls of Aigues-Mortes. There are nine individually appointed, en-suite and air-conditioned rooms, with a swimming pool and free indoor parking. **€106**

**Azur Bord de Mer** Place Justin, La Grande Motte ☎ 04 67 56 56 00, ⓦ hotelazur.net. Set dramatically on the

extremity of the quay, this is the most appealing among the town's dozen or so near-identical hotels, its en-suite rooms featuring flatscreen TV and queen beds. **€90**

**Camping le Garden** Av de la Petite Motte, La Grande Motte ☎ 04 67 56 50 09, ⓦ legarden.fr. A good campsite with excellent facilities a couple of minutes' walk from the beach (two-night minimum in high season). Closed Nov–April. **€44**

## Sète

Some 28km southeast of Montpellier, twenty minutes away by train, **SÈTE** has been an important port for three hundred years. The upper part of the town straddles the slopes of the Mont St-Clair, which overlooks the vast Bassin de Thau, a breeding ground of mussels and oysters, while the lower part is intersected by waterways lined with tall terraces and seafood restaurants. Sète's crowded and vibrant pedestrian streets are scattered with café tables, and the town has a lively workaday bustle in addition to its tourist activity. Things are at their height during the summer *joutes nautiques* (see box below).

A short climb up from the harbour is the **cimetière marin**, the sailors' cemetery, where poet Paul Valéry is buried. Near the cemetery, the small **Musée Paul Valéry**, 148 rue Denoyer (April–Oct daily 9.30am–7pm; Nov–March Tues–Sun 10am–6pm; €7; ☎ 04 99 04 76 16, ⓦ museepaulvalery-sete.fr), and the **Éspace Brassens**, 67 bd Camille Blanc (June–Sept daily 10am–6pm; Oct–May Tues–Sun 10am–noon & 2–6pm; €5; ☎ 04 99 04 76 26, ⓦ espace-brassens.fr), dedicated to the locally born singer-songwriter George Brassens, will be of little interest to non-fans. More intriguing is the found art collection at the **Musée International des Arts Modestes** at 23 Quai Maréchal de Lattre de Tassigny (July & Aug daily 10am–noon & 2–6pm; Sept–June closed Mon; €5; ☎ 04 67 18 64 00, ⓦ miam.org).

**12**

## ARRIVAL AND INFORMATION

**SÈTE**

**By train** The *gare SNCF* (ⓦ ter-sncf.com), on the main Nîmes-Toulouse line, lies 1km north of the tourist office on place André Cambon.

**By bus** Regular buses to Montpellier (3–15 daily; 1hr 5min) arrive at the *gare routière*, on quai de la République, on the eastern edge of the town centre.

**By ferry** Ferries for Morocco (1–2 weekly) and Mallorca (1–3 weekly) depart from the *gare maritime* at 4 quai

d'Alger (☎ 04 67 46 68 00).

**Tourist office** 60 Grand'rue Mario-Roustan (April–Oct daily 9.30am–6/7pm; Nov–March Mon–Fri 9.30am–5.30pm, Sat 9.30am–12.30pm & 2–5.30pm, Sun 9.30am–1pm; ☎ 04 67 74 71 71, ⓦ ot-sete.fr). They have a good array of English-language information, and sell the €14 "City Pass" that gives entry to all three of the town's museums.

## ACCOMMODATION AND EATING

**Grand Hôtel** 17 quai de Lattre-de-Tassigny ☎ 04 67 74 71 77, ⓦ legrandhotelsete.com. This artily renovated hotel, dating from 1882, combines *belle époque* splendour with modern touches. Rooms are luxurious, service is impeccable, and amenites include a pool and gym. **€100**

★ **L'Orque Bleu** 10 quai Aspirant-Herber ☎ 04 67 74 72 13, ⓦ hotel-orquebleue-sete.com. A charmingly sophisticated B&B/hotel overlooking the main canal and fishing port. Request a canal-side room for an ideal vantage for water-jousting. Rooms have internet, en-suite bath and satellite TV. **€94**

---

### JOUTES NAUTIQUES

**Water-jousting** is a venerable Languedoc tradition that pits boat-borne jousting teams against each other in an effort to unseat their opponents. Two sleek boats, each manned by eight oarsmen and bearing a lance-carrying jouster, charge at each other on a near head-on course. As the boats approach, the jousters attempt to strike their adversary from his mount. There are about a dozen *sociétés des joutes* in Sète itself, and you can see them in action all through the summer.

★ **La Palangrotte** Rampe Paul Valéry ☎ 04 67 74 80 35. This local standby is famous for its mussels and bouillabaisse and solid wine list. Reservations recommended. Meals from €25. Tues & Wed–Sat

noon–2pm & 7–9.30pm, Sun noon–2pm.
**Villa Salis** 7 rue du Général Revest ☎ 04 67 53 46 68, ⓦ fuaj.org. The HI hostel is high up on the hill above town. Closed Dec to mid-March. **€20**

## Agde and around

Midway between Sète and Béziers, at the western end of the Bassin de Thau, the old town of **AGDE** is the most interesting of the coastal towns. Originally Phoenician, and maintained by the Romans, it thrived for centuries on trade with the Levant. Outrun as a seaport by Sète, it later degenerated into a sleepy fishing harbour.

Today, it's a major tourist centre with a good deal of charm, notably in the narrow back lanes between rue de l'Amour and the riverside, where fishing boats tie up. There are few sights apart from the impressively fortified **cathedral**, though the **waterfront** is attractive, and by the bridge you can watch the Canal du Midi slip modestly into the River Hérault on the very last leg of its journey from Toulouse to the Bassin de Thau and Sète.

### Cap d'Agde

**CAP D'AGDE** lies to the south of Mont St-Loup, 7km from Agde. The largest (and by far the most successful) of the newer resorts, it sprawls out from the volcanic mound of St-Loup in an excess of pseudo-traditional buildings that offer every type of facility and entertainment – all of which are expensive. It is perhaps best known for its colossal **Village Naturiste**, one of the largest in France, with the best of the beaches, space for 20,000 visitors, and its own restaurants, banks, post offices and shops. Access is possible if you're not actually staying there (visitors to 8pm only; €15 per car, €6 on foot; ☎ 04 62 32 16 51, ⓦ villagenaturiste-agde.com). If you have time to fill, head for the **Musée de l'Éphèbe**, Mas de la Clape (Sept–June Wed–Mon 9am–noon & 2–6pm, July & Aug daily 9.30am–6.30pm; €4.70; ☎ 04 6794 69 60), which displays antiquities discovered locally, including many unique and rare pieces drawn from the sea around here.

### ARRIVAL AND INFORMATION
AGDE AND AROUND

**By train** The *gare SNCF* is at the end of av Victor-Hugo. Destinations Avignon (12 daily; 1hr 40min–2hr 19min); Narbonne (16 daily; 30min); Nîmes (16 daily; 1hr 10min); Perpignan (12 daily; 1hr 10min); Toulouse (8 daily; 1hr 45min–2hr 15min).

**By bus** Hourly buses run between Agde and Cap d'Agde, stopping at the *gare SNCF*, the bridge and La Promenade.

**Tourist office** Rond-point du Bon Accueil, the roundabout at the entrance to Cap d'Agde, travelling from the *cité*

(April, May & Sept daily 9am–12.30pm & 2–7pm; June–Aug daily 9am–7/8pm; Oct & Nov daily 9am–noon & 2–5/6pm; Dec–March Mon–Sat 9am–noon & 2–5/6pm; ☎ 04 67 01 04 04, ⓦ capdagde.com).

**Boat tours** Boat trips of the Canal du Midi and the coast are organized by Le Millésime (from €6; ☎ 04 67 01 71 93, ⓦ agde-croisiere-peche.com), Trans Cap (from €6; ⓦ transcapcroisieres.com) and Agde Croisières (€18/day; ☎ 04 67 21 38 72, ⓦ agde-brescou-croisieres.com).

### ACCOMMODATION

**Le Donjon** Place Jean Jaurès ☎ 04 67 94 12 32, ⓦ hotelagde.com. The best deal in the old town, just a short walk from the *gare SNCF*. Set in a renovated medieval building, the en-suite rooms are comfortable and colourful. Garage parking is available for a fee. **€48**

**La Voile d'Or** Place du Globe, Cap d'Agde ☎ 04 67 01 04 11, ⓦ lavoiledor.com. This modern resort-style place may lack atmosphere but offers spacious rooms with private terraces and lots of amenities. It has two pools and is a stroll away from the seaside. Closed mid-Nov to Feb. **€132**

### EATING

**Le Jardin de Beaumont** Rte de Florensac ☎ 04 67 21 19 23, ⓦ beaumont-holidays.com. A wine *domaine* 3km north of Agde, where you can dine on tapas and local specialites, and enjoy excellent wines indoors or out. *Menus* €16–25. July & Aug daily noon–2pm & 7–10pm; Sept–June Thurs–Sat noon–2pm & 7pm, Sun–Wed noon–2pm.

**La Table de Stéphane** 2 rue du Moulins à Huile ☎ 04 67 26 45 22, ⓦ latabledestephane.com. This famous local restaurant, set about 2km east of Agde's old town, features elaborate creations such as jellied oysters in squid ink. *Menus* from €45. Tues–Fri noon–2pm & 7–9.30pm, Sat 7–9.30pm, Sun noon–2pm.

# Southern Languedoc

**Southern Languedoc** presents an exciting and varied landscape, its coastal flats stretching south from the mouth of the Aude towards Perpignan, interrupted by occasional low, rocky hills. Just inland sits **Béziers**, its imposing cathedral set high above the languid River Orb, girded in the north by the amazingly preserved Renaissance town of **Pézenas** and in the south by the pre-Roman settlement of the **Ensérune**. It's also a gateway to the spectacular uplands of the **Monts de l'Espinouse** and the **Parc Naturel Régional du Haut Languedoc**, a haven for ramblers. Just south of Béziers, the ancient Roman capital of **Narbonne** guards the mouth of the Aude. Following the course of this river, which is shadowed by the historic **Canal du Midi**, you arrive at the quintessential medieval citadel, the famous fortress town of **Carcassonne**. Once a shelter for renegade **Cathar** heretics, this is also a fine departure point for the Cathar castles – a string of romantic ruins.

## Béziers

Though no longer the rich city of its nineteenth-century heyday, **BÉZIERS** has admirable panache. The town is the capital of the Languedoc **wine** country and a focus for the **Occitan** movement, as well as being the birthplace of Resistance hero **Jean Moulin**. Today local resistance takes the form of the CRIV, a radical clandestine group championing the area's besieged vintners, which occasionally employs modest but violent acts of terrorism. The town is also home to two great Languedocian adopted traditions: English **rugby** and the Spanish **corrida**, both of which are followed with a passion. The best time to visit is during the mid-August **feria**, a raucous four-day party that can be enjoyed even if bullfighting isn't to your taste.

**12**

### Cathédrale St-Nazaire

Plan des Albigeois • ☎ 04 67 76 50 80

The finest view of the Old Town is from the west, as you come in from Carcassonne: crossing the willow-lined River Orb by the Pont-Neuf, you can look upstream at the sturdy arches of the **Pont-Vieux**, above which rises a steep-banked hill crowned by the **Cathédrale St-Nazaire** which, with its crenellated towers, resembles a castle more than a church. The best approach to the cathedral is up the medieval lanes at the end of Pont-Vieux, rue Canterelles and passage Canterellettes. Its architecture is mainly Gothic, the original building having burned down in 1209 during the sacking of Béziers, when Armand Amaury's crusaders massacred some seven thousand people at the church of the Madeleine for refusing to hand over about twenty Cathars. "Kill them all", the pious abbot is said to have ordered, "God will recognize his own!"

From the top of the cathedral **tower**, there's a superb view out across the vine-dominated surrounding landscape. Keep an eye on small children, however, lest they slip through the potentially perilous gaps in the wall. Next door, you can wander through the ancient **cloister** and out into the shady **bishop's garden** overlooking the river.

### Musée des Beaux-Arts

Place de la Révolution • Tues–Sun: July & Aug 10am–5/6pm • €2.90; ticket includes entrance to Hôtel Fayet • ☎ 04 67 28 38 78, ⓦ ville-beziers.fr/culture/02.cfm

Steps away from the cathedral, **place de la Révolution** is home to the **Musée des Beaux-Arts** which, apart from an interesting collection of Greek Cycladic vases, won't keep you long.

### Musée du Biterrois

Caserne Saint-Jacques Rampe du 96ème • Tues–Sun: July & Aug 10am–5/6pm • €2.90 • ☎ 04 67 36 81 61, ⓦ ville-beziers.fr

The **Musée du Biterrois** holds an important collection ranging from locally produced pottery to funerary monuments and artefacts dredged from ancient shipwrecks, but the highlight is the "treasure of Béziers" – a rich cache of silver platters found in a nearby field.

## ARRIVAL AND INFORMATION

**By train** From the *gare SNCF* on bd Verdun, the best way into town is through the landscaped gardens of the Plateau des Poètes opposite the station entrance and up the allées Paul-Riquet.

Destinations Agde (18 daily; 45min); Arles (10–14 daily; 2hr 10min); Avignon (4–10 daily; 2hr); Bédarieux (4–8 daily; 40min); Carcassonne (22 daily; 45min–1hr 45min); Clermont-Ferrand (3 daily; 6–7hr); Marseille (8 daily; 3hr 10min); Millau (4–6 daily; 2hr); Montpellier (26 daily; 45min); Narbonne (18 daily; 14min); Nîmes (20 daily; 1hr 15min); Paris (30 daily; 4hr 30min–12hr); Perpignan (18 daily; 40min–1hr); Sète (23 daily; 25min).

**By bus** The *gare routière* (☎ 04 67 28 36 41, ⓦ busoccitan

.com) is on Place de Gaulle, at the northern end of the *allées*. Destinations Agde (2 daily; 4–6 daily in summer; 25min); Bédarieux (generally up to 2 daily; 1hr); Castres (2 daily; 2hr 50min); La Salvetat (generally up to 2 daily; 2hr 10min); Mazamet (2 daily; 2hr); Pézenas (4–11 daily; 32min); St-Pons-de-Thomières (4 daily; 1hr 20min).

**Tourist office** A new tourist office is slated to open at 2 place Gabriel Péri in 2013 (daily 9am–6/7pm; ☎ 04 67 76 20 20, ⓦ beziers-mediterranee.com).

**Bike rental** If you fancy pottering along the Canal du Midi, rent a bike at La Maison du Canal, 32 bd Pasteur ☎ 04 67 62 18 18, ⓦ maisonducanal.fr) beside the Pont-Neuf, south of the *gare SNCF*.

## ACCOMMODATION

**Les Berges du Canal** 2120 rte de Narbonne ☎ 04 67 39 36 09, ⓦ lesbergesducanal.com. The nearest campsite to Béziers is outside Villeneuve-lès-Béziers, about 4km southeast of the town centre. Closed Nov–Feb. €21

**Impérator** 28 allées Paul-Riquet ☎ 04 67 49 02 25, ⓦ hotel-imperator.fr. A notch above the rest but still an excellent deal, this hotel is set in a gracious renovated

mansion. Rooms come with en-suite bath, TV and air-conditioning. €83

**Des Poètes** 80 allées Paul-Riquet ☎ 04 67 76 38 66, ⓦ hoteldespoetes.net. Set at the southern end of the allées overlooking a garden, this basic but pleasant hotel offers free garage parking and free bike loan, and comfortable, if plain, rooms. €45

## EATING

**L'Ambassade** 22 bd de Verdun ☎ 04 67 76 06 24, ⓦ restaurant-lambassade.com. Béziers's top-rated restaurant, under the direction of well-known chef, Patrick Orly, and sommelier Karim Rabatel. Cuisine is elaborate *terroir* with a wide selection of meat and fish dishes. *Menus*

€29–65. Tues–Sat noon–2pm & 7–9.30pm.

★ **Le Cep d'Or** 2 Impasse de la Notarie ☎ 04 67 49 28 09. A bistro with a charming old-fashioned air, serving mostly seafood. *Menus* €15–23. Mon–Sat noon–2pm & 7–9pm, Sun 10am–noon. Closed Mon out of season.

# Pézenas

**PÉZENAS** lies 18km east of Béziers on the old N9. Market centre of the coastal plain, it looks across to rice fields and shallow lagoons, hazy in the heat and dotted with pink flamingos. The town was catapulted to glory when it became the seat of the parliament of Languedoc and the residence of its governors in 1465, and reached its zenith in the late seventeenth century when the prince Armand de Bourbon made it a "second Versailles". The legacy of this illustrious past can be seen in the town's exquisite array of fourteenth- to seventeenth-century mansions. Pézenas also plays up its association with **Molière**, who visited several times with his troupe in the mid-seventeenth century, when he enjoyed the patronage of Prince Armand, and put on plays at the **Hôtel d'Alfonce** on rue Conti.

## Musée Vulliod St-Germain

3 rue Albert Paul Allies • June–Sept Tues–Sun 10am–noon & 3–7pm; Oct–May Tues–Sun 10am–noon & 2–5pm • €2.50 • ☎ 04 67 98 90 59, ⓦ ville-pezenas.fr

Although Molière features in the eclectic **Musée Vulliod St-Germain**, housed in a sixteenth-century palace tucked away in the north end of the old town, it's the grand salon, with its Aubusson tapestries and seventeenth- and eighteenth-century furniture, that steals the show.

## The town mansions

The tourist office, at the main entrance to the Old Town, distributes a guide to all the town's eminent houses, taking in the former **Jewish ghetto** on rue des Litanies and rue Juiverie, but you can just as easily follow the explanatory plaques posted all over the centre, starting at the east end of rue François-Outrin where it leaves the town's main square, place du 14-juillet.

### ARRIVAL AND INFORMATION
PÉZENAS

**By bus** The *gare routière* is opposite the square on the riverbank, with buses to Montpellier, Béziers and Agde.

**Tourist office** Place des États du Languedoc (July & Aug Mon, Tues, Thurs & Sat 9am–7pm, Wed & Fri 9am–10pm, Sun 10am–7pm; Sept–June Mon–Sat 9am–noon &

2–6pm, Sun 10am–noon & 2–5pm; ☎04 67 98 36 40, ⓦ pezenas-tourisme.fr).

**Market** There's a huge market each Sat on cours Jean Jaurès, along the river.

### ACCOMMODATION

**Molière** 18 place du 14-juillet ☎04 67 98 14 00, ⓦ hotel-le-moliere.com. Charming nineteenth-century hotel on the edge of the old town, with en-suite rooms (with internet) and a lovely old salon. **€79**

**Le Saint Germain** 6 av Paul Vidal ☎04 67 98 14 00, ⓦ hotel-saintgermain.com. Functional, but with a small pool and private parking, and en-suite rooms decorated in cool, muted colours. **€70**

### EATING

Anyone with a sweet tooth should sample two local delicacies: flavoured sugar-drops called *berlingots*, and *petits pâtés* – bobbin-shaped pastries related to mince pies, reputedly introduced by the Indian cook of Clive of India, who stayed in Pézenas in 1770.

**Les Palmiers** 50 rue de Mercière ☎04 67 09 42 56. A beautiful and welcoming establishment serving inventive Mediterranean-style food. This is not haute

cuisine, but the menu features a variety of excellently prepared dishes. A full meal will set you back around €30. Mon–Sat noon–2pm & 7–9.30pm.

# Narbonne and around

On the Toulouse–Nice main train line, 25km west of Béziers, is **NARBONNE**, once the capital of Rome's first colony in Gaul, Gallia Narbonensis, and a thriving port in classical times and the Middle Ages. Plague, war with the English, and the silting up of its harbour finished it off in the fourteenth century. Today, it's a pleasant provincial city with a small but well-kept Old Town, dominated by the great truncated choir of its cathedral and bisected by a grassy esplanade on the banks of the Canal de la Robine.

## The Horreum

7 Rue Rouget de Lisle • Daily: June–Sept 10am–6pm; Oct–May 10am–noon & 2–5pm • €6 • ☎04 68 32 45 30, ⓦ mairie-narbonne.fr

One of the few Roman remnants in Narbonne is the **Horreum**, at the north end of rue Rouget-de-l'Isle, an unusual underground grain store divided into a series of small chambers leading off a rectangular passageway.

## Cathédrale St-Just-et-St-Pasteur

Rue Armand Gauthier • **Salle du Trésor** July–Sept daily (except Tues morning) 10–11.45am & 2–5.45pm; Oct–June daily 2–5pm • €2.20 • ☎04 68 32 09 82, ⓦ narbonne-tourisme.com

At the opposite end of Rouget-de-l'Isle from the Horreum, close to the attractive tree-lined banks of the **Canal de la Robine**, is Narbonne's other principal attraction, the enormous Gothic **Cathédrale St-Just-et-St-Pasteur**. With the Palais des Archevêques and its 40m-high keep, it forms a massive pile of masonry that dominates the restored lanes of the Old Town. In spite of its size, this is actually only the choir of a much more ambitious church, whose construction was halted to avoid wrecking the city walls. The immensely tall interior has some beautiful fourteenth-century stained glass in the chapels on the northeast side of the apse and imposing Aubusson tapestries – one of the most valuable of these is kept in the **Salle du Trésor**, along with a small collection of ecclesiastical treasures.

## Museum of Art and Archaeology Museum

Place de l'Hôtel-de-Ville • Daily: June–Sept 10am–6pm; Oct–May 10am–noon & 2–5pm • €6 • ☎ 04 68 65 15 60, Ⓦ narbonne-tourisme.com

The **place de l'Hôtel-de-Ville**, next to the cathedral, is dominated by the great towers of St-Martial, the Madeleine and Bishop Aycelin's keep. From there the passage de l'Ancre leads through to the **Palais des Archevêques** (Archbishops' Palace), which houses a fairly ordinary **Museum of Art** and a good **Archaeology Museum**, whose interesting Roman remains include a massive 3.5m wood and lead ship's rudder, and a huge mosaic.

## Abbey de Fontfroide

Fontfroide, 15km southwest of Narbonne • Guided tours daily: April–June & Sept 10am–12.15pm & 1.45pm–5.30pm; July & Aug 10am–6pm; Oct 10am–12.15pm & 1.45pm–4.45pm; Nov–March 10am–noon & 2–4pm • €10 • ☎ 04 68 41 02 26, Ⓦ fontfroide.com

A good side trip from Narbonne – just 15km southwest, but impossible without transport of your own – is the lovely **Abbey de Fontfroide**, which enjoys a beautiful location tucked into a fold in the dry cypress-clad hillsides. The extant buildings go back to the twelfth century, with some elegant seventeenth-century additions in the entrance and courtyards, and were in use from their foundation until 1900, first by Benedictines, then Cistercians. It was one of the Cistercian monks, Pierre de Castelnau, whose murder as papal legate set off the Albigensian Crusade against the Cathars in 1208.

Visits to the restored abbey are only possible on a **guided tour**. Star features include the cloister, with its marble pillars and giant wisteria creepers, the church itself, some fine ironwork and a rose garden. The stained glass in the windows of the lay brothers' dormitory consists of fragments from churches in north and eastern France damaged in World War I.

**12**

### ARRIVAL AND INFORMATION
### NARBONNE AND AROUND

**By train** Narbonne is on the main train lines to Perpignan, Toulouse and Nîmes; the *gare SNCF* is at 1 bd Frédéric Mistral on the northwest side of town.

**By bus** Buses to Gruissan (3–6 daily; 45min) and Narbonne-Plage (2–8 daily; 45min) stop at the *gare routière*, next to the train station.

**Tourist office** 31 rue Jean Jaurès, next to the cathedral (April to mid-Sept daily 9am–7pm; mid-Sept to March Mon–Sat 10am–12.30pm & 1.30–6pm, Sun 9am–1pm; ☎ 04 68 65 15 60, Ⓦ narbonne-tourisme.fr).

### ACCOMMODATION

★ **Grand Hôtel du Languedoc** 22 bd Gambetta ☎ 04 68 65 14 74, Ⓦ hoteldulanguedoc.com. Set in a dignified nineteenth-century house in the heart of the old town, with elegant en-suite rooms. There is secure parking and the reception is open 24hr. **€64**

**Les Mimosas** Chaussée de Mandirac ☎ 04 68 49 03 72, Ⓦ lesmimosas.com. The nearest campsite is 6km south of Narbonne on the Étang de Bages (there is no public transport). **€35**

**MJC Centre International de Séjour** Place Salengro ☎ 04 68 32 01 00, Ⓦ cis-narbonne.com. The best budget accommodation in town is this modern, friendly and completely accessible youth hostel. **€22.60**

**Will's Hotel** 23 av Pierre-Sémard ☎ 04 68 90 44 50, Ⓦ willshotel-narbonne.com. A homely backpackers' favourite near the station, set in a 150-year-old house. Spacious rooms feature a/c and en-suite showers. The management is very welcoming and English is spoken. **€61**

### EATING

★ **L'Ecrivesse s'Alsace** 1 av Pierre-Sémard ☎ 04 68 65 10 24, Ⓦ restaurant-lecrevisse.com. This is Narbonne's best restaurant, hands down, featuring mammoth servings of excellent *terroir* and northeastern French dishes, plus local seafood – baked *loup de mer* is the house speciality. Meals from €20. Mon, Tues & Thurs–Sat noon–2pm & 7–10pm. Closed part Feb and 4 weeks in summer.

**L'Estagnol** 5 Cours Mirabeau ☎ 04 68 65 09 27, Ⓦ lestagnol.fr. Across the canal from the old town, this local favourite attracts the crowds with its simple, good-value food. *Menus* €11–32. Mon–Sat noon–3pm & 7.30–11.30pm.

**FROM TOP** PONT DU GARD (P.644); ST-GUILHEM VILLAGE (P.649) >

## Parc Naturel Régional du Haut Languedoc

Embracing Mont Caroux in the east and the Montagne Noire in the west, the **Parc Naturel Régional du Haut Languedoc** is the southernmost extension of the Massif Central. The west, above Castres and Mazamet, is Atlantic in feel and climate, with deciduous forests and lush valleys, while the east is dry, craggy and calcareous. Except in high summer you can have it almost to yourself. Buses serve the Orb valley – where you'll find the small, unremarkable town of Bédarieux – and cross the centre of the park to **La Salvetat** and **Lacaune**, but you really need transport of your own to make the most of it.

### Olargues

Near the eastern edge of the park sits the medieval village of **OLARGUES**, scrambling up the south bank of the Jaur above its thirteenth-century single-span bridge. The steep twisting streets, presumably almost unchanged since the bridge was built, lead up to a thousand-year-old belfry crowning the top of the hill. With the river and gardens below, the ancient and earth-brown farms on the infant slopes of Mont Caroux beyond, and swifts swirling round the tower in summer, you get a powerful sense of age and history.

### St-Pons-de-Thomières

**ST-PONS-DE-THOMIÈRES**, 18km west of Olargues, is on the Béziers–Castres and Béziers–La Salvetat bus routes, as well as the Bédarieux–Mazamet route. This is the "capital" of the park, with the **Maison du Parc** housed in the local **tourist office**. Sights include the **cathedral** (July & Aug 8am–6pm; Sept–June Wed 9am–2pm, Thurs–Tues 9am–6pm) – a strange mix of Romanesque and classical – and a small and reasonably interesting **Musée de Préhistoire Régionale**, which is across the river from the tourist office (July to mid-Sept Tues 10am–noon & 3–6pm; April–June Thurs–Sun 3–6pm; €3.50; ☎04 67 97 22 61).

### The park's uplands

The uplands of the park are wild and little travelled, dominated by the towering peak of **Mont Caroux** and stretching west along the ridge of the **Monts de l'Espinouse**. This is prime hiking territory, where thick forest of stunted oak alternates with broad mountain meadows, opening up on impressive vistas. Civilization appears again to the west in the upper Agout valley, where **Fraïsse** and **La Salvetat** have become thriving bases for outdoor recreation, and to the north, at the medieval spa town of **Lacaune**. There's no transport crossing the uplands, but the D180 takes you from Le Poujol-sur-Orb, 2km west of Lamalou-les-Bains, to Mont Caroux and L'Espinouse.

#### Into the Agout valley

The D180 is the most spectacular way to climb into the park. Soon after leaving the main highway, you'll pass the **Forêt des Écrivains-Combattants**, named after the French writers who died in World War I. Just above the hamlet of Rosis, the road levels out in a small mountain valley, whose slopes are brilliant yellow with broom in June. Continuing north, the D180 climbs another 12km above deep ravines, offering spectacular views to the summit of **L'Espinouse**. The Col de l'Ourtigas is a good place to stretch your legs and take in the grandeur. Here the landscape changes from Mediterranean cragginess to marshy moor-like meadow and big conifer plantations, and the road begins to descend west into the valley of the River Agout. It runs through tiny Salvergues, with its plain workers' cottages and a striking fortress-church; Cambon, where the natural woods begin; and postcard-pretty **Fraïsse-Sur-Agout**.

#### La Salvetat-Sur-Agout

**LA SALVETAT-SUR-AGOUT** is an attractive mountain town 10km west of Fraïsse between the artificial lakes of La Raviège and Laouzas. Built on a hill above the river, with car-wide streets and houses clad in huge slate tiles, it's usually half asleep except at holiday time, when it becomes a busy outdoor activities centre.

## Lacaune and around

**LACAUNE** makes a pleasant stop if you're crossing the park. Set 45km east of Castres, surrounded by rounded wooded heights, it's very much a mountain town. It was one of the centres of Protestant Camisard resistance at the end of the seventeenth century, when its inaccessibility was ideal for clandestine worship. The air is fresh, and the town, though somewhat grey in appearance because of the slates and drab stucco common throughout the region, is cheerful enough.

From Lacaune to Castres the most agreeable route is along the wooded **Gijou valley**, following the now defunct train track, past minuscule Gijounet and **LACAZE**, where a nearly derelict **château** strikes a picturesque pose in a bend of the river.

## ARRIVAL AND INFORMATION     PARC NATUREL RÉGIONAL DU HAUT LANGUEDOC

### BÉDARIEUX
**By train and bus** The *gare SNCF* in place Pierre Seymard on the southwest edge of the old town, meets trains from Béziers (4–6 daily; 35–45min), and buses from Béziers (Mon–Sat 3 daily; 1hr 30min), Montpellier (1–4 daily; 1hr 25min) and St-Pons via Olargues (1–4 daily; 40min–1hr 10min).
**Tourist office** Place aux Herbes (Mon–Fri 9am–noon & 2–6pm, Sat 9am–noon; ☎ 04 67 95 08 79, 🌐 bedarieux.fr).

### OLARGUES
**Tourist office** Av de la Gare (April–June & Sept Tues–Sat 9am–noon & 2–6pm; July & Aug Mon–Sat 9am–1pm & 3.30–7pm, Sun 9am–1opm; Oct–March Tues–Sat 10am–noon & 2–5pm; ☎ 04 67 97 71 26, 🌐 olargues.org).

### ST-PONS-DE-THOMIÈRES
**By bus** There are buses to St-Pons from Castres (Mon–Sat 1–4 daily; 1hr–1hr 30min) and La-Salvetat (Mon–Sat 2 daily; 40min).

### LA SALVETAT-SUR-AGOUT
**Tourist office** Place des Archers (June & Sept Mon–Fri 9am–noon & 2–6pm, Sat 10am–noon & 2–6pm, Sun 10am–12.30pm; July & Aug Mon–Fri 9am–1pm & 2–7pm, Sat 10am–12.30pm & 3–6pm, Sun 10am–12.30pm; Nov–May Mon–Fri 9am–noon & 2–6pm; ☎ 04 67 97 64 44, 🌐 salvetat-tourisme.fr).

### LACAUNE
**By bus** Buses from Castres stop at Lacaune (Mon–Sat 1–4 daily; 50min).
**Tourist office** Place de la République (mid-June to mid-Sept Mon–Fri 9am–12.30pm & 2–6.30pm, Sat & Sun 10am–noon & 2–6.30pm; mid-Sept to mid-June Mon–Sat 9/10am–noon & 2–5pm; ☎ 05 63 37 04 98, 🌐 lacaune .com). You can rent bikes here.

## ACCOMMODATION AND EATING

### BEDARIEUX
**La Forge** 22 av Abbé Tarroux ☎ 04 67 95 13 13. An excellent restaurant with a cosy, vaulted dining-room and *terroir menus* from €16. Tues & Thurs–Sat noon–2pm & 7–9.30pm, Mon 7–9.30pm, Wed & Sun noon–2pm. Closed part Nov & part Jan.
**De l'Orb** Parc Phoros, Rte de Saint Pons ☎ 04 67 23 35 90, 🌐 hotel-orb.com. This is the town's only hotel: a decent, if basic, place. Located on the south end of town along av Jean Jaurès, about 500m south of the Pont Vieux. All rooms are en suite. €51

### OLARGUES
**La Baous** North of Olargues ☎ 04 67 97 71 50, 🌐 campingolargues.com. This beautiful, riverside campsite is just a 5min walk north of town. Closed

Sept–April. €13.60
★ **Les Quatr' Farceurs** Rue de la Comporte (☎ 04 67 97 81 33, 🌐 olargues.co.uk). This friendly, English-owned B&B is widely recognized as one of the area's best accommodation options. The rooms are comfortable, if basic, and the abundant home-cooked meals (€25) are accompanied by free-flowing wine. €47

### ST-PONS-DE-THOMIÈRES
★ **Bergeries de Ponderach** 1km east of town ☎ 04 67 97 02 57, 🌐 bergeries-ponderach.fr. Deluxe accommodation in a luxurious seventeenth-century country estate with beautifully decorated rooms; the larger ones have kitchenettes. There is a big pool and an excellent restaurant with *menus* from €16. €85
**Les Cerisiers du Jaur** Les marbrières du Jaur ☎ 04 67 97

34 85, ⓦ cerisierdujaur.com. The well-equipped municipal campsite is on the main road east to Bédarieux. **€23**

#### LA SALVETAT-SUR-AGOUT
**La Plage** Lac de la Raviège ⓣ 04 67 97 69 87, ⓦ pageloisirs.com/hotel-la-plage. Inexpensive rooms and generous portions of home-cooked local food (from €12.50) on offer at this small lakeside hotel 1km from the town centre. **€52**

#### LACAUNE
**Calas** 4 place de la Vierge ⓣ 05 63 37 03 28, ⓦ pageloisirs.com/calas. This small hotel's main draw is not the pool or the comfortable and well-equipped rooms, but its highly praised, fourth-generation bistro, where house specialities include pigeon and pigs' feet with truffles. *Menus* €15–38. Restaurant Easter–Oct daily noon–1.30pm & 7.30–9pm; Oct–Easter Sun–Thurs noon–1.30pm & 7.30–9pm, Fri & Sat noon–1.30pm. **€40**

**Domaine Le Clot** Les Vidals ⓣ 05 63 37 03 59, ⓦ domaineleclot.com. The basic but beautifully sited municipal campsite is on the Murat road. Closed Nov–March. **€18.15**

## Carcassonne

Right on the main Toulouse–Montpellier train link, **CARCASSONNE** couldn't be easier to reach. For anyone travelling through this region it is a must – one of the most dramatic, if also most-visited, towns in the whole of Languedoc. Carcassonne owes its division into two separate "towns" to the wars against the Cathars. Following Simon de Montfort's capture of the town in 1209, its people tried in 1240 to restore their traditional ruling family, the Trencavels. In reprisal, King Louis IX expelled them from

**12**

### THE CANAL DU MIDI

The **Canal du Midi** runs for 240km from the River Garonne at Toulouse via Carcassonne to the Mediterranean at Agde. It was the brainchild of **Pierre-Paul Riquet**, a minor noble and tax collector, who succeeded in convincing Louis XIV (and more importantly, his first minister, Colbert) of the merits of linking the Atlantic and the Mediterranean via the Garonne.

The work, begun in 1667, took fourteen years to complete, using tens of thousands of workers. The crux of the problem from the engineering point of view was how to feed the canal with water when its high point at Naurouze, west of Carcassonne, was 190m above sea level and 58m above the Garonne at Toulouse. Riquet responded by building a system of reservoirs in the Montagne Noire, channelling run-off from the heights down to Naurouze. He spent the whole of his fortune on the canal and, sadly, died just six months before its inauguration in 1681.

The canal was a success and sparked a wave of prosperity along its course, with traffic increasing steadily until 1857, when the Sète–Bordeaux railway was opened, reducing trade on the canal to all but nothing. Today, the canal remains a marvel of engineering and beauty, incorporating no fewer than 99 locks (*écluses*) and 130 bridges, almost all of which date back to the first era of construction. The canal has, since its construction, been known for its lovely place trees lining the riverbank. Sadly, a wilt infection was discovered in 2006 and since then the trees have systematically been cut down. They will be replaced however, the view will not be the same for many of the years to come. You can follow it by road, and many sections have foot or bicycle paths, but the best way to see it is, of course, by boat. Outfits in all the major ports rent houseboats and barges, and there are many cruise options to choose from as well.

**Boat rental and cruises** Crown Blue Line (ⓣ 04 68 94 52 72, ⓦ crownblueline.com) or Locaboat (ⓣ 03 86 91 72 72, ⓦ locaboat.com), both have a number of branches in Languedoc and the Midi. For a green option, try the solar-powered 14-berth barges (accessible for passengers with mobility issues) available from Naviratous (from €700/week ⓣ 04 68 46 37 98, ⓦ naviratous2.com).

**Information** Voies Navigables de France, 2 Port St-Étienne in Toulouse (ⓣ 05 61 36 24 24, ⓦ vnf.fr); they also have English-speaking offices at the major canal ports.

the **Cité**, only permitting their return on condition they built on the low ground by the River Aude – what would become the **ville basse**.

A major summertime event worth catching is the **Festival de Carcassonne** from late June to mid-August, featuring world-class dance, theatre and music. The high point is the mammoth fireworks display on Bastille Day (July 14).

## The Cité

To reach the Cité from the *ville basse*, take bus #2 from outside the station, or a *navette* from Square Gambetta; you can walk it in less than 30min, crossing the Pont-Vieux and climbing rue Barbacane, past the church of St-Gimer to the sturdy bastion of the Porte d'Aude (this is effectively the back entrance – the main gate is Porte Narbonnaise, on the east side)

The attractions of the well-preserved and lively *ville basse* notwithstanding, everybody comes to Carcassonne to see the **Cité**, the double-walled and turreted fortress that crowns the hill above the River Aude. From a distance it's the epitome of the fairy-tale medieval town. Viollet-le-Duc rescued it from ruin in 1844, and his "too-perfect" restoration has been furiously debated ever since. It is, as you would expect, a real tourist trap. Yet, in spite of the chintzy cafés, crafty shops and the crowds, you'd have to be a very stiff-necked purist not to be moved at all.

### Château Comtal

1 rue Viollet-le-Duc • Daily: April–Sept 9.30am–6.30pm; Oct–March 9.30am–5pm; guided tours only, several in English • €8.50 • ☎ 04 68 11 70 70, ⓦ carcassonne.monuments-nationaux.fr

There is no charge for admission to the streets or the grassy *lices* – "lists" – between the walls, though cars are banned from 10am to 6pm. However, to see the inner fortress of the **Château Comtal** and walk the walls, you'll have to join a **guided tour**.

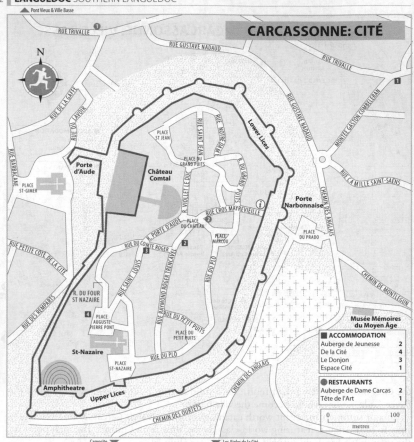

These assume some knowledge of French history, and point out the various phases in the construction of the fortifications, from Roman and Visigothic to Romanesque and the post-Cathar adaptations of the French kings.

### St-Nazaire

Place St-Nazaire • Mon–Fri 8.45am–12.45pm & 1.45–5/6pm, Sat & Sun 8.45–10.30am & 2–5/6pm • Free • ☎ 04 68 10 24 30 • ⓦ carcassonne.org

Don't miss the beautiful **church of St-Nazaire**, towards the southern corner of the Cité at the end of rue St-Louis. It's a serene combination of nave with carved capitals in the Romanesque style and a Gothic choir and transepts, along with some of the loveliest stained glass in Languedoc. In the south transept is a tombstone believed to belong to Simon de Montfort. You can also climb the **tower** for spectacular views over the Cité.

### ARRIVAL AND DEPARTURE
CARCASSONNE

**By plane** Carcassonne Airport lies just west of the city (☎ 04 68 71 96 46, ⓦ carcassonne.aeroport.fr). A *navette* (€5; hourly; 15min) leaves from outside the terminal and stops at the *gare SNCF*, square Gambetta and the Cité; a taxi

to the centre will cost €8–15.

**By train** The *gare SNCF* is in the *ville basse* on the north bank of the Canal du Midi at the northern limits of the old town.

Destinations Arles (4–8 daily; 2hr 40min–3hr 30min); Béziers (22 daily; 45min–1hr 45min); Bordeaux (18–22 daily; 3hr 20min–4hr 30min); Limoux (16 daily; 25min); Marseille (12–18 daily; 3hr 20min–5hr 30min); Montpellier (18 daily; 1hr 30min–4hr); Narbonne (22 daily; 35min); Nîmes (26 daily; 2hr 5min–3hr 10min); Quillan (6 daily; 1hr 15min); Toulouse (22 daily; 45min–1hr).

**By bus** The *gare routière* is a series of bus stops, with no actual building, located on bd de Varsovie on the northwest side of town, south of the canal.

## INFORMATION

**Tourist office** 28 rue Verdun (April–June, Sept & Oct Mon–Sat 9am–6pm, Sun 9am–1pm; July & Aug 9am–7pm; Nov–March Mon–Sat 9am–12.30pm & 1.30–6pm; ☎04 68 10 24 30, ⓦcarcassonne-tourisme.com). There's also an annexe (April–Oct daily 9am–5/6/7pm; Nov–March Sat & Sun 9am–5pm) just inside Porte Narbonnaise, the main gate to the Cité.

**Discount pass** If you are planning on visiting other medieval sites near Carcassonne (including the Cathar castles), you might buy the Passeporte aux Sites du Pays Cathares (€2), which gives you a discounted admission price to many castles and monuments.

## ACCOMMODATION

**Auberge de Jeunesse** Rue Trencavel ☎04 68 25 23 16, ⓦfuaj.org; map opposite. This modern, clean hostel, in the heart of the Cité, offers the cheapest accommodation in town and tends to get booked up well in advance. **€21.60**

**Campsite la Cité** Rte St-Hilaire ☎04 68 10 01 00, ⓦcampingcitecarcassonne.com; map p.661. Tucked away amid parkland to the south of town, the local campsite can be reached by local bus (line #8) or on foot (about 20min) from the Cité. Closed mid-Oct to March. Minimum stay of one week in July & Aug. **€27**

★ **De la Cité** Place Auguste-Pierre Pont ☎04 68 71 98 71, ⓦhoteldelacite.com; map opposite. Carcassonne's luxury option, with prices to match, featuring rooms and suites in an opulent medieval manor house, with a heated swimming pool and stunning views from the battlemented walls. **€358**

**Le Donjon** 2 rue Comte-Roger ☎04 68 11 23 00, ⓦhotel-donjon.fr; map opposite. A shade less luxurious than the *Cité* and a good deal less expensive, this hotel offers four-star amenities in a medieval building near the castle. The rooms are spacious and airy. **€150**

**Espace Cité** 132 rue Trivalle ☎04 68 25 24 24, ⓦhotelespacecite.fr; map opposite. Just outside the main gate of the Cité, and offering Carcassonne's best value for money – excellent location, en-suite rooms, mod cons and efficient service at reasonable prices. Rates include an all-you-can-eat breakfast buffet. **€80**

**Du Soleil Terminus** 2 av de Maréchal-Joffre ☎04 68 25 25 00, ⓦsoleilvacances.com; map p.661. A station-side hotel of decaying steam-age luxury, with a splendid *fin-de-siècle* facade. There is also a fitness centre with a pool, sauna, and hot tub, and bike rental available. **€120**

## EATING

**Auberge de Dame Carcas** 3 place du Château ☎04 68 71 23 23, ⓦdamecarcas.com; map opposite. A traditional bistro offering cassoulet and other regional dishes. *Menus* €15–26. Daily: July & Aug 11.30am–3pm & 6.30–11pm; Sept–June noon–2pm & 7–10pm.

★ **L'Écurie** 43 bd Barbès ☎04 68 72 04 04, ⓦrestaurant-lecurie.fr; map p.661. Sophisticated local cuisine with adventurous touches, such as roast lamb with thyme and garlic. *Menus* €15–30. Mon–Sat noon–1.30pm & 7–9.30pm; Sun noon–1.30pm.

**Roberto Rodriguez** 39 rue Coste Reboulh ☎04 68 47 37 80, ⓦrestaurantrobertrodriguez.com; map p.661. Carcassonne's most flamboyantly experimental restaurant combines local, fresh ingredients in inventive permutations. What's on offer changes according to season and the chef's inclinations, with *menus* at €40–70. Mon, Tues & Thurs–Sat noon–2.30pm & 7–9.30pm; Wed noon–2.30pm.

**Tête de l'Art** 37bis rue Trivalle ☎04 68 47 36 36; map opposite. This cheerful place has an arty atmosphere and excellent *terroir menus* from €16 to €34 with a filling vegetarian option at €13. Mon–Sat noon–2pm & 7–10pm.

# Castelnaudary

Some 36km west of Carcassonne, on the main road from Toulouse, **CASTELNAUDARY** is one of those innumerable French country towns that boasts no particular sights but is nonetheless a pleasure to spend a couple of hours in, having coffee or shopping in the market. Today it serves as an important commercial centre for the rolling Lauragais farming country hereabouts, as it once was for the traffic on the Canal du Midi. In fact,

12

the most flattering view of the town is still that from the canal's **Grand Bassin**, which makes it look remarkably like a Greek island town, with its ancient houses climbing the hillside from the water's edge. Castelnaudary's chief claim to fame is as the world capital of **cassoulet**, which, according to tradition, must be made in an earthenware pot from Issel (a *cassolo*) with beans grown in Pamiers or Lavelanet, and cooked in a baker's oven fired with rushes from the Montagne Noire.

## INFORMATION CASTELNAUDARY

**Tourist office** Place de la République (Mon–Sat 9.30am–noon & 2–6pm; ☎04 68 23 07 73, ⓦ castelnaudary-tourisme.com).

## ACCOMMODATION AND EATING

**La Belle Époque** 55 rue Général-Dejean ☎04 68 23 39 72, ⓦ labelleepoque-castelnaudary.com. This is one of the best places to try Castelnaudary's signature dish, the cassoulet. Otherwise there is a broad selection of regional meat, fish, and vegetarian options. *Menus* from €19. July & Aug daily noon–2pm & 7–9.30pm; April–June & Sept–Nov Thurs–Mon noon–2pm & 7–9.30pm;

Nov–March Mon & Thurs noon–2pm, Fri–Sun noon–2pm & 7–9.30pm.

**Du Canal** 88 av Arnaut-Vidal ☎04 68 94 05 05, ⓦ hotelducanal.com. A comfortable and beautifully located canalside hotel with large rooms. There is secure parking, a splendid terrace, and guests have use of a fridge and freezer. Family rooms are also available. **€70**

# The Montagne Noire

There are two good routes from Carcassonne north into the **Montagne Noire**, which forms the western extremity of the Parc Naturel Régional du Haut Languedoc: Carcassonne–Revel and Carcassonne–Mazamet by the valley of the Orbiel. Neither is served by public transport, but both offer superlative scenery.

## Montolieu

**MONTOLIEU**, semi-fortified and built on the edge of a ravine, has set itself the target of becoming France's **secondhand book capital**, with its shops overflowing with dog-eared and antiquarian tomes. Drop in to the Librairie Booth, by the bridge over the ravine, for English-language titles.

## Saissac

**SAISSAC**, 8km beyond Montolieu, is an upland village surrounded by conifers and beechwood, interspersed with patches of rough pasture, with gardens terraced down its steep slopes. Remains of towers and fortifications poke out among the ancient houses, and on a spur below the village stand the romantic ruins of its castle and the church of St-Michel.

## St-Papoul Abbey

April–June, Sept & Oct daily 10–11.30am & 2–5.30pm; July & Aug daily 10am–6.30pm; Nov–March Sat, Sun & hols 10–11.30am & 2–6.30pm • €3.50 • ☎04 68 94 97 75, ⓦ www.saint-papoul.fr

Some 14km west of Saissac on the D103 (or just a few kilometres southwest of the *Bout du Monde* campsite), the ancient village of **ST-PAPOUL**, with its walls and Benedictine **abbey**, makes for a gentle side trip. The abbey is best known for the sculpted corbels on the exterior of the nave, executed by the "Master of Cabestany". These can be viewed free at any time, although the interior of the church and its pretty fourteenth-century cloister are also worth a peek.

## Revel

The "main" D629 road winds down through the forest past the Bassin de St-Férréol, which was constructed by Riquet to supply water to the Canal du Midi, and on to **REVEL**. Revel is a *bastide* dating from 1342, featuring an attractive arcaded central square with a superb wooden-pillared medieval *halle* in the middle. Now a prosperous market town (Saturday is market day), it makes an agreeably provincial stopover.

### Châteaux de Lastours

16km north of Carcassonne • Feb, March, Nov & Dec Sat, Sun & hols 10am–5pm; April–June & Sept daily 10am–6pm; July & Aug daily 9am–8pm; Oct daily 10am–5pm • €5 • ☎ 04 68 77 56 02, ⓦ les4chateaux-lastours.lwdsoftware.net

The most memorable site in the **Montaigne Noire** is the **Châteaux de Lastours**, the most northerly of the Cathar castles. There are, in fact, four castles here – their ruined keeps jutting superbly from a sharp ridge of scrub and cypress that plunges to rivers on both sides. The two oldest, Cabaret (mid-eleventh century) and Surdespine (1153), fell into de Montfort's hands in 1211, after their lords had given shelter to the Cathars. The other two, Tour Régine and Quertinheux, were added after 1240, when the site became royal property, and a garrison was maintained here as late as the Revolution. A path winds up from the roadside, bright in early summer with iris, cistus, broom and numerous other plants.

| ACCOMMODATION AND EATING | THE MONTAGNE NOIRE |
|---|---|
| **Auberge du Midi** 34 bd Gambetta, Revel ☎ 05 61 83 50 50, ⓦ hotelrestaurantdumidi.com. A hotel and restaurant in a refined old nineteenth-century mansion, with basic amenities but very friendly and welcoming owners. It also has the town's best restaurant, where you can dine on *terroir* cuisine inside or on a shaded terrace. *Menus* €19–45. Restaurant daily noon–2pm & 7–10pm. **€51** | **Domaine du Lampy-Neuf** 4km north of Saissac on the D4 ☎ 04 68 24 46 07, ⓦ domainelampy-neuf.com. This lakeside estate, set amongst the rich woods of the Montaigne Noire, features its own arboretum. It offers beautiful if basic rooms, as well as excellent regional meals (€25) for guests. An ideal base for exploring the region. **€75** |

12

# Western Languedoc

**Toulouse**, with its sunny, cosmopolitan charms, is not only the main town in **Western Languedoc** but also a very accessible kick-off point for anywhere in the southwest of France. Of the places nearby, **Albi**, with its highly original cathedral and comprehensive collection of Toulouse-Lautrec paintings, is the number-one priority, and once you've made it that far, it's worth the hop to the well-preserved medieval town of **Cordes**. West of Toulouse the land opens up into the broad plains of the **Gers**, a sleepy and rather dull expanse of wheat fields and rolling hills. Those in search of a solitary, little-visited France will enjoy its uncrowded monuments, especially any fond lover of rich terrines and Armagnac.

## Toulouse

**TOULOUSE** is one of the most vibrant provincial cities in France. Long an **aviation** centre – St-Exupéry and Mermoz flew out from here on their pioneering airmail flights over Africa and the Atlantic in the 1920s – Toulouse is now home to Aérospatiale, the driving force behind Concorde, Airbus and the Ariane space rocket. Moreover, the city's 110,000 students make it second only to Paris as a **university** centre.

This is not the first flush of pre-eminence for Toulouse. From the tenth to the thirteenth centuries the counts of Toulouse controlled much of southern France. They maintained a resplendent court, renowned especially for its troubadours, the poets of courtly love whose work influenced Petrarch, Dante and Chaucer and thus the whole course of European poetry. The arrival of the hungry northern French nobles of the Albigensian Crusade put an end to that; in 1271 Toulouse became crown property.

The beautiful old city – the **Ville Rose**, pink not only in its brickwork, but also in its left-leaning politics – lies within a rough hexagon clamped round a bend in the wide,

# TOULOUSE

● **BAR**
Bodega-Bodega    4

● **CAFÉS**
Bibent    6
Le Café des Artistes    10
Le Florida    5
Jour de Fête    3

● **RESTAURANTS**
Les Abattoirs Chez Carmen    12
La Bascule    13
Benjamin    9
Faim des Haricots    11
Les Jardins de l'Opéra    7
Michel Sarran    8
Au Pois Gourmand    1
Le Sept Place St-Sernin    2

■ **CLUBS**
L'Ambassade    3
Bodega-Bodega    2
Le Cri de la Mouette    1
Shanghaï Express    4
L'Ubu Club    5

■ **LIVE MUSIC**
Le Bikini    7
Zénith    6

■ **ACCOMMODATION**
Albert 1er    7
Des Ambassadeurs    2
Beausejour    5
Camping de Rupé    1
Castellane    8
Le Clochez de Rodez    4
Grand Hôtel de l'Opéra    10
Ours Blanc    6
St-Sernin    3
Wilson Square    9

## Church of Les Jacobins

69 rue Pargaminières • Daily 9am–7pm • Free • ☎ 05 61 22 21 92, Ⓦ jacobins.mairie-toulouse.fr

A short distance west of place du Capitole, on rue Lakanal, is the church of **Les Jacobins**. Constructed in 1230 by the Order of Preachers (Dominicans), which St Dominic had founded here in 1216 to preach against Cathar heretics, the church is a huge fortress-like rectangle of unadorned brick, buttressed – like Albi cathedral – by plain brick piles, quite unlike what you'd normally associate with Gothic architecture. The interior is a single space divided by a central row of ultra-slim pillars from whose minimal capitals spring an elegant splay of vaulting ribs – 22 from the last in line – like palm fronds. Beneath the altar lie the bones of the philosopher St Thomas Aquinas. On the north side, you step out into the calming hush of a **cloister** with a formal array of box trees and cypress in the middle, and its adjacent art **exhibition hall**.

## St-Sernin

Place St-Sernin • Daily 10am–6pm • Free; ambulatory & crypt €2 • ☎ 05 61 11 02 22, Ⓦ basilique-st-sernin-toulouse.fr

From the north side of place du Capitole, **rue du Taur** leads past the belfry wall of **Notre-Dame-du-Taur**, whose diamond-pointed arches and decorative motifs are the acme of Toulousain bricklaying skills, to place St-Sernin. Here you're confronted with the largest Romanesque church in France, the **basilica of St-Sernin**, begun in 1080 to accommodate the passing hordes of Santiago pilgrims, and one of the loveliest examples of its genre. Its most striking external features are the octagonal brick belfry with rounded and pointed arches, diamond lozenges, colonnettes and mouldings picked out in stone, and the apse with nine radiating chapels. Entering from the south, you pass under the Porte Miégeville, whose twelfth-century carvings launched the influential Toulouse school of sculpture. Inside, the great high nave rests on brick piers, flanked by double aisles of diminishing height, surmounted by a gallery running right around the building. The fee for the **ambulatory** is worth it for the exceptional eleventh-century marble reliefs on the end wall of the choir and for the extraordinary wealth of reliquaries in the spacious **crypt**.

**12**

## Musée St-Raymond

1 Ter place St-Sernin • Daily 10am–6/7pm • €3 • ☎ 05 61 22 31 44, Ⓦ saintraymond.toulouse.fr

Right outside the basilica of St-Sernin is the city's archeological museum, **Musée St-Raymond**, housed in what remains of the block built for poor students of the medieval university. It contains a large collection of objects ranging from prehistoric to Roman, as well as an excavated necropolis in the basement.

## Cité de l'Espace

Av Jean Gonord, beside exit 17 of the A612 *périphérique* on the road to Castres • Feb–Aug daily 9am–5/7pm • €23, under-5s free • ☎ 08 20 37 72 23 • Ⓦ cite-espace.com • Bus #19 from place Marengo (school hols only)

At the **Cité de l'Espace**, out in the suburbs to the east, the theme is space and space exploration, including satellite communications, space probes and, best of all, the opportunity to walk inside a mock-up of the Mir space station – fascinating, but chilling. Many of the exhibits are interactive and you could easily spend a half-day here, especially if you're with children.

## Aérospatiale's Usine Clément Ader

10 av Georges-Guynemer • Times vary; Guided tours only, normally in French; apply in advance (a few days for EU citizens, two weeks for others) • €10–14.50 • ☎ 05 34 39 42 00, Ⓦ taxiway.fr

**Aérospatiale's Usine Clément Ader**, in the western suburbs, is where Airbus passenger jets are assembled, painted and tested before taking their maiden flights from next-door Blagnac airport. The informative tours include a climb high above the eerily quiet assembly bays where just one hundred people, ably assisted by scores of computerized robots, churn out the A380Airbus, a two-storey superliner that dwarfs even the Jumbo.

In 2014, **Aeropscopia**, a major aerospace museum, is expected to open in Blagnac. Check for news at ⓦtaxiway.fr.

## ARRIVAL AND DEPARTURE

**By plane** Aéroport Toulouse-Blagnac (☏05 61 42 44 00 or ☏05 24 61 80 00, ⓦtoulouse.aeroport.fr) is 5km northwest of the town centre. An airport shuttle (every 20min 5am–8.20pm, returning 7.35am–12.15am; €5; tickets can be bought from driver) puts you down at the bus station (with stops on allées Jean-Jaurès and place Jeanne-d'Arc).

**By train** The *gare SNCF*, better known to locals as *gare Matabiau*, is at 80 bd Pierre Semard (☏08 36 35 35 35). To reach the city centre takes just 5min by métro to Capitole, or 20min on foot (turn left out of the station, cross the canal and head straight down allées Jean-Jaurès).

Destinations Albi (17 daily; 1hr); Auch (18–20 daily; 1hr 15min–2hr 30min); Ax-les-Thermes (6 daily; 1hr 55min);

Bayonne (18–22 daily; 2hr 25min–3hr 45min); Bordeaux (18–22 daily; 2hr 30min); Castres (11 daily; 1hr 5min); Foix (13 daily; 47min–1hr 15min); La-Tour-de-Carol (6 daily; 2hr 30min); Lourdes (8–16 daily; 1hr 40min); Lyon (14–18 daily; 4–6hr); Marseille (22 daily; 3hr 30min–6hr); Mazamet (11 daily; 1hr 30min–1hr 55min); Paris (13 daily; 5hr 20min–6hr 45min); Pau (6–10 daily; 2hr–2hr 30min); Tarascon-sur-Ariège (13 daily; 1hr 20min); Tarbes (6–13 daily; 1hr 45min).

**By bus** The *gare routière* (☏05 61 61 67 67) is next to the train station, on bd Pierre-Sémard.

Destinations Albi (12–16 weekly; 2hr 40min); Carcassonne (1 daily; 2hr 20min); Castres (8–12 weekly; 1hr 40min–2hr).

## GETTING AROUND

**Transport passes** Tisseo-Connex (☏05 61 41 70 70; ⓦtisseo.fr) tickets (€1.60) cover one hour's transport by métro and city buses within the city centre.

**Taxi** Capitole ☏05 34 25 02 50. For taxis to the airport call ☏05 61 30 02 54.

**Bike rental** The municipal bike system, VéloToulouse (subscribe for €1.20/day, €5/week; ⓦvelo.toulouse.fr), rents bikes for free for up to 30min (around €2/hr thereafter) from over 200 automated stations.

## INFORMATION

**Tourist office** Square Charles-de-Gaulle (June–Sept Mon–Sat 9am–7pm, Sun 10am–5.15pm; Oct–May Mon–Fri 9am–6pm, Sat 9am–12.30pm & 2–6pm, Sun 10am–12.30pm & 2–5pm; ☏05 61 11 02 22, ⓦtoulouse-tourisme.com). The Capitole métro stop is right outside.

**Discount pass** The Toulouse en Liberté card (€25) offers discounts at a range of hotels, museums, cultural events and shops, and free cocktails at selected restaurants. Each card is valid for one year, for two adults and two children.

## ACCOMMODATION

**Albert 1ᵉʳ** 8 rue Rivals ☏05 61 21 17 91, ⓦhotel-albert1.com. This small, comfortable and good-value hotel is set in a quiet side street just off the Capitole and close to the central market in place de Victor-Hugo. Check for special weekend deals. **€59**

**Des Ambassadeurs** 68 rue de Bayard ☏05 61 62 65 84, ⓦhotel-des-ambassadeurs.com. Very friendly little hotel just down from the station. All rooms have TV, en-suite bath and phone – a surprisingly good deal given the price. **€54**

**Beausejour** 4 rue Caffarelli ☏05 61 62 77 59, ⓦhotelbeausejourtoulouse.com. Basic, but dirt cheap, and with a great copper-balconied facade and soundproofed rooms. Best of the hotels in the slightly dodgy but engagingly gritty neighbourhood around place de Belfort. **€39**

**Camping de Rupé** Chemin du Pont du Rupé ☏05 61 70 07 35, ⓦcamping-toulouse.com. Toulouse's nearest campsite. Take bus #59, to the "Rupé" stop. Reception open 9am–12.30pm & 4–8pm, year-round. Car €2.10 extra. **€19**.

**Castellane** 17 rue Castellane ☏05 61 62 18 82, ⓦcastellanehotel.com. A cheerful hotel with a wide selection of room sizes and types – most are bright and quiet. One of the few wheelchair-accessible hotels in this price range. **€82**

★ **Le Clochez de Rodez** 14 place de Jeanne-d'Arc ☏05 61 62 42 92, ⓦhotel-clocher-toulouse.com. Comfortable and central, with secure parking and all mod cons. Despite its size, it exudes a very personal hospitality. **€80**

**Grand Hôtel de l'Opéra** 1 place du Capitole ☏05 61 21 82 66, ⓦgrand-hotel-opera.com. Originally a seventeenth-century convent, the *grande dame* of Toulouse's hotels presides over the place du Capitole. The rich decor, peppered with antiques and artwork, underlines the atmosphere of sophistication, and there's a fitness centre. Substantial online discounts. **€190**.

**Ours Blanc** 25 place de Victor-Hugo ☏05 61 21 62 40, ⓦhotel-oursblanc.com. Right by the covered market and steps from the Capitole, this welcoming hotel is one of

**12**

the city's better bargains, with comfortable, functional rooms. **€75**

**St-Sernin** 2 rue St-Bernard ☎ 05 61 21 73 08, ⓦ hotelstsernin.com. Nicely renovated old hotel in one of the best districts of the Old Town, around the basilica – close to all the action, but far enough away to provide peace in the evening. **€84**.

**Wilson Square** 12 rue d'Austerlitz ☎ 05 61 21 67 57, ⓦ hotel-wilson.com. Clean and well-kept place at the top end of rue Austerlitz. The hotel is not long on character but it's comfortable and well outfitted, with en-suite bathrooms a/c and a lift. Also a great patisserie at street level. **€68**

## EATING AND DRINKING

Place Arnaud-Bernard, a popular arty hangout, is a great place to lounge in a café, while place du Capitole is the early evening meeting place. Place St-Georges remains popular, though its clientele is no longer convincingly bohemian, and place Wilson also has its enthusiasts. For lunch, a great informal option is the row of five or six small restaurants jammed in on the mezzanine floor above the gorgeous food market in place de Victor-Hugo, off boulevard de Strasbourg. They are all closed on Monday, and cost as little as €12 for market-fresh *menus*. The food and atmosphere are perfect.

### CAFÉS

**Bibent** 5 place du Capitole ☎ 08 99 96 56 79, ⓦ maisonconstant.com/fr_bibent.htm. On the south side of the square, this is Toulouse's most distinguished café, with exuberant plasterwork, marble tables and cascading chandeliers. Daily 7am–midnight.

**Le Café des Artistes** 13 place de la Daurade ☎ 08 99 96 58 28. Lively young café overlooking the Garonne. A perfect spot to watch the sun set on warm summer evenings, as floodlights pick out the brick buildings along the *quais*. Mon–Sat 8am–2am, Sun noon–9pm.

**Le Florida** 12 place du Capitole ☎ 05 61 23 94 61, ⓦ leflorida-capitole.fr. Relaxed café with a retro air. One of the most pleasant places to hang out on the central square. Daily 6am–2am.

**Jour de Fête** 43 rue du Taur ☎ 05 61 23 36 48. Trendy tearoom and brasserie with a small streetside patio. Friendly service and a young university crowd. Tues–Sat noon–midnight.

### RESTAURANTS

**Les Abbatoirs Chez Carmen** 97 allée Charles-de-Fitte ☎ 05 61 42 04 95, ⓦ chezcarmen.fr. Family-run for two generations, this is one of the last of the traditional slaughterhouse-side meat emporia, with a reputation for top-of-the-line intestinal delicacies, as well as calves' brains and pigs' feet. *Menus* from €21. Sept–July Tues–Sat noon–2pm & 7–9pm.

**La Bascule** 14 av Maurice-Hauriou ☎ 05 61 52 09 51. A Toulouse institution. Its chrome interior is pure Art Deco and the food well prepared and presented. The menu includes regional dishes like cassoulet, *foie de canard* and oysters from the Bay of Arcachon. Meals €25 and up. Closed Sat lunch & Sun.

**Benjamin** 7 rue des Gestes ☎ 05 61 22 92 66. A long-standing institution for economical *terroir* food; service is pleasant and professional, although the atmosphere is

somewhat anonymous. There's a wide selection of duck-based lunch and dinner *menus* from €17–23. Daily noon–2.30pm & 7.30–11pm.

**Faim des Haricots** 3 rue du Puits Vert ☎ 05 61 22 49 25, ⓦ lafaimdesharicots.fr. Toulouse's best vegetarian option, with generous *formules* starting at €15. Daily noon–2.30pm & 7–10.30pm. Closed first half Aug.

**Les Jardins de l'Opéra** 1 place du Capitole ☎ 05 61 21 05 56, ⓦ lesjardinsdelopera.com. The *Grand Hôtel's* restaurant is Toulouse's best and most luxurious. If you fancy a splurge you will pay for it – a basic *menu* starts at €19 at lunch, and dinner can run to €100 – but the food is outstanding. Tues–Sat noon–2pm & 8–10pm. Closed part Aug.

★ **Michel Sarran** 21 bd Armand-Duportal ☎ 05 61 12 32 32, ⓦ michel-sarran.com. Justifiably renowned *gastronomique* restaurant, a 15min walk from the place du Capitole (follow rue des Lois and rue des Salenques to the end, and turn left). Imaginative dishes with a strong Mediterranean streak are served with style and warmth. *Menus* from €49 at lunch and €98 at dinner. Mon, Tues, Thurs & Fri noon–1.45pm & 8–9.45pm, Wed 8–9.45pm. Closed part Aug.

**Au Pois Gourmand** 3 rue Émile-Heybrard ☎ 05 34 36 42 00, ⓦ pois-gourmand.fr. Great location in a riverside nineteenth-century house with a beautiful patio. The quality French cuisine does not come cheap, but is of a high standard, and the *carte* presents a pleasant departure from purely regional dishes. *Menus* from €37. Take bus #66 or #14 from métro St-Cyprien-République. Mon–Sat 7.30–9.30pm.

★ **Le Sept Place St-Sernin** 7 place St-Sernin ☎ 05 62 30 05 30, ⓦ 7placesaintsernin.com. A small house behind the basilica conceals a lively and cheerful restaurant serving inventive and original cuisine with a constantly changing *carte*, followed by dazzling desserts. *Menus* from €38. Mon–Fri noon–1.45pm & 7.30–9.45pm, Sat 7.30–10pm.

**12**

## NIGHTLIFE AND ENTERTAINMENT

### CLUBS

**L'Ambassade** 22 bd de la Gare ☎ 05 62 47 24 73. Downbeat club where funk and soul rule. Live jazz on Sun nights. Mon–Fri 7pm–2am, Sat & Sun 7pm–5am.

**Bodega-Bodega** 1 rue Gabriel-Péri ☎ 05 61 63 03 63. The old *Telegraph* newspaper building makes a superb venue for this bar-restaurant, which hosts a hugely popular club after 10pm. Mon–Fri & Sun 7pm–2am, Sat 7pm–4am.

**Le Cri de la Mouette** Place Héraklès ☎ 05 62 30 05 28, ⓦ lecridelamouette.com. Popular club featuring reggae, rock, funk and soul. Cover from €5. Daily 11pm–5am.

**Shanghaï Express** 12 rue de la Pomme ☎ 05 61 23 37 80, ⓦ shanghai-club.fr. One of the city's most established gay and lesbian clubs, which attracts a mixed crowd including transvestites and transsexuals. Wed–Sun midnight–7am.

**L'Ubu Club** 16 rue St-Rome ☎ 05 61 23 26 75, ⓦ facebook.com/pages/LUbu-Club/55060665459. Long-standing pillar of the city's dance scene, which remains as popular as ever. Wed–Sat 8pm–2am.

### LIVE MUSIC

**Le Bikini** 55 chemin des Étroits, rte de Lacroix-Falgarde ☎ 05 62 24 09 50, ⓦ lebikini.com. On the city's southern outskirts, this is *the* hangout for Toulouse rockers, and a prime venue for live gigs. Thurs–Sun 8pm–2am.

**Zénith** 11 av Raymond Badiou ☎ 05 62 74 49 49. The city's biggest concert venue (with 9000 seats), specializing in rock. At métro Arènes.

### THEATRE

**Cave-Poésie René Gouzenne** 71 rue du Taur ☎ 05 61 23 62 00, ⓦ cave-poesie.com. Home to decidedly bohemian literary workshops, concerts and gatherings. Hours vary.

**Théâtre de la Cité** 1 rue Pierre-Baudis ☎ 05 34 45 05 05, ⓦ tnt-cite.com. Live theatre featuring a varied programme of top-notch French and foreign productions.

**Odyssud** 4 av du Parc, Blagnac ☎ 05 61 71 75 15, ⓦ odyssud.com. Major venue featuring both theatre and opera. Take bus #66.

## DIRECTORY

**Consulates** Canada, 10 rue Jules de Resseguier (☎ 05 61 52 19 06, ⓔ consulat.canada-st_pierreetmiquelon @amb-canada.fr); USA, 25 allées Jean-Jaurès (☎ 05 34 41 36 50, ⓦ france.usembassy.gov). Closest British Consulate is in Bordeaux, at 353 bd Wilson (☎ 05 57 22 21 10; ⓦ ukinfrance.fco.gov.uk); there is an Honorary Consulate in Toulouse (☎ 05 61 30 37 91).

**Health** For medical emergencies contact SAMU (☎ 115). The network of university hospitals has facilities all over the city. For non-emergencies check their website for the appropriate centre (ⓦ chu-toulouse.fr). For a pharmacy out of hours, try Pharmacie de Nuit, 70–76 allées Jean-Jaurès, entry on rue Arnaud-Vidal (daily 8pm–8am ☎ 05 61 62 38 05).

# Albi

**ALBI**, 77km and an hour's train ride northeast of Toulouse, is a small industrial town with two unique sights: a museum containing the most comprehensive collection of **Toulouse-Lautrec**'s work (Albi was his birthplace); and a remarkable **Gothic cathedral**. Its other claim to fame comes from its association with Catharism; though not itself an important centre, it gave its name – Albigensian – to both the heresy and the crusade to suppress it.

## Cathédrale Ste-Cécile

Place Ste-Cécile • Daily: June–Sept 9am–6pm; Oct–May 9am–noon & 2–6pm • Choir €2; treasury €2; choir & treasury €3 • ☎ 05 63 43 23 43, ⓦ catholique-tarn.cef.fr

**Cathédrale Ste-Cécile**, begun about 1280, dwarfs the town like some vast bulk carrier run aground, the belfry its massive superstructure. The comparison sounds unflattering, and this is not a conventionally beautiful building; it's all about size and boldness of conception. The sheer plainness of the exterior is impressive on this scale, and it's not without interest: arcading, buttressing, the contrast of stone against brick – every differentiation of detail becomes significant. During July and August there are free **organ recitals** here (Wed 5pm & Sun 4pm); the tourist office can supply information.

## Musée Toulouse-Lautrec

Place Ste-Cécile • April to late June & Oct daily 9/10am–noon & 2–6pm; July & Aug daily 9am–6pm; Oct–March Wed–Mon 10am–noon & 2–5/6pm • €5.50 • ☎ 05 63 49 48 70, ⓦ museetoulouselautrec.net

Next to the cathedral, a powerful red-brick castle, the thirteenth-century **Palais de la Berbie**, houses the superb **Musée Toulouse-Lautrec**. It contains paintings, drawings,

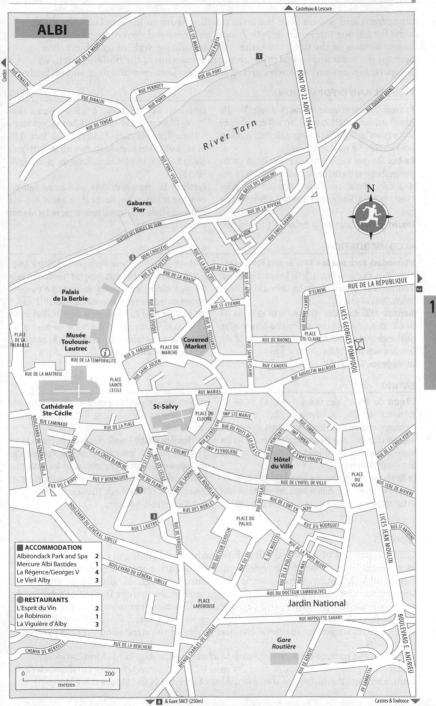

ALBI

Castelnau & Lescure

River Tarn

Gabares Pier

Palais de la Berbie

Musée Toulouse-Lautrec

Covered Market

Cathédrale Ste-Cécile

St-Salvy

Hôtel du Ville

Jardin National

Gare Routière

**ACCOMMODATION**
| Albirondack Park and Spa | 2 |
| Mercure Albi Bastides | 1 |
| La Régence/Georges V | 4 |
| Le Vieil Alby | 3 |

**RESTAURANTS**
| L'Esprit du Vin | 2 |
| Le Robinson | 1 |
| La Viguière d'Alby | 3 |

0 — 200 metres

Cordes

RUE RINALDI

RUE DE LA MADELEINE

RUE STE MARIE

RUE STE PORTA

RUE DU PORT

PONT DU 22 AOUT 1944

RUE EDOUARD BRANLY

RUE PERROTY

RUE PORTA

RUE RINALDI

RUE DU TENDAT

RUE BASSE DES MOULINS

RUE DE LA RIVIÈRE

RUE EMILE GRAND

RUE ALBON

RUE DE LA RÉPUBLIQUE

SENTIER DES BERGES DU TARN

QUAI CHOISEUL

RUE D'ENGUEYSSE

RUE DE LA GRAL'OLE COTE

RUE DE LA VIGNE

RUE ST-AFRIC

D'ELBENE

RUE BONNE-CAMBE

LICES GEORGES POMPIDOU

RUE DE LA BUADE

RUE ST-ETIENNE

PLACE STE-CLAIRE

RUE DE LA SOUQUE

RUE DE RHONEL

RUE FARGUES

RUE POISSANTS

RUE SAINTE-CLAIRE

RUE CANDEIL

RUE AUGUSTIN MALROUX

PLACE DE LA TREBAILLE

RUE DE LA TEMPORALITE

PLACE DU MARCHE

RUE DE LA MAITRISE

RUE SAINT JULIEN

PLACE SAINTE CECILE

RUE MARIES

RUE CAMINADE

RUE DE PRETRES

RUE DE LA PIALE

PLACE DU CLOITRE

IMP STE MARIE

RUE TIMBAL

RUE DE LA CROIX VERTE

BOULEVARD DU GENERAL SIBILLE

RUE DE LA CROIX BLANCHE

RUE DE L'OULMET

RUE DU PUITS DE LA BAL'E

IMP TIMBAL

RUE STE CLAIRE

IMP PEYROLIERE

RUE DES PENITENTS

IMP D'EMPEYRALOTS

RUE DU 6 BIOU

RUE P BERENGUIER

RUE DU PLANCAT

RUE DE SAUNAL

RUE BOUQUERANE

RUE DE L'HOTEL DE VILLE

PLACE DU VIGAN

RUE SERE DE RIVIERE

RUE T LAUTREC

RUE DES NOBLES

RUE DU PALAIS

RUE DE L'ORT EN SALVY

RUE DU BOURGUET

RUE ST ANTOINE

RUE DE PEROUSSE

PLACE DU PALAIS

LICES JEAN MOULIN

BOULEVARD DU GENERAL SIBILLE

RUE DOCTEUR DEVOISIN

RUE DU SEL

R. DES MUETTES

RUE DE LA VIOLETTE

RUE DU MAIL

RUE DE LA PORTE NEUVE

PLACE LAPEROUSE

RUE DU DOCTEUR CAMBOULIVES

RUE HIPPOLYTE SAVARY

CHEMIN DE MERVILLE

RUE DE LA BERCHERE

AVENUE CHARLES-DE-GAULLE

AV GAMBETTA

AV DE GENEVE

BOULEVARD E. ANDRIEU

12

lithographs and posters from the artist's earliest work to his very last – an absolute must for anyone interested in *belle époque* seediness and, given the predominant Impressionism of the time, the rather offbeat painting style of its subject. But perhaps the most impressive thing about this museum is the building itself, its parapets, gardens and walkways giving stunning views over the river and its bridges.

## ARRIVAL AND INFORMATION
ALBI

**By train** Trains from Cordes-Vindrac (3–4 daily; 1hr–1hr 30min) and Toulouse (16 daily; 1–2hr) pull in to the *gare SNCF* on place Stalingrad; it's a 10min walk north into town along avs Maréchal-Joffre and de-Gaulle.

**By bus** The *gare routière*, on place Jean-Jaurès on the southeast edge of the Old Town, meets buses from Castres (6–8 daily; 50min) and Cordes (Mon–Sat 1–4 daily; 35min). Some SNCF buses leave from here, others from the *gare*.

**Tourist office** Palais de la Berbie (Oct to mid-June

Mon–Sat 9am–12.30pm & 2–6/6.30pm, Sun 10am–12.30pm & 2.30–5pm; mid-June to Sept Mon–Sat 9am–7pm, Sun 10am–12.30pm & 2.30–5pm; ☏ 05 63 36 36 00, ⊛ albi-tourisme.fr). They sell the "Albi Pass", giving free or discounted admission to the town's sights (€6.50).

**Festivals** The town hosts three good annual festivals, dedicated to jazz in May, theatre at the end of June and beginning of July, and classical music at the end of July and beginning of August.

## ACCOMMODATION

**Albirondack Park and Spa** 31 allée de la Piscine ☏ 05 63 60 37 06, ⊛ albirondack.fr. Set in a wooded glade near town, this beautiful campsite also has cabins and Airstream trailers. Open all year. **€28**

**Mercure Albi Bastides** 41 rue Porta ☏ 05 63 47 66 66, ⊛ lemoulin-albi.fr. Understated luxury in an eighteenth-century mill overlooking the banks of the Tarn, and with views of the Cathedral. **€98**

**La Régence/Georges V** 27–29 av Maréchal Joffre

☏ 05 63 54 24 16, ⊛ hotelgeorgev.com. These long-established twin hotels, occupying old townhouses near the train station, are currently undergoing a complete renovation and are due to reopen in summer 2013. **€55**

★ **Le Vieil Alby** 25 rue Toulouse-Lautrec ☏ 05 63 54 14 69, ⊛ levieilalby.com. A real find in the heart of old Albi – cheap and comfortable, with a friendly owner and excellent home-cooked food. **€50**

## EATING

**L'Esprit du Vin** 11 quai Choiseul ☏ 05 63 54 60 44, ⊛ lespritduvin-albi.com. Perhaps Albi's best, this prestigious *restaurant gastronomique* boasts an excellent wine selection including vintages made especially for the house. *Menus* from €23 at lunch, €60 dinner. Tues–Sun noon–1pm & 8–9pm.

**Le Robinson** 142 rue Édouard Branly ☏ 05 63 46 15 69. Set in the woods just upriver from the old town, this restaurant's environs alone make it worth a visit. Ideal for

children, especially when the weather is good. *Menus* from €17. Wed–Sun noon–2.30pm & 7–9.30pm. Closed Nov–March.

**La Viguière d'Alby** 7 rue Toulouse-Lautrec ☏ 05 63 54 76 44. An Albigeois *terroir* institution long affiliated with the European Gastronomic Association. Try *lou tastou* (the local tapas) or in winter enjoy fire-cooked specialities. *Menus* from €17 at lunch. Fri–Tues noon–2pm & 7–9.30pm, Thurs 7–9.30pm.

# Cordes

**CORDES**, perched on a conical hill 24km northwest of Albi, and just a brief trip away by train and bus, is one of the region's must-see sights. Founded in 1222 by Raymond VII, Count of Toulouse, it was a **Cathar** stronghold, and the ground beneath the town is riddled with tunnels for storage and refuge in time of trouble. As one of the southwest's oldest and best-preserved *bastides*, complete with thirteenth- and fourteenth-century houses climbing steep cobbled lanes, Cordes is inevitably a major tourist attraction: medieval banners flutter in the streets and artisans practise their crafts.

The **Musée Charles-Portal**, 1 rue Saint-Michel (July & Aug Wed–Mon 2–6pm; Easter–June, Sept & Oct Sat & Sun 2–6pm; €2.50; ⊛ musee-charles-portal.asso-web .com) recounts the history of the town. Also of interest is the **Musée d'Art Moderne et**

**Contemporain** (daily: mid-March to mid-Nov 10am–12.30pm & 2–6.30pm; €3.50; ☎05 63 56 14 79, ⓦmairie.cordessurciel.fr), which features works by the figurative painter Yves Brayer, who lived here from 1940.

# Castres

In spite of its industrial activities, **CASTRES**, 40km south of Albi and 55km east of Toulouse, has kept a lot of its charm in the streets on the right bank of the Agout and, in particular, the riverside quarter where the old tanners' and weavers' houses overhang the water. The centre is a bustling, businesslike sort of place, with a big morning **market** on Saturdays on place Jean-Jaurès.

## Musée Goya

Hôtel de Ville • July & Aug daily 10am–6pm; Sept–June Tues–Sun 9am–noon & 2–5/6pm • €3 • ☎05 63 71 59 30, ⓦville-castres.fr

Next to the rather unremarkable old cathedral, the former bishop's palace holds the Hôtel de Ville and Castres' **Musée Goya**, home to the biggest collection of Spanish paintings in France outside the Louvre. Goya is represented by some lighter political paintings and a large collection of engravings, while other famous Iberian artists on show include Murillo and Velázquez.

## Musée Jean-Jaurès

2 place Pelisson • July & Aug daily 10am–6pm; Sept–June Tues–Sun 9am–noon & 2–5/6pm • €1.50 • ☎05 63 72 01 01, ⓦamis-musees-castres.asso.fr/jaures/museejaures.htm

Getting to the **Musée Jean-Jaurès**, dedicated to the city's famous native son, takes you through the streets of the Old Town, past the splendid seventeenth-century **Hôtel Nayrac**, on rue Frédéric-Thomas. The slightly hagiographic museum pays well-deserved tribute to one of France's boldest and best political writers, thinkers and activists of modern times.

### ARRIVAL AND INFORMATION                          CASTRES

**By train** The *gare SNCF* lies 1km southwest of the town centre on av Albert-1er. Trains and SNCF buses arrive from Toulouse (11 daily; 1hr 5min).

**By bus** The *gare routière* is on place Soult, with bus services to Albi (6–8 daily; 50min), Lacaune (Mon–Sat 1–4 daily 50min), Revel (Mon–Sat 1–6, 45min) St-Pons (Mon–Sat 1–4 daily; 1hr–1hr 30min), Toulouse (8–12 weekly; 1hr 40min–2hr).

**Tourist office** Beside the Pont Vieux at 3 rue Milhau-Ducommun (Sept–June Mon–Sat 9.30am–12.30pm & 2–6pm; July & Aug Mon–Sat 9.30am–6.30pm & 2.30–5pm, Sun 2.30–4.30pm; ☎05 63 62 63 62, ⓦtourisme-castres.fr). You can buy the Passe Tourisme (€4.50) here; it gives reductions on museums, shops and restaurants.

### ACCOMMODATION

**Camping du Gourjade** Rte de Roquecourbe ☎05 63 59 33 51, ⓦcampingdegourjade.net. The municipal campsite is in a riverside park 2km northeast of town on the road to Roquecourbe; it's accessible by river-taxi (return €5). Closed Oct–March. €15

★ **Renaissance** 17 rue Victor-Hugo ☎05 63 59 30 42, ⓦhotel-renaissance.fr. This cosy three-star hotel in the heart of old Castres has a variety of rooms, including junior suites. Expect wooden floors and comfortable furnishings. €74.

**Rivière** 10 quai Tourcaudière ☎05 63 59 04 53, ⓦpagesperso-orange.fr/hotelriviere. A basic, welcoming and good-value option with tidy if nondescript rooms, the best of which have views over the Agout. €49

### EATING AND DRINKING

**La Mandragore** 1 rue Malpas ☎05 63 59 51 27. This local favourite is praised both for its *gastronomique* cuisine, its *terroir* standbys, and its wine selection. Dine inside or on the terrace. *Menus* €14–30. Tues–Sat noon–2pm & 7–9pm.

**Le Médiéval** 44 rue Milhau-Ducommun ☎05 63 51 13 78. A homely little restaurant with a great atmosphere, friendly staff and a riverside location. *Menus* from €18. Tues–Sun noon–2pm & 7–9pm.

12

# The Gers

West of Toulouse, the *département* of **Gers** lies at the heart of the historic region of Gascony. In the long struggle for supremacy between the English and the French in the Middle Ages it had the misfortune to form the frontier zone between the English base at Bordeaux and the French at Toulouse. The attractive if unspectacular rolling agricultural land is dotted with ancient, honey-stoned farms. Settlement is sparse and – with the exception of **Auch**, the capital – major monuments are largely lacking, which keeps it well off the beaten tourist trails.

The region is perhaps best known for its stout-hearted mercenary warriors – of whom Alexandre Dumas' d'Artagnan and Edmond Rostand's Cyrano de Bergerac are the supreme literary exemplars – its rich cuisine (Gers is the biggest producer of **foie gras** in the country), and its **Armagnac**.

## Auch

The sleepy provincial capital of the Gers, **AUCH** is most easily accessible by rail from Toulouse, 78km to the east. The **Old Town**, which is the only part worth exploring, stands on a bluff overlooking the tree-lined River Gers, with the **cathedral** towering dramatically over the town.

### Cathédrale Ste-Marie

Rue Arnaud de Moles • Daily: mid-July to Aug 8.30am–6.30pm; Sept–June 8.30/9am–noon & 2–5/6pm; closed during services • €2 • ☎ 06 30 41 19 38, ⓦ www.auch-tourisme.com

The **Cathédrale Ste-Marie** makes a trip to Auch worthwhile. Although not finished until the latter part of the seventeenth century, it is built in broadly late Gothic style, with a classical facade. Of particular interest are the choir stalls and the stained glass; both were begun in the early 1500s, though the windows are of clearly Renaissance inspiration, while the choir remains Gothic. The eighteen windows, unusual in being a complete set, parallel the scenes and personages depicted in the stalls. They are the work of a Gascon painter, Arnaud de Moles, and are equally rich in detail.

### The Old Town

Immediately south of the cathedral, in the tree-filled place Salinis, is the 40m-high **Tour d'Armagnac**, which served as an ecclesiastical court and prison in the fourteenth

---

## ARMAGNAC

**Armagnac** is a dry, golden brandy distilled in the district extending into the Landes and Lot and Garonne *départements*, divided into three distinct areas: Haut-Armagnac (around Auch), Ténarèze (Condom) and Bas-Armagnac (Éauze), in ascending order of output and quality. Growers of the grape like to compare brandy with whisky, equating malts with the individualistic, earthy Armagnac distilled by small producers, and blended whiskies with the more consistent, standardized output of the large-scale houses. Armagnac grapes are grown on sandy soils and, importantly, the wine is distilled only once, giving the spirit a lower alcohol content but more flavour. Aged in local black oak, Armagnac matures quickly, so young Armagnacs are relatively smoother than corresponding Cognacs.

Distilled originally for medicinal reasons, Armagnac has many claims heaped upon it. Perhaps the most optimistic are those of the priest of Éauze de St-Mont, who held that the eau de vie cured **gout** and hepatitis. More reasonably, he also wrote that it "stimulates the spirit if taken in moderation, recalls the past, gives many joys, above all else, conserves youth. If one retains it in the mouth, it unties the tongue and gives courage to the timid."

Many of the producers welcome visitors and offer tastings, whether you go to one of the bigger *chais* (storehouse) of Condom or Éauze, or follow a faded sign at the bottom of a farm track. For more **information**, contact the Bureau National Interprofessionnel de l'Armagnac (ⓦ cognacnet.com/armagnac).

century. Descending from here to the river is a **monumental stairway** of 234 steps, with a statue of d'Artagnan gracing one of the terraces. From place de la République, in front of the cathedral's main west door, rue d'Espagne connects with rue de la Convention and what is left of the narrow medieval stairways known as the **pousterles**, which give access to the lower town. On the north side of place de la République, the tourist office inhabits a splendid, half-timbered fifteenth-century house on the corner with rue Dessoles, a pedestrianized street that has an array of fine buildings.

### Musée des Jacobins

4 Place Louis Blanc • Feb, March, Nov & Dec Mon–Fri 2–5pm; Sat & Sun 10am–noon & 2–5pm; April–Oct daily 10am–noon & 2–6pm • €4 • ☎ 05 62 05 22 89, ⓦ www.auch-tourisme.com

Just down the steps to the east of rue Dessoles, on place Louis-Blanc, the former convent, now the **Musée des Jacobins**, houses one of the best collections of pre-Columbian and later South American art in France. Also of interest is its small collection of traditional Gascon furniture, religious artefacts and Gallo-Roman remains.

## ARRIVAL AND INFORMATION                                                                    AUCH

**By train** The *gare SNCF* is on av Pierre Mendès across the river from the cathedral, a 10min walk east.

**By bus** The *gare routière* is next to the train station. Destinations Bordeaux (1 daily; 3hr 40min); Condom (1–2 daily; 40min); Lectoure (4–8 daily; 40min); Montauban (generally up to 3 daily; 2hr); Tarbes (3–4 daily; 2hr); Toulouse (1–4 daily; 1hr 30min).

**Tourist office** 1 rue Dessoles (May to mid-July & mid-Aug to Sept Mon–Sat 9.15/10am–noon & 2–6pm, Sun 10am–12.15pm; mid-July to mid-Aug Mon–Sat 9.30am–6.30pm, Sun 10am–12.15pm & 3–6pm; Sept & Nov–April Mon–Sat 9.15/10am–noon & 2–6pm; Oct Sun 10am–12.15pm; ☎05 62 05 22 89, ⓦwww .auch-tourisme.com).

## ACCOMMODATION

**Château les Charmettes** 21 rte de Duran ☎05 62 62 10 10, ⓦchateaulescharmettes.com. The best hotel in the area, in a country estate 2km northwest of the town centre. Amenities include a pool, jacuzzi, tennis courts, and a stunning garden setting. An ideal base for exploring the region. **€160**

**De France** 2 place de la Libération ☎05 62 61 71 71, ⓦwww.hoteldefrance-auch.com. Right by the *mairie*

and only a few minutes' walk west of the cathedral, this beautiful old hotel has a variety of rooms, all en suite. The restaurant is good, too (see below). Excellent value. **€80**

**De Paris** 38 av de la Marne ☎05 62 63 26 22, ⓔhotelparis.auch@orange.fr. A basic but clean budget option near the stations, with a garage. Closed Nov. **€33**

## EATING

**De France** 2 place de la Libération ☎05 62 61 71 71, ⓦwww.hoteldefrance-auch.com. This well-regarded hotel restaurant tilts towards the *gastronomique*. There is also a separate brasserie serving less complex and less expensive dishes. Weekday lunch *menus* from €18, although à la carte will set you back considerably more.

Tues–Fri 10am–noon & 7–9pm, Sat 7–9pm, Sun 10am–noon.

**La Table d'Oste** 7 rue Lamartine ☎05 62 05 55 62. Good Gascon and Languedocian cuisine, including foie gras, duck, cassoulet and stuffed chicken. *Menus* €16–24. Mon 7–9.30pm, Tues–Sat noon–2pm & 7–9.30pm.

12

# The Massif Central

CIRQUE DE NAVACELLES

**13**

# The Massif Central

Thickly forested and sliced by numerous rivers and lakes, the once volcanic uplands of the Massif Central are geologically the oldest part of France and culturally one of the most firmly rooted in the past. Industry and tourism have made few inroads here, and the people remain rural and somewhat taciturn, with an enduring sense of regional identity.

The Massif Central takes up a huge portion of the centre of France, but only a handful of towns have gained a foothold in its rugged terrain: **Le Puy**, spiked with theatrical pinnacles of lava, is the most compelling, with its steep streets and majestic cathedral; the spa town of **Vichy** has an antiquated elegance and charm; even heavily industrial **Clermont-Ferrand**, the biggest town in the Massif, has a certain cachet in the black volcanic stone of its historic centre and its stunning physical setting beneath the **Puy de Dôme**, a 1464m-high volcanic plug. There is pleasure, too, in the unpretentious provinciality of **Aurillac** and in the untouched medieval architecture of smaller places like **Murat, Besse, Salers, Orcival, Sauveterre-de-Rouergue** and **La Couvertoirade**, and in the hugely influential abbey of **Conques**. But, above all, this is a region where you come to see the landscapes rather than towns, churches or museums.

Many of France's greatest rivers rise in the Massif Central: the **Dordogne** in the Monts-Dore, the **Loire** on the slopes of the Gerbier de Jonc in the east, and in the Cévennes the **Lot** and the **Tarn**. It is these last two rivers that create the distinctive character of the southern parts of the Massif Central, dividing and defining the special landscapes of the *causses*, or limestone plateaux, with their stupendous gorges. This is territory tailor-made for walkers or lovers of the **outdoors**.

## Auvergne

The heart of the Massif Central is the **Auvergne**, a wild and unexpected scene of extinct volcanoes (*puys*), stretching from the grassy domes and craters of the **Monts-Dômes** to the eroded skylines of the **Monts-Dore**, and the deeply ravined **Cantal mountains** to the forest of darkly wooded pinnacles surrounding Le Puy. It's one of the poorest regions in France and has long remained outside the main national lines of communication: much of it is higher than 1000m and snowbound in winter.

If travelling by public transport, you'll probably have to pass through **Clermont-Ferrand**, the Auvergne capital, and with its dramatic historical associations – it was the site of Pope Urban II's speech, which launched the First Crusade in 109 – the city certainly doesn't disappoint. The small towns in the spectacular **Parc Naturel Régional des Volcans d'Auvergne**, like **Orcival, Murat** and **Salers**, are attractive; at **St-Nectaire** you can see a beautiful small church displaying the distinct Auvergnat version of Romanesque; and even **St-Flour** and **Aurillac** have an agreeable provincial insularity.

CONQUES

# Highlights

**❶ Puy de Dôme** Some 400m above Clermont-Ferrand, this long-extinct volcano offers staggering vistas of the Massif Central. **See p.686**

**❷ Le Puy-en-Velay** Built on volcanic rocks, this ancient town offers intriguing reminders of how similar the Byzantine and Romanesque styles once were. **See p.697**

**❸ Conques** Modern pilgrims trek to this monastery town, once an important way station on the route to Santiago de Compostela. See p.705

**❹ The Millau viaduct** Designed by Sir Norman Foster, the viaduct is a miracle of modern engineering. **See p.708**

**❺ Canoeing** The river gorge of the Tarn provides excellent opportunities for kayaking and canoeing. **See p.710**

**❻ Gorges de l'Ardèche** From the natural bridge at Pont d'Arc, the rushing Ardèche has carved out a dramatic descent through wooded and cave-riddled cliffs. **See p.718**

**HIGHLIGHTS ARE MARKED ON THE MAP ON P.682**

# Clermont-Ferrand and around

**13**

The most dramatic approach to **CLERMONT-FERRAND** is from the Aubusson road or along the scenic rail line from Le Mont-Dore, both of which cross the chain of the Monts-Dômes just north of the Puy de Dôme. Descending through the leafy western suburbs, you get marvellous views of the black towers of the **cathedral**, which sits atop the volcanic stump that forms the hub of the Old Town.

Although its location is magnificent, almost encircled by the wooded and grassy volcanoes of the **Monts-Dômes**, in the twentieth century the town was a typical smokestack industrial centre, the home base of Michelin tyres. Today, however, focusing on the service industries and with two universities, Clermont-Ferrand is very different. Many of the old factories have been demolished, avenues have widened for tramways, and derelict blocks have become shopping malls. As a result, the old centre has a surprisingly hip and youthful feel, with pavement bars packed out in the evenings, as the boutiques and galleries that have sprung up start to wind down for the day. While the town's central **place de Jaude** is largely a monument to garish modernism, the cafés are well placed to take in the morning sun. Here students gather with their laptops and iPads to take advantage of the free wi-fi connection offered in the square.

For one week in February, during the **International Short Film Festival** (⊛clermont -filmfest.com), Clermont-Ferrand becomes as renowned in the film world as Cannes.

## Some history

Clermont-Ferrand's roots, both as a spa and a communications and trading centre, go back to Roman times. It was just outside the town, on the plateau of Gergovia to the south, that the Gauls, under **Vercingétorix**, won their only victory against Julius Caesar's invading Romans. In the Middle Ages, the rival towns of Clermont and Montferrand were ruled respectively by a bishop and the count of Auvergne. Louis XIII united them in 1630, but it was not until the rapid industrial expansion of the late nineteenth century that the two really became indistinguishable.

## Cathédrale Notre-Dame de l'Assomption

**Cathedral** Mon–Sat 7.30am–noon & 2–6pm, Sun and holidays 9.30am–noon & 3–7.30pm **Tour de la Bayette** Mon–Sat 9–11.15am & 2–5.15pm, Sun 3–5.30pm • €1.50 • ⊛ cathedrale-catholique-clermont.cef.fr

As you enter the appealing medieval quarter, clustered in a characteristic muddle

---

### THE FOOD OF THE MASSIF CENTRAL

Don't expect anything very refined from the cuisine of the Auvergne and Massif Central: it's solid peasant food, as befits a traditionally poor and rugged region. The best-known dish is **potée auvergnate**, a kind of cabbage soup, with added potatoes, pork or bacon, beans and turnips – easy to make and very nourishing. Another popular cabbage dish is **chou farci**: cabbage stuffed with pork and beef and cooked with bacon.

Two potato dishes are very common – **la truffade** and **l'aligot**. For *truffade*, the potatoes are sliced and fried in lard, then fresh Cantal cheese is added; for an *aligot*, the potatoes are puréed and mixed with cheese. Less palatable for the squeamish is **tripoux**, usually a stuffing of either sheep's feet or calf's innards, cooked in a casing of stomach lining. **Fricandeau**, a kind of pork pâté, is also wrapped in sheep's stomach.

**Clafoutis** is a popular fruit tart in which the fruit is baked with a batter of flour and egg simply poured over it. The classic fruit ingredient is black cherries, though pears, blackcurrants or apples can also be used.

The Auvergne and the Ardèche in the east produce some wines, though these are not of any great renown. **Cheese**, however, is a different story. In addition to the great cow's milk cheeses – St-Nectaire (see p.691), Laguiole, Cantal, Fourme d'Ambert and Bleu d'Auvergne – this region also produces the prince of all cheeses, **Roquefort**, made from sheep's milk at the edge of the Causse du Larzac (see p.711).

**13**

around the cathedral, Clermont's status as a *ville noire* becomes immediately apparent. The colour is not due to pollution, but to the black volcanic rock used to make many of its buildings. The **Cathédrale Notre-Dame de l'Assomption** stands at the centre and highest point of the Old Town, with its dark and sombre walls built from local lava. Begun in the mid-thirteenth century, it was not finished until the nineteenth, under the direction of Viollet-le-Duc, who was the architect of the west front and those typically Gothic spires. The gloomy interior is startlingly illuminated by the brilliantly coloured rose windows in the transept and the stained-glass windows in the choir, most of which date back to the fourteenth century. Remnants of medieval frescoes survive, too: a particularly beautiful Virgin and Child adorns the right wall of the Chapelle Ste-Madeleine and an animated battle scene between the Crusaders and Muslims unfolds on the central wall of the Chapelle St-Georges. On a fine day it's worth climbing the **Tour de la Bayette**: you look back over the rue des Gras to the Puy de Dôme looming dramatically over the city, with white morning mist retreating down its sides.

### Basilique Notre-Dame-du-Port

Rue du Port • Daily 8am–7pm • Free

Northeast of the cathedral, down the elegant old rue du Port, stands Clermont's other great church, the Romanesque **Basilique Notre-Dame-du-Port** – a century older than the cathedral and in almost total contrast, built from softer arkose stone in pure Auvergnat Romanesque style. Check out the Madonna and Child in the tympanum of the south door in the strangely stylized local form. Both figures are stiff and upright, the Child more like a dwarf than an infant. It was near here (in all probability in place Delille) that Pope Urban II called for the First Crusade in 1095, preaching to a vast crowd who received his speech with shouts of *Dios lo volt* (Occitan for "God wills it"), which became the battle cry of the crusaders.

### The Michelin Adventure

32 rue du clos Four • Sept–June Tues–Sun 10am–6pm; July & Aug daily 10am–7pm • €9 • ☎ 04 73 98 60 60, ⓦ aventure-michelin.com

It feels somewhat incongruous that this French provincial capital is the world headquarters of a colossal global brand. **The Michelin Adventure**, in the old Michelin factory, is an enjoyable place to learn about one of the most innovative industries in France – and one that is still going strong. The company, which invented not only the radial tyre but also the folding map, originated in 1829 thanks partly to the ingenuity of Charles Mackintosh, the Scotsman of waterproof raincoat fame, whose niece married Édouard Daubrée, a Clermont sugar manufacturer, and brought with her ideas about making rubber goods that she had learnt from her uncle. In 1889, the company became Michelin and Co, just in time to catch the development of the automobile and the World War I aircraft industry. The Michelin Adventure runs through the rest of the story: how the company rode the wave of the car boom; how it started producing maps in 1900 to inform customers where to find petrol; and how they started adding restaurants nearby and rating them with stars. Finally, of course, there is Michelin Man himself: the only marketing mascot that has survived unchanged for more than a century.

### Musée Bargoin

45 rue Ballainvilliers • Tues–Sat 10am–noon & 1–5pm, Sun 2–7pm • €5, €9 with the Muséum Henri Lecoq and Musée d'Art Roger-Quilliot • ☎ 04 73 42 69 70

Elegant **Rue Ballainvilliers**, with its sombre eighteenth-century facades, leads to the **Musée Bargoin**. Archeological finds on display here include some fascinating domestic items: Roman shoes, baskets, bits of dried fruit, glass and pottery, as well as a remarkable burial find from nearby Martres-de-Veyre, dating back to the second century AD. There is also a diverse collection of tapestries and textiles.

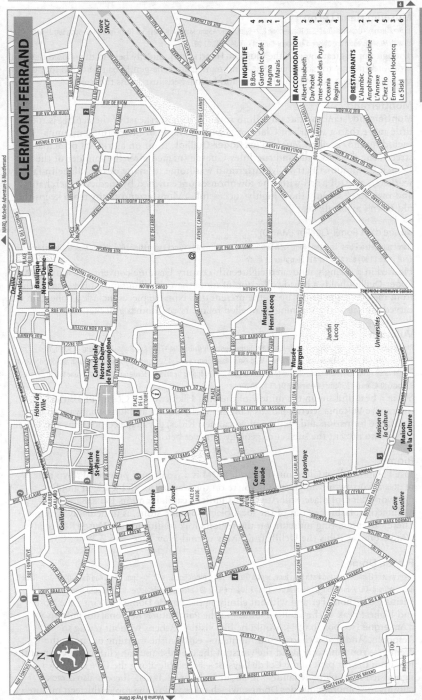

**13**

## Muséum Henri Lecoq

15 rue Bardoux • Oct–April Tues–Sat 10am–noon & 2–5pm, Sun 2–5pm; May–Sept Tues–Sat 10am–noon & 2–6pm, Sun 2–6pm • €5 or €9 with Musée Bargoin and Musée d'Art Roger-Quilliot • ☎ 04 73 42 32 00

Though not of great interest, the **Muséum Henri Lecoq**, directly behind the Musée Bargoin, is devoted mainly to natural history – and named after the gentleman who also founded the public garden full of beautiful trees and formal beds just across the street.

## Montferrand

**Montferrand**, standing out on a limb some 2.5km northeast of the centre, is today little more than a suburb of Clermont, with a couple of interesting museums including the excellent **Musée d'Art Roger-Quilliot**. Built on a grid, its principal streets, rue de la Rodade and rue Jules-Guesde (named after the founder of the French Communist Party – Montferrand was home to many of the Michelin factory workers), are still lined with fine townhouses once owned by medieval merchants and magistrates. Only the – highly successful – Montferrand **rugby team** keeps the old town's name alive.

### Musée d'Art Roger-Quilliot (MARQ)

Place Louis-Deteix • Tues–Fri 10am–6pm, Sat & Sun 10am–noon & 1–6pm • €5 or €9 with Musée Bargoin and Muséum Henri Lecoq • ☎ 04 73 16 11 30 • Bus #1, #9 or #16 from place de Jaude

Housed in a daringly renovated eighteenth-century Ursuline convent, the **Musée d'Art Roger-Quilliot** holds a broad collection of more than two thousand works of art dating from medieval times right up to the present day. Notable pieces include a collection of carved capitals and a stunning enamelled reliquary of Thomas à Becket.

## Vulcania

Rte de Mazayes, St-Ours-les-Roches • April–June daily 10am–6pm; July daily 10am–7pm; Aug Thurs–Tues 10am–7.30pm, Wed 10am–11pm; Sept to mid-Nov & last half of March Wed–Sun 10am–6pm • €21–24.50 depending on season; English audioguide €2.50 • ☎ 04 73 19 70 00, ⓦ vulcania.com • A *navette* leaves the gare SNCF, stopping by place de Jaude on its way (mid-June to mid-Sept daily 9.15am, 10.45am & 12.30pm; €4 return; ☎ 04 73 42 20 20)

Set in a beautiful site in the middle of the *puys* 17km west of Clermont-Ferrand, the interactive **Vulcania** science park is a big hit with families and kids who want to learn about the formation and lifetime of volcanoes. Rides, geysers, electric trains and films all serve to present the subject of geology as never before.

## Riom

Just 15km north of Clermont-Ferrand, **RIOM** is a sedate and provincial town that makes a worthwhile lunch stop if you're on the way up to Vichy. It's an aloof, old-world kind of place, still Auvergne's judicial capital, and its Renaissance architecture, fashioned out of the local black volcanic stone, is undeniably striking. There's an interesting museum on the region's folk traditions, the **Musée Régional d'Auvergne**, at 10bis rue Delille (mid-May to mid-Nov Tues–Sun 2–4pm; €3).

## Puy de Dôme

15km west of Clermont Ferrand **Path** May, June, Sept & Oct Sat, Sun & public holidays 12.30–5pm; July & Aug daily 10am–5pm **Rack Railway** April–Oct 7am–midnight; Nov–March 8am–7.30pm; €9.50; ⓦ panoramiquedesdomes.fr • ⓦ puydedome.com

Visiting Clermont-Ferrand without climbing the **Puy de Dôme** (1465m), the closest and highest peak of the Monts-Dômes, in the **Parc Naturel Régional des Volcans d'Auvergne** (see box, p.691), would be like visiting Athens without seeing the Acropolis. And if you choose your moment – early in the morning or late in the evening – you can easily avoid the worst of the crowds. You can climb to the top of the Puy from the car park of the **Col de Ceyssat** – accessible along the D941 and clearly signposted from place de Jaude – in about an hour (2.3km). There is also a rack railway, the **Panoramique des Dômes**, which takes you to the top in thirteen minutes; a *navette* runs to the entrance from the *gare SNCF* via place de Jaude (7 daily mid-June to mid-Sept; €2.80 return; ☎04 73 44 68 68).

The result of a volcanic explosion about 10,000 years ago, the Puy is a steep 400m from base to summit. Although the weather station buildings and enormous television mast are pretty ugly close up, the staggering views and sense of airy elevation more than compensate. Even if Mont Blanc itself is not always visible way to the east – it can be if conditions are favourable – you can see huge distances, all down the Massif Central to the Cantal mountains. Above all, you get a bird's-eye view of the other volcanic summits to the north and south, largely forested and including the perfect 100m-deep grassy crater of the **Puy de Pariou**.

Just below the summit are the scant remains of a substantial **Roman temple**, dedicated to the god Mercury, some of the finds from which are displayed in Clermont-Ferrand's Musée Bargoin (see p.684).

## ARRIVAL AND INFORMATION — CLERMONT-FERRAND AND AROUND

**By plane** The city airport (☎04 73 62 71 00, ⓦclermont-aeroport.com), at Aulnat, 7km east, serves mainly domestic flights. A local bus (#20; €1.40 one way) connects with the train station.

Destinations Southampton (April–Oct 1–2 weekly; 2hr 30min; FlyBe).

**By train** The *gare SNCF* is on av de l'Union Soviétique, a 10min bus journey from place de Jaude, at the western edge of the cathedral hill. There are buses to the centre (€1.40). A taxi costs around €10.

Destinations Aurillac (5 daily; 2hr 25min); Lyon (5–7 daily; 2hr 30min); Le Puy (up to 4 daily; 2hr 10min); Marseille (1 daily; 7hr 10min); Mende (4 daily; 2hr 40min–3hr); Millau (1 daily; 5hr); Murat (6–7 daily; 1hr 40min); Nevers (8 daily; 1hr 35min); Nîmes (4 daily; 5hr 10min); Paris Bercy (8 daily 3hr–3hr 30 min); Riom (2–4 hourly; 10min); St-Flour (1 daily; 2 hr); Toulouse(1 daily; 6hr); Vichy (every 15–30min; 30min).

**By bus** The intercity *gare routière* is at place Gambetta–Les Salins (☎04 73 93 13 61; ⓦgare-routiere-clermont-fd.com), though some buses stop by the *gare SNCF*.

Destinations Le Mont-Dore (4–5 daily; 2hr 45min); Nîmes (1 daily; 7hr); St-Étienne (2 daily; 2hr 50min); St Flour (1 daily; 1hr 10min).

**Tourist office** Place de la Victoire (Sept–June Mon–Fri 9am–6pm, Sat & Sun 10am–1pm & 2–6pm; July & Aug Mon–Fri 9am–7pm, Sat & Sun 10am–7pm; ☎04 73 98 65 00, ⓦclermont-fd.com).

**Internet** *S@X*, 11 av Carnot (Mon–Fri 8am–7pm, closed Aug; ☎04 73 14 99 74; €4/hr). There is free wi-fi in place de Jaude.

## GETTING AROUND

**City transport** Everywhere in Clermont-Ferrand is accessible by bus, *navette* or tram. There's a city transport information kiosk, Boutique T2C, at 24 bd Charles-de-Gaulle (☎04 73 28 70 00). For city bus and tram timetables check ⓦt2c.fr.

**By bike** With 60km of routes in special lanes along the tram line, the city is a joy for cyclists, although not always flat. Cycles are available at extremely low prices (€3/day) from Moovicité, opposite the *gare SNCF* (Mon–Fri 7am–3pm, Sat 8am–3pm, ⓦmoovicite.com).

## ACCOMMODATION

**Albert Elisabeth** 37 av Albert-Elisabeth ☎04 73 92 47 41, ⓦhotel-albertelisabeth.com. Well-run, a/c family hotel that's handy for the station. With pastel rooms, it offers parking (€6.50), with breakfast for €7.90. Special weekend rates. **€58**

**Dav'hotel** 10 rue des Minimes ☎04 73 93 31 49, ⓦdavhotel.fr. Tucked away in a small street behind the place de Jaude, this is the best-value hotel in the centre. Rooms adjoining *Le Cosmic* bar tend to be noisy, so specify a quiet room unless you want to hang out till closing time (which is not such a hardship). Breakfast €9.80. **€64**

★ **Inter-hôtel des Puys** 16 place Delille ☎04 73 91 92 06, ⓦhoteldespuys.com. A modern, three-star offering spacious rooms, some with balconies. Its first-rate gourmet restaurant and breakfast room has splendid views of the town and the Puy de Dôme. There's an indoor garage. Breakfast €14. **€116**

**Oceania** 82 bd François Mitterrand ☎04 73 29 59 59, ⓦoceaniahotels.com. A central, quiet four-star with laundry and a covered garage (€15/day). Its standard (cheaper) rooms have showers only, with just a low partition separating the bathroom from the bedroom; choose the family suites if you can. There's a good restaurant, too (closed Sat, and Sun lunch). Large breakfast buffet €17. **€182**

**Regina** 14 rue Bonnabaud ☎04 73 93 48 40, ⓦhotel-foch-clermont.com. Behind the striking brick-and-volcanic-stone facade an elegant spiral staircase leads up to fresh, clean rooms. Paid parking available in a garage opposite. Breakfast €7. **€59**

**13**

## EATING

The best restaurants in Clermont-Ferrand are around the conspicuously modern covered food market, in place St-Pierre just off rue des Gras.

### CLERMONT-FERRAND

**L'Alambic** 6 rue Ste-Claire ☎ 04 73 36 17 45, ✆ alambic .restaurant.online.fr. A *terroir* restaurant with a high-end feel, excellent food and service, and mid-range prices. Try the *trouffade* for €19 or the cassoulet with Puy lentils for €20. Mon & Wed 7–10.15pm, Tues & Thurs–Sat noon–2pm & 7–10.15pm; closed 15 July–15 Aug.

**Amphitryon Capucine** 50 rue Fontgiève ☎ 04 73 31 38 39, ✆ amphitryoncapucine.com. Great service, quality products and good-value *menus*, especially the *menu Esquisse* at €28. Tues–Sat noon–2pm & 7.30–9.30pm.

**L'Annexe** 1 rue de Courpière ☎ 04 73 92 50 00, ✆ l-annexe-restaurant.com. Converted from a printing office, this inventive restaurant, with an open kitchen, is a local favourite. Lunch *menus* from €17, dinner from €28. Tues–Thurs noon–1.30pm & 7.30–10.30pm, Fri noon–1.30pm & 7.30–11pm, Sat 7.30–11pm.

**Chez Flo** 18 rue du Cheval Blanc ☎ 04 73 31 11 52, ✆ chezflo.fr. Difficult to find but worth it: a low-ceilinged, cosy brasserie with smiling service and excellent-value local cuisine. Basic *menu* €13.90, but go, if you can, for the three-course *gourmet menu* at €24. Tues noon–1.30pm, Wed–Sat noon–1.30pm & 7.30–9.30pm.

★ **Emmanuel Hodencq** 6 place St-Pierre ☎ 04 73 31 23 23, ✆ hodencq.com. The city's finest restaurant, with one Michelin star, has a pleasantly airy dining room and Auvergnat *menus* from €39. Cooking classes are offered every Sat morning (€135). Tues–Sat noon–1.30pm & 7.30–9.30pm.

**Le Sisisi** 16 rue Massillon ☎ 04 73 14 04 28, ✆ lesisisi .com. Cool, contemporary bistro, with stripped wooden floors, that's popular with night owls due to its late hours. Mains €18, lunchtime *menus* €13.50. Booking recommended. Tues–Fri noon–2pm & 8.30–11pm, Sat 8.30–11pm.

### RIOM

**Le Magnolia** 11 av du Commandant Madeline ☎ 04 73 38 08 25, ✆ lemagnolia.fr. Riom's finest restaurant, offering local cuisine with *menus* for €23–40. Tues–Fri noon–2pm & 7–9pm, Sat 7–9pm, Sun noon–2pm.

## DRINKING AND NIGHTLIFE

**B.Box** 29 rue de l'Eminée ☎ 04 73 28 59 74, ✆ bboxclub .com. The city's main club, in the industrial heartland of Pardieu, with notoriously long queues due to its big-name international DJs. Get there before midnight; it's accessible by tram (stop "Lycée Lafayette"), with special hourly shuttles heading back to the centre after 3am. €10 includes one drink; free on Thurs free. Thurs–Sun & nights before holidays 11pm–5am.

**Garden Ice Café** 48 place de Jaude ☎ 04 73 93 40 97, ✆ gardenicecafe.com. Great service and friendly banter in this sports bar-brasserie facing place de Jaude. Dishes from €15 and *assiettes* €11. Daily noon–midnight.

**Le Marais** 49 rue Fontgiève ☎ 04 73 40 06 56, ✆ lemaraisbar.com. Clermont's main gay and lesbian venue has theme nights during the week – from karaoke to drag shows – and disco *soirées* on Fri and Sat. Tues–Sun 8pm–2am.

**Magma** 10 place de la Victoire ☎ 04 75 37 18 93. The best of many good bar-brasseries on this square, with long kitchen hours, a young clientele and great double-decker hamburgers for €15. Ask for the Auvergnat cola. Daily 10am–1.30am.

# Vichy

**VICHY,** 50km north of Clermont-Ferrand, is famous for two things: its World War II puppet government under Marshal Pétain, and its curative sulphurous **springs**, which attract thousands of ageing and ailing visitors, or *curistes*, every year. The town is almost entirely devoted to catering for its largely elderly, genteel population, which swells several-fold in summer, though attempts are being made to rejuvenate Vichy's image by appealing to a younger, fitness-conscious generation. Still, with Clermont-Ferrand's nightlife so close, the young people aren't flocking here, except perhaps in July and August when **Des Célestines**, the rather good riverside **beach**, becomes a big draw.

There's a real *fin-de-siècle* atmosphere about Vichy, and the best reason to come is to see its fine *belle époque*, Art Nouveau and Art Deco **architecture**. The tourist office offers several afternoon **tours** (in French) showcasing different periods and also a brochure with suggested walking tours. If you are strolling on your own, you'll find the most striking examples in and around the **rue de Russie**, **rue de Belgique** and **rue Alquié** and around the old town between the church of **St Blaise**, the river and the **Sources des Célestines**.

## Parc des Sources

Vichy revolves around the **Parc des Sources**, a stately tree-shaded park that takes up most of the centre. At its north end stands the **Hall des Sources** (mid-Feb to Dec Mon–Sat 7am–5.30pm; free), an enormous iron-framed greenhouse in which people sit and chat or read newspapers, while the various waters emerge from a large tiled stand in the middle, beside the just-visible remains of the Roman foundation. The *curistes* line up to get their prescribed cupful, and for 25c you can join them. The Célestins is the only spring whose water is bottled and widely drunk: if you're up for a taste experience, try the other five. They are progressively more sulphurous and foul, with the Source de l'Hôpital, which has its own circular building at the far end of the park, almost unbelievably nasty. Each of the springs is prescribed for a different ailment and the tradition is that, apart from the Célestins, they must all be drunk on the spot in order to work – a dubious but effective way of drawing in the crowds.

## Grand Établissement Thermal

Esplanade Napoléon III • Various treatments available; a price list is offered at reception

Directly behind the Hall des Sources, on the leafy **Esplanade Napoléon III**, is the enormous, Byzantine-style **Grand Établissement Thermal**, the former thermal baths, decorated with Moorish arches, gold-and-blue domes and blue ceramic panels of voluptuous mermaids. All that remains of the original baths is the grand entrance hall, with its fountain and two beautiful murals, *La Bain* and *La Source*, from 1903. The arcades leading off either side of the hall, once the site of gyms and treatment rooms, now house expensive boutiques.

## Parc de Napoléon III and around

There are four parks on the right bank of the Allier, providing pleasant, wooded river walks. The most famous is the **Parc de Napoléon III**, an English garden created for Napoléon III. Not far from here, at 3 rue Sainte-Cécile, the old town boasts the strange **church of St-Blaise**, actually two churches in one, with a stunning 1931 Art Deco Notre-Dame-des-Malades attached to the original seventeenth-century church. Inside there's an Auvergne Black Virgin which stands surrounded by plaques offered by grateful worshippers who were cured by the sulphurous waters.

### ARRIVAL AND INFORMATION                                           VICHY

**By train** The *gare routière* is a 10min walk from the centre, on the eastern edge at the end of rue de Paris.
Destinations Clermont-Ferrand (1–3 hourly; 30min); Paris Bercy (8 daily; 2hr 50min).
**By bus** Buses, including services from Ambert (4 daily; 2hr), pull in to the *gare routière* on the corner of rue Doumier and rue Jardet, by the central place

Charles-de-Gaulle. There's public transport information on ☎ 04 70 30 17 30.
**Tourist office** 19 rue du Parc (April–June & Sept Mon–Sat 10am–noon & 2–6pm, Sun 3–6pm; July & Aug Mon–Sat 10am–7pm, Sun 2.30–7pm; Oct–March Mon–Sat 10am–noon & 2–6pm; ☎ 04 70 98 71 94, ⟨w⟩ vichy-tourisme.com).

### ACCOMMODATION

**De Cognac** 22 rue du M Gallieni ☎ 04 70 32 15 58, ⟨w⟩ hoteldecognac-vichy.com. If you can cope with the surly owners, this is the best dirt-cheap option, and without the dirt. Nice rooms by the river beach, with colourful and cheerful furnishings. Breakfast €6. Closed mid-Nov to mid-April. €39

★ **La Demeure d'Hortense** 62 av du President Doumer ☎ 04 70 96 73 66, ⟨w⟩ demeure-hortense.fr. A *fin-de-siècle* mansion – the Italian Embassy during the Vichy

period – converted into a high-end B&B with antique Third Republic furnishings and themed rooms. Breakfast included; take it in the flower-filled back patio and relax. €115
**Midland** 4 rue de l'Intendance ☎ 04 70 97 48 48, ⟨w⟩ hotel-midland.com. The most pleasant of several good-value lodgings in the city, this friendly, quiet, grand neo-Baroque hotel sports the excellent restaurant *Le Derby's*, as well. Breakfast €9; check the full or half-board options. Closed mid-Nov to mid-April. €65

**13**

## EATING AND DRINKING

In addition to the hotel-restaurants listed above, there are several brasseries and cafés in the area around the junction of rue Clemenceau and rue de Paris.

**Jacques Decoret** 15 rue du Parc ☎04 70 97 65 06, ⓦjacquesdecoret.com. A must-try establishment, with eclectic dishes drawing on flavours from places as diverse as Oaxaca and Marseille. *Menus* €40–170. Thurs–Mon 12.15–1.25pm & 8–9.25pm. Closed last two weeks of Aug and first week of Sept.

**Le Montreize** 22 place d'Allier ☎04 70 59 99 44. Everyone's favourite Vichy restaurant, offering traditional dishes – and best known for the Auvergnat burger (€13), made with local beef, bacon and cheese sauces. *Menus* from €18. Tues–Sat noon–1.30pm & 7–9pm.

**La Table d'Antoine** 8 rue Burnol ☎04 70 98 99 71, ⓦlatabledantoine.com. A good, affordable option, under chef Antoine Suillat, for haute cuisine. *Menus* from €19.90, with an all-lobster option at €63.50. Tues–Sat 12.15–1pm & 7.30–9pm (8.30pm in winter), Sun 12.15–1pm.

## SHOPPING

★ **Galerie de l'Opera** 6 rue du Casino ☎04 70 31 90 27, ⓦperso.wanadoo.fr-galerie.opera.vichy. One of the delights of a visit to Vichy is hunting for *objets d'art*; this is the best shop, with the highly knowledgeable Alain Cannet de Valdere at your service. Wed–Sun noon–6pm, Mon & Tues by appointment only.

# The Monts-Dore

The **Monts-Dore**, part of the Parc Naturel Régional des Volcans d'Auvergne (see p.691), lie about 50km southwest of Clermont. Volcanic in origin – the main period of activity was around five million years ago – they are much more rugged and more obviously mountainous than their gentler, younger neighbours, the Monts-Dômes. Their centre is the precipitous, plunging valley of the River Dordogne, which rises on the slopes of the **Puy de Sancy**, at 1885m the highest point in the Massif Central, just above the little town of **Le Mont-Dore**.

## Le Mont-Dore

Squeezed out along the narrow wooded valley of the infant Dordogne, grey-slated **LE MONT-DORE** is the gateway to the region. An altogether wholesome and civilized sort of place, it's a long-established spa resort, with Roman remains testifying to just how old it is. Its popularity goes back to the eighteenth century, when roads replaced the old mule paths and made access possible, but reached its apogee with the opening of the railway around 1900.

### Établissement Thermal

Day passes from €49

The **Établissement Thermal** – the baths, which give Le Mont-Dore its *raison d'être* – are in the middle of town and certainly worth visiting. Early every morning, the *curistes* stream into the neo-Byzantine halls – an extravaganza of tiles, striped columns and ornate ironwork – hoping for a remedy in this self-proclaimed "world centre for treatment of asthma".

### Puy de Sancy

For walkers the principal attraction of Le Mont-Dore is the nearby **Puy de Sancy** (1885m), whose jagged skyline blocks the head of the Dordogne valley, 3km away. Accessible by **cable car** since 1936 (April, May & Sept daily 9am–12.30pm & 1.30–5pm; July & Aug daily 9am–6pm; Oct & autumn school holidays Sat & Sun 9am–noon 1.30–5pm; €8.50), it's one of the busiest tourist sites in the country.

### Orcival

Some 27km southwest of Clermont and about 20km north of Le Mont-Dore, lush pastures and green hills punctuated by the abrupt eruptions of the *puys* enclose the

## PARC DES VOLCANS D'AUVERGNE

The **Parc Naturel Régional des Volcans d'Auvergne** consists of three groups of extinct volcanoes – the **Monts-Dômes** (see p.686), the **Monts-Dore** and the **Monts du Cantal** – linked by the high plateaux of Artense and the Cézallier. It's big, wide-open country, sparsely populated, and in spite of their relative ruggedness, there are few crags or rock faces. The steep upper slopes, grassy and treeless, are known as *montagnes à vaches* (mountains for cows), traditionally providing pasture for the cows that produce **St-Nectaire** cheese. You can still see the (now mainly ruined) primitive stone huts, or *burons*, of their herdsmen, scattered along the slopes.

**Maison du Parc** Château de Montlosier, 20km southwest of Clermont-Ferrand ☏ 04 73 65 64 26, ⓦ parc-volcans-auvergne.com. The park headquarters oversees various subsidiary *maisons du parc*, each devoted to different themes or activities: fauna and flora, the lives of the herdsmen, peat bogs and so on. April, Oct & Christmas holidays Tues–Sun 9am–12.30pm & 1.30–5pm; May 9.30am–12.30pm & 1.30–5.30pm; June–Sept daily 9.30am–12.30pm & 1.30–6.30pm.

small village of **ORCIVAL**. A pretty, popular place, founded by the monks of La Chaise-Dieu (see p.700) in the twelfth century, it makes a suitable base for hiking in the region.

### Notre-Dame d'Orcival

Daily 8am–noon & 2–7pm • Free

Orcival is dominated by the stunning Romanesque church of **Notre-Dame d'Orcival**, built from dark-grey volcanic stone and fanned with tiny chapels. Once a major parish, it counted no fewer than 24 priests in the mid-1200s, and the ironwork on the north door, with its curious forged human head motif, dates from that era. Inside, attention focuses on the choir, neatly and harmoniously contained by the semicircle of pillars defining the ambulatory. Mounted on a stone column in the centre is the celebrated **Virgin of Orcival**, a gilded and enamelled twelfth-century statue; she has been the object of a popular cult since the Middle Ages and is still carried through the streets on Ascension Day.

## St-Nectaire and around

**ST-NECTAIRE** lies 26km southeast of Orcival, midway between Le Mont-Dore and Issoire. It comprises the old village of **St-Nectaire-le-Haut**, overlooked by the magnificent Romanesque **church of St Nectaire** and the tiny spa of **St-Nectaire-le-Bas**, whose main street is lined with grand but fading *belle époque* hotels. Among the town's other curiosities are a couple of caverns, and the **Maison du Fromage**.

For walks out of St-Nectaire, take the D150 past the church through the old village towards the **Puy de Mazeyres** (919m), and turn up a path to the right for the final climb to the summit (1hr), where you get a superb aerial view of the surrounding country. Alternatively, follow the D966 along the Couze de Chambon valley to **SAILLANT**, where the stream cascades down a high lava rock face in the middle of the village.

### Basilica of St-Nectaire

Daily: April–Oct 9am–7pm; Nov–March 10am–5pm

Like the church in Orcival and Notre-Dame-du-Port in Clermont, the Basilica of St-Nectaire is one of the most striking examples of the Auvergne's Romanesque architecture. The carved capitals around the apse retain the tantalizing hues of the paint that once covered the whole interior, while the church's treasures, guarded in the north transept, include a magnificent gilded bust of St Baudime (the third-century missionary of the Auvergne and parish-founder), a polychrome *Virgin in Majesty* and two enamelled plaques, all dating from the twelfth century.

## ST-NECTAIRE CHEESE

The cheese of **St-Nectaire** has been growing in reputation ever since Louis XIV had it regularly served at his table; only cheeses made from herds grazing in a limited area to the south of the Monts-Dore are entitled to the *appellation contrôlée*. The cheese is made in two stages. First, a white creamy cheese or *tomme* is produced. This is matured for two to three months in a cellar at a constant temperature; the resulting mould on the skin produces the characteristic smell, taste and whitish or yellowy-grey colour.

There are two kinds of St-Nectaire cheese: **fermier** and **laitier**. The *fermier* is the strongest and tastiest, and some of it is still made entirely on local farms. Increasingly, however, farmers make the *tomme* and then sell it on to wholesalers for the refining stage. The *laitier* is more an "industrial" product, made from the milk of lots of different herds, and then sold onto a cooperative or cheese manufacturer for its final stages.

### Maison du Fromage

Daily: March–June 10am–noon & 2–7pm; July & Aug 10am–7pm; Sept 10am–noon & 2–6pm; Oct–Nov 2–6pm • €5.50 • ☎ 04 73 88 57 96

Find an exhibition on the cheese-making process and a chance to visit a cheese-ripening cellar at the **Maison du Fromage** you'll. The countryside is notable for its menhirs and other prehistoric megaliths; the tourist office (see below) has information on how to find them.

### Besse

Fifteen or so kilometres south of St-Nectaire, and 11km south of the sleepy little village of Murol, **BESSE** is one of the prettiest and oldest villages in the region. Its fascinating winding streets of lava-built houses – some fifteenth-century – sit atop the valley of the Couze de Pavin, with one of the original fortified town **gates** still in place at the upper end of the village.

Besse became wealthy due to its role as the principal market for the farms on the eastern slopes of the Monts-Dore, and its cooperative is still one of the main producers of St-Nectaire cheese (see box above). The annual **festivals** of the Montée and Dévalade, marking the ascent of the herds to the high pastures in July and their descent in autumn, are still celebrated by the procession of the Black Virgin of Vassivière from the **church of St-André** in Besse to the chapel of **La Vassivière**, west of **Lac Pavin**, and her journey back again in autumn (July 2 and the first Sun after Sept 21).

### Lac Pavin and around

**Lac Pavin** lies 5km west of Besse, on the way to the purpose-built downhill ski resort of **SUPER-BESSE** (both are connected to Besse by an hourly *navette*). It's a perfect volcanic lake, filling the now wooded crater. The **GR30** goes through, passing by the **Puy de Montchal**, whose summit (1407m) gives you a fine view over several other lakes and the rolling plateau south towards **ÉGLISENEUVE-D'ENTRAIGUES**, 13km away by road, where the Parc des Volcans' **Maison du Fromage** gives a detailed account of the making of the different Auvergne cheeses (mid-May to June & Sept Wed 9.30am–12.30pm, Sat 2–5pm; July & Aug Mon–Sat 9.30am–12.30pm & 2–6.30pm, Sun and holidays 10.30am–12.30pm & 2–5pm; free; ☎ 04 73 22 30 83).

### ARRIVAL AND INFORMATION

#### LE MONT-DORE

**By train** The *gare SNCF* is at av Guyot Dessaigne at the entrance to the town; a 10min walk down av Michelet gets you to the centre. The track to Clermont-Ferrand will be being maintained in 2013.

**By bus** The *gare routière* is next to the *gare SNCF*. In winter there are early morning/late evening special ski shuttles between here, Clermont-Ferrand and Vichy.

Destinations Clermont-Ferrand (3–4 daily; 2hr 45min); Sancy (June–Aug 1–4 daily; 15min).

**Tourist office** 25 av de la Libération (Mon–Sat 9.30am–noon & 2–6pm, Sun & hols 10am–noon & 2–4pm; ☎ 04 73 65 20 21, ⊕ mont-dore.com). The helpful staff will advise you about walking and cycling possibilities, as well as offer excursions to otherwise inaccessible places in the area.

## ACCOMMODATION AND EATING

### LE MONT-DORE

**Grand Hôtel** 2 rue Meynadier ☎04 73 65 02 64, ⓦhotel-mont-dore.com. A stately nineteenth-century mansion belonging to the charming Patrick and Murielle Perrot, who will organize everything for you. Good off-season offers. Breakfast €8. **€69**

**Helvétia** 5 rue de la Saigne ☎04 73 65 26 73, ⓦhelvetia-mont-dore.fr. Simple, very welcoming hotel by the river, offering good half- and full-board rates. Breakfast €5. Closed mid-Oct to mid-Dec. **€40**

### ORCIVAL

**Camping de la Haute-Sioule** St-Bonnet-Près-Orcival ☎04 73 65 83 32, ⓦcamping-auvergne.info. Some 5km north of the village on a hillside with wonderful views of the surrounding mountains, this is a delightful base for the summer season. Closed Oct–April. **€16**

### ST NECTAIRE

**Les Bains Romains** ☎04 73 88 57 00, ⓦhotel-bains -romains.com. Near the town centre, this top-notch hotel, converted from a spa, offers elegant sitting areas, chic

bedrooms and plush swimming pool. The restaurant is also very good (*menus* from €25). Breakfast €14. **€120**

**De la Paix** ☎04 73 88 49 07, ⓦhotel-delapaix.net. This hotel, at the base of the GR30 footpath below the church, offers comfortable rooms and a reasonably priced restaurant (*menus* from €15). Breakfast €8. Closed Jan, March & 25 Oct–26 Dec. **€50**

### MUROL

**De Paris** Rue de la Vieille Tour ☎04 73 88 60 09, ⓦhoteldeparis-murol.com. A solid, dependable hotel, with bright, well-furnished rooms and a restaurant serving local specialities. The half-board offers are excellent, and there are big discounts for multi-night stays. Picnic baskets for walkers €12, breakfast €9. Closed mid-Nov to Feb. **€70**

### BESSE

**Hostellerie du Beffroy** 24 rue Abbé-Blot ☎04 73 79 50 08, ⓦlebeffroy.com. Atmospheric hotel with a striking hexagonal tower and heavy antique French furnishings. The restaurant is more modern-looking, with excellent *menus* from €28. Breakfast €12, private parking €12. **€65**

# The Monts du Cantal

The Cantal Massif forms the most southerly extension of the Parc des Volcans. Still nearly 80km in diameter and once 3000m high, it is one of the world's largest (albeit extinct) volcanoes, shaped like a wheel without a rim. The hub of the **Monts du Cantal** is formed by the three great conical peaks that survived the erosion of the original single cone: **Plomb du Cantal** (1855m), **Puy Mary** (1787m) and **Puy de Peyre-Arse** (1686m).

From this centre a series of deep-cut wooded valleys radiates out like spokes. The most notable are the **valley of Mandailles** and the **valleys of the Cère and Alagnon** in the southwest, where the road and rail line run, and in the north the **valleys of Falgoux and the Rhue**. Between the valleys, especially on the north side, are huge expanses of gently sloping grassland, including the **Plateau du Limon**. This grassland has for centuries been the mainstay of life in the Cantal, as summer pasture for the cows whose milk makes the firm yellow Cantal cheese which is pressed in the form of great crusty drums. But this tradition has long been in serious decline; as elsewhere, many of the herds are now beef cattle and tourism is on the increase, in particular walking, horseriding and skiing.

## Aurillac

**AURILLAC**, the lively provincial capital of the Cantal, lies on the west side of the mountains, 98km east of Brive and 160km from Clermont-Ferrand. Though it has good mainline train connections and has a population of around 30,000, it remains one of the most out-of-the-way French provincial capitals. The annual **international street theatre festival** (ⓦaurillac.net), held in the last week in August, attracts performers from all over Europe and fills the town with rather more exotic characters than are normally to be seen in these provincial parts.

The most interesting part of Aurillac is the kernel of old streets, now largely pedestrianized and full of good shops, just north of the central **place du Square**. **Rue Duclaux** leads through to the attractive **place de l'Hôtel-de-Ville**, where big markets are held (Wed & Sat) in the shadow of the handsome grey-stone **Hôtel de Ville**, built in Neoclassical style in 1803. Beyond it, the continuation of **rue des Forgerons** leads to

**13**

## ROUTE DES CRÊTES

The sinuous and spectacular **Route des Crêtes** (mountain ridge road) on the D35 between Aurillac and Tournemire (30km) gives you the best view of the Cantal mountain range, and reaches a pass at the Col de Bruel (1308m). Good stops include Croix de Cheules, for a commanding view over the valleys below, and the village of St-Jean-de-Dône, which has an original Templar chapel. From Tournemere you can return to Aurillac via St-Cernin or continue to Salers. The road closes in the winter; check in Aurillac before you set off.

the beautiful little **place St-Géraud**, with its round twelfth-century fountain overlooked by a Romanesque house that was probably part of the original abbey guesthouse, and the externally rather unprepossessing **church of St-Géraud**, which nonetheless has a beautifully ribbed late Gothic ceiling (only open during Mass).

### Muséum des Volcans

Rue Château Saint-Etienne • Mid-June to Aug Mon–Sat 10am–6.30pm & Sun 2–6.30pm; Sept to mid-June Tues–Sat 2–6pm • €4 • ☎ 04 71 48 07 00

On a steep bluff overlooking the east end of town towers the eleventh-century keep of the Château St-Étienne. The keep holds the town's most worthwhile museum, the **Muséum des Volcans**, which has a good section on the relationship between humankind and volcanoes and a splendid view over the mountains to the east.

### ARRIVAL AND INFORMATION                                        AURILLAC

**By train** The *gare SNCF* is on place Sémard, a 10min walk from the central place du Square along av de la République and rue de la Gare.

Destinations Clermont-Ferrand (4 daily; 2hr 20min); Toulouse (3 daily; 3hr 50min).

**By bus** The *gare routière* is next to the *gare SNCF*. Bus

timetables to local destinations are online at ☎ stabus.fr.

**Tourist office** 7 rue des Carmes (Easter–June & Sept Mon–Sat 9am–noon & 1.30–6.30pm, last two Suns in June 10.30am–12.30pm; July & Aug Mon–Sat 9am–7pm, Sun 10am–4pm; Oct–April Mon–Sat 9.30am–noon & 1.30–5.30pm; ☎ 04 71 48 46 58, ☎ iaurillac.com).

### ACCOMMODATION

★ **La Chapellerie** 8 rue de Noailles ☎ 06 80 24 23 33, ☎ un-jour-en-auvergne.com. Bang in the middle of the historic centre and a stone's throw from the Hôtel de Ville, this townhouse, built in 1350 has been renovated with lots of atmosphere; a medieval road ran through what is now the kitchen. Rooms don't have TVs. Breakfast included. **€150**

**Grand Hôtel de Bordeaux** 2 av République ☎ 04 71 48 01 84, ☎ hotel-de-bordeaux.fr. An Aurillacoise institution for 150 years, set in a nineteenth-century mansion. They offer good three-star accommodation and

attentive service. Breakfast €11. **€88**

**Rocher de Cerf** Super-Lioran, 40km southwest of Aurillac ☎ 04 71 49 50 14, ☎ lerocherducerf.com. A pretty spa chalet with all its rooms offering memorable views of the Monts de Cantal. Half-board packages for two are very competitive. Breakfast €8. **€90**

**Le Square** 15 place du Square ☎ 04 71 48 24 72, ☎ cantal-hotel.com. Smart, comfortable hotel near the tourist office, with a pizzeria (rather than a restaurant) attached. Breakfast €7.50. **€51**

### EATING AND DRINKING

★ **L'Arsène sur Cour** 18 rue Arsène Vermenouze ☎ 04 71 48 01 69, ☎ aurillac-restaurant.com. Don't miss out on this restaurant. It offers not only a €17 *menu* of local specialities such as *pounti* (baked cabbage loaf with

prunes), but also Alsatian *tartiflettes*, Savoyard fondues and *pierrades* (Auvergnat meats cooked on hot stones). Book ahead in summer to get an outside table. Tues–Thurs noon –2.30pm & 7–9pm, Fri & Sat noon–2.30pm & 7–10pm.

## Salers

**SALERS** lies 42km north of Aurillac, at the foot of the northwest slopes of the Cantal and within sight of the Puy Violent. Scarcely altered in size or aspect since its sixteenth-century heyday, it remains an extraordinarily homogeneous example of the architecture of that time. If things appear rather grand for a place so small, it's because the town became the administrative centre for the highlands of the Auvergne in 1564 and home of its magistrates. Exploiting this history is really all it has left, but Salers still makes a very worthwhile visit.

If you arrive by the Puy Mary road, you'll enter town by the **church**, which is worth a look for the super-naturalistic statuary of the *Entombment of Christ* (1496). From here, the cobbled **rue du Beffroi** leads uphill, under the massive clock tower, and into the central **place Tyssandier-d'Escous**. This is a glorious little square, surrounded by fifteenth-century mansions with pepper-pot turrets, mullioned windows and carved lintels, among them the **Maison des Templiers**, which houses the small **Musée de Salers**.

Before you leave, head out to the **Promenade de Barrouze** for the view out across the surrounding green hills and the Puy Violent.

### Musée de Salers

Rue des Templiers • April–June & Sept Wed–Mon 10.30am–noon & 2–7.30pm; July & Aug daily 10.30am–noon & 2–7.30pm • €3 • ☎ 04 71 40 75 97

Though the **Musée de Salers** itself is rather dull, with exhibitions on the Salers cattle breed, traditional costumes and the local cheesemaking industry, it's worth having a look at the vaulted ceiling of the entrance passageway, with its carved lions and heads of saints, such as St John the Baptist framed by wild flowing hair.

| INFORMATION | SALERS |
|---|---|

**Tourist office** Place Tyssandier-d'Escous (daily 9.30am–7pm; ☎ 04 71 40 58 08, ⟨w⟩ salers-tourisme.fr).

### ACCOMMODATION AND EATING

**Le Gerfaut** Rte du Puy-Mary ☎ 04 71 40 75 75, ⟨w⟩ salers -hotel-gerfaut.com. Luxurious yet affordable, with stunning views and a small swimming pool, this is probably the best option in Salers. The restaurant offers meals to residents, with half-board options. Breakfast €11.50 Closed Nov–Easter. **€88**

**Des Remparts** Promenade de Barrouze ☎ 04 71 40 70 33, ⟨w⟩ salers-hotel-remparts.com. A very good hotel, with large comfortable rooms, in the centre of the village. Its excellent restaurant specializes in Auvergnat cuisine (*menus* from €14). Breakfast €10. Closed mid-Oct to mid-Dec. **€84**

## Murat

**MURAT**, on the eastern edge of the Cantal, is the closest town to the high peaks and a busy little place, its cafés and shops uncharacteristically bustling for this region. It is also the easiest to access, lying on the N122 road and main train line, about 40km southwest of Salers. Rather than any particular sight, it's the ensemble of grey-stone houses that attracts, many dating from the fifteenth and sixteenth centuries. Crowded together on their medieval lanes, they make a magnificent sight, especially as you approach from the St-Flour road, with the backdrop of the steep basalt cliffs of the **Rocher Bonnevie**, once the site of the local castle and now surmounted by a huge white statue of the Virgin Mary. Facing the town, perwtched on the distinctive mound of the **Rocher Bredons**, by the village of **Albepierre**, there's the lovely Romanesque **Église de Bredons** (July & Aug, arrange a viewing at the mairie of Albepierre or call ☎ 04 71 20 02 80) which contains some fine eighteenth-century altarpieces.

### Maison de la Faune

Place de l'Hôtel de Ville • June Mon–Sat 10am–noon & 2–6pm; July & Aug Mon–Sat 10am–noon & 2–6pm, Sun 2–6pm • €4.70 • ☎ 04 71 20 00 52

One of the finest of Murat's old houses, open to the public in summer as the **Maison de la Faune**; it's full of stuffed animals and birds illustrating the wildlife of the Parc des Volcans.

| ARRIVAL AND INFORMATION | MURAT |
|---|---|

**By train** The *gare SNCF* is on the main road, av du Dr-Mallet.

**Tourist office** 2 rue du Faubourg Notre-Dame (Oct–March Mon–Sat 10am–noon & 2–6pm; April–June & Sept Mon–Sat 9am–noon & 2–6pm; July & Aug Mon–Sat 9.30am–6.30pm, Sun & holidays 10am–12.30pm & 2.30–5.30pm; ☎ 04 71 20 09 47, ⟨w⟩ officedetourismepaysdemurat .com).

**13**

## ACCOMMODATION AND EATING

**Les Messageries** 18 av du Dr-Mallet ☎ 04 71 20 04 04, ⓦ hotel-les-messageries.com. Comfortable hotel with family rooms, a gym, a skating ring in winter and a restaurant serving good hearty meals (€28–34), including home-made *terrines* and fruit tarts. In high season (Feb & Aug) half-board is compulsory and a two-night stay the minimum. Breakfast included. **€80**

**Les Stalapos** Rue du Stade ☎ 04 71 20 01 83, ⓦ camping-murat.com. A cheerful, shady municipal campsite below the *gare SNCF*, with free wi-fi throughout and lots of good facilities. Closed Oct–April. **€7.80**

## St-Flour

Seat of a fourteenth-century bishopric, **ST-FLOUR** stands dramatically on a cliff-girt basalt promontory above the River Ander, 92km west of Le Puy and 92km south of Clermont-Ferrand. Prosperous in the Middle Ages because of its strategic position on the main road from northern France to Languedoc and the proximity of the grasslands of the Cantal, whose herds provided the raw materials for its tanning and leather industries, it fell into somnolent decline in modern times, only partially reversed in the last thirty-odd years.

While the lower town that has grown up around the station is of little interest, the wedge of old streets that occupies the point of the promontory surrounding the cathedral has considerable charm. The best time to come is on a Saturday morning when the **Old Town** fills up with **market stalls** selling sausages, cheese and other local produce. If you're in a car, you can park it in the chestnut-shaded square, **Les Promenades**. The narrow streets of the Old Town lead off from Les Promenades and converge on the **place d'Armes**, with its **cathedral**, some attractive old arcaded buildings housing a couple of cafés, and the town's two **museums**.

### Cathédrale St-Pierre

Place d'Armes • Daily 9am–6pm • Free

The fourteenth-century **Cathédrale St-Pierre** backs onto the edge of the cliff, with a terrace giving good views out over the countryside. The plain grey volcanic exterior is rather severe; inside, however, you will see fine ceiling vaulting and a number of works of art, most notably a carved, painted woodcarving of a Black Christ with a strikingly serene expression, dating from the thirteenth century.

### Musée Alfred Douët

17 place d'Armes • May–Sept daily 10am–noon & 2–6pm; April Mon–Sat 10am–noon & 2–6pm; closes 5pm on holidays • €3.50 with the Musée de la Haute-Auvergne • ☎ 04 71 60 44 99, ⓦ musee-douet.com

At the north end of the place d'Armes, in a fine fourteenth-century building, the **Musée Alfred Douët** houses a private collection of French, Italian and Flemish artworks as well as tapestries, weapons and antique furniture. The view from the cliffs behind the museum gives a sense of St-Flour's impregnable position.

### Musée de la Haute-Auvergne

1 place d'Armes • May–Sept daily 10am–noon & 2–6pm; April Mon–Sat 10am–noon & 2–6pm • €3.50 with the Musée Alfred Douët • ☎ 04 71 60 22 32

At the south end of the place d'Armes, the current Hôtel de Ville, formerly the bishop's palace (1610), houses the interesting **Musée de la Haute-Auvergne**, whose collections include some beautifully carved Auvergnat furniture and exquisitely made traditional musical instruments, such as the *cabrette*, a kind of accordion peculiar to the Auvergne.

## ARRIVAL AND INFORMATION                                    ST-FLOUR

**By train** The *gare SNCF* is on av Charles-de-Gaulle in the lower town. A few trains from Clermont-Ferrand and Aurillac stop here, but most journeys involve changing at Neussargues onto a SNCF bus, which can drop you off on the Promenades in the Old Town, saving you the walk up.

**Tourist office** 17bis place d'Armes (May, June & Sept Mon–Sat 9am–12.30pm & 2–6.30pm, Sun & hols 10am–12.30pm & 2.30–5.30pm; July & Aug Mon–Sat 9am–12.30pm & 1.30–7pm, Sun 10am–12.30pm & 2.30–5.30pm; Oct–April Mon–Sat 9am–noon & 2–6pm; ☎ 04 71 60 22 50, ⓦ saint-flour.com).

## ACCOMMODATION

**Grand Hôtel de l'Europe** 12–13 Cours Spy-des-Ternes ⊤04 71 60 03 64, ⓦsaint-flour-europe.com. Well-sited hotel just outside the historic centre in front of the main free municipal car park. All rooms have panoramic views, satellite TV and safes. The good restaurant serves local recipes. Breakfast €9. **€55**

**La Maison des Planchettes** 7 rue des Planchettes ⊤04 71 60 10 08, ⓦmaison-des-planchettes.com. Magnificent, old-style, basic hotel which offers half-board for as low as €59.30. The good Auvergnat restaurant attached has *menus* from €12.90. Breakfast included with the half-board option only. **€35**

# Le Puy-en-Velay

Right in the middle of the Massif Central, **LE PUY-EN-VELAY**, often shortened to Le Puy, is one of the most remarkable towns in the whole of France, with a landscape and architecture that are totally theatrical. Slung between the higher mountains to east and west, the countryside erupts in a chaos of volcanic acne: everywhere is a confusion of abrupt conical hills, scarred with dark outcrops of rock and topknotted with woods. Even in the centre of the town, these volcanic thrusts burst through. Le Puy is also somewhat inaccessible: the three main roads out all cross passes more than 1000m high, which causes problems in winter.

In the past, Le Puy enjoyed influence and prosperity because of its ecclesiastical institutions, which were supported in part by the production of the town's famous green lentils. It was – and in a limited way, still is – a centre for pilgrims embarking on

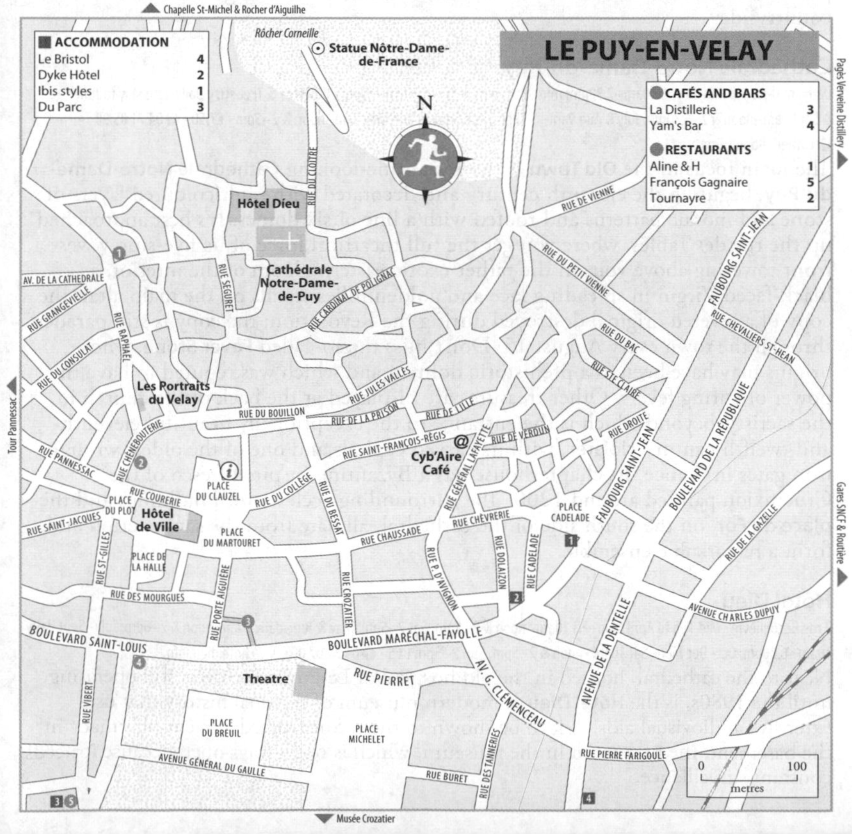

**13**

the 1600km trek to **Santiago de Compostela**. (History has it that Le Puy's Bishop Godescalk was the first pilgrim to make the journey, in the tenth century.) The specific starting point is **place du Plot** (also the scene of a lively Saturday market) and rue St-Jacques. Recently, however, Le Puy has fallen somewhat on hard times, and its traditional industries – tanning and lace – have essentially gone bust. However, in the maze of steep cobbled streets and steps that terrace the **Rocher Corneille**, lacemakers still do a fine trade, with their doilies and lace shawls hanging enticingly outside souvenir shops. If you happen to be here in the third week of September you are in luck: the five-day **King of the Birds** festival engulfs the Old Town in a colourful feast of Renaissance costumes (ⓦ roideloiseau.com).

### Notre-Dame-de-France

**Climb** Daily: April 9am–6pm; May, June & Sept 9am–7pm; July & Aug 9am–7.30pm; Oct to mid-Nov 10am–5pm • €3 •
☎ 04 71 04 11 33

It would be hard to lose your bearings in Le Puy – wherever you go there's no losing sight of the **Notre-Dame-de-France**, the colossal, brick-red statue of the Virgin and Child that towers above the town on the **Rocher Corneille**, 755m above sea level and 130m above the lower town. The Virgin was cast in 1860 from 213 guns captured at Sebastopol and painted red to match the tiled roofs below. You can climb up to the statue's base and, irreverent though it may seem, even up inside it. From here you get stunning views of the city, the church of St-Michel atop its needle-pointed pinnacle a few hundred metres northwest, and the surrounding volcanic countryside.

### Cathédrale Notre-Dame-du-Puy

Daily: mid-Aug to mid-June 6.30am–7.30pm; mid-June to mid-Aug 6.30am–10pm • **Cloister & Treasury** Daily: late May to June
& Sept 9am–noon & 2–6.30pm; July & Aug 9am–6.30pm; late Sept to late May 9am–noon & 2–5pm • €7.50 • ☎ 04 71 05 98 74,
ⓦ cathedraldupuy.org

The main focus in the **Old Town** is the Byzantine-looking **Cathédrale Notre-Dame-du-Puy**, begun in the eleventh century and decorated with multicoloured layers of stone and mosaic patterns and roofed with a line of six domes. It's best approached up the rue des Tables, where you get the full theatrical force of its five-storey west front towering above you. In the rather exotic eastern gloom of the interior, a black-faced Virgin in spreading lace and golden robes stands on the main altar, the copy of a revered original destroyed during the Revolution; the copy is still paraded through the town every August 15. Don't miss the so-called **Fever Stone**, whose origins may have been as a prehistoric dolmen and which was reputed to have the power of curing fevers. Other treasures are displayed at the back of the church in the sacristy, beyond which is the entrance to the exceptionally beautiful eleventh- and twelfth-century **cloister**, with its carved capitals and one of the oldest wrought iron gates in France. Its chapterhouse has a Byzantine-inspired fresco of the Crucifixion painted around 1200. The surrounding ecclesiastical buildings and the **place du For**, on the south side of the cathedral, all date from the same period and form a remarkable ensemble.

### Hôtel Dieu

2 rue Becdelièvre • Mid-Feb to April Mon–Fri 10am–noon & 2–5pm, Sat 2–5pm; May & June daily 10am–noon & 2–6pm; July–Sept daily
10am–6.30pm; Oct–Dec Mon–Sat 10am–noon & 2–5pm, Sun 2–5pm • €5 • ☎ 04 71 07 00 00, ⓦ hoteldieu.info

Next to the cathedral, housed in the old hospital of Le Puy, which was still operating until the 1980s, is the **Hôtel Dieu**, a modern museum of regional history that uses extensive audiovisual aids. Ask to be shown to the reconstructed ancient pharmacy in the basement, the best room in the museum, which is not always open because it needs constant surveillance.

## Chapelle- St-Michel

Daily: Feb to mid-March 2–5pm; mid-March to April & Oct to mid-Nov 9.30am–noon & 2–5.30pm; May–Sept 9am–6.30pm; Christmas hols 2–5pm • €3

It's a fifteen-minute, signposted walk from the cathedral to the **Chapelle- St-Michel**, perched atop the 82m-high needle-pointed lava pinnacle of the **Rocher d'Aiguilhe**. The little Romanesque church, built on Bishop Godescalk's return from his pilgrimage to Santiago de Compostela and consecrated in 962, is a beauty in its own right, and its improbable situation atop this striking pinnacle of rock is quite extraordinary – it's a long haul up 265 steps to the entrance.

## ARRIVAL AND INFORMATION
## LE PUY-EN-VELAY

**By train** The *gare SNCF* is on place Maréchal-Leclerc, around a 15min walk from the central place du Clauzel.
**Destinations** St-Etienne-Lyon (7–8 daily; 2hr–2hr 30min); Clermont-Ferrand (up to 4 daily; 2hr 10min); Lyon (up to 3 daily; 2hr 40min); St Étienne (10–11 daily; 1hr 30min).
**By bus** The *gare routière* faces the *gare SNCF* on place Maréchal-Leclerc. There is one direct train daily to Clermont-Ferrand (2hr 30min), but most involve

changing on to a SNCF train at St Georges D'Aurac or Issoire.
**Tourist office** 2 place du Clauzel (Easter–June & Sept Mon–Sat 8.30am–noon & 1.30–6.15pm, Sun 10am–noon & 2–5.30pm; July & Aug Mon–Sat 8.30am–7pm, Sun 10am–noon & 2–5.30pm; Oct–Easter Mon–Sat 8.30am–noon & 1.30–6.15pm, Sun 10am–noon; ☎04 71 09 38 41, ⓦot-lepuyenvelay.fr). They offer free wi-fi.

## ACCOMMODATION

**Le Bristol** 7–9 av Foch ☎04 71 09 13 38, ⓦhotelbristol-lepuy.com. A former pilgrims' hostel, in one of the area's oldest buildings. The restaurant offers regional dishes from €11.90. Good half-board options. Breakfast €9. **€67**
**Dyke Hôtel** 37 bd Maréchal-Fayolle ☎04 71 09 05 30, ⓦdykehotel.fr. This basic two-star is always popular because of its range of services, so book well ahead. Parking €6. Breakfast €6.50. **€58**
**Ibis Styles** 47 bvd Maréchal Fayolle ☎04 71 09 32 36 ⓦlepuy-hotels.com. The garish soullessness of this

hotel is compensated for by the range of services on offer and its convenient location, especially for drivers. The *chambres familiales* are great value. Guests receive a 10 percent reduction in the attached restaurant, *Taverne de Maître Kanter*. Garage €6. Breakfast included. **€111**
★ **Du Parc** 4 av Clément-Charbonnier ☎04 71 02 40 40 ⓦhotel-du-parc-le-puy.com. A four-star option tucked south of the centre in a quiet street; it offers just fifteen minimalist rooms, which have all the facilities you might require and more. Breakfast €14, garage €7. **€92**

## EATING AND DRINKING

**Aline & H** 11–13 rue des Tables ☎04 71 00 40 72. Aline is from Gabon and H (Henriette) is her mother, but you wouldn't know it from the traditional food served in this superbly situated restaurant in the heart of the old town. The pilgrim's *menu* (sausage with lentils, a selection of cheeses and a glass of wine) is a steal at €16. Daily noon–3pm & 6–10.30pm.
★ **La Distillerie** 29 place du Breuil ☎04 71 04 91 12. Le Puy's most atmospheric pub/brasserie, tucked away from the main street in its own shaded terrace, offers an impressive selection of regional speciality beers and liqueurs. *Plat du jour* €9.70. Daily 8.30am–1am; food served noon–2pm & 7–9.30pm.
★ **François Gagnaire Restaurant** 4 av Charbonnier ☎04 71 02 75 55, ⓦfrancois-gagnaire-restaurant.com. Serving the most creative cuisine in the Haute-Loire, combining flavours such as pigeon and lobster in one dish,

this is a one-star Michelin restaurant belonging to the *Du Parc* hotel – even if you're a guest you'll still have to book, when you reserve a room. *Menus* €37–150 (the latter with wine). Sept–June Tues 7.30–9.30pm, Wed–Sat noon–1.30pm & 7.30–9.30pm, Sun noon–1.30pm; July & Aug Sun–Tues 7.30–9.30pm, Wed–Sat noon–1.30pm & 7.30–9.30pm.
**Tournayre** 12 rue Chènebouterie ☎04 71 09 58 94, ⓦrestaurant-tournayre.com. A local favourite, located in a seventeenth-century building and specializing in regional food (*menus* €25–68). Tues & Thurs–Sat noon–1.30pm & 7–9pm, Sun noon–1.30pm. Closed two weeks in early Sept & last week of Sept.
**Yam's Bar** 1 place aux Laines ☎04 61 09 72 36. A lively brasserie for an evening drink and the best place to try the local green lentil beer, which is also available in many of Le Puy's nightspots. Daily 7am–1am.

**13**

## SHOPPING

★ **Les Portraits du Velay** 10 rue Raphaël ☎04 71 06 00 94, ⓦdentelledepuy.com. Shopping in Le Puy means buying traditional lace and embroidery goods; this shop, opened by lacemaker Didier in 1998, offers the best selection. Mon–Sat 9am–noon & 2–7pm.

# North of Le Puy

**North of Le Puy**, the D906 crosses a vast and terminally depopulated area of pine-clad uplands – now the **Parc Naturel Régional Livradois-Forez** – and continues all the way to Vichy, via the historic town of **La Chaise-Dieu** and the old industrial centre of **Ambert**.

## La Chaise-Dieu

The little town of **LA CHAISE-DIEU** is renowned for the **Abbey church of St-Robert** whose square towers dominate the town. An old diesel **panoramic train** runs between here and Ambert (daily July & Aug; €18 return; ☎04 73 82 43 88, ⓦagrivap.fr); a leisurely and hugely enjoyable way to see the region.

### Abbey church of St-Robert

**Abbey church** Jan Sat 10am–noon & 2–5pm, Sun 2–5pm; Oct–April Tues–Sat 10am–noon & 2–5pm, Sun 2–5pm; May & Sept Mon–Sat 10am–noon & 2–6pm, Sun 2–5pm; June Mon–Sat 9am–noon & 2–6pm, Sun 2–6pm; July to mid-Aug Mon–Sat 9am–7pm, Sun 2–7pm • €4 **Place de l'Echo** Easter–Sept daily 10am–6pm; Oct–Easter Mon–Sat 10am–5pm • Free • ☎04 71 00 06 06, ⓦabbaye-chaise-dieu.com

Founded in 1044 and restored in the fourteenth century at the expense of Pope Clement VI, who had served as a monk here, the Abbey church was destroyed by the Huguenots in 1562, burnt down in 1692, and remained unfinished when the Revolution brought a wave of anticlericalism. It was only really finished in the twentieth century. Its interior contains the tomb of Clement VI, some magnificent Flemish tapestries of Old and New Testament scenes hanging in the choir – which also boasts some fine Gothic stalls – and a celebrated fresco of the **Danse Macabre**, depicting Death plucking at the coarse plump bodies of 23 living figures, representing the different classes of society. "It is yourself", says the fifteenth-century text below.

The remarkable **Salle de l'Echo**, part of the Abbey complex, was once used for hearing confession from the sick and dying. The acoustics are such that two people can turn their backs on each other, stand in opposite corners and still have a perfectly audible conversation just by whispering.

## Ambert

Some 25km north of La Chaise-Dieu, the little town of **AMBERT** was, from the fourteenth to eighteenth centuries, the centre of papermaking in France. It especially supplied the printers of Lyon, a connection that brought the region into contact with new ideas, in particular the revolutionary teachings of the Reformed Church. In the still-operating **Richard-de-Bas paper mill**, just east of town, the **Musée Historique du Papier** (daily: July & Aug 9.30am–7pm; Sept–June 9am–12.30pm & 2–6pm; €6.90; ☎04 73 82 03 11, ⓦwww.richarddebas .com) features exhibits on everything from papyrus to handmade medieval samples.

| **INFORMATION AND TOURS** | **NORTH OF LE PUY** |
|---|---|

**Tourist office** Place de la Mairie, La Chaise-Dieu (May, June & Sept Tues–Sun 10am–noon & 2–6pm; July & Aug daily 10am–12.30pm & 2–7pm; Oct–April Tues & Thurs–Sat 10am–noon & 2–5pm, Wed 10am–noon; ☎04 71 00 01 16, ⓦla-chaise-dieu.info).

## ACCOMMODATION AND EATING

**De La Casadei** Place de l'Abbaye, La Chaise-Dieu ☎04 7100 00 58, ⓦhotel-la-casadei.com. A comfortable hotel that doubles as an umbrella art gallery (you'll simply have to see it). Its restaurant is also very good, with *truffade* and Puy lentil specialities (€15). Breakfast €9. **€49**

**OPPOSITE** GORGES DE L'ARDÈCHE >

**13**

# The southwest

In the southwestern corner of the Massif Central, the landscapes start to change and the altitude begins to drop. The wild, desolate moorland of the **Aubrac** is cut and contained by the savage gorges of **the Lot and Truyère rivers**, in the confluence of which lies the unspoiled village of **Entraygues** ("between the waters" in Occitan). To the south, the arid, but more southern-feeling, plateaux form a sort of intermediate step to the lower hills and coastal plains of Languedoc.

The town of **Rodez**, the capital of the old province of the **Rouergue** – renamed Aveyron after the Revolution – also has much more of a Mediterranean feel, with its pink sandstone cathedral offering a stark contrast to the dark volcanic structures of the Auvergne. The town is certainly worth a visit, though its attractions need not keep you for more than a day. The two great architectural draws of the southwest are **Conques**, with its medieval village and magnificent abbey, which owes its existence to the Santiago pilgrim route (now the GR65), and the perfect little *bastide* of **Sauveterre-de-Rouergue**.

## The Aubrac mountains

The **Aubrac** lies to the south of St-Flour, east of the valley of the River Truyère and north of the valley of the Lot. It's a region of bleak, windswept uplands with long views and huge skies, dotted with glacial lakes and granite villages hunkered down from the weather. The highest points are between 1200m and 1400m, and there are more cows up here than people; you see them grazing the boggy, peaty pastures, divided by dry-stone walls and turf-brown streams. There are few trees, save for a scattering of willow and ash and the occasional stand of hardy beeches on the tops, and only the abandoned shepherds' huts testify to more populous times. It's an area that's invisible in bad weather, but which, in good conditions, has a raw beauty, little disturbed by tourism or modernization.

### Aubrac and around

The marathon **GR65** from Le Puy to Santiago de Compostela in Spain crosses the Aubrac mountains from northeast to southwest en route to Conques. The tiny village of **AUBRAC**, which gave its name to the region, owes its existence to this Santiago pilgrim route; around 1120, a way station was opened here for the express purpose of providing shelter for the pilgrims on these inhospitable heights. Little remains today, beyond the windy **Tour des Anglais**.

The waymarked **Tour d'Aubrac** footpath does a complete circuit of the area in around ten days, starting from the town of **AUMONT-AUBRAC**, 40km from Aubrac and a much better option for accommodation.

### St-Urcize

In the wildest and most starkly beautiful part of the Aubrac region, the close-huddled village of **ST-URCIZE**, 13km north of Aubrac, hangs off the side of the valley of the River Lhère; it has a lovely Romanesque church at its centre and a poignant World War I **memorial**. The village is ghostly out of season; most of the unspoiled granite houses are owned by people who live elsewhere.

### Laguiole

Seventeen kilometres west of St-Urcize, **LAGUIOLE** passes for a substantial town in these parts; if you don't have a car your only chance of getting in or out of town is on the morning bus to Rodez. Derived from the Occitan word for "little church", it's a name that now stands for knives and cheese.

## LAGUIOLE: KNIVES AND CHEESE

Laguiole **knives**, which draw hordes of French to the town's many shops, are characterized by a long, pointed blade and bone handle that fits the palm; the genuine article should bear the effigy of a bee stamped on the clasp that holds the blade open. The industry started here in the nineteenth century, then moved to industrial Thiers, outside Clermont-Ferrand, before returning in 1987. At this point, the Société Laguiole (the only outlet for the genuine article) opened a Philippe Starck-designed factory on the St-Urcize road, with a giant knife projecting from the roof of the windowless all-aluminium building. They have a shop on the main through-road, on the corner of the central marketplace (Ⓦ www.forge-de-laguiole.com).

Laguiole's **cheesemaking** tradition (Ⓦ laguiole-online.com) dates back to the twelfth century; unpasteurized cow's milk is formed into massive cylindrical cheeses, and aged up to eighteen months. To sample or buy, try the factory outlet on the north edge of town.

## ACCOMMODATION AND EATING

### AUBRAC AND AROUND

**Chez Camillou** 10 rue du Languedoc, Aumont Aubrac ☎ 04 66 42 80 22, Ⓦ hotel-camillou.com. Finding a great, comfortable three-star hotel in the proverbial middle of nowhere is priceless; finding its excellent hotel restaurant *Cyril Attrazic* is little short of a miracle. Closed mid-Nov to mid-March. **€80**

**De la Dômerie** Aubrac ☎ 05 65 44 28 42, Ⓦ hotel domerie.com. Friendly hotel, in the same family for generations, with each room decorated and furnished in a different style. Try the Aubrac steak in the restaurant. Breakfast €12. Closed mid-Nov to Jan. **€70**

**Relais de Peyre** 9 rue du Languedoc, Aumont Aubrac ☎ 04 66 42 85 88, Ⓦ lerelaisdepeyre.com. Less grand than the *Chez Camillou* opposite, but no less comfortable, this hotel also has a good-value restaurant serving a juicy entrecote steak for just €20. Breakfast €8. Closed Jan. **€48**

### ST-URCIZE

**Guy Prouhèze** 2 rte de Languedoc ☎ 04 66 42 80 07,

## THE AUBRAC MOUNTAINS

Ⓦ prouheze.com. Excellent-value hotel featuring a famed *gastronomique* restaurant (*menu* €60; closed Sun lunch & Mon) along with two other good restaurants: the upmarket *Prouhèze* and the rustic *Le Compostelle* (*menu* €22.90). Many special offers available online. Closed Dec–March. Breakfast €13. **€90**

### LAGUIOLE

**Aubrac** 17 allée Amicale ☎ 05 65 44 32 13, Ⓦ hotel -aubrac.fr. A café, hotel and restaurant in the centre of Laguiole, offering a wide range of rooms from singles to six-person family suites. Breakfast €8.50. **€45**

**Auguy** 2 allée Amicale ☎ 05 65 44 31 11, Ⓦ hotel -auguy.fr. Newly refurbished hotel, with a good restaurant with a *menu terroir* from €22. Breakfast €11. Closed Jan to mid-Feb. **€70**

**Noù4** Rue Bardière ☎ 05 65 51 68 30, Ⓦ nou4.izihost .com. The tiny *Noù4*, a cross between a café-restaurant, boutique and hotel, also offers ski lessons in winter. Rooms are on the small side, but cosy. Breakfast €6. **€56**

# Rodez

A particularly beautiful and out-of-the-way stretch of country lies on the southwest of the Massif Central, bordered roughly by the valley of the **River Lot** in the north and the **Viaur** in the south. The upland areas are open and wide, with views east to the mountains of the Cévennes and south to the Monts de Lacaune and the Monts de l'Espinouse. The only place of any size, accessible on the main train and bus routes, is Aveyron's capital, **RODEZ**, an active and prosperous town with a charming, renovated centre and a fine **cathedral**.

## The Old Town

Built on high ground above the River Aveyron, the **Old Town**, dominated by the massive red sandstone **Cathedral of Notre-Dame**, is visible for kilometres around. All approaches lead to the **place d'Armes**. From the back of the cathedral to the north and the south, a network of well-restored medieval streets connects place de-Gaulle, place de la Préfecture and the attractive place du Bourg, with its fine sixteenth-century houses. In place Foch, just south of the cathedral, the Baroque chapel of the old **lycée** is worth a look for its amazing painted ceiling, while in **place Raynaldy**, the modern **Hôtel de Ville** and the **médiathèque** quite successfully graft modern styles onto old buildings.

**13**

## Cathedral of Notre-Dame

Place d'Armes • Daily 9am–6.30pm • Free

The **Cathedral of Notre-Dame**, with its plain, fortress-like west front, sits next to the seventeenth-century bishop's palace on the place d'Armes – both buildings were incorporated into the town's defences. The Gothic cathedral, its plain facade relieved only by an elaborately flowery rose window, was begun in 1277 and took three hundred years to complete. Towering over the square is the cathedral's 87m **belfry**, decorated with fabulous pinnacles, balustrades and statuary. The impressively spacious interior, architecturally as plain as the facade, is adorned with a magnificently extravagant seventeenth-century walnut organ loft and fifteenth-century choir stalls.

## Musée Fenaille

Place Raynaldy • Sept–June Tues, Thurs & Fri 10am–noon & 2–6pm; July & Aug daily 10am–6pm • €3; €4 with the Musée Denys Puech • ☎ 05 65 73 84 30, ⓦ musee-fenaille.com

The **Musée Fenaille** is the main museum in Rodez, holding an impressive permanent collection of historical artefacts found in Aveyron, and hosting temporary exhibitions each summer showcasing the work of local artists. The big attraction is the top floor, which is devoted to carved **menhirs** dating back more than three thousand years; don't miss the anthropomorphic Neolithic statue-menhir of the Dame de Saint-Sernin.

## Musée Denys Puech

Place George Clemenceau • Tues–Fri 10am–noon & 2–6pm, Sat & Sun 2–6pm • €2.50; €4 with the Musée Fenaille • ☎ 05 65 77 89 60

Behind place Raynaldy, the **Musée Denys-Puech** has a permanent collection celebrating the work of Denis Puech (1854–1942), one of the most important post-Rodin French sculptors, and presents three special exhibitions of contemporary art per year.

### ARRIVAL AND INFORMATION — RODEZ

**By plane** Rodez airport is 7km north of town. There is no shuttle to Rodez; a taxi costs €20 (20min).
Destinations London Stansted (1hr 45min; Ryanair); Dublin (3hr; Ryanair).

**By train** The gare SNCF is on bd Joffre, on the northern edge of town.
Destinations Mende (up to 1 daily; 2hr 30min); Millau (hourly; 1hr 25min); Toulouse (hourly; 2hr 20min).

**By bus** The *gare routière* (☎ 05 65 68 11 13) is on av Victor-Hugo.
Destinations Conques (up to 2 daily; 1hr 50min); Entrayges (up to 2 daily; 1hr 10min); Laguiole (1 daily; 1hr 30min).

**Tourist office** 24 Bd Denys Puech (July & Aug Mon–Sat 9am–12.30pm & 1.30–6.30pm, Sun 10am–noon; Sept–June Mon–Sat 9am–12.30pm & 1.30–6pm; ☎ 05 65 75 76 77, ⓦ ot-rodez.fr).

### ACCOMMODATION

**Du Clocher** 4 rue Séguy ☎ 05 65 68 10 16, ⓦ hotel-clocher.com. Hotel with a nice yellow and ochre colour scheme and stylish rooms with large plasma screens. Great half-board option. Breakfast €8. **€62**

**Mercure Rodez Cathédrale** 1 av Victor Hugo ☎ 05 65 68 55 19, ⓦ accorhotels.com. With a beautiful 1930s Art Deco facade, this four-star hotel provides stylish accommodation by the cathedral (for a real Art Deco

experience, pop in to the *Brasserie Broussy* next door). Its wi-fi signal can be picked up in the place d'Armes. Some free parking places. Breakfast €12.50. **€110**

**La Tour Maje** 1 bd Gally ☎ 05 65 68 34 68, ⓦ hoteltourmaje.fr. A comfortable three-star in a modern building rather incongruously tacked onto a medieval tower. Breakfast €12. **€70**

### EATING AND DRINKING

**Bistro Les Colonnes** 6 place d'Armes ☎ 05 65 68 00 33. The safe choice: a great place to view the cathedral (especially at night), long hours, and large portions. *Menus* start at €11 and cocktails at €5. Sun–Wed 8am–1am, Thurs–Sat 8am–2am; kitchen closes at 10.30pm, 9pm Sun.

**Le Bistroquet** 17 rue du Bal ☎ 05 65 68 74 75. Traditional French restaurant with good salads and grills for

around €15 – and they even dare to go to medium for steaks. Tues–Sat noon–2pm & 7–9pm; closed Feb.

**Goûts et Couleurs** 38 rue Bonald ☎ 05 65 42 75 10, ⓦ goutsetcouleurs.com. *The* place to go for gourmet food is this classy one-star Michelin restaurant with *menus* by chef Jean-Luc Fau starting at €29. Wi-fi available. Mon & Tues noon–2pm, Wed–Sat noon–2pm & 7–9pm.

**Le Kiosque** 6 rue Planard ☎05 65 68 56 21, ⓦlekiosque-rodez.fr. With a brilliant location in the middle of Rodez's Jardin du Foirail, this restaurant focuses on seafood and fish (six oysters €10; sixteen shrimps €9) but also offers a variety of local *menus* such as the Aveyronnais for €21.50. Tues & Thurs–Sat noon–2pm &

7.30–9.45pm, Sun 7.30–9.45pm.

**La Taverne** 23 rue de l'Embergue ☎05 65 42 14 51, ⓦtavernerodez.com. One of the cheapest places to sample local cuisine (speciality is the *choux farcis*) with an attractive terrace at the back. *Menus* from €8.50; takeaway available. Mon–Sat noon–2pm & 7–9.30pm.

## Sauveterre-de-Rouergue

Forty kilometres southwest of Rodez, **SAUVETERRE-DE-ROUERGUE** (ⓦsauveterre.free.fr) makes the most rewarding side trip in this part of Aveyron if you have your own vehicle. It is a perfect, otherworldly *bastide*, founded in 1281, with a large, wide central square, part cobbled, part gravelled, and surrounded by stone and half-timbered houses built over arcaded ground floors. Narrow streets lead off to the outer road, lined with stone-built houses the colour of rusty iron. On summer evenings, *pétanque* players come out to roll their *boules* beneath chestnut and plane trees, while swallows and swifts swoop and dive overhead.

**ACCOMMODATION AND EATING**                    **SAUVETERRE-DE-ROUERGUE**

**La Grappe d'Or** Bd Lapérouse Tour de Ville ☎05 65 72 00 62 ⊜guy.gayubar@orange.fr. A charming hotel whose restaurant offers an excellent *menu* at €12, with dishes like *gésiers chauds* and *tripoux*, and, for dessert, cheese, ice cream and *fouace* (a sweet cake). Breakfast €6. Hotel closed Nov–March; restaurant open all year. **€37**

**Le Sénéchal** At the entrance to the village ☎05 65 71 29 00, ⓦhotel-senechal.fr. Four-star business hotel with an indoor pool, conference rooms and an excellent restaurant with *menus* at €27–120. Breakfast €16. Closed Jan to mid-March. **€150**

## Conques

**CONQUES**, 37km north of Rodez, is one of the great villages of southwest France. It occupies a spectacular position on the flanks of the steep, densely wooded gorge of the little **River Dourdou**, a tributary of the Lot. It was its **abbey** that brought Conques into existence, after a hermit called Dadon settled here around 800 AD and founded a community of Benedictine monks, one of whom is said to have pilfered the relics of the martyred girl, Sainte-Foy, from the monastery at Agen. Known for her ability to cure blindness and liberate captives, Ste Foy's presence brought the pilgrims flocking, earning the abbey a prime place on the pilgrimage route to Santiago de Compostela.

The **village** is very small, largely depopulated and mainly contained within medieval **walls**, parts of which still survive, along with three of its **gates**. The houses date mainly from the late Middle Ages, and the whole ensemble of cobbled lanes and stairways is a pleasure to stroll through. There are two main streets, the old **rue Haute**, or "upper street", which was the route for the pilgrims coming from Estaing and Le Puy and passing onto Figeac and Cahors through the **Porte de la Vinzelle**; and the lane, now **rue Charlemagne**, which leads steeply downhill through the **Porte de Barry** to the river and the ancient **Pont Romain**, with the little **chapel of St-Roch** off to the left, from where you get a fine view of the village and church.

In August, Conques hosts a prestigious **classical music festival**, most of the concerts taking place at the abbey church.

### The Abbey Church of Ste-Foy

**Church** Daily 7.30am–10pm • Free **Treasury** April–Sept 9.30am–12.30pm & 2–6.30pm; Oct–March 10am–noon & 2–6pm • €6.20 including Musée Fau (see p.706)

At the village's centre, dominating the landscape, stands the Romanesque **Abbey Church of Ste-Foy**, begun in the eleventh century, whose giant pointed towers are echoed in those of the medieval houses clustered tightly around it. Its plain,

### THE TREASURY OF CONQUES

Conques Abbey's most prized asset is its hoard of extraordinarily rich, bejewelled medieval **reliquaries**, including a statue known as the *A of Charlemagne*, because it is thought to have been the first in a series given by the emperor to monasteries he founded. But it is the astonishing gilded **statue of Ste-Foy**, parts of which are as old as the fifth century, that is the highlight of any visit: seated, with a blank expression, it looks more like an Inca idol than the work of a Catholic artist. Writing in 1010, a cleric named Bernard d'Angers gave an idea of the effect of these wonders on medieval pilgrims: "The crowd of people prostrating themselves on the ground was so dense it was impossible to kneel down… When they saw it [Ste-Foy] for the first time, all in gold and sparkling with precious stones and looking like a human face, the majority of the peasants thought that the statue was really looking at them and answering their prayers with her eyes." The treasure is kept in a room adjoining the now ruined cloister; in addition, the **Musée Fau**, in the cathedral square, holds a miscellany of sixteenth-century and later tapestries, furnishings and medieval statues.

fortress-like facade rises on a small cobbled square beside the tourist office and pilgrims' fountain, the slightly shiny silver-grey schist prettily offset by the greenery and flowers of the terraced gardens.

In startling contrast to this plainness, the elaborately sculpted *Last Judgement* in the **tympanum** above the door admonishes all who see it to eschew vice and espouse virtue. Christ sits in judgement in the centre, with the chosen on his right hand, among them Dadon the hermit and the emperor Charlemagne. Meanwhile, his left hand directs the damned to Hell, which is as usual, so much more graphically and interestingly portrayed, with all its gory tortures, than the bliss of Paradise which is depicted in the bottom left panel.

The **interior** was designed to accommodate large numbers of pilgrims, channeling them down the aisles and round the ambulatory. From here they could contemplate Ste Foy's relics displayed in the choir, encircled by a lovely wrought-iron screen, still in place. There is some fine carving on the capitals, especially in the triforium arches; to see them, climb to the organ loft, which gives you a superb perspective on the whole interior.

On summer evenings, around 9.30pm, the abbey church hosts organ and piano concerts at the **Nocturne des Tribunes** (May–Sept daily; tickets from the tourist office, €5; no children under 12) – a stunning way to experience the beauty of the place.

### European Centre for Medieval Art and Civilization

Daily 9.30am–noon & 1.30–5pm • Free • ☎ 05 65 71 24 00, ⓦ ceacm.com

Climbing the road on the far side of the valley brings you to the rather grandiose-sounding **European Centre for Medieval Art and Civilization**, hidden in a bunker right at the top of the hill. Along with a small permanent collection of medieval artefacts, they also feature temporary exhibitions.

### ARRIVAL AND INFORMATION                                                     CONQUES

**By car** You need a car to reach Conques. There's a car park 450m outside the village centre as you arrive from the D901 (€3).

**Tourist office** Rue Henri Paraye (daily: April–Sept 9.30am–12.30pm & 2–6.30pm; Oct–March 10am–noon & 2–6pm; ☎ 05 65 72 85 00, ⓦ tourisme-conques.fr). Guided tours leave from here (1 or 2 daily; €4).

### ACCOMMODATION AND EATING

**Auberge St-Jacques** At the centre of Conques ☎ 05 65 72 86 36, ⓦ aubergestjacques.fr. Near the abbey church, this good-value, old-fashioned hotel also has a popular restaurant, with *menus* from €11.50. Breakfast €8.50. **€53**

**Camping Beau Rivage** On the banks of the Dourdou, 400m below Conques ☎ 05 65 69 82 23, ⓦ camping conques.com. A simple, efficient campsite with a pretty good restaurant and a few cottages available for rent as well (€45). Breakfast €6. Closed Oct–March. **€19.50**

**Moulin de Cambelong** Le Moulin 1 Conques ❶ 05 65 72 84 77, ⓦ moulindecambelong.com. A four-star hotel with rooms that have spacious wooden balconies with great views of the river. Its one-star Michelin restaurant, under chef d'Hervé Busset, specializes in duck dishes (lunchtime *menu* from €28 Mon–Fri, otherwise €55). Breakfast €20. **€290**; river view **€360**

★ **St Foy** Opposite the abbey church ❶ 05 65 69 84 03, ⓦ hotelsaintfoy.fr. Beautiful airy rooms, some with a view, and a good restaurant serving food in the beautifully shaded patio. Wi-fi access only around reception area. Breakfast €13, garage €15. **€97**

**De la Terrasse** Vieillevie, 6km east of Conques ❶ 04 71 49 94 00, ⓦ hotel-terrasse.com. A good hotel with an even better restaurant (*menus* €22–37), a pretty sun terrace and a small pool. Canoe rental is also available. Closed mid-Nov to March. Breakfast €9.50 **€50**

## The upper Lot valley

The most beautiful stretch of the **Lot Valley** is the 21.5km between the bridge of Coursavy, below **Grand-Vabre** (just north of Conques), and **Entraygues**: deep, narrow and wild, with the river running full and strong, as yet unaffected by the dams higher up, with scattered farms and houses high on the hillsides among long-abandoned terracing. The shady, tree-tunnelled road is level and not heavily used, making it ideal for cycling.

### Entraygues and around

Lying right where the Lot meets the equally beautiful River Truyère, **ENTRAYGUES**, with its riverside streets and attractive grey houses, has an airy, open feel that belies its mountain sleepiness. The brown towers of a thirteenth-century **château** overlook the meeting of the waters, and a magnificent four-arched **bridge** of the same date crosses the Truyère a little way upstream, alongside the ancient tanners' houses.

#### Château de Calmont d'Olt

Espalion, 10km south of Entraygues • Daily: May, June & Sept 10am–noon & 2–6pm; July & Aug 10am–7pm; school hols 2–6pm • €8 in summer, otherwise €5.50 • ⓦ chateaucalmont.org

The **Château de Calmont d'Olt** is a rough and atmospheric old fortress dating from the eleventh century, on the very peak of an abrupt bluff, 535m high and a stiff 1km climb above the town of **ESPALION** on the south bank – its views of the town and the country beyond are unbeatable. Regular childrens activities include demonstrations of medieval siege engines and artillery.

| INFORMATION | ENTRAYGUES AND AROUND |
|---|---|

**Tourist office** Place de la République (April–June & Sept Mon–Sat 10am–12.15pm & 2–6pm; July & Aug Mon–Sat 9.30am–12.30pm & 3–7pm, Sun & holidays 10am–12.30pm; Oct–March Mon 2–6pm, Tues–Fri 10am–12.15pm & 2–6pm, Sat to 5pm); ❶ 05 65 44 56 10, ⓦ tourisme-entraygues.com). Here you'll get information about walking, mountain biking and canoeing in the area.

### ACCOMMODATION AND EATING

**Du Centre** 1 place de la Republique ❶ 05 65 44 51 19, ⓦ hotelducentre-12.com. One of those wonderful, friendly hotels that you find in rural France, offering everything with a smile: spotless rooms, a shady terrace, a bar and a restaurant offering family cooking with *menus* €12–36. Breakfast €7. **€45**

**Lion d'Or** 6 Tour de Ville ❶ 05 65 44 50 01, ⓦ hotel -lion-or.com. First-rate hotel with a covered swimming pool and garden, assorted family-friendly amenities and attached restaurant (*menu du terroir* €18). Breakfast €8. Closed mid-Nov to March. **€48**

# Les Causses

The **Parc Régional des Grands Causses** merges naturally with the **Causses and Cévennes** UNESCO Heritage Site and it is only human administrators who have artificially separated one from the other. The park, most of which lies in the

**13**

---

### GRAND VIADUC DE MILLAU

The **Grand Viaduc de Millau** is an astonishing 2.5km-long viaduct supported by seven enormous pillars which, at times, puncture the cloud level (the highest reaches 326m, taller than the Eiffel Tower). Designed by Sir Norman Foster, engineered by Michel Virlogeux and built by Eiffage, a construction firm that traces its heritage back to Gustave Eiffel, it is as much a work of art as it is a vital link from Paris to the Languedoc coast. There is a signposted belvedere off the D991 out of Millau just before you reach the A75 *autoroute*.

---

*département* of **Lozère**, is sculpted by the canyon of **Gorges du Tarn**, where the deep limestone cliffs are a barrier to even mobile signals. Moulded over millennia, this is a spectacular country of narrow valleys, granite gorges and small villages built precariously on slopes such as the **Cirque of Navacelles**. The gateway to it all is the appealing town of **Millau**; further south the village of **Roquefort-Sur-Soulzon** is home to the famed cheese, while the **Cistercian Abbey de Silvanès** and the Templar village of **La Couvertoirade** provide history in spades.

## Millau

The lively town of **MILLAU** occupies a beautiful site in a bend of the River Tarn at its junction with the Dourbie. It's enclosed on all sides by impressive white cliffs, formed where the rivers have worn away the edges of the *causses*, especially on the north side, where the spectacular table-top hill of the **Puech d'Andan** stands sentinel over the town. Millau owes its original prosperity to its position on the ford where the Roman road from Languedoc to the north crossed the Tarn, marked today by the truncated remains of a medieval **bridge** surmounted by a watermill jutting out into the river beside the modern bridge.

From the Middle Ages until modern times, thanks to its proximity to the sheep pastures of the *causses*, the town was a major manufacturer of **leather**, especially gloves. Although outclassed by cheaper producers in the mass market, Millau still leads in the production of top-of-the-range goods.

The town's clean and well-preserved old streets have a summery, southern charm. Whether you arrive from the north or south, you'll find yourself sooner or later in **place du Mandarous**, the main square, where avenue de la République, the road to Rodez, begins. South of here, the **old town** is built a little way back from the river to avoid floods and is contained within an almost circular ring of shady boulevards. **Rue Droite** cuts through the centre of the old town, linking its three squares: place Emma-Calvé, place des Halles and place Foch.

### Place Foch

The rue Droite cuts through the centre, linking three squares: place Emma-Calvé, place des Halles and place Foch. The prettiest by far is **place Foch**, with its café shaded by two big plane trees and its houses supported on stone pillars; some date back to the twelfth century. In one corner, the **church of Notre-Dame** is worth a look for its octagonal Toulouse-style belfry, originally Romanesque.

#### Musée de Millau

Place Foch · Oct–June Mon–Sat 10am–noon & 2–6pm; July & Aug daily 10am–6pm; Sept daily 10am–noon & 2–6pm · €5.40 · ☏ 05 65 59 01 08, ⓦ museedemillau.fr

The very interesting **Musée de Millau**, housed in the Hôtel de Pégayrolles, a stately eighteenth-century mansion, has thirty exhibition rooms focusing on the bizarre combination of archeology and gloves. Here you can see the magnificent red pottery of the Graufesenque works (see p.709), as well as the complete skeleton of a 180-million-year-old plesiosaurus.

## Place Emma-Calvé and around

**Belfry** 16 rue Droite April–Sept daily 10am–noon & 2–6pm • €3.60 • ☏ 05 65 59 01 08

**Place Emma-Calvé** and the adjoining **place du Beffroi** have been subject to some questionable attempts at reconciling old stonework with contemporary urban design. The **clock tower** by the Post Office on place du Beffroi is worth a climb for the great all-round view. Take a look also in the streets off the square – rue du Voultre, rue de la Peyrollerie and their tributaries – for a sense of the old working-class and bourgeois districts.

## La Graufesenque

Av Louis Balsan, 2km southeast of the centre just upstream on the south bank of the Tarn • July & Aug Tues–Sun 10am–12.30pm & 2.30–7pm; May, June & Sept Tues–Sun 10am–noon & 2–6pm; Oct–Dec, March & April Tues–Sun 10am–noon & 2–5pm • €4.30 • ☏ 05 65 60 11 37, ⓦ graufesenque.com

Clear evidence of the town's importance in Roman times (when it was called Condatomagus) can be seen in the **La Graufesenque** Gallo-Roman site, whose renowned bright red terracotta wares (*terra sigillata*) were distributed throughout the Roman world. This is the archeological site only; the finds can be seen in the Musée de Millau (see p.708).

### ARRIVAL AND INFORMATION
MILLAU

**By train** The *gare SNCF* is on rue de Belfort; it's a walk of around 10min down rue Alfred-Merle to the main square, place du Mandarous.

Destinations Clermont-Ferrand (1 daily; 5hr); Rodez (10 daily; 1hr 25min).

**Tourist office** Place du Beffroi (July & Aug Mon–Sat 9am–7pm, Sun 9.30am–4pm; Sept–June Mon–Sat 9am–12.30pm & 2–6.30pm, Sun 9.30am–4pm; ☏ 05 65 60 02 42, ⓦ millau-viaduc-tourisme.fr).

### ACCOMMODATION

**De la Capelle** 7 place de la Fraternité ☏ 05 65 60 14 72, ⓦ hotel-millau-capelle.com. Modern and rather cheerily American in look and feel, this hotel, with good views of the Puech d'Andan, is a good-value option, especially for families; double rooms can sleep up to four people. Breakfast €7. **€60**

**Des Causses** 56 av Jean-Jaurès ☏ 05 65 60 03 19, ⓦ hotel-des-causses.com. Set in an attractive building, this two-star hotel is known in the area for its traditional restaurant (Mon–Sat; from €30) that features local variations on lamb sweetbreads and tripe. Reception is closed 11am–5pm. Breakfast €9. **€79**

**Emma Calvé** 28 rue Jean-Jaurès ☏ 05 65 60 13 49, ⓦ millau-hotel-emmacalve.com. The most atmospheric hotel in the area, this used to be the home of the eponymous popular nineteenth-century French singer and its decor and furnishings are evocative of the time. Breakfast €6. **€52**

**Les Érables** Rte de Millau-Plage ☏ 05 65 59 15 13, ⓦ campingleserables.fr. A shaded, three-star campsite, not overly crowded and near a leisure centre. Free wi-fi at reception. Closed Oct–March. **€17**

### EATING AND DRINKING

**La Braconne** 7 place Foch ☏ 05 65 60 30 93, ⓦ restaurant-la-braconne.fr. In an eighteenth-century vaulted hall, this traditional restaurant serves local charcuterie and cheese plates. Excellent service. *Menus* from €19. Tues–Sat 12.15–2pm & 7.30–9.30pm (10pm in July & Aug), Sun 12.15–2pm.

**La Loco** 33 av Gambetta ☏ 05 75 85 60 05. A popular place, good for a drink, coffee or dinner, with late hours and live music on summer evenings. Sun–Thurs 3.30pm–1am, Fri–Sat 3.30pm–2am.

**La Mangeoire** 10 bd de la Capelle ☏ 05 65 60 13 16, ⓦ restaurantmillau.com. Restaurant serving grilled fish, oysters, meat and game dishes, with *menus* from a *formule du jour* at €15 right up to €49. Tues–Sun noon–2pm & 7–10pm.

# The Gorges du Tarn

Millau is the gateway to the spectacular **Gorges du Tarn**, which cuts through the limestone plateaux of the Causse de Sauveterre and the Causse Méjean in a precipitous trench 400–500m deep and 1000–1500m wide. Its sides, cloaked with woods of feathery pine and spiked with pinnacles of eroded rock, are often sheer and always very

**13**

steep, creating within them a microclimate in sharp distinction to the inhospitable plateaux above. The permanent population is tiny, though there's plenty of evidence of more populous times in the abandoned houses and once-cultivated terraces.

The most attractive section of the gorge runs northeast for 53km from the pretty village of **LE ROZIER**, 21km northeast of Millau, to **ISPAGNAC**. A narrow and very twisty road follows the left bank of the river from Le Rozier, but it's not the best way to see the scenery. For drivers, the best views are from the road to St-Rome-de-Dolan above Les Vignes, and from the roads out of La Malène and the attractive **STE-ÉNIMIE**. But it is far nicer to **walk**, or hire a **boat** (see below). There are two beautiful **caves** about 25km up the Jonte river from Le Rozier.

### Aven Armand

Daily: March to early July & Sept to mid-Nov 10am–noon & 1.30–5pm; early July & Aug 9.30am–6pm • Guided visits only; €9.45 • ☎ 04 66 45 61 31, ⓦ aven-armand.com

**Aven Armand**, on the edge of the Causse Méjean, is fitted with a funicular that takes you more than 100m underground. Its great attraction is the hundreds of stalagmite columns, including the world's tallest stalagmite towering 30m above the cave floor.

### The Grotte de Dargilan

Daily: Easter–June & Sept 10am–5.30pm; July & Aug 10am–6.30pm; Oct 2–4.30pm (10am–4.30pm in French school holidays) • Guided tours only; €8.70 • ☎ 04 66 45 60 20, ⓦ grotte-dargilan.com

The **Grotte de Dargilan**, on the south side of the river on the edge of the Causse Noir, known as the "pink cave" from the colour of its iron oxide deposits, is supposed to be one of France's most beautiful stalactite caverns. Grey Manganese salts mix with pure white stalactites and occasional brown and yellow ochre ferrous hues to give some delicate drapery effects on its walls.

---

**GETTING AROUND**                                             **THE GORGES DU TARN**

**By boat** Better than driving around the Gorges du Tarn is to walk, or follow the river's course by boat or canoe; for rental try Le Soulio (mid-June to mid-Sept 10am–2.30pm; ☎ 04 66 48 81 56, ⓦ le-soulio.com).

**ACCOMMODATION AND EATING**

**Auberge de la Cascade** St-Énimie ☎ 04 66 48 52 82, ⓦ aubergecascade.com. Hotel with panoramic views, a good bar and restaurant (*menus* €17.50–36). The full-board option is only marginally more expensive than half-board. One of the few options in the area offering disabled access. Closed Nov–Easter. **€49**

**Auberge du Moulin** St-Énimie ☎ 04 66 48 53 08, ⓦ aubergedumoulin.free.fr. An old converted stone mill where all rooms have views of either the Tarn or the lush garden. Good restaurant with a range of *menus* from €13.50–36. Breakfast €8.50. Closed Nov–Easter. **€60**

**Grand Hôtel des Voyageurs** Le Rozier ☎ 05 65 62 60 09, ⓦ grandhoteldesvoyageurs.fr. You can get excellent value at this friendly and unpretentious hotel; if you are travelling alone, half-board at €55, including breakfast, is just €10 more than the price of a room. Closed Nov–Easter. **€45**

**Le Vallon** Ispagnac ☎ 04 66 44 21 24, ⓦ hotel-vallon .com. A small hotel with an excellent *terroir* restaurant (from €16), offering family-size rooms and good-value half-board from €43 per person. They also own a small campsite, 200m from the hotel (€10). Breakfast €6.50. Closed Nov–March. **€45**

## South of Millau

On the edge of the Parc Régional des Grands Causses, the cheesemaking village of **Roquefort-sur-Soulzon** and the medieval **Abbey of Sylvanés** are relatively isolated spots, best visited on a return trip from Millau, if you are prepared to drive through some of the most rural and bucolic parts of France.

The main *autoroute* heads southeast and traverses the barren and windswept **Causse du Larzac**. Two photo-opportunities lie not far off the highway: the quaint village of **La Couvertoirade** and the great panoramic vision of the **Cirque de Navacelles**.

## ROQUEFORT CHEESE

**Roquefort** cheese is given its special flavour by the **fungus**, *penicillium roqueforti*, that grows exclusively in the fissures in the rocks in the surrounding valley. While the sheep's milk used to make the cheese comes from different flocks and dairies as far afield as the Pyrenees, the crucial fungus is grown right here, on bread. Just 2g of powdered fungus is enough for 4000 litres of milk, which in turn makes 330 Roquefort cheeses; they are matured in Roquefort's many-layered cellars, first unwrapped for three weeks and then wrapped up again. It takes three to six months for the full flavour to develop.

In you want to find out more, you can visit a few cheese manufacturers in the area. Visits, which start with a short film, followed by a tour of the cellars and a tasting, are free.

**Gabriel Coulet** 5 av de Lauras ☎ 05 65 59 90 21, ⓦ gabriel-coulet.fr. Jan Sat & Sun 9.30–11.50am & 1.30–4.50pm; Feb, March & Oct–Dec daily 9.30–11.50am & 1.30–4.50pm; April–June & Sept daily 9.30am–5.50pm; July & Aug daily 9am–6.50pm.

**Papillon** 8 av de Lauras ☎ 05 65 58 50 08, ⓦ visite-roquefort-papillon.com. Daily: April–June & Sept 10–11.15am & 2–5.15pm; July & Aug 10am–6.15pm; Oct–March 10–11.15am & 2–4.15pm.

## Roquefort-sur-Soulzon

Twenty-one kilometres south of Millau is the village of **ROQUEFORT-SUR-SOULZON**, which has little to it apart from its cheese. Almost every building is devoted to the cheese-making process.

### Abbey de Silvanès

Silvanès • Jan to mid-March & mid-Nov to mid-Dec Mon–Fri 9.30am–12.30pm & 2–6pm; mid-March to June & Sept to mid-Nov daily 9.30am–12.30pm & 2–6pm; July & Aug daily 9.30am–1pm & 2–7pm • €2.50 • ☎ 05 65 98 20 20, ⓦ sylvanes.com

Deep in the isolation of the *causses*, 26km south of Roquefort, squats the twelfth-century Cistercian **Abbey de Silvanès**, founded in 1137 and the first Cistercian house in the region. Having largely survived the depredations of war and revolution, the abbey serves today as a centre for sacred music and dance from the world over. Although you'll have to manage your own transport, it's worth visiting not only for the evocative setting, but also for the excellently preserved thirteenth-century church and the surviving monastic buildings, including a refectory and scriptorium dating back to the 1100s.

**ACCOMMODATION AND EATING**          **SILVANÈS ABBEY**

**Château de Gissac** Gissac, 4.5km northwest of Silvanès Abbey ☎ 05 65 98 14 60, ⓦ chateau .gissac.com. A magnificent, moderately priced, sixteenth-century château, with a landscaped French garden and a heated pool, offering half- and full-board. Breakfast €10. **€75**

## La Couvertoirade

**LA COUVERTOIRADE**, 45km south of Millau, is billed as a perfect "Templar" village, although in fact its present remains post-date the dissolution of that Order in the late thirteenth century. It's still a striking site, completely enclosed by its towers and walls and almost untouched by renovation. Its forty remaining inhabitants live by tourism, and you have to pay to walk around the **ramparts** (daily: March & Oct to mid-Nov 10am–noon & 2–5pm; April, June & Sept 10am–noon & 2–6pm; July & Aug 10am–7pm; €3; English audioguide €5; ☎ 05 65 58 55 59, ⓦ lacouvertoirade.com). Just outside the walls on the south side is a *lavogne*, a paved water hole of a kind seen all over the *causse* for watering the flocks whose milk is used for Roquefort cheese.

## The Cirque de Navacelles

Some 5km south of La Couvertoirade, you can turn off at **Le Caylar** to drive another 20km south on the stunning road to **ST-MAURICE-NAVACELLES**, a small and sleepy hamlet centring on a fine World War I memorial by Paul Dardé. From here, head north to the

**13**

**Cirque de Navacelles**, 10km away on the D25 past the beautiful ruined seventeenth-century sheep farm of *La Prunarède*. The cirque is a widening in the 150m-deep trench of the Vis gorge, formed by a now dry loop in the river that has left a neat pyramid of rock sticking up in the middle like a wheel hub. An ancient and scarcely inhabited hamlet survives in the bottom – a bizarre phenomenon in an extraordinary location, and you get literally a bird's-eye view of it from the edge of the cliff above.

## The Margeride

The wild, rolling and sparsely populated wooded hills of the **Margeride**, east of Aubrac and Aveyron, are best visited in conjunction with the Causses, although strictly speaking not part of that region. Using your own transport, take the D4, a slow but spectacular route east (92km) to Le Puy, crossing the forested heights of **Mont Mouchet**, at 1465m the highest point of the Margeride. A side turning, the D48 (signposted), takes you to the national **Resistance monument**. It is sited by the woodman's hut that served as HQ to the local Resistance commander in June 1944. Here, resistance fighters battled to delay German reinforcements moving north to strengthen resistance to the D-Day landings in Normandy.

The Margeride also has two wildlife parks – **Wolves Of Gévaudan**, in Hameu de Ste-Lucie (daily: April–June, Sept & Oct 10am–6pm; July & Aug 10am–7pm; Nov, Dec & Feb 10am–5pm; €7.50; ☎04 66 32 09 22, ⓦloupsdugevaudan.com) and, 40km northeast, the **European Bison Reserve** at Ste-Eulalie-en-Margeride (daily: April–June & Sept to mid-Nov 9.30am–6pm; July & Aug 9.30am–7pm; mid-Dec to Feb 10am–5pm; €13; ☎04 66 31 40 40, ⓦbisoneurope.com). **St-Alban-sur-Limagnole**, a quiet village conveniently situated between the two, is a good spot for lunch or an overnight stay.

---

**ACCOMMODATION AND EATING** | **THE MARGERIDE**

★ **Relais St Roch** Chemin du Carreiru, St-Alban-sur-Limagnole ☎04 66 31 55 48, ⓦrelais-saint-roch.fr. Housed in a nineteenth-century mansion built in pink arkose stone, this four-star hotel, its rooms decorated with Genovese velvet and cherry furniture, can best be admired from the pool. The restaurant, *La Petite Maison*, has an exceptional, gut-busting three-course bison menu (€64). Breakfast €17. **€144**

---

# The Cévennes and Ardèche

The **Cévennes** mountains and **River Ardèche** form the southeastern defences of the Massif Central, overlooking the Rhône valley to the east and the Mediterranean littoral to the south. The bare upland landscapes of the inner or western edges are those of the central Massif. The outer edges, Mont Aigoual and its radiating valleys and the tributary valleys of the Ardèche, are distinctly Mediterranean: deep, dry, and clothed in forests of sweet chestnut, oak and pine.

---

### THE STEVENSON TRAIL

In 1878, the author Robert Louis Stevenson took a walking trail through Haute-Loire, Ardèche, Lozère and the Cévennes with Modestine, a donkey he bought in Le Monastier-sur-Gazeille near Le Puy and sold at journey's end in the former Protestant stronghold of St-Jean-du-Gard. The journey is described in *Travels with a Donkey* (see p.1028), a book that has captured the imagination of so many with its line "I travel for travel's sake; the great affair is to move." Today you can follow the **Chemin de Stevenson** in a variety of ways: walking it, while a car transports your luggage (La Malle Postale; ☎04 71 04 21 79, ⓦlamallepostale. com); on a packaged hike (Cévennes Évasion Voyage Nature; ☎04 66 45 18 31, ⓦcevennes-evasion.com); or even by renting a donkey (Chik'Anes; ☎04 71 08 30 07, ⓦchikanes.com). For more information and a full list of operators, check ⓦchemin-stevenson.org.

Remote and inaccessible country until well into the twentieth century, the region has bred rugged and independent inhabitants. For centuries it was the most resolute stronghold of Protestantism in France, and it was in these valleys that the persecuted Protestants put up their fiercest resistance to the tyranny of Louis XIV and Louis XV. In World War II, it was heavily committed to the Resistance, while after 1968, it became the domain of hippies – some of whom remain.

# The Parc National des Causses et Cévennes and around

The **Parc National des Causses et Cévennes** was created in 1970 to protect and preserve the life, landscape, flora, fauna and architectural heritage of the Cévennes. North to south, it stretches from **Mende** on the Lot to **Le Vigan** and includes both **Mont Lozère** and **Mont Aigoual**. Access, to the periphery at least, is surprisingly easy, thanks to the Paris–Clermont–Alès–Nîmes train line and the Montpellier–Mende link. In July and August, it's wise to book ahead for **accommodation**; otherwise you could find yourself sleeping outdoors; the **main information office** for the park is at Florac (see p.714).

## Mende

Capital of the Lozère *département*, **MENDE** lies well down in the deep valley of the Lot at the northern tip of the Parc des Cévennes, and 40km north of Florac, with train and bus links to the Paris–Nîmes and Clermont–Millau lines. It's an attractive southern town, though much of its charm is lost in the newly commercialized streets of the city centre. However, what Mende lacks in authenticity it makes up for in practicality: it's a great place to buy last-minute supplies before you head off to the mountains.

Otherwise, aside from visiting the **cathedral**, you could take a quiet wander in the old town's minuscule squares and narrow medieval streets, with their bulging houses. In **rue Notre-Dame**, which separated the Christian from Jewish quarters in medieval times, the thirteenth-century house at no. 17 was once a synagogue. If you carry on down to the river, you'll see a thirteenth-century stone bridge, the **Pont Notre-Dame**, with its worn cobbles.

### The cathedral

Daily 9am–7pm • Free

Standing against the haze of the mountain background, Mende's main landmark, the **cathedral**, owes its construction to Pope Urban V, who was born locally. Although work began in 1369, progress was hampered by war and natural disasters and the building wasn't completed until the end of the nineteenth century. Inside is a handsome choir, and, suspended from the clerestory, eight great Aubusson tapestries, depicting the life of the Virgin. She's also present in one of the side chapels of the choir in the form of a statue made from olive wood, thought to have been brought back from the Middle East during the crusades.

**ARRIVAL AND INFORMATION**

MENDE

**By train** The *gare SNCF* lies in place de la Gare across the river, 600m north of the centre.
Destinations Clermont-Ferrand (3 daily; 3hr 10min); Nîmes (4 daily; 3hr 15min); St-Flour (4 daily; 2hr).
**By bus** Buses, most of which are local, leave from the *gare SNCF*.
Destinations Clermont-Ferrand (2 daily; 3hr 20min); Le

Puy (Mon–Sat 1 daily; 1hr 20min); Rodez (up to 1 daily 2hr 30min).
**Tourist office** Place du Foirail (June & Sept Mon–Sat 9am–noon & 2–6pm; July & Aug Mon–Sat 9am–7pm, Sun 10am–5pm; Oct–May Mon–Fri 9am–noon & 2–6pm, Sat 9am–noon; ✆04 66 94 00 23, ⓦot -mende.fr).

**ACCOMMODATION AND EATING**

**De France** 9 bd Lucien-Arnault ✆04 66 65 00 04, ⓦhoteldefrance-mende.com. Central and comfortable

hotel with private parking – essential in Mende. The large, white sparkling rooms have good facilities, including

**13**

refined restaurant offering French cuisine on *menus* from €29. Breakfast €11. Closed Christmas to mid-Jan. **€95**
**Pont-Roupt** 2 av du 11-novembre ☎ 04 66 65 01 43, ⓦ hotel-pont-roupt.fr. A 5min walk from the centre and

facing the river, this classy hotel offers an indoor pool, terrace, spa and good restaurant; dishes include *truite au lard* and *salade au Roquefort*. *Menus* from €24. Buffet breakfast €12. **€88**

## Mont Lozère and around

**Mont Lozère** is a windswept and desolate barrier of granite and yellow grassland, rising to 1699m at the summit of **Finiels**. It is still grazed by herds of cows, but in nothing like the numbers of bygone years when half the cattle in Languedoc came up here for their summer feed. Snowbound in winter and wild and dangerous in bad weather, it has claimed many a victim among lost travellers. In some of the squat granite hamlets on the northern slopes, like **Servies**, **Auriac** and **Les Sagnes**, you can still hear the bells, known as *clochers de tourmente*, that tolled in the wind to give travellers some sense of direction when the cloud was low.

If you're travelling by car from Mende, the way to the summit is via the village of **LE BLEYMARD**, about 30km to the east on the bank of the infant River Lot. From Le Bleymard, the D20 winds 7km up through the conifers to join up with the GR7, which has taken a more direct route from Le Bleymard. This is the route that Stevenson took, waymarked as the "Tracé Historique de Stevenson". Road and footpath run together as far as the **Col de Finiels**, where the GR7 strikes off on its own to the southeast. The source of the River Tarn is about 3km east of the Col, the summit of Lozère 2km to the west. From the Col, the road and Stevenson's route drop down in tandem, through the lonely hamlet of **FINIELS** to the village of Le Pont-de-Montvert.

### Le Pont-de-Montvert

At the pretty but touristy village of **LE PONT-DE-MONTVERT**, a seventeenth-century **bridge** crosses the Tarn by a stone tower that once served as a tollhouse. In this building in 1702, the Abbé du Chayla, a priest appointed by the Crown to reconvert the rebellious Protestants enraged by the revocation of the Edict of Nantes, set up a torture chamber to coerce the recalcitrant. Incensed by his brutality, a group of rebels led by one Esprit Séguier attacked and killed him on July 23. Reprisals were extreme; nearly twelve thousand were executed, thus precipitating the Camisards' guerrilla war against the state. At the edge of the village, there's a museum on the life and character of the region, the **Maison du Mont Lozère** (daily: April–Sept 10.30am–12.30pm & 2.30–6.30pm; €3.50; ☎ 04 66 45 80 73, ⓦ culture.lozere.fr).

## Florac

Situated 39km south of Mende, **FLORAC** lies in the bottom of the trench-like valley of the Tarnon, just short of its junction with the Tarn. Behind the village rises the steep wall that marks the edge of the Causse Méjean. When you get here, you will have already passed the frontier between the northern and Mediterranean landscapes; the dividing line seems to be the **Col de Montmirat** at the western end of Mont Lozère. Once you begin the descent, the scrub and steep gullies and the tiny abandoned hamlets, with their houses oriented towards the sun, speak clearly of the south.

The village, with some two thousand inhabitants, is strung out along the left bank of the Tarnon and the main street, **avenue Jean-Monestier**. There's little to see, though the close lanes of the village up towards the valley side have their charms, especially the plane-shaded **place du Souvenir**. In summer it is worth visiting the Thursday **market**, when you'll find the tiny streets packed with merchants and local produce.

**INFORMATION**                                                    **FLORAC**

**Centre d'Information du Parc National des Cévennes** Maison du Parc, 6bis place du Palais

(Easter–June, Sept & Oct daily 9.30am–12.15pm & 1.30–5.30pm; July & Aug daily 9am–6.30pm;

Nov–Easter Mon–Fri 2.30–6pm; ☎ 04 66 49 53 00, ⓦ cevennes-parcnational.fr). A red schist castle above the village houses the Maison du Parc, which has a wide stock of brochures about the region, from its flora, fauna and traditions to local activities and routes for walkers, cyclists, canoeists and horseriders. It also provides a list of *gîtes d'étape* in the park and can provide information for anyone following Stevenson's route (see p.712), including where to hire a donkey.

**Tourist office** 33 av Jean-Monestier (April–Oct Mon–Sat 9am–12.30pm & 2–6.30pm, Sun 10am–1pm; ☎ 04 66 45 01 14, ⓦ vacances-cevennes.com). The office provides details on guided treks around the national park.

**Mountain bike rental** Cévennes Evasion, 1 place Boyer (☎ 04 66 45 18 31, ⓦ cevennes-evasion.com; €18/day). They also offer a Stevenson trail (see p.712) bike route.

## ACCOMMODATION AND EATING

**Les Gorges du Tarn** 48 rue du Pêcher ☎ 04 66 45 00 63, ⓦ hotel-gorgesdutarn.com. An airy and sunny hotel that also offers self-catering apartments for weekly stays. Its *Adonis* restaurant (daily 7–8.30pm) is worth visiting even if you don't stay; it offers a variety of *menus* from €19–29. Breakfast €9. Closed Nov–Easter. **€60**

**Grand Hôtel du Parc** 47 av Jean-Monestier ☎ 04 66 45 03 05, ⓦ grand-hotel-du-parc-48.com. A fantastic three-star with a pool, a large, pleasant garden and an excellent restaurant with *menus* from €19–38. Buffet breakfast €8.50. Closed Nov–Easter. **€53**

## Mont Aigoual

You can travel up the beautiful valley of the Tarnon to the **Col de Perjuret**, where a right turn will take you on to the **Causse Méjean** and to the strange rock formations of **Nîmes-le-Vieux**, and a left turn along a rising ridge a further 15km to the 1565m summit of **Mont Aigoual** (GR6, GR7, GR66). From the latter, it is said that you can see a third of France, from the Alps to the Pyrenees, with the Mediterranean coast from Marseille to Sète at your feet. It's not a craggy summit, although the ground drops away pretty steeply into the valley of the River Hérault on the south side, but the view and the sense of exposure to the elements is dramatic enough. At the summit an **observatory** which has been in use for more than a century. A small but interesting **exhibition** (May–Sept daily 10am–6pm; free) shows modern weather-forecasting techniques alongside displays of old barometers and weather vanes.

The **descent** to Le Vigan by the valley of the Hérault is superb; a magnificent twisty road follows the deepening ravine through dense beech and chestnut woods, to come out at the bottom in rather Italianate scenery, with tall, close-built villages and vineyards beside the stream.

## ACCOMMODATION AND EATING                                        MONT AIGOUAL

**Les Bruyères** Valleraugue ☎ 04 67 82 20 06, ⓦ hotelvalleraugue.com. In a leafy riverside setting in the charming village of Valleraugue, this three-star hotel has a pool, bar, children's playroom, parking (€7/day) and big, airy rooms. Breakfast €8. Closed Nov–April. **€50**

**Du Touring** L'Espérou ☎ 04 67 82 60 04, ⓦ hotel-restaurant-touring.com. A family hotel, just below the summit, with rooms that have the rustic feel of a log cabin. Breakfast €7, half-board €47pp, restaurant *menus* from €14.50; this is a good place to try the *aligot* sausage. Free private parking. Closed April & Dec. **€50**

## Le Vigan

Just 64km from Montpellier and 29km from St-Guilhem-le-Desert, **LE VIGAN** makes a good starting point for exploring the southern part of the Cévennes. It's a leafy, cool and thoroughly agreeable place, at its liveliest during the **Fête d'Isis** at the beginning of August and the colossal **fair** that takes over the Parc des Châtaigniers for a couple of days in September.

The prettiest part of the town is around the central **place du Quai**, shaded by lime trees and bordered by cafés and brasseries. From here it's just a two-minute walk south, down rue Pierre-Gorlier, to the gracefully arched **Pont Vieux**. Beside it stands the **Musée Cévenol**.

**13**

### Musée Cévenol

Jan–March, Nov & Dec Wed–Fri 10am–noon & 2–5pm; April–June, Sept & Oct Wed–Fri 10am–noon & 2–6pm; July & Aug Wed–Mon 10am–1pm & 3–6.30pm • €4.50 • ☎ 04 67 81 06 86, ☖ viganais.free.fr

The **Musée Cévenol** offers a well-presented look at traditional rural occupations in the area, including woodcutting, butchery, shepherding and wolf-hunting. There's also a room devoted to the area's best-known twentieth-century writer, André Chamson, whose novels are steeped in the traditions and countryside of the Cévennes. Interestingly, Coco Chanel also features: she had local family connections and it seems found inspiration for her designs in the *cévenol* silks.

## INFORMATION

**Tourist office** Place du Marché (July & Aug Mon–Sat 9am–12.30pm & 2–6pm, Sun and public holidays 10am–12.30pm; Nov–Easter Mon–Fri 9am–12.30pm & 2–6pm, Sat 9am–12.30pm; Easter–June, Sept & Oct Mon–Fri 9am–12.30pm & 2–6pm, Sat 9am–12.30pm & 3–6pm; ☎ 04 67 81 01 72, ☖ cevennes-meridionales.com).

## ACCOMMODATION AND EATING

**Auberge Cocagne** Avèze ☎ 04 67 81 02 70, ☖ auberge-cocagne-cevennes.com. An early seventeenth-century building belonging to a friendly French couple, this is a *hotel de charme* more than worthy of its name. Restaurant *menus* from €16. Closed parking. Breakfast €8. Closed mid-Dec to mid-Feb. **€65**

**Mas de la Prairie** Av Sargeant Triaire ☎ 04 67 81 80 80, ☖ masdelaprairie.fr. Comfortable hotel with many amenities including a swimming pool and a restaurant with *menus* from €17–25. Good half- and full-board options. Closed mid-Nov to April. **€52**

**Val de l'Arre** 2km upriver from Le Vigan ☎ 04 67 81 02 77, ☖ valdelarre.com. A shaded riverside campsite near Le Vigan, on the opposite bank. Facilities include wi-fi (not free), a snack bar, shops that offer local produce and a pool. Closed Nov–March. **€21**

## St-Jean-du-Gard and around

Some 58 winding kilometres northeast of Le Vigan, **ST-JEAN-DU-GARD** was the centre of Protestant resistance during the Camisard war in 1702–04. It straggles along the bank of the River Gardon, crossed by a graceful, arched eighteenth-century bridge, and a number of picturesque old houses that still survive along the main street, **Grande-Rue**.

### Musée des Vallées Cévenoles

95 Grande-Rue • April–June, Sept & Oct daily 10am–12.30pm & 2–7pm; July & Aug daily 10am–7pm; Nov–March Tues–Thurs 9am–noon & 2–6pm, Sun 2–6pm • €5 • ☎ 04 66 85 10 48, ☖ museedesvalleescevenoles.pagesperso-orange.fr

One of St-Jean-du-Gard's old houses contains the splendid **Musée des Vallées Cévenoles**, a museum of local life with displays of tools, trades, furniture, clothes, domestic articles and a fascinating collection of pieces related to the silk industry. The silk-spinning work was done by women, in factories, and lists of regulations on display give some idea of the tough conditions in which they had to work.

### The Musée du Désert

Mas Soubeyran, near Mialet • Daily: March–June & Sept–Nov 9.30am–noon & 2–6pm; July & Aug 9.30am–6.30pm • €5.50 • ☎ 04 66 85 02 72, ☖ museedudesert.com

Signposts at St-Jean direct you to the museum at **MAS SOUBEYRAN**, a minuscule hamlet of beautiful rough-stone houses in a gully above the village of Mialet, about 8km east of St-Jean. The **Musée du Désert** is in the house that once belonged to Rolland, one of the Camisards' self-taught but most successful military leaders, and it remains much the same as it would have looked in 1704, the year he died. It catalogues the appalling sufferings and sheer dogged heroism of the Protestant Huguenots in defence of their freedom of conscience; and the "desert" they had to traverse between the Revocation of the Edict of Nantes in 1685 and the promulgation of the Edict of Tolerance in 1787, which restored their original rights (full emancipation came with the Declaration of the Rights of Man in the first heady months of the Revolution in 1789).

Unsurprisingly, the brutality the Protestants faced led to armed rebellion, inspired by the prophesying of the lay preachers who had replaced the banished priests, calling for a holy war. The rebels were hopelessly outnumbered, however, and the revolt was ruthlessly put down in 1704. Memorabilia on display includes documents, private letters and lists of those who died for their beliefs, including five thousand who died as galley slaves (*galériens pour la foi*) and the women who were immured in the Tour de Constance prison in Aigues-Mortes.

### Prafrance

Twelve kilometres southeast of St-Jean towards Anduze, **PRAFRANCE** is noteworthy for **La Bambouseraie** (daily: March & Oct 9.30am–6pm; April–Sept 9.30am–7pm; Nov 9.30am–5pm; €8.60 last entry 30min before close; ☏04 66 61 70 47, ⓦbambouseraie .com), an extraordinary and appealing garden consisting exclusively of bamboos of all shapes and sizes; the project was started in 1855 by local entrepreneur Eugène Mazel. An easy way to get here is to take the **steam train** (see below) from St-Jean-du-Gard; it takes just ten minutes.

| **INFORMATION** | **ST-JEAN-DU-GARD AND AROUND** |
|---|---|
| **Tourist office** Place Rabaut St-Étienne (July & Aug Mon–Sat 9am–12.30pm & 2.30–6pm, Sun 10am–12.30pm; Sept–June Mon–Fri 9am–noon & 1.30–5pm, Sat and holidays 10am–noon; ☏04 66 85 32 11, | ⓦtourisme-saintjeandugard.fr). They can advise you about the steam train between St-Jean and Anduze (June–Sept 4 daily; April, May & Oct 3 daily Tues–Thurs, Sat & Sun; €14 return). |

| **ACCOMMODATION AND EATING** | |
|---|---|
| **L'Orange** Place de la Revolution ☏04 66 86 05 52, ⓦhotelorange.com. Housed in a seventeenth-century stone building where Stevenson stayed in 1879, this is a | popular choice if only for its sense of history and atmosphere. The restaurant has a good reputation, too, with *menus* from €17.50. Breakfast from €8. **€59** |

## Northern Ardèche

North of the Cévennes, the Ardèche river starts carving the gorge towards the southeast within sloping forests of pine, spruce and, lower down, **chestnut** trees. This is a land of beautiful villages, some, such as **Vogüé**, **Jaujac** or **Antraigues-sur-Volane** etched onto the volcanic basalt slopes. Chestnut cream, chestnut biscuits and a very drinkable 21 percent proof chestnut liqueur are all available to taste in **Aubenas**, the main administrative centre, but the town lacks good hotels, so it is best visited on a day-trip.

If you want to stay in the northern Ardèche, nearby **VALS-LES-BAINS** and **NEYRAC-LES-BAINS** are better options. Apart from the thermal spas that dominate the area, this is where you will also find the regional **Bourganel Brewey** (ⓦbieres-bourganel.com) with – surprise – its chestnut-flavoured beer.

### Aubenas

Some 91km southeast of Le Puy, **AUBENAS** sits high on a hill overlooking the middle valley of the River Ardèche. The central knot of streets with their cobbles and bridges, occupying the highest point of town around **place de l'Hôtel-de-Ville**, have great charm, particularly towards place de la Grenette and place 14-Juillet. Place de l'Hôtel-de-Ville is dominated by the eleventh-century **château**, from which the local *seigneurs* ruled the area right up until the Revolution (guided tours June & Sept Tues–Sat 10.30am & 2.30pm; July & Aug daily 11am, 2pm, 3pm, 4pm & 5pm; Oct–May Tues, Thurs & Sat 2pm; €3.50). There's a magnificent view of the Ardèche snaking up the valley from under an arch beside the castle. Other sights include the heavily restored thirteenth-century **St-Laurent church**, which has the curious seventeenth-century hexagonal **Dôme Bênoit chapel** (only accessible on a 2hr town tour, July & Aug Mon–Fri 5pm; €3.50).

## INFORMATION

### NORTHERN ARDÈCHE

**AUBENAS**
**Tourist office** 4 bd Gambetta (July & Aug Mon–Sat 9am–noon & 2–7pm, Sun 9am–1pm; Sept–June Mon–Sat 9am–noon & 2–6pm; ☎ 04 75 89 02 03, ⓦ aubenasvals .com). One of the best tourist offices for maps and information on the whole of the Ardèche.

## ACCOMMODATION AND EATING

★ **Le Carré des Maîtres** 6 av P. Ribeyre, Vals-les-Bains ☎ 04 75 94 00 89, ⓔ carre-des-maitres @wanadoo.fr. A great wine bar with a good selection of local Rhône wines and a back terrace overlooking a stream. The daily set *menu* is always guaranteed to be top quality (€21). April to mid-Nov daily noon–2.30pm & 6–10.30pm.

★ **Chateau Clement** Vals-les-Bains ☎ 04 75 87 40 13, ⓦ chateauclement.com. A family-friendly Third Republic château with carved walnut wood-panelling and a huge double revolution staircase leading to rooms ranging from the super-modern to the highly traditional. Rates include breakfast and views over the valley of Vals-les-Bains, and the weekly rates for family suites and self-catering apartments are fantastic value. **€170**

**Du Levant** Neyrac-les-Bains ☎ 04 75 36 41 07, ⓦ hotel-levant.com. An old coach-house in the same family for six generations, also housing the famous restaurant by Claude Brioude (*menus* €19–39). The hotel offers half- or full-board. Breakfast €9. **€86**

# The Gorges de l'Ardèche

The **Gorges de l'Ardèche** begins at the **Pont d'Arc**, a very beautiful 54m-high arch that the river has cut for itself through the limestone, just downstream from **VALLON**, itself 39km south of Aubenas. The gorge continues for about 35km to **ST-MARTIN-D'ARDÈCHE** in the valley of the Rhône.

The gorge winds back and forth, much of the time dropping 300m straight down to the almost dead-flat scrubby Plateau des Gras. It's beautiful, but a tourist trap; the road following the rim, with spectacular viewpoints at regular intervals, is jammed with traffic in **summer**, when you should book accommodation well in advance. The river, down at the bottom, which is where you really want to be to appreciate the grandeur of the canyon, is likewise packed with canoes in high season.

## Aven Marzal

Signposted from the main Ardèche gorge road **Caves** Mid-March to June & Oct to mid-Nov daily 10.30am–5.30pm; July & Aug daily 9.30am–7pm; visits approximately every 20min in July and Aug, falling to 4 per day in other months • €8, joint ticket with zoo €14.40 **Zoo** Mid-Feb to mid-March daily 2–4.30pm; mid-March to June & Oct to mid-Nov daily 10.30am–5.30pm; July & Aug daily 9.30am–7pm • €8; joint ticket with caves €14.40 • ☎ 04 75 04 12 45, ⓦ aven-marzal.com

The Ardèche plateau is riddled with caves. **Aven Marzal**, a stalactite cavern north of the main gorge road, has a prehistoric **zoo**, filled with reconstructions of dinosaurs and various friends, but the frequency of actual visits to the cave depends on the number of people who are present on any one day.

## Aven Orgnac

Signposted from Orgnac L'Aven • 90min tours daily: Feb & March 10am–noon & 2–4.45pm; April, June & Sept 10am–noon & 1.30–5.30pm; July & Aug 9.30am–6pm; Oct to mid-Nov 10am–noon & 2–4.30pm • €10 • ☎ 04 75 38 65 10, ⓦ orgnac.com

Best of the area's caves, to the south of the gorge, is the **Aven Orgnac**, one of France's most spectacular and colourful stalactite formations. In addition to the normal tours, you can also opt for two "*visites spéléologiques*", which are hard-core caving tours that last either three or eight hours; reserve two weeks ahead. There's also a very good prehistory museum (re-opening in summer 2013), the **Cité de la Préhistoire**.

## Chauvet Cave Museum

Rue de Miarou, Vallon • Mid-March to June & Sept to mid-Nov Tues–Sun 10am–noon & 2–5.30pm; July & Aug 10am–1pm & 3–7pm • €2.70 • ☎ 04 75 37 17 68, ⓦ prehistoireardeche.com

The most important cave in the Ardèche, France, and arguably in the world, is the **Chauvet cave**, which features in Werner Herzog's award-winning 2010 documentary

*The Cave of Forgotten Dreams*; it and can be spotted from the car park in the Pont d'Arc. The discovery in 1994 of this immense natural prehistoric sanctuary amazed archeologists: it contained no less than 425 individual animal paintings of exceptional quality and technique dating back 36,000 years. Sadly, you cannot visit the cave, but a duplicate is being created nearby, due to open in 2014. In the meantime, a **museum** in Vallon contains some artefacts from the cave and includes an awe-inspiring film made by the local explorers who found it.

## ARRIVAL AND INFORMATION

**By bus** The Vallon bus station is by the tourist office. In July & Aug there is a free daily shuttle from Vallon to Pont d'Arc (9.30am–6.50pm every 30–50min; last return from Pont d'Arc 7.30pm).
Destinations Aubenas (Mon–Sat 2–5 daily; 1hr 45min); Avignon (1 daily; 1hr 30min).

## THE GORGES DE L'ARDÈCHE

**Tourist office** 1 Place de l'Ancienne Gare, Vallon (April, May & Oct Mon–Fri 9am–noon & 2–5pm, Sat 9am–noon & 2–4pm; June–Sept Mon–Sat 9am–7pm, Sun 9am–5pm; Nov–March Mon–Fri 9am–noon & 2–5pm, Sat 9am–noon; ☎04 75 88 04 01, ⓦ vallon -pont-darc.com).

## ACCOMMODATION

Finding accommodation in the area can be a problem during the high season. This is really a place to get back to nature, so camping is the best option.

★ **Le Belved'R** Rte des Gorges de l´Ardèche ☎04 75 88 00 02, ⓦ le-belvedere-hotel.com. Close to the Pont d'Arc, this is the hotel to stay in if you want to be in the middle of the gorge. All facilities are provided, as well as activities on the river. Try its unbeatable two-day off-season "Forget it all" package, which offers full-board, hiking and kayaking for €95 per person. Breakfast €8. **€89**
**Camping L'Ardechois** Vallon-Pont-d'Arc ☎04 75 88 06 63, ⓦ ardechois-camping.com. Palatial and award-winning campsite with the option of private bathrooms,

two swimming pools, restaurants, takeaways, entertainment and sports activities; especially focused on families and children. Closed Oct–Easter. **€49**
**Le Manoir du Raveyron** Rue Henri-Barbusse, Vallon ☎04 75 88 03 59, ⓦ manoir-du-raveyron.com. The best hotel near Vallon – 300m from the centre of the village – this is a converted sixteenth-century manor house with a beautiful, scenic backdrop and a good restaurant (daily 7–9pm; *menus* €28). Breakfast included. Closed Nov to mid-March. **€80**

# The Alps and Franche-Comté

WALKING NEAR MONT BLANC

# The Alps and Franche-Comté

14

The wild and rugged landscape of the Alps, formed by the collision of continental tectonic plates over tens of millions of years, and the eroding actions of multiple glaciers and fast-flowing rivers, contains some of Europe's most stunning mountain landscapes. King of all it surveys, and Europe's highest peak, is Mont Blanc, which sits pretty over the Chamonix valley below, itself the region's premier sporting playground. On offer are some of the most thrilling outdoor activities on the continent, from world-class skiing and mountain climbing, to superb road cycling and the most gentle of valley walks. While resorts like Chamonix absorb the lion's share of adrenaline-seeking visitors to the Alps, there are excellent alternatives, notably the Queyras and Écrins national parks.

Yet you'll also find plenty of charming towns and villages and towns to explore, notably **Grenoble**, the economic capital of the Alps, which possesses a vibrant nightlife and lively cultural scene. **Chambéry**, too, offers stimulating cultural attractions alongside some wonderful Italianate architecture, while easy-going **Annecy** is a town whose picture-postcard lakeside setting is sure to delight. Close by, the genteel spa resort of **Aix-le-Bains** presents further possibilities for lake-bound fun, as does **Lake Geneva**, whose pristine shoreline is punctuated by well turned-out towns and villages like **Evian** and **Yvoire**. Further south, **Briançon**, one of the highest towns in Europe, offers Vauban's formidable fortress as a reminder of the tumultuous past of this region on France's eastern frontier.

The region of **Franche-Comté**, which lies to the northwest of Lake Geneva, was once ruled by the Grand Dukes of Burgundy, and annexed by France in the late seventeenth century. The four *départements* of Franche-Comté – the Territoire de Belfort, the Haute-Saône, the Doubs and the Jura are generally far more rural and less touristy than those in Rhone-Alpes. The region's capital, **Besançon**, is an attractive town built around imposing fortifications, developed by the French military engineer Vauban (see box, p.735) during the late 1600s.

Lying in the rich agricultural valley to the south of Besançon, the quiet town of **Lons-le-Saunier** provides a gateway to the Jura mountains to the east. Composed of gentle, forested slopes in the west, of more sheer crags in the east and of high-forested plateaux in between, these mountains have long been popular for cross-country skiing, but the varied terrain also provides plenty of good trails for hikers. Note that the official *département* of Jura in the south of Franche-Comté does not contain the whole

CABLE CARS IN CHAMONIX

# Highlights

**❶ Skiing and snowboarding** Test your skills from December to April in any number of world-class resorts, like Chamonix, Méribel and Val d'Isère. **See p.733, p.755 & p.747**

**❷ Parc Naturel Régional du Queyras** Walk or drive through the empty mountain landscapes of the Queyras to St-Véran, one of the highest villages in Europe. **See p.739**

**❸ Annecy** Take a leisurely cruise on Annecy's beautiful lake and wander through the narrow lanes of its historic Old Town. **See p.746**

**❹ Aiguille du Midi** Brave one of the world's highest cable-car ascents for a spectacular view of Mont Blanc, the highest peak in Europe. See p.756

**❺ Lake Geneva** Enjoy the sedate pleasures of Évian and Yvoire on the French side of this huge and scenic lake, or hop on one of the frequent ferries to Switzerland. **See p.758**

**❻ Besançon** Explore the imposing Citadelle, the intriguing museums and the inviting cafés of the capital of Franche-Comté. **See p.761**

**❼ Jura Mountains** Far less visited than the Alps, this sublimely forested landscape is perfect for an abundance of outdoor pursuits, in particular cross-country skiing, hiking and mountain biking. **See p.767**

HIGHLIGHTS ARE MARKED ON THE MAP ON P.724

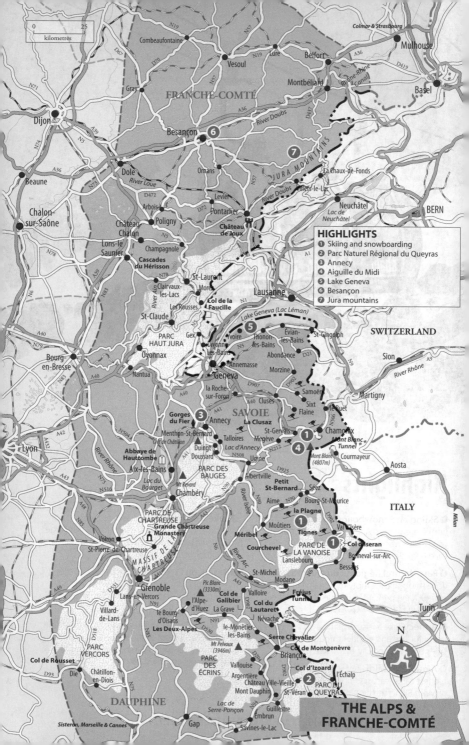

of the mountain range commonly known as the Jura; these mountains also stretch northward into the Doubs *département* as well as into Switzerland. A particular highlight in these mountains is the **Région des Lacs**, which possesses beautiful lakes, pine forests and small farming communities as well as ski resorts. At the northern tip of the region is the historic town of **Belfort**, is a rewarding destination in itself, and, one that makes a handy base for exploring the area.

## INFORMATION

**THE ALPS AND FRANCHE-COMTÉ**

**Getting around** Travelling around the Alps and Franche-Comté is relatively easy, with frequent trains between the major towns and resorts, while during the skiing season of December to April and the summer months of July and August, more bus services become available. The more remote areas of the Alps and Jura are difficult to reach without a car, but anyway are best explored on foot or by bicycle. Drivers should remember that some high passes in the east of the region, including the Col du Galibier and the Col de l'Iseran, can remain closed well into June. This can force you to make long detours into Italy via expensive Alpine tunnels.

**Useful websites** ⓦ rhonealpes-tourisme.com and ⓦ savoie-mont-blanc.com provide excellent introductions to the region. For the Franche-Comté area, check out ⓦ franche-comte.org.

**Accommodation** Many of the hotels outside the main towns – and in particular the ski resorts – are often seasonal (closed in late spring and late autumn) and invariably over-priced, though booking ahead will often get you the best deals. There are plentiful campsites as well as hostels and *refuges* (huts), the former mostly open year-round, the latter generally open between mid-June and September.

# Grenoble

Set serenely at the confluence of the Drac and Isère rivers, **GRENOBLE**, the self-styled "capital of the Alps", is, at just 213m above sea level, France's lowest city, watched over by the snowcapped peaks of the Belledonne, Vercors and Chartreuse massifs. It's a vibrant and cosmopolitan place, home to more than 60,000 students and a lively cultural scene, while at its centre is a quirky maze of streets, where modern and medieval buildings are packed close together. Its restaurants and cafes, meanwhile, provide relaxing spots in which to sit and admire the grandeur of this fantastic mountain setting.

---

## HIKING AND CLIMBING IN THE ALPS AND FRANCHE-COMTÉ

There are seven national or regional parks in the area covered by this chapter: Vanoise, Chartreuse, Bauges, Écrins, Queyras, Vercors and Haut Jura. All of these contain gentle day-walks and more demanding treks – not least classic long-distance paths like the Tour du Mont Blanc – which require one or two weeks' walking. Most of these routes are clearly marked and dotted with *refuge* huts; the routes are also described in high detail by the Topo-guides guidebooks (see p.47). Nonetheless, even the most experienced walkers or skiers treat these mountains and their unpredictable weather conditions with due respect. Even low-level walks in the Alps during summer often require a good level of fitness and specialist equipment, such as crampons or ice axes. You should take account of the weather conditions (which can vary considerably between the valleys and peaks), of the potentially debilitating effects of high altitude, and of the serious danger of avalanches.

The Alps was the first great centre for European rock climbers in the nineteenth century and still offers countless routes that can be enjoyed by both novices and world-class climbers. A more recent development has been the creation of *Via Ferrata* courses, in which wires and ladders are bolted onto the rock so that even inexperienced climbers (wearing harnesses and ropes) can make ascents which would otherwise be impossible for them. There are *via ferrata* courses being developed across the whole region, but at present two of the largest centres for this popular sport are at Serre Chevalier and in the Parc National des Écrins.

The **Bureau Info Montagne** office in Grenoble and the **Office de Haute Montagne** in Chamonix can provide information on the best guides and the most up-to-date information on all the GR paths and the best *via ferrata* courses, while local tourist offices often produce detailed maps of walks in their own areas.

Settled by the Celtic Allobroges tribe, who called their settlement Curaro, it was renamed Gratianopolis by the Romans in the fourth century and became the seat of a bishop. The city was annexed by France in the fourteenth century, and it was here, far from Paris, that a local uprising in 1788 (known as the Journée des Tuiles) initiated the French Revolution. Grenoble is the final stop on the Route Napoléon; the French emperor arrived here on March 7, 1815, declaring "Before Grenoble, I was an adventurer. In Grenoble, I was a prince." The prosperity of the city was originally founded on glove-making, but in the nineteenth century its economy diversified to include industries as varied as mining and hydroelectric power, while more recently it has forged a reputation as a centre for scientific research in the electronic and nuclear industries.

## The téléphérique

Quai Stéphane-Jay • Times are complex but it's roughly May–Sept daily 9.30am–11.45pm, Mon from 11am; April & Oct Tues–Sun 9.30am–11.45pm; Nov–Feb Tues–Sun 11am–6.30pm, Fri & Sat till 11.45pm • €7.10 return• ☏ 04 76 44 33 65, Ⓦ bastille-grenoble.com

The best way to start your tour of the city is to take the **téléphérique** to **Fort de la Bastille** on the steep slopes above the northern bank of the Isère. One of the world's first urban cable cars, built in 1934, it's a hair-raising ride as you're whisked swiftly into the air in a transparent glass ball towards the Bastille 263m above. The journey is not for those of a claustrophobic disposition, though one alternative is to climb the steep footpath from the St-Laurent church on the northern bank of the Isère. For the more adventurous, there's a *via ferrata* along the walls leading up to the Bastille, comprising two fairly difficult stages, each around forty-five minutes long. If you fancy having a go, contact the Maison de la Montagne (see p.729).

## Fort de la Bastille

The **Bastille's** main draw is its spectacular **views**. At your feet, the Isère flows under old bridges which join the St-Laurent quarter (a home for Italian immigrants in the later 1800s) on the northern bank of the river to the nucleus of the medieval town. Even this far south, if you look northeast on a clear day you can see the distant white peaks

---

### FOOD AND DRINK IN THE ALPS AND FRANCHE-COMTÉ

Most characteristic of Alpine cuisine is the liberal amount of cheese made from the local cow, ewe and goat milk. The *fromageries* of Franche-Comté and the Northern Alps are full of cheeses like Roblochon, Tome des Bauges, Emmental, Chèvre, Comté and Beaufort. These are found not just in the famous fondue, but also *raclette* and *tartiflette* (both cheese-based dishes served with ham and potatoes). Other cheeses worth seeking out include the smooth blue-veined Bleu de Gex, produced exclusively in the Pays de Gex region, and creamy Saint Marcellin, from the Grenoble area.

Many restaurants feature **fish** (notably salmon and trout) from the Alpine lakes and use locally grown herbs, like thyme, basil and rosemary. These herbs are particularly in evidence in the Southern Alps around Briançon, where they are often used to flavour the *saucisson* (cured sausage), which you'll find in many a morning shopping market.

The region produces many light and fruity varieties of **wine**, of which the most popular is the dark red Mondeuse, with its faint taste of raspberries. By contrast, the expensive *vin jaune* from the Jura is a potent, golden wine, made from Sauvignon grapes with a fermentation process similar to that of sherry – it remains in the cask for 6–10 years before being bottled. *Vin jaune* is a favourite accompaniment for the local cheeses of Franche-Comté, and is used in speciality dishes such as *poulet au vin jaune* (chicken in a creamy sauce flavoured by the wine). It's also worth sampling some regional **liqueurs**. The most famous of these is undoubtedly **Chartreuse**, the drink produced by Carthusian monks since the sixteenth century, which contains 130 different herbs and is known as the "elixir of life", while Chambéry is famous for its high-quality **vermouth**, including the unique Chambéryzette, flavoured with strawberries.

## GRENOBLE

— Tramline

▪ - - - ◀ Téléphérique

0    250
metres

**▼ 9 & 10**

| ◼ ACCOMMODATION | | Institut | 3 | ◆ CAFÉS AND RESTAURANTS | | La Gazzetta | 5 | ● BARS | |
|---|---|---|---|---|---|---|---|---|---|
| D'Angleterre | 7 | Institut | 3 | L'Auberge Napoléon | 8 | La Gazzetta | 5 | L'assemblage | 6 |
| Auberge de Jeunesse | 10 | Suisse | | Café de la Table Ronde | 2 | Maison Bourbon | 4 | La Boîte à Sardines | 1 |
| Camping Le Bois | | et Bordeaux | 2 | La Casse Croute à Dédé | 7 | Le Petit Rousseau | 9 | | |
| de Cornage | 9 | Terminus | 1 | Chardon Bleu | 10 | | | ◼ CLUB | |
| De L'Europe | 5 | Touring | 6 | La Ferme à Dédé | 3 | | | Le Café des Arts | 1 |
| Le Grand | 4 | Victoria | 8 | | | | | | |

of Mont Blanc further up the deep valley of the Isère. To the east, snowfields gleam in the high gullies of the Belledonne massif (2978m). To the southeast is the peak of Le Taillefer (2807m), while further to the south you can make out the mountain pass which the famous Route Napoléon crosses on its way northwards from the Mediterranean. This was the road towards Paris that Napoleon took after his escape from Elba in March 1815. Finally, to the west you can admire Moucherotte (1901m), the highest peak of the Vercors massif, and the mountain which most seems to dominate the city beneath.

## Musée des Troupes de Montagne

Tues–Sun 11am–6pm, closed Jan • €3, including audioguide • ☎ 04 76 00 92 25

Although the well-preserved nineteenth-century fortifications were never tested in battle, part of the Fort de la Bastille now houses the **Musée des Troupes de Montagne**. Dedicated to the history of the French mountain troops, the first alpine units were formed in 1888, since which time they've been engaged in many major combat situations, not least both World Wars, while more recent missions have included Bosnia and Afghanistan. The equipment and uniform on display testify to the exacting terrain and conditions the Chasseurs Alpins, or "Les diables bleus" (The Blue Devils), are often required to operate in.

**14**

## Musée Dauphinois

30 rue Maurice-Gignoux • Daily except Tues: June–Aug 10am–7pm; Sept–May 10am–6pm • Free • ☎ 04 57 58 89 01

Up a steep cobbled path opposite the St-Laurent footbridge, the **Musée Dauphinois** is located in a former convent, and is devoted to the history, arts and crafts of the Dauphiné province. In the basement, there's a Baroque chapel with grey and gold wall paintings depicting episodes from the New Testament and scenes from the life of St-François-de-Sales, the convent's founder. In the museum proper, there's plenty of information on the lives of the rugged and self-sufficient Dauphinois mountain people, but perhaps the most memorable exhibit details the evolution of skiing in the area over the last four thousand years, right through to the modern winter sports that came to Grenoble when it hosted the 1968 Winter Olympics.

## Musée Archéologique Grenoble Saint-Laurent

Place St-Laurent • June–Aug daily 10am–7pm; Sept–May Wed–Mon 10am–6pm • Free • ☎ 04 76 44 78 68

Housed within the former **Église St-Laurent** is the superbly renovated **Musée Archéologique**, whose spectacular hoard of grave goods was unearthed from some 1500 graves. Evidence points to pagan and Christian worship dating back as far as the fourth century, with earthenware, jewellery and coins among the many precious items recovered. Its centrepiece, though, is an eighth-century crypt and a medieval cloister.

## The Old Town

The narrow streets of the **Old Town** on the southern bank of the Isère, particularly around places Grenette, Vaucanson, Verdun and Notre-Dame, make up the liveliest and most colourful quarter of the city. Here, too, there is plenty of cultural interest, not least one of France's most renowned art collections.

### Musée de Grenoble

5 place de Lavalette • Daily except Tues 10am–6.30pm • €5 • ☎ 04 76 63 44 44, ⓦ museedegrenoble.fr

A vast modern complex down by the riverbank, the **Musée de Grenoble** is home to one of the country's most prestigious art collections. The classical wing has a fine spread of masterpieces spanning the thirteenth to nineteenth centuries. Pieces by Rubens, Veronese, and Canaletto take centre stage in the first few rooms, followed by nineteenth-century luminaries Gauguin, Renoir, and local hero, Henri Fantin-Latour. Once you've absorbed those, there is still a further two dozen or so rooms of twentieth-century and modern art to negotiate, including works by Chagall, Matisse, Picasso and Warhol, to name but a few. If you can summon the energy, take a peek at the basement collection of Egyptian antiquities.

### Musee de l'Ancien Évêché

2 rue Trés-Cloitres • Mon, Tues, Thurs & Fri 9am–6pm, Wed 1–6pm, Sat & Sun 11am–6pm • Free • ☎ 04 76 03 15 25

Housed in the old bishop's palace, the **Musee de l'Ancien Évêché** offers a brisk tour through Grenoble's history from the Stone Age onwards. The remains of the Roman town walls and a fifth-century **baptistry** are on show in the basement, while upstairs you will find the oldest human skull found in the Alps, dating back 11,000 years, Iron Age jewellery and many Roman artefacts, including a colourful mosaic floor panel depicting a pair of parrots. The absence of any English captioning does, however, dilute the experience somewhat.

### Musée de la Résistance et de la Déportation de l'Isère

14 rue Hébert • Daily: July & Aug 10am–7pm, Tues 1.30–7pm; Sept–June 9am–6pm, Tues 1.30–6pm • Free • ☎ 04 76 42 38 53

As sobering as it is insightful, the excellent **Musée de la Résistance et de la Déportation de l'Isère** relates the history of the Nazi occupation of the Dauphiné, from where some 2600 people were deported, including a thousand Jews. Alongside the wealth of poignant and personal wartime memorabilia, the role of the Resistance fighters is given due prominence, Isére being one of the major centres of the Resistance movement in France during World War II. The combination of guerrilla warfare activities, intelligence, and clandestine publications such as *Les Allobroges* were all, ultimately, key to ensuring Allied success.

## ARRIVAL AND DEPARTURE                                                     GRENOBLE

**By plane** Grenoble-Isère airport (☎ 04 76 65 48 48, ⓦ grenoble-airport.com) is 45km to the northwest of the city. Buses run hourly from the airport to the *gare routière* in Grenoble (45min; €12.50), and in winter, there are also frequent buses between the airport and the ski resorts of Les Deux-Alpes and L'Alpe d'Huez (1hr 30min; €40).

**By train** The *gare SNCF* is at the western end of avenue Félix-Viallet, just ten minutes' walk from the centre.

**Destinations** Annecy (frequent; 2hr); Briançon, changing at Gap (6 daily; 4hr 20min); Chambéry (frequent; 1hr); Lyon (frequent; 1hr 30min); Paris-Lyon (several daily; 3hr).

**By bus** The *gare routière* is next to the *gare SNCF*.

**Destinations** L'Alpe d'Huez (1–2 daily; 40min); Le Bourg-d'Oisans (6 daily; 1hr); Briançon (3 daily; 2hr 40min); Chambéry (frequent; 2hr); Col du Lautaret (3 daily; 1hr 50min); La Grave (3 daily; 1hr 30min); St-Pierre-de-Chartreuse (6 daily; 1hr 10min).

## INFORMATION

**Tourist office** In the ugly concrete building at 14 rue de la République (May–Sept Mon–Sat 9am–6.30pm, Sun 10am–1pm & 2–5pm; Oct–April Mon–Sat 9am–6.30pm, Sun 10am–1pm; ☎ 04 76 42 41 41, ⓦ grenoble-tourisme.com).

**Maison de la Montagne** Behind the tourist office, at 3 rue Raoul-Blanchard, is the "House of the Mountains" (Mon–Fri 9.30am–12.30pm & 1–6pm, Sat 10am–1pm & 2–5pm; ☎ 04 76 44 67 03, ⓦ grenoble-montagne.com). Its highly informed staff can offer walking suggestions and

detailed information on *refuges* (including taking bookings), as well as arrange guides for various outdoor activities. Maps are also sold here.

**Grenoble Passes** If you're in town for more than a day or two, it could be worth buying the full Grenoble Pass from the tourist office (€15.50). This gives you a guided tour of the Old Town, admission to the Musée de Grenoble, a return trip on the *téléphérique* and a ride on the inevitable *petit train*. Cheaper passes, giving you a choice of either two (€11.50) or three (€13.50) of the above options are also available.

## GETTING AROUND

With the exception of the hilly north bank of the Isère, Grenoble is compact and flat enough to negotiate by foot. That said, there's a useful bus and tram system in place should you start to flag.

**Public transport** This comprises four tram lines – the most useful of which are lines A and B which pass outside the train station – in addition to a host of bus lines. You can pick up the handy tram and bus map at the public transport office (TAG), which is located in the same building as the tourist office.

**Tickets** A single ticket costs €1.50, but better value is the one-day *Visitag* (€4.10). If you're staying longer, consider the three-day *Visitag* (€9.90) or a *carnet* of ten (€12.30).

Tickets for buses can be bought from the driver, but tickets for trams must be bought at machines outside tram stations or at the TAG office.

**Bike rental** Metrovélo in the underpass of the *gare SNCF*, place de la Gare; €5 per day, including helmet and lock; ☎ 08 20 22 38 38, ⓦ metrovelo.fr. There's also an excellent little fold-out map (Le Plan du cycliste urbain) available.

**Taxi** Grenoblois 14 rue de la République ☎ 04 76 54 42 54. Provides a 24hr radio taxi service.

## ACCOMMODATION

**D'Angleterre** 5 place Victor-Hugo ☎ 04 76 87 37 21, ⓦ hotel-angleterre-grenoble.com. The red telephone booth in the reception aside, there's little else purporting to be English here, but this is a solid, if slightly pricey, central option. Rooms are modestly sized, though the Jacuzzi baths, DVD players, and tea- and coffee-making facilities are nice extra touches. Free overnight parking. Breakfast €13. **€120**

**Auberge de Jeunesse** 10 av de Grésivaudan ☎ 04 76 09 33 52, ✉ grenoble@fuaj.org. This modern hostel provides simple meals, but also has good kitchen facilities

and is near a supermarket. It's 5km south of the city centre in a large park in Echirolles; bus #1 to the "Quinzaine" stop or tram A to "La Rampe". Breakfast included. From **€19**

**Camping Le Bois de Cornage** 110 Chemin du Camping, Vizille ☎ 06 83 18 17 87, ⓦ campingvizille .com. Around 15km from the city centre, this three-star campsite has a swimming pool and restaurant on site. Take bus #3000 from the *gare routière* in Grenoble and get off at stop "Place du Chateau" in Vizille. Open May–Oct. Chalets are available by the week and sleep five people. Camping **€15.90**, chalet **€520 per week**

14

**14**

**De L'Europe** 22 place Grenette ☎ 04 76 46 16 94, ⓦ hoteleurope.fr. With its stuccoed facade and elegant, wrought-iron balconies, Grenoble's oldest hotel promises much, but the rooms themselves are on the simple side. Still, they're well turned out and the location overlooking a central square is a good one. There are also cheaper rooms with washbasin only. Breakfast €9. €85

**Le Grand** 5 rue de la République ☎ 04 76 51 22 59, ⓦ grand-hotel-grenoble.fr. By far the city's most luxurious hotel, albeit one with a slightly inflated sense of its own importance. The triple-glazed rooms are surprisingly modest in size, though boast sumptuous beds with the crispest of linen, grey silk curtains, and glass fronted cupboards – the dazzling bathrooms, meanwhile, are tiled brilliant-white and feature walk-in showers. Expect the likes of salmon and foie gras for breakfast (€15). €140

**Institut** 10 rue Barbillon ☎ 04 76 46 36 44, ⓦ institut-hotel.fr. Two blocks in from the train station, this friendly two-star hotel provides small and functional but artfully decorated rooms, and on the whole represents pretty good value for money. Triples and quads available too. Breakfast €7. €67

**Suisse et Bordeaux** 6 place de la Gare ☎ 04 76 47 55 87, ⓦ hotel-sb-grenoble.com. Opposite the railway station, this grand nineteenth-century building – take a look up at the fabulous tiled facade – houses decently sized, though rather spartan rooms, some in need of a lick of paint. Breakfast is served from 6am for early risers. Note that the entrance is on avenue Felix Viallet. Breakfast €7. €66

**Terminus** 10 place de la Gare ☎ 04 76 87 24 33, ⓦ terminus-hotel-grenoble.fr. Although more expensive than you'd expect from a train station hotel, it's in the *Best Western* fold so a certain standard is guaranteed, and this is undoubtedly the best option in the vicinity; large, generously furnished rooms, all fully soundproofed with a/c. Breakfast €12. €99

**Touring** 26 av Alsace Lorraine ☎ 04 76 46 24 32, ⓦ france-touring-hotel.com. Overlooking one of the main tramlines into the city centre, this greying building has seen better days, but it offers a range of cheapish rooms, either with showers or bathtubs. Breakfast €7.50. €52

**Victoria** 17 rue Thiers ☎ 04 76 46 06 36, ⓦ hotelvictoriagrenoble.com. This simple but clean, cheap and comfortable two-star hotel offers a bunch of rooms in two buildings set apart within a small courtyard. Rooms with shared WCs are slightly cheaper. Closed Aug. Breakfast €7. €50

## EATING, DRINKING AND NIGHTLIFE

### CAFÉS AND RESTAURANTS

**L'Auberge Napoléon** 7 rue Montorge ☎ 04 76 87 53 64, ⓦ auberge-napoleon.fr. The city's most upmarket, if not most well-regarded, restaurant, offering fine evening-only cuisine such as foie gras with pistachio and muscat wine jelly, and white cheese mousse with blueberry sorbet. The heavily glassed and mirrored decor might be a bit much for some, but it's all part of the package. Starters €12, mains €25. Closed first two weeks Aug. Mon–Sat 7.30–10pm.

**Café de La Table Ronde** 7 place St-André ☎ 04 76 44 51 41, ⓦ restaurant-tableronde-grenoble.com. Allegedly France's second oldest café, founded in 1739, this has always been a hotspot for writers, artists and tourists. The mirrored interior is an atmospheric place to linger over a coffee, but when the sun comes out, the terrace is as enjoyable a place as any to down a beer or two. Daily noon–2pm & 7–11pm. Closed Sun in winter.

★ **Le Casse Croute à Dédé** Place Ste-Claire ☎ 04 76 89 93 80. Thick wedges of broccoli and blue cheese quiche, walnut and ham pie, stuffed potatoes, fondant cakes and fruit tarts are just some of the over-the-counter tempters at this super sit-down or takeaway restaurant, and all for around €5 too. The playful, alpine-themed decor and unfailingly helpful, beret-wearing staff add an even bigger dollop of charm to this place. Daily 9am–11pm.

**Chardon Bleu** 23 av Alsace Lorraine ☎ 04 76 12 05 93, ⓦ auchardonbleu.com. Big, bold and bright glass-fronted café-cum-patisserie that doles out a whole lot more besides home-made pastries and coffee, namely quiches, lasagne, and a tasty little *pâté en croute*, as well as breakfasts (€6) and a *plat du jour* (€12.50). Park yourself down on a stool at one of the simple plastic tables or take your grub with you. Mon–Sat 6.45am–7.45pm.

★ **La Ferme à Dédé** 1 place aux Herbes ☎ 04 76 54 00 33, ⓦ restaurantlafermeadede.com. You could be forgiven for thinking you were halfway up a mountain in this fun, almost Lyonnais bouchon-style restaurant, with its red-and-white-checked tablecloths and randomly scattered alpine junk. Big menu featuring hearty sausage casseroles, gooey Savoyarde fondues, and local favourites, *raclette* and *tartiflette*. Packed to the gills most nights. Starters €9, mains €13. Mon–Sat noon–2pm & 7–10pm.

**La Gazzetta** 30 av Félix Viallet ☎ 04 76 50 22 22, ⓦ la -gazzetta.fr. A cut above your average Italian, *La Gazzetta* offers sublimely crafted dishes like mushroom and foie gras ravioli, and pasta stuffed with truffles on a bed of rocket. The risotto dishes are also worth a shot, or you could just settle for a pizza. The black and orange colour scheme, big bay windows and mezzanine-level seating lend the place a with-it, lounge-like vibe. Pizza €9, pasta €11. Mon–Fri noon–2pm & 7–10pm, Sat 7–10pm.

**Maison Bourbon** 3 place Notre-Dame ☎ 04 76 54 57 93, ⓦ boulangerie-patisserie-bourbon.fr. Popular take-away patisserie selling freshly made sandwiches, quiches, and other savouries, as well as countless little cakes and tarts. Mon–Sat 6am–8pm, Sun 6am–6.30pm.

**Le Petit Rousseau** 3 rue Jean Jaques Rousseau ☎ 04 76 62 04 18. Diminutive place tucked away down a little side street off place St-Claire, featuring white, rough-hewn walls, cool blue spotlights, and perfectly set tables. Expect dishes like salmon and cream *ravioles*, and seared foie gras with apples. *Menus* from €24. Starters €13, mains €17. Daily noon–2pm & 7–10.15pm.

### BARS

**L'assemblage** Place Ste-Claire ☎04 76 15 39 31, ⓦ lassemblage.fr. Admire the beautifully boxed wines lining the walls of this classy wine bar as you take a seat at the central island bar and savour a vintage *vierre du vin* (around €5) with a tasty tapenade or two. You can buy bottles to take away too. Tues–Fri 6–11pm, Sat & Sun 10am–1pm.

**La Boîte à Sardines** 1 place Claveyson ☎04 76 44 27 84. Cool name, cool place – which just about sums up the "Box of Sardines", a quirky, easy-going watering hole where you can sup on a crisp draught Belgian beer (€3.50–6) or a mojito while contemplating the rather peculiar decor. Daily noon–late.

**Le Café des Arts** 36 rue St-Laurent ☎04 76 54 65 31, ⓦ lecafedesarts38.fr. Entertainment-wise, there's little reason to visit the north bank, but this place is the exception. From Thursdays through to Saturdays, there's a humdinger of a live music programme, from African blues and Balkan jazz to classical and chanson. On music nights, you can have dinner and watch the concert for just €18. Mon–Sat 8pm–midnight.

### DIRECTORY

**Bookshops** BD Fugue, rue Jean-François Hache (Mon 10am–7pm, Tues–Sat 9.30am–7pm), is the place to go for French-language comic books, and it also has a super little Tintin-themed café. Librairie des Alpes, 1 rue Casimier Perier, has an excellent collection of coffee-table books on the Alps.

**Car hire** All the following have outlets at or opposite the *gare SNCF*: AVIS ☎08 20 61 16 51; Europcar ☎08 25 88 70 90; Hertz ☎04 76 86 55 80; Rent-a-Car, 10 place de la Gare ☎04 76 86 27 60.

**Festivals** Grenoble's premier annual event is Cabaret Frappé (ⓦ cabaret-frappe.com), a week-long celebration of contemporary jazz, soul, world and experimental music

held at venues around town in late July. In keeping with the musical vibe, the superb Détours de Babel, in late March, proposes a different theme each year, for example, Music and Politics, or Music and Identity.

**Internet** Pl@net On-Line, 1 place Vaucanson (Mon–Sat 9am–midnight).

**Health** Centre Hospitalier Universitaire (CHU) ☎04 76 76 50 25; ambulance Alp'Azur (a private ambulance company) ☎04 76 21 11 11.

**Pharmacy** There are several large pharmacies in the centre which have long opening hours. Pharmacie Victor Hugo, 2 bd Agutte Sembat (daily 8am–8pm) ☎04 76 46 04 15.

**Police** 36 bd Maréchal-Leclerc ☎04 76 60 40 40.

# The Chartreuse massif

ⓦ chartreuse-tourisme.com

Nestling a short way north of Grenoble, the **Chartreuse massif** is a place of spectacular landscapes, including sharp limestone peaks, mountain pastures and large areas of pine forest. Designated in 1995 as the **Parc Naturel Régional de Chartreuse** the landscape provides wonderful opportunities for all manner of recreational pursuits. The **Maison de la Montagne** office in Grenoble (see p.729) can offer advice on many of these activities, and also publishes descriptions of the various hiking routes in the area.

## The Grande Chartreuse Monastery and Musée de la Grande Chartreuse

The massif's main local landmark is the **Grande Chartreuse Monastery**, situated up the narrow Gorges des Guiers Morts, southeast of St-Laurent-du-Pont, and some 35km from Grenoble. Carthusian monks and nuns seek a life of contemplation following the example of their founder, the eleventh-century monk St Bruno, a life which involves long periods of solitude, silence, work and prayer. Members of the order live in cells and meet only for Mass and a weekly communal meal, eaten in silence. Since 1605, however, the Carthusians have also become famous as the producers of various **Chartreuses**, powerfully alcoholic herbal elixirs ranging from the better-known green and yellow variants to a number of gentler fruit and nut liqueurs. The monastery is not open to the public, but near the village of **ST-PIERRE-DE-CHARTREUSE**, 5km back on the Grenoble road, you can visit the **Musée de la Grande Chartreuse** (April, Oct & early Nov Mon–Fri 1.30–6pm, Sat & Sun 10am–6pm; May–Sept daily 10am–6.30pm; €7.70 including audioguide; ☎04 76 88 60 45, ⊛musee-grande-chartreuse.fr), formerly La Correrie monastery, which illustrates the life of the Carthusian Order.

## Voiron

For those interested in the local liqueurs, a visit to **VOIRON**, 30km west of the park and on the train line from Grenoble to Lyon, is most definitely in order. Here, you'll find the **Caves de la Chartreuse** (10 bd Edgar Kofler; April–Oct daily 9–11.30am & 2–6.30pm; Nov–March Mon–Fri 9–11.30am & 2–5.30pm; free; ☎04 76 05 81 77, ⊛chartreuse.fr), where the "elixir of life" has been bottled since 1737. These days, the herbs (some 130 of them) are picked, crushed and mixed in great secrecy at the monastery by just two monks, before being transferred to the distillery here in Voiron. It is the monks, too, who decide when the liquor is ripe for bottling, which is typically several years into the maturation process. Following an informative 3D film on the history of the monastery and the secret manuscript with the recipe of the original liqueur (which dates from 1605), you are taken through the world's largest liqueur cellars – built in 1860 and some 160 metres long – before the real highlight of the tour; a tasting of one of the beverages themselves.

## Le Bourg-d'Oisans

Connecting Grenoble to Briançon, the **N91** twists through the precipitous valley of the Romanche and over the **Col du Lautaret** (2058m), which is kept open all year round and crossed at least a couple of times a day (and more often during the skiing season) by the Grenoble–Briançon bus. The first major settlement on the route, **LE BOURG-D'OISANS** (known as "Le Bourg"), 20km southeast of Grenoble, is of no great interest in itself, but it sits in a beautiful position in the valley and is a good base for summer sports. It's particularly popular with cyclists.

### INFORMATION                                      LE BOURG D'OISANS

**Tourist office** On quai Girard, by the river in the middle of town (July & Aug daily 9am–7pm; Sept–June Mon–Sat 9am–noon & 2–6pm; ☎04 76 80 03 25, ⊛bourgdoisans .com); you can pick up lots of excellent information on hiking routes here.
**Maison du Parc National des Écrins** Rue Gambetta

(daily July & Aug 8am–noon & 3–7pm; Sept–June Mon–Fri 8am–noon & 2–5.30pm; ☎04 76 80 00 51); they can also advise on hiking possibilities within the park boundary.
**Bicycle rental** Road and mountain bikes from Au Cadre Rouges, 20 rue du Général de Gaulle (☎04 76 80 13 81), for €22 per day; they also do repairs.

## La Grave

Continuing on the N91 towards La Grave past the modern ski resort of **Les Deux-Alpes**, you'll pass two waterfalls issuing from the north side of the valley: early summer run-off enhances the 300m plume of the **Cascade de la Pisse**, while, 6km further on is the near-vertical fall of churning whitewater called the **Saut de la Pucelle** ("the virgin's leap") – a breathtaking sight.

**LA GRAVE**, 18km on from the Barrage du Lac du Chambon, lies at the foot of the Col du Lautaret, facing the majestic glaciers of the north side of **La Meije** (3984m). While it lies at the heart of a large and testing ski area, La Grave, with its small collection of stone buildings, could not be a more different environment than Les Deux-Alpes. In addition to the skiing opportunities, it's also a good base for walkers and climbers; the **GR54** passes to the northwest of the village, and there are also two equipped *via ferrata* courses nearby (an easier one at Arsine and a tougher course at the Mines du Grand Clot).

**14**

## SKIING IN THE ALPS

With their long and varied runs, extensive lift networks, and superb après-ski, the French Alps offer some of the best skiing not just in Europe, but the world. Skiing first became a recreational sport here in the early 1900s but the industry really began to boom in the Alps during the 1960s with the construction of dozens of high-altitude, purpose-built resorts that ensured good lasting snow cover. Some of these resorts have their detractors: the modern architects often created sprawling concrete settlements that had little in common with the traditional farming villages lower in the valleys, and in so doing they earned France a lasting reputation for "ski factories". Nonetheless, few can knock the efficiency of these resorts. They have an abundance of hotels, equipment outlets and ski schools, while at many you can simply clip your skis on at the hotel door and be skiing on some of the most challenging pistes on earth within minutes.

Although downhill is the most common form of the sport at all the resorts, **cross-country** or **nordic skiing** has become increasingly popular on gentler slopes (particularly around Morzine and in the Parc Naturel Régional du Queyras), while there are also several famous routes for **ski touring** (a form of cross-country skiing with uphill sections and across much longer distances), not least the **Haute Route** between Chamonix and Zermatt (Switzerland) and the **Grande Traversée des Alps**, which leads south from Thonon-les-Bains on Lake Geneva through several national parks. There are also plenty of opportunities for **snowboarding** with many resorts having developed snow parks expressly for snowboarders.

The ski **season** runs from December to late April, with high season over Christmas and New Year, February half-term and (to a lesser extent) Easter.

If you don't want to walk, then an easier way of appreciating the stunning vistas is provided by the *télécabine* (mid-June to early Sept & late Dec to early May; €22 return), which rises sharply from the centre of the village to the 3200m summit of **Le Rateau**, just west of La Meije. The 35-minute ride is value for money considering that the view of the barely accessible interior of the Écrins is normally seen only by the most intrepid mountaineers. The lift also provides access to acres of off-piste skiing, and the freezing conditions of the mountain's northerly face make it ideal for ice climbing.

From La Grave it's only 11km to the top of the **Col du Lautaret**, a pass which is generally kept clear for traffic during the winter months, despite its high altitude (2057m). Around the col is a huge expanse of meadow long known to botanists for its glorious variety of Alpine flowers, which are seen at their best in mid-July.

**INFORMATION**                                                       **LA GRAVE**

**Bureau des Guides** Place du Téléphérique (mid-Dec to mid-May & mid-June to mid-Sept; ☎04 76 79 90 21, ⓦguidelagrave.com). Provides guides for the different hiking paths in the area, as well as guides for activities such as caving, canyoning and mountain biking.

# The Hautes-Alpes

The **Hautes-Alpes** make up the area of high mountains to the southeast of Grenoble and south of the Massif de la Vanoise. To the east lies the Italian border and to the south, the Alpes de Provence. The region is sliced in two by the Durance valley, with the **Parc National des Écrins** lying on the western side of the divide and the **Parc Naturel Régional du Queyras** on the eastern. At the head of the Durance valley, where the Guisane and Durance rivers converge, has the ancient fortified city of **Briançon** which makes an excellent base for exploring the surrounding region.

## Briançon

Located 100km east of Grenoble along the N91, **Briançon** is the capital of the Écrins and one of Europe's highest towns at 1350m above sea level. The town is essentially split between the steep, narrow streets of the **ville haute** (also known as the Cité Vauban), which sits high above the urban spread of the modern and charmless lower town (**ville basse**), itself of little interest save for the **Télécabine de Prorel**, which shoots up from avenue René-Froger, linking Briançon with the Serre Chevalier ski resort. It also provides a head start to mountain walkers (Dec–April & July–Aug; €11.40 return).

## Ville Haute

French-language tours Mon–Sat (€6) usually start at 3pm from the porte Pignerol; English-language tours on Sun also at 3pm (€7)

The **ville haute** looms on the cusp of a rocky outcrop high above the Durance and Guisane valleys. Fortified originally by the Romans to guard the road from Milan to Vienne, it's encircled by lofty ramparts and sheer walls constructed by the French architect and soldier Sébastien Le Preste de Vauban in the seventeenth century.

The highest point of the fortifications is the **citadelle**, which looks over the strategic intersection of five valleys and guards the start of the climb to the desolate and windswept **Col de Montgenèvre**, one of the oldest and most important passes into Italy. There are four **gates**: portes Dauphine and Pignerol lie to the north, porte d'Embrun to the southwest and porte de la Durance to the east. If you come by car the best option is to park at the **Champ de Mars** at the top of the hill and enter the town through the porte Pignerol. From here the narrow main street, Grande Rue – known as the *grande gargouille* because of the "gurgling" stream running down the middle – tips steeply downhill, bordered by mostly eighteenth-century houses. Almost halfway down and to the right is the sturdy **collegiate church**, designed under the supervision of Vauban, again with an eye to defence. Beyond it, there's a fantastic **view** from the walls, especially on a clear starry night, when the snows on the surrounding barrier of mountains give off a silvery glow. Continuing further down Grande Rue, and turning left, you'll find the blocky **Cordeliers church**, Briançon's sole surviving medieval building; it's only occasionally open to visitors, but there are some colourful, well-preserved fifteenth-century murals inside.

### ARRIVAL AND INFORMATION
BRIANÇON

**By train** The *gare SNCF* is on avenue de la République in the *ville basse*, 1.5km south of the old city. Local buses #1 and #3 (€1) link the station and the Champ de Mars in the *ville haute*.
Destinations (train) Embrun (6 daily; 45min); Gap (6 daily; 1hr 25min); Grenoble (2 daily; 4hr); Marseille (4 daily; 5hr 30min).
Destinations (bus) Col du Lautaret (3 daily; 50min); Gap (8 daily; 1hr 45min); La Grave (3 daily; 1hr 10min); St-Véran via Guillestre (1–2 daily; 1hr 40min); Vallouise via Argentière (1 daily; 2hr).
**Tourist office** In the *ville haute* at 1 place du Temple, close to the porte Pignerol gateway (July & Aug daily

9am–7pm; Sept–June Mon–Sat 9am–noon & 2–6pm, Sun 10.15am–12.15pm & 2.30–5pm; ☎04 92 21 08 50, ⓦot-briancon.fr).
**Bureau des Guides** In the Central Parc in the *ville basse* (July & Aug 10am–noon & 4–7pm; Sept–June 5–7pm; ☎04 92 20 15 73, ⓦguides-briancon.fr), this is the place to head to for information about outdoor activities in the mountains.
**Maison du Parc National des Écrins** Place Médecin-Général-Blanchard in the *ville haute* (July & Aug daily 10am–noon & 3–7pm; Sept–June Mon–Fri 2–6pm; ☎04 92 21 08 49, ⓦecrins-parcnational.fr), provides maps for those venturing into the nearby Écrins massif.

### ACCOMMODATION

There's a half-decent choice of hotels in town, although most are located down in the dull *ville basse*, with just a couple of options in the Old Town.

**Auberge de la Paix** 3 rue Porte Méane ☎04 92 21 37 43, ⓦauberge-de-la-paix.com. Secreted away within the Old Town walls, this thirteen-room townhouse certainly doesn't lack for character or charm, with its creaky floorboards and wonky doors. The quirky, colourfully painted rooms are all different from one another, and variously sleep between two and five, some with bunks. Breakfast €8. **€65**
**Camping des Cinq Vallées** St Blaise ☎04 92 21 06 27,

ⓦcamping5vallees.com. Located 2km south of the town, this welcoming campsite has all the facilities you'd expect of a three-star site, including heated outdoor pool, shop, laundry and pizzeria. June–Sept. Camping **€18.60**, mobile home **€600** per week
**De la Chaussée** 4 rue Centrale ☎04 92 21 10 37, ⓦhotel-de-la-chaussee.com. Super *ville basse* option offering a slice of alpine chic amid the modern, grey

surrounds; pine-panelled walls and ceilings, chunky wooden furnishings, sliding wooden doors and sweet little bathrooms with cute sinks and wood-framed mirrors. Breakfast €9. **€72**

**Des Remparts** 14 av Vauban ☎ 04 92 21 08 73, Ⓦ hotel-des-remparts.com. The location, just inside the Porte Pignerol, is fabulous, and it's as cheap as chips, but the rooms, some of which have a shower and some just a sink, are extremely basic at best. The bar is the reception. Breakfast €6. **€35**

**Du Soleil** Central Parc ☎ 04 92 20 37 47, Ⓦ soleilvacances .com. Briançon's largest hotel, also known as the *Parc Hotel*, occupies most of the lower town's small central park, and while the rooms are nothing out of the ordinary, they're generously proportioned and do have splendid views of the surrounding mountains. Breakfast €10. **€70**

**14**

## EATING AND DRINKING

When it comes to eating and drinking, make tracks for the *ville haute*, which is chock-a-block with cafés and restaurants, though some of these can be rather hit and miss.

**Le Panier Alpin** 50 Grande Rue ☎ 04 92 20 54 65. For something light, this gorgeous, and very arty, *épicerie*-cum-tearoom is just the ticket. An *assiette dégustation*, consisting of a selection of local cheeses, cured meats and salad, will set you back just €11.90, or just rest up with a *grand crème* or sticky chocolate fondue (€4). The adjoining shop sells a mouthwatering variety of local foodstuffs. July & Aug & Dec–April daily 10am–11pm, rest of year Tues–Sat 10am–7pm.

**Le Passé Simple** 3 rue Porte Méane ☎ 04 92 21 37 43. Traditional mountain dishes are the bill of fare at the good-looking in-house restaurant of *Auberge de la Paix*, for example, mountain trout in fried butter, or duck breast with red fruit sauce and cottage cheese. The gut-busting *Menu Vauban* (€26) reprises dishes from the seventeenth-century (roast potatoes with ham and cheese, veal escalope, and *pudding au pain*). Menus from €19. Starters €9, mains €16. Daily noon–3pm & 7–10.30pm.

**Le Rustique** 35 rue du Pont d'Asfeld ☎ 04 92 21 00 10, Ⓦ restaurantlerustique.com. For a taste of the delicious local trout, head to this cheerfully decorated restaurant just off the main drag; have it fried, grilled or baked, and accompanied by almond and cream, red berries, or calvados. Their own particular *Menu Vauban* (€35) features nettle soup and salmon among the dishes. Menus from €25. Starters €11, mains €17. Wed–Sun noon–2pm & 7–10pm.

**Les Templiers** 20 rue du Temple ☎ 04 92 20 29 04. Vaulted restaurant right next to the tourist office serving up regional staples like *raclettes*, fondues and *tourtons*, stuffed ravioli parcels popular in the mountain areas. Menus from €19. Starters €8, mains €16. Wed–Sun noon–2pm & 7–10pm.

# The Parc National des Écrins and Vallouise

The Écrins national park is worth a trip for the sheer variety of sports that it offers in a much less crowded setting than Mont Blanc. The best base for exploring the area is the village of **Vallouise**, 19km southwest of Briançon on the D902. From Vallouise, there are several excellent shorter walks that take you into the heart of the Écrins or you can follow the GR54, which makes a circuit of the park and passes through the village.

Vallouise itself centres around the Romanesque **church of St Etienne**, which has a gorgeous, partly frescoed porch. The buildings lining the two or three streets fanning out from here are typical of the region; striking, three-storey farmhouses consisting of a vaulted ground floor (for livestock), a first-floor living quarter, and an upper floor which would have served as a granary.

---

## VAUBAN AND HIS FORTRESSES

The citadelle in Briançon is just one example (albeit a spectacular one) of the many fortifications built on France's eastern borders by **Sébastien Le Preste de Vauban** (1633–1707), a Marshal and engineer in the army of Louis XIV. In all, Vauban built 33 fortresses and strengthened countless others in order to defend the new lands won by **Louis**, the so-called **"Sun King"**, during the wars of the seventeenth century. Vauban was highly innovative in the design of his fortresses, which were often built in the shape of a star so that the various defensive bastions could defend each other with covering fire. The other spectacular fortifications planned and constructed by him in the Alps and Franche-Comté are the citadelles at Besançon and Mont-Dauphin. Twelve of Vauban's fortresses, dotted around France, are now included on UNESCO's World Heritage List.

**14**

Reaching Vallouise by public transport is difficult: your best bet is to take a train from Briançon to L'Argentière-la-Bessée, from where you could either hitch or hang around for one of the very infrequent buses to Vallouise.

**Tourist office** Place de l'Église (Tues–Sat 9am–noon & 2–6pm; ☎ 04 92 23 36 12, ⊚ paysdesecrins.com).
**Bureau des Guides** Hut in the main car park (☎ 04 92 23 32 29, ⊚ guides-ecrins.com).
**Maison du Parc des Écrins** Located on the road that

turns left before you enter Vallouise, and has all the information you need on the park, including local hikes (May to mid-June Tues–Sun 2–6pm, mid-June to Aug daily 10am–noon & 2–6pm, Sept–April Tues–Fri 1.30–5.30pm; ☎ 04 92 23 58 08).

### ACCOMMODATION AND EATING

**Les Vallois** Rière Point ☎ 04 92 23 33 10, ⊚ lesvallois .com. Pleasant chalet-style accommodation down by the river offering pine-heavy rooms, some of which feature a balcony overlooking the hotel garden, and swimming pool.

The combined bar/restaurant is worth a stop if you're feeling peckish and offers a good-value *plat du jour* for €9.90 and *menus* from €15. Breakfast €9. **€70**

# Briançon to the Queyras

The direct road from Briançon to Queyras (the D902) is a beautiful route that ascends steeply to the 2360m **Col d'Izoard** before descending into the **Casse Déserte**, a wild, desolate region with an abundance of scree running down from the peaks above. If the Col d'Izoard is closed (or if you don't fancy driving on the high, winding mountain roads), you can reach the Queyras from the north or the south on the N94.

## Mont-Dauphin

Guided tours July & Aug daily 10am, 3pm & 4pm; June & Sept daily 10am & 3pm; Oct–May Tues–Sun 3pm • €7.50 • Regular trains from Briançon stop at the *gare SNCF* in Mont Dauphin, though the station is situated down on the main road, from where it's a long uphill slog to reach the fortress.

From Briançon, the River Durance meanders through a wide valley following the N94 until, some 30km later, the brooding grey fortress of **MONT-DAUPHIN** hoves into view. Spread across the wide Plateau des Milles Vents ("a thousand winds"), and with commanding views towards the Durance and the Guil, Mont-Dauphin was constructed in 1692, and so named after the eldest son of King Louis XIV, upon whose orders Vauban was requested to build it. Sizing up its gargantuan walls, it's not difficult to see why this was considered the ideal spot from which to repel the Duke of Savoie's advancing troops. Crossing the moat, you enter the village via the thick-set porte de Briançon, from where the main road spears down to the porte D'Embrun. The grid-like streets fanning out from here, lined with houses built from the local pink Guillestre marble, are well inhabited today, with the odd café in situ to cater to passing tourists.

## Embrun

From Mont-Dauphin, the River Durance continues alongside the N94 for 17km to **EMBRUN**, an attractive little town of narrow streets on a rocky bluff above the Durance and an excellent base if you want to spend a longer time exploring the Parc du Queyras. Embrun has been a fortress town for centuries. Emperor Hadrian made it the capital and main religious centre for this region, and from the third century to the Revolution it was the seat of an archbishopric.

### Cathédrale Notre-Dame and Tour Brune

Guided tours in English of the cathedral and treasury mid-June to mid-Sept Thurs at 10am • €4.50, must be booked at the tourist office (see opposite) **Tour Brune**: Mid-June to mid-Sept Tues–Sat 10am–12.30pm & 3–6.30pm, Sun 9am–noon

Embrun's chief sight is its twelfth-century **cathédrale Notre-Dame**, the largest in the French Alps, which has inspired numerous imitations throughout the region. The elaborate main porch, guarded by stone lions, and the fifteenth-century rose window, are especially impressive. The interior, meanwhile, is striking for its wide Gothic arches and rib-vaulted ceiling, which is composed of alternate bands of black and white bricks. Just behind the cathedral is the formidable-looking **Tour Brune** (Brown Tower) which was built in the thirteenth-century as a watchtower, though today it hosts exhibitions run by the Écrins National Park.

### Lac de Serre-Poncon

Embrun nestles at the northeastern corner of the **Lac de Serre-Ponçon,** a wide expanse of water created by the damming of the Durance in the late 1950s (completed in 1961), thus making it one of the largest man-made lakes in Europe. The lake is a great spot to indulge in water-bound activities such as canoeing, waterskiing and windsurfing; the best place to organize such activities is **Savines-Le-Lac,** 10km southwest of Embrun on the southern shore. This is also the place from where most of the lake cruises depart.

**14**

### ARRIVAL AND INFORMATION

### EMBRUN

**By train and bus** The *gare SNCF* and *gare routière* are a five-minute walk east of town on Place de la Gare. There are daily trains and buses from Embrun to Briançon, as well as to Guillestre and Mont-Dauphin.

**Tourist office** Inside the former chapel of the Cordeliers on place Général-Dosse (Mon–Sat 8.30am–noon & 2–6.30pm; ☏ 04 92 43 72 72, ⓦ tourisme-embrun.com),

which is itself notable for the beautiful medieval frescoes which adorn the walls and ceilings. Staff can provide information on nearby walking routes, as well as on the wide range of other locally available outdoor activities including rafting, sailing and climbing, and watersports on nearby Lac de Serre-Ponçon.

### ACCOMMODATION

**Camping Le Vielle Ferme** ☏ 04 92 43 04 08, ⓦ campingembrun.com. Located at the southern end of town, this is the most comfortable and most conveniently sited campsite in the area. There's an on-site restaurant, and they also organise lots of river activities. Two- and three-bed apartments sleeping up to six also available. May–Sept. Camping €27, apartments €385 per week.

**De la Mairie** Place Barthelon ☏ 04 92 43 20 65, ⓦ hoteldelamairie.com. Occupies a sunny location on the town's main square. There are two categories of room available; the rather boring, pine-walled Montagnarde rooms, and the considerably more appealing (and not

much more expensive) Gustavienne rooms, complete with cool saloon doors that separate bedroom and bathroom. Breakfast €9.50. €65

★ **Le Pigeonnier** 2 rue Victor Maurel ☏ 04 92 43 89 63, ⓦ pigeonnier.net. This gorgeous seventeenth-century house, set within lush, Mediterranean-style gardens, offers three stunning rooms, each furnished with parquet flooring, marble fireplace, floor-to-ceiling drapes, and a chaise longue. The bathrooms, meanwhile, are enormous and magnificent, fitted with double sinks and stand-alone baths. Factor in a host of other delightful little touches, and the expense seems worth it. €130

### EATING

**L'Ogow** 72 rue de la liberte ☏ 04 92 43 58 84. A smiling Tintin cut-out welcomes you to this accommodating restaurant which relies on regional specialities like *tourtons*

and *ravioles*. If the weather's warm, head for the sunny terrace out back. Starters €10, mains €12. Daily noon–2.30pm & 7–10pm.

# Gap

Sitting some 10km west from Savines-Le-Lac via the N94 is the departmental capital, **GAP**, a small, pleasant town on the Route Napoléon, whose origins reach back to Roman times. Gap prospered in the Middle Ages, partly thanks to its position on the pilgrim route to Santiago de Compostela, but suffered badly in the sixteenth-century Wars of Religion, and was burnt to the ground by the invading forces of the Duke of Savoy in 1692. Today the pedestrianized streets of the walled Old Town are lined with elegant, mainly eighteenth-century buildings and social life revolves around the café-filled place Jean-Marcellin. The house where Bonaparte spent a night in March 1815 is just off the square at 19 rue de France (look for the mural on the facade). Gap's massive Romanesque-style **cathedral** on place St-Arnoux, was completed in 1904, and incorporates elements from older churches, including marble altars and carved wooden angels.

**14**

## Musée Départemental

6 av Maréchal Foch • July to mid-Sept daily 10am–noon & 2–6pm; mid-Sept to June Wed–Fri & Mon 2–5pm, Sat & Sun 2–6pm • Free • ☎ 04 92 51 01 58

Located beyond the walled town, the **Musée Départemental** houses an intermittently stimulating collection of local Iron Age and Roman archeological finds, folk crafts and paintings. The most interesting exhibits are the exquisitely carved *coffre*, wooden trunks from the Queyras region which would have been used either as safes or were purely for ornamental purposes; look out, too, for the miniature versions of these. Down in the basement, a mummified infant's foot takes centre stage.

### Domaine de Charance and Pic de Charance

A few kilometres north of the town centre (and accessible via free shuttle buses in July and August) are the lovely gardens of the **Domaine de Charance** (free), which, at around 1000m, offer fantastic views over the surrounding countryside and Gap's famous apple and pear orchards. The grand eighteenth-century château is closed to visitors, but the beautiful terraced gardens, featuring numerous apple trees and 500 species of roses are worth the trip alone. Behind the château is a wilder "English" garden, woodland and photogenic lake. Reasonably fit walkers can follow the trail from here to the **Pic de Charance** (1852m), which should take around three hours.

### ARRIVAL AND INFORMATION
                                                                    GAP

**By train** The *gare SNCF* is just east of the centre on avenue des Alpes.
Destinations Briançon (6 daily; 1hr 25min); Grenoble (4 daily; 2hr 15min).
**Tourist office** At the western end of the Old Town at 2 cours Frédéric Mistral (July & Aug Mon–Sat 9am–7pm, Sun 10am–1pm; Sept–June Mon–Fri 9am–noon & 2–6pm,

Sat 9am–4pm; ☎ 04 92 52 56 56, ⓦ gap-tourisme.fr). It can provide information on nearby mountain-biking routes and the airborne activities, such as paragliding, parachuting and hot-air ballooning, for which the surrounding region is especially well known. The tourist office also offers free bike rental.

### ACCOMMODATION

**La Cloche** 2 place Alsace-Lorraine ☎ 04 92 51 02 52. Eight rather austere rooms above an Old Town café offer rooms with and without shower and next to nothing by way of furnishings. Still, you get a TV, and there are some decent views of the square from the shuttered windows. Breakfast €5. **€33–46**
**Station Gap-Bayard** ☎ 04 92 50 16 83, ⓦ gap-bayard .com. You'll need your own transport to get here, as it's 7km north of town on RN85, but the best thing about staying in one of these clean and bright rooms – including

eight-bed dorms – are the fantastic views over a stunning golf course (green fee €48). Half-board from **€35**
**Les Trois Chardon Bleus** 26 av du Commandant Dumont ☎ 06 52 67 09 41, ⓦ troischardonbleus.fr. A delightful, family-run guesthouse ten-minutes' walk northeast of the centre, with three sweet rooms packed with simple homely charms; wall pictures, potted plants, little fluffy towels and so on. A little tricky to find as it's set back from the road and behind a gate. **€79**

### EATING

**Diversion** place Jean-Marcellin ☎ 04 92 52 08 20. The square's most fun place to eat and drink, featuring a train track suspended above the main dining area, and American car number plates and street signs plastering the walls. Alternatively, plonk yourself outside on the terraced seating and tuck into some *moules frites* or a savoury-filled crêpe. Starters €9, mains €12. Daily 6am–1am.
**Le Lavandin** 1 La Placette ☎ 04 92 51 15 46. Sweet little rustically decorated restaurant offering an appealing choice of light dishes such as salads, quiches and omelettes (€8.50–11), as well as a wide range of tasty home-made

pastries and desserts (€5). Mon–Sat noon–2pm & 7–9pm; also closed Wed eve.
**La Menthe Poivrée** 20 rue du Centre ☎ 09 52 77 55 73. Hidden away just off place Grenette, "The Peppermint" is Gap's standout restaurant, though it's not nearly as expensive as it's smart, shallow-vaulted interior might suggest – and what's more, with just half a dozen tables, there's ample room to relax. And the food's not half-bad either, with exemplary dishes like lobster ravioli, and *filet mignon* in a herb crust. Starters €10, mains €15. Daily except Wed noon–2pm & 7.30–10pm.

# Parc Régional du Queyras

Ⓦ queyras.com

Spreading southeast of Briançon to the Italian border, the **Parc Régional du Queyras** is much more Mediterranean in appearance than the mountains to the north, with only shallow soils and low scrub covering the mountainsides. The open land along the park's rolling roads makes it particularly enjoyable to spend a few hours driving up to **St-Véran**, an Alpine village near the Italian border. There are some good walking opportunities: the **GR58** or **Tour du Queyras** path runs through St-Véran on its circuit of the park, and the **GR5** passes Ceillac and Arvieux on its way from Briançon towards Embrun.

14

## Guillestre

The road into the Queyras park follows the River Guil from Mont-Dauphin. The first stop is **GUILLESTRE**, a pretty mountain village that only really comes to life in summer. Its houses, in typical Queyras style, have open granaries on the upper floors and its sixteenth-century church has an intriguing porch (reminiscent of the cathedral at Embrun) with squatting lions carved from limestone.

### INFORMATION AND ACCOMMODATION — GUILLESTRE

**Tourist office** Place Salva (Mon–Sat 9am–noon & 2–6pm; also July & Aug Sun 9am–noon & 3–7pm; Ⓣ 04 92 24 77 61, Ⓦ guillestre-tourisme.com) can advise on all aspects of visiting the Queyras.
**Le Catinat Fleuri** Ⓣ 04 92 45 07 62, Ⓦ catinat-fleuri.com.

A 5min walk uphill from the tourist office. The rooms here, like the building itself, are rather plain, but the complex does boast two superb pools (one indoor, one outdoor), verdant gardens and spots for camping. Breakfast €7. **€64**

## Château Queyras and around

July & Aug daily 9am–9pm, May, June & Sept Tues–Sun 10am–5.30pm • €7 • Ⓣ 04 92 21 98 58, Ⓦ fortqueyras.com

Continuing along the D947 from Guillestre, you'll come to the fortress of **Château-Queyras** which bars the way so completely that there's scarcely room for the road to squeeze around its base. There was probably a fortification of some kind here in the fourteenth century, though it wasn't until Vauban got his hands on it in the early eighteenth century that it took on its present shape. Just beyond the fort is **CHÂTEAU-VILLE-VIEILLE**, a small village with a few old houses and a church still intact. A right turn here takes you towards St-Véran, but if you stay on the road parallel to the river Guil, you will pass through the villages of Aiguilles, Abriès and L'Échalp (all with *gîtes d'étape*), to the **Belvédère du Viso**, close to the Italian border and the **Monte Viso**, at 3841m the highest peak in the area.

## St-Véran

Seven kilometres south of Château-Ville-Vieille lies **ST-VÉRAN**, which at 2042m is one of the highest villages in Europe. Its houses are part stone part timber, and the seventeenth-century **Église de St-Véran** stands prettily on the higher of the two streets, with its white tower silhouetted against the bare crags on the other side of the valley. The **GR58** passes south of the village; waymarked and easy to follow, the path eventually turns right down to the river, before continuing up the opposite bank through woods of pine and larch till the chapel of Notre-Dame-de-Clausis. There, above the line of trees, it crosses to the right bank of the stream and ends in the **Col de Chamoussière** (2884m), about three and a half hours from St-Véran. The ridge to the right of the col marks the frontier with Italy.

### INFORMATION AND ACCOMMODATION — ST-VÉRAN

**Tourist office** Halfway down the main high street (Mon–Sat 9am–12.30pm & 2–5.30pm; also open Sun in high season; Ⓣ 04 92 45 82 21, Ⓦ saintveran.com). In July and August, *Petit Mathieu* buses (Ⓣ 04 92 46 71 56) link the village with the *gare SNCF* in Guillestre, although it's best to contact the tourist office for the most up-to-date times.

**Les Chalets du Villard** Ⓣ 04 92 45 82 88, Ⓦ leschaletsduvillard.fr. One of the most tranquil places to stay in the village, offering spacious studio apartments with kitchen facilities and private terraces, as well as a spa and restaurant on site. Mid-Dec to April & June to mid-Sept. Two people sharing **€106**

**14**

# Chambéry and around

Nestling in a valley to the north of the Chartreuse Massif, the town of **CHAMBÉRY** commands the entrance to the mountain passes which lead towards Italy, and has thus held an important strategic position for the various armies and merchants who have crossed the Alps over the centuries. The town grew up around the château built by Count Thomas of Savoie in 1232, and became the Savoyard capital, enjoying a golden age in the fourteenth and fifteenth centuries. Although superseded as capital by Turin in 1562, it remained an important commercial and cultural centre, and the philosopher Rousseau spent some of his happiest years in the town during the 1730s. Only incorporated into France in 1860, modern Chambéry is a bustling provincial town with a wealth of grand Italianate architecture and a strong sense of its regional identity.

Around 13km north of Chambéry is the spa resort of **Aix-les-Bains**, with its famous thermal baths, as well as the **Lac du Bourget**, one of the best sites in the country for watersports.

## Fontaine des Éléphants and rue de Boigne

Halfway down the broad, leafy boulevard de la Colonne is Chambéry's most famous monument, the extravagant and somewhat off-scale **Fontaine des Éléphants**. The fountain was erected in 1838 in homage to Général Comte de Boigne (1751–1830), a local boy who amassed a fortune working as a mercenary in India and subsequently used much of his vast wealth to fund major urban developments in his home town. Appropriately enough, de Boigne has a street named after him, hence **rue de Boigne**, which, with its elegant colonnades, is immediately reminiscent of Turin. At its bottom end, Rue de Boigne opens up on to the café-lined **place St-Léger**, which hosts a **flea market** on the second Saturday of every month. Heading east along place St-Léger you'll come to the fine old **rue de la Croix-d'Or**, the hub of aristocratic Chambéry in the seventeenth century and now home to numerous restaurants.

## Musée Savoisien and Cathédrale St-François

A few paces from the Fontaine des Éléphants, the **Musée Savoisien** on Square de Lannoy de Bissy (Mon & Wed–Sun 10am–noon & 2–6pm; €3; ☎04 79 33 44 48) chronicles the history of Savoie from the Bronze Age onwards. Despite the rather dry presentation, it has its moments, with a diverse mix of Iron Age pottery, Roman bronzes, and paintings. The museum's centrepiece, however, is the Cruet Mural, a remarkably well-preserved set of thirteenth-century wall paintings depicting battle scenes and life at the royal court. The building itself is a former Franciscan monastery, hence the lovely little cloister. The town's main ecclesiastical sight is right by the museum; the **cathédrale St-François**, which dates from the 1400s but has an interior decorated in elaborate nineteenth-century trompe l'oeil.

## Château des Ducs de Savoie

May, June & Sept Tues–Sun 2.30pm; July & Aug daily 10.30am, 2.30pm, 3.30pm & 4.30pm; Oct–April Tues–Sun 2.30pm • €2.50 • ☎04 79 60 20 40

A massive and imposing structure, the **Château des Ducs de Savoie** was once the main home of the Dukes of Savoy, and is now occupied by the prefecture; the interior is only accessible by guided tours, which begin from the adjacent place du Château. The **Sainte-Chapelle**, in the internal courtyard, was once the repository of the Turin Shroud; it was damaged in a fire here in 1532 and was transferred to the Duke's new court in Turin in 1578.

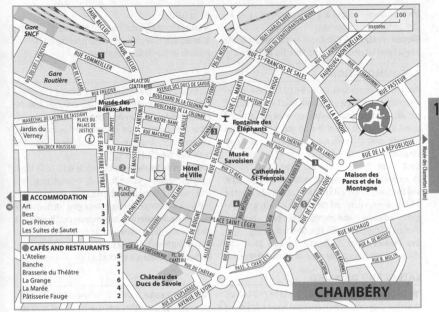

Map legend:

**■ ACCOMMODATION**

| Art | 1 |
| Best | 3 |
| Des Princes | 2 |
| Les Suites de Sautet | 4 |

**● CAFÉS AND RESTAURANTS**

| L'Atelier | 5 |
| Banche | 3 |
| Brasserie du Théâtre | 1 |
| La Grange | 6 |
| La Marée | 4 |
| Pâtisserie Fauge | 2 |

**CHAMBÉRY**

## Musée des Beaux-Arts

Place du Palais de Justice • Mon & Wed–Sun 10am–noon & 2–6pm • Free, €3 for exhibitions • ☏ 04 79 33 75 03

The small but beautifully presented **Musée des Beaux-Arts** is largely devoted to works by lesser-known Italian artists from the Renaissance; the pride of the collection is the fifteenth-century *Portrait of a Young Man*, attributed to Paolo Uccello. The remainder of the collection is given over to French painters from the late nineteenth and early twentieth centuries, with the emphasis, not surprisingly, on bucolic lake and mountain scenes, such as *Vue du Lac du Bourget* by Ginain.

## Musée des Charmettes

Chemin des Charmettes • April–Sept daily except Tues 10am–noon & 2–6pm; Oct–March daily except Tues 10am–noon & 2–4.30pm • Free • ☏ 04 79 33 39 44

Two kilometres south of town on the rustic chemin des Charmettes is Rousseau's Chambéry address, **Les Charmettes**. This country cottage is now home to the **Musée des Charmettes**, a museum focused on Rousseau's writing and domestic life. The house is beautifully furnished in the style of the day, while the walls of the downstairs dining and music rooms manifest Italian-style trompe l'oeil paintings, though these were completed after Rousseau's time. Adjacent to the house, the lovely formal gardens – with abundant herbs and fruits – are laid out just as Rousseau would have remembered them. He only lived here a short while (1736–42), with his companion Madame de Warens, but claimed to have "savoured a century of life and a complete and pure happiness" in this isolated and tranquil location. Look out for open-air events taking place here on summer evenings.

### ARRIVAL AND INFORMATION                                   CHAMBÉRY

**By train** The *gare SNCF* is on rue Sommeiller, 500m north of the Old Town.

Destinations Aix-les-Bains (frequent; 15min); Annecy (frequent; 45min); Bourg-St-Maurice (several daily; 2hr);

Geneva (4 daily; 1hr 30min); Grenoble (frequent; 45min); Lyon (frequent; 1hr 30min); Paris-Lyon (several daily; 3hr).

**Tourist office** 5 place du Palais de Justice (July & Aug Mon–Sat 9am–6.30pm, Sun 10am–1pm; Sept–June

Mon–Sat 9am–12.30pm & 2–6pm; ☎04 79 33 42 47, ⓦchambery-tourisme.com).

**Bicycle rental** La Vélostation is an excellent bike hire scheme located at the gare SNCF (€3 for half a day, €5 for full day).

**Market** Chambéry's main food market, selling everything from regional cheeses to live poultry, sets up on Place du Palais de Justice on Saturday mornings.

## ACCOMMODATION

**Art** 154 rue Sommeiller ☎04 79 62 37 26, ⓦarthotel -chambery.com. A few paces along from the train station, the *Art* has functional though not wholly unattractive rooms that come in one of two categories (standard and comfort), most of which are either road or rail facing. Breakfast (€8.50) is served from 5.30am. **€56**

**Best** 9 rue Denfert-Rochereau ☎04 79 85 76 79, ⓦbesthotel.fr. It's not exactly run through with character, and the rooms do feel a little barren, but plans are afoot for a full scale renovation, and the location is pretty good. The more expensive apartments here have balconies overlooking the place du Théâtre. Breakfast €9. **€74**

**Des Princes** 4 rue de Boigne ☎04 79 33 45 36, ⓦhoteldesprinces.eu. The sense of colonial grandeur is unmistakable in the Indian-themed decor of this refined hotel. The rooms are a real mix of styles and tastes, from the heavily wood and timber-furnished, alpine-style rooms, to those with sharper, more contemporary design features, such as frosted glass doors that separate the bedroom and bathroom. Breakfast €10. **€88**

**Les Suites de Sautet** 6 rue Métropole ☎06 16 83 16 64, ⓦhotel-chambery-sautet.fr. Nicely secreted away in a little courtyard, this eighteenth-century townhouse conceals two large and gorgeously decorated rooms which combine old-style classic charm with contemporary chic. There's also a library/lounge (from where you can borrow DVDs to watch on your flatscreen TV), and a sumptuous breakfast, prepared by the friendly owners, is included. **€120**

## EATING AND DRINKING

★ **L'Atelier** 59 rue de la République ☎04 79 70 62 39, ⓦatelier-chambery.com. Former post house that's now a trendy bistro comprising two vividly coloured rooms and an easy-going wine bar. Sophisticated and contemporary lunch and evening *menus* (€28) with dishes like cappuccino of cauliflower soup, and saddle of rabbit roasted with mustard and foie gras; alternatively, pop along for tapas night on a Tuesday. Starters €8, mains €15. Tues–Sat noon–2pm & 7.30–10pm.

**Banche** 10 place de l'Hôtel de Ville ☎04 79 85 36 10. Chambéry's oldest restaurant has been here in some form or other since the sixteenth century, and it remains a welcoming little place, offering a brief menu of typical brasserie dishes like *steak frites* and *moules*. Starters €8, mains €15. Tues–Sat noon–2pm & 7.30–10pm.

**Brasserie du Théâtre** 14 rue Denfert-Rochereau ☎04 79 25 56 10. This traditional café/brasserie with outdoor seating, attached to the venerable theatre, is a popular place for locals to enjoy afternoon coffees and evening aperitifs. They also serve light meals. *Plats du jour* from €9. Mon–Sat noon–2pm & 7–10pm.

**Pâtisserie Fauge** 6 place Genève ☎04 79 33 36 77. Savoury bites, sandwiches, and *galettes*, as well as an eye-popping selection of artfully presented cakes and chocolates, are just some of the tasters available at this perky patisserie which has both indoor and outdoor seating. Tues–Sat 8am–7pm, Sun 8am–2pm.

**La Grange** 33 place Monge ☎04 79 85 60 31, ⓦrestaurantlagrange.com. One of a clutch of restaurants in this little quarter, a homely, thick-wood panelled restaurant offering a variety of Savoyard specialities like *raclette* and *croziflette*, though you'll find most diners chomping their way through one of the deliciously sticky fondues. *Menus* from €23. Starters €10, mains €15. Mon–Sat 11.45am–1.45pm & 7–10.30pm.

**La Marée** 44 av Pierre Lanfrey ☎04 79 69 02 78, ⓦrestaurant-lamaree.com. If seafood is your bag, then *La Marée* should be your first port of call; cod, sea bass and lobster are standard plates, but you can't beat the supremely tasty, and just a little spicy, bouillabaisse. *Menus* from €24. Mon–Sat noon–2pm & 7–10pm.

# Aix-les-Bains

Thirteen kilometres north of Chambéry is **AIX-LES-BAINS**, one of France's premier spa resorts. The town's waters have been famous for their healing qualities since Roman times but most of the elegant buildings here date from Aix's *belle époque* heyday of the late 1800s, when members of European high society dropped by to relax and take the waters; Queen Victoria was a frequent visitor. These days, Aix-les-Bains is a sedate and genteel place, with thousands of French pensioners descending on the town throughout

**CLOCKWISE FROM TOP LEFT** ECRINS NATIONAL PARK (P.735); SNOWBOARDING IN THE TROIS VALLÉES, SAVOIE (P.747); VAL THORENS, SAVOIE (P.747) >

the year for state-funded thermal treatments. The spa centre, **Les Thermes Nationaux d'Aix-les-Bains** (daily 10am–7.45pm; ☎04 79 35 38 50, ⊛thermaix.com; weekdays €19, weekends €21) was formerly housed in the impressive (though now sadly redundant) Art Deco building on place Maurice-Mollard, but these days you'll find it at **Thermes Chevalley**, a five-minute walk uphill behind here. There are also some parks to amble through and plenty of cafés where you can sit back with a *pastis* and watch the world go slowly by. Aix is also the best base for enjoying the sights and outdoor activities at the nearby **Lac du Bourget** (see below).

## Arc de Campanus and the Musée Lapidaire

The activities and sights of the town are focused around place Maurice-Mollard, where the most eye-catching landmark is **Arc de Campanus**, a Roman arch erected in the first century BC as a funerary monument. The large Roman baths that once stood near here are said to have incorporated over 24 kinds of marble; of the surviving ruins in the square (some of which back on to the *mairie*), the most intact is the Temple de Diane, a rectangular monument which now houses the **Musée Lapidaire** (daily 10am–noon & 1.30–6pm; closed Tues pm; €5), where there's a small collection of Gallo-Roman ceramics and statues.

## Musée Faure

10 bd des Côtes • Mon & Wed–Sun 10am–noon & 1.30–6pm • €4.70 • ☎04 79 61 06 57

Heading west from place Maurice-Mollard, up rue Divat, you'll come to an elegant roadside villa which now houses the marvellous **Musée Faure**. Named after the eponymous pharmacologist, the gallery holds a relatively small but superb collection of nineteenth-century Impressionist art, featuring works by Sisley, Sargent, Pissarro and Cézanne, whose grey-skied *Vue de Bonnières* was one of the painter's first attempts at a landscape. There are some lovely Degas pastels too, in particular *Danseuses Mauve* (Ballerinas in Mauve). Degas' versatility is evident from one or two of his sculptures up on the second floor, which is otherwise dominated by Rodin pieces.

## Lac du Bourget

It's 2km from the town centre to the Grand Port on the Lac du Bourget, but if that's too long a walk, bus #2 departs every 30min from outside the tourist office in Aix-les-Bains (see opposite), passing the *gare SNCF* on the way. Note also that, between April and October, the ubiquitous Petit Train trundles down to the lake hourly between 2pm & 6pm (€7)

Connected to the River Rhône by the Canal de Savières, the **Lac du Bourget** is France's biggest natural lake, at 18km long and 3.5km wide, and a place of great beauty, a protected wildlife reserve and home to the now scarce European beaver. "Nowhere could one find such perfect concord between water, mountains, earth and sky", enthused the nineteenth-century French writer Balzac, and it's clear what attracted him and so many other poets and artists to this place. The lake's "Côte Sauvage" rises

---

### WATERSPORTS ON LAC DU BOURGET

Whatever your favourite watersport, the Lac du Bourget is likely to have a club and good facilities available. Here are a few options:

**Sailing** Seek out Club Nautique Voile d'Aix-les-Bains on boulevard Barrier at the Grand Port (☎04 79 34 10 74, ⊛cnva.com; 5 half-day sessions for €150).

**Waterskiing** Contact the Ski Club Nautique, at Baie de Mémard to the north of the Grand Port (☎06 46 65 31 81, ⊛aixlesbainskinautique.com; €34 for a lesson).

**Kayaking and rowing** On offer at the Entente Nautique Aviron d'Aix-les-Bains, 22 av Daniel Rops (☎04 79 88 12 07, ⊛aviron.ena.free.fr; €15 for a 2hr session).

**Boat trips** Bateaux du Lac du Bourget (☎04 79 63 45 00, ⊛compagniedesbateauxdulac.fr) run daily sightseeing cruises on the lake between April and October (1–1hr 30min; €11.80–14.50), as well as more expensive lunch, dinner and evening cruises.

precipitously above the sparkling blue water on its western bank, which is dominated at its southern end by the looming presence of the **Dent du Chat** (1390m).

There are daily boat trips (30min) to the picturesque **Abbaye d'Hautecombe** (audioguide tours in English and other languages; Mon & Wed–Sun 10–11.15am & 2–5pm; €3; ☎04 79 54 58 80) on the western side of the lake. The abbey is the final resting place of many members of the Savoie royals, including the last king and queen of Italy, Umberto II de Savoie and his wife Marie-José. The Abbaye lies close to the village of St-Pierre de Curtille, and is also accessible to cars via the D18 road.

14

## ARRIVAL AND INFORMATION AIX-LES-BAINS

**By train** The *gare SNCF* in Aix-les-Bains is on the southern side of the town centre on boulevard Président-Wilson, from where it's a brief stroll up avenue Charles-de-Gaulle to the central place Maurice-Mollard.

**Tourist office** Inside the enormous former spa building on place Maurice-Mollard (daily: June–Aug 9am–6.30pm; Feb–May & Sept 9am–noon & 2–6pm; Oct–Jan 9am–noon & 2–5.30pm, closed Sun; ☎04 79 88 68 00, ⍟aixlesbains.com).

## ACCOMMODATION

**Aix-les-Bains Hostel** Promenade du Sierroz ☎04 79 88 32 88, ⍟aix-les-bains@fuaj.org. In a fab location just a stone's throw from the lake, this well-equipped hostel offers four- five- and six-bedded dorms, as well as doubles. Breakfast included. Feb–Oct. Dorms €22, doubles €28

**Bristol** 8 rue du Casino ☎04 79 35 08 14, ⍟bristol savoie.com. Big hotel which, in the main, is frequented by package-holidays tourists – but that's not to say it's not good value. There's not a lot to choose between the standard and classic rooms, but they're all decently sized, have firm beds, and some overlook a pleasant garden. Breakfast €9.50, or for €2 more, you can have it brought to your room. Mid-March to mid-Nov. €65

**Camping du Sierroz** Boulevard Robert Barrier ☎04 79 61 21 43, ⍟campingsierroz.com. Some 400m along from the hostel, this is the largest and best kept of the several lakeshore campsites. Facilities include shop and restaurant, and plenty of play areas for kids. Mid-March to mid-Nov. €17.50

★ **Le Carre d'Aix** 94 rue du Casino ☎04 79 35 13 89, ⍟hotel-carre-daix-bains.fr. Elegant, privately run hotel with nineteen idiosyncratic rooms spread over four floors leading off a fine, wrought-iron spiral staircase. The walls and fabrics are coloured in gorgeous shades of chocolate brown and charcoal grey, though it's the quirky furnishings and assorted accoutrements garnered from the owner's travels that steal the show; for example in one room you might find an old leather trunk, and in another an old-fashioned telephone. Breakfast €7. €48

**Savoy** 21 av Charles de Gaulle ☎04 79 35 13 33, ⍟hotel-savoy-aixlesbains.com. It's not nearly as grand as it sounds, but this welcoming hotel, in a renovated nineteenth-century building, provides high-ceilinged, parquet-floored rooms, some with shower and toilet, some without – the latter therefore with shared corridor facilities. Breakfast €7.50. €36

## EATING AND DRINKING

**L'Arbre à Palabres** 12 place du Revard ☎04 79 88 39 37. About 50m down from place Maurice-Mollard, there's not much that this tidy cafe/pizzeria doesn't do; burgers, salads, *moules*, and the full range of Savoyard specialities. It's also a good spot for an early morning pick-me-up, with decent coffee and a reasonably substantial breakfast going for €5. Starters €9, mains €13. Daily 8am till late.

**Le Petit Café** 102 rue de Genève ☎04 79 35 07 67. Sitting pretty on a little cobbled square, this neat, mirror-lined café is the perfect place to rest up over lunch; savoury tarts, salads, hot sandwiches, burgers and desserts, or a *plat du jour* for €7.90. Mon–Sat 7am–8pm, Sun 8am–noon.

**La Rotonde** Square Jean Moulin ☎04 79 35 00 60, ⍟rotonde-aixlesbains.com. Perched on the edge of the park, the smart and spacious *Rotonde* packs them in for its extensive *menus*, including some excellent wok-prepared dishes, tartare and carpaccio plates, and more offbeat choices like clafoutis with chorizo, and tiramisu with parmesan. If you just fancy a drink, take a seat inside the lounge bar. *Menus* from €18.50. Starters €8, mains €16. Daily noon–2pm & 7–10.30pm.

# The Isère valley and the Vanoise

The **Massif de la Vanoise**, a rugged set of mountains east of Chambéry, rises to heights of over 3500m, and offers challenging routes for skiers, particularly along the steep slopes of the **Isère valley**. The glacier-capped southeast quadrant of the Vanoise forms

## WALKING IN THE PARC NATIONAL DE LA VANOISE

The **Parc National de la Vanoise** (Ⓦ vanoise.com) occupies the eastern end of the Vanoise Massif. It's extremely popular, with over 500km of marked paths, including the **GR5**, **GR55** and **GTA** (Grande Traversée des Alpes), and numerous *refuges* along the trails. For in-depth information on the various routes, head for the tourist offices in Val d'Isère, Bourg-St-Maurice and Méribel.

To cross the park, you can take the **GR55** from the Lac de Tignes and over the **Col de la Vanoise.** You can then connect with the **GR5**, which brings you out at the southern end of the park in the town of Modane. There are countless shorter but equally beautiful walks in the park. Settlements in the Arc Valley, like Bessans, are good bases to start exploring the park, but even the ski resorts of Tignes, Val d'Isère and Méribel are good starting points.

the **Parc National de la Vanoise**, where hikers will find some of the most spectacular GR trails in France. The easiest road access to the Massif is from Chambéry or Grenoble, although driving the winding and precipitous old highways from Annecy or Chamonix is an adventure in itself.

The A43 from Chambéry cuts between the Massif des Bauges to the north and the Vanoise to the south, following the path of the lower Isère River as it flows down from Albertville. Following the river by road from here involves a 180km journey south, north and south again back to its source high in the mountains near the **Col de l'Iseran** (2770m), close to the Italian frontier. From Albertville, the N90 climbs southeast along the bends of the Isère River for 50km to Moûtiers, the turn-off for the massive **Les Trois Vallées** ski region. At Moûtiers, the river course swings northeast and following it will lead you to **Bourg-St-Maurice**, the town at the midpoint of the upper Isère valley. At Séez, a couple of kilometres further east, the road comes to an important junction: the N90 continues to climb steeply towards the **Col du Petit St-Bernard** (2188m), while the D902 heads south towards **Val d'Isère**.

## The Col de l'Iseran

From the ski resort of Val d'Isère, the **D902** veers south from the river and climbs towards the **Col de l'Iseran** (2770m), the highest pass with a paved road in the Alps. Despite the dangers of weather and the arduous climb, the pass has been used for centuries, mainly because it is by far the quickest route between the remote upper valleys of the Isère and Arc. From October to June, the pass is blocked by snow, but in summer, it's a must-see sight for tourists with cars, who have the option of moving on to the much less touristy villages of the **Arc Valley** that lie beyond the pass. If the weather is good and you are reasonably fit, you should consider walking from here along a steep path to the **Pointe des Lessières** (3041m), which offers beautiful views of the Vanoise Massif, as well as the fearsome Italian side of Mont Blanc.

# Annecy

Lying 50km to the south of Lake Geneva, **ANNECY**, set on a sparkling turquoise lake, the Lac d'Annecy, is one of the most beautiful and popular resort towns of the French Alps. It enjoyed a brief moment of political and religious importance in the early sixteenth century, when Geneva embraced the Reformation and the Catholic bishop, François de Sales, decamped here with a train of ecclesiastics and a prosperous, cultivated elite.

These days, the delights of the town lie not just in its historical monuments, like the imposing château on the hill or the stronghold of the Palais de l'Île closer to the lake, but also in the stunning scenery. Annecy's Old Town is a bewitching warren of passages and arcaded houses that date from the sixteenth century and are divided by peaceful little branches of the **Canal du Thiou**. Many of the houses here are ringed by canalside railings overflowing with geraniums and petunias in summer; added to the cool shade offered by the arcades, these flowers make the town's pedestrianized streets a delight to wander around on a sunny afternoon.

## The Château

**Musée and observatoire** Place du Château • June–Sept daily 10.30am–6pm; Oct–May daily except Tues 10am–noon & 2–5pm • €5 • ☎ 04 50 33 87 30

From rue de l'Île on the Canal du Thiou's south bank, the narrow rampe du Château leads up to the **Château**, the former home of Genevois counts and the dukes of Nemours, a junior branch of the house of Savoy. There has been a castle on this site since the eleventh century, but the Nemours found the old fortress a little too rough for their taste and added more refined living quarters in the sixteenth century. These now house the collections of the **Musée Château** and **Observatoire Régional des Lacs Alpins**. In the latter, there are some intriguing exhibits about the geology and marine life of the local lakes, while the former contains folk art and handicrafts from across the region. The main attractions, however, are the castle itself and the views it provides of the lake below. Concerts are regularly held in the ballroom during summer.

## Rue Ste-Claire and the cathedral

At the base of the château is **rue Ste-Claire**, the main street of the Old Town, with arcaded shops and houses, as well as plentiful cafés and restaurants. Running parallel to rue Ste-Claire, on the other side of the canal, is rue Jean-Jacques Rousseau which passes the city's **cathedral**, where Rousseau once sang as a chorister. It was in Annecy that Rousseau met Madame de Warens and eventually converted to Catholicism.

## Palais de l'Île

Serenely pitched between two bridges in the middle of the Canal du Thiou, the photogenic **Palais de l'Île** is the town's signature landmark. A small twelfth-century

---

### SKIING IN THE SAVOIE

Unquestionably, the Savoie region offers some of the world's greatest skiing. To begin with, there's **Les Trois Vallées** (ⓦ les3vallees.com), one of the world's largest linked skiing areas, with endless off-piste possibilities. Its four component resorts are glitzy **Courchevel** (ⓦ courchevel.com), which also has by far the finest restaurants of any French ski resort; ugly and family-oriented **Les Menuires** (ⓦ lesmenuires.com); **Val Thorens** (ⓦ valthorens.com), favoured by younger crowds and the snowboarding set; and **Méribel** (ⓦ meribel.net), traditionally dominated by British tourists, and which therefore perhaps explains its status as the party capital of the Three Valleys. Despite the British imports, though, the small wooden chalets which climb the eastern side of the valley do manage to give the resort a traditional Savoyard feel. Less well known is the **Paradiski** ski area, on the slopes above Bourg-St-Maurice, which comprises the resorts of **Les Arcs** (ⓦ lesarcs.com) and **La Plagne** (ⓦ la-plagne .com), linked together by a giant double-decker *téléphérique* that swings over the Ponthurin valley. The former is accessible from the town via a funicular railway, and offers excellent snow and terrain for all levels, while La Plagne is made up of ten resorts high above the Isère valley, with plenty of opportunities for both beginners and more advanced skiers. Beyond here, the world-famous resort of **Val d'Isère** (ⓦ valdiscre.com), site of the 1992 Olympic downhill, offers some of the most varied and demanding skiing in the country, including year-round skiing on its glacier.

**ANNECY**

**BARS**
| | |
|---|---|
| Brasserie l'Abbaye | 2 |
| Café des Arts | 6 |
| Le Munich | 9 |

**CAFÉS AND RESTAURANTS**
| | |
|---|---|
| Après la plage | 4 |
| Auberge du Lyonnais | 5 |
| Le Cochon à l'Oreille | 8 |
| Au Fidèle Berger | 3 |
| La Part des Anges | 1 |
| Le Petit Zinc | 7 |

**ACCOMMODATION**
| | |
|---|---|
| Alexandra | 3 |
| Allobroges Park | 1 |
| Des Alpes | 2 |
| Auberge de la Jeunesse | 9 |
| Camping Le Belvédère | 4 |
| Central | 7 |
| Du Château | 8 |
| Palais de l'Isle | 6 |
| Splendid | 5 |

Lac d'Annecy

Île des Cygnes

CHAMP DE MARS

LES JARDINS DE L'EUROPE

Embarcadère for lake cruise

Hôtel de Ville

St-François

Compagnie de Bateaux (Boat tour office)

PLACE AUX BOIS

Planète Telecom

Centre Bonlieu

St-Maurice

Palais de l'Île

Château

Notre Dame Church

Cathédrale

Gare SNCF

Gare Routière

Roul'ma Poule (Bicycle shop)

Plage d'Albigny

Plage de Marquisats

Basilique de la Visitation, 8 & 9

N

0 — 100 metres

QUAI DE LA TOURNETTE
RUE DES MARQUISATS
AVENUE DU TRÉSUM
RUE DE LA PROVIDENCE
QUAI BAYREUTH
QUAI NAPOLÉON III
QUAI JULES PHILIPPE
PROMENADE JACQUET
Canal du Vassé
RUE ST-MAURICE
QUAI PERRIÈRE
CÔTE PERRIÈRE
RUE DE CHARMOIX
QUAI EUSTACHE CHAPPUIS
RUE JEAN JAURÈS
RUE SOMMEILLER
AVENUE D'ALBIGNY
RUE DU LAC
RUE DU COLLÈGE CHAPUISIEN
RUE GRENETTE
RUE FILATERIE
RUE PERRIÈRE
RAMPE DU CHÂTEAU
CH. DE LA TOUR LA REINE
RUE DU PÂQUIER
RUE VAUGELAS
RUE CARNOT
RUE DE LA PAIX
RUE SOMMEILLER
RUE JEAN-JACQUES ROUSSEAU
QUAI DE L'ÉVÊCHÉ
RUE STE-CLAIRE
RUE DE L'ÉVÊCHÉ
ESCALIER DU CHÂTEAU
CHEMIN DES REMPARTS
RUE DE LA RÉPUBLIQUE
FAUBOURG DES BALMETTES
RUE DE LA POSTE
RUE ROYALE
RUE DES GLIÈRES
RUE DE LA GARE
Canal du Thiou
PROMENADE DU ST-EXUPÈRE
AVENUE DU LOVENCHY
RUE DE LA GARE
RUE DE L'INDUSTRIE
AVENUE DE BROGNY
AVENUE BOUVARD
AVENUE DE CHEVÈNES
AVENUE DE CHAMBÉRY
AVENUE D'ALÉRY
PROMENADE LOUIS LACHENAL
AVENUE DU RHÔNE
AVENUE DU RHÔNE
PROMENADE DU ST-SÉPULCRE
AVENUE LOUIS LACHENAL

stronghold, beautifully constructed out of the local stone, it variously served as a fortified residence, mint, court and prison; it last functioned as the last of these during World War II, and you can still read the graffiti left by French Resistance prisoners. It now houses the **Centre d'Interprétation de l'Architecture et du Patrimoine de l'Agglomération d'Annecy** (June–Sept daily 10.30am–6pm; Oct–May daily except Tues 10am–noon & 2–5pm; €3.50, a combined ticket for the Palais de l'Île and the Musée-Château costs €6.60; ☎04 50 65 08 14), a museum with several French-language audiovisual presentations on urban environments in the region.

**14**

## Basilica of the Visitation

20 av de la Visitation • Daily 7am–noon & 2–7pm • **Museum** Daily 9am–noon & 2–5pm • Free

A stroll south on rue des Marquisats leads along the lake to the free, grassy **plage de Marquisats**. Alternatively, take avenue de Trésum up towards the **Basilica of the Visitation**. Built in the 1920s, the Basilica houses the remains of both St François de Sales and St Jane de Chantal, held in Art Deco-style reliquaries in front of the altar. There's a tiny museum displaying some of the saints' personal belongings, and panoramic views of the town below.

### ARRIVAL AND INFORMATION
ANNECY

**By train** The *gare SNCF* and complex is just a 5min walk northwest of the town centre.

Destinations Aix-les-Bains (frequent; 30min); Chambéry (frequent; 45min); Chamonix via St-Gervais (3 daily; 3hr); Grenoble (hourly; 2hr); Lyon (hourly; 2hr); Paris-Lyon (several daily; 4hr).

**By bus** The *gare routière* is part of the complex involving the *gare SNCF*.

Destinations Geneva (2 daily; 1hr 15min); Lyon (5 daily; 2hr).

**Tourist office** Inside the Centre Bonlieu, a modern civic centre at 1 rue Jean-Jaurès (Mon–Sat 9am–6.30pm; mid-May to mid-Sept also Sun same hours; ☎04 50 45 00 33, ⓦlac-annecy.com). Guided tours of the Old Town take place in July and August on Tuesdays and Fridays at 4pm, departing from the tourist office (€6).

**Bicycle rental** There's excellent bike rental (as well as kayaks and paddleboards) at Roul' ma poule, 4 rue des Marquisats (☎04 50 27 86 83, ⓦroulmapoule.com).

**Festival** Annecy plays host to the superb International Animated Film Festival each June, which showcases a wide range of animated films from around the world.

**Internet access** Planète Telecom at 2 rue Jean-Jaurès (Mon–Sat 10am–7pm).

### ACCOMMODATION

**Alexandra** 19 rue Vaugelas ☎04 50 52 84 33, ⓦhotelannecy-alexandra.fr. A good-value option midway between the stations and the Old Town. The rooms – some of which have balconies overlooking a canal – are quite simple, with unfussy but clean, modern furnishings. Breakfast €8. **€73**

**Allobroges Park** 11 rue Sommeiller ☎04 50 45 03 11, ⓦallobroges.com. A solid and comfortable three-star set back from the road in its own little courtyard. The warm, thickly carpeted rooms enjoy lots of light thanks to high windows, and there's a snazzy little lobby bar where you can enjoy a nightcap before hitting the sack. Breakfast €9.50. **€90**

**Des Alpes** 12 rue de la Poste ☎04 50 45 04 56, ⓦhotelannecy.com. A warm welcome awaits at this diminutive hotel not far from the *gare SNCF*. Chalet-style rooms with pine-laced walls and just about every other bit of furniture culled from some sort of timber. Triples and quads available. Breakfast €8. **€75**

**Auberge de Jeunesse** 4 rte du Semnoz ☎04 50 45 33 19, ⓔannecy@fuaj.org. Serene, forest-fringed location overlooking the lake 2km away from the town

---

#### BEACH LIFE

If you (or, as is more likely, the kids) have had enough of traipsing around town, then you might consider retreating to one of Annecy's two excellent, albeit grassy, **beaches**. One is located over on the northeast corner, near the *Imperial Hotel*, while the other – which is shallower and therefore much better suited to families – is on the western shore just south of the port. Both are open roughly mid-June to mid-September, have shower and toilet facilities, and are fully supervised.

14

centre, with good facilities, including internet access and kitchens. Mid-Jan to Nov. Dorms **€20.60**

**Camping Le Belvédère** 8 rte du Semnoz ✆ 04 50 45 48 30, ✉ camping@ville-annecy.fr. The municipal campsite is just a 10min walk south from the Old Town; facilities include laundry and on-site bar. April to mid-Oct. **€16.10**

**Central** 6 rue Royale ✆ 04 50 45 05 37, ⓦ hotelcentralannecy.com. While the exterior of this one-star hotel promises little, inside you will find a cheerily run affair offering fourteen occasionally garish, but never dull, rooms, some of which have shared toilet and shower facilities. Rooms either look out over a quiet courtyard or down on to one of the town's canals. Breakfast €6. **€60**

**Du Château** 16 Rampe du Château ✆ 04 50 45 27 66, ✉ hotelduchateau@noos.fr. Situated a few paces down from the château, sixteen cottage-like rooms inform this handsome nineteenth-century stone building high above the terracotta tiled-roofs of the Old Town; chunky wooden bedsteads, wicker chairs and pretty, home-made textiles are all standard features. Breakfast €7. **€70**

**Palais de l'Isle** 13 rue Perrière ✆ 04 50 45 86 87, ⓦ palaisannecy.com. In a pitch-perfect setting right by the canal in the heart of the Old Town, the *Palais* is a labyrinth of narrow corridors concealing crisp, designer-furnished rooms painted in either yellow or sky blue, some of which overlook the canal, others the street. Breakfast €13. **€120**

**Splendid** 4 quai Eustache Chappuis ✆ 04 50 45 20 00, ⓦ splendidhotel.fr. In an enviable spot overlooking the grassy expanse of the Champ de Mars, the *Splendid* is one of the more expensive options in town, but its polished, burgundy-and-black-coloured rooms, and big, tiled bathrooms with oversized mirrors are pretty much what you'd expect for the price. Tea- and coffee-making facilities are a welcome touch too. Breakfast €13.50. **€120**

## EATING AND DRINKING

The town's restaurants are, on the whole, pretty commendable, though the string of establishments by the canal along quai Perrière are apt to serving unimaginative fodder for the tourist masses. Elsewhere, there are few more enjoyable things to do on a warm summer's evening in Annecy than to park yourself down by one of the canalside cafés and soak up the local architecture. Away from here, rue Ste-Claire offers some promising possibilities for a late-night drink or two.

### CAFÉS AND RESTAURANTS

★ **Après la plage** 2 place Saint-Maurice ✆ 04 50 51 46 64. Local, organically sourced food is the theme at this fabulous little restaurant with funky mismatched tables and chairs coloured in lustrous pinks and cool greys and blacks. Gazpacho and courgette crumble are typically fresh and fun dishes, though there are plenty of meaty treats on the menu, in particular veal, beef and salmon. Starters €10, mains €20. Tues–Sun noon–2pm & 7–10pm.

**Auberge du Lyonnais** 9 rue de la République ✆ 04 50 51 26 10, ⓦ fauberge-du-lyonnais.com. Upscale canalside joint that excels in the wet stuff, including langoustines, oysters, crabs and clams from the sea, and fresh fish hauled daily from the lake. Lamb and beef dishes are also served. Starters €20, mains €25. Mon–Sat 9.15am–7pm, Sat 9am–7.30pm.

**Le Cochon à l'Oreille** Quai Perrière ✆ 04 50 45 92 51, ⓦ cochon-annecy.com. Slightly weird-looking place – unless you're into porcelain pigs, of which there are hundreds – which might explain the preponderance of pork on the menu. Kids will love it, as might the parents, as there are excellent baby-changing facilities here. Starters €8, mains €15. Daily noon–2pm & 7–10pm; closed Mon mid-Nov to mid-April.

**Au Fidèle Berger** 2 rue Royale ✆ 04 50 45 00 32. Genteel, ever-busy *salon de thé* that makes for a nice spot to relax with a coffee or pot of Darjeeling, though while you're here it'd be remiss not to sample one of their deliciously creamy pastries. Breakfasts and light dishes, such as salads, are also on the menu. Mon–Fri 9.15am–7pm, Sat 9am–7.30pm.

**La Part des Anges** 23 rue Sommeiller ✆ 04 50 60 07 14, ⓦ restaurant-lapartdesanges.com. Slick restaurant and wine bar sited well away from the tourist track and catering to a more discerning crowd. You'll find the likes of salmon carpaccio with mint oil, and risotto *cremeux* with white truffle oil on the menu, alongside tried and trusted classics like chocolate fondant, *crème brûlée* and *tarte tatin*. The restaurant itself looks impressive, heavily mirrored walls bearing down on black-cloth-covered tables and velvet cushioned seating. Starters €9.50, mains €18. Closed first three weeks August. Tues–Sat 11am–3pm & 6–10.30pm; wine bar opens at 6pm.

**Le Petit Zinc** 11 rue Pont Morens ✆ 04 50 51 12 93. This popular little bistro is one of the better canal side places to indulge in the local Savoyard favourites, particularly some excellent fondues. Starters €8, mains €16. Daily 11.30am–2.30pm & 6.30–10.30pm.

### BARS

**Brasserie l'Abbaye** 4 rue du Pâquier ✆ 04 50 45 12 88, ⓦ abbaye-annecy.com. This lively brick-lined bar/brasserie also has a large outdoor terrace where you can kick back with one of their Belgian brews, though they're not cheap at around €5 a pop. Light munchies available too, like pizza and *moules marinières*. Daily 8am–1am.

**Café des Arts** 4 passage de l'Isle ☏ 04 50 51 56 40. Despite its position right in the heart of the tourist zone, this mellow café-bar remains a true local's favourite. Chill out on the sunny cobbled terrace with an espresso, or cool off inside the brick-lined bar with a pint, particularly on Wednesdays when there's live music. Daily 10am–midnight.

**Le Munich** 1 quai Perrière ☏ 04 50 45 02 11, ⓦ lemunich.com. Vaguely reminiscent of a Bavarian beer hall, *Le Munich* is where the serious drinking takes place; around a dozen of or so draught beers, mostly German (Krombacher, Munchen) and Belgian (including Trappist beers); and to soak it all up, get your chops around one of their monster-sized burgers, like the no-nonsense Fat Bastard. Closed Jan. Daily 8am–2am.

**14**

# Around Annecy

While the tourist crowds that flock to Annecy in the summer high season may only be bearable for a day or two, there are plenty of places around the lake to escape to and run wild. As well as **boat tours**, **cycling** is an especially enjoyable means of appreciating the beauty of the Lac d'Annecy. Cycling the 40km road circuit of the lake is a very popular Sunday morning activity among sporty Annéciens; a traffic-free cycle route follows the west shore down to Faverges. The surrounding hills offer walking and mountain-biking excursions to suit all levels of ability and fitness. Experienced walkers should enjoy the relatively undemanding ascent of **La Tournette** (2351m) on the eastern side of the lake, while gentler walks and cycle routes are plentiful in the forested **Semnoz mountains** on the lake's west side. This is also a great spot for tandem paragliding. Ten kilometres west of Annecy, the **Gorges du Fier** are among the most spectacular and beautiful natural gorges in France.

## Château de Menthon

May, June & Sept Fri–Sun & hols 2–6pm; July & Aug daily noon–6pm • €8 • ☏ 04 50 60 12 05

Close to the village of **MENTHON-ST-BERNARD** on the eastern shore of the lake is the grand, turreted **Château de Menthon**. The fortress has been inhabited since the twelfth century and was the birthplace of St Bernard, the patron saint of mountaineers – indeed, the castle remains in the hands of the de Menthon family. In the nineteenth century, however, it was extensively renovated in the romantic Gothic revival style and now possesses an impressive library containing some 12,000 books. On weekends, costumed actors relate the château's history.

## The Gorges du Fier

Daily: mid-March to mid-June & mid-Sept to mid-Oct 9.30am–6.15pm; mid-June to mid-Sept 9.30am–7.15pm • €5 • ☏ 04 50 46 23 07, ⓦ gorgesdufier.com

Some 10km west of Annecy, the River Fier has cut a narrow crevice through the limestone rock at the **Gorges du Fier**, which is signposted off the D14 at Lovagny. It's an awe-inspiring landscape of often bizarre geology, with eroded cliff faces, narrow rock fissures and curiously sculpted boulders, all formed by the rushing waters of the river below. Once you are inside the 300m-long gorge, you traverse a high-level walkway pinned to the gorge side. The crevice is so narrow that when it rains heavily the water can rise by around 25m in just a few hours. There's a shop, café and free car park on site.

---

## LAC D'ANNECY CRUISES

A **lake cruise** is the most peaceful way to travel between Annecy and the other settlements around the lake. Compagnie des Bateaux, 2 place aux Bois (☏ 04 50 51 08 40, ⓦ annecy-croisieres.com), runs several boats daily from the quai Napoléon III, including a one-hour trip (€13.10), and a two-hour jolly which briefly stops off at various points around the lake (€16.80). They also run 2–3hr cruises which include lunch or dinner (as well as dancing in the evening) on the MS *Libellule*; prices start at €51 for a lunch cruise and €54 for a dinner cruise.

**14**

# Mont Blanc

Fifty kilometres to the east of Annecy on the Swiss and Italian borders looms **Mont Blanc** (4807m), Western Europe's highest peak. First climbed in 1786 by Jacques Balmat and Michel-Gabriel Paccard, two intrepid gentlemen from Chamonix, the mountain and its surrounding valleys are now the biggest tourist draw to the Alps.

The closest airport is in Geneva, but if you're coming from France then Annecy is the easiest city from which to approach the mountain, and, of the two road routes, the one east via the Megève is the more picturesque. The two main approach roads to Mont Blanc come together at Le Fayet, a village just outside St-Gervais-les-Bains, where the **Tramway du Mont Blanc** begins its 75-minute haul to the **Nid d'Aigle** (2375m), a vantage point on the northwest slope (€27.40 return; ⓦcompagniedumontblanc.com). Experienced mountaineers can press on from here along the famous Goûter ridge to the summit of Mont Blanc itself.

If you are heading into Italy from Chamonix, the most direct road is the N205, which takes you south out of Chamonix, then through the 11.6km **Mont Blanc Tunnel** (one-way €35.10, return €43.70), and brings you out on the road to Aosta and Milan.

## Chamonix-Mont-Blanc

The bustling, cosmopolitan town of **CHAMONIX** (known officially as Chamonix-Mont-Blanc) is the primary French base for outdoor activities on or around Mont Blanc. "Cham" throngs with visitors throughout the year, and although it may have long since had its village identity submerged in a sprawl of tourist development, flashy restaurants and boutiques, the stunning backdrop of glaring snowfields, eerie blue glaciers and ridges of sharp peaks that surround Mont Blanc are ample compensation.

Naturally, the mountains provide the main sights and activities, but on days when the bad weather sets in, there are a few things to do in town. Otherwise, it's a case of just chilling out in one of the town's many convivial restaurants or bars.

### Musée Alpin, Espace Tairraz and Richard Bozon Sports Centre

The **Musée Alpin** (daily: mid-Dec to mid-June 3–7pm; mid-June to Oct 2–7pm; €5; ☎04 50 53 25 93) on avenue Michel-Croz is full of exhibits which detail the life of the valley since the first tourists began to arrive in the eighteenth century and also has displays on mountaineering equipment. The **Espace Tairraz** (daily: mid-Dec to mid-June 3–7pm; mid-June to Oct 2–7pm; ☎04 50 55 53 93) exhibition centre on Esplanade Saint-Michel, meanwhile, hosts temporary photography exhibitions of the mountains, plus a permanent collection of crystals. The **Richard Bozon Sports Centre**, to the west of the town centre at 214 av de la Plage (hours vary; ☎04 50 53 23 70), has ice-skating, a pool, sauna and hammam, a climbing wall and tennis and squash courts.

**ARRIVAL AND DEPARTURE**          **CHAMONIX-MONT-BLANC**

**By train and bus** The *gare SNCF* and *gare routière* are on Rue des Allobroges, a short walk to the south of place du Triangle-de-l'Amitié. In the ski season and from mid-June to August, there's a free bus shuttle service (Les Mulets) between place du Mont Blanc to Chamonix Sud and place de l'Aiguille du Midi.

Destinations (train) Annecy via St Gervais (6 daily; 2hr 20min).
Destinations (bus) Geneva (2 daily; 2hr); other resorts in the Chamonix-Mont-Blanc area: Argentière (12 daily; 20 min); Les Houches (frequent; 20min).

**INFORMATION**

**Tourist office** 85 place du Triangle-de-l'Amitié (daily: mid-April to mid-Dec 9am–12.30pm & 2–6pm, mid-Dec to April 8.30am–7pm; ☎04 50 53 00 24, ⓦchamonix.com).

**Compagnie des Guides** Inside the Maison de la Montagne at 190 place de l'Église (daily 8.30am–noon & 3.30–7pm; ☎04 50 53 00 88, ⓦchamonix-guides.com); established in 1821, this excellent organization can provide guides for just about every mountain activity going, from off-piste skiing, snowshoeing and heli-skiing in the winter, to hiking, mountaineering and rock climbing in the summer; they offer a superb summer programme for kids too (ⓦcham-aventure.com). The same building houses the Office de Haute Montagne (Mon–Sat 9am–noon & 3–6pm, also Sun in July & Aug; ☏04 50 53 22 08, ⓦohm-chamonix.com), where you can get details and suggestions for all the local hiking routes, advice on *refuges*, as well as up-to-the-minute information on weather conditions.

**Useful website** ⓦchamonix.net is also an excellent source of information on the town.

**Bicycle rental** Any number of places in town offer bike rental, though one particularly good outfit is Zero G, 90 av Ravanel le Rouge (daily 9am–12.30pm & 3.30–7pm; ☏04 50 53 01 01).

**Internet** Wi-fi outside the tourist office on place du Triangle-de-l'Amitié.

**14**

## ACCOMMODATION

There's plenty of accommodation to go around in Chamonix, but given the volume of tourist traffic in and around town, you'd do well to book in advance, whatever the time of year. The tourist office also offers a reservation service (☏04 50 53 23 33, ⓦreservation.chamonix.com), which can find you a room at even the busiest times. High season in Chamonix is February to March and July and August, with some establishments closing in May and October. If you're staying in a Chamonix hotel or at the hostel, then you should receive a free *Carte d'Hôte* on arrival; this guest card entitles you to free transport on the resort's public buses and on the SNCF train line between Servoz and Vallorcine.

**Auberge de Jeunesse**127 montée Jacques-Balmat, Les-Pèlerins-en-Haut ☏04 50 53 14 52, ⓔchamonix @fuaj.org. This large hostel, 2.5km out of the town centre, has two- four- and six bedded rooms, and although there's no communal kitchen, they do offer cheap, three-course meals in the evening (€12). Bus #3 to the "Auberge de Jeunesse" stop, just below the hostel. Mid-May to Sept & Dec–April. Breakfast included. Dorms **€22.70**

**Camping La Mer de Glace** 200 chemin de la Bagna, Les Praz ☏04 50 53 44 03, ⓦchamonix-camping.com. This beautifully secluded site, 2km northeast of Chamonix, offers decent facilities including laundry, kids' play area, internet room and a small pizza hut. May–Sept. **€23**

**Le Chamonix** 11 rue de l'Hôtel de Ville ☏04 50 53 11 07, ⓦhotel-le-chamonix.com. This long-standing climbers and hikers hotel is creaking at the seams a bit

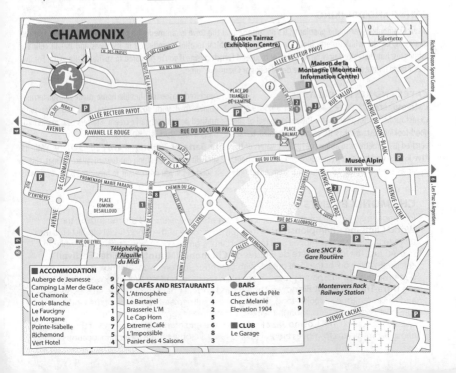

**CHAMONIX**

ACCOMMODATION
| | |
|---|---|
| Auberge de Jeunesse | 9 |
| Camping La Mer de Glace | 6 |
| Le Chamonix | 2 |
| Croix-Blanche | 3 |
| Le Faucigny | 1 |
| Le Morgane | 7 |
| Pointe-Isabelle | 7 |
| Richemond | 5 |
| Vert Hotel | 4 |

CAFÉS AND RESTAURANTS
| | |
|---|---|
| L'Atmosphère | 7 |
| Le Bartavel | 4 |
| Brasserie L'M | 2 |
| Le Cap Horn | 5 |
| Extreme Café | 6 |
| L'Impossible | 8 |
| Panier des 4 Saisons | 3 |

BARS
| | |
|---|---|
| Les Caves du Pèle | 5 |
| Chez Melanie | 1 |
| Elevation 1904 | 9 |

CLUB
| | |
|---|---|
| Le Garage | 1 |

**14**

these days, but it has a good selection of doubles, triples and quads (some with bunks), and a friendly welcome is assured. Breakfast €8. **€82**

**Croix-Blanche** 81 rue Vallot ☎04 50 53 00 11, ⓦbestmontblanc.com. Dating from 1793, the *Croix-Blanche* is the oldest surviving hotel in Chamonix, and its rooms still manage to combine an old-fashioned elegance with contemporary comfort. Breakfast €10. **€85**

★ **Le Faucigny** 118 place de l'Eglise ☎04 50 53 01 17, ⓦhotelfaucigny-chamonix.com. A gem of a hotel within a few paces of the main square, Le Faucigny has 28 crisply decorated rooms furnished in white-tinted pine and smart greys, with those on the second floor positioned under the Mansard roof. At 4pm each day, you can pop down to the library-like lounge and help yourself to some complementary tea, coffee and cake along with a newspaper, and you can also enjoy the spa, complete with Jacuzzi and sauna. Breakfast €11. **€150**

**Le Morgane** 145 av de l'Aiguille du Midi ☎04 50 53 57 15, ⓦmorgane-hotel-chamonix.com. Sophisticated, and very expensive, hotel, with minimalist rooms conceived in wood and stone and coloured in muted browns and beiges. There's also a gorgeous basement pool, sauna and hammam, while the top-floor terrace offers superb views of Mont Blanc. Free bike rental. Breakfast €15. **€195**

**Pointe-Isabelle** 165 av Michel Croz ☎04 50 53 12 87, ⓦpointe-isabelle.com. While this unprepossessing place just two-minutes' walk from the *gare SNCF* is far from inspiring – much of it could certainly do with a makeover – this is just about the cheapest option in town, hence reasonable value for money. Closed first three weeks in May and Nov to mid-Dec. Wi-fi costs extra. Breakfast €12. **€68**

**Richemond** 228 rue Docteur Paccard ☎04 50 53 08 85, ⓦrichemond.fr. An imposing early twentieth-century structure set back from the busy main street, the *Richemond* has been managed by the same family for three generations, hence its rather old-fashioned, but still very charming, manner. The rooms are a mix of old and new, while the five "Alpinist" rooms on the top floor are prepared with hikers in mind (basic with shared showers), and cost roughly half the price of a standard double. Closed mid-April to mid-June, and mid-Sept to mid-Dec. **€112**

**Vert Hotel** 964 rte des Gaillands ☎04 50 53 13 58, ⓦverthotel.com. Around 1km west of the town centre, close to the Lac du Gaillands, the "Green Hotel" mostly attracts a youthful, sporty crowd, drawn here by the simple but clean and decently priced double, twin and quad rooms (all en-suite) and fabulous lounge bar, which can turn into quite a party place. Bus #1 stops just outside. Rates on Fri and Sat are around €10 more. Breakfast €9. **€65**

## EATING AND DRINKING

Given Chamonix's year-round popularity, it's no surprise that the town is rammed with places to eat and drink, and the quality is, on the whole, pretty high. Chamonix's geographical location is reflected in its Swiss and Italian culinary influences, but there's certainly no shortage of high-end French cuisine if you're prepared to spend a little extra. For live music head for the pubs and clubs of rue des Moulins or Chamonix Sud.

### CAFÉS AND RESTAURANTS

**L'atmosphère** 123 Place Balmat ☎04 50 55 97 97, ⓦrestaurant-atmosphere.com. The main appeal of this good-looking restaurant is its covered balconied terrace perched just a metre or so above the rushing waters of the Arve River – and there's a tremendous wine cellar to boot. As far as the food goes, take your pick from beautifully conceived seasonal dishes like home-made venison terrine, guinea fowl with rosemary juice, and cod fillet with mashed potato and garlic cream. Starters €12, mains €20. Daily noon–2pm & 7.30–11pm.

**Le Bartavel** 26 Bartavel ☎04 50 53 97 19. With its sprawling terrace edging out towards place Balmat, this is a solid bet if you don't want to break the bank. Pizza and

---

## CHAMONIX EVENTS

Inevitably, many of the town's biggest annual events revolve around the mountains; the **World Climbing Championships** in mid-July sees some of the world finest alpinists roll into town to tackle a series of speed and technical climbs on an enormous artificial wall, while, in mid-August, the four-day **Fête de Guides de Chamonix (Mountain Guides Festival)** celebrates the work of the local guides, with live music, folklore events, climbing demonstrations, and a grand procession to bless the ropes and ice axes. Two weeks later, it's the **Ultra-Trail du Mont Blanc**, which starts and ends in Chamonix but also crosses Swiss and Italian territory; at 166km-long, this single stage ultra-marathon is one of the world's toughest endurance tests, though the best athletes manage to complete it in a remarkable twenty hours or so. The **Cosmo Jazz Festival** at the end of July attracts some of the world's finest jazz musicians to venues around town as well as some terrific mountain locations.

## SKIING IN CHAMONIX

Despite its fame, Chamonix is not the most user-friendly of ski resorts and access to the slopes relies on shuttle buses, trains or a car. For advanced skiers, however, it's probably one of the best places in the Alps since it offers an impressive range of challenging runs and off-piste itineraries. It's not so much a single resort as a chain of unconnected ski areas set along both sides of the Chamonix valley and dominated by Mont Blanc. The **Brévent** and **Flégère** areas on the southern slopes both have a good variety of pistes and provide some fine views of the Mont Blanc massif across the valley, while **Argentière–Les Grands Montets** is a colder, north-facing area that is well-suited to advanced skiers. The famous **Vallée Blanche** can be accessed by cable car from the Aiguille du Midi; skiing here involves a 20km descent which passes many crevasses and is not patrolled, so a guide is strongly recommended. Closer to Chamonix itself, the **Les Planards** and **Le Savoy** areas require artificial snow and snow cannons to stay open, but they are good spots for beginners to hone their technique. There are plenty of **ski schools** in Chamoix, which provide lessons for skiers and snowboarders, as well as guides. The ESF office (☎04 50 53 22 57, ⓦesf-chamonix) is situated in the Maison de la Montagne; the guides here hold special lessons on the famous runs of the Vallée Blanche.

**14**

pasta form the mainstay of a long menu which also features crêpes and *grillades*. Daily 11.30am–11.30pm.

**Brasserie L'M** 81 rue Joseph Vallot ☎04 50 53 58 30. The multicoloured outdoor seating is the most striking feature of this central brasserie-cum-tapas bar, not least because of the marvellous views it affords of Mont Blanc. Big choice of Savoyard dishes alongside a lengthy tapas menu (€2–4 each), which is arguably a better reason to come here. Starters €10, mains €15. Daily noon–11pm.

**La Cap Horn** 74 rue des Moulins ☎04 50 21 80 80, ⓦcaphorn-chamonix.com. The entrance to this most contemporary of restaurants is through a fine timber-framed porch, a theme continued inside with three floors of wood and slate and a slightly peculiar mix of alpine and nautical decor. Home-made fish soup with garlic mayo, cod and smoked salmon rillette, and meats grilled on hot stones, are the sort of dishes to expect. Starters €10, mains €18. Daily noon–2.30pm & 7–10pm.

**Extreme Café** 21 Place Balmat. Popular daytime café with a dozen or so outdoor tables in a cracking location on Chamonix's main square. Good for light lunches (bagels, wraps, waffles), fresh fruit smoothies and shakes, and fresh, hot coffee. Daily 8am–7pm.

**L'Impossible** 9 chemin du Cry ☎04 50 53 20 36, ⓦrestaurant-impossible.com. Well worth the 10min walk from the town centre for its cosy farmhouse interior and thrilling dishes like suckling pig with gorgonzola, polenta and sweet red onion, and custard-filled doughnuts with balsamic vinegar ice cream. Plenty of inventive non-carnivorous options too. Starters €13, mains €25. Daily 7–10.30pm. Closed Nov & Tues in May–June & Sept–Oct.

★ **Panier des 4 Saisons** 262 rue Docteur Paccard ☎04 50 53 98 77, ⓦrestaurant-panierdes4saisons .com. Ignore the rather uninviting location up a grubby side alley, this lovely restaurant rustles up some of the finest food in town; honey caramelized roast duck breast with turnip mousse, roasted deer fillet with quince purée, and for veggies, there's a scrummy goat cheese ravioli in leek fondue. Starters €12, mains €25. Mon–Sat noon–2pm & 7.30–10.30pm.

### BARS AND CLUBS

**Les Caves du Pèle** 74 rue des Moulins ☎04 50 21 80 80. Kick back with a cocktail or a glass of red wine, and a plate of tapas, in the sophisticated basement wine-bar-cum-jazz club of *Le Cap Horn*. Music most nights, usually DJs or live jazz sessions.

**Chez Melanie** 11 rue de l'Hôtel de Ville. Below Le Chamonix hotel (see p.753), this eternally popular bar has several beers on tap (50cl for €5–7) and provides a nice spot to watch the world go by in the adjacent place de l'Église. Closed May & Nov.

**Elevation 1904** 259 av Michel Croz ☎04 50 53 00 52. Whether it's an early-morning cappuccino or a pint at sundown, you'll find all the cool dudes hanging out on the al fresco terrace of this buzzing little bar opposite the train station. Daily 8am–midnight.

**Le Garage** 213 av de l'Aiguille-du-Midi ☎06 72 43 92 83, ⓦnightclublegarage.com. Chamonix's biggest and most banging nightclub, with resident house DJ Dawa spinning the discs alongside a regular crop of visiting international DJs. Daily 1–4am.

# Excursions in the Chamonix Valley

Alongside the walking and skiing opportunities around Chamonix, there are several exhilarating excursions using the various ski lifts and mountain railways; it may be worth getting a **multipass** that covers all the lifts in the area (€52.20 for 24 hours, €65.90/76.10 for two/three consecutive days). These can be purchased online, at the tourist office, or at the foot of each cable-car ascent.

## Aiguille du Midi téléphérique

May to mid-June & Sept 8am–5pm; mid-June to Aug 7am–5pm, Oct 8.30am–4pm; Jan–April 8.30am–4.30pm • €45.60 return, advance reservations €2 • ☎ 04 50 53 22 75, ⓦ compagniedumontblanc.com

Easily the most famous excursion in the area is the **téléphérique** to the **Aiguille du Midi** (3842m), one of the longest cable-car ascents in the world, rising 3000m above the valley floor in two extremely steep stages – anyone even remotely suffering from vertigo should forget about this particular excursion. Although the trip is absurdly expensive, penny-pinching by buying a ticket only as far as the Plan du Midi (2310m) is a waste of money: go all the way or not at all. If you do go up, make the effort to be on your way before 9am, as the summits tend to cloud over towards midday, and huge crowds may force you to wait for hours if you try later. Take warm clothes – even on a summer's day it'll be below zero at the top – and sunblock is also advisable to protect against the glare off the snow.

The Aiguille is an exposed granite pinnacle on which a restaurant and the *téléférique* dock are precariously balanced. The view is incredible. At your feet is the snowy plateau of the **Col du Midi**, with the glaciers of the Vallée Blanche and Géant sloping down the mountainside. From the Aiguille, the Three Monts climbing route takes mountaineers up the steep snowfield and exposed ridge to the summit of Mont Blanc with its final cap of ice. On the horizon lies rank upon rank of snow- and ice-capped monsters receding into the distance. Perhaps most impressive of all is the view from east to south, in which the Aiguille Verte, Triollet and the Jorasses, with the Matterhorn and Monte Rosa, form a cirque of needle-sharp peaks and sheer crags.

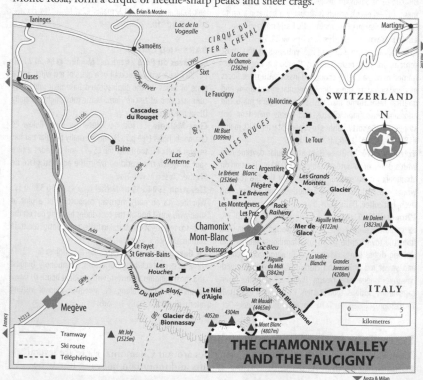

THE CHAMONIX VALLEY
AND THE FAUCIGNY

---

## CLIMBING MONT BLANC AND THE TOUR DU MONT BLANC

Climbing Mont Blanc is not a task that should be undertaken lightly, as testified by the number of lives claimed by the mountain each year. It is a semi-technical climb and fast-changing weather conditions mean that a guide is essential. There are several different routes, the most popular of which is the Gouter ridge route (three days), which ascends from the Nid d'Aigle at the top of the Tranway du Mont Blanc. The best season for climbing the mountain is mid-June to September (when the majority of refuges are also open), but even in this period, it should only be attempted by fit, acclimatized and well-prepared mountaineers.

The classic way for walkers to admire Mont Blanc without putting themselves through the dangers of an ascent is to undertake the **Tour du Mont Blanc**, a 250km circuit of the mountain across French, Swiss and Italian terrain. The trail normally takes eight to twelve days, during which you can either camp or stay at the *refuges* (€20–25) en route. Many of the *refuges* provide food and other supplies, but it's worth checking the latest details with the **Office de Haute Montagne** in Chamonix, which can also provide maps of the route. Even in early July, many of the passes on the route can still be covered in snow, so walkers should carry crampons and heavy-duty waterproofs. Several tour companies in Chamonix can provide guides for the walk, though the venerable Compagnie des Guides (see p.752) is your best bet.

**14**

## Montenvers rack railway

Daily: May–June & Sept–Oct 8.30am–5pm; July & Aug 8am–6pm; Nov–April 10am–4pm; closed Oct • €20.30 return • ☎ 04 50 53 22 75, ⓦ compagniedumontblanc.com

If you haven't tired of superb panoramic views, you can make for the **Montenvers rack railway**, a train service which has been running up from Chamonix to the Mer de Glace (1913m) on the flanks of Mont Blanc since 1908; indeed the advent of the Montenvers rack railway effectively signalled the beginning of Alpine tourism in the region. Taking around twenty minutes, the little train chugs its way up to the "Sea of Ice", which, at 7km long and nearly 2000m at its widest point, is by far the largest glacier in the Alps. At the top you have the option of walking for twenty minutes or taking a short cable-car ride (an additional €6) down into an **ice cave** freshly carved out of the Mer de Glace every summer – this is usually open between mid-June and September. Another excellent possibility is to make the relatively easy hike from Montenvers to the Plan du Midi (2hr) and take the cable car back down to Chamonix from there.

## Hiking and climbing

There are countless excellent **shorter walks** around Chamonix, including many on the northern side of the valley amid the lower but nonetheless impressive peaks of the **Aiguilles Rouges**. One easy, picturesque trail takes you from the village of Les Praz (just to the northeast of Chamonix itself) to **Lac Blanc**. Take the *téléférique* from Les Praz to Flégère and then the gondola to L'Index (a combined ticket is €21). The walk to the lake and back from L'Index takes around 2hr 30min and requires good walking boots.

## The Faucigny and the Cirque du Fer-à-Cheval

To the north of Chamonix is the **Faucigny**, a region of wide glacial valleys, gentle forested slopes and peaceful little villages that seem a world away from the party atmosphere of the resorts further south. **Samoëns**, lying 15km away from Chamonix, is one such village; despite its relatively low altitude, it has become popular with **skiers** thanks to a short transfer time from Geneva and its proximity to the Grand Massif ski area (particularly the purpose-built resort of **Flaine**) via the Express du Grand Massif, a *télécabine* to the south of the village.

If you head east from Samoëns along the D907, you follow the valley as it narrows into the Gorges des Tines before opening out again at another delightful little village, **SIXT-FER-À-CHEVAL**. This pretty village lies on the confluence of two branches of the river Giffre: the Giffre-Haut, which comes down from Salvagny, and the Giffre-Bas, which flows all the way from the **Cirque du Fer-à-Cheval**. The cirque is a horseshoe-shaped ridge famed for the rugged beauty of its cliffs and waterfalls, and it is this which makes the journey away from Chamonix truly memorable.

The cirque begins about 6km from Sixt and you can reach it easily via the footpath on the left bank of the Giffre-Bas. It is a vast semicircle of limestone walls, up to 700m in height and 4–5km long, from which spring countless waterfalls, particularly in the summer months. The left-hand end of the cirque is dominated by a huge spike of rock known as La Corne du Chamois (The Goat's Horn). At its foot the valley of the Giffre bends sharply north to its source in the glaciers above the Fond de la Combe. The bowl of the cirque is thickly wooded except for a circular meadow in the middle where the road ends.

**14**

# Lake Geneva

The crescent-shaped expanse of **Lake Geneva** (known as Lac Léman in France) is some 73km long, 14km wide and an impressive 310m deep; it has always been a natural border with Switzerland to the north. Even in summer, the lake is subject to violent storms, yet the experience of sailing across its waters on a calm day is delightful, and should not be missed. On the French side of the lake, the spa resort of **Évian-les-Bains** (of bottled water fame) and the picturesque village of **Yvoire** are the main sites of interest. **Thonon-les-Bains**, a larger town situated between these two landmarks, is the starting point of the renowned touring route, the **Route des Grandes Alpes**, and a gateway to the beautiful Chablais region to the south of the lake. North of the lake, close to the Swiss border, is the peaceful spa town of **Divonne-Les-Bains**, and the green pastures of the Pays de Gex region, renowned for its blue cheese and scenic hiking and cycling routes.

## Évian-Les-Bains

The most well-known French spa resort on Lake Geneva, **ÉVIAN** maintains a clinical orderliness that wouldn't be out of place on the opposite side of the water. The spa aside – which is currently being renovated – there are a certainly a couple of attractions that merit an afternoon's sightseeing, although simply taking a stroll along the waterfront, or a leisurely trip on the lake is good enough reason to spend some time here.

### The Waterfront

Elegantly laid out with squares of immaculately mown grass, perfectly clipped hedges and colourful flowerbeds, the waterfront strip is the town's focal point. Its main promenade is fronted by a quartet of fine *belle époque* buildings, not least the grand, glazed brick and stone **Palais Lumière**, built as a pump-room in 1902 and adorned with gorgeous stained-glass windows and Art Nouveau frescoes – today it's a cultural centre, hosting regular exhibitions. Next door is the **town hall**, the former summer residence of celebrated photographer Antoine Lumière (see p.784), while, a little further along is the prepossessing **theatre** building which has been functioning as such since 1885. Completing this showy line-up of buildings, and which no self-respecting spa resort would be without, is the **casino** (1912), topped by a "Neo-Byzantine" dome and elegant scalloped arcade.

### Pré-Curieux Water Gardens

3 boats daily: 10am, 1.45pm, 3.30pm in July & Aug; May, June & Sept boats run at the same times Wed–Sun only • €11 for boat trip and tour of gardens • ☎ 04 50 70 15 44, ⓦ precurieux.com

Situated by the lake on the town's western outskirts and accessible only by a boat that leaves from the centre of Évian are the **Pré-Curieux** water gardens. Set around a colonial-style house, where you can views some displays, these picturesque lakeside

**LAKE GENEVA FERRIES**

Évian is an excellent base for exploring other towns around the lake, thanks to the Compagnie General de Navigation (CGN) **ferries** (☎84 81 18 48, ⊛cgn.ch) which depart from the port here every day. These head towards several destinations, including Lausanne (19 daily; €29.60 return) and Geneva (2 daily; €60.90 return) in Switzerland, as well as Yvoire (3 daily; €40 return) and Thonon-les-Bains (4 daily; €24.40 return) on the French side.

**14**

gardens are divided into various water-based ecosystems (including ponds, marshes and a waterfall), each of which exhibits different forms of plant and animal life. Tickets for the gardens are available at the small kiosk in front of the casino and boats leave from the nearby quay.

### The Funicular

Rue du Port • Mid-May to Sept daily 10am–6.40pm • Free • ☎ 04 50 26 35 35.

One thing not to miss is the town **funicular**, which departs from its gorgeous little Art Nouveau station behind the Palais Lumiere and rattles its way uphill to the suburb of Neuvecelle, some 750m distant. Opened in 1907 to transport guests from the Cachat spring up to the *Évian Royal Hotel* (see below), the line then closed in the 1960s, remaining dormant for the best part of three decades before being extended (there are now six stops) and re-opened in 2002. The best way to experience it is to ride to the top, grab a drink at the hut, and then walk back down, the path more or less following the line of the funicular. Bikes can be transported on the trailer, also free of charge.

### Source Cachat

The mineral water for which Évian is famous is now bottled at an industrial estate in Amphion, 3km along the lakeside (contact ☎04 50 84 86 54 for one of the 4 daily tours between mid-June & Sept; €3), but you can admire the **Source Cachat** on avenue des Sources, which gushes away behind the Évian company's former offices on rue Nationale – itself a fine bit of Art Nouveau architecture, though now sadly redundant. Make sure you do as the locals do and take a bottle along, though there is often a bit of a scrum around the fountain from whence the nicely chilled water spouts.

### ARRIVAL AND INFORMATION — ÉVIAN-LES-BAINS

**By train** The *gare SNCF* lies on the hill a 10min walk to the southwest of the town centre on avenue de la Gare.
**Destinations** Annecy via Annemasse (several daily; 2hr); Geneva via Annemasse (several daily; 1hr); Thonon-les-Bains (frequent; 10min).
**By bus** The *gare routière*, from which you can catch buses to Thonon-les-Bains and Yvoire, is next to the tourist office on quai Baron de Blonay.
**Tourist office** Place d'Allinges (May, June & Sept Mon–Fri 9am–noon & 2–6.30pm, Sat 9.30am–12.30pm &

2.30–6.30pm, Sun 10am–noon & 3–6pm; July & Aug Mon–Fri 9.30am–6.30pm, Sat & Sun 10am–6pm; Oct–April Mon–Fri 9am–noon & 2–6pm, closes 5pm on Sat, closed Sun; ☎ 04 50 75 04 26, ⊛eviantourism.com); there's free internet here.
**Bike and canoe hire** Takamaka, 1 place du Port (July & Aug daily 9am–noon & 2–6pm, rest of year Mon–Fri only; ☎ 04 50 73 80 98) offers bike rental (€16 per day), as well as tandem canoes (€35).

### ACCOMMODATION

**Littoral** 9 av de Narvik ☎04 50 75 64 00, ⊛hotel -littoral-evian.com. Rooms at this personable little hotel are neatly fashioned either in thick pine wood or a slightly more contemporary style, but the best thing going for this place is its super position near the water, which ensures that many of the rooms have head-on lake views. Breakfast €9.50. **€80**

**Evian Royal Resort** ☎04 50 26 85 00, ⊛evian royalresort.com. Unbridled luxury begets this venerable

resort hotel situated a short way south of town. It actually comprises two hotels, the larger, five-star *Royal*, and the four-star *Ermitage*, though both boast rooms of the very highest order. There's also a stunning golf course to hand. Breakfast €25. *Royal* **€295** *Ermitage* **€170**

**Evian Express** 32 av de la Gare ☎04 50 75 15 07, ⊛hotel-evianexpress.com. Appropriately named joint positioned directly opposite the *gare SNCF*, this welcoming, warmly run place is the antithesis of your average station hotel; bright, boldly coloured and spotless rooms sleeping two- to four people, some of which have fantastic lake views – and it's the cheapest option in town. Reception open 8am–noon & 2–9pm. Breakfast €8. €66

**De France** 59 rue Nationale ☎ 04 50 75 00 36, ⊛ hotel-france-evian.com. Distinguished eighteenth-century building overlooking one of the town's biggest squares, concealing a mix of fairly ordinary rooms and a bunch of larger, more polished rooms, which aren't actually that much more expensive. Breakfast €8.50. €75

## EATING AND DRINKING

**14**

**Instant Gourmand** 10 rue de l'Eglise ☎ 04 50 04 74 98, ⊛ instantgourmand.fr. Fabulous backstreet restaurant with barely half a dozen tables, inside and out, but with an intriguing little menu featuring the likes of pan-fried skate with tandoori yoghurt sauce, and clafoutis *cerise* and balsamic vinegar. Starters €11, mains €20. Tues–Sat noon–2pm & 7.30–10.30pm.

**Le Pizza** 4 place Charles De Gaulle ☎ 04 50 75 05 36, ⊛ lapizzaevian.com. The name is hardly inspiring, and there's little to suggest that there's anything particularly special about this place, but the pizzas – many made with crème fraiche – are absolutely cracking, and go for around €8. Mon & Wed–Sun noon–2pm & 7–11pm.

# Yvoire

Occupying a picture-postcard setting 25km to the west of Évian is the absurdly pretty medieval village of **YVOIRE**, where narrow cobbled lanes lined with artisan shops and chunky stone-built houses slope down to the water's edge, and every street corner seemingly abounds with colourful flowers. Although the village heaves with day-trippers – notably Japanese – in the summer months, you can still find some peace and quiet. Today the most visible reminder of Yvoire's medieval past is the old **castle** along with the two stone gateways, both dating from the fourteenth century.

## Labyrinthe-Jardin des Cinq Sens

Rue de Lac · April–May & Sept to early Oct Tues–Sun 11am–6pm; June–Aug daily 10am–7pm · €10 · ☎ 04 50 72 88 80

Yvoire's one main attraction is the **Labyrinthe-Jardin des Cinq Sens**, a display of immaculate formal gardens designed to stimulate each of the five senses: fruit bushes appeal to your tastebuds; the foliage in the Jardin des Textures encourages you to touch; geraniums provide vivid colours; lilies and honeysuckle produce attractive perfumes, while the central aviary is filled with birdsong.

## ARRIVAL AND INFORMATION

**YVOIRE**

In the absence of a train or bus station most people make their way here by car, hence the preponderance of car parks located just outside the medieval core.

**Boat trips** From Port du Plaisance a regular stream of ferries make the short trip to Nyon (€20.90 return) on the opposite side of the lake, with less regular ferries to Lausanne (€50.50) and Geneva (€37.40).
**Tourist office** Place de la Mairie (Oct–March Mon–Fri

9.30am–12.30pm & 1.30–5pm; April–June & Sept Mon–Sat 9.30am–12.30pm & 1.30–5pm, Sun noon–4pm; July & Aug daily 9.30am–6.30pm; ☎ 04 50 72 80 21, ⊛ yvoiretourism.com). Guided visits of the village can be organized here.

---

## THE ROUTE DES GRANDES ALPES

Winding its way over mountain passes and secluded valleys all the way from Thonon-les-Bains to Menton on the Mediterranean coast is the most renowned tourist route of the French Alps, the 684km **Route des Grandes Alpes**. The route crosses six Alpine passes over 2000m, three of which – the Col de la Cayolle, the Col de l'Izoard and the Col de Vars – were only paved in 1934. The complete route opened in 1937 and has been a popular touring route for drivers, walkers and cyclists ever since. It can be covered in a couple of days by car, but only by rushing through the stunning mountain landscapes and intriguing settlements (including Morzine, Valloire, Briançon and Barcelonnette) that line the route.

## ACCOMMODATION AND EATING

**Le Jules Verne** ⏱ 04 50 72 80 08, ⓦ hoteljulesverne .com. Most of the rooms in this upmarket hotel, superbly located down by the port, face lakewards, while those down on the ground floor have the added bonus of their own little terraced garden. In a nod to the eponymous explorer, the breakfast room is decked out with colourful hot-air balloons. Mid-Feb to Oct. Breakfast €15. **€130**

**La Traboule** Grande Rue ⏱ 04 50 72 83 73, ⓦ la -traboule.fr. While it can't boast a grand lakeside setting like most of Yvoire's restaurants, this is a beautiful-looking place with little potted flowers adorning immaculately laid

tables. Inevitably lake fish (in particular perch fillet) take pride of place, but there are also some superb cheese-based dishes on the menu. Starters €11, mains €18. Daily noon–2pm & 7–10pm.

**Le Vieux Logis** Grande Rue ⏱ 04 50 72 80 24, ⓦ levieuxlogis.com. Tucked away in the heart of the medieval village, this sweet little family-run hotel and restaurant offers plenty of charm, even though the furnishings are nothing particularly special. Mid-Feb to Nov. Breakfast €9. **€85**

# Besançon

The capital of Franche-Comté, **BESANÇON**, is an attractive town of handsome stone buildings that sits between the northern edge of the Jura mountains and a loop of the wide River Doubs. It is this natural defensive position that has defined the town's history. Besançon was briefly a Gallic fortress before Caesar smashed the Gauls' resistance in 58 BC. Strong outer walls were developed during the Middle Ages and the indefatigable military engineer Vauban added the still-extant Citadelle in the seventeenth century in order to guard the natural breach in the river, and a large French army presence remained in the area until well into the twentieth century.

For the most part, visitors are unlikely to stray far from the Old Town which is squeezed into a tight loop of the Doubs. Its pedestrianized streets and narrow walkways conceal a wealth of good museums and cosy cafés. From the tourist office on the far side of the river, the **rue de la République** leads across the pont de la République and into the heart of the Old Town, to the central **place du 8 septembre** and the sixteenth-century **Hôtel de Ville**. The principal street, **Grande-Rue**, cuts across place du 8 septembre along the line of an old Roman road. At its north-western end is another bridge, the modern **Pont Battant**, a replacement for the original Roman bridge into the city, which (in a testament to Roman engineering) survived until 1953. Just before the bridge is the liveliest part of town, filled with inviting cafés and bars.

## Musée des Beaux-Arts et d'Archéologie

Place de la Révolution • Daily except Tues 9.30am–noon & 2–6pm • €5 • ⏱ 03 81 87 80 49

In the main square just off the northern end of Grand-Rue, the **Musée des Beaux-Arts et d'Archéologie** exhibits a fabulous hoard of Egyptian antiquities, notably a beautiful wood-stuccoed and painted sarcophagus, in addition to some fine Roman mosaics and bronzes. The fine art collection, meanwhile, spans the late fifteenth- to early twentieth centuries, with key works by Rembrandt, Renoir and Matisse.

## Musée du Temps

96 Grande-Rue • Tues–Sat 9.15am–noon & 2–6pm • €5, free Sun • ⏱ 03 81 87 81 50

Horologists will delight in the comprehensive display of clocks at the **Musée du Temps**, housed inside the sixteenth-century **Palais Granvelle**. Packed with interactive exhibits on the important local clock-making industry, which reached its zenith here in the nineteenth century, there are all manner of fabulous timepieces to admire, from exquisitely produced watches and table clocks to grandfather clocks and navigational instruments. The museum's star exhibit, however, is Foucault's Pendulum, a seventeen-metre high apparatus conceived by the eponymous physicist as a means of demonstrating how the earth rotated.

14

14

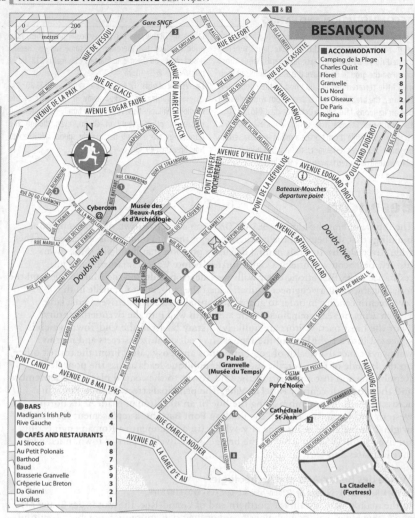

## Castan Square and Porte Noire

A plaque at no.140 Grande-Rue indicates that this house was the birthplace of Victor Hugo, in 1802. Across the way stands the idyllic **Castan Square**, which takes its name from the archeologist who, in 1870, discovered the remains of what was most probably a Roman theatre – fronted by eight Corinthian columns of varying height, it's now a delightful English-style garden. Just beyond here is the **Porte Noire** ("Black Gate"), something of a misnomer for this almost whiter than white triumphal arch built in the second century AD in honour of Emperor Marcus Aurelius. Given its age, the ornamentation is remarkable, particularly on the inside of the arch and recesses on the other side.

## Cathédrale St-Jean and Horloge Astronomique

**Horloge Astronomique** Hourly guided visits in French; April–Sept daily except Tues 9.50–11.50am & 2.50–5.50pm; Oct–Dec & Feb–March daily except Tues & Wed same hours · €3

Through the arch is the eighteenth-century **Cathédrale St-Jean** (closed Tues), whose spare but imposing interior manifests high Romanesque arches leading upwards to a magnificent rib-vaulted ceiling. The principal interest here, though, is the **Horloge Astronomique**, a remarkable astronomical clock built between 1858 and 1860 which contains some 30,000 parts and indicates over a hundred terrestrial and celestial positions.

## The Citadelle
99 rue des Fusillés de la Résistance • Daily: April–June & Sept–Oct 9am–6pm; July & Aug 9am–7pm; Nov–March 10am–5pm; Nov & Dec closed Tues • €9.20, includes entrance to all museums; €2 for audioguide • ☎ 03 81 87 83 33, ⓦ citadelle.com

A steep fifteen-minute climb from the cathedral (or bus #17 if you don't fancy that), Vauban's vast and spectacular **citadelle** lords it over the Old Town below. There's much to see and do here, and you could quite easily spend several hours exploring the walls, turrets and ditches that Vauban left as traps for any potential assailants, not to mention several museums and a **zoo**, which has been cleverly incorporated into the fortification trenches.

Inevitably, the **Musée de la Résistance et de la Déportation** is a rather sobering affair, though it does a superb job detailing the activities of the wartime resistance movement, both locally and throughout France. The **Musée Comtois**, meanwhile, has some lovely displays pertaining to the lives and traditions of the local populace, with collections of pottery, furniture and puppets, and a magnificent assemblage of seventeenth- and eighteenth-century cast-iron firebacks. Squarely one for the kids, the **Musée d'Histoire Naturelle** contains an aquarium, insectarium and noctarium.

## ARRIVAL AND INFORMATION                                             BESANÇON

**By train** The *gare SNCF* is at the end of avenue Maréchal-Foch, a 10min walk north of the Old Town, while the *gare de Besançon Franche-Comté* TGV station (part of the new high speed LGV Rhin-Rhône line) is some 10km north of town; trains connect the two stations roughly every 60–90min. Destinations Bourg-en-Bresse (4 daily; 1hr 30min); Dijon (several daily; 1hr); Paris-Lyon (5 daily; 2hr 30min).

**By bus** There is an extensive bus network, with several major stops, including one at the *gare SNCF*.

**Tourist office** The main tourist office is on the northern bank by the Pont de la République at 2 place de la Première

Armée Française (Mon–Sat 10am–6pm; ☎ 03 81 80 92 55, ⓦ besancon-tourisme.com). There's a more central branch in the Hôtel de Ville on place du 8 septembre (daily 10am–6pm, Oct–April closes at 1pm on Sun, same phone), which also has internet access.

**Bicycle rental** Bikes can be hired from some thirty Velocité stations dotted around town.

**River boats** On the other side of the Pont de la République from the tourist office is the departure point for cruise boats (4 times daily July & Aug; €11), which follow the Doubs on its course around the outer limits of the town centre.

## ACCOMMODATION

**Camping de la Plage** 12 rte du Belfort, Chalezeule ☎ 03 81 88 04 26, ⓦ campingdebesancon.com. Located 5km out of town, this campsite has a restaurant, pool and plenty of opportunities for various sporting activities. Free wi-fi throughout the site. April–Sept. €17

★ **Charles Quint** 3 rue du Chapître ☎ 03 81 82 05 49, ⓦ hotel-charlesquint.com. Wonderful ivy-clad hotel set in an eighteenth-century building next to the Cathédrale St-Jean, with nine sublime, parquet-floored rooms complete with Italian showers. Breakfast (€12) can be taken in the courtyard, where you'll also find a swimming pool. €89

**Florel** 6 rue de la Viotte ☎ 03 81 80 41 08, ⓦ hotel-florel .fr. Easily the most appealing of the three hotels opposite the *gare SNCF*, *Florel* offers bright, modern rooms, each fashioned in a different colour, while the more expensive deluxe rooms also have a private terrace. Breakfast €9. €69

**Granvelle** 13 rue du Général Lecourbe ☎ 03 81 81 33 92, ⓦ hotel-granvelle.fr. Set in a quieter corner of the Old

Town, the rooms here are a bit dated, but comfortable enough, and, curiously, all windows are fitted with electric shutters rather than curtains. Breakfast €8. €60

**Du Nord** 8 rue Moncey ☎ 03 81 81 34 56, ⓦ hotel-du -nord-besancon.com. Central hotel with comfortable, high-ceilinged rooms painted in strong oranges and reds, and furnished to a decent standard, though the street-facing ones can be a little noisy. Breakfast €8. €61

**Les Oiseaux** 48 rue des Cras ☎ 03 81 40 32 00, ⓔ fjtlesoiseaux@yahoo.fr. A 15min walk from the *gare SNCF* along rue de Belfort, but difficult to find; head for the tourist office, where you can catch the #5 bus and get off at the "Les Oiseaux" stop, which is next to the hostel. Singles, doubles and triples only, and although there's no communal kitchen, breakfast is included in the price. Singles €25; doubles €40

**De Paris** 33 rue des Granges ☎ 03 81 81 36 56, ⓦ besanconhoteldeparis.com. The high, brown plastic chairs lining the reception corridor are a bit weird, but that aside, this former coaching inn has infinite class; tastefully decorated rooms with big plump beds, thick curtains and soft carpets, and super-shiny bathrooms. Other facilities include a gym, lounges and private car park. Breakfast €11.50. **€81**

**Regina** 91 Grande-Rue ☎ 03 81 81 50 22, ⓦ besancon-regina.fr. Located right in the heart of town, yet the *Regina* still feels quite private, set back in a courtyard off the road. The rooms are bang on average and a little on the dark side, but perfectly acceptable. Note that there are four floors but no lift. Breakfast €7. **€62**

## EATING AND DRINKING

### CAFÉS AND RESTAURANTS

★ **Al Sirocco** 1 rue Chifflet ☎ 03 81 82 24 05. This always buzzing pizzeria looks great with its glazed, wood-framed windows that open up onto the street, and its earthy wooden furniture. Pizzas are prepared in a large brick-fired oven before being delivered steaming hot to your table; deliciously fresh pasta dishes too. Tues–Sat noon–2pm & 7–10pm.

**Au Petit Polonais** 81 rue des Granges ☎ 03 81 81 23 67. Founded in 1870, this veteran of the Besançon restaurant scene provides a small but tasty range of standard brasserie-type fare, such as hamburger and fries, and quiche and salad. Starters €9. mains €14. Tues–Sun noon–2pm & 7–10pm.

**Barthod** 20–24 rue Bersot ☎ 03 81 82 27 14, ⓦ barthod.fr. With a classy wine shop at the entrance, it's little surprise that wine is as important as the food at this marvellously refined restaurant. Some delicious steak and duck main courses to enjoy, or take your pick from one of the extensive range of *menus* €20–58, one of which features Lyonnais bouchon-style dishes. Starters €15, mains €20. Tues–Sat noon–2pm & 7–10pm.

**Baud** 4 Grande-Rue ☎ 03 81 81 20 12. This glittering *chocolatier*-cum-café provides an irresistible array of cakes, pastries and chocolates to nibble on, as well as light meals like eggs Florentine (€9.80) and lots of teas and coffees. Tues–Sat 7.30am–7.30pm, Sun 7.30am–1pm.

**Brasserie Granvelle** Place Granvelle ☎ 03 81 81 05 60. It's not particularly outstanding, but its location in a shady little park with outdoor seating makes it an agreeable spot to sit with a glass of wine or enjoy the simple *plats du jour* (€9) or pizzas (€11). Daily 8am–11pm.

**Crêperie Luc Breton** 7 rue Luc Breton ☎ 03 81 81 13 45. This stylish central crêperie provides *galettes* galore, such as smoked salmon and crème fraiche, as well as a stack of sweet and savoury crêpes, some of quite exotic proportions, like caramelized apples, raisins and cinnamon with calvados (€4–9). Mon–Sat noon–2pm & 7–11pm.

**Da Gianni** 9 rue Richebourg ☎ 03 81 81 42 96. There are some superb Italian restaurants in town, but this place really takes some beating. Sparky, enthusiastically staffed place serving scrummy antipasti, like calamari carpaccio, steaming bowls of pasta (€12), thin crust pizzas (€11), and genuinely excellent Italian ice cream. Reservations advised. Mon–Sat noon–2pm & 7–10pm.

**Lucullus** 46 rue Battant ☎ 03 81 81 57 45. Just over the Pont Battant in the "new town", the effortlessly good-looking *Lucullus* offers a brilliant menu of local specialities such as chicken cooked in *Marc du Jura* wine, *cassolette d'escargots*, and *saucisses de morteau* (smoked sausage) with a cheese fondue. *Menus* €16–35. Starters €10, mains €16. Daily noon–1.30pm & 7–10pm; closed Tues eve & Wed & Sat lunchtime.

### BARS

**Madigan's Irish Pub** 17 place du 8 septembre ☎ 03 81 81 17 44. Lively, good-time party place where you can sup on a range of French and international beers (€5 for 50cl), or select from one of the brews of the moment. Mon–Sat 10am–2am, Sun 2pm–1am.

**Rive Gauche** 2 quai Vauban ☎ 03 81 61 99 57, ⓦ brasserie-rive-gauche.com. This sociable riverside café-bar with outdoor seating is a popular place for locals to gather over an evening aperitif or a cold beer on a hot day. They also serve light meals and simple *menus* from €10. Daily 8am–midnight.

# Lons-le-Saunier and around

The origins of the sleepy little spa town and departmental capital of **LONS-LE-SAUNIER** date back to Roman times, although most of the old town was destroyed by a fire in the early seventeenth century, and much of the old town you see today dates mainly from the 1700s. Lons was once a major, and very prosperous, centre for winemaking and salt production, and the legacy of this era can still be seen in the grand townhouses and public buildings. These days it's a rather quiet place, but there's a handful of sights worth spending a lazy afternoon looking over. A good day to visit is Thursday, as that's when people from all over roll into town for the enormous **market**.

The ideal place to start your tour of the town is the sunny **place de la Liberté**, where the theatre clock at the eastern end chimes a familiar half-dozen notes from *La Marseillaise* to honour Lons' most famous citizen, Rouget de Lisle; he composed the anthem during his time as a campaigner in the French revolutionary army during the early 1790s.

## Musée Rouget de Lisle

24 rue du Commerce • July & Aug: Mon–Fri 10am–noon & 2–6pm, Sat & Sun 2–5pm • €1 • ⓣ 03 84 47 29 16

Running north from place de la Liberté is the attractive colonnaded thoroughfare of **rue du Commerce**, where you'll find some of Lons' oldest buildings. No. 24 is the house where de Lisle was born, in 1760, and now accommodates the **Musée Rouget de Lisle**; as well as lots of personal effects, it's also of interest for its fine eighteenth-century interior and furnishings.

## Musée des Beaux Arts and La Maison de la Vache qui Rit

At the northern end of rue du Commerce at place Philibert de Chalon stands the **Musee des Beaux Arts** (Tues–Fri 2–5pm, Sat & Sun 2–6pm, €2, ⓣ 03 84 47 64 30), which houses an intermittently interesting collection of nineteenth-century sculptures, including those of the local artist Jean-Joseph Perraud. Spreadable cheese enthusiasts, meanwhile, might be tempted to continue north to 25 rue Richebourg to **La Maison de la Vache qui Rit** (April–June & Sept–Oct Tues–Fri 2–6pm, Sat & Sun 10am–6pm; July & Aug daily 10am–7pm; Dec & Feb–March Sat & Sun 10am–6pm, €7.50, ⓣ 03 84 43 54 10), a multimedia museum dedicated to the locally produced Laughing Cow cheese. Returning south along rue Richebourg to avenue Jean-Moulin, you'll come to a statue of de Lisle himself. It was created by Frédéric Bartholdi, the man who designed New York's Statue of Liberty.

## Spa Lédonia

4 rue de Pavigny • Mon–Fri 10am–7pm, Sat 9am–7pm, Sun 9am–1pm • Spa treatments from €20 • ⓣ 03 84 24 38 18, ⓦ valvital.fr

A left turn at the Lisle statue leads to the peaceful, tree-lined **Parc Édouard Guenon**, where you'll find the delightfully ornate *fin-de-siècle* **Spa Lédonia**, or mineral baths. The baths are now run by **Thermes Valvital**, and have a sauna, Turkish bath and Jacuzzi.

### ARRIVAL AND INFORMATION — LONS-LE-SAUNIER

**By train** The *gare SNCF* is on bd Gambetta, a ten-minute walk south of place de la Liberté; head straight down avenue Aristide Briand (opposite the station entrance) to reach the centre.

Destinations Annecy via Lyon (5 daily; 3hr 30min); Belfort via Besançon (several daily; 3hr); Besançon (frequent; 1hr); Geneva via Bourg-en-Bresse (3 daily; 2hr 30min); Paris-Lyon via Bourg-en-Bresse (4 daily; 3hr).

**Tourist office** In the theatre building on place du 11 novembre (July & Aug Mon–Sat 9am–12.30pm & 1.30–6pm; Sept–June Mon–Fri 9am–noon & 2–6pm, Sat 10am–noon & 2–4pm; ⓣ 03 84 24 65 01, ⓦ ot.lons-le-saunier.com).

### ACCOMMODATION

**Au Terminus** 37 av Aristide-Briand ⓣ 03 84 24 41 83, ⓦ hotel-terminus-lons.com. A decent station hotel, and not that dissimilar to the *Gambetta* (see above) just a few doors along, though the rooms here are a touch brighter, and it's slightly cheaper making it better value on the whole. Breakfast €8. **€52**

**Gambetta** 4 bd Gambetta ⓣ 03 84 24 41 18, ⓦ hotel-gambetta-lons.com. A friendly, family-run place directly opposite the *gare SNCF*, with high-ceilinged a/c rooms with modern furnishings. Breakfast €7.50. **€58**

**Du Parc** 9 av Jean Moulin ⓣ 03 84 86 10 20, ⓦ hotel-parc.fr. The most central option, overlooking the main square, and although the furnishings are a bit plastic, the rooms are well-kept. There's also a popular restaurant downstairs, as well as parking for cars and bikes. Breakfast €7.50. **€62**

**Parenthèse** 186 chemin du Pin ⓣ 03 47 55 44, ⓦ hotel-jura.com. If you've got wheels, and a bit more cash to spare, then this lovely, isolated hotel, some 2km north of Lons in the pretty little village of Chille is perfect. Super smart rooms, each one named after, and displaying a piece of work by, a well-known artist. Excellent spa facility including a gorgeous pool. Breakfast €12. **€99**

## EATING AND DRINKING

**L'Arc-en-Ciel** 1 place Philibert de Chalon ☎ 03 84 86 06 64. You can't miss this super little restaurant opposite the Musée des Beaux Arts, thanks to its outrageously fun decor – stripey painted walls, spotted drapes, and variously coloured glasses and bowls. Organically sourced vegetables and meats provide for a short but tasty menu of salads and burgers. Or just pop by for a coffee. Mon–Sat 10am–9pm.

★ **La Comédie** 65 place de la Comédie ☎ 03 84 24 20 66. Understatedly smart-looking restaurant with Venetian-style ball masks adorning the burgundy/grey walls, nicely spaced out tables, and a delightful wood-decked terrace

out back. The menu is far from exhaustive, but dishes like foie gras medallions with pistachio, and oven-roasted langoustine will more than satisfy. Starters €15, mains €20. Tues–Sat noon–2pm & 7–10pm.

**Pelen** 1 rue Saint Désiré ☎ 03 84 24 31 39. For truly indulgent pastries and chocolates, don't miss this place just off place de la Liberté, which, in addition to the ground-floor chocolate shop (cakes around €3.50), has an upstairs tearoom with a short lunch menu including roast quail and salads, and an outdoor kiosk selling ices. Mon–Fri 8.30am–12.15pm & 2.30–7pm, Sat till 5.15pm, Sun till 12.30pm.

# The Région des Lacs

If you drive east for 20km along the N78 road from Lons, you'll enter the **Région des Lacs**, an area of woods, pastures and lakes strung out along the valley of the River Ain. During the journey, the road begins its ascent to the peaks and gorges that define the border with Switzerland. With each bend in the climbing road, the views down to the tiny villages become all the more impressive. Some of the lakes charge parking fees during the day, but after 6pm, when the crowds and swimming supervisors have gone home, they are deserted and serenely peaceful – the perfect place for an evening picnic at sunset.

## Clairvaux-Les-Lacs

The Région des Lac's main town is **CLAIRVAUX-LES-LACS**. It's here that the River Ain flows into the northern tip of the serpentine **Lac de Vouglans**, which is dammed 25km downstream. The **Grand Lac**, just south of town, is the focus of summer resort activity, with a beach area and watersports facilities. It's calm and scenic, in spite of all the camping activity going on around it.

## INFORMATION AND ACCOMMODATION                         CLAIRVAUX-LES-LACS

**Office du Tourisme du Pays des Lacs** 36 Grande-Rue (Mon–Fri 9am–noon & 2–6pm, Sat 9am–noon; also May–Aug Sat till 6pm, and July & Aug Sun 10am–noon; ☎ 03 84 25 27 47, ⌨ juralacs.com), is the place to find information about the region and outdoor activities such as boat and bike rental and the 46 hiking routes in the area.

**La Chaumière du Lac** Grand Lac ☎ 03 84 25 81 52, ⌨ juralacs.com/adherents/lachaumiere.    Good-value lakeside hotel with twelve rooms providing simple comforts, plus a restaurant serving local fish and cheese (*menus* €15–35). Breakfast €7. April–Sept. **€52**

## Lac de Chalain and around

Some 16km north of Clairvaux, near the village of **DOUCIER** and surrounded by hills, **Lac de Chalain** is, a much more impressive setting. It's also a very popular spot for **camping**, hence the prices can be high.

One reason this area is so popular with campers is its proximity to the **Cascades du Hérisson** (⌨ cascades-du-herisson.fr), the septet of waterfalls that has become one of the Jura's best-known natural spectacles. If you are **driving**, you can reach the main car park for the Cascades by passing through Val-Dessous, a village just to the southeast of Doucier, and then heading for the Parking de l'Éventail. A well-signposted path takes you from the car park to the highest of the falls, which descend a breathtaking 255m over just 7km. A gentle walk of around ten minutes from the car park leads to the prettiest of the falls, the **Éventail**. If you continue upstream, you'll arrive at the **Grand Saut** fall, where the water plummets down a sheer drop of some sixty metres. If you follow the pathway behind the waterfall, you can ascend a steep trail as it leads past

---

### CROSS-COUNTRY SKIING AND MOUNTAIN BIKING IN FRANCHE-COMTÉ

The high plateaux of the Jura mountains (Ⓦjura-tourism.com) guarantee good snow cover in winter, but they also lack the steep gradients of the Alpine peaks further to the south; it is this high but level terrain which has made the Jura into France's most popular destination for **cross-country skiing**, or *ski de fond*. The goal of any superfit *fondeur* is the 175km **Grande Traversée du Jura** (GTJ), which crosses the high plateau from Villers-le-Lac to Giron, a town in the south of the Parc Naturel Régional Haut Jura.

The same gentle topography and established infrastructure that enable cross-country skiing have made this region an ideal high-summer venue for **mountain biking**, with hundreds of waymarked cross-country skiing pistes used out of season as trails for adventurous mountain bikers. The 360km **GTJ–VTT**, which starts near Montbéliard (just to the south of Belfort), has become the greatest long-distance biking challenge in the area. Many people cycle on the road; there aren't many cars, so if you can handle the hills, then go for it.

**14**

---

several smaller springs as well as a drinks kiosk; from here another path leads south to the village of Bonlieu. Finally, the path ends at the uppermost fall, which is known as **Saut Girard**, close to the village of **ILAY**. In all, the walk should take around three hours for reasonably fit walkers.

## Les Rousses

A couple of kilometres before the frontier with Switzerland is the ski resort of **LES ROUSSES**, an outstanding area for cross-country skiing. Les Rousses is also very handy for hikers looking to explore the **Parc Naturel Régional du Haut-Jura** (Ⓦparc-haut-jura .fr), the regional park which runs south from Champagnole across the southern Jura mountains. There are several **GR** footpaths which can be accessed from Les Rousses. **GR9** passes through here as it moves along the crest of the ridge towards the Col de la Faucille; the **GR559**, a route which takes you on a tour of the lakes of Franche-Comté, begins here and ends in Lons-le-Saunier; even the much longer **GR5** passes within a few kilometres of the resort.

### INFORMATION
LES ROUSSES

**Tourist office** 495 rue Pasteur (July & Aug, and mid-Dec to mid-March daily 9am–noon & 2–6pm; mid-March to June, and Sept to mid-Dec Mon–Sat 9am–noon & 2–6pm; ☎03 84 60 04 31, Ⓦlesrousses.com) can provide information on the local skiing conditions. The ESF is also based in the tourist office (☎03 84 60 01 61); their ski instructors organize lessons focusing specifically on cross-country skiing techniques.

### ACCOMMODATION

**Auberge de Jeunesse** 3.5km outside Les Rousses in Le Bief-de-la-Chaille ☎03 84 60 02 80, ✉les-rousses @fuaj.org. Decent hostel located in an old farmhouse by a stream. Late Dec to March & mid-May to mid-Sept. Breakfast included. **€18.50**

**La Ferme du Père Francois** 214 rue Pasteur ☎03 84 60 34 62, Ⓦperefrancois.fr. The warm, family-run *"Farm of Father François"* hotel offers smart, beautifully lit rooms featuring lots of solid pine furnishings and inviting red-and-white checked bedspreads and curtains. There's a very good restaurant here too. Breakfast €12. **€90**

**Du Village** 344 rue Pasteur ☎03 84 34 12 75, Ⓦhotelvillage.fr. Close by *La Ferme* (see above), this neat building can't be accused of lacking colour, from the shocking-pink reception area, to the rooms, with their richly painted walls and multicoloured bedspreads. Triples and quads too. Good value. Breakfast €7. **€56**

## Château-Chalon

Some 10km to the north of Lons on the N83 road towards Besançon, the route known locally as the **Route des Vins du Jura**, you come to a turn-off on the D120 for **Voiteur**. This is an unremarkable provincial town, but just beyond it is one of the prettiest villages in Franche-Comté. **CHÂTEAU-CHALON** is a delight to wander around, with a beautiful church, the twelfth-century **Église Saint Pierre**, and a medieval keep, which is all that remains of the grand Benedictine Abbey which once stood here. As well as holding a stunning position on top of a high rocky outcrop, the village is also noted for the unique variety of *vin jaune*, and there are several vineyards operating around the town. A good choice if you want to sample a range of local and regional wines is the vineyard of Jean Berthet-Bondet on the rue de la Tour (contact the vineyard to organize a tour; ☎03 84 44 60 48, Wberthet-bondet.net), which offers tasting sessions.

**14**

## Poligny

Lying at the southern end of the Culée de Vaux valley, the attractive little town of **POLIGNY** is the cheese capital of Franche-Comté, and you'll find three superb *fromageries* on place des Déportés, the lovely, café-fringed main square. There's another cheese shop on Rue Notre-Dame, opposite the **Église Notre-Dame**, which is just one example of several fine medieval churches scattered along the valley. Standing in an overgrown grass square, and featuring a marvellous steeple, this one dates from the eleventh century.

### Maison du Comté

Av de la Résistance • Hourly guided tours April–June & Sept–Oct Tues–Sun 2pm, 3.15pm & 4.30pm; July & Aug daily 10am, 11.30am & 2.15–5.15pm • €4 • ☎03 84 87 78 40

Cheese afficionados won't want to miss the **Maison du Comté**, an old *fromagerie* that's now the headquarters of the Comité Interprofessional du Gruyère du Comté, France's favourite cheese. The guided tour begins with a twenty-minute film (with English subtitles), followed by various displays, animated models and, best of all, a tasting session.

### INFORMATION AND ACCOMMODATION
POLIGNY

**Tourist office** Place des Déportés (Mon–Fri 9.30am–12.30pm & 1.30–5.30pm, Sat 9.30am–12.30pm & 2–5pm; July & Aug also Sun 9.30am–12.30pm; ☎03 84 37 24 21, Wville-poligny.fr); pick up one of their handy little self-guided leaflets outlining the town's surprisingly numerous historical sites.

**De la Vallee Heureuse** Rte de Genève ☎03 84 37 12

13, Whotelvalleeheureuse.com. Located around 800m east of town in a lovely old converted mill, and while it's not cheap, the rooms are beautifully designed (some with balcony), and the hotel possesses excellent facilities, namely indoor and outdoor pools, sauna, Jacuzzi and restaurant. Breakfast €14. **€125**

## Arbois

Serious wine-lovers should head for **ARBOIS**, 10km to the north of Poligny. Wine emporia line the central place de la Liberté, all of which entreat you to sample the unusual local reds, whites and rosés in the shop windows. Of these local wines, the sweet *vin de paille* is the rarest; the name derives from its grapes, which are dried on beds of straw during the production process, thus giving the wine a strong aftertaste.

### Musée de la Vigne et du Vin

March–June, Sept & Oct daily except Tues 10am–noon & 2–6pm; July & Aug daily 10am–noon & 2–6pm; Nov–Feb daily except Tues 2–6pm • €3.50 • ☎03 84 66 40 45

A few kilometres south of town on the D469 is the Château Pécauld, where you'll find the **Musée de la Vigne et du Vin**, which details the development and production of wine in the Jura. The surrounding vineyards illustrate the work of the local wine-growers, while the cellars and galleries trace the changing methods of wine production over the years. The château also has wine-tasting sessions, which must be booked in advance (☎03 84 66 40 53, Wchateaupecauld.com).

### Maison de Louis Pasteur

83 rue de Courcelles • April to mid-Oct daily guided tours 9.45am–5pm • €6 • ☎ 03 84 66 11 72

At the far end of rue de Corcelles, just by the bridge, stands the **Maison de Louis Pasteur**, a former tannery and childhood home of the eponymous scientist, who, in 1885, discovered the rabies vaccine – indeed, a local nine-year old boy by the name of Joseph Meister became the first, fortunate, recipient of the vaccine that same year. Born in nearby Dole, but schooled in Arbois, Pasteur regularly returned to the house in adulthood, eventually re-settling here following the death of his father in 1865. On view are many of his personal effects, as well as his laboratory, bedroom and lounge, complete with billiard table.

**14**

### ARRIVAL AND INFORMATION

ARBOIS

**By train** The *gare SNCF* is a 20min walk northwest of town on avenue de la Gare; head straight down avenue Pasteur, then rue de Corcelles to reach the centre.

**Tourist office** 17 rue de l'Hôtel de Ville (Mon–Sat 9am–12pm & 2–6pm, also from Easter Sun 10am–noon;

July & Aug Mon–Sat 9am–12.30pm & 2–6.30pm, Sun 10am–noon & 3–6pm; ☎ 03 84 66 55 50, ⓦ arbois.com); staff can provide details of vineyards in the area that offer tasting sessions of local wine.

### ACCOMMODATION AND EATING

**La Balance Mets et Vins** 47 rue de Courcelles ☎ 03 84 37 45 00, ⓦ labalance.fr. Great-looking restaurant located on the main road close to Maison de Louis Pasteur, with copper-tinted walls and brick pillars running its length. The chef here prepares many of his dishes with the local drink, for example, stuffed pigeon and *vin de paille*, and saddle of rabbit stuffed with dried fruits and cooked in Franche beer. *Menus* €20–55. Starters €14, mains €21. Daily noon–2pm & 7–10pm; closed Tues evening & Wed.

**Camping Les Vignes** avenue Général-Leclerc ☎ 03 84 25 26 19, ⓦ odesia-arbois.com. Large, well-maintained municipal site 1km east of the centre, with grocery store, snack bar, swimming pool and play areas. Open mid-April to Sept. **€16.70**

**Jean-Paul Jeunet** 9 rue de l'Hôtel de Ville ☎ 03 84 66 05 67, ⓦ jeanpauljeunet.com. Fantastically classy boutique hotel offering twelve rooms of unbridled luxury; lush green carpets, beautifully patterned armchairs and fancy artwork inform the bedrooms, while bright white designer sinks and walk-in showers are the most striking aspects of the gloriously shiny bathrooms. Breakfast €16.50. **€125**

**Les Messageries** 2 rue de Courcelles ☎ 03 84 66 15 45, ⓦ hoteldesmessageries.com. Located in an old stone townhouse full of character, though the rooms are now a little dated despite the odd splash of colour and occasional wall print. There are also cheaper rooms without shower. Breakfast €11. **€69**

# Belfort

Nestled in the gap between two mountain ranges – the Vosges to the north and the Jura to the south – lies **BELFORT**, a town assured of a place in French hearts for its history as an insurmountable stronghold on this obvious route for invaders. The town is remembered particularly for its long resistance to a siege during the 1870 Franco–Prussian War; it was this resistance that spared it the humiliating fate of being annexed into the German empire, a fate suffered by much of neighbouring Alsace-Lorraine. The commanding officer at the time was one Colonel Denfert-Rochereau (known popularly as the "Lion of Belfort"), who earned himself the honour of numerous street names throughout the country, as well as that of a Parisian square and métro station.

On your way up to the castle, look out for an 11m-high red sandstone **lion** carved out of the rock face. It was designed by Frédéric Bartholdi, of Statue of Liberty fame, as a monument to commemorate the 1870 siege, and was completed in 1880.

## Musée d'Histoire

Daily except Tues: April–May 10am–noon & 2–6pm; June–Sept 10am–6pm; Oct–March 10am–noon & 2–5pm • €2 • ☎ 03 84 90 40 70

Finding your way around Belfort is easy enough. The town is sliced in two by the River Savoureuse: the **new town** to the west is the commercial hub; lying beneath

**14**

> ## EUROCKÉENNES
>
> First staged in 1989, today Eurockéennes (🌐 eurockeennes.fr) is one of France's biggest and most diverse annual rock festivals, attracting top international artists as well as plenty of up-and-coming French acts. The three-day festival takes place over the first weekend in July in a lovely setting on the shores of the Lac du Malsaucy, 6km northeast of Belfort, and the vibe is suitably relaxed and friendly, despite crowds of 100,000 or more. There's a free campsite nearby with 12,000 spaces for those who want the full rock festival experience.

the impressive edifice of the red **Citadelle** on the eastern side is the quieter **Old Town**. This fortress was built by Vauban on the site of a medieval keep, of which only a single tower to the north of the castle remains. There are excellent views of Belfort's Old Town and of the surrounding countryside from up here. Vauban was also responsible for a new set of fortifications surrounding Belfort, and from the castle you can see how these moulded the Old Town into a pentagonal shape. The street plan is still largely unchanged. The Citadelle now houses the **Musée d'Histoire**, which displays exhibits on the town's military history, as well as many Bronze and Iron Age artefacts.

## Musée des Beaux-Arts and Donation Maurice Jardot

Art-lovers should head to the **Musée des Beaux-Arts** (daily except Tues: April–May 10am–noon & 2–6pm; June–Sept 10am–6pm; Oct–March 10am–noon & 2–5pm; €2; ☎ 03 84 22 16 73), located in Tour 41 in the lower part of the fortifications, where paintings by the likes of Dürer and Doré and sculptures by Rodin and Carrière are on display.

Also worth a visit is the **Donation Maurice Jardot** (8 rue de Mulhouse; same times as Musée d'Histoire; €2; ☎ 03 84 90 40 70), on the northern edge of the new town. It was founded at the behest of Maurice Jardot, an associate of Daniel-Henry Kahnweiler, one of the most noted art dealers of the twentieth century; when Jardot died in 1997, he left 150 works of art to the town, including some by Chagall, Braque and Picasso.

### ARRIVAL AND INFORMATION
BELFORT

**By train** The *gare SNCF* and departure point for local buses is at the end of Faubourg-de-France, the main shopping street in the new town.

Destinations Besançon (frequent; 1hr 15min); Montbéliard (frequent; 15min); Mulhouse (8 daily; 30min); Paris-Est (5 daily; 4hr); Strasbourg (3 daily; 2hr).

**Tourist office** 2 rue Clemenceau (Mon–Sat 9am–6.30pm, mid-June to mid-Sept also Sun 10am–1pm; ☎ 03 84 55 90 90, 🌐 belfort-tourisme.com). To reach the tourist office from the *gare SNCF*, walk for ten minutes down Faubourg-de-France as far as the river, then turn left and walk along quai Charles-Vallet until you reach rue Clemenceau. Free internet access is available at the tourist office.

### ACCOMMODATION

**Boreal** 2 rue du Comte de la Suze ☎ 03 84 22 32 32, 🌐 hotelboreal.com. Although a little on the pricey side, this quietly located new town hotel offers large, airy and smoothly furnished rooms, and is a popular stopover with business travellers. Breakfast €7. **€120**

**Camping International de l'Étang des Forges** Rue du Général-Béthouart ☎ 03 84 22 54 92, 🌐 camping -belfort.com. The best local campsite, a few km north of the Old Town next to Lake Forges; here you'll find decent amenities, including a grocery store, swimming pool, volleyball court and snack bar. April–Sept. **€16**

**Grand Hôtel du Tonneau d'Or** 1 rue Général Reiset ☎ 03 84 58 57 56, 🌐 tonneaudor.fr. The lobby of this hotel, housed in an impressive building dating from 1902, is quite something; a monumental Neoclassical staircase with stained-glass windows either side. The rooms are spacious and pleasingly modern. Breakfast €13. **€80**

**Résidence Madrid** 6 rue de Madrid ☎ 03 84 21 39 16, 🌐 fjtbelfort.org. Belfort's large hostel is located 1km west of the railway line, with singles, doubles, dorms and studios, plus a communal kitchen and restaurant. Open year-round. Dorms **€17**

**Saint-Christophe** Place d'Armes ☎03 84 55 88 88, ⓦhotelsaintchristophe.com. In an historic building at the heart of the Old Town, the *Saint-Christophe* has neat, colourfully painted rooms, though some are a little on the boxy side. Breakfast €8.50. **€70**

## EATING AND DRINKING

**Café du Commerce** 6 Faubourg-de-France ☎03 99 54 55 37. The most enjoyable place in town to sit down with a coffee or linger with a beer and watch the world go by on the main pedestrian street. Mon–Sat 7am–1am.

**Finnegans** 6 bd Carnot ☎03 84 28 20 28. Down near the river, an ever-busy Irish pub, with lots of beers on tap (€3.50 for 25cl) and the occasional live band to ramp things up a bit. Tues–Sat 2pm–1am, Sun 5pm–midnight.

**Molière** 6 rue de l'Etuve ☎03 84 21 86 38. For more sophisticated fare, and more upscale surrounds, *Molière* is the place to go in Belfort; here you can sample some fabulous dishes, in particular some delicious game and fish. Starters €12, mains €19, *menus* €22–70. Daily noon–1.30pm & 7–10pm; closed Wed.

14

# The Rhône valley

A TRADITIONAL LYON BOUCHON

# The Rhône valley

The Rhône valley stretches down from the compelling city of Lyon, the second biggest city in France, to just north of Orange, in Provence. The north–south route of ancient armies, medieval traders and modern rail and road, the valley has experienced some industalization, but this has done little to affect the verdant, vine-dotted beauty of the countryside. Following the River Rhône is of limited appeal, with the exception of the scenic stretch of vineyards and fruit orchards between the Roman city of Vienne and the distinctly southern city of Valence. The nougat capital of Montélimar, further south still, also wears its charms well. But the big magnet is, of course, the gastronomic paradise of **LYON**, with its unrivalled concentration of world-class restaurants.

**15**

## GETTING AROUND

Getting up and down the Rhône Valley couldn't be simpler, with plentiful trains – both regional and TGV – plying the route between Lyon and Montélimar. Travelling by car will, inevitably, allow you to dictate things at your own pace, though having your own wheels is pretty much imperative if you wish to explore the Beaujolais region, as bus services here are virtually non-existent.

# Lyon

Viewed from the Autoroute du Soleil, the first impression of **LYON** is of a major confluence of rivers and roads, around which only petrochemical industries thrive. In fact, from the sixteenth century right up until the postwar dominance of metalworks and chemicals, silk was the city's main industry, generating the wealth that left behind a multitude of Renaissance buildings. But what has stamped its character most on Lyon is the commerce and banking that grew up with its industrial expansion. Today, with its eco-friendly tram system, high-tech industrial parks home to international companies, Lyon is a modern city *par excellence*.

Most French people find themselves here for business rather than for recreation: it's a get-up-and-go place, with an almost Swiss sense of cleanliness, order and efficiency. But as a manageable slice of urban France, Lyon certainly has its charms. Foremost among these is **gastronomy**; there are more restaurants per Gothic and Renaissance square metre of the old town than anywhere else on earth, and the city could form a football team with its superstars of the international chef circuit.

The city offers superb cultural attractions, too, from a raft of fine churches, notably the mighty Basilica Notre Dame up on Fourvière, to half a dozen exceptional museums, chief amongst them the **textile museum**, the constantly absorbing **Gallo-Roman museum**, and the wonderful **Gadagne museum**, with its marvellous puppetry displays. Urban explorers, meanwhile, will enjoy staking out Lyon's distinctive older quarters and

# Highlights

**❶ Traboules** Follow in the footsteps of the plucky Resistance fighters, and explore Lyon's dark and winding *traboules*, hidden away behind hulking doorways. **See p.780**

**❷ Musée Gallo-Romain** Vienne is run through with Roman remains, though this vast plot, across the river in St-Romain-en-Gal, offers the most intriguing insight into the daily life and domestic architecture of Roman France. See p.783

**❸ Lyon's restaurants** Food is king here, with award-winning chefs and Michelin stars galore, though for an alternative take on Lyonnais cuisine, make a beeline for one of the city's famous bouchons. **See p.788**

**❹ Beaujolais** Take a trip around this verdant countryside dotted with pretty hilltop villages and lush vineyards yielding some of the country's most distinctive wines, such as Cru Beaujolais. **See p.792**

**❺ Montélimar nougat** Without doubt, the best place to gorge on the moreish bonbon made of sweet honey and crunchy nuts. **See p.800**

**HIGHLIGHTS ARE MARKED ON THE MAP ON P.776**

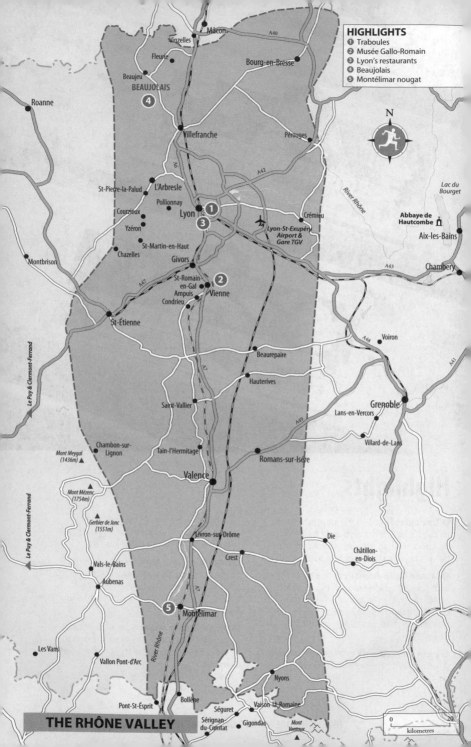

N

Roanne

Mâcon

Vinzelles

Fleurie

Bourg-en-Bresse

Beaujeu

**BEAUJOLAIS**
4

A40

Villefranche

Pérouges

River Rhône

Lac du Bourget

St-Pierre-la-Palud

L'Arbresle

Pollionnay

Courzieux

Lyon

1
3

A42

Crémieu

Lyon-St-Exupéry Airport & Gare TGV

Abbaye de Hautcombe

Aix-les-Bains

Yzéron

St-Martin-en-Haut

Chazelles

Givors

Montbrison

St-Romain-en-Gal

Ampuis

Condrieu

2

Vienne

A47

A43

Chambery

St-Étienne

Beaurepaire

Hauterives

A48

Voiron

Saint-Vallier

Grenoble

Lans-en-Vercors

A49

Villard-de-Lans

A41

Le Puy & Clermont-Ferrand

Chambon-sur-Lignon

Mont Meygal (1436m) ▲

Tain-l'Hermitage

Valence

Romans-sur-Isère

Mont Mézenc (1754m) ▲

Gerbier de Jonc (1551m) ▲

Livron-sur-Drôme

Die

Châtillon-en-Diois

Crest

Le Puy & Clermont-Ferrand

Vals-le-Bains

Aubenas

5

Montélimar

Les Vans

Vallon Pont-d'Arc

River Rhône

Nyons

Pont-St-Ésprit

Bollène

Séguret

Vaison-la-Romaine

Sérignan-du-Comtat

Gigondas

Mont Ventoux ▲

0                    20
kilometres

# THE RHÔNE VALLEY

its winding, secret *traboules*. As if that weren't enough, Lyon's nightlife, cinema and theatre, its antique markets, music and other cultural festivities might tempt you to stay just that little bit longer.

Lyon is organized into nine arrondissements. Of most interest to visitors is the **Presqu'île** (1$^{er}$ and 2$^e$ arrondissements), the tongue of land between the rivers Saône and Rhône, and **Vieux Lyon** (5$^e$) on the west bank of the Saône, where the Romans built their capital of Gaul, Lugdunum. To the north of the Presqu'île is the old silk-weavers' district of **La Croix-Rousse** (4$^e$). Other well-touristed areas include modern Lyon on the east bank of the Rhône (3$^e$), at the heart of which is the bustling commercial area around Part-Dieu, and, north of here, **Parc de la Tête d'Or**, the city's main green space.

## The Presqu'île

The Presqu'île, or peninsula, is most visitors' first port of call. Its dominant feature is **place Bellecour**, whose pink gravelly acres were first laid out in 1617, and which offer fabulous views up to the looming bulk of Notre-Dame de Fourvière. The southern portion of the peninsula starts around Perrache station, beyond which a huge regeneration project has smartened up the previously down-at-heel confluence district.

Running south from place Bellecour is **rue Auguste-Comte** which is full of antique shops selling heavily framed eighteenth-century art works; **rue Victor-Hugo**, is a pedestrian precinct full of chic shops, continues north of place Bellecour on rue de la République, all the way up to the back of the Hôtel de Ville.

To the north of place Bellecour at the top of quai St-Antoine is the **quartier Mercière**, the old commercial centre of the town, with sixteenth- and seventeenth-century houses lining rue Mercière, and the **church of St-Nizier**, whose bells used to announce the nightly closing of the city's gates. In the silk-weavers' uprising of 1831, workers fleeing the soldiers took refuge in the church, only to be massacred. Today, traces of this working-class life are almost gone, edged out by bars, restaurants and designer shops, the latter along rue du Président Edouard-Herriot and the long pedestrian rue de la République in particular.

### Musée Historique des Tissus and Musée des Arts Décoratifs

34 rue de la Charité • Tues–Sun 10am–5.30pm • €10 • ☎ 04 78 38 42 00, ⑩ musee-des-tissus.com

The fine **Musée Historique des Tissus**, housed in the eighteenth-century former town palace of the Duke of Villeroy, doesn't quite live up to its claim to cover the history of decorative cloth through the ages, but it does have brilliant collections from certain periods. Particularly outstanding are the exhibits from Egypt and Persia, notably a remarkably well-preserved baby's bonnet, and a quite gorgeous Persian silk kaftan gilded with silver metal wrapped threads. The main hall is given over to oversized carpets from Ottoman Turkey and the once all-powerful Iranian Safavid dynasty, while upstairs, Chinese tapestries and Japanese kimonos are the most prominent items on show.

The stuff produced in Lyon itself reflects the luxurious nature of the silk trade: seventeenth- to nineteenth-century hangings and chair covers, including hangings from Marie-Antoinette's bedroom at Versailles, from Empress Josephine's room at Fontainebleau and from the palaces of Catherine the Great of Russia. There are also some lovely twentieth-century pieces – including Sonia Delaunay's *Tissus Simultanés* – and couture creations from Worth to Mariano Fortuny, Paco Rabanne and Christian Lacroix.

The adjoining **Musée des Arts Décoratifs** is something of an anti-climax after the textile museum, with its rather dour displays of faïence, porcelain, furniture and eighteenth-century rooms removed from old houses in the Presqu'île. There is, though, a collection of superb modern silverware by noted architects, including Richard Meier and Zaha Hadid.

15

15

BARS
Ninkasi 7
Le Sirius Berges du Rhône 5

CAFÉ
Mokxa 3

RESTAURANTS
Daniel et Denise 4
La Mère Brazier 2
Paul Bocuse 1
Rue le Bec 6

River Soâne

River Rhône

Cuire

Musée d'Art Contemporain

Saierie Vivante

Parc de la Tête d'Or

Hénan

4e

LA CROIX-ROUSSE

PLACE DE CROIX-ROUSSE

Croix-Rousse

1er

Croix Pâquet

St-Polycarpe

6e

Foch

Masséna

TERREAUX

Hôtel de Ville

Opéra

Musée des Beaux Arts

Hôtel de Ville-Louis Pradel

VIEUX LYON

Basilique Notre-Dame de Fourvière

Fourvière

5e

Cordeliers Bourse

PRESQU'ÎLE

BROTTEAUX

Les Halles de Lyon Paul Bourse

Auditorium Maurice-Ravel

Préfecture

Place Guichard Bourse du Travail

Vieux Lyon

Minimes-Théâtre Romain

Minimes

St-Just

Bellecour

PLACE BELLECOUR

2e

Guillotière

Saxe-Gambetta

Ampère Victor Hugo

PLACE CARNOT

Centre d'Échanges Lyon-Perrache

Perrache

7e

Gare SNCF de Perrache

Centre d'Histoire de la Résistance et de la Déportation

Jean Macé

0        500
metres

Gerland

Port Edouard Herriot

A6 to Dardilly, Mâçon & Paris

A7 to Clermont-Ferrand & Valence

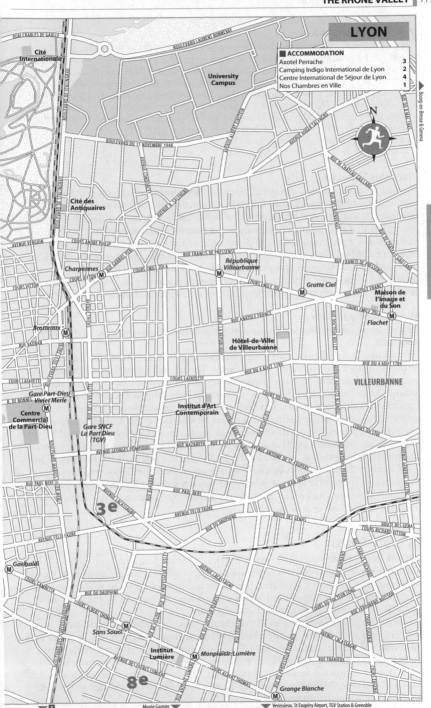

LYON

**ACCOMMODATION**

| | |
|---|---|
| Axotel Perrache | 3 |
| Camping Indigo International de Lyon | 2 |
| Centre International de Séjour de Lyon | 4 |
| Nos Chambres en Ville | 1 |

15

**15**

---

**LYON'S MURALS**

Lyon's fascination with **mural art** can be traced back to the 1970s, when a group of students thought it a good idea to introduce some colour to the city's grimescape, while simultaneously bringing art to the masses. The Musée Garnier murals aside, the easiest ones to track down are the Mur des Canuts in Croix-Rousse, a brilliant, illusory piece depicting everyday life of the district's inhabitants, including, of course, the old silk-weavers; La Fresque des Lyonnais on the corner of rue de la Martinière and Quai St Vincent, which honours Lyon's most famous citizens, such as the Lumiére brothers, Garnier and Bocuse; and La bibliothéque (The City Library), just down the road on the corner of rue de la Platiére and Quai de la Pecherie. Check out ⓦ cite-creation.com for more information.

---

## Place des Terreaux

Flanked by cafés and bars, elongated **place des Terreaux** has as its focal point a monumental nineteenth-century **fountain**. Originally intended for residence in Bordeaux, it was designed by Bartholdi, of Statue of Liberty fame, although the rows of watery jets that sprout up unexpectedly across the rest of the square are a modern addition. The square's eastern end is dominated by the even more monumental **Hôtel de Ville**, its facade crawling with ostentatious statuary. Just off place des Terreaux, behind the Hotel de Ville is Lyon's **opera house**, radically redesigned in 1993 by Jean Nouvel. Its original Neoclassical elevations are now topped by a huge glass Swiss roll of a roof, and the interior's now entirely black with silver stairways climbing into the darkness.

### Musée des Beaux-Arts

20 place des Terreaux • Mon, Wed, Thurs, Sat & Sun 10am–6pm, Fri 10.30am–6pm • €7; audioguide included • ☎ 04 72 10 17 40, ⓦ mba-lyon.fr

Housed in a former Benedictine abbey, the collections of the **Musée des Beaux-Arts** are second in France only to those in the Louvre. The museum is organized roughly by genre, with nineteenth- and twentieth-century sculpture in the ex-chapel on the ground floor. The first floor houses a particularly interesting collection of Egyptian artefacts including coffins, amulets and stone tablets, in addition to a selection of medieval French, Dutch, German and Italian woodcarving and antiquities, coins and *objets d'art*. Upstairs, twentieth-century painting is represented by Picasso and Matisse, and there are also works by Braques, a brace of Bonnards and a gory Francis Bacon. The nineteenth century is covered by the Impressionists and their forerunners, Corot and Courbet; there are works by the Lyonnais artists Antoine Berjon and Fleury Richard, and from there you can work your way back through Rubens, Zurbarán, El Greco, Tintoretto and more. Keep an eye out for Rembrant's earliest known work from 1625, *The Stoning of St Steven*.

## La Croix-Rousse

**La Croix-Rousse** is the old silk-weavers' district and spreads up the steep slopes of the hill above the northern end of the Presqu'île. Although increasingly gentrified, it's still predominantly a working-class area, but barely a couple of dozen people operate the modern high-speed computerized looms that are kept in business by the restoration and maintenance of France's palaces and châteaux.

Along with Vieux Lyon, it was in this district that the **traboules** flourished. Officially the *traboules* are public thoroughfares during daylight hours, but you may find some closed for security reasons. The long climb up the part-pedestrianized **Montée de la Grande Côte**, however, still gives an idea of what the *quartier* was like in the sixteenth century, when the *traboules* were first built. One of the original *traboules*, **Passage Thiaffait** on rue Réné-Leynaud, has been refurbished to provide premises for young couturiers.

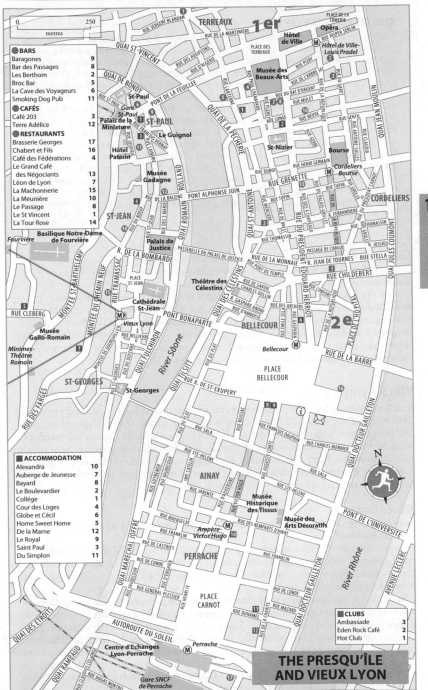

**THE PRESQU'ÎLE AND VIEUX LYON**

15

**BARS**
Baragones 9
Bar des Passages 8
Les Berthom 2
Broc Bar 5
La Cave des Voyageurs 6
Smoking Dog Pub 11

**CAFÉS**
Café 203 3
Terre Adélice 12

**RESTAURANTS**
Brasserie Georges 17
Chabert et Fils 16
Café des Fédérations 4
Le Grand Café
 des Négociants 13
Léon de Lyon 7
La Machonnerie 15
La Meunière 10
Le Passage 8
Le St Vincent 1
La Tour Rose 14

**ACCOMMODATION**
Alexandra 10
Auberge de Jeunesse 7
Bayard 8
Le Boulevardier 2
Collège 1
Cour des Loges 4
Globe et Cécil 6
Home Sweet Home 5
De la Marne 12
Le Royal 9
Saint Paul 3
Du Simplon 11

**CLUBS**
Ambassade 3
Eden Rock Café 2
Hot Club 1

## THE SILK STRIKE OF 1831

Though the introduction of the Jacquard loom of 1804 made it possible for one person to produce 25cm of silk in a day instead of taking four people four days, **silk workers**, or *canuts* – whether masters or apprentices, and especially women and child workers – were badly paid whatever their output. As the price paid for a length of silk fell by over fifty percent, attempts to regulate the price were ignored by the dealers, even though hundreds of skilled workers were languishing in debtors' jails.

On November 21, 1831, the *canuts* called an all-out **strike**. As they processed down the Montée de la Grande Côte with their black flags and the slogan "Live working or die fighting", they were shot at and three people died. After a rapid retreat uphill they built barricades, assisted by half the National Guard, who refused to fire cannon at their "comrades of Croix-Rousse". Following three days of battle, and with the bourgeoisie running scared, the *canuts'* employers called upon outside aid, and 30,000 extra troops arrived to quash the rebellion. Some 600 people were killed or wounded, and in the end the silk industrialists were free to pay whatever pitiful fee they chose, but the uprising was one of the first instances of organized labour taking to the streets during the most revolutionary fifty years of French history.

15

## Soierie Vivante

21 rue Richan • Tues 2–6.30pm, Wed–Sat 9am–noon & 2–6.30pm; guided tours 2pm & 4pm • €5 • ☎ 04 78 27 17 13, Ⓦ soierie-vivante.asso.fr • Mº Croix-Rousse

One of the few remaining silk worker's ateliers in Lyon is the former trimming workshop of one Madame Létourneau, now run by **Soierie Vivante** (Living Silk Association). A tour of the workshop includes a demonstration of the three beautiful Jacquard looms dating from 1870, the only ones of this type still functioning in Lyon. If you can't make it along for a demonstration, you can still have a nose around, and there's also a gift shop selling some lovely silk wares.

# Vieux Lyon

Reached by one of the three *passerelles* (footbridges) crossing the Saône from Terreaux and the Presqu'île, **Vieux Lyon** is made up of the three villages of St-Jean, St-Georges and St-Paul at the base of the hill overlooking the Presqu'île. South of place St-Paul, the cobbled streets of Vieux Lyon, pressed close together beneath the hill of **Fourvière**, form a backdrop of Renaissance and medieval facades, bright night-time illumination and a swelling chorus of well-dressed Lyonnais in search of supper or a midday splurge.

## Musée Gadagne

1 place du Petit Collège • Wed–Sun 11am–6.30pm • €6 each or €8 for both museums, including audioguide • ☎ 04 78 42 03 61, Ⓦ gadagne.musees.lyon.fr

Housed in a splendid fifteenth-century Renaissance mansion, the **Musée Gadagne** comprises two very fine museums. Two floors are given over to the **Musée d'Histoire de Lyon**, which offers a comprehensive chronological overview of the city's development, from antiquity to the modern day.

Better still is the **Musée des Marionnettes du Monde**, showcasing the many different forms of puppetry from both France and around the world, including Venetian glove puppets, Javanese rod puppets, and Chinese shadow puppets. In France, puppet theatres first appeared in the sixteenth-century, developing strong regional identities, as here in Lyon, around the turn of the nineteenth century, particularly with the advent of shadow and paper theatres. Pride of place in the collection goes to the nineteenth-century Lyonnais creations, Guignol and Madelon – the French equivalents of Punch and Judy, who also make an appearance.

## Cathédrale St-Jean
Place St Jean • Mon–Fri 8am–noon & 2–7.30pm, Sat, Sun & holidays 8am–noon & 2–5pm • Free

Standing on the square of the same name is the twelfth- to fifteenth-century **Cathédrale St-Jean**, whose imposing facade lacks most of its statuary as a result of various wars and revolutions. The interior is conspicuously bland, save for some lovely thirteenth-century stained glass above the altar and in the rose windows of the transepts, and a fourteenth-century astronomical clock in the northern transept; its mechanism is cloaked by a beautiful Renaissance casing and is capable of computing moveable feast days (such as Easter) until the year 2019. On the strike of noon, 2pm, 3pm and 4pm the figures of the Annunciation go through an automated set piece, heralded by the lone bugler at the top of the clock.

## Musée Gallo-Romain
17 rue Cléberg • Tues–Sun 10am–6pm • €4 (Thurs free) • ☎ 04 72 38 49 30, ⓦ musees-gallo-romains.com • Funicular Fourvière/Minimes

Well worth the short trek up to Fourvière, the underground **Musée Gallo-Romain** showcases exhibits from prehistoric times to 7 AD, the sheer number and splendour of which serve to underline Roman Lyon's importance. Among the many highlights is a fragment of the so-called "Claudian Table", a fine bronze engraving of a speech by the Lyon-born Emperor Claudius, discovered in 1528 by a Lyonnais cloth-maker. Elsewhere look out for a superb Bronze Age processional chariot, and some remarkably well-preserved mosaics – "In The Circus", for example, recalls the city's standing as one of Roman Gaul's most popular centres of entertainment.

**15**

## Roman Theatres
6 rue de l'Antiquaille • Mid-April to mid-Sept 7am–9pm; mid-Sept to mid-April 7am–7pm • free • Funicular Minimes

These antiquities consist of two ruined **theatres** dug into the hillside – the larger of which was built by Augustus in 15 BC and extended in the second century by Hadrian to seat 10,000 spectators. Nowadays, they are the focal point for the **Nuits de Fourvière** music and film festival each summer.

## Basilique Notre-Dame de Fourvière
Place du Fourvière • Daily 8am–7pm • Rooftop tours 2.30pm & 4pm: April, May, Oct Wed & Sun; June–Sept daily; Nov 2.30pm & 3.30pm; 1hr 15min • Rooftop tours €5 • ☎ 04 78 25 13 01 • Funicular Fourvière

A hulking, incredibly ornate wedding cake of a church, the **Basilique Notre-Dame de Fourvière** was built, like the Sacré-Coeur in Paris, in the aftermath of the 1871 Commune to emphasize the defeat of the godless socialists. And like the

---

### TOP TRABOULES

All around Lyon lurk *traboules*, alleyways and tunnelled passages originally built to provide shelter from the weather for the silk-weavers as they moved their delicate pieces of work from one part of the manufacturing process to another. The streets running down from boulevard de la Croix-Rousse, as well as many in Vieux Lyon, are intersected by these *traboules*. Usually hidden by plain doors, they are impossible to distinguish from normal entryways, proving an indispensable escape network for prewar gangsters and wartime Resistance fighters. Look out for subtle signs on the walls indicating the presence of a *traboule*.

**Vieux Lyon** Find the aptly named *longue traboule*, a dark winding passage connecting 27 rue de Boeuf with 54 rue St-Jean.

**Vieux Lyon** A *traboule* lies behind the door of 28 rue St-Jean, leading to the serene courtyard of a fifteenth-century palace.

**La Croix-Rousse** Go up rue Réné-Leynaud, passing St-Polycarpe on your right, then take rue Pouteau via a *passage*. Turn right into rue des Tables Claudiennes, and enter no. 55 emerging opposite 29 rue Imbert-Colomes. Climb the stairs into 14bis, cross three courtyards and climb the steps, where you finally arrive at place Colbert.

Sacré-Coeur, its hilltop position has become a defining element in the city's skyline. The interior is currently enveloped in scaffolding, and will be for some time, but down in the crypt there's some beautifully executed stonework, plus an ornate turquoise mosaic ceiling in the apse. The observation tower is presently closed but a rooftop tour is a vertigo-worthy replacement – if you can't stomach that, you can take in the magnificent citywide views from the esplanade. From here, the **montée St-Barthélémy** footpath winds back downhill to Vieux Lyon through the hanging gardens.

# Modern Lyon

On the skyline from Fourvière, you can't miss the gleaming pencil-like skyscraper that belongs to Lyon's home-grown Crédit Lyonnais bank. This is the centrepiece of **Part-Dieu**, a business-culture-commerce hub which includes one of the biggest public libraries outside Paris, a mammoth concert hall and a busy shopping centre. While it's not the most aesthetically pleasing area, you don't have to go far to enjoy some culture.

**15**

### Halles de Lyon Paul Bocuse

102 cours Lafayette • Market Tues–Thurs 7am–12.30pm & 3–7pm, Fri & Sat 7am–7pm, Sun 7am–2pm • Trolleybus #3, stop "Les Halles Paul Bocuse"

Named in honour of Lyon's celebrated chef, the **Halles indoor market** has been a temple of food since 1859 (albeit one relocated here in 1971), with goodies ranging from oysters and truffles to spiced sausages and cheeses, as well as chocolate, confectionery, wine and much more. There are plenty of possibilities for tasting too, though whether you're buying or eating here, it's not cheap. Bocuse himself is a regular visitor.

### Parc de la Tête d'Or

Trolleybus #1, stop "Parc Tête d'Or Churchill"

For some respite from the urban scene, do as the locals do and head for the **Parc de la Tête d'Or**, a vast green space pressed up against the Rhône. Here you'll find an enormous boating lake, rose gardens, a botanical garden, a small zoo and lots of amusements for kids.

### Cité Internationale and Musee d'Art Contemporain

81 quai Charles-de-Gaulle • Wed–Fri 11–6pm, Sat & Sun 10am–7pm • €8 • ☎ 04 72 69 17 17, Ⓦ mac-lyon.com • Trolleybus #1, stop "Musée d'Art Contemporain"

Overlooked by the bristling antennae of the international headquarters of Interpol, the **Cité Internationale** is made up of glass-heavy luxury apartments, slick restaurants, and the **Palais des Congres** conference centre. The complex is also home to the **Musée d'Art Contemporain**, a grand, white building with an imposing Neoclassical facade designed by Renzo Piano. It hosts excellent temporary exhibitions as well as the Lyon art biennial in every odd-numbered year.

### Institut Lumière

25 rue du Premier-Film • Tues–Sun 10am–6.30pm • €6.50 • ☎ 04 78 78 18 95, Ⓦ institut-lumiere.org • M° Monplaisir-Lumière

Film buffs won't want to miss the enlightening **Institut Lumière**, housed within the grandiose Art Nouveau villa that was, for a period, the home of Antoine Lumière, father of Auguste and Louis, two of the earliest pioneers of film. The emphasis here is very much on the earliest forms of photographic techniques, which subsequently paved the way for film. Prize exhibits include early magic lanterns, the first cinematograph (1885), and the first ever autochromes, or colour plates, one of which is a picture of Antoine's third daughter relaxing in the Winter Garden. Don't miss the stunning collection of photos by celebrated Lumière photographer, Gabriel Veyre – the quality is so good that it's hard to believe they were taken in the 1930s. Meanwhile, in the basement projection room, you can view some entertaining cinematic clips including the first film, *Les Sorties des Usines Lumière*, showing workers leaving the Lumière factory. In the theatre across the way, several different films are shown nightly.

## Centre d'Histoire de la Résistance et de la Déportation

14 av Berthelot • Wed–Fri 9am–5.30pm, Sat & Sun 9.30am–6pm • €4 • ☎ 04 78 72 23 11, ⓦ chrd.lyon.fr • M° Perrache/Jean-Macé

Housed within the former military medical school used by the Gestapo during World War II, the **Centre d'Histoire de la Résistance et de la Déportation** makes for a sobering but worthwhile visit. In addition to a library of books, videos, memoirs and other documents recording experiences of resistance, occupation and deportation to the camps, there's an exhibition space housed over the very cellars and cells in which Klaus Barbie, the Gestapo boss of Lyon, tortured and murdered his victims. Barbie was brought back from Bolivia and tried in Lyon in 1987 for crimes against humanity; the centrepiece of the exhibition is a moving and unsettling 45-minute video of the trial in which some of his victims recount their terrible ordeal.

## Musée Garnier

4 rue des Serpollieres • Tues–Sun 2–6pm • €6 • ☎ 04 78 75 16 75, ⓦ museeurbaintonygarnier.com • Tram #4, stop "États-Unis Musée Tony Garnier"

One of France's most influential urban planners, Lyon-born Tony Garnier (1869–1948), was responsible for many of the city's key architectural sites, though his presence looms particularly large in the rather anonymous 8ᵉ arrondissement. The **Musée Garnier** is not a museum in the conventional sense, rather it's an open-air exhibition of murals painted on the ends of apartment blocks, each one depicting a period of the city's history, such as the factory workers at the old blast furnaces, or some of Garnier's many architectural contributions, like Stade Gerland, the hospital, or the abattoir (now the Halle Tony Garnier). Garnier actually designed and lived in the squat building opposite the museum and, fittingly, there's a mural of the great man close by.

## ARRIVAL AND DEPARTURE | LYON

### BY PLANE

**Lyon-Saint Exupéry International Airport** (☎ 08 26 80 08 26, ⓦ lyonaeroports.com) is 25km to the southeast of the city, just off the Grenoble *autoroute*. Taxi aside (€40–45), the only way of reaching the city centre is the Rhône Express tram (every 15–30min 5am–12.40am; €14), which terminates at Part-Dieu train station. Note that there are no services from the airport's TGV station into Lyon. There are also regular buses from the airport to Grenoble, Chambery and Annecy.

### BY TRAIN

Central Lyon has two train stations: Gare de Perrache on the Presqu'île is used mainly for ordinary trains rather than TGVs; and Part-Dieu (TGV) is in the 3ᵉ arrondissement to

the east of the Presqu'île. Some TGV trains from Paris give the option of getting off at either station.

**Destinations** (from La Part-Dieu or Perrache) Arles (4 daily; 2hr 40min); Avignon (hourly; 2hr–2hr 40min); Avignon TGV (hourly; 1hr 10min); Bourg-en-Bresse (10 daily; 55min–1hr 30min); Clermont-Ferrand (12 daily; 2hr 20min–2hr 50min); Dijon (1–2 hourly; 2hr); Grenoble (every 30min; 1hr 15min–1hr 50min); Lille-Europe (8 daily; 3hr 10min); Marseille (frequent; 1hr 40min–3hr 45min); Montélimar (10 daily; 1hr 35min); Orange (11 daily; 2hr 5min); Paris (every 30min; 2hr); Paris CDG Airport (9 daily; 2hr 10min); Meximieux (for Pérouges) (hourly; 30min); St-Étienne 3–4 hourly; 50min–1hr); Valence (frequent; 1hr 10min); Valence TGV (frequent; 35min); Vienne (frequent; 20–40min); Villefranche (frequent; 25–40min).

## INFORMATION

**Tourist office** The main tourist office stands on the southeast corner of place Bellecour (daily 9am–6pm; ☎ 04 72 77 69 69, ⓦ lyon-france.com). There's also a small information office in Terminal 2 of the airport.

**Guided tours** Numerous guided tours are offered by the

tourist office; for example, the silk tour explores the former silk workers district of Croix-Rousse, while another tour delves into the complex web of Lyon's famous *traboules*. Tours usually last 2hr and cost €10 (free with Lyon City Card; see box, p.786).

## LYON CITY CARD

The great-value **Lyon City Card** (€21, €31 or €41 for one, two or three days) grants unlimited access to the métro, bus and tramway, nineteen museums (including the Roman ruins in St-Romain-en-Gal; see p.796), guided city tours and river cruise trips. The card is available from the tourist office and the major TCL offices.

## GETTING AROUND

With the exception of reaching Vieux-Lyon and the Croix-Rousse district, it's pretty easy to get around on foot in Lyon.

**Public transport** This comprises four métro lines, four tram lines, as well as trolleybuses, buses and two funiculars (*ficelle*). The métro runs 5am–12.15am, but some bus lines terminate as early as 8pm. You can pick up handy métro, tram and bus map at any of the city transport (TCL) offices around the city.

**Tickets** A single ticket costs €1.60, but better value is the one-day *Ticket Liberté* (€4.90), or a *carnet* of ten (€14.30). A single ride on the funicular costs €2.40. Tickets, which can be bought at machines outside métro and tram stations or at any of the TCL offices, are valid for one hour after they have been validated on board.

**Car rental** All the main car hire companies have offices at the airport and at Perrache and Part-Dieu train stations. Note that car rental outlets at the airport are situated on the opposite side to the main terminals, and accessed via a shuttle bus.

**Bike rental** Vélo'v (w velov.grandlyon.com) is a pick-up and drop-off bike hire scheme with stations all over the city. After subscribing (€1 for one day, €3 for seven days), the first hour is €1, and it's €2 for every 30min thereafter.

**Boat trips** Lyon City Boat (Naviginter), 13bis quai Rambaud, 2ᵉ ☏ 04 78 42 96 81, w naviginter.fr. Leaving from quai des Célestins, boats run up the Saône to Île Barbe or down to the confluence with the Rhône (April & Sept–Oct Tues–Sun; May–Aug daily; €9.50). The same company offers lunch and dinner cruises from €48.

**Taxis** TCLO (☏ 06 10 63 38 77, w tclo.fr) or Taxi Radio Lyon (☏ 04 72 10 86 60, w taxilyon.com).

## ACCOMMODATION

Lyon has an abundance of accommodation, with a healthy stock of hotels and an increasing number of *chambres d'hôtes*. The greatest concentration of hotels is in the Presqu'île, particularly in the 2ᵉ arrondissement between place Bellecour and Perrache station. The following are marked on the map on p.781, unless otherwise stated.

### HOTELS

**Alexandra** 49 rue Victor-Hugo, 2ᵉ ☏ 04 78 37 75 79, w hotel-alexandra-lyon.fr; Mᵒ Ampère Victor-Hugo. Entranced via a brick passageway, just off a lively pedestrian zone, this decent hotel possesses thirty or so almost identically furnished rooms: warm bedrooms and designer bathrooms coloured in cool greys and blacks with splashes of red. The seven rooms to the rear – one of which is a family room with a mezzanine – have direct access to a sunny wood-decked terrace. Breakfast €8. **€89**

**Axotel Perrache** 12 rue Marc Antoine Petit, 2ᵉ ☏ 04 72 77 70 70, w hotel-lyon.fr/perrache; Mᵒ Perrache; map pp.778–779. Instantly recognizable by its boldly painted murals depicting famous Lyon landmarks and events, this three-star hotel comes with few frills, but the rooms are tidy and it's bang in between Perrache station and the burgeoning confluence district. The downstairs bar contains a pool table. Breakfast €10. **€75**

**Bayard** 23 place Bellecour, 2ᵉ ☏ 04 78 37 39 64, w hotelbayard.fr; Mᵒ Bellecour. Sister hotel to the Alexandra (see above), the even more accomplished *Bayard* occupies an enviable spot across from the enormous main square. Differently styled rooms are available, though the square-facing ones are the most appealing, featuring high ceilings, parquet flooring and period furnishings. Breakfast €12. **€119**

**Le Boulevardier** 5 rue de la Fromagerie, 1ᵉʳ ☏ 04 78 28 48 22, w leboulevardier.fr; Mᵒ Cordeliers. A rare central budget find, the rooms here are generally fairly spartan – low-slung beds, small desk and a chair or two – but they're clean and bright, and the bathrooms are up to scratch. Note, though, that the stairs are steep and there's no lift, while the downstairs bar (which functions as reception) can get noisy. Breakfast €6. **€53**

★ **Collège** 5 place St-Paul, 5ᵉ ☏ 04 72 10 05 05, w college-hotel.com; Mᵒ Vieux-Lyon. There's much that'll make you smile about this wonderful school-themed hotel, from the chairs plastered to the facade to the library-like reception and the breakfast room furnished like a classroom. The concept is continued in the completely all-white rooms (including the TVs), with lockers for cupboards and recycled school desks for tables. Better still, each floor has a vintage refrigerator stocked with complimentary drinks. Breakfast €6. **€125**

**Cour des Loges** 2–8 rue du Boeuf, 5ᵉ ☏ 04 72 77 44 44, w courdesloges.com; Mᵒ Vieux-Lyon. Lyon's most luxurious residence is set in a seventeenth-century former Jesuit college, at the centre of which is a stunning glazed atrium. The sixty or so rooms are predominantly fashioned in decadent Renaissance style, roughly half of which have mezzanine-level flooring and wet-room-style open spaces with attractive metal-framed showers. A spa with pool, sauna and Turkish bath round things off in some style. **€250**

★ **Globe et Cécil** 21 rue Gasparin, 2ᵉ 04 78 42 58 95, globeetcecilhotel.com; Mº Bellecour. No one room is the same in this welcoming, family-run hotel near place Bellecour, which is some feat given that there are more than sixty of them. Each one is appointed with the sort of careful touch and individuality that you might find in your own home, so expect to find vibrant colours, wrought-iron or carved wooden bedsteads, oak bureaus, marble fireplaces and the like. **€189**

**Home Sweet Home** 6 rue Cléberg, 5ᵉ 04 72 32 15 66, home-sweet-home-lyon.com; Mº Vieux Lyon/Minimes. Sweet and quirky guesthouse just 100m down the road from the Musée Gallo-Romain, with three pretty rooms bursting with colour and providing super views across town, though bathroom facilities are shared. The friendly lady owner provides a substantial breakfast which you can enjoy on the little terrace. Note that the sign on the wall says Villa Romaine – just buzz in. **€58**

**De la Marne** 78 rue de la Charité, 2ᵉ 04 78 37 07 46, hoteldelamarne.fr; Mº Perrache. Despite the rather grubby exterior, this friendly, well-managed hotel is actually not a bad place to bed down for the night, and it's one of the cheapest lodgings going in the Presqu'île. Twenty-three perky rooms available, though you'd do well to plump for one in the courtyard annexe, which is not only quieter but also possesses a family room and another with fully adapted wheelchair facilities. **€63**

★ **Nos Chambres en Ville** 12 rue René Leynaud, 2ᵉ 04 78 27 22 30, chambres-a-lyon.com; Mº Croix Paquet; map pp.778–779. Secreted away up in Croix-Rousse, this former silkweaver's residence has been converted into a warm and welcoming guesthouse. The three cleverly conceived rooms (two with shower, one with bath) manifest the original grey stone walls and exposed beams, but there are also touches of contemporary chic. Similarly, the communal lounge area – which guests are invited to use – has been sensitively renovated. Tricky to find as there's no sign outside, but you'll be given a code to punch in when you reserve. Closed Aug. **€89**

**Le Royal** 20 place Bellecour, 2ᵉ 04 78 37 57 31, lyonhotel-leroyal.com; Mº Bellecour. A landmark building since its inception as Lyon's first hotel in 1893, *Le Royal* remains a cut above most places in town. Rooms are impeccably styled in one of two colour schemes – red or blue – and are upholstered throughout with Toile de Jouy fabrics. The service is first class, and nothing is too much trouble for the obliging staff. Breakfast €21. **€145**

**Saint Paul** 6 rue de la Lainerie, 5ᵉ 04 78 28 13 29, hotelstpaul.fr; Mº Vieux Lyon. Occupying a superb Old Town location, in one of the city's oldest buildings (possibly late fourteenth-century), this age-old hotel is well worth a punt. The more functional rooms to the rear face inwards onto a darkened courtyard, so receive little light, while those at the front are larger, brighter and have retained the original beamed ceilings. For late risers, continental breakfast (€7) is served until midday. **€75**

**Du Simplon** 11 rue Duhamel, 2ᵉ 04 78 37 41 00, hoteldusimplon.com; Mº Perrache. The unprepossesing exterior actually conceals a homely, and very popular, little hotel, run by a friendly lady with a penchant for cherries, as evidenced by the many cherry-adorned *objets* in the lounge and breakfast room. The rooms, meanwhile, are cosily decorated in different colours, and although a touch boxy and with smallish bathrooms, are meticulously clean. **€86**

### HOSTELS AND CAMPSITE

**Auberge de Jeunesse (Vieux Lyon)** 41–45 montée du Chemin Neuf, 5ᵉ 04 78 15 05 50, lyon@fuaj.org; Mº Vieux-Lyon/Minimes. Modern hostel set in a steep part of the Old Town with great views over Lyon. Dorms sleep four- to six people, and there's a kitchen for use, as well as a laundry. If you want to avoid the climb from Vieux Lyon métro station get the funicular to Minimes. Breakfast included. **€22**

**Camping Indigo International de Lyon** Dardilly 04 78 35 64 55, camping-indigo.com; map pp.778–779. North along the A6 from Lyon or by bus #89 (stop "Camping International") from the gare de Vaise. Alternatively #3 from Hôtel de Ville. Pleasant, green site with plenty of pitches, as well as wood/canvas tents sleeping five, and mobile homes sleeping two- to- six. There's also a restaurant and a laundry. Open year round. Camping **€19.90**; wood/canvas tent **€61**; mobile home **€85**

**Centre International de Séjour de Lyon** 103 bd États-Unis, 8ᵉ 04 37 90 42 42, cis-lyon.com; map pp.778–779. Large, modern hostel with lots of beds, situated just out of earshot of the main ring road. Quads, triples, doubles and singles are available, all with shower and sink, some also with toilet. Bus #32 from Perrache or #36 from Part-Dieu, stop "États-Unis-Beauvisage". Open 24hr, check-in from 2.30pm. Breakfast included. Dorms **€18–20**, doubles **€22–34**

### EATING AND DRINKING

Few cities anywhere in Europe, let alone France, can rival Lyon for the quality of its food, and at any given time there are typically more than a dozen restaurants with one or more Michelin stars. However, while these temples of gastronomy continue to raise standards, the humble bouchon remains as popular as ever, and really is an experience not to be missed – note that some of the more upscale restaurants are closed on Saturdays and Sundays, with others closing on Mondays. More

## THE BOUCHON

No visit to Lyon is complete without a visit to a **bouchon**, the traditional Lyonnais eating establishment. Its provenance most likely comes from the time when inns serving wine would attach small bundles of straw to their signs, indicating that horses could be cared for (*bouchonnés*) while the coachmen went inside to have a drink. The food may not be to everyone's taste – *andouillette* (hot cooked tripe sausage) and *pieds de veau* (calves' feet) are typical staples – but the dishes are usually beautifully cooked and they're wonderfully convivial places. While many bouchons claim to be authentic, only 22 are certified, the best of which are to be found in the Presqu'île.

surprisingly, Lyon doesn't have a particularly strong café culture, though there are plenty of places to sip an espresso on place des Terreaux and the streets of Vieux Lyon. the following are marked on the map on p.781, unless otherwise stated.

**15**

### CAFÉS

**Café 203** 9 rue du Garet, 1er ☎04 78 28 66 65; M° Hôtel-de-Ville. Apparently, this engaging street corner café takes its name from the classic Peugeots parked out front. Whatever its provenance, it's a good deal of fun and just the ticket for a daytime caffeine shot or an evening mojito, plus juicy burgers and cheap *plats du jour* all day. Daily 7am–1am.

★ **Mokxa** 3 rue de l'Abbé Rozier, 1er ☎04 27 01 48 71; M° Croix-Paquet; map pp.778–779. Decent coffee is hard to find in Lyon, so it's no surprise that this cheerful little café, on a sunny little square in Croix-Rousse, has gained a loyal following, particularly among the laptop crowd (there's wi-fi). Very reasonably priced flat whites, cappuccinos, chai lattes and similar served by knowledgeable staff. Tues–Fri 8am–7pm, Sat 9am–7pm, Sun 2–9pm (closed last Sun in the month).

**Terre Adélice** 1 place de la Baleine, 5e ☎04 78 03 51 84; M° Vieux-Lyon. Sparkling ice-cream parlour on a pretty Old Town square, though it's the sorbets that the locals really come here for. Choose, if you can, from over one hundred flavours, from the sublime (chestnut, vine peach, wild strawberry), to the ridiculous (cucumber, goats' cheese). One scoop €2.50, two scoops €4. April–Oct daily noon–midnight, Nov–March Wed–Sun noon–7pm.

### RESTAURANTS

**Brasserie Georges** 30 cours de Verdun, 2e ☎04 72 56 54 54, ⊛brasseriegeorges.com; M° Perrache. Row upon row of crisply laid tables with red leather seating, and friezes poised above the heavily mirrored walls, make for quite a setting in this cavernous Art Deco brasserie founded in 1836. *Choucroutes* are the house speciality, though the local pork and pistachio sausages are also worth trying. Starters €12, mains €20. Mon–Thurs 11.30am–11.30pm, Fri & Sat till 12.30am.

★ **Café des Fédérations** 8–10 rue Major-Martin, 1er ☎04 78 28 26 00, ⊛lesfedeslyon.com; M° Hôtel-de-Ville. One of Lyon's most enduring and celebrated bouchons, serving the earthiest of Lyonnais specialities such as marinated tripe and black pudding, and veal brains fried in butter provençal. Cheerful green-and-white-checked tables are complemented by rough wooden floorboards and jovial pictures on the walls. A good time is guaranteed here. Starters €12, mains €15. Mon–Sat noon–2pm & 7–10pm.

**Chabert et Fils** 11 rue des Marronniers, 2e ☎04 78 37 01 94, ⊛chabertrestaurant.fr; M° Bellecour. Noisy, chaotic and a great deal of fun, this age-old bouchon is the pick of the many restaurants packed along this street. It offers much more than just the usual bouchon staples, for example, *coq au vin* with polenta, and smoked salmon with lemon whipped cream – unusually, the menu is also available in English. Starters €9, mains €14. Mon–Thurs & Sun noon–2pm & 7–11pm, Fri & Sat till 11.30pm.

★ **Daniel et Denise** 156 rue de Créqui, 3e ☎04 78 60 66 53, ⊛daniel-et-denise.fr; M° Place Guichard; map pp.778–779. If you've only got time to try one bouchon, make it this one. Run by charismatic *meilleur ouvrier de France*, Joseph Viola, this little corner restaurant will charm your socks off from the moment you step inside the old-fashioned interior, with its red-and-white-check-clothed tables, tiled flooring, and copper pots dangling from the walls. On the menu are deliciously tasty dishes like sirloin of Angus beef with black pepper and cognac, and poached pears with red wine and orange peel – though do not leave without trying a slice of Viola's *pâté en croute*, a sensational crusty foie gras and sweetbread paté. Starters €12, mains €16. Mon–Fri noon–2pm & 7–10pm. Closed Aug.

**Le Grand Café des Négociants** 1 place Francisque Régaud, 2e ☎04 78 42 50 05, ⊛lesnegociants.com; M° Cordeliers. Despite its unenviable position on a busy junction, this venerable old place – dating from 1864 – is always rammed, be it the sumptuously gilded brasserie, serving both regional and traditional dishes (and continental and American-style breakfasts), or the bustling outdoor terrace – the ideal spot for a beer. Traditional *menu* €30, regional *menu* €34. Starters €11, mains €20. Daily 7am–1am; restaurant noon–midnight.

**Léon de Lyon** 1 rue Pléney, 1er ☎04 72 10 11 12, ⊛bistrotsdecuisiniers.com; M° Hôtel-de-Ville. The distinctive orange and green stained-glass frontage conceals a distinguished brasserie serving original culinary creations as well as traditional Lyonnais recipes. There's plenty of seating inside, but in warmer weather the pavement terrace is a more convivial spot to dine. Starters €10, mains €20. Closed first three weeks Aug. Daily noon–2.30pm & 7–11pm.

**La Machonnerie** 36 rue Tramassac, 5$^e$ ☎04 78 42 24 62, ⊛lamachonnerie.com; M° Vieux-Lyon. The pick of the Old Town bouchons, *La Machonnerie* is the sister restaurant to *Daniel et Denise* (see above), hence its almost identical menu; beef cheek confit in Beaujolais wine, veal liver with parsley, and so on – there's also an English menu to aid you. The tightly packed ranks of neat red-and-white-check-clothed wooden tables look terrific. Starters €12, mains €16. Menu €27. Tues–Sat noon–2pm & 7–10pm.

★ **La Mère Brazier** 12 rue Royale, 1$^{er}$ ☎04 78 23 17 20, ⊛lamerebrazier.fr; M° Croix-Paquet; map pp.778–779. Established in 1921 by Mme Brazier, one of the original Méres Lyonnaises (see box below) and the first woman to attain three Michelin stars, this magnificent restaurant is now headed up by superstar chef Mathieu Viannay. This is about as good, and as expensive, as it gets in Lyon, with a menu as brilliant as it is bold, for example poached Bresse chicken with black truffles under its skin. Starters €35, mains €50. Mon–Fri noon–2pm & 7.30–11pm. Closed Aug.

**La Meunière** 11 rue Neuve, 1$^{er}$ ☎04 78 28 62 91, ⊛la .meuniere.free.fr; M° Hôtel-de-Ville. Dyed-in-the-wool bouchon whose happily careworn demeanour is manifest in age-old furnishings and faded wall prints. Seating is arranged around a central "guest" table laded with various cuts of meat, cheeses and patés, while the menu features the likes of chicken in vinegar sauce, black pudding with apple, and pistachio loaf sausage. Good fun and good value. Starters €9, mains €12. Tues–Sat noon–2pm & 7–10pm.

**Paul Bocuse** 40 rue de la Plage, Collonges-au-Mont-d'Or ☎04 72 42 90 90, ⊛bocuse.com; map pp.778–779. Some 9km north of the city, on the west bank of the Saône, you can't miss the oversized signage proclaiming Lyon's most famous restaurant, named after its celebrity chef-owner. High-end French gastronomy is the bill of fare, and Bocuse himself delivers exquisitely crafted dishes such as scallop of foie gras in verjus sauce, and veal sweetbreads with crayfish, though you will, inevitably, be paying through the nose. Starters €40, mains €55. *Menus* from €145. Daily noon–2pm & 8–10pm.

**Le Passage** 8 rue du Platre, 1$^{er}$ ☎04 78 28 11 16, ⊛le-passage.com; M° Hôtel-de-Ville. Thick burgundy velvet drapes, mahogany framed mirrors and sultry red lighting inform this striking, and very romantic, restaurant. Thoughtfully crafted dishes like fresh roasted codfish filet with cauliflower cream, and rabbit leg with veal marrow should get the tastebuds going. Starters €16, mains €20. *Menus* from €35. Tues–Fri noon–2pm & 7.30–10pm, Sat till 11pm. Closed Aug.

**Le St Vincent** 6 place Fernand-Rey, 1$^{er}$ ☎04 72 07 70 43; M° Hôtel-de-Ville. Kick back on the terrace of this sweet little restaurant and enjoy the comings and goings on this arty, tree-shaded square. Relatively simple but beautifully prepared food like farmhouse chicken with mushrooms and plates of charcuterie. Starters €13, mains €25. Mon–Sat noon–2pm & 7.30–10pm.

**Rue le Bec** 43 quai Rambaud, 2$^e$ ☎04 78 92 87 87, ⊛nicolaslebec.com; M° Perrache; map pp.778–779. Headed up by superstar chef, Nicolas Le Bec, this classiest of venues, down in the increasingly high profile confluence district, attempts to replicate a shopping street (hence the name), with a bakery, butchers, fishmongers and so on, and a menu fashioned in similar style. It's a big space, which can make it feel a little impersonal, but when full, it generates a terrific buzz, particularly in summer when the riverfront terrace opens up for barbecues. Starters €10, mains €20. Mon–Sat noon–2pm & 7.30–10pm.

**La Tour Rose** 22 rue du Boeuf, 5$^e$ ☎04 78 92 69 10, ⊛latourrose.fr; M° Vieux-Lyon. Wonderful-looking restaurant comprising two, colour-themed dining areas; the pebble-floored, conservatory-like La Salle Blue, and the gorgeous, oak-beamed La Salle Blanche, which formerly existed as part of an old chapel. Expect fantastically creative concoctions like hazelnut crust with foie gras and asparagus, and pineapple poached in lemongrass with green tea sorbet. Starters €10, mains €25. *Menus* from €30. Tues–Sat noon–2pm & 7.30–10pm.

**15**

---

## THE MÉRES LYONNAISES

Lyon's standing as one of the world's finest gastronomic destinations is in no small part down to the **Méres Lyonnaises**, or "Mothers of Lyon". Originally house cooks for the middle and upper classes, many of these women ultimately became surplus to requirements, so instead opened up their own businesses, serving food that combined grand bourgeoisie cuisine with more humble fare of the kind you might find in a bouchon, hence dishes such as pullet hen with black truffles, and pike *quenelle* casserole. Leading the way were women like Mère Fillioux and Mère Eugene Brazier, the latter establishing her eponymous restaurant (see above) on rue Royale, which is also where Paul Bocuse completed his apprenticeship.

## NIGHTLIFE AND ENTERTAINMENT

Lyon packs a pretty mean punch when it comes to nightlife and entertainment, with a wide range of bars and clubs, alongside some great live music, opera and theatre. The best places to wander if you are looking for a bar are rue Mercière, the area around place des Terreaux and the Opéra and the streets of Vieux Lyon, though increasingly popular are the river boat bars along the banks of the Rhône.

Lyon's cinematic history is also extremely rich, thanks largely to the pioneering work of the Lumière brothers (see p.784). For avant-garde, classic and obscure films, usually in their original language, check the listings for the cinemas CNP Terreaux, Bellecour, Fourmi Lafayette, Opéra and Ambiance.

For listings (though only in French), pick up a copy of the free weekly newspaper *Le Petit Bulletin* from tourist offices and outlets citywide, or there's the weekly *Lyon Poche* (ⓦlyonpoche.com), also available from newsagents (€1). The following are marked on the map on p.781, unless otherwise stated.

### BARS AND CLUBS

**Ambassade** 4 rue Stella, 2ᵉ ☎04 78 42 23 23, ⓦambassade-club.com; Mᵒ Cordeliers. One of the best and hippest places to party in Lyon, this uber-cool club features top DJs bashing out heavy house beats and hip-hop, as well as soul, electronica and Nu-disco. Wed–Sat 11pm–4am.

**Baragones** 5 place St-Paul, 5ᵉ ☎04 72 10 05 05; Mᵒ Vieux Lyon. Cheery bar adjoining the *Collége* (see p.786) serving *goneries* (French-style finger foods) and fine wine by the glass or bottle. In the same vein as the hotel, the recycled school fixtures and fittings lend the joint a respectably cool vintage vibe. Tues–Sat 4pm–midnight.

★ **Bar des Passages** 8 rue de Platre, 1ᵉʳ ☎04 78 28 11 16, ⓦle-passage.com; Mᵒ Hôtel-de-Ville. Intimate, utterly seductive wine bar set against a gothic backdrop of leather seating, candle-topped tables, and soft red lights. A glass of wine can be anything from €5 to €15 although in such luxurious surroundings you might just be tempted to splash out on champagne. Tues–Sat 6pm–2am.

**Broc Bar** 20 rue Lanterne, 1ᵉʳ ☎04 78 30 82 61; Mᵒ Hôtel-de-Ville. There's nothing obviously exciting about this street corner café-cum bar, with its battered-looking red and yellow tables and chairs, but the terrace is invariably packed with punters idly chatting over a daytime coffee or an evening beer. Mon 7.30am–9pm, Tues–Sat 7.30am–1am, Sun 10am–9pm.

**Les Berthom** 24 rue Pizay, 1ᵉʳ ☎09 62 25 14 34, ⓦlesberthom.fr; Mᵒ Hôtel-de-Ville. An industrial aesthetic prevails at this good-time bar, with exposed brick walls and ceilings, stripped wooden flooring and chunky wooden stools and tables. The beer, meanwhile, is strictly of the Belgian variety. Mon–Fri 5pm–midnight, Sat & Sun 2pm–2am.

**La Cave des Voyageurs** 7 place St-Paul, 5ᵉ ☎04 78 28 92 28, ⓦlacavedesvoyageurs.free.fr; Mᵒ Vieux Lyon. Earthy, two-floored brick-lined wine bar serving 450 varieties of wine from all over France that you can taste and take away; better still, enjoy a glass with a plate of charcuterie. Tues–Sat 11am–1am.

**Eden Rock Café** 68 rue Mercière, 1ᵉʳ ☎04 78 38 28 18, ⓦedenrockcafe.com; Mᵒ Cordeliers. One of the city's better live music venues, staging straight down the line

rock music, with the same band typically playing on consecutive nights from Thursday through to Saturday. Sun–Wed 4.30pm–1am, Thurs–Sat 4.30pm–3am.

**Hot Club** 26 rue du Lanterne, 1ᵉʳ ☎04 78 39 54 74, ⓦhotclubjazz.com; Mᵒ Hôtel-de-Ville. Hidden away down a seedy side street, the unsuspecting entrance conceals a fine vaulted cellar playing host to a nightly programme of jazz, swing, blues and funk, and has been doing so since 1948. Tickets €5–10. Tues–Sat 9pm–1am; closed July & Aug.

★ **Ninkasi** 267 rue Marcel Mérieux, 7ᵉ ☎04 72 76 89 00, ⓦninkasi.fr; Mᵒ Gerland; map pp.778–779. Ninkasi is actually a collective of some half a dozen bars scattered across the city, though this, the original bar down in the Gerland district, remains the most prominent. A high-spirited crowd is drawn here nightly to down a few refreshing house brews and soak up some cracking music, be it live bands or world-renowned DJs. Mon–Wed 10am–1am, Thurs 10am–2am, Fri & Sat 10am–4am, Sun 10am–midnight.

**Le Sirius Berges du Rhône** Opposite 4 quai Augagneur, 3ᵉ ☎04 78 71 78 71; Mᵒ La Guillotière; map pp.778–779. Laidback boat bar on the River Rhône with an impressive roster of DJs, a diverse programme of live music, including world, rock, and soul, and jazz jam sessions on Tuesdays. Friendly staff and late opening too. Daily 2pm–3am.

**Smoking Dog Pub** 16 rue Lainerie, 5ᵉ ☎04 78 28 38 27, ⓦsmoking-dog.com; Mᵒ Vieux Lyon. The name says it all; hugely popular, faux-English pub with a large TV screen showing live sporting events including Premiership football, plus a pub quiz every Tuesday. Beyond the air of masculinity, however, the book-filled shelves lining the walls lend the place an air of serenity. Daily 2pm–1am.

### THEATRE, MUSIC AND FILM

**Institut Lumiére** 25 rue de Premier-Film, 8ᵉ ☎04 78 78 18 95, ⓦinstitut-lumiere.org; Mᵒ Montplaisir-Lumière. Housed in the former "Hangar" on the site of the old Lumière factories, this superbly renovated theatre offers a terrifically varied programme of film, both domestic and foreign. Tickets €7.50.

**Opera house** Place de la Comédie, 1ᵉʳ ☎08 26 30 53 25, ⓦopera-lyon.com; Mᵒ Hôtel-de-Ville. One of the

best opera houses in France, it's also home to the well regarded Lyon Opera Ballet company. Cheap tickets are sold just before performances begin.

**Théâtre des Célestins** Place des Célestins, 2ᵉ ☏ 04 72 77 40 00, ⓦ celestins-lyon.org; Mᵒ Bellecour. Beautiful, gilded residence on a lovely little square staging less radical stuff than most places but offering a highly competent

programme of works nonetheless.

**Théâtre National Populaire** 8 place Lazare-Goujon ☏ 04 78 03 30 00, ⓦ tnp-villeurbanne.com; Mᵒ Gratte-Ciel. Located a short way east of the city centre in Villeurbanne, the TNP stands as Lyon's most prominent theatre, staging the biggest, blowsiest productions.

## DIRECTORY

**Health** Samu – emergency medical attention ☏ 15; Police ☏ 17; SOS Médecins ☏ 04 78 83 51 51. Hospitals: Croix-Rousse, 93 Grand rue de la Croix Rousse ☏ 04 72 07 10 46; Hôpital Edouard-Herriot, 5 place d'Arsonval, 3ᵉ (☏ 04 72 11 76 45). For house calls contact the medical referral centres (☏ 04 72 33 00 33).

**Internet** Planète Net Phone, 21 rue Romarin, 1ᵉʳ (Mon–Fri 10am–10pm, Sat til 9pm); Raconte Moi de la Terre, 38 rue Thomassin, 2ᵉ (Mon–Sat noon–7.30pm).

**Lesbian and gay Lyon** ARIS (Accueil Rencontres Informations Services), 13 rue des Capucins (☏ 04 78 27 10 10), is a gay and lesbian centre organizing various activities and producing a useful scene guide. Online listings and activities are posted at the Forum Gai et Lesbien (ⓦ fgllyon.org). Lyon celebrates lesbian and gay pride in mid-June.

**Police** The main commissariat is at 47 rue de la Charité, 2ᵉ ☏ 04 78 42 26 56.

# Pérouges

Thirty-four kilometres northeast of Lyon, on the N84 is **PÉROUGES**, a lovely village of cobbled alleyways and ancient houses. Its charm has not gone unnoticed by the French film industry either – historical dramas such as *The Three Musketeers* were filmed within its fortifications – nor by some of the residents, who have fought long and hard for preservation orders on its most interesting buildings. The result is an immaculate work of conservation. Local traditional life is also thriving in the hands of a hundred or so workers who still weave locally grown hemp.

The simple and beautiful church of **Marie-Madeleine**, close to the medieval gate that serves as the entry-point to Pérouges, is worth an exploration. Built around 1440 its style is pimarily early Gothic with Romanesque features. The central square, the **place du Halle**, and Pérouges' main street, the **rue du Prince**, have some of the best-preserved French medieval remains. The **lime tree** on place du Halle is a symbol of liberty, planted in 1792.

### ARRIVAL AND INFORMATION PÉROUGES

**By train** From Lyon, you will arrive at the train station in Meximieux from where it's a 10min walk to Pèrouges.

**Tourist office** 1 rue de Geneve (Tues & Thurs

9.30am–noon & 3–6pm, Wed 9.30am–noon, Fri & Sat 2.30–6pm; ☏ 04 74 23 36 72, ⓦ perouges.org).

### ACCOMMODATION AND EATING

**Auberge du Coq** Rue des Rondes ☏ 04 74 61 05 47. Those with a modest wallet should head for this pretty, stone-walled restaurant, where good value *menus* are available from €17; snail casserole and *coq au vin, cuisses de grenouilles* (frogs' legs), or roast chicken with mushrooms are standards. Do sample the local speciality, the deliciously sugary *galette Pérouginne*. Tues 7–10.30pm, Wed–Sat noon–2pm & 7–10.30 pm, Sun noon–2pm.

**Hostellerie de Pérouges** Place du Tilleul ☏ 04 74 61 00 88, ⓦ hostelleriedeperouges.com. This hotel, lodging within a cluster of gorgeous medieval houses scattered around the square, has a range of rooms from three- to four-stars, though all are prepared to an exceptionally high standard – four poster beds and period furnishings are typical features. Breakfast €17. **€130**

# Beaujolais

Around 30km northeast of Lyon, the countryside becomes increasingly hilly as you approach the **Beaujolais** region, where the light, fruity red wines hail from. Fashionable to drink when it is young, Beaujolais is made from the Gamay grape, which thrives on the area's granite soil. Of the three Beaujolais appellations, the best are the crus, which come from the northern part of the region between St-Amour and Brouilly. If you have your own transport, you can follow the cru trail that leads up the D68 to St-Amour, before wending your way along the D31. Beaujolais Villages produces the most highly regarded nouveau, which comes from the middle of the region, while plain Beaujolais are produced in the vineyards southwest of Villefranche-sur-Saône.

## Oingt

There are any number of delightful Beaujolais villages you could head for, but if time is a limiting factor, then head to **Oingt**, around 15km southwest of Villefranche (see p.793). Oingt is typical of the villages in this "Golden Stones" region, so called because of the distinctive ochre-yellow colour of its buildings. The narrow, sun-dappled streets of this splendidly fortified village lead up to the evocative **church of St Matthews,** and, across the way, the chunky, circular observation tower, from where there are superlative views of the surrounding vineyards. Arts and crafts also play a big part in village life here, and you'll find workshops liberally scattered throughout the streets.

**15**

## Villefranche

Thirty-five kilometres north of Lyon, **Villefranche** is both an excellent base for an exploration of the Beaujolais region and a worthwhile destination in itself. Rue Nationale is the long, gently dipping main axis of town, where you'll find smart shops, cafés and patisseries, and the striking **church of Notre-Dame**, which has a fine tower with a soaring spire and ferocious-looking gargoyles. Secreted away behind many of the handsome two-and three-storey buildings lining rue Nationale are some beautifully restored Renaissance courtyards, like the **Italian House**, at no. 407, which features a superb wooden gallery with a spiral staircase leading to a watchtower – some of these courtyards you can enter freely, but for others you should contact the tourist office (see below), who can arrange guided tours. If you're planning on visiting the Beaujolais region and want to gather a picnic, try the superb **covered market** on boulevard Jean-Jaurès.

### ARRIVAL AND INFORMATION                                           VILLEFRANCHE

**By train** The train station is on place de la Gare, from where it's an easy 5min walk down rue de la Gare to the main street, rue Nationale.

**Tourist office** Just off rue Nationale, at 96 rue de la Sous-Préfecture (May–Sept Mon–Fri 9am–6pm, Sat 9am–12.30pm & 1.30–6pm; Oct–April Mon–Fri 10am–5pm, Sat 10am–12.30pm & 1.30–5pm; ☎04 74 07 27 40, ⓦvillefranche-beaujolais.fr); the friendly staff are more than willing to assist with any aspect of visiting the Beaujolais wine region.

### ACCOMMODATION, EATING AND DRINKING

**Bar 91** 91 rue Stalingrad ☎04 74 03 14 10. If you can't make it to the Beaujolais region, then a quick stop at this vibrant, modern wine bar near the station will be some compensation. A slick wood and brick aesthetic with mismatched tables and chairs, floor-to-ceiling windows through which to soak up the sun, tasting sessions, live music and kiddie-friendly facilities make this a super little place. You can also pick up a *plat du jour* for €8.50. Tues–Sat 11am–10pm.

**Plaisance** 96 avenue de la Libération ☎04 74 65 33 52, ⓦhotel-plaisance.com. Accomplished *Best Western* hotel at the southern end of town (fronting the large car park), offering decently sized, smartly furnished rooms in assorted fetching colours (plum, lime green, turquoise), some with bath, some with shower. €95

# Vienne

As you head south from Lyon on the A7, a twenty-kilometre stretch of oil refineries and factories, steel and chemical works may well tempt you to make a beeline for the lavender fields of Provence further south. However, a short detour off the *autoroute* leads to **VIENNE**, which, along with **St-Romain-en-Gal** (see p.796), just across the river, once prospered as Rome's major wine port and entrepôt on the Rhône.

Many Roman monuments survive to attest to this past glory, while several important churches recall Vienne's medieval heyday: it was a bishop's seat from the fifth century and the home town of twelfth-century Pope Calixtus II. The town has undoubtedly maintained its character and sense of purpose, and the compact old quarter makes for enjoyable wandering. Moreover, Vienne takes great pride in hosting Jazz à Vienne, one of the country's foremost **international jazz festivals**, which takes place in the first two weeks of July (ⓦ jazzavienne.com) and stars some of the very best musicians in the world.

## The Roman monuments

**15**

Roman monuments are scattered liberally around the streets of Vienne, including the magnificently restored **Temple d'Auguste et de Livie**, a perfect, scaled-down version of Nîmes' Maison Carrée, on place du Palais, and the remains of the **Jardin Archéologique de Cybèle**, off place de Miremont, which were discovered as recently as 1938 on the site of a former hospital.

### Théâtre Antique

Rue du Cirque • April–Aug daily 9.30am–1pm & 2–6pm; Sept & Oct Tues–Sun 9.30am–1pm & 2–6pm; Nov–March Tues–Fri 9.30am–12.30pm & 2–5pm, Sat & Sun 1.30–5.30pm • €2.40, or €6 combined ticket (see box below) • ☎ 04 74 85 39 23

Best of all the Roman monuments in Vienne is the magnificent **Théâtre Antique**, sited at the base of Mont Pipet to the north of town. Built around 40AD, in its heyday it could seat up to 13,000 spectators, making it one of the largest such venues in Roman antiquity. While it's a bit of a slog to get up here, it's definitely worth the effort for the view of the town and river from the very top seats. Better still, the theatre is a quite superb venue for the many concerts held in Vienne throughout the summer, not least during the Jazz Festival.

## Musée Archéologique Église St-Pierre

Place St Pierre • April–Oct Tues–Sun 9.30am–1pm & 2–6pm; Nov–March Tues–Fri 9.30am–12.30pm & 2–5pm, Sat & Sun 1.30–5.30pm • €2.80 or €6 combined ticket • ☎ 04 74 85 20 35

The **Musée Archéologique Église St-Pierre** stands on the site of one of France's first cathedrals, the origins of which date from the fifth century. The building has suffered much reconstruction and abuse since, including a stint as a factory in the nineteenth century, though the monumental portico of the former church is still striking. Today, the cool, haunting interior retains the atmosphere of an architectural salvage yard, housing substantial but broken chunks of Roman columns, capitals and cornices, though there are some splendid fresco fragments and mosaics to admire.

---

**VIENNE MUSEUM PASS AND AUDIOGUIDE**

The Musée Gallo-Romain de Saint-Roman-en-Gal, Théâtre Antique, Église and Cloître de St-André-le-Bas, Musée des Beaux-Arts et d'Archéologie, Musée de la Draperie and Musée Archéologique St-Pierre can be visited on a **single ticket** (€6), which can be picked up at any of the sites and is valid for 48 hours. Audioguides (€5), available from the tourist office, will give you more information on the city's glorious past at each of the main temples and ruins.

## Cathédrale St-Maurice

Place St Paul • Daily 8.30am–6pm • Free

Completely out of proportion with its surrounds, the monumental **Cathédrale St-Maurice** was pieced together between the eleventh and sixteenth centuries – hence the somewhat unwieldy facade, a combination of Romanesque and Gothic, which appears as if its upper half has been dumped on top of a completely alien building. The interior, with its 90m-long vaulted nave, is impressive though, spare and elegant, with some modern stained-glass windows and traces of fifteenth-century frescoes.

## Église and Cloître de St-André-le-Bas

Place du Jeu-de-Paume • April–Oct Tues–Sun 9.30am–1pm & 2–6pm; Nov–March Tues–Fri 9.30am–12.30pm & 2–5pm, Sat & Sun 1.30–5.30pm • €2.80 or €6 combined ticket • ☎ 04 74 85 18 49

The **Église** and **Cloître de St-André-le-Bas** on place du Jeu de Paume, a few streets north of the cathedral, date from the ninth and twelfth centuries. The back tower of the church, on rue de la Table Ronde, is a remarkable monument, studded with tiny carved stone faces, while the cloister is entered via a small garden a few paces across from the church; beyond the room where temporary exhibits are held, this beautiful little Romanesque affair manifests slender, chalky columns and walls decorated with local tombstones, some dating from the fifth century.

### ARRIVAL AND INFORMATION

**VIENNE**

**By train** The train station is at the top of cours Brillier, which runs down to the riverfront.

**Tourist office** At the bottom of cours Brillier, next to the pretty Jardin du 8 Mai 1945 (Mon 10.30am–noon & 1.30–6pm, Tues–Sat 9am–noon & 1.30–6pm, Sun 9am–noon &

2–6pm; ☎ 04 74 53 80 30, ⓦ vienne-tourisme.com).

**Bike hire** Available from the tourist office, which is particularly useful if you're pushed for time and want to visit St-Romain-en-Gal. €3 for half a day, €5 per day.

### ACCOMMODATION

**Auberge de Jeunesse** 11 quai Riondet ☎ 04 74 53 21 97. Close to the centre of town on the other side of the gardens from the tourist office, this ageing hostel has several large dorms, as well as triples and doubles, all with shared shower and toilet facilities. Open for reservations Mon–Thurs 5–8pm, Fri 8am–noon. Breakfast is not available but there is a kitchen. **€15**

**Grand Hôtel de la Poste** 47 cours Romestang ☎ 04 74 85 02 04, ⓦ hoteldelapostevienne.com. The building is

beginning to show its age, and the rooms are a little frayed around the edges, but it's clean, fairly priced, and the location, overlooking a pretty, tree-lined *cours*, is perfect. Triples, quads and family rooms also available. Breakfast €8.50. **€70**

**Le Pyramide** 14 bd Fernand Point ☎ 04 74 53 01 96, ⓦ lapyramide.com. Part of the prestigious Relais & Chateaux group, this gorgeous hotel offers twenty immaculately turned out rooms, ranging from standard to superior. Breakfast €22. **€200**

### EATING

**Le Cloitre** 2 rue des Cloitres ☎ 04 74 31 93 57. Nicely tucked in next to the Cathédrale St-Maurice, this unassuming but polished little restaurant serves traditional dishes like foie gras alongside some interesting variations on fish and many of the classic desserts such as crème brulée and panna cotta. Starters €9.50, mains €14. Mon–Fri noon–2pm & 7.30–10pm, Sat 7.30–10pm.

**Le Pyramide** 14 bd Fernand Point ☎ 04 74 53 01 96, ⓦ lapyramide.com. *Le Pyramide* was one of France's premier restaurants in the 1930s, when its then-owner, Fernand Point, garnered three Michelin stars. Today, with two stars to its name, this magnificent establishment remains one of the hottest addresses around, and if you're

willing to stump up, you can feast on the likes of spit-roast lamb with violet mustard, and a warm Gran Marnier soufflé. In summer meals are served out on the garden terrace, which looks sublime with its neatly clipped hedges and colourful flowerbeds. *Menus* from €60. Starters €45, mains €65. Thurs–Tues noon–2pm & 7–10pm.

**Le Table de César** Musée Gallo-Romain ☎ 04 74 53 74 06. Easy-going riverside restaurant in the same building as the museum (see p.796), with a smart glass-fronted terrace perched above the promenade. It serves a gamut of dishes, from salads and pizzas to sea-fish starters and grilled beef mains, but is equally a cool spot to chill out with a beer. Lunch *menu* €18. Starters €9, mains €14. Daily noon–3pm & 7–11pm.

# St-Romain-en-Gal: Musée Gallo-Romain

Saint-Romain-En-Gal • Tues–Sun 10am–6pm • €4 or €6 combined ticket, free Thurs audioguide included • ☎ 04 74 53 74 01, ⓦ musees-gallo-romains.com.

Across the Rhône from Vienne, several hectares of Roman ruins constitute the site of **ST-ROMAIN-EN-GAL**, also the name of the modern town surrounding it. Before exploring the excavations, you enter the vast glass and steel building holding the **Musée Gallo-Romain**, which is dominated by some superb mosaics, though those on display are just a fraction of the 250 or so that were discovered along the river bank; the most outstanding example is the olive green coloured Punishment of Lycurgus, which is placed in a separate room on the upper floor.

The site itself – discovered as recently as 1968 – attests to a significant community dating from the first century BC to the third AD, and comprises domestic houses, a craftsmen's district including the significant remains of a fulling mill, a commercial area with market halls and warehouses, and, most impressive of all, the wrestlers' baths, complete with marble toilets displaying some remarkable frescoes.

**15**

# St-Étienne

**ST-ÉTIENNE**, 51km southwest of Lyon, was until recently a bland town. Almost entirely industrial, it is a major armaments manufacturer, enclosed for kilometres around by mineworkings, warehouses and factory chimneys. Like many other industrial centres, it fell on hard times, and the demolition gangs have moved in to raze its archaic industrial past. Only in the last decades has equilibrium been restored thanks to a concerted programme to revitalize the town. Today the centre is quite cheerful, buoyed by several small museums.

## Musée d'Art Moderne

La Terrasse Wed–Mon 10am–6pm • €5, free every first Sun of the month • ☎ 04 77 79 52 52, ⓦ mam-st-etienne.fr.

A justified detour for anyone with an interest in twentieth-century art, the museum stands at the terminus of tram T2 from St-Étienne's central station. It is quite an unexpected treasure house of contemporary work, both pre- and post-World War II, with a good modern American section in which Andy Warhol and Frank Stella figure prominently, along with work by Rodin, Matisse, Léger and Ernst. There are many rooms filled entirely with French art, imaginatively laid out to exciting effect.

## Musée d'Art et d'Industrie

2 place Louis-Comte, daily 10am–6pm • €4.70 • ☎ 04 77 49 73 00, ⓦ musee-art-industrie.saint-etienne.fr

A fine museum on St-Étienne's industrial background, including the development of the revolutionary Jacquard loom, which has an impressive exhibition of arms and armour.

### ARRIVAL AND INFORMATION
ST-ÉTIENNE

**By plane** Apart from the airport in Lyon (see p.785), St-Etienne is also served by a local international airport, Saint-Etienne (ⓦ saint-etienne.aeroport.fr), 10km north of the town. It is 20min from the centre with the airport bus.

**By train** The main *gare* is at Châteaucreux in the new business quarter, 10min away from the centre by tram. However there are four more stations in St-Etienne depending on the direction of the destinations. Take care to check which one you are leaving from/arriving at.

**Destinations** Lyon (3–4 hourly; 50min–1hr); Paris (10 daily; 2hr 45min–3hr 30min); Le Puy-en-Velay (1 hourly; 1hr 30min).

**Tourist office** 16 av de la Libération (Mon–Sat 10am–12.30pm & 2–6.30pm; July & Aug also Sun 10am–12.30pm; ☎ 04 77 49 39 00, ⓦ saint-etienne tourisme.com). The office is around ten minutes' walk from Châteaucreux station along avenue Denfert-Rochereau. All brochures are available to download from its website.

**Bicycle rental** There are thirty 24/7 rental points around town (pre-registration only; ☎ 09 69 32 42 00, ⓦ velivert.fr).

## ACCOMMODATION

**Le Cheval Noir** 11 rue François-Gillet ☎ 04 77 33 41 72, ⓦ www.hotel-chevalnoir.com. Totally renovated in 2009, this hotel is strikingly painted in the brightest of colours. Breakfast €8. __€65__

**Terminus du Forez** 31 av Denfert-Rochereau ☎ 04 77 32 48 47, ⓦ hotel-terminusforez.com. Central, funky 3-star *Logis Hotel* with two different decors: Egyptian or

Neoclassical. Free parking, good restaurant and, amazingly, breakfast available 24/7 for €8. __€74__

**La Tour** 3 rue Mercière ☎ 04 77 32 28 48, ⓦ hoteldelatour.fr. Large beds, satellite TV and good service in the main hotel and the four attached self-catering flats for 1–6 people. Two special needs rooms available. Café-croissant breakfast €5. __€44__

## EATING

**L'Agapee** 7 rue Robert ☎ 04 77 41 74 55, ⓦ restaurant -lagapee.fr. The latest cool restaurant-cum-bistro in the city, in the hands of Mr and Mme Lenormand since 2011, offering highly imaginative cuisine. Three-course dinner

*menus* from €28 and a great wine list that draws heavily from the Rhône and Burgundy. Tues–Sat noon–2pm & 7–10pm; Sun lunch by reservation only. Closed last two weeks in Aug.

**15**

# Between Vienne and Valence

Between Vienne and Valence are some of the oldest, most celebrated **vineyards** in France: the renowned Côte Rotie, Hermitage and Crozes-Hermitage *appellations*. If you've got any spare luggage space, it's well worth stopping to pick up a bottle from the local co-op; even their *vin ordinaire* is superlative and unbelievably cheap, considering its quality. Just south of Ampuis on the west bank, 8km south of Vienne, is the tiny area producing one of the most exquisite and oldest French white wines, Condrieu, and close by is one of the most exclusive – Château-Grillet – an *appellation* covering just this single château (by appointment; ☎ 04 74 59 51 56).

Between **St-Vallier** and **Tain l'Hermitage**, the Rhône becomes more scenic, with the Alps looming into view soon after Tain. In spring you're more likely to be conscious of orchards everywhere rather than vines. Cherries, pears, apples, peaches and apricots, as well as bilberries and strawberries, are cultivated in abundance and sold at roadside stalls.

## Tain-l'Hermitage

**TAIN-L'HERMITAGE**, accessible from both the N7 and the A7, is unpretentious and uneventful, but if you have a weakness for wine or chocolate, you'll love this place. If your visit happens to fall on the last weekend in February you can try out wines from 78 vineyards in the Foire aux Vins des Côtes du Rhône Septentrionales, and on the third weekend of September, the different wine-producing villages celebrate their cellars in the **Fête des Vendanges**. But at any time of the year you can go bottle-hunting along the N86 for some 30km north of Tain along the right bank, following the *dégustation* signs and then crossing back over between Serrières and Chanas. Tain also boasts the oldest suspension bridge over the Rhône, on the opposite side of which is pretty **Tournon-Sur-Rhone**, which marks the border with the Ardeche region.

### Cave de Tain

22 rte de Larnage • Mon–Sat 9am–12.30pm & 2–6.30pm, Sun 10am–12.30pm & 2–6pm • ☎ 04 75 08 20 87, ⓦ cavedetain.com

There are cellars all over town where you can taste and buy wine but, for ease and expertise, head to the **Cave de Tain**, where they have all the wines of the distinguished Hermitage and Crozes-Hermitage *appellations* you'll ever need, and at ridiculously low prices too. There are excellent English notes throughout, as well as a tasting area where you're welcome to sample any of the wines on display. From the *gare SNCF*, walk down avenue Dr Durand before turning left along rue du Noir and then rue Louis Pinard – it's signposted from there.

## Valrhona

14 av du Président-Roosevelt • Mon 10am–7pm, Tues–Sat 9am–7pm • ☎ 04 75 07 90 62, ⓦ valrhona.com

As you go along the main RN7, beyond the junction with the RN95, the irresistable waft of cocoa signals the famous **Valrhona Chocolaterie**. Founded in 1922, Valrhona has become one of the world's leading chocolate manufacturers, and there's even a school for chocolate chefs here. The shop itself offers limitless tasting possibilities (reason alone to visit), though it's inconceivable that you'll leave empty-handed.

### ARRIVAL AND INFORMATION

**By train** The train station is on avenue Dr Durand, from where it's a five-minute walk down to the main road, avenue Jean-Jaurès.

**Tourist office** Across avenue Jean-Jaurès, next to the church

**TAIN SUR L'HERMITAGE**

at place du 8-mai-1945 (Sept–May Mon–Sat 9.30am–noon & 2–6pm; June–Aug Mon–Sat 9.30am–7pm, Sun 9.30am–noon; ☎ 04 75 08 06 81, ⓦ ot-payshermitage.com); they can provide you with an extensive list of vineyards.

### ACCOMMODATION AND EATING

**Les 2 Côteaux** 18 rue Joseph-Péala ☎ 04 75 08 33 01, ⓦ hotel-les-2-coteaux-26.com. Superbly located down by the suspension bridge, the "Two Hillsides" offers eighteen cool, sunlit rooms, though there's little by way of decor; those facing the river cost a little more, but are well worth it. Wi-fi costs extra. Breakfast €9. **€62**

**Pavillon de L'Ermitage** 69 av Jean-Jaurès ☎ 04 75 08 65 00, ⓦ pavillon-ermitage.com. The exterior and lobby are unlikely to solicit much enthusiasm, and it's a little overpriced, but the differently coloured rooms are

decently sized, and come with extras like tea- and coffee-making facilities. There's an outdoor pool too. Breakfast €11. **€105**

**Le Quai** 17 rue Joseph-Péala ☎ 04 75 07 05 90, ⓦ le -quai.com. Opposite *Les 2 Côteaux*, hence with similarly lovely views of the Rhône from its breezy terrace, this upmarket but unstuffy restaurant serves delicious, inventive cuisine like duck breast accompanied with a fig and raspberry vinegar tart and fried mushrooms. Starters €12, mains €17. Daily noon–2pm & 7–10pm.

## Hauterives

**Palais Idéal** 8 rue du Palais • Daily: Jan & Dec 9.30am–12.30pm & 1.30–4.30pm; Feb, March, Oct & Nov 9.30am–12.30pm & 1.30–5.30pm; April–June & Sept 9am–12.30pm & 1.30–6.30pm; July & Aug 9am–12.30pm & 1.30–7pm • €5.50, joint ticket with Musée International de la Chaussure, €7.20 • ☎ 04 75 68 81 19, ⓦ facteurcheval.com.

**HAUTERIVES**, 25km northeast of Tain, is a small unspoilt village, save for one remarkable creation – the manic, surreal **Palais Idéal** built by a local postman by the name of Ferdinand Cheval (1836–1912). The house is truly bizarre, a bubbling frenzy reminiscent of the *modernista* architecture of Spain, with features that recall Thai or Indian temples. The eccentric building took thirty years to carve, and Cheval designed the equally bizarre tombstone nearby. Various Surrealists have paid homage to the building and psychoanalysts have given it much thought, but it defies all classification.

## Romans-sur-Isère

Like Hauterives, **ROMANS-SUR-ISÈRE**, 27km further south and 15km east of the Rhône at Tain, is dominated by one thing; its shoemaking industry, which was to the fore here in the nineteenth century. Otherwise, the old town is pleasant enough, peppered with the inevitable shoe shops as well as establishments offering Romans' two other specialities – this time gastronomic: *pogne*, a ringed spongy bread flavoured with orange water, and *ravioles*, small cornflour-based ravioli with a cheese filling.

### Musèe International de la Chaussure

2 rue Ste-Marthe • Jan–April & Oct–Dec Tues–Sat 10am–5pm; May, June & Sept 10am–6pm; July & Aug Mon–Sat 10am–6pm; year-round Sun 2.30–6pm • €5, or joint ticket with Palais Idéal, €7.20 • ☎ 04 75 05 51 81, ⓦ villes-romans.com.

Housed in the former Convent of the Visitation, the vast **Musèe International de la Chaussure** traces the history of shoemaking and tanning throughout the ages, accompanied by a staggering 16,000 items of footwear from around the world. Your toes will curl in horror at the extent to which women have been immobilized by their footwear from ancient times to the present on every continent, while at the same time you can't help but admire the craziness of some of the creations. Among the highlights of the collection are some mummified feet from ancient Egypt, and a pair of boots as worn by Napoleon. If inspired to replenish your own shoe stock, drop in to the Charles Jourdan factory shop at 1 bd Voltaire or the large shopping outlet, Marques Avenue, along avenue Gambetta.

| ARRIVAL AND INFORMATION | ROMANS-SUR-ISÈRE |
|---|---|
| **Train station** The train station (which is named Romans-Bourg de Pèage, after its sister town across the river) is a 5min walk north of central place Charles de Gaulle on place Carnot. **Tourist office** 62 bd Gambetta (July & Aug Mon–Fri | 9am–6.30pm, Sat 9am–6pm; Sept–June Mon–Fri 9am–12.30pm & 1.30–6pm, Sat 9am–6pm, also mid-May to mid-Sept Sun 9.30am–12.30pm; ☎04 75 02 28 72, ⓦromans-tourisme.com). |

| ACCOMMODATION | |
|---|---|
| **L'Oree du Parc** 6 av Gambetta ☎04 75 70 26 12, ⓦhotel-oreeparc.com. Housed in a 1920s mansion a short walk from town, this is about as restful an option as | you could wish for; ten silky smooth rooms, some of which overlook a leafy garden complete with pool and terrace. Breakfast €11. **€88** |

# Valence

At an indefinable point along the Rhône, there's an invisible sensual border, and by the time you reach **VALENCE**, you know you've crossed it. The quality of light is different and the temperature higher, bringing with it the scent of eucalyptus and pine, and the colours and contours suddenly seem worlds apart from the cold lands of Lyon and the north.

Valence is the obvious place to celebrate your arrival in the **Midi** (as the French call the south), a spruce town made up of tidy boulevards, large public areas and fresh-looking facades as well as a very pleasant old quarter. Although there's little in the way of sights, the town holds some outstanding restaurants, as well as many convivial bars in which to while away a few hours in the sun.

## Cathédrale St-Apollinaire

The focus of Vieux Valence, the **Cathédrale St-Apollinaire**, was consecrated in 1095 by Pope Urban II (who proclaimed the First Crusade), and largely reconstructed in the seventeenth century. More work was carried out later, including the horribly mismatched nineteenth-century tower, but the interior still preserves its original Romanesque grace – especially the columns around the ambulatory.

## The côtes

Between the cathedral and **Église de St-Jean** at the northern end of Grande-Rue, which has preserved its Romanesque tower and porch capitals, are some of the oldest and narrowest streets of Vieux Valence. They are known as **côtes**: côte St-Estève just northwest of the cathedral; côte St-Martin off rue du Petit-Paradis; and côte Sylvante off rue du Petit-Paradis' continuation, rue A.-Paré. Diverse characters who would have walked these steep and crooked streets include Rabelais, a student at the university founded here in 1452 and suppressed during the Revolution, and the teenage Napoleon Bonaparte, who began his military training as a cadet at the artillery school.

## Maison des Têtes and the Maison Dupré-Latour

Though Valence lacks the cohesion of the medieval towns and villages further south, it does have several vestiges of the sixteenth-century city, most notably the Renaissance

**Maison des Têtes** at 57 Grande-Rue. Try to have a look at the ceiling in the passageway here (office hours only), where sculpted roses transform into the cherub-like heads after which the palace is named. Also worth a look is the **Maison Dupré-Latour**, on rue Pérollerie, which has a superbly sculptured porch and spiral staircase.

## ARRIVAL AND INFORMATION

**Train and bus stations** The *gare SNCF* and *gare routière* are just a 5min walk from the old town on rue Denis Papin. Note that the TGV station is 10km northeast of Valence, along the *autoroute* to Romans, though regional trains do stop here too. Regular shuttles and trains connect the *gare TGV* with the *gare SNCF*.

**Destinations** Gap Grenoble (frequent; 1hr–1hr 40min);

### VALENCE

Lyon (frequent; 1hr 10min); Montélimar (frequent; 30min); Tain l'Hermitage (frequent; 10min); Vienne (frequent; 50min).

**Tourist office** 11 bd Bancel, the main thoroughfare (June–Sept Mon–Sat 9.30am–6.30pm, Sun 10.30am–3.30pm; Oct–May Mon–Sat 9.30am–12.30pm & 1.30–6pm, Sun 10.30am–1.30pm; ☎ 04 75 44 90 40, ⓦ valencetourisme.com).

## ACCOMMODATION

**De France** 16 Général-de-Gaulle ☎ 04 75 43 00 87, ⓦ hotel-valence.com. A super-smart establishment on the main boulevard with fully soundproofed rooms decorated in tasteful palettes such as lime green and mauve, while the sumptuous beds certainly invite a good night's sleep. Little touches like proper coffee machines round things off beautifully. In warmer weather breakfast (€13) can be taken on the summery terrace. Small dogs welcome too. **€90**

**De Lyon** 23 av Pierre-Semard ☎ 04 75 41 44 66, ⓦ hoteldelyon.com. A stock two-star bang opposite the train station, offering averagely sized rooms, decorated mostly in white to offset the brightly coloured bedspreads. There are also rooms for families and rooms with wheelchair-accessible bathrooms. Breakfast €7. **€63**

**Les Négociants** 27 av Pierre-Semard ☎ 04 75 44 01 86, ⓦ hotel-lesnegociantsvalence.com. Cheaper and marginally more appealing than *De Lyon* next door, this chic little hotel features softly lit, a/c rooms with minimalist, chocolate-brown-coloured furnishings and shuttered windows to help insulate from passing traffic. Breakfast €7. **€50**

## EATING AND DRINKING

**Chez Grand-Mère** 3 place de la Pierre ☎ 04 75 62 09 98. Set on a pretty, tree-shaded square, this homely, timber-framed restaurant – complete with retro junk – lets diners make up their own three-course *formule* from anything chalked up on the board for just €19.80. Local dishes feature highly, such as the baked tomato and basil *ravioles*. Starters €8, mains €15. Tues–Sat noon–2pm & 7–10pm.

★ **L'Épicerie** 18 place Saint Jean ☎ 04 75 42 74 46. The pick of the town centre restaurants, comprising three contrasting but equally gorgeous dining areas. The restaurant's long-time resident chef, Pierre Séve, is just as likely to take and deliver your order, which could include the likes of salad with bacon and ravioli *grillotteés*, saddle of rabbit stuffed with crayfish, or iced nougat. *Menus* from €25. Starters €12, mains €18. Closed mid-July to mid-Aug. Mon–Fri noon–2pm & 7–10pm, Sat 7–10pm.

**Le Marché** 6 place des Clercs ☎ 04 75 60 00 18. Kick back and soak up the rays on this sun-drenched square near the cathedral with an espresso or one of the several refreshing German draught beers (€4.50/pint). Tues–Fri 10am–2am, Sat 9am–2am, Sun 11am–6pm.

**Pic** 285 av Victor Hugo ☎ 04 75 44 15 32, ⓦ pic-valence .fr. Overseen by three Michelin-starred chef Anne Sophie Pic (granddaughter of the restaurant's founder), this is not an experience you'll forget in a hurry, and with prices on a par with a short haul flight, nor will your wallet. Technically brilliant, sumptuously tasting food, including the restaurant's signature dish, sea bass with Aquitaine caviar. *Menus* €90–320. Significantly less bank-busting is *Le 7* bistro, which features a beautiful three-course *menu* for €30. Tues–Sat noon–2pm & 7.30–10.30pm. Le 7 daily same times.

# Montélimar

If you didn't know it before, you'll soon realize what makes the attractive town of **MONTÉLIMAR**, 40km south of Valence, tick: nougat. Shops and signs everywhere proclaim the glory of the stuff, which has been made here for centuries. The *vieille ville* is made up of narrow lanes that radiate out from the main street, **rue Pierre-Julien**, which runs from the one remaining medieval **gateway** on the nineteenth-century ring of boulevards at place St-Martin, south past the **church of Sainte-Croix**, and on to place Marx-Dormoy.

## Musée de la Miniature

19 rue Pierre Julien • July & Aug daily 9.30am–noon & 2–6pm; Sept–Dec & mid-Feb to June Wed–Sun 2–6pm • €3 • ☎ 04 75 53 79 24

Located opposite the post office, the small but utterly charming **Musée de la Miniature** is the one attraction to visit if you're short of time. Viewed through microscopes, many of these delightful 1/12 scale miniatures are highly amusing, such as the violin-playing grasshopper, and a pair of mosquitoes playing chess; look out, too, for an exquisite model of Noah's Ark, made entirely from paper.

## Château des Adhémar

Plateau de Narbonne • April–Oct 10am–noon & 2–6pm; Nov–March Wed–Mon 2–6pm • €3.50 • ☎ 04 75 00 62 30

High above the old town, the impressive **Château des Adhémar** originally belonged to the family after whom the town ("Mount of the Adhémars") was named. The castle is mostly fourteenth-century, but also boasts a fine eleventh-century chapel with some patchy frescoes, and twelfth-century living-quarters, which is now used exclusively for contemporary art exhibitions. It's a stiff little walk up here, but there are lovely views from the ramparts.

## Fabrique et Musée d'Arnaud Soubeyran

Zone Commerciale Sud (RN7) • Mon–Sat 9am–7pm, Sun 10am–noon & 2.30–6.30pm • Free • ☎ 04 75 51 01 35 • Bus line 1 from outside the train station towards Soleil Levant; stop "A. Pontaimery"

If the sheer number of places offering nougat still hasn't sated your appetite, then pay a visit to the **Fabrique et Musée d'Arnaud Soubeyran**, where they'll show you how they concoct eighty tonnes of the stuff each year – the essential ingredients being lavender honey and almonds from Provence, vanilla and pistachios. There's also a fun museum outlining the history of nougat, while the shop sells many flavours, including delicious orange and lavender, as well as a stack of other sweet-toothed tempters.

### ARRIVAL AND INFORMATION     MONTÉLIMAR

**By train** The *gare SNCF* is on the western side of town, from where it's a 5min walk through the gardens to the main boulevard.

**Tourist office** A 10min walk from the station on Montée Saint-Martin (Allées Provençales) (Mon–Sat 9am–12.30pm & 1.30–6pm; ☎ 04 75 01 00 20, ⓦ montelimar-tourisme.com).

### ACCOMMODATION AND EATING

**Le 45éme** 4 rue de 45e ☎ 04 75 01 80 20. Modern, vaguely arty, glass-fronted bistro just behind the tourist office that suffices for a range of salads, pasta and risotto dishes, in addition to meaty treats like pork ribs and beef fillets. *Menus* from €14. Starters €6, mains €14. Daily noon–2pm & 7–10pm.

**Méli-Mélo** 22 rue de Quatre Alliances ☎ 04 75 51 85 55. Look out for the ceramic tiles on the facade of this terrific little "bio" restaurant in the old quarter, which serves up wholesome organic dishes including chicken couscous with seasonal vegetables. Starters €8, mains €14. Tues–Sat noon–2pm & 7–10pm.

**Sphinx** 19 bd Marre-Desmarais ☎ 04 75 01 86 64, ⓦ sphinx-hotel.fr. Initially, this place doesn't hold out much promise, but enter the courtyard and you'll discover a quite lovely seventeenth-century townhouse accommodating classically furnished, predominantly red, rooms with the snazziest of bathrooms and a host of neat little touches. The husband and wife owners couldn't be more helpful. Breakfast €7.50. **€70**

15

# Provence

LAVENDER FIELDS NEAR THE LUBERON

# Provence

Arguably the most irresistible region in France, Provence ranges from the snow-capped mountains of the southern Alps to the delta plains of the Camargue, and boasts Europe's greatest canyon, the Gorges du Verdon. Fortified towns guard its ancient borders; countless villages perch defensively on hilltops; and great cities like Arles, Aix and Avignon are full of cultural glories. The sensual inducements of Provence include sunshine, food and wine, and the heady perfumes of Mediterranean vegetation. Small wonder it has for so long attracted the rich and famous, the artistic and reclusive, and ever-growing throngs of summer visitors.

The Mediterranean shoreline of Provence is covered separately in our Côte d'Azur chapter (see pp.860–929). Away from the coastal resorts, **inland Provence** remains remarkably unscathed. Evidence of its many inhabitants – Greeks, Romans, raiding Saracens, schismatic popes, and an endless succssion of competing counts and princes – remains everywhere apparent. Provence only became fully integrated into France in the nineteenth century and, though just a tiny minority speak the **Provençal** language, the accent is distinctive even to a foreign ear. In the east, the rhythms of speech become clearly Italian.

Unless you have months to expore, the main difficulty in visiting Provence is choosing where to go. In the west, along the **Rhône valley**, are the Roman cities of **Orange**, **Vaison-la-Romaine**, and **Arles**, and the papal city of **Avignon**, with its fantastic summer festival. **Aix-en-Provence**, the mini-Paris of the region, was home to Cézanne, for whom the **Mont Ste-Victoire** was an enduring subject, while Van Gogh is forever linked with **St-Rémy** and Arles. The **Gorges du Verdon**, the **Parc National du Mercantour** along the Italian border, **Mont Ventoux** northeast of Carpentras, and the flamingo-filled lagoons of the **Camargue** offer stunning and widely disparate landscapes.

## GETTING AROUND
PROVENCE

Much the fastest way to get to and around Provence is on the high-speed TGV trains, which stop at Orange, Avignon and Aix en route to Marseille. Note, however, that TGV stations tend to be a long way outside the towns they nominally serve, and distinct from the *gares SNCF* used by the useful network of slower local trains. A couple of lines that originate in Nice make great sightseeing routes into the mountains – the Train des Merveilles up to Tende (see p.858), and the narrow-gauge Chemins de Fer de Provence to Digne-les-Bains (see p.853). To explore the mountains and rural areas in any depth, however, there's no substitute for a car.

CAMARGUE HORSES

# Highlights

**❶ Avignon** The former city of the popes complements its monuments and museums by staging a dynamic annual theatre festival. **See p.814**

**❷ Medieval hilltop villages** Les Baux and Gordes are the most famous, but many others are equally picturesque, and much less frequented. **See p.827**

**❸ Arles** With its impressive Roman remains, delightful ancient core, and intimate association with van Gogh, Arles is an under-appreciated gem. **See p.828**

**❹ La Camargue** The marshland of the Rhône delta is home to white horses, flamingos and unearthly landscapes. **See p.833**

**❺ Aix-en-Provence** This beautiful city is a wonderful place for café idling, and hosts the region's most vibrant markets. **See p.843**

**❻ Les Gorges du Verdon** The largest canyon in Europe, with stunning views and a full range of hikes. **See p.849**

**❼ Haute-Provence** The Parc National du Mercantour and the Vallée des Merveilles are Alpine gems off the beaten path. **See p.853**

**HIGHLIGHTS ARE MARKED ON THE MAP ON P.806**

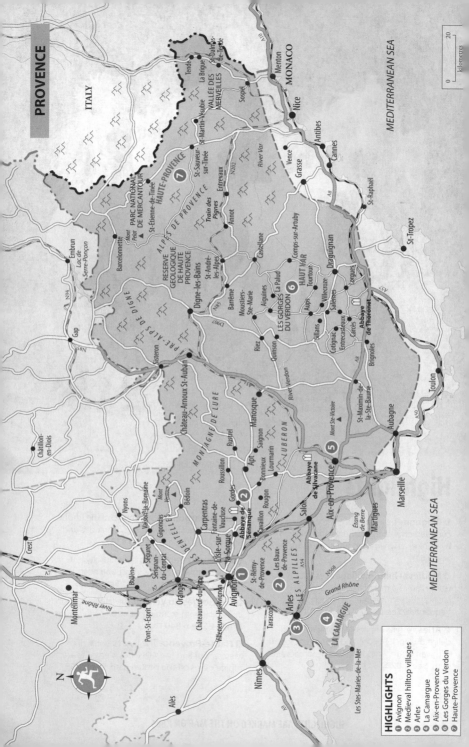

# PROVINCE

ITALY

MEDITERRANEAN SEA

MEDITERRANEAN SEA

MONACO

Menton
Nice
Antibes
Cannes
St-Raphaël
St-Tropez

Toulon
Marseille
Martigues
Étang de Berre

Aubagne
Aix-en-Provence
St-Maximin-de-la-Ste-Baume
Mont Ste-Victoire ▲

Abbaye de Thoronet
Brignoles
Draguignan
Lorgues
Carcès
Entrecasteaux
Salernes
Cotignac
Sillans
Aups
Villecroze
Tourtour
Comps-sur-Artuby
HAUT VAR
La Palud
Aiguines
LES GORGES DU VERDON
Moustiers-Ste-Marie
Quinson
Riez
Barrême
Castellane
Annot
Entrevaux
St-André-les-Alpes
Train des Pignes
Digne-les-Bains

RÉSERVE GÉOLOGIQUE DE HAUTE PROVENCE

ALPES DE PROVENCE

HAUTE-PROVENCE

St-Sauveur-sur-Tinée
St-Étienne-de-Tinée
St-Martin-Vésubie
VALLÉE DES MERVEILLES
La Brigue
St-Dalmas-de-Tende
Tende
Sospel
Vence
Grasse
River Var

PARC NATIONAL DE MERCANTOUR
Mont Pelat ▲
Barcelonnette
Embrun
Lac de Serre-Ponçon
Gap
PRÉ-ALPES DE DIGNE

Château-Arnoux St-Auban
Sisteron
MONTAGNE DE LURE
Banon
Forcalquier
Manosque
Apt
Saignon
Lourmarin
Bonnieux
LUBERON
Rougon
Roussillon
Gordes
Abbaye de Sénanque
Fontaine-de-Vaucluse
Abbaye de Silvacane
Salon
Cavaillon
L'Isle-sur-la-Sorgue
Carpentras
Bédoin
Mont Ventoux
Vaison-la-Romaine
Nyons
DENTELLE
Gigondas
Séguret
Sérignan-du-Comtat
Orange
Châteauneuf-du-Pape
Villeneuve-lès-Avignon
Avignon
St-Rémy-de-Provence
Les Baux-de-Provence
LES ALPILLES
Tarascon
Arles
Nîmes
Alès
Pont-St-Esprit
Bollène
Montélimar
River Rhône
Crest
Châtillon-en-Diois
Grand Rhône
LA CAMARGUE
Les Stes-Maries-de-la-Mer

N

0    20
kilometres

## HIGHLIGHTS
1. Avignon
2. Medieval hilltop villages
3. Arles
4. La Camargue
5. Aix-en-Provence
6. Les Gorges du Verdon
7. Haute-Provence

# West Provence

The richest area of Provence, the Côte d'Azur apart (see p.862), is the **west**. Most of the large-scale production of fruit, vegetables and wine is based here, in the low-lying plains beside the Rhône and the Durance rivers. The only heights are the rocky outbreaks of the Dentelles and the Alpilles, and the narrow east–west ridges of Mont Ventoux, the Luberon and Mont Ste-Victoire. The two dominant cities of inland Provence, **Avignon** and **Aix**, both have rich histories and stage lively contemporary festivals; Arles, Orange and Vaison-la-Romaine hold impressive Roman remains. Around the Rhône delta, the **Camargue** is a unique self-contained enclave, as different from the rest of Provence as it is from anywhere else in France.

## Orange

Thanks to its spectacular **Roman theatre**, the small town of **ORANGE**, west of the Rhône 20km north of Avignon, is famous out of all proportion to its size. Founded as Aurisio in 35 BC, it became associated with the fruit and colour in the eight century, when Charlemagne made it the seat of the counts of Orange, a title that passed to the Dutch crown in the sixteenth century.

Now known as the Théâtre Antique, the **Roman theatre** is the one must-see attraction. Otherwise, with its medieval street plan, fountained squares, ancient porticoes and courtyards, and Thursday-morning market, Orange is attractive to stroll around, and makes a quiet base for exploring the region.

**16**

### Théâtre Antique

**Archeological site** Daily: March & Oct 9.30am–5.30pm; April, May & Sept 9am–6pm; June–Aug 9am–7pm; Nov–Feb 9.30am–4.30pm • €8.50 including Musée d'Art et Histoire; €7.50 for last hour of each day • ☎ 04 90 51 70 60, Ⓦ theatre-antique.com

The enormous wall of the **Théâtre Antique** dominates Orange's medieval centre. Said to be the world's best-preserved Roman theatre, it's the only one with its stage wall still

---

### PROVENÇAL FOOD AND DRINK

The appetizing cuisine of Provence bursts with Mediterranean influences. **Olives** are a defining ingredient, whether appearing in sauces and salads, tarts and pizzas; mixed with capers in *tapenade* paste, and spread on bread or biscuits; or simply accompanying the traditional Provençal aperitif of *pastis*. Another Provençal classic, **garlic**, is used in pistou, a paste of olive oil, garlic and basil, and *aïoli*, the name for both a garlic mayonnaise and the dish in which it's served with salt cod.

Vegetables – tomatoes, capsicum, aubergines, courgettes and onions – are often made into **ratatouille**, while **courgette flowers** (*fleurs de courgettes farcies*), stuffed with pistou or tomato sauce, are an exquisite local delicacy.

Sheep, taken up to the mountains in summer, provide the staple **meat**; you'll find the finest, *agneau de Sisteron*, roasted with Provençal herbs as *gigot d'agneau aux herbes*. **Fish** is especially prominent on traditional menus, with freshwater trout, salt cod, anchovies, sea bream, monkfish, sea bass and whiting all common, along with wonderful seafood such as clams, periwinkles, sea urchins and oysters.

**Sweets** include almond *calissons* from Aix and candied fruit from Apt, while the **fruit** – melons, white peaches, apricots, figs, cherries and Muscat grapes – is unbeatable. **Cheeses**, such as Banon, wrapped in chestnut leaves and marinated in brandy, and the aromatic Picadon, from the foothills of the Alps, are invariably made from goat's or ewe's milk.

The best **wines** come from around the Dentelles, notably Gigondas, and from Châteauneuf-du-Pape. To the east are the light, drinkable, but not particularly special wines of the Côtes du Ventoux and the Côtes du Lubéron *appellations*. With the exception of the Côteaux des Baux around Les Baux, and the Côtes de Provence in the Var *département*, the best wines of southern Provence come from along the coast.

---

### THE CHORÉGIES

When Orange's **choral festival**, the **Chorégies** (☎ 04 90 34 24 24, ⓦ choregies.asso.fr), began in 1879, it marked the first performance at the Théâtre Antique in 350 years. The festival these days consists of one or two opera performances or orchestral concerts each week in July. Tickets cost from €23 to €263. Other concerts, performances and film shows throughout the year are listed on ⓦ theatre-antique.com.

---

standing. Later a fort, slum and prison before its reconstruction in the nineteenth century, the Théâtre now hosts musical performances in summer and is also open as an archeological site.

Spreading a colossal 36m high by 103m wide, its outer face resembles a monstrous prison wall, despite the ground-level archways leading into the backstage areas. Inside, an excellent audioguide paints an evocative picture of its history and architecture. The enormous **stage**, originally sheltered by a mighty awning, could accommodate throngs of performers, while the acoustics allowed a full audience to hear every word.

Though missing most of its original decoration, the inner side of the wall above the stage is extremely impressive. Below columned niches, now empty of their statues, a larger-than-life statue of Augustus, raising his arm in imperious fashion, looks down centre stage. Seating was allocated strictly by rank; an inscription "EQ Gradus III" (third row for knights) remains visible near the orchestra pit.

The best **viewpoint** over the entire theatre, on St-Eutrope hill, can be accessed without paying from both east and west. As you look down towards the stage, the ruins at your feet are those of the short-lived seventeenth-century castle of the princes of Orange. Louis XIV had it destroyed in 1673, and the principality of Orange was officially annexed to France forty years later.

### Musée d'Art et Histoire

Rue Madeleine Roch • Daily: March & Oct 9.45am–12.30pm & 1.30–5.30pm; April, May & Sept 9.15am–6pm; June–Aug 9.15am–7pm; Nov–Feb 9.45am–12.30pm & 1.30–4.30pm • €5.50, or €8.50 with Théâtre Antique • ☎ 04 90 50 17 60, ⓦ theatre-antique.com

The **Musée d'Art et Histoire**, across from the Théâtre, covers local history from the Romans onwards, and also hosts temporary exhibitions. Artefacts taken from the Théâtre complex include the largest known Roman land-survey maps, carved on marble, along with a couple of sphinxes and a mosaic floor.

### Arc de Triomphe

Av de l'Arc de Triomphe • 24hr access

Orange's second major Roman monument, the impressive, triple-bayed **Arc de Triomphe**, occupies a lozenge-shaped traffic island north of the centre. Built around 20 BC, its intricate friezes and reliefs celebrate the victories of the Roman Second Legion against the Gauls.

### ARRIVAL AND INFORMATION                           ORANGE

**By train** The *gare SNCF* is on av Frédéric Mistral, 800m east of the centre.
Destinations Avignon (17 daily; 15min); Paris (2 daily; 2hr 30min).

**By bus** The *gare routière* is on bd Edouard-Daladier, 250m east of the theatre.
Destinations Carpentras (3 daily; 40–45min); Châteauneuf-du-Pape (3 daily; 25min); Séguret (10 daily; 40min); Sérignan (7 daily; 15min); Vaison (10 daily; 40–50min).

**By car** Parking is very limited in the city centre; for short stays, park along cours Aristide Briand, or overnight in the underground car park east of the theatre near the bus station.

**Tourist office** 5 cours Aristide Briand (April–June & Sept Mon–Sat 9am–6.30pm, Sun 10am–1pm & 2–6.30pm; July & Aug Mon–Sat 9am–7.30pm, Sun 10am–1pm & 2–7pm; Oct–March Mon–Sat 10am–1pm & 2–5pm; ☎ 04 90 34 70 88, ⓦ otorange.fr).

16

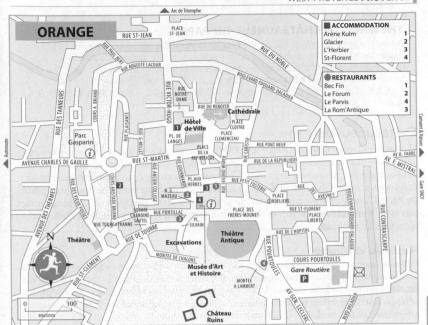

ORANGE

**ACCOMMODATION**
| | |
|---|---|
| Arène Kulm | 1 |
| Glacier | 2 |
| L'Herbier | 3 |
| St-Florent | 4 |

**RESTAURANTS**
| | |
|---|---|
| Bec Fin | 1 |
| Le Forum | 2 |
| Le Parvis | 4 |
| La Rom'Antique | 3 |

16

## ACCOMMODATION

**Arène Kulm** 8 place de Langes ☎04 90 11 40 40, ⓦhotel-arene.fr. Very presentable hotel, with spacious rooms, with a pool and an Italian restaurant, on a quiet, pedestrianized (though not especially attractive) square. The cheapest rooms are in a separate annexe. Annexe **€70**; main hotel **€105**

**Glacier** 46 cours Aristide Briand ☎04 90 34 02 01, ⓦle-glacier.com. Comfortable, cosy Provençal-style rooms – think yellows and blues with pretty quilts and floral curtains. All en suite and a/c, they vary widely in size and amenities. Good breakfasts in the little pavement café downstairs. Closed Nov–Feb Fri–Sun. *Économique* **€50**; standard **€60**

**L'Herbier** 8 place aux Herbes ☎04 90 34 09 23, ⓦlherbierdorange.com. A good budget option, set in a seventeenth-century house overlooking a pretty square near the theatre. Rooms are simple and clean; all have at least showers, and the family rooms are good value. **€59**

**St-Florent** 4 rue du Mazeau ☎04 90 34 18 53, ⓦhotel-orange-saintflorent.com. Very central, inexpensive hotel, with appealingly kitsch decor and a wide range of rooms; some have four-poster beds, all are en suite, and there are some extremely cheap singles. **€57**

## EATING AND DRINKING

**Bec Fin** Rue Segond Weber ☎04 90 34 05 10. Large restaurant, sprawled along a narrow alley with slender views of the theatre. Hearty salads and tasty pizzas for around €12, plus a good €28 dinner *menu* featuring gazpacho, slow-cooked bream and a delicious dessert. Mon–Sat noon–2pm & 7.30–10pm.

**Le Forum** 3 rue du Mazeau ☎04 90 34 01 09. Small, intimate restaurant where *menus* (from €29) revolve around seasonal ingredients; in January, truffles feature heavily, while in May, it's asparagus. Often booked up, so reserve ahead. Mon & Tues 7.30–9.30pm, Thurs–Sun noon–2pm & 7.30–9.30pm.

**Le Parvis** 55 cours Pourtoules ☎04 90 34 82 00. The town's best Provençal food, though the service can be very

slow. Straight from the market, ingredients are whipped up into tempting, good-value dishes such as pikeperch with asparagus *millefeuille*. Lunch *menus* from €14.50, dinner from €28 for three courses. Tues–Sat noon–1.30pm & 7.30–9.15pm; closed last 3 weeks in Nov & last 3 weeks in Jan.

**La Rom'Antique** 5 place Silvain, rue Madeleine Roch ☎04 90 51 67 06, ⓦla-romantique.com. Stylish modern restaurant immediately east of the Roman theatre, serving a €22 *menu* that features a delicious chickpea gazpacho. A few outdoor tables complement the cool, crisp a/c indoor dining room. June–Sept Tues–Fri & Sun noon–2pm & 7.30–9.30pm, Sat 7.30–9.30pm; Oct–May Tues–Fri noon–2pm & 7.30–9.30pm, Sat 7.30–9.30pm, Sun noon–2pm.

> ### THE WINES OF CHÂTEAUNEUF-DU-PAPE
>
> During the first weekend of August, the **Fête de la Véraison** celebrates the ripening of the grapes, with free tasting stalls throughout the village, as well as parades, dances, and equestrian contests. At other times, free **tastings** are available all around the village. The best selection of wines is at **La Maison des Vins**, 8 rue du Maréchal Foch (daily: mid-June to mid-Sept 10am–7pm; mid-Sept to mid-June 10.30am–noon & 2–6.30pm; ☎04 90 83 70 69, ⓦvinadea.com).

## Châteauneuf-du-Pape

The large village of **CHÂTEAUNEUF-DU-PAPE**, between Avignon and Orange, takes its name from the summer palace of the Avignon popes. Its rich ruby-red **wine** ranks among the most renowned in France. Commercial activity centres on the main road that loops around Châteauneuf's small central hill. Walk up from the busy little **place du Portail**, and you're swiftly in a tangle of sleepy, verdant alleyways. A couple of intact castle walls still crown the top of the hill, but they simply define a hollow shell, freely accessible at all times.

### Musée du Vin Brotte

Bd Pierre-de-Luxembourg • Daily: May to mid-Oct 9am–1pm & 2–7pm; mid-Oct to April 9am–noon & 2–6pm • Free • ☎04 90 83 70 07

The best place to learn about local wines of Châteauneuf-du-Pape is the **Musée du Vin Brotte**, southwest of the centre. As well as providing a good historical overview of the wine industry, covering regional geology, it illustrates traditional tools and techniques, offers free tasting, and sells the Brotte family's own wine.

### INFORMATION
### CHÂTEAUNEUF-DU-PAPE

**Tourist office** Place du Portail (June–Sept Mon–Sat 9.30am–6pm; Oct–May Mon, Tues & Thurs–Sat 9.30am–12.30pm & 2–6pm; ☎04 90 83 71 08, ⓦccpro.fr /tourisme).

### ACCOMMODATION AND EATING

**Garbure** 3 rue Joseph-Ducos ☎04 90 83 75 08, ⓦla -garbure.com. Cosy, very central village hotel, with eight cheerful rooms and an excellent restaurant, with dinner *menus* from €28 and terrace seating. Restaurant closed Sun & Mon, hotel closed three weeks in Nov. **€76**
**Le Verger des Papes** 4 montée du Château ☎04 90 83 50 40, ⓦvergerdespapes.com. This delightful hilltop restaurant, well away from the traffic near the château, serves traditional food on a peaceful panoramic terrace with *menus* at €19 for lunch, €30 for dinner. July & Aug Mon–Sat noon–2pm & 7.30–9.30pm, Sun noon–2pm; Sept–May Tues–Sat noon–2pm & 7.30–9.30pm, Sun noon–2pm.

## Vaison-la-Romaine

The charming old town of **VAISON-LA-ROMAINE**, 27km northeast of Orange, is divided into two distinct halves, connected by a single-arched Roman bridge across the River Ouvèze. Throughout its history, Vaison's centre has shifted from one side to the other. Now known as the **Haute Ville**, and topped by a ruined twelfth-century castle, the steep, forbidding hill south of the river was the site of the original Celtic settlement. The **Romans**, however, built their homes on the flatter land north of the river. That's now the modern town centre, so the medieval Haute Ville remains a self-contained and largely unspoiled village.

### Roman ruins

Av Général-de-Gaulle • Daily: Feb, Nov & Dec 10am–noon & 2–5pm; March & Oct 10am–12.30pm & 2–5.30pm; April & May 9.30am–6pm; June–Sept 9.30am–6.30pm • €8 with cathedral cloisters

Vaison's two excavated **Roman residential districts** lie either side of the main road through the town centre. While you can peek through the railings for free, you'll get a much better sense if you pay for admission, which also enables you to visit the excellent museum.

### Vestiges de Puymin

The eastern portion of Vaison's archeological district, the **Vestiges de Puymin**, stretches up a gentle hillside. The ground plans of several mansions and houses are discernible in the foreground, while higher up the **museum** holds all sorts of detail and decoration unearthed from the ruins. Everyday artefacts include mirrors of silvered bronze, lead water pipes, weights and measures, taps shaped as griffins' feet and dolphin doorknobs, and there are also some impressive statues and stelae. A tunnel through the hillside leads to an ancient Roman **theatre**, which still seats seven thousand people during the July **dance festival** (ⓦvaison-danses.com)

### Vestiges de la Villasse

Vaison's smaller, western Roman ruins, the **Vestiges de la Villasse**, reveal a clear picture of the layout of a comfortable, well-serviced Roman town. As well as a row of arcaded shops, they include patrician houses (some with mosaics still intact), a basilica and the baths.

## Haute Ville

From the south side of the **Pont Romain**, the sturdy ancient bridge across the River Ouvèze, a cobbled lane climbs upwards towards place du Poids and the fourteenth-century gateway to the medieval **Haute Ville**. More steep zigzags take you past the Gothic gate and overhanging portcullis and into the heart of this sedately quiet, largely uncommercialized *quartier*. All the squares hold pretty fountains and flowers, and right at the top, from the twelfth- to sixteenth-century **castle**, you'll have a great view of Mont Ventoux. Every Tuesday in summer, Vaison's **market** spreads up into the Haute Ville.

**16**

### ARRIVAL AND INFORMATION

VAISON-LA-ROMAINE

**By bus** The *gare routière* is on av des Choralies, east of the centre.
Destinations Avignon (3 daily; 1hr 25min); Orange (10 daily; 40–50min).

**Tourist office** Place du Chanoine-Sautel, between the two Roman sites; free wi-fi (mid-May to June Mon–Fri

9.30am–1pm & 2–5.45pm, Sat 9.30am–noon & 2–5.45pm, Sun 9.30am–noon; July & Aug Mon–Fri 9.30am–6.45pm, Sat & Sun 9.30am–12.30pm & 2–6.45pm; Sept to mid-May Mon–Sat 9.30am–noon & 2–5.45pm, Sun 9.30am–noon & 2–5.45pm; ☎04 90 36 02 11, ⓦvaison-la-romaine.com).

### ACCOMMODATION

★ **Le Beffroi** Rue de l'Évêché ☎04 90 36 04 71, ⓦle -beffroi.com. Beautiful, luxurious sixteenth-century residence in a lovely setting in the Haute Ville, with a pool, and a great restaurant where the terrace enjoys unsurpassable views over the valley. Hotel closed Feb–March; restaurant closed Tues, and Nov–March. **€115**

**Burrhus** 1 place Montfort ☎04 90 36 00 11, ⓦburrhus .com. Large, modern if somewhat characterless rooms in the heart of town, with tiled floors and very comfortable beds. It can be noisy at weekends, but the sunny breakfast balcony is a real plus. **€65**

**Camping du Théâtre Romain** Chemin du Brusquet, off av des Choralies, quartier des Arts ☎04 90 28 78 66,

ⓦcamping-theatre.com. Small, four-star campsite, 500m northeast of the centre and 150m from the Roman theatre, with good facilities and an emphasis on peaceful family fun. Reserve well ahead in summer. Closed early Nov to mid-March. **€22.50**

★ **L'Évêche** 14 rue de l'Évêche ☎04 90 36 13 46, ⓦeveche.free.fr. This lovely B&B, in the Haute Ville, has comfortable modern rooms and a homely atmosphere. Enjoy coffee and croissants on the little terrace at the back. **€84**

**La Fête en Provence** Place du Vieux Marché ☎04 90 36 36 43, ⓦhotellafete-provence.com. Gorgeous, comfortable rooms and apartments, surrounding a pool and flower-decked patio, in the Haute Ville. **€75**

### EATING AND DRINKING

**L'Auberge de la Bartavelle** 12 place Sus-Auze ☎04 90 36 02 16. A lively place in an otherwise drab square in the modern town, with decent and affordable specialities from southwest France – rabbit ravioli, *confit de canard* and the like – on *menus* from €16 at lunch, €22 at dinner.

Black-and-white photos honour Provençal novelist and film-maker Marcel Pagnol. Feb–Dec Tues–Thurs, Sat & Sun noon–1.30pm & 7.30–9.30pm, Fri 7.30–9.30pm.

**Le Brin d'Olivier** 4 rue de Ventoux ☎04 90 28 74 79. Welcoming Provençal restaurant, serving lunch *menus*

from €18 and dinner *menus* from €29. It's down towards the river, though its pretty courtyard has no views. Mon, Tues, Thurs, Fri & Sun noon–1.30pm & 7.30–9.30pm; Wed & Sat 7.30–9.30pm; closed Wed Oct–June.
**La Lyriste** 45 cours Taulignan ☏ 04 90 36 04 67. On this quiet boulevard, just north of place Montfort, the *Lyriste* stands out for its changing, high-quality *menus*, based around themes like cheese, exotic fruits or scallops. The simple €19 *menu découverte* is great value. Tues & Thurs–Sun noon–1.30pm & 7.30–9.30pm, Wed 7.30–9.30pm.

## Mont Ventoux

**MONT VENTOUX**, whose outline repeatedly appears upon the horizon from the Rhône and Durance valleys, rises some 20km east of Vaison. White with snow, black with storm-cloud shadow or reflecting myriad shades of blue, the barren pebbles of the uppermost 300m are like a weathervane for all of western Provence. Winds can accelerate to 250km per hour around the meteorological, TV and military masts and dishes on the summit, but if you can stand still for a moment the view in all directions is unbelievable.

Long renowned as among the most fearsome challenges on the Tour de France, the climb up Mont Ventoux is attempted by hundreds of **cyclists** each day in summer. Most start at one of two small towns low on its western flanks – **MALAUCÈNE**, on the D938 10km southeast of Vaison, or livelier **BEDOIN**, another dozen kilometres southeast. The D974 loops between the two via the summit of Mont Ventoux, a total haul of 42km; the anticlockwise circuit from Bedoin offers a marginally gentler gradient. Coming this way, you reach a stone cairn 1km short of the very top, well above the tree line, that commemorates British cyclist **Tom Simpson**, who died here in 1967 from heart failure on one of the hottest days ever recorded in the Tour de France. According to race folklore his last words were "Put me back on the bloody bike."

## Dentelles de Montmirail

Running northeast to southwest between Vaison and Carpentras, the jagged hilly backdrop of the **DENTELLES DE MONTMIRAIL** is best appreciated from the contrasting landscape of level fields, orchards and vineyards lying to their south and west. The range is named after lace (*dentelles*) – the limestone protrusions were thought to resemble the contorted pins on a lace-making board – though the alternative connection with teeth (*dents*) is equally appropriate.

The area is best known for its wines. On the western and southern slopes lie the wine-producing villages of **Gigondas**, **Séguret**, **Beaumes-de-Venise**, **Sablet**, **Vacqueyras** and, across the River Ouvèze, **Rasteau**. Each carries the distinction of having its own individual *appellation contrôlée* within the Côtes du Rhône or Côtes du Rhône Villages areas: in other words, their wines are exceptional.

### Séguret

The star Dentelles village is **SÉGURET**, whose name means "safe place" in Provençal. This alluring spot, 9km southwest of Vaison-la-Romaine, blends into the side of a rocky cliff; a ruined castle soars high above. Amid its steep cobbled streets, vine-covered houses and medieval structures, look out for an old stone laundry and a belfry with a one-handed clock. The **Fête des Vins et Festival Provençal Bravade** in the last two weeks of August involves processions for the Virgin Mary and the patron saint of wine growers.

### Gigondas

**GIGONDAS**, 14km southwest of Seguret, is a worthwhile stop, its main draw being its exquisite **red wine**, which is strong with an aftertaste of spice and nuts. Sampling the varieties could not be easier; the **Syndicat des Vins** runs a *caveau des vignerons* (daily 10am–noon & 2–6pm) in place de la Mairie where you can taste and ask advice about the produce from forty different *domaines*.

**16**

## INFORMATION

### GIGONDAS

**Tourist office** Place du Portail (April–June, Sept & Oct Mon–Sat 10am–12.30pm & 2.30–6pm; July & Aug

## ACCOMMODATION AND EATING

### SÉGURET

**Bastide Bleue** Rte de Sablet ☎ 04 90 46 83 43, ⓦ bastidebleue.com. This delightful rural villa, at the foot of the hill below Séguret, offers simple but attractive en-suite rooms, plus a pool. Its rustic dining room, closed Tues & Wed in low season, serves good *menus* from €27 in the evening. Rates include breakfast. **€85**

### GIGONDAS

**Les Florets** Rte des Dentelles ☎ 04 90 65 85 01, ⓦ hotel-lesflorets.com. Charming hotel, 2km north of Gigondas towards Séguret, with elegant and very comfortable rooms and an excellent restaurant (closed

## DENTELLES DE MONTMIRAIL

Mon–Sat 10am–12.30pm & 2.30–6.30pm, Sun 10am–1pm; Nov–March Mon–Sat 10am–noon & 2–5pm; ☎ 04 90 65 85 46, ⓦ gigondas-dm.fr).

Wed) that serves *menus* from €25 lunch, €32 dinner. Closed Jan to mid-March. **€110**

**Gîte d'Etape des Dentelles** Le village ☎ 04 90 65 80 85, ⓦ gite-dentelles.com. This simple, inexpensive *gîte*, at the entrance to the village, offers two large shared dorms, ten very plain double rooms, and one triple, none of them en suite. Closed Jan & Feb. Dorms **€15**, doubles **€34**

**L'Oustalet** Place du Village ☎ 04 90 65 85 30, ⓦ restaurant-oustalet.fr. Thanks to a dynamic young chef, this modern restaurant, with seating indoors and out on a pleasant shaded terrace, offers the best dining in the village centre. Full dinner *menus* start at €39. Tues–Sat noon–1.30pm & 7.30–9.15pm; also Sun noon–1.30pm in summer.

# Carpentras

The faded provincial town of **CARPENTRAS** dates back to 5 BC, when it was the capital of a Celtic tribe. The Greeks who founded Marseille came to Carpentras to buy honey, wheat, goats and skins, and the Romans had a base here. For a brief period in the fourteenth century, it became the papal headquarters and gave protection to Jews expelled from France.

In Carpentras today, immaculately restored squares and fountains alternate with decayed streets of seventeenth- and eighteenth-century houses, some forming arcades over the pavement.

## Synagogue du Carpentras and around

Place Juiverie • Mon–Thurs 10am–noon & 3–5pm, Fri 10am–noon & 3–4pm; closed Jewish holidays • Free • ☎ 04 90 63 39 97

A seventeenth-century construction on fourteenth-century foundations, the **Synagogue du Carpentras** is the oldest surviving place of Jewish worship in France. The **Porte Juif**, on the southern side of the fifteenth-century **Cathédrale St-Siffrein** nearby, is so named because Jews used to pass through it to enter the cathedral in chains. Inside, they would be unshackled as converted Christians.

## ARRIVAL AND INFORMATION

**CARPENTRAS**

**By bus** Buses arrive either at the *gare routière* on place Terradou (from Avignon, Vaison, and other points north and west), or on av Victor-Hugo (from Marseille, Aix and Cavaillon). Destinations Cavaillon (2–5 daily; 45min); Gigondas (1–3 daily; 30min); L'Isle-sur-la-Sorgue (5 daily; 20min); Marseille (3 daily; 1hr 15min–2hr 5min); Orange (3 daily;

40–45min); Vaison (4 daily; 45min).
**Tourist office** 97 place du 25 aout 1944 (July & Aug Mon–Sat 9am–1pm & 2–7pm, Sun 9.30am–1pm; Sept–June Mon & Wed–Sat 9.30am–12.30pm & 2–6pm, Tues 9.30am–12.30pm & 3–6pm; ☎ 04 90 63 00 78, ⓦ carpentras-ventoux.com).

## ACCOMMODATION

**Comtadin** 65 bd Albin-Durand ☎ 04 90 67 75 00, ⓦ le -comtadin.com. Nicely restored traditional hotel, a short walk west of the tourist office, offering light, double-glazed rooms and a sunny breakfast patio. **€90**

**Fiacre** 153 rue Vigne ☎ 04 90 63 03 15, ⓦ hotel-du -fiacre.com. Grand eighteenth-century townhouse, with a central courtyard; nicely decorated rooms, two with terraces; and friendly owners. **€72**

16

**Logis des Jeunes du Comtat Venaissin** 200 rue Robert-Lacoste ☎ 04 90 67 13 95, ⊕ carpentras-ventoux .com. Simple accommodation in 4- or 5-bed dorms, 2km southeast of the centre near the Pierre de Coubertin sports centre. Pool, table tennis, and a cafeteria. **€14.50**

**Lou Comtadou** Rte St-Didier, 881 av Pierre-de-Coubertin ☎ 04 90 67 03 16, ⊕ campingloucomtadou.

com. Very pleasant, well equipped four-star campsite, in shaded rural surroundings 1km south of the centre. Closed Nov–Feb. **€24**

**Malaga** 37 place Maurice-Charretier ☎ 04 90 60 57 96, ⊕ lemalaga@orange.fr. Eight clean en-suite rooms, rather kitsch but perfectly satisfactory for budget travellers, above a decent central brasserie. **€40**

### EATING AND DRINKING

**Chez Serge** 90 rue Cottier ☎ 04 90 63 21 24, ⊕ chez -serge.com. Sleek bistro serving daily *plats* on its tree-shaded terrace. The lunch *menu* is €15, and dinner *menus* start at €34, with a major emphasis on truffles; there's also a wide selection of €10 pizzas. Daily noon–2pm & 7.30–10pm.

**Patisserie Jouvaud** 40 rue de l'Evêche ☎ 04 90 63 15 38. This cosy tearoom and patisserie, which also has three tables

on the pedestrian street outside, makes a fabulous stopoff for tea and cakes. Daily 10am–8pm.

**Petite Fontaine** 13/17 place du Colonel Mouret ☎ 04 90 60 77 83, ⊕ lapetitefontaine84.fr. Cheery restaurant, beside a little fountain, that serves delicious fresh food, with a €25 *menu*. Mon, Tues & Thurs–Sat noon–1.30pm & 7.30–9.30pm.

# Avignon

Capital of the Catholic Church during the early Middle Ages and for centuries a major artistic centre, **AVIGNON** remains an unmissable destination. During the **Festival d'Avignon** in July, it becomes *the* place to be in Provence.

Low medieval **walls** still encircle Avignon's old centre, as it nestles up against a ninety-degree bend in the Rhône river. Their gates and towers restored, the ramparts dramatically mark the historic core off from the formless sprawl of the modern city beyond. Despite their menacing crenellations, however, they were never a formidable defence. The major monuments occupy a compact quarter up against the river, just beyond the principal **place de l'Horloge**, at the northern end of rue de la République, the chief axis of the old town.

Yes, Avignon can be dauntingly crowded, and stiflingly hot, in summer. But it's worth persevering, not simply for the colossal **Palais des Papes**, home to the medieval popes, and its fine crop of museums and ancient churches, but also the sheer life and energy that throbs through its lanes and alleyways.

---

## POPES AND ANTIPOPES – THE INTRIGUING HISTORY OF AVIGNON

The first **pope** to come to Avignon, **Clement V**, was invited by the astute King Philippe le Bel in 1309, ostensibly to protect him from impending anarchy in Rome. In reality, Philip saw a chance to extend his power by keeping the pope in Provence, during what came to be known as the Church's "Babylonian captivity". Clement's successor, **Jean XXII**, who had previously been bishop of Avignon, re-installed himself happily in the episcopal palace. The next Supreme Pontiff, **Benedict XII**, acceded in 1334; accepting the impossibility of returning to Rome, he replaced the bishop's palace with an austere fortress, now known as the **Vieux Palais**.

Though Gregory XI finally moved the Holy See back to Rome in 1378, this didn't mark the end of the papacy here. After Gregory's death in Rome, dissident local cardinals elected their own pope in Avignon, provoking the Western Schism, a ruthless struggle for control of the Church's wealth. That lasted until **Benedict XIII** – now officially deemed to have been an **antipope** – fled into self-exile near Valencia in 1409. It was Benedict who built Avignon's walls in 1403, when under siege by French forces loyal to Rome. Avignon itself remained papal property until the Revolution.

As home to one of Europe's richest courts, fourteenth-century Avignon attracted princes, dignitaries, poets and raiders, who arrived to beg from, rob, extort and entertain the popes. According to Petrarch, the overcrowded, plague-ridden papal entourage was "a sewer where all the filth of the universe has gathered".

## Palais des Papes

Daily: first half of March 9am–6.30pm; mid-March to June & mid-Sept to Oct 9am–7pm; July & first half of Sept 9am–8pm; Aug 9am–9pm; Nov–Feb 9.30am–5.45pm; last ticket 1hr before closing • €10.50, or €13 with Pont St-Bénézet; €8.50/10 with Avignon Passion pass (see p.820) • ☎ 04 32 74 32 74, ⓦ palais-des-papes.com

Avignon's vast **Palais des Papes** soars above the cobbled place du Palais at the north end of the walled city, overlooking the curving Rhône. Although the palace was built primarily as a fortress, and equipped with massive stone vaults and battlements, the two pointed towers that hover above its gate are incongruously graceful. Inside, so little remains of its original decoration and furnishings that the denuded interior leaves hardly a whiff of the corruption and decadence of fat, feuding cardinals and their mistresses; the thronging purveyors of jewels, velvet and furs; the musicians, chefs and painters competing for patronage; and the riotous banquets and corridor schemings.

### Vieux Palais

Steered by multimedia audioguides, visits to the Palais des Papes begin in the original **Vieux Palais**, constructed from 1335 onwards, under Benedict XII. The first building you enter, the **Pope's Tower**, is accessed via the vaulted **Treasury**, where the Church's deeds and finances were handled. Four large holes in the floor of the smaller downstairs room, now covered by glass, held the papal gold and jewels. The same cunning storage device was used in the **Chambre du Camérier** or Chamberlain's Quarters, off the Jesus Hall upstairs. In the adjoining **Papal Vestiary**, the Pope had a small library and would dress before receiving sovereigns and ambassadors in the **Consistoire** of the Vieux Palais, on the other side of the Jesus Hall.

On the floor above, the **kitchen** offers powerful testimony to the scale of papal gluttony. Major feasts were held in the **Grand Tinel**, or dining room, where only the pope was allowed to wield a knife. During the conclave that elected a new pope, the cardinals were locked into this room, adjourning to conspire in chambers to the south and west.

### Palais Neuf

Despite its name, the **Palais Neuf** is only a few years newer than the Vieux Palais – it was erected by the next Pope, Clement VI. Both his bedroom and his study, the **Chambre du Cerf**, bear witness to his secular concerns, and provide the tour's first dash of colour. The walls in the former are adorned with wonderful entwined oak- and vine-leaf motifs, the latter with superb hunting and fishing scenes. Austerity resumes in the cathedral-like proportions of the **Grande Chapelle**, or **Chapelle Clementine**, beyond, and in the **Grande Audience**, its twin in terms of volume on the floor below.

The circuit also includes a walk along the roof terraces, which offer such tremendous views that it's worth heading up a little higher to the rooftop café even when the signs insist it's closed.

## Petit Palais

Daily except Tues 10am–1pm & 2–6pm • €6 • ☎ 04 90 86 44 58, ⓦ petit-palais.org

Immediately north of the Palais de Papes, the **Petit Palais** contains a first-rate collection of thirteenth- to fifteenth-century painting and sculpture, mostly by masters from northern Italian cities. Visitors can watch as the masters wrestle with and finally conquer the representation of perspective – a revolution from medieval art, where the size of figures depended on their importance rather than position within the picture.

## Pont St-Bénézet

Daily: first half of March 9am–6.30pm; mid-March to June & mid-Sept to Oct 9am–7pm; July & first half of Sept 9am–8pm; Aug 9am–9pm; Nov–Feb 9.30am–5.45pm; last ticket 1hr before closing • €4.50, or €13 with Palais des Papes • ☎ 04 32 74 32 74, ⓦ palais-des-papes.com

Now merely jutting halfway out to the Île de Barthelasse, the twelfth-century **Pont St-Bénézet** originally reached all the way to Villeneuve, and was the only bridge to

▲ 1

Boat to Île de
la Barthelasse

Swimming
Pool

Pont St-Bénézet

BOULEVARD DE LA LIGNE

ÎLE DE LA BARTHELASSE

CHEMIN DE L'ÎLE PIOT

ⓘ Porte du Rocher

Rocher des
Doms

CHEMIN DE BAGATELLE

3

4

BOULEVARD DU RHÔNE

RUE REMPART DU RHÔNE

RUE LIMAS

RUE FERRUCE

Petit
Palais

Cathédrale
Notre-Dame-
des-Doms

Cinema
Utopia

1

2

Villeneuve-lès-Avignon ◀

Free Parking ◀

PONT DALADIER

CHEMIN DE L'ÎLE PIOT

RUE LIMASSET

RUE GRANDE FUSTERIE

RUE DE LA BALANCE

2

PLACE DU
PALAIS

CHEMIN DE L'ÎLE PIOT

RUE LIMAS

RUE DES GROTTES

RUE CHIRON

3

Porte de l'Oulle

RUE ST-ÉTIENNE

Conservatoire
de Musique

PLACE
CRILLON

R. BARONCELLI

5

RUE VILAR

Palais des
Papes

7

RUE PETROLERIE

PLACE
CHÂTAIGNES

River Rhône

ALLÉE DE L'OULLE

BOULEVARD DE L'OULLE

RUE DE LA PLAISANCE

6

RUE DU MAIL

RUE PETITE FUSTERIE

3

RUE RACINE

Opéra

6

Hôtel de
Ville

PLACE DE
L'HORLOGE

RUE DE MONS

4

Maison
Jean Vilar

RUE BANASTERIE

RUE BANASTERIE

16

PASSAGE DE L'ORATOIRE

RUE JOSEPH VERNET

St-Agricol

RUE ST-AGRICOL

9

RUE FÉLIX GRAS

Palais
du Roure

PLACE DE
CHANGE

8

St-Pierre

PLACE
CARNOT

RUE DES MARCHANDS

PLACE DE LA
PRINCIPALE

RUE DU VIEUX-

RUE SAINT-THOMAS D'AQUIN

RUE ST-ANDRÉ

RUE PTE. CALADE

RUE VIALA

RUE DU ROURE

RUE DE LA RÉPUBLIQUE

RUE BANCASSE

RUE GALANTE

RUE FIGUIÈRE

RUE COLLÈGE DE LA CROIX

RUE VICTOR HUGO

Musée
Calvet

RUE BASILE

RUE DE LA BOUQUERIE

St-Didier

RUE DU ROI RENE

Musée
Vouland

RUE D'ANNANELLE

RUE SAINT-ANDRÉ

RUE LANTERNE

Musée
Requien

RUE HORACE VERNET

PLACE
ST-DIDIER

Mediathèque
Ceccano

RUE DES 3 FAUCONS

Porte
St-Dominique

RUE BOISSERIN

Musée
Lapidaire

RUE F. MISTRAL

Musée
Angladon

RUE DES ÉTUDES

BOULEVARD ST-DOMINIQUE

RUE VÉLOUTERIE

RUE ST-CHARLES

RUE JOSEPH VERNET

RUE VIOLETTE

Collection
Lambert

9

RUE DU PORTAIL BOQUIER

COURS JEAN-JAURÈS

ⓘ

13

Agricole
Perdiguier

RUE DES LICES

PLACE DES
CORPS
SAINTS

14

RUE ST-MICHEL

BOULEVARD RASPAIL

10

RUE DE L'OBSERVANCE

RUE ST-CHARLES

BOULEVARD RASPAIL

RUE AGRICOL PERDIGUIER

TCRA
Office

RUE DE LA BOURSE

11

Porte
St-Roch

RUE DU REMPART SAINT-ROCH

AVENUE L. DE TASSIGNY

Anc. Couvent
des Célestins

Nîmes ◀

BOULEVARD ST-ROCH

COURS PRES KENNEDY

Porte de
la République

RUE PAUL-MÉRINDOL

AVENUE EISENHOWER

Porte
St-Charles

AVENUE DE BLANCHISSAGE

BOULEVARD ST-ROCH

AVENUE MONCLAR-NORD

AVIGNON

PLACE DE LA
RÉPUBLIQUE

Gare SNCF

Gare
Routière

▼ Gare TGV

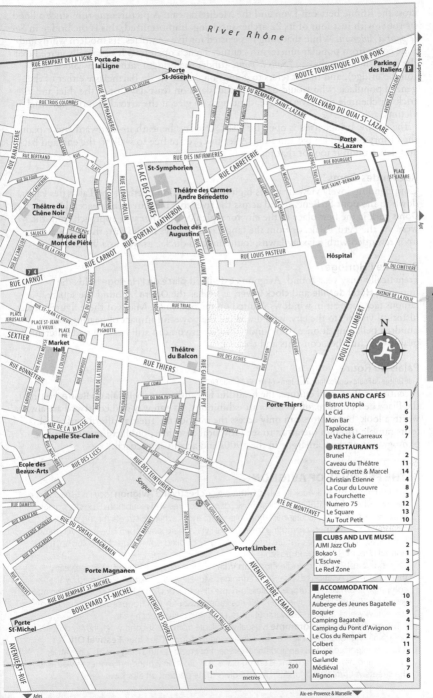

**River Rhône**

Orange & Carpentras

Parking
des Italiens P

RUE REMPART DE LA LIGNE

Porte de
la Ligne

Porte
St-Joseph

ROUTE TOURISTIQUE DU DR PONS

RUE TROIS COLOMBES

RUE JOSEPH

RUE DU REMPART SAINT-LAZARE

BOULEVARD DU QUAI ST-LAZARE

AVENUE DES ITALIENS

RUE PALAPHARNERIE

RUE PERSIL

RUE TAMISEY

RUE DE LA TOUR

Apt

RUE BANASTERIE

RUE BERTRAND

RUE DES INFIRMIERES

Porte
St-Lazare

RUE DU FOUR

RUE STE-CATHERINE

RUE 3
PLATS

RUE CARRETERIE

RUE GEORGES MAULIER

RUE BOURGUET

PLACE
ST-LAZARE

R. SAUCES

RUE SIGOUETTE

RUE CAMPANE

RUE LEDRU-ROLLIN

St-Symphorien

RUE SAINT-BERNARD

Théâtre du
Chêne Noir

PLACE DES CARMES

Théâtre des Carmes
Andre Bénedetto

RUE DE LA CARREE

RUE PICPUS

Musée du
Mont de Piété

RUE PORTAIL MATHERON

Clocher des
Augustins

RUE BARALLERIE

RUE POMMIER

Hôpital

RUE DE L'AMELIER

RUE DE LA CROIX

RUE CARNOT

RUE GUILLAUME PUY

RUE LOUIS PASTEUR

AV. DU CIMETIERE

7 4

RUE CARNOT

RUE DU CHAPEAU ROUGE

RUE PONT TROUCA

RUE HOTEL DAME DES SEPT

AVENUE DE LA FOLIE

16

PLACE
JERUSALEM

RUE ST-JEAN LE VIEUX

RUE TRIAL

PLACE
PIGNOTTE

RUE BON PASTEUR

N

SEXTIER

PLACE ST-JEAN
LE VIEUX

PLACE
PIE

10

Market
Hall

RUE PETITE MEUSE

RUE DE L'OLIVIER

RUE AMPHOUX

RUE DU FOUR DE LA TERRE

Théâtre
du Balcon

RUE DES ECOIES

RUE BUFFON

POULLOURS

BOULEVARD LIMBERT

RUE BONNETERIE

RUE THIERS

RUE GRIVOLAS

RUE PHILOMARDE

RUE COMU

Porte Thiers

RUE DE LA MASSE

RUE FRANCK

RUE GUILLAUME PUY

RUE DU BON PASTEUR

RUE ROQUILLE

Chapelle Ste-Claire

RUE NOEL BIRET

RUE ST-CHRISTOPHE

Ecole des
Beaux-Arts

RUE DES LICES

RUE DES TEINTURIERS

RUE CASSAN

RTE DE MONTFAVET

RUE DAMETTE

Sorgue

RUE BON MARTINET

RUE GUILLAUME PUY

12

RUE BARACANE

RUE DU PORTAIL MAGNANEN

RUE TARASQUE

Porte Limbert

RUE GRANDE MONNAIE

RUE DE L'AIGROLON

Porte Magnanen

AVENUE PIERRE SEMARD

Porte
St-Michel

RUE DU REMPART ST-MICHEL

BOULEVARD ST-MICHEL

AVENUE ST-RUF

AVENUE DES SOURCES

AVENUE DE LA TRILLADE

0          200
metres

Arles

Aix-en-Provence & Marseille

● **BARS AND CAFÉS**
| | |
|---|---|
| Bistrot Utopia | 1 |
| Le Cid | 6 |
| Mon Bar | 5 |
| Tapalocas | 9 |
| Le Vache à Carreaux | 7 |

● **RESTAURANTS**
| | |
|---|---|
| Brunel | 2 |
| Caveau du Théâtre | 11 |
| Chez Ginette & Marcel | 14 |
| Christian Étienne | 4 |
| La Cour du Louvre | 8 |
| La Fourchette | 3 |
| Numero 75 | 12 |
| Le Square | 13 |
| Au Tout Petit | 10 |

■ **CLUBS AND LIVE MUSIC**
| | |
|---|---|
| AJMI Jazz Club | 2 |
| Bokao's | 1 |
| L'Esclave | 3 |
| Le Red Zone | 4 |

■ **ACCOMMODATION**
| | |
|---|---|
| Angleterre | 10 |
| Auberge des Jeunes Bagatelle | 3 |
| Boquier | 9 |
| Camping Bagatelle | 4 |
| Camping du Pont d'Avignon | 1 |
| Le Clos du Rempart | 2 |
| Colbert | 11 |
| Europe | 5 |
| Garlande | 8 |
| Médiéval | 7 |
| Mignon | 6 |

cross the Rhône between Lyon and the Mediterranean. A picturesque ruin since a flood in 1668, with just four of its 22 arches surviving, immortalized, this is the bridge in *Sur le pont d'Avignon*. While that song has existed for five centuries, its modern words and tune come from popular nineteenth-century French operettas. It's generally agreed that the lyrics should really say "*Sous le pont*" (under the bridge) rather than "*Sur le pont*" (on the bridge), and that it refers to goings-on on the Île de Barthelasse either of the general populace, who would dance on the island on feast days, or of the thief and trickster clientele of a tavern there, dancing with glee at the arrival of more potential victims.

The narrow bridge itself is open for visits. Displays beneath its landward end explain the history of both bridge and song. After that, you're free to walk to the end and back, and dance upon it too for that matter.

## Rocher des Doms

Commanding lovely views from its high hilltop position north of the Palais des Papes, down to the pont St-Bénézet and across the river to Villeneuve, the peaceful **Rocher des Doms** park is the best place in the city for a picnic. Whether you approach from the west, via the Petit Palais, or from the tangle of alleyways to the east, the steep climb up is rewarded with relaxing lawns, fountains and ducks, as well as a little café.

## Place de l'Horloge

Frenetically busy year-round, Avignon's café-lined **place de l'Horloge** holds the imposing **Hôtel de Ville** and **clock tower**, as well as the **Opéra**. Around the square, famous faces appear in windows painted on the buildings. Many of these figures depict historical visitors to the city, who described the powerful impact of hearing over a hundred bells ring at once. On Sunday mornings you can still hear myriad different peals from churches, convents and chapels.

## Palais du Roure

3 rue Collège du Roure • Guided tours Tues 3pm • €4.60 • ☎ 04 90 80 80 88

A centre for Provençal culture, the beautiful fifteenth-century **Palais du Roure**, south of the Place de l'Horloge, often hosts art exhibitions. Its gateway and courtyard are always worth a look, but visitors can only access the interior on Tuesday afternoons, when tours ramble through the attics to see Provençal costumes, publications and presses, photographs of the Camargue in the 1900s and an old stagecoach.

---

### THE FESTIVAL OF AVIGNON

Starting in the second week in July, the three-week **Festival d'Avignon** focuses especially on theatre, while also featuring classical music, dance, lectures and exhibitions. The city's great buildings make a spectacular backdrop to performances, while its streets throng with bright-eyed performers promoting their shows. Everywhere stays open late, and everything from accommodation to obscure fringe events gets booked up very quickly; doing anything normal becomes virtually impossible.

Founded in 1947 by actor-director **Jean Vilar**, the festival has included, over the years, theatrical interpretations as diverse as Euripides, Molière and Chekhov, performed by companies from across Europe. While big-name directors draw the largest crowds to the main venue, the Cour d'Honneur in the Palais des Papes, lesser-known troupes and directors also stage new works, and the festival spotlights a different culture each year.

The main **festival programme** is usually available from the second week in May on ⓦ festival-avignon.com; tickets go on sale around mid-June. The fringe **Festival Off** (ⓦ avignonleoff.com) adds an additional element of craziness and magic, with innovative, obscure and bizarre performances taking place in more than a hundred venues as well as in the streets. A *Carte Public Adhérent* for €16 gives thirty percent off all shows.

## Place Pie and around

Avignon's main **pedestrianized area** stretches between the chainstore blandness of rue de la République and the jaw-dropping modern **market hall** on **place Pie**, active every morning except Monday. **Rue des Marchands** and **rue du Vieux-Sextier** have their complement of chapels and late medieval mansions, while the Renaissance **church of St-Pierre** on place St-Pierre (Mon–Wed & Sun 10am–1pm; Thurs–Sat 10am–1pm & 2–6pm) has superb doors, sculpted in 1551, and an altarpiece dating from the same period. To the south on place St-Didier, more Renaissance art is on show in the fourteenth-century **church of St-Didier** (daily 8am–6.30pm), chiefly *The Carrying of the Cross* by Francesco Laurana, commissioned by King René of Provence in 1478.

South of place Pie is the **Chapelle Ste-Claire**, where the poet Petrarch first saw and fell in love with Laura, during the Good Friday service in 1327. A little way east, the atmospheric **rue des Teinturiers** was a centre for calico printing during the eighteenth and nineteenth centuries. The cloth was washed in the Sorgue canal, which still runs alongside, though the four of its mighty watermills that survive no longer turn.

## Musée Angladon

5 rue Labourer • Mid-April to mid-Nov Tues–Sun 1–6pm; mid-Nov to mid-April Wed–Sun 1–6pm • €6 • ☎ 04 90 82 29 03, ⓦ angladon.com

The **Musée Angladon** preserves the private collection of *couturier* Jacques Doucet. Apart from Antonio Forbera's extraordinary *Le Chavalet du Peintre*, a trompe l'oeil painting from 1686 depicting the artist's easel, complete with sketches and palette as well as work in progress, the older works are largely unexceptional. Doucet's contemporary collection, however, includes Modigliani's *The Pink Blouse*, various Picassos, including a self-portrait from 1904, and Van Gogh's *The Railroad Cars*, his only Provençal painting on permanent display in the region.

## Musée Calvet

65 rue Joseph-Vernet • Daily except Tues 10am–1pm & 2–6pm • €6, or €7 with Musée Lapidaire • ☎ 04 90 86 33 84, ⓦ musee-calvet-avignon.com

The excellent, airy **Musée Calvet** is housed in a lovely eighteenth-century palace. Highlights include a wonderful gallery of languorous nineteenth-century marble sculptures, among them Bosio's *Young Indian*; the Puech collection of silverware and Italian and Dutch paintings; and works by Soutine, Manet and Joseph Vernet, as well as Jacques-Louis David's subtle, moving *Death of Joseph Barra*. It also holds much more ancient artefacts, like enigmatic stelae from the fourth-century BC, carved with half-discernible faces, and Bronze Age axes.

## Musée Lapidaire

27 rue de la République • Daily except Mon 10am–1pm & 2–6pm • €2, or €7 with Musée Calvet • ☎ 04 90 84 75 38, ⓦ musee-calvet-avignon.com

At the **Musée Lapidaire**, a former Baroque chapel is home to larger pieces from the archeological collection of its sister museum, the Musée Calvet. Besides Egyptian statues and Etruscan urns, it abounds in Roman and Gallo-Roman sarcophagi, and early renditions of the mythical Tarasque (see p.831).

## Collection Lambert

5 rue Violette • July & Aug daily 11am–7pm; Sept–June Tues–Sun 11am–6pm • €7 • ☎ 04 90 16 56 20, ⓦ collectionlambert.com

Avignon's major contemporary art gallery, the thoughtfully curated **Collection Lambert**, is home to artworks lovingly amassed by Yvon Lambert. The superb space houses large-scale temporary exhibitions, one of which each year is devoted to a specific contemporary artist, and work from previously featured artists is also shown. The permanent display includes pieces created by Jean-Michel Basquiat for Lambert's Paris gallery in 1988, as well as work by Cy Twombly, Anselm Kiefer and Roni Horn.

**16**

## ARRIVAL AND DEPARTURE

**By train** Avignon's *gare SNCF* is just outside the walls south of the old city. Do not confuse it with the separate TGV station, 2km south, and linked by shuttles to and from cours Président-Kennedy (daily, 2–4 hourly; departures from station 6.22am–11.27pm, from town 5.46am–11.14pm; €3; ⓦ tcra.fr); a taxi into town (call ☎ 04 90 82 20 20) can cost €15 or more.

Destinations from gare SNCF Arles (hourly; 20–45min); Lyon (12 daily; 2hr 30min); Marseille (14 daily; 1hr 5min); Orange (17 daily; 15min); Valence (12 daily; 1hr 20min).

Destinations from TGV Aix-en-Provence TGV (22 daily; 20min); Lille-Europe (5 daily; 4hr 30min); London St Pancras (summer 1 on Sat only: 5hr 53min); Marseille (every 30min; 30min); Paris (17 daily; 2hr 40min); Valence TGV (9 daily; 30–40min).

**By bus** Avignon's *gare routière* is alongside the *gare SNCF*, just outside the walls south of the old city.

Destinations Aix (6 daily; 1hr 15min); Arles (7 daily; 1hr); Carpentras (frequent; 35–45min); Digne (3–4 daily;

3hr–3hr 30min); Fontaine-de-Vaucluse (4 daily; 55min); L'Isle-sur-la-Sorgue (10 daily; 40min); Orange (every 30–45min; 50min); St-Rémy (8 daily; 40min); Vaison (3 daily; 1hr 25min).

**By plane** Avignon-Caumont Airport, 8km southeast of the centre (☎ 04 90 81 51 51, ⓦ avignon.aeroport.fr), is connected with Birmingham, Exeter, and Southampton on Flybe (ⓦ flybe.com), and with London City Airport on Cityjet (ⓦ cityjet.com).

**By car** Driving into Avignon involves negotiating a nightmare of junctions and one-way roads. Two free, guarded car parks, neither of which stays open at night, are connected with the centre by free shuttles: Île Piot (Mon–Fri 7.30am–8.30pm, Sat 1.30–8.30pm), on the Île de la Barthelasse between Avignon and Villeneuve, and Parking des Italiens (Mon–Sat 7.30am–8.30pm), beside the river northeast of the old town. Parking within the walls is expensive; check whether your hotel offers free or discounted parking.

## GETTING AROUND

**By bus** The main TCRA local bus stops are on cours Président-Kennedy and outside Porte de l'Oulle facing the river (tickets €1.20 each; book of ten €10; one-day pass €3.60; ⓦ tcra.fr).

**By ferry** Free river ferries cross from east of Pont St-Bénézet to the Île de la Barthelasse, site of the city's campsites (March & Oct Wed 2–5.30pm, Sat & Sun 10am–noon & 2–5.30pm;

April–June & Sept daily 10am–12.30pm & 2–6.30pm; July & Aug daily 11am–9pm).

**By bike** Provence Bike, east of the *gare SNCF* at 7 av St-Ruf (☎ 04 90 27 92 61, ⓦ provence-bike.com), rents bicycles, scooters and motorbikes.

**By taxi** There is a taxi rank on place Pie (☎ 04 90 82 20 20, ⓦ taxis-avignon.fr).

## INFORMATION AND TOURS

**Tourist office** 41 cours Jean-Jaurès (April–June & Aug–Oct Mon–Sat 9am–6pm, Sun 9.45am–5pm; July Mon–Sat 9am–7pm, Sun 10am–5pm; Nov–March Mon–Fri 9am–6pm, Sat 9am–5pm, Sun 10am–noon; ☎ 04 32 74 32 74, ⓦ avignon-tourisme.com).

**Avignon Passion passports** These free passes, distributed by tourist offices in Avignon and Villeneuve-lès-Avignon, are a great deal. After paying the full admission for the first museum you visit, holders and family receive

discounts of 10–50 percent on admssion to all subsequent local museums. Valid for fifteen days, the pass also gives discounts on tourist transport such as riverboats and bus tours.

**Boat trips** In summer, from just south of place Crillon, Cruises Mireio (☎ 04 90 85 62 25, ⓦ mireio.net) offer 45min river trips on the Rhône (April–June & Sept daily 2pm, 3pm & 4.15pm; July & Aug daily 2pm, 3pm, 4pm, 5pm & 6pm; €8), as well as dinner cruises (€35.50–68).

## ACCOMMODATION

### HOTELS AND B&BS

**Angleterre** 29 bd Raspail ☎ 04 90 86 34 31, ⓦ hotelangleterre.fr. In the quiet southwest corner of the old city, well away from night-time noise, this is a traditional hotel with plain, low-priced rooms, many of them very small but equipped with reasonable bathrooms. **€75**

★ **Boquier** 6 rue du Portail Boquier ☎ 04 90 82 34 43, ⓦ hotel-boquier.com. Extremely welcoming little hotel near the tourist office, with funkily decorated, widely differing, and consistently inexpensive en-suite rooms, some very small, some sleeping three or four. **€60**

★ **Le Clos du Rempart** 35 rue Crémade ☎ 04 90 86 39 14, ⓦ closdurempart.com. Delightful B&B in a pretty nineteenth-century house behind the Palais des Papes, with two large, luxurious and very peaceful en-suite rooms; there's a wonderful wisteria-covered breakfast terrace and a hammock to doze in on sunny afternoons. **€160**

**Colbert** 7 rue Agricol Perdiguier ☎ 04 90 86 20 20, ⓦ avignon-hotel-colbert.com. At the south end of town, handy for local trains and buses, with warmly and imaginatively decorated rooms, mostly large and all a/c, a pleasant central courtyard, and helpful owners. Rates drop significantly in low season. Closed Nov to mid-March. **€100**

**Europe** 12 place Crillon ☎04 90 14 76 76, ⓦheurope
.com. Very comfortable upscale hotel, in a sixteenth-
century townhouse. Unpretentiously classy, it's set back in
a shaded courtyard, with bright, modern, soundproofed
rooms, home-made breakfasts and an excellent
restaurant. **€209**

**Garlande** 20 rue Galante ☎04 90 80 08 85, ⓦhotel
degarlande.com. Stylish little family-run hotel, in a
pedestrian street near the Palais des Papes. The eleven
generally spacious rooms offer Provençal touches and a
decent bathroom. **€92**

**Médiéval** 15 rue Petite Saunerie ☎04 90 86 11 06,
ⓦhotelmedieval.com. Very central hotel in a fine
seventeenth-century townhouse, with reasonable rates
and a lovely garden courtyard but rather plain, dated
rooms of varying sizes. **€72**

**Mignon** 12 rue Joseph Vernet ☎04 90 82 17 30,
ⓦhotel-mignon.com. The decor may be a little fussy for
some tastes, but this small hotel is amazing value for
money considering its spotless little rooms and fantastic
location on a chic street. Closed Jan. **€71**

### HOSTEL AND CAMPSITES

**Auberge des Jeunes Bagatelle** Camping Bagatelle,
25 allées Antoine-Pinay, Île de la Barthelasse ☎04 90
86 30 39, ⓦcampingbagatelle.com. Rather basic hostel
facilities in the grounds of the well-equipped *Camping
Bagatelle* site. Beds in two-, four- or six-person dorms, plus
private rooms sleeping from two to four, with and without
en-suite facilities; all rates include breakfast. Dorms **€19**,
doubles **€51**

**Camping Bagatelle** 25 allées Antoine-Pinay, Île de la
Barthelasse ☎04 90 86 30 39, ⓦcampingbagatelle
.com. Wooded, three-star campsite, with laundry facilities,
a shop and café. It's the closest to the city centre, visible as
you cross the Daladier bridge from Avignon; take bus #20
from the post office, or a 15min walk from place de
l'Horloge. Open all year. **€22**

**Camping du Pont d'Avignon** Île de la Barthelasse
☎04 90 80 63 50, ⓦcamping-avignon.com. Well
shaded four-star site, with a lovely pool, on the island
directly facing Pont St-Bénézet across the river, a fair walk
from the centre on bus route #20. Closed Nov to mid-
March. **€24**

## EATING AND DRINKING

### RESTAURANTS

★ **Au Tout Petit** 4 rue d'Amphoux ☎04 90 82 38 86,
ⓦautoutpetit.fr. Popular acclaim has ensured that this
market-area restaurant, specializing in, as they put it,
"*cuisine re-créative*", is no longer as "*petit*" as the name
suggests. Served indoors only, the food remains
imaginative, fresh and unbeatable; the service brisk and
efficient; and the owner extremely friendly. Two-course
lunch *formule* for €12, dinner *menus* from €17. Tues–Sat
noon–2pm & 6.30–10pm.

**Brunel** 46 rue de la Balance ☎04 90 85 24 83. This
cheerful restaurant, with a flowery terrace near the
Palais des Papes, serves superb regional dishes,
including *bourride*, with a *plat du jour* for €12.50 and
dinner *menus* from €32.50. Tues–Sat noon–1.30pm &
7.30–9pm.

**Caveau du Théâtre** 16 rue des Trois Faucons ☎04 90
82 60 91, ⓦcaveaudutheatre.com. Friendly bistro, with
pretty painted walls, jolly red tables out on the street, and
occasional live jazz, serving delicious dishes like market-
fresh fish baked with licorice (€14.50) or huge mixed salads
(€15). Lunch *menu* €14, dinner *menus* €19 and €23. Mon–
Fri noon–2.30pm & 7pm–midnight, Sat 7pm–
midnight; closed 2nd half of Aug.

**Chez Ginette & Marcel** 27 place des Corps-Saints ☎04
90 85 58 70. The most attractive of several restaurants on
this lively, youthful little square; if you sit outside, be sure
to venture inside, to see a funky evocation of a 1950s'
French grocery. €5 *tartines* and salads are the speciality;
you can get a substantial meal for well under €10, while

breakfast, including a *tartine* of course, is just €6. Mon–Sat
9am–midnight.

★ **Christian Étienne** 10 rue de Mons ☎04 90 86
16 50, ⓦchristian-etienne.fr. Avignon's best-known
gourmet restaurant, housed in a twelfth-century mansion,
with a terrace overlooking the place du Palais, and offering
such mouthwatering Provençal delights as a whole *menu*
devoted to tomatoes, or autumn vegetables – with meat
and fish, naturally – or lobster with ginger, asparagus and
sesame seeds followed by orange and carrot macaroons
with almond sorbet. Dinner *menus* range from €70–115,
but you can sample its pleasures for €31 at lunchtime.
Tues–Sat noon–1.30pm & 7–9.15pm.

**La Cour du Louvre** 23 rue St-Agricol ☎04 90 27 12 66,
ⓦlacourdulouvre.com. Hidden peacefully away from the
old-town bustle in a delightful interior courtyard at the end
of a *cour*, with a romantic atmosphere and good
Mediterranean cooking. *Menus* from €26 for lunch – when
there's also a €13.50 *plat du jour* – and €36 for dinner. Mon–
Sat noon–2.15pm & 7–10pm.

**La Fourchette** 17 rue Racine ☎04 90 85 20 93. Bright,
busy yet refined restaurant serving up classic and sophisticated
fish and meat dishes – try the tasty sardines marinated in
coriander – on €32 and €42 dinner *menus*. Mon–Fri 12.15–
1.45pm & 7.15–9.45pm; closed first 3 wks in Aug.

**Numero 75** 75 rue Guillaume Puy ☎04 90 27 16 00,
ⓦnumero75.com. Housed in a beautiful nineteenth-
century mansion, with indoor and garden seating, this
smart restaurant serves Provençal dinner *menus* from
€32.50, but offers a €14.50 lunchtime *plat du jour*. Mon–

**16**

Sat noon–1.45pm & 7.30–9.30pm.

**Le Square** Square Agricol Perdiguier ☎04 06 21 86 71 94. There's little exceptional about the food in this outdoor brasserie, sprawling in a spacious park behind the tourist office, but it makes a great spot for a summer-morning coffee, or a simple lunchtime salad or *plat* for under €10. Daily 8am– sunset.

## CAFÉS

**Bistrot Utopia** 4 rue Escalier Ste-Anne ☎06 37 57 52 31. In the shadow of the Palais des Papes, around the back, this café has exhibitions on its walls, live jazz some nights, and adjoins a good cinema. Mon–Fri noon–1am, Sat & Sun 2pm–1am.

**Mon Bar** 17 rue Portail Matheron. Pleasantly old-fashioned café, not far east of the place du Palais and steeped in the lore of Avignon, with a laidback atmosphere. Mon–Sat 7am–8pm, Sun 1–8pm.

## BARS

**Le Cid** 11 place de l'Horloge ☎04 90 82 30 38, ⓦlecidcafe.com. Trendy mixed gay/straight bar and terrace that opens at the crack of dawn, and keeps going long after the rest of place de l'Horloge has closed for the night. Daily 6.30am–1pm.

**Tapalocas** 15 rue Galante ☎04 90 82 56 84, ⓦtapalocas-avignon.com. Tapas at under €3 each, plus Spanish music, sometimes live, in a large, atmospheric bar. Daily 11.45am–1am.

**Le Vache à Carreaux** 14 rue Peyrollerie ☎04 90 80 09 05, ⓦvache-carreaux.com. This intimate, homely wine bar styles itself a "restaurant de fromage et vins", and cheese is indeed prominent on the food menu, with large €9 salads as well as €12 baked half-camemberts. Mon–Fri noon–2pm & 7–10.30pm, Sat 7–11.30pm, Sun noon–2pm & 7–11.30pm.

## NIGHTLIFE AND ENTERTAINMENT

Though Avignon saves a lot of its energy for the festival, the city is busy with nightlife and cultural events all year round, particularly café-theatre, and plenty of classical concerts are performed in churches, usually for free.

**16**

### LIVE MUSIC AND CLUBS

**AJMI Jazz Club** La Manutention, 4 rue Escalier Ste-Anne ☎04 90 86 08 61, ⓦjazzalajmi.com. This popular club, above *Bistrot Utopia*, hosts major acts and adventurous new jazz and improvised music year-round. Hours vary.

**Bokao's** 9 bis bd du Quai St-Lazare ☎04 90 82 47 95, ⓦbokaos.fr. Mainstream, youth-oriented club, in a converted barn across from the river just outside the walls, with outdoor space as well, and playing an eclectic mix of music styles. Thurs–Sat 10pm–5am.

**L'Esclave** 12 rue du Limas ☎04 90 85 14 91, ⓦesclavebar.com. Avignon's gay and lesbian bar, with regular DJs, drag shows and karaoke nights at ground level, and more secluded areas upstairs. Tues–Sun 11pm until dawn.

**Le Red Zone** 25 rue Carnot ☎04 90 27 02 44, ⓦredzonebar.com. Sweaty, very crimson club where DJs play anything from salsa to electro. Sun & Mon 10pm–3am, Tues–Sat 9pm–3am.

### THEATRE AND CINEMA

**Cinéma Utopia** La Manutention, 4 rue Escalier Ste-Anne ☎04 90 82 65 36, ⓦcinemas-utopia.org. Part of a hip converted warehouse complex that also includes the *Bistrot Utopia* and *AJMI Jazz Club*, this wildly popular venue shows a busy repertory programme of world cinema.

**Opéra** Place de l'Horloge ☎04 90 82 81 40, ⓦoperatheatredavignon.fr. The season at Avignon's most prestigious venue for classical opera and ballet runs from October to June.

**Théâtre du Balcon** 38 rue Guillaume-Puy ☎04 90 85 00 80, ⓦtheatredubalcon.org. A venue staging everything from African music and twentieth-century classics to contemporary theatre.

**Théâtre des Carmes André Benedetto** 6 place des Carmes ☎04 90 82 20 47, ⓦtheatredescarmes.com. Set up by, and now named after, one of the founders of Festival Off, this theatre specializes in avant-garde performances.

**Théâtre du Chêne Noir** 8 bis rue Ste-Catherine ☎04 90 86 58 11, ⓦchenenoir.fr. Programmes at this eclectic theatre range anywhere between mime, musicals and Molière.

## DIRECTORY

**Emergencies** Doctor/ambulance ☎15; hospital, Centre Hospitalier H. Duffaut, 305 rue Raoul-Follereau (☎04 32 75 33 33, ⓦch-avignon.fr); night chemist ☎3237, ⓦ3237.fr.

**Markets** Flea market: place des Carmes (Sun morning).

Flowers: place des Carmes (Sat morning). Food: in the covered halls on place Pie (Tues–Fri until 1.30pm; Sat & Sun until 2pm).

**Police Municipale** 13 quai St-Lazare ☎08 00 00 84 00 or ☎04 90 85 13 13.

# Villeneuve-lès-Avignon

Pretty and prosperous, though little more than a village at its core, **VILLENEUVE-LÈS-AVIGNON** (also spelled Villeneuve-lez-Avignon) climbs a rocky escarpment above the west bank of the Rhône, looking down across the river upon its older and larger neighbour from behind far more convincing fortifications. Despite ongoing rivalry, Villeneuve has effectively been a suburb of Avignon for most of its history, holding palatial residences constructed by the cardinals and a great monastery founded by Pope Innocent VI.

To this day, Villeneuve is technically a part of Languedoc and not Provence. It might be better known were it further from Avignon, whose monuments it almost matches in scale. It is, however, a very different – and really rather sleepy – kind of place, where daily activity centres around the lovely little place Jean-Jaurès. As such, it retains a timelessness that bustling Avignon inevitably lacks. Whatever time of year you visit it's certainly worth a day spent exploring.

**Market** days in Villeneuve's place Charles-David are Thursday, for food, and Saturday for bric-a-brac.

## Fort St-Andre

**Fort St-Andre** Daily: April to mid-May & last 2 weeks of Sept 10am–1pm & 2–5.30pm; mid-May to mid-Sept 10am–1pm & 2–6pm; Oct–March 10am–1pm & 2–5pm • €5.50, €4.50 with Avignon Passion pass (see p.820) • ☏ 04 90 25 45 35, ⓦ fort-saint-andre .monuments-nationaux.fr **Abbey** Tues–Sun: April–Sept 10am–12.30pm & 2–6pm; Oct–March 10am–12.30pm & 2–5pm • €5, €4 with Avignon Passion pass • ☏ 06 71 42 16 90, ⓦ abbaye-saint-andre.com

Originally, Villeneuve-lès-Avignon was enclosed within the walls of the enormous **Fort St-André**, on a rise to the east. Then, in 1770, the course of the Rhône shifted 1km south, and the fort lost its strategic importance. Now a hollow shell, it can be reached by climbing either from place Jean-Jaurès, or up the steeper rue Pente Rapide, a cobbled street that leads from the north side of place Charles-David.

Once through the fort's vast white walls, via a bulbous, double-towered gateway, you're on what used to be the town's narrow main street. Buying a ticket for the fort itself allows you to continue up the street, passing tumbledown ruins, and then walk along the parapets, where a cliff-face terrace offers tremendous views across the river. You can also pay separately to visit its former **abbey**, which as well as more views has gardens of olive trees, ruined chapels, lily ponds and dovecotes.

## La Chartreuse du Val du Bénédiction

58 rue de la République • April–June daily 9.30am–6.30pm; July & Sept daily 9am–6.30pm; Aug daily 9am–7.30pm; Oct–March Mon–Fri 9.30am–5pm, Sat & Sun 10am–5pm • €7.70, €6.10 with Avignon Passion pass (see p.820) • ☏ 04 90 15 24 24, ⓦ chartreuse.org

One of France's largest Carthusian monasteries, **La Chartreuse du Val du Bénédiction**, spreads below the Fort St-André. Founded by the sixth Avignon pope, Innocent VI, it was sold after the Revolution. Today its buildings are totally unembellished, and except for the Giovanetti frescoes in the chapel, all its artworks have been dispersed. Visitors can wander around unguided, through the three cloisters, the church, chapels, cells and communal spaces, though there's little to see. It's one of the best venues of the Festival of Avignon (see p.818).

## Musée Pierre-de-Luxembourg

3 rue de la République • Tues–Sun: Feb, March & Oct–Dec 10am–noon & 2–5pm; April–Sept 10am–12.30pm & 2–6.30pm • €3.20, €2.20 with Avignon Passion pass (see p.820) • ☏ 04 90 27 49 66

The **Musée Pierre-de-Luxembourg**, just off the central place Jean-Jaurès, holds treasures from the fourteenth-century **Église Collégiale Notre-Dame** nearby, including a rare fourteenth-century smiling Madonna and Child carved from a single tusk of ivory. Paintings taken from the Chartreuse include the stunning *Coronation of the Virgin*, painted in 1453 by Enguerrand Quarton.

16

## Tour Philippe-le-Bel

Tues–Sun: Feb, March, & Oct 2–5pm; April–Sept 10am–12.30pm & 2.30–6.30pm • €2.20, €1.70 with Avignon Passion pass (see p.820) •
☏ 04 32 70 08 57

The stout **Tour Philippe-le-Bel**, beside the main road from Avignon south of the centre, was built to guard the western end of Avignon's Pont St-Bénézet. The tricky climb to the top is rewarded with an overview of Villeneuve and Avignon.

### ARRIVAL AND INFORMATION VILLENEUVE-LÈS-AVIGNON

**By bus** The #11 bus (every 30min) takes 10min to ply between Villeneuve's place Charles-David and Avignon's cours Président-Kennedy.

**Tourist office** Place Charles-David (April–June, Sept & Oct Mon–Sat 9am–12.30pm & 2–6pm; July Mon–Fri

10am–7pm, Sat & Sun 10am–1pm & 2 30–7pm; Aug daily 9am–12.30pm & 2–6pm; Nov–March Mon–Sat 9.30am–12.30pm & 2–5pm; ☏ 04 90 25 61 33, ⍵ tourisme-villeneuvelezavignon.fr).

### ACCOMMODATION

★ **L'Atelier** 5 rue de la Foire ☏ 04 90 25 01 84, ⍵ hoteldelatelier.com. Very tasteful rooms in a charming sixteenth-century house with a central stone staircase bathed in light, plus huge open fireplaces and a delightful well-shaded courtyard garden with terraces. Closed Jan. **€89**

**Camping Municipal de la Laune** Chemin St-Honoré ☏ 04 90 25 76 06, ⍵ camping-villeneuvelezavignon .com. A spacious, well-shaded three-star site off the D980, north of both town and fort near the sports stadium and munipal swimming pool. Closed mid-Oct to March. **€15.75**

**Jardin de la Livrée** 4bis rue Camp de Bataille ☏ 04 90 26 05 05, ⍵ la-livree.fr. Clean, comfortable B&B rooms in an old house in the centre of the village, with a swimming pool and an appealing Mediterranean restaurant (closed Mon) that serves an €18 lunch *menu*

and a €26 dinner *menu*. The one drawback is the noise of passing trains. **€92**

**Prieuré** 7 place du Chapitre ☏ 04 90 15 90 15, ⍵ leprieure.com. If you fancy being surrounded by tapestries, finely carved doors, old oak ceilings and other baronial trappings, this old priory surrounded by a peaceful flower-filled garden is indisputably the first choice. The restaurant serves Provençal cuisine with a gourmet twist. Closed Jan to mid-Feb & Nov. **€242**

**YMCA** 7bis chemin de la Justice ☏ 04 90 25 46 20, ⍵ ymca-avignon.com. Beautifully situated hostel overlooking the river. Balconied rooms for one to four people, with and without en-suite facilities, and available both as dorms and as private rooms, plus an open-air swimming pool. Stop "Pont d'Avignon" on buses heading from Avignon to Villeneuve, "Gabriel Péri" in the other direction. Dorms **€23**, doubles **€32**

### EATING AND DRINKING

Most of Villeneuve's restaurants are special-treat places for day-trippers from Avignon, though there is a handful of pleasant little cafés on place Jean-Jaurès where you can enjoy a simple snack with your drink.

**La Banaste** 28 rue de la République ☏ 04 90 25 64 20. Bountiful Provençal and Languedocien *terroir* meals. More pleasant indoors than on the cramped roadside terrace. *Menus* from €24 (two courses), €30 (three). July to mid-Aug daily noon–2pm & 7–9.30pm, mid-Aug to June daily except Thurs noon–2pm.

★ **Les Jardins d'Été de la Chartreuse** Cloître St-Jean, La Chartreuse ☏ 04 90 15 24 23,

⍵ chartreuse.org. A truly memorable experience; in summer only, you can thread your way through the labyrinthine old monastery to find this open-air restaurant in a secluded courtyard. Some tables have lovely sunset views. Friendly service and *menus* of substantial Provençal cuisine from €19 for lunch, €28 for dinner, plus early-evening drinks and snacks. June–Aug daily noon–2.30pm & 6–9.30pm.

## St-Rémy-de-Provence

The dreamy, little-changed community of **ST-RÉMY-DE-PROVENCE**, where Van Gogh painted some of his most lyrical works, nestles against the northern base of the Alpilles, 30km from either Arles or Avignon. St-Rémy is a beautiful spot, centring on a charmingly low-key old town, the **Vieille Ville**, an enchanting tangle of narrow lanes and ancient alleyways interspersed with peaceful little squares. Despite the presence of several boutiques and restaurants, it's all surprisingly sleepy. There's not even a café where you can sit and watch the world go by; instead virtually all the town's commercial life takes place on the four busy boulevards that ring the entire ensemble.

Several exceptional sites and attractions lie within walking distance to the south: Van Gogh's hospital of **St-Paul-de-Mausole**, a **Roman arch**, and the ruins of the ancient city of **Glanum**.

## St-Paul-de-Mausole

Av Vincent-van-Gogh • Daily: April–Oct 9.30am–7pm; Oct–March 10.15am–4.45pm • €4 • ☎ 04 90 92 77 00, ⊛ cloitresaintpaul -valetudo.com

The former monastery of **St-Paul-de-Mausole**, where **Vincent van Gogh** was a voluntary psychiatric patient between May 1889 and May 1890, stands just under 2km south of St-Rémy's old town. Visiting is a profoundly moving experience. Amazingly enough, it's still a psychiatric hospital, and although tourists are kept well clear of the active area, you get a real sense of its ongoing work. Displays in the church and cloisters contrast Van Gogh's diagnosis and treatment with modern-day practices, and you can see a mock-up of his former room and walk in the glorious gardens, planted with lavender and poppies. Vincent was allowed to wander around the town and Alpilles, so long as he stayed within an hour's walk of the hospital. Art therapy forms a major component of current treatment, and patients' work is sold in the on-site shop.

## Glanum

Rte des Baux-de-Provence, 1600m south of central St-Rémy • April–Aug daily 10am–6.30pm; Sept Tues–Sun 10am–6.30pm; Oct–March Tues–Sun 10am–5pm • €7.50, car parking €2.50 • ⊛ glanum.monuments-nationaux.fr

The impressive ancient settlement of **GLANUM** was dug from the alluvial deposits at the foot of Alpilles. This site originally held a Neolithic homestead, before the Gallo-Greeks, probably from Massalia (Marseille), built a city here between the second and first centuries BC. Then the Gallo-Romans constructed yet another town, which lasted until the third century AD; a Roman triumphal arch and mausoleum still stand beside the main road nearby, known as Les Antiques and freely accessible around the clock.

A footpath drops from the site entrance to run through the ruins of Glanum itself, which can be hard to decipher. Greek levels can be most readily distinguished from the Roman by the stones: the earlier civilization used massive hewn rocks, as opposed to the smaller, more accurately shaped stones preferred by the Romans.

At the site's southern end, where it narrows into a ravine, a Greek edifice stands around the **spring** that made this location so desirable. Steps lead down to a pool, with a slab above for the libations of those too sick to descend. Traces of a prehistoric settlement that also depended on this spring survive up the hill to the west. The Gallo-Romans directed the water through canals to heat houses and, of course, to the **baths** that lie near the site entrance.

## ARRIVAL AND INFORMATION                                    ST-RÉMY-DE-PROVENCE

**By bus** The main bus stop is in place de la République, on the eastern edge of the old town.

Destinations Arles (8 daily; 50min); Avignon (8 daily; 40min); Les Baux (4 daily; 15min).

**Tourist office** Place Jean-Jaurès, just south of the old town (mid-March to June & Sept to mid-Oct Mon–Sat

9am–12.30pm & 2–6.30pm, Sun 10am–12.30pm; June–Sept Mon–Sat 9am–12.30pm & 2–7pm, Sun 10am–12.30pm & 2.30–5pm; mid-Oct to mid-March Mon–Sat 9am–12.30pm & 2–5.30pm; ☎ 04 90 92 05 22, ⊛ saintremy-de-provence.com).

## ACCOMMODATION

**Canto Cigalo** 8a chemin de Canto Cigalo ☎ 04 90 92 14 28, ⊛ cantocigalo.com. Very nice, peaceful country villa hotel, beside the canal a 20min walk southeast of the old town, with good-sized rooms, some with a/c, and cricket-themed decor (as in the insect, not the sport), plus

a pool and plenty of outdoor space on the terrace and in the large gardens. **€69**

**Mas de Nicolas** Av Plaisance du Touch ☎ 04 90 92 27 05, ⊛ camping-masdenicolas.com. Spacious and shady four-star municipal site with its own pool, 800m

**16**

from the centre on a turning off the rte de Mollèges. Closed Nov to mid-March. **€25**

**Pegomas** 3 av Jean-Moulin ☎04 90 92 01 21, ⓦcampingpegomas.com. The nearest site to the town centre, this three-star option, 1km east towards Cavaillon, has a pool, a bar and a small shop. Closed late Oct to mid-March. **€25.50**

★ **Le Soleil** 35 av Pasteur ☎04 90 92 00 63, ⓦwww.hotelsoleil.com. Very welcoming hotel, set back from the main road a short walk south of the centre, with a pool and private parking. Nice, simple rooms; a bar but no restaurant;

and three self-contained apartments. Closed early Nov to late March. **€70**

★ **Sous les Figuiers** 3 av Taillandier ☎04 32 60 15 40, ⓦhotel-charme-provence.com. Gorgeous place just north of the old town, run by a creative duo (a photographer and a painter). Of the fourteen well-appointed rooms, the best eleven cost extra, and have their own private garden terraces; there are no TVs, but there's a swimming pool and an on-site artist's studio (art classes available). Closed mid-Jan to mid-March. **€92**

## EATING AND DRINKING

**L'Aile ou la Cuisse** 5 rue de la Commune ☎04 32 62 00 25. Very romantic, upscale restaurant in the old town, with a pricey à la carte menu of main dishes at €26–35, as well as a deli that sells posh picnic items and delectable jams and olive oils. Tues–Sun noon–1.30pm & 7.30–9.30pm.

**Cinecitta** 4bis rue Estrine ☎04 90 92 82 20, ⓦwww.artemoda-cinecitta.fr. Strangely, this restaurant is attached to an Italian boutique, with tables set out among the clothes racks. The main dining area, however, is in a pleasant enclosed courtyard, where you can enjoy a flexible selection of Italian and Mediterranean specialities. Portions on the *menus* are enormous; the €16 *Cinema* is great value, the €29 *Gourmand* consistently delicious. April–Sept daily noon–3pm & 7pm–midnight; Oct–March Wed, Thurs & Sun noon–3pm & 7pm–midnight, Fri & Sat noon–3pm & 7pm–midnight.

**Grain de Sel** 25 bd Mirabeau ☎04 90 92 00 89, ⓦgraindesel-resto.com. Inside, this place looks like a glitzy big-city jazz lounge; outside, it's a pavement bistro

like most of its neighbours. As a restaurant the concept is a little confusing: either order à la carte, in which case conventional French starters cost around €15, *plats* more like €25, or get a *Grande Assiette*, for around €28, which is a very big plate filled with hot and cold dishes to eat in whatever order you fancy. The food is excellent, ranging from salmon tartare with a wasabi mousse to duck in pastry parcels. Mon–Sat noon–1.30pm & 7.30–9.30pm, Sun noon–1.30pm.

**Taberna Romana** Glanum, av van-Gogh ☎04 90 92 65 97, ⓦtaberna-romana.com. This self-styled Roman restaurant, serving authentic Roman dishes, makes a very nice open-air lunch spot, overlooking the ruins of Glanum from a well-shaded terrace. You don't have to pay to go in, and in fact you can see the ruins pretty well from here for free. The food itself is zestful and a bit different, with a large mixed plate of, say, *samsa* (spicy olives), *cicerona* (chickpeas) and goat's cheese for €18, or a *matza*, which closely resembles a chicken wrap, for €9. They also serve "Roman beer". April–Oct Tues–Sun 10am–6.30pm.

**16**

# Les Baux-de-Provence

The distinctly unreal fortified village of **LES BAUX-DE-PROVENCE** perches atop the Alpilles ridge, 15km northeast of Arles. The ruins of its eleventh-century **castle** merge almost imperceptibly into the plateau, whose rock is both foundation and part of the structure. The village itself, straggling over the hilltop just below, is a too-good-to-be-true collection of sixteenth- and seventeenth-century churches, chapels and mansions. To avoid the crowds of summer day-trippers, it's best to turn up late in the day.

## The château

Daily: March–June 9am–7.15pm; July & Aug 9am–8.15pm; Sept–Nov 9.30am–6pm; Dec–Feb 10am–5pm; last entry 1hr before closing • April–Sept €9; Oct–March €7; audioguide in English available • ☎04 90 54 55 56, ⓦchateau-baux-provence.com

The only entrance to the enormous **château** at Les Baux is via turnstiles at the end of the main village street. These lead first to open ground below the walls, which is scattered with replica siege engines and catapults, and then to footpaths over and through buildings that include the ruins of the feudal castle demolished on Richelieu's orders, the partially restored **Chapelle Castrale** and the **Tour Sarrasine**. The higher you climb, the more spectacular the views become.

## The Carrières de Lumières

D27, 500m north of Les Baux • Daily: April–Sept 10am–6pm; Oct–March 10am–5pm • €8.50 • ☎ 04 90 54 47 37, ⓦ carrieres-lumieres.com

It's said that Dante took his inspiration for the nine circles of the *Inferno* from the **Val d'Enfer** (Valley of Hell), immediately north of Les Baux. Jean Cocteau used its contorted rocks and bauxite quarries as a location for his 1959 film, *Le Testament d'Orphée*. Those quarries have now been turned into an audiovisual experience called the **Carrières de Lumières**. Projection is continuous, so you don't have to wait to go in. Images are projected over the floor, ceilings and walls of the vast rectangular caverns, accompanied by music that resonates strangely in the captured space. The precise content changes each year, but makes little difference; the experience is mind-blowing.

### INFORMATION

### LES-BAUX-DE-PROVENCE

**Tourist office** Maison du Roy, rue Porte Mage, at the start of Grande-Rue (daily: May–Sept Mon–Fri 9am–6pm, Sat & Sun 10am–5.30pm; Oct–April Mon–Fri 9.30am–5pm, Sat & Sun 10am–5.30pm; ☎ 04 90 54 34 03, ⓦ lesbauxdeprovence.com).

### ACCOMMODATION AND EATING

**Hostellerie de la Reine Jeanne** ☎ 04 90 54 32 06, ⓦ la-reinejeanne.com. The only moderately priced hotel in the village, near the tourist office. Very friendly staff, simple rooms with views of the citadel, and good *menus* starting at €27. Closed mid-Jan to mid-Feb. **€56**

**Le Prince Noir** rue de l'Orme ☎ 04 90 54 39 57, ⓦ leprincenoir.com. An eccentric B&B in the home of an artist, in the uppermost house in the village. Choose between the one comfortable bedroom or the two luxurious suites; two-night minimum stay. **€95**

**Les Variétés** 29 rue du Trencat ☎ 04 90 54 55 88. The best-value restaurant in town has a lovely interior courtyard and sells good salads and pasta dishes for around €10. March–Sept daily noon–2pm & 7–9pm.

## Arles

With its sun-kissed golden stone, small-town feel and splendid setting on the east bank of the Rhône, **ARLES** ranks high among southern France's loveliest cities. It's also one of the oldest, with the extraordinary Roman amphitheatre at its heart, **Les Arènes**, simply the most famous of several magnificent monuments. Originally a Celtic settlement, Arles later became the Roman capital of Gaul, Britain and Spain. For centuries, the port of Arles prospered from trade up the Rhône, especially when enemies blockaded its eternal rival, Marseille. Decline set in with the arrival of the railways, however, and the town where **Van Gogh** spent a lonely and miserable period in the late nineteenth century was itself inward-looking and depressed.

Thankfully, however, Arles today is pleasantly laidback – at its liveliest on Saturdays, when Camargue farmers come in for the weekly **market** – and a delightful place simply to stroll around. Its compact central core, tucked into a ninety-degree curve in the river, is small enough to cross on foot in a few minutes. While ancient ruins are scattered everywhere, the heart of the Roman city, the **place du Forum**, remains the hub of popular life. Medieval Arles, on the other hand, centred on what's now the place de la République, the pedestrianized site of both the **Cathédrale St-Trophime** and the Hôtel de Ville. The one area where the city's former **walls** have survived lies to the east, in a quiet and attractive little corner. Sadly, the **riverfront**, once teeming with bars and bistros, was heavily damaged during World War II.

---

### THE RENCONTRES INTERNATIONALES DE LA PHOTOGRAPHIE

Europe's most prestigious annual photography festival, Arles' **Rencontres Internationales de la Photographie** (ⓦ www.rencontres-arles.com) takes over more than a dozen venues throughout the city between July and late September. Visitors can either pay €3.50–11 for admission to a single exhibition, or buy passes – €27 for one day, €35 for the whole festival – from ticket offices in the place de la République and elsewhere.

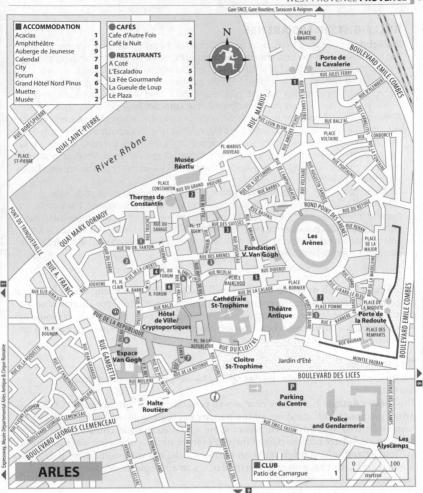

| ■ **ACCOMMODATION** | | ● **CAFÉS** | |
|---|---|---|---|
| Acacias | 1 | Cafe d'Autre Fois | 2 |
| Amphithéâtre | 5 | Café la Nuit | 4 |
| Auberge de Jeunesse | 9 | ● **RESTAURANTS** | |
| Calendal | 7 | A Coté | 7 |
| City | 8 | L'Escaladou | 5 |
| Forum | 4 | La Fée Gourmande | 6 |
| Grand Hôtel Nord Pinus | 6 | La Gueule de Loup | 3 |
| Muette | 3 | Le Plaza | 1 |
| Musée | 2 | | |

**ARLES**

**16**

| ■ **CLUB** | |
|---|---|
| Patio de Camargue | 1 |

## Roman Arles

Arles is still recognizable as the **Roman** city thrust to greatness when Julius Caesar built an entire fleet here within a month. After using the ships to win control of Rome, he devastated Marseille for supporting his enemy Pompey, and Arles became a major port. The Mediterranean was closer to the city then, and the wheat fields of the Camargue became known as the "granary of Rome". Arles' relative isolation after the empire crumbled allowed its heritage to be preserved.

### Les Arènes

Daily: March, April & Oct 9am–6pm; May–Sept 9am–7pm; Nov–Feb 10am–5pm • €6 with Théâtre Antique • ☎ 04 90 49 36 74, Ⓦ www.arenes-arles.com

Constructed at the end of the first century AD, the dramatic amphitheatre known as **Les Arènes** was the largest Roman building in Gaul. Looming above the city, it measures 136m long by 107m wide; its two tiers of sixty arches each (the lower Doric, the upper Corinthian) were originally topped by a third, and thirty thousand spectators

---

## BULLFIGHTS IN LES ARÈNES

**Bullfighting**, or more properly *tauromachie* ("the art of the bull"), comes in two styles in Arles and the Camargue. In the local **courses camarguaises**, held at *fêtes* from late spring to early autumn (the most prestigious of which is Arles' Cocarde d'Or, on the first Monday in July), *razeteurs* pluck ribbons and cockades tied to the bulls' horns, cutting them free with special barbed gloves. In this gentler bullfight, people are rarely injured and the bulls are not killed.

More popular, however, are the brutal Spanish-style **corridas** (late April, early July & Sept at Arles), consisting of a strict ritual leading to the all-but-inevitable death of the bull. After its entry into the ring, the bull is subjected to the *bandilleros* who stick decorated barbs in its back, the *picadors*, who lance it from horseback, and finally, the *torero*, who endeavours to lead the bull through a graceful series of movements before killing it with a single sword stroke to the heart. In one *corrida* six bulls are killed by three *toreros*, for whom injuries (sometimes fatal) are not uncommon.

While outsiders may disapprove, *tauromachie* has a long history here, and offers a rare opportunity to join in local life. It's also a great way to experience Arles' Roman arena in use. Assorted bullfighting events are staged at Les Arènes between Easter and October each year, including non-fatal *courses camarguaises* at 5.30pm each Wednesday & Friday from early July until late August; ticket prices range from €10 for the *courses camarguaises* up to €97 for a prime spot at a *corrida* (ⓦ www.arenes-arles.com).

---

would cram beneath its canvas roof to watch gladiator battles. During the Middle Ages, it became a fortress, sheltering over two hundred dwellings and three churches; now it's once more used for entertainment. While it's impressive from the outside, it's only worth paying for admission when a performance – a bullfight (see above), perhaps or a concert – is taking place.

### Théâtre Antique

Daily: March, April & Oct 9am–noon & 2–6pm; May–Sept 9am–7pm; Nov–Feb 10am–noon & 2–5pm • €6 with Les Arènes • ☎ 04 90 18 41 20

The **Théâtre Antique** is nowhere near as well preserved as the amphitheatre. Only one pair of columns is still standing, all the statuary has been removed, and the sides of the stage are littered with broken chunks of stone. Quarried to build churches after the Romans left, it later became part of the city's fortifications – one wing was turned into the **Tour Roland**, whose height gives an idea where the top seats would have been. While there's little to see on an ordinary day, it's an atmospheric venue for performances and festivals.

### Cryptoportiques

Accessed via Hôtel de Ville, place de la République • Daily: March, April & Oct 9am–noon & 2–6pm; May–Sept 9am–noon & 2–7pm; Nov–Feb 10am–noon & 2–5pm • €3.50

Arles' most unusual – and spookiest – Roman remains, the **Cryptoportiques**, are reached via stairs that descend from inside the Hôtel de Ville. No one knows quite what these huge, dark and dank underground galleries were; they may have simply propped up one side of the town's level open forum, which stood above. Empty now, they're gloriously atmospheric for a fifteen-minute subterranean stroll.

### Thermes de Constantin

Rue du Grand-Prieuré • Daily: March, April & Oct 9am–noon & 2–6pm; May–Sept 9am–noon & 2–7pm; Nov–Feb 1–5pm • €3 • ☎ 04 90 49 36 74

Only the ruins of the **Thermes de Constantin**, Provence's largest Roman baths, remain of the emperor's palace that extended along the Rhône waterfront. You can see the heating system beneath a thick floor and the divisions between the different areas, but there's nothing to help you imagine the original. The most striking feature, the elegant high wall of an apse that sheltered one of the baths, in alternating stripes of orange brick and grey masonry, is best viewed from outside.

### Les Alyscamps

Av des Alyscamps • Daily: March, April & Oct 9am–noon & 2–6pm; May–Sept 9am–7pm; Nov–Feb 10am–noon & 2–5pm • €3.50 • ☎ 04 90 49 36 74

Arles's Roman necropolis, known as **Les Alyscamps**, lies a few minutes' walk south of boulevard des Lices. Originally much larger, it was regarded as the most hallowed Christian burial ground in all Europe long after the Roman era had ended; until the twelfth century, mourners far upstream would launch sumptuous coffins to float down the Rhône, for collection at Arles. Only one alleyway now survives, while the finest of its sarcophagi and statues have long since disappeared. Nonetheless, ancient tombs still line the shaded walk, as painted by Van Gogh, and the tranquil stroll ends at the Romanesque church of **St-Honorat**, which is wonderfully simple, and cool on a hot day.

### Musée Départemental Arles Antique

Av 1<sup>era</sup> Division France Libre • Daily except Tues 10am–6pm • €6, free first Sun of each month • ☎ 04 13 31 51 03, ⊛ arles-antique.cg13.fr

The superb **Musée Départemental Arles Antique**, the best place to get an overall sense of Roman Arles, stands southwest of the centre. Open-plan, flooded with light and immensely spacious, it starts with regional prehistory, then leads through the Roman era. The story of Arles is traced from Julius Caesar's legionnaire base up to the height of its importance as a fifth-century trading centre. At that time, Emperor Honorius could say "the town's position, its communications and its crowd of visitors is such that there is no place in the world better suited to spreading, in every sense, the products of the earth". Excellent models show Arles' changing layout, while thematic displays explore topics like medicine, industry and agriculture.

The museum is positioned on the axis of the second-century **Cirque Romaine**, an enormous chariot racetrack that stretched back 450m and seated twenty thousand spectators. Little is now discernible on the ground, however.

The museum's imminent **expansion** will focus on Arles' Roman port.

## Cathédrale St-Trophime

Place de la République • **Cathedral** Mid-April to June Mon–Sat 8am–noon & 2–6pm; Sun 9am–1pm & 3–7pm; July–Sept Mon–Sat 8am–noon & 3–7pm, Sun 9am–1pm & 3–7pm; Oct to mid-April daily 8am–noon & 2–6pm • Free **Cloisters** Daily: March, April & Oct 9am–noon & 2–6pm; May–Sept 9am–7pm; Nov–Feb 10am–noon & 2–5pm • €3.50, €6 with Les Arènes

Arles' **Cathédrale St-Trophime** is simply one inconspicuous facade among many on place de la République. Superb twelfth-century Provençal stone carving around its doorway depicts the Last Judgement, trumpeted by angels playing with the enthusiasm of jazz musicians. Inside, the high nave is decorated with d'Aubusson tapestries, while there's more Romanesque and Gothic stone carving in the beautiful **cloisters**, reached by a separate entrance to the right.

## Musée Réattu

10 rue du Grand-Prieuré • Tues–Sun: July–Sept 10am–7pm; Oct–June 10am–12.30pm & 2–6.30pm • €7 • ☎ 04 90 49 37 58, ⊛ museereattu.arles.fr

The must-see **Musée Réattu**, in a beautiful fifteenth-century priory beside the river, centres on 57 ink and crayon sketches by Pablo Picasso, made between December 1970 and February 1971. Among the split faces, clowns and hilarious mythical Tarasque, there's a beautifully simple portrait of Picasso's mother, painted from life in 1923. Other twentieth-century pieces include *Odalisque*, Zadkine's polychromed sculpture of a woman playing a violin, and Mario Prassinos' black-and-white studies of the Alpilles.

**16**

## VAN GOGH IN ARLES

On February 21, 1888, **Vincent van Gogh** arrived in Arles from Paris, to be greeted by snow and a bitter Mistral wind. Within a year, he painted such celebrated canvases as *The Sunflowers*, *Van Gogh's Chair*, *The Red Vines* and *The Sower*. He always lived near the station, staying first at the *Hotel Carrel*, 30 rue de la Cavalarie, then the *Café de la Gare*, and finally the so-called "Yellow House", at 2 place Lamartine.

Van Gogh found few kindred souls in Arles, but managed to persuade **Paul Gauguin** to join him in October. Their relationship quickly soured when the November weather forced them to spend more time indoors. Precisely what transpired on the night of December 23, 1888 may never be known. According to Gauguin, Van Gogh, feeling threatened by his friend's possible departure, attacked first Gauguin and then himself. He cut off the lower part of his **left ear**, wrapped it in newspaper, and handed it to a prostitute. Gauguin duly left Arles, and although Vincent's wound soon healed, his mental health swiftly deteriorated. In response to a petition from thirty of his neighbours, he was packed off to the **Hôtel-Dieu** hospital, from where he moved on to St-Rémy (see p.825).

None of Van Gogh's paintings remains in Arles, and the Yellow House was destroyed by World War II bombing. Vestiges of the city that he knew survive, however. Behind the Réattu museum, lanterns line the river wall where he'd wander, wearing candles on his hat, watching the night-time light: *The Starry Night* shows the Rhône at Arles, while the distinctive Pont Langlois drawbridge survives on the southern edge of town. The Hôtel-Dieu hospital itself, on rue du Président-Wilson, is now the **Espace Van Gogh**, housing a *mediathèque* and university departments, with a bookshop and a *salon de thé* in the arcades.

The **Fondation Vincent van Gogh** is due to open a large exhibition and research facility on rue du Dr-Fanton. As well as displaying contemporary works inspired by Van Gogh, it hopes to arrange temporary loans of paintings by the artist himself. For details, visit ⓦfondation -vincentvangogh-arles.org.

**16**

## ARRIVAL AND INFORMATION ARLES

**By train** Arles' *gare SNCF* is on av Pauline Talabot, a few blocks north of Les Arènes.
Destinations Avignon (17 daily; 20min); Avignon TGV (2 daily; 20min); Lyon (7–9 daily; 2hr 30min); Marseille (23 daily; 45min–1hr); Nîmes (7 daily; 30min); Paris (2 daily; 4hr); Tarascon (4 daily; 10min).

**By bus** Most buses arrive at the unstaffed *gare routière* on av Pauline Talabot, but local services stop on bd Georges Clemenceau, east of rue Gambetta.
Destinations Aix (7 daily; 1hr 30min); Avignon (7 daily; 1hr); Avignon TGV (10 daily; 55min); Les Baux (5 daily; 40min); Nîmes (11 daily; 1hr 5min);

Stes-Maries-de-la-Mer (9 daily; 50min); St-Rémy (8 daily; 50min); Tarascon (10 daily; 20min).

**By car** Drivers are better off parking on the periphery, such as in the "Centre" car park on bd des Lices, than venturing into the central maze of narrow one-way streets.

**Tourist office** Bd des Lices (Easter–June & Sept daily 9am–6.45pm; July & Aug daily 9am–7.45pm; Oct–Easter Mon–Sat 9am–4.45pm, Sun 10am–1pm; ☏04 90 18 41 20, ⓦarlestourisme.com).

**Bike rental** Europbike, 5 rue Marius Jouveau (☏06 38 14 49 50, ⓦeuropbike-provence.net).

## ACCOMMODATION

**Acacias** 2 rue de la Cavalerie ☏04 90 96 37 88, ⓦhotel -acacias.com. Modern, simple but cheerfully decorated – and soundproofed – rooms in a friendly hotel, not far from the train station. Closed late Oct to March. **€76**

★ **Amphithéâtre** 5–7 rue Diderot ☏04 90 96 10 30, ⓦhotelamphitheatre.fr. Very central hotel, where the spacious and beautifully decorated a/c rooms feature warm colours, tiles and wrought ironwork, and large well-equipped bathrooms; the four-person rooms and suites are good value. **€67**

**Auberge de Jeunesse** 20 av du Maréchal-Foch ☏04 90 96 18 25, ⓦfuaj.org/arles. Old-style hostel, 500m south

of the centre – from the *gare SNCF*, take bus #3 to stop "Clemenceau" – with rock-hard beds in large dorms, and spartan facilities. Rates include breakfast. Bike hire available. Reception 7–10am & 5–11pm (midnight in summer). Closed mid-Dec to mid-Feb. **€18.50**

**Calendal** 5 rue Porte-de-Laure ☏04 90 96 11 89, ⓦlecalendal.com. Welcoming hotel, overlooking the Théâtre Antique and glowing at sunset, with bright a/c rooms around a pleasant shaded garden; rates include access to the indoor spa. **€119**

**City** 67 rte de Crau ☏04 90 93 08 86, ⓦcamping-city .com. The closest campsite to town, 1.5km southeast on the Crau bus route, this three-star is not very attractive, but there's a certain amount of shade, and a pool. Closed Oct– March. **€19**

**Forum** 10 place du Forum ☎04 90 93 48 95, ⓦhotelduforum.com. This venerable hotel, in Arles' most appealing little square, offers plain but tasteful and reasonably spacious rooms, plus a bar that's barely changed since Picasso hung out here fifty years ago. There's even a tiny pool. **€80**

**Grand Hôtel Nord Pinus** 14 place du Forum ☎04 90 93 44 44, ⓦnord-pinus.com. Chic, luxurious rooms in a grand mansion dominating a pretty, lively square in the heart of the old town. Much favoured by the *vedettes* of the bullring, it's decorated with trophies and photos. **€175**

★ **Muette** 15 rue des Suisses ☎04 90 96 15 39, ⓦhotel-muette.com. Charming old stone hotel, close to Les Arènes, where the tasteful, tranquil rooms are decked out in beiges and creams, with rough-hewn terracotta-tiled floors and lots of Van Gogh touches, down to the (artificial) sunflowers on the tables. Nice buffet breakfast, and friendly management. Closed Jan & Feb. **€84**

**Musée** 11 rue du Grand-Prieuré ☎04 90 93 88 88, ⓦhoteldumusee.com. Small, good-value, family-run place, in a quiet seventeenth-century mansion, with a pretty, flower-filled terrace, and its own art gallery. Closed Jan & first fortnights of March & Dec. **€65**

## EATING AND DRINKING

### RESTAURANTS

**A Coté** 21 rue des Carmes ☎04 90 47 61 13, ⓦbistro-acote.com. The most affordable of three all-but adjoining restaurants belonging to chef Jean-Luc Rabanel, along a tiny but very central alleyway, this informal bistro has pleasant outdoor seating. Open from breakfast onwards, it serves full *menus* from €29, but also mouthwatering tapas such as aubergine caviar from around €8, and varying *plats* from €18. Daily 9am–midnight.

**L'Escaladou** 23 rue Porte-de-Laure ☎04 90 96 70 43. Behind its old-fashioned facade, near the upper side of the Théâtre Antique, this local favourite holds three substantial dining rooms. Some dismiss it as a tourist trap; it can be noisy and not exactly romantic, and the service is perfunctory at times, but the honest local food is delicious. *Menus* from €19; magnificently garlicky fish specials include a sumptuous €28 Arlesian bouillabaisse. Mon, Tues & Fri–Sun noon–1.30pm & 7.30–9.30pm, Thurs 7.30–9.30pm.

**La Fée Gourmande** 39 rue Dulau ☎04 90 18 26 57. Great-value home cooking in a friendly, slightly kitsch environment, with *menus* and *plats* from just €13. The house speciality is melt-in-your-mouth slow-cooked lamb. Wed–Sun noon–1.30pm & 7.30–9.30pm.

★ **La Gueule de Loup** 39 rue des Arènes ☎04 90 96 96 69. Cosy stone-walled restaurant, with the open kitchen plus four tables downstairs, and the main dining room upstairs. Elaborate and delicate Provençal dishes include a courgette-blossom mousse and turbot on a bed of puréed aubergine. *Menus* from €13 at lunch, €25 at dinner. Mon 7.30–9.30pm, Tues–Sat noon–1.45pm & 7.30–9.30pm.

**Le Plaza** 28 rue du Dr-Fanton ☎04 90 96 33 15. Smart but very friendly place, also known as *La Paillote*, with a good €21 *menu* full of Provençal starters and main courses such as *papillote de taureau* (bull), and a €33 *menu* of house specialities, with no choice. Reserve for outdoor seating. Mon & Thurs–Sun noon–1.20pm & 7–9.30pm, Tues 7–9.30pm, Wed noon–1.20pm.

### CAFÉS

**Café d'Autre Fois** 22 rue de la Liberté ☎06 09 24 39 59, ⓦcafedautrefois.com. Close to the heart of things, this coffee bar has a laidback atmosphere and its outdoor terrace is a welcome escape. Organic espressos and pricey but refreshing all-fruit smoothies (the 75cl size costs €6.70), plus breakfast for €4.40 and salads or *plats* for around €8. Daily 7.30am–7pm.

**Café la Nuit** 11 place du Forum ☎04 90 96 44 56. Immortalized by Van Gogh – though it's not his *Café la Nuit*, which was near the station – this long-established café remains *the* place to enjoy Arles' pretty central square. Have a drink on the terrace and you'll find yourself in quite a few holiday snaps; don't eat here though, the food is very poor. Daily 8am–11pm.

## NIGHTLIFE

**Patio de Camargue** 51bis Chemin Barriol ☎04 90 49 51 76, ⓦchico.fr. Arles was the original base for the world-conquering Gipsy Kings group. Founder-member Chico now runs this riverfront restaurant-cum-music venue, 1km southwest of the centre, which puts on regular dinner concerts. Typically on Saturday nights, they cost upwards of €50; check website for schedules.

# The Camargue

Spreading across Rhône delta, defined by the Petit Rhône to the west, the Grand Rhône to the east, and the Mediterranean to the south, the drained, ditched and now protected land known as the **CAMARGUE** is distinct from the rest of Provence. With land, lagoon and sea sharing the same horizontal plain, its horizons appear infinite, its boundaries unseen.

16

16

# THE CAMARGUE

**Map legend:**
- Footpaths
- Digues
- Border of Parc
- Régional de Camargue

**Places and features on the map:**

Port-St-Louis-du-Rhône

They de la Gracieuse

Plage Napoléon

La Palissade

Etg. de Grande Palun

Saltworks

Plage de Piémanson

Ferry

Saltworks

Salin-de-Giraud

Etang de Faraman

Le Sambuc

Musée du Riz

D36

Grand Rhône

Vieux Rhône

La Capelière

Centre d'Ecologie

Etang du Fournelet

Etang du Fangassier

Etang du Gr. Rascaillon

Etg. du Vaisseau

Etang du Galabert

Etang du Beauduc

Villeneuve

D36

D37

RÉSERVE NATIONALE DE CAMARGUE

Beauduc Lighthouse

Gageron

PARC NATUREL RÉGIONAL DE CAMARGUE

Etang de Vaccarès

Etang du Lyon

Mas de la Camargue

Musée de la Camargue

Méjanes

BOIS DES RIÈGES

RÉSERVE DES IMPÉRIAUX

Albaron

D37

Etang de Malagroy

Etang de Consecanière

Cacharel

Etang dit L'Impérial

Les Stes-Maries-de-la-Mer

D570

Pioch-Badet

Etang de Gines

D85A

Centre de Gines

D570

D38B

D38A

Parc Ornithologique

Pont de Gau

PETITE CAMARGUE

Pont de Sylvéreal

D85

Aigues-Mortes

MEDITERRANEAN SEA

N

0          5
kilometres

---

## BULLS, BIRDS AND BEAVERS: CAMARGUAIS WILDLIFE

The Camargue is a treasure trove of bird and animal species, both wild and domestic. Its most famous denizens are its **bulls** and the **white horses**, both of which roam in semi-liberty. Born dark brown or black, the Camargue horse turns white in around its fourth year.

An estimated 2500 of the region's **gardians** or herdsmen – ten percent of them women – remain active. A hardy bunch, they play a major role in preserving Camarguais traditions. Their traditional homes, or *cabanes*, are thatched, windowless one-storey structures, with bulls' horns over the door to ward off evil spirits. Throughout the summer, the *gardians* are kept busy, with spectacles involving bulls and horses in every village arena; winter is a good deal harder.

Camargue **wildlife** ranges from wild boars, beavers and badgers, tree frogs, water snakes and pond turtles, to marsh and seabirds and birds of prey. The best season for **birdwatching** lasts from April to June. Of the region's fifty thousand or so **flamingos**, ten thousand remain in winter (Oct–March), when the rest migrate to Africa.

---

The whole of the Camargue is a Parc Naturel Régional, which sets out to balance tourism, agriculture, industry and hunting against the indigenous ecosystems. When the Romans arrived, the northern part of the Camargue was a forest; they felled the trees to build ships, then grew wheat. These days, especially since the northern marshes were drained and re-irrigated after World War II, the main crop is **rice**.

The Camargue is split into two separate sections by the large **Étang du Vaccarès**, a lagoon that's out of bounds to visitors. Most people focus their attention on the western Camargue, home to the sizeable town of **Stes-Maries-de-la-Mer**, and also commercial attractions such as wildlife parks and activity operators. It is possible, however, to take a quick look at both the western and eastern halves of the Camargue within a single day.

**16**

### The western Camargue: the road to Stes-Maries

The **western** side of the Camargue is busy all summer with tourists, who flock down its main artery, the D570, towards **Stes-Maries-de-la-Mer**. Take the time to explore the marshes and dunes en route, or follow the waterfront nature trails.

#### Musée de la Camargue

D570, 10km southwest of Arles • Feb, March & Oct–Dec daily except Tues 10am–12.30pm & 1–5pm; April–Sept daily 9am–12.30pm & 1–6pm • €4.50, under-18s free • ☎ 04 90 97 10 82, ⊕ parc-camargue.fr

Adjoining the main Camargue **information centre**, the **Musée de la Camargue** documents the history, traditions and livelihoods of the Camarguais people, with particular emphasis on rice, wine and bulls. Its excellent displays are not very accessible if you don't read French.

#### Parc Ornithologique de Pont de Gau

Pont de Gau, 4km north of Stes-Maries • Daily: April–Sept 9am–sunset; Oct–March 10am–sunset • €7.50 • ☎ 04 90 97 82 62, ⊕ parcornithologique.com

The **Parc Ornithologique de Pont de Gau** makes a great stop before you reach Stes-Maries. Paths lead around and over three separate lagoons in a thirty-acre marsh, making birdwatching easy. Flamingos are abundant, while some less easily spotted species, such as owls and vultures, are kept in aviaries.

### Les Stes-Maries-de-la-Mer

Although most Camargue visitors head straight to **LES STES-MARIES-DE-LA-MER**, 37km southwest of Arles, this attractive but commercialized seaside village has much more in common with France's other Mediterranean beach resorts than with the wild and empty land that surrounds it.

Stes-Maries is most famous for its annual **gypsy festival** on May 24–25, when Romanies celebrate **Sarah**, their patron saint. She was the Egyptian servant of the two "Maries" in the town's name: **Mary Jacobé**, the aunt of Jesus, and **Mary Salomé**, mother of two of the Apostles, who were said to have landed here in a boat without sails and oars after being driven out of Palestine.

A line of **beaches**, sculpted into little crescents by stone breakwaters and busy with bathers and windsurfers in summer, stretches away west from Stes-Maries' central core of white-painted, orange-tiled houses, while the pleasure **port** to the east offers boat trips to the lagoons and fishing expeditions. The town **market** takes place on place des Gitans every Monday and Friday.

## Church of Stes-Maries

Place Jean XXIII • **Rooftop** Daily: July & Aug Mon–Sat 10am–sunset, Sun 1pm–sunset; March–June & Sept to mid-Nov Mon–Sat 10am–12.30pm & 2pm–sunset, Sun 2pm–sunset • €2.20

The spiders-web tangle of streets and alleyways at the heart of old Stes-Maries opens out into spacious squares around the grey-gold Romanesque **Church of Stes-Maries**. Fortified in the fourteenth century in response to frequent attacks by pirates, the church has beautifully pure lines and fabulous acoustics. Its high, barrel-vaulted interior provided shelter for all the villagers; it even holds its own freshwater well.

At the far end, steps lead up to the altar or down to the low **crypt**, where the tinselled, sequined and dark-skinned statue of Sarah is surrounded by candles, while two bones are displayed in a tabernacle nearby.

Although you can't climb to the top of the tower, you can pay to scramble onto and over the church roof, for great views over the town.

## The eastern Camargue

Cut through by the final canalized stretch of the Grand Rhône, the little-visited **eastern** side of the Camargue is less agricultural and more industrial, but holds its own share of wildlife reserves and tranquil refuges, as well as the quiet little village of **Salin-de-Giraud**.

**Salt** evaporation was first undertaken here by the Romans, and the Camargue now holds one of the biggest saltworks in the world. Saltpans and pyramids add an extra-terrestrial feel to the landscape.

## La Capelière

D36B, 23km south of Arles • April–Sept daily 9am–1pm & 2–6pm; Oct–March daily except Tues 9am–1pm & 2–5pm • €3 • ☎ 04 90 97 00 97, ⓦ reserve-camargue.org

**La Capelière**, the information centre for the eastern Camargue, holds faded displays on Camargue wildlife and how to see it. Outside, a short but excellent 1.5km initiation trail circles a small lagoon, and there are superb **birdwatching** opportunities from camouflaged hides equipped with telescopes.

### ARRIVAL AND INFORMATION
### THE CAMARGUE

**LES STES-MARIES-DE-LA-MER**

**By bus** Buses from Arles (9 daily; 50min) arrive at the north end of place Mireille, 400m short of the sea.

**Tourist office** 5 av Van-Gogh, on the seafront (daily: Jan,

Feb, Nov & Dec 9am–5pm; March & Oct 9am–6pm; April–June & Sept 9am–7pm; July & Aug 9am–8pm; ☎ 04 90 97 82 55, ⓦ saintesmaries.com).

### TOURS AND ACTIVITIES

**River trips** The paddle steamer *Le Tiki III* offers 90min trips from the mouth of the Petit Rhône, 2.5km west of Les Stes-Maries-de-la-Mer (mid-March to Oct 1–5 daily; €12; ☎ 04 90 97 81 68, ⓦ tiki3.fr), and the *Camargue* from the port in Stes-Maries (mid-March to mid-Oct 1–4 daily; ☎ 04 90 97

84 72, ⓦ bateau-camargue.com).

**Horseriding** Around thirty Camargue farms offer horseriding, costing from €16/hr up to €85/day. You can find full lists at ⓦ saintesmaries.com, ⓦ promenades-a-cheval.com and ⓦ camargue.fr.

16

**Cycling** Bikes can be rented in Les Stes-Maries-de-la-Mer from Le Vélociste, which is back from the sea on place Mireille (☎ 04 90 97 83 26, ⓦ www.levelociste.fr).

**Canoeing and kayaking** Canoes and kayaks are available from Kayak Vert in Sylvéréal, 17km northwest of

Les Stes-Maries-de-la-Mer (from €10 for 1hr; ☎ 04 66 73 57 17, ⓦ kayakvert-camargue.fr).

**Jeep safaris** Camargue Safari (☎ 04 90 93 60 31, ⓦ www .safari-4x4-gallon.camargue.fr) offer jeep safaris, starting from Arles or Stes-Maries, for €36 and upwards.

## ACCOMMODATION

**Bleu Marine** 15 av du Dr-Cambon, Les Stes-Maries-de-la-Mer ☎ 04 90 97 71 00, ⓦ hotel-bleu-marine.com. Friendly, peaceful retreat at the western end of town, with simple but immaculate rooms, a nice pool and easy parking. **€70**

**Cacharel** Rte de Cacharel, 4km north of Stes-Maries ☎ 04 90 97 95 44, ⓦ hotel-cacharel.com. Sixteen luxurious rooms in one of the Camargue's oldest farms, with open fires to warm you in winter, a pool to cool off in summer, and horseriding available year-round, but no restaurant. **€131**

**Camping Le Clos du Rhône** Rte d'Aigues-Mortes, 800m west of central Stes-Maries ☎ 04 90 97 85 99, ⓦ camping-leclos.fr. Busy four-star site at the mouth of the Petit Rhône, west of Stes-Maries along an easy seaside path, with a pool, laundry and shop. Closed early Nov to April. **€25.50**

**Hostellerie du Pont de Gau** Rte d'Arles, Pont de Gau, 4km north of Stes-Maries ☎ 04 90 97 81 53, ⓦ pontdegau.camargue.fr. Old-fashioned Camarguais decor and an excellent restaurant, 4km north of

Stes-Maries near the Parc Ornithologique. Rates include breakfast. Closed Jan to mid-Feb. **€70**

★ **Mangio Fango** Rte d'Arles, Les Stes-Maries-de-la-Mer ☎ 04 90 97 80 56, ⓦ hotelmangiofango.com. Tranquil farmhouse, overlooking the Étang des Launes, with a Mediterranean twist. Stylish, comfortable rooms – get one at the back, with a balcony, if at all possible – pricey restaurant, and a pool surrounded by lush green foliage. Closed Dec–March, except Christmas & New Year. **€135**

**Mas de Pioch** Pioch-Badet, 10km north of Stes-Maries ☎ 04 90 97 50 06, ⓦ masdepioch.com. Great-value B&B in a converted nineteenth-century hunting inn just off the main road north of Stes-Maries. Large rooms and a pool. Book well in advance. **€51**

★ **Mediterranée** 4 av F-Mistral, Les Stes-Maries-de-la-Mer ☎ 04 90 97 82 09, ⓦ mediterraneehotel.com. Decked out in jolly flowers, this welcoming hotel has pretty Provençal-style rooms – sleeping up to four – and is on the main restaurant street, seconds from the sea. The cheapest rooms share toilets, and there are some well priced four-person options. **€45**

**16**

## EATING AND DRINKING

The only Camargue town to hold a significant concentration of restaurants is Les Stes-Maries-de-la-Mer. Of a summer evening, it gets very lively indeed, with the *terrasses* of its restaurants and bars sprawling out across the streets and squares, and flamenco or gypsy-jazz guitarists and buskers everywhere. Camarguais specialities include *tellines*, tiny shiny shellfish served with garlic mayonnaise; *gardianne de taureau*, bull's meat cooked in wine, vegetables and Provençal herbs; eels from the Vaccarès; rice, asparagus and wild duck; and *poutargue des Stes-Maries*, a mullet roe dish.

**La Bouvine** 1 place Esprit Pioch, Les Stes-Maries-de-la-Mer ☎ 04 90 97 87 09. Very large restaurant on Stes-Maries' main dining street, with lots of outdoor seating and a choice of pretty much any French or Spanish dish you care to mention, from paella (€12) to bouillabaisse (€54 for two), plus a €15 *menu* featuring *gardianne de taureau*. Daily except Thurs noon–2pm & 7–10pm.

**Casa Romana** 6 rue Joseph-Roumanille, Les Stes-Maries-de-la-Mer ☎ 04 90 97 83 33. Friendly Provençal restaurant, with outdoor seating on a side street near the church. Two daily €12.50 *plats du jour* at lunchtime, such as mussels or *taureau*, also feature on an €18.50 set *menu*; the evening *menu* is €22. Feb–Dec Tues 5.30–10pm, Wed–Sun noon–2pm & 7–10pm.

# The River Sourgue

As you head east from Avignon to the Luberon, try to find time to pause at two delightful spots on the River Sorgue: the pretty market town of **L'Isle-sur-la-Sorgue**, and **Fontaine-de-Vaucluse**, which guards the river's source a little further east.

## L'Isle-sur-la-Sorgue

**L'ISLE-SUR-LA-SORGUE**, 30km east of Avignon, straddles five branches of the River Sorgue, with little canals and waterways running through and around the centre. Its waters were once filled with otters and beavers, eels, trout and crayfish, and turned the power wheels of a medieval cloth industry. Tanneries, dyeing works, and subsequently silk and paper manufacturing, all ensured considerable prosperity for the "island".

Nowadays, the blackened waterwheels turn for show only, and the mills and tanneries stand empty. In summer, though, L'Isle is a cheerful place, particularly on Sundays, when people arrive for its well-known **antiques market**, which centres on the Village des Antiquaires on avenue de l'Égalité and spills out onto the boulevards.

While claims to be the Venice of Provence may stretch a point, L'Isle-sur-la-Sorgue is a pleasant waterside place to spend an afternoon. The central **place de l'Église** and **place de la Liberté** offer reminders of past prosperity, most obviously in the Baroque seventeenth-century **church** (Tues–Sat: July & Aug 10am–noon & 3–6pm, Sun 3–6pm; Sept–June 10am–noon & 3–5pm), the richest religious edifice for miles around.

## Fontaine-de-Vaucluse

The source of the River Sorgue is a mysterious tapering fissure, 7km east of L'Isle-sur-la-Sorgue at the foot of towering 230m cliffs. Among the most powerful natural springs in the world, and compellingly beautiful into the bargain, it's a hugely popular tourist attraction. All access is via a gentle 500m footpath from the ancient riverside village of **FONTAINE-DE-VAUCLUSE**. Both the village and the full length of the path are heavily (albeit reasonably tastefully) commercialized, but it's still a gorgeous spot, with the glorious green river cascading beneath thickly wooded slopes.

**16**

### INFORMATION

THE RIVER SOURGUE

**L'ISLE-SUR-LA-SORGUE**

**Tourist office** Place de l'Église (Mon–Sat 9am–12.30pm & 2.30–6pm; Sun 9am–12.30pm; ☎ 04 90 38 04 78, ⓦ oti-delasorgue.fr).

**FONTAINE-DE-VAUCLUSE**

**Tourist office** On the riverside footpath (May–Sept daily 10am–1pm & 2–6pm; Oct–April Mon–Sat 9.30am–12.30pm & 1.30–5.30pm, Sun 1.30–5.30pm; ☎ 04 90 20 32 22, ⓦ oti-delasorgue.fr).

### ACCOMMODATION AND EATING

**L'ISLE-SUR-LA-SORGUE**

**Bistrot de l'Industrie** 2 quai de la Charité ☎ 04 90 38 00 40. This traditional old bistro serves decent €10 *plats du jour* and *menus* from just €13, at secluded riverside tables. Mon–Fri 11am–11pm, Sat 11am–10pm.

**La Prévôté** 4 rue J.J. Rousseau ☎ 04 90 38 57 29, ⓦ la-prevote.fr. Set around a quiet courtyard behind the church, this charming hotel offers five rooms decked out in beautiful terracotta tiles, wooden beams and Provençal quilts. Its small, superb restaurant, downstairs in the old sacristy, serves top-quality *menus* from €22 for lunch, €39 at dinner. Rates include breakfast. Restaurant closed Mon lunch, all Tues, & Wed lunch. **€160**

**FONTAINE-DE-VAUCLUSE**

★ **Auberge La Figuière** ☎ 04 90 20 37 41, ⓦ la-figuiere.fr. Simple but attractive B&B rooms in the village

centre, with terracotta tiles, tasteful Provençal furnishings and excellent walk-in showers. The restaurant downstairs serves a great-value €23 *menu* in a pleasant flowery courtyard. No credit cards for rooms. Closed Oct to mid-Feb. **€51**

**Restaurant Philip** Chemin de la Fontaine ☎ 04 90 20 31 81. This gorgeous riverside spot is sure to catch your eye as you walk up to the spring. At the very least, it's worth enjoying a quick drink on the bar section of its long, peaceful terrace, but the food is a lot better than you might expect, with full *menus* starting at €27. Easter–Sept daily noon–9pm.

**L'Hotel du Poète** Just below the main D25 on the river's north bank ☎ 04 90 20 34 05, ⓦ hoteldupoete.com. Despite its uninspiring exterior, this former water mill offers luxurious accommodation, with large, comfortable rooms and a pool, but no restaurant. Closed Dec to mid-March. **€95**

## The Luberon

East of Avignon and north of Aix, the beautiful wine-growing, lavender-carpeted valley of the **Luberon** has long been a favoured escape for well-heeled Parisians, Dutch and

## PARC NATUREL RÉGIONAL DU LUBERON

With the aim of conserving the natural fauna and flora and limiting development, much of the Luberon has been designated as the **Parc Naturel Régional du Luberon**. It's administered by the **Maison du Parc**, 60 place Jean-Jaurès in Apt (Mon–Fri 8.30am–noon & 1.30–6pm; April–Aug also Sat 8.30am–noon; ☎ 004 90 04 42 00, ⓦ parcduluberon.fr). **Vélo Loisir en Luberon** (ⓦ veloloisirluberon.com), a consortium of hotels, campsites and cycle hire and repair shops, promotes cycle tourism throughout the region.

British, not to mention artists. The Luberon's northern face is damper and more alpine in character than the Mediterranean-scented southern slopes, and gets extremely cold in winter. It's almost all wooded, except for the summer sheep pastures at the top, and there's just one main route across, the Combe de Lourmarin. In addition to the valley's one sizeable town, likeable **APT**, countless small **villages** cling stubbornly to the Luberon foothills. With their impossibly narrow cobbled streets, tumbledown houses strewn with flowers, and sun-baked *places*, they make wonderful days out and even better places to stay.

## Apt

The only town base for exploring the Luberon, bustling little **APT** has one of the oldest cathedrals in Provence. It's especially worth visiting on a Saturday for the lively **market** when, as well as every imaginable Provençal edible, there are barrel organs, jazz musicians and stand-up comics on show.

**16**

## Saignon

Despite being perhaps Luberon's most enchanting village, tiny, immaculate **SAIGNON**, 4km southeast of Apt, remains somewhat undiscovered on the tourist circuit. For a breathtaking overview of the surrounding splendour, follow signs up to **Le Rocher**.

## Bonnieux

It's very easy to get lost among the narrow, twisting lanes of **BONNIEUX**, built on several interlocking levels, 12km southwest of Apt. If all else fails, head to the top of the hill and dinky twelfth-century *église haute* where there are marvellous views across the valley. **Market day** is Friday.

## Ménerbes

Surrounded by sweeping countryside and perched on a hill 23km southwest of Apt, the village **MÉNERBES** boasts a fine collection of medieval and Renaissance-era houses and a dominant sixteenth-century citadelle. **Market day** is Thursday.

### Maison de la Truffe et des Vins

Place de l'Horloge • Daily: April–Oct 10am–12.30pm & 2.30–6.30pm; Nov–March 3–6pm • ☎ 04 90 72 38 37, ⓦ vin-truffe-luberon.com

If you're feeling overwhelmed by the multitude of local road signs directing you to wine-tasting *caves* or *châteaux*, head for the elegant **Maison de la Truffe et des Vins**, which sells wines from all three of Luberon's *appellations* for the same price as at the wholesalers. They arrange wine and truffle-tasting.

## Gordes and around

**GORDES**, 20km west of Apt or 12km north of Ménerbes, is an incredibly picturesque Provençal village much favoured by Parisian media personalities, film directors, artists and the like. A cluster of magnificent, honey-coloured buildings clinging to a sheer rockface, it's a spectacular sight. **Market day** is Tuesday.

At the top of the village, a church and houses surround a mighty twelfth- to sixteenth-century **château**, housing the paintings of the contemporary Flemish artist **Pol Mara**, who lived locally (daily 10am–noon & 2–6pm; €4).

## Village des Bories

3.5km east of Gordes, off the D2 · Daily 9am–sunset · €6 · ☎ 04 90 72 03 48, ⓦ gordes-village.com

A collection of peculiar dry-stone dwellings on the hillside east of Gordes is known as the **Village des Bories**. Although such buildings were first constructed in the Bronze Age, most of these constructions – sheep-pens, wine vats, bread-ovens and the like – date from the eighteenth century, and were inhabited until little more than a hundred years ago.

## Abbaye de Sénanque

D177, 4km north of Gordes · Self-guided visits Feb to mid-Nov Mon–Sat 9.45–11am; mid-Nov to Jan Mon–Sat 2.30–5pm; 1hr guided tours, in French, to a very intricate schedule, ranging from 10 daily in summer to 2 in winter; first tour 10.10am May–Aug, 10.30am Feb–April & Oct to mid-Nov, last usually at 4.30pm; mid-Nov to Dec the only tours are at 2.15pm & 3.30pm; closed Sun morning all year, and much of Jan; reservations essential · €7 · ☎ 04 90 72 05 72, ⓦ www.senanque.fr

Set amid much-photographed lavender fields in a deep cleft in the hills, the twelfth-century Cistercian **Abbaye de Sénanque** is still active as a monastery. You can visit the church, cloisters and all the main rooms of this substantial and austere building; a shop sells the monks' produce, including liqueur, honey and lavender essence.

## Abbaye de Silvacane

**16**

D561A, 29km south of Apt · June–Sept daily 10am–6pm; Oct–May daily except Tues 10am–1pm & 2–5pm · €7.50 · ☎ 04 42 50 41 69, ⓦ abbaye-silvacane.com

Drivers en route between Aix-en-Provence and Apt pass close to the ancient Cistercian **Abbaye de Silvacane**, contemporary with that of Sénanque, just south of the Durance. After a long history of abandonment and evictions, the abbey is once again a monastic institution. Isolated from the surrounding villages on the bank of the Durance, its architecture has hardly changed over the last seven hundred years; you can visit the stark, pale-stoned splendour of the church, its cloisters and surrounding buildings.

## Roussillon

The houses in the village of **ROUSSILLON**, 10km east of Gordes, radiate all the different shades of the seventeen ochre tints once quarried here. As colourful as an artist's palette itself, the town attracts a multitude of painters, potters and sculptors, whose works are on show and for sale throughout the town. **Market day** is Thursday.

## Conservatoire des Ocres

Feb–June & Sept–Nov daily 9am–6pm; July & Aug daily 9am–7pm; Dec & Jan Wed–Sun 9am–6pm · €6, includes optional guided tour · ☎ 04 90 05 66 69, ⓦ okhra.com

To find out more about the ochre industry, head to the **Conservatoire des Ocres**, which demonstrates the various washing, draining, settling and drying procedures, and also hosts fascinating exhibitions.

## The Sentiers des Ocres

Daily mid-Feb to Dec; hours change monthly, up to 9am–7.30pm in July & Aug · €2.50 · ⓦ roussillon-provence.com

A pretty natural park full of colourful and oddly shaped rocks and pinnacles, the **Sentiers des Ocres** provides a fine opportunity to admire the lovely ochre hues of the Luberon – and to stretch your legs. From the entrance next to Roussillon's cemetery, simply follow the sandy, colour-coded walks.

**CLOCKWISE FROM TOP LEFT** AVIGNON (P.814); LES GORGES DU VERDON (P.849); MARKET IN AIX (P.844); PALAIS DES PAPES, AVIGNON (P.815) >

## ARRIVAL AND INFORMATION

### APT

**By bus** Buses from Aix (2 daily; 1hr 45min) stop at the *gare routière* on av de la Libération, east of the centre, but also drop passengers in the central place de la Bouquerie.

**Tourist office** 20 av Philippe-de-Girard (July & Aug Mon–Sat 9.30am–1pm & 2.30–7pm, Sun 9.30am–12.30pm; May, June & Sept Mon–Sat 9.30am–12.30pm & 2.30–6.30pm, Sun 9.30am–12.30pm; Oct–April Mon–Sat 9.30am–12.30pm & 2–6pm; ☎04 90 74 03 18, 🅦luberon-apt.fr).

**Bike hire** Luberon Cycles, 86 quai du Général Leclerc (☎04 90 74 17 16).

### MENERBES

**Tourist office** Maison de la Truffe et des Vins, place de l'Horloge (Daily: April–Oct 10am–12.30pm & 2.30–6.30pm; Nov–March 3–6pm; 🅦vin-truffe-luberon.com).

### GORDES

**Tourist office** In the château (Mon–Sat 9am–noon & 2–6pm, Sun 10am–noon & 2–6pm; ☎04 90 72 02 75, 🅦gordes-village.com).

### ROUSSILLON

**Tourist office** Place de la Poste (Mon–Sat 10am–noon & 1.30–5pm; ☎04 90 05 60 25, 🅦roussillon-provence.com).

## ACCOMMODATION

### APT

**Auberge du Luberon** 17 quai Léon-Sagy ☎04 90 74 12 50, 🅦aubergeluberon.sitew.com. Neat little hotel-restaurant in a lovely, secluded but very central position beside the river. The seven en-suite rooms are spruce and comfortable, if slightly old-fashioned. **€70**

**Camping Les Cèdres** 63 impasse de la Fantasie ☎04 90 74 14 61, 🅦camping-les-cedres.fr. Pleasant, shady and very inexpensive little campsite, within easy walking distance of the centre across the bridge from place St-Pierre. Closed mid-Nov to mid-Feb. **€9.50**

**Le Couvent** 36 rue Louis Rousset ☎04 90 04 55 36, 🅦loucouvent.com. This pretty former convent, now run as a guesthouse, is Apt's most attractive option, with five stylish, simple, spacious rooms. Rates include breakfast. **€95**

### SAIGNON

**Auberge du Presbytère** Place de la Fontaine ☎04 90 74 11 50, 🅦auberge-presbytere.com. Saignon's finest hotel stands on its dreamy, rose-covered central square. Its sixteen lovely and widely varying rooms are cosy and comfortable, and there's a rather pricey, but good, restaurant (closed Wed) with a full dinner *menu* at €38. Closed mid-Jan to mid-Feb. **€65**

**La Bastide du Jas** Rue du Jas ☎04 90 04 88 27, 🅦labastidedujas.com. Restored rural farmhouse, set amid rambling gardens at the bottom of the village, with glorious, homely rooms and studios (two-bed studio €1200 per week), along with a swimming pool. **€76**

## EATING

### APT

**Les Délices de Léa** 87 rue de la République ☎04 90 74 32 77. Apt's best-value restaurant for a satisfying meal – assuming you haven't stuffed yourself with chocolates and candied fruit, the local speciality – has outdoor tables, and

### BONNIEUX

**Bastide de Capelongue** Chemin des Cabanes ☎04 90 75 89 78, 🅦capelongue.com. Incredibly luxurious hotel at the top of the village, which offers beautiful bedrooms, sitting rooms, terraces and pool. Its chef, Edouard Loubet, has received two Michelin stars and concocts gloriously insubstantial delicacies, such as duck breast with cauliflower mousse, at rather more substantial prices. **€250**

⭐ **Mas del Sol** Chemin des Foulans ☎04 90 75 94 80, 🅦chambres-dhotes-bonnieux-luberon.com. Immaculate B&B, 2.5km northwest of the village centre towards Goult, run by a friendly young couple and offering five modern rooms with a pool. **€145**

### GORDES

**Bastide de Gordes** Le village ☎04 90 72 12 12, 🅦bastide-de-gordes.com. Luxurious hotel, built into the ramparts of the old village. Some rooms have vaulted ceilings, there's a lavish spa as well as an outdoor pool, and the terrace boasts stunning views. **€300**

### ROUSSILLON

**Le Clos de la Glycine** Place de la Poste ☎04 90 05 60 13, 🅦luberon-hotel.com. Swanky hotel-restaurant in the heart of the hill village, where several of the sumptuous rooms enjoy fabulous views over the valley, and a fine restaurant serves *menus* from €29. **€130**

**Les Rêves d'Ocres** Rte de Gordes ☎04 90 05 60 50, 🅦hotel-revesdocres.com. Charming, ochre-coloured hotel, where the nicest of the sixteen rooms have private terraces, and there's a very relaxing garden. **€80**

*menus* from €17. Tues–Sat noon–1.30pm & 7.30–9.30pm.

### MÉNERBES

**Café Veranda** 101 rue Marcellin Poncet ☎04 90 72 72 33. Rather stylish contemporary restaurant, with seating indoors as well as on the eponymous panoramic veranda. Lunch *menu* €16, dinner *menus* from €32, and also large deli plates for less than €20. Tues–Sun noon–1.30pm & 7–9.30pm.

**Le Galoubet** 104 rue Marcellin Poncet ☎04 90 72 36 08. Quiet but popular little restaurant, serving good-quality, traditional Provençal dishes. The lunch *menu* is €14, typical daily *plats* more like €18. Daily except Wed

noon–1.30pm & 7.30–9.15pm.

### GORDES

**L'Artégal** Place du Château ☎04 90 72 02 54. Romantic village restaurant, in a beautiful setting facing the château, and serving fabulous food on *menus* from €35. Mid-March to Dec Mon & Thurs–Sun noon–1.30pm & 7.30–9.30pm, Tues 7.30–9.30pm.

## Aix-en-Provence

Were it not for the great metropolis of Marseille, just 30km south, **AIX-EN-PROVENCE** would be the dominant city of central Provence. Historically, culturally and socially,

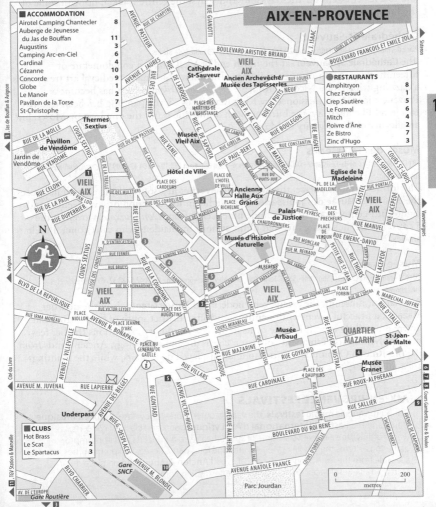

AIX-EN-PROVENCE

ACCOMMODATION
| | |
|---|---|
| Airotel Camping Chantecler | 8 |
| Auberge de Jeunesse du Jas de Bouffan | 11 |
| Augustins | 3 |
| Camping Arc-en-Ciel | 6 |
| Cardinal | 4 |
| Cézanne | 10 |
| Concorde | 9 |
| Globe | 1 |
| Le Manoir | 2 |
| Pavillon de la Torse | 7 |
| St-Christophe | 5 |

RESTAURANTS
| | |
|---|---|
| Amphitryon | 8 |
| Chez Feraud | 1 |
| Crep Sautière | 5 |
| Le Formal | 6 |
| Mitch | 4 |
| Poivre d'Âne | 2 |
| Ze Bistro | 7 |
| Zinc d'Hugo | 3 |

CLUBS
| | |
|---|---|
| Hot Brass | 1 |
| Le Scat | 2 |
| Le Spartacus | 3 |

the two cities are moons apart, and for visitors the tendency is to love one and hate the other. Aix is more immediately attractive, a stately and in parts pretty place that's traditionally seen as conservative. The proudest moment in its history was its fifteenth-century heyday as an independent fiefdom under the beloved King René of Anjou, while in the nineteenth century it was home to close friends Paul Cézanne and Émile Zola. Today, the youth of Aix dress immaculately; hundreds of foreign students, particularly Americans, come to study here; and there's a certain snobbishness, almost of Parisian proportions.

Known as **Vieil Aix**, the tangle of medieval lanes at the city's heart is a great monument in its entirety, an enchanting ensemble that's far more compelling than any individual building or museum it contains. With so many streets alive with people; so many tempting restaurants, cafés and shops; a fountained square to rest in every few minutes; and a backdrop of architectural treats from the sixteenth and seventeenth centuries, it's easy to while away days at a time enjoying its pleasures. On Saturdays, and to a lesser extent on Tuesdays and Thursdays, the centre is taken up with some of the finest **markets** in Provence.

### Cathédrale St-Sauveur

Place des Martyrs-de-la-Résistance • Daily 7.30am–noon & 2–6pm • ⓦ cathedrale-aix.net

The **Cathédrale St-Sauveur**, at the north end of Vieil Aix, is a conglomerate of fifteenth- to sixteenth-century buildings. The finest of its many medieval art treasures is a dazzling triptych by Nicolas Froment, *Le Buisson Ardent*, which has become a Provençal icon. Commissioned by King René in 1475, the painting has been restored to a jewel-like intensity; the burning bush of the title is not the one seen by Moses, but an allegory of the virginity of Mary.

### Musée des Tapisseries

28 place des Martyrs-de-la-Résistance • Daily except Tues 10am–noon & 2–6pm • €3.10 • ☎ 04 42 23 09 91, ⓦ museum-aix-en-provence.org

The former bishop's palace, the **Ancien Archevêché**, just south of the cathedral, houses the enjoyable **Musée des Tapisseries**. Highlights in its collection of seventeenth- and eighteenth-century tapestries include nine scenes from *Don Quixote*, woven in the 1730s. In one, he's being divested of his armour by maidens who can't conceal their smiles.

### Musée Granet

Place St-Jean-de-Malte • Tues–Sun: June–Sept 11am–7pm; Oct–May noon–6pm • €6 • ☎ 04 42 52 88 32, ⓦ museegranet-aixenprovence.fr

Aix's largest museum, the extensively modernized **Musée Granet**, is in the **quartier Mazarin**, a peaceful seventeenth-century residential district south of cours Mirabeau. You're most likely to visit for one of its high-class temporary exhibitions (higher fees may apply), but its permanent collection covers art and archeology. Ancient finds from the pre-Roman Oppidum d'Entremont are displayed downstairs, while the paintings are a mixed bag.

---

#### AIX-EN-PROVENCE FESTIVALS

During the annual **music festivals**, the varied contemporary showcase of **Aix en Musique** (June) and the **Festival International d'Art Lyrique** (opera and classical concerts; last two weeks of July), the alternative scene – of street theatre, rock concerts and impromptu gatherings – turns the whole of Vieil Aix into one long party. Tickets and programmes are available from the festival offices in the Palais de **l'Ancien Archevêché** on place des Martyrs-de-la-Résistance ( ☎ 04 34 08 02 17, ⓦ festival-aix.com).

**Paul Cézanne**, who studied in this building when it was an art school, is represented by minor canvases such as *Bathsheba*, *The Bathers* and *Portrait of Madame Cézanne*, assorted student pieces, and even one of his paint-encrusted palettes. There's also a small Rembrandt self-portrait; a similarly small Picasso from 1937, *Femme au Ballon*; several Giacomettis and a couple of Morandis; and a whole room of depictions of ruins by François Granet (1775–1849), whose original collection formed the nucleus of the museum.

## Atelier Cézanne

9 av Paul-Cézanne • April–June & Sept daily 10am–noon & 2–6pm; July & Aug daily 10am–6pm; Oct, Nov & March daily 10am–noon & 2–5pm; Dec–Feb Mon–Sat 10am–noon & 2–5pm; daily English tour 5pm (April–Sept) or 4pm (Oct–March) • €5.50 • ☎ 04 42 21 06 53, Ⓦ atelier-cezanne.com • Bus #1

While Paul Cézanne used many studios in and around Aix, he finally had a house built for the purpose in 1902, overlooking the city from the north. It was here that he painted the *Grandes Baigneuses*, the *Jardinier Vallier* and some of his greatest still lifes. The **Atelier Cézanne** remains exactly as it was at the time of his death in 1906: coat, hat, wineglass and easel, the objects he liked to paint, his pipe, a few letters and drawings … everything save the pictures he was working on.

## Jas de Bouffan

Rte de Galice, 4km west of central Aix • Open for 45min guided tours only: April, May & Oct Tues, Thurs & Sat French tours 10.30am, noon & 3.30pm, English tour 2pm; June–Sept daily French tours 10.30am, noon & 3.30pm, English tour 2pm; Nov–Dec Wed & Sat French tour 10am, no English tour • €5.50 • Ⓦ cezanne-en-provence.com • Bus #6

When Paul Cezanne was 20 years old, his father bought an elegant Provençal manor known as the **Jas de Bouffan**. It remained in the family for forty years; now somewhat shabby, it's open for guided tours. Somewhat reluctantly, Cezanne senior gave his son free rein to paint the walls of the drawing room, but all traces have now been removed and dispersed. The rambling gardens and duck-filled pond outside were often the subject of Cezanne's paintbrush.

## Oppidum d'Entremont

3km north of central Aix • Daily except Tues 9am–noon & 2–6pm; Sept–April, closed 1st & 3rd Mon of month • Free • Ⓦ entremont .culture.gouv.fr • Bus #20 from cours Sextius

The **Oppidum d'Entremont** is the site of a Gallic settlement built more than two hundred years before the Romans established the city. You'll find the remains of a fortified enclosure, as well as excavations of the residential and commercial quarters of the town. Statues and trinkets unearthed at the site are displayed in the Musée Granet in central Aix.

## ARRIVAL AND INFORMATION
### AIX-EN-PROVENCE

**By train** As well as a *gare SNCF*, on rue Gustave Desplace, Aix is served by a TGV station, 10km southwest of town, from which regular minibuses (every 30min: daily 4am–11.30pm; €5) run to the *gare routière* in town.

Destinations from gare SNCF Marseille (every 20–30min; 30–45min).

Destinations from TGV Avignon TGV (22 daily; 20min); Marseille (frequent; 15min); Paris (8 daily; 3hr); Paris CDG Airport (4 daily; 3hr 30min).

**By bus** The *gare routière* is on av de l'Europe, on the south side of the old town.

Destinations Apt (2 daily; 1hr 45min); Arles (7 daily; 1hr 30min); Avignon (6 daily; 1hr 15min); Carpentras (3–4 daily; 1hr 30min); Cavaillon (4 daily; 1hr 20min); Marseille (very frequent; 30–50min); Sisteron (3 daily; 2hr).

**By car** Driving into Aix can be confusing: the entire ring of boulevards encircling the old town is essentially one giant roundabout, circulating anticlockwise; hotels are signposted off in yellow. Parking in the old town is pretty nightmarish; the ring is probably the best bet for on-street parking, while good underground car parks are dotted around the boulevards.

**Tourist office** 2 place Général-de-Gaulle (June & Sept daily 8.30am–8pm; July & Aug 8.30am–9pm; Sept–May Mon–Sat 8.30am–7pm, Sun 10am–1pm & 2–6pm; ☎ 04 42 16 11 61, Ⓦ aixenprovencetourism.com).

## ACCOMMODATION

For accommodation between mid-June and the end of July – festival time – it's essential to reserve a hotel room at least a couple of months in advance. The tourist office offers online bookings on ⓦ aixenprovencetourism.com.

### HOTELS

**Augustins** 3 rue de la Masse ☎04 42 27 28 59, ⓦ hotel-augustins.com. Classy central hotel, housed in a fourteenth-century monastery on the southern edge of the old core; the rooms are dependably comfortable, though they don't quite live up to the promise of the public areas, and the breakfast is skimpy for the €10 price. **€99**

**Cardinal** 22–24 rue Cardinale ☎04 42 38 32 30, ⓦ hotel-cardinal-aix.com. Clean, peaceful and welcoming establishment with 29 great-value, antique-furnished a/c rooms, including six very fancy suites in an annexe just up the street. **€75**

**Cézanne** 40 av Victor-Hugo ☎04 42 27 28 59, ⓦ hotelaix.com/cezanne. Smart modern boutique hotel, close to the *gare SNCF*, offering opulent bedrooms styled in honour of local boy Cézanne. Breakfast is €19.50 extra, but at least there's free parking. **€185**

**Concorde** 68 bd du Roi-Réné ☎04 42 26 03 95, ⓦ hotel-aixenprovence-concorde.com. Inexpensive family-run hotel, a short walk southeast of the centre on the busy ring road, with simple, clean soundproofed rooms and private parking. The cheapest rooms have showers but not toilets. **€64**

**Globe** 74 cours Sextius ☎04 42 26 03 58, ⓦ hotelduglobe.com. There's a slight chain-like feel to this large hotel, a 10min walk from the centre, but the standard rooms are adequate, and there are also some much cheaper "student" singles – not en suite – and family rooms. Modern breakfast room and rooftop terrace. Closed mid-Dec to mid-Jan. **€82**

**Le Manoir** 8 rue d'Entrecasteaux ☎04 42 26 27 20, ⓦ hotelmanoir.com. Comfortable, quirkily old-fashioned hotel in a remarkably peaceful central location, in its own garden courtyard, with free parking. The lack of a/c in these relatively small rooms can be a problem in high summer. Breakfast in the sixteenth-century cloister. **€70**

**Pavillon de la Torse** 69 cours Gambetta ☎04 42 27 90 15, ⓦ latorse.com. Grand five-room B&B, set in supremely tranquil grounds with an infinity pool, a 15min walk southeast of the centre. English-speaking hosts, free parking. **€150**

**St-Christophe** 2 av Victor-Hugo ☎04 42 26 01 24, ⓦ hotel-saintchristophe.com. Comfortable 1930s-style place above a popular brasserie, close to the station and cours Mirabeau; some rooms have private terraces, the cheapest have showers not baths. **€97**

### HOSTEL AND CAMPSITES

**Airotel Camping Chantecler** 41 av du Val St-André, rte de Nice ☎04 42 26 12 98, ⓦ campingchantecler.com. Spacious campsite, set in a big park 2km southeast of the centre on bus #3, surrounding a Provençal country house and featuring a large pool and a restaurant that's open for all meals. Open all year. **€21**

**Auberge de Jeunesse du Jas de Bouffan** 3 av Marcel-Pagnol ☎04 42 20 15 99, ⓦ auberge-jeunesse-aix.fr. Rather institutional-looking hostel, 2km west of the centre, with small dorm rooms, a restaurant, baggage deposit, tennis and volleyball courts, as well as parking. Catch bus #2 to stop "V. Vasarély". Closed mid-Dec to mid-Jan. **€22.50**

**Camping Arc-en-Ciel** 50 av Malacrida, Pont des Trois Sautets ☎04 42 26 14 28, ⓦ campingarcenciel.com. Located 2km southeast of town on bus #3, near the *Chantecler* site, this small, clean fifty-pitch site has very good facilities, including a pool, plus shopping close at hand. No credit cards. Closed Oct–March. **€20**

## EATING

Aix is stuffed full of restaurants. Place des Cardeurs, northwest of the Hôtel de Ville, consists of little but restaurant, brasserie and café tables, while rue de la Verrerie running south from the Hôtel de Ville and place Ramus hold an immense number of Indian, Chinese and North African restaurants. Rue des Tanneurs is a good street for low budgets.

**Amphitryon** 2 rue Paul Doumer ☎04 42 26 54 10, ⓦ restaurant-amphitryon.fr. This excellent restaurant, serving eclectic cuisine on a flower-drenched terrace in a grotty side street of old Aix, won't break the bank. *Menus* from €22 at lunch, €30 at dinner (when the €39.50 option offers the day's market specialities). Tues–Sat noon–1.30pm & 7.30–9.30pm; closed second half Aug.

**Chez Feraud** 8 rue du Puits-Juif ☎04 42 63 07 27. Classy, romantic Provençal restaurant in a quiet corner near the Hôtel de Ville, serving chickpea salad with tapenade, grilled sea bass with fennel, and *pieds et paquets* on a superb €30 *menu*. Sept–July Tues–Sat noon–1.30pm & 7–10pm.

**Crep Sautière** 18 rue de Bédarrides ☎04 42 27 91 60. Delicious, fresh crêpes (from €5) to take away or enjoy while squashed into the cosy, vaulted and often packed restaurant. Tues–Sat noon–2.30pm & 7pm–midnight.

**Le Formal** 32 rue Espariat ☎04 42 27 08 31, ⓦrestaurant-leformal.fr. You could easily miss this inconspicuous central restaurant, housed in a medieval cellar (which means, unfortunately, that it's entirely indoors). Don't let the name put you off; "Formal" is the surname of the chef, not a description of the ambience. Beautifully presented contemporary cuisine is served on *menus* priced from €38 to €76, though you can get a two-course lunch, including a mini-bouillabaisse, for €22. Tues–Fri noon–1.30pm & 7.30–9.30pm, Sat 7.30–9.30pm.

**Mitch** 26 rue des Tanneurs ☎04 42 26 63 08, ⓦmitchrestaurant.com. Chic, intimate contemporary restaurant in the old town, open for dinner only and serving changing *menus* at €25–45 that depend on each day's freshest market ingredients. Indoor and outdoor seating. Mon–Sat 7.30–9.30pm.

★ **Poivre d'Âne** 40 place des Cardeurs ☎04 42 21 32 66, ⓦrestaurantlepoivredane.com. Small, dinner-only restaurant on the fringes of the popular place des Cardeurs, with seating inside and out. Book ahead to enjoy great-value, wide-ranging set *menus* of creative local cuisine, from €29 to €45. Daily 7.30–9.30pm; closed Wed in winter.

**Ze Bistro** 7 rue de la Couronne ☎04 42 39 81 88, ⓦzebistro.com. Creative, relaxed old-town bistro, serving the freshest fish and local produce in simple surroundings, best sampled on good-value *menus* from €25 for lunch, €37 for dinner. Sept–July Tues–Fri 12.30–1.30pm & 7.30–9.30pm, Sat 7.30–9.30pm.

**Zinc d'Hugo** 22 rue Lieutaud ☎04 42 27 69 69, ⓦzinc-hugo.com. Snug wine bar with inventive cuisine. €22 gets you a delicious *assiette comptoire* of ham, cheeses and salad; there's a €25 set *menu*; and mains like tuna steak with raspberry balsamic vinegar cost €20–26. Tues–Sat noon–2.30pm & 7pm–midnight.

### NIGHTLIFE

The nightlife scene in Aix divides readily between well-heeled visitors and the city's large student population. Local youth tends to congregate around the fountains and cafés near cours Mirabeau until midnight. Later on, the bars along shabby rue Verrerie get going.

**Hot Brass** Chemin d'Eguilles, Celony ☎04 42 21 05 07, ⓦhotbrassaix.com. Top music venue, 5km northwest of town, that books big-name live acts and DJs. Fri & Sat 10.30pm–6am.

**Le Scat** 11 rue de la Verrerie ☎04 42 23 00 23, ⓦscatclub.free.fr. Eclectic, cave-like late-night club, nominally jazz but putting on live music of all genres. Tues–Sat 11pm until late.

**Le Spartacus** Rte de Rans, La Malle, Cabries ☎06 63 00 33 90, ⓦspartacus-club.com. Located southwest of Aix, en route to Marseille, this electro club attracts a huge gay contingent from both cities. Fri & Sat 11pm until late.

# Central Provence

In **central Provence**, it's the landscapes rather than the towns that dominate. The gentle hills and tranquil villages of the **Haut-Var** make for happy exploration by car or bike, before the foothills of the Alps close in around the citadelle town of **Sisteron** and **Dignes-les-Bains** further east.

The most exceptional geographical feature is the **Gorges du Verdon** – Europe's answer to the Grand Canyon. So long as you have your own transport, good bases for exploring the majestic peaks, cliffs and lakes of this spectacular area include the small market town of **Aups**, south of the Gorges, and to the northeast, **Castellane**, a centre for sports and activities.

## Aups

The neat and very pleasant village of **AUPS**, 90km northeast of Aix, makes an ideal base for drivers touring the Haut-Var or the Grand Canyon du Verdon. While holding all the facilities visitors might need, it remains a vibrant, lived-in community, still earning its living from agriculture, and at its best on Wednesdays and Saturdays, when **market** stalls fill its central squares and the surrounding streets.

Aups centres on three ill-defined and inter-connected **squares**: place Frédéric-Mistral, the smaller place Duchâtel slightly uphill to the left, and the tree-lined gardens of place Martin Bidouré to the right. Beyond these, the tangle of old streets, and the sixteenth-century clock tower with its campanile, make it an enjoyable place to explore.

## INFORMATION

**Tourist office** Place Frédéric-Mistral (May–June & Sept Mon–Sat 8.45am–12.15pm & 2–5.30pm; July & Aug Mon–Sat 9am–12.30pm & 3.30–7pm, Sun 9am–12.30pm; Oct–April Mon, Tues, Thurs & Fri 8.45am–12.15pm & 1.30–5pm, Wed & Sat 8.45am–12.15pm; ☎04 94 84 00 69, ⓦaups-tourisme.com).

## ACCOMMODATION AND EATING

★ **Auberge de la Tour** Rue Aloisi ☎04 94 70 00 30, ⓦaubergedelatour.net. Appealing and great-value hotel, where the tasteful, airy, well-equipped rooms sleep up to four, and surround a sunny, peaceful, plant-filled courtyard restaurant that serves good *menus* from €19.50. Closed Oct–March, restaurant also closed Tues Sept–June. €55

**Camping Les Prés** Rte de Tourtour ☎04 94 70 00 93, ⓦcampinglespres.com. Well-shaded two-star site, off allée Charles-Boyer 300m southeast of the centre. Open all year, with a bar, snack bar and pool. €19

**Grand Hôtel** Place Duchâtel ☎04 94 70 10 82, ⓦgrand-hotel-aups.com. Traditional village hotel, just off the main square, with six plain but adequate en-suite rooms, including some that sleep up to four. The efficient garden restaurant in front serves excellent *menus* at €15.50–27, and there's a nice bar. €50

★ **St-Marc** Rue Aloisi ☎04 94 70 06 08, ⓦlesaintmarc.com. Rickety, earthy, but very character-ful old rooms (sleeping up to five; not all en suite) in a former olive-oil mill overlooking a tiny little square and above a good restaurant, with a €21 dinner *menu* and pizzas cooked over a wood fire. Closed Tues & Wed Sept–June, plus second half Nov. €40

## Haut-Var villages

The **villages** of the Haut-Var are among the prettiest in all Provence. Bask in their tranquillity and beauty, wander the maze-like lanes and admire the glorious, verdant landscape. The main historical sight is the serene **Abbaye de Thoronet**.

### Villecroze

It would be easy to drive straight through charming **VILLECROZE**, 8km southeast of Aups, without realizing its lovely, peaceful old quarter was even there. The inconspicuous walled medieval village, immediately south of the main D557, is a joy to stroll around, with its lovely vaulted stone arcades.

Villecroze sits beneath a water-burrowed cliff, on its northern side. The **gardens** around the base are delightfully un-Gallic and informal, and intriguing **grottoes** in its flanks are open to visitors in summer (April & May Sat & Sun 2–6pm; June–Sept Wed & Fri–Sun 2–6pm; July & Aug daily 10.30am–12.30pm & 2.30–7pm; €2.50; ☎04 94 67 50 00).

### Salernes

Compared with Villecroze, **SALERNES**, 5km west, is quite a metropolis, with a thriving tile-making industry and enough near-level irrigated land for productive agriculture. Twenty or so studios and shops, large and small, sell a huge range of **pottery** and **tiles**, while on Sunday and Wednesday a **market** takes place beneath the ubiquitous plane trees on the *cours*.

### Sillans-le-Cascade

Tiny **SILLANS-LE-CASCADE**, 9km southwest of Aups, is a sleepy little village that has clung on to a brief stretch of ancient ramparts. Down below, on the Bresque River, a stunning **waterfall**, reached by a twenty-minute walk along a delightful and clearly signed path from the main road, gushes into a turquoise pool that's perfect for swimming.

## Cotignac

**COTIGNAC**, 15km southwest of Aups, is the Haut-Var village *par excellence*, with a shaded main square for *pétanque* and passages and stairways bursting with begonias, jasmine and geraniums leading through a cluster of medieval houses. More gardens sprawl at the foot of the bubbly rock cliff that forms the back wall of the village, threaded with troglodyte walkways.

## Abbaye du Thoronet

Off the D79, 16km southeast of Cotignac • April–Sept Mon–Sat 10am–6.30pm, Sun 10am–noon & 2–6.30pm; Oct–March Mon–Sat 10am–1pm & 2–5pm, Sun 10am–noon & 2–5pm • €7.50 • ☎ 04 94 60 43 90, ⓦ thoronet.monuments-nationaux.fr

The last of the three great Cistercian monasteries of Provence, the **Abbaye du Thoronet**, remains even less scarred by time than Silvacane and Sénanque. During the Revolution, it was kept intact as a remarkable monument of history and art; it's now used occasionally for concerts. It was first restored in the 1850s, while a more recent campaign has brought it to clear-cut perfection. The interior spaces, delineated by walls of pale rose-coloured stone, are inspiring.

| INFORMATION | HAUT-VAR VILLAGES |
|---|---|

### SALERNES

**Tourist office** Place Gabriel-Péri (July & Aug Mon–Fri 9.30am–6.30pm, Sat 9.30am–7pm, Sun 9.30am–1pm; Sept–June Tues–Sat 9.30am–12.30pm & 2–6pm; ☎ 04 94 70 69 02, ⓦ ville-salernes.fr).

### COTIGNAC

**Tourist office** 475 rte de Carcès (Tues–Fri 9am–12.30pm & 2–5.30pm, Sat 9am–12.30pm & 2–5pm; ☎ 04 94 04 61 87, ⓦ ot-cotignac.provenceverte.fr).

## ACCOMMODATION AND EATING

### VILLECROZE

★ **La Bohème** Villecroze ☎ 04 94 70 80 04. Delightful, very floral cafe and tearooms, just inside the walls of the medieval enclave, with tables out on the alley. Breakfast (€6) is served, along with cooked brunches, afternoon tea, smoothies and cakes. Daily 9am–1pm & 4–7pm.

**Le Colombier** Rte de Draguignan ☎ 04 94 70 63 23, ⓦ lecolombier-var.com. Very charming hotel-restaurant, south of the village along the D557, with six sizeable and tastefully decorated rooms with terraces, and a lovely peaceful garden. *Menus* in the restaurant (closed Sun eve & Mon) start at €29. Closed mid-Nov to mid-Dec. €90

### SALERNES

**L'Odyssée** 5 rue des 4 Coins ☎ 04 94 67 56 43, ⓦ restaurant-83-salernes-var.com. Friendly, high-class restaurant with seating on the main square, serving changing daily menus that focus on local, and especially organic, produce; *plats* like beef tartare or risotto typically cost €15–18. Concerts and theatre performances in winter. Daily except Thurs noon–1.30pm & 7.30–9.30pm.

### SILLANS-LE-CASCADE

**Les Pins** 1 Grand Rue ☎ 04 94 04 63 26, ⓦ restaurant-lespins.com. The five simple en-suite rooms in this attractive hotel-restaurant, beside the main road, are well priced but very ordinary; the food, served on a colourful patio, is considerably better, with lunch at €18 and dinner *menus* from €24. €50

### COTIGNAC

**Restaurant du Cours** 18 cours Gambetta ☎ 04 94 04 78 50. Sun-kissed pavement restaurant – not to be confused with *Brasserie du Cours* – at the heart of the village's social life, decked out with bright yellow tablecloths and serving top-quality *menus* that start at €13 for lunch and range from €17 to €30 in the evening. Despite the sign, it's not a hotel. Daily except Wed noon–2pm & 7.30–9pm.

★ **Le Temps de Pose** Place de la Mairie ☎ 04 94 77 04 69 17. This quaint, flower-bedecked café on a quiet square makes an ideal spot for breakfast, a light lunch or a reviving cup of tea. Tasty, fresh sandwiches and quiches cost around €8; a large salad or daily *plat* more like €10. Daily 10.30am–10pm.

# The Gorges du Verdon

Also widely known as the Grand Canyon du Verdon, the breathtaking beauty and majesty of the **Gorges du Verdon** almost matches its American counterpart, albeit on a much smaller scale. Peppered with spectacular viewpoints, plunging crevices up to

16

Comps-sur-Artuby & Draguignan ▲

Comps-sur-Artuby & Draguignan ▲

◄ Castellane

◄ Moustiers-Ste-Marie & Riez

D955

Pont de Soleils

River Jabron

Trigance

D955

D90

D71

D71

Clue de Carejuan

Rougon

Point Sublime

CORNICHE SUBLIME

Balcons de la Mescla

D23

Belvédère de l'Escalès

Couloir Samson

ROUTE DES CRÊTES

Sentier Martel

River Verdon

Pont de l'Artuby

R. Artuby

Belvédère du Tilleul

Belvédère des Glacières

Falaise des Cavaliers

D17

La Palud-sur-Verdon

ℹ

CORNICHE SUBLIME

Chalet de la Maline

Passerelle de l'Estellié (Closed)

D23

D952

GR4

CORNICHE SUBLIME

COULOIR SAMSON

D952

CORNICHE SUBLIME

D71

Mayreste

GR4

River Verdon

Pont du Galetas

Col d'Illoire

D952

D957

D71

D619

D957

Aiguines

D957

Lac de Ste-Croix

N

**GORGES DU VERDON**

0 ─── 2 kilometres

700m deep, and glorious azure-blue lakes, the area is absolutely irresistible; try not to leave Provence without spending at least a day here. The river falls from Rougon at the top of the gorge, disappearing into tunnels, decelerating for shallow, languid moments and finally exiting in full, steady flow at the **Pont du Galetas**. Alongside, the huge artificial **Lac de Sainte-Croix** is great for swimming when the water levels are high; otherwise the beach becomes a bit sludgy.

With so many hairpin bends and twisting, narrow roads, it takes a full, rather exhausting day to **drive** right round the Gorges. Many visitors choose instead between tracing either its north or south rim. The entire circuit being 130km long, this is **cycling** country only for the preternaturally fit.

Local outfitters and guides offer **activities** including climbing, rafting, canoeing, canyoning, cycling and horseriding.

### Moustiers-Ste-Marie

The loveliest village on the fringes of the gorge, **MOUSTIERS-STE-MARIE** occupies a magnificent site near its western end. Set high enough to command fine views down to the Lac de Sainte-Croix, it straddles a plummeting stream that cascades between two golden cliffs. A mighty star slung between them on a chain, originally suspended by a returning Crusader, completes the perfect picture.

Moustiers gets crowded in summer, when visitors throng its winding lanes and pretty bridges, and fill its stores and galleries. To escape, puff your way up to the aptly named chapel of **Notre-Dame de Beauvoir**, high above the village proper.

### The north rim

The spectacular and tortuous D952 runs more or less parallel to the **north rim** of the gorge for 45km east from Moustiers to Castellane. For the best close-up views, head south near the village of **La Palud-sur-Verdon** halfway along, and follow the **Route des Crêtes** to the lip of the abyss.

#### La Palud-Sur-Verdon

Peace, tranquillity and breathtaking scenery reign supreme in the principal pit stop along the northern rim, **LA PALUD-SUR-VERDON**, 20km southeast of Moustiers. Even if you're just passing through, take the time to wander around the narrow, rambling streets and enjoy a meal or drink at a traditional restaurant or café.

#### The Route des Crêtes

To admire the very best of the Gorges du Verdon, detour off the D952 onto the dramatic **Route des Crêtes**, which loops away both from the centre of La Palud, and from another intersection a short distance east. There's nothing to stop you driving straight off into the abyss on its highest stretches, and at some points you look down a sheer 800m drop to the sliver of water below. As the mid-section of the Route des Crêtes is one-way (westbound only), to see it all you have to start from the more scenic eastern end. The road closes each winter from November 15 to March 15.

### The south rim

The aptly named **Corniche Sublime** follows the southern rim between **AIGUINES**, perched high above the **Lac de Sainte-Croix** 14km south of Moustiers, and **COMPS-SUR-ARTUBY**, 40 km east. As this road was built expressly to provide jaw-dropping and hair-raising views, drivers with any fear of heights – and of course their passengers – are best advised not to come this way.

### Castellane

Huddled at the foot of a sheer 180m cliff, the rather severe-looking town of **CASTELLANE** serves as the eastern gateway for visitors to the Gorges du Verdon,

**16**

17km southwest. In summer, thanks to its wide range of restaurants, hotels and cafés, it enjoys an animation rare in these parts.

Houses in Castellane's old quarter, the *vieille ville*, are packed close together; some lanes are barely shoulder-wide. A footpath from behind the parish church winds its way up to the clifftop chapel of Notre-Dame du Roc. Twenty to thirty minutes should see you at the top; you won't actually see the gorge, but there's a good view of the river disappearing into it and the mountains circling the town.

## INFORMATION

### MOUSTIERS-STE-MARIE

**Parc Naturel Région du Verdon** Overall information on the Park. Domaine de Valx (☎04 92 74 68 00, ⓦparcduverdon.fr) Overall information on the park.

**Tourist office** Place de l'Église (March, Oct & Nov daily 10am–noon & 2–5.30pm; April–June daily 10am–12.30pm & 2–6pm; July & Aug Mon–Fri 9.30am–7pm, Sat & Sun 9.30am–12.30pm & 2–7pm; Sept daily 10am–12.30pm & 2–6.30pm; Dec–Feb daily 10am–noon & 2–5pm; ☎04 92 74 67 84, ⓦmoustiers.fr).

### LA PALUD-SUR-VERDON

**Bureau des Guides** Grande Rue (hours erratic; ☎04 92 77 30 50, ⓦescalade-verdon.fr); this is the best place to find out about guided walks, climbing, canyoning, rafting and other activities.

## THE GORGES DU VERDON

**Tourist office** The Maison des Gorges du Verdon, in the central château, incorporates the tourist office and has displays on the gorge (daily except Tues: mid-March to mid-June and mid-Sept to mid-Nov 10am–noon & 4–6pm; mid-June to mid-Sept 10am–1pm & 4–7pm; ☎04 92 77 32 02, ⓦlapaludsurverdon.com; exhibition €4).

### AIGUINES

**Tourist office** Allées de Tilleul (July & Aug Mon–Sat 8.30am–6pm, Sun 10am–noon & 2–6pm; Sept–June Mon–Fri 9am–noon & 2–5pm; ☎04 94 70 21 64, ⓦaiguines.com).

### CASTELLANE

**Tourist office** Rue Nationale (May, June & Sept Mon–Sat 9am–noon & 2–6pm, Sun 10am–1pm; July & Aug daily 9am–7.30pm; Oct–April Mon–Sat 9am–noon & 2–6pm; ☎04 92 83 61 14, ⓦcastellane.org).

## ACCOMMODATION AND EATING

### MOUSTIERS-STE-MARIE

**Le Colombier** Quartier St-Michel ☎04 92 74 66 02, ⓦle-colombier.com. Very comfortable, good-value hotel on the main road, 600m below the village centre. The cheapest rooms are in the older orginal building, with larger and fancier options in a motel-style annexe, and there's a pleasant garden and pool, but no restaurant. Closed Nov–March. **€78**

### LA PALUD-SUR-VERDON

**Auberge de Jeunesse** Rte de la Maline ☎04 92 77 38 72, ⓦfuaj.org. Beautifully sited, nicely modernized hostel, poised on the hillside 500m south of the village, offering beds in rooms that sleep from two to six. Rates include breakfast. Closed Oct–March. **€18.50**

**Perroquet Vert** Grande Rue ☎04 92 77 33 39, ⓦleperroquetvert.com. Right in the village centre, this townhouse B&B offers three plain but comfortable bedrooms plus simple meals, and also serves as a shop-cum-rendezvous for climbers and walkers. Closed Nov–March. **€53**

### AIGUINES

**Altitude 823** Grande Rue ☎04 98 10 22 17, ⓦhotel-altitude823-verdon.com. The best of the nine rooms in this small hotel-restaurant, at the hairpin bend where the main road reaches the centre, enjoy far-reaching views down to the lake. Rates include breakfast. Closed Nov to mid-March. **€103**

**Le Galetas** Quartier Vernis ☎04 94 70 20 48, ⓦaiguines.com/galetas. Aiguines' large and rather plain municipal campsite is a long way down from the village, almost within diving distance of the lake. Closed mid-Oct to March. **€12.50**

**Grand Canyon du Verdon** Falaise des Cavaliers ☎04 94 76 91 31, ⓦhotel-canyon-verdon.com. Perched atop a dramatic precipice on the Corniche Sublime, 20km east of Aiguines, this has to be the finest place to stay on the south side – so long as you don't suffer from vertigo. The restaurant (closed Tues eve & Wed except July & Aug) serves good meals on *menus* from €24. Rates are for compulsory *demi-pension*. Closed Nov–March. **€125**

### CASTELLANE

★ **Commerce** Place Marcel Sauvaire ☎04 92 83 61 00, ⓦhotel-du-commerce-verdon.com. Comfortable and very central, Castellane's finest hotel has recently modernized rooms that sleep up to four, plus a small pool. Its restaurant (closed Mon) serves wonderful food, both indoors and outside. Closed Nov–Feb. **€100**

> ### THE CHEMINS DE FER DE PROVENCE
>
> Also known as the **Train des Pignes**, in honour of the pine-cones originally used as fuel, the narrow-gauge **Chemins de Fer de Provence** connects Digne-les-Bains with Nice, with stops including Annot and St-André-les-Alpes. It's a stupendous ride, taking 3hr 30min in total for a one-way fare of €20.30; the scenery en route includes glittering rivers, lush dark-green forests, dramatic cliff faces, and plunging gorges. For full details, see ⓦ trainprovence.com.

## Alpes de Haute-Provence

North of Castellane, the **Route Napoléon** passes through the barren scrubby rocklands of the **Alpes de Haute-Provence**. The road was built in the 1930s to commemorate the great leader's journey north through Haute-Provence on return from exile on Elba in 1815, in the most audacious and vain recapture of power in French history. Using mule paths still deep with winter snow, Napoleon and his seven hundred soldiers forged ahead towards **Digne-les-Bains** and **Sisteron** on their way to Grenoble – a total of 350km – in just six days. One hundred days later, he lost the battle of Waterloo, and was subsequently dispatched to the island of St Helena for permanent exile.

### Digne-les-Bains

By far the largest community in the Provençal Alps, the faded spa town of **DIGNE-LES-BAINS**, is best seen as a convenient base for trips into the mountains, rather than a destination in its own right, though it does feature one interesting **museum**.

#### Musée Alexandra David-Néel

27 av du Maréchal Juin • Tours daily 10am, 2pm & 3.30pm • Free • ☎ 04 92 31 32 38, ⓦ alexandra-david-neel.org

The **Musée Alexandra David-Néel** is dedicated to the memory of an extraordinary, tenacious explorer who spent more than fourteen years travelling the length and breadth of Tibet. David-Néel lived out the remainder of her life in this house, eventually dying in 1969, aged almost 101. It's stuffed with photographs tracing her journeys, as well as Tibetan ornaments, masks and paintings.

### Sisteron

**SISTERON**, 25km northwest of Digne on the Route Napoléon, was the most important mountain gateway to Provence. The site has been fortified since time immemorial; even now, half-destroyed by the Anglo-American bombardment of 1944, its magnificent **citadelle** (April–Nov daily 9am–dusk; €6) stands as a fearsome sentinel over the city and the solitary bridge across the River Durance. The views from the ramparts, built in 1370, are breathtaking, while a small **historical museum** lies just inside, and further up the vertiginous late medieval chapel, **Notre-Dame-du-Château**, has been restored to its Gothic glory.

### ARRIVAL AND INFORMATION ALPES DE HAUTE-PROVENCE

#### DIGNE-LES-BAINS

**By train** The gare Chemin de Fer de la Provence (see above), with trains to and from Nice (4 daily; 3hr 30min), is on av Pierre Sémard, on the west bank of the river.

**By bus** The *gare routière* is on *rond point* du 11 Novembre 1918.

Destinations Aix (4 daily; 2hr); Avignon (3 daily; 3hr 30min); Barcelonnette (2 daily; 1hr–1hr 30min); Sisteron (3 daily; 1hr 15min).

**Tourist office** Rond point du 11 Novembre 1918 (July &

Aug Mon–Sat 8am–7pm, Sun 9.30am–noon & 3.30–5.30pm; Sept–June Mon–Sat 9am–noon & 2–6pm, Sun 9.30am–noon & 3.30–5.30pm; ☎ 04 92 36 62 62, ⓦ ot-dignelesbains.fr).

#### SISTERON

**Tourist office** Place de la République (July & Aug Mon–Sat 9am–7pm, Sun 10am–5pm; Sept–June Mon–Sat 9am–noon & 2–5pm; ☎ 04 92 61 36 50, ⓦ sisteron.fr).

**16**

## ACCOMMODATION AND EATING

### DIGNE-LES-BAINS

**Central** 26 bd Gassendi ☎04 92 31 31 91, ⓦlhotel -central.com. Spacious, comfortable budget hotel, on a bustling street in the heart of town near the tourist office. The cheapest of its simple antique-furnished rooms lack en-suite facilities. €48

★ **Le Chaudron** 40 rue de l'Hubac ☎04 92 31 24 87. This excellent old-town restaurant, run by a very friendly husband-and-wife team, offers pavement seating in summer, a cosy upstairs dining room in winter. *Menus*, from €21 to €32.50, focus on substantial baked dishes from their wood-fired oven. Mon, Tues & Fri–Sun noon–1.30pm & 7.30–9.15pm.

**Villa Gaia** 24 rte de Nice ☎04 92 31 21 60, ⓦhotel -villagaia-digne.com. Stately, peaceful eighteenth-century country house, 3km southwest of the centre and offering ten very comfortable guest rooms of varying sizes, along with spa facilities. There's no public restaurant, but you can have dinner for €26. Closed Nov to mid-April. €92

### SISTERON

**Les Becs Fins** 16 rue Saunerie ☎09 63 51 44 80, ⓦpro.pagesjaunes.fr/restaurant-becs-fins. Top-notch regional cuisine, infused with flavours of the mountains, on an attractive pedestrian street. Fish is the chief speciality, on four daily changing *menus* priced from €25. July & Aug daily noon–1.30pm & 7.30–9pm; Sept–June Tues–Sat noon–1.30pm & 7.30–9pm, Sun noon–1.30pm.

**La Citadelle** 126 rue Saunerie ☎04 92 61 13 52, ⓦhotel-lacitadelle.com. Cheap, clean rooms beside the river – be sure you get one with a view of the imposing landscape – plus a decent restaurant. €40

**Grand Hôtel du Cours** Allée de Verdun ☎04 92 61 04 51, ⓦhotel-lecours.com. This old-fashioned, family-run hotel, just a few steps from the cathedral, is the perfect place to appreciate the genteel charms of Sisteron, and has a good restaurant. Closed Jan & Feb. €80

# 16 Northeast Provence

Depending on the season, the **northeastern corner of Provence** can be two different worlds. In winter, the sheep and shepherds find warmer pastures, leaving the snowy heights to horned mouflons, chamois and the perfectly camouflaged ermine. The villages where shepherds came to summer markets are battened down for the long, cold haul, while modern conglomerations of Swiss-style chalet houses, sports shops and nightclubs come to life around the ski lifts. The seasonal dichotomy is especially evident in towns like **Colmars-les-Alpes** and **Barcelonnette**.

The **Alpes-Maritimes** make up much of northeastern Provence, encompassing much of the magnificent **Parc National du Mercantour**, which runs south of Barcelonnette to the Italian border villages of Tende, Breil-sur-Roya and Sospel.

## Colmars-les-Alpes

Even when it's spookily empty, out of season, the charming village of **COLMARS-LES-ALPES** makes an ideal journey's break on the western periphery of the Parc National du

---

### THE PARC NATIONAL DU MERCANTOUR

The **Parc National du Mercantour** is a long, narrow band of mountains, near the Italian border, that runs for 75km from south of Barcelonnette to Sospel, 16km north of the Mediterranean. A haven for wildlife, it holds colonies of chamois, mouflon, ibex and marmots, breeding pairs of golden eagles and other rare birds of prey, great spotted woodpeckers and hoopoes, blackcocks and ptarmigan. In recent years grey wolves, which disappeared in the 1930s, have returned from neighbouring Italy. The flora too is special, with unique species of lilies, orchids and Alpine plants, including the rare multi-flowering saxifrage.

Numerous paths cross the park, including the GR5 and GR52, with *refuge* huts providing basic food and bedding for hikers. The **Maisons du Parc** in Barcelonnette, St-Étienne-de-Tinée and St-Martin-Vésubie can provide maps and accommodation details as well as advice on footpaths and weather conditions; see also ⓦmercantour.eu. Camping, lighting fires, picking flowers, playing radios or disturbing the delicate environment is strictly outlawed.

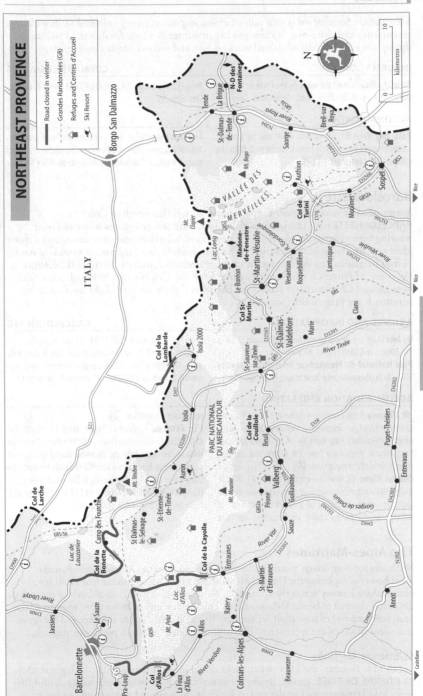

**NORTHEAST PROVENCE**

Road closed in winter
Grandes Randonnées (GR)
Refuges and Centres d'Accueil
Ski Resort

Borgo San Dalmazzo

ITALY

N-D des Fontaines
Tende
La Brigue
St-Dalmas-de-Tende
Saorge
Breil-sur-Roya
River Roya
N204
D6204

Mt. Bego
Authion
Moulinet
Sospel
D2566
D2204
D2566
D2566
Nice

VALLÉE DES MERVEILLES

Mt. Capier
Lac Long
Col de Turini
D70
Nice

Madone-de-Fenestre
St-Martin-Vésubie
Venanson
Roquebillière
Lantosque
River Vésubie
D2565
GR5

Le Boréon
Col St-Martin
St-Dalmas-Valdeblore
Clans
Marie
D2205
River Tinée

Isola 2000
Col de la Lombarde
D97
Isola
St-Sauveur-sur-Tinée
D2205
GR5

Col de la Larche
Jausiers
River Ubaye
D900
Loc de Lauzanier
Col de la Bonette
Camp des Fourches
St-Dalmas-le-Selvage
St-Étienne-de-Tinée
Auron
Mt. Ténibre
GR5/56
D2205

PARC NATIONAL DU MERCANTOUR

Mt. Mounier
Col de la Couillole
Beuil
D28
D902
D202
Entrevaux
Puget-Théniers
D4202
D4202

Mt. Pelat
Loc d'Allos
GR56
Col de la Cayolle
Entraunes
St-Martin-d'Entraunes
Valberg
Péone
GR52a
Guillaumes
Sauze
Gorges de Daluis
River Var
D2202
D902
D908
Annot

Le Sauze
Barcelonnette
D900
Pra-Loup
Col d'Allos
La Foux d'Allos
Allos
Ratery
D908
Colmars-les-Alpes
Beauvezer
River Verdon
Thorame
D202
N202
Castellane

Gap

16

0  10 kilometres
N

Mercantour. Secreted away in a valley behind imposing, honey-coloured walls and large seventeenth-century *portes*, it comes to life in winter as a base for skiers, as well as during the summer festivals (third week in July and second Sunday in August).

## INFORMATION

COLMARS-LES-ALPES

**Tourist office** Outside the walls, by the Porte de la Lance (July & Aug daily 8am–7pm; Sept–June Tues–Sat 9am–12.15pm & 2–5.45pm; ☏ 04 92 83 41 92, ⊛ colmars -les-alpes.fr).

## ACCOMMODATION

**Bois Joly** ☏ 04 92 83 40 40. Small and very scenic campsite, amid the riverside trees a 10min walk from the village. Closed Oct–April. **€11.70**

**Le France** ☏ 04 92 83 42 93. Colmars' one hotel, just across the D908 opposite the walled town, with a garden restaurant that serves pizza in summer. Closed Jan to late Feb. **€51**

# Barcelonnette

Surrounded by majestic snow-capped mountains, 44km north of Colmars, **BARCELONNETTE** is an immaculate little place, with sunny squares where old men wearing berets play *pétanque*. All the houses have tall gables and deep eaves, and a more ideal spot for doing nothing would be hard to find. It owes its Spanish-sounding name, "Little Barcelona", to its foundation in the thirteenth century by Raimond Béranger IV, count of Provence, whose family came from the Catalan city. Although snow falls here around Christmas and stays until Easter, and there are several ski resorts nearby, summer is the main tourist season.

## ARRIVAL AND INFORMATION

BARCELONNETTE

**By bus** There are are bus connections with Digne (2 daily; 1hr 30min) and Gap (4 daily; 1hr 30min).
**Parc National du Mercantour information centre** 10 av de la Libération (mid-June to mid-Sept daily 10am–

noon & 3–7pm; ☏ 04 92 81 21 31, ⊛ mercantour.eu).
**Tourist office** Off place Frédéric Mistral (July & Aug daily 9am–12.30pm & 1.30–7.30pm; Sept–June Mon–Sat 9am–noon & 2–6pm; ☏ 04 92 81 04 71, ⊛ barcelonnette.com).

## ACCOMMODATION AND EATING

★ **L'Azteca** 3 rue François-Arnaud ☏ 04 92 81 46 36, ⊛ azteca-hotel.fr. Extremely pleasant hotel, in a nineteenth-century villa built by an emigrant returned from Mexico, steps away from the centre and enjoying superb views of the mountains. **€88**
**Cheval Blanc** 12 rue Grenette ☏ 04 92 81 00 19, ⊛ chevalblancbarcelonnette.com. Inexpensive, central *Logis de France*, consisting of a rambling labyrinth of widely varying rooms above an attractive bar and

restaurant. Closed Nov. **€66**
**L'In Attendu** 4 place St-Pierre ☏ 04 92 31 30 95, ⊛ linattendu-restaurant.com. Great-value Provençal restaurant on a peaceful and otherwise empty square, with a snug dining room and a handful of tables beneath the clock tower of the St-Pierre church. The one dinner *menu* changes daily, with two courses for €18 and three for €21. Daily noon–1.30pm & 7.30–9.30pm.

# The Alpes-Maritimes

With an economy driven mostly by tourism, the towns of the **Alpes-Maritimes** make great bases for exploring the Parc du Mercantour. From Barcelonnette (the D64) it's a breathtaking journey across the Cime de la Bonette pass, which at an altitude of more than 2800m is claimed to be the highest road in Europe. It's only open for three months of the year, from the end of June until September. The air is cold even in summer and the green and silent spaces of the approach to the summit, circled by barren peaks, are magical.

## St-Étienne-de-Tinée

South of la Bonette, the D64 switchbacks down into the Tinée valley. Its highest town, **ST-ÉTIENNE-DE-TINÉE**, springs awake for sheep fairs, held twice every summer, and the Fête de la Transhumance at the end of June. At the west end of town off boulevard d'Auron, a cable car then chair lift climb to the summit of **La Pinatelle**, linking the village to the ski resort of **AURON**.

In **summer** a handful of the lifts are open to hikers and mountain bikers (July & Aug; €9/day; ⓦauron.com) while in **winter** skiers come to enjoy the 42 pistes (€30/day).

## St-Martin-Vésubie

In the lovely little town of **ST-MARTIN-VÉSUBIE**, 60km southeast of St-Étienne-de-Tinée in the Vésubie valley, a cobbled, narrow street with a channelled stream runs through the old quarter beneath the overhanging roofs and balconies of Gothic houses.

The annual highlight at the *Alpha* **wolf reserve** in Le Boréon, a small, scenic mountain retreat 8km north, comes in spring, when visitors can see newborn wolf cubs (July & Aug daily 10am–6pm, last admission 4.30pm; mid-April to June, Sept, Oct & school hols daily 10am–5pm, last admission 3.30pm; €12; ☎04 93 02 33 69, ⓦalpha-loup.com).

| INFORMATION | THE ALPES-MARITIMES |
|---|---|

**ST-ÉTIENNE-DE-TINÉE**

**Tourist office** 1 rue des Communes-de-France (daily 9am–noon & 2–5pm; ☎04 93 02 41 96, ⓦauron.com).
**Maison du Parc** At the northern end of the village (daily: July & Aug 9.30am–noon & 2–6pm; Oct–May 9.30am–noon & 2–5.30pm; ☎04 93 02 42 27; ⓦmercantour.eu).

**ST-MARTIN-DE-VÉSUBIE**

**Tourist office** Place Félix-Faure (July & Aug daily 9am–12.30pm & 2–7.30pm; Sept–June Mon–Sat 10am–12.30pm & 2–6pm, Sun 10am–12.30pm; ☎04 93 03 21 28, ⓦsaintmartinvesubie.fr).

## ACCOMMODATION

**ST-ÉTIENNE-DE-TINÉE**

**Camping du Plan d'Eau** ☎04 93 02 41 57, ⓦcampingduplandeau.com. Small, summer-only municipal site, in a nice verdant location at the edge of the village, beside a little lake and near the Maison du Parc. Closed Oct to mid-May. **€9.90**
**Regalivou** 8 bd d'Auron ☎04 93 02 49 00, ⓦleregalivou.free.fr. Lively hotel-restaurant, perched above the village centre with a large terrace, and open year round. Fourteen en-suite rooms and a hearty dining room. **€75**

**ST-MARTIN-DE-VÉSUBIE**

**Châtaigneraie** Allée de Verdun ☎04 93 03 21 22, ⓦraiberti.com. Imposing, summer-only hotel, set in lovely gardens near the village centre. Comfortable en-suite rooms, many with balconies, that sleep up to five, plus a pool and a good restaurant. Closed Oct–May. **€70**

16

# The Roya valley

The thickly forested **Roya valley** runs from Col de Tende on the French–Italian border down to Breil-sur-Roya. The roads that follow the river are narrow and steep, so driving is usually slow. In the **upper** valley, the highlight is the **Vallée des Merveilles**, a jumble of

---

### EXPLORING THE VALLÉE DES MERVEILLES

The first recorded visitor to stumble on the **Vallée des Merveilles**, a fifteenth-century traveller who had lost his way, described it as "an infernal place with figures of the devil and thousands of demons scratched on the rocks". That's a pretty accurate description, except that some of the carvings are of animals, tools, people working and mysterious symbols, dated to some time in the second millennium BC.

The valley is best approached from **ST-DALMAS-DE-TENDE**, 4km south of Tende. The easiest route is the 10km hike (6–8hr there and back) that starts at *Les Mesches Refuge*, 8km west on the D91. The engravings are beyond the *Refuge des Merveilles*. Note that certain areas are out of bounds unless accompanied by an official guide – and remember that blue skies and sun can quickly turn into violent hailstorms and lightning, so go prepared, properly shod and clothed, and take your own food and water. For details of **guided walks**, contact the tourist office in Tende (see p.858).

lakes and tumbled rocks on the western flank of Mont Bego. Down in the **lower** valley, don't miss the sleepy Italianate town of **Sospel**.

## Tende

**TENDE**, the highest town on the Roya, guards the access to the Col de Tende, which connects Provence with Piedmont but is now bypassed by a road tunnel. As recently as 1947, it still belonged to Italy. While not especially attractive, it's a busy little place that has plenty of cheap accommodation, places to eat, bars and shops.

### Musée des Merveilles

Av 16 Septembre 1947 • July–Sept daily 10am–6.30pm; Oct–June daily except Tues 10am–5pm; closed 2 weeks in March & 2 weeks in Nov • Free • ☎ 04 93 04 32 50, ⊛ museedesmerveilles.com

Tende's beautifully designed **Musée des Merveilles** details the geology, archeology and traditions of the Vallée des Merveilles. Alongside dioramas depicting the daily lives of Copper- and Bronze-Age peoples, reproductions of the rock designs are displayed, with attempts to decipher the beliefs and myths that inspired them. Whether or not you go to the valley itself, the museum provides an invaluable insight into an intriguing subject, though you'll need reasonable French to understand the displays.

## La Brigue

Pretty **LA BRIGUE**, 6km southeast of Tende, makes a good base for visits to the Vallée des Merveilles. While you're here, make the trip 4km east to the sanctuary of **Notre-Dame-des-Fontaines** (daily 9.30am–7pm; €2.50). From the exterior this looks like a graceful retreat, but inside it's more like a slasher movie: all its fifteenth-century frescoes, ranging from Christ's torment on the Cross to devils claiming their victims and, ultimate gore, Judas's disembowelment, are full of violent movement and colour.

## Sospel

The best place to take a relaxed break in the lower Roya valley is **SOSPEL**, a dreamy Italian-looking town that spans the gentle River Bévéra 36km south of St-Dalmas-de-Tende. Its main street, avenue Jean-Médecin, follows the Bévéra on its southern bank; halfway down the thirteenth-century **Vieux Pont** spans the river. Much of the town centre is made up of dark, narrow lanes, but **place St-Michel** at its heart is a riot of colourful Baroque facades and arcaded houses, dominated by the Cathédrale St-Michel.

---

### ARRIVAL AND INFORMATION

THE ROYA VALLEY

**TENDE**

**By train** The Train des Merveilles, designed for sightseers and offering English commentary in summer, leaves Nice daily at 9.24am, and reaches Tende at 11.05am (€25 return). Regular ordinary trains run along the same line, which also passes through La Brigue.
**Tourist office** 103 av 16 Septembre 1947 (daily 9am–noon & 2–6pm; ☎ 04 93 04 73 71, ⊛ tendemerveilles.com).

**LA BRIGUE**

**Tourist office** Place St-Martin (daily 9am–12.30pm &

2–5.30pm; ☎ 04 93 79 09 34, ⊛ labrigue.fr).

**SOSPEL**

**By train** The *gare SNCF* is southeast of town on av A-Borriglione.
Destinations La Brigue (1–3 daily; 50min); Nice (4 daily; 50min); St-Dalmas-de-Tende (3 daily; 45min); Tende (3 daily; 55min).
**Tourist office** 19 av Jean-Médecin (Mon–Fri 9am–6pm, Sat & Sun 9am–5pm; ☎ 04 93 04 15 80, ⊛ sospel-tourisme.com).

### ACCOMMODATION AND EATING

**TENDE**

**La Marguerita** 19 av du 16 Septembre ☎ 04 93 04 60 53. Popular pizzeria, with beams strung with dried herbs

and garlic, stuffed foxes on the walls, and a good range of Italian specialities. Daily noon–2pm & 7.30–9.30pm; closed Tues Oct–June.

**Miramonti** 5 rue Antoine Vassalo ☎04 93 04 61 82, ⓦlemiramonti-restaurant.fr. Inexpensive and very central hotel-restaurant that's handy for the station. The cheapest of its six clean, plain rooms lack en-suite facilities. Closed mid-Nov to mid-Dec. €39

### LA BRIGUE

**Le Mirval** 3 rue Vincent-Ferrier ☎04 93 04 63 71, ⓦlemirval.com. Large, renovated century-old *Logis de France* by the bridge, offering eighteen rooms overlooking the Levenza stream, and decent food in its light conservatory dining room. Closed Nov–March. €48

### SOSPEL

**Étrangers** 7 bd de Verdun ☎04 93 04 00 09, ⓦsospel.net. Smart hotel, just across the town's eastern bridge, with a pool; its riverfront restaurant (closed Tues & Wed lunch) serves *menus* from €25. Closed Dec–Feb. €70

**Le Mas Fleuri** Quartier La Vasta ☎04 93 04 14 94, ⓦcamping-mas-fleuri.com. The closest of the four local campsites, 2km upstream along the D2566, this two-star site has a pool. Closed Oct–March. €16.40

**Relais du Sel** 3 bd de Verdun ☎04 93 04 00 43. Attractive restaurant at the east end of town, where you dine on a terrace that's well below street level and just above the river. Excellent *menus* at €23 and €33. Also open as a tearoom in the afternoons. Tues–Sat noon–2pm & 7–10pm, Sun noon–2pm.

**16**

# The Côte d'Azur

ROUTE DES CRÊTES

**17**

# The Côte d'Azur

The Côte d'Azur polarizes opinion like few places in France. To some it remains the most glamorous of all Mediterranean playgrounds; to others, it's an overdeveloped victim of its own hype. Yet at its best – in the gaps between the urban sprawl, on the islands, in the remarkable beauty of the hills, the impossibly blue water after which the coast is named and in the special light that drew so many artists to paint here – it captivates still.

The ancient city of **Marseille** possesses its own earthy magnetism, while right on its doorstep there's swimming and sailing in the pristine waters of the **Calanques national park**. To the east the family resorts of **La Ciotat** and **St Raphaël**, sedate **Hyères** and Roman **Fréjus** hold their own in the face of huge media hype, while true Mediterranean magic is to be found in the scented vegetation, silver beaches, secluded islands and medieval perched villages like **Grimaud** and **La Garde Freinet**. You can escape to the wonderful unspoilt landscapes of the **Îles d'Hyères**, with some of the best flora and fauna in Provence, then contrast the beachcomber charm of **La Croix Valmer** with the flashy ebullience of its overhyped neighbour, **St Tropez** – unmissable if only for a day-trip, though you need to be prepared to contend with huge crowds in summer.

Once an inhospitable shore with few natural harbours, the seventy-odd kilometres of the Riviera between **Cannes** and **Menton** blossomed in the nineteenth century as foreign aristocrats began to winter in the region's mild climate. In the interwar years the toffs were gradually supplanted by new elites – film stars, artists and writers – and the season switched to summer. Nowadays, the **Riviera** is an uninterrupted sprawl of hotels, serried apartment blocks and secluded villas, with liner-sized yachts bobbing at anchor. Attractions remain, however, notably in the legacies of the artists who stayed here: Bonnard, Picasso, Léger, Matisse, Renoir and Chagall. **Nice** has real substance as a major city, while **Monaco** intrigues visitors with its tax-haven opulence and comic-opera independence.

The months to avoid are July and August, when room prices soar, overflowing campsites become health hazards and locals get short-tempered, and November, when many museums, hotels and restaurants close.

## GETTING AROUND
## THE CÔTE D'AZUR

**By bus** Regular buses run along much of the coast, but heavy traffic makes it extremely slow in high season.
**By train** Frequent trains link the major cities along the coast. Note that the main rail line turns inland between Toulon and Fréjus.

**By bike** Though you can cycle, distances between destinations are large, and you probably won't get very far unless you're Tour de France material.
**By car** Driving around the Côte d'Azur is by far the easiest and most convenient option.

LES CALANQUES

# Highlights

**❶ Vieux Port, Marseille** The old trading port, with its restaurants, beautiful sunsets and nightlife, attracts the most colourful characters in southern France. **See p.865**

**❷ Les Calanques** The limestone cliffs between Marseille and Cassis make for excellent hikes leading to isolated coves in which to go swimming. **See p.877**

**❸ Îles de Port-Cros and St-Honorat** These well-preserved islands offer a glimpse of what much of the coast must have looked like a hundred years ago. **See p.881 & p.899**

**❹ Massif des Maures** This undeveloped range of hazy coastal hills is a world apart from the glitz and glamour of the Côte. **See p.886**

**❺ Fondation Maeght** Modern art, architecture and landscape fuse to create a stunning visual experience. **See p.910**

**❻ Nice** The Riviera's capital of street life is laidback, surprisingly cultured and easy to enjoy, whatever your budget. **See p.912**

**HIGHLIGHTS ARE MARKED ON THE MAP ON P.864**

**17**

### FOOD AND WINE OF THE CÔTE D'AZUR

As part of Provence, the **Côte d'Azur** shares its culinary fundamentals of olive oil, garlic and herbs, gorgeous vegetables and fruits, goat's cheeses and, of course, the predominance of fish. The fish soups – Marseilile's **bouillabaisse**, and **bourride**, accompanied by a garlic and chilli-flavoured mayonnaise known as *rouille* – are served all along the coast, as are **fish** covered with Provençal herbs and grilled over an open flame. **Seafood** – from spider crabs to clams, sea urchins to crayfish, crabs, lobster, mussels and oysters – are piled onto huge *plateaux de fruits de mer*, which may not reflect this coast's harvest but do demonstrate the luxury associated with it.

The **Italian influence** is strong, from ravioli stuffed with spinach to thin-crust pizzas and every sort of pasta as a vehicle for anchovies, olives, garlic and tomatoes. Nice has its own specialities, such as *socca*, a chickpea flour pancake, *pissaladière*, a pizza-like tart with anchovies and black olives, *salade niçoise* and *pan bagnat*, both of which combine egg, olives, salad, tuna and olive oil, and mesclun, a salad of bitter leaves: consequently, Nice is about as good a spot to enjoy cheap street food as you'll find. *Petits farcis* – stuffed aubergines, peppers or tomatoes – are a standard feature on Côte d'Azur *menus*.

The best of the Côte **wines** come from Bandol: Cassis too has its own *appellation*, and around Nice the Bellet wines are worth discovering. Fancy cocktails are a Côte speciality, but *pastis* is the preferred tipple.

# Marseille

In recent years **MARSEILLE** has undergone a renaissance. France's greatest port has shaken off much of its old reputation for sleaze and danger to attract a wider range of visitors. What they discover is an earthy, vibrant city, where the attractions of a major metropolis meet those of the coast, its hitherto down-at-heel appearance scrubbed up for its stint as European Capital of Culture 2013. The march of progress is not, however, relentless: too often last year's prestige civic project becomes this year's broken, bottle-strewn fountain. But that's Marseille. If you don't like your cities gritty, it may not be for you. See beyond its occasional squalor, though, and chances are you will warm to this cosmopolitan, creative place.

### Some history

Founded by the Greeks some two and a half millennia ago, the most renowned and populated metropolitan area in France after Paris and Lyon has both prospered and been ransacked over the centuries. It has lost its privileges to French kings and foreign armies, recovered its fortunes, suffered plagues, religious bigotry, republican and royalist terror and had its own Commune and Bastille-storming. It was the march of Marseillaise revolutionaries to Paris in 1792 that gave the *Hymn of the Army of the Rhine* its name of *La Marseillaise*, later to become the national anthem. Occupied by the Germans during World War II, it became a notably cosmopolitan place in the postwar years, when returning *pieds noirs* (European settlers from Algeria) were joined by large communities of Maghreb origin and by migrants from the Comoros archipelago, a former French colony in the Indian Ocean.

### The Vieux Port and around

The cafés around the **Vieux Port**, where glistening fish are sold straight off the boats on quai des Belges, are wonderful spots to observe the city's street life. Particularly good in the afternoon is the north (Le Panier) side, where the terraces are sunnier and the views better. A free **ferry** (10am–1.15pm & 2–7pm) shuttles across the port from the Hôtel de Ville on the north side to the quai de Rive Neuve opposite.

**17**

### Fort St-Nicolas

Two **fortresses** guard the harbour entrance. The construction of **St-Nicolas**, on the south side of the port, represented the city's final defeat as a separate entity: Louis XIV ordered the new fort to keep an eye on the city after he had sent in an army, suppressed the city's council, fined it, arrested all opposition and set ludicrously low limits on Marseille's subsequent expenditure and borrowing.

### Basilique St-Victor

3 rue de l'Abbaye • Daily: 9am–7pm • Crypt €2 • ☎ 0496112260, ⓦ saintvictor.net

A short way inland from the Fort St-Nicolas, above the Bassin de Carénage, is Marseille's oldest church, the **Basilique St-Victor**. Originally part of a monastery founded in the fifth century on the burial site of various martyrs, the church was built, enlarged and fortified – a vital requirement given its position outside the city walls – over a period of two hundred years from the middle of the tenth century. It looks and feels like a fortress, though the interior has an austere power and the **crypt** is a fascinating, crumbling warren containing several sarcophagi, including one with the remains of St Maurice.

### Musée des Civilisations d'Europe et de la Méditerranée (MuCEM)

Fort St-Jean • ⓦ mucem.org

**Fort St-Jean**, on the north side of the harbour, dates from the Middle Ages, when Marseille was an independent republic; the building is undergoing conversion and the addition of a modernist extension by Algerian-born architect Rudy Ricciotti to create the new national **Musée des Civilisations d'Europe et de la Méditerranée (MuCEM)**, scheduled to open in 2013.

## Notre-Dame-de-la-Garde

Rue Fort du Sanctuaire • Daily: summer 7am–7.15pm; winter 7am–6.15pm • ☎ 04 91 13 40 80, ⓦ notredamedelagarde.com • Bus #60 or tourist train from Vieux Port

The best view of the Vieux Port is from the **Palais du Pharo**, on the headland beyond Fort St-Nicolas, or, for a wider angle, from **Notre-Dame-de-la-Garde**, the city's Second Empire landmark atop the La Garde hill. It is the highest point of the city – and the most distinctive – crowned by a monumental gold Virgin that gleams to ships far out at sea. Inside, model ships hang from the rafters while the paintings and drawings depict the shipwrecks, house fires and car crashes from which the Virgin has supposedly rescued grateful believers.

## Le Panier

To the north of the Vieux Port is the oldest part of Marseille, **Le Panier**, where, up until the last war, tiny streets, steep steps and houses of every era formed a *vieille ville* typical of the Côte. In 1943, however, with Marseille under German occupation, the quarter

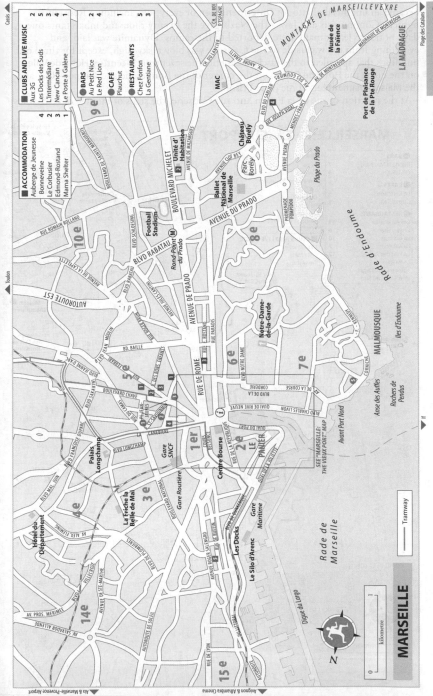

**17**

became an unofficial ghetto for **Untermenschen** of every sort, including Resistance fighters, Communists and Jews. The Nazis gave the twenty thousand inhabitants one day's notice to leave; many were deported to the camps. Dynamite was laid, and everything from the waterside to rue Caisserie was blown sky-high, except for three old buildings that appealed to the fascist aesthetic: the seventeenth-century **Hôtel de Ville**, on the quay; the **Hôtel de Cabre**, on the corner of rue Bonneterie and Grande-Rue; and the **Maison Diamantée**, on rue de la Prison.

At the junction of rue de la Prison and rue Caisserie, the steps of montée des Accoules

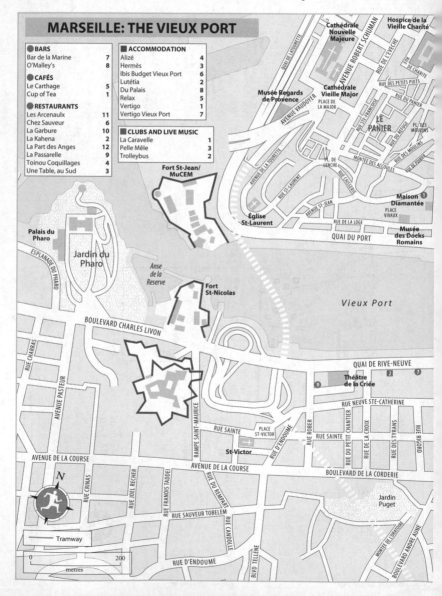

lead up to **place de Lenche**, site of the Greek *agora* and a good café stop. What's left of old Le Panier is above here, though many of the tenements have been demolished.

## Hospice de la Vieille Charité

2 rue de la Charité • **Musée d'Archéologie Méditerranéenne** Tues–Sun 10am–6pm • €3 • Ⓦ musee-archeologie-mediterraneenne .marseille.fr **Musée des Arts Africains, Océaniens et Amérindien** Tues–Sun 10am–6pm • €3 • Ⓦ maaoa.marseille.fr

At the top of rue du Réfuge stands the restored **Hospice de la Vieille Charité**, a seventeenth-century workhouse with a gorgeous Baroque chapel surrounded by

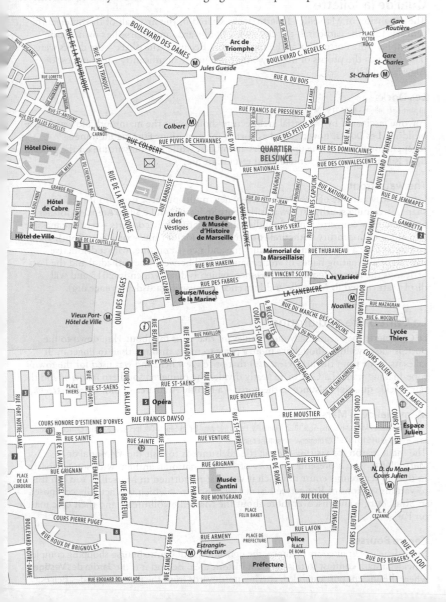

**17**

columned arcades; only the tiny grilled exterior windows recall its original use. It's now a cultural centre, a venue for temporary exhibitions and contains two museums: the **Musée d'Archéologie Méditerranéenne**, that has some very beautiful pottery and glass and an Egyptian collection with a mummified crocodile; and the **Musée des Arts Africains, Océaniens et Amérindiens,** with beautiful objets from as far afield as Mali and Vanuatu, and a room devoted to Mexico.

## Quai de la Joliette

The expansion of Marseille's **Joliette docks** started in the first half of the nineteenth century. Like the cathedral, the city's wide boulevards and Marseille's own Arc de Triomphe – the **Porte d'Aix** at the top of cours Belsunce/rue d'Aix – the docks were paid for with the profits of military enterprise, most significantly the conquest of Algeria in 1830.

### Les Docks

10 place de la Joliette • ☎ 04 91 90 04 69, ⓦ les-docks.fr

Anyone fascinated by industrial architecture should visit the mammoth old warehouse building, **Les Docks**, now restored as part of the ambitious **Euroméditerranée** regeneration scheme. The upper floors are offices, while the long arcade on the ground floor is being converted for retail and restaurant use.

### The waterfront

On the seaward side of Les Docks a lively new multi-purpose waterfront is taking shape, stretching southwest towards the Fort St-Jean from **Le Silo d'Arenc** – a former grain silo now converted into an auditorium for large-scale concerts – past the massive late nineteenth-century **Cathédrale de la Nouvelle Major** (Tues–Sat 10am–7pm), architecturally a blend of neo-Romanesque and neo-Byzantine, with a distinctive pattern of alternating bands of stone. Sandwiched between the cathedral and the Fort St-Jean is the **Musée Regards de Provence**, which is due to open in 2013 and will display art related to Marseille and Provence (ⓦ museeregardsdeprovence.org).

## La Canebière and around

**La Canebière**, the occasionally tatty boulevard that runs for about 1km down to the port, is the city's hub, though it's more a place to move through than to linger in. It takes its name from the hemp (*canabê*) that once grew here and was used for the town's rope-making trade. La Canebière neatly divides the moneyed southern *quartiers* and the ramshackle **quartier Belsunce** to the north – a mainly Arab area of old, narrow streets.

### Mémorial de la Marseillaise

25 rue Thubaneau • Mid-June to mid-Sept 10am–6pm daily; Feb to mid-June & mid-Sept to Dec Tues–Sun 2–6pm • €7; free English audioguide • ☎ 04 91 91 91 97, ⓦ memorial-marseillaise.com

The main reason for visiting the quartier Belsunce is to visit the **Mémorial de la Marseillaise**, which presents the story of France's national anthem with some panache in the old real tennis court in which it was first performed in Marseille. You can listen to various versions of Rouget de Lisle's 1792 anthem – which was actually composed in Strasbourg – and discover more about the Marseille volunteers and their epic march on Paris.

### Centre Bourse

Immediately west of cours Belsunce, the ugly but useful **Centre Bourse** shopping complex provides a stark contrast to this tatty but historic area. Behind it is the **Jardin des Vestiges**, where the ancient port extended, curving northwards from the present quai des Belges.

Excavations have revealed a stretch of the Greek port and bits of the **city wall** with the bases of three square towers and a gateway, dated to the second or third century BC.

### Musée d'Histoire de Marseille

Centre Bourse • Ⓦ centre-bourse.com

Within the Centre Bourse, the **Musée d'Histoire de Marseille** presents finds from excavations of the Jardin des Vestiges, including a third-century wreck of a Roman trading vessel. Refurbishment and extension of the museum, allied to restoration of the Jardin des Vestiges, will double the previous exhibition space in 2013.

### Musée de la Marine

Palais de la Bourse • Daily 10am–6pm • €2 • Ⓣ 04 91 39 33 21

At the Vieux Port end of La Canebière is the **Musée de la Marine**, housed in the Neoclassical stock exchange and with a superb collection of shipbuilders' models, including the legendary 1930s liner *Normandie* and Marseille's own prewar queen of the seas, the *Providence*.

## The Palais Longchamp and around

22 bd Longchamp • **Musée des Beaux-Arts** Ⓦ musee-des-beaux-arts.marseille.fr **Musée d'Histoire Naturelle** Tues–Sun 10am–6pm • €5 • Ⓣ 04 91 14 59 50, Ⓦ museum-marseille.org • Mᵒ Longchamp–Cinq-Avenues or Tramway 2 same stop

The **Palais Longchamp**, 2km east of the port at the end of boulevard Longchamp, forms the grandiose conclusion of an aqueduct that once brought water from the Durance to the city. The palace's north wing holds the city's **Musée des Beaux-Arts**, which includes works by Rubens, Jordaens, Corot and Signac and devotes one room to the nineteenth-century satirist from Marseille, Honoré Daumier. At the time of research the museum was closed for renovation. The palace's southeastern wing is occupied by the **Musée d'Histoire Naturelle**, where the oldest of the collection of stuffed animals and fossils dates back to the eighteenth century.

### Musée Grobet-Labadié

140 bd Longchamp • Tues–Sun 10am–6pm • €3 • Ⓦ musee-grobet-labadié.marseille.fr • Mᵒ Longchamp–Cinq-Avenues or Tramway 2 same stop

Opposite the Palais Longchamp, the **Musée Grobet-Labadié** is an elegant late nineteenth-century townhouse filled with exquisite *objets d'art*, representing the tastes of a typical family from Marseille's affluent merchant class at its zenith. It also stages temporary exhibitions.

## South of La Canebière

The prime shopping district of Marseille is encompassed by three streets running **south from La Canebière**: rue Paradis, rue St-Ferréol and **rue de Rome**. The most elegant boutiques and galleries cluster in the area around the **Musée Cantini**.

### Musée Cantini

19 rue Grignan • Ⓣ 04 91 54 77 75, Ⓦ musee-cantini.marseille.fr

Fauvists and Surrealists are well represented at the **Musée Cantini**, a good little museum of modern art, along with works by Matisse, Léger, Picasso, Ernst, Le Corbusier, Miró and Giacometti.

### Cours Julien

Mᵒ Notre-Dame-du-Mont–Cours-Julien

A few blocks east of rue de Rome is one of the most pleasant places to idle in the city, **cours Julien**, with its pools, fountains, pavement cafés and boutiques, buried

**17**

under graffiti and populated by Marseille's bohemian crowd and diverse immigrant community. Streets full of bars and music shops lead east to **place Jean-Jaurès**, locally known as "la Plaine", where the market is a treat, particularly on Saturdays.

## The corniche and around

For the corniche, take bus #83 from the Vieux Port; the quickest way to the beaches is by bus #19 from métro Rd-Pt-du-Prado

The most popular stretch of sand close to the city centre is the **plage des Catalans**, a few blocks south of the Palais du Pharo. This marks the beginning of Marseille's **corniche**, avenue J.-F.-Kennedy, which follows the cliffs past the dramatic statue and arch of the **Monument aux Morts des Orients**.

South of the monument, steps lead down to a picturesque inlet, **Anse des Auffes**, where there are small fishing boats beached on the rocks and narrow stairways leading nowhere. The corniche then turns inland, bypassing the **Malmousque peninsula**, whose coastal path gives access to tiny bays and rocky beaches – perfect for swimming when the mistral wind is not blowing. The corniche ends at the **Parc Balnéaire du Prado**, the city's main sand beach.

## Parc Borély

**Park** Daily 6am–9pm **Botanical garden** Daily: March–Oct 10am–noon & 1–6pm; Nov–Feb 10am–12.30pm & 1.30–4.30pm • €3

A short way up **avenue du Prado** from the beach, avenue du Park-Borély leads into the city's best green space, the **Parc Borély**, which has a boating lake, rose gardens, palm trees and a botanical garden.

The eighteenth-century **Château Borély** itself is scheduled to reopen in June 2013 as a museum of decorative arts to house collections hitherto scattered in various locations across the city.

## The Château d'If

Mid-May to mid-Sept daily 9.30am–6.10pm; mid-Sept to March Tues–Sun 9.30am–4.45pm; April to mid-May daily 9.30am–4.45pm • €5.50 • ⓦ if.monuments-nationaux.fr • Boats depart quai des Belges on the Vieux Port (every 35–55min; 25min; €10.10; ⓦ frioul-if-express.com)

The **Château d'If**, on the tiny island of If, is best known as the penal setting for Alexandre Dumas' **The Count of Monte Cristo**. Having made his watery escape after fourteen years of incarceration as the innocent victim of treachery, the hero of the piece, Edmond Dantès, describes the island thus: "Blacker than the sea, blacker than the sky, rose like a phantom the giant of granite, whose projecting crags seemed like arms extended to seize their prey". In reality, most prisoners went insane or died before leaving. The sixteenth-century castle and its cells are horribly well preserved, and the views back towards Marseille are fantastic. Note that **ferries** may not run when the mistral blows because it's too difficult to land.

## MAC

69 av d'Haïfa • Tues–Sun 10am–6pm • €3 • Bus #23, stop "Ste-Anne-Haïfa" or #45 from Mᵒ Rd-Pt-du-Prado, stop "Haïfa Marie-Louise"

Between Montredon and **boulevard Michelet**, the main road out of the city, is the contemporary art museum, **MAC**. The permanent collection includes works from the 1960s to the present day by Buren, Christo, Klein, Niki de Saint Phalle, Tinguely and Warhol, as well as Marseillais artists César and Ben.

# Unité d'Habitation

**17**

Bus #21 from M° Rd-Pt-du-Prado to "Le Corbusier"

Set back just west of boulevard Michelet stands a building that broke the mould, Le Corbusier's seventeen-storey block of flats, the **Unité d'Habitation**, designed in 1946 and completed in 1952. It's also known as the Cité Radieuse, and many architects the world over have tried to imitate it. Up close, its revolutionary example is apparent: at ground level the building is decorated with Le Corbusier's famous human figure, the Modulor; on the third floor there is a hotel (see p.874) and restaurant. Take the lift to the top to view the iconic rooftop recreation area; it's here that Le Corbusier's ocean liner inspiration is most obvious.

## ARRIVAL AND DEPARTURE

## MARSEILLE

**By plane** The city's airport, the Aéroport Marseille-Provence (☎04 42 14 14 14, ⓦmarseille-airport.com), is 20km northwest of the city, linked to the *gare SNCF* by bus (every 20min 5.10am–12.10am; every 15min at peak times; €8).

**Destinations** Bristol (3 weekly; 1hr 50min); Dublin (3 weekly; 2hr 5min); Edinburgh (2 weekly; 2hr 30min); London Gatwick (5 daily; 1hr 50min); London Stansted (daily; 2hr 5min); Montréal (4 weekly; 8hr 55min); Paris CDG (7 daily; 1 hr 30min); Québec (1 weekly; 8hr).

**By train** The *gare SNCF St-Charles* (☎3635) is on the northern edge of the 1er arrondissement on square Narvik. From the station, a monumental staircase leads down to bd d'Athènes and on to La Canebière, Marseille's main street.

**Destinations** Aix-en-Provence (every 30–40min; 35–45min); Aix-en-Provence TGV (every 20min–1hr;

12min); Arles (every 30min–1hr; 42min–1hr); Avignon (every 30min–1hr; 30–35min); Cannes (every 30min–1hr; 2hr 5min); Cassis (every 30min–1hr; 25min); Fréjus (1 daily; 1hr 36min); La Ciotat (every 20min–1hr; 30–35min); Les Arcs for Draguignon (12 daily; 1hr 20min); Lyon Part-Dieu (every 30min–1hr; 1hr 40min); Nice (every 30min–1hr; 2hr 30min); Paris Gare de Lyon (hourly; 3hr 17min); St Raphaël (every 30min–1hr; 1hr 37min–1hr 47min); Salon (hourly; 53min); Sisteron (6 daily; 1hr 50min–2hr 10min).

**By bus** The *gare routière* is alongside the train station on place Victor Hugo (☎0810 000).

**Destinations** Aix-en-Provence (every 20min; 30min); Cassis (10 daily; 40–50min).

**By ferry** SNCM, 61 bd des Dames (☎32 60; ⓦsncm.fr) runs ferries to Corsica, Tunisia and Algeria.

## GETTING AROUND

### BY PUBLIC TRANSPORT

**Bus, tram and metro** Marseille has an efficient public transport network (ⓦrtm.fr). The métro runs from 5am until 10.30pm on weekdays and until after midnight at weekends; trams run from 5am to after midnight.

**Information** You can get a plan of the transport system from most métro stations' *points d'accueil* (daily 6.50am–7.40pm) or at the RTM office at the Centre Bourse (6 rue des Fabres; Mon–Fri 8.30am–6pm).

**Tickets and passes** Flat-fee tickets for buses, trams and the métro can be used for journeys combining all three as long as they take less than 1hr. You can buy individual tickets (€1.50) from bus and tram drivers, and from métro ticket offices or machines on métro stations and tram stops. Two-journey *Tickets 2 Voyages* (€3) and ten-journey *Cartes 10 Voyages* (€12.80) can be bought from métro stations, RTM kiosks and shops displaying the RTM sign. Consider also the good-value one-day *Pass Journée* (€5) and

three-day *Pass 3 Jours* (€10.50), available from the same outlets. Tickets must be punched in the machines on the bus, on tramway platforms or at métro gates.

**Ferry** RTM runs a ferry between the Vieux Port and Pointe Rouge in the south of the city for easier access to the beaches and *calanques* (March to mid-Sept hourly 7am–7pm).

### BY BIKE

Blue bicycles belonging to Le Vélo scheme (ⓦlevelo-mpm .fr) can be rented from the 130 self-service rental points throughout the city using a bank card (€1 for seven-day membership, after which first 30min is free; €1 for each additional 30min). Mountain bikes can be rented from Tandem, 16 av du Parc Borély (☎04 91 22 64 80).

### BY TAXI

Taxi Radio Marseille (☎04 91 02 20 20); Taxi Marseillais ☎04 (☎04 91 92 92 92).

## INFORMATION

**Tourist office** 4 La Canebière (Mon–Sat 9am–7pm, Sun & public hols 10am–5pm; ☎0826 500 500, ⓦmarseille-tourisme.com), down by the Vieux Port.

**Marseille City Pass** If you intend visiting several of

Marseille's museums it's worth considering this pass, which for €22 (one day) or €29 (two days) includes free admission to museums, city guided tours, entry to the Château d'If and free travel on métros and buses.

**17**

## ACCOMMODATION

### HOTELS

**Alizé** 35 quai des Belges, 1er ☎04 91 33 66 97, ⓦalize-hotel.com; map p.868–869. Comfortable, attractive two-star hotel on the Vieux Port. Public areas are a little gloomy but rooms are modern, soundproofed and a/c; the more expensive ones look out onto the Vieux Port. €109

**Le Corbusier** Unité d'Habitation, 280 bd Michelet, 8e ☎04 91 16 78 00, ⓦhotellecorbusier.com; map p.867. Landmark hotel on the third floor of this renowned architect's iconic high-rise with fabulous views and a variety of room styles, from simple studios to elegant mini-suites with access to a large eighth-floor balcony. €70

**Edmond-Rostand** 31 rue Dragon, 6e ☎04 91 37 74 95, ⓦhoteledmondrostand.com; map p.867. Friendly *Logis de France*-affiliated two-star centrally located in the antiques district, a short walk uphill from the Vieux Port. Simple but comfortable, smallish a/c rooms with contemporary furnishings. €86

**Hermes** 2 rue Bonneterie 2e ☎04 96 11 63 63, ⓦhotelmarseille.com; map pp.868–869. Two-star in a superb position just off the Vieux Port, with plain but comfortable rooms with flatscreen TV. Some have terraces and views and there's a roof terrace with fabulous views over the Vieux Port. €90

**Ibis Budget Vieux Port** 46 rue Sainte, 1er ☎08 92 68 05 82, ⓦetaphotel.com; map pp.868–869. This budget chain hotel is worth a stay for its location alone, close to the Vieux Port. Situated in a historic building, some of the rooms have timber beams – it's incredibly popular, so book ahead. €63

**Lutétia** 38 allée Léon-Gambetta, 1er ☎04 91 50 81 78, ⓦhotelmarseille.com; map pp.868–869. Pleasant two-star just off La Canebière, with soundproofed and a/c rooms with flatscreen TV. Cheaper rooms have showers; some Superior rooms have larger beds and there are two singles. €72

★ **Mama Shelter** 64 rue de la Loubière, 6e ☎04 84 35 20 00, ⓦmamashelter.com; map p.867. Eagerly awaited Marseille sister of the hip Paris original, combining stylish design and boutique hotel comforts – including iMacs for TV, internet and free on-demand movies – with budget prices. There's a restaurant and bar on site and on-site parking. €79

**Du Palais** 26 rue Breteuil, 6e ☎04 91 37 78 86, ⓦhoteldupalaismarseille.com; map pp.868–869. Nicely appointed three-star hotel in a good location a short walk from the Vieux Port. The standard rooms are a little small, but all are soundproofed and a/c. €95

**Relax** 4 rue Corneille, 1er ☎04 91 33 15 87, ⓦhotelrelax.fr; map pp.868–869. Homely and very friendly budget hotel, right next to the Opéra and near all the action. Public areas are a little overstuffed in style; rooms are simpler, a/c and soundproofed. Prices are keen for the central location. €60

### HOSTELS

**Auberge de Jeunesse Bonneveine** Impasse Bonfils, av J.-Vidal, 8e ☎04 91 17 63 30, ⓦfuaj.org; map p.867. Friendly hostel just 200m from the plage du Prado. Facilities include internet access, restaurant and bar, and the decor is attractive and modern. Rates include breakfast. Reception 6am–1am. Closed mid-Dec to mid-Jan. Mo Rd-Pt-du-Prado, then bus #44 (direction "Floralia Rimet", stop "Place Bonnefon") or night bus #583 from Vieux Port. €21

★ **Vertigo** 42 rue des Petites Maries, 1er ☎04 91 91 07 11, ⓦhotelvertigo.fr; map pp.868–869. Funky backpacker hotel and hostel near the train and bus stations, with simple, stylish decor, youthful staff, and a bar in the lobby. En-suite double rooms fill up fast, so book those in advance. Dorms €25.40; doubles €60

★ **Vertigo Vieux Port** 38 rue Fort Notre Dame, 7e ☎04 91 54 42 95, ⓦhotelvertigo.fr; map pp.868–869. This sister hostel to *Vertigo* (above) has a similarly cool atmosphere, with accommodation in simple twin rooms or small mixed or all-female dorms, all en suite. Rates include breakfast. Dorms €25; twins €60

## EATING

Good restaurant hunting grounds include cours Julien or place Jean-Jaurès (international options), the Vieux Port (touristy and fishy), the Corniche and plage du Prado (glitzy and pricey). Rue Sainte is good for smart, fashionable dining close to the Vieux Port.

### CAFÉS AND BARS

**Bar de la Marine** 15 quai de Rive-Neuve, 1er ☎04 91 54 95 42; map pp.868–869. A favourite bar for Vieux Port lounging, and inspiration for Pagnol's celebrated Marseille trilogy. It's open from breakfast: at lunchtime you might tuck into a €10 *salade niçoise* or €12 *plat du jour*; in the evening tapas anchor down the mojitos and wine. Daily 7am–2am.

**Le Carthage** 8 rue d'Aubagne, 1er ☎04 91 54 72 85; map pp.868–869. They sell Tunisian sandwiches from €4, but it's the tempting piles of sticky North African pastries (from €1.30) that draw the eye at this diminutive, traditional *salon de thé* close to the marche des Capucins. Mon–Sat 7am–8pm, Sun 7am–noon.

**Cup of Tea** 1 rue Caisserie, 2e ☎04 91 90 84 02; map pp.868–869. A gorgeous Le Panier bookshop and *salon de* *thé* strategically located midway up the climb from the Vieux Port to the Vieille Charité. Huge selection of teas including green tea or rooibos from €3.50; coffee from €1.60. Mon–Sat 8.30am–7pm.

★ **Plauchut** 168 La Canebière, 1er ☎04 91 48 06 67, ⓦplauchut.com; map p.867. Beautiful old *pâtissier-chocolatier-glacier* and *salon de thé*, established in 1820, selling delicious home-made ice cream, croissants, *calissons* and *macarons*, plus *pogne* (a type of brioche) and traditional *navettes* – a hard orange-scented biscuit – from €1. Tues–Sun 8am–8pm.

## RESTAURANTS

★ **Les Arcenaulx** 25 cours d'Estienne-d'Orves, 1er ☎04 91 59 80 30, ⓦles-arcenaulx.com; map pp.868–869. This classy place has an atmospheric and intellectual vibe, as it's also a bookshop; there's a €20 lunch *menu* and a six-course *menu découverte* for €59; otherwise, expect to pay around €17 for the likes of *tartare de boeuf* with frites and mesclun. Mon–Sat noon–11pm.

**Chez Sauveur** 10 rue d'Aubagne, 1er ☎04 91 54 33 96, ⓦchezsauveur.fr; map pp.868–869. Established in 1943, this modest Sicilian restaurant close to the marché des Capucins is renowned locally for the excellent wood-fired pizzas, including a few made with *brousse*, a type of goat's cheese. Prices from around €9.50. Tues–Sat 11am–2pm & 7–10.30pm.

**Chez Fonfon** 140 Vallon des Auffes, 7e ☎04 91 52 14 38, ⓦchez-fonfon.com; map p.867. There's no debate about the quality of the bouillabaisse (€47) here, for this chic restaurant overlooking a small fishing harbour is one of an elite band guarding the true recipe of the dish. Mon 7.15–9.45pm, Tues–Sat noon–1.45pm & 7.15–9.45pm.

**La Garbure** 9 cours Julien, 6e ☎04 91 47 18 01, ⓦrestaurant-marseille-lagarbure.com; map pp.868–869. Rich specialities from southwest France, including duck cassoulet or duck confit with ceps in this wonderfully romantic and stylish restaurant. Three-course *menu* at €26; otherwise main courses cost around €15 and up. Booking advised. Mon–Fri 12.30–2.30pm & 7.30–11pm, Sat 7.30–11pm.

**La Gentiane** 3 rue des Trois-Rois, 6e ☎04 91 42 88 80; map p.867. Resolutely French and traditional, with dishes like duck breast with ceps; the service is friendly and the food is superb. Great bohemian location, parallel to cours Julien. *Menus* from around €20. Tues–Sat 7.30pm–11pm.

**La Kahena** 2 rue de la République, 2e ☎04 91 90 61 93; map pp.868–869. Great Tunisian restaurant just off the Vieux Port, with a bright interior, elaborate patterned tiles, couscous from €10 and *brochettes* with salad and *frites* from €12. There are a few North African bottles on the wine list. Daily noon–2.30pm & 7.30–10.30pm.

★ **La Part des Anges** 33 rue Sainte, 1er ☎04 91 33 55 70, ⓦlapartdesanges.com; map pp.868–869. Wonderful *cave de vins* serving hearty food and cheese platters, from a chalked-up daily menu, to mop up the classy wines; *plats* from around €13.50. Wines are listed by region and the selection changes daily. Mon–Sat 9am–2am, Sun 9am–1pm & 6pm–2am.

**La Passarelle** 52 rue Plan Fourmiguier, 7e ☎04 91 33 03 27, ⓦrestaurantlapassarelle.fr, map pp.868–869. Relaxed and informal restaurant tucked behind La Criée, with a short, daily changing seasonal menu featuring the likes of baked *daurade*, courgette flower *beignets* and lamb chops. Main courses around €18. The garden terrace is one of the prettiest (and most peaceful) in the city. Daily noon–2pm & 6–10.30pm.

**Toinou Coquillages** 3 cours Saint-Louis, 1er ☎08 11 45 45 45, ⓦtoinou.com; map pp.868–869. Popular with locals and visitors alike for the choice of more than forty types of shellfish, served in the restaurant and sold fresh from the counter at the front. Lunchtime *moules-frites formule* €14.90; oysters from €8.40 for six. Sun–Tues 11.30am–10.30pm, Wed & Thurs 11.30am–11pm, Sat 11.30am–midnight.

**Une Table, au Sud** 2 quai du Port, 2e ☎04 91 90 63 53, ⓦunetableausud.com; map pp.868–869. Stylish, Michelin-starred gastronomic restaurant overlooking the Vieux Port. Chef Lionel Lévy's contemporary take on Provençal cooking includes his signature dish, bouillabaisse milkshake (€18). Two-course daily changing lunch *menu* €29, otherwise *menus* start at €71. Tues–Thurs noon–2.30pm & 7–10pm, Fri & Sat noon–2.30pm & 7pm–midnight.

## DRINKING

**Au Petit Nice** 28 place Jean-Jaurès, 1er ☎04 91 48 43 04; map p.867. A Marseille institution in the most bohemian quarter of the city. The terrace is the place to head for on Saturday during the market, with a great selection of reasonably priced beers (from €2.30 *pression*, €3 in bottles). Tues–Fri 11am–2am, Sat & Sun 8am–2am.

**O'Malley's** 9 quai de Rive-Neuve, 1er ☎04 91 33 65 50; map pp.868–869. Classic expat-friendly Irish pub on the Vieux Port, with the familiar Celtic trappings plus live music every Thursday at 9.30pm and daily happy hour (5–9pm),

when pints are €4.50. Wed & Thurs 4pm–3am, Fri & Sat 4pm–4am, Sun–Tues 4pm–2am.

**Le Red Lion** 231 av Pierre-Mendès-France, 8e ☎04 91 25 17 17, ⓦpub-redlion.com; map p.867. Large British-style pub close to plage Borély, with a big selection of beers including Kronenbourg, Grimbergen and Guinness; draught beer from €5.50. The interior is dark and cavernous, though when the sun shines everyone crowds onto the narrow terrace at the front. Mon–Fri 4pm–2am, Sat & Sun 4pm–4am.

## NIGHTLIFE AND ENTERTAINMENT

Marseille's nightlife has something for everyone. Of the various free local arts newspapers the free fortnightly *Ventilo* and *Sortir* are the most useful; pick them up from tourist offices, museums and cultural centres, from the Virgin Megastore at 75 rue St-Ferréol, or FNAC in the Centre Bourse: these two – and the tourist office's ticket bureau – are the best places for tickets and information.

### LIVE MUSIC AND CLUBS

**La Caravelle** 34 quai du Port, 2e ☎04 91 90 36 64, ⓦlacaravelle-marseille.com; map pp.868–869. Café, bar and cabaret on the first floor of the *Hôtel Bellevue* with portside views. Live jazz on Wednesdays and Fridays from 9pm except in summer. Daily 7am–1am.

**Les Docks des Suds** 12 rue Urbain V, 2e ☎04 91 99 00 00, ⓦdocks-des-suds.org; map p.867. Vast warehouse that hosts Marseille's annual Fiesta des Suds world music festival (October) and is a regular live venue for hip-hop, electro and world music.

**L'Intermédiare** 63 place Jean-Jaurès, 6e ☎06 20 72 86 24; map p.867. Loud, hip club and bar with regular live bands and DJs and a highly eclectic music policy, ranging from rock to electro, hip house, dancehall, reggae and world music.

**Pelle Mêle** 8 place aux Huiles, 1er; map pp.868–869. Intimate and lively jazz club and piano bar just off the Vieux Port, with frequent live sets. Drinks prices are – by Marseille standards – a little on the high side, with a big range of whiskies from €9. Mon–Sat 6pm–2am.

**Le Poste à Galène** 103 rue Ferrari, 5e ☎04 91 47 57 99, ⓦleposteagalene.com; map p.867. Intimate and popular venue with regular live pop, folk, jazz, rock and electro, plus 1980s and 1990s DJ nights (Saturdays at 11pm; €6) and a bar.

**Trolleybus** 24 quai de Rive-Neuve, 7e ☎04 91 54 30 45, ⓦletrolley.com; map pp.868–869. Atmospheric bar and club in a series of vaulted seventeenth-century catacombs that once housed an arsenal; DJ nights have an emphasis on electro but there are also regular live gigs. Free Thurs & Fri, Sat €10 with *conso* (free drink). Thurs–Sat midnight–6am.

### GAY AND LESBIAN CLUBS

**Aux 3G** 3 rue St-Pierre, 5e ☎04 91 48 76 36, ⓦaux3g .site-forums.com; map p.867. Marseille's only lesbian bar, close to La Plaine market and regularly packed for its weekend DJ nights, when they spin anything from dance music to eighties hits. Gay men are also welcome. Thurs 7pm–midnight, Fri & Sat 7pm–2am.

**New Cancan** 3–7 rue Sénac, 1er ☎04 91 48 59 76, ⓦnewcancan.com; map p.867. It's pretty cheesy, but the *New Cancan* is nevertheless Marseille's only gay disco and something of a local institution, with regular Sunday cabaret nights. Entry with *conso* Fri & Sun €10, Sat €16–18. Fri–Sun midnight–dawn, plus Thurs in Aug.

### THEATRES AND CONCERT HALLS

**Ballet National de Marseille** 20 bd Gabès, 8e ☎04 91 32 72 72, ⓦballet-de-marseille.com. The home venue of the famous dance company, founded in 1972 by Roland Petit. Now under the direction of Fréderic Flamand, the company also performs at the Opéra and at La Criée theatre, as well as touring worldwide.

**Espace Julien** 39 cours Julien, 6e ☎04 91 24 34 10, ⓦespace-julien.com. Vibrant, municipally run arts centre staging everything from live comedy to jazz, electro and rock bands. There's a large main auditorium and a second, more intimate venue, the *Café Julien*.

**La Friche la Belle de Mai** 41 rue Jobin, 3e ☎04 95 04 95 04, ⓦlafriche.org. Interdisciplinary arts complex occupying a former industrial site in the north of the city, hosting theatre, dance, live music, circus, puppetry and art exhibitions.

**Opéra** 2 rue Molière, 1er ☎04 91 55 11 10, ⓦopera .marseille.fr. High opera and symphony concerts by the Orchestre Philharmonique de Marseille in a magnificent setting, part Neoclassical, part Art Deco. There are good last-minute deals on unsold tickets. The opera repertoire tends towards the classical – Bizet, Rossini, Verdi.

**Le Silo d'Arenc** 35 quai Lazaret, 2e ☎04 91 90 00 00, ⓦsilo-marseille.fr. 1920s-built former dockside grain silo converted into a 2000-seat multi-purpose concert venue, hosting everything from ballet to rock, swing and jazz-funk.

**Théâtre National la Criée** 30 quai de Rive-Neuve, 7e ☎04 91 54 70 54, ⓦtheatre-lacriee.com. Marseille's most prestigious stage for drama, home base of the Théâtre National de Marseille and occasional venue for ballet.

### CINEMAS

**Château de la Buzine** 56 traverse de la Buzine, 11e ☎04 91 43 91 23, ⓦchateaudelabuzine.com. It's a long trek from the centre, but the villa that Pagnol dreamed of turning into a *cinémathèque* is now exactly that – and a fantastic place to see his classic films. Matinées and evening screenings; tickets €6.90. Bus #50 from Castellane to La Valentine, then bus #51.

**Les Variétés** 37 rue Vincent Scotto, 1er ☎08 92 68 95 97. Five-screen art-house cinema just of La Canebière that frequently shows undubbed (*v.o*) English-language and other foreign films. There's also a bar and exhibition area. Tickets €8.

## DIRECTORY

**Consulates** UK, 24 av du Prado, 6ᵉ (☎04 91 15 72 10); USA, place Varian Fry, 6ᵉ (☎04 91 54 92 00).
**Health** Ambulance ☎15; doctors ☎3624; 24hr casualty departments at Hôpital de la Conception, 147 bd Baille, 5ᵉ (☎04 91 38 00 00); medical emergencies for travellers SOS Voyageurs, Gare St-Charles, 3ᵉ (☎04 91 62 12 80).

**Lost property** 41 bd de Briançon, 3ᵉ (☎04 91 14 68 97).
**Pharmacy** Pharmacie de la République, 7 rue de la République, 2ᵉ (bilingual; Mon–Fri 9am–7.30pm, Sat 9.30am–7pm; ☎04 91 91 90 32 27).
**Police** Commissariat Central, 2 rue Antoine-Becker, 2ᵉ (24hr; ☎04 91 39 80 00).

# Cassis

Many people rate chic little **CASSIS**, 23km east of Marseille, as the best resort this side of St-Tropez; hemmed in by cliffs, its development has been necessarily modest, making it a pleasant stop-over or day-trip from Marseille. Be sure to try the local Cassis white wines.

The spectacular clifftop **route des Crêtes** links Cassis with La Ciotat; regular belvederes allow you to stop and take the perfect shot of distant headlands receding into the sunset – vertigo permitting. The route is closed during high winds.

## The calanques

Boat trips from around €15 • Forest fire information ☎08 11 20 13 13 • If walking, call the information line before setting out as from June to September access is controlled according to a colour-coded alert level: orange means free access, red means access 6–11am only and black means the massifs are closed altogether

Portside posing and sunbathing aside, don't miss a boat trip to the **calanques** – pristine fjord-like inlets that cut deep into the limestone cliffs between Cassis and Marseille, recently declared a national park. Several companies operate from the port; be prepared for rough seas. If you're feeling energetic, follow the well-marked GR98 footpath from Port-Miou on the western side of the town. It's about ninety-minutes' walk to the furthest and best *calanque*, **En Vau**, where you can reach the shore. The water is deep blue and swimming between the cliffs is pure heaven. The fire risk is high; smoking and fires are prohibited and you're advised not to attempt the walk in high winds. There are no refreshment stops either, so take water.

## ARRIVAL AND INFORMATION CASSIS

**By bus** Buses from Marseille (9 daily; 45min) arrive at rond point du Gendarmerie from where it's a short walk to the port and beach.
**By train** The *gare SNCF* is 3.5km from town, connected by bus (7.15am–8.25pm every 35min–1hr; 20min).
**Destinations** Bandol (every 30min–1hr; 18min); La Ciotat (every 30min–1hr; 6min); Marseille (every 20min–1hr; 25–30min); St Cyr/Les Lecques (every 30min–1hr; 12min).
**Tourist office** Quai des Moulins (March, April & Oct

Mon–Sat 9am–12.30pm & 2–6pm, Sun 10am–12.30pm; May, June & Sept Mon–Sat 9am–6.30pm, Sun 9.30am–12.30pm & 3–6pm; July & Aug Mon–Sat 9am–7pm, Sun 9.30am–12.30pm & 3–6pm; Nov–Feb Mon–Sat 9.30am–12.30pm & 2–5pm, Sun 10am–12.30pm; ☎08 92 25 98 92, ⓦot-cassis.com).
**Activities** You can hire kayaks or boats in Cassis, sometimes including a skipper, and there are a couple of diving outfits; the tourist office has details.

## ACCOMMODATION

**Le Cassidien** 7 av Victor-Hugo ☎04 42 01 72 13, ⓦhotel-le-cassidien.fr. Just back from the port, this newly renovated hotel has ten small, attractive modern rooms with simple decor, en-suite shower rooms. Rooms are double glazed and a/c. Good value for the standard. **€70**
**Les Cigales** Inland just off the D559 on the edge of the village ☎04 42 01 07 34, ⓦcampingcassis.com. Cassis' only campsite is a two-star affair, and a 15min walk from

the port, with free wi-fi and 250 pitches. Closed mid-Nov to mid-March. **€19**
**Le Commerce** 12 rue St-Clair ☎04 42 01 09 10, ⓦhotel-lecommerce.fr. A handy budget option just uphill from the quayside, offering basic en-suite comforts with rooms sleeping one to four; some rooms have sea views. There is also a cottage, which sleeps up to 19 people. Closed Dec to mid-Feb. **€50**
**La Fontasse** 12km west of Cassis ☎04 42 01 02 72,

ⓦ fuaj.org. Solar-powered eco-friendly hostel in the hills above the *calanques*. It's pretty basic: there are no showers, you'll need to bring your own food and will be expected to help with chores. You can hike here along the GR98. Not bookable online. Reception 8–10am & 5–9pm. Closed Dec to mid-March. **€12.50**

**Les Roches Blanches** Av des Calanques ⓣ 04 42 01 09 30, ⓦ roches-blanches-cassis.com. Cassis' best hotel is in an idyllic setting amid pines on the Presqu'île, west of the port. Rooms have contemporary decor, bathrooms and a/c and many have either a balcony or terrace. There's a pool, plus direct access to the sea. **€150**

### EATING AND DRINKING

**Le Chaudron** 4 rue Adolphe Thiers ⓣ 04 42 01 74 18, ⓦ resto-lechaudron.skyrock.com. Esteemed, old family-run bistro in the streets behind the port, with modern decor, pasta from €13 and duck breast with honey and lavender on the *carte*. Menus €25 and €34. Wed–Mon from 7.15pm.

**Le Clos des Arômes** 10 rue Abbé P. Mouton ⓣ 04 42 01 71 84, ⓦ le-clos-des-aromes.com. Classic Provençal cooking in a simple, rustic dining room or in a pretty garden, with dishes like *daube à l'ancienne*, *pieds et paquets* and *pissaladière*. Menus €21 or €38. Feb–Dec Mon, Tues, Fri & Sat noon–1.30pm & 7.15–9.30pm, Wed, Thurs & Sun 7.15–9.30pm.

# La Ciotat

Cranes still loom over the little port of **LA CIOTAT**, where vast oil tankers were once built. Today, the unpretentious town relies on tourism and yachting and is less a place for sightseeing than relaxing, with a lively waterfront and good, sandy beaches on the eastern side of the port. The streets of the old town, apart from **rue Poilus**, are uneventful, though the increasing numbers of boutiques and *immobiliers* reflect the change from shipyard to pleasure port.

## The Eden Cinema

Corner bd A.-France and bd Jean-Jaurès • Closed for renovation; contact tourist office (ⓦ tourisme-laciotat.com) for information

In 1895, **Auguste and Louis Lumière** filmed the first moving pictures in La Ciotat – the town's main claim to fame. The world's oldest movie house, the **Eden Cinema**, still stands today, the subject of a €5 million restoration project to coincide with Marseille's stint as European Capital of Culture. The town has an annual film festival and the brothers are also commemorated by a monument on plage Lumière.

## Parc du Mugel

Daily: April–Sept 8am–8pm; Oct–March 9am–6pm • Bus #30, stop "Mugel"

Take a walk through the **Parc du Mugel**, with its strange cluster of rock formations on the promontory beyond the shipyards. A path leads up through overgrown vegetation to a narrow terrace overlooking the sea. If you continue on bus #30 to Figuerolles you can reach the **Anse de Figuerolles** *calanque* down the avenue of the same name, and its neighbour, the **Gameau**.

### ARRIVAL AND INFORMATION

**By train** The *gare SNCF* is 5km from the town but bus #40 is frequent at peak times and gets you to the Vieux Port in around 20min.

**Destinations** Bandol (every 30min–1hr; 10–21min); Cassis (every 20min–1hr; 6min); Marseille (every 20min–1hr; 33min); St Cyr-Les Lecques (every 30min–1hr; 5min).

**Tourist office** Bd Anatole-France (June–Sept Mon–Sat 9am–8pm, Sun 10am–1pm; Oct–May Mon–Sat 9am–noon & 2–6pm; ⓣ 04 42 08 61 32, ⓦ tourisme-laciotat.com).

**Boat trips** For a day-trip, Île Verte Navette makes the crossing to the islet of Île Verte (daily: May–June & Sept hourly 10am–noon & 3–5pm; July & Aug hourly 9am–7pm; April & Oct enquire at Vieux Port or call; €11 return; ⓣ 06 63 59 16 35, ⓦ laciotat-ilverte.com). Catamaran Le Citharista runs trips to the *calanques* of Cassis and Marseille from quai Ganteaume, sometimes in a glass-bottomed boat (late March to end Oct except during bad weather; up to 8 daily in high season; €16–28; ⓣ 06 09 35 25 68).

## ACCOMMODATION

**La Marine** 1 av Fernand Gassion ☎04 42 08 35 11, ⓦhotellamarine.free.fr. About the cheapest you'll get in La Ciotat, nothing fancy but close to the port and cheerful enough for the price. Some rooms sleep three or four; cheaper options don't have shower or WC. **€36**

**Miramar** 3 bd Beaurivage, La Ciotat-Plage ☎04 42 83 33 79, ⓦmiramarlaciotat.com. Comfortable family-run hotel in the beach suburb of La Ciotat-Plage, right on the palm-fringed seafront, with a/c en-suite rooms, some with balconies. There's also a restaurant. **€105**

**La Rotonde** 44 bd de la République ☎04 42 08 67 50, ⓦwww.hotel-larotonde-ciotat.fr. Good-value non-smoking two-star 200m from the port. Standard rooms have private bath and flatscreen TV, the cheapest share WC, and around half the 31 rooms have balconies. **€48**

**Le Soleil** 751 av Emile Bodin ☎04 42 71 55 32, ⓦcamping-dusoleil.com. The most central of La Ciotat's three campsites, around 1500m from the beach and harbour, this two-star has an on-site restaurant and takeaway. Camping **€20**, mobile homes from **€460** per week; bungalows from **€480** per week

## EATING AND DRINKING

**De la Vigne a l'Olivier** 44 quai François Mitterand ☎04 86 33 27 02. Classy restaurant/café and wine bar at the far side of the port, with seafood salads from €10 and wines by the glass from €3. There's a lunchtime *formule* of pasta and wine for €12. Tues–Sat 9am–7.30pm, Sun 9am–1.30pm.

**Roche Belle** Corniche du Liouquet ☎04 42 71 47 60, ⓦroche-belle.fr. In an idyllic setting near the sea between Bandol and Les Lecques, with a shady terrace and dishes like fillet of beef with morel sauce and potato *galette*. There's a three-course *menu* at €35 and they serve Bandol wines. Main courses from around €22. Sept–June Mon–Sat noon–1.30pm & 7.30–9.30pm; July & Aug Mon & Tues 7.30–9.30pm, Wed–Sat noon–1.30pm & 7.30–9.30pm.

# Bandol and around

Across La Ciotat bay are the fine sand and shingle beaches of **Les Lecques**, an offshoot of the inland town of **St-Cyr-Sur-Mer**, to which it is fused by modern suburbs. From the Port de la Madrague at the eastern end of Les Lecques' bay a signposted 10km **coastal path** runs through a stretch of secluded beaches and unspoilt *calanques* to the unpretentious resort of **BANDOL**. Inland, *dégustation* signs announce the *appellation* Bandol, whose **vineyards** produce some of the best wines on the Côte. The reds are highly reputed; the pale rosé is sublime on a warm summer's evening. To taste or buy, visit the **Oenothèque des Vins de Bandol**, place Lucien Artaud, opposite the casino on the seafront (Mon–Sat 10am–1pm & 3–7pm, Sun 10am–1pm; ☎04 94 29 45 03, ⓦmaisondesvins-bandol.com).

## ARRIVAL AND INFORMATION                        BANDOL AND AROUND

**By train** St Cyr/Les Lecques station is in St-Cyr-Sur-Mer, 2km inland; irregular buses link it with Les Lecques. Bandol station is uphill from the port; infrequent free shuttle buses link it with Embarcadère, close to the tourist office. Destinations from Les Lecques Bandol (every 30min–1hr; 6min); La Ciotat (every 20min–1hr; 4min).

Destinations from Bandol Toulon (for Hyères; every 30min–1hr; 15min).

**Tourist office** On Bandol's quayside at allée Vivien (July & Aug daily 9am–7pm; Sept–June Mon 9am–noon & 3–6pm, Tues–Sat 9am–noon & 2–6pm; ☎04 94 29 41 35, ⓦbandol.fr).

## ACCOMMODATION

**Golf Hotel** Plage de Rènecros, Bandol ☎04 94 29 45 83 ⓦgolfhotel.fr. Pleasant two-star on this pretty sandy cove just a short walk from Bandol. Secure parking. **€84**

**Le Key Largo** 19 corniche Bonaparte, Bandol ☎04 94 29 46 93, ⓦhotel-key-largo.com. Simple, bright rooms right by the sea near the port. Some have balconies and sea views. **€78.60**

# Hyères and around

**HYÈRES** is the oldest resort on the Côte, listing Queen Victoria and Tolstoy among its early admirers. Set back from the coast, it lost out when the focus of tourism switched

**17**

from winter convalescence to the beach. Today it exports cut flowers and exotic plants – the most important being the date palm, which graces every street – and it's a garrison town. Walled, medieval **old Hyères** perches on the slopes of Casteou hill, 5km from the sea; below it lies the **modern town**, with its elegant villas in fanciful pseudo-Moorish styles; avenue Gambetta is its main north–south axis. At the coast, the **Presqu'île de Giens** is leashed to the mainland by an isthmus, known as **La Capte**, and a parallel sand bar enclosing salt flats.

## The lower vieille ville

From place Clemenceau, a medieval gatehouse – the **Porte Massillon** – opens into the *vieille ville* on rue Massillon which is lined with tempting shops selling fruit and vegetables, chocolate, soaps, olive oil and wine. It ends at **place Massillon**, a perfect Provençal square with terraced cafés overlooking the twelfth-century **Tour des Templiers** (April–Oct daily except Tues 10am–noon & 4–7pm; Nov–March Wed–Sun 10am–noon & 2–5pm; free), the remnant of a Knights Templar fort elegantly converted into exhibition space for contemporary art.

## The upper vieille ville

Behind the Tour des Templiers, rue Ste-Catherine leads uphill to place St-Paul, from which you have a panoramic view over the Golfe de Giens. Wide steps fan out from the Renaissance door of the former collegiate **church of St-Paul** (April–Oct Wed–Sat 9am–noon & 2–6pm, Sun 10am–noon; Nov–March Wed–Sat 9am–noon & 2-6.30pm; Sun 10am–noon; free), whose distinctive belfry is pure Romanesque, as is the choir, though the simplicity of the design is masked by the collection of votive offerings hung inside. To the right of St-Paul, a Renaissance house bridges rue St-Paul, its turret supported by a pillar rising beside the steps. Through this arch you can head up rue Ste-Claire to **Parc Ste-Claire** (daily 8am–5/6/7pm; free), the exotic gardens around **Castel Ste-Claire**, once home to the American writer Edith Wharton. Cobbled paths continue up the hill towards the **Parc St-Bernard** (daily 8am–5/6/7pm; free) which is full of almost every Mediterranean flower known.

### Villa Noailles and around

Montée de Noailles • July–Sept Mon, Wed, Thurs, Sat & Sun 2–7pm, Fri 4–10pm; Oct–June Mon, Wed, Thurs, Sat & Sun 1–6pm, Fri 3–8pm • Free • ☎ 04 98 08 01 98, ⍟ villanoailles-hyeres.com

The **Villa Noailles**, a Cubist mansion enclosed within part of the old citadel walls, was designed by Mallet-Stevens in the 1920s and housed all the luminaries of Dada and Surrealism. It now hosts contemporary art and design exhibitions. Still further up the hill are the immaculate remains of the eleventh-century **castle**, whose keep and ivy-clad towers give stunning views out to the Îles d'Hyères and east to the Massif des Maures.

## The Hyères coast

If you're keen on the ancient history of this coast, the **Site Archéologique d'Olbia** in Almanarre is worth a visit for its Greek, Roman and medieval remains, including those of the abbey of Saint-Pierre de l'Almanarre (July & Aug daily 9.30am–noon & 3.30pm–7pm; April–June, Sept & Oct Mon & Wed–Sat 9.30am–noon & 2–5.30pm; Nov–March call to reserve; €2.50; ☎04 94 65 51 49). Along the eastern shore of the isthmus linking Hyères to the **Presqu'île de Giens** there are plenty of sandy **beaches**. Alternatively, take the **route du Sel** (closed 9pm–5am, and mid-Nov to mid-April) along the western shore for a glimpse of the flamingos on the adjoining saltpans and of the kitesurfers at the southern end of the windy plage de l'Almanarre.

# The Îles d'Hyères

The wild, scented greenery and fine sand beaches of the **Îles d'Hyères** are a reminder of what much of the mainland was like half a century ago. You can **stay** on all three main islands, though accommodation is scarce, coveted and expensive. Visitors should observe signs forbidding smoking (away from the ports), flower-picking and littering. The fire risk in summer is extreme: at times large sections of the islands are closed off and visitors must stick to marked paths.

A haven from tempests in ancient times, then the peaceful home of monks and farmers, the **Îles d'Hyères** became, from the Middle Ages, the target of piracy and coastal attacks. The three main islands, **Porquerolles**, **Port-Cros** and **Levant**, are covered in half-destroyed, rebuilt or abandoned forts, dating from the sixteenth century to the twentieth, when the German gun positions on Port-Cros and Levant were put out of action by the Americans. Porquerolles and Levant still have a military presence, which has helped prevent development. The islands' fragile environment is protected by the Parc National de Port-Cros and the Conservatoire Botanique de Porquerolles.

## Île de Porquerolles

The most easily accessible island is **Île de Porquerolles**, whose village, also called **PORQUEROLLES**, has a few hotels and restaurants, plenty of cafés, a supermarket and fruit stall and interminable games of *boules*. It dates from a nineteenth-century military settlement, and still focuses around the central **place d'Armes**. In summer it teems with day-trippers, but there is some activity all year round. This is the only cultivated island, with a few olive groves and three Côtes de Provence *domaines*, which you can visit.

Porquerolles is big enough to find yourself alone amid its stunning landscapes. The **lighthouse**, south of the village, and the *calanques* to its east make good destinations for an hour's walk, though the southern shoreline is mostly cliffs, with scary paths meandering close to the edge through exuberant maquis scrub.

### Maison du Parc

Daily: July & Aug 9.30am–12.30pm & 2.30–6.30pm; Feb–June, Sept & Oct 9.30am–12.30pm & 2–6pm • Free

Just off the path to the lighthouse at the southern end of the village is the **Maison du Parc** which has a garden of palms from around the world, information on the national park's activities and tours of the nearby Mediterranean botanic garden of **Le Hameau** (groups only; on application).

### The beaches

The most fabled (and distant) of the beaches is the **plage Notre-Dame**, 3km northeast of the village just before the *terrain militaire* on the northeastern tip. The nearest to the village is the sandy **plage de la Courtade**, which you pass on the way to Notre Dame. Facilities are minimal – there are earth toilets and places to park bikes at Courtade. The much smaller **plage d'Argent** on the west of the island has a pleasant **restaurant**.

## Île de Port-Cros

The dense vegetation and hills of **Île de Port-Cros** (ⓦportcrosparcnational.fr) make its exploration much tougher than Porquerolles, though it's less than half the size – take water with you. Aside from ruined forts and the handful of buildings around the port, the only intervention is the classification labels on some of the plants and the extensive network of paths; you're not supposed to stray from these and it would be difficult to do so given the thickness of the undergrowth. The entire island is a protected zone, and has the richest fauna and flora of all the islands. Kestrels, eagles and sparrowhawks nest here; there are shrubs that flower and bear fruit at the same time, and more common species like broom, lavender, rosemary and heather flourish. One kilometre from the port (and a 45min walk) is the nearest beach, **plage de la Palud**; it takes rather longer to reach Mont Vinaigre, the island's highest point, via the **Vallon de la Solitude** – a

**17**

three-hour round trip. From here there are views over the island's south coast and the islet of Gabinière. Except for those close to the beaches, the island's 30km of paths are all liable to close during times of high fire risk.

## Île du Levant

The **Île du Levant** – ninety percent of it a missile testing range – is almost always humid and sunny. Cultivated plant life goes wild, with the result that giant geraniums and nasturtiums climb 3m hedges, overhung by gigantic eucalyptus trees and yuccas. The tiny bit of the island spared by the military is the **nudist colony** of **HELIOPOLIS**, set up in the 1930s.

### ARRIVAL AND DEPARTURE

HYÈRES AND AROUND

#### HYÈRES

**By plane** Hyères-Toulon airport (☎ 0825 018 387, ⓦ toulon-hyeres.aeroport.fr) lies between Hyères and Hyères-Plage, 3km from the centre, to which it's connected by an infrequent bus service (#102).

Destinations London City (2 weekly in summer; 2hr); London Stansted (5 weekly in summer; 2hr 5 min); Paris Orly (daily; 1hr 25min).

**By train** The *gare SNCF* is on place de l'Europe, with frequent buses (#29, #39 or #67) to the town centre, 1.5km north.

Destinations Toulon (8 daily; 22min).

**By bus** The *gare routière* is on place Mal-Joffret, two blocks south of the entrance to the old town (☎ 04 94 03 87 03, ⓦ reseaumistral.com).

Destinations Le Lavandou (8 daily; 35min); St Tropez (8 daily; 2hr); Toulon (frequent; 1hr); Tour Fondue (for Porquerolles: every 1–2hr; 30min).

#### ÎLES D'HYÈRES

**From Bandol** Quai d'Honneur. Three weekly excursions to Porquerolles in summer; the trip includes 6hr on the island

(☎ 04 94 32 51 41, ⓦ atlantide1.com).

**From La Tour Fondue** Presqu'île de Giens. The closest port to Porquerolles; all year round to Porquerolles (☎ 04 94 58 21 81, ⓦ tlv-tvm.com).

**From Le Lavandou** *Gare maritime* (☎ 04 94 71 01 02, ⓦ vedettesilesdor.fr). The closest port to Port-Cros and Levant, with year-round services to both and services to Porquerolles (daily July & Aug; 3 weekly April to early Oct). The same line runs less frequent seasonal services from Cavalaire and La Croix Valmer to Port Cros and Porquerolles.

**From La Londe** Port Miramar. Services to Porquerolles and Port Cros (April to mid-Nov; ☎ 04 94 05 21 14, ⓦ bateliersdelacotedazur.com).

**From Port d'Hyères** Hyères-Plage. Services to Port-Cros and Levant all year (☎ 04 94 57 44 07, ⓦ tlv-tvm.com).

**From St-Raphaël** Quai Nomy, Vieux Port. Excursions to Porquerolles (July & Aug weekly ☎ 04 94 95 17 46, ⓦ bateauxsaintraphael.com).

**From Toulon** Quai Cronstadt. Summer trips to Porquerolles (May–Sept ☎ 04 94 46 24 65, ⓦ lesbateliers delarade.com).

### INFORMATION

#### HYÈRES

**Tourist office** Near the *gare routière* at Rotonde du Park Hôtel, av de Belgique (July & Aug daily 9am–7pm; Sept–June Mon–Fri 9am–6pm, Sat 9am–4pm; ☎ 04 94 01 84 50, ⓦ hyeres-tourisme.com).

**Bike rental** Holiday Bikes, 10 rue Jean d'Agrève, near port Saint-Pierre (☎ 04 94 38 79 45, ⓦ holiday bikes.fr).

#### ÎLE DE PORQUEROLLES

**Tourist office** There's a booth by the harbour in Porquerolles (April–Sept daily 9am–5.30pm; Oct–March 9am–12.30pm; ☎ 04 94 58 33 76, ⓦ porquerolles.com), where you can get basic maps – for €2 you'll get an info pack and much better one from the Maison du Parc (see p.881).

**Bike rental** There are several outlets in Porquerolles including La Bécane, rue de la Poste (☎ 04 94 58 36 00) and L'Indien, place d'Armes (☎ 04 94 58 30 39).

### ACCOMMODATION

#### HYÈRES

**Le Calypso** 36 av de la Méditerranée ☎ 04 94 58 02 09, ⓦ lecalypso.fr Basic and friendly hotel close to Port Saint Pierre, handy for the beach and for trips to the islands. The 11 rooms have double glazing and flatscreen TVs; some also have a terrace or small garden. **€49**

**Camping Bernard** Rue des Saraniers 5 ☎ 04 94 66 30 54, ⓦ campingbernard.fr. Two-star campsite just

50m from the sea in Le Ceinturon, with 100 pitches and plenty of shade; facilities include a barbecue area, washing machine, snack bar and children's games. Closed Oct–Easter. **€20.20**

**Camping Clair de Lune** 27 av du Clair de Lune ☎ 04 94 58 20 19, ⓦ campingclairdelune.fr. Three-star campsite and caravan park on the Presqu'île de Giens, with free wi-fi. They also have bungalows and mobile homes. Closed mid-Nov to early Feb. Camping €28; two-berth caravans €325 per week, mini bungalow €359 per week

**Du Soleil** Rue du Rempart ☎04 94 65 16 26, ⓦhotel -du-soleil.fr. Twenty assorted en-suite rooms in a renovated house at the top of the *vieille ville*, close to parc St Bernard and the Villa Noailles. Decor is simple, and the location peaceful. €94

### ÎLE DE PORQUEROLLES

**L'Arche de Porquerolles** 12 rue de la Ferme ☎04 94 58 33 71, ⓦlarchedeporquerolles.com. Eleven modernized, a/c rooms above a restaurant in the village with modern decor, en-suite showers, wooden floors and flatscreen TVs. Some rooms also have terraces and sea views. Closed mid-Nov to March. €170

**Les Medes** 2 rue de la Douane ☎04 94 12 41 24, ⓦhotel -les-medes.fr. Quite smart, modern three-star hotel close to place d'Armes with a/c and a garden with an artificial waterfall. Closed early Nov to late Dec. €165

### ÎLE DE PORT-CROS

**Le Manoir** ☎04 94 05 90 52, ⓦhotel-lemanoirportcros .com. The island's principal hotel, in a leafy garden beneath tall eucalyptus and with a pool. Doubles with shower;

half-board only. Main courses in its *restaurant gastronomique* from €28. Closed Nov–March. €185 per person

**Provençale** ☎04 94 05 90 43, ⓦhostellerie -provencale.com. En-suite, a/c rooms above a restaurant, with terrace or balcony. More luxurious rooms have sea views and access to a swimming pool. Half-board only Closed mid-Nov to March. €145 per person

### ÎLE DU LEVANT

**La Brise Marine** ☎04 94 05 91 15, ⓦlabrisemarine .net. One of the better-value options, this small hotel has fourteen simple en-suite rooms with sea views. There's a pool and a restaurant (open for lunch only). Closed Nov– Easter. €85

**Héliotel** ☎04 94 00 44 88, ⓦheliotel.net. Larger and a bit more fancy than the *Brise Marine*, this three-star hotel has a pool, a terrace with sea views and a restaurant (two course *formule* €16, three courses €19). Rooms have a/c. €120

**La Pinède** ☎04 94 05 92 81, ⓦcampingdulevant.free .fr. The island's campsite has a pool, jacuzzi and sauna and also rents out bungalows and an apartment with kitchen and private terrace. Closed Oct–March. Camping €30, bungalows from €70, apartment €135

## EATING AND DRINKING

### HYÈRES

**Le Bistrot de Marius** 1 place Massillon ☎04 94 35 88 38. One of the nicest options in the *vieille ville*, with dishes like octopus *daube* with polenta and rouille and lamb tagine with olives and lemon on its *carte*. Menus €19–26. Wed–Sun noon–2pm & 7–10.30pm.

**Les Jardins de Bacchus** 32 av Gambetta ☎04 94 65 77 63, ⓦbacchushyeres.com. Creative fusion cooking in the modern town with dishes like fillet of beef glazed with honey and mustard or roast sea bass with artichokes and fondant courgettes. Evening *menus* €22 and €29; lunch *menus* €14 and €19. Tues–Sat noon–1.30pm & 7.30–9.30pm.

★ **Les Jardins de Saradam** 35 av de Belgique ☎04 94 65 97 53. Reliable North African restaurant close to the *gare routière* with a pretty garden and filling couscous and

tagines on offer from around €13. Book ahead. Sept–June Tues–Sat noon–2pm & 7–9.30pm, Sun noon–2pm; July & Aug daily 7–9.30pm.

### ÎLE DE PORQUEROLLES

**L'Olivier** Le Mas du Langoustier ☎04 94 58 30 09, ⓦlangoustier.com. If you want gourmet cuisine you'll need to make the trek to the idyllic and Michelin-starred restaurant of the *Mas du Langoustier* hotel in the west of the island, with *menus* starting from €62 and dishes like lobster and foie gras cannelloni on the *carte*. May–Sept daily 12.30–2pm & 7–9.30pm.

**La Plage d'Argent** Plage d'Argent ☎04 94 58 32 48, ⓦplage-dargent.com. Right on the beach, serving salads from around €17 and seafood from around €21, plus snacks. April–Sept daily noon–3.30pm.

# The Corniche des Maures

The Côte really gets going with the resorts of the **Corniche des Maures**, where multimillion-dollar residences lurk in the hills, luxurious yachts bob in the bays, and seafront prices become alarming.

The Corniche itself is spectacular, with beaches that shine silver (from the mica crystals in the sand), tall dark pines, oaks and eucalyptus to shade them, glittering rocks of purple, green and reddish hue and chestnut-forested hills keeping winds away. No wonder the French president's official retreat, the Fort de Bregançon, is here – close to Bormes-les-Mimosas.

## 17 Bormes-les-Mimosas

Seventeen kilometres east of Hyères, chic **BORMES-LES-MIMOSAS** is medieval in flavour, with a ruined but restored **castle** at the summit of its hill, protected by spiralling lines of pantiled houses backing onto immaculately restored flights of steps. The mimosas here, and all along the Côte d'Azur, are no more indigenous than Porsches: the tree was introduced from Mexico in the 1860s, but the town still has some of the most luscious climbing flowers of any Côte town, and in summer, the displays of bougainvillea and oleander are impressive.

### ARRIVAL AND INFORMATION

**By bus** Buses from Hyères stop at Pin below the medieval village, from where there's a free shuttle bus daily in summer; otherwise, you'll have to walk up.
Destinations La Croix Valmer (up to 8 daily; 45min); Le Lavandou (up to 8 daily; 10min); St Tropez (up to 8 daily; 1hr 5min).

**Tourist office** Place Gambetta (April–June & Sept daily 9.30am–12.30pm & 2.30–6.30pm, 7pm in July and Aug; Oct–March Mon–Sat 9am–12.30pm & 2–5.30pm; ☎04 94 01 38 38, ⓦbormeslesmimosas.com).

### ACCOMMODATION

**Bellevue** Place Gambetta ☎04 94 71 15 15, ⓦbellevuebormes.com. Simple but attractive hotel/restaurant at the entrance to the medieval village with a/c en-suite rooms with wi-fi, flatscreen TV and safe. Full or half-board available. Closed mid-Nov to late Jan. €50

**Hostellerie du Cigalou** Place Gambetta ☎04 94 41 51 27, ⓦhostellerieducigalou.com. Classy three-star hotel opposite the *Bellevue*, and a member of *Châteaux & Relais de France*. It has a mimosa-shaded swimming pool and twenty tastefully decorated, a/c rooms with bath, safe and flatscreen TV. €189

**Clau Mar Jo** 895 chemin de Bénat ☎04 94 71 53 39, ⓦwww.camping-clau-mar-jo.fr. Four-star mobile-home park just below the main road between the village and Le Lavandou, with good facilities including a swimming pool, children's play area and *boules* pitch. Closed mid-Sept to mid-June. From €721 per week for 4 in high season

### EATING AND DRINKING

**La Cassole** 1 ruelle du Moulin ☎04 94 71 14 86. Provençal specialities in unpretentious surroundings on a pretty terrace in the medieval village. Three-course *menu* €28, otherwise €15 and up for the likes of sautéed chicken with chorizo and green olives. Mon–Sat 7.30–9pm or later.

**Pâtes…et Pâtes** Place du Bazar ☎04 94 64 85 75, ⓦbormeslesmimosas.com/patesetpates. At the foot of the medieval village, this restaurant serves good pasta from around €9.50, with a big choice of sauces; fancier dishes include the four-cheese ravioli with cream sauce for €14.90. Sept–June Fri–Tues noon–1.45pm & 7–9.15pm, Wed noon–1.45pm; July & Aug Wed–Mon 7–9.15pm.

**La Tonnelle de Gil Renard** Place Gambetta ☎04 94 71 34 84, ⓦla-tonnelle-bormes.com. Rather chic, *Gault Millau*-listed restaurant at the entrance to the old village, with dishes like veal kidneys sautéed with port sauce and polenta or aioli with seasonal vegetables. *Menus* from €19, otherwise around €20. Oct–April Fri–Tues noon–1.30pm & 7.15–9.30pm; May–June & Sept Thurs–Tues noon–1.30pm & 7.15–9.30pm; July & Aug Thurs–Tues 7.15–9.30pm.

## Le Lavandou and around

**LE LAVANDOU**, a few kilometres east of Bormes, is a pleasantly unpretentious seaside town known for its good beaches. Its name derives from *lavoir* or "wash-house" rather than "lavender". From the central promenade of quai Gabriel-Péri the sea is all but invisible thanks to the pleasure boats moored at the three harbours; demand from restaurateurs also keeps a few fishing boats in business. There's a sandy beach in town, but the fabled silver sands are to the east at **Aiguebelle, Le Rossignol, Cavalière, Pramousquier** and across the municipal boundary in **Le Canadel** and **Le Rayol**. It's hardly open countryside, but this is one of the most unspoilt sections of the Côte, with a well-made cycle track parallel to the coast road. You can follow the sinuous D27 up to the Col du Canadel for breathtaking views and beautiful cork-oak woodland and, in Le Rayol, visit a superb garden, the **Domaine de Rayol** (daily: July & Aug 9.30am–7.30pm; April–June, Sept & Oct 9.30am–6.30pm; Nov–March

9.30am–5.30pm; €9; ☎04 98 04 44 00, ⓦdomainedurayol.org), which has plants from differing parts of the world that share the Mediterranean climate.

**17**

| ARRIVAL AND INFORMATION | LE LAVANDOU AND AROUND |
|---|---|

**By bus** Buses from Bormes and Hyères stop at the *gare routière* on av de Provence.
Destinations La Croix Valmer (up to 8 daily; 35min); Rayol Canadel (up to 8 daily; 15min); St Tropez (up to 8 daily; 55min).

**Tourist office** Opposite the port at quai Gabriel-Péri (Mon, Wed & Thurs–Sat 9am–12.30pm & 2.30–7pm, Tues 9.30am–12.30pm & 2.30–7pm, Sun 9.30am–12.30pm & 3.30–6.30pm; ☎04 94 00 40 50, ⓦ ot-lelavandou.fr).

## ACCOMMODATION AND EATING

**L'Oustaou** 20 av Général-de-Gaulle ☎04 94 71 12 18, ⓦlavandou-hotel-oustaou.com. Le Lavandou's best budget option – a clean, family-run two-star in the town centre, just minutes from the beach and port. It's well known and gets busy, so it might be worth booking ahead. **€56**

**La Plage** 14 rue des Trois-Dauphins ☎04 94 05 80 74, ⓦlhoteldelaplage.com. Classy, modernized two-star hotel right on the pretty sandy cove of Aiguebelle, with uncluttered modern decor, a restaurant (three-course *menu* €22.90) and a broad terrace with bar. Rooms have en-suite bath and a/c. **€90**

# La Croix-Valmer

Beyond Le Rayol the corniche climbs through 3km of open countryside, scarred almost every year by fires. As abruptly as this wilderness commences, it ends with the sprawling family resort of **Cavalaire-sur-Mer**. From here another exceptional stretch of coastline, dressed only in its natural covering of rock and woodlands, is visible across the Baie de Cavalaire. This is the **Domaine de Cap Lardier**, a wonderful coastal conservation area around the southern tip of the St-Tropez peninsula, easily accessible from **LA CROIX-VALMER**. The resort's rather characterless centre is 2.5km from the sea; vineyards between the two produce a very decent Côte de Provence.

| ARRIVAL AND INFORMATION | LA CROIX-VALMER |
|---|---|

**By bus** Buses stop at the Plage du Débarquement and at the Croix de Constantin in the village. A free shuttle bus connects the village centre with plage de Gigaro (June–Sept every 45min).
Destinations Hyères (7 daily; 1hr 15min); Le Lavandou (7 daily; 35min); St Tropez (up to 8 daily; 20min).

**Tourist office** 287 rue Louis Martin, just up from the junction of the D559 and D93 (July & Aug daily 10am–7pm; April–June & Sept Mon–Sat 9am–noon & 2–6pm, Sun 9am–noon; Oct–March Mon–Fri 9am–noon & 2–6pm, Sat 9am–noon; ☎04 94 55 12 12, ⓦlacroixvalmer.fr).

## ACCOMMODATION

**Le Château de Valmer** Rte de Gigaro ☎04 94 55 15 15, ⓦchateauvalmer.com. Luxurious old mansion in an idyllic setting between pines, palms and vines just back from the plage de Gigaro, with 42 rooms plus cottages on the estate and a few treehouses. Spa and leisure facilities include an indoor pool, sauna, hammam and gym. Closed Oct–April. **€355**
**La Ricarde** Bd de St Raphaël, plage du Débarquement ☎04 94 79 64 07, ⓦhotel-la-ricarde.com. A good-value

family-run *chambres d'hôte* just 150m from the beach, with eight tasteful and individually styled, a/c rooms with en-suite shower and WC. Closed Nov–Feb. **€73**
**Sélection** 12 bd de la Mer ☎04 94 55 10 30, ⓦ selectioncamping.com. Four-star campsite, 400m from the sea and with excellent facilities including a heated pool, bar, restaurant, takeaway, shop and plenty of activities. Closed mid-Oct to mid-March. **€42**

## EATING AND DRINKING

**L'Italien/Pepe le Pirate** Plage de Gigaro ☎04 94 79 67 16, ⓦlesmoulinsdepaillas.com. Two-in-one restaurant near the conservation area. It's quite smart and formal at lunch (two-course *menu* €29) and more casual in

the evening, with a menu dominated by pasta and pizza (from €10). The adjacent *restaurant gastronomique*, *Brigantine*, is run by the same people. Mid-May to Sept daily 12.15–2pm & 7.30–9pm.

**17**

# The Massif des Maures

Between Hyères and Fréjus the coast's bewitching hinterland is the wooded, hilly **Massif des Maures**. The highest point of these hills stops short of 800m, but the quick succession of ridges, the sudden drops and views, and the curling, looping roads, are pervasively mountainous. In spring, the sombre forest is enlivened by millions of wild flowers and the roads are busy with cyclists; in winter, this is the haunt of hunters. Amid the brush crawl the last of the Hermann's tortoises, once found along the entire northern Mediterranean coast.

## Collobrières and around

At the heart of the Massif is the ancient village of **COLLOBRIÈRES**, reputed to have been the first place in France to learn from the Spanish that a certain tree plugged into bottles allows a wine industry to grow. From the Middle Ages until supplanted by the sweet chestnut, cork production was the major business here.

### Confiserie Azuréenne

Bd Koenig • Daily 9.30am–12.30pm & 1.30–6.30pm • ☎ 04 94 48 07 20, ⓦ confiserieazureenne.con

Collobrières' church, *mairie* and houses don't seem to have changed much for a century, but the **Confiserie Azurienne** exudes efficiency and modernity in the manufacture of all things chestnut: ice cream, jam, nougat, purée and *marrons glacés*. There's an exhibition that explains the production process and a small terrace on which to enjoy the delicious ice cream.

### La Chartreuse de la Verne

Off the D14 • Feb–May & Oct–Dec daily except Tues 11am–5pm; June–Sept daily except during high fire risk 11am–6pm • €6 • ☎ 04 94 43 48 28 or ☎ 04 94 48 08 00 for fire-risk information, ⓦ diocese-frejus-toulon.com/Monastere-Notre-Dame-de-Clemence • If you arrive by car, you have to park at the new visitor car park, several hundred metres back from the monastery

Hidden in the forest, 12km from Collobrières towards Grimaud, is a huge and now largely restored twelfth-century monastery, **La Chartreuse de la Verne**, abandoned at the time of the Revolution. These days it looks a little too pristine, though there's no denying the wonder of its setting.

## Grimaud

**GRIMAUD**, 25km east of Collobrières along the twisting D14 and more easily reached from St-Tropez or La Croix Valmer, is a film set of a **village perché**. The cone of houses enclosing the eleventh-century church and culminating in the ruins of a medieval castle appears as a single, perfectly unified entity, though the effect of timelessness is undermined by the (handy) glass lift that whisks visitors up into the village from the main road. The most vaunted street is the arcaded **rue des Templiers**, which leads up to the Romanesque **Église de St-Michel** and a house of the Knights Templar, while the view from the **castle** ruins (free) is superb. Back on the main road through the village is a small folk museum, the **Musée des Arts et Traditions Populaires** (May–June & Sept Mon–Sat 2.30–6pm; July & Aug Tues–Sat 2.30–6pm; Oct–April Mon–Sat 2–5.30pm; free; ☎ 04 94 43 39 29).

### Port Grimaud

The entrance is well signed off the N98

Grimaud's celebrated coastal extension, **PORT GRIMAUD**, stands at the head of the Golfe de St-Tropez, just north of La Foux. Created in the 1960s with waterways for roads and with yachts everywhere, it's exquisitely tasteful, though surrounded by car parks rather than lavender fields and with a mild air of artificiality. The inhabitants include a certain Joan Collins. You don't have to pay to visit, but you can't explore properly without hiring a boat (€25 for 30min) or joining a boat tour (€5.50).

## La Garde-Freinet

The peaceful village of **LA GARDE-FREINET**, set in forested hills 10km northwest of Grimaud, was founded in the late twelfth century by people from the nearby villages of Saint Clément and Miremer. The original fortified settlement sat further up the hillside, and the foundations of the **fortress** are still visible above the village beside the ruins of a fifteenth-century castle (take the path from La Planette car park at the northwestern end of the village). The medieval charm, easy walks to stunning panoramas and twice weekly **market** (Wed and Sun) make it an alluring spot, and many ex-pats have bought property here. Happily, though, attempts to "do a St-Tropez" by making it trendy and expensive seem – thus far – doomed to failure.

| ARRIVAL AND INFORMATION | THE MASSIF DES MAURES |
|---|---|

### COLLOBRIÈRES

**By bus** Collobrières is served by infrequent buses from Hyères (1 daily; 90min) and Toulon (1–2 daily; 1hr 45min).
**Tourist office** Bd Charles-Caminat (Tues, Wed, Fri & Sat 9am–noon & 3–5pm; ☏ 04 94 48 08 00, ⌨ collobrieres -tourisme.com). They can supply details of walks in the surrounding hills.

### GRIMAUD

**By bus** Buses link St-Tropez to Grimaud (up to 6 daily; 25min) and Port Grimaud (up to 10 daily; 20min). There are also connections from Grimaud village to La Garde-Freinet (3 daily; 15min).
**Tourist office** On the RD558 next to the lift up to the old village (Mon–Sat: April–June & Sept 9am–12.30pm & 2.30–6pm; July & Aug 9am–12.30pm & 3–7pm; Oct– March 9am–12.30pm & 2–5.30pm; ☏ 04 94 55 43 83, ⌨ grimaud-provence.com).

### LA GARDE-FREINET

**By bus** Buses from Grimaud (up to 4 daily; 15min) and St-Tropez (up to 4 daily; 40min–1hr 5min) arrive at parking du Stade on the main road at the entrance to the village.
**Tourist office** Chapelle St Jean, place de l'Hôtel de Ville (April–June, Sept & Oct Mon–Sat 9am–12.30pm & 2–6pm; July & Aug Mon–Sat 9am–1pm & 3–6.30pm, Sun 9am–1pm; Nov–March Mon–Fri 9am–12.30pm & 2–5.30pm; ☏ 04 94 43 67 41, ⌨ www.la-garde-freinet -tourisme.fr). They can provide details for the entire Maures region, including suggested walks and hikes (in English), such as the spectacular 21km GR9 route des Crêtes.
**Conservatoire du Patrimoine** Next door to the tourist office on place de l'Hôtel de Ville (Tues–Sat 10am–12.30pm & 2.30–5.30pm). They organize guided walks on local topics and have exhibits on local history.

| GETTING AROUND | |
|---|---|

**On foot** Much of the Massif is inaccessible even to walkers. However, the GR9 footpath follows the highest and most northerly ridge from Pignans on the N97 past Notre-Dame- des-Anges, La Sauvette, La Garde-Freinet and down to the head of the Golfe de St-Tropez.

**By bike** For cyclists, the D14 that runs for 42km through the middle, parallel to the coast, from Pierrefeu-du-Var, north of Hyères, to Cogolin near St-Tropez, is manageable and stunning, climbing from 150m to 411m above sea level.

| ACCOMMODATION | |
|---|---|

### COLLOBRIÈRES

**Camping Municipal St Roch** On the eastern side of the village near place Charles-de-Gaulle ☏ 04 94 48 08 00, ⌨ collobrieres-tourisme.com. Fairly basic campsite (bookings only through the tourist office), open summer only. *Camping sauvage* is forbidden. **€9.40**
**Des Maures** 19 bd Lazare Carnot ☏ 04 94 48 07 10, ⌨ hoteldesmaures.fr. Simple but spacious and very good-value rooms above a restaurant and bar in the centre of the village, facing the river at the back. Competitive half-board available. **€33**

★ **Notre Dame** 15 av de la Libération ☏ 04 94 48 07 13, ⌨ hotel-notre-dame.eu. Surprisingly chic for the deeply rural location, this trendy boutique-style hotel has ten individually decorated rooms with huge bathrooms plus a lovely patio restaurant by the river that offers excellent wines. **€98**

### GRIMAUD

**Le Coteau Fleuri** Place des Pénitents ☏ 04 94 43 20 17, ⌨ coteaufleuri.fr. Fourteen rooms above an excellent restaurant (see p.888) in a peaceful corner of the medieval

**17**

village. Cheaper rooms lack a/c and have shower rather than bath; more expensive ones have views across open countryside. **€99**

### LA GARDE-FREINET

**Camping de Bérard** 5km along the RD558 to Grimaud ☎ 04 94 43 21 23, ⓦ campingberard.com. Three-star campsite with a swimming pool, free wi-fi, a shop, restaurant and bar, plus musical evenings and plenty of

games facilities. Closed Nov–Feb. **€13.70**

**Le Mouron Rouge** Quartier Le Défend Nord, 1km north of La Garde Freinet ☎ 04 94 43 66 33, ⓦ lemouronrouge.com. Lovely *chambres d'hôte* in a rustic setting, with well-equipped apartments (for 2–5 people), studios (2–4 people) and a double room with private terrace. There's a *boules* pitch and a large pool. Double **€110**, apartments **€155**, studios **€130**

## EATING

### COLLOBRIÈRES

**La Petite Fontaine** 6 place de la République ☎ 04 94 48 00 12. Congenial and affordable *Gault Millau*-listed restaurant with an excellent reputation, serving classic Provençal dishes on €26 and €31 *menus*. It gets booked up fast. Tues–Sat noon–2pm & 7.30–9pm, Sun noon–2pm.

**Les Vignerons de Collobrières** Near *Hôtel Notre-Dame* at the western entrance to the village ☎ 04 94 48 07 26. A good place to buy the local Côtes de Provence wines. Mon 2–6pm, Tues–Sat 8.30am–noon & 2–6pm.

### GRIMAUD

**Le Coteau Fleuri** Place des Pénitents ☎ 04 94 43 20 17, ⓦ coteaufleuri.fr. In a tranquil spot, this good hotel restaurant offers a two-course lunch *menu* at €24, with

three courses at €27. Mid-Dec to Oct 12.15–10pm; closed Tues except July & Aug.

### LA GARDE-FREINET

**Le Carnotzet** 7 place du Marché ☎ 04 94 43 62 73. Lively bar, art gallery and restaurant with a terrace on the village's most exquisite square. *Plats du jour* from €14, *menu* €24; occasional live jazz July–Sept. Wed–Mon noon–2.30/3.30pm & 5.30–11.30pm, Tues noon–2.30/3.30pm.

**La Faucado** Av de l'Esplanade ☎ 04 94 43 60 41. *Restaurant gastronomique* with mains around €35; it's overpriced, but serves beautiful dishes like fillet of beef with port or lamb *brochette* from local produce in a pretty garden setting. Daily noon–2pm & 7–10pm; closed Tues outside high season.

# St-Tropez and around

As the summer playground of Europe's youthful rich, **ST-TROPEZ** is among the most overhyped – and in July and August overcrowded – spots in the Mediterranean. It remains undeniably glamorous, its vast yachts and infamous champagne "spray" parties creating an air of hedonistic excess in high summer. Alas, partaking of its designer charms can seriously dent your budget at any time of the year.

### Some history

The **origins** of St-Tropez are unremarkable: a fishing village that grew up around a port founded by Marseille's Greeks, destroyed by Saracens in 739 and finally fortified in the late Middle Ages. Its sole distinction was its inaccessibility: stuck on a small peninsula that never warranted proper roads, reached only by boat till the end of the nineteenth century.

Soon after, bad weather forced the painter **Paul Signac** to moor in St-Tropez. He promptly decided to build a house there, to which he invited his friends. Matisse was one of the first to accept, with Bonnard, Marquet, Dufy, Dérain, Vlaminck, Seurat and Van Dongen following suit, and by World War I St-Tropez was an established **bohemian** hangout. The 1930s saw a new influx, of writers as much as painters: Cocteau, Colette and Anaïs Nin, whose journal records "girls riding bare-breasted in the back of open cars". In 1956, Roger Vadim filmed Brigitte Bardot here in **Et Dieu ... Créa la Femme**; the cult of Tropezian sun, sex and celebrities promptly took off and the place has been groaning under the weight of visitors ever since.

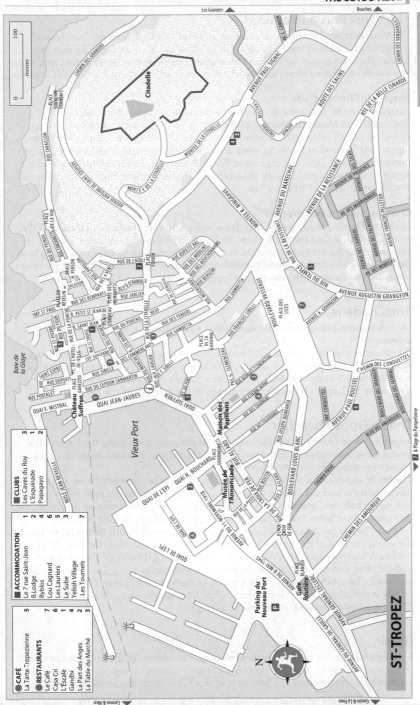

**17**

# The Vieux Port and around

The **Vieux Port**, rebuilt after its destruction in World War II, defines the French word *frimer*, which means to stroll ostentatiously in places like St-Tropez. You'll either love it or hate it. The other pole of St-Tropez's life, south of the Vieux Port, is **place des Lices**, where you can sit on benches in the shade of the plane trees and watch, or join, the *boules* games.

## Musée de l'Annonciade

2 rue de l'Annonciade • Dec–Oct daily except Tues 10am–noon & 2–6pm • €5 • ☎ 04 94 17 84 10, ⓦ saint-tropez.fr

The marvellous **Musée de l'Annonciade** occupies a deconsecrated sixteenth-century chapel on place Georges-Grammont, right on the Vieux Port. It features works by Signac, Matisse and most of the other artists who worked here: you'll see grey, grim, northern views of Paris, Boulogne and Westminster, and then local, brilliantly sunlit scenes by the same brushes – the museum is unrivalled outside Paris for its collection of French art between 1890 and 1940.

## Château Suffren and around

Up from the port, at the end of quai Jean-Jaurès, you enter place de l'Hôtel-de-Ville, where you'll find the **Château Suffren**, built in 980 by Count Guillaume 1$^{er}$ of Provence, and the very pretty *mairie*. A street to the left leads down to the rocky **baie de la Glaye**, while straight ahead rue de la Ponche passes through an ancient gateway to place du Revelin above the exceptionally pretty **fishing port** and its tiny beach.

# The Citadelle

1 Montée de la Citadelle • Daily: April–Sept 10am–6.30pm; Oct–March 10am–12.30pm & 1.30–5.30pm • €2.50 • ☎ 04 94 97 59 43, ⓦ saint-tropez.fr

If you turn inland from the sea and walk upwards, you finally reach the open space around the beautiful sixteenth-century **Citadelle**, worthwhile chiefly for the glorious views of the gulf and the town – views which haven't changed much since they were painted by St-Tropez's bohemian newcomers in the first half of the last century.

# The St-Tropez beaches

Transport from St-Tropez is provided by a minibus service in summer from place des Lices to Salins (5 daily; 15min), or bus #7705 to Ramatuelle (6 daily in summer; 9min); by car, you'll have to pay high parking charges at all the beaches – the approach roads are designed to make it impossible to park for free on the verge

The beach within easiest walking distance of St-Tropez is **Les Graniers**, below the citadelle just beyond the port des Pêcheurs along rue Cavaillon. From there, a path follows the coast around the **baie des Canebiers**, with its small beach, to Cap St-Pierre, Cap St-Tropez, the very crowded **Les Salins** beach and right round to Tahiti-Plage, about 11km away.

Tahiti-Plage is the start of the almost straight, 5km north–south **Pampelonne** beach, the world initiator of the topless bathing cult. The water is shallow for 50m or so, and the beach is exposed to the wind, and sometimes scourged by dried sea vegetation and garbage. **Bars** and restaurants line the beach, all with patios and sofas, serving cocktails, gluttonous ice creams and full-blown meals. **Le Club 55** on boulevard Patch (☎04 94 55 55 55) is the original and most famous, while **Nikki Beach**, route de l'Epi (☎04 94 79 82 04, ⓦnikkibeach.com), is the celebrity hangout.

# Gassin

In delightful contrast to the overcrowded coast, the interior of the **St-Tropez peninsula** remains undeveloped, thanks to government intervention, complex ownerships and the value of some local wines. The best view of this richly green countryside is from the

**17**

hilltop village of Gassin, just 8km from St Tropez. **GASSIN** is the shape and size of a ship perched on a summit; once an eighth-century Muslim stronghold, it's an excellent place for a big dinner, outside by the village wall where you can sit and enjoy a spectacular panorama east over the peninsula.

## ARRIVAL AND DEPARTURE

### ST-TROPEZ AND AROUND

**By bus** Buses drop you at the *gare routière* on av Général-de-Gaulle.

Destinations Hyères (up to 8 daily; 1hr 40min); Le Lavandou (up to 8 daily; 1hr 5min); Ste-Maxime (up to 13 daily; 45min), Saint Raphaël (up to 11 daily; 1hr 35min).

**By car** Beware of driving to St-Tropez in summer – traffic jams start in earnest at Ste-Maxime, where the D25 from the *autoroute* joins the coast road; it can take 2hr to crawl the

remaining 16km into St-Tropez. There is (paid) parking in the vast Parking du Nouveau Port at the entrance to the village.

**By ferry** The quickest way to reach St Tropez in summer – except by helicopter – is the ferry from Ste-Maxime (see p.894) on the opposite side of the gulf (mid-Feb to Dec, every 15min in high season; 15min). In summer there are also ferries from Port Grimaud, Les Issambres and Cogolin's marina (☎ 04 94 49 29 39, ⓦ bateauxverts.com).

## INFORMATION

**Tourist office** Quai Jean-Jaurès (daily: April–June, Sept & Oct 9.30am–12.30pm & 2–7pm; July & Aug 9.30am–1.30pm & 3–7.30pm; Oct [after les Voiles] to March 9.30am–12.30pm & 2–6pm; ☎ 04 94 97 45 21, ⓦ ot-saint-tropez.com). In high season there's also an

office at the Parking du Nouveau Port.

**Bike rental** Bikes and motorbikes can be rented at Rolling Bikes, 12 av G.-Leclerc (☎ 04 94 97 09 39, ⓦ rolling-bikes.com).

## ACCOMMODATION

You'll be lucky to find a room in high season. The tourist office can help (€10), but – transport permitting – you might be better off staying elsewhere. A lot of the classiest accommodation is out of town on the peninsula – there's no price advantage, but you may gain in tranquillity what you lose in convenience; some outlying hotels run shuttle services into town. Camping is geared more towards glamping in fancy chalets than pitches for tents.

**Le 7 Rue Saint-Jean** 7 rue Saint-Jean ☎ 06 16 05 21 76, ⓦ aucoeurdesainttropez.com. Stylish *chambres d'hôte* with two individually decorated rooms in the oldest part of the village. The larger of the two is a duplex with views of the citadelle and sea; it sleeps up to three. **€135**

**B. Lodge** 23 rue de l'Aïoli ☎ 04 94 97 06 57, ⓦ hotel-b -lodge.com. Overlooking the citadelle, this attractive boutique-style hotel is in a quieter setting than places in the centre and has stylish decor and its own bar. Lack of a/c in cheaper rooms is a downside, and there's no parking. **€140**

**Byblos** Av Paul-Signac ☎ 04 94 56 68 00, ⓦ byblos .com. A member of the *Leading Hotels of the World* group, the *Byblos* is a perennial favourite if money really is no object and you need to be with the in-crowd. Closed Nov–March. **€700**

**Lou Cagnard** 18 av Paul-Roussel ☎ 04 94 97 04 24, ⓦ hotel-lou-cagnard.com. The best budget option. Nineteen Provençal-style rooms – fifteen of them with a/c – in

a relatively tranquil location with a garden and secure private parking. Seven-night minimum stay in July and Aug. **€75**

**Les Lauriers** Rue du Temple ☎ 04 94 97 04 88, ⓦ hotel -les-lauriers.com. Just behind place des Lices, this friendly, relaxed two-star has eighteen a/c rooms and a pleasant garden. Relatively good value for Saint Tropez. Closed Nov–April. **€90**

**Le Sube** 15 quai Suffren ☎ 04 94 97 30 04, ⓦ hotelsube .net. One of St Tropez's oldest-established hotels, right in the thick of the action, with 25 rooms, a/c and a bar. Some – more expensive – rooms offer fantastic views over the port. Closed mid-Nov to Easter. **€140**

**Yelloh Village Les Tournels** Rte de Camarat, 3km from Ramatuelle ☎ 04 94 55 90 90, ⓦ tournels.com. Four-star campsite with an extensive, heated outdoor pool with water slides, plus an indoor pool and spa. It's more geared to chalet lets than tents, but they do welcome campers too. Closed Jan to mid-March. **€59**

## EATING AND DRINKING

### ST-TROPEZ

St-Tropez restaurants are notoriously expensive, with style over substance almost an art form. Avoid the Vieux Port if you're on a tight budget; better value is to be found in the streets behind it, particularly up towards the church and Citadelle.

**Le Café** Place des Lices ☎ 04 94 97 44 69, ⓦ lecafe.fr. Old-school, landmark brasserie with a terrace facing onto place des Lices. *Menu* €30 with classics like *soupe de poissons* and *daube de boeuf*; lunchtime *formule* €18. *Boules* can be borrowed for a game of *pétanque* in the square. Daily 8am–2am.

**Casa Cri** 12 rue Berny ☎04 94 97 42 52. Classy if rather pricey Italian, set in a lovely courtyard garden down a quiet side street just back from the Vieux Port. Pasta dishes from €16; meat dishes such as *scaloppine* in white wine sauce from around €22. Mid-April to June & Sept to mid-Oct Tues–Sun from 7.30pm; July & Aug daily from 7.30pm.

**l'Escale** 9 quai Jean-Jaurès ☎04 94 97 00 63, ⓦalpazurhotels.com. Upmarket seafood restaurant and lounge on the Vieux Port with a stylish beige-and-white interior. Pasta dishes from around €23, *plats* from €26 and – if you're pushing the boat out – *plateaux de fruits de mer* kicking off at €68. Daily noon–2.30pm & 8.30–10.30pm.

**Gandhi** 3 quai de l'Épi ☎04 94 97 71 71, ⓦgandhisai .com. Near the parking du Nouveau Port, this small, busy Indian restaurant offers a few fusion dishes like fillet of rascasse in masala sauce alongside the familiar vindaloos and biryanis. Lunch *formule* €16.50, most dishes around €12. Tues & Thurs–Sun noon–2pm & 7–10.30pm, Mon & Wed 7–10.30pm.

**La Part des Anges** 6 rue de l'Église ☎04 94 96 19 50. Very pleasant little restaurant serving decent food at modest prices in a pretty, atmospheric lane just down from St-Tropez's church, with pasta from €11 and fish dishes from around €13. There's also a three-course dinner *menu*. Daily except Wed noon–3pm & 7–11pm.

**La Table du Marché** 11 rue des Commerçants ☎04 94 97 01 25. Smart but casual place offering dishes like chicken Caesar salad for €12, club sandwiches for €16 and *plats du jour* from the chalked-up menu for around €14. May–Oct noon–3pm & 7–11pm.

**La Tarte Tropezienne** 36 rue G.-Clemenceau ☎04 94 97 71 42, ⓦtropezienne.com. Patisserie claiming to have invented the rather sickly but moreish eponymous sponge and custard cake (€2.90 for an enormous slice), though you no longer have to come to St-Tropez to sample it – the company is now a chain. Good, too, for cheap takeaway lunch *formules* (€5.90). Daily 6.30am–7.30pm.

**GASSIN**

⭐ **Bello Visto** 9 place des Barrys ☎04 94 56 17 30, ⓦbellovisto.eu. Good Provençal specialities on a €28 *menu*, with dishes like endive *tarte tatin* with honey and pine nuts or john dory with saffron. They have rooms, also. April–Oct noon–2pm & 7–10pm.

**NIGHTLIFE**

In season St-Tropez stays up late. The *boules* games on place des Lices continue well after dusk and the portside spectacle doesn't falter until the early hours.

**Les Caves du Roy** Byblos, av du Maréchal Foch ☎04 94 56 68 00, ⓦlescavesduroy.com. Still the place to see and be seen, the *Caves du Roy* is the place to rub shoulders with rap stars and supermodels. Music is a mix of current dance hits and oldies from the seventies and eighties. €28 with *conso*. July & Aug nightly midnight–dawn; Sept to mid-Oct & mid-April to June Fri & Sat only.

**L'Esquinade** 2 rue du Four ☎04 94 97 87 44, ⓦfacebook.com/discotheque.esquinadesainttropez.

Gay-friendly club spinning house, disco, R&B and world music. Unlike most of St Tropez's clubs it's open year-round.

**Papagayo** Port de Saint Tropez ☎04 94 97 95 95, ⓦpapagayo-st-tropez.com. Fifty-year-old veteran of the St-Tropez nightlife scene with a restaurant terrace (*plats* from €19) overlooking the yachts. Club entry from €25 with *conso*. May–Aug midnight to 5/6am; restaurant noon–midnight.

# Ste-Maxime

Facing St-Tropez across its gulf, **STE-MAXIME** is the perfect Côte stereotype: palmed corniche and enormous pleasure-boat harbour, beaches crowded with bronzed windsurfers and water-skiers, and an Art Deco casino presiding over the seafront. It sprawls a little too much – merging with its northern neighbours to create a continuous suburban strip up to Fréjus. But though hardly as colourful as St-Tropez, it's less pretentious and the beaches are cleaner. If your **budget** denies you the pleasures of watersports, you might find Ste-Maxime a little lacking in diversions. You can, at least, eat at reasonable cost, since there are plenty of crêperies, *glaciers* and snack places along the central avenue Charles-de-Gaulle. There's also an **Aqualand** water park with all manner of ingenious water slides just off the D25 Le Muy road north of town, though this isn't cheap, either (mid-June to early Sept daily 10am–6/7pm; €25, children €18.50; ⓦaqualand.fr).

**17**

## The Ste-Maxime beaches

For the spenders, the east-facing **plage de la Nartelle**, 5km east from the centre towards Les Issambres, is the strip of sand to head for. Here, at **Barco Beach** (Ⓦbarcobeach.com) and its four neighbours, you'll pay for shaded, cushioned comfort, watersports and grilled fish; drinks will be brought to your mattress and a pianist plays as dusk falls. A kilometre or so further on, **plage des Éléphants** recalls the town's link to Jean de Brunhoff – creator of Babar the elephant –who had a holiday home in Ste-Maxime.

## The markets

Ste-Maxime's *vieille ville* has several good **markets**: a covered flower and food market on rue Fernand-Bessy (July & Aug Mon–Sat 8am–1pm & 4.30–8pm, Sun 8am–1pm; Sept–June Tues–Sun 8am–1pm); a daily fish market on the port (8am–noon); a Thursday morning food market on place du Marché; a weekly flea market on promenade Simon Lorière (Wed 8am–6pm) and arts and crafts in the pedestrian streets (mid-June to mid-Sept daily 4–11pm).

## Musée du Phonographe et de la Musique Mécanique

Parc St Donat, rte de Muy • Wed–Sun: May, June & Sept 10am–noon & 4–6pm; July & Aug 10am–noon • €3 • ☎ 04 94 96 50 52

High up in the Massif des Maures on the road to Le Muy, some 10km north of Ste-Maxime, the marvellous **Musée du Phonographe et de la Musique Mécanique** is the result of one amazing woman's forty-year obsession with collecting audio equipment. She has amassed a wide selection of automata, musical boxes and pianolas, plus one of Thomas Edison's "talking machines" dating from 1878.

### ARRIVAL AND INFORMATION

STE-MAXIME

**By bus** Buses from St-Tropez (up to 12 daily; 35min–1hr) and Saint Raphaël (up to 12 daily; 50min) stop outside the tourist office (see below).
**By ferry** If you're heading for St-Tropez from Ste-Maxime, an alternative to the bus is to go by boat (see p.892).

**Tourist office** 1 promenade Simon-Lorière (June–Aug daily 9am–1pm & 3–7pm; Sept–May Mon–Sat 9am–noon & 2–6pm; ☎ 04 94 55 75 55, Ⓦ sainte-maxime.com).
**Bike rental** ADA/Holiday Bikes, 16 bd Frédéric-Mistral (☎ 04 94 96 16 25, Ⓦ holiday-bikes.com).

### ACCOMMODATION

**Auberge Provençale** 19 rue Aristide-Briand ☎ 04 94 55 76 90, Ⓦ sainte-maxime.com. Central and very welcoming, this simple, greenery-swathed budget hotel has doubles with showers, a/c and some triples and rooms for four. There's also a restaurant with tables in the pretty garden. **€50**
**Castellamar** 8 av G.-Pompidou ☎ 04 94 96 19 97, Ⓦ hotelcastellamar.wordpress.com. The best of the cheaper hotels, on the west side of the river, but still close to the town centre and the sea, with a bar, lounge and tree-shaded terrace. Closed mid-Oct to mid-March. **€67**

**Les Cigalons** 34 av di Croiseur Léger le Malin ☎ 04 94 96 05 51, Ⓦ campingcigalon.com. Two-star seaside campsite east of town, just 50m from the beach, with wi-fi, children's games and *boules*. It also rents out holiday bungalows. Closed mid-Oct to early April. Camping **€27**, bungalows per week from **€550**
**De la Poste** 11 bd Frédéric-Mistral ☎ 04 94 96 18 33, Ⓦ hotelleriedusoleil.com. Smart, very central three-star hotel with Cuban-themed decor and a pool. There are various categories and styles of room but all have a/c and either bath or shower. Closed most of Dec. **€145**

### EATING

**De la Belle Aurore** 5 bd Jean-Moulin ☎ 04 94 96 02 45, Ⓦ belleaurore.com. Elegant *restaurant gastronomique* with a stunning setting on the water's edge with views across to St-Tropez. There's a three-course *menu*; otherwise it's around €38 for a main course. April to mid-Oct Mon 12.30–2.30pm, Tues 12.30–2.30pm & 7.30–9.15pm.

Closed Wed outside high season.
**La Dérive** 14 rue Courbet ☎ 06 12 43 30 75. Lively brasserie with a smart terrace in an atmospheric part of the old town. Pasta from €14, meat dishes from €15 and fish from around €18. There's a sister restaurant, *La Petite Dérive*, next door. Daily lunch & dinner.

# Fréjus and around

FRÉJUS – along with its neighbour **ST-RAPHAËL**, 3km east – dates back to the Romans. It was established as a naval base under Julius Caesar and Augustus, and its ancient port – known as Forum Julii – consisted of 2km of quays connected by a walled canal to the sea (which was considerably closer then). After the battle of Actium in 31 BC, the ships of Antony and Cleopatra's defeated fleet were brought here. Little remains of the Roman walls that circled the city, and the once-important port silted up and was filled in after the Revolution. Today you can see a scattering of **Roman remains**, along with the medieval **Cité Episcopale**, or cathedral complex, which takes up two sides of **place Formigé**, the marketplace and heart of both contemporary and medieval Fréjus.

The area between Fréjus and the sea is now the suburb of **Fréjus-Plage**, with a vast 1980s marina, **Port-Fréjus**. Both Fréjus and Fréjus-Plage merge with St-Raphaël, which in turn merges with **Boulouris** to the east.

## The Roman remains

A tour of the Roman remains gives you a good idea of the extent of Forum Julii, but they are scattered throughout and beyond the town centre and take a full day to get around. Turning right out of the *gare SNCF* and then right down boulevard Severin-Decuers brings you to the **Butte St-Antoine**, against whose east wall the waters of the port would have lapped, and which once was capped by a fort. It was one of the port's defences, and one of the ruined **towers** may have been a lighthouse. A path around the southern wall follows the quayside (some stretches are visible) to the medieval **Lanterne d'Auguste**, built on the Roman foundations of a structure marking the entrance of the canal into the ancient harbour. If you retrace your steps back to the centre, you'll come to rue des Moulins, and the arcades of the **Porte d'Orée**, positioned on the former harbour's edge alongside what was probably a **bath complex**.

### The amphitheatre

Rue Henri Vadon • Tues–Sun: May–Oct 9.30am–12.30pm & 2–6pm; Nov–April 9.30am–12.30pm & 2–5pm • €2 • ☎ 04 94 51 34 31, ⓦ frejus.fr

Taking a left turn from the station, passing the Roman **Porte des Gaules** and heading along rue Henri-Vadon, brings you to the **amphitheatre**, with a capacity of around ten thousand. Fit to host concerts again after a refurbishment in 2012, its upper tiers have been reconstructed, but the vaulted galleries on the ground floor are largely original.

### The Roman theatre and around

Rue du Théâtre Romain • Tues–Sun: May–Oct 9.30am–12.30pm & 2–6pm; Nov–April 9.30am–12.30pm & 2–5pm • €2 • ☎ 04 94 53 58 75, ⓦ frejus.fr

The **Roman theatre** is north of the old town. Its original seats have long gone, though it's still used for shows in summer. To the northeast, in the parc Aurelienne at the far end of avenue du XVème-Corps-d'Armée, six arches are visible of the 40km **aqueduct**, which was once as high as the ramparts.

## The cathedral complex

Cathedral, cloisters and baptistry 48 rue du Cardinal Fleury • Oct–May Tues–Sun 9am–noon & 2–5pm; June–Sept daily 9am–6.30pm • €5.50; guided tours in English available • ☎ 04 94 51 26 30, ⓦ cathedrale-frejus.monuments-nationaux.fr Musée Archéologique Tues–Sun: May–Oct 9.30am–12.30pm & 2–6pm; Nov–April 9.30am–12.30pm & 2–5pm • €2 • ☎ 04 94 52 15 78, ⓦ frejus.fr

The oldest part of the **cathedral complex** is the **baptistry**, built in the fourth or fifth century and so contemporary with the decline of the city's Roman founders. Its two doorways are of different heights, signifying the enlarged spiritual stature of the

**17**

baptized. Bits of the early Gothic **cathedral** may belong to a tenth-century church, but its best features, apart from the bright diamond-shaped tiles on the spire, are Renaissance: the choir stalls, a wooden crucifix on the left of the entrance and the intricately carved doors with scenes of a Saracen massacre, only opened for the guided tours. The most engaging component of the whole ensemble, however, are the **cloisters**. In a small garden of scented bushes around a well, slender twelfth-century marble columns support a fourteenth-century ceiling painted with apocalyptic creatures. The treasures of the **Musée Archéologique**, on the upper storey of the cloisters, include a complete Roman mosaic of a leopard and a copy of a double-headed bust of Hermes.

## St-Raphaël

Fréjus' neighbour **ST-RAPHAËL** became fashionable at the turn of the twentieth century, but lost many of its *belle époque* mansions and hotels to World War II bombardment. All the same, you may prefer to stay here rather than in Fréjus for its livelier, family-friendly atmosphere and easy access to the **beaches,** which stretch west of the port into Fréjus-Plage and east of the Jardin Bonaparte to the modern **Marina Santa Lucia**, which offers opportunities for every kind of watersport. When you're tired of sea and sand, you can lose whatever money you have left at the **Casino Barrière** (ⓦlucienbarriere.com) on Square de Gand overlooking the Vieux Port.

### The Vieille Ville

The **Vieille Ville**, beyond place Carnot on the inland side of the railway line, is no longer the town's commercial focus but a good place to stroll and browse. The fortified Romanesque church of **San Raféu** on rue des Templiers, has fragments of the Roman aqueduct that brought water from Fréjus in its courtyard, along with a local **history and underwater archeology museum** (Tues–Sat 9am–noon & 2–6pm; free; ⓦmusee-saintraphael.com). You can climb to the top of the fortified tower to views the town and sea.

## Notre-Dame-de-Jerusalem

Rte de Cannes • Tues–Sun: May–Oct 9.30am–12.30pm & 2–6pm; Nov–April 9.30am–12.30pm & 2–5pm • Free • ☎ 04 94 53 27 06

Just off the RN7 at La Tour de Mare, 5.6km from the centre of Fréjus, is the last of Jean Cocteau's artistic landmarks, the chapel of **Notre-Dame-de-Jerusalem**. Conceived as the church for a failed artistic community, the octagonal building was not completed until after Cocteau's death in 1963, and the interior was completed to Cocteau's plans by Edouard Dermit. The Last Supper scene inside includes a self-portrait of Cocteau.

### ARRIVAL AND DEPARTURE

**FRÉJUS AND AROUND**

**FRÉJUS**

**By train** Trains to St-Raphaël are much more frequent than those to Fréjus, so it's often easiest to alight there and take the #3, #4, #5, #6, #7 or #14 Agglobus, which run frequently between the two towns (15min). There are also trains between St-Raphaël and Fréjus *gare SNCF*, which is on the south side of the *vieille ville* (9 daily; 3–4min).

**By bus** The *gare routière* is on the east side of the town centre

### OUTDOOR FUN AROUND FRÉJUS

Around Fréjus, rugged terrain for **cyclists** is found in the forested hills of the **Massif de l'Esterel** to the northeast of town; there are more than 100km of signposted trails in and around Fréjus. The tourist office in St Raphael (see p.897) sells a **map/guide** to the Esterel for €8.50. There are also cycle trails at the **Base Nature François Leotard** (daily: mid-June to Oct 8am–midnight; mid-Sept to mid-June 8am–11pm; free; ☎ 04 94 51 91 10), a large public park just west of Port-Fréjus on the coast, as well as a beach, a public swimming pool and sports pitches. Opposite the Base Nature is Fréjus' water park, **Aqualand**, with all manner of water slides and pools (ⓦaqualand.fr).

at Clos de la Tour close to the tourist office (☎ 04 94 53 78 46).

## ST-RAPHAËL

**By train** St Raphaël's *gare SNCF*, on the Marseille–Ventimiglia line, is on rue Waldeck-Rousseau in the centre of town.

Destinations Cannes (every 10–30min; 24–40min); Fréjus

(9 daily; 3–4min); Nice (every 10–30min; 55min–1hr 15min).

**By bus** The *gare routière* is at 100 rue Victor Hugo, across the rail line behind the train station.

Destinations Fréjus (frequent; 15–20min); Ste-Maxime (up to 16 daily; 50min); St Tropez (up to 12 daily; 1hr 25min–1hr 55min).

## INFORMATION

### FRÉJUS

**Tourist office** Le Florus II, 249 rue Jean-Jaurès (June–Sept daily Mon–Fri 9am–1pm & 2–7pm; Oct–May Mon–Sat 9.20am–noon & 2–6pm; ☎ 04 94 51 83 83, ⓦ frejus.fr).

**Passes** If you're planning to visit most of Fréjus' sights, it may be worth getting the seven-day Fréjus' Pass (€4.60), which gives access to the amphitheatre, Roman theatre and Musée Archéologique, or the Pass Intégral (€6.60), which adds access to the cathedral cloisters and baptistry.

**Bike rental** Holiday Bikes, 238 av de Verdun (☎ 04 94 44 22 37, ⓦ holidaybikes.fr).

**Market days** Wed and Sat.

### ST-RAPHAËL

**Tourist office** Quai Albert-1er (July & Aug daily 9am–7pm; Sept–June Mon–Sat 9am–12.30pm & 2–6.30pm; ☎ 04 94 19 52 52, ⓦ saint-raphael.com).

**Boat trips** Les Bateaux de Saint Raphaël offer boat trips to St-Tropez and the *calanques* of the Esterel coast from quai Nomy on the south side of the Vieux Port (ticket office April & May Mon–Sat 9am–noon & 2–5pm, Sun 2–5pm, June & Sept daily 9am–noon & 2–5pm; July & Aug Mon–Thurs & Sat 9am–7pm, Fri 9am–7pm & 9–10.30pm, Sun 9–11.45am & 1.30–7pm; Oct Mon 2–5pm, Tues–Sat 9am–noon & 2–5pm; ☎ 04 94 95 17 46, ⓦ bateauxsaintraphael.com).

## ACCOMMODATION

### FRÉJUS

**Les Acacias** 370 rue Henri-Giraud, 2.5km from the old town, close to the pagoda Hong Hien ☎ 04 94 53 21 22, ⓦ campingacacias.fr. Leafy, moderate-sized three-star campsite with 83 pitches, children's play facilities, a swimming pool and spa. Closed Nov–March. **€36.50**

**Aréna** 145 rue de Général-de-Gaulle ☎ 04 94 17 09 40, ⓦ hotel-frejus-arena.com. Comfortable three-star hotel in three buildings grouped around a pool and luxuriant garden, close to the *gare SNCF*. Rooms have flatscreen TV and a/c. There's also a good restaurant. **€130**

**Auberge de Jeunesse Fréjus/Saint Raphaël** 627 chemin du Counillier ☎ 04 94 53 18 75, ⓦ fuaj.org. Fréjus' hostel is set amid 10 hectares of umbrella pines 2km northeast of the centre. It's close to the pagoda Hong Hien and served by the infrequent bus #10 from St Raphaël *gare routière*. Reception 8–11am & 5.30–9.30pm. Closed Christmas and New Year. **€19.60**

**Le Bellevue** Place Paul-Vernet ☎ 04 94 17 12 20, ⓦ hotelbellevue-frejus.com. Basic two-star hotel with fairly simple, a/c rooms above a bar next to the bus station and a large car park. **€69**

**Le Flore** 35 rue Grisolle ☎ 04 94 51 38 35, ⓦ hotelleflore.com. The nicest budget option in the old town is this pretty, wisteria-clad two-star. It won't win any

awards for decor but rooms have shower and WC, a/c and flatscreen TV. **€60**

### ST-RAPHAËL

**Agay Soleil** 1152 bd de la Plage, Agay ☎ 04 94 82 00 79, ⓦ agay-soleil.com. Three-star campsite on the horseshoe-shaped bay of Agay, east of St Raphaël on the breathtaking corniche de l'Esterel, with mobile homes and chalets to rent as well as pitches. Closed Nov to late March. **€29.80**

**Bellevue** 22 bd Felix Martin ☎ 04 94 19 90 10, ⓦ hotel-bellevue-saintraphael.com. Budget two-star hotel in the town centre. It's nothing fancy but rooms do have a/c, flatscreen TV. It smells nice, being above a bakery, and it's open all year round. **€55**

**Excelsior** 192 Bd Félix Martin ☎ 04 94 95 02 42, ⓦ excelsior-hotel.com. The handsome old *Excelsior* is one of the rare seafront survivors from Saint Raphaël's prewar heyday, with 40 tastefully decorated a/c rooms plus a restaurant and English-style pub. More expensive rooms have sea views. **€160**

**Du Soleil** 47 bd du Domaine du Soleil ☎ 04 94 83 10 00, ⓦ hotel-dusoleil.com. Charming non-smoking hotel occupying a very pretty old villa east of the town centre. Rooms have flatscreen TV, bath or shower and most have a balcony or terrace. Bus #8 to Les Plaines. **€88**

## EATING, DRINKING AND ENTERTAINMENT

### FRÉJUS

**Brasserie Hermès** 15 place Formigé ☎ 04 94 17 26 02. Unpretentious and affordable brasserie with a terrace

facing the cathedral. There's a €13.50 two-course lunchtime *formule* and a big choice of salads and pizza from around €9, plus a few pasta dishes at slightly higher prices.

**17**

Daily 11am–11pm.

**Cadet Rousselle** 25 place Agricola ☎04 94 53 36 92. Perennially popular crêperie with a wide choice of sweet crêpes and savoury galettes and a three-course weekday menu for €13. They also serve main-course-sized salads from €6. Tues, Wed & Fri–Sun noon–1.30pm & 6.30–8.30pm, Thurs 6.30–8.30pm.

**Le Jardin de l'Aréna** 145 rue de Général-de-Gaulle ☎04 94 17 09 40, ⑩hotel-frejus-arena.com. You can dine on the leafy terrace at the Aréna hotel's restaurant gastronomique, and enjoy dishes like prawns with mesclun and balsamic caramel or lobster with olive oil and bisque. Menus €23–38. Sun & Tues–Fri noon–2pm & 7–9.30pm, Sat & Mon 7–9.30pm.

**ST-RAPHAËL**

**Le Bishop** 84 rue Jean Aicard ☎04 94 95 04 63 Popular restaurant dishing up the Provençal staples at reasonable prices, a couple of blocks back from the beach. Niçois-style tripe €13, andouillette €13; menus from €19.90. Mon–Sat noon–2pm & 7–10pm.

**Blue Bar** 133 rue Jules Barbier ☎04 94 95 15 87. There's a big range of Belgian beers from €5.20 at this unpretentious, pubby place on the seafront. Cocktails start at around €7.20 and they serve fancy ice creams (€6.50), inexpensive snacks and salads. Daily 7am–3am.

**La Brasserie** 6 av de Valescure ☎04 94 95 25 00, ⑩labrasserietg.fr. Traditional Provençal dishes are cooked to a high standard at this smart modern restaurant on the edge of the vieille ville. Bourride €18.90, aioli €17.90; pieds et paquets Marseille-style €14.90. Mon–Sat noon–2.30pm & 7–11pm.

**Elly's** 54 rue de la Liberté ☎04 94 83 63 39, ⑩elly-s .com. Elegant restaurant serving the likes of seared tournedos of tuna with truffled gnocchi or fillet beef with bordelaise sauce, with fancy Bordeaux and Burgundies alongside Provençal wines. Menus €30–65. Mon–Sat 7–9.30pm, Sun noon–1.30pm & 7–9.30pm.

**La Réserve** Promenade René Coty ☎06 09 87 25 58, ⑩la-reserve.fr. Swish seafront disco, improbably situated beneath a road junction, that attracts some big-name international DJs. Entry with conso €15, spirits priced by the bottle, beers €9. Summer nightly 11.30pm–7am; winter Fri & Sat only.

# Cannes and around

With its immaculate seafront hotels and exclusive beach concessions, glamorous yachts and designer boutiques, **CANNES** is in many ways the definitive Riviera resort, a place where appearances count, especially during the **film festival** in May, when the orgy of self-promotion reaches its annual peak. The ugly seafront Palais des Festivals is the heart of the film festival but also hosts conferences, tournaments and trade shows. Despite its glittery image Cannes works surprisingly well as a big seaside resort, with plenty of free, sandy public beaches. You'll find the non-paying **beaches** to the west of Le Suquet towards the suburb of **La Bocca** along the **plages du Midi**, though there's also a tiny public section of beach on **Plage de la Croisette**, just east of the Palais des Festivals.

Alternatively, you can explore the old aristocratic suburbs La Croix des Gardes and La Californie, once populated by Russian and British royals. Just offshore, the peaceful **Îles de Lérins** – **Ste-Marguerite** and **St-Honorat** – offer a sublime, easily accessible contrast to the frenetic town, while further out are the towns of **Vallauris**, with its interesting Picasso connections, and **Grasse**, famed for its perfume.

## Promenade de la Croisette

**Promenade de la Croisette** is certainly the sight to see, with its palace hotels – the Martinez and Carlton – on one side and their private beaches on the other. It's possible to find your way down to the beach without paying, but not easy (you can of course walk along it below the rows of sun beds). The hotel beaches are where you're most likely to spot a star or topless hopeful during the film festival – or at least the paparazzi crowding around them.

## Le Suquet

The old town, known as **Le Suquet** after the hill on which it stands, provides a great panorama of the curve of Cannes' bay. On its summit stand the remains of the fortified priory lived in by Cannes' eleventh-century monks, and the beautiful twelfth-century **Chapelle Ste-Anne**.

## Musée de la Castre

Place de la Castre • April & May Tues–Sun 10.30am–1.15pm & 2.15–5.45pm; June–Sept daily 10am–5.45pm; Oct–March Tues–Sun 10.30am–1.15pm & 2.15–4.45pm • €6 • ☎ 04 93 38 55 26, Ⓦ cannes.travel

The **Musée de la Castre**, in the remains of Cannes' eleventh-century priory, holds an extraordinary collection of musical instruments from all over the world, along with pictures and prints of old Cannes and an ethnology and archeology section.

# Îles de Lérins

The **Îles de Lérins** would be lovely anywhere, but at just fifteen minutes' ferry ride from frantic Cannes, they're not far short of paradise. Of the two, **Ste-Marguerite** is busier than its neighbour, **St-Honorat**, whose abbey is often used for spiritual retreats.

## Île Ste-Marguerite

**Île Ste-Marguerite** is beautiful, and large enough for visitors to find seclusion by following the trails that lead away from the congested port, through the Aleppo pines and woods of evergreen oak that are so thick they cast a sepulchral gloom. The western end is the most accessible, but the lagoon here is brackish, so the best places to swim are along the rocky southern shore, reached most easily along the **allée des Eucalyptus**. The channel between Ste-Marguerite and St-Honorat is, however, a popular anchorage for yachts, so you're unlikely to find solitude.

### Fort Ste-Marguerite

April–May Tues–Sun 10.30am–1.15pm & 2.15–5.45pm; June–Sept 10am–5.45pm; Oct–March Tues–Sun 10.30am–1.15pm & 2.15–4.45pm • €6, includes museum • ☎ 04 93 38 55 26, Ⓦ cannes.travel

Dominating the island is the **Fort Ste-Marguerite**, a Richelieu commission that failed to prevent the Spanish occupying both of the islands between 1635 and 1637. Later, Vauban rounded it off, presumably for Louis XIV's *gloire* – since the strategic value of enlarging a fort facing the mainland without upgrading the one facing the sea is pretty minimal. There are cells to see, including the one in which Dumas' **Man in the Iron Mask** is supposed to have been held, and the **Musée de la Mer**, containing mostly Roman local finds but also remnants of a tenth-century Arab ship.

## Île St-Honorat

Owned by monks almost continuously since its namesake and patron founded a monastery here in 410 AD, **Île St-Honorat**, the smaller southern island, was home to a famous bishops' seminary, where St Patrick trained before setting out for Ireland. There are a couple of places to eat but no bars, hotels or cars: just vines, lavender, herbs and olive trees mingled with wild poppies and daisies, and pine and eucalyptus trees shading the paths beside the white rock shore. The present **abbey** buildings (Ⓦ abbayedelerins.com) date mostly from the nineteenth century, though some vestiges of the medieval and earlier constructions remain in the austere church and the cloisters. You can visit the eleventh-century fortified monastery on the water's edge and the abbey church, see the chapels dotted around the island and purchase the abbey's sought-after wines and liqueurs.

# Vallauris

Pottery and Picasso are the attractions of **VALLAURIS**, an otherwise unremarkable town in the hills above Golfe-Juan, 6km northeast of Cannes. It was here that Picasso first began to use clay, thereby reviving the town's traditional craft. Today the main street,

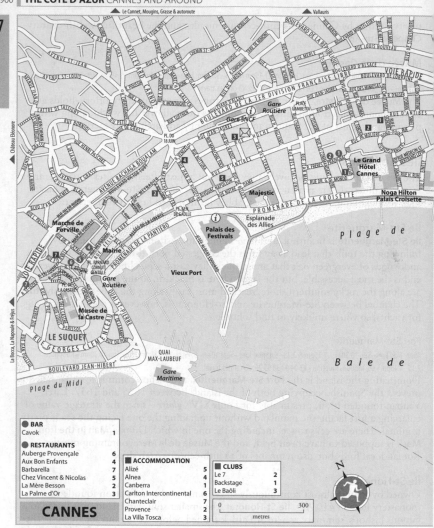

**CANNES**

● **BAR**
Cavok ......................................... 1

● **RESTAURANTS**
Auberge Provençale ................ 6
Aux Bon Enfants ...................... 4
Barbarella ................................. 7
Chez Vincent & Nicolas ......... 5
La Mère Besson ....................... 2
La Palme d'Or ........................... 3

■ **ACCOMMODATION**
Alizé ......................................... 5
Alnea ........................................ 4
Canberra .................................. 1
Carlton Intercontinental ....... 6
Chanteclair .............................. 7
Provence .................................. 2
La Villa Tosca .......................... 3

■ **CLUBS**
Le 7 ........................................... 2
Backstage ................................ 1
Le Baôli .................................... 3

0 ———————————— 300
metres

**avenue Georges-Clemenceau**, sells nothing but pottery, much of it garish bowls or figurines that could feature in souvenir shops anywhere. The bronze statue of **Man with a Sheep**, the artist's gift to the town, stands in the main square, place Paul Isnard, beside the church and castle.

### The Musée National Picasso

Place de la Libération du 24 Août 1944 • Daily July & Aug 10am–7pm; Sept–June daily except Tues 10am–12.15pm & 2–5/6pm • €3.25, includes Musée de la Céramique/Musée Magnelli • ☎ 04 93 64 71 83, ⓦ musee-picasso-vallauris.fr

In 1952, Picasso was asked to decorate the deconsecrated early medieval **chapel** in the castle courtyard; his subject was war and peace. The space, now the **Musée National Picasso**, is tiny, with the architectural simplicity of an air-raid shelter, and at first it's easy to be unimpressed by the painted panels covering the vault – as many critics still

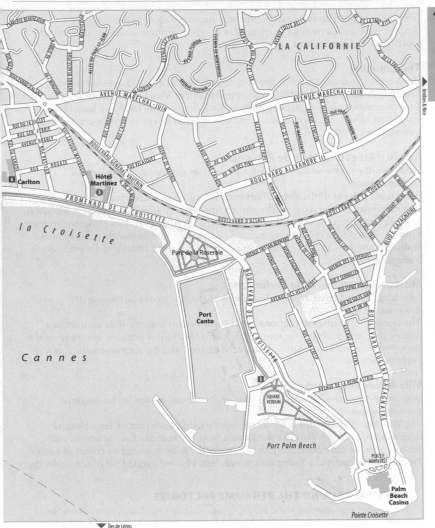

La Croisette

Cannes

Carlton

Hôtel Martinez

Parc de la Roseraie

Port Canto

Port Palm Beach

Palm Beach Casino

Pointe Croisette

Îles de Lérins

are – since the work looks mucky and slapdash, with paint-runs on the plywood panel surface. But stay a while and the passion of this violently drawn display of pacifism slowly emerges. The ticket also gives admission to the **Musée de la Céramique** in the castle itself, which exhibits Picasso's and other ceramics and the **Musée Magnelli,** which exhibits works by the Florentine painter Alberto Magnelli, a contemporary of Picasso.

## Grasse

**GRASSE**, 16km inland from Cannes and an easy day-trip from the coast, has been the world capital of *parfumiers* for almost three hundred years. These days it promotes a fragrant image of a medieval hill town surrounded by scented flowers, though in truth, the glamour of this friendly place is mostly bottled, and the **perfume** industry is at

**17**

pains to keep quiet about modern, unromantic innovations and techniques. Though the main purpose of coming here is to buy perfume, there are also several worthwhile small **museums**.

### The cathedral

Place du Petit Puy • Oct–June Mon–Sat 9.30–11.30am & 3–5.30pm; July–Sept daily Sat 9.30–11.30am & 3–6.30pm • Free

The twelfth-century **cathedral**, at the opposite end of Vieux Grasse from the Place aux Aires, contains various valuable paintings, including one by local boy Jean-Honoré Fragonard, three by Rubens and a wondrous triptych by the sixteenth-century Niçois painter Louis Bréa.

### Musée d'Art et d'Histoire de Provence

2 rue Mirabeau • May–Sept Mon–Sat 10am–7pm; Oct–March Tues–Sat 11am–6pm; April Mon–Sat 11am–6pm • Free • Ⓦ museesdegrasse.com

The **Musée d'Art et d'Histoire de Provence** is housed in a luxurious townhouse commissioned by the sister of the eighteenth-century aristocratic radical Mirabeau as a place to entertain. As well as all the gorgeous fittings and an eighteenth-century kitchen, the eclectic collections include eighteenth- to nineteenth-century faïence from Apt and Le Castellet, Mirabeau's death mask, a tin bidet and six prehistoric bronze leg bracelets.

### Musée International de la Parfumerie

8 place du Cours; May–Sept Mon–Sat 10am–7pm; Oct–March Tues–Sat 11am–6pm; April Mon–Sat 11am–6pm • €4 • Ⓦ museesdegrasse.com

The fascinating **Musée International de la Parfumerie** is a worthwhile adjunct to a factory visit, and probably far more informative. It displays perfume bottles from the ancient Greeks via Marie Antoinette to the present, and has a reconstruction of a perfume factory.

### Villa-Musée Fragonard

23 bd Fragonard • May–Sept Mon–Sat 10am–7pm; Oct–March Tues–Sat 11am–6pm; April Mon–Sat 11am–6pm • Free • Ⓦ museesdegrasse.com

The **Villa-Musée Fragonard** is where the celebrated Rococo painter Jean-Honoré Fragonard returned to live after the Revolution. The staircase has impressive wall paintings by his son Alexandre-Evariste, while the salon is graced by copies of **Love's Progress in the Heart of a Young Girl**, which Jean-Honoré painted for Madame du Barry.

---

### SNIFFING AROUND THE PERFUME FACTORIES

There are ten **parfumeries** in and around Grasse, most of them making not perfume but essences-plus-formulas, sold to Dior, Lancôme, Estée Lauder and the like, who make up their own brand-name perfumes.

The ingredients that the "nose" – as the creator of the perfume's formula is known – has to play with include resins, roots, moss, beans, bark, civet (a secretion from the cat-like civet), ambergris (whale vomit), bits of beaver and musk from Tibetan goats. You can visit three local **showrooms** for free, with overpoweringly fragrant shops and guided tours, in English, of the traditional perfume factory setup (the actual working industrial complexes are strictly out of bounds).

**Fragonard** 20 bd Fragonard Ⓦ fragonard.com. Feb–Oct daily 9am–6pm; Nov–Jan 9am–12.30pm & 2–6pm.

**Galimard** 73 rte de Cannes Ⓦ galimard.com. June–Sept 9am–7.30pm; Oct–May 9am–12.30pm & 2.30–7pm.

**Molinard** 60 bd Victor-Hugo Ⓦ molinard.com. April–Sept daily 9am–6.30/7pm; Oct–March Mon–Sat 9.30am–1pm & 2–6.20pm.

## ARRIVAL AND DEPARTURE

### CANNES

**By train** The *gare SNCF* is on rue Jean-Jaurès, five blocks north of the Palais des Festivals on the seafront.

Destinations Antibes (every 10–30min; 9–13min), Grasse (hourly; 25–30min); Nice (every 10–20min; 31–41min); St Raphaël (up to 32 daily; 21–38min).

**By bus** There are two *gares routières*: one on place B.-Cornut-Gentille between the *mairie* and Le Suquet, serving coastal destinations; and the other, next to the *gare SNCF*, for buses inland. Bus Azur (☎ 08 25 82 55 99; ⓦ busazur.com; €1) runs 24 lines and six night buses, serving all of Cannes and the surrounding area.

Destinations Antibes (every 15–20min; 35min); Grasse (every 20min; 40–50min); Nice (every 15–20min; 1hr 55min); Vallauris (every 45min; 15min).

### ÎLES DE LÉRINS

Boats for both islands leave from Cannes' Quai des Îles at the seaward end of the quai Max-Laubeuf.

**To St-Honorat** Compagnie Planaria (May–Sept 10 daily; winter 8 daily; the last boat back to Cannes leaves 5pm in winter & 6/7pm in summer; €13; ☎ 04 92 98 71 38,

## INFORMATION

### CANNES

**Tourist offices** There are three tourist offices in Cannes (all ☎ 04 92 99 84 22, ⓦ cannes.travel): Palais des Festivals, 1 bd de la Croisette (daily: March–June, Sept & Oct 9am–7pm; July & Aug 9am–8pm; Nov–Feb 10am–7pm); at the train station (Mon–Sat 9am–1pm & 2–6pm); and at 1 rue Pierre-Sémard in Cannes-La Bocca (Tues–Sat: July & Aug 9am–12.30pm & 3.30-7pm; Sept–June 9am–noon & 2.30–6.30pm).

**Bike rental** Bikes can be hired from Elite Rent a Bike, 32 av Maréchal Juin (☎ 04 93 94 30 34), or Holiday Bikes, 44 bd Lorraine (☎ 04 97 06 07 07, ⓦ holidaybikes.fr).

## ACCOMMODATION

### CANNES

**Alizé** 29 rue Bivouac Napoleon ☎ 04 97 06 64 64, ⓦ hotel-alize-cannes.fr. A central hotel with large, renovated and soundproofed rooms with a/c and cable TV – great value in the lower end of this price range. **€92**

**Alnea** 20 rue Jean de Riouffe ☎ 04 93 68 77 77, ⓦ hotel-alnea.com. Centrally located two-star with pleasant service and simple but colourful and well-equipped rooms. **€85**

★ **Canberra** 120 rue d'Antibes ☎ 04 97 06 95 00, ⓦ hotel-cannes-canberra.com. Classy, understated and intimate four-star hotel with elegant, 50s-inspired decor and large rooms with a/c and flatscreen TV. There's a heated pool in the garden plus a sauna, gym, restaurant and cocktail bar. **€196**

**Carlton Intercontinental** 58 La Croisette ☎ 04 93 06 40 06, ⓦ ichotelsgroup.com. Legendary landmark *belle*

ⓦ lerins-sainthonorat.com).

**To Ste-Marguerite** Three companies – Horizon (☎ 04 92 98 71 36, ⓦ horizon-lerins.com), Riviera Lines (☎ 04 92 98 71 31, ⓦ riviera-lines.com) and Trans Côte d'Azur (☎ 04 92 98 71 30, ⓦ trans-cote-azur.com) – run to Ste-Marguerite (up to 18 daily 7.30am–5.30pm; €12/€12.50).

### VALLAURIS

**By bus** Regular buses from Cannes (#18 from the *gare routière* by the *gare SNCF*) and from Golfe-Juan SNCF arrive at the rear of the château.

Destinations Antibes (every 45–50min; 30min); Cannes (every 45min; 15min).

### GRASSE

**By bus** Grasse's *gare routière* is just north of the old town at place de la Buanderie.

Destinations Cannes (every 20min; 40–50min); Nice (every 35–50min; 1hr 30min).

**By train** Trains from Cannes (hourly; 25–30min) arrive at Grasse's *gare SNCF*, south of the *vieille ville*; it's a stiff walk uphill, so take bus #2, #4 or #5 into town.

### VALLAURIS

**Tourist office** Square du 8 Mai 1945, at the opposite end of the town centre from the museums (July & Aug daily 9am–7pm; Sept–June Mon–Sat 9am–12.15pm & 1.45–6pm; ☎ 04 93 63 82 58, ⓦ vallauris-golfe-juan.fr). The main tourist car park is also here.

### GRASSE

**Tourist office** 22 cours Honoré-Cresp (July–Sept daily 9am–7pm; Oct–June Mon–Sat 9am–12.30pm & 2–6pm; ☎ 04 93 36 66 66, ⓦ grasse.fr).

*époque* seafront palace hotel that featured in Hitchcock's *To Catch a Thief*. Rooms are decorated in a tasteful but conservative style, with pay-per-view movies, voicemail and TV internet browser, plus individually controlled a/c. **€390**

**Chanteclair** 12 rue Forville ☎ 04 93 39 68 88, ⓦ hotelchanteclair.fr. About as cheap as you'll get in the centre of Cannes, right next to the old town, and with a private courtyard where you can eat breakfast. Rooms are small but all have shower; most also have WC. **€75**

**Provence** 9 rue Molière ☎ 04 93 38 44 35, ⓦ hotel-de-provence.com. Charmingly decorated and well-appointed three-star hotel just off rue d'Antibes, with pale colours, a/c, a bar and a luxuriant garden. Some rooms have balconies and the suite deluxe has a large terrace. **€140**

**17**

**La Villa Tosca** 11 rue Hoche ☎ 04 93 38 34 40, ⓦ villa -tosca.com. Smartly renovated three-star hotel a few blocks from the sea, with well-equipped, a/c rooms with TV; some also have balconies. There is a cheaper two-star sister hotel – the *PLM* – a few doors down. **€125**

## GRASSE

**Le Patti** Place du Patti ☎ 04 93 36 01 00, ⓦ hotelpatti.com. Just below the bus station and on the edge of the old town, this two-star hotel has Provençal-style decor and 73 a/c rooms with bath or shower. **€95**

## EATING AND DRINKING

### CANNES

Cannes has restaurants catering for every budget, with Rue Meynadier, Le Suquet and quai St-Pierre being the best places to look. You can buy your own food in the Forville market two blocks behind the *mairie* (daily except Mon 7am–1pm).

**Auberge Provencale** 10 rue Saint-Antoine, Le Suquet ☎ 04 92 99 27 17, ⓦ auberge-provencale.com. Established in 1860, this stylish restaurant is the oldest in Cannes. It serves Niçois specialities and creative dishes like crème brûlée with foie gras or sea bream with black olives, tomato, basil and saffron potatoes. *Menu* €29; two-course lunch *formule* €20. Daily noon–2.15pm & 7–11.15pm.

**Aux Bons Enfants** 80 rue Meynadier. Small, friendly and rustic, this family-run stalwart – established in 1920 – serves very reliable Provençal cuisine with *menus* at €26 and dishes like octopus with saffron potatoes or hazelnut and foie gras terrine. Cash only. Jan–Nov Tues–Sat noon–2pm & 7–9.30pm.

★ **Barbarella** 16 rue Saint Dizier, Le Suquet ☎ 04 92 99 17 33, ⓦ barbarellarestaurant.fr. Stylish, fun and gay-friendly, with Philippe Starck ghost chairs on the terrace and a cosmopolitan fusion *menu* with Asian and other influences in dishes like cod fillet in ginger crust with baby vegetables. *Menus* from €29. Tues–Sat eves, until midnight.

**Chez Vincent & Nicolas** 90 rue Meynadier ☎ 04 93 68 35 39. Slightly quirky and original choice, with a lovely setting in a square just off the main street. The scallops wrapped in bacon are worth a try. Meat or fish mains start at around €16. Daily 6.30–11.30pm.

**La Mère Besson** 13 rue des Frères Pradignac ☎ 04 93 39 59 24. This smart, long-established restaurant in the thick of the nightlife quarter is an old Cannes favourite, with dishes like chicken with parsley cream or mesclun salad with lardons. *Menus* €28. Sept–June Mon–Fri 7–10.30pm; Mon–Fri noon–2pm & 7–10.30pm during festivals or exhibitions.

**La Palme d'Or** *Hôtel Martinez*, 73 bd de la Croisette ☎ 04 92 98 74 14. The place to go and celebrate if you've just won a film festival prize; it has held two Michelin stars for more than twenty years. Lunch *menu* €68; evening *menus* start at €95. Tues–Sat 12.30–2pm & 8–10pm.

### ÎLES DE LÉRINS

Taking a picnic to the islands is a good idea, particularly out of season, though there are reasonably priced snack stalls, two restaurants on Ste-Marguerite (May–Sept) and one on St-Honorat near the landing stage (daily for lunch; closed Nov to mid-Dec).

### GRASSE

**La Bastide Saint Antoine** 48 rue Henri-Dunant ☎ 04 93 70 94 94, ⓦ jacques-chibois.com. The best place to eat in Grasse is the Michelin-starred restaurant at this elegant small hotel, which serves *cuisine gourmande* with a Provençal twist in dishes like lobster bouillabaisse-style with olives. Lunch *menus* €59; otherwise *menus* from €169. Daily noon–2pm & 8–10pm.

**Gazan** 3 rue Gazan ☎ 04 93 36 22 88. Bustling restaurant, strategically located between the museums and the cathedral, with dishes like entrecote with café de Paris butter or beef fajitas with pepper cream; *plats du jour* €1, two-course lunchtime *formule* €15. Mon–Thurs lunch, Fri & Sat lunch & dinner.

**Maison Venturini** 1 rue Marcel-Journet ☎ 04 93 36 20 47. *Confiserie* where you can buy *fougassettes* – a sweet flatbread flavoured with orange blossom (€1.60). They also sell candied fruits, candied rose petals and Marseille-style *navettes* (€3 a pack). Tues–Sat 9am–12.30pm & 3–6.30pm.

## NIGHTLIFE

### CANNES

There are tons of trendy, exclusive bars and clubs, especially in the grid of streets bounded by rue Macé, rue V. Cousin, rue Dr G.-Monod and rue des Frères Pradignacs.

**Le 7** 7 rue Rouguière ☎ 06 09 55 22 79, ⓦ facebook .com/cabaretdiscotheque.leseptcannes?ref=ts. Gay disco and cabaret club just off rue Félix Faure, with drag shows on Fri and Sat. Free entry. Daily midnight–dawn; opens 5.30pm during the film festival.

**Backstage** 17 rue Gérard Monod ⓦ backstage-cannes .com. The biggest and flashiest of the trendy restaurant/ bar/clubs in the tight little knot of streets between rue d'Antibes and la Croisette, with dramatic black decor, and live music and cabaret Mon–Thurs. Main courses from €17 up, cocktails €10. Mon–Sat 6pm–5am.

**Le Baôli** Port Pierre Canto ☎ 04 93 43 03 43, ⓦ lebaoli

.com. If you want to rub shoulders with celebrities and big-name international DJs, head to this exclusive exotic (and expensive) outdoor disco-restaurant with palms lit up at night – dress the part. April–Oct daily; Nov–March Sat & Sun: restaurant (€70/80) from 8pm, club midnight–5am.

**Cavok** 19 rue des Frères Pradignacs ☎ 09 62 53 60 04. Smaller than the average Cannes nightspot and with chilled music, this is a good place to relax from the hustle and bustle of these streets. Cocktails €10. Daily in season, otherwise Tues–Sat 5pm–2.30am.

# Antibes and around

Graham Greene, who lived in **ANTIBES** for more than twenty years, considered it the only place on this stretch of coast to have preserved its soul. And although Antibes and its twin, **Juan-les-Pins**, have not escaped the overdevelopment that blights the region, they have avoided its worst excesses. Antibes itself is a pleasing old town, extremely animated, with one of the finest **markets** on the coast and the best **Picasso collection** in its ancient seafront castle; and the southern end of the **Cap d'Antibes** still has its woods of pine, in which some of the most exclusive mansions on the Riviera hide. North of Antibes is lovely **Biot**, with its fascinating Fernand Léger connections.

## Musée Picasso

Place Mariejol • Mid-June to mid-Sept Tues–Sun 10am–6pm, plus July & Aug Wed & Fri until 8pm; mid-Sept to mid-June Tues–Sun 10am–noon & 2–6pm • €6 or €10 with other municipal museums • ☎ 04 92 90 54 20, ⓦ antibes-juanlespins.com

Lording it over the Antibes ramparts and the sea, the sixteenth-century **Château Grimaldi** is a beautifully cool, light space, with hexagonal terracotta floor tiles, windows over the sea and a terrace garden filled with sculptures by Germaine Richier, Miró, César and others. In 1946 Picasso was offered the dusty building as a studio. Several extremely prolific months followed before he moved to Vallauris (see p.899), leaving all his Antibes output to what is now the **Musée Picasso**. Although Picasso donated other works later on, the bulk of the collection belongs to this one period. Picasso himself is the subject of works here by other painters and photographers, including Man Ray, Hans Hartung and Bill Brandt; there are also anguished canvases by Nicolas de Staël, who stayed in Antibes for a few months from 1954 to 1955.

## Cathédrale d'Antibes

Rue du Saint-Esprit

Alongside the castle is the **Cathédrale d'Antibes**, built on the site of an ancient temple. The choir and apse survive from the Romanesque building that served the city in the Middle Ages while the nave and stunning ochre facade are Baroque. Inside, in the south transept, is a sumptuous medieval altarpiece surrounded by immaculate panels of tiny detailed scenes.

## Cap d'Antibes

**Plage de la Salis**, the longest Antibes beach, runs along the eastern neck of **Cap d'Antibes**, with no big hotels squatting its sands – amazingly rare on the Riviera. To

---

**ANTIBES MARKET**

One block from the sea, the morning **covered market** (June–Aug daily 6am–1pm; Sept–May closed Mon) overflows with Provençal goodies and cut **flowers**, the traditional and still-flourishing Antibes business. In the afternoons a **craft market** (mid-June to Sept Tues–Sun 3pm–midnight; Oct to mid-June Fri–Sun only) takes over, and when the stalls pack up, café tables take their place.

the south, at the top of chemin du Calvaire, there are superb views from the **Chapelle de la Garoupe** (daily 10am–noon & 2.30–5pm; ⓦgaroupe.free.fr), which contains Russian spoils from the Crimean War and hundreds of **ex votos**. To the west, on boulevard du Cap between chemins du Tamisier and G.-Raymond, you can wander around the **Jardin Thuret** (Mon–Fri: summer 8am–6pm; winter 8.30am–5.30pm; free), botanical gardens belonging to a national research institute. Back on the east shore, further south, lies a second public beach, **plage de la Garoupe**. From here a footpath follows the shore to join the chemin des Douaniers.

### Around the Southern Cap

At the southern end of the Cap d'Antibes, on avenue L.D. Beaumont, stands the grandiose **Villa Eilenroc** (April–June Wed & Sat 10am–5pm; July–Sept Wed, Sat & Sun 3–7pm; Oct–March Wed & Sat 1–4pm; €2, Oct–March free), designed by Charles Garnier, architect of the casino at Monte-Carlo, and surrounded by lush gardens. There are more sandy coves and little harbours along the western shore, where you'll also find the **Musée Naval**, at the end of avenue J.-F.-Kennedy in a former Napoleonic coastal battery; it presents changing exhibitions on maritime themes (mid-June to mid-Sept Tues–Sun 10am–6pm; mid-Sept to mid-June Tues–Sat 10am–4.30pm; €3). Much of the southern tip of the **cap** is a warren of private roads, including the area around the fabled **Hotel du Cap Eden Roc** and the so-called "bay of millionaires".

## Juan-les-Pins

**JUAN-LES-PINS**, less than 2km from the centre of Antibes, had its heyday in the interwar years, when the summer season on the Riviera first took off and the resort was the haunt of film stars like Charlie Chaplin, Maurice Chevalier and Lilian Harvey, the polyglot London-born musical star who lingered here until 1968, long after her fame had faded. Juan-les-Pins isn't as glamorous as it once was either, though it still has a casino and a certain cachet, and the beaches are sand.

## Biot

The *village perché* of **BIOT**, 8km north of Antibes, is where Fernand Léger lived for a few years at the end of his life. The village itself – famous for its hand-blown bubble glass – is beautiful, full of craft shops and ateliers selling everything from glassware to fine art and handbags.

### Musée Fernand Léger

316 chemin du Val de Pôme • Daily except Tues: May–Oct 10am–6pm; Nov–April 10am–5pm • €5.50 (€7.50 during temporary exhibitions) • ☎ 04 92 91 50 30, ⓦmusee-fernandleger.fr • Bus #10 (every 20–40 min; 30min) to stop "F. Leger"

A stunning collection of the artist's intensely life-affirming works, created between 1905 and 1955, is on show at the **Musée Fernand Léger**. The museum is just east of the village on the chemin du Val de Pôme, and if you're using public transport it is best reached by bus.

---

#### JAZZ À JUAN

Juan's **international jazz festival** – known simply as Jazz à Juan and by far the best in the region (ⓦjazzjuan.com) – is held in the middle two weeks of July in the central pine grove, the **Jardin de La Pinède**, and **square Gould** above the beach by the casino. A Hollywood-style walk of fame immortalizes various jazz greats at la Pinede, set into the pavement.

**By train** Antibes' *gare SNCF* lies north of the old town at the top of av Robert-Soleau. Turn right out of the station and a 3min walk along av R.-Soleau will bring you to place de Gaulle.
Destinations Cannes (up to 5/hr; 7–10min); Nice (up to 5/hr; 20–25 min).

**By bus** The *gare routière* is east of the train station on place Guynemer, with frequent buses between the two. Local Envibus services link Antibes to its neighbours: bus #2 goes to Cap d'Antibes, bus #3(o) to Juan-les-Pins and #10 to Biot.
Destinations Cap d'Antibes (every 40min; 9min); Juan-les-Pins (every 40min; 6min), Biot (every 20–35 min; 25min).

**Tourist office** 11 place de Gaulle (July & Aug daily 9am–7pm; Sept–June Mon–Fri 9am–12.30pm & 1.30–6pm, Sat 9am–noon & 2–6pm, Sun 10am–12.30pm & 2–6pm; ☏ 04 97 23 11 11, ⊚ antibesjuanlespins.com). There's an annex in Juan-les-Pins.

**Bike rental** Bikes can be hired from Holiday Bikes, 93 bd Wilson in Juan-les-Pins (☏ 04 93 20 90 20).

**Bookshop** Heidi's English Bookshop, 24 rue Aubernon (Tues–Sat 10am–7pm, Sun & Mon 11am–6pm; ☏ 04 93 34 74 11) is the best-stocked English bookshop on the coast.

## ACCOMMODATION

### ANTIBES

**La Jabotte** 13 av Max Maurey, Antibes ☏ 04 93 61 45 89, ⊚ jabotte.com. Just a short walk from the plage de la Salis, this gay-friendly place has beautifully decorated rooms in vibrant, cheerful colours – book in advance. The cheapest double has a shower, but shared WC facilities. **€101**

**Logis de la Brague** 1221 rte de Nice ☏ 04 93 33 54 72, ⊚ camping-logisbrague.com. As with all campsites near Antibes, this three-star site is north of the city in the *quartier* of La Brague (bus #10 or one train stop to "Gare de Biot"); this one is closest to the station. Closed Oct–April. **€17**

**La Marjolaine** 15 av du Docteur Fabre, Juan-les-Pins ☏ 04 93 61 06 60. Seventeen traditionally styled rooms in a beautiful a/c villa with a leafy terrace and a handy location between Juan les Pins train station and the beach. Closed Nov to late Dec. **€90**

**Le Mas Djoliba** 29 av de Provence, Antibes ☏ 04 93 34 02 48, ⊚ hotel-djoliba.com. Three-star *Logis de France* with a pool, *boules* and a fabulous garden; it's a great hideaway from the bustle of town and not too far from the beach. Closed mid-Nov to early March. **€154**

**De la Pinède** 7 av Georges Gallice, Juan-les-Pins ☏ 04 93 61 03 95, ⊚ hotel-pinede.com. Renovated, friendly two-star hotel in the centre of Juan-les-Pins, just a short walk from the beach, with a small sun terrace. Closed Nov to mid-Feb. **€119**

**Relais International de la Jeunesse "Caravelle 60"** 272 bd de la Garoupe, Cap d'Antibes ☏ 04 93 61 34 40, ⊚ clajsud.fr. As it is right by the beach, you must book well in advance to secure a bed at this popular hostel. Bus #2 stops right outside. Closed Oct–March. **€28**

**Le Relais du Postillon** 8 rue Championnet, Antibes ☏ 04 93 34 20 77, ⊚ relaisdupostillon.com. In Antibes old town, this charming gay-friendly two-star above a low-key bar feels like an old inn, with its individually styled rooms and lots of exposed stonework. **€114**

### BIOT

**Des Arcades** 16 place des Arcades ☏ 04 93 65 01 04. Book well in advance to stay in this appealing old hotel/restaurant in the medieval centre of the village, full of old-fashioned charm and with huge rooms and an excellent restaurant, which doubles as an art gallery. Very good value for this neck of the woods. **€55**

## EATING, DRINKING AND ENTERTAINMENT

Antibes' old town is rich in eating and drinking options; Juan-les-Pins isn't quite so well-endowed, but does have several discos and cocktail bars. In Biot, the best place to eat is in the *Des Arcades* hotel restaurant (see above).

**De Bacon** 664, bd de Bacon, Cap d'Antibes ☏ 04 93 61 50 02, ⊚ restaurantdebacon.com. With excellent fish and a sea view, this locally renowned restaurant offers a €55 set lunch; otherwise, *menus* from €85 except during high season. April–Oct Tues 7.30–10pm, Wed–Sun noon–2pm & 7.30–10pm.

**Brûlot** 3 rue Frédéric Isnard, Antibes ☏ 04 93 34 17 76, ⊚ brulot.fr. A stalwart of the restaurant scene in Antibes' old town, dishing up classic regional dishes like *socca*, *salade niçoise* and tripe. Lunch *formule* €12.90, *menus* €19–42. Mon–Wed dinner, Thurs–Sat lunch & dinner.

**Le Pam–Pam** 137 bd Wilson, Juan-les-Pins ☏ 04 93 61 11 05, ⊚ pampam.fr. Perennially popular cocktail bar with a Polynesian-meets-Brazilian ambience and frequent live music and dance spectacles. Fruit and gewgaw-bedecked cocktails from €9.60. Daily 3pm–4.30am.

**La Passagère** *Hotel Belles Rives*, 33 bd Edouard Baudoin, Juan-les-Pins ☏ 04 93 61 02 79, ⊚ bellesrives.com. Modern Mediterranean delights using regional produce served in lovely, restored Art Deco surroundings with wonderful views over the bay; *retour du marché menu* €70, otherwise mains €45–58. March–Dec daily noon–2.30pm & 8–10.30pm; closed Mon & Tues outside high season.

17

**Les Vieux Murs** 25 promenade Amiral-de-Grasse, Antibes ☎04 93 34 06 73, wlesvieuxmurs.com. *Restaurant gastronomique* serving classy food, like salt cod with shavings of Iberian ham or poached veal with artichokes, in a perfect setting on the castle ramparts. Lunch *menu* from €29, dinner *menu* €34–90. Tues–Sun 12.30–2pm & 7.30–10pm.

# Above the Baie des Anges

Between Antibes and Nice, the **Baie des Anges** laps at a long stretch of undistinguished twentieth-century resorts. The old towns, such as **Cagnes**, lie inland. Cagnes is associated with Renoir – as is **St-Paul-de-Vence**, which houses the wonderful modern art collection of the Fondation Maeght. **Vence** has a small chapel decorated by Matisse, and is a relaxing place to stay.

## Cagnes

**CAGNES** is a confusing agglomeration, consisting of the seaside district of **Cros-de-Cagnes**, the immaculate medieval village of **Haut-de-Cagnes** overlooking the town from the northwest, and **Cagnes-sur-Mer**, the traffic-choked town centre wedged between the two.

### Les Collettes – the Musée Renoir

Chemain des Colettes • Closed for renovation until July 2013; collections on temporary view in Chateau Grimaldi • ⓦ cagnesurmer.fr • Bus #49 from Cagnes-sur-Mer bus station

**Les Collettes**, the house that Renoir had built in 1908 and where he spent the last twelve years of his life, is now a **museum**, encompassing the house and olive and rare orange groves surrounding it. One of the two studios in the house – north-facing to catch the late afternoon light – is arranged as if Renoir had just popped out. Albert André's painting, *A Renoir Painting*, shows the ageing artist hunched over his canvas, plus there's a bust of him by Aristide Maillol, and a crayon sketch by Richard Guido. Bonnard and Dufy were also visitors to Les Collettes; Dufy's *Hommage à Renoir*, transposing a detail of *Le Moulin de la Galette*, hangs here. Renoir's own work is represented by several sculptures, some beautiful watercolours and ten paintings from his Cagnes period.

### Château Grimaldi

Place Grimaldi, Haut-de-Cagnes • Daily except Tues: 10am–noon & 2–5/6pm • €4 • ☎ 04 92 02 47 30 • Free shuttle bus #44 from bus station; by foot, it's a steep ascent from av. Renoir along rue Général-Bérenger and montée de la Bourgade

Arty **Haut-de-Cagnes** lives up to everything dreamed of in a Riviera *village perché*. The ancient village backs up to a crenellated feudal **château** which has a stunning Renaissance interior, housing museums of local history, olive cultivation, the **donation Solidor** – a diverse collection of paintings of the famous cabaret artist Suzy Solidor – plus an **olive museum** and exhibition space for **contemporary art**.

### ARRIVAL AND INFORMATION                                    CAGNES

**By train** The *gare SNCF* Cagnes-sur-Mer (one stop from the *gare SNCF* Cros-de-Cagnes) is southwest of the centre alongside the *autoroute*; turn right on the northern side of the *autoroute* along avenue de la Gare to head into town. The sixth turning on your right, rue des Palmiers, leads to the tourist office.
Destinations Antibes (every 20–30min; 11min); Cannes (every 20–30min; 23min); Nice (every 15–30min; 15min).
**By bus** Buses #42, #49, #56 and #200 all make the short

run from the *gare SNCF* to the *gare routière* on square Bourdet.
Destinations Cannes (every 15–20min; 57min); Nice (every 15–20min; 38min).
**Tourist office** 6 bd Maréchal-Juin (July & Aug Mon–Sat 9am–12.30pm & 2–6pm; Sept–June Mon–Fri 9am–noon & 2–6pm, Sat 9am–noon; ☎04 93 20 61 64, ⓦcagnes-tourisme.com). There's a second office close to the château in Haut-de-Cagnes.

**CLOCKWISE FROM TOP LEFT** FONDATION MAEGHT (P.910); MOULES-FRITES, CASSIS; VIEUX NICE (P.878) >

**17**

## ACCOMMODATION

**Aéva** 22–23 promenade de la Plage ☏ 04 93 73 39 52, Ⓦ hotel-aeva.fr. Stylishly revamped seafront hotel in Cros de Cagnes. Elegant, modern, a/c en-suites have soundproofing, satellite TV and safes. There's a classy restaurant facing the sea, and a separate *aparthotel*, too. **€100**

**Le Val Fleuri** 139 chemin Vallon des Vaux ☏ 04 93 31 21 74, Ⓦ campingvalfleuri.fr. Two-star campsite approximately 4km from the sea (bus #41) with a heated pool, snack bar and children's play area. They also rent out studio flats and mobile homes. Closed mid-Oct to Jan. **€23**

## EATING, DRINKING AND ENTERTAINMENT

The best places to eat are in Haut-de-Cagnes. In early July Cagnes celebrates all manner of sea-related activities as part of the Fête de la Saint-Pierre et de la Mer; in early August there is free street theatre on place du Château and on the seafront, and in late August, there's a bizarre square *boules* competition down montée de la Bourgade.

**Fleur de Sel** 85 montée de la Bourgade ☏ 04 92 20 33 33, Ⓦ restaurant-fleurdesel.com. This restaurant serves dishes such as langoustines in creamy risotto and tournedos of beef with duck foie gras and black truffle sauce; *menus* from €33. April–Sept daily except Wed from 7.30pm; Oct–March Mon, Tues & Fri–Sun from 7.30pm.

**Josy-Jo** 2 rue du Planastel ☏ 04 93 20 68 76, Ⓦ restaurant-josyjo.com. Charming restaurant in the space that served as Soutine's workshop in the interwar years, with an oleander-shaded terrace and refined Provençal dishes. *Menus* €29–42, otherwise around €25 for main courses à la carte. July & Aug Mon–Sat dinner only; Sept–June Tues–Sat lunch & dinner.

# St-Paul-de-Vence

The fortified village of **ST-PAUL-DE-VENCE** is home to one of the best artistic treats in the region: the remarkable **Fondation Maeght**, created in the 1950s by Aimé and Marguerite Maeght, art collectors and dealers who knew all the great artists who worked in Provence.

## Fondation Maeght

623 Chemin des Gardettes • Daily: July–Sept 10am–7pm; April & May 10am–6pm; Oct–March 10am–1pm & 2–6pm • €14 • ☏ 04 93 32 81 63, Ⓦ fondation-maeght.com

Through the gates of the **Fondation Maeght** is a sublime fusion of art, modern architecture and landscape. Alberto Giacometti's *Cat* stalks along the edge of the grass; Miró's *Egg* smiles above a pond; it's hard not to be bewitched by the Calder mobile swinging over watery tiles, by Léger's *Flowers, Birds and a Bench* on a sunlit rough stone wall, or by the clanking tubular fountain by Pol Bury. The building itself is superb: multi-levelled, flooded with daylight and housing a fabulous collection of works by Braque, Miró, Chagall, Léger and Matisse, among others. Not everything is exhibited at any one time, apart from what is permanently featured in the garden.

## The vieux village

St-Paul-de-Vence's other famous sights are in the busy but beautiful **vieux village**. The hotel-restaurant **La Colombe d'Or** at the entrance to the village is celebrated for the art on its walls, donated in lieu of payment for meals by the then-impoverished Braque, Picasso, Matisse and Bonnard in the lean years following World War I – though it doesn't exactly encourage casual visitors. You could instead make the pilgrimage to the simple grave of **Marc Chagall** on the right-hand side of the little **cemetery** (open during daylight hours) at the southern end of the village, running the gauntlet of the boutiques and galleries on rue Grande to get there.

## ARRIVAL AND DEPARTURE                                      ST-PAUL-DE-VENCE

**By bus** The Nice–Vence bus #400 has two stops in St-Paul: alighting at the Fondation Maeght stop, the first on the way up from Nice, the Fondation is a left turn up the hill from the roundabout; from the village centre, head uphill along the steep street opposite the entrance to the village itself.

**Destinations** Nice (every 35min–1hr; 1hr 3min); Vence (every 35min–1hr; 10min).

**La Colombe d'Or** Place du Général-de-Gaulle ☏ 04 93 32 80 02, ⓦla-colombe-dor.com. Famous for its stellar collection of modern art, the *Colombe d'Or* also has a *restaurant gastronomique*, valet parking, a heated outdoor pool, sauna and gardens, plus 13 rooms and 12 apartments. Closed Nov to Christmas. **€295**

# Vence

Long one of the less pretentious of Côte d'Azur towns, **VENCE** is slowly succumbing to a chi-chi makeover. Blessed with ancient houses, gateways, fountains, chapels and a **cathedral** containing Roman funeral inscriptions and a Chagall mosaic, in the 1920s it became a haven for painters and writers: André Gide, Raoul Dufy, D.H. Lawrence (who died here in 1930 while being treated for tuberculosis contracted in England) and Marc Chagall were all long-term visitors, along with **Matisse** whose work is the reason most people come.

## Chapelle du Rosaire

466 av Henri-Matisse • Mid-Dec to mid-Nov Mon, Wed & Sat 2–5.30pm, Tues & Thurs 10–11.30am & 2–5.30pm • €4 • ☏ 04 93 58 03 26

Towards the end of World War II, Matisse moved to Vence to escape Allied bombing of the coast, and his legacy is the exciting **Chapelle du Rosaire**, off the road to St-Jeannet, which leaves the town from carrefour Jean-Moulin at the top of avenue des Poilus. The chapel was his last work – consciously so – and not, as some have tried to explain, a religious conversion. "My only religion is the love of the work to be created, the love of creation, and great sincerity", he said in 1952 when the five-year project was completed.

The drawings on the chapel walls – black outline figures on white tiles – were executed by Matisse with a paintbrush fixed to a 2m-long bamboo stick specifically to remove his own stylistic signature from the lines. He succeeded in this to the extent that many people are disappointed, not finding the "Matisse" they expect. Yet it is a total work – every part of the chapel is Matisse's design – and one that the artist was content with.

## Château de Villeneuve Fondation Emile Hugues

2 place du Frêne • Tues–Sun: 10am–12.30pm & 2–6pm • €7 • ☏ 04 93 58 15 78, ⓦmuseedevence.com

On place du Frêne, by the western gateway in Vieux Vence, the fifteenth-century **Château de Villeneuve Fondation Emile Hugues** provides a beautiful temporary exhibition space for the works of artists such as Matisse, Dufy, Dubuffet and Chagall.

VENCE

**By bus** Vence's *gare routière* is at place Maréchal Juin, a short walk from the tourist office.

Destinations Nice (every 35min–1hr; 55min–1hr 10min); St-Paul-de-Vence (every 35min–1hr; 5min).

**Tourist office** Place du Grand-Jardin (July & Aug Mon–Sat 9am–7pm, Sun 10am–6pm; March–June, Sept & Oct Mon–Sat 9am–6pm; Nov–Feb Mon–Sat 9am–5pm; ☏ 04 93 58 06 38, ⓦvence.fr).

**Le 2 des Portiques** 2 rue des Portiques ☏ 04 93 24 42 58, ⓦle2vence.fr. Four stylish a/c rooms – including a junior suite and a loft with private roof terrace – in a *chambres d'hote* in the heart of Vieux Vence, above a bistro with live music in the evenings. **€90**

**Domaine de la Bergerie** 1330 chemin de la Sine ☏ 04 93 58 09 36, ⓦcamping-domainedelabergerie.com. Three-star campsite 3km west of town off the road to

Tourettes-sur-Loup, with a pool and *pétanque* pitch. They also rent small chalet-like pods (€40). Closed mid-Oct to late March. **€24.50**

**Villa Roseraie** Av Henri-Giraud ☏ 04 93 58 02 20, ⓦvillaroseraie.com. Three-star comforts in a villa that dates from 1929, with a palm-fringed pool, a garden, private parking and a bar. The rooms are decorated in Provençal style and some have private patio or terrace. **€107**

**La Farigoule** 15 av Henri-Isnard ☏ 04 93 58 01 27, ⓦlafarigoule-vence.fr. This very pretty restaurant – with

white limed beams inside and a courtyard garden – is a good bet for a special meal, with *menus* at €29 and €45 and

**17**

Côtes de Provence wines. High season Tues–Sun noon–1.30pm & 7.30–9.30pm; closed Tues outside high season.
**Le Pêcheur du Soleil** 1 place Godeau ☎ 04 93 58 32 56,

ⓦ pecheurdusoleil.com. Tiny place in Vieux Vence with a huge choice of pizzas from €11, salads from €6.50 and omelettes from €8.50. Feb–Nov Tues–Sat noon–2pm & 7–9pm, Sun noon–2pm.

# Nice

The capital of the Riviera and fifth largest city in France, **NICE** lives off a glittering reputation. Far too large to be considered simply a beach resort, it has all the advantages and disadvantages of a major city: superb culture, shopping, eating and drinking, but also crime, graffiti and horrendous traffic, all set against a backdrop of blue skies, sparkling sea and sub-tropical greenery kept lush by sprinklers.

Popularized by English aristocrats in the eighteenth century, Nice reached its zenith in the *belle époque* of the late nineteenth century, and has retained its historical styles almost intact: the medieval rabbit warren of **Vieux Nice**, the Italianate facades of **modern Nice** and the rich exuberance of **fin-de-siècle residences** dating from when the city was Europe's most fashionable winter retreat. It has mementos from its time as a Roman regional capital, and earlier still, when the Greeks founded the city. The **museums** are a treat for art lovers, and though its politics are conservative Nice doesn't feel stuffy; it has a highly visible lesbian and gay community and spirited nightlife. Of late Nice has been smartening up its act with extensive **refurbishment** of its public spaces and the construction of an ultra-modern **tramway**. Conservative it may be, but Nice does not rest on its laurels.

## Parc de la Colline du Château

Daily 8am–6/7/8pm according to season • Take the lift by the Tour Bellanda at the eastern end of quai des États-Unis (June–Aug 9am–8pm, April, May & Sept 9am–7pm; Oct–March 10am–6pm), or climb the steps from rue de la Providence or montée du Château in the old town

For initial orientation, fantastic sea and city views and the scent of Mediterranean vegetation, head for the **Parc de la Colline du Château**. It's where Nice began, as the ancient Greek city of Nikaïa, hence the mosaics and stone vases in mock Grecian style. Despite the name, there's no château, just wonderful views over the scrambled rooftops and gleaming mosaic tiles of Vieux Nice and along the sweep of the promenade des Anglais.

## Vieux Nice

**Vieux Nice** has been much gentrified in recent years, but the restaurants, boutiques and little art galleries still coexist with humbler shops, there's washing strung between the tenements, and away from the showpiece squares a certain shabbiness lingers. Tourism now dominates Vieux Nice: throbbing with life day and night in August, much of it seems deserted in November. It is best explored on foot.

### NICE ORIENTATION

Shadowed by mountains that curve down to the Mediterranean east of its port, Nice divides fairly clearly between old and new. **Vieux Nice**, the old town, groups about the hill of **Le Château**, its limits signalled by **boulevard Jean-Jaurès**, built along the course of the River Paillon. Along the seafront, the celebrated **promenade des Anglais** runs a cool 5km until forced to curve inland by the sea-projecting runways of the airport. The central square, **place Masséna**, is at the bottom of the modern city's main street, **avenue Jean-Médecin**, to the north is the exclusive hillside suburb of **Cimiez**, while the port lies on the eastern side of **Le Château**.

The central square is **place Rossetti**, where the soft-coloured Baroque **Cathédrale de Ste-Réparate** (Mon–Fri 9am–noon & 2–6pm, Sat 9am–noon & 2–7.30pm, Sun 9am–1pm & 3–6pm; ⓦcathedrale-nice.com) just manages to be visible in the concatenation of eight narrow streets. There are cafés to relax in, and a fabulous ice-cream parlour, *Fenocchio*, with an extraordinary choice of flavours.

## Cours Saleya

The old town's real magnet is **cours Saleya** and the adjacent place Pierre-Gautier and place Charles-Félix. These wide-open, sunlit spaces – fringed with grandiloquent municipal buildings and Italianate chapels – are the site of the city's main **market**. Café and restaurant tables fill the *cours* on summer nights, and presiding over it all is the baroque **Chapelle de la Miséricorde** (Tues 2.30–5pm) with its elliptical nave and exceptionally rich ornamentation. The **market** on the Cours is a treat, with gorgeous, colourful displays of fruit, vegetables, cheeses and sausages, plus cut flowers and potted roses, mimosa and other scented plants. On Monday the stalls sell bric-a-brac and secondhand clothes.

## Palais Lascaris

15 rue Droite • Daily except Tues 10am–6pm • Free • ☎ 04 93 62 72 40, ⓦ palais-lascaris-nice.org

Grandest survivor of Vieux Nice's baroque town mansions is the **Palais Lascaris**, a seventeenth-century palace built by the Duke of Savoy's Field-Marshal, Jean-Paul Lascaris, whose family arms, engraved on the ceiling of the entrance hall, bear the motto "Not even lightning strikes us". It's all very sumptuous, with frescoes, tapestries and chandeliers, along with a five-hundred-strong collection of historic musical instruments.

# Place Masséna and around

The stately, largely pedestrianized **place Masséna** is the hub of the new town, built in 1835 across the path of the River Paillon. A balustraded terrace and steps on the south of the square lead to Vieux Nice; the new town lies to the north. A short walk to the west lie the **Jardins Albert 1ᵉʳ**, where the Théâtre de Verdure occasionally hosts concerts, including the annual jazz festival.

## Avenue Jean-Médecin to rue Masséna

Running north from place Masséna, **avenue Jean-Médecin** is the city's nondescript main shopping street, cheered up slightly by the revamped Nice-Étoile **shopping complex** between rue Biscarra and boulevard Dubouchage; there are branches of FNAC and Virgin nearby for books, CDs and concert tickets. **Designer** boutiques sit west of place Masséna on rue du Paradis and rue Alphonse Karr. Both these streets intersect with the pedestrianized **rue Masséna** and the end of **rue de France** – true holiday territory, all ice-cream parlours and big brasseries, and always crammed.

## Musée d'Art Moderne et d'Art Contemporain

Promenade des Arts • Tues–Sun 10am–6pm • Free • ☎ 04 97 13 42 01, ⓦ mamac-nice.org

The covered course of the Paillon northeast of place Masséna is the site of the city's more recent prestige projects. Most appealing of these is the marble **Musée d'Art Moderne et d'Art Contemporain**, or MAMAC, which has rotating exhibitions of avant-garde French and American movements from the 1960s to the present. New Realism (smashing, burning, squashing and wrapping the detritus or mundane objects of everyday life) and Pop Art feature strongly with works by Warhol, Klein, Lichtenstein, César, Arman and Christo.

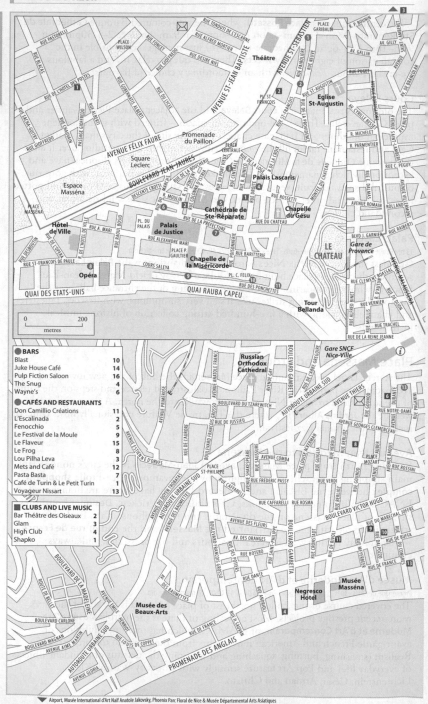

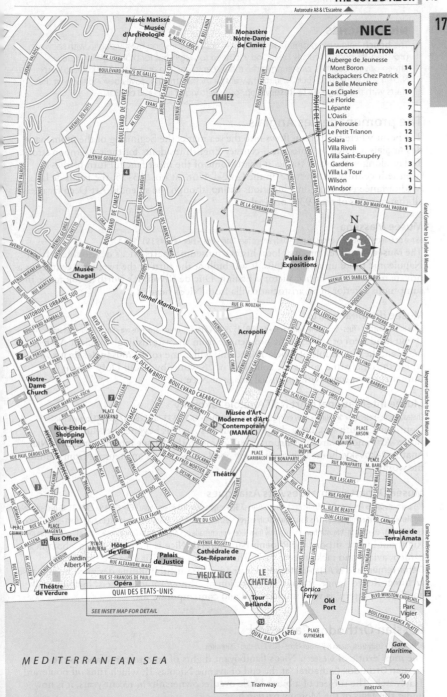

**NICE**

■ **ACCOMMODATION**

| | |
|---|---|
| Auberge de Jeunesse Mont Boron | 14 |
| Backpackers Chez Patrick | 5 |
| La Belle Meunière | 6 |
| Les Cigales | 10 |
| Le Floride | 4 |
| Lépante | 7 |
| L'Oasis | 8 |
| La Pérouse | 15 |
| Le Petit Trianon | 12 |
| Solara | 13 |
| Villa Rivoli | 11 |
| Villa Saint-Exupéry Gardens | 3 |
| Villa La Tour | 2 |
| Wilson | 1 |
| Windsor | 9 |

MEDITERRANEAN SEA

**17**

---

**NICE BEACHES**

The **beach** below the promenade des Anglais is all pebbles and mostly public, with showers provided. It's not particularly clean and you need to watch out for broken glass. There are fifteen private beaches, clustering at the more scenic, eastern end of the bay close to Vieux Nice. If you don't mind rocks, you might want to try the string of coves beyond the port that starts with the **plage de la Réserve**, opposite Parc Vigier (bus #20 or #30).

---

## The promenade des Anglais

The point where the Paillon flows into the sea marks the beginning of the **promenade des Anglais**, created by nineteenth-century English residents for their afternoon strolls. Today, along with lots of traffic, it boasts some of the most fanciful turn-of-the-twentieth-century architecture on the Côte d'Azur. At nos. 13–15, the Palais de la Méditerranée is once again a luxurious **casino**, though the splendid Art Deco facade is all that remains of the 1930s original.

### Musée Masséna

65 rue de France/35 promenade des Anglais • Daily except Tues 10am–6pm • Free • ☎ 04 93 91 19 10

The **Musée Masséna**, the city's local history museum, charts Nice's development from Napoleonic times up to the 1930s. It was built at the turn of the twentieth century as a private residence for Prince Victor d'Essling, Duc de Rivoli. It's worth a look to see the sumptuous interior of an aristocratic villa from Nice's heyday.

### Musée des Beaux-Arts

33 av des Baumettes • Tues–Sun 10am–6pm • Free • ☎ 04 92 15 28 28, ⓦ musee-beaux-arts-nice.org • Bus #23, stop "Grosso"

If you head 1km or so down the promenade from the astonishingly opulent *Negresco Hotel* and head a couple of blocks inland you will come to the **Musée des Beaux-Arts**, where the chief attraction is the collection of 28 works by Raoul Dufy, who is intimately connected with the visual image of Nice.

### Musée International d'Art Naïf Anatole Jakovsky

Château Sainte-Hélène, av de Fabron • Daily except Tues 10am–6pm • Free • ☎ 04 93 71 78 33 • Bus #23, stop "Fabron/Art Naïf"

Continuing southwest along the promenade des Anglais beyond the Musée des Beaux-Arts and towards the airport, you'll come to the **Musée International d'Art Naïf Anatole Jakovsky**, home to a surprisingly good collection of amateur art from around the world.

### Musée Départemental des Arts Asiatiques

405 promenade des Anglais • **Park** Daily: April–Oct 9.30am–7.30pm; Nov–March 9.30am–6pm • €2 • ☎ 04 92 29 77 01, ⓦ parc-phoenix. org **Musée Départemental des Arts Asiatiques** Daily except Tues: May to mid-Oct 10am–6pm; mid-Oct to April 10am–5pm • Free • ☎ 04 92 29 37 00 • Exit St-Augustin from the highway from Nice or promenade des Anglais from Cannes, or bus #9, #10 or #23 from Nice

Right out by the airport, the **Phoenix Parc Floral de Nice** is a cross between a botanical garden, aviary and tacky theme park. The best reason to visit is to see the **Musée Départemental des Arts Asiatiques**, located in a beautiful building designed by Japanese architect Kenzo Tange. It houses a collection of ethnographic artefacts, including silk goods and pottery, as well as traditional and contemporary art.

## Russian Orthodox Cathedral

Av Nicolas-II • Daily 9am–noon & 2–6pm • Free • Bus #17, stop "Tzaréwitch"

The most exotic of western Nice's flamboyant flights of architectural fancy is the **Russian Orthodox Cathedral**, at the end of avenue Nicolas-II, which runs off boulevard Tsaréwitch. The subject of a bitter battle over its ownership in recent years, it is now under the aegis of the Moscow patriarchate.

# Cimiez

**17**

Bus #15, #17 or #22, stop "Arènes/Musée Matisse"

Packed with vast *belle époque* piles, many of them former hotels, the northern suburb of **Cimiez** has always been posh. The heights of Cimiez were the social centre of the local elite some 1700 years ago, when the town was capital of the Roman province of Alpes-Maritimae. Part of a small amphitheatre still stands, and excavations of the **Roman baths** have revealed enough detail to distinguish the sumptuous and elaborate facilities for the top tax official and his cronies, the plainer public baths and a separate complex for women. All the finds, plus an illustration of the town's history up to the Middle Ages, are displayed in the **Musée d'Archéologie**, 160 av des Arènes (daily except Tues 10am–6pm; free; ☎04 93 81 59 57).

## Musée Matisse

164 av des Arènes de Cimiez • Daily except Tues 10am–6pm • Free • ☎ 04 93 81 08 08, ⓦ musee-matisse-nice.org

The seventeenth-century villa lying between the Roman excavations and the arena is the **Musée Matisse**. Matisse spent his winters in Nice from 1916 onwards, and then from 1921 to 1938 rented an apartment overlooking place Charles-Félix. It was here that he painted his most sensual, colour-flooded canvases of odalisques posed against exotic draperies. As well as the Mediterranean light, Matisse loved the cosmopolitan aspect of Nice and the presence of fellow artists Renoir, Bonnard and Picasso in neighbouring towns. He died in Cimiez in November 1954, aged 85.

## Monastère Notre-Dame de Cimiez and around

Place du Monastère • **Church** Mon–Sat 9am–6pm • Free **Gardens** Daily: June–Aug 8am–8pm; April, May & Sept 8am–7pm; Oct–March 8am–6pm • Free

The Roman remains and the Musée Matisse back onto an old olive grove, at the eastern end of which are the sixteenth-century buildings and exquisite gardens of the **Monastère Notre-Dame de Cimiez**. The oratory has brilliant murals illustrating alchemy, while the church houses three masterpieces of medieval painting by Louis and Antoine Bréa. On the north side of the monastery is the **Cemetery** of Cimiez (daily: May–Aug 8am–6.45pm; March, April, Sept & Oct 8am–5.45pm; Nov–Feb 8am–4.45pm); the simple tomb of **Matisse** is signposted on the left-hand side.

## Musée Chagall

Av du Docteur Ménard • Daily except Tues: May–Oct 10am–6pm; Nov–April 10am–5pm • €5.50, €7.50 during temporary exhibitions • ☎ 04 93 53 87 20, ⓦ musees-nationaux-alpesmaritimes.fr • Bus #22, stop "Musée Chagall"

At the foot of Cimiez hill, just off boulevard Cimiez, **Chagall's Biblical Message** is housed in a **museum** built specially for the work and opened by the artist in 1972. The rooms are light, white and cool, with windows allowing you to see the greenery of the garden beyond the indescribable shades between pink and red of the *Song of Songs* canvases. The seventeen paintings are all based on the Old Testament and complemented with etchings and engravings.

---

**ARRIVAL AND DEPARTURE** **NICE**

**By plane** Aeroport Nice Côte d'Azur (☎0820 423 333, ⓦ nice.aeroport.fr), which has flights from most regional British airports, New York, Montréal and Paris, is at the western end of the promenade des Anglais. Two fast buses connect with the city: #99 goes to the *gare SNCF* on av Thiers (every 30min 8am–9pm); #98 goes to the *gare routière* (every 20min 5.52am–11.37am). A €4 day-pass is needed for either. The slower regular bus #23 (€1; last bus 8.50pm) also serves the *gare SNCF* from the airport. Taxis are plentiful and cost about €22–32 into town.

**By train** Nice's *gare SNCF* (☎3635) is on av Thiers on the northern edge of the city centre next to the *voie rapide*. Destinations Antibes (2–6/hr; 18–29 min); Cannes (2–6/hr; 27–42min); Marseille (17 daily; 2hr 32min–2hr 45min); Menton (1–4/hr; 28–35min); Monaco (1–4/hr; 15–22min); St Raphaël (every 30min–1hr; 53min–1hr 15min); Sospel (9 daily; 48 min); Villefranche (1–4/hr; 6min).

**By bus** Buses pull in along av Félix Faure near place Masséna.

**17**

Destinations Antibes (every 10–20min; 50min); Cannes (every 10–20min; 1hr 30 min); Grasse (every 25–45min; 1hr 35min); Menton (up to 5/hr; 1hr 25min); Monaco (up to 5/hr; 43 min); St-Paul-de-Vence (every 30min–1hr; 1hr); Vence (every 30min–1hr; 1hr 10min).

**By ferry** Ferries to Corsica are run by SNCM, quai du Commerce (☎ 04 93 13 66 59, ⊛ sncm.fr) and Corsica Ferries, quai du Commerce (☎ 0825 095 095, ⊛ corsica-ferries.fr).

## GETTING AROUND

**By bus and tram** Buses and trams in Nice and surrounding towns are provided by Lignes d'Azur, 3 place Masséna (Mon–Fri 7.30am–6.45pm, Sat 8.30am–6pm; ☎ 08 1006 1006, ⊛ lignesdazur.com). A single tram line loops in a "V" shape from the northern suburbs through the city centre to the northeastern suburbs. Buses are frequent until early evening (roughly 7.30–9.15pm), after which five Noctrambus night buses serve most areas from Station Bermand, close to place Masséna until 1.10am; the tram continues until 12.50am to Las Planas and until 1.35am to Pont Michel. You can buy a single ticket (€1) or a day-pass (€4) on the bus; ten-journey multipasses (€10) and seven-day passes (€15) are available from *tabacs*, kiosks, newsagents and from the Lignes d'Azur office, where you can also pick up a free route map.

**By taxi** Central Taxi Riviera (☎ 04 93 13 78 78, ⊛ taxis-nice.fr); Taxis Niçois Indépendants (☎ 04 93 88 25 82).

**By bike** Nice has an on-street bicycle rental scheme, Vélo Bleu (⊛ velobleu.org), with 120 rental stations scattered throughout the city. You have to sign up online or at the bike station (€1/day, €5/week; ☎ 04 30 00 30 01), after which the first 30min is free; it costs €1 for the next 30min and €2/hr thereafter. Payment is by credit card. If you want to hire a mountain bike, electric bike, scooter or motorbike, try Holiday Bikes, 23 rue de Belgique (☎ 04 93 16 01 62, ⊛ holidaybikes.fr).

**Car rental** Major commercial agencies are based at the airport and *gare SNCF*. You can rent an electric car using the Autobleue rental scheme (⊛ auto-bleue.org). There are 42 rental stations around the city. Registration fee is €25, after which the hourly rate is €8, or €50/day.

## INFORMATION

**Tourist office** At the *gare SNCF* on av Thiers (mid-June to mid-Sept Mon–Sat 8am–8pm, Sun 9am–7pm; mid-Sept to mid-June Mon–Sat 8am–7pm, Sun 10am–5pm; ☎ 0892 707 407, ⊛ en.nicetourisme.com). There are annexes at 5 promenade des Anglais (mid-June to mid-Sept Mon–Sat 8am–8pm, Sun 9am–7pm; mid-Sept to mid-June Mon–Sat 9am–6pm) and at terminal 1 of the airport: (April–Sept daily 9am–8pm; Oct–March Mon–Sat 9am–6pm).

## ACCOMMODATION

Before hunting for accommodation, it's worth taking advantage of the online reservation service on the tourist office website. The area around the station teems with cheap hotels, some of them seedy, though there are a few gems. Sleeping on the beach is illegal and for campsites you'll need to head west to Cagnes sur Mer (see p.908).

### HOTELS

**Les Cigales** 16 rue Dalpozzo ☎ 04 97 03 10 70, ⊛ hotel-lescigales.com. Clean, a/c and renovated three-star hotel 150m from the promenade des Anglais, with soundproofed en-suite rooms with satellite TV and safe, plus a sun terrace for guests. Good value for the price and location. **€99**

★ **Le Floride** 52 bd de Cimiez ☎ 04 93 53 11 02, ⊛ hotel-floride.fr. Clean, friendly, good value two-star hotel in Cimiez, with some spacious en-suite doubles and a few cheap singles with WC and shower. There's no a/c – which might be an issue in high season – but rooms have fans. Private parking. **€67**

**Lépante** 6 rue Lépante ☎ 04 93 62 20 55, ⊛ hotellepante.com. Gay-friendly two-star hotel in a refurbished, central *belle époque* building, with a/c and a first-floor sunny balcony with lots of seating. Decor is traditional, but there's a wide variety of room types and tariffs. **€99**

★ **L'Oasis** 23 rue Gounod ☎ 04 93 88 12 29, ⊛ hotelniceoasis.com. Tucked off the street in a peaceful garden setting, this freshly renovated three-star has nice, upgraded and a/c rooms, secure private parking and an outdoor terrace where you can take breakfast in fine weather. **€109**

---

## THE CHEMINS DE FER DE PROVENCE

The **Chemins de Fer de Provence** runs one of France's most scenic and fun railway routes, from the Gare de Provence on rue Alfred-Binet (4 daily; 3hr 15min). The line runs up the Var valley into the hinterland of Nice to Digne-les-Bains, and climbs through some spectacular scenery as it goes. There are also special steam train excursions on Sundays in summer. For more, see ⊛ trainprovence.com).

**La Pérouse** 11 quai Rauba-Capeu ☏ 04 93 62 34 63, ⓦ hotel-la-perouse.com. The best-situated hotel in central Nice, at the foot of Le Château, and with a rooftop pool and fabulous views over the promenade des Anglais and Baie des Anges. Rooms have marble bathrooms and individually controlled a/c. **€290**

**Le Petit Trianon** 11 rue Paradis ☏ 04 93 87 50 46, ⓦ lepetittrianon.fr. Prettily renovated, in a modern yet slightly frou-frou style that matches the name, these a/c and soundproofed rooms have a great location in an old apartment block in the pedestrian zone close to the beach. **€95**

**Solara** 7 rue de France ☏ 04 93 88 09 96, ⓦ hotelsolara .com. Simple but attractive a/c rooms on the fourth and fifth floors of a building in the pedestrian shopping area close to the beach, accessed by a tiny lift. Rooms on the fifth floor have balconies. Good value and central. **€85**

**Villa Rivoli** 10 rue Rivoli ☏ 04 93 88 80 25, ⓦ villa -rivoli.com. Sweet hotel in a *belle époque* building a short walk from the promenade des Anglais and beach, with refurbished, a/c en-suite rooms with pretty, traditional decor. Some rooms have small balconies; parking is available. **€80**

**Villa la Tour** 4 rue de la Tour ☏ 04 93 80 08 15, ⓦ villa -la-tour.com. The only hotel in the heart of Vieux Nice, with 14 a/c en-suite rooms with satellite TV and safe, including a few with balconies or views over the city. Room styles (and rates) vary quite widely. There's also a roof terrace. **€59**

**Wilson** 39 rue de l'Hotel des Postes ☏ 04 93 85 47 79, ⓦ hotel-wilson-nice.com. A stylish and gay-friendly budget guesthouse on the third floor in a great location, with a quirky fingerprint entry system and individually themed rooms, the cheapest of which have washbasin only. **€45**

**Windsor** 11 rue Dalpozzo ☏ 04 93 88 59 35, ⓦ hotelwindsornice.com. Smart boutique-style and gay-friendly "art hotel" with individually styled rooms,

some with frescoes, and many of them quite striking. There's also a spa with sauna and steam bath, and small pool in a partially shaded garden, overgrown with bamboo. **€128**

**HOSTELS**

**Auberge de Jeunesse Mont Boron** Rte Forestière du Mont-Alban ☏ 04 93 89 23 64, ⓦ fuaj.org. HI hostel 4km from the centre of town, just off the Moyenne Corniche on the forested slopes of Mont Boron. Take bus #14 from J.C. Bermond (direction "place du Mont-Boron", stop "L'Auberge"); the last bus that runs as far as the hostel leaves at 7.30pm. Reception 7am–noon & 5pm–midnight. Rates include breakfast. Closed Nov–May. **€19.60**

**Backpackers Chez Patrick** First floor (there is another hostel downstairs), 32 rue Pertinax ☏ 04 93 80 30 72, ⓦ backpackerschezpatrick.com. Clean, a/c hostel close to the station. There are no cooking facilities but there's a fridge and washing machine, a safe, and no curfew. Accommodation is in four- to six-bed dorms or doubles. Dorms **€30**, doubles **€70**

**La Belle Meunière** 21 av Durante ☏ 04 93 88 66 15, ⓦ bellemeuniere.com. Efficient, clean and friendly backpacker hotel in a lovely old bourgeois house, with accommodation in double, twin, triple or four-bed rooms, or dorms that sleep up to five. There's a laundry service, private parking and a terrace at the front; public areas have recently been spruced up. Dorms **€22**, doubles **€76**

★ **Villa Saint-Exupery Gardens** 22 av Gravier ☏ 04 93 84 42 83, ⓦ vsaint.com. Well-equipped, family-run hostel in an old nunnery, some way out of central Nice, with bar, internet, kitchen and laundry facilities. Tram from Place Masséna direction "Las Planas", stop "Comte de Falicon"; staff will pick you up from there. There's also a sister hostel in the city centre. Dorms **€30**, twins **€90**

**EATING**

**Don Camillo Créations** 5 rue des Ponchettes ☏ 04 93 85 67 95, ⓦ doncamillo-creations.fr. Elegant, modern *restaurant gastronomique* between Vieux Nice and the château, with contemporary Niçois/Italian cooking and dishes like roast langoustines with *cèpes* or foie gras marinated in Sauternes on a €45 *menu*. Tues–Sat noon– 2.30pm & 7–10.30pm.

**L'Escalinada** 22 rue Pairolière ☏ 04 93 62 11 71, ⓦ escalinada.fr. Good Niçois specialities at this old restaurant at the foot of a stepped side-street in Vieux Nice: stuffed sardines with mesclun €15.50, courgette fritters €13, *plats du jour* from €15, *menu* €26. Service is efficient, but occasionally a bit gruff. Daily lunch & dinner.

★ **Fenocchio** 2 place Rossetti ☏ 04 93 80 72 52, ⓦ fenocchio.fr. A firm Vieux Nice favourite, this excellent *glacier* serves a vast range of ice creams, with flavours like

salty caramel, violet or beer sorbet alongside more familiar offerings. On warm nights, skip the restaurant desserts and head here instead. One scoop €2, two €3.50. Daily 9am–midnight.

**Le Festival de la Moule** 20 cours Saleya ☏ 04 93 62 02 12. If you like mussels, come to this unpretentious all-you-can-eat *moules-frites* place on cours Saleya. There are ten sauces to choose from, and a pot is €14.90 with free refills; they also serve pasta and grilled fish. Daily 11am–11pm.

**Le Flaveur** 25 rue Gubernatis ☏ 04 93 62 53 95, ⓦ flaveur .net. Friendly gastro restaurant with creative dishes, such as lobster with green curry and coconut milk or maki-style *jamon Serrano*, that make this a new local favourite. *Menus* €45–70. Tues–Fri lunch and dinner, Sat dinner only.

**Le Frog** 2 rue Milton Robbins ☏ 04 93 85 85 65, ⓦ frog -restaurant.fr. Quirky, trendy little restaurant close to the

**17**

opera serving up inventive variations on classic French cooking, with dishes like duck foie gras with fig ice cream or warm goat's cheese salad with truffles & apple. *Menu* €19 including a glass of wine. Tues–Sun noon–2pm & 7–11pm, Mon 7–11pm.

**Lou Pilha Leva** 10 rue Collet ☎ 04 93 13 99 08. One of a number of places in Vieux Nice where you can try street food *à la niçois* at rock-bottom prices: *socca* costs €2.80, *pissaladière* €3, *petits farcis* €5.70. You can take away or eat at the benches outside. Daily 11am–9.30pm, later in summer.

**Mets and Café** 28 rue Assalit ☎ 04 93 80 30 85. Busy lunchtime-only budget brasserie close to many of the backpacker hostels, serving up traditional French food and with a €9.80 lunchtime *formule*. Mon–Sat 11.30am–3pm.

**Pasta Basta** 18 rue de la Préfecture ☎ 04 93 80 03 57. No-frills pasta place with eleven types of fresh and three dried pasta varieties and a choice of twenty sauces. Pasta from €4.80, sauce from €3.50, and rough wine by the *pichet* from €4. Try the *merda de can* – buckwheat gnocchi. Daily noon–10.30pm.

**Café de Turin & Le Petit Turin** 5 place Garibaldi ☎ 04 93 62 29 52, ⓦcafedeturin.fr. A local institution, the *Café de Turin* has spread into the premises next door so that it dominates one corner of place Garibaldi. The emphasis is on raw seafood, with *panachés* of *fruits de mer* from €34, plus a few shellfish-based cooked options. They don't take reservations, so be prepared to queue. Daily 8am–10pm.

★ **Voyageur Nissart** 19 rue Alsace Lorraine ☎ 04 93 82 19 60, ⓦvoyageurnissart.com. Excellent food like *maman* used to make, in a setting that couldn't be more typically French – chequered tablecloths and all. *Menus* start at €16.50; one focuses on Niçois specialities like *daube* and *petits farcis*. Tues–Fri & Sun noon–2.30pm & 7–10.30pm, Sat 7–10.30pm.

## NIGHTLIFE AND ENTERTAINMENT

Vieux Nice is the centre of Nice's pub and club scene, much of it anglophone in character. As for nightclubs, bouncers judging how much you're going to spend, or exclusive membership lists, are the rule. There are two big casinos – the Casino Ruhl (1 promenade des Anglais; ☎ 04 97 03 12 22) and the Palais de la Méditerranée (15 promenade des Anglais; ☎ 04 92 14 68 21). Nice's lesbian and gay scene is active, and for lesbian and gay visitors the city has a relaxed feel. The annual Pink Parade takes place in early summer. The Mardi Gras Carnival opens the year's events in February (ⓦnicecarnaval .com), with the second week of July taken up by the Nice Jazz Festival (ⓦnicejazzfestival.fr for info).

### BARS

**Blast** 8 place Charles Felix ☎ 04 93 80 00 50. The vast terrace of this lively bar is an ideal vantage point for observing the comings and goings on cours Saleya. There's finger food to soak up the €8.50 cocktails, draught beers start at €4 and bottled Belgian beer at €6.50. Daily from 8pm.

**Juke House Café** 8 rue Defly ☎ 04 93 80 02 22. Tiny, American-style cocktail and tapas bar that draws a young crowd. Happy hour is 6–8pm; otherwise, cocktails cost upwards of €8 and beers start at €3.30. The food menu is a mix of tapas, burgers and salads, and as the name suggests, there's a jukebox. Tues–Sat noon–midnight.

★ **Pulp Fiction Saloon** 7 rue Emmanuel Philibert at place du Pin ☎ 04 93 55 25 35. Stylish new lesbian and gay bar on a corner site in the newly emerging "petit Marais" gay district along rue Bonaparte, with black decor, skull-and-crossbones wallpaper and Philippe Starck "Ghost" chairs on the terrace. Bottled beers €4.50. Tues–Sat noon–12.30pm, Sun & Mon 5–12.30pm.

**The Snug** 22 rue Droite ☎ 04 93 80 43 22, ⓦsnugand cellar.com. Smaller and more low-key than most of Nice's Irish bars, with a friendly, pubby atmosphere, live music on Mondays and Guinness and Kilkenny to drink. *Pression* beer from €2.80; they also serve food, including a Sunday roast. Daily noon–12.30am.

**Wayne's** 15 rue de la Préfecture, ☎ 04 93 13 46 99, ⓦwaynes.fr. This big, boisterous bar is one of the lynchpins of the Vieux Nice nightlife scene, very popular with Anglophone expats and with sport on big-screen TVs plus regular live rock bands. Daily noon–2am.

### CLUBS AND LIVE MUSIC

**Bar Théâtre des Oiseaux** 65 rue de l'Abbaye ☎ 04 93 80 21 93, ⓦbardesoiseaux.com. Named for the birds that once nested in the loft of this bar, which serves Niçois tapas (4 for €10) and cocktails (€7 up). There's also an old-fashioned small cabaret stage. A good place to hear traditional French chanson. Bar Mon–Sat lunch & dinner; theatre Wed & Thurs from 8.30pm, Fri & Sat from 9pm.

**Glam** 6 rue Eugène Emanuel ☎ 06 60 55 26 61, ⓦleglam .org. Nice's liveliest lesbian and gay club, with guest DJs, a dance and pop-oriented music policy and theme nights ranging from bears to underwear. Entry with *conso* €10 Fri, €13 Sat; free on Sun. Fri–Sun 11pm–4.30am.

**High Club** 45 promenade des Anglais ☎ 06 16 95 75 87, ⓦhighclub.fr. Large seafront disco that attracts big-name international DJs and live PAs. There's also an eighties-themed club, *Studio 47*, that targets the over-25s, plus a lesbian and gay-friendly club, *Sk'high*. Expect to pay €10, except for the occasional free nights. Fri–Sun 11.45pm–6am.

★ **Shapko** 5 rue Rossetti ☎ 09 54 94 69 31, ⓦshapko .com. Intimate and friendly Vieux Nice music bar on two levels, with a relaxed crowd and eclectic live music, from slap bass jazz to live electronica, plus Mexican bar food. Wed–Sun 7pm–12.30am.

## DIRECTORY

**Consulates** Canada, 2 place Franklin (☎ 04 93 92 93 22); USA, 7 av Gustave-V (☎ 04 93 88 89 55).
**Health** Riviera Medical Services (English-speaking doctors; ☎ 04 93 26 12 70); Hôpital St-Roch, 5 rue

Pierre-Dévoluy (☎ 04 92 03 33 33).
**Pharmacy** 66 av Jean Médecin (Mon–Sat 24hr, Sun 7pm–8am; ☎ 04 93 62 54 44).
**Police** 1 av Maréchal Foch (☎ 04 92 17 22 22).

# The Corniches

Three **corniche roads** run east from Nice to the independent principality of Monaco and to Menton, the last town of the French Riviera. Each provides a superb means of seeing the most mountainous stretch of the Côte d'Azur. Napoleon built the **Grande Corniche** on the route of the Romans' Via Julia Augusta, and the **Moyenne Corniche** dates from the first quarter of the twentieth century, when aristocratic tourism on the Riviera was already causing congestion on the lower, coastal road, the **Corniche Inférieure**. The upper two are the classic location for car commercials, and for movie car crashes. Real deaths occur too – most notoriously Princess Grace of Monaco – a bitter irony, since the corniches had been the backdrop to one of her greatest film successes, *To Catch a Thief*.

## The Corniche Inférieure

Although buses take all three corniche roads, the train runs only along the lower, **Corniche Inférieure**, and if you don't have your own transport this is the easiest route to take. The attractions include the pretty resorts of **Villefranche-sur-Mer** and **Beaulieu-sur-Mer** and two remarkable villas that hark back to the Riviera's aristocratic heyday.

### Villefranche-sur-Mer

**VILLEFRANCHE-SUR-MER** is on the far side of Mont Alban from Nice. The cruise liners attracted by its beautiful bay can somewhat spoil the ambience, but as long as your visit doesn't coincide with the sudden rush of a shore excursion, the **old town**, with its fishing boats, sixteenth-century citadelle and the covered medieval **rue Obscure** running beneath the houses, is a charming place to while away an afternoon.

#### Chapelle de St-Pierre

Tues–Sun: spring & summer 10am–noon & 3–7pm; autumn & winter 10am–noon & 2–6pm • €2.50

Villefranche's tiny harbour is overlooked by the medieval **Chapelle de St-Pierre**, decorated by Jean Cocteau in 1957 in shades he described as "ghosts of colours". The drawings portray scenes from the life of St Peter and homages to the women of Villefranche and the gypsies. The chapel is used just once a year, on June 29, when fishermen celebrate the feast day of St Peter and St Paul with a Mass.

#### Villa Éphrussi

Saint-Jean-Cap-Ferrat • Mid-Feb to June, Sept & Oct daily 10am–6pm; July & Aug daily 10am–7pm; Nov to mid-Feb Mon–Fri 2–6pm, Sat & Sun 10am–6pm • €12, €18 with Villa Kérylos • ☎ 04 93 01 33 09, ⓦ villa-ephrussi.com

On the main road along the neck of the **Cap Ferrat peninsula**, between Villefranche and Beaulieu, stands the **Villa Éphrussi**, surrounded by elaborate gardens. Built in 1912 for a Rothschild heiress, it overflows with decorative art, paintings, sculpture and artefacts ranging from the fourteenth to the nineteenth centuries, and from European to Far Eastern origins.

#### Villa Kérylos

Impasse Gustave Eiffel, Beaulieu-sur-Mer • Mid-Feb to June, Sept & Oct daily 10am–6pm; July & Aug daily 10am–7pm; Nov–Feb Mon–Fri 2–6pm, Sat & Sun 10am–6pm • €10, €18 with Villa Éphrussi • ☎ 04 93 01 01 44, ⓦ villa-kerylos.com • The villa is a 5min walk from Beaulieu train station

**17**

The main reason to visit attractive, *belle époque* **BEAULIEU-SUR-MER** is the **Villa Kérylos,** a near-perfect reproduction of an ancient Greek villa that's on the seafront, just east of the casino. Théodore Reinach, the archeologist who had it built in 1900, lived here for twenty years, in the manner of an Athenian citizen, taking baths with his male friends and assigning separate suites to women.

## The Moyenne Corniche

Of the three Corniche roads east of Nice, the **Moyenne Corniche** is the most photogenic, a real cliff-hanging, car-chase highway. Eleven kilometres from Nice, the medieval village of **EZE** winds round its conical rock just below the corniche. No other *village perché* is more infested with pseudo-artisans and others catering to rich tourists, and it requires a major mental feat to recall that the tiny vaulted passages and stairways were designed with defence in mind. At the summit, a cactus garden, the **Jardin Exotique** (daily: Feb–March 9am–5pm; April & May 9am–6pm; June & Sept 9am–7pm; July & Aug 9am–7.30pm; Oct 9am–5.30pm; Nov–Jan 9am–4.30pm; €6, €13.50 with Villa Éphrussi; ⒲eze-tourisme.com) covers the site of the former castle.

## The Grande Corniche

At every other turn on the **Grande Corniche**, you're invited to park your car and enjoy a *belvédère*. At certain points, such as **Col d'Eze**, you can turn off upwards for even higher views; bus #82 goes here.

### Trophée des Alpes

Av Albert 1ᵉʳ, La Turbie • Tues–Sun: mid-May to mid-Sept 9.30am–1pm & 2.30–6.30pm; mid-Sept to mid-May 10am–1.30pm & 2.30–5pm • €5.50 • ☎ 04 93 41 20 84, ⒲ monuments-nationaux.fr • Infrequent buses (Mon–Sat; #116) from Nice

Eighteen stunning kilometres from Nice, you reach the village of **LA TURBIE** and its **Trophée des Alpes**, a huge monument raised in 6 BC to celebrate the subjugation of the tribes of Gaul. Originally a statue of Augustus Caesar stood on the 45m-high plinth, which was pillaged, ransacked for building materials and blown up over the centuries. Painstakingly restored in the 1930s, it now stands statueless, 35m high; viewed from a distance, it still looks imperious.

### Roquebrune

As the Grande Corniche descends towards Cap Martin, it passes the eleventh-century castle of **ROQUEBRUNE**, its village nestling round the base of the rock. The **castle** (daily: Jan & Oct–Dec 10am–12.30pm & 2–5pm; Feb–May 10am–12.30pm & 2–6pm; June–Sept 10am–12.30pm & 2–7pm; €4.50) has been kitted out enthusiastically in medieval fashion, while the tiny vaulted passages and stairways of the village are almost too good to be true. One thing that hasn't been restored is the vast millennial **olive tree** that lies just to the east of the village on the chemin de Menton.

### Cap Martin

Southeast of Roquebrune old town is the peninsula of **Cap Martin**, with a **coastal path** giving access to a wonderful shoreline of white rocks, secluded beaches and wind-bent pines. The path is named after **Le Corbusier**, who spent several summers in Roquebrune. He drowned off Cap Martin in 1965 and his grave – designed by himself – is in the **cemetery** (square J near the flagpole), high above the old village.

**ACCOMMODATION AND EATING** THE CORNICHES

**THE CORNICHE INFÉRIEURE**

**La Darse** 32 av du Général de Gaulle ☎ 04 93 01 72 54, ⒲ hoteldeladarse.com. Two-star hotel, west of the train station and near the citadelle and the sea, with renovated a/c rooms, some with sea-facing balconies and some sleeping up to four. Closed mid-Nov to March. **€76**

**La Grignotière** 3 rue du Poilu ☎04 93 76 79 83. An affordable option in Villefranche's old town, with fillet of sea bream Provençal-style or *salade niçoise* on a three-course *menu* (€16) and pizza from €9; otherwise, main courses from around €10. April–Oct daily lunch & dinner.

**Riviera** 6 rue Paul Doumer ☎04 93 01 04 92, ⓦhotel-riviera.fr A tempting, economical option, this family-run three-star hotel is right in the centre, close to the Villa Kérylos and the sea. Tastefully decorated rooms have a/c and double glazing. **€70**

**THE GRANDE CORNICHE**

**Café de la Fontaine** 4 av Général de Gaulle, La Turbie ☎04 93 28 52 79. Excellent bistro on the main road through La Turbie, run by the same team as the two-Michelin-starred *Hostellerie Jérôme* in the old villages and with a chalked-up selection of classic dishes like roast *gigot* of lamb or *daube de boeuf* with carrots; main courses from €15. Daily 7am–midnight.

**Les Deux Frères** Place des Deux Frères, Roquebrune ☎04 93 28 99 00, ⓦlesdeuxfreres.com. The best-located hotel in Roquebrune village, worth booking in advance to try to get a sea-view room; there are just nine a/c rooms, varying widely in style and price. The hotel also has a good restaurant with €28 and €48 *menus*. Restaurant Tues–Sat noon–1.30pm & 7.30–9.30pm, Sun noon–1.30pm. **€75**

# Monaco

Viewed from a distance, there's no mistaking the cluster of towers that is **MONACO**. Postwar redevelopment rescued the tiny principality from economic decline but elbowed aside much of its previous prettiness – not for nothing was **Prince Rainier**, who died in 2005, known as the Prince Bâtisseur ("Prince Builder"). This tiny state, no bigger than London's Hyde Park, retains its comic opera independence: it has been in the hands of the autocratic Grimaldi family since the thirteenth century, and in theory would become part of France were the royal line to die out. It is home to six thousand British expats – including Roger Moore and Shirley Bassey – out of a total population of around 36,000. Along with its wealth, Monaco latterly acquired a reputation for wheeler-dealer **sleaze**. On his accession in 2005, the US-educated Prince Albert II set about trying to get the principality off an OECD list of uncooperative tax havens, declaring he no longer wished Monaco to be known – in the words of Somerset Maugham – as "a sunny place for shady people".

The oldest part of the principality is **Monaco-Ville**, around the palace on the rocky promontory, with the **Fontvieille** marina in its western shadow. **La Condamine** is the old port on the other side of the promontory; the ugly bathing resort of **Larvotto** extends to the eastern border; and **Monte-Carlo** is in the middle.

One time not to visit is during the Formula 1 **Monaco Grand Prix** in May – no viewpoint is accessible without a ticket and prices soar to ridiculous levels.

## Monte-Carlo

**MONTE-CARLO** is where the real money is flung about, and its famous **casino** demands to be seen. Adjoining it is the gaudy **opera house**, and around the palm-tree-lined place du Casino are more casinos, palace-hotels and *grands cafés*. The American Bar of the **Hôtel de Paris** is *the* place for the elite to meet, while the turn-of-the-twentieth-century **Hermitage** has a beautiful Gustave Eiffel iron-and-glass dome.

### Casino de Monte-Carlo

Place du Casino • **Salons Européens** Open from 2pm • €10 **Salons Privés** May & June Fri & Sat from 8pm; July & Aug Mon–Fri daily from 8pm • €20 • ☎ +377 98 06 21 75, ⓦmontecarlocasinos.com • Bus #1, #2 or #6

Entrance to **Casino de Monte-Carlo** is restricted to over-18s and you may have to show

---

**PHONING MONACO**

Monaco's international code is 00377 and numbers have eight digits (omit 0 when dialling from outside the principality).

**17**

your passport; dress code is rigid, with shorts and T-shirts frowned upon, though most visitors are scarcely the last word in designer chic. Skirts, jackets and ties are obligatory for the more interesting sections. Bags and large coats are checked at the door. The first gambling hall is the **Salons Européens** where slot machines surround the American roulette, craps and blackjack tables, the managers are Vegas-trained and the lights are low. Above this slice of Nevada, however, the decor is *fin-de-siècle* Rococo extravagance, while the ceilings in the adjoining Pink Salon Bar are adorned with female nudes smoking cigarettes. The heart of the place is the **Salons Privés**. To get in, you have to look like a gambler. Rather larger and more richly decorated than the European Rooms, the atmosphere is of intense concentration.

### Villa Sauber

17 av Princesse Grace • Daily: June–Sept 11am–7pm; Oct–May 10am–6pm • €6 • ☎ +377 98 98 91 26, ⓦ nmnm.mc

The **Villa Sauber** is one of the few surviving *belle époque* villas in the principality, set amid concrete apartment blocks. It comprises one half of the **Nouveau Musée National**, and presents interesting temporary art exhibitions, often on Monaco-related themes.

## Monaco-Ville

The old town of **MONACO-VILLE** (bus #1 or #2) has been spared the developers' worst. On place du Palais you can watch the **changing of the guard** at 11.55am, then take a self-guided tour around the Lilliputian **Palais Princier** (April–Oct daily 10am–6pm; €8;

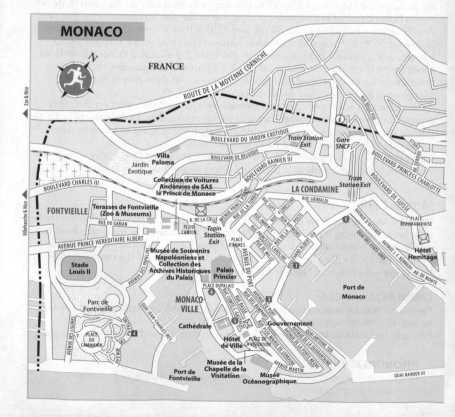

+377 93 25 18 31, palais.mc) – the voice on the audioguide is Prince Albert himself. Afterwards, examine Napoleonic relics at the **Musée des Souvenirs Napoléoniens et Collection des Archives Historiques du Palais** on the same square (Jan–April & Dec 10.30am–5pm; May–Oct 10am–6.15pm; €4); see the tombs of Prince Rainier and Princess Grace in the nineteenth-century **cathedral** (daily 8.30am–6/7pm; free) and even watch "Monaco the movie", at the **Monte-Carlo Story** on the Parking des Pêcheurs (on the hour: Jan–June & Sept–Nov 2–5pm; July & Aug 2–6pm; €8; monaco-memory.com).

## Musée de la Chapelle de la Visitation
Place de la Visitation • Tues–Sun 10am–4pm • €3 • +377 93 500 700

The **Musée de la Chapelle de la Visitation** displays part of Barbara Piasecka Johnson's collection of religious art, a small but exquisite collection including works by Zurbarán, Rubens and Vermeer. It's well worth a visit.

## Musée Océanographique
Av Saint-Martin • Daily: April–June & Sept 9.30am–7pm; July & Aug 9.30am–7.30pm; Oct–March 10am–6pm • €14 • +377 93 15 36 00, oceano.org

One of Monaco's best sights is the aquarium in the basement of the imposing **Musée Océanographique**, where the fishy beings outdo the weirdest Kandinsky or Hieronymus Bosch creations. A serious scientific institution as well as a visitor attraction, the museum celebrated its centenary in 2010.

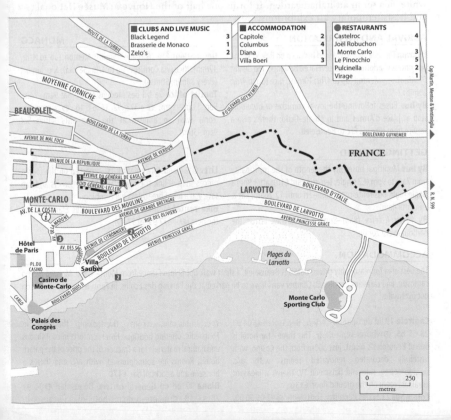

**17**

# Fontvieille

**FONTVIEILLE**, below the rock of Monaco-Ville, has a number of interesting museums: the **Musée Naval** (daily 10am–6pm; €4), containing 250 model ships; the **zoo** (March–May 10am–noon & 2–6pm; June–Sept 9am–noon & 2–7pm; Oct–Feb 10am–noon & 2–5pm; €5), with exotic birds, hippopotamuses and lemurs; and the museum of stamps and coins, the **Musée des Timbres et des Monnaies** (daily: July & Aug 9.30am–6pm; Sept–June 9.30am–5pm; €3; ⓦ oetp-monaco.com), which has rare stamps, money and commemorative medals dating back to 1640.

## Collection de Voitures Anciennes de SAS le Prince de Monaco

Les Terrasses de Fontvieille • Daily 10am–6pm • €6 • ☎ +377 92 05 28 56

**The Collection de Voitures Anciennes de SAS le Prince de Monaco** is an enjoyable miscellany of old and not-so-old cars, with everything from a 1928 Hispano-Suiza worthy of Cruella de Ville to Princess Grace's elegant 1959 Renault Florida Coupé.

## Jardin Exotique and around

62 bd du Jardin-Exotique • Daily: mid-May to mid-Sept 9am–7pm; mid-Sept to mid-May 9am–6pm or dusk • €7 • ☎ +377 93 15 29 80, ⓦ jardin-exotique.mc • Bus #2

High above Fontvieille there are breathtaking panoramas of the coast as far as Italy from the **Jardin Exotique**, where cacti and succulents alternate with mineral-rich caverns. Close by is the Villa Paloma, 56 bd du Jardin-Exotique (daily: June–Sept 11am–7pm; Oct–May 10am–6pm; €6; ☎ +377 98 98 48 60, ⓦ nmnm.mc), a dazzling white villa set in an Italian garden. It forms one half of the **Nouveau Musée National**, and hosts temporary art exhibitions.

### ARRIVAL AND INFORMATION

**By train** The *gare SNCF* is wedged between bd Rainier III and bd Princess Charlotte and has several exits, signposted clearly. **Destinations** Menton (up to 4/hr; 10min); Nice (up to 4/hr; 20min).

**By bus** Buses following the lower corniche or *autoroute* stop at place d'Armes and in Monte-Carlo; there's also a service from Nice via Èze to Beausoleil.

**Destinations** Èze (6 daily; 15min); Menton (up to 4/hr; 42min); Nice (via Corniche, up to 4/hr; 58min); Nice airport (every 30min; 50min).

**Tourist office** 2a bd des Moulins (Mon–Sat 9am–7pm, Sun 11am–1pm; ☎ +377 92 16 61 16, ⓦ visitmonaco .com) with an annexe at the *gare SNCF* (Tues–Sat 9am–5pm).

### GETTING AROUND

**By bus** Municipal buses ply the length of the principality from 7am to 9pm (€2 single; ten-trip card €10); after 9pm a single night bus route runs (Mon–Fri until 12.20am; Sat & Sun until 4am).

**By ferry** A ferry (8am–8pm; €2) shuttles across the harbour every 20min.

**Lifts** Clean and convenient lifts – marked on the tourist office's map – link the lower and higher streets and can save you a lot of breathless hill climbing.

**Bike rental** Monte-Carlo-Rent, quai des États-Unis, on the port (☎ +377 99 99 97 79).

### ACCOMMODATION

The best area for reasonably priced hotels is Beausoleil, a short walk uphill into France from Monte-Carlo. Monaco has no campsite, and caravans are illegal. Camper vans have to be parked at the Parking des Écoles, in Fontvieille, and even then not overnight.

**Capitole** 19 bd du Général-Leclerc, Beausoleil ☎ 04 93 28 65 65, ⓦ whotel-capitole.fr. This three-star hotel is one of Beausoleil's nicest, just 300m from the Casino, with tastefully decorated renovated rooms with a/c, soundproofing, safe and flatscreen TV. There's a pleasant breakfast room on the ground floor. **€130**

**Colombus** 23 av des Papalins, Fontvieille ☎ 92 05 90 00,

ⓦ columbusmonaco.com. Overlooking the sea in Fontvieille, offering boutique hotel comforts in cool shades and natural materials for a fraction of the price of the palace hotels. Rooms are soundproofed, with a/c, and there's a brasserie and a cocktail bar. **€170**

**Diana** 17 bd du Général-Leclerc, Beausoleil ☎ 04 93 78 47 58, ⓦ monte-carlo.mc/hotel-diana-beausoleil.

The least expensive option in Beausoleil. It's a little tired, but it's soundproofed and has a/c and it's very close to Monte-Carlo's sights. Cheapest rooms have washbasin and bidet but no WC. **€50**

**Villa Boeri** 29 bd du Général-Leclerc, Beausoleil

☏ 04 93 78 38 10, ⊚ hotelboeri.com. Cheerful Beausoleil cheapie almost hidden behind a screen of oleander, with a nice shady terrace. The a/c rooms are soundproofed, with satellite TV and bath or shower and WC. **€78**

## EATING AND DRINKING

**Castelroc** Place du Palais ☏ +377 93 30 36 68, ⊚ restaurant-castelroc.com. Opposite the Palais Princier with a terrace overlooking Fontvieille, this smart restaurant isn't cheap, but it's a good place to sample traditional Monegasque dishes like *barbajuans* – samosa-like triangles stuffed with Swiss chard and cheese. Mains €25. Feb, March & Oct to mid-Dec daily noon–3pm; April–Sept Sun–Fri noon–3pm.

**Joël Robuchon Monte Carlo** *Hôtel Metropole*, 4 av de la Madone ☏ +377 93 15 15 10, ⊚ metropole.com. The inventive, refined Mediterranean-accented cooking of this two-Michelin-starred restaurant is under the aegis of one of France's most respected chefs. It may not be the very grandest dining room in the principality, but it's pretty close. Lunch €49–79, Discovery *menu* €119. Daily 12.15–2pm & 7.30–11pm.

**Le Pinocchio** 30 rue Comte-Félix-Gastaldi ☏ +377 93 30 96 20. A reliable, good-value Italian in a narrow street

in Monaco-Ville dishing up hearty portions from a long menu of antipasti and pasta, including *vitello tonnato* with salad for €15 and penne *alla sorrentina* for €13. Feb–Dec daily until 11.30pm.

**Pulcinella** 17 rue du Portier ☏ +377 93 30 73 61, ⊚ pulcinella.mc. Traditional Italian restaurant between the Casino and Larvotto beach. The view – of a motorway flyover – isn't the best, but the food is relatively good value for the location. *Salade niçoise* €15, risotto with *cèpes* €18; more elaborate dishes include breaded veal Milanese and roast sea bass. Daily noon–2pm & 7.30–11pm.

**Virage** 1 quai Albert 1ᵉʳ ☏ +377 93 50 77 21, ⊚ virage .mc. Light-flooded, glassy modern restaurant on the port, serving simple bistro-type food including salads, risotto and fish: *fritti misto* with tartare sauce or roast chicken with five spices, for example. Around €21 or more. Daily noon–11.30pm & for Sun brunch 11.30am–5pm.

## DRINKING AND NIGHTLIFE

**Black Legend** Rte de la Piscine ☏ +377 93 30 09 09, ⊚ black-legend.com. A portside restaurant and lounge bar that morphs into a disco and live music venue as the evening progresses, with an emphasis on black American music. DJ sets nightly from 7.30–11.30pm in summer, after which the club proper gets going – until 5am.

**Brasserie de Monaco** 36 rte de la Piscine ☏ +377 97 98 51 20, ⊚ brasseriedemonaco.com. Situated on the port and with Monaco's only beer brewed on the premises – including wheat beers and amber ale – this

smart place is often guested by internationally known DJs and there are occasional live bands. Pints €7. Daily 11am–5am.

**Zelo's** 10 av Princesse Grace, atop the Grimaldi Forum ☏ +377 99 99 25 50, ⊚ zelosworld.com. Stylish combination of a restaurant, lounge, DJ bar and disco, with a sea-facing terrace and plush interior complete with chandeliers. Occasional sets from internationally known DJs. Daily 6–9pm for a light food menu; club continues until 2.30am.

# Menton

Of all the Côte d'Azur resorts, **MENTON**, ringed by mountains, is the warmest and most Italianate, being right on the border. In 1861 a British doctor, James Henry Bennet, published a treatise on the benefits of Menton's mild climate to tuberculosis patients, and soon thousands of well-heeled sufferers were flocking here in the vain hope of a cure. Menton's biggest event of the year is the **Fête du Citron** in February, when the lemon-flavoured bacchanalia includes processions of floats decorated entirely with the fruit.

## Musée Jean Cocteau Collection Séverin Wunderman

2 quai de Monléon · Daily except Tues 10am–6pm · €6 for museum and bastion; temporary exhibitions €5, combi ticket for all €8 · ☏ 04 89 81 52 50, ⊚ museecocteaumenton.fr

The **promenade du Soleil** runs along the pebbly beachfront of the Baie du Soleil, stretching from the quai Napoléon-III past the casino towards Roquebrune. The most

**17**

---

### THE GARDENS OF GARAVAN

A trip to the luxuriant **gardens** of **Garavan**'s villas makes a pleasant break from the beach.

**Les Colombières** North of bd de Garavan. The best of Garavan's gardens, privately owned, and designed by the artist Ferdinand Bac between 1918 and 1927. Ask at the tourist office about summer tours or contact Service du Patrimoine (☎04 92 10 97 10).

**Fontana Rosa** Av Blasco-Ibañez ☎04 92 41 76 95. The former home of the Spanish author Vincente Blasco-Ibañez, bright with ceramic decoration. Guided tours Mon & Fri 10am; €6.

---

diverting building is the striking new structure opened in 2011 to house the **Musée Jean Cocteau Collection Séverin Wunderman,** which exhibits all facets of the polymath artist's work from before World War I to the 1950s; it also mounts temporary exhibitions. You can also visit the seventeenth-century bastion by the quai Napoléon-III nearby, restored according to Cocteau's plans between 1958 and 1963. It contains ceramics and pictures of his Mentonaise lovers in the *Inamorati* series.

## Église St-Michel and around

Parvis de la Basilique St-Michel • Mon–Fri 10am–noon & 3–5.15pm, Sat & Sun 3–5.15pm

As the *quai* bends around the western end of the Baie de Garavan from the Cocteau museum, a long flight of pebbled steps leads up into the **vieille ville** to the **Parvis de la Basilique**, an attractive Italianate square hosting concerts in summer and giving a good view out over the bay. The frontage of the **Église St-Michel** proclaims its Baroque supremacy in perfect pink-and-yellow proportions; climbing a few steps further will reward you with the beautiful facade of the **chapel of the Pénitents-Blancs** in apricot and white (the chapel can be visited in summer as part of a guided tour; contact tourist office for details).

## The crumbling cemetery

Daily: May–Sept 7am–8pm; Oct–April 7am–6pm; free

Menton's crumbling **cemetery** at the top of the old town on the site of the town's château, is hauntingly sad – many of the young tuberculosis sufferers who ended their days in Menton are buried here – but also bewitchingly beautiful, with views along the coast into Italy.

## Palais Carnolès

3 av de la Madone • Daily except Tues 10am–noon & 2–6pm • Free • Bus #7

An impressive collection of paintings from the Middle Ages to the twentieth century are displayed in the **Palais Carnolès**, the old summer residence of the princes of Monaco. Of the early works, the *Madonna and Child with St Francis* by Louis Bréa is exceptional. The most recent include canvases by Graham Sutherland, who spent some of his final years in Menton.

### ARRIVAL AND INFORMATION                                    MENTON

**By train** Menton's *gare SNCF* is at the end of av de la Gare, off av de Verdun/ Boyer, a broad double boulevard that bisects the modern part of town.
Destinations Monaco (every 15–30min; 11min); Nice (every 15–30min; 35min).

**By bus** The *gare routière* is north of the *gare SNFC* on av de Sospel, which is the northern continuation of av de Verdun.

Destinations Monaco (up to 5/hr; 32min); Nice (up to 5/hr; 1hr 30min); Nice airport (hourly; 1hr).

**Tourist office** 8 av Boyer (mid-Sept to June Mon–Sat 8.30am–12.30pm & 2–6pm, Sun 9am–12.30pm; July to mid-Sept daily 9am–7pm; ☎04 92 41 76 76, ⓦtourisme-menton.fr).

## ACCOMMODATION

**Camping St-Michel** 1 rte des Ciappes ☎04 93 35 81 23, ⓦwww.hotelmenton.fr/hotel-menton/menton-camping-saint-michel. Menton's municipal campsite sits in an olive grove overlooking the town. It's a gruelling walk uphill, so take the bus (#6 via les Ciappes or #903) from the *gare routière*. No bookings. Closed mid-Oct to March, except for the Fête du Citron. **€19.80**

★**Lemon** 10 rue Albert-1er ☎04 93 28 63 63, ⓦhotel-lemon.com. Newly renovated budget hotel a couple of minutes' walk from the train station, run by a friendly young couple. Simple but modern en-suite rooms, and a pretty garden. A good choice at the price. **€59**

**Moderne** 1 cours George V ☎04 93 57 20 02, ⓦhotel-moderne-menton.com. Good-value two-star between the *gare SNCF* and the tourist office. The a/c and soundproofed rooms have cable TV; some have balconies. The decor isn't as up-to-the-minute as the name might suggest, but it's comfortable enough. **€90**

**Napoléon** 29 porte de France, Baie de Garavan ☎04 93 35 89 50, ⓦnapoleon-menton.com. Menton's smartest hotel is modern, friendly and right on the seafront between the old town and Italian border, with understated contemporary decor, a private beach, and an ice-cream parlour 100m from the hotel, and a bar and pool on site. **€175**

## EATING AND DRINKING

**Le Bruit qui Court** 31 quai Bonaparte ☎04 93 35 94 64, ⓦlebruitquicourt.fr. Foie gras is a speciality at this smart restaurant facing the port and plage des Sablettes, but there's a lot of fish on offer too – John Dory with béarnaise sauce, grilled salmon with fennel – plus lamb with *herbes de Provence*. Menu €23. Wed–Sat noon–1.30pm & 7pm–late, Tues 7pm–late.

**Côté Sud** 15–17 quai Bonaparte ☎04 93 84 03 69. One of the more promising budget options facing the port, with stylish modern decor, a vast selection of pizzas from €7.50, pasta from €9.50 and main course salads around €11; meat or fish mains from around €14.50. Daily 7am–midnight.

**Mirazur** 30 av Aristide Briand ☎04 92 41 86 86, ⓦmirazur.fr. Rising culinary star Mauro Colagreco has bagged two Michelin stars for this swish 1930s-style dining room by the Italian border; it's one of the Riviera's hottest culinary tickets. Three courses €85; €29 two-course weekday lunch. Mid-July to Aug Tues–Sun 7.15–10pm, Sat & Sun noon–3pm; Sept to mid-July Wed–Sun noon–3pm & 7.15–10pm.

# Corsica

CAMPOMORO, GOLFE DE VALINCO

# Corsica

More than three million people visit Corsica each year, drawn by the mild climate and some of the most diverse landscapes in all Europe. Nowhere in the Mediterranean has beaches finer than the island's perfect half-moon bays of white sand and transparent water, or seascapes more dramatic than the red porphyry Calanches of the west coast. Even though the annual visitor influx now exceeds the island's population nearly ten times over, tourism hasn't spoilt the place: there are a few resorts, but overdevelopment is rare and high-rise blocks are confined to the main towns.

**Bastia**, capital of the north, was the principal Genoese stronghold, and its fifteenth-century citadelle has survived almost intact. It's a purely Corsican city, and commerce rather than tourism is its main concern. Also relatively undisturbed, the northern Cap Corse harbours inviting sandy coves and fishing villages such as **Macinaggio** and **Centuri-Port**. Within a short distance of Bastia, the fertile region of the Nebbio contains a scattering of churches built by Pisan stoneworkers, the prime example being the Cathédral de Santa Maria Assunta at the appealingly chic little port of **St-Florent**.

To the west of here, **L'Île-Rousse** and **Calvi**, the latter graced with an impressive citadelle and fabulous sandy beach, are major targets for holiday-makers. The spectacular **Scandola nature reserve** to the southwest of Calvi is most easily visited by boat from the tiny resort of **Porto**, from where walkers can also strike into the wild **Gorges de Spelunca**. **Corte**, at the heart of Corsica, is the best base for exploring the mountains and gorges of the interior which form part of the **Parc Naturel Régional** that runs almost the entire length of the island.

Sandy beaches and rocky headlands punctuate the west coast all the way down to **Ajaccio**, Napoleon's birthplace and the island's capital, where pavement cafés and palm-lined boulevards teem with tourists in summer. Slightly fewer make it to nearby **Filitosa**, greatest of the many prehistoric sites scattered across the south. **Propriano**, the area's principal resort, lies close to stern **Sartène**, former seat of the wild feudal lords who once ruled this region and still the quintessential Corsican town.

More megalithic sites lie south of Sartène on the way to **Bonifacio**, a comb of ancient buildings perched atop furrowed white cliffs at the southern tip of the island. Equally popular, **Porto-Vecchio** provides a springboard for excursions to the amazing beaches of the south. The eastern plain has less to boast of, but the Roman site at **Aléria** is worth a visit for its excellent museum.

## Brief history

Set on the western Mediterranean trade routes, Corsica has always been of strategic and commercial appeal. Greeks, Carthaginians and Romans came in successive waves, driving native Corsicans into the interior. The Romans were ousted by Vandals, and for the following thirteen centuries the island was attacked, abandoned, settled and sold as

GORGES DE LA RESTONICA

# Highlights

**❶ Plage de Saleccia** Soft white shell sand, turquoise water and barely a building in sight. See **p.947**

**❷ Calvi** Corsica's hallmark resort, framed by snow peaks and a spectacular blue gulf. See **p.949**

**❸ The GR20** Gruelling 170km footpath, which takes in spectacular mountain scenery – but is only for the fit. See **p.952**

**❹ Girolata** The last fishing village on the island still inaccessible by road, set against a backdrop of red cliffs and dense maquis. See **p.954**

**❺ Les Calanches de Piana** A mass of terracotta-red porphyry, eroded into dogs' heads, witches and devils. See **p.958**

**❻ Filitosa menhirs** Among the Western Mediterranean's greatest archeological treasures, unique for their carved faces. See **p.969**

**❼ Boat trips from Bonifacio** Catch a *navette* from the harbour visited by Odysseus for imposing views of the famous chalk cliffs and *haute ville*. See **p.977**

**❽ Corte** A nationalist stronghold, with loads of eighteenth-century charm and a rugged mountain setting. See **p.981**

**HIGHLIGHTS ARE MARKED ON THE MAP ON P.934**

a nation state, with generations of islanders fighting against foreign government. In 1768 France bought Corsica from Genoa, but nearly two-and-half centuries of French rule have had a limited effect and the island's Baroque churches, Genoese fortresses, fervent Catholic rituals and a Tuscan-influenced indigenous language and cuisine show a more profound affinity with Italy.

Corsica's uneasy relationship with the mainland has worsened in recent decades. Economic neglect and the French government's reluctance to encourage Corsican language and culture spawned a nationalist movement in the early 1970s, whose clandestine armed wing – the FLNC (Fronte di Liberazione Nazionale di a Corsica) – and its various offshoots have been engaged ever since in a bloody conflict with the state. The violence seldom affects tourists but signs of the "troubles" are everywhere, from the graffiti-sprayed road signs to the bullet holes plastering public buildings.

Relations between the island's hardline nationalists and Paris may be perennially fraught, but there's little support among ordinary islanders for total independence. Bankrolled by Paris and Brussels, Corsica is the most heavily subsidized region of France. Moreover, Corsicans are exempt from social security contributions and the island as a whole enjoys preferential tax status, with one-third of the permanent population employed in the public sector. Increasingly, nationalist violence is seen as biting the hand that feeds it.

Opinion, however, remains divided on the best way forward for the island. While the centre-Right UMP (Union Pour un Mouvement Populaire) party pushes for an all-out promotion of tourism as a socio-economic cure-all, local nationalist groups resist large-scale development, claiming it will irrevocably damage the pristine environment visitors come to enjoy. Such opposition achieved resounding popular support in the territorial elections of 2010, in which the nationalists gained an historic 35 percent of the vote thanks largely to their anti-development policies. This, however, was not enough to win them control of L'Assemblée Corse, which went by a narrow margin to Paul Giacobbi's centre-Left coalition.

**18**

---

## THE FOOD AND DRINK OF CORSICA

It's the herbs – thyme, marjoram, basil, fennel and rosemary – of the maquis (the dense, scented scrub covering lowland Corsica) that lend the island's cuisine its distinctive aromas.

You'll find the best **charcuterie** in the hills of the interior, where pork is smoked and cured in the cold cellars of village houses – it's particularly tasty in Castagniccia, where wild pigs feed on the chestnuts which were once the staple diet of the locals. Here you can also taste chestnut fritters (*fritelli a gaju frescu*) and chestnut porridge (*pulenta*) sprinkled with sugar or eau de vie. **Brocciu**, a soft mozzarella-like cheese made with ewe's milk, is found everywhere on the island, forming the basis for many dishes, including omelettes and cannelloni. *Fromage corse* is also very good – a hard **cheese** made in the sheep- and goat-rearing central regions, where *cabrettu à l'istrettu* (kid stew) is a speciality.

**Game** – mainly stews of hare and wild boar but also roast woodcock, partridge and wood pigeon – features throughout the island's mountain and forested regions. Here blackbirds (*merles*) are made into a fragrant pâté, and eel and trout are fished from the unpolluted rivers. **Sea fish** like red mullet (*rouget*), bream (*loup de mer*) and a great variety of shellfish is eaten along the coast – the best crayfish (*langouste*) comes from around the Golfe de St-Florent, whereas oysters (*huîtres*) and mussels (*moules*) are a speciality of the eastern plain.

Corsica produces some excellent, and still little-known, **wines**, mostly from indigenous vine stocks that yield distinctive, herb-tinged aromas. Names to look out for include: Domaine Torraccia (Porto-Vecchio); Domaine Fiumicicoli (Sartène); Domaine Saparale (Sartène); Domaine Gentille (Patrimonio); Domaine Leccia (Patrimomio); and Venturi-Pieretti (Cap Corse). In addition to the usual whites, reds and rosés, the latter also makes the sweet muscat for which Cap Corse was renowned in previous centuries. Another popular aperitif is the drink known as Cap Corse, a fortified wine flavoured with quinine and herbs. Note that **tap water** is particularly good quality in Corsica, coming from the fresh mountain streams.

**18**

## GETTING THERE

### BY FERRY

The French company, SNCM – along with its freight subsidiary CMN – dominates ferry services to Corsica. In addition, two smaller operators – Corsica Ferries and La Méridionale – run services from Nice, Marseille and Toulon to Calvi, L'Île Rousse, Ajaccio, Propriano and Bastia. Crossings take between seven and twelve hours on a regular ferry, and from two and a half to three and a half hours on the giant hydrofoil ("NGV", or *navire à grande vitesse*).

**Fares** Fares fluctuate according to the season, with the lowest between October and May; during July and August ticket prices more than quadruple. A one-way crossing for a foot passenger costs anything from €10 to €125 per person, plus €60 to €285 per vehicle, depending on the date of the journey.

**Tickets** You can book SNCM and CNM tickets via their central reservation desk (☎ 08 36 67 95 00, ⓦ www.sncm.fr). For Corsica Ferries contact ☎ 04 95 32 95 95/ⓦ corsica-ferries.co.uk, or for La Méridionale ☎ 08 10 20 13 20, ⓦ lameridionale.fr. Note that reservations are essential for journeys in July and August.

### BY AIR

Direct flights to Corsica depart from several major French cities, including Paris, Marseille, Lyon and Nice. The largest operators are Air France (ⓦ airfrance.fr) and Air Corsica (ⓦ aircorsica.com), who fly to Bastia, Ajaccio, Calvi and Figari year round. In addition, easyJet (ⓦ easyjet.com) fly daily from Paris to Bastia and Ajaccio, and XL Airways (ⓦ www .xlairways.com) fly to Figari during the summer season.

**Fares** Return fares start at around €100 low season with easyJet, and peak at around €400 for weekend departures with Air France in July and August.

## GETTING AROUND

### BY CAR

With public transport woefully inadequate, the most convenient way of getting around Corsica is by rental car. All the big firms have offices at airports and towns across the island, allowing you to collect and return vehicles in different places. Even if your budget won't stretch to a week, it's worth renting for a couple of days to explore remote beaches and the back roads of the interior.

### BY BUS

Bus services are fairly frequent between Bastia, Corte and Ajaccio, and along the east coast from Bastia to Porto-Vecchio and Bonifacio. Elsewhere in the island, services tend to peter out in the winter months or are relatively infrequent. Getting accurate timetable information for bus services can also be difficult – the best way to check information is at a tourist office or, better still, online at ⓦ corsicabus.org.

**Fares and timetables** Prices are reasonable: tickets for the 3hr trip between Bastia and Ajaccio cost €21. Rundowns of journey times and frequencies appear in the relevant accounts throughout this chapter.

### BY TRAIN

Corsica's diminutive train, the *Micheline* or *Trinighellu* (little train; ⓦ ter-sncf.com), rattles through the mountains from Ajaccio to Bastia via Corte, with a branch line running northwest to Calvi. At the time of writing, schedules were badly disrupted after a new batch of locomotives had been removed from service only a couple of years after their introduction, due to premature wear on their wheels – though the new trains should, all being well, be back in service again by the time you read this.

**Fares and timetables** At €22.60 for a single journey between Bastia and Ajaccio, fares are a tiny bit pricier than travelling the same route by bus. Again, the latest timetable information and fares appear on ⓦ corsicabus.org.

# Bastia and around

The dominant tone of Corsica's most successful commercial town, **BASTIA**, is one of charismatic dereliction, as the city's industrial zone is spread onto the lowlands to the south, leaving the centre of town with plenty of aged charm. The old quarter, known as the Terra Vecchia, comprises a tightly packed network of haphazard streets, flamboyant Baroque churches and lofty tenements, their crumbling golden-grey walls set against a backdrop of maquis-covered hills.

The city dates from Roman times, when a base was set up at Biguglia to the south, beside a freshwater lagoon. Little remains of the former colony, but the site merits a day-trip for the well-preserved pair of Pisan churches at Mariana, rising from the southern fringes of Poretta airport. Bastia began to thrive under the Genoese, when wine was exported to the Italian mainland from Porto Cardo, forerunner of Bastia's Vieux Port, or Terra Vecchia. Despite the fact that in 1811 Napoleon appointed Ajaccio capital of the island, initiating a rivalry between the two towns which exists to this day, Bastia soon established a stronger

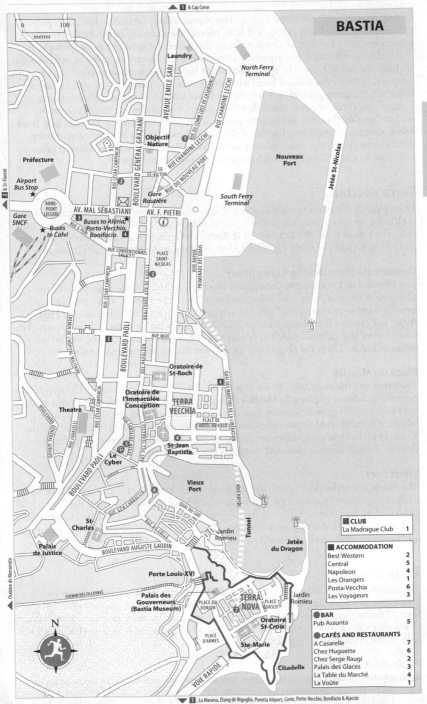

**BASTIA**

Laundry

North Ferry
Terminal

AVENUE EMILE SARI

RUE DU COMM LUCE DE CASABLANCA

RUE CHANOINE LESCHI

Objectif
Nature

BOULEVARD GÉNÉRAL GRAZIANI

RUE CHANOINE LESCHI

RUE CÉSAR CAMPINCHI

SQ
ST-VICTOR

RUE CHANOINE LESCHI

Nouveau
Port

Préfecture

RUE DU NOUVEAU PORT

Jetée St-Nicolas

Airport
Bus Stop

ROND-
POINT
LECLERC

AV. MAL SÉBASTIANI

Gare
Routière

South Ferry
Terminal

Gare
SNCF

RUE G PERI

AV. F. PIETRI

Buses to
Aléria,
Porto-Vecchio,
Bonifacio

Buses
to Calvi

PLACE
SAINT-
NICOLAS

RUE CONVENTIONNEL
SALICETI

PROMENADE DES QUAIS

VOIE RAPIDE

BOULEVARD PAOLI

RUE CÉSAR CAMPINCHI

BOULEVARD GÉN RAP

RUE MIOT

RUE NAPOLEON

CHEMIN DE L'HOPITAL MILITAIRE

Oratoire de
St-Roch

QUAI DES MARTYRS DE LA LIBÉRATION

Oratoire de
l'Immaculée
Conception

TERRA
VECCHIA

Theatre

BOULEVARD GÉNÉRAL GIRAUD

RUE CÉSAR CAMPINCHI

RUE FAVALELLI

RUE DES TERRASSES

PLACE DE
HÔTEL DE VILLE

St-Jean
Baptiste

Le
Cyber

@

BOULEVARD PAOLI

Vieux
Port

VOIE RAPIDE

St-
Charles

RUE GEN CARBUCCIA

Jardin
Romieu

QUAI DU SUD

RUE DE LA COLLE

Palais
de Justice

BOULEVARD AUGUSTE GAUDIN

Jetée
du Dragon

Tunnel

Oratoire de Monserato

Porte Louis-XVI

CHEMIN DES FILLIPINES

Palais des
Gouverneurs
(Bastia Museum)

PLACE DU
DONJON

TERRA
NOVA

PLACE
GUASCO

Jardin
Romieu

Oratoire
St-Croix

PLACE
D'ARMES

Ste-Marie

N

Citadelle

VOIE RAPIDE

0    100
metres

▲ 1 & Cap Corse

◀ 2 & St-Florent

▼ 1 , La Marana, Étang de Biguglia, Poretta Airport, Corte, Porto-Vecchio, Bonifacio & Ajaccio

| **CLUB** | |
| --- | --- |
| La Madrague Club | 1 |

| **ACCOMMODATION** | |
| --- | --- |
| Best Western | 2 |
| Central | 5 |
| Napoleon | 4 |
| Les Orangers | 1 |
| Posta-Vecchia | 6 |
| Les Voyageurs | 3 |

| **BAR** | |
| --- | --- |
| Pub Assunta | 5 |

| **CAFÉS AND RESTAURANTS** | |
| --- | --- |
| A Casarelle | 7 |
| Chez Huguette | 6 |
| Chez Serge Raugi | 2 |
| Palais des Glaces | 3 |
| La Table du Marché | 4 |
| La Voûte | 1 |

18

trading position with mainland France. The Nouveau Port, created in 1862 to cope with the increasing traffic with France and Italy, became the mainstay of the local economy, exporting chiefly agricultural products from Cap Corse, Balagne and the eastern plain.

The centre of Bastia is not especially large, and all its sights can easily be seen in a day without the use of a car. The spacious **place St-Nicolas** is the obvious place to get your bearings: open to the sea and lined with shady trees and cafés, it's the main focus of town life. Running parallel to it on the landward side are boulevard Paoli and rue César-Campinchi, the two main shopping streets, but all Bastia's historic sights lie within **Terra Vecchia**, the old quarter immediately south of place St-Nicolas, and **Terra Nova**, the area surrounding the Citadelle. Tucked away below the imposing, honey-coloured bastion is the much-photographed **Vieux Port**, with its boat-choked marina encircled by crumbling eighteenth-century tenement buildings.

## Terra Vecchia

From place St-Nicolas the main route into Terra Vecchia is **rue Napoléon**, a narrow street with some ancient offbeat shops and a pair of sumptuously decorated chapels on its east side. The first of these, the **Oratoire de St-Roch**, is a Genoese Baroque extravagance built in 1604, with walls of finely carved wooden panelling and a magnificent gilt organ.

### Oratoire de L'Immaculée Conception

The **Oratoire de L'Immaculée Conception** was built in 1609 as the showplace of the Genoese in Corsica, who used it for state occasions. The austere white-marble facade belies a flamboyant interior of gilt and velvet, whose centrepiece (behind the High Altar) is a copy of Bartolomé Esteban Murillo's celebrated depiction of the Immaculate Conception (the original hangs in Madrid's El Prado museum). During the British rule of the island in 1795, the chapel was used as the seat of the regional parliament.

### Place du Marché

The **place de l'Hôtel-de-Ville**, to the rear of the Oratoire de L'Immaculée Conception, is commonly known as **place du Marché** after the lively farmers' market that takes place here each morning, from around 7am until 2pm. Dominating the south end of the square is the **church of St-Jean-Baptiste**, an immense ochre edifice that dominates the Vieux Port. Its twin campaniles are iconic of the city, but the interior – a hideous Rococo overkill of multicoloured marble – is less impressive.

### Vieux Port

The oldest and most photogenic part of Bastia is the **Vieux Port** – a secretive zone of dark alleys, vaulted passageways and seven-storey houses packed around the base of the church of St-Jean-Baptiste. Site of the original Roman settlement of Porto Cardo, the harbour later bustled with Genoese traders, but since the building of the ferry terminal and commercial docks to the north it has become a backwater.

## Terra Nova

The military and administrative core of old Bastia, **Terra Nova** (or the citadelle) is focused on **place du Donjon**, which gets its name from the squat round tower that formed the nucleus of Bastia's fortifications: it was used by the Genoese to incarcerate Corsican patriots, among them the nationalist rebel Sampiero Corso in 1657, who was held in the dungeon for four years.

### Palais des Gouverneurs

**Musée de Bastia** July to mid-Sept Tues–Sun 10am–7.30pm, April–June & mid-Sept to Oct Tues–Sun 10am–6pm, Nov–March Tues–Sat 9am–noon & 2–5.30pm • €5 • ⓦ musee-bastia.com.

Facing the place du Donjon is the impressive fourteenth-century **Palais des Gouverneurs**, a building with a distinctly Moorish feel originally built for the Genoese governor and bishop. It became a prison after the French transferred the capital to Ajaccio, and was then destroyed during a British attack of 1794 (in which an ambitious young captain named Horatio Nelson played a decisive part). The subsequent rebuilding was not the last, as parts of it were mistakenly blown up by American B-52s in the bungled attack of 1943 which devastated the city centre on the day after the island's liberation. Today, the Palais hosts the expensively revamped **Musée de Bastia**, a state-of-the-art museum charting the city's evolution as a trade and artistic centre. Its collection includes part of Cardinal Fesch's famous hoard of Renaissance art (see p.964).

**18**

### Église Ste-Marie and Oratoire Sainte-Croix

If you cross the place du Donjon and follow rue Notre-Dame you come out at the **Église Ste-Marie**. Built in 1458 and overhauled in the seventeenth century, the church was the cathedral of Bastia until 1801, when the bishopric was transferred to Ajaccio. Inside, its principal treasure is a small silver statue of the Virgin (housed in a glass case on the right wall as you face the altar), which is carried through Terra Nova and Terra Vecchia on August 15, the Festival of the Assumption. Immediately behind Ste-Maire in rue de l'Évêché stands the **Oratoire Sainte-Croix**, a sixteenth-century chapel decorated in Louis XV style, with lashings of rich blue paint and gilt scrollwork. It houses another holy item, the *Christ des Miracles*, a blackened oak crucifix much venerated by Bastia's fishermen.

## L'Oratoire de Monserato

One of Bastia's most extraordinary monuments, the **Oratoire de Monserato**, lies a pleasant two-kilometre uphill walk from the town centre. The building itself looks unremarkable from the outside, but its interior houses the much revered **Scala Santa**, a replica of the Holy Steps of the Basilica of Saint John of Lateran in Rome. Penitents who ascend it on their knees as far as its high altar may be cleansed, or so it is believed, of all sins, without the intercession of a priest.

### ARRIVAL AND DEPARTURE

**BASTIA**

#### BY FERRY
**Nouveau Port** All ferries arrive and depart from the Nouveau Port, just a five-minute walk from place St-Nicolas and the centre of town. Toilet facilities are inside the South Terminal, where there's a left luggage counter (*consigne*; closed at the time of writing due to terrorist threat). Taxis queue outside at disembarkations times.

**Ferry offices** Corsica Ferries, Palais de Mer, 5bis, rue Chanoine-Leschi and sales counter at Nouveau Port, South Terminal ☎ 08 25 09 50 95, ⓦ corsicaferries.com; Mobylines (for departures to Italian ports), Sarl Colonna D'Istria & Fils, 4 rue Luce de Casablanca, just behind the Nouveau Port ☎ 04 95 34 84 94, ⓦ www.mobylines.com; SNCM, Nouveau Port ☎ 04 95 54 66 99, ⓦ sncm.fr; La Méridionale, Port de Commerce ☎ 048 10 20 13 20, ⓦ lameridionale.fr.

#### BY PLANE
Bastia's Poretta Airport (☎ 04 95 54 54 54, ⓦ www.bastia .aeroport.fr) is 16km south of town, just off the route nationale (N193). Shuttle buses to and from the centre

coincide with flights; the stop at the airport (marked by a single post with a small timetable on it) is easy to miss – it stands immediately outside the terminal concourse, 20m from the exit. Tickets cost €9. You can be dropped at the north side of Bastia's square, place St-Nicolas, or at the terminus outside the train station. These are also the departure points for travellers heading in the other direction (ie, out to the airport). Taxis charge a hefty €50/60 (day/ evenings and nights after 7pm) for the 20–30min trip.

#### BY BUS
Bastia doesn't have a proper bus station, which can cause confusion, with services arriving and departing from different locations around the north side of the main square. Roughly speaking, services to Ajaccio, Corte and smaller, rural destinations – including Cap Corse and St-Florent – operate out of the *gare routière*, at the north end of place St-Nicolas behind the Hôtel de Ville. Buses for Bonifacio, Porto-Vecchio and services to the east coast can be picked up outside the Rapides Bleus office, at the roadside opposite the main post office on avenue Maréchal-Sébastiani.

**18**

Services for Calvi via L'Île Rousse depart from outside the train station. Departure points are marked on our map, but should be checked in advance at the tourist office.

Destinations Ajaccio (2 daily; 3hr); Aléria/Cateraggio (2 daily; 1hr 30min); Calvi (2 daily; 2hr); Centuri (3 weekly; 2hr); Corte (2–3 daily; 1hr 15min); Erbalunga (hourly; 30–50min); L'Île Rousse (2 daily; 1hr 30min); Porto-Vecchio (2 daily; 3hr); St-Florent (2 daily; 45min–1hr).

## INFORMATION

**Tourist office** At the north end of place St-Nicolas (June to mid-Sept daily 8am–8pm; mid-Sept to May Mon–Sat 8am–6pm, Sun 9am–1pm; ☏04 95 54 20 40, ⊛bastia -tourisme.com), but don't expect advice about other parts of the island; the staff are basically there to hand out glossy leaflets, bus timetables and free fold-out maps, nothing more.

**Health** Centre Hospitalier, Furiani ☏04 95 59 11 11.
**Internet** Le Cyber, Rue des Jardins, just behind the Vieux Port (daily 10am–2am).
**Left luggage** The *consigne* at the Nouveau Port terminal is currently closed, but you can leave bags at Objectif Nature, rue Notre Dame-de-Lourdes (just north of place St-Nicolas) for €3/day.

## GETTING AROUND

**Taxis** There are ranks outside the *gare routière*, train station and Nouveau Port. Otherwise call direct: Bleus Bastiais (☏04 95 32 70 70); Taxis Radio Bastiais (☏04 95 34 07 00).
**Bike rental** Objectif Nature, rue Notre Dame-de-Lourdes (☏04 95 32 54 34, ⊛objectif-nature-corse.com) rent

cycles for €10/18 per half-day/full day.
**Car rental** Avis (Ollandini), 40 bd Paoli ☏04 95 31 95 64, airport ☏04 95 54 55 46; Europcar, 1 rue du Nouveau-Port ☏04 95 31 59 29, airport ☏04 95 30 09 50; Hertz, square St-Victor ☏04 95 31 14 24, airport ☏04 95 30 05 00.

## ACCOMMODATION

**Best Western** Av Zuccarelli ☏04 95 55 05 10, ⊛bestwestern-corsica-hotels.com. Hardly the most characterful option, but rates are highly competitive, and the location (on the hill above town) attractive, and rooms spacious for the price. Central a/c. **€70**

⭐ **Central** 3 rue Miot ☏04 95 31 69 72, ⊛www .centralhotel.fr. Eighteen pleasantly furnished rooms (plus a handful of larger studios), with textured walls and sparkling bathrooms, just off the southwest corner of place St-Nicolas. By far the most pleasant and best-value place to stay in the centre. Advance reservation essential. **€80**

**Napoleon** 43/45 bd Paoli ☏04 95 31 60 30, ⊛hotel -napoleon-bastia.fr. Smartly renovated 2-star in a central location. The rooms are all well air-conditioned and have small fridges. Welcoming management by Bastia standards. Copious breakfasts included. **€80**

**Les Orangers** Miomo, 5km north of town ☏04 95 33 24 09, ⊛camping-lesorangers.com The most convenient campsite if you're relying on public transport; frequent buses leave from the top of place St-Nicolas opposite the tourist office. April–Oct. **€25**

**Posta-Vecchia** Quai-des-Martyrs-de-la-Libération ☏04 95 32 32 38, ⊛hotelpostavecchia.com. The only hotel in the Vieux Port, and good value, with views across the sea from the (pricier) rooms at the front. There are smaller, cheaper options in the old block across the lane; all have a/c. **€75**

**Les Voyageurs** 9 av Maréchal-Sébastiani ☏04 95 34 90 80, ⊛hotel-lesvoyageurs.com. Smart three-star near the train station, done out in pale yellow and with two categories of differently themed rooms ("Jules Verne", "Indians" & "Cinema"): the larger, more expensive ones have baths instead of showers. No views to speak of, but fine for a night or two. Secure parking and central a/c. **€95**

## EATING, DRINKING & NIGHTLIFE

Lined with smart café-restaurants, place St-Nicolas is the place to be during the day, particularly between noon and 3pm, when the rest of town is deserted. Along boulevard Paoli and rue César-Campinchi, chi-chi *salons de thé* offer elaborate pâtisseries, local chestnut flan and doughnuts (*beignets*). The Casanis factory is on the outskirts in Lupino, so pastis is indisputably the town's tipple – order a "Casa" and you'll fit in well. A couple of cheesy discos, and unwelcoming bars, offer some nightlife, but you'll have to search hard for a crowded venue outside weekends in summer. The best source of information about all events is the daily local paper *Corse-Matin*.

### CAFÉS AND RESTAURANTS

⭐ **A Casarelle** 6 rue Ste-Croix ☏04 95 32 02 32. Innovative Corsican-French cuisine (swordfish steaks in flaky pastry with aubergine and mint, for example) served on a terrace on the edge of the citadelle. The chef's specialities are traditional dishes of the Balagne, such as *casgiate* (nuggets of

fresh cheese baked in fragrant chestnut leaves) or the rarely prepared *storzapretti* – balls of brocciu spinach and herbs in tomato sauce. *Menu* at €32 for lunch. April–Nov daily noon–3pm & 7pm–late; closed Dec–March.

**Chez Huguette** Rue de la Marine, Vieux Port ☏04 95 31 37 60, ⊛chezhuguette.fr. A cut above the competition on the Vieux Port, this place should be your first choice if you want to splash out on seafood to remember. The location on the quayside, facing St-Jean-Baptiste, is perfect, and the cooking sublime, from the Étang de Diane oysters to their impeccably fresh catch of day and – if you're really not counting your euros – their exquisite Cap Corse lobster, which could set you back as much as €200 for a large one (for two). Reservation recommended. Mon–Sat noon–3pm & 7–10.30pm, & Sun mid-June to Aug.

**Chez Serge Raugi** 2bis rue Capanelle, off bd Général Graziani, at the north end of place St-Nicolas ☎04 95 31 22 31. Corsica's greatest ice-cream maker, from an illustrious line of local *glaciers*. Tables on a cramped pavement terrace or upstairs on an even smaller mezzanine floor. In winter, they also do a legendary chickpea tart to take away. Daily 10am–7pm.

**Palais des Glaces** Place St-Nicolas ☎04 95 35 05 01. One of the few dependable lunch spots on the main square, frequented as much by Bastiais as visitors. Their good-value €19 *menu corse*, served under swish awnings beneath the plane trees, often includes the house favourite: fish bruschettas. Daily 7am–late.

**La Table du Marché** Place du Marché ☎04 95 31 64 25. Offering far better value than most places on the nearby Vieux Port, this smart terrace restaurant serves a tempting €30 *menu regional* featuring local crayfish, east-coast oysters

and *filets du St Pierre*. The à la carte menu is dominated by fancier gastro seafood, and is much more expensive. Mon–Sat noon–3pm & 7–10.30pm, plus Sun in July & Aug.

**La Voûte** 6 rue Luce-de-Casabiance ☎04 95 32 47 11. Just north of place St-Nicolas, this place is a favourite local lunch spot, offering great value, simple three-course *menus* from €20–25 which might include fresh seafood spaghetti or grilled lamb fillet with maquis herbs; and the house terrine is great. You can eat indoors in an attractive, stone-vaulted dining room, or outside on a noisier balcony overlooking the ferry port. Mon–Sat noon–2.30pm & 7–11pm.

**BARS AND CLUBS**

**La Madrague Club** Lucciani, 10km south of Bastia on the airport road ☎04 95 33 36 83. This is currently the only *boîte* (club) of note in the city. It attracts a mainly teenage crowd, and you'll need a car to get there. Entry is free but drinks extortionate, at around €10 for a Pietra beer. Fri–Sun 9pm–late.

**Pub Assunta** 4 rue Fontaine-Neuve ☎04 95 34 11 40. Large and lively bar in the heart of the old quarter that serves as an *avant-boîte* for the city's partygoers on weekends, and gets packed out with visitors during the summer. They serve light meals as well as drinks. Live music three nights/week in season. Mon–Sat noon–3pm & 6pm–midnight.

## South of Bastia

Fed by the rivers Bevinco and Golo, the **ÉTANG DE BIGUGLIA**, to the south of the city, is the largest lagoon in Corsica, and one of its best sites for rare migrant birds. The Roman town of **MARIANA**, on the southern shore of the *étang*, can be approached by taking the turning for Poretta airport, 16km along the N193, or the more scenic coastal route through **LA MARANA**. Mariana was founded in 93 BC as a military colony, but today's houses, baths and basilica are too ruined to be of great interest. It's only the square baptistry, with its remarkable mosaic floor decorated with dancing dolphins and fish looped around bearded figures representing the four rivers of paradise, that warrants a detour.

Adjacent to Mariana stands the **church of Santa Maria Assunta**, known as **La Canonica**. Built in 1119 close to the old capital of Biguglia, it's the finest of around three hundred churches built by the Pisans in their effort to evangelize the island. Modelled on a Roman basilica, the perfectly proportioned edifice is decorated outside with Corinthian capitals plundered from the main Mariana site and with plates of Cap Corse marble. Another ancient church, **San Parteo**, built in the eleventh and twelfth centuries, stands 300m further south.

# Cap Corse

Until Napoléon III had a coach road built around **Cap Corse** in the nineteenth century, the promontory was effectively cut off from the rest of the island, relying on Italian maritime traffic for its income – hence its distinctive Tuscan dialect. Many Capicursini later left to seek their fortunes in the colonies of the Caribbean, which explains the distinctly ostentatious mansions, or *palazzi*, built by the successful émigrés (nicknamed

**18**

"les Américains") on their return. For all the changes brought by the modern world, Cap Corse still feels like a separate country, with wild flowers in profusion, vineyards and quiet, traditional fishing villages.

Forty kilometres long and only fifteen across, the peninsula is divided by a spine of mountains called the Serra, which peaks at **Cima di e Folicce**, 1324m above sea level. The coast on the east side of this divide is characterized by tiny ports, or *marines*, tucked into gently sloping river-mouths, alongside coves which become sandier as you go further north. The villages of the western coast are sited on rugged cliffs, high above the rough sea and tiny rocky inlets that can be glimpsed from the corniche road.

## GETTING AROUND                                    CAP CORSE

**By bus** The main villages on Cap Corse are connected to Bastia's *gare routière* by bus. Services are fairly frequent during the summer, but drop off considerably between October and May. Running up the east coast to Pietracorbara, the Bastia municipal bus company, STIB (☎ 04 95 31 06 65, see ⊕ corsicabus.org/busBastia/BIA_Sisco.html), lays on hourly services from Monday to Saturday, the first departing at 6.30am. Transports Micheli (☎ 04 95 35 14 64) also runs two daily services all the way to Macinaggio. It's advisable to check all timings before departure via the Bastia tourist office or online at ⊕ corsicabus.org.

# Erbalunga

Built along a rocky promontory 10km north of Bastia, the small port of **ERBALUNGA** is the highlight of the east coast, with its aged, pale buildings stacked like crooked boxes behind a small harbour and ruined Genoese watchtower. A little colony of French artists lived here in the 1920s, and the village has drawn a steady stream of admirers ever since. Come summer it's transformed into something of a cultural enclave, with concerts and art events adding a spark to local nightlife. The town is most famous, however, for its Good Friday procession, known as the **Cerca** (Search), which evolved from an ancient fertility rite. Hooded penitents, recruited from the ranks of a local religious brotherhood, form a spiral known as a *Granitola*, or snail, which unwinds as the candlelit procession moves into the village square.

## ACCOMMODATION                                    ERBALUNGA

★ **Castel Brando** On the main square ☎ 04 95 30 10 30, ⊕ castelbrando.com. Shaded by a curtain of mature date palms, this elegant, stone-floored *palazzu* is like a *belle époque* backdrop to a classic Visconti movie. The rooms are furnished in period, with the welcome addition of air conditioning, a lovely pool, spa and ample parking. Open mid-March to mid-Nov. **€135**

## EATING AND DRINKING

**A Piazzetta** In the tiny square behind the harbour ☎ 04 95 33 28 69. The village's budget alternative, serving quality pizzas, veal in Cap Corse liqueur, excellent *moules-frites* and possibly Corsica's best sorbets. *Menus fixes* at €16 and €19; count on €25–20 à la carte. July–Aug daily noon–3pm & 7–11pm; Sept–June closed Tues.

★ **Le Pirate** On the harbourside ☎ 04 95 33 24 20, ⊕ restaurantlepirate.com. Well-heeled Bastiais flock year round to this Michelin-starred restaurant on the waterfront for its famous *haute gastronomie*. Local seafood and meat delicacies dominate their set *menus* (€42/75/90 for lunch/dinner). Daily noon–3pm & 7–11pm.

# Macinaggio

A port since Roman times, well-sheltered **MACINAGGIO**, 20km north of Erbalunga, was developed by the Genoese in 1620 for the export of olive oil and wine to the Italian peninsula. The Corsican independence leader, Pascal Paoli, landed here in 1790 after his exile in England, whereupon he kissed the ground and uttered the words "*O ma patrie, je t'ai quitté esclave, je te retrouve libre*" ("Oh my country, I left you as a slave, I rediscover you a free man"). There's not much of a historic patina to the place nowadays, but with its packed **marina** and line of colourful seafront awnings, Macinaggio has a certain appeal, made all the stronger by its proximity to some of the wildest landscape on the Corsican coast.

Another reason to linger is to sample the superb **Clos Nicrosi** wines, grown in the terraces above the village, which you can taste at the domaine's little shop on the north side of the Rogliano road, opposite the *U Ricordu* hotel.

**18**

## Site Naturel de la Capandula

North of the town lie some beautiful stretches of sand and clear sea – an area demarcated as the **Site Naturel de la Capandula**. A marked footpath, known as **Le Sentier des Douaniers** (see box below) because it used to be patrolled by customs officials, threads its way across the hills and coves of the reserve, giving access to an area that cannot by reached by road. The **Baie de Tamarone**, 2km along this path, is a good place for diving and snorkelling. Just behind the beach, the *piste* forks: follow the left-hand track for twenty minutes and you'll come to a stunning arc of turquoise sea known as the **rade de Santa Maria**, site of the isolated Romanesque **Chapelle Santa-Maria**. The bay's other principal landmark is the huge **Tour Chiapelle**, a ruined three-storeyed watchtower dramatically cleft in half and entirely surrounded by water.

**INFORMATION** MACINAGGIO

**Tourist office** Located in the port (☎04 95 35 40 34, ⓦmacinaggiorogliano-capcorse.fr; July & Aug Mon–Sat 9am–noon & 2.30–7pm, Sun 9am–noon, Sept Mon–Sat 9am–noon & 2.30–6pm, Sun 9am–noon, Oct–May Mon–Fri 9am–noon & 2–5pm).

**Boat trips** The San Paulu launch runs a twice-daily shuttle service for walkers between Macinaggio and Centuri-Port (July & Aug; by reservation only; €15), as well as half-day excursions to outlying beauty spots (€24). Timetables are published online at ⓦsanpaulu.com, and on leaflets at the tourist office. You can also phone the company direct on ☎04 95 35 07 09.

**ACCOMMODATION**

**U Libecciu** Rte de la Plage ☎04 95 35 43 22, ⓦwww.u-libecciu.com. The only commendable option in Macinaggio is this welcoming, modern two-star, located down the lane leading from the marina to the plage de Tamarone. Smallish rooms without balconies, or larger ones with terraces. Mid-March to mid-Nov. **€115**

**U Stazzu** 1km north of the harbour, signposted off the Rogliano road ☎04 95 35 43 76, ⓦcamping-u-stazzu .jimdo.com. Basic site on the edge of the village. The ground slopes and is rock hard, but it's cheap, there's ample shade and easy access to the nearby beach; the site's little café serves particularly good breakfasts and pizzas. May to mid-Sept. **€19**

---

### LE SENTIER DU DOUANIER

The roadless northern tip of Cap Corse is among the few stretches of coastline on the island crossed by a waymarked path, **Le Sentier du Douanier**. Following the yellow splashes of paint, it's possible to follow it all the way from Macinaggio to Centuri-Port (or vice versa) in seven to eight hours, taking in the picturesque Santa Maria and Agnello towers en route.

The **tourist office** (see above) in Macinaggio will furnish you with a free **map** and route description. Being mostly flat, the route presents no great physical challenges, although you should be aware of the force of the sun along this stretch of coast. In July and August, set off at dawn and aim to rest up in the shade (of which there's precious little) between 11.30am and 4pm. **Water** can also be a problem as there are no springs.

## EATING AND DRINKING

**Osteria di u Portu** Facing the marina ☎ 04 95 35 40 49. Unassuming harbourfront bistro where you can dine on fish straight off local boats, suckling lamb stew and tender free-range veal – at honest prices (*menus* from €22–27). April–Sept daily noon–3pm & 7–11pm. Oct–March closed eves, except Sat.

**Le Vela d'Oro** Down a narrow alleyway running off the little square, opposite the port ☎ 04 95 35 42 46. Capcorsin seafood specialities – such as local crayfish in home-made spaghetti – served in a cosy dining room decorated with old nautical maps. *Menus* from €17. Daily mid-Feb–Dec noon–3pm & 7–10pm. Closed Wed out of season.

**18**

# Centuri-Port

When Dr Johnson's biographer, James Boswell, arrived here from England in 1765, the former Roman settlement of **CENTURI-PORT** was a tiny fishing village, recommended to him for its peaceful detachment from the dangerous turmoil of the rest of Corsica. Not much has changed since Boswell's time: Centuri-Port exudes tranquillity despite a serious influx of summer residents, many of them artists who come to paint the fishing boats in the slightly prettified harbour, where the grey-stone wall is highlighted by the green serpentine roofs of the encircling cottages, restaurants and bars. The only drawback is the beach, which is disappointingly muddy and not ideal for sunbathing.

## ACCOMMODATION AND EATING                                      CENTURI-PORT

**Hôtel-Restaurant du Pêcheur** Rue du Port ☎ 04 95 35 60 14. Basic, but appealing hotel in the old-school Mediterranean mode: no TVs or a/c, but idyllic views out of its shuttered, front-side rooms over the harbour (ask for No.4). Everything's impeccably clean, the beds are comfy and the staff genuinely welcoming. Great little seafood restaurant on the ground floor, ten steps from the water. Easter to mid-Nov. **€70**

**La Jetée** At entrance to the port ☎ 04 95 35 64 46,

Ⓦ la-jetee.net. The *Jetée* has 14 spacious, airy rooms, most with balconies overlooking the harbour. Furnishings are bland but adequate, and there's a busy, good-value terrace restaurant tacked on the back. April–Oct. **€80**

**Vieux Moulin** At the entrance to the village ☎ 04 95 35 60 15, Ⓦ le-vieux-moulin.net. Centuri's most stylish option: a converted *maison d'Américain* with a wonderful terrace and attractively furnished en-suite rooms. March–Oct. **€85**

# Nonza

Set high on a black rocky pinnacle that plunges vertically into the sea, the village of **NONZA**, 18km south of Centuri, is one of the highlights of the Cap Corse shoreline. It was formerly the main stronghold of the da Gentile family, and the remains of their **fortress** are still standing on the overhanging cliff. Reached by a flight of six hundred steps, Nonza's long grey **beach** is discoloured as a result of pollution from the now disused asbestos mine up the coast. This may not inspire confidence, but the locals insist it's safe (they take their own kids there in summer), and from the bottom you get the best view of the tower, which looks as if it's about to topple into the sea.

## ACCOMMODATION                                                      NONZA

**Casa Lisa** At the bottom of the village ☎ 04 95 37 83 52, Ⓦ casalisa.free.fr. Gorgeous rooms with exposed beams, original tiled floors and shuttered windows looking across the gulf to the Désert des Agriates. Cards not accepted. April–Oct. **€70**

**Casa Maria** Chemin de la Tour ☎ 04 95 37 80 95,

Ⓦ casamaria-corse.com. Four pleasantly furnished rooms (and one pricier family suite), housed in a restored schist building above the square. Breakfast is served on a delightful outdoor terrace with lovely views. Cards not accepted. April–Oct. **€85–95**

# The Nebbio (U Nebbiu)

Taking its name from the thick mists that sweep over the region in winter, the **Nebbio** has for centuries been one of the most fertile parts of the island, producing honey, chestnuts and some of the island's finest wine. An amphitheatre of rippled chalk hills, vineyards and cultivated valleys surrounds the area's main town, **St-Florent**, half an hour's drive west over the mountain from Bastia at the base of Cap Corse. Aside from EU subsidies, the major money earner here is viticulture: the village of **Patrimonio** is the wine-growing hub, with *caves* offering *dégustations* lined up along its main street.

St-Florent is the obvious base for day-trips to the beautifully preserved Pisan church of Santa Maria Assunta, just outside the town, and the **Désert des Agriates**, a wilderness of parched maquis-covered hills across the bay whose rugged coastline harbours one of Corsica's least accessible, but most picturesque, beaches.

18

### GETTING AROUND

THE NEBBIO

**By bus** The principal public transport serving the Nebbio is the twice-daily bus from Bastia to St-Florent, operated by

Transports Santini (☎ 04 95 37 02 98). Timings can be checked at ⚙ corsicabus.org, or at the tourist office in St-Florent.

## St-Florent

Viewed from across the bay, **ST-FLORENT** (San Fiurenzu) appears as a bright line against the black tidal wave of the Tenda hills, the pale stone houses seeming to rise straight out of the sea, overlooked by a squat circular citadelle. It's a relaxing town, with a decent beach and a good number of restaurants, but the key to its success is the **marina**, which is jammed with expensive boats throughout the summer. Neither the tourists, however, nor indeed St-Florent's proximity to Bastia, entirely eclipse the air of isolation conferred on the town by its brooding backdrop of mountains and scrubby desert.

In Roman times, a settlement called Cersunam – referred to as Nebbium by chroniclers from the ninth century onwards – existed a kilometre east of the present village. The ancient port was eclipsed by the harbour that developed around the new Genoese citadelle in the fifteenth century, which prospered as one of Genoa's strongholds, and it was from here that Paoli set off for London in 1796, never to return.

### Place des Portes and the citadelle

**Place des Portes**, the centre of village life, has café tables facing the sea in the shade of plane trees, and in the evening fills with strollers and *pétanque* players. The fifteenth-century circular **citadelle** can be reached on foot from place Doria at the seafront in the old quarter. Destroyed by Nelson's bombardment in 1794, it was renovated in the 1990s and affords superb views from its terrace.

### Church of Santa Maria Assunta

July–Aug daily 9am–noon & 3–6.30pm; Sept–June Tues–Sat 9am–noon & 3–6.30pm; off season, key obtainable through tourist office • €2

Just a kilometre to the east of the town down a small lane running off place des Portes, on the original site of Cersanum, you come to the **church of Santa Maria Assunta** – the so-called "cathedral of the Nebbio" – a fine example of Pisan Romanesque architecture. Built in warm yellow limestone, the building has gracefully symmetrical blind arcades decorating its western facade, and at the entrance twisting serpents and wild animals adorning the pilasters on each side of the door. In the nave, immediately to the right of the entrance stands a glass case containing the mummified figure of St Flor, a Roman soldier martyred in the third century.

### ARRIVAL

ST-FLORENT

**By bus** Transports Santini buses (☎ 04 95 37 02 98) run from Bastia's *gare routière* to St-Florent twice daily (except Sun) leaving at 11am and 6pm (except Oct–May Wed & Sat, when they leave at noon & 5.30pm), pulling into the village car park behind the marina. This is also the departure point for return buses to Bastia, which from June to September

leave at 7am and 2pm, and at 6.50am and 1.30pm from October until May. The journey takes one hour.

**Tickets** You can purchase tickets on the bus or book in advance from Transports Santini's travel agency on St-Florent's main street, rue du Centre, just below the post office.

**18**

> ## BOAT TRIPS TO THE DESERT
>
> Excursion boats run out of St-Florent marina to the superb beaches – Loto (see opposite) and Saleccia (see opposite) – across the bay in the Désert des Agriates (see opposite). The *Agriate Express* (☎ 06 10 38 27 65; ⊚ corse-croisieres.com) and *Popeye* (☎ 04 95 37 19 07; ⊚ lepopeye .com) leave at regular intervals throughout the day, returning around 4pm (or later in July & Aug); tickets cost €17 for the return trip.

### INFORMATION

**Tourist office** Next to the post office at the top of the village (July & Aug Mon–Fri 8.30am–12.30pm & 2–7pm, Sat & Sun 9am–noon & 3–6pm; Sept–June Mon–Fri 9am–noon & 2–5pm, Sat 9am–noon; ☎ 04 95 37 06 04, ⊚ corsica -saintflorent.com), 100m north of place des Portes.

**Internet** There's a small cyber café just off the square, on the left (north) side of the road leading to Santa Maria

Assunta. The photography shop opposite the turning also offers internet access.

**Shops and services** The large Spar, next to the bridge in the marina, is the best-stocked supermarket in the area, and stays open on Sundays in the summer. Every other facility you could possibly want for a beach, camping or watersports holiday is available at the cavernous Corse Plaisance next door.

### ACCOMMODATION

**Camping Kallisté** Rte de la Plage ☎ 04 95 37 03 08, ⊚ campingkalliste.fr. Closest to town and most congenial. Closed Oct–May. **€26**

**Du Centre** Rue de Fornellu ☎ 04 95 37 00 68. Refreshingly unpretentious, old-fashioned place of a kind that's fast disappearing on the island. The modest rooms, all en suite and with showers, are kept impeccably clean by the feisty Mme Casanova. Ask for "côté jardin". **€70**

**De l'Europe** Place des Portes ☎ 04 95 37 00 03, ⊚ hotel-europe2.com. Swankily refurbished old building in the village centre next to the square, with original flagstone floors and modern comforts. Rooms are on the small side for the price, but all are en suite and well aired, and some overlook the marina. **€80**

**Maloni** On the Bastia road, 2km northeast of town ☎ 04 95 37 14 30, ⊚ malonihotel.com. An excellent little budget hotel, especially popular with bikers, with simple but pleasant en-suite rooms opening on to a leafy garden. **€65**

**Maxime** Rte d'Oletta, just off place des Portes ☎ 04 95 38 39 39. Bright, modern hotel in the centre. Rooms to the rear of the building have French windows and little balconies overhanging a small water channel. Closed Dec–Jan. **€85**

**U Palazzu** Serenu Oletta ☎ 04 95 37 00 68, ⊚ upalazzuserenu.com. Beautiful art-boutique hotel in a restored seventeenth-century mansion on the edge of a pretty hill village 6km inland. Works by Anish Kappor, Wendy Wischer and others adorn the nine rooms. The pool is heated, and there's a small restaurant and spa on site. **€370**

### EATING

**L'Europe** St-Florent marina ☎ 04 95 35 32 91. Local meat, seafood and pasta specialities are the mainstays of this rather fancy but good-value bistro on the waterfront, where you can dine on tables overlooking the port. Menus from €20; count on €30 à la carte. Easter–Oct daily noon–2.30pm & 7–11pm, Nov–Easter closed Mon, Tues & Sun eve.

**La Gaffe** St-Florent marina ☎ 04 95 37 00 12. One of the town's top seafood restaurants, where you can order

sumptuous devilfish stew on a bed of tagliatelle, with mains €15–30, or *menus* at €29 and €60. July & Aug, daily noon–2.30pm & 7–11pm, Sept–June closed Tues.

**La Rascasse** St-Florent marina ☎ 04 95 37 06 09, ⊚ restaurant-la-rascasse.fr. Renowned for its imaginative spins on local seafood: lobster cannelloni, mussel and chestnut fritters, and rock fish sautéed in cured ham. Mains €25–35; *menu* at €39. Mid-March to Oct daily noon–2.30pm & 7–11pm.

## Patrimonio (Patrimoniu)

As you leave St-Florent by the Bastia road, the next village you come to, after 6km, is **PATRIMONIO**, centre of the first Corsican wine region to gain *appellation contrôlée* status. Apart from the renowned local muscat, which can be sampled in the village or at one of the *caves* along the route from St-Florent, Patrimonio's chief asset is the sixteenth-century **church of St-Martin**, occupying its own little hillock and visible for kilometres around. The colour of burnt sienna, it stands out vividly against the rich green vineyards and chalk hills. In a garden 200m south of the church stands a limestone **statue-menhir** known as U Nativu, a late megalithic piece dating from

900–800 BC. A carved T-shape on its front represents a breastbone, and two eyebrows and a chin can also be made out.

The U Nativu menhir takes pride of place next to the stage at Patrimonio's annual open-air guitar festival (ⓦfestival-guitare-patrimonio.com), held in the last week of July next to the church, when performers and music aficionados from all over Europe converge on the village.

## The Désert des Agriates

Extending westwards from the Golfe de St-Florent to the mouth of the Ostriconi River, the **Désert des Agriates** is a vast area of uninhabited land, dotted with clumps of cacti and scrub-covered hills. It may appear inhospitable now, but during the time of the Genoese this rocky moonscape was, as its name implies, a veritable breadbasket (*agriates* means "cultivated fields"). In fact, so much wheat was grown here that the Italian overlords levied a special tax on grain to prevent any build-up of funds that might have financed an insurrection. Fires and soil erosion eventually took their toll, however, and by the 1970s the area had become a total wilderness.

Numerous crackpot schemes to redevelop the Désert have been mooted over the years – from atomic weapon test zones to concrete Club-Med-style resorts – but during the past few decades the government has gradually bought up the land from its various owners (among them the Rothschild family) and designated it as a protected nature reserve.

### The beaches

A couple of rough pistes wind into the desert, but without some kind of 4WD vehicle the only feasible way to explore the area and its rugged coastline, which includes two of the island's most beautiful **beaches**, is on foot. From St-Florent, a pathway winds northwest to **plage de Perajola**, just off the main Calvi highway (N1197), in three easy stages. The first takes around 5hr 30min, and leads past the famous **Martello tower** and much-photographed **plage de Loto** to **plage de Saleccia**, a huge sweep of soft white sand and turquoise sea that was used as a location for the invasion sequences in the film *The Longest Day*. From plage de Saleccia, it takes around three hours to reach the second night halt, **plage de Ghignu**, where a simple *gîte d'étape* (see below) provides basic facilities. The last stretch to Perajola can be covered in under six hours. Note that the only water sources along the route are at Saleccia and Ghignu, so take plenty with you.

### GETTING THERE

Excursion boats leave at regular intervals throughout the day from the jetty in St-Florent marina (€17 return), ferrying passengers across the gulf to and from plage de Loto. For current timetables, go to ⓦlepopeye.com or ⓦcorse-croisieres.com.

### ACCOMMODATION

**Paillers du Ghignu** Plage de Ghignu ☎04 95 57 10 10. This superbly remote *gîte d'étape* offers the most far-flung accommodation in coastal Corsica. Housed in a converted shepherd's hut close to the shoreline, its only facilities are basic bunks, hot showers and toilets – you'll need to bring a sleeping bag, food and drink. April–Sept. Bunks **€10**

**U Paradisu** Plage de Saleccia ☎04 95 37 82 51, ⓦcamping-uparadisu.com. Well set up campsite with pitches for tents in shady scrub behind the dunes, plus a scattering a delightful drystone cottages with bunks for coast walkers May–Sept. Bunks **€26**

# The Balagne (A Balagna)

The **Balagne**, the region stretching west from the Ostriconi valley as far as the red-cliffed wilderness of Scandola, has been renowned since Roman times as "Le Pays de l'Huile et Froment" (Land of Oil and Wheat). Backed by a wall of imposing, pale grey mountains, the characteristic outcrops of orange granite punctuating its spectacular coastline shelter a string of idyllic beaches, many of them sporting ritzy marinas and holiday complexes. These, along with the region's two honeypot towns, **L'Île Rousse** and **Calvi**, get swamped in summer, but the scenery more than compensates. In any case, Calvi, with its cream-coloured citadelle, breathtaking white-sand bay and mountainous backdrop, should not be missed.

# L'Île Rousse

**18**

Developed by Pascal Paoli in the 1760s as a "gallows to hang Calvi", the port of **L'ÎLE ROUSSE** (Isula Rossa) simply doesn't convince as a Corsican town, its palm trees, smart shops, neat flower gardens and colossal pink seafront hotel creating an atmosphere that has more in common with the French Riviera. Pascal Paoli had great plans for his new town on the Haute-Balagne coast, which was laid out from scratch in 1758 as a port to export the olive oil produced in the region. A large part of it was built on a grid system, quite at odds with the higgledy-piggledy nature of most Corsican villages and towns. Thanks to the busy trading of wine and oil, it soon began to prosper and, two and a half centuries later, still thrives as a successful port. These days, however, the main traffic consists of holiday-makers, lured here by brochure shots of the nearby beaches. This is officially the hottest corner of the island, and the town is deluged by sun-worshippers in July and August. Given the proximity of Calvi, and so much unspoilt countryside, it's hard to see why you should want to stop here for longer than it takes to have lunch or a coffee on the square.

## Place Paoli

All roads in L'Île Rousse lead to **place Paoli**, a shady square that's open to the sea and has as its focal point a fountain surmounted by a bust of "U Babbu di u Patria" ("Father of the Nation"), one of many local tributes to Pascal Paoli. There's a French-ified covered **market** at the entrance to the square, which hosts a popular artisan-cum-antiques sale on Saturday mornings, while on the west side rises the grim facade of the **church of the Immaculate Conception**.

## Île de la Pietra

To reach the **Île de la Pietra**, the islet that gives the town its name, continue north from the top of the promenade, passing the station on your left. Once over the causeway, you can walk through the crumbling mass of red granite as far as the lighthouse at the far end, from where the view of the town is spectacular, especially at sundown, when you get the full effect of the red glow of the rocks.

## The town beach

Immediately in front of the promenade, the **town beach** is a crowded Côte d'Azur-style strand, blocked by ranks of sun loungers and parasols belonging to the row of lookalike café-restaurants behind it. Two much more enticing beaches, **Bodri** and **Giuncheto**, lie a couple of kilometres around the headland to the west; you can get there on the four to six daily tramway services shuttling between L'Île Rousse and Calvi.

---

**ARRIVAL AND DEPARTURE** **L'ÎLE ROUSSE**

**By train** The train station (☎ 04 95 60 00 50) is on route du Port, 500m south of where the ferries arrive. Two services daily run to and from Bastia, Corte and Ajaccio, and a seasonal tramway (June–Sept; see ⓦ corsica-bus.org for timetables) rattles along the coast to and from Calvi via the beaches and villages en route.

**By bus** The Bastia–Calvi bus, operated Mon–Sat by Les Beaux Voyages (☎ 04 95 65 11 35, ⓦ lesbeauxvoyagesencorse

.com), stops just south of place Paoli in the town's main thoroughfare, avenue Piccioni. Tickets can be purchased from the driver.

**By ferry** Passenger ferries from Nice, Marseille and Toulon, and Italian port of Savona, dock at the quayside on the northwest side of the centre, a 10min walk from the town centre.

## INFORMATION

**Tourist office** On the south side of place Paoli (April–June & Sept–Oct Mon–Fri 9am–noon & 2–5pm; July & Aug daily 9am–1pm & 2.30–7.30pm; ☏ 04 95 60 04 35, ⓦ balagne-corsica.com).

**Internet** Movie Store (Mon–Sat 10am–midnight, Sun 2pm–midnight), diagonally opposite the supermarket on the crossroads where the *route nationale* cuts through the centre of town.

## ACCOMMODATION

**Le Bodri** 3km west off the main Calvi road ☏ 04 95 16 19 70, ⓦ campinglebodri.com. Slap on a beach, this large campsite can be reached direct by rail – ask for "l'arrêt Bodri". Although rammed in summer, it's pleasantly quiet outside the *grandes vacances*. April–Sept. **€19**

**Cala di L'Oru** Bd Pierre Pasquini ☏ 04 95 60 14 75, ⓦ hotel-caladiloru.com. Smart two-star, swathed in greenery, on the outskirts of town. The rooms are functional without being bland, and a good-sized pool is a welcome bonus. Generous discounts low- and mid-season. April–Oct. **€130**

**Le Grillon** 10 av Paul-Doumer ☏ 04 95 60 00 49, ⓦ hotel-grillon.net. The best cheap hotel in town, just 1km from the centre on the St-Florent/Bastia road. Nothing special, but quiet and immaculate. April–Oct. **€67**

**Les Oliviers** 1km east of town ☏ 04 95 60 19 92, ⓦ camping-oliviers.com. Well-shaded site on the eastern outskirts, sandwiched between the highway and cliffs. April–Sept. **€17.50**

**Santa Maria** Rte du Port ☏ 04 95 63 05 05, ⓦ hotelsantamaria.com. Next to the ferry port and affiliated to the *Best Western* chain, this is one of the larger and better-value three-star places. Their a/c rooms have small balconies or patios opening onto a garden and pool, and there's exclusive access to a tiny pebble beach. **€165**

**Splendid** 4 bd Valéry-François ☏ 04 95 60 00 24, ⓦ le -splendid-hotel.com. Well-maintained, 1930s-style building with a small curvi-form pool and some sea views from upper floors; restrained tariffs, given the central location. Open mid-March to Dec. **€105**

## EATING AND DRINKING

Though there's an abundance of mediocre eating places in the narrow alleys of the old town, a few restaurants do stand out, some offering stylish gourmet *menus* and others serving superb fresh seafood. The best cafés are found under the plane trees lining the southern side of place Paoli.

**L'Escale** Rue Notre Dame ☏ 04 95 60 10 53. Giant fresh mussels, prawns and crayfish from the east coast *étangs* are the thing here, served in various *menus* (€16–29) on a spacious terrace looking across the tramway line to the bay. Brisk, courteous service, copious portions and for once the house white (by the glass or *pichet*) is palatable. The *menu pêcheur* (a mixed platter) is especially good value. Daily noon–2.30pm & 7–11pm.

**L'Ostéria** Place Santelli ☏ 04 95 60 08 39. On a quiet backstreet in the old quarter, this established Corsican speciality restaurant offers a great-value set *menu* (€25), featuring courgette fritters, *soupe de nos villages*, tarragon-scented *gratin d'aubergines*, stuffed sardines and fresh pan-fried prawns. You can sit in a vaulted room adorned with farm implements or on the shaded terrace. Daily noon–2.30 & 7–11pm.

**Le Pasquale Paoli** 2 place Paoli ☏ 04 95 46 67 70, ⓦ pasquale-paoli.com. One of the few restaurants on the island to have earned a Michelin star. Gastronomic renditions of Corsican standards are its forté: the octopus in olive oil and lemon confit is hard to top, and there are plenty of wonderful vegetarian options. Count on around €70–100 à la carte. Closed: lunchtime July–Aug; Mon lunchtime Nov–Feb; Sun eve & Wed Oct–May.

# Calvi

Seen from the water, **CALVI** is a beautiful spectacle, with its three immense bastions topped by a crest of ochre buildings, sharply defined against a hazy backdrop of mountains. Located twenty kilometres west along the coast from L'Île Rousse, the town began as a fishing port on the site of the present-day *ville basse* below the citadelle, and remained just a cluster of houses and fishing shacks until the Pisans conquered the island in the tenth century. Not until the arrival of the Genoese, however, did the town become a stronghold when, in 1268, Giovaninello de Loreto, a Corsican nobleman, built a huge citadelle on the windswept rock overlooking the port and named it Calvi. A fleet commanded by Nelson launched a brutal two-month attack on the town in 1794; he left saying he hoped never to see the place again, and very nearly didn't see anywhere else again, having sustained the wound that cost him his sight in one eye.

The French concentrated on developing Ajaccio and Bastia during the nineteenth century, and Calvi became primarily a military base. A hangout for European glitterati in the 1950s, the town these days has the ambience of a slightly kitsch Côte d'Azur resort, whose glamorous marina, souvenir shops and fussy boutiques jar with the down-to-earth villages of its rural hinterland. It's also an important base for the French Foreign Legion's parachute regiment, the 2e REP, and immaculately uniformed legionnaires are a common sight around the bars lining avenue de la République.

Social life in Calvi focuses on the restaurants and cafés of the **quai Landry**, a spacious seafront walkway linking the marina and the port. This is the best place to get the feel of the town, but the majority of Calvi's sights are found within the walls of the **citadelle**.

## The citadelle

"Civitas Calvis Semper Fidelis" – always faithful – reads the inscription of the town's motto, carved over the ancient gateway into the fortress. The best way of seeing the citadelle is to follow the ramparts connecting the three immense bastions, the views from which extend out to sea and inland to Monte Cinto. Within the walls the houses are tightly packed along tortuous stairways and narrow passages that converge on the place d'Armes. Dominating the square is the **Cathédrale St-Jean-Baptiste**, set at the highest point

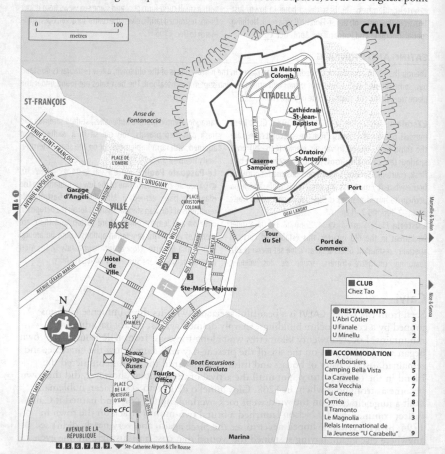

of the promontory. This chunky ochre edifice was founded in the thirteenth century, but was partly destroyed during the Turkish siege of 1553 and then suffered extensive damage twelve years later, when the powder magazine in the governor's palace exploded. It was rebuilt in the form of a Greek cross. The church's great treasure is the **Christ des Miracles**, which is housed in the chapel on the right of the choir; this crucifix was brandished at marauding Turks during the 1553 siege, an act which reputedly saved the day.

## La Maison Colomb

To the north of place d'Armes in rue de Fil stands **La Maison Colomb**, the shell of a building which Calvi believes – as the plaque on the wall states – was Christopher Columbus's birthplace, though the claim rests on pretty tenuous, circumstantial evidence. The house itself was destroyed by Nelson's troops during the siege of 1794, but as recompense a statue was erected in 1992, the five-hundredth anniversary of Columbus's "discovery" of America; the date of this historic landfall, October 12, is now a public holiday in Calvi.

## The beach

Calvi's **beach** sweeps round the bay from the end of quai Landry, but most of the first kilometre or so is owned by bars which rent out sun loungers for a hefty price. To avoid these, follow the track behind the sand, which will bring you to the start of a more secluded stretch. The sea might not be as sparklingly clear as at many other Corsican beaches, but it's warm, shallow and free of rocks.

### ARRIVAL AND DEPARTURE                                    CALVI

**By plane** Ste-Catherine Airport, served by domestic and international flights, lies 7km south of Calvi (☎ 04 95 65 88, ⓦ www.calvi.aeroport.fr); the only public transport into town is by taxi, which shouldn't cost more than €25 weekdays (or €30 on weekends).

**By train** The train station (Gare CFC ☎ 04 95 65 00 61), on avenue de la République close to the marina, is the terminus for regular long-distance trains to Bastia and Ajaccio, as well as villages and resorts along the route of the seasonal tramway.

Destinations Ajaccio (2 daily; 4hr 10min); Bastia (2 daily; 3hr min); Corte (2 daily; 2hr 24min); L'Île Rousse (2–10 daily; 30min).

**By bus** Buses to and from Bastia and towns along the north coast (Les Beaux Voyages ☎ 04 95 65 11 35;

year-round Mon–Sat) stop outside the train station on place de la Porteuse d'Eau, whereas those from Porto, run by SAIB (mid-May to June & mid-Sept to end Sept Mon–Sat, July–mid-Sept daily; ☎ 04 95 22 41 99) work from the roadside behind the marina.

Destinations Bastia (1 daily; 1hr 45min–2hr 15min); L'Île Rousse (2 daily; 40min); Porto (1 daily; 2hr 30min).

**By boat** Ferries, including NGV hydrofoils, dock at the Port de Commerce at the foot of the citadelle. Tramar (aka "CCR"), agents for SNCM, are on the quai Landry (☎ 04 95 65 00 63); Corsica Ferries' office is over in the Port de Commerce (☎ 04 95 65 43 21).

Destinations Nice (2–5 weekly; 8hr overnight or 2hr 40min via NGV).

### INFORMATION

**Tourist office** Quai Landry (mid-June to Sept daily 9am–7pm; Oct to mid-June Mon–Fri 9am–noon & 2–5.30pm, Sat 9am–noon; ☎ 04 95 65 16 67, ⓦ balagne -corsica.com).

**Bicycle rental** Garage d'Angeli, rue Villa-Antoine, on the

left just west of place Christophe-Colomb (☎ 04 95 65 02 13, ⓦ garagedangeli.com), from €13 per day. Take along your credit card or passport, which they'll need to secure the deposit.

### ACCOMMODATION

Accommodation is easy to find in Calvi except during the jazz festival (third week of June).

**Les Arbousiers** Rte de Pietra-Maggiore ☎ 04 95 65 04 47, ⓦ arbousiers.com. Large, ochre-painted place set back from the main road, 1km south of town and 150m from the beach, with very well maintained,

reasonably priced rooms ranged around a quiet courtyard. **€81**

**Camping Bella Vista** Rte de Pietra-Maggiore, 1km southeast of the centre (700m inland from the beach)

**18**

☎04 95 65 11 76, ⊕www.camping-bellavista.com. The best option for backpackers as it's much closer to the centre of town than the competition – though you pay a couple of euros per night extra for the privilege. Plenty of shade, nice soft ground and clean toilet blocks. Closed Nov–March. **€24**

**La Caravelle** Marco Plage, 1km south of centre ☎04 95 65 95 50, ⊕hotel-la-caravelle.com. An impeccably clean, modern hotel virtually on the beach, with ground-floor rooms set around a garden; those on the first floor are more luxurious. Buffet breakfasts served on a sunny patio, and there's a nice bar-restaurant. Good value in this bracket considering the location, quality of the property and service. **€162**

**Casa Vecchia** Rte de Santore ☎04 95 65 09 33, ⊕hotel-casa-vecchia.com. Small chalets set in a leafy garden, 500m south of town, and 200m from the beach. Half-board obligatory in July & Aug. Friendly management. May–Sept. **€90**

★ **Du Centre** 14 rue Alsace-Lorraine ☎04 95 65 02 01. Old-fashioned pension, with a hospitable owner, occupying a former police barracks in a narrow, pretty street near Église Ste-Marie-Majeure and harbourside. Its rooms are large for

the price, but plain with shared WC. The cheapest option in town – by a long chalk. Open June–Oct. **€50**

**Cyrnea** Rte de Bastia ☎04 95 65 03 35, ⊕hotel-cyrnea.fr. Large budget hotel, a twenty-minute walk south of town, and 300m from the beach. Good-sized rooms for the price, all with bathrooms and balconies (ask for one with "vue montagne" to the rear), and there's even a pleasant pool. Outstanding value for money, especially in high season. Open April–Nov. **€85**

**Il Tramonto** Rte de Porto ☎04 95 65 04 17, ⊕hotel-iltramonto.com. Excellent little budget hotel, with clean, comfortable and light rooms on the far north side of town. Definitely worth splashing out on one with "vue mer", which have little terraces and a superb panorama over Punta de la Revellata. **€75**

★ **Le Magnolia** Rue Charming ☎04 95 65 19 16, ⊕hotel-le-magnolia.com. Nineteenth-century town house with *belle époque* decor and the atmosphere of an elegantly old-fashioned pension, set behind high walls in the heart of the historic quarter. The eponymous magnolia tree shades a lovely terrace restaurant where breakfast is served in the mornings. Welcoming management. **€120**

## THE GR20

Winding some 170km from Calenzana (12km from Calvi) to Conca (22km from Porto-Vecchio), the **GR20** is Corsica's most demanding long-distance footpath. Only one-third of the 18,000 to 20,000 hikers who start it each season complete all sixteen stages, which can be covered in ten to twelve days if you're in good physical shape – if you're not, don't even think about attempting this route. Marked with red-and-white splashes of paint, it comprises a series of harsh ascents and descents, sections of which exceed 2000m and become more of a scramble than a walk, with stanchions, cables and ladders driven into the rock as essential aids. The going is made tougher by the necessity of carrying a sleeping bag, all-weather kit and two or three days' food with you. That said, the rewards more than compensate. The GR20 takes in the most spectacular mountain terrain in Corsica and along the way you can spot the elusive mouflon (mountain sheep), glimpse lammergeier (a rare vulture) wheeling around the crags, and swim in ice-cold torrents and waterfalls.

The first thing you need to do before setting off is get hold of the Parc Régional's indispensable **Topo-guide**, published by the Fédération Française de la Randonnée Pédestre, which gives a detailed description of the route, along with relevant sections of IGN contour maps, lists of refuges and other essential information. Most good bookshops in Corsica stock them, or call at the park office in Ajaccio (see p.965).

The route can be undertaken in either **direction**, but most hikers start in the north at Calenzana, tackling the most demanding *étapes* early on. The hardship is alleviated by extraordinary mountainscapes as you round the Cinto massif, skirt the Asco, Niolo, Tavignano and Restonica valleys, and scale the sides of Monte d'Oro and Rotondo. At Vizzavona on the main Bastia–Corte–Ajaccio road, roughly the halfway mark, you can call it a day and catch a bus or train back to the coast, or press on south across two more ranges to the needle peaks of Bavella.

**Accommodation** along the route is provided by **refuges**, where, for around €13–17, you can take a hot shower, use an equipped kitchen and bunk down on mattresses. Usually converted *bergeries*, these places are staffed by wardens during the peak period (June–Sept). Advance reservations can be made online via the national park (PNRC) website, ⊕parc-corse .org, for an advance payment of €5 per bed; any un-booked places are allocated on a first-come-first-served basis, so be prepared to bivouac if you arrive late. Another reason to be

**Relais International de la Jeunesse "U Carabellu"**
4km from the centre of town on rte Pietra-Maggiore
☎ 04 95 65 14 16, ⓦ clajsud.fr. Follow the N197 for 2km,
turn right at the sign for Pietra-Maggiore, and the hostel

– two little houses with spacious, clean dormitories,
looking out over the gulf – is in the village another 2km
further up the lane. Book in advance. May–Oct. Beds
**€20/31** (B&B/half-board)

## EATING AND DRINKING

### RESTAURANTS

**L'Abri Côtier** Quai Landry, but entrance on rue Joffre
☎ 04 95 46 00 04. Mostly seafood dishes (such as sea bass
with fennel) and pizzas (from €16), served on a lovely
terrace looking out to sea. Their set *menus* (€19–40) and
*suggestions du jour* are invariably the best deals. March–
Oct daily noon–2.30pm & 7–11pm.

★ **U Fanale** Rte de Porto, just outside the centre of
town on the way to Punta de la Revellata ☎ 04 95 65
18 82, ⓦ ufanale.com. Worth the walk out here for their
delicious, beautifully presented Corsican specialities –
mussels or lamb simmered in ewe's cheese and white
wine, a fine *soupe Corse*, and melt-in-the-mouth *fiadone*
(traditional flan). *Menus* €20–25 plus a full à la carte
choice (count on €35), and pizzas from €15. You can dine
outside in the garden or inside their *salle panoramique*,
with views across the bay to Punta de la Revellata.

March–Dec daily noon–2.30pm & 7–11pm; closed
Tues lunchtime.

**U Minellu** Off bd Wilson, nr Ste-Marie-Majeure ☎ 04 95
65 05 52. Wholesome Corsican specialities served in a
narrow stepped alley, or on a shady terrace with pretty
mosaic tables. Their *menu* features baked lamb, cannelloni
*al brocciu*, spider crab dressed "à la Calvaise", and a cheese
platter – good value at €22. March–Oct daily noon–
2.30pm & 7–11pm.

### CLUB

**Chez Tao** Rue St-Antoine, in the citadelle ☎ 04 95 65
00 73, ⓦ cheztao.com. Legendary nightclub, opened in
the wake of the Bolshevik Revolution by a Muslim White
Russian, and long the haunt of the Riviera's glitterati. Now
turned into a pricey piano bar from 11.30pm–2am, after
which DJs take over. June–Sept daily 10am–4am.

18

---

on the trail soon after dawn is that it allows you to break the back of the *étape* before 2pm,
when clouds tend to bubble over the mountains and obscure the views.

The **weather** in the high mountains is notoriously fickle. A sunny morning doesn't necessarily
mean a sunny day, and during July and August violent storms can envelop the route without
warning. It's therefore essential to take good wet-weather gear with you, as well as a hat,
sunblock and shades. In addition, make sure you set off on each stage with adequate **food** and
**water**. At the height of the season, most *refuges* sell basic supplies (*alimentation* or *ravitaillement*),
but you shouldn't rely on this service; ask hikers coming from the opposite direction where their
last supply stop was and plan accordingly (basic provisions are always available at the main
passes of Col de Vergio, Col de Vizzavona, Col de Bavella and Col de Verde). The refuge wardens
(*gardiens*) will be able to advise you on how much water to carry at each stage.

Finally, a word of **warning**: each year, injured hikers have to be air-lifted to safety off remote
sections of the GR20, normally because they strayed from the marked route and got lost.
Occasionally, fatal accidents also occur for the same reason, so always keep the paint splashes
in sight, especially if the weather closes in – don't rely purely on the many cairns that
punctuate the route, as these sometimes mark more hazardous paths to high peaks.

### GETTING TO THE TRAILHEAD

Getting to **Calenzana** from Calvi, trailhead for the GR20, is no easy feat given the sporadic
nature of public transport. It's straightforward enough during the summer holidays (July to
early Sept), when two daily buses leave from the Porteuse d'Eau roundabout in Calvi (2.30pm
& 7.30pm; €8, plus €1 for luggage); but for the rest of the year, this service only operates once
daily in termtime on Mondays, Tuesdays, Thursdays and Fridays (3.45pm). Timetables may be
consulted at ⓦ corsicabus.org, or by direct via the bus company, Beaux Voyages (3 rue Joffre;
☎ 04 95 65 11 35, ⓦ corsicar.com).

If you find yourself heading off to the GR20 on a day when the bus isn't running, you can jump
in an expensive cab (around €45 from Calvi airport or Lumio, the nearest train station to
Calenzana), or, if you're part of a group, hire a car for the day, drive your fellow walkers to Calenzana
and catch a cab yourself back up the hill after dropping the car off. Be warned, if you're tempted to
cover the stretch on foot, that the road makes a seriously unpleasant, and in places downright
dangerous, walk – especially at night (when, inevitably, the taxi fare rises to around €60).

**18**

# The Réserve Naturel de Scandola

The extraordinary **Réserve Naturel de Scandola** takes up the promontory dividing the Balagne from the Golfe de Porto. Composed of striking red porphyry granite, its sheer cliffs and gnarled claw-like outcrops were formed by Monte Cinto's volcanic eruptions 250 million years ago, and subsequent erosion has fashioned shadowy caves, grottoes and gashes in the rock. Scandola's colours are as remarkable as the shapes, the hues varying from the charcoal grey of granite to incandescent rusty purple.

The headland and its surrounding water were declared a nature reserve in 1975 and now support significant colonies of seabirds, dolphins and seals, as well as 450 types of seaweed and some remarkable fish such as the grouper, a species more commonly found in the Caribbean. In addition, nests belonging to the rare Audouin's gull are visible on the cliffs, and you might see the odd fish eagle (*Balbuzard pêcheur*) – there used to be only a handful of nesting pairs at one time, but careful conservation has increased their numbers considerably over the past two decades.

## GETTING THERE — RÉSERVE NATUREL DE SCANDOLA

**By boat** Scandola is off-limits to hikers and can be viewed only by boat (Colombo Lines ☎ 04 95 62 32 10, ⊚ colombo-line.com), which means taking one of the daily excursions from Calvi or Porto. These leave morning and afternoon from Calvi, and from Porto at various intervals throughout the daytime and early evening (April–Oct), the first two stopping for two hours at Girolata (see below) and returning in the late afternoon. It's a fascinating journey and well worth the steep fare, although it's a good idea to take a picnic if you're on a tight budget, as the restaurants in Girolata are very pricey.

## Girolata

Connected by a mere mule track to the rest of the island (1hr 30min on foot from the nearest road), the tiny fishing haven of **GIROLATA**, immediately east of Scandola, has a dreamlike quality that's highlighted by the vivid red of the surrounding rocks. A short stretch of stony beach and a few houses are dominated by a stately watchtower, built by the Genoese later in the seventeenth century in the form of a small castle on a bluff overlooking the cove. For most of the year, this is one of the most idyllic spots on the island, with only the odd yacht and party of hikers to threaten the settlement's tranquillity. From June to September, though, daily boat trips from Porto and Calvi ensure the village is swamped during the middle of the day, so if you want to make the most of the scenery and peace and quiet, walk here and stay a night in one of the *gîtes*.

The head of the Girolata trail is at **Bocca à Crocce** (Col de la Croix), on the Calvi–Porto road, from where a clear path plunges downhill through dense maquis and forest to a flotsam-covered cove known as **Cala di Tuara** (30min). The more rewarding of the two tracks that wind onwards to Girolata is the gentler one running left around the headland, but if you feel like stretching your legs, follow the second, more direct route uphill to a pass.

## ACCOMMODATION — GIROLATA

**La Cabane du Berger** On the beach ☎ 04 95 20 16 98. Basic *gîte d'étape* offering a choice of accommodation in dorms or small wood cabins in the garden behind (these accommodate two people); you can also put your tent up here. Meals are served in their quirky wood-carved bar, but the food isn't up to much. May–Oct; no cards. Dorms €40 (half-board obligatory)

**Le Cormoran Voyageur** Among the houses at the north end of the cove ☎ 04 95 20 15 55. Eighteen dorm spaces and a small restaurant overlooking the boat jetty. July & Aug; no cards. Dorms €40 (half-board obligatory)

## EATING

Unless you're staying at one of the *gîtes*, you'll be better off paying a little extra to eat at one of the two restaurants just up the steps. For a quick bite before heading back up the path, look no further than the little Bastella shop down on the beach, which sells tasty Corsican pasties (*bastelles*), filled with spinach, onions and brocciu.

**Le Bel Ombra** ☎ 04 95 20 15 67. The pricier of the village's two places to eat, with a terrace overlooking the bay where you can tuck into fresh local seafood specialities, including fresh Scandola lobster. *Menus* at €19 & 27. No cards. April–Sept. Daily noon–3pm & 6.30–10.30pm.

**Le Bon Espoir** Next door to *Le Bel Ombra* (see opposite) ☎ 04 95 10 04 55. Same view, similar seafood menu, only slightly lower prices than its neighbour, because the fish comes straight off the patron's own boat. April–Sept daily noon–3pm & 6.30–10.30pm.

# Porto (Portu) and around

18

The overwhelming proximity of the mountains, combined with the pervasive eucalyptus and spicy scent of the maquis, give **PORTO**, 30km south of Calvi, a uniquely intense atmosphere that makes it one of the most interesting places to stay on the west coast. Except for a watchtower erected here by the Genoese in the second half of the sixteenth century, the site was only built upon with the onset of tourism since the 1950s; today the village is still so small that it can become claustrophobic in July and August, when overcrowding is no joke. Off season, the place becomes eerily deserted, so you'd do well to choose your times carefully; the best months are May, June and September.

The crowds and traffic jams tend to be most oppressive passing the famous **Calanches**, a huge mass of weirdly eroded pink rock just southwest of Porto, but you can easily sidestep the tourist deluge in picturesque **Piana**, which overlooks the gulf from its southern shore, or by heading inland from Porto through the **Gorges de Spelunca**. Forming a ravine running from the sea to the watershed of the island, this spectacular gorge gives access to the equally grandiose **Forêt d'Aïtone**, site of Corsica's most ancient Laricio pine trees and a deservedly popular hiking area. Throughout the forest, the river and its tributaries are punctuated by strings of *piscines naturelles* (natural swimming pools) – a refreshing alternative to the beaches hereabouts. If you're travelling between Porto and Ajaccio, a worthwhile place to break the journey is the clifftop village of **Cargèse** where the two main attractions are the Greek church and spectacular beach.

## Vaïta and the marina

Eucalyptus-bordered **route de la Marine** links the two parts of the resort. The village proper, known as **Vaïta**, comprises a strip of supermarkets, shops and hotels 1km from the sea, but the main focus of activity is the small **marina**, located at the avenue's end.

---

### BOAT TRIPS FROM PORTO

Tickets for the daily **boat excursions** to the **Réserve Naturelle de Scandola** via **Girolata**, and to the **Calanches de Piana**, are available in advance direct from the operators (not from the tourist office), who have stalls outside their associated hotels in the marina. Working out of the Hôtel Monte Rossu, just off the square, is J.B. Rostini's Porto Linea (April–Oct: for Scandola and Girolata, daily departures 9am & 2pm; €45; Calanches de Piana evening cruises 5 daily; €25; ☎ 04 95 26 11 50, ⊛ portolinea.com). One of their vessels, the *Mare Nostrum*, carries only twelve people. Its diminutive size can be a disincentive if there's a big swell, but allows the boat to enter narrow defiles and caves in the Calanches unreachable by the competition, plus you gain a more vivid sense of the sea. The rival Compagnie Nave Va has a much larger boat, which accommodates up to 150 people. They operate from the Hôtel Cyrnée, just behind the tourist office (April–Oct: Scandola and Girolata daily 9.30am, 1.30pm & 2.30pm, €37; Calanches de Piana daily 4.15pm & 5.30pm; €25; ☎ 04 95 26 15 16, ⊛ naveva.com). Both these boats leave from Porto marina. Finally, the operator from the Hotel du Golfe at the foot of the tower, Via Mare (☎ 06 07 28 72 72, ⊛ viamare-promenades.com) run the largest boat of all, with daily trips to Scandola (9.15am & 2pm; €37) and the Calanches (5.45pm; €25), or longer tours combining both (3pm; €45). Reduced tariffs for **children** apply to all these excursions. Tickets should be booked at least a day in advance.

**18**

Overlooking the entrance to the harbour is the much-photographed **Genoese Tower** (May, June & Sept daily 9am–7pm, July–Aug 9am–9pm, €2.50), a square chimney-shaped structure that was cracked by an explosion in the seventeenth century, when it was used as an arsenal. An awe-inspiring view of the crashing sea and maquis-shrouded mountains makes it worth the short climb. Occupying a converted powder house down in the square opposite the base of the tower is the **Aquarium de la Poudrière** (May, June & Sept daily 8am–7pm, July–Aug 8am–10pm, €5.50), where you can view the various species of sea life that inhabit the gulf, including grouper, moray eels and sea horses.

## The beach

The **beach** consists of a pebbly cove south beyond the shoulder of the massive rock supporting the tower. To reach it from the marina, follow the little road that skirts the rock, cross the wooden bridge which spans the River Porto on your left, then walk through the car park under the trees. Although it's rather rocky and exposed, and the sea very deep, the great crags overshadowing the shore give the place a vivid, wild atmosphere.

### ARRIVAL AND INFORMATION                                          PORTO

**By bus** Buses from Calvi, via Galéria, and from Ajaccio, via Cargèse, pull into the junction at the end of route de la Marine, opposite the Banco supermarket, en route to the marina. Timetables are posted at the stops themselves, and at the tourist office.

**Tourist office** Porto's tourist office is down in the marina (May, June & Sept daily 9am–6pm; July & Aug daily 9am–7pm; Oct–April Mon–Fri 9am–5pm; ☎04 95 26 10 55, ⓦ porto-tourisme.com), and is of use primarily as a source of Topo-guides and brochures for hikes in the area.

**Diving and sea kayaking** The clear waters of the gulf offer superlative diving. There are two schools, both working out of the marina next to the footbridge: the Méditerranée Porto Sub (☎06 14 94 08 44, ⓦ portoplongeecorse.fr) and the Centre de Plongée du Golfe (☎04 95 26 10 29, ⓦ plongeeporto.com). Both run courses for beginners and will take out more experienced divers with their own equipment; you can also fill your gas bottles here. In addition, the Centre de Plongée du Golfe have unsinkable canoes for rent – ideal for paddling into the hidden coves around Porto.

### ACCOMMODATION

Competition between hotels is more cut-throat in Porto than in any other resort on the island. During slack periods towards the beginning and end of the season, most places engage in a full-on price war, pasting up cheaper tariffs than their neighbours – all of which is great for punters. In late July and August, however, the normal high rates prevail.

**Le Belvédère** Porto marina ☎04 95 26 12 01, ⓦ hotel-le-belvedere.com. This three-star is the smartest of the hotels overlooking the marina, with great views from its comfortable rooms and terraces of Capo d'Orto. Reasonable rates given the location. €75

**Brise de Mer** On the left of rte de la Marine as you approach tower from the village, opposite the telephone booths ☎04 95 26 10 28, ⓦ brise-de-mer.com. A large, old-fashioned place with very friendly service and a congenial terrace restaurant. Worth spending an extra €4–5 for a room at the back, which have the best views. April to mid-Oct. €70

**Camping Les Oliviers** At the east end of the village, next to the bend in the main road ☎04 95 26 14 49, ⓦ camping-oliviers-porto.com. Top-notch two-star site, boasting a huge, multilayered pool. April–Nov. €27

**Camping Sol e Vista** At the main road junction near the supermarkets ☎04 95 26 15 71, ⓦ camping-sole-e-vista.com. A superb location on shady terraces ascending a steep hillside with a small café at the top. Great views of Capo d'Orto cliffs opposite, and immaculate toilet blocks. April–Nov. €23

**Le Colombo** At the top of the village opposite the turning for Ota ☎04 95 26 10 14, ⓦ hotel-colombo-porto.com. An informal, sixteen-room hotel overlooking the valley, decorated in sea-blue colours with driftwood and flotsam sculpture. The rooms are functional but clean and airy, and there's a well-shaded garden for breakfast. April to mid-Oct. €90

**Le Golfe** At the base of the rock in the marina ☎04 95 26 12 31, ⓦ hotel-le-golfe-porto.com. Small, cosy and unpretentious; every room has a balcony with a sea view. Among the cheapest at this end of the village. May–Oct. €45

★ **Le Maquis** At the top of the village just beyond the Ota turning ☎04 95 26 12 19, ⓦ hotel-lemaquis.com.

FROM TOP CALVI (P.949); DÉSERT DES AGRIATES (P.947) >

A perennially popular, impeccably well-maintained budget hotel; rooms are basic, but comfortable enough, and they give good off-season discounts. Advance booking recommended; rates double in Aug; at other times, tariffs stay under €50 per double. **€94**

### EATING AND DRINKING

The overall standard of restaurants in Porto is poor, with overpriced food and indifferent service the norm, particularly during high season. There are, however, three noteworthy exceptions:

**Le Maquis** In the hotel of the same name (see p.956). Honest, affordable home cooking served in a cosy bar or on a tiny terrace that hangs over the valley. Their good-value €22 *menu* includes delicious scorpion fish in mussel sauce. Mid-March to Oct daily noon–2.30pm & 6–11pm.

**La Mer** Opposite the tower ☎04 95 26 11 27. Porto's posh option, and one of the finest seafood restaurants in the area, with fish fresh from the gulf, imaginatively prepared and served in an ideal setting. *Menus* range from €20–40 and it's best to reserve early for a seat with a view. Easter–Oct daily noon–2.30pm & 6.30–11pm.

**Le Sud** In the marina ☎04 95 26 14 11. Simple and delicious cooking from around the Mediterranean ("cuisine de tous les suds") served on a stylish teak deck overlooking the marina. Count on €35–40 for two courses plus wine and coffee. Easter–Sept daily noon–3pm & 6–11pm.

## The Calanches

The UNESCO-protected site of the **Calanches**, 5km southwest of Porto, takes its name from *calanca*, the Corsican word for creek or inlet, but the outstanding characteristics here are the vivid orange and pink rock masses and pinnacles which crumble into the dark blue sea. Liable to unusual patterns of erosion, these tormented rock formations and porphyry needles, some of which soar 300m above the waves, have long been associated with different animals and figures, of which the most famous is the Tête de Chien (Dog's Head) at the north end of the stretch of cliffs. Other figures and creatures conjured up include a Moor's head, a monocled bishop, a bear and a tortoise.

One way to see the fantastic cliffs of the Calanches is by boat from Porto (see p.955). Alternatively, you could drive along the corniche road that weaves through the granite archways on its way to Piana. Eight kilometres along the road from Porto, the *Roches Bleues* café is a convenient landmark for walkers.

### Piana

Picturesque **PIANA** occupies a prime location overlooking the Calanches, but for some reason does not suffer the deluge of tourists that Porto endures. Retaining a sleepy feel, the village comprises a cluster of pink houses ranged around an eighteenth-century church and square, from the edge of which the panoramic views over the Golfe de Porto are sublime.

### ACCOMMODATION AND EATING

PIANA

**Les Roches Rouges** Rte de Porto ☎04 95 27 81 81, ⓦ lesrochesrouges.com. Having lain empty for two decades, this elegant old *grand hôtel* rising from the eucalyptus canopy on the outskirts was restored with most of its original fittings and furniture intact, and possesses loads of *fin-de-siècle* style. The rooms are huge and light, with large shuttered windows, but make sure you get one facing the water. Non-residents are welcome to drop in for a sundowner on the magnificent terrace, or for a meal in the fresco-covered restaurant, whose *menus gastronomiques* (€34–70), dominated by local seafood delicacies, are as sophisticated as the ambience. Count on €70–80 for three courses à la carte. April–Oct. **€136**

## The Gorges de Spelunca

Spanning the 2km between the villages of **Ota** and **Évisa**, a few kilometres inland from Porto, the **Gorges de Spelunca** are a formidable sight, with bare orange granite walls, 1km deep in places, plunging into the foaming green torrent created by the confluence of the rivers Porto, Tavulella, Onca, Campi and Aïtone. The sunlight, ricocheting across the rock walls, creates a sinister effect that's heightened by the dark jagged

> ## CALANCHES WALKS
>
> The rock formations visible from the road are not a patch on what you can see from the waymarked **trails** winding through the Calanches, which vary from easy ambles to strenuous stepped ascents. An excellent leaflet highlighting the pick of the routes is available free from tourist offices. Whichever one you choose, leave early in the morning or late in the afternoon to avoid the heat in summer, and take plenty of water.
>
> • **Walk one** The most popular walk is to the Château Fort (1hr), which begins at a sharp hairpin in the D81, 700m north of the *Café Roches Rouges* (look for the car park and signboard at the roadside). Passing the famous Tête de Chien, it snakes along a ridge lined by dramatic porphyry forms to a huge square chunk of granite resembling a ruined castle. Just before reaching it there's an open platform from where the views of the gulf and Paglia Orba, Corsica's third highest mountain, are superb – one of the best sunset spots on the island – but bring a torch to help find the path back.
>
> • **Walk two** For a more challenging extension to Walk one (see above), begin instead at the *Roches Rouges Café*. On the opposite side of the road, two paths strike up the hill: follow the one on your left nearest the stream (as you face away from the café), which zigzags steeply up the rocks, over a pass and down the other side to rejoin the D81 in around 1hr 15min. About 150m west of the spot where you meet the road is the trailhead for the Château Fort walk with more superb views.
>
> • **Walk three** A small oratory niche in the cliff by the roadside, 500m south of *Café Roches Rouges*, contains a Madonna statue, Santa Maria, from where the wonderful *sentier muletier* (1hr) climbs into the rocks above. Before the road was blasted through the Calanches in 1850, this old paved path, an extraordinary feat of workmanship supported in places by dry-stone banks and walls, formed the main artery between the villages of Piana and Ota. After a very steep start, the route contours through the rocks and pine woods above the restored mill at Pont de Gavallaghiu, emerging after one hour back on the D81, roughly 1.5km south of the starting point. Return by the same path.

needles of the encircling peaks. The most dramatic part of the gorge can be seen from the road, which hugs the edge for much of its length.

## Évisa

ÉVISA's bright orange roofs emerge against a lush background of chestnut forests about 10km from Ota, on the eastern edge of the gorge, and the village makes the best base for hiking in the area. Situated 830m above sea level, it caters well for hikers and makes a pleasant stop for a taste of mountain life – the air is invariably crisp and clear, and the food particularly good.

### ACCOMMODATION

**Camping Acciola** 3km out of Évisa ☎ 04 95 26 23 01, ⓦ acciola.com. A small site, in the depths of nowhere, with a café-bar and great panorama over the mountains. Take the D84 for 2km, and turn right at the T-junction towards Cristinacce; *Acciola* lies another 400m on your left. **€18**

**La Châtaigneraie** On the west edge of the village on the Porto road ☎ 04 95 26 24 47, ⓦ hotel-la-chataigneraie.com. Set amid chestnut trees, this traditional schist and granite building is the best option in the village, with a dozen smart, cosy rooms in an annexe around the back of the main building. On the front side, a pleasant little restaurant serves mountain cooking such as wild boar stew with *pulenta* made from local chestnuts. The *patronne* is American, so English is spoken. Mid-April to mid-Oct. **€65**

### EATING

**A Tràmula** In the middle of the village ☎ 04 95 26 24 39. Traditional local cuisine – quality charcuterie, veal's tongue in *vin de myrthe*, chestnut crêpes and other delights – with ingredients sourced in or from the farms in the immediate area. Ask for a table on the tiny balcony overlooking the valley. Mains €11–20; *menu* at €24. April–Sept daily noon–3pm & 6–10.30pm; Oct–March, eves only.

**18**

## Cargèse (Carghjese)

Sitting high above a deep blue bay on a cliff scattered with olive trees, **CARGÈSE**, 20km southwest of Porto, exudes a lazy charm that attracts hundreds of well-heeled summer residents to its pretty white houses and hotels. The full-time locals, half of whom are descendants of Greek refugees who fled the Turkish occupation of the Peloponnese in the seventeenth century, seem to accept with nonchalance this inundation – and the proximity of a large Club Med complex – but the best times to visit are May and late September, when Cargèse is all but empty.

### The Roman Catholic and Greek churches

Two churches stand on separate hummocks at the heart of the village, a reminder of the old antagonism between the two cultures (resentful Corsican patriots ransacked the Greeks' original settlement in 1715 because of the newcomers' refusal to take up arms against their Genoese benefactors). The **Roman Catholic church**, built for the minority Corsican families in 1828 and one of the latest examples of Baroque in Corsica, with a trompe l'oeil ceiling. The **Greek church**, however, is the more interesting of the two: a large granite Neo-Gothic edifice built in 1852 to replace a building that had become too small for its congregation. Inside, the outstanding feature is an unusual iconostasis, a gift from a monastery in Rome, decorated with uncannily modern-looking portraits. Behind it hang icons brought over from Greece with the original settlers – the graceful Virgin and Child, to the right-hand side of the altar, is thought to date as far back as the twelfth century.

### Plage de Pero

The best beach in the area, **plage de Pero**, is 2km north of the village – head up to the junction with the Piana road and take the left fork down to the sea.

### ARRIVAL AND INFORMATION  CARGÈSE

**By bus** SAIB buses (☎04 95 22 41 99, ⓦauto carsiledebeaute.com) pass through Cargèse en route to and from Ajaccio and Porto, stopping outside the tiny main square in the centre of the village. The service runs three times daily from July to mid-Sept, twice daily on Mon–Sat in May, June and from mid- until the end Sept, and twice daily Mon–Sat from Oct–April.

**Tourist office** The village's tourist office stands on rue Dr-Dragacci (daily: July–Sept 9am–noon & 4–7pm; Oct–June 3–5pm; ☎04 95 26 41 31, ⓦcargese.net).

**Boat trips** Launch trips to the Calanches and Scandola run daily out of Cargèse in season, costing €33/50 respectively (☎04 95 28 02 66, ⓦnaveva.com). Tickets may be purchased on departure or, to secure a place in high season, in advance from the tourist office (see above).

### ACCOMMODATION

**Camping Torraccia** 4km north of Cargèse on the main road ☎04 95 26 42 39, ⓦcamping-torraccia.com. Well shaded under olive groves, its best pitches are at the top of the hill, looking inland towards Capo Vitullo (1331m); they also have simple wood cabins that can be rented on a daily basis out of season, or by the week from late June to August. **€22**

**Le Continental** Top of the village, near the turning for plage de Pero ☎04 95 26 42 24, ⓦcontinentalhotel .free.fr. Mostly sea-facing rooms (not all en suite) overlooking the main road just past place St-Jean. Clean, efficient, and good value. **€74**

**Cyrnos** Rue de la République ☎04 95 26 49 47, ⓦtorraccia.com. Simple hotel on the main street offering smallish and plain but clean rooms with mountain or sea views; the glass-partitioned balconies of the vue mer rooms look out over the church to the bay. The same family also has bargain wood chalets up the hill near *Camping Torraccia* (see opposite). **€58**

**De France** Rue Colonel-Fieschi ☎04 95 26 41 07. The rock-bottom option: a bit dark and noisy (the front rooms open onto the main road), but unbelievably cheap, even in August. **€50**

★ **Les Lentisques** plage de Pero ☎04 95 26 42 34, ⓦleslentisques.com. Head down the lane dropping downhill from the junction at the top of the village to reach this congenial, family-run three-star. Nestled in the dunes behind the area's nicest beach, it has a large, breezy breakfast hall and ten simple rooms (fully en suite and sea-facing), and there's also a fair-sized pool. **€106**

**Punta e Mare** Up the lane past the Spar supermarket ☎04 95 26 44 33, ⓦlocations-cargese.com. Secluded, unpretentious hotel tucked away on the quiet outskirts of the village. There's ample parking, and the rooms, though on the small side, are well kept and have little loggias. **€90**

**St Jean** Overlooking the crossroads ☎ 04 95 26 46 68, ⊛ lesaintjean.com. Smart rooms, some with sea views, balconies and self-catering facilities. Rates fall to €50 per double off-peak. **€100**

## EATING AND DRINKING

A fair number of restaurants are scattered about the village, as well as the standard crop of basic pizzerias, but the most tempting places to eat are down in the harbour.

**Le Cabanon de Charlotte** In the marina ☎ 06 81 23 66 93. Local seafood served on a raised teak deck overlooking the jetty. Menus at €21–30; or you can go for their copious seafood tapas. Live polyphony sessions take place in high season. Feb–Nov daily noon–2.30 & 6–11pm.

**U Rasaghiu** In the marina ☎ 04 95 26 48 60. Slightly more competitively priced than its neighbour, Le

Cabanon de Charlotte, this serves local specialtiés corses, seafood dishes (including lobster in garlic sauce) in its restaurant and huge pizzas to eat in or takeaway (€10–15) in the adjacent bistro wing. They also lay on live polyphony music two or three evenings each week in season. Menus at €18–25. Feb–Nov daily noon–2.30 & 6–11pm.

# Ajaccio (Aiacciu)

Edward Lear claimed that on a wet day it would be hard to find so dull a place as **AJACCIO**, a harsh judgement with an element of justice. The town has none of Bastia's sense of purpose and can seem to lack a definitive identity of its own, but it is a relaxed and good-looking place, with an exceptionally mild climate, and a wealth of smart cafés, restaurants and shops.

Although it's an attractive idea that Ajax, hero of the Trojan War, once stopped here, the name of Ajaccio actually derives from the Roman *Adjaccium* (place of rest), a winter stopoff point for shepherds descending from the mountains to stock up on goods and sell their produce. This first settlement was destroyed by the Saracens in the tenth century, and modern Ajaccio grew up around the citadelle founded in 1492. **Napoleon** gave the town international fame, but though the self-designated *Cité Impériale* is littered with statues and street names related to the Bonaparte family, you'll find the Napoleonic cult has a less dedicated following here than you might imagine: the emperor is still considered by many Ajacciens as a self-serving Frenchman rather than as a Corsican.

Since the early 1980s, Ajaccio has gained an unwelcome reputation for nationalist violence. The most infamous terrorist atrocity of recent decades was the murder, in February 1998, of the French government's most senior official on the island, Claude Erignac, who was gunned down as he left the opera. However, separatist violence rarely (if ever) affects tourists, and for visitors Ajaccio remains memorable for the things that have long made it attractive – its battered old town, relaxing cafés and the encompassing view of its glorious bay.

The core of the **old town** – a cluster of ancient streets spreading north and south of **place Foch**, which opens out to the seafront by the port and the marina – holds the most interest. Nearby, to the west, **place de Gaulle** forms the modern centre and is the source of the main thoroughfare, **cours Napoléon**, which extends parallel to the sea almost 2km to the northeast. West of place de Gaulle stretches the modern part of town fronted by the **beach**, overlooked at its eastern end by the citadelle.

## Place Foch

Once the site of the town's medieval gate, **place Foch** lies at the heart of old Ajaccio. A delightfully shady square sloping down to the sea, it gets its local name – place des Palmiers – from the row of palms bordering the central strip. Dominating the top end, a fountain of four marble lions provides a mount for the inevitable statue of Napoleon.

**18**

## NAPOLEON AND CORSICA

**Napoleon Bonaparte** was born in Ajaccio in 1769, a year after the French took over the island from the Genoese. They made a thorough job of it, crushing the Corsican leader Paoli's troops at Ponte Nuovo and driving him into exile. Napoleon's father Carlo, a close associate of Paoli, fled the scene of the battle with his pregnant wife in order to escape the victorious French army. But Carlo's subsequent behaviour was quite different from that of his former leader – he came to terms with the French, becoming a representative of the newly styled Corsican nobility in the National Assembly, and using his contacts with the French governor to get a free education for his children.

At the age of 9, Napoleon was awarded a scholarship to the **Brienne military academy**, an institution specially founded to teach the sons of the French nobility the responsibilities of their status, and the young son of a Corsican Italian-speaking household used his time well, leaving Brienne to enter the exclusive **École Militaire** in Paris. At the age of 16 he was commissioned into the artillery. When he was 20 the Revolution broke out in Paris and the scene was set for a remarkable career.

Always an ambitious opportunist, Napolean obtained leave from his regiment, returned to Ajaccio, joined the local Jacobin club and – with his eye on a colonelship in the Corsican militia – promoted enthusiastically the interests of the Revolution. However, things did not quite work out as he had planned, for **Pascal Paoli** had also returned to Corsica.

Carlo Bonaparte had died some years before, and Napoleon was head of a family that had formerly given Paoli strong support. Having spent the last twenty years in London, Paoli was pro-English and had developed a profound distaste for revolutionary excesses. Napoleon's French allegiance and his Jacobin views antagonized the older man, and his military conduct didn't enhance his standing at all. Elected second-in-command of the volunteer militia, Napoleon was involved in an unsuccessful attempt to wrest control of the citadelle from royalist sympathizers. He thus took much of the blame when, in reprisal for the killing of one of the militiamen, several people were gunned down in Ajaccio, an incident which engendered eight days of civil war. In June 1793, Napoleon and his family were chased back to the mainland by the Paolists.

Napoleon promptly renounced any special allegiance he had ever felt for Corsica. He Gallicized the spelling of his name, preferring Napoléon to his baptismal Napoleone. And, although he was later to speak with nostalgia about the scents of the Corsican countryside, he put the city of his birth fourth on the list of places he would like to be buried.

A humbler effigy occupies a niche high on the nearest wall – a figurine of Ajaccio's patron saint, **La Madonnuccia**, dating from 1656, a year in which Ajaccio's local council, fearful of infection from plague-struck Genoa, placed the town under the guardianship of the Madonna in a ceremony conducted on this spot.

### Salon Napoléonien

Mid-June to mid-Sept Mon–Sat 9–11.45am & 2–5.45pm; mid-Sept to mid-June Mon–Fri 9–11.45am & 2–4.45pm • €2.50

At the northern end of place Foch stands the **Hôtel de Ville** of 1826. Its first-floor is given over to the **Salon Napoléonien**, which contains a replica of the ex-emperor's death mask, along with a solemn array of Bonaparte family portraits and busts. A smaller medal room has a fragment from Napoleon's coffin and part of his dressing case, plus a model of the ship that brought his body back from St Helena.

## South of place Foch

The south side of place Foch, standing on the former dividing line between the poor district around the port and the bourgeoisie's territory, gives access to **rue Bonaparte**, the main route through the latter quarter. Built on the promontory rising to the citadelle, the secluded streets in this part of town – with their dusty buildings and hole-in-the-wall restaurants lit by flashes of sea or sky at the end of the alleys – retain more of a sense of the old Ajaccio than anywhere else.

## Maison Bonaparte

Place Letizia • April–Sept Mon daily 9am–noon & 2–6pm; Oct–April Tues–Sun 9am–noon & 2–4.45pm • €6/7 winter/summer • ⓘ 094 95 21 43 89, ⓦ musee-maisonbonaparte.fr

Napoleon was born in what's now the colossal **Maison Bonaparte**, on place Letizia, off the west side of rue Napoléon. The house passed to Napoleon's father in the 1760s and here he lived, with his wife and family, until his death. But in May 1793, the Bonapartes were driven from the house by Paoli's partisans, who stripped the place down to the floorboards. Requisitioned by the English in 1794, Maison Bonaparte became an arsenal

**18**

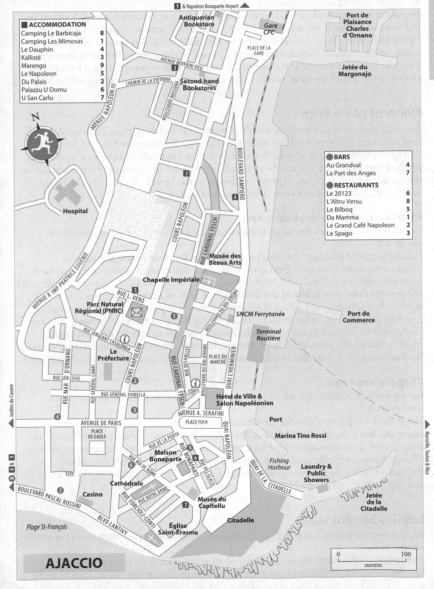

**ACCOMMODATION**

| | |
|---|---|
| Camping Le Barbicaja | 8 |
| Camping Les Mimosas | 1 |
| Le Dauphin | 4 |
| Kallisté | 3 |
| Marengo | 9 |
| Le Napoleon | 5 |
| Du Palais | 2 |
| Palazzu U Domu | 6 |
| U San Carlu | 7 |

**BARS**

| | |
|---|---|
| Au Grandval | 4 |
| La Part des Anges | 7 |

**RESTAURANTS**

| | |
|---|---|
| Le 20123 | 6 |
| L'Altru Versu | 8 |
| Le Bilboq | 5 |
| Da Mamma | 1 |
| Le Grand Café Napoleon | 2 |
| Le Spago | 3 |

**AJACCIO**

and a lodging house for English officers until Napoleon's mother Letizia herself funded its restoration. Owned by the state since 1923, the house now bears few traces of the Bonaparte family's existence. One of the few original pieces of furniture left in the house is the wooden sedan chair in the hallway – the pregnant Letizia was carried back from church in it when her contractions started. The upper floors house an endless display of portraits, miniatures, weapons, letters and documents.

## 18 The cathedral

Mon–Sat 8am–1.30pm & 2.30–6pm; no tourist visits on Sun

Napoleon was baptized in 1771 in the **cathedral**, on rue Forcioli-Conti. Modelled on St Peter's in Rome, it was built in 1587–93 on a much smaller scale than intended, owing to lack of funds – an apology for its diminutive size is inscribed in a plaque inside, on the wall to the left as you enter. Inside, to the right of the door, stands the font where he was dipped at the age of 23 months. Before you go, take a look in the chapel to the left of the altar, which houses a gloomy Delacroix painting of the Virgin.

# North of place Foch

The dark narrow streets backing onto the port to the north of place Foch are Ajaccio's traditional trading ground. Each weekday and Saturday morning (and on Sundays during the summer), the square directly behind the Hôtel de Ville hosts a small **fresh produce market** where you can browse and buy top-quality fresh produce from around the island, including myrtle liqueur, wild-boar sauces, ewe's cheese from the Niolo valley and a spread of fresh vegetables, fruit and flowers.

## Palais Fesch: Musée des Beaux Arts

May–Sept Mon, Wed & Sat 10.30am–6pm, Thurs, Fri & Sun noon–6pm; Oct–April Mon, Wed & Sat 10am–5pm, Thurs, Fri & Sat noon–5pm • €8

Behind here, the principal road leading north is **rue Cardinal-Fesch**, a delightful meandering street lined with boutiques, cafés and restaurants. Halfway along, set back from the road behind iron gates, stands Ajaccio's – indeed Corsica's – finest art gallery, the resplendent **Palais Fesch: Musée des Beaux Arts**. Cardinal Joseph Fesch was Napoleon's step-uncle and bishop of Lyon, and he used his lucrative position to invest in large numbers of paintings, many of them looted by the French armies in Holland, Italy and Germany. His bequest to the town includes seventeenth-century French and Spanish masters, but it's the Italian paintings that are the chief attraction: Titian, Bellini, Veronese, Botticelli and Michelangelo are all represented in state-of-the-art air-conditioned galleries.

## Chapelle Impériale

May–Sept Mon, Wed & Sat 10.30am–6pm, Thurs, Fri & Sun noon–6pm; Oct–April Mon, Wed & Sat 10am–5pm, Thurs, Fri & Sat noon–5pm • €1.50

You'll need a separate ticket for the **Chapelle Impériale**, which stands across the courtyard from the Musée des Beaux Arts. With its gloomy monochrome interior the chapel itself is unremarkable, and its interest lies in the crypt, where various members of the Bonaparte family are buried. It was the cardinal's dying wish that all the Bonaparte family be brought together under one roof, so the chapel was built in 1857 and the bodies – all except Napoleon's – subsequently ferried in.

# Les Îles Sanguinaires

Municipal buses (line #5) run three times hourly to Punta della Parata from cours Napoleon and place De Gaulle, passing a string of small beaches en route

The largest of the islets, Mezzo Mare (or Grande Sanguinaire), is topped by a lighthouse where Alphonse Daudet spent ten days in December 1862. Tufts of gorse, a square watchtower (la Tour de Castellucciu) and crashing surf give the place a dramatic air. Without the luxury of your own vessel, the only way to get a close look at them is to join the daily boat excursion from Porticcio and Ajaccio run by Nave Va (see below). You can, however, enjoy the iconic view of the islands from **Punta della Parata**, the narrow, rocky headland facing them from the mainland. A ten-minute clamber from the car park at the road's end takes you up to the **Tour de la Parata**, a 12m-tall watchtower built of dark grey granite in 1608. One of the last of its kind erected by the Genoese to guard the coast against Barbary pirates, it sports the rusting remains of Corsica's first aerial telegraph, installed in the latter half of the eighteenth century.

**18**

## ARRIVAL AND DEPARTURE                                    AJACCIO

### BY PLANE
Served by domestic and international flights, Ajaccio's Napoléon Bonaparte (formerly Campo dell'Oro) Airport (☎04 95 23 56 56, ⚑2a.cci.fr/Aeroport_Napoleon _Bonaparte_Ajaccio.html.fr) is 8km south of town around the bay. Shuttle buses, or *navettes* (three per hour 6.30am–10.45pm; ☎04 95 23 29 41) provide an inexpensive link with the centre, stopping on cours Napoléon, the main street – tickets cost €5 one-way, and the journey takes around 20min. The best place to pick up buses from the centre to the airport is the car park adjacent to the main bus station (*terminal routière*). Taxis charge around €20 for the trip, or slightly more on Sundays, holidays and after 7pm.

### BY BOAT
Ferries dock at the Terminal Maritime on quai L'Herminier (daily 6am–8pm; ☎04 95 29 66 99). Facilities are limited to a toilet and waiting area, where Corsica Ferries has a booking counter; the other two have offices nearby (see below). There's no left luggage here at present.
**Ferry offices** Corsica Ferries, counter inside the Terminal Maritime (☎08 25 09 50 95, ⚑corsicaferries.com); La Méridionale, on the quayside a 5min walk north of the

terminal building along bd Sampiero (☎08 10 20 13 20, ⚑lameridionale.fr); SNCM's office is opposite the main ferry terminal (☎3260, ⚑sncm.fr).
**Destinations** Marseille (4–7 weekly; 11–12hr overnight, or 4hr 30min NGV); Nice (1–5 weekly; 12–13hr overnight); Toulon (2–4 weekly; 10hr overnight).

### BY BUS
Long-distance buses work from the lay-by outside the Terminal Maritime. All of the various companies have booking and information counters inside the departures hall (to the right of the building as you enter).
**Destinations** Bastia (2–3 daily; 3hr); Bonifacio (2–3 daily; 3hr 15min); Cargèse (2–3 daily; 1hr); Corte (2 daily; 1hr 45min); Évisa (1–3 daily; 2hr 20min); Porto (1–2 daily; 2hr); Porto-Vecchio (2–5 daily; 3hr 30min); Propriano (2–6 daily; 1hr 50min); Sartène (2–6 daily; 2hr).

### BY TRAIN
The gare CFC lies almost a kilometre north along bd Sampiero (☎04 95 23 11 03, ⚑ter-sncf.com), a continuation of the quai l'Herminier.
**Destinations** Bastia (4 daily; 3hr 30min); Calvi (2 daily; 4hr); Corte (4 daily; 1hr 30min); L'Île Rousse (2 daily; 3hr 35min).

## INFORMATION

**Tourist office** Place du Marché, behind the Hôtel de Ville (April–June & Sept Mon–Sat 8am–7pm, Sun 9am–1pm; July & Aug Mon–Sat 8am–8.30pm, Sun 9am–1pm & 4–7pm; Oct–March Mon–Fri 8.30am–6pm, Sat 8.30am–noon; ☎04 95 51 53 03, ⚑ajaccio-tourisme.com). They hand out large free glossy maps and posts transport timetables for checking departure times.
**National Park Office** Anyone planning a long-distance hike should head for the office of the national parks

association, the Parc Naturel Régional de Corse, 2 rue Sergeant-Casalonga, around the corner from the préfecture on cours Napoléon (Mon–Fri 8am–noon & 2–6pm; ☎04 95 51 79 00, ⚑parc-corse.org), where you can buy Topo-guides, maps, guidebooks and leaflets.
**Hospital** Centre Hospitalier, 27 av Impératrice-Eugénie ☎04 95 29 90 90; for an ambulance, call ☎15.
**Internet** Free in the lobby of the *Hotel Kallisté* on cours Napoléon.

## GETTING AROUND

**Car rental** Rent-a-Car, at the *Hôtel Kallisté*, 51 cours Napoléon (☎04 95 51 34 45) and the airport (☎04 95 23 56 36); and Avis-Ollandini, 1 rue Colonna d'Istria (☎04 95 23 92 50) and the airport (☎04 95 21 28 01).
**Bus** The most useful of the Municipal bus routes crisscrossing the city is line #5, which runs a few times hourly from cours

Napoléon and place De Gaulle to the Îles Sanguinaires.
**Boat trips** Nave Va (☎04 95 51 31 31, ⚑naveva.com) operate popular gulf cruises from Ajaccio's Marina Tino Rossi, departing at 2.30pm. Tickets cost €34. The same firm also runs longer day-trips north as far as Scandola, and south around the coast to Bonifacio.

## ACCOMMODATION

Ajaccio suffers from a dearth of inexpensive accommodation, but there are a fair number of mid- and upscale places. Whatever your budget, it's essential to book ahead, especially for weekends between late May and September, when beds are virtually impossible to come by at short notice.

**Camping Le Barbicaja** 4.5km west along the route des Sanguinaires ☎04 95 52 01 17. Close to the beach and easier to reach by bus (#5 from place de Gaulle) than *Les Mimosas* (see below), but more crowded, and altogether grottier. April–Oct. **€24**

**Camping Les Mimosas** 3km northwest of town ☎04 95 20 99 85, ⓦcamping-lesmimosas.com. A shady and well-organized site with clean toilet blocks, friendly management and fair rates – though a long trudge if you're loaded with luggage. May–Oct. **€23**

**Le Dauphin** 11 bd Sampiero ☎04 95 21 12 94, ⓦledauphinhotel.com. No-frills place opposite the port de Commerce, above a bar that's straight out of a French crime flick, complete with pinball machine and old men sipping *pastis* under a cloud of Gauloise smoke. Various categories of rooms, some on the grotty side for the price, but their budget options in an adjacent building (with shared showers and toilets) are among the cheapest beds in town. Includes breakfast. **€75**

★ **Kallisté** 51 cours Napoléon ☎04 95 51 34 45, ⓦhotel-kalliste-ajaccio.com. Efficient, hip hotel in an eighteenth-century tenement, with plenty of parking space. Soundproofed rooms for up to four people, all with cable TVs and bathrooms. Internet facilities in lobby, and the staff speak English. Year round. **€95**

★ **Marengo** 12 bd Mme-Mère ☎04 95 21 43 66, ⓦhotel-marengo.com. A 10min walk west of the centre, up a quiet side street off bd Mme-Mère. Slightly boxed in by tower blocks, but it's a secluded, quiet and pleasant small hotel (with only 16 rooms) away from the city bustle, offering bargain rates. Mid-March to mid-Nov. **€70**

**Le Napoleon** 4 rue Lorenzo-Vero ☎04 95 51 54 00, ⓦhotel-napoleon-ajaccio.fr. Dependable upper mid-scale hotel slap in the centre of town, on a side road off cours Napoléon, in a revamped Second Empire building. Comfortable, very welcoming and good value for the location, though peak season tariffs are high. **€123**

**Du Palais** 5 av Bévérini-Vico ☎04 95 22 73 68, ⓦhoteldupalaisajaccio.com. Recently re-furbished mid-scale place, a 10min walk north of the centre, within easy reach of the train station. The rooms are on the small side, but they're impeccably clean. Ask for one at the rear of the building if you want peace and quiet. **€85**

**Palazzu U Domu** 17 rue Bonaparte ☎04 95 50 00 20, ⓦpalazzu-domu.com. The only place resembling a boutique hotel in Ajaccio, housed in a former mansion of the Pozzo di Borgo clan. Using natural materials such as teak and slate, it manages to fuse Imperial elegance with contemporary designer chic. The effect of all the dark wood and stone is a touch sombre and some of the rooms are on the gloomy side, but this is as cool as accommodation in the Imperial City gets, and it's right in the middle of the old quarter (all the other luxury hotels are well out of town). **€300**

**U San Carlu** 8 bd Danielle-Casanova ☎04 95 21 13 84, ⓦhotel-sancarlu.com. Sited opposite the citadelle and close to the beach, this three-star hotel is the poshest option on the waterfront, with sunny, well-furnished rooms, all fully a/c, and a special suite for disabled guests in the basement – but no parking. Closed Dec. **€86**

## EATING, DRINKING AND ENTERTAINMENT

At mealtimes, the alleyways and little squares of Ajaccio's old town become one large, interconnecting restaurant terrace lit by rows of candles. All too often, however, the breezy locations and views of the gulf mask indifferent cooking and inflated prices. With the majority of visitors spending merely a night or two here in transit, only those places catering for a local clientele attempt to provide real value for money. Bars and cafés jostle for pavement space along cours Napoléon, generally lined with people checking out the promenaders, and on place de Gaulle, where old-fashioned cafés and *salons de thé* offer a still more sedate scene. If you fancy a view of the bay, try one of the flashy cocktail bars that line the seafront on boulevard Lantivy, which, along with the casino, a few cinemas and a handful of overpriced clubs, comprise the sum total of Ajaccio's nightlife.

### RESTAURANTS

**Le 20123** 2 rue Roi-de-Rome ☎04 95 21 50 05, ⓦ20123.fr. Decked out like a small hill village, complete with fountain and parked Vespa, the decor here's a lot more frivolous than the food: serious Corsican gastronomy features on a single €34 *menu*. Top-notch cooking, and organic AOC wine. Noon–2.30pm & 6.30–11pm. Closed Mon, except in July & Aug.

**L'Altru Versu** Les Sept Chapelles, rte des Sanguinnaires ☎04 95 50 05 22, ⓦlaltruversu.com. Classy Corsican speciality place hosted by one of the island's top young chefs. The menu is a mouthwatering array of traditional fare given a gourmet twist: sea-bass soufflé with brocciu and fresh mint, chestnut tagliatelle. *Menus* €35–42; count on €55–85 à la carte. Daily noon–2.30pm & 6.30–11pm.

**Le Bilboq** Av des Glacis, just off place Foch ☎ 04 95 51 35 40. The eponymous patron (a former fisherman and boxer) of this legendary seafood joint is Ajaccio's undisputed "lobster king", and there's no point in coming here to eat anything but local langouste, served grilled with spaghetti. Dine al fresco on a narrow alley terrace, or inside, regaled by music of Tino Rossi (which, unlike the lobster, is definitely an acquired taste). Count on €50–70 per head for three courses, plus wine. Daily 6.30–11pm.

**Da Mamma** Passage Guinghetta ☎ 04 95 21 39 44. Tucked away down a narrow passageway connecting cours Napoléon and rue Cardinal-Fesch. Authentic but affordable Corsican cuisine – such as *cannelloni al brocciu*, roast kid and seafood – on set *menus* from €15 to €30 served in a stone-walled dining room or under a rubber tree in a tiny courtyard. Tues–Sat noon–2.30pm & 6.30–11pm, Mon 6.30–11pm.

**Le Grand Café Napoleon** 10 cours Napoléon ☎ 04 95 21 42 54. With its studiously Second Empire decor, this is Ajaccio's most genteel meeting place. Drop by for a pastry at the chi-chi *salon de thé*, or dine in Napoléon III splendour in the restaurant. *Menus* €18–45; or around €50–60 for three courses, plus wine. Daily noon–2.30pm & 6.30–11pm.

**Le Spago** 1bis rue av Emmanuel Arena ☎ 04 95 21 15 71. Thanks largely to its idiosyncratic designer interior, this funky little lounge restaurant has become one of Ajaccio's hippest places to eat. Techno DJs and local bands frequently enliven meals, and the modern Corsican food is reasonably priced. Try their tasty *raclette*, or Bonifacien-style baked aubergine; and leave room for one of the tempting desserts. Mains €13–24. Mon–Fri noon–2.30pm & 6.30–10.30pm, Sat noon–11pm.

### BARS

**Au Grandval** 4 rue Maréchal Ornano. This local bar off the place de Gaulle is worth a visit for its collection of antique photos of Ajaccio (mostly evocative portraits). Daily 8am–late.

**La Part des Anges** Diamant II, bd Lantivy ☎ 04 95 21 29 34. Lively wine bar below the place de Gaulle, near the Casino, popular with a bourgeois 18–30 crowd. Live jazz and DJs on Fri & Sat during the summer. At lunchtime it doubles as a gastro-bar, serving inventive light bites (€18–20 per head). Daily 11.30am–late.

# Le Golfe de Valinco

From Ajaccio, the vista of whitewashed villas and sandy beaches lining the opposite side of the gulf may tempt you out of town when you first arrive. On closer inspection, however, **Porticcio** turns out to be a faceless string of leisure settlements for Ajaccio's smart set, complete with tennis courts, malls and flotillas of jet-skis. Better to skip this stretch and press on south along the *route nationale* (RN194) which, after scaling the **Col de Celaccia**, winds down to the stunning **Golfe de Valinco**. A vast blue inlet bounded by rolling, scrub-covered hills, the gulf presents the first dramatic scenery along the coastal highway. It also marks the start of militant and Mafia-ridden south Corsica, more closely associated with vendetta, banditry and separatism than any other part of the island. Many of the mountain villages glimpsed from the roads hereabouts are riven with age-old divisions, exacerbated in recent years by the spread of organized crime and nationalist violence. But the island's seamier side is rarely discernible to the hundreds of thousands of visitors who pass through each summer, most of whom stay around the small port of **Propriano**, at the eastern end of the gulf. In addition to offering most of the area's tourist amenities, this busy resort town lies within easy reach of the menhirs at **Filitosa**, one of the western Mediterranean's most important prehistoric sites.

**GETTING AROUND**          **THE GOLFE DE VALINCO**

The Golfe de Valinco region is reasonably well served by public transport, with buses running four times per day between Ajaccio and Bonifacio, via Propriano and Sartène. Note, however, that outside July and August there are no services along this route on Sundays.

## Propriano (Pruprià)

Tucked into the narrowest part of the Golfe de Valinco, the small port of **PROPRIANO**, 57km southeast of Ajaccio, centres on a fine natural harbour that was exploited by the ancient Greeks, Carthaginians and Romans, but became a prime target for Saracen pirate raids in the sixteenth century, when it was largely destroyed. Redeveloped in the 1900s, it now boasts a thriving marina, and handles ferries to Toulon, Marseille and Sardinia.

## The beaches

During the summer, tourists come here in droves for the area's **beaches**. The nearest of these, **plage de Lido**, lies 1km west, just beyond the Port de Commerce, but it's nowhere near as pretty as the coves strung along the northern shore of the gulf around **Olmeto plage**. You can reach Olmeto on the three daily buses from Propriano to Porto.

### ARRIVAL AND INFORMATION

PROPRIANO

**By boat** Ferries from the mainland and Sardinia dock in the Port de Commerce, a 10min walk from rue du Général-de-Gaulle, the town's main street. The SNCM office is on quai Commandant-L'Herminier (☎ 04 95 76 04 36).

**By bus** Buses go from the roadside next to the church on rue de la Miséricorde/Montée de l'Eglise, above the village centre.

**Destinations** Ajaccio (2–4 daily; 1hr 50min); Bonifacio (2–4 daily; 1hr 35min); Porto-Vecchio (2–4 daily; 1hr 45min); Sartène (2–4 daily; 20min).

**Tourist office** Inside the harbour-master's office in the marina (June & Sept Mon–Sat 9am–noon & 3–7pm; July & Aug daily 8am–8pm; Oct–May Mon–Fri 9am–noon & 2–6pm; ☎ 04 95 76 01 49, ⊕ sartenaisvalinco.com).

### ACCOMMODATION

**Arcu di Sole** Rte de Baracci ☎ 04 95 76 05 10, ⊕ arcudisole.fr.st. A large modern pink building with green shutters, just off the main Ajaccio road, 3km west of town (turn inland by the Total petrol station). The ground-floor rooms have little balconies; those to the rear are pleasantly shaded. No views to speak of, but there's a garden pool, gourmet restaurant, tennis courts and mini-golf for the kids. April–Oct. **€118**

**Beach Hôtel** Av Napoléon ☎ 04 95 76 17 74, ⊕ perso .wanadoo.fr/beach.hotel. Spacious and comfortable en-suite rooms in a four-storey block overlooking the Port de Commerce and plage du Phare. **€89**

**Bellevue** Av Napoléon ☎ 04 95 76 01 86, ⊕ hotel -bellevue-propriano.com. The cheapest central hotel, halfway down av Napoléon and bang opposite the marina; all rooms have balconies with a view of the gulf and are cheerfully decorated. The bar is lively and popular with locals. **€95**

**Camping Colomba** 3km northeast along rte de Baracci ☎ 04 95 76 06 42, ⊕ camping-colomba.com. Take the right-hand turning off the main road by the Total petrol station to reach this medium-sized, peaceful three-star with good facilities (including a pizzeria) and plenty of shade – the best of the sites are within walking distance of town. April to mid-Oct. **€20.50**

**Gîte d'Étape U Fracintu** 7km northeast of Propriano at Burgo ☎ 04 95 76 15 05, ⊕ gite-hotel-valinco.fr. One of the largest hikers' hostels in Corsica, with room for 65 people in 2- and 3-bed rooms. Lovely views across the valley from its terrace, and right next to the Mare a Mare Sud trailhead. Advance booking essential. May–Oct. Doubles **€55**

**Lido** Between plage du Phare and plage de L'Arena Blanca, on the west edge of town ☎ 04 95 76 06 37, ⊕ le-lido.com. This low-rise hotel on the outskirts which dates from the 1930s, had a major face-lift a few years back but still possesses more character than most of the competition. That said, its rooms, ranged around a cool courtyard with rear terraces jutting on the sand behind, are ridiculously overpriced in high season. **€130**

### EATING AND DRINKING

Propriano has more than its fair share of duff restaurants – most of them lining the marina. The swish terraced establishments on the waterfront along avenue Napoléon can be relied upon for fresh croissants at breakfast and maybe a pizza, but few live up to their location when it comes to serious cooking. For that, you'll have to stick to the places reviewed below.

★ **Chez Charlot** Viggianello, 4.4km east up the D19 ☎ 04 95 76 00 06. Down-to-earth village cuisine – Corsican soup, veal bruschettas, stuffed courgettes, roast pork, tripe, rabbit stew and pan-fried snapper – offered on a superb-value €23 menu. You can eat indoors or out on a narrow terrace next to the church which surveys the entire gulf. Daily noon–2.30 & 6.30–11pm.

**Le Croco d'Île** 7 quai L'Herminier ☎ 04 95 73 27 85. Dependable pizzeria on the quayside next to where the ferries dock. A bit out of the way, but the wood-fired pizzas are juicy and they do a range of sensibly priced grilled meats, as well as seafood. Live music most evenings in summer. *Menus* €16–20. Daily noon–2.30pm & 6–11pm.

**No Stress Café – Bischof** 24 av Napoléon ☎04 95 51 2 77 08. This place occupies a prime spot, with great views over the harbour from its rear terraces. Charcoal-grilled local meat specialities are their forté, but they also do a mean prawn risotto and proper pizzas for those on tighter budgets. *Menus* €20–25. Daily noon–2.30pm & 6–11pm.

★**Tempi Fa** 7 Rue Napoleon ☎04 95 76 06 52, ⊚tempi-fa.com/. Done out in rustic Corsican style, with exposed stone walls and sides of ham dangling from the rafters, *Tempi* Fa functions as a local produce boutique by day and a lively tapas bar in the evenings, where you can order plates of top-notch charcuterie, local cheese, Alta Rocca olives and Rizzanese wines, while perched on stools around old barrels on the terrace or inside a cosy dining hall with antique tiled floors and wooden ceilings. Tapas *assiettes* €9–13; *menus* €13.50–24. March–Dec daily 11.30am–2.30pm & 6pm–late.

**Terra Cotta** 29 av Napoléon ☎04 95 74 23 80. The town's swankiest restaurant, with tables in a cool, Moroccan-style bistro, or out on a seafront terrace. The cooking is uncompromisingly sophisticated, using only the freshest local seafood, and the service smiling. *Formules* at lunchtime from €22; count on €60–70 à la carte; reservations recommended in the evenings. Mid-June to mid-Sept Mon–Sat noon–3pm & 6.30–11pm, closed Sun lunchtime; mid-March to mid-June & mid-Sept to mid-Nov closed Sun.

## Filitosa

Easter–Oct 8am–sunset, out of season by arrangement only • €7 • ☎04 95 74 00 91, ⊚filitosa.fr

Set deep in the countryside of the fertile Vallée du Taravo, the extraordinary **Station Préhistorique de Filitosa**, 17km north of Propriano, comprises a wonderful array of statue-menhirs and prehistoric structures encapsulating some eight thousand years of history. There's no public transport to the site; vehicles should be parked in the small car park five-minutes' walk from the entrance in the village.

Filitosa was settled by Neolithic farming people who lived here in rock shelters until the arrival of navigators from the east in about 3500 BC. These invaders were the creators of the menhirs, the earliest of which were possibly phallic symbols worshipped by an ancient fertility cult. When the seafaring people known as the Torréens (after the towers they built on Corsica) conquered Filitosa around 1300 BC, they destroyed most of the menhirs, incorporating the broken stones into the area of dry-stone walling surrounding the site's two *torri*, or towers, examples of which can be found all over the south of Corsica. The site remained undiscovered until a farmer stumbled across the ruins on his land in the late 1940s.

### The Filitosas

**Filitosa V** looms up on the right shortly after the main entrance to the site. The largest statue-menhir on the island, it's an imposing spectacle, with clearly defined facial features and a sword and dagger outlined on the body. Beyond a sharp left turn lies the *oppidum* or central monument, its entrance marked by the **eastern platform**, thought to have been a lookout post. The cave-like structure sculpted out of the rock is the only evidence of Neolithic occupation and is generally agreed to have been a burial mound. Straight ahead, the Torréen **central monument** comprises a scattered group of menhirs on a circular walled mound, surmounted by a dome and entered by a corridor of stone slabs and lintels. Nobody is sure of its exact function.

Nearby **Filitosa XIII** and **Filitosa IX**, implacable lumps of granite with long noses and round chins, are the most impressive of the menhirs. Filitosa XIII is typical of the figures made just before the Torréen invasion, with its vertical dagger carved in relief – **Filitosa VII** also has a clearly sculpted sword and shield. Filitosa **VI**, from the same period, is remarkable for its facial detail. On the eastern side of the central monument stand some vestigial Torréen houses, where fragments of ceramics dating from 5500 BC were discovered; they represent the most ancient finds on the site, and some of them are displayed in the museum.

**18**

**18**

### The western monument

The **western monument**, a two-roomed structure built underneath another walled mound, is thought to have been some form of Torréen religious building. A flight of steps leads to the foot of this mound, where a footbridge opens onto a meadow that's dominated by five statue-menhirs arranged in a semicircle beneath a thousand-year-old olive tree. A bank separates them from the quarry from which the megalithic sculptors hewed the stone for the menhirs – a granite block is marked ready for cutting.

### The museum

The **museum** is a downbeat affair, but the artefacts themselves are fascinating. The major item here is the formidable **Scalsa Murta**, a huge menhir dating from around 1400 BC and discovered at Olmeto. Like other statue-menhirs of this period, this one has two indents in the back of its head, which are thought to indicate that these figures would have been adorned with headdresses. Other notable exhibits are **Filitosa XII**, which has a hand and a foot carved into the stone, and **Trappa II**, a strikingly archaic face.

# Sartène (Sartè) and around

Prosper Mérimée famously dubbed **SARTÈNE** *"la plus corse des villes corses"* ("the most Corsican of Corsican towns"), but the nineteenth-century German chronicler Gregorovius put a less complimentary spin on it when he described it as a "town peopled by demons". Sartène hasn't shaken off its hostile image, despite being a smart, better-groomed place than many small Corsican towns. The main square, Place Porta, doesn't offer many diversions once you've explored the enclosed *vielle ville*, and the only time of year Sartène teems with tourists is at Easter for **U Catenacciu**, a Good Friday procession that packs the main square with onlookers.

Close to Sartène are some of the island's best-known **prehistoric sites**, most notably Filitosa, the megaliths of **Cauria** and the **Alignement de Palaggiu** – Corsica's largest array of prehistoric standing stones – monuments from which are displayed in the town's excellent museum.

## Place Porta and Santa Anna

**Place Porta** – its official name, place de la Libération, has never caught on – forms Sartène's nucleus. Once the arena for bloody vendettas, it's now a well-kept square opening onto a wide terrace. Flanking the north side is the **church of Ste-Marie**, built in the 1760s but completely restored to a smooth granitic appearance. Inside the church, the most notable feature is the weighty wooden cross and chair carried through the town by hooded penitents during the Easter **Catenacciu** procession.

A flight of steps to the left of the **Hôtel de Ville**, formerly the governor's palace, leads past the post office to a ruined **lookout tower** (*échauguette*), which is all that remains of the town's twelfth-century ramparts. This apart, the best of the *vieille ville* is to be found behind the Hôtel de Ville in the **Santa Anna** district, a labyrinth of constricted passageways and ancient fortress-like houses. Featuring few windows and often linked to their neighbours by balconies, these houses are entered by first-floor doors which would have been approached by ladders – dilapidated staircases have replaced these necessary measures against unwelcome intruders.

## Musée départemental de préhistoire corse et d'archéologie

Daily 9am–7pm • €5 • ⓦ prehistoire-corse.org

A noteworthy attraction in Sartène is the recently revamped **Musée départemental de préhistoire corse et d'archéologie**. Exhibits comprise mostly Neolithic and Torréen pottery fragments, with some bracelets and glass beads from the Iron Age, and painted ceramics from the thirteenth to sixteenth centuries.

## ARRIVAL AND INFORMATION

**By bus** Arriving in Sartène by bus, you'll be dropped either at the top of avenue Gabriel-Péri or at the end of cours Général-de-Gaulle.

**Tourist office** Cours Soeur Amélie (summer only Mon–Fri 9am–noon & 2.30–6pm; ☎04 95 77 15 40, ⓦoti-sartenaisvalinco.com).

## ACCOMMODATION

**18**

**Domaine de Croccano** 3km down the D148 ☎04 95 77 11 37, ⓦcorsenature.com. This gorgeous eighteenth-century farmhouse, hidden in a fold of the Rizzanese Valley, has breathtaking views over the Sartenais from its vine-covered terraces. Tariffs hover around €90 per double, although in July & August you have to stay for a minimum of one week (€714). **€90**

**U Farrandu** 1km down the main Propriano road ☎04 95 73 41 69. Pleasant, friendly and well-shaded site just

off the main road. May–Oct. **€20**

**U San Damianu** Just across the bridge from the vieille ville, beneath the convent of the same name ☎04 95 70 55 41, ⓦsandamianu.fr. A three-star occupying a plum spot with spectacular views over the town and valley. It's a bit bland, but offers all the comforts and amenities you'd expect for a hotel in this class, including a lovely pool and teak sun terrace. **€162**

## EATING

In addition to the restaurants listed below, cafés cluster around place Porta, and are great places for crowd-watching.

**Auberge Santa Barbara** 2km out of town on the Propriano road ☎04 95 77 09 66, ⓦsantabarbara.fr. This smart Corsican gourmet restaurant on the outskirts does gastro versions of Sartenais dishes from both the coast and interior: langoustine salad, roast pigeon with wild myrtle berries, *courgettes al brocciu*, and divine *milles feuilles aux fruits rouges* – in addition to Mme Lovich's legendary *flan grandemère*. You can wait for your table in a comfy sofa under the palms, while enjoying the views of

the *vielle ville*. Easter–mid-Oct, daily noon–3pm & 6.30–11pm.

**Restaurant du Cours ("Chez Jean")** 20 cours Soeur Amélie ☎04 95 77 19 07. Wholesome, honest *cuisine sartenaise* (pork stews, stuffed courgettes and local liver sausage grilled over an open fire), as well as inexpensive pizzas, served in a stone-walled inn. In winter they cook in the open hearth. House *menus* €16–25. Daily noon–3pm & 6.30–11pm.

# The megalithic sites

Sparsely populated today, the rolling hills of the southwestern corner of Corsica are rich in prehistoric sites. The megaliths of **Cauria**, standing in ghostly isolation 10km southwest from Sartène, comprise the Dolmen de Fontanaccia, the best-preserved monument of its kind on Corsica, while the nearby alignments of **Stantari** and **Renaggiu** have an impressive congregation of statue-menhirs.

More than 250 menhirs can be seen northwest of Cauria at **Palaggiu**, another rewardingly remote site. Equally wild is the coast hereabouts, with deep clefts and coves providing some excellent spots for diving and secluded swimming.

As you snake your way through the maquis, the **Dolmen de Fontanaccia** eventually comes into view on the horizon, crowning the crest of a low hill amid a sea of vegetation. A blue sign at the parking space indicates the track to the dolmen, a fifteen-minute walk away.

Known to the locals as the **Stazzona del Diavolu** (Devil's Forge), a name that does justice to its enigmatic power, the Dolmen de Fontanaccia is in fact a burial chamber from around 2000 BC. This period was marked by a change in burial customs – whereas bodies had previously been buried in stone coffins in the ground, they were now placed above, in a mound of earth enclosed in a stone chamber. What you see today is a great stone table, comprising six huge granite blocks nearly 2m high, topped by a stone slab that remained after the earth eroded away.

The twenty "standing men" of the **Alignement de Stantari**, 200m to the east of the dolmen, date from the same period. All are featureless, except two which have roughly sculpted eyes and noses, with diagonal swords on their fronts and sockets in their heads where horns would probably have been attached.

Across a couple of fields to the south is the **Alignement de Renaggiu**, a gathering of forty menhirs standing in rows amid a small shadowy copse, set against the enormous granite outcrop of Punta di Cauria. Some of the menhirs have fallen, but all face north to south, a fact that seems to rule out any connection with a sun-related cult.

**18**

### GETTING THERE                                      THE MEGALITHIC SITES

**By car** To reach the Cauria megalithic site, you need to turn off the N196 about 2km outside Sartène, at the Col de l'Albitrina (291m), taking the D48 towards Tizzano. Four kilometres along this road a left turning brings you onto a winding road through maquis. Keep going until you see the Dolmen de Fontanaccia, about 2km later.

## Palaggiu

The **Alignement de Palaggiu** holds the largest concentration of menhirs in Corsica. Stretching in straight lines across the countryside like a battleground of soldiers, the 258 menhirs include three statue-menhirs with carved weapons and facial features – they are amid the first line you come to. Dating from around 1800 BC, the statues give few clues as to their function, but it's a reasonable supposition that proximity to the sea was important – the famous Corsican archeologist Roger Grosjean's theory is that the statues were some sort of magical deterrent to invaders.

### GETTING THERE                                                  PALAGGIU

**By car** To reach the Palaggiu by road (there are no buses covering this route), regain the D48 and head southwards past the Domaine la Mosconi vineyard (on your right, 3km after the Cauria turn-off), 1500m beyond which a green metal gate on the right side of the road marks the turning. From here a badly rutted dirt track leads another 1200m to the stones, lost in the maquis, with vineyards spread over the hills in the half-distance.

# Bonifacio (Bonifaziu) and around

**BONIFACIO** enjoys a superbly isolated location at Corsica's southernmost point, a narrow peninsula of dazzling white limestone creating a town site unlike any other. The much-photographed **haute ville**, a maze of narrow streets flanked by tall Genoese tenements, rises seamlessly out of sheer cliffs that have been hollowed and striated by the wind and waves, while on the landward side the deep cleft between the peninsula and the mainland forms a perfect natural harbour. A haven for boats for centuries, this inlet is nowadays a chic marina that attracts yachts from around the Med. Its geography has long enabled Bonifacio to maintain a certain temperamental detachment from the rest of Corsica, and the town today remains distinctly more Italian than French in atmosphere. It retains Renaissance features found only here, and its inhabitants have their own dialect based on Ligurian, a legacy of the days when this was practically an independent Genoese colony.

Such a place has its inevitable drawbacks: exorbitant prices, overwhelming crowds in July and August and a commercial cynicism that's atypical of Corsica as a whole. However, the old town forms one of the most arresting spectacles in the Mediterranean, and warrants at least a day-trip. If you plan to come in peak season, try to get here early in the day before the bus parties arrive at around 10am.

## Montée Rastello

At the end of the café-lined **quai Comparetti**, just before the **port commercial** where ferries leave for Sardinia, a flight of steps – **Montée Rastello** – lead uphill to the **haute ville**. The climb is rewarded by a magnificent view of the white limestone cliffs tapering

**18**

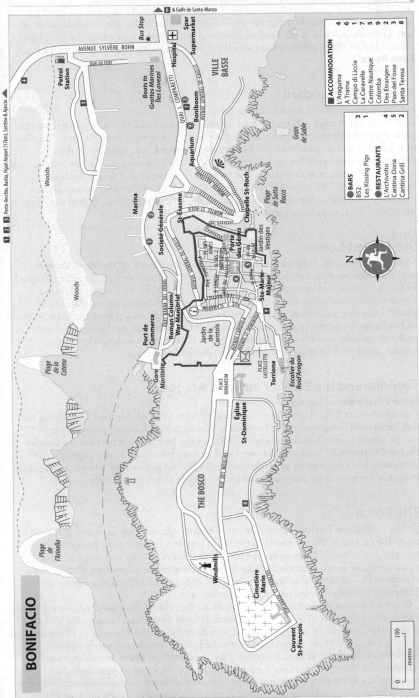

# BONIFACIO

**6** & Golfe de Santa-Manza

**1 2 3** Porto-Vecchio, Bastia, Figari Airport (17km), Sartène & Ajaccio

Sardinia

N

Bus Stop

Spar
Supermarket

AVENUE SYLVÈRE BOHN

QUAI DU PORT

Petrol
Station

Hospital

Boats to
Grottes Marines
Îles Lavezzi

QUAI J. COMPARETTI

AVENUE GÉNÉRAL DE GAULLE

Bonboom

VILLE
BASSE

Grain
de Sable

Aquarium

Marina

Plage
de Sutta
Rocca

Chapelle St-Roch

St-Erasme

Société Générale

MONTÉE ST-ROCH

Porte
des Gênes

Jardin des
Vestiges

Woods

Ste-Marie-
Majeur

Port de
Commerce

Roman Column/
War Memorial

QUAI BANDA DEL FERRO

Jardin de
la Carotols

Plage
de la
Catena

Gare
Maritime

PLACE
BIRKHAKEM

PLACE
CASTELLETTO

Torrione

Escalier du
Roi d'Aragon

Woods

Église
St-Dominique

THE BOSCO

RUE DES MOULINS

Plage
de
l'Arinella

Windmills

Cimetière
Marin

Couvent
St-François

metres
0        100

**ACCOMMODATION**
| L'Araguina | 4 |
| A Trama | 6 |
| Campo di Liccia | 7 |
| La Caravelle | 5 |
| Centre Nautique | 9 |
| Colomba | 3 |
| Des Etrangers | 2 |
| Pian del Fosse | 3 |
| Santa Teresa | 8 |

**BARS**
| B52 | 3 |
| Les Kissing Pigs | 1 |

**RESTAURANTS**
| L'Archivolto | 4 |
| Cantina Doria | 5 |
| Cantina Grill | 2 |

to Capu Persutau, and the huge lump of fallen rock-face called the Grain de Sable. The tiny **Chapelle St-Roch**, at the head of steps, was built on the spot where the last plague victim died in 1528; another, narrower stone staircase twists down to the tiny beach of **Sutta Rocca**.

## Bastion de l'Étendard

April–June & Sept Mon–Sat 10am–5.30pm; July & Aug daily 9am–9pm • €2.50

Montée St-Roch takes you up the final approach to the citadelle walls, entered via the great **Porte des Gênes**, once the only gateway to the *haute ville*. It opens on to the place des Armes, where you can visit the **Bastion de l'Étendard**, sole remnant of the fortifications destroyed during a siege in 1554. While exploring the narrow streets, look out for flamboyant marble escutcheons above the doorways and double-arched windows separated by curiously stunted columns. Many of the older houses did not originally have doors; the inhabitants used to climb up a ladder which they would pull up behind them to prevent a surprise attack.

## Ste-Marie-Majeure

Cutting across rue du Palais de Garde brings you to the church of **Ste-Marie-Majeure**, originally Romanesque but restored in the eighteenth century, though the richly sculpted belfry dates from the fourteenth century. The facade is hidden by a loggia where the Genoese municipal officers used to dispense justice in the days of the republic. The church's treasure, a fragment of the True Cross, was saved from a shipwreck in the Straits of Bonifacio; for centuries after, the citizens would take the relic to the edge of the cliff and pray for calm seas whenever storms raged. It is kept under lock and key in the sacristy, along with an ivory cask containing relics of St Boniface.

## Torrione and the Escalier du Roi d'Aragon

Escalier du Roi d'Aragon June–Sept daily 11am–5.30pm • €2.50

Rue Doria leads towards the Bosco (see below); at the end of this road a left down rue des Pachas will bring you to the **Torrione**, a 35-metre-high lookout post built in 1195 on the site of Count Bonifacio's castle. Descending the cliff from here are the **Escalier du Roi d'Aragon**'s 187 steps, which were said to have been built in one night by the Aragonese in an attempt to gain the town in 1420, but in fact they had already been in existence for some time and were used by the people to fetch water from a well.

## The Bosco

To the west of the Torrione lies the **Bosco**, a quarter named after the wood that used to cover the far end of the peninsula in the tenth century. In those days a community of hermits dwelt here, but nowadays the limestone plateau is open and desolate. The entrance to the Bosco is marked by the **Église St-Dominique** (admission €2.50), a rare example of Corsican Gothic architecture – it was built in 1270, most probably by the Templars, and later handed over to the Dominicans.

Beyond the church, rue des Moulins leads on to the ruins of three **windmills** dating from 1283, two of them decrepit, the third restored. Behind them stands a memorial to the 750 people who died when a troopship named *Sémillante* ran aground here in 1855, on its way to the Crimea, one of the many disasters wreaked by the notoriously windy straits.

The tip of the Bosco plateau is occupied by the **Cimetière Marin**, its white crosses standing out sharply against the deep blue of the sea. Open until sundown, the cemetery is a fascinating place to explore, with its flamboyant mausoleums displaying a jumble of architectural ornamentations. Next to the cemetery stands the **Couvent**

St-François, allegedly founded after St Francis sought shelter in a nearby cave – the story goes that the convent was the town's apology to the holy man, over whom a local maid had nearly poured a bucket of slops. Immediately to the south, the **Esplanade St-François** commands fine views across the bay to Sardinia.

## ARRIVAL AND DEPARTURE

**By car** Most of the town's car parks lie to the left of the marina as you arrive. The municipal ones charge around €5 per half-day; launch operators also have their own lots further down the lane towards Pertusato, where you can park for free if you buy a ticket for one of their boat trips.

**By bus** Buses drop passengers in the marina, next to the tourist office.

Destinations Ajaccio (2 daily; 3hr 30min); Bastia (2–4 daily; 3hr 25min); Porto-Vecchio (1–4 daily; 30–40min);

### BONIFACIO

Propriano (2–4 daily; 1hr 40min); Sartène (2 daily; 1hr 25min).

**By plane** Figari airport, 17km north of Bonifacio (☎ 04 95 71 10 10, ⓦ 2a.cci.fr), handles flights from mainland France and a few charters from the UK. There's a seasonal bus service operated by Transports Rossi (☎ 04 95 71 00 11) that in theory should meet incoming flights, stopping at Bonifacio en route to Porto-Vecchio; otherwise, your only option is to take a taxi into town – around €50.

**18**

## INFORMATION

**Tourist office** The tourist office in the *haute ville*, at the bottom of rue F. Scamaroni (July–Sept daily 9am–7pm; Oct–June Mon–Fri 9am–noon & 2–5pm; ☎ 04 95 73 11 88, ⓦ bonifacio.fr) has audioguides for hire in English and French (€5 for 1hr 30min tour).

**Care hire** Cars may be rented from Avis, quai Banda del Ferro (☎ 04 95 73 01 28); Citer, quai Noel-Beretti (☎ 04 95 73 13 16); Hertz, quai Banda del Ferro (☎ 04 95 73 06 41). All of the above also have branches at Figari airport.

**Banks** If you need to change money, note the ATM at Bonifacio's only bank, the Société Générale on the quai Comparetti, frequently runs out of bills, so get there early in the day. Aside from the rip-off *bureaux de change* dotted around town, the only other source of cash is the post office up in the *haute ville* (Mon–6am–6pm, Sat 6am–noon).

**Internet** Scara Lunga Quai Comparetti (daily 7am–10pm; ☎ 04 95 73 55 45).

## ACCOMMODATION

Finding a place to stay can be a chore, as the hotels are quickly booked up in high season; for a room near the centre, reserve well in advance, and brace yourself for a lot of noise at night if you nab a room on the quayside – Bonifacio becomes a proper party town when the Italians descend in August. Better still, save yourself the trouble, and a considerable amount of money, by finding a room somewhere else and travelling here for the day; tariffs in this town are the highest on the island. The same applies to the large campsites dotted along the road to Porto-Vecchio, which can get very crowded.

**L'Araguina** av Sylvère-Bohn ☎ 04 95 73 02 96, ⓦ campingaraguina.fr. The closest campsite to town, but unwelcoming, cramped in season, and with inadequate washing and toilet facilities. Avoid unless desperate – though its undoubtedly the most convenient if you're backpacking. April–Sept. **€17.50**

**A Trama** 1.5km from Bonifacio along the Rte de Santa Manza ☎ 04 95 73 17 17, ⓦ a-trama.com. Discreet three-star, hidden behind a screen of maquis, palms, pines and dry-stone chalk walls. The chalet rooms, all with private terraces, are grouped around a garden and pool; some could do with modernizing, but the lovely outside space is ample compensation, especially if you're travelling with kids, and there's a classy restaurant (*Le Clos Vatel*). Expensive in high summer, but more affordable off season. **€200**

**Campo di Liccia** 3km north towards Porto-Vecchio ☎ 04 95 73 03 09, ⓦ campingdiliccia.com. Well shaded and large, so you're guaranteed a place. April–Oct. **€17**

**La Caravelle** 35 quai J. Comparetti ☎ 04 95 73 00 03, ⓦ hotelrestaurant-lacaravelle-bonifacio.com.

Long-established place in prime location on the quayside, whose standard rooms are on the small side for the price, though clean and with modern bathrooms, and there's ample guest parking. The real downside is the discotheque next door, which blasts music until 2am in high season. April–Oct. **€134**

**Centre Nautique** On the marina ☎ 04 95 73 02 11, ⓦ centre-nautique.com. Chic but relaxed hotel on the waterfront, fitted out with mellow wood and nautical charts. All rooms are stylishly furnished and consist of two storeys connected with a spiral staircase, though their breakfasts (€12) are a rip-off – you get much better value at the quayside cafés. **€200**

**Colomba** Rue Simon Varsi ☎ 04 95 73 73 44, ⓦ hotel-bonifacio-corse.fr. The only hotel worthy of note in the thick of the old quarter occupies a smartly renovated medieval tenement on one of the *haute ville's* prettiest streets. It offers ten classically furnished, en-suite rooms, some with shuttered widows opening to magnificent sea views. Parking available. April–Oct. **€165**

**18**

**Des Étrangers** 4 av Sylvère-Bohn ☎04 95 73 01 09, ⓦhoteldesetrangers.fr. Simple rooms (the costlier ones have TV and a/c) facing the main road, just up the main Porto-Vecchio road from the port. Nothing special, but good value for Bonifacio, especially in July & Aug. April–Oct. **€75**

**Pian del Fosse** 4km out of town on the rte de Santa Manza ☎04 95 73 16 34. Big three-star site that's very peaceful and quiet in June & September, and well placed for the beaches. April to mid-Oct. **€19**

**Santa Teresa** Quartier St-François ☎04 95 73 11 32, ⓦhotel-santateresa.com. Large, modern and efficient three-star on the clifftop overlooking the Cimetière Marin, noteworthy for its stupendous views across the straits to Sardinia. Not all the rooms are sea-facing, though, so ask for "vue mer avec balcon" when you book. April–Oct. **€160**

## EATING, DRINKING AND NIGHTLIFE

Eating possibilities in Bonifacio might seem unlimited, but it's best to avoid the chintzy restaurants in the marina, few of which merit their exorbitant prices. For a snack, try the boulangerie-pâtisserie *Faby*, 4 rue St-Jean-Baptiste, in the *haute ville*, a tiny local bakery serving Bonifacien treats such as *pain des morts* (sweet buns with walnuts and raisins) and *migliacis* (buns made with fresh ewe's cheese), in addition to the usual range of spinach and brocciu *bastelles*, baked here in the traditional way – on stone. For a scrumptious, budget Bonifacien breakfast you can buy a *pain de morts* warm out of the oven at the *Pâtisserie Sorba* (follow the smell of baking bread to the bottom of the Montée Rastello steps) and take it to *Bar du Quai* a couple of doors down.

### RESTAURANTS

**L'Archivolto** Rue de l'Archivolto ☎04 95 73 17 58. With its candlelit, antique- and junk-filled interior, this would be the most commendable place to eat in the *haute ville* were the cooking a little less patchy and the prices fairer. But it still gets packed out – reservations are recommended. Lunch *menus* around €19–25; evening à la carte only, around €35–40 for three courses. Easter–June & Sept–Oct Mon–Sat noon–3pm & 6–11pm; July & Aug daily noon–3pm & 6–11pm.

**★ Cantina Doria** 27 rue Doria ☎04 95 73 50 49, ⓦcantinagrill.fr. Down-to-earth Corsican specialities at down-to-earth prices. Their popular three-course €18 *menu* – which includes the house speciality, aubergines *à la bonifacienne* – offers unbeatable value for the *haute ville*, though you'll soon bump up your bill if you succumb to the temptations of the excellent wine selection. June to mid-Sept daily noon–3pm & 6–11pm; March–May & mid-Sept to Oct closed Sat.

**Cantina Grill** Quai Banda del Ferro ☎04 95 70 49 86, ⓦcantinagrill.fr. Same patron as the popular Cantina Doria (see above) in the citadelle, but down in the marina and with a better choice of seafood (octopus risotto, swordfish steaks, fish soup). They also do succulent grillades with a selection of different sauces. The food is dependably fresh, well prepared and presented, and the prices great value. June to mid-Sept daily noon–3pm & 6–11pm; March–May & mid-Sept to Oct closed Sat.

### BARS

**B52** Quai Comparetti ⓦfacebook.com/B52cafe bonifacio. Hippest of the waterfront lounge bars, hosting DJs on weekends and throughout peak season. Mid-June to mid-Sept daily 8pm–2am.

**Les Kissing Pigs** Quai Banda del Ferro ☎04 95 73 56 99. Curiously themed wine bar boasting the world's largest collection of kissing pig photos and other snout-related ephemera. They serve all the island's top wines (by the glass and carafe, as well as bottle), accompanied by fragrant *charcuterie maison* (try the pungeant two-year-old *figatellu*), grillades, flans and salads. *Menus* €15–22. Daily 11am–late.

# Around Bonifacio

There are impressive views of the citadelle from the **cliffs** at the head of the montée Rastello (reached via the pathway running left from the top of the steps), but they're not a patch on the spectacular panorama from the sea. Throughout the day, a flotilla of excursion **boats** (see box opposite) ferries visitors out to the best vantage points, taking in a string of caves and other landmarks only accessible by water en route, including the **Îles Lavezzi**, the scattering of small islets where the troop ship *Sémillante* was shipwrecked in 1855, now designated as a nature reserve. The whole experience of bobbing around to an amplified running commentary is about as touristy as Bonifacio gets, but it's well worth enduring just to round the mouth of the harbour and see the *vieille ville*, perched atop the famous chalk cliffs. The Lavezzi islets themselves are surrounded by wonderfully clear sea water, offering Corsica's best snorkelling. On your way back, you skirt the famous **Île Cavallo**, or "millionaire's island", where the

## BOAT TRIPS FROM BONIFACIO

From the moment you arrive in Bonifacio, you'll be pestered by touts from the many boat companies running excursions out of the harbour. There are more than a dozen of these, but they all offer more or less the same routes, at the same prices.

Lasting between thirty and forty-five minutes, the shorter trips take you out along the cliffs to the *grottes marines* (sea caves) and *calanches* (inlets) below the old town; tickets cost €15–20 depending on the demand and how well you can haggle.

Longer excursions out to the **Îles Lavezzi**, part of the archipelago to the east of the straits of Bonifacio, cost around €25–35. Most companies offer a shuttle (*navette*) service, allowing you to spend as much time as you like on the islands before returning. Boats go out past the Grain de Sable and Phare du Pertusato and then moor at the main island of **Lavezzi**, beside the **cimetière Achiarino**. Buried in two walled cemeteries are the victims of the *Sémillante* shipwreck of 1855, in which 773 crew members and soldiers bound for the Crimean War were drowned after their vessel was blown onto the rocks.

Classified as a nature reserve since 1982, the islets are home to several rare species of **wild flower**, and offer fabulous **snorkelling** and some exquisite shell-sand **beaches**. A network of footpaths runs between them, well waymarked, as you're not permitted to wander off into the fragile vegetation.

18

likes of Princess Caroline of Monaco and other French and Italian glitterati have luxury hideaways.

### The beaches

The **beaches** within walking distance of Bonifacio are generally smaller and less appealing than most in southern Corsica. For a dazzling splash of turquoise, you'll have to follow the narrow, twisting lane east of town in the direction of Pertusatu lighthouse, turning left when you see signs for **Piantarella**, Corsica's kitesurfing hotspot. A twenty-minute walk south around the shore from there takes you past the remains of a superbly situated Roman villa to a pair of divine little coves, Grand Sperone and Petit Sperone – both shallow and perfect for kids.

Another superb beach in the area is **Rondinara**, a perfect shell-shaped cove of turquoise water enclosed by dunes and a pair of twin headlands. Located 10km north (east of N198), it's sufficiently off the beaten track to remain relatively peaceful (outside school holidays). Facilities are minimal, limited to a smart wooden beach restaurant, paying car park and campsite (see below). Shade is at a premium, so come armed with a parasol.

### ACCOMMODATION
THE BEACHES

**Camping Rondinara** Rondinara beach ☎ 04 95 70 43 15, ⓦ rondinara.fr. Facilities at Rodinara beach are minimal but include this well set up campsite, which boasts its own pool, bar, pizzeria and grocery store, and is only a minute's walk from the sand. Mid-May to Sept. **€21**

# Porto-Vecchio and around

Set on a hillock overlooking a beautiful deep blue bay, **PORTO-VECCHIO**, 25km north of Bonifacio, was rated by James Boswell as one of "the most distinguished harbours in Europe". It was founded in 1539 as a second Genoese stronghold on the east coast, Bastia being well established in the north. The site was perfect: close to the unexploited and fertile plain, it benefited from secure high land and a sheltered harbour, although the mosquito population spread malaria and wiped out the first Ligurian settlers within months. Things began to take off mainly thanks to the cork industry, which still thrived well into the twentieth century. Today most revenue comes from tourists, the vast majority of them well-heeled Italians who flock here for the fine outlying **beaches**. To the northwest, the little town of **Zonza** makes a good base for exploring the dramatic forest that surrounds one of Corsica's most awesome road trips, the **route de Bavella**.

Around the centre of town there's not much to see, apart from the well-preserved **fortress** and the small grid of **ancient streets** backing onto the main place de la République. East of the square you can't miss the **Porte Génoise**, which frames a delightful expanse of sea and saltpans and through which you'll find the quickest route down to the modern marina, which is lined with cafés and restaurants.

## ARRIVAL AND INFORMATION

**By plane** Figari airport, 28km southwest, is served by weekly charter flights to various destinations in northern Europe, and by domestic departures to several cities on the French mainland. During the summer, a bus leaves three or four times daily from the marina; tickets cost €1 single. Timetable information appears online at ⓦ corsicabus.org, or contact Transports Rossi direct on ☎ 04 95 71 00 11. Taxis charge €40–50, depending on the time of day.

**By bus** Porto-Vecchio doesn't have a bus station; instead, the various companies who come here stop and depart outside their agents' offices on the edge of the *haute ville*.

Destinations Ajaccio (2–4 daily; 3hr 30min); Bastia (2 daily; 2hr 45min–3hr); Bonifacio (1–4 daily; 30–40min); Propriano (2–4 daily; 1hr 40min); Sartène (2–4 daily; 1hr 35min).

**Tourist office** Porto-Vecchio's efficient tourist office (May–Sept Mon–Sat 9am–8pm, Sun 9am–1pm; Oct–May Mon–Fri 9am–12.30 & 2–6pm; ☎ 04 95 70 09 58, ⓦ ot-portovecchio.com) is on the east side of Rue Générale Leclerc.

## ACCOMMODATION

As most visitors staying in this region during the summer come for fly-drive villa holidays, hotel accommodation is thin on the ground, especially at the bottom end.

**Goéland** Port de Plaisance ☎ 04 95 70 14 15, ⓦ hotelgoeland.com. Charming hotel, set in on a little man-made beach looking across the gulf, with large rooms, some of which have teak terraces overlooking the water. Rates include breakfast; and food served on the waterfront lawn is wonderful. **€230**

**Holzer** 12 rue Jean-Jaurès/rue Jean-Nicoli ☎ 04 95 70 05 93, ⓦ hotel-holzer.com. Labyrinthine place with airless, boxed-in rooms, but immaculately clean and very central. **€145**

**Matonara** Just north of the centre at the Quatre-Chemins intersection ☎ 04 95 70 37 05, ⓦ lamatonara .com. Lying within easy reach of the Hyper U supermarket, this is the most easily accessible site in the area. Pitches are shaded by stands of cork trees. Bring plenty of mozzie repellent. May–Oct. **€15.50**

**Mistral** Rue Jean-Nicoli ☎ 04 95 70 08 53, ⓦ lemistral .eu. Comfortable mid-range two-star, slightly removed from the noisy centre of town. Classier than the *Panorama* (see below) opposite, and fully a/c. **€145**

**Panorama** 12 rue Jean-Nicoli ☎ 04 95 70 07 96. Basic pension-style place just above the old town, with parking spaces and various types of rooms (nos. 8 and 9 on the top floor are the cosiest, though without toilets). Not all that well maintained, but usually the cheapest in town. **€90**

★ **San Giovanni** 2km south of Porto-Vecchio on the D659 towards Arca ☎ 04 95 70 22 25, ⓦ hotel-san -giovanni.com. Thirty comfortable chalet-style rooms set in landscaped gardens, with a heated pool, jacuzzi, sauna, tennis court, ping pong table and children's games area. It's well run, peaceful and great value. **€135**

## EATING AND DRINKING

**A Furana** Rue Borgo ☎ 04 95 70 58 03. Fragrant local cuisine served in a vaulted Genoese dining hall, or on a romantic terrace boasting panoramic gulf views. Count on €26–30 for three courses à la carte. Daily noon–3pm & 6–10.30pm.

**U Corsu** Port de Commerce ☎ 04 95 70 13 91. Plenty of other places to eat are clustered around the marina and *port de commerce*, but none rustle up pizzas more delectable than those served here. Reserve early for a sea view on their *pieds dans l'eau* terrace. *Formules* from €19–

24; or around €35–40 à la carte. Daily March–Oct noon–3pm & 6–10.30pm.

**U Sputinu** Rue Guidice de Cinarce ☎ 04 95 10 78 05. The pièce de résistance of this Corsican speciality place on the little square opposite the church is their copious *grande assiette* – a selection of quality charcuterie, cheese, spinach pasties (*chaussons herbes*) and savoury fritters (*migliacciu*) – served on rustic wooden plates. Daily except Sun March–Oct noon–3pm & 6–10.30pm.

# Golfe de Porto-Vecchio

Much of the coast of the **Golfe de Porto-Vecchio** and its environs is characterized by ugly development and hectares of swampland, yet some of the clearest, bluest sea and whitest beaches on Corsica are also here. The most frequented of these, Palombaggia and Santa Giulia, can be reached by **bus** from the town in summer, timetables for which are posted in the tourist office (see above) and online at ⓦcorsicabus.org; at other times you'll need your own transport. The same applies to the **Casteddu d'Araggiu**, one of the island's best-preserved Bronze Age sites, which stands on a ledge overlooking the gulf to the north of town.

## The beaches

A golden semicircle of sand edged by short twisted umbrella pines and red rocks, the **plage de Palombaggia** is south Corsica's trademark beach, and indisputably one of the most beautiful bays in Europe. Come here outside the school holidays and you'll find it hard to resist the striking colours and serene, clear water. But in summer the crowds can be simply overwhelming. One possible compromise is to press on south to two other smaller, less famous beaches just beyond Palombaggia – **Cala di la Folaca** and the **plage d'Acciaju** – where the sand is just as white and the water equally translucent. Narrow access lanes and pistes drop down to them from the main road at regular intervals, but the best way to enjoy this exquisite string of coves is by walking along them.

A few kilometres further south along the same road takes you over the Bocca di l'Oru to the plage de **Santa Giulia**, a spectacular white-sand beach and turquoise bay. The presence of several sprawling holiday villages and facilities for windsurfing and other watersports ensure large crowds from early in the season, but the colours alone warrant a detour. Shallow and crystal-clear, the water is especially good for little ones.

North of Porto-Vecchio, the first beach worth a visit is **San Ciprianu**, a half-moon bay of white sand, reached by turning left off the main road at the Elf petrol station. Carry on for another 7km, and you'll come to the even more picturesque beach at **Pinarellu**, an uncrowded, long sweep of soft white sand with a Genoese watchtower and, like the less inspiring beaches immediately north of here, benefiting from the spectacular backdrop of the Massif de l'Ospédale.

## Casteddu d'Arragiu

The coast between Porto-Vecchio and Solenzara is strewn with **prehistoric monuments**. The most impressive of these, **Casteddu d'Araggiu**, lies 12km north along the D759. From the site's car park (signposted off the main road), it's a twenty-minute stiff uphill climb through maquis and scrubby woodland to the ruins. Built in 2000 BC, the *casteddu* consists of a complex of chambers built into a massive circular wall of pink granite from the top of which the views over the coastal belt are superb.

---

### THE DOMAINE DE TORRACCIA

A short way inland from Pinarellu, the hamlet of Lecci, on the main Porto-Vecchio–Bastia highway, marks the turning for one of Corsica's finest vineyards, the **Domaine de Toraccia.** Produced with traditional vine stock and labour-intensive organic cultivation methods, its flagship cuvée is the Oriu, a dense, smoky *vin de garde* that's the ideal accompaniment to local mountain charcuterie and ewe's cheese. Made from hundred-percent Vermentino, Torraccia's white, by contrast, is bone dry and tinged with herb – perfect with seafood.

You can sample the domaine's full list – along with their equally delicious olives and olive oil – at the **vineyard** itself (Mon–Sat 8am–noon & 2–6pm; free), where there's an engaging exhibition of old Corsican photographs to peruse. With the exception of the Oriu, they're all available *en vrac* (straight out of the *cuves* in demi-jars) at less than half the bottle price.

**18**

## The route de Bavella

Starting from just north of the resort of **Solenzara** on the east coast, and winding 40km through the mountains to the picture-postcard-pretty mountain village of **ZONZA**, the D268 – known locally as the **route de Bavella** – is perhaps the most dramatic road in all Corsica. The road penetrates a dense expanse of old pine and chestnut trees as it rises steadily to the **Col de Bavella** (1218m), where a towering statue of **Notre-Dame-des-Neiges** marks the windswept pass itself. An amazing panorama of peaks and forests spreads out from the col: to the northwest the serrated granite ridge of the Cirque de Gio Agostino is dwarfed by the pink pinnacles of the Aiguilles de Bavella; behind soars Monte Incudine.

## Bavella

Just below the Col de Bavella the seasonal hamlet of **BAVELLA** comprises a handful of congenial cafés, corrugated-iron-roofed chalets and hikers' hostels from where you can follow a series of waymarked **trails** to nearby viewpoints. Deservedly the most popular of these is the two-hour walk to the **Trou de la Bombe**, a circular opening that pierces the Paliri crest of peaks. From the car park behind the *Auberge du Col* follow the red-and-white waymarks of GR20 for 800m, then head right when you see orange splashes.

# Aléria

Built on the estuary at the mouth of the River Tavignano on the island's east coast, 40km southeast of Corte along the N200, **ALÉRIA** was first settled in 564 BC by a colony of Greek Phocaeans as a trading port for copper and lead, as well as wheat, olives and grapes. After an interlude of Carthaginian rule, the Romans arrived in 259 BC, built a naval base and re-established its importance in the Mediterranean. Aléria remained the east coast's principal port right up until the eighteenth century. Little is left of the historic town except Roman ruins and a thirteenth-century Genoese fortress, which stands high against a background of chequered fields and green vineyards. To the south, a strip of modern buildings straddling the main road makes up the modern town, known as **Cateraggio**, but it's the village set on the hilltop just west of here that's the principal focus for visitors.

## The Site

**Musée Jerome Carcopino** Mid-May to Sept daily 8am–noon & 2–7pm; Oct to mid-May Mon–Sat 8am–noon & 2–5pm • €2

Before looking around the ruins of the ancient city, set aside an hour for the **Musée Jerôme Carcopino**, housed in the Fort Matra. It houses remarkable finds from the **Roman site**, including Hellenic and Punic coins, rings, belt links, elaborate oil lamps decorated with Christian symbols, Attic plates and a second-century marble bust of Jupiter Ammon. Etruscan bronzes fill another room, with jewellery and armour from the fourth to the second century BC.

A dusty track leads from here to the Roman site itself (closes 30min before museum; same ticket), where most of the excavation was done as recently as the 1950s. Most of the site still lies beneath ground and is undergoing continuous digging, but the balneum (bathhouse), the base of Augustus's triumphal arch, the foundations of the forum and traces of shops have already been unearthed.

**GETTING THERE** ALÉRIA

**By bus** Aléria/Cateraggio can be reached on any of the daily buses running between Bastia and the south of the island via the east coast.

## EATING

**Aux Coquillages de Diana** 1.2km north of Aléria: look for a signboard on the right (east) side of the road pointing the way down a surfaced lane ☎ 04 95 57 04 55, ⓦ www.auxcoquillagesdediana.fr. This famous seafood restaurant, resting on stilts above the water, is the place to sample the local Nustale oysters, hauled fresh each day from the nearby Étang de Diane lagoon. It serves a great-value €27 seafood platter, featuring clams, mussels and a terrine made from dried mullet's eggs called *poutargue* – the kind of food one imagines the Romans must have feasted on when they farmed the *étang* two millennia ago. June–Sept daily noon–3pm & 6.30–10.30pm; Oct–May open daily for lunch & dinner.

# Corte (Corti) and around

Stacked up the side of a wedge-shaped crag against a spectacular backdrop of granite mountains, **CORTE** epitomizes *l'âme corse*, or "Corsican soul" – a small town marooned amid a grandiose landscape, where a spirit of dogged patriotism is never far from the surface. Corte has been the home of Corsican nationalism since the first National Constitution was drawn up here in 1731, and was also where **Pascal Paoli**, "U Babbu di u Patria" ("Father of the Nation"), formed the island's first democratic government later in the eighteenth century. Self-consciously insular and grimly proud, it can seem an inhospitable place at times, although the presence of the island's only university lightens the atmosphere noticeably during termtime, when the bars and cafés lining its long main street fill with students. For the outsider, Corte's charm is concentrated in the tranquil *haute ville*, where the forbidding **citadelle** – site of a modern **museum** – presides over a warren of narrow, cobbled streets.

## Haute ville

The old **haute ville**, immediately above Corte's main street, cours Paoli, centres on the **Place Gaffori**, which is dominated by a statue of General Gian-Pietru Gaffori pointing vigorously towards the church. On its base a bas-relief depicts the siege of the Gaffori house by the Genoese, who attacked in 1750 when the general was out of town and his wife Faustina was left holding the fort. Their residence still stands, right behind, and you can clearly make out the bullet marks made by the besiegers.

For the best view of the citadelle, follow the signs uphill to the viewing platform, the **Belvédère**, which faces the medieval tower, suspended high above the town on its pinnacle of rock and dwarfed by the immense crags behind. The platform also gives a wonderful view of the converging rivers and encircling forest – a summer bar adds to the attraction.

Just above place Gaffori, left of the gateway to the citadelle, stands the **Palais National**, a great, solid block of a mansion that's the sole example of Genoese civic architecture in Corte. Having served as the seat of Paoli's government for a while, it became the Università di Corsica in 1765, offering free education to all (Napoleon's father studied here). The university closed in 1769 when the French took over the island after the Treaty of Versailles, not to be resurrected until 1981. Today several modern buildings have been added, among them the Institut Universitaire d'Études Corses, dedicated to the study of Corsican history and culture.

## The Museu di a Corsica and citadelle

April to June 21 & Sept 21 to Oct daily except Tues 10am–6pm; June 22 to Sept 20 daily 10am–8pm; Nov–March Tues–Sat 10am–6pm • €5.30 • ⓦ www.usee-corse.com

The monumental gateway just behind the Palais National leads from place Poilu into Corte's Genoese citadelle, whose lower courtyard is dominated by the modern

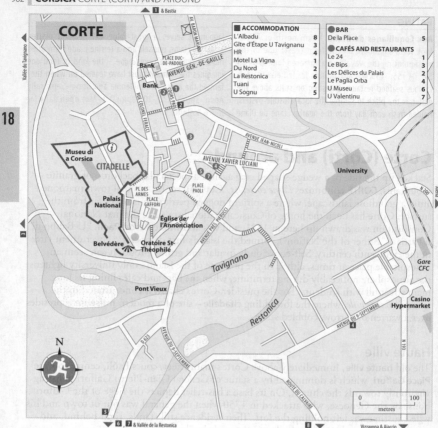

**CORTE**

| ■ ACCOMMODATION | |
|---|---|
| L'Albadu | 8 |
| Gîte d'Étape U Tavignanu | 3 |
| HR | 4 |
| Motel La Vigna | 1 |
| Du Nord | 2 |
| La Restonica | 6 |
| Tuani | 7 |
| U Sognu | 5 |

| ● BAR | |
|---|---|
| De la Place | 5 |

| ● CAFÉS AND RESTAURANTS | |
|---|---|
| Le 24 | 1 |
| Le Bips | 3 |
| Les Délices du Palais | 2 |
| Le Paglia Orba | 4 |
| U Museu | 6 |
| U Valentinu | 7 |

buildings of **Museu di a Corsica**, a state-of-the-art museum housing the collection of ethnographer Révérend Père Louis Doazan, a Catholic priest who spent 27 years amassing a vast array of objects relating to the island's traditional transhumant and peasant past: principally old farm implements, craft tools and peasant dress.

The museum's entrance ticket also admits you to Corte's principal landmark, the **citadelle**. The only such fortress in the interior of the island, the Genoese structure served as a base for the Foreign Legion from 1962 until 1984, but now houses a pretty feeble exhibition of nineteenth-century photographs. It's reached by a huge staircase of Restonica marble, which leads to the medieval tower known as the **Nid d'Aigle** (Eagle's Nest). The fortress, of which the tower is the only original part, was built in 1420, and the barracks were added during the mid-nineteenth century. These were later converted into a prison, in use as recently as World War II, when the Italian occupiers incarcerated Corsican Resistance fighters in tiny cells. Adjacent to the cells is a former **watchtower** which at the time of Paoli's government was inhabited by the hangman.

## ARRIVAL AND DEPARTURE CORTE

**By bus** Buses running to and from Ajaccio and Bastia, operated by Eurocorse Voyages (☎04 95 21 06 30) stop outside *Bar Le Majestic* at the top of cours Paoli. Services to and from Porto and Évisa with Autocars Mordiconi (☎04 95 48 00 04) work from outside the train station (see below). Destinations Ajaccio (2 daily; 1hr 45min–2hr); Bastia (2 daily; 1hr 15min); Évisa (4 daily; 2hr); Porto (1 daily; 2hr 30min).

**By train** The *gare CFC* (☎ 04 95 46 00 97) is at the foot of the hill near the university.

Destinations Ajaccio (4 daily; 1hr 50min); Bastia (4 daily; 1hr 35min); Calvi (2 daily; 2hr 30min); L'Île Rousse (2 daily;

1hr 40min).

**By car** For those who are driving, the best place to park is at the top of avenue Jean-Nicoli, the road which leads into town from Ajaccio.

## INFORMATION

**Tourist office** Just inside the main gates of the citadelle, near the museum (July & Aug Mon, Wed & Sat 10am–5pm, Tues, Thurs & Fri 9am–7pm; Sept–June Mon–Fri 9am–noon

& 2–6pm; ☎ 04 95 46 26 70, ⓦ www.corte-tourisme.com). In the same building is the information office of the Parc Régional (same hours and phone number).

## ACCOMMODATION

★ **L'Albadu** Ancienne rte d'Ajaccio, 2.5km southwest of town ☎ 04 95 46 24 55, ⓦ hebergement -albadu.fr. Simply furnished rooms with showers (shared toilets) on a working farm-cum-equestrian centre. Warm family atmosphere, beautiful horses, fine views and Corsican speciality food (for a bargain €48 half-board). Advance reservation essential. There's also a perfect little camping area which is basic, but much nicer than any of the town sites. April–Oct. **€48** per person (half-board obligatory)

**Gîte d'Étape U Tavignanu** ("Chez M. Gambini") Behind the citadelle ☎ 04 95 46 16 85. Run-of-the-mill hikers' hostel with small dorms and a relaxing garden terrace that looks over the valley. Peaceful, secluded, and the cheapest place to stay after the campsites. Follow the signs for the Tavignano trail (marked with orange spots of paint) around the back of the citadelle. Breakfast included. Easter to mid-Oct. **€18**

**HR** Allée du 9-Septembre ☎ 04 95 45 11 11, ⓦ hotel-hr .com. This converted concrete-block gendarmerie, 200m southwest of the gare CFC, looks grim from the outside, but its 125 rooms are comfortable enough and its rates rock-bottom; bathroom-less options are the best deal. No credit cards. **€45**

**Motel A Vigna** Chemin de Saint-Pancrace ☎ 04 95 46 02 19. Tucked away on the leafy northern edge of town, this small but rather swish students' hall of residence is vacated between early June and the end of September and

converted into a motel. The rooms are simple and lacking character by Corte standards, but clean and all en-suite, with balconies. June–Sept. **€60**

**Du Nord** 22 cours Paoli ☎ 04 95 46 00 33, ⓦ hoteldunord-corte.com. Pleasant, clean place right in the centre, with oodles of Second Empire charm. Its variously priced rooms are large for the tariffs. **€102**

★ **La Restonica** Vallée de la Restonica, 2km southwest from town ☎ 04 95 46 09 58, ⓦ auberge restonica.com. Sumptuous comfort in a wood-lined riverside hotel set up by a former French-national footballer, Dominique Colonna. Hunting trophies, old paintings, salon with open fireplace and leather-upholstered furniture create an old-fashioned atmosphere, and there's a large pool and garden terrace. **€100**

★ **Tuani** Vallée de la Restonica, 7km southeast ☎ 04 95 46 11 65, ⓦ campingtuani.com. Too far up the valley without your own car, but the wildest and most atmospheric of the campsites around Corte, overlooking a rushing stream, deep in the woods. Ideally placed for an early start on Monte Rotondo. Basic facilities, although they do have a cheerful little café serving good bruschettas and other hot snacks. Mid-April to mid-Sept. **€18.50**

**U Sognu** Rte de la Restonica ☎ 04 95 46 09 07. At the foot of the valley, a 15min walk from the centre. Has a good view of the citadelle, plenty of poplar trees for shade, and toilets in a converted barn. There's also a small bar and restaurant (in summer). May–Sept. **€15**

## EATING AND DRINKING

★ **Le 24** 24 cours Paoli ☎ 04 95 46 02 90. Served by an enthusiastic young crew against a backdrop of vaulted stone walls and stylish designer furniture, the food in this hip Corsican speciality place is innovative yet full of traditional flavours: pan-fried foie gras with chestnut crumble; salmon rolled in onion seeds with creamy red-onion velouté sauce; sublime chocolate mousse. Menus €21–28; or around €40 à la carte. March to mid-Feb daily noon–2.30pm & 6–10.30pm.

**Le Bips** 14 cours Paoli ☎ 04 95 46 06 26. Popular budget restaurant on the main drag, serving fragrant, copious pasta dishes, salads, steaks and some local specialities at down-to-earth rates. Hidden away in an

eighteenth-century cellar, it's tricky to find: you have to cut down a back alley of the main street to a rear door. And expect to wait for a table unless you arrive early. Mains €12–25. Daily noon–2.30pm & 6–10.30pm.

**Les Délices du Palais** Cours Paoli. Frilly little crêperie-cum-*salon-de-thé* whose bakery sells a selection of delicious Corsican patisserie: try their colzone (spinach pasties) or brocciu baked in flaky chestnut-flour pastry. Mon–Sat 9am–2pm & 4–6pm.

**Le Paglia Orba** 1 av Xavier-Luciani ☎ 04 95 61 07 89. Quality Corsican cooking at restrained prices, served on a terrace overlooking the street. Most people come for their succulent pizzas (€10–15), but there is also plenty of choice à la carte, particularly for vegetarians. Pan-fried veal served with *storzapretri* (nuggets of brocciu and herbs) is their *plat de* résistance. *Menus* from €18. Mon–Sat noon–2.30pm & 6–10.30pm.

**De la Place** Place Paoli. On the shady side of the main square, this is the place to hole up for a spot of crowd-watching over a *barquettes de frites* (a pile of chips) and draught Pietra. Daily 8am–10pm.

**U Museu** Rampe Ribanelle in the haute ville at the foot of the citadelle, 30m down rue Colonel-Feracci ☎04 95 61 08 36, ⓦrestaurant-umuseu.com. Congenial and well-situated place on a terrace at the foot of the citadelle

walls. Try the €21 *menu corse*, featuring lasagne in wild boar sauce, trout, and tripettes. Great value for money, and the house wines are local AOC. June–Sept daily noon–2.30pm & 6–10.30pm, Oct–May closed Sun.

**U Valentinu** 1 place Paoli ☎04 95 61 19 65. This great little Italian restaurant on the main street serves Corte's best pizzas, baked to perfection in a wood oven. The dining hall's spacious, staff friendly, portions copious and prices reasonable. Go for one of their Corsican speciality options, featuring mountain charcuterie and ewe's cheese. Mains €8–19. Daily noon–2.30pm & 6–10.30pm.

# Central Corsica

**Central Corsica** is a nonstop parade of stupendous scenery, and the best way to immerse yourself in it is to get onto the region's ever-expanding network of trails and forest tracks. The ridge of granite mountains forming the spine of the island is closely followed by the epic **GR20** footpath, which can be picked up from various villages and is scattered with refuge huts, most of them offering no facilities except shelter. For the less active there are also plenty of roads penetrating deep into the **forests** of Vizzavona, La Restonica and Rospa Sorba, crossing lofty passes that provide exceptional views across the island. The most popular attractions in the centre, though, are the magnificent **gorges** of **La Restonica** and **Tavignano**, both within easy reach of Corte.

## Gorges du Tavignano

A deep cleft of ruddy granite beginning 5km to the west of Corte, the **Gorges du Tavignano** offers one of central Corsica's great walks, marked in yellow paint flashes alongside the broad cascading River Tavignano. You can pick up the trail from opposite the Chapelle Sainte-Croix in Corte's *haute ville* and follow it as far as the Lac de Nino, 30km west of the town, where it joins the GR20.

**ACCOMMODATION**                                                     **CENTRAL CORSICA**

**A Sega** ☎06 10 71 77 26. Situated at 1192m amid glorious pine forest, this ranks among Corsica's best-run *refuges* and serves as a welcome stop off on the long trek up the valley to Lac de Nino. It takes around 3.5–4hr to reach on foot (there's no access road), and offers dorm

beds, bivouac, filling breakfasts and evening meals and can supply packed lunches (€12). Dorm beds have to be booked through the PNRC website (ⓦparc-corse.org); meals in advance by phone. Bivouac €5, dorms €12, half-board in bivouac €40, half-board in dorm €50

## Gorges de la Restonica

The glacier-moulded rocks and deep pools of the **Gorges de la Restonica** make the D936 running southwest from Corte the busiest mountain road in Corsica – if you come in high summer, expect to encounter traffic jams all the way up to the car park at the **Bergeries de Grotelle**, 15km from Corte. **Minibuses** run from Corte to the Bergeries, costing €13; taxis charge around €40. The gorges begin after 6km, just beyond where the route penetrates the **Forêt de la Restonica**, a glorious forest of chestnut, Laricio pine and the tough maritime pine endemic to Corte. Not surprisingly, it's a popular place to walk, picnic and bathe in the many pools fed by the cascading torrent of the River Restonica, easily reached by scrambling down the rocky banks.

From the *bergeries*, a well-worn path winds along the valley floor to a pair of beautiful glacial lakes. The first and larger, **Lac de Melo**, is reached after an easy hour's hike through the rocks. One particularly steep part of the path has been fitted with security chains, but the scramble around the side of the passage is perfectly straightforward, and much quicker. Once past Lac de Melo, press on for another forty minutes along the steeper marked trail over a moraine to the second lake, **Lac de Capitello**, the more spectacular of the pair. Hemmed in by vertical cliffs, the deep turquoise-blue pool affords fine views of the Rotondo massif on the far side of the valley, and in clear weather you can spend an hour or two exploring the surrounding crags.

18

RODIN'S *THE THINKER*

# Contexts

# History

Ever since Julius Caesar observed that "Gaul" was divided into quite distinct parts, and then conquered and unified the country, France has been perceived as both a nation and a collection of fiercely individualistic *pays*, or localities. The two Frances have often come into conflict. Few countries' governments have centralized as energetically, or have imposed such radical change from above. Equally, few peoples have been so determined to hold on to their local traditions. Charles de Gaulle famously complained that it was impossible to govern a country with 246 different kinds of cheeses. Yet each of those cheesemaking regions, as de Gaulle was well aware, was proud to belong to the kind of impossibly, quarrelsomely traditional nation that could have so many cheeses.

The themes of nationalism and localism, of central control and popular resistance, of radicalism and conservatism, continue to define France today. What follows is necessarily a brief account of major events in the country's past.

## Caves to Celts

Traces of human existence are rare in France until about 50,000 BC. Thereafter, beginning with the stone tools of the Neanderthal "Mousterian civilization", they become ever more numerous, with an especially heavy concentration of sites in the Périgord region of the Dordogne, where, near the village of Les Eyzies, remains were discovered in 1868 of a late Stone Age people, subsequently dubbed "Cro-Magnon". Flourishing from around 25,000 BC, these cave-dwelling hunters seem to have developed quite a sophisticated culture, the evidence of which is preserved in the beautiful paintings and engravings on the walls of the region's caves.

By 10,000 BC, human communities had spread out widely across the whole of France, and by about 7000 BC, **farming and pastoral communities** had begun to develop. By 4500 BC, the first **dolmens** (megalithic stone tombs) showed up in Brittany, while dugout canoes dating back to the same epoch have been unearthed in Paris. It seems that a thriving trade followed the rivers, while the land between was heavily forested.

By 1800 BC, the **Bronze Age** had arrived in the east and southeast of the country, and trade links had begun with Spain, central Europe, southern Britain and around the Mediterranean – **Greek colonists** founded Massalia (Marseille) in around 600 BC.

The first Celts made an appearance in around 500 BC. Whether these were the same people known to the Romans as "long-haired" Gauls isn't certain. Either way, the inhabitants of France were far from shaggy-haired barbarians. The Gauls, as they became known, invented the barrel and soap and were skilful manufacturers and prolific traders – as was proved by the "chariot tomb" of **Vix**, where the burial goods included rich gold jewellery, a metal-wheeled cart and elaborate Greek vases.

| 1,800,000 BC | 400,000 BC | 28,000–30,000 BC |
| --- | --- | --- |
| Appearance of first stone tools in France | Traces of fire left at Terra Amata, Nice | Chauvet cave in Archèche is painted; Neanderthals disappear |

## Roman Gaul

By 100 BC the **Gauls** had established large **hilltop towns with merchant communities**. The area equivalent to modern **Provence** became a Roman colony in 118 BC and, in 58 BC, when **Julius Caesar** arrived to complete the Roman conquest of Gaul, there were perhaps fifteen million people living in the area now occupied by modern France. **Tribal rivalries** made the Romans' job of conquering the north fairly easy, and when the Gauls finally united under **Vercingétorix** in 52 BC, it only made their defeat at the battle of **Alésia** more final.

This **Roman victory** was one of the major turning points in the history of France, fixing the frontier between Gaul and the Germanic peoples at the Rhine, thus saving Gaul from disintegrating because of internal dissension and making it a Roman province. During the five centuries of peace that followed, the Gauls farmed, manufactured and traded, became urbanized and educated – and learnt Latin. The emperor Augustus founded numerous cities – including Autun, Limoges and Bayeux – built roads and settled Roman colonists on the land. Vespasian secured the frontiers beyond the Rhine, thus ensuring a couple of hundred years of peace and economic expansion.

Serious **disruptions** of the Pax Romana only began in the third century AD. Oppressive aristocratic rule and an economic crisis turned the destitute peasantry into gangs of marauding brigands – precursors of the medieval *jacquerie*. But most devastating of all, there began a series of incursions across the Rhine frontier by various restless **Germanic tribes**, the first of which, the Alemanni, pushed down as far as Spain, ravaging farmland and destroying towns.

In the fourth century the reforms of the emperor **Diocletian** secured some decades of respite from both internal and external pressures. Towns were rebuilt and fortified, foreshadowing feudalism and the independent power of the nobles. By the fifth century, however, the Germanic invaders were back: **Alans**, **Vandals** and **Suevi**, with **Franks** and **Burgundians** in their wake. While the Roman administration assimilated them as far as possible, granting them land in return for military duties, they gradually achieved independence from the empire.

## The Franks and Charlemagne

By 500 AD, the **Franks**, who gave their name to modern France, had become the dominant invading power. Their most celebrated king, **Clovis**, consolidated his hold on northern France and drove the Visigoths out of the southwest into Spain. In 507 he made the until-then insignificant little trading town of Paris his capital and became a Christian, which inevitably hastened the **Christianization** of Frankish society.

Under the succeeding **Merovingian** dynasty the kingdom began to disintegrate until, in 732, **Charles Martel** reunited the kingdom and saved western Christendom from the northward expansion of Islam by defeating the Spanish Moors at the **battle of Poitiers**.

In 754 Charles's son, Pepin, had himself crowned king by the pope, thus inaugurating the **Carolingian dynasty** and establishing for the first time the principle of the divine right of kings. His son was **Charlemagne**, who extended Frankish control over the whole of what had been Roman Gaul, and far beyond. On Christmas Day in 800, he was crowned emperor of the **Holy Roman Empire**, though the kingdom again fell apart following his death in squabbles over who was to inherit various parts of his empire. At

| 18,000–15,000 BC | 7,000 BC | 3,600 BC | 1,800 BC |
|---|---|---|---|
| Lascaux cave art, Dordogne: artistic peak of the Upper Paleolithic | Neolithic farming begins | The first megaliths appear in Brittany | Start of the Bronze Age; walled citadelles built |

the Treaty of Verdun in 843, his grandsons agreed on a division of territory that corresponded roughly with the extent of modern France and Germany.

Charlemagne's administrative system had involved the royal appointment of counts and bishops to govern the various provinces of the empire. Under the destabilizing attacks of Norsemen/Vikings (who evolved into the Normans) during the ninth century, Carolingian kings were obliged to delegate more power and autonomy to these **provincial governors**, whose lands, like **Aquitaine** and **Burgundy**, already had separate regional identities as a result of earlier invasions. Gradually the power of these governors overshadowed that of the king, whose lands were confined to the Île-de-France. When the last Carolingian died in 987, it was only natural that they should elect one of their own number to take his place. This was **Hugues Capet**, founder of a dynasty that lasted until 1328.

## The rise of the French kings

The years 1000 to 1500 saw the gradual extension and consolidation of the power of the **French kings**, accompanied by the growth of a centralized administrative system and bureaucracy. Foreign policy was chiefly concerned with restricting papal interference in French affairs and checking the English kings' continuing involvement in French territory. Conditions for the overwhelming majority of the population, meanwhile, remained remarkably unchanged.

Surrounded by vassals much stronger than themselves, **Hugues Capet** and his successors remained weak throughout the eleventh century, though they made the most of their feudal rights. At the beginning of the twelfth century, having successfully tamed his own vassals in the Île-de-France, Louis VI had a stroke of luck. **Eleanor**, daughter of the powerful duke of Aquitaine, was left in his care on her father's death, so he promptly married her off to his son, the future Louis VII. The marriage ended in divorce, however, and in 1152 Eleanor married Henry of Normandy, shortly to become **Henry II** of England. Thus the **English** crown gained control of a huge chunk of French territory, stretching from the Channel to the Pyrenees. Though their fortunes fluctuated over the ensuing three hundred years, the English rulers remained a perpetual thorn in the side of the French kings, with a dangerous potential for alliance with any rebellious French vassals.

**Philippe Auguste** (1179–1223) made considerable headway in undermining English rule by exploiting the bitter relations between Henry II and his three sons, one of whom was **Richard the Lionheart**. By the end of his reign Philippe had recovered all of Normandy and the English possessions north of the Loire.

For the first time, the royal lands were greater than those of any other French lord. The foundations of a systematic administration and civil service had been established in **Paris**, and Philippe had firmly and quietly marked his independence from the papacy by refusing to take any interest in the **crusade** against the heretic Cathars of Languedoc. When Languedoc and Poitou came under royal control in the reign of his son Louis VIII, France was by far the greatest power in western Europe.

## The Hundred Years' War

In 1328 the Capetian monarchy had its first succession crisis, which led directly to the ruinous **Hundred Years' War** with the English. Charles IV, last of the line, had only

| **600 BC** | **450 BC** | **58–52 BC** | **406 AD** |
| --- | --- | --- | --- |
| Greek colonists found Massalia (Marseille) | Arrival of the Gauls | Julius Caesar conquers Gaul | Frank and Germanic tribes settle |

daughters as heirs, and when it was decided that France could not be ruled by a queen, the English king, **Edward III** claimed the throne of France for himself – on the grounds that his mother was Charles's sister.

The French chose **Philippe, Count of Valois**, instead, and Edward acquiesced for a time. But when Philippe began whittling away at his possessions in Aquitaine, Edward renewed his claim and embarked on war. With its population of about twelve million, France was the far richer and more powerful country, but its army was no match for the superior organization and tactics of the English. Edward won an outright victory at **Crécy** in 1346 and seized the port of Calais as a permanent bridgehead. Ten years later, his son, the Black Prince, actually took the French king, Jean le Bon, prisoner at the **battle of Poitiers**.

Although by 1375 French military fortunes had improved to the point where the English had been forced back to Calais and the Gascon coast, the strains of war and administrative abuses, as well as the madness of Charles VI, caused other kinds of damage. In 1358 there were **insurrections** among the Picardy peasantry (the *jacquerie*) and among the townspeople of Paris under the leadership of Étienne Marcel. Both were brutally repressed, as were subsequent risings in Paris in 1382 and 1412.

When it became clear that the king was mad, two rival camps began to vie for power: the **Burgundians**, led by the king's cousin and Duke of Burgundy, Jean sans Peur, and the **Armagnacs**, who gathered round the Duke of Orléans, Charles's brother. The situation escalated when Jean sans Peur had Orléans assassinated, and when fighting broke out between the two factions, they both called on the English for help. In 1415 Henry V of England inflicted another crushing defeat on the French army at **Agincourt**. The Burgundians seized Paris, took the royal family prisoner and recognized Henry as heir to the French throne. When Charles VI died in 1422, the English and their Burgundian allies assumed control of much of France, leaving the young French heir, the Dauphin Charles, barely clinging on to a rump state around the Loire Valley.

The French state might well have been finally exterminated had it not been for the arrival at court, in 1429, of **Joan of Arc**, a 17-year-old peasant girl who promised divine support for an aggressive military campaign. The English were driven back from their siege of Orléans, the Dauphin crowned as Charles VII at Reims in July 1429, Paris was retaken in 1436 and the English finally driven from France altogether (except for a toehold at Calais) in 1453. Joan's own end was less triumphant: she fell into the hands of the Burgundians and was burnt at the stake for heresy in 1431 (see p.365).

From the 1450s, court life was centred on pleasure-seeking in the Loire valley. Even for the peasantry life grew less hard. The threats of war and plague steadily receded, and from 1450 the harvests did not fail for seventy unbroken years. The population began to grow again, and a kind of peasant aristocracy took shape in the form of the smallholder *fermiers*. In the towns, meanwhile, the *aisés*, or well-to-do merchants and artisans, began to form the basis of what would become the bourgeoisie.

By the end of the fifteenth century, Dauphiné, Burgundy, Franche-Comté and Provence were under royal control, and an effective standing army had been created. The taxation system had been overhauled, and France had emerged from the Middle Ages a rich, powerful state, firmly under the centralized authority of an absolute monarch.

| 732 AD | 800 AD | 987 AD | 1152 |
|---|---|---|---|
| Northward advance of the Moors halted at Battle of Poitiers | Charlemagne crowned Holy Roman Emperor | Capetian Dynasty founded by Hugues Capet | England's Henry II marries Eleanor of Aquitaine |

# The Wars of Religion

After half a century of self-confident but inconclusive pursuit of military glory in Italy, brought to an end by the **Treaty of Cateau-Cambrésis** in 1559, France was plunged into another period of devastating internal conflict. The **Protestant** ideas of Luther and Calvin had gained widespread adherence among all classes of society, despite sporadic brutal attempts by François I and Henri II to stamp them out.

**Catherine de Médicis**, acting as regent for her son, later Henri III, implemented a more tolerant policy, provoking violent reaction from the ultra-Catholic faction led by the **Guise** family. Their massacre of a Protestant congregation coming out of church in March 1562 began a civil **War of Religion** that, interspersed with ineffective truces and accords, lasted for the next thirty years.

Well organized and well led by the Prince de Condé and Admiral Coligny, the **Huguenots** – French Protestants – kept their end up very successfully, until Condé was killed at the battle of Jarnac in 1569. Three years later came one of the blackest events in the memory of French Protestants, even today: the **massacre of St Bartholomew's Day**. Coligny and three thousand Protestants who had gathered in Paris for the wedding of Marguerite, the king's sister, to the Protestant Henri of Navarre were slaughtered at the instigation of the Guises, and the bloodbath was repeated across France, especially in the south and west where the Protestants were strongest.

In 1584 Henri III's son died, leaving his brother-in-law, **Henri of Navarre**, heir to the throne, to the fury of the Guises and their Catholic league, who seized Paris and drove out the king. In retaliation, Henri III murdered the Duc de Guise, and found himself forced into alliance with Henri of Navarre, whom the pope had excommunicated. In 1589 Henri III was himself assassinated, leaving Henri of Navarre to become Henri IV of France. It took another four years of fighting and the abjuration of his faith for the new king to be recognized. "Paris is worth a Mass," he is reputed to have said.

Once on the throne, Henri IV set about reconstructing and reconciling the nation. By the **Edict of Nantes** of 1598, the Huguenots were accorded freedom of conscience, freedom of worship in certain places, the right to attend the same schools and hold the same offices as Catholics, their own courts and the possession of a number of fortresses as a guarantee against renewed attack, the most important being La Rochelle and Montpellier.

# Kings and cardinals

In the seventeenth century, France was largely ruled by just two kings, **Louis XIII** (1610–43) and **Louis XIV** (1643–1715). In the *grand siècle*, as the French call it, or "Great Century", the state grew ever stronger, ever more centralized, and ever more embodied in the person of the king. France also expanded significantly, with frontiers secured in the Pyrenees, on the Rhine and in the north; conflict with the neighbouring Habsburg kings of Spain and Austria, however, helped exhaust the state's resources.

Louis XIII had the good fortune to be served by the extraordinarily capable minister **Cardinal Richelieu**, who began his services by crushing a revolt led by Louis XIII's brother Gaston, Duke of Orléans. He then confronted Protestantism. Believing that the Protestants' retention of separate fortresses within the kingdom was a threat to security, and the absolute power of the king, he attacked and took La Rochelle in 1627.

| 1163 | 1328 | 1346 | 1348–1352 |
| --- | --- | --- | --- |
| Cornerstone laid of Notre Dame de Paris, France's pre-eminent Gothic cathedral | Start of the Hundred Years War with the English | Edward III is victorious at Battle of Crécy | The Black Death ravages France |

Although he was unable to extirpate their religion altogether, Protestants were never again to present a military threat.

Richelieu also actively promoted economic self-sufficiency – **mercantilism** – by encouraging the growth of the luxury craft industries. France was to excel in textile production right up to the Revolution. On the foreign front, he built up the navy and granted privileges to companies involved in establishing **colonies** in North America, Africa and the West Indies. He adroitly kept France out of actual military engagement, meanwhile, by funding the Swedish king and general, Gustavus Adolphus, to make war against the Habsburgs in Germany. When in 1635 the French were finally obliged to commit their own troops, they made significant gains against the Spanish in the Netherlands, Alsace and Lorraine, and won Roussillon for France.

### The Sun King

Richelieu died just a few months before Louis XIII in 1642. As Louis XIV was still an infant, his mother, Anne of Austria, acted as regent, served by Richelieu's upstart protégé, **Cardinal Mazarin**, who was hated just as much as his predecessor by the traditional aristocracy and the *parlements*. They were anxious that their privileges, including the collection of taxes, would be curtailed. Spurred by these grievances, which were in any case exacerbated by the ruinous cost of the Spanish wars, various groups in French society combined in a series of revolts, known as the **Frondes**. The first Fronde, in 1648, was led by the *parlement* of Paris, which resented royal oversight of tax collection. It was quickly followed by an aristocratic Fronde, supported by various peasant risings round the country. All were suppressed easily enough.

In 1659 Mazarin successfully brought the Spanish wars to an end. Two years later, **Louis XIV** came of age, declaring that he would rule without a first minister. He embarked on a long struggle to modernize the administration. The war ministers, Le Tellier and his son Louvois, provided Louis with a well-equipped and well-trained professional army that could muster some 400,000 men by 1670. But the principal reforms were carried out by **Colbert**, who tackled corruption, set up a free-trade area in northern and central France, established the French East India Company, and built up the navy with a view to challenging the commercial supremacy of the Dutch.

Alongside his promotion of wise governance, Louis XIV certainly liked to gild his own throne, earning himself the title Le Roi Soleil, the **"Sun King"**. His grandiosity was expressed in two ruinously expensive forms: his extravagant new royal palace at Versailles and incessant military campaigns. His war against the Dutch, in 1672, ultimately resulted in the acquisition of Franche-Comté and a swathe of Flanders, including the city of Lille. In 1681 he simply grabbed Strasbourg, and got away with it.

In 1685, under the influence of his very Catholic mistress, Madame de Maintenon, the king removed all privileges from the **Huguenots** by revoking the Edict of Nantes. The result was devastating. Many of France's most skilled artisans, its wealthiest merchants and its most experienced soldiers were Protestants, and they fled the country in huge numbers – over 200,000 by some estimates. Protestant countries promptly combined under the auspices of the League of Augsburg to fight the French. Another long and exhausting war followed, ending, most unfavourably for Louis XIV, in the **Peace of Rijswik** (1697).

No sooner was this concluded than Louis became embroiled in the question of who was

| 1415 | 1431 | 1562 | 1572 |
|---|---|---|---|
| King Henry V of England inflicts crushing defeat at Battle of Agincourt | Jean d'Arc burned at the stake | Guise family massacres Protestants to start 30-year War of Religion | St Bartholomew's Day Massacre, Paris |

to succeed the moribund Charles II of Spain as ruler of the Habsburg domains in Europe. William of Orange, now king of England as well as ruler of the Dutch United Provinces, organized a Grand Alliance against Louis. The so-called **War of the Spanish Succession** broke out and dragged on until 1713, leaving France totally impoverished. The Sun King, finally, was eclipsed. He died in 1715, after ruling for 72 years over a country that had grown to dominate Europe, and had become unprecedentedly prosperous, largely because of colonial trade. Louis XIV's power and control, however, had masked growing tensions between central government and traditional vested interests.

## Louis XV and the parlements

Louis XIV had outlived both his son and grandson. His successor, **Louis XV**, was only 5 when his great-grandfather died. During the **Regency**, the traditional aristocracy and the *parlements* scrambled to recover a lot of their lost power and prestige. An experiment with government by aristocratic councils failed, however, and attempts to absorb the immense national debt by selling shares in an overseas trading company ended in a huge collapse. When the prudent and reasonable **Cardinal Fleury** came to prominence upon the regent's death in 1726, the nation's lot began to improve (though the disparity in wealth between the countryside and the towns continued to increase). The Atlantic seaboard towns grew rich on slavery and trade with the American and Caribbean colonies, though in the middle of the century France lost out to England in the **War of Austrian Succession** and the **Seven Years War** – both in effect contests for control of America and India. The need to finance the wars led to the introduction of a new tax, the Twentieth, which was to be levied on everyone. The *parlement*, which had successfully opposed earlier taxation and fought the Crown over its religious policies, dug its heels in again, leading to renewed conflict over Louis' pro-Jesuit religious policy.

The division between the *parlements* and the king and his ministers only sharpened during the reign of **Louis XVI**, which began in 1774. Strangely enough, the one radical attempt to introduce an effective and equitable tax system led directly to the Revolution. Calonne, finance minister in 1786, tried to get his proposed tax approved by an **Assembly of Notables**, a device that had not been employed for more than a hundred years. His purpose was to bypass the *parlement*, which could be relied on to oppose any radical proposal. The attempt backfired, the *parlement* demanding a meeting of the **Estates-General**, representing the nobles, the clergy and the bourgeoisie – this being the only body competent to discuss such matters. As law and order began to break down, the king gave in and agreed to summon the Estates-General on May 17, 1789.

# Revolution and empire

Against a background of deepening economic crisis and general misery, the Estates-General proved unusually radical. On June 17, 1789, the Third Estate – the representatives of the bourgeoisie – seized the initiative and declared itself the National Assembly, joined by some of the lower clergy and liberal nobility. Louis XVI appeared to accept the situation, and on July 9 the National Constituent Assembly declared itself. However, the king then called in troops, unleashing the anger of the people of Paris, the **sans-culottes** (literally, "without trousers").

| 1598 | 1661 | 1664 | 1685 |
|---|---|---|---|
| Edict of Nantes grants Huguenots freedom of worship | Louis XIV, the "Sun King", comes of age; start of Absolute Monarchy | First performance of Molière's Tartuffe | Louis revokes the Edict of Nantes, forcing mass exodus of Huguenot soldiers, artisans and merchants |

On July 14 the *sans-culottes* stormed the fortress of the **Bastille**, symbol of the oppressive nature of the king's **"ancien régime"**. Throughout the country, peasants attacked landowners' châteaux, destroying records of debt and other symbols of oppression. On the night of August 4, the Assembly abolished the feudal rights and privileges of the nobility – a momentous shift of gear in the Revolutionary process. Later that month they adopted the **Declaration of the Rights of Man**. In December church lands were nationalized.

Bourgeois elements in the Assembly tried to bring about a compromise with the nobility, with a view to establishing a constitutional monarchy, but these overtures were rebuffed. Émigré aristocrats were already working to bring about foreign invasion to overthrow the Revolution. In June 1791 the king was arrested trying to escape from Paris. The Assembly, following an initiative of the wealthier bourgeois **Girondin** faction, decided to go to war to protect the Revolution.

On August 10, 1792, the *sans-culottes* set up a **Revolutionary Commune** in Paris and imprisoned the king, marking a radical turn in the Revolution. A new National Convention was elected and met on the day the ill-prepared Revolutionary armies finally halted the Prussian invasion at Valmy. A major rift swiftly developed between the more moderate **Girondins** and the **Jacobins** and *sans-culottes* over the abolition of the monarchy. The radicals carried the day, and, in January 1793, Louis XVI was executed. By June, the Girondins had been ousted.

**Counter-Revolutionary forces** were gathering in the provinces and abroad. A Committee of Public Safety was set up as chief organ of the government. Left-wing popular pressure brought laws on general conscription and price controls and a deliberate policy of secularization, and **Robespierre** was pressed onto the Committee as the best hope of containing the pressure from the streets, marking the beginning of the **Terror**.

As well as ordering the death of the hated queen, **Marie Antoinette**, Robespierre felt strong enough to guillotine his opponents on both Right and Left. But the effect of so many rolling heads was to cool people's faith in the Revolution; by mid-1794, Robespierre himself was arrested and executed, and his fall marked the end of radicalism. More conservative forces gained control of the government, deregulating the economy, limiting suffrage and establishing a five-man executive Directory, in 1795.

## Napoleon

In 1799, **General Napoleon Bonaparte**, who had made a name for himself as commander of the Revolutionary armies in Italy and Egypt, returned to France and took power in a coup d'état. He became First Consul, with power to choose officials and initiate legislation. He redesigned the tax system, created the Bank of France, replaced the power of local institutions by a corps of *préfets* answerable to himself, and made judges into state functionaries – in short, laid the foundations of the modern French administrative system.

Although alarmingly revolutionary in the eyes of the rest of Europe, Napoleon was no Jacobin. He restored unsold property to émigré aristocrats, reintroduced slavery in the colonies, and recognized the Church once more. The authoritarian, militaristic nature of his regime, meanwhile, became more and more apparent. In 1804 he crowned himself **emperor** in the presence of the pope.

The tide began to turn in 1808. Spain, which was then under the rule of Napoleon's brother, rose in revolt, aided by the British, and in 1812, Napoleon threw himself into

| 1759 | 1762 | 1789 | 1793 |
|---|---|---|---|
| Voltaire publishes his magnum opus, *Candide* | Rousseau's *Du Contrat Social* revolutionizes political thought | French Revolution ends the monarchy | Marie Antoinette is guillotined on the Place de la Concorde, nine months after her husband, Louis XVI |

the disastrous **Russian campaign**. He reached Moscow, but the long retreat in terrible winter conditions annihilated his veteran Grande Armée. The nation was now weary of the burden of unceasing war and in 1814 Napoleon was forced to abdicate by a coalition of European powers. They installed **Louis XVIII**, brother of the decapitated Louis XVI, as monarch. In a last effort to recapture power, Napoleon escaped from exile in Elba and reorganized his armies, only to meet final defeat at **Waterloo** on June 18, 1815. Louis XVIII was restored to power.

## Restorations and revolutions

In the **White Terror**, which followed Napoleon's downfall, aristocrats attempted to wipe out all trace of the Revolution and restore the *ancien régime*. Louis XVIII resisted these moves, however, at least until the Duc de Berry was assassinated in an attempt to wipe out the Bourbon family. In response to reactionary outrage, the king was forced to dismiss his moderate royalist minister, Decazes. Censorship became more rigid and education was once more subjected to the authority of the Church. Then, in 1824, Louis was succeeded by the thoroughly reactionary **Charles X**, who pushed through a law indemnifying émigré aristocrats for property lost during the Revolution.

When the liberal opposition won a majority in the elections of 1830, the king dissolved the Chamber and restricted the already narrow suffrage. Barricades went up in the streets of Paris. Charles X abdicated and parliament was persuaded to accept **Louis-Philippe**, Duc d'Orléans, as king. On the face of it, divine right had been superseded by popular sovereignty as the basis of political legitimacy. The **1814 Charter**, which upheld Revolutionary and Napoleonic reforms, was reaffirmed, censorship abolished, the tricolour restored as the national flag, and suffrage widened.

However, the **Citizen King**, as he was called, had somewhat more absolutist notions about being a monarch. He began the colonization of Algeria and resisted attempts to enfranchise even the middle ranks of the bourgeoisie. A growing economic crisis brought bankruptcies, unemployment and food shortages, helping to radicalize the growing urban working class, whose hopes of a more just future received a theoretical basis in the **socialist writings** and activities of Blanqui, Fourier, Louis Blanc and Proudhon, among others.

### 1848 and the Second Republic

In February 1848 workers and students took to the streets, and when the army fired on a demonstration and killed forty people, civil war appeared imminent. The Citizen King fled to England, a provisional government was set up and a **republic** proclaimed. The government quickly extended the vote to all adult males – an unprecedented move for its time. But by the time elections were held in April, a new tax designed to ameliorate the financial crisis had antagonized the countryside, and a massive conservative majority was re-elected. Three days of bloody street fighting at the barricades followed, when General Cavaignac, who had distinguished himself in the suppression of Algerian resistance, turned the artillery on the workers. More than 1500 were killed and 12,000 arrested and exiled.

A reasonably democratic constitution was drawn up and elections called to choose a president. To everyone's surprise, Louis-Napoléon, nephew of the emperor, romped home. In spite of his liberal reputation, he restricted the vote again, censored the press

| 1795 | 1804 | 1815 | 1848 |
|---|---|---|---|
| Rouget de Lisle's La Marseillaise adopted as French national anthem | Napoleon crowned Emperor | Napoleon defeated at Waterloo; the monarchy is re-established | Founding of the Second Republic |

## PARIS UNDER SIEGE

On September 1, 1870, when news of Napoleon III's surrender to Kaiser Wilhelm at the Battle of Sédan reached Paris, it was, ironically, greeted with **jubilation** rather than dismay. George Sand declared the fall of the Second Empire "a third awakening", while crowds poured on to the streets to sing the Marseillaise, confident that with the end of the bellicose regime the Prussian invaders would pack up and turn for home. What none of the merrymakers realized, however, was that the Prussian armies were on the brink of encircling their city and intent on crushing it.

The siege was regarded as a bit of a joke at the start. Secure behind a ten-metre-tall wall reinforced by 93 bastions, earthworks and landmines, Parisians had stockpiled grain, while huge herds of sheep and oxen grazed in the Bois de Boulogne – a scene as bucolic as it was ominous.

Within a month, however, the joke had turned sour. The authorities had grossly under-provisioned. Fresh meat and bread quickly ran out. The bourgeoisie were forced to slaughter their carriage horses and pets (and even – famously – the contents of the municipal zoo, including its much loved elephants). The working classes, meanwhile, resorted to mice and sewer rats, growing hungrier and more restless with each passing day.

Entirely cut off from the rest of the country for over three months, the city's only means of communication with the war cabinet in Tours were hastily constructed **hot-air balloons**. Some of these red-striped behemoths were blown out to sea and never seen again. Others pitched up in Prussia. One even landed on the snow-covered mountains of Norway. But the majority, having survived fusillades from the enemy lines, made haphazard landings in rural France, where their pilots, precious mail sacks and carrier pigeons were spirited away by local patriots.

As a the chill of the worst winter in living memory began to bite, however, indiscriminate bombardment from Herr Krupp's massive guns stationed on the outskirts sapped what little will remained. By early January, the world's most glittering and sophisticated city – home to Zola, Hugo, Renoir and Degas, which only two years previously had hosted the Great Exhibition – had been brought to its knees.

Bismarck's plan had always been to choke the capital from outside, and in the end, dissent from inside Paris rather than the shells raining upon it brought about the end of the siege. After months of relentless cold and starvation, the Red Clubs and 350,000-strong National Guard – their ranks swollen by members of an angry, politicized underclass consigned by Haussmann's rebuilding of Paris to slum quarters on the city's fringes – lost patience with the ineffectual leadership of General Trochu and threatened **rebellion**. To avert a bloodbath, Trochu secretly dispatched a message to Bismarck requesting an armistice.

The Prussian terms were harsh, and intended to humiliate. After a triumphant ceremony at the Palace of Versailles where the **surrender** was formally accepted, 30,000 Uhlans staged a victory march down the Champs-Elysées. This ordeal, coupled with crippling reparations, contributed in no small part to the punitive conditions later imposed on Germany in the Treaty of Versailles – one of the principal causes of World War II.

and pandered to the Catholic Church. In 1852, following a coup and further street fighting, he had himself proclaimed **Emperor Napoléon III**.

## Empire and Commune

Napoléon III's authoritarian regime oversaw rapid growth in industrial and economic power. When he came to power, over half the country subsisted on the land (a figure down from three-quarters at the Revolution), two-thirds of road traffic took the form of a mule and France itself remained a semi-continent made up as much of wilderness

| 1832 | 1851 | 1852 | 1857 |
|------|------|------|------|
| Chopin performs his debut concert in Paris | Louis Napoléon stages coup d'état | Baron Haussmann hired to rebuild the French capital | Charles Baudelaire publishes *Les Fleurs du Mal* |

– forests, mountains, moorlands and grassy wastes – as land under cultivation. The peasant population was overwhelmingly enmired in debt, poverty and hunger: in 1865, life expectancy for those who made it to 5 years old was 51 years.

Industrialization, however, was now under way, and the explosive expansion of the railways began to lift the provinces out of their previous isolation. By 1888, 22,000 miles of track had been laid. Disaster, however, was approaching in the shape of the **Franco–Prussian** war. Involved in a conflict with Bismarck and the rising power of Germany, Napoléon III declared war. The French army was quickly defeated and the emperor himself taken prisoner in 1870. The result at home was a universal demand for the proclamation of a **third republic**. The German armistice agreement insisted on the election of a national assembly to negotiate a proper peace treaty. France lost Alsace and Lorraine and was obliged to pay hefty war reparations.

Outraged by the monarchist majority re-elected to the new Assembly and by the attempt of its chief minister, Thiers, to disarm the National Guard, the people of Paris created their own municipal government known as **the Commune**. However, it had barely existed two months before it was savagely crushed. On May 21, the **"semaine sanglante"** began in which government troops fought with the Communards street by street, massacring around 25,000, the last of them lined up against the wall of Père Lachaise cemetery and shot. It was a brutal episode that left a permanent scar on the country's political and psychological landscape.

### The Third Republic

In the wake of the Commune, competing political factions fought it out for control. Legitimists supported the return of a Bourbon to the throne, while Orléanists supported the heir of Louis-Philippe. Republicans, of course, would have none of either. Thanks in part to the intransigence of the Comte de Chambord, the Bourbon claimant who refused to accept a constitutional role, the Third Republic was declared. The Crown Jewels were sold off in 1885, and France never again seriously considered having a monarch.

### The War years

In the years preceding **World War I**, the country enjoyed a period of renewed prosperity. Yet the conflicts in the political fabric of French society remained unresolved. With the outbreak of war in 1914, France found itself swiftly overrun by Germany and its allies, and defended by its old enemy, Britain. The cost of the war was even greater for France than for the other participants because it was fought largely on French soil. Over a quarter of the eight million men called up were either killed or injured; industrial production fell to sixty percent of the prewar level. This – along with memories of the Franco–Prussian war of 1870 – was the reason that the French were more aggressive than either the British or the Americans in seeking war reparations from the Germans.

In the postwar struggle for recovery the interests of the urban working class were again passed over, save for Clemenceau's eight-hour-day legislation in 1919. As the **Depression** deepened in the 1930s, Nazi power across the Rhine became ever more menacing. In 1936, the Left-wing **Front Populaire** won the elections with a handsome majority,

| 1870–1871 | 1888 | 1889 | 1903 |
|---|---|---|---|
| Franco–Prussian War and Siege of Paris lead to the bloodbath of the Commune | After a fight with Gauguin in Arles, painter Vincent Van Gogh cuts off his own ear | Eiffel Tower is built | The first ever Tour de France is staged |

## THE DREYFUS AFFAIR

From 1894, the **Dreyfus Affair** dramatically widened the split between Right and Left. Captain Dreyfus was a Jewish army officer convicted of spying for the Germans and shipped off to the penal colony of Devil's Island. It soon became clear that he had been framed – by the army itself – yet they refused to reconsider his case. The affair immediately became an issue between the anti-Semitic, Catholic Right and the Republican Left, with Radical statesman Clemenceau, Socialist leader Jean Jaurès and novelist Émile Zola coming out in favour of Dreyfus. Charles Maurras, founder of the fascist Action Française – precursor of Europe's Blackshirts – took the part of the army.

Dreyfus was officially rehabilitated in 1904, but in the wake of the affair the more radical element in the Republican movement began to dominate the administration, bringing the army under closer civilian control and dissolving most of the religious orders. In 1905 the Third Republic affirmed its anti-clerical roots by introducing a law on the separation of church and state.

ushering in **Léon Blum,** France's first socialist and first Jewish Prime Minister. He pushed through progressive reforms, but his government quickly fell – and the Left would remain out of power until 1981. France meanwhile, had more pressing concerns, as it was drawn into war by the German invasion of Poland, in September 1939.

### World War II

For eight months, France waited out what it called a *drôle de guerre*, or "funny kind of war". Then, in May 1940, Germany attacked – with terrifying speed. In just six weeks, France was overrun as the government fled south, along with up to ten million refugees, or roughly a quarter of the population. **Maréchal Pétain**, a conservative veteran of World War I, emerged from retirement to sign an armistice with Hitler and head the collaborationist **Vichy government**, which ostensibly governed the southern part of the country, while the Germans occupied the strategic north and the Atlantic coast. Pétain's prime minister, Laval, believed it was his duty to adapt France to the new authoritarian age heralded by the Nazi conquest of Europe.

There has been endless controversy over who collaborated, how much and how far it was necessary. One thing at least is clear: Nazi occupation provided a good opportunity for out-and-out French fascists to track down Communists, Jews, Resistance fighters, freemasons – all those who they considered "alien" bodies in French society. While some Communists were involved in the **Resistance** right from the start, Hitler's attack on the Soviet Union in 1941 brought them into the movement on a large scale. Resistance numbers were further increased by young men taking to the hills to escape conscription as labour in Nazi industry. General de Gaulle's radio appeal from London on June 18, 1940, resulted in the Conseil National de la Résistance, unifying the different Resistance groups in May 1943.

Although British and American governments found him irksome, **de Gaulle** was able to impose himself as the unchallenged spokesman of the Free French. Even the Communists accepted his leadership. Representatives of his provisional government moved quickly into liberated areas of France behind the Allied advance after D-Day, thereby saving the country from localized outbreaks of civil war – and saving France, in de Gaulle's view, from the threat of Communist uprising.

| 1907 | 1900–1904 | 1913 |
|---|---|---|
| The game of *pétanque* is invented in La Ciotat on the Côte d'Azur | Pablo Picasso resides at the Bateau Lavoir in Paris: his 'Blue Period' | Marcel Proust completes the first volume of *À la recherche du temps perdus* (*Remembrance of Things Past*) |

## The aftermath of war

France emerged from the war demoralized, bankrupt and bomb-wrecked. Almost half its people were peasants, still living off the land, and its industry was in ruins. Under a new constitution, in which **French women** were granted the vote for the first time, elections resulted in a large and squabbling Left-wing majority. De Gaulle resigned in disgust. The new **Fourth Republic** was weak and fractious, but thanks in part to American aid in the form of the Marshall Plan, France achieved enormous industrial **modernization and expansion** in the 1950s. The country opted to remain in the US fold, but at the same time aggressively and independently pursued **nuclear technology**, finally detonating its own atom bomb in early 1960. France also took the lead in promoting closer **European integration**, a process culminating in 1957 with the creation of the European Economic Community.

## Colonial wars

On the surrender of Japan to the Allies in 1945, **Vietnam**, the northern half of the French Indochina colony, came under the control of Ho Chi Minh and his Communist organization, Vietminh. An eight-year armed struggle ended with French defeat at Dien Bien Phu and partition of the country at the Geneva Conference in 1954 – at which point the Americans took over in the south, with well-known consequences.

In the same year the **Algerian war of liberation** began. The French government was legally, economically and, it felt, morally committed to maintaining its rule over Algeria. Legally, the country was a *département*, an integral part of France, and the million-odd settlers, or **pieds noirs**, were officially French. And there was oil in the south. By 1958, half a million troops, most of them conscripts, had been committed to a bloody and brutal war that cost some 700,000 lives.

By 1958, it began to seem as if the government would take a more liberal line towards Algeria. In response, hard-line Rightists among the settlers and in the army staged a putsch and threatened to declare war on France. General de Gaulle let it be known that in its hour of need and with certain conditions – that is, stronger powers for the president – the country might call upon his help. Thus, on June 1, 1958, the National Assembly voted him full powers for six months and the Fourth Republic came to an end.

# De Gaulle and his successors

As prime minister, then newly powerful president of the **Fifth Republic**, de Gaulle wheeled and dealed with the *pieds noirs* and Algerian rebels. Meanwhile the war continued, and violence in France – including a secret massacre of two hundred demonstrating French Algerians in Paris in 1961 – escalated. Eventually, in 1962, a referendum gave an overwhelming "yes" to **Algerian independence**, and *pieds noirs* refugees flooded into France. At the same time, a French labour shortage led to massive recruitment campaigns for workers in North Africa, Portugal, Spain, Italy and Greece. When the immigrants arrived in France, however, they found themselves under-paid, ill-housed and discriminated against both socially and officially.

De Gaulle's leadership was haughty and autocratic in style, and his quirky strutting on the world stage irritated France's partners. He blocked British entry to the European Economic Community, cultivated the friendship of the Germans, rebuked the US for

| 1914–1918 | 1919 | 1926 |
|---|---|---|
| World War I causes massive casualties in northeastern France | Treaty of Versailles restores territories lost in the Franco–Prussian War | Coco Chanel launches her "little black dress" in American Vogue |

its imperialist policies in Vietnam, withdrew from NATO, refused to sign a nuclear test ban treaty and called for a "free Québec".

Still, the sudden over-boiling of **May 1968** took everyone by surprise. Beginning with student protests at the University of Nanterre, outside Paris, the movement of revolt rapidly spread to the Sorbonne and out into factories and offices. On the night of May 10, barricades went up in the streets of the Quartier Latin in Paris, and the CRS (riot police) responded by wading in. A **general strike** followed, and within a week more than a million people were out, marching under vaguely radical slogans. De Gaulle appealed to the nation to elect him as the only effective barrier against Left-wing dictatorship, and dissolved parliament. The "silent majority", frightened and shocked by *les événements* – "the events", as they were nervously called – voted massively in his favour. When the smoke cleared, little had changed.

## Pompidou and Giscard

Having petulantly staked his presidency on the outcome of yet another referendum (on a couple of constitutional amendments) and lost, de Gaulle once more took himself off to his country estate and retirement. He was succeeded as president in 1969 by his business-oriented former prime minister **Georges Pompidou** and then, in 1974, by **Valéry Giscard d'Estaing**, who announced that his aim was to make France "an advanced liberal society". But, aside from reducing the voting age to 18 and liberalizing divorce laws, little progress was made. Giscard fell foul of various scandals and fell out with his ambitious prime minister, **Jacques Chirac**, who set out to challenge the leadership with his own RPR Gaullist party.

The Left seemed well placed to win the coming 1978 elections, until the fragile union between the Socialists and Communists cracked, the latter fearing their roles as the coalition's junior partners. The result was another Right-wing victory, with Giscard able to form a new government, grudgingly supported by the RPR. Law and order and immigrant controls were the dominant features of Giscard's second term.

## The Mitterrand and Chirac era

When **François Mitterrand** won the presidential elections over Giscard in 1981, inaugurating the first Socialist government for decades, expectations were sky high. By 1984, however, the flight of capital, inflation and budget deficits had forced a complete turnaround, and the 1986 parliamentary election saw the Right, under Jacques Chirac, winning a clear majority in parliament. Thus began a period marked by what the French call **cohabitation**, in which the head of state (the president) and head of government (the prime minister) belong to opposite sides of the political divide.

As Prime Minister, Chirac embarked on a policy of privatization and monetary control, but the greatest change of the era was instituted by Mitterrand. In 1992, the president staked his reputation on the **Maastricht referendum** on creating closer political union in Europe. The vote was carried by a narrow margin in favour. On the whole, poorer rural areas voted "No" while rich urbanites and political parties voted "Yes". Only the extreme end of the political spectrum, the Communists and the Front National, remained determinedly anti-Europe.

In the 1990s, emerging scandals over cover-ups, corruption and the dubious war records of senior politicians tainted both the major parties, and Mitterrand tottered on

| 1929 | 1934 | 1935 |
|---|---|---|
| The start of the Great Depression; Jean-Paul Sartre meets Simone de Beauvoir at the École Normale in Paris | Gypsy guitarist Django Rheinhardt and violin virtuoso Stephane Grappelli form the Hot Club de France Quintette | Edith Piaf's breakthrough performance at *Le Gerny* nightclub |

to the end of his presidential term, looking less and less like the nation's favourite uncle. Several mayors ended up in jail, but it seemed as if the Paris establishment was above the law. By the time Mitterrand finally stepped down, he had been the French head of state for fourteen years, during a period when crime rose and increasing numbers of people found themselves excluded from society by racism, poverty and homelessness. Support for extreme Right policies propelled Jean-Marie Le Pen's Front National from a minority faction to a serious electoral force.

### Chirac's first presidency

Elected as president in 1995 and winning a second mandate in 2002, Chirac showed himself every bit as astute a politician as Mitterrand, and no less prone to scandal and controversy. An early sign of the rocky road ahead came when his Prime Minister, Alain Juppé, introduced **austerity measures**, designed to prepare France for European monetary union. Reforms to pensions and healthcare spending provoked a series of damaging strikes in 1995 and 1996, and led to growing popular disenchantment with the idea of closer European integration.

The **Front National** played up their image of standing up for the small man against the corrupt political establishment, and at municipal elections in June 1995 gained control of three towns, including the major port of Toulon. The **Algerian bomb attacks** which rocked Paris in the mid-1990s – designed to punish France for supporting Algeria's anti-Islamist military government – further played into the hands of the far Right and diminished public confidence in the government as guardian of law and order.

Feeling increasingly beleaguered and unable to deliver on the economy, Chirac called a snap parliamentary election in May 1997. His gamble failed spectacularly, and he was forced into a weak **cohabitation** with a Socialist parliament headed by **Lionel Jospin**, who promptly introduced the 35-hour working week, a 50:50 gender quota for representatives of political parties and, in 1999, the **Pacs** or Pacte Civile de Solidarité, a contract giving cohabiting couples, particularly gay couples, almost the same rights as married people.

### Skeletons in the mayoral cupboard

The most persistent **corruption scandals** focused on the finances of the Paris town hall, dating back to the 1980s. In 1995 it was revealed that Alain Juppé had rented a luxury flat in Paris for his son at below-market rates, and in 1998 the conservative Paris mayor **Jean Tiberi** was implicated in a scam involving subsidized real estate and fake town-hall jobs – with real salaries – for party activists and relatives. Prosecutors edged ever closer to Chirac himself. In 2001 the president was accused of using some three million francs in cash from illegal sources to pay for luxury holidays, and in 2003 it was revealed that in eight years in office as mayor of Paris he and his wife had run up grocery bills of 2.2 million euros – over half of which had been reimbursed in cash. When investigating magistrates tried to question Chirac he claimed presidential immunity, a position that was upheld by France's highest court. But finally, in late 2011, the old fox was run to ground, charged with creating fictional jobs for political cronies and friends in need. The jury found him guilty and Chirac, by then 79 years old, was given a two-year suspended prison sentence for embezzelling public funds, abuse of trust and illegal conflict of interest. Due to his age and status as former head of state, he was not required to go to prison.

| 1939–1945 | 1948 | 1954–1962 | 1959 |
|---|---|---|---|
| World War II; Paris and northern France occupied by Nazis; the south is ruled by the puppet Vichy regime | Citroën unveils the iconic 2CV motor car | Algerian War of Independence | François Truffaut's *Les Quatre Cent Coups* (The 400 Blows) epitomizes French Nouvelle Vague (New Wave) cinema |

## The election earthquake

In the run-up to the **presidential elections of 2002**, everyone in France assumed that the race was between Chirac and Jospin. Both far Left and far Right were damagingly split – and Front National leader, **Jean-Marie Le Pen**, had lost much support for punching a woman Socialist candidate in 1998. Lionel Jospin's hopes had been bolstered by the election of Socialist **Bertrand Delanoë** as Mayor of Paris in March 2001 but in the run-up to the elections the economy began to falter, unemployment was once more on the rise and fears over crime were widespread. Chirac talked up issues of immigration and law and order and when the results of the first round came through, Jospin had been beaten into third place by Le Pen – leaving Chirac and Le Pen to stand against each other in the final run-off in May.

The result was widely referred to as an "earthquake", shaking voters out of their disillusioned apathy. On May 1, 800,000 people packed the boulevards of Paris to protest against Le Pen and Socialists called on their supporters to vote for Chirac. He duly swept the board and, in the **ensuing parliamentary elections**, his new Right-wing party, the **Union for a Presidential Majority**, swept convincingly to power. In an attempt to address widespread concerns about lack of representation and government accountability, one of Chirac's first measures was a **devolution** bill, giving more power to 26 regional assemblies and ending centuries of central government steadily accruing power to itself.

## Iraq, Muslims and climate change

In March 2003, a reinvigorated Chirac declared that he would wield France's Security Council veto if the US tried to table a resolution that contained an ultimatum leading to war in Iraq. Both the nationalist Right and anti-imperialists on the Left lapped it up in an orgy of anti-Americanism, and even some international observers applauded France's principled defence of international law, or perhaps of European power. Others saw Chirac's actions as cynical political posturing.

Either way, the result was an almighty spat that seriously damaged the cherished Franco–American relationship. One thing France's tough stance wasn't based on was any particularly pro-Arab or pro-Islamic bias, despite the presence of 5 million or more **Muslims** in France – the largest community in Europe. During 2003, Chirac presided over a government setting expulsion targets for illegal immigrants and enacting a hugely controversial bill – though it was backed by almost two-thirds of the population and passed in parliament by 494 votes to 36 – banning "ostensibly religious" signs, notably Islamic headscarves, from schools and hospitals. Proposing the measure in December 2003, Chirac avowed that "Secularity is one of the republic's great achievements … We must not allow it to be weakened."

In 2003 **climate change** also bludgeoned its way onto the headlines, due to Parisian temperatures in August regularly topping 40ºC (104ºF) – more than ten degrees above the average maximum for that time of year. Fifteen thousand people died. No one seemed willing to take responsibility for doing anything about it.

## Reforms, resistance and riots

Faced with an ageing population, unemployment flatlining at around ten percent and a budget deficit persistently exceeding the eurozone's three-percent ceiling, the newly confident Right decided it would reform the public sector once and for all. First to go

| 1961 | 1968 | 1981 | 1995 |
|------|------|------|------|
| Johnny Hallyday's cover of *Let's Twist Again* tops every chart in Europe | Student revolts and national strike cripple the country | Mitterrand becomes President of the Republic | Chirac voted President |

under the knife would be the state's generous pensions and unemployment benefits, then worker-friendly hiring and firing rights, and finally the world-leading health service. Most of France saw the programme less as prudent milk-rationing and more as getting their sacred cows ready to be sent off to slaughter. By mid-May 2003, two million workers were out on strike; and on May 26 half a million protested in the streets of Paris. And this was only in defence of pensions.

In the regional elections of March 2004, the electoral map turned a furious pink. Then, in the referendum of May 2005, 55 percent of French voters rejected the proposed new EU constitution when all the major political parties had urged them to vote "Yes". French voters, it seemed, did not want to join the new, economically liberal, globalized world.

Neither did disaffected French youths. In October 2005, two teenagers in a run-down suburb outside Paris were electrocuted while hiding from police they believed were chasing them. Local anger led speedily to three weeks of nightly, nationwide riots and confrontations. Youths torched cars, buses, schools and even police and power stations – anything connected with the hated state. Almost 9000 vehicles and property worth €200 million went up in smoke, and almost 2900 people had been arrested. The ambitious Interior Minister, Nicolas Sarkozy, demanded the neighbourhoods be cleaned with power-hoses. Young people who actually lived in the "hot" suburbs saw the main cause as anger at **racism** and social and economic exclusion. Many of the worst-affected areas were home to communities of largely African or North-African origin, where youth unemployment runs as high as fifty percent – double the already high average among young people.

Even as the *banlieue* burned, Prime Minister Dominique de Villepin attempted to tackle the problem of youth unemployment and economic stagnation by giving small companies the right to dismiss new employees without having to give cause. This looked suspiciously like neoliberal or "Anglo-Saxon" capitalism. So, in October 2005, a million workers across the country marched against the new labour law. When, in early 2006, the laws were to be extended to all companies employing workers under the age of 26, the young responded with fury. In March, students in Paris **occupied the Sorbonne**, in conscious imitation of May 1968. And just as in 1968, people protested across France in their millions – only this time in the hope not that France would radically change, but that everything would stay the same. On April 10, Dominique de Villepin withdrew the law.

## Sarko

In the wake of the employment rights debacle, Nicolas Sarkozy, by now known popularly (and not affectionately) as "Sarko", was confirmed as the UMP's candidate for the 2007 presidential election. By a narrow margin, he defeated his centrist Socialist rival, **Ségolène Royal**. He had promised ongoing, radical reform, but major surprises followed his victory. First, he appointed a notably conciliatory cabinet. Next, his wife left him, and he took up with the model, singer and Euro-jetsetter Carla Bruni, marrying her in February 2008. Suddenly, the media spotlight was on his Presidency, and it was asking more questions about the lifts in his shoes than his economic policies.

Then came the global financial crisis of 2008–09. Suddenly, the "Anglo-Saxon" form of market-led, laissez-faire capitalism seemed exactly what French socialists had always

| 1998 | 2002 | 2003 | 2005 |
|---|---|---|---|
| Zidane's dream team beat Brazil 3-0 in the FIFA World Cup, then win the UEFA Euros two years later | The Euro replaces French Franc | Severe heat wave leaves 15,000 dead | Urban riots by immigrant communities across the country |

said it was: a debt-fuelled castle built on sand. In response, Sarkozy performed an astonishing political about-turn, pledging to wield the power of the state to ensure stability. Strong-state *dirigisme* was back. National reform, again, would have to wait. France never teetered on the edge of banking meltdown like its Atlantic rivals, but it was hit by recession nonetheless. In 2009, unemployment in France began racing towards the ten percent figure.

The usual **corruption scandals**, meanwhile, started to circle over Sarkozy's beleaguered administration. In 2009, his former political associate Dominique de Villepin was tried for his alleged role in the Clearstream affair, a supposed smear campaign in which a fake list of dodgy bank accounts, containing Sarkozy's name, was passed to an investigating judge. Rumours surfaced of kickbacks from French arms sales to Pakistan, allegedly used to fund Eduoard Balladur's election campaign in the mid-1990s. Sarkozy was later accused of becoming a "French Berlusconi", by putting pressure on his powerful media friends to ensure a compliant press. Then members of his party were accused of accepting illegal donations from the L'Oréal heir and France's wealthiest woman, Liliane Bettencourt. In July 2010, Sarkozy himself was forced into making an unprecedented TV address to deny ever receiving money stuffed into an envelope – none of which did much to bolster the popularity of a leader widely perceived, with his jet-set lifestyle and glamorous marriage, as having lost touch with the Man in the Street.

As France's public debt spiralled and industrial output plummeted through 2011, the "President of the Rich" was increasingly seen as failing to deliver on his electoral pledges, while standing by as the mega-wealthy benefitted from tax breaks and legal loopholes.

### "Mr Normal"

It was to distinguish himself from his adversary's high-rolling lifestyle that Socialist Party candidate, **François Hollande**, declared himself "Mr Normal" in the run-up to the 2012 elections. A moderate social-democrat from the central French province of Corrèze, Hollande had served as First Secretary of his party, but had long remained in the shadow of his wife, former presidential candidate, Ségolène Royal. The marriage, however, collapsed shortly after Royal's bid for the presidency in 2007, when it emerged that Hollande was involved with a *Paris Match* political journalist, Valérie Trierweiler.

In spite of the interest in his private life, Hollande went on to emerge victorious from the 2012 battle with Sarkozy for the French presidency – an acrimonious campaign in which the far-Right National Front candidate, Marine Le Pen, shocked many by polling nearly 18 percent of the vote.

When the Socialist Party won an outright majority in the parliamentary elections soon after, Hollande's new administration had the mandate it needed to push through the keystones of its manifesto: a 75 percent tax on earnings over €1 million, and rapid expansion of the state sector as a means of stimulating growth. In his refusal to use the word "austerity", Hollande was showing himself to be in step with the French electorate, but at odds with his opposite number in Berlin, Angela Merkel. The debate over which approach will ultimately prove most effective in solving the Euro crisis continues to dominate political life in France – a country whose economic future is far less certain than the impressive margin of victory with which Hollande and his party swept to power in 2012.

| 2007 | 2011 | 2012 |
| --- | --- | --- |
| Nicolas Sarkozy wins Presidential election | The Muslim veil, or hejab, is banned in French schools | François Hollande defeats Sarkozy in closely fought Presidential election |

# Art

Since the Middle Ages, France has held – with occasional gaps – a leading position in the history of European painting, with Paris, above all, attracting artists from the whole continent. The story of French painting is one of richness and complexity, partly due to this influx of foreign painters and partly due to the capital's stability as an artistic centre.

## Beginnings

In the late Middle Ages, the itinerant life of the nobles led them to prefer small and transportable works of art; splendidly **illuminated manuscripts** were much praised and the best painters, usually trained in Paris, continued to work on a small scale until the fifteenth century. Many illuminators were also panel painters, and foremost among them was **Jean Fouquet** (c.1420–81). Born in Tours in the Loire valley he became court painter to Charles VIII, drawing from both Flemish and Italian sources and utilizing the new fluid oil technique that had been perfected in Flanders.

Two other fifteenth-century French artists could be said to represent distinctive northern and southern strands. **Enguerrand Quarton** (c.1410–c.1466) was the most famous Provençal painter of the time. His *Coronation of the Virgin*, which hangs at Villeneuve-lès-Avignon, ranks as one of the first city/landscapes in the history of French painting: Avignon itself is faithfully depicted and the Mont Ste-Victoire, later to be made famous by Cézanne, is recognizable in the distance. The Master of Moulins, active in the 1480s and 1490s, was noticeably more northern in temperament, painting both religious altarpieces and portraits commissioned by members of the royal family or the fast-increasing bourgeoisie.

## Mannerism and Italian influence

At the end of the fifteenth and the beginning of the sixteenth centuries, the French invasion of Italy brought both artists and patrons into closer contact with the Italian Renaissance.

The most famous of the artists who were lured to France was **Leonardo da Vinci** who spent the last three years of his life (1516–19) at the court of François I. From the Loire valley, which until then had been his favourite residence, the French king moved nearer to Paris, where he had several palaces decorated. Italian artists were once again called upon, and two of them, **Rosso** and **Primaticcio**, who arrived in France in 1530 and 1532, respectively, were to shape the artistic scene in France for the rest of the sixteenth century.

Both artists introduced to France the latest Italian style, **Mannerism**, with its emphasis on the fantastic, the luxurious and the large-scale decorative. It was first put to the test in the revamping of the palace at Fontainebleau, and most French artists worked at the château at some point in their career, or were influenced by its homogeneous style, leading to what was subsequently called the **School of Fontainebleau**.

**Antoine Caron** (c.1520–1600), who often worked for Catherine de Médicis, the widow of Henri II, contrived complicated allegorical paintings in which elongated figures are arranged within wide, theatre-like scenery packed with ancient monuments and Roman statues. Even the Wars of Religion, raging in the 1550s and 1560s, failed to rouse French artists' sense of drama, and representations of the many massacres then going on were detached and fussy in tone.

Portraiture tended to be more inventive, and very French in its general sobriety. The portraits of **Jean Clouet** (c.1485–1541) and his son **François** (c.1510–72), both official painters to François I, combined sensitivity in the rendering of the sitter's features with a keen sense of abstract design in the arrangement of the figure, conveying with great clarity social status and giving clues to the sitter's profession.

## The seventeenth century

In the **seventeenth century**, Italy continued to be a source of inspiration for French artists, most of whom were drawn to Rome – at that time the most exciting artistic centre in Europe, dominated by Italian painters such as Michelangelo Merisi da Caravaggio and Annibale Carracci.

Some French painters like **Moise Valentin** (c.1594–1632) worked in Rome and were directly influenced by Caravaggio; others, such as the great painter from Lorraine, **Georges de la Tour** (1593–1652), benefitted from his innovations at one remove, gaining inspiration from the Utrecht Caravaggisti who were active at the time in Holland. La Tour produced deeply felt religious paintings in which figures appear to be carved out of the surrounding gloom by the magical light of a candle. Sadly, his output was very small – just some forty or so works in all.

Humble subjects and attention to naturalistic detail were also important aspects of the work of the **Le Nain brothers**, especially **Louis** (1593–1648), who depicted with great sympathy, but never with sentimentality, the condition of the peasantry. He chose moments of inactivity or repose within the lives of the peasants, and his paintings achieve timelessness and monumentality by their very stillness. The other Italian artist of influence, the Bolognese **Annibale Carracci** (d. 1609), impressed French painters not only with his skill as a decorator but, more tellingly, with his ordered, balanced landscapes, which were to prove of prime importance for the development of the classical landscape in general, and in particular for those painted by **Claude Lorrain** (1604/5–82). Born in Lorraine, Claude studied and travelled in Italy, which would provide him with subjects of study for the rest of his life. His landscapes are airy compositions in which religious or mythological figures are lost within an idealized, Arcadian nature, bathed in tranquil light.

Landscapes, harsher and even more ordered, but also recalling the Arcadian mood of antiquity, were painted by the other French painter who elected to make Rome his home, **Nicolas Poussin** (1594–1665). Like Claude, Poussin selected his themes from the rich sources of Greek, Roman and Christian myths and stories; unlike Claude, however, his figures are not subdued by nature but rather dominate it, in the tradition of the masters of the High Renaissance, such as Raphael and Titian, whom he greatly admired. Poussin only briefly returned to Paris, called by the king, Louis XIII, to undertake some large decorative works quite unsuited to his style or character.

Many other artists visited Italy, but most returned to France, the luckiest to be employed at the court to boost the royal images of Louis XIII and XIV and their respective ministers, Richelieu and Colbert. **Simon Vouet** (1590–1649), **Charles Le Brun** (1619–90) and **Pierre Mignard** (1612–95) all performed that task with skill, often using ancient history and mythology to suggest flattering comparisons with the reigning monarch.

The official aspect of their works was paralleled by the creation of the new **Academy of Painting and Sculpture** in 1648, an institution that dominated the arts in France for the next few hundred years, if only by the way artists reacted against it. **Philippe de Champaigne** (1602–74), a painter of Flemish origin, alone stands out at the time as remotely different, removed from the intrigues and pleasures of the court and instead strongly influenced by the teaching and moral code of Jansenism, a purist and severe form of the Catholic faith. But it was the more courtly, fun-loving portraits and paintings by such artists as Mignard that were to influence most of the art of the following century.

# The early eighteenth century

The semi-official art encouraged by the foundation of the Academy became more frivolous and light-hearted in the **eighteenth century**. The court at Versailles lost its attractions, and many patrons now were to be found among the hedonistic bourgeoisie and aristocracy living in Paris. History painting, as opposed to genre scenes or portraiture, retained its position of prestige, but at the same time many artists tried their hands at landscape, genre, history or decorative works, often merging aspects of one genre with another. **Salons**, at which painters exhibited their works, were held with increasing frequency and bred a new phenomenon in the art world – the art critic.

Possibly the most complex personality of the eighteenth century was **Jean-Antoine Watteau** (1684–1721). Primarily a superb draughtsman, Watteau's use of soft and yet rich, light colours reveals how much he was struck by the great seventeenth-century Flemish painter Rubens. His subtle depictions of dreamy couples, often seen strolling in delicate, mythical landscapes, are known as "*Fêtes Galantes*". They convey a mood of melancholy and poignancy largely lacking in the works of followers such as Nicolas Lancret and J.-B. Pater.

The work of **François Boucher** (1703–70) was probably more representative of the eighteenth century: the pleasure-seeking court of Louis XV found the lightness of morals and colours in his paintings immensely congenial. Boucher's virtuosity is seen at its best in his paintings of women, always rosy, young and fantasy-erotic. **Jean-Honoré Fragonard** (1732–1806) continued this exploration of licentious themes but with an exuberance, a richness of colour and a vitality (*The Swing*) that was a feast for the eyes and raised the subject to a glorification of love. Far more restrained were the paintings of **Jean-Baptiste-Siméon Chardin** (1699–1779), who specialized in homely genre scenes and still lifes, painted with a simplicity that belied his complex use of colours, shapes and space to promote a mood of stillness and tranquillity. **Jean-Baptiste Greuze** (1725–1805) chose stories that anticipated reaction against the laxity of the times; the moral, at times sentimental, character of his paintings was all-pervasive, reinforced by a stage-like composition well suited to cautionary tales.

# Neoclassicism

This new seriousness became more severe with the rise of **Neoclassicism**, a movement for which purity and simplicity were essential components of the systematic depiction of edifying stories from the classical authors. Roman history and legends were the most popular subjects. Many of the paintings of **Jacques-Louis David** (1748–1825) are reflections of republican ideals and of contemporary history, from the *Death of Marat* to events from the life of Napoleon, who was his patron. For the emperor and his family, David painted some of his most successful portraits – *Madame Recamier* is not only an exquisite example of David's controlled use of shapes and space and his debt to antique Rome, but can also be seen as a paradigm of Neoclassicism.

Two painters, **Jean-Antoine Gros** (1771–1835) and **Baron Gérard** (1770–1837), followed David closely in style and in themes (portraits, Napoleonic history and legend), but often with a touch of softness and heroic poetry that pointed the way to Romanticism.

**Jean-Auguste-Dominique Ingres** (1780–1867) was a pupil of David; he also studied in Rome before coming back to Paris to develop the purity of line that was the essential and characteristic element of his art. His effective use of it to build up forms and bind compositions can be admired in conjunction with his recurrent theme of female nudes bathing, or in his magnificent and stately portraits that depict the nuances of social status.

# Romanticism

Completely opposed to the stress on drawing advocated by Ingres, two artists created, through their emphasis on colour, form and composition, pictures that look forward to the later part of the nineteenth century and the Impressionists. **Théodore Géricault** (1791–1824), whose short life was dominated by the heroic vision of the Napoleonic era, explored dramatic themes of human suffering in such paintings as *The Raft of the Medusa*, while his close contemporary, **Eugène Delacroix** (1798–1863), epitomized the **Romantic movement** – its search for emotions and its love of nature, power and change.

Delacroix was deeply aware of tradition, and his art was influenced, visually and conceptually, by the great masters of the Renaissance and the seventeenth and eighteenth centuries. In many ways he may be regarded as the last great religious and decorative French painter, but through his technical virtuosity, freedom of brushwork and richness of colours, he can also be seen as the essential forerunner of the Impressionists.

Other painters working in the Romantic tradition were still haunted by the Napoleonic legends, as well as by North Africa (Algeria) and the Middle East, which had become better known to artists and patrons alike during the Napoleonic wars. These were the subjects of paintings by **Horace Vernet** (1789–1863), **Théodore Chassériau** (1819–56) and the enormously popular but now little-regarded giant of old-fashioned Classicism, **Jean-Louis-Ernest Meissonier** (1815–91).

Among their contemporaries was **Honoré Daumier** (1808–79): very much an isolated figure, influenced by the boldness of approach of caricaturists, he was content to depict everyday subjects such as a laundress or a third-class rail car – caustic commentaries on professions and politics that work as brilliant observations of the times.

## Landscape painting and realism

The first part of the **nineteenth century** saw nature, unadorned by artistic conventions, became a subject for study. Running parallel to this was the realization that painting could be the visual externalization of the artist's own emotions and feelings. **Jean-Baptiste-Camille Corot** (1796–1875) started to paint landscapes that were influenced as much by the unpretentious and realistic country scenes of seventeenth-century Holland as by the balanced compositions of Claude. His loving and attentive studies of nature were much admired by later artists, including Monet.

At the same time, a whole group of painters developed similar attitudes to landscape and nature, helped greatly by the practical improvement of being able to buy oil paint in tubes rather than as unmixed pigments. Known as the **Barbizon School** after the village on the outskirts of Paris around which they painted, they soon discovered the joy and excitement of *plein-air* (open-air) painting. **Théodore Rousseau** (1812–67) was their nominal leader, his paintings of forest undergrowth and forest clearings displaying an intimacy that came from the immediacy of the image. **Charles-François Daubigny** (1817–78), like Rousseau, often infused a sense of drama into his landscapes.

**Jean-François Millet** (1814–75) is perhaps the best-known associate of the Barbizon group, though he was more interested in the human figure than simple nature. Landscapes, however, were essential settings for his figures; indeed, his most famous pictures are those exploring the place of people in nature and their struggle to survive. *The Sower*, for instance, reflected a typical Millet theme, suggesting the heroic working life of the peasant. As is so often the case for painters touching on new themes or on ideas that are uncomfortable to the rich and powerful, Millet enjoyed little success during his lifetime, and his art was only widely appreciated after his death.

The moralistic and romantic undertone in Millet's work was something that **Gustave Courbet** (1819–77) strove to avoid. After an initial resounding success in the Salon exhibition of 1849, he endured constant criticism from the academic world and patrons alike, his scenes of ordinary life regarded as unsavoury and wilfully ugly. Breaking with the Salon tradition, Courbet put on a private exhibition of some forty of his works. Inscribed on the door in large letters was one word: "**Realism**".

# Impressionism

Like Courbet, **Edouard Manet** (1832–83) was strongly influenced by Spanish painters. Unlike Courbet, however, he never saw himself as a rebel or avant-garde painter – yet his technique and his themes were both new and shocking. Manet used bold contrasts of light and very dark colours, giving his paintings a forcefulness that critics often took for a lack of sophistication. And his detractors saw much to decry in his reworking of an old subject originally treated by the sixteenth-century Venetian painter, Giorgione, *Le Déjeuner sur l'Herbe*. Manet's version was shocking because he placed naked and dressed figures together, and because the men were dressed in the costume of the day, implying a pleasure party too specifically contemporary to be "respectable".

Manet's most successful pictures are reflections of ordinary life in bars and public places, where respectability was certainly lacking. To Manet, painting was to be enjoyed for its own sake and not as a tool for moral instruction – in itself an outlook that marked a definite break with the past. From the 1870s, Manet began to adopt the new techniques of painting out-of-doors, and his work became lighter and freer. He began to be seen as a much-admired member of a burgeoning group of mould-breaking young painters, alongside **Claude Monet** (1840–1926). Born in Le Havre, Monet came into contact with **Eugène Boudin** (1824–98), whose colourful beach scenes anticipated the way the Impressionists approached colour. Monet discovered that, for him, light and the way in which it builds up forms and creates an infinity of colours was the element that governed all representations. Under the impact of Manet's bright hues and his unconventional attitude ("art for art's sake"), Monet soon began using pure colours side by side, blended together to create areas of brightness and shade.

In 1874, a group of thirty artists exhibited together for the first time. Among them were some of the best-known names of this period of French art: Degas, Monet, Renoir, Pissarro. One of Monet's paintings was entitled *Impression: Sun Rising*, a title that was singled out by the critics to ridicule the colourful, loose and unacademic style of these young artists. Overnight they became, derisively, the "**Impressionists**".

**Camille Pissarro** (1830–1903) was slightly older than most of them and seems to have played the part of an encouraging father figure, always keenly aware of any new development or new talent. Not a great innovator himself, Pissarro was a very gifted artist whose use of Impressionist technique was supplemented by a lyrical feeling for nature and its seasonal changes. But it was really with **Monet** that Impressionist theory ran its full course: he painted and repainted the same motif under different light conditions, at different times of the day, and in different seasons, producing whole series of paintings such as *Grain Stacks*, *Poplars* and, much later, his *Water Lilies*.

**Auguste Renoir** (1841–1919), who started life as a painter of porcelain, was swept up by Monet's ideas for a while, but soon felt the need to look again at the old masters and to emphasize the importance of drawing. Renoir regarded the representation of the female nude as the most taxing and rewarding subject that an artist could tackle. Like Boucher in the eighteenth century, Renoir's nudes are luscious, but rarely, if ever, erotic – although in his later paintings they can become cloyingly, almost overpoweringly, sweet. Better were his portraits of women fully clothed, both for their obvious and innate sympathy and for their keen sense of design.

**Edgar Degas** (1834–1917) was yet another artist who, although he exhibited with the Impressionists, did not follow their precepts very closely. The son of a rich banker, he was trained in the tradition of Ingres: design and drawing were an integral part of his art, and, whereas Monet was fascinated mainly by light, Degas wanted to express movement in all its forms. His pictures are vivid expressions of the body in action, usually straining under fairly exacting circumstances – dancers and circus artistes were among his favourite subjects, as well as more mundane depictions of laundresses and other working women.

Like so many artists of the day, Degas had his imagination fired by the discovery of **Japanese prints**, which could for the first time be seen in quantity. These provided him with new ideas of composition, not least in their asymmetry of design and the use of large areas of unbroken colour. **Photography**, too, had an impact, if only because it finally liberated artists from the task of producing accurate, exacting descriptions of the world.

Degas' extraordinary gift as a draughtsman was matched only by that of the Provençal aristocrat **Henri de Toulouse-Lautrec** (1864–1901). Toulouse-Lautrec, who had broken both his legs as a child, was unusually small, a physical deformity that made him particularly sensitive to free and vivacious movements. A great admirer of Degas, he chose similar themes: people in cafés and theatres, working women and variety dancers all figured large in his work. But, unlike Degas, Toulouse-Lautrec looked beyond the body, and his work is scattered with social comment, sometimes sardonic and bitter. In his portrayal of Paris prostitutes, there is sympathy and kindness; to study them better he lived in a brothel, revealing in his paintings the weariness and sometimes gentleness of these women.

## Post-Impressionism

Though a rather vague term, as it's difficult to date exactly when the backlash against Impressionism took place, **Post-Impressionism** represents in many ways a return to more formal concepts of painting – in composition, in attitudes to subject and in drawing.

**Paul Cézanne** (1839–1906), for one, associated only very briefly with the Impressionists and spent most of his working life in relative isolation, obsessed with rendering, as objectively as possible, the essence of form. He saw objects as basic shapes – cylinders, cones, and so on – and tried to give his painting a unity of texture that would force the spectator to view it not so much as a representation of the world but rather as an entity in its own right, as an object as real and dense as the objects surrounding it. It was this striving for pictorial unity that led him to cover the entire surface of the picture with small, equal brush strokes which made no distinction between the textures of a tree, a house or the sky.

The detached, unemotional way in which Cézanne painted was not unlike that of the seventeenth-century artist Poussin, and he found a contemporary parallel in the work of **Georges Seurat** (1859–91). Seurat was fascinated by current theories of light and colour, and he attempted to apply them in a systematic way, creating different shades and tones by placing tiny spots of pure colour side by side, which the eye could in turn fuse together to see the colours mixed out of their various components. This **pointillist** technique also had the effect of giving monumentality to everyday scenes of contemporary life.

While Cézanne, Seurat and, for that matter, the Impressionists sought to represent the outside world objectively, several other artists – the **Symbolists** – were seeking a different kind of truth, through the subjective experience of fantasy and dreams. **Gustave Moreau** (1840–98) represented, in complex paintings, the intricate worlds of the romantic fairy tale, his visions expressed in a wealth of naturalistic details. The style of **Puvis de Chavannes** (1824–98) was more restrained and more obviously concerned with design and the decorative. And a third artist, **Odilon Redon** (1840–1916), produced some weird and visionary graphic work that especially intrigued Symbolist writers; his less frequent works in colour belong to the later part of his life.

The subjectivity of the Symbolists was of great importance to the art of **Paul Gauguin** (1848–1903). He started life as a stockbroker who collected Impressionist paintings, a Sunday artist who gave up his job in 1883 to dedicate himself to painting.

During his stay in Pont-Aven in Brittany, Gauguin worked with a number of artists who called themselves the **Nabis**, among them **Paul Sérusier** and **Émile Bernard**. He began exploring ways of expressing concepts and emotions by means of large areas of colour and powerful forms, and developed a unique style that was heavily indebted to his knowledge of Japanese prints and of the tapestries and stained glass of medieval art.

His search for the primitive expression of primitive emotions took him eventually to the Pacific, where, in Tahiti, he found some of his most inspiring subjects.

A similar derivation from Symbolist art and a wish to exteriorize emotions and ideas by means of strong colours, lines and shapes underlies the work of **Vincent Van Gogh** (1853–90), a Dutch painter who came to live in France. Like Gauguin, with whom he had an admiring but stormy friendship, Van Gogh started painting relatively late in life, lightening his palette in Paris under the influence of the Impressionists, and then heading south to Arles where, struck by the harshness of the Mediterranean light, he turned out such frantic expressionistic pieces as *The Reaper* and *Wheatfield with Crows*. In all his later pictures the paint is thickly laid on in increasingly abstract patterns that follow the shapes and tortuous paths of his deep inner melancholy.

**Édouard Vuillard** (1868–1940) and **Pierre Bonnard** (1867–1947) explored the Nabi artists' interest in Japanese art and in the decorative surface of painting. They produced intimate images in which figures and objects blend together in complicated patterns. In the works of Bonnard, in particular, the glowing design of the canvas itself becomes as important as what it's trying to represent.

## Fauvism, Cubism, Surrealism

The **twentieth century** kicked off to a colourful start with the **Fauvist** exhibition of 1905, an appropriately anarchic beginning to a century which, in France above all, was to see radical changes in attitudes towards painting. The painters who took part in the exhibition included, most influentially, **Henri Matisse** (1869–1954), **André Derain** (1880–1954), **Georges Rouault** (1871–1958) and **Albert Marquet** (1875–1947), and they were quickly nicknamed the Fauves (Wild Beasts) for their use of bright, wild colours that often bore no relation whatsoever to the reality of the object depicted. Skies were just as likely to be green as blue since, for the Fauves, colour was a way of composing, of structuring a picture, and not necessarily a reflection of real life. Raoul Dufy (1877–1953) used Fauvist colours in combination with theories of abstraction to paint an effervescent industrial age.

Fauvism was just the beginning: the first decades of the twentieth century was a time of intense excitement and artistic activity in Paris, and painters and sculptors from all over Europe flocked to the capital to take part in the liberation from conventional art that individuals and groups were gradually instigating. This loose, cosmopolitan grouping of artists gradually became known as the **École de Paris**, though it was never a "school" as such. **Pablo Picasso** (1881–1973) was one of the first to arrive in Paris – from Spain, in 1900. He soon started work on his first Blue Period paintings, which describe the sad and squalid life of itinerant actors in tones of blue. Later, while Matisse was experimenting with colours and their decorative potential, Picasso came under the sway of Cézanne and his organization of forms into geometrical shapes. He also learned from so-called "primitive", and especially African, sculpture, and out of these studies came a painting that heralded a definite new direction, not only for Picasso's own style but for the whole of modern art – *Les Demoiselles d'Avignon*. Executed in 1907, this painting combined Cézanne's analysis of forms with the visual impact of African masks.

It was from this semi-abstract picture that Picasso went on to develop the theory of **Cubism**, inspiring artists such as **Georges Braque** (1882–1963) and **Juan Gris** (1887–1927), another Spaniard, and formulating a whole new movement. The Cubists' aim was to depict objects not so much as they saw them but rather as they knew them to be: a bottle and a guitar were shown from the front, from the side and from the back as if the eye could take in all at once every facet and plane of the object. Braque and Picasso first analysed forms into these facets (analytical Cubism), then gradually reduced them to series of colours and shapes (synthetic Cubism), among which a few recognizable symbols such as letters, fragments of newspaper and numbers appeared. The complexity of different planes overlapping one another made the deciphering of

Cubist paintings sometimes difficult, and the very last phase of Cubism tended increasingly towards abstraction.

Spin-offs of Cubism were many: such movements as **Orphism**, headed by **Robert Delaunay** (1885–1941) and **Francis Picabia** (1879–1953), who experimented not with objects but with the colours of the spectrum. **Fernand Léger** (1881–1955), one of the main exponents of the so-called School of Paris, exploited his fascination with its smoothness and power of colour spectrum to create geometric and monumental compositions of technical imagery that were indebted to both Cézanne and Cubism.

The war, meanwhile, had affected many artists: in Switzerland, **Dada** was born out of the scorn artists felt for the petty bourgeois and nationalistic values that had led to the bloodshed. It was best exemplified in the work of the Frenchman **Marcel Duchamp** (1887–1968), who selected everyday objects ("ready-mades") and elevated them, without modification, to the rank of works of art simply by putting them on display – his most notorious piece was a urinal which he called *Fontaine* and exhibited in New York in 1917. His conviction that art could be made out of anything would be hugely influential.

Dada was a literary as well as an artistic movement, and through one of its main poets, André Breton, it led to the inception of **Surrealism**. It was the unconscious and its dark unchartered territories that interested the Surrealists: they derived much of their imagery from Freud and even experimented in words and images with free-association techniques. Strangely enough, most of the "French" Surrealists were foreigners, primarily the German **Max Ernst** (1891–1976) and the Spaniard **Salvador Dalí** (1904–89), though Frenchman **Yves Tanguy** (1900–55) also achieved international recognition. Mournful landscapes of weird, often terrifying images evoked the landscape of nightmares in often very precise details and with an anguish that went on to influence artists for years to come. **Picasso**, for instance, shocked by the massacre at the Spanish town of Guernica in 1936, drew greatly from Surrealism to produce the disquieting figures of his painting of the same name.

## Towards Nouveau Réalisme

At the outbreak of **World War II** many artists emigrated to the US, where the economic climate was more favourable. France was no longer the artistic melting pot of Europe, though Paris itself remained full of vibrant new work. Sculptors like the Romanian **Brancusi** (1876–1957) and the Swiss **Giacometti** (1886–1966) lived most of their lives in the city. Reacting against the rigours of Cubism, many French artists of the 1940s and 1950s opened themselves instead to the language and methods of American Abstract Expressionism, emanating from a vibrant New York. French painters such as **Pierre Soulages** (b.1919) and **Jean Dubuffet** (1901–85) pursued **Tachisme**, also known as **l'Art informel**. Dubuffet was heavily influenced by **Art Brut** – that is, works created by children, prisoners or the mentally ill. He produced thickly textured, often childlike paintings, pioneering the depreciation of traditional artistic materials and methods, fashioning junk, tar, sand and glass into the shape of human beings. His work (which provoked much outrage) influenced the French-born American, **Arman** (1928–2005), and **César** (1921–98), both of whom made use of scrap metals – their output ranging from presentations of household debris to towers of crushed and compressed cars.

These artists, among others, began to constitute what would be seen as the last coherent French art movement of the century: **Nouveau Réalisme**. A phenomenon largely of the late 1950s and 1960s, this movement rejected traditional materials and artistic genres, and concentrated instead on the distortion of the objects and signs of contemporary culture. It is often compared to Pop Art. Nouveau Réaliste sculpture is best represented by the works of the Swiss **Jean Tinguely** (1925–91), whose work was concerned mainly with movement and the machine, satirizing technological civilization. His most famous work, executed in collaboration with **Niki de Saint Phalle**

(1926–2002), is the exuberant fountain outside the Pompidou Centre, featuring fantastical birds and beasts shooting water in all directions.

A founder member of Nouveaux Réalisme, though resisting all classification was **Yves Klein** (1928–1962) who laid the foundations for several currents in contemporary art. He is seen as a precursor of minimalism thanks to his exhibition "Le Vide" in 1958, in which he redefined the void and the immaterial as having a pure energy. He was fascinated by the colour blue, which he considered to possess a spiritual quality. He even patented his own colour, International Klein Blue, employing it in a series of "body prints" in which he covered female models with paint, thus prefiguring performance art.

## Conceptual and contemporary

The chief legacy of Surrealism in 1960s France was the way in which avant-garde artists regularly banded together – and often quickly disbanded – around ideological or conceptual manifestos. These groups were not art schools as such, more conscious experiments in defining and limiting what art could be, in the search for political or theoretical meaning – in search, some would say, of coherence. One of the first such self-constituted groups of the 1960s, **GRAV** (Groupe de recherche d'art visuel) played with abstraction in the form of mirrors, visual tricks and **kinetic art** – which had a strong heritage in France from Duchamp and Alexander Calder. Among the leading figures were **François Morellet** (b.1926), who focused on geometric works, and the Argentine-born **Julio Le Parc** (b.1928). GRAV's goal, as its 1963 *Manifesto* declared, was to demystify art by tricking the spectator into relaxing in front of the artwork.

Perhaps the most significant group launched itself in January 1967, when Daniel Buren, Olivier Mosset, Michel Parmentier and Niele Toroni removed their own works from the walls of the Salon de la Jeune Peinture, in protest against the reactionary nature of painting itself – and, paradoxically, to reaffirm the relevance of painting as an art form existing in itself, without interpretation. It was an early taste of the politics of 1968. The works of **BMPT** – the name was taken from the four men's surnames – focused on abstract colour, often in regular patterns. The best-known of the four, **Daniel Buren** (b.1938), caused a furore in 1985–86 with his installation in the courtyard of the Palais Royal that consisted of numerous black-and-white, vertically striped columns of differing heights. Now, however, this one-time *enfant terrible* has become one of France's most respected living artists.

Following BMPT's lead, the geometrically abstract **Supports-Surfaces** group emerged in Nice in 1969, founded by **Daniel Dezeuze** (b.1942), **Jean-Pierre Pincemin** (1944–2005) and **Claude Villat** (b.1936), among others. The group stressed the importance of the painting as object – as paint applied to a surface.

The 1977 opening of the Musée Nationale d'Art Moderne, in Paris's Pompidou Centre, was a sign of the increased state support that French contemporary art was beginning to attract – a support that would be hugely boosted in the early 1980s by the active buying policy of the Socialist government. The landmark Pompidou exhibition of 1979, *Tendances de l'art en France*, showed artists in three groupings. The first was broadly abstract, the second, figurative. It was the third, however, which would look most prophetic of future directions; it focused on **conceptual artists**, many of them working with unconventional materials. This third group included the BMPT iconoclasts, along with three artists who would become landmark figures in French contemporary art: **Christian Boltanski** (b.1944) and **Annette Messager** (b.1943) – who were then husband and wife – and **Bertrand Lavier** (b.1949). All three work with found objects: Boltanski's often harrowing work has even employed personal property lost in public places, while Messager has drawn on toys and needlework to create unsettling works, often challenging perceptions of women. Lavier, meanwhile, is best known for playing with art and reality – principally by applying paint to industrial objects.

A quintessentially French reaction to minimalist and conceptual art emerged in 1981 with **Figuration Libre**, a movement which absorbed comic-strip art and graffiti in an explosion of punk creativity. Among the key figures were **Jean-Charles Blais** (b.1956), **Robert Combas** (b.1957), **François Boisrond** (b.1959) and **Herve di Rosa** (b.1959). Despite such breakout movements, the juggernaut of conceptual art continued to roll on through the last two decades. Large-scale installation has become important, particularly in the works of **Jean-Marc Bustamante** (b.1952) and **Jean-Luc Vilmouth** (b.1952), who have been known to co-opt buildings, resulting in a blurring of the aesthetic and the functional. Artists crossing and re-crossing generic boundaries is another ongoing theme. Bustamante, for example, whose principal medium is photography, collaborated for four years with the sculptor Bernard Bazile (b.1952) under the name **Bazile Bustamante**.

A new generation of artists is using non-traditional media, including video, photography, electronic media and found objects. Recent work could hardly be more diverse, but a common thread seems to be the use of films and installations which explore the relationships between reality and fiction, between interiority and the exterior world – ideas which resonate in the films, puppet shows and "public interventions" of **Pierre Huyghe** (b.1962). Huyghe is often associated with – and has worked with – the Algerian-born **Philippe Parreno** (b.1964), who in 2006 co-directed (with Douglas Goedon) a feature film which followed the footballer Zinédine Zidane for ninety minutes of relentless close-up. Two other associated artists are **Dominique Gonzalez-Foerster** (b.1965), who works with films, photographs, installations and even métro stations and shop windows to create worlds where fantasy and reality seem to overlap, and **Claude Closky** (b.1963), whose "books" and videos restructure everyday flotsam and jetsam. Closky has declared, "My work bears on all that daily life has made banal, on things that are never called into question." Similarly eclectic in his choice of media is **Fabrice Hybert** (b.1961), who has created the world's largest-ever bar of soap (at 22 tons) and a working television studio. His playful, interactive work taps into what he describes as the "enormous reservoir of the possible". **Sophie Calle** (b.1953) blends texts and photographs; among her most publicized works have been her intimate documentations of the lives of both strangers and – after she asked her mother to hire a private detective for the purpose – Calle herself.

In such a multimedia milieu, some critics have claimed that painting is moribund in France. Bucking this trend is the celebrated Lyonnais painter **Marc Desgrandchamps** (b.1960). He may work with traditional oils, but Desgrandchamps is hardly a traditionalist. His figures often appear partially transparent, or are presented as fragments, thus overlaying the perception of reality with doubt and disquiet.

# Architecture

France's architectural legacy reflects the power and personality of Church and the state, the "great men" vying to outdo their peers with lavish statements in stone. Many of France's architectural trends were born in Italy – Romanesque, Renaissance and Baroque – but they were refined and developed in uniquely French ways. Rococo grew from Baroque, Neoclassicism came from the Renaissance, and Art Nouveau was a brilliant, confused jumble of Baroque features combined with the newly developed cast-iron industry. France's last great architectural flowerings can be seen in the work of the early twentieth-century Modernists, Auguste Perret and Le Corbusier, but the contemporary scene is potentially as exciting, with Jean Nouvel and Christian de Portzamparc as its pre-eminent stars.

## The Romans

The **Romans**, who had colonized the south of France by around 120 BC, were fine town-planners, linking complexes of buildings with straight roads punctuated by decorative fountains, arches and colonnades. They built essentially in the Greek style, and their large, functional buildings were concerned more with strength and solidity than aesthetics. A number of substantial Roman building works survive: in **Nîmes** you can see the Maison Carrée, the best-preserved Roman temple still standing, and the Temple of Diana, one of just four vaulted Roman temples in Europe. Gateways remain at **Autun**, **Orange**, **Saintes** and **Reims**, and largely intact amphitheatres can be seen at Nîmes and **Arles**. The **Pont du Gard** aqueduct outside Nîmes is still a magnificent and ageless monument of civil engineering, built to carry the town's fresh water over the gorge, and Orange has its massive theatre, with Europe's only intact Roman facade. There are excavated archeological sites at **Glanum** near **St-Rémy**, **Vienne**, **Vaison-la-Romaine** and **Lyon**.

## Romanesque

Charlemagne's ninth-century **Carolingian dynasty** attempted to revive the symbols of civilized authority by recourse to Roman models. Of this era, very few buildings remain, though the motifs of arch and vault and the plan of semicircular apse and basilican nave and aisles would be hugely influential.

The style later dubbed "**Romanesque**" (*Roman* in French, as opposed to *Romain* which, confusingly, means Roman/classical) only really developed from the eleventh century onwards. Classical Roman architecture was not so much a direct model as a distant inspiration, filtered partly through the Carolingian heritage and partly through Byzantine models – as imported by returning crusaders and arriving artisans from Italy. The new style was also shaped by the particular needs of monastic communities, which began to burgeon in the period, and the requirements of pilgrims, who began to tour shrines in ever-greater numbers.

The key characteristics of Romanesque are thick walls with small windows, round arches on Roman-style piers and columns, and a proliferation of stone sculpture and wall paintings – these last often being the first victims of wear-and-tear and iconoclasm. Romanesque is as diverse as the various regions of France. In the south, the classical inheritance of Provence is strong, with stone barrel vaults, aisleless naves and domes. **St-Trophime** at Arles (1150) has a porch directly derived from Roman models and, with the church at St-Gilles nearby, exhibits a delight in carved ornament peculiar to the south at this time. The presence of the wealthy and powerful Cluniac order, in Burgundy, made this region a veritable powerhouse of architectural experiment, while the south was the readiest route for the introduction of new cultural developments. The pointed arch and vault are probably owed to Spanish Muslim sources, and appear first in churches such as **Notre-Dame** at Avignon, Notre-Dame-la-Grande at Poitiers, the cathedral at **Autun** and **Ste-Madeleine** at Vézelay (1089–1206).

In Normandy, the nave with aisles is more usual, capped by twin western towers. The emphasis in general is on mass and size, and geometrical design is favoured over figurative sculpture. The **Abbaye aux Hommes** at Caen (1066–77) is typical – and also contains many of the elements later identified as "Gothic", notably ribbed vaults and spires.

## Gothic

The reasons behind the development of the **Gothic style** (twelfth to sixteenth centuries) lie in the pursuit of the sublime; to achieve great height without apparent great weight would seem to imitate religious ambition. Its development in the north is partly due to the availability of good building stone and soft stone for carving, but perhaps more to the growth of royal aspiration and power based in the Île de France, which, allied with the papacy, stimulated the building of the great **cathedrals** of Paris, Bourges, Chartres, Laon, Le Mans, Reims and Amiens in the twelfth and thirteenth centuries.

The Gothic phase is said to begin with the building of the choir of the **abbey of St-Denis** near Paris in 1140. In France, the style reigned supreme until the end of the fifteenth century. Architecturally, it encompasses the development of spacious windows of coloured glass and the flying buttress, a rib of external stone that resists the outward push of the vaulting. But, above all, French Gothic is characterized by verticality.

In the south, as at Albi and Angers, the great churches are generally broader and simpler in plan and external appearance, with aisles often almost as high as the nave. Many secular buildings survive – some of the most notable in their present form being the work of Viollet-le-Duc, the pre-eminent nineteenth-century restorer – and even whole towns, for example **Carcassonne** and **Aigues Mortes**; **Avignon** has the bridge and the papal palace.

Even castles began to lend themselves to the disappearing walls of the Gothic style, as windows steadily increased in size in response to more settled times. Fine Gothic stone-carving was applied to doors and windows, and roofscapes came alive with balustrades, sculpted gables and exquisite leadwork finials and ridges. Some of the most elaborate châteaux, as at **Châteaudun** and **Saumur**, in the Loire valley, were veritable palaces. Yet they still incorporated the old defensive feudal tower in their design, perhaps in the form of a elaborately sculpted open staircase. In the Dordogne region, a series of colonial settlements, the **bastides**, or fortified towns, are a refreshing antidote to triumphal French bombast.

## Renaissance

French military adventures in Italy in the early sixteenth century hastened the arrival of a new style borrowing heavily from the Italian **Renaissance**. The persistence of Gothic traditions, however, and the necessity of steep roofs and tall chimneys in the more northerly climate, gave the newly luxurious castles, or châteaux, a distinctively French emphasis on the vertical line, with an elaboration of detail on the facade at the expense of the clear modelling of form.

Gradually, these French forms were supplanted by a purely classical style – a development embodied by the **Louvre** palace, which was worked over by all the grand names of French architecture from Lescot in the early sixteenth century, via François Mansart and Claude Perrault in the seventeenth, to the later years of the nineteenth century.

At Blois and **Maisons Lafitte** (1640), Mansart began to experiment with a new suavity and elegance, attitudes that appear again in the eighteenth century in the townhouses of the Rococo period. On the other hand, **Claude Perrault** (1613–88), who designed the great colonnaded east front of the Louvre, gives an austere face to the official architecture of despotism, magnificent but far too imperial to be much enjoyed by common mortals. The high-pitched roofs, which had been almost universal until then, are replaced here by the classical balustrade and pediment, the style grand but cold and supremely secular. Art and architecture were at the time organized by boards and academies, including the Académie Royale d'Architecture, and style and employment were strictly controlled by royal direction. With such a limitation of ideas at the source of patronage, it's hardly surprising that there was a certain dullness to the era.

## Baroque

In a similar way to the preceding century, the churches of the **seventeenth and eighteenth centuries** have a coldness quite different from the German, Flemish and Italian **Baroque**. When the Renaissance style first appeared in the early sixteenth century, there was no great need for new church building, the country being so well endowed from the Gothic centuries. **St-Étienne-du-Mont** (1517–1620) and **St-Eustache** (1532–89), both in Paris, show how old forms persisted with only an overlay of the new style.

It was with the Jesuits in the seventeenth century that the Church embraced the new style in order to combat the forces of rational disbelief. In Paris the churches of the **Sorbonne** (1653) and **Val-de-Grâce** (1645) exemplify this, as do a good number of other grandiose churches in the **Baroque** style, from **Les Invalides** at the end of the seventeenth century to the **Panthéon** of the late eighteenth century. Here is the Church triumphant, rather than the state, but no more beguiling.

The architect of Les Invalides was **Jules Hardouin Mansart**, a product of the Académie Royale d'Architecture, which harked back to the ancient, classical tradition. Mansart also greatly extended the palace of **Versailles** and so created the CinemaScope view of France with that seemingly endless horizon of royalty. As an antidote to this pomposity, the **Petit Trianon** at Versailles is as refreshing now as it was to Louis XV, who had it built in 1762 as a place of escape for his mistress. This is even more true of that other pearl formed of the grit of boredom in the enclosed world of Versailles – **La Petite Ferme**, where Marie Antoinette played at being a milkmaid, which epitomizes the Arcadian and "picturesque" fantasy of the painters Boucher and Fragonard.

The lightness and charm that was undermining official grandeur with Arcadian fancies and **Rococo** decoration was, however, snuffed out by the Revolution. There's no real Revolutionary architecture: the necessity of order and authority soon asserted itself and an autocracy every bit as absolute returned with Napoleon, drawing on the old grand manner but with a stronger trace of the stern old Roman.

In Paris it was not the democratic Doric but the imperial Corinthian order that re-emerged triumphant in the church of the **Madeleine** (1806) and, with the **Arc de Triomphe** like some colossal paperweight, reimposed the authority of academic architecture in contrast to the fancy-dress structures of contemporary Regency England.

## The nineteenth century

The restoration of legitimate monarchy after the **fall of Napoleon** stimulated a revival of interest in older Gothic and early Renaissance styles, which offered a symbol of dynastic reassurance not only to the state but also to the newly rich. So in the private and commercial architecture of the nineteenth century these earlier styles predominate – in mine-owners' villas and bankers' headquarters.

From 1853, the overgrown and insanitary medieval capital was ruthlessly transformed into an urban utopia. In half a century, half of Paris was rebuilt. Napoléon III's authoritarian government provided the force – land was compulsorily purchased and boulevards bulldozed through old quarters – while banks and private speculators provided the cash. The poor, meanwhile, provided the labour – and were shipped out to the suburban badlands in their tens of thousands to make way for richer tenants. The presiding genius was Napoléon III's architect-in-chief, **Baron Haussmann** (1809–91). In his brave new city, every apartment building was seven storeys high. Every facade was built in golden limestone, often quarried from under the city itself, with unobtrusive Neoclassical details sculpted around the windows. Every second and fifth floor had its wrought-iron balcony and every lead roof sloped back from the street front at precisely 45 degrees.

Competing with Haussmann's totalitarian sobriety was a voluptuous, exuberant **neo-Baroque** strain, exemplified by Charles Garnier's Opéra in Paris (1861–74), and a third, engineering-led approach, embodied in the official **School of Roads and Bridges**. The teachings of Viollet-le-Duc, the great restorer who reinterpreted Gothic style as pure structure, led to the development of new techniques out of which "modern" architectural style was born. Iron was the first significant new material, often used in imitation of Gothic forms and destined to be developed as an individual architectural style in America. In the enormously controversial **Eiffel Tower** (1889), France set up a potent symbol of things to come.

## Le Corbusier to Art Deco

The sinuous, organic **Art Nouveau** style, which was at the height of fashion around the turn of the nineteenth and twentieth centuries, quickly found its winding way onto the facades of many Parisian buildings, including the department stores Printemps and La Samaritaine. The most famous expression of the style, however, is the entrances to the Paris métro, whose twisting metal railings and antennae-like orange lamps were deeply controversial when **Hector Guimard** first designed them in the 1900s. Few of the early entrances now remain, however (**Place des Abbesses** is one), partly because conservatives fought back under **Charles Garnier**, architect of the Opéra Garnier. He demanded classical marble and bronze porticoes for every station; his line was followed, on a less grandiose scale, wherever the métro steps surfaced by a major monument, thereby putting Guimard out of a job.

Even as Art Nouveau sought lithe and living forms, brutal **Modernism** powered ahead. Towards the end of the nineteenth century, France pioneered the use of reinforced concrete, most notably in buildings by **Auguste Perret**, such as his 1903 apartment house at 25 rue Franklin in Paris. Perret and other **modernists** designed gigantic skyscraper avenues and suburban rings, which now look like totalitarian horror-movie sets.

The more acceptable face of Modernism, in the 1920s and 30s, was the simple geometry of the modern or International Style, which was allied to the glamorous **Art Deco look**; you're most likely to come across it in the capital, either on apartment block facades or in mega-projects such as the Palais de Tokyo.

The greatest proponent of this style was **Le Corbusier**. His stature may now appear diminished by the ascendancy of a blander style in concrete boxing, as well as by the significant technical and social failures of his buildings – not to mention his total disregard for historic streets and monuments – but he remains France's most influential modern architect. Surprisingly few of his works were ever built, but the **Cité Radieuse** in Marseille and plenty of lesser examples in Paris bear witness to the ideas of the man largely responsible for changing the face and form of buildings throughout the world.

# Contemporary

The miserable 1950s and 1960s buildings found all over the country are probably best skipped over. From the 1970s onwards, however, France again established itself as one of the most exciting patrons of international **contemporary architecture**. The **Pompidou Centre**, by **Renzo Piano** and **Richard Rogers**, derided, adored and visited by millions, maximizes space by putting the service elements usually concealed in walls and floors on the outside. It is one of the great contemporary buildings in western Europe – for its originality, popularity and practicality.

In the 1980s, under President Mitterrand's grandiose *grands projets*, it was decided that the axis from the Louvre to the Arc de Triomphe was to be extended westwards towards the **Grande Arche de la Défense**, symbol of the new La Défense business district. Designed by Von Spreckelsen, it isn't really an arch but a huge hollow cube. At the other end of the axis stands Ieoh Ming Pei's glass **pyramid** in the Cour Napoléon, the main entrance to the Louvre. Hugely controversial at first, it's now widely accepted and admired.

As part of the wider reorganization of the Louvre, the **Ministry of Finance** decamped to a new building in **Bercy** designed by Paul Chemetov and nicknamed the "steamboat" because of its titanic length and its anchoring in the Seine. Formerly full of wine warehouses, Bercy is now extensively redeveloped. Also in the Parc de Bercy stands Frank Gehry's (architect of Bilbao's Guggenheim Museum) free-form, exuberant **American Centre**. Another mega-project from broadly the same era is the **Parc de la Villette** complex, which was built on the site of an old abattoir. It houses the Cité des Sciences, Bernard Tschumi's 21 *"folies"* of urban life and the **Cité de la Musique** concert hall and conservatoire complex, designed by acclaimed architect Christian de Portzamparc to be like a symphony, its various sections creating a harmonious ensemble.

Perhaps the least successful of Mitterrand's grand projects was the **Bibliothèque Nationale**. Designed by Dominique Perrault, it's made up of four L-shaped tower blocks, resembling four open books, set around an inaccessible sunken garden. The most outstanding, by contrast, is arguably the **Institut du Monde Arabe**. Designed by **Jean Nouvel**, France's most eminent contemporary architect, it ingeniously marries high-tech architecture and motifs from traditional Arabic culture. Jean Nouvel's airy, green-themed buildings continue to multiply in Paris, from the Fondation Cartier, with its glass wall, to the curving, light-filled **Quai Branly** museum, surrounded by a lush garden which was designed by Gilles Clément, who landscaped the Parc André Citroën.

Paris continues to find space for new architecture. The futuristically twisting double-ribbon of the **Passerelle Simone de Beauvoir** now bridges the Seine opposite Perrault's Bibliothèque. Upstream, the University Paris 7 is now installed in the massive **Grands Moulins de Paris** and **Halle aux Farines**, and a new school of architecture – appropriately enough – resides in the handsomely arched, late nineteenth-century **SUDAC** building. Christian de Portzamparc's blade-like **Tour Granite** is now one of the most distinctive silhouettes in the La Défense skyline, a vigorous foil to the incised cylinders of the twin Société Générale towers. Jakob Macfarlane's **Cité de la Mode et du Design** has a lime-green glass tube apparently pouring through it. And at the time of writing, Frank Gehry's **Fondation Louis Vuitton pour la Création** was slowly taking shape in the Bois de Boulogne; judging by the plans, Gehry's fantasy looks less like the advertised "cloud of glass" than a glazed armadillo which has burst out of its own skin.

In **Marseille** there's Will Alsop's mammoth seat of regional government, while the first cathedral to be built in France since the nineteenth century, the **Cathédrale d'Évry**, masterminded by Swiss Mario Botta and finished in 1995, is a huge cylindrical red-brick tower which, besides being a place of worship, houses an art centre, concert hall and cinema screen. The new **European Parliament** building in **Strasbourg**, designed by the Architecture Studio group, was finished in 1997. A huge, boomerang-shaped structure with a glass dome and metal tower, it sits across the river from the eccentric, high-tech Richard Rogers-designed **European Court of Human Rights**.

Museums across the country continue to attract innovative architects. In **Nîmes**, Norman Foster's **Carré d'Art** modern art museum (1993) is characterized by its simple transparent design, while his **Musée de Préhistoire des Gorges du Verdon** (2001) in **Provence** uses local materials – part of the museum is folded into the landscape and blends on one side into an existing stone wall, while the entrance hall resembles the very caves the museum celebrates.

The country's ever-advancing **transport network** has fuelled some of the most state-of-the-art design and engineering in Europe, as in **Roissy**, around the Charles-de-Gaulle airport, and at **Euralille**, the large complex around Lille's TGV/Eurostar station, masterminded by Dutch architect Rem Koolhaas. Most dramatic of all is the **Millau Viaduct**, a bridge so huge in scale and ambition that its impact could almost be described as geographical. Designed by engineer Michel Virlogeux and Norman Foster's firm, and opened in December 2004, its sleekness belies its size: the largest of its soaring white pylons is actually taller than the Eiffel Tower.

Even as they push towards a high-tech future, the French are particularly good at preserving the past – too good, some would say. A passion for restoring "*la patrimoine*" results in many fine old buildings being practically rebuilt – the dominant restoration theory in France is to restore to perfection rather than halt decay. More often than not, restoration is carried out by the **Maisons de** Compagnonnage, the old craft guilds, which have maintained traditional building skills, handing them down from master to apprentice (and never to women), while also taking on new industrial skills.

## Futures

In 2009 the government invited ten leading architectural firms to submit proposals for **Le Grand Pari** – the Greater, Greener Paris of the future. The architects envisioned new "*Grands Axes*", avenues as radical as any bulldozed by Haussmann – but in this case linking city and *banlieue*. President Sarkozy favoured high-speed rail links down the Seine towards the port of Le Havre; Richard Rogers called for a green network covering the train lines leading out of the northern stations; Christian de Portzamparc wanted a high-speed elevated train running circles around the ring road. The radical Left-wing architect Roland Castro mildly proposed that perhaps the suburbs might have their share of government offices and cultural institutions.

Meanwhile, real works progress apace in **Paris**, and beyond. From 2010, the capital's old, murky underground mall of **Les Halles** is being transformed by architect David Mangin into light-filled spaces under a giant glass roof. Also in 2010, the Louvre began work on its annex of glossy pavilions, sited in the northern town of Lens (it is a modest partner to the equally new Abu Dhabi annex, designed by – who else – Jean Nouvel), while the Pompidou Centre has opened its own curvaceously geometric satellite in **Metz**, designed by Shigeru Ban and Jean de Gastines to echo the shape of a Chinese hat. In the Défense business district, the **Tour Phare**, a bold eco-scraper, will rival the height of the Eiffel Tower by 2017. Jean Nouvel's **Tour sans Fins** or "endless tower", has been cancelled, however. It was supposed to dissipate its 425m in the clouds above La Défense; in the end, it was the budget which dissipated, along with the economy. Others may replace it, however: in 2008, ominously, Paris's city council dropped the legal ban on skyscrapers. The capital may yet lose its radical uniformity.

# Cinema

The first (satisfied) cinema audience in the world was French. Screened to patrons of the Grand Café, on Paris's boulevard des Capucines, in December 1895, Louis Lumière's single-reelers may have been jerky documentaries, but they were light-years ahead of anything that had come before. Soon after, Georges Méliès' magical-fantastical features were proving a big hit with theatre audiences, and the twin cinematic poles of Realism and Surrealism had been established. France took to cinema with characteristic enthusiasm and seriousness. Ciné-clubs were formed all over the country, journals were published, critics made films and film-makers became critics. The avant-garde wing of French cinema acquired the moniker of French Impressionism, a genre characterized by directors such as Louis Delluc, Jean Epstein and Abel Gance, who used experimental, highly visual techniques to express altered states of consciousness. It was only a short step from here to the all-out Surrealism of the artist-polymath Jean Cocteau, and the Spanish director Luis Buñuel.

Towards the end of the 1920s, histrionic adaptations of novels, epic historical dramas and broad comedies attracted mass audiences, but the silent heyday ended abruptly with the advent of sound in 1929. Most silent stars faded into obscurity, but a number of directors successfully made the transition, notably Jean Renoir, the son of the painter, René Clair, Julien Duvivier, Jean Gremillon and Abel Gance. Among the newcomers were Jean Vigo, who died young in 1934, and Marcel Carné, who worked with the powerful scripts of the poet Jacques Prévert. The film-makers of the 1930s developed a bold new style, dubbed **Poetic Realism** for its pessimism, powerful visual aesthetic – high-contrast, often nocturnal – and devotion to "realistic", usually working-class, settings.

In 1936 the collector Henri Langlois set up the **Cinémathèque Française**, dedicated to the preservation and screening of old and art films – an indication of the speed with which the "*septième art*" had found its niche within the pantheon of French culture. Langlois played an important role in saving thousands of films from destruction during the war, but the Occupation had surprisingly little effect on the industry. Renoir and Clair sought temporary sanctuary in Hollywood, and domestic production dipped, but hundreds of films continued to be made in Vichy France at a time when audiences sought the solace and comfort of the cinema in record numbers.

Postwar and pre-television, the late 1940s and early 1950s was another boom time for French cinema. Poetic Realism morphed into **film noir**, whose emphasis on darkness and corruption gave birth in turn to the thriller, a genre exemplified by the films of Henri-Georges Clouzot and Jean-Pierre Melville. During this period the mainstream cinema industry became highly organized and technically slick, and older directors such as Clair, Renoir and Jacques Becker made superbly controlled masterpieces spanning genres as diverse as thrillers, comedies and costume dramas.

The first shot of the coming revolution – a warning shot only – was fired by the acerbic young critic François Truffaut, writing in the legendary film magazine, **Les Cahiers du cinéma**, in the mid-1950s. In opposition to what he and fellow critics dubbed *la tradition de qualité*, Truffaut envisaged a new kind of cinema based on the independent vision of a writer-director, an *auteur* (author), who would make films in a purer and more responsive manner. Directors such as Melville and Louis Malle – who made his first film with the diver Jacques Cousteau – were beginning to make moves in this direction, but Truffaut's vision was only fully realized towards the end of the decade, when the **Nouvelle Vague** ("New Wave") came rolling in. Claude Chabrol's *Les Cousins*, Truffaut's own *Les Quatre-cents coups*, Eric Rohmer's *Le Signe du lion*, Alain Resnais' *Hiroshima, mon amour* and Jean-Luc Godard's *À Bout de souffle* were all released in 1959. The trademark freedom of these *auteur*-directors' films – loosely scripted, highly individualistic and typically shot on location – ushered in the modern era.

The 1960s was the heyday of the *auteur*. Truffaut established his pre-eminent status by creating an extraordinary oeuvre encompassing science fiction, thriller, autobiography and film noir, all his films characteristically elegant and excitingly shot. But the "new wave" hadn't carried all before it: René Clément, Henri-Georges Clouzot and even Jean Renoir were still working throughout the decade; Jean-Pierre Melville continued shooting his characteristically noir **films policiers** (crime-thrillers); and the Catholic director Robert Bresson carried on making films on his favourite theme of salvation. And Jacques Tati, the maverick genius behind the legendary comic character M. Hulot, made two of his greatest and most radical quasi-silent films, *Playtime* and *Trafic*, at either end of the 1960s.

The 1970s is probably the least impressive decade in terms of output, but a shot in the arm was delivered in the 1980s by the **Cinéma du Look**, a genre epitomized in the films of Jean-Jacques Beineix, Luc Besson and Leos Carax. Stylish, image-conscious and postmodern, films such as *Diva* and *Betty Blue* owed much to the look of American pulp cinema and contemporary advertising. Meanwhile, throughout the 1980s and into the 1990s, high-gloss costume dramas – historical or adaptations of novels – were the focus of much attention. Often called **Heritage Cinema**, the best films of this genre are the superbly crafted creations of Claude Berri, though Jean-Pierre Rappeneau's *Cyrano de Bergerac* is probably the internationally recognized standard-bearer. At the other end of the scale lies **cinéma beur**: naturalistic, socially responsible and low-budget films made by French-born film-makers of North African origin – *les beurs* in French slang. The newest trends in contemporary art cinema follow a related path of social realism. In recent years, a number of younger directors, notably Mathieu Kassovitz, have made films set in the deprived suburbs (*la banlieue*), creating a number of sub-genres that have been acclaimed variously as **New Realism**, **cinéma de banlieue** and **le jeune cinéma** ("young cinema").

Today, France remains the second-largest exporter of films in the world. The industry's continued health is largely due to the intransigence of the French state, which continues to protect and promote domestic cinema as part of its policy of **l'exception culturelle** – despite the complaints of the free-marketeers who would have the French market "liberalized". Half of the costs of making a feature film in France are paid for by state subsidies, levied on television stations, box-office receipts and video sales. Currently, American-made films capture around fifty percent of the French market, while home-grown productions make up around forty percent. But the future looks promising: recent years have seen the number of films made in France rise to almost two hundred a year, most of them domestically funded.

Note that the **films reviewed below** are only intended to point out a few landmarks of French cinema; we can't review every Godard film nor cover every significant director. As such, they can all be considered as highly recommended. Alternative English titles are given for those films renamed for the main foreign release.

## CINEMA PRE-1945

★ **L'Atalante** *Jean Vigo, 1934.* Aboard a barge, a newly married couple struggle to reconcile themselves to their new situation. Eventually, the wife, Juliette, tries to flee, but is brought back by the unconventional deck-hand, Père Jules, superbly portrayed by the great Michel Simon. This sensual and naturalistic portrait of a relationship was made just before Vigo died, and is his only feature film.

**La Belle équipe/They Were Five** *Julien Duvivier, 1936.* A group of unemployed workers wins the lottery and sets up a cooperative restaurant. The version with an upbeat conclusion was a huge hit with contemporary audiences; Duvivier himself preferred his darker ending. Jean Gabin stars as the defeated hero, as in Duvivier's other greats, *La Bandéra* (1935) and the cult classic, *Pépé-le-Moko* (1937).

**Un Chien andalou/An Andalusian Dog** *Luis Buñuel, 1929.* Made in collaboration with Salvador Dali, this short opens with a woman's eye being cut into with a razorblade. While it doesn't get any less weird or shocking for the rest of its twenty-minute length, it's surprisingly watchable – when it came out, it was a big hit at Paris's Studio des Ursulines cinema. Buñuel further developed his Surrealist techniques in the feature-length talkie *L'Age d'or* (1930).

★ **Les Enfants du Paradis** *Marcel Carné, 1945.* Probably the greatest of the collaborations between Carné and the poet-scriptwriter, Jacques Prévert, this film is set in the low-life world of the popular theatre of 1840s Paris. Beautiful and worldly actress Garance (the great Arletty) is loved by arch-criminal Lacenaire, ambitious actor Lemaître, and brilliant, troubled mime Baptiste – unforgettably played by the top mime of the 1940s, Jean-Louis Barrault. The outstanding character portrayals and romantic, humane ethos are reminiscent of a great nineteenth-century novel.

**Le Jour se lève/Daybreak** *Marcel Carné, 1939.* This brooding classic from the Poetic Realist stable has Jean Gabin, the greatest star of the era, playing another of his iconic working-class hero roles. After shooting his rival, the villainous old music-hall star Valentin, François (Gabin) is holed up in his guesthouse bedroom. In the course of the night, he recalls the events that led up to the murder. Also stars the great female idol of the 1930s, Arletty, and a superb script by the poet Jacques Prévert. Carné's *Hôtel du Nord* (1938) and *Quai des brumes* (1938) are in a similar vein.

**Le Million** *René Clair, 1931.* In 1930 Clair had made the first great French talkie, *Sous les toits de Paris*, but it wasn't until *Le Million* that the true musical film was born. A hunt for a lost winning lottery ticket provides plenty of opportunity for madcap comedy, suspense and romance.

★ **La Règle du jeu/The Rules of the Game** *Jean Renoir, 1939.* Now hailed as the foremost masterpiece of the prewar era, this was a complete commercial failure when it was released. The Marquis de la Chesnaye invites his wife, mistress and a pilot friend to spend a weekend hunting and partying in the countryside. Matching the four are a group of four servants with similarly interweaved love lives. Renoir himself plays Octave, who moves between the two groups. A complex, almost farcical plot based around misunderstanding and accusations of infidelity moves inexorably towards disaster.

## POSTWAR CINEMA

**Ascenseur pour l'échafaud/Elevator to the Gallows/Frantic** *Louis Malle, 1957.* This thriller is Louis Malle's remarkable debut. Two lovers (Jeanne Moreau and Maurice Ronet) murder the woman's husband but get trapped by a series of unlucky coincidences. Beautifully shot – especially when Jeanne Moreau wanders through the streets of Paris, accompanied by Miles Davis' superb original score – and as breathtaking as any Hitchcock film.

★ **La Belle et la bête/Beauty and the Beast** *Jean Cocteau, 1946.* Cocteau's theatrical rendition of the "Beauty and the Beast" tale teeters on the edge of the surreal, but the pace is as compelling as any thriller. *Orphée* (1950) is more widely considered to be the director's masterpiece, a surreal retelling of the Orpheus tale in a setting strongly redolent of wartime France.

**Casque d'or/Golden Marie** *Jacques Becker, 1952.* Becker's first great film depicts the ultimately tragic romance between a gangster and a beautiful, golden-haired prostitute, portrayed with legendary seductiveness by Simone Signoret. Underneath the love story lurks the moral corruption of a brilliantly re-created turn-of-the-century Paris. Becker went on to make the seminal crime thriller, *Touchez pas au grisbi/Honour Among Thieves* (1953).

★ **Un Condamné à mort s'est échappé/A Man Escaped** *Robert Bresson, 1956.* A prisoner, Fontaine (François Leterrier), calmly plans his escape from prison,

working with a painstaking slowness that is brilliantly matched by the intensely absorbed camerawork. Working with real locations and amateur actors, Bresson echoed the work of the Italian Neo-realists, and foreshadowed the work of the Nouvelle Vague directors. Sometimes entitled *Le Vent souffle où il veut*.

**Et ... Dieu créa la femme/And God Created Woman** *Roger Vadim, 1956.* This film should be called "And Roger Vadim created Brigitte Bardot", as its chief interest is not its harmless plot – love and adultery in St-Tropez – but its scantily clad main actress, who spends most of the time sunbathing and dancing in front of fascinated males. Deemed "obscene" by the moralizing authorities of the time, it helped liberate the way the body was represented in film.

**Les Jeux interdits** *René Clément, 1952.* A small Parisian girl loses her parents and her dog in a Stuka attack on a column of refugees, and is rescued and befriended by a peasant boy. Together, they seek solace from the war by building an animal cemetery in an abandoned barn. This moving meditation on childhood and death extracted two remarkable performances from the child actors.

**Le Salaire de la peur/The Wages of Fear** *Henri-Georges Clouzot, 1953.* This is the tensest, most suspense-driven of all the films made by the "French Hitchcock", focusing on four men driving an explosive-laden lorry hundreds of miles to a burning, third-world oil field. Tight and shatteringly sustained right up to the magnificent finale.

★ **Les Vacances de Monsieur Hulot/Mr Hulot's Holiday** *Jacques Tati, 1951.* The slapstick comic mime Jacques Tati created his most memorable character in Hulot, the unwitting creator of chaos and nonchalant hero

of this gut-wrenchingly funny film. So full of brilliantly conceived and impeccably timed sight gags that you hardly notice the innovative absence of much dialogue or plot. Groundbreaking cinema, and superlative entertainment. The later *Mon oncle* (1958) has an edgier feel, adopting a distinctly critical attitude to modern life.

## THE NOUVELLE VAGUE

**A Bout de souffle/Breathless** *Jean-Luc Godard, 1959.* This is the film that came nearest to defining the Nouvelle Vague: insolent charm, cool music and sexy actors. Jean-Paul Belmondo is a petty criminal, Michel, while Jean Seberg plays Patricia, his American girlfriend. The film's revolutionary style, with its jerky, unconventional narrative, abrupt cuts and rough camerawork, proved one of the most influential of the twentieth century.

**Les Cousins/The Cousins** *Claude Chabrol, 1959.* The Balzac-inspired plot centres around Charles (Gérard Blain), an earnest provincial student, who comes to live in Neuilly with his glamorous cousin Paul (Jean-Claude Brialy). A near-caricature of the Nouvelle Vague – idle students in the Quartier Latin, extravagant parties, convertible cars and exciting music.

**Hiroshima, mon amour** *Alain Resnais, 1959.* On her last days of shooting a film in Hiroshima, a French actress (Emmanuelle Riva) falls in love with a Japanese architect (Eiji Okada). Gradually, she reveals the story of her affair with a German soldier during the Occupation, and her subsequent disgrace. Based on an original script by

Marguerite Duras, Resnais' first film masterfully weaves together past and present in a haunting story of love and memory.

★ **Ma Nuit chez Maude/My Night at Maud's** *Eric Rohmer, 1969.* Rohmer's career-long obsessions with sexuality, conversation, existential choices and the love triangle are given free rein in this moody, lingering portrait of a flirtation. Jean-Louis Trintignant plays a handsome egotist who, during the course of one long night, is drawn into a strange and inconclusive relationship with his friend's friend, the hypnotically attractive Maude (Françoise Fabian).

★ **Les Quatre-cents coups/The 400 Blows** *François Truffaut, 1959.* A young *cinéphile* and critic turned film-maker, François Truffaut triumphed at the 1959 Cannes film festival with this semi-autobiographical film, showing a Parisian adolescent (Jean-Pierre Léaud) trying to escape his lonely, loveless existence, and slowly drifting towards juvenile delinquency. Léaud's poignant performance, and Truffaut's sensitive, sympathetic observation, make this one of the most lovable films of the Nouvelle Vague.

## COMEDY AND SATIRE

**Belle de jour** *Luis Buñuel, 1966.* Catherine Deneuve plays Séverine, who lives out her sexual fantasies and obsessions in a brothel. At first sight, this is a far cry from Buñuel's prewar collaborations with Dalí, though the film moves away from the initial acerbic comedy towards surrealism.

**Bienvenue chez les Ch'tis** *Danny Boon 2008.* The highest-grossing French film of all time, written and starring Danny Boon, has been largely ignored by the Anglophone world – largely because its humour is all-but un-translatable. It follows the fate of a postal manager sent from his cushy job in the south of France to one in the rainy north near Dunkirk, where the culture – and particularly impenetrable dialect, or ch-ti, of the locals– fuels many a pun and hilarious misunderstanding. The film had French audiences rolling in the aisles for months, and though the English subtitles inevitably fall short, it's worth persevering with for an insight into Gallic attitudes to regional differences.

★ **La Cage aux folles/Birds of a Feather** *Edouard Molinaro, 1978.* Renato runs a cabaret nightclub at which his boyfriend, Albin, is the headlining drag act. When Renato's son, Laurent, decides to get married, the couple are drawn into an escalating farce as they try to present

themselves as a conventional mother-and-son couple to Laurent's conservative in-laws. A supremely camp international hit.

**Le Fabuleux destin d'Amélie Poulain/Amélie** *Jean-Pierre Jeunet, 2001.* This sentimental, feel-good portrait of a youthful ingenue wandering around a romanticized Montmartre was a worldwide hit. Amélie (Audrey Tatou) is on a mission to help the world find happiness; her own is harder to fix up.

★ **La Grande vadrouille/Don't Look Now ... We're Being Shot At!** *Gérard Oury, 1966.* For forty years, until the release of *Bienvenue Chez Les Ch'tis*, "The Big Jaunt" was France's biggest ever hit movie. Set in wartime Paris, it centres on three Allied soldiers parachuting down on a hapless conductor and decorator, played by stars Bourvil and Louis de Funès. In their desperation to be rid of the parachutists, the pair end up leading them to the free zone.

**Intouchables/The Untouchables** *Olivier Nakache 2011.* Based on the book *You Changed My Life* by Abdel Sellou, *Intouchables* has proved the feel-good blockbuster of the past few years, and one of the most successful French movies ever, shifting 19 million tickets in its first 16 weeks. It follows the story of Driss, a young, unemployed

Senegalese man from the Parisian *banlieue*, who inadvertently finds himself taken on as the carer of a millionaire tetraplegic, Phillipe. As the unlikely bond between the two grows, both lives are transformed, with predictable consequences – and what must be the cheesiest ending in the history of French cinema.

**Playtime** *Jacques Tati, 1967*. Tati once more plays Hulot, cinema's most radical slapstick creation. From a simple premise – he is showing a group of tourists round a futuristic Paris – he creates an intimately observed and perfectly controlled farce. Just as the city has somehow been transformed into a refined and faceless world of glass and steel, Tati's comedy has become infinitely subtle and reflective.

**Les Visiteurs/The Visitors** *Jean-Marie Poiré, 1993*. A medieval knight and his squire are transported to present-day France, where they discover their castle has been turned into a country hotel by their descendants. The earthly comic encounters between time-travellers and modern middle-classes make for an extremely funny comedy of manners. French audiences so loved being sent up that this became the third most successful film in French history.

**Zazie dans le métro/Zazie** *Louis Malle, 1960*. In one of his few comedies, Malle successfully rendered novelist Raymond Queneau's verbal experiments by using cartoon-like visual devices. Ten-year-old Catherine Demongeot is perfect as the delightfully rude little girl driving everybody mad; and the film offers some great shots of Paris, climaxing in a spectacular scene at the top of the Eiffel Tower.

## DRAMAS/THRILLERS/FILMS POLICIERS

**L'Armée des ombres/The Army in the Shadows** *Jean-Pierre Melville, 1969*. A small group of Resistance fighters, played by Yves Montand, Simone Signoret and Jean-Pierre Meurisse, are betrayed, questioned and then released. The tight, minimalist style creates a suffocating tension which culminates in an unforgettable conclusion.

⭐ **Le Boucher/The Butcher** *Claude Chabrol, 1969*. A young schoolteacher in a tiny southwest village lives in an apartment above her school. Her loneliness is eased by a surprising fledgling romance with the local butcher – a kindly yet sinister figure – until a sequence of schoolgirl murders sows doubt in her mind. This would be gripping as a portrayal of village life even without the underlying tension and lurking violence.

⭐ **Caché/Hidden** *Michael Haneke, 2005*. The smooth bourgeois life of literary TV presenter Georges (Daniel Auteuil) and his wife Anne (Juliette Binoche) is disrupted when they receive a chillingly innocuous videotape of their own home under surveillance. In what has been widely read as a metaphor for France's attitude to its own colonial past, Georges is forced to confront a childhood friend, Majid (Maurice Bénichou), and his own troubled conscience.

**Coup de Torchon/Clean Slate** *Bertrand Tavernier, 1981*. The setting is colonial West Africa, 1938. Ineffective, humiliated police chief Cordier (Philippe Noiret) decides to take murderous revenge on his wife, her lover, his mistress's husband and the locals he views as uniformly corrupt. As much an extremely black comedy as a true thriller.

⭐ **Irréversible** *Gaspar Noé, 2002*. One of the more disturbing films ever made: not just for the nightmarish rape and murder scenes but for the evisceration of the most terrifying elements of the male sexual psyche. A giddy, swooping camera traces the events of one night backwards in time from a brutal murder to a post-coital couple (Vincent Cassel and Monica Bellucci) getting ready for a party.

**Monsieur Hire** *Patrice Leconte, 1989*. A slow-moving, unsettlingly erotic psychological thriller. Michel Blanc plays the spookily impassive Monsieur Hire, a voyeur who witnesses his neighbour's boyfriend commit a murder, and becomes the prime suspect.

**Ne le dis à personne/Tell No one** *Guillaume Canet, 2006*. Disturbing psycho-thriller in which a doctor who is slowly rebuilding his life after the murder of his wife, eight years earlier, is suddenly implicated in two fresh murders. To complicate matters further, he is sent evidence that his wife is still alive. As much *Mulholland Drive* as *Frantic*, and more exciting than either.

⭐ **Pierrot-le-fou** *Jean-Luc Godard, 1965*. Godard's fascination with American pulp fiction is most brilliantly exploited in this highly charged and deeply sophisticated thriller. Accidentally caught up in a murderous gangland killing, Ferdinand (Jean-Paul Belmondo) flees with his babysitter (Godard's then-wife, Anna Karina) to the apparent safety of a Mediterranean island. The bizarre and tragic denouement is one of the great scenes of French cinema.

**Des dieux et des homes/Of Gods and Men** *Xavier Beauvois, 2010*. When seven Trappist monks were kidnapped from the monastery of Tibhirine in Algeria and assassinated in 1996, the outcry in France was universal. Until their abduction, the monks had for decades lived in harmony with the Muslim population around them. This multi-award-winning drama recounts the story of their murder and its aftermath, focusing on the Trappists' relationship with their captors and with the Algerian government, as external events conspire to transform a peaceful situation into a violent tragedy.

## FILMS D'AMOUR

⭐ **L'Ami de mon amie/Boyfriends and Girlfriends** *Eric Rohmer, 1987*. Two glossy young women in a flashy new town outside Paris – Cergy-Pontoise – become friends. While Blanche is away, Léa falls in love with

Blanche's boyfriend Alexandre; when Blanche comes back, she in turn falls in love with Léa's boyfriend, Fabien. Behind the light comedy and seemingly inconsequential dialogue lurks a profound film about love and free will.

**Baisers volés/Stolen Kisses** *François Truffaut, 1968.* The third of Truffaut's five-part semi-autobiographical sequence, which began with *Les Quatre-cents coups*, is probably the simplest and most delightful. Returning from military service, idealistic young Antoine Doinel (Jean-Pierre Léaud) mooches about Paris while working variously as a hotel worker, private detective and TV repairman. Through various amorous and bizarre adventures he slowly finds his way back towards the girl he loved and left behind.

**La Belle noiseuse** *Jacques Rivette, 1991.* "The beautiful troublemaker" originally stretched to four hours, though the more commonly screened "Divertimento" cut is half that length. A washed-out painter (the splendidly stuttering Michel Piccoli) lives in the deep south with his wife (Jane Birkin). An admiring younger painter offers his beautiful girlfriend (Emmanuelle Béart) as a nude model. Her fraught sittings become the catalyst for all the latent tensions in the two relationships to quietly explode.

**Un Coeur en hiver/A Heart in Winter/A Heart of Stone** *Claude Sautet, 1992.* In this thoughtful, fresh *ménage à trois* scenario, violinist Camille (Emmanuelle Béart) is paired first with Maxime (André Dussolier), a violin-shop owner, and then with loner Stéphane (Daniel Auteuil), the chief craftsman. As the title "A Heart in Winter" suggests, this is a moody but ultimately sentimental film about love, and the fear of love.

**Le Dernier métro/The Last Metro** *François Truffaut, 1980.* This huge commercial success stars Catherine Deneuve and Gérard Depardieu as two actors who fall in love while rehearsing a play during the German Occupation. Wartime Paris is evoked through lavish photography and a growing feeling of imprisonment inside the confined space of the theatre. Swept the Césars that year, for Best Film, Director, Actor and Actress.

⭐ **Le Mari de la coiffeuse/The Hairdresser's Husband** *Patrice Leconte, 1990.* Leconte's film about a man who grows up obsessed with hairdressers, and ends up marrying one, epitomizes the best in French romantic film-making. A quirky, subtle and engagingly twisted portrait of an obsessive relationship.

**Les Parapluies de Cherbourg/The Umbrellas of Cherbourg** *Jacques Demy, 1964.* Demy's most successful film also gave Catherine Deneuve one of her first great roles. It is an extraordinarily stylized musical, shot in bright, artificial-looking colours, and entirely sung rather than spoken. Demy disturbingly twists the traditional cheerfulness of the musical genre to give a dark, bitter ending to this story of love and abandonment, set during the Algerian war.

⭐ **Trois Couleurs: Rouge/Three Colours: Red** *Krzysztof Kieslowski, 1994.* The final part of Polish-born director's Kieslowski's "tricolore" trilogy is perhaps the most satisfying, though to get the most out of the powerful denouement, in which all the strands are pulled together through a series of chances and accidents, you really need to have watched *Bleu* and *Blanc* as well. A young model, Valentine (Irène Jacob), runs over a dog and traces its owner, a reclusive retired judge (Jean-Louis Trintignant) who assuages his loneliness by tapping his neighbours' phone calls. The film's "colour" is expressed through presiding red-brown tones and the theme of *fraternité*, the third principle of the French Republic.

## HERITAGE CINEMA

⭐ **Cyrano de Bergerac** *Jean-Paul Rappeneau, 1990.* It's hard to know what's finest about this extravagantly romantic film: Rostand's original story, set in seventeenth-century France, or Gérard Depardieu's landmark performance as the big-nosed swashbuckler-poet, Cyrano, who hopelessly loves the brilliant and beautiful Roxanne. The film's panache is matched by the verse dialogue – brilliantly rendered into English subtitles by Anthony Burgess. Hilarious, exciting and sublimely weepy.

⭐ **Jean de Florette** *Claude Berri, 1986.* This masterful adaptation of Marcel Pagnol's novel created the rose-tinted genre, *cinema du patrimoine*. In the gorgeous setting of inland, prewar Provence, Gérard Depardieu plays a deformed urban refugee struggling to create a rural utopia. He is opposed by the shrewd peasant Papet (Yves Montand) and a simpleton, Ugolin (Daniel Auteuil), who dreams of giant fields of carnations. The excellent sequel, *Manon des Sources* (1987), launched the stellar career of the improbably pouting Emmanuelle Béart.

**Au Revoir les enfants/Goodbye, Children** *Louis Malle, 1987.* Malle's autobiographical tale is one of the finest film portraits of the war, and of school life in general. It is minutely observed, and desperately moving without being unduly sentimental. Three Jewish boys are hidden among the pupils at a Catholic boys' boarding school. Eventually, the Gestapo discover the ruse.

**La Vie En Rose** *Olivier Dahan 2007.* The star of this internationally acclaimed biopic, Marion Cotillard, won an Oscar for her compelling portrayal of the Parisian chanteuse, Edith Piaf – the first French woman to be honoured with an Academy Award for Best Actress – as well as BAFTAs and Golden Globes. The gongs were well deserved. Adopting a fractured narrative approach, the film flits with sustained intensity between the "Little Sparrow's" early life in Paris to the events leading up to and surrounding her death, framed by a stirring rendition of Piaf's iconic song, *Je ne regrette rien* – a much more deft and memorable ending than it sounds.

## CINÉMA DU LOOK

★ **37°2 le matin/Betty Blue** *Jean-Jacques Beineix, 1986.* Pouty Béatrice Dalle puts on a compellingly erotic performance as Betty, a free-thinking girl who lives in a beach house with struggling writer Zorg. The film opens in romantic mood with a sustained and passionate sex scene but rapidly spirals towards its disturbing ending. The film's intense and sometimes weird stylishness, along with its memorable score, made it an international hit.

**Les Amants du Pont-Neuf** *Léos Carax, 1991.* Homeless painter Michèle (Juliette Binoche) is losing her sight. One day, on Paris's Pont-Neuf, she meets an indigent, fire-eating acrobat (Denis Lavant), and they tumble together into a consuming love, madly played out against the background of their life on the streets. An intense and beautiful film.

★ **Delicatessen** *Jean-Pierre Jeunet/Marc Caro, 1991.* Set in a crumbling apartment block in a dystopian fantasy city – Occupation Paris meets comic book – a grotesque local butcher murders his assistants and sells them as human meat, until his daughter falls in love with the latest butcher boy and the subterranean vegetarian terrorists find out. Hilarious and bizarre in equal measure, with superb cameos from the neighbours.

**Subway** *Luc Besson, 1985.* The favoured urban-nocturnal setting of the *cinéma du look* is given its coolest expression in *Subway.* A hock-headed Christophe Lambert is hunted by police and criminals alike for a cache of documents he shouldn't have. He hides out in the Paris métro where he manages to form a rock band – before being found by Isabelle Adjani. Film noir meets MTV.

## NEW REALISM: BEUR, BANLIEUE AND JEUNE

**Comme une image/Look at Me** *Agnès Jaoui, 2004.* Agnès Jaoui manages to be both sensitive and hard-hitting in this exploration of the dysfunctional relationship between a self-conscious, under-confident daughter (Marilou Berry) and her monstrously egotistical, literary lion of a father – a role played superbly by Jean-Pierre Bacri, who co-wrote the script with Jaoui.

**La Haine/Hate** *Mathieu Kassovitz, 1995.* The flagship film of the *cinéma de banlieue*, films of the tough suburbs, centres on three friends: Hubert, of black African origin; Saïd, a *beur* (from North Africa); and Vinz, who is white and has Jewish roots – and a gun. They spend a troubled night wandering Paris before heading back to the *banlieue* and a violent homecoming. Brilliantly treads the line between gritty realism and street cool – the fact that it's shot in black-and-white helps, as does the soundtrack from French rapper MC Solaar, among others.

**Hexagone** *Malik Chibane, 1991.* Shooting in just 24 days, and using amateur actors, Chibane somehow pulled off exactly what he planned: to raise the profile of the new generation of *beurs*. The story is a simple enough rite-of-passage tale focused on five young friends who get in trouble, but the recurring motif of the sacrifice of Abraham gives it a thoughtful twist. The street-slang peppered script and cinematography – strong on handheld shots of the inner-city landscape – are superb.

★ **Un prophète** *Jacques Audiard, 2009.* A prison movie that becomes a gangland thriller, this film is lifted beyond the confines of either genre by its bitter political message and by its magnificent anti-hero, the *naïf*-but-turned-ruthless young Arab man played brilliantly by Tahir Rahim.

★ **La Ville est tranquille/The Town Is Quiet** *Robert Guédiguian, 2000.* Notwithstanding its title, this harrowing film describes the dysfunctional society of a far-from-quiet city – Marseille – focusing on the hardships of Michèle (Ariane Ascaride), a 40-year-old woman working in a fish factory while fighting to save her heroin-addict daughter. After a series of light, happy tales, Robert Guédiguian magnificently turns here to a more realistic and political tone.

# Books

The most highly recommended books in this selection are marked by a ★ symbol.

## TRAVEL

**Marc Augé** *In the Metro*. A philosophically minded anthropologist descends deep into metro culture and his own memories of life in Paris. Brief and brilliant.

**Walter Benjamin** *The Arcades Project*. An all-encompassing portrait of Paris from 1830 to 1870, in which the *passages* are used as a lens through which to view Parisian society. Never completed, Benjamin's magnum opus is a kaleidoscopic assemblage of essays, notes and quotations, gathered under such headings as "Baudelaire", "Prostitution", "Mirrors" and "Idleness".

**Adam Gopnik** *Paris to the Moon*. Intimate and acutely observed essays from the Paris correspondent of the New Yorker on society, politics, family life and shopping.

**Julien Green** *Paris*. A collection of very personal sketches and impressions of the city, by an American who has lived all his life in Paris, writes in French, and is considered one of the great French writers of the century. Bilingual text.

**Richard Holmes** *Footsteps*. A marvellous mix of objective history and personal account, such as the tale of the author's own excitement at the events of May 1968 in Paris, which led him to investigate and reconstruct the experiences of the British in Paris during the 1789 Revolution.

**Michael de Larrabeiti** *French Leave*. In the summer of 1949, aged just 15, Michael de Larrabeiti set off on his own by bicycle to Paris from the UK. This book provides a wonderfully evocative testimony to his love of France as he looks back over fifty years of working and travelling throughout the country.

**Robert Louis Stevenson** *Travels with a Donkey*. Mile-by-mile account of Stevenson's twelve-day trek in the Haute Loire and Cévennes uplands with the donkey Modestine. His first book, *Inland Voyage*, took him round the waterways of the north.

## HISTORY

### GENERAL

★ **Eric Hazan** *The Invention of Paris*. Weighty but utterly compelling "psychogeographical" account of the city, picking over its history *quartier* by *quartier* in a thousand aperçus and anecdotes.

★ **Alistair Horne** *Seven Ages of Paris*. Highly readable narrative by the great British historian and journalist, tracing the capital's history from the twelfth century to the death of de Gaulle in 1969. Its brilliance lies in Horne's love of the quirky, and often seedy, side of life, where fashion, celebrity, street culture and a host of incidental characters combine to create a rich tableau that tells you a lot more than comparable academic histories.

**Colin Jones** *The Cambridge Illustrated History of France*. A political and social history of France from prehistoric times to the mid-1990s, concentrating on issues of regionalism, gender, race and class. Good illustrations and a friendly, non-academic writing style.

★ **Colin Jones** *Paris: Biography of a City*. Jones focuses tightly on the actual life and growth of the city, from the Neolithic past to the future. Five hundred pages flow by easily, punctuated by thoughtful but accessible "boxes" on characters, streets and buildings whose lives were especially bound up with Paris's, from the Roman *arènes* to Zazie's métro. The best single book on the city's history.

★ **Ross King** *The Judgement of Paris*. High-octane account of the artistic culture wars of the 1860s and 1870s, focusing on the fascinating parallel lives of the well-established painter Meissonier and the radical upstart Manet.

★ **Graham Robb** *The Discovery of France*. Captivating, brilliant study of France which makes a superb antidote to the usual narratives of kings and state affairs. With affection and insight, and in fine prose, Robb describes a France of vast wastes inhabited by "faceless millions" speaking mutually unintelligible dialects, and reveals how this France was gradually discovered and, inevitably, "civilized".

★ **Graham Robb** *Parisians: An Adventure History of Paris*. Robb's equally compelling meanderings through the history of the nation's capital approaches the familiar from some beguilingly oblique angles, casting characters as diverse as Napleon, Baudelaire, Haussmann, Hitler and Proust across a range of uniquely Parisian settings. The result reads like sparkling modern novel, filled with revelations and fine storytelling.

**Robert Tombs & Isabelle Tombs** *That Sweet Enemy: The British and the French from the Sun King to the Present*. A fascinating, original and mammoth study of a strangely intimate relationship. The authors are a French woman and her English husband, and they engage in lively debate between themselves. Covers society, culture and personalities, as well as politics.

### THE MIDDLE AGES AND RENAISSANCE

**Natalie Zemon Davis** *The Return of Martin Guerre*. A vivid account of peasant life in the sixteenth century and a perplexing and titillating hoax in the Pyrenean village of Artigat.

★ **J.H. Huizinga** *The Waning of the Middle Ages.* Primarily a study of the culture of the Burgundian and French courts – but a masterpiece that goes far beyond this, building up meticulous detail to re-create the whole life and mentality of the fourteenth and fifteenth centuries.

**R.J. Knecht** *The French Renaissance Court.* The definitive work by a genuine authority. Not exactly a racy read, but successfully mixes high politics with sharp detail on life at court life, backed up by plentiful illustrations.

★ **Marina Warner** *Joan of Arc.* Brilliantly places France's patron saint and national heroine within historical, spiritual and intellectual traditions.

### EIGHTEENTH AND NINETEENTH CENTURIES

**Vincent Cronin** *Napoleon.* An enthusiastic and engagingly written biography of France's Emperor.

★ **Christopher Hibbert** *The French Revolution.* Well-paced and entertaining narrative treatment by a master historian.

**Alistair Horne** *The Fall of Paris.* A very readable and humane account of the extraordinary period of the Prussian siege of Paris in 1870 and the ensuing struggles of the Commune.

★ **Ross King** *The Judgement of Paris: The Revolutionary Decade That Gave the World Impressionism.* Lively account of the stormy early years when the Impressionists were refused entry to official exhibitions.

★ **Lucy Moore** *Liberty: The Lives and Times of Six Women in Revolutionary France.* This original book follows the lives of six influential – and very different women – through the Revolution, taking in everything from sexual scandal to revolutionary radicalism.

★ **Ruth Scurr** *Fatal Purity: Robespierre and the French Revolution.* This myth-busting biography of the "remarkably odd" figure of the man they called The Incorruptible, and who went on to orchestrate the notorious Terror, ends up being one of the best books on the Revolution in general.

### TWENTIETH CENTURY

**Marc Bloch** *Strange Defeat.* Moving personal study of the reasons for France's defeat and subsequent caving-in to fascism. Found among the papers of this Sorbonne historian after his death at the hands of the Gestapo in 1942.

**Carmen Callil** *Bad Faith: A Forgotten History of Family and Fatherland.* This quietly angry biography of the loathsome Louis Darquier, the Vichy state's Commissioner for Jewish Affairs, reveals the banality of viciousness in wartime France.

★ **Geoff Dyer** *The Missing of the Somme.* Structured round the author's visits to the war graves of northern France, this is a highly moving meditation on the trauma of World War I and the way its memory has been perpetuated.

**Jonathan Fenby** *The General: Charles de Gaulle and the France He Saved.* This monumental but utterly readable biography does not always get under the famously private president's skin, but does show how de Gaulle not only shaped but embodied the ideals and ambitions of the postwar nation – or a certain, proudly, idealistically reactionary segment of it, at least.

**Ian Ousby** *Occupation: The Ordeal of France 1940–1944.* Revisionist 1997 account which shows how relatively late resistance was, how widespread collaboration was, and why.

## SOCIETY AND POLITICS

**Julian Barnes** *Something to Declare.* This journalistically highbrow collection of 18 essays on French culture – films, music, the Tour de France, and, of course, Flaubert – wears its French-style intellectualism on its sleeve, but succeeds in getting under the skin anyway.

**Mary Blume** *A French Affair: The Paris Beat 1965–1998.* Incisive and witty observations on contemporary French life by the *International Herald Tribune* reporter who was stationed there for three decades.

★ **Jonathan Fenby** *On the Brink.* While the country isn't perhaps quite as endangered as the title suggests, this provocative book takes a long, hard look at the problems facing contemporary France, from unemployment to corruption in its self-serving, self-selecting ruling class.

★ **Mark Girouard** *Life in the French Country House.* Girouard meticulously re-creates the social and domestic life that went on between the walls of French châteaux, starting with the great halls of early castles and ending with the commercial marriage venues of the twentieth century.

**Tim Moore** *French Revolutions: Cycling the Tour De France.* A whimsical bicycle journey along the route of the Tour by a genuinely hilarious writer. Lots of witty asides on Tour history and French culture.

**Jim Ring** *Riviera: The Rise and Rise of the Cote d'Azur.* A fascinating portrait of France's most anomalous region, taking in its discovery by aristocratic pleasure-seekers in the nineteenth century, the golden years of the 1920s when it was the playground of artists, film stars and millionaires, and the inevitable fall from grace.

★ **Charles Timoney** *Pardon My French: Unleash Your Inner Gaul.* Incisive and often very droll dissection of contemporary culture through the words and phrases that the French use all the time. Looks and maybe sounds like a gift book, but it's rather brilliant.

**Gillian Tindall** *Célestine: Voices from a French Village.* Intrigued by some nineteenth-century love letters left behind in the house she has bought in Chassignolles, Berry, Tindall researches the history of the village back to the 1840s. A brilliant, warm-hearted piece of social history.

**Lucy Wadham** *The Secret Life of France*. Funny and insightful insider-eye view of the French, written by an expat who married one of them. Particularly good on women and female culture, and generally more intelligent than most in this genre.

## ART, ARCHITECTURE AND POETRY

**Philip Ball** *Universe of Stone: Chartres Cathedral and the Triumph of the Medieval Mind*. Ball gets hopelessly sidetracked into potted histories of all kinds of aspects of medieval life, but at the core of this book is a fascinating letter of love to an extraordinary building.

★ **André Chastel** *French Art*. Authoritative, three-volume study by one of France's leading art historians. Discusses individual works of art – from architecture to tapestry, as well as painting – in some detail in an attempt to locate the Frenchness of French art. With glossy photographs and serious-minded but readable text.

★ **David Cairns** *Berlioz: The Making of an Artist 1803–1832*. The multiple-award winning first volume of Cairns' two-part biography is more than just a life of the passionate French composer, it's an extraordinary evocation of post-Napoleonic France and its burgeoning Romantic culture.

**Theodore Zeldin** *The French*. A wise and original book that attempts to describe a country through the prism of the author's intensely personal conversations with a fascinating range of French people. Chapter titles include "How to be chic" and "How to appreciate a grandmother".

★ **John Richardson** *The Life of Picasso*. No twentieth-century artist has ever been subjected to as much scrutiny as Picasso receives in Richardson's brilliantly illustrated biography. Three of an expected four volumes have been published to date.

**Stephen Romer** (editor) *20th-Century French Poems*. A collection of around 150 French poems spanning the whole of the century. Although there's no French text, many of the translations are works of art in themselves, consummately rendered by the likes of Samuel Beckett, T.S. Eliot and Paul Auster.

**Rolf Toman** (editor) *Romanesque: Architecture, Sculpture, Painting*. Huge, sumptuously illustrated volume of essays on every aspect of the genre across Europe, with one chapter specifically devoted to France.

## GUIDES

**David Abram** *Corsica Trekking: GR20*. Comprehensive guide to France's most redoubtable *Grande Randonée*, with detailed maps and coverage of the island's history, geography and culture.

**Glynn Christian** *Edible France*. A guide to food rather than restaurants: regional produce, local specialities, markets and best shops for buying goodies to bring back home. Dated, but still reliable for the provinces, if not Paris.

**Cicerone** *Walking Guides*. Neat, durable guides with detailed route descriptions. Titles include *Tour of Mont Blanc; Chamonix-Mont Blanc; Tour of the Oisans (GR54); French Alps (GR5); The Way of Saint James (GR65); Tour of the Queyras; The Pyrenean Trail (GR10); Walks and Climbs in the Pyrenees; Walking in the Alps*.

**Philippe Dubois** *Where to Watch Birds in France*. Maps, advice on when to go, habitat information, species' lists – everything you need.

★ **David Hampshire** *Living and Working in France*. An invaluable guide for anyone considering residence or work in France; packed with ideas and advice on job hunting, bureaucracy, tax, health and so on. Usually updated every two years.

**Richard Holmes** *Fatal Avenue: A Traveller's History of the Battlefields of France and Flanders 1346–1945*. Excellent combination of guidebook and storytelling from a renowned military historian.

# French

French can be a deceptively familiar language because of the number of words and structures it shares with English. Despite this, it's far from easy, though the bare essentials are not difficult to master and can make all the difference. Even just saying "Bonjour Madame/Monsieur" and then gesticulating will often get you a smile and helpful service. People working in tourist offices, hotels and so on almost always speak English and tend to use it when you're struggling to speak French.

## Pronunciation

One easy rule to remember is that **consonants** at the ends of words are usually silent: the most obvious example is Paris, pronounced "Paree", while the phrase *pas plus tard* (not later) sounds something like "pa-plu-tarr". The exception is when the following word begins with a vowel, in which case you generally run the two together: *pas après* (not after) becomes "pazaprey". Otherwise, consonants are much the same as in English, except that: *ch* is always "sh", *c* is "s", *h* is silent, *th* is the same as "t", and *r* is growled (or rolled). And to complicate things a little, *ll* after *i* usually sounds like the "y" in yes – though there are exceptions, including common words like *ville* (city), and *mille* (thousand). And *w* is "v", except when it's in a borrowed English word, like *le whisky* or *un weekend*.

**Vowels** are the hardest sounds to get exactly right, but they rarely differ enough from English to make comprehension a problem. The most obvious differences are that *au* sounds like the "o" in "over"; *aujourd'hui* (today) is thus pronounced "oh-jor-dwi". Another one to listen out for is *oi*, which sounds like "wa"; *toi* (to you) thus sounds like "twa". Lastly, adding "m" or "n" to a vowel, as in *en* or *un*, adds a nasal sound, as if you said just the vowel with a cold.

### PHRASEBOOKS AND COURSES

**Rough Guide French Phrasebook** Mini dictionary-style phrasebook with both English–French and French–English sections, along with cultural tips, a menu reader and downloadable scenarios read by native speakers.

**Breakthrough French** One of the best teach-yourself courses, with three levels to choose from. Each comes with a book and CD-ROM.

**The Complete Merde! The Real French You Were Never Taught at School.** More than just a collection of swearwords, this book is a passkey into everyday French,

and a window into French culture.

**Oxford Essential French Dictionary** Very up-to-date French–English and English–French dictionary, with help on pronunciation and verbs, and links to free online products.

**Michel Thomas** A fast-paced and effective audio course that promises "No books. No writing. No memorizing", with an emphasis on spoken French, rather than conjugating verbs and sentence construction. ⓦmichelthomas.com /learn-french.

## Basic words and phrases

French nouns are divided into masculine and feminine. This causes difficulties with adjectives, whose endings have to change to suit the nouns they qualify – you can talk about *un château blanc* (a white castle), for example, but *une tour blanche* (a white tower). If you're not sure, stick to the simpler masculine form – as used in this glossary.

## ESSENTIALS

| | | | |
|---|---|---|---|
| hello (morning or afternoon) | bonjour | big | grand |
| | | small | petit |
| hello (evening) | bonsoir | more | plus |
| good night | bonne nuit | less | moins |
| goodbye | au revoir | a little | un peu |
| thank you | merci | a lot | beaucoup |
| please | s'il vous plaît | inexpensive | pas cher/bon marché |
| sorry | pardon/Je m'excuse | expensive | cher |
| excuse me | pardon | good | bon |
| yes | oui | bad | mauvais |
| no | non | hot | chaud |
| OK/agreed | d'accord | cold | froid |
| help! | au secours! | with | avec |
| here | ici | without | sans |
| there | là | entrance | entrée |
| this one | ceci | exit | sortie |
| that one | celà | man | un homme |
| open | ouvert | woman | une femme (pronounced "fam") |
| closed | fermé | | |

## NUMBERS

| | | | |
|---|---|---|---|
| 1 | un | 21 | vingt-et-un |
| 2 | deux | 22 | vingt-deux |
| 3 | trois | 30 | trente |
| 4 | quatre | 40 | quarante |
| 5 | cinq | 50 | cinquante |
| 6 | six | 60 | soixante |
| 7 | sept | 70 | soixante-dix |
| 8 | huit | 75 | soixante-quinze |
| 9 | neuf | 80 | quatre-vingts |
| 10 | dix | 90 | quatre-vingt-dix |
| 11 | onze | 95 | quatre-vingt-quinze |
| 12 | douze | 100 | cent |
| 13 | treize | 101 | cent-et-un |
| 14 | quatorze | 200 | deux cents |
| 15 | quinze | 300 | trois cents |
| 16 | seize | 500 | cinq cents |
| 17 | dix-sept | 1000 | mille |
| 18 | dix-huit | 2000 | deux mille |
| 19 | dix-neuf | 5000 | cinq mille |
| 20 | vingt | 1,000,000 | un million |

## TIME

| | | | |
|---|---|---|---|
| today | aujourd'hui | now | maintenant |
| yesterday | hier | later | plus tard |
| tomorrow | demain | at one o'clock | à une heure |
| in the morning | le matin | at three o'clock | à trois heures |
| in the afternoon | l'après-midi | at ten thirty | à dix heures et demie |
| in the evening | le soir | at midday | à midi |

## DAYS AND DATES

| | | | |
|---|---|---|---|
| January | janvier | March | mars |
| February | février | April | avril |

| | | | |
|---|---|---|---|
| May | mai | Tuesday | mardi |
| June | juin | Wednesday | mercredi |
| July | juillet | Thursday | jeudi |
| August | août | Friday | vendredi |
| September | septembre | Saturday | samedi |
| October | octobre | August 1 | le premier août |
| November | novembre | March 2 | le deux mars |
| December | décembre | July 14 | le quatorze juillet |
| Sunday | dimanche | November 23 | le vingt-trois novembre |
| Monday | lundi | 2013 | deux mille treize |

## TALKING TO PEOPLE

When addressing people a simple *bonjour* is not enough; you should always use *Monsieur* for a man, *Madame* for a woman, *Mademoiselle* for a young woman or girl. This has its uses when you've forgotten someone's name or want to attract someone's attention. "Bonjour" can be used well into the afternoon, and people may start saying "bonsoir" surprisingly early in the evening, or as a way of saying goodbye.

| | | | |
|---|---|---|---|
| Do you speak English? | Parlez-vous anglais? | ... South African | ... sud-africain[e] |
| How do you say it in French? | Comment ça se dit en français? | I understand | Je comprends |
| | | I don't understand | Je ne comprends pas |
| What's your name? | Comment vous appelez-vous? | Could you speak more slowly? | S'il vous plaît, parlez moins vite |
| My name is ... | Je m'appelle ... | How are you? | Comment allez-vous?/ Ça va? |
| I'm ... | Je suis ... | | |
| ... English | ... anglais[e] | Fine, thanks | Très bien, merci |
| ... Irish | ... irlandais[e] | I don't know | Je ne sais pas |
| ... Scottish | ... écossais[e] | Let's go | Allons-y |
| ... Welsh | ... gallois[e] | See you tomorrow | À demain |
| ... American | ... américain[e] | See you soon | À bientôt |
| ... Australian | ...australien[ne] | Leave me alone (aggressive) | Laissez-moi tranquille |
| ... Canadian | ... canadien[ne] | | |
| ... a New Zealander | ... néo-zélandais[e] | Please help me | Aidez-moi, s'il vous plaît |

## FINDING THE WAY

| | | | |
|---|---|---|---|
| bus | autobus/bus/car | ticket office | vente de billets |
| bus station | gare routière | how many kilometres? | combien de kilomètres? |
| bus stop | arrêt | how many hours? | combien d'heures? |
| car | voiture | hitchhiking | autostop |
| train/taxi/ferry | train/taxi/bac or ferry | on foot | à pied |
| boat | bâteau | Where are you going? | Vous allez où? |
| plane | avion | I'm going to ... | Je vais à ... |
| shuttle | navette | I want to get off at ... | Je voudrais descendre à ... |
| train station | gare (SNCF) | the road to ... | la route pour ... |
| platform | quai | near | près/pas loin |
| What time does it leave? | Il part à quelle heure? | far | loin |
| What time does it arrive? | Il arrive à quelle heure? | left | à gauche |
| a ticket to ... | un billet pour ... | right | à droite |
| single ticket | aller simple | straight on | tout droit |
| return ticket | aller retour | on the other side of | à l'autre côté de |
| validate/stamp your ticket | compostez votre billet | on the corner of | à l'angle de |
| | | next to | à côté de |
| valid for | valable pour | behind | derrière |

| in front of | devant | all through roads (road sign) | toutes directions |
|---|---|---|---|
| before | avant | other destinations (road sign) | autres directions |
| after | après | | |
| under | sous | upper town | ville haute/haute ville |
| to cross | traverser | lower town | ville basse/basse ville |
| bridge | pont | Old Town | vieille ville |
| town centre | centre ville | | |

## QUESTIONS AND REQUESTS

The simplest way of asking a question is to start with *s'il vous plaît* (please), then name the thing you want in an interrogative tone of voice. For example:

| Where is there a bakery? | S'il vous plaît, la boulangerie? | Can we have a room for two? | S'il vous plaît, une chambre pour deux? |
|---|---|---|---|
| Which way is it to the Eiffel Tower? | S'il vous plaît, la route pour la Tour Eiffel? | Can I have a kilo of oranges? | S'il vous plaît, un kilo d'oranges? |

## QUESTION WORDS

| where? | où? | why? | pourquoi? |
|---|---|---|---|
| how? | comment? | at what time? | à quelle heure? |
| how many/how much? | combien? | what is/which is? | quel est? |
| when? | quand? | | |

## ACCOMMODATION

| a room for one/ two persons | une chambre pour une/ deux personne(s) | sheets | draps |
|---|---|---|---|
| a double bed | un grand lit/ un lit matrimonial | blankets | couvertures |
| | | quiet | calme |
| a room with two single beds/twin | une chambre à deux lits | noisy | bruyant |
| | | hot water | eau chaude |
| a room with a shower | une chambre avec douche | cold water | eau froide |
| | | Is breakfast included? | Est-ce que le petit déjeuner est compris? |
| a room with a bath | une chambre avec salle de bain | I would like breakfast | Je voudrais prendre le petit déjeuner |
| for one/two/three nights | pour une/deux/trios nuits | I don't want breakfast | Je ne veux pas de petit déjeuner |
| Can I see it? | Je peux la voir? | | |
| a room on the courtyard | une chambre sur a cour | bed and breakfast | chambres d'hôte |
| a room over the street | une chambre sur la rue | Can we camp here? | On peut camper ici? |
| first floor | premier étage | campsite | camping/terrain de camping |
| second floor | deuxième étage | | |
| with a view | avec vue | tent | tente |
| key | clé | tent space | emplacement |
| to iron | repasser | hostel | foyer |
| do laundry | faire la lessive | youth hostel | auberge de jeunesse |

## DRIVING

| service station | garage |
|---|---|
| service | service |
| to park the car | garer la voiture |
| car park | un parking |
| no parking | défense de stationner/ stationnement interdit |
| petrol/gas station | poste d'essence |
| fuel | essence |

---

### SIGN LANGUAGE

**Défense de ...** It is forbidden to ...
**Fermé** closed
**Ouvert** open
**Rez-de-chaussée (RC)** ground floor
**Sortie** exit

| | | | |
|---|---|---|---|
| unleaded | sans plomb | the battery is dead | la batterie est morte |
| leaded | super | plug (for appliance) | prise |
| diesel | gazole | to break down | tomber en panne |
| oil | huile | petrol can | bidon |
| air line | ligne à air | insurance | assurance |
| put air in the tyres | gonfler les pneus | green card | carte verte |
| battery | batterie | traffic lights | feux rouges |

## HEALTH MATTERS

| | | | |
|---|---|---|---|
| doctor | médecin | pain | douleur |
| I don't feel well | Je ne me sens pas bien | it hurts | ça fait mal |
| medicines | médicaments | chemist/pharmacist | pharmacie |
| prescription | ordonnance | hospital | hôpital |
| I feel sick | Je suis malade | condom | préservatif |
| I have a headache | J'ai mal à la tête | morning-after pill/ | pilule du lendemain |
| stomach ache | mal à l'estomac | emergency contraceptive | |
| period | règles | I'm allergic to … | Je suis allergique à … |

## OTHER NEEDS

| | | | |
|---|---|---|---|
| bakery | boulangerie | tobacconist | tabac |
| food shop | alimentation | stamps | timbres |
| delicatessen | charcuterie, traiteur | bank | banque |
| cake shop | patisserie | money | argent |
| cheese shop | fromagerie | toilets | toilettes |
| supermarket | supermarché | police | police |
| to eat | manger | telephone | téléphone |
| to drink | boire | cinema | cinéma |
| tasting, eg wine | dégustation, tasting | theatre | théâtre |
| camping gas | camping gaz | to reserve/book | réserver |

## RESTAURANT PHRASES

| | | | |
|---|---|---|---|
| I'd like to reserve a table for two people, at eight thirty | Je voudrais réserver une table pour deux personnes à vingt heures et demie | Waiter! (never "garçon") | Monsieur/Madame!/ s'il vous plaît! |
| I'm having the €30 set menu | Je prendrai le menu à trente euros | the bill/check please | l'addition, s'il vous plaît |

# Food and dishes

## BASIC TERMS

| | | | |
|---|---|---|---|
| l'addition | bill/check | entrée | starter |
| beurre | butter | formule | lunchtime set menu |
| bio or biologique | organic | fourchette | fork |
| bouteille | bottle | fumé | smoked |
| carafe d'eau | jug of water | gazeuse | fizzy |
| la carte | the menu | lait | milk |
| chauffé | heated | le menu | set menu |
| couteau | knife | moutarde | mustard |
| cru | raw | oeuf | egg |
| cuillère | spoon | offert | free |
| cuit | cooked | pain | bread |
| emballé | wrapped | pimenté | spicy |
| à emporter | takeaway | plat | main course |

| | |
|---|---|
| poivre | pepper |
| salé | salted/savoury |
| sel | salt |
| sucre | sugar |
| sucré | sweet |
| table | table |
| verre | glass |
| vinaigre | vinegar |

## SNACKS

| | |
|---|---|
| un sandwich/ | a sandwich |
| une baguette | |
| jambon beurre | with ham and butter |
| au fromage | with cheese, no butter |
| mixte | with ham and cheese |
| au pâté (de campagne) | with pâté (country-style) |
| croque-monsieur | grilled cheese and ham |
| | sandwich |
| panini | toasted Italian sandwich |
| tartine | buttered bread or open |
| | sandwich, often with |
| | jam |
| oeufs | eggs |
| au plat | fried |
| à la coque | boiled |
| durs | hard-boiled |
| brouillés | scrambled |
| omelette | omelette |
| nature | plain |
| aux fines herbes | with herbs |
| au fromage | with cheese |
| salade de tomates | tomato salad |
| salade verte | green salad |

## PASTA (*PÂTES*), PANCAKES (*CRÊPES*), TARTES AND COUSCOUS

| | |
|---|---|
| nouilles | noodles |
| pâtes fraîches | fresh pasta |
| crêpe au sucre/aux oeufs | pancake with sugar/eggs |
| galette | buckwheat pancake |
| pissaladière | tart of fried onions with |
| | anchovies and black |
| | olives |
| tarte flambée | thin pizza-like pastry |
| | topped with onion, |
| | cream and bacon |
| couscous | steamed semolina grains, |
| | usually served with |
| | meat or veg, chickpea |
| | stew and chilli sauce |
| couscous Royale | couscous with spicy |
| | merguez sausage, |
| | chicken and beef or |
| | lamb kebabs |

## SOUPS (*SOUPES*)

| | |
|---|---|
| bisque | shellfish soup |
| bouillabaisse | soup with five fish |
| bouillon | broth or stock |
| bourride | thick fish soup |
| consommé | clear soup |
| garbure | potato, cabbage and |
| | meat soup |
| pistou | parmesan, basil and garlic |
| | paste added to soup |
| potage | thick vegetable soup |
| potée auvergnate | cabbage and meat soup |
| rouille | red pepper, garlic and |
| | saffron mayonnaise |
| | served with fish soup |
| soupe à l'oignon | onion soup with a rich |
| | cheese topping |
| velouté | thick soup, usually fish or |
| | poultry |

## STARTERS (*HORS D'OEUVRES*)

| | |
|---|---|
| assiette de charcuterie | plate of cold meats |
| assiette composée | mixed salad plate, usually |
| | cold meat and veg |
| crudités | dressed raw vegetables |
| hors d'oeuvres | combination of the above |
| | often with smoked or |
| | marinated fish |

## FISH (*POISSON*), SEAFOOD (*FRUITS DE MER*) AND SHELLFISH (*CRUSTACES OR COQUILLAGES*)

| | |
|---|---|
| anchois | anchovies |
| anguilles | eels |
| barbue | brill |
| baudroie | monkfish or |
| | anglerfish |
| bigourneau | periwinkle |
| brème | bream |
| cabillaud | cod |
| calmar | squid |
| carrelet | plaice |
| claire | type of oyster |
| colin | hake |
| congre | conger eel |
| coques | cockles |
| coquilles | scallops St-Jacques |
| crabe | crab |
| crevettes grises | shrimp |
| crevettes roses | prawns |
| daurade | sea bream |
| éperlan | smelt or whitebait |
| escargots | snails |
| flétan | halibut |

| | |
|---|---|
| friture | assorted fried fish, often like whitebait |
| gambas | king prawns |
| hareng | herring |
| homard | lobster |
| huîtres | oysters |
| langouste | spiny lobster |
| langoustines | saltwater crayfish (scampi) |
| limande | lemon sole |
| lotte de mer | monkfish |
| loup de mer | sea bass |
| maquereau | mackerel |
| merlan | whiting |
| moules (marinières) | mussels (with shallots in white wine sauce) |
| oursin | sea urchin |
| palourdes | clams |
| poissons de roche | fish from shoreline rocks |
| praires | small clams |
| raie | skate |
| rouget | red mullet |
| saumon | salmon |
| sole | sole |
| thon | tuna |
| truite | trout |
| turbot | turbot |
| violet | sea squirt |

## FISH DISHES AND TERMS

| | |
|---|---|
| aïoli | garlic mayonnaise |
| anchoïade | anchovy paste or sauce |
| arête | fish bone |
| assiette de pêcheur | assorted fish |
| beignet | fritter |
| darne | fillet or steak |
| la douzaine | a dozen |
| frit | fried |
| friture | deep-fried small fish |
| fumé | smoked |
| fumet | fish stock |
| gigot de mer | large fish baked whole |
| grillé | grilled |
| hollandaise | butter and vinegar sauce |
| à la meunière | in a butter, lemon and parsley sauce |
| mousse/mousseline | mousse |
| pané | breaded |
| poutargue | mullet roe paste |
| quenelles | light dumplings |

## MEAT (VIANDE) AND POULTRY (VOLAILLE)

| | |
|---|---|
| agneau (de pré-salé) | lamb (grazed on salt marshes) |
| andouille | cold pork and tripe sausage |
| andouillette | hot, cooked tripe sausage |
| bavette | flank-like steak |
| boeuf | beef |
| boudin blanc | sausage of white meats |
| boudin noir | black pudding |
| caille | quail |
| canard | duck |
| caneton | duckling |
| contrefilet | sirloin roast |
| coquelet | cockerel |
| la cuisson? | how would sir/madam like his/her steak done? |
| dinde/dindon | turkey |
| entrecôte | rib steak |
| faux filet | sirloin steak |
| foie | liver |
| foie gras | (duck/goose) liver |
| gibier | game |
| gigot (d'agneau) | leg (of lamb) |
| grenouilles (cuisses de) | frogs' (legs) |
| langue | tongue |
| lapin/lapereau | rabbit/young rabbit |
| lard/lardons | bacon/diced bacon |
| lièvre | hare |
| merguez | spicy, red sausage |
| mouton | mutton |
| museau de veau | calf's muzzle |
| oie | goose |
| onglet | tasty, flank-like steak |
| os | bone |
| poitrine | breast |
| porc | pork |
| poulet | chicken |
| poussin | baby chicken |
| rillettes | pork mashed with lard and liver |
| ris | sweetbreads |
| rognons | kidneys |
| rognons blancs | testicles |
| sanglier | wild boar |
| steak | steak |
| tête de veau | calf's head (in jelly) |
| tournedos | thick slices of fillet |
| tripes | tripe |
| tripoux | mutton tripe |
| veau | veal |
| venaison | venison |

## MEAT AND POULTRY DISHES AND TERMS

| | |
|---|---|
| aïado | roast shoulder of lamb stuffed with garlic and other ingredients |
| aile | wing |
| blanquette, daube, estouffade, hochepôt, navarin, ragoût | types of stew |
| blanquette de veau | veal in cream and mushroom sauce |
| boeuf bourguignon | beef stew with Burgundy, onions and mushrooms |
| brochette | kebab |
| carré | best end of neck, chop or cutlet |
| cassoulet | casserole of beans, sausages and duck/ goose |
| choucroute | sauerkraut with peppercorns, sausages, pork and ham |
| civet | game stew |
| confit | meat preserve |
| coq au vin | chicken slow-cooked with wine, onions and mushrooms |
| côte | chop, cutlet or rib |
| cuisse | thigh or leg |
| en croûte | in pastry |
| épaule | shoulder |
| farci | stuffed |
| au feu de bois | cooked over wood fire |
| au four | baked |
| garni | with vegetables |
| gésier | gizzard |
| grillade | grilled meat |
| grillé | grilled |
| hâchis | chopped meat or mince hamburger |
| magret de canard | duck breast |
| marmite | casserole |
| médaillon | round piece |
| mijoté | stewed |
| pavé | thick slice |
| pieds et paques | mutton or pork tripe and trotters |
| poêlé | pan-fried |
| poulet de Bresse | chicken from Bresse |
| râble | saddle |
| rôti | roast |
| sauté | lightly fried in butter |
| steak au poivre (vert/rouge) | steak in a black peppercorn sauce (green/red peppercorn) |
| steak tartare | raw chopped beef, topped with a raw egg yolk |
| tagine | North African casserole |
| viennoise | fried in egg and bread crumbs |

## TERMS FOR STEAKS

| | |
|---|---|
| bleu | almost raw |
| saignant | rare |
| à point | medium rare |
| bien cuit | well done |
| très bien cuit | ruined |

## GARNISHES AND SAUCES

| | |
|---|---|
| américaine | sauce of white wine, cognac and tomato |
| auvergnat | with cabbage, sausage and bacon |
| béarnaise | sauce of egg yolks, white wine, shallots and vinegar |
| beurre blanc | sauce of white wine and shallots, with butter |
| bonne femme | with mushroom, bacon, potato and onions |
| bordelaise | in a red wine, shallot and bone-marrow sauce |
| boulangère | baked with potatoes and onions |
| bourgeoise | with carrots, onions, bacon, celery and braised lettuce |
| chasseur | sauce of white wine, mushrooms and shallots |
| châtelaine | with artichoke hearts and chestnut purée |
| diable | strong mustard seasoning |
| façon | in the style of … |
| forestière | with bacon and mushroom |
| fricassée | rich, creamy sauce |
| mornay | cheese sauce |
| pays d'auge | cream and cider |
| périgourdine | sauce with foie gras and possibly truffles |
| piquante | with gherkins or capers, vinegar and shallots |
| provençale | sauce of tomatoes, garlic, olive oil and herbs |
| savoyarde | with gruyère cheese |

## VEGETABLES (*LÉGUMES*), GRAINS (*GRAINS*), HERBS (*HERBES*) AND SPICES (*ÉPICES*)

| | |
|---|---|
| ail | garlic |
| anis | aniseed |
| artichaut | artichoke |
| asperge | asparagus |
| avocat | avocado |
| basilic | basil |
| betterave | beetroot |
| blette/bette | Swiss chard |
| cannelle | cinnamon |
| capre | caper |
| cardon | cardoon |
| carotte | carrot |
| céleri | celery |
| champignons, cèpes, ceps, girolles, chanterelles, pleurotes | mushrooms |
| chou (rouge) | (red) cabbage |
| choufleur | cauliflower |
| concombre | cucumber |
| cornichon | gherkin |
| échalotes | shallots |
| endive | chicory |
| épinards | spinach |
| estragon | tarragon |
| fenouil | fennel |
| fèves | broad beans |
| flageolets | flageolet beans |
| gingembre | ginger |
| haricots | beans |
| verts | green beans |
| rouges | kidney beans |
| laurier | bay leaf |
| lentilles | lentils |
| maïs | maize (corn) |
| menthe | mint |
| moutarde | mustard |
| oignon | onion |
| panais | parsnip |
| persil | parsley |
| petits pois | peas |
| piment rouge/vert | red/green chilli pepper |
| pois chiche | chickpeas |
| pois mange-tout | mange-tout |
| pignons | pine nuts |
| poireau | leek |
| poivron (vert, rouge) | sweet pepper (green, red) |
| pommes de terre | potatoes |
| primeurs | spring vegetables |
| radis | radish |
| riz | rice |
| safran | saffron |
| sarrasin | buckwheat |
| thym | thyme |
| tomate | tomato |
| truffes | truffles |

## VEGETABLE DISHES AND TERMS

| | |
|---|---|
| à l'anglaise | boiled |
| beignet | fritter |
| duxelles | fried mushrooms and shallots with cream |
| farci | stuffed |
| feuille | leaf |
| fines herbes | mixture of tarragon, parsley and chives |
| gratiné | browned with cheese or butter |
| à la grecque | cooked in oil and lemon |
| jardinière | with mixed diced vegetables |
| mousseline | mashed potato with cream and eggs |
| à la parisienne | sautéed potatoes, with white wine and shallot sauce |
| parmentier | with potatoes |
| petits farcis | stuffed tomatoes, aubergines, courgettes and peppers |
| râpée | grated or shredded |
| à la vapeur | steamed |
| en verdure | garnished with green vegetables |

## FRUIT (*FRUIT*) AND NUTS (*NOIX*)

| | |
|---|---|
| abricot | apricot |
| acajou | cashew nut |
| amande | almond |
| ananas | pineapple |
| banane | banana |
| brugnon, nectarine | nectarine |
| cacahouète | peanut |
| cassis | blackcurrant |
| cérise | cherry |
| citron | lemon |
| citron vert | lime |
| datte | date |
| figue | fig |
| fraise (de bois) | strawberry (wild) |
| framboise | raspberry |
| fruit de la passion | passion fruit |
| grenade | pomegranate |
| groseille | redcurrant |
| mangue | mango |
| marron | chestnut |

| | | | |
|---|---|---|---|
| melon | melon | chèvre | goat's cheese |
| mirabelle | small yellow plum | clafoutis | heavy custard and fruit |
| myrtille | bilberry | | tart |
| noisette | hazelnut | crème Chantilly | vanilla-flavoured and |
| noix | walnuts; nuts | | sweetened whipped |
| orange | orange | | cream |
| pamplemousse | grapefruit | crème fraîche | sour cream |
| pastèque | watermelon | crème pâtissière | thick, eggy pastry- |
| pêche | peach | | filling |
| pistache | pistachio | crêpe suzette | thin pancake with orange |
| poire | pear | | juice and liqueur |
| pomme | apple | fromage blanc | cream cheese |
| prune | plum | gaufre | waffle |
| pruneau | prune | glace | ice cream |
| raisin | grape | Île flottante/oeufs | whipped egg-white |
| reine-claude | greengage | à la neige | floating on custard |
| | | macaron | macaroon |
| **FRUIT DISHES AND TERMS** | | madeleine | small sponge cake |
| agrumes | citrus fruits | marrons Mont Blanc | chestnut purée and cream |
| beignet | fritter | | on a rum-soaked |
| compôte | stewed fruit | | sponge cake |
| coulis | sauce of puréed fruit | palmier | caramelized puff pastry |
| crème de marrons | chestnut purée | parfait | frozen mousse, |
| flambé | set aflame in alcohol | | sometimes ice cream |
| frappé | iced | petit-suisse | a smooth mixture of |
| | | | cream and curds |
| **DESSERTS (DESSERTS), PASTRIES** | | petits fours | bite-sized cakes/ |
| **(PÂTISSERIE) AND CHEESES (FROMAGES)** | | | pastries |
| brebis | sheep's milk cheese | plâteau de fromages | cheeseboard |
| bombe | moulded ice-cream | poires belle hélène | pears and ice cream in |
| | dessert | | chocolate sauce |
| brioche | sweet breakfast roll | tarte tatin | upside-down apple |
| charlotte | custard and fruit in a | | tart |
| | lining of almond biscuits | yaourt/yogourt | yoghurt |
| | or sponge | | |

# Glossary of architectural terms

These are either terms you'll come across throughout this book, or come up against while travelling around.

**abbaye** abbey

**ambulatory** passage round the outer edge of the choir of a church

**apse** semicircular termination at the east end of a church

**Baroque** mainly seventeenth-century style of art and architecture, distinguished by ornate Classicism

**basse ville** lower town

**bastide** walled town

**capital** carved top of a column

**Carolingian** dynasty (and art, sculpture etc) named after Charlemagne; mid-eighth to early tenth centuries

**château** mansion, country house, castle

**château fort** castle

**chevet** east end of a church

**choir** the eastern part of a church between the altar and nave, used by the choir and clergy

**Classical** architectural style incorporating Greek and Roman elements: pillars, domes, colonnades, etc, at its height in France in the seventeenth century and revived, as Neoclassical, in the nineteenth century

**clerestory** upper storey of a church, incorporating the windows

**cloître** cloister

**donjon** castle keep

**église** church

**flamboyant** florid, late (c.1450–1540) form of Gothic

**Gallo-Roman** from the Roman era in France

**Gothic** late medieval architectural style characterized by pointed arches, verticality and light

**haute ville** upper town

**hôtel (particulier)** mansion or townhouse

**Merovingian** dynasty (and art etc) ruling France and parts of Germany from sixth to mid-eighth centuries

**narthex** entrance hall of church

**nave** main body of a church

**porte** gateway

**Renaissance** classically influenced art/architectural style imported from Italy to France in the early sixteenth century

**retable** altarpiece

**Roman** Romanesque (easily confused with Romain, which means Roman)

**Romanesque** early medieval architecture distinguished by squat, rounded forms and naive sculpture, called Norman in Britain

**stucco** plaster used to embellish ceilings etc

**tour** tower

**transepts** transverse arms of a church

**tympanum** sculpted panel above a church door

**voussoir** wedge-shaped stones used in an arch or vault

# Small print and index

## A ROUGH GUIDE TO ROUGH GUIDES

Published in 1982, the first Rough Guide – to Greece – was a student scheme that became a publishing phenomenon. Mark Ellingham, a recent graduate in English from Bristol University, had been travelling in Greece the previous summer and couldn't find the right guidebook. With a small group of friends he wrote his own guide, combining a highly contemporary, journalistic style with a thoroughly practical approach to travellers' needs.

The immediate success of the book spawned a series that rapidly covered dozens of destinations. And, in addition to impecunious backpackers, Rough Guides soon acquired a much broader readership that relished the guides' wit and inquisitiveness as much as their enthusiastic, critical approach and value-for-money ethos.

These days, Rough Guides include recommendations from budget to luxury and cover more than 200 destinations around the globe, as well as producing an ever-growing range of eBooks and apps.

Visit **roughguides.com** to see our latest publications.

## Rough Guide credits

**Editors**: Lucy Kane and Samantha Cook
**Layout**: Pradeep Thapliyal
**Cartography**: Katie Bennett
**Picture editor**: Roger Mapp
**Proofreader**: Susanne Hillen
**Managing editor**: Monica Woods
**Assistant editor**: Prema Dutta
**Photographers**: David Abram, Lydia Evans,
Jean-Christophe Godet, Michelle Grant and Greg Ward
**Production**: Charlotte Cade

**Cover design**: Jess Carter, Pradeep Thalipyal
**Editorial assistant**: Olivia Rawes
**Senior pre-press designer**: Dan May
**Design director**: Scott Stickland
**Travel publisher**: Joanna Kirby
**Digital travel publisher**: Peter Buckley
**Reference director**: Andrew Lockett
**Publishing director (Travel)**: Clare Currie
**Commercial manager**: Gino Magnotta
**Managing director**: John Duhigg

## Publishing information

This thirteenth edition published March 2013 by
**Rough Guides Ltd**,
80 Strand, London WC2R 0RL
11, Community Centre, Panchsheel Park,
New Delhi 110017, India
**Distributed by the Penguin Group**
Penguin Books Ltd,
80 Strand, London WC2R 0RL
Penguin Group (USA)
375 Hudson Street, NY 10014, USA
Penguin Group (Australia)
250 Camberwell Road, Camberwell,
Victoria 3124, Australia
Penguin Group (NZ)
67 Apollo Drive, Mairangi Bay, Auckland 1310,
New Zealand
Penguin Group (South Africa)
Block D, Rosebank Office Park, 181 Jan Smuts Avenue,
Parktown North, Gauteng, South Africa 2193
Rough Guides is represented in Canada by Tourmaline
Editions Inc. 662 King Street West, Suite 304, Toronto,
Ontario M5V 1M7
Printed in Singapore by Toppan Security Printing Pte. Ltd.

## Help us update

We've gone to a lot of effort to ensure that the thirteenth
edition of **The Rough Guide to France** is accurate and up-
to-date. However, things change – places get "discovered",
opening hours are notoriously fickle, restaurants and
rooms raise prices or lower standards. If you feel we've got
it wrong or left something out, we'd like to know, and if
you can remember the address, the price, the hours, the
phone number, so much the better.

Please send your comments with the subject line
"**Rough Guide France Update**" to @ mail@uk.roughguides
.com. We'll credit all contributions and send a copy of the
next edition (or any other Rough Guide if you prefer) for
the very best emails.

Find more travel information, connect with fellow
travellers and book your trip on ⊛ roughguides.com

## Acknowledgements

**Brian Catlos** Thanks to Nuria Silleras-Fernandez; Germen Soriguera Duocastillo; Marta La Torre Tafanell; Mike Lane; Helene Aznar; Beatriz de Rivera Marinello; and Jane O. Lindsay.

**Mary Anne Evans** At the following tourist boards, thanks to Sarah Flook (Champagne-Ardennes); Claude Chaboud (Picardy); Delphine Bartier (Nord); and Benoît Diéval (Pas-de-Calais).

**Emma Gibbs** Thanks to everyone who helped me with my research, especially Sarah Chambers, Paul and Belinda Patterson, Arjan and Marije Capelle, Micheline Morisson-neu, Claire and Typhanie at *Clos la Boëtie*, Florence and Christophe at *Le Jardins de Brantôme*, Fiona Hilliard, and Estelle at *Le Vieux Logis*. Big thanks also to Lucy Kane for getting me out there, to Sam Cook for being an excellent and patient editor, and to Matthew, as always, for his constant encouragement and support.

**Norm Longley** would like to offer a special thank you to Lucy Kane for her inordinate patience throughout. Massive thanks to Isabelle Faure in Lyon and Florine Verjus in Chambéry for their invaluable assistance. Thanks are also due to Marine Guy in Lyon, Céline Grison in Villefranche, Céline Guillermin and Gérard Charpin in Chambéry, Frédérique Alléon in Evian, Julie Thiebaud in Besançon, and Pascal Boscher and family in Gap.

**John Malathronas** Thanks to Françoise Graive, Office de Tourisme, Clermont Ferrand; Jessica Poole, Maison de la Région Languedoc Roussillon–London; Philippe Gendre and Cécile Bassville, Office de Tourisme, Vichy; Isabelle Pfeffer, Aurillac; Cécile Mathiaud, Christine Muller-Wille, Morgane Grillot and Veronique Beigenger, Office de Tourisme, Bourgogne; Carine Buch, Tourism-Lorraine;

Anne-Sophie Le Bigot, Autun; Arnaud Lizeray, Comité Régional du Tourisme Midi-Pyrénées; Anouck Sittre, Tourism Alsace; Anne-Frédérique Gerard, Vins de Bourgogne (BIVB); Phil Partridge, Rhino Car Hire; Florence Bucciacchio, Dijon Tourist Office; France Grenouillet, Amnéville-les-Thermes; Lucile Clara, Ardèche Tourism Development; Vanessa Michy, Tourism Auvergne; Jean-Paul Grimaud, Tourism Office, Le Puy-en-Velay; Patricia, Lucy and Philip Hawkes, Château de Missery; Sylvie Favat, Cantal Tourisme; Franck Chrétien, Chablis; Anne Bossuyt, Office de Tourisme, Sens; Bertrand Devillard, Mercurey; Vincent Jacquot, Meuse Tourism; Pascale Clément and Florent Luyt, Joigny; Nathalie Desarmenien, Beaune.

**Natalia O'Hara** Thanks to Didier Descamps for on the ground research, James O'Hara for fact-checking, Nathalène Arnoux for help in Arcachon, Don Pangburn for researching Bordeaux viniculture and Xavier Le Carboulec for his tour of Cap Ferret. At the tourist boards, thanks to Sophie Cousin, Fabienne Couton-Laine, Gillian Green, Karin Labardin, Christine Lacaud, Sarah Manser and Sandrine Pailloncy. Many thanks to those who provided hospitality, and especially Veronique Daudin, Angélique Daure-Dumayet, Bernard Le Gouil, Leslie Kellen, James Martin, Denise Méry, Monique Potel, Ann Roberts, Clarissa Schaefer, and Erika and Patrice Vignial, who welcomed us into their homes. Warm thanks to editor Lucy Kane, and to my researcher and friend Natalie Pangburn.

**Greg Ward** Thanks to Nicolas Caron, José and Flavia De Mello, Alexis Dubosc, Christopher Jones, Jane Mercer, Liz Thorold, Jean-Jacques Violo, and, especially, Carmel and Graham Ramsay for their wonderful hospitality.

## Readers' letters

Thanks to all the readers who have taken the time to write in with comments and suggestions (and apologies if we've inadvertently omitted or misspelt anyone's name):

David Andrews; James Austin-Smith; Anna Bonavia; Debbie Bramley; Ian Daines; Richard Fearn; Chris and Jill Hore; Judy Hubbard; Alysson Jackson; Moire Lennox; Françoise More; Michelle and Alaistair Palmer; Dez Paradise; Anthony and Janet Peter; Maria Sahitu; Natie Shevel; Jalin Somaiya; David Warden; Joseph Wright.

## Photo credits

All photos © Rough Guides except the following:
(Key: t-top; c-centre; b-bottom; l-left; r-right)

# Index

Maps are marked in grey

## R

## Q

# Map symbols

The symbols below are used on maps throughout the book

| | | | | | | | |
|---|---|---|---|---|---|---|---|
| ✈ | Airport | 🎿 | Skiing | 🏰 | Château | - - - - | Cable car/téléphérique |
| Ⓜ | Métro station | 🦃 | Wildlife park/nature reserve | ◠ | Cave | —— | Tram route |
| Ⓡ | RER station | 🐘 | Zoo | ∴ | Ruin | — · — · | Ferry route |
| Ⓣ | Tram stop | 🏊 | Swimming pool | ⛩ | Fort/castle | ▬▬▬ | Pedestrian road |
| P | Parking | ⊤ | Gardens/fountain | ⚑ | Standing stone | - - - - | Footpath |
| ★ | Bus stop | ☉ | Statue/memorial | ⚵ | Viewpoint | —— | Wall |
| ⛴ | Boat/ferry | 🏛 | Monument | ⚱ | Waterfall | ◼ | Building |
| ⛽ | Fuel station | ♦ | Place of interest | ⛰ | Mountain range | ⛪ | Church |
| ⊠ | Post office | ⊠ | Gate | ▲ | Mountain peak | ▢ | Market |
| ⓘ | Tourist office | 🗼 | Lighthouse | ▬▬■ | Railway | ▨ | Park |
| @ | Internet access | ⚔ | Battlefield | ▬▬■ | TGV line | ▢ | Beach |
| ✚ | Hospital | 🏚 | Abbey | ▪▪▪▪▪ | Funicular | ⊞ | Cemetery |
| ⛑ | Race circuit | ⛩ | Monastery | | | | |

## Listings key

| | |
|---|---|
| ◼ | Accommodation |
| ● | Café/Restaurant/Bar |
| ◼ | Club/Venue |
| ● | Shop |

# Find your perfect place to stay in France

Enjoy more space, privacy and luxury
in a holiday home rental

Over 120,000 gites, villas & chateaux in France and 320,000+ properties
worldwide available to rent direct from owners and agents

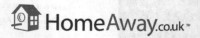 HomeAway.co.uk™

Own a holiday home? Find out how much you could earn today, visit HomeAway.co.uk/tellmemore